P9-CRM-358

THE
SOTHEBY'S
WINE
ENCYCLOPEDIA

THE
SOTHEBY'S
WINE
ENCYCLOPEDIA

TOM STEVENSON

LONDON, NEW YORK, MELBOURNE, MUNICH, DELHI

5th edition (2011)

DORLING KINDERSLEY
PROJECT EDITOR Andrew Roff
SENIOR ART EDITOR Jane Ewart
MANAGING EDITOR Dawn Henderson
MANAGING ART EDITOR Christine Keilty
SENIOR JACKETS CREATIVE Nicola Powling
US EDITORS Shannon Beatty, Margaret Parrish
SENIOR PRODUCTION EDITOR Jennifer Murray
SENIOR PRODUCTION CONTROLLER Alice Sykes
CREATIVE TECHNICAL SUPPORT Sonia Charbonnier

This edition produced for Dorling Kindersley by
SANDS PUBLISHING SOLUTIONS
PROJECT EDITOR David Tombesi-Walton
ART EDITOR Simon Murrell
INDEXER John Noble

Originally produced for Dorling Kindersley by
COOLING BROWN LTD

First American edition, 1988
This edition, 2011
Published in the United States by
DK Publishing
375 Hudson Street
New York, New York 10014

12 13 14 15   10 9 8 7 6 5 4 3 2

002–183378–Nov/2011

Published in Great Britain by Dorling Kindersley Limited.

A catalog record for this book is available from the Library of Congress.

ISBN: 9780756686840

DK books are available at special discounts when purchased in
bulk for sales promotions, premiums, fund-raising, or educational use.
For details, contact: DK Publishing Special Markets, 375 Hudson Street,
New York, New York 10014 or SpecialSales@dk.com.

Color reproduction by Colourscan, Singapore
Printed and bound by Hung Hing, China

Tom Stevenson can be found at www.wine-pages.com/guests/tom/intro.htm

Discover more at
www.dk.com

CONTENTS

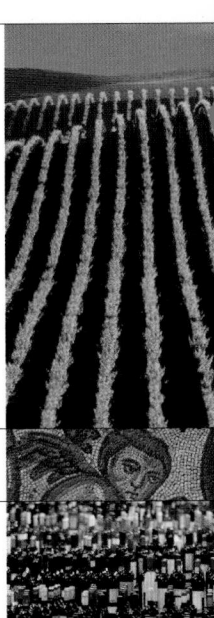

FACTORS AFFECTING TASTE AND QUALITY

The Factors Affecting Taste and Quality boxes appear on the introductory pages of countries, regions, or districts. The taste guides (Appellations, Producers, and Wine Styles) follow these introductions.

FACTORS AFFECTING TASTE AND QUALITY

 LOCATION

 CLIMATE

 ASPECT

 SOIL

 VITICULTURE AND VINIFICATION

 GRAPE VARIETIES

TASTE GUIDE SYMBOLS

ﭏ When to drink for optimum enjoyment. This is usually given as a range (such as 3–7 years) from the date of the vintage. "Upon purchase" is for wines that should be both bought and drunk while young. "Upon opening" is for fortified wines that can keep for many years but, contrary to popular belief, do not keep well once opened.

🍇 Grape varieties used.

♔ The 10 (or fewer) greatest wines for the type or style indicated.

✓ Recommended producers, vineyards, and wines.

STAR RATING SYSTEM

Stars are given for a producer's general quality and do not necessarily apply to each wine produced. When a producer has neither stars nor a cross, this indicates an acceptable but not outstanding standard.

Half-stars indicate intermediate ratings.

★ Wines that excel within their class or style.

★★ Very exceptional wines. The local equivalent of a Bordeaux super-second. *See* Micropedia, p688.

★★★ The best wines that money can buy, without any allowances made for limitations of local style and quality.

◉ A producer of organic wines.

Ⓑ A producer of biodynamic wines.

❶ Wines of exceptional value for money, whether they are inexpensive or not.

The following are seldom used, as there is a bias towards including producers than can be recommended.

❷ Wines that are inconsistent, or too rustic, or judgement has been reserved for a stated reason.

❸ Underperformers for their category or style.

Key to symbols
How good a wine producer is and why a wine tastes the way it does are the twin pillars of this encyclopedia – thus, Factors Affecting Taste and Quality and Star Rating System are two of its two most regular features.

FOREWORD

by Serena Sutcliffe MW,
head of Sotheby's International Wine Department

WINE BOOKS ARE A BIT LIKE WINE ITSELF: they should age with grace. However, books have an advantage over wine in that they can be refreshed and updated, whereas topping up bottles is, in my view, undesirable. While that process is fine for a cask, a bottle should always keep its integrity.

The honesty and aims of this book have been a constant since it was first published. Now, with this new edition, real knowledge has been synthesized and honed to a high degree, with a worldwide view that is breathtaking in its scope. Whether I need Romanian label language, information on the Hilltops area of New South Wales, or a guide to who is growing what and where in China, I can reach for *The Sotheby's® Wine Encyclopedia* with total confidence. And do believe me when I say that professionals have arms as long as amateurs; no one person can ingest everything that is happening in both wine production and wine consumption, although Tom Stevenson might be that one individual. Try to trip him up with a query on Thailand – he will come up trumps.

Seeing as many cellars as I do, I am amazed that, in the days of the Internet and Kindle, there is often a smattering of wine books among the bins and bottles. It is as if wine lovers like the reassurance and proximity of the written word when they are roaming around their cellar, contemplating what they might want to drink that evening or deciding what to buy to fill the gaps.

There is a real advantage in reading a book in which all the information has been filtered by a single, highly experienced author, and I sense that this has been part of the success of this encyclopedia. Compendium books can lack focus and cohesion, whereas one knows where Tom Stevenson is coming from (a pretty high place, one feels!), and the sheer weight of his lifetime with wine and his ability to unearth and disseminate facts seep through the pages.

Above all, though, the purpose of this book is to enhance enjoyment of drinking wine – a noble pursuit if ever there was one.

Serena Sutcliffe

IN WITH THE NEW

TWENTY-TWO YEARS AGO, when the first edition of *The Sotheby's®
Wine Encyclopedia* was published, the world of wine was a such a
relatively simple place that it was possible for those in the know to
visualize the entire global industry in their mind's eye. Now, the very
thought of the intricate and convoluted way in which wine has spread
both vertically, within the major winemaking regions, and horizontally,
across so many other countries, is enough to make even the most
knowledgeable heads spin. If there is one thing that can help us
remain anchored while contemplating this ever-growing morass of
vinous information, it is a sense of place for wine, and the only way
to project that is with maps. If readers can sit in an armchair, sip a
delicious wine, look at a map, and say, "Ah, that's where it comes
from," then I have done my job. That is why my focus has always
been on trying to map every single wine appellation, whether official
or not, rather than detailing on which hillside a specific wine is
grown, which I leave to other, more specialized books. With this
edition, I am more satisfied than I have ever been with the extent of cartographic coverage, through both
updating existing maps and creating new ones. Just look at, for example, Greece, Romania, Israel, South
Africa, North Africa, and Asia. And I do not think there is another book available that can claim to have
mapped every single Italian DOC or all existing US AVAs, but *The Sotheby's® Wine Encyclopedia* can.

Varieties and Chronology

One big change in this edition has been the addition of the ABC of Grape Varieties, and I must highlight the
role of Lyn Parry in achieving this. Without her groundwork, I would never have been able to contemplate,
let alone complete, such a huge expansion of the old Glossary of Grape Varieties. It has long been an
ambition of mine to include every grape variety and synonym mentioned throughout the encyclopedia,
but it was such a mammoth task simply to go through the book and list them that I put it off – until
this edition, that is, when I commissioned Lyn to construct a list and, in the process, to resolve any
contradictions, conflicts, spelling differences, or other discrepancies that might exist. With the number
of grape varieties having grown organically over two decades, I suspected there would be plenty of
inconsistencies, and as Lyn will attest, I was not wrong! When she presented the final listing, it was
so long that I seriously considered shelving it for a future edition, but I knuckled down, and I think
it has been worth the trouble. It will also become a rod for my own back,
because the listing of grapes can only be harvested from the existing
edition; thus, the ABC of Grape Varieties will always require expansion
and will always run one edition behind.

A totally new feature in this fifth edition is A Chronology of Wine.
How do you get a meaningful history into an encyclopedia such as this
without it doubling the size of the book and making for heavy reading?
Well, this chronology is my answer, and I hope readers find it as
fascinating to dip into as I do.

May 2011

EASTERN HORIZONS
by Serena Sutcliffe MW

Why do people make wine? While there are undoubtedly altruists and fanatics among this motley band, the vast majority of winemakers – and vineyard and winery owners – are involved in this historic profession to earn a living. And if this is to be achieved, they have to sell the wine they produce. Increasingly, those who make it are also deeply involved in marketing their wine, since there is no better person to do this successfully than the person who knows it best.

IN RECENT YEARS, the trend has been to create ever more direct links between château, estate, or domaine and the wine-consuming public. Modern methods of communication have further contracted the space between winery and dining table, and now it is just as likely that a kind host will regale you with stories about the wine he is serving as the producer himself. Books like these make everyone an expert! We have, therefore, seen a huge number of winemakers fanning out across the globe to promote and show their wines.

The clamour to taste wines with the people responsible for crafting them has been an international phenomenon, and while it has undoubtedly augmented the profits of the airline companies, it has also made wine more immediate and more "real" to audiences that, a decade or two ago, regarded it as peripheral – if they considered it at all.

The huge advance of wine drinking in Asia has been the chief beneficiary of this vineyard-to-glass approach. Wine appreciation has gone to a different level, and swathes of forests have suffered as commentators strive to find the answers to changing demand and the exponential rise in the price of very fine wines. When I look at the patronizing way, only a year or two ago, in which the West derided Asians for adding sugary drinks (I will not even allow myself to mention the brands!) to their wine and then compare that with the wonderful wine-and-food dinners to which I now go in Hong Kong, Beijing, Shanghai, Taipei, and Singapore, I feel embarrassed on behalf of my part of the world.

Singapore, in fact, started the ball rolling more than a quarter of a century ago, and its attitude was exactly in tune with the huge local gastronomic enthusiasm and experience: wine was there to augment the pleasure of the food. This is very much a part of Chinese culture – like the French, they can be enjoying one meal while discussing another! Until quite recently, everyone thought that classic wines needed classic French food as a background, but this has changed dramatically, and most people in Asia feel confident enough to proffer a series of marvellous Chinese dishes while plying you with their best

BIG PRICE
Sotheby's auctioneer Jamie Ritchie selling one of the bottles of Château Lafite Rothschild 1869 that went for $232,692 at Sotheby's Hong Kong in October 2010.

wines. With the exciting diversity of widely differing regions all over the Chinese mainland and, indeed, throughout Asia as a whole, the wealth of choice in raw materials is enormous.

SOUGHT-AFTER LABELS AND BOTTLES
Much has also been made of Asian attitudes to wine-label snobbery, as if it were a trait peculiar to them; pretty well everyone is prone to "label pride". More constructively, people realize that pouring good wine can win friends and influence people – anything that oils the wheels of life is fine by me. At first, this can lead to a fairly narrow category of wines that is deemed dignified enough to be served to one's peers, but each month in Asia seems to show that more names are being added to the list and a wider spectrum of bottles is regarded as desirable and worthy of a place at the banquet.

At Sotheby's, we have been at the forefront of the Asian wine boom, reaching, in 2011, the extraordinary record of 15 consecutive 100 per cent-sold white-glove wine auctions in Hong Kong. Demand for wine from Asian collectors played an important part in fuelling Sotheby's overall global wine total of $88.27 million in 2010, the highest figure in the company's 40 years of wine sales. The Lafite Ex-Cellars sale in Hong Kong set a new record for a single standard-sized bottle at auction when a bottle of Château Lafite Rothschild 1869 sold for $232,692, joining our record for a bottle in any format (a jeroboam of Mouton Rothschild 1945, which fetched $310,700 in 2007 in New York) and any wine lot at auction (50 cases of Mouton 1982, which sold for $1,051,600 in 2006 in New York).

GOING EAST
Serena Sutcliffe MW with a selection of the highlights from Sotheby's first sale of a new era of wine auctions in Hong Kong, April 2009.

THE INTERNATIONAL ARENA

As wine drinking becomes a given, encompassing all continents and myriad cultures, it is rewarding to give some thought to national tastes, if indeed they can be identified. The most facile assumption with regard to Asia was that wine had to be red – after all, anything that can bring us luck and health has to be recommended. People also like long-lived wines, hoping perhaps that something of this quality will rub off on ourselves, and wines that have a track record. Thus, the centuries-old reputation of Bordeaux châteaux in the front line, First Growths in prime position, has real psychological importance. Then, there is an identifiable hierarchy of châteaux (think 1855) that helps concentrate the mind. Even if we do not agree with it, we can argue about it. More prosaically, there is also a considerable quantity of Bordeaux – enough to make a market.

So, Bordeaux took, and takes, pride of place in the Asian arena. But when wine took off in England in medieval times, Bordeaux was first in the door there. And when North America woke up to fine wine in the second part of the 20th century – guess what – Bordeaux led from the front. We have to admit it: internationally, at the top end of the wine pyramid, Bordeaux reigns supreme. And we like it; it delivers the goods, in terms of complexity, depth, and flavour. We find it fascinating to compare châteaux and vintages and to watch it develop. What is more, we love talking about it – a factor that is not to be underestimated.

NATIONAL PALATES

There is a school of thought that suggests that more "sophisticated" wine drinkers subsequently turn to Burgundy, and there is a grain of intellectual superiority in knowing the names of growers who make hundreds, not thousands, of cases from tiny plots of vineyard. The taste of Pinot Noir at its most sublime is pretty marvellous, too. So, Domaine de la Romanée-Conti has become pivotal in Asia, drawing other domaines into the magnetic circle and thus aggravating further the difficulties of supply for everyone else. My tip in 2011 is to turn to the Rhône Valley before more names there become iconic.

White wines are now permitted at table in Asia, and the obvious partnership of white Burgundy with all the superb seafood one finds throughout Eastern countries is established. Champagne is welcomed before wine dinners, and different house styles are discussed with authority. Sweet wines have a way to go, as this is not dessert territory, but there are adventurous spirits who know how to sip and appreciate them.

Are there really national palates? Every cross-continental tasting that has been essayed seems to come to very hazy conclusions. And these palates change and expand – perhaps sometimes like the drinkers themselves! One just has to look at, for example, the growth in consumption of Austrian wines in the UK, particularly in the restaurant sector, to witness a new departure and a willingness to embrace new scents and flavours. I am on a mission

YQUEM VERTICAL
Serena Sutcliffe MW and Pierre Lurton, managing director of Château d'Yquem, outside the château. Sotheby's London auctioned historic wines from the cellars of Château d'Yquem in April 2008, when a 70-vintage vertical collection, comprising 136 bottles, sold for £368,000 ($724,371).

STAR OF 45
This jeroboam (4.5 litres) of Château Mouton Rothschild 1945 was sold for $310,700 by Sotheby's New York in February 2007.

to bring to the fore some of the delicious red and white Greek wines that are now being made, although I suspect that it might take more than my lifetime to see a range of Agiorgitiko reds being shown over roast duck in a far-flung corner of Asia.

Wine drinking needs open minds, and if this leads me to Slovenian Pinot Grigio with my *sashimi*, so much the better.

MOVING AND CHANGING

We all know that no situation ever remains static and that there is no room for complacency. Prices must have a realistic base, from both a quality and an availability point of view. In the end, the consumer makes the price, just as he chooses the books he will read – and we hope this book makes his shortlist! Overheating is as bad for a market as it is for a wine, and everyone should bear in mind the rollercoaster tendencies of economic history.

Counter-balancing this is the indisputable fact that the wine trade has never been more international. Of all the fascinating figures we garner for our part of the market, this one gives me the most cause for optimism: in our 2010 London sales, our buyers came from 43 countries. Couple this with the 14 major languages in which this encyclopedia has been published in its 20-odd years, and we see that wine is continuing its ascent as a global phenomenon.

FACTORS *affecting*
TASTE AND QUALITY

In the introductory text for countries, regions, or districts, a tinted panel provides a quick-reference guide to the fundamental factors that determine the quality and style of the wines produced in that area: location, climate, aspect, soil, viticulture and vinification, and grape varieties. The first four listed are the constant factors that determine the ability to grow grapes anywhere; viticulture and vinification affect the potential quality of those grapes and the style of the wines they produce; while the choice of grape varieties decides the basic taste of the wine that can be made, which brings us to the winemaker, who is the idiosyncratic joker in the pack.

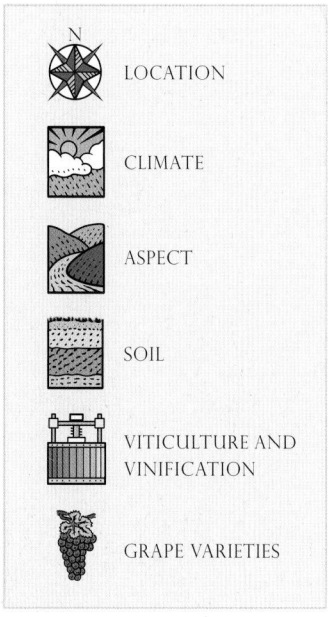

NAPA VALLEY
Most of the Napa Valley is flat, fertile, and highly productive, but parts of it have a very different topography. Where the vines follow rolling hills, the aspect changes, altering the amount of light and heat received.

LOCATION

The location of a vineyard determines whether its climate is suitable for viticulture. The same grape grown in the same area can make two totally different wines, yet due to other factors affecting quality, different grapes grown continents apart may produce two wines that are very similar.

THE VAST MAJORITY of the world's wine-producing areas, including all of the classic and most successful wine regions, are located in the temperate zones, between 10°C (50°F) and 20°C (68°F), where *Vitis vinifera* is capable of producing premium quality wine grapes. If you look at the Wine by Latitude map (*see below*), you will notice that most of the vineyards in both hemispheres are found between 30° and 50° of latitude. While these two latitudinal bands correspond approximately to the northern and southern temperate zones, they can never represent precise parameters, since altitude, prevailing winds, ocean currents, and the penetration of sea fog into coastal valleys influence the temperatures experienced beyond such simplicities as distance from the sun and the angle of its rays. Look at the isotherm map (Wine by Temperate Zones, *opposite top*), and you can see the true extent of the northern and southern temperate zones. According to wine-loving climatologist Dr Gregory Jones, whose studies have focused on a slightly different thermal zone (12–22°C [54–72°F]), the line for the lower annual temperature has shifted 80–240 kilometres (50–150 miles) polewards in both hemispheres. This has been due to an increase of 1.7°C (3.1°F) in the average growing-season temperature in Europe and, over a similar time period (1948–2004), an increase of 1.5°C (2.7°F) in the western USA, driven mostly by increases in minimum temperatures. This might take the crisp, acidic edge off the coolest-climate wines (eg, in Germany's Mosel), which, over the passage of time, will inevitably become fractionally softer than they used to be – but such generic changes to the potential taste profile of any given area will be partly hidden by the evolutionary style change of the wine producers themselves, who are intentionally harvesting riper fruit anyway. Since many consumers have turned to – or have become conditioned by – softer, fatter, and sometimes sweeter wines, it is

TERRACED VINEYARDS OVERLOOKING THE RHINE
Vines beside bodies of water benefit from the sun's rays reflecting off the water – an advantage in areas where the climate is cooler.

debatable just how much difference brought about by this they will notice. The increase in minimum temperatures has also opened up greater quality potential for vineyards that were perhaps on the wrong side of the viticultural periphery (such as England) and will, if the current trend continues, offer serious opportunities to other areas that were once well outside the bounds of commercial viticulture (such as Scandinavia).

Most of the world's finest wines are produced in west-coast locations, which tend to be cooler and less humid than east-coast areas, due to ocean currents and their accompanying winds (*see* Ocean Currents map, *opposite*). Forests and mountain ranges protect the vines from wind and rain. A relatively close proximity to forests and large masses of water can influence the climate through transpiration and evaporation, providing welcome humidity in times of drought, although they can encourage rot. Thus, some factors can have both positive and negative effects.

WINE BY LATITUDE
The most important areas of cultivation in both the northern and southern hemispheres lie mainly between latitudes 30° and 50°.

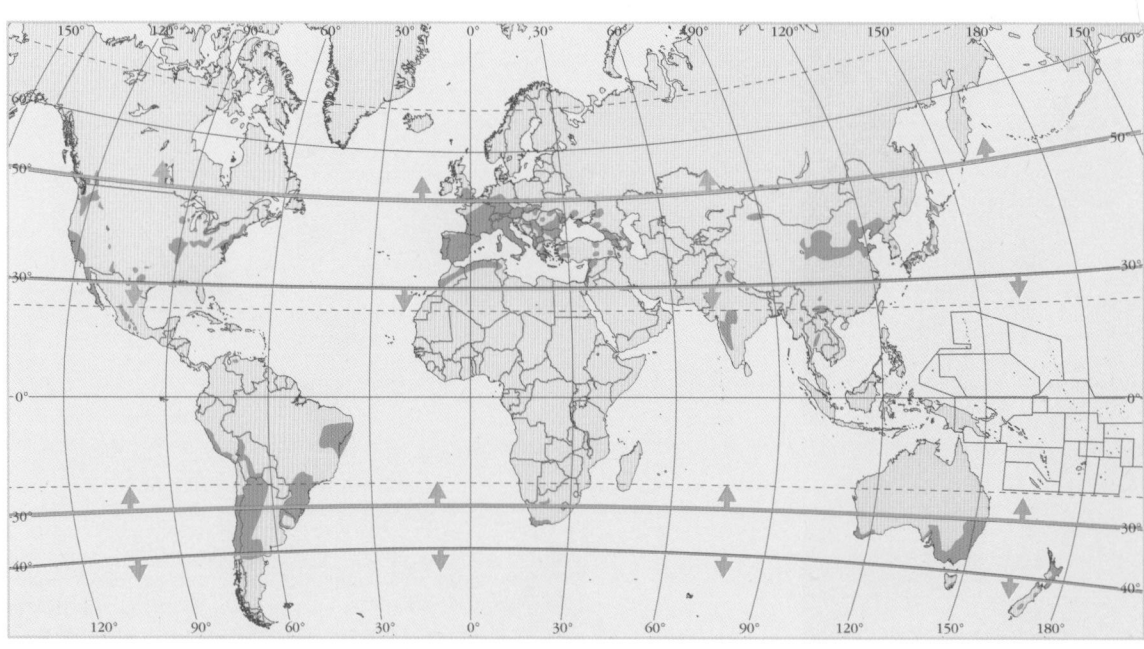

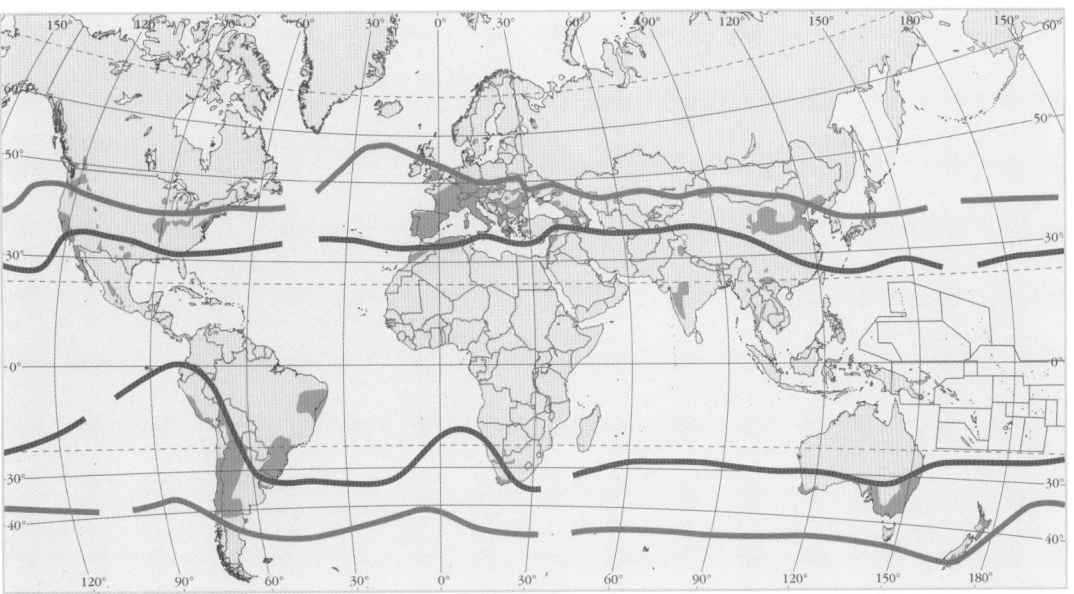

WINE BY TEMPERATE ZONES
With the boundaries adjusted for temperature rather than latitude, these temperate zones clearly contain even more of the world's vineyards. The factors that determine the widening and narrowing of this band include altitude and ocean currents (see below).

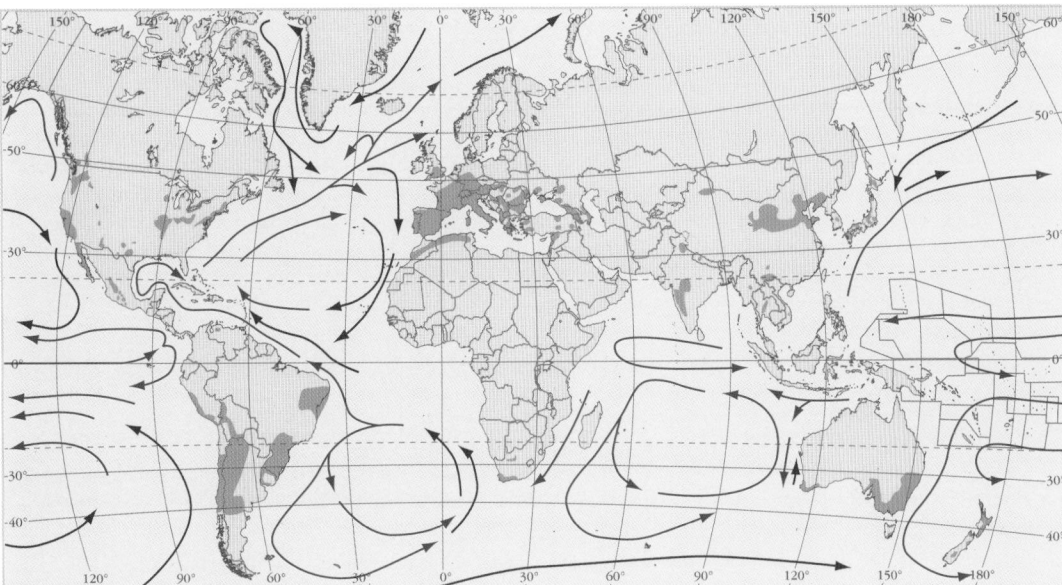

OCEAN CURRENTS (BELOW)
The ocean's currents link together to form the Global Ocean Conveyor Belt, which effectively controls the global climate and thereby dictates where grapevines can be cultivated. The currents work by a mechanism known as thermohaline circulation, which is driven by temperature (thermo) and salt (haline), although they are also tweaked by the pull of the moon. An illustration of the profound effect of ocean currents on climate is the Younger Dryas Event 13,000 years ago, when the glacial Lake Agassiz melted. This immense glacial lake was located in the centre of North America and covered an area that was larger than all of the modern Great Lakes today. When it drained off through the Mississippi Delta, the volume of fresh water was so vast and sudden that it cut off the Gulf Stream in its prime, causing the last full-blown Ice Age. Compare all three maps on these pages, and it is easy to see how the Peru (or Humboldt) Current can push the 20°C (68°F) isotherm so far up the South American coast – thanks, also, to altitude – and how the Gulf Stream enables viticulture to survive in England.

ASPECT

The aspect of a vineyard refers to its general topography – which direction the vines face, the angle and height of any slope, and so on – and how this interrelates with the climate.

There are few places in the world where winemaking grapes – as opposed to table grapes – are successfully grown under the full effect of a prevailing climate. The basic climatic requirements of the vine are usually achieved by manipulating local conditions, keeping sunshine, sun strength, drainage, and temperature in mind.

Sunshine
In the northern hemisphere, south-facing slopes (and north-facing slopes in the southern hemisphere) attract more hours of sunshine and are therefore cultivated in cooler areas. In hotter regions, the opposite facing slopes tend to be cultivated.

Sun strength and drainage
Because of the angle, vines on a slope absorb the greater strength of the sun's rays. In temperate regions the sun is not directly overhead, even at noon, so its rays fall more or less perpendicular to a slope. Conversely, on flat ground the sun's rays are dissipated across a wider area, so their strength is diluted. (The plains are also susceptible to flooding and have soils that are usually too fertile, yielding larger crops of correspondingly inferior fruit.) Lake- and river-valley slopes are well suited for vines because rays are also reflected from the water.

A sloping vineyard also affords natural drainage. However, hilltop vines are too exposed to wind and rain, and their presence, instead of a forest covering, deprives vines below of protection. Forested hilltops not only supply humidity in times of drought, but absorb the worst of any torrential rain that could wash away the topsoil below.

Temperature
While slopes are very desirable sites, it should be remembered that for every 100 metres (330 feet) above sea level, the temperature falls 1°C (1.8°F). This can result in an extra 10 to 15 days being needed for the grapes to ripen, and because of the extra time, the acidity will be relatively higher. Thus, a vineyard's altitude can be a very effective way of manipulating the quality and character of its crop. Riverside and lakeside slopes also have the advantages of reflected sunlight and the water acting as a heat reservoir, releasing at night heat that has been stored during the day. This not only reduces sudden drops in temperature that can be harmful, but also lessens the risk of frost. However, depressions in slopes and the very bottoms of valleys collect cold air, are frost-prone, and slow growth.

CLIMATE

Climate and weather are the most important factors that influence the growth of grapes for quality wines. Climate is determined by geographical location (and that is subject to the ocean currents), whereas weather is the result of how nature decides to affect that climate on a daily basis. In other words, climate is what it should be; weather is what it is.

A GROWER MUST SELECT A REGION with an amenable climate and hope that nature does not inflict too many anomalies. Although some vines survive under extreme conditions, most – and all classic – grapevines are confined to two relatively narrow climatic bands, as illustrated under Location (*see* pp14–15), and require a sympathetic combination of heat, sunshine, rain, and frost.

HEAT
Vines will not provide grapes suitable for winemaking if the annual mean temperature is less than 10°C (50°F). The ideal mean temperature is 14° to 15°C (57° to 59°F), with an average of no less than 19°C (66°F) in the summer and -1°C (30°F) in the winter. In order for the vines to produce a good crop of ripe grapes, the minimum heat-summation, measured in "degree-days" with an average of above 10°C (50°F) over the growing season, is 1,000° (using °C to calculate) or 1,800° (using °F to calculate). Below are the degree-day totals over the growing season for a variety of vineyards from around the world.

AREA/REGION	DEGREE-DAYS, CELSIUS (FAHRENHEIT)
Trier, Mosel, Germany	945 (1,700)
Bordeaux, France	1,320 (2,375)
McLaren Vale, South Australia	1,350 (2,425)
Russian River, California, USA	2,000 (3,600)

SUNSHINE
While light is required for photosynthesis, the most important biological process of green plants, there is sufficient light for this even in cloudy conditions. For vinegrowing, however, sunshine is needed more for its heat than its light. Approximately 1,300 hours is the minimum amount of sunshine required per growing season, but 1,500 hours is preferable.

AREA/REGION	SUNSHINE
Bordeaux, France	1,427 hours
Trier, Mosel, Germany	1,576 hours
McLaren Vale, South Australia	1,765 hours
Russian River, California, USA	2,100 hours

RAINFALL
A vine requires 68 centimetres (27 inches) of rain per year. Ideally, most of the rain should fall in the spring and the winter, but some is needed in the summer too. Vines can survive with less water if the temperature is higher, although rain in warm conditions is more harmful than rain in cool conditions. A little rain a few days before the harvest will wash the grapes of any sprays and is therefore ideal if followed by sun and a gentle, drying breeze. Torrential rain, however, can split berries and cause fungus.

Below are annual rainfall figures for a variety of vineyards from around the world.

AREA/REGION	RAINFALL
McLaren Vale, South Australia	60 cm (24 in)
Trier, Mosel, Germany	65 cm (26 in)
Bordeaux, France	90 cm (36 in)
Russian River, California, USA	135 cm (53 in)

FROST
Surprising as it may seem, some frost is desirable, providing it is in the winter, as it hardens the wood and kills spores and pests that the bark may be harbouring. However, frost can literally kill a vine, particularly at bud-break and flowering (*see* p24).

VINTAGE
The anomalies of a vintage can bring disaster to reliable vineyards and produce miracles in unreliable ones. A vintage is made by weather, as opposed to climate. While the climate may be generally good, uncommon weather conditions can sometimes occur. In addition to this, the vintage's annual climatic adjustment can be very selective; on the edge of a summer hailstorm, for example, some vineyards may be destroyed and produce no wine at all, while others are virtually unharmed and produce good wine. Vines situated between the two might be left with a partial crop of fruit that could result in wines of an exceptional quality if given a further two to three months of warm sunshine before the harvest, because reduced yields per vine produce grapes with a greater concentration of flavour.

CLIMATIC CONDITIONS

Favourable
• A fine, long summer with warm, rather than hot, sunshine ensures that the grapes ripen slowly. Such weather leads to a good acid–sugar balance.
• A dry, sunny autumn is essential for ripening grapes and avoiding rot; but, again, it must not be too hot.
• The winter months from November to February (May to August in the southern hemisphere) are climatically flexible, with the vine able to withstand temperatures as low as -20°C (-4°F) and anything other than absolute flood or drought.
• Within the above parameters, the climate must suit the viticultural needs of specific grape varieties – for example, a cooler climate for Riesling, hotter for Syrah, and so on.

Unfavourable
• Major dangers are frost, hail, and strong winds, all of which can denude a vine and are particularly perilous when the vine is flowering or the grapes are ripening and at their most susceptible.
• Rain and/or cold temperatures during the flowering may cause imperfect fertilization, which results in a physiological disorder called *millerandage*. The affected grapes contain no seeds and will be small and only partially developed when the rest of the cluster is fully matured.
• Persistent rain at, or immediately before, the harvest can lead to rot or dilute the wine, both of which can cause vinification problems.
• Sun is not often thought of as a climatic danger, but just as frost can be beneficial to the vine, so sun can be harmful. Too much sun encourages the sap to go straight past the embryo grape clusters to the leaves and shoots. This causes a physiological disorder called *coulure*, which is often confused with *millerandage*. It is totally different, although both disorders can appear together due to the vagaries of climate. Most seeds suffering from *coulure* drop to the ground, and those that remain do not develop.
• Excessive heat during the harvest rapidly decreases the acid level of grape juice and makes the grapes too hot, creating problems during fermentation. It is especially difficult to harvest grapes at an acceptable temperature in very hot areas, such as South Africa. As a result, some wine estates harvest the grapes at night, when the grapes are at their coolest.

SOIL

Topsoil is of primary importance to the vine because it supports most of its root system, including most of the feeding network. Subsoil always remains geologically true. Main roots penetrate several layers of subsoil, whose structure influences drainage, the root system's depth, and its ability to collect minerals.

THE METABOLISM OF THE VINE is well known, and the interaction between it and the soil is generally understood. The ideal medium in which to grow vines for wine production is one that has a relatively thin topsoil and an easily penetrable (and therefore well-drained) subsoil with good water-retaining characteristics. The vine does not like "wet feet", so drainage is vital, yet it needs access to moisture, so access to a soil with good water retention is also important. The temperature potential of a soil, its heat-retaining capacity, and its heat-reflective characteristics affect the ripening period of grapes: warm soils (gravel, sand, loam) advance ripening, while cold soils (clay) retard it. Chalk falls between these two extremes, and dark, dry soils are obviously warmer than light, wet soils. High-pH (alkaline) soils, such as chalk, encourage the vine's metabolism to produce sap and grape juice with a relatively high acid content. The continual use of fertilizers has lowered the pH level of some viticultural areas in France, and these are now producing wines of higher pH (less acidity).

THE MINERAL REQUIREMENTS OF THE VINE
Just as various garden flowers, shrubs, and vegetables perform better in one soil type as opposed to another, so too do different grape varieties. Certain minerals essential to plant growth are found in various soils. Apart from hydrogen and oxygen (which are supplied as water), the most important soil nutrients are

nitrogen, which is used in the production of a plant's green matter; phosphate, which directly encourages root development and indirectly promotes an earlier ripening of the grapes (an excess inhibits the uptake of magnesium); potassium, which improves the vine's metabolism, enriches the sap, and is essential for the development of the following year's crop; iron, which is indispensable for photosynthesis (a lack of iron will cause chlorosis); magnesium, which is the only mineral constituent of the chlorophyll molecule (lack of magnesium also causes chlorosis); and calcium, which feeds the root system, neutralizes acidity and helps create a friable soil structure (although an excess of calcium restricts the vine's ability to extract iron from the soil and therefore causes chlorosis).

HILLS NEAR SANCERRE
In the spring, vineyards give the rolling countryside in France's Loire Valley a speckled appearance. Most soils in the area are dominated by clay or limestone.

GUIDE TO VINEYARD SOILS

To the wine amateur, the details of geology are not always important; what matters is how soil affects the growth of vines. If one clay soil is heavier or more silty, sandy, or calcareous, that is relevant. But there is enough jargon used when discussing wine to think of mixing it with rock-speak.

Acid soil Any soil that has a pH of less than 7 (neutral). Typical acidic soils that are acidic due to their parent rock include brown or reddish-brown, sandy loams or sands, volcanic soils, and any igneous or silicate-rich soil. Neutral soils can become acidic from too much humus or acid rain. Acid soils are low in calcium and magnesium, with negligible amounts of soluble salts and reduced phosphorous availability.

Aeolian soil Sediments deposited by wind (eg, loess).

Albariza White-surfaced soil formed by diatomaceous deposits, found in southern Spain.

Alberese A compact clay and limestone found in the Chianti region.

Albero Synonymous with albariza.

Albian A type of schist found in Maury, Roussillon.

Alkaline soil Any soil that has a pH of more than 7 (neutral). Typical alkaline soils include chalk and any calcareous soils.

Alluvial deposits (noun – alluvium) Material that has been transported by river and deposited. Most alluvial soils contain silt, sand, and gravel and are highly fertile.

Aqueous rocks One of the three basic rock forms (*see* Rock). Also called sedimentary or stratified.

Arenaceous rocks Formed by the deposits of coarse-grained particles, usually siliceous, and often decomposed from older rocks (eg, sandstone).

Arène A coarse, granitic sand ideally suited to the Gamay, arène is found in the Beaujolais region.

Argillaceous soils This term covers a group of sedimentary soils, commonly clays, shales, mudstones, siltstones, and marls.

Argovian marl A chalky, clay-like marl found in many parts of the Côte des Beaune.

Arkose A red, Triassic sandstone consisting of feldspar, quartz, and clay minerals, arkose is often found in the Côtes d'Auvergne and parts of Beaujolais (eg, St-Amour).

Aubuis Found in the Touraine district of the Loire and highly rated for Chenin Blanc in Vouvray and Montlouis, aubuis is a stony mix of permeable, fertile, calcareous clays that are said to be well suited to white grape varieties.

Barro A similar soil to albariza but brown in colour, sandier, and with less diatomaceous content. While Palomino grapes are grown on albariza soil, barro is reserved for Pedro Ximenez grapes.

Basalt material This accounts for as much as 90 per cent of all lava-based volcanic rocks. It contains various minerals, is rich in lime and soda, but not quartz, the most abundant of all minerals, and it is poor in potash.

Bastard soil A *bordelais* name for medium-heavy, sandy-clay soil of variable fertility.

Bauxite As well as being a valuable ore mined for aluminium production, bauxite is found in limestone soils of Coteaux de Baux-de-Provence.

Block-like soil Referring to the soil structure, "block-like" indicates an angular or slanting arrangement of soil particles.

Boulbènes A *bordelais* name for a very fine siliceous soil that is easily compressed and hard to work. This "beaten" earth covers part of the Entre-Deux-Mers plateau.

Boulder *See* Particle size

Calcareous clay Argillaceous soil with carbonate of lime content that neutralizes the clay's intrinsic acidity. Its low temperature also delays ripening, so wines produced on this type of soil tend to be more acidic.

Calcareous soil Any soil, or mixture of soils, with an accumulation of calcium and magnesium carbonates. Essentially alkaline, it promotes the production of acidity in grapes, although the pH of each soil will vary according to its level of "active" lime. Calcareous soils are cool, with good water retention. With the exception of calcareous clays (*see* above), they allow the vine's root system to penetrate deeply and provide excellent drainage.

Carbonaceous soil Soil that is derived from rotting vegetation under anaerobic conditions. The most common carbonaceous soils are peat, lignite, coal, and anthracite.

Chalk A type of limestone, chalk is a soft, cool, porous, brilliant-white, sedimentary, alkaline rock that encourages grapes with a relatively high acidity level. It also allows the vine's roots to penetrate and provides excellent drainage, while at the same time retaining sufficient moisture for nourishment. One of the few finer geological points that should be adhered to is that which distinguishes chalk from the numerous hard limestone rocks that do not possess the same physical properties.

Clay A fine-grained argillaceous compound with malleable, plastic characteristics and excellent water-retention properties. It is, however, cold, acid, offers poor drainage, and, because of its cohesive quality, is hard to work. An excess of clay can stifle the vine's root system, but a proportion of small clay particles mixed with other soils can be advantageous.

Clayey-loam A very fertile version of loam, but heavy to work under wet conditions, with a tendency to become waterlogged.

Cobble *See* Particle size

Colluvial deposits (noun – colluvium) Weathered material transported by gravity or hill-wash.

CHALK
Pristine white chalk on the Côtes des Blancs.

Crasse de fer Iron-rich hard-pan found in the Libournais area of France. Also called *machefer*.

Crystalline May be either igneous (eg, granite) or metamorphic.

Dolomite A calcium-magnesium carbonate rock. Many limestones contain dolomite.

Entroques Type of hard limestone found in Burgundy (eg, Montagny).

Feldspar or **Felspar** One of the most common minerals, feldspar is a white- or rose-coloured silicate of either potassium-aluminium or sodium-calcium-aluminium and is present in a number of rocks, including granite and basalt.

Ferruginous clay Iron-rich clay.

Flint A siliceous stone that stores and reflects heat and is often associated with a certain "gun-flint" smell that sometimes occurs in wines, although this is not actually proven and may simply be the taster's auto-suggestion.

Gabbro A dark, coarse-grained igneous rock found in Muscadet.

Galestro Rocky, schistous clay soil commonly found in most of Tuscany's best vineyards.

Glacial moraine A gritty scree that has been deposited by glacial action.

Gore A pinkish, decomposed, granitic arenaceous soil found in Beaujoalais, St Joseph, and Côtes Roannaise.

Gneiss A coarse-grained form of granite.

Granite A hard, mineral-rich rock that warms quickly and retains its heat. Granite contains 40 to 60 per cent quartz and 30 to 40 per cent potassium feldspar, plus mica or hornblende, and various other minerals. It has a high pH that reduces wine acidity. Thus, in Beaujolais, it is the best soil for the acidic Gamay grape. It is important to note that a soil formed from granite is a mixture of sand (partly derived from a disintegration of quartz and partly from the decomposition of feldspar with either mica or hornblende), clay, and various carbonates or silicates derived from the weathering of feldspar, mica, or hornblende.

Gravel A wide-ranging term that covers siliceous pebble of various sizes that are loose, granular, airy, and afford excellent drainage. Infertile, it encourages the vine to send its roots down deep in search of nutrients. Gravel beds above limestone subsoils produce wines with markedly more acidity than those above clay.

Greensand A dark greenish coloured, glauconite-rich sand of Cretaceous origin found in some vineyards in southeast England. Greensand is used as a water softener, which is ironic considering that it is found over chalk subsoil, known for its hard water.

Greywacke Argillaceous rocks that could have been formed as recently as a few thousand years ago by rivers depositing mudstone, quartz, and feldspar. Commonly found in Germany, South Africa, and New Zealand.

Gypsum Highly absorbent, hydrated calcium-sulphate that was formed during the evaporation of sea-water.

Gypsiferous marl A marly soil permeated with Keuper or Muschelkalk gypsum fragments, which improve the soil's heat-retention and water-circulation properties.

Hard-pan A dense layer of clay that forms if the subsoil is more clayey than the topsoil at certain depths. As hard-pans are impermeable to both water and roots, they are not desirable too close to the surface but may provide an easily reachable water-table if located deep down. A sandy, iron-rich hard-pan known as iron-pan is commonly found in parts of Bordeaux.

GRAVEL
Château de France, Léognan, Gironde.

Hornblende A silicate of iron, aluminium, calcium, and magnesium, it constitutes the main mineral found in basalt and is a major component of granite and gneiss.

Humus Organic material that contains bacteria and other micro-organisms that are capable of converting complex chemicals into simple plant foods. Humus makes soil fertile; without it, soil is nothing more than finely ground rock.

Igneous rock One of the three basic rock forms (*see* Rock), igneous rocks are formed from molten or partially molten material. Most igneous rocks are crystalline.

Iron-pan A sandy, iron-rich hard-pan.

Jory A volcanic soil, primarily basalt, which is in turn a hard and dense soil that often has a glassy appearance. One of the two primary soil types found in Oregon's Willamette Valley, particularly on the lower foothills, such as the Dundee Hills, where Pinot Noir excels.

Keuper Often used when discussing wines in Alsace, Keuper is a stratigraphic name for the Upper Triassic period and can mean marl (varicoloured, saliferous grey, or gypsiferous grey) or limestone (ammonoid).

Kimmeridgian soil A greyish-coloured limestone originally identified in, and so named after, the village of Kimmeridge in Dorset, England. A sticky, calcareous clay containing this limestone is often called Kimmeridgian clay.

Lacustrine limestone A freshwater limestone that forms at the bottom of lakes. Lacustrine-limestone soils have been found on Pelee Island and the Niagara district of Ontario, Yakima Valley in Washington, and Quincy in the Loire Valley.

Lignite The "brown coal" of Germany and the "black gold" of Champagne, this is a brown carbonaceous material intermediate between coal and peat. Warm and very fertile, it is mined and used as a natural fertilizer in Champagne.

Limestone Any sedimentary rock consisting essentially of carbonates. With the exception of chalk, few limestones are white, with grey- and buff-coloured probably the most commonly found limestone in wine areas. The hardness and water retention of this rock vary, but being alkaline it generally encourages the production of grapes with a relatively high acidity level.

Loam A warm, soft, crumbly soil with roughly equal proportions of clay, sand, and silt. It is perfect for large-cropping mediocre-quality wines but too fertile for fine wines.

Loess An accumulation of wind-borne, mainly silty material, that is sometimes calcareous but usually weathered and decalcified. It warms up relatively quickly and also has good water-retention properties.

Machefer *See* **Crasse de fer**

Macigno Hard grey-blue sandstone found in the Chianti region.

Marl A cold, calcareous clay-like soil (usually 50 per cent clay content) that delays ripening and adds acidity to wine.

Marlstone Clayey limestone that has a similar effect to marl.

Metamorphic rocks One of the three basic categories of rock (*see* Rock), this is caused by great heat or pressure, often both.

Mica A generic name encompassing various silicate minerals, usually in a fine, decomposed-rock format.

Millstone Siliceous, iron-rich, sedimentary rock.

Moraine *See* Glacial moraine

Mudstone A sedimentary soil similar to clay but without its plastic characteristics.

Muschelkalk Often used when discussing wines in Alsace, Muschelkalk is a stratigraphic name for the Middle Triassic period and can mean anything from sandstone (shelly, dolomitic, calcareous, clayey, pink, yellow, or millstone) to marl (varicoloured or fissile), dolomite, limestone (crinoidal or grey), and shingle.

Oolite A type of limestone.

Oolith A term used for small, round, calcareous pebbles that have grown through fusion of very tiny particles.

Palus A *bordelais* name for a very fertile soil of modern alluvial origin that produces medium-quality, well-coloured, robust wines.

Particle size The size of a rock determines its descriptive name. No handful of soil will contain particles of a uniform size, unless it has been commercially graded, of course, so all such descriptions can only be guesstimates, but it is worth noting what they should be, otherwise you will have nothing to base your guesstimates on. According to the Wentworth-Udden scale, they are: boulder (greater than 256mm), cobble (64mm–256mm), pebble (4mm–64mm), gravel (2mm–4mm), sand (1/16mm–2mm), silt (1/256mm–1/16mm) and clay (smaller than 1/256mm). Notice that even by this precise scale, Wentworth and Udden have allowed overlaps, thus a 1/16mm particle might either be sand or silt and, of course, sub-divisions are possible within each group, as there is such a thing as fine, medium, or coarse sand and even gritty silt.

Pebble *See* Particle size

Pelite Fine-grained clayey-quartz sedimentary rock found in Banyuls.

Peperite Limestone or marly rock found on Madeira and along Idaho's Snake River Valley that has been ejected by volcanic activity and is literally "peppered" with tiny peppercorn-like grains of basalt.

Perlite A fine, powdery, light, and lustrous substance of volcanic origin with similar properties to diatomaceous earth.

Perruches Very stony, flinty clays combined with silica, perruches soils warm up quickly and are said to be why Sauvignon Blanc grown on them have a flinty taste.

Phtanite Dark-coloured sedimentary rock bearing stratas of quartz crystals, found in Savennières and Coteaux du Layon

Platy soil Referring to the soil structure, "platy" indicates a horizontal alignment of soil particles.

Porphyry A coloured igneous rock with high pH.

Precipitated salts A sedimentary deposit. Water charged with acid or alkaline material, under pressure of great depth, dissolves various mineral substances from rocks on the sea-bed, which are then held in solution. When the water flows to a place of no great depth or is drained away or evaporates, the pressure is reduced, the minerals are no longer held in solution and precipitate in deposits that may be just a few centimetres or several thousand metres deep. There are five groups: oxides, carbonates, sulphates, phosphates, and chlorides.

Prism-like soil Referring to the soil structure, "prism-like" indicates a columnar or vertical arrangement of soil particles.

Pudding stones A term used for a large, heat-retaining conglomerate of pebbles.

Quartz The most common and abundant mineral, quartz is the crystalline form of silica. It is found in various sizes and in almost all soils, although sand and coarse silt contain the largest amount. Quartz has a high pH, which reduces wine acidity, but quartz that is pebble-sized or larger, stores and reflects heat, which increases alcohol potential.

Red earth *See* Terra rossa

Rock A rock may be loosely described as a mass of mineral matter. There are three basic types of rock: igneous, metamorphic, and sedimentary (or aqueous or stratified).

Ruedas Red sandy-limestone soil found in the Montilla-Moriles region of Spain.

Ruffe A fine-grained, brilliant-red sandstone soil rich in iron-oxide, ruffe is found in parts of the Languedoc region of France, particulary the Vin de Pays des Coteaux de Salagou.

Safres A sandy-marl found in the southern Rhône Valley.

Saibro A decomposed red tufa soil that is highly regarded in Madeira.

Sand Tiny particles of weathered rocks and minerals that retain little water but constitute a warm, airy soil that drains well and is supposedly phylloxera-free.

Sandstone Sedimentary rock composed of sand-sized particles that have either been formed by pressure or bound by various iron minerals.

Sandy-loam Warm, well-drained, sand-dominated loam that is easy to work and suitable for early-cropping grape varieties.

Schist Heat-retaining, coarse-grain, laminated, crystalline rock that is rich in potassium and magnesium but poor in nitrogen and organic substances.

Scree Synonymous with colluvium deposits.

Sedimentary rock One of the three basic rock forms (*see* Rock), it includes arenaceous (eg, sandstone), argillaceous (eg, clay), calcareous (eg, limestone), carbonaceous (eg, peat, lignite, or coal), siliceous (eg, quartz), and the five groups of precipitated salts, (oxides, carbonates, sulphates, phosphates, and chlorides). Sedimentary rocks are also called aqueous or stratified.

Shale Heat-retaining, fine-grain, laminated, moderately fertile sedimentary rock. Shale can turn into slate under pressure.

Shingle Pebble- or gravel-sized particle rounded by water-action.

Siliceous soil A generic term for acid rock of a crystalline nature. It may be organic (such as flint) or inorganic (quartz) and have good heat retention, but no water retention unless found in a finely ground form in silt, clay, and other sedimentary soils. Half of the Bordeaux region is covered with siliceous soils.

Silt A very fine deposit, with good water retention. Silt is more fertile than sand but is cold and offers poor drainage.

Slate Hard, often dark grey (but can be any colour between brown and bluish grey), fine-grain, plate-like rock formed under pressure from clay, siltstone, shale, and other sediments. It warms up quickly, retains its heat well, and is responsible for many fine wines, most notably from the Mosel.

Slaty-schist A sort of half-formed slate created under lower temperature and pressure than fully formed slate.

Spiroidal soil Referring to the soil structure, "spiroidal" indicates a granular or crumb-like composition of soil particles.

Steige A type of schist found on the north side of Andlau in Alsace, it has metamorphosed with the Andlau granite and is particularly hard and slaty. It has mixed with the granitic sand from the top of the Grand Cru Kastelberg and makes a dark, stony soil.

Stone This word should be used with rock types, such as limestone and sandstone, but is often used synonymously with pebble.

Stratified rock One of the three basic rock forms (*see* Rock); also called sedimentary or aqueous.

Terra rossa A red, clay-like, sometimes flinty sedimentary soil that is deposited after carbonate has been leached out of limestone. It is often known as "red earth".

Terres blanche Steep Kimmeridgian marls in Sancerre.

Tufa A limestone concretion that forms via water dripping through gaps in limestone, tufa is typical of the soil of Orvieto, Umbria, and is also found in Montalcino, Tuscany, as well as the Langhe region of Piedmont.

Tuff Rocks formed by fractured or water-bound material ejected by volcanic activity, tuff drains well and is found in Taburno, Campania, in Italy; Balatonfüred-Csopak, Balatonfelvidék and Balatonboglár around Lake Balaton in Hungary; and the Galilee region of Israel, particularly Upper Galilee and the Golan Heights.

Tuffau A buff-coloured, sandstone-rich, otherwise chalky limestone as found in the Loire, particularly around Touraine, and used in the construction of many of its châteaux.

Volcanic soils Derived from two sources, volcanic soils are lava-based (the products of volcanic flow) and vent-based (material blown into the atmosphere). Some 90 per cent of lava-based rocks and soils are comprised of basalt, while others include andesite, pitchstone, rhyolite, and trachyte. Vent-based matter has either been ejected as molten globules, cooled in the air, and dropped to earth as solid particles (pumice), or as solid material and fractured through the explosive force with which it was flung (tuff).

Willakenzie A silty clay-loam colluvium, this is one of the two primary soil types found in Oregon's Willamette Valley.

TERRA ROSSA
The red soil of Wynns, Coonawarra, South Australia.

VITICULTURE AND VINIFICATION

WINEMAKERS GET ALL THE GLORY, but their success depends on the grapes they use. Vinification is an art and a science, but it is the art and science of damage limitation. Viticulture is all about preparation and providing the potential, which is why those who control the vineyards of successful wines are the true wine heroes.

It is always possible to raise the quality in the vineyard, often by a significant amount, but once the grapes are harvested, the potential of the wine is capped and cannot be raised. The winemaker's job is, therefore, one of containment and, when things do not go right, mounting a search-and-rescue mission. As the late Johnny Hugel once put it, "As soon as the grape is removed from the vine, it is exposed to the air, the clock starts ticking, and the winemaker's job becomes a race against time."

In the ideal domaine, where the grapes are carefully picked by hand, placed into small trays to prevent them from being crushed under their own weight, and the vines are close enough to the winery that all the trays are delivered to the press house within an hour (which is highly unlikely), the winemaker is already dealing with grapes that have effectively started to deteriorate. Even in a perfectly run ideal winery, the grapes probably represent no more than 95–97 per cent of their potential at the time of picking, and the most talented winemakers on earth would struggle to make a wine that goes into the bottle at anything close to 90 per cent, with most wines much closer to 80 per cent. By comparison, it is relatively easy to double the potential quality in the vineyard through the choice of grape variety and/or specific clones of that grape variety, the choice of rootstock, where the vines are planted, the planting density, how the vines are pruned and cared for, and when and how they are harvested. Instead of struggling to produce a 90 per cent potential wine, after improvements in the vineyard, a few years later the winemaker could put his or her feet up and churn out something closer to the equivalent of 180 per cent of the quality he or she used to deliver.

While it is the variety of grape that determines the basic flavour of a wine, it is the way the variety is grown that has the most profound effect on the quality of the wine.

VINE TRAINING

In vine training, it is absolutely crucial to ensure that no cane ever touches the ground. Should a cane find its way to the ground, its natural inclination is to send out suckers that will put down roots.

WITHIN TWO OR THREE YEARS the majority of the grafted vine's above-ground network would be dependent not upon grafted roots, but upon the regenerated root system of the producing vine. Not only would this have the effect of putting

the vine at the mercy of phylloxera, but, ironically, that part of the vine still receiving its principal nourishment from the grafted hybrid rootstock would send out its own shoots and, unchecked by any sort of pruning, these would produce hybrid fruit. Therefore, the fundamental reason for training and pruning a vine is to avoid phylloxera and to ensure that the purity of the fruiting stock is maintained.

The manner in which a vine is trained will guide the size, shape, and height of the plant towards reaping maximum benefits from the local conditions of aspect and climate. Vines can be trained high to avoid ground frost, or low to hug any heat that may be reflected by stony soils at night. There may be a generous amount of space between rows to attract the sun and avoid humidity. On the other hand, vines may be intensively cultivated to form a canopy of foliage to avoid too much sun.

STYLES OF VINE TRAINING

Within the two basic systems of cane training and spur training, hundreds of different styles are employed, each developed for a reason, and all having their own advantages and disadvantages. In order to discern the style used in a particular vineyard, it is always best to look at the vines between late autumn and early spring when the branches are not camouflaged with leaves. In the illustrations below, which are not drawn to scale, vines are shown as they appear during their winter dormancy, with the following season's fruiting canes shown in green. For cane-trained systems, a green-brown tint has been used to pick out the one-year-old wood used as next season's main branch.

Bush vine – *Spur-training system*

An unsupported version of the Gobelet system (*see below left*), the term "bush vine" originated in Australia, where a few old vineyards – usually planted with Grenache – are still trained in this fashion. Bush vines are traditional in Beaujolais (where both supported and unsupported methods are referred to as Gobelet) and they are commonly found throughout the most arid areas of the Mediterranean. Being unsupported, the canes often flop downwards when laden with fruit, giving the vine a sprawling, straggly look. In the Beaujolais *crus*, the total number of canes on a vine is restricted to between three and five, but in other, less controlled, wine areas a Bush Vine may have as many as 10 canes. This method is only suitable for training low-vigour vines.

Chablis – *Spur-training system*

As the name implies, this style of vine training was originally developed in the Chablis district, although the method employed there now is, in fact, the Guyot Double. Champagne is the most important winemaking region to employ the Chablis system for training vines; there, it is used for more than 90 per cent of all the Chardonnay grown. Either three, four, or five permanent branches may be cultivated, each one being grown at yearly intervals. This results in a three-year-old vine (the minimum age for AOC Champagne) having three branches, a four-year-old having four branches, and so forth. The distance between each

---

BASIC SYSTEMS OF VINE TRAINING

There are two basic systems of vine training: cane training and spur training, of which there are many local variations. Cane-trained vines have no permanent branch because all but one of the strongest canes (which will be kept for next season's main branch) are pruned back each year to provide a vine consisting of almost entirely new growth. Apart from the trunk, the oldest wood on a cane-trained vine is the main branch and that is only ever one year old. This system gives a good spread of fruit over a large area, and allows easier regulation of annual production, because the number of fruiting buds can be increased or decreased. With spur training there is no annual replacement of the main branch, thus a solid framework is formed. It is easy, therefore, to know which basic training system has been applied to a vine simply by looking at the main branch. Even if you cannot recognize the specific style of training, if the main branch is thin and smooth, you will know that it has been cane trained, whereas if it is thick, dark, and gnarled, it has been spur trained.

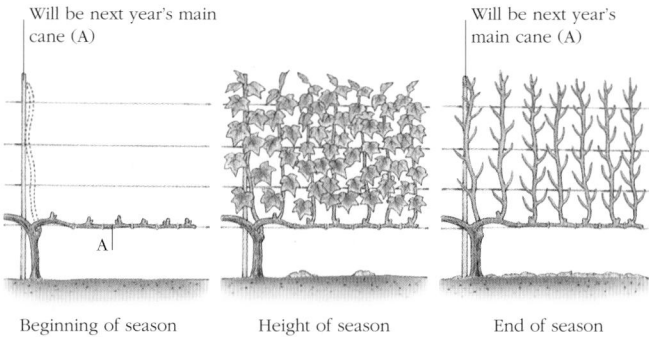

Will be next year's main cane (A)   Will be next year's main cane (A)

Beginning of season   Height of season   End of season

GUYOT – AN EXAMPLE OF CANE TRAINING
In the winter, the main horizontal cane is cut off and the spare cane (A) is bent horizontally to be tied to the bottom wire, where it will become next season's main cane. Another shoot close to the trunk will be allowed to grow as next season's spare cane.

Beginning of season   Height of season   End of season

GOBELET – AN EXAMPLE OF SPUR TRAINING
The main canes on a spur-trained vine are all permanent, and will only be replaced if they are damaged. Only the year-old shoots are pruned back.

vine in the same row determines the eventual life of the oldest branch because, when it encroaches upon the next vine, it is removed and a new one cultivated from a bud on the main trunk.

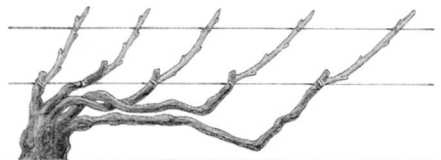

The Chablis spur-training system is, in effect, little more than a slanting bush vine unsupported by a central post.

Cordon de Royat - *Spur-training system*
This is to Champagne's Pinot Noir what the Chablis system is to its Chardonnay and is nothing more complicated than a spur-trained version of Guyot Simple (*see below*). There is even a double variant, although this is rarely cultivated purely for its own ends, its primary reason for existence being to replace a missing vine on its blind side. When, after their winter pruning, they are silhouetted against the sky, Cordon de Royat vines look very much like columns of gnarled old

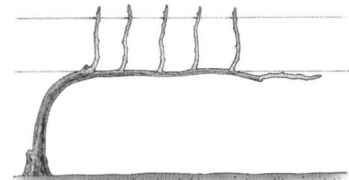

men in perfect formation; they all face forward, bent almost double, as if with one arm dug into the pit of the back and the other seeking the support of a stick.

Geneva Double Curtain
- *Spur-training system*
This downward-growing, split-canopy system was developed by Professor Nelson Shaulis of the Geneva Experimental Station in New York state in the early 1960s to increase the volume and ripening of locally grown Concord grapes. Since then, GDC, as it is often referred to, has been adopted all over the world (particularly in Italy). However, unlike Concord varieties, classic *vinifera* vines have an upward-growing tendency, which makes the system more difficult to apply. Successful results are obtained by shoot positioning, which can either be accomplished via a movable wire (as in Scott Henry, *see opposite*), by hand, or even by machine. Yields from GDC are 50 per cent higher than those from the standard VSP trellis (*see opposite*), and the system offers increased protection from frosts (due to height above ground). It is ideal for full mechanization of medium- to high-vigour vineyards on deep fertile soils (low-vigour vines do not benefit).

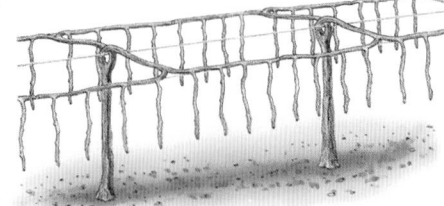

Guyot - *Cane-training system*
Developed by Jules Guyot in 1860, both the double and simple forms shown here represent the most conservative style of cane training possible. It is the least complicated concept for growers to learn and, providing the number of fruiting canes and the number of buds on them are restricted, Guyot is the easiest means of restraining yields. Even when growers abuse the system, it is still the most difficult vine-training method with which to pump up production. This system is commonly

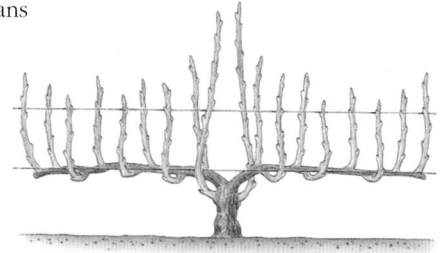

used in Bordeaux, where the number of canes and buds are restricted by AOC rules (although, like most French bureaucratic systems, much depends on self-regulation – I have never seen an INAO inspector in the middle of a vineyard checking the variety of vines or counting them, let alone counting the number of canes or buds on canes!). Guyot is also used for some of the finest wines throughout the winemaking world, both Old and New.

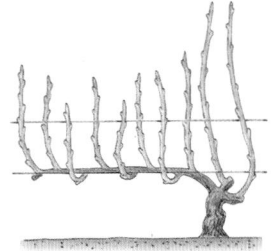

Lyre - *Spur-training system*
Also known as the "U" system, the canopy is divided, so as to allow a better penetration of light (thereby improving ripeness levels) and air (thereby reducing the incidence of cryptogamic disorders). Although it was developed in Bordeaux, the Lyre system is more common in the New World, where vine vigour is a problem, although not a major one. As with all split-canopy systems, the Lyre method is of no use whatsoever for low-vigour vineyards. Some growers have successfully adapted Lyre to cane training.

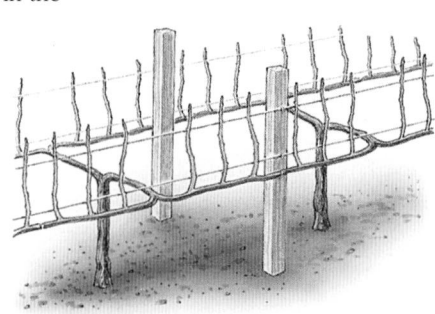

Minimal Pruning - *Spur-training system*
A wild, unruly mass that contains a central thicket of unpruned dead wood, which by definition has no disciplined form and is therefore impossible to illustrate. Some of the central thicket may be mechanically removed in the winter, but will still be a tangled mass. Initially, several canes are wrapped loosely around a wire, either side of the trunk, about 1.5 to 2 metres (5 to 6 feet) off the ground. The vine is then left to its own devices, although if necessary some of the summer shoots will be trimmed to keep the fruit off the ground. Some growers give up quite quickly because yields can initially be alarmingly high and as the volume increases, so the quality noticeably deteriorates. However, if they are patient, the vine eventually achieves a natural balance, reducing the length of its shoots and, consequently, the number of fruiting nodes on them. Although mature minimally pruned vines continue to give fairly high yields, the quality begins to improve after two or three years. By the sixth or seventh year the quality is usually significantly superior to the quality achieved before minimal pruning was introduced – and the quantity is substantially greater. The ripening time needed by the grapes also increases, which can be an advantage in a hot climate, but disastrous in a cool one, particularly if it is also wet. Furthermore, after a number of years, the mass of old wood in the central thicket and the split-ends of machine-pruned cane ends surrounding it can make the vine vulnerable to various pests and diseases, especially rot and mildew, which is why minimally pruned vines in wet areas like New Zealand are more heavily pruned than they are in the hotter areas of Australia – such as Coonawarra and Padthaway – where minimal pruning first emerged and is still used to great effect.

Pendelbogen - *Cane-training system*
Also known as the "European Loop", or "Arc-Cane Training", this vine-training system, which is a variant of the Guyot Double (*see left*), is most popular in Switzerland and the flatter Rhine Valley areas of Germany and Alsace, although it can also be found in

Mâcon, British Columbia, and Oregon. By bending the canes in an arch, Pendelbogen has more fruit-bearing shoots than the Guyot Double system, thereby providing higher yields. The arching does promote better sap distribution, which helps the production of more fruit, but it can also reduce ripeness levels, making the prime motive for adopting Pendelbogen one of economy, not of quality.

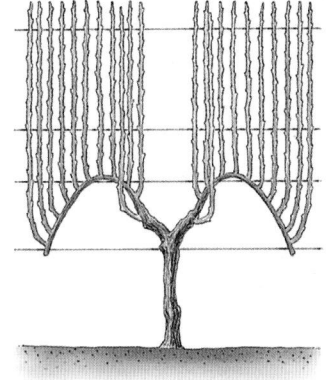

Scott Henry – *Cane-training system*

Developed by Scott Henry at the Scott Henry Vineyard in Oregon, this system effectively doubles the fruiting area provided by Guyot Double. It also offers a 60 per cent increase in fruiting area over the standard VSP Trellis system (*see right*). Scott Henry not only provides larger crops, but riper, better quality fruit – and because the canopy is split and, therefore, less dense, the wines are less herbaceous, with smoother tannins. Increased yields and increased quality may seem unlikely, but Kim Goldwater of Waiheke Island has records to prove it; and as Goldwater Estate is consistently one of New Zealand's best red wines, that is good enough for me. When I have asked growers who have tried the Scott Henry method why they have given it up, they invariably reply "Have you ever tried to grow vine shoots downwards? It doesn't work!". However, the downward-growing shoots actually grow upwards for most of the season. They are separated from the other upward-growing shoots by a moveable wire that levers half the canopy into a downwards position. The secret of this system's success is to move the wire no earlier than two or three weeks before the harvest, which gives the canes no time to revert and, with the increasing weight of the fruit, no inclination. In areas where grazing animals coexist with vines (as sheep do in New Zealand, for instance), the fact that both halves of the canopy are a metre (two feet) or so above the ground most of the time allows under-vine weeds and water-shoots to be controlled without herbicides or manual labour, without fear of the crop being eaten in the process. Scott Henry is found mainly in the New World and is becoming increasingly popular.

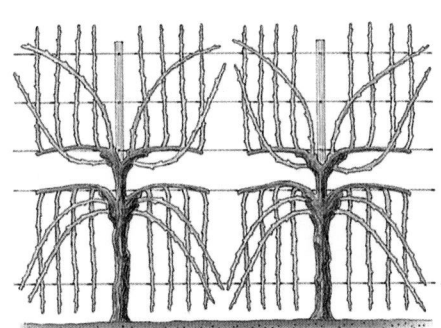

Scott Henry – *Spur-training system*

When the Scott Henry cane-training system is adapted to spur training, each vine has two permanent spurs instead of four annual canes and produces either top canopies or bottom canopies, but not both. The vines are pruned at alternating heights to replicate the effect of cane training, and all canopies grow upwards until

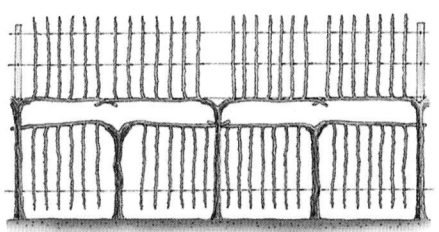

those on the lower vines are eventually levered downwards to the position shown here. The detailed structure of the Scott Henry system is almost impossible to identify when the vines are shrouded in foliage.

Sylvos – *Spur-training system*

This is like Guyot Double, only the trunk is much longer – up to 2 metres (6 feet) – the main branches are permanent, and the fruiting canes are tied downwards, not upwards. Sylvos requires minimal pruning and is simple to maintain, lending itself to mechanization, but yields are low, unless pruned very lightly. *Vinifera* varieties do not like being forced downwards, but shoot positioning has been introduced by growers in Australia (where it is called "Hanging Cane") and New Zealand. The system was originally conceived by Carlo Sylvos in Italy, where it is still very popular and is sometimes operated without a bottom wire, the canes falling downwards under their own weight. The main disadvantage is the dense canopy, which makes the vines prone to bunch-rot.

Sylvos (Hawke's Bay variant) – *Spur-training system*

This version of the Sylvos system was developed by Gary Wood of Montana Wines in the early 1980s on a Hawke's Bay vineyard belonging to Mark Read. The difference between this and the similar Scott Henry system is that it has two main spurs instead of four. With alternate fruiting canes on the same spur trained upwards then downwards, the canopy is more open, and grape clusters are farther apart. This reduces bunch-rot significantly and facilitates better spray penetration. Yields are increased by as much as 100 per cent. The only disadvantage is the longer ripening time needed, which is a risk in areas where late harvests have their dangers.

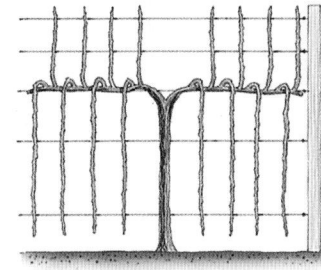

VSP Trellis – *Cane-training system*

The VSP or Vertical Shoot Positioned trellis is widely used, particularly in New Zealand, where it is commonly referred to as the "standard" trellising system. With the fruiting area contained within one compact zone on wires of a narrow span, it is ideally suited to mechanized forms of pruning, leaf removal, harvesting, and spraying, but it is prone to high vigour and shading. This is a very economic method and, when properly maintained, it is capable of producing good (but not top) quality wines. VSP is only suitable for low-vigour vines. A spur-trained version with just two main spurs is commonly encountered in France and Germany.

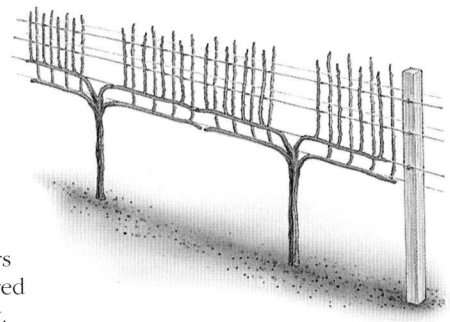

VITICULTURAL SPRAYS

The use of sprays was once confined to protecting the vine against pests and diseases and for controlling weeds, but they now have additional uses. Foliar feeds supply nutrients direct to the vine, while other sprays halt the growth of foliage, rendering summer pruning unnecessary. Some sprays deliberately induce two disorders called *millerandage* and *coulure* to reduce the yield and, hopefully, increase the quality.

ANNUAL LIFE-CYCLE OF THE VINE

The calendar of events by which any well-established vine seeks to reproduce, through the production of grapes, is outlined below, with a commentary on *how the vine is cultivated to encourage the best grapes for winemaking. The vine's year starts and finishes with the end and approach of winter.*

FEBRUARY Northern hemisphere
AUGUST Southern hemisphere

1. Weeping

Weeping is the first sign of the vine awakening after a winter of relative dormancy. When the soil at a depth of 25 centimetres (10 inches) reaches 10.2°C (50°F), the roots start collecting water and the sap in the vine rises, oozing out of the cane ends which were pruned in winter, in a manifestation called "weeping". This occurs suddenly, rapidly increases in intensity, and then decreases gradually. Each vine loses between half and five-and-a-half litres (10 pints) of sap. Weeping is the signal to prune for the spring growth. However, this poses a problem for the grower because the

As the soil warms up the vine awakes, pushing sap out of its cane ends.

vine, once pruned, is at its most vulnerable to frost. But waiting for the danger of frost to pass wastes the vine's preciously finite energy and retards its growth, delaying the ripening of the fruit by as much as 10 days, and thus risking exposure of the fruit to autumn frosts later on.

MARCH to APRIL Northern hemisphere
SEPTEMBER to OCTOBER Southern hemisphere

2. Bud-break

In the spring, some 20 to 30 days after the vine starts to weep, the buds open. Different varieties bud-break at different times; there are early bud-breakers and the same variety can bud-break at different times in different years due to climatic changes. The type of soil can also affect the timing; clay, which is cold, will retard the process, while sand, which is warm, will promote it. Early bud-break varieties are susceptible to frost in northerly vineyards (southerly in the southern hemisphere), just as late-ripeners are vulnerable

Buds begin to open at a time determined by variety and climate.

to autumn frosts. In the vineyard, pruning continues into March (September in the southern hemisphere). The vines are secured to their training frames, and the earth that was ploughed over the grafting wound to protect it in the winter is ploughed back, aerating the soil and levelling off the ground between the rows.

APRIL to MAY Northern hemisphere
OCTOBER to NOVEMBER Southern hemisphere

3. Emergence of shoots, foliage, and embryo bunches

Following bud-break, foliage develops and shoots are sent out. In mid-April (mid-October in the southern hemisphere), after the fourth or fifth leaf has emerged, tiny green clusters form. These are the flowers which, when they bloom, will develop into grapes. Commonly called embryo bunches, they are the first indication of the potential size of a crop. In the vineyard, spraying to ward off various vine pests, or cure diseases and other disorders, starts in May (November), and continues until the harvest. Many of these sprays are combined with systemic

Embryo bunches, the vine's flowers, form.

fertilizers to feed the vine directly through its foliage. These spraying operations are normally done by hand or tractor, but may sometimes be carried out by helicopter if the slopes are very steep or the vineyards too muddy to enter. At this time of year the vine can be affected by *coulure* or *millerandage* (see p16).

MAY to JUNE Northern hemisphere
NOVEMBER to DECEMBER Southern hemisphere

4. Flowering of the vine

The embryo bunches break into flower after the 15th or 16th leaf has emerged on the vine. This is normally about eight weeks after the bud-break and involves pollination and fertilization, and lasts for about 10 days. The weather must be dry and frost-free, but temperature is the most critical requirement. A daily average of at least 15°C (59°F) is needed to enable a vine to flower and between 20° and 25°C (68° and 77°F) is considered ideal. Heat summation, however, is more important than temperature levels, so the length of day

The 10 days in which the vine flowers is a vulnerable period.

has a great influence on the number of days the flowering will last. Soil temperature is more significant than air temperature, so the soil's heat-retaining capacity is a contributory factor. Frost is the greatest hazard, and many vineyards are protected by stoves or sprinkling systems.

JUNE to JULY Northern hemisphere
DECEMBER to JANUARY Southern hemisphere

5. Fruit set

After the flowering, the embryo bunches rapidly evolve into true clusters. Each fertilized berry expands into a grape, the first visible sign of the actual fruit that will produce the wine. This is called fruit set. The number of grapes per embryo bunch varies from variety to variety, as does the percentage that actually set into grapes. The panel below illustrates this. In the vineyard, spraying continues and summer pruning (cutting away some bunches) will concentrate the vine's energy on making fruit. In

Clearly recognizable grapes begin to form.

some vineyards this is the time for weeding, but in others the weeds are allowed to grow as high as 50 centimetres (20 inches) before they are mown and ploughed into the soil to break up the soil and provide the vines with excellent green manure.

VARIETY	BERRIES PER EMBRYO BUNCH	GRAPES IN A RIPE CLUSTER	PERCENTAGE OF FRUIT SET
Chasselas	164	48	29%
Gewürztraminer	100	40	40%
Pinot Gris	149	41	28%
Riesling	189	61	32%
Sylvaner	95	50	53%

AUGUST Northern hemisphere
JANUARY Southern hemisphere

6. Ripening of the grapes

As the grape develops its fleshy fruit, very little chemical change takes place inside the berry until its skin begins to turn a different colour – the process known as *véraison*. Throughout the grape's green stage, the sugar and acid content remains the same, but during August (January in the southern hemisphere), the ripening process begins in earnest – the skin changes colour, the sugar content dramatically increases, and the hard malic acid diminishes as the riper tartaric acid builds up. Although the tartaric acid

The grapes begin to change colour – the sign of true ripening.

content begins to decline after about two weeks, it always remains the primary acid. It is at this stage that the grape's tannins are gradually hydrolysed. This is a crucial moment because only hydrolysed tannins are capable of softening as a wine matures. In the vineyard, spraying and weeding continue, and the vine's foliage is thinned to facilitate the circulation of air and thus reduce the risk of rot. Care must be taken not to remove too much foliage as it is the effect of sunlight upon the leaves, not the grapes, that causes the grapes to ripen.

AUGUST to OCTOBER Northern hemisphere
FEBRUARY to MARCH Southern hemisphere

7. Grape harvest

Grapes are picked at a time determined by the winemaker.

The harvest usually begins mid- to late September (mid- to late February in the southern hemisphere) and may last for a month or more, but, as is the case with all vineyard operations, the timing is earlier nearer to the equator and is dependent on the weather. Picking may, therefore, start as early as August (February) and finish as late as November (April). White grapes ripen before black grapes and must, in any case, be harvested a little bit earlier to achieve a higher acidity balance.

NOVEMBER to DECEMBER Northern hemisphere
APRIL to MAY Southern hemisphere

8. Grapes affected by Botrytis cinerea

These rotting grapes are soon to be harvested for sweet botrytized wine.

In November the sap retreats to the protection of the vine's root system. As a result, the year-old canes begin to harden and any remaining grapes, cut off from the vine's metabolic system, start to dehydrate. The concentrated pulp that they become is subject to severe cold. This induces complex chemical changes in a process known as *passerillage*. In specialized sweet-wine areas the grapes are deliberately left on the vine to undergo this quality-enhancing experience and, in certain vineyards with suitable climatic conditions, growers pray for the appearance of *Botrytis cinerea*, or "noble rot".

DECEMBER to JANUARY Northern hemisphere
MAY to JUNE Southern hemisphere

9. Eiswein

Grapes that are still on the vine may yet become wine.

In Germany, it is possible to see grapes on the vine in December and even January. This is usually because the grower has hoped for *Botrytis cinerea*, or *Edelfäule* as it is called in Germany, but it has failed to occur on some grapes. Should frost or snow freeze the grapes, they can be harvested to produce *Eiswein*, one of the world's most spectacular wines. As it is only the water that freezes, this can be skimmed off once the grapes are pressed in order to leave a super-concentrated unfrozen pulp that produces *Eiswein*.

HARVESTING AND PRESSING

When to pick is one of the most crucial decisions a grower has to make each year. It varies according to the grape variety, the location of the vineyard, and the style of wine that is to be made.

MULTIPLE OPTIONS
The Willmes Sigma press can be hermetically sealed for maceration, micro-oxygenation, or inert-gas operation.

WHITE WINE GENERALLY BENEFITS from the extra acidity of earlier harvested grapes, but they also need the varietal aroma and richness that can only be found in ripe grapes. It is essential to get the balance right. Red wine requires relatively less acidity, although it is still important, and profits from the increased colour, sugar, and tannin content of later harvested grapes.

Growers must also take the vagaries of the weather into account. Those who have the nerve to wait for perfectly ripe grapes every year can produce exceptional wines in even the poorest vintages, but they also run the risk of frost, rot, or hail damage, which can totally destroy an entire year's income. Those who never take a chance may harvest healthy grapes, but in poor years they risk an unripe crop and mediocre wine.

MECHANICAL HARVESTING
The subject of mechanical harvesting is a contentious one. The advantages of mechanization are dramatically reduced labour costs and a quick harvest of the entire crop at optimum ripeness, but the vineyard has to be adapted to the machine chosen, and the reception and fermentation facilities must be enlarged to cope with the greater amounts and quicker throughput, which is costly. Disadvantages relate to compacting the soil, the efficiency of the machinery, and the quality of the wine.

As the machines beat the vine trunks with rubber sticks, the grapes drop onto a conveyor along with leaves and other matter, most of which is ejected as the fruit is sorted on its way to the hold. Apart from the waste that inevitably remains with the harvested grapes – which is becoming less as machines become more sophisticated – the main disadvantage of mechanical harvesting is the inability of a machine to distinguish between the ripe and the unripe, or to sort the healthy from the diseased or plain rotten (the first thing to drop from any plant when shaken). This can be achieved manually, though, and the latest machines are capable of sorting the fruit. From a practical point of view, it would seem that this method of harvesting is better for red wine than it is for white wine, particularly sparkling, because it splits the grapes. This encourages oxidation and a loss of aromatics and, when harvesting black grapes for white sparkling wine, results in an undesirable coloration of the juice.

It is well known that machine harvesting is widely employed in New World countries like Australia, but few realize just how prevalent it is in France, where more than 60 per cent of the wines are machine harvested.

PRESSING
In the race against time to get the grapes from the vineyard to the winery, everything possible should be done to cosset the fruit. Ideally, the winery and the vineyards are close, and the grapes are transported in stackable plastic crates that are small enough to prevent damage from their own weight.

When grapes arrive at the winery, white varieties are destemmed and immediately pressed, whereas black grapes are crushed and kept in contact with their skins while they ferment (to extract colour and tannins). Some aromatic white varieties might also be crushed and kept in contact with their skins, but they will be pressed immediately prior to fermentation. Two famous exceptions are for Champagne (where the grapes, both white and black, are not destemmed before pressing) and Beaujolais Nouveau (for which whole clusters are neither destemmed nor crushed but kept under carbon dioxide pressure in a vat, where they undergo an aerobic intracellular fermentation). Some red wines are made with a percentage of whole-cluster fermentation, while others are made without the free-run juice (juice that runs freely from the grapes under their own weight as they are piled into a press), which gives more colour and structure to a wine because of the higher ratio of skins to remaining juice.

There are various types of press. First, they break down into continuous and batch presses. A continuous press usually operates on the principle of an Archimedes screw, which applies increasingly higher pressure as the grapes move through the press to exit in a never-ending bone-dry fibrous sausage of skins, seeds, and stalks. This is the harshest of the pressing processes, and as such it is primarily used for high-volume, low-cost wines. Batch presses are the most common form of press found in the majority of wineries and are essentially divided into two types: hydraulic plate presses (horizontal and vertical) and pneumatic (horizontal). The former category is most effectively illustrated by Vaslin, a firm whose name is synonymous with hydraulic presses. Hydraulic presses have their uses, particularly the vertical bunch presses, and the technology is much better than it was in the 1970s, when Vaslin horizontal hydraulic presses were everywhere. A horizontal press consists of a perforated cylinder containing plates either end. Grapes are loaded through a closeable hatch, and the press rotates to remove any free-run juice, after which the two metal plates move towards each other, squeezing the grapes between, with the juice exiting through the holes in the perforated cylinder. The vertical hydraulic press, or basket press, is the oldest design of press known but is particularly useful in Champagne and for limited-production wines (because this type of press can be produced in the smallest sizes).

Pneumatic presses are the softest-pressing and consist of a central or side rubber bladder that is inflated by compressed air, squashing the grapes against the perforated sides of the cylindrical press, where the juice escapes through holes. Top-quality pneumatic presses include those by Bücher, Willmes, and Magnum. The latest development in pneumatic presses involves flooding it with an inert gas such as nitrogen, carbon dioxide, or argon.

However softly grapes are pressed, there is no getting away from the fact that it is a destructive process traditionally carried out in an oxygen-rich environment; as such, it represents the first crisis point for any winemaker anxious to avoid the onset of oxidation. Pressing grapes in an inert-gas environment seeks to eliminate much of this risk. On the other hand, there are times when winemakers deliberately oxidize grape juice prior to fermentation (for either stylistic reasons or technical reasons).

HUMAN IMPACT

The winemaker, and that includes the winegrower, can maximize or minimize the fruits of nature by his or her intervention. Time and again I have seen that neighbouring winemakers can make wines of widely varying quality using virtually the same raw product and technology.

CHEMICAL ANALYSES OF THE WINES IN QUESTION may be virtually indistinguishable, yet one wine will have all the definition, vitality, and expression of character that the other lacks. Why does this occur? Because it is always the winemakers with passion who are able to produce the finer, more characterful wines. Many inferior wines are made by the misuse of up-to-date technology, and I have seen dedicated winemakers produce absolutely spellbinding wines using totally inadequate or inferior equipment. If the test is between passionless, high-tech wine and wine made by an ill-equipped genius, the genius always wins, but employing a few caring oenologists (not all are) in the largest modern winery can make all the difference. Some winemakers have even been known to sleep by their vats during a particularly difficult fermentation, so that they are on hand to make any adjustments immediately if anything goes wrong. From the grower who never hesitates to prune the vine for low yields yet always agonizes over the optimum time to harvest, to the winemaker who literally nurses the wines through each and every stage of fermentation and maturation and bottles at precisely the right time and at exactly the correct temperature, the human element is most seriously the joker in the pack when it comes to factors affecting the taste and quality of the wines produced.

THE JOKER AT WORK

There are many examples of the human joker changing the taste and quality of wine for either good or bad, but few practices have had such a widespread negative impact on modern winemaking as picking grapes by so-called physiological ripeness. This pseudo-scientific term (*see* Alsace, p235) has assumed an almost religious reverence among winemakers, turning former dry white-wine areas into preserves of increasingly sweet concoctions, and where there were once red wines brimming with vibrant fruit and finesse, we now have dark, dense wines full of nothing but dead fruit, the size and power of which we are expected to find awesome.

Other notable bad jokes include putting the best Chardonnay in new oak throughout the New World, which only hides the grape's best attributes, and using leftover wines for so-called unoaked Chardonnay, when logic tells us it should be the opposite way around: put the lesser wines in the oak to hide their imperfections, and leave the best Chardonnays unoaked to reveal every facet of their beauty! Whether oak or other winemaking techniques are used – lees stirring, acidifying, malolactic, carbonic maceration, or whatever – their tell-tale aromas should not be noticeable. At worst, they should play no more than a minor supporting role in a seamless presentation of the wine. It should be the wine, not the technique used to make the wine, that leaps out of the glass as soon as you pick it up. Yet some of these jokers deliberately show off their techniques, creating not complexity or finesse but the vinous equivalent of a painting by numbers; they make it so obvious how their wines are made. The good jokers are those winemakers who are seeking elegance and finesse over weight and alcohol – those who aspire to make wines with extraordinary great length, not due to their sheer size but because they know that the real skill is in achieving a balance required to provide length, no matter how light in weight the wine might be.

RANDALL GRAHM
Probably the wine world's biggest joker, Randall Grahm of Bonny Doon Vineyard in Santa Cruz, California, has even macerated grape juice on crushed rock from different soils in his search for the meaning of terroir.

VINIFICATION

Although the internationalization of winemaking techniques is a topic that is always much discussed, methods of production can still vary greatly not just from country to country, but from region to region, and quite commonly even from grower to grower within the same village.

IN WINEMAKING, much depends upon whether traditional values are upheld or innovations are sought and, for the latter, whether the technology is available. Whatever the winemaker decides, certain principles will, essentially, remain the same. These are described below, followed by sections on styles of wine and the processes common or unique to each one.

THE DIMINISHING QUALITY FACTOR

The quality of the grapes when they are harvested represents the maximum potential of any wine that can be made from them. However, a winemaker will never be able to transfer 100 per cent of this inherent quality to the wine, because deterioration sets in from the moment a grape is disconnected from the vine's metabolism. Furthermore, the very process of turning grapes into wine is necessarily a destructive one, so every action taken by the winemaker, however quality-conscious he or she may be, will inevitably erode some of the wine's potential. Winemakers, therefore, can only attempt to minimize the loss of potential quality.

It is relatively easy to retain approximately 80 per cent of the potential quality of a wine, but very difficult to preserve every percentile point after that. It is also relatively easy to double or even triple the basic grape quality by better selection of vineyard sites, improved training methods, the use of superior clones, correct rootstock, and a reduction in yields. As a result, research has long since swung from the winery back to the vineyard.

That said, oenological practices are still important and how they are employed will have a profound effect not only on quality, but also on the style of the wine produced.

PRINCIPLES OF VINIFICATION

With modern technology, good everyday-drinking wines can be made anywhere that grapes are grown. When such wines are not made, the reason is invariably a lack of equipment and expertise or an absence of self-respect. Finer quality wines require vineyards that have a certain potential and winemakers with a particular talent. When not even good everyday-drinking wines are made from fine wine vineyards, it is usually due to a combination of excessive yields and poor winemaking, and there is no excuse for either.

FERMENTATION

The biochemical process that transforms fresh grape juice into wine is called fermentation. Yeast cells excrete enzymes that convert natural fruit sugars into almost equal quantities of alcohol and carbonic gas. This process ceases when the supply of sugar is exhausted or when the alcoholic level reaches a point that is toxic for the yeast enzymes (usually 15 to 16 per cent, although certain strains can survive at 20 to 22 per cent). Traditionally, winemakers racked their wine from cask to cask (*see opposite*) until they were sure that fermentation had stopped, but there are now many other methods that halt fermentation artificially. These can involve the use of heat, sulphur dioxide, centrifugal filtration, alcohol, pressure, or carbonic gas.

- **Heat** There are various forms of pasteurization (for table wines), flash-pasteurization (for finer wines), and chilling operations that are used to stabilize wine. These operate on the basis that yeast cells are incapacitated at temperatures above 36°C (97°F), or below -3°C (26°F), and that yeast enzymes are destroyed above 65°C (149°F). Flash-pasteurization subjects wines to a temperature of about 80°C (176°F) for between 30 seconds and one minute, whereas fully fledged pasteurization involves lower temperatures of 50 to 60°C (122 to 140°F) for a longer period.

- **Addition of sulphur dioxide or sorbic acid** Dosing with one or more aseptic substances will kill off the yeasts.

- **Centrifugal filtration or filtration** Modern equipment is now capable of physically removing all the yeasts from a wine, either by filtration (simply pouring the wine through a medium that prevents certain substances passing through) or by centrifugal filtration (a process that separates unwanted matter from wine – or grape juice, if used at an earlier stage – by so-called "centrifugal force").

- **Addition of alcohol** Fortification raises the alcohol content to a level toxic to yeast.

- **Pressure** Yeast cells are destroyed by pressure in excess of eight atmospheres (the pressure inside a Champagne bottle is around six atmospheres).

- **Addition of carbonic gas (CO_2)** Yeast cells are destroyed in the presence of 15 grams per litre or more of carbonic gas. (There are just over 10 grams per litre in a fully sparkling wine.)

THE USE OF SULPHUR

Sulphur is used in winemaking from the time the grapes arrive at the winery until just before the wine is bottled. It has several properties, including anti-oxidant and aseptic qualities, that make it essential for commercial winemaking. To some extent, all wines are oxidized from the moment the grapes are pressed and the juice is exposed to the air, but the rate of oxidation must be controlled. This is where sulphur is useful, because it has a chemical attraction for the tiny amounts of oxygen that are present in wine. One molecule of sulphur will combine with two molecules of oxygen to form sulphur dioxide (SO_2), or fixed sulphur. Once it is combined with the sulphur, the oxygen is neutralized and can no longer oxidize the wine. More oxygen will be absorbed by wine during the vinification process, of course, and there will also be a small head of air between the wine and the cork after bottling. It is for this reason that wines are bottled with a set amount of free sulphur (the amount of the total sulphur content that is not fixed). Occasionally a winemaker claims that sulphur is completely

---

YEAST THE FERMENTER

The yeasts used for fermentation may be divided into two categories: cultured yeasts and natural yeasts.

Cultured yeasts are nothing more than thoroughbred strains of natural wine yeasts that have been raised in a laboratory. They may be used because the juice has been cleansed of all organisms, including its yeasts, prior to fermentation; or because the winemaker prefers their reliability, or for a specific purpose, such as withstanding higher alcohol levels or the increased osmotic pressure that affects bottle-fermented sparkling wines.

Natural yeasts are to be found adhering to the *pruina*, a waxy substance that covers the skin of ripe grapes and other fruits. By the time a grape has fully ripened, the coating of yeasts and other micro-organisms, commonly referred to as the "bloom", contains an average of 10 million yeast cells, although only one per cent – or just 100,000 cells – are so-called "wine-yeasts". A yeast cell is only microscopic, yet under favourable conditions it has the ability to split 10,000 sugar molecules every second during fermentation.

superfluous to the winemaking process, but whereas low-sulphur regimes are actually to be encouraged, wines produced without it are usually dire or have a very short shelf-life.

One famous wine that claimed not to use any sulphur was so long-lived that I had a bottle independently analysed, only to find that it did contain sulphur. The quantity was small, but far too significant to have been created during fermentation (which is possible in tiny amounts). It was, therefore, an example of how effective a low-sulphur regime can be. Methods of reducing the level of SO_2 are well known, the most important being a very judicious initial dosage because a resistance to sulphur gradually builds up and, as a result, later doses always have to be increased.

Some wines can be over-sulphured and, although they are less common than they used to be, they are by no means rare. Over-sulphured wines are easily recognizable by their smell, which ranges from the slight whiff of a recently ignited match (which is the clean smell of free sulphur) to the stench of bad eggs (which is H_2S, where the sulphur has combined with hydrogen – literally the stuff of stink-bombs). When H_2S reacts with ethyl alcohol or one of the higher alcohols, foul-smelling compounds called mercaptans are formed. They can smell of garlic, onion, burnt rubber, or stale cabbage, depending on the exact nature of the compound. Mercaptans are extremely difficult for the winemaker to remove and can ruin a wine, which illustrates just how important it is to maintain a low-sulphur regime.

MALOLACTIC FERMENTATION

Malolactic fermentation is sometimes known as the secondary fermentation, but this is an inappropriate description. The malolactic, or "malo" (as it is sometimes called), is a biochemical process that converts the "hard" malic acid of unripe grapes into two-parts "soft" lactic, or "milk", acid (so-called because it is the acid that makes milk sour) and one-part carbonic gas. Malic acid is a very strong-tasting acid, which reduces during the fruit's ripening process. However, a significant quantity persists in ripe grapes, and, although reduced by fermentation, also in wine.

The quantity of malic acid present in a wine may be considered too much and the smoothing effect of replacing it with just two-thirds the quantity of the much weaker lactic acid is often desirable. This smoothing effect is considered vital for red wine, beneficial for fuller, fatter, more complex whites, and optional for lighter, crisper whites and certain styles of sparkling wine.

To ensure that the malo can take place, it is essential that specific bacteria are present. These are found naturally on grape skins among the yeasts and other micro-organisms, but commercially prepared bacteria may also be used. To undertake their task, they require a certain warmth, a low level of sulphur, a pH of between 3 and 4, and a supply of various nutrients found naturally in grapes.

STAINLESS STEEL OR OAK?

The use of stainless-steel and oak containers for fermentation and maturation is not simply dependent on the cost (*see right*). The two materials produce opposing effects upon wine, so the choice is heavily dependent upon whether the winemaker wants to add character to a wine or to keep its purity.

A stainless-steel vat is a long-lasting, easy-to-clean vessel made from an impervious and inert material that is ideally suited to all forms of temperature control. It has the capacity to produce the freshest wines with the purest varietal character. An oak cask has a comparatively limited life, is not easy to clean (it can never be sterilized), makes temperature control very difficult, and is neither impervious nor inert. It allows access to the air, which encourages a faster rate of oxidation, but also causes evaporation, which concentrates the flavour. Vanillin, the essential aromatic constituent of vanilla pods, is extracted from the oak by oxidation and, with various wood lactones and unfermentable sugars, imparts a distinctive, sweet and creamy vanilla nuance to wine. This oaky

STAINLESS-STEEL VATS
Stainless steel is the cornerstone of modern winemaking technology. The bands around each tank contain a coolant to regulate fermentation temperatures.

character takes on a smoky complexity if the wine is allowed to go through its malolactic fermentation in contact with the wood, and becomes even more complex, and certainly better integrated, if the wine has undergone all or most of its alcoholic fermentation in cask. Oak also imparts wood tannins to low tannin wine, absorbs tannins from tannic wine, and can exchange tannins with some wines. Oak tannins also act as catalysts, provoking desirable changes in grape tannins through a complex interplay of oxidations.

POST-FERMENTATION PROCEDURES

Numerous procedures can take place in the winery after fermentation and, where applicable, malolactic fermentation, have ceased. However, the five most basic procedures are racking, fining, cold stabilization, filtration, and bottling.

Racking

Draining the clear wine off its lees, or sediment, into another vat or cask is known as "racking" because of the different levels, or racks, on which the wine is run from one container into another. In modern vinification, this operation is usually conducted several times during vat or cask maturation. The wine gradually throws off less and less of a deposit. Some wines, such as Muscadet sur lie, are never racked.

Fining

After fermentation, wine may look hazy to the eye. Even if it does not, it may still contain suspended matter that threatens cloudiness in the bottle. Fining usually assists the clarification of wine at this stage. In addition, special fining agents may be employed to remove unwanted characteristics. When a fining agent is added to wine,

---

THE COST OF NEW OAK

Two hundred 225-litre (49-gallon) oak casks with a total capacity of 450 hectolitres (9,900 gallons) cost between four and 10 times the cost of a single 450-hectolitre (9,900-gallon) stainless-steel vat. After two years of much higher labour costs to operate and maintain the large number of small units, the volume of wine produced in the oak casks is 10 per cent less because of evaporation, and the winemaker faces the prospect of purchasing another 200 casks.

it adheres to cloudy matter by physical or electrolytic attraction, creating tiny clusters (known as colloidal groups), which drop to the bottom of the vat as sediment. The most commonly encountered fining agents are egg white, tannin, gelatine, bentonite, isinglass, and casein. Winemakers have their preferences and individual fining agents also have their specific uses: positively charged egg white fines out negatively charged matter, such as unwanted tannins or anthocyanins, while negatively charged bentonite fines out positively charged matter, such as protein haze and other organic matter.

Cold stabilization

When wines are subjected to low temperatures, a crystalline deposit of tartrates can form a deposit in the bottle. Should the wine be dropped to a very low temperature for a few days before bottling, this process can be precipitated, rendering the wine safe from the threat of a tartrate deposit in the bottle. For the past 25 years, cold stabilization has been almost obligatory for cheap commercial wines, and it is now increasingly used for those of better quality as well. This trend is a pity because the crystals are, in fact, entirely harmless and their presence is a completely welcome indication of a considerably more natural, rather than heavily processed, wine.

Filtration

Various methods of filtration exist, and they all entail running wine through a medium that prevents particles of a certain size from passing through. Filtration has become a controversial subject in recent times, with some critics claiming that anything that removes something from wine must be bad. Depending on who you listen to, this "something" is responsible for a wine's complexity, body, or flavour. However, although it is undeniable that filtration strips something from a wine, if it is unfiltered, it will throw a much heavier deposit and do so relatively quickly. The mysterious "something" is, therefore, purged from all wines at some time or other, whether they are filtered or not, and whether the critics like it or not. Filtration, like so many things, is perfectly acceptable if it is applied in moderation. The fact that many of the world's greatest wines are filtered is a testament to this.

I prefer less or no filtration, as do most quality-conscious winemakers. This is not because of any romantic, unquantifiable ideal; it is simply because I prefer wine to be as unprocessed and as natural as possible. This is a state that can only be achieved through as much of a hands-off approach as the wine will allow. Generally, the finer the wine, the less filtration required, as consumers of expensive wines expect sediment and are prepared

FROM GRAPE TO GLASS

Virtually every ingredient of a fresh grape can be found in the wine it makes, although additional compounds are produced when wine is made and any sedimented matter is disposed of before it is bottled. The most significant difference in the two lists below is the disappearance of fermentable sugar and the appearance of alcohol, although the constituents will vary according to the variety and ripeness of the grape and the style of wine produced.

THE "INGREDIENTS" OF FRESH GRAPE JUICE

Percentage by volume

73.5	Water	
25	Carbohydrates, of which:	
	20%	Sugar (plus pentoses, pectin, inositol)
	5%	Cellulose
0.8	Organic acids, of which:	
	0.54%	Tartaric acid
	0.25%	Malic acid
	0.01%	Citric acid (plus possible traces of succinic acid and lactic acid)
0.5	Minerals, of which:	
	0.25%	Potassium
	0.05%	Phosphate
	0.035%	Sulphate
	0.025%	Calcium
	0.025%	Magnesium
	0.01%	Chloride
	0.005%	Silicic acid
	0.1%	Others (aluminium, boron, copper, iron, molybdenum, rubidium, sodium, zinc)
0.13	Tannin and colour pigments	
0.07	Nitrogenous matter, of which:	
	0.05%	Amino acids (arginine, glutamic acid, proline, serine, threonine, and others)
	0.005%	Protein
	0.015%	Other nitrogenous matter (humin, amide, ammonia, and others)
Traces	Mainly vitamins (thiamine, riboflavin, pyridoxine, pantothenic acid, nicotinic acid, and ascorbic acid)	

WATER INTO WINE

The individual flavouring elements in any wine represent barely 2 per cent of its content. Although we can determine with great accuracy the amount and identity of 99 per cent of these constituents, the mystery is that if we assembled them and added the requisite volume of water and alcohol, the result would taste nothing like wine, let alone like the specific wine we would be trying to imitate.

THE "CONTENTS" OF WINE

Percentage by volume

86	Water	
12	Alcohol (ethyl alcohol)	
0.4	Glycerol	
Organic acids, of which:		
	0.20%	Tartaric acid
	0.15%	Lactic acid
	0.05%	Succinic acid (plus traces of malic acid citric acid)
0.2	Carbohydrates (unfermentable sugar)	
0.2	Minerals, of which:	
	0.075%	Potassium
	0.05%	Phosphate
	0.02%	Calcium
	0.02%	Magnesium
	0.02%	Sulphate
	0.01%	Chloride
	0.005%	Silicic acid
	Traces	Aluminium, boron, copper, iron, molybdenum, rubidium, sodium, zinc
0.1	Tannin and colour pigments	
0.045	Volatile acids (mostly acetic acid)	
0.025	Nitrogenous matter, of which:	
	0.01%	Amino acids (arginine, glutamic acid, proline, serine, threonine, and others)
	0.015%	Protein and other nitrogenous matter (humin, amide, ammonia, and others)
0.025	Esters (mostly ethyl acetate, but traces of numerous others)	
0.004	Aldehydes (mostly acetaldehyde, some vanillin, and traces of others)	
0.001	Higher alcohols (minute quantities of amyl plus traces of isoamyl, butyl, isobutyl, hexyl, propyl, and methyl may be present)	
Traces	Vitamins (thiamine, riboflavin, pyridoxine, pantothenic acid, nicotinic acid, and ascorbic acid)	

to decant. Delicate reds, such as Pinot Noir, should be the least filtered of all, as I swear they lose fruit just by looking at them, and they certainly lose colour – that, at least, is quantifiable. No wine with extended barrel-ageing should ever require filtration – just a light, natural fining.

Each filtration is expensive and time-consuming, thus even producers of the most commercial, everyday wines (which even filtration critics accept must be filtered) should keep these operations to a minimum. The principle means of achieving this is by ensuring the best possible clarification by settling and racking. Fining (see p29) should always take precedence, as it is both kinder on the wine and much cheaper than filtering. There are four basic types of filtration: Earth, Pad, Membrane, and Crossflow.

• **Earth Filtration** This system is primarily used after racking for filtering the wine-rich lees that collect at the bottom of the fermentation tank. A medium, usually kieselguhr (a form of diatomaceous earth), is continuously fed into the wine and used with either a Plate and Frame Filter or a Rotary Drum Vacuum Filter. Both types of filter are precoated with the medium, but in a Plate and Frame Filter, the wine and medium mix is forced, under pressure, through plates, or screens, of the medium, in a manner similar to that of any other filter. For the Rotary Drum Vacuum Filter, however, the precoat adheres to the outside of a large perforated drum by virtue of the vacuum that is maintained inside. The drum revolves through a shallow bath into which the wine is pumped and literally sucks the wine through the precoat into the centre, where it is piped away. The advantage of this system is that on one side of the shallow bath there is a scraper that constantly shaves the coating on the drum to the desired thickness. The medium thus falls into the wine, with which it mixes, and is then sucked back on to, and through, the drum. It is a continuous process and a very economical one, as the amount of medium used is limited. In a Plate and Frame Filter, the medium is enclosed and eventually clogs up, requiring the operation to be stopped, and the equipment to be dismantled and cleaned before the process can resume.

• **Pad Filtration** Also called Sheet Filtration, this requires the use of a Plate and Frame Filter with a variable number of frames into which filter pads or sheets can slide. Before it was outlawed in the 1970s, these used to be made of asbestos. They now contain numerous filtration mediums, ranging from diatomaceous earth to regular cellulose pads, the latter of which are the most commonly used medium. Special filter formats include active carbon (to remove unwanted colour, which is frowned upon for all but the most commercial, high-volume wines) and electrostatically charged pads. These are designed to attract any matter that is suspended in the wine, most of which will possess a negative or positive charge. It is claimed that these electrostatically charged pads are more effective in filtering out matter than the same pads without a charge.

• **Membrane Filtration** This is also called Millipore because the membranes contain microscopic holes capable of removing yeasts and other micro-organisms. As these holes account for 80 per cent of the sheet's surface, the throughput of wine can be extremely fast provided it has undergone a light pre-filtration. Both filtration and pre-filtration can now, however, be done at the same time with new Millipore cartridge filters. These contain two or more membranes of varying porosity, thus the coarser ones act as a screen for those with the most minuscule holes. Many producers will not put a full-bodied wine through a membrane filter because it filters down to such a microscopic level that it is thought to remove too much of the body.

• **Crossflow Filtration** Originally designed to purify water, a crossflow filter varies from the others (with the exception of the Rotary Drum Vacuum Filter) because it is self-cleaning and never clogs up. The wine flows across the membrane, not into it, so only some of it penetrates. Most of it returns to the chamber from which it came and, because it flows very fast, takes with it any matter filtered out by the membrane.

BOTTLING

When visiting larger producers, automated bottling lines are the wine journalist's *bête noire*. They get faster and more complex each year and, having invested vast sums in the very latest bottling line, it is understandable that proprietors are eager to show off their new high-tech toy. However, as John Arlott once told me, as he resolutely refused to set foot in the bottling hall of Piper-Heidsieck, "I have not written a single word about bottling lines in my life and I'm not going to start now". They make a very dull experience and inevitably break down just as one's host boasts that it is the fastest bottling line in the world, but their smooth operation most days of the week is essential if the wine is to remain as fresh as possible in the bottle. All that readers need to know is that the bottles should be sterile; that fully-automated lines cork, capsule, label, and box the wines; and that there is a device to detect any impurities before the bottles are boxed. All European systems either print on the label, or laser-print directly on to the bottle, a lot number that identifies the date each batch was bottled. This means that in an emergency, a specific batch can be recalled, rather than the entire production having to be cleared from every wholesaler and retailer stocking a particular line.

FORTIFIED WINES

Any wine, dry or sweet, red or white, to which alcohol has been added is classified as a fortified wine, whatever the inherent differences of vinification may be. Still wines usually have a strength of 8.5 to 15 per cent alcohol; fortified wines a strength of 17 to 24 per cent. The spirit added is usually, but not always, brandy made from local wines. It is totally neutral, with no hint of a brandy flavour. The amount of alcohol added, and exactly when and how it is added, is as critical to the particular character of a fortified wine as is its grape variety or area of production. *Mutage*, early fortification, and late fortification are all methods that may be used to fortify wines.

MUTAGE

This is the addition of alcohol to fresh grape juice, which prevents fermentation and produces fortified wines, known as *vins de liqueurs* in France, such as Pineau des Charentes in the Cognac region, Floc de Gascogne in Armagnac, Macvin in the Jura, and Ratafia in Champagne.

EARLY FORTIFICATION

This is the addition of alcohol after fermentation has begun, and it is often done in several small, carefully measured, timed doses spread over several hours or even days. The style of fortified wine being made will dictate exactly when the alcohol is added, and the style itself will be affected by the variable strength of the grapes from year to year. On average, however, alcohol is added to port after the alcohol level has reached 6 to 8 per cent, and added to the *vins doux naturels* of France, such as Muscat de Beaumes de Venise, at any stage between 5 and 10 per cent.

LATE FORTIFICATION

This is the addition of alcohol after fermentation has ceased. The classic drink produced by this method is sherry, which is always vinified dry, with any sweetness added afterwards.

AROMATIZED WINES

With the exception of Retsina, the resinated Greek wine, aromatized wines are all fortified. They also all have aromatic ingredients added to them. The most important aromatized wine is vermouth, which is made from neutral white wines of 2 to 3 years of age, blended with an extract of wormwood (vermouth is a corruption of the German *Wermut*, meaning "wormwood"), vanilla, and various other herbs and spices. Although the earliest example of vermouth dates back to 16th-century Germany and the first commercial vermouth (Punt e Mes, created by Antonio Carpano of Turin) to 1786, the notion of adding herbs and spices to wine was prevalent in Roman times and goes back at least as far as ancient Egypt. Italian vermouths are produced in Apulia and Sicily, and French vermouths in Languedoc and Roussillon. Chambéry is a delicate generic vermouth from the Savoie and Chambéryzette is a red-pink version flavoured with alpine strawberries, but such precise geographical aromatized wines are rare. Most, in fact, are made and sold under internationally recognized brands such as Cinzano and Martini. Other well-known aromatized wines include Amer Picon, Byrrh, Dubonnet (both red and white), Punt e Mes, St-Raphael, and Suze.

RED WINEMAKING

On arrival at the winery, the grapes are usually crushed and destemmed, although it was once accepted practice to leave the stems for a more tannic wine. However, stem tannins are too harsh and fail to soften as the wine matures. The modern winemaker can include a small quantity of stems if the grape variety requires extra structure or if the vintage needs firming up.

FERMENTATION

After the grapes are destemmed and lightly crushed, they are pumped into a vat, where fermentation may begin as early as 12 hours or as late as several days later. Even wines that will be cask-fermented must start off in vats, whether they are old-fashioned oak *foudres* or modern stainless-steel tanks. This is because they must be fermented along with a *manta*, or cap, of grapeskins. To encourage fermentation, the juice may be heated and selected yeast cultures or partially fermented wine from

another vat added. During fermentation, the juice is often pumped from the bottom of the vat to the top and sprayed over the *manta* to keep the juice in contact with the grapeskins. This ensures that the maximum colour is extracted. Other methods involve the *manta* being pushed under the fermenting juice with poles. Some vats are equipped with crude but effective grids that prevent the *manta* from rising; others rely on the carbonic gas that is given off during fermentation to build up pressure, releasing periodically and pushing the *manta* under the surface. Another system keeps the *manta* submerged in a "vinimatic", a sealed, rotating stainless-steel tank, based on the cement-mixer principle.

The higher the temperature during fermentation, the more colour and tannin will be extracted; the lower the temperature, the better the bouquet, freshness, and fruit will be. The optimum temperature for the fermentation of red wine is 29.4°C (85°F). If it is too hot, the yeasts produce certain substances (decanoic acid, octanoic acids, and corresponding esters) that inhibit their own ability to feed on nutrients and cause the yeasts to die. It is, however, far better to ferment hot fresh juice than to wait two weeks (which is normal in many cases) to ferment cooler but stale juice. The fuller, darker, more tannic, and potentially longer-lived wines remain in contact with the skins for anything

RIPE SANGIOVESE GRAPES
Varieties with tightly packed bunches such as Sangiovese can struggle to bring colour to a wine even when they are ripe. This can be remedied by blending from a particularly dark-skinned colour, such as the aptly named Colorino, which is traditionally used for this purpose in Tuscany, or by draining off the free-run juice so that the ratio of skin to juice is increased.

CARBONIC MACERATION

There are several variations of carbonic maceration (known in French as *macération carbonique*), a technique used almost exclusively for making red wine, involving an initial fermentation under pressure of carbonic gas. The traditional method, dating back at least 200 years, was to put the uncrushed grapes in a closed container where, after a while, a natural fermentation would take place inside the grapes. When the grapes eventually exploded, filling the container with carbonic gas, a normal fermentation continued and the grapes macerated in their own skins. Today the grapes are often placed in vats filled with carbonic gas from a bottle. Carbonic maceration produces light wines with good colour, soft fruit, and a "peardrop" aroma.

HOW RED WINE IS MADE

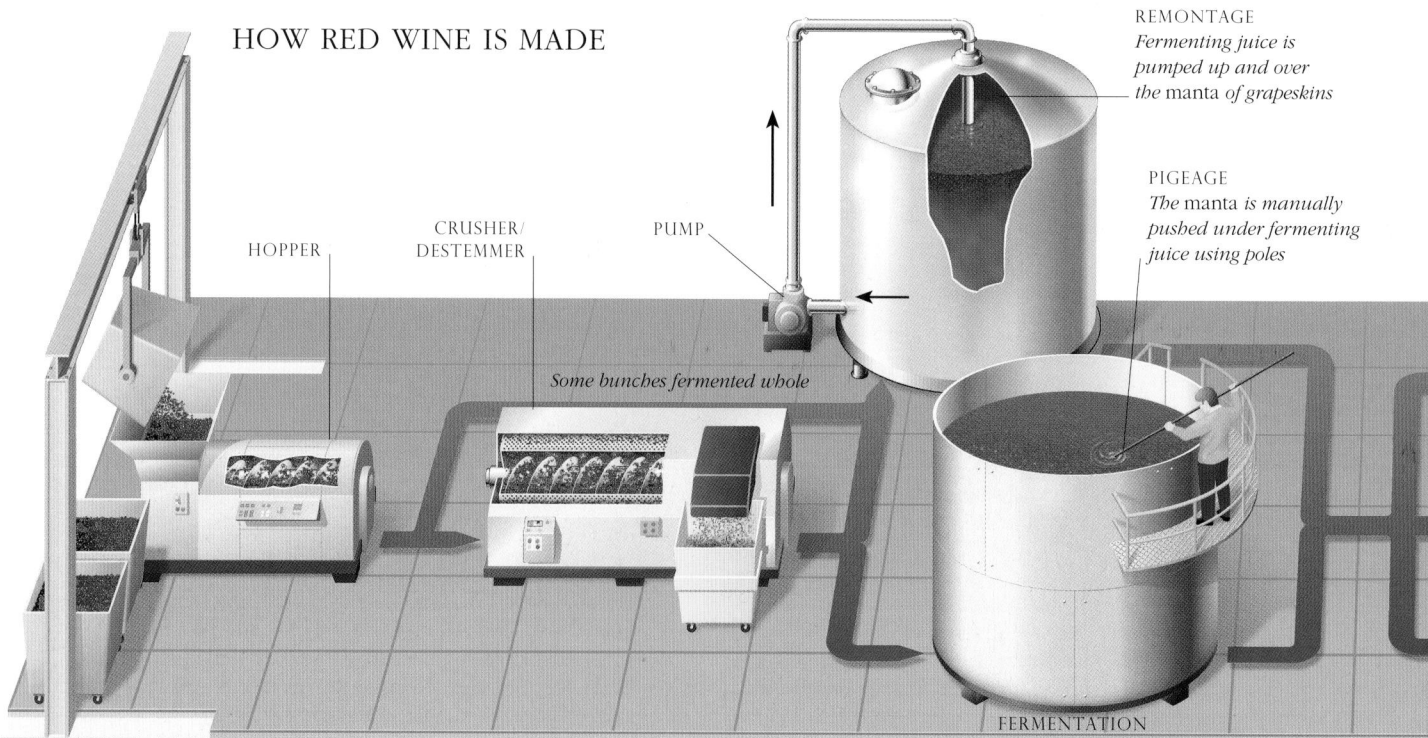

HOPPER

CRUSHER/ DESTEMMER

PUMP

Some bunches fermented whole

REMONTAGE
Fermenting juice is pumped up and over the manta *of grapeskins*

PIGEAGE
The manta *is manually pushed under fermenting juice using poles*

FERMENTATION

between 10 and 30 days. Lighter wines, on the other hand, are separated from the skins after only a few days.

VIN DE GOUTTE AND VIN DE PRESSE

The moment the skins are separated from the juice, every wine is divided into two: free-run wine, or *vin de goutte*, and press wine, or *vin de presse*. The free-run juice runs out of the vat when the tap is opened. The remains – the *manta* of grapeskins, pips, and other solids – are put into a press to extract the very dark, extremely tannic "press wine". The free-run wine and the press wine are then pumped into separate vats or casks depending on the style of the wine being made. These wines then undergo their malolactic conversion separately and are racked several times, fined, racked again, blended, then fined and racked once more before bottling.

QUINTA DO CENTRO
The fermentation tanks in Richard Mayson's Portuguese winery are all small enough to ferment his wines on a block-by-block basis. Note how they stand well clear of the ground to facilitate drainage by gravity.

ROSÉ WINES

With the exception of pink Champagne, most of which is made by blending white wine with red, all quality rosés are produced by bleeding, pressing, or limited maceration. A true-bled, or *saignée*, rosé is made from the juice that issues from black grapes pressed under their own weight. This is a sort of *tête de cuvée*, which, after fermentation, is a very pale *vin gris* colour but has a rich, fruity, and exquisitely fresh flavour. Pressed rosé is made by pressing black grapes until the juice takes on enough colour. It, too, has a pale *vin gris* colour but lacks the true richness of a *tête de cuvée* rosé. Limited maceration is the most common method used in the production of rosé. During this process, rosé is made in exactly the same way as red wine, except that skin-contact is limited to what is sufficient to give the desired pink tint. (All shades of rosé exist, ranging from a barely perceptible hint of colour to *clairet*, or almost red.) Some superior rosé wines that have been made using this last method are virtually by-products of red-wine production. In certain areas that lack the appropriate climate for deep red wines, some free-run juice might be run off in order to produce rosé, thus leaving a greater ratio of colouring pigment in the juice that remains.

BLENDING
CHÂTEAU D'ESCLANS
The idea that only wines such as Champagne are blended is misguided, because even the smallest-production single-vineyard wines have to be blended, as the assemblage *of this high-quality Provence rosé illustrates. Furthermore, it is a matter not simply of selecting the best wines but also of achieving just the right balance of fruit, acidity, oak, and malolactic, so that none of these characteristics stands proud in the final blend.*

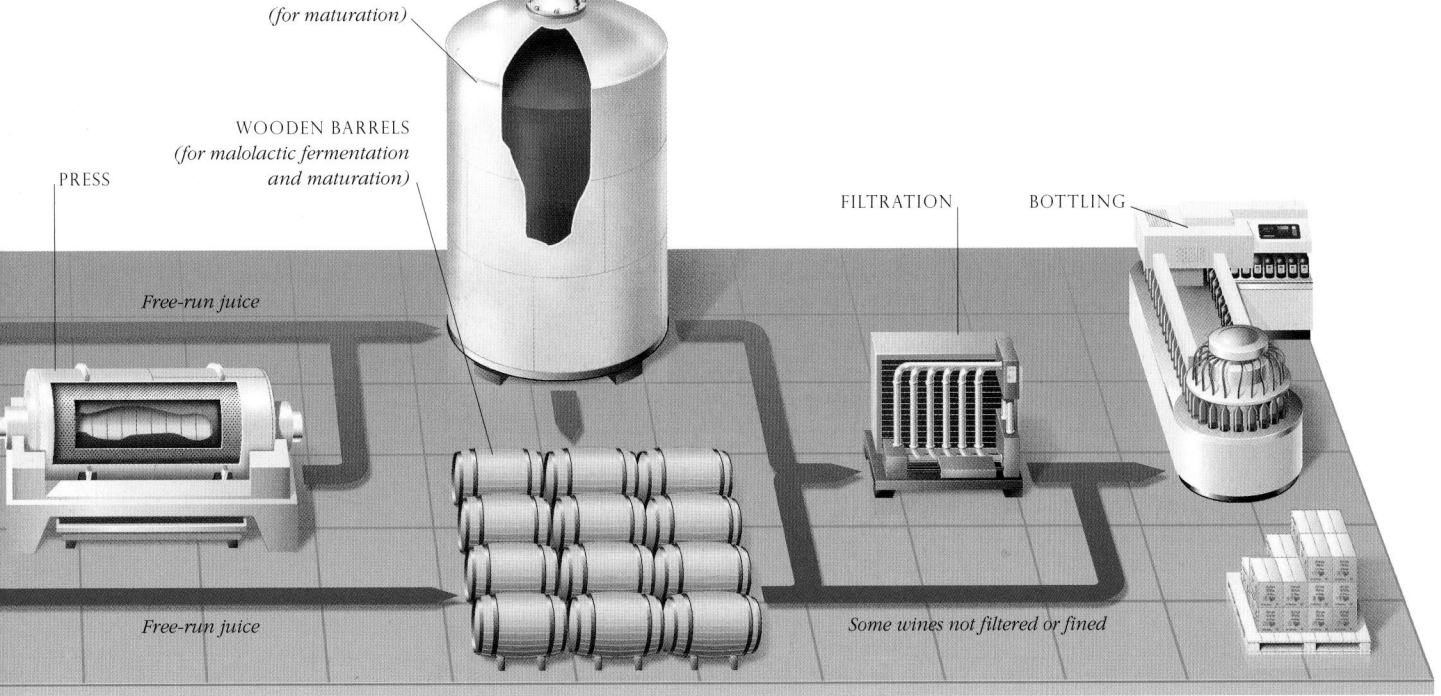

STAINLESS-
STEEL TANK
(for maturation)

WOODEN BARRELS
*(for malolactic fermentation
and maturation)*

PRESS

Free-run juice

Free-run juice

FILTRATION

BOTTLING

Some wines not filtered or fined

WHITE WINEMAKING

Until fairly recently, it could be said that two initial operations distinguished the white-winemaking process from the red one: first, an immediate pressing to extract the juice and separate the skins; and second, the purging, or cleansing, of this juice.

FOR WHITE WINES OF EXPRESSIVE VARIETAL CHARACTER, however, the grapes are now often crushed and then macerated (sometimes in a vinimatic) for 12 to 48 hours to extract the aromatics that are stored in the skins. The juice that is run out of the vinimatic, and the juice that is pressed out of the macerated pulp left inside it, then undergoes cleansing and fermentation like any other white wine.

With the exception of wines macerated in a vinimatic, the grapes are either pressed immediately on arrival at the winery or lightly crushed and then pressed. The juice from the last pressing is murky, bitter, and low in acidity and sugar, so only the first pressing, which is roughly equivalent to the free-run juice in red wine, together with the richest elements of the second pressing, should be used for white-wine production. Once pressed, the juice is pumped into a vat, where it is purged, or cleansed, which in its simplest form means simply leaving the juice to settle so that particles of grapeskin and any other impurities fall to the bottom. This purging may be helped by chilling, adding sulphur dioxide and, possibly, a fining agent. Light filtration and centrifugation may also be applied during this process.

After cleansing, the juice is pumped into the fermenting vat, or directly into barrels if the wine is to be cask-fermented. The addition of selected yeast cultures occurs more often in the production of white wine because of the wine's limited contact with the yeast-bearing skins and the additional cleansing that reduces the potential amount of wine yeasts available.

The optimum temperature for fermenting white wine is 18°C (64°F), although many winemakers opt for between 10°C and 17°C

CAMEL VALLEY REICHENSTEINER
Some white-wine varieties are better eaten than fermented. Celebrity chef Rick Stein enjoyed eating Reichensteiner grapes off the vine at Camel Valley so much that he dubbed the variety "Ricksteiner" on his television programme.

(50°F and 63°F), and it is actually possible to ferment wine at temperatures as low as 4°C (39°F). At the lower temperatures, more esters and other aromatics are created, less volatile acidity is produced, and a lower dose of sulphur dioxide is required; on the other hand, the resulting wines are lighter in body and contain less glycerol.

With acidity an essential factor in the balance of fruit and, where appropriate, sweetness in white wines, many products are not permitted to undergo malolactic conversion and are not bottled until some 12 months after the harvest. Oak-matured wines – which, incidentally, always undergo malolactic conversion – may be bottled between 9 and 18 months, but wines that are made especially for early drinking are nearly always racked, fined, filtered, and bottled as quickly as the process will allow in order to retain as much freshness and fruitiness as possible.

HOW WHITE WINE IS MADE

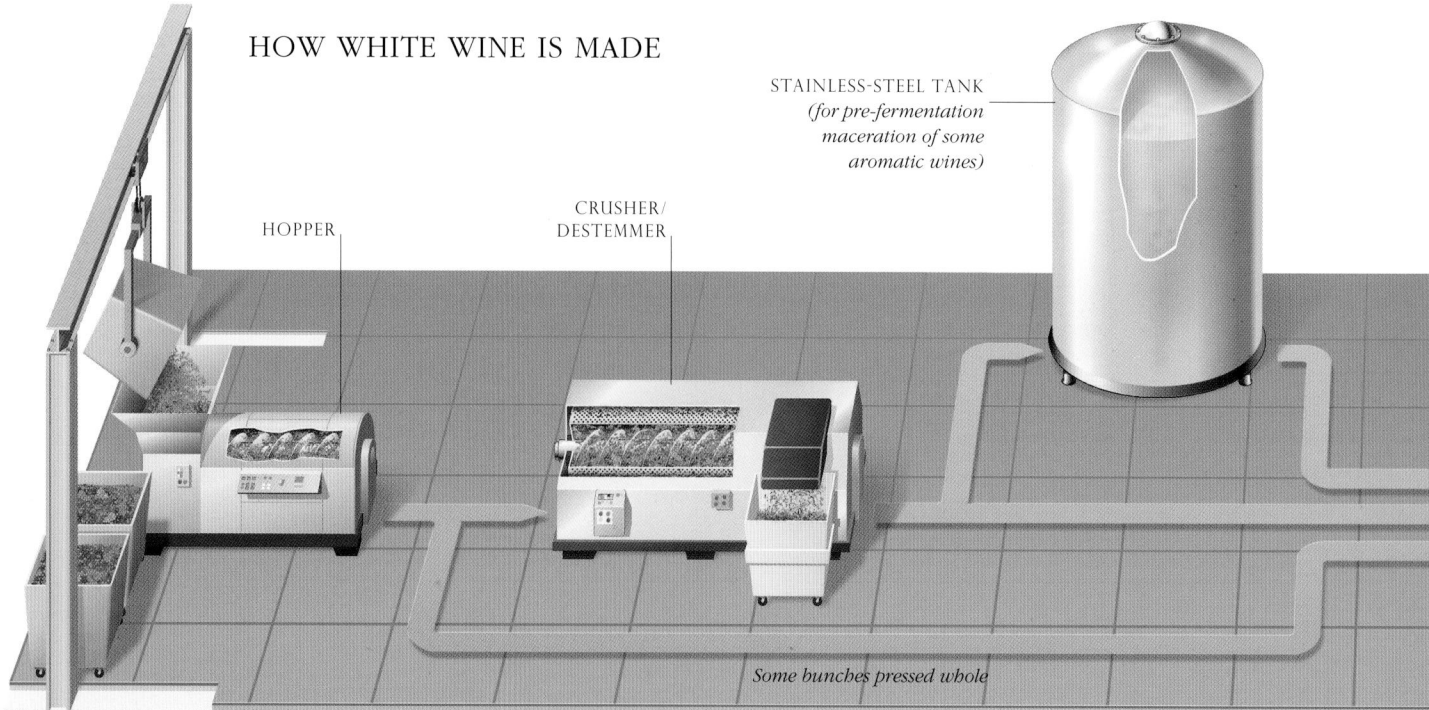

STAINLESS-STEEL TANK
(for pre-fermentation maceration of some aromatic wines)

HOPPER

CRUSHER/
DESTEMMER

Some bunches pressed whole

WHITE-WINEMAKING TECHNIQUES

Some of the following winemaking techniques can be used for red wine as well as white, but without the benefit of a red wine's lengthy maceration on skins, a white wine inevitably needs more techniques for those who want to tweak the outcome. However, the higher the quality and the more specific the *terroir*, the less hands-on a winemaker needs to be to express the grapes grown and a sense of place.

Acidification Unless you do this all the time, acidification is not easy to get right, but when performed proficiently, it can be the saving of what would otherwise be a flabby wine. It also increases perceived freshness and reduces SO_2 requirements. Even the greatest wines have benefited from acidification.

Back-blending A judicious addition of fresh, sterile-filtered juice after fermentation can increase freshness and fruitiness with minimal increase in residual sweetness.

Blanc de noirs A red wine is only red because it has been macerated on its own skins. With very rare exceptions (ie, *teinturier* grapes), black varieties have clear juice, so making white wine from them is no big deal. It is not new either – the *champenois* have been doing it for centuries, and *blanc de noirs* Champagnes are consistently the best rendition of this style. Other *blanc de noirs* wines can and do work, but usually only when produced by someone has been inspired to make such a wine. Far too many *blanc de noirs* are produced from grapes that, for one reason or another, were harvested before the skins had developed sufficient pigments to make a half-decent red wine, and the white wine alternative is often disappointing.

Cool fermentation The lower the temperature, the more freshness, less volatile acidity (VA), and less need for SO_2. But for every degree of temperature below 18°C (64°F), there is a trade-off between increasing these advantages and reducing fruit and body. At the lowest temperatures, the amount of amyl acetate produced becomes noticeable, though, as the aromas go from banana through peardrop to nail varnish.

Enzymes The use of enzymatic preparations to affect the biochemical pathways in white winemaking has been on the increase since the mid-1990s. Enzymes are used for improving the pressing or maceration (by reducing the risk of earthy or grassy notes) and increasing the filterability of musts and wines (by increasing clarification), but most attention has been directed towards the flavour-altering capabilities of these preparations, particularly for aromatic grape varieties such as Riesling, Gewürztraminer, and Muscat. Lafazym Arom, for example, is supposed to increase various terpenoid compounds (*see* Micropedia), but whether it and other similar enzymatic preparations have a significant effect on the right terpenes is open to question. It is difficult to judge the effect of these enzymes on either Gewürztraminer or Muscat, but there are reports that they give an inappropriate Turkish-delight floral aroma to Riesling.

Lees stirring What the French call *bâtonnage*, lees stirring has been taken over by certain New World winemakers who hamfistedly stir the lees in their barrel-fermented Chardonnays too frequently and too long, until the wine becomes dominated by overtly rich, dairy-like aromas. *Bâtonnage* was developed to prevent the formation of hydrogen sulphide (*see* Egg, in the Taste and Aroma Chart, p79, as well as the Micropedia). When practised with a light hand, it should merely endow a wine with a barely perceptible umami-like (*see* p74) amplitude that is more textural than taste, with no vulgar telltale aromas.

Malolactic Thanks to the diacetyl, this can produce anything from big and buttery to "baby sick", but malolactic should never be noticeable on the nose – just a creamy texture at the back of the palate. *See also* Non-malolactic.

Micro-oxygenation The oxidation of wine is not only inevitable but desirable, to smooth out the tannins and open up the fruit during winemaking, or simply as part of the maturation process in barrel or bottle. Only the rate of oxidation determines a fault. The role of artificial micro-oxygenation (the introduction of a constant stream of minuscule oxygen bubbles into a wine) has replaced the traditional methods of exposing wine to air (such as that deliberately practised when racking a wine) and has become ubiquitous in the technological environment of premium winemaking.

Non-malolactic For crisp grapes (Sauvignon Blanc, Riesling, etc) and aromatic varieties (Riesling, Gewürztraminer, etc), malolactic is the last thing needed. By avoiding it, the natural acidity is enhanced, and any minerality of fruit is retained.

Oak ageing It is always preferable to barrel-ferment, but ageing part or all of a wine in oak barrels following fermentation in stainless-steel tanks is cheaper. If this can be achieved with a low-key malolactic in the barrel, then the oak-aged wine will be better integrated than a wine that has gone through malolactic in tank.

VA lift Tweaking the volatile acidity in a wine to lift the fruity notes of its aroma and intensify fruitiness on the palate must be undertaken with great care, as a touch too much can reveal acrid notes of acetic acid (vinegar).

Wild-yeast ferment It's debatable how many claimed wild-yeast ferments have been fermented by wild yeasts to any significant degree, unless the fermentations have been carried out in a closed and controlled environment, as research has shown that the yeast that gets into every nook and cranny of the cleanest press-house and winery (the true terror yeast) will always take over the fermentation after the first 2 or 3° of alcohol. True wild-yeast ferments supposedly run the risk of excessive volatile acidity and are famed for their "funky" flavours.

Winter bottling When wines are bottled in the winter, they retain more of their residual carbonic gas, which can heighten the sense of acidity without being *pétillant* as such. This practice best suits crisper, non-malolactic, unoaked, more mineral styles of white wine. For cheaper wines, a similar effect can be created all year around by sparging the wines with CO_2 as they are bottled.

Yeast manipulation Although everything ultimately depends on the initial ingredients in the grape juice being fermented, many of those ingredients are neutral precursors to very specific aromas that can only be activated by certain biochemical processes that yeast cells are capable of initiating. Bearing that in mind and the fact that yeasts are responsible, through those biochemical processes, for more than 40 per cent of all the aromatic compounds found in wine, and it becomes clear that the choice of whether to use a proprietary can have a profound effect on the type of wine produced – for example, Zymaflore VL3 from Laffort promotes the production of 4MMP (the Sauvignon Blanc varietal aroma), 3MH (citrus), and 3MHA (passion fruit).

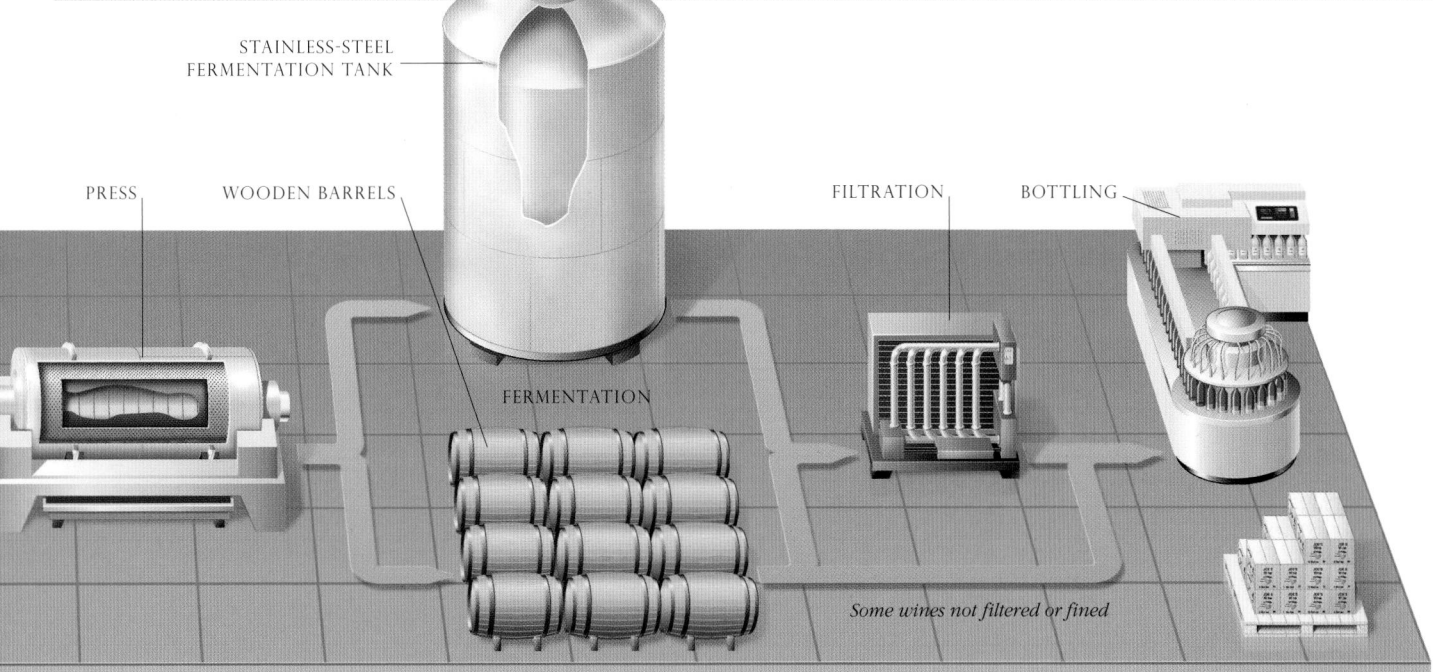

PRESS WOODEN BARRELS STAINLESS-STEEL FERMENTATION TANK FILTRATION BOTTLING

FERMENTATION

Some wines not filtered or fined

SPARKLING WINEMAKING

When grape juice is fermented, sugar is converted into alcohol and carbonic gas. For still wines, the gas is allowed to escape, but if it is prevented from doing so – by putting a lid on a vat or a cork in a bottle – it will remain dissolved in the wine until the lid or cork is removed, when the gas will be released to rush out of the wine in the form of bubbles. The production of all natural sparkling wines is based on this essential principle, using one of four different methods: méthode champenoise, bottle-fermented, méthode rurale, *and* cuve close. *They can also be made by injecting the bubbles.*

MÉTHODE CHAMPENOISE

Also referred to as *méthode traditionnelle* or *méthode classique* (France), *metodo classico* (Italy), and *Cap Classique* (South Africa), this term indicates a sparkling wine that has undergone a second fermentation in the bottle in which it is sold. A label may refer to a wine being "Individually fermented in this bottle", which is the beautifully simple American equivalent of *méthode champenoise*.

After the first fermentation, which might or might not include malolactic or partial malolactic, the *assemblage* takes place. This usually occurs in the first few months of the year following the harvest. At its most basic, and without taking into consideration any particular house style, it is a matter of balancing the characteristics of different wines produced in different places (far and wide or even merely different parts of a single vineyard) and, possibly, different grape varieties. For non-vintage Champagne and increasingly for other serious sparkling wines, the *assemblage* also involves the use of reserve wines. These are, quite literally, wines that are kept in reserve from previous years. The idea that reserve

wines are primarily used to make *cuvées* conform to a particular house style no matter what the quality or character of the base-wine year is a misconception. The job of reserve wine is, if anything, closer to that of the *dosage* in that both make a sparkling wine easier to drink at a younger age. Reserve wines also provide a certain richness, fullness, and mellowed complexity, which is why it is generally considered that the more reserve wines are added, the better. However, unless kept on their yeast, reserve wines can dilute the autolysis process (*see opposite*); thus, there may come a point when potential finesse is traded for instant complexity.

THE SECOND FERMENTATION AND REMUAGE

The second fermentation is the essence of the *méthode champenoise* and is the only way to produce a fully sparkling wine. After the blended wine has undergone its final racking, the *liqueur de tirage*, or bottling liquor, is added. This is a mixture of still Champagne, sugar, selected yeasts, yeast nutrients, and a clarifying agent. The amount of sugar added depends on the degree of effervescence required and the amount of natural sugar in the wine. The wines are bottled (usually in May or thereabouts) and capped with a temporary closure. The second fermentation can take between ten days and three months, after which the bottles can be transferred to *pupitres* to undergo *remuage*. A *pupitre* consists of a pair of heavy, hinged, rectangular boards, each containing 60 holes, which have been cut at an angle to enable the bottle to be held by the neck in any position between horizontal and vertical (neck pointing downwards). *Remuage* is a method of riddling the bottles to loosen sediment, encouraging it to move to the neck of the bottle, where it collects. By hand this takes about eight weeks, although many companies now have computerized 504-bottle pallets that perform the task in just eight days. A technique involving the use of porous yeast capsules, which trap the sediment inside them, reduces *remuage* to a mere eight seconds, but this is seldom used. After *remuage*, the wine undergoes a period of ageing *sur point* (in a fully inverted position) before the sediment is removed.

HOW SPARKLING WINE IS MADE

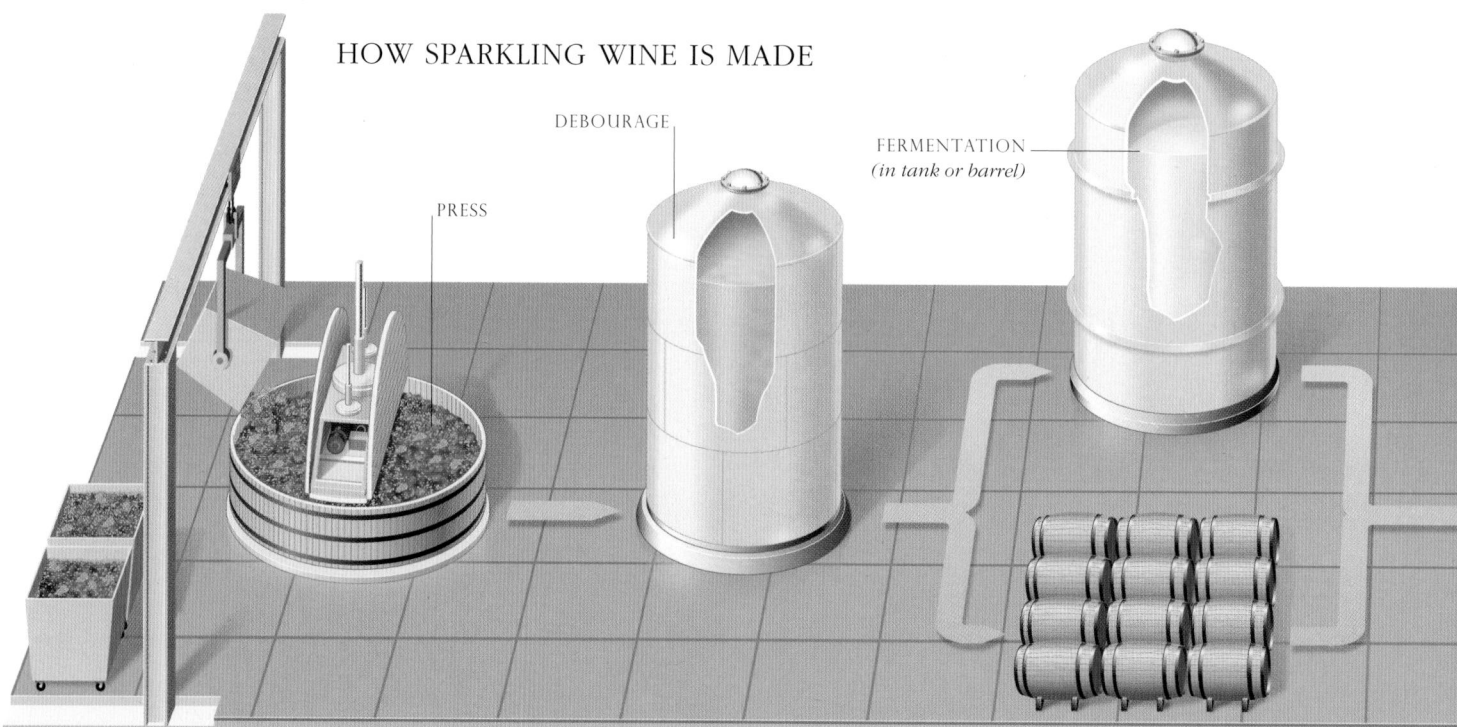

DEBOURAGE

FERMENTATION
(in tank or barrel)

PRESS

PUPITRES AT CA' DEL BOSCO
Bottles of Cuvée Annamaria Clementi, quite probably Italy's greatest sparkling wine, are riddled manually in pupitres *before disgorgement.*

AGEING ON LEES AND AUTOLYSIS

Ageing a sparkling wine on its lees improves its quality because the sediment contains dead yeast cells that break down by autolysis, which contributes to the wine's inimitable "Champagny" character. The optimum duration of yeast ageing depends on the quality of the wine and how it has been processed. Although most Champagnes require at least three years and few sparkling wines produced outside of Champagne benefit from as much as three years, there are many exceptions. Some Champagnes are at their best between 18 months and two years on yeast, while a number of serious sparkling wines can improve for up to a decade. After a sparkling wine's specific optimum time on lees, the complexity stops building, and the wine simply remains fresher than earlier-disgorged wine, since its toasty and biscuity aromas, which require oxygen molecules to evolve, are suppressed in the reductive environment on yeast.

DISGORGEMENT AND DOSAGE

Disgorgement is the removal of the sediment from the wine, which is normally collected in a plastic pot. The normal modern method is known as *dégorgement à la glace*, which involves the immersion of the bottle neck in a shallow bath of freezing brine. This causes

OTHER SPARKLING-WINEMAKING METHODS

Bottle-fermented
This refers to a wine produced through a second fermentation in a bottle but (and this is the catch) not necessarily in the bottle in which it is sold. It may have been fermented in one bottle, transferred to a vat, and, under pressure at -3°C (26°F), filtered into another bottle. This is also known as the "transfer method".

Méthode rurale
This refers to the precursor of *méthode champenoise*, which is still used today, albeit only for a few obscure wines. It involves no second fermentation, the wine being bottled before the first alcoholic fermentation is finished.

Cuve close, Charmat method, or tank method
This is used for the bulk production of inexpensive sparkling wines that have undergone a second fermentation in large tanks before being filtered and bottled under pressure at -3°C (26°F). Contrary to popular belief, there is no evidence to suggest this is an intrinsically inferior way of making sparkling wine. It is only because it is a bulk production method that it tends to attract mediocre base wines and encourage a quick throughput. I genuinely suspect that a *cuve close* produced from the finest base wines of Champagne and given the autolytic benefit of at least three years on its lees before bottling might well be indistinguishable from the "real thing".

Carbonation
This is the cheapest method of putting bubbles into wine and simply involves injecting it with carbon dioxide. Because this is the method used to make lemonade, it is incorrectly assumed that the bubbles achieved through carbonation are large and short-lived. They can be, and fully sparkling wines made by this method will indeed be cheapskates, but modern carbonation plants have the ability to induce the tiniest of bubbles, even to the point of imitating the "prickle" of wine bottled *sur lie*.

the sediment to adhere to the base of the plastic pot, enabling the bottle to be turned upright without disturbing the sediment. When the crown-cap is removed, the semi-frozen sediment is ejected by the internal pressure of the bottle. Only a little wine is lost, as the wine's pressure is reduced by its lowered temperature.

Before corking, bottles are topped up to their previous level, and *liqueur d'expédition* is added. In all cases except for *Nature* and some *Extra Brut*, this *liqueur* includes a small amount of sugar: the younger the wine, the greater the *dosage* of sugar required to balance its acidity. A *Brut* champagne may have between 0 and 12 grams of residual sugar per litre (the upper limit was 15 grams per litre until 2009), but it should have at least 6 grams if it is likely to be cellared, unless the producer intends for it to develop oxidatively.

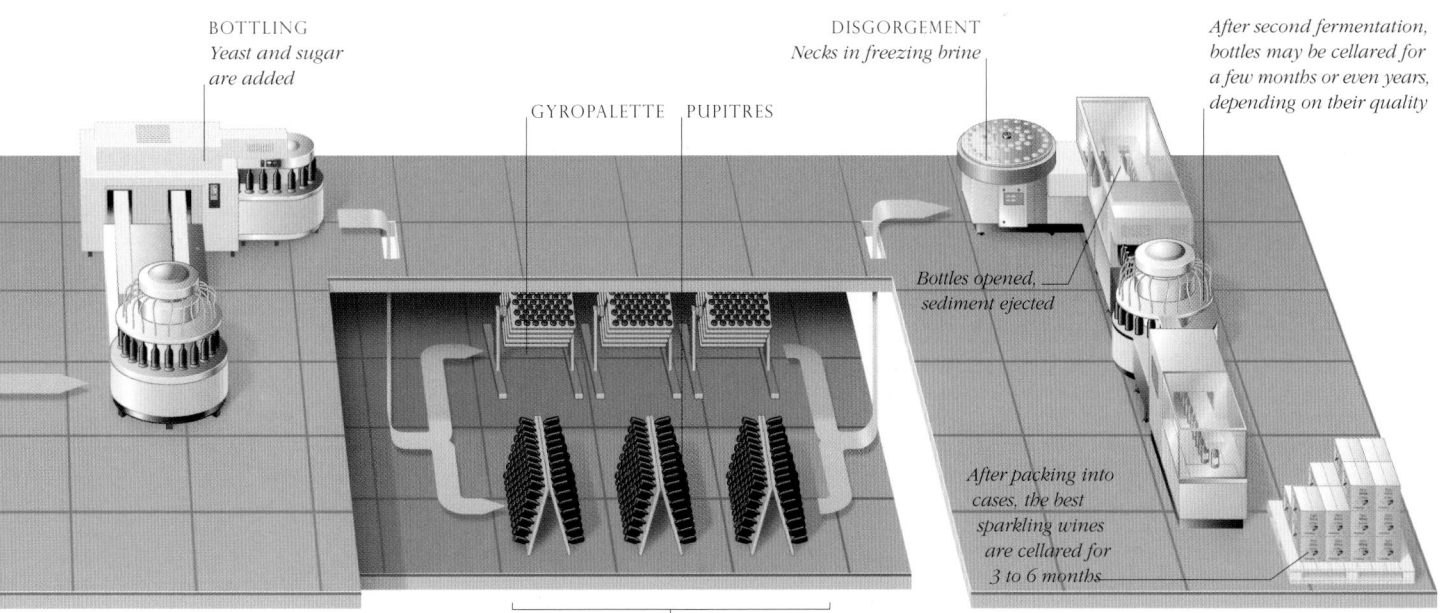

BOTTLING
Yeast and sugar are added

GYROPALETTE PUPITRES

DISGORGEMENT
Necks in freezing brine

After second fermentation, bottles may be cellared for a few months or even years, depending on their quality

Bottles opened, sediment ejected

After packing into cases, the best sparkling wines are cellared for 3 to 6 months

REMUAGE

THE CHOICE OF OAK

I have seen the question only once in print, yet it is the most fundamental question that could possibly be asked: why oak? Why, out of all the woods around the world, is oak and, to any significant degree, only oak used for barrelmaking?

THE ANSWER IS THAT OTHER WOODS are either too porous or contain overpowering aromatic substances that unpleasantly taint the wine. It is not entirely true to say that only oak is used in winemaking; chestnut, for example, is occasionally found in the Rhône and elsewhere, but it is so porous and so tannic that it is usually lined with a neutral substance, rendering the wood no different from any other lined construction material (such as concrete). A beech variety called *rauli* used to be popular in Chile until its winemakers, suddenly exposed to international markets, soon discovered they had become so used to the wood that they had not realized that it gave their wines a musty joss-stick character. Large, redwood tanks are still used in California and Oregon, but they are not greatly appreciated and, as the wood cannot be bent very easily, it is not practical for small barrels. Pine has a strong resinous character that the Greeks seem to enjoy, although they have had 3,000 years to acquire the taste. Most tourists try Retsina, but very few continue to drink it by choice when they return home. Moreover, it is made by adding resin, with no direct contact with the wood and, apart from an oddity called "Tea Wine", produced on La Palma in the Canary Islands, no wine to my knowledge is produced in barrels made of pine. Eucalyptus also has a resinous affect, acacia turns wine yellow, and hardwoods are impossible to bend and contain aromatic oils that are undesirable.

White oak, on the other hand, is easily bent, has a low porosity, acceptable tannin content, and mild, creamy aromatic substances that either have an intrinsic harmony with wine or, like the Greeks, we have grown accustomed to the effect.

LARGE OR SMALL?

The size of the cask is critical to its influence because the smaller it is, the larger the oak-to-wine ratio, and a greater oaky flavour it imparts. A 200-litre *barrique* has, for example, one-and-a-half times the internal surface area of oak for every litre of wine as a 500-litre cask. Traditional sizes for *barriques* range from 205 litres in Champagne, to 225 litres in Bordeaux and Spain, 228 litres in Burgundy, and 300 to 315 litres in Australia and New Zealand.

AN OAK BARREL

The staves of a barrel are held together by metal hoops, which are sometimes positioned at slightly different distances, depending on the traditions of the cooper, or *tonnelier*, in question. There may be a red colour between the two innermost hoops, but this is merely where some winemakers wish to conceal their own dribble marks around the bung by dyeing the entire middle area with wine,

which can look very impressive. When fermenting white wines, the bung is always uppermost and, even with a good ullage, or space, the hole may be left open during the most tumultuous period, but will be sealed with an air-lock valve when the fermentation process settles down and will remain closed during the malolactic fermentation. After racking, when all wines undergo several months of maturation, the barrels are filled to the very top, and positioned so that the tightly sealed bung is to one side, visually reminding cellar-workers that the casks are full.

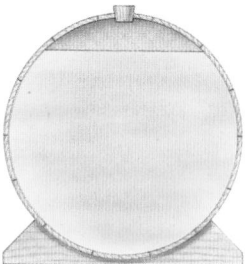 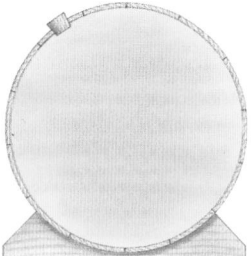

FERMENTING POSITION   MATURATION POSITION

Square barrels were even developed to increase the ratio of oak-to-wine and, although treated as a novelty, were actually more practical and economical than normal casks. More practical because they make more efficient use of storage space, and more economical because their straight sides could be reversed to create a new oak barrel from an old one. An Australian firm even built a square stainless-steel tank with two oak panels made from oak staves that could be replaced, reversed, and adjusted in size to give different oak-to-wine ratios. However, all such barrels became superfluous, with the advent and widespread use of oak chips.

CHIPS OFF THE OLD BLOCK

Using old oak barrels for the finest *barrique*-fermented or *barrique*-matured wines is a question of style rather than a consideration of cost. But for less expensive wines, it is almost entirely a question of economics, as barrels can double, for example, the cost of a *vin de pays*.

The use of new oak *barriques* for just a small percentage of a wine blend can add a certain subliminal complexity to it, although not the overt oakiness that so many people find attractive, yet so few are willing to pay very much for. Oak chips or shavings are the answer. Although generally believed to be a fairly recent phenomenon, the use of oak chips was sufficiently widespread by 1961 to warrant statutory controls in the United States. In fact, as a by-product of barrelmaking, today's ubiquitous chip probably has an equally long, if somewhat more covert, history. Oak chips have been one of the most potent weapons in the New World's armoury, producing relatively inexpensive, but distinctly premium-quality, wines to conquer international markets. This has been particularly evident in Australia, where flying winemakers have

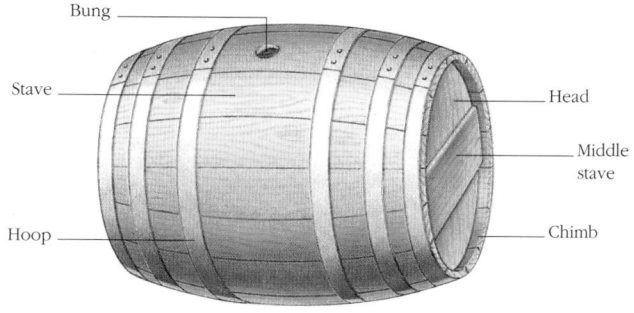

Bung

Stave

Hoop

Head

Middle stave

Chimb

AMERICAN OAK DUST
Light toast

FRENCH OAK CHIPS
Medium toast

AMERICAN OAK CHIPS
High toast

FRENCH OAK "APPELLATIONS"

Some winemakers swear by a particular variety of French oak, but most are suspicious of barrels that claim to be from one specific forest. Tronçais, for example, is one of the most famous oak forests, but the Tronçais forest supplies just 2 per cent of all French oak and, if every barrel claiming to be from there actually did so, the forest would have disappeared long ago.

Perhaps the Bordelais, who are the most experienced in buying new French oak, realized

this centuries ago, as they have traditionally purchased barrels made from "mixed staves" (ie, various forests).

Most winemakers buy from a particular cooper because they like their barrels. This usually has less to do with their construction than with the seasoning of the wood and the toasting of the barrels. Most barrels are not only made on a mix-and-match basis, but the mix of staves is likely to vary from year to year. This is because oak is

sold by auction, and coopers buy on quality, not name. It is more important who owns the forest than where it is located, because known sources, such as the *Office National des Forêts*, which is the only purveyor of *Haute Futaie* oak and which only sells *Haute Futaie* oak, can guarantee a consistency that a private proprietor, even with good wood, cannot. Therefore, some companies, such as Seguin Moreau, follow a policy of buying only *Haute Futaie* oak.

---

not only perfected oak chip wines, but by the early 1990s had exported the techniques to virtually every winemaking country in the world. Some experiments have demonstrated that wine matured with oak chips used in old barrels is "virtually indistinguishable" from the same wine stored in new oak. The range of oak chip products is now very comprehensive, covering the entire range of oak varieties and different toast levels. Some are even impregnated with malolactic bacteria. If a wine label mentions oak, but not *barriques*, barrels, or casks, it is probably a clue that oak chips have been employed in the winemaking and, if the wine is cheap, you can bet on it.

ANYONE FOR TOAST?

Toasting is one operation in the barrelmaking process that has a very direct effect on the taste of the wine. In order to bend the staves, heat is applied in three stages: warming-up (*pre-chauffrage*), shaping (*cintrage*), and toasting (*bousinage*), each of which browns, or chars, the internal surface of the barrel. However, it is only the last stage – *bousinage* – that determines the degree of toasting. During toasting, furanic aldehydes (responsible for "roasted" aromas) reach their maximum concentration, the vanilla aroma of vanillin is heightened, and various phenols, such as eugenol (the chief aromatic constituent of oil of cloves),

BOUSINAGE
The final barrel-firing operation puts a light, medium, or heavy toast on the inner surface.

add a smoky, spicy touch to the complexity of oak aromas in wine.

There are three degrees of toasting: light, medium, and heavy. A light toasting is used by winemakers who seek the most natural oak character (although it is not as neutral as using staves that have been bent with steam); medium varies between a true

medium, which suits most red wine demands, and the so-called medium-plus, which is the favourite for fermenting white wines; the third, a heavy toast, dramatically reduces the coconutty-lactones and leaves a distinctly charred-smoke character that can be overpowering unless used only as a small component in a blend. Furthermore, with time, the high carbon content of heavily toasted barrels can leach the colour out of some wines, so they tend to be used for white wines (often big, brash Chardonnays), although heavy toast is best suited to maturing Bourbon whiskey.

THE DIFFERENT OAKS

Both American and European oaks are used for winemaking. The aromatics of fast-growing, wide-grained American white oak, *Quercus alba*, are more pungent, while there are more tannins, finer in texture, in slow-growing, tight-grained European brown oaks, *Quercus robur* (syn pedunculate oak), and *Quercus sessilis* (syn *Quercus petraea* and *Quercus rouvre*). Much of the appealing, if obvious, coconut character in American oak is also due to the very different barrelmaking techniques used in the US.

Unlike European oak, American is sawn, not split. This ruptures the wood cells, releasing aromatic substances, especially vanillin and up to seven different lactones, which together explain the coconut aroma. American oak is also kiln-dried, which concentrates the lactones, while European oak is seasoned outside for several years, a process that leaches out some of the most aromatic substances, and reduces the more aggressive tannins. The whole process tends to accentuate the character of American oak, while subduing that of European oak.

Many French winemakers consider American oak vulgar. Even so, a little-known fact is that in ultra-conservative Bordeaux, at least 60 châteaux are experimenting with it. Coconut-flavoured claret is by no means a foregone conclusion, but oak is expensive, a little sawn *Quercus alba* goes a long way, and a small percentage of American oak, either as barrels or mixed staves, could, in fact, significantly reduce the percentage of new oak needed each year.

LIGHT TOAST   MEDIUM TOAST   HEAVY TOAST

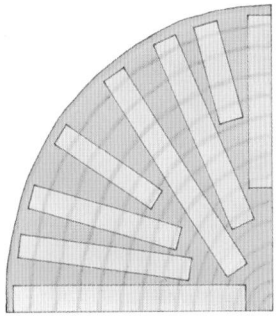
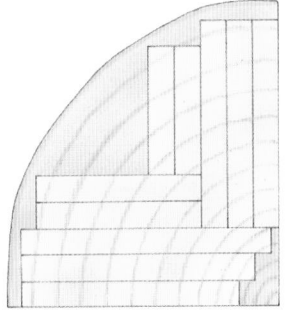

EUROPEAN SPLIT VERSUS AMERICAN SAWN
After the bark has been stripped from a log destined for barrelmaking, it will be split (in Europe) or sawn (in the United States) into quarters. The examples above clearly show that it is more economical to saw staves from a quarter, as opposed to splitting them. This is the major reason why American oak barrels cost half the price of European ones.

REGIONAL OAK VARIETIES

For winemaking, the tighter the size of the oak grain, the better. The slower the tree grows, the tighter the grain – thus, cooler-climate European oak is older and tighter-grained than warmer-climate American oak. Of the European oaks, forest oak (*Quercus sessilis*) is preferred to solitary oak trees (*Quercus robur*) because its branches start higher and the trunk is longer and straighter. Solitary oaks grow faster and have a larger grain because they tend to grow in fertile soil where there is more water. *Quercus sessilis* is also preferred to *Quercus robur* because it is four times richer in aromatic components.

AMERICAN *Quercus alba*

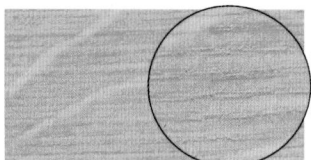

This oak covers most of the eastern US. Some winemakers think that Minnesota and Wisconsin are the best, while others find them too tannic and consider Appalachian oak, particularly from Pennsylvania, to be superior. Other popular oaks are Ohio, Kentucky, Mississippi, and Missouri. All are white oaks, fast-growing, wide-grained, with lower tannin (except for Oregon) than any European brown oaks, but with higher, sweeter, more coconutty aromatics. *Quercus alba* is favoured for traditional Rioja, Australian Shiraz, and California Zinfandel.

OREGON *Quercus gariana*

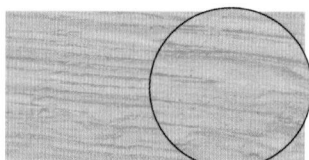

Although a white oak, *Quercus gariana* has a significantly tighter grain than *Quercus alba*. Relatively few barrels have been made from Oregon oak, and it has always been sawn, making it hard to evaluate the claim that it is similar to European oak. In 1996, however, barrels were made from split, open-air seasoned Oregon oak, so watch this space.

ALLIER *Quercus sessilis*

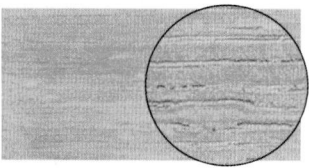

Tight-grained with well-balanced, medium tannin and aromatics, Allier is highly regarded.

ARGONNE *Quercus sessilis*

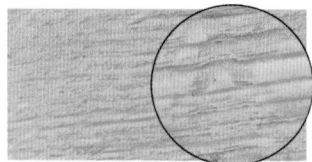

Tight-grained with low aromatics and tannin, this oak was used for Champagne before the advent of stainless-steel. Now seldom used.

AMERICAN OAK FORESTS

EUROPEAN OAK FORESTS

BOURGOGNE *Quercus sessilis*

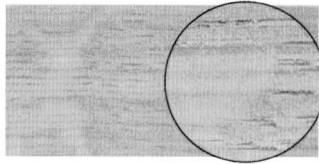

Tight-grained with high tannin and low aromatics, most of this oak goes to Burgundian cellars.

LIMOUSIN *Quercus robur*

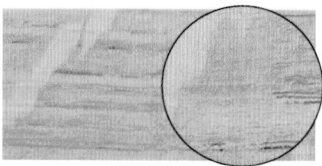

Wider-grained with high tannin and low aromatics, this oak used to be favoured for Chardonnay, but is most widely used for brandy.

NEVERS *Quercus sessilis*

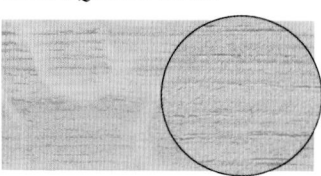

Tight-grained with well-balanced, medium tannin and aromatics, Nevers is highly regarded.

TRONÇAIS *Quercus sessilis*

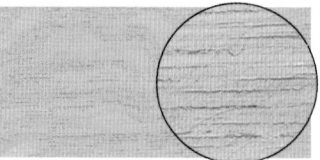

The tightest-grained and, with Vosges, the highest tannin content, Tronçais grows in the Allier forest. It is highly suitable for long-term maturation, owing to its understated aromatics, and has been long sought after.

VOSGES *Quercus sessilis*

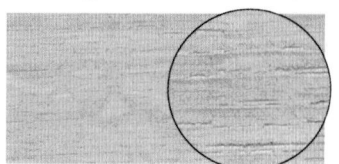

The tight grain, very high tannin content, and understated but slightly spicy aromatics make Vosges an especially well-balanced oak for winemaking. It is underrated, particularly in its home region of Alsace, where even though few winemakers use *barriques*, those who do ironically seem to experiment with virtually every French forest except the one that is actually on their own doorstep. Vosges is especially popular in California and New Zealand, where some winemakers think it is similar to Allier and Nevers. Vosges deserves to receive greater recognition.

BALKAN *Quercus robur*

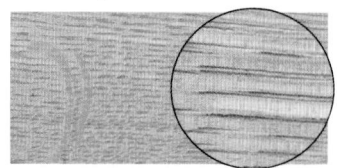

Often called Slavonian or Yugoslav oak, the grain is tight, with medium tannin and low aromatics. Balkan oak is popular for large oval casks, particularly in Italy. Diminishing use due to recent troubles.

PORTUGUESE *Quercus gariana*

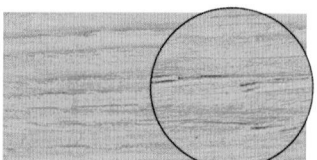

Cooperage oak (*Quercus gariana*) is far less of a commercial concern in Portugal than stunted cork-industry oak (*Quercus suber*), but the former's medium-grain wood has good aromatic properties, making it preferable in Portugal itself, where it is much cheaper than French oak.

RUSSIAN *Quercus sessilis*

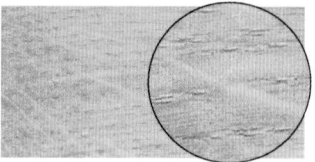

Tight-grained with low aromatics and easy to confuse with French oak under blind conditions, this was the major oak in Bordeaux during the 19th century and up until the 1930s. Thus all the great old vintages owe something to it. Thanks to investment from Seguin Moreau, which set up a cooperage in the Adygey region near the Black Sea, French producers have begun to use Russian oak again, although it is mysteriously just 10 per cent cheaper than French.

BARRELMAKERS

There are approximately 800,000 barrels produced every year around the world, with no fewer than 550,000 made in France. Most are constructed from French oak, but some French-coopered barrels are made from American and Eastern European oak, just as some American coopers build French oak barrels in the USA. There has also been a growth in so-called hybrid barrels, produced from both French and American oak.

SINCE THE TURN OF THE 21ST CENTURY, many French *tonnelleries* have stopped selling their French oak barrels by the name of individual forests, opting instead to offer oak selected on the basis of grain tightness. Although they swear that grain is the ultimate arbiter of quality for oak and claim that selling by grain provides better consistency of product and greater ease of verification, this practice is more likely to be the result of a crackdown by the French authorities investigating oak-origin fraud within individual *tonnelleries*. (It is true that a simple inspection of the croze can show the tightness of grain, whereas who can tell what forest a particular barrel comes from without expensive analysis?)

GRAIN OF TRUTH

Selling solely by grain is wrong on many levels. Discarding such famous names as Allier, Limousin, Nevers, Tronçais, and Vosges – which have, over centuries, created the enviable reputation of French oak around the world – in favour of something that is as generic as grain is madness. It is like abandoning famous wine names such as Bordeaux and Burgundy in favour of a generic descriptor like "body". Despite the French wine industry's many faults, that just wouldn't happen, and a small number of *tonneliers*, such as Vincent and Jérôme Damy, refuse to abandon these world-famous forest names. Those barrelmakers who are adamant about the primacy of grain point out that the grain of oak varies from tree to tree within the same forest. They are probably right, but so what? What is to stop them from specifying the forest and grain? Or just specifying the forest and a variation of grain? Or specifying the grain first and naming the mix of forests used? Maybe they are missing a marketing opportunity; maybe there is a niche in the market for an Allier-Nevers blend or a Limousin-Tronçais-Vosges blend, just as there is for Cabernet-Shiraz or a Grenache-Syrah-Mourvèdre? This would at least keep the famous names of French forests alive. What it all boils down to is transparency and the oak equivalent of what Australian winemakers call "truth in labelling". Any *tonnellerie* found guilty of oak-origin fraud ought to be prosecuted – it's as simple as that. Yet some of the most vociferous proponents of not using forest names claim full traceability of forest origin. If that is so, why not proudly stamp it on every barrel?

> ### DID YOU KNOW?
>
> Contrary to popular belief, the finer the oak's grain, the greater its porosity. This might sound counter-intuitive, but the warmer the weather, the quicker the growth – and the quicker the growth, the wider the grain. Although summer growth is quicker, it is also harder and more dense than spring growth, due to its hotter, drier growing environment. In cooler climates, where there is not as much summer growth, the incidence of less dense, tighter-grained, but more porous spring growth is significantly higher. The tighter the grain, the greater the micro-oxidation and, therefore, the more softening the effect on the tannins in a wine; thus, the tighter grain, the greater its winemaking reputation. Most European oak is much tighter-grained than American oak, and Tronçais – which has the narrowest trunks and greatest proportion of spring wood to summer wood of all French forests – has the tightest grain, hence the greatest reputation.

A SELECTION OF THE BEST AND MOST WIDELY ENCOUNTERED
BARRELMAKERS

AQUITAINE
Cazouls-Les-Beziers, Languedoc, France
Annual production: 40,000 barrels
Established at Bellebat in the Entre-Deux-Mers, Tonnellerie d'Aquitaine has been supplying First Growth Bordeaux châteaux since 1860, all oak air-seasoned for two to three years. Traditional Bordeaux and Burgundian barrels and puncheons are produced in French oak only, all air-seasoned for two to three years. Aquitaine recommends Allier and Tronçais for ageing Pinot Noir, Chardonnay, or Syrah 15–24 months; Nevers and Bertranges for ageing Pinot Noir, Merlot, Cabernet Sauvignon, or Cabernet Franc 12–18 months; Vosges for ageing Syrah or Grenache 9–16 months; and Belleme, Jupilles, and Berce for ageing white wines (Sauvignon Blanc, Chardonnay, or Viognier) and lighter reds (Sangiovese, Syrah, or Merlot) 8–12 months in barrel.

BERNARD
Lignières Sonneville, Cognac, France
Annual production: 6,500 barrels
This third generation *cognaçais tonnellerie* was established in 1936, and its modern, computer-controlled facility still uses a conventional brazier firing to toast the barrels. Hogsheads and puncheons are produced in addition to the classic Bordeaux and Burgundian barrels that are traditional in these parts. Winemakers who use these barrels talk about their exceptional consistency of performance.

BERTHOMIEU
La Charité-sur-Loire, Loire, France
Annual production: confidential
All barrels are constructed from a blend of Allier, Centre-France, Nevers, and Vosges oaks. (Berthomieu also does a "Hybride" barrel with French staves and American heads.) This *tonnellerie* has developed a unique toasting system that combines steaming with firing to provide an exceptionally deep heat penetration by opening the pores of the staves. Winemakers like the elegant results using Berthomieu barrels, appreciating the sweetness and mouthfeel when vinifying whites and roasted coffee-bean and floral components when ageing reds.

BILLON
Beaune, Burgundy, France
Annual production: 12,000 barrels
Founded in 1947 and run today by Vincent Damy, a third-generation *tonnelier*, Billon is a sister company to Damy under Les Tonnelleries de Bourgogne, which is owned by Vincent's father, Jacques Damy. Billon specializes in oak from specific and hard-to-source forests such as Bertranges, Cher, Citeaux, Jupilles, and Jura. Its barrels are often used for Pinot Noir in New Zealand, where winemakers have begun using Billon for Chardonnay and Syrah. Billon seasons its oak in the open for two to three years, dependent on climatic conditions. Winemakers like the sweet spiciness that Billon barrels bring to their wines. Billon also produces barrels in acacia and chestnut.

T W BOSWELL
See World Cooperage

BOUTES
Beychac et Caillau, Bordeaux, France
Annual production: 28,000 barrels
Since 1880, this family-owned *tonnellerie* in Entre-Deux-Mers has specialized in Allier oak, air-seasoned in Allier itself and toasted longer and at lower temperatures than most other barrels. These are produced in three qualities: the conventional "Tradition" (18–24

months' seasoning and manual toasting) and "Selection" (minimum of three years' seasoning, with computer-controlled toasting) and the somewhat unconventional "Grande Réserve" barrels (which appeal to winemakers who want new barrels but only for micro-oxygenation, not the aromas of new oak). Boutes also assembles barrels made from fine-grain oak grown in various other European countries (notably Romania) and American oak (from Ohio, Missouri, and Kentucky).

BULGARIAN OAK
Skutare, Southern Region, Bulgaria

Annual production: 500 barrels

Bulgaria represents the fourth-largest reserves of oak forests in Europe, and Bulgarian Oak (aka Balkan Oak and Teres Tonnellerie) supplies, among others, Trentadue and Gallo wineries. All Bulgarian oak is air-seasoned for between two and three years and slow-toasted over open fire. Some of the latest products include Bulgarian-coopered barrels made from American and French oak.

CADUS
Ladoix-Serrigny, Burgundy, France

Annual production: 17,000 barrels

Founded in 1996, Cadus was conceived by Vincent Bouchard of Bouchard Cooperage, an international barrel broker, with Maison Jadot and the Vicard *tonnellerie* as its major shareholders. Cadus is managed by François "Paquito" Barbier, a *tonnelier* with more than 30 years' experience. Although one of the two original goals was to produce the best custom-made barrels available for Chardonnay and Pinot Noir, Cadus barrels are now used with many other varietals that require the subtle influence of fine-grained oak. The other goal was to study the impact of different climates on the seasoning of staves. All oak is air-seasoned for a minimum of 30 months, with toasting strictly controlled by time and temperature. Winemakers find that Cadus barrels shine the spotlight on the fruit in their wines, ramping up the richness on the palate.

DAMY
Meursault, Burgundy, France

Annual production: 20,000 barrels

A father-and-son handcrafted operation, this *tonnellerie* was founded in 1946 is now managed by third-generation Jérôme Damy, who has moved the business into a new, ultra-modern facility. Damy offers a choice of oak from Burgundy, Allier, Vosges, Cher, Centre de France, Limousin, Nevers, and Tronçais, as well as American and Hungarian oak. Its barrels are highly regarded in France for Chardonnay, which is why they are to be found in more than 80 per cent of the cellars in the Côte de Beaune, especially Puligny-Montrachet and Meursault. In New Zealand, Damy is widely used for Pinot Noir. This *tonnellerie* developed the "Long Toast" for preserving grape aromas in Chardonnay and delicate red wines. Winemakers enjoy the soft, floral effect of Damy oak, which always supports and never dominates.

DARGAUD & JAEGLE
Romanèch-Thorins, Burgundy, France

Annual production: 24,000 barrels

Founded in 1921, this family-owned *tonnellerie* in modern premises does not buy trees or split wood, believing that effective quality control can be made only at stave stage. All Dargaud & Jaegle's barrels are therefore made from bought-in staves. The spiciness, purity of fruit, and roundness that these barrels bring to the palate makes Dargaud & Jaegle a favourite of many white-wine specialists. The company also produces barrels in chestnut.

DEMPTOS
Saint-Caprais-de-Bordeaux, France

Annual production: 75,000 barrels

Founded in 1825, Demptos remained a family-owned business for more than 160 years, opening up a subsidiary cooperage in the Napa Valley in 1982, just seven years prior to a takeover by François Frères. In 1989, Jean François, the owner of François Frères, pulled his son Jérôme out of business school and put him in charge of Demptos; Jérôme now runs the entire François Frères group, which has subsidiaries in Spain, Hungary, South Africa, and the USA. Demptos's top-of-the-range "Réserve" oak barrel is produced from the company's finest tight-grained oak; its "Essencia" barrel is comprised exclusively of selected high norisoprenoidal (ie, most aromatic) oak; and each barrel in the Demptos D'Collection is supposed to enhance a specific grape variety.

ERABLE
See Saury

EUROPEAN COOPERS
Bátaapáti, Szekszárd, Hungary

Annual production: 2,800 barrels

Established in 1997 with Antinori the major shareholder, European Coopers uses only Hungarian oak sourced from the Zemplen Hills in the Tokaj region and the Mecsek Hills near Pécs. The oak is aged for three years and toasted by hand using traditional fire pots. These barrels are sold under the Kádárok brand and are said to have less oak impact than French barrels, tending to highlight natural fruit aromas and soften the harsher phenolics.

FRANÇOIS FRÈRES
Saint Romain, Burgundy, France

Annual production: confidential

Established in 1910 by Joseph François, this family-run Burgundian *tonnellerie* is now under the control of fourth-generation Jérôme François, whose empire includes either exclusive or partial ownership of eight cooperages and three stave mills. All toasting is strictly controlled by time and temperature. These barrels are definitely not shy in showing their presence in a wine, but many winemakers adore the integration of rich, smoky-creamy aromatics that François Frères barrels can add to their wines. "Exclusive" and "Privilege" casks are aged three years, "Classic" is aged two years, and "Horizon" is made from Hungarian oak. François Frères also owns Demptos.

GILLET
Saint Romain, Burgundy, France

Annual production: 10,000 barrels

This artisanal *tonnellerie* was established by Claude Gillet in 1966, who did not even have his own workshop until 1978. Gillet sources French oak from Allier, Bertranges, Centre de France, Châtillonnais, Limousin, Nevers, and Vosges but also uses American oak from Missouri and Eastern European oak from Romania. Most barrels are multisourced and sold by grain, traditional size, and shape, but some, such as the Bordeaux Château Ferrés, are made exclusively from Allier. Understandably for a Burgundian *tonnellerie*, Gillet's barrels were once used only for Chardonnay and Pinot Noir, but New World producers are now having success with Sauvignon Blanc, Sémillon, Shiraz, and Viognier. Gillet barrels are generally thought to be very elegant, with low-key extraction of flavours, yet capable of providing a sweet, floral kiss to a wine.

KÁDÁROK
See European Coopers

LAGLASSE
Varize, Lorraine, France

Annual production: confidential

Established in 1986 by Alain Laglasse, this small, family-owned

TOASTING AND SHAPING
This barrelmaker is toasting a barrel over a fire pot. The burning wood chips in the pot give off a "flavour" that helps style the wine. The barrel is also shaped at this time.

business specializes in neutral barrels and alternative oak usage. It moved to new premises near Metz in 1998 and supplies Billon and Damy with some of their staves. Laglasse uses only Vosges oak seasoned for one year.

LEROI
See Saury

MERCIER
Barbezieux, Charente-Maritime, France

Annual production: 10,000–15,000 barrels

Strategically located between Bordeaux and Cognac, Mercier was established in 1960. Traditional Bordeaux and Burgundy barrels are made from oak that has been air-seasoned for a minimum of two years. Some winemakers find these barrels too dominant, while those who have worked the longest with Mercier believe that the oak is heavy-handed only in the first few months, after which the wines settle down beautifully, particularly for the more powerful reds. Mercier has launched three speciality barrels: "Delicate White", "Delicate Pinot", and the top-of-the-range three-year-aged "F de Mercier".

MERCUREY
Mercurey, Burgundy, France

Annual production: 16,000 barrels

A Burgundian *tonnellerie* with a *champenois* heart, this business was established in 1992 by Nicolas Tarteret, the owner of a sawmill at Aix-en-Othe, west of Troyes, the ancient capital of Champagne, not far from Estissac, where Nicolas's father Philippe Tarteret set up the first sawmill in Champagne. Just two years after the business was founded on two barrels a day, Bruno Lorenzon of Domaine Lorenzon was so impressed by the quality that he personally developed export markets for Mercurey barrels in Australia, Canada, New Zealand, and South Africa. All oak is sourced within 100 km (60 miles) of the company's sawmill in Aix-en-Othe and air-seasoned for at least two years. Mercurey offers a number of special toasts, including the "Chalk Selection", which involves a light toasting of specially selected oak grown on chalky soils.

MILLET
Galgon, Bordeaux, France

Annual production: confidential

This small, family-owned *tonnellerie* was founded in 1952 in Puisseguin by Guy Millet, whose son Dominique took over in 1995 and moved the business to new premises five years later. As might be expected, these barrels are made very much in the Bordeaux tradition and are sought out by winemakers for Merlot and Cabernet in various countries.

MISTRAL BARRELS
Sonoma, California, USA

Annual production: confidential

Established in 1995, the Chilean-owned Mistral Barrels produces two brands – "Mistral" itself and "Odysé" – and either may be constructed from French (fine-grain Allier and Vosges) or American (Missouri and Kentucky), both of which have been air-seasoned for 30 months. The difference between the two is that the "Mistral" barrel is water-steam bent and fine-toasted, while "Odysé" is water-steam bent and convection-toasted. Steam bending avoids carbonization, and convection toasting takes this one step further, as "Odysé" barrels are toasted by purified hot air without open fire, utilizing Mistral's own trademarked process, which avoids smoke or charring; they say this eliminates potentially harmful contaminants. Mistral is fast becoming the Madonna of the barrelmaking world. First, they reinvent the ancient art of steam bending, then they reinvent toasting as a convection process – and just as that gets popular, they reinvent it over again as the "Ambrosia Flavor Boost", which promises to be even sweeter, even more complex, and more intense than "Odysé" and can be ordered not only for any barrel but for anything, from staves to oak dust! In 2001, Mistral reinvented the zigzag barrel renovation system, whereby 24–28 narrow new oak staves can be inserted through (and removed from) the bung-hole. Other zigzag systems require the removal of the head for insertion and removal, which is hardly winemaker-friendly, so this was a particularly welcome reinvention.

MORLIER
Saint-Estèphe, Bordeaux, France

Annual production: 3,000 barrels

A true artisanal *tonnelier*, Morlier provides barrels to some of the most famous Bordeaux châteaux, including at least one First Growth (Latour).

NADALIÉ
Ludon-Médoc, Bordeaux, France

Annual production: confidential

A family-owned *tonnellerie* for five generations, Nadalié has supplied Bordeaux châteaux with barrels since 1910 and now produces the full range of traditional Bordeaux and Burgundian barrels. Nadalié uses French, Hungarian, and American oak (from its own Megnin Mills in Pennsylvania) and has operated its own cooperage in Calistoga, California, since 1980, the oldest French-style manufacturing cooperage in the Americas. The company also owns Tonnellerie Marsannay, which offers barrels from specific forests (Allier, Bertranges, Jupilles, Nevers, Tronçais, and Vosges).

ODYSÉ
See Mistral Barrels

OKANAGAN BARREL WORKS
Oliver, British Columbia, Canada

Annual production: confidential

Here's a heart-warming story about a guy who takes it on the chin, doesn't complain, and moves quickly to seize the day. In 1996, Cal Craik, the future founder of this enterprise, was out of work in Vancouver. Cal always fancied living in the Okanagan Valley, but there was no job to go to. However, there was no job in Vancouver either and, with his wife a full-time mother, nothing to stop him, so he upped sticks and moved to the Oliver, where on a whim he built and sold wooden gift boxes to local wineries to feed the family and pay the mortgage. One evening, he was sharing a drink with his neighbour, who said what a shame it was that there was no one in the Okanagan Valley selling, repairing, or refurbishing wine barrels. (Unbelievably, the last cooperage to operate in Canada, the Sweeney Cooperage, had closed up in the early 1980s.) After a quick trip to Napa, Cal came back as the local representative for the Demptos Napa Cooperage. He also brought back a few used barrels and set to work trying to figure out how to take them apart and put them back together again. Once he'd solved that, Cal designed and constructed a specially built machine to shave out the insides of old barrels, to give them a bit more life. In 1998, Cal met Chris Scott, who had started importing oak barrels from Central Europe, and the two decided to team up as the Okanagan Barrel Works, which now makes barrels from French (Centre de France) and American (Pennsylvania) oak. The wood is air-seasoned for a minimum of two years.

OREGON BARREL WORKS
McMinnville, Oregon, USA

Annual production: 800 barrels

Established in 1996 by Rick DeFerrari – the first (and still the only) person to hand-split Oregon oak for making barrels – Oregon Barrel Works makes hand-split barrels, seasoned for three years in the open and coopered in traditional Bordeaux or Burgundian style. To further refine the Oregon oak taste profile, Oregon Barrel Works initiated a water-immersion programme in 2006, whereby the wood is rinsed three times prior to coopering, and has combined this with a new slow-toasting process. In 2007, Oregon Barrel Works introduced a range of French oak barrels from specific vineyards (Bertranges, Centre de France, Chatillon, Fontainebleau, Nevers, and Vosges), all seasoned three years in the open in France but coopered in McMinnville, where they are marketed under the Tonnellerie DeFerrari trade name.

QUINTESSENCE
Beychac et Caillau, Bordeaux, France

Annual production: confidential

In addition to traditional Bordeaux and Burgundian barrels made from French, Slovakian, and American (Missouri Ozark) oak, this *tonnellerie* also produces a "Fleur de Quintessence" constructed from extra-fine-grain Tronçais and Jupilles oak. Part of World Cooperage with TW Boswell.

RADOUX
Jonzac, Charente-Maritime, France

Annual production: confidential

Robert Radoux established himself as an artisanal *tonnelier* at Jonzac, north of Bordeaux, in 1947, with a business that was developed into Tonnellerie Radoux in 1982 by his son Christian. The latter opened his own stave mill in 1987, also setting up cooperages in Stellenbosch, South Africa, that same year and in Rioja, Spain, and Santa Rosa, California, in 1994. Radoux has recently introduced crosscut staves for more extraction and developed a device called Oakscan, which measures tannin levels in staves and is used on every stave produced by the company to sort them by tannin. Radoux's standard French barrels are air-seasoned for one to two years and sold by grain, but bespoke barrels can be seasoned longer and produced from a specific forest. "Blend Limited Edition" is the top of the range and made from Eastern European and American (Minnesota, Missouri, and Appalachian) oak. Radoux and its sister company Seguin-Moreau form the major part of the cooperage division of Oneo, the largest barrelmaker in the world (formerly known as Sabaté Diosos).

ROUSSEAU
Couchey, Burgundy, France

Annual production: confidential

Rousseau's barrels can be seen when visiting many Burgundy cellars, particularly in the Côte de Nuits. To decipher their marks: HBE is Vosges; HBC is selected from oak rich in polysaccharides and vanillin; HB is a mix of Centre de France and Vosges; and HB36 is an undisclosed mix of forests air-seasoned for 36 months. Rousseau also sells an "Expert" range, which comprises "Video" and "Piano" for white wines and "Allegro" and "Forte" for reds. All four are constructed from a blend of oaks involving different mixes of fine- and medium-grain oak, and all are double toasted. ("Forte" is high-toasted; "Allegro" is a long, deep, high-temperature, medium-plus toast; and the other two are long, low-temperature, medium-low toast.) All except the "Forte" are designed to give a restrained, balanced impact that enhances the wine's fruit. Single-forest barrels are made from Bertranges, Châtillon, and Tronçais. Winemakers like the rich, creamy sweetness that Rousseau barrels bring to white wines (some believe this enhances tropical-fruit aromas) and the rich dark-chocolate aromas in red wines.

SAINT MARTIN
Pecarrere, Buzet, France

Annual production: 14,000 barrels

This business was established in 1945 as an artisanal *tonnelier* for Armagnac producers but developed into the Bordeaux market by the 1950s and started exporting in 1997. All oak is from Allier, Vosges, and other selected French forests and is air-seasoned for a minimum of two years (three for limited production of pure Tronçais).

SAURY
Brive, Corrèze, France

Annual production: 40,000 barrels

Established in 1873 and still family-owned, this firm purchased two other *tonnelleries* in 2006, both in Cognac: Leroi (dating back to 1773 and formerly belonging to Martell, to which Leroi still sells 80 per cent of its 13,000 barrel production) and Erable. These additions made Saury the fifth-largest cooperage in the world. All oak is air-seasoned for two to three years. Saury also produces water-immersion barrels, which are rinsed prior to cooperage and aptly branded "Immersion". Some winemakers of well-structured reds, such as Syrah and Zinfandel, like the way that Saury barrels have minimal impact upon varietal structure.

SEGUIN MOREAU
Chagny, Burgundy, France

Annual production: 90,000 barrels

Tonnellerie Moreau was established in 1838; Tonnellerie Seguin was established in 1870. After Rémy Martin became the sole owner of Seguin in 1972, Moreau was purchased, and the two companies were merged. Today, Seguin Moreau has one stave mill in France plus three cooperages: one in Charente, one in Burgundy, and one in Napa. It is the largest individual barrelmaker in the world, and with its sister company Radoux, it forms the major part of the cooperage division of Oneo, the largest barrelmaking group in the world (formerly known as Sabaté Diosos). For the giant of the barrelmaking world, Seguin Moreau makes some beautiful barrels, which can be seen when visiting the cellars of some of the world's greatest wines (such as châteaux Cheval Blanc, Haut Brion, Latour, Margaux, Mouton Rothschild, and Yquem, Domaine Ramonet in Burgundy, and Krug in Champagne). As might be expected, Seguin Moreau uses oak from a large range of sources – first and foremost France (from where they assemble a classic blend of Haute Futaie forests, including Allier, Tronçais, Nevers, and Centre de

France), then Eastern Europe (Hungary, Slovakia, and Romania), Russia (Republic of Adygea), and the USA (the Appalachians and the Midwest forests of Minnesota, Iowa, and Missouri). The company makes all the classic barrel shapes, sizes, and types, all toasted for various durations at different temperatures. On these barrels you might see one of the following: "SVT" (Sélection Vendanges Tardives), made from ultra-tight-grain oak that has been seasoned in the open for 18–36 months and designed with sweet wines in mind; "SC" (Sélection Cabernet), very tight grain, for ageing all red Bordeaux varietals over extended periods; "SR" (Sélection Rouge), described as a workhorse for all red wines requiring 15–18 months in barrel; "SB" (Sélection Blanc), restricted to a medium-long toasting for white-wine ageing requiring oak character; "ST" (Sélection Terroir), designed to have minimum oak impact, allowing an expression of fruit and terroir over 8–12 months ageing in barrel; "BGC" (Bourgogne Grand Cru), made from very tight-grain oak and designed with ultra-premium white and red wines in mind, with up to 18 months in barrel; "CP" (Chagny Pinot), toasted in Burgundian style to enhance sweet oak tannins in red-wine varietals not requiring long ageing; "CW" (Chagny White), the same Burgundian-style toasting but on oak with a medium- to semi-tight-grain oak, for faster expression of oak on white wines, particularly Chardonnay, where less barrel ageing is required; and "Grand Domaine", which is the red-wine equivalent of "CW". Seguin Moreau is famous – some might say infamous – for its U-Stave system, whereby the inside of the barrel consists of a continuous series of grooves, 10 mm wide and 5 mm deep, that increases the ratio of oak surface to wine by 75 per cent. No winemaker ever uses U-Stave barrels for 100 per cent of any wine, but some find the odd barrel can create an extremely useful blending component.

SIRUGUE
Nuits-Saint-Georges, Burgundy, France

Annual production: confidential

Sirugue was established at Morey-Saint-Denis in 1903 by Félix Sirugue, whose father Victor Sirugue was the *tonnelier* for Maison Thomas-Massot at Gevrey Chambertin, later moving to Nuits-Saint-Georges. In the 1950s, when the introduction of cement tanks dramatically reduced the demand, Félix's son Emile looked abroad for sales; thanks to James Zellerbach, the American industrialist who made the first barrel-fermented California Chardonnay (Hanzell 1957 Chardonnay), this *tonnellerie* opened up sales of French oak to the USA. Still family-owned and run by Félix's grandchildren, Sirugue

very traditionally produces just four types of barrel, although kosher versions are available. Winemakers who use Sirugue find that these barrels have typically subtle smoky vanillin aromas, amplifying the fruit in white wines and adding spice to red wines.

SUD-OUEST
Brens, Gaillac, France

Annual production: confidential

As part of the Sylvaboise group since 1988, Sud-Ouest has exclusive access to three sawmills and two stavemills. In addition to the traditional Bordeaux and Burgundian barrels of various sizes produced in either French or American oak, Sud-Ouest also offers the "Alliance F" (which is composed of French staves with American heads) and "Alliance A" (American staves with French heads) and is one of the few *tonnelleries* to produce acacia barrels.

SYLVAIN
Saint Denis de Pile, Bordeaux, France

Annual production: confidential

This business was established in 1957 by Gérard Sylvain, who opened a small barrel-repair workshop in Libourne. Under Gérard's son Jean-Luc, the company moved to a full production facility in Saint Denis de Pile, just north of the St-Émilion district. Sylvain uses exclusively French oak from 150–200-year-old trees in several forests, including Tronçais, Bercé, Fontainebleau, and Haguenau. It produces Bordeaux barrels (including "Château Tradition" and "Château Ferré") in three types: "Réserve" (top of the range, very fine grain); "Sélection" (might include some *Quercus robur*, fine grain, recommended for powerful, tannic wines); and "Blanc" (a fine-grain barrel developed for the balance and elegance of white wine).

TARANSAUD
Cognac, France

Annual production: confidential

Established at Juillac-le-Coq in 1932 by Roger Taransaud, whose family have been *tonneliers* since 1672, the business moved to Cognac in 1937. Taransaud was taken over in 1972 by Cognac producer Hennessy, which sold the firm on to its current owners, the Pracomtal family, who built a new cooperage. The Pracomtal family owns the Chêne group, which also includes Jacques Garnier (a *tonnellerie* in Charente-Maritime), Canton (a Kentucky-based cooperage combining American oak and "French know-how"), and Thalés (reconditioned barrels), and co-owns the Kádár Hungary cooperage. All oak is air-seasoned for between two and three years, depending on the thickness of the staves (12 months for every 10 mm). This is very much a red-wine *tonnelerie*. The 350-litre "Export" barrel is recommended for

grapes like Syrah, Zinfandel, Petit Verdot, and Grenache, while the 400-litre "Export" barrel is built for varieties such as Barbera, Nebbiolo, Syrah, and Sangiovese. Winemakers who use Taransaud barrels often say they like the smoky-roasted coffee-bean aromas they impart.

VICARD
Cognac, France

Annual production: 70,000 barrels

This sixth-generation *tonnellerie* was founded in Cognac by Paul Vicard, whose son Jean was named Best Craftsman in France in 1965. Vicard is the largest single-site cooperage in France, spread over 12 ha (30 acres), including a 6-ha (15-acre) wood yard that is due to be expanded to 8 ha (20 acres). The company uses French, Eastern European, and American oak, with the American oak sourced exclusively from Missouri but aged in Cognac, where the climate is better suited to seasoning in the open. Toasting is carried out by a fully automated, patented state-of-the-art process to guarantee a specific temperature, duration, and percentage of humidity during firing. Vicard owns three stave mills (Merrains de France, Merrains de Cognac, and Merrains du Périgord), and its barrels are best suited to red wines, particularly Merlot, Cabernet Sauvignon, and Cabernet Franc.

WORLD COOPERAGE
Napa, California, USA

Annual production: confidential

Established in 1912 by Thomas Walton Boswell, World Cooperage (aka Cooperages 1912 and Tonnellerie du Monde) owns the Quintessence *tonnellerie* in Bordeaux, which is supplied by its own sawmill at Monthureux-sur-Saône. World Cooperage is still owned by the Boswell family, who make and sell barrels under two brands: World Cooperage and the upmarket TW Boswell range. The company's traditional barrels are made from extra-fine-grain French or fine- or extra-fine-grain American (Missouri Ozark) oak, plus hybrids of American oak staves and French heads. All oak is a minimum of two years' air-seasoned, with a limited availability of 36 months. The TW Boswell range consists of traditional barrels, made from French, Slovakian, and American (Missouri Ozark) oak, in its "Legacy" range; the "Polonyi Blanc" barrel for full-bodied white wine and "Polonyi Rouge" for red wines, both from Slovakian oak; the "Appellation Series" ("Médoc", "Côte d'Or", "Côtes du Rhône", and "Pinotage"); and "Eau" for its water-immersion barrels. All TW Boswell oak is air-seasoned for 30 months, with a limited availability of 36 months. All the French and European oak is extra-fine grain, and the American oak can be extra-fine grain by special order.

GRAPE VARIETIES

The grape variety used for a wine is the most influential factor in determining its taste. The factors that influence the inherent flavour of any grape variety are the same as those that determine the varietal taste of any fruit.

THE VITIS FAMILY

The vine family is a large and diverse family of plants ranging from the tiny pot-plant Kangaroo Vine to Virginia Creeper. The Wine Vine Tree (*see below*) shows how *Vitis vinifera*, the classic winemaking species, relates to the rest of the vine family. The *Vitis vinifera* is one of many belonging to the genus *Euvitis*. Other species in this genus are used for rootstock.

Upon close examination, readers who possess earlier editions of this book might notice that I have slightly pruned the Wine Vine Tree. *Euvitis* (or *Euvites*) and *Muscadinia* used to be classified as sub-genera of *Vitis*, but *Muscadinia* is now considered to be its own genus because of the difference in the number of its chromosomes. Without this sub-genus, *Euvitis* becomes redundant and only *Vitis* remains. Furthermore, after several revisions, the number of genera in the botanical family *Vitaceae* has risen from 10 to 17, although Professor Markus Keller, author of *The Science of Grapevines* (Academic Press, 2010), which lists 17 genera, told me, "I may have to revise the number down to 15, 14, 12, even as low as 6, or perhaps up to 19 for the next edition, as the botanical classification in this area is in a constant state of flux!"

SIZE

The smaller the fruit, the more concentrated the flavour will be. Thus most classic grape varieties, such as Cabernet Sauvignon and Riesling, have small berries, although some varieties that rely more on elegance than power of concentration, such as the Pinot Noir,

may yield large berries. Many varieties are known as *petit* or *gros* something, and it is usually the *petit* that is the better variety – Petit Vidure is Cabernet Sauvignon; Gros Vidure, Cabernet Franc.

SKIN STRUCTURE

The skin contains most of the aromatic characteristics with which we associate the varietal identity of any fruit. Its construction and thickness is, therefore, of paramount importance. For example, the thick-skinned Sauvignon Blanc produces an aromatic wine that, when ripe, varies in pungency from "peach" in a warm climate to "gooseberry" in a cool climate, and when underripe varies in herbaceousness, ranging from "grassy" to "elderflower" and even "cat's pee". Meanwhile the thin-skinned Sémillon produces a rather neutral wine, although its thin skin makes it susceptible to noble rot and is thus capable of producing one of the world's greatest botrytized sweet wines, with mind-blowing aromatics.

SKIN COLOUR AND THICKNESS

A dark-coloured, thick-skinned grape, such as Cabernet Sauvignon, produces very deep-coloured wines, while the lighter-coloured, thin-skinned grapes, such as Merlot, produce a less intense colour.

ACID–SUGAR RATIO AND OTHER ELEMENTS

The grape's sugar content dictates the wine's alcohol level and the possibility of any natural sweetness; together with the acidity level, this determines the balance. The proportions of a grape's other constituents, or their products after fermentation, form the subtle nuances that differentiate the varietal characters. Although soil, rootstock, and climate have an effect on the ultimate flavour of the grape, the genetics of the vine dictate the end result.

ROOTSTOCK

Hundreds of rootstock varieties have been developed from various vine species, usually *Vitis berlandieri*, *V riparia*, or *V rupestris* (all genus *Vitis*) because they are the most phylloxera-resistant. The precise choice of rootstock is dependent on its suitability to the vinestock on which it is to be grafted, as well as on its adaptability to the geographical location and soil type. The choice can increase or decrease a vine's productivity, and thus has a strong effect upon the quality of the wine produced from the grapes: generally, the lower the quantity, the higher the quality.

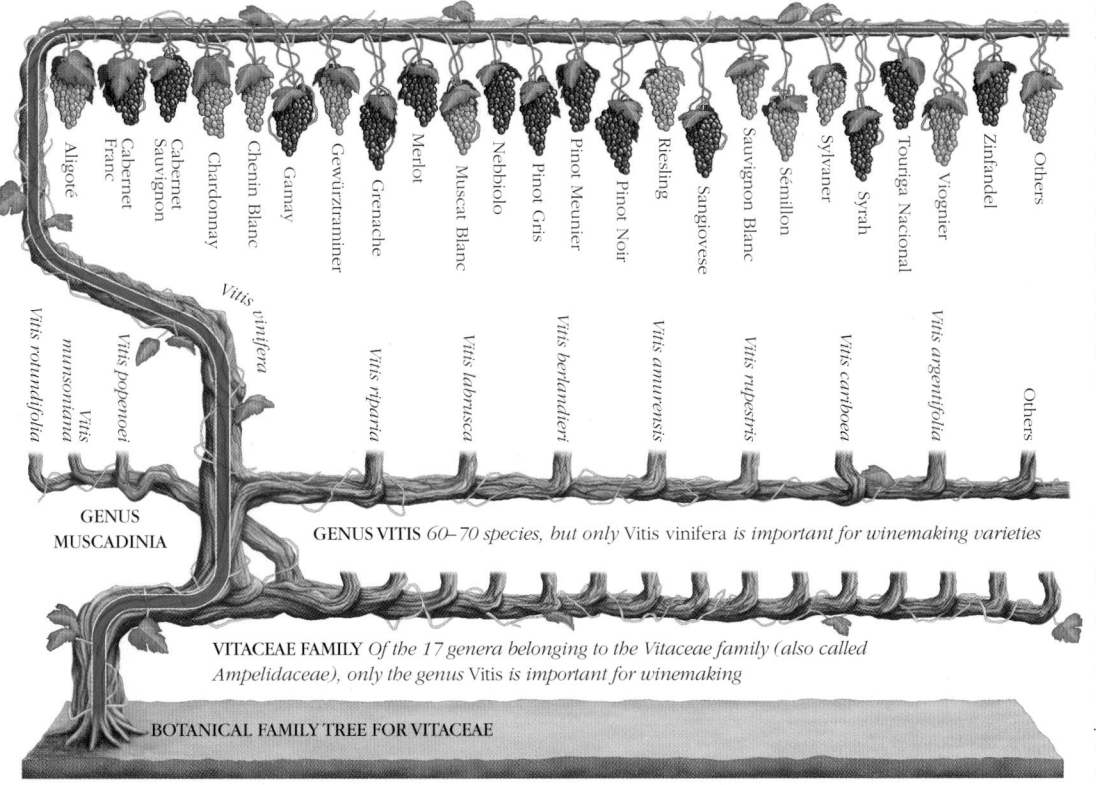

GENUS MUSCADINIA

GENUS VITIS *60–70 species, but only* Vitis vinifera *is important for winemaking varieties*

VITACEAE FAMILY *Of the 17 genera belonging to the Vitaceae family (also called Ampelidaceae), only the genus* Vitis *is important for winemaking*

BOTANICAL FAMILY TREE FOR VITACEAE

THE WINE VINE TREE
The blue line running from the ground traces the parentage of Vitis vinifera, *the species from which all classic winemaking grapes come. Although* Vitis vinifera *is the most important species of the genus* Vitis, *wine is made from grape varieties from other species, notably* Vitis labrusca, *native to North America and, more recently,* Vitis amurensis.

ABC OF GRAPE VARIETIES
INCLUDING SYNONYMS

It is estimated that there are more than 10,000 grape varieties in current commercial production, but this could well include the same grapes under other names. With the relatively short and recent experience of DNA fingerprinting, it is thought that the real number might come down closer to 5,000.

This glossary has grown since it was first introduced in 1988, and that first version was itself an expansion of my two-part feature "An ABC of Grape Varieties", published in *Decanter* in 1981. For ease of use, the list of synonyms has been integrated with the grape variety entries, and all names have been listed alphabetically, regardless of colour, so you have only one section to search.

CROSSES AND HYBRIDS
A cross between grape varieties within one species is called a cross, and a cross between varieties from different species is a hybrid. Cross the same grape varieties more than once and the odds are that the new strains produced will not be the same. Thus *Sylvaner* **x** *Riesling* is the parentage not only of the Rieslaner but also of the Scheurebe, two totally different grapes. It is also possible to cross a variety with itself and produce a different grape. In the following glossary, the parentage of crosses and hybrids is always in *italic*.

Prior to our intervention in the process, most varieties originated by spontaneous crossing (most grapevines are hermaphrodite, but the flowers can be fertilized by the pollen from another variety to create a spontaneous cross) or as seedlings (when a grape drops to the ground and a seedling springs forth, it will never replicate the vine that produced it; thus, a new variety will always result).

CLONES AND CLONING
Within varietal limitations, intensive selection can produce a vine to suit specific conditions, such as to increase yield, resist certain diseases, or to thrive in a particular climate. Identical clones of this vine can then be replicated an infinite number of times by micro-biogenetic techniques. Clones are named by number and initial. For instance, "Riesling clone 88Gm" is the 88th clone of the Riesling variety produced at Geisenheim (Gm), the German viticultural research station. A "localized" clone is a vine that has evolved naturally under specific conditions within a particular environment. These may be named first by grape variety and then by locality and referred to as sub-varieties. However, the name of the original variety is often entirely forgotten with the passing of time, so that the variety acquires a new name altogether.

Ⓢ GRAPE VARIETY SYNONYMS

Many varieties of grape are known by several different synonyms. The Malbec grape, for example, has at least 34 different names, including Pressac, Auxerrois, Balouzet, Cot, Estrangey, and Grifforin. The Chasselas officially has 213 synonyms. This would not be too confusing if the synonyms applied, uniquely, to the same grape variety, but unfortunately this is not the case. The Malbec is again a good example: a black grape, it is known as the Auxerrois in Cahors, but in Alsace and Chablis, the Auxerrois is a white grape, while in other parts of France, the Malbec is known as the Cahors!

Synonyms relating to localized clones or sub-varieties are often regarded as singularly separate varieties in their own right. The Italian Trebbiano, itself a synonym for the French Ugni Blanc, has many sub-varieties recognized by the Italian vine regulations. Also, many synonyms revolve around the name of another grape variety, although they are not necessarily related. Ampelographers distinguish between "erroneous" and "misleading" synonyms. The former refers to varieties that have mistakenly been given the name of another, totally different variety, whereas the latter refers to varieties whose names suggest, incorrectly, that they are related to another variety – for example, the Pinot Chardonnay, which is Chardonnay, and not remotely related to any Pinot variety whatsoever.

OVERVIEW OF GRAPE COLOURS

Ⓦ WHITE VARIETIES
Most white grapes actually range from a pale green (higher-acid skin sap) to an amber-yellow (lower acidity).

Ⓜ MID-COLOURED VARIETIES
Between black grapes and white grapes, there are numerous mid-coloured varieties. The French sub-divide this category into *rouge*, *rosé*, and *gris*, but similar distinctions could be made within either black or white grape categories, which would confuse more than clarify; thus, all mid-coloured varieties here are classified as one.

Ⓑ BLACK VARIETIES
Black grapes vary from dark, ruddy red (higher-acid skin sap) to blue-black (lower acidity). While white wine can be made from most black grapes, because their juice is clear and uncoloured, red wine can be made only from black grapes, since it is the pigments in their skin, called anthocyanins, that give the wine its colour.

Ⓣ TEINTURIER VARIETIES
A *teinturier* variety literally means a "dyer" grape, so called because not only is its skin coloured, but so is its red-coloured juice. Without having to rely on highly phenolic anthocyanins, red wines produced from *teinturier* grapes can be deeply coloured with very little tannin, which can be an odd taste sensation unless crafted well (ie, blended with other grape varieties, aged in oak to extract wood tannins, and so on).

Note The majority of varieties mentioned in the text below are cross-referenced, but readers will occasionally come across some references, particularly of varieties indicated as parents or distant relatives of various crosses and hybrids, that lead to dead ends. This is for purely practical purposes, as they would lead to ever more obscure entries, culminating in a far longer list of little more practical use.

KEY

Ⓦ *White grape variety*

Ⓜ *Mid-coloured grape variety*

Ⓑ *Black grape variety*

Ⓣ *Teinturier grape variety*

Ⓢ *Synonym*

Ⓢ **Abbondosa** Synonym for Nuragus

Ⓑ **Abbuoto** Incorrectly linked to the ancient Roman wine Caecuban (because this is a black grape, while Caecuban was a white renowned for turning "fire-coloured" as it aged), Abbuoto produces a deep-coloured, full-flavoured red with a tannic edge that repays ageing in oak and being blended with at least one other variety to bring smoothness and intensity, such as Villa Matilde's excellent Cecubo.

Ⓑ **Abouriou** This grape produces a Gamay-like red wine, as well as gallons of inexpensive rosé, in southwestern France.

Ⓢ **Acadie** Synonym for L'Acadie

Ⓑ **Ada Karasi** or **Adakarasi** A Turkish grape traditionally used for producing a red but mostly makes rosé wines called Buyulubag.

Ⓑ **Agiorgitiko** An excellent indigenous Greek grape variety that is responsible for the rich and often oak-aged wines of Nemea, the Agiorgitiko (meaning "the grape of St George") is one of the most widely planted grape varieties in Greece. The best Agiorgitiko has a spicy richness to the fruit, and the greater the altitude at which it is grown, the more defined the spiciness becomes. This is a variety that can withstand the heat, but the cooler it is within the realms of a warm climate, the more it repays.

Ⓑ Aglianico This is the grape that made the famous Falernum of ancient Rome, the modern equivalent of which is typically dark and rustically rich. Many smoother examples are gradually being crafted by passionate winemakers, but there is never any getting away with the muscular structure of this grape. It is, after all, part of its attraction.

Ⓢ Agostina *See* Fiano.

Ⓦ Airén This very ordinary-quality Spanish grape is the widest planted white wine grape in the world in terms of area. However, as most Airén is grown in arid areas of Spain at between half and one-third of the density of most other grape varieties, it would slip down to third or fourth widest grown in terms of the number of vines in the ground. Grown for its good acidity in hot climates, it has a neutral character that makes it ideal for brandy and useful for tweaking white-wine blends in La Mancha.

Ⓦ Ak Dimrit or **Akdimrit** Technically a synonym for Dimrit Beyaz, but Ak Dimrit, literally meaning white Dimrit, is the more common usage. Grown in the Central Anatolia and Mediterranean Coast regions. Also used for the production of *raki*.

Ⓦ Albana This was the first Italian white grape to be accorded DOCG status back in 1987, yet it still struggles to deliver wines of an internationally acceptable standard. Producers such as Bissoni, Umberto Cesari, Leone Conti, Gallegati, and Fattoria Zerbina have all produced very good *passito* wines, but given the lengths that winemakers have to go to produce a true straw wine, they should be good. It's a bit like noble rot or *Eiswein*. You put any grapes through that, even Thompson Seedless, and you can expect something good. If Albana is one of the greatest white wine grapes from one of the greatest wine countries in the world, then it should be able to show its class in an unadulterated dry wine style, but so far only Stefano Ferrucci and

Fattoria Monticino Rosso have made an Albana di Romagna *secco* that stands out. And they stand out against the rest, not when compared to the world's great dry white wines. At the time of writing they have had 23 years to practise, and a couple of flashes in the pan have done nothing to alter my original conclusion that the Albana is merely a high-yielding grape that makes a rather rustic, almost common wine.

Ⓢ Albanella Synonym for Ugni Blanc

Ⓢ Albariño Synonym for Alvarinho

Ⓦ Albarola Native to northwestern Italy, this grape is mostly known as the principal variety for the Cinque Terre DOC, which is better known for its dramatic scenery than its slightly aromatic, light dry white wine.

Ⓢ Alcayata Synonym for Mourvèdre

Ⓑ Aleatico A Muscat-like variety grown principally in southern Italy and, to a lesser extent, Tuscany, Aleatico usually produces vivid red sweet wine that may be fortified or not. This grape crops up far and wide, from Corsica to Elba, and California to Australia.

Ⓑ Alfrocheiro Preto This Portuguese grape is a blending component in the red wines of Alentejo, Dão, Estremadura and Terras do Sado.

Ⓣ Alicante Bouschet or **Alicante Henri Bouschet** The full name of this variety is Alicante Henri Bouschet, but it is invariably referred to simply as Alicante Bouschet, even though other Alicante Bouschets exist, such as (Alicante Bouschet) Précoce, Tardif, and à Longues Grappes. *Petit Bouschet* x *Grenache* cross, this is a *teinturier* grape, with vivid, red juice. It was a favourite during Prohibition, when the rich colour of its juice enabled bootleggers to stretch wines with water and sugar. Alicante Bouschet is used primarily for Port-style wines today, and is seldom seen as a varietal table wine. The secret of a good Alicante Bouschet table wine is in achieving the tannins, structure, and mouthfeel that are compatible with its naturally inky-purple colour.

Many moons ago, Angelo Papagni's death-defying Alicante Bouschet was not to be missed, and Coturri and Jim Clendenen (with Il Podere dell'Olivos) have at times dabbled very successfully with this variety. The organically minded Topolos is the only consistently high-quality producer of Alicante Bouschet nowadays.

Ⓑ Alicante Ganzin This *Aramon Rupestris Ganzin* x *Alicante Bouschet* hybrid was bred in France by Victor Ganzin in 1886. Although tiny amounts are grown in France and the USA, this *teinturier* vine is seldom used for anything other than breeding other varieties.

Ⓦ Aligoté *See box, below.*

Ⓦ Altesse The finest of Savoie's traditional varieties, this grape makes delightfully rich and fragrant wines.

Ⓢ Altra Uva Synonym for Ortrugo

Ⓑ Alvarelhão A minor Spanish grape that is also one of Port's lesser varieties. A few parcels of this vine can be found in Victoria and New South Wales, Australia, although it is not highly regarded in that country.

Ⓦ Alvarinho The classic Vinho Verde grape, although it might not rank as a classic grape variety *per se*.

Ⓦ Amigne An old Swiss variety found in pockets of the Valais.

Ⓑ Ancellota An Italian variety used to deepen the colour of Lambrusca in Emilia-Romagna, Ancellota is also grown in Argentina, where Zucardi has successfully produced a pure varietal version for many years.

Ⓑ André This *Limberger* x *St-Laurent* cross is primarily grown in the Czech Republic's Velkopavlovická region, where there is even an André Vine Trail. Also found in Germany's Saale-Unstrut region.

Ⓢ Ansolia Synonym for Inzolia

Ⓢ Ansonica Synonym for Inzolia

Ⓢ Aragnan Synonym for Picardan

Ⓢ Aragones or **Aragonés** Synonyms for Alicante Bouschet, Grenache, and Tempranillo

Ⓢ Aragonêz Synonym for Tempranillo

Ⓢ Aramon This used to be the most widely planted vine in France. Although rapidly declining, there is still, even today, more of this variety in the Languedoc region alone than there is of famous varieties such as Pinot Blanc, Riesling, or Viognier growing throughout the entire country. Aramon produces an undistinguished wine, as does its rarely encountered siblings Aramon Blanc and Aramon Gris.

Ⓦ Arban, Arbane, or **Arbanne** An ancient but minor Champagne grape variety that was supposed to be so noticeable in the tiniest proportion in Aube wines in the 19th century that when local winegrowers walked into a *cuverie* they would immediately detect it and exclaim, "Ah, Arbanne!" Currently undergoing a mini-revival in Champagne along with other permitted ancient

varieties. Also found in the Vin de Pays des Coteaux de Coiffy between the Aube and Alsace. Arbanne Noir and Arbanne Rouge exist but are rarely encountered.

Ⓦ Arbois Authorized for various Loire wines, including Vouvray, where a handful of producers use its intrinsically high acidity to tweak the acidity of their sweeter wines in hotter years.

Ⓑ Arinarnoa This *Merlot* x *Petit Verdot* cross was created at Montpellier in 1956 but has only just started to be cultivated seriously beyond France and Lebanon since the late 1990s. It can now be found in Australia, Chile, Italy, Spain, Switzerland, and even China.

Ⓦ Arinto The Arinto is one of Portugal's potentially excellent white grapes. Its use in the small district of Bucelas is to make a crisp, lemony wine that ages well. Four different localized clones are formally recognized: Arinto de Bucelal, Arinto de Colares, Arinto do Dão, and Arinto no Douro.

Ⓦ Arneis Literally meaning "little rascal", this Piedmontese grape was so named because of its erratic ripening. Once threatened by commercial extinction, this delicately aromatic variety is now extremely fashionable.

Ⓦ Arrufiac Formerly a primary grape for Pacherenc du Vic-Bilh and Côtes de Saint-Mont, Arrufiac is high-yielding, rich in sugar, but low in character and finesse and has thus been reduced to secondary status.

Ⓢ Arvino Synonym for Gaglioppo

Ⓑ Aspiran or **Aspiran Noir** Once widely planted, the Aspiran is rarely found today, although a little is used as a minor blending component in Minervois. Blanc, Gris, and Rosé varieties also exist but are even more rarely encountered.

Ⓦ Asprinio An ancient variety known from Etruscan times, this grape is best known today for Asprinio di Aversa DOC in Campania, where the vine is trained up poplar trees to a height of 13.7 metres (45 feet) to produce fresh, crisp, dry white wines that are still, *frizzantino*, or *frizzante*.

Ⓢ Asprino Synonym for Asprinio

Ⓢ Aspro Synonym for Xynisteri

Ⓦ Assyrtiko One of the better-quality indigenous varieties of Greece, the classic example of this variety is to be found on Santorini, although the super-*terroir* character of the island's volcanic-ash soil can be too pungent for unconditioned palates, and Pavlidis Assyrtiko from Drama might be more enjoyable for most wine drinkers.

Ⓢ Aubaine Synonym for Chardonnay

Ⓑ Aubun This grape used to be a minor blending component in Cabardès and Côtes of Vivarais, but it was always more of a bland variety used to pad out a wine than provide any useful ability to tweak

ALIGOTÉ
A thin-skinned grape of unexceptional quality grown in Burgundy and Bulgaria. It makes tart wines of moderate alcoholic content, but in exceptionally hot years they can have good weight and richness. The variety's best wines come from certain Burgundian villages, especially Bouzeron, where the quality may be improved by the addition of a little Chardonnay.

a blend. Consequently, it has been banned since 1995.

Ⓦ **Aurore** The most useful character of this *Seibel 5279* x *Seibel 29* hybrid is its very blandness, which has often been used to mute (as best as it can) the extrovert foxiness of Lambrusca wines.

Ⓢ **Auvernat** Synonym for Pinot Noir

Ⓢ **Auvernat Blanc** Synonym for Muscadelle

Ⓢ **Auvernat Gris** Synonym for Pinot Gris or Pinot Meunier

Ⓦ **Auxerrois** At home in Alsace, Luxembourg, and England, Auxerrois makes a fatter wine than Pinot Blanc, so suits cooler situations. Its musky richness has immediate appeal, but it is inclined to low acidity and blowsiness in hotter climates.

Ⓢ **Auxerrois** Synonym for Malbec

Ⓢ **Auxerrois Gris** Synonym for Pinot Gris

Ⓢ **Auxois** Synonym for Chardonnay and Pinot Gris

Ⓢ **Avello** Synonym for Picpoul Blanche

Ⓦ **Avesso** A mildly aromatic, otherwise quite bland and lightweight Portuguese variety used for both Vinho Verde and Rios do Minho.

Ⓢ **Avillo** Synonym for Picpoul Blanche

Ⓢ **Axina de Margiai** or **Axina de Poporu** Synonym for Nuragus

Ⓑ **Băbeaskă** or **Băbeaskă Neagră** Found mostly in the Nicoreşti region of Romania, where it is capable of producing a deep-coloured, spicy red wine.

Ⓦ **Bacchus** A (*Riesling* x *Sylvaner*) x *Müller-Thurgau* cross that is one of Germany's more superior crosses, Bacchus is refreshingly aromatic with zesty grapey fruit that can be a delight to drink when produced in cooler climes, such as Camel Valley in England.

Ⓑ **Baco** or **Baco Noir** One of the more successful red hybrids, particularly when grown in Ontario or the Atlantic Northeast, where the this grape can be relied upon to produce a decent medium-bodied red and can also churn out the odd nugget of gold that shows surprising smoky-spicy finesse. There are legions of Baco varieties, all produced in the 19th century by François Baco, but the very first Baco (*Folle Blanche* x *Riparia Grand Glabre*), aka Baco Noir or Baco 1, is the Baco that most hybrid winemakers and wine writers refer to. Most of the other Baco varieties are referred to simply by numbers. A few have their own primary names, such as Petit Boue, Baco, Bakouri, Caperan, Cazalet, Celine, Douriou, Estellat, Olivar, Rescape, and Totmur, but they were all originally registered as numbered Baco hybrids.

Ⓢ **Baco 1** Synonym for Baco Noir

Ⓑ **Baga** Principal grape variety for Bairrada, where it produces firm

tannic reds, but the wines are developing more accessible fruit and softer tannins with new viticultural and winemaking practices.

Ⓢ **Banatski Rizling** Synonym for Welschriesling

Ⓢ **Bangalore Blue** Synonym for Isabelle

Ⓜ **Barbarossa** or **Barbarossa Rosé** A light-red grape found in the Piedmont, Liguria, and Tuscany, which are home to the best-known localized clones of this variety: Barbarossa di Finale (aka Barbarossa di Liguria), Barbarossa di Piemonte (aka Barbarossa di Conegliano), and Barbarossa di Toscana (aka Barbarossa di Lucca). Barbarossa is also a synonym for Sangiovese, as in Barbarossa Il Dosso from Fattoria Paradiso in Emilia-Romagna, while Barbarossa Précoce is a synonym for Chasselas Rosé, and Barbarossa Verduna is synonym for Grec Rosé.

Ⓜ **Barbaroux** or **Barbaroux Rosé** This grape is found in Provence (AOCs of Cassis and Vin de Provence) and Corsica (AOCs of Ajaccio and Vin de Corse, and Vin de Pays de L'Île de Beauté), where it either makes rosés or is used to lighten the reds that can get a bit heavy this far south. Barbaroux is listed as a singular variety and separated from the Piemontese Barbaroux by some ampelographers, but this has not been established by DNA fingerprinting, and with Provence a stepping stone between the Piedmont and Corsica, and the Italian heritage of most Corsican grapes, the jury must still be out on this one.

Ⓑ **Barbera** A prolific Italian variety grown in Piedmont, the Barbera makes light, fresh, fruity wines that are sometimes very good. Because of its refreshing acidity, this grape can perform exceptionally well in warmer, New World climes.

Ⓦ **Baroque** or **Barroque** A herbaceous Colombard-like white wine grape from southwestern France, where it is primarily responsible for Tursan, Vin de Pays des Terroirs Landais.

Ⓑ **Bastardo** This is the classic Port grape and is identified as the Trousseau, an ancient variety once widely cultivated in the Jura, France.

Ⓢ **Beaunois** Synonym for Chardonnay or Pinot Blanc

Ⓑ **Beichun**, **Beihong**, and **Beimei** Three of the more successful of the so-called "Bei" series of *Muscat Hamburg* x *Vitis amurensis Ruprecht* hybrids, which were bred in China to combat severe winter temperatures and yield extraordinarily high sugar, these varieties now account for some 7,000 hectares (17,300 acres), mostly in the southern regions of the country.

Ⓑ **Béquignol** This old Bordeaux variety is rarely encountered in France today but is still widely grown in Argentina, where it produces soft, deeply coloured red wines. Béquignol is also a synonym for the Fer.

CABERNET FRANC
Grown all around the world, but especially in Bordeaux, Cabernet Franc fares best as Bouchet in St-Emilion and at Pomerol, across the Dordogne River, where Cabernet Sauvignon is less well represented. It is grown under neutral conditions, and while it might not be easy to distinguish any significant varietal differences between the two Cabernets – suited, as they are, to different situations – the Cabernet Franc tends to produce a slightly earthy style of wine that is very aromatic but has less fine characteristics on the palate when compared to the Cabernet Sauvignon.

Ⓢ **Bernard** Synonym for Prié Blanc

Ⓦ **Beverdino** A minor grape used in the Colli Piacentini primarily as a major component in some of its *vin santo*, but also allowed as a secondary variety in Monterosso Val d'Arda, Beverdino makes a full yet soft wine with neutral fruit.

Ⓢ **Bianca Fernanda** Synonym for Cortese

Ⓢ **Biancame** or **Bianchello** Synonyms for Albana

Ⓢ **Bianchetta** or **Bianchetto** Synonyms for Albarola

Ⓢ **Bianchino** Synonym for Montuni

Ⓦ **Bianco d'Alessano** One of the latest-ripening varieties in CSIRO's collection at Marbein in Victoria, Australia, demonstrating why this grape manages to hold on to decent acidity levels in even the hottest climes, but it merely makes bland, undistinguished wine as a pure varietal. In its native Apulia, Bianco d'Alessano is a secondary variety in the DOCs of Gravina, Lizzano, Locorotondo, and Martina Franca, but most vines are planted outside these areas, where the harvest is mopped up by vermouth producers.

Ⓦ **Biancolella** This Campanian variety is mostly grown on the island of Ischia but is also used as a component of DOCs Campi Flegrei and Penisola Sorrentina. Its wines are quite neutral.

Ⓢ **Biancolelle** Synonym for Biancolella

Ⓢ **Bical** Synonym for Borrado des Moscas

Ⓢ **Bical Tinto** Synonym for Touriga Nacional

Ⓢ **Bidure** Synonym for Cabernet Franc and Cabernet Sauvignon

Ⓢ **Black Alicante** Synonym for Trincadeira Preta

Ⓢ **Black Hamburg** Synonym for Muscat Hamburg and Schaiva Grossa

Ⓢ **Black Malvoisie** Synonym for Cinsault

Ⓢ **Black Muscat** or **Black Muscat of Alexandria** Synonyms for Muscat Hamburg

Ⓢ **Black Portugal** Synonym for Trincadeira Preta

Ⓑ **Black Spanish** This grape is having something of a minor revival in Texas, where it was widely grown in the 1830s to make a Port-like wine. This is known and sold as Lenoir in Texas, and Lenoir is a synonym for the Jacquez, which is either a natural *aestivalis* x *vinifera* hybrid, according to the Vitis database, or a so-called *Vitis bourquiniana* (*aestivalis* x *cinerea* x *vinifera*), according to the great ampelographer Pierre Galet. To confuse things further, there is another Black Spanish grape that is cultivated in the United States and that turns out to be a variety called Ohio, which is another *Vitis bourquiniana* and, even more confusingly, it sometimes masquerades as Lenoir or Jacquez! The Black Spanish in Texas can be quite dense but tastes a bit diffused and sometimes earthy.

Ⓢ **Blanc d'Anjou** Synonym for Chenin Blanc

Ⓢ **Blanc Doux** Synonym for Sémillon

Ⓢ **Blanc Fumé** Synonym for Sauvignon Blanc

Ⓢ **Blanc de Morgex** or **Blanc de la Salle** Synonyms for the Prié Blanc

Ⓢ **Blanc Select** Synonym for Ondenc

Ⓢ **Blanc de Troyes** Synonym for Aligoté

Ⓢ **Blanc Verdet** Synonym for Arbois

Ⓢ **Blanc Vert** Synonym for Sacy

Ⓢ **Blauburgunder** Synonym for Pinot Noir

Ⓢ **Blauer Portugieser** Synonym for Portugieser

Ⓑ **Blauer Wildbacher** Found in the Veneto region of Italy and Western Styria in Austria, the Blauer Wildbacher makes some nice fresh, crisp, dry rosé wines and even a few outlandish fizzy reds, but the light-bodied still reds are much less interesting.

ⓢ **Blaufränkisch** Synonym for Limberger

Ⓦ **Boal** or **Boal Branco** The richest and fattest of Madeira's four classic grape varieties, Boal is also grown for wines produced on the Portuguese mainland in the DO appellations of Carcavelos and Lagos, and the IPRs of Chaves and Valpaços in the Trás-os-Montes region.

Ⓦ **Bombino** or **Bombino Bianco** Widely planted throughout central and southern Italy, where it has often been mistaken for Trebbiano. (The Trebbiano referred to as Abruzzese, Bianco di Chieti, Campolese, d'Abruzzo, di Avessano [sic], di Macerata, di Teramo, d'Ora, d'Oro, and Dorato di Teramo are all Bombino.) This is a tough-skinned grape that is highly resistant to parasites, diseases, and adverse climatic conditions. The Bombino is most at home in Emilia-Romagna, where it is known as the Pagadebit and produces a firmer-structured, more alcoholic wine than elsewhere and is sold in dry, semi-sweet, still and *frizzante* styles under the Pagadebit di Romagna DOC. This grape also plays a useful role as a blending component in the DOCs of Biferno and Pentro di Iserinia in Moloise, and Gravina, Leverano, Locorotondo, and San Severo in Apulia.

Ⓑ **Bombino Nero** Less widely planted and less well regarded than its white sibling, this grape is a secondary variety for the DOC of Lizzano (Apulia).

ⓢ **Bonarda** Synonym for Bonarda variants, a confusing mess of incorrect synonyms and other varieties such as Corbeau Noir, Croatina, and Uva Rara.

Ⓦ **Bonarda Bianca** The white Bonarda is seldom seen outside of Argentina, where it is merely used as a bulk blending variety.

ⓢ **Bonarda di Borgomasino** Synonym for Bonardina

ⓢ **Bonarda di Gattinara** Synonym for Croatina and Uva Rara

ⓢ **Bonarda a Grandes Grappes**, **Bonarda dell'Astigiano**, **Bonarda del Monferrato**, **Bonarda di Asti**, **Bonarda di Chieri**, **Bonarda di Gattinara**, **Bonarda di Piemonte**, **Bonarda du Piémont**, **Bonarda Nera**, or **Bonarda Nero** Synonyms for Bonarda Piemontese

ⓢ **Bonarda Macun** or **Bonarda Rotunda** Synonyms for Durasa

ⓢ **Bonarda Novarese** Synonym for Uva Rara

Ⓦ **Bonarda di Piava** A minor blending component occasionally encountered in the Veneto region of Italy.

Ⓑ **Bonarda Piemontese** Traditionally used to support Nebbiolo in such DOC wines as Bramaterra, Gattinara, and Ghemme, it also makes pure varietal wine under the Piemonte DOC. But this native Italian grape is cultivated on a far greater scale in Argentina, where it is most successful in Syrah-Bonarda blends.

ⓢ **Bonarda di Rovescala**, **Bonarda Grossa**, or **Bonarda Pignola** Synonyms for Croatina

ⓢ **Bonarda Viretta** Synonym for Zanello

Ⓑ **Bondola** An indigenous Swiss variety that can be used for rather rustic reds on its own, the Bondola is at its best when blended with Bonarda, Freisa, and other local varieties in wines.

ⓢ **Bordelais** Synonym for Baroque

Ⓦ **Borrado des Moscas** A Dão grape, literally called "fly droppings", Borrado des Moscas retains high natural acidity at high alcohol levels, making it well suited to white winemaking in hot areas.

ⓢ **Bouboulenc** Synonym for Malvoisie

Ⓑ **Bouchalès** More commonly known as Prolongeau in parts of Bordeaux, Bouchalès is the primary name for this grape, which used to be a permitted variety in Blaye and basic Bordeaux appellations. Now

almost extinct, but Cuvée A & A from Chateau de la Vieille Chapelle is a stunning revival made from recently identified 100-year-old vines. It's like a dense *garagiste* Merlot, and for legal reasons it claims to be Merlot, but it's pure Bouchalès.

ⓢ **Bouchet** Synonym for Cabernet Franc and Cabernet Sauvignon

Ⓦ **Bourboulenc** Found throughout southern France but particularly in the Rhône, where it is an authorized variety for several AOCs, most famously Châteauneuf-du-Pape, Bourboulenc is a late-ripening variety. This gives it the ability to retain good acid levels, which is the reason why it is so useful for tweaking blends. This is also one of the varieties James Busby took to Australia in 1832 after touring French and Spanish vineyards.

Ⓦ **Bouvier** A modest-quality variety in Austria and one which, as Ranina, produces the "Tiger's Milk" wine of Slovenia.

ⓢ **Bouviertraube** Synonym for Bouvier

ⓢ **Bovale** Synonym for Mourvèdre

Ⓑ **Brachetto** This Muscat-like variety produces the highly fragrant, sweet, and sumptuous Brachetto d'Acqui DOC, the red wine equivalent of a top Asti.

Ⓦ **Branco sem Nome** A minor Port variety, this *Malvasia Fina* x *Malvasia Grossa* cross is capable of adding some fragrance and structure in tiny quantities.

Ⓑ **Braquet** or **Braquet Noir** This grape is grown in a small area of Provence, where it is one of the primary varieties authorized for the production of red and rosé wines under the Bellet AOC. A Braquet Blanc and Braquet Gris exist, but Braquet Blanc is also a synonym for Jurançon Blanc.

ⓢ **Braquet des Jardins** Synonym for Brachetto

ⓢ **Brown Muscat** Synonym for Muscat Blanc à Petits Grains

Ⓑ **Brugnola** A secondary variety for Valtellina Rosso DOC in Lombardy and for Bosco Eliceo DOC in Emilia-Romagna (where this grape is known as the Fortana or Fortana Nera), Brugnola produces a firm but not full-bodied red wine with high acid levels, which is why one of its synonyms is Uva d'Aceto (meaning "vinegar grape"!), but it does make this variety useful for tweaking blends.

Ⓑ **Brun Argenté** This grape is allowed for the AOCs of Côtes du Rhône, Côtes du Rhône Villages, Gigondas, Rasteau, and Vacqueyras. The decrees for these appellations use the synonyms of both Camarèse and Vaccarèse in all cases. As these are uniquely synonyms for Brun Argenté, not any other variety, this grape is in fact authorized twice.

ⓢ **Brunello** Synonym for Sangiovese

Ⓑ **Brun-Fourca** or **Brun-Fourcat** One of the secondary varieties used

for red, white, and rosé wines under the Palette AOC of Provence.

ⓢ **Bual** Synonym for Boal Branco

ⓢ **Burgundi Gamet** or **Burgundi Kék** Synonyms for Gamay

ⓢ **Burgundi Mic** Synonym for Pinot Noir

ⓢ **Burgundi Nagyszemu** Synonym for Gamay

ⓢ **Burgundske Sede** or **Burgundské Modré** Synonyms for Pinot Gris

ⓢ **Buzetto** Synonym for Ugni Blanc

ⓢ **Cabarnelle** Synonym for Carmenère

Ⓑ **Cabernet Franc** See box, *opposite.*

ⓢ **Cabernet Gris** Synonym for Cabernet Franc

Ⓑ **Cabernet Pfeffer** A grape of disputed origins. The French call this Pfeffer Cabernet (aka Fer Servadou), whereas the Americans have transposed the French name into Cabernet Pfeffer, which for Anglo-Saxons slips off the tongue easily and is more rational. There are various opinions as to its origins in the USA, the most plausible being a 19th-century cross (but no one knows what with or who made the cross, and cannot be more precise than a 100-year-old span). Only two US sources of this variety exist today: the 100-year-old Wirz Family vineyard in Monterey's Cienega Valley, California, and one of Casa Nuestra's vineyards in Oakville, where the vines were planted in the 1940s.

Ⓑ **Cabernet Sauvignon** See box, *below.*

ⓢ **Cagnina** Synonym for Mondeuse

Ⓑ **Calabrese** The true Calabrese (it is also a synonym for Sangiovese and, particularly, Nero d'Avola) is widely grown in Italy, especially on Sicily, where it is probably a native variety, although its name means "Calabrian". Used primarily as a secondary variety in the Sicilian DOCs of Faro and Marsala.

ⓢ **Calito du Languedoc** Synonym for Braquet

Ⓑ **Calitor** or **Calitor Noir** One of the minor Rhône grapes that is steadily being grubbed up, due to its high yields, light colour, and neutral character, Calitor is also one of the varieties James Busby took to Australia in 1832, although only the odd vine survives there today. Calitor Blanc and Calitor Gris exist. Calitor is also a synonym for Brachetto.

ⓢ **Camaralet** Synonym for Camaraou

Ⓦ **Camaraou** A secondary variety for the AOCs of Béarn and Jurançon in southwest France.

ⓢ **Camarate**, **Câmarate** or **Camarate Tinto** Under its Casculho synonym, the Camarate is one of the lesser Port grapes, but it is planted throughout the rest of Portugal, particularly in the Alentejo, where it performs better as a secondary variety in various unfortified red wines. Camarate is

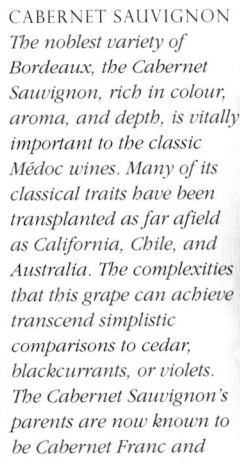

CABERNET SAUVIGNON
The noblest variety of Bordeaux, the Cabernet Sauvignon, rich in colour, aroma, and depth, is vitally important to the classic Médoc wines. Many of its classical traits have been transplanted as far afield as California, Chile, and Australia. The complexities that this grape can achieve transcend simplistic comparisons to cedar, blackcurrants, or violets. The Cabernet Sauvignon's parents are now known to be Cabernet Franc and Sauvignon Blanc.

CHARDONNAY

The greatest non-aromatic dry white wine grape in the world, despite the proliferation of cheap, identikit Chardonnay wines that are churned out globally, hence its "ABC" reputation. This classic variety is responsible for producing the greatest white Burgundies and is one of the three major grape types used in the production of Champagne.

CHENIN BLANC

A variety that acquired its name from Mont-Chenin in the Touraine district in about the 15th century but can be traced back to Anjou, around AD 845. The grape has a good acidity level, thin skin, and a high natural sugar content, making it very suitable for either sparkling or sweet wines, although some dry wines, notably Savennières, are made from it.

---

also a synonym for Fernão Pires, Rabigato, and Tamares.

Ⓢ **Camarèse** Synonym for Brun Argenté

Ⓑ **Campbell's Early** Sounding more like a potato than a grape, this *Moore Early* x (*Belvidere* x *Muscat Hamburg*) hybrid is grown in very marginal wine-grape regions, such as Japan's Miyazaki Prefecture, where the conditions are not unlike those of Florida. The grapes are very large, and the wine produced has a pronounced exotic character that some might think better suited to wine jelly than wine itself. Campbell's Early is also the most widely grown grape variety in South Korea. Under its synonym Island Belle, this variety is also grown on Stretch Island, Washington State.

Ⓢ **Campolese** Synonym for Ugni Blanc

Ⓑ **Canaiolo** or **Canaiolo Nero** This native Tuscan grape is a secondary variety for wines such as Carmignano, Chianti, and Vino Nobile di Montepulciano but is capable of producing a soft, fruity red wine in a pure varietal format. Also found in Umbria, where it is traditionally blended with Sangiovese.

Ⓢ **Caniolo** Synonym for Canaiolo

Ⓢ **Cannamelu** Synonym for Guarnaccia

Ⓢ **Cannonadu**, **Cannonao**, **Cannonatu**, **Cannonau**, and **Canonau** Synonyms for Grenache

Ⓢ **Cape Riesling** Although not commercialized as such, the Crouchen is still commonly referred to in South Africa as Cape Riesling.

Ⓢ **Caprettone** Synonym for Coda del Volpe

Ⓜ **Cardinal** This *Flame Tokay* x *Ribier* cross is still grown in France, Spain, Morocco, Australia, and Argentina, although it has a neutral flavour and low acids.

Ⓑ **Carignan** or **Carignan Noir** A Spanish grape grown extensively in southern France and California. One of its synonyms – Mataro – is a common name for the Mourvèdre, which also provides a well-coloured wine, but one that is not quite as harsh. A Carignan Blanc and Gris also exist.

Ⓢ **Carignane**, **Carignano**, and **Cariñena** Synonyms for Carignan

Ⓑ **Carmenère** An old *bordelais* variety that was almost extinct, until it was discovered in Chile posing as Merlot, and then in Franciacorta, where it was pretending to be Cabernet Franc (interestingly, one of Carmenère's synonyms is Grand Vidure, while one of Cabernet Franc's names is Gros Vidure).

Ⓑ **Carnelian** A *Grenache* x (*Carignan* x *Cabernet Sauvignon*) cross developed in the 1930s by Professor Olmo for use in the hot continental climate of California's Central Valley, this grape produces rather rustic reds that do not compare to those of Ruby Cabernet or Rubired, two other Olmo crosses. The potential quality of Carnelian has yet to rise above the *blanc de noirs* sparkling wine produced by Tedeschi Vineyard in Hawaii.

Ⓦ **Carricante** The major grape in Etna DOC, Carricante usually produces a neutral-flavoured white wine unless planted at higher altitudes, where in the hands of a gifted winemaker such as Planeta, Carricante can have excellent acidity, with stunning minerality and finesse. Although various synonyms include the name Catarratto, Carricante is not related to the true Catarratto, which is in fact a secondary variety in the Etna DOC.

Ⓑ **Cascade** This *Seibel 7042* x *Seibel 5409* hybrid is a prolific producer of light coloured, undistinguished red wine.

Ⓢ **Casculho**, **Castelão da Bairrada**, **Castelão do Nacional**, **Castelão do Nosso**, **Castelão Nacional**, and **Castelão Nosso** Synonyms for Camarate

Ⓢ **Castelão de Cova da Beira** Synonym for Trincadeira Preta

Ⓢ **Castelão Frances** Synonym for Periquita

Ⓢ **Castelão Nacional** Synonym for Camarate

Ⓢ **Castelão Real** Synonyms for Camarate

Ⓑ **Castets** Originally from southwest France, having possibly travelled over the Pyrenees from Spain, this variety is almost extinct and rarely

encountered beyond a few parcels in Palette AOC of Provence.

Ⓢ **Catalan** Synonym for Carignan or Mourvèdre

Ⓦ **Catarratto** This the secondary variety in the wines of Etna and is far more widely planted across Sicily than Carricante, the primary grape in that DOC.

Ⓜ **Catawba** A *labrusca* x *vinifera* cross that was once so famous that Henry Longfellow felt compelled to write an ode to it (*see* Ohio, p588), this grape has the *labrusca*'s characteristically foxy aroma. It is still grown in Ohio today and also widely cultivated in New York State, Michigan, North Carolina, Kansas, the Ozarks, and even Indiana, all of which continue to produce and sell pure Catawba varietal wine.

Ⓢ **Ceubo** Synonym for Abbouto

Ⓣ **Centurion** A *teinturier* grape.

Ⓢ **Cercial** Synonym for Esgana Cão

Ⓜ **Cereza** High-yielding Argentinian varietal that can be quite aromatic but lacks fruit and body, thus is mostly used as a blending component.

Ⓑ **Cesanese** This variety is found in Latium, where it makes numerous medium-bodied red wines of no special quality in all styles, from dry to sweet, and still to sparkling.

Ⓑ **César** A minor grape variety of moderate quality that is still used in some areas of Burgundy, most notably for Bourgogne Irancy. Just 5 or 10 percent of César can make a positive contribution when it is carefully blended with Pinot Noir, but any more will have a negative effect.

Ⓑ **Chambourcin** The rot-resistance of this grape is formidable, enabling it to yield half-decent Beaujolais-like wines even when contending with bracing sea breezes and lashing rain. This might not be my favourite grape, but I have tasted drinkable Chambourcin from as far afield as Illinois, Kansas, Kentucky, Michigan, Missouri, Nebraska, Pennsylvania, and Virginia in the USA; in Canada; and in the Granite Belt and Hastings Valley in Australia. And even Madagascar in the Indian Ocean!

Ⓦ **Chardonel** Known as "Chard in Hell" to many a wine judge forced to taste its wines, Chardonel is a *Seyval* x *Chardonnay* cross made by

Cornell University in 1953, but not released until 1990. So far the wines produced have been more bland than even the most anonymous Chardonnay.

Ⓦ **Chardonnay** See box, above.

Ⓦ **Chasan** Created by Paul Truel at INRA's Domaine de Vassal in 1958, this *Palomino* x *Chardonnay* cross is slightly aromatic with low acidity. Chasan is best bottled and consumed early, when a bare prickle of carbonic gas will enhance its freshness and crispness.

Ⓦ **Chasselas** or **Chasselas Blanc** Responsible for the best-forgotten Pouilly-sur-Loire wines (not to be confused with Pouilly-Blanc Fumé), this variety is at its modest best in Alsace and Switzerland's Valais (where it is known as the Fendant). Primarily a good eating grape. There are a dozen or more very minor true sub-varieties of Chasselas, but Chasselas Doré and Chasselas Vert are just synonyms, even though they are officially listed as separate varities in several appellations. Chasselas has no fewer than 213 synonyms.

Ⓢ **Chasselas Doré**, **Chasselas Roux**, or **Chasselas Vert** Synonyms for Chasselas Blanc

Ⓢ **Chenel** Synonym for Chenin Blanc and Ugni Blanc

Ⓦ **Chenin Blanc** See box, above.

Ⓢ **Chiavennasca** Synonym for Nebbiolo

Ⓑ **Ciliegiolo** A secondary variety for various wines in Tuscany, Umbria, and the Marches, the Ciliegiolo is also known as the Sangiovese Polveroso – and with some justification it appears, since DNA fingerprinting has identified its parentage as *Sangiovese* x *Muscat Rouge de Madere*.

Ⓑ **Cinsault** A prolific grape found mainly in southern Rhône and Languedoc-Roussillon vineyards, where it makes robust, well-coloured wines. It is best blended, as happens at Châteauneuf-du-Pape, for example.

Ⓢ **Cinsaut** Synonym for Cinsault

Ⓦ **Clairette** or **Clairette Blanche** A sugar-rich, intrinsically flabby grape best known for its many wines of southern France. It is the Muscat though, not the Clairette, which is chiefly responsible for the "Clairette de Die" in the Rhône.

(S) **Clairette à Grains Ronds** Synonym for Ugni Blanc

(W) **Clairette à Gros Grains** A variant of Clairette Blanche bred by Antoine Besson and grown in parts of Provence.

(S) **Clairette à Petits Grains** Synonym for Clairette Blanche

(M) **Clairette Rosé** Compared to Clairette Blanche, the only difference is the colour of skin at the time of ripeness. Very seldom encountered, but there are pockets in the Rhône, primarily in Lirac and Tavel.

(S) **Clairette de Trans** Synonym for Clairette Blanche

(S) **Clare Riesling** Synonym for Crouchen

(S) **Clevner** Synonym for Pinot Blanc

(S) **Coda di Pecora** Synonym for Coda del Volpe

(W) **Coda del Volpe** A minor Campanian grape variety whose main claim to fame is as the primary variety for Vesuvio Lacryma Christi.

(W) **Códega** This Portuguese variety is grown in Transmontano, where it is usually blended into the wines of Chaves and Valpaços. Any black grape claiming to be Códega will in fact be Malvasia Grossa.

(S) **Colombar** Synonym for Colombard

(W) **Colombard** This produces thin, acidic wine ideal for the distillation of Armagnac and Cognac. It has also adapted well to the hotter winelands of California and South Africa, where its high acidity is a positive attribute. It can produce fresh, lively, everyday-drinking white wines with zesty fruit in the Aquitaine, France.

(S) **Colombier** Synonym for Colombard or Sémillon

(B) **Colorino** Widely grown in Tuscany, particularly in Valdarno, Val d'Elsa, and the Val di Pesa, where this variety provides very loose bunches of small grapes that are easily aerated and thus, with their thick skins, are resistant to rot. This enables the production of deep-coloured wines in poor years when Sangiovese and other varieties with tightly packed bunches struggle to bring much colour to a wine, hence the Colorino name.

(W) **Completer** A rare Swiss variety of ancient origin, this grape should be called the Malanstraube but is better known as Completer in Graubünden, where it makes a fascinating, rich, Auslese-style wine.

(B) **Concord** The widest-cultivated variety in North America outside of California, this *Vitis labrusca* variety has an extremely pronounced foxy flavour.

(B) **Cornalin** or **Cornalin d'Aosta** This old Italian variety is virtually extinct in its native Valle d'Aosta and rarely encountered elsewhere, except for a few patches in the

Valais, where it produces a rich and concentrated red wine. Although also known as the Humagne Rouge, this variety is not related to the Humagne Blanc.

(B) **Cornifesto** A Portuguese variety grown in the Transmontano region for the wines of Valpaços.

(W) **Cortese** A widely planted Piemontese variety that makes soft-textured, dry white wines that may or may not be slightly *frizzantino* when young.

(B) **Corvina** This variety is widely planted in the Veneto region, where it is the mainstay of Valpolicella and is blended into many other wines. Too easily capable of light-coloured, lightweight reds with simple tart cherry and almond fruit with a touch of bitterness, Corvina needs to be restricted in the vineyard and nurtured in the winery to produce something special.

(S) **Corvinone** Synonym for Corvina

(S) **Cot** Synonym for Malbec

(M) **Coucieira** This is a lesser Port variety, due to its light colour and neutral flavour. No relation to the black-skinned Cousoeira, which is a separate variety.

(B) **Counoise** The colour and spice of Counoise can often play an instrumental, if minority, role in some wines of Châteauneuf-du-Pape, where it is one of the 13 permitted varieties. Also widely grown throughout the southern Rhône, neighbouring Languedoc, and Provence. Beware that Counoise is also a synonym for Aubun, a completely different variety.

(S) **Courbu Blanc** and **Courbu Noir** Secondary varieties in many wines of southwestern France, the back-skinned sibling is rarely encountered.

(B) **Criolla** There is no such thing as true Criolla. This is not so much a variety as a loose family of grapes that has evolved throughout South America since the Spanish missionaries arrived in the wake of the conquistadors. The first grape variety the missionaries brought with them was, unsurprisingly, the so-called Mission Grape (aka Criolla Chica or, in Chile, the Pais). This was crossed either spontaneously or, in some cases, possibly by design, with other varieties brought from Spain (primarily Muscat d'Alexandrie and Tempranillo) to form many localized Criolla, such as Criolla Grande. These new Criollas were then spread to other vineyards by later settlers, where they could well have been crossed with each other. Much research into South America's Criolla varieties has been conducted, but not enough to give a complete picture. The Criolla or Pais name, plain and simple, has thus been given to many variants, the parents of which have yet to be identified, so that a grape simply labelled "Criolla" (or "Pais") in one country or a part of one country is not necessarily the same as a "Criolla" (or "Pais") found

elsewhere, although they all have a propensity to produce a fairly similar style of rustic red wines that may or may not have a slight aromatic character.

(S) **Criolla Chica** The scientific designation for the Mission Grape.

(M) **Criolla Grande** An Argentine descendant of Mission Grape, this mildly aromatic *Mission Grape x Muscat d'Alexandrie* cross is the second most widely cultivated mid-coloured grape in the world (after Pinot Gris).

(S) **Crna Moravka** Synonym for Limberger

(B) **Croatina** A Croatian variety that has found itself at home in Italy, particularly Lombardy and Piedmont, the Croatina is capable of producing well-coloured, soft and fruity red wines. It has been confused with the Bonarda and even Nebbiolo in the past.

(W) **Crouchen** Widely cultivated, particularly in Australia and South Africa, this variety used to be widely but incorrectly sold as Clare or Cape Riesling. Recent efforts to standardize varietal labelling to fall in line with EU regulations have reduced this practice, but it is still referred to by those traditional but false Riesling names.

(S) **Cruina** Synonym for Corvina

(S) **Csabagyöngye** Synonym for Perl Von Csaba

(S) **Cynthiana** Synonym for Norton

(W) **Damaschino** This Sicilian grape has a neutral character and is allowed as a secondary variety in Alcamo DOC but usually ends up in Marsala blends. A little is grown in the Barossa Valley, where it is known as Farana and was previously mistaken for Ugni Blanc.

(T) **Deckrot** This *Pinot Gris x Teinturier Färbertraube* cross is a *teinturier* grape mainly grown in Germany, where it is used to add colour to local red wines.

(W) **Delaware** This American hybrid of uncertain parentage was developed in Frenchtown, New Jersey, and propagated in Delaware, Ohio, in the mid-19th century. Although grown in New York State and Brazil, it is far more popular in Japan.

(W) **Devin** A *Gewürztraminer x Veltliner Rotweiss* cross grown in the Tokajská region of Slovakia for non-Tokajské wines.

(W) **Dimiat** An under-rated Bulgarian variety grown in the Dunavska Raunina and Thrakiiska Nizina regions, where the Dimiat can produce fresh, tangy white wines. The Dimiat Tcherven is a Russian mid-coloured variety.

(S) **Dimrit** Within the Dimrit family, there is the Akdimrit (or white Dimrit) and Karadimrit (or black Dimrit).

(B) **Dolcetto** Under-rated variety found in northwestern Italy, where it is often over-cropped, but can be delightful when yields are restricted.

(S) **Dona Branca** Synonym for Roupeiro

(S) **Donzelinha, Donzelynho,** and **Donzelinho** Synonyms for Donzelinho Branco and Donzelinho Tinto

(W) **Donzelinho Branco** The true Donzelinho Branco is a white Port variety, but it is also a synonym for Rabigato.

(S) **Donzelinho de Castelo, Donzelinho de Portugal, Donzelinho do Castello,** or **Donzelinho Macho** Synonyms for Donzelinho Tinto

(S) **Donzelino de Castille** Synonym for Trousseau

(S) **Donzelinho do Galego, Donzelinho Gallego,** or **Donzelinho Roxo** Synonyms for Donzelinho Rosa

(M) **Donzelinho Rosa** A minor Port variety.

(B) **Donzelinho Tinto** A Port variety and minor grape for Douro DOC wines.

(B) **Dornfelder** A *Helfensteiner x Heroldrebe* cross that produces light-to-medium-bodied reds with a malleable fruit character, Dornfelder is grown mostly in the Pfalz, Rheinhessen, and Württemberg regions of Germany, but can also be found in England and other marginal grape-growing areas of the world.

(S) **Doucillon** Synonym for Bourboulenc

(S) **Drupeggio** Synonym for Canaiolo

(T) **Dunkelfelder** The parentage of this *teinturier* grape is uncertain but thought to be *Färbertraube x Blauer Portugieser*, which might account for one of its synonyms, the Färbertraube Frölich. The dark wines produced from this variety are typically all colour and no flavour, without the tannin structure expected of any red wine, unless tannin-adjusted.

(B) **Duras** A Gaillaçoise grape grown throughout southwest France as a secondary yet useful blending component, but at home in the Gaillac AOC, where it is the primary variety, albeit still blended. The Duras produces medium-sized clusters of small grapes with high sugar levels, but its rustic peppery fruit needs support.

(W) **Durello** This Italian variety has good but not exceptional acidity and is used mostly to produce Monti Lessini Durello DOC, a sometimes good but never exceptional sparkling wine in the Veneto.

(B) **Dureza** Apart from a few vines in the experimental vineyards of Domaine de Vassal in Montpellier, this minor Ardèche variety is for all practical purposes extinct but deserves to be preserved for no other reason than it was one of the parents that gave birth to the Syrah.

(S) **Durif** Technically the primary name, this variety is, however, better known as Mourvèdre.

(S) **Dusty Miller** Synonym for Pinot Meunier

(S) **Early Burgundy** Synonym for Abouriou

(S) **Edeltraube** Synonym for Gewürztraminer

(W) **Ehrenfelser** A *Riesling* x *Sylvaner* cross, the Ehrenfelser has turned out to be a *cul-de-sac* in British Columbia, Canada, where it remains the preserve of a few die-hards.

(W) **Elbling** This variety was once held in high esteem in Germany and France. The major Mosel grape in the 19th century, it is now mostly confined to the Ober-Mosel where its very acid, neutral flavour makes it useful for German *Sekt*. In Alsace it was *Knipperlé* and its former position was such that one of the *grand cru* Guebwiller slopes was named after it.

(W) **Emerald Riesling** A *Muscadelle* x *Riesling* cross, this grape was developed for cultivation in California by Professor Olmo of UC-Davis fame as the sister to his Ruby Cabernet cross.

(W) **Emir** Used for rustic local white wines, often fizzy, sometimes aged in oak, in the Central Anatolian region of Turkey, where it is often blended with the Narince grape.

(W) **Encruzado** An important Dão variety, Encruzado is an under-rated grape with fine fruit and excellent acidity.

(W) **Erbaluce** This Italian variety is at its best around Caluso in Piedmont, where it truly favours the production of *passito* wines.

(S) **Ermitage** Synonym for Marsanne

(W) **Esgana Cão** Better known as Madeira's classic Sercial grape, Esgana Cão (meaning "dog strangler"!) is the official primary name for this variety, which was once erroneously reputed to be a distant relative of the Riesling. This grape produces a lean, dry white wine with relatively high acidity and emphatic minerality, which translates into the driest and most assertive of Madeira's fortified wine styles.

(S) **Esgana Cão** Synonym for Touriga Franca

(S) **Etraire** Synonym for Persan

(S) **Etraire Blanche** Synonym for Verdesse

(B) **Etraire de la Dui** This Savoie grape originated in the Isère *département* and is cultivated throughout the region, where it likes clayey-limestone soils and has the potential to produce well-coloured, full-bodied red wines.

(W) **Ezerjó** A distinctive Hungarian variety that is also grown in northern Serbia, Austria, Bulgaria, China, Czech Republic, Romania, Slovakia, and Ukraine, but is at its best in the Mór district west of Budapest, where Ezerjó (which means "a thousand good things") is crisp and racy with excellent minerality. Also used for cheaper sweet wines.

(S) **Faber** Synonym for Faberebe

(W) **Faberrebe** A *Weissburgunder* x *Müller-Thurgau* cross grown in Germany, where it produces a fruity wine with a distinctive light Muscat aroma.

(W) **Falanghina** Widely planted throughout Campania, where it is both a primary and a secondary variety in many DOCs, Falanghina produces round and fruity wines in still and fizzy formats.

(W) **Favorita** In Portugal this is the offspring of *Tamares* x *Muscat d'Alexandrie*, but in Italy, where the Favorita name is far more famous, particularly in Piedmont, it is a synonym for Vermentino.

(S) **Fehérburgundi** Synonym for Pinot Blanc

(S) **Feiner Weisser Burgunder** Synonym for Chardonnay

(S) **Fendant** Synonym for Chasselas

(B) **Fer** This vine has very hard wood that is notoriously difficult to prune, hence its name (meaning "iron"). The Fer is grown throughout southwest France, where it is often blended with Tannat, Malbec, or Cabernet grapes.

(W) **Fernão Pires** Widely grown throughout Portugal, this grape produces fresh, floral-grapey style wines with citrus-Muscat type fruit and good acidity. A mid-coloured sibling called Fernão Pires Rosado exists.

(W) **Feteasca Alba** or **Feteasca Regala** A Moldovan variety that is so widely cultivated in Romania that many Romanian winemakers consider it to be native to that country, the Feteasca Regala is an under-rated grape that has the potential to produce distinctive dry white wines. A little is grown in Australia, where it is appreciated for maintaining good acidity levels while ripening.

(B) **Feteasca Negra** Less prolific than Feteasca Alba, but even more under-rated.

(S) **Fetjaska** and **Fetyaska** Synonym for Feteasca

(W) **Fiano** This Campanian variety has been known since ancient Roman times, when it was called *Vitis apiana*. Fiano wines have a distinctive floral aroma and honeyed flavour, best illustrated by the top wines of Fiano di Avellino DOCG. There is no black variant; Fiano Rosso is a synonym for Aglianico and Agostina.

(M) **Flora** This California *Sémillon* x *Gewürztraminer* cross was bred by the famed Professor Olmo and has a tendency to produce overly exotic, often extremely blowsy wines, but it works well in a sparkling wine like Schramsberg's Crémant Demi-Sec, which is 100 per cent Flora, and as a blend, such as Brown Brothers Orange Muscat & Flora. If a red-skinned Flora is encountered, it will not be any relation but will in fact be a *vinifera* x *labrusca* hybrid that was bred in 1850 by A M Sprangler of Philadelphia.

GAMAY
The mass-produced wine of this famous grape from Beaujolais has a tell-tale "peardrop" aroma, indicative of its carbonic-maceration style of vinification. These wines should be drunk very young and fresh, although traditionally vinified wines from Beaujolais' 10 classic crus can be aged like other red wines and, after 10 or 15 years, develop Pinot Noir traits. This may be because the grape is an ancient, natural clone of Pinot Noir. In France, Gamay Beaujolais is the synonym for true Gamay.

(S) **Folgosão** Synonym for Terrantez

(W) **Folle Blanche** Traditionally used for the distillation of Armagnac and Cognac, the Folle Blanche grape also produces the Gros Plant wine of the Loire Valley. It can produce fresh, lively, everyday-drinking white wines with zesty fruit in the Aquitaine, France.

(S) **Folle Noire** Synonym for Valdiguié

(S) **Fortana** Synonym for Brugnola, Jurançon Noir, and Négrette

(W) **Francavidda** A south Italian variety capable of producing a delicate, dry white made in the Ostuni DOC, Apulia.

(S) **Francavilla** Synonym for Francavidda

(S) **Franken**, **Franken Riesling**, or **Frankenriesling** Synonyms for Sylvaner

(S) **Frankenthaler** Synonym for Schiava Grossa

(S) **Frankinja Crna** or **Frankinja Modra** Synonyms for Gamay

(S) **Frankisch** Synonym for Gewürztraminer

(S) **Frankovka**, **Frankovka Modrá**, **Frankova**, or **Frankovka Modrǎ** Synonyms for Limberger

(S) **Frappato** Synonym for Nerello

(B) **Freisa** The Freisa d'Asti has been known for centuries and was a favourite of King Victor Emmanuel, who drank these fruity reds as dry, still wines, although much of the production today is sweet and fizzy. Freisa is produced in Chieri and other areas of Piedmont, where it typically has an aroma of raspberry and rose petals. This variety, which is descended from Nebbiolo, is also grown in Veneto and Switzerland.

(S) **French Colombard** Synonym for Colombard

(W) **Friulano** This is better known as the Sauvignonasse, which literally means "Sauvignon-like" or "Sauvignon-ish" but it's not very Sauvignon-ish and is not, in fact, any relation to Sauvignon Blanc, even though another one of its synonyms is Sauvignon Vert. The high-yielding Sauvignonasse is perhaps most infamously grown in Chile, where it used to masquerade as Sauvignon Blanc until the mid-1990s, even though the wines were terrible. It was also once quite widely grown in California, as was the Sauvignon Vert, but as a synonym for Muscadelle, not Sauvignonasse. Although the Sauvignonasse and the Friulano are one and the same variety, when grown in Friuli-Venezia Giulia the Friulano (previously more commonly known as the Tocai Friulano) produces an altogether more enjoyable wine in both pure and blended formats. It is now turning up all over the place, and winemakers are making a real effort to produce wines of genuine quality and interest, such as the Friulano made by Channing Daughters in New York State. One day someone is going to make the following advice redundant by producing a truly excellent Sauvignonasse, but for now it is possible to say that wherever you come across Sauvignonasse it should be avoided, but wherever this grape is known as Friulano, you stand a good chance of finding something decent to drink.

(S) **Friularo** Synonym for Raboso

(S) **Fromenteau Blanc** Synonym for Roussanne and Savagnin Blanc

(S) **Fromenteau Gris** Synonym for Pinot Gris

(S) **Fromenteau Rouge** Synonym for Gewürztraminer

(S) **Fromentot** Synonym for Pinot Gris

(S) **Frontignac** Synonym for Muscat Blanc à Petits Grains

(B) **Frühburgunder** A lighter-bodied, delicately aromatic mutation of Pinot Noir that evolved in and around the village of Bürgstadt in the Franken, the Frühburgunder nearly became extinct in the 1970s because of its variable yields, but dedicated growers have deliberately restricted yields to coax some exquisitely elegant wines from this grape, which is at its best in southern Baden, the Pfalz, and the Ahr.

Ⓜ **Frühroter Veltliner** Not black as such, this grape has a darker skin than the more widely encountered Roter Veltliner, but like that grape, the Frühroter is not a true Veltliner and can in fact trace its parentage back to Silvaner and Roter Veltliner itself. This variety has in excess of 130 synonyms, many of which are incorrectly attributed to Malvasia.

Ⓢ **Fruttana** Synonym for Brugnola

Ⓑ **Fuella** A secondary variety in the blends of Lavilledieu in southwest France and Bellet in Provence.

Ⓢ **Fumé Blanc** Synonym for Sauvignon Blanc

Ⓑ **Fumin** A minor variety that produces a robust red on its own but can be a useful blending component, adding structure to wines such as Torrette in the Valle d'Aosta DOC.

Ⓦ **Furmint** This strong, distinctively flavoured grape is the most important variety used to make Tokaji in Hungary. However, the Furmint's potential is not only for botrytized sweet wine. If its best clones are sought out and their wines crafted by talented winemakers, this variety could do for Hungary what Grüner Veltliner has done for Austrian dry white wines. Although it has a very different varietal character, this grape has a similar aptitude to Grüner Veltliner in its ability to produce both profoundly complex, oak-fermented wines and a leaner, more mineral style.

Ⓑ **Gaglioppo** An ancient variety, the Gaglioppo is the most widely planted black grape in Calabria, where it is often blended with the Greco Noir to produce full, fresh, *chiaretto*-style wines. Its *Sangiovese* x *Mantonico di Bianco* parentage has only recently been discovered by DNA fingerprinting, yet one of its synonyms is Mantonico Nero, indicating that local growers had an inkling of its origins long before the term DNA had been invented.

Ⓢ **Gaioppo** Synonym for Gaglioppo

Ⓦ **Galbena** This Moldovan variety is often found in Romania. It's full name is Galbena de Odobesti, and it is known by 33 different synonyms. But not all Galbena is Galbena, since the name is also an incorrect synonym for Furmint and Fetească Regălă.

Ⓢ **Galbena Ourata** or **Galbenă Uriasa** Synonyms for Galbena

Ⓢ **Gallioppa** or **Galloppo** Synonyms for Lacrima

Ⓢ **Gamaret** This Swiss *Gamay Noir* x *Reichensteiner* cross was first released in 1970, but serious commercial cultivation did not take place until the 1990s. As a pure varietal, Gamaret is typically light, yet reasonably well structured, with spicy red fruits. At its best, Gamaret has more fruit and body.

Ⓑ **Gamay** or **Gamay Noir** *See box, opposite.*

Ⓢ **Gamay Beaujolais** Synonym for Abouriou and the true Gamay

Ⓢ **Gamay Blanc** or **Gamay Blanc à Feuille Rond** Synonyms primarily Melon de Bourgogne, Chenin Blanc and Chardonnay

Ⓣ **Gamay de Bouze** or **Gamay Teinturier de Bouze** The widest-planted Gamay Teinturier, this variety is believed to have originated in Bouze-lès-Beaune in Burgundy, although most of its 310 hectares (765 acres) are now located in the Loire. Both Gamay de Bouze and Gamay de Chaudenay were permitted for most of the Loire VDQS appellations, and they are still allowed in the production of various *vins de pays* including Vin de Pays d'Urfé and Vin de Pays du Val de Loire (formerly Jardin de la France). Teinturier grapes are supposed to have less finesse than red wines that derive their colour from the skins, yet Domaine de la Charmoise Les Cépages Oubliés from Henri Marionnet is a pure varietal Gamay de Bouze that can be very good indeed.

Ⓢ **Gamay Castille** Synonym for Gamay Castille Mutation Blanche

Ⓣ **Gamay de Chaudenay** or **Gamay Teinturier de Chaudenay** Almost as widely planted as Gamay de Bouze, approximately 250 hectares (615 acres) of this *teinturier* grape are currently grown in France. For a pure Gamay de Chaudenay, try Clos de la Bruyère Elément Terre from Julien Courtois, a near neighbour of Henri Marionnet. *See* Gamay de Bouze.

Ⓢ **Gamay de Couchey** Synonym for Gamay Teinturier Fréaux.

Ⓢ **Gamay Noir** or **Gamay Noir à Just Blanc** Synonym for Gamay

Ⓣ **Gamay Teinturier** Synonym for any coloured-juice Gamay, especially Gamay de Bouze and Gamay de Chaudenay, but also including Gamay Castille, Gamay Teinturier Fréaux, and Gamay Teinturier Mouro.

Ⓣ **Gamay Teinturier Fréaux** Named after Antoine Fréaux, who first identified this grape growing at Couchey in the Côte de Nuits, though it is now mostly confined to the upper reaches of the Loire, and there are now just 70 hectares (170 acres) left in France. Technically not allowed for the production of wine, but it's still in some vineyards and they don't bother weeding out the fruit. In 2009, stem cells were taken from this variety, the coloured juice of which is apparently loaded with powerful antioxidants and free-radical scavengers and used for UV skin-protection products.

Ⓢ **Gamza** Synonym for Kadarka

Ⓦ **Garganega** The principal grape used in the production of Soave. At its best, this grape is capable of producing both dry and sweet wines that are surprisingly rich for their delicate balance.

Ⓢ **Garnacha** or **Garnacha Noir** Although the primary name for this variety, Garnacha is better known as Grenache beyond the boundaries of Spain.

Ⓢ **Garnacha Blanca** Synonym for Grenache Blanc

Ⓢ **Gewurztraminer** Umlaut-less usage in France, particularly Alsace. *See* Gewürztraminer.

Ⓦ **Gewürztraminer** *See box, left.*

Ⓑ **Girò** A minor Italian grape mostly confined to Sardinia, where it is also known as the Girò Rosso di Spagna, reflecting the belief of some that it might have Spanish origins.

Ⓦ **Glera** This is the grape we have all come to know as Prosecco, but the name of which was changed in 2010 to Glera, when the sparkling wine of the same name and grape variety was elevated from DOC to DOCG status. Prosecco is now officially accepted exclusively as a wine appellation, and some ampelographers record Glera as this variety's primary name. This vine is thought to have originated in the village of Prosecco (now a coastal suburb of Trieste), where it was known as Glera, after which it was transplanted to the Colli Euganei in Veneto, where it was called Serprina. Only when it reached the Conegliano-Valdobbiadene region, north of Venice and south of the Dolomites, did this variety assume its Prosecco identity, having been named as such by Malvolti Francesco in 1772. However, Malvolti alleged that the Prosecco had been growing in the Conegliano-Valdobbiadene area since 700, and further claimed that it was the grape used for the ancient Roman wine known as "Pucinum", although there is no documentation explaining how he arrived at either of these two wild conclusions. The historical waters surrounding the origin of this vine are also muddied by the fact that a grape known as the Prosecco Nostrale is none other than the Malvasia Bianca Lunga (the Malvasia of Chianti), so Prosecco has been consistently mistaken for Malvasia over the ages, and vice versa, meaning claims of origin could easily be misleading. The Glera grape makes a very uninspiring still wine, except as a *vin de paille*, and in terms of sparkling wine gains nothing from time on yeast or, indeed, post-disgorgement ageing. It works best when tank-fermented and sold as young and as fresh as possible, as DOCG Prosecco is.

Ⓦ **Goldburger** Developed in 1922 by Professor Fritz Zweigelt, this *Welschriesling* x *Orangetraube* is primarily used in Austrian white wine blends.

Ⓢ **Gordo Blanco** Synonym for Muscat d'Alexandrie

Ⓦ **Gouais** or **Gouais Blanc** This mundane vine produces sour grapes that do not make a very pleasant wine. In the Middle Ages, Gouais vines were planted around a vineyard so that its sour grapes might deter animals and grape thieves. However, with Pinot Fin Teinturier, another unremarkable grape, the Gouais has given birth to numerous classic varieties, including one of the world's greatest grapes – Chardonnay.

Ⓢ **Gouveio** or **Gouveio Real** Synonyms for Verdelho

Ⓑ **Graciano** An important variety used in the production of Rioja, where a small amount lends richness and fruit to a blend, Graciano is still a seriously under-rated grape.

Ⓢ **Grande Vidure** Synonym for Carmenère

Ⓣ **Grand Noir de la Calmette** This *Aramon* x *Petit Bouschet teinturier* grape was developed in 1855 at Domaine de la Calmette by Henri Bouschet of Alicante Bouschet fame.

Ⓦ **Grasă** or **Grasă de Cotnari** A very old Moldovan variety often used for sweet wines due to its susceptibility to noble rot, this grape is often confused with the Hungarian Furmint, which has 118 synonyms, including Grasă and

GEWÜRZTRAMINER
At its most clear-cut and varietally distinctive in Alsace (where it is never spelled with an umlaut), this variety produces very aromatic wines that are naturally low in acidity. The Gewürztraminer's famous spiciness is derived from terpenes, which are found in the grape's skins. The grapes have to be ripe, otherwise the wine will just have a soft rose-petal character, and the wine must not be acid-adjusted, otherwise the spice will lack breadth and potential spicy complexity. All classic Gewürztraminer wines need bottle age to reveal their true spice-laden aromas.

GRENACHE

The Grenache is grown in southern France, where it is partly responsible for the wines of Châteauneuf-du-Pape, Tavel, and many others. It is the mainstay of Rioja, makes Port-style and light rosé wines in California, and is also grown in South Africa. Its wines are rich, warm, and alcoholic, sometimes too much so, and require blending with other varieties. The true Grenache has nothing to do with the Grenache de Logroño of Spain, which is, in fact, the Tempranillo or Tinto de Rioja. Some sources say the Alicante (a synonym of the Grenache) is the Alicante Bouschet (or plain Bouschet in California), but this too is misleading.

Grasă de Cotnari. This could possibly be because both varieties originated not in Moldova or in Hungary, but in Romania's Transylvania region.

Ⓢ **Grauburgunder, Grauerburgunder,** or **Grauer Burgunder** Synonyms for Pinot Gris

Ⓢ **Grauklevner** Synonym for Pinot Gris

Ⓢ **Gray Riesling** Synonym for Trousseau Gris

Ⓢ **Grecanico** Synonym for Garganega

Ⓢ **Grechetto** and **Greco** These are often used synonymously for each other, which is incorrect as they are totally different varieties. Both Grechetto and Greco have black and white variants, but no mid-coloured variants. The Grechetto Rosa is just a synonym for Grechetto Rosso, while the pink-skinned Greco Rosso is not even Greco but a very obscure Spanish variety called Malaga Rosie. There is a raft of synonyms with a place name attached that can either be true Grechetto or Greco but may also be synonyms for Malvasia, Trebbiano (Ugni Blanc) or other grapes.

Ⓑ **Grechetto** or **Grechetto Blanco** The true white Grechetto is grown further north than the Greco, mainly in Umbria, where it forms part of the blend for Orvieto and numerous other wines. Sportoletti produces a fresh, crisp, stainless-steel fermented pure Grechetto that benefits from no malolactic in Assisi DOC.

Ⓑ **Grechetto Rosso** The true black Grechetto grows a little further south, in Latium, where Andrea Occhipinti produces a fruit-driven pure Grechetto Rosso just north of Rome.

Ⓢ **Greco, Greco Ad Acini Picoli, Greco Bianco delle Marche, Greco Castellano, Greco delle Marche, Greco Fino, Greco Maceratino,** or **Greco Montecchiese** Synonyms for Maceratino

Ⓢ **Greco Nero** The true black Greco is far more widely planted in Italy than its more famous white variant and makes everyday-drinking cherry-coloured reds and rosés. Probably at its best in Calabria, where it is often blended with Gaglioppo.

Ⓦ **Greco di Tufo** The true white Greco is more famous than the true black Greco, even though it often plays no more than a supporting role in many Italian wines. The two most famous exceptions are Greco di Tufo DOCG, which can be a delightfully delicate dry white wine when made by the likes of Feudi di San Gregorio, and Greco di Bianco DOC, which is a *passito* wine of mostly uninspiring quality except in the hands of the gifted Umberto Ceratti, when it can be absolutely vivacious.

Ⓦ **Green Hungarian** The primary name for this Hungarian variety is Putzscheere, but it is better known as Green Hungarian. Small pockets of this vine are to be found in Hungary, Romania, and California. It is usually hidden in a blend, but Weibel of California is probably the only producer that still makes a pure varietal wine from this grape, although Green Hungarian has disappeared from the label to be replaced by "GH".

Ⓑ **Grenache** or **Grenache Noir** See box, above.

Ⓦ **Grenache Blanc** This is the white Grenache variant that is widely planted in France and Spain. It is an ancient Spanish variety with the potential to produce a good-quality, full-bodied wine.

Ⓜ **Grenache Gris** Of all the Spanish Garnacha variants, this is grown more in France than Spain, or anywhere else for that matter. Grenache Gris can be highly aromatic, with a touch of spice.

Ⓢ **Grey Riesling** Synonym for Trousseau Gris

Ⓑ **Grignolino** This Italian variety originates from the Asti region and typically produces lightly tannic red wines with a slightly bitter aftertaste under the Grignolino d'Asti DOC.

Ⓦ **Grillo** The original Marsala variety, Grillo is still considered the best for that fortified wine, but it is also found throughout the rest of Sicily, where it is either blended or, mostly, makes an undistinguished soft, dry white wine, although the best can have a gentle, floral aroma, with tropical fruits on the palate and a touch of spice on the finish.

Ⓦ **Gringet** A minor white variety found in the Savoie, where it contributes to the blend of still and, mostly, sparkling wines. Not to be confused with Gringet, a synonym for the Savagnin Blanc.

Ⓦ **Gris de Salces** Curiously, this is a white grape variety and an incorrect synonym for the Trouseau Gris, a true mid-coloured variety.

Ⓑ **Grolleau** or **Grolleau Noir** A prolific grape with a high natural sugar content, it is important for the bulk production of Anjou rosé, but rarely interesting in terms of quality. Both Grolleau and Groslot are used throughout the Loire – for instance, it's Grolleau in Anjou, but Groslot in the Fiefs Vendée, but both are pronounced the same, and both are the same variety. Internationally, Grolleau is the accepted standard, with Groslot its most important synonym. Grolleau Blanc exists but is rarely encountered.

Ⓜ **Grolleau Gris** Just 450 hectares (1,110 acres) and declining in the Loire compared to 2,500 hectares (6,180 acres) of Grolleau Noir.

Ⓢ **Gropello** Synonym for Rossignola

Ⓑ **Groppello** At home in Breganze on the opposite bank of Lake Garda to Valpolicella, Groppello is definitely better suited to the pure varietal format. When blended with Sangiovese, Marzemino, or Barbera, as often happens, the results seldom equal, let alone exceed, the sum of their parts. The original localized clone, the Groppello Gentile, is considered superior to the Groppello San Stefano or Groppello Mocasina, both of which are also grown in the Lake Garda area. A white version exists but is seldom encountered.

Ⓢ **Gros Blanc** Synonym for the Prié Blanc

Ⓢ **Groslot** Synonym for Grolleau

Ⓢ **Groslot Gris** Synonym for Grolleau Gris

Ⓢ **Groslot Noir** Synonym for Grolleau Noir

Ⓢ **Gros Manseng** Grown in southwestern France, where with the Petit Manseng it contributes to many wines, dry and sweet, but is most famous for producing the legendary and succulently sweet Jurançon Moelleux. Curiously, the Gros Manseng grapes are as small as, if not smaller than, those of the Petit Manseng, and in terms of wine character they are very similar, producing wines with a certain nervosity of fruit. There is far more Gros Manseng cultivated in France than Petit Manseng, and late-harvest Gros Manseng tends to be more *passerillé*, whereas the smaller percentage of Petit Manseng will attract more noble rot.

Ⓢ **Gros Noir** Synonym for César

Ⓢ **Gros Noiren** Synonym for Pinot Noir

Ⓢ **Gros Plant** Synonym for Folle Blanche

Ⓢ **Grosse Clairette** Synonym for Bourboulenc or Picardan

Ⓢ **Gross Vernatsch** or **Grossvernatsch** Synonyms for Schiava Grossa

Ⓢ **Grünedel, Grüner Silvaner, Grünfrankisch,** and **Grünling** Synonyms for Sylvaner

Ⓦ **Grüner Veltliner** This is the most important wine grape in Austria, where it commonly produces fresh, well-balanced wines, with a light, fruity, sometimes slightly spicy, flavour. Top-quality Grüner Veltliner from the Wachau can have a penetrating ground white pepperiness. Some of the very top-quality wines have become too fat and heavy, whereas others are the equal of great Chardonnays. A number of unoaked Grüner Veltliners from the finest sites can have a beautiful minerality that sometimes verges on Riesling in character.

Ⓢ **Guarnaccia** If the grapes are black, this is a synonym for Perricone, Tintora, and Vernaccia Nera. But if the grapes are white, it is Vernaccia Bianca.

Ⓦ **Guarnaccia** or **Guarnaccia Bianca** The true Guaranaccia is a white variety used to soften the Gaglioppo-based red wines of Pollino DOC in Calabria.

Ⓢ **Gutedel** Synonym for Chasselas

Ⓦ **Gutenborner** This *Müller-Thurgau* x *Chasselas* cross is grown in Germany and England. It produces grapes with intrinsically high sugar levels, but makes rather neutral wines.

Ⓢ **Gwäss** Synonym for Gouais

Ⓢ **Habitant Blanc** Synonym for L'Acadie

Ⓢ **Hanepoot** Synonym for Muscat d'Alexandrie

Ⓦ **Hárslevelü** This Hungarian grape is the second most important Tokaji variety. It produces full, rich, and powerfully perfumed wines.

Ⓢ **Heunisch Weiss** Synonym for Gouais

Ⓦ **Humagne Blanc** or **Humagne Blanche** No relation to the Humagne Rouge, which is also grown in the Valais of Switzerland, where this variety originated, the Humagne Blanc has lost its capsicum aroma now that it is being grown at lower yields. Never alcoholic, the wines from this grape can be deceptively full and rich, with hints of exotic fruit on the palate and sometimes a touch of spice on the finish. A mid-coloured Humagne Gris exists.

Ⓢ **Humagne Rouge** Synonym for Cornalin

Ⓢ **Hunter Riesling** Although not commercialized as such, Sémillon is still commonly referred to in Australia as Hunter Riesling.

Ⓦ **Huxelrebe** A *Chasselas* x *Muscat Courtillier* cross that is grown in Germany and England, and is capable of producing good-quality wine. At its best, the Huxelrebe has a herbaceous-grapefruit bite with a hint of elderflower that can go very "cat's pee" in cold or wet years.

Ⓢ **Ianculella** or **Ianculillo** Synonyms for Biancolella

Ⓦ **Impigno** This Italian variety makes light, delicate dry white in Ostuni DOC, where it is blended with Francavidda.

Ⓢ **Incrocio Bruni 54** Synonym for *Verdicchio* x *Sauvignon Blanc*

Ⓢ **Incrocio Manzoni 215** Synonym for *Prosecco* x *Cabernet Sauvignon*

Ⓢ **Incrocio Manzoni 6013** Synonym for *Riesling* x *Pinot Blanc*

Ⓢ **Incrocio Terzi** Synonym for *Barbera* x *Cabernet Franc*

Ⓦ **Inzolia** This Marsala grape is also capable of producing surprisingly light and delicate dry wines in Sicily. Also a blending component for Elba DOC in Tuscany, where this variety is known as Ansonica.

Ⓦ **Irsai Olivér** This Hungarian *Pozsonyi* x *Perl Von Csaba* cross was created in 1930 and produces a very fresh, aromatic wine with grapey fruit, but it is intrinsically too soft without a bit of judicious blending or being bottled with a bit of residual gas to provide a crispy-crunchy impression that lifts the finish.

Ⓢ **Iskendiriye Misketi** Synonym for Muscat d'Alexandrie

Ⓢ **Isabelle** Synonym for Valdiguié

Ⓢ **Italianski Rizling** or **Italiansky Rizling** Synonyms for Welschriesling

Ⓦ **Jacquère** or **Jacquère Blanche** The work-horse grape of the Savoie, the Jacquère is subject to rot, has a neutral flavour and high acidity.

Ⓢ **Johannisberg Riesling** Synonym for Riesling

Ⓑ **Joubertin** A minor Savoie grape, of which there is very little left in France but still a few hectares in Argentina.

Ⓦ **Jurançon Blanc** This minor variety is found in southwest France, where it is authorized for Pineau des Charentes AOC, Vin de Pays du Comté Tolosan, and Armagnac. Although Braquet Blanc and Brachetto Bianco are both synonyms for the Jurançon Blanc, it is not related to either grape.

Ⓑ **Jurançon Noir** This grape used to be permitted for Cahors and even has Cahors as one of its synonyms,

but it was a high-yielding variety that produced an undistinguished wine and was thus banned.

Ⓑ **Kadarka** Hungary's most widely cultivated grape variety is grown throughout the Balkans. It was once thought to be the same as the Zinfandel, but this theory no longer persists. It makes pleasant, light, and fruity wine.

Ⓢ **Kalabaki** or **Kalambaki** Synonyms for Limnio

Ⓦ **Kanzler** A *Müller-Thurgau* x *Sylvaner* cross that produces a good Sylvaner substitute in the Rheinhessen.

Ⓢ **Karachi Gulabi** Synonym for Muscat Hamburg

Ⓑ **Kara Dimrit** or **Karadimrit** Technically synonyms for Dimrit Beyaz, but Kara Dimrit (or Karadimrit), literally meaning "red Dimrit", is the more common usage. Grown in the Central Anatolia and Mediterranean Coast regions. Also used for the production of *raki*.

Ⓢ **Kékfrankos** Synonym for Limberger

Ⓑ **Kékporto** Synonym for Portugieser or Blauer Portugieser

Ⓦ **Kerner** A *Trollinger* x *Riesling* cross that produces wines with a high natural sugar content and good acidity, but a very light aroma. Like Müller-Thurgau, Kerner has been planted in too many former Riesling vineyards to have much sympathy for it.

Ⓢ **Klein Reuschling**, **Kleinberger**, **Kleiner Räuschling**, or **Kleinergelber** Synonyms for Elbling

Ⓢ **Klevener de Heiligensteiner** Synonym for Savagnin Rosé

Ⓢ **Klevner** Synonym for Pinot Blanc or Pinot Noir

Ⓢ **Knipperlé** Synonym for Elbling

Ⓣ **Kolor** This *teinturier* grape is a *Pinot Gris* x *Teinturier Färbertraube* cross that was developed at the Freiburg Research Institute in Germany.

Ⓜ **Koshu** Although commonly viewed as a Japanese variety, the Koshu originated in Asia Minor, moving to China via the Silk Route, before Buddhists took it to Japan, where it has been cultivated in the Yamanashi district since at least the 8th century. Until the turn of the millennium, this grape was used only to make sweet wine or disappeared into modern Japanese blends, but producers have started to hone a pure Koshu in its own inimitable dry style, which would be an acquired taste for most Western palates but is revered and very much in vogue on its home market.

Ⓦ **L'Acadie** Specifically created at Vineland in Ontario for the harsh winters and short, hot summers of Nova Scotia, this hybrid is named after 17th-century Acadian French who settled in the Annapolis Valley of that province. L'Acadie has proved some degree of competence as a very minor blending component in some

sparkling-wine *cuvées* produced by Benjamin Bridge in Nova Scotia's Gaspéron Valley.

Ⓑ **Lacrima** or **Lacrima Nera** Primarily known for producing a soft, medium-bodied red wine in the Marches province of Ancona, under the DOC Lacrima di Morro d'Alba. Lacrima (or Lacryma) Christi del Vesuvio is not made from the Lacrima grape, even though one of its very few synonyms is Raisin de Vesuve. Various localized clones, both black and white exist, but beware: Lacrima is also a synonym for Asprinio, Gaglioppo, and Sangiovese.

Ⓢ **Lafnetscha** Synonym for Completer

Ⓑ **Lagrein** An ancient Alto Adige variety, Lagrein was well known to Pliny, who called it Lageos, and is now known to be s spontaneous cross of *Schiava Gentile* x *Teroldego*. This underrated grape has distinctively rich and chunky fruit with relatively high acid levels when young, but it is capable of developing a silky-smooth finesse after a few years in bottle. Also good for rosé and used as a blending component throughout the region.

Ⓑ **Lambrusco** This covers a multitude of sub-varieties, all of which essentially produce simplistic wine, primarily in Emilia-Romagna, where it is fizzed up, cherry-coloured, and cherry-flavoured. Lambrusco Salamino is by far the most widely planted, followed by Marani, Gasparossa, and then, at a slightly lower level, Foglia Frastagliata and Sorbara. Beyond this, there are small pockets of numerous other sub-varieties, mostly black but occasionally mid-coloured, such as Pedunculo Rossa and Sorbara a Foglia Rossa. To add to the confusion, each sub-variety also has several synonyms.

Ⓢ **Landroter** Synonym for Cornalin

Ⓢ **Languedocien** Synonym for Picpoul Blanche

Ⓦ **Lauzet** A minor white variety that is used as a blending component in southwest France.

Ⓢ **Leányka** Synonym for Fetjaska

Ⓦ **Lela** A Serbian *Welschriesling* x *Kunbarat* hybrid developed in 1977 to provide extreme winter hardiness, thanks to the Kunbarat, which is itself part Amurensis.

Ⓢ **Lemberger** Synonym for Limberger

Ⓦ **Len de l'El** Flavoursome, naturally sugar-rich grape that is used in Gaillac.

Ⓑ **Léon Millot** One of the better hybrid grapes, this *Millardet et Grasset* x *Goldriesling* cross (exactly the same parentage as the Maréchal Foch) has produced some honourable reds, most notably in Ontario and the USA's Atlantic Northeast states.

Ⓑ **Liatiko** An important Greek grape, Liatiko is the primary variety for the wines of Dafnés and Sitia on Crete.

Ⓑ **Limberger** An Austrian variety (also called Blaufränkisch) that makes a relatively simple, light red wine. This grape is also grown in the Atlantic Northeast, where it is more commonly referred to as Lemberger (a name that is also used elsewhere, erroneously, as a synonym for Gamay).

Ⓑ **Limnio** An ancient variety known to Hesiodos and Polydeuctes as Limnia, this grape originated on the island of Limnos, where its importance has diminished in recent times. Limnio is today found in northern Greece, in Rapsani, Halkidiki, and Mount Athose, where it is more of a blending component than a stand-alone variety. A late-ripening grape, Limnio has a tendency to show herbaceous pyrazines when not fully ripe but has the potential to provide good colour and body.

Ⓢ **Limniona** Synonym for Limnio

Ⓢ **Lipovina** Synonym for Hárslevelű

Ⓢ **Listán** Synonym for Palomino Fino

Ⓑ **Listán Negro** Opinion is divided over whether this grape, which is found mostly in the Canary Islands, is in fact the Palomino Negro, but some ampelographers do not list any synonyms for Palomino Negro, and the five official synonyms listed for Listán Negro do not bear any resemblance to Palomino. Whatever its upbringing, Listán Negro has so far made only modest, everyday red wines at best.

Ⓦ **Liza** A Serbian *Kunleany* x *Pinot Gris* hybrid developed in the 1970s to provide extreme winter hardiness, thanks to the Kunleany, which is itself part Amurensis.

Ⓢ **Lladoner** Synonym for Grenache

Ⓢ **Lladoner Pelut** Synonym for Grenache Gris

Ⓦ **Loureiro** Considered one of the best two Vinho Verde grapes with Alvarinho, Loureiro is much higher cropping, but it was compared to Muscat in the 19th century and, at lower yields, has the potential to provide fine floral aromatics.

Ⓢ **Macabeu** Synonym for Macabéo

Ⓦ **Macabéo** This is a Spanish variety used to "lift" a sparkling Cava blend and give it freshness. Bearing the name of Viura, it is also responsible for some of the best fresh, unoaked white Rioja.

Ⓢ **Maccabeu** Synonym for Macabéo

Ⓦ **Maceratino** An old Marches variety, Maceratino produces at best a light, delicate dry white wine, but more often something far more neutral. Due to its variability, this grape has historically been mistaken for Greco and Verdicchio.

Ⓢ **Mâconnais** Synonym for Altesse

Ⓦ **Madeleine Angevine** This is a *Précoce de Malingre* x *Madeleine Royale* cross that is grown quite successfully in England, where it produces a characteristically light-bodied, aromatic wine in some of the country's most northerly vineyards.

Ⓢ **Madiran** Synonym for Tannat

Ⓢ **Magliocc** Synonym for Gaglioppo

Ⓑ **Malbec** This grape is traditionally used in Bordeaux blends in order to provide colour and tannin. It is also grown in the Loire, Cahors, and Mediterranean regions, among many others, and was the grape responsible for the "black wine of Cahors" – a legendary name, if not wine, in the 19th century. However, Cahors is now made from a blend of grapes and is an infinitely superior wine to its predecessor.

Ⓢ **Malmsey** or **Malvagia** Synonyms for Malvasia Bianca and Pinot Gris

Ⓢ **Malvagia** Synonym for Malvasia

Ⓢ **Malvasia** A large and confusing family of true Malvasia and wannabees, further complicated by the fact that Malvasia is a common synonym for Pinot Gris, and an occasional synonym for Branco sem Nome, Códega, Marufo (black variety), Roupeiro, Tamares, Torrontés, Trincadeira Preta (black variety), and Teneron.

Ⓢ **Malvasia Babosa** (Portuguese, possibly the same as Malvasia Branco de São Jorge), **Malvasia Bianca di Basilicata** (Italian), **Malvasia Bianca di Piemonte** (Italian, aka Malvasia Greca, Moscato Greco Nell'Astiniano), **Malvasia Bianca Lunga** (Italian, aka Malvasia Bianca di Bari, Malvasia Bianca di Toscana, Malvasia Cannilunga, Malvasia Cannilunga di Novoli, Malvasia de Chianti, Malvasia del Chianti, Malvasia di Arezzo, Malvasia di Brolio, Malvasia di San Nicandro, Malvasia di Trieste, Malvasia Lunga, Malvasia Piccola Lunga, Malvasia Pugliese Bianca, Malvasia Toscana, Malvasia Trevigna Verace), **Malvasia Branco de São Jorge**, **Malvasia Candida** (Italian via Crete, aka Malvasia Bianca di Candia, Malvasia de Madere, Malvasia Fina de Madere, Malvazija Kanida), **Malvasia de Lazarote** (Spanish), **Malvasia de Oerias** (Portuguese), **Malvasia de Porto** (Portuguese), **Malvasia de Setúbal** (Portuguese), **Malvasia del Lazio** (Italian, aka Malvasia Col Puntino, Malvasia Gentile, Malvasia Nostrale, Malvasia Puntinata), **Malvasia di Candia Aromatica** (aka Malvasia Bianca Aromatica, Malvasia di Alessandria, Malvasia di Candia, Malvasia di Candia a Sapore Moscato), **Malvasia di Candia a Sapore Semplice, Malvasia di Napoli** (Italian), **Malvasia di Sardegna** (Italian, aka Malvasia de Sitges, Malvasia delle Lipari, Malvasia di Bosa, Malvasia di Lipari. Malvasia di Ragusa, Malvasia di Sardegna, Malvasia di Sitjes [sic], Malvasija de Doubrovnik Blanche, Malvoisie de Liparie, Malvoisie de Sitges, Malvoisie Doubrovatchka), **Malvasia Istriana** (Italian, aka Malvasia d'Istria, Malvasia del Carso, Malvasia del Lazio, Malvasia di Ronchi, Malvasia Friulana, Malvasia Istriana, Malvasia Nostrale, Malvasia Puntinata, Malvasika Istarska Bijela, Malvazija Istarska, Malvazija Istarska Bijela, Malvoisie de l'Istrie), **Malvasia Moscatel Fonte Grande** (Portuguese, aka Fonte Grande), **Malvasia Nostrana** (Italian), **Malvasia Parda** (Italian) These are not synonyms but are all recognized as singular localized clones of Malvasia Bianca (with their own synonyms in parentheses).

Ⓢ **Malvasia Belaia** Synonym for Agostenga

Ⓦ **Malvasia Bianca** The true Malvasia Bianca is an Italian variety of possibly Greek origin. This grape is widely grown in Italy, France, and Spain. There are also fairly sizeable plantations in Brazil and the USA, with pockets in most other wine countries. The wines produced are typified by their full body and distinctive, almost musky aroma, but the most famous Malvasia is, of course, Malmsey Madeira.

Ⓢ **Malvasia a Bonifacio** Synonym for Vermentino

Ⓢ **Malvasia Branca** In addition to being a synonym for Malvasia Bianca, this is also a synonym for Códega.

Ⓢ **Malvasia di Casorzo** (Italian, aka Malvasia Casorzo, Malvasia Nera di Casale, Malvasia Nera di Casorzo, Malvasia Nera di Piemonte, Moscatellina), **Malvasia di Castelnouvo del Bosco, Malvasia di Schierano** (Italian, aka Malvasia a Grappolo Corto, Malvasia di Casorzo, Malvasia di Castelnouvo), **Malvasia Nera di Basilicata** (Italian), **Malvasia Nera di Basilicata** (Italian), **Nera di Bolzano** (Italian), **Malvasia Nera di Brindisi** (Italian, aka Malvasia di Bitonto, Malvasia di Trani, Malvasia Nera di Bari, Malvasia Nera di Candia, Malvasia Nera di Lecce), **Malvasia Nera Lunga** (Italian, aka Moscatella Nell'Alessandrina), and **Malvasia Preta** (Portuguese, aka Moireto do Dão) These are not synonyms but are all recognized as singular localized clones of Malvasia Nera.

Ⓢ **Malvasia Comun, Malvasia de Colares, Malvasia de la Rioja, Malvasia de Rioja, Malvasia de Roja, Malvasia Fina, Malvasia Grossa, Malvasia Riojana, Malvazija Bela**, and **Malvaziya Fina** Synonyms for Malvasia Bianca

Ⓢ **Malvasia Corada** or **Malvasia Fina de Douro** Synonyms for Vital

Ⓢ **Malvasia Fina** In addition to being a synonym for Malvasia Bianca, this is also a synonym for Arinto, Douradinha and Trebbiano Toscano.

Ⓢ **Malvasia Fina Roxa** (Portuguese, aka Assario Roxo, Malvasia Roxa) and **Malvasia Trigueira** These are not synonyms but are all recognized as singular localized clones of Malvasia Grigia.

Ⓜ **Malvasia Grigia** Rarely encountered Spanish variety.

Ⓢ **Malvasia Grossa** Synonym for Malvasia di Sardegna and Códega and Vermentino

Ⓢ **Malvasia Grosso** Synonym for Códega and Dona Branca

Ⓢ **Malvasia de Manresa** Synonym for Garganega

Ⓑ **Malvasia Nera** Although not as widely cultivated as Malvasia Bianco, this Italian variety is the most aromatic of all Malvasia variants.

Ⓢ **Malvasia Nera Agglomerata, Malvasia Nera di Bari, Malvasia Nera di Candia, Malvasia Odorossima**, or **Malvoisie Noire Musquée** Synonyms for Malvasia Nera

Ⓢ **Malvaisia Rei** Synonym for Palomino

Ⓢ **Malvasia Rey** Synonym for Trincadeira Preta

Ⓢ **Malvasia Riojana** Synonym for Malvasia Bianca and Subirat-Parent

Ⓜ **Malvasia Rosa** A mutation of Malvasia di Candia Aromatica, Malvasia Rosa was bred by Mario Fregoni at the Instituto di Frutti-Viticoltura in 1967.

Ⓢ **Malvasia Rossa** or **Malvazija Crvena** Synonyms for Malvasia Rosa

Ⓢ **Malvazia Krasnaja** Synonym for Muscat Rouge de Madere

Ⓢ **Malvazija Bela** or **Malvaziya Fina** Synonyms for Malvasia Bianca

Ⓢ **Malvoisie** Synonym for Malvasia and Pinot Gris

Ⓢ **Malvoisie Rosé** Synonym for Frühroter Veltliner

Ⓢ **Mammola** or **Mammolo** Synonyms for Sciaccarello

Ⓑ **Mandelaria** A tannic Greek variety that is grown on Crete, Paros, and Rhodes, where it is either softened by other varieties or used to provide the backbone of a blend.

Ⓢ **Manosquin** Synonym for Téoulier

Ⓑ **Manseng Noir** Little-known black-skinned sibling of the Gros and Petit Manseng, the Manseng Noir is also grown in southwest France, where it contributes to the fresh and fruity red-wine blends of Béarn.

Ⓢ **Mantonico Nero** Synonym for Gaglioppo

Ⓑ **Maratheftiko** An indigenous Cypriot grape, this underrated variety has the capability to produce wines of good colour with a rich, spicy black-fruit flavour.

Ⓑ **Maréchal Foch** One of the better hybrid grapes, this *Millardet et Grasset* x *Goldriesling* (exactly the same parentage as the Léon Millot) cross has produced some honourable reds, most notably in Ontario and the USA's Atlantic Northeast states.

Ⓑ **Mare's Nipple** This Turkish variety was presented to Emperor Tai-Tsung of China in 674, when it was recorded that the purple grapes hung in bunches up to 60 centimetres (24 inches) long and made a "fiery" wine.

Ⓢ **Maria Gomes** Synonym for Fernão Pires

Ⓦ **Mariensteiner** A *Sylvaner* x *Rieslaner* cross that is grown in Germany and is generally considered superior to the Sylvaner.

Ⓦ **Marsanne** This grape makes fat, rich, full wines and is one of the two major varieties used to produce the rare white wines of Hermitage and Châteauneuf-du-Pape.

Ⓑ **Marselan** One of the better new varieties, this *Cabernet Sauvignon* x *Grenache Noir* cross was created in 1961 and has become relatively widely planted in France since the new millennium, despite being restricted to Vins de Table (now Vins de France) and Vins de Pays. It has raspberry-blackcurrant fruit with a touch of smokiness and makes a straightforward yet substantial wine.

Ⓑ **Marsigliana** A minor blending grape in Calabria. A Marsigliana Bianco exists, but this is also a synonym for a Lebanese grape also known as Afus Ali.

Ⓢ **Maru** Synonym for Mare's Nipple

Ⓑ **Marzemino** This grape variety was probably brought to Italy from Slovenia by the Romans. By the 18th century, it had achieved sufficient fame for Mozart to use it in his opera Don Giovanni as a preliminary to the seduction of Zerlina. A Marzemino cluster typically provides large, loosely bunched grapes that make aromatic, early-drinking red wines, either as a pure varietal in Trentino or blended in several other DOCs.

Ⓢ **Mataro** Synonym for Mourvèdre and Carignan

Ⓦ **Mauzac** A late-ripening grape with good natural acidity, grown in southwest France, Mauzac is flexible in the wines it produces, but is used for sparkling wine and is particularly suitable for sweet sparkling wine in Limoux.

Ⓜ **Mauzac Rosé** The mid-coloured Mauzac variant is mostly restricted Gaillac sparkling wines and *vins de pays* in the Comté Tolosan.

Ⓑ **Mavro, Mavroud,** or **Mavrud** Probably at its best in Assenovgrad, Bulgaria, where this grape produces dark, dry, plummy-spicy red wine that can age well.

Ⓑ **Mavrodaphne** The most famous example of this grape is Mavrodaphne of Patras, a rich, sweet, red liqueur wine with a velvety smooth, sweet-oak finish. There is an affinity between Mavrodaphne and oak that reveals itself even when this variety is playing a supporting role, as it does in Gentilini's Syrah.

Ⓜ **Mayolet** A minor blending component in the Valle d'Aosta

Ⓦ **Mayorquin** A secondary variety in the wines of Bellet, Provence.

Ⓢ **Mazuelo** Synonym for Carignan

Ⓑ **Melnik** Technically Shiroka Melnishka Ioza is the primary name for this Bulgarian variety, but most wine professionals, including those in the Bulgarian wine industry, refer to this grape simply as Melnik. It makes a well-coloured, smooth and richly flavoured red wine that may be soft or tannic, depending on how it was made.

Ⓦ Melon de Bourgogne This variety was transplanted from Burgundy to Nantais where it replaced less hardy vines after the terrible winter of 1709. Most famous for its production of Muscadet. When fully ripe, it makes very flabby wines, lacking in acidity, although curiously it can be successful in California's warmer climes.

Ⓢ Menu Pineau or **Menu Pineau de Vouvray** Synonyms for Arbois

Ⓢ Meragus Synonym for Nuragus

Ⓑ Mérille A minor blending component in Bergerac and the Frontonnais, Mérille is also a synonym for Bouchalès.

Ⓑ Merlot See box, below.

Ⓦ Merlot Blanc An undistinguished variety, this grape was banned in the wines of Blaye and Bourg in 1997 but is still allowed for the generic white-wine appellations of Bordeaux and Bordeaux Supérieur.

Ⓢ Meslier Synonym for Luglienga Bianca, Meslier Saint Francois (spontaneous *Gouais* x *Chenin Blanc* cross), Roublot, and Welschriesling. See Petit Meslier.

Ⓢ Meunier Synonym for Pinot Meunier

Ⓦ Mila A Serbian *Kunleany* x *Muscat Ottonel* hybrid developed in 1977 to provide extreme winter hardiness, thanks to the Kunleany, which is itself part Amurensis.

Ⓑ Milgranet A secondary variety authorized for the red-wine blends of Lavilledieu in southwest France but almost extinct. An even more rarely encountered white Milgranet exists.

Ⓣ Millefleurien A localized *teinturier* clone of Gamay de Fréaux, this grape is restricted to a few vineyards around the village of Millefleur in Auvergne.

Ⓦ Misket This can either be a singular variety of Ukrainian Muscat

or a generic synonym for Muscat, mostly Bulgarian.

Ⓜ Misket Cherven The Misket Cherven or Red Misket is the most widely planted Misket variety in Bulgaria, where it produces fresh, light, aromatic white wines.

Ⓑ Misket Dunavski (*Chaouch Blanc* x *Muscat Hamburg*), **Misket Ran** (*MAI 3* x *Cardinal*), **Misket Rusenski** (*Muscat Hamburg* x *Cardinal*), **Ran Hamburgski Misket** (*Yulski Biser* x *Muscat Hamburg*) Black-skinned Misket crosses developed and grown in Bulgaria.

Ⓦ Misket Kailachki (*Muscat Hamburg* x *Villard Blanc* hybrid), **Misket Markovski** ([*Terra Promesa* x *Muscat Ottonel*] x *Muscat Ottonel*), **Misket Plovdivski** ([*Caush* x *Marsilsko Ranno*] x *Italia*), **Misket Sandanski** (*Siroka Melniska* x [*Tamyanka* x *Cabernet Sauvignon*]), **Misket Trakijski** (*Dimiat* x *Perl Von Csaba*), **Misket Varnenski** (*Dimiat* x *Riesling*), **Misket Vratchanskii** (*Corna Alba* x *Muscat Blanc a Petits Grains*) White-skinned Misket crosses developed and grown in Bulgaria.

Ⓑ Mission Grape This is the first variety the Spanish missionaries planted in the wake of the conquistadors, and it is still widely cultivated throughout South America and Mexico, where it is mostly used for rustic reds consumed by locals or lost in cheap mega-blends.

Ⓢ Modrý Portugal Synonym for Portugieser or Blauer Portugieser

Ⓦ Molette The true Molette is a minor white variety rarely encountered outside of the Savoie region of eastern France. If the grapes are black, then Molette will be a synonym for Mondeuse.

Ⓑ Molinara A minor blending component in northeast Italy.

Ⓢ Monaca Synonym for Monica

Ⓢ Monastrell Synonym for Mourvèdre

Ⓑ Mondeuse This variety may have originally hailed from Friuli in northeastern Italy, where it is known as the Refosco. It is now planted as far afield as the Savoie in France, parts of the USA, including California, and in Switzerland, Italy, Argentina, and Australia, where it is often an important constituent of the fortified Port-type wines.

Ⓦ Mondeuse Blanche A minor white-wine variety rarely encountered outside the Savoie region of eastern France, the greatest claim to fame this grape has is as one of the two parents of the classic Syrah (the other parent being the equally nondescript Dureza!).

Ⓑ Monica This Sardinian variety produces a fragrant red wine that may be dry or sweet, fortified or not.

Ⓑ Montepulciano A late-ripening variety that performs best in the Abruzzi region of Italy, where its wines are very deep in colour, and can either be full of soft, fat, luscious fruit, or made in a much firmer, more tannic, style.

Ⓢ Montonico Nero Synonym for Gaglioppo

Ⓢ Montù Synonym for Montuni

Ⓦ Montuni This variety is found in Emilia-Romagna, where it makes light, dry, or sweet still or sparkling white wine with a slightly bitter finish.

Ⓢ Morellino Synonym for Sangiovese

Ⓑ Moreto or **Moreto d'Alentejo** A minor but widely planted Portuguese variety, Moreto is only an average Port grape but is more useful when blended into numerous unfortified dry red wines.

Ⓢ Moreto do Dão Synonym for Camarate and Malvasia Preta

Ⓢ Moreto Mortagua Synonym for Trincadeira Preta

Ⓢ Morillon Synonym for Pinot Noir

Ⓢ Morillon Taconé Synonym for Pinot Meunier

Ⓦ Morio-Muskat This *Sylvaner* x *Pinot Blanc* cross is widely grown in the Rheinpfalz and Rheinhessen of Germany. It has always been intriguing how neutral parents could produce such a powerfully aromatic offspring, but now that we know that the Traminer is one of Sylvaner's parents, the answer is obviously in the genes.

Ⓢ Morrastel Synonym for Graciano

Ⓢ Moscadello Synonym for Muscat Blanc à Petits Grains and Muscat Selvatico

Ⓢ Moscatel A generic Spanish synonym for almost any Muscat variety

Ⓢ Moscatel Dorado Synonym for Muscat Blanc à Petits Grains

Ⓦ Moscatel Galego A good quality white Port grape, Moscatel Galego is also known as Moscatel do Douro. A black variant also exists.

Also a synonym for Muscat Blanc à Petits Grains and Muscat Noir à Petits Grains.

Ⓢ Moscatel Gordo or **Moscatel Gordo Blanco** Synonyms for Muscat d'Alexandrie

Ⓢ Moscatel Grano Menudo or **Moscatel Menudo Bianco** Synonyms for Muscat Blanc à Petits Grains

Ⓢ Moscatel de Málaga or **Moscatel Romano** Synonyms for Muscat d'Alexandrie

Ⓢ Moscatel Rosé Synonym for Muscat Rosé à Petits Grains

Ⓢ Moscatel Samsó or **Moscatel de Setúbal** Synonyms for Muscat d'Alexandrie

Ⓢ Moscato A generic Italian synonym for almost any Muscat variety

Ⓢ Moscato d'Asti or **Moscato di Canelli** Synonyms for Muscat Blanc à Petits Grains

Ⓢ Moskhatos Synonym for Misket

Ⓢ Mourisco A confusing mishmash of varieties and synonyms clarified below. In Spain, rather than Portugal, when the Mourisco name is unqualified by anything else and the grapes are white, it will be a synonym for Palomino.

Ⓢ Mourisco Arsello Synonym for Cayetana Blanca

Ⓢ Mourisco de Braga Synonym for Mourisco de Semente

Ⓦ Mourisco Branco A minor and mediocre white Port variety.

Ⓢ Mourisco du Douro Synonym for Marufo

Ⓢ Mourisco Portalegre Synonym for Cayetana Blanca

Ⓑ Mourisco de Semente A minor Port variety that is not as highly regarded as Mourisco de Trevões, the Mourisco de Semente grapes are fat, low in colour and acid, but rich in sugar, limiting their use to tawny style.

Ⓢ Mourisco Tinto or **Mourisco Vero** Synonyms for Marufo

Ⓑ Mourisco de Trevões A minor Port variety but with grapes that are slightly smaller and more highly regarded than those of the Mourisco de Semente.

Ⓑ Mourvèdre Although Monastrell is its primary name, this variety is better known outside Spain as Mourvèdre – an excellent-quality grape that has been used more than other lesser varieties in Châteauneuf-du-Pape. The Mourvèdre is grown extensively throughout southern France and, under the name of Mataro, has become one of Australia's widest-cultivated black grapes, although it is a declining force in southern California.

Ⓑ Mouyssaguès A rarely encountered blending variety from southwest France.

Ⓢ Müller Rebe, Müller Schwarzriesling, or **Müllerrebe** Synonym for Pinot Meunier

Ⓦ Müller-Thurgau This variety was bred at Geisenheim in 1882 by

MERLOT
Infamously ridiculed in the film Sideways, *Merlot produces nicely coloured wines, soft in fruit but capable of great richness. It is invaluable in Bordeaux, bringing fruity lusciousness and a velvet quality to wines that might otherwise be rather hard and austere. It is the chief grape in Château Pétrus, which is the top name in Pomerol.*

Professor Hermann Müller, who hailed from the canton of Thurgau in Switzerland, and was named after him by August Dern in 1891. It was originally believed to be a *Riesling* x *Sylvaner* cross, but not a single plant has ever reverted to Sylvaner, and the closest resemblance to it is the Rabaner, a *Riesling (clone 88Gm)* x *Riesling (clone 64Gm)*. At one time, this seemed to confirm the theory that the Müller-Thurgau was a self-pollinated Riesling seed, but recent DNA analysis has revealed the true parentage to be *Riesling* x *Madeleine Royale*. It is more prolific than the Riesling, has a typically flowery bouquet and good fruit, but lacks the Riesling's characteristic sharpness of definition. Although Müller-Thurgau has a justifiably important position in the production of cheap German *Tafelwein*, its cultivation in the classic Riesling vineyards of the Mosel has devalued that great wine region. It is widely planted in English and New Zealand vineyards, although in both cases the acreage devoted to it has shrunk markedly since the 1990s.

ⓢ **Munica** Synonym for Monica

ⓢ **Muristrellu** Synonym for Monastrell

ⓦ **Muscadelle** A singular variety that has nothing to do with the Muscat family, although it does have a musky aroma and there is, confusingly, a South African synonym for the Muscat – the Muskadel. In Bordeaux, small quantities of this grape add a certain lingering "after-smell" to some of the sweet wines, but the Muscadelle is at its sublime best in Australia, where it is called the Tokay and produces a rich and sweet "liqueur wine".

ⓢ **Muscadelle des Nantes** Synonym for Baroque

ⓢ **Muscadet** Synonym for Melon de Bourgogne

ⓢ **Muscadine** A generic term for any variety belonging to *Vitis rotundifolia* (eg, Scuppernong).

ⓢ **Muscadine Red** Synonym for Chasselas Rosé

Ⓑ **Muscardin** One of Châteauneuf-du-Pape's 13 permitted varieties, Muscardin produces a light-coloured red wine with good aromatic qualities. It is an authorized grape for many other wines throughout the Rhône but is not widely planted.

ⓢ **Muscat** Synonym for every Muscat variety and sub-variety

ⓦ **Muscat d'Alexandrie** An extremely important grape in South Africa, where it makes mostly sweet, but some dry, wines. In France, it is responsible for the fortified wine Muscat de Rivesaltes (a very tiny production of unfortified dry Muscat is also made in Rivesaltes), and the grape is also used for both wine and raisin production in California.

Ⓑ **Muscat Bailey** or **Muscat Bailey-A** A complex *Bailey* x *Muscat Hamburg* Japanese hybrid, where Bailey is the American *Big Extra* x *Triumph* hybrid, Big Extra is *Big Berry* x *Triumph*, Big Berry is from *Vitis L.* (one of the 17 genera belonging to the genus *Vitis*). and Triumph is *Concord* x *Chasselas Musque*. This convoluted cross was developed to withstand Japan's wet and windy climate, which it achieves. In so doing, though, it has resulted in wine that is more Muscat than red, which would be fine in itself, but to deliver a Japanese red wine that can be compared to the tannin structure of Western models, it is often blended with Merlot or Cabernet, and the effect is mesmerizingly weird, with two taste profiles that mix no better than oil and water!

ⓢ **Muscat Blanc à Petits Grains** *See* Muscat à Petits Grains.

ⓦ **Muscat Fleur d'Oranger** A spontaneous cross of *Muscat Blanc à Petits Grains* x *Chasselas Blanc* occasionally encountered in California and Australia, where it is known as Orange Muscat and has produced some high-quality, early-drinking wines.

ⓢ **Muscat Gordo Blanco** Synonym for Muscat d'Alexandrie

ⓢ **Muscat de Hambourg** Synonym for Muscat Hamburg

Ⓑ **Muscat Hamburg** This *Schiava Grossa* x *Muscat d'Alexandrie* cross is a better table grape than wine grape but is widely planted and used for dessert wines.

ⓦ **Muscat Ottonel** One of the mysteries of wine-grape history, this was first thought to be a cross of East European origin because of its proliferation in Romania and Hungary, and the fact that one of its two parents, Muscat d'Eisenstadt, obviously had Austrian connotations (Eisenstadt being the state capital of Burgenland). The name, though, turned out to be misleading, since Muscat d'Eisenstadt, a black table-grape variety, was developed by Jean-Pierre Vibert of Angers in France. Vibert was better known as a master rose breeder (ranked by some as the greatest French rose breeder of the 19th century) and, as such, was well acquainted with the use of such fanciful names for his creations. However, it is now thought that Muscat Ottonel is a cross between Chasselas and Muscat Précoce de Saumur, not Muscat d'Eisenstadt, and that it was bred by Moreau-Robert, who were successors to Vibert, in 1852. Initially, the date looked perfect because Vibert retired in 1951, but it transpired that Moreau-Robert could not have bred this cross in 1852 because, although Vibert sold his business to Robert, his *jardinière en chef*, in 1851, Moreau (who presumably became the major shareholder from the order of their trading name) did not enter the business until 1853! On the other hand, Muscat Lierval was registered as a cross developed by Vibert in 1855, four years after he retired, so the dates do not necessarily tell the whole story. Muscat Ottonel may have been developed in 1852, but by the time it was registered the business could have changed its trading name. What remains a mystery is why

breeders from Angers would want to cross any variety with a Muscat from Saumur, particularly when the breeder in question already has three Muscats of his own and would go on to produce more? There is no evidence that Muscat Ottonel was bred from Muscat Précoce de Saumur; all the earliest records cite Muscat d'Eisenstadt, which Vibert had developed and commercialized in 1842. More than 45 per cent of all Muscat Ottonel today is grown in Austria, and most of this is in Burgenland, the capital of which is Eisenstadt. No DNA fingerprinting exists, and until it does, it is safest to consider this variety to be a *Chasselas* x *Muscat d'Eisenstadt* cross. It has a very clean, fresh, grapey-Muscatty aroma, and because of its relative hardiness, it continues to replace the more difficult-to-grow but potentially more intense, complex, and age-worthy Muscat à Petits Grains in Alsace.

ⓦ **Muscat à Petits Grains** See box, left.

ⓢ **Muscat Rosé à Petits Grains** *See* Muscat à Petits Grains.

ⓦ **Muskat Moravské** A *Muscat Ottonel* x *Prachttraube 23/33* cross developed and grown in the Czech Republic.

ⓢ **Muskat Ottonel** Synonym for Muscat Ottonel

ⓢ **Muskateller** or **Muskotály** Synonyms for Muscat Blanc à Petits Grains

ⓢ **Muskotály Kék** Synonym for Muscat Noir à Petits Grains

ⓢ **Nagi-Burgundi** or **Nagyburgundi** Synonym for Pinot Noir

ⓢ **Napa Gamay** Synonym for Valdiguié

ⓦ **Narince** Used for rustic local white wines, often fizzy, sometimes aged in oak, in the Central Anatolian region of Turkey, where it is often blended with the Emir grape.

ⓦ **Nasco** This Sardinian variety makes finely scented, delicate, dry and sweet white wines that can also be *liquoroso*.

⑤ **Nascu** Synonym for Nasco

⑤ **Naturé** Synonym for Savagnin

Ⓑ **Nebbiolo** See box, opposite.

⑤ **Nebbiolo di Gattinara** Synonym for Croatina

⑤ **Négret** Synonym for Mouyssaguès

Ⓑ **Négrette** Known for its deep, dark colour, Négrette is grown in the Pays Nantais, Fiefs Vendée, Frontonnais, and Haute Garonne. There is also a little bit planted in the San Benito, California, where Wild Horse Winery has produced a pure varietal wine for many years.

⑤ **Negri** Synonym for Malbec

Ⓑ **Negroamaro** This Apulian grape makes dark, potentially bitter red wines that used to be sold in bulk for blending but are starting to acquire their own reputation in the wines of Alezio, Brindisi, Leverano, Lizzano, Matino, Nardo, and Salice Salentino, not to mention contributing to many more.

⑤ **Negron** Synonym for Mourvèdre

Ⓑ **Nerello** Interesting black grape widely grown on Sicily, where it is one of the varieties used for Marsala but has more individual potential than that and produces full reds and fruity rosés. Nerello is also found in Calabria.

⑤ **Nerino** Synonym for Sangiovese

⑤ **Nero d'Avola** Synonym for Calabrese

Ⓦ **Neuburger** This Austrian *Roter Veltliner* x *Sylvaner* cross excels on chalky soil, where it can make full-bodied wines with a typically nutty flavour in all categories of sweetness. Also grown in the Czech Republic.

⑤ **Neuburské** Synonym for Neuburger

Ⓑ **Neyret** This variety is used as a blending component in northwest Italy.

Ⓦ **Niagara** This *Concord* x *Cassady* is a native American *labrusca* x *labrusca* cross and can be ruinously foxy, the only exception being the award-winning Solera Cream Sherry from the St Julian Wine Company in Michigan, which not only has no hint of foxiness, but as a Sherry-type wine it is indisputably world-class!

⑤ **Niedda** Synonym for Monica

Ⓑ **Nielluccio** Widely used as a primary variety for reds and in Provence and Corsica.

⑤ **Niura d'Avola** Synonym for Calabrese

Ⓦ **Noblessa** This is a low-yielding *Madeleine Angevine* x *Sylvaner* cross grown in Germany, which produces grapes with a high sugar level.

Ⓦ **Nobling** A *Sylvaner* x *Chasselas* cross grown in Baden, Germany, its grapes have high sugar and acidity levels.

Ⓑ **Nocera** A minor Sicilian grape that contributes to the wines of Faro DOC.

⑤ **Noiren** Synonym for Pinot Noir

Ⓑ **Norton** At one time, Norton and Cynthiana were thought to be different varieties, although they have since been identified as one and the same. As Norton grows wild in Richmond, Virginia, where Dr D N Norton propagated grapes in the early 19th century, and this variety became commercially available under the Norton name in 1830, it is generally assumed that it was named after him. Cynthiana gained its name when the same variety was sent from Arkansas to William Robert Prince, the famed nurseryman at Flushing on Long Island. Described accurately by some of its proponents as "The Real American Grape" because, unlike Zinfandel, Norton (or Cynthiana) is native to the USA, this is pure *Vitis aestivalis*, not *vinifera*, and it is not in slightest bit foxy. Norton yields very small grapes with a high pip ratio, necessitating *déstelage* to avoid excessively harsh tannins in the wine. Acidity is high, with an unusually high proportion of malic acidity, and the wine has the unnerving ability seemingly to "stain" glass! That said, the best examples are good, and it is the only wild grape capable of producing fine wine.

Ⓦ **Nosiola** At one time the least known of Trentino's traditional grapes because it is mostly used for *vin santo*, Nosiola has made some interesting dry white varietal wines in recent years.

Ⓑ **Notar Domenico** or **Notar Domenico** Rarely encountered beyond its native land in Upper Salento, this loose-bunched variety is used as a blending component only.

Ⓦ **Nuragus** A Sardinian grape that produces dry, semi-sweet, and *frizzante* white wines under the Cagliari DOC.

⑤ **Nuragus Trebbiana** Synonym for Nuragus

⑤ **Nusco** Synonym for Nasco

⑤ **Nzolia** Synonym for Inzolia

Ⓑ **Oeillade** A minor grape variety in the southern Rhône and Languedoc regions, where it is now mostly used for blending into *vins de pays*.

⑤ **Oesterreicher** Synonym for Sylvaner

⑤ **Ojo de Liebre** Synonym for Tempranillo

⑤ **Olasz Riesling**, **Olasz Rizling**, **Olaszriesling**, **Olaszrizling**, or **Olaszrizling** Synonyms for Welschriesling

⑤ **Olivella** Synonym for Sciascinoso

⑤ **Olivese** Synonym for Asprinio

Ⓦ **Ondenc** A grape once widely planted in southwest France and popular in Bergerac, it is now grown more in Australia than in France. Its acidity makes it useful for sparkling wines.

⑤ **Oporto** Synonym for Portugieser

Ⓦ **Optima** Developed in 1970, this (*Riesling* x *Sylvaner*) x *Müller-Thurgau* cross is already widely grown in Germany because it ripens even earlier than the early-ripening Müller-Thurgau.

⑤ **Orange Muscat** Synonym for Muscat Fleur d'Oranger

Ⓦ **Orion** This *Optima* x *Villard Blanc* cross is perhaps the least inspiring of four recent hybrids that have been allowed by the EU for the production of wine because the percentage of non-*vinifera* is too tiny to be of any significance.

⑤ **Oriou** Synonym for Petit Rouge

⑤ **Ormeasco** Synonym for Dolcetto

Ⓦ **Ortega** A *Müller-Thurgau* x *Siegerrebe* cross that is grown in both Germany and England, its aromatic grapes have naturally high sugar and make a pleasantly fragrant and spicy wine.

Ⓦ **Ortrugo** A minor variety used in Emilia-Romagna for still and sparkling wine under the Colli Piacentini DOC.

⑤ **Ottavianello** Synonym for Cinsault

⑤ **Paarl Riesling** Although not commercialized as such, the Crouchen is still commonly referred to in South Africa as Cape Riesling.

⑤ **Pacali** Synonym for Monica

⑤ **Pagadebit**, **Pagadebiti**, or **Pagedebito** Synonym for Bombino Bianco and (if a black variety) Plavak Mali

⑤ **Pagadebit Crni**, **Pagadebit Mali**, **Pagadebit Pravi**, **Pagadebit Veliki**, or **Pagadebit Zelenjak** Synonyms for Plavak Mali

⑤ **Paien** Synonym for Gewürztraminer

⑤ **Pais** Synonym for the Mission Grape

⑤ **Pallagrello Bianco** Synonym for Coda del Volpe

⑤ **Palombina Nera** Synonym for Piedirosso

Ⓦ **Palomino** or **Palomino Fino** The classic Sherry grape variety, Palomino occupies more than 90 per cent of all the vineyards in Jerez, where its combination of low alcohol and acidity is perfect for that particular fortified-wine style. Known elsewhere in Spain as Listan, Palomino is used as a minor component in cheap Australian and South African blends (both unfortified and fortified) and has even produced Ecuador's first drinkable dry white wine.

Ⓜ **Pamid** This is the most widely cultivated of Bulgaria's indigenous mid-coloured grape varieties. It makes light and fruity quaffing wine.

⑤ **Pampanino** Synonym for Pampanuto

Ⓦ **Pampanuto** An undistinguished variety grown in Apulia.

⑤ **Pansá Bianca** Synonym for Xarel-lo

Ⓦ **Parellada** The major white grape variety of Catalonia, used for still wines and sparkling Cava, in which it imparts a distinctive aroma and is used to soften the firm Xarel-lo grape.

Ⓦ **Pascal Blanc** A minor blending variety in the Rhône, Pascal Blanc is being phased out of the Côtes du Ventoux and Côtes du Vivarais by 2014 but is still allowed in Rasteau and Cassis.

⑤ **Passale** Synonym for Monica

⑤ **Passerina** Synonym for Albana

⑤ **Pâté Noir** Synonym for Salvador

Ⓦ **Pecorino** A blending component used for undistinguished white wines in Italy's Marches and to soften some reds in Calabria.

⑤ **Pecoui-Touar** Synonym for Calitor

⑤ **Pedepalumb** Synonym for Piedirosso

Ⓑ **Pedro Ximénez** or **PX** Some unfortified wines are produced from this classic Sherry grape, but they lack acidity and character to stand on their own and are therefore swallowed up by such mega-sized blends that they are lost. Although its primary use in Sherry is as a sweetening agent (typically with 360 grams of residual sugar per litre), there has been a certain vogue for limited releases of very old PX sweetening wines, sold as the ultimate dessert wine. Huge, dark, deep, and powerfully rich, these special PX wines are piled high with complex, raisiny Muscovado flavours that can be compared in quality, weight, and intensity with only some of the oldest and rarest Australian liqueur Muscats.

Ⓦ **Perderná** Average-quality blending component for white Port.

⑤ **Per'e Palumme** Synonym for Piedirosso

Ⓑ **Periquita** Widely grown throughout Portugal, from Lisbon to the Douro, this grape can be far too astringent if not harvested on tannin ripeness but has the potential to make great red wines, as well as being a good-quality Port variety.

Ⓦ **Perle** A *Gewürztraminer* x *Müller-Thurgau* cross, this grape can survive winter temperatures as low as -30°C (-22°F), and produces a light, fragrant, and fruity wine, but in low yields.

Ⓦ **Perl Von Csaba** This *Madeleine Angevine* x *Muscat Fleur d'Orange* cross was created in Hungary in 1904 and is grown in small pockets in Hungary, France, and Argentina.

Ⓑ **Perricone** This Sicilian variety has started to shine since the introduction of the Sacha di Perricone IGT, when growers started cropping at lower levels and winemakers took more care in their vinification, including using oak barrels. With a little extra ripeness, the red fruit flavours of cherry, redcurrant, and raspberry typically found in Perricone can gravitate to denser, more black-fruit notes without being too alcoholic.

Ⓦ **Perrum** This high-yielding, rot-resistant grape is a minor blending variety in various parts of Portugal, while in Spain, Perrum is a synonym for Palomino.

Ⓑ Persan Minor red variety grown in the Savoie region.

Ⓢ Petit Arvine Synonym for Arvine

Ⓢ Petit Blanc Synonym for the Prié Blanc

Ⓢ Petit Blanche Synonym for Biancolella

Ⓣ Petit Bouschet This *Aramon Noir* x *Teinturier du Cher* hybrid is another *teinturier* cross bred by Louis Bouschet at Domaine de la Calmette by Henri Bouschet of Alicante Bouschet fame. Petit Bouschet is also a synonym for Cabernet Sauvignon and Alicante Bouchet.

Ⓑ Petit-Brun A minor blending component for the red and rosé wines of the Palette AOC in Provence.

Ⓢ Petit Cabernet Synonym for Cabernet Sauvignon

Ⓦ Petite Arvine This old Valais variety makes a rich, dry white, with a distinctive grapefruit character and good acidity in Switzerland, where it also adapts well to sweeter, late-harvest styles. In the Valle d'Aosta, Italy, the Petite Arvine produces a lighter, more fragrant dry white.

Ⓑ Petite Sirah An ancient cross between Peloursin and Syrah, the Petite Sirah seems more at home in California than its native France, where it has often been mistaken for Syrah. A synonym for Durif.

Ⓢ Petite-Vidure Synonym for Cabernet Sauvignon

Ⓦ Petit Manseng Grown in southwestern France, where with the Gros Manseng it is known primarily for producing the legendary Jurançon Moelleux. Less widely grown than the Gros Manseng, the Petit Manseng curiously does not have smaller grapes, although the berry size is still very small. Another curiosity is that Petit Manseng is extremely resistant to grey rot yet susceptible to noble rot, whereas late-harvested Gros Manseng grapes tend to be *passerillé*.

Ⓦ Petit Meslier An ancient Champagne variety and spontaneous cross of *Gouais* x *Savagnin Blanc*, the Petit Meslier is one of the permitted varieties for Vin de Pays des Coteaux de Coiffy and is making a small revival in Champagne itself.

Ⓢ Petit Pineau Synonym for Arbois

Ⓑ Petit Rouge A low-yielding variety in the Valle d'Aosta, where it is capable of producing deep, dark, highly perfumed red wines. There have been moves to change the name of this grape to Oriou (one of its many synonyms) because of the misconception that the "Petit" refers to its quality, even though it refers to the size of berry, and most classic varieties have smaller, rather than larger, grapes.

Ⓑ Petit Verdot A grape that has been used to good effect in Bordeaux because it is a late ripener, bringing acidity to the overall balance of a wine. Certain modern techniques of viticulture and vinification have rendered it less valuable, which might prove to be a pity, because it also produces a characterful, long-lived, and tannic wine when it is sufficiently ripe.

Ⓦ Petra A Serbian *Kunbarat* x *Pinot Noir* hybrid developed in the 1970s to provide extreme winter hardiness, thanks to the Kunbarat, which is itself part Amurensis.

Ⓦ Phoenix One of four recent hybrids that have been allowed by the EU for the production of wine because the percentage of non-*vinifera* is too tiny to be of any significance. A *Bacchus* x *Villard Blanc*, Phoenix has a slightly muted Bacchus aroma with a touch of herbaceous character in the fruit.

Ⓦ Picardan or **Picardan Blanc** Although the primary name according to some ampelographers is Araignan, this variety is best known as the Picardan, one of Châteauneuf-du-Pape's 13 permitted varieties, even if it plays only an occasional minor role in some Châteauneuf-du-Pape *blanc*. Picardan is also one of the Bourboulenc's synonyms, and Grosse Clairette is a synonym for both Bourboulenc and Picardan, illustrating why these two singular varieties have often been confused for one another. Although a Picardan Noir exists, it is not related, but Picardan Noir is also a synonym for both Bouchalès and Cinsault.

Ⓦ Picolit Typically produces grossly over-rated and horrendously over-priced sweet wine in Italy.

Ⓦ Picpoul, Picpoul Blanche, or **Picpoul de Pinet** Widely planted in the southern Rhône and Languedoc, Picpoul is one of the 13 varieties authorized for Châteauneuf-du-Pape and produces a delicate dry white under the Coteaux du Languedoc – Picpoul de Pinet AOC. It is also a synonym for Folle Blanche.

Ⓑ Picpoul Noir High sugar levels make this a useful blending component for the wines of Corbières, Coteaux du Tricastin, Côtes-du-Rhône, Côtes-du-Ventoux, Languedoc, Minervois, and Vacqueyras. Picpoul Noir is also a synonym for Calitor.

Ⓢ Pied di Colombo Synonym for Piedirosso

Ⓑ Pigato This Italian variety is grown in Liguria but probably originated from Greece. Capable of producing full-flavoured, nicely aromatic, early-drinking red wines.

Ⓢ Pignatello Synonym for Perricone

Ⓑ Pignerol Minor Provençal grape used as a blending component in the red and rosé wines of Bellet AOC.

PINOT GRIS
The widest-cultivated and fastest-expanding mid-coloured grape in the world, this variety undoubtedly at its best in Alsace, where it can produce succulent, rich, and complex wines of great quality and a spiciness seldom found elsewhere. When coupled with an acidity that is lower than that of Pinot Blanc, an absence of spicy varietal definition will invariably be due to high yields. This is why Pinot Grigio in northeast Italy generally lacks the intensity of Alsace Pinot Gris, although both use the same clones.

Ⓑ Pignola Valtellina or **Pignola Valtellinese** Blending component in the Valtellina Superiore DOCG.

Ⓢ Pignoletto Synonym for Perricone

Ⓜ Pineau d'Aunis This grape is best known for its supporting role in the production of Rosé d'Anjou. A *teinturier* variant also exists.

Ⓢ Pineau Blanche de Loire or **Pineau de la Loire** Synonyms for Chenin Blanc

Ⓢ Pineau Rouge Synonym for Pineau d'Aunis

Ⓢ Pineau de Saumur Synonym for Grolleau

Ⓦ Pinella Although only a minor Veneto variety, Pinella has its own varietal appellation under the Colli Euganei DOC.

Ⓢ Pinello Synonym for Pinella

Ⓑ Pinotage A *Pinot Noir* x *Cinsault* cross developed in 1925, it occupies an important position in South African viticulture, where its rustic and high-toned wine is greatly appreciated. If this variety has the

potential that some South Africans believe, then they should actively encourage its spread throughout as many wine areas across the world, and benefit from as wide experimentation, as possible.

Ⓢ Pinot Aigret Synonym for Rufete

Ⓢ Pinot d'Anjou or **Pinot d'Aunis** Synonyms for Pineau d'Aunis

Ⓢ Pinot Beurot or **Pinot Burot** Synonyms for Pinot Gris

Ⓢ Pinot Bianco Synonym for Pinot Blanc

Ⓦ Pinot Blanc A variety that is perhaps at its best in Alsace, where it is most successful, producing fruity, well-balanced wines with good grip and alcohol content. It also has excellent potential in northern Italy as Pinot Bianco. Plantings are gradually diminishing worldwide.

Ⓢ Pinot Blanc Cramant or **Pinot Blanc Chardonnay** Synonyms for Chardonnay

Ⓢ Pinot Blanco Synonym for Chenin Blanc

PINOT MEUNIER
An important variety in Champagne, where vinified white gives more upfront appeal of fruit than the Pinot Noir when young and is therefore essential for young Champagnes. Its characteristics are more immediate in appeal but less fine than those of the Pinot Noir. The Pinot Meunier is extensively cultivated in the Marne Valley area of Champagne, where its resistance to frost makes it the most suitable vine. Its synonym Plant de Brie illustrates just how far west of Champagne (as we know it today) the old vineyards used to extend. Research carried out in 2008 clearly indicates that not all Pinot Meunier kept in nursery collections is even from the same varietal family, as some bore close resemblance to Pinot Noir, while others did not and, to quote, "several Meunier samples from different collections showed different genotypes" (ie, they were different varieties). It is now found all over the place and can make very Pinot Noir-like red wine.

Pinot Blanc Vrai Synonym for Pinot Blanc

Pinot Branco Synonym for Pinot Blanc

Pinot Chardonnay Synonym for Chardonnay

Pinot Droit or **Pinot Fin** Synonyms for Pinot Noir

Pinot d'Evora Synonym for Carignan

Pinot Fin Teinturier or **Pinot Teinturier** This Pinot Noir with its coloured juice has so far produced undistinguished wine, but with Gouais Blanc, another unremarkable variety, it has fathered one of the world's greatest grapes, the Chardonnay.

Pinot Fleri Synonym for Mourvèdre

Pinot Giallo Synonym for Chardonnay

Pinot Grigio Synonym for Pinot Gris

Pinot Gris See box, opposite.

Pinot Liébault A natural localized clone of Pinot Noir first identified in Grand Cru Les Charmes, Gevrey Chambertin, in 1810, Pinot Liébault's propensity for higher yields has been widely exaggerated, as it is only moderately higher-cropping than the most widely planted Pinot Noir clones.

Pinot de la Loire Synonym for Chenin Blanc

Pinot Meunier See box, opposite.

Pinot Nero Synonym for Pinot Noir

Pinot Noir See box, below.

Pinot Noiren Synonym for Pinot Noir

Pinot Noir Précoce Synonym for Frühburgunder

Pinot d'Orléans Synonym for Beaunoir

Pinot Rouge Synonym for Dameron

Pinot St George Synonym for Négrette

Pinot Vache Synonym for Mondeuse

Pinot Verdet Synonym for Arbois

Plant d'Arbois Synonym for Poulsard Blanc

Plant d'Arles Synonym for Cinsault

Plant d'Aunis Synonym for Pineau d'Aunis

Plant de Brie Synonym for Pinot Meunier

Plant Dore, **Plant Doré** or **Plant Fin** Synonyms for Pinot Noir

Plant Noir Synonym for Mondeuse

Pinot Noir Luissant Synonym for Pinot Noir

Ploussard Synonym for Poulsard Blanc and Poulsard Noir

Portoghese Synonym for Portugieser or Blauer Portugieser

Portugal Synonym for Tinto Amarella

Portugieser One of the most widely planted black varieties in Germany, the Portugieser is thought to have originated in the Danube district of Austria, not in Portugal as its name suggests. It makes a very ordinary, extremely light red wine, so it is often vinified white in bad years to blend with white wines that are too acidic. In addition to Germany and Austria, the Portugieser is also found in Italy, France, the Czech Republic, Hungary, Romania, and Croatia. Never say never, they say, but despite there being at least 87 different synonyms for this grape, with 33 of those referring to Portugal, I have never seen this grape growing in that country.

Poulsard or **Poulsard Noir** Grown in the Jura, where it contributes to various appellations, Poulsard Noir is the most commonly encountered Poulsard and has the capability of producing complex Burgundian-style wines, but it seldom does and probably needs slightly warmer climes to excel. A more aromatically spicy sub-variety exists, the Poulsard Noir Musquet, which was originally and erroneously thought to be a Muscat variety, when it was known as the Muscat Pelosard Noir. A little Poulsard Noir Musquet is grown in Hungary.

Poulsard Blanc Rarely encountered, undistinguished white version of the Jura's more famous Poulsard Noir.

Poulsard Musqué Synonym for Poulsard Noir Musquet

Poulsard Rosé or **Poulsard Rouge** Rarely encountered, undistinguished mid-coloured version of the Jura's more famous Poulsard Noir.

Praça Average-quality white Port variety.

Premetta Minor Italian variety found in the Valle d'Aosta where it produces slightly tannic, bright cherry-red wines.

Prié Blanc This Italian variety produces light, delicate, sometimes sparkling white wine and is almost exclusively found in the Valle d'Aosta, although it is also grown in the Swiss Valais.

Primitivo Synonym for Zinfandel

Procanico Synonym for Ugni Blanc

Prolongeau Synonym for Bouchalès and Malbec

Prosecco Synonym for Glera

Prugnolo Synonym for Sangiovese

Pugnet Synonym for Nebbiolo

Pulciano Synonym for Grechetto

PX Synonym for Pedro Ximénez

Rabaner This Riesling (clone 88Gm) x Riesling (clone 64Gm) cross has the dubious honour of being the variety that most resembles the Müller-Thurgau.

Rabigato This is the main white Port grape variety. It is also known as Rabo da Ovelha, or "ewe's tail", and is grown in the Douro Valley for unfortified wines under the name Donzelinho Branco.

Rabo de Ovelha Synonym for Rabigato

Rabo de Ovelha Tinto Synonym for Trincadeira Preta

Raboso This underrated variety is indigenous to the Veneto region, where it can make excellent-value red wines that are full of sunny fruit. There are two distinct, localized clones, Raboso del Piave and Raboso Veronese. Raboso del Piave is the most widely planted and is most often used as a pure varietal. Raboso Veronese is the more productive; and while it does not have the same richness or positive character, it is a very effective blending component. Raboso Veronese is also found in Argentina. This clone should not be confused with Raboso Piava, which is a synonym for Durella, or Raboso Piave, the synonym for Béquignol Noir.

Raffiat This is a minor, undistinguished blending component in southwest France.

Ragusan Synonym for Asprinio

Ramisco Famously grown ungrafted in trenches dug out of the sandy dunes of Sintra, Portugal, where it produces Colares, which is as tough as old boots.

Räuschling Synonym for Elbling

Red Misket Synonym for Misket Cherven

Red Muscadel Synonym for Muscat Rosé à Petits Grains

Refosco This ancient Italian variety is a native of the Friuli-Venezia Giulia region of northern Italy, where it makes dark, spicy red wines. There are 11 distinctly individual localized clones, of which Refosco dal Peduncolo Rosso is the oldest, most highly regarded, and

PINOT NOIR

This is one of the classic varieties of Champagne, although its greatest fame lies in Burgundy. The Pinot Noir has 258 official synonyms, and there are innumerable Pinots that are not related. In a study by Regner et al in 2000, it was concluded that "results suggest that Pinot was derived from a cross of Schwarzriesling x Traminer", which would make Meunier an even earlier heterogenously distinct variety, rather than (as previously thought) a variant of Pinot Noir, which itself is widely regarded as one of the very oldest identifiable grapevines. Regner's data is not inconsistent with the proposed parentage, but neither is it compelling, and to make matters worse, a subsequent scientific paper (Salmaso et al) claimed that Regner et al "proposed Riesling Renano and Traminer as the progenitors of Pinot Nero", when clearly they had not. What this will morph into once these findings hit the Internet is anybody's guess, but don't take any notice of claims that the Riesling has anything to do with the Pinot Noir's parentage. In the right place, under ideal climatic conditions, the Pinot Noir can produce the richest, most velvet-smooth wines in the world. Depending on climate and ripeness, its flavour can range from cherries to strawberries. Great Pinot Noir is also made in California (notably Russian River and Santa Barbara), Oregon, and Central Otago, New Zealand. While individual producers in the New World are making progress in trying to replicate the extraordinary balance of weight, finesse, and complexity that this grape can achieve in the truly great grands crus of Burgundy, there is a feeling that most of even the best Pinot Noir wines produced outside Burgundy are all barely more than "varietal wines" and that, when this is taken to its extreme, they become "fruit-bombs". Having stated that, it should be remembered that the worst grand cru Burgundies do not even qualify as "fruit-bombs"; thus, even in the greatest terroirs, the Pinot Noir is extremely unforgiving.

most widely cultivated, followed by Refosco Nostrano, aka Refoscono. The other clones are Refosco Barbeano, Refosco Boton, Refosco Chiozza, Refosco d'Istria, Refosco degli Ucelli, Refosco Guarnieri, Refosco Runcis, and Refosco Scodavacca. With just three exceptions, any other Refosco will probably be a synonym of one of these clones and most likely will refer to Refosco dal Peduncolo Rosso, which has the most synonyms. The three exceptions are Refosco as a synonym for Mondeuse and Terrano, and any white Refosco, which would merely be an incorrect synonym for the Ezerjó of Hungary.

Ⓑ Regent One of four recent hybrids that have been allowed by the EU for the production of wine because the percentage of non-*vinifera* is too tiny to be of any significance. A *Diana* x *Chambourcin* cross, Regent is supposed to provide a wine with good body and a touch of spice, although even the best of the samples I have tasted have been uninspiring. It is surprisingly widely planted in Germany and is also finding favour in Switzerland and the UK.

Ⓦ Regner The parents of this *Luglienca Bianca* x *Gamay* cross are a curious combination. Why anyone would consider crossing a table grape with the red wine grape of Beaujolais to create a German white wine variety is a mystery. Predictably it produces sugar-rich grapes and mild, Müller-Thurgau-like wines.

Ⓦ Reichensteiner Affectionately known as the "Rick Steiner" at Camel Valley, a Cornish vineyard that has long supplied the restaurants of local celebrity chef Rick Stein, this *Müller-Thurgau* x *Madeleine Angevine* x *Calabreser-Fröhlich* cross is grown in Germany and England. Its sugar-rich grapes produce a mild, delicate, somewhat neutral, Sylvaner-like wine.

Ⓢ Rhine Riesling Synonym for Riesling

Ⓦ Rhoditis This grape is used as a supporting variety in the making of Retsina, a use only eclipsed by its suitability for the distilling pot!

Ⓦ Ribolla or **Ribolla Gialla** An important blending component grown in the Friuli-Venezia Giulia region of northern Italy. Ribolla Nera exists, but this name is also a synonym for the Schioppetino.

Ⓦ Rieslaner A *Riesling* x *Sylvaner* cross mainly grown in Franken, Germany, where it produces sugar-rich grapes and full-bodied, rather neutral wines.

Ⓦ Riesling See box, right.

Ⓢ Riesling Italico Synonym for Welschriesling

Ⓢ Riesling Renano Synonym for Riesling

Ⓢ Riesling x Sylvaner or **Rivaner** Synonyms for Müller-Thurgau

Ⓦ Rkatsiteli An old Georgian variety, this grape is also grown in Moldova, Bulgaria, and in very small parcels in Australia, Russia, Italy, and elsewhere.

Ⓦ Robola Confined to the island of Cephalonia, this is a good-quality Greek grape that is at its best when its minerality is encouraged.

Ⓢ Rolle Synonym for Vermentino

Ⓦ Romorantin An obscure variety that is confined to the Loire Valley, Romorantin can trace its ancestry back to a natural *Gouais Blanc* x *Pinot Fin Teinturier* cross and is thus a sibling of Auxerrois, Chardonnay, Gamay, Melon de Bourgogne, Sacy, *et al*. This grape is capable of producing a delicate, attractive, and flowery wine if it is not over-cropped.

Ⓑ Rondo One of four recent hybrids that have been allowed by the EU for the production of wine because the percentage of non-*vinifera* is too tiny to be of any significance. A *Zarya Severa* x *St-Laurent* cross with both Saperavi and Amurensis in the parentage of Zarya Severa, this grape is more useful (disease resistance, winter hardiness, and good colour) than outstanding.

Ⓢ Rooi Grenache Synonym for Grenache

Ⓢ Rossanella Synonym for Molinara

Ⓢ Rossara Synonym for Molinara and Schiava Lombarda

Ⓦ Rossese There is one recognized local clone, Rossese di Campochiesa, but Rossese di Dolceacqua and Rossese d'Albenga are just synonyms for Rossese Bianco (if the grapes white). Rossese is also an incorrect synonym for Vermentino, just as Rossese Nericcio and Rossese Nero are for Tibouren. There is no true black-skinned Rossese.

Ⓑ Rossignola A minor blending component for Valpolicella.

Ⓢ Rossola Synonym for Roter Veltliner

Ⓢ Rossola Nera Synonym for Mourvèdre

Ⓑ Rotberger A *Schiava Grossa* x *Riesling* cross. The parents seem an odd couple, but the offspring is surprisingly successful, producing some excellent rosé wines.

Ⓜ Roter Veltliner Not related to the Grüner Veltliner, although both are Austrian varieties; DNA fingerprinting has discovered the Roter Veltliner parentage to be *Rotgipfler* x *Neuburger*. No coloured Veltliner variant has yet been identified. The rosé-coloured Roter Veltliner, which is lighter in shade than the distinctly red-coloured Frühroter Veltliner, is in fact descended from this variety (*Roter Veltliner* x *Silvaner*).

Ⓦ Rotgipfler This Austrian variety makes a robust, full-bodied, spicy white wine of not dissimilar character to the Zierfandler, which is often made into a dry style, although the semi-sweet Rotgipfler

of Gumpoldskirchen is probably the most famous rendition of this grape.

Ⓦ Roupeiro Technically, its primary name is Síria, but this grape is better known as Roupeiro. It is grown all over Portugal but is considered most noble in Alentejo, where it produces soft, full, well-rounded white wines.

Ⓦ Roussanne One of two major varieties used to produce the rare white wines of Hermitage and Châteauneuf-du-Pape in France's Rhône Valley, this grape makes the finer, more delicate wines, while those made from the Marsanne tend to be fatter and richer.

Ⓦ Roussette Commonly associated with Savoie, the true Roussette is, however, the Roussette of the Rhône, which is a good-quality grape that produces a rich, full-bodied wine. A Savoie wine that states Roussette on the label (eg, Roussette de Savoie) will definitely have Altesse inside the bottle, another good-quality grape, but lighter in body with higher acidity and more minerality.

Ⓦ Roussette d'Ayze The only Roussette in Savoie, the Roussette d'Ayze, aka Chasselas d'Ayze and Clairette du Midi, is an undistinguished grape used as a blending component in very ordinary sparkling wine.

Ⓣ Royalty This *Alicante Ganzin* x *Trousseau Noir* hybrid is a *teinturier* grape that was developed in California, where it is grown to no great success in the hot Central Valley.

Ⓑ Rubin This Bulgarian *Nebbiolo* x *Syrah* cross was developed in 1944 and produces interesting, spicy-cherry fruit that even has a touch of cracked black pepper but is perhaps a tad too alcoholic to rival either of its very classy parents.

Ⓣ Rubired Possibly the most successful *teinturier* grape bred so far, Rubired was once restricted to Port-style fortified wines (useful for its high ratio of acid to colour), but

this *Alicante Ganzin* x *Tinta Cão* hybrid is being increasingly used in unfortified red wines in California and Australia.

Ⓑ Ruby Cabernet This *Cabernet Sauvignon* x *Carignan* cross was produced by Professor Olmo of UC Davis. Its origination date is often misquoted, so, to clarify, this grape was bred in 1936, first fruited in 1940, and made its first wine in 1946. Although one of the more successful *Cabernet Sauvignon* x *Carignan* crosses, this variety nevertheless inherited far more of the Carignan's genes than the Cabernet's, like all the rest. The Ruby Cabernet is highly resistant to heat and drought, but its most useful attribute is probably the ability to survive high winds, when the metabolic system of most other vines shuts down. Primarily grown in California, but with a fairly significant hectarage in South Africa and Australia, and just a smattering in Spain and Argentina, the Ruby Cabernet typically provides a rather one-dimensional red wine with characteristic cherry fruit. Attempts to achieve anything more are usually blighted by too much oak or over-extraction, but there have been exceptions, notably Flagstone's Ruby in the Dust (South Africa) and, to a lesser extent, Rimfire (Australia).

Ⓑ Ruché Best known for producing Ruché di Castagnole Monferrato DOC, the Ruché is a rather mysterious grape of unknown but presumed Piedmontese origin that generally makes a light ruby-coloured wine with an aromatic twist, although through reduced yields, much darker, richer wines not dissimilar to Nebbiolo, only more aromatic, can be achieved.

Ⓑ Rufete A high-yielding, low-quality Portuguese grape for red wine, due to its low acidity. It is, however, a good blending component in the production of Port.

Ⓢ Ruländer Synonym for Pinot Gris

RIESLING

The classic German grape produces a zesty, citrus, intensely flavoured wine of great mineral complexity, length, and longevity. When grown on certain soils, the terpenes in Riesling benefit from bottle-age and can, after several years, develop a so-called petrolly bouquet. Alsace and Austria make most (not all) of the best dry Riesling. In Australia, the wine from this grape has, by and large, a simplistic lime-fruit character that is prone to going petrolly in a relatively short while but lacks the finesse and complexity of truly classic petrolly aromas. However, great Australian Rieslings do exist, made in traditional areas such as Grosset's Polish Hill in the Clare Valley, Holmoak in Tasmania (where the 2005 is a standout), and Frogmore Creek FGR (for a delicate, Mosel-like balance of sweetness), also in Tasmania.

SAGRANTINO
An Umbrian grape that was almost extinct until its revival in the 1980s, which directly led to the 1992 upgrading of Montefalco Sagrantino to DOCG. Traditionally this variety makes both dry and sweet passito reds. The name is supposed to have derived from sagra *or "festival", suggesting that the wines it yields were originally reserved for feast days.*

(S) **Rulandské Bílé** Synonym for Pinot Blanc

(S) **Rulandské Modrý** Synonym for Pinot Noir

(S) **Rulandské Šedé** Synonym for Pinot Gris

(S) **Ryzlink Rýnský** Synonym for Riesling

(S) **Ryzlink Vlašsky** Synonym for Welschriesling

(W) **Sacy** A minor grape variety that produces bland "stretching" wine and is grown in small quantities in the Chablis district. Its high acidity could make it very useful in the production of sparkling wines.

(B) **Sagrantino** See box, above.

(T) **Salvador** This French *teinturier* grape is a *Munson Noir* (aka *Jaeger 70*) x *vinifera* hybrid that is mostly planted in California's Central Valley, with small amounts found in Australia, Bulgaria, Brazil, India, Mexico, and Romania. The juice is coloured and pulpy, but not gelatinous as some sources suggest.

(B) **Samarrinho** A good-quality Port variety.

(B) **Sangiovese** This variety is most famously known as the principal variety used for Chianti, which at its most basic should provide plenty of quaffing juicy cherry, raspberry, and plummy fruit flavours. At one time, Sangiovese was marked by an astringency at best, a metallic finish at worst, but since the cultivation of lower-yield clones, its potential has gone through the roof in terms of complexity and finesse.

(S) **Sangiovese dell'Ottavi** Synonym for Uva Fina

(S) **Sangiovese Polveroso Bonechi** Synonym for Ciliegiolo

(S) **Sangioveto** Synonym for Sangiovese

(T) **Saperavi** The origins of this Georgian *teinturier* grape are unclear, but its once fearsome wine is gradually becoming clearer. Symphony Wines in Australia's King Valley also produces a Saperavi, and with a nice touch of irony, David Nelson, an Australian winemaker, and Lado Uzunashvilli, a Georgian-Australian winemaker, have done much to improve the Saperavi in Georgia since 2001. Recognized localized clones are Saperavi Atenis, Saperavi Bezhashvilis, Saperavi Budeshuriseburi, Saperavi Grdzelmtevana, Saperavi Guriis, Saperavi Kartlis, Saperavi Pachkha, and Saperaviseburi.

(S) **Saperavi de Kachet, Saperavi de Kachetie,** and **Saperavi Patara** Synonyms of Saperavi, not localized clones.

(S) **Saperavi Ochanuri** Not a Saperavi; synonym for Otskhanuri Sapere.

(S) **Sauvignon** Synonym for Sauvignon Blanc

(W) **Sauvignon Blanc** See box, below.

(M) **Sauvignon Gris** An extremely muted sibling with none of Sauvignon Blanc's gooseberry character, a little Sauvignon Gris is still found in the Saint-Bris AOC of Burgundy, but there is not much left in its native Bordeaux these days. Where it does exist, such as at Château Ducla, it is so subtle in varietal style that it is easily dominated by the more extrovert Sauvignon Blanc, as in that château's Expérience XII *cuvée*. In the 19th century, it was transplanted from Bordeaux to Chile, where it has miraculously survived. Miraculously because, although no *vinifera* variety likes "wet feet", the sensitivity of Sauvignon Gris to wet soils is almost at a phobic level and, until relatively recently, all Chilean vineyards existed only because they were flood-irrigated. Most Sauvignon Gris these days seems to come from Chile, where it grows particularly well in the Leyda Valley. It is a variety that is on the up, albeit in a strictly limited production, throughout the wine world, generated as a backlash to the über-success of Sauvignon Blanc's extrovert style. It is being replanted in France and has even started to appear in Marlborough, the New World heartland of Sauvignon Blanc, where it has been showcased by none other than Montana.

(S) **Sauvignon Rosé** Synonym for Sauvignon Gris

(S) **Sauvignon Vert** Synonym for Muscadelle and Friulano

(S) **Sauvignonasse** Synonym for Friulano

(W) **Savagnin Blanc** This grape is a non-aromatic Traminer Weiss, and subjected to ageing under *flor*, the Savagnin Blanc is responsible for the Sherry-like *vin jaune* of the Jura, of which the best known is Château Chalon.

(M) **Savagnin Rosé** This is the non-aromatic Traminer Rosé (from which the highly aromatic Gewürztraminer evolved), and it grows primarily in the village of Heiligenstein, Alsace, where it is known as the Klevener de Heiligenstein. It was almost extinct in the 1950s, with just 15 ares (ie, 0.15 hectares, or barely more than one-third of an acre) surviving, but with renewed interest this has grown to more than 40 hectares (100 acres).

(W) **Savatiano** Although used primarily for *retsina*, the highly drought-resistant Savatiano is grown all over Greece as white-wine insurance against a lack of rainfall. Pure non-resinated Savatiano is not unknown (such as the unfortunately named Kanza from Attica, the heartland of the resinated version), but due to its low acidity it usually forms part of a blend.

(W) **Scheurebe** A *Riesling* x *Sylvaner* cross, this is one of the best of Germany's new varieties. When ripe, it makes very good aromatic wines, but, if it is harvested too early, very herbaceous cat's pee.

(B) **Schiava** The so-called Schiava family is only just being classified. DNA research has determined that 22 Schiava cultivars can in fact be grouped into five genetically unrelated groups according to their geographical origin: Valtellina, Bergamo, Brescia, and Alto Adige in Italy, and the Swabian hills of Württemberg. It was concluded that the term Schiava (or "slave") referred to a similar cultivation practice in contiguous regions rather than any common genetic background.

(S) **Schiava di Bergamo** Synonym for Schiava Lombarda

(W) **Schiava Bianca** Least encountered of the Schiava family (and not DNA tested), this minor variety is an occasional blending component in Lombardy and the Alto Adige.

(S) **Schiava di Como** or **Schiava di Varese** Synonyms for Schiava Lombarda

(B) **Schiava Gentile** Supposedly the best Schiava, this is the most widely cultivated variety in the Alto Adige, where it produces mostly light-coloured, light-bodied red of undistinguished quality, sometimes with an almond character to the fruit and a light bitterness on the finish. The best wines are Alto Adige DOC, especially Colli di Bolzano and Santa Maddalena, yet they are merely soft, fruity, and early-drinking. Usually much better if bolstered by other varieties such as Lagrein or Pinot Nero.

(M) **Schiava Grigia** Seldom encountered mid-coloured variant of the Schiava family (but not DNA tested). Most Schiava Grigia that does exist is to be found in the Alto Adige.

(B) **Schiava Grossa** The least appreciated of the Schiava clan, most Schiava Grossa is cultivated in the Alto Adige.

(B) **Schiava Lombarda** One of the lesser Schiava varieties, Schiava Lombarda is most often used as a blending component in the wines of Bergamasca and Valcalepio Rosso.

(S) **Schiava Media** Synonym for Schiava Gentile

(B) **Schiava Meranese** One of the lesser Schiava varieties, Schiava Meranese is most often used as a blending component in the wines of Bergamasca and Valcalepio Rosso.

(S) **Schiava Piccola** or **Schiava Rot** Synonyms for Schiava Gentile

(S) **Schilcher** Synonym for Blauer Wildbacher

SAUVIGNON BLANC
Sauvignon Blanc is at its best defined in New Zealand, particularly Marlborough, and is still a long way from achieving a similar level of quality and consistency in its home location of the Loire Valley. It is improving in Bordeaux, where it is also used in Sauternes and Barsac blends. Some exciting wines have begun to emerge from the Cape winelands, South Africa (ignoring those that are artificially flavoured), but California remains hugely disappointing, even though its vines are the same Sauvignon Blanc clone as New Zealand's.

SÉMILLON

In Sauternes and Barsac, this is the grape susceptible to "noble rot". Some say its aroma is reminiscent of lanolin, but as pure lanolin is virtually odourless, the comparison hardly conveys the Sémillon's distinctive bouquet. For dry wine, this grape is at its best in Australia, particularly the Hunter Valley, where its lime fruit takes to oak like a duck to water, whereas bottle-aged Sémillon can be sublime even after several decades.

SYLVANER

Originally from Austria, this variety is widely planted throughout Central Europe. It is prolific, early maturing, and yields the dry wines of Franken and Alsace. It is also widely believed to be the Zierfandler of Austria. Sylvaner has a tart, earthy, yet neutral flavour, which takes on a tomato-like richness in the bottle. This grape is now known to be the offspring of the Österreichisch Weiss and Traminer. Angelo Puglisi of Ballandean Estate in the Granite Belt of Queensland has consistently produced the world's greatest Sylvaner with cane cutting and late harvests.

Ⓑ **Schioppetino** An ancient Friulian variety, Schioppetino was nearly extinct until it suddenly became fashionable in the 1980s. When not harvested at full ripeness, Schioppetino can be just another medium-bodied wine hinting unimpressively at cherries. But when harvested ripe, this grape produces much rounder wines, with blacker fruit and a fine, cracked-pepper aroma. Rarely seen beyond the boundaries of Friuli, but Holdredge Wines grows Schioppetino at its MacBryde Vineyard in the Russian River and produces a pure varietal wine from it.

Ⓢ **Schioppettino** Synonym for Schioppetino

Ⓦ **Schönberger** A *Spätburgunder* x *(Chasselas Rosé x Muscat Hamburg)* cross, this grape is grown in Germany and England. It produces sugar-rich grapes that make wine with good aromatic qualities but low acidity.

Ⓢ **Schwartzriesling** Synonym for Pinot Meunier

Ⓑ **Sciaccarello** A Corsican variety of typically Italian origin, the Sciaccarello grape has aromatics and acidity that are comparable to those of the Tibouren in Provence. It is, in fact, the same grape as the Mammolo (Tuscany), which is traditionally blended with Sangiovese. In Corsica, the Sciaccarello is blended into the AOCs of Ajaccio, Patrimonio, and Vin de Corse Porto Vecchio, adding a distinctive floral aroma to the wines. This variety is seldom encountered outside Corsica, Tuscany, and a few other isolated parts of Italy, but as the Mammolo, the odd few vines can be found in Mudgee, Australia.

Ⓦ **Scuppernong** This is not a *Vitis vinifera*, but a native American *Vitis rotundifolia*, thus a so-called Muscadine. Scuppernong's large and cherry-like grapes produce an extraordinary, disturbingly exotic, and most unusual wine. Yet it was from these grapes that "Captain" Paul Garrett first made his notorious, best-selling Virginia Dare wine from a string of East Coast wineries in the 1900s. Unless conditioned from birth to Scuppernong grapes, the extremely foxy wine they make will at best be off-putting to most wine consumers today. A black-skinned Scuppernong exists but is less widely cultivated.

Ⓦ **Sémillon** *See box, above.*

Ⓢ **Sercial** Synonym for Esgana Cão

Ⓢ **Serène** Synonym for Syrah

Ⓢ **Serprina** or **Serprino** Synonym for Glera

Ⓦ **Seyval Blanc** This *Seibel 5656* x *Seibel 4986* hybrid is the most successful of the many Seyve-Villard crosses. It is grown primarily in New York State and England, where it produces the better wine (whereas Vidal grown in New York State is superior to English-grown Vidal). Although seldom accomplished, this grape can produce high-quality sparkling wine, as demonstrated on occasions by Three Choirs' non-vintage Classic Cuvée.

Ⓢ **Shiraz** Synonym for Syrah

Ⓢ **Shiroka Melnishka Ioza** Synonym for Melnik

Ⓜ **Siegerrebe** This is a *Madeleine Angevine* x *Gewürztraminer* cross, a grape that was once widely grown in Germany. Also found in England and elsewhere, Siegerrebe is primarily grown in cool, potentially wet climates for its early ripening capability and high sugar yield. It can have very good aromatic character but unfortunately has very low acidity.

Ⓢ **Silvaner**, **Silvain Vert**, or **Silván** Synonyms for Sylvaner

Ⓢ **Sousão** or **Souzão** Synonym for Vinhão and Donzelinho Tinto

Ⓢ **Spätburgunder** Synonym for Pinot Noir

Ⓢ **Spergola** Synonym for Sauvignon Blanc

Ⓢ **St Emilion** Synonym for Ugni Blanc

Ⓑ **St-Laurent** This is a French variety but widely planted in Austria, Hungary, and the Czech Republic, where it is appreciated for its soft tannins and Pinot-like character.

Ⓦ **St Pepin** A relatively recent *Elmer Swenson 114* x *Syval Blanc* hybrid, the St. Pepin is primarily cultivated in the Atlantic Northeast and other marginal viticultural areas of the USA, where this grape benefits from early ripening and is capable of surviving winter temperatures in excess of -32°C (-25°F). St Pepin typically produces fruity, but unexciting semi-sweet white wines but can be stretched to some intriguing limits, such as the 2003 Very Late Harvest at Wollersheim in Wisconsin, which had an aroma that veered from almost roast parsnip into emulsion paint and threaded itself all the way through the wine's oily sweetness. Actually, it was not as bad as that sounds!

Ⓢ **Steen** Synonym for Chenin Blanc

Ⓢ **Sultana** or **Sultaniye** Synonyms for Thompson Seedless

Ⓦ **Susumaniello** This historic descendant of Sangiovese is currently under-rated and plays only a minor blending role for the wines of Brindisi and Ostuni DOCs in Apulia. It could have much greater potential.

Ⓢ **Svatovav'rinecke** or **Svätovavrinecké** Synonyms for St-Laurent

Ⓦ **Sylvaner** or **Sylvaner Blanc** *See box, above.*

Ⓜ **Sylvaner Rouge** A few hectares of this rare red sub-variety exist in Germany; and in Alsace, JosMeyer used to produce a pure Sylvaner Rouge up to 2001, but the vines were grubbed up after it was banned. Quite why is difficult to comprehend because it is a slightly tastier version of the primary Sylvaner Blanc. Relatively recently, however, the ban was in part reversed, with up to 10 per cent Sylvaner Rouge allowed in any Sylvaner varietal. If JosMeyer cannot persuade the authorities to allow a pure Sylvaner Rouge in the future, they intend to release one as a *vin de table* registered under the name of Peaurouge ("Redskin").

Ⓢ **Sylvánske Zelené** Synonym for Sylvaner

Ⓦ **Symphony** Plantations of this *Muscat d'Alexandrie* x *Grenache*

SYRAH

Because the name of this variety derived from Shiraz (which Australia has adopted), the capital of Fars, the idea arose that it must have originated in Persia. We now know it is pure French in its breeding, being the progeny of two minor varieties, the Mondeuse Blanche and Dureza. The Syrah makes fashionably dark-coloured red wines in many countries. The wines from this variety are generally perceived to one of two basic styles: the classic French (sometimes referred to as the north European) style, with its black, cracked-peppercorn fruit and a certain astringency in its formative years; or the bigger, brasher, distinctively oaky, New World classic, as epitomized by Barossa Shiraz.

Gris cross rapidly increased in California in the mid-1990s, althouth it was developed by Professor Olmo as long ago as 1940. The wine it makes is usually off-dry with a distinctly flowery-grapey Muscat aroma.

ⓑ **Syrah** *See box, opposite.*

ⓢ **Szilváni** Synonym for Sylvaner

ⓢ **Szürkebarát** Synonym for Pinot Gris

ⓢ **Talia** Synonym for Ugni Blanc

ⓢ **Tămaioasă** or **Tamianka** Synonyms for Muscat Blanc

ⓑ **Tannat** This grape originated from the Basque region, and has the potential to produce deeply coloured, tannic wines of great longevity (although there are certain modern methods of vinification that often change the traditional character of Tannat wines). The variety's best-known wines are the attractive red Madiran and Irouléguy. A little Tannat wine is used for blending purposes in and around the town of Cahors.

ⓑ **Tarrango** This *Touriga Nacional* **x** *Thompson Seedless* cross is a high-yielding Australian variety that is capable of producing fresh, fruity, Beaujolais-style wines.

ⓦ **Tazzelenghe** This grape variety takes its name from the Friulian dialect word for *tazzalingua*, Italian for "a sharpness on the tongue," and refers not to the tingle of any residual carbonic gas, but to the wine's tannic structure.

ⓑ **Tempranillo** *See box, above.*

ⓢ **Teneddu** Synonym for Biancolella

ⓑ **Téoulier** A minor blending component in the reds and rosés of Provence.

ⓑ **Teroldego** This grape is thought to have originated in the Rotaliano area of the Alto Adige, where today it produces a surprisingly dark, full, and distinctive wine for a naturally high-yielding vine. In youth, the wines can be chewy, with a tannic raspberry richness, but this softens with age, eventually attaining a silky-violety finesse.

ⓢ **Terrano** Synonym for Refosco

ⓦ **Terrantez**, **Terrantez da Madeira**, or **Terrantez de Madere** This is a white grape variety, although you might be forgiven for thinking otherwise if you have a beautiful brick-red 20-year-old Terrantez Madeira in your hand. Although virtually extinct on the island of Madeira today, it is possible to find numerous old releases, and the occasional pure Terrantez is still produced from time to time. When produced as Madeira, this grape is highly perfumed, providing a rich, powerfully flavoured, tangy-sweet wine with a typically drier finish. Terrantez is also a synonym for Cascal and Donzelinho Branco.

ⓦ **Terret Blanc** A minor blending component in Languedoc, even for rosés and reds, for which this grape has traditionally been used as an ameliorator.

ⓢ **Terret-Bourret** Synonym for Terret Gris

ⓦ **Terret Gris** An excellent and interesting blending component in the Languedoc, where old vines are capable of producing full-bodied wines with slightly spiced aromatic notes.

ⓑ **Terret Noir** The least encountered of the Terret varieties, this is one of the 13 permitted varieties for Châteauneuf-du-Pape, despite there being less than half a hectare (1.25 acres) in the entire region. It has a spicy-floral aroma, relatively high acidity, and has not yet been fully exploited.

ⓑ **Terret Ramenée** A minor blending component for rosés and reds in the Languedoc.

ⓦ **Thompson Seedless** I suspect that this variety crops up in many more wines than we might be led to expect, but perhaps its greatest claim to fame was the first *cuvées* of Omar Khayyam, the Indian sparkling wine. Those earliest wines were produced in the 1980s by fizzmaking genius Raphael Brisbois, who crafted such a good sparkler in its day that its marketeers (not Brisbois himself) had little trouble convincing wine journalists it was made from Chardonnay. Not bad for a grape better known as sultana, not merely because it is something we imagine more suited to Granny's fruitcake than any wine product, but also because its firm flesh and lack of seeds make the sultana a difficult grape to press.

ⓑ **Tibouren** An aromatic black-skinned grape that produces lightly coloured but relatively acidic red wine, better suited to the production of rosé.

ⓢ **Tibourenc** Synonym for Tibouren

ⓢ **Tignolo** Synonym for Sangiovese

ⓦ **Timorasso** First produced as a pure varietal wine by Walter Massa in the upper Val Curone of Piedmont, when a *grappa* producer by the name of Antonella Bocchino became interested in this grape from 19th-century documents and tracked down a plot growing on Massa's estate. Bocchino asked Massa to press the Timorasso separately but was interested only in making *grappa* with the pressings, which left Massa with juice, so he made the first Timorasso. Over the years, he has crafted the wine so that Vigneti Massa's Timorasso from the Colli Tortonesi is now a masterpiece of balance between body, richness, and minerality.

ⓢ **Tinta Amarela** or **Tinta Amarella** Synonyms for Trincadeira Preta

ⓢ **Tinta Bairrada** Synonym for Baga

ⓢ **Tinta Barca** Synonym for Tinta da Barca and Touriga Franca

ⓑ **Tinta da Barca** A seriously under-rated old Port variety that produces dark, rich, concentrated wine. This grape is also known as Tinta Barca, but it should not be confused with the lowly Tinta de Barca.

ⓢ **Tinta de Barca** Synonym for Mourisco de Semente

ⓑ **Tinta Barroca** The wine produced by this top-quality Port grape is quite precocious and therefore useful for younger-drinking Ports or to dilute Port blends that are too tannic and distinctive.

ⓢ **Tinta Bastardeira** Not related to the Bastardo, this is a synonym for Cornifesto.

ⓢ **Tinta Cão** Synonym for Tinto Cão

ⓑ **Tinta Carvalha** A minor blending component for both fortified and unfortified wines in the Douro, Tinta Carvalha is considered to be too light in body and colour to be much use in Port blends, but it is favoured by some Portuguese-owned producers, who traditionally make a much lighter style of Port. When they get the blend right, there is nothing lacking or insubstantial in those wines – just pure finesse.

ⓢ **Tinta Fina** Synonym for Alicante Bouschet, Baga, and Grand Noir

ⓢ **Tinta Francesa** Synonym for Grand Noir

ⓑ **Tinta Francisca** Two different grape varieties are known by this name. First, there is the seldom-encountered minor Port grape variety of undistinguished quality, which gets its name from historic stories of its French origin (supposedly brought to Portugal by Robert Archibald, founder of Quinta do Roriz). Second is the French *teinturier* grape with many synonyms, two of which are, intriguingly, Portugal and Oporto, but it is not the same as the true Oporto variety called Tinta Francisca, the grapes of which have a clear juice.

ⓑ **Tinta Grossa** A popular variety grown in the Vidigueira region, whereas elsewhere in the Alentejo it is merely used as blending fodder. Tinta Grossa is also a synonym for Tinta Barroca and Marufo.

ⓢ **Tinta Martins** Synonym for Tinto Martins

ⓢ **Tinta do Minho** Synonym for Donzelinho Tinto

ⓢ **Tinta Muida** Synonym for Graciano

ⓑ **Tinta Negre** or **Tinta Negre Mole** This Madeira grape was planted as an improvement to the illegal hybrid varieties it replaced. And an improvement it was, but it is nonetheless a low-quality variety that is several classes below the truly classic grapes of Madeira. Cheap Madeira made from this grape is sold in bulk to France, Germany, and Belgium.

ⓢ **Tinta Negreda** Synonym for Tinta Negre Mole

ⓢ **Tinta Roriz** Synonym for Tempranillo

ⓢ **Tintilla** Synonym for Monica

ⓢ **Tintinha** Synonym for Petit Bouschet

ⓑ **Tinto Cão** This is a top-quality Port variety, a small proportion of which can add finesse and complexity to a blend, but this is not easy to pull off in the Douro Valley. Tinto Cão enjoys a cooler environment than most other authorized Port grapes; it requires training on wires to produce a decent crop; and it is a late ripener in one of the world's hottest wine valleys. This variety is also excellent for unfortified Douro wines, either as part of a blend or as a pure varietal.

ⓑ **Tinto Martins** A seldom encountered minor Port grape variety of undistinguished quality.

ⓢ **Tocai Friulano** Synonym for Friulano

ⓢ **Tocai Rosso** Synonym for Grenache

TEMPRANILLO
This is the most important variety in Rioja, where it is traditional to blend the grapes, although many pure Tempranillo wines of excellent quality are made. It is capable of producing long-lived wines of some finesse and complexity. It is also an important variety on the other side of the Iberian peninsula, where it is known as Tinta Roriz in the north and Aragonêz in the south. Tempranillo could do well in parts of Portugal, but its role is usually confined to that of a blending component, and we have to look to the New World before we find any non-Spanish wine areas taking this grape seriously. It is found in California, and a small amount grows in Oregon and even New Mexico, but it is in Australia where it produces by far the greatest number of pure varietal wines. It is also grown in Egypt, without much luck, and Thailand, where it is more successful.

Ⓢ **Tokay** Synonym for Muscadelle

Ⓢ **Tokay** Synonym for Pinot Gris

Ⓦ **Torrontés** Various different naturalized clones of this lightly aromatic grape are found throughout South America, particularly in Argentina, but the most predominant are firstly the Torrontés Riojano, then Torrontés Sanjuanino. DNA fingerprinting has revealed the parentage of both to be the Mission Grape and Muscat d'Alexandrie. Neither has any relation to the Torrontés grown in Spain (where Torrontés is the local synonym for the Arbillo Blanco).

Ⓢ **Touriga** Synonym for Touriga Nacional

Ⓦ **Touriga Branca** A minor white Port variety of undistinguished quality.

Ⓑ **Touriga Brasileira** A minor Port variety of undistinguished quality

Ⓑ **Touriga Franca** This classic Port grape is no relation of the Touriga Nacional. Its wine is less concentrated, but of fine quality.

Ⓢ **Touriga Francesa** Synonym for Touriga Franca

Ⓑ **Touriga Nacional** The finest Port grape in the entire Douro, it produces fantastically rich and tannic wine, with masses of fruit, and is capable of great longevity and complexity.

Ⓢ **Tramin** or **Traminer** Synonyms for Savagnin Blanc

Ⓢ **Traminer Aromatico, Traminer Aromatique, Traminer Musqué, Traminer Parfumé, Traminer Rosé, Traminer Rosso, Traminer Roz,** or **Traminer Rozovy** Synonyms for Gewürztraminer

Ⓦ **Traminette** A *Joannes Seyve 23–416* x *Gewürztraminer* hybrid that was developed by Cornell University and released in 1996. Since then, it has been planted here and there throughout the Atlantic Northeast. Some American winemakers consider it superior to Gewürztraminer because of its significantly higher acidity, but this interferes with aromatics, which are more "spiky" than the Gewürztraminer's classic broad-spice bouquet. Notwithstanding this, there have been successes, even if they are few and far between. Generally perceived as a cool-climate grape, the Traminette's high acidity does, however, raise the question of whether it might not fare much better in the warmer climes of California.

Ⓢ **Tramini** or **Tramini Piros** Synonyms for Gewürztraminer

Ⓢ **Trebbiano** Although the primary name, this variety is better known outside Italy as Ugni Blanc.

Ⓢ **Trebbiano Abruzzese, Trebbiano Bianco di Chieti, Trebbiano Campolese, Trebbiano d'Abruzzo, Trebbiano di Avessano, Trebbiano di Macerata, Trebbiano di Teramo, Trebbiano d'Ora, d'Oro,** and **Trebbiano Dorato di Teramo** Not true

Trebbiano, these are all synonyms for Bombino Bianco.

Ⓢ **Trebbiano Casale, Trebbiano di Parenzo, Trebbiano di Piemonte, Trebbiano di Spagna, Trebbiano Dorato, Trebbiano Dorato Citta' Sant Angelo, Trebbiano Emiliano, Trebbiano Giallo, Trebbiano Modenese, Trebbiano Perugino, Trebbiano Romagnolo, Trebbiano Spoletino,** and **Trebbiano Toscano** All singular localized clones of Trebbiano. *See Ugni Blanc.*

Ⓢ **Trebbiano di Luna** Synonym for Verdicchio

Ⓢ **Trebbiano Rosa** or **Trebbiano Rosso** Synonyms for Ugni Rosé

Ⓢ **Tresallier** Synonym for Sacy

Ⓑ **Tressot** An ancient spontaneous *Duras* x *Petit Verdot* cross that is almost extinct, except for a few vines growing in the Yonne district of France, where its wines are typically thin, weak, and without any merit.

Ⓦ **Trincadeira das Pratas** The white Trincadeira is less widely planted than the black Trincadeira and not so highly regarded.

Ⓑ **Trincadeira Preta** One of the best Port grapes, this variety was imported by James Busby into Australia, where it is better known as Tinta Amarella and used to soften wine blends. In the Douro itself, this variety is known as Tinta Amarela (with just one "l") but is more commonly known as Trincadeira Preta elsewhere in Portugal. When yields are restricted, this grape has the potential to produce wines of great finesse and fragrance.

Ⓑ **Triomphe d'Alsace** An unexceptional hybrid that was bred but outlawed in Alsace, this *Millardet et Grasset* x *Knipperlé* cross is often purchased by non-French growers who think they are growing a true Alsace variety.

Ⓢ **Trollinger** Synonym for Schiava Grossa

Ⓑ **Trousseau** or **Trousseau Noir** *See box, above.*

Ⓢ **Trousseau Blanc** Synonym for Gris de Salces

Ⓜ **Trousseau Gris** This grape is now more widely grown in Portugal, Argentina, California, and New Zealand than in its traditional home of the northern Jura, France. It is yet another grape that has been erroneously tagged with the Grey Riesling name in the New World but does not resemble classic Riesling in the slightest.

Ⓢ **Uarnaccia** Synonym for Guarnaccia

Ⓦ **Ugni Blanc** A variety that usually makes light, even thin, wines that have to be distilled, the Ugni Blanc is ideal for making Armagnac and Cognac. There are a few exceptions, but most wines are light, fresh, and quaffing at their very best. Known as the Trebbiano in Italy, Ugni Blanc is also

incorrectly used as a synonym for the Spanish Viura (Macabéo) and Portuguese Douradinha.

Ⓜ **Ugni Rosé** or **Ugni Rouge** More often encountered in Italy as the Trebbiano Rosa or Trebbiano Rosso, a little Ugni Rosé is, however, found in Provence, primarily as a minor blending component in the Palette AOC.

Ⓢ **Ull de Llebre** Synonym for Tempranillo

Ⓢ **Uva d'Aceto** Synonym for Brugnola

Ⓢ **Uva Asprina** Synonym for Asprinio

Ⓢ **Uva Canina** Synonym for Sangiovese

Ⓢ **Uva d'Oro** Synonym for Brugnola

Ⓑ **Uva Rara** Widely cultivated in the Novarese province northwest of Milan, where it is a major variety in the red wines of Colline Novarese DOC and its medium-bodied, soft, fruity wines benefit from the structure and added complexity of the Nebbiolo grape.

Ⓢ **Uva di Spagna** Synonym for Carignan

Ⓑ **Uva di Troia** This Apulian grape variety has no connection with the town of Troia in Apulia's northern province of Foggia, but refers to ancient Troy, whence it originated. It was brought to the region by the first Greeks to settle in the Taranto area and is best exemplified today by the medium-bodied, ruby-coloured, everyday-quality red wines produced under the Rosso Bartletta DOC, although it plays a good supporting role throughout Apulia.

Ⓢ **Vaccarèse** Synonym for Brun Argenté

Ⓑ **Valdiguié** An undistinguished variety in France, where it was once planted widely and known also as the Folle Noire by those who thought it was a dark-skinned sibling of the Folle Blanche. Valdiguié was permitted in Vin de Marcillac until 1990, when it was

promoted from VDQS to Marcillac AOC and the inferior varieties were rightly banned. In warmer climes such as California, however, this grape comes into its own, producing a nice quaffing red that is far fruitier than most of the true Gamay produced in Beaujolais.

Ⓢ **Varnenski Misket** Synonym for Misket Varnenski

Ⓢ **Veltliner** Synonym for Rossol

Ⓢ **Veltliner Frühroter** Synonym for Frühroter Veltliner

Ⓢ **Veltlínské Červené** Synonym for Roter Veltliner

Ⓢ **Veltlinske Zelene** Synonym for Grüner Veltliner

Ⓦ **Verdeca** At its most expressive in the Locorotondo DOC, where, with Bianco d'Alessano, it produces light, fresh, fruity, dry white wines of good everday quality, the Verdeca grape has often been mistaken for Verdicchio in the past.

Ⓦ **Verdelho Branco** A successful grape variety for making white wines in Australia in recent years, and possibly connected to the Verdello of Italy, Verdelho is best known, however, as a classic grape variety grown on the Portuguese island of Madeira for the island's fortified wine. (A Verdelho *tinto* also exists on the island but is almost extinct.)

Ⓦ **Verdesse** Grown in the Savoie region of Eastern France, this variety has good acidity and a crisp, light, fresh and floral aroma.

Ⓢ **Verdet** Synonym for Arbois

Ⓦ **Verdicchio** or **Verdicchio Bianco** As well as being used to make Verdicchio wine, this grape is also employed for blending.

Ⓢ **Verdicchio Femmina, Verdicchio Peloso, Verdicchio Tirolese,** or **Verdicchio Verde** Not Verdicchio; these are all synonyms for Verdeca.

Ⓢ **Verdicchio Marina, Verdicchio Marino, Verdicchio Sirolese,** or **Verdicchio Tirolese** Not Verdicchio; these are all synonyms for Maceratino.

Ⓢ **Verdicchio Nera** Synonym for Greco Nero

Ⓢ **Verdurino** Synonym for Bianco d'Alessano

Ⓦ **Verduzzo** Widely grown in the Friuli-Venezia Giulia region of Italy, where the Verduzzo plays an important blending role in many dry white wines, this grape responds particularly well to dessert-styles wines, such as Ramandolo in the Colli Orientali del Friuli DOC or Roberto Scubla's Passito "Cratis" Scubla.

Ⓦ **Vermentino** Cultivated throughout the Rhône, Provence, and Corsica, where it makes a light, dry, remarkably fragrant white wine. Two of the best examples of this grape are Domaine de Garbelle Vin de pays du Var Vermentino and Domaine Saint Hilaire Vermentino Vin de Pays d'Oc, both unpretentious, highly drinkable, refreshing dry white wines.

Ⓢ **Vermentino de Corse** Synonym for Códega

Ⓢ **Vernaccia di Austera, Vernaccia di San Vero Milis**, or **Vernaccia Solarussa** Synonyms for Vernaccia di Oristano

Ⓑ **Vernaccia Nera** One of the primary varieties for Ischia DOC, where this grape is known as Guarnaccia, which produces a robust, fruity red wine.

Ⓦ **Vernaccia di Oristano** No relation to Vernaccia di San Gimignano, this is the most widely cultivated of all so-called Vernaccia grapes, with most of it growing between Cabras and Baratili on the island of Sardinia, where it produces various types of wine, the most famous of which is unfortified, Sherry-like wine aged under *flor* in chestnut barrels.

Ⓦ **Vernaccia di San Gimignano** No relation to Vernaccia di Oristano, this Tuscan grape produces deliciously crisp and vibrantly fruity DOCG wines.

Ⓢ **Vernaccia di Toscana** Synonym for Vernaccia di San Gimignano

Ⓢ **Vernaccia Trentina** Synonym for Bianchetta Trevigiana

Ⓢ **Vernatsch** Synonym for Schiava Grossa

Ⓢ **Vernatsch Weiss** Synonym for Vernaccia Bianca

Ⓦ **Vespaiolo** Pure varietal wines are produced from this grape in the Breganze DOC.

Ⓑ **Vespolina** This Piedmontese variety is a natural offspring of the Nebbiolo grape. In addition to pure varietal wines made under the Colline Novaresi DOC, it may be blended with Nebbiolo in wines such as Bramaterra and Ghemme.

Ⓦ **Vidal Blanc** This *Ugni Blanc* x *Rayon d'Or* cross produces a better wine in Ontario and New York State than it does in England (whereas Seyval Blanc grown in England is superior to that grown in either New York State or Ontario). In recent times, Vidal Blanc has become famed for its prolific production of Ice Wine in Ontario, although most have noticeably high volatile acidity.

Ⓢ **Vidure** Synonym for Cabernet Sauvignon

Ⓑ **Vien de Nus** An old Valle d'Aosta variety, Vien de Nus is a blending component in the wines of Arnad-Montjovat, Enfer d'Arvier, Torrette, and, primarily, Nus itself.

Ⓦ **Villard Blanc** This *Seibel 6468* x *Seibel 6905* hybrid is the widest cultivated of the Seyve-Villard crosses in France. Its slightly bitter, iron-rich wine cannot be compared with the attractive wine of the Seyve-Villard 5276, commonly known as Seyval Blanc.

Ⓣ **Vinhão** In the Minho, this Portuguese *teinturier* variety is rated as the best grape for red Vinho Verde, but it is probably better known in the Douro, where, as Sousão, it donates colour and acidity to a Port blend.

Ⓦ **Viognier** See box, below.

Ⓦ **Viosinho** Considered one of the best white Port varieties for body and flavour, Viosinho is also used as a blending component in the various still wines of Douro, Planalti Mirandês, and Trás-os-Montes, but it can be heavy in an unfortified format, unless grown at high altitudes.

Ⓦ **Vital** A not-so-vital, characterless grape, despite being an authorized variety for many Portuguese wines.

Ⓢ **Viura** Synonym for Macabéo

Ⓢ **Vrachanski Misket** Synonym for Misket Varnenski

Ⓢ **Weissburgunder** Synonym for Pinot Blanc

Ⓦ **Welschriesling** No relation whatsoever to the true Riesling, this variety is still grown in Austria, Italy, and Brazil, producing ordinary medium-dry to medium-sweet white wines.

Ⓢ **White Muscadel** Synonym for Muscat à Petits Grains

Ⓢ **White Riesling** Synonym for Riesling

Ⓢ **Wildbacher** Synonym for Blauer Wildbacher

Ⓢ **Wrotham Pinot** Synonym for Pinot Meunier

Ⓦ **Würzer** This German *Gewürztraminer* x *Müller-Thurgau* cross was one of the last developed by George Scheu, the breeder of Scheurebe. Early ripening with a strong spicy aroma but highly susceptible to rot and on the decline.

Ⓦ **Xarel-lo** A Spanish grape variety vital to the sparkling Cava industry, Xarel-lo makes firm, alcoholic wines.

Ⓦ **Xynisteri** This Cypriot grape is the most widely planted on the island, and its wines are best drunk young if at all. Also spelled Xinisteri, and also known as Aspro.

Ⓑ **Xinomavro** (most commonly) or **Xynomavro** *Xyno* means "acid", and *mavro* is "black", an indication of how dark and long-lived the wines of this excellent Greek variety can be. Xinomavro is a late ripener, which helps it retain excellent acidity levels at harvest. Naoussa is the heartland for this variety, but it makes beautiful wine in other parts of Greece and could potentially excel throughout the New World, should any Greek expats want to give it a try.

Ⓢ **Zagarese** Synonym for Zinfandel

Ⓢ **Zierfandler** Synonym for Sylvaner

Ⓜ **Zierfandler Rot** A minor Austrian variety capable of producing a full-bodied, flavourful dry white wine. Also a synonym for Sylvaner Rouge.

Ⓦ **Zierfandler Weiss** A minor Hungarian variety, listed by some ampelographers as a separate singular variety that is not related to the Austrian Zierfandler. However, with no DNA evidence one way or the other, and with much Austrian and Hungarian vinestock sharing a very close history, the jury remains out on this one.

Ⓑ **Zinfandel** See box, below.

Ⓢ **Zingarello** Synonym for Zinfandel

Ⓦ **Zlata** A Serbian *Irsai Oliver* x *Kunleany* hybrid developed in the 1970s to provide extreme winter hardiness, thanks to the Kunleany, which is itself part Amurensis.

Ⓑ **Zweigelt** This *St-Laurent* x *Limberger* cross is grown primarily in its native Austria but is also widely grown in Hungary and the Czech Republic, with pockets also found in Germany, Canada, and England. The norm for this high-yielding variety is rather light and lacklustre, but when yields are restricted, the wines can be big and soft, with peppery fruit.

Ⓢ **Zweigeltrebe** Synonym for Zweigelt

VIOGNIER

This individual, shy-bearing variety used to be confined to a tiny part of the Rhône Valley, where it produced the famous wines of Condrieu and Château Grillet. Although this variety crept out to Australia in the 1970s, the real explosion did not occur until the 1990s in Languedoc-Roussillon and California. At its best, Viognier has a lush, aromatic quality, with a distinctive peachy character, but it is all too often over-oaked. Without the searing effect of the Gewürztraminer's spicy backbone, this variety's intrinsically low acidity produces a wine that can be too soft and exotic for those with palates that prefer higher-acid, more mineral styles.

ZINFANDEL

Once thought to be the only indigenous American Vitis vinifera *grape, Zinfandel has now been positively identified by Isozyme "fingerprinting" as the Primitivo grape of southern Italy. However, the origins of this grape are Croatian, where it is known as the Crljenak Kastelanski. Depending on the vinification method used, Zinfandel can produce many different styles of wine – from rich and dark, to light and fruity or* nouveau *style. They can be dry or sweet; white, rosé, or red; dessert or sparkling.*

STORING AND SERVING WINE

Do you have to worry about how and where to store wine? Not really. More than 95 per cent of wine is ready to drink straight from the shelf and most is actually consumed within 24 hours of purchase. How concerned should you be about how to serve a particular wine? Much less than you think. Not all, but certainly most, of how and why we drink wines the way we do can be put down to conditioning, and much of that is over-fussy.

STORAGE

If you do not have a cellar – and most people do not – then there really is no need to store wine. However, if you want to keep a few bottles for convenience, common sense will tell you to place it somewhere relatively cool and dark. On the other hand, if you are determined to build up a cellar of wine (and for the enthusiast, there is nothing more enjoyable), then there are some very important factors to consider, principally temperature and light.

TEMPERATURE

While 11°C (52°F) is supposed to be the perfect storage temperature for wine, anything between 5°C and 18°C (40°F and 65°F) will in fact suffice for most styles of wines, providing there is no great temperature variation over a relatively short period of time. Higher temperatures increase the rate of oxidation in a wine, therefore a bottle of wine stored at 18°C (65°F) will gradually get "older" than the same wine stored at 11°C (52°F). However, a constant 15°C (59°F) is far kinder to a wine than erratic temperatures between 5°C and 18°C (40°F and 65°F). Changes in temperature cause the cork to shrink and expand, which can loosen the closure's grip on the inner surface of the bottle's neck, rendering the wine liable to oxidation.

LIGHT

All wines are affected negatively by the ultraviolet end of the light spectrum, but some of the harmful photo-chemical effects this causes can be reversed by cellaring a light-affected wine in darkness for a few months. Brown or dead-leaf coloured wine bottles offer more natural protection from ultraviolet light than those that are made of traditional green glass – but dark green is better than light green, whereas blue and clear are the most vulnerable (which is why Roederer Cristal is wrapped in protective yellow cellophane).

OTHER FACTORS

A certain humidity (between 60 and 70 per cent) is essential to keep the cork moist and flexible. This is one reason why long-term storage in a domestic refrigerator should be avoided – the refrigeration process de-humidifies. Several days in a refrigerator is okay, but much longer than this, and the cork will start to dry out.

The position in which a wine bottle is stored is also extremely important: most wines should be stacked on their sides to keep their corks moist, and therefore fully swollen and airtight. Exceptions to this rule are sparkling wines and any wine that has been sealed with a screw-cap. Champagne and any other sparkling wine may be safely stored in an upright position because the carbonic gas (CO_2) trapped in the space between the top of the wine and the base of the cork provides more than enough. Screw-caps require no moistening, of course.

SERVING WINE

Traditionally, white wines have been served chilled and red wines at room temperature, or *chambré*. At higher temperatures, the odorous compounds found in all wines are more volatile, so the practice of serving full-bodied red wines *chambré* has the effect of releasing more aromatics into the bouquet.

One major effect of chilling wine is that more carbonic gas is retained at lower temperatures. This enhances the crispness and freshness and tends to liven the impression of fruit on the palate. It is thus beneficial to chill a youthful white wine but absolutely vital to serve a sparkling wine well chilled, as this keeps it bubbling longer. However, the now widespread use of refrigerators and central heating means that white wines are frequently served too cold, and red wines too warm.

Over-chilling wine kills its flavour and aroma, as well as making the cork difficult to remove because the wax on a cork adheres to the bottle. Over-warm wine, on the other hand, is bland to taste. The rough guide below is more than you need to know. I prefer not to complicate life with specific temperatures and simply think in terms of "putting a chill on" white or rosé wines and "taking the chill off" red wines.

WINE TYPE	SERVING TEMPERATURE
Sparkling (red, white, and rosé)	4.5–7°C (40–45°F)
White	7–10°C (45–50°F)
Rosé and light-bodied red	10–12.5°C (50–55°F)
Medium-bodied red	12.5–15.5°C (55–60°F)
Full-bodied red	15.5–18°C (60–65°F)

RAPID CHILLING AND INSTANT CHAMBRÉ

It is fine to chill wine in a refrigerator for a few days, but not long term because the cork may stick. Ten or 15 minutes in the deep-freeze has never done a wine any harm. The belief that this practice "burns" a wine is unfounded; the cold creeps evenly into the bottle by exactly the same principle as with rapid-chill sheaths.

Unlike cooling, warming a wine by direct heat is not an even process; whether standing a bottle by a fire or putting it under a hot tap, some of the wine gets too hot, leaving the rest too cold. The best way of "taking the chill off" is 30 to 90 seconds in a microwave on low to medium power. The duration and power setting will depend on the storage temperature of the wine to *chambré*, personal preference (which itself can change according to the climate and time of year), and, of course, the power of the

A PERFECT CELLAR
The modern wine collector's perfect cellar includes climate control, UV-protected glass panelling, a professional spittoon, glass storage, and an aluminium rack to accommodate both regular and oversized bottles without shredding any labels.

microwave in question. A microwave is ideal because the process is so gentle, involving no heat as such, merely the vibration of water molecules, which warm up as they rub together.

DECANTING

With increasing age, many wines – especially reds – throw a natural sediment of tannins and colouring pigments that collect in the base or along the side of the bottle. Most sediment is loose and fine, but you may encounter a thin film of dark-coloured sediment adhering to the inside of the bottle. Often this is just a patch, with the shoulder being a favoured location for some reason, but occasionally it can be found to cover almost the entire bottle. The degree of adhesion varies but can at times be very stubborn, as anyone who has tried to rinse out such bottles will testify. The technical description of this bloom is an insoluble complex polymer of pigmented tannins and protein. It is not known why it affects some wines and not others, but it does appear to be more commonly found in high-pH red wines from exceptional vintages or hotter climes generally.

Both red and white wines, particularly white, can also shed a crystalline deposit due to a precipitation of tartrates. The precipitations can appear on the end of the cork that is in contact with the wine, too. Although all these deposits are harmless, their appearance is distracting and decanting will be necessary to remove them.

Preparing the bottle and pouring the wine

Several hours prior to decanting, move the bottle into an upright position. So doing allows the sediment lying along the side of the bottle to fall to the bottom. Cut away the top half a centimetre or so of the foil capsule. This could well reveal a penicillin growth or, if the wine is an old vintage, a fine black deposit, neither of which will have had contact with the wine, but to avoid any unintentional contamination when removing the cork it is wise to wipe the lip of the bottle neck and the top of the cork with a clean, damp cloth. Insert a corkscrew and gently withdraw the cork. Place a clean finger covered in tissue inside the top of the bottle and carefully remove any pieces of sediment, cork, or any tartrate crystals adhering to the inside of the neck, then wipe the lip of the bottle neck with a clean, dry cloth.

Lift the bottle slowly in one hand and the decanter in the other and bring them together over a light source, such as a candle or torch, to reveal any sediment as the wine is poured. Aim to pour the wine in a slow, steady flow so that the bottle does not jerk and wine does not "gulp for air". Such mishaps will disturb the sediment, spreading it through a greater volume of liquid.

Once the wine is decanted, the next question is whether to serve it in the decanter or to rinse out the bottle, allow it to stand upside down to drip dry, then refill the original bottle. If the label is in good condition, I often serve the wine in its own bottle. I think the original bottle is the best possible vessel from which to pour a wine, and it allows people to see what they are drinking.

Filtering dregs

Personally, I flout tradition by pouring cloudy dregs through a fine-grade coffee filter paper. I always attempt to decant the maximum volume, thereby filtering the minimum, and no one has ever been able to tell the difference under blind conditions.

ALLOWING WINE TO BREATHE

Wine "feeds" on the small amount of air trapped inside the bottle between the wine and the cork, and on the oxygen naturally absorbed by the wine itself. It is during this slow oxidation that various elements and compounds are formed or changed in a complex chemical process known as maturation. Allowing a wine to breathe is, in effect, creating a rapid, but less sophisticated, maturation. Breathing may be beneficial to certain still wines for several reasons, only some of which are known. The only generalization that tends to hold true is that breathing is likely to improve young, full-bodied, tannic red wines.

The fact that restaurants invariably decant older vintages has given rise to a belief that older vintages must be allowed to breathe. But this is misleading – and such actions can be detrimental to the wine. A good sommelier will always decant any wine that has a sediment (and should, if he knows his or her wines, suggest decanting younger wines that are known to benefit from breathing), but any breathing of older vintages just because they have a sediment will not be intentional. Indeed, the older the wine, the more delicate it is, and the more likely it is that it will be on its last legs and should be consumed as soon after opening as possible. While it is true that some extremely venerable wines can build in the glass over many hours, you will always have that option however soon after opening you taste it; whereas if you leave it to breathe regardless, such a narrow window of opportunity will be lost forever.

OPENING AND SERVING A BOTTLE OF CHAMPAGNE

OPENING

• Remove the foil from the bulbous top end of the neck. Quite often there is a little foil tail sticking out, which you merely pull. Failing this, you may have to look for the circular imprint of the end of the wire cage, which will have been twisted, folded upwards, and pressed into the neck. When you find this, simply pull it outwards – this will rip the foil, enabling you to remove a section from just below the level of the wire cage.

• Holding the bottle upright at an angle, keep one hand firmly on the cork to make sure it will not surprise you by shooting out, untwist the wire with the other hand, and loosen the bottom of the wire cage so that there is a good space all round. A good tip is not to remove the wire cage, not only because that is when most bottles fire their corks unexpectedly, but also because it acts as a good grip, which you need when a Champagne cork is stuck tight.

• Transfer your grip on the cork to the other hand, which should completely enclose the cork and cage, and, holding the base of the bottle with your other hand, twist both ends in opposite directions. As soon as you feel pressure forcing the cork out, try to hold it in, but continue the twisting operation until, almost reluctantly, you release the cork from the bottle. The mark of a professional is that the cork comes out with a sigh, not a bang.

OPENING

SERVING

• With just a little bit of practice, it will soon become clear that pouring from a Champagne bottle, particularly a magnum, is easier to achieve with just one hand, your thumb in the punt and your fingers spread beneath the bottle for support. The correct way to pour any sparkling wine is directly into a standing *flûte* or glass, not to tilt the glass as if you are pouring a lager. Recent research and common sense tell us that the "lager method" will preserve the carbonic gas content of a Champagne, but the *mousse* of a youthful non-vintage needs a little taming, and the softest, silkiest *mousse* will always enhance the more complex character of a mature vintage Champagne.

HOLDING

POURING

WINE GLASSES

Over the past 20 years, wine glasses have moved from regional tradition to technical shapes, with today's emphasis clearly placed on physical and aesthetic qualities that have been engineered to suit specific styles of wine.

IN THE 19TH AND EARLY 20TH CENTURIES, the so-called traditional styles of wine glass evolved on a regional basis, but these shapes were primarily for recognition purposes, in much the same way that the different regional shapes of wine bottle were developed. Their suitability to the wines in question was not considered to be as relevant as the ability to discern what glass a particular wine should be poured into at the table; consequently, most traditional wine glasses have turned out to be the wrong shape and size, with rims that are much too thick. The first manufacturer to design stemware (as wine glasses have been collectively known since the 1920s) to suit the technical demands and aromatic virtues of specific styles of wine was Riedel. Although established in 1756, this family-owned company only set the wine world alight in 1973, with its Sommeliers collection of 10 specially designated wine glasses. Riedel had created some media attention with its Burgundy Grand Cru glass in 1958 and Bordeaux Grand Cru in 1961, capable of holding well over a bottle of wine each, and although they formed part of the Sommeliers collection, it was the size, precision, and design of the other eight glasses that grabbed the most attention 15 years later.

Aesthetics are always a serious consideration for any hedonistic pursuit, particularly one as subjective as wine. The proportions of

AESTHETICS
The glass on the left has the edge for tasting a high-quality sparkling wine and is also very good for drinking. The flute on the right is almost as good for tasting and will offer some aesthetically minded consumers even more pleasure at the table.

a glass and, especially, the fineness of the glass at the rim play an important role in the appreciation of wine. Put a *cru classé* Bordeaux in a small, squat Paris goblet with a bulbous, rolled rim, and drinking it will not be as pleasurable as drinking the same wine from any precision-made wine glass, whether manufactured by Riedel, Schott Zweisel, or whoever. Although a *vin de table* cannot be transformed into a *grand cru* by the glass you drink it from, an inexpensive, good-value wine can seemingly be infused with a certain class and finesse by the quality-enhancing effects of crisp, modern stemware of sufficient size to swirl the wine around, the right shape to capture and present the aromatics, and precision cut of the rim, which is the last contribution the glass provides as the wine is taken into our mouth; it is this tactile impression that plays with our perception of finesse.

All high-quality stemware brings an extra dimension to wine, whichever manufacturer we choose, but having tested almost every glass in every range of every top-quality brand over the past three years, I am left in no doubt that Riedel's Sommeliers range is the best – and for me, regardless of body or sweetness, the Hermitage is the best for tasting and drinking all red-wine styles; the Loire, for tasting and drinking all white-wine styles; the Vintage Champagne, for tasting all sparkling-wine styles; and the Champagne flute, for drinking all sparkling-wine styles. I could easily live with just these four glasses, but I adore Orrefors's Difference range and have a soft spot for Mikasa's avant-garde Oenology range. Indeed, I would be happy with any of the glasses recommended below. It's just that the Riedel Sommeliers range has the edge when it comes to delivering finesse through the rim. There are other factors involved, of course, such as shape and size, which are essential for aesthetics and aromatics, but where two glasses are similar in shape and size, Riedel always wins on finesse.

Lobmeyer
This Viennese glassmaker was established in 1823 and is probably far better known for its lighting glassware than wine glasses, although it has many stemware ranges. Most, however, are straight-sided, overly ornate, or simply inappropriate. For wine lovers, Lobmeyer's hand-blown, lead-free 276 range stands out.
Particularly recommended:
276 Champagne B, 276 Champagne flute

Mikasa
A US firm that was taken over by the French-owned Arc International, Mikasa is uniquely known for its development of Kwarx, an extraordinary "glass material" that is often described as unbreakable. It looks like glass, feels like glass, and rings like glass, but that's where the similarity ends. Kwarx glasses might not be indestructible, but they are almost unbreakable. I regularly amaze people by clashing two together, then bashing one on the kitchen worktop, and dropping it on the floor. I don't want to be the party pooper, but just occasionally one snaps, and curiously that can happen when the glass is in ordinary use, not being smashed about. Even more curiously, the break is always in the same place, on the stem, about 1 centimetre (½ inch) above the base. So, enjoy these glasses, bash them about for fun and to shock, but do not be misled into thinking they will never break. Every glass I have ever tested eventually goes milky in the dishwasher, but Mikasa Kwarx glasses take much longer than all others. I'm not impressed by the Grand Cru range of crystal glasses or the Select range of traditional-shaped glasses in Kwarx, but I do like the Oenology range of Kwarx glasses.
Particularly recommended:
Oenology Champagne Flute, Oenology 55cl Red

Orrefors

This Swedish firm, whose hand-blowing skills date back to 1742, produces beautiful, top-quality Scandinavian stemware. Orrefors's exquisitely elegant Difference range stands out.

Particularly recommended:
Difference Crisp Wine, Difference Primeur Wine

Riedel

Established in Bohemia in 1756, Riedel make the world's best stemware. The funny thing is, the design of each of its wine glasses is right for all the wrong reasons. Riedel designed each glass to deliver wine to a certain part of the tongue in the belief that, in hitting or missing the dedicated taste receptors for sweetness, sourness, acidity, and bitterness, they would be able to manipulate how we perceive a wine in a very fundamental way. We now know, of course, that separate taste zones do not exist, but the so-called tongue taste map (*see p74*) was the accepted truth in 1973, when these glasses were launched. Nonetheless, Riedel has designed some great stemware. The company now offers a ridiculous number of ranges, but the original hand-blown lead-crystal Sommeliers range still stands out, not just within this manufacturer's raft of ranges, but against all others around the world. With a few exceptions, the Sommeliers glasses come with the highest possible recommendation. The Rheingau, Alsace, Sherry, and Vintage Port are too small for my liking; the Rosé just doesn't work; and unless you are the most garish of *nouveau riche*, you will find the bucket-sized Burgundy Grand Cru and Bordeaux Grand Cru somewhat vulgar – but the other 13 glasses are impeccable. I also love the curvy lines and long, elegant machine-pulled stems of the Vitis range. Riedel owns Spiegelau.

Particularly recommended:
Sommeliers Hermitage, Sommeliers Loire, Sommeliers Vintage Champagne, Sommeliers Champagne

Rosenthal

Established at Selb, Germany, in 1879, Rosenthal leans towards dinnerware and has produced several inappropriate wine-glass designs alongside some truly serious stemware, particularly in its Studio Line. The Fuga part of this line includes the top-of-the-range Bordeaux Grand Cru and Burgundy Grand Cru, which are too large, as is often the case; but the White Wine Robust makes a perfect all-rounder. If you like Mikasa's Oenology range, you'll love the Red Wine and Champagne glasses in Rosenthal's TAC 02 range, but they are not made from Kwarx, so don't think you can bash them together and get away with it!

Particularly recommended:
Fuga Red Wine Robust, TAC 02 Red Wine, TAC 02 Champagne

Schott Zweisel

This German glassmaker was established in 1872, and its hand-blown, lead-free Zweisel 1872 The First range is the one to go for. It was designed in collaboration with the 2004 world champion sommelier Enrico Bernardo, who has combined inspired performance with elegance and a brilliance of lustre in these stylish glasses.

Particularly recommended:
The First Rioja, The First Riesling, The First Champagne (1332/77)

Spiegelau

This firm's history goes way back to at least 1521, when the German glassmaking factory of Spiegelau was mentioned in a will. The company was taken over by Nachtmann in 1990 and has been part of the Riedel group since 2004, when Nachtmann was purchased by Riedel. These glasses are often viewed as Riedel's cheaper secondary brand, but Riedel produces its own cheaper ranges and purchased Spiegelau for its quality, not its price, and because Nachtmann was Riedel's biggest competitor. My favourite range is VinoVino, which boasts the world's first machine-pulled stem and provides the feel of hand-blown stemware at machine-blown prices. For a Champagne glass, however, I prefer Spiegelau's hand-blown Grand Palais.

Particularly recommended:
VinoVino Bordeaux, VinoVino Burgundy, Grand Palais Champagne

Steger

Berlin-based sommelier Peter Steger designed the excellent-value OneForAll machine-blown, lead-free tasting glasses. They have a bulbous bowl and a tall, narrow "chimney" opening.

Particularly recommended:
OneForAll Red

Stölzle

Established in 1433, German glassmaker Stölzle produces brilliant machine-blown, machine-pulled stemware in its Grandezza range, from which the Bordeaux makes an ideal all-round red-wine glass, while the Grandezza Red Wine is perfect for white wine! The new hand-blown QI range is like a more curvy version of Mikasa's Oenology glasses.

Particularly recommended:
Grandezza Bordeaux, Grandezza Red Wine, QI Burgundy, Exquisit Royal Champagne

Zalto

The Austrian Zalto Denk'Art range stole the show at *Stern* magazine's 2009 invitation taste-off between 10 stemware manufacturers. Forget the firm's claim that the success of these glasses is all down to the 24°, 48°, or 72° angled slope of their bowls being the triumvirate of angles on which the Earth tilts on its axis, thus they possess almost magical qualities. These glasses are just exceptionally well designed to capture aromatics. Some might find the straight sides of the angular design more proficient than elegant, but there is no denying that technical proficiency.

Particularly recommended:
White Wine, Bordeaux, Champagne

IDEAL RED-WINE GLASS
The perfectly proportioned swell of the bowl allows this glass to be filled halfway and still have plenty of room for heftier red-wine aromatics to accumulate.

WHITE AND MORE
Slightly smaller, this white-wine glass is also ideal for dessert and fortified wines, which should never be served in traditional small glasses.

THE TASTE OF WINE

The difference between tasting and drinking is similar to test-driving a car you may buy and the relish of driving it afterwards. One is a matter of concentration, as you seek out merits and faults, while the other is a more relaxed and enjoyable experience. Almost anyone can learn to taste wine.

WHEN TASTING A WINE, it is important to eliminate all distractions, especially comments made by others; it is all too easy to be swayed. The wine should be tasted and an opinion registered before any ensuing discussions. Even at professionally led tastings, the expert's job is not to dictate but to educate, putting into perspective other people's natural responses to smells or tastes through clear and concise explanation. The three "basics" of wine-tasting are sight, smell, and taste, known as "eye", "nose", and "palate".

THE SIGHT, OR "EYE", OF A WINE

The first step is to assess the wine's limpidity, which should be perfectly clear. Many wines throw a deposit, but this is harmless if it settles to yield a bright and clear wine. If it is cloudy or hazy, the wine should be discarded. Tiny bubbles that appear on the bowl or cling persistently to the edge of the glass are perfectly acceptable in a few wines, such as Muscadet *sur lie* and Vinho Verde, but probably indicate a flaw in most other still wines, particularly if red and from classic Old World regions.

The next step is to swirl the wine gently around the glass. So-called "legs" or "tears", thin sinewy threads of wine that run down the side of the glass, may appear. Contrary to popular belief, they are not indicative of high glycerol content, but are simply the effect of alcohol on wine's viscosity, or the way the wine flows. The greater the alcohol content, the less free-flowing, or more viscous, the wine actually becomes.

The colour of wine

Natural light is best for observing a wine's colour, the first clue to its identity once its condition has been assessed. Look at the wine against a white background, holding the glass at the bottom of the stem and tilting it away from you slightly. Red wines vary in colour from *clairet*, which is almost rosé, to tones so dark and opaque that they seem black. White wines range from a colourless water-white to deep gold, although the majority are a light straw-yellow colour. For some reason, there are very few rosé wines that are truly pink in colour, the tonal range extending from blue-pink, through purple-pink, to orange-pink. Disregard

VISUAL EXAMINATION
Unless it has an extreme colour or hue, the appearance of a wine is the least interesting aspect of a tasting note for most readers, which is why most authors use colour descriptions sparingly. However, the eye is one of the most important sensory organs for professional tasters (such as Joanna Simon, above) as even the most subtle shade or nuance can provide numerous clues to the wine's identity.

NOSING A WINE
As we smell most flavours, rather than taste them, a good sniff tells us a lot about a wine. But refrain from continuously sniffing, as this will dull your sense of smell. Take one good sniff, then pause for thought. Do not rush on to tasting the wine. Remember that no smells are specific to wine – they can all be compared to something familiar, but you need time to work out what they are.

HOW WE TASTE SMELLS

All tastes other than sweetness, sourness, bitterness, saltiness, and umami are detected as aromas by receptors on the olfactory bulb, which transmits the data directly to the brain, where we are fooled into believing that the aromas are in fact complex tastes, or flavours. That explains why we lose so much of our ability to taste when our nose is blocked by a cold. The perception of all aroma-based flavours is influenced by one or more of the five basic tastes, as well as temperature and touch. The warmer the wine, the more aromas are given off, and the more flavour we perceive (thus melting ice-cream has more flavour than frozen ice-cream). The sense of touch should not be underestimated, as texture can be very influential. The smoother something is, the more creamy it tastes. Imagine a smooth, creamy toffee; now imagine a toffee made with exactly the same ingredients but grainy in texture – not so creamy, is it? A watery wine gives us an entirely different taste sensation compared to a more viscous wine with theoretically the same aromas and basic tastes. Add some fizziness, and the taste parameters change even further, as will the strength of *mousse* and the size of bubble.

DID YOU KNOW?

An average human being has about 10,000 taste buds, and within each of those there are around 100 taste receptors, making a total of around one million taste receptors. Most of these are on the tongue, but some are also present on the soft or upper palate, the insides of the cheeks and lips, and around the back of the throat and upper throat.

The tongue itself reveals very little – just five basic tastes: sweetness, sourness (or acidity), bitterness, saltiness, and umami. The concept whereby these basic tastes are perceived by receptors in specific parts of the tongue (such as sweetness on the tip, acidity on the sides, etc) has now been thoroughly debunked. Apart from these five basic taste perceptions, we smell tastes rather than taste them. Any food or drink emits odorous vapours in the mouth that are automatically conveyed to the roof of the nasal passages. Here the olfactory bulb examines, discerns, and catalogues them – as they originate from the palate, the natural inclination is to perceive them as tastes. For many of us, it is difficult to believe that we taste with an organ located behind the eyes at the top of the nose, but when we eat ice-cream too quickly, we painfully experience precisely where the olfactory bulb is, as the chilly ice-cream aromas literally freeze this acutely delicate sensory organ (*see* How We Taste Smells, *left*). The texture of a wine also influences its taste; the prickly tactile sensation of carbon dioxide, for example, heightens our perception of acidity, while increased viscosity softens it.

any impression about a wine's colour under artificial lighting because it will never be true – fluorescent light, for example, makes a red wine appear brown.

Factors affecting colour

The colour and tonal variation of any wine, whether red, white, or rosé, is determined by the grape variety. It is also influenced by the ripeness of the actual grapes, the area of production, the method of vinification, and the age of the wine. Dry, light-bodied wines from cooler climates are the lightest in colour, while fuller-bodied or sweeter-styled wines from hotter regions are the deepest. Youthful red wines usually have a purple tone, whereas young white wines may hint of green, particularly if they are from a cooler climate. The ageing process involves a slow oxidation that has a browning effect similar to the discoloration of a peeled apple that has been exposed to the air.

THE SMELL, OR "NOSE", OF A WINE

Whenever an experienced taster claims to be able to recognize in excess of 1,000 different smells, many wine lovers give up all hope of acquiring even the most basic tasting skills. Yet they should not be discouraged. Almost everybody can detect and distinguish over 1,000 different smells, the majority of which are ordinary, everyday odours. Ask anyone to write down all the smells they can recognize and most will be able to list several hundred without really trying. Yet a far greater number of smells are locked away in our brains waiting to be triggered.

The wine-smelling procedure is quite simple: give the glass a good swirl, put your nose into the glass, and take a deep sniff. While it is essential to take a substantial sniff, it is not practicable to sniff the same wine again for at least two minutes. This is because each wine activates a unique pattern of nerve ends in the olfactory bulb; these nerve ends are like small candles that are snuffed out when activated and take a little time to reactivate. As a result, subsequent sniffs of the same smell can reveal less and less, yet it is perfectly feasible to smell different smells, therefore different wines, one after the other.

THE TASTE, OR "PALATE", OF A WINE

As soon as one sniffs a wine the natural reaction is to taste it, but do this only after all questions concerning the nose have been addressed. The procedure is simple, although it may look and sound rather strange to the uninitiated. Take a good mouthful and draw air into the mouth through the wine; this makes a gurgling sound, but it is essential to do it in order to magnify the wine's volatile characteristics in the back of the throat.

MAGNIFYING THE TASTE OF A WINE
The tongue discerns only sweetness, sourness, bitterness, saltiness, and umami (see Micropedia). Every other "taste" we smell. By drawing air through a mouthful of wine, the volatilized aromas are taken into the back of the throat, where they are picked up by the olfactory bulb, which automatically analyses them and transmits the information to the brain as various so-called flavours.

WHAT IS A SUPERTASTER?

The term "supertaster" was coined by Linda Bartoshuk at Yale Medical School in 1991 to refer to those who are supersensitive to various tastes, particularly bitterness. They are supersensitive because they have more taste buds than the rest of us, but it is more of a super-burden than a super-power. Around 50 per cent of the population are normal tasters, 25 per cent are so-called non-tasters, and 25 per cent are supertasters. Women are more likely to be supertasters than men, so although 25 per cent of the population are supertasters, by gender this breaks down as 35 per cent of women and 15 per cent of men. Also, Asians are more likely to be supertasters than Caucasians. Everything tastes bland to non-tasters, so they smother their food in sauces and spices. Supertasters are particularly sensitive to bitterness and dislike strong, bitter foods like raw broccoli, grapefruit juice, coffee, and dark chocolate. So, is a supertaster a super wine taster? No – the normal tannin content of all the world's greatest red wines would be far too bitter for a supertaster to bear, let alone enjoy.

QUALITY AND TASTE: WHY OPINIONS DIFFER

Whether you are a novice or a Master of Wine, it is always personal preference that is the final arbiter when you are judging wine. The most experienced tasters can often argue endlessly over the relative merits and demerits of certain wines.

We all know that quality exists, and more often than not agree which wines have it, and yet we are not able to define it. Lacking a solid definition, most experienced tasters would happily accept that a fine wine must have natural balance and finesse and show a definite, distinctive, individual character within its own type or style.

If we occasionally differ on the question of the quality of wine, should we disagree on what it tastes like? We may love or hate a wine, but surely the taste we perceive is the same? Surprisingly, the answer is no, it isn't.

Conveying specific taste characteristics from the mind of one person to that of another is difficult enough, whether one is writing a book or simply discussing a wine at a tasting. Much of this difficulty lies in the words we choose, but the problem is not confined to semantics. Even in a world of perfect communication, conveying impressions of taste would still be an inexact art because of the different threshold levels at which we pick up fundamental tastes and smells, and because of the various tolerance levels at which we enjoy them. Because individuals require different quantities of acidity, tannin, alcohol, sugar, esters, and aldehydes in a wine before actually detecting them, the same wine has, literally, a different taste for each of us. In the unlikely event of people having the same threshold for every constituent and combination of constituents, disagreement would probably ensue because we also have different tolerance levels; therefore, some of us would enjoy what others dislike because we actually like the tastes and smells they dislike. Thresholds and tolerance levels vary enormously; the threshold for detecting sweetness, for example, varies by a factor of five, which explains the "sweet tooth" phenomenon, and there are an infinite number of tolerance levels. Apply this to every basic aroma and flavour, and it is surprising that we agree on the description of any wine.

THE DEBUNKED TONGUE TASTE MAP

The concept whereby the original four basic tastes were detected by receptors found only in specific parts of the tongue, the so-called tongue taste map (*right*), has now been thoroughly debunked.

The origins of the tongue taste map can be traced back to a PhD thesis written by D P Hanig and published in *Philosophische Studien* in 1901, but he did not conceive it. The graphs in Hanig's raw data reveal variations in sensitivity to the four basic tastes around the tongue, but these variations were so tiny as to be insignificant for any practical purposes. Furthermore, Hanig's data did not reveal distinct areas, as they overlapped each other. The subtlety of this variation and the overlapping of zones was lost in 1942, when Hanig's paper was translated at Harvard by Edwin Garrigues Boring, upon whose work the tongue taste map was established. It was not until 1974 that Boring's error was uncovered by Virginia Collings, who re-examined Hanig's original data. The fact that this was not mentioned by Amerine & Roessler in their otherwise seminal work *Wines: Their Sensory Evaluation* some two years later, illustrates how long it took the wine trade to abandon the tongue taste map, despite the work of other scientists specializing in basic tastes, especially Linda Bartoshuk since 1993.

Labels on tongue diagram: Bitter, Sour, Salt, Sweet

WHAT IS UMAMI?

The term umami (meaning "deliciousness") was coined in 1908, when Professor Kikunae Ikeda identified it as the fifth basic taste, isolating monosodium glutamate (MSG) as the active chemical compound responsible. Ikeda immediately patented the manufacturing process for extracting MSG from wheat flour, and the first commercially available MSG became available under the trade name Ajinomoto (meaning "at the origin of flavour") in 1909. It was later discovered that MSG was not exclusively responsible for the umami taste but worked in a synergistic fashion with other substances, such as disodium inosinate and disodium guanylate, which occur naturally in meat, fish, vegetables, and dairy products. Although MSG is tasteless, it increases the flavour of these other substances by six- to eightfold, resulting in the so-called umami taste.

Although the concept of umami has been accepted throughout much of Asia since the early 20th century, it did not achieve scientific credence until 2002, when Charles Zuker and Nick Ryber identified taste receptors on the tongue that were capable of detecting amino acids. One amino acid we detect in this way is glutamic acid, and MSG is a salt of glutamic acid. It is found in protein-rich foods such as meat (particularly bacon), cheese (particularly Parmesan), soy sauce, mushrooms, broths, and stocks. In the 1950s, when scientists began to analyse the Eastern concept of umami, various English-language descriptors were applied, such as "amplitude", "mouth-fullness", and "bloom". Perhaps the most appropriate one-word translation is "moreish", but a more complete description would be "a comforting and fulfilling brothy savouriness". The difficulty in assigning a simple yet precise, distinctive, stand-alone taste descriptor (such as sweetness, sourness, acidity, or bitterness) is indicative of how umami is not an obvious basic taste. From a totally unscientific perspective, the richness and complexity of umami makes it an ideal candidate for the sort of taste we smell. Even from a scientific standpoint, umami hardly fits in with the singularity of hypothesis that scientists normally apply to basic tastes.

HOW TO ASSESS A WINE

I thought long and hard about whether to drop this section, as the ability to make wines of almost every type, style, and depth of colour has spread across the planet since the mid-1980s when the Sample Tasting was developed. Does it have any relevance today?

A NUMBER OF WINE PROFESSIONALS, particularly former World Champion Sommeliers, told me that whereas all types of wine are indeed more widely produced today, the logical process of questions and answers required to identify a wine under blind-tasting conditions remains very much the same. Arriving at a correct answer is far more difficult and requires much wider tasting experience than before, but everyone I spoke to told me that without understanding the underlying principles expressed below, it would be impossible. So the section remains. Just try to apply an "over the horizon" radar when considering geographic origin.

SIGHT
Look at the colour: is it deep or pale, is there a positive quality to it, a specific hue that reminds you of a particular grape variety, the growing climate, or the area of production? Is the colour vivid and youthful, or is there browning that might suggest its age? What does the rim, or meniscus, indicate? Does it retain the intensity of colour to the rim of the glass, which suggests a quality product or warmer clime, or does it fade to an unimpressive, watery finish?

A SAMPLE TASTING

This chart provides a few examples from a whole range of the possible options that are open in the complex business of tasting. It also demonstrates that it is possible to approach the task systematically and rationally. When tasting, it is important to keep your options open until you have assessed the sight, smell, and taste of the wine. At each stage you should be seeking to confirm at least one of the possibilities that has arisen during the previous stage. Be confident and do not be afraid to back your own judgement – it is the only way to learn.

 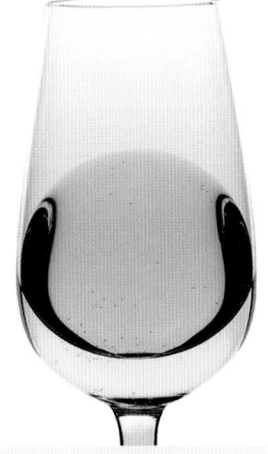  

SIGHT
The clear, well-defined garnet colour of medium intensity suggests only moderately hot climatic origins. The tinge of purple on the meniscus could indicate youth.

SMELL
This is dominated by the distinctive peardrop aroma of carbonic maceration, hallmark of all but the best *cru* Beaujolais. Often mistaken for the varietal aroma of Gamay (from which Beaujolais is made), the aroma is characteristic of all wines fermented in this way. If this is a Beaujolais, the colour suggests something more serious than a lighter basic Beaujolais or Nouveau.

TASTE
The balance between fruit, acidity, and alcohol confirms that this is Beaujolais. The good depth of spicy-grapey fruit beneath the pervasive peardrop character indicates that it is better-than-average.

CONCLUSION
Grape variety Gamay
Region Beaujolais
Age 2 to 3 years old
Comment Beaujolais Villages

SIGHT
Water-white, this wine has obvious cool climatic origins, although the tiny bubbles collecting on the glass suggest it could be a Vinho Verde; however, the palest usually have a tell-tale hint of straw colour. Probably a modest *Qualitätswein* from the Mosel region of Germany.

SMELL
This is not Vinho Verde. Its crisp, youthful, sherbet aroma is typical Mosel Riesling. Considering its colour, the nose would confirm that this is probably a *Qualitätswein*, or a *Kabinett* at most, of a modest vintage, but from a very good grower who is possibly as high up as the Saar tributary.

TASTE
Youthful, tangy fruit with the flower of the Riesling still evident. More flavour than expected, and a nice dry, piquant finish with a hint of peach on the aftertaste.

CONCLUSION
Grape variety Riesling
Region Mosel
Age about 18 to 24 months
Comment *Kabinett*, top grower

SIGHT
Intense, almost black colour that is virtually opaque. Obviously from a thick-skinned grape variety like the Syrah, which has ripened under a very hot sun. Australia's Swan Valley or France's Rhône Valley? California?

SMELL
As intense on the nose as on the eye. Definitely Syrah, and judging by its spicy aroma with hints of herbal scrub, almost certainly from the northern Rhône. Australia and California can now be ruled out. More massive than complex, it must be from an exceptional vintage.

TASTE
Powerful and tannic, the spicy-fruit flavour is rich with blackberries, blackcurrants, plums, and cinnamon. Beginning to develop, but has a long way to go. This is a high-quality Rhône Syrah, but without quite the class of Hermitage, or the finesse of Côte Rôtie.

CONCLUSION
Grape variety Syrah
Region Cornas, Rhône Valley
Age about 5 years old
Comment top grower, great year

SIGHT
The brick-red colour and watery meniscus immediately suggest a young Bordeaux of *petit-château* quality. But first impressions can deceive – more evidence is needed.

SMELL
An attractive violet aroma with a restrained hint of soft, spicy fruit. Nothing contradicts my impressions, although the lack of blackcurrant suggests that the wine is a Bordeaux with a high proportion of Merlot rather than Cabernet Sauvignon.

TASTE
The palate perfectly reflects the nose. This is a medium-bodied, modest claret of no great age. However, the fruit is well rounded and the soft tannin structure indicates that in little more than another 2, possibly 3, years it will be at its peak.

CONCLUSION
Grape variety Merlot-dominated blend
Region Bordeaux
Age 2 years old
Comment *petit château* or good generic

SMELL

If the first impression is very heady, is the wine fortified? (Classic fortified wines, such as port, sherry, and Madeira, do have easily recognizable characteristics, but it can still be difficult to distinguish between a robust wine with a naturally high alcohol level produced in a hot country and a fortified wine.) Does the wine have any distinctive aromas, or are they obscure or bland, or simply reticent? Does the wine smell as youthful or as mature as it appears to the eye? Is it smooth and harmonious, suggesting the wine is ready to drink? If so, should it be drunk? If it is not ready, can you estimate when it will be? Is there a recognizable grape variety aroma? Are there any creamy coffee, coconut, or vanilla hints to suggest that it has been fermented or aged in new oak? If so, which region ages such wine in oak? Is it a simple wine or is there a degree of complexity? Are there any hints as to the area of production? Is its quality obvious or do you need confirmation on the palate?

TASTE

This should reflect the wine's smell and confirm any judgements you have already made. Should. But human organs are fallible, not least so the brain, so keep an open mind. Be prepared to accept contradiction as well as confirmation. Ask yourself all the questions you asked on the nose, but before you do, ask what your palate tells you about the acidity, sweetness, and alcoholic strength.

If you are tasting a red wine, its tannin content can be revealing. Tannin is derived from the grape's skin, and the darker and thicker it is, and the longer the juice macerates with the skins, the more tannin there will be in the wine. A great red wine will contain so much tannin that it will literally pucker the mouth, while early-drinking wines will contain little.

If you are tasting a sparkling wine, on the other hand, its mousse, or effervescence, will give extra clues. The strength of the mousse will determine the style – whether it is fully sparkling, semi-sparkling, or merely *pétillant* – and the size of the bubbles will indicate the quality; the smaller they are, the better.

CONCLUSION

Just try to name the grape variety and area of origin, and give some indication of the age and quality of the wine. Wise tasters do not risk their credibility by having a stab at anything more specific, such as the producer or vineyard, unless he or she is 100 per cent sure. In the Master of Wine examination, marks are given for correct rationale, even if the conclusion that is drawn is wrong, while it has been known for a candidate to name the wine in precise detail but, because of defective reasoning, to receive no score at all. Wine tasting is not a matter of guessing, it is about deduction, and getting it wrong should be encouraged as that is the only way to learn.

   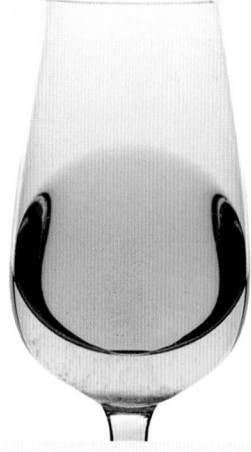

SIGHT
This distinctive yellow-gold colour retains its intensity to the rim. Various possibilities: a sweet wine, a full-bodied dry wine, a mature wine, or something obscure like Retsina. If none of these, it could be a Gewürztraminer.

SMELL
Gewürztraminer! Full, rich, and spicy, the aroma hits you between the eyes and the first instinct is to think of Alsace. Usually you will be right, but bear in mind the possibility of a top grower in the Rheinpfalz or Austria. If the aroma were muted, it might be Italian; if exotic, Californian or Australian. This, however, seems to be a classic example of a ripe Alsace vintage of perhaps 4 years of age.

TASTE
A rich-flavoured wine; full, fat, and fruity with well-developed spice and a soft, succulent finish. Evidently made from very ripe grapes.

CONCLUSION
Grape variety Gewürztraminer
Region Alsace
Age about 4 to 5 years old
Comment very good quality

SIGHT
Stunning colour, more distinctive even than the Gewürztraminer, the old gold immediately suggests a full, rich, and probably very sweet wine. Sauternes springs to mind, but Austria, or even an oddity from Australia are also possible.

SMELL
This has the amazingly full, rich, and opulent nose of a botrytized wine. Anyone who dislikes sweet wine should smell a wine like this before giving up on it altogether. A touch of creamy-spicy oak rules out Austria and its maturity, probably between 10 and 15 years, probably disposes of Australia.

TASTE
Everything is here from peaches, pineapple, and cream to the honeyed aromatics of a fairly mature wine. Only a classic Sauternes can have such intense flavours, yet possess such great finesse.

CONCLUSION
Grape variety mostly Sémillon
Region Sauternes
Age about 15 years old
Comment *premier cru*, great vintage

SIGHT
The orange-pink of this wine almost certainly pins it to Provence or Tavel, although, if the orange hue is not indicative of the style and vinification of the wine, it could be almost any over-the-hill rosé.

SMELL
Put the dunce's hat on and stand in the corner! The high-toned Pinot Noir aroma dismisses the firm conviction of a Tavel or Provence rosé. But what is it? It is not oxidized, so it cannot be an otherwise obvious wine that has gone over. Is the orange hue a clue to its origin? More information is needed; must taste the wine.

TASTE
Definitely Burgundian, but with a very distinctive, piquant Pinot Noir taste. At its peak now, but certainly not on the way down. By eliminating what it cannot be, only Rosé de Marsannay fits the bill.

CONCLUSION
Grape variety Pinot Noir
Region Burgundy
Age 4 to 5 years old
Comment medium quality

SIGHT
This sparkling wine has an attractive, lively, lemon-yellow colour. Not young, but not old, its mousse is evident, but its power and size of bubble cannot be assessed without tasting it. Its star-bright limpidity just makes it look like a fine wine.

SMELL
Its quality is immediately evident, with the autolytic characteristics of a wine with several years on its first cork (in contact with its lees prior to disgorgement), which eliminates every possibility other than a fine Champagne. It has the zippy tang of ripe Chardonnay grapes. This must be a Champagne *blanc de blancs* with a high proportion of wine from the Côte des Blancs.

TASTE
A gently persistent mousse of ultra-fine bubbles. The fresh, lively flavour has a long finish but needs five years more to reach perfection.

CONCLUSION
Grape variety Chardonnay
Region Champagne
Age about 5 years old
Comment top quality

TASTES AND AROMAS

A taste chart is a useful mind-jogging aid for identifying elusive aromas and flavours that you may have encountered in a wine but cannot quite put a name to.

EVEN SEASONED WINE TASTERS experience this. Logically, though, anything the brain recognizes must be well known to it, and the odds are it is an everyday aroma or flavour, rather than something obscure. Therefore, it is not the aroma itself that is elusive, merely its name. This is not surprising, since we all have the sensory profile of more than a thousand everyday aromas locked away in our brains; the difficulty lies in accessing the information. I realized

this long ago, which is why my personal tasting books always have a list of mind-jogging aromas and flavours. When I am on my travels and find that I cannot immediately identify a flower, fruit, or spice, I run my finger down the list until my brain connects with the aroma I am trying to discern.

HOW TO USE THE CHART

If you know the category (flower, fruit, spice, etc) of the aroma you are looking for, use the mind-jogging chart below to pinpoint the specific aroma you are trying to pinpoint. Take the glass in one hand, swirl the wine, and take a sniff. If it is a flavour you are seeking, take a sip, while methodically running a finger through the list that starts overleaf, until you come to the right one.

MIND-JOGGING CHART

Fruity	Citrus	Orange
		Lime
		Lemon
		Grapefruit
	Berry	Blackberry
		Raspberry
		Strawberry
		Blackcurrant/cassis
	Orchard/stone fruit (pitted fruit)	Cherry
		Apricot
		Peach
		Apple
	Tropical fruit	Banana
		Melon
		Pineapple
	Dried fruit	Fig
		Prune
		Raisin
	Other	Foxy/jelly
		Amylic/peardrop
Vegetative	Fresh	Cut green grass
		Bell pepper
		Eucalyptus
		Mint
	Canned/cooked	Green beans
		Asparagus
		Artichoke
	Dried	Hay/Straw
		Tea
		Tobacco
Chemical	Petroleum	Tar
		Plastic
		Kerosene/petrol
		Diesel
	Sulphur	Rubbery
		Bad eggs
		Natural gas
		Truffle
		Garlic
		Skunk
		Cabbage
		Burnt match
		Sulphur dioxide
		Wet dog
	Pungent	Nail varnish
		Vinegar
		Skunk
		Garlic

Woody	Burnt	Coffee
		Smoky
		Burnt toast
	Resinous	Vanilla
		Eucalyptus
		Cedar
		Oak
	Phenolic	Bacon
		Phenolic
		Medicinal
Microbiological	Yeasty	Christmas cake
		Acacia
	Lactic	Creamy
		Buttery
		Yoghurt
		Sauerkraut
		Sweaty
	Other	Horsey
		Mousey
Caramel	Caramel	Honey
		Butterscotch
		Butter
		Soy sauce
		Chocolate
		Molasses
Earthy	Dry undergrowth	Dusty
		Truffle
		Mushroom
	Mouldy	Mouldy
		Musty/Mildew
Floral	Floral	Elderflower
		Orange blossom
		Rose
		Violet
		Geranium
Spicy	Spicy	Cloves
		Black pepper
		Ginger
		Aniseed
		Liquorice
Oxidative	Nutty	Almond
		Walnut
		Hazelnut
	Oxidative	Dried fruits
		Biscuity (cookie-like)
	Oxidizing	Sherry
	Oxidized	Vinegar

THE ORIGIN OF EVERYDAY AROMAS IN WINE

Although no wines actually contain fruits (other than grapes, of course), flowers, vegetables, herbs, spices *et al*, it is perfectly reasonable to use their aromas and flavours when describing wines. To the uninitiated, it might sound rather fanciful to say that a wine is buttery, but diacetyl, which is used as an artificial flavouring to make margarine smell and taste buttery, is created naturally in wine as a by-product of the malolactic process. Wines, in fact, contain varying amounts of many chemical compounds that can be linked directly to a vast number of characteristic aromas or flavours.

Some of the compounds involved can evoke different aromas depending on the levels found and the presence of other compounds

that can also exert an influence; and various unrelated compounds can induce a very similar aroma. The amount involved can be minuscule; a strong presence of the aromatic compounds responsible for peas and bell peppers or capsicums of the green variety can be detected, for example, at levels of one part in 100 billion!

Do not get carried away in the search for these aromas and flavours. It is far more important to concentrate on just one or two descriptors than to record a fruit cocktail or potpourri of aromas and flavours. When you read elaborate descriptions (not too many in this book, I hope), just ask yourself what such concoctions would actually smell like and whether it would be possible to discern any of their component parts.

Note Whether we perceive any of a wine's characteristics as aromas or flavours, technically they are all aromas (*see* p73). However, textural and tactile impressions made in the mouth, and true tastes sensed by the tongue (sweetness, acidity or sourness, bitterness, saltiness, and umami), also

influence our perception. Where specific chemical compounds are known to be responsible for an aroma or flavour, they are mentioned, and are italicized so that those who are interested can identify the possible cause, while those who are not can skim across without interruption to the text.

TASTE AND AROMA CHART

ACACIA
This is the flowery autolytic aroma on a recently disgorged sparkling wine. It can be found in other white wines (paratolylmethyl ketone).

ALMOND
Considered part of the varietal character of Gamay, fresh and toasted almond is also commonly found in all types of wine (acetoin, acetophenone), especially when aged in oak (benzaldehyde), whereas a bitter almond aroma (also benzaldehyde) is often detected in sparkling wines and red carbonic-maceration wines.

ANISEED
This is characteristic of a Bas Rhin Riesling but can be found in almost any wine red or white (anethole).

APPLE
Apple is a white-wine aroma that ranges from green apple (malic acid) in under-ripe wines to soft, red-apple flavours in riper wines, where 50-odd known compounds might or might not be responsible.

APPLE, BRUISED
See Oxidative.

APPLE BLOSSOM
This aroma is typical of youthful Riesling (p-ansic acid, amyl acetate).

APPLE PEEL
This is a pithy apple character (ethyl hexanoate, n-hexyl, n-butanoate, hexyl hexanoate).

APRICOT

A pithy apricot character is less ripe and more bottle-aged than peachiness, which is a finer, juicier, more succulent fruitiness. Apricot is often found in Loire or German whites (4-decanolide, amyl propoanate).

ASPARAGUS
Asparagus is common in Sauvignon Blanc made from over-ripe grapes or kept too long in bottle. Some people adore this style, but most do not. It can develop into canned peas aroma (isobutyl or segbutyl). In a wine without any pyrazine character, it will be dimethyl disulphide, otherwise definitely 2-Methoxy-3-isobutylpyrazine.

BABY SICK
This classic aroma informs of excessive malolactic (diacetyl or lactic acid).

BANANA
Banana is found in cool-fermented whites and reds made by carbonic maceration (amyl acetate or isoamyl acetate, also known as "banana oil" and "pear oil", which, in excess, can lead to a nail-varnish aroma). A more profound banana character found on the aftertaste of Alsace Pinot Gris or Gewurztraminer is the precursor to bottle-aged spiciness.

BAND-AID
This sticking-plaster aroma is one of the four olfactory defects known collectively as phenol off-flavour, or "poff" (vinyl-4-phenol).

BARNYARD
See Horsey.

BEETROOT
This fruity-vegetal earthiness may be found in some red wines, mostly Pinot Noir grown in unsuitable areas, and aged too long in bottle, or Cabernet Franc (geosmin).

BELL PEPPER OR CAPSICUM
This can be found in a slightly grassy-herbaceous Sauvignon, a Loire Cabernet Franc, or a Cabernet Sauvignon from high-vigour vines. It used to be a big problem in New Zealand (2-Methoxy-3-isobutylpyrazine).

BILBERRY
See Blueberry.

BISCUITY (COOKIE-LIKE)
Found in fine-quality, well-matured Champagnes, biscuitiness is the post-disgorgement bottle-aroma that typifies Pinot Noir, although many pure Chardonnay Champagnes develop a creamy-biscuitiness (acetal, acetoin, diacetyl, benzoic aldehyde, and undecalactone).

BLACKBERRY
This is detectable in ripe Pinot Noir in the black-fruit stage beyond strawberry (ethyl caprylate, ethyl hexanoate, ethyl butyrate, amyl propionate).

BLACKCURRANT
Characteristic of classic Cabernet, blackcurrant is also found in grapes such as Carmenère and Syrah, particularly when bottle-aged (ethyl acetate, ethyl formate, various acids and esters).

BLUEBERRY
Also known as bilberry or whortleberry, this fruit gives an aroma that is much softer, more perfumed, and less intensely flavoured than blackcurrant (possibly hexanoate).

BREADY
The second stage of autolysis, as the flowery acacia-like aromas take on more substance and a certain creaminess (diacetyl, undecalactone, or paratolylmethyl ketone).

BROAD BEAN (FAVA BEAN)
A typical Sauvignon Blanc aroma between bell pepper and fresh green pea. It is also found in Cabernet Sauvignon (2-Methoxy-3-isobutylpyrazine).

BUBBLEGUM
Found in cool-fermented whites and reds made by carbonic maceration (amyl acetate or isoamyl acetate, also known as "banana oil" or "pear oil", which, in excess, can lead to a nail-varnish aroma).

BURNT MATCH
A burnt match aroma is the clean, if somewhat choking, whiff produced by free sulphur. This is not a fault as such in a young or recently bottled wine, and it can be dispersed by swirling the wine around in the glass (sulphur dioxide).

BURNT RUBBER
This is a serious wine fault created by the reaction between ethyl alcohol and hydrogen sulphide, another wine fault, which produces a foul-smelling compound called ethylmercaptan.

BUTTER
This characteristic is usually found in Chardonnay, and is caused by diacetyl, an artificial flavouring that is used by the food industry, but it is also produced naturally during the malolactic process (also undecalactone). It is inappropriate for classic sparkling wine, so the champenois utilize special low-diacetyl-forming bacteria.

BUTTERSCOTCH
Butterscotch is produced when very ripe, exotically fruity white wines are aged in well-toasted new oak *barriques*, and is most commonly found in New World wines (cyclotene, diacetyl, maltol, or undecalactone).

CABBAGE OR CAULIFLOWER

The presence of cabbage or cauliflower usually denotes a Chardonnay wine or a wine from the Pinot family. Some people think mature unfiltered Burgundy should have this aroma, or even one that is farmyardy or evocative of manure (methylmercaptan).

CANDLE WAX
Candle wax is a more accurate descriptor for Sémillon wines than the more commonly employed lanolin, since lanolin possesses no smell, even though it has a connotation of one (aprylate, caproate, or ethyl capryate).

CARAMEL
This may be either a mid-palate flavour in young wines aged in new *barriques* or, as in tawny port, an aftertaste achieved through considerable ageing in used barrels (cyclotene or maltol).

CARDBOARD
This characteristic can literally be produced by storing glasses in a cardboard box. It may also be caused by heavy-handed filtration or by leaving a wine to mature for too long in old wood. The glue-ridden smell of wet cardboard can be either TCA or mercaptan.

CARNATION
This is one of the four olfactory defects known collectively as phenol off-flavour, or "poff". Although perceived as a defect in wines from most grape varieties, it is said to contribute in a positive sense the varietal aroma of Gewürztraminer (vinyl-4-guaiacol).

CAT'S PEE
The is the elderflower aroma taken to the extreme in Sauvignon Blanc, probably due to unripe grapes (4-Mercapto-4-methylpentan-2-one).

CEDARY OAK
This is not as silly as it sounds. Various oak lactones have a cedary aroma, particularly in American oak, but this is also a common descriptor for Bordeaux, so it is assumed it can come from French oak, too.

CHEESE
Occasionally, a wine can have a clean cheese aroma (Emmental or blue-veined being most common), but a strong cheesy smell will be the result of a bacterial fault (ethyl butryrate or S-ethythioacetate).

CHERRY

Tart, red cherries are classic in cool-climate Pinot Noir, while black cherries can be part of the complexity of a great Cabernet or Syrah (cyanhydrin benzaldehyde).

CHOCOLATE OR CHOCOLATE-BOX
This is the aroma or flavour typical of youngish Cabernet Sauvignon or Pinot Noir wines, when they are rich and soft with a high alcohol content and low acidity level. It may also be detected as part of the complexity of a mature wine or be due to various oak lactones.

CINNAMON
Part of the aged complexity of many fine red wines, especially Rhône, cinnamon is also found in oak-aged whites, particularly Gewürztraminer or those made from botrytized grapes (cinnamic aldehyde).

CITRUS FRUIT
This is a very common taste descriptor in France, where agrume is attributed to the fresh complexity of many young white wines. It is often more complex than a specific citrus fruit aroma (one or more of limonene, citonellol, linalool).

CLEMENTINE
See Mandarin.

CLOVE
Clove is found in wines that have been matured or aged in new oak *barriques*, which gain this aroma during the process of being toasted (*see* p39). In addition, clove is found in Gewürztraminer from certain *terroirs*, such as Soultzmatt and Bergbieten in Alsace (eugenol or eugenic acid from oak if not an aromatic variety).

COCONUT
This characteristic is another found in great old Champagne. Pungent coconutty aromas are also produced by various wood lactones that are most commonly found in American oak, notably Cis G-Octa Lactone (could also be capric acid).

COFFEE
A sign of a great old Champagne, maybe 20- or 50-year-old or more, coffee is now increasingly found on the finish of inexpensive red wines made with medium- or high-toast American oak chips.

CURRANT LEAF
Although associated with Sauvignon Blanc, this herbaceous character can be found in any wine made from under-ripe grapes or grapes from high-vigour vines. Can be green and mean on the finish.

DRIED FRUIT
The aroma of sultanas or currants is most commonly found in Italian Recioto or Amarone wines, and sometimes a yeast-complexed aroma in a Pinot Noir-dominant Champagne, whereas the aroma of raisins is characteristic of fortified Muscat.

EARTHY
Wines can have an earthiness on the palate that some people incorrectly attribute to the *terroir*, but this undesirable taste is unclean and not expressive of origin (geosmin).

EGG, HARD-BOILED OR ROTTEN
Sulphur is added to wine in order to prevent oxidation, which it does by fixing itself to any oxygen that is present in the wine but, if it fixes with hydrogen, it creates hydrogen sulphide, which smells of hard-boiled or rotten eggs.

ELDERFLOWER
Found in wines made from aromatic grape varieties, elderflower is good only when the aroma is clean and fresh, and the fruit ripe, but can verge on cat's pee when the grapes are unacceptably under-ripe (pyrazines).

EUCALYPTUS
This aroma is noticeable in many Australian Cabernet Sauvignon and Shiraz wines, and could originate from leaves falling off eucalyptus trees into grape-pickers' baskets (eucalyptol).

FENNEL
A softer, more subtle, slightly herbal rendition of aniseed (anethole).

FIG

A fig-like aroma is sometimes a characteristic of potential complexity in a youthful Chardonnay and may be found in combination with nuances of apple or melon (ethyl propionate, isobutyl acetate).

FLINTY
This is a subjective connotation for the finest Sauvignon Blanc.

FLORAL
This generic flowery aroma is usually light and fresh (linalool, 2-phenylethanol, methyl 2-methylpropanoate, various aldehydes).

FLOWERY-FRUITY
In terms of development, this could be viewed as a few months' more bottle-age than "floral" (ß-damascenone, ethyl hexanoate).

FOXY
Foxy is the term used to describe the very distinctive, cloyingly sweet, and perfumed character of certain indigenous American grape varieties (methyl anthranilate or ethyl anthranilate).

GARLIC

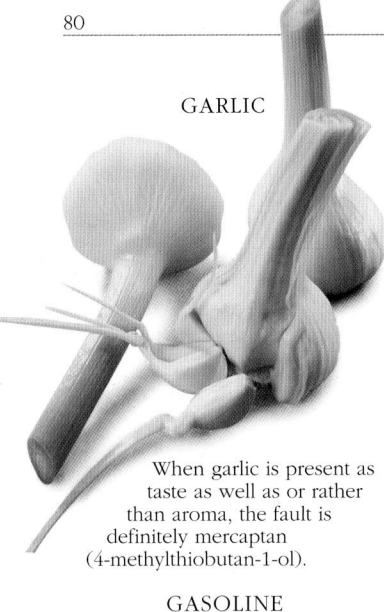

When garlic is present as taste as well as or rather than aroma, the fault is definitely mercaptan (4-methylthiobutan-1-ol).

GASOLINE
See Petrol.

GERANIUM
Commonly a sweet wine fault (2-ethoxyhexa-3, 5-diene), but also the sign of an Asti that is too old (geraniol degradation), it is always distinctive (also glycyrrhizin or hexanedienol).

GINGERBREAD
Found in mature Gewürztraminer of the highest quality, when the true spiciness of this variety is mellowed by bottle-age (citronellal, citronellol, eugenol, geranial, geraniol, linalool, nerol, myrcene).

GOOSEBERRY
The classic aroma of a truly ripe, yet exceedingly fresh, crisp, and vibrant Sauvignon Blanc, gooseberry is most widely found in white wines from New Zealand, particularly Marlborough (4-MMP, aka 4-mercapto-4-methylpentan-2-one).

GRAPE

Few wines are actually grapey, but grapiness is found in cheap German wines, young Gewürztraminer, and Muscat or Muscat-like wines (ethyl caprylate, ethyl heptanoate, and ethyl perargonate).

GRAPEFRUIT
Grapefruit is found in the Jurançon Sec and Alsace Gewürztraminer, German or English Scheurebe and Huxelrebe, and Swiss Arvine wines (3-mercaptohexanol or a combination of terpenes, such as linalool and citronellal).

GRASS, FRESHLY CUT
Can be aggressive, but if fresh, light, and pleasant, it is a positive attribute of deliberately early-picked Sauvignon Blanc or Sémillon grapes (methoxy-pyrazine hexenal or hexanedienol).

HAY
Like dull, flat, or oxidized grassiness, the hay characteristic can be found in sparkling wines that have undergone a slight oxidation prior to their second fermentation (linalool oxides).

HAZELNUT
Discovered as recently as 2000, roasted hazelnut from time in oak is 2-acetylthiazole. This characteristic is part of the complexity of mature white Burgundy and Champagne (undecalactone, 4-methylthiazole, trimethylpyrazine or diacetyl).

HERBACEOUS
Overt herbaceousness is a sign of under-ripeness or an over-vigorous canopy, although an understated herbaceousness can add an attractive dimension to some early-drinking wines (various pyrazines).

HONEY
Almost every fine white wine becomes honeyed with age, but particularly great Burgundy, classic German Riesling, and botrytized wines (phenylethylic acid).

HORSEY
Once thought to be part of a wine's complexity, then believed to be a mercaptan fault, the horsey (or barnyard or sweaty-saddle) aroma is now known to be a Brettanomyces fault and one of the four olfactory defects known collectively as phenol off-flavour, or "poff" (ethyl-4-phenol).

JAM
Any red wine can be jammy, but Grenache has a particular tendency towards raspberry jam, while Pinot Noir has a distinct tendency to evoke strawberry jam. A jammy flavour is not typical of a really fine wine, but can be characteristic of a wine that is upfront and lip-smacking.

KEROSENE
See Petrol.

LAVENDER
Lavender is often found with lime on Australian wines, particularly Riesling, Muscat, or sparkling wines, and occasionally in German Riesling and even Vinho Verde.

LEATHER
A dry, almost tactile impression of leather can be a complex element of many high-quality wines and should not be confused with the more pungent sweaty-saddle aroma (see Horsey). Leather can be a pure alcohol aroma "peeping" through the fruit.

LEMON

Not as distinctive in wine as freshly cut lemon would suggest, many young white wines have simple, ordinary, almost mild lemony fruit or acidity (limonene or citronellal).

LILAC
The lilac characteristic is found in some herbaceous reds and peppery Rhônes. It can be overpowering in Muscadine (α-terpineol).

LILY OF THE VALLEY
This floral characteristic is found in New World Gewürztraminer (linalool).

LIME

A truly distinctive aroma and flavour found in good-quality Australian Sémillon and Riesling; in the latter, it often turns to lavender in bottle (limonene, citronellal, or linalool).

LIME TREE (LINDEN)
Youthful Riesling typically has this characteristic (hotrienol).

LINDEN
See Lime tree.

LIQUORICE
This can be part of the complexity of red, white, and fortified wines of great concentration, particularly those that are made from late-harvested or sun-dried grapes (geraniol or glycyrrhizin).

LYCHEE
Fresh lychee is depicted as the classic varietal character of Gewürztraminer, but is not as widely encountered as commonly imagined, whereas tinned lychee is commonly found in precocious white wines from off-vintages. Fresh lychee aroma is the product of at least 12 different compounds, the most dominant of which is cis-rose oxide.

MACAROONS
The almondy-coconutty taste of macaroons is a typical characteristic of a great old Champagne, being similar to a coconutty taste, but sweeter and more complex (undecalactone or capric acid).

MALT
More at home as a beer aroma, malt is unwelcome rather than unpleasant in wine. The most common occurrence of malt is in a sparkling wine that has either had too long on its lees or has undergone a less-than-ideal autolysis. (3-methylbutanal, 3-methylbutanol involving lactobacillus, 3-hydroxy-2-methyl-4-pyrone, aka maltol, gives the most distinctive maltiness and can develop into a blue-cheese aroma.)

MAGNOLIA
Although characteristic of a Muscadine grape variety actually called Magnolia, this distinctly floral aroma can also be found in wines made from other grapes (geranyl acetone).

MANDARIN OR CLEMENTINE

A softer yet zestier and more defined aroma than simple orange, mandarin or clementine can be found in Muscat or Riesling of exceptional complexity and finesse (ethyl octanoate, ethyl decanoate, isoamyl alcohol, ethyl hexanoate and isoamyl acetate).

MANURE
This aroma is a very extreme form of the "farmyardy" aroma, which some people (not this author) believe to be characteristic of great Pinot Noir. Certain New World winemakers try to emulate this aroma in their wines, but it is probably a fixed-sulphur fault, and quite possibly a mercaptan.

MELON
A characteristic of young, cool-fermented, New World Chardonnay, melon may be found in combination with nuances of apple or fig (limonene, citronellal, or linalool).

MINT

Although it is occasionally found in Bordeaux, mint is actually far more redolent in full-bodied New World reds, particularly Californian Cabernet (especially Napa) and Coonawarra Shiraz (l-carvone, menthol, menthone, menthyl acetate).

MOUSE

The mousey aroma was once thought to be a *Brettanomyces* fault but is now known to be a *Lactobacillus* fault that can only occur when lysine is present in the wine (acetyl-tetrahydrpyridines).

MUSCAT

The fresh, grapey aroma of the Muscat grape is an aromatic characteristic that can occasionally be found in wines made from other varieties, but it usually defines a Muscat wine and is the only grapey-grape aroma in the winemaking world (essentially a combination of geraniol, linalool, and nerol).

MUSHROOM

A beautifully clean mushroom aroma is an indication of Pinot Meunier in a fine old Champagne, but if the aroma is musty, it will be a contamination fault such as infected staves or a corked wine.

MUSTY

This has a drier perception than "mouldy" – the difference as in a dry, musty church and a damp, mouldy cellar. Although both could be due to infected staves, "mouldy" can also come from grapes affected by botrytis, although it is more likely to be grey rot than brown (2,4,6-trichloroanisole, or TCA)

NAIL POLISH

Nail polish is the pungent, peardrop aroma produced by intensive carbonic maceration. It is found on the worst Beaujolais Nouveau (amyl acetate or isoamyl acetate, otherwise known as "banana oil" or "pear oil").

NUTS

This ranges from the generic nuttiness of mature Burgundy, and the walnuts or hazelnuts in Champagne blanc de blancs, to the almondy fruit of young Italian red (acetoin, diacetyl, or undecalactone).

NUTTINESS

See Oxidative.

OAK

Used on its own, the term oak is so generic as to be almost meaningless and should be qualified to indicate the type of oakiness, such as coffee-oak, creamy oak, lemony oak, spicy oak, sweet oak and vanilla oak (various oak lactones). *See also* Cedary oak.

ONION

This aroma indicates a very unpleasant fault and can range from rubbery onion (ethanethiol) to pungent raw onion, garlic, or burnt rubber onion (diethyl disulphide).

ORANGE

A good blind-tasting tip is that orange can be found in Muscat, but never Gewürztraminer. It is also found in some fortified wines and Ruby Cabernet (limonene, citronellal, or linalool).

ORANGE BLOSSOM

This is typical of youthful dry Muscat (anisic acid, limonene, citronellol).

OXIDATIVE

This characteristic can range from bruised apple to Sherry (acetaldehyde) in a still wine, and nutty in a sparkling wine. "Oxidative" can be positive for those who like the style, forming part of the complexity. But when the word "oxidized" is used in a description of a wine, it is only in a negative sense.

PARAFFIN

See Petrol.

PASSION FRUIT

An intense New Zealand Sauvignon Blanc aroma, a touch of passion fruit adds to the complexity of a wine, but too much can push the varietal aroma into sweaty-armpit mode (mercaptohexanol).

PEACH

Found in ripe Riesling and Muscat, very ripe Sauvignon Blanc, true Viognier, Sézannais Champagne, New World Chardonnay, and botrytized wines (piperonal or undecalactone).

PEANUT

At low levels and with a pleasant popcorn hint, this characteristic is found in some Banyuls, Port, and Bordeaux, but a more pungent peanut aroma comes from ladybird or Asian ladybug taint, usually machine-harvested, where just one ladybird in a vat can be responsible for the peanut off-odour (adaline, adalinine, and 2-isopropyl-3-methoxypyrazine).

PEAR

Pear is found in cool-fermented whites and reds made by carbonic maceration (amyl acetate or isoamyl acetate, also known as "banana oil" or "pear oil", which, in excess, can lead to a nail-varnish aroma).

PEAS, CANNED

Common in Sauvignon Blanc made from over-ripe grapes or kept too long in bottle. Some people adore this style, but most do not. Can develop from an asparagus aroma (isobutyl or segbutyl). *See* Asparagus.

PEAS, FRESH

The fresh green-pea aroma found in Sauvignon Blanc is closer to broad bean than it is to tinned peas or asparagus (2-Methoxy-3-isobutylpyrazine).

PEBBLE, WET

Not an aroma or taste as such, this sensation is reminiscent of the salivating effect produced when sucking a wet pebble and is indicative of Sauvignon Blanc of exceptional finesse.

PEPPERCORN

Many young reds have a basic peppery character, but Syrah evokes the distinctive fragrance of crushed black peppercorns (rotundone), while for top-quality Grüner Veltliner, it is ground white pepper.

PETROL

The so-called petrol (kerosene, gasoline, or paraffin) aroma is a well-known varietal characteristic of a classic, racy Riesling wine of some maturity. It does not literally smell or taste of petrol, but it is an instantly recognizable aroma descriptor that experienced tasters use without pretension. The active chemical compound responsible for the petrol aroma has been identified as trimethyldihydronaph-thalene, or TDN for short. TDN develops during the bottle-ageing process through the degradation of beta carotene, an antioxidant that is itself derived from lutein, another antioxidant. The ratio of beta carotene to lutein is higher in Riesling than in any other white grape variety. Studies show that the lower the pH of a wine, the higher its potential for developing TDN, thus its propensity to develop in warmer climes. The longer it takes for the petrol aromas to emerge, the more finesse they have. Interestingly, cork absorbs 40 per cent of TDN; ergo, screwcaps preserve petrol aromas.

PINEAPPLE

Pineapple is found in very ripe Chardonnay, Chenin Blanc, and Sémillon, especially in the New World, and almost any botrytized wine. It implies good acidity for the ripeness (ethyl caprylate or butyl butyrate).

PLASTIC OR POLYTHENE

This not uncommon off-odour is possibly caused by benzohiazole or unsaturated olefins.

POPCORN

This can be a malolactic aroma, but *see also* Peanut.

POTATO PEELINGS

More earthy and less fruity than beetroot, potato peelings is found in a wide range of red wines, and could be an indication of infected staves or corkiness (geosmin).

QUINCE OR QUINCE JELLY

This is a classic reductive aroma (dimethyl sulphide, dimethyl disulphide).

RAISIN

The raisin aroma is commonly found in fortified wines, particularly Muscat (ß-damascenone).

RASPBERRY

This is sometimes found in Grenache, Loire Cabernet, Pinot Noir, and Syrah (evolving into blackcurrant in bottle) (ethyl acetate, ethyl formate, various acids and esters).

REDCURRANT

Youthful Pinot Noir, probably cool-climate grown, commonly has redcurrant aromas, but it is also sometimes found in young New World Cabernet Sauvignon and even Merlot.

RHUBARB

Some yeasts (eg, Lalvin 71B-1122) tend to produce a rhubarb-like fruitiness, particularly in wines that have undergone carbonic maceration (3-mercaptohexanol).

ROSE
Rose petals can be found in many wines, particularly delicate Muscats and understated Gewürztraminers (damascanone, diacetyl, geraniol, irone, nerol, or phenylethylic acid/rose oxide).

RUBBER
This is a fixed-sulphur fault (carbon disulphide) or a mercaptan (ethanethiol), whereas burnt rubber can be either a sulphur fault (diethyl sulphide) or a mercaptan (thiophen-2-thiol; although at low concentrations, this can give a wonderful roast-coffee aroma).

SAUERKRAUT
The lactic smell of a wine that has undergone excessive malolactic, sauerkraut is actually even less acceptable in wine than the sour milk or sour cream aroma (diacetyl or lactic acid).

SHERRY
This is the tell-tale sign of excessive acetaldehyde, which could turn a wine into vinegar unless it is sherry or another type of fortified wine, which will be protected by its high alcohol content.

SKUNK
Once smelled, never forgotten, the pungent, highly resinous skunk aroma is a methyl mercaptan fault (dimethylethanethiol).

SMOKE
Smoke is a complexity that might be varietal, as in the case of Syrah, but can be induced by stirring less during barrel fermentation, suggesting that the wine has not been racked, fined, or filtered (guaiacol or 4-ethylguaiacol).

SMOKY-SPICY
Although this can be part of a wine's complexity, it may also be one of the four olfactory defects known collectively as phenol off-flavour, or "poff" (ethyl-4-guaiacol).

SOAPY
A youthful soapiness in white wines, particularly Riesling, can indicate potential complexity, but too distinctive a soapiness is a fault (caprylate, caproate, ethyl caprate).

SOUR MILK OR SOUR CREAM
The lactic smell of a wine that has undergone excessive malolactic, the sour-milk character may develop into a more pronounced sauerkraut aroma (diacetyl or lactic acid); *see also* Sauerkraut.

SPICY
Many wines have a hint of spiciness, which is more exotic than peppery, but, after a few years' bottle-age, the spiciness of Gewürztraminer should almost burn the palate.

STABLE
See Horsey.

STAGNANT WATER
This is a mercaptan fault (methanethiol).

STRAWBERRY
Succulent, ripe strawberry fruit is found in classic Pinot Noir from a warm climate or top vintage. It is also found in Loire Cabernet (ethyl acetate, ethyl formate, various acids and esters).

SUMMER FRUITS
This aroma can be either a more complex or less distinct medley of raspberry, strawberry, blackberry, and blackcurrant (ethyl acetate, ethyl butyrate).

SWEATY
An unattractive sweaty-armpit aroma can be the result of many compounds found in wine, but the best documented is when passion fruit in Sauvignon Blanc goes sweaty (mercaptohexyl acetate).

SWEATY SADDLE
See Horsey.

TAR
Like liquorice with a touch of smoke, a tarry aroma in some full-bodied reds, typically Barolo and northern Rhône, could indicate a wine that has not been racked, fined, or filtered.

TOAST
Toastiness is commonly associated with Chardonnay and mature

Champagne, particularly *blanc de blancs*, but it can be found in many wines. Toastiness can either be a slow-developing bottle-aroma or an instant gift of new oak (furanic aldehydes). Current theory among research chemists is that the toastiness in Chardonnay wines is technically a fixed-sulphur fault, although it is a fault that many wine lovers have come to enjoy.

TOBACCO
The tobacco aroma is often found in mature reds, particularly Bordeaux, or big New World reds (3-oxy-a-ionol, ß-damascenone, hydroxy-ß-damascenone).

TOFFEE
This is less creamy and more oxidative than caramel (various oak lactones).

TOMATO

We tend to think of tomato as a vegetable, but it is really a fruit and, although not a common feature in wines, it is found in bottle-aged Sylvaner and, with blood-orange, in Ruby Cabernet. Also found in Merlot, Pinot Noir, and various Italian wines (trans-2-pentanal).

TOMATO LEAF
This characteristic is the distinctive aroma of deliberately oxidized Sauvignon Blanc juice prior to fermentation (2-isobutylthiazole).

TROPICAL FRUIT
Usually found in New World whites, particularly Chardonnay, tropical-fruit aromas can also be found in Viognier, exotic Riesling, or Old World wines, such as Champagne from Sézanne or mature bottles of exceptionally hot vintages (ß-damascenone).

TRUFFLE

While truffle is often cited as part of the profound complexity of a great wine, if it is noticeable, it is a fixed-sulphur fault (dimethyl sulphide).

VANILLA
Probably vanillin from new oak, although vanillin is also found in cork. Various vanillin-based compounds also have vanilla aromas, and a hint of vanilla can be due to unrelated compounds present in wines that have seen no oak or cork. DDMP has a vanilla-sugar aroma and is a product of Maillard reactions during the toasting of oak barrels (vanillin, vanillyl acetate, acetovanillone, ethyl vanillate, methyl vanillate, guaiacol, furylacetone, 4-ethylguaiacol, 2,3-dihydro-2,5-dihydroxy-6-methyl-4-H-pyran-4-one, aka DDMP).

VEGETAL
Although unattractive sounding, vegetal can be either negative or positive (trans-2-hexenol).

VINEGAR
This is a classic volatile-acidity fault (acetic acid).

VIOLET

Violets can often be found as part of the finesse on the finish of Cabernet-based red wines, notably Bordeaux, especially from Graves. It is possibly more tactile-based than a volatile aroma (ionones).

WET DOG OR WET WOOL
These aromas are heat-generated volatile sulphur faults involving the retro-Michael reaction of methional, which is thermally unstable and evolves rapidly into acrolein and methanethiol, which are responsible for the so-called wet-dog and wet-wool aromas and a stronger cooked-cauliflower smell.

WHORTLEBERRY
See Blueberry.

YEAST-COMPLEXED
Yeasty aromas are not welcome and are rarely encountered, but yeast-complexed aromas are, especially in Champagne, where they give a chewy creaminess to the fruit and encourage many different aromatic characters, such as dried fruit, developing into Christmas cake for yeast-complexed Pinot Noir.

FAULT FINDING

SYMPTOM	CAUSE	REMEDY
Bits of floating cork	You are the cause, and this is not a corked wine! Tiny bits of cork have become dislodged when opening the bottle.	Fish them out and drink the wine. If it happens frequently, buy a Screwpull corkscrew.
Sediment	All wines shed a deposit in time; most are drunk before they do.	Decant the bottle.
Coating on the inside of the bottle	Full-bodied reds from hot countries or exceptionally hot vintages in cool-climate countries are prone to shedding a deposit that adheres to the inside of the bottle.	You can check to see whether the wine pours clear. However, there is bound to be some loose sediment and, even when there is not, it is always safest to decant.
Cloudy haze	If it is not sediment, it will not drop out and is either a metal or protein haze.	Seek a refund. Home winemakers can try bentonite but, although this removes a protein haze, it could make a metal haze worse!
A film or slick on the surface	This is an oil slick caused by glasses or a decanter. Either they have not been properly rinsed or a minuscule amount of grease has come from the glass-cloth used to polish them.	Use detergent to clean glasses and rinse them thoroughly in hot water. Never use a glass-cloth for anything other than polishing glasses and never dry them with general-purpose tea towels.
Still wine with tiny bubbles clinging to the glass	An unwanted second fermentation or malolactic can make some still wines as fizzy as Champagne.	If the wine is really fizzy, then take it back, but if the fault is just a spritz or prickle, use a Vacu-vin to suck the gas out.
Asparagus or canned-peas aromas	Sauvignon Blanc from over-ripe grapes or kept too long in bottle.	No technical fault – buy a more recent vintage next time.
Cabbage, cauliflower, farmyardy, or manure aromas	Technically a fault (methylmercaptan), but half the wine trade would argue it is part of the complexity of some wines, particularly Burgundy.	Some retailers will refund you, but those who have personally selected this "traditional" style may not.
Currant leaf aromas or flavours	Caused by under-ripe grapes or high-vigour vines, this may be deliberate if wine is from a hot country and green on the finish.	Not a fault as such, although it is not exactly good winemaking so, if you cannot force yourself to drink the wine, throw it away.
Bubblegum, peardrops, or nail-varnish aromas	Produced by cool-fermentation in white wines and carbonic maceration in reds, and found in the worst Beaujolais Nouveau.	This is not a fault, so drink the wine or give it away.
Burnt match aromas (or a tickle in the nose or throat)	The clean whiff of free sulphur, which protects the wine, as opposed to fixed-sulphur faults, which have a pungent stench.	Swirl the glass or pour the wine vigorously into a jug and back into the bottle to disperse the aroma through aeration.
Burnt rubber or skunk	A serious wine fault created when ethyl alcohol reacts with hydrogen sulphide, a fixed-sulphur fault, to form a foul-smelling compound called ethylmercaptan.	Take the wine back for a full refund.
Cardboard aromas	This can be due to storing glasses in a cardboard box, heavy-handed filtration, or leaving a wine too long in old wood.	If the wine is still cardboardy in a clean, untainted glass, you could seek a refund, but may have to put it down to experience.
Cheese aromas	Occasionally a wine has a clean cheese aroma (Emmental or blue-veined being most common), but a real cheesy smell will be a bacterial fault (ethyl butryrate or S-ethythioacetate).	Take the wine back for a full refund.
Earthy aromas	Unclean, but not exactly a known fault.	As the wine was probably purchased by someone who thought it had a *goût de terroir*, you are unlikely to get a refund.
Hard-boiled or rotten-egg aromas	Sulphur is added to wine to prevent oxidation by fixing itself to any oxygen, but if it fixes with hydrogen it creates hydrogen sulphide, which is the stuff of stink bombs.	Theoretically, if you put a brass or copper object into the wine, the smell should drop out as a very fine brown sediment, but frankly it is quicker and easier to ask for a refund.
Geranium aromas	In a sweet wine, this is a sorbic acid and bacterial infection fault. In Asti or any other Muscat wine, the geraniol that gives the wine its classic flowery-peach character has degraded with age.	Take the wine back for a full refund.
Maderized (in any wine other than Madeira)	Maderization is undesirable in any ordinary, light table wine. Such a wine will have been affected by light or heat, or both.	Take the wine back for a full refund, unless you have kept it under bad conditions yourself.
Mushroom aromas	A clean mushroom aroma indicates Pinot Meunier in a fine old Champagne but, if musty, it will be a contamination fault.	If a contamination fault, take the wine back for a full refund.
Musty aromas, as in an old church	The wine is corked (or at least it is suffering from a corky taint).	Smell the wine an hour later: a corked wine will get worse and you should seek a refund. Harmless bottle mustiness disappears.
Mousy aromas	Caused by *Brettanomyces* yeast and malolactic bacteria, this is feared in the New World, but some Old World wineries use *Brettanomyces* yeast deliberately to add to a wine's complexity.	Give it to someone you do not like.
Onion or garlic aromas	A serious wine fault created when ethyl alcohol reacts with hydrogen sulphide, a fixed-sulphur fault, to form a foul-smelling compound called ethylmercaptan.	Take the wine back for a full refund.
Sauerkraut aromas	The smell of a wine that has undergone excessive malolactic, this is more unacceptable than sour milk or sour cream aromas.	Take the wine back for a full refund.
Sherry aromas (in any wine other than sherry)	Excessive acetaldehyde: the wine is oxidized. An ordinary wine with excessive acetaldehyde turns into vinegar, but sherry and other fortified wines are protected by a high alcohol content.	Take the wine back for a full refund.
Vinegar aromas	The distinctive aroma of acetic acid: the wine has oxidized.	Use it for salad dressing.

A CHRONOLOGY OF WINE

In a work that casts its net as
far and wide as this book, it would be
impossible to provide anything approaching
a comprehensive historical coverage
without doubling its size and price.
Where space is limited, the usual solution is to
opt for a very selective history, choosing just
two or three pivotal topics to summarize. But
when an entire book devoted to the history of
any subject ends up being a compromise, such
an approach becomes so eclectic as to be
meaningless. The chronological format is also
a compromise – indeed, it is by definition a
compromise – but that is its advantage. It was
conceived to be a compromise. Instead of
choosing two or three pivotal topics to
summarize, why not try to cover as many topics
as possible in as few words as possible?
A Chronology of Wine is the sort of history that
anyone would want to dip in and out of, and
by interspersing important historical events with
the odd bizarre wine-related fact, I hope I have
made it a fun read, too. Just as the Micropedia
(*see* p688) has taken more than two decades
to evolve from its more modest origin as a
glossary of tasting and technical terms,
so it is expected that this chronology will
grow over forthcoming revisions.

ANCIENT GRAPES
These grape-picking putti *feature in a mosaic
at Villa Romana del Casale, Sicily, dating
from the late 3rd to early 4th centuries.*

Notes

1. Where dates are approximate periods or carbon dated, the oldest possible date is given.
2. Geographical locations preceding events are the modern-day equivalents.

500 million BC	A distant relative of *Vitis vinifera* is speculated to be *Ampelopsis*, a climbing vine that existed when Earth had only one land mass, the supercontinent known as Pangaea.
200 million BC	Postulated appearance of *Vitis vinifera sylvestris*, the Eurasian wild grape, bearing fruit that would be black or dark red. All wine grapes we know today are descended from this single wild-grape variety. White grapes are highly unlikely at this juncture.
50 million BC	The oldest fossilized remains of *Vitis vinifera sylvestris* date from this period.
2.5 million BC	Several pockets of *Vitis vinifera sylvestris* survive during the Quaternary Ice Age, including, it is believed, in an area somewhere between the Black Sea and southern Caspian Sea, from where modern viticulture eventually spreads.
200,000 BC	Postulated appearance of the first white mutations of *Vitis vinifera sylvestris*.
21,000 BC	**Israel:** Remains of *Vitis vinifera sylvestris* carbon dated to this period are found at the Ohalo II site on the southwest shore of the Sea of Galilee, in Israel's Rift Valley.
8500 BC	**Armenia, Azerbaijan, Georgia, Turkey:** The first *vinifera* (*Vitis vinifera vinifera*) is domesticated by the earliest agricultural societies of Neolithic humans for fresh and dried grapes. • As the vine spreads through the Fertile Crescent (Mesopotamia and Levant) and beyond, it adapts to local conditions, from which distinctly separate grape varieties will emerge.
7000 BC	**China:** Residue of the oldest-known alcoholic product in carbon-dated storage jar found at Jiahu, a Neolithic village in the Yellow River Valley, fermented from rice, honey, and either grapes or hawthorn, possibly both.
6700 BC	**Middle East:** Desertification commences due to changes in the Earth's orbit and a tilt of its axis. Prior to this, the lands into which *vinifera* spread were green and lush.
6000 BC	**Georgia:** Wine residue in a carbon-dated storage jar found at Shulveri was the oldest-known wine in 2003.
5400 BC	**Iran:** Wine residue in a carbon-dated storage jar found at Hajji Firuz was the oldest-known wine in 1995.

Hajji Firuz storage jar

4000 BC	**Lebanon:** Estimated arrival of viticulture in the northern part of Canaan that is now Lebanon. Wine plays an important role in the culture of both the Canaanites and the Phoenicians, their successors. **Armenia:** In January 2011, the world's oldest "winery" was discovered in the cave complex at the Areni-1 archaeological site. A shallow trough about 1 metre (3 feet) across had been positioned to drain into a deep vat. This is thought to be a *lagar* for treading grapes. *Vinifera* grape seeds, remains of pressed *vinifera* grapes, fermentation jars, a cup, and a drinking bowl were also discovered inside the cave.
3150 BC	**Egypt:** More than 700 wine jars buried in the U-j tomb of Scorpion I, the earliest-known king of Egypt's Protodynastic Period, at Abydos. The wine is laced with pine resin, figs, and various herbs, including balm, coriander, mint, and sage.
3100 BC	**Egypt:** The word for wine exists in ancient Egyptian as *irp* (written using the eye symbol "ir" followed by the mat symbol "p"). • The world's earliest "wine labels" are stamped into clay on sealed wine jars later found in the tomb of King Den at Abydos, certifying that the wine they contained was produced at a vineyard dedicated to Horus. • By this time, wine jars are standardized in shape and volume (10, 20, and

	30 litres), sealed with a wet-clay stopper that is spread down over the shoulder of the vessel to create a tight seal. • Tomb paintings show vines grown in raised troughs to avoid wasting precious irrigation resources and trained into arbours for easy harvesting.
3000 BC	**Iran:** Wine residue in a carbon-dated storage jar found at Godin Tepi was the oldest-known wine in 1991.
2550 BC	**Egypt:** A wine known as Chassut Red produced by vintner Sekem-Ka is reputed not to be ready to drink until it has aged 100 years!
2500 BC	**Egypt:** Illustration in a tomb at Saqqara depicts an early Egyptian bag press being squeezed by twisting poles. • Estimated earliest use of cork stoppers.

Egyptian bag press

2400 BC	**Egypt:** Various mosaics from the Fourth Dynasty show grapes and wine production.
2137 BC	**China:** The earliest-recorded eclipse occurs, according to *The Shu King*. This volume also documents the execution of two royal astronomers, Hsi and Ho, for failing to predict the eclipse because they had drunk too much rice wine.
2000 BC	**Greece:** Viticulture is introduced by Phoenician and Egyptian traders to the Cycladic and Minoan (Cretan) civilizations of ancient Greece.
1600 BC	**Iran:** Glassmaking emerges in Mesopotamia.
1520 BC	**Egypt:** Painted scenes in the tomb of Amenhotep I depict the entire winemaking process, from harvesting and treading the grapes, through fermentation and storage in sealed jars with a hole drilled in the top (obviously to facilitate the escape of carbon dioxide, since these holes are later stopped with clay), which are then carried individually in net slings and transported by boat.
1450 BC	**Egypt:** Tomb illustration of wine being siphoned off its sediment and blended in preparation for, it is supposed, a banquet, though it could equally be for rebottling into fresh wine jars.
1345 BC	**Egypt:** Of the 26 wines later buried with Tutankhamun, five are from this vintage, including a "sweet wine" from the House of Aton on the Western River, produced by chief vintner Aperershop.
1344 BC	**Egypt:** The first white wine is made near Alexandria, its residue later found in one of the amphorae in Tutankhamun's tomb.
1330 BC	**Egypt:** Paintings in the tomb of Parennefer, adviser to Akhenaten, illustrate a primitive but effective form of air conditioning, since wine jars are stored in wet sand and fanned to keep cool. Although the reason for this practice is unknown, it would have slowed the fermentation, resulting in fruitier wines.
1200 BC	**Greece:** Greek viticulture is at its peak. Vines are trained in parallel rows, just as they are today, with care taken to ensure proper spacing between each vine. At least six different methods of pruning and training are employed, the choice depending on the variety of grape, type of soil, and wind strength. The classic wines of ancient Greece were great indeed, relative to their era, and worthy of note in the writings of Hippocrates, Homer, Plato, Pliny, Virgil, and many others.
1153 BC	**Egypt:** Rameses III is buried with more than 20,000 jars of wine. He had previously listed 513 vineyards as belonging to the temple of Amun-Ra.
1000 BC	**Italy:** Viticulture is introduced to southern Italy by the Greeks.
800 BC	**France, Spain, Portugal:** Viticulture is introduced by Phoenician traders.
750 BC	**Tunisia:** Viticulture and winemaking are believed to have commenced here when Phoenician traders founded the city of Carthage, which Greco-Roman legend puts at 814 BC. However, no Phoenician artefact older than 750 BC has been found west of Phoenicia's Levant origins.
700 BC	**Spain:** Archeological evidence found of Phoenician winemaking in Valdepeñas.

650 BC	**Greece:** It is customary to drink wine mixed with water. Under the first Greek laws to be codified, Zaleucus decrees that anyone caught drinking undiluted wine shall be put to death.
620 BC	**Greece:** Under Draco's "Draconian law", anyone caught stealing grapes will face the death penalty.
600 BC	**France:** The Phocaeans (Greeks from the Ionian city of Phocaea in Anatolia, now Turkey) establish the port of Marseilles and introduce viticulture to the Gauls (ancient French). **Bulgaria, Moldova, Romania, Ukraine:** Vineyards are established by the Greeks.
500 BC	**Algeria, Morocco:** Viticulture probably established by the Carthaginians (Phoenician descendants). **France, Spain, Portugal:** Viticulture has been introduced by the Romans by this date. Although some vines were planted much earlier by Phoenicians, it was the Romans who established vineyards farther inland and started flourishing wine industries in most of Europe's classic wine regions. Initially, this was not for commercial purposes but merely to sustain the Roman army.
450 BC	**Greece:** The world's first wine laws regulating quality are introduced.
425 BC	**Greece:** The world's first wine law setting the earliest harvesting date is introduced.
424 BC	**Greece:** Herodotus, the world's first true historian, writes about casks of "palm wood filled with wine" being moved by boat to Babylon, invoking the possibility that the art of cooperage might have been invented by the ancient Mesopotamians, not the Celts as is generally accepted.
400 BC	**Spain:** Viticulture established on Ibiza by the Carthaginians (Phoenician descendants).
300 BC	**Spain, Portugal:** Viticulture is introduced to Tarragona, Rioja, Duero, and Douro.
250 BC	**Syria, Iran:** Glassblowing is invented.
128 BC	**China:** *Vinifera* vines are introduced by General Chang, who plants seeds at the Imperial Palace in Chang An (now called Xian).
121 BC	**Italy:** This legendary Roman vintage is named the Opimian vintage, after Lucius Opimius, Rome's consul at the time, and is noted for a large harvest of exceptionally high quality, now believed to be due to the grapes shrivelling on the vine. Falernian is the greatest wine of this vintage, and although there are several documented examples of Falernian Opimian being drinkable at the age of 100 years or more, this would be contested by Cicero, who in 46 BC declared that, at 75 years old, "the Opimian is already too old to drink".
50 BC	**France:** With all of Gaul under Roman occupation, the Romans discover the barrel and the art of cooperage, a Celtic invention (but *see* 424 BC).
19 BC	**Israel:** A large Roman two-handled wine amphora is sent from Italy to King Herod. It is found in an ancient garbage dump near the synagogue of Masada in 1996.
AD 43	**England:** The Romans brought the vine to England, and by this date every important villa had its own vineyard.
AD 65	**France, Italy, Spain:** The 12-book set *De Re Rustica* is completed by Lucius Junius Columella; it is the most comprehensive documented record of Roman viticulture that has survived to this day. Columella tells us that "many vineyards" yielded as much as 15 *cullei* per *jugera* (300 hl/ha), although some modern references give the impression that only 3 *cullei* per *jugera* (60 hl/ha) were the norm, but that was the yield at which Columella considered a vineyard to be unprofitable and recommended uprooting. Columella indicates that there were already many distinctly different varieties of grape and demonstrates that there was a keen and widespread sense of matching the most appropriate vine to a given terroir among farmers, who "assign to a fat and fertile land a vine that is slender and not too productive by nature; to lean land, a prolific vine; to heavy soil, a vigorous vine that puts forth much wood and foliage;

Castle remains, Masada

	to loose and rich soil, one that has few canes". Farmers were also aware of how to avoid rot: "He will know that it is not proper to commit to a damp place a vine with thin-skinned fruit and exceptionally large fruit, but one with fruit that is tough-skinned, small, and full of seeds."
AD 79	**Italy:** Pompeii is laid to waste by the eruption of Vesuvius. The town is preserved forever, which is how we know it boasted more than 160 bars selling wine and food. With a mere 10,000 inhabitants, and bars less than 10 m (30 ft) apart in places, Pompeii demonstrates that dining out is not merely a modern trend.
100	**Italy:** The city of Rome swells to 1 million inhabitants and has to import wine from Gaul and Iberia, despite the expansion of Italian vineyards.
250	**France, Italy:** As the flow of wine from France to Rome increases, the Romans realize the advantages of wooden casks over amphorae for transporting wine. From this juncture, casks become the vessel of choice for wine, and cooperage spreads throughout the Roman Empire.
674	**China:** Chinese wine is first documented (but *see* 128 BC).
760	**France:** St Fulrade is reputed to have brought the Pinot Noir to the village of St-Hippolyte from Italy (but *see* 1894).
802	**Western and Central Europe:** Charlemagne bans "leaded wine". The addition of lead was to make a sour wine taste sweet, a hangover from Roman times, when wines were sweetened with concentrate, and lead vessels were preferred for boiling down the concentrate because copper vessels left a bitter taste.
1001	**USA:** The first native American vines are identified by a German called Tyrker, who accompanied Viking Leif Ericson on a voyage of discovery to Newfoundland, Canada, and Northeast America, almost 500 years before Christopher Columbus. According to the *Grœnlendinga Saga*, a tale first documented in the *Flateyjarbók* manuscript between 1387 and 1394, Tyrker found what he described as *vinber*, or wine berries, having told Ericson, "I was born where there is no lack of either grapes or vines." Ericson gave Newfoundland the name Vinland. While this was written nearly 400 years after the alleged event, it was more than 100 years before Columbus "discovered" America; and in 1075 – more than 400 years before Columbus – Adam of Bremen wrote in *Descriptio Insularum Aquilonis* that the name Vinland comes from the huge amount of grapes growing there. Furthermore, a Viking settlement has now been unearthed in Newfoundland – not conclusive but convincing.
1086	**England:** The *Domesday Book* records some 40 significantly sized vineyards in England.
1152	**England, France:** The marriage between king-to-be Henry II and Eleanor of Aquitaine starts a special relationship between Bordeaux and England that continues to this day.
1232	**France:** This is such a hot year in Alsace that it is possible to fry eggs on paving stones.
1255	**France:** The crop in Alsace is so huge that, after filling all available casks, excess wine had to be used for mixing mortar.
1268	**Italy:** The "nibiol" vineyards of the Rivoli estate in Turin are believed to be the first mention of Nebbiolo (*see also* 1292).
1292	**Italy:** First recorded spelling of Nebbiolo is documented in Alba.

Pompeii wine counter

The Domesday Book

1307	**England:** There are claims that cork was shipped to England as early as this, possibly directly to Edward II from his cousin, King Diniz of Portugal.
1330	**France:** The first documented mention of Chardonnay is by the Cistercian monks, who planted it (and no other variety) at Clos de Vougeot in Burgundy.
1335	**Italy:** A document written by Francesco Scacchi dating from this year is later claimed, in the 20th century, as proof that the world's first sparkling wine was made in Italy. It turns out to be no more than a warning of the ill effects of a spoiled wine that has either not stopped fermenting or has accidentally started to re-ferment.
1375	**France:** The first documented mention of Pinot Noir is in Burgundy.
1385	**Italy:** Giovanni di Pietro Antinori of Florence branches out from his family's lucrative silk and wool business to become a winemaker.
1418	**Portugal:** The island of Madeira is discovered by João Gonçalves Zarco.

João Gonçalves Zarco

1435	**Germany:** The first Riesling vines to be documented are purchased by Klaus Kleinfisch, the administrator of Rüsselsheim Castle, which is on the opposite bank of the River Main to the villages of Hochheim and Florsheim in the Rheingau but, ironically, no longer makes any wine. Widespread claims that the "storage inventory of the counts of Katzenelnbogen lists the purchase of six barrels of Riesling from a Rüsselsheim vintner" are false.
1455	**Portugal:** Alves da Mosto writes about the vines on Madeira producing "more grapes than leaves" with "clusters of extraordinary size".
1458	**France:** Grapes in Alsace ripen by 21 May!
1470	**Germany:** French monks take the Pinot Noir to the Rheingau.
1477	**France:** The first varietal wine, Riesling (then spelled Rissling), appears in Alsace.
1478	**England:** According to Shakespeare, the Duke of Clarence was drowned in a barrel of Malmsey in the Tower of London. There is no evidence of Madeira being shipped to England as early as this (*see* 1537), although it was obviously well known by the Bard's time.
1484	**France:** The Alsace crop is so large that prices plummet, and 50 litres of wine cost as little as one egg.
1487	**Germany:** A Prussian royal decree requires wines to be preserved with sulphur burned on wood chips.
1490	**Spain:** Wine areas are extensively planted during the supposedly abstemious rule of the Moors.
1500	**France:** Muscat and Traminer are mentioned in Alsace.
1505	**France:** The greatest vintage of the 16th century.
1515	**Portugal, France:** The first Madeira – dry and unfortified – is shipped to Francis I in France.
1521	**Mexico:** The first vines on the American continent are planted by the Spanish.
1524	**Mexico:** Hernando Cortez, the governor of New Spain, orders every Spaniard holding a grant of land to plant annually 1,000 vines per each native forced labourer for a period of five years.
1531	**France:** Later claims that a document of this date detailing that Benedictine monks of St-Hilaire in Limoux produced intentionally sparkling wine are untrue (*see* 1544).
1535	**Canada:** French explorer Jacques Cartier discovers the first native Canadian vines when he finds a large island in the St Lawrence River that is totally overrun by wild vines (Île d'Orléans).
1537	**Portugal, England:** The first documented shipment of Madeira to England mentions a dry unfortified wine called "malvoisie of the Isle of Madeer".
1544	**France:** Upon later inspection, the document that many sources refer to as detailing that Benedictine monks of St-Hilaire in Limoux produced sparkling wine dates from this year, not 1531, and contains no mention

	of any effervescence, only that the bottles used were a different shape and the price the wine achieved was higher. Irrationally (but not unprofitably), this is what local Limoux producers have convinced themselves is proof of a sparkling wine.
1548	**Chile:** The first vines are planted by Spanish conquistador Francisco Pizarro y González.
1554	**Argentina:** The first vines are planted at Santiago del Estero by Juan Cidrón, a Catholic priest.
1560	**Spain:** The first Spanish wine laws are introduced (for Rioja).
1564	**USA:** French Huguenots produce the first American wine from Scuppernong grapes at Fort Caroline, 21 km (13 miles) northeast of what will be Jacksonville, Florida, which is ironically destined to become the least viticultural state in the country. **Canada:** It is theorized that Jesuit missionaries would have planted vines upon arrival in Canada.

Sir Francis Drake raids Cádiz

1587	**Spain, England:** Sherry shoots to fame in England following the daring raid on Cádiz by Sir Francis Drake, who sets alight the Spanish fleet and makes off with 3,000 casks of it.
1590	**Italy:** The Sangiovese is first documented as "Sangiogheto" in Tuscany. **Hungary:** A Tokaji from this vintage is possibly the earliest documented noble-rot wine, according to a report dated 1856.
1595	**Mexico:** Philip II of Spain prohibits any further planting of vines in New Spain (the colonies) to protect exports of Spanish wines.
1597	**Mexico:** The country's first winery is established by a royal decree of Philip II dated 19 August 1597 to Don Lorenzo Garcia of the San Lorenzo Hacienda. Still in existence, it is now Casa Madera.
1599	**England:** Cork stoppers are used in wine bottles in England by this date at the latest, according to *As You Like It*, which Shakespeare is supposed to have written in 1599 or 1600, although it was not published until 1623 (*see* 1685).
1606	**Hungary:** The oldest-known existence of a noble-rot wine is a Tokaji from this vintage. A Warsaw wine merchant known as Fukier (called Fugger in the 17th century, and now a famous restaurant) still possessed 328 bottles when the city was invaded in World War II. But when Warsaw was "liberated" by the Russians, they found only 300 bottles of 1668 and a thousand or so from the vintages of 1682, 1737, 1783, and 1811 (but *see* 1590).
1615	**England:** A ban on charcoal burning is introduced to preserve forests for the English fleet. Coal-fired glass is thus found to be significantly stronger than wood-fired glass, as favoured by the French.
1630	**Hungary:** Szepsi Laczkó Máté describes the method for producing Tokaji wine from botrytized grapes.
1631	**France:** The greatest vintage of the 17th century.
1638	**Portugal:** The first Port house is established: C N Kopke & Co.
1642	**USA:** The first vines in what will become New York State are planted by the Dutch.
1644	**France:** First mention of Pinot Gris (as Grauklevner) in Alsace.
1655	**South Africa:** The first vines are planted by Van Riebeek.
1657	**USA:** The first attempt at Prohibition dates back this far, when the General Court of Massachusetts makes it illegal to sell strong liquor "whether known by the name of rumme, strong water, wine, brandy, etc".
1658	**USA:** In the last year of his life, Oliver Cromwell offers by an Act of Assembly 10,000 lb (4,535 kg) of tobacco to whoever "shall first make two tunne of wine raised out of a vineyard made in this colony". This prize was never claimed, and it quietly dropped in 1685, when it was eventually realized that winegrowing would never succeed.
1659	**South Africa:** First wine made by Van Riebeek.

1662	**England:** The first intentionally sparkling wine in the world is documented by Christopher Merret, six years before Dom Pérignon takes up his post as winemaker at the abbey of Hautvillers in Champagne.
1663	**France, England:** Samuel Pepys drinks "Ho Bryan" (Château Haut-Brion), the first branded or single-estate wine documented since Roman times.
1668	**France:** Dom Pérignon takes up his post as cellarmaster at the abbey of Hautvillers.

Dom Pérignon

1673	**England:** The world's first wine auction is held.
1676	**England:** Sparkling Champagne is so popular in England that it is mentioned in English literature (*The Man of Mode* by Sir George Etheridge), 42 years before it was documented in France and 53 years before the first Champagne house is established.
1679	**South Africa:** Simon van der Stel complains about the "revolting sourness" of South African wines.
1680	**South Africa:** Simon van der Stel plants 100,000 vines in Constantia.
1685	**France:** Dom Pérignon is believed to have brought cork from Spain.
1688	**South Africa:** French Huguenots emigrate to the Cape and establish vineyards in the Franschhoek Valley.
1709	**France:** Louis XIV orders the frozen vineyards of the Loire-Atlantique to be replanted with Melon Blanc (Muscadet).
1716	**Italy:** The country's first wine laws are introduced (Chianti).
1718	**France:** The first documented mention of sparkling Champagne in France refers to its initial appearance some 20 years earlier.
1724	**France:** The first claim is made that it was "Dom Pérignon who found the secret of making white sparkling wine".
1729	**France:** Ruinart, the first Champagne house, is founded.
1750	**Spain:** The world's first cork-stopper factory opens in Anguine.
1761	**South Africa:** Constantia wines are exported to Europe.
1766	**England:** Wine from this date is included in the very first Christie's auction (*see* 1965 and 1966).
1768	**England:** The Great Vine (Black Hambourg, aka Schiava Grossa) is planted by Capability Brown at Hampton Court. By 2010, it fills an entire greenhouse from a single trunk and requires a large field next to the greenhouse to remain fallow to sustain its roots.

The Great Vine

1769	**USA:** The first vines planted in California by Franciscan monks in San Diego are the so-called Mission grapes (Criolla), brought from Mexico, but there is no documented evidence of wine produced until 1782.
1775	**Germany:** The practice of late harvesting is born at Schloss Johannisberg following the delay of a messenger from the prince-bishop of Fulda. Since 1718 it had been customary not to start the harvest at Schloss Johannisberg until it was announced in writing by the prince-bishop, but the messenger sent out in 1775 was delayed for 14 days. When the messenger finally turned up, many of the grapes were rotten, and it was feared the wine would be ruined. Instead, it was so special that Schloss Johannisberg started to produce late-harvest (*Spätlese*) wines on a regular basis. Just three years later, Thomas Jefferson writes about how Schloss Johannisberg stands out: "It has none of the acid of Hochheim and other Rheniss grapes … 1775 is the best!"
1782	**USA:** California wine is first documented. It was produced at San Juan Capistrano by Fathers Pablo de Mugártegui and Gregorio Amurrió, from vines transported by Don José Camacho, commander of the supply ship *San Antonio*.
1783	**Germany:** The country's first sparkling wines are made in the Rhine (*see* 1791).

1786	**USA:** The first commercial vineyard and winery in America is established near Philadelphia by Frenchman Peter Legaux of the Pennsylvania Vine Company.
1788	**South Africa:** The dessert wines of Constantia achieve legendary status throughout Europe. **Australia:** The first vineyard is planted at Farm Cove in New South Wales by the first governor, Captain Arthur Phillip, with vines brought from Rio de Janeiro and the Cape of Good Hope. • Nine vines are planted by William Bligh of HMS Bounty at the eastern end of Adventure Bay on Bruny Island. This is much farther south than Tasmanian vines grow today; consequently, it is no surprise that they had not survived when Bligh returned in 1791 (*see* 1823).
1790	**USA:** President George Washington serves Champagne to Senator Johnson of South Carolina before the Champagne houses start shipping to America.
1791	**Germany:** The first mention of a sparkling German wine is recorded in *Intelligenziablatt* by Johann Funcke, who states that sparkling wine has been made in the Rhine since 1783.
1793	**France:** The temperature recorded in Alsace on 21 June is -20°C (-4°F)!
1794	**Germany:** The first recorded *Eiswein* is produced in Franconia, although both Pliny and Martial document wines produced from frozen grapes in Roman times.
1799	**Ukraine:** The country's first sparkling wine is supposedly produced by Peter Simon Pallas, a German professor of natural history, in the Crimean town of Sudak.
1801	**France:** Thanks to Jean-Antoine Chaptal, the amount of sugar added to wine to increase its potential alcoholic strength (chaptalization) or sparkling (as in Champagne) can now be accurately quantified.
1803	**Germany:** Napoleon conquers the Rhine region, taking its vineyards from the Church and dividing them between several families, who are told to produce the lightest, most flavourful white wines in the world.
1806	**France:** One year after the death of her husband, the widow Clicquot invents the precursor to the *pupitre*, a kitchen table with holes cut in its top, and begins *remuage* (riddling) experiments.
1808	**USA:** The country's first temperance organization is formed. Although the Temperance Society of Moreau and Northumberland sought to eliminate the sale and drinking of spirits (except for medical purposes), in its earliest days it only wanted to temper the consumption of other less alcoholic beverages, not ban them – so they said.

Temperance Society founders: Rev L Armstrong, Dr B J Clark, Gardner Stow, and James Mott

1811	**Canada:** Johann Schiller establishes the first Canadian winery in the area of Mississauga, now known as Cooksville, Ontario.
1813	**USA:** The Massachusetts Society for the Suppression of Intemperance similarly seeks to discourage, not prohibit, "hard liquor" (spirits).
1816	**USA:** The first "dry legislation" is enacted, prohibiting Sunday sales of any form of alcohol in Indiana.
1817	**USA:** Governor Sola reports 53,687 grape-bearing vines growing in Los Angeles.
1818	**France:** Antoine Müller, the *chef de caves* at Champagne Veuve Clicquot, perfects *remuage* by taking the Grande Dame's kitchen table one huge step closer to being a fully fledged *pupitre* by cutting the holes at an angle of 45 degrees.
1820	**France:** The first sparkling Burgundy is produced by J Laussere of Nuits-St-George.
1822	**France:** Louis Pasteur is born in the small wine village of Dole in the Jura region (*see* 1857 and 1864). **USA:** Postulated earliest date by which George Gibbs could have imported Zinfandel vines from the Schönbrunn collection in Vienna, Austria, which logically should have included Crljenak Kastelanski (Zinfandel) because Schönbrunn was supposed to have housed every variety grown in the Austro-Hungarian Empire. Many of the vines received by Gibbs were not named, though, and Crljenak Kastelanski was not among those that were.

	Australia: The first Australian wine documented is made in New South Wales by Gregory Blaxland from vines planted at Ermington, a few kilometres down river from Captain Phillip's second vineyard (*see* 1788). **South Africa:** Of just over 22 million vines growing in the Cape vineyards, 21 million are the "green grape", aka Sémillon.
1823	**Australia:** The first vineyard in Tasmania is planted by Bartholomew Broughton at Prospect Farm (but *see* 1788 and 1956).
1824	**Australia:** In this year, some believe, James Busby plants the first Hunter Valley vineyard at Kirkton, run by his brother-in-law William Kelman. Other sources suggest the vineyard is established in 1825 or 1830 (the Kelman Winery celebrated its 100th anniversary in 1930). Certainly, Busby arrived with cuttings in 1824, and there is no record of their being lost or destroyed.
1825	**USA:** The first vines in what will become Washington State are planted at Fort Vancouver on the Columbia River by traders working for the Hudson's Bay Company. **Slovakia:** The country's first sparkling wine is produced by messrs Hubert and Habermann near Pozsony (today Bratislava), then part of Hungary.
1826	**Germany:** George Kessler at Esslingen is generally accepted as the first German sparkling-wine producer (but *see* 1783 and 1791).
1827	**France:** In *Oenologie Française*, Jean-Alexandre Cavoleau claims that Hermitage is purchased by the Bordeaux wine trade to blend with its own wines.
1829	**Australia:** The first vineyard in Western Australia is planted by Thomas Waters, a veteran winemaker from South Africa, at Olive Farm in the Swan Valley. **Switzerland:** The country's first sparkling wine is produced by Louis-Edouard Mauler at the Abbey of St-Pierre in Môtiers, Neufchâtel.
1830	**USA:** The "Black Zinfardel" catalogued by nurseryman William Prince, owner of the Linnaean Botanic Gardens on Long Island, is presumably Zinfandel, although the etymological origin of Zinfardel is unknown. (It could have been confused in cataloguing with Zierfandler, a white Austrian variety.) The "Black Zinfardel" is later sold as Zinfindal and Zinfendel (*see* 1846). **Australia:** The first Cabernet Sauvignon, Riesling, and Verdelho in Australia are planted by William Macarthur at Camden Park near Penrith in New South Wales.
1833	**USA:** The first commercial winery in California is established by *bordelais* Jean-Louis Vignes.
1834	**France:** Phylloxera is found on European oak trees by French entomologist Boyer de Fonscolombe, who classifies and names the genus, but the deadly native American *Phylloxera vastatrix* (hereafter referred to in this chronology simply as phylloxera) is not yet identified. **Australia:** The first vineyard in Victoria is planted by William Ryrie in the Yarra Valley.
1836	**Australia:** The first vineyard in South Australia is planted by John Barton Hack at Chichester Gardens, North Adelaide. **USA:** The first vines in Napa are planted by George Yount (who gave his name to Yountville) in a vineyard he named Napanook, now part of Dominus Estate.
1841	**Australia:** The first vines in the Barossa are planted by Joseph Gilbert at Pewsey Vale.
1842	**Austria:** The first Austrian sparkling wine is produced by Robert Schlumberger in Vienna. **USA:** The first American sparkling wine is produced by Nicholas Longworth in Cincinnati. **England:** The original screw-type Kilner jar, the earliest precursor to the screwcap, is invented by John Kilner of Yorkshire.
1843	**Australia:** The country's first sparkling wine is produced by James King Irrawing in the Hunter Valley (*see also* 1883 and 1920). **USA:** Portland, Maine, is the first American city to go dry.

Phylloxera vastatrix

1846	**USA:** The first documented use of the Zinfandel spelling is by viticulturist J F Allen.
1851	**USA:** Maine is the first American state to go dry. The Maine Law, as it becomes known, is the model for other states to outlaw the sale of alcohol. **Spain:** The first Spanish sparkling wine is produced by Antoni Gali Comas.
1852	**USA:** This is when, according to Arpad Haraszthy, Zinfandel was introduced to California by his father, the legendary Agoston Haraszthy, who first planted it at Las Flores, south of San Francisco, and took it with him wherever he went. However, Arpad wrote this account 30 years after the event, while just six years after, in 1858, Agoston failed to mention Zinfandel in his famous *Report on Grapes and Wine of California*. Nor did he mention the variety later that year, when he wrote a long letter to the State Agricultural Society describing his activities at Buena Vista Farm (*see* 1866). • Those who debunk Haraszthy consider that either Captain Frederick W Macondray or William Robert Prince was the first to bring Zinfandel to California. Certainly Macondray was one of two exhibitors of Zinfandel at the Mechanics' Institute Fair in San Francisco in 1857, and the vines had to have been established at least two years prior to that. Interestingly, Macondray and Haraszthy were neighbours.
1854	**USA:** The first vines are planted in Oregon in the Rogue River Valley.
1855	**France:** Bordeaux's famed classification is first published.
1856	**USA:** The boom in the economy and population created by the Gold Rush of the previous 10 years fuels demand for wine and provides both the capital and the entrepreneurs to kick-start the California wine industry, increasing the number of vines grown from 1.5 million in 1856 to 8 million in 1862. • San Francisco vintners start exporting California wines to England, Germany, Russia, and China.
1857	**USA:** Agoston Haraszthy establishes Buena Vista Winery in Sonoma, California, planting 165 different varieties of vine imported from Europe. **France:** Louis Pasteur discovers the role of yeast in the fermentation process.

Louis Pasteur

1858	**USA:** It is speculated that phylloxera reached California by this date (but *see* 1873). • John L Mason patents what could be described as an American version of the Kilner jar (*see* 1842).
1860	**France:** Before anyone has ever heard about phylloxera, Léo Laliman, a viticulturist in Bordeaux, recommends grafting classic *vinifera* vines on to American rootstock as a protection against oidium (powdery mildew).
1861	**USA:** Mary Todd Lincoln, the wife of Abraham Lincoln, starts the practice of serving American wines at the White House.
1862	**France:** Unknown to anyone at the time, phylloxera-infested vines are planted in a *clos* in Roquemaure (now part of AOC Lirac) in the Rhône (*see* 1874 Veuve Borty's confession).
1863	**England:** Phylloxera is identified at Kew Gardens on vines imported from America.
1864	**France:** Louis Pasteur discovers microbial growths in wine and invents pasteurization as a means of combating spoiled wine.
1866	**USA:** The first documented evidence of Zinfandel as a wine comes from Thomas Hart Hyatt, the editor of *California Rural Home Journal*, who describes a Buena Vista wine made "mostly from Mission, Zinfindal [sic], and Black St Peter" (*see* 1852).
1868	**France:** Professor Jules-Émile Planchon of the Montpellier School of Agriculture (hereafter referred to simply as Montpellier) identifies phylloxera as the cause of vineyards dying in the Rhône and deduces that infection spreads via cuttings imported from America by *vignerons* in search of hardy vines to experiment with following the havoc wreaked by oidium (powdery mildew) in the 1840s and 1850s (*see* 1860). **Argentina:** Professor Pouet introduces Cabernet Sauvignon, Malbec, and Merlot from Bordeaux.

1869	**France**: Baron Paul Thénard tries to kill phylloxera with carbon bisulphide-filled trenches. He not only succeeds in killing the bugs but also kills the vines! • Louis Faucon, the owner of a small phylloxera-infested vineyard on a tributary of the Rhône, suffers one calamity after another when his vineyard is severely flooded but is delighted to discover, once the flood has receded, that all the phylloxera has drowned. His vines immediately pick up, and later that year, Faucon enjoys a good harvest (*see* 1874 Faucon).
1870	**France**: The French government offers a prize of 20,000 francs to the inventor of a cure for phylloxera. • The first varietal Sylvaner wine is produced in Alsace (the year that Germany assumed sovereignty). **USA**: Thomas Munson, whose destiny it is to save the vineyards of France, becomes only the second person to graduate from a new college that would eventually become the University of Kentucky. • California overtakes Missouri and Ohio to become the largest winegrowing state in the USA.
1871	**France**: Phylloxera spreads throughout the entire Rhône Valley and reaches Bordeaux, Languedoc, and Provence. **Portugal**: Phylloxera reaches Portuguese vineyards. **Turkey**: Phylloxera reaches Turkish vineyards. Although mostly used for table grapes, the first vineyard infected had been planted with Bordeaux vines (imported by Kösé Riza Efendi).
1872	**France**: The first experiments to graft classic *vinifera* varieties on to American rootstock are conducted at Montpellier. **Austria**: Phylloxera reaches Austrian vineyards (Klosterneuberg).
1873	**Switzerland**: Phylloxera reaches Swiss vineyards. **France**: Planchon travels to America to research phylloxera. **USA**: The first phylloxera identified in California is found in a Sonoma vineyard (but *see* 1858).
1874	**France**: Veuve Borty, the widow of a wine merchant in Roquemaure (*see* 1862), confesses to Professor Planchon that in 1862 her late husband had been given a gift of some "exotic" vines by a friend who had brought them with him from New York. Her husband had planted them in a walled garden, but the following year he noticed that Grenache and Alicante vines in the same garden had started to wither; then, in 1864 and 1865, they heard about vines in surrounding vineyards mysteriously dying. • Louis Faucon presents his paper *Sur la Maladie de la Vigne et sur Son Traitement par le Procédé de la Submersion* to the Académie des Sciences in Paris. He recommends flooding a vineyard for at least 40 days, which is discovered to be effective, but only temporarily, since it does not prevent reinfection. Flooding is also very expensive, requiring an enormous infrastructure of dikes, gates, pipes, steam-powered pumps, and of course an abundant supply of water. Even then, not all vineyards can be flooded. Most of the greatest sites are all on slopes to some extent. Furthermore, growers are acutely aware that *vinifera* vines do not like "wet feet"; consequently, it is debatable how many times a vineyard might withstand flooding, if indeed it was capable of flooding and its owners could afford multiple remedies. • The French government increases its prize for a cure for phylloxera from 20,000 francs (*see* 1870) to 300,000 francs and commissions Montpellier to evaluate all submissions.
1875	**Spain**: Phylloxera reaches Spanish vineyards. **France**: Phylloxera reaches Corsica, western Loire, and southern Burgundy. • Professor Millardet of Bordeaux starts work on hybrid rootstocks (*see* 1887). **Serbia**: Phylloxera is identified at Pancsova (now Pancevo), just east of Belgrade. **USA**: The first screw-sealed bottle is invented by William T Fry of Brooklyn, New York, who develops a male-threaded *collerette* that encircles the neck of the bottle, on to which a female-threaded top is screwed.
1877	**France**: Of the 696 remedies for phylloxera submitted in response to the French government's prize of 300,000 francs, Montpellier considers 317 worthy of evaluation and puts them to the test in a nearby infested vineyard (Las Sorres). Only two remedies have any effect on phylloxera – potassium sulphide dissolved in human urine, and the direct application of sulphide – but neither method is fully effective, and what control they do achieve is only temporary, since neither solution prevents reinfestation. • The first reference in Champagne to the addition of a liqueur to promote a second fermentation is made by Professor Robinet in Epernay, 215 years after Merret's paper to the Royal Society (*see* 1662). • A sparkling Sauternes from Messrs Normandin Sparkling Sauternes Manufactory, in the tiny Charentes village of Châteauneuf, receives a gold medal at the Concours Régional d'Angoulême.

	USA: French scientist Pierre Viala is tasked with saving Cognac from phylloxera and visits Thomas Munson in Denison, Texas, where the two agree the most appropriate American rootstock to graft the region's vines. Munson starts shipping cuttings to France and gears up production for future shipments.
1878	**USA**: The first true screwcap (a moulded metal cap fitting over a screw moulded into the glass neck of the bottle) is patented by August Voege of Brooklyn, New York, in June 1878, and a variant is patented by John K Chase of New York in September 1878. Both are described as an "improvement in screwcaps for bottles", indicating that cruder screwcaps were in prior use. **France**: Phylloxera has invaded 39 *départements*, killing off 370,000 ha (914,300 acres) of vineyard and infecting another 250,000 ha (617,800 acres). • The first-ever instances of downy mildew in Europe appear in France, having crossed the Atlantic on American vines imported to defeat phylloxera. • Lermat-Robert et Cie of Bordeaux enters a sparkling Barsac at the Paris Exhibition. • Henry Vizetelly tastes "sparkling Chambertin, Romanée, and Vougeot of the highest order" at the Paris Exhibition.
1879	**France**: State-licensed nurseries are established to mass produce rootstocks. **Italy**: Phylloxera reaches Italian vineyards.
1880	**France**: All vineyard regions with the exception of Champagne and Alsace (then part of Germany) are infested by phylloxera. • The addition of a *liqueur de tirage* starts to be become widespread in Champagne. Prior to this, most Champagne was rendered sparkling by bottling before the first fermentation had ceased, a haphazard judgment that often resulted in a massive loss of production from exploding bottles. • The first sparkling wine in Alsace (then part of Germany) is produced by a small grower in Guebwiller called Dirler. **Slovenia**: Phylloxera reaches Pisece and Bizeljsko in the Bizeljsko-Sremic area. **Italy**: Phylloxera reaches Sicily. **USA, France**: Swiss-born Hermann Jaeger, the father of direct-producing hybrid vines and owner of a nursery vineyard at New Switzerland, in the southwest Ozark region of Missouri, has shipped many of the "millions upon millions of American cuttings" that had been imported by France to replant phylloxera-infested vineyards. • US state legislation requires the University of California to commence research and instruction in viticulture and winemaking. • The first mention of the use of agglomerated cork is in a US patent for protective headgear issued to Abraham Moses.
1881	**France**: At the International Phylloxera Congress held in Bordeaux, the consensus is that the only viable long-term solution for vineyards continuing to grow classic *vinifera* varieties is to graft them on to American rootstock. Direct-producing hybrid vines also present a viable long-term solution, but whatever anyone thinks about the wines they produce, everybody agrees that they cannot replicate the classic quality, character, and style of famous French wines. **Germany**: Phylloxera reaches German vineyards. **Australia**: Australia's first "sparkling burgundy" is rosé coloured and produced from Pinot Noir grapes by Auguste d'Argent at the Victorian Champagne Company in Melbourne (*see* 1920).
1882	**Germany**: Carl Wienke invents the Waiter's Friend, which becomes the workhorse corkscrew for sommeliers all over the world and remains so for more than 100 years. *The Waiter's Friend*
1883	**USA**: The first commercial winery in Texas, the Val Verde Winery, is established at Del Rio by Italian immigrant Frank Qualia. **Algeria**: Aware of the devastation caused by phylloxera in France and the plans to build the vineyards of Algeria into a second viticultural France, the colonial government imposes a strict law requiring growers to report any potential symptoms. • The French are the first to experiment with cool fermentation, in a bid to improve the odds for winemaking in such a hot country (but *see* 1330 BC). **Australia**: Roseworthy College is established for agricultural studies but does not yet include winemaking (*see also* 1843 and 1920).

1884	**France:** The refrigerated bath required for *disgorgement à la glace* is invented by a Belgian, Armand Walfart; the system is first used in the same year by Champagne Henri Abelé. **Algeria:** In a further bid to protect Algeria from phylloxera, all imports of vines, fruits, and fresh vegetables are banned.
1885	**Algeria:** Phylloxera is discovered at Sidi-Bel-Abbès and Tlemcen. **New Zealand:** Phylloxera reaches New Zealand. **Israel:** The country's first commercial winery, Carmel Winery, is established by Baron Edmond James de Rothschild at Zikhron Ya'akov.
1886	**South Africa:** Phylloxera reaches South Africa.
1887	**France:** The first completely successful rootstock, 41B, a Chasselas x Berlandieri cross, is launched at the Mâcon Wine Congress by its breeder, Professor Millardet.
1888	**USA:** Thomas Munson is made a Chevalier of the Légion d'Honneur by the French government for his part in saving the French wine industry by supplying millions of American vines for grafting purposes. The French send a delegation to Denison, Texas, to present Munson with this award (*see also* 1870 USA and 1877 USA). **Peru:** Phylloxera reaches Peruvian vineyards.
1889	**Austria:** Phylloxera has destroyed more than 42,000 ha (104,000 acres). **England:** Most references credit Dan Rylands of Hope Glass Works in Barnsley as the inventor of the screwcap at this date, but the Americans got there more than a decade earlier (*see* 1878).
1890	**France:** Bordeaux and Burgundy commence a complete replanting of their vineyards with grafted vines. **Australia:** The first vines are planted in Coonawarra by John Riddoch at Yallum. • The first vines are planted in the Margaret River Valley by the Cullen family at Bunbury. **Czech Republic:** Phylloxera reaches Šatov, in the Znojmo district of Moravia. **India:** This is the earliest date by which phylloxera is speculated to have reached India. This country's emerging British-built wine industry was killed off by phylloxera in the 1990s.
1891	**USA:** The crown cap (aka crown cork, and originally called the Crown Cork Tin Bottle Cap) is invented by William Painter of Maryland and sold by his employee, King Camp Gillette, who would go on to invent the disposable safety razor.
1892	**Israel:** Phylloxera destroys the vines at Carmel, the country's only vineyard (*see* 1885). **China:** First *vinifera* vines are taken to China by Chinese businessman Zhang Bishi.
1893	**France:** Wine production exceeds pre-phylloxera level for the first time.
1894	**France:** Phylloxera finally reaches Champagne. **Italy:** First mention of Pinot Nero (aka Pinot Noir) in Italy being grown in Trentino and the Alto Adige.
1895	**Portugal:** All Portuguese vineyard areas are infested with phylloxera. The northern areas are worst affected, destroying 32,000 ha (79,000 acres) in the Douro region alone. **USA:** Mass production of wine bottles becomes possible following the invention of an automatic glass-blowing machine by Michael Owens of the Libby Glass Company in Toledo, Ohio (*see* 1903). **Algeria:** Only the Alger *département* is free of phylloxera. *Michael Owens*
1898	**Greece:** Phylloxera reaches Thessaloniki. **Australia:** Experimental cool fermentation is undertaken.
1901	**Australia:** The first documented mention of Malbec is by Isaax Himmelhoch, who has planted it at his Grodno vineyard at Liverpool, near Sydney.
1903	**USA:** The first fully automatic bottle-making machine, "The Owens Machine", goes operational (*see* 1895). **Algeria:** Despite phylloxera penetrating almost all of Algeria, the French manage to increase Algerian vineyards from just 15,000 ha (37,000 acres) in 1878 to 167,000 ha (412,600 acres) by 1903.
1904	**France:** Phylloxera reaches Alsace (then part of Germany).
1907	**France:** The Charmat Method is invented by Eugène Charmat.
1908	**USA:** The viticultural department of the University of California moves to Davis.
1909	**USA:** Charles McManus is said to have invented agglomerate cork closures. **Croatia:** Phylloxera is discovered in Dalmatia.
1910	**China:** A French priest converts a Beijing church graveyard into a vineyard and small winery called Shangyi (*see* 1949 and 1987).
1912	**Macedonia:** Phylloxera is found in Macedonian vineyards. **South Korea:** Phylloxera reaches Korea (table grapes).
1914	**France:** Phylloxera has destroyed 1 million ha (2.47 million acres) of French vineyards since 1875.
1920	**USA:** More than 30 states are already totally dry by the time the Eighteenth Amendment to the Constitution is officially ratified, enforcing Prohibition throughout the entire USA. Despite this, 100 wineries continue production under strict federal control for medicinal purposes, for sacramental wines, and to make "salted wine" for cooking. **Australia:** It is unknown when Australia's "sparkling burgundy" evolved from a rosé-coloured Pinot Noir *cuvée* with a touch of sweetness to a seriously sweet, deep-coloured, pure Shiraz fizz, but it is believed that Great Western (which had been producing the lighter style since 1890) was the instigator and that the change in grape variety and style began in or around 1920 (*see also* 1843 and 1883).
1921	**Luxembourg:** The country's first sparkling wine is produced by Bernard-Massard.
1933	**USA:** National Prohibition ends. • E & J Gallo is established; it will become the world's largest wine producer from the 1960s until Constellation Brand is formed (*see* 2003).
1934	**USA:** The Wine Institute is incorporated, and California introduces state wine standards. • Frank Schoonmaker and Tom Marvel publish *The Complete Wine Book*, in which they urge American winemakers to plant better vine varieties, adopt better winemaking standards, and sell honest, informatively labelled wines, rather than relying on borrowed European names.
1935	**France:** Introduction of the AOC system. **Tunisia:** Phylloxera reaches Tunisia and destroys all vines there.
1936	**Australia:** Roseworthy College launches the nation's first winemaking course.
1939	**USA:** Frank Schoonmaker starts sourcing and selling varietal wines from California, New York, and Ohio. Growers in all these states, but particularly California, start to replant their vineyards with classic *vinifera* varieties as soon as it is evident that Schoonmaker's wines are attracting a significant premium. The New World varietal wine trend begins.
1944	**France:** In his capacity as the Vichy mayor of Paris, Pierre Taittinger, founder of Champagne Taittinger and the far-right Jeunesses Patriotes, persuades General von Choltitz, the German governor of Paris, to defy Hitler's order to destroy the city.
1945	**South Africa:** Nederburg Première Cuvée is the country's first *cuve close* sparkling wine (*see* 1971).
1948	**Italy:** The first vintage of Sassicaia, the first of the so-called super-Tuscans, is harvested (*see also* 1971).
1949	**China:** The Shangyi in Beijing is taken over by the Chinese government (*see* 1910 and 1987).
1951	**Australia:** The first (experimental) vintage of the legendary Penfold's Grange is harvested.
1956	**Australia:** The first vines in Tasmania's modern viticultural era are planted by Jean Miguet at La Provence (now called, for legal reasons, Providence).
1957	**USA:** When James Zellerbach – industrialist, financier, head of the Marshall Plan mission in Italy, and US ambassador to Italy – makes the first Chardonnay at his Hanzell vineyard in Sonoma, he leaves nothing to chance, building a small but high-tech, gravity-fed winery full of gleaming, temperature-controlled, stainless-steel vats equipped with inert-gas blanketing that is way ahead of its time. He is also the first to insist on French oak barrels. When the Hanzell 1957 Chardonnay is

released and found by critics to have a "complex French flavour", other wineries start ordering French oak. While some eventually go back to American oak for most or all of their wines, the French oak standard has been set for premium Chardonnay in California. • Ukrainian viticulturist Konstantin Frank does something that Americans thought impossible: he successfully grows *vinifera* grapes in New York State.

1958
USA: The University of California issues a report on suitable rootstock, recommending the high-yielding AxR#1 as "the nearest approach to an all-purpose stock", despite admitting that it had "only moderate phylloxera resistance". The clock for the second coming starts ticking.
Russia: A large part of the Fukier Tokaji collection (*see* 1606), which had been missing since the beginning of World War II, turns up at an extraordinary tasting laid on by Marshall Zhukov for his personal friend General Alan Shapley, deputy commander of the US Marine Corps. The vintages include 1811, 1783, 1737, 1682, and 1668 but unfortunately no 1606!

1960
Argentina: When Moët & Chandon establishes Bodegas Chandon, which will make and sell Champaña, it is the beginning of the end of Champagne's integrity in its defence against others abusing its appellation (*see* 1993 and 2007).

1961
France: This is the greatest postwar Bordeaux vintage. • By the 1980s, the market performance of this vintage of Château Palmer will have led to the creation of the "super-second" concept, whereby some high-performing châteaux that are not First Growths start achieving prices close to First Growth prices and, as Palmer demonstrates, super-seconds do not necessarily have to be Second Growths.

1963
Australia: The first Cabernet Sauvignon is planted in the Hunter Valley.
Portugal: This is the greatest postwar Port vintage.

1965
USA: The first commercial use of mechanical harvesting takes place in New York State, but experimental machines have been tested in California and elsewhere since the early 1950s.
England: Christie's makes plans to reopen a wine department.

Mechanical harvesting

1966
England: Michael Broadbent MW is hired to head Christie's new wine department, exactly 200 years after its first wine auction (*see* 1766).
USA: Robert Mondavi opens his Napa Valley winery.

1967
USA, Italy: Dr Austin Goheen of UC Davis visits Bari in Puglia and is so reminded of Zinfandel when tasting the local Primitivo that he takes back cuttings to grow side by side with Zinfandel. They appear to be identical.
Australia: The country's first vines of the modern era are planted at Vasse Felix by Dr Tom Cullity.

1968
France: Vins de Pays regulations are established.

1969
Armenia: Phylloxera reaches Armenian vineyards.
USA: Schramsberg's first rosé sparkling wine is produced from 100% Gamay (a grape that was permitted in the Aube region of Champagne until 1949).

1971
Australia: The first Chardonnay is planted in the Hunter Valley. • The first vines in the Canberra District are planted by two doctors, Dr Edgar Riek (at Cullarin, on the northwest shore of Lake George) and Dr John Kirk (at Clonakilla Vineyard, in Murrumbateman).
Italy: The first vintage of Tignanello, the second so-called super-Tuscan (*see* 1948).
England: Hugh Johnson's *The World Atlas of Wine* is published, establishing for the very first time a sense of place for everyone who drinks wine. People like Frank Schoonmaker have been trying to get across such a notion since the 1930s, but until Johnson the most this amounted to was a line drawing of minimal detail. Now they can sit back in an armchair, sip a delicious wine, and find out precisely where it came from on a beautiful, full-colour, highly detailed map.
South Africa: Kaapse Vonkel is widely cited in South Africa itself as the country's first sparkling wine produced by the *méthode champenoise*, yet one of the most reliable of those sources, *The Complete Book of*

South African Wine, also states in the very next paragraph, "In earlier days in the Cape, all sparkling wines were made this way, but with the perfection of tank fermentation, bottle fermentation all but disappeared." The first South African sparkling wine was probably produced in the 19th century, but exactly when and by whom is not yet known (*see also* 1945).

1973
France: The first Vins de Pays are available to purchase.
USA: Domaine Chandon establishes the first French sparkling-wine venture in California, at Yountville in Napa County.

1975
USA: Zinfandel and Primitivo are declared to be one and the same following isozyme "fingerprinting" by Wade Wolfe, a PhD student at UC Davis, where both varieties have been growing side by side since 1967.
Italy: Talento Metodo Classico sparkling wines are established.
England: Colin Parnell and Tony Lord launch *Decanter* magazine.
Australia: While teaching viticulture at Roseworthy Agricultural College, Dr Richard Smart introduces the concept of vineyard region homoclime matching, arguing that if climate and, especially, temperature are so important in affecting the composition of grapes and, thus, the style and quality of wine, then why not, for example, look in Australia for similar climates (homoclimes) to those of famous French regions?

1976
France, USA: Steven Spurrier holds the famous Judgment of Paris wine tasting that pits the best California wines against the best French wines.
USA: The concept of AVAs (Approved Viticultural Areas, often referred to as American Viticultural Areas) is considered by the ATF (Bureau of Alcohol, Tobacco and Firearms).
England: The first English sparkling wine is made by two different producers in the same year: Felsted and Pilton Manor.

1977
Australia: Andrew Pire introduces a humidity index to a homoclime-like analysis of Australian wine regions for his PhD thesis at the University of Sydney.

1978
USA: Robert Parker launches *The Wine Advocate*, introducing his 100-point rating system, and the wine world will never be the same again. • The regulations for AVAs are established and differ from the French AOC concept in that, although there must be some topographical and climatical homogeneity of growing zone, there is no attempt to control what grape varieties are grown, how vines should be cultivated, or what style of wine must be produced.

1979
USA: In *The Myth of the Universal Rootstock*, Lucie T Morton wonders why the AxR#1 rootstock became the rootstock of choice for the California wine industry, when the French, who developed it, had long since concluded that AxR#1 and all other *vinifera rupestris* rootstocks are dangerously low in resistance. • Marvin Shanklin buys *Wine Spectator* and turns it into the most successful wine magazine in the world.

1980
USA: The first AVA is established in Augusta, Missouri.
Australia: Dr Richard Smart and Dr Peter Dry of Roseworthy Agricultural College publish their climate classification for Australian viticultural regions, establishing the concept of homoclimes in the public domain. This also includes the first strictly defined meaning of water deficit (calculated over the growing season as the difference between rainfall and estimated vineyard water use).
China: The Tianjin Winery and Rémy Martin launch the Dynasty brand in the first joint Franco-Chinese wine venture.

1981
USA: The Napa Valley is the second AVA to be established.

1982
India: Raphael Brisbois of Piper Heidsieck Technology advises Sham Chougule to establish his Champagne Indage (later changed to Chateau Indage) sparkling-wine vineyard and winery of the modern Indian viticultural era at Narayangaon, in the Sahyadri Mountains north of Puna.

1983
Germany: The Charta organization promoting dry Riesling is founded in the Rheingau.
USA: A new biotype of phylloxera hits Napa and Sonoma vineyards grafted on to AxR#1 rootstock.

1984
England: Robert Joseph and Charles Metcalfe establish the International Wine Challenge (IWC), the first truly international wine competition. Despite being set in a country with no wine-producing industry of its own to speak of, the IWC attracts thousands of wines from countries whose producers had been reluctant to let judges in other wine-producing countries make qualitative assessments about their competitors' wines.
Cyprus: Phylloxera reaches Cypriot vineyards.

1985	**USA:** The Bureau of Alcohol, Tobacco, Firearms, and Explosives rules that Zinfandel may not be used as a synonym for Primitivo, declaring there is not enough evidence to prove Zinfandel and Primitivo are the same. • The first Rhône varieties are planted in California (by Phelps). **Austria:** The "anti-freeze scandal" is misreported by the media as a health scare. It was a scandal, and its greedy perpetrators did untold damage to the reputation of the Austrian wine industry for the next 10 years or so, but it was not a health scare. Ethylene glycol is anti-freeze and highly lethal, but the illegal additive used was diethylene glycol, which is less toxic than alcohol. The more diethylene glycol added, the more alcohol is displaced, and the less toxic the wine becomes! **Australia:** Domaine Chandon establishes its sparkling-wine venture in Victoria's Yarra Valley (*see* 1989).
1986	**Italy:** At least 22 Italians die and 90 others are hospitalized after drinking wine contaminated with methanol. Six suspects are named, and millions of gallons of wine are disposed of.
1987	**China:** The Shangyi winery in Beijing is renamed the Beijing Friendship Winery and, in partnership with Pernod-Ricard, launches the Dragon Seal brand.
1988	**England:** Stuart and Sandy Moss, two Americans from Chicago, purchase Nyetimber, ignore all advice, and kick-start a golden age for English sparkling wine.

Nyetimber vineyard

1989	**Australia:** By Domaine Chandon's third vintage, Tony Jordan has already surpassed the quality established by Domaine Chandon's California operation, even though the latter had a 12-year head-start (*see* 1985).
1991	**Australia:** Dr Richard Smart and colleagues offer a worldwide homoclime-matching service, using computers and international climate databases. **USA:** The French Paradox gets its first mention on the CBS show *60 Minutes*, hosted by Morley Shafer. Within weeks, US sales of red wine have increased 44 per cent, and Gallo's Hearty Burgundy is put on allocation. **England, Chile:** The British publication *Wines & Spirits* reveals that Chile is selling eight times more Sauvignon Blanc than it could possibly produce.
1992	**Germany:** Hans-Peter Frericks sues wine collector Meinhard Görke (aka Hardy Rodenstock) over alleged fake wine. The Munich state court finds that Görke has "adulterated the wine or knowingly offered adulterated wine". Görke appeals, and the pair file criminal complaints against each other for defamation. The action for fraud and the two defamation cases are eventually settled out of court.
1993	**France, South America:** Moët & Chandon admits under pressure that there is no law that requires their subsidiaries to use Champagne or Champaña on its sparkling wines produced in Argentina or Brazil, despite claiming this in numerous court battles around the world (*see* 1960 and 2007). • Château Couhins-Lurton becomes the first Bordeaux *cru classé* to be sealed with a screwcap.
1994	**France:** This is the first vintage when some *bordelais* harvest by tannin ripeness. **USA:** Using DNA typing, Professor Carole Meredith, a plant geneticist at UC Davis, establishes conclusively that Zinfandel and Primitivo are genetically the same.
1995	**France:** Michel Bettane, one of the country's top wine writers, declares, "Today, *appellation contrôlée* guarantees neither quality nor authenticity."
1997	**USA:** An estimated 6,700 ha (16,500 acres) of infected vineyards in Napa and 4,000 ha (10,000 acres) in Sonoma have been uprooted and replanted since the 1983 phylloxera attack. • Professor Carole Meredith uses DNA "fingerprinting" to determine that only four of the seven Petite Sirah vines in the UC Davis collection are in fact Petite Sirah. Two are Durif and one is pure Syrah. **China:** The country's first sparkling wines are produced by Frenchman Denis Degache using 1993 reserve wines. **Azerbaijan:** Phylloxera reaches Nagorno-Karabakh.

2000	**USA:** The 1997 Plumpjack Reserve is sold in two formats, one sealed with a cork, as per normal, and the other sealed with a screwcap. Both are exactly the same wine, but the screwcap is $10 per bottle more expensive. A point is being made.
2001	**Australia, New Zealand:** Dr Richard Smart identifies homoclimes of Martinborough and Marlborough in New Zealand and uses the same principle to search for vineyard locations at Tamar Ridge Estate in Tasmania. Typically, homoclime searches are initially conducted using only monthly maximum and minimum temperatures over the growing season, leaving other data layers – such as rainfall, humidity, sunshine, and calculated moisture stress – to be factored in later for the searches that are most likely to bear fruit. Other data, such as soils, may also be added.
2002	**USA:** Two American scientists, Charles Zuker and Charles Ryber, confirm the Japanese concept of umami, a satisfying savouriness that is the fifth of the five basic tastes recognized by the palate, alongside sweetness, sourness, saltiness, and bitterness. **France:** François Mauss, head of the Grand Jury of European Tasters, describes much of Beaujolais as "not proper wine" and its producers of "consciously commercializing a *vin de merde*".
2003	**USA, Australia:** E & J Gallo is overtaken as the world's largest wine producer when Constellation Brands is formed by merging Canandaigua, the second-largest wine producer in the USA, and BRL Hardy, the second-largest wine producer in Australia.
2004	**USA:** Following the release of the American comedy film *Sideways*, US sales of Pinot Noir increase, while sales of Merlot drop. • Michigan fizz fanatic Larry Mawby launches a sparkling wine called Sex, after submitting as a joke an application for the name and being totally shocked when the federal authorities officially gave him permission (but *see* 2005).
2005	**USA:** Larry Mawby's Sex might have got past the normally puritanical federal authorities in the USA (*see* 2004), but the sparkling wine is refused entry into the UK by the Portman Group, the wine trade's self-regulatory body, which deems it "sexually suggestive", even though there is no illustration or text to suggest that it is meant to be anything other than sex as in gender. However, the Portman Group is perfectly happy to allow many emphatically suggestive labels such as Old Tart, which is illustrated and contains descriptive text full of *double entendres*. **China:** Phylloxera is suddenly rampant in Jiading and Shanghai.

Larry Mawby's Sex

2006	**USA:** Billionaire Bill Koch sues millionaire Meinhard Görke (aka Hardy Rodenstock) over a bottle of "Lafitte 1787" engraved with "Th. J." (supposedly standing for Thomas Jefferson), claiming that he has scientific proof that the wine is a fake and that the initials have been engraved by an electronic tool. A default judgment was entered against Görke in May 2010 because, as a German citizen, he refused to participate (*see also* 1992), but in March 2011 the US District Court of New York threw out Koch's case – not because the bottle was not a fake, but because Koch knew it was a fake when he bought it. **Australia:** Cullen, in the Margaret River, becomes the country's first carbon-neutral winery.
2007	**France, South America:** More than a decade after Moët & Chandon admitted there is no legal requirement for its subsidiaries to prostitute its own Champagne on bottles of South American sparkling wine, this unprincipled practice has stopped (*see* 1960 and 2007).
2008	**USA, England, France:** The film *Bottle Shock* is released. This comedy drama is loosely based on the Judgment of Paris tasting (*see* 1976). • Prince Charles converts his 38-year-old Aston Martin DB6 (a 21st-birthday present from the Queen) to run on bioethanol fuel distilled from surplus English wine; it now gets 1.6 km (1 mile) for 4.5 bottles of wine.
2010	**Finland:** A cache of 168 bottles of Champagne from the 1830s is recovered from a shipwreck in Finland's Åland archipelago. Identified as Champagne Juglar (a brand belonging to Champagne Jacquesson since 1829) and Veuve Clicquot, they are the oldest Champagnes ever tasted – golden in colour, sweet to taste, and extraordinarily fresh for nearly 200 years old.

The WINES of
THE WORLD

AROUND THE WORLD, consumers have continued their gradual move upmarket in quality, switching from white wine to red and Old World to New in the process. If there is any deviation in these trends, it is that some Old World wine countries are staging something of a rally, but so far this has only slowed the drift, not stopped it. Although consumption in some countries has stopped declining, the underlying problem remains surplus production. This is a global phenomenon, but because Europe produces and consumes more than the rest of the world put together, it is a much bigger problem for European countries. Furthermore, it could get worse as of 2016, when the EU is due to scrap planting restrictions.

A WORLD OF WINE
Thousands of wines from all over the world stand ready for tasting during the 27th International Wine Challenge in London.

A WORLD OF WINE

At just over 280 million hectolitres (hl), world wine production has increased by 12 per cent in the past 10 years, but with global wine consumption averaging 240 million hl, there has never been so much surplus production.

ALMOST EVERY COUNTRY produces more wine than it can consume and export, but Europe accounts for more than 80 per cent of the world's surplus production. This problem was created by the Common Agricultural Policy (CAP), which encouraged deliberate overproduction throughout the second half of the 20th century. Even though the wine regime under CAP was altered in 1999 to combat this practice, it has had little impact on the benefit-grabbing growers that the original policy had already bred. They still found it much easier and more profitable to grow huge volumes of the poorest-quality grapes in the sure knowledge that any undrinkable wines would be carted off for so-called crisis distillation. Depending on which report you read, this practice was costing member states between half a billion and two billion euros annually, which was why the EU also allocated half a billion euros a year to grub up uncompetitive vines. Twelve years down the line, the overproduction situation is worse, not better, which is pretty scary, because crisis distillation is due to end in 2012, and from 2016 all restrictions on planting vines are supposed to be removed. From this date, all vineyards will have to sink or swim on the basis of their commercial competitiveness, without any state-subsidized support. However, seeing is believing with the EU – thus, cynics among us might expect these reforms to fail, and extensions to these deadlines will be the first step.

BEWARE OF ALL-CONSUMING FACTS

Statistics for *per capita* wine consumption are notoriously unreliable. Even supposedly the same statistic (ie, *per capita* consumption for the same country in the same year) can vary in different documents and tables from the same organization. There are many anomalies at work. The Luxembourgois, to quote one major reference, "leave everyone else standing" when it comes to wine consumption, but the Belgians and Germans use their country as a giant superstore, buying up wine, cigarettes, and petrol in bulk because of the significantly lower taxes. The trade is so vast and Luxembourg's population so small that this cross-border trading distorts the imbibing prowess of the Luxembourgois, so precisely where they fit in the *per capita* scheme of things is debatable. By contrast, the population of France is so large that the trade makes no difference, and the Luxembourg trade would, in any case, be offset by cross-Channel transactions. Holiday-resort islands, principalities, and tax havens with small populations, such as the Turks and Caicos Islands, Andorra, and the Cayman Islands, are prone to similar distortions, with much of the wine enjoyed by tourists rather than inhabitants. Quite why the Vatican City should top the chart is anybody's guess, although it is well known for its catholic taste. Small discrepancies may be due to the use of different 12-month periods, with some organizations using pure annual figures, while others use mid-year to mid-year and differing statistical adjustments. Such tables therefore generally provide a good overview, rather than a detailed picture.

INTERNATIONALIZATION?

Some critics are obsessed by what they see as a growing internationalization of wine. This is often ascribed to the spread of such ubiquitous grapes as Chardonnay and Cabernet Sauvignon, especially into new and emerging regions, and often at the expense of indigenous varieties. It is also attributed to a perceived homogenization in style due to technology, flying winemakers, and schools of oenology, where winemakers are all taught to sing from the same sheet. Anyone who has to taste thousands of wines for a living gets "Chardonnayed out" far too frequently these days, but I believe there are good reasons not to be so pessimistic.

Those ubiquitous grapes

They were a necessary evil. It was not that long ago when it was a relief to taste a fresh young Chardonnay in parts of Languedoc-Roussillon, let alone Spain, southern Italy, Sardinia, Greece, and much more obscure wine-producing regions of the world. As recently as the early 1980s, it was almost impossible to discern whether many such areas had any potential whatsoever. Was the dire quality in these places caused by what were (then) unknown grape varieties, by the way that the vines were grown and harvested, a lack of quality winemaking experience, or the crude conditions under which the wines were produced? For anyone setting out to improve quality in these viticultural backwaters, the obvious place to start was in the vineyard and, equally obviously, Chardonnay was the best choice.

While Chardonnay might get a hard time in the press these days, this was not always the case. If readers consult books and articles written in the

WORLD WINE PRODUCTION (THOUSAND HECTOLITRES)

COUNTRY (POSITION 10 YEARS AGO)	2008	2007	2006	2005	2004	2003	2002	2001	2000	1999
1. Italy (2)	51,500	49,631	50,566	50,556	53,000	44,090	44,600	52,290	54,070	58,070
2. France (1)	45,692	52,127	53,400	50,500	57,386	47,350	52,000	55,770	59,740	60,240
3. Spain (3)	36,781	38,290	36,158	35,300	43,162	36,000	34,440	30,940	41,790	32,680
4. USA (4)	24,274	25,125	24,298	23,500	20,109	23,500	25,400	23,000	25,000	20,690
5. Argentina (5)	15,013	15,046	15,396	15,222	15,465	11,200	12,150	15,840	12,540	15,890
6. Australia (8)	14,750	9,620	14,628	14,001	13,811	11,800	12,200	10,770	8,590	8,510
7. China (7)	14,500	14,000	13,000	11,050	12,467	10,860	10,800	10,800	10,500	10,260
8. Germany (6)	10,363	9,000	9,256	9,100	10,047	8,290	10,180	9,080	10,080	12,290
9. South Africa (9)	10,300	10,200	10,130	8,310	9,279	7,610	7,610	7,610	6,950	7,970
10. Chile (12)	8,690	8,280	8,450	7,886	6,301	5,750	5,750	5,650	6,670	4,810
11. Portugal (10)	6,049	7,542	7,267	6,645	7,475	6,800	6,270	7,430	6,690	7,810
12. Romania (11)	5,288	5,015	2,602	3,800	6,166	5,460	5,000	5,500	5,460	6,500
13. Russia (18)	5,000	5,000	5,000	4,200	4,000	4,100	3,430	3,430	3,230	2,903
14. Moldova (21)	3,650	3,600	3,597	2,400	2,620	2,400	2,100	1,400	2,020	1,332
15. Greece (13)	3,337	3,874	3,997	4,093	4,295	4,950	5,000	4,280	4,600	3,680
16. Hungary (14)	3,222	3,144	3,103	3,100	4,340	4,200	3,800	5,410	4,300	3,340
17. Brazil (15)	3,000	3,000	2,372	2,850	3,925	4,000	3,200	3,200	3,000	3,190
18. Ukraine (16)	2,400	2,400	2,460	2,400	2,400	2,390	2,668	2,800	2,912	3,007
19. Austria (19)	2,300	2,300	2,256	2,259	2,735	3,250	2,600	2,530	2,340	2,800
20. New Zealand (22)	2,052	1,476	1,332	1,022	1,192	550	890	533	602	606
21. Bulgaria (17)	1,800	1,757	1,708	1,961	2,327	2,400	2,390	2,606	2,700	3,001
22. Croatia (20)	1,600	1,600	1,592	2,600	2,600	2,600	2,200	2,040	1,890	2,090
Other	12,337	12,673	12,467	15,895	14,281	13,030	13,192	14,251	17,826	8,341
World TOTAL	283,898	284,700	285,035	278,650	299,383	262,580	267,870	277,160	293,500	280,010

Source: COPS; CIES; Wine Institute (USA); TDA; and individual national statistics

1980s, they will discover Chardonnay to be universally revered as one of the greatest white wine grapes in the world. Furthermore, its ability to transplant varietal characteristics to myriad soils and climates throughout the world was considered uncanny and, if anything, served to confirm its nobility. Jancis Robinson waxed lyrical about Chardonnay in her seminal work *Vines, Grapes and Wines* (1986), and even today only the most prejudiced wine drinker would deny that the best white Burgundies rank among the very greatest of dry white wines. If a winemaker in a lowly area of southern France, an Aegean island, or parts of China could not produce a half-decent wine out of the world's greatest, best-travelled grape variety, the vineyards in question would have been written off long ago.

Decline of indigenous varieties

Far from being under the threat of decline, these varieties owe their survival to the likes of Chardonnay and Cabernet Sauvignon muscling in on their areas of production. Had the so-called international varieties not achieved a certain success, these areas would have been grubbed up long ago (between 1980 and 1994, the area under vine throughout the world plummeted from over 10 million hectares to less than 8 million, this loss almost entirely stemming from the Old World). Having demonstrated a suitability for viticulture via yardsticks like Chardonnay, local winemakers started to apply the standards learned to the indigenous varieties that had once been the underperformers. In the New World, of course, there are virtually no indigenous grapes suited to winemaking, but again the experience with benchmark international varieties has encouraged growers in new and emerging wine areas to experiment with other European varieties. In both Old and New Worlds, there is too much ordinary Chardonnay being made, but it is only too much for critics and wine enthusiasts, because if it were too much for most consumers, the wines would not exist. If more consumers develop a deeper interest, the market will adapt – so perhaps wine critics should spend more time communicating.

Homogenization of style

Technology is what you make of it. It can enable vast volumes of technically correct wines to be produced with more fruit and fresher flavours, thus enticing greater numbers of consumers to migrate from popular to finer wines, and that's not a bad thing. When the best technology is combined with the best traditions, it can also improve the quality and expressiveness of highly individual wines, and that's not bad either.

What about so-called flying winemakers? Are they responsible for homogenization in style? I cannot imagine how they can be, as they make less than one per cent of one per cent of the world's wine. What flying winemakers have done is to leave a certain level of cleanliness and competence in their wake, and to show winemakers in underperforming wineries what can be achieved. They have also created a reverse flow in terms of where winemakers go to seek practical experience. Over the past 30 years, New World winemakers had gone to Europe

to pick up tips on fruit handling and winemaking techniques; now the most inquisitive Europeans go to Australia, New Zealand, or California to learn.

As for schools of oenology, it used to be *de rigueur* to have the likes of Bordeaux, Dijon, or Montpellier on a winemaker's CV, but now the university faculties at Roseworthy (Australia) and Davis (USA) are the fashion, as much in Europe as the New World itself. There might be a danger that these schools are producing technically correct oenologists trained not to take risks, rather than winemakers whose passion is intimately entwined with the sort of risk-taking that can result in something truly special. However, ultimately, it is better for a winemaker to understand what he or she is doing, though even that statement has its exceptions, with many a self-taught winemaker who has never opened a book on oenology producing some of the world's most stunning wines.

PER CAPITA CONSUMPTION – HIGHEST CONSUMING COUNTRIES (LITRES PER PERSON PER YEAR)

COUNTRY	2008	2007	2006	2005	2004	2003	2002	2001	2000	1999
1. Vatican City*	66.7	53.9	59.4	62.0	66.7					
2. Norfolk Island*	57.4	59.1	54.5	50.3	58.2					
3. France	53.2	53.2	53.6	55.1	54.6	55.4	56.0	56.9	55.9	57.2
4. Luxembourg *	52.7	52.7	52.7	53.5	55.4	55.8	60.9	59.4	65.1	62.8
5. Andorra*	51.8	51.9	56.4	60.1	63.0					
6. Italy	50.1	48.0	46.4	46.5	48.7	51.1	51.0	50.0	51.0	51.5
7. Portugal	44.3	44.8	45.2	45.5	46.3	52.6	43.0	47.0	46.0	48.0
8. Slovenia	43.8	43.8	43.8	43.8	29.9	44.4	31.2	31.1	35.4	28.3
9. Falkland Islands*	42.0	60.4	50.8	14.3	25.6					
10. Croatia	41.2	41.2	41.2	41.3	41.3	39.5	42.1	43.2	42.0	47.0
11. Turks and Caicos Islands*	39.1	33.1	27.3	10.2	9.9					
12. Cayman Islands*	36.9	37.0	40.2	27.8	34.4					
13. Switzerland	36.2	36.6	36.8	37.9	39.0	41.4	41.8	43.1	43.5	43.5
14. Hungary	35.1	35.1	35.1	35.1	30.9	31.6	36.0	35.1	34.0	32.0
15. Spain	32.9	33.3	33.4	33.9	34.4	33.6	29.6	30.0	32.0	34.0
16. Greece	32.8	32.8	32.8	33.6	30.9	22.3	33.9	34.0	34.0	35.2
17. Austria	30.3	29.6	29.3	29.3	29.3	29.4	29.8	28.5	30.5	30.6
18. Guatemala	29.2	33.7	29.7	24.3	23.5					
19. Denmark	27.5	27.5	28.1	28.6	29.6	31.8	32.0	31.2	30.9	29.8
20. Argentina	26.8	27.3	27.8	27.5	27.8	32.1	36.1	36.3	37.8	38.7
Major (population and/or winemaking) countries only										
23. Belgium	25.3	25.3	24.9	24.4	23.9	25.3	24.3	24.2	23.4	23.0
24. Romania	25.1	25.1	24.9	10.7	26.0	22.6	25.3	25.5	23.2	22.7
26. Uruguay	24.9	25.06	25.2	25.3	24.7	22.1	32.8	31.9	32.0	32.0
27. Germany	24.1	24.1	24.2	24.1	24.1	24.4	24.2	24.0	23.1	23.0
28. Australia	22.7	22.7	22.5	22.3	21.5	21.3	21.2	20.5	20.5	20.4
29. New Zealand	21.8	21.6	21.3	20.0	18.9	17.0	17.1	16.7	17.0	16.3
30. Netherlands	21.7	21.5	21.3	21.1	20.3	22.1	22.5	21.0	19.5	15.9
34. United Kingdom	19.1	19.2	19.3	19.8	17.7	17.9	17.6	17.0	15.3	17.2
36. Bulgaria	18.3	18.28	18.3	18.3	18.3	17.7	21.3	21.4	21.4	21.4
39. Ireland	17.2	17.2	17.4	16.8	13.8	14.7	13.0	12.8	11.6	9.8
40. Chile	16.1	16.1	16.1	16.4	15.8	16.1	15.9	16.0	18.8	18.6
42. Sweden	15.5	15.8	16.2	17.0	14.7	16.9	16.0	15.9	13.5	13.6
44. Norway	13.7	13.6	13.5	13.2	12.5	12.4	11.3	10.9	10.3	9.9
47. Canada	12.2	12.1	12.1	11.5	10.9	10.9	9.1	9.0	8.8	8.6
48. Slovakia	11.0	11.0	11.0	11.0	11.0	11.0	11.9	11.8	11.7	8.2
56. Macedonia	9.8	9.8	9.8	9.8	9.8	10.8	23.7	23.8	23.8	23.8
57. USA	9.7	9.6	9.1	8.8	8.5	8.1	9.7	9.3	8.3	8.3
59. Finland	8.5	8.5	8.5	9.4	9.0	8.7	23.5	21.9	20.6	19.5
60. Czech Republic	8.0	8.0	8.0	8.0	8.0	11.5	10.6	8.7	6.6	6.3
61. South Africa	7.9	7.8	7.8	7.8	7.9					
65. Russia	7.5	7.4	7.4	7.4	7.1					
86. Lebanon	3.5	3.5	3.5	3.5	3.5					
95. Japan	1.9	1.8	1.9	2.0	2.0					
98. Brazil	1.8	1.8	1.8	2.0	1.7					
112. Israel	1.1	1.1	1.1	1.1	1.1					

Sources: Australian Wine Bureau; Wine Institute (USA); CIES; OIV; IVV; TDA; Statec.
* *See Beware of all-consuming facts, facing page*

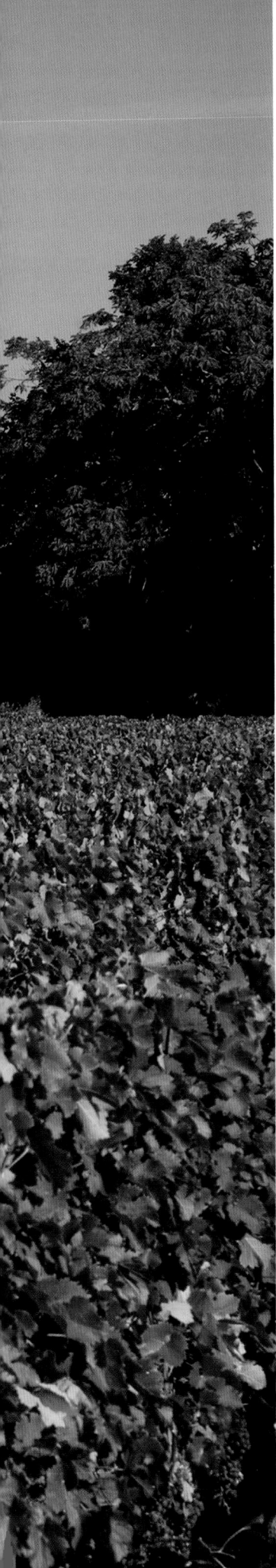

The WINES of
FRANCE

FRENCH WINES ARE REGARDED as the best
in the world, and a thread of this belief is
even shared by France's fiercest New World
competitors. Although the winemakers of
Australia and California, for instance, no longer
try to copy famous French wine styles, they
still consider them benchmarks. The great
French wine regions are a fortunate accident
of geography, climate, and *terroir*. No other
winemaking country in the world has such a
wide range of cool climates; this factor has
enabled France to produce the entire spectrum
of classic wine styles – from the crisp sparkling
wines of Champagne through the smooth
reds of Burgundy to the rich sweet wines of
Sauternes. Over many centuries of trial and
error, the French have discovered that specific
grapes are suited to certain soils, and through
this, distinctive regional wine styles have
evolved, so that every wine drinker knows
what to expect from a bottle of Bordeaux,
Burgundy, Champagne, or Rhône. This has
been the key to success for French wines.

VIEUX CHÂTEAU CERTAN
*This château is the oldest known growth
in Pomerol – hence its prefix. It has belonged to
the Thienpont family since 1924.*

FRANCE

The success of French wine has been built on deservedly famous regions that have been enshrined by Appellation d'Origine Contrôlée (AOC) *laws, but the unwillingness to police this system in any meaningful sense has gradually debased historic reputations at the precise point in history when New World producers have been eager to establish their own wines.*

FRANCE HAS A TOTAL OF 872,000 hectares (2,153,800 acres) under vine, including 70,000 hectares (172,900 acres) for Cognac and 6,000 hectares (14,820 acres) for Armagnac, and produces an average of almost 53 million hectolitres (588 million cases) of wine every year. Since the mid-1980s, French wine production has dropped by 27 per cent in response to a move away from the lower-quality end of the spectrum, as consumers have begun to drink less wine, but of better quality. How that quality is classified is the most contentious issue facing the French wine industry.

HOW FRENCH WINE IS CLASSIFIED
In 1935, when the Institut National des Appellations d'Origine (INAO) was established, France became the first nation to set up a countrywide system for controlling the origin and quality of its wines, although individual wine areas outside France had put in place quality controls much earlier (Chianti in 1716 and Rioja in 1560). INAO's task was to devise the geographical limits of appellations and to enforce the regulations governing them.

Appellation d'Origine Contrôlée (AOC)
There are now more than 480 separate AOCs, covering almost 474,000 hectares (1,171,300 acres), and producing just over 26 million hectolitres (288 million cases) of wine. The AOC laws regulate the grape varieties used, viticultural methods, harvest and yield restrictions, minimum alcohol content, and winemaking

FRENCH WINE AT A GLANCE

BY CLASSIFICATION
Appellation d'Origine Contrôlée (AOC or AC)
Exactly 51% of total French wine production – 20% exported, 80% consumed within France

Vin de Pays
Almost 28% of total French wine production – 20% exported, 80% consumed within France

Vin de France
Just over 6% of total French wine production – 16% exported, 84% consumed within France

Grape Brandy
Very nearly 15% of total French wine production is distilled into Cognac, Armagnac, and other grape brandies – 15% exported, 85% consumed within France

BY TYPE
Red wine
Just over 65% of total French wine production – 30% exported, 70% consumed within France

White wine
21.5% of total French wine production – 55% exported, 45% consumed within France

Rosé wine
6.5% of total French wine production – 25% exported, 75% consumed within France

Sparkling wine
Just under 6% of total French wine production – 50% exported, 50% consumed within France

Fortified wine
Just under 1% of total French wine production – 20% exported, 80% consumed within France

techniques for each area. Although the laws are supposed to control the quality of each wine by having it pass an official analysis and tasting, the latter of these has become something of a farce, since panels of tasting judges are composed of the very people who actually make the wine. Furthermore, the wines are not tasted and passed on a tank by tank basis, the absence of which is probably responsible for most of the very worst AOC wines on the shelf. Virtually all the producers I know admit that only those wines with faults – and obvious ones at that – are likely to be rejected, with no account taken of either quality or whether a wine reflects the character of the grapes used or expresses any particular regional style. Some were honest enough to explain that most people are too afraid to start the ball rolling on the issue of

AOP OR AOC?

Even wine magazines have published incorrect or incomplete articles trying to explain Europe's new appellation designations. It's all very simple, really. Contrary to popular belief, *Appellation d'Origine Protégée* (AOP) will not replace *Appellation d'Origine Contrôlée* (AOC). AOP (or PDO – Protected Designation of Origin – in English) is not the replacement for any national designations; it is the replacement for VQPRD (QWPSR in English), which is the official EU classification under which AOC, DO, DOC, QmP, *et al* fall. This is not being pedantic. The national designations will remain on the label, and although producers *could* use AOP (PDO or their own national equivalent) on the label, they do not have to and are not likely to, any more than you were likely to find VQPRD (QWPSR or other national equivalents) on wine labels prior to the change. There have been a few instances of VQPRD appearing on a label in the past, but literally a handful. It was used, but on the capsule, not the label, and only on the capsule of French wines sold in France, where you would see a green VQPRD seal on the capsule. The tiny lettering on this green seal will change from VQPRD to AOP, and if you had not read this, you probably would not have noticed any change. That's how little difference it will make to the appellation of the wines you will buy in future.
Indication Géographique Protégée (IGP or PGI – Protected Geographical Indication – in English) is the new designation for the *Vin de Pays*, and in theory there is exactly the same lack of obligation to use it on the label as there is for AOP. However, in practice IGP might become more commonplace on labels than AOP. There are various marketing reasons for this. For a start, the IGP stamp looks like an additional, higher-quality, more *terroir*-specific qualification, whereas it's more of an "either/or" for AOP and AOC. It also does no harm that IGP has a similar ring to Italy's IGT (*Indicazione di Geografica Tipica*).

CHÂTEAU DE MONBAZILLAC
This 16th-century Renaissance château is set up high and has a commanding view over the Dordogne. It produces the top-of-the-range wines for the local cooperative, just a few kilometres down the road.

FRANCE
The coloured areas on this map identify the 10 main wine-producing regions of France, where the areas of Appellation d'Origine Contrôlée, *which cover 474,000 hectares (1.2 million acres), are concentrated. However, the country has more than 800,000 hectares of vineyards in total, and many good, everyday-drinking wines are made in other parts of the country. See also* Vin de Pays *maps, pp298, 299.*

DID YOU KNOW?

• There are over 147,000 vineyard owners in France, just over 95,000 of whom make and sell wine, of whom more than 58,000 are producers of AOC wines.

• 62 per cent of all French vineyards are machine harvested.

• 3.3 per cent of all French vineyards are farmed organically or biodynamically.

• 45 per cent of all French wine is processed by 774 *cave coopératives*.

• Merlot is the most planted grape variety of any colour in France.

• Ugni Blanc is the widest planted white grape variety in France.

Bordeaux *See also p109*	The Rhône Valley *See also p263*	—— *Département* boundary
Burgundy *See also p182*	Jura, Bugey, and Savoie *See also p274*	▲ Height above sea level (metres)
Champagne *See also pp216, 218*	Southwest France *See also p278*	
Alsace *See also p236*	Languedoc-Rousillon *See also p285*	
The Loire Valley *See also p247*	Provence and Corsica *See also p294*	

0 20 40 60 80 100 miles
0 50 100 150 km

quality or style for fear that someone whose wine has already been rejected might seek revenge by rejecting other wines indiscriminately. It is little surprise, therefore, that only around 2 or 3 per cent of wines fail to pass such sham tastings.

The tasting system is obviously deficient, as evidenced by the glut of very poor-quality AOCs that are put on the shelf every year. The best AOC wines are still superb, but without some sort of overhaul of the system (*see* Challenging tradition, p104), the onus remains very much on the knowledge of consumers to discern the reputation of individual producers.

On a more positive note, INAO has instituted tougher controls in the vineyards that could result in distillation of the entire crop of any grower who exceeds the *Plafond Limité de Classement* (PLC). The PLC is the absolute maximum yield for any AOC. This is usually set at 20 per cent above the base yield, which may itself be adjusted upwards on an annual basis by, normally, some 10–15 per cent. INAO has formed local "work

committees" to visit vineyards, to detect any aberrations. Essentially, but not exclusively, they will be looking for signs of overproduction, and if found, they will tell the grower (depending on the time of year) to prune, green-harvest, or thin the bunches. Later in the year, the grower could have his entire crop declassified if he has not done as requested. In future years, such an offender might not be given the opportunity to rectify any overcropping and could have his entire crop carted off for distillation for inadequate pruning. Of course, the efficacy of this initiative will be dependent upon how tough the "work committees" actually are, and, like AOC tasting panels, these will be comprised of fellow winegrowers, so....

Vin de pays

There are 154 *vin de pays*, or "country wine", appellations, covering 206,000 hectares (509,000 acres), and producing an annual average of just over 14 million hectolitres (166 million cases). Officially established in 1968, the *vins de pays* did not become a marketable reality until 1973, when the rules for production were fixed. They were created, quite simply, by authorizing some *vins de table* to indicate their specific geographic origin and, if desired, the grape varieties used, but the effect was more profound than that. For a long while, it was even obligatory for these wines to carry the term "Vin de Table" in addition to their *vin de pays* appellation, but this regulation was discontinued in 1989 and Vin de Table itself was replaced by Vin de France in 2009. Allowing producers of potentially superior table wine areas to declare, for the first time, the origin and content of their wines gave back a long-lost pride to the best growers, who started to care more about how they tended their vines and made their wines, and began to uproot low-quality varieties, replant with better ones, and restrict yields.

There are four categories of *vin de pays*, each with its own controls, but all regulated by the Office National Interprofessionnel des Vins (ONIVINS), which is due to be merged with INAO. Although every *vin de pays* must have a specified origin on the

---

VINS DE PRIMEUR

We tend to think of Beaujolais Nouveau as the only *vin de primeur*, or "new wine", but there are no fewer than 55 different wines that are allowed by AOC regulations to be sold in the year they are harvested, and 25 of these must be labelled *primeur* or *nouveau*. They are made in a style that is at its peak in the first year of its life. So, for those who like drinking wine when it has only just stopped fermenting, why not look out for the following?

1. Anjou Gamay
2. Beaujolais (red or rosé)
3. Beaujolais Supérieur (red or rosé)
4. Beaujolais-Villages (red or rosé)
5. Beaujolais with village name but not *cru* (red or rosé)
6. Bourgogne (white only)
7. Bourgogne Aligoté (white only)
8. Bourgogne Grand Ordinaire (white only)
9. Cabernet d'Anjou (rosé)
10. Cabernet de Saumur (rosé)
11. Coteaux du Languedoc (red or rosé)
12. Coteaux du Lyonnais (red, white, or rosé)
13. Coteaux du Tricastin (red, white, or rosé)
14. Côtes-du-Rhône (red sold only as a *vin de café* or rosé)
15. Côtes du Roussillon (red, white, or rosé)
16. Côtes du Ventoux (red, white, or rosé)
17. Gaillac (red Gamay or white)
18. Mâcon (white or rosé)
19. Mâcon Supérieur (white only)
20. Macon-Villages (white only)
21. Macon with village name (white only)
22. Muscadet
23. Muscadet de Sèvre et Maine
24. Muscadet des Coteaux de la Loire
25. Muscadet Côtes de Grand-Lieu
26. Rosé d'Anjou
27. Tavel (rosé only)
28. Touraine Gamay (red only)
29. Touraine (rosé only)

The following wines may be sold from 1 December after the harvest without any mention of *primeur* or *nouveau*:

1. Anjou (white only)
2. Bergerac (white or rosé, but not red)
3. Blayais (white only)
4. Bordeaux (*sec*, rosé, or *clairet*)
5. Buzet (white or rosé)
6. Cabernet d'Anjou (rosé)
7. Cabernet de Saumur (rosé)
8. Corbières (white or rosé)
9. Costières de Nîmes (white or rosé)
10. Coteaux d'Aix-en-Provence (white or rosé)
11. Coteaux du Languedoc (white or rosé)
12. Coteaux Varois (white or rosé)
13. Côtes de Bourg (white only)
14. Côtes de Duras (white or rosé)
15. Côtes du Marmandais (white or rosé)
16. Côtes de Provence (white or rosé)
17. Côtes-du-Rhône (white or rosé)
18. Côtes du Ventoux (white or rosé)
19. Entre-Deux-Mers (white only)
20. Faugères (rosé only)
21. Graves (white only)
22. Graves de Vayres (white only)
23. Jurançon Sec
24. Minervois (white or rosé)
25. Montravel (white or rosé)
26. Muscadet
27. Muscadet de Sèvre et Maine
28. Muscadet des Coteaux de la Loire
29. Muscadet Côtes de Grand-Lieu
30. Premières Côtes de Blaye (white only)
31. Rosé d'Anjou
32. Rosé de Loire
33. St-Chinian (rosé only)
34. Ste-Foy-Bordeaux (white only)
35. Saumur (white only)
36. Touraine (white only)

BACK TO BASICS

France has taken the opportunity of the EU's new wine regime (*see* AOP or AOC? p100) to shake up its own national system. All appellations have been given the chance to turn back the clock. It must be understood that each AOC was created merely as an official endorsement of local tradition. Some of those local traditions were less principled than others, and over the years these imperfect rules have been added to – and in some cases, bent – in order to placate local politics. Each appellation has been given the opportunity to go back to the basic EU wine-regime requirements or to add further restrictions to those rules as they see fit. Many appellations were carrying so much extra baggage that they gladly grabbed the chance to simplify the day-to-day lives of everyone involved. At the same time, France has dropped its VDQS appellations, which were technically VQPRD (now AOP). As VQPRD, they were the equivalent of AOC in the eyes of the EU; thus, each VDQS was given the option of applying for AOC or Vin de Pays. It was assumed that most would go for the more prestigious AOC but some might feel their needs were better served by the greater flexibility of the IGP. At one time, Gros Plant Nantais was the only appellation going for IGP, but in the end its producers chose AOC, as did every former VDQS.

Reports that Vin de Table will be scrapped are misleading. Those wines still exist, but the name is changing to Vin de France. The wines under this new designation will be able to mention the vintage and grape variety but not any more specific a geographic area than France. However, if the wine is sold by a small domaine producer, the address will be a big clue, because the odds are that the Vin de France will be from one or more of the appellations that his other wines are sold under. For larger producers, the attraction is to blend wines from different regions and to sell them under a designation that is far more attractive to consumers than Vin de Table, with a more informative label. What would you buy – a non-vintage Vin de Table or Cabernet Sauvignon 2009 Vin de France? They could both be the same, but at least you know what you are buying with Vin de France. This will still house most of the poorest-quality French wines, but it should develop into a very interesting category. Expect to see it grow.

BREAKDOWN OF FRENCH WINE PRODUCTION MEASURED IN HECTOLITRES

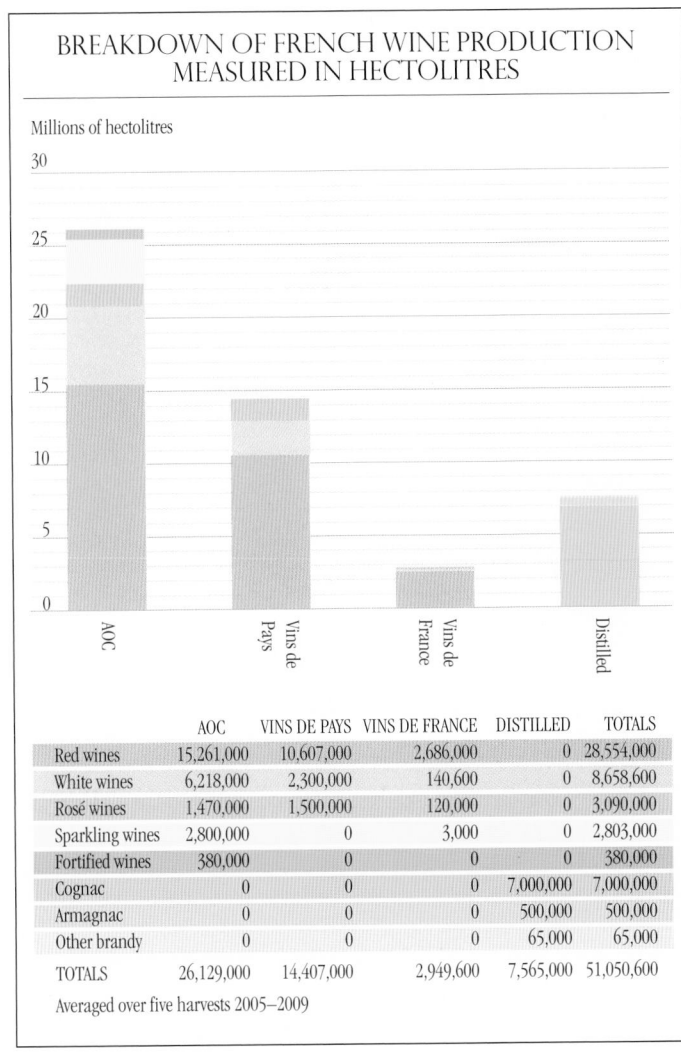

Millions of hectolitres

	AOC	VINS DE PAYS	VINS DE FRANCE	DISTILLED	TOTALS
Red wines	15,261,000	10,607,000	2,686,000	0	28,554,000
White wines	6,218,000	2,300,000	140,600	0	8,658,600
Rosé wines	1,470,000	1,500,000	120,000	0	3,090,000
Sparkling wines	2,800,000	0	3,000	0	2,803,000
Fortified wines	380,000	0	0	0	380,000
Cognac	0	0	0	7,000,000	7,000,000
Armagnac	0	0	0	500,000	500,000
Other brandy	0	0	0	65,000	65,000
TOTALS	26,129,000	14,407,000	2,949,600	7,565,000	51,050,600

Averaged over five harvests 2005–2009

FRENCH WINE PRODUCTION BY TYPE

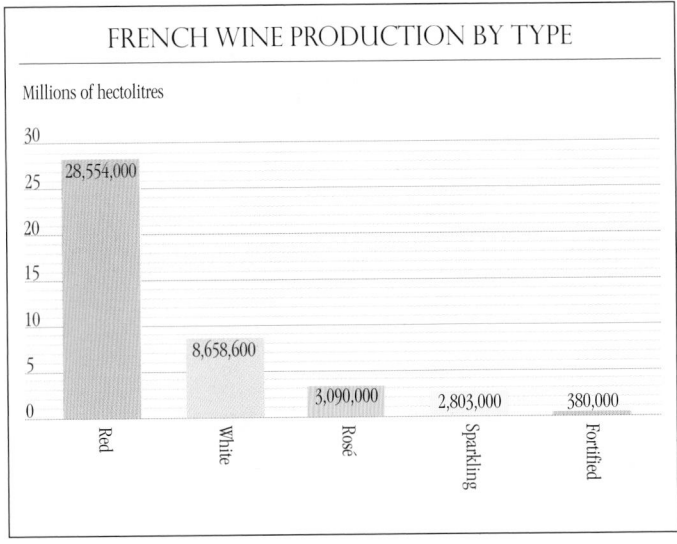

Millions of hectolitres

Red 28,554,000 · White 8,658,600 · Rosé 3,090,000 · Sparkling 2,803,000 · Fortified 380,000

label, a wide range of grape varieties can be used and high yields are allowed. A certain flexibility on choice of grape varieties allows innovation, a character-building trait that has been denied winemakers under the AOC regime, but the high yields permitted have also caused many an unprincipled producer to jump on the relatively lucrative *vin de pays* bandwagon, thus the quality can vary greatly. This is, nevertheless, a most interesting category of wines, often infiltrated by foreign winemakers producing some of the most exciting, inexpensive, and upfront-fruity wines.

Many *vins de pays* are, of course, bland and will never improve, but some will make it up the hierarchical ladder to full AOC status. Certain individual producers, such as the Guiberts of Mas de Daumas Gassac and the Dürrbachs of Domaine de Trévallon, could not care less about AOC status, as they happen to be making wines under the less draconian *vin de pays* system. They already have reputations as good as those of the finest French appellations and demand even higher prices than some expensive AOC wines. For a description of the various *vin de pays* categories, a map showing the areas producing *vins de pays*, and profiles of every *vin de pays* along with their finest producers, see pp298–309.

Vin de France

Formerly Vin de Table Français, this category encompasses just over 55,000 hectares (a little under 136,000 acres) of unclassified vineyards in France, producing an annual average of nearly 3 million hectolitres (more than 33 million cases) of Vin de France, (although this also includes a variable volume of grape juice, grape concentrate, and wine vinegar). This compares with a production of 34 million hectolitres (510 million cases) in the mid-1990s and is evidence of the trend away from the lower end of the market.

Vin de France, like *vin de table*, is the bottom of the quality ladder, but its wines do not have to be bad. Just as the less strict regulations give *vins de pays* the flexibility to produce some outstanding wines that would not normally be permitted in their area of origin, so the even less strict Vin de France regulations give Vin de France even more flexibility to pull something really special out of the bag. We saw the possibility of such wines even under the old *vin de table* regulations, when **Zind** (a mouthwatering blend of Auxerrois, Pinot Blanc, and Chardonnay from three exceptional *lieux-dits* produced by Zind Humbrecht in Alsace) and historical wines such as **Libre Expression** (effectively a late-harvest version of Rivesaltes from Domaine Cazes that is dry and not fortified) and **Muscat de Petit Grains Passerillé Vendange d'Octobre** (a top-class oak-aged dessert wine produced from shrivelled grapes grown on old vines) commanded higher prices and exuded more quality and individual style than most AOC wines produced in the same area.

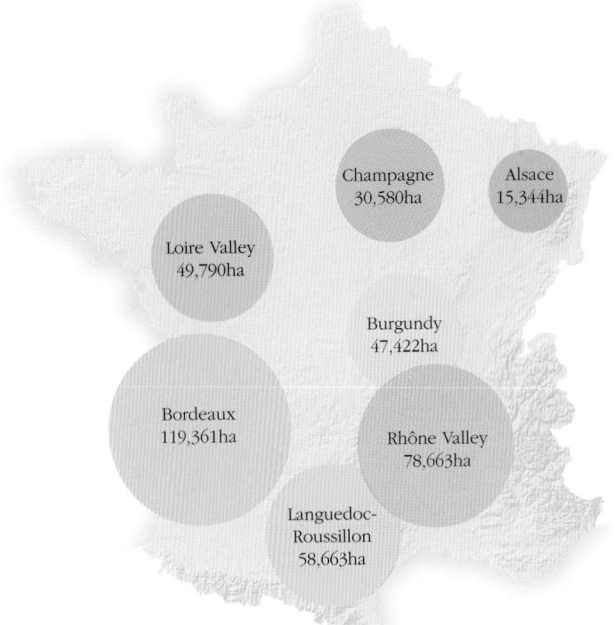

MAJOR AOC WINE-PRODUCING REGIONS
From this map, it is easy to discern the relative size of production of the seven most important wine regions of France.

Champagne 30,580ha · Alsace 15,344ha · Loire Valley 49,790ha · Burgundy 47,422ha · Bordeaux 119,361ha · Rhône Valley 78,663ha · Languedoc-Roussillon 58,663ha

CHALLENGING TRADITION

The French establishment has been slow to wake up to the fact that the AOC classification was not AOK, but they have started to think the unthinkable: change. When the late René Renou, director of INAO (the man in charge of running the entire French appellation system), proposed a super-appellation that would be bestowed on wines of "demonstrably superior quality", he shook the very foundations of French culture – tradition. This country produces both the best and the worst wines in the world because of its fixation with tradition, but whereas the French are always willing to preserve the best traditions, they are loath to banish the worst. Even when the need to do so is staring them in the face.

In 1995 Michel Bettane, one of France's top wine writers, was quoted as saying: "Today, *appellation contrôlée* guarantees neither quality nor authenticity." At the time, Alain Berger was the director of INAO, and when pressured he caused uproar by confessing that: "One can find on the market scandalously poor products with the *appellation contrôlée* halo." But was anything done? Of course not. For Renou to confirm the situation, and propose a solution, was a unique event. However, a fundamental shake-up to the system that gave birth to wine regimes throughout Europe threatened the moral authority of French wine, thus Renou's proposals have been met with hostility in some quarters, while in others they are viewed as absolutely necessary.

Those who support Renou are, essentially, a quality-conscious minority, while those who oppose include the worst of the worst, although the vast majority simply feel so safe with their traditions that they do not wish to rock the boat.

Initially, there was good news and bad news: the good news being that the Burgundians were for it, the bad being that the *bordelais* were not. However, the good news turned out to be bad, as evidenced by the supposedly pro-Renou Jean-François Delorme,

who as president of the Bureau Interprofessionnel des Vins de Bourgogne (BIVB), commented: "Of course, all of Burgundy's AOCs would be super-AOCs." If all Burgundy were of the quality of Romanée Conti, Leroy, or Leflaive, no one would argue, but much too much is no better than *vin ordinaire*, while – as with every wine region – some wines can be almost undrinkable. So no, a pan-Burgundian application for super-AOCs would not be very super at all.

Being no fool, Renou allowed his historic proposal to "slip out" in London, where he could count on its radical aims receiving widespread objective approval, before presenting the plan in detail to the INAO's 80-member National Committee. He later provided more details about his super-appellation, which he now called *Appellation d'Origine Contrôlée d'Excellence* (AOCE), and threw another spanner in the traditionalist works by introducing the novel concept in the form of his proposed new *Site et Terroir d'Excellence* (STE) appellation.

On past experience, the odds always were that a compromise would be sought. That the aims would become so fudged, and the regulations so watered-down, that they will not simply be ineffective, but will probably be detrimental to the future of French wine. And that is precisely what has happened, but these new appellations and the reasons why they were rejected need exploring in more detail so that French wine lovers can at least know what Renou's good intentions were. Readers will then be able to appreciate how the French catastrophically missed this opportunity, and why the growers and government minister involved deserve to reap whatever ill fortune they have sown.

The BIVB was the first to support Renou's initiative, but Delorme's unrealistic position was disowned by its members, who turned out to be so hostile to the idea of AOCEs that Burgundy was given until "early 2005 at the latest" to present

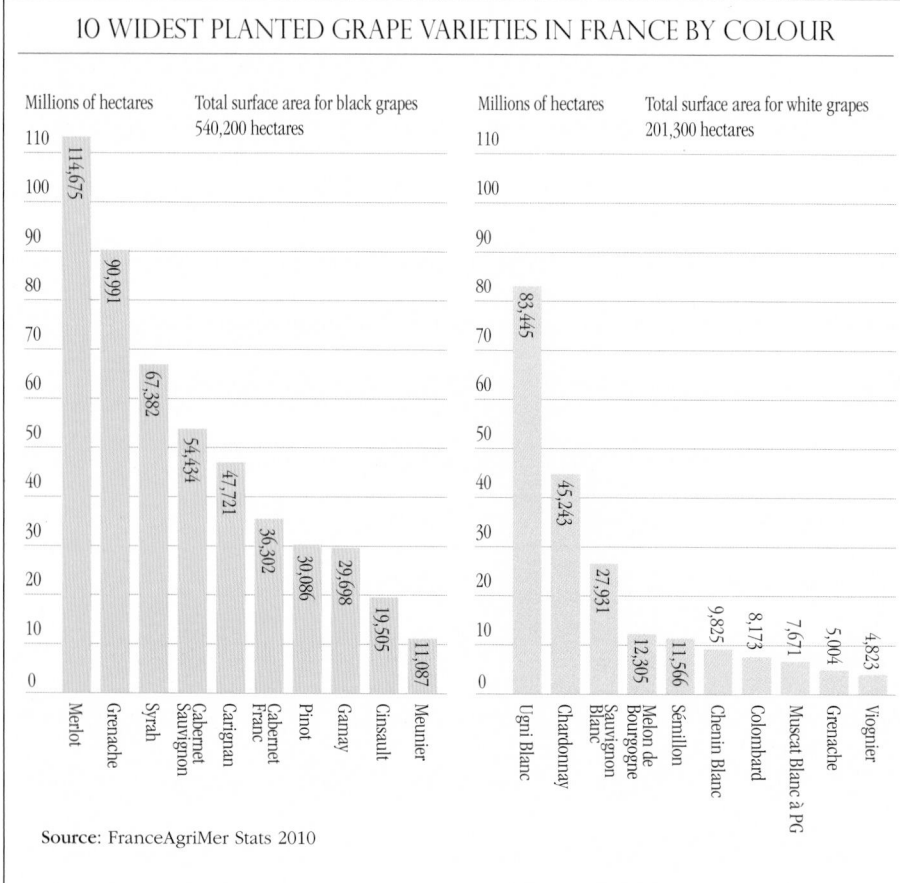

10 WIDEST PLANTED GRAPE VARIETIES IN FRANCE BY COLOUR

Millions of hectares — Total surface area for black grapes 540,200 hectares

Variety	Hectares
Merlot	114,675
Grenache	90,991
Syrah	67,382
Cabernet Sauvignon	54,434
Carignan	47,721
Cabernet Franc	36,302
Pinot	30,086
Gamay	29,698
Cinsault	19,505
Meunier	11,087

Millions of hectares — Total surface area for white grapes 201,300 hectares

Variety	Hectares
Ugni Blanc	83,445
Chardonnay	45,243
Sauvignon Blanc	27,931
Melon de Bourgogne	12,305
Sémillon	11,566
Chenin Blanc	9,825
Colombard	8,173
Muscat Blanc à PG	7,671
Grenache	5,004
Viognier	4,823

Source: FranceAgriMer Stats 2010

PINOT NOIR GRAPES
The Holy Grail of red winemakers, the Pinot Noir is the most finicky of all black grapes to work with, but when successful, it can produce velvety red wines of stunning purity, finesse, and length.

the INAO's president with modifications and solid proposals for putting such plans in place. They would not get the chance. The chop would come much earlier than that.

But what exactly did the Burgundians – and, in fact, growers from almost every wine region – object to? The AOCE designation would be granted only to areas that committed to a series of strict regulations in virtually every facet of vineyard management and winemaking, including lower yields, higher planting density, harvesting (manual or machines), ageing (oak barrels or chips), grape varieties, wines judged by tasting panels, and so on. To become eligible for an AOCE, a minimum of 75 per cent of the producers in an appellation would have to approve the tighter regulations, at which point any unwilling grower would be coerced to follow the majority and abide by the new regulations. INAO would review each appellation's status as an AOCE every five years.

There were two obvious flaws. First, if it is up to the wine producers of an appellation to decide by voting whether it is to be an AOC or AOCE, it cannot work. A truly famous wine that is offered the opportunity of claiming super-appellation status is one thing, but an ordinary wine that assumes super-appellation status simply because the majority of its growers vote for it would be pointless. Equally, if the growers of a truly famous wine did not grab such a chance with both hands, they would deserve to suffer the decline that would inevitably ensue, although there were many objectors who did not think that far ahead. In Chablis, for example, which is a truly famous wine region, one person with a short-term view is Jean Durup. He sits on the INAO National Committee, and was reported as saying that he didn't think the AOC would want to change its standards and adopt stricter rules because "we are the world's most famous white wine, and there is no crisis in Chablis". What would the next generation of Chablis growers think in 20 years' time, once the AOCE status of other white Burgundies had become well established? It would surely not be unreasonable for consumers at that juncture to assume that plain old Chablis AOC was simply not in the same class as Burgundy's AOCEs. The second potential flaw in the system was the panel tastings, because if they were to be conducted by the producers themselves, the results would be as worthless as those for AOC wines (*see* p100).

SITE ET TERROIR D'EXCELLENCE

As for the brand-new STE classification, this was a truly inspired concept and, as such, its demise has been an even greater tragedy. STE was designed to recognize the exceptional effort put in by serious, quality-conscious producers in relatively modest or otherwise generally unambitious appellations. Individual wineries could receive the STE label if their wines are much better wines than those of most other producers in the appellation. Renou had intimated that INAO was likely to approve hundreds of STE wineries. What an opportunity the French have lost to fight back on the super-premium stage.

Jean-Michel Aubinel, who represents growers in Mâcon, clearly did not think so. He was reported as saying the scheme would entrench rivalry between neighbouring properties, if applied to one and not the other. Well, that's the whole idea Monsieur: it is called competition. How else does anyone in any sphere strive to improve? But then, perhaps the AOC is meant only to guarantee mediocrity. Denis Dubourdieu of Château Reynon in Premières Côtes de Bordeaux was far more upbeat, pointing out that: "The STE concept appears to be the truly original point of the proposal. You can spend 20 years claiming you do better than most in one of Bordeaux's lesser-known satellite appellations, but the STE will give you status, and it will stimulate producers to make excellent wines." Well, Denis, my readers know about your top-performing wines, but it looks as though you'll have to spend another 20 years telling the rest of the world.

FRANCE "SHOT IN FOOT"

A Bordeaux campaign to "drink less, drink better" was banned in 2004, after the National Association for the Prevention of Alcoholism (NAPA) took the Conseil Interprofessionnel des Vins de Bordeaux (CIVB) to court. Any rational person would have to question the motives of an organization that is so opposed to people drinking less, but better wine that it would drag them into a court of law. If NAPA seeks prohibition, it should do so openly. Furthermore, any rational person would also have to question the motives behind a law under which a court is obliged to declare that "drink less, drink better" is illegal because it "incites people to purchase wine". Why should inciting people to purchase less, better-quality wine be against the law? One of the Bordeaux posters was also declared illegal because it depicted someone drinking wine. According to this warped law, it is legal to display an alcoholic product on a poster, but not legal to display that product being consumed. What are people supposed to think they should do with such a product after purchasing it?

The law in question is the Loi Evin, enacted in January 1991, and named after Claude Evin, a minister in the Rocard government. And so, finally, we must question this man's motives. Why, when Evin presented his proposal to the French parliament, did he do so under the banner of "In the case of alcohol, only abuse is dangerous"? Certainly not to mislead parliament. The National Assembly was informed precisely how far beyond the curbing of abuse this law extended, and was thus as guilty as the infamous Evin. So, if the minister was not hiding the draconian powers of his legislation behind such a misleading slogan from parliament, who was he hiding them from? The French people?

Other French governments have inherited the Loi Evin, but had done nothing to curb its excesses until July 2004, when to get around its advertising restrictions, Hervé Gaymard, the French agricultural minister, announced plans to reclassify wine as a "food". This was quickly followed by a report requested by Prime Minister Raffarin on how to boost the "struggling wine industry" through advertising "without undermining the principles of consumer protection" in the Loi Evin.

In fact, the Loi Evin has no principles of consumer protection – it has no principles, period. It is not of the making of any current French government, so they should stop trying to fudge a dodgy compromise, and simply revoke the Loi Evin on the grounds of its being against the national interest.

In conclusion, AOCEs and STEs would have re-invented and re-invigorated the French appellation system. Renou's proposals represented one of just four options. The second was to fudge them, the third was to do nothing at all, and the fourth was to scrap the "control-freak" element of French appellations altogether, bringing them more in line with New World thinking. There are good reasons why the fourth option should have been considered, such as: Why shouldn't people grow what they like, where they like? What does it matter what system of vine training a grower employs? Why try to control yields when the consumer will be the final arbiter of whether a producer will survive? Surely all that is necessary is the New World concept of truth in labelling: if a wine claims to be made from a particular variety, grown in a specific place, in a certain year, then that is what the wine should be. All good reasons – but there is a little Francophile part of me that wants to see the AOC concept survive, and to do that it needs re-inventing from time to time. So what did they choose? The fudge, of course. The French cannot resist fudge, particularly when it comes sugar-wrapped.

At a three-hour crisis meeting between the French minister of agriculture, Hervé Gaymard, and representatives of the French wine industry on 21 July 2004, Renou's proposals were discarded because they made French wine more complicated at a time when it needs to become more accessible (granted, sorting the chaff from the wheat does tend to make the chaff less accessible! – TS). Gaymard stressed that there would be "tighter" controls for the production of AOC wines, to ensure that they were genuine *vins de terroir*, which represented "the top of the range", and were product-driven rather than consumer-driven (a flaw-free implementation of AOCE and STE would have achieved these very aims – TS). Gaymard's proposals were presented to each of the regional interprofessional bodies with a view to becoming effective with the 2006 harvest, along with a 50 per cent increase in government aid for wine promotion overseas (the sugar coating – TS).

FRENCH LABEL LANGUAGE

FRONT- AND BACK-LABEL DEFINITIONS

Année Literally year, this will refer to the vintage.

Appellation d'Origine Contrôlée Top official classification, commonly referred to as AOC (*see* p100).

Barriques Small oak barrels of approximately 225 litres capacity.

Blanc White.

Blanc de blancs Literally "white of whites", a white wine made from white grapes, a term that is often, but not exclusively, used for sparkling wines.

Blanc de noirs Literally "white of blacks", a white wine made from black grapes, a term that is often, but not exclusively, used for sparkling wines. In the New World, the wines usually have a tinge of pink, often no different from a fully-fledged rosé, but a classic *blanc de noirs* should be as white as possible without artificial means.

Brut Normally reserved for sparkling wines, *brut* literally means raw or bone dry, but in practice there is always some sweetness and so can at the most only be termed dry.

Cave coopérative Cooperative cellars where members take their grapes at harvest time, and the wines produced are marketed under one label. Basic products will often be blended, but top of the range wines can be from very specific locations. A lot of cooperative wines can be ordinary, but the best cooperatives usually offer exceptional value.

Cépage This means grape variety, and is sometimes used on the label immediately prior to the variety, thus 'Cépage Mauzac' means that the wine is made from the Mauzac grape variety.

Châtaignier Chestnut (occasionally used to make barrels).

Château Literally "castle" or "mansion", but whereas many wines do actually come from magnificent edifices that could truly be described as châteaux, many that claim this description are merely modest one-storey villas, some are no more than purpose-built *cuveries*, while a few are actually tin sheds! The legal connotation of a château-bottled wine is the same as for any domaine-bottled wine.

Chêne Oak (commonly used to make barrels).

Clairet A wine that falls somewhere between a dark rosé and a light red wine.

Climat A single plot of land with its own name, located within a specific vineyard.

Clos Synonymous with *climat*, except this plot of land is either enclosed by walls, or was once.

Côte, côtes Literally slope(s) or hillside(s) of one contiguous slope or hill, but in practical terms often no different from Coteau, coteaux.

Coteau, coteaux Literally slope(s) or hillside(s) in a hilly area that is not contiguous, but in practical terms often no different from Côte, côtes.

Crémant Although traditionally ascribed to a Champagne with a low-pressure and a soft, creamy mousse, the term has now been phased out in Champagne as part of the bargain struck with other French sparkling wines that have agreed to drop the term *méthode champenoise*. In return they have been exclusively permitted to use this old Champagne term to create their own appellations, such as Crémant de Bourgogne, Crémant d'Alsace etc.

Cru or **crû** Literally means a growth or plot of land, this term usually implies that it has been officially designated in some way, such as a *cru bourgeois*, *cru classé*, *premier cru* or *grand cru*.

Cru bourgeois An officially designated growth below *cru classé* in the Médoc.

Cru classé An officially classified vineyard in the Médoc and Provence.

Cuve A vat, *cuve* should not be confused with *cuvée*.

Cuve close A sparkling wine that has undergone second fermentation in a vat, *cuve close* is synonymous with Charmat or Tank Method.

Cuvée Originally the wine of one *cuve* or vat, but now refers to a specific blend or product which, in current commercial terms, will be from several vats, this term is used most commonly, but not exclusively, in Champagne.

Dégorgé or **dégorgement** Found on some sparkling wines, this term will be followed by the date when the wine was disgorged of the yeast sediment that has built up during its second fermentation in bottle.

Demi-muid A large oval barrel, usually made of oak, with a capacity of 300 litres (600 litres in Champagne).

Demi-sec Literally semi-dry, but actually tastes quite sweet.

Domaine Closer to estate than vineyard, as a domaine can consist of vineyards scattered over several appellations in one region. The wine in the bottle must come from the domaine indicated on the label. Some former "châteaux" have changed to "domaine" in recent years.

Doux A sweet wine.

Encépagement The proportion of grape varieties in a blend or *cuvée*.

Elevage par X or **eleveur X** Refers to the traditional function of a *négociant* (X), who has not made the wine initially, but purchased it, after which the *négociant* will age, possibly blend, bottle and sell the wine.

Elevée en … Aged in ….

Elevée et mise en bouteille par X The wine was aged and bottled by X, but none or only part of the wine was produced by X.

Foudre A large wooden cask or vat.

Fûts Barrels, but not necessarily small ones.

Grand cru Literally "great growth", this term indicates the wine has come from a truly great vineyard (which, to put it in context, a lousy producer can make a hash of) in regions such as Burgundy and Alsace, where its use is strictly controlled. In Champagne, *grand cru* is much less meaningful, as it applies to entire villages, which might contain most of the best vineyards in the region, but where lesser vineyards also exist.

Grand vin This term has no legal connotation whatsoever, but when used properly in Bordeaux, *grand vin* applies to the main wine sold under the château's famous name, and will have been produced from only the finest barrels. Wines excluded during this process go into second, third and sometimes fourth wines that are sold under different labels.

Lie French for lees: *sur lie* refers to a wine kept in contact with its lees.

Lieu-dit A named site, this term is commonly used for a wine from a specific, named site.

Médaille Medal: *médaille d'or* is gold medal, *médaille d'argent* is silver, and *médaille de bronze* is bronze.

Méthode ancestrale A sweet sparkling wine from Limoux that is produced by a variant of *méthode rurale*, a process that involves no secondary fermentation, the wine being bottled before the first alcoholic fermentation has finished.

Méthode champenoise Contrary to popular belief, this term is not banned in the EU. It is expressly reserved for Champagne, the producers of which seldom bother to use it (cannot say never because I saw it once!). *Méthode champenoise* is the process whereby an effervescence is produced through a secondary fermentation in the same bottle it is sold in.

Méthode classique One of the legal terms for a sparkling wine made by the *méthode champenoise*.

Méthode deuxième fermentation, traditionnelle, méthode traditionnelle classique Legal terms for a sparkling wine made by the *méthode champenoise* (*méthode deuxième fermentation* is used only in Gaillac).

Millésime, millésimé Refers to the vintage year.

Mis en bouteille au domaine or **à la propriété** or **le château** Bottled at the domaine/property/ château indicated on the

AOC

VIN DE FRANCE

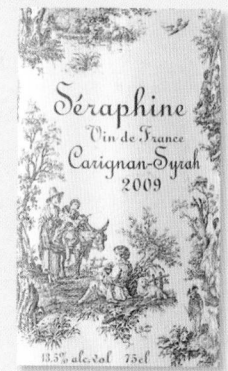

VIN DE PAYS

CHAMPAGNE

label (the wine must have been made exclusively from grapes grown there).

Mis en bouteille par … Bottled by … (not necessarily made by).

Mistelle Fresh grape juice that has been muted with alcohol before any fermentation can take place.

Moelleux Literally "soft" or "smooth", this term usually implies a rich, medium-sweet style in most French areas, except the Loire, where it is used to indicate a truly rich, sweet botrytis wine, thereby distinguishing it from *demi-sec*. This term was due to be obligatory in Alsace for wines that have a minimum residual sugar of 12 g/l (9 g/l for Riesling), but it was dropped after being vetoed by growers.

Monopole With one exception, this means that the wine comes from a single vineyard (usually a *grand cru*) that is under the sole ownership of the wine producer in question. The exception is Champagne Heidsieck & Co Monopole, which is just a trading name.

Mousse The effervescence of a sparkling wine.

Mousseux Sparkling, found only on cheap fizz.

Négociant Literally a trader or merchant, this name is used by wine producers whose business depends on buying in raw materials (the name is derived from the traditional practice of negotiating with growers to buy grapes and/or wine, and with wholesalers and retailers to sell wine).

Négociant-éleveur Wine firm that buys in ready-made wines for *élevage*.

Négociant-propriétaire A *négociant* who owns vineyards and probably offers a range of its own produced wines.

Non filtré The wine has not been filtered, thus is liable to drop a sediment much earlier than most other wines, and should always be decanted.

Oeil de perdrix Literally "partridge eye" and refers to a rosé-coloured wine.

Perlant Very slightly sparkling, even less so than *pétillant*.

Pétillance, pétillant A wine with enough carbonic gas to create a light sparkle.

Premier cru Literally a "first growth", the status of a *premier cru* is beneath that of *grand cru* but only of relevance in areas where the term is controlled, such as Burgundy and Alsace. In Champagne, *premier cru* is much less meaningful, as it applies to entire villages, of which there are far too many, and in which much lesser vineyards also exist.

Produit Product, as in Product of …

Propriétaire-récoltant Grower-producer whose wine will be made exclusively from his own property.

Récolte Refers to the vintage year.

Réserve Ubiquitous and meaningless.

Rosé Pink.

Rouge Red.

Rubis Sometimes seen on rosé wines, particularly, but not exclusively, on darker styles.

Saignée A rosé wine produced by "bleeding" off surplus liquid from either the press or the fermenting vat.

Sec Dry, but in a sparkling wine this will have more sweetness than a *brut*.

Sélection de grains nobles A rare, intensely sweet, wine in Alsace made from selected botrytized grapes.

Sélection par X Selected, but not produced or bottled by X.

Supérieur As part of an appellation (eg, Mâcon Supérieur as opposed to Mâcon plain and simple), this refers not so much to a superior quality than – possibly – a superior alcoholic strength (the minimum criteria being 0.5 per cent ABV higher than the minimum for the same appellation without the Supérieur appendage).

Sur lie Refers to wines, usually Muscadets, that have been kept on their lees and have not been racked or filtered prior to bottling. This enhances the fruit of the normally bland Melon de Bourgogne grape used in Muscadet, often imparting a certain liveliness.

Tête de cuvée No legal obligation, but this term strongly suggests that a wine has been produced exclusively from the first flow of juice during the pressing, which is the highest in quality with the most acids, sugars and minerals.

Tonneau A large barrel, traditionally four times the size of a *barrique*.

Trie Usually used to describe the harvesting of selected overripe or botrytized grapes by numerous sweeps (or *tries*) through the vineyard.

Union coopérative A regional collective of local cooperatives.

Vendange tardive Late harvest, implying a sweet wine.

Vieilles vignes Supposedly from old vines, implying lower yields and higher concentration.

No legal parameters apply, but most reputable producers would not dream of using the term unless the vines are at least 35 to 50 years old.

Vieillissement Ageing.

Vigne Vine.

Vigneron Literally a vineyard worker, but often used to denote the owner-winemaker.

Vignoble Vineyard.

Vin Wine.

Vin de l'année Synonymous with *vin primeur*.

Vin doux naturel. A fortified wine, such as Muscat de Beaumes de Venise, that has been muted during fermentation, after it has achieved between 5 and 8 per cent alcohol.

Vin de France Lowest official classification, immediately below *vin de table* (see p103).

Vin de glace French equivalent of *Eiswein* or Icewine.

Vin gris A delicate, pale version of rosé.

Vin jaune The famous "yellow wine" of the Jura derives its name from the honey-gold colour that results from its deliberate oxidation beneath a Sherry-like *flor*. The result is quite similar to an aged *fino* Sherry, although *vin jaune* is not fortified.

Vin de liqueur A fortified wine that is muted with alcohol before fermentation can begin.

Vin mousseux Literally means sparkling wine without any connotation of quality one way or the other, but because all fine sparkling wines in France utilize other terms, it should be taken to mean a cheap, low-quality fizz.

Vin nouveau Synonymous with *vin primeur* – as in Beaujolais Nouveau.

Vin de paille Literally "straw wine", this is a complex sweet wine produced by leaving late-picked grapes to dry and shrivel while hanging from rafters over straw mats.

Vin de Pays Official classification, usually precedes the actual *vin de pays* name, such as Vin de Pays des Collines de la Moure. Vin de Pays is above Vin de France (see p102).

Vin primeur A young wine sold within weeks of the harvest, and meant to be drunk within the year. Beaujolais Primeur is the most commonly known example, but numerous other AOCs are allowed to be sold in this fashion (see box, p102), as is every *vin de pays*.

Vin d'une nuit A rosé or very pale red wine that is allowed contact with its grapeskins for one night only.

BORDEAUX

Bordeaux is an area in an almost-perfect viticultural situation on the west coast of France and benefits from the ultimate marketing tool – a château-based classification system that was established more than 150 years ago.

THE NEW MILLENNIUM appears to be just as taxing for Bordeaux's reputation as the last decade of the 20th century turned out to be. Rain-drenched harvests towards the end of the 1990s challenged Bordeaux's claim to be the ultimate viticultural paradise, while the depressingly poor quality of its generic wines attracted almost as much bad publicity as the grossly inflated prices of modest vintages from the top châteaux. The weather might have improved in the first few years of the 21st century, but the quality of generic Bordeaux has remained abysmal, prices continue to rise almost in direct relation to the drop in sales – and then the unimaginable happened: the renowned US wine critic Robert Parker failed to appear for the *primeur* tastings in March 2003.

But all is not lost – Christian Delpeuch, the new head of the Conseil Interprofessionel des Vins de Bordeaux (CIVB), has mooted the possibility of declassifying some of the weaker Bordeaux wines into a wider *vin de pays*, which could then be bolstered by stronger wines from outside the region, but traditional to the southwest, such as the deep, dark Tannat. Delpeuch is the managing director of Ginestet, the region's biggest trader, and seems to have a good understanding of the more commercial end of Bordeaux's business. He has suggested the creation of a Vins de Pays d'Aquitaine category for the Bordeaux region, under which varietal wines could be marketed. Far from detracting from the classic wines of Bordeaux, this would in fact improve their quality through stricter selection. As for the very top end of the market, the *bordelais* can once again sleep easy in their beds, as Robert Parker returned for the *primeur* tastings in 2004.

OVERVIEW
The Bordeaux appellation and the Gironde *département* are geographically one and the same. Moreover, the Gironde is the largest *département* in France, and Bordeaux is the largest source of quality wines in the world. There are 8,650 vineyard proprietors working almost 120,000 hectares (280,000 acres), producing 6.4 million hectolitres (over 71 million cases) of Bordeaux wine (85 per cent red, 3 per cent rosé, and 12 per cent white) under 60 different appellations every year. Although there are fewer than 9,000 vineyard owners, there are 10,000 châteaux and more than 12,000 château names appearing on Bordeaux labels. While some producers own a number of different châteaux, the problem is compounded by the use of more than one name for each château. According to a decree dating back to 1921, only one château name per property may be used, and because this regulation was by and large ignored, a new decree was issued in 1993 reiterating the rule. As only the French are wont to do, a second name is allowed if it was in use prior to 1983, even though it was illegal at that juncture!

THE CHÂTEAU SYSTEM AND MERCHANT POWER
Prior to the concept of château wine estates, the land was worked on a crop-sharing basis. This feudal system slowly changed from the late 17th century onwards. As the *bordelais* brokers developed the habit of recording and classifying wines according to their cru, or growth (that is to say their geographical origin), and the prices they fetched, the reputations of individual properties became established.

The 19th century saw the rise of the *négociant*, or merchant, in Bordeaux. Many *négociants* were of English origin, and some firms were established by Scottish, Irish, Dutch, or German businessmen. The best château wines were not consumed by the French themselves; they were the preserve of other northern European countries. Thus foreign merchants had an obvious advantage over their French counterparts. Yearly, in spring, these *négociants* took delivery of young wines in cask from the various châteaux and matured them in their cellars prior to shipping. They were therefore responsible for their *élevage*, or upbringing, and came to be known as *négociants-éleveurs*, eventually becoming the middlemen found in every aspect of wine trading. Many foreign buyers found it more convenient to deal through a *négociant* than directly with the wine producer, and often they had no alternative, since a number of châteaux were owned by, or were exclusive to, certain *négociants*.

THE MODERN BORDEAUX WINE TRADE
It was perhaps inevitable that the historically powerful and family-owned négociant-éleveur firms would eventually become a spent force. They lacked the resources required to adequately finance the huge increase in demand for Bordeaux in the 1960s, and those that did not founder during the oil crisis of the early to mid-1970s fell prey to the economic depressions of the following two decades.

As proud old firms were either taken over or went bankrupt, so the power shifted from the *négociants* to the châteaux, and in order to cope with a boom in world markets, many Bordeaux properties expanded their vineyards or added large, shiny new fermentation facilities. Many of these projects were financed with bank loans when interest rates were low. When sales slumped and interest rates shot up, the repayments became unbearable.

DID YOU KNOW?
Less than 10 per cent of Bordeaux producers sell more than 90 per cent of Bordeaux wine (mostly as brands).

VOLUME V. REPUTATION
Very few Bordeaux wines are produced from great vineyards. As the table below illustrates, the famous appellations represent a relatively small amount of the *bordelais vignoble*, and the classified growths a minuscule proportion of that. Yet it could be argued that the reputation of Bordeaux has been built upon a fraction of its *cru classé* or *grand cru classé* – the best performers. Bordeaux is a great wine region, but not all Bordeaux is great wine.

Districts	Surface Area Expressed as a percentage of Bordeaux vineyards
Bordeaux (red)	36.8
Bordeaux Supérieur (red)	10.0
Médoc (red, non cru classé)	11.0
Médoc (red, cru classé)	2.4
Graves (red)	3.1
Saint-Émilion (red)	4.2
Saint-Émilion (red, grand cru classé)	0.8
Saint-Émilion satellites (red)	2.7
Pomerol (red)	0.7
Lalande de Pomerol (red)	1.0
Fronsac (red)	1.1
Various côtes (red)	14.4
Dry white	8.3
Sweet white	3.4

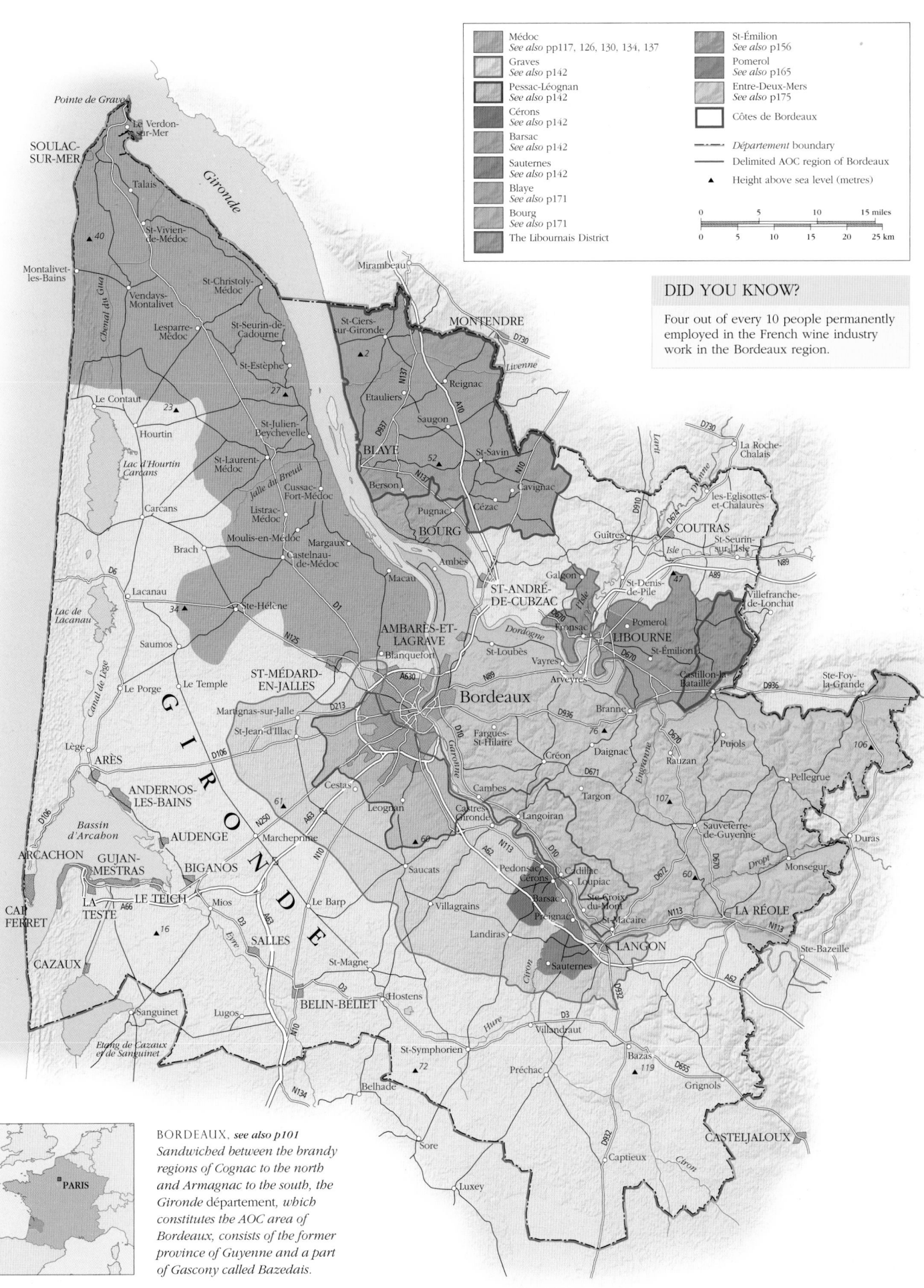

Legend

Médoc *See also pp117, 126, 130, 134, 137*	St-Émilion *See also p156*
Graves *See also p142*	Pomerol *See also p165*
Pessac-Léognan *See also p142*	Entre-Deux-Mers *See also p175*
Cérons *See also p142*	Côtes de Bordeaux
Barsac *See also p142*	
Sauternes *See also p142*	*Département* boundary
Blaye *See also p171*	Delimited AOC region of Bordeaux
Bourg *See also p171*	▲ Height above sea level (metres)
The Libournais District	

0 5 10 15 miles
0 5 10 15 20 25 km

DID YOU KNOW?

Four out of every 10 people permanently employed in the French wine industry work in the Bordeaux region.

BORDEAUX, *see also p101*
Sandwiched between the brandy regions of Cognac to the north and Armagnac to the south, the Gironde département, *which constitutes the AOC area of Bordeaux, consists of the former province of Guyenne and a part of Gascony called Bazadais.*

PARIS

Consequently, apart from a few entrepreneurial owners, power then shifted from châteaux to investors – not only banks but insurance groups, pension funds, and the like.

In today's market, therefore, the *négoce* has much less influence than before, with its *élevage* role primarily restricted to branded wines. The *élevage* of fine *cru classé* wine is either handled by the individual château itself or dispensed with by selling wines ridiculously young through French supermarkets or through the worldwide *en primeur* trade (*see* p112). Additionally, a number of château owners have carved out little empires, collecting estates or developing their own *négociant* businesses.

THE CLASSIFICATION OF BORDEAUX WINES

Of all the Bordeaux classifications that exist, it is the 1855 Classification that is meant whenever anyone refers to "The Classification". It was commissioned by the Bordeaux Chamber of Commerce, which was required by the government of the Second Empire to present a selection of its wines at the 1855 Exposition Universelle in Paris. For their own ends, the brokers of the Bordeaux Stock Exchange traditionally categorized the most famous Bordeaux properties on the basis of the prices they fetched, so they were charged by the Chamber of Commerce to submit a "complete list of classified red Bordeaux wines, as well as our great white wines". The classifications listed in the boxes on this page and the facing page give the 19th-century names in the original form as listed by the brokers on 18 April 1855. The frequent absence of the word château has been followed, as has the circumflex in *crû*, and the use of *second crû* for red wines and *deuxième crû* for whites.

THE CLASSIC GRAPE VARIETIES OF BORDEAUX

Contrary to what one might expect, it is Merlot, not Cabernet Sauvignon, that is the most important grape variety in Bordeaux. Cabernet Sauvignon represents less than 24 per cent of black grapes cultivated in Bordeaux, whereas Merlot accounts for more than 63 per cent. It is nearer the truth, therefore, to say that Cabernet Sauvignon gives backbone to Merlot, rather than to suggest that Merlot softens Cabernet Sauvignon (which is the old adage). Although Château Mouton-Rothschild contains no less than 90 per cent Cabernet Sauvignon, it is an exception, as even on the Médoc's hallowed ground, where it is blasphemy to mention the name of Merlot, 40 per cent of the vines grown are of that variety. Château Pétrus (*see* p168), one of the most expensive wines in the world, contains 95 per cent Merlot, without any Cabernet Sauvignon at all. Cabernet Sauvignon is a classic grape, quite

THE MERLOT GRAPE VARIETY
More than twice as much Merlot as Cabernet Sauvignon grows in Bordeaux.

THE 1855 CLASSIFICATION OF THE WHITE WINES OF THE GIRONDE

PREMIER CRU SUPÉRIEUR
(Superior First Growth)
Yquem, Sauternes

PREMIERS CRUS
(First Growths)
Latour Blanche, Bommes
(now *Château La Tour Blanche*)
Peyraguey, Bommes
(now two properties: *Château Lafaurie-Peyraguey* and *Château Clos Haut-Peyraguey*)
Vigneau, Bommes
(now *Château Rayne-Vigneau*)
Suduiraut, Preignac
Coutet, Barsac
Climens, Barsac
Bayle, Sauternes
(now *Château Guiraud*)
Rieusec, Sauternes
(now *Château Rieussec*, Fargues)
Rabeaud, Bomme
(now two properties: *Château Rabaud-Promis* and *Château Sigalas-Rabaud*)

DEUXIÈMES CRUS
(Second Growths)
Mirat, Barsac
(now *Château Myrat*)
Doisy, Barsac (now three properties: *Château Doisy-Daëne*, *Château Doisy-Dubroca*, and *Château Doisy-Védrines*)
Pexoto, Bommes (now part of *Château Rabaud-Promis*)
D'arche, Sauternes
(now *Château d'Arche*)
Filhot, Sauternes
Broustet Nérac, Barsac
(now two properties: *Château Brousset* and *Château Nairac*)
Caillou, Barsac
Suau, Barsac
Malle, Preignac
(now *Château de Malle*)
Romer, Preignac (now two properties: *Château Romer* and *Château Romer-du-Hayot*, Fargues)
Lamothe, Sauternes (now two properties: *Château Lamothe* and *Château Lamothe-Guignard*)

---

possibly the greatest red-wine grape in the world, but its importance for Bordeaux is often overstated.

Sémillon is the most important white grape variety grown in Bordeaux. It is significant both in terms of its extent of cultivation and quality. This grape variety is susceptible to botrytis, the "noble rot" that results in classic Sauternes and Barsac. It is therefore considered to be the world's greatest sweet-wine grape. Sémillon also accounts for most of the fine dry white wines of Bordeaux, but these are relatively few and lack prestige. Sauvignon Blanc plays the supporting role in the production of sweet wines, and is used to a greater or lesser degree for dry wines. Many of the less expensive dry white wines are pure Sauvignon Blanc varietals.

VARIETAL CONTRIBUTIONS TO A CUVÉE

The Cabernet Sauvignon is the most complex and distinctive of all black Bordeaux grapes. It has a firm tannic structure, yet with time reveals a powerful, rich, and long-lasting flavour. Wines from this grape can have great finesse; their bouquets often possess a "blackcurrant" or "violets" character. Cabernet Franc has similar characteristics to Cabernet Sauvignon, but may also have a leafy, sappy, or earthy taste depending on where it is cultivated. It does, however, shine through as the superior variety when grown in St-Émilion and Pomerol, and can compete on even terms with its more famous cousin in parts of Graves. Merlot is soft, silky, and sometimes opulent. It is a grape that charms, and can make wines with lots of juicy-rich and spicy fruit. Petit Verdot is a late-ripener with a naturally high acidity, while Malbec has a thick skin that is rich in colour pigments. Small amounts of Petit Verdot and Malbec were traditionally used to correct the colour and acidity of a blended wine. The cultivation and use of these two varieties for this purpose has been on the decline for the past 20 years owing to the various modern techniques of viticulture and vinification. The white Sémillon grape provides a wine naturally rich in flavour and high in alcohol. It makes succulent sweet white wines that are capable of great longevity. Its intrinsically low acidity makes it less suitable for producing dry wines, but in exceptional circumstances the highest quality Sémillon does make a fine dry white wine – if matured in new oak. This enhances the aromatic character of the wine and gives it a firm structure without which it would be too "fat" and "flabby".

The Sauvignon Blanc in Bordeaux is soft, delicate, and easy to drink. It does not have the same bite as it does in the Loire vineyards of Sancerre or Pouilly-Fumé, but the varietal character is more pronounced today, with a crisper, fresher style than it was a few years ago. Early harvesting, pre-fermentation maceration on the grape skins to draw out the aromatics, and longer, cooler fermentation in stainless steel have all combined to produce a far more interesting, medium-quality, dry white wine.

FERMENTATION AND MATURATION
Although some properties producing *crus classés* retain their wooden vats for the fermentation process (more because they lack the funds to re-equip than for any idealistic reasons), hardly any of them actually invest in new oak vats, preferring those made of stainless steel. The one startling exception is Château Margaux. This great property has spent more money, following the advice of the legendary oenologist Professor Peynaud, than any other château in Bordeaux. This is puzzling because it was principally at his recommendation that virtually everyone else in Bordeaux invested in stainless steel.

ADDING VIN DE PRESSE
One technique that is more characteristic of red winemaking in Bordeaux than in any other region is the addition of a certain amount of *vin de presse*. This is produced after the wine has

THE VINIFICATION PROCESS
The proportion of grape varieties grown and the intrinsic potential of a château's terroir determine the basic quality and character of Bordeaux's finest wines. However, this region's best châteaux hone their styles by manipulating the vinification process. This can include adding up to 15 per cent vin de presse; grape-skin contact (for up to a month); maturation, which used to take 3 to 5 years, but now takes 15 to 18 months; and a percentage of new oak, always the hallmark of Bordeaux's premiers crus.

completed its alcoholic fermentation and has undergone malolactic conversion. The wine is drawn off its lees into casks and the residue of skin and pips at the bottom of the vat is pressed. Normally this requires two pressings: the first *vin de presse* is the best and represents about 10 per cent of the total wine produced, the second provides a further 5 per cent. *Vin de presse* is relatively low in alcohol, very dark, and extremely tannic. In a wine made for early drinking, *vin de presse* would be harsh and unpleasant, but with the structure of a classic oak-matured Bordeaux, it gives extra body and increases longevity.

THE 1855 CLASSIFICATION OF THE RED WINES OF THE GIRONDE

They say *terroir* never changes, but that is to ignore the human impact – and so much has changed since 1885. Nearly all châteaux have increased their vineyards by either expansion or purchasing a neighbouring property, quite often both, meaning some châteaux have had their vineyards split or totally absorbed. Furthermore, the grapevines grown have changed, polarizing from maybe as many as a dozen varieties to Cabernet Sauvignon, Merlot, Cabernet Franc, and, to a much lesser extent, Petit Verdot. Go back to the Médoc in 1855, and there are many places you would not recognize. However, the 1855

Classification had little to do with *terroir* and everything to do with money, posing the fascinating question, Where would these châteaux figure in a price-based classification today? The 1855 Classification is replicated below, and the number before each producer indicates how they would be classed today according to the data provided by Benjamin Lewin MW in his book *What Price Bordeaux?* (Vendange Press, 2009). Zero implies a classification below Fifth Growth. In the second part of the box are the 14 unclassified wines, including second wines, that would qualify for *cru classé* status.

PREMIERS CRUS
(First Growths)
(1) Château Lafite, Pauillac (now *Château Lafite-Rothschild*)
(1) Château Margaux, Margaux
(1) Château Latour, Pauillac
(1) Haut-Brion, Pessac (Graves)

SECONDS CRUS
(Second Growths)
(1) Mouton, Pauillac (now *Château Mouton-Rothschild* and a first growth since 1973)
(3) Rauzan-Ségla, Margaux
(5) Rauzan-Gassies, Margaux
(2) Léoville, St-Julien (now three properties: châteaux (2) *Léoville-Las-Cases*, (3) *Léoville-Poyferré*, and (3) *Léoville-Barton*)
(5) Vivens Durfort, Margaux (now *Château Durfort-Vivens*)
(3) Gruau-Laroze, St-Julien (now *Château Gruaud-Larose*)
(3) Lascombe, Margaux (now *Château Lascombes*)
(3) Brane, Cantenac (now *Château Brane-Cantenac*)
(2) Pichon Longueville, Pauillac (now two properties: *Château Pichon-Longueville-Baron* and *Château Pichon-Longueville-Comtesse-de-Lalande*)
(2) Ducru Beau Caillou, St-Julien (now *Château Ducru-Beaucaillou*)
(2) Cos Destournel, St-Estèphe (now *Château Cos d'Estournel*)
(2) Montrose, St-Estèphe

TROISIÈMES CRUS
(Third Growths)
(4) Kirwan, Cantenac
(4) Château d'Issan, Cantenac
(4) Lagrange, St-Julien
(3) Langoa, St-Julien (now *Château Langoa-Barton*)
(4) Giscours, Labarde
(4) St-Exupéry, Margaux (now *Château Malescot-St-Exupéry*)
(0) Boyd, Cantenac (now two properties: (0) *Château Boyd-Cantenac* and (5) *Château Cantenac Brown*)
(2) Palmer, Cantenac
(4) Lalagune, Ludon (now *Château La Lagune*)
(0) Desmirail, Margaux
(4) Dubignon, Margaux (no longer in existence, but some of these original vineyards now belong to (4) *Château Malescot-St-Exupéry*, (2) *Château Palmer*, and (1) *Château Margaux*)
(3) Calon, St-Estèphe (now *Château Calon-Ségur*)
(5) Ferrière, Margaux
(0) Becker, Margaux (now *Château Marquis d'Alesme-Becker*)

QUATRIÈMES CRUS
(Fourth Growths)
(4) St-Pierre, St-Julien (now *Château St-Pierre-Sevaistre*)
(3) Talbot, St-Julien

(4) Du-Luc, St-Julien (now *Château Branaire-Ducru*)
(4) Duhart, Pauillac (at one time *Château Duhart-Milon Rothschild*, but now *Château Duhart-Milon*, although still Rothschild-owned)
(0) Pouget-Lassale, Cantenac (now *Château Pouget*)
(0) Pouget, Cantenac (now *Château Pouget*)
(0) Carnet, St-Laurent (now *Château La Tour-Carnet*)
(5) Rochet, St-Estèphe (now *Château Lafon-Rochet*)
(4) Château de Beychevele, St-Julien (now *Château Beychevele*)
(4) Le Prieuré, Cantenac (now *Château Prieuré-Lichine*)
(5) Marquis de Thermes, Margaux (now *Château Marquis-de-Terme*)

CINQUIÈMES CRUS
(Fifth Growths)
(3) Canet, Pauillac (now *Château Pontet-Canet*)
(0) Batailley, Pauillac (now two properties: (0) *Château Batailley* and (5) *Château Haut-Batailley*)
(3) Grand Puy, Pauillac (now *Château Grand-Puy-Lacoste*)
(0) Artigues Arnaud, Pauillac (now *Château Grand-Puy-Ducasse*)
(2) Lynch, Pauillac (now *Château Lynch-Bages*)
(0) Lynch Moussas, Pauillac

(5) Dauzac, Labarde
(5) Darmailhac, Pauillac (now *Château d'Armailhac*)
(5) Le Tertre, Arsac (now *Château du Tertre*)
(5) Haut Bages, Pauillac (now *Château Haut-Bages-Libéral*)
(0) Pédésclaux, Pauillac (now *Château Pédésclaux*)
(0) Coutenceau, St-Laurent (now *Château Belgrave*)
(0) Camensac, St-Laurent
(5) Cos Labory, St-Estèphe
(4) Clerc Milon, Pauillac
(0) Croizet-Bages, Pauillac
(0) Cantemerle, Macau

The following 14 wines would appear on today's classification but did not exist in 1855.

(3) Forts de Latour
(3) Pavillon Rouge de Margaux
(3) Clos du Marquis
(3) Carraudes de Lafite
(4) Haut Marbuzet
(4) Sociando Mallet
(5) Tourelle Longueville
(5) Alto Ego de Palmer
(5) Phélan Ségur
(5) Gloria
(5) Pibran
(5) Siran
(5) Labégorce
(5) Ormes de Pez

BUYING EN PRIMEUR

WHAT IS BUYING EN PRIMEUR?

This is a method of investing in Bordeaux wines by buying the wine before it is bottled. It is no longer something I subscribe to. Every château in Bordeaux attempts to pre-sell a certain amount of its wine production in the first year of the wine's life, although it will not be bottled and shipped until it is three or, perhaps, four years old.

APPROXIMATED BLENDS

The wines tasted by the trade and upon which *en primeur* offers are based will be approximated blends, which is to say that they will consist of several different casks in roughly the proportion of grape variety that will make up the final *grand vin*. Yet no matter how honest and accurate the winemaker tries to be, this can never be a true representation of the final wine. Winemakers do not know what the final proportions of grape varieties will be. Much depends on whether every

barrel matures as expected, and how strict the selection is when it comes to rejecting wines not fit for making the *grand vin*.

WINE SALES BY MAIL ORDER

The first sales usually begin in the spring after the vintage, shortly after merchants from all over the world have spent a hectic week tasting hundreds of wines barely six months old. Cask samples (wine bottled from the cask) of the best wines are taken back to their home markets for tasting by the trade and key private buyers. This can be as early as March, although June is the most popular month and it is at around then that mail-order offers go out with vivid descriptions of the wines and how they are likely to mature.

WHY BUY EN PRIMEUR?

It is only worth buying a wine that you cannot touch for three or four years (and probably should

not drink for at least another three or four years after that), if you know it will be unavailable by any other means or, when it does become available, that it is likely to cost significantly more at that time.

WHICH WINES SHOULD YOU BUY?

Wine lovers are better advised to take up offers to buy *en primeur* wines such as Cornas from the Rhône, which never seem to be available when ready to drink. As far as investments are concerned, there is only one piece of advice I can give, and that is to stick to "blue-chip" wines in top vintages. It does not matter whether cask samples of Latour, Mouton, Pétrus, Yquem, and so on bear any resemblance to the final bottled product, they will always be a good investment, and from a wine drinker's point of view, there is no point in gambling on any other Bordeaux *en primeur*.

OAK CASK MATURATION

After fermentation and prior to bottling, all the best red Bordeaux are matured in 225-litre (59-gallon) Bordeaux oak casks called *barriques*. The duration of this operation and the percentage of new oak casks used should depend entirely on the quality and structure of the wine, and this will vary according to the vintage. The bigger the wine, the more new oak it can take and the longer maturation it will need. The greatest wines – all the *premiers crus* – require at least 18 to 24 months in 100 per cent new oak to reach maturity. Other fine-quality Bordeaux wines do not need so much time, perhaps only 12 to 18 months, and do not benefit from 100 per cent new oak; between 30 and 50 per cent may be enough. If you get the chance, put your nose into a new oak cask before it has been used. The wonderful creamy-smoky, vanilla-and-charcoal aroma is the very essence of what should come through when a fine wine has been properly matured in oak.

PAST, PRESENT, AND FUTURE

During the early 1980s, the idea of "second wines" – always a factor in the production of the finest Bordeaux growths – began to catch on among the properties producing *crus bourgeois*, enabling

BARRELS IN A BORDEAUX CHAI
These new oak barriques *at Château Langoa-Barton contain the wines of Château Léoville-Barton. (Léoville-Barton has no chai of its own.) Both properties belong to the Barton family, who are of British descent.*

modest estates to make much better wines through stricter selection of their *grands vins*. Towards the end of the 1980s, "green harvesting", or crop-thinning, became *de rigueur* for all quality-conscious châteaux (even though the Romans considered such practices essential 2,000 years ago!).

However, the most significant advance in Bordeaux over the past 20 years came in 1994, when a decision was taken to harvest grapes according to tannin ripeness, rather than sugar-acidity ripeness. Unripe tannins are not hydrolysed; they are hard and will never soften, whereas ripe tannins are hydrolysed, have a certain suppleness from day one, and will always soften. This phenomenon has long been known, but precisely when it occurs can vary from region to region, and year to year. In Bordeaux tannin ripeness has been under study since 1986 by Vincent Dupuch, who discovered that grapes deemed physiologically ripe in Bordeaux by their sugar-acidity ratio actually possessed a high proportion of unripe tannins.

In 1994, many *bordelais* harvested according to Dupuch's tannin ripeness parameters and were surprised to discover the optimum moment to pick was, in fact, much later than they had previously thought. This means not only that many Bordeaux wines will be riper, but also that by determining ripeness in this way, the winemaker is aware of the precise phenolic content, and this allows the fine-tuning of maceration and fermentation for each batch of grapes.

The 21st century will see a continuation in the rise of super-premium boutique wines, particularly from St-Émilion. However, the increase in the density of vines to raise general standards in several Bordeaux appellations has been delayed. According to decrees issued in 1994, these new standards were to be fast-tracked, but this was fudged by new decrees in 1998, which let some areas off the hook, making higher-density planting not legally enforceable until 2025.

Meanwhile, the volume of dry white Bordeaux has dropped, leaving fewer producers making superior wines. Once the poorest cousin in Bordeaux, dry whites are better today than they have ever been. This applies across the board, from the lowliest Entre-Deux-Mers to the finest classified growth, even to the point where the 1993 Château Couhins-Lurton became the first ever Bordeaux *cru classé* to be sealed with a screwcap.

In a move to inform the public, and increase the region's profile among consumers of wines that do not include the Bordeaux name in the appellation (from Bourg to Blaye, and Fronsac to Pauillac *et al*), all wines must include "Vin de Bordeaux" or "Grand Vin de Bordeaux" on the label.

RECENT BORDEAUX VINTAGES

2010 This year has had the bad luck to be a very good – possibly very great – vintage that follows on the heels of the extraordinary 2009. However, the potential greatness of 2010 started early, when it suffered from *coulure* at fruit set (as did 1961), and the style of the wine will forever be marked by its very dry summer, with hardly any rain in August. This resulted in a small crop, 20 to 30 per cent down across the region, of small berries with very thick skins and (because of beneficial rain at the start of September) good phenolic ripeness. The 2010s are bigger and heftier than the 2009s, but at this stage they do not appear to be as fine or as consistent across the appellations. Thus, I would suggest that, although probably a great vintage, 2010 is not as great as 2009.

2009 This is without doubt one of the greatest Bordeaux vintages on record, and the 2009 reds on both banks (although a tad stronger on the left bank) are at least as good as the 2005s but bigger in every sense, with more fruit, more tannin, and more acidity. The greatest 2009s are totally *terroir*-driven, while the greatest 2005s

are more man-made. This is the 1961 of modern times. With a vintage this great, you do not need many words, as the wines will do all the talking. Sauternes and Barsac have been surprisingly underrated by some, but have no fear: this is one of the all-time great botrytis vintages.

2008 An Indian summer saved Bordeaux, following a rather miserable July and August. The hot and dry weather from September through to October produced clear skies into which the heat flew during the night, creating a significant diurnal difference that favoured Cabernet Sauvignon more than any other variety. Not that the Merlot did not fare well; some great Pomerols were produced. Generally this vintage provided a healthy crop of an excellent quality, hallmarked by fine aromatics from those cool nights during the vital *véraison* period. Good but not exceptional dry white wines. Barsac was marginally better than Sauternes, but both lack botrytis richness.

2007 Forget the reds (well most of them) – this is a white-wine vintage. The best that can be

said about the reds is that it is an extremely varied vintage, thus by definition some good wines have been made; the best of those are soft and seductive, early-drinking wines. The whites, on the other hand, are wonderful – from some of the best dry whites in memory, to the best Sauternes and Barsacs since 2001.

2006 A bizarre year in which July was too hot, August too cool, September much too wet, and the generally high humidity a pain for all, including the *sauternais* at times. With rot, unripe grapes, and raisined berries in abundance, strict selection during the harvest was essential. The best wines will be extremely elegant, but few and far between, with relatively modest natural alcohol levels. This year favoured Merlot over Cabernet Sauvignon, thus right bank over left, although those who restricted yields heavily declassified wines into their second and third labels. For reds, therefore, this is an extremely variable vintage; but for white wines, 2006 is something of a revelation, particularly for Sauternes, Barsac, and other late-picked sweet wines.

BORDEAUX'S BEST GENERIC BRANDS

Bordeaux has the greatest reputation for red wine in the world, but as in all regions, ordinary wines do exist. In fact, the majority of wines produced in any region is very ordinary, and Bordeaux is no exception. Remember that more than money separates Mouton Cadet from Château Mouton-Rothschild. While the former might be the most famous of all generic Bordeaux brands, it is merely the blended product of relatively inferior wines grown anywhere within the vast *départemental* appellation of Bordeaux, while the latter is a selection of one of the finest wines grown on a single estate – a *premier cru classé* in the small, communal AOC of Pauillac.

In the following top 10 best-selling Bordeaux brands, there is a big drop in volume between the top three, which turnover more than 3 million cases in total every year, whilst the rest can barely manage 500,000 cases between them.

[1] Mouton Cadet; [2] Malesan (Castel); [3] Baron de Lestac (Castel); [4] Dourthe No.1; [5] Marquis de Chasse (Ginestet); [6] Premius Exigence (Yvon Mau); [7] Calvet Reserve; [8] Sirius (Maison Sichel); [9] Mascaron (Ginestet); [10] Michel Lynch (Jean Michel Cazes).

Branded generic Bordeaux wine can be a disappointing introduction to the world's greatest wine region, so the following brands are suggested as reliable choices.

CORDIER
What they used to call "good luncheon claret" in the old days.

LA COUR PAVILLON
One of the most reliable and underrated generic Bordeaux wines on the market at the moment. Made at Château Loudenne, this wine always displays good fruit, but possesses enough structure to keep for a while.

DOURTHE NO.1
Probably the best, largest-selling branded Bordeaux available.

KRESSMAN MONOPOLE BLANC
This is one of the few big white Bordeaux blends to show any distinctive character.

MAÎTRE D'ESTOURNEL
This has the same connection to Château Cos d'Estournel as "Mouton Cadet" has to Château Mouton-Rothschild, which is absolutely non-existent as far as the wine is concerned, but both brands hope to sell on the back of their respective château name. There is, however, a fundamental difference between the two, of course: "Maître d'Estournel" happens to be an expressive, early-drinking wine that can also take a few years in bottle, whereas "Mouton Cadet" is mutton dressed up as lamb.

MICHEL LYNCH
Produced by Michel Cazes of Château Lynch-Bages in an unashamedly up-front, fruity style. Red, white, and rosé are all thoroughly recommended.

PREMIUS EXIGENCE
Produced by Yvon Mau, the step up between the premium Premius and Premius Exigence is about as big as it can get for two wines sharing the

same brand. The stricter selection of grapes and no-expense-spared handling shows through in the richer, oak-layered fruit.

SICHEL SIRIUS
This is as serious as it sounds. An excellent oak-aged generic Bordeaux, it will improve for a further year or two in bottle.

THOMAS BARTON RÉSERVE
This superb range of district-level brands (Graves Blanc, Médoc, Saint-Émilion, Sauternes, Margaux, and the limited-edition Privée Médoc) has quickly established a reputation for its exceptionally exciting generic wines.

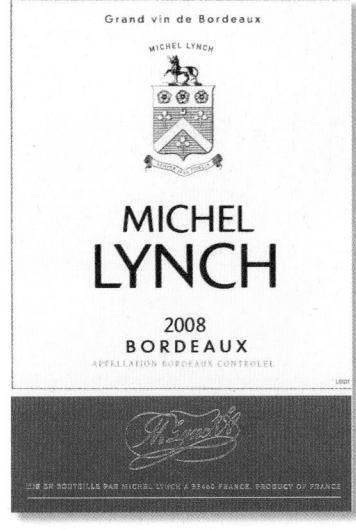

THE APPELLATIONS OF GENERIC
BORDEAUX

BORDEAUX AOC

Wines carrying the generic appellation may come from any AOC vineyard in the entire Gironde. Some of the most interesting wines are from classic areas where the more specific appellation is confined to a precise style: such as a red Bordeaux produced by a château in Sauternes. If the wine is a brand, it should be ready to drink. If it is a château wine, the address should reveal its origin, and the price will be an indication of its quality and a guide to when it should be drunk.

RED Most are simply dry luncheon claret styles, made for early drinking and usually softened by a high Merlot content.

🍇 Cabernet Sauvignon, Cabernet Franc, Carmenère, Merlot, Malbec, Petit Verdot

⌛ 1–5 years

WHITE All medium-dry basic white Bordeaux contain at least 4 grams of residual sugar per litre, and have a certain sweetness. It is by far the most variable appellation category, with many dull wines. If the wine contains less than 4 grams of residual sugar per litre, the Bordeaux appellation must be qualified by "Sec". These dry whites are also variable, but most of the best wines of the appellation are found among them. They may be sold from 1 December without any mention of *primeur* or *nouveau*.

🍇 Sémillon, Sauvignon, Muscadelle plus up to 30% in total of Merlot Blanc, Colombard, Mauzac, Ondenc, Ugni Blanc

⌛ 1–2 years

ROSÉ When made by individual properties, this medium-dry, medium-bodied wine can be attractive. These wines may be sold from 1 December following the harvest without any mention of *primeur* or *nouveau*.

🍇 Cabernet Sauvignon, Cabernet Franc, Carmenère, Merlot, Malbec, Petit Verdot

⌛ Immediately

BORDEAUX ROSÉ AOC

The theory is that this appellation is reserved for wine deliberately produced as rosé, while "Bordeaux Clairet" is for a light-coloured red wine. Both may simply be labelled "Bordeaux AOC". For technical details, *see* Bordeaux AOC.

BORDEAUX SEC AOC

White Bordeaux with less than 4 grams of residual sugar per litre (*see* Bordeaux AOC).

BORDEAUX SUPÉRIEUR AOC

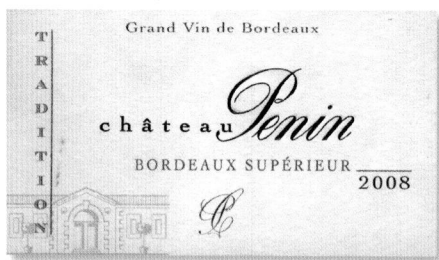

Technically superior to Bordeaux AOC by only half a degree of alcohol for *rouge* and two degrees for *blanc*, yet most of these wines do seem to have a greater consistency of quality, and therefore value. All generics are variable, but this one is less so than most.

RED These dry, light-bodied or medium- to full-bodied wines vary a lot but are generally fuller and richer than most red wines using the basic Bordeaux appellation.

🍇 Cabernet Sauvignon, Cabernet Franc, Carmenère, Merlot, Malbec, Petit Verdot

⌛ 2–6 years

WHITE Dry or sometimes sweet, light- to medium-bodied white wines that are little seen.

🍇 Sémillon, Sauvignon, Muscadelle plus up to 30% in total of Merlot Blanc, Colombard, Mauzac, Ondenc, Ugni Blanc; the proportion of Merlot Blanc must not exceed 15%

⌛ 1–2 years

CÔTES DE BORDEAUX

The proposal for this new combined appellation (March 2009) can be traced back as far as 1975, when growers felt they stood a better chance of survival together than apart, following the economic depression of the early 1970s. At that time, there were six established appellations involved in the project, but Graves des Vayres dropped out because the term "Côtes" had never been part of its identity, and Côtes de Bourg parted company when its members became concerned about possible confusion with the Premières Côtes de Bordeaux. The result is probably even more confusing than the Côtes de Bourg growers feared, as the Premières Côtes de Bordeaux district is now part of Cadillac Côtes de Bordeaux (along with Côtes de Bordeaux Saint-Macaire, Loupiac, and Sainte-Croix-du-Mont), and all four Côtes de Bordeaux-named districts are located in three equidistant blocks 40 kilometres (25 miles) from each other and separated by a clutch of other AOCs. There is nothing to suggest why these four AOCs should be connected with each other and everything to indicate that Bordeaux or Bordeaux Supérieur would be a more appropriate linkage – an option that was (and still is) open to some of these wines anyway. The Côtes de Bordeaux appellation plain and simple may be used only for red wines.

For Blaye Côtes de Bordeaux, *see* p173; Cadillac Côtes de Bordeaux, p176; Castillon Côtes de Bordeaux, p154; and Francs Côtes de Bordeaux, p154.

RED In theory, these could be a blend of any two or more of four appellations, so are impossible to describe in any generic terms at this juncture.

🍇 Cabernet Sauvignon, Cabernet Franc, and Merlot, plus secondary varieties Malbec, Carmenère, and Petit Verdot

CRÉMANT DE BORDEAUX AOC

This was introduced in 1990 to replace the old Bordeaux Mousseux AOC (which was phased out on 31 December 1995). Changing the appellation has done nothing to change the product because, like its predecessor, Crémant de Bordeaux is merely a modest and inoffensive fizz. It lacks the spirit and expressiveness to stand out from the sea of far cheaper, but equally boring, sparkling wines that exist almost everywhere. I have tasted much better from areas far less suited to sparkling wine than Bordeaux.

SPARKLING WHITE Varies from dry to sweet and light- to medium-bodied, but is almost always bland.

🍇 Sémillon, Sauvignon, Muscadelle, Ugni Blanc, Colombard, Cabernet Sauvignon, Cabernet Franc, Carmenère, Merlot, Malbec, Petit Verdot

⌛ 1–2 years

SPARKLING ROSÉ The authorities should have taken advantage of the introduction of a new appellation to allow the inclusion of white grapes for this style, as this would potentially have improved the quality.

🍇 Cabernet Sauvignon, Cabernet Franc, Carmenère, Merlot, Malbec, Petit Verdot

⌛ 2–3 years

THE WINE PRODUCERS OF
BORDEAUX AND BORDEAUX SUPÉRIOR

BORDEAUX

CHÂTEAU BEAULIEU
Le Gay
★

Brilliant value until 2005, then a step up in quality. This is one to watch – definitely a future star. But make sure you get in before the price shoots up!

CHÂTEAU BERTINERIE
Cavignac

A serious rosé, pleasantly romantic, with delicately rich, floral fruit on the palate and a smooth finish.

CHÂTEAU CARSIN
Rions

Popular in the UK; influenced by the New World.

CHÂTEAU COURTEY
St-Macaire
★ ⓥ

Intensely flavoured old-style wines, with quite a remarkable bouquet.

CHÂTEAU FAUGAS
Cadillac

Well-balanced reds with attractive berry-fruit flavours.

CHÂTEAU DU GRAND MOUËYS
Capian

Consistently elegant red wines.

CHÂTEAU GRAND VILLAGE
Mouillac

Rich and easy Merlot-dominated,

oak-aged red, and a good second wine under the "Beau Village" label.

CHÂTEAU DE HAUX
Haux

Gorgeously ripe, dry white wine, with very fresh and elegant fruit.

CHÂTEAU LAGROSSE
Tabanac
★☆**V**

Elegant, ripe, and long, with lemony-rich, oaky fruit.

CHÂTEAU LAPÉYÈRE
Cadillac

Well-structured red, dominated by Cabernet Sauvignon.

CHÂTEAU DE LUGUGNAC
Pellegrue

Romantic 15th-century château making attractive, firm, and fleshy red that can show some finesse.

CHÂTEAU MARJOSSE
Branne
☆**V**

This is Pierre Lurton's home, where he makes lush and up-front reds with creamy-silky fruit and a beautiful dry white.

CHÂTEAU MORILLON
Monségur
★☆**V**

Rich, fat, and juicy wines.

CHÂTEAU PLAISANCE
Capian

This château makes excellent, lightly rich Bordeaux Blanc Sec from 50-year-old vines and fermented in oak.

CHÂTEAU DE PLASSAN
Tabanac
★☆**V**

The basic Bordeaux Blanc Sec has fresh, swingeing Sauvignon fruit, while the more expensive Bordeaux Blanc Sec, which is fermented and aged in oak, has lovely creamy fruit and a fine, lemony-vanilla finish.

CHÂTEAU POUCHAUD-LARQUEY
La Réole
◉

Full and rich red with lots of fruit.

CAVE DE QUINSAC
La Tresne

Delicately coloured, light-bodied, rosé-style wines sold as clairet.

CHÂTEAU RENON
Langoiran
★☆**V**

This is a pleasantly fresh and floral Sauvignon-style wine.

CHÂTEAU REYNON
Cadillac
★☆**V**

This is a star-performing château that produces cru classé dry white

wine under the auspices of Denis Dubourdieu. The elite Vieilles Vignes *cuvée* is quite extraordinary, but everything produced here can be relied upon, right down to the aptly named "Le Second de Reynon". Also very good red.

CHÂTEAU ROC-DE-CAYLA
Targon

Easy-drinking, well-balanced reds with good fruit and some finesse.

LE ROSÉ DE CLARKE
Castelnau-de-Médoc

From Château Clarke, this has all the fragrance expected from a classic dry rosé.

CHÂTEAU THIEULEY
Créon
★☆**V**

These are medium-bodied, elegant reds that possess more than just a hint of cask-ageing. Also fine, fresh, floral, and fruity white wines.

CHÂTEAU TIMBERLAY
St-André-de-Cubzac
★☆**V**

Deep-coloured, full of flavour, but not without a certain elegance.

BORDEAUX SUPÉRIEUR

CHÂTEAU DES ARRAS
St-André-de-Cubzac
★☆**V**

Deep-coloured wines with good structure and lots of chunky fruit.

CHÂTEAU LA COMBE-CADIOT
Blanquefort
★☆**V**

Well-coloured wines with a big bouquet; oaky with delicious fruit.

CHÂTEAU FONCHEREAU
St-Loubès
★☆**V**

Well-structured, finely balanced *vins de garde* of extremely good quality.

CHÂTEAU FOUCHÉ
Bourg-sur-Gironde

This wine is firm yet has fat, juicy fruit and a smooth finish.

CHÂTEAU LA GRANGE-LES-TOURS
St-André-de-Cubzac

Well-made, full, flavoursome wines.

CHÂTEAU GREE LAROQUE
St-Ciers-d'Abzac
★

Elegantly rich wines, with succulent, beautifully focused fruit supported by fine-grained tannins.

CHÂTEAU GROSSOMBRE
Branne
★☆**V**

Nicely concentrated, very good red wine which will improve for 12 to 18 months, and represents exceptional value.

CHÂTEAU JEAN FAUX
Ste-Radegonde
★

An ancient wine property that once belonged to the Knights Templars, Château Jean Faux has been brought back to life by wine-loving *tonnelier* Pascal Collotte, with the advice of top consultant Stéphane Derenoncourt.

CHÂTEAU LATOUR
Sauveterre-de-Guyenne

These medium-bodied wines have consistently good fruit, smooth flavour, and make a cheap punt to get the "latour" name on the table!

CHÂTEAU LAVILLE
St-Loubès

Rich, tannic, and powerfully structured wines with spicy fruit.

MARQUIS DE BOIRAC
Castillon-la-Batille
★☆**V**

Super value *coopérative* wine with a big, oaky aroma and fruit to match.

CHÂTEAU MÉAUME
Coutras

Alan Johnson-Hill used to be a UK wine merchant before settling north of Pomerol. Since then, he has gained a reputation for cleverly tailoring this red Bordeaux to young British palates.

CHÂTEAU LA MICHELERIE
St-André-de-Cubzac

Another property producing a big, tannic style of wine.

CHÂTEAU LES MOINES-MARTIN
Galgon

This is a well-made wine for reasonably early drinking, with an attractive bouquet, round fruit, and fine balance.

CHÂTEAU PÉNIN
Génissac
★★☆

Dark fruits and dark colour. The quality from this château has been nothing short of *cru classé* standard since the turn of the century.

CHÂTEAU PEY LA TOUR
Salleboeuf
★☆**V**

From the Dourthe stable, the Réserve is always a deeply impressive, almost pure varietal Merlot wine.

CHÂTEAU DE PIERREDON
Sauveterre-de-Guyenne
★☆**V**

Cabernet Sauvignon-dominated Bordeaux from the Haut-Benauge.

CHÂTEAU LE PIN BEAUSOLEIL
St-Ciers-d'Abzac
★

Originally named Le Pin, this ancient property was purchased in 1997 by Arnaud Pauchet, who renovated and renamed it. He soon started making a name for his wine, with the help of consultant Stéphane Derenoncourt. He sold it in 2002 to Dr Michael Hallek, who retained Derenoncourt.

ROSÉ DE LASCOMBES
Margaux

Refreshing, fruity rosé of excellent character, quality, and finesse.

CHÂTEAU DE SEGUIN
La Tresne

Look out for the Cuvée Prestige, which is rich and smoother than the basic Château de Seguin.

CHÂTEAU TOUR-DE-L'ESPÉRANCE
Galgon
★☆**V**

This is soft and smooth wine, full of fat, ripe, and juicy fruit, yet not without finesse.

CHÂTEAU TOUR PETIT PUCH
St-Germain-du-Puch
★☆**V**

Attractively coloured, well-made wines, with a touch of spice.

CHÂTEAU DE LA VIEILLE CHAPELLE
Lugnon-et-l'Île-du-Carney
★☆

Try La Cuvée A&A, which is the world's very last pure Bouchalès (Prolongeau).

CHÂTEAU DE LA VIEILLE TOUR
St-Michel-Lapujade
★☆**V**

Consistently rich and smooth, even in notoriously harsh vintages.

CHÂTEAU VIEUX MOULIN
Villegouge

Well-rounded, long, supple wines, of consistently fine quality.

THE MÉDOC

If the Médoc was in California, its growers would no doubt be criticized for cultivating such a relatively flat area, and so-called experts would encourage them to go up into the hills of Blaye, where they will find true terroir. *That is, after all, exactly what the Romans thought. The style of wine alters more radically over short distances in the Médoc than in any other French red wine district.*

THE WINES ARE MILD and unexceptional immediately northwest of Bordeaux, but from Ludon onwards they become progressively more characterful, acquire finesse, and – after Margaux – gain considerable body. Beyond St-Estèphe, the firmness of body of the wines eventually turns to coarseness, and their finesse fades.

The Médoc takes its name from the Latin phrase *medio aquae* – "between the waters" – referring to the Gironde estuary and the Atlantic Ocean. It is a long, thin strip of prized vines, extending northwest from the city limits of Bordeaux to the Pointe de Grave. At its centre is the classic area of Bordeaux, where the vast majority of the most famous châteaux are located, and yet this was the last major district of Bordeaux to be cultivated. While winemaking in the Libournais district of St-Émilion began as early as the Roman occupation, it was another thousand years before scattered plots of vines spread along the Médoc. Across the large, brown expanse of water called the Gironde, the Romans viewed Bourg and considered its hilly area far more suitable for growing vines. At that time the marshland of the Médoc was difficult to cross and impossible to cultivate. Today, the Médoc is the envy of winemakers the world over and Bourg is merely a source of inexpensive, if good-value, basic Bordeaux.

THE MÉDOC STYLE: VARIATIONS ON A THEME

The four famous communes of Margaux, St-Julien, Pauillac, and St-Estèphe, plus the two lesser-known but developing communes of Listrac and Moulis, are to be found in a region within the Médoc known as the Haut-Médoc, where the wines are fine, firm, and fleshy. The Haut-Médoc begins at the southern outskirts of the city of Blanquefort, along the northern reaches of the Graves district where the wines are fairly neutral. The greatest wines of the Haut-Médoc are found in the area beginning at Ludon with Château la Lagune – the first *cru classé* encountered moving north from Blanquefort. Fine *crus bourgeois* are to be found in this area as well.

The wines at Margaux are soft and velvety and full of charm, although they are very much *vins de garde* and will improve well with age. The wines of St-Julien are elegant with a very pure flavour. They have the delicate touch of Margaux, yet lean closer to Pauillac in body. The wines of Pauillac are powerful, often

FACTORS AFFECTING TASTE AND QUALITY

LOCATION
The Médoc lies on the left bank of the Gironde estuary, stretching northwest from Bordeaux in the south to Soulac in the north.

CLIMATE
Two large masses of water either side of the Médoc – the Atlantic and the Gironde – act as a heat-regulator and help provide a microclimate ideal for viticulture. The Gulf Stream generally gives the Médoc mild winters, warm summers, and long, sunny autumns. The district is protected from westerly and northwesterly winds by the continuous coastal strip of pine forest that runs roughly parallel to the Médoc.

ASPECT
Undulating hillsides with knolls and gentle slopes are characteristic of the Médoc. The best vineyards can "see the river" and virtually all areas of the Haut-Médoc gradually slope from the watershed to the Gironde. Marshy areas, where vines cannot be grown, punctuate most communes.

SOIL
Similar topsoils lie over different subsoils in the Médoc. Its topsoils are typically outcrops of gravel, consisting of sand mixed with siliceous gravel of varying particle size. Subsoils may contain gravel and reach a depth of several metres, or may consist of sand, often rich in humus, and some limestone and clay.

VITICULTURE AND VINIFICATION
Only red wines can use the Médoc appellation. Mechanical harvesting is commonplace and all grapes are destalked prior to fermentation in tanks, or in vats increasingly made of stainless steel. Skin contact lasts for one to two weeks, although some châteaux have reverted to the once standard four weeks.

GRAPE VARIETIES
Primary varieties: Cabernet Franc, Cabernet Sauvignon, Merlot
Secondary varieties: Carmenère, Malbec, Petit Verdot

BARRELMAKING AT LAFITE-ROTHSCHILD
Wines are aged in new oak at Château Lafite-Rothschild, although for a shorter length of time than in the past. The barrels are made with great care in a time-honoured, traditional manner.

DISTRIBUTION OF MÉDOC CRUS CLASSÉS THROUGHOUT THE APPELLATIONS

APPELLATION	GROWTHS					
	1ST	2ND	3RD	4TH	5TH	TOTAL
Haut-Médoc	0	0	1	1	3	5
St-Estèphe	0	2	1	1	1	5
Pauillac	3	2	0	1	12	18
St-Julien	0	5	2	4	0	11
Margaux	1	5	10	3	2	21
TOTAL	4	14	14	10	18	60

having a rich blackcurrant flavour with hints of cedar and tobacco. These are wines of great finesse, and Pauillac can be considered the greatest appellation of the Médoc. St-Estèphe includes many minor growths of rustic charm and a few classic wines, and technology is changing the robustness of its spicy wines to richness.

Beyond St-Estèphe lies the commune of St-Seurin-de-Cadourne, whose wines are entitled to use the Haut-Médoc appellation, after which the appellation becomes simply AOC Médoc. This area, formerly known as the Bas-Médoc, has a lesser reputation than the Haut-Médoc. However, many exceptional wines are made here: the triangle formed by St-Yzans, Lesparre, and Valeyrac contains such outstanding minor growths as Loudenne, Potensac, la Cardonne, Blaignan, les Ormes-Sorbet, la Tour-St-Bonnet, la Tour-de-By, and Patache d'Aux. In general the style is more simplistic than in the Haut-Médoc.

PROPORTION OF AOC AREA UNDER VINE REPRESENTED BY CRUS CLASSÉS

APPELLATION	UNDER VINE HA	(ACRES)	CRUS CLASSÉS HA	(ACRES)	REPRESENTS
Médoc	5,652	(13,966)	–		No crus classés
Haut-Médoc	4,596	(11,357)	379	(1,039)	8% of AOC, 11% of crus classés
Listrac	597	(1,475)	–		No crus classés
Moulis	603	(1,490)	–		No crus classés
St-Estèphe	1,214	(3,000)	248	(680)	20% of AOC, 7% of crus classés
Pauillac	1,212	(2,995)	1,063	(2,914)	88% of AOC, 32% of crus classés
St-Julien	920	(2,273)	740	(2,028)	80% of AOC, 22% of crus classés
Margaux	1,489	(3,679)	884	(2,423)	59% of AOC, 26% of crus classés
TOTAL	**16,283**	**(40,235)**	**3,314**	**(9,084)**	20% of all Médoc AOCs, 99% of all crus classés*

* Not 100% because Château Haut-Brion was included in the 1855 Classification

THE FIGHT FOR GRAVEL

The best soils for vine-growing also happen to be the most suitable for gravel quarrying. After the war, in the absence of any legislation, gravel quarrying started in abandoned vineyards. Once the gravel was gone, the opportunity to reclaim the area as a vineyard was lost. There is plenty of gravel in the Gironde estuary itself, but it is more profitable to take it from an open pit. Quarrying companies will continue to plunder the Médoc's finite resources until the government agrees to protect them, but past administrations have shown little interest.

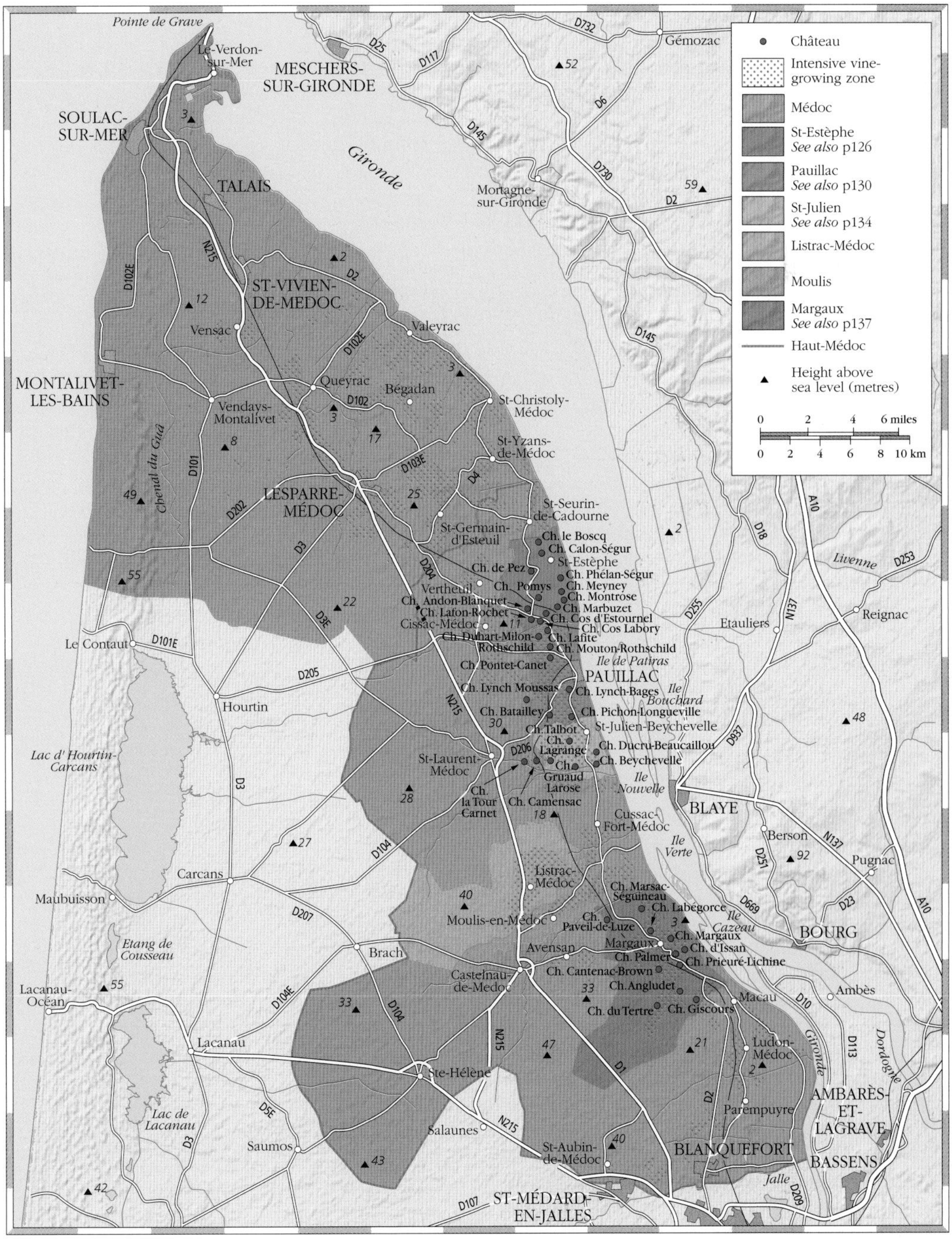

THE MÉDOC, *see also p109*

The Médoc, a narrow strip of land between the Gironde estuary and the Atlantic Ocean, stretches northwards from the city of Bordeaux to the Pointe de Grave. The climate is Bordeaux's mildest, moderated by both the estuary and the ocean.

CRU BOURGEOIS – A CLASS STRUGGLE!

It's all change as far as the *bourgeois* growths are concerned. The original Cru Bourgeois Classification of 1932 had been carried out by Bordeaux wine brokers – as, in fact, had the famous 1855 Classification – and this recognized no fewer than 444 Médoc properties divided into three hierarchal levels: *crus bourgeois exceptionnel* (six properties), *crus bourgeois supérieur* (99 properties) and the basic *crus bourgeois* (339 properties). Although this worked well enough for three decades, there were only 94 *cru bourgeois* properties remaining by the 1960s, the others having been grubbed up, abandoned, or consolidated. Furthermore, although authorized by the Bordeaux Chamber of Commerce, this classification had never been submitted for ministerial ratification, thus the term *cru bourgeois* was not recognized by the French government and therefore had little meaning. In 1962, the surviving properties established the Syndicat des Crus Bourgeois and set about establishing a new classification, which made an initial assessment of 101 *crus bourgeois* in 1966, and this was expanded to 124 in 1978. Although the 94 surviving properties had widened their scope to include other châteaux, the classification did exclude a number of highly regarded châteaux. Additionally, those selected as the very best (*cru bourgeois exceptionnel*) and generally superior (*cru bourgeois supérieur*) were not allowed to use those terms, as the Common Market regulations of 1979 permitted only the words *cru bourgeois*. Being French, they used the terms anyway. However, they were not the only ones flouting the law, as many of those demoted in 1978 from one of the higher ranks they had previously enjoyed continued to use their 1932 status, while the term *cru bourgeois* was often used for second wines, unclassified properties, and even châteaux outside of the Médoc in Blaye, Bourg, and Sauternes.

It was obvious that the legal situation had to be rectified, but it was not until November 2000 that a new *cru bourgeois* law could be agreed and ratified by ministerial decree. This legislation required the classification to be reassessed every 12 years, and the first such reassessment took place in June 2003, when just 247 of the 490 châteaux that applied were successful. Such a high failure rate indicated a level of seriousness often lacking in most forms of French wine assessment, whether for classifications, AOC acceptance, or whatever. No classification will ever be perfect, as there will always be deserving producers who are excluded – not simply due to a flaw in the system or errors of judgment, but because they might simply have abstained from the process. Overall, however, the judging panel on this occasion got it right. Inevitably, some château owners objected to the outcome, and none more so that Jean-François Mau, who was "outraged" by the exclusion of his Château Preuillac. Mau had purchased this property in 1998, but the panel tasted wines from the vintages of 1994 to 1999 only, which is why he was so critical of the process, stating, "It is a huge injustice to be judged on the past and not present performance." Mau had a point. The past is important, but it should be evaluated within the context of more recent vintages: is the trend for improvement or decline? As this classification required reassessment every 12 years, it would seem logical to assess the 12 immediately previous vintages, and had that been the case, Château Preuillac would no doubt have been included. The objections achieved critical mass in 2007, when, after an acrimonious series of legal challenges and counter-challenges, a total of 77 aggrieved châteaux appeared before Jean-Pierre Valeins, the magistrate of Bordeaux's administrative court of appeal. Although Valeins admitted that it was not a case of who was right and who was wrong, he had no hesitation in annulling the classification – a decision that was subsequently endorsed by the French government. The magistrate revealed that four of the 18 members on the classification panel had direct ties to a number of châteaux included in the 2003 classification, but essentially his decision came down to the fact that, in a classification, all the wines are judged in relation to each other. As Valeins told *Decanter* magazine, "You cannot reconsider some without the rest. You have to start all over."

In November 2009, the French government ratified a decree for the latest incarnation of *cru bourgeois*. This annual scheme was called the Reconnaissance system, whereby the term *cru bourgeois* – and *cru bourgeois* only – will be awarded to châteaux on an exclusively vintage-by-vintage basis. In the first of a two-step process open to all properties in the Médoc, the *cuverie* of all applicants is subjected to a quality-control check (a process that will be repeated every five years), and any successful château may submit its wine for annual blind assessment by an independently audited panel of impartial tasters. The wines are tasted two years after they were made, at the time of bottling, and this is the only obvious flaw in an otherwise impressive new system, as the wine could be adversely affected by the bottling process. It would make far more sense to insist on a minimum ageing period between bottling and shipping and to taste the wines after they have had sufficient time to settle in bottle.

Compared to the 247 successful applicants out of the 490 châteaux that applied for *cru bourgeois* status in 2003, the number qualifying for *cru bourgeois* in 2008, the first Reconnaissance vintage (243 out of 290 submitted), would make the cynic think that the French are back to their old tricks. However, you can see this is not so when you look a bit deeper. The first thing that should give readers a clue is that the 243 successful applicants in 2008 are almost the same as the 247 in 2003. Most of the other 240-odd châteaux have not improved their game and probably never will under their current ownership; consequently, they either accepted that it would not be worth the effort and cost of applying, or their *cuveries* failed the quality-control check. Some might up their game as the term *cru bourgeois* re-establishes itself as price-enhancing brand name. There are also some highly regarded properties that previously held the status of *cru bourgeois exceptionnel* or *cru bourgeois supérieur* and did not see the value in applying for what was effectively a lower-grade title for the 2008 vintage. The very best of those are probably right and can no doubt make a better go of it by building their own brand. Those that cannot might return to the fold. But even taking into account all the properties that will make a concerted effort to improve quality – including previously unclassified châteaux under new ownership – I cannot see Alliance membership rising above 350 or the number of successful *cru bourgeois* in any one vintage topping 320. I might be wrong, and if I am because of a genuine increase in quality, I hope I am.

In the meantime, since the 2003 classification strictly selected only nine *crus bourgeois exceptionnel* and none participated in the Cru Bourgeois Reconnaissance, I have listed them below.

Château Chasse-Spleen (Moulis-en-Médoc, AOC Moulis)

Château Haut-Marbuzet (Saint-Estèphe, AOC Saint-Estèphe)

Château Labégorce Zédé (Soussans, AOC Margaux) – now absorbed by Château Labégorce

Château Les Ormes de Pez (Saint-Estèphe, AOC Saint-Estèphe)

Château de Pez (Saint-Estèphe, AOC Saint-Estèphe)

Château Phélan Ségur (Saint-Estèphe, AOC Saint-Estèphe)

Château Potensac (Ordonnac, AOC Médoc)

Château Poujeaux (Moulis-en-Médoc, AOC Moulis)

Château Siran (Labarde, AOC Margaux)

THE APPELLATIONS OF
THE MÉDOC

HAUT-MÉDOC AOC

This AOC encompasses the Médoc's four finest communes – Margaux, St-Julien, Pauillac, and St-Estèphe – as well as the less well-known Listrac and Moulis communes. Wines produced outside these six appellations but within the Haut-Médoc are not generally as thrilling, although infinitely superior to those of Médoc. Among these very reliable wines are a few great-value *crus classés* and many high-quality *crus bourgeois*, but although Haut-Médoc is a name to look out for on the label of château-bottled wines, it counts for little on a generic.

RED These dry wines have a generosity of fruit tempered by a firm structure, and are medium- to full-bodied.

🍇 Cabernet Sauvignon, Cabernet Franc, Merlot, Malbec, Petit Verdot, Carmenère

🍷 6–15 years (*crus classés*); 5–8 years (others)

LISTRAC-MÉDOC AOC

Significant funds have been invested in a number of high-performance châteaux in this commune, although its heavy clay soil does not have anything like as much potential as the gravel ridges found in the most famous Médoc appellations.

RED These dry, medium- to full-bodied wines have the fruit and finesse of St-Julien combined with the firmness of St-Estèphe. The most successful wines tend to have a large proportion of Merlot, which enjoys the Haut-Médoc's clay soil.

🍇 Cabernet Sauvignon, Cabernet Franc, Carmenère, Merlot, Malbec, Petit Verdot

🍷 5–10 years

MARGAUX AOC

The best Margaux are potentially the greatest wines in the whole of Bordeaux, but this is an appellation that covers five communes encompassing a great diversity of soil and some of its wines not unnaturally have a tendency to disappoint. Margaux benefits enormously from having a namesake château, which is unique in Bordeaux, and the fact that this property sets the most extraordinarily high standards has done no harm to the reputation and price of these wines generally. The phenomenal success of Château Margaux has, however, unfairly raised expectations of many lesser-quality châteaux in the area, but those critics who widely accuse proprietors of sacrificing quality for quantity could not be further from the truth. There are individual châteaux that overproduce and therefore fail to achieve their full potential, but excessive volume is not typically the problem with this appellation, since it has

the lowest yield per hectare of the four famous Médoc AOCs.

RED Exquisite, dry, medium-bodied, and sometimes full-bodied, wines that can be deep-coloured and fabulously rich, yet they have great finesse and a silky finish.

🍇 Cabernet Sauvignon, Cabernet Franc, Carmenère, Merlot, Malbec, Petit Verdot

🍷 5–20 years (*crus classés*); 5–10 years (others)

MÉDOC AOC

Technically, this appellation covers the entire Médoc, but most wines actually come from north of the Haut-Médoc in the area which was formerly called the Bas-Médoc. Its vineyards have undergone a rapid and extensive expansion since the mid-1970s.

RED The best of these dry, medium-bodied wines are similar in style to good Haut-Médocs, although the style is less sophisticated.

🍇 Cabernet Sauvignon, Cabernet Franc, Carmenère, Merlot, Malbec, Petit Verdot

🍷 4–8 years

MOULIS AOC *or*
MOULIS-EN-MÉDOC AOC

One of the two communal appellations located on the Atlantic side of the Médoc, Moulis-en-Médoc is smaller and potentially more interesting than its neighbour Listrac. Like Listrac, it has no *cru classé* châteaux, despite adjoining Margaux, the appellation that has the highest number of such properties in the Médoc.

RED These dry, medium-bodied, sometimes full-bodied, wines have more power than those of Margaux, but far less finesse.

🍇 Cabernet Sauvignon, Cabernet Franc, Carmenère, Merlot, Malbec, Petit Verdot

🍷 5–12 years

PAUILLAC AOC

This commune vies with Margaux as the most famous appellation, but is without doubt the most rock solid and consistent of Bordeaux AOCs, while its *premiers crus* of Latour, Lafite, and Mouton make it the most important.

RED Dark and virtually opaque, great Pauillac is a dry, powerfully constructed wine, typically redolent

of blackcurrants and new oak. It might be unapproachable when young, but is always rich with fruit when mature. Although it does not have the grace of great Margaux, Pauillac brings power and style together to produce wines of incomparable finesse for their size.

🍇 Cabernet Sauvignon, Cabernet Franc, Carmenère, Merlot, Malbec, Petit Verdot

🍷 9–25 years (*crus classés*); 5–12 years (others)

ST-ESTÈPHE AOC

The potential of St-Estèphe is exemplified by Cos d'Estournel, which is one of the best *deuxièmes crus* in the Médoc, but the strength of this appellation lies in its range of *crus bourgeois*. The area under vine is slightly less than that of Margaux, which has the largest area, but St-Estèphe has far more unclassified châteaux, and even the best wines are wonderfully cheap.

RED If Pauillac is the stallion of the four famous appellations, St-Estèphe must be the shire-horse. These dry, full-bodied wines are big and strong, yet not without dignity. St-Estèphe demands affection and, with the rich fruit of a sunny year, deserves it. These most enjoyable, sweet-spice and cedary wines can have lots of honest, chunky fruit. Cos d'Estournel is the thoroughbred of the commune.

🍇 Cabernet Sauvignon, Cabernet Franc, Carmenère, Merlot, Malbec, Petit Verdot

🍷 8–25 years (*crus classés*); 5–12 years (others)

ST-JULIEN AOC

St-Julien is the smallest of the four famous appellations and the most intensively cultivated, with almost 50 per cent of the commune under vine. There are no first growths, but there are as many as five seconds, and the standard and consistency of style is very high. This AOC overlaps part of the commune of Pauillac, and, historically, châteaux Latour and Pichon-Longueville-Comtesse-de-Lalande could as easily have become St-Julien AOC as Pauillac AOC.

RED These are dry, medium-bodied, sometimes full-bodied, wines that have purity of style, varietal flavour, and can be long-lived. Well balanced and elegant, these wines fall somewhere between the lushness that is typical of Margaux and the firmer structure of Pauillac.

🍇 Cabernet Sauvignon, Cabernet Franc, Carmenère, Merlot, Malbec, Petit Verdot

🍷 6–20 years (*crus classés*); 5–12 years (others)

THE WINE PRODUCERS OF
THE MÉDOC

CHÂTEAU D'AGASSAC
AOC Haut-Médoc
★★✩ ❤

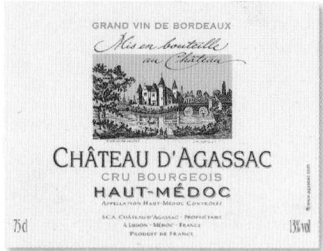

This is one of the best unclassified wines in the Haut-Médoc. The wine is matured in wood for 15 months, with one-third new oak.

RED Dark-coloured, plummy wine, with a lot of soft, ripe fruit.

🍇 Cabernet Sauvignon 47%, Merlot 50%, Petit Verdot 3%

🍷 4–10 years

Second wine: *Château Pomiès-Agassac*

CHÂTEAU D'AURI LHAC
AOC Haut-Médoc
★

A relative newcomer that has quickly developed a cult following. The grapes are machine harvested, and the wine is matured in wood for 12 months, with 35 per cent new oak.

RED A flashy, huge, dark, and dense wine with masses of fruit to balance the ripe tannins and extrovert oak.

🍇 Cabernet Sauvignon 56%, Merlot 38%, Cabernet Franc 3%, Petit Verdot 3%

🍷 5–15 years

Second wine: *Château La Fagotte*

CHÂTEAU BEAUMONT
AOC Haut-Médoc
✩ ❤

A large property that consistently produces wines of good quality. This wine is matured in wood for 12 months, with 30 per cent new oak.

RED These are aromatically attractive wines with elegant fruit and supple tannin.

🍇 Cabernet Sauvignon 60%, Merlot 35%, Cabernet Franc 2%, Petit Verdot 3%

🍷 4–8 years

Second wine: *Château d'Arvigny*
Other wine: *Tours de Beaumont*

CHÂTEAU
BEL-AIR LAGRAVE
AOC Moulis
✩ ❤

This growth was classified *cru bourgeois* in 1932, but not included in the Syndicat's 1978 list. The wine is matured in wood for 18 to 20

months, with 70 per cent new oak.

RED These vividly coloured wines have a fine bouquet and a firm tannic structure.

🍇 Cabernet Sauvignon 60%, Merlot 35%, Petit Verdot 5%

🍷 8–20 years

Second wine: *Château Peyvigneau*

CHÂTEAU BELGRAVE
AOC Haut-Médoc 5ème Cru Classé
★★✩ ❤

Situated on a good gravel bank behind Château Lagrange, the wine, which is matured in wood for 24 months with up to 50 per cent new oak, has improved consistently throughout the 1990s.

RED A good balance of blackcurrant fruit and ripe acidity, with much more supple tannin structure than used to be the case, and vanilla overtones of new oak.

🍇 Cabernet Sauvignon 55%, Merlot 32%, Cabernet Franc 12%, Petit Verdot 1%

🍷 8–16 years

Second wine: *Diane de Belgrave*

CHÂTEAU BEL-ORME-
TRONQUOY-DE-LALANDE
AOC Haut-Médoc
★

This property has a confusingly similar name to Château Tronquoy-Lalande, St-Estèphe. Steady improvement since the mid-1990s has turned the once four-square character of these wines into a more classically structured style. This wine is matured in wood for 12 to 14 months, with 10 per cent new oak.

RED These are firm, fruity, classically structured wines.

🍇 Cabernet Sauvignon 35%, Merlot 55%, Cabernet Franc 10%

🍷 7–15 years

CHÂTEAU BERNADOTTE
AOC Haut-Médoc
★★✩ ❤

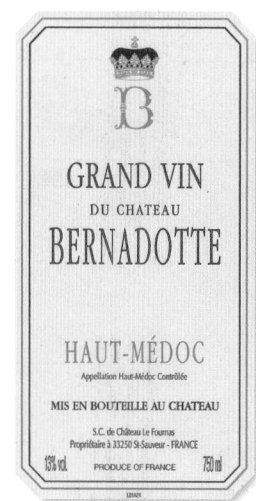

Consistently performing above its class, this château is situated on fine, gravelly ground that once had the right to the Pauillac appellation and formed part of a *cru classé*. The quality has improved since the property was purchased in 1996 by the redoubtable Mme Lencquesaing, who also owns Pichon-Longueville-Comtesse-de-Lalande. This wine is now matured in wood for 12 months, with 30 per cent new oak.

RED These wines are very stylish, with lush Cabernet fruit backed up by the creamy richness of new oak.

🍇 Cabernet Sauvignon 62%, Merlot 36%, Cabernet Franc, Petit Verdot 2%

🍷 6–12 years

Second wine: *Château Le Fournas Bernadotte*

CHÂTEAU
BISTON-BRILLETTE
AOC Moulis
★★✩ ❤

This top-quality Moulis property ages its wines in wood for 12 to 15 months, with up to 35 per cent new oak.

RED Wines that are very rich in colour and fruit with a full, spicy-cassis character and a supple tannin structure.

🍇 Cabernet Sauvignon 55%, Merlot 40%, Malbec 2%, Petit Verdot 3%

🍷 5–15 years

Second wine: *Château Biston*
Other wine: *Château Graveyron*

CHÂTEAU
BOUQUEYRAN
AOC Moulis
✩ ❤

A big improvement in quality and value since this 13-hectare (32-acre) property was leased by Philippe Porcheron of nearby Château Rose Saint-Croix. Wines are matured in wood for 18 months with up to 50 per-cent new oak. La Fleur de Bouqueyran is a superior *cuvée*.

RED Lovely deep-coloured, deep-flavoured wines of not inconsiderable style and finesse.

🍇 Cabernet Sauvignon 41%, Merlot 57%, Petit Verdot 2%

🍷 5–10 years

Second wine: *Les Tourelles de Bouqueyran*

CHÂTEAU
LE BOURDIEU VERTHEUIL
AOC Haut-Médoc

Situated between Vertheuil and St-Estèphe, this château was classified *cru bourgeois* in 1932, but not included in the Syndicat's 1978 list. This wine is matured in wood for 12 months, with 30 per cent new oak.

RED Well-coloured, full-bodied wines of robust character that are not lacking in charm.

🍇 Cabernet Sauvignon 60%, Merlot 25%, Cabernet Franc 10%, Petit Verdot 5%

🍷 7–15 years

Second wine: *Château Haut-Brignays*

Other wines: *Château La Croix des Sablons, Château Victoria-Picourneau*

CHÂTEAU BRANAS
GRAND POUJEAUX
AOC Moulis
★★✩

These excellent and rapidly improving wines are aged in wood for 18 months, with 100 per cent new oak.

RED Thanks to an increase in Merlot, this wine has plenty of accessible fruit, charming aromatic properties, and increasing finesse.

🍇 Cabernet Sauvignon 50%, Merlot 45%, Petit Verdot 5%

🍷 5–12 years

Second wine: *Clos des Demoiselles*

CHÂTEAU BRILLETTE
AOC Moulis
★★✩ ❤

This château's name reputedly derives from its glinting, pebbly soil. The wine is matured in wood for 12 months, with 40 per cent new oak.

RED These are attractively coloured wines of full but supple body, with delightful summer-fruit and vanilla aromas. Easily equivalent to *cru classé* quality.

🍇 Cabernet Sauvignon 40%, Merlot 48%, Cabernet Sauvignon 9%, Petit Verdot 3%

🍷 5–12 years

CHÂTEAU
CAMBON-LA-PELOUSE
AOC Haut-Médoc
✩

Under the same ownership as Château Grand Barrail-Lamarzelle-Figeac, this estate was classified *cru bourgeois* in 1932, but not included in the Syndicat's 1978 list. This wine is matured in wood for 12 months, with 45 per cent new oak.

RED Soft, medium- to full-bodied wines with fresh and juicy flavours.

🍇 Cabernet Sauvignon 30%, Merlot 50%, Cabernet Franc 20%

🍷 3–8 years

Other wine: *Château Trois Moulins*

CHÂTEAU CAMENSAC
AOC Haut-Médoc 5ème Cru Classé
★ Ⓥ

Situated behind Château Belgrave, this property was renovated in the mid-1960s by the new owners, the Forner brothers, who are of Spanish origin, and later established Marquès de Cáceres in Rioja. Camensac began making wine equivalent to its classification in the late 1970s, and since 1995 has been performing beyond its class. It is matured in wood for 17 to 20 months, with 35–70 per cent new oak.

RED Well-structured wine, with a medium weight of fruit and a certain amount of finesse.

🍇 Cabernet Sauvignon 60%, Merlot 40%

🍷 8–20 years

Second wine: *La Closerie de Camensac*

Other wine: *Le Bailly de Camensac*

CHÂTEAU CANTEMERLE
AOC Haut-Médoc 5ème Cru Classé
★ ★☆ Ⓥ

In 1980, new stainless-steel fermentation vats replaced the old wooden ones that had been responsible for some stingy vintages. Also discarded were all the old casks, so the 1980 vintage was uniquely matured in 100 per cent new oak. The wine is normally matured in wood for 18 to 20 months, with one-third new oak. It is currently performing above its classification.

RED Deliciously rich wines of fine colour, creamy-oaky fruit, beautiful balance, and increasing finesse.

🍇 Cabernet Sauvignon 50%, Merlot 40%, Cabernet Franc 5%, Petit Verdot 5%

🍷 8–20 years

Second wine: *Villeneuve de Cantemerle*

CHÂTEAU CAP-LÉON-VEYRIN
AOC Listrac
★

Simply called Château Cap-Léon originally, the vines of this property are planted in two plots of clay-gravel soil over marl.

RED Deep-coloured, full-bodied, richly flavoured wines with high extract levels and a good balance of tannin.

🍇 Cabernet Sauvignon 35%, Merlot 60%, Petit Verdot 5%

🍷 5–12 years

CHÂTEAU LA CARDONNE
AOC Médoc
★ Ⓥ

This property was purchased by the Rothschilds of Lafite in 1973 and has since been expanded and renovated. This wine is matured in wood for 12 months, with 50 per cent new oak.

RED These are attractive, medium-bodied wines with a good, grapey perfume and a silky texture, made in an elegant style.

🍇 Cabernet Sauvignon 45%, Merlot 50%, Cabernet Franc 5%

🍷 6–10 years

CHÂTEAU CARONNE-STE-GEMME
AOC Haut-Médoc
★☆ Ⓥ

This property is situated south of Château Lagrange – a superb island of vines on a gravel plateau. Matured in wood for 12 months, with 25 per cent new oak.

RED Full-bodied wines rich in flavour with undertones of creamy oak, and a supple tannin structure.

🍇 Cabernet Sauvignon 65%, Merlot 33%, Petit Verdot 2%

🍷 8–20 years

Second wine: *Château Labat*

CHÂTEAU CASTÉRA
AOC Médoc
★☆ Ⓥ

The original château was reduced to ruins by the Black Prince in the 14th century. This wine is matured in wood for 12 months, with one-third new oak.

RED Soft-textured, medium-bodied wines best drunk relatively young.

🍇 Cabernet Sauvignon 45%, Merlot 45%, Cabernet Franc 7%, Petit Verdot 3%

🍷 4–8 years

Second wine: *Château Bourbon La Chapelle*

Other wines: *Château Moulin de Buscateau, La Chapelle du Castera*

CHÂTEAU CHANTELYS
AOC Médoc
★☆ Ⓥ

Owner Christine Courrian Braquissac brings a gentle touch to the naturally firm wines of this district.

RED Well-coloured, medium-bodied, gently rich-flavoured wines of some elegance.

🍇 Cabernet Sauvignon 55%, Merlot 40%, Petit Verdot 5%

🍷 3–8 years

Second wine: *Château Gauthier*

CHÂTEAU CHARMAIL
AOC Haut-Médoc
★ Ⓥ

The wines from this château have improved dramatically since its excellent 1996 vintage, and continue to perform well in blind tastings. This wine is matured in wood for 12 months, with 30 per cent new oak.

RED Rich, spicy, and long, with well-rounded, ripe tannins.

🍇 Cabernet Sauvignon 30%, Cabernet Franc 20%, Merlot 48%, Petit Verdot 2%

🍷 3–7 years

Second wine: *Château Tours de Charmail*

CHÂTEAU CHASSE-SPLEEN
AOC Moulis
★ ★ Ⓥ

The proprietor of this quality-conscious property also owns the *cru classé* Château Haut-Bages-Libéral and the excellent unclassified growth of Château la Gurgue in Margaux. The wine is matured in wood for 18 months with 40 per cent new oak, and is usually of *cru classé* quality. Certainly, it well deserves being recently classified as one of only nine *crus bourgeois exceptionnels*.

RED Full-bodied wines of great finesse, vivid colour, with a luxuriant, creamy-rich flavour of cassis and chocolate with warm, spicy-vanilla undertones. Easily equivalent to *cru classé* quality.

🍇 Cabernet Sauvignon 70%, Merlot 25%, Petit Verdot 5%

🍷 8–20 years

Second wines: *L'Oratoire de Chasse-Spleen, L'Ermitage de Chasse-Spleen, L'Orangeraie de Chasse-Spleen*

CHÂTEAU CISSAC
AOC Haut-Médoc
★ Ⓥ

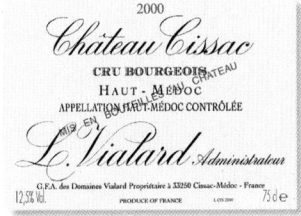

Château Cissac is always good value, especially in hot years. It is fermented in wood and matured in cask with no *vin de presse*. This wine is matured in wood for 18 months, with up to 50 per cent new oak.

RED These are deep-coloured, well-flavoured, full-bodied wines made in a vin de garde style.

🍇 Cabernet Sauvignon 75%, Merlot 20%, Petit Verdot 5%

🍷 8–20 years

Second wine: *Château Les Reflets du Cissac*

Other wine: *Château Abiet*

CHÂTEAU CITRAN
AOC Haut-Médoc

This substantial-sized property was once run by Château Coufran, then passed into Japanese ownership, under the Fujimoto company, which invested in improvements in the vineyard and winery. In 1997, it was taken back into French ownership, under the auspices of Groupe Taillan, and is run personally by Céline Villars. This wine is matured in wood for 12 to 14 months, with 40 per cent new oak.

RED A once solid, if plodding, Médoc of robust character, the style has become more accessible since the mid-1990s, and since the new millennium has shown a true plumpness of fruit, with not inconsiderable finesse.

🍇 Cabernet Sauvignon 58%, Merlot 42%

🍷 5–15 years

Second wine: *Moulins de Citran*

CHÂTEAU LA CLARE
AOC Médoc
★☆ Ⓥ

A well-established property that is receiving renewed attention of late. Approximately 30 per cent of the wine is matured in wood for 23 months, with 5–10 per cent new oak.

RED A rich, nicely coloured, medium-bodied wine with some spicy finesse.

🍇 Cabernet Sauvignon 57%, Merlot 36%, Cabernet Franc 7%

🍷 4-8 years

Second wines: *Laveline, Gentilhomme*

CHÂTEAU CLARKE
AOC Listrac
★ Ⓥ

This estate's vines were dug up and its château pulled down in 1950. All was abandoned until 1973, when it was purchased by Baron Edmond de Rothschild. He completely restored the vineyard and installed an ultra-modern winery. Since the 1981 vintage, it has become one of the Médoc's fastest-rising stars. The wine is fermented in stainless steel and matured in wood for 12 to 18 months, with up to 80 per cent new oak.

RED Well-coloured wines have a good measure of creamy-smoky oak, soft fruit, and increasing finesse.

🍇 Cabernet Sauvignon 40%, Merlot 60%

🍷 7–25 years

Second wine: *Château Granges des Domaines Edmond de Rothschild*

CHÂTEAU COUFRAN
AOC Haut-Médoc
★☆ Ⓥ

These wines are matured in wood for 13 to 18 months, with 25 per cent new oak.

RED Frank and fruity, this medium- to full-bodied wine has a chunky, chocolaty flavour, which is dominated by Merlot.

🍇 Cabernet Sauvignon 15%, Merlot 85%, Petit Verdot 5%

🍷 4–12 years

Second wine: *Domaine de la Rose-Maréchale*

CHÂTEAU DUTRUCH GRAND POUJEAUX
AOC Moulis
★ Ⓥ

Dutruch is one of the best Grand Poujeaux satellite properties. It also makes two other wines from the specific-named plots "La Bernède" and "La Gravière". Matured in wood for 12 months, with 25 per cent new oak.

RED These are fine, full-bodied wines of excellent colour, fruit, and finesse.

🍇 Cabernet Sauvignon 45%, Merlot 50%, Petit Verdot 5%

🍷 7–15 years

Other wines: *La Bernède-Grand-Poujeaux, La Gravière-Grand-Poujeaux*

CHÂTEAU FONRÉAUD
AOC Listrac

This splendid château has south-facing vineyards situated on and around a knoll, Puy-de-Menjon. This wine is matured in wood for 12 to 18 months, with one-third new oak.

RED Attractive medium- to full-bodied wines of good fruit and some style.

🍇 Cabernet Sauvignon 55%, Merlot 42%, Petit Verdot 3%

🍷 6–12 years

Second wine: *La Tourelle de Château Fonréaud*

CHÂTEAU FOURCAS DUPRÉ
AOC Listrac
★ Ⓥ

A charming house, with vineyards situated on gravel over iron-pan soil, which can excel in hot years. This wine is matured in wood for 12 months, with one-third new oak.

RED The good colour, bouquet, and tannic structure of these wines is rewarded with rich fruit in good years.

🍇 Cabernet Sauvignon 44%, Merlot 44%, Cabernet Franc 10%, Petit Verdot 2%

🍷 6–12 years

CHÂTEAU FOURCAS HOSTEN
AOC Listrac
★ Ⓥ

Under multinational ownership (French, Danish, and American) since 1972, the winemaking facilities here have been renovated. The wines are matured in wood for 12 months, with one-third new oak.

RED Deeply coloured and full-bodied wines, rich in fruit and supported by a firm tannic structure, although the style is becoming more supple, and can even be quite fat in ripe years like 1982.

🍇 Cabernet Sauvignon 45%, Merlot 45%, Cabernet Franc 10%

🍷 8–20 years

Second wine: *Les Cèdres d'Hosten*

CHÂTEAU LES GRANDS CHÊNES
AOC Médoc
★✿ Ⓥ

The quality here has been excellent since the mid-1990s, but has taken another step up since 1999, when the château was purchased by Bernard Magrez, one of the joint owners of Château Pape Clément. Magrez runs this property personally. The wine is matured in wood for 12 to 15 months, with one-third new oak (except for its 100 per cent new oak "Prestige Cuvée").

RED Lush and charming, with opulent fruit and fine acidity balance.

🍇 Cabernet Sauvignon 65%, Merlot 30%, Cabernet Franc 5%

🍷 6–15 years

Other wine: ☑ *Château Les Grands Chênes Prestige Cuvée*

CHÂTEAU GRESSIER GRAND POUJEAUX
AOC Moulis
★ Ⓥ

This château was classified *cru bourgeois* in 1932, but not in 1978. It has in recent years produced successful wines that compare well with good *crus classés*. This wine is matured in wood for 24 months, with one-third new oak.

RED Full-bodied wines with plenty of fruit and flavour. Well worth laying down.

🍇 Cabernet Sauvignon 50%, Merlot 30%, Cabernet Franc 10%, Petit Verdot 10%

🍷 6–12 years

CHÂTEAU GREYSAC
AOC Médoc
★ Ⓥ

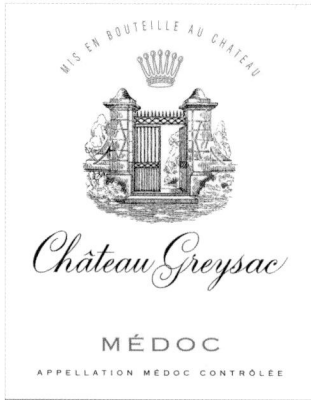

Since it was purchased by the late Baron de Gunzbourg in 1973, the facilities of this château have undergone extensive modernization. The quality of the wine is excellent and its future promising. This wine is matured in wood for 12 months, with 25 per cent new oak.

RED Stylish, medium-bodied wines with silky-textured, ripe-fruit flavours.

🍇 Cabernet Sauvignon 45%, Merlot 45%, Cabernet Franc 5%, Petit Verdot 5%

🍷 6–10 years

CHÂTEAU HANTEILLAN
AOC Haut-Médoc
★ Ⓥ

Under the keen direction of Catherine Blasco, this large property produces a consistently fine wine, and her achievements have been consolidated by the new winemaking facilities. This wine is matured in wood for 12 months, with 30 per cent new oak.

RED The wine has a fine colour, spicy bouquet with underlying vanilla-oak tones, ripe fruit, and supple tannins.

🍇 Cabernet Sauvignon 50%, Merlot 41%, Cabernet Franc 5%, Petit Verdot 4%

🍷 6–12 years

Second wine: *Château Larrivaux Hanteillan*

CHÂTEAU LACOMBE-NOILLAC
AOC Haut-Médoc
★✿ Ⓥ

Jean-Michel Lapalu's property boasts some of the most northerly vines in the Médoc. The wine is matured in wood for 6 months, with 15 per cent new oak.

RED Elegant, medium-bodied wines of surprising style and finesse for the location.

🍇 Cabernet Sauvignon 58%, Cabernet Franc 6%, Merlot 32%, Petit Verdot 4%

🍷 4–10 years

Second wine: *Château Les Traverses*
Other wine: *Château Les Traverses La Franque*

CHÂTEAU LA LAGUNE
AOC Haut-Médoc 3ème Cru Classé
★✿ Ⓥ

Owned by the Ducellier family of Champagne Ayala, the immaculate vineyard of this fine château is the first *cru classé* encountered after leaving Bordeaux, and is situated on sand and gravel soil. The château itself was completely renovated in 2003. This wine is matured in wood for 16 to 18 months, with 100 per cent new oak.

RED These wines are deep-coloured with complex cassis and stone-fruit flavours intermingled with rich, creamy-vanilla oak nuances. They are full-bodied but supple.

🍇 Cabernet Sauvignon 60%, Merlot 20%, Cabernet Franc 10%, Petit Verdot 10%

🍷 5–30 years

Second wine: *Moulin de Lagune*

CHÂTEAU DE LAMARQUE
AOC Haut-Médoc
★ Ⓥ

This large and constantly improving property is owned and run by Pierre-Gilles and Marie-Hélène Gromand-Brunet d'Évry. The vineyard was systematically replanted in the 1960s and is currently at its optimum age for both quality and volume. While it will gradually decline in yield, the quality should continue to improve. The wine is matured in wood for 12 to 15 months, with one-third new oak.

RED This wine has the supple style of a modern Médoc, with plenty of real fruit flavour, and an enticingly perfumed bouquet.

🍇 Cabernet Sauvignon 46%, Merlot 25%, Cabernet Franc 24%, Petit Verdot 5%

🍷 5–12 years

Second wine: *D de Lamarque*
Other wines: *Réserve du Marquis d'Évry, Noblesse Oblige (saigné rosé)*

CHÂTEAU LAMOTHE-CISSAC
AOC Haut-Médoc
★ Ⓥ

An up-and-coming wine from one of Bordeaux's oldest properties, Lamothe-Cissac is matured in wood for 12 to 14 months, with 20 per cent new oak. It has recently started to outperform Cissac.

RED Classically proportioned, Cabernet-dominated wines of excellent potential longevity.

🍇 Cabernet Sauvignon 70%, Merlot 26%, Petit Verdot 4%

🍷 4–16 years

CHÂTEAU LANESSAN
AOC Haut-Médoc
★✿ Ⓥ

Supposedly missed out from the 1855 classification because the owner forgot to submit samples, or could not be bothered, this château was later classified *cru bourgeois* in 1932, but not included in the Syndicat's 1978 list. The grapes are machine harvested, and the wines are matured in wood for 15 months, with no claim of any new oak.

RED Big, intensely flavoured wines of deep, often opaque, colour and a quality that closely approaches that of a *cru classé*, requiring a similar minimum ageing before its fruit shows through.

🍇 Cabernet Sauvignon 75%, Merlot 20%, Cabernet Franc 1%, Petit Verdot 4%

⌇— 7–20 years

Second wine: *Domaine de Ste-Gemme*

CHÂTEAU LAROSE-TRINTAUDON
AOC Haut-Médoc
★★ⓥ

This is the largest estate in the Médoc and was under the same ownership as Château Camensac until 1986, during which time vast sums were spent on renovation. The standard of these wines, which are matured in wood for 12 months with 25 per cent new oak, is as high as it has ever been.

RED Medium-bodied, and sometimes full-bodied, wines with an elegantly rich flavour of juicy summer fruits, vanilla, and truffles, backed up by supple tannins. Larose-Perganson is more of a *tête de cuvée* than a second wine. Representing just 15 per cent of the total production, this wine is exclusively from the oldest vines and the grapes are all hand-picked, in contrast to Larose-Trintaudon, which is machine-picked.

🍇 Cabernet Sauvignon 65%, Merlot 30%, Cabernet Franc 5%

⌇— 6–15 years

Second wine: *Larose Saint-Laurent*

Other wines: ✓ *Château Larose-Perganson, Les Hauts de Trintaudon*

CHÂTEAU LESTAGE-DARQUIER
AOC Moulis
★★ⓥ

This is the least encountered of the many Poujeaux châteaux (formerly sold as Château Lestage-Darquier-Grand-Poujeaux), but well worth digging out. This wine is matured in wood for 9 to 12 months, with 100 per cent one-year-old oak.

RED Densely coloured wines, rich in bouquet and fruit, with a powerful structure.

🍇 Cabernet Sauvignon 50%, Merlot 45%, Cabernet Franc 2%, Petit Verdot 2%

⌇— 8–20 years

CHÂTEAU LIVERSAN
AOC Haut-Médoc
★ⓥ

The estate of Château Liversan was purchased in 1984 by Prince Guy de Polignac, when it was inexorably

linked with Champagne Pommery, but was first leased and then sold to the owners of Patache d'Aux. The vineyard is on fine, sandy gravel over a limestone subsoil, just 3 kilometres (almost 2 miles) from Lafite and Mouton-Rothschild. The wine is fermented in stainless steel and matured in wood for 12 months, with 25 per cent new oak.

RED Rich and flavourful wines, of full body and some style. They are gaining in class with each vintage.

🍇 Cabernet Sauvignon 49%, Merlot 38%, Cabernet Franc 10%, Petit Verdot 3%

⌇— 7–20 years

Second wine: *Les Charmes des Liversan*

CHÂTEAU LOUDENNE
AOC Médoc

This pink-washed, Chartreuse-style château, with its lawns running down to the Gironde, once belonged to W and A Gilbey, who ran it in a style that harked back to the last days of the British Empire. It was sold to Jean-Paul Lafragette in 1999. The wine is matured in wood for 15 to 18 months, with 25 per cent new oak. Loudenne also produces a dry white wine that is attractive when drunk one to two years after the harvest.

RED Full-bodied wines with a spicy-blackcurrant bouquet, sometimes silky and hinting of violets, with underlying vanilla oak, a big mouthful of rich and ripe fruit, excellent extract, and great length.

🍇 Cabernet Sauvignon 45%, Merlot 45%, Cabernet Franc 7%, Malbec 2%, Petit Verdot 1%

⌇— 5–15 years

Second wines: *Château Lestagne, Pavillon de Loudenne*

CHÂTEAU MALESCASSE
AOC Haut-Médoc
★★ⓥ

CRU BOURGEOIS

CHATEAU MALESCASSE

HAUT-MÉDOC

APPELLATION HAUT-MÉDOC CONTRÔLÉE

S.A. CHATEAU MALESCASSE
PROPRIÉTAIRE À LAMARQUE · GIRONDE · FRANCE
MIS EN BOUTEILLES AU CHÂTEAU

12,5% Vol   750 ml

Entirely replanted between 1970 and 1992, Château Malescasse was purchased midway through this process by the owner of Pontet-Canet and Lafon-Rochet, only to be sold to Alcatel Alsthon once completed. The wine is matured in wood for 16 months, with 30 per cent new oak.

RED Firm, dependable, good-value claret, getting better with each vintage.

🍇 Cabernet Sauvignon 55%, Merlot 35%, Cabernet Franc 10%

⌇— 4–8 years

Second wine: *Le Closerie de Malescasse*

CHÂTEAU DE MALLERET
AOC Haut-Médoc
★ⓥ

Château de Malleret is a vast estate, which incorporates a stud farm with two training race-tracks and stables for both hunting and racing. The vineyard boasts 60 hectares (148 acres). This wine is matured in wood for 12 to 16 months, with up to 50 per cent new oak.

RED Delightful wines of good bouquet, medium body, and juicy-rich fruit. Improving.

🍇 Cabernet Sauvignon 65%, Merlot 30%, Cabernet Franc 3%, Petit Verdot 2%

⌇— 5–12 years

CHÂTEAU MAUCAILLOU
AOC Moulis
★★ⓥ

Château Maucaillou is consistently one of the best-value wines produced in Bordeaux. This wine is matured in wood for 18 months, with up to 80 per cent new oak.

RED Deep-coloured, full-bodied wine with masses of velvety-textured fruit, beautiful cassis and vanilla flavours, and supple tannins.

🍇 Cabernet Sauvignon 55%, Merlot 36%, Cabernet Franc 2%, Petit Verdot 7%

⌇— 6–15 years

Second wine: *Château Cap de Haut-Maucaillou*

Other wine: *Château Duplessis-Fabre*

CHÂTEAU MAUCAMPS
AOC Haut-Médoc
★ⓥ

Situated between Macau itself and the *cru classé* Cantemerle to the south, this château makes superb use of its 15 hectares (37 acres) of fine, gravelly vineyards. This wine is matured in wood for 16 months, with up to 40 per cent new oak.

RED Always a deep-coloured, full-bodied wine with plenty of fruit flavour supported by supple tannins.

🍇 Cabernet Sauvignon 50%, Merlot 40%, Petit Verdot 10%

⌇— 5–12 years

Second wine: *Clos de May*

CHÂTEAU LE MEYNIEU AOC
Haut-Médoc
★ⓥ

This property is under the same ownership as Château Lavillotte, which is situated in St-Estèphe. The deep-coloured wine is not filtered before it is bottled.

RED This is a deep, dark, brooding wine of dense bouquet and solid fruit which promises much for the future.

🍇 Cabernet Sauvignon 62%, Merlot 30%, Cabernet Franc 8%

⌇— 7–15 years

CHÂTEAU MOULIN-À-VENT
AOC Moulis

One-third of the property of Château Moulin-à-Vent overlaps the commune of Listrac, but its appellation is still Moulis. This wine is matured in wood for 20 months, with 25 per cent new oak.

RED Medium-bodied wines with an elegant bouquet and a full flavour.

🍇 Cabernet Sauvignon 60%, Merlot 35%, Petit Verdot 5%

⌇— 7–15 years

Second wine: *Moulin-de-St-Vincent*

CHÂTEAU NOAILLAC
AOC Médoc
★ⓥ

Under the same ownership as Château La Tour de By. The wine is matured in wood for up to 12 months, with 15 per cent new oak.

RED Deliciously fruity style, underpinned by a discreet use of oak.

🍇 Cabernet Sauvignon 55%, Merlot 40%, Petit Verdot 5%

⌇— 3–8 years

Second wines: *Moulin de Noaillac, La Rose Noaillac, Les Palombes de Noaillac*

CHÂTEAU LES ORMES-SORBET
AOC Médoc
★ⓥ

Owned by the Boivert family since 1764. The wine today is matured in wood for 18 to 20 months, with one-third new oak.

RED Once reputed for its characterful wines of substantial body, dense fruit, and positive flavour, this château has made an increasingly opulent style, with fine aromatics, since the early 1990s, fully justifying its 2003 *cru bourgeois supérieur* classification.

🍇 Cabernet Sauvignon 65%, Merlot 30%, Petit Verdot 2%, Carmenère 1%

⌇— 4–15 years

Second wine: *Château de Conques*

CHÂTEAU PALOUMEY
AOC Haut-Médoc
★ⓥ

An old property that enjoyed fame in the 19th century, but was grubbed up and forgotten until the current owner, Martine Cazeneuve, replanted it in 1990. The wine is matured in wood for 12 to 15 months, with one-third new oak.

RED Deliciously rich and ripe, fruit-driven style that is underpinned by a nicely restrained use of oak, with exceptional finesse for such young vines. Can only get better!

Cabernet Sauvignon 55%, Merlot 40%, Cabernet Franc 5%

☐ 4–8 years

Second wines: *Les Ailes de Paloumey, Château Haut-Carmaillet*

CHÂTEAU PATACHE-D'AUX
AOC Médoc
★ ✔

This old property once belonged to the Aux family, descendants of the counts of Armagnac, but was purchased by a syndicate headed by Claude Lapalu in 1964. Although Patache-d'Aux is always reliable, it has performed particularly well since its stunning 1990 vintage. The wine is matured in wood for 12 months, with 25 per cent new oak.

RED Stylish, highly perfumed, medium-bodied wine with very accessible fruit.

Cabernet Sauvignon 70%, Merlot 20%, Cabernet Franc 7%, Petit Verdot 3%

☐ 4–8 years

Second wine: *Le Relais de Patache-d'Aux*

Other wine: *Les Chevaux de Patache-d'Aux*

CHÂTEAU PEYRABON
AOC Haut-Médoc
★ ✔

Virtually unknown until 1998, when it was purchased by Millesima (formerly Les Vins des Grands Vignobles), Château Peyrabon is matured in wood for 18 months, with one-third new oak.

RED Sturdy style, but not lacking in fruit, and usually very good value.

Cabernet Sauvignon 57%, Merlot 37%, Cabernet Franc 5%, Petit Verdot 1%

☐ 5–10 years

Second wines: *Lapiey, Château Le Fleur Peyrabon*

Other wines: *Château Pierbone, Domaine du Roman*

CHÂTEAU PLAGNAC
AOC Médoc

Owned by Domaines Cordier since 1972, this property has produced consistently good-value red Bordeaux since the end of that decade. The wine is matured in wood for 12 months.

RED Full-bodied and full-flavoured, with some breed; lots of up-front Merlot fruit, and a smooth finish.

Cabernet Sauvignon 65%, Merlot 35%,

☐ 4–10 years

Second wine: *Château Haut de Plagnac*

CHÂTEAU PONTEY
AOC Médoc
★ ★ ✔

Owned by the Bordeaux négociant Quancard family, this château occupies an excellent location on a gravel plateau. The wines are

matured in wood for 12 months, with one-third new oak.

RED These wines have always been cleverly constructed and brimming with lush, oaky fruit, but they are even more lush than before.

Cabernet Sauvignon 45%, Merlot 55%

☐ 3–12 years

Second wine: *Château Vieux Prezat*

Other wine: *Château Pontey Caussan*

CHÂTEAU POTENSAC
AOC Médoc
★ ★ ✔

This property is under the same ownership as Château Léoville-Las-Cases in St-Julien, and its wines often aspire to *cru classé* quality, fully justifying the *cru bourgeois exceptionnel* classification in 2003. The wine is fermented in stainless steel, then matured in wood for 18 months, with 20 per cent new oak.

RED Classy, full-bodied wines of a lovely brick-red colour, with lots of fruit and underlying chocolate and spice flavours.

Cabernet Sauvignon 60%, Merlot 25%, Cabernet Franc 15%

☐ 6–15 years

Second wine: *Château Lassalle*

Other wines: *Château Gallais-Bellevue, Goudy la Cardonne*

CHÂTEAUX POUJEAUX
AOC Moulis
★ ★ ✔

After Chasse-Spleen, this château produces the best wine in Moulis and is easily the equivalent of a good *cru classé*. Hence it was no surprise that it was classified as one of only nine *crus bourgeois exceptionnels* in 2003.

RED Full-bodied and deep-coloured wine with a very expansive bouquet and creamy-rich, spicy fruit.

Cabernet Sauvignon 50%, Merlot 40%, Cabernet Franc 5%, Petit Verdot 2%

☐ 10–25 years

Second wine: *Château La Salle-de-Poujeaux*

CHÂTEAU PREUILLAC
AOC Médoc
★ ✔

Purchased in 1998 by Yvon Mau, who has sold his eponymously named *négociant* business to

Freixenet in a bid to build up a portfolio of estate properties. A lot of money and attention was devoted to renovating the property, reducing yields, and updating the vinification facilities, which is why director Jean-Christophe Mau was upset not to have been included in the 2003 *cru bourgeois* classification (*see* p118), although there is no doubt that it will succeed at the next reclassification (2015). Certainly, if the current rate of improvement can be maintained, this château will do very well. The grapes are hand-picked then sorted on tables, and the wines are fermented in stainless steel (2001 was the first), then matured in wood for 18 months, with 20 per cent new oak.

RED The creamy cassis and chocolaty fruit in these wines is a testament to Mau's efforts. Preuillac used to be rather rustic, but now shows more finesse with each and every vintage, particularly from 2003.

Cabernet Sauvignon 54%, Merlot 44%, Cabernet Franc 2%

☐ 4–12 years

CHÂTEAU RAMAGE-LA-BATISSE
AOC Haut-Médoc
★ ✔

This property has excelled itself since the late 1980s, making wines of remarkable quality–price ratio which are matured in wood for 14 months, with 50 per cent new oak.

RED Rich, well-flavoured, oaky wines that are immediately attractive in light years and ridiculously inexpensive *vins de garde* in the best vintages. Not unlike a poor man's Lynch-Bages (which in turn I have called a poor man's Latour!).

Cabernet Sauvignon 70%, Merlot 23%, Cabernet Franc 5%, Petit Verdot 2%

☐ 7–15 years

Second wine: *Le Terrey*

Other wine: *Château Dutellier*

CHÂTEAU ROLLAN DE BY
AOC Médoc
★ ★

A new cult wine on the Bordeaux scene, it is matured in wood for 18 months, with 60 per cent new oak.

The wine has a string of blind tasting victories. The Château Haut-Condessas is a super-selection, with 100 per cent new oak.

RED Lots of up-front fruit, but long and classy, with plenty of finesse. Not big and, surprisingly, not over-oaked.

Cabernet Sauvignon 20%, Merlot 70%, Petit Verdot 10%

☐ 4–12 years

Other wine: *Château Fleur de By*

CHÂTEAU ST-BONNET
AOC Médoc
★

Some 53 of this important estate's 85 hectares are planted with vines (130 of 210 acres). The wine is matured in wood for 18 months, with 25 per cent new oak.

RED Full-flavoured wines of promising quality and immediate aromatic appeal.

Merlot 50%, Cabernet Sauvignon 28%, Cabernet Franc 22%

☐ 5–10 years

CHÂTEAU ST-PAUL
AOC Haut-Médoc
★ ✔

Up-and-coming vineyard pieced together from parcels previously owned by two St-Estèphe châteaux. This wine is matured in wood for 18 months, with 25 per cent new oak.

RED Plump, fruit-driven reds of good class and finesse, with a long finish.

Cabernet Sauvignon 60%, Merlot 35%, Cabernet Franc 5%

☐ 4–12 years

CHÂTEAU SÉNÉJAC
AOC Médoc
★ ✔

This property changed hands in 1999. The wine is matured in wood for 18 months, with 25 per cent new oak (up to 100 per cent for its prestige *cuvée* Karolus).

RED A firm, full-flavoured wine of excellent longevity, Sénéjac is not, however, for the faint-hearted, especially in its rather stern youthful years. The Karolus is bigger, richer, and more concentrated.

Cabernet Sauvignon 60%, Merlot 25%, Cabernet Franc 14%, Petit Verdot 1%

☐ 5–15 years

Second wine: *Artique de Sénac*

Other wine: ✔ *Karolus*

CHÂTEAU SIGOGNAC
AOC Médoc
✪

Owned by Colette Bonny, this wine is matured in wood for 12 months, with 20 per cent new oak.

RED Consistently good-value, lunchtime claret of some elegance.

🍇 Merlot 50%, Cabernet Sauvignon 28%, Cabernet Franc 22%

🍷 3–8 years

Second wine: *Château La Croix du Chevalier*

CHÂTEAU SOCIANDO-MALLET
AOC Haut-Médoc
★★✪

This property has been making a name for itself since 1970, when Jean Gautreau raised standards to near *cru classé* quality. The quality of Sociando-Mallet has continued to increase throughout the 1990s, when between 80 and 100 per cent new oak became the norm. Its owners did not bother to submit wines for the 2003 reclassification, since it already achieves a higher price than a number of *cru classé* wines, but it is undoubtedly at least *cru bourgeois exceptionnel* in quality, if not name.

RED These are powerfully built wines that are rich in colour and extract. Often totally dominated by vanilla oak in their youth, they are backed up with plenty of concentrated cassis fruit.

🍇 Cabernet Sauvignon 55%, Merlot 42%, Cabernet Franc 2%, Petit Verdot 1%

🍷 10–25 years

Second wine: *La Demoiselle de Sociando-Mallet*

CHÂTEAU SOUDARS
AOC Médoc
★✪

Soudars was formed by the combination of several parcels of rock-strewn land that had become overgrown with brambles until Eric Miailhe took over the property in 1973 and spent several years clearing it. The wine is fermented in stainless steel, and matured in wood for 12 to 14 months, with up to 40 per cent new oak.

RED Excellent, well-coloured wines of good structure and accessible fruit.

🍇 Cabernet Sauvignon 49%, Merlot 50%, Cabernet Franc 1%

🍷 5–10 years

Second wine: *Château Marquis de Cadourne*

CHÂTEAU LE TEMPLE
AOC Médoc
★✪

Starting to live up to its reputation in the early 1900s, when it was known as "Lafite of the Bas-Médoc", this wine is matured in wood for 12 months, with 22 per cent new oak.

RED Increasingly lush and fruit-dominant, without losing its classic, tannin structure.

🍇 Cabernet Sauvignon 60%, Merlot 35%, Petit Verdot 5%

🍷 7–15 years

Second wine: *Château Bairac*
Other wine: *Château La Croix des Sablons*

CHÂTEAU LA TOUR DE BY
AOC Médoc
★✪

The tower of Tour de By was once a lighthouse. The wine is of very good quality; it is matured in wood for 16 months, with up to 30 per cent new oak.

RED These deeply coloured, full-bodied, richly flavoured wines have good spicy fruit, backed up by a firm tannic structure.

🍇 Cabernet Sauvignon 60%, Merlot 36%, Cabernet Franc 4%

🍷 6–12 years

Second wine: *Château La Roque-de-By*

Other wines: *Château Moulin de Roque, Château Moulin de la Roque*

CHÂTEAU LA TOUR-CARNET
AOC Haut-Médoc
4ème Cru Classé

This charming, 13th-century miniature moated castle has a well-kept vineyard. Its wines used to be lacklustre, but have been transformed by the new owner, Bernard Magrez of Pape-Clément, who purchased the property in 1999. The wine is now matured in wood for 12 to 18 months, with 60 per cent new oak.

RED Much riper, more opulent fruit, with some lush new oak in a supporting role, this wine has the richness of flavour it used to lack, with improvements noticeable from one year to the next.

🍇 Cabernet Sauvignon 53%, Merlot 33%, Cabernet Franc 10%, Petit Verdot 4%

🍷 5–15 years

Second wine: *Douves de Carnet*

CHÂTEAU TOUR HAUT-CAUSSAN
AOC Médoc
★★☆

An up-and-coming property owned by Philippe Courrian, who also makes wine in Corbières. The grapes are all hand-harvested, and the wine is matured in wood for 12 months, with one-third new oak.

RED Rich, well-coloured wines with a great concentration of fruit and nicely integrated, creamy oak.

🍇 Cabernet Sauvignon 50%, Merlot 50%

🍷 4–10 years

Second wine: *Château Landotte*

CHÂTEAU TOUR SAINT-BONNET
AOC Médoc
★✪

Situated on fine, gravelly ridges, this property was known as Château la Tour Saint-Bonnet-Cazenave in the 19th century. This wine is matured in wood for 18 months, with 50 per cent new oak.

RED Firm, full-flavoured, well-coloured wines of consistent quality.

🍇 Cabernet Sauvignon 45%, Merlot 45%, Malbec 5%, Petit Verdot 5%

🍷 7–15 years

Second wine: *Château La Fuie-Saint-Bonnet*

CHÂTEAU VERDIGNAN
AOC Haut-Médoc
✪

Since 1972, the property of the Miailhe family, who continue to improve the quality. The wine is fermented in stainless steel and matured in wood for 12 to 14 months, with 30 per cent new oak.

RED Medium-bodied, fruity wines, made in a soft and silky style.

🍇 Cabernet Sauvignon 50%, Merlot 45%, Cabernet Franc 5%

🍷 5–10 years

Second wine: *Château Plantey-de-la-Croix*

CHÂTEAU VILLEGORGE
AOC Haut-Médoc
★✪

This château was classified *cru bourgeois* in 1932. It was purchased by Lucien Lurton in 1973, but he then resigned from the Syndicat and, therefore, the château was not included in its 1978 list, although it is superior to a few that were. He was succeeded by his daughter, Marie-Louise, the present incumbent, who has continued improving the quality, achieving *supérieur* status in the 2003 reclassification. The wine is matured in wood for 10 to 24 months, with up to 30 per cent new oak.

RED Full-bodied wines, with a lovely colour, increasingly lush and opulent fruit, understated, creamy oak, and an increasing spicy finesse.

🍇 Cabernet Sauvignon 40%, Merlot 60%

🍷 6–12 years

Second wine: *Reflet de Villegeorge*

VINEYARDS THRIVING IN THE MÉDOC
In ancient Roman times this area was considered too marshy for cultivation, yet today it is one of the most prized areas under vine in the world, envied by winemakers worldwide.

SAINT-ESTÈPHE

Although St-Estèphe can be considered the least sexy of the Médoc's famous four appellations, it has an abundance of high-quality bourgeois growths, which make it indubitably the "bargain basement" of Bordeaux wines.

WITH ONLY FIVE *CRUS CLASSÉS* covering a mere 6 per cent of the commune, St-Estèphe is a rich source of undervalued clarets, where the prices paid by wine drinkers are unlikely to be sent soaring by wine investors. Enthusiasts rather than speculators will benefit from the fact that no fewer than four of the Médoc's nine *crus bourgeois exceptionnels* are to be found in this commune.

CHÂTEAU COS D'ESTOURNEL

St-Estèphe might lack *crus classés*, but it is not lacking in class. If it had only one *cru classé* – the stunning, stylish Château Cos d'Estournel – St-Estèphe would still be famous. The reputation of

this château soared after Bruno Prats took over control in 1971. Essentially, this success can be put down to his maximizing the true potential of Cos d'Estournel's exceptional *terroir*, a superb, south-facing ridge of gravel with perfect drainage.

HARVEST, CHÂTEAU COS D'ESTOURNEL
The bizarre eastern façade of this purpose-built winery overlooks the vineyards. The château was owned by perfectionist Bruno Prats before it was sold to the Bernard Taillan group in October 1998.

ST-ESTÈPHE PROFILE

Appellation area
Covers parts of the commune of St-Estèphe only

Size of commune
3,757 ha (9,284 acres)

AOC area under vine
1,214 ha (3,000 acres), 32% of the commune

Surface area of *crus classés*
248 ha (613 acres), 6.5% of commune, 20.5% of AOC

Special comments
Approximately 5 ha (12.5 acres) of vineyards within St-Estèphe are classified as AOC Pauillac

ST-ESTÈPHE CRU CLASSÉ STATISTICS

***Crus classés* in AOC St-Estèphe**
Five châteaux (by number: 8% of *crus classés* in the Médoc) with 248 ha (613 acres) of vineyards (by area: 7.5% of *crus classés* in the Médoc and 20.5% of this AOC)

1ers crus classés
None

2èmes crus classés
Two châteaux (by number: 14% of *2ème crus classés* in the Médoc) with 132 ha (326 acres) of vineyards (by area: 14% of *2ème crus classés* in the Médoc)

3èmes crus classés
One château (by number: 7% of *3ème crus classés* in the Médoc) with 53 ha (131 acres) of vineyards (by area: 9% of *3ème crus classés* in the Médoc)

4èmes crus classés
One château (by number: 10% of *4ème crus classés* in the Médoc) with 45 ha (111 acres) of vineyards (by area: 8% of *4ème crus classés* in the Médoc)

5èmes crus classés
One château (by number: 5.5% of *5ème crus classés* in the Médoc) with 18 ha (44 acres) of vineyards (by area: 2% of *5ème crus classés* in the Médoc)

FACTORS AFFECTING TASTE AND QUALITY

LOCATION
St-Estèphe is the most northerly of the four classic communes of the Médoc. It is situated 18 kilometres (11 miles) south of Lesparre, bordering the Gironde.

CLIMATE
As for the Médoc (*see* p116).

ASPECT
St-Estèphe has well-drained, well-sited, softly sloping vineyards. The southeast-facing crest of gravel overlooks Château Lafite-Rothschild in Pauillac and is relatively steep for the Médoc.

SOIL
The topsoil is gravelly and more fertile than in communes further south, with clay subsoil exposed in parts, consisting of clay beds, stony-clay, and limestone over iron-pan.

VITICULTURE AND VINIFICATION
Only the red wines have the right to the appellation in this commune. With increasing emphasis placed on the Merlot grape, which can now account for up to 50 per cent of the vines cultivated in some châteaux, reduced use of *vin de presse*, and improved vinification techniques, these wines are becoming far more accessible in less sunny years. During the vinification, all grapes must be destalked, and duration of skin contact averages three weeks. Maturation in cask currently varies between 15 and 24 months.

GRAPE VARIETIES
Primary varieties: Cabernet Franc, Cabernet Sauvignon, Merlot
Secondary varieties: Carmenère, Malbec, Petit Verdot

Those vineyards on heavier soil with less gravel and more clay tend to produce more rustic wines.

MODERN ST-ESTÈPHE

Most wines from St-Estèphe have always been well structured, with natural longevity, but they now have more lushness of fruit, which allows the wines to be accessible when relatively young. It was once essential to buy only the greatest vintages and wait 20 years or more before drinking them. The increasing use of the Merlot grape as well as Cabernet Sauvignon and Cabernet Franc, and a tendency to favour vinification techniques that extract colour and fruit in preference to the harsher tannins, provide richer, fruitier, and eminently drinkable wines in most vintages.

ST-ESTÈPHE, *see also p109*
Of the Haut-Médoc's four best-known communes, St-Estèphe is the most northerly, although the actual AOC area covers only part of the commune.

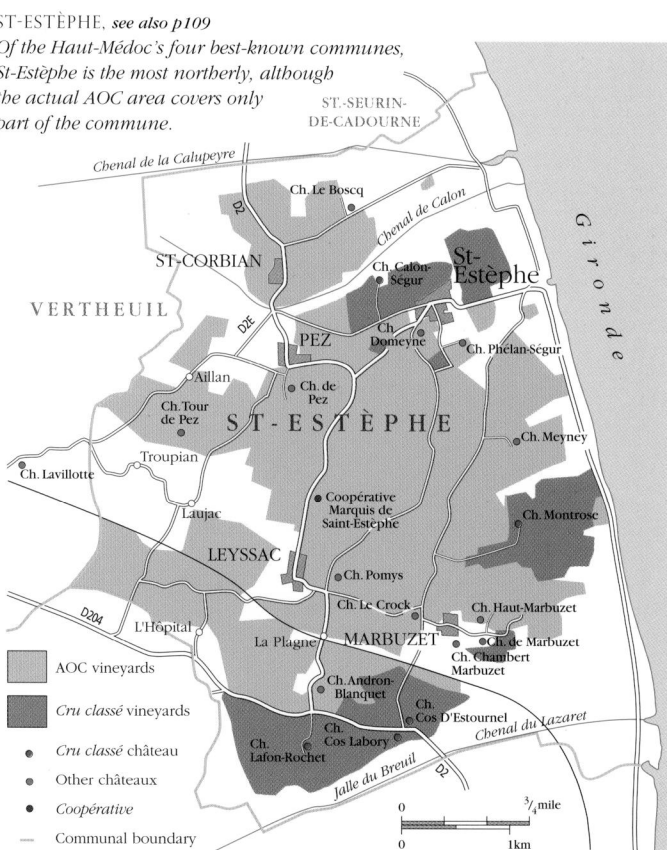

THE WINE PRODUCERS OF
SAINT-ESTÈPHE

CHÂTEAU ANDRON-BLANQUET
★ V

Under the same ownership as Château Cos Labory, the vineyards of this property are situated above the gravel crest of *cru classé* châteaux that overlook Château Lafite-Rothschild in Pauillac. This wine is matured in wood for 12 months, with 25 per cent new oak.

RED An exceptionally well-made wine that consistently rises above its *petit château* status. Fermented and matured in cask, it has good fruit and a distinctive style.

🍇 Cabernet Sauvignon 40%, Merlot 35%, Cabernet Franc 25%

🍷 4–10 years

Second wine: *Château St-Roch*
Other wine: *Château Blanquet*

CHÂTEAU BEAU-SITE
★ V

This property should not be confused with Château Beau-Site Haut-Vignoble, a lesser St-Estèphe. This wine is matured in wood for 16 to 18 months, with 50 per cent new oak.

RED A stylish, medium-bodied, sometimes full-bodied, wine that often has an elegant finish reminiscent of violets.

🍇 Cabernet Sauvignon 70%, Merlot 30%

🍷 3–10 years

CHÂTEAU LE BOSCQ
★✫ V

This property has always produced good wine, but quality increased dramatically in the 1980s. It was taken over by Dourthe-Kressman in 1995.

RED Superbly aromatic, almost exotic, full-bodied wine that is elegant and rich with the flavour of summer fruits, and is nicely backed up with new oak.

🍇 Cabernet Sauvignon 42%, Merlot 51%, Petit Verdot 7%

🍷 5–12 years

Second wine: *Héritage de Le Boscq*

CHÂTEAU CALON-SÉGUR
3ème Cru Classé
★✫ V

From the Gallo-Roman origins of this château grew the community of St-Estèphe. The first wine estate in the commune, it used to boast "*Premier Cru de St-Estèphe*" on its label until other producers objected. This wine is matured in wood for 18 months, with 50 per cent new oak.

RED Full, fruity, well-structured wine that has a creamy, rich flavour.

It is of consistently good quality and improves well in bottle.

🍇 Cabernet Sauvignon 50%, Merlot 35%, Cabernet Franc 10%, Petit Verdot 5%

🍷 3–20 years

Second wine: *Marquis de Ségur*

CHÂTEAU CAPBERN GASQUETON
★ V

This property is under the same ownership as Château Calon-Ségur. The vineyards are found north and south of the village of St-Estèphe. This wine is matured in wood for 18 months, with 30 per cent new oak.

RED Medium-weight, ripe, and fruity wine of consistent quality; it is mellowed by 24 months in wood.

🍇 Cabernet Sauvignon 50%, Merlot 35%, Cabernet Franc 15%

🍷 4–12 years

CHÂTEAU CHAMBERT-MARBUZET
★✫ V

Technically faultless, hand-harvested wine produced in limited quantities from the sister château of Haut-Marbuzet. Many would rate it easily equivalent to a *cru classé*. This wine is matured in wood for 18 months, with 50 per cent new oak.

RED Aromatically attractive, medium-bodied, sometimes full-bodied, wine. It is rich, ripe, and fruity, with plenty of caramel-oak and sufficient tannin to age well.

🍇 Cabernet Sauvignon 70%, Merlot 30%

🍷 3–10 years

Second wine: *Château Grand-Village Capbern*

CHÂTEAU COS D'ESTOURNEL
2ème Cru Classé
★★★ V

This was one of the very first super-seconds to emerge and this was the achievement of one man, Bruno Prats, although he would claim it to be teamwork. In 1998 Prats was forced by French tax laws to sell out to Groupe Taillan, who in 2001 sold it on to Michel Reybier, a Geneva-based food manufacturer. Cos d'Estournel has no château as such, merely a bizarre façade to the winery with huge, elaborately carved oak doors that once adorned the palace of the Sultan of Zanzibar. Bruno Prats' son Jean-Guillaume manages the property for Reybier, and the wine is made in the same careful way that his father introduced. This involves some of the wine being fermented in stainless steel, but all of it is matured in cask for 18 to 24

months, with 100 per cent new oak for big years, and up to 70 per cent for lighter vintages.

RED A rich, flavoursome, and attractive wine of full body, great class, and distinction; without doubt the finest wine in St-Estèphe. It is uniquely generous for the appellation and capable of amazing longevity, even in the poorest years. This is a complex wine with silky fruit and great finesse.

🍇 Cabernet Sauvignon 60%, Merlot 40%

🍷 8–20 years

Second wine: *Les Pagodes de Cos*

CHÂTEAU COS LABORY
5ème Cru Classé
★

Until the late 19th century, this property formed part of Château Cos d'Estournel. During the 1920s, it was purchased by distant cousins of Madame Audoy, the current owner. The wine is matured in wood for 15 to 18 months, with one-third new oak.

RED These wines used to be merely light and elegant with a certain degree of finesse, even when at their best. However, recent vintages have displayed a very welcome change to a distinctly fuller, fruitier, and fatter style.

🍇 Cabernet Sauvignon 55%, Merlot 35%, Cabernet Franc 5%, Petit Verdot 5%

🍷 5–15 years

Second wine: *Château Charme Labory*

CHÂTEAU LE CROCK
★✫ V

This property is under the same ownership as Château Léoville-Poyferré of St-Julien, and was promoted to *supérieur* status in the 2003 reclassification. This hand-harvested wine is matured in wood for 18 months, with 20 per cent new oak.

RED These dark-coloured, substantial wines have surged in quality since 1995 under the personal guidance of Michel Rolland.

🍇 Cabernet Sauvignon 58%, Merlot 24%, Cabernet Franc 12%, Petit Verdot 6%

🍷 6–15 years

Second wine: *Château Croix Saint-Estèphe*
Other wine: *Château Fatin*

CHÂTEAU DOMEYNE
★✫ V

This property was not classified *cru bourgeois* in 1932, nor was it listed by the Syndicat in 1978, but it

certainly should have been. This wine is matured in wood for 18 months, with 40 per cent new oak.

RED These are typically deep-coloured, rich-flavoured wines that have an excellent marriage of fruit and oak. They are smooth and well-rounded wines that can be drunk while fairly young.

🍇 Cabernet Sauvignon 60%, Merlot 35%, Cabernet Franc 5%

🍷 3–8 years

CHÂTEAU FAGET
★ V

Château Faget was classified *cru bourgeois* in 1932, but was not included in the Syndicat's 1978 list. However, this *coopérative*-produced wine is now superior to some that were included. This hand-harvested wine is matured in wood for 12 months, with one-third new oak.

RED This is a well-made wine that gives a solid mouthful of flavour, and ages well.

🍇 Cabernet Sauvignon 60%, Merlot 30%, Cabernet Franc 10%

🍷 6–10 years

CHÂTEAU HAUT-MARBUZET
★★ V

This is one of several properties belonging to Henri Duboscq. These wines receive 18 months in 100 per cent new oak, which is extremely rare even for *cru classé* châteaux.

RED These full-bodied, deep-coloured wines are packed with juicy fruit, backed up by supple tannin. They are marked by a generous buttered-toast and creamy-vanilla character.

🍇 Merlot 50%, Cabernet Sauvignon 40%, Cabernet Franc 10%

🍷 4–12 years

Second wine: *Tour de Marbuzet*

CHÂTEAU LA HAYE
★ V

New equipment, 25 per cent new oak casks every year, and a fair proportion of old vines combine to produce some exciting vintages at this property.

RED Always limpid, this medium-bodied, sometimes full-bodied, wine is rich in colour and flavour, well balanced, and lengthy, with vanilla-oak evident on the finish.

🍇 Cabernet Sauvignon 50%, Merlot 42%, Petit Verdot 8%

🍷 5–8 years

Second wine: *Fief de la Haye*

CHÂTEAU LAFON-ROCHET
4ème Cru Classé
★ ♥

When Guy Tesseron purchased this vineyard, which is situated on the borders of Pauillac, in 1959, he embarked on a project to increase the proportion of Cabernet Sauvignon grapes used in the wine. However, this proved to be a mistake for Lafon-Rochet's *terroir* and has been rectified in recent years. The wine produced here is matured in wood for 18 months, with up to 50 per cent new oak.

RED More fruit and finesse from the mid-1990s onwards.

🍇 Cabernet Sauvignon 55%, Merlot 40%, Cabernet Franc 5%

🍷 5–12 years

Second wine: ✓ *Numero 2*

CHÂTEAU LAVILLOTTE
★ ☆ ♥

This star-performing *petit château* gives good value. This wine is matured in wood for 16 months, with up to 40 per cent new oak.

RED These are dark-coloured wines with a deep and distinctive bouquet. Smoky, full-bodied, intense, and complex.

🍇 Cabernet Sauvignon 72%, Merlot 25%, Petit Verdot 3%

🍷 5–12 years

Second wine: *Château Aillan*

CHÂTEAU DE MARBUZET
☆

Under the same ownership as Cos d'Estournel, Marbuzet used to include the wines rejected from the *grand vin* of that "super-second". However, all the wine from this château has been produced exclusively from its own 17-hectare (42-acre) vineyard since 1994. The wine is matured in wood for 12 to 14 months in used barrels.

RED These elegant, medium-bodied, and sometimes full-bodied, wines are well balanced and have good fruit and a supple finish.

🍇 Cabernet Sauvignon 40%, Merlot 60%

🍷 4–10 years

Second wine: *Château Charme Labory*

LE MARQUIS DE SAINT-ESTÈPHE
★ ♥

This wine is produced by the conscientious Cave Coopérative Marquis de Saint-Estèphe, who mature it in wood for 12 months, with a whopping 70 per cent new oak.

RED A consistently well-made, good-value, usually medium-bodied (although sometimes full-bodied) wine, with increasingly more noticeable oak.

🍇 Cabernet Sauvignon 65%, Merlot 25%, Cabernet Franc 3%, Malbec 3%, Petit Verdot 4%

🍷 3–6 years

CHÂTEAU MEYNEY
★ ♥

This château is consistent in managing to produce fine wines in virtually every vintage.

RED These wines used to be big, beefy, chunky, and chewy, and required at least 10 years in bottle. They have changed, and for the better, acquiring a silky-textured finesse and ageing gracefully without so many years in bottle.

🍇 Cabernet Sauvignon 67%, Merlot 25%, Cabernet Franc 5%, Petit Verdot 3%

🍷 5–25 years

Second wine: *Prieuré de Meyney*

CHÂTEAU MONTROSE
2ème Cru Classé
★ ★ ♥

This "youngest" of the *cru classé* vineyards, this property grew out of an inconsequential plot of vines retained by a M Dumoulin, the former owner of Calon-Ségur, when he sold that château in 1824. These vines were on a 5–6 hectare (12–15 acre) plot of land called Escargeon, which for some reason he changed to Montrose the very next year. There are rumours about the origin of this new name, but no one really knows the true story. What we do know, however, is that by 1855, Montrose had grown to 96 hectares (237 acres), as Dumoulin bought and exchanged parcels of land from and with his neighbours. Despite the new-found importance of Montrose, Calon-Ségur was still considered by locals to be its superior, thus there was much surprise when Montrose was classified as a *deuxième cru classé*, above *troisième cru* Calon-Ségur. The wines are matured in wood for 19 months, with 50 per cent new oak.

RED The inhibiting factor at Montrose had always been its "stemmy" tannins. A vintage of exceptional richness and fatness was required to overcome the aggressive character produced by these tannins. The excellent 1994 gave me hope that this château has started to harvest the grapes when they are tannin-ripe (*see* p112) and

was applying more specific maceration techniques. Happily, my hopes were not dashed, and Montrose's performance since the mid-1990s has clearly demonstrated that this wine is a true *deuxième cru classé*.

🍇 Cabernet Sauvignon 65%, Merlot 25%, Cabernet Franc 10%

🍷 8–25 years

Second wine: ✓ *La Dame de Montrose*

CHÂTEAU LES ORMES DE PEZ
★ ★ ♥

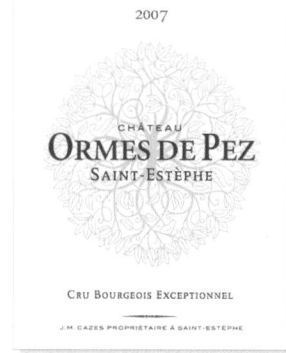

Owner Jean-Michel Cazes of Château Lynch-Bages in Pauillac installed new stainless-steel vats in 1981 and has raised the quality of these wines from good to sensational. Matured in wood for at least 12 to 15 months, with 50 per cent new oak, this relatively cheap wine is easily equivalent to a good *cru classé*.

RED Dark and fruity, yet capable of ageing with a herbal complexity.

🍇 Cabernet Sauvignon 65%, Merlot 25%, Cabernet Franc 10%

🍷 3–15 years

CHÂTEAU DE PEZ
★ ★ ♥

This property was purchased by Louis Roederer of Champagne in 1995. The wines are fermented in wooden vats, then matured in small casks for 18 months, with 40 per cent new oak. These wines are easily the equivalent of *cru classé* quality.

RED Consistently one of the best *bourgeois* growths in the entire Médoc. A medium-bodied wine, it has a rich fruit flavour and good tannic structure, and can mature into a sublime, cedary wine.

🍇 Cabernet Sauvignon 45%, Merlot 44%, Cabernet Franc 8%, Petit Verdot 3%

🍷 6–20 years

CHÂTEAU PHÉLAN-SÉGUR
★ ☆ ♥

This château was purchased in 1984 by its present owners, the Gardinier family, one year after selling Champagnes Pommery and Lanson. In retrospect, it is quite clear to see that there have been two steps up

in quality; the first in 1988 and the second in 1999, with obvious consolidation achieved during the intervening decade, with serious investment going into the infrastructure of vineyard and winery. Now one of the best-value wines in the Médoc, this wine is matured in wood for 16 months, with 50 per cent new oak.

RED Increasingly stylish wines of good colour and a certain plumpness of fruit, without loss of true St-Estèphe structure. Unlike most other success stories in the commune, this has not been achieved by increasing Merlot; the reverse, in fact.

🍇 Cabernet Sauvignon 60%, Merlot 35%, Cabernet Franc 5%

🍷 5–10 years

Second wine: *Franck Phélan*

Other wine: *Croix Bonis*

CHÂTEAU POMYS
★ ☆ ♥

This property was classified *cru bourgeois* in 1932, but was not included in the 1978 list, although it is superior to a few that were. This hand-harvested wine is matured in wood for 15 months, with 30 per cent new oak.

RED Substantial wines with good fruit and tannin balance.

🍇 Cabernet Sauvignon 50%, Merlot 35%, Cabernet Franc 15%

🍷 3–10 years

Other wine: *Château Saint-Louis*

CHÂTEAU TOUR DE PEZ
★ ☆ ♥

The huge investments made since this château changed hands in 1989 paid off in 2003 when it was promoted to *crus bourgeois supérieur*. This wine is matured in wood for 16 to 18 months, with 50 per cent new oak.

RED Consistently elegant, medium-bodied wine with good, plump, fleshy fruit.

🍇 Cabernet Sauvignon 45%, Cabernet Franc 10%, Merlot 40%, Petit Verdot 5%

🍷 3–7 years

Second wine: *T de Tour de Pez*

Other wines: *Château les Hauts de Pez, Château L'Hereteyre Château Haut-Coutelin*

CHÂTEAU TRONQUOY-LALANDE
★ ♥

Owned by Arlette Castéja-Texier with active input from the Dourthe-Kressman winemaking team.

RED This wine can be dark and tannic, but as from the 1996 vintage it has displayed more fruit and finesse.

🍇 Cabernet Sauvignon 45%, Merlot 45%, Petit Verdot 10%

🍷 3–7 years

PAUILLAC

If any Bordeaux appellation can be described as "big, black, and beautiful", it is Pauillac – the commune most famous for the three premiers crus of Latour, Lafite, and Mouton. If the wine is allowed to evolve slowly, it achieves an astonishing degree of finesse for its weight.

PAUILLAC IS, HOWEVER, an appellation of quite surprising contrasts. Although it boasts three-quarters of the Médoc's *premiers crus*, it also contains two-thirds of the region's *cinquièmes crus*. Very little lies between these two extremes, and former *crus bourgeois* are, therefore, the exception rather than the rule. Cabernet Sauvignon is at its most majestic in Pauillac, and while the much-vaunted blackcurrant character of this grape may be elusive in many clarets, it is certainly very much in evidence in Pauillac. In this wine, the cassis character is always beautifully balanced by a tannic structure.

PAUILLAC STATISTICS

Crus classés in AOC Pauillac
18 châteaux (by number: 30% of *crus classés* in the Médoc) with 1,063 ha (2,627 acres) of vineyards (by area: 32% of *crus classés* in the Médoc and 88% of this AOC)

1ers crus classés
3 châteaux (by number: 75% of *1ers crus classés* in the Médoc) with 264 ha (652 acres) of vineyards (by area: 76% of *1ers crus classés* in the Médoc)

2èmes crus classés
2 châteaux (by number: 14% of *2èmes crus classés* in the Médoc) with 155 ha (383 acres) of vineyards (by area: 16.5% of *2èmes crus classés* in the Médoc)

3èmes crus classés
None

4èmes crus classés
1 château (by number: 10% of *4èmes crus classés* in the Médoc) with 70 ha (173 acres) of vineyards (by area: 12.5% of *4èmes crus classés* in the Médoc)

5èmes crus classés
12 châteaux (by number: 67% of *5èmes crus classés* in the Médoc) with 574 ha (1,418 acres) of vineyards (by area: 63% of *5èmes crus classés* in the Médoc)

Note: Only Margaux has more *cru classé* châteaux than Pauillac, and no communal AOC has a greater concentration of *cru classé* vines.

CHÂTEAU LATOUR
Due to radical changes in vinification techniques introduced in the 1960s, Château Latour became the most consistent of Bordeaux's great premiers crus classés. It produces the archetypal Pauillac wine, which balances weight with finesse.

FACTORS AFFECTING TASTE AND QUALITY

 LOCATION
Pauillac is sandwiched
between St-Estèphe to the north
and St-Julien to the south.

CLIMATE
As for the Médoc (see p116)

ASPECT
Pauillac consists of two large,
low-lying plateaux, one to the
northwest of the town of Pauillac,
the other to the southwest.
Exposure is excellent, and both
drain down gentle slopes,
eastwards to the Gironde,
westwards to the forest, or north
and south to canals and streams.

SOIL
Pauillac's two plateaux are
massive gravel beds, reaching a
greater depth than any found
elsewhere in the Médoc.

The water drains away before the
iron-pan subsoil is reached.
St-Sauveur consists of shallow sand
over a stony subsoil to the west,
and gravel over iron-pan (or more
gravel) in the centre and south.

**VITICULTURE AND
VINIFICATION**
Only red wines have the right to the
Pauillac appellation. Some *vin de
presse* is traditionally used by most
châteaux. Skin contact duration
averages between 3 and 4 weeks,
and maturation in cask currently
varies between 18 and 24 months.

GRAPE VARIETIES
Primary varieties: Cabernet
Franc, Cabernet Sauvignon, Merlot
Secondary varieties: Carmenère,
Malbec, Petit Verdot

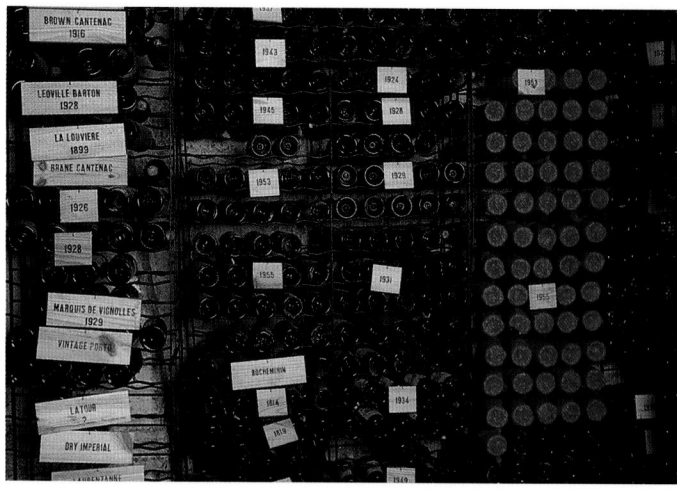

CAVEAU PRIVÉ, CHÂTEAU PICHON-LONGUEVILLE-
COMTESSE-DE-LALANDE
*One wall of the château's private cellars encapsulates a winemaking history,
particularly of Bordeaux, stretching back nearly 200 years.*

PAUILLAC PROFILE

Appellation area
Covers parts of the commune of
Pauillac, plus 34 ha (84 acres) in
St-Sauveur, 16 ha (40 acres) in
St-Julien, 5 ha (12.4 acres) in
St-Estèphe, and 1 ha (2.5 acres)
in Cissac

Size of commune
2,539 ha (6,274 acres)

AOC area under vine
1,212 ha (2,995 acres) 48% of
commune

Surface area of *crus classés*
1,063 ha (2,627 acres), 42% of
commune, 88% of AOC

PAUILLAC, *see also p109*
*Blessed with three premiers crus, Lafite-Rothschild and
Mouton-Rothschild in the north, and Latour to the south,
Pauillac is sandwiched between St-Estèphe
and St-Julien.*

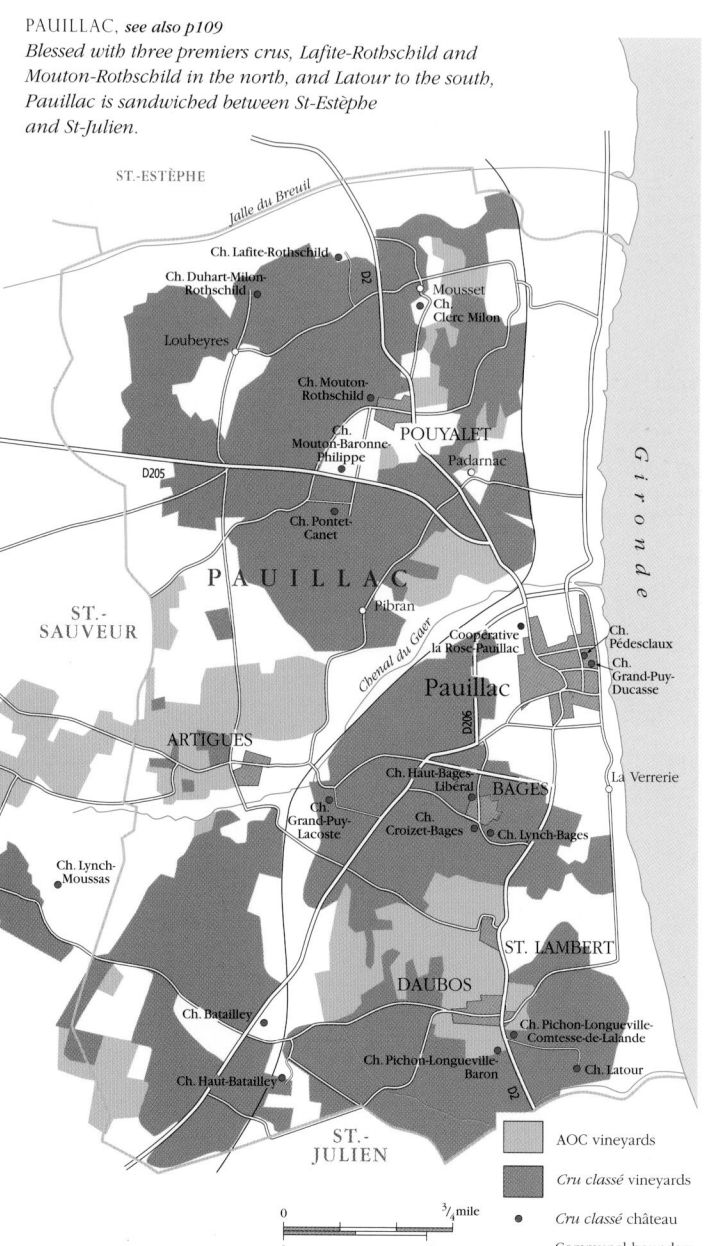

PAUILLAC
*The town of Pauillac, the largest of the Médoc, sits on the west bank of the
Gironde. Despite its size and position, it retains a quiet, rural character.*

THE WINE PRODUCERS OF

PAUILLAC

CHÂTEAU D'ARMAILHAC
5ème Cru Classé
★★☆

Baron Philippe de Rothschild purchased Château Mouton d'Armailhac in 1933. In 1956 he renamed it Château Mouton Baron-Philippe. In 1975 it was changed to Mouton-Baronne-Philippe in honour of the baron's late wife. In 1991 it reverted to d'Armailhac, but without the Mouton tag because the baron believed the wine to be in danger of assuming second wine status due to the overwhelming prestige of Mouton-Rothschild. This property borders that of Mouton, and one of Baron Philippe's reasons for acquiring it was to provide an easier, more impressive access to the famous *premier cru*. The wines, which are matured in wood for 16 months, with 25 per cent new oak, are produced with the same care and consideration. Despite this attention, I have criticized the "austere, light and attenuated style" of Château d'Armailhac in the past, which "proves that even money cannot buy *terroir*", but within limits improvements can always be made, and by tweaking harvesting and vinification techniques, owners Baron Philippe de Rothschild SA produced the greatest wine this property has ever known in 2000. That was an extraordinary vintage, but the style shift and giant stride in quality continued in 2001, 2002, and 2003.

RED Since 2000, much riper tannins, and a more supple structure has given this wine more velvety fruit than previous vintages had established. The start of a new era.

🍇 Cabernet Sauvignon 52%, Merlot 26%, Cabernet Franc 20%, Petit Verdot 2%

🍷 6–15 years

CHÂTEAU BATAILLEY
5ème Cru Classé
★★☆ ✪

This is a château that responds well to sunny years and produces underrated and undervalued wine. The 1985 was possibly the best

bargain in Bordeaux, and the 1986 is probably even better. This wine is matured in wood for 18 months, with 60 per cent new oak.

RED This wine has sometimes been rustic and too assertive in the past, but now shows its class with fine, succulent fruit supported by a ripe tannic structure and a complex creamy-oak aftertaste.

🍇 Cabernet Sauvignon 70%, Merlot 25%, Cabernet Franc 3%, Petit Verdot 2%

🍷 10–25 years

Second wine: *Château Haut-Bages Monpelou*

CHÂTEAU CLERC MILON
5ème Cru Classé
★

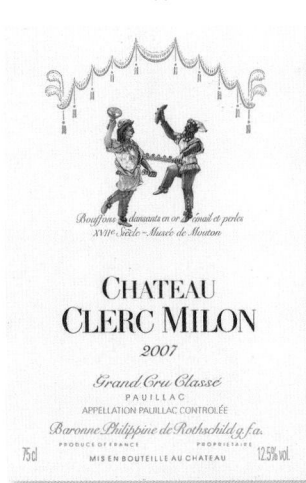

This property was purchased by Baron Philippe de Rothschild in 1970. After more than a decade of investment and quite a few disappointing vintages along the way, it came good in 1981, achieved sensational quality in 1982, and now consistently performs well above its classification. This wine, which is matured in wood for 18 months with one-third new oak, is one worth watching.

RED A deep-coloured, medium-bodied, sometimes full-bodied, wine with cassis-cum-spicy-oak aromas and rich berry flavours well balanced by ripe acidity.

🍇 Cabernet Sauvignon 70%, Merlot 20%, Cabernet Franc 10%

🍷 10–20 years

CHÂTEAU COLOMBIER-MONPELOU
★☆ ✪

In the third edition of *Bordeaux and its Wines*, published in 1874, this property was described as a *quatrième cru*. Of course, it was never classified as such, but its recent *cru bourgeois supérieur* achievement is about right. This wine is matured in wood for 16 months, with 40 per cent new oak.

RED Rich, spicy, fruit with fine Cabernet characteristics, backed up by good, ripe tannic structure and vanilla-oaky undertones.

🍇 Cabernet Sauvignon 55%, Merlot 35%, Cabernet Franc 5%, Petit Verdot 5%

🍷 5–12 years

Other wines: *Château Grand Canyon, Château Pey la Rose, Château Coubersant, Château de Puy la Rose*

CHÂTEAU CORDEILLAN-BAGES
★

Jean-Michel Cazes of Château Lynch-Bages was the driving force behind the group of growers from the Médoc who renovated Château de Cordeillan, turning it into an extensive complex comprising a hotel, restaurant, and wine school. With only a very small production from just two hectares of vineyards this hand-harvested wine that is produced by the Lynch-Bages winemaking team is matured in wood for up to 15 months, with a massive 100 per cent new oak.

RED As dark and as dense as might be expected from a wine produced with the Lynch-Bages influence, with smoky oak, tobacco plant, and violet aromas weaving their way through the chocolaty Cabernet fruit.

🍇 Cabernet Sauvignon 70%, Merlot 20%, Cabernet Franc 10%

🍷 3–8 years

CHÂTEAU CROIZET-BAGES
5ème Cru Classé
★☆ ✪

Under the same ownership as Château Rauzan-Gassies of Margaux, and situated on the Bages plateau, Croizet-Bages is a classic example of a "château with no château". Its wine is matured in wood for 18 months and although not unattractive, it lacks class and rarely excites. Improvements started slowly in the mid-1990s, then stepped up a gear at the turn of the millennium.

RED Not one of the most deeply coloured Pauillacs, this medium-bodied wine has always been easy-drinking, but has been more stylish since 1999, gaining both in gravitas and finesse.

🍇 Cabernet Sauvignon 37%, Cabernet Franc 30%, Merlot 30%, Malbec and Petit Verdot 3%

🍷 6–12 years

Second wine: *Enclos de Moncabon*

CHÂTEAU DUHART-MILON-ROTHSCHILD
4ème Cru Classé
★★☆

Another "château with no château", Duhart-Milon was purchased by the Lafite branch of the Rothschild family in 1962. Its wines prior to this date were almost entirely Petit Verdot, and so only in abnormally hot years did it excel with this late-ripening grape, which is traditionally cultivated for its acidity. Interestingly, in the near-tropical heat of 1947, Duhart-Milon managed to produce a wine that many considered to be the best of the vintage. The Rothschilds expanded these vineyards bordering Lafite and replanted them with the correct combination of varieties to suit the *terroir*. In 1994 Charles Chevalier arrived, and since 1996 he has moved these wines up a gear. The wine is matured for at least 18 months in wood, with 50 per cent new oak.

RED These wines are elegantly

perfumed, deliciously rich in creamy-oaky fruit, and have exceptional balance and finesse.

🍇 Cabernet Sauvignon 80%, Merlot 20%

🍶 8–16 years

Second wine: *Moulin de Duhart*

CHÂTEAU LA FLEUR-MILON

A "château with no château", La Fleur-Milon produces a wine accumulated from various parcels of vines bordering such prestigious properties as Lafite, Mouton, and Duhart-Milon. This wine is matured in wood for 18 months, with one-third new oak.

RED A consistently firm, solid, and decent sort of wine, which somehow fails to live up to the favoured origins of its vines.

🍇 Cabernet Sauvignon 45%, Cabernet Franc 20%, Merlot 35%

🍶 4–10 years

Other wines: *Château Chanteclerc-Milon, Château Buisson-Milon*

CHÂTEAU FONBADET
★ ❂

This growth was classified *cru bourgeois* in 1932, but was not included in the Syndicat's 1978 list, although it is superior to a few that were, and achieved due recognition in the 2003 reclassification. Many of the vines are in excess of 80 years old, with an average age of 50 years for the entire 20-hectare (50-acre) vineyard. This hand-harvested wine is matured in wood for 18 months, with 30 per cent new oak. Great-value Pauillac.

RED This typical Pauillac has a deep, almost opaque colour, an intense cassis, cigar-box, and cedarwood bouquet, a concentrated spicy, fruit flavour with creamy-oak undertones, and a long finish.

🍇 Cabernet Sauvignon 60%, Merlot 20%, Cabernet Franc 15%, Malbec and Petit Verdot 5%

🍶 6–15 years

Other wines: *Château Haut-Pauillac, Château Padarnac, Château Montgrand-Milon, Château Tour du Roc-Milon, Pauillac*

CHÂTEAU GRAND-PUY-DUCASSE
5ème Cru Classé
★ ★ ❂

Under the same owners as Château Rayne-Vigneau in Sauternes, this property produces an undervalued wine that comes from various plots scattered across half the commune. One of the best value, improving *cru classé* wines available, this wine is matured in wood for 18 to 24 months, with up to 40 per cent new oak.

RED Well-balanced, relatively early-drinking, medium-bodied, sometimes full-bodied, wine of classic Pauillac cassis character and more suppleness than is usual for this commune.

🍇 Cabernet Sauvignon 61%, Merlot 39%

🍶 5–10 years

Second wine: *Prélude à Grand-Puy Ducasse*

Other wine: *Château Artigues-Arnaud*

CHÂTEAU GRAND-PUY-LACOSTE
5ème Cru Classé
★ ★ ❂

Under the same ownership as Château Ducru-Beaucaillou, Grand-Puy-Lacoste is going from strength to strength under the skilful guidance of François-Xavier Borie. The wine is matured in wood for 18 months, with 50 per cent new oak.

RED Deep-coloured with complex cassis, cigar-box spice, and vanilla bouquet, with lots of fruit, length, and finesse.

🍇 Cabernet Sauvignon 75%, Merlot 25%

🍶 10–20 years

Second wine: *Lacoste-Borie*

CHÂTEAU HAUT-BAGES-LIBÉRAL
5ème Cru Classé
★

Under the same ownership as the bourgeois growth of Château Chasse-Spleen in Moulis and the excellent unclassified Château la Gurgue in Margaux, this dynamic property is currently producing sensational wines. They are matured for 16 months in wood, with up to 40 per cent new oak.

RED Dark, full-bodied wines with masses of concentrated spicy-cassis fruit, great tannic structure, and ripe, vanilla oak. In a word – complete.

🍇 Cabernet Sauvignon 80%, Merlot 17%, Petit Verdot 3%

🍶 8–20 years

Second wine: *Chapelle de Bages*

CHÂTEAU HAUT-BATAILLEY
5ème Cru Classé
★ ❂

This property is under the same ownership as châteaux Grand-Puy-Lacoste and, in St-Julien, Ducru-Beaucaillou. When the Borie family purchased Château Batailley in 1942, this part of the vineyard was given to one son, while the bulk of the property, including the château itself, was given to the other. The wine is matured in wood for 20 months, with one-third new oak.

RED Haut-Batailley is well-coloured and medium-bodied and shows more elegance and finesse than Batailley, although it can lack the latter's fullness of fruit.

🍇 Cabernet Sauvignon 65%, Merlot 25%, Cabernet Franc 10%

🍶 7–15 years

Second wine: *Château La Tour l'Aspic*

Other wine: *Château La Couronne*

CHÂTEAU LAFITE-ROTHSCHILD
1er Cru Classé
★ ★ ★

Since 1994 this famous château, the vineyard of which includes a small plot in St-Estèphe, has been run along traditional lines and with fastidious care by Charles Chevalier for Baron Eric of the French branch of the Rothschilds. The St-Estèphe portion of the Lafite vineyard is allowed to bear the Pauillac appellation, having been part of the Lafite-Rothschild estate for several hundred years. A change of style occurred in the mid-1970s, when the decision was taken to give the wines less time in cask, but under Chevalier they have gone into hyperdrive and are often the very best of the *premiers crus*. Well into the first decade of the new millennium, Lafite is arguably the best performing of all *premiers crus*. This hand-harvested wine is matured in wood for 20 months, with 100 per cent new oak.

RED Not the biggest of the *premiers crus*, but Lafite is nevertheless textbook stuff: a rich delicacy of spicy fruit flavours, continuously unfolding, supported by an array of creamy-oak and ripe tannins; a wine with incomparable finesse.

🍇 Cabernet Sauvignon 70%, Merlot 25%, Cabernet Franc 3%, Petit Verdot 2%

🍶 25–50 years

Second wine: ✓ *Carruades de Lafite*

Other wine: *Moulin des Carruades*

CHÂTEAU LATOUR
1er Cru Classé
★ ★ ★

The Pearson Group (which owns the publisher of this book) was accused by the French of turning a Bordeaux *premier cru* into a dairy when temperature-controlled, stainless-steel vats were installed in 1964. These French critics conveniently ignored the fact that Château Haut-Brion had done the same three years earlier. Pearson actually owned just over half of Latour at the time and Harveys of Bristol owned a quarter. Together, they paid less than £1 million (around $2.8 million) for almost 80 per cent of this *premier cru*. It was a bargain, for, although they invested heavily in renovating the vineyards and winery, Allied-Lyons (owners of Harvey's) paid almost £60 million ($108 million) in 1989 for Pearson's share, valuing the entire property at £110 million ($198 million). Allied-Lyons lost out, however, when in 1993 they needed to liquidate various shareholdings to finance takeovers and sold Latour to François Pinault, the French industrialist, for £86 million ($140 million). Pinault appointed Frédéric Engerer, a graduate of one of France's top business schools, as the new young president of Latour. He has revolutionized working practices in both the vineyard and winery and with Frédéric Ardouin, his new, even younger winemaker at his side, the change in gear at Latour promised to be as dramatic as it was at Margaux. This hand-harvested wine is matured in wood for 18 months, with 100 per cent new oak.

RED Despite its close proximity to the neighbouring commune of St-Julien, Latour is the archetypal Pauillac. Its ink-black colour accurately reflects the immense structure and hugely concentrated flavour of this wine. If Lafite is the ultimate example of finesse, then Latour is the ideal illustration of how massive a wine can be while still retaining great finesse.

🍇 Cabernet Sauvignon 75%, Merlot 20%, Cabernet Franc and Petit Verdot 5%

🍷 15–60 years

Second wine: ✓ *Les Forts de Latour*

Other wine: *Pauillac de Latour*

CHÂTEAU LYNCH-BAGES
5ème Cru Classé
★★✓

This château is sited on the edge of the Bages plateau, a little way out of Pauillac. It is on the southern fringe of the small town of Bages. Jean-Michel Cazes produces wines that some people describe as "poor man's Latour (or Mouton)". Well, that cannot be such a bad thing, but if I were rich, I would drink as many *cinquièmes crus* from this château as *premiers crus* from elsewhere. No expense was spared in building the new vinification and storage facilities at this château, and since 1980 the successes in off-vintages have been extraordinary, making it more consistent than some *deuxièmes crus*. This hand-harvested wine is matured in wood for 12 to 15 months, with 50 per cent new oak.

RED An intensely deep purple-coloured wine of seductive character that is packed with fruit and has obvious class. It has a degree of complexity on the nose, a rich, plummy flavour, supple tannin structure, and a spicy, blackcurrant and vanilla aftertaste.

🍇 Cabernet Sauvignon 75%, Merlot 15%, Cabernet Franc 10%

🍷 8–30 years

Second wine: ✓ *Château Haut-Bages-Avérous*

Other wine: *Blanc de Lynch-Bages* (rare "Médoc" white wine)

CHÂTEAU LYNCH-MOUSSAS
5ème Cru Classé
★

Owned by Emile Castéja of Borie-Manoux, this property has been renovated and the wines could well improve. The wine is matured in wood for 18 months, with 60 per cent new oak.

RED After a false start in the mid-1980s, when an exceptionally stylish 1985 turned out to be exactly that (an exception), this château continued to produce light, rather insubstantial wines of no specific character or quality, but with better selection, riper fruit, less time in

cask, and more than twice the amount of new oak Lynch-Moussas used to receive, it has made significantly better wines since the mid-1990s.

🍇 Cabernet Sauvignon 75%, Merlot 25%

🍷 4–8 years

Second wine: *Château Haut-Madrac*

CHÂTEAU MOUTON-ROTHSCHILD
1er Cru Classé
★★★

The famous case of the only wine ever to be officially reclassified since 1855, Baron Philippe de Rothschild's plight ended with Mouton's status being justly raised to *premier cru* in 1973. Through promotion of Mouton's unique character, he was probably responsible for elevating the Cabernet Sauvignon grape to its present high profile. Part of his campaign to keep this château in the headlines was the introduction of a specially commissioned painting for the label of each new vintage. The hand-harvested wine is matured in wood for up to 22 months, with 100 per cent new oak.

RED It is difficult to describe this wine without using the same descriptive terms as those used for Latour, but perhaps the colour of Mouton reminds one more of damsons and the underlying character is more herbal, sometimes even minty. And although it ages just as well as Latour, it becomes accessible slightly earlier.

🍇 Cabernet Sauvignon 77%, Merlot 11%, Cabernet Franc 10%, Petit Verdot 2%

🍷 12–60 years

Second wine: *Le Petit Mouton de Mouton-Rothschild*

Other wines: *Aile d'Argent* (another rare "Médoc" white)

CHÂTEAU PEDESCLAUX
5ème Cru Classé

Little-seen *cru classé* produced from two very well-situated plots of vines, one bordering Lynch-Bages,

the other between Mouton-Rothschild and Pontet-Canet. Most of its exported production goes to Belgium. It is matured in wood for 18 months, with 50 per cent new oak. Wine rejected for the *grand vin* is blended into the wine of Château Belle Rose, a *cru bourgeois* under the same ownership.

RED Full, firm, traditional style of Pauillac that is slow-maturing and long-lasting.

🍇 Cabernet Sauvignon 65%, Merlot 25%, Cabernet Franc 5%, Petit Verdot 5%

🍷 15–40 years

Second wine: *Château Haut-Pardanac*

CHÂTEAU PICHON-LONGUEVILLE BARON PICHON-LONGUEVILLE
2ème Cru Classé
★★★

The smaller of the two Pichon vineyards and until very recently the less inspiring, although many experts reckoned the *terroir* of Pichon-Baron to be intrinsically superior to that of its neighbour, the star-performing Pichon-Comtesse. Indeed, 15 years ago, I even suggested that Madame de Lencquesaing should buy this château and cast her seemingly irresistible spell on what would inevitably be the still greater *terroir* of the two properties combined. Whether she had such an ambition, or even the cash to consider it, AXA-Millésimes got there first, and has been remarkably successful at conjuring the most incredible quality from Pichon-Baron. Essentially by reducing Cabernet Sauvignon in favour of Merlot and almost tripling the amount of new oak used, AXA has ensured that Pichon-Baron now lives up to its potential. The wine is matured in wood for 15 to 18 months, with 80 per cent new oak.

RED Intensely coloured, full-bodied wine with concentrated spicy-cassis fruit backed up by supple tannins, which are rich and heady with smoky-creamy oak and complexity. True super-second quality.

🍇 Cabernet Sauvignon 60%, Merlot 35%, Cabernet Franc 4%, Petit Verdot 1%

🍷 8–25 years

Second wine: ✓ *Les Tourelles de Longueville*

CHÂTEAU PICHON LONGUEVILLE COMTESSE-DE-LALANDE
2ème Cru Classé
★★★

There is a limit to the quality of any wine and this is determined by the potential quality of its grapes. But at Pichon-Comtesse (as it is known), the formidable Madame de Lencquesaing demands the maximum from her *terroir* – and

consistently gets it. The wine is matured in wood for 20 months, with 50 per cent new oak.

RED This temptress is the Château Margaux of Pauillac. It is silky-textured, beautifully balanced, and seductive. A wine of great finesse, even in humble vintages.

🍇 Cabernet Sauvignon 45%, Merlot 35%, Cabernet Franc 12%, Petit Verdot 8%

🍷 10–30 years

Second wine: ✓ *Réserve de la Comtesse*

Other wines: *Les Gartieux*

CHÂTEAU PONTET-CANET
5ème Cru Classé
🅑★★

The reputation of this château has suffered in recent decades, but many thought the situation would be reversed when Guy Tesseron purchased the property in 1975. The 1985 vintage gave a glimmer of hope, but it was not until 1995 that the breakthrough occurred, and the 1998 vintage is nothing less than outstanding. Definitely one to watch, this hand-harvested wine is matured in wood for 15 to 20 months, with 60 per cent new oak.

RED Since the mid-1990s, these wines have been fruity and graceful with a rich, smooth, oaky touch.

🍇 Cabernet Sauvignon 68%, Merlot 20%, Cabernet Franc 10%, Malbec 2%

🍷 6–12 years

Other wine: Les Hauts de Pontet

CHÂTEAU LA TOUR-PIBRAN
★✓

This growth was classified *cru bourgeois* in 1932, but was not in the Syndicat's 1978 list, although it is superior to a few that were.

RED This wine has bags of blackcurranty fruit, yet retains the characteristic Pauillac structure and firm finish. The superb 1985 is not unlike a "mini-Mouton".

🍇 Cabernet Sauvignon 75%, Merlot 15%, Cabernet Franc 10%

🍷 6–16 years

SAINT-JULIEN

The commune's fame is disproportionate to its size, since it is smaller than any of the other three classic Médoc appellations – St-Estèphe, Pauillac, or Margaux.

St-Julien has no *premiers crus*, although some châteaux sometimes produce wines that are undeniably of *premier cru* quality. Nor *cinquièmes crus*. The concentration of its 11 *crus classés* in the middle of the classification is St-Julien's real strength, enabling this commune justly to claim that it is the most consistent of the Médoc appellations; these quintessential clarets have a vivid colour, elegant fruit, superb balance, and great finesse.

It is perhaps surprising that wines from 16 hectares (40 acres) inside St-Julien's borders may be classified as AOC Pauillac, particularly in view of the perceived difference in style between these appellations. This illustrates the "grey area" that exists when communal boundaries overlap the historical borders of great wine estates, and highlights the existence and importance of blending, even in a region reputed for its single-vineyard wines. We should not be too pedantic about communal differences of style: if these borders of the Médoc followed local history, Château Latour, the most famous château of Pauillac, would today be in St-Julien – and that makes me wonder how the wines of this commune might be described under such circumstances.

FACTORS AFFECTING TASTE AND QUALITY

LOCATION
St-Julien lies in the centre of the Haut-Médoc, 4 kilometres (2.5 miles) south of Pauillac.

CLIMATE
As for the Médoc (*see* p116).

ASPECT
The gravel crest of St-Julien slopes almost imperceptibly eastwards towards the village and drains into the Gironde.

SOIL
Fine, gravel topsoil of good-sized pebbles in vineyards within sight of the Gironde. Further inland, the particle size decreases and the soil begins to mix with sandy loess. The subsoil consists of iron-pan, marl, and gravel.

VITICULTURE AND VINIFICATION
Only red wines have the right to the appellation. All grapes must be destalked. Some *vin de presse* may be used according to the needs of the vintage. Skin contact duration averages 2 to 3 weeks and most châteaux allow 18 to 22 months' maturation in cask.

GRAPE VARIETIES
Primary varieties: Cabernet Franc, Cabernet Sauvignon, Merlot
Secondary varieties: Carmenère, Malbec, Petit Verdot

SAINT-JULIEN CRU CLASSÉ STATISTICS

Crus classés in AOC St-Julien
Eleven châteaux (by number: 18% of *crus classés* in the Médoc) with 740 ha (1,829 acres) of vineyards (by area: 22% of *crus classés* in the Médoc and 80% of this AOC)

1ers crus classés
None

2èmes crus classés
Five châteaux (by number: 36% of *2èmes crus classés* in the Médoc) with 366 ha (904 acres) of vineyards (by area: 39% of *2èmes crus classés* in the Médoc)

3èmes crus classés
Two châteaux (by number: 14% of *3èmes crus classés* in the Médoc) with 128 ha (316 acres) of vineyards (by area: 22% of *3èmes crus classés* in the Médoc)

4èmes crus classés
Four châteaux (by number: 40% of *4èmes crus classés* in the Médoc) with 246 ha (608 acres) of vineyards (by area: 44% of *4èmes crus classés* in the Médoc)

5èmes crus classés
None

SAINT-JULIEN PROFILE

Appellation area
Covers part of the commune of St-Julien only

Size of commune
1,554 ha (3,840 acres)

AOC area under vine
920 ha (2,273 acres), 59% of commune

Surface area of crus classés
740 ha (1,829 acres), 48% of commune, 80% of AOC

Special comments
Some 16 ha (40 acres) of St-Julien are classified as AOC Pauillac

ST-JULIEN-BEYCHEVELLE
The Médoc's most consistent appellation has two small villages as its major centres, St-Julien-Beychevelle itself and, to the south, Beychevelle.

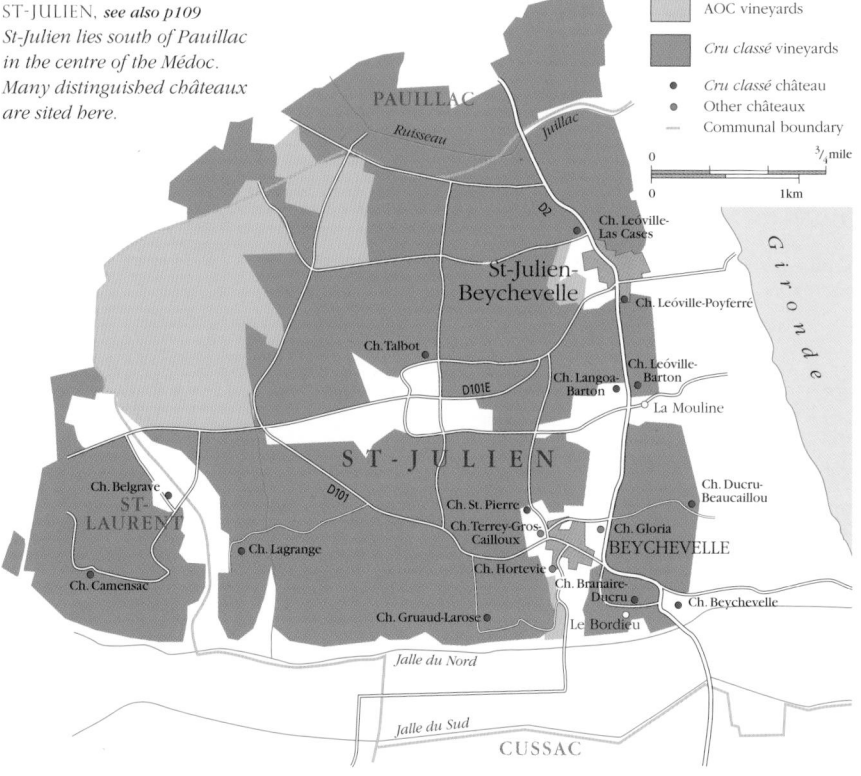

ST-JULIEN, *see also p109*
St-Julien lies south of Pauillac in the centre of the Médoc. Many distinguished châteaux are sited here.

AOC vineyards
Cru classé vineyards
• *Cru classé* château
○ Other châteaux
— Communal boundary

PAUILLAC
Ruisseau
Juillac
D2
Ch. Leóville-Las Cases
St-Julien-Beychevelle
Ch. Leóville-Poyferré
Ch. Talbot
Ch. Leóville-Barton
Ch. Langoa-Barton
La Mouline
D101E
ST-JULIEN
D101
Ch. Ducru-Beaucaillou
Ch. Belgrave
ST-LAURENT
Ch. St. Pierre
Ch. Gloria
Ch. Terrey-Gros Cailloux
BEYCHEVELLE
Ch. Lagrange
Ch. Hortevie
Ch. Camensac
Ch. Branaire-Ducru
Ch. Beychevelle
Ch. Gruaud-Larose
Le Bordieu
Jalle du Nord
Jalle du Sud
CUSSAC
Gironde
0   ³⁄₄ mile
0   1km

THE WINE PRODUCERS OF
SAINT-JULIEN

CHÂTEAU BEYCHEVELLE
4ème Cru Classé
★★

The immaculate and colourful gardens of this château never fail to catch the breath of passers-by. Beychevelle also boasts one of the most famous legends of Bordeaux: its name is said to be a corruption of "basse-voile", the command to "lower sail". This arose because the Duc d'Épernon, a former owner who was also an admiral of France, apparently required the ships that passed through the Gironde to lower their sails in respect. His wife would then wave her kerchief in reply. This story, however, is not true. Épernon actually held the title of Baron de Beychevelle prior to being made the Amiral de Valette, and did not actually live at Beychevelle. I prefer the story of the sailors who lowered their trousers and revealed their sterns, which shocked the duchess but made her children laugh. The wines are matured in wood for 20 months with 40 per cent new oak.

RED Medium- to full-bodied wines of good colour, ripe fruit, and an elegant oak and tannin structure. They can be quite fat in big years.

🍇 Cabernet Sauvignon 59%, Merlot 30%, Cabernet Franc 8%, Petit Verdot 3%

🍷 12–20 years

Second wine: ✓ *Amiral de Beychevelle*

Other wine: *Les Brulières de Beychevelle*

CHÂTEAU BRANAIRE-DUCRU
4ème Cru Classé
★☆ ⓥ

The vineyards of this château are situated further inland than those of Beychevelle and Ducru-Beaucaillou and its soil contains more clay and iron-pan than theirs, so the wine here is fuller and can be assertive, although never austere. It is matured in wood for 18 months, with up to 50 per cent new oak, and is remarkably consistent.

RED This is a quite full-bodied wine, which is richly flavoured and can show a certain chocolate character in big years. It has a distinctive bouquet that sets it apart from other St-Juliens.

🍇 Cabernet Sauvignon 75%, Merlot 20%, Cabernet Franc 5%

🍷 12–25 years

Second wine: *Duluc*

CHÂTEAU LA BRIDANE

The owners of this property have maintained a vineyard here since the 14th century.

RED Attractive, fruity, medium-bodied wine that is easy to drink.

🍇 Cabernet Sauvignon 55%, Merlot 45%

🍷 3–6 years

CHÂTEAU DUCRU-BEAUCAILLOU
2ème Cru Classé
★★☆

One of the super-seconds, the quality of this classic St-Julien château, the flagship property of the Borie empire, is both legendary and inimitable. In both good years and bad it remains remarkably consistent and, although relatively expensive, the price fetched falls short of those demanded by *premiers crus*, making it a relative bargain. The wine is matured in wood for 20 months, with 50 per cent new oak.

RED This wine has a fine, deep colour that can belie its deft elegance of style. There is richness of fruit, complex spiciness of oak, great finesse, and exquisite balance.

🍇 Cabernet Sauvignon 65%, Merlot 25%, Cabernet Franc 10%

🍷 15–30 years

Second wine: *La Croix*

CHÂTEAU DU GLANA
★☆ ⓥ

This property is under the same ownership as Château Plantey in Pauillac and Château la Commanderie in St-Estèphe.

RED Du Glana is normally an unpretentious and medium-weight wine, but it excels in really hot years, when it can be deliciously ripe and juicy.

🍇 Cabernet Sauvignon 68%, Merlot 25%, Petit Verdot 5%, Cabernet Franc 2%

🍷 3–6 years

CHÂTEAU GLORIA
★

Gloria excites opposite passions in wine drinkers: some consider it the equal of several *cru classé* wines – even superior in some cases – while others believe it earns an exaggerated price based on the reputation of merely a handful of vintages. Certainly the owners saw nothing to be gained by entering this wine for consideration in the 2003 reclassification, although it should have easily made *cru bourgeois supérieur* status had they done so. The wine is matured in wood for 12 months, with 40 per cent oak.

RED A deep plum-coloured, full-bodied wine with masses of fruit and a rich, exuberant character.

🍇 Cabernet Sauvignon 65%, Merlot 25%, Cabernet Franc 5%, Petit Verdot 5%

🍷 12–30 years

Second wine: *Peymartin*

Other wine: *Haut-Beychevelle-Gloria*

CHÂTEAU GRUAUD-LAROSE
2ème Cru Classé
★★ ⓥ

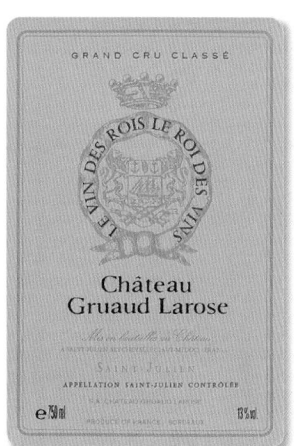

This large property produces consistently great wines of a far more solid structure than most other St-Julien wines. Anyone who has tasted the supposedly mediocre 1980 Sarget de Gruaud-Larose (made from the wines rejected from the grand vin) will realize the true potential of Château Gruaud-Larose in any year. If anything, the quality of Gruaud-Larose is still improving.

RED Full-bodied, rich, and plummy wine with masses of fruit. Its spicy blackcurrant flavour is supported by a structure of ripe tannins.

🍇 Cabernet Sauvignon 57%, Merlot 30%, Cabernet Franc 7%, Petit Verdot 4%, Malbec 2%

🍷 10–40 years

Second wine: ✓ *Sarget de Gruaud-Larose*

Other wines: *La Roseraie de Gruaud-Larose, Chevalier de Gruaud-Larose*

CHÂTEAU HORTEVIE
★★☆ ⓥ

There is no château as such on this property. This tiny vineyard's wine is made at Château Terrey-Gros-Cailloux by Henri Pradère, the owner of both properties.

RED This is a silky-soft, rich, and succulent wine of excellent quality. This great-value wine is easily equivalent to *cru classé* quality.

🍇 Cabernet Franc and Cabernet Sauvignon 70%, Merlot 25%, Petit Verdot 5%

🍷 7–15 years

CHÂTEAU DE LACOUFOURQUE

This tiny 1.25-hectare (3-acre) vineyard is mentioned not because of its past performance but because it is unique in Bordeaux in being a 100 per cent Cabernet Franc varietal, and it should be preserved.

RED This wine is sold in bulk as generic St-Julien, which makes it impossible to make generalizations about its character.

🍇 Cabernet Franc 100%

CHÂTEAU LAGRANGE
3ème Cru Classé
★★☆ ⓥ

When the Ban de Vendanges was held at this Japanese-owned château in 1986, everyone realized that the Japanese were not simply content to apply state-of-the-art technology; they seriously intended to make Lagrange the best-quality wine in St-Julien. They could well succeed in this ambition. The formidable Bordeaux oenologist Professor Peynaud has dubbed Lagrange a "dream estate", and describes its vinification centre as "unlike any other in the whole of Bordeaux". Each vat is, according to Peynaud, a "wine-making laboratory". The wine spends 18 months in wood, with up to 60 per cent new oak.

RED A deeply coloured wine with intense spicy-fruit aromas. It is full-bodied, silky-textured, and rich, with an exquisite balance and finish.

🍇 Cabernet Sauvignon 65%, Merlot 28%, Cabernet Franc and Petit Verdot 7%

🍷 8–25 years

Second wine: ✓ *Les Fiefs de Lagrange*

CHÂTEAU LALANDE-BORIE
★ ⓥ

Under the same ownership as the illustrious Château Ducru-Beaucaillou, Lalande-Borie is an inexpensive introduction to the wines of St-Julien.

RED These are well-coloured wines, dominated by rich, blackcurranty

Cabernet Sauvignon flavours. Some vintages are fat and juicy, while others are more ethereal and tannic.

🍇 Cabernet Sauvignon 65%, Merlot 25%, Cabernet Franc 10%

🍷 5–10 years

CHÂTEAU LANGOA-BARTON
3ème Cru Classé
★ 🅥

This beautiful château was known as Pontet-Langlois until 1821, when it was purchased by Hugh Barton, grandson of "French Tom" Barton, the founder of Bordeaux négociant Barton & Guestier, and is now run by Anthony Barton. Both Langoa-Barton and Léoville-Barton are made here using very traditional techniques. The wine is matured in wood for 24 months, with a minimum of one-third new oak.

RED Attractive, easy-drinking wine with good fruit and acidity. It is lighter than the Léoville and can sometimes taste a little rustic in comparison, but has gained a degree of extra elegance and finesse in recent years.

🍇 Cabernet Sauvignon 70%, Merlot 20%, Cabernet Franc 8%, Petit Verdot 2%

🍷 10–25 years

Second wine: 🗸 *Lady Langoa* (a blend of Langoa-Barton and Léoville-Barton formerly sold simply as "St-Julien")

CHÂTEAU LÉOVILLE-BARTON
2ème Cru Classé
★★★½ 🅥

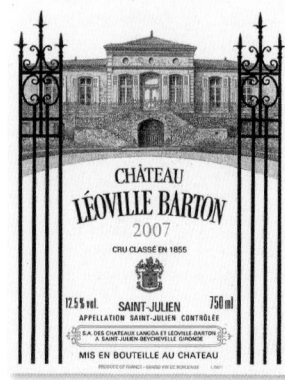

A quarter of the original Léoville estate was sold to Hugh Barton in 1826, but the château remained in the hands of the Léoville estate and is now called Château Léoville-Las Cases (*see below*). This wine is made by Anthony Barton at Langoa-Barton (*see left*). It is matured in wood for 24 months, with a minimum of one-third new oak. Although it is the better of the two Barton estates, it has been considered significantly beneath the standard set by Léoville-Las Cases – since the late 1980s, however, it has performed equally as well. A great château in ascendancy.

RED Excellent wines of great finesse and breeding; they are darker, deeper, and richer than the Langoa-Barton, which is itself of very good quality. With maturity, a certain cedarwood complexity develops in this wine and gradually overwhelms its youthful cassis and vanilla character.

🍇 Cabernet Sauvignon 70%, Merlot 20%, Cabernet Franc 8%, Petit Verdot 2%

🍷 15–30 years

Second wine: 🗸 *Lady Langoa* (a blend of Langoa-Barton and Léoville-Barton formerly sold simply as "St-Julien")

CHÂTEAU LÉOVILLE-LAS CASES
2ème Cru Classé
★★★½

The label reads "Grand Vin de Léoville du Marquis de Las Cases", although this wine is commonly referred to as "Château Léoville-Las Cases". This estate represents the largest portion of the original Léoville estate. This is a great wine, and it certainly qualifies as one of the super-seconds, while "Clos du Marquis" is one of the finest second wines available and probably the best value St-Julien. The grand vin spends 18 months in wood, with 50 per cent new oak.

RED This dark, damson-coloured, full-bodied, and intensely flavoured wine is complex, classy, and aromatically stunning. A skilful amalgam of power and finesse.

🍇 Cabernet Sauvignon 65%, Merlot 19%, Cabernet Franc 13%, Petit Verdot 3%

🍷 15–35 years

Second wine: 🗸 *Clos du Marquis*
Other wines: *Domaine de Bigarnon*

CHÂTEAU LÉOVILLE POYFERRÉ
2ème Cru Classé
★★½

This property once formed a quarter of the original Léoville estate, and probably suffers from being compared to the other two châteaux, whose properties were also part of Léoville – Léoville-Barton and Léoville-Las Cases. Yet in the context of St-Julien as a

whole, it fares very well, and since 1982 it has had some extraordinary successes. Since the involvement of Michel Rolland from the mid-1990s, quality has gone up another gear. Wine is matured in wood for 18 months, with one-third new oak.

RED This wine has always been tannic, but is now much fuller in fruit, richer in flavour, and darker in colour, with oaky nuances.

🍇 Cabernet Sauvignon 65%, Merlot 30%, Cabernet Franc 5%

🍷 12–25 years

Second wine: *Moulin-Riche*

CHÂTEAU MOULIN-DE-LA-ROSE
★ 🅥

This vineyard is well situated, being surrounded by *crus classés* on virtually all sides. Its wine is fermented in stainless steel and aged in cask for 18 months, with 25 per cent new oak.

RED This attractively aromatic wine is unusually concentrated and firm for a minor St-Julien, but rounds out well after a few years in bottle.

🍇 Cabernet Sauvignon 65%, Merlot 25%, Petit Verdot 8%, Cabernet Franc 2%

🍷 6–12 years

CHÂTEAU ST-PIERRE
4ème Cru Classé
★ ½ 🅥

This property was bought in 1982 by Henri Martin, who owns the bourgeois growth Château Gloria. The wine is matured in wood for between 18 and 20 months, with 50 per cent new oak.

RED Once an astringent, coarse wine; now ripe, fat, and full of cedarwood, spice, and fruit.

🍇 Cabernet Sauvignon 70%, Merlot 20%, Cabernet Franc 10%

🍷 8–25 years

Second wine: *Saint-Louis-le-Bosq*
Other wine: *Clos d'Uza*

CHÂTEAU TALBOT
4ème Cru Classé
★ ½ 🅥

Named after the English Commander who fell at the Battle of Castillon in 1453, this property remains under Cordier family ownership, while its sister château Gruaud-Larose now belongs to Groupe Taillan. To contrast the style of these two St-Juliens is justifiable,

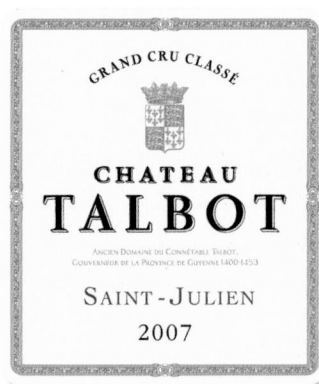

but to compare their quality is not: Château Talbot is a great wine and closer to the style of a classic St-Julien, but intrinsically it does not have the quality nor the consistency of Château Gruaud-Larose. Talbot is matured in wood for between 15 and 18 months, with one-third new oak.

RED A graceful wine, medium-bodied, with elegant fruit, gently structured by ripe oak tannins and capable of considerable finesse.

🍇 Cabernet Sauvignon 66%, Merlot 24%, Cabernet Franc 3%, Petit Verdot 5%, Malbec 2%

🍷 8–30 years

Second wine: 🗸 *Connétable Talbot*
Other wine: *Caillou Blanc*

CHÂTEAU TERREY-GROS-CAILLOUX
★ ½ 🅥

This establishment is under the same ownership as Château Hortevie (whose wine it also makes) and is itself a top-performing property.

RED This beautifully coloured, medium- to full-bodied wine always has rich fruit and is often equivalent to a good *cru classé*.

🍇 Cabernet Sauvignon 65%, Merlot 30%, Petit Verdot 5%

🍷 5–12 years

CHÂTEAU TEYNAC
★ 🅥

This fine gravel vineyard once formed part of *cru classé* Château St-Pierre.

RED Well-balanced, medium- to full-bodied wine with good spice and a firm tannin structure.

🍇 Cabernet Sauvignon 65%, Merlot 35%

🍷 6–10 years

MARGAUX

Situated in the south of the Médoc district, Margaux is the most famous of all Bordeaux appellations. While it bathes in the reflected glory of its name-sake premier cru, *it is also the largest and least consistent of the four classic Médoc appellations.*

WHILE THE OTHER THREE great Médoc AOCs – St-Estèphe, Pauillac, and St-Julien – are connected in one unbroken chain of vineyards, Margaux stands alone to the south, with its vines spread across five communes – Labarde, Arsac, and Cantenac to the south, Margaux in the centre, and Soussans to the north. Margaux and Cantenac are the most important communes and, of course, Margaux contains the *premier cru* of Château Margaux itself. Cantenac has a slightly larger area under vine and no fewer than eight classified growths, including the star-performing Château Palmer, which was partly owned by the late Peter Sichel.

Margaux and Pauillac are the only appellations in the Médoc with *premier cru* vineyards, but only Margaux can boast vineyards in all five categories of the classification. It also has more *cru classé* châteaux than any other Médoc appellation, including an impressive total of 10 *troisièmes crus*.

FACTORS AFFECTING TASTE AND QUALITY

LOCATION
In the centre of the Haut-Médoc, some 28 kilometres (17 miles) northwest of Bordeaux, encompassing the communes of Cantenac, Soussans, Arsac, and Labarde in addition to Margaux itself.

CLIMATE
As for the Médoc (*see* p116).

ASPECT
One large, low-lying plateau centring on Margaux, plus several modest outcrops that slope west towards the forest.

SOIL
Shallow, pebbly, siliceous gravel over a gravel subsoil interbedded with limestone.

VITICULTURE AND VINIFICATION
Only red wines have the right to the appellation. All grapes must be destalked. On average, between 5 and 10 per cent *vin de presse* may be used in the wine, according to the needs of the vintage. Skin contact duration averages 15 to 25 days, with the period of maturation in cask currently varying between 18 and 24 months.

GRAPE VARIETIES
Primary varieties: Cabernet Franc, Cabernet Sauvignon, Merlot
Secondary varieties: Carmenère, Malbec, Petit Verdot

MARGAUX CRU CLASSÉ STATISTICS

Crus classés in AOC Margaux
Twenty-one châteaux (by number: 35% of *crus classés* in the Médoc) with 884 ha (2,184 acres) of vineyards (by area: 26.5% of *crus classés* in the Médoc and 59% of this AOC)

1ers crus classés
One château (by number: 25% of *1ers crus classés* in the Médoc) with 82 ha (203 acres) of vineyards (by area: 23.5% of *1ers crus classés* in the Médoc)

2èmes crus classés
Five châteaux (by number: 36% of *2èmes crus classés* in the Médoc) with 281 ha (694 acres) of vineyards (by area: 30% of *2èmes crus classés* in the Médoc)

3èmes crus classés
Ten châteaux (by number: 71% of *3èmes crus classés* in the Médoc) with 306 ha (756 acres) of vineyards (by area: 54% of *3èmes crus classés* in the Médoc)

4èmes crus classés
Three châteaux (by number: 30% of *4èmes crus classés* in the Médoc) with 125 ha (309 acres) of vineyards (by area: 22% of *4èmes crus classés* in the Médoc)

5èmes crus classés
Two châteaux (by number: 11% of *5èmes crus classés* in the Médoc) with 90 ha (222 acres) of vineyards (by area: 10% of *5èmes crus classés* in the Médoc)

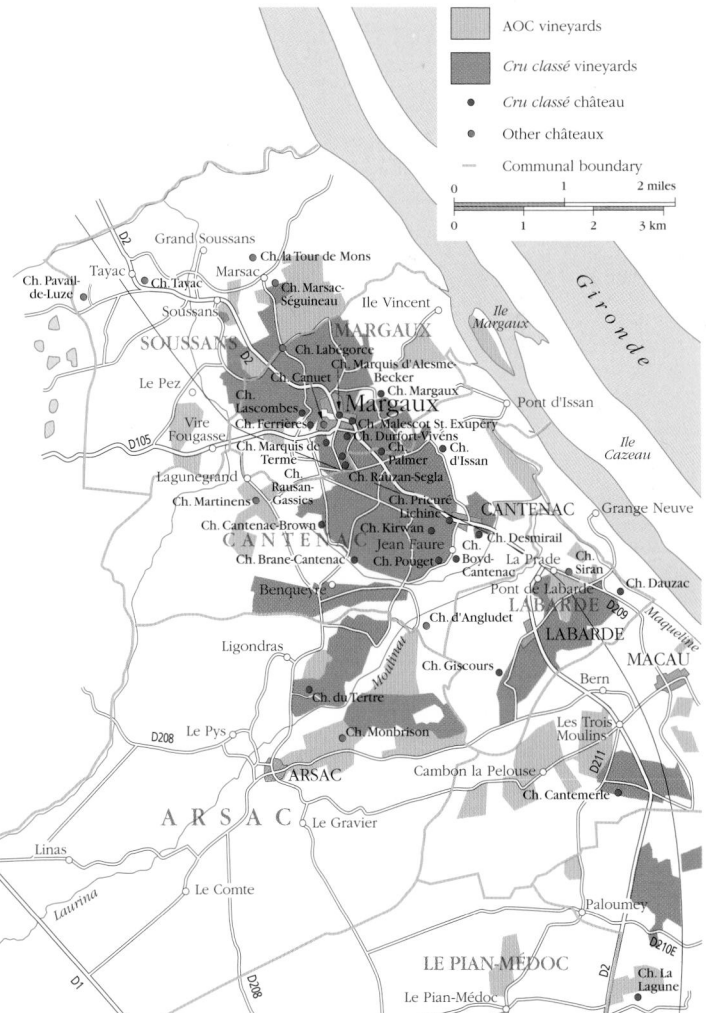

Key:
- AOC vineyards
- *Cru classé* vineyards
- *Cru classé* château
- Other châteaux
- Communal boundary

MARGAUX, *see also p109*
Of the classic Médoc appellations, Margaux – the most famous – stands alone to the south, and can boast more cru classé *châteaux than any of the others.*

CHÂTEAU MARGAUX
Margaux's celebrated premier cru *vineyards are matched by the grandeur of the building itself. Both the building and the wine are justifiably famous.*

MARGAUX PROFILE

Appellation covers: parts of the communes of Arsac, Cantenac, Labarde, Margaux, and Soussans as follows.

REGION	SIZE OF COMMUNE	AOC AREA UNDER VINE	VINE AREA AS PROPORTION OF COMMUNE	VINE AREA AS PROPORTION OF APPELLATION
Arsac	3,219 ha (7,954 acres)	225 ha (556 acres)	7%	15%
Cantenac	1,417 ha (3,502 acres)	411 ha (1,016 acres)	27%	28%
Labarde	475 ha (1,174 acres)	120 ha (296 acres)	24%	8%
Margaux	843 ha (2,083 acres)	432 ha (1,067 acres)	48%	29%
Soussans	1,558 ha (3,850 acres)	301 ha (744 acres)	18%	20%
TOTAL	7,512 ha (18,562 acres)	1,489 ha (3,679 acres)	19%	100%

Total size of all five communes: 7,512 ha (18,562 acres)
Total AOC area under vine: 1,489 ha (3,679 acres) (20% of communes)
Surface area of *crus classés*: 884 ha (2,184 acres) (12% of communes, 59% of AOC)

AN OUTSTANDING WINE

If the massive Pauillac wines of Château Latour and Château Mouton are an object lesson in how it is possible to bombard the senses with power and flavour, and yet retain quite remarkable finesse, then the exquisite wines of Margaux at their very best are perfect proof that complexity does not necessarily issue from an intense concentration of flavour.

However, this is not to suggest that Margaux wines do not actually possess some concentration; indeed, Château Margaux has a particularly remarkable concentration of flavour, and it remains the quintessential wine of this appellation.

NEW CELLAR AT CHÂTEAU MARGAUX
Evidence of the investment made in Château Margaux since the late 1970s is the refurbished wine store and its full complement of new oak barrels.

SOUTIRAGE CHÂTEAU MARGAUX
As the wine matures in the barrel its clarity is checked regularly. It spends between 18 and 24 months in new oak.

CHÂTEAU CANTENAC BROWN
This third growth was originally part of Château Boyd, but after the Boyds and Browns – who were joined by marriage in the late 18th century – had a family crisis, the property was divided into Château Boyd-Cantenac and Château Cantenac Brown.

CHÂTEAU D'ANGLUDET
Angludet, home of the Sichel family, dates back to Bertrand d'Angludet, who in 1313 swore allegiance to Edward II of England. Owned by Sichel from 1960 till 1999, this property exudes its English heritage, with swans gliding on the brook at the bottom of the garden.

THE WINE PRODUCERS OF
MARGAUX

CHÂTEAU D'ANGLUDET
★☆

This château is owned by the Sichel family, who are also part-owners of the star-performing Château Palmer. Since the late 1980s this château has established itself as *cru classé* quality. It will be interesting to see what the next decade brings. The wine is matured in wood for 12 months, with up to one-third new oak.

RED Vividly coloured, medium- to full-bodied wines with excellent fruit, finesse, and finish – classic Margaux.

🍇 Cabernet Sauvignon 55%, Merlot 35%, Petit Verdot 10%

🍷 10–20 years

Second wine: *La Ferme d'Angludet*
Other wine: *Clairet d'Angludet*

CHÂTEAU D'ARSAC

Until recently, this was the only property in Arsac not to benefit from the Margaux appellation. Since a change in ownership this estate has expanded its vineyards from just over 11 hectares (27 acres) to 102 (252 acres), of which 40 (100 acres) are now classified as Margaux. The wines are matured in wood for 12 to 18 months, with 20 per cent new oak.

RED These are deep-coloured, full-bodied wines.

🍇 Cabernet Sauvignon 80%, Merlot 15%, Cabernet Franc 5%

🍷 7–15 years

Second wine: *Château Ségur-d'Arsac*
Other wine: *Château Le Monteil-d'Arsac*

CHÂTEAU BEL-AIR MARQUIS D'ALIGRE
Ⓥ

Château Bel-Air Marquis d'Aligre was classified *cru bourgeois* in 1932, but was not included in the Syndicat's 1978 list, although it is superior to a few that were. The vineyard has limestone subsoil and only organic fertilizers are used.

RED Well-made wines of fine colour, elegant fruit, with a distinctive style are produced by Château Bel-Air Marquis d'Aligre.

🍇 Merlot 35%, Cabernet Sauvignon 30%, Cabernet Franc 20%, Petit Verdot 15%

🍷 6–12 years

Second wine: *Château Bel-Air-Marquis-de-Pomereu*

CHÂTEAU BOYD-CANTENAC
3ème Cru Classé

Château Boyd-Cantenac is a property producing traditional-style

wines from old vines. The wine is made at owner M Guillemet's other property, Château Pouget, under the supervision of Professor Peynaud. It is matured in wood for 24 months, with 30 per cent new oak and, in my opinion, would benefit from more Merlot and no Petit Verdot.

RED Full-bodied, firm wine of good colour that needs a long time in bottle to soften. The mediocre 1980 was particularly successful.

🍇 Cabernet Sauvignon 70%, Merlot 20%, Cabernet Franc 5%, Petit Verdot 5%

🍷 12–20 years

CHÂTEAU BRANE-CANTENAC
2ème Cru Classé
★☆Ⓥ

This property is a superb plateau of immaculately kept vines situated on gravel over limestone and is owned and run by Henri Lurton. The wine is matured in wood for 18 months, with 25 to 30 per cent new oak.

RED These stylish wines have a smoky-cream and new-oak bouquet, deliciously rich fruit, and finesse on the palate. They are top-quality wines, velvety and beautifully balanced.

🍇 Cabernet Sauvignon 70%, Cabernet Franc 15%, Merlot 13%, Petit Verdot 2%

🍷 8–25 years

Second wine: *Le Baron de Brane*
Other wines: *Domaine de Fontarney, Château Notton*

CHÂTEAU CANTENAC BROWN
3ème Cru Classé

Ever since I drank a 50-year-old half-bottle of 1926 Cantenac Brown in splendid condition, I have had a soft spot for this château, which has, frankly, been disproportionate to the quality of its wines. Despite heavy investment after being purchased by AXA in 1989, these wines have not noticeably improved. However, that did not stop Syrian-born, British-based property billionaire Simon Halabi from snapping up this château for a rumoured £50 million ($86 million) in 2006. At the time, he insisted that the aim was to invest further in Cantenac Brown,

to make it one of the best wines in Margaux.

RED A similar weight to Brane-Cantenac, but with a less velvety and generally more rustic style.

🍇 Cabernet Sauvignon 65%, Merlot 25%, Cabernet Franc 10%

🍷 10–25 years

Second wine: *Canuet*
Other wine: *Lamartine*

CHÂTEAU CHARMANT

This property was not classified as a *cru bourgeois* in 1932, nor listed by the Syndicat in 1978, but it certainly deserves recognition today.

RED An elegant wine with plenty of fruit and a soft finish. It makes delightful drinking when young.

🍇 Cabernet Sauvignon 60%, Merlot 35%, Cabernet Franc 5%

🍷 3–8 years

CHÂTEAU DAUZAC
5ème Cru Classé
★

Now owned by MAIF and managed by Vignobles André Lurton, the quality of the wines from this château has steadily increased since the mid-1990s. The wine, which is matured in wood for 16 to 18 months with one-third new oak, is steadily improving.

RED Ruby-coloured, medium-bodied, round, and attractively fruity wines that are easy to drink.

🍇 Cabernet Sauvignon 65%, Merlot 25%, Cabernet Franc 5%, Petit Verdot 5%

🍷 6–12 years

Second wine: *Labarde*
Other wine: *La Bastide*

CHÂTEAU DESMIRAIL
3ème Cru Classé
☆

A "château with no château" (because the building that was its château was purchased by Château Marquis d'Alesme-Becker), Desmirail has been on the ascent since its purchase by the Lurton family, but it still has a way to go before it becomes a true *troisième cru*. It is owned and run by Denis Lurton, while oenologist Professor Peynaud advises. The wine is matured in wood for 20 months, with 25 to 50 per cent new oak.

RED A medium-bodied wine that is nicely balanced, with gentle fruit flavours and supple tannins. It is well made and gradually gaining in finesse.

🍇 Cabernet Sauvignon 80%, Merlot 10%, Cabernet Franc 9%, Petit Verdot 1%

🍷 7–15 years

Second wine: *Château Baudry*
Other wine: *Domaine de Fontarney*

CHÂTEAU DEYREM-VALENTIN

This château was classified *cru bourgeois* in 1932, but was not included in the Syndicat's 1978 list, although it is superior to a few that were. Its vineyards adjoin those of Château Lascombes.

RED Honest, medium-bodied, fruity wine of some elegance.

🍇 Cabernet Sauvignon 45%, Merlot 45%, Cabernet Franc 5%, Petit Verdot 5%

🍷 4–10 years

CHÂTEAU DURFORT-VIVENS
2ème Cru Classé
★Ⓥ

Owned by Gonzague Lurton, who is married to Claire Villars, the administrator of châteaux Chasse-Spleen and Haut-Bages-Libéral. Dufort-Vivens has become one of the best-value *cru classé* wines of Margaux since the mid-1990s. This property matures its wine in wood for 18 to 20 months, with up to one-third new oak.

RED Higher tannic structure than Brane-Cantenac, but without the luxurious new-oak character, and with less fruit and charm. The 1985 was particularly rich and impressive.

🍇 Cabernet Sauvignon 82%, Cabernet Franc 10%, Merlot 8%

🍷 10–25 years

Second wine: *Second de Durfort*
Other wine: *Domaine de Curé-Bourse*

CHÂTEAU FERRIÈRE
3ème Cru Classé
★Ⓥ

When managed by Château Lascombes this was little more than second-label status, but it has gained in both exposure and quality since this property was purchased by the Villars family.

RED Quick-maturing wine of medium weight and accessible fruit.

🍇 Cabernet Sauvignon 75%, Merlot 20%, Petit Verdot 5%

🍷 4–8 years

Second wine: *Les Remparts de Ferrière*

CHÂTEAU GISCOURS
3ème Cru Classé
★★☆

This property is situated in the commune of Labarde. It was purchased in 1952 by the Tari family, who have restored the château, the vineyard, and the quality of its wine to their former glory. In 1995 the château was sold to Eric Albada Jelgerms, a Dutch businessman who has at least maintained the quality

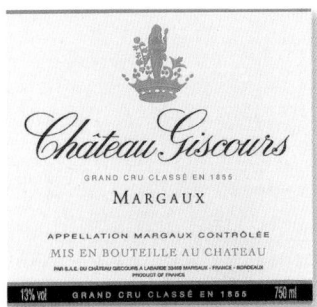

and arguably improved it. The wine is matured in wood for 20 to 34 months, with 50 per cent new oak.

RED Vividly coloured wine, rich in fruit and finesse. Its vibrant style keeps it remarkably fresh for years.

🍇 Cabernet Sauvignon 75%, Merlot 22%, Cabernet Franc 2%, Petit Verdot 1%

🍷 8–30 years

Second wine: *La Sirène de Giscours*
Other wine: *Cantelaude*

CHÂTEAU LA GURGUE

This property was classified *cru bourgeois* in 1932, but not included in the 1978 list, although it is superior to a few that were. Its proprietor also owns *cru classé* Haut-Bages-Libéral and *cru bourgeois exceptionnel* Chasse-Spleen.

RED Soft, elegant, medium-bodied wine of attractive flavour and some finesse, improving since 2000.

🍇 Cabernet Sauvignon 70%, Merlot 25%, Petit Verdot 5%

🍷 4–12 years

CHÂTEAU D'ISSAN
3ème Cru Classé
★★

This beautiful 17th-century château is frequently cited as the most impressive in the entire Médoc, and its remarkable wines, matured in wood for 18 months, with up to one-third new oak, are consistently just as spectacular.

RED This wine really is glorious! Its luxuriant bouquet is immediately seductive, its fruit is unbelievably rich and sumptuous. A great wine of great finesse.

🍇 Cabernet Sauvignon 85%, Merlot 15%

🍷 10–40 years

Second wine: *Blason d'Issan*
Other wine: *De Candel*

CHÂTEAU KIRWAN
3ème Cru Classé
★☆🅥

Château Kirwan is a well-run and improving property owned by the Bordeaux négociant Schröder & Schÿler with Michel Rolland consulting. The wine is matured in wood for 18 to 24 months, with up to 50 per cent new oak.

RED Deep-coloured, full-bodied, rich and concentrated wines that are well made and gaining in generosity, riper tannins, and

new oak influence with each passing vintage.

🍇 Cabernet Sauvignon 40%, Merlot 30%, Cabernet Franc 20%, Petit Verdot 10%

🍷 10–35 years

Second wine: *Les Charmes de Kirwan*

CHÂTEAU LABÉGORCE
★★🅥

This château was classified *cru bourgeois* in 1932, but not included in the 1978 list. Since Hubert Perrodo, a wine-loving oil tycoon, purchased Labégorce in 1989, the quality and price of its wines have increased steadily. Matured in wood for 18 months, with up to one-third new oak. Labégorce has purchased neighbouring Château Labégorce-Zédé, which ceased production after the 2008 vintage, when its 22 hectares (54 acres) were absorbed by this château.

RED Well-coloured wine with good balance of concentration and finesse.

🍇 Cabernet Sauvignon 55%, Merlot 40%, Cabernet Franc 5%

🍷 5–15 years

Second wine: *Zédé de Labégorce*

CHÂTEAU LABÉGORCE-ZÉDÉ
★★🅥

Classified *cru bourgeois* in 1932, but not included in the 1978 list, although it is one of the best non-*cru classé* wines of the commune. This château was absorbed by Château Labégorce and no longer exists. The last vintage was 2008. This profile remains for those of you who encounter vintages of Château Labégorce-Zédé.

RED Fine flavour and great length, combined with a certain complexity, give the wines of this château an edge over those of Labégorce.

🍇 Cabernet Sauvignon 50%, Merlot 35%, Cabernet Franc 10%, Petit Verdot 5%

🍷 5–15 years

Second wine: *Château de l'Amiral*

CHÂTEAU LASCOMBES
2ème Cru Classé
★★

The wines of this large property have always been good, yet they have improved dramatically under René Vanatelle. It was Vanatelle who recognized that only 50 of Lascombes' 83 hectares (125 of 208 acres) were of authentic *deuxième cru* potential. He therefore segregated the vineyard and sold the lesser wines as Château Segonnes. This accounted for the noticeable step up in quality in the 1980s. Then in 1997, the year before he retired, Vanatelle introduced a true second wine, Chevalier des Lascombes, which has pushed standards up yet another gear, before handing over to Bruno Lemoine, formerly of Montrose. The

wine is matured in wood for 14 to 20 months, with one-third new oak.

RED Full-bodied, rich, and concentrated wine with ripe fruit, a lovely cedarwood complexity, and supple tannin.

🍇 Cabernet Sauvignon 55%, Merlot 40%, Petit Verdot 5%

🍷 8–30 years

Second wine: *Chevalier Lascombes*
Other wines: *Château Segonnes, Gombaud, Rosé de Lascombes, Vin Sec Chevalier Lascombes*

CHÂTEAU MALESCOT ST-EXUPÉRY
3ème Cru Classé
★

English-owned until 1955, when it was purchased by Roger Zuger, whose brother owns Château Marquis-d'Alesme-Becker. The wine is matured in wood for 18 months, with 20 per cent new oak.

RED Richer, more complex wines have been produced since 1996.

🍇 Cabernet Sauvignon 50%, Merlot 35%, Cabernet Franc 10%, Petit Verdot 5%

🍷 8–25 years

Second wines: *Château De Loyac, La Dame de Malescot*
Other wine: *Balardin*

CHÂTEAU MARGAUX
1er Cru Classé
★★★🅥

This is the most famous wine in the world and, since its glorious rebirth in 1978, the greatest. Its quality may occasionally be matched, but it is never surpassed. Purchased in 1977 for 72 million francs by the late André Mentzelopoulos, who spent an equal sum renovating it, this fabulous jewel in the crown of the Médoc is now run by his daughter, Corinne Mentzelopoulos. Both Château Margaux and its second wine, "Pavillon Rouge", are vinified in oak vats and matured for 18 to 24 months in 100 per cent new oak.

RED If finesse can be picked up on the nose, then the stunning and complex bouquet of Château Margaux is the yardstick. The softness, finesse, and velvety texture of this wine belies its depth. Amazingly rich and concentrated, with an elegant, long, and complex finish supported by ripe tannins and wonderful smoky-creamy oak aromas. This is as near perfection as we will ever get.

🍇 Cabernet Sauvignon 75%, Merlot 20%, Cabernet Franc and Petit Verdot 5%

🍷 15–50 years

Second wine: *Pavillon Rouge du Château Margaux*
Other wine: *Pavillon Blanc du Château Margaux*

CHÂTEAU MARQUIS D'ALESME
3ème Cru Classé

Like Château Malescot St-Exupéry, this was English-owned until purchased by Jean-Claude Zuger, who also purchased the maison of neighbouring Desmirail to act as its château. The wine is matured in wood for 12 months, with one-sixth new oak. Purchased by Hubert Perrodo of Château Labégorce just before his untimely death in a skiing accident in 2006, this château has dropped "Becker" from its label.

RED Austere and charmless wines from my point of view, although they have their admirers. They are well made, but lack sufficient selection, although the *terroir* has potential.

🍇 Cabernet Sauvignon 40%, Merlot 30%, Cabernet Franc 20%, Petit Verdot 10%

🍷 8–20 years

Second wine: *Marquise d'Alesme*

CHÂTEAU MARQUIS D'ALESME-BECKER

Same wine as Château Marquis d'Alesme, but the new owners have removed the Becker name from recent vintages. *See* Château Marquis d'Alesme.

CHÂTEAU MARQUIS-DE-TERME
4ème Cru Classé

Situated next to Château Margaux, this once majestic estate developed the reputation for producing tight, tannic, one-dimensional wines, but its quality has picked up since the late 1970s and has been performing extremely well since 1983. The wine is matured in wood for 24 months, with one-third new oak.

RED Appears to be developing a style that is ripe and rich, with definite and delightful signs of new oak. The 1984 was quite a revelation.

🍇 Cabernet Sauvignon 60%, Merlot 30%, Petit Verdot 7%, Cabernet Franc 3%

🍷 10–25 years

Second wine: *Terme des Goudat*

CHÂTEAU MARSAC-SÉGUINEAU

This property was classified *cru bourgeois* in 1932, but not included in the 1978 list, although it is superior to a few that were. The vineyards of this château include some plots that originally belonged to a *cru classé*.

RED Medium- to full-bodied wines of good bouquet and a soft style.

🍇 Cabernet Sauvignon 65%,
Merlot 35%

🍷 5–12 years

Second wine: *Château Gravières-de-Marsac*

CHÂTEAU MONBRISON
★❷❤

These vineyards used to be part of *cru classé* Château Desmirail; the wines were excellent 15 years ago, and now vie with those of true *cru classé* standard.

RED This château's second label offers a brilliant selection of beautifully deep-coloured wines with spicy-oak, super-rich juicy fruit, and a fine structure of supple tannin.

🍇 Merlot 35%, Cabernet Franc 30%, Cabernet Sauvignon 30%, Petit Verdot 5%

🍷 8–15 years

Second wine: *Château Cordat*

CHÂTEAU MONTBRUN

Château Montbrun was classified *cru bourgeois* in 1932, but not included in the Syndicat's 1978 list, although it is superior to a few that were. This used to be part of *cru classé* Château Palmer.

RED Beautifully made, ripe, and juicy, medium- to full-bodied, Merlot-dominated wines.

🍇 Merlot 75%, Cabernet Franc and Cabernet Sauvignon 25%

🍷 5–12 years

CHÂTEAU PALMER
3ème Cru Classé
★★★

Only Château Margaux outshines this property, jointly owned by Belgian, French, and British (the Sichel family) interests. Château Palmer 1961 and 1966 regularly fetch prices at auction that equal those fetched by the *premiers crus*. Judged at the very highest level, it could be more consistent. It is usually excellent, but not always astonishing – although when it is, it can stand shoulder to shoulder with *premiers crus* in a blind tasting. A true super-second that promises to achieve even greater heights since the introduction of Alto Ego, a sort of super-premium of second wines, in 1998. The wine is matured in wood for 18 to 24 months, with one-third new oak.

RED Almost opaque-coloured, with masses of cassis fruit and an exceedingly rich, intense, and complex construction of creamy, spicy, cedarwood, and vanilla flavours.

🍇 Cabernet Sauvignon 50%, Merlot 40%, Cabernet Franc 7%, Petit Verdot 3%

🍷 12–35 years

Second wines: *Alto Ego, Réserve du Général*

CHÂTEAU PONTAC-LYNCH
★❷

This property was classified *cru bourgeois* in 1932, but not included in the Syndicat's 1978 list, although it is superior to a few that were. The vineyards are well-situated, and surrounded by *crus classés*.

RED Richly perfumed, deeply coloured, full-bodied wines of good structure.

🍇 Cabernet Sauvignon and Merlot 47%, Cabernet Franc 45%, Petit Verdot 8%

🍷 6–15 years

Second wine: *Pontac-Phénix*

CHÂTEAU POUGET
4ème Cru Classé
❾

Under the same ownership as Boyd-Cantenac, this property houses the winemaking and storage facilities for both châteaux. The wine is matured in wood for 22 to 24 months, with 30 per cent new oak.

RED Well-coloured, full-bodied wine with good depth of flavour. Good, but not great, and could be more consistent.

🍇 Cabernet Sauvignon 70%, Merlot 17%, Cabernet Franc 8%, Petit Verdot 5%

🍷 10–25 years

CHÂTEAU PRIEURÉ-LICHINE
4ème Cru Classé
★

The late Alexis Lichine purchased Château Prieuré in 1951 and added his name to it. To develop the small run-down vineyard, he bought various prized plots of vines from Palmer, Kirwan, Giscours, Boyd-Cantenac, Brane-Cantenac, and Durfort-Vivens – some 60 hectares (148 acres). The composite classification must be higher than its official status – the wines certainly are. Lichine's son Sacha ran the property until 1999, when he sold it. The current owners, the Ballande family, have steadily improved the quality under top consultant Stéphane Derenoncourt. The wines are matured in wood for 19 months, with one-third new oak.

RED Well-coloured, full-bodied wines, plummy and rich, with good blackcurrant fruit supported by supple tannins and a touch of vanilla-oak.

🍇 Cabernet Sauvignon 54%, Merlot 39%, Cabernet Franc 2%, Petit Verdot 5%

🍷 7–20 years

Second wine: *De Clairefont*

CHÂTEAU RAUZAN-GASSIES
2ème Cru Classé
★

Until the French Revolution of 1789, this property and Château Rauzan-Ségla were one large estate. The globe-trotting Professor Peynaud was brought in to steer this wine back on course in the early 1980s, but he failed miserably. Jean-Louis Camp, formerly of Loudenne, seems to be having more success, albeit limited. The wine is matured in wood for 17 to 20 months, with 20 per cent new oak, although there is little evidence of it on the palate.

RED The 1996 and 1998 suggested an upturn in quality, and this has been partly realized in vintages like 2000 and 2002, but the quality is still frustratingly patchy.

🍇 Cabernet Sauvignon 40%, Merlot 39%, Cabernet Franc 20%, Petit Verdot 1%

🍷 7–15 years

Second wine: *Enclos de Moncabon*

CHÂTEAU RAUZAN-SÉGLA
2ème Cru Classé
★★

The quality of this once-disappointing château began to lift in the 1980s due to significant investment in the property from its owner, the Bordeaux négociant house of Eschenauer, which also instigated a far stricter selection of the *grand vin*. In 1994 Rauzan-Ségla was sold to Chanel, the under-bidder for Latour (sold by Allied-Lyons to the French industrialist François Pinault). Since then key personnel from the *premier cru* have been brought in to keep the improvements in full swing. The wine is matured in wood for 20 months, with 50 per cent new oak, and is currently one of Bordeaux's top-performing *deuxièmes crus*.

RED In classic years, this wine is deep and dark, with a powerful tannic construction, and more than enough intensely flavoured fruit to match. Lesser vintages are dark for the year, but much more lush, with softer tannins.

🍇 Cabernet Sauvignon 65%, Merlot 30%, Cabernet Franc 5%

🍷 15–30 years

Second wine: *Ségla*
Other wines: *Lamouroux*

CHÂTEAU SIRAN
★★❤

The vineyard is well situated, with immaculately manicured vines that border those of châteaux Giscours and Dauzac. The wine is matured in wood for 24 months, with one-third new oak, in air-conditioned cellars. Owned by the Miailhe de Burgh family, who are direct descendents of Sir Patrick Sarsfield, the daring Irish Jacobite who gave William of Orange such a bloody nose.

RED Stylish, aromatic wines of good

body, creamy-spicy fruit, length, and obvious class. Easily equivalent to *cru classé* quality.

🍇 Cabernet Sauvignon 40%, Merlot 35%, Petit Verdot 20%, Cabernet Franc 5%

🍷 8–20 years

Second wine: *Château Bellegarde*
Other wine: *Château St-Jacques*

CHÂTEAU TAYAC

As Bernard Ginestet, whose family owned Château Margaux for 40 years, once wrote, "this is one of the largest of the smaller properties, and one of the smallest of the larger".

RED Firm, medium- to full-bodied wines of good character, although somewhat rustic; they tend to be coarse in lesser years.

🍇 Cabernet Sauvignon 65%, Merlot 25%, Cabernet Franc 5%, Petit Verdot 5%

🍷 6–12 years

CHÂTEAU DU TERTRE
5ème Cru Classé
★★

An underrated *cru classé*, this château has well-situated vineyards. It is under the same ownership as Giscours since 1998. The wine is matured in wood for 24 months, with 25 per cent new oak.

RED Although the scent of violets is supposed to be common to Margaux wines, this is one of the few in which I pick it up. The wine is medium- to full-bodied, rich in fragrant fruit, and has excellent balance, with obvious class.

🍇 Cabernet Sauvignon 85%, Cabernet Franc 5%, Merlot 10%

🍷 8–25 years

CHÂTEAU LA TOUR DE MONS

These wines are aged in wood for 22 months, with 20 per cent new oak and have improved enormously since the late 1980s. Easily equivalent to *cru classé* quality.

RED As richly flavoured as ever, but without the tannins or acidity that used to be this wine's pitfall.

🍇 Cabernet Sauvignon 45%, Merlot 40%, Cabernet Franc 10%, Petit Verdot 5%

🍷 10–30 years

Second wine: *Château Richeterre*

CHÂTEAU DES TROIS-CHARDONS
★❤

A tiny production of very high-quality wine from a château named after the current owner, a Monsieur Chardon, and his two sons.

RED Ultra-clean, soft, fruity but serious wines of some finesse and well-defined Margaux character.

🍇 Cabernet Sauvignon 50%, Merlot 40%, Cabernet Franc 10%

🍷 6–15 years

GRAVES, CÉRONS, SAUTERNES, AND BARSAC

The finest red Graves wines are produced in Pessac-Léognan, good red and improving dry white wines in the centre of Graves, and the great sweet wines of Sauternes and Barsac in the south. The emphasis in production is on classic red wines.

THE SILKY-SMOOTH red wines of the Graves district have been famous since the Middle Ages, when they were protected by local laws that punished those who dared to blend them with other Bordeaux wines. Château Haut-Brion was the only red wine outside the Médoc to be classified in 1855, and such was its reputation that it was placed alongside the *premiers crus* of Latour, Lafite, and Margaux. Beneath Haut-Brion, there are a few great wines equivalent in quality to *deuxième* or *troisième cru*, but only a few.

The relative lack of superstars in Graves is offset by a higher base quality of wine and greater consistency of performance in the red wines at least. There are 43 communes in this appellation. Much the best are Léognan, Talence, and Pessac, after which Martillac and Portets are the most outstanding, followed by Illats and Podensac. All the greatest wines are therefore in the north of the Graves district, amid the urban sprawl of Bordeaux, and this presents something of a problem. The once-peaceful left bank of the Garonne is slowly and inexorably disappearing. As the city bursts outwards, more rural vineyards are encircled by the concrete jungle, and many quite simply vanish. How many

Bordeaux aficionados who fly directly to the airport in Mérignac stop to consider the cost of such progress? In 1908 there were 30 winemaking properties in the commune of Mérignac; today there is just one – Château Picque-Caillou. The conurbated communes of Cadaujac, Gradignan, Léognan, Martillac, Mérignac, Pessac, Talence, and Villenave d'Ornon have lost 214 wine châteaux over the same period.

THE PROBLEM OF WHITE GRAVES SOLVED

While the quality and reputation of the red wines have always been well established, white Graves had a serious identity problem that came to a crisis point in the mid-1980s. Although fine white Graves were being produced, most of it was in the northern communes, but they were tarred with the same brush as the worst white wines from further south. It was not simply a north–south divide; there was also an identity problem – should they be making rich, oak-aged blends or light and fluffy Sauvignon Blanc? Paradoxically, the worst wines came from some of the best properties in the north, produced by winemakers who either did not know how to, or did not care to, clean up their act, as they continued to sell tired, over-sulphured, oxidized, and flabby wines on the back of their decaying reputations.

An official north-south divide, however, proved to be the solution for, since 1987, when the Pessac-Léognan AOC was introduced, things have never looked better for Graves. The Pessac-Léognan appellation is a single appellation for both red and white wines from the communes Cadaujac, Canéjan, Gradignan, Léognan, Martillac, Mérignac, Pessac, St-Médard-d'Eyrans, Talence, and Villenave d'Ornon. This has had the effect of giving the northern châteaux the official quality recognition they both wanted

GRAVES, CÉRONS, SAUTERNES, AND BARSAC, *see also p109*
The winemaking area that includes Graves, Cérons, Sauternes, and Barsac forms a swathe that sweeps down from Bordeaux, parallel with the Garonne.

VINES AT HAUT-BRION
Rose bushes at the end of each row act as a pest early-warning system.

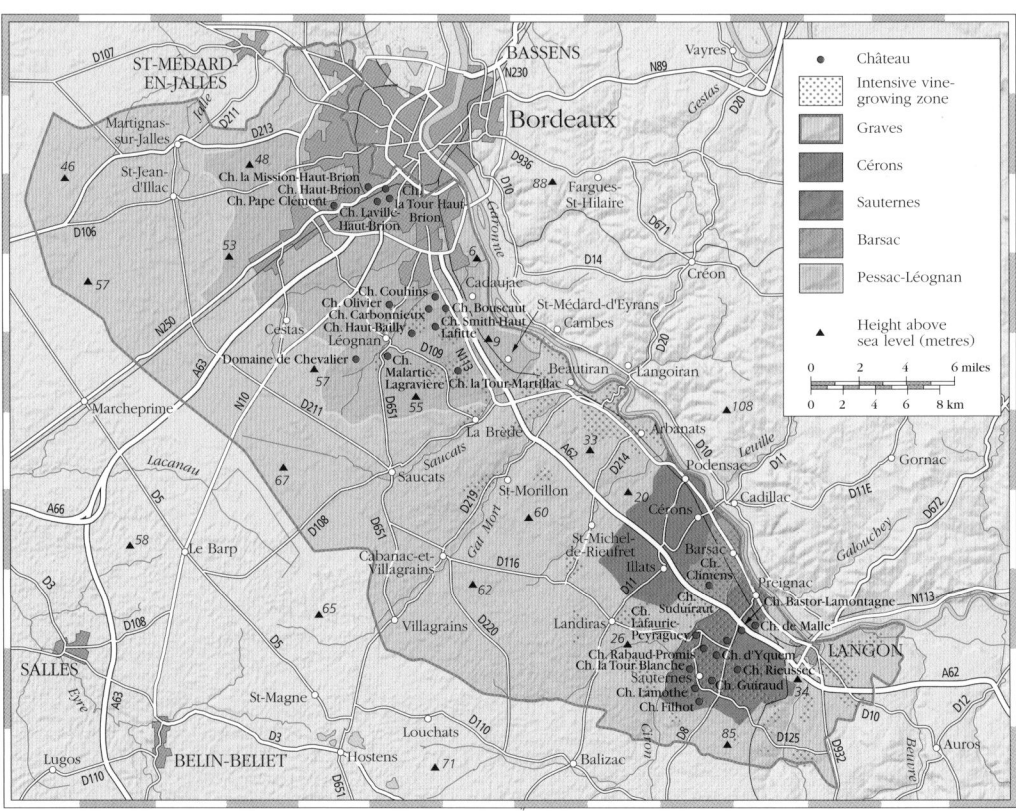

FROM GRAPE TO GLASS

The only Graves property to be classified in 1855 was Château Haut-Brion. The Syndicat, for the defence of the Graves appellation, wanted to create its own classification but was prevented from doing so until the 1921 law was changed in 1949. The first classification was not made until 1953, and this itself was later modified in 1959.

Distinction is made between red wines and white wines, but no attempt at ranking between the various growths is made – they all have the right to use the term *cru classé*. It can be seen from the 535 hectares (1,320 acres) of classified properties listed below that this represents not much more than 13 per cent of the total 4,350 hectares (10,745 acres) of delimited vineyards planted in the Graves and Pessac-Léognan appellation.

RED WINES	COMMUNE	AREA CURRENTLY UNDER VINE HECTARES	(ACRES)
Château Bouscaut	Cadaujac	47 ha	(116 acres)
Château Carbonnieux	Léognan	50 ha	(124 acres)
Domaine de Chevalier	Léognan	40 ha	(99 acres)
Château de Fieuzal	Léognan	65 ha	(161 acres)
Château Haut-Bailly	Léognan	30 ha	(74 acres)
Château Haut-Brion	Pessac	48 ha	(119 acres)
Château La Mission-Haut-Brion	Pessac	27 ha	(67 acres)
Château Latour-Haut-Brion	Talence	5 ha	(12 acres)
Château La Tour-Martillac	Martillac	35 ha	(86 acres)
Château Malartic-Lagravière	Léognan	46 ha	(114 acres)
Château Olivier	Léognan	45 ha	(111 acres)
Château Pape-Clément[1]	Pessac	30 ha	(74 acres)
Château Smith-Haut-Lafitte[1]	Martillac	44 ha	(109 acres)
TOTAL AREA UNDER VINE		**512 HA**	**(1,265 ACRES[2])**

WHITE WINES	COMMUNE	AREA CURRENTLY UNDER VINE HECTARES	(ACRES)
Château Bouscaut	Cadaujac	7 ha	(17 acres)
Château Carbonnieux	Léognan	42 ha	(104 acres)
Domaine de Chevalier	Léognan	5 ha	(12 acres)
Château de Fieuzal	Léognan	10 ha	(25 acres)
Château Couhins-Lurton[3]	Villenave	13 ha	(32 acres)
Château Haut-Brion	Pessac	3 ha	(10 acres)
Château La Tour-Martillac	Martillac	10 ha	(25 acres)
Château Laville-Haut-Brion	Talence	3 ha	(10 acres)
Château Malartic-Lagravière	Léognan	7 ha	(17 acres)
Château Olivier	Léognan	10 ha	(25 acres)
TOTAL AREA UNDER VINE		**110 HA**	**(277 ACRES[2])**

NOTES

[1] *These châteaux also produce a dry white wine, but only the red is classified as cru classé.*

[2] *These figures are not precise conversions of the hectare totals, but are column totals and differ because of rounding up.*

[3] *This château also produces a red wine, but only the white is classified as cru classé.*

VINEYARDS AT CHÂTEAU D'YQUEM
Here, the winter vineyard shows the characteristic sandy-pebbly clay topsoil and the system of wires and stakes that supports the vines. Yquem's clay subsoil contains 100 kilometres (62 miles) of terracotta pipes, which were laid down at the end of the 19th century to provide perfect drainage.

THE GLOWING TINTS OF CHÂTEAU D'YQUEM
Château d'Yquem vintages, stretching back from a bottle of the 1980. The younger wines are a rich gold with a greenish tinge, deepening to old gold and amber with the older vintages.

CHÂTEAU D'YQUEM: THE INNER COURTYARD
A huge stone well dominates the square central courtyard of this beautiful château, which comprises disparate elements dating from the 15th, 16th, and 17th centuries.

and deserved. It was a bit slow to start off – after all, Pessac-Léognan hardly trips off the tongue and there were worries about its marketability. There is still a tendency to put Graves on labels, and use Pessac-Léognan to qualify the wine as if it were a higher classification of Graves, which for all practical purposes it is.

Once the châteaux realized that foreign markets were picking up on the superior connotation of Pessac-Léognan, use of the appellation soon became widespread. Whether by their own volition or due to peer pressure, many of the underperformers have become the most quality-conscious châteaux in the appellation, and it has spurred producers in the south to improve their wines. They do not like being considered inferior, and as they intend to prove they are not, the consumer can only gain.

CÉRONS

This is an area situated within the boundaries of Graves. It is the stepping stone between dry white Graves, and sweet white Sauternes and Barsac. The châteaux of Cérons have been given the official right to make both red and white Graves, Graves Supérieur (which may be dry but is usually sweet) and, of course, the sweet wine of Cérons – a wine that has enjoyed a modest reputation for nearly 200 years. In fact, only 20 per cent of the production in this area is sold as Cérons, since the appellation covers three communes, those of Illats, Podensac, and Cérons itself. Many of the vineyards comprise scattered plots, some of which are partially planted with acacias.

SAUTERNES AND BARSAC

The gap between ordinary sweet white wines and the great wines of Sauternes and Barsac is as wide as that between sweet and dry wines. What creates this gap is something called "complexity" –

TRADITIONAL HORSE-DRAWN PLOUGH
At Château d'Yquem work-horses are used to help plough the topsoil between the rows, both after the harvest and again in March.

to find out what that is, sample the aroma of a glass of mature Sauternes. The wines produced in Sauternes are not only the world's most luscious, but also the most complex wines. I have seen hardened men who resolutely refuse to drink anything sweeter than lemon juice go weak at the knees after one sniff of Château Suduiraut, and I defy the most stubborn and bigoted anti-sweet wine drinker not to drool over a glass of Château d'Yquem 1967. Astonishingly, there are dissenters, but for me Yquem is by far the best wine of these two appellations, Sauternes and Barsac. The battle for second place is always between the soft, luscious style of Suduiraut, and the rich, powerful character of Rieussec, with Climens, Nairac, and the non-classified growths of Gilette and de Fargues in close pursuit. Guiraud has the potential to go right to the top, and with so many châteaux seriously improving, they could all end up chasing each other for the number two spot.

The "noble rot"

Yquem might be the ultimate sweet white wine, but many other great wines are made in these two small areas tucked away in the Bordeaux backwaters. What gives all these wines their hallmark of complexity is, literally, a lot of rot – namely "noble rot", or the fungal growth *Botrytis cinerea*. The low-lying hills of Sauternes and, to a lesser extent, of Barsac, together with a naturally warm but humid climate, provide a natural breeding ground for botrytis, the spores of which are indigenous to the area. They remain dormant in the vineyard soil and on vine bark until they are activated by suitable conditions – alternate moisture and heat (the early-morning mist being followed by hot, mid-morning sunshine). The spores latch on to the skin of each grape, replacing its structure with a fungal growth and feeding on moisture from within the grape. They also devour five-sixths of the grape's acidity and one-third of its sugar, but as the amount of water consumed is between one-half and two-thirds, the effect is to concentrate the juice into a sticky, sugar-rich pulp. A healthy, ripe grape with a

potential of 13 per cent alcohol is thus converted into a mangy-looking mess with a potential of between 17.5 per cent and 26 per cent. The spread of botrytis through a vineyard is neither orderly nor regular, and the harvest may take as long as ten weeks to complete, with the pickers making various sorties, or *tries*, through the vineyard. On each *trie*, only the affected grapes should be picked, but care must be taken to leave some rot on each bunch to facilitate its spread. The longer the growers await the miraculous "noble rot", the more the vines are prone to the ravages of frost, snow, hail, and rain, any of which could destroy an entire crop.

The viticulture of Sauternes and Barsac is the most labour-intensive of any region. The yield is very low, officially a maximum of 25 hectolitres per hectare (112 cases per acre), about half that in the Médoc, and the levels achieved in the best châteaux are much lower, around 15 to 20 hectolitres per hectare (67 to 90 cases per acre). At Yquem it is even less, the equivalent of one glass per vine. On top of all this, the vinification is, at the very least, difficult to handle, and maturation of a fine sweet wine demands a good proportion of very expensive new oak.

Variations in character

Not all the sugar is used up during fermentation, even when a wine of perhaps 14 to 15 per cent alcohol is made. The remaining unfermented sugar, often between 50 and 120 grams per litre, gives the wine its natural sweetness. However, unlike Sauternes' German counterparts, its alcohol level is crucial to its character. Its strength, in harmony with the wine's sweetness, acidity, and fruit give it a lusciousness of concentration that simply cannot be matched. Its complexity is not, however, the effect of concentration, although an increased mineral level is no doubt an influence. Complexity is created by certain new elements that are introduced into the grape's juice during the metabolic activities of its botrytis – glycerol, gluconic acid, saccharic acid, dextrin, various oxidizing enzymes, and an elusive antibiotic substance called "botrycine".

It is easy to explain how these components of a botrytized wine that form its inimitably complex character can vary. When tasting wine from different *tries* at the same château, the intensity of botrytized character varies according to the "age" of the fungus when the grapes are harvested. Wines made from the same percentage of botrytized grapes collected at the beginning and end of the harvest are noticeably mute compared to those in the middle when the rot is at its most rampant. If it is not surprising that youthful *Botrytis cinerea* has an undeveloped character, the same cannot be said of late-harvested. Many people believe that the longer botrytis establishes itself, the more potent its effect, but this is not true.

CHÂTEAU DE FARGUES
The original family home of the Lur-Saluces family is now a ghostly ruin. The family moved to Yquem in 1785 upon its union with the De Sauvage family.

THE "POURRITURE NOBLE", OR NOBLE ROT
A bunch of Sémillon grapes ready for the first trie. *Some of the grapes are still unaffected by the fungus, some are affected and discoloured but not shrivelled, others are dried, withered, and covered with the fungus bloom.*

FACTORS AFFECTING TASTE AND QUALITY

LOCATION
The left bank of the Garonne river, stretching southeast from just north of Bordeaux to 10 kilometres (6 miles) east of Langon. Cérons, Sauternes, and Barsac are tucked into the southern section of the Graves district.

CLIMATE
Very similar to the Médoc, but fractionally hotter and with slightly more rainfall. In Sauternes and Barsac it is mild and humid, with an all-important autumnal alternation of misty mornings and later sunshine, the ideal conditions for "noble rot".

ASPECT
The suburbs of Bordeaux sprawl across the northern section of this district, becoming more rural beyond Cadaujac. Graves has a much hillier terrain than the Médoc, with little valleys cut out by myriad streams that drain into the Garonne. Some of the vineyards here are quite steep. The communes of Sauternes, Bommes, and Fargues are hilly, but Preignac and Barsac, on either side of the Ciron – a small tributary of the Garonne – have gentler slopes.

SOIL
Travelling south through the district, the gravelly topsoil of Graves gradually becomes mixed with sand, then with weathered limestone and eventually with clay. The subsoil also varies, but basically it is iron-pan, limestone, and clay, either pure or mixed. Cérons has a stony soil, mostly flint and gravel, over marl; there is reddish clay-gravel over clay, or gravelly iron-pan in Sauternes, and clay-limestone over clay-gravel in Fargues. The gravel slopes of Bommes are sometimes mixed with heavy clay soils, while the plain is sandy clay with a reddish clay or limestone subsoil. Preignac is sand, gravel, and clay over clay-gravel in the south, becoming more alluvial over sand, clay, and limestone closer to Barsac. Where the classified growths of Barsac are situated, the soil is clay-limestone over limestone, elsewhere the topsoil mingles with sandy gravel.

VITICULTURE AND VINIFICATION
Some châteaux add a certain amount of *vin de presse* to the red wine. The *cuvaison* varies between eight and 15 days, although some Graves châteaux permit 15–25 days. Maturation in cask is generally between 15 and 18 months. The sweet white wines of Sauternes and Barsac are made from several tries of late-harvested, overripe grapes which, ideally, have "noble rot". Destalking is usually unnecessary. The fermentation of grape juice so high in sugar content is difficult to start and awkward to control, but it is usually over within two to eight weeks. The exact period of fermentation depends upon the style desired. Many of the best wines are matured in cask for one and a half to three and a half years.

GRAPE VARIETIES
Primary varieties: Cabernet Franc, Cabernet Sauvignon, Merlot, Sauvignon Blanc, Sémillon
Secondary varieties: Malbec, Muscadelle, Petit Verdot

The rewards, the reality, and the future

A good Sauternes is the most arduous, expensive, and frustrating wine in the world to produce – and what is the winemaker's reward? Very little, I'm afraid. Apart from Château d'Yquem – not only the greatest Sauternes but some would argue the greatest wine *per se* – the wines of this region fail to realize their true worth. This is predictable in a world where the trend is towards lighter and drier styles of wine, and may have a positive short-term effect for Sauternes aficionados, for it means a cheaper supply of their favourite wine. In the long term, however, this is not a positive way to operate, and some proprietors simply cannot afford to go on. The Comte de Pontac uprooted all the vines at his *deuxième cru* Château de Myrat in Barsac, and even the ever-optimistic Tom Heeter, former owner of Château Nairac, once said, "You have to be at least half-crazy to make a living out of these wines." We certainly do not deserve the luscious wines of Sauternes and Barsac if we continue to ignore them, but if the authorities had more sense, and the owners more business acumen, these wines could literally become "liquid gold".

The only way ahead

The vineyards of Sauternes and Barsac should also be allowed to sell red and dry white wines under the Graves appellation. If this is a right accorded to modest Cérons, why not to its illustrious neighbours? Many châteaux already make red and dry white wines, but they are sold under the cheaper "Bordeaux" appellation. Tom Heeter was right, the proprietors must be half-crazy, because their motivation for producing these alternative products is to subsidize the cost of making their botrytized wine, when they should be trying to supplement their income. Given the incentive of a superior appellation, the châteaux should concentrate on making the finest red and dry white wines every year. Only when conditions appear favourable should some of the white grape crop be left on the vine, with fingers crossed for an abundance of *Botrytis cinerea*. Instead of these châteaux investing in new oak for modest vintages, they should utilize the casks for the red and the dry white. The result would be a tiny amount of the world's most luscious wine, maybe three or four years in ten. It would no longer be necessary to attempt the impossible task of selling an old-fashioned image to young wine drinkers; the limited supply would outstrip the current demand. After 30 years of watching this area's vain attempts to win over popular support for its wines, I have come to accept the view of Comte Alexandre de Lur-Saluces, proprietor of Château d'Yquem. When asked to justify the price of Yquem, he simply said his wines are not made for everyone; they are made for those who can afford them.

THE APPELLATIONS OF
GRAVES, CÉRONS, SAUTERNES, AND BARSAC

BARSAC AOC

The commune of Barsac is one of five that have the right to the Sauternes appellation. (The others are Preignac, Fargues, Bommes, and Sauternes itself.) Some generic wines sold in bulk may take advantage of this, but all individual properties are sold as Barsac. The wine must include overripe botrytized grapes harvested in *tries*.

WHITE Luscious, intensely sweet wines similar in style to Sauternes, but perhaps lighter in weight, slightly drier, and less rich. As in Sauternes, 1983 is one of the best vintages of the 20th century.

🍇 Sémillon, Sauvignon Blanc, Muscadelle

🍷 6–25 years for most wines; between 15–60 years for the greatest

CÉRONS AOC

These inexpensive wines from an area adjacent to Barsac are the best value-for-money sweet wines in Bordeaux. They must include overripe botrytized grapes harvested in *tries*.

WHITE Lighter than Barsac, but often just as luscious, the best of these wines can show true botrytis complexity.

🍇 Sémillon, Sauvignon Blanc, Muscadelle

🍷 6–15 years for most wines

GRAVES AOC

This appellation begins at the Jalle de Blanquefort, where the Médoc finishes and runs for 60 kilometres (37 miles) along the left bank of the Garonne. Almost two-thirds of the wine is red, and is consistently high in quality and value.

RED I was brought up on the notion that with full maturity a Graves reveals itself through a certain earthiness of character. Experience has taught me the opposite. The biggest Graves from hot years can have a denseness that may combine with the smoky character of new oak to give the wine a roasted or tobacco-like complexity, but Graves is intrinsically clean. Its hallmark is its vivid fruit, clarity of style, silky texture, and hints of smoke.

🍇 Cabernet Sauvignon, Cabernet Franc, Merlot
   Secondary grape varieties: Malbec, Petit Verdot

🍷 6–15 years

WHITE This is the disappointing half of the appellation: light- to full-bodied, from pure Sauvignon to pure Sémillon (with all proportions of blends in between, flabby to zingy, and unoaked to heavily-oaked). Pay strict attention to the château profiles on the following pages. These wines may be sold from 1 December following the harvest without any mention of *primeur* or *nouveau*.

🍇 Sémillon, Sauvignon Blanc, Muscadelle

🍷 1–2 years for modest wines; 8–20 years for the best

GRAVES SUPÉRIEUR AOC

Some surprisingly good would-be Barsacs lurk under this appellation that is rarely seen yet accounts for more than a fifth of all white Graves produced.

WHITE This wine can be dry, but most is a sweet style, similar to Barsac.

🍇 Sémillon, Sauvignon Blanc, Muscadelle

🍷 6–15 years

PESSAC-LÉOGNAN AOC

Introduced in September 1987, this appellation covers the ten best communes that have the right to the Graves AOC, and it is not by chance that it also encompasses 55 of the best estates, including all the *crus classés*. The technical requirements are similar to Graves except that the Carmenère may be used for red wines; white wines must contain at least 25 per cent Sauvignon Blanc and a slightly stricter yield. If you are not sure which château to buy in the Graves, it is worth remembering this appellation and paying a premium for it.

RED Soft, silky reds of great violety elegance, and not lacking either concentration or length. Most have been aged in a percentage of new oak, which adds a smoky or tobacco-like complexity.

🍇 Cabernet Sauvignon, Cabernet Franc, Merlot, Malbec, Petit Verdot, Carmenère

🍷 6–20 years

WHITE The serious styles are invariably oaked these days, with oodles of flavour, often tropical and fruity, with a firm acid structure. These wines may be sold from 1 December following the harvest without any mention of *primeur* or *nouveau*.

🍇 A minimum of 25% Sauvignon Blanc, plus Sémillon, Muscadelle

🍷 Usually 3–8 years, but up to 20 years for the best

SAUTERNES AOC

The much hillier communes of Bommes, Fargues, and Sauternes produce the richest of all Bordeaux's dessert wines, while the châteaux in the lower-lying, flatter Preignac make wines very close in style to Barsac. The wine must include overripe botrytized grapes harvested in *tries*.

WHITE Golden, intense, powerful, and complex wines that defy the senses and boggle the mind. They are rich in texture, with masses of rich, ripe, and fat fruit. Pineapple, peach, apricot, and strawberry are some of the lush flavours that can be found, and the creamy-vanilla character of fruit and new oak matures into a splendid honeyed sumptuousness that is spicy and complex. Above all, these wines are marked by the distinctive botrytis character.

🍇 Sémillon, Sauvignon Blanc, Muscadelle

🍷 10–30 years for most wines; between 20 and 70 years for the greatest

---

THE WINE PRODUCERS OF
GRAVES AND CÉRONS,

CHÂTEAU D'ARCHAMBEAU
Illats
★ ✶ ♥

Sited in Podensac, one of the communes of Cérons, this fine property is owned by Dr Jean Dubourdieu, nephew of Pierre Dubourdieu of Doisy-Daëne, a *deuxième cru* in Barsac. He produces a fine-quality, fragrant, and attractively aromatic red wine, which has the typical silky Graves texture. The deliciously fresh, crisp, and fruity dry white Graves is better than some efforts by certain *cru classé* châteaux. His soft, fruity Cérons is *moelleux* with the emphasis more on perfume than richness.

Second wines: *Château Mourlet, Château La Citadelle*

CHÂTEAU LA BLANCHERIE
La Brède
◉ ✶ ♥

This fresh and lively dry white Graves is cool fermented, and has plenty of juicy fruit flavour balanced with ripe acidity.

CHÂTEAU LA BLANCHERIE-PEYRAT
La Brède
◉ ✶ ♥

The red wine of La Blancherie is sold under this label. It is a medium- to full-bodied wine that is matured in casks and has an engaging, spicy bouquet and a rich, fruity flavour.

CHÂTEAU BOUSCAUT
Cadaujac
Cru Classé (red and white)
★ ✶

Belongs to Sophie and Louis Lurton. The red wine is matured in wood for 18 months, with 25 per cent new oak. The white wine is fermented and matured for up to six months in 100 per cent new oak.

RED Until the 1980s this wine was big, tough, and tannic with little charm. Recent vintages have shown increasing suppleness, but the wine still struggles to find form. The second wine, Château Valoux, is a really excellent wine for its class.

🍇 Merlot 55%, Cabernet Sauvignon 35%, Cabernet Franc 5%, Malbec 5%

🍷 8–20 years

Second wine: *Château Valoux*

WHITE This dry, medium-bodied white wine has exotic fruit flavours supported by gentle oak.

🍇 Sémillon 70%, Sauvignon 30%

🍷 5–10 years

CHÂTEAU CARBONNIEUX
Léognan
Cru Classé (red and white)
★ ✶ ♥

This is the largest wine estate in Graves. The white wine, the better known of the two styles, is cool-fermented in stainless steel and matured in 100 per cent new oak for three months.

RED I frankly did not care for this wine until the splendid 1985

vintage, which seduced me with its creamy-oak nose, silky-textured fruit, and supple tannin, but similar joys have been few and far between.

Cabernet Sauvignon 55%, Merlot 30%, Cabernet Franc 10%, Malbec, and Petit Verdot 5%

⊢— 6–18 years

WHITE Once solid and uninspiring, this wine has really come into its own since the early 1990s. From this time Château Carbonnieux has been lush and creamy with well-integrated new oak and not a little finesse.

Sauvignon 60%, Sémillon 40%

⊢— 2–5 years

Second wine: *Château La Tour Léognan*

CHÂTEAU DE CARDAILLAN
Toulenne
★✓❶

Under the same ownership as Château de Malle, this is a *deuxième cru* Sauternes in the commune of Preignac. This excellent property produces a technically brilliant red Graves with a voluptuous blackcurrant flavour, which develops quickly, yet ages well.

Cabernet Sauvignon 80%, Merlot 20%

CHÂTEAU LES CARMES-HAUT-BRION
Pessac
★

From 1584 until the French Revolution in 1789, this property belonged to the white friars Carmes, hence the name. This soft, Merlot-dominated wine has always been in the shadow of its more famous neighbour, Haut-Brion, and always will, but there has been a noticeable shift upwards in quality.

CHÂTEAU DE CÉRONS
Cérons

This 17th-century château, which makes an attractively light, sweet white Cérons, is owned by Jean Perromat, owner of Mayne-Binet, de Bessanes, Ferbos, Ferbos-Lalanette in Cérons, and Prost in Barsac.

CHÂTEAU DE CHANTEGRIVE
Podensac
★✓❶

This château produces a substantial quantity of an excellent, soft, and fruity red Graves (Cabernet Sauvignon 50 per cent, Merlot 40 per cent, Cabernet Franc 10 per cent) that is matured in wooden vats for six months and then transferred to casks for a further 12 months with 20 per cent new oak. It also produces an elegant, aromatic, cool-fermented dry white Graves that is produced entirely from the first pressing (Sémillon 60 per cent, Sauvignon 30 per cent, Muscadelle 10 per cent).

The proprietor also owns Château d'Anice.

Second wine: *Château Mayne-Lévêque*

Other wine: *Château Bon-Dieu-des-Vignes*

DOMAINE DE CHEVALIER
Léognan
Cru Classé (red and white)
★★★✓❶

One of the top three Graves after Haut-Brion, this extraordinary property gives me more pleasure than any other in this AOC. It utilizes the most traditional methods to produce outstanding red and dry white wine. Fermenting the red wine at a temperature as high as 32°C (89°F) might encourage some problems elsewhere, but under the meticulous care of those at the Domaine de Chevalier, this practice, designed to extract the maximum tannins and colouring material, is a positive advantage. The red wine is matured in wood for up to 24 months, with 50 per cent new oak. The white wine is fermented and matured in wood for 18 months, with up to 25 per cent new oak. Stéphane Derenoncourt has been consulting (red wine) since 2003.

RED Deep-coloured, medium-to-full or full-bodied wines, stunningly rich in fruit and oak, with intense cedarwood and tobacco overtones, yet subtle, seductive, and full of finesse. These are wines of great quality, longevity, and complexity.

Cabernet Sauvignon 65%, Merlot 30%, Cabernet Franc 5%

⊢— 15–40 years

WHITE Even better than the red, but produced in frustratingly small quantities, this star-bright, intensely flavoured dry wine is almost fat with exotic fruit and epitomizes finesse.

Sauvignon 70%, Sémillon 30%

⊢— 8–20 years

CHÂTEAU CHICANE
Toulenne

This châteaux is typical of the large number of properties in the area that consistently make an excellent basic Graves. Here is an elegant, medium-bodied red wine, with a bouquet of violets, and heaps of clean, silky-smooth fruit.

CLOS FLORIDÈNE
Pujols-sur-Ciron
★★✓

Owned by Bordeaux's white wine revolutionary, Denis Dubourdieu, who is producing a sensational dry white Graves (Sémillon 70 per cent, Sauvignon 30 per cent) from this small estate. The red Clos Floridène (Cabernet Sauvignon 80%, Merlot 20%) possesses an extraordinary combination of rich fruit and elegant new oak, and is the equivalent of a top *cru classé*.

Second wine: *Second de Floridène*

CLOS SAINT-GEORGES
Illats
★✓

This property produces a small amount of red Graves, but is most famous for its scintillating sweet Graves Supérieur. A stunningly rich and flavoursome wine, full of botrytis complexity.

CHÂTEAU COUHINS
Villenave-d'Ornon
Cru Classé (white only)

The Institut National de La Récherche Agronomique (INRA) and Lucien Lurton share this estate. INRA produces a separate wine, which is cool fermented with no maturation in wood.

WHITE Clean, crisp, and fruity dry white wines that are well made.

Sauvignon 50%, Sémillon 50%

⊢— 2–4 years

Note Château also produces a red Graves, but it is not a *cru classé*.

CHÂTEAU COUHINS-LURTON
Villenave-d'Ornon
Cru Classé (white only)
★✓❶

The highest-performing half of the Couhins estate owned by André Lurton. The wine is fermented and matured in 100 per cent new oak.

WHITE Delicious dry wines that have all the advantages of freshness and fruitiness, plus the complexity of oak. Surprisingly fat for pure Sauvignon.

Sauvignon 100%

⊢— 3–8 years

Second wine: *Château Cantebau*

CHÂTEAU DE CRUZEAU
St-Médard-d'Eyrans
★✓

Situated on a high, south-facing crest of deep, gravel soil, this property belongs to André Lurton, owner of Château Couhins-Lurton, the high-performance white Graves *cru classé*. De Cruzeau makes 18,000 cases of full-bodied red Graves (Cabernet Sauvignon 60 per cent, Merlot 40 per cent) that is ripe and velvety with a spicy-cedarwood complexity.

This château also produces around 5,000 cases of a fine-quality white Graves (Sauvignon 90 per cent, Sémillon 10 per cent) that after some five years of maturation, develops an intense citrous bouquet and flavour.

CHÂTEAU FERRANDE
Castres

A large property that, like so many in Graves, makes better red wine than white. The red wine (Cabernet Sauvignon 35 per cent, Merlot 35 per cent, Cabernet Franc 30 per cent) is a consistently good-quality, chocolaty Graves that is matured in wood for 15 to 18 months, with 10

to 15 per cent new oak. The dry white Graves (Sémillon 60 per cent, Sauvignon 35 per cent, Muscadelle 5 per cent) is somewhat less inspiring.

CHÂTEAU DE FIEUZAL
Léognan
Cru Classé (red only)
★★

This property occupies the highest and best exposed gravel crest in the commune. The vineyard and the château are immaculate, which is reflected in the style of its wines.

RED A deeply coloured, full-bodied, rich, stylish wine with typical Graves silky texture and ample finesse.

Cabernet Sauvignon 60%, Merlot 30%, Malbec 5%, Petit Verdot 5%

⊢— 12–30 years

Second wine: *L'Abeille de Fieuzal*

Note De Fieuzal also produces a rich, exotic, and oaky dry white wine that is not *cru classé*, yet is one of the finest white Graves produced.

GRAND ENCLOS DU CHÂTEAU DE CÉRONS
Cérons
★✓❶

This property, entirely enclosed by a wall, once formed the largest part of the estate of Château de Cérons. The wines produced here – far superior to those of Château de Cérons, and possibly the best of the appellation – are fat and rich, with good ageing potential and some complexity. The proprietor also makes dry white wines at nearby Château Lamouroux.

DOMAINE DE LA GRAVE
Portets
★✓

Formerly owned by maestro Peter Vinding-Diers, the Danish-born, Australian-trained winemaker who isolated the famous "RZ" yeast strain. Vinding-Diers sold this property along with Landiras to van Quikelberg in 1998. The wines are for medium-term consumption, with a very soft, vibrantly fruity, easy-to-drink red and a lovely oak-aged white.

CHÂTEAU HAURA
Illats

Château Haura produces wines under the Cérons appellation. Although not as consistent as it should be, it can sometimes produce a fine, honey-sweet wine with some distinction and concentration. The residence on this property is known as Château Hillot and red and dry white Graves are sold under this name that come from vines contiguous with those of Haura. The proprietor also owns Château Tucau in Barsac.

CHÂTEAU HAUT-BAILLY
Léognan
Cru Classé (red only)
★★★✫Ⓥ

This château's well-kept vineyard is located on an excellent gravel crest bordering the eastern suburbs of Léognan. This red Graves is matured in wood for up to 20 months, with 50 per cent new oak.

RED The class of fruit and quality of new oak is immediately noticeable on the creamy-ripe nose of this medium-bodied wine. Never block-busting stuff, but always elegant and stylish.

🍇 Cabernet Sauvignon 60%, Merlot 30%, Cabernet Franc 10%

🍷 12–25 years

Second wine: Le Pardre de Haut-Bailly

CHÂTEAU HAUT-BRION
Pessac
Cru Classé (red and white)
★★★

In 1663 this famous château was mentioned in Pepys's diary as "Ho Bryan". It has been under American ownership since 1935, when it was purchased by Clarence Dillon, the banker. The parent company is called Domaine Clarence Dillon, and Dillon's granddaughter, the Duchesse de Mouchy, is the president. Jean Delmas is the technical director. The red wine is fermented in stainless steel and matured in wood for 24 to 27 months, with 100 per cent new oak. The white wine is fermented and matured in 100 per cent new oak. The second wine used to be Bahans Haut-Brion but is now sold as Le Clarence Haut-Brion.

RED This supple, stylish, medium- to full-bodied wine has a surprisingly dense flavour for the weight, and a chocolaty-violet character. The ideal commercial product, it develops quickly and ages gracefully.

🍇 Cabernet Sauvignon 55%, Merlot 25%, Cabernet Franc 20%

🍷 10–40 years

Second wine: Le Clarence Haut-Brion

Other wine: Le Clarté de Haut-Brion

WHITE This is not one of the biggest white Graves, but it is built to last. It is sumptuous, oaky, and teeming with citrus and exotic fruit flavours.

🍇 Sauvignon 50%, Sémillon 50%

🍷 5–20 years

CHÂTEAU LANDIRAS
Landiras

M and Mme van Quikelberg purchased this property in 1998. Production is four-fifths white and potentially of *cru classé* quality.

CHÂTEAU LARRIVET-HAUT-BRION
Léognan
★★

Originally called Château Canolle, the name was at one point changed to Château Haut-Brion-Larrivet. Larrivet is a small stream that flows through the property, and Haut-Brion means "high gravel", referring to the gravel plateau west of Léognan on which the vineyard is situated.

Château Haut-Brion took legal action over the re-naming, and since 1941 the property and its wines have been known as Château Larrivet-Haut-Brion. The red wine (Cabernet Sauvignon 55 per cent, Merlot 45 per cent), which is matured in wood for 18 months with 25 per cent new oak, is certainly *cru classé* standard, being a well-coloured and full-bodied Graves with good flavour, spicy-cedarwood undertones, and a firm tannic structure. The white wine (Sauvignon Blanc 85 per cent, Sémillon 15 per cent) has leapt in quality since 1996.

CHÂTEAU LAVILLE-HAUT-BRION
Talence
Cru Classé (white only)
★★

Since 1983, this small vineyard has been owned by Clarence Dillon, American proprietor of Château Haut-Brion. This "château with no château" is thought of as the white wine of La Mission. The wine is fermented and matured in cask. This label has become extinct now that the wine is sold as Château La Mission-Haut-Brion Blanc, but the profile remains for readers who encounter vintages in this name.

WHITE Until 1982, the style was full, rich, oaky, and exuberant, tending to be more honeyed and spicy with a floral finesse since 1983. Both styles are stunning and complex.

🍇 Sauvignon 60%, Sémillon 40%

🍷 6–20 years

CHÂTEAU LA LOUVIÈRE
Léognan
★★★Ⓥ

Part of André Lurton's Graves empire, this château has made a smart about-turn since 1985 as far as the quality of its red wine goes. A string of dull, lifeless vintages have come to an end with the beautiful, deep, and vividly coloured wines of the years 1985 and 1986. There was another step up in quality in the mid-1990s, since when this has been a truly splendid, full-bodied red Graves that is rich in spicy-blackcurranty fruit and new oak (Cabernet Sauvignon 70 per cent, Merlot 20 per cent, Cabernet Franc 10 per cent). The white wines of Château La Louvière have always been excellent, but even here there has been a gigantic leap in quality. These are exciting and complex wines that deserve to be among the very best *crus classés*.

Second wine: Château Coucheroy

Other wines: "L" de Louvière (dry white), Château Les Agunelles, Château Cantebau, Château Clos-du-Roy, Château Le Vieux-Moulin

CHÂTEAU MAGENCE
St-Pierre-de-Mons
✫Ⓥ

A good property making 5,000 cases of a supple, well-perfumed, red wine (Cabernet Sauvignon 40 per cent, Cabernet Franc 30 per cent, Merlot 30 per cent) and 10,000 cases of attractive, aromatic, cool-fermented dry white Graves (Sauvignon 64 per cent, Sémillon 36 per cent).

CHÂTEAU MALARTIC-LAGRAVIÈRE
Léognan
Cru Classé (red and white)
★★

This 20-hectare (50-acre) vineyard forms a single block around the château. An underrated property, which has consistently produced much higher quality wines since the 1980s. The red wine is fermented in stainless steel at a low temperature (16°C/61°F), and matured in wood for 20 to 22 months, with one-third new oak. The white wine is now matured in 100 per cent new oak for seven to eight months.

RED Rich, garnet-coloured with an opulent sweet-oak nose, penetrating flavour, and supple tannin structure.

🍇 Cabernet Sauvignon 50%, Cabernet Franc 25%, Merlot 25%

🍷 7–25 years

WHITE Recent vintages of this once lacklustre white Graves prove the worth of new oak. It is not difficult to mistake this honey-rich, ripe, and succulent wine for pure Sémillon.

🍇 Sauvignon 100%

🍷 5–12 years

CHÂTEAU MAYNE-BINET
Cérons

Proprietor Jean Perromat also owns several other châteaux, namely De Cérons, De Bessanes, Ferbos, and Ferbos-Lalanette in Cérons and Château Prost in Barsac. At Mayne-Binet he produces a fine sweet white Cérons.

CHÂTEAU MILLET
Portets
★Ⓥ (red only)

The red is a deep, dark-coloured wine made in a traditional style with a dense flavour of concentrated spicy fruit. Although it has a firm tannin structure, this quickly rounds out with a few years in bottle. There is a dry white Graves, but it lacks the boldness and character of the red.

Other wine: Château Du Clos Renon

CHÂTEAU LA MISSION-HAUT-BRION
Pessac
Cru Classé (red only)
★★★✫

Under the ownership of Henri Woltner, this was the pretender to the throne of Graves. Little wonder, then, that Clarence Dillon of Haut-Brion snapped it up when the opportunity arose in 1983. The red wine is matured in wood for 24 months, with 50 per cent new oak.

RED Despite different winemaking techniques, Dillon's La Mission is no less stunning than Woltner's. Both styles are deeper, darker, and denser than any other wine Graves can manage. They are essentially powerful wines that require great bottle-age, but they do lack finesse.

🍇 Cabernet Sauvignon 60%, Merlot 30%, Cabernet Franc 10%

🍷 15–45 years

WHITE This was sold as Château Laville-Haut-Brion until 2009, when it metamorphosed into this château's white sibling – and what a vintage to choose for the change, effectively doubling the price of this wonderful but already extremely expensive wine. Clear-cut floral minerality at the front of the palate; deep, rich, and honeyed on the finish.

Second wine: La Chapelle de la Mission-Haut-Brion

CHÂTEAU OLIVIER
Léognan
Cru Classé (red and white)
✫

There has never been any doubt about this château's *terroir*, which has as much potential as any Graves *cru classé*, but it was one of the appellation's most disappointing producers until 1990. Since then progress has been agonizingly slow and patchy, but recent vintages have revived hopes that this remains a château to watch. The red wine is matured in wood for 18 months; the white wine up to three months, with 100 per cent new oak.

RED The fruit is now easier-drinking and the oak, which used to be aggressive, more supple and creamy.

🍇 Cabernet Sauvignon 70%, Merlot 30%

WHITE This wine actually began to sparkle as early as 1985, with some quite outstanding vintages in the 1990s, since when has been an added freshness, real fruit flavour, and some positive character developing.

🍇 Sémillon 65%, Sauvignon 30%, Muscadelle 5%

🍷— 3–7 years

CHÂTEAU PAPE-CLÉMENT

Pessac
Cru Classé (red only)
★★

After a disastrous period in the 1970s and early 1980s, Pape-Clément began to improve in 1985 and 1986, due to stricter selection of the *grand vin* and the introduction of a second wine. Some critics rate these two vintages highly, and they were very good wines, but when examined in the context of the enormous potential of this vineyard, my brain tells me they were not at all special, even if my heart wants them to be.

The trio of 1988, 1989, and 1990 wines turned out to be the best this château has produced since 1953, although they are nowhere near as great and still not special at the very highest level of Graves wine. However, even in the string of lesser vintages Bordeaux experienced in the early 1990s, Pape-Clément managed to produce good wines, and with 1995, 1996, 1998, and 1999, it has truly regained the reputation of its former glory years. The red wine from this château is matured in wood for 24 months, with a minimum of 50 per cent new oak.

RED Medium-bodied wines of excellent deep colour, a distinctive style, and capable of much finesse.

🍇 Cabernet Sauvignon 67%, Merlot 33%

Second wine: *Le Clémentin*

Note This château also produces a little non-*cru classé* white Graves, made from equal proportions of Sémillon, Sauvignon, and Muscadelle.

CHÂTEAU RAHOUL

Portets

The wine produced by Château Rahoul is not quite as exciting as it was in the 1980s, when the property was home to – although never owned by – the maestro, Peter Vinding-Diers (*see* Domaine de la

Graves and Château Landiras). However, both red and white wines are still reliable sources of very good value oak-aged Graves.

Second wine: *Château Constantin*
Other wine: *Petit Rahoul*

CHÂTEAU RESPIDE-MÉDEVILLE

Toulenne
★ ♥

Christian Médeville, the man responsible for Château Gilette, the rising star of Sauternes, produces excellent wines here using a totally different wine philosophy. Both the red and the white are fine examples of the best of modern vinification combined with new oak. The red is a well-coloured wine with rich, ripe fruit, some spice, and a creamy, new-oak aftertaste, good for early drinking. The white is a rich, creamy-vanilla concoction with soft, succulent fruit and a fat finish.

CHÂTEAU DU ROCHEMORIN

Martillac
★ ♥

Originally called "La Roche Morine" (the Moorish rock), this estate has a history that extends at least as far back as the eighth century when Bordeaux was defended by the Moors from attacking Saracens. Another château belonging to André Lurton, Rochemorin produces a fine, elegant, fruity red Graves that is well balanced and has a good spicy finish (Cabernet Sauvignon 60 per cent, Merlot 40 per cent). Rochemorin also produces a very clean and correct dry white Graves.

CHÂTEAU DE ROQUETAILLADE LA GRANGE

Mazères
★☆ ♥

This is a very old property, that produces some 12,000 cases of an attractive, well-coloured red Graves that has an aromatic bouquet and a delicious spicy-cassis flavour. This wine is made from Merlot 40 per cent, Cabernet Sauvignon 25 per cent, Cabernet Franc 25 per cent,

Malbec 5 per cent, and Petit Verdot 5 per cent. Its firm, tannic structure means it matures gracefully over 15 or more years. The white wine, which is made from Sémillon 80 per cent, Sauvignon 20 per cent, is less successful.

Second wine: *Château de Carolle*
Other wines: *Château de Roquetaillade-le-Bernet*

CHÂTEAU DU SEUIL

Cérons

Up-and-coming Graves property producing fine, elegant reds and fruity, oak-aged whites, both proving to be of increasingly excellent value.

CHÂTEAU SMITH-HAUT-LAFITTE

Martillac
Cru Classé (red only)
★☆ ♥

The reputation of these wines began to soar under consultant Michel Rolland, but the quality has stepped up another gear since 2001, when Stéphane Derenoncourt took over. The red wine matures in wood for 18 months, with 50 per cent new oak.

RED These wines are now in a richer style with creamy-oak undertones and up-front fruit.

🍇 Cabernet Sauvignon 69%, Merlot 20% Cabernet Franc 11%

🍷— 8–20 years

Second wine: *Les Hauts-de-Smith-Haut-Lafitte*

Note A white Graves is also made. It is not a *cru classé*, yet ironically now considered one of the finest white wines in Pessac-Léognan.

CHÂTEAU LA TOUR-HAUT-BRION

Talence
Cru Classé (red only)
★★

This château is situated close to Château La Mission-Haut-Brion. By 1980 wine sold under the label of this château was merely regarded as the Second Wine of Château La Mission-Haut-Brion. All the grapes from both vineyards were vinified

together, and the two wines made by selection. However, after acquisition by Domaine Clarence Dillon in 1983, some 4.5 hectares (11 acres) of vines were delimited as Château La Tour-Haut-Brion, and from 1984 all its wines can be said to be from one specific site. The wine is matured in wood for 24 months, with 50 per cent new oak.

RED This very dark, tannic, full-bodied wine is full of chocolaty, tannic fruit above an earthy-smoky bitterness of undeveloped extract. Despite its awesome attack of flavour it shows great finesse.

🍇 Cabernet Sauvignon 60%, Merlot 30%, Cabernet Franc 10%

🍷— 20–40 years

CHÂTEAU LA TOUR-MARTILLAC

Martillac
Cru Classé (red and white)
◉★☆

This property has its own herd of cattle to supply manure for the château's strictly "organic" wine. Its red wine is not as consistent as the very best Graves and tends to lack charm in cask. These factors make it an underrated wine. It is matured in wood for 18 to 22 months with one-third new oak. The white is fermented in stainless steel, and matured in 100 per cent new oak.

RED Not big or bold wines with immediate appeal; the reds are elegant with some finesse. The fruit in recent vintages has tended to be a bit plumper, but in bottle these wines develop creamy-oak flavour.

🍇 Cabernet Sauvignon 60%, Merlot 25%, Cabernet Franc 6%, Malbec 5%, Petit Verdot 4%

🍷— 8–20 years

Second wine: *Château La Grave-Martillac*

WHITE The stunning 1986 vintage heralded a new era of exciting dry whites. This is very fresh, elegant wine, the fruit gently balanced by complex nuances of oak.

🍇 Sémillon 55%, Sauvignon 35%, Muscadelle 3%, old diverse varieties 7%

🍷— 4–8 years

THE WINE PRODUCERS OF
SAUTERNES AND BARSAC

CHÂTEAU D'ARCHE

Sauternes
2ème Cru Classé
★ ♥

This property dates from 1530. It was known as Cru de Bran-Eyre until it was bought by the Comte d'Arche in the 18th century. It has been inconsistent. The wine sees up to 50 per cent new oak.

WHITE The successful Château d'Arche is an elegantly balanced wine that is more in the style of

Barsac than Sauternes. It is sweet, rich, and has complex botrytis flavours, which often puts it on par with a *premier cru*, although it is less plump than most Sauternes. Easily equivalent to a classed growth in quality and the Crème de Tête is even better.

🍇 Sémillon 80%, Sauvignon 15%, Muscadelle 5%

🍷— 8–25 years

Second wine: *Cru de Braneyre*
Other wine: *d'Arche-Lafaurie*

CHÂTEAU BASTOR-LAMONTAGNE

Preignac
★☆ ♥

A large property that deserves *deuxième cru* status. The wine is matured in wood for up to 36 months, with 10 to 15 per cent new oak. Lighter years such as 1980, 1982, and 1985 lack botrytis but are successful in an attractive mellow, citrus style. Big years such as 1983 lack nothing: the wines are full,

rich, and stylish with concentrated botrytis flavour and ample class. 1989, 1990, 1996, 1997, 1998, and 1999 all very successful.

Second wine: *Les Remparts du Bastor*

CHÂTEAU BOUYOT

Barsac
★☆ ♥

Jammy Fonbeney, the winemaker at this little-known property, is producing some stunning wines that deserve recognition. They have classic Barsac elegance, light in body, but not in flavour, with rich pineapple and creamy botrytis fruit, some spice, and fine length.

CHÂTEAU BROUSTET
Barsac 2ème Cru Classé
★ ❤

The wine produced at Château Broustet is matured in wood for 20 months with what was until recently just 10 per cent new oak, but this increased to 40 per cent after the 1986 vintage.

WHITE Chateau Broustet can be a delightful wine, with a fruit-salad-and-cream taste, a very elegant balance, and some spicy-botrytis complexity.

🍇 Sémillon 63%, Sauvignon 25%, Muscadelle 12%

🍷 8–25 years

Second wine: *Château de Ségur*

CHÂTEAU CAILLOU
Barsac
2ème Cru Classé
★ ✦ ❤

This château gets its name from the *cailloux*, the stones that are brought to the surface during ploughing. These have been used to enclose the entire 15-hectare (37-acre) vineyard and to provide hardcore for the tennis courts. M Bravo, the owner, has run out of uses but he is still churning them up. This is not one of the better-known *deuxièmes crus*, but it consistently produces wines of a very high standard, and so deserves to be.

WHITE A rich, ripe, and spicy-sweet Barsac with concentrated botrytis flavours underscored by refined oak. Not the fattest of Barsacs, but made in the richer rather than lighter style.

🍇 Sémillon 90%, Sauvignon 10%

🍷 8–30 years

Second wine: *Petit-Mayne*
Other wines: *Cru du Clocher* (red), *Château Caillou Sec* (dry white), *Rosé St-Vincent* (dry rosé)

CHÂTEAU DE LA CHARTREUSE
Preignac
★ ❤

This is the same stunning wine as Château Saint-Amande, but under a different exclusive label. *See also* Château Saint-Amande.

CHÂTEAU CLIMENS
Barsac
1er Cru Classé
★★✦

Under the ownership of Bérénice Lurton, this property has long been considered one of the top wines of both appellations. The wine is matured in wood for 24 months with up to one-third new oak.

WHITE The fattest of Barsacs, yet its superb acidity and characteristic citrous style give it an amazingly fresh and zippy balance. This wine has masses of creamy-ripe botrytis fruit supported by good cinnamon and vanilla-oak flavours.

🍇 Sémillon 98%, Sauvignon 2%

🍷 10–40 years

Second wine: *Les Cyprès de Climens*

CHÂTEAU CLOS HAUT-PEYRAGUEY
Bommes
1er Cru Classé
★★

Originally part of Château Lafaurie-Peyraguey, this property has been owned by the Pauly family since 1934. A good dose of sulphur dioxide used to be the method of stopping fermentation at Clos Haut-Peyragey and the bouquet was often marred by an excess of sulphur. Thankfully, this has not been evident since the 1985 vintage, when coincidentally, the wines began to benefit from some new oak. The wine is now matured in wood for 18 months, with up to 25 per cent new oak.

WHITE This wine now flaunts a positively eloquent bouquet, and has a rich flavour with complex botrytis creamy-oak nuances – very stylish.

🍇 Sémillon 83%, Sauvignon 15%, Muscadelle 2%

🍷 8–25 years

Second wine: *Château Haut-Bommes*

CHÂTEAU COUTET
Barsac
1er Cru Classé
★★

This château is usually rated a close second to Climens, but in fact it is capable of matching it in some vintages and its occasional production of tiny quantities of *tête de cuvée* called "Cuvée Madame" often surpasses it. It is fermented and matured for 24 months in cask with 30 to 50 per cent new oak. The dry white "Vin Sec" is an AOC Graves and very disappointing.

WHITE This wine has a creamy vanilla-and-spice bouquet, an

initially delicate richness that builds on the palate, good botrytis character, and oaky fruit.

🍇 Sémillon 75%, Sauvignon 23%, Muscadelle 2%

🍷 8–25 years (15–40 years for Cuvée Madame)

Other wines: *Cuvée Madame, Vin Sec du Château Coutet*

CHÂTEAU DOISY-DAËNE
Barsac
2ème Cru Classé
★★ ❤

Owner Pierre Dubourdieu cool ferments this wine in stainless steel until the desired balance of alcohol and sweetness is achieved, and then matures it in 100 per cent new oak for a short while. The wine also undergoes various low-sulphur techniques. The result is a wine equal to a Barsac *premier cru*.

WHITE This is a wine of great floral freshness and elegance, with a delightful honeyed fragrance of deliciously sweet fruit, delicate botrytis character, hints of creamy oak, and perfect balance.

🍇 Sémillon 100%

🍷 8–20 years

Second wine: *Château Cantegril*
Other wine: *Vin Sec de Doisy-Daène*

CHÂTEAU DOISY-DUBROCA
Barsac
2ème Cru Classé
◉

This property is run in conjunction with Climens, and is the smallest part of the original Doisy estate. But the wine, although consistent, is not in the same class as Doisy-Daëne, let alone Climens. It is matured in cask for 24 to 30 months with 25 per cent new oak.

🍇 Sémillon 90%, Sauvignon 10%

🍷 6–15 years

Second wine: *La Demoiselle de Doisy*

CHÂTEAU DOISY-VÉDRINES
Barsac
2ème Cru Classé
★★✦ ❤

This is the original and largest of the three Doisy châteaux. It is owned by Olivier Castéja, the head of Bordeaux *négociant* Roger Joanne. The wine is matured in wood for 18 months with one-third new oak.

WHITE This wine was somewhat lacklustre until 1983, since when it has exploded with character. Rich, ripe, and oaky, with a concentrated botrytis complexity.

🍇 Sémillon 80%, Sauvignon 20%

🍷 8–25 years

Other wine: *Château La Tour-Védrines*

CHÂTEAU DE FARGUES
Fargues
★★

The eerie ruin of Château de Fargues is the ancestral home of the Lur-Saluces family. The small production of ultra-high-quality wine is made by essentially the same fastidious methods as Yquem, including fermentation and maturation in 100 per cent new oak. It is powerful and viscous, very rich, succulent, and complex, with a fat, toasty character (Sémillon 80 per cent, Sauvignon 20 per cent). Easily equivalent to a classed growth.

CHÂTEAU FILHOT
Sauternes
2ème Cru Classé
★

The beautiful Château Filhot was built between 1780 and 1850. This splendid château has a potentially great vineyard that consistently produces boring wine. Investment is required on a large scale in nearly every department: the proportion of Sémillon should be increased, the number of *tries* should be increased, the wine should contain more botrytized grapes and should be matured in cask, with some new oak.

WHITE At best these are well-made, simply fruity, and sweet.

🍇 Sémillon 60%, Sauvignon 37%, Muscadelle 3%

CHÂTEAU GILETTE
Preignac
★

Christian Médeville rejects modern marketing methods, preferring instead to keep his precious nectar (made from Sémillon 94 per cent, Sauvignon 4 per cent, Muscadelle 2 per cent) in vats under anaerobic conditions for an amazing 20 years before bottling and selling it. The Crème de Tête is *premier cru* quality with a powerful bouquet and intense flavour of liquorice and peaches and cream, followed by a long barley-sugar aftertaste. The Crème de Tête deserves ★★, but I am less impressed with Château Gilette's regular bottlings (if, indeed, any bottling at this property can be so described!).

CHÂTEAU GUIRAUD
Sauternes
1er Cru Classé
★★

This property has been on the up since 1981, when the Narby family of Canada purchased it. The château and vineyards were in a very run-down state. Narby dug up much of the Sauvignon and planted Sémillon, then totally re-equipped the winery and renovated the château. Only Yquem is on as high ground as Guiraud and as drainage is a key factor affecting the quality of the greatest Sauternes, where heavy clay soils dominate, the potential for this wine is very exciting and one that has been skilfully exploited with the help of Xavier Plantey, ex-manager of Château la Gaffelière. The wine is matured in wood for 30 months with at least 50 per cent new oak. The first vintages of the dry white Vin Blanc Sec "G" were dull, but subsequent efforts have improved.

WHITE After two dismal decades, great Sauternes arrived at this château with the classic 1983 vintage, the first true botrytis wine under Narby's ownership. Guiraud is now plump with Sémillon fruit and fat with botrytis character. A deliciously sweet wine with luxuriant new oak, complexity, and considerable finesse.

Sémillon 70%, Sauvignon 30%

12–35 years

Second wine: *Le Dauphin*
Other wine: *Vin Blanc Sec "G"* (dry white)

CHATEAU HAUT-BOMMES
Bommes

The owner, Jacques Pauly, prefers to live here rather than at his *premier cru* Château Clos Haut-Peyraguey. Occasionally the wine used to excel for an unclassified growth; the recent improvements at Château Clos Haut-Peyraguey augur well for the future.

CHÂTEAU LES JUSTICES
Preignac
★ Ⓥ

Under the same ownership as the star-performing Château Gilette, but here Christian Médeville gives his wines only four years ageing in vats. Les Justices is a consistent wine of excellent quality that is riper and fruitier than Gilette and the equivalent of a *deuxième cru*.

CHATEAU LAFAURIE-PEYRAGUEY
Bommes
1er Cru Classé
★★★ Ⓥ

As with Cordier properties, this wine shows remarkable consistency. It is matured in wood for between 18 and 20 months with up to 50 per cent new oak.

WHITE The combination of botrytis and oak is like pineapples and peaches and cream in this elegant wine that keeps fresh and retains an incredibly light colour in old age.

Sémillon 98%, Sauvignon 2%

8–30 years

CHÂTEAU LAMOTHE-DESPUJOLS
Sauternes
2ème Cru Classé

In 1961 the Lamothe vineyard was split in two. The section belonging to Jean Despujols has been the most disappointing half up until the 1985 vintage, but it has really come into its own since 1990.

WHITE Fuller, richer, and sweeter than previously expected, and in an oily, fuller bodied style, with overtly attractive tropical fruit character.

Sémillon 70%, Sauvignon 20%, Muscadelle 10%

CHÂTEAU LAMOTHE-GUIGNARD
Sauternes
2ème Cru Classé
★ Ⓥ

The Guignards are really trying to achieve something with their section of the Lamothe vineyard. It was called Lamothe-Bergey until the name was changed in 1981. The wine is matured in wood for 24 months with 20 per cent new oak.

WHITE Rich, spicy, and concentrated wines of full body and good botrytis character.

Sémillon 85%, Muscadelle 10%, Sauvignon 5%

7–20 years

CHÂTEAU LIOT
Barsac
★ Ⓥ

This wine is elegant, with light but fine botrytis character and creamy vanilla of new oak – probably the equivalent of a *deuxième cru* in quality and is excellent value. Owner Jean-Nicol David also produces Château Saint-Jean, a dry white Graves, and Château Pinsas, a fruity red Graves.

CHÂTEAU DE MALLE
Preignac
2ème Cru Classé

Dry white wine is produced under the "Chevalier de Malle" label, and red Graves from contiguous vineyards under the Château du Cardaillan label. While this vineyard does not shine every year (1989 and 1990 are its best-ever vintages), when it does, it can be superb value.

WHITE These are firm, well-concentrated wines often influenced more by passerillage than botrytis. Delicious, rich, and luscious.

Sémillon 75%, Sauvignon 22%, Muscadelle 3%

7–20 years

Second wine: *Château St-Hélène*
Other wine: *Chevalier de Malle*

CHÂTEAU DU MAYNE
Barsac
Ⓥ

There is a good proportion of old vines at this property which adds concentration and weight to these wines, which are fatter than the norm for Barsac. Owned by the Sanders family of the splendid Château Haut-Bailly of Graves.

CHÂTEAU MÉNOTA
Barsac
Ⓥ

This quaint old property – with its historic towers and ramparts – has exported its wines to England since the 16th century. Château Ménota produces very good Barsac, despite the unusually high proportion of Sauvignon Blanc (60 per cent).

CHATEAU NAIRAC
Barsac
2ème Cru Classé
★ ★

Tom Heeter established the practice of fermenting and maturing his wine in up to 100 per cent new oak – Nevers for vanilla and Limousin for backbone – and his perfectionist ex-wife, Nicole Tari, has continued this format with great success.

WHITE These are rich and oaky wines that require ample ageing to show true finesse. With enough bottle maturity the tannin and vanilla harmonize with the fruit, and the rich botrytis complexity emerges.

Sémillon 90%, Sauvignon 6%, Muscadelle 4%

8–25 years

CHÂTEAU PERNAUD
Barsac
★ Ⓥ

This property was once part of the Sauvage d'Yquem estate. It was then owned by the Lur-Saluces family, but was abandoned after the oidium fungus devastated Bordeaux in the late 18th century. It has been completely replanted and renovated, and is now building up something of a reputation. This slightly richer style of Barsac (Sémillon 70 per cent, Sauvignon 25 per cent, Muscadelle 5 per cent) has a typically elegant balance and is certainly a wine to watch.

CHÂTEAU RABAUD-PROMIS
Bommes
1er Cru Classé
★ ★

The wines of this once-grand property used to be awful. It was sad to see the vineyard, château, and wine so neglected. What a joy to witness such a dramatic change. It began with the 1983; and the vintages are now something special.

WHITE A lovely gold-coloured wine with full, fat, and ripe botrytis character on the bouquet and palate.

Sémillon 80%, Sauvignon 18%, Muscadelle 2%

8–25 years

CHÂTEAU RAYMOND-LAFON
Sauternes

As I wrote in the last edition, it is easy to understand how people can get carried away by the idea of a vineyard so close to Yquem as Raymond-Lafon, especially when its owner, Pierre Meslier, was régisseur at Yquem. This was, however, an overrated and overpriced wine in the mid-1980s, and although things have improved since the 1989 and 1990 vintages, it is performing at only *deuxième cru* level and is consequently overrated and overpriced. Now that the style has been cleaned up and plumped out, Raymond-Lafon (Sémillon 80 per cent, Sauvignon 20 per cent) is a nice Sauternes, but not worth three times the price of Rieussec or two-and-a-half times as much as Climens.

CHÂTEAU RAYNE-VIGNEAU
Bommes
1er Cru Classé
★

The quality of Rayne-Vigneau had plummeted to dismal depths until 1985. The wine is now matured in wood for 24 months with 50 per cent new oak. It has a higher Sémillon content than the statistics would suggest, due to the 5,000 cases of dry Sauvignon Blanc that are sold as "Rayne Sec".

WHITE Château Rayne-Vigneau is now a very high-quality wine that has an elegant peachy ripeness to its botrytis character.

Sémillon 65%, Sauvignon 35%

8–25 years

Second wine: *Clos l'Abeilley*
Other wines: *Rayne Sec*

CHÂTEAU RIEUSSEC
Fargues
1er Cru Classé
★★★

This fine property promises to make even better wine since its acquisition by Domaines Rothschild in 1984. None of the Sauvignon produced here is used for Château Rieussec (it goes in the "R"), effectively making the wine 96 per cent Sémillon. It is barrel-fermented and cask matured for 18 to 30 months with 50 per cent new oak.

WHITE This wine is one of the richest and most opulent of Sauternes, with intense pineapple fruit and a heavily botrytized character.

Sémillon 75%, Sauvignon 22%, Muscadelle 3%

12–35 years

Second wines: *Clos Labère, Mayne des Carmes*

Other wine: *"R" de Château Rieussec* (dry white)

CHÂTEAU DE ROLLAND

Barsac
★☆ ✪

Buy at leisure at Château de Rolland, where you can stop over at the B&B in the vineyard and relax in the swimming pool.

WHITE Fresh and elegant, with a particular emphasis on fruit. An improving Barsac, produced by the Guignard family, which also owns the excellent Château de Roquetaillade-La-Grange at Mazères in Graves.

🍇 Sémillon 80%, Sauvignon 15%, Muscadelle 5%

🍷 5–8 years

CHÂTEAU ROMER

Fargues
2ème Cru Classé
✪

The original Romer estate was divided in 1881, and at just 5 hectares (13 acres) this is the smallest part. I have never come across the wine.

🍇 Sémillon 50%, Sauvignon 40%, Muscadelle 10%

CHÂTEAU ROMER-DU-HAYOT

Fargues
2ème Cru Classé
✪

Monsieur André du Hayot owns these 10 hectares (25 acres) of vines on a fine clayey-gravel crest that was once part of the original Romer estate. The wines are little seen, but represent very good value.

WHITE Fresh, not oversweet, fruit-salad and cream style, with light botrytis character and an elegant balance.

🍇 Sémillon 70%, Sauvignon 25%, Muscadelle 5%

🍷 5–12 years

CHÂTEAU ROUMIEU

Barsac
★ ✪

This property, which borders the classified growths of Climens and Doisy-Védrines, has produced luscious sweet wines of a richer than normal style in some vintages (Sémillon 90 per cent, Sauvignon 10 per cent).

CHÂTEAU ROUMIEU-LACOSTE

Barsac
★ ✪

A Dubourdieu property producing consistently fine Barsac (Sémillon 80 per cent, Sauvignon 20 per cent) with good botrytis concentration.

CHÂTEAU SAINT-AMANDE

Preignac
★ ✪

An elegant and stylish wine (Sémillon 67 per cent, Sauvignon 33 per cent) that is very attractive when young, yet some vintages have potentially excellent longevity

and are often equivalent to a classed growth in quality. Part of the production of this property is sold under the Château de la Chartreuse label.

Second wine: *Château de la Chartreuse*

CHÂTEAU SIGALAS-RABAUD

Bommes
1er Cru Classé
★☆

This is the largest part of the original Rabaud estate. The proprietor contracted Cordier to manage this property as from 1995 and the wines have already shown a marked improvement.

WHITE A stylish early-drinking wine with an elegant botrytis bouquet and deliciously fresh fruit on the palate.

🍇 Sémillon 85%, Sauvignon 15%

🍷 6–15 years

CHÂTEAU SIMON

Barsac
2ème Cru Classé

A combination of modern and traditional methods produces a mildly sweet wine from Sémillon 70 per cent, Sauvignon 30 per cent. Most Sauternes and Barsacs are aged in Nevers or Limousin oak. Sometimes Allier is used, but at Simon they mature the wine in Merrain oak for two years.

CHÂTEAU SUAU

Barsac
2ème Cru Classé

The vineyard belongs to Roger Biarnès, who makes the wine at his Château Navarro in Cérons because the original château is under different ownership. Furthermore, this is not the same property as Château Suau at Capian, on the opposite bank of the Garonne, almost directly north.

WHITE This attractive, fresh, and fragrantly fruity wine has a gentle citrus-and-spice botrytis complexity. Improvement noted in the 2005 vintage.

🍇 Sémillon 80%, Sauvignon 10%, Muscadelle 10%

🍷 6–12 years

CHÂTEAU SUDUIRAUT

Preignac
1er Cru Classé
★★★☆

This splendid 17th-century château, with its picturesque parkland, effectively evokes the graceful

beauty found in its luscious wines. Suduiraut's superb 100-hectare (245-acre) vineyard enjoys a good susceptibility to "noble rot", and adjoins that of Yquem. The wines went through an inconsistent patch in the 1980s, but have improved dramatically under the watchful eye of Jean-Michel Cazes's AXA insurance group. The wines are fermented and matured in cask for 24 months, with at least one-third new oak.

WHITE Soft, succulent, and sublime, this is an intensely sweet wine of classic stature. It is rich, ripe, and viscous, with great botrytis complexity that benefits from good bottle-age.

🍇 Sémillon 80%, Sauvignon 20%

🍷 8–35 years

Second wine: *Castelnau de Suduiraut*

CHÂTEAU LA TOUR BLANCHE

Sauternes
1er Cru Classé
★★☆

This property was placed at the head of the *premiers crus* in 1855, when only Yquem was deemed to be superior, but until relatively recently it failed to live up to this reputation. Even at its lowest ebb, few critics would have denied that these vineyards truly possessed great potential, but the wines were ordinary. This was made all the more embarrassing by the fact that the state-owned La Tour Blanche was a school of agriculture and oenology that was supposed to teach others how to make Sauternes. This depressing situation began to change, however, in the mid-1980s when Château la Tour Blanche started increasing the proportion of Sémillon, picking much riper grapes, and implementing stricter selection in both vineyard and chais. Fermentation is in wood (with up to 90 per cent new oak but averaging 25 per cent in most years), and the results have been exciting with excellent wines produced in 1988, 1989, 1990 (its greatest ever), 1994, 1995, 1996, 1997, and 1998.

WHITE These are now so rich they are almost fat and bursting with plump, ripe, juicy fruit and oodles

of complex botrytis character.

🍇 Sémillon 78%, Sauvignon 19%, Muscadelle 3%

🍷 8–20 years

Second wine: *Mademoiselle de Saint-Marc*

CHÂTEAU D'YQUEM

Sauternes
1er Cru Supérieur
★★★

This most famous of all châteaux belonged to the English crown from 1152 to 1453. It then passed into the hands of Charles VII, King of France. In 1593 Jacques de Sauvage acquired tenant's rights to the royal property and in 1711 his descendants purchased the fiefdom of Yquem. In 1785 it passed into the hands of the Lur-Saluces family. The *tries* tradition was kept alive at Yquem when it was long forgotten by other noble châteaux. Like Pétrus, one of Yquem's "secrets" is its pickers. They are all skilled; they know what to pick and, just as important, what to leave. The gap between *tries* can vary from three days to several weeks. Housing and feeding 120 pickers for several weeks of inactivity is not cheap.

The property has been run with passionate care by succeeding generations, although LVMH (which owns Moët & Chandon in Champagne) purchased a majority shareholding in 1999 (after three years of acrimony between members of the Lur-Saluces family). Alexandre Lur-Saluces lost his independence, but won a handsome contract to remain in his former home. He is still very much in charge.

In 1972 the harvest consisted of 11 *tries* spread over 71 days. In that year no wine was sold as Château d'Yquem. This is not to say that Yquem's fastidious attention to selection and quality does not pay off in some poor vintages. But in good years, because of the strict selection in the vineyard, the amount of wine that is finally used is as high as 80 to 90 per cent. The wines are matured for up to 42 months with 100 per cent new oak. Other *terroirs* in Sauternes and Barsac are potentially comparable, but, no matter how conscientious their owners, none makes the same sacrifices as Yquem.

WHITE This wine represents the ultimate in richness, complexity, and class. No other botrytis wine of equal body and concentration has a comparable finesse, breeding, and balance. Some of the characteristic aromas and flavours include peach, pineapple, coconut, nutmeg, and cinnamon, with toasty-creamy vanilla and caramel flavours of new oak.

🍇 Sémillon 80%, Sauvignon 20%

🍷 20–60 years

Other wines: *"Y" de Château d'Yquem* (dry white)

THE LIBOURNAIS AND FRONSADAIS

The right bank of the Dordogne River, known as the Libournais district, is red-wine country. Dominated by the Merlot grape, the vineyards here produce deep-coloured, silky- or velvety-rich wines of classic quality in the St-Émilion and Pomerol regions, in addition to wines of modest quality, but excellent value and character, in the "satellite" appellations that surround them.

IN THE MID-1950S, many Libournais wines were harsh, and even the best AOCs did not enjoy the reputation they do today. Most growers believed that they were cultivating too much Cabernet Sauvignon and Malbec for their particular *terroir* and decided that they should plant more vines of Cabernet Franc. A few growers argued for the introduction of Merlot, which was allowed by the regulations, because it would give their wines the suppleness they desired. Even if they could have agreed on united action, changing the *encépagement* of an entire district would have been a very long-term project, as well as being extremely expensive. However, in 1956, frost devastated the vineyards, forcing the Libournais growers into action. With poor, short crops inevitable for some years to come, prices soared, enabling them to carry out the massive replanting which, ironically, they could not have afforded prior to the crisis. This devastation led to the wholesale cultivation of Merlot and Cabernet Franc, which established a completely different style of wines, providing the catalyst for the spectacular post-war success of St-Émilion and Pomerol.

THE GARAGISTE EFFECT

In 1979, Jacques Thienpont, owner of Pomerol's classy Vieux Château Certan, unintentionally created what would become the *"vin de garagiste"* craze, when he purchased a neighbouring plot of land, and created a new wine called Le Pin. With a very low yield, 100 per cent Merlot, and 100 per cent new oak, the decadently rich Le Pin directly challenged Pétrus, just 1 kilometre (0.6 mile) away. It was widely known that Thienpont considered Vieux Château Certan to be at least the equal of Pétrus, and he could certainly claim it to be historically more famous, but Pétrus regularly got much the higher price, which dented his pride. So Le Pin was born, and although he did not offer his fledgling wine at the same price as Pétrus, it soon trounced it on the auction market. In 1999, a case of 1982 Le Pin was trading at a massive £11,550 ($18,650), while a case of 1982 Château Pétrus could be snapped up for a "mere" £7,800 ($12,600). By 2003, the Pétrus had traded up to a mind-boggling £16,215 ($26,190) and yet Le Pin sold for £27,490 ($44,400). Unfortunately, Jacques Thienpont died in 1985, long before his little experiment yielded such crazy prices. By the late 1980s, however, Le Pin's extraordinary financial success had became so obvious to a number of *vignerons* in neighbouring St-Emilion that they attempted to replicate it with small plots of land in their own appellation: Jean-Luc Thunevin with Château de Valandraud (first vintage 1991), Gérard and Dominique Bécot with Château La Gomerie (first vintage 1995), von Neipperg with Château La Mondotte (first vintage 1996), Francis Gaboriaud with Château L'Hermitage (first vintage 1997), Alain and Françoise Raynaud with Château Quinault l'Enclos (first vintage 1997),

THE LIBOURNAIS DISTRICT, *see also p109*
This great red-wine area includes St-Émilion, Pomerol, and their satellites. In the Libournais district, the Merlot grape reigns supreme, its succulent fruit essential to the local style.

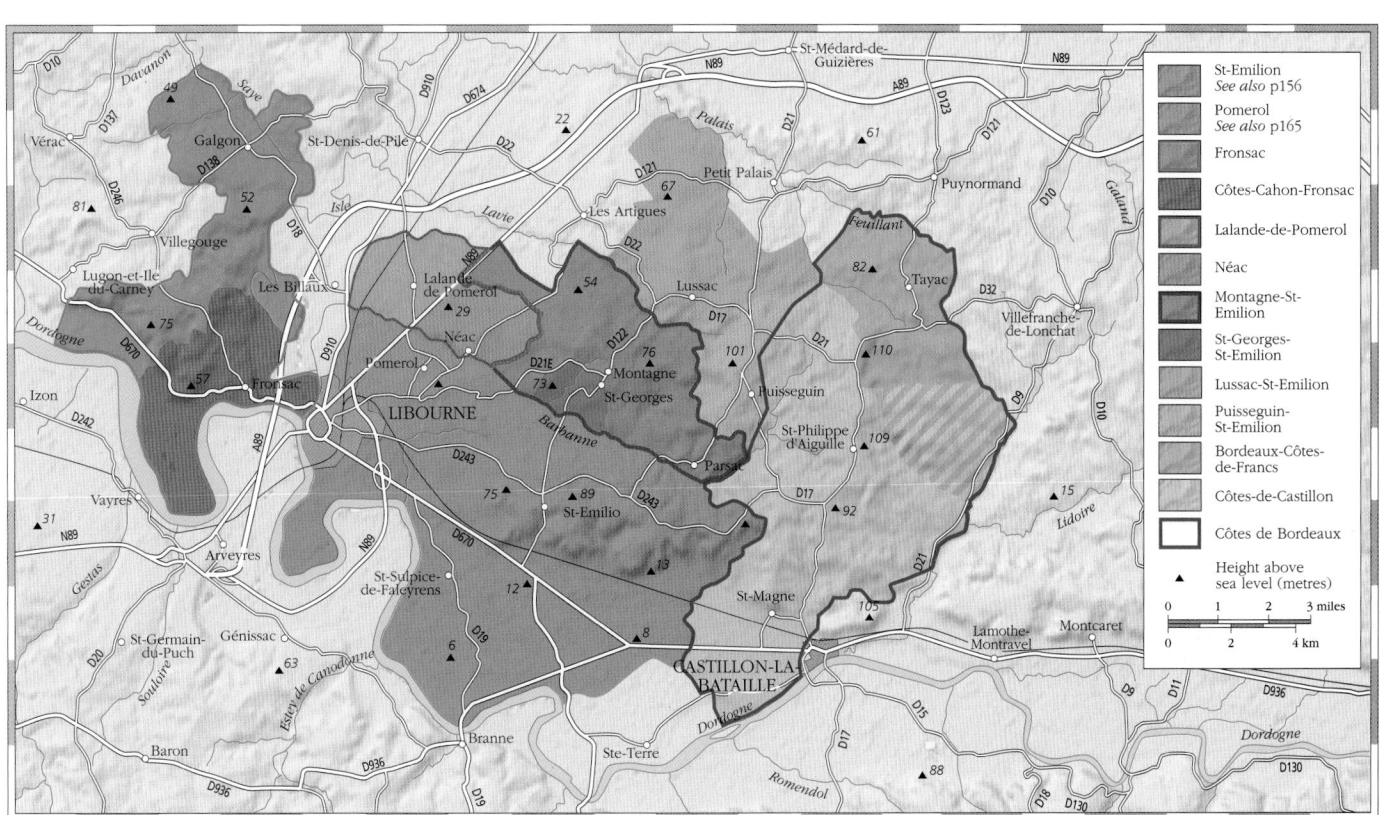

and Château Teyssier with Le Dôme (first vintage 1998). But it was Le Pin's cellar, which is truly a garage under a battered farmhouse, that inspired French wine writer Michel Bettane to coin the phrase "*vins de garage*". It is interesting how this new breed of wines has polarized critics into opposite camps, as if there is something intrinsically right or wrong with producing wine on a small scale. Because that is all it is, and the *garagistes* are popping up in the Graves, the Médoc, and well beyond the borders of Bordeaux. While some consumers (all wealthy) are happy to pay any price demanded for these wines, others seem to take offence at the very mention of the word *garagiste*. Both positions are bizarre. Besides, where do you draw the line between a *vin de garage* and an honest *lieu-dit* wine? Oh dear Jacques and Michel: what have you started?

THE SATELLITE APPELLATIONS OF ST-ÉMILION AND POMEROL

The wines of Lussac, Montagne, Parsac, Puisseguin, Sables, and St-Georges were once sold as St-Émilion, but in 1936 these outer areas were given their own AOCs. This was done to protect the image of the greatest St-Émilion châteaux, but through the historical use of this famous name these areas won the right to attach the name of St-Émilion to theirs. The tiny Sables area was later reclaimed by the St-Émilion AOC, and in 1972 a new appellation, Montagne-St-Émilion, was created. This appellation, which covered a large region, could be adopted by growers who had previously used either Parsac-St-Émilion AOC or St-Georges-St-Émilion AOC, but the executive order that created Montagne-St-Émilion AOC in 1972 did not disband either of these smaller appellations.

So, a situation arose in which growers could choose between two very similar AOCs. In 1993, however, Parsac-St-Émilion was finally disbanded, since it was noticed that virtually all the producers of Parsac-St-Émilion were not using the original AOC but opting for Montagne-St-Émilion AOC. Many growers in St-Georges-St-Émilion, however, were still using the original appellation, and so disbanding this would not have been so simple. All five combined St-Émilion AOCs would in fact benefit from merging, since they all produce wines of essentially similar nature, under identical regulations.

THE GENERIC APPELLATIONS OF
THE LIBOURNAIS AND FRONSADAIS

BORDEAUX-CÔTES-DE-FRANCS AOC

This forgotten area's vineyards are contiguous with those of Puisseguin-St-Émilion and Lussac-St-Émilion, and have a very similar clay-limestone over limestone and iron-pan soil. The Bordeaux Supérieur version of these wines differs only in its higher alcohol level.

RED These are essentially robust, rustic, full-bodied wines that are softened by their high Merlot content.

🍇 Cabernet Franc, Cabernet Sauvignon, Malbec, Merlot

🍷 5–10 years

WHITE Little-seen dry, semi-sweet, and sweet wines of clean, fruity character.

🍇 Sauvignon Blanc, Sémillon, Muscadelle

🍷 5–10 years

BORDEAUX-CÔTES-DE-FRANCS LIQUOREUX AOC

This style of Bordeaux-Côtes-de-Francs wine must by law be naturally sweet and made from overripe grapes that possess at least 223 grams of sugar per litre. The wines must have a minimum level of 11.5 per cent alcohol and 27 grams of residual sugar per litre.

WHITE Rich, genuinely *liquoreux* wines; only tiny amounts are made.

🍇 Sauvignon Blanc, Sémillon, Muscadelle

🍷 5–15 years

BORDEAUX SUPÉRIEUR CÔTES-DE-FRANCS AOC

See Bordeaux-Côtes-de-Francs AOC

CANON-FRONSAC AOC

See Côtes-Canon-Fronsac AOC

CASTILLON CÔTES DE BORDEAUX AOC

The boundary and technical requirements for this red-wine-only appellation are precisely the same as for Côtes-de-Castillon.

CÔTES-CANON-FRONSAC AOC

Fronsac AOC and Côtes-Canon-Fronsac AOC will no doubt be the next wines to be "discovered" by budget-minded Bordeaux drinkers. The best of these wines are Côtes-Canon-Fronsac AOC, sometimes called Canon-Fronsac AOC. With lower yields and stricter selection, these wines could equal all but the best of St-Émilion and Pomerol.

RED Full-bodied, deep-coloured, rich, and vigorous wines with dense fruit, fine spicy character, plenty of finesse, and good length.

🍇 Cabernet Franc, Cabernet Sauvignon, Malbec, Merlot

🍷 7–20 years

CÔTES-DE-CASTILLON AOC

This is an attractive hilly area squeezed between St-Émilion, the Dordogne River, and the Dordogne *département*. Its wine has long been appreciated for quality, consistency, and value. These wines used to be sold as Bordeaux and Bordeaux Supérieur wine until the 1989 vintage, when Côtes-de-Castillon received its own AOC status.

RED Firm, full-bodied, fine-coloured wines with dense fruit and finesse.

🍇 Cabernet Franc, Cabernet Sauvignon, Carmenère, Malbec, Merlot, Petit Verdot

🍷 5–15 years

FRANCS CÔTES DE BORDEAUX AOC

The boundary and technical requirements for this appellation are precisely the same as for Bordeaux Côtes-de-Francs. The wines may be red or white (dry, semi-sweet, and sweet).

FRONSAC AOC

This generic appellation covers the communes of La Rivière, St-Germain-la-Rivière, St-Aignan, Saillans, St-Michel-de-Fronsac, Galgon, and Fronsac.

RED These full-bodied, well-coloured wines have good chunky fruit and a fulsome, chocolaty character. Not quite the spice or finesse of Côtes-Canon-Fronsac, but splendid value.

🍇 Cabernet Franc, Cabernet Sauvignon, Malbec, Merlot

🍷 6–15 years

LALANDE-DE-POMEROL AOC

This good-value appellation covers the communes of Lalande-de-Pomerol and Néac. No matter how good they are, even the best are but pale reflections of classic Pomerol.

RED Firm, meaty Merlots with lots of character but without Pomerol's texture and richness.

🍇 Cabernet Franc, Cabernet Sauvignon, Malbec, Merlot

🍷 7–20 years

LUSSAC-ST-ÉMILION AOC

A single-commune appellation 9 kilometres (5.5 miles) northeast of St-Émilion.

RED The wines produced on the small gravelly plateau to the west of this commune are the lightest, but have the most finesse. Those produced on the cold, clayey lands to the north are robust and earthy, while those from the clay-limestone in the southeast have the best balance of colour, richness, and finesse.

🍇 Cabernet Franc, Cabernet Sauvignon, Carmenère, Malbec, Merlot

⌇ 5–12 years

MONTAGNE-ST-ÉMILION AOC

This appellation includes St-Georges-St-Émilion, a former commune that is today part of Montagne-St-Émilion. St-Georges-St-Émilion AOC and Montagne-St-Émilion AOC are the best of all the appellations that append "St-Émilion" to their names.

RED Full, rich, and intensely flavoured wines that mature well.

🍇 Cabernet Franc, Cabernet Sauvignon, Malbec, Merlot

⌇ 5–15 years

NÉAC AOC

This appellation has not been employed since the proprietors have been allowed to use the Lalande-de-Pomerol appellation. *See* Lalande-de-Pomerol AOC.

POMEROL AOC

The basic wines of Pomerol fetch higher prices than those of any other Bordeaux appellation. The average Merlot content of a typical Pomerol is around 80 per cent.

RED It is often said that these are the most velvety-rich of the world's classic wines, but they also have the firm tannin structure that is necessary for successful long-term maturation and development. The finest also have surprisingly deep colour, masses of spicy-oak complexity, and great finesse.

🍇 Cabernet Franc, Cabernet Sauvignon, Malbec, Merlot

⌇ 5–10 years (modest growths) 10–30 years (great growths)

PUISSEGUIN-ST-ÉMILION AOC

This commune has a clay-limestone topsoil over a stony subsoil and the wines it produces tend to be more rustic than those of the Montagne-St-Émilion AOC.

RED These are rich and robust wines with a deep flavour and lots of fruit and colour, but they are usually lacking in finesse.

🍇 Cabernet Franc, Cabernet Sauvignon, Carmenère, Malbec, Merlot

⌇ 5–10 years

ST-ÉMILION AOC

These wines must have a minimum of 10.5 per cent alcohol, but in years when chaptalization (the addition of sugar to grape juice to increase alcohol content) is allowed, there is also a maximum level of 13 per cent.

RED Even in the most basic St-Émilions the ripe, spicy-juiciness of the Merlot grape should be supported by the firmness and finesse of the Cabernet Franc. The great châteaux achieve this superbly: they are full, rich, and concentrated, chocolaty and fruit-cakey.

🍇 Cabernet Franc, Cabernet Sauvignon, Carmenère, Malbec, Merlot

⌇ 6–12 years (modest growths) 12–35 years (great growths)

ST-GEORGES-ST-ÉMILION AOC

Along with the Montagne region of Montagne-St-Émilion, this is the best parish of the outer areas.

RED These are deep-coloured, plummy wines with juicy, spicy fruit, and good supporting tannic structure.

🍇 Cabernet Franc, Cabernet Sauvignon, Malbec, Merlot

⌇ 5–15 years

SATELLITE APPELLATIONS IN THE ST-ÉMILION AREA
It would make sound commercial sense if all the St-Émilion satellites (Lussac-St-Émilion, Puisseguin-St-Émilion, and St-Georges-St-Émilion) were combined under the Montagne St-Émilion appellation.

SAINT-ÉMILION

The Romans were the first to cultivate the vine in St-Émilion, a small area that has exported its wines to various parts of the world for over eight hundred years. In the first half of the twentieth century it lapsed into obscurity, but in the last fifty years it has risen like a phoenix.

ST-ÉMILION AS WE KNOW IT is a phenomenon of the post-war era, but there are many reminders of this wine's ancient past – from the famous Château Ausone, named after the Roman poet Ausonius, to the walled hilltop village of St-Émilion itself, which has survived almost unchanged since the Middle Ages. In contrast, the Union des Producteurs, the largest single-appellation *coopérative* in France, is a graphic illustration of the best in modern, technologically sophisticated wine production. Today, there are over a thousand *crus* within 10 kilometres (6 miles) of the village of St-Émilion that may use this appellation.

THE APPEAL OF ST-ÉMILION WINES

For those who find red wines too harsh or too bitter, St-Émilion, with its elegance and finesse, is one of the easiest with which to make the transition from white to red. The difference between the wines of St-Émilion and those of its satellites is comparable to the difference between silk and satin, whereas the difference between St-Émilion and Pomerol is like the difference between silk and velvet: the quality is similar, but the texture is not – although, of course, we must be humble about categorizing such complex entities as wine areas. It could justifiably be argued that the *graves* (gravelly terrain) that produces two of the very best St-Émilions – Châteaux Cheval-Blanc and Figeac – has more in common with Pomerol than with the rest of the appellation.

THE QUESTION OF QUALITY

The diverse nature of St-Émilion's soil has led to many generalizations that attempt to relate the quantity and character of the wines produced to the soils from which they come. Initially the wines were lumped into two crude categories, *côtes* (literally "hillside" or "slope") and *graves* (literally "gravelly terrain"). The term *côtes* was supposed to describe fairly full-bodied

CHÂTEAU FIGEAC
Without doubt in a class of its own within Class B of premiers grands crus classés, Château Figeac has long fought to be classified with Ausone and Cheval Blanc.

FACTORS AFFECTING TASTE AND QUALITY

LOCATION
St-Émilion is on the right bank of the Dordogne, 50 kilometres (80 miles) east of Bordeaux.

CLIMATE
The climate is less maritime and more continental than that of the Médoc, with a greater variation in daily temperatures – there is also slightly more rain during spring, and substantially less during summer and winter.

ASPECT
The village of St-Émilion sits on a plateau where vines grow at an altitude of 25 to 100 m (80 to 330 ft). These vineyards are quite steep, particularly south of the village where two slopes face each other. The plateau heads eastwards as hilly knolls. North and west of the village, the vineyards are on flatter ground.

SOIL
St-Émilion's soil is extremely complex (*see* The question of quality, *left*) and is part of the area known as "Pomerol-Figeac *graves*" that encompasses the châteaux Cheval Blanc and Figeac.

VITICULTURE AND VINIFICATION
Some of the *vin de presse*, usually the first pressing only, is considered necessary by many châteaux. Skin-contact usually lasts for 15–21 days, but may last up to four weeks. Some wines spend as little as 12 months in cask, but the average is nearer to 15–22 months.

GRAPE VARIETIES
Primary varieties: Cabernet Franc, Cabernet Sauvignon, Merlot
Secondary varieties: Carmenère, Malbec

A LARGE PRODUCTION

If you look at the map of the entire Bordeaux region (*see* p109) you will be amazed by how small this appellation of a thousand châteaux really is. It is a surprising but regular occurrence that an appellation as small as St-Émilion produces more wine than all the famous appellations of the Médoc combined – St-Estèphe, Pauillac, St-Julien, and Margaux.

SAINT-ÉMILION
Most of the highest-classified châteaux are located on the slopes around Saint-Émilion itself or to the northwest, where they neighbour the vineyards of Pomerol.

THE CLASSIFICATION OF ST-ÉMILION

St-Émilion wines were first classified in 1958, with the intention that the classification be revised every 10 years according to the performance of properties during the previous decade. Three basic categories were established: *premier grand cru classé*, *grand cru classé*, and *grand cru*. Of the 12 châteaux that were originally classified *premiers grands crus classés*, Ausone and Cheval-Blanc were placed in a superior subsection. The rest were listed alphabetically, not qualitatively, as were the 64 *grands crus classés*. The classification was revised in 1969, 1985 (some six years late), and again in 1996 and 2006 – which brought the reclassification period back to that anticipated. After the legal challenges, the 2006 classification was annulled – well, sort of – and the 1996 reinstated – sort of – until a new classification is introduced for the 2012 vintage. The 2006 classification kicked out 11 properties and brought in another four, but four of the 11 demoted properties took exception and made a legal fight. Much like the *cru bourgeois* classification fiasco (*see* p118), the only long-term solution was to set up a scrupulously fair reclassification under water-tight conditions and to agree a temporary situation that appeased everyone in the meantime. Unlike the *cru bourgeois*, the new St-Émilion classification will be revised every 10 years. It does, after all, infer a *grand cru classé title*, which must be imbued with some sort of longevity if its superior *terroir*-based status is to be believed. This new classification will be conducted under the auspices of seven INAO members, none of whom are from Bordeaux, let alone St-Émilion, and they will blind-taste 10 vintages (1999 to 2008, for 2012 classification) or 15 vintages if a promotion from *grand cru classé* to *premier grand cru classé* is envisaged. The tasting results will contribute at least 50 per cent of the final decision, with the balance accounted for by criteria such as quality of technical equipment, hygiene of the winery and historic reputation of the château and its wine.

In order to preclude the possibility of further legal challenges, the system has a built-in appeals procedure, allowing any individual property to appeal against its classification without challenging the entire classification. In order to have a clear run-up to the new 2012 classification, it was agreed to reinstate all the 2006 demotions and revert to the 1996 (although some properties have disappeared, *see below*) but additionally to take in all of the promotions from the 2006 classification. That makes everyone sufficiently happy to let INAO get on with its work.

Beware the distinction between *grand cru* (unclassified growths) and *grand cru classé* (classified growths) because the difference is considerable. In St-Émilion, *grand cru* merely indicates a minimum alcoholic strength 0.5% higher than that required by the basic St-Émilion appellation, and a slightly lower yield. Any producer may apply for a *grand cru*, and hundreds do so. It is not a classification, but merely an adjunct to the appellation, and would be more accurately conveyed as a new appellation called St-Émilion Supérieur, since the difference between St-Émilion and *grand cru* is akin to that between basic Bordeaux and Bordeaux Supérieur.

ST-ÉMILION CLASSIFICATIONS OF 1958, 1969, 1985, 1996, AND 2006
Incorporating vineyard soil classification

PREMIER GRAND CRU CLASSÉ CLASS A

1 Château Ausone
   Soil: *Côte and St-Émilion plateau*
2 Château Cheval Blanc
   Soil: *Graves and ancient sand*

PREMIER GRAND CRU CLASSÉ CLASS B

3 Château l'Angélus [7]
   Soil: *Pied de côte and ancient sand*
4 Château Beau-Séjour Bécot [1, 7]
   Soil: *St-Émilion plateau and côte*
5 Château Beauséjour (Duffau Lagarosse)
   Soil: *Côte*
6 Château Bélair [12]
   Soil: *St-Émilion plateau and côte*
17 Château Bellevue [11]
   Soil: *Côte and St-Émilion plateau*
7 Château Canon
   Soil: *St-Émilion plateau and côte*
8 Château-Figeac
   Soil: *Graves and ancient sand*
9 Clos Fourtet
   Soil: *St-Émilion plateau and ancient sand*
10 Château la Gaffelière
   Soil: *Côte, pied de côte*
11 Château Magdelaine
   Soil: *St-Émilion plateau, côte, and pied de côte*
12 Château Pavie
   Soil: *Côte and St-Émilion plateau*
64 Château Pavie Macquin [10]
   Soil: *St-Émilion plateau, côte, and sandy gravel*
79 Château Troplong Mondot [10]
   Soil: *St-Émilion plateau*
13 Château Trottevieille
   Soil: *St-Émilion plateau*

GRAND CRU CLASSÉ

14 Château l'Arrosée
   Soil: *Côte*
15 Château Baleau (now Château Côte de Baleau) [1, 3]
   Soil: *Côte and ancient sand*
16 Château Balestard la Tonnelle
   Soil: *St-Émilion plateau*

- Château Bellefont-Belcier [13]
   Soil: *St-Émilion plateau*
18 Château Bergat
   Soil: *Côte and St-Émilion plateau*
19 Château Berliquet [2]
   Soil: *Côte and pied de côte*
20 Château Cadet-Bon [1, 8, 11]
   Soil: *St-Émilion plateau and côte*
21 Château Cadet-Piola
   Soil: *St-Émilion plateau and côte*
22 Château Canon-la-Gaffelière
   Soil: *Pied de côte and sandy-gravel*
23 Château Cap de Mourlin
   Soil: *Côte and ancient sand*
- Château la Carte [4]
   Soil: *St-Émilion plateau and ancient sand*
- Château Chapelle-Madeleine [5]
   Soil: *Côte and St-Émilion plateau*
24 Château le Châtelet [9]
   Soil: *Côte and ancient sand*
25 Château Chauvin
   Soil: *Ancient sand*
26 Château Clos des Jacobins
   Soil: *Côte and ancient sand*
27 Château la Clotte
   Soil: *Côte*
28 Château la Clusière
   Soil: *Côte*
29 Château Corbin
   Soil: *Ancient sand*
30 Château Corbin Michotte
   Soil: *Ancient sand*
31 Château la Couspaude [1, 8]
   Soil: *St-Émilion plateau*
32 Château Coutet [1]
   Soil: *Côte*
- Château le Couvent [6]
   Soil: *St-Émilion plateau*
33 Couvent des Jacobins [3]
   Soil: *Ancient sand and pied de côte*
34 Château Croque Michotte [9]
   Soil: *Ancient sand and graves*
35 Château Curé Bon la Madeleine
   Soil: *St-Émilion plateau and côte*
36 Château Dassault [3]
   Soil: *Ancient sand*

- Château Destieux [13]
   Soil: *Côte*
37 Château la Dominique
   Soil: *Ancient sand and graves*
38 Château Faurie de Souchard [11]
   Soil: *Pied de côte*
- Château Fleur Cardinale [13]
   Soil: *St-Émilion plateau*
39 Château Fonplégade
   Soil: *Côte*
40 Château Fonroque
   Soil: *Côte and ancient sand*
41 Château Franc-Mayne
   Soil: *Côte*
42 Château Grand Barrail Lamarzelle Figeac [9]
   Soil: *Ancient sand*
43 Château Grand Corbin [14]
   Soil: *Ancient sand*
44 Château Grand-Corbin-Despagne [14]
   Soil: *Ancient sand*
45 Château Grand Mayne
   Soil: *Côte and ancient sand*
46 Château Grandes Murailles [1, 8]
   Soil: *Côte and ancient sand*
47 Château Grand-Pontet
   Soil: *Côte and ancient sand*
48 Château Guadet St-Julien
   Soil: *St-Émilion plateau*
49 Château Haut-Corbin
   Soil: *Ancient sand*
50 Château Haut-Sarpe [3]
   Soil: *St-Émilion and St-Christophe plateaux and côtes*
51 Château Jean Faure [1]
   Soil: *Ancient sand*
52 Château Laniote [3]
   Soil: *Ancient sand and pied de côte*
53 Château Larcis Ducasse
   Soil: *Côte and pied de côte*
54 Château Larmande
   Soil: *Ancient sand*
55 Château Laroque [8]
   Soil: *St-Émilion plateau and côte*
56 Château Laroze
   Soil: *Ancient sand*
57 Clos la Madeleine [9]
   Soil: *St-Émilion plateau and côte*
58 Château la Marzelle [11] (now Château Lamarzelle)
   Soil: *Ancient sand and graves*

59 Château Matras [3]
   Soil: *Pied de côte*
60 Château Mauvezin
   Soil: *St-Émilion plateau and côte*
- Château Monbousquet [13]
   Soil: *Côte*
61 Château Moulin du Cadet
   Soil: *Côte and ancient sand*
62 Clos de l'Oratoire [3]
   Soil: *Pied de côte*
63 Château Pavie Décesse
   Soil: *St-Émilion plateau and côte*
65 Château Pavillon-Cadet [9]
   Soil: *Côte and ancient sand*
66 Château Petit-Faurie-de-Soutard [11]
   Soil: *Ancient sand and côte*
67 Château le Prieuré
   Soil: *St-Émilion plateau and côte*
68 Château Ripeau
   Soil: *Ancient sand*
69 Château St-Georges (Côte Pavie)
   Soil: *Côte and pied de côte*
70 Clos St-Martin
   Soil: *Côte and ancient sand*
71 Château Sansonnet [9]
   Soil: *St-Émilion plateau*
72 Château la Serre
   Soil: *St-Émilion plateau*
73 Château Soutard
   Soil: *St-Émilion plateau and côte*
74 Château Tertre Daugay [3, 11]
   Soil: *St-Émilion plateau and côte*
75 Château la Tour Figeac
   Soil: *Ancient sand and graves*
76 Château la Tour du Pin Figeac [11, 15] (Owner: Giraud-Belivier)
   Soil: *Ancient sand and graves*
77 Château la Tour du Pin Figeac [11] (Owner: Moueix)
   Soil: *Ancient sand and graves*
78 Château Trimoulet
   Soil: *Ancient sand and graves*
- Château Trois-Moulins [4]
   Soil: *St-Émilion plateau and côte*
80 Château Villemaurine [11]
   Soil: *St-Émilion plateau*
81 Château Yon-Figeac [11]
   Soil: Ancient sand

See overleaf for chart notes and an explanation of soil types.

wines that develop quickly; the term *graves*, fuller, firmer, and richer wines that take longer to mature.

The simplicity was appealing, but it ignored the many wines produced on the stretch of deep sand between St-Émilion and Pomerol, and those of the plateau, which has a heavier topsoil than the *côtes*. It also failed to distinguish between the eroded *côtes* and the deep-soiled bottom slopes. But most importantly, it ignored the fact that many châteaux are spread across more

than one soil type (*see* the list of classified growths, *previous page*) and that they have various other factors of *terroir*, such as aspect and drainage, which affect the character and quality of a wine (*see* Soil Survey of St-Émilion, *below*).

The map below shows the positions of the 81 classified châteaux of St-Émilion, listed with their soil types (*see previous page*). Châteaux la Carte, Chapelle-Madeleine, le Couvent, and Trois-Moulins are listed but do not appear on the map (*see* Notes, *below*).

SOIL SURVEY OF ST-ÉMILION

The map below shows the area covered by *premier grand cru classé* and *grand cru classé* châteaux. Each soil type is described (*right*) and colour keyed on the map. The numbered châteaux are listed on the previous page.

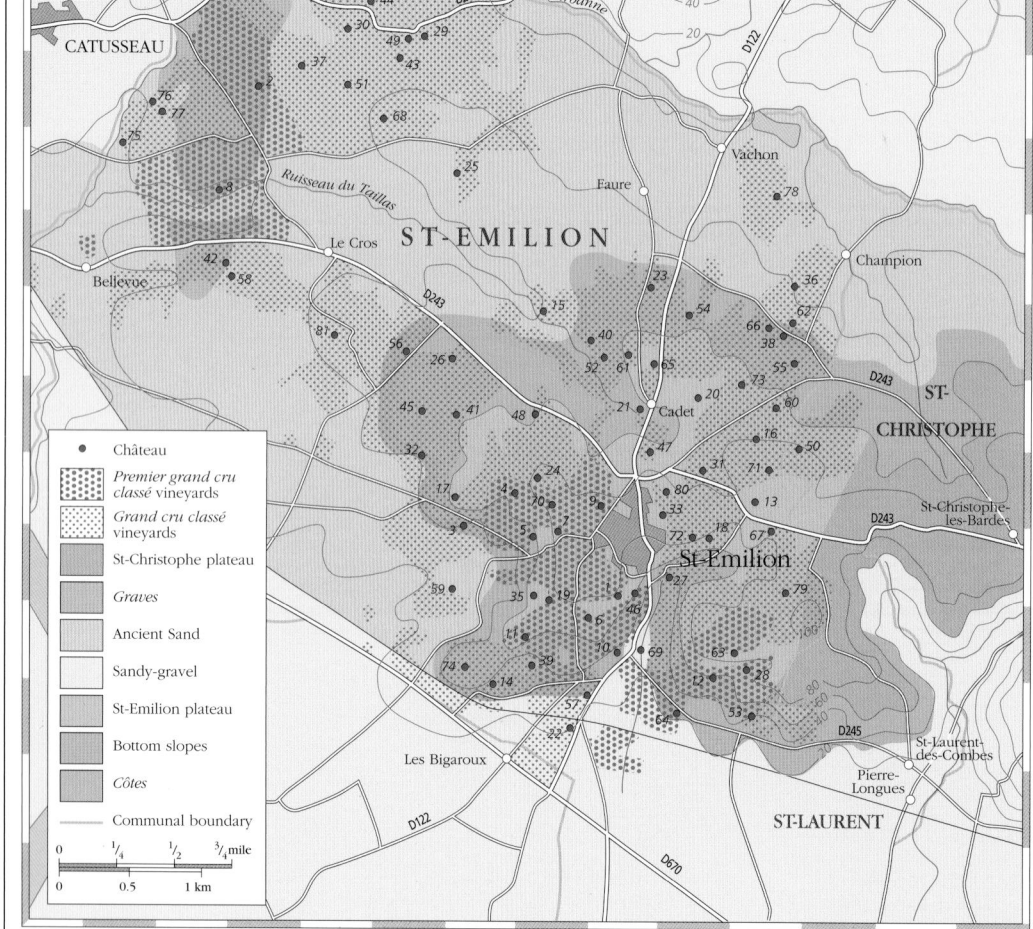

ST-CHRISTOPHE PLATEAU
Clay-limestone and clay-sand topsoil over limestone and *terra rossa* subsoil (a red, clay-like, limestone soil).

GRAVES
Deep gravel topsoil with a subsoil of large-grain sand over a very deep, hard, and impermeable sedimentary rock called *molasse*. The gravel is similar to that found in the Médoc.

ANCIENT SAND
Thick blanket of large-grain sand over a subsoil of *molasse*. The bulk of this sand extends northeast from the village of St-Émilion towards Pomerol. Although this area seems to have a gentle slope all round it, and the sand is very permeable, the *molasse* below is flat and impermeable. The water collects, saturating root systems and increasing soil acidity. Some châteaux benefit greatly from underground drainage pipes.

SANDY-GRAVEL
Sandy and sandy-gravel topsoil over sandy-gravel, ferruginous gravel, and iron-pan.

ST-ÉMILION PLATEAU
Shallow clay-limestone and clay sand, shell debris, and silt topsoil over eroded limestone subsoil.

BOTTOM SLOPES
The gentler bottom slopes of the *côtes* have a deep, reddish-brown, sandy-loam topsoil over yellow sand subsoil.

CÔTES
The lower-middle to upper slopes of the *côtes* have a shallow, calcareous, clay-silty-loam topsoil with a high active lime content. Quite sandy on the middle slopes, the topsoil thins out higher up. The subsoil is mostly *molasse*, not the impermeable type found under the ancient sand and *graves*, but a weathered, absorbent *molasse* of limestone or sandstone.

NOTES

[1] One *premier grand cru classé* and six *grands crus classés* demoted in the 1985 revision.

[2] This property was not in the original 1958 classification, nor was it included in the 1969 revision, but was awarded *grand cru classé* status in 1985.

[3] These properties were not in the original 1958 classification, but were awarded *grand cru classé* status in the 1969 revision.

[4] These two properties were merged with *premier grand cru classé* Château Beau-Séjour-Bécot in 1979. Wines bearing both labels can be found up to the 1978 vintage, and it is possible that they might reappear sometime in the future, particularly as the expansion of Château Beau-Séjour-Bécot vineyard was primarily responsible for its demotion in the 1985 classification.

[5] This property was merged with *premier grand cru classé* Château

Ausone in 1970. Wines with this label can be found up to the 1969 vintage.

[6] This property changed hands prior to the 1985 revision and did not apply to be considered; it was not demoted, but simply ignored.

[7] Properties promoted to *premier grand cru classé* (B) in 1996.

[8] Properties promoted to *grand cru classé* in 1996.

[9] Properties demoted in 1996.

[10] Properties promoted to *premier grand cru classé* (B) in 2006.

[11] Properties demoted in 2006 but reinstated until at least 2012.

[12] Now Château Bélair-Monange.

[13] Included for first time in 2006 and remains until at least 2012, even though the 2006 classification has been annulled.

[14] Demoted in 1996 but included in 2006.

[15] Now Château la Tour du Pin, the "Figeac" having been dropped by the new owners (Bernard Arnault and Albert Frère of Château Cheval Blanc).

THE WINE PRODUCERS OF
SAINT-ÉMILION

CHÂTEAU ANGÉLUS
Premier Grand Cru Classé (B)
★★

This is a large property with a single plot of vines on the south-facing *côtes*. At one time the château produced wines in the old "farmyard" style, but that ended with the 1980 vintage. Two-thirds of the wine is matured for 14 to 16 months in wood with 100 per cent new oak. This château is a rising star, and was promoted to *premier grand cru classé* (B) in 1996.

RED This is a soft, silky, and seductive wine. The luxury of new oak is having a positive effect on the quality, character, and ageing potential of this wine.

🍇 Cabernet Franc 50%, Merlot 45%, Cabernet Sauvignon 5%

🍷 7–20 years

Second wine: *Carillon de l'Angélus*

CHÂTEAU L'ARROSÉE
Grand Cru Classé
★☆♥

This property sits on the *côtes* above the local *coopérative*. Through excellent selection of only its finest grapes, it has consistently produced wines that are a class above those of many of its peers. Under new ownership (Roger Caille) since 2003.

RED A voluptuous bouquet, and soft, creamy-rich fruit backed up by supple oak tannin.

🍇 Merlot 50%, Cabernet Sauvignon 35%, Cabernet Franc 15%

🍷 5–15 years

Second wine: *Les Coteaux du Château l'Arrosée*

CHÂTEAU AUSONE
Premier Grand Cru Classé (A)
★★★

After gifted winemaker Pascal Delbeck took control of Château Ausone in 1975, this prestigious property produced wines of stunning quality, and it now deserves its superstar status. In 1997, after a power struggle between the two owners, Alain Vauthier took control, sacked Delbeck and hired Michel Rolland as consultant. The vineyard of Château Ausone has a privileged southeast exposure and its vines are fairly established at between 40 and 45 years of age. They are capable of yielding very concentrated wines, which are then matured in wood for between 16 and 22 months, with 100 per cent new oak.

RED These rich, well-coloured wines have opulent aromas and scintillating flavours. They are full in body, compact in structure, and refined in character, with masses of spicy-cassis fruit and creamy-oak undertones. These wines are the quintessence of class, complexity, and finesse.

🍇 Cabernet Franc 50%, Merlot 50%

🍷 15–45 years

CHÂTEAU BALESTARD LA TONNELLE
Grand Cru Classé
★

The label of this wine bears a 15th-century poem by François Villon that cites the name of the château. One-third of the wine is matured in 100 per cent new oak for up to 24 months, one-third is aged in two-year-old barrels, and the remainder rests in stainless-steel vats until bottling, when it is all blended together.

RED The gentle, ripe aromas of this wine belie its staunchly traditional style. It is a full-bodied wine of great extract, tannin, and acidity that requires time to soften, but it has masses of fruit, and so matures gracefully.

🍇 Merlot 65%, Cabernet Franc 20%, Cabernet Sauvignon 10%, Malbec 5%

🍷 10–30 years

Second wine: *Les Tourelles de Balestard*

CHÂTEAU BEAUSÉJOUR
(Owner: Duffau-Lagarosse)
Premier Grand Cru Classé (B)
★★

These little-seen wines consistently underwhelmed critics until the 1980s, since when Château Beauséjour began to produce darker, fuller wines with more class, but I was not that impressed until the stellar class 2000 vintage.

RED Lovely rich wine, with concentrated fruit, and great potential longevity from 2000 onwards.

🍇 Merlot 50%, Cabernet Franc 25%, Cabernet Sauvignon 25%

🍷 7–15 years

Second wine: *La Croix de Mazerat*

CHÂTEAU BEAU-SÉJOUR BÉCOT
Premier Grand Cru Classé (B)
★★

Since 1979, this property has almost doubled in size by merging with two *grands crus classés, Château la Carte and Château Trois Moulins*. In 1985, Beau-Séjour Bécot was the only *premier grand cru classé* to be demoted in the revision of the St-Émilion classification. The demotion was not due to its quality or performance, which were consistently excellent, but because of its expansion. In 1996 this château was promoted and is once again a *premier grand cru classé* (B). The wine is fermented in stainless steel and matured in wood for 18 months, with 90 per cent new oak.

RED Once lightweight and high-tone, this wine is now full, rich, and truly characterful. The silky Merlot fruit develops quickly, but is backed up with creamy new oak.

🍇 Merlot 70%, Cabernet Franc 15%, Cabernet Sauvignon 15%

🍷 7–25 years

Second wine: *La Tournelle des Moines*

CHÂTEAU BÉLAIR
Premier Grand Cru Classé (B)
★★

Pascal Delbeck, the winemaker formerly of Château Ausone, lives here and makes the wine with the same care and attention that he used to apply at Ausone. The wine is matured in wood for 16 to 20 months. Up to half is aged in new oak. This is one of the very best *premiers grands crus*.

RED This is a deep-coloured, full-bodied wine with a rich flavour of plums, chocolate, black cherries, and cassis. It has great finesse.

🍇 Merlot 60%, Cabernet Franc 40%

🍷 10–35 years

Second wine: *Roc Blanquet*

CHÂTEAU BELLEVUE
★★☆

This small property was originally called Fief-de-Bellevue and belonged to the Lacaze family from 1642 to 1938. Up to and through the 1990s, Bellevue was an underperformer at best, but since 2000 the wines have shown their true class under manager Nicolas Thienpont and ace consultant Stéphane Derenoncourt. So to be demoted from *grand cru classé* in 2006 was perverse.

RED Beautifully ripe fruit, sleek, with great finesse, and remarkably evocative of its *terroir*.

🍇 Merlot 67%, Cabernet Franc 16.5%, Cabernet Sauvignon 16.5%

🍷 5–10 years

CHÂTEAU BERGAT
Grand Cru Classé
❓

This small vineyard is jointly owned by Emile Castéja and the Preben Hansen family.

RED Medium-bodied, with ample fruit for easy drinking, and hints of oak on the finish.

🍇 Merlot 50%, Cabernet Franc 40%, Cabernet Sauvignon 10%

🍷 4–6 years

CHÂTEAU BERLIQUET
Grand Cru Classé
★☆

The only property upgraded to *grand cru classé* in 1985. The wine is fermented in stainless steel vats and matured in wood for 18 months, with 30 per cent new oak.

RED These are deep, dark, and dense wines with spicy-cassis fruit and good vanilla oak.

🍇 Merlot 70%, Cabernet Franc and Cabernet Sauvignon 30%

🍷 10–30 years

CHÂTEAU CADET-BON
★

This property was demoted from *grand cru classé* in 1985, reinstated in 1996, then demoted again in 2006! The last demotion was not as bewildering as Bellevue, but it was surprising nonetheless. However, under the wine wizardry of Stéphane Derenoncourt these wines stepped up another gear since 2004, ensuring that Cadet-Bon will be promoted once again in 2016.

RED From the 1990s until 2003, this wine was not the richest on the block, but it had an ampleness that made for easy, early drinking. Since 2004 there has been increasing richness, with a very fine, elegant tannin structure.

🍇 Merlot 60%, Cabernet Franc 40%

🍷 7–20 years

CHÂTEAU CADET-PIOLA
Grand Cru Classé
★

This property usually shows great consistency and exquisite style. Up to 50 per cent of the wine is matured in new oak.

RED These are full-bodied, intensely flavoured wines with powerful, new-oak character and great tannic strength.

🍇 Merlot 51%, Cabernet Sauvignon 28%, Cabernet Franc 18%, Malbec 3%

🍷 12–25 years

Second wine: *Chevalier de Malte*

CHÂTEAU CANON
Premier Grand Cru Classé (B)
★★ ✪

Many years ago, this château used to produce a second wine called "St-Martin-de-Mazerat", which was the old parish name before Château Canon was absorbed by St-Émilion. Excellent wines were made under Eric Forner and although he sold out in 1996 the quality has been maintained. In summer 2000 the new owners, Chanel Inc, bought the nearby property Curé Bon la Madeleine with INAO agreement to incorporate it into Canon from the 2000 vintage. So goodbye Curé Bon! The *grand vin*, fermented in oak vats and matured in wood for 20 months with 50 per cent new oak, is one of the best of St-Émilion's *premiers grands crus classés*.

RED These wines have a deep purple colour, an opulent cassis bouquet, and are very rich and voluptuous on the palate with masses of juicy Merlot fruit and spicy-complexity.

🍇 Merlot 55%, Cabernet Franc 40%, Cabernet Sauvignon 4%

🍷 8–30 years

Second wine: *Clos J Kanon*

CHÂTEAU CANON-LA-GAFFELIÈRE
Grand Cru Classé
★★ ☆

Owned since 1985 by Comte von Neipperg, Château Canon-la Gaffeliére is one of the oldest properties in St-Émilion. Its wines were fermented in stainless-steel vats until wooden vats were installed in 1997, and the quality soared the very next year. Malolactic fermentation is carried out in barrel and the wines are matured for 18 months, with up to 50 per cent new oak.

RED This wine has been on form since 1998. It has been really plump, displaying vivid, concentrated, spicy fruit, and finishing with creamy oak.

🍇 Merlot 65%, Cabernet Franc 30%, Cabernet Sauvignon 5%

🍷 8–20 years

Other wines: *Côte Mignon-la-Gaffelière*

CHÂTEAU CAP DE MOURLIN
Grand Cru Classé
★

Until 1982 there were two versions of this wine, one bearing the name of Jacques Capdemourlin and one that of Jean Capdemourlin. This property is run by Jacques. The wine is matured in wood for up to 24 months, with one-third new oak.

RED An improving, attractive, well-made, medium-bodied wine, with exquisitely fresh fruit, and a smooth finish.

🍇 Merlot 60%, Cabernet Franc 25%, Cabernet Sauvignon 12%, Malbec 3%

🍷 6–15 years

Second wine: *Mayne d'Artagnan*

CHÂTEAU LA CARTE
Grand Cru Classé

Since 1980, the vineyards of this property have been merged with those of *premier grand cru classé* Château Beau-Séjour-Bécot.

CHÂTEAU CHAPELLE-MADELEINE
Grand Cru Classé until 1996

Since 1971, these vineyards have been merged with those of *premier grand cru classé* Château Ausone.

CHÂTEAU CHAUVIN
Grand Cru Classé
★

This property's wine is matured in wood for 18 months, with one-third new oak. It is difficult to find, but its quality makes it deserving of better distribution.

RED When on form, Château Chauvin can have excellent colour, an aromatic bouquet, full body, and plummy fruit. More hits than misses these days, as the wines are made with an increasing degree of finesse.

🍇 Merlot 60%, Cabernet Franc 30%, Cabernet Sauvignon 10%

🍷 4–10 years

Second wine: *Chauvin Variation*

CHÂTEAU CHEVAL BLANC
Premier Grand Cru Classé (A)
★★★

The unusual aspect of this great wine is its high proportion of Cabernet Franc, which harks back to the pre-1956 era. Switching to a majority of Merlot vines was advantageous for most Libournais properties but keeping a proportion of 60 per cent Cabernet Franc was even better for Château Cheval Blanc. In 1998 this château was bought by two businessmen, Albert Frère from Belgium and Bernard Arnault, the head of LVMH. The wine is matured in wood for 20 months, with 100 per cent new oak.

RED These wines have all the sweet, spicy richness one expects from a classic St-Émilion property situated on *graves*.

🍇 Cabernet Franc 60%, Merlot 37%, Malbec 2%, Cabernet Sauvignon 1%

🍷 12–40 years

Second wine: *Le Petit Cheval*

CLOS FOURTET
Premier Grand Cru Classé (B)
★★ ☆ ✪

This property had an inconsistent record, but has steadily improved throughout the 1990s. The wines are matured in wood for 12 to 18 months, using 70 per cent new oak.

RED Opulent and medium-bodied with silky Merlot fruit, gaining in complexity and finesse.

🍇 Merlot 60%, Cabernet Franc 20%, Cabernet Sauvignon 20%

🍷 6–12 years

Second wine: *Domaine de Martialis*

CHÂTEAU CLOS DES JACOBINS
Grand Cru Classé
★

Clos des Jacobins, which is kept in the impeccable style to which all the Cordier properties are accustomed, is impressive even during "off-vintages".

RED These are rich, fat wines, bursting with chocolate and black-cherry flavours.

🍇 Merlot 85%, Cabernet Franc 10%, Cabernet Sauvignon 5%

🍷 8–25 years

CLOS DE L'ORATOIRE
Grand Cru Classé
★★

This property belongs to Stephan von Neipperg, who has developed a cult following for this wine. The wine is matured in wood for 18 months, with one-third new oak.

RED These fine, full-flavoured wines tend to have great concentration and style.

🍇 Merlot 75%, Cabernet Franc 25%

🍷 7–15 years

CLOS ST-MARTIN
Grand Cru Classé
★

These wines are made at Château Côte Baleau alongside those of that property and those of Château Grandes Murailles. Of these three wines, only Clos St-Martin retained *grand cru classé* status after the reclassification of 1985. It is aged in wood with 25 per cent new barrels every four years.

RED Vivid colour with ripe Merlot fruit, silky texture, and elegant style.

🍇 Merlot 75%, Cabernet Franc 25%

🍷 6–15 years

CHÂTEAU LA CLOTTE
Grand Cru Classé

This property is under the same ownership as the Logis de la Cadène restaurant in St-Émilion, where much of its wine is sold. The Libournais *négociant* Jean-Pierre Moueix takes three-quarters of the crop.

RED Although not as consistent as some *grands crus classés*, when successful this estate can make attractive and elegant wines with lots of soft, silky fruit that are a match for its peers.

🍇 Merlot 70%, Cabernet Franc 30%

🍷 5–12 years

CHÂTEAU LA CLUSIÈRE
Grand Cru Classé

This is a small enclave within the property of Château Pavie and is under the same ownership as Pavie and Château Pavie Décesse. This wine is fermented in stainless steel vats and matured in wood (two-year-old barrels from Château Pavie) for up to 24 months.

RED This wine has a certain elegance, but lacks finesse and has a high-tone style that does not appeal to me. To be fair, I must point out that those who appreciate this style often find la Clusière solid and characterful.

🍇 Merlot 70%, Cabernet Franc 20%, Cabernet Sauvignon 10%

🍷 5–10 years

CHÂTEAU CORBIN
Grand Cru Classé
★ ☆

This property has the same owners as Château Grand Corbin – the Corbin estate, which is now divided into five separate properties bordering the Pomerol district. The wine is fermented in stainless steel and one-third of the production is matured in 100 per cent new oak.

RED Deep-coloured, full-bodied, and deliciously rich, but rather rustic for a classified growth.

🍇 Merlot 67%, Cabernet Franc and Cabernet Sauvignon 33%

🍷 6–12 years

Other wines: *Latour Corbin, Château Corbin-Vieille-Tour*

CHÂTEAU CORBIN MICHOTTE
Grand Cru Classé
★

This is one of five Corbin and two Michotte estates! This wine is fermented in stainless steel and some is matured in wood, with one-third new oak.

RED A dark, deeply flavoured, full-bodied wine that has rich, juicy Merlot fruit and some finesse.

🍇 Merlot 65%, Cabernet Franc 30%, Cabernet Sauvignon 5%

🍷 6–15 years

Second wine: *Les Abeilles*

CHÂTEAU CÔTE DE BALEAU
Grand Cru Classé until 1985
★

This property was unjustly demoted from its *grand cru classé* status in the 1985 revision. Côte de Baleau deserves its former classification and is under the same ownership as Château Grandes Murailles and Clos St-Martin, the former of which was also unfairly demoted. This wine is aged in wood and 25 per cent of the barrels are renewed every four years.

RED Full, rich, and well-balanced wines that have good fruit, some fat, and an attractive underlying vanilla character.

🍇 Merlot 70%, Cabernet Sauvignon 20%, Cabernet Franc 10%

🍷 4–12 years

Second wine: *Des Roches Blanches*

CHÂTEAU LA COUSPAUDE
Grand Cru Classé
★

This property was demoted from its *grand cru classé* status in 1985 but, following a string of good vintages, was promoted back to its original classification in 1996, since when the quality has continued to improve. The wine is matured in wood, with up to 80 per cent new oak.

RED This wine now has lots of upfront, juicy-Merlot fruit with an increasing amount of finesse.

🍇 Merlot 60%, Cabernet Franc and Cabernet Sauvignon 40%

🍷 3–7 years

Second wine: *Hubert*

CHÂTEAU COUTET
Grand Cru Classé until 1985
❷

This property was demoted from its *grand cru classé* status in 1985. It has a record of producing finer wines than la Couspaude (*see* previous entry), but unfortunately has the same lack of consistency.

RED Most vintages have a light but elegant style, with a firm tannin structure.

🍇 Cabernet Franc 45%, Merlot 45%, Cabernet Sauvignon 5%, Malbec 5%

🍷 4–8 years

COUVENT DES JACOBINS
Grand Cru Classé
★

The wine from the young vines of this property is not included in its *grand vin*, but is used to make a second wine called "Château Beau Mayne". One-third of the production is matured in wood, with 100 per cent new oak.

RED The delicious, silky-seductive fruit in this consistently well-made wine is very stylish and harmonious.

CHÂTEAU CROQUE MICHOTTE
Grand Cru Classé until 1996
◉★

This property certainly deserves its former *grand cru classé* status. The wine is fermented in stainless steel and matured in wood for between 18 and 24 months, with up to one-third new oak.

RED A delightful and elegant style of wine, brimming with juicy, soft, and silky Merlot fruit.

🍇 Merlot 80%, Cabernet Franc and Cabernet Sauvignon 20%

🍷 5–12 years

CHÂTEAU CURÉ BON LA MADELEINE
Grand Cru Classé

Surrounded by *premiers grands crus classés* such as Ausone, Belair, and Canon, this property has had an excellent record, but was absorbed by Château Canon in the summer of 2000.

CHÂTEAU DASSAULT
Grand Cru Classé
★✯

This property was promoted to *grand cru classé* in the 1969 revision of the 1954 St-Émilion classification. It has an excellent record and more than deserves its classification. The wine is fermented in stainless steel and matured in wood for 12 months, with one-third of the casks being new oak, and undergoes as many as six rackings. With its beautifully understated Lafite-like label, Dassault's presentation is perfect.

RED Supremely elegant wines that always display a delicate marriage of fruit and oak in perfect balance, with fine acidity and supple tannin.

🍇 Merlot 65%, Cabernet Franc 20%, Cabernet Sauvignon 15%

🍷 8–25 years

Second wine: *Merissac*

CHÂTEAU LA DOMINIQUE
Grand Cru Classé
★★

This property, one of the best of the *grands crus classés*, is situated close to Château Cheval Blanc on the *graves* in the extreme west of St-Émilion. The wine is fermented in stainless-steel vats that are equipped with grilles to keep the *marc* (residue of seeds, stalks, and skin) submerged during the *cuvaison* (skin-contact fermentation). It is matured in wood for 24 months, with 50 per cent new oak.

RED Very open and expressive wines that are plump and attractive, full of ripe, creamy fruit with elegant underlying oak.

🍇 Merlot 60%, Cabernet Franc 15%, Cabernet Sauvignon 15%, Malbec 10%

🍷 8–25 years

Second wine: *St-Paul de la Dominique*

CHÂTEAU FAURIE DE SOUCHARD

This lacklustre underperformer was demoted from *grand cru classé* in 2006.

RED Recent vintages have increased in concentration and colour, but the wines are not special.

🍇 Merlot 65%, Cabernet Franc 26%, Cabernet Sauvignon 9%

🍷 4–7 years

Other wines: *Cadet-Peychez*

CHÂTEAU–FIGEAC
Premier Grand Cru Classé (B)
★★★

Some critics suggest that the unusually high proportion of Cabernet Sauvignon in the *encépagement* (varietal blend) of this great château is wrong, but owner Thierry de Manoncourt refutes this. He has bottles of pure varietal wines produced at Figeac going back 30 years. As far as I am concerned, his blended *grand vin* says it all every year. This château belongs with the elite of Ausone and its *graves* neighbour, Cheval Blanc. The wine is matured in wood for 18 to 20 months, with 100 per cent new oak.

RED Impressively ripe, rich, and concentrated wines with fine colour, a beautiful bouquet, stunning creamy-ripe fruit, great finesse, and a wonderful spicy complexity.

🍇 Merlot 30%, Cabernet Franc 35%, Cabernet Sauvignon 35%

🍷 12–30 years

Second wine: *La Grange Neuve*

CHÂTEAU FONPLÉGADE
Grand Cru Classé

Under the same ownership as Château la Tour du Pin Figeac, this property belongs to Armand Moueix, cousin of Jean-Pierre Moueix of Château Pétrus *et al*. The wine is matured in wood for 12 to 15 months, using one-third new oak.

RED I used to find this wine astringent and vegetal, earthy even, but then it appeared to pick up, only to lapse. There have been so many false starts in its perceived improvement that I no longer expect any consistency. Even though the best vintages (1982, 1990, 2000, and 2001) have been delightfully clean and attractive, literally bursting with the soft, ripe, juicy fruit flavours of raspberries and strawberries, mostly this is an austere, tannic wine with attenuated fruit, and lacking style.

🍇 Merlot 60%, Cabernet Franc 35%, Cabernet Sauvignon 5%

🍷 5–12 years

Second wine: *Clos Goudichaud*

CHÂTEAU FONROQUE
Grand Cru Classé
Ⓑ

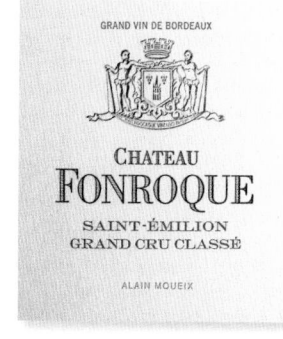

Located just northwest of St-Émilion itself, this secluded property has belonged to the négociant J-P Moueix since 1931. The wine is matured in wood for 24 months.

RED This is a deep-coloured, well-made wine with a fine plummy character that shows better on the bouquet and the initial and middle palate than on the finish.

🍇 Merlot 70%, Cabernet Franc 30%

🍷 6–15 years

CHÂTEAU LA GAFFELIÈRE
Premier Grand Cru Classé (B)
★★✯

This property belongs to Comte Léo de Malet-Roquefort, who also owns the very old estate of Château Tertre Daugay, a *grand cru classé*. After a string of aggressive, ungenerous vintages, Gaffelière has produced increasingly excellent wines since the mid-1980s. The wine is matured in wood for 18 months, with 100 per cent new oak.

RED These wines are concentrated and tannic, but they now have much more finesse, fat, and mouth-tingling richness than previously.

🍇 Merlot 65%, Cabernet Franc 20%, Cabernet Sauvignon 15%

🍷 12–35 years

Second wine: *Clos la Gaffelière*
Other wine: *Roquefort*

CHÂTEAU LA GOMERIE
Grand Cru
★★

Owned by Gérard and Dominique Bécot of Beau-Séjour-Bécot fame, I rather get the impression that the tiny production of this 100 per cent Merlot vinified in 100 per cent new oak is the vinous equivalent of sticking one finger up to the authorities. The unfair demotion of Beau-Séjour-Bécot in 1985 (rectified in 1996) was a cruel and unjustified blow to the Bécots, who had improved the quality of their wine. By producing an unclassified super-premium St-Émilion that demands and receives a higher price than its own *premier grand cru classé*, the Bécots have demonstrated that the classification is meaningless.

RED Masses of rich, ripe Merlot fruit dominate this wine, despite its 100 per cent new oak. A stunning wine that deserves its cult following.

🍇 Merlot 100%

🍷— 4–18 years

CHÂTEAU GRAND-CORBIN-DESPAGNE
Grand Cru Classé
☉★🅥

This part of the Corbin estate was bought by the Despagne family – hence the name. It was demoted in the 1996 St-Émilion Classification but reinstated in 2006. The wine is fermented in stainless steel and matured in wood for up to 18 months, with some new oak.

RED A well-coloured wine of full and rich body with plenty of creamy fruit and oak, supported by supple tannin.

🍇 Merlot 90%, Cabernet Franc 10%

🍷— 7–25 years

Second wine: *Reine-Blanche*

CHÂTEAU GRAND MAYNE
Grand Cru Classé
★☆🅥

This château ferments its wine in stainless-steel vats and ages it in wood with 80 per cent new oak.

RED This is a firm, fresh, and fruity style of wine that had a rather inconsistent reputation until the 1990s when the wines have had much more richness than in previous years.

🍇 Merlot 50%, Cabernet Franc 40%, Cabernet Sauvignon 10%

🍷— 4–10 years

Second wine: *Les Plantes du Mayne*
Other wines: *Cassevert, Château Beau Mazerat*

CHÂTEAU GRANDES MURAILLES
Grand Cru Classé
★

This property was demoted from its *grand cru classé* status in 1985, unjustly I think. The wines produced here are better and more consistent than those of many châteaux that were not demoted at that time. Château Grandes Murailles was, however, promoted back to its previous status in the 1996 St-Émilion Classification. It is under the same ownership as Château Côte de Baleau and Clos St-Martin, the former of which was also unfairly demoted. The wine is fermented in stainless steel vats and matured in wood for 20 months, using up to 25 per cent new oak.

RED These elegant, harmonious wines have good extract and a supple tannin structure that quickly softens. They are a delight to drink when relatively young, although they also age gracefully.

🍇 Merlot 60%, Cabernet Franc 20%, Cabernet Sauvignon 20%

🍷— 5–20 years

CHÂTEAU GRAND-PONTET
Grand Cru Classé
★☆🅥

Since 1980 this property has been under the same ownership as Château Beau-Séjour Bécot. The wine is matured in wood for 12–18 months with 50 per cent new oak.

RED After a string of very dull vintages, this property is now producing full-bodied wines of fine quality and character. They are fat and ripe, rich in fruit and tannin, with delightful underlying creamy-oak flavours.

🍇 Merlot 60%, Cabernet Franc and Cabernet Sauvignon 40%

🍷— 6–15 years

CHÂTEAU GUADET ST-JULIEN
Grand Cru Classé
★

This property deserves its status. The wines are matured in wood for 18 to 20 months, using up to one-third new oak.

RED These are wines that show the silky charms of Merlot very early, and then tighten up for a few years before blossoming into finer and fuller wines.

🍇 Merlot 75%, Cabernet Franc and Cabernet Sauvignon 25%

🍷— 7–20 years

CHÂTEAU HAUT-CORBIN
Grand Cru Classé
★

This wine is matured in wood for 24 months, with up to 20 per cent new oak. Same ownership as Canteneste, with a string of good vintages since the 1990s.

🍇 Merlot 70%, Cabernet Franc and Cabernet Sauvignon 30%

Second wine: *Vin d'Edouard*

CHÂTEAU HAUT-SARPE
Grand Cru Classé
★

Although not one of the top performers, this château certainly deserves its status. The wine is matured in wood for 20 to 22 months, using 25 per cent new oak.

RED Elegant, silky, and stylish medium-bodied wines that are best appreciated when young.

🍇 Merlot 70%, Cabernet Franc 30%

🍷— 4–8 years

CHÂTEAU L'HERMITAGE

Owned by Véronique Gaboriaud, a friend of *garagiste* Jean-Luc Thunevin, this well-sited property produces just 750 cases annually, with wines matured in 100 per cent new oak.

RED So succulent and luscious is the fruit, and so supple the tannins, that this wine is accessible from a remarkably youthful age, yet will still improve.

🍇 Merlot 60%, Cabernet Sauvignon 40%

🍷— 5–15 years

CHÂTEAU JEAN FAURE
Grand Cru Classé until 1985

This property was demoted from its *grand cru classé* status in 1985. I have not tasted vintages beyond 1983. The wine is matured in wood for 24 months, with 25 per cent new oak.

RED These wines have good colour and easy, attractive, supple fruit.

🍇 Cabernet Franc 60%, Merlot 30%, Malbec 10%

🍷— 3–8 years

CHÂTEAU LAMARZELLE
★

Under the same ownership as Grand Barrail Lamarzelle Figeac, this property preserved its classification in 1996, while the other château was demoted – only to follow suit in 2006.

RED Forward, fruity wines that have improved throughout the 1990s.

🍇 Cabernet Franc 80%, Merlot 20%

🍷— 3–7 years

CHÂTEAU LANIOTE
Grand Cru Classé
★

An old property that incorporates the "Holy Grotto" where St-Émilion lived in the 8th century. The wine is fermented and matured in wood with 25 per cent new oak.

RED Stylish medium-bodied wines, with plenty of fresh, elegant fruit.

🍇 Merlot 70%, Cabernet Franc 20%, Cabernet Sauvignon 10%

🍷— 6–12 years

CHÂTEAU LARCIS DUCASSE
Grand Cru Classé
★☆

This property, whose vineyard is situated on the Côte de Pavie, matures its wine in vat and wood for 24 months.

RED Fuller, richer wines in the 1990s, particularly in the best years.

🍇 Merlot 65%, Cabernet Franc and Cabernet Sauvignon 35%

🍷— 4–8 years

CHÂTEAU LARMANDE
Grand Cru Classé
★☆

Consistently one of the best *grands crus classés* in St-Émilion, fermented in stainless-steel vats and matured in wood for 12 to 18 months, with 35 to 50 per cent new oak.

RED These superb wines are typified by their great concentration of colour and fruit. They are rich and ripe with an abundancy of creamy cassis and vanilla flavours that develop into a cedarwood complexity.

🍇 Merlot 65%, Cabernet Franc 30%, Cabernet Sauvignon 5%

🍷— 8–25 years

Second wine: *Le Cadet de Larmande*
Other wine: *Des Templiers*

CHÂTEAU LAROQUE
Grand Cru Classé
★

Made a *grand cru classé* in 1996, this is one of three *grands crus classés* châteaux that are not situated in the commune of St-Émilion itself.

RED As smooth and fruity as might be expected, with good tannic edge and increasing oak influence.

🍇 Merlot 80%, Cabernet Franc 15%, Cabernet Sauvignon 5%

🍷— 4–16 years

Second wine: *Les Tours de Laroque*

CHÂTEAU LAROZE
Grand Cru Classé
★🅥

This 19th-century château was named Laroze after a "characteristic scent of roses" was found in its wines. The wine is matured in wood for one to three years.

RED The wine does have a soft and seductive bouquet, although I have yet to find "roses" in it. It is an immediately appealing wine of some finesse that is always a delight to drink early.

🍇 Merlot 50%, Cabernet Franc 45%, Cabernet Sauvignon 5%

🍷— 4–10 years

CHÂTEAU MAGDELAINE
Premier Grand Cru Classé (B)
★★🅥

This could be considered the Pétrus of St-Émilion. It is the grandest St-Émilion estate in the Jean-Pierre Moueix Libournais empire, but as fine as the *terroir* is, and as much as Moueix does to extract maximum quality, the *w*ine falls short of Pétrus. The wine matures in wood for 18 months, with a third new oak.

RED These well-coloured wines have excellent concentration, yet great finesse and a certain delicacy. The flavour is multi-layered with a long, elegant, and complex finish.

🍇 Merlot 80%, Cabernet Franc 20%

🍷— 10–35 years

CHÂTEAU MATRAS
Grand Cru Classé
★☆

This wine is matured in tank for 12 months, followed by 12 months in one-third new oak.

RED Fine, floral, and firm.

🍇 Cabernet Franc 60%, Merlot 40%

🍷— 6–15 years

CHÂTEAU MAUVEZIN
Grand Cru Classé
★☆

This property deserves its *grand cru classé* status. The wine is fermented and matured in new oak.

RED Some stunningly supple vintages since 2001, showing great oak-laden, aromatic finesse.

🍇 Cabernet Franc 50%, Merlot 40%, Cabernet Sauvignon 10%

⌛ 7–15 years

CHÂTEAU MONBOUSQUET
Grand Cru Classé
★★☆

This was hypermarket owner Gérard Perse's first venture into wine and he openly admits that he bought the property because of its beauty, rather than out of any detailed analysis of its viticultural potential. That said, he has, with the help of consultant Michel Rolland, taken this château to unbelievable heights and, having done so, set about analysing what could and should be purchased in St-Émilion from a purely viticultural perspective. He set his sights on Pavie and Pavie Décesse, which he purchased in 1998 and 1997. Monbousquet remains his home.

RED Voluptuous, velvety, and hedonistic, these wines lack neither complexity nor finesse, but they are so delicious to drink that their more profound qualities easily slip by. Or should that be slip down?

🍇 Cabernet Sauvignon 10%, Cabernet Franc 40%, Merlot 50%

⌛ 4–15 years

CHÂTEAU MONDOTTE
Grand Cru
★★

Since the 1996 vintage, Stephan von Neipperg's unclassified *vin de garage* has surpassed the quality and price of his excellent *grand cru classé* Château Canon-la-Gaffelière. Low yield, 100 per cent oak and ludicrous prices.

RED Extraordinary colour, density, and complexity for a wine that is not in the slightest bit heavy and makes such charming and easy drinking.

🍇 Cabernet Franc 10%, Merlot 90%

⌛ 5–20 years

CHÂTEAU MOULIN DU CADET
Grand Cru Classé
◉★Ⓥ

This château, which is farmed by the Libournais *négociant* J-P Moueix, is consistently one of the best *grands crus classés*. The wine is matured in wood for 18 months, with a small proportion of new oak.

RED These wines have good colour, a fine bouquet, delightfully perfumed Merlot fruit, excellent finesse, and some complexity. They are not full or powerful, but what they lack in size, they more than make up for in style.

🍇 Merlot 85%, Cabernet Franc 15%

⌛ 6–15 years

CHÂTEAU PAVIE
Premier Grand Cru Classé (B)
★★Ⓥ

This top-performing château was purchased in 1998 along with Pavie Décesse and La Clusière by Gérard Perse. Perse used to own a group of hypermarkets, but his love of fine wine began to take over his working life in 1993, when he purchased Monbousquet. The link between Pavie under its previous owners, the Valette family, and now is Michel Rolland, who has been retained as consultant. Although Pavie has produced some of the greatest wines of St-Émilion in recent decades, the obvious advantage for Rolland is that Perse has poured a small fortune into new installations. The wine is matured in wood for 18 to 24 months, with 100 per cent new oak.

RED Great, stylish wines packed with creamy fruit and lifted by exquisite new oak. Fabulous concentration since 1998, without losing any finesse, although I will keep an open mind about the 2003 for a decade or so!

🍇 Merlot 60%, Cabernet Franc 30%, Cabernet Sauvignon 10%

⌛ 8–30 years

CHÂTEAU PAVIE DÉCESSE
Grand Cru Classé
★★☆

This property was under the same ownership as Château Pavie when the Valette family were the owners, and still is under Perse. Although it is not one of the top *grands crus classés*, it is consistent and certainly worthy of its status.

RED Huge seachange in colour, quality, and concentration in the 1998 and 1999 vintage.

🍇 Merlot 60%, Cabernet Franc 25%, Cabernet Sauvignon 15%

⌛ 6–12 years

CHÂTEAU PAVIE MACQUIN
Premier Grand Cru Classé (B)
★★☆

This property was named after Albert Macquin, a local grower who pioneered work to graft European

vines on to American rootstock. These wines noticeably improved throughout the 1990s, with Nicolas Thienpont of Vieux Château Certan overseeing the production.

RED Much richer, with more fruit and new oak in recent years.

🍇 Merlot 75%, Cabernet Franc and Cabernet Sauvignon 25%

⌛ 4–8 years

CHÂTEAU PETIT-FAURIE-DE-SOUTARD
★★

Some poor wines produced in the mid-1990s and at the turn of the millennium resulted in demotion from *grand cru classé* in 2006, but great improvements from 2003 to 2005 should mean reinstatement in 2016. Half of its production is matured in wood for up to a year.

RED This wine has soft, creamy aromas on the bouquet, some concentration of smooth Merlot fruit on the palate, a silky texture, and a dry, tannic finish. It is absolutely delicious when young but gains a lot from a little bottle-age.

🍇 Merlot 60%, Cabernet Franc 30%, Cabernet Sauvignon 10%

⌛ 3–8 years

CHÂTEAU PIPEAU
Grand Cru
★Ⓥ

Up and coming château, Pipeau is matured in wood for 18 months, with 50 per cent new oak.

RED Rich, stylish and quite striking wines that are full of fruit, underpinned by creamy-smoky oak, and easier to drink younger than most St-Émilions.

🍇 Merlot 80%, Cabernet Franc 10%, Cabernet Sauvignon 10%

⌛ 4–10 years

CHÂTEAU LE PRIEURÉ
Grand Cru Classé
★☆

This property is under the same ownership as Château Vray Croix de Gay in Pomerol and Château Siaurac in Lalande-de-Pomerol. The wine produced here is matured in wood for 18 to 24 months, with 25 per cent new oak.

RED Light but lengthy wines of some elegance that are best enjoyed when young and fresh.

🍇 Merlot 60%, Cabernet Franc 30%, Cabernet Sauvignon 10%

⌛ 4–8 years

Second wine: *L'Olivier*

QUINAULT L'ENCLOS
Grand Cru
★Ⓥ

Increasingly impressive since being purchased by Dr Alain Raynaud in 1997, this wine is matured in wood for 18 months, with 100 per cent new oak.

RED Exceptionally concentrated and complex.

🍇 Merlot 80%, Cabernet Franc 10%, Cabernet Sauvignon 5%, Malbec 5%

⌛ 6–20 years

CHÂTEAU ST-GEORGES (CÔTE PAVIE)
Grand Cru Classé
★

Owned by Jacques Masson, this small property's vineyard is well situated, lying close to those of châteaux Pavie and la Gaffelière. The wine is fermented in stainless steel and matured in wooden casks for 24 months.

RED This is a delicious medium-bodied wine with plump, spicy-juicy Merlot fruit, made in an attractive early-drinking style that does not lack finesse.

🍇 Merlot 50%, Cabernet Franc 25%, Cabernet Sauvignon 25%

⌛ 4–8 years

CHÂTEAU SANSONNET
Grand Cru Classé until 1996
❷

Supposedly purchased in 1999 by François d'Aulan, the former owner of Piper-Heidsieck and the master puppeteer behind numerous wine-related deals ever since. One of my spies reports that the previous owner is still there. If d'Aulan is serious about taking this château on, then we can expect some investment and improvement. However, if it's just part of one of his deals, don't hold your breath.

RED This wine is inconsistent and many vintages lack concentration, but the 1982, even though it was very light for the year, remains supple and attractive.

🍇 Merlot 60%, Cabernet Franc 20%, Cabernet Sauvignon 20%

⌛ 3–7 years

CHÂTEAU LA SERRE
Grand Cru Classé
★Ⓥ

This is another property that is improving tremendously in quality. It occupies two terraces on St-Émilion's limestone plateau, one in front of the château and one behind. The wine is fermented in lined concrete tanks and matured in wood for 16 months with a small proportion of new oak.

RED This wine initially charms, then goes through a tight and sullen period, making it reminiscent of Château Guadet St-Julien. Their styles, however, are very different. When young, this is quite a ripe and plump wine, totally dominated by new oak. In time, the fruit emerges to form a luscious, stylish wine of some finesse and complexity.

🍇 Merlot 80%, Cabernet Franc 20%

⌛ 8–25 years

Second wine: *Menuts de la Serre*

CHÂTEAU SOUTARD
Grand Cru Classé
★ ☆ ❤

The large and very fine château on this estate was built in 1740 for the use of the Soutard family in summer. Vines have grown here since Roman times. The wine of Soutard is matured in wood for 18 months, with up to one-third new oak casks.

RED This dark, muscular, and full-bodied wine is made in true *vin de garde* style, which means it improves greatly while ageing. It has great concentrations of colour, fruit, tannin, and extract. With time it can also achieve great finesse and complexity.

🍇 Merlot 65%, Cabernet Franc 30%, Cabernet Sauvignon 5%

🍷 12–35 years

Second wine: *Clos de la Tonnelle*

CHÂTEAU TERTRE DAUGAY
Grand Cru Classé
★ ☆

This property was purchased in 1978 by Comte Léo de Malet-Roquefort, the owner of *premier grand cru classé* Château la Gaffelière. The wine of Château Tertre Daugay, which is matured in wood with one-third new oak, is excellent and is getting better by the vintage.

RED These wines are rich, plump, and fruity with a fine bouquet, ripe underlying oak, great finesse, and surprising longevity.

🍇 Merlot 60%, Cabernet Franc 30%, Cabernet Sauvignon 10%

🍷 7–20 years

Second wine: *De Roquefort*

Other wine: *Moulin du Biguey*

CHÂTEAU TERTRE-RÔTEBOEUF
★★

François Mitjavile's cult wine is yet more proof that the only important classification is made by the consumer. This was considered to be outrageously expensive before Mondotte. The price has not gone down, but in France you can get four or five bottles of Tertre-Rôteboeuf for the cost of one bottle of Mondotte.

RED Huge, oaky, complex, and cultish: the Leonetti of St-Émilion!

🍇 Cabernet Franc 20%, Merlot 80%

🍷 5–20 years

CHÂTEAU LA TOUR FIGEAC
Grand Cru Classé
★ ☆

This property was attached to Château Figeac in 1879 and today it is one of the best of the *grands crus classés*. The wine is matured in wood for 18 months, with one-third new oak.

RED These are fat and supple wines with a very alluring bouquet and masses of rich, ripe cassis fruit gently supported by smoky-creamy oak.

🍇 Merlot 60%, Cabernet Franc 40%

🍷 4–8 years

CHÂTEAU LA TOUR DU PIN FIGEAC
(Giraud-Bélivier)
❷

This property is run by André Giraud, who also owns Château le Caillou in Pomerol. Unfortunately, these wines have never impressed me and so I am unable to recommend them.

🍇 Merlot 75%, Cabernet Franc 25%

CHÂTEAU LA TOUR DU PIN FIGEAC
(Moueix)
★★

This property is one of the best of the *grands crus classés*. It is now part of the Armand Moueix stable of châteaux. The wine is matured in wood for 12 to 15 months, with one-third new oak.

RED These consistently well-made wines always show a beautiful balance of spicy-juicy Merlot fruit, creamy oak, and supple tannin.

🍇 Merlot 60%, Cabernet Franc 30%, Cabernet Sauvignon and Malbec 10%

🍷 6–15 years

CHÂTEAU TRIMOULET
Grand Cru Classé
★

This is an old property overlooking St-Georges–St-Émilion. The wine is matured in wood for 12 months, with 100 per cent new oak.

RED This well-coloured wine has an overtly ripe and fruity aroma, lots of creamy-oaky character, a fruit flavour, and supple tannin.

🍇 Merlot 60%, Cabernet Franc 20%, Cabernet Sauvignon 20%

🍷 7–20 years

CHÂTEAU TROIS-MOULINS
Grand Cru Classé

These vineyards have been incorporated with those of Château Beau-Séjour Bécot since 1979.

CHÂTEAU TROPLONG MONDOT
Premier Grand Cru Classé (B)
★★

This property is owned by Claude Valette and is run by his daughter Christine. Half the production is matured in wood for 18 months with 80 per cent new oak.

RED Since the introduction of temperature-controlled fermentation and a second wine in 1985, some critics have believed the quality of this wine to be on a par with that of a *premier grand cru classé*, but for me, Troplong Mondot came on stream with the sensational 1988, 1989, 1990, 1992, and 1996 (those between being merely excellent!).

🍇 Merlot 65%, Cabernet Franc and Malbec 20%, Cabernet Sauvignon 15%

🍷 4–8 years

Second wine: *Mondot*

CHÂTEAU TROTTEVIEILLE
Premier Grand Cru Classé (B)
★ ☆

This property has the reputation of producing a star wine every five years or so, interspersed by very mediocre wines indeed, but has been made very consistent since 1985, and now makes true *premier grand cru classé* quality wine every year. The wine is matured in wood for 18 months, with up to 100 per cent new oak.

RED The quality has dramatically improved since the mid-1980s. It has fabulous Merlot-fruit richness with new oak and the power of a true *premier grand cru classé*.

🍇 Merlot 50%, Cabernet Franc 40%, Cabernet Sauvignon 10%

🍷 8–25 years (successful years only)

CHÂTEAU VALANDRAUD
Grand Cru
★★

Owned by Jean-Luc Thunevin, Château Valandraud is one of St-Émilion's best-known *vins de garage*, although it has grown from its original small plot of 0.6 hectares (1.5 acres) to 4.5 hectares (11 acres), making it more of a *parc de stationnement*.

RED Wines that even Gary Figgins of Leonetti in Washington state might complain were too oaky!

🍇 Merlot 70%, Cabernet Franc 30%

🍷 6–25 years

CHÂTEAU VILLEMAURINE

Château Villemaurine belongs to Robert Giraud, which is a *négociant* concern owning not only this property, but also some 20 other *petits châteaux* in various Bordeaux districts. The wine is matured in wood for 18 to 24 months, with 50 per cent new oak. Demoted from *grand cru classé* in 2006.

RED These are full-bodied wines of excellent, spicy Merlot fruit, good underlying oak, and firm structure.

🍇 Merlot 70%, Cabernet Sauvignon 30%

🍷 8–25 years

Other wines: *Maurinus, Beausoleil*

CHÂTEAU YON-FIGEAC
★

This important property situated near Pomerol was demoted, surprisingly, in 2006. The wine is matured for 18 months with 100 per cent new oak.

RED This wine was merely attractive and easy-to-drink until 1997, since when it has shown admirable concentration of rich, spicy fruit of increasing complexity and finesse.

🍇 Merlot 80%, Cabernet Franc 20%

🍷 6–20 years

THE BEST OF THE REST

With more than a thousand châteaux in this one district, it not practical to feature every recommendable wine, thus I list here the best of the rest: châteaux that consistently make wine that stands out for either quality or value, sometimes both. Those marked with a star sometimes produce wines that are better than many *grands crus classés*.

*Château Bellefont-Belcier†
*Château Belregard-Figeac
*Château La Bienfaisance
*Château Cantenac (since 2002)
*Château Carteau Côtes Daugay
*Château Le Castelot
*Château Le Châtelet
Château Cheval Noir
*Château la Commanderie
*Château Destieux†
*Château Faugères
*Château Ferrand-Lartique (since 2003)

*Château la Fleur
*Château Fleur Cardinale†
*Château Fleur-Cravignac
*Château la Fleur Morange
Château la Fleur Pourret
*Château Fombrauge
*Château Fourtet (since 2001)
Château Franc Bigoroux
Château Grand Barrail Lamarzelle-Figeac
Château Grand Champs
*Château la Grave Figeac
*Château Haut Brisson
*Château Haut Plantey
*Château Haut-Pontet

*Haut-Quercus
Clos Labarde
Château Lapelletrie
*Château Laroque
*Lucia
*Château Magnan la Gaffelière
*Château Monbousquet
*Château Moulin-St-Georges
Château Patris
*Château Pavillon Figeac
*Château Petit-Figeac
Château Petit-Gravet
*Château Petit Val
Château Peyreau

*Château Pindefleurs
*Château Plaisance
Château de Pressac
Château Puy Razac
Château Roc Blanquant
*Château Rol Valentin (since 1999)
*Château Rolland
*Château Rolland-Maillet
Château Sansonnet
*Château Teyssier
Château Tour St-Christophe

† Promoted to *grand cru classé* in 2006.

POMEROL

The most velvety and sensuous clarets are produced in Pomerol, yet the traveller passing through this small and rural area, with its dilapidated farmhouses at every turn, few true châteaux and no really splendid ones, must wonder how this uninspiring area can produce such magnificently expensive wines.

THE PROSPERITY OF RECENT YEARS has enabled Pomerol's properties to indulge in more than just an extra lick of paint, but renovation can only restore, not create, and Pomerol essentially remains an area with an air of obscurity. Even Château Pétrus, which is the greatest growth of Pomerol and produces what for the last twenty years has been consistently the world's most expensive wine, is nothing more than a simple farmhouse.

There has been no attempt to publish an official classification of Pomerol wines, but Vieux Château Certan was considered to be its best wine in the 19th century. Nowadays, however, Pétrus is universally accepted as the leading growth. It commands prices that dwarf those of wines such as Mouton and Margaux, so could not be denied a status equivalent to that of a *premier cru*. Indeed, Le Pin has become considerably more expensive than Pétrus itself. If, like the 1885 classification, we classify Pomerol according to price, next would come Lafleur, followed by a group including L'Évangile, La Fleur-Pétrus, La Conseillante, Trotanoy and a few others, all of which can cost as much as a Médoc First Growth. It is difficult to imagine, but Pomerol was ranked as an inferior sub-appellation of St-Émilion until it obtained its independent status in 1900. Even then it was a long hard struggle, since even Pétrus did not become sought after until the mid-1960s.

FACTORS AFFECTING TASTE AND QUALITY

LOCATION
Pomerol is a small rural area on the western extremity of the St-Émilion district, just northeast of Libourne.

CLIMATE
The same as for St-Émilion (*see* p156).

ASPECT
This modest mound, with Château Pétrus and Château Vieux Certan situated at its centre, is the eastern extension of the Pomerol-Figeac *graves* (gravelly terrain). The vines grow on slightly undulating slopes that, over a distance of 2 km (1.2 miles), descend from between 35 and 40 m above sea level (115 and 130 ft) to 10 m (33 ft).

SOIL
Pomerol's soil is sandy to the west of the national highway and to the east, where the best properties are situated on the sandy-gravel soil of the Pomerol-Figeac *graves*. The subsoil consists of an iron-pan known as *crasse de fer* or *machefer*,

with gravel in the east and clay in the north and centre. The château of Pétrus lies in the very centre of the Pomerol-Figeac *graves*, on a unique geological formation of sandy-clay over *molasse* (sandstone).

VITICULTURE AND VINIFICATION
Some of Pomerol's châteaux use a proportion of *vin de presse* according to the requirement of the vintage. At Pétrus, the *vin de presse* is added earlier than is normal practice, in order to allow it to mature with the rest of the wine – this is believed to reduce harshness. The duration of skin-contact is usually between 15 and 21 days, but is sometimes as brief as ten days or as long as four weeks. The wines stay in cask for between 18 and 20 months.

GRAPE VARIETIES
Primary varieties: Cabernet Franc, Cabernet Sauvignon, Merlot
Secondary variety: Malbec

THE VINEYARDS OF VIEUX CHÂTEAU CERTAN
After Château Pétrus, this is one of the best wine-producing properties in Pomerol. A quaint signpost marks the boundary of the vineyard.

POMEROL, *see also p153*
The sleepy area of Pomerol and Lalande-de-Pomerol fans out above the riverside town of Libourne. None of the so-called "châteaux" is particularly imposing: among the most attractive are Château Nénin and Vieux Château Certan.

• The best château
• Other outstanding châteaux
• Selected great châteaux
— Communal boundary

THE WINE PRODUCERS OF

POMEROL

CHÂTEAU BEAUREGARD
★★ Ⓥ

An American architect who visited Pomerol after World War I built a replica of Beauregard called "Mille Fleurs" on Long Island, New York. Quality changed dramatically at Beauregard in 1985, two years before the arrival of Michel Rolland, who followed 1985's superb wine with others and was generally responsible for turning this château around. The wine is matured in wood for 24 months with 60 per cent new oak.

RED Firm, elegant, and lightly rich wine with floral-cedarwood fruit.

🍇 Merlot 48%, Cabernet Franc 44%, Cabernet Sauvignon 6%, Malbec 2%

🍷 5–10 years

Second wine: *Le Benjamin de Beauregard*

CHÂTEAU BONALGUE

This small property lies on gravel and sand northwest of Libourne. The wine is matured in wood.

RED This medium- to full-bodied wine has always been of respectable quality with a frank attack of refreshing fruit flavours, a supple tannin structure, and a crisp finish.

🍇 Merlot 65%, Cabernet Franc and Cabernet Sauvignon 30%, Malbec 5%

🍷 5–10 years

Second wine: *Burgrave*

CHÂTEAU LE BON PASTEUR
★

This good and steadily improving wine is matured in wood for 24 months, with 35 per cent new oak.

RED These intensely coloured, full-bodied, complex wines are packed with cassis, plum, and black-cherry flavours.

🍇 Merlot 75%, Cabernet Franc 25%

🍷 8–25 years

CHÂTEAU BOURGNEUF-VAYRON
★Ⓥ

This property is situated close to Château Trotanoy. It has an honourable, if not exciting, record and a 10-hectare (25-acre) vineyard.

RED Made in a quick-maturing style with soft fruit and a light herbal finish.

🍇 Merlot 85%, Cabernet Franc 15%

🍷 4–8 years

CHÂTEAU LA CABANNE
★

This is a fine estate producing increasingly better wine. The wine is matured in wood for 18 months, with one-third new oak.

RED These medium-bodied, sometimes full-bodied, wines have fine, rich, chocolaty fruit.

🍇 Merlot 60%, Cabernet Franc 30%, Malbec 10%

🍷 7–20 years

Second wine: *Domaine de Compostelle*

CHÂTEAU CERTAN DE MAY DE CERTAN
★★

This can be a confusing wine to identify because the "De May de Certan" part of its name is in very small type on the label and it is usually referred to as "Château Certan de May". It is matured in wood for 24 months, with 50 per cent new oak.

RED This is a firm and tannic wine that has a powerful bouquet bursting with fruit, spice, and vanilla.

🍇 Merlot 65%, Cabernet Franc 25%, Cabernet Sauvignon and Malbec 10%

🍷 15–35 years

CHÂTEAU CLINET
★☆

This wine, which is matured in wood with one-third new oak, has undergone a revolution in recent years. It used to disappoint those looking for the typically fat, gushy-juicy style of Pomerol, and critics often blamed this on the wine's high proportion of Cabernet Sauvignon. The 1985 vintage was more promising (a touch plumper than previous vintages, with more juicy character), so Clinet's previous lack of typical Pomerol character was evidently not entirely due to the blend of grape varieties, although the vineyard has since undergone a radical change in varietal proportions. There was talk of a turnaround in quality beginning with the 1986 vintage, but it was not until the stunning 1989 and 1990 vintages that we really saw this wine take off. There has, however, been inconsistency, going through phases of better, and not so good, quality, although currently on the up.

RED Château Clinet is now producing exceedingly fine, rich, ripe wine with ample, yet supple tannin structure mixed with oaky tannins to produce a creamy-herbal-menthol complexity.

🍇 Merlot 75%, Cabernet Sauvignon 15%, Cabernet Franc 10%

🍷 7–20 years

CLOS DU CLOCHER
★☆ Ⓥ

This belongs to the Libournais *négociant* Audy. The wine is rotated in thirds between new oak, one-year-old casks, and vat, and is one of the most undervalued Pomerols.

RED These are deliciously deep-coloured, attractive, medium-bodied, sometimes full-bodied, wines that have plenty of plump, ripe fruit, a supple structure, intriguing vanilla undertones, and plenty of finesse.

🍇 Merlot 80%, Cabernet 20%

🍷 8–20 years

Second wine: *Esprit de Clocher*

Other wine: *Château Monregard-Lacroix*

CLOS L'ÉGLISE
★☆

There are several "Église" properties in Pomerol. The wine from this one is matured in wood for 24 months, with some new oak.

RED A consistently attractive wine with elegant, spicy Merlot fruit and firm structure; it is eventually dominated by violet Cabernet perfumes.

🍇 Merlot 55%, Cabernet Sauvignon 25%, Cabernet Franc 20%

🍷 6–15 years

Second wine: *La Petite Église*

CLOS RENÉ
★Ⓥ

This property is situated just south of l'Enclos on the western side of the N89. The wine is matured in wood for 24 months with up to 15 per cent new oak. An underrated wine, it represents good value.

RED These wines have a splendid spicy-blackcurrant bouquet, plenty of fine plummy fruit on the palate, and a great deal of finesse. They are sometimes complex in structure, and are always of excellent quality.

🍇 Merlot 60%, Cabernet Franc 30%, Malbec 10%

🍷 6–12 years

Other wine: *Moulinet-Lasserre*

CHÂTEAU LA CONSEILLANTE
★★☆

If Pétrus is rated a "megastar", this property must be rated at least a "superstar" in the interests of fairness. The wine is matured in wood for 20 to 24 months, with 50 per cent new oak.

RED This wine has all the power and concentration of the greatest wines of Pomerol, but its priorities

are its mindblowing finesse and complexity.

🍇 Cabernet Franc 45%, Merlot 45%, Malbec 10%

🍷 10–30 years

CHÂTEAU LA CROIX
★

This property's wine is matured in wood for 20 to 24 months.

RED These attractive wines are quite full-bodied, yet elegant and quick-maturing, with fine, spicy Merlot fruit.

🍇 Merlot 60%, Cabernet Sauvignon 20%, Cabernet Franc 20%

🍷 5–10 years

Second wine: *Le Gabachot*

CHÂTEAU LA CROIX DE GAY
★

This property is situated in the north of Pomerol on sandy-gravel soil, and the wine is matured in wood for 18 months, with up to 100 per cent new oak.

RED Used to be somewhat lightweight, but attractive, with easy-drinking qualities, the fruit in Croix de Gay has plumped-up in recent vintages.

🍇 Merlot 80%, Cabernet Sauvignon 10%, Cabernet Franc 10%

🍷 4–8 years

Other wines: *Château le Commandeur, Vieux-Château-Groupey*

CHÂTEAU LA CROIX-ST-GEORGES
★

Under the same ownership as Château La Croix-de-Gay, this wine is matured in wood for 18 months, with 100 per cent new oak.

RED Rich, soft and seductive.

🍇 Merlot 95%, Cabernet Franc 5%

🍷 4–10 years

Other wines: *Château le Commandeur, Vieux-Château-Groupey*

CHÂTEAU DU DOMAINE DE L'ÉGLISE

This is the oldest estate in Pomerol. The wine is matured in wood for 18 to 24 months, with one-third new oak.

RED This is another attractive, essentially elegant wine that is light in weight and fruit.

Merlot 90%, Cabernet Franc 10%

4–8 years

CHÂTEAU L'ÉGLISE-CLINET
★★

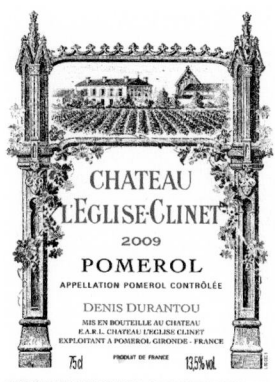

The wine produced by Château L'Église-Clinet, which is matured in wood for up to 24 months with as much as 50 per cent new oak, is fast becoming one of the most exciting Pomerols. Quality in overdrive since the 1990s.

RED These are deeply coloured wines with a rich, seductive bouquet and a big, fat flavour bursting with spicy blackcurrant fruit and filled with creamy-vanilla oak complexity.

Merlot 80%, Cabernet Franc 20%

8–30 years

Second wine: *La Petite l'Église*

CHÂTEAU L'ENCLOS
★ⓥ

The vineyard is situated on an extension of the sandy-gravel soil from the better side of the N89. The wine is matured in wood for 20 months, with a little new oak.

RED These are deliciously soft, rich, and voluptuous wines, full of plump, juicy Merlot fruit and spice.

Merlot 80%, Cabernet Franc 19%, Malbec 1%

7–15 years

CHÂTEAU L'ÉVANGILE
★★★⯪

Situated close to two superstars of Pomerol, Vieux Château Certan and Château la Conseillante, this château produces stunning wines that are matured in wood for 15 months with 40 per cent new oak.

RED Dark but not brooding, these fruity wines are rich, and packed with summer fruits and cedarwood. More Merlot and new oak

since 1998 has given the wine more generosity.

Merlot 78%, Cabernet Franc 22%

8–20 years

CHÂTEAU FEYTIT-CLINET
★

J-P Moueix, who is not this château's owner, does produce the wine and sells it on an exclusivity basis. Some vines are over 70 years old. The wine is matured in wood for 18 to 22 months.

RED Consistently well-coloured and stylish wines that are full of juicy plum and black-cherry flavours.

Merlot 80%, Cabernet Franc 20%

7–15 years

CHÂTEAU LA FLEUR-DE-GAY
★★⯪

Owned by the Raynaud family, with the ubiquitous Michel Rolland consulting, this wine is matured in wood for 18 months, with 100 per cent new oak.

RED Big, concentrated fuit underpinned by firm tannic structure.

Merlot 100%

8–20 years

CHÂTEAU LA FLEUR-PÉTRUS
★★

Château La Fleur-Pétrus, producer of one of the best Pomerols, is situated close to Château Pétrus, but on soil that is more gravelly. Four hectares (10 acres) of Château le Gay were purchased in 1994 and incorporated in this property, fattening out the style. The wine is matured in wood for 18 to 22 months.

RED Although recent vintages are relatively big and fat, these essentially elegant wines rely more on exquisiteness than richness. They are silky, soft, and supple.

Merlot 80%, Cabernet Franc 20%

6–20 years

CHÂTEAU LE GAY
★ⓥ

This is another château exclusive to the Libournais *négociant* J-P Moueix. The wine is matured in wood for 18 to 22 months.

RED Firm and ripe, this big wine is packed with dense fruit and coffee-toffee oak.

Merlot 70%, Cabernet Franc 30%

10–25 years

CHÂTEAU GAZIN
★⯪ⓥ

This château's record was disappointing until the stunning 1985 vintage, and it has been on a roll ever since, having abandoned harvesting by machine, introduced new, thermostatically controlled vats, and employed various quality-enhancing practices, not the least being a second wine, which

enables stricter selection of grapes. The wine is matured in wood for 18 months with up to one-third new oak.

RED Marvellously ripe and rich wine with plump fruit. It should have a great future.

Merlot 80%, Cabernet Franc 15%, Cabernet Sauvignon 5%

8–20 years

Second wine: *Hospitalet de Gazin*

CHÂTEAU LA GRAVE
★

The gravelly vineyard of this property has an excellent location. The Trignant de Boisset element of this château's name has been dropped. It is owned by Christian Moueix and farmed by J-P Moueix. The wine is matured in wood with 25 per cent new oak.

RED Supple, rich and fruity, medium-bodied wines of increasing finesse.

Merlot 85%, Cabernet Franc 15%

7–15 years

CHÂTEAU HOSANNA
★⯪ⓥ

This property was called Château Certan-Marzelle until 1956 and was purchased in 1999 by Jean-Paul Moueix, with Christian Moueix in control. Almost immediately 4 hectares (10 acres) of less well-positioned vineyards were sold to Nénin and strict selection imposed on the 1999 vintage. Watch this space! The wine is matured in wood for 24 months, with 15 per cent new oak.

RED These ripe, voluptuous wines become darker and denser since 1999.

Merlot 67%, Cabernet Franc and Cabernet Sauvignon 33%

8–20 years

Second wine: *Clos du Roy*
Other wine: *Château Certan-Marzelle*

CHÂTEAU LAFLEUR
★★★⯪

This property has a potential for quality second only to Château Pétrus itself, but it has a very inconsistent record. The quality and concentration of the wines have soared since 1985.

RED This is a well-coloured wine with a rich, plummy-porty bouquet, cassis fruit, a toasty-coffee oak complexity and great finesse.

Cabernet Franc 50%, Merlot 50%

10–25 years

Second wine: *Les Pensées de Lafleur*

CHÂTEAU LAFLEUR-GAZIN
★

This property has been run by the J-P Moueix team on behalf of its owners since 1976. It produces a wine that is matured in wood for 18 to 22 months.

RED Well-made wines of good colour and bouquet, supple structure, and some richness and concentration.

Merlot 70%, Cabernet Franc 30%

6–15 years

CHÂTEAU LAGRANGE
★ⓥ

Not to be confused with its namesake in St-Julien, this property belongs to the firm J-P Moueix. The wine is aged in wood for 18 to 22 months, with some new oak.

RED The recent vintages of this full-bodied wine have been very impressive, with an attractive and accessible style.

Merlot 90%, Cabernet Franc 10%

8–20 years

CHÂTEAU LATOUR À POMEROL
★★ⓥ

Château Latour à Pomerol now belongs to the last surviving sister of Madame Loubat, Madame Lily Lacoste (owner of one-third of Château Pétrus). The wine is matured in wood with 25 per cent new oak.

RED These deep, dark wines are luscious, voluptuous, and velvety. They have a great concentration of fruit and a sensational complexity of flavours.

Merlot 90%, Cabernet Franc 10%

12–35 years

CHÂTEAU MAZEYRES
★

Two-thirds of this wine is matured in wood with 40 per cent new oak, and one-third is aged in vat.

RED These elegant wines are rich, ripe, and juicy, and have silky Merlot fruit and some oaky finesse.

Merlot 70%, Cabernet Franc 30%

5–12 years

CHÂTEAU MOULINET
★ⓥ

This large estate belongs to Armand Moueix. The wine is matured in wood for 18 months, with one-third new oak.

RED These red wines are attractively supple with a light, creamy-ripe fruit and oak flavour.

🍇 Merlot 60%, Cabernet Sauvignon 30%, Cabernet Franc 10%

🍷 5–10 years

CHÂTEAU NÉNIN
★

A large and well-known property between Catussau and the outskirts of Libourne. The wine has had a disappointing record, but there has been a noticeable improvement since this property was purchased by Jean-Hubert Delon in 1997, who added 4 hectares (10 acres) from Certan-Giraud.

RED No similarity to Nenin of the past, vintages from 1998 onwards have been increasingly full, deep, and concentrated, with a lush, opulent fruit, and a silky finish.

🍇 Merlot 75%, Cabernet Franc 25%

🍷 5–18 years

Second wine: 🗸 *Fugue de Nenin*

CHÂTEAU PETIT-VILLAGE
★★

This property borders Vieux Château Certan and Château La Conseillante, and it therefore has the advantage of a superb *terroir* and a meticulous owner. The result is a wine of superstar quality, even in poor years. Petit-Village is matured in wood for 18 months with at least 50 per cent of the casks made from new oak.

RED These wines seem to have everything. Full and rich with lots of colour and unctuous fruit, they have a firm structure of ripe and supple tannins and a luscious, velvety texture. Classic, complex, and complete.

🍇 Merlot 80%, Cabernet Franc 10%, Cabernet Sauvignon 10%

🍷 8–30 years

CHÂTEAU PÉTRUS
★★★

The Libournais *négociant* Jean-Pierre Moueix was in technical control of this estate from 1947 until his death at the age of 90 in March 2003. Before the previous owner, Madame Loubat, died in 1961, she gave one-third of Pétrus to Monsieur Moueix. She had no children, just two sisters who were not on the best of terms, so Madame Loubat wisely gave Moueix the means of ensuring that family disagreements would not be able to harm the day-to-day running of Château Pétrus. In 1964 Moueix purchased one of the other two shares and his family has controlled the destiny of this world-famous château ever since.

RED The low acidity of Château Pétrus makes it an intrinsically soft wine which, when combined with the inherent lusciousness of the Merlot grape, enables Pétrus to produce intensely coloured, super-concentrated wines that would otherwise be too harsh to drink.

🍇 Merlot 95%, Cabernet Franc 5%

🍷 20–50 years

CHÂTEAU LE PIN
★★

This tiny property was purchased in 1979 by the late Jacques Thienpont. The yield is very low, the wine is fermented in stainless steel and matured in wood for 18 months with 100 per cent new oak.

RED These oaky wines are very full-bodied, and powerfully aromatic with a sensational spicy-cassis flavour dominated by decadently rich, creamy-toffee, toasty-coffee oak. Those who are not convinced by Le Pin keep asking whether there is enough concentration in these wines to match the oak; my guess is that there is, and that their wonderfully voluptuous style belies their true size and structure, but it will be a long time before we really know the answer.

🍇 Merlot 100%

🍷 10–40 years

CHÂTEAU PLINCE
★♥

This property is owned by the Moreau family, but its wines are sold by the Libournais *négociant* J-P Moueix. It is matured in vats for six months and in wood for 18 months, with 15 per cent new oak.

RED These wines are fat, ripe, and simply ooze with juicy Merlot flavour. Although they could not be described as aristocratic, they are simply delicious.

🍇 Merlot 75%, Cabernet Franc 20%, Cabernet Sauvignon 5%

🍷 4–8 years

CHÂTEAU LA POINTE
♥

After hoping that the mid-1980s would prove to be a turning point in the reputation of this important château, it now seems that this did not happen until 1998, although there is still a lot of room for improvement, before La Pointe can be described as a truly lush Pomerol.

RED Lightweight, lacklustre wines until 1998, when they have shown more fruit, with plummy-chocolaty overtones. Getting there.

🍇 Merlot 80%, Cabernet Franc 15%, Malbec 5%

🍷 5–12 years

Second wine: *La Pointe Riffat*

CHÂTEAU ROUGET
★♥

One of the oldest properties in Pomerol. The proprietor also owns the neighbouring estate of Vieux Château des Templiers. The wine is matured in wood for 24 months.

RED Château Rouget produces excellent red wines with a fine bouquet and elegant flavour. Fat and rich, with good structure and lots of ripe fruit, they are at their most impressive when mature.

🍇 Merlot 90%, Cabernet Franc 10%

🍷 10–25 years

CHÂTEAU DE SALES
★♥

At 48 hectares (119 acres), this is easily the largest property in the Pomerol appellation. It is situated in the very northwest of the district. Despite an uneven record, it has demonstrated its potential and inherent qualities on many occasions and the wine, which is matured in wood for 18 months with 35 per cent new oak, is one to watch for the future.

RED When successful, these wines have a penetrating bouquet and a palate jam-packed with deliciously juicy flavours of succulent stone-fruits such as plums, black cherries, and apricots.

🍇 Merlot 70%, Cabernet Franc 15%, Cabernet Sauvignon 15%

🍷 7–20 years

Second wine: *Château Chantalouette*

Other wine: *Château de Délias*

CHÂTEAU DU TAILHAS

The wines of this château are matured in wood for 18 months with 50 per cent new oak.

RED Consistently attractive, with silky Merlot fruit and creamy oak.

🍇 Merlot 80%, Cabernet Franc 10%, Cabernet Sauvignon 10%

🍷 5–12 years

CHÂTEAU TAILLEFER

This potentially excellent property belongs to Bernard Moueix. The wines are matured in wood for between 18 and 22 months, with the addition of some new oak.

RED At best these wines are attractively light and fruity, revealing their potential, but more often than not they are simply light and dilute. The 2000 was the best vintage this château has produced, but it was very difficult not to make fine wine that year.

🍇 Merlot 55%, Cabernet Franc 30%, Cabernet Sauvignon 15%

🍷 4–8 years

Second wine: *Clos Toulifaut*

CHÂTEAU TROTANOY
★★★

Some consider this to be second only to Château Pétrus, although in terms of price L'Évangile and Lafleur have overtaken it. The wine is matured in wood for up to 24 months, with 50 per cent new oak.

RED This inky-black, brooding wine has a powerful bouquet and a rich flavour, which is supported by a firm tannin structure and a complex, creamy-toffee, spicy-coffee oak character.

🍇 Merlot 90%, Cabernet Franc 10%

🍷 15–35 years

VIEUX CHÂTEAU CERTAN
★★★

This was once regarded as the finest-quality growth in Pomerol. It has not so much dropped its standards as witnessed the rapid rise of a new star – Pétrus – and all its pretenders. Vieux Château Certan remains one of Bordeaux's great wines. This wine is matured in wood for 18 to 24 months with up to 60 per cent new oak.

RED This is an attractive, garnet-coloured, full-bodied wine that has a smouldering, smooth, and mellow flavour. It displays great finesse and complexity of structure.

🍇 Merlot 50%, Cabernet Franc 25%, Cabernet Sauvignon 20%, Malbec 5%

🍷 12–35 years

Second wine: *La Gravette de Certan*

CHÂTEAU LA VIOLETTE
★

In the same way as Château Laroze in St-Émilion is said to be named after its aroma of roses, so this château is named after its aroma of violets – or so the story goes. It is located in Catussau and its vineyards are scattered about the commune. The wine, matured in wood for up to 24 months, can be inconsistent, but I think it has great potential.

RED I have not tasted this wine as frequently as I would like, but I can enthusiastically recommend the best vintages, when they have a rich and jubilant flavour of Merlot fruit, which is ripe and fat.

🍇 Merlot 95%, Cabernet Franc 5%

🍷 5–15 years

CHÂTEAU VRAY CROIX DE GAY

A small property on good gravelly soil next to Château le Gay and under the same ownership as Château le Prieuré. The wine is matured in wood in 18 months.

RED The wine can be full, rich, chocolate- and black-cherry-flavoured, with the best vintages showing more fat and oak.

🍇 Merlot 80%, Cabernet Franc 15%, Cabernet Sauvignon 5%

🍷 5–10 years

THE WINE PRODUCERS OF THE FRONSADAIS AND THE
SAINT-ÉMILION AND POMEROL SATELLITES

DOMAINE DE L'A
AOC Bordeaux-Côtes-de-Castillon
★✫🅑

The home of ace consultant Stéphane Derenoncourt, and unlike plumbers and decorators, he does not neglect his own property. Sleek and rich, early drinking, yet benefits from several years' additional ageing, and it's biodynamic. A future star!

CHÂTEAU D'AIGUILHE
AOC Bordeaux-Côtes-de-Castillon
★✫Ⓥ

Purchased in 1998 by Stephan von Neipperg, who has restored the property. Super since 1999.

Second wine: *Seigneurs d'Aiguible*

CHÂTEAU DES ANNEREAUX
AOC Lalande-de-Pomerol

Attractive, fruity, medium-bodied wines of some elegance.

CHÂTEAU BARRABAQUE
AOC Côtes Canon-Fronsac
★✫Ⓥ

Situated on the mid-*côte*, this 80 per cent Merlot has really shone since the late 1990s. Excellent Cuvée Prestige is the *crème de la crème* here.

CHÂTEAU BEL-AIR
AOC Puisseguin-St-Émilion

This property makes generous, fruity, early-drinking wines.

CHÂTEAU DE BEL-AIR
AOC Lalande-de-Pomerol
★Ⓥ

One of the best of the appellation, this property has fine, sandy gravel.

CHÂTEAU BELAIR-MONTAIGUILLON
AOC St-Georges-St-Émilion
★Ⓥ

Consistently rich, deliciously fruity. The best wine selected from old vines and matured in cask, including some new oak, is sold as Château Belair-St-Georges.

CHÂTEAU DE BELCIER
AOC Bordeaux-Côtes-de-Francs and Bordeaux Supérieur Côtes-de-Francs

This property produces fruity wines that can claim the Côtes de Castillon or Côtes de Francs appellations.

CHÂTEAU CALON
AOC Montagne-St-Émilion and AOC St-George-St-Émilion

This château is under the same ownership as the *grand cru classé* Château Corbin-Michotte. The wine is good quality, with a juicy style, and very Merlot in character. Part of this vineyard falls within the St-George-St-Émilion area and this produces the best wine.

CHÂTEAU CANON
AOC Côtes Canon-Fronsac
★✫Ⓥ

This is one of several Fronsadais properties formerly owned, and still managed by, J-P Moueix. It was sold to Jean Galland in September 2000. It produces one of the best wines in this appellation from 100 per cent Merlot (40 years old).

CHÂTEAU CANON DE BREM
AOC Côtes Canon-Fronsac
★Ⓥ

No longer owned by J-P Moueix, Château Canon de Brem was sold to Jean Halley, the CEO of, and major shareholder in, Carrefour, in September 2000. It produces fine, firm, and flavoursome *vins de garde* that are deep coloured and powerful, yet complex and spicy.

CHÂTEAU CAP DE MERLE
AOC Lussac-St-Émilion
★✫Ⓥ

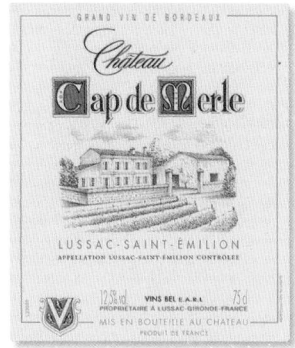

Château Cap de Merle is wine guru Robert Parker's best Lussac performer for the 1981, 1982, and 1983 vintages. These wines today remain consistently good value.

CHÂTEAU CARLES
AOC Fronsac
★Ⓥ

This producer's primary wine is attractive and juicy, but it is the 1.5 blockbusting 95 per cent Merlot selection, sold as Château Haut Carles, that really stands out here.

Other wine: *Château Haut Carles*

CHÂTEAU CASSAGNE-HAUT-CANON
AOC Côtes Canon-Fronsac
★Ⓥ

Château Cassagne-Haut-Canon produces a selection of rich, full, fat, fruitcake-flavoured wines that are especially attractive when they are still young.

CHÂTEAU LES CHARMES-GODARD
AOC Bordeaux-Côtes-de-Castillon
★Ⓥ

Brilliant, soft, silky wines of elegance and richness since 1999.

CHÂTEAU DE CLOTTE
AOC Bordeaux-Côtes-de-Castillon and AOC Bordeaux Supérieur Côtes-de-Castillon
★Ⓥ

This property has the right to both the Côtes-de-Castillon and Côtes-de-Francs appellations, but uses only the former.

CHÂTEAU LA CROIX CANON
AOC Côtes Canon-Fronsac
✫Ⓥ

Another former Moueix property that was sold to Jean Halley, the CEO of, and major shareholder in, Carrefour, yet it is managed by the established team. Attractive, Merlot-dominated wines are full of juicy fruit.

CHÂTEAU DU COURLAT
AOC Lussac-St-Émilion

These are spicy-tannic wines with good fruit flavours.

CHÂTEAU COUSTOLLE VINCENT
AOC Côtes Canon-Fronsac

Château Coustolle Vincent's wines are well-flavoured, and matured in up to 20 per cent new oak.

CHÂTEAU DALEM
AOC Fronsac
★✫Ⓥ

These soft and velvety wines develop quickly but have finesse and are among the very best of their appellation.

CHÂTEAU DE LA DAUPHINE
AOC Fronsac
✫

This property has been sold to Jean Halley, the CEO of, and major shareholder in, Carrefour, but is still run by the Moueix team, who produce fresh and fruity wines that mature in oak, 20 per cent of which is new.

CHÂTEAU DURAND LAPLAIGNE
AOC Puisseguin-St-Émilion

The excellent-quality wine produced by Château Durand Laplaigne is grown using clay-and-limestone soil, with a strict selection of grapes, and modern vinification techniques.

CHÂTEAU LA FLEUR DE BOÜARD
AOC Lalande-de-Pomerol
★Ⓥ

Very good wines, getting much better since this property was purchased by the owner of Angelus in 1998.

Second wine: *Château La Fleur St-Georges*

CHÂTEAU FONTENIL
AOC Fronsac
★✫Ⓥ

This rich, velvety 90 per cent Merlot high-flyer has lashings of new oak and is from Michel Rolland's own property.

CHÂTEAU GRAND-BARIL
AOC Montagne-St-Émilion

Attractive, fruity wine made by the agricultural school in Libourne.

CHÂTEAU GRAND ORMEAU
AOC Lalande-de-Pomerol
★Ⓥ

A rich and lusciously fruity wine that is matured in 50 per cent new oak, Grand Ormeau is very classy for its appellation.

Second wine: *Château d'Haurange*

CHÂTEAU GUIBEAU-LA FOURVIEILLE
AOC Puisseguin-St-Emilion
★✫Ⓥ

Much investment has gone into this property, the wines of which are now considered to be the best in Puisseguin.

Second wines: *Le Vieux Château Guibeau, Château La Fourvieille*

CHÂTEAU HAUT-CHAIGNEAU
AOC Lalande-de-Pomerol
★Ⓥ

Look out for Château Le Sergue 1.5, which is selected from this property's best wines and matured in 80 per cent new oak. A poor man's Mondotte?

Other wines: *Château Le Sergue*

CHÂTEAU HAUT-CHATAIN
AOC Lalande-de-Pomerol
★✫Ⓥ

Fat, rich, and juicy wines with definite hints of new-oak vanilla are made by Château Haut-Chatain.

CHÂTEAU LES HAUTS-CONSEILLANTS
AOC Lalande-de-Pomerol

Château les Hauts-Conseillants is another fine Néac property.

Other wine: *Château les Hauts-Tuileries* (export label)

CHÂTEAU HAUT-TUQUET

AOC Bordeaux-Côtes-de-Castillon and
AOC Bordeaux Supérieur
Côtes-de-Castillon

This wine is consistently good.

CHÂTEAU JEANDEMAN

AOC Fronsac

This château produces fresh, fruity wine with good aroma.

CHÂTEAU JUNAYME

AOC Côtes Canon-Fronsac
★ ⓥ

Well-known wines of finesse.

CHÂTEAU DES LAURETS

AOC Puisseguin-St-Émilion

The appellation's largest property.

Other wines: *Château la Rochette, Château Maison Rose*

CHÂTEAU DE LUSSAC

AOC Lussac-St-Émilion

Château de Lussac produces well-balanced, early-drinking wine.

CHÂTEAU DU LYONNAT

AOC Lussac-St-Émilion

The appellation's largest property.

Other wines: *La Rose Peruchon*

CHÂTEAU MAISON BLANCHE

AOC Montagne-St-Émilion
◉

Château Maison Blanche produces attractive wine that is easy to drink.

CHÂTEAU MAQUIN-ST-GEORGES

AOC St-Georges-St-Émilion

This wine is 70 per cent Merlot.

Other wine: *Château Bellonne-St-Georges*

CHÂTEAU MAUSSE

AOC Côtes Canon-Fronsac

Wines with good aroma and flavour.

CHÂTEAU MAYNE-VIEIL

AOC Fronsac

Easy-drinking wines with good Merlot spice and fruit.

CHÂTEAU MAZERIS

AOC Côtes Canon-Fronsac

There is an unusually high proportion of Cabernet Sauvignon in these wines.

CHÂTEAU MILON

AOC Lussac-St-Émilion
★ ⓥ

A château that produces a fine-quality, full, yet fragrant, wine.

CHÂTEAU MONCETS

AOC Lalande-de-Pomerol
★ ⓥ

This Néac property makes a fine, rich, and elegant Pomerol lookalike.

CHÂTEAU MOULIN HAUT-LAROQUE

AOC Fronsac

Well-perfumed, quite fat wines with lots of fruit and good tannin.

CHÂTEAU MOULIN NEUF

AOC Bordeaux-Côtes-de-Castillon and
AOC Bordeaux Supérieur
Côtes-de-Castillon
★ ⓥ

These wines regularly win medals.

CHÂTEAU LA PAPETERIE

AOC Montagne-St-Émilion

Wines with a rich nose and a big fruit-filled palate.

CHÂTEAU DU PONT DE GUESTRES

AOC Lalande-de-Pomerol
★ ⓥ

This château produces full, ripe, fat wines of good quality.

CHÂTEAU LA PRADE

AOC Bordeaux-Côtes-de-Francs
✰

Increasing quality since 2000.

CHÂTEAU LE PUY

AOC Bordeaux-Côtes-de-Francs and
AOC Bordeaux Supérieur
Côtes-de-Francs
◉★ⓥ

Red wines from this property are rustic and overtly fruity.

CLOS PUY ARNAUD

AOC Bordeaux-Côtes-de-Castillon
★

Owner-winemaker Thierry Valette produces increasingly concentrated, yet extremely approachable wines since 2000.

CHÂTEAU PUYCARPIN

AOC Bordeaux-Côtes-de-Castillon and
AOC Bordeaux Supérieur
Côtes-de-Castillon

This property produces a well-made red, and a little dry white.

CHÂTEAU PUYGUERAUD

AOC Bordeaux-Côtes-de-Francs and
AOC Bordeaux Supérieur
Côtes-de-Francs

Aromatically attractive wines with good colour and supple fruit.

CHÂTEAU RICHELIEU

AOC Fronsac
★Ⓑ

Excellent since 2003. The 2005 is stunning, especially the wonderfully lush and satisfying prestige cuvée "La Favorite de Richelieu".

Second wine: *Trois Musketeers*

CHÂTEAU DE LA RIVIÈRE

AOC Fronsac
★✰ⓥ

Magnificent wines that are built to last: they are rich, tannic, and fruity, and matured in up to 40 per cent new oak.

CHÂTEAU ROBIN

AOC Bordeaux-Côtes-de-Castillon and
AOC Bordeaux Supérieur
Côtes-de-Castillon
✰ⓥ

Château Robin produces award-winning red wines.

CHÂTEAU LA ROCHE-GABY

AOC Côtes Canon-Fronsac
★ⓥ

Château La Roche-Gaby produces intensely flavoured, attractive, and well-structured wines, which are designed to have a long life.

CHÂTEAU ROCHER-BELLEVUE

AOC Bordeaux-Côtes-de-Castillon and
AOC Bordeaux Supérieur
Côtes-de-Castillon
Ⓑ✰ⓥ

A good St-Émilion look-alike that regularly wins medals.

Other wines: *La Palène, Coutet-St-Magne*

CHÂTEAU ROUDIER

AOC Montagne-St-Émilion
★✰ⓥ

Quality wines that are well-coloured, richly flavoured, finely balanced, and long and supple.

CHÂTEAU LA ROUSSELLE

AOC Fronsac
ⓥ

Lovely rich, ripe, elegant wines since 2003.

CHÂTEAU SIAURAC

AOC Lalande-de-Pomerol

Fine, firm, and fruity wines.

CHÂTEAU STE-COLOMBE

AOC Bordeaux-Côtes-de-Castillon
★ⓥ

This château was purchased in 1999 by Gérard Perse of Pavie *et al* and Alain Raynaud of La Croix-de-Gay. These wines look very promising indeed.

CHÂTEAU ST-GEORGES

AOC St-Georges-St-Émilion
★✰ⓥ

Super quality wine of great finesse.

CHÂTEAU TARREYO

AOC Bordeaux-Côtes-de-Castillon and
AOC Bordeaux Supérieur
Côtes-de-Castillon

Château Tarreyo (Gascon for "knoll of stones") is sited on a limestone mound, as its name suggests.

CHÂTEAU THIBAUD-BELLEVUE

AOC Bordeaux-Côtes-de-Castillon and
AOC Bordeaux Supérieur
Côtes-de-Castillon

Medium-bodied, fruity red wine.

CHÂTEAU TOUMALIN

AOC Côtes Canon-Fronsac

Fresh, fruity wine from a property under the same ownership as Château La Pointe in Pomerol.

CHÂTEAU TOUR-DU-PAS-ST-GEORGES

AOC St-Georges-St-Émilion
✰ⓥ

An excellent and inexpensive entrée into the world of *premier cru* claret.

CHÂTEAU DES TOURELLES

AOC Lalande-de-Pomerol
★ⓥ

Fine wines with vanilla undertones.

CHÂTEAU TOURNEFEUILLE

AOC Lalande-de-Pomerol
★✰ⓥ

This rich, long-lived wine is the best of the appellation.

CHÂTEAU DES TOURS

AOC Montagne-St-Émilion
✰ⓥ

The largest property in the appellation. The wine is big, full, and fleshy, yet soft and easy to drink.

CHÂTEAU LA VALADE

AOC Fronsac
✰ⓥ

Elegant, aromatic, and silky-textured wines, which are made exclusively from Merlot grapes.

CHÂTEAU LA VIEILLE CURE

AOC Fronsac
★✰

Very fresh and velvety with delightful floral, summer fruit aromas, these wines are at the very top of their appellation. The 1998 is stunning.

VIEUX-CHÂTEAU-ST-ANDRÉ

AOC Montagne-St-Émilion
★✰ⓥ

A soft, exciting wine, full of cherry, vanilla, and spice flavours.

CHÂTEAU LA VILLARS

AOC Fronsac
★ⓥ

Soft, fat, and juicy wines of excellent quality, one-third of which are matured in new oak.

CHÂTEAU VRAY-CANON-BOYER

AOC Côtes Canon-Fronsac

This château produces a fruity, medium-bodied wine that is attractive for early drinking from 90 per cent Merlot grapes.

BOURG AND BLAYE

Ninety-five per cent of the wine produced in Bourg and Blaye is good-value red. Tiny Bourg makes more wine than its five-times-larger neighbour, Blaye, and most of the vines grown in Blaye come from a cluster of châteaux close to the borders of Bourg.

AS ONE WOULD EXPECT of an area that has supported a settlement for 400,000 years, Bourg has a close-knit community. Comparatively recently, the Romans used neighbouring Blaye as a *castrum*, a fortified area in the defence system that shielded Bordeaux. According to some sources, the vine was cultivated in Bourg and Blaye as soon as the Romans arrived. Vineyards were certainly flourishing here long before those of the Médoc, just the other side of the Gironde.

Bourg is a compact, heavily cultivated area with pretty hillside vineyards at every turn. The vine is less important in Blaye, which has other interests, including a caviar industry based at its ancient fishing port where sturgeon is still a major catch. The south-facing vineyards of Blaye are mostly clustered in the countryside immediately bordering Bourg and, despite the similarity of the countryside, traditionally produce slightly inferior wines to those of Bourg. The D18 motorway appears to be a

FACTORS AFFECTING TASTE AND QUALITY

LOCATION
The vineyards fan out behind the town of Bourg, which is situated on the right bank of the confluence of the Dordogne and the Garonne, some 20 kilometres (12.5 miles) north of Bordeaux. Blaye is a larger district that unfolds beyond Bourg.

CLIMATE
These two areas are less protected than the Médoc from westerly and northwesterly winds, and have a higher rainfall.

ASPECT
Bourg is very hilly with vines cultivated on steep limestone hills and knolls up to a height of 80 m (260 ft). In the southern section of Blaye the country is rich and hilly, with steep slopes overlooking the Gironde that are really just a continuation of those in Bourg. The northern areas are gentle and the hills lower, with marshes bordering the viticultural areas.

SOIL
In Bourg the topsoil is clay-limestone or clay-gravel over a hard limestone subsoil, although in the east the subsoil sometimes gives way to gravel and clay. The soil in Blaye is clay or clay-limestone over hard limestone on the hills overlooking the Gironde, getting progressively sandier going east.

VITICULTURE AND VINIFICATION
There are many grape varieties here, some of which are far too inferior or unreliable to contribute to the quality of these wines, particularly the whites. Bourg produces the best reds, Blaye the best whites, but there is relatively little white wine made in both appellations – even Blaye is 90 per cent red and Bourg is in excess of 99 per cent red. Very few *petits châteaux* in both areas can afford the use of casks, let alone new ones, and much of the wine in Bourg is made by one of its five *coopératives*.

GRAPE VARIETIES
Primary varieties: Cabernet Franc, Cabernet Sauvignon, Merlot, Sauvignon Blanc, Sémillon
Secondary varieties: Béguignol, Chenin Blanc, Colombard, Folle Blanche, Malbec, Merlot Blanc, Muscadelle, Petit Verdot, Prolongeau (Bouchalès), Ugni Blanc

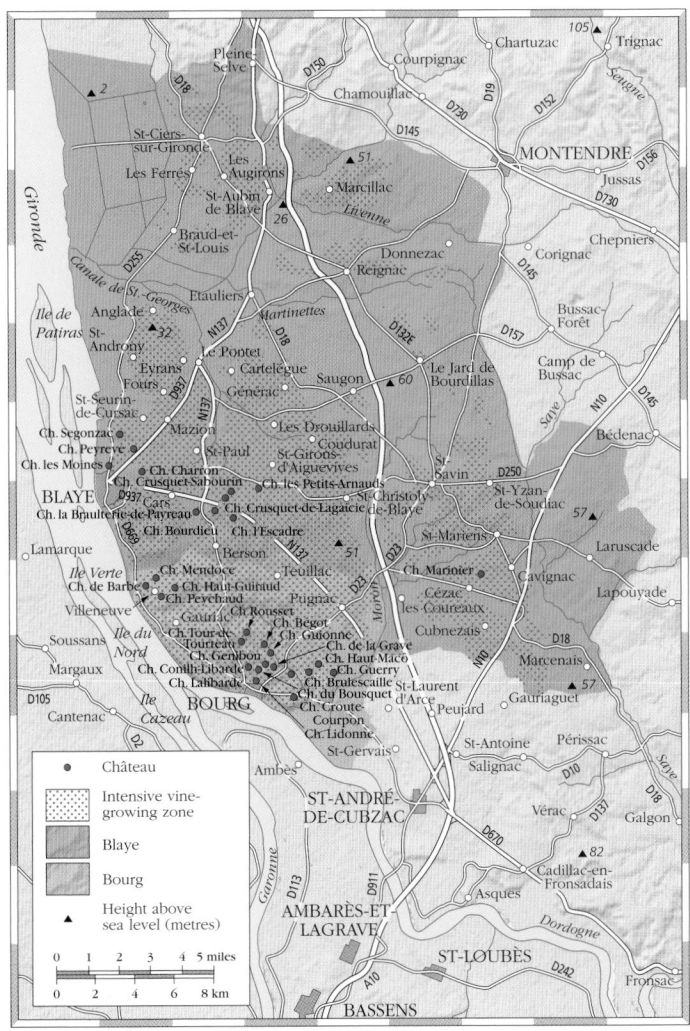

Château
Intensive vine-growing zone
Blaye
Bourg
Height above sea level (metres)

0 1 2 3 4 5 miles
0 2 4 6 8 km

THE TOWN OF BLAYE
The attractive fishing port of Blaye with, in the foreground, the ruins of its ancient citadel guarding against the approach of marauders from the sea.

BOURG AND BLAYE, *see also p109*
Most of the best growths of Bourg and Blaye are clustered behind the respective ports that give this wine-producing area its name. Bourg, the smaller area, has a higher concentration of vineyards and generally produces the better wines.

barrier beyond which the less intensely cultivated hinterland takes on a totally different topography, where the more expansive scenery is dotted with isolated forests.

THE POTENTIAL OF BOURG AND BLAYE
To the Romans, these south-facing vineyards overlooking the Gironde seemed the ideal place to plant vines. Indeed, the quality achieved today in these vineyards would have surpassed the most optimistic hopes of those past masters of the vine. However, by today's expectations, Bourg and Blaye have been relegated to a viticultural backwater. This is a pity, as there are some exciting quality wines being made here. Perhaps when the world has woken up to the gems in Canon-Fronsac, more curious consumers might turn their attention to the better producers in this district. As soon as wine lovers are prepared to pay higher prices for these wines, so its proprietors will be able to restrict yields, improve vinification techniques, and indulge in a percentage of new oak.

CHENIN BLANC IN BORDEAUX
The Chenin Blanc of Loire fame (or infamy, as the case may be) is allowed in the white wines of Bourg, albeit restricted to a maximum of 10 per cent. However, in the AOCs of Blayais and Côtes de Blaye (but not Premières Côtes de Blaye), this interloper from the north has a free run, or could have, if a producer wanted to market a pure Chenin Blanc varietal wine. I have never been a fan of Chenin Blanc in the Loire, except in those idyllic vintages when the sublime *moelleux* style can be produced in quantity, and it is very hard not to produce liquid magic. The problem with Chenin in the Loire is that it grows like weed, but rarely has the degree of sunshine this grape likes to luxuriate in. Combine that with the inclination of far too many growers to over-yield and season it with those who have less than clinically clean vinification habits, and it is clear why Loire Chenin, particularly dry Loire Chenin, has such a poor reputation. On the other hand, even cheap, mass-produced Chenin Blanc wines in the New World have lovely, ripe tropical-fruit flavours. Not all of them, of course, the New World has its good, bad, and ugly too, but I believe that the longer hours of warmer sunshine in Bordeaux could produce some excellent dry Chenin wines. A pure Chenin Blanc Bordeaux would indeed be a novelty.

VINEYARDS ALONG THE DORDOGNE AT BOURG
The Romans planted these south-facing vineyards, believing this to be a far more ideal place to grow vines than on the other side of the confluence of the Dordogne and Garonne estuaries where, understandably, they failed to realize the possibilities of the Médoc concealed beyond its virtually impenetrable marshes.

CHÂTEAU SEGONZAC, ST-GENÈS-DE-BLAYE
A short distance from the fortress of Blaye, these sweeping vineyards belong to Château Segonzac, a wine estate created in 1887 by Jean Dupuy, the owner of Le Petit Parisien, the largest-circulation newspaper in the world at the time.

THE APPELLATIONS OF
BOURG AND BLAYE

The appellations in this area are very confusing for the consumer. There is no reason why just two AOCs – Côtes de Blaye and Côtes de Bourg – could not be used for all the wines produced here.

BLAYAIS AOC
See Blaye AOC

BLAYE AOC

Blaye or Blayais is a large and diverse appellation of variable quality.

RED Few properties cultivate obscure varieties such as Prolongeau and Béguignol, thus many utilize the prestigious sounding Premières Côtes de Blaye AOC, hence hardly anyone bothers to sell the wine under this plain appellation.

🍇 Cabernet Sauvignon, Cabernet Franc, Merlot, Malbec, Prolongeau, Béguignol, Petit Verdot

🍷 3–7 years

WHITE Since 1997 Ugni Blanc has dominated, with Merlot Blanc and Folle Blanche banned. The ripeness level has been lowered from 170 to 153 grams of sugar, with no more than 4 grams residual allowed in the finished wine, and a maximum of 12.5% alcohol imposed, thus ensuring fresher, crisper wines. These wines may be sold from 1 December following the harvest without any mention of *primeur* or *nouveau*.

🍇 Ugni Blanc plus up to 10% in total of Folle Blanche, Colombard, Chenin Blanc, Sémillon, Sauvignon Blanc, Muscadelle

🍷 1–2 years

BLAYE CÔTES DE BORDEAUX AOC

The boundary and technical requirements for this appellation are precisely the same as for the Premières Côtes de Blaye. The wines may be red or dry white.

BOURG AOC

Also called Bourgeais, this appellation, which covers both red and white wines, has fallen into disuse because the growers prefer to use the Côtes de Bourg AOC, which is easier to market but conforms to the same regulations. *See also* Côtes de Bourg AOC.

BOURGEAIS AOC
See Bourg AOC

CÔTES DE BLAYE AOC

Unlike the Bourg and Côtes de Bourg appellations, which cover red and white wines, Côtes de Blaye is white only. Blaye, however, may be red or white.

WHITE As much white Côtes de Blaye is produced as basic Blaye. The wines are similar in style and quality.

🍇 Merlot Blanc, Folle Blanche, Colombard, Chenin Blanc, Sémillon, Sauvignon Blanc, Muscadelle

🍷 1–2 years

CÔTES DE BOURG AOC

Bourg is one-fifth the size of Blaye, yet it traditionally produces a greater quantity and, more importantly, a much finer quality of wine than that produced at Blaye.

RED Excellent-value wines of good colour, full of solid, fruity flavour. Many are very stylish indeed.

🍇 Cabernet Sauvignon, Cabernet Franc, Merlot, Malbec

🍷 3–10 years

WHITE A very small quantity of this light, dry wine is produced and sold each year. It may be sold from 1 December following the harvest without any mention of *primeur* or *nouveau*.

🍇 Sémillon, Sauvignon Blanc, Muscadelle, Merlot Blanc, Colombard, plus up to 10% Chenin Blanc

🍷 1–2 years

PREMIÈRES CÔTES DE BLAYE AOC

This covers the same area as Blaye and Côtes de Blaye, but only classic grapes are used and the minimum alcoholic strength is higher. The area has very good potential for producing quality wines.

RED There are one or two excellent properties that use a little new oak.

🍇 Cabernet Sauvignon, Cabernet Franc, Merlot, Malbec

🍷 4–10 years

WHITE Dry, light-bodied wines that may have a fresh, lively, grapey flavour.

🍇 Sémillon, Sauvignon Blanc, Muscadelle

🍷 1–2 years

THE WINE PRODUCERS OF
BOURG

CHÂTEAU DE BARBE
Villeneuve

Château de Barbe is a property that makes substantial quantities of light-styled, Merlot-dominated, gently fruity red wines, which are easy to drink.

CHÂTEAU BÉGOT
Lansac

This property produces some 5,000 cases of agreeably fruity red wine, which is best drunk young.

CHÂTEAU DU BOUSQUET
Bourg-sur-Gironde
★ Ⓥ

This large, well-known château produces some 40,000 cases of red wine of excellent value for money. The wine is fermented in stainless steel and aged in oak, has a big bouquet, and a smooth feel.

CHÂTEAU BRULESCAILLE
Tauriac

Château Brulescaille's vineyards are very well-sited and produce agreeable wines for early drinking.

CHÂTEAU CONILH-LIBARDE
Bourg-sur-Gironde

Soft, fruity red wines are made at this small vineyard overlooking Bourg-sur-Gironde and the river.

CHÂTEAU CROUTE-COURPON
Bourg-sur-Gironde

A small but recently enlarged estate, it produces honest, fruity red wines.

CHÂTEAU EYQUEM
Bayon-sur-Gironde

Owned by the serious winemaking Bayle-Carreau family, which also owns several other properties, this wine is not normally, however, purchased for its quality. It is enjoyable as a light luncheon claret, but the real joy is in the spoof of serving a red "Yquem".

CHÂTEAU FALFAS
Bourg-sur-Gironde
Ⓑ ★ Ⓥ

Owned by John and Vonique Cochran, whose biodynamic wines are consistently rich, mid-term drinkers of no little finesse.

CHÂTEAU GÉNIBON
Bourg-sur-Gironde

This small vineyard produces attractive wines that have all the enjoyment upfront and are easy to drink.

CHÂTEAU GRAND-LAUNAY
Teuillac
★ Ⓥ

This property has been developed from the vineyards of three estates: Domaine Haut-Launay, Château Launay, and Domaine les Hermats. Mainly red wine is produced, although a very tiny amount of white is also made. The star-performing wine at this château is a superb, special reserve *cuvée* of red that is sold under the Château Lion Noir label.

CHÂTEAU DE LA GRAVE
Bourg-sur-Gironde
★ Ⓥ

An important property situated on one of the highest points of Bourg-sur-Gironde, it produces a large quantity of light, fruity Malbec-influenced red wine and a very tiny amount of white.

CHÂTEAU GUERRY
Tauriac
★ Ⓥ

Some 10,000 cases of really fine wood-aged red wines are produced at this château. The wines have good structure, bags of fruit, and a smooth, elegant flavour.

CHÂTEAU GUIONNE
Lansac

These are easy-drinking wines, full of attractive Merlot fruit, good juicy flavour, and some finesse. A little white wine of some interest and depth is also made.

CHÂTEAU HAUT-MACÔ
Tauriac

This rustic red wine is full of rich, fruity flavours, and good acidity. The proprietors also own a property called Domaine de Lilotte in Bourg-sur-Gironde producing attractive,

early-drinking red wines under the Bordeaux Supérieur appellation.
Other wine: Les Bascauds

CHÂTEAU HAUT-ROUSSET
Bourg-sur-Gironde

Some 12,000 cases of decent, everyday-drinking red wine and 1,000 cases of white are produced at this fairly large property. The red wines from a small vineyard close by are sold under the Château la Renardière label.

CHÂTEAU DE LIDONNE
Bourg-sur-Gironde
★

This very old property produces an excellent-quality red wine, powerfully aromatic and full of Cabernet character. Its name comes from the 15th-century monks who looked after the estate and offered lodgings to passing pilgrims: "Lit-Donne" or "Give Bed".

CHÂTEAU PEYCHAUD
Teuillac
★ 🅥

These fruity red wines are easy to drink when young. A little white is also made. It is under the same ownership as Château Peyredoulle and Château le Peuy-Saincrit.

CHÂTEAU ROC DE CAMBES
Bourg-sur-Gironde
★★☆

You can expect to pay five times the price of any other Côtes de Bourg for this blockbuster, which is made by François Mitjavile, the owner of Tertre-Rôteboeuf. However, some vintages are worth it.

CHÂTEAU ROUSSET
Samonac
★ 🅥

A fine estate of gravel vineyards producing lightly rich, juicy, Merlot-dominated wines of some finesse; they are perfect to drink when two or three years old.

CHÂTEAU SAUMAN
Villeneuve

These immaculate vineyards produce a good-quality red wine for medium-term maturity. The proprietor also owns the red-wine producing Domaine du Moulin de Mendoce in the same commune.

CHÂTEAU TOUR-DE-TOURTEAU
Samonac
★ 🅥

This property was once part of Château Rousset. However, the wines are definitely bigger and richer than those of Rousset.

THE WINE PRODUCERS OF

BLAYE

CHÂTEAU BARBÉ
Cars
★☆ 🅥

This château produces well-made, and overtly fruity red and white wines. Château Barbé is one of several properties owned by the Bayle-Carreau family (see also La Carelle).

CHÂTEAU BOURDIEU
Berson

This old and well-known property produces Cabernet-dominated red wines of a very firm structure that receive time in oak. Seven hundred years ago this estate was accorded the privilege of selling "clairet", a tradition it maintains today by ageing the blended production of various vineyards in oak. The white wines are of improving quality.

CHÂTEAU LA CARELLE
St-Paul

More than 11,000 cases of agreeable red wines and just 1,500 cases of white are made at this property. The owner also runs Châteaux Barbé.

CHÂTEAU CHARRON
St-Martin-Lacaussade
★☆ 🅥

These very attractive, well-made, juicy-rich, Merlot-dominated red wines are matured in oak, some of which is new. A small amount of white wine is also made.

CHÂTEAU CRUSQUET-DE-LAGARCIE
Cars
★ 🅥

A tremendously exciting, richly styled red wine: deep coloured, bright, big, full of fruit, vanilla, and spice. A small amount of dry white wine is sold as "Clos-des-Rudel" and an even smaller quantity of sweet white wine as "Clos-Blanc de Lagarcie". The châteaux Les-Princesses-de-Lagarcie and Touzignan, also in Cars, are under the same ownership.

CHÂTEAU L'ESCADRE
Cars
★☆ 🅥

These elegant red wines are well-coloured, full, and fruity. They can be enjoyed young, but also improve with age. A small amount of fruity white wine is produced.
Second wine: Château la Croix

CHÂTEAU GIGAULT CUVÉE VIVA
Mazion
★★☆ 🅥

Amazing richness and opulence of fruit for the price.

DOMAINE DU GRAND BARRAIL
Plassac
🅥

This château makes a fine-quality red wine that attracts by its purity of fruit. A little white wine is produced. The proprietor also owns Château Gardut-Haut-Cluzeau and Domaine du Cavalier in Cars.

CHÂTEAU LES GRANDS MARÉCHAUX
St-Girons d'Aiguevives
★ 🅥

Bags of black fruit for your bucks.

CHÂTEAU DU GRAND PIERRE
Berson
★ 🅥

This property can produce tremendous value medium- to full-bodied red wine with sweet, ripe fruit. Fresh, zesty, dry white wine of agreeable quality is also made.

CHÂTEAU HAUT BERTINERIE
Cubnezais
★★☆ 🅥

The consistent class of this wine, with its silky fruit and beautifully integrated oak, makes it stand out above the rest as the best-value dry white currently made in Bordeaux.

CHÂTEAU DE HAUT SOCIONDO
Cars

Agreeably light and fruity red and white wines are made here.

CHÂTEAU LES JONQUEYRES
St-Paul-de-Blaye
★★ 🅥

This château produces lush Merlot-dominated reds with lots of well-integrated creamy oak. The wines are impeccably produced.

CHÂTEAU LACAUSSADE SAINT MARTIN "TROIS MOULINS"
St-Martin Lacaussade
★ 🅥

Owned by Jacques Chardat, but managed and marketed by Vignobles Germain, both the sumptuous red and classy dry white benefit from 100 per cent new oak.

CHÂTEAU LAMANCEAU
St-Androny

Production at this property is entirely red and of an excellent standard: richly coloured wine full of the juicy spice of Merlot.

CHÂTEAU MAINE-GAZIN "LEVENNE" VIEILLES VIGNES
Plassac
★ 🅥

With one-third new oak, this 90 per cent Merlot wine is rich, sumptuous, and above its class.

CHÂTEAU MARINIER
Cézac
★☆ 🅥

Twice as much red wine as white is produced. The red is agreeably fruity, but the white is much the better wine: smooth, well balanced, lightly rich, and elegant. Red and rosé wines are also produced under the Bordeaux appellation.

CHÂTEAU MENAUDAT
St-Androny
★ 🅥

These are extremely attractive, full, and fruity red wines.

CHÂTEAU LES MOINES
Blaye

A red-only château, producing a light- to medium-bodied, fresh and fruity wine for easy drinking.

CHÂTEAU LES PETITS ARNAUDS
Cars
★☆ 🅥

Attractively aromatic red wines, pleasingly round and fruity. Dry white Blaye and a moelleux white.

CHÂTEAU PEYREDOULLE
Berson
★ 🅥

This 15th-century property produces mainly good-quality red wine, although some white is made. The proprietors also own Château Peychaud in the Bourgeais commune of Teuillac and the Bordeaux AOC of Château le Peuy-Saincrit.

CHÂTEAU PEYREYRE
St-Martin-Lacaussade
★ 🅥

This château produces rich-flavoured reds of some finesse. Bordeaux Rosé is also made.

CHÂTEAU SEGONZAC
St-Genès-de-Blaye
★ 🅥

Château Segonzac's easy-drinking red wines are light, well made, fresh, firm, and agreeably fruity.

ENTRE-DEUX-MERS

Entre-Deux-Mers, which literally means "between two seas" is situated between the Dordogne and Garonne rivers. It is Bordeaux's largest district, and produces inexpensive dry white wines and an increasing volume of excellent value-for-money red wines that are entitled to the Bordeaux, Bordeaux Supérieur, and Premières-Côtes-de-Bordeaux appellations.

TECHNOLOGICAL PROGRESS in winemaking occurred earlier and more quickly in Entre-Deux-Mers than in any other district of Bordeaux. As early as the 1950s and 1960s, there was a grass-roots viticultural movement to drop the traditional low vine-training systems and adopt the revolutionary "high-culture" system that contrasted with the methods common throughout Bordeaux. These new vineyard techniques were followed in the 1970s by a widespread adoption of cool-fermentation techniques. With fresh, light, and attractively dry white wines being made at many châteaux, the major export markets suddenly realized it would be easier to sell the name Entre-Deux-Mers rather than continue to sell what had become boring Bordeaux Blanc. This was even better if the wine could boast some sort of individual *petit château* personality.

THE "HIGH-CULTURE" SYSTEM OF VINE TRAINING
Entre-Deux-Mers in the late 1940s and early 1950s was a sorry place. The wines were sold in bulk, ending up as anonymous Bordeaux Blanc, and much of the decline in the Bordeaux region was centred on this district. But the new post-war generation of

CHÂTEAU BONNET
In 1898 this vineyard was acquired by Léonce Recapet, one of the first to carry out replanting after the devastation of the Gironde vineyard by phylloxera at the turn of the century. His son-in-law François Lurton succeeded him, and in 1956 his grandson, André Lurton, became the owner.

winegrowers was not content with this state of affairs. Although times were difficult and the economy was deteriorating, the young, technically minded *vignerons* realized that the district's compressed *boulbènes* soil, which was choking the vines, could not be worked by their ancestors' outdated methods, and they therefore took a considerable financial risk to rectify the situation. They grubbed up every other row of vines, thus increasing the spacing between the rows, and trained the plants on a "high-culture" system similar to that practised further south in Madiran and Jurançon (also in

LOUPIAC CHURCH
The local church stands alongside the vineyards of Château Loupiac, which are situated on the right bank of the Garonne.

ENTRE-DEUX-MERS, *see also p101*
The varied countryside of this district spreads out between the rivers Dordogne and Garonne as their paths diverge. The Premières Côtes form a narrow strip along the south side.

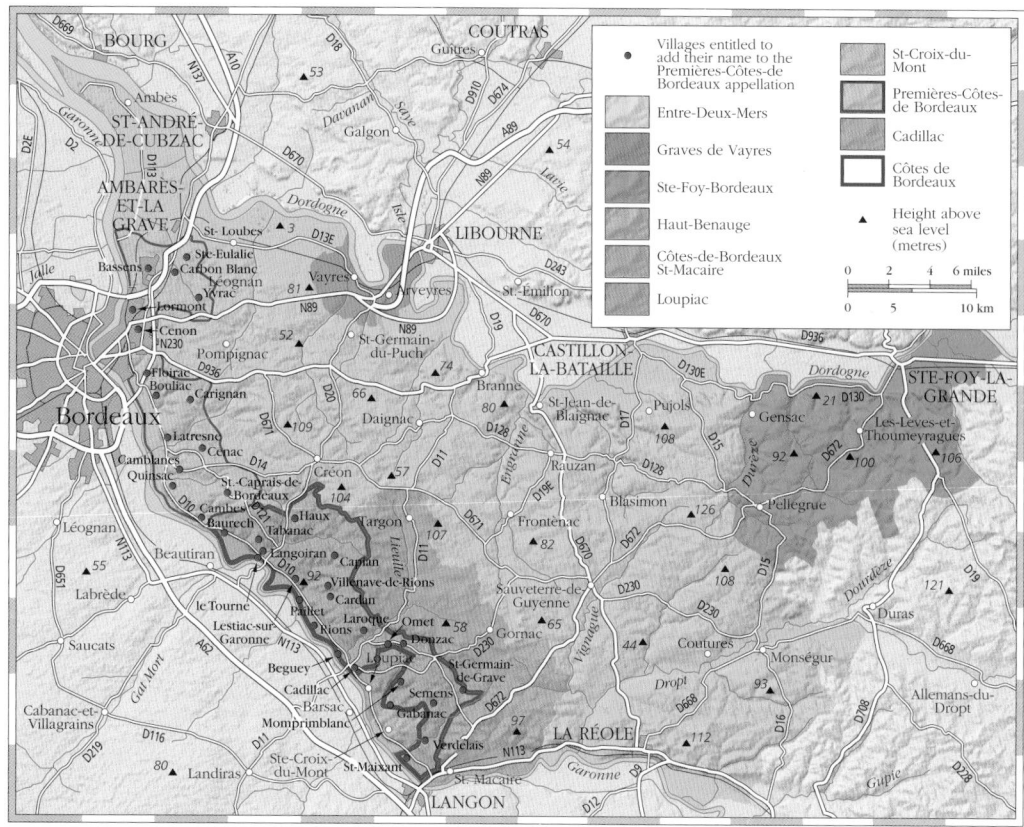

FACTORS AFFECTING TASTE AND QUALITY

LOCATION
A large area east of Bordeaux between the Garonne and Dordogne rivers.

CLIMATE
More blustery and wetter than the Médoc; areas near the rivers are liable to flood.

ASPECT
Quiet and very attractive countryside of vine-covered hillsides, orchards, and meadows.

SOIL
Very varied topsoils, ranging from alluvium by the river to gravel on some hillsides and crests, and clay-gravel or clay-limestone on various plateaux. At the western end of the district a soil called *boulbènes* dominates. This is extremely fine and sandy and has a tendency to compress into an impermeable barrier. Vines must be grafted on to special rootstock in order to be productive in such soil. Much of the subsoil is limestone or limestone-based, but sandy-clay, clay-and-limestone rubble, a quarry stone called *aslar*, and *ribot* – a sandstone containing gravel and iron deposits – are also found.

VITICULTURE AND VINIFICATION
This area is famed for its "high and wide" method of vine training, which was developed in the early 1950s and is similar to the Lenz Moser system used in Austria. Greater emphasis is now placed on the Sauvignon grape and cool fermentation in stainless-steel vats.

GRAPE VARIETIES
Primary varieties: Muscadelle, Sauvignon Blanc, Sémillon
Secondary varieties: Colombard, Mauzac, Merlot Blanc, Ugni Blanc

Austria where it was originally conceived and was called the Lenz Moser system). This system allowed machinery to work the land and break up the soil. It also increased the canopy of foliage, which intensified chlorophyll assimilation and improved ripening.

COOL FERMENTATION
In the 1970s, university-trained personnel at the well-funded Entre-Deux-Mers *coopératives* invested in temperature-controlled stainless-steel vats and led the way in cool-fermentation techniques. Prior to this, fermentation temperatures were often in excess of 28°C (83°F), but it was soon discovered that the lower the temperature, the more aromatic compounds were released. They discovered that fermentation could take place at temperatures as low as 4°C (39°F), although the risk of stuck-fermentation (when the fermentation process stops) was greater at such low temperatures. It soon became clear that the ideal fermentation temperature was somewhere between 10°C (50°F) and 18°C (64°F). This increased the yield of alcohol and important aromatic and flavour compounds. It also reduced both the loss of carbonic gas and the presence of volatile acidity and required less sulphur dioxide. In the mid-1980s it was confirmed that 18°C (64°F) is the optimum temperature for fermentation. Lower temperatures also produce amylic aromas, which in small quantities are fine, but the lower the temperature, the more the wine is dominated by these nail-varnish aromas.

THE APPELLATIONS OF
ENTRE-DEUX-MERS

BORDEAUX HAUT-BENAUGE AOC

Situated above the Premières Côtes, opposite Cérons, this area corresponds to the ancient and tiny county of Benauge. To claim this appellation, as opposed to Entre-Deux-Mers-Haut-Benauge, the grapes are restricted to the three classic varieties and must be riper, with a minimum sugar level of 195 grams per litre instead of 170 grams per litre. The yield is 10 per cent lower, and the minimum alcoholic level is 1.5 per cent higher.

WHITE Dry, medium-sweet, and sweet versions of this light-bodied, fruity wine may be made.

🍷 Sémillon, Sauvignon Blanc, Muscadelle

⌛ 1–3 years for dry and medium-sweet wines; 3–6 years for sweet wines

CADILLAC AOC

Of the trio of sweet-wine areas on the right bank of the Garonne, Cadillac is the least known. It encompasses 21 communes, 16 of which form the canton of Cadillac, yet very little wine is produced under this appellation – just one-fifth of that made in Loupiac, or one-tenth of that made in Ste-Croix-du-Mont. The regulations state that the wines must be made from botrytized grapes harvested in successive *tries*, but there is little evidence of this in the wines, which at best have the character of *passerillage*. The *terroir* could produce wines of a much superior quality, but it would be costly to do so, and sadly, this appellation does not fetch a high enough price to justify the substantial investment needed.

WHITE Attractive honey-gold wines with fresh, floral aromas and a semi-sweet, or sweet, fruity flavour.

🍷 Sémillon, Sauvignon Blanc, Muscadelle

⌛ 3–8 years

CADILLAC CÔTES-DE-BORDEAUX AOC

This is a bit of a misnomer. The boundaries for the other three Côtes de Bordeaux appellations are exactly the same as the AOC with which they are prefixed (ie, Côtes de Blaye for Blaye, Côtes de Castillon for Castillon, and Côtes de Francs for Francs), but Cadillac Côtes de Bordeaux encompasses not only Cadillac but also Premières-Côtes-de-Bordeaux, Côtes-de-Bordeaux St-Macaire, Loupiac, and Ste-Croix-du-Mont. Despite the proliferation of wine styles within these AOCs, the wines for Cadillac Côtes-de-Bordeaux must be red only.

CÔTES-DE-BORDEAUX-ST-MACAIRE AOC

These little-seen wines come from an area at the eastern extremity of the Premières-Côtes-de-Bordeaux. Of the 2,300 hectares (6,000 acres) of vineyards that may use this appellation, barely 30 hectares (75 acres) bother to do so.

WHITE Medium-bodied, medium-sweet, or sweet wines that are attractive in a fruity way, but unpretentious.

🍷 Sémillon, Sauvignon Blanc, Muscadelle

⌛ 1–3 years

ENTRE-DEUX-MERS AOC

This is the largest district in the region, and after the generic Bordeaux Blanc, it is its greatest-volume white-wine appellation. Entre-Deux-Mers has a growing reputation for exceptional-value wines of a high technical standard.

WHITE Crisp, dry, light-bodied wines that are fragrant, aromatic, and usually predominantly Sauvignon Blanc. These are clean, cool-fermented wines. They may be sold from 1 December following the harvest without any mention of *primeur* or *nouveau*.

🍷 At least 70 per cent Sémillon, Sauvignon Blanc, and Muscadelle, plus a maximum of 30 per cent Merlot Blanc and up to 10 per cent in total of Colombard, Mauzac, and Ugni Blanc

⌛ 1–2 years

ENTRE-DEUX-MERS-HAUT-BENAUGE AOC

These wines are drier than those of the Bordeaux-Haut-Benauge appellation, and their blends may include a greater number of grape varieties, although the same nine communes comprise both appellations. The wines comply with the less rigorous regulations of Entre-Deux-Mers and, consequently, this AOC produces four times the volume of wine than does Bordeaux-Haut-Benauge. Entre-Deux-Mers-Haut-Benauge has so far produced only dry wines, with the exception of 1983, when a luscious vintage arrived that was easy to make into sweet wines.

WHITE These dry wines are very similar to those of Entre-Deux-Mers.

🍷 At least 70 per cent Sémillon, Sauvignon Blanc, and Muscadelle, plus a maximum of 30 per cent Merlot Blanc and up to 10 per cent in total of Colombard, Mauzac, and Ugni Blanc

⌛ 1–3 years

GRAVES DE VAYRES AOC

An enclave of gravelly soil on the left bank of the Dordogne, this appellation produces a substantial quantity of excellent-value red and white wines.

RED These are well-coloured, aromatic, medium-bodied wines with fragrant, juicy-spicy, predominantly Merlot fruit. They are richer than those found elsewhere in Entre-Deux-Mers.

🍇 Cabernet Sauvignon, Cabernet Franc, Carmenère, Merlot, Malbec, Petit Verdot

🍷— 4–10 years

WHITE Mostly dry and off-dry styles of fresh, fragrant, and fruity wines made for early drinking. Occasionally, sweeter styles are made. These wines may be sold from 1 December following the harvest without any mention of *primeur* or *nouveau*.

🍇 Sémillon, Sauvignon Blanc, and Muscadelle plus a maximum of 30 per cent Merlot Blanc

🍷— 1–3 years

LOUPIAC AOC

This appellation is located on the right bank of the Garonne, opposite Barsac. It is by far the best sweet-wine appellation in Entre-Deux-Mers and its wines are always excellent value. According to the regulations, Loupiac must be made with the "assistance" of overripe botrytized grapes and, unlike Cadillac, these wines often have the honeyed complexity of "noble rot". The best Loupiac wines come from vineyards with clay-and-limestone soil.

WHITE Luscious medium- to full-bodied wines that are sweet or intensely sweet, honey-rich, and full of flavour. They can be quite complex, and in suitable years have evident botrytis character.

🍇 Sémillon, Sauvignon Blanc, Muscadelle

🍷— 5–15 years (25 in exceptional cases)

PREMIÈRES-CÔTES-DE-BORDEAUX AOC

60-kilometre (37-mile) strip of southwest-facing slopes covering 170 hectares (420 acres) of vines scattered through 37 communes, each of which has the right to add its name to this appellation. They are: Bassens, Baurech, Béguey, Bouliac, Cadillac, Cambes, Camblanes, Capian, Carbon Blanc, Cardan, Carignan, Cenac, Cenon, Donzac, Floirac, Gabarnac, Haux, Langoiran, Laroque, Lestiac, Lormont, Monprimblanc, Omet, Paillet, Quinsac, Rions, Sémens, St-Caprais-de-Bordeaux, St-Germain-de-Graves, St-Maixant, Ste-Eulalie, Tabanac, Le Tourne, La Tresne, Verdelais, Ville-nave de Rions, and Yvrac.

RED The best red wines come from the northern communes. These well-coloured, soft, and fruity wines are a cut above basic Bordeaux AOC.

🍇 Cabernet Sauvignon, Cabernet Franc, Carmenère, Merlot, Malbec, Petit Verdot

🍷— 4–8 years

WHITE Since the 1981 harvest, no dry wines have been allowed under this generally unexciting appellation. They must have at least some sweetness, and most are in fact semi-sweet. Simple, fruity wines, well made for the most part, but lacking character.

🍇 Sémillon, Sauvignon Blanc, Muscadelle

🍷— 3–7 years

STE-CROIX-DU-MONT AOC

This is the second-best sweet-white appellation on the right bank of the Garonne, and it regularly produces more wine than Barsac. Like Loupiac

wines, these wines must be made with the "assistance" of overripe botrytized grapes. They have less honeyed complexity of "noble rot" than Loupiac wines, but often have more finesse.

WHITE Fine, viscous, honey-sweet wines that are lighter in body and colour than Loupiac wines. Excellent value when they have rich botrytis character.

🍇 Sémillon, Sauvignon Blanc, Muscadelle

🍷— 5–15 years (25 in exceptional cases)

STE-FOY-BORDEAUX AOC

Until relatively recently, Ste-Foy-Bordeaux was known primarily for its white wines, but it now produces as much red as white. There is a high proportion of "organic" winemakers in this area.

RED Ruby-coloured, medium-bodied wines made in a soft, easy-drinking style.

🍇 Cabernet Sauvignon, Cabernet Franc, Merlot, Malbec, Petit Verdot

🍷— 3–7 years

WHITE Mellow, semi-sweet wines of uninspiring quality, and fresh, crisp dry white wines that have good aroma and make attractive early drinking. These wines may be sold from 1 December following the harvest without any mention of *primeur* or *nouveau*.

🍇 Sémillon, Sauvignon Blanc, and Muscadelle, and up 10 per cent in total of Merlot Blanc, Colombard, Mauzac, and Ugni Blanc

🍷— 1–3 years

THE WINE PRODUCERS OF
ENTRE-DEUX-MERS

CHÂTEAU ARNAUD-JOUAN

Cadillac

AOC Premières-Côtes-de-Bordeaux and AOC Cadillac

★☆�V

This large, well-situated vineyard makes interesting, attractive wines.

DOMAINE DU BARRAIL

Monprimblanc

AOC Premières-Côtes-de-Bordeaux and AOC Cadillac

★☆�V

Both the red Premières Côtes and sweet white Cadillac produced at this property are worth watching.

CHÂTEAU DE BEAUREGARD

AOC Entre-Deux-Mers and AOC Bordeaux-Haut-Benauge

The red and white wines are well-made. The red has good structure, but is softened by the spice of the Merlot.

CHÂTEAU BEL-AIR

Vayres

AOC Graves de Vayres

Most of the wines made here are red and well-coloured. They are aromatic wines of a Cabernet character.

CHÂTEAU BIROT

Béguey

AOC Premières-Côtes-de-Bordeaux and AOC Cadillac

★☆�V

Popular for its easy-drinking whites, this property also produces well-balanced red wines of some finesse.

CHÂTEAU LA BLANQUERIE

Mérignas

AOC Entre-Deux-Mers

Dry white wine with a Sauvignon character and a fine finish.

CHÂTEAU BONNET

Grézillac

AOC Entre-Deux-Mers

★★☆

This top-performing Entre-Deux-Mers château is owned by André Lurton. It produces crisp, fresh, and

characterful white wines, and soft, fruity, extremely successful (Bordeaux Supérieur) red.

Second wine: *Le Colombey*
Other wines: *Tour-de-Bonnet, Château Gourmin, Château Peyraud*

CHÂTEAU BRÉTHOUS

Camblanes-et-Meynac

AOC Premières-Côtes-de-Bordeaux and AOC Cadillac

★�V

The red wines are forward and attractive, yet well-structured, while the whites are succulent and sweet.

CHÂTEAU CANET

Guillac

AOC Entre-Deux-Mers

★�V

These excellent white wines are clean and crisp, with good fruit and an elegant balance.

CHÂTEAU CAYLA

Rions

AOC Premières-Côtes-de-Bordeaux

★�V

The reds are elegant and accessible with just a touch of new oak.

CHÂTEAU DE CÉRONS

Cérons

AOC Cérons

★�V

Jean Perromat also owns Château d'Arche, and consistently produces superb, white botrytized wines.

Other wine: De Calvimont (dry white)

DOMAINE DE CHASTELET

Quinsac

AOC Premières-Côtes-de-Bordeaux and AOC Cadillac

★�V

Domaine de Chastelet produces red wine that is delicious, yet firm and complex, with very well-balanced blackcurrant fruit flavours and a hint of vanilla oak.

CLOS BOURGELAT

Cérons

AOC Cérons

★☆�V

These botrytized wines have great aroma, finesse, and complexity.

CLOS JEAN
Loupiac

AOC Loupiac

The wines produced by Clos Jean are similar quality to those of Château du Cros, but more refined and ethereal in character.

CHÂTEAU LA CLYDE
Tabanac

AOC Premières-Côtes-de-Bordeaux and AOC Cadillac

★❖

These aromatic, deep-coloured, ruby-red wines show good spice and fruit. The white has finesse and balance.

CHÂTEAU DU CROS
Loupiac

AOC Loupiac

★❖

The fine, fat, succulent sweet wines of this château are among the best of the appellation.

CHÂTEAU DINTRANS
Ste-Eulalie

AOC Premières-Côtes-de-Bordeaux and AOC Cadillac

This château produces attractive, nicely coloured, fruity red wines.

CHÂTEAU DE L'ESPLANADE
Capian

AOC Premières-Côtes-de-Bordeaux

Produced by Patrick and Sabine Bayle of Château Plaisance, these primarily Merlot wines are cheaper and simpler than those of Château Plaisance, but are easy-drinking nevertheless. They are also sold under the Château Florestan label.

CHÂTEAU FAYAU
Cadillac

AOC Premières-Côtes-de-Bordeaux and AOC Cadillac

This château produces succulent sweet wines in addition to red, clairet, and dry white wines.

Other wine: Clos des Capucins

CHÂTEAU FLORESTAN
See Château de l'Esplanade

CHÂTEAU FONGRAVE
Gornac

AOC Entre-Deux-Mers

These dry white wines have a fresh and tangy taste.

Second wine: Château de la Sablière Fongrave (red wines)

CHÂTEAU DE GORCE
Haux

AOC Premières-Côtes-de-Bordeaux and AOC Cadillac

This château produces fruity reds and fresh, floral whites.

CHÂTEAU GOUDICHAUD
Vayres

AOC Graves de Vayres

This property also extends into St-Germain-du-Puch in Entre-Deux-Mers, where it produces some very respectable wines.

CHÂTEAU GOUMIN
Dardenac

AOC Entre-Deux-Mers

Goumin is another successful André Lurton château. It produces up to 10,000 cases of pleasant, soft, fruity red wine and 5,000 cases of white wine that is slightly fuller than other similar Lurton products.

GRAND ENCLOS DU CHÂTEAU DE CÉRONS
Cérons

AOC Cérons

★

Although historically part of Château de Cérons, this is not under the same ownership. The original estate belonged to the Marquis de Calvimont, but was split in two by the route from Bordeaux to Spain, which was constructed in 1875. The marquis then sold the property in three separate lots, one of which was called Grand Enclos and was purchased by the Lataste family, who are still the owners today. The white wines of Grand Enclos are equally as rich and potentially complex as those of Château de Cérons itself (which is so called because it retains the marquis' château).

CHÂTEAU GRAND MONEIL
Salleboeuf

AOC Entre-Deux-Mers

★❖

Barely more than a thousand cases of white, but 35,000 cases of excellent-quality, soft, quaffing red.

CHÂTEAU DU GRAND MOUËYS
Capian

AOC Premières-Côtes-de-Bordeaux

★❖

Excellent-value reds for medium-term ageing are currently made at this château.

CHÂTEAU GRAVELINES
Sémens

AOC Premières-Côtes-de-Bordeaux and AOC Cadillac

★❖

This large property produces equal quantities of excellent red and white wines.

CHÂTEAU GROSSOMBRE
Branne

AOC Entre-Deux-Mers

★❖

The daughter of André Lurton runs this property, which produces lush yet elegant white wines and a beautifully concentrated red, the latter of which is sold under the Bordeaux Supérieur AOC and must be one of Bordeaux's greatest bargains.

CHÂTEAU DU GUA
Ambarès-et-Lagrave

AOC Premières-Côtes-de-Bordeaux and AOC Cadillac

★

An attractive, well-structured red wine is produced from this 8-hectare (20-acre) vineyard of fine gravel.

CHÂTEAU HAUT-BRIGNON
Cénac

AOC Premières-Côtes-de-Bordeaux and AOC Cadillac

★

This property has been steadily improving since the late 1980s, producing a soft, velvety red and crisp, dry white, plus one of Cadillac's better wines.

CHÂTEAU DE HAUX
Haux

AOC Premières-Côtes-de-Bordeaux

★★❖

These red and white wines are gorgeously ripe and ready to drink, absolutely fresh, and very elegant, and, under the Château Frère label, a fabulous oak-fermented white is also produced. Probably the top-performing château in the Premières Côtes for both red and white.

CHÂTEAU HOSTENS PICANT
Grangeneuve Nord

★❖

Since the current owners Nadine and Yves Picant purchased this property in 1986, broke off relations with the local cooperative, and built their own winery, this château has not looked back. The top wine, LVCVLLVS Cuvée d'Exception, is ★★ quality, but the "basic" grand vin is excellent, and the refreshing dry white and rosé (sold as the seldom-seen AOC Bordeaux Clairet) offer deliciously good value.

CHÂTEAU DU JUGE
Haux

AOC Premières-Côtes-de-Bordeaux and AOC Cadillac

These promising red wines are easy drinking, and full of juicy fruit flavours. Decent, if unexciting whites are also made.

CHÂTEAU DU JUGE
Cadillac

AOC Premières-Côtes-de-Bordeaux and AOC Cadillac

Respectable red and dry white wines are produced at Château du Juge, and in some years, a little sweet white wine of high quality is also made. Both red and white wines are extraordinarily good value.

CHÂTEAU LABATUT
St-Maixant

AOC Premières-Côtes-de-Bordeaux and AOC Cadillac

★

The red wines are aromatic and full of flavour, while the sweet white wines are exceptional quality. Decent dry white is also produced.

CHÂTEAU LAFITTE
Camblanes-et-Meynac

AOC Premières-Côtes-de-Bordeaux and AOC Cadillac

Nothing like the real thing (the famous premier cru), of course, but the wine is decent, well structured, and capable of improving with age – a cheap way to get a Château Lafitte on the table, even if it is not the Château Lafite.

CHÂTEAU LAFUE
Cadillac

AOC Ste-Croix-du-Mont

Attractive, sweet white wines with more of a fruity than a botrytis character. Nearly a quarter of the production is red wine.

CHÂTEAU LAMOTHE
Haux

AOC Premières-Côtes-de-Bordeaux and AOC Cadillac

Some exceptionally good wines have been produced in recent years at this château, which derives its name from "La Motte", a rocky spur that protects the vineyard.

CHÂTEAU LAROCHE BEL AIR
Baurech

AOC Premières-Côtes-de-Bordeaux

Absolutely delicious-drinking reds under the basic Château Laroche label, and an even better selection of oak-aged reds under Laroche Bel Air.

CHÂTEAU LATOUR
St-Martin-du-Puy
AOC Entre-Deux-Mers

From this ancient château, parts of which date back to the 14th century, 10,000 cases of attractive, well-balanced, smooth red Bordeaux Supérieur are produced every year. This château's technically sound wines often win prizes and enable its devotees to claim that they can afford to drink Château Latour every day, at minimum expense.

CHÂTEAU LATOUR
Camblanes-et-Meynac
AOC Premières-Côtes-de-Bordeaux and AOC Cadillac

This is another everyday-drinking claret with this prestigious name.

CHÂTEAU LAUNAY
Soussac
AOC Entre-Deux-Mers

This large property produces 40,000 cases of a fresh dry white wine and 15,000 cases of a red wine sold under the "Haut-Castanet" label.

Other wines: *Bradoire, Château Dubory, Château Haut-Courgeaux, Château La Vaillante*

CHÂTEAU LAURETTE
Cadillac
AOC Ste-Croix-du-Mont
☆

This property is under the same ownership as Château Lafue, and run along similar lines.

CHÂTEAU LOUBENS
Cadillac
AOC Ste-Croix-du-Mont
★

This château produces rich, liquorous, superbly balanced sweet white wines. Dry white wines are sold as "Fleur Blanc", and a little red wine is also made.

Other wine: *Fleur Blanc de Château Loubens*

CHÂTEAU LOUPIAC-GAUDIET
Loupiac
AOC Loupiac

Fine, honey-rich sweet wines hinting of crystallized fruit are produced here.

CHÂTEAU LOUSTEAU-VIEIL
Cadillac
AOC Ste-Croix-du-Mont
★

This property produces richly flavoured, high-quality sweet wines.

CHÂTEAU MACHORRE
St-Martin-de-Sescas
AOC Côtes-de-Bordeaux-St-Macaire
☆

The sweet white wine of this château has an attractive, fresh, fruit-salad flavour and is one of the best examples of the appellation. Very respectable red and dry Sauvignon wines are also produced, which are sold under the Bordeaux appellations.

CHÂTEAU DES MAILLES
Cadillac
AOC Ste-Croix-du-Mont

Some outstanding sweet wines are produced at Château des Mailles, but the wines can occasionally be disappointing.

CHÂTEAU LA MAUBASTIT
AOC Ste-Foy-de-Bordeaux
◉

Some 5,000 cases of white and 2,000 of red, both "organic" wines, are sold under the Bordeaux appellation.

CHÂTEAU MORLAN-TUILIÈRE
St-Pierre-de-Bat
AOC Entre-Deux-Mers-Haut-Benauge and Bordeaux Haut-Benauge
Ⓑ

One of the best properties of the area, producing a vibrant, crystal-clear Entre-Deux-Mers-Haut-Benauge, a Bordeaux Supérieur in the *moelleux* style, and a fairly full-bodied red AOC Bordeaux.

CHÂTEAU MOULIN DE LAUNAY
Soussac
AOC Entre-Deux-Mers

Despite the vast quantity produced, the dry white wine is crisp and fruity, and of a very fine standard. A little red is also produced.

Other wines: *Plessis, Château Tertre-de-Launay, Château de Tuilerie, Château la Vigerie*

CHÂTEAU MOULIN DE ROMAGE
AOC Ste-Foy-de-Bordeaux

This château produces equal quantities of "organic" red and white.

DOMAINE DU NOBLE
Loupiac
AOC Loupiac

This property consistently produces fine botrytized wines that combine sweetness and strength with elegance and a fresh, long finish.

CHÂTEAU PETIT-PEY
St-André-du-Bois
AOC Côtes-de-Bordeaux-St-Macaire

Good, sweet white St-Macaire and agreeably soft red AOC Bordeaux are made at this property.

CHÂTEAU PEYREBON
Grézillac
AOC Entre-Deux-Mers

Produces red and white wine in almost equal quantities. The dry white is fine and flavoursome.

CHÂTEAU PEYRINES
Mourens
AOC Entre-Deux-Mers-Haut-Benauge and Bordeaux Haut-Benauge
★☆

The vineyard of this château has an excellent southern exposure and produces fruity red and white wines.

CHÂTEAU DE PIC
Le Tourne
AOC Premières-Côtes-de-Bordeaux

The basic red is a lovely, creamy-sweet, easy-drinking, fruity wine. A superb oak-aged red under the *Cuvée* Tradition label is also made.

CHÂTEAU PICHON-BELLEVUE
Vayres
AOC Graves de Vayres

The red wines are variable, but the dry whites are delicate and refined.

CHÂTEAU PLAISANCE
Capian
AOC Premières-Côtes-de-Bordeaux

The *Cuvée* Tradition, in which the wine is aged in oak and is unfiltered, gives rich, ripe fruit with supple tannin structure and smoky oak.

Other wines: *De l'Esplanade, Château Florestin*

CHÂTEAU DE PLASSAN
Tabanac
AOC Premières-Côtes-de-Bordeaux

The basic red has a lot of character, with cherry-minty undertones in riper years. However, the fuller, more complex *cuvée spéciale* is worth paying for, particularly if you want a wine to accompany food.

CHÂTEAU PONTETTE-BELLEGRAVE
Vayres
AOC Graves de Vayres

This property has a reputation for subtly flavoured, dry white wines.

CHÂTEAU PUY BARDENS
Cambes
AOC Premières-Côtes-de-Bordeaux

This top-performing château produces reds with sweet, ripe, fat fruit and a soft, velvety finish.

CHÂTEAU LA RAME
Cadillac
AOC Ste-Croix-du-Mont

One of the top wines of the appellation, La Rame can have fruit, with cream and honey flavours.

CHÂTEAU REYNON-PEYRAT
Béguey
AOC Premières-Côtes-de-Bordeaux

This property produces a superb, oak-aged Premières Côtes red wine, and two dry white wines under the Château Reynon label.

CHÂTEAU RICAUD
Loupiac
AOC Loupiac

The wines of Château Ricaud are once again the best in the Loupiac appellation. They suffered a significant decline under the previous proprietor, but have at last recovered, and now display great class under new ownership.

CHÂTEAU DE LA SABLIÈRE-FONGRAVE
Gornac
AOC Entre-Deux-Mers-Haut-Benauge and Bordeaux Haut-Benauge

Sold as a Bordeaux Supérieur, the red wine of Château de la Sablière-Fongrave is fairly robust and requires time in bottle to soften. A much better quality dry white is produced and sold under the Entre-Deux-Mers appellation.

CHÂTEAU TANESSE
Langoiran
AOC Premières-Côtes-de-Bordeaux and AOC Cadillac

A Cordier property, Château Tanesse produces a decent Cabernet-dominated red, and fine-quality, Sauvignon-style dry white.

CHÂTEAU DES TASTES
Cadillac
AOC Ste-Croix-du-Mont
★Ⓥ

The sweet white wine is truly exciting; luxurious in texture, with creamy-rich flavours showing the classic complex character of botrytis.

CHÂTEAU TERFORT
Cadillac
AOC Ste-Croix-du-Mont
☆

A small amount of excellent sweet white wine is produced by Château Terfort.

CHÂTEAU THIEULEY
La Sauve
AOC Entre-Deux-Mers
☆

Château Thieuley is owned by Professor Courselle, a former Médoc professor of viticulture and oenology. His dry white combines good fruit flavour with a fine Sauvignon style, while the red is good and silky.

CHÂTEAU DE TOUTIGEAC
Targon
AOC Entre-Deux-Mers-Haut-Benauge and Bordeaux Haut-Benauge
☆Ⓥ

Château de Toutigeac is a well-known property that produces full, rich red wine. It is made for early drinking, and is the best the château produces.

BURGUNDY

Villages with double-barrelled names are the key to Burgundy's greatest wines. You cannot become an expert overnight, but if you remember that the second part of every double-barrelled Burgundian village is one of its best vineyards, you will instantly know some of Burgundy's greatest wines.

THIS IS BECAUSE these villages hijacked the names of their most famous vineyards, so that humble village wines could sell on the back of the finest grands crus. The village of Gevrey was the first to do this when in 1848 it took the name of its Chambertin vineyard to become Gevrey-Chambertin. Say "Burgundy" and most people think of the famous wines of the Côtes de Nuits and Côtes de Beaune, but Burgundy stretches from Chablis, which is close to the Aube vineyards of Champagne, down to Beaujolais, which is in the Rhône *département*. In fact, the Côtes de Nuits and Côtes de Beaune account for less than 10 per cent of Burgundy, while even a much-reduced Beaujolais represents a third of the region's entire production. Problems with the quality of so much Beaujolais led to the *vin de merde* story by *Lyon Mag* in 2001, but few people outside of Beaujolais's own backyard would have heard of this if 56 cooperatives had not decided to sue the local rag. Within a short time, wine lovers all over the world discovered that *Lyon Mag* had described 1.1 million cases of Beaujolais as *vin de merde* because no one wanted it; consequently, it had to be distilled (*see* p212). Since the case came to light, the figures speak for themselves, as production has plummeted by more than 50 per cent at the bottom of the Beaujolais market. The best Beaujolais today is better than it has ever been, but as it became impossible to get rid of the cheapest and nastiest Beaujolais, producers began to sell it as Bourgogne AOC – perfectly legal, but it began damaging the generic reputation of Burgundy itself, prompting calls to remove Beaujolais from the Burgundy region altogether. Even though it is made from an entirely different grape variety grown way down in the Rhône, that was never going to happen, but the pressure it brought to bear on the situation did force through changes in the AOCs. As from the 2011 vintage, wines from the Beaujolais district can no longer be sold under the Bourgogne AOC and must be sold as Coteaux Bourgignons AOC (formerly called Bourgogne Ordinaire or Bourgogne Grand

VIRÉ, MÂCONNAIS
Viré is the most ubiquitous of Mâcon's village appellations, but it nevertheless makes consistently fine wines.

Ordinaire). This appellation is open to wines from all over the Burgundy region but, in practice, will primarily be produced from Gamay grown in Beaujolais. Additionally, a new generic appellation, Bourgogne Côte d'Or AOC, has been created for wines exclusively from the Côte d'Or.

Burgundy still produces the world's greatest Chardonnay and Pinot Noir wines, and the only Gamay wines ever to achieve classic status, but it is increasingly debased by a growing number of lacklustre, sometimes quite disgusting, mass-market wines that rely solely upon the reputation of the famous Burgundian names, which their producers then abuse to sell low-quality wines at high prices.

Burgundy, or *Bourgogne* as it is known in French, is an area rich in history, gastronomy, and wine, but unlike the great estates of Bordeaux, the finest Burgundian vineyards are owned by a proliferation of smallholders. Prior to 1789, the church owned most of the vineyards in Burgundy, but these were seized and broken up as a direct result of the Revolution, which was as much anti-church as anti-aristocracy. While in Bordeaux, although some of the large wine estates were owned by the aristocracy, many

RECENT BURGUNDY VINTAGES

2010 Apart from rampant rot in the Chardonnay of the southern Côtes de Beaune, the whites are generally better than the reds, with fine balance, good fruit, and a distinctive, crisp finish. The reds will require careful selection, particularly at village and regional level, but the best *grands* and *premiers crus* have good colour and plenty of fruit. It's not a particularly ripe vintage, though, and a green meanness is likely to rear its ugly head in many of the less successful wines. Beaujolais is surprisingly good, with dark colour and plenty of early-drinking fruit.

2009 This is a vintage that is so easy to drink when young that doubts can easily set in as to the wine's staying power. But when a lush and full vintage happens naturally in European vineyards, and there is great finesse to match

the charm, such balance should tell us to be confident about the wine's potential longevity. This is definitely a great vintage of extraordinary quality, including the best Beaujolais in almost 40 years. The general quality of whites is on par with the 2005s but with more individual highlights.

2008 This is an inconsistent vintage for reds, with the Côte de Nuits much better than the Cote de Beaune, although Pommard does stand out. However, even the best red wines are more varietal than complex. This is more of a white-wine vintage, with some potentially long-lived wines produced, due in many cases to high malic-acid levels.

2007 Definitely a white-wine vintage, although some attractive, lighter-bodied reds were

produced. The wines were exceptional in Mâcon and Côte Chalonnaise, and very good in Beaujolais, with elegant reds in the Côte d'Or, but fleshier in the Côte de Nuits than in the Côtes de Beaune.

2006 Some great wines were produced in Chablis, which was the most successful Burgundian district in 2006. Generally, this is a white-wine vintage all round, with whites outperforming reds in the Côte de Beaune, Côte de Nuits, Côtes Chalonnaise, and, as to be expected, the Mâconnais. Best reds are in the early-drinking style with only a modest capacity to age, and most are to be found in the Côtes Chalonnaise. Beaujolais did well, too.

were owned by the *bourgeoisie*, who, because of their long association with the English, were anti-papist, and so escaped the full wrath of the Revolution. In Burgundy the great vineyards were further fragmented by inheritance laws, which divided the plots into smaller and smaller parcels. Consequently, many *crus*, or growths, are now owned by as many as 85 individual growers. The initial effect of this proprietorial carve-up was to encourage the supremacy of *le négoce*. Few commercial houses had been established prior to the mid-18th century because of the difficulty of exporting from a land-locked area, but with better transport and no opposition from land-owning aristocracy, merchant power grew rapidly. A network of brokers evolved in which dealers became experts on very small, localized areas.

As ownership diversified even further, it became a very specialized, and therefore rewarding, job to keep an up-to-date and comprehensive knowledge of a complex situation. The brokers were vital to the success of a *négociant*, and the *négoce* himself was essential to the success of international trade and therefore responsible for establishing the reputation of Burgundy.

THE ROLE OF THE NÉGOCIANT

Until the early 1980s, virtually all Burgundy would be sold through *négociants* and, although many of them had their own vineyards, these wines were seldom domaine-bottled. Faced with the rise of domaine-bottled Burgundies from small growers, most of the old-fashioned merchants were devoured by Boisset (*see* Did You Know? box), which has become the largest merchant of its kind. Boisset might survive by marketing a mass of different labels, particularly in the supermarket sector or at the bottom end of the restaurant market, but the recent hiring of Pascal Marchand indicates that it has changed its strategy. Marchand is the French-Canadian whose wine-wizardry enabled the quality at Domaine Comte Armand to soar in the second half of the 1990s. By enticing him away to set up and run Domaine de la Vougeraie, Boisset has shown a determination to join the ranks of the few traditional *négociants* who can be said to be top-performing. These currently include Bouchard Père, Drouhin, Louis Jadot, and Leroy, who have not only enlarged their own domaines but have also taken an increasingly proactive role in the vineyards of their suppliers,

GRAND CRU VALMUR, CHABLIS
At the very heart of Chablis' grands crus lies Valmur. Bordered by Grenouilles and Vaudésir on one side and Les Clos on the other, this vineyard is renowned for the fine bouquet and rich flavour of its wines.

DID YOU KNOW?

In 2009, Burgundy *super-négociant* head Jean-Charles Boisset married Gina Gallo, the grand-daughter of California's Julio Gallo.

tending now to buy in grapes or must rather than wines. Until this new strategy evolved, the purchase of wine rather than grapes was the major difference between the old-style *négociant* and the new-wave growers-cum-merchants. The best of the latter include the likes of Jean-Marc Boillot, Michel Colin, Bernard Morey, and Sauzet, who tend to buy grapes to expand their range of single-vineyard wines, in contrast to the old-style merchant, who still churns out examples from nearly every village under the Burgundian sun.

The decline of the old-style merchant is clearly highlighted by domaine-bottling statistics. Today, as much as 90 per cent of all *grand cru* wines (and 50 per cent of all *premiers crus*) are domaine bottled, although – tellingly – only 24 per cent of the entire production of Burgundy is domaine bottled.

BURGUNDY'S RICH DIVERSITY

Chablis in the north of Burgundy produces the crispest white Chardonnay wines in the world and is geographically closer to Champagne, of which it was once a part, than to the rest of Burgundy. After travelling more than 100 kilometres (60 miles) southwest from Champagne, we reach the great Burgundy districts of the Côte d'Or: the Côte de Nuits is encountered first, followed by the Côte de Beaune.

If you associate Nuits with "night" or "darkness" and Beaune with "bone-white", then you will easily remember which area is most famous for which wine: for although both *côtes* make excellent red and white wines, most of the greatest red Burgundies come from the Côte de Nuits, whereas most of the greatest white Burgundies come from the Côte de Beaune.

CORTON, CÔTE DE BEAUNE
Capped by the Bois de Corton, this magnificent slope produces the Côte de Beaune's most famous red wines and minuscule amounts of Corton Charlemagne, possibly the greatest of all white Burgundies.

BURGUNDY, *see also p101*

The route between Dijon and Lyon is studded with the illustrious names of the great growths of Burgundy. Above this north-south band are the Yonne appellations that include Chablis.

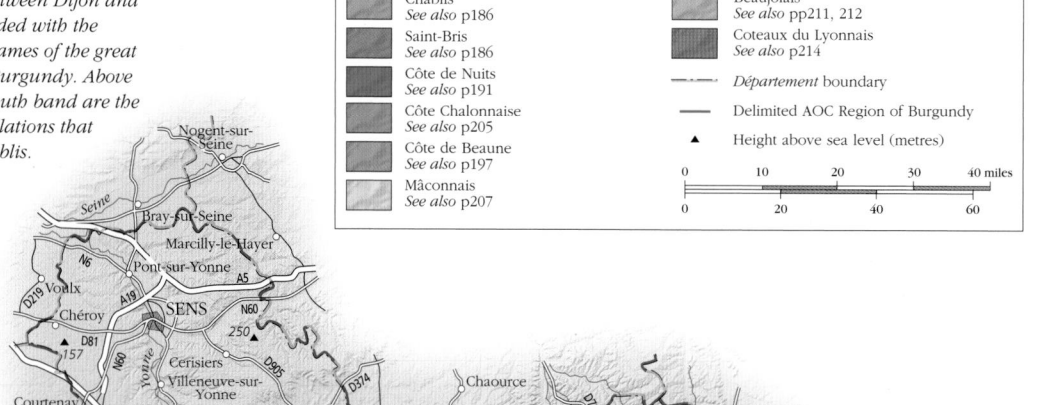

Chablis *See also p186*	Beaujolais *See also pp211, 212*
Saint-Bris *See also p186*	Coteaux du Lyonnais *See also p214*
Côte de Nuits *See also p191*	- - - - *Département* boundary
Côte Chalonnaise *See also p205*	—— Delimited AOC Region of Burgundy
Côte de Beaune *See also p197*	▲ Height above sea level (metres)
Mâconnais *See also p207*	

DID YOU KNOW?

The *super-négociant* Boisset currently owns the following:

- Jean-Claude Boisset (Côte de Nuits)
- Bouchard Aîné & Fils (Côte de Beaune)
- F Chauvenet (Côte de Nuits)
- Château du Grand Talencé (Beaujolais)
- Jaffelin (Côte de Beaune)
- Benoît Lafont (Beaujolais)
- Mommessin (Beaujolais)
- J Moreau & Fils (Chablis)
- Morin Père & Fils (Côte de Nuits)
- Joseph Pellerin (Beaujolais)
- Pierre Ponnelle (Côte de Beaune)
- Ropiteau Frères (Côte de Beaune)
- Thomas-Bassot (Côte de Nuits)
- Thorin (Beaujolais)
- Charles Vienot (Côte de Nuits)
- Domaine de la Vougeraie (Côte de Nuits)

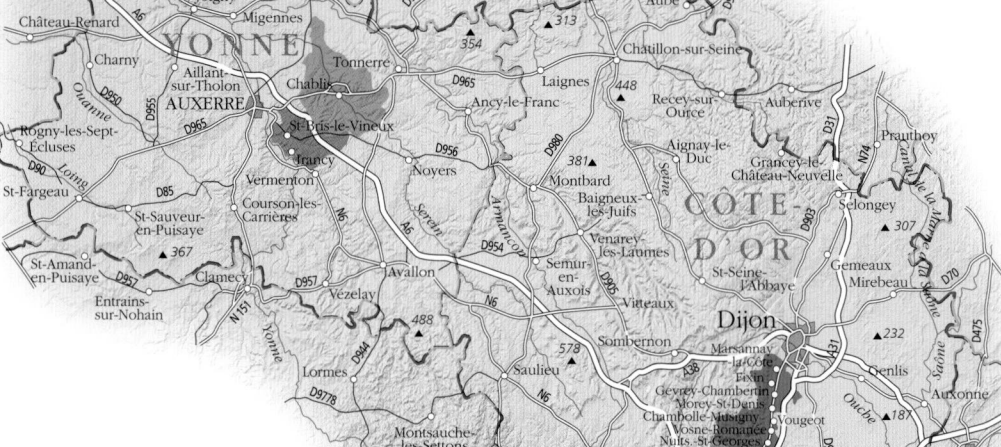

BURGUNDY AT A GLANCE

% OF ALL BURGUNDY	DISTRICT	HECTOLITRES (CASES)	PRODUCTION		
			RED/ROSÉ	WHITE	(GRANDS CRUS)
18	Generic AOCs	412,098 (4,578,867)	56	44	–
6	Crémant AOCs	130,606 (1,451,178)	8	92	–
12	Chablis	289,104 (3,212,267)	–	100	1.80%
4	Côte de Nuits	83,079 (923,100)	96	4	11.00%
1	Hautes-Côtes de Nuits	25,000 (277,778)	97	3	–
8	Côtes de Beaune	175,024 (1,944,711)	63	37	4.00%
1	Hautes-Côtes de Beaune	33,000 (366,667)	98	2	–
3	Côte Chalonnaise	79,737 (885,967)	52	48	–
15	Mâconnais	342,356 (3,803,956)	15	85	–
33	Beaujolais	759,000 (8,433,333)	99	1	–
100	TOTAL	2,329,004[1] (25,877,822[1])	58[2]	42[2]	–

[1] These totals might not tally with each other due to rounding of numbers above
[2] Average percentage for region

VINEYARD AND CHÂTEAU OF RULLY
With the most northerly AOC vineyards of the Côte Chalonnaise, Rully produces excellent dry Chardonnay wines and some pleasant red wines as well.

The Côte Chalonnaise, or Mercurey, region – probably the least-known, but certainly the best-value, wine district of Burgundy – produces similar, if somewhat less classic, red and white styles to those in the Côte de Beaune. Softer still are the primarily white wines of Mâcon, where Pouilly Fuissé AOC rules supreme. (Note: this wine should never be confused with Pouilly Fumé AOC in the Loire.)

Still in Burgundy, but further south, is the Beaujolais region, which is in the Rhône *département*, although its soft, light, fluffy, fruity red wines are far removed from the archetypal full-bodied red wines that we immediately think of as coming from the Rhône Valley.

Beaujolais can be delicious, but most of it is not. Whereas Beaujolais Nouveau was never meant to be considered as a serious wine, it is now a joke, and far too many of even the best Beaujolais *cru* wines are simply overpriced, but that is all part of Burgundy's rich tapestry.

THE GENERIC APPELLATIONS OF
BURGUNDY

BOURGOGNE AOC

Many writers consider Bourgogne AOC to be too basic and boring to warrant serious attention, but for me it is the most instructive of all Burgundy's appellations. If a producer cares about the quality of the *Bourgogne*, how much more effort does that producer put into making higher-quality wines? I delight in finding a delicious, easy-to-drink *Bourgogne*, and I often get more of a kick discovering one that will improve for several years than I do from a superior appellation that should age well, considering its famous name and high price. Light-red/dark-rosé wines may be sold as Bourgogne Clairet AOC, but the style is outmoded and the appellation rarely seen.

RED Despite the grape varieties that may be used to make this wine, the only *Bourgogne* worth seeking out is that with the flavour and aroma of pure Pinot Noir. Many producers indicate the grape variety on the label.

🍇 Pinot Noir, Pinot Gris, Pinot Liébault plus, in the Yonne district, César, Tressot, and Gamay (if from one of the original nine *crus Beaujolais* – but not Régnié)

🍷⤳ 2–5 years

WHITE There are a lot of boring white wines made under this appellation, and unless you have access to something more interesting like the wine from J-F Coche-Dury or another top grower, it is probably safer to buy an inexpensive Mâcon AOC. The once over-performing Bourgogne Blanc Clos du Château du Meursault, which was often better than Château du Meursault itself (which is Meursault AOC), is now one of Burgundy's under-performers

(along with Château de Meursault!). These wines may be sold as *primeur* or *nouveau* as from the third Thursday of November following the harvest.

🍇 Chardonnay, Pinot Blanc

🍷⤳ 1–4 years

ROSÉ The wines produced under this appellation are acceptable, but they are never special – it is the least exciting category of *Bourgogne*.

🍇 Pinot Noir, Pinot Gris, Pinot Liébault, plus, in the Yonne district, César and Tressot

🍷⤳ 1–4 years

✓ **Bourgogne Rouge** *Robert Arnoux* • *Ghislaine Barthod* • *Bertagna* • *Jean-Marc Boillot* • *Pascal Bouley* • *Carré-Courbin* • *Sylvain Cathiard* • *Château de Chamilly* • *Philippe Charlopin* • *Christian Clerget* • *J-F Coche-Dury* • *de la Combe* • *Joseph Drouhin* • *Alex Gambal* • *Anne Gros* • *Henri Jayer* • *Michel Juillot* • *Pierre Labet* • *Labouré-Roi* • *Michel Lafarge* • *Marie-Hélène Laugrotte* • *Dominique Laurent* • *Olivier Leflaive* • *Lucien Lemoine* • *Leroy* ❽ *Hubert Lignier* • *Catherine et Claude Maréchal* (Cathérine, Gravel) • *Jean-Philippe Marchand* • *Mauperthuis* (Grande Réserve) • *Olivier Merlin* (Les Cras) ◉ • *Denis Mortet* • *Lucien Mouzard* • *de Perdrix* • *des Pitoux* • *de la Pousse d'Or* • *Daniel Rion & Fils* • *Michel & Patrice Rion* • *Nicolas Rossignol* • *Emmanuel Rouget* • *Tollot-Beaut* • *Vallet Frères* • *A & P de Villaine* ◉ • *de la Vougeraie* ❽ (Terres de Familles)
Bourgogne Blanc *Jean-Baptiste Béjot* • *Simon Bize & Fils* • *Jean-Marc Boillot* • *Jean-Marc Brocard* (Cuvée Jurassique) • *J-F Coche-Dury* • *Coste-Caumartin* • *Alex Gambal* • *Patrick Javillier* • *François Jobard* • *Labouré-Roi* • *Michel Lafarge* • *Hubert Lamy* •

Leflaive ❽ • *Olivier Leflaive* • *Lucien Lemoine* • *Lorenzon* • *Catherine et Claude Maréchal* • *Bátrice & Gilles Mathias* • *Olivier Merlin* ◉ • *Pierre Morey* ❽ • *Antonin Rodet* • *Georges Roumier* • *Michel Rouyer* (Domaine du Petit-Béru) • *Tollot-Beaut* • *Henry de Vézelay* • *A & P de Villaine* ◉
Bourgogne Rosé *Abbaye du Petit Quincy* • *Philippe Defrance* • *Elise Villiers*

Note For other local generic wines *see*:
Chablis Bourgogne Chitry AOC, Bourgogne Coulanges-la-Vineuse AOC, Bourgogne Côtes d'Auxerre AOC, Bourgogne Côte Saint-Jacques AOC, Bourgogne Épineuil AOC, Bourgogne Vézelay AOC (p188)

• **Côte de Nuits** and **Hautes-Côtes de Nuits** Bourgogne Hautes-Côtes de Nuits AOC, Bourgogne Le Chapitre AOC, Bourgogne Montrecul AOC (p192)

• **Côte de Beaune** and **Hautes-Côtes de Beaune** Bourgogne La Chapelle Notre-Dame AOC, Bourgogne Hautes-Côtes de Beaune AOC (p200)

• **Côte Chalonnaise** Bourgogne Côte Chalonnaise AOC, Bourgogne Côtes du Couchois AOC (p205)

BOURGOGNE ALIGOTÉ AOC

The finest Bourgogne-Aligoté wines come from the village of Bouzeron in the Mercurey region, which has its own appellation (*see also* Bouzeron AOC, p206). With the exception of the wines below, the remaining Aligoté can be improved by adding *crème de cassis*, a local blackcurrant liqueur, to create an aperitif known as a "Kir".

WHITE Dry wines that are usually thin, acid, and not very pleasant: bad examples are even worse and are becoming widespread. When good, however, Aligoté can make a refreshing change from Burgundy's ubiquitous Chardonnay wines. However, even among the top producers, this grape seems to inflict its own inconsistency. Any one of the following recommended producers could make the greatest Aligoté of the vintage one year, then turn out something very ordinary the next year. Bourgogne Aligoté may be sold as *primeur* or *nouveau* from the third Thursday of November following the harvest.

🌿 Aligoté and a maximum of 15% Chardonnay

🍷 1–4 years

✓ *d'Auvenay* ❸ • *Bersan* • *Marc Brocard* • *Arnaud Ente* • *Naudin-Ferrand* • *de la Folie* • *Alex Gambal* • *Ghislaine et Jean-Hughes Goisot* • *François Jobard* • *Daniel Largeot* • *Catherine et Claude Maréchal* • *Edmond Monot* • *Alice et Olivier Moor* • *Jacky Renard* • *de la Sarazinière* (Clos des Bruyères) • *Thévenot-le-Brun & Fils* • *Vignerons des Terres Secrètes* (Château des Moines) • *A & P de Villaine* ◉

BOURGOGNE CÔTE D'OR AOC

This new appellation, as from the 2012 harvest, applies to red, white, and rosé wines produced from grapes grown exclusively on specified plots restricted to the Côte d'Or *département* (ie, the Côte de Nuits and Côte de Beaune), with tougher criteria than the basic Bourgogne AOC for yields, ripeness levels, and so on. At the time of writing, INAO was still in the process of delimiting the boundaries for Bourgogne Côte d'Or AOC, which should end up being the best *Bourgogne* on the market. However, there is no guarantee; undrinkable *grand cru* Burgundy exists, so we will have to wait and see.

BOURGOGNE GAMAY AOC

This new appellation from the 2012 vintage preserves Gamay under the *Bourgogne* label but will be restricted to vineyards within the 10 *crus* Beaujolais.

BOURGOGNE GRAND-ORDINAIRE AOC

See Coteaux Bourguignons AOC

BOURGOGNE MOUSSEUX AOC

Since December 1985 this appellation has been limited to, and remains the only outlet for, sparkling red Burgundy.

SPARKLING RED A favourite fizzy tipple in the pubs of pre-war Britain. This wine's sweet flavour is very much out of step with today's sophisticated consumers.

🌿 Pinot Noir, Gamay, plus, in the Yonne district, César and Tressot

🍷 Upon purchase

BOURGOGNE ORDINAIRE AOC

See Coteaux Bourguignons AOC

BOURGOGNE PASSE-TOUT-GRAINS AOC

Made from a *mélange* of Pinot Noir and Gamay grapes, *passe-tout-grains* is the descendant of an authentic peasant wine. A grower would fill his vat with anything growing in his vineyard and ferment it all together. Thus *passe-tout-grains* once contained numerous grape varieties. The Pinot Noir and Gamay varieties were, however, the most widely planted, and the wine naturally evolved as a two-grape product. Up until 1943, a minimum of one-fifth Pinot Noir was enforced by law; now the minimum is one-third.

RED Many *passe-tout-grains* used to be drunk too early, as the better-quality examples require a few years of bottle-ageing to show the aristocratic influence of their Pinot Noir content. With an increase in Pinot Noir production and more modern vinification techniques, more producers have begun making softer, less rustic *passe-tout-grains*, which are easier to drink when young. They remain relatively modest wines.

🌿 Pinot Noir plus a maximum of one-third Gamay and a combined maximum of 15% Chardonnay, Pinot Blanc, and Pinot Gris

🍷 2–6 years

ROSÉ This dry, pink version is worth trying.

🌿 A maximum of one-third Gamay plus Pinot Noir and Pinot Liébault

🍷 1–3 years

✓ *Robert Chevillon* • *Edmond Cornu & Fils* • *Michel Lafarge* • *Laurent Ponsot* (former Volpato old vines) • *Lejeune* • *Daniel Rion & Fils*

COTEAUX BOURGUIGNONS AOC

The name of this appellation has altered since the 2011 vintage, when no wines made in the Beaujolais district could be declassified into Bourgogne AOC but had to be sold under the lower-quality Bourgogne Ordinaire or Bourgogne Grand-Ordinaire. This was as a result of complaints from Côte d'Or producers that inferior Gamay sold under Burgundy's name was damaging their reputation. Forced to accept this demotion, but not wanting to be lumbered with the "ordinary" or "very ordinary" tag, Beaujolais producers settled for Coteaux Bourguignons as a mutually acceptable compromise. Although this appellation is open to wines from all over the Burgundy region, in all likelihood the reds will be primarily produced from Gamay grown in Beaujolais.

RED No wines produced under this appellation at the time of writing.

🌿 A minimum of 85% Gamay, Pinot Noir, and (in the Yonne *département* only) César, plus Chardonnay, Pinot Blanc, and Pinot Gris, with a maximum in total of 10% Gamay de Bouze and Gamay de Chaudenay

WHITE No wines produced under this appellation at the time of writing.

🌿 Aligoté, Chardonnay, Melon de Bourgogne, Pinot Blanc, Pinot Gris

ROSÉ No wines produced under this appellation at the time of writing.

🌿 A minimum of 85% Gamay, Pinot Noir, and (in the Yonne *département* only) César, plus Chardonnay and Pinot Blanc, but only if part of a field blend with the black varieties

CRÉMANT DE BOURGOGNE AOC

This appellation was created in 1975 to supersede the Bourgogne Mousseux AOC, which failed to inspire a quality image because the term "*mousseux*" also applied to cheap sparkling wines. Bourgogne Mousseux is now for red wines only. The major production centres for Crémant de Bourgogne are the Yonne, Region de Mercurey, and the Mâconnais. There are already many exciting wines, and the quality is certain to improve as more producers specialize in cultivating grapes specifically for sparkling wines, rather than relying on excess or inferior grapes, as was traditional in Burgundy.

SPARKLING WHITE Dry but round, the styles range from fresh and light to rich and toasty.

🌿 Pinot Noir, Pinot Gris, Pinot Blanc, Chardonnay, Sacy, Aligoté, Melon de Bourgogne, and a maximum of 20% Gamay

🍷 3–7 years

SPARKLING ROSÉ Until now the best pink Crémant produced outside of Champagne has come from Alsace. Good examples are made in Burgundy, but have not realized their potential.

🌿 Pinot Noir, Pinot Gris, Pinot Blanc, Chardonnay, Sacy, Aligoté, Melon de Bourgogne, and a maximum of 20% Gamay

🍷 2–5 years

✓ *Caves de Bailly* • *André Bonhomme* • *Paul Chollet* • *André Delorme* • *Cave de Lugny* • *Roux Père* • *Caves de Viré*

THE CHABLIS DISTRICT

Chablis is one of Burgundy's two classic white-wine areas, yet this island of vines is closer to Champagne than to the rest of Burgundy, and its Chardonnay grape is grown on soils and under climatic conditions that are more champenois *than* bourguignon.

LIKE CHAMPAGNE, CHABLIS owes much of its success to a cool and uncertain northern climate that puts viticulture on a knife-edge. This is a source of constant worry and not a little diabolical wine, but when everything comes together just right, Chablis can produce the most electrifying Chardonnay in the world.

Known as the "Golden Gate", this area has the advantage of being the inevitable first stop for anyone visiting the Burgundy region by car, whether directly from Paris or via Champagne. Situated in the Yonne *département*, much of which once formed part of the ancient province of Champagne, Chablis gives the distinct impression of an area cut off not simply from the rest of Burgundy but from the rest of France. Indeed, the great *négociants* of the Côte d'Or rarely visit Chablis and have never made any significant penetration into what appears to be a closed-shop trade.

THE VARYING STYLES OF CHABLIS
The traditional description of Chablis is of a wine of clear, pale colour with a green hue around the rim. It is very straight and positive, with an aggressive, steely character, very direct attack, and a high level of acidity that needs a few years to round out.

THE TOWN OF CHABLIS
Above the town of Chablis, the vines face southeast and southwest, clinging to hills along the banks of the Serein, a small tributary of the Yonne. These are the grand cru *vineyards that make this district's finest wines.*

This description, however, rarely applies, as much has changed in the way these wines are made at both ends of the quality spectrum.

Thirty-five years ago most Chablis did not undergo malolactic fermentation. The wines that resulted had a naturally high acidity, and were hard, green, and ungenerous in their youth, although they often matured into wines of incomparable finesse. Now, most

FACTORS AFFECTING TASTE AND QUALITY

LOCATION
Chablis is isolated halfway between Beaune and Paris, 30 kilometres (19 miles) from the southernmost vineyards of Champagne, but 100 kilometres (60 miles) from the rest of Burgundy.

CLIMATE
This area has a semi-continental climate with minimal Atlantic influence, which results in a long, cold winter, a humid spring, and a fairly hot, very sunny summer. Hail storms and spring frosts are the greatest hazards.

ASPECT
All the *grands crus* are located on one stretch of southwest-facing slopes just north of Chablis itself, where the vineyards are at a height of between 150 and 200 metres (490 to 660 feet). Apart from the southwest-facing slopes of Fourchaume and Montée de Tonnerre, the *premier cru* slopes face southeast.

SOIL
This area is predominantly covered with calcareous clay, and the traditional view is that of the two major types, Kimmeridgian and Portlandian, only the former is suitable for classic Chablis, but

this is neither proven nor likely. Geologically they have the same Upper Jurassic origin. Any intrinsic geographical differences should be put down to aspect, microclimate, and the varied nature of the sedimentary beds that underlie and interbed with the Kimmeridgian and Portlandian soils.

VITICULTURE AND VINIFICATION
The vineyards in Chablis have undergone rapid expansion, most particularly in the generic appellation and the *premiers crus*, both of which have doubled in size since the early 1970s. Mechanical harvesting has now found its way to the *grands crus* slopes of Chablis, but smaller producers still pick by hand. Most Chablis is fermented in stainless steel, but oak barrels are making a comeback, although too much new oak fights against the lean, austere intensity of the Chardonnay grown in this district.

GRAPE VARIETIES
Primary variety: Chardonnay
Secondary varieties: Aligoté, César, Gamay, Melon de Bourgogne, Pinot Beurot (Pinot Gris), Pinot Blanc, Pinot Liébault, Sauvignon Blanc, Sacy, Tressot

MACHINE-HARVESTING AT DOMAINE STE-CLAIRE IN PRÉHY
Machine-harvesting, which can lower the quality of white wines in particular, is widespread in Chablis, even on the grands crus. The technique is most appropriate at Préhy, where the vineyards are of lesser quality.

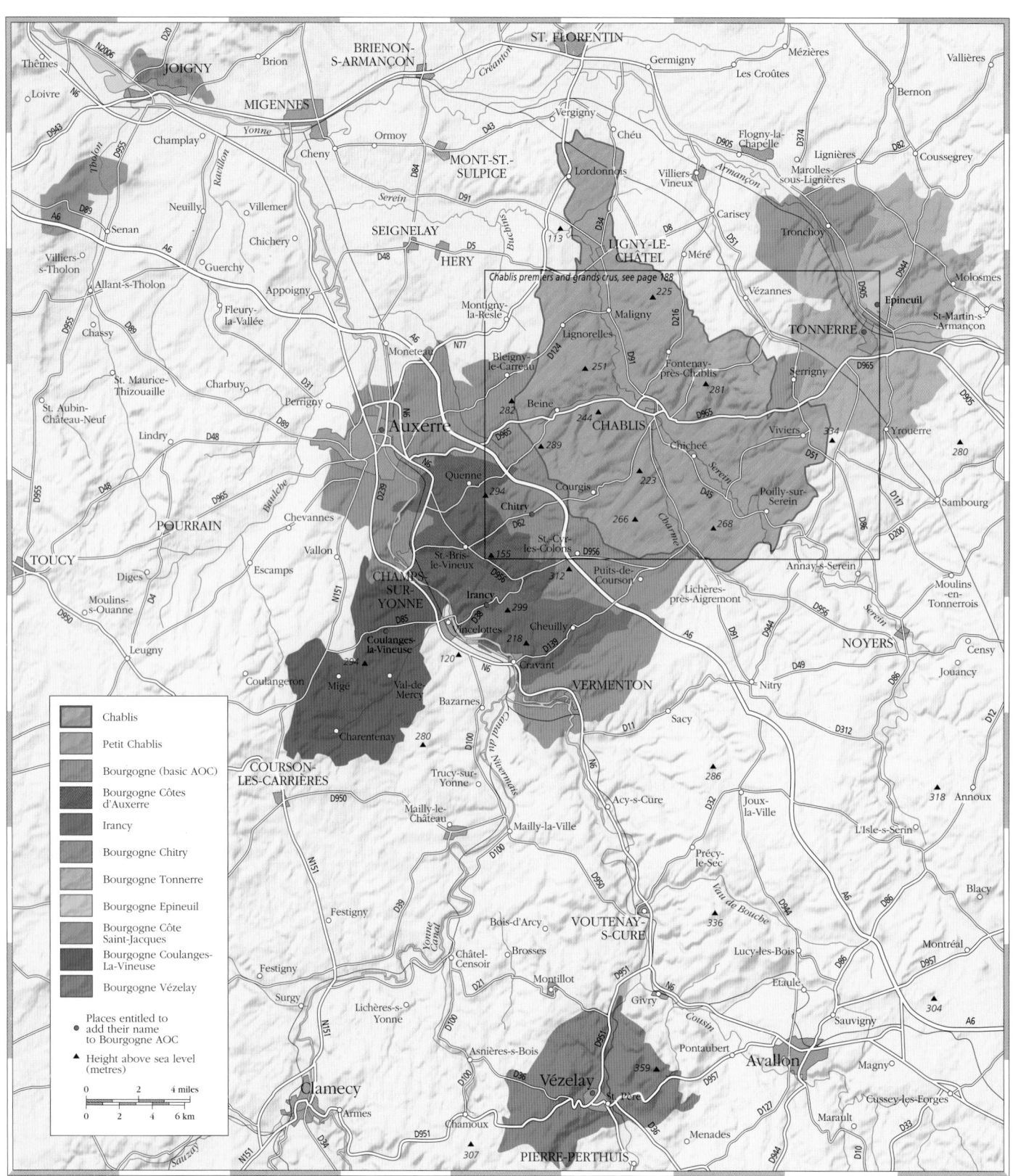

CHABLIS DISTRICT

Overlooked by its grands crus *and surrounded by* premiers crus,
Chablis (highlighted on the map) lies at the centre of its eponymous
wine-producing area, which is geographically and climatically
closer to Champagne than to the rest of Burgundy.

Chablis wines undergo malolactic fermentation and cold stabilization, which is used to precipitate tartrates (although some wines fermented or matured in small oak casks do not), making the wine fuller, softer, and rounder.

At the top end of the market, there are two distinctly different schools. Some wines are fermented in stainless steel and bottled early to produce the most direct and attacking style, while others are fermented in wood and matured in casks with an increasing amount of new oak. Writers often describe the unoaked, stainless-steel-fermented Chablis as traditional, but these vats were introduced in the 1960s, so it cannot be a well-established tradition. The oak barrel is much older, of course, and thus far more traditional, but what the critics really mean is that new oak has never been a feature of Chablis winemaking; therefore, the crisp, clean style of Chablis fermented in stainless steel is closer to the original style: traditional by default. Obviously, the most authentic style of Chablis is the wine that is made in old or, more accurately, well-used casks. The traditional Chablisienne cask, known as a *feuillette*, is only half the size of a normal Burgundian barrel, thus has twice the effect, but not being new oak, this would be an oxidative effect, not creamy-vanilla or other aromatics. However, the more rapid oxidative effect of the *feuillette* does explain why the wines were traditionally bottled early, retaining the minerality of the fruit, and invariably imparting a slight spritz, further separating the style of these wines from Chardonnay produced in the Côte d'Or.

What makes the divide between oaked and unoaked Chablis even wider is the fact that the leaner, more mineral style of wine produced in this district can fight against the effects of new oak, whereas the fatter, softer, more seductive wines of the Côte d'Or embrace it with open arms. Recognizing that some people enjoy new oak characteristics, the recommendations in this book include producers of the best oaky Chablis. However, the trend for new oak peaked sometime in the late 1990s. Nowadays, even producers known for the oakiest Chablis have been holding back, to promote the minerality meant to be expressive of the *terroir*.

There has always been a certain inconsistency about Chablis, which is only to be expected given its uncertain climate, and this has never deterred its devotees. However, things have gone from bad to worse over the last 15 years, and it is not the weather that has always been to blame – it is the increasing yields by greedy producers and sloppy winemaking. There are still great joys to be had with the best and most passionately produced of Chablis, from the lowliest appellation to the greatest *grands crus*, but wine buyers must be increasingly vigilant.

OTHER WINES OF YONNE

Other than Chablis, the two best-known wines of the Yonne are the red wines of Bourgogne Irancy AOC and the white Saint-Bris AOC, made from the Sauvignon Blanc grape – a trespasser from the Loire. Other grapes peculiar to the Yonne are the César and Tressot, which are black, and the Sacy, which is white. None is permitted in any Burgundian appellation other than AOC Bourgogne from Yonne, and they are not even widely cultivated here. César is the most interesting of these varieties, albeit rather rustic. It is a low-yielding vine that produces a thick, dark, tannic wine, although Simonnet-Febvre makes one of the better examples. César grows best at Irancy and can make a positive contribution when it is carefully blended with Pinot Noir. Just 5 or 10 per cent of César is required, but a few growers use as much as 20 per cent and this tends to knock all the elegance out of the light-bodied local Pinot Noir. The Tressot is thin, weak, and without any merit, but this blank canvas together with the advantage of its typically high yield made it the obvious partner to the César in bygone times. Occasionally encountered, it usually tastes like a thin, coarse Beaujolais. This district's other viticultural oddity is the steadily declining Sacy, a high-yielding white grape that produces acidic, neutrally flavoured wines best used in Crémant de Bourgogne, although most of it has traditionally been sold to Germany for making *Sekt*.

FOURCHAUME
Just north of Chablis itself, Fourchaume is one of only two premier cru slopes that face southwest. The other is Montée de Tonnerre. It is probably no coincidence that, out of a total of 17 Chablis premiers crus, these vineyards are always among the top three.

THE GRANDS CRUS OF CHABLIS
The slopes of the district's greatest vineyards rise quietly and majestically on the other side of the Serein river beyond the northern outskirts of Chablis itself.

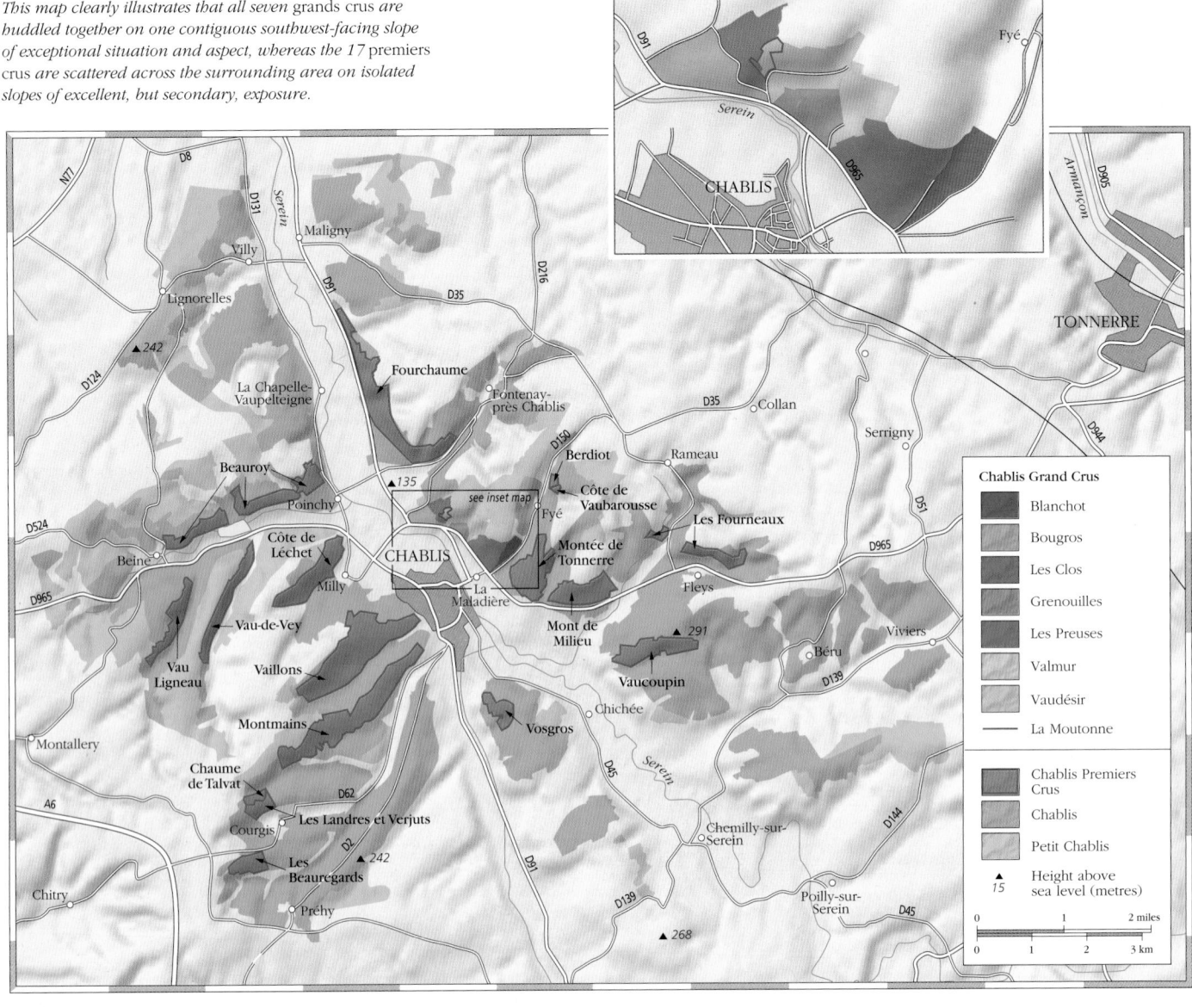

CHABLIS GRANDS AND PREMIERS CRUS
This map clearly illustrates that all seven grands crus are huddled together on one contiguous southwest-facing slope of exceptional situation and aspect, whereas the 17 premiers crus are scattered across the surrounding area on isolated slopes of excellent, but secondary, exposure.

Chablis Grand Crus

- Blanchot
- Bougros
- Les Clos
- Grenouilles
- Les Preuses
- Valmur
- Vaudésir
- La Moutonne

- Chablis Premiers Crus
- Chablis
- Petit Chablis

▲ Height above sea level (metres)
15

0   1   2 miles
0 1   2   3 km

THE APPELLATIONS OF
THE CHABLIS DISTRICT

BOURGOGNE CHITRY AOC

A true single-village appellation, in that only vines in Chitry qualify. This village neighbours St-Bris-le-Vineux to the northeast, and its vineyards are comprised of 27 hectares (67 acres) of black grapes, and 27 hectares (67 acres) of white grapes. Generally, the reds are least interesting, whereas the whites can be modestly successful, with their attractive, fresh-lemony fruit and an occasional aromatic hint on the nose and finish. Chalmeau and Thibaut are the best performers here.

🐾 Pinot Noir, Pinot Liébault, Pinot Gris, César, Tressot, Chardonnay, Pinot Blanc

🍷 Upon purchase

✓ *Patrick & Christine Chalmeau* (blanc only) • *Griffe* (blanc only) • *Jean-Baptiste Thibaut* (rouge only) • *Marcel Giraudon* (rouge only)

BOURGOGNE CÔTE SAINT-JACQUES AOC

One of four local Bourgogne appellations created in the 1990s (*see also* Bourgogne La Chapelle Notre Dame, p200; Bourgogne Le Chapitre, p192; and Bourgogne Montrecul, p192). Côte Saint-Jacques overlooks Joigny, which has the most northerly vineyards in Burgundy. Vines were first permitted to grow here for basic Bourgogne AOC in 1975, but just a few hectares were planted. Currently the largest vineyard owner is Alain Vignot, whose father pioneered winemaking in the area, but the local *coopérative*, which also has vineyards here, is planting a large proportion of the 90 hectares (220 acres) that were officially classified as Côte Saint-Jacques. At the present time, the area barely manages to produce a light-bodied white wine, although Vignot makes a *vin gris* from Pinot Noir and Pinot Gris, which Joigny was famous for in pre-phylloxera

times. What they need here is the true Auxerrois of Alsace (which has no connection with nearby Auxerre). The reasoning would be exactly the same as for Alsace, where more Auxerrois is used to make so-called Pinot Blanc wine the further north the vineyards are situated. In the Côte de Nuits it would be too fat and spicy, but in Joigny it would simply bring some generosity to the wines.

RED Michel Lorain's Clos des Capucins outclasses the rest of this appellation with its good colour and truly expressive fruit.

🐾 Pinot Noir, Pinot Liébault, Pinot Gris, César, Tressot

🍷 1–3 years

WHITE Not worth buying.

🐾 Chardonnay, Pinot Blanc

🍷 Upon purchase

ROSÉ There are a handful of pure Pinot Gris wines

made elsewhere in Burgundy, but they are usually white wines, whereas the tradition here is to make a rosé or *vin gris* from this variety, either pure (Alain Vignot) or blended.

🍇 Pinot Noir, Pinot Liébault, Pinot Gris, César, Tressot

🍷 Upon purchase

✓ *Michel Lorain* (rouge only) • *Alain Vignot* (rouge and rosé only)

BOURGOGNE CÔTES D'AUXERRE AOC

Overlapping the Saint-Bris appellation, Côte d'Auxerre covers various parcels of vines scattered throughout the hillsides overlooking Augy, Auxerre-Vaux, Quenne, St-Bris-le-Vineux, and in part of Vincelottes that does not qualify for Irancy.

RED With the exception of Bersan or Ghislaine & Jean-Hugues Goisot in a good vintage, these wines are invariably disappointingly light and dilute.

🍇 Pinot Noir, Pinot Liébault, Pinot Gris, César, Tressot

🍷 Upon purchase

WHITE Ghislaine & Jean-Hugues Goisot make a range of different Côtes d'Auxerre, and their Corps de Garde and Gondonne *cuvées* usually outclass the rest of the competition, although Bailly-Lapierre gives Goisot a good run for its money in some years (such as 2002).

🍇 Chardonnay, Pinot Blanc

🍷 Upon purchase

ROSÉ Light, fresh, easy-drinking rosé that is better than a lot of supposedly finer AOCs.

🍇 Pinot Noir, Pinot Liébault, Pinot Gris, César, Tressot

🍷 Upon purchase

✓ *Bailly-Lapierre* • *Bersan* • *Patrice Fort* • *Ghislaine & Jean-Hugues Goisot* • *Tabit & Fils*

BOURGOGNE COULANGES-LA-VINEUSE AOC

The far-flung borders of Coulanges-la-Vineuse encompass no fewer than six communes in addition to its own: Charentenay, Escolives-Sainte-Camille, Migé, Mouffy, Jussy, and Val-de-Mercy. Vines cover almost 60 hectares (148 acres), of which only 4 hectares (10 acres) are planted with white varieties.

RED Most of these wines are primarily Pinot Noir with a small dash of César. Most are simply frank and fruity, although the best can be quite rich, with truly expressive fruit.

🍇 Pinot Noir, Pinot Liébault, Pinot Gris, César, Tressot

🍷 1–3 years

WHITE Not worth buying.

🍇 Chardonnay, Pinot Blanc

🍷 Upon purchase

ROSÉ Not tasted.

🍇 Pinot Noir, Pinot Liébault, Pinot Gris, César, Tressot

🍷 Upon purchase

✓ *Le Clos du Roi* (rouge only) • *Jean-Luc Houblin* (rouge only) • *Jean-Pierre Maltoff* (rouge only) • *Alain Rigoutat* (rouge only)

BOURGOGNE ÉPINEUIL AOC

A true single-village appellation, Épineuil consists of 85 hectares (210 acres) of hillside vineyards on the banks of the Armançon River, overlooking

Tonnerre, northeast of Chablis. Planted mostly with Pinot Noir, there are just 6 hectares (15 acres) of white grapes, with La Chablisienne the most important producer.

RED Most are light and undistinguished, but the Domaine de l'Abbaye du Petit Quincy makes a much darker version, especially its Côte de Grisey and Côte de Grisey Cuvée Juliette, which many consider to be the finest wines of Épineuil. Neither light nor dark, the ruby-coloured wine produced by the local *coopérative*, La Chablisienne, is probably the most consistent wine in the appellation.

🍇 Pinot Noir, Pinot Liébault, Pinot Gris, César, Tressot

🍷 1–5 years

WHITE Few wines deliver more than a straightforward fresh, crisp, dry white of fairly neutral character.

🍇 Chardonnay, Pinot Blanc

🍷 Upon purchase

ROSÉ At its best, this can be a deliciously fresh, easy-drinking rosé.

🍇 Pinot Noir, Pinot Liébault, Pinot Gris, César, Tressot

🍷 Upon purchase

✓ *Abbaye du Petit Quincy* • *La Chablisienne* • *Eric Dampt* (white only) • *Dominique Gruhier* • *Alain Mathias*

BOURGOGNE TONNERRE AOC

This appellation was created in 2006 for pure Chardonnay wine from the Armançon Valley, immediately east of Chablis. Vines have grown here since the 9th century and had, by the start of the 19th century, extended to more than 2,000 hectares (5,000 acres). These vineyards were destroyed by phylloxera in the 1890s and not replanted until 1987, when local grower Bernard Dampt planted the first Tonnerre vines of modern times.

WHITE Lighter and more ethereal than Chablis, with flashes of brilliance when the vintage is right.

🍇 Chardonnay

🍷 1–2 years

✓ *Dampt*

BOURGOGNE VÉZELAY AOC

This appellation southeast of the main Chablis district covers some 64 hectares (158 acres) of vines on the steep upper slopes (above the frost-line) overlooking the village of Vézelay itself.

WHITE At its most basic level, not worth buying, but top-performing white wines from these appellations are superior to the lower end of Chablis, which is relatively much more expensive. They are invariably pure Chardonnay, yet rarely taste like Chablis, being softer and smoother. Marc Meneau is the top producer here.

🍇 Chardonnay, Pinot Blanc

🍷 1–3 years

✓ *Marc Meneau* • *Elise Villiers*

CHABLIS AOC

With careful selection, basic Chablis can be a source of tremendous-value, classic 100 per cent Chardonnay wine, particularly in the best vintages. However, the appellation covers a relatively large area with many vineyards that do not perform well, and there are far too many mediocre winemakers. Basic Chablis needs to come

from the most favourable locations, where the grower restricts the yield and the winemaker selects only the best wines; it is not an appellation in which short cuts can be taken. Cheap Chablis can be dire, even in superior appellations; better therefore to pay for a top *cuvée* of basic Chablis than to be seduced by a cut-price *premier cru*. However, La Chablisienne's Vieilles Vignes is not the consistent superstar it used to be. (*See also* Chablis Premier Cru and Petit Chablis AOC.)

WHITE When successful, these wines have the quintessential character of true Chablis – dry, clean, green, and expressive, with just enough fruit to balance the "steel".

🍇 Chardonnay

🍷 2–6 years

✓ *Christian Adine* • *Baillard* • *Billaud-Simon* • *Jean-Marc Brocard* • *La Chablisienne* • *de Chantemerle* • *Jean Collet* • *de la Concierge* • *Jean Defaix* • *René & Vincent Dauvissat* • *Jean-Paul Droin* (especially Vieilles Vignes) • *Gérard Duplessis* • *William Fèvre de la Maladière* • *Jean-Pierre Grossot* • *Michel Laroche* • *Olivier Leflaive* • *Château de Ligny* • *des Malandes* (especially Tour de Roi) • *Louis & Anne Moreau* (especially Domaines de Biéville and Cèdre Doré) • *Sylvain Mosnier* (Vieilles Vignes) • *Gilbert Picq* (Vieilles Vignes) • *François Raveneau*

CHABLIS GRAND CRU AOC

The seven *grands crus* of Chablis are all located on one hill that overlooks the town of Chablis itself. They are Blanchot, Bougros, Les Clos, Grenouilles, Les Preuses, Valmur, and Vaudésir. One vineyard called La Moutonne is not classified in the appellation as a *grand cru*, but the authorities permit the use of the coveted status on the label because it is physically part of other *grands crus*. In the 18th century La Moutonne was in fact a 1-hectare (2.5-acre) *climat* of Vaudésir, but under the ownership of Louis Long-Depaquit, its wines were blended with those of three other *grands crus* (namely, Les Preuses, Les Clos, and Valmur). This practice came to a halt in 1950 when, in a bid to get La Moutonne classified as a separate *grand cru*, Long-Depaquit agreed to limit its production to its current location, which cuts across parts of Vaudésir and Les Preuses. Its classification never actually took place, but the two *grands crus* that it overlaps are probably the finest of all.

WHITE Always totally dry, the *grands crus* are the biggest, richest, most complex of all Chablis and should always boast great minerality. However, many are overwhelmed by new oak. Their individual styles depend very much on how the winemaker vinifies and matures the wine, but when well made they are essentially as follows: **Blanchot** has a floral aroma and is the most delicate of the *grands crus* (Michel Laroche's Réserve de l'Obédiance is the greatest Chablis *grand cru* I have tasted, taking richness to the very limit, while not losing sight of true Chablis structure, crispness, minerality, and finesse); **Bougros** has the least frills of all the *grands crus*, but is vibrant with a penetrating flavour; **Les Clos** is rich, luscious, and complex with great mineral finesse and beautiful balance; **Grenouilles** should be long and satisfying, yet elegant, racy, and aromatic; **Les Preuses** gets the most sun and is vivid, sometimes exotic, quite fat for Chablis, yet still expressive and definitely complex, with great finesse; **Valmur** has a fine bouquet, rich flavour, and smooth texture; **Vaudésir** has complex, intense flavours that display great finesse and spicy complexity; and **La Moutonne** is fine, long-flavoured, and wonderfully expressive.

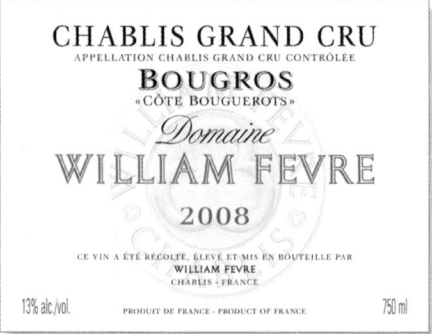

🔲 Chardonnay

🍷 6–20 years

✓ **Blanchot** *Billaud-Simon* (Vieilles Vignes) • *Michel Laroche* • *Raveneau* • *Domaine Vocoret* **Bougros** *William Fèvre* • *Joseph Drouhin* • *de la Maladière* • *Michel Laroche* **Les Clos** *Billaud-Simon* • *La Chablisienne* • *René & Vincent Dauvissat* • *Jean-Paul Droin* • *Joseph Drouhin* • *Caves Duplessis* • *William Fèvre* • *Michel Laroche* • *de la Maladière* • *Domaines des Malandes* • *Louis Michel* • *J Moreau* (lieu-dit Clos des Hospices) • *Pinson* • *Raveneau* • *Servin* **Grenouilles** *La Chablisienne* (Château Grenouilles) • *Louis Michel* **La Moutonne** *Long-Depaquit* **Les Preuses** *Billaud-Simon* • *Joseph Drouhin, René & Vincent Dauvissat* • *William Fèvre* **Valmur** *Jean Collet* • *Jean-Paul Droin* • *William Fèvre* • *Olivier Leflaive* • *Raveneau* **Vaudésir** *Billaud-Simon* • *La Chablisienne* • *Jean-Paul Droin* • *Joseph Drouhin* • *William Fèvre* • *Michel Laroche* • *des Malandes* • *Louis Michel*

CHABLIS PREMIER CRU

Premiers crus: Les Beauregards, Beauroy, Berdiot, Chaume de Talvat, Côte de Jouan, Côte de Léchet, Côte de Vaubarousse, Fourchaume, Les Fourneaux, Montée de Tonnerre, Montmains, Mont de Milieu, Vaillons, Vaucoupin, Vau-de-Vey (or Vaudevey), Vau Ligneau, and Vosgros. Unlike the *grands crus*, the 17 *premiers crus* of Chablis are scattered among

the vineyards of 15 surrounding communes, and the quality and style is patchy. Montée de Tonnerre is the best *premier cru* throughout the different producers and across the many vintages. One of its *lieux-dits*, Chapelot, is considered by many to be the equivalent of a *grand cru*. After Montée de Tonnerre, Côte de Léchet, Les Forêts (which is a *climat* within Montmains), Fourchaume, Mont de Milieu, and Vaillons vie for second place.

WHITE Dry wines that can vary from light- to fairly full-bodied, but should always be finer and longer-lasting than wines of the basic Chablis appellation, although without the concentration of flavour expected from a *grand cru*.

🔲 Chardonnay

🍷 4–15 years

✓ **Les Beauregards** *Jean-Marc Brocard* **Beauroy** *Sylvain Mosnier* **Berdiot** *None* **Chaume de Talvat** *None* **Côte de Jouan** *Michel Cobois* **Côte de Léchet** *Jean-Paul Droin* • *Jean Defaix* • *Sylvain Mosnier* **Côte de Vaubarousse** *None* **Fourchaume** *Billaud-Simon* • *La Chablisienne* • *de Chantemerle* • *Jean-Paul Droin* • *Gérard Duplessis* • *Jean Durup* • *William Fèvre* (Côte de Vaulorent) • *Lamblin & Fils* • *Michel Laroche* (Vieilles Vignes) • *des Malandes* • *Louis Michel* • *Francine & Olivier Savary* • *Verget* **Les Fourneaux** *Jean-Pierre Grossot* • *Louis & Anne Moreau* **Montée de Tonnerre** *Billaud-Simon* • *Jean-Paul Droin* (Vieilles Vignes) • *Caves Duplessis, William Fèvre* • *Louis Michel* • *Raveneau* (including Chapelot and Pied d'Aloue lieux-dits) • *Guy Robin* **Montmains** *La Chablisienne* • *René & Vincent Dauvissat* (La Forest [sic] lieu-dit) • *Jean-Paul Droin, Caves Duplessis* • *des Malandes* • *des Marronniers* • *Louis Michel* • *Georges Pico, Pinson* • *Raveneau* (Butteaux lieu-dit) • *Guy Robin* (Butteaux lieu-dit) • *Robert Vocoret* (La Fôret lieu-dit) **Mont de Milieu** *Barat* • *Billaud-Simon* (especially Vieilles Vignes) • *La Chablisienne* • *Jean Collet* • *Jean-Pierre Grossot* • *de Meulière* • *Pinson* **Vaillons** *Barat* • *Billaud-Simon* • *R & V Dauvissat* (Séchet lieu-dit) • *Jean Defaix* • *Jean-Paul Droin* • *Gérard Duplessis* • *Michel Laroche* (Vieilles Vignes) • *François Raveneau* • *Verget* **Vaucoupin** *Jean-Pierre Grossot* **Vau-de-Vey** *Jean Durup* • *Michel Laroche* **Vau Ligneau** *Thierry Hamelin* • *Louis & Anne Moreau* **Vosgros** *Jean-Paul Droin* • *Gilbert Picq*

IRANCY AOC

Irancy was promoted from Bourgogne Irancy to full village AOC status in its own right in 1999. This red-wine-only appellation encompasses 160 hectares (395 acres) in Irancy and neighbouring villages of Cravant and Vincelottes.

RED Irancy is supposed to be the "famous" red wine of Chablis, but it is not really that well known and is not even the best local red wine. Michel Lorain's Côte Saint-Jacques Clos des Capucins, and Domaine de l'Abbaye du Petit Quincy's Côte de Grisey Cuvée Juliette are both consistently superior to the best Irancy, though the latter do possess a certain richness of fruit that most examples of this modest appellation lack. Original Irancy was a pure César wine: Anita and Jean-Pierre Colinot make the most interesting example (Les Mazelots César).

🔲 Pinot Noir, Pinot Gris, César

🍷 1–3 years

✓ *Léon Bienvenu* • *Benoît Cantin* (Cuvée Emiline) • *Roger Delaloge* • *Anita & Jean-Pierre Colinot* (Palotte, Les Mazelots, Les Mazelots César, Les Bessys, Côte-de-Moutier) • *Roger Delalogue* • *Christophe Ferrari* (rouge only) • *Félix* • *Saint-Germain* (La Bergère)

PETIT CHABLIS AOC

A depreciatory appellation that covers inferior soils and expositions within the same area as generic Chablis, with the exception of Ligny-le-Châtel, Viviers, and Collan. Although I have found four more reliable producers than last time, this appellation should be downgraded to VDQS or uprooted. The rumour is that it will be phased out, but do not misunderstand: this does not mean that they will uproot the vines, simply that this inferior land will instead produce Chablis, albeit of a *petit vin* quality.

WHITE Apart from the occasional pleasant surprise, most are mean and meagre dry wines of light to medium body. The producers below provide most of the pleasant surprises.

🔲 Chardonnay

🍷 2–3 years

✓ *Jean-Marc Brocard* • *Jean Durup* • *Vincent Gallois* • *Thierry Hamelin* • *Francine & Olivier Savary*

SAINT-BRIS AOC

This wine is as good as most Sauvignon Blanc AOCs, and considerably better than many other white AOCs made from lesser grape varieties. Twenty-five years ago I did not believe it possible that Sauvignon de St-Bris would ever overcome Burgundy's Chardonnay-chauvinism to rise to the ranks of Appellation Contrôlée, but in 2003, Sauvignon de St-Bris VDQS was promoted to Saint-Bris AOC (retrospectively applied to the 2001 vintage).

WHITE Fine wet-grass or herbaceous aromas, full smoky-Sauvignon flavours, and a correct, crisp, dry finish. Made from the rare Sauvignon Gris, Ghislaine & Jean-Hugues Goisot's Cuvée du Corps de Garde Gourmand Fié Gris is the best, most consistent, and most unusual wine in this appellation, while the same producer's "straight" Sauvignon is easily the top thoroughbred Sauvignon Blanc.

🔲 Sauvignon Blanc, Sauvignon Gris

🍷 2–5 years

✓ *Jean-Marc Brocard* • *Robert Defrance* • *Félix* • *Ghislaine & Jean-Hugues Goisot* • *Erick Lavallée* • *Jacky Renard*

CÔTE DE NUITS AND HAUTES-CÔTES DE NUITS

The Côte de Nuits is essentially a red-wine area (with one or two extraordinary whites), and with 22 of Burgundy's 23 red grands crus, it is the place par excellence for Pinot Noir.

THE CÔTE D'OR, or "golden slope", is the departmental name for both the Côte de Nuits and the Côte de Beaune. Firmness and weight are the key words to describe the wines produced here, and these characteristics intensify as the vineyards progress north. A string of villages with some of the richest names in Burgundy – Gevrey-Chambertin, Chambolle-Musigny, Vosne-Romanée, and Nuits-St-Georges – these slopes ring up dollar signs in the minds of merchants throughout the world. Ironically, the most famous appellations also produce some of Burgundy's worst wines.

CÔTE DE NUITS AND HAUTES-CÔTES DE NUITS, *see also p182*
The best vineyards of the Côte de Nuits form a tighter, more compact strip than those of the Côte de Beaune (see also p197), and the wines produced are tighter, with more compact fruit.

CLOS ARLOT OF DOMAINE DE L'ARLOT
Purchased in 1987 by the AXA group, Domaine de l'Arlot is one of the most consistent quality producers in Nuits-St-Georges, making text-book Pinot Noir and, from its monopole Clos Arlot, tiny amounts of sublime white wine.

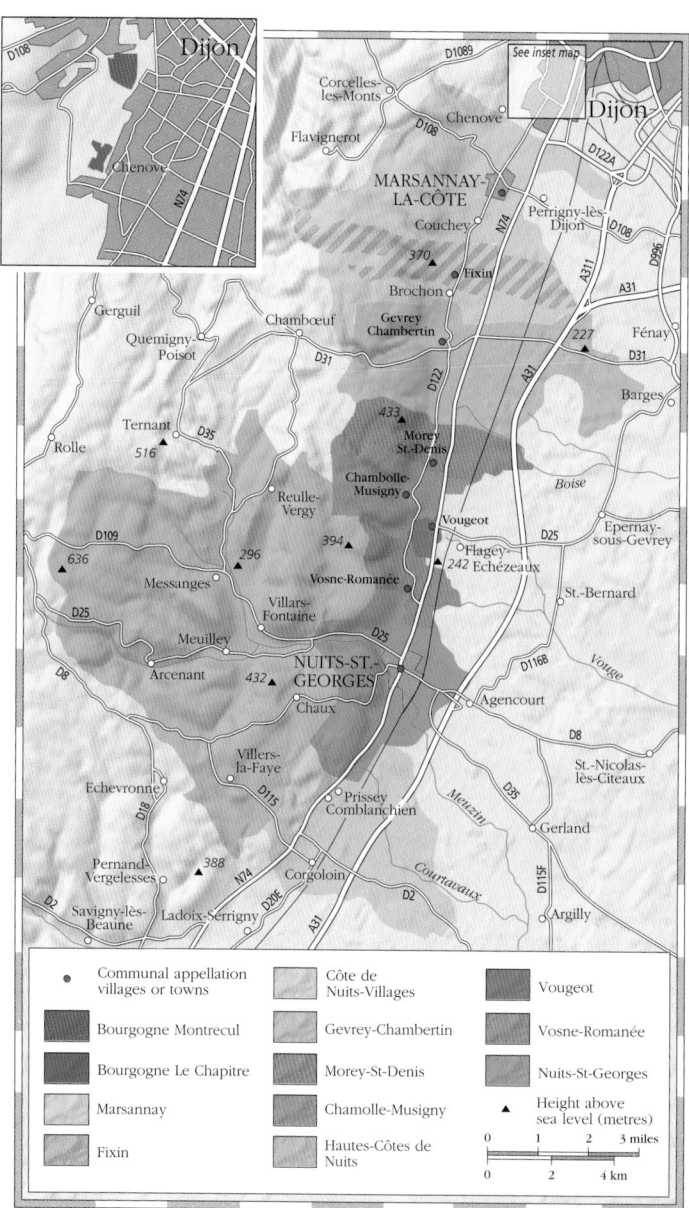

Communal appellation villages or towns

Bourgogne Montrecul

Bourgogne Le Chapitre

Marsannay

Fixin

Côte de Nuits-Villages

Gevrey-Chambertin

Morey-St-Denis

Chamolle-Musigny

Hautes-Côtes de Nuits

Vougeot

Vosne-Romanée

Nuits-St-Georges

▲ **Height above sea level (metres)**

0   1   2   3 miles

0   2   4 km

FACTORS AFFECTING TASTE AND QUALITY

LOCATION
The Côte de Nuits is a narrow, continuous strip of vines stretching from Dijon to just north of Beaune, with the Hautes-Côtes de Nuits in the southwestern hinterland.

CLIMATE
Semi-continental climate with minimal Atlantic influence, which results in a long, cold winter, a humid spring, and a fairly hot, very sunny summer. Hail is its greatest natural hazard and heavy rain is often responsible for diluting the wines and causing rampant rot.

ASPECT
A series of east-facing slopes which curve in and out to give some vineyards northeastern, some southeastern aspects. The vines grow at an altitude of between 225 and 350 metres (740 to 1,150 feet) and, apart from Gevrey-Chambertin and Prémeaux-Prissey, those vineyards that have the right to the village and higher appellations rarely extend eastwards beyond the RN 74 road.

SOIL
A subsoil of sandy-limestone, which is exposed in places, but usually covered by a chalky scree mixed with marl and clay particles on higher slopes and richer alluvial deposits on lower slopes. Higher slopes sometimes have red clay.

VITICULTURE AND VINIFICATION
The vines are trained low to benefit from heat reflected from the soil at night. For red wines, the grapes are almost always destemmed and the juice is kept in contact with the skins for between eight and ten days. Less than three per cent of the wine produced is white, but this is mostly high quality and traditionally cask fermented. The best wines are matured in oak.

GRAPE VARIETIES
Primary varieties: Chardonnay, Pinot Noir
Secondary varieties: Aligoté, Gamay, Melon de Bourgogne, Pinot Beurot (Pinot Gris), Pinot Blanc, Pinot Liébault

CONFRÉRIE DES CHEVALIERS DU TASTEVIN

After the three terrible vintages of 1930, 1931, and 1932, and four years of world slump following the Wall Street Crash of 1929, Camille Rodier and Georges Faiveley formed the Confrérie des Chevaliers du Tastevin to revive Burgundy's fortunes. They named the brotherhood after the traditional Burgundian *tastevin*, a shallow, dimpled, silver tasting-cup with a fluted edge.

The first investitures took place on 16 November 1934 in a cellar in Nuits-St-Georges; the Confrérie now boasts thousands of members in numerous foreign chapters and averages 20 banquets a year at Château du Clos de Vougeot. Until the late 1980s, wines bearing the distinctive Tastevin label used to be a useful means of quickly identifying wines within basic appellations that have risen above their modest status, but the selection gradually became less rigorous, with some decidedly underperforming wines slipping through. In recent years, however, there appears to be more consistency, once again making the Tastevinage label worth watching out for.

THE APPELLATIONS OF
CÔTE DE NUITS AND HAUTES-CÔTES DE NUITS

Note Each *grand cru* of Côte de Nuits has its own appellation and is listed individually below. However, the *premiers crus* do not, and are therefore listed under the appellation of the village in which the vineyards are situated. *Premiers crus* that are virtually contiguous with *grand cru* vineyards are in *italics*; they are possibly superior to those that do not share a boundary with one or more *grand crus*, and generally superior to those that share boundaries with village AOC vineyards.

BONNES MARES AOC
Grand Cru

Bonnes Mares is the largest of the two *grands crus* of Chambolle-Musigny. It covers 13.5 hectares (34 acres) in the north of the village, on the opposite side to Musigny, the village's other *grand cru*, and extends a further 1.5 hectares (3.5 acres) into Morey-St-Denis.

RED A fabulous femininity of style with sheer depth of flavour give something rich and luscious, yet complex and complete.

🍇 Pinot Noir, Pinot Gris, Pinot Liébault

🍷⟼ 12–25 years

✓ *d'Auvenay* ❽ • *Bouchard Père & Fils* • *Dujac* • *R Groffier* • *Dominique Laurent* • *J F Mugnier* • *Christophe Roumier* • *Georges Roumier* • *Nicolas Potel* • *Comte Georges de Vogüé*

BOURGOGNE LA CHAPITRE AOC

One of the Côte de Nuits' two Bourgogne *lieux-dits* created in 1993, La Chapitre is located at Chenove, between Marsannay and Dijon. According to Anthony Hanson (in his book *Burgundy*), the wines of Chenove once fetched higher prices than those of Gevrey (Chenove's most famous vineyard is Clos du Roi, of which Labouré-Roi took management in 1994), but the only example I have tasted (Domaine Bouvier) was not special.

BOURGOGNE HAUTES-CÔTES DE NUITS AOC

A source of good-value wines, these vineyards have expanded since the 1970s, and the quality is improving noticeably. Half-red/half-rosé wines may be sold as Bourgogne Clairet Hautes-Côtes de Nuits AOC, but the style is outmoded and the appellation rarely encountered.

RED Medium-bodied and medium- to full-bodied wines with good fruit and some true Côte de Nuits character. The wines from some growers have fine oak nuances.

🍇 Pinot Noir, Pinot Liébault, Pinot Gris

🍷⟼ 4–10 years

WHITE Just 5 per cent of the production is dry white. Most have a good weight of fruit, but little finesse.

🍇 Chardonnay, Pinot Blanc

🍷⟼ 1–4 years

ROSÉ Little-seen, but those that have cropped up have been dry, fruity, and delicious wines of some richness.

🍇 Pinot Noir, Pinot Liébault, Pinot Gris

🍷⟼ 1–3 years

✓ *Bertagna* • *J-C Boisset* • *Yves Chaley* • *Guy*

Dufouleur • *Michel Gros* • *Robert Jayer-Gilles* • *de Montmain* • *Naudin-Ferrand* • *Thévenot-le-Brun & Fils* • *Alain Verdet* ❽ • *Thierry Vigot-Battault*

BOURGOGNE MONTRECUL
or MONTRE-CUL *or*
EN MONTRE-CUL AOC

The other Bourgogne *lieu-dit* in this district is actually located on the outskirts of Dijon. Some might think this is a wine to moon over, but the only wine I have tasted (again Domaine Bouvier) was again not special. If no one is going to produce something exciting under these Bourgogne *lieux-dits*, why bother with them in the first place?

CHAMBERTIN AOC
Grand Cru

This is one of the nine *grands crus* of Gevrey-Chambertin. All of them (quite legally) add the name Chambertin to their own and one, Clos de Bèze, actually has the right to sell its wines as Chambertin.

RED Always full in body and rich in extract, Chambertin is not, however, powerful like Corton, but graceful and feminine with a vivid colour, stunning flavour, impeccable balance, and lush, velvety texture.

🍇 Pinot Noir, Pinot Gris, Pinot Liébault

🍷⟼ 12–30 years

✓ *Bouchard Père & Fils* • *Vincent Girardin* • *Leroy* ❽ • *Denis Mortet* • *Henri Rebourseau* • *Armand Rousseau* • *Jean Trapet Père & Fils*

CHAMBERTIN-CLOS
DE BÈZE AOC
Grand Cru

Another Gevrey-Chambertin *grand cru*. The wine may be sold simply as Chambertin, the name of a neighbouring *grand cru*, but Chambertin may not call itself Clos de Bèze.

RED This wine is reputed to have a greater finesse than Chambertin but slightly less body. It is just as sublime.

🍇 Pinot Noir, Pinot Gris, Pinot Liébault

🍷⟼ 12–30 years

✓ *Bouchard Père & Fils* • *Bruno Clair* • *Faiveley* • *R Groffier* • *Louis Jadot* • *Dominique Laurent* • *Lucien Lemoine* • *Armand Rousseau*

CHAMBOLLE-MUSIGNY AOC

This village is very favourably positioned, with a solid block of vines nestled in the shelter of a geological fold.

RED Many of these medium- to fairly full-bodied wines have surprising finesse and fragrance for mere village wines.

🍇 Pinot Noir, Pinot Gris, Pinot Liébault

🍷⟼ 8–15 years

✓ *Ghislaine Barthod* • *Sylvain Cathiard* (Les Clos de L'Orme) • *Dujac Père* • *J F Mugnier* • *Géantet Pansiot* • *Perrot-Minot* • *Daniel Rion & Fils* • *Georges Roumier* • *Comte Georges de Vogüé*

CHAMBOLLE-MUSIGNY
PREMIER CRU AOC

Premiers crus: *Les Amoureuses*, *Les Baudes*, Aux Beaux Bruns, *Les Borniques*, Les Carrières, Les Chabiots, Les Charmes, Les Châtelots, *La Combe d'Orveau*, Aux Combottes, Les Combottes, Les Cras, Derrière la Grange, Aux Echanges, Les Feusselottes, *Les Fuées*, Les Grands Murs, Les Groseilles, Les Gruenchers, Les Hauts Doix, *Les Lavrottes*, Les Noirots, Les Plantes, Les Sentiers.

The outstanding *premier cru* is Les Amoureuses, with Les Charmes a very respectable second.

RED The best have a seductive bouquet and deliciously fragrant flavour.

🍇 Pinot Noir, Pinot Gris, Pinot Liébault

🍷⟼ 10–20 years

✓ *Amiot-Servelle* (Amoureuses) • *Ghislaine Barthod* • *Jean-Claude Boisset* • *Confuron-Cotétidot* • *R Groffier* • *Moine Hudelot* • *Dominique Laurent* • *Lucien Lemoine* • *Leroy* ❽ • *Denis Mortet* • *Mugnier* • *Perrot-Minot* • *Laurent Ponsot* • *Michelle & Patrice Rion* • *Christophe Roumier* • *Georges Roumier* • *Comte Georges de Vogüé*

CHAPELLE-CHAMBERTIN
AOC
Grand Cru

This is one of the nine *grands crus* of Gevrey-Chambertin, comprised of two *climats* called En la Chapelle and Les Gémeaux.

RED The lightest of all the *grands crus*, with a delightful bouquet and flavour.

🍇 Pinot Noir, Pinot Gris, Pinot Liébault

🍷⟼ 8–20 years

✓ *Louis Jadot* • *Jean Trapet Père & Fils*

CHARMES-CHAMBERTIN AOC
Grand Cru

The largest Gevrey-Chambertin *grand cru*, part of the vineyard is known as Mazoyères, from which Mazoyères-Chambertin has evolved.

RED Soft, sumptuous wines with ripe-fruit flavours and pure Pinot character, although some slightly lack finesse.

🍇 Pinot Noir, Pinot Gris, Pinot Liébault

🍷 10–20 years

✓ *Denis Bachelet • Chanson Camille Giroud • Confuron-Cotétidot • Claude Dugat • Bernard Dugat-Py • Frédéric Magnien • Géantet-Pansiot • Vincent Girardin • Perrot-Minot • Sérafin Père & Fils • Joseph Roty • Christophe Roumier • Armand Rousseau • Taupenot-Merme • de la Vougeraie* ❸

CLOS DE BÈZE AOC

An alternative appellation for Chambertin-Clos de Bèze. *See* Chambertin-Clos de Bèze AOC.

CLOS DES LAMBRAYS AOC
Grand Cru

This vineyard was classified as one of the four *grands crus* of Morey-St-Denis only as recently as 1981, although the previous owner used to put *"grand cru classé"* (illegally) on the label.

RED The vineyard was replanted under new ownership and now produces fine, elegant wines with silky fruit of a good, easily recommendable quality.

🍇 Pinot Noir, Pinot Gris, Pinot Liébault

🍷 10–20 years

✓ *des Lambrays*

CLOS DE LA ROCHE AOC
Grand Cru

Covering an area of almost 17 hectares (42 acres), Clos de La Roche is twice the size of the other *grands crus* of Morey-St-Denis.

RED A deep-coloured, rich, and powerfully flavoured *vin de garde* with a silky texture. Many consider it the greatest *grand cru* of Morey-St-Denis.

🍇 Pinot Noir, Pinot Gris, Pinot Liébault

🍷 10–20 years

✓ *Jean-Claude Boisset • Dujac • Leroy* ❸ *• Lucien Lemoine • Hubert Lignier • Michel Magnien & Fils • Ponsot • Armand Rousseau*

CLOS ST-DENIS AOC
Grand Cru

This is the *grand cru* that the village of Morey attached to its name when it was the best growth in the village, a position now contested by Clos de la Roche and Clos de Tart.

RED Strong, fine, and firm wines with rich liquorice and berry flavours that need time to come together.

🍇 Pinot Noir, Pinot Gris, Pinot Liébault

🍷 10–25 years

✓ *Bertagna • Philippe Charlopin-Parizot • Philippe Charlopin • Dujac • Louis Jadot • Lucien Lemoine • Michel Magnien & Fils • Ponsot • Nicolas Potel*

CLOS DE TART AOC
Grand Cru

This is one of the four *grands crus* of Morey-St-Denis. It is entirely owned by the *négociant* Mommessin. In addition to Clos de Tart itself, a tiny part of the Bonnes Mares *grand cru* also has the right to this appellation.

RED This *monopole* yields wines with a penetrating Pinot flavour, to which Mommessin adds such a spicy-vanilla character from 100 per cent new oak

that great bottle maturity is required for a completely harmonious flavour.

🍇 Pinot Noir, Pinot Gris, Pinot Liébault

🍷 15–30 years

✓ *Mommessin*

CLOS DE VOUGEOT AOC
Grand Cru

The only *grand cru* of Vougeot, it is a massive 50-hectare (123-acre) block of vines with no fewer than 85 registered owners. It has been described as "an impressive sight, but a not very impressive site". This mass ownership situation has often been used to illustrate the classic difference between Burgundy and Bordeaux, where an entire vineyard belongs to one château and so the wine can be blended to a standard quality and style every year.

RED With individual plots ranging in quality from truly great to very ordinary, operated by growers of varying skills, it is virtually impossible to unravel the intrinsic characteristics of this *cru*. Its best wines, however, have lots of silky Pinot fruit, an elegant balance, and a tendency towards finesse rather than fullness.

🍇 Pinot Noir, Pinot Gris, Pinot Liébault

🍷 10–25 years

✓ *Robert Arnoux • Joseph Drouhin • René Engel • Faiveley • Jean Grivot • Anne Gros • Michel Gros • Alain Hudelot-Noëllat • Louis Jadot • Dominique Laurent • Leroy* ❸ *• Méo-Camuzet • Mugneret-Gibourg • Nicolas Potel • Château la Tour • de la Vougeraie* ❸

CLOS VOUGEOT AOC
See Clos de Vougeot AOC

CÔTE DE NUITS-VILLAGES AOC

This appellation covers the wines produced in one or more of five communes: Fixin and Brochon, situated in the north of the district, and Comblanchien, Corgoloin, and Prissy in the south.

RED Firm, fruity, and distinctive wines made in true, well-structured Côte de Nuits style.

🍇 Pinot Noir, Pinot Gris, Pinot Liébault

🍷 6–10 years

WHITE Very little is made – just 4 hectolitres (44 cases) in 1985 – and I have never encountered it.

🍇 Chardonnay, Pinot Blanc

✓ *de l'Arlot • Michel Esmonin • Gachot-Monot • Naudin-Ferrand • Daniel Rion & Fils (Le Vaucrain)*

ECHÉZEAUX AOC
Grand Cru

This 30-hectare (74-acre) vineyard is the larger of the two *grands crus* of Flagey-Echézeaux and is comprised of 11 *climats* owned by no fewer than 84 smallholders.

RED The best have a fine and fragrant flavour that relies more on delicacy than power, but too many deserve no more than a village appellation.

🍇 Pinot Noir, Pinot Gris, Pinot Liébault

🍷 10–20 years

✓ *Robert Arnoux • Albert Bichot* (Clos Frantin) *• Confuron-Cotétidot • Dujac • Engel • Faiveley • Forey Père & Fils • Vincent Girardin • Jean Grivot • A-F Gros • Louis Jadot • Robert Jayer-Gilles • Lucien Lemoine • Mongeard-Mugneret • Mugneret-Gibourg • de la Romanée-Conti • Emmanuel Rouget • Fabrice Vigot*

FIXIN AOC

Fixin was at one time the summer residence of the dukes of Burgundy.

RED Well-coloured wines that can be firm, tannic *vins de garde* of excellent quality and even better value.

🍇 Pinot Noir, Pinot Gris, Pinot Liébault

🍷 6–12 years

WHITE Rich, dry, and concentrated wines that are rare, but exciting and well worth seeking out. Bruno Clair shows what Pinot Blanc can produce when it is not over-cropped.

🍇 Chardonnay, Pinot Blanc

🍷 3–8 years

✓ *Bart • Berthaut • Bruno Clair • Pierre Gelin • Philippe Joliet • Mongeard-Mugneret*

FIXIN PREMIER CRU AOC

Premiers crus: Les Arvelets, Clos du Chapitre, Aux Cheusots, Les Hervelets, Le Meix Bas, La Perrière, Queue de Hareng (located in neighbouring Brochon), En Suchot, Le Village. The best *premiers crus* are La Perrière and Clos du Chapitre. Clos de la Perrière is a monopoly owned by Philippe Joliet that encompasses En Souchot and Queue de Hareng as well as La Perrière itself.

RED Splendidly deep in colour and full in body with masses of blackcurrant and redcurrant fruit, supported by a good tannic structure.

🍇 Pinot Noir, Pinot Gris, Pinot Liébault

🍷 10–20 years

WHITE I have not encountered any, but it would not be unreasonable to assume that it might be at least as good as a basic Fixin *blanc*.

✓ *Berthaut • Pierre Gelin • Philippe Joliet • Mongeard-Mugneret*

GEVREY-CHAMBERTIN AOC

Famous for its *grand cru* of Chambertin, the best growers also produce superb wines under this appellation. Some vineyards overlap the village of Brochon.

RED These well-coloured wines are full, rich, and elegant, with a silky texture and a perfumed aftertaste reminiscent of the pure fruit of Pinot Noir.

🍇 Pinot Noir, Pinot Gris, Pinot Liébault

⌛ 7–15 years

✓ *Denis Bachelet • Alain Burguet • Philippe Charlopin • Confuron-Cotétidot • Drouhin-Laroze • Bernard Dugat-Py • Dujac • Dujac Père • Labouré-Roi • Marc Roy* (Vieilles Vignes, Clos Prieur) *• Denis Mortet • Géantet Pansiot*

GEVREY-CHAMBERTIN PREMIER CRU AOC

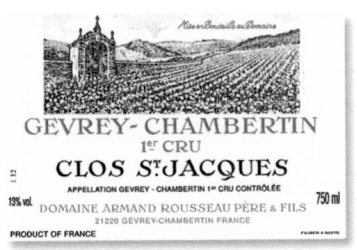

Premiers crus: Bel Air, La Bossière, Les Cazetiers, Champeaux, *Champitennois,* Champonnet, Clos du Chapitre, *Cherbandes, Au Closeau,* Combe au Moine, *Aux Combottes, Les Corbeaux,* Craipillot, En Ergot, Etournelles (or Estournelles), Fonteny, Les Goulots, Lavaut (or Lavout St-Jacques), *La Perrière, Petite Chapelle,* Petits Cazetiers, *Plantigone* (or *Issarts*), Poissenot, *Clos Prieur-Haut* (or *Clos Prieure*), La Romanée, Le Clos St-Jacques, Les Varoilles.

RED These wines generally have more colour, concentration, and finesse than the village wines, but, with the possible exception of Clos St-Jacques, do not quite match the *grands crus*.

🍇 Pinot Noir, Pinot Gris, Pinot Liébault

⌛ 10–20 years

✓ *Alain Burguet • Bruno Clair • Drouhin-Laroze • Claude Dugat • Bernard Dugat-Py • Dujac • Frédéric Esmonin • Michel Esmonin • Faiveley • Jean-Claude Fourrier • Herezstyn • Louis Jadot • Lucien Lemoine • Denis Mortet • Philippe Nadeff • Géantet Pansiot • Michelle & Patrice Rion • Joseph Roty • Armand Rousseau • Sérafin • Jean Trapet Père & Fils*

GRANDS ECHÉZEAUX AOC
Grand Cru

The smaller and superior of the two *grands crus* of Flagey-Echézeaux, this area is separated from the upper slopes of the Clos de Vougeot by a village boundary.

RED Fine and complex wines that should have a silky bouquet, often reminiscent of violets. The flavour can be very round and rich, but is balanced by a certain delicacy of fruit.

🍇 Pinot Noir, Pinot Gris, Pinot Liébault

⌛ 10–20 years

✓ *Engel • Gros Frère & Sœur • François Lamarche • Mongeard-Mugneret • de la Romanée-Conti*

LA GRANDE RUE AOC
Grand Cru

The newest *grand cru* of Vosne-Romanée, La Grande Rue was generally considered to have the best potential of all the *premiers crus* in this village. Officially upgraded in 1992, although the quality of wine produced by its sole owner, François Lamarche, was erratic to say the least. The *terroir* is, however, undeniably superior for a *premier cru*

and as Lamarche has been on form since its promotion, perhaps the cart should come before the horse sometimes.

RED When Lamarche gets this right, the wine is well coloured with deep, spicy-floral, black cherry fruit.

🍇 Pinot Noir, Pinot Gris, Pinot Liébault

⌛ 7–15 years

✓ *Lamarche*

GRIOTTES-CHAMBERTIN AOC
Grand Cru

The smallest of the nine *grands crus* of Gevrey-Chambertin.

RED The best growers produce deep-coloured, delicious wines with masses of soft-fruit flavours and all the velvety texture that could be expected of Chambertin itself.

🍇 Pinot Noir, Pinot Gris, Pinot Liébault

⌛ 10–20 years

✓ *Joseph Drouhin • Claude Dugat • Frédéric Esmonin • Jean-Claude Fourrier • Louis Jadot • Ponsot • Joseph Roty*

LATRICIÈRES-CHAMBERTIN AOC
Grand Cru

One of the nine *grands crus* of Gevrey-Chambertin, situated above the Mazoyères *climat* of Charmes-Chambertin. A tiny part of the adjoining *premier cru*, Aux Combottes, also has the right to use this AOC.

RED Solid structure and a certain austerity connect the two different styles of this wine (early-drinking and long-maturing). They sometimes lack fruit and generosity, but wines from the top growers recommended below are always the finest to be found.

🍇 Pinot Noir, Pinot Gris, Pinot Liébault

⌛ 10–20 years

✓ *Drouhin-Laroze • Faiveley • Leroy ⑧ • Ponsot • Jean Trapet Père & Fils*

MARSANNAY AOC

This village, situated in the very north of the Côte de Nuits, has long been famous for its rosé and has recently developed a reputation for its red wines. In May 1987 it was upgraded to full village AOC status from its previous appellation of Bourgogne Marsannay. There is talk of a classification of Marsannay that would result in a new Marsannay *premier* cru AOC. This would be at least as justifiable as Maranges *premier cru* in the Côte de Beaune, not so much in the sense that either village has vineyards of truly *premier cru* quality, but it is at least useful in highlighting the better vineyards.

RED Firm and fruity wines with juicy redcurrant flavours, hints of liquorice, cinnamon and, if new oak has been used, vanilla.

🍇 Pinot Noir, Pinot Gris, Pinot Liébault

⌛ 4–8 years

WHITE Mostly light and tangy, early-drinking wines, although the top wines made in a suitable vintage, by the likes of Charles Audoin and Louis Jadot, are a lot richer, creamier and offer serious ageing potential.

🍇 Chardonnay

⌛ 2–5 years

ROSÉ These dry wines are rich, rather than light and fragrant. Packed with ripe fruit flavours that can include blackberry, blackcurrant, raspberry and

cherry, they are best consumed young, although people do enjoy them when the wine has an orange tinge and the fruit is over-mature.

🍇 Pinot Noir, Pinot Gris, Pinot Liébault

⌛ 1–3 years

✓ *Charles Audoin • René Bouvier • Bernard Coillot* (Les Boivins) *• Louis Jadot • Denis Mortet* (Les Longeroies) *• Géantet Pansiot* (Champ Perdrix)

MAZIS-CHAMBERTIN AOC
Grand Cru

Sometimes known as Mazy-Chambertin. One of the nine *grands crus* of Gevrey-Chambertin.

RED These complex wines have a stature second only to Chambertin and Clos de Bèze. They have a fine, bright colour, super-silky finesse, and a delicate flavour that lasts.

🍇 Pinot Noir, Pinot Gris, Pinot Liébault

⌛ 10–20 years

✓ *d'Auvenay ⑧ • Bernard Dugat-Py • Frédéric Esmonin • Faiveley • Jean-Michel Guillon • Lucien Lemoine • Leroy ⑧ • Bernard Maume • Philippe Nadeff • Joseph Roty • Armand Rousseau*

MAZOYÈRES-CHAMBERTIN AOC

An alternative appellation for Charmes-Chambertin. *See* Charmes-Chambertin AOC.

MOREY-ST-DENIS AOC

This excellent little wine village tends to be overlooked. The fact that it is situated between two world-famous places, Gevrey-Chambertin and Chambolle-Musigny, coupled with the fact that Clos St-Denis is no longer considered to be Gevrey-Chambertin's top *grand cru*, does little to promote the name of this village.

RED The best of these village wines have a vivid colour, a very expressive bouquet, and a smooth flavour with lots of finesse. A Morey-St-Denis from a domaine such as Dujac can have the quality of a top *premier cru*.

🍇 Pinot Noir, Pinot Gris, Pinot Liébault

⌛ 8–15 years

WHITE Dujac produces an excellent Morey-St-Denis *blanc*, but more interesting, although less consistent, is Ponsot's Monts Luisants *blanc*. Although Monts Luisants is a *premier cru*, the upper section from which this wine comes is part of the village appellation (the southeastern corner is classified *grand cru* and sold as Clos de la Roche!). When Ponsot gets the Monts Luisants *blanc* right, it can be a superbly fresh, dry, buttery-rich wine and some writers have compared it to a Meursault.

🍇 Chardonnay, Pinot Blanc

⌛ 3–8 years

✓ *Pierre Amiot • Philippe Charlopin • Dujac • Dujac Père • Hubert Lignier • Michel Magnien • Perrot-Minot • Ponsot • Georges Roumier*

MOREY-ST-DENIS PREMIER CRU AOC

Premiers crus: Clos Baulet, Les Blanchards, La Bussière, *Les Chaffots, Aux Charmes, Les Charrières, Les Chénevery,* Aux Cheseaux, *Les Faconnières, Les Genevrières,* Les Gruenchers, *Les Millandes, Monts Luisants, Clos des Ormes,* Clos Sorbè, Les Sorbès, Côte Rôtie, La Riotte, *Les Ruchots,* Le Village.

RED These wines should have all the colour, bouquet, flavour, and finesse of the excellent village wines plus an added expression of *terroir*. The best *premiers crus* are: Clos des Ormes, Clos Sorbè, and Les Sorbès.

🍇 Pinot Noir, Pinot Gris, Pinot Liébault

🍷 10–20 years

WHITE The only white Morey-St-Denis I know is from the upper section of Monts Luisants belonging to Ponsot (*see* Morey-St-Denis AOC). To my knowledge, no other white Morey-St-Denis *premier cru* is made.

🍇 Chardonnay

✓ *Pierre Amiot • Dujac • Herezstyn • Hubert Lignier • Frédéric Magnien* (Les Ruchots) *• Perrot-Minot • Georges Roumier*

MUSIGNY AOC
Grand Cru

Musigny is the smaller of Chambolle-Musigny's two *grands crus*. It covers some 10 hectares (25 acres) on the opposite side of the village to Bonnes Mares.

RED These most stylish of wines have a fabulous colour and a smooth, seductive, and spicy bouquet. The velvet-rich fruit flavour constantly unfolds to reveal a succession of taste experiences.

🍇 Pinot Noir, Pinot Gris, Pinot Liébault

🍷 10–30 years

WHITE Musigny *blanc* is a rare and expensive dry wine produced solely at Comte Georges de Vogüé. It combines the steel of a Chablis with the richness of a Montrachet, although it never quite achieves the quality of either.

🍇 Chardonnay

🍷 8–20 years

✓ *Joseph Droubin • Louis Jadot • Leroy ⓑ • J-F Mugnier* (Château de Chambolle-Musigny) *• Christophe Roumier • Georges Roumier • Comte Georges de Vogüé*

NUITS AOC
See Nuits-St-Georges AOC

NUITS PREMIER CRU AOC
See Nuits-St-Georges Premier Cru AOC

NUITS-ST-GEORGES AOC

More than any other, the name of this town graphically projects the image of full flavour and sturdy structure for which the wines of the Côte de Nuits are justly famous.

RED These are deep-coloured, full, and firm wines, but they can sometimes lack the style and character of wines from Gevrey, Chambolle, and Morey.

🍇 Pinot Noir, Pinot Gris, Pinot Liébault

🍷 7–15 years

WHITE I have not tasted this wine. (*See* white Nuits-St-Georges Premier Cru.)

✓ *de l'Arlot • R Chevillon • J Chauvenet • J-J Confuron • Confuron-Cotétidot • Thibault Liger-Belair • Bertrand Marchard de Gramont • A Michelot • des Perdrix • Daniel Rion & Fils*

NUITS-ST-GEORGES PREMIER CRU AOC

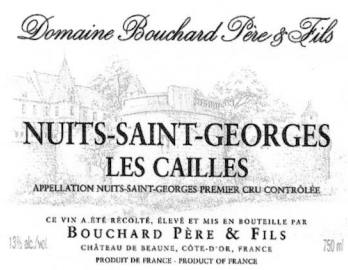

Premiers crus: Les Argillats, Les Argillières*, Clos Arlot*, Aux Boudots, Aux Bousselots, Les Cailles, Les Chaboeufs, Aux Chaignots, Chaine-Carteau (or Chaines-Carteaux), Aux Champs Perdrix, Clos des Corvées*, Clos des Corvées Pagets*, Aux Cras, Les Crots, Les Damodes, Les Didiers, Les Forêts* (or Clos des Forêts St-Georges*), Les Grandes Vignes*, Château Gris, Les Hauts Pruliers, Clos de la Maréchale*, Aux Murgers, Aux Perdrix*, En la Perrière Noblet (or En la Perrière Noblot), Les Perrières, Les Porets, Les Poulettes, Les Procès, Les Pruliers, La Richemone, La Roncière, Rue de Chaux, Les St-Georges, Clos St-Marc (or Aux Corvées), Les Terres Blanches, Aux Thorey, Les Vallerots, Les Vaucrains, Aux Vignerondes.
*In the village of Prémeaux-Prissey.

RED These wines have a splendid colour, a spicy-rich bouquet, and a vibrant fruit flavour which can be nicely underpinned with vanilla.

🍇 Pinot Noir, Pinot Gris, Pinot Liébault

🍷 10–20 years

WHITE Henri Gouges's La Perrière is dry, powerful, almost fat, with a spicy-rich aftertaste. The vines used for this wine were propagated from a mutant Pinot Noir that produced bunches of both black and white grapes. Gouges cut a shoot from a white-grape-producing branch of the mutant vine in the mid-1930s, and there is now just under half a hectare (just over one acre) of the vines planted by Gouges, none of which have ever reverted to producing black grapes.

🍇 Chardonnay, Pinot Blanc

🍷 5–10 years

✓ *Bertrand Ambroise • de l'Arlot • Robert Arnoux • Bouchard Père & Fils • Jean Chauvenet* (Les Perrières) *• Robert Chevillon • J-J Confuron • Confuron-Cotétidot • Dubois & Fils • Faiveley • Forey Père & Fils • Henri Gouges • Jean Grivot • Alain Hudelot-Noëllat • Robert Jayer-Gilles • Dominique Laurent • Philippe & Vincent Léchenaut • Leroy ⓑ • Thibault Liger-Belair • Alain Michelot • Mugneret-Gibourg • Gérard Mugneret • Gilles Remoriquet • Daniel Rion & Fils • Michelle & Patrice Rion • Patrice Rion • Antonin Rodet • Jean Tardy • de la Vougeraie ⓑ*

RICHEBOURG AOC
Grand Cru

One of the six *grands crus* at the heart of Vosne-Romanée's vineyards.

RED This is a gloriously rich wine that has a heavenly bouquet and is full of velvety and voluptuous fruit flavours.

🍇 Pinot Noir, Pinot Gris, Pinot Liébault

🍷 12–30 years

✓ *Jean Grivot • Anne Gros • Alain Hudelot-Noëllat • Leroy ⓑ • Méo-Camuzet • de la Romanée-Conti*

LA ROMANÉE AOC
Grand Cru

This vineyard is owned by the Liger-Belair family, but the wine was matured, bottled, and sold by Bouchard Père & Fils until 2002, when Louis-Michel Liger-Belair took over. Less than 1 hectare (2.5 acres), it is the smallest *grand cru* of Vosne-Romanée.

RED This is a full, fine, and complex wine that might not have the voluptuous appeal of a Richebourg, but that certainly has the class to age gracefully.

🍇 Pinot Noir, Pinot Gris, Pinot Liébault

🍷 12–30 years

✓ *Bouchard Père & Fils • Vicomte Liger-Belair*

ROMANÉE-CONTI AOC
Grand Cru

This Vosne-Romanée *grand cru* is under 2 hectares (5 acres) in size and belongs solely to the famous Domaine de la Romanée-Conti.

RED As the most expensive Burgundy in the world, this wine must always be judged by higher standards than all the rest. Yet I must admit that I never fail to be amazed by the stunning array of flavours that continuously unfold in this fabulously concentrated and utterly complex wine.

🍇 Pinot Noir, Pinot Gris, Pinot Liébault

🍷 15–35 years

✓ *de la Romanée-Conti*

ROMANÉE-ST-VIVANT AOC
Grand Cru

The largest of the six *grands crus* on the lowest slopes and closest to the village.

RED This is the lightest of the fabulous *grands crus* of Vosne-Romanée, but what it lacks in power and weight it makes up for in finesse.

🍇 Pinot Noir, Pinot Gris, Pinot Liébault

🍷 10–25 years

VINEYARDS OF CLOS DE VOUGEOT ON THE CÔTE DE NUITS
The Château du Clos de Vougeot has played a big part in the region's wine industry for many years.
However, the 50 hectares (123 acres) of vineyards surrounding the château are split into more than 80 plots.

✓ *Robert Arnoux • Sylvain Cathiard • J-J Confuron • Joseph Drouhin • Follin-Arbelet • Alain Hudelot-Noëllat • Lucien Lemoine • Leroy ❸ • de la Romanée-Conti*

RUCHOTTES-CHAMBERTIN AOC
Grand Cru

This is the second-smallest of the nine *grands crus* of Gevrey-Chambertin. It is situated above Mazis-Chambertin and is the last *grand cru* before the slope turns to face north.

RED Normally one of the lighter Chambertin lookalikes, but top growers like Roumier and Rousseau seem to achieve a bagful of added ingredients in their splendidly rich wines.

🍇 Pinot Noir, Pinot Gris, Pinot Liébault

🍷 8–20 years

✓ *Frédéric Esmonin • Mugneret-Gibourg • Christophe Roumier • Georges Roumier • Armand Rousseau*

LA TÂCHE AOC
Grand Cru

SOCIÉTÉ CIVILE DU DOMAINE DE LA ROMANÉE-CONTI
PROPRIÉTAIRE A VOSNE-ROMANÉE (COTE-D'OR) FRANCE
LA TÂCHE
APPELLATION LA TÂCHE CONTROLÉE
19.789 Bouteilles Récoltées
LES ASSOCIES-GERANTS
BOUTEILLE Nº 00000
ANNÉE 2001
Mise en bouteille au domaine

One of Vosne-Romanée's six *grands crus*, this fabulous vineyard belongs to the world-famous Domaine de la Romanée-Conti (DRC), which also owns the Romanée-Conti *grand cru*.

RED While this wine is indeed extremely rich and very complex, it does not in comparative terms quite have the richness of Richebourg, nor the complexity of Romanée-Conti. It does, however, have all the silky texture anyone could expect from

the finest of Burgundies, and no other wine surpasses La Tâche for finesse.

🍇 Pinot Noir, Pinot Gris, Pinot Liébault

🍷 12–30 years

✓ *de la Romanée-Conti*

VOSNE-ROMANÉE AOC

This is the most southerly of the great villages of the Côte de Nuits. Some Vosne-Romanée vineyards are in neighbouring Flagey-Echézeaux. This village includes the Romanée-Conti vineyard.

RED Sleek, stylish, medium-bodied wines of the purest Pinot Noir character and with the silky texture so typical of the wines of this village.

🍇 Pinot Noir, Pinot Gris, Pinot Liébault

🍷 10–15 years

✓ *Robert Arnoux • Sylvain Cathiard • Bruno Clavelier • Engel • Confuron-Cotédidot • Bernard Dugat-Py* (Vieilles Vignes) *• Forey Père & Fils • Jean Grivot • Anne Gros • Michel Gros • Méo-Camuzet • Mugneret-Gibourg • Perrot-Minot • Emmanuel Rouget • Fabrice Vigot*

VOSNE-ROMANÉE PREMIER CRU AOC

Premiers crus: Les Beaux Monts, Les Beaux Monts Bas*, Les Beaux Monts Hauts*, Les Brûlées, Les Chaumes, La Combe Brûlées, *La Croix Rameau, Cros-Parantoux*, Les Gaudichots, Les Hauts Beaux Monts, *Aux Malconsorts*, En Orveaux*, Les Petits Monts, Clos des Réas, Aux Reignots, Les Rouges du Dessus*, Les Suchots.
*These *premier cru* vineyards of Vosne-Romanée are actually in Flagey-Echézeaux.

RED These are well-coloured wines with fine aromatic qualities that are often reminiscent of violets and blackberries. They have a silky texture and a stylish flavour that is pure Pinot Noir. The best *premiers crus* to look out for are: Les Brûlées, Cros-Parantoux, Les Petits-Monts, Les Suchots, and Les Beaumonts (an umbrella name for the various Beaux Monts, high and low).

🍇 Pinot Noir, Pinot Gris, Pinot Liébault

🍷 10–20 years

✓ *de l'Arlot • Robert Arnoux • Albert Bichot (Clos Frantin) • Sylvain Cathiard • Confuron-Cotétidot • Engel • Jean Grivot • Alain Hudelot-Noëllat • S Javouhey • Henri Jayer • Lamarche • Lucien Lemoine • Leroy ❸ • Vicomte Liger-Belair • Méo-Camuzet • Gérard Mugneret • Perrot-Minot • Nicolas Potel • Daniel Rion & Fils • Michelle & Patrice Rion • Emmanuel Rouget*

VOUGEOT AOC

The modest village wines of Vougeot are a relative rarity, this appellation covering less than 5 hectares (12 acres), which is less than one-tenth of the area encompassed by the Clos de Vougeot *grand cru* itself.

RED Little-seen, fine-flavoured, well-balanced wines that are overpriced due to their scarcity. It is better to buy a *premier cru*.

🍇 Pinot Noir, Pinot Gris, Pinot Liébault

🍷 8–20 years

WHITE A rarity.

✓ *Bertagna • Mongeard-Mugneret*

VOUGEOT PREMIER CRU AOC

Premiers crus: Les Crâs, Clos de la Perrière, Les Petits Vougeots, La Vigne Blanche. The *premiers crus* are located between Clos de Vougeot and Musigny and, from a *terroir* point of view, should produce much better wines.

RED Can be nicely coloured, medium bodied, and have an attractive flavour with a good balance and a certain finesse.

🍇 Pinot Noir, Pinot Gris, Pinot Liébault

🍷 10–20 years

WHITE A clean, rich, and crisp wine of variable quality, called Clos Blanc de Vougeot, is produced by L'Héritier Guyot from the *premier cru* of La Vigne Blanche.

🍇 Chardonnay, Pinot Blanc

🍷 4–10 years

✓ *Bertagna* (Clos de la Perrière *monopole*) *• Choppin • Lamarche • de la Vougeraie ❸ (Clos du Prieuré monopole)*

CÔTE DE BEAUNE AND HAUTES-CÔTES DE BEAUNE

Pinot Noir in the Côte de Beaune is renowned for its softness and finesse, characteristics that become more evident as one progresses south through the region, but with seven of Burgundy's eight white grands crus *this is really Chardonnay country, and the wines produced are the richest, longest-lived, most complex, and stylish white wines in the world.*

ENTERING THE CÔTE DE BEAUNE from the Nuits-St-Georges end, the most immediately visible viticultural differences are its more expansive look and the much greater contrast between the deep, dark, and so obviously rich soil found on the inferior eastern side of the RN 74 road and the scanty patches of pebble-strewn

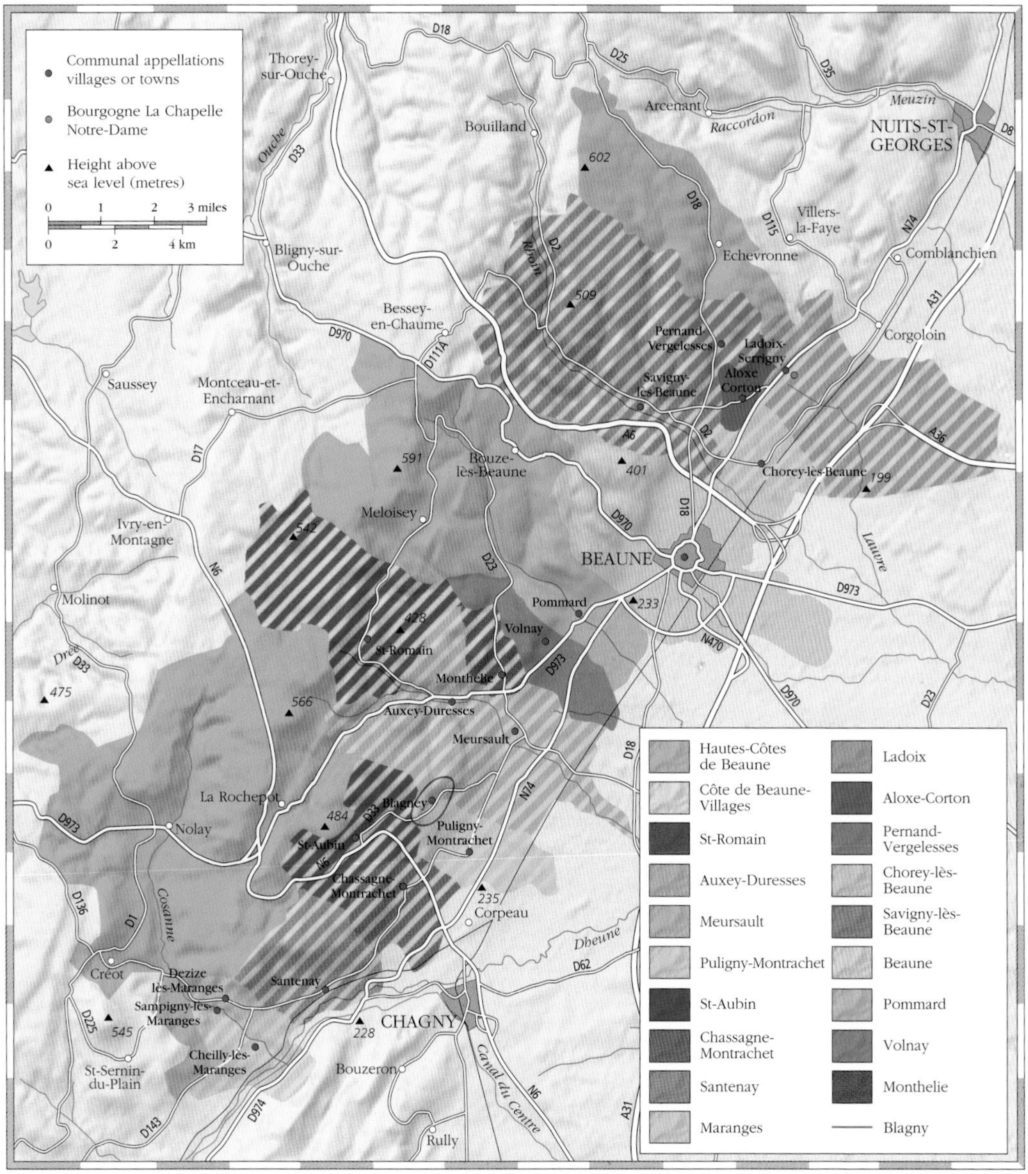
Communal appellations villages or towns
Bourgogne La Chapelle Notre-Dame
Height above sea level (metres)
0 1 2 3 miles
0 2 4 km
Thorey-sur-Ouche
Ouche
D33
Bouilland
D18
D25
D35
Arcenant
Raccordon
Meuzin
NUITS-ST-GEORGES
D8
602
D18
Rhoin
D2
D115
Villers-la-Faye
N74
Comblanchien
Bligny-sur-Ouche
Echevronne
509
A31
Corgoloin
Bessey-en-Chaume
D970
D111A
Pernand-Vergelesses
Ladoix-Serrigny
Savigny-lès-Beaune
Aloxe-Corton
Saussey
Montceau-et-Echarnant
A6
D2
A36
D17
591
Bouze-lès-Beaune
401
Chorey-lès-Beaune
199
Ivry-en-Montagne
542
Meloisey
D970
D18
Lauve
D23
BEAUNE
N6
Molinot
Pommard
233
D973
428
St-Romain
Volnay
N470
Dree
D33
D973
Monthelie
D970
475
566
Auxey-Duresses
D23
Meursault
D18
La Rochepot
Blagny
D973
Nolay
484
D33
N74
St-Aubin
Puligny-Montrachet
N6
Chassagne-Montrachet
D136
D1
Cosanne
235
Corpeau
Dheune
D62
Creot
Dezize-lès-Maranges
Santenay
Sampigny-lès-Maranges
D225
545
228
CHAGNY
Canal du Centre
Cheilly-lès-Maranges
St-Sernin-du-Plain
Bouzeron
N6
A31
D974
D143
Rully
Hautes-Côtes de Beaune
Côte de Beaune-Villages
St-Romain
Auxey-Duresses
Meursault
Puligny-Montrachet
St-Aubin
Chassagne-Montrachet
Santenay
Maranges
Ladoix
Aloxe-Corton
Pernand-Vergelesses
Chorey-lès-Beaune
Savigny-lès-Beaune
Beaune
Pommard
Volnay
Monthelie
Blagny

CÔTE DE BEAUNE VINEYARDS
The slopes of the Côte de Beaune vineyards are generally a little gentler than those of the Côte de Nuits. In both areas, Pinot Noir and Chardonnay vines are planted, but it is here that Chardonnay is king.

DOMAINE SA

LADOIX-SERRIGNY
Situated to the west of Aloxe-Corton, parts of Ladoix-Serrigny are encompassed by that village's appellations, including the grands crus *of Corton and Corton-Charlemagne.*

CÔTE DE BEAUNE AND HAUTES-CÔTES DE BEAUNE, ***see also p182***
The Côte d'Or is a hilly ridge that follows the trajectory of the Autoroute du Soleil. Most of the village and Hautes-Côtes appellations are clustered between Nuits-St-Georges in the north and Chagny in the south.

thick drift that cover the classic slopes west of the road.
It is often said that the slopes of the Côte de Beaune are gentler
than those of the Côte de Nuits, but there are many parts that
are just as sheer, although the best vineyards of the Côte de
Beaune are located on the middle slopes, which have a gentler
incline. The steeper upper slopes produce good but generally
lesser wines in all cases, except the vineyards of Aloxe-Corton –
which are, anyway, more logically part of the Côte de Nuits
than the Côte de Beaune.

FACTORS AFFECTING TASTE AND QUALITY

LOCATION
The Côte de Beaune abuts the Côte de Nuits on its southern tip and stretches almost 30 kilometres (18 miles) past the town of Beaune to Cheilly-lès-Maranges. Its vines are contiguous, although those of the Hautes-Côtes de Beaune in the western hinterland are divided into two by the Côte de Beaune vineyards of St-Romain.

CLIMATE
This area has a slightly wetter, more temperate climate than the Côte de Nuits and the grapes tend to ripen a little earlier. Hail is still a potential hazard, but less so, with wet winds and heavy rain being a greater nuisance.

ASPECT
Comprised of a series of east-facing slopes, up to 2 kilometres (just over 1 mile) wide, which curve in and out to give some vineyards northeastern aspects, and others southeastern aspects. Here the vines grow at an altitude of between 225 and 380 metres (740 to 1,250 feet) on slightly less steep slopes than those of the Côte de Nuits. South of Beaune, no vines with the right to the village (and higher) appellations extend past the RN 74 road on to the flat and fertile ground beyond.

SOIL
A limestone subsoil with sporadic beds of oolitic ironstones with flinty clay and calcareous topsoils. Light-coloured marl topsoil is found in the vineyards of Chassagne and Puligny.

VITICULTURE AND VINIFICATION
The vines are trained low to benefit from heat reflected from the soil at night. In the south of the district, the system employed is similar to that used in parts of Champagne and slightly different from elsewhere on the Côte de Beaune. For red wines, the grapes are almost always destemmed and the juice kept in contact with the skins for between eight and ten days. Classic white wines are cask fermented and the best wines, both red and white, matured in oak. The flavour of the Pinot Noir grape can easily be overwhelmed by oak so it always receives less new-oak maturation than Chardonnay does.

GRAPE VARIETIES
Primary varieties: Chardonnay, Pinot Noir
Secondary varieties: Aligoté, Gamay, Melon de Bourgogne, Pinot Beurot (Pinot Gris), Pinot Blanc, Pinot Liébault

THE HOSPICES DE BEAUNE LABEL

This distinctive label indicates that the wine comes from vineyards belonging to the Hospices de Beaune, a charitable institution that has cared for the sick and poor of Beaune since 1443. Half a millennium of gifts and legacies has seen the accumulation of vineyards that now total some 62 hectares (153 acres) of *premiers crus* and *grands crus*.

Since 1859 these wines have been sold by auction and, because of the publicity gained by this annual event, the prices fetched are now generally much higher than the going rate. We consumers must be prepared to pay a relatively higher price for these wines and help the cause.

After some criticism of the unreliability of certain wines, a new *cuverie* was built at the rear of the famous Hôtel-Dieu, known for its magnificent Flemish-crafted roof. All the wines are now matured in new oak casks. There remain, however, the variations that result from the different *élevages* of the various casks of the same *cuvée*. At the most innocent level, these may result from one *négociant* giving his wine more or less cask-maturation than another, and temperature and humidity levels can also radically change the wine's alcohol and extract content. The cellar management of less scrupulous firms may also be a consideration.

After the wines have been auctioned, they become the full responsibility of the purchaser.

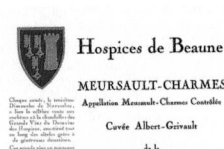

THE HOSPICES DE BEAUNE CUVÉES
RED WINES

CUVÉE CLOS DES AVAUX
AOC Beaune
Unblended Les Avaux

CUVÉE BILLARDET
AOC Pommard
A blend of Petits Epenots, Les Noizons, Les Arvelets, Les Rugiens

CUVÉE BLONDEAU
AOC Volnay
A blend of Champans, Taille Pieds, Ronceret, En l'Ormeau

CUVÉE BOILLOT
AOC Auxey-Duresses
Unblended Les Duresses

CUVÉE BRUNET
AOC Beaune
A blend of Les Teurons, La Mignotte, Les Bressandes, Les Cents Vignes

CUVÉE SUZANNE CHAUDRON
AOC Pommard
Unblended Pommard

CUVÉE MADELEINE COLLIGNON
AOC Mazis-Chambertin
Unblended Mazis-Chambertin

CUVÉE RAYMOND CYROT
AOC Pommard
A blend of Pommard and Pommard premier cru

CUVÉE CYROT-CHAUDRON
AOC Beaune
Unblended Beaune Les Montrevenots

CUVÉE GEORGES KRITTER
AOC Pommard
Unblended Clos de la Roche

CUVÉE DAMES DE LA CHARITÉ
AOC Pommard
A blend of Les Epenots, Les Rugiens, Les Noizons, La Refène, Les Combes Dessus

CUVÉE DAMES HOSPITALIÈRES
AOC Beaune
A blend of Les Bressandes, La Mignotte, Les Teurons, Les Grèves

CUVÉE MAURICE DROUHIN
AOC Beaune
A blend of Les Avaux, Les Grèves, Les Boucherottes, Champs Pimont

CUVÉE CHARLOTTE DUMAY
AOC Corton
A blend of Renardes, Les Bressandes, Clos du Roi

CUVÉE FORNERET
AOC Savigny-lès-Beaune
A blend of Les Vergelesses, Aux Gravains

CUVÉE FOUQUERAND
AOC Savigny-lès-Beaune
A blend of Basses Vergelesses, Les Talmettes, Aux Gravains, Aux Serpentières

CUVÉE GAUVAIN
AOC Volnay
A blend of Les Santenots, Les Pitures

CUVÉE ARTHUR GIRARD
AOC Savigny-lès-Beaune
A blend of Les Peuillets, Les Marconnets

CUVÉE GUIGONE DE SALINS
AOC Beaune
A blend of Les Bressandes, En Sebrey, Champs Pimont

CUVÉE HUGUES ET LOUIS BÉTAULT
AOC Beaune
A blend of Les Grèves, La Mignotte, Les Aigrots, Les Sizies, Les Vignes Franches

CUVÉE LEBELIN
AOC Monthélie
Unblended Les Duresses

CUVÉE JEHAN DE MASSOL
AOC Volnay-Santenots
Unblended Les Santenots

CUVÉE GÉNÉRAL MUTEAU
AOC Volnay
A blend of Volnay-le-Village, Carelle sous la Chapelle, Cailleret Dessus, Les Frémiets, Taille Pieds

CUVÉE DOCTEUR PESTE
AOC Corton
A blend of Les Bressandes, Les Chaumes et la Voierosse, Clos du Roi, Les Fiètres, Les Grèves

CUVÉE RAMEAU-LAMAROSSE
AOC Pernand-Vergelesses
Unblended Les Basses Vergelesses

CUVÉE NICOLAS ROLIN
AOC Beaune
A blend of Les Cents Vignes, Les Grèves, En Genêt

CUVÉE ROUSSEAU-DESLANDES
AOC Beaune
A blend of Les Cent Vignes, Les Montrevenots, La Mignotte, Les Avaux

WHITE WINES

CUVÉE DE BAHÈZRE DE LANLAY
AOC Meursault-Charmes
A blend of Les Charmes Dessus, Les Charmes Dessous

CUVÉE BAUDOT
AOC Meursault-Genevrières
A blend of Genevrières Dessus, Les Genevrières Dessous

CUVÉE PHILIPPE LE BON
AOC Meursault-Genevrières
A blend of Genevrières Dessus Les Genevrières Dessous

CUVÉE PAUL CHANSON
AOC Corton-Vergennes
Unblended Corton-Vergennes

CUVÉE DAMES DE FLANDRES
AOC Bâtard-Montrachet
Unblended Bâtard-Montrachet

CUVÉE GOUREAU
AOC Meursault
A blend of Le Poruzot, Les Pitures, Les Cras

CUVÉE ALBERT GRIVAULT
AOC Meursault-Charmes
Unblended Les Charmes Dessus

CUVÉE JEHAN HUMBLOT
AOC Meursault
A blend of Le Poruzot, Grands Charrons

CUVÉE LOPPIN
AOC Meursault
Unblended Les Criots

CUVÉE FRANÇOISE POISARD
AOC Pouilly-Fuissé
Unblended Pouilly-Fuissé

CUVÉE FRANÇOISE-DE-SALINS
AOC Corton-Charlemagne
Unblended Corton-Charlemagne

THE APPELLATIONS OF
THE CÔTE DE BEAUNE AND HAUTES-CÔTES DE BEAUNE

Notes 1. All the *grands crus* of Côte de Beaune have their own separate appellations and are therefore listed individually below. However, the *premiers crus* do not, and are therefore listed under the appellation of the village in which the vineyards are situated. *Premiers crus* that are virtually contiguous with *grand cru* vineyards are italicized; they are possibly superior to those that do not share a boundary with one or more *grands crus*, and generally superior to those that share boundaries with village AOC vineyards.
2. Leflaive plain and simple refers to Domaine Leflaive, while Olivier Leflaive is the *négociant*.

ALOXE-CORTON AOC
This village is more Côte de Nuits than Côte de Beaune, as its 99 per cent red-wine production suggests.

RED These deeply coloured, firm-structured wines with compact fruit are reminiscent of reds from northern Côte de Nuits. They are excellent value for money.

🍇 Pinot Noir, Pinot Gris, Pinot Liébault

⌛ 10–20 years

WHITE Very little Aloxe-Corton *blanc* is made, but Daniel Senard makes a lovely buttery-rich, concentrated pure Pinot Gris wine (which, although it is definitely a white wine, makes it red according to the regulations!).

🍇 Chardonnay

⌛ 4–8 years

✓ *Edmond Cornu & Fils* • *P Dubreuil-Fontaine* • *Follin-Arbelet* • *Maurice Martray* • *Daniel Senard* • *Tollot-Beaut*

ALOXE-CORTON PREMIER CRU AOC
Premiers crus: Les Chaillots, *La Coutière**, Les Fournières, Les Guérets, *La Maréchaude**, *Clos des Maréchaudes*, Les Maréchaudes, Les Meix (or Clos du Chapitre), *Les Moutottes**, *Les Paulands, Les Petites Lolières**, *La Toppe au Vert**, *Les Valozières*, Les Vercots.

*Premier cru vineyards of Aloxe-Corton in Ladoix-Serrigny.

RED These wines can have an intense bouquet and a firm, spicy fruit flavour. The best *premiers crus* are Les Fournières, Les Valozières, Les Paulands, and Les Maréchaudes.

🍇 Pinot Noir, Pinot Gris, Pinot Liébault

⌛ 10–20 years

WHITE I have never encountered any.

✓ *Cachat-Ocquidant & Fils* (Les Machaudes) • *Capitain-Gagnerot* • *Antonin Guyon* • *André Masson* • *Prince Florent de Mérode*

AUXEY-DURESSES AOC
A beautiful village, set in an idyllic valley behind Monthélie and Meursault.

RED Attractive wines not very deep in colour, but with a softness of fruit and a little finesse.

🍇 Pinot Noir, Pinot Gris, Pinot Liébault

⌛ 6–12 years

WHITE Medium-bodied wines with a full, spicy-nutty flavour, like that of a modest Meursault.

🍇 Chardonnay, Pinot Blanc

⌛ 3–7 years

✓ *Robert Ampeau* • *d'Auvenay* ⓑ • *Jean-Pierre Diconne* • *Alain Gras* • *Louis Jadot* • *Henri Latour* • *Olivier Leflaive* • *Leroy* ⓑ • *Prunier* (all and sundry) • *Dominique & Vincent Roy* • *Jean-Marc Vincent* (Les Hautes)

AUXEY-DURESSES PREMIER CRU AOC
Premiers crus: Bas des Duresses, Les Bretterins, La Chapelle, Climat du Val, Les Duresses, Les Écusseaux, Les Grands-Champs, Reugne.

RED The *premiers crus* provide nicely coloured soft wines with good finesse. The best have fine redcurrant Pinot character with the creamy-oak of cask maturity.

🍇 Pinot Noir, Pinot Gris, Pinot Liébault

⌛ 7–15 years

WHITE Excellent value, smooth, and stylish wines in the Meursault mould.

🍇 Chardonnay, Pinot Blanc

⌛ 4–10 years

✓ *Armand* • *Jean-Pierre Diconne* • *Michel Prunier* • *Vincent Prunier*

AUXEY-DURESSES-CÔTES DE BEAUNE AOC
Alternative appellation for red wines only. *See* Auxey-Duresses AOC.

BÂTARD-MONTRACHET AOC
Grand Cru
This *grand cru* is situated on the slope beneath Le Montrachet and overlaps both Chassagne-Montrachet and Puligny-Montrachet.

WHITE Full-bodied, intensely rich wine with masses of nutty, honey-and-toast flavours. It is one of the best dry white wines in the world.

🍇 Pinot Chardonnay (*sic*)

⌛ 8–20 years

✓ *Jean-Marc Boillot* • *Bouchard Père & Fils* • *Jean-Noël Gagnard* • *Vincent Girardin* • *Louis Latour* • *Leflaive* ⓑ • *Marc Morey* • *Pierre Morey* ⓑ • *Michel Niellon* • *Paul Pernot* • *Ramonet* • *Antonin Rodet* • *Étienne Sauzet*

BEAUNE AOC
Beaune gives its name to village wines and *premiers crus*, but not to any *grands crus*.

RED These soft-scented, gently fruity wines are consistent and good value.

🍇 Pinot Noir, Pinot Gris, Pinot Liébault

⌛ 6–14 years

WHITE An uncomplicated dry Chardonnay wine with a characteristic soft finish.

🍇 Chardonnay, Pinot Blanc

⌛ 3–7 years

✓ *Bouchard Père & Fils* • *Bertrand Darviot* • *Dominique Laurent* (Vieilles Vignes) • *Machard de Gramont* • *Tollot-Beaut* • *de la Vougeraie* ⓑ

BEAUNE PREMIER CRU AOC
Premiers crus: Les Aigrots, Aux Coucherias (or Clos de la Féguine), Aux Cras, Clos des Avaux, Les Avaux, Le Bas des Teurons, Les Beaux Fougets, Belissand, Les Blanches Fleurs, Les Boucherottes, Les Bressandes, Les Cents Vignes, Champs Pimont, Les Chouacheux, l'Écu (or Clos de l'Écu), Les Epenottes (or Les Epenotes), Les Fèves, En Genêt, Les Grèves, Clos Landry (Clos Ste-Landry), Les Longes, Le Clos des Mouches, Le Clos de la Mousse, Les Marconnets, La Mignotte, Montée Rouge, Les Montrevenots, En l'Orme, Les Perrières, Pertuisots, Les Reversées, Clos du Roi, Les Seurey, Les Sizies, Clos Ste-Anne (or Sur les Grèves), Les Teurons, Les Toussaints, Les Tuvilains, La Vigne de l'Enfant Jésus, Les Vignes Franches (or Clos des Ursules).

RED The best *crus* are medium-bodied with a delightfully soft rendition of Pinot fruit and lots of finesse. Look out for Faiveley's Clos de L'Écu, a *monopole* purchased at the time of writing. I expect Faiveley will want to make some sort of quality statement here.

🍇 Pinot Noir, Pinot Gris, Pinot Liébault

⌛ 10–20 years

WHITE These wines have lovely finesse and can display a toasty flavour more common to richer growths. Domaine Jacques Prieur's Champs Pimont has stood out lately.

🍇 Chardonnay, Pinot Blanc

⌛ 5–12 years

✓ *Arnoux Père & Fils* • *Jean-Claude Boisset* • *Bouchard Père & Fils* • *Chanson Père & Fils* (Clos de Fèves, Clos des Mouches) • *Joseph Drouhin* • *Camille Giroud* • *Louis Jadot* • *Jaffelin* • *Michel Lafarge* • *Louis Latour* • *René Monnier* • *Bernard Morey* • *Albert Morot* • *Michel Picard* • *Jacques Prieur* • *Tollot-Beaut*

BIENVENUES-BÂTARD-MONTRACHET AOC
Grand Cru
This is one of Puligny-Montrachet's four *grands crus*.

WHITE Not the fattest dry wines from this village, but they have great finesse, immaculate balance, and some of the nuttiness and honey-and-toast flavours expected in all Montrachets.

🍇 Chardonnay

⌛ 8–20 years

✓ *Louis Carillon & Fils* • *Chartron et Trebuchet* • *Vincent Girardin* • *Louis Latour* • *Leflaive* ⓑ • *Paul Pernot* • *Ramonet* • *Étienne Sauzet*

BLAGNY AOC
A red-only appellation from Blagny, a tiny hamlet shared by the communes of Meursault and Puligny-Montrachet.

RED These rich, full-flavoured, Meursault-like red wines are underrated.

🍇 Pinot Noir, Pinot Gris, Pinot Liébault

⌛ 8–15 years

✓ *Robert Ampeau* • *Matrot*

BLAGNY PREMIER CRU AOC

Premiers crus: La Garenne (or Sur la Garenne), Hameau de Blagny (in Puligny-Montrachet), La Jeunelotte, La Pièce sous le Bois, Sous Blagny (in Meursault), Sous le Dos d'Ane, Sous le Puits.

RED These rich wines have even more grip and attack than basic Blagny.

🍇 Pinot Noir, Pinot Gris, Pinot Liébault

🍷 10–20 years

✓ *Robert Ampeau • François Jobard • Larue (Sous le Puits) • Leflaive ❸ • Matrot*

BLAGNY-CÔTE DE BEAUNE AOC

Alternative appellation for Blagny. *See* Blagny AOC.

BOURGOGNE LA CHAPELLE NOTRE-DAME AOC

One of three Bourgogne *lieux-dits* created in 1993. La Chapelle Notre Dame is located in Serrigny, which is just east of Ladoix. Red, white, and rosé may be produced according to the same grapes and rules as for Bourgogne AOC (*see* p183). P Dubreuil-Fontaine has produced a wine from this *lieu-dit* for many years. It has always been decent, not special, but capable of improving in bottle. André and Jean-René Nudant also makes a light, fresh red from this appellation.

BOURGOGNE HAUTES-CÔTES DE BEAUNE AOC

This appellation is larger and more varied than Hautes-Côtes de Nuits. Half-red/half-rosé wines may be sold as Bourgogne Clairet Hautes-Côtes de Beaune AOC, but the style is outmoded and the appellation rarely encountered.

RED Ruby-coloured, medium-bodied wines with a Pinot perfume and a creamy-fruit finish.

🍇 Pinot Noir, Pinot Gris, Pinot Liébault

🍷 4–10 years

WHITE Not very frequently encountered, but Guillemard-Dupont's pure Pinot Beurot (Pinot Gris) is rich, dry, and expressive. Its grape variety makes it a very pale white, red, or rosé according to the regulations!

🍇 Chardonnay, Pinot Blanc

🍷 1–4 years

ROSÉ Pleasantly dry and fruity wines with some richness and a soft finish.

🍇 Pinot Noir, Pinot Gris, Pinot Liébault

🍷 1–3 years

✓ *Contat-Grange • Jean Joliot & Fils • Didier Montchovet • Claude Nouveau • Naudin-Ferrand*

CHARLEMAGNE AOC
Grand Cru

This white-only *grand cru* of Aloxe-Corton overlaps Pernand-Vergelesses and is almost, but not quite, identical to the *grand cru* of Corton-Charlemagne.

CHASSAGNE-MONTRACHET AOC

These village wines have a lesser reputation than those of Puligny-Montrachet.

RED Firm, dry wines with more colour and less softness than most Côte de Beaune reds.

🍇 Pinot Noir, Pinot Gris, Pinot Liébault

🍷 10–20 years

WHITE An affordable introduction to the great wines of Montrachet.

🍇 Chardonnay, Pinot Blanc

🍷 5–10 years

✓ *Bernard Colin & Fils • Fontaine-Gagnard • Jean-Noël Gagnard • Marquis de Laguiche • Château de la Maltroye • Bernard Morey • Jean-Marc Morey*

CHASSAGNE-MONTRACHET PREMIER CRU AOC

Premiers crus: Abbaye de Morgeot, Les Baudines, *Blanchot Dessus*, Les Boirettes, Bois de Chassagne, Les Bondues, La Boudriotte, Les Brussonnes, En Cailleret, La Cardeuse, Champ Jendreau, Les Champs Gain, La Chapelle, Clos Chareau, Les Chaumées, Les Chaumes, Les Chenevottes, Les Combards, Les Commes, Ez Crets, Ez Crottes, *Dent de Chien*, Les Embrazées, Les Fairendes, Francemont, La Grande Borne, La Grande Montagne, Les Grandes Ruchottes, Les Grands Clos, Guerchère, Les Macherelles, *La Maltroie*, Les Morgeots, Les Murées, Les Pasquelles, Petingeret, Les Petites Fairendes, Les Petits Clos, Les Pitois, Les Places, Les Rebichets, En Remilly, La Romanée, La Roquemaure, Clos St-Jean, Tête du Clos, Tonton Marcel, Les Vergers, *Vide Bourse*, Vigne Blanche, Vigne Derrière, En Virondot.

RED The wines of Chassagne-Montrachet have the weight of a Côte de Nuits and the softness of a Côte de Beaune.

🍇 Pinot Noir, Pinot Gris, Pinot Liébault

🍷 10–25 years

WHITE Flavoursome dry wines, but lacking the finesse of those in the neighbouring appellation of Puligny.

🍇 Chardonnay, Pinot Blanc

🍷 6–15 years

✓ *Guy Amiot & Fils • Roger Belland* (Morgeot Clos Pitois *monopole*) • *Blain-Gagnard • Bernard Colin & Fils • Marc Colin • Vincent Dancer • Michel Colin-Deléger* (due to a split in this domaine, look out for Bruno Colin and Philippe Coil) • *Fontaine-Gagnard • Jean-Noël Gagnard • Gagnard-Delagrange • Vincent Girardin • Gabriel et Paul Jouard • Vincent et François Jouard • Louis Latour • Olivier Leflaive • Lucien Lemoine • Château de la Maltroye • Bernard Moreau & Fils • Marc Morey • Michel Niellon • Roux • Verget*

CHASSAGNE-MONTRACHET-CÔTE DE BEAUNE AOC

Alternative appellation for red wines only. *See* Chassagne Montrachet AOC.

CHEVALIER-MONTRACHET AOC
Grand Cru

This is one of Puligny-Montrachet's four *grands crus*.

WHITE Fatter and richer than Bienvenues-Bâtard-Montrachet, this wine has more explosive flavour than Bâtard-Montrachet.

🍇 Chardonnay

🍷 10–20 years

✓ *d'Auvenay ❸ • Bouchard Père & Fils • Vincent Dancer • Georges Deléger • Vincent Girardin • Louis Jadot • Leflaive ❸ • Marc Morey • Michel Niellon*

CHOREY-LÈS-BEAUNE AOC

This satellite appellation of Beaune produces exciting, underrated wines.

RED Although next to Aloxe-Corton, Chorey has all the soft and sensuous charms that are quintessentially Beaune.

🍇 Pinot Noir, Pinot Gris, Pinot Liébault

🍷 7–15 years

WHITE Less than one per cent of the wines produced in this village are white.

✓ *Arnoux Père & Fils • Maillard Père & Fils • Maurice Martray • Tollot-Beaut*

CHOREY-LÈS-BEAUNE CÔTE DE BEAUNE AOC

Alternative appellation for red wines only. *See* Chorey-lès-Beaune AOC.

CORTON AOC
Grand Cru

This is one of the *grands crus* of Aloxe-Corton (it extends into Ladoix-Serrigny and Pernand-Vergelesses). Corton is the only *grand cru* in the Côte de Beaune that includes red and white wines and thus parallels the Côte de Nuits *grand cru* of Musigny. The following 20 *climats* may hyphenate their names (with or without the prefix) to the Corton appellation: Les Bressandes, Le Charlemagne, Les Chaumes, Les Chaumes et la Voierosse, Les Combes, Le Corton, Les Fiètres, Les Grèves, Les Languettes, Les Maréchaudes, Les Miex, Les Meix Lallemand, Les Paulands, Les Perrières, Les Pougets, Les Renardes, Le Rognet-Corton, Le Clos de Roi, Les Vergennes, La Vigne au Saint. So it is possible to get a red Corton-Charlemagne. Beware: Corton is one of the least dependable *grands crus* for quality. When it is great, it is wicked, but production is vast (3,500 to 3,800 hectolitres per year) – over twice the volume of the huge, over-producing Clos de Vougeot, and more than one-quarter of all the red *grand cru* wine produced in both the Côte de Nuits and Côte de Beaune.

RED These wines may sometimes appear intense and broody in their youth, but, when fully mature, a great Corton has such finesse and complexity that it can stun the senses.

🍇 Pinot Noir, Pinot Gris, Pinot Liébault

🍷 12–30 years

WHITE A medium- to full-bodied wine with a fine, rich flavour.

🍇 Chardonnay

🍷 10–25 years

✓ *Arnoux Père & Fils • Bouchard Père & Fils • Chevalier Père & Fils* (Rognet) • *Vincent Girardin • Antonin Guyon • Louis Jadot • Leroy ❸ • Bonneau du Martray • Faiveley • Michel Juillot • Prince Florent de Mérode • Jacques Prieur • Rapet Père & Fils • Comte Daniel Senard • Tollot-Beaut*

CORTON-CHARLEMAGNE AOC
Grand Cru

This famous *grand cru* of Aloxe-Corton extends into Ladoix-Serrigny and Pernand-Vergelesses. Although the best Corton-Charlemagne is incomparable, there is so much produced that consumers can pay a lot of money for relatively disappointing wine. At an average of 2,280 hectolitres, the production of Corton-Charlemagne represent more than two out of every three bottles of all the *grand cru* white wines produced in both the Côte de Nuits and Côte de Beaune.

WHITE At its natural best, this is the most sumptuous of all white Burgundies. It has a fabulous concentration of rich, buttery fruit flavours, a dazzling balance of acidity, and delicious overtones of vanilla, honey, and cinnamon.

🍇 Chardonnay

🍷 5–25 years

✓ *Bertrand Ambroise • Bonneau du Martray • Bouchard Père & Fils • J-F Coche-Dury • Joseph Drouhin • Genot-Boulanger • Vincent Girardin • Antonin Guyon • Louis Jadot • Patrick Javillier • Michel Juillot • Louis Latour • Olivier Leflaive • Lucien Lemoine • Jacques Prieur • Rapet Père & Fils • Remoissenet Père & Fils • Christophe Roumier*

CÔTE DE BEAUNE AOC

Wines that are entitled to the actual Côte de Beaune appellation are restricted to a few plots on the Montagne de Beaune above Beaune itself.

RED These are fine, stylish wines that reveal the purest of Pinot Noir fruit. They are produced in the soft Beaune style.

🍇 Pinot Noir, Pinot Gris, Pinot Liébault

🍷 10–20 years

WHITE Little-seen, dry basic Beaune.

🍇 Chardonnay, Pinot Blanc

🍷 3–8 years

✓ *Lycée Agricole & Viticole de Beaune*

CÔTE DE BEAUNE-VILLAGES AOC

While AOC Côte de Nuits-Villages covers red and white wines in a predominantly red-wine district, AOC Côte de Beaune-Villages applies only to red wines in a district that produces the greatest white Burgundies!

RED Excellent-value fruity wines, made in true soft Beaune style.

🍇 Pinot Noir, Pinot Gris, Pinot Liébault

🍷 7–15 years

✓ *Bernard Bachelet & Fils • Coron Père & Fils • Lequin Roussot*

CRIOTS-BÂTARD-MONTRACHET AOC

Grand Cru

The smallest of Chassagne-Montrachet's three *grands crus*.

WHITE This wine has some of the weight of its great neighbours and a lovely hint of honey-and-toast richness, but it is essentially the palest and most fragrant of all the Montrachets.

🍇 Pinot Chardonnay (*sic*)

🍷 8–20 years

✓ *d'Auvenay* ❸ *• Joseph Belland • Blain-Gagnard • Vincent Girardin • Olivier Lamy*

LADOIX AOC

Parts of Ladoix-Serrigny have the right to use the Aloxe-Corton Premier Cru appellation or the *grands crus* of Corton and Corton-Charlemagne. Ladoix AOC covers the rest of the wine produced in the area.

RED Many wines are rustic versions of Aloxe-Corton, but there are some fine grower wines that combine the compact fruit and structure of a Nuits with the softness of a Beaune.

🍇 Pinot Noir, Pinot Gris, Pinot Liébault

🍷 7–20 years

WHITE Just 5 per cent of the production is white and it is not very well distributed.

🍇 Chardonnay, Pinot Blanc

🍷 4–8 years

✓ *Capitain-Gagnerot • Edmond Cornu & Fils • François Gay & Fils • Maurice Martray • Prince Florent de Mérode*

LADOIX PREMIER CRU AOC

Premiers crus: Basses Mourottes, Bois Roussot, Les Buis, Le Clou d'Orge, La Corvée, Les Gréchons, *Hautes Mourottes*, Les Joyeuses, La Micaude, En Naget, *Rognet et Corton*.

These *premier cru* vineyards were expanded from 14 to 24 hectares (35 to 59 acres) in 2000.

RED These wines are decidedly finer in quality and deeper in colour than those with the basic village appellation.

🍇 Pinot Noir, Pinot Gris, Pinot Liébault

🍷 7–20 years

WHITE Prince Florent de Mérode of de Serrigny makes the only white Ladoix Premier Cru I know: Ladoix Hautes Mourottes blanc.

✓ *Bertrand Ambroise • Capitain-Gagnerot • Edmond Cornu & Fils • Prince Florent de Mérode • Naudin-Ferrand • André Nudant & Fils • G & P Ravaut*

LADOIX-CÔTE DE BEAUNE AOC

See Ladoix AOC

Alternative appellation for red wines only.

MARANGES AOC

In 1989 Maranges AOC replaced three separate appellations: Cheilly-lès-Maranges AOC, Dézize-lès-Maranges AOC, and Sampigny-lès-Maranges AOC, a trio of villages sharing the once moderately famous *cru* of Marange, which is on a well-exposed hillside immediately southwest of Santenay. The red wines may also be sold as Côte de Beaune AOC or Côte de Beaune-Villages AOC. Production used to be erratic, with most of the wine (including much of that qualifying for *premier cru*) sold to *négociants* for blending into Côte de Beaune-Villages, but two or three dedicated growers are beginning to get the name around.

RED Wines with a very pure Pinot perfume, which are developing good colour and body.

🍇 Pinot Noir, Pinot Gris, Pinot Liébault

🍷 2–7 years

WHITE Rarely produced in any of the three villages and never in Dézize-lès-Maranges, as far as I am aware, although it is allowed.

✓ *Fernand Chevrot • Contat-Grange • Jaffelin • René Martin • Edward Monnot • Claude Nouveau*

MARANGES CÔTE DE BEAUNE AOC

Alternative appellation for red wines only.
See Maranges AOC.

MARANGES PREMIER CRU AOC

Premiers crus: Clos de la Boutière, La Croix aux Moines, La Fussière, Le Clos des Loyères, Le Clos des Rois, Les Clos Roussots.

Some of these *climats* officially designated as *premiers crus* are a bit of a puzzle. Clos de la Boutière, for example, was originally just plain old La Boutière, and Les Clos Roussots once adjoined a *premier cru* called Les Plantes de Marange, but was never classified as one itself. According to maps prior to the merging of the three appellations, Les Plantes de Marange, Maranges, and En Maranges were the authentic names of the most important vineyards in the area classified as *premier cru*, but they have since adopted less repetitive *lieux-dits*, and such revisionism is probably justified from a marketing aspect.

RED The best examples are well coloured, with a good balance of fruit, often red fruits, and a richer, longer finish than those wines bearing the basic Maranges appellation.

🍇 Pinot Noir, Pinot Gris, Pinot Liébault

WHITE Rarely encountered.

🍇 Chardonnay, Pinot Blanc

✓ *Bernard Bachelet & Fils • Fernand Chevrot • Contat-Grangé • Edward Monnot • Claude Nouveau*

MEURSAULT AOC

While the greatest white Côte de Beaune is either Montrachet or Corton-Charlemagne, Meursault is probably better known and is certainly more popular.

RED This is often treated as a novelty, but it is a fine wine in its own right, with a firm edge.

🍇 Pinot Noir, Pinot Gris, Pinot Liébault

🍷 8–20 years

WHITE Even the most basic Meursault should be deliciously dry with a nutty-buttery-spice quality added to its typically rich flavour.

🍇 Chardonnay, Pinot Blanc

🍷 5–12 years

✓ *Robert Ampeau • d'Auvenay* ❸ *• Pierre Boisson • Bouchard Père & Fils • Boyer-Martenot • Alain Coche-Bizouard • J-F Coche-Dury • Vincent Dancer • Jean-Philippe Fichet • Henri Germain* (Limozin) *• Albert Grivault • Patrick Javillier • François Jobard • Rémy Jobard • Comte Lafon* ❸ *• Michelot* (any Michelot, hyphenated or otherwise, with a Meursault address) *• François Mikulski • Pierre Morey* ❸ *• Guy Roulot*

MEURSAULT PREMIER CRU AOC

Premiers crus: Aux Perrières, Les Bouchères, Les Caillerets, Les Charmes-Dessous (or Les Charmes-Dessus), Les Chaumes de Narvaux, Les Chaumes des Perrières, Les Cras, Les Genevrières-Dessous (or Les Genevrières-Dessus), Les Gouttes d'Or, La Jeunelotte, Clos des Perrières, Les Perrières-Dessous (or Les Perrières-Dessus), La Pièce sous le Bois, Les Plures, Le Porusot, Les Porusot-Dessous (or Le Porusot-Dessus), Clos des Richemont (or Cras), Les Santenots Blancs, Les Santenots du Milieu, Sous Blagny, Sous le Dos d'Âne.

RED Finer and firmer than the basic village wines, these reds need plenty of time to soften.

🍇 Pinot Noir, Pinot Gris, Pinot Liébault

🍷 10–20 years

WHITE Great Meursault should always be rich. Their various permutations of nutty, buttery, and spicy Chardonnay flavours may often be submerged by the honey, cinnamon, and vanilla of new oak until considerably mature.

🍇 Chardonnay, Pinot Blanc

🍷 6–15 years

✓ *d'Auvenay* ❽ • *Bouchard Père & Fils* • *Michel Bouzereau & Fils* • *J-F Coche-Dury* • *Vincent Dancer* • *Henri Germain* • *Vincent Girardin* • *Albert Grivault (Clos des Perrières)* • *Patrick Javillier* • *François Jobard* • *Comte Lafon* ❽ • *Jean Latour Labille* • *Leroy* ❽ • *Martelet de Cherisey* (Meursault-Blagny) • *Matrot* • *Mazilly Père & Fils* (Les Meurgers) • *Michelot* (any Michelot, hyphenated or otherwise, with a Meursault address) • *Pierre Morey* ❽ • *Alain Patriarche* (Les Grands Charrons) • *Jacques Prieur* • *Hubert de Montille* (Château de Puligny-Montrachet, Les Pruzots) • *Remoissenet Père & Fils* • *Guy Roulot*

MEURSAULT-BLAGNY PREMIER CRU AOC

Premiers crus: La Jeunelotte, La Pièce sous le Bois, Sous Blagny, Sous le Dos d'Âne.

An alternative appellation for Meursault wines from vineyards in the neighbouring village of Blagny. The wines must be white, otherwise they claim the Blagny Premier Cru appellation. *See* Meursault Premier Cru AOC.

MEURSAULT-CÔTE DE BEAUNE AOC

Alternative red-wine-only appellation for Meursault. *See* Meursault AOC.

MEURSAULT-SANTENOTS AOC

This is an alternative appellation for Meursault Premier Cru that comes from a part of the Volnay-Santenots appellation. *See* Volnay-Santenots AOC.

MONTHÉLIE AOC

Monthélie's wines, especially the *premiers* crus, are probably the most underrated in Burgundy. A few years ago there was a silly fuss over whether there should be an accent on the first "e" in Monthélie, and a number of authoritative references differ. The definitive answer – in black and white from the mayor of the village, and the president of the local *syndicat* for Monthélie – is yes, there should be.

RED These excellent wines have a vivid colour, expressive fruit, a firm structure, and a lingering, silky finish.

🍇 Pinot Noir, Pinot Gris, Pinot Liébault

🍷 7–15 years

WHITE Relatively little white wine is produced.

🍇 Chardonnay, Pinot Blanc

🍷 3–7 years

✓ *Eric Boigelot* • *Denis Boussey* • *Eric Boussey* • *J-F Coche-Dury* • *Paul Garaudet* • *Comte Lafon* ❽ • *Monthélie-Douhairet* • *Annick Parent*

MONTHÉLIE PREMIER CRU AOC

Premiers crus: Le Cas Rougeot, Les Champs Fulliot, Les Duresses, Le Château Gaillard, Le Clos Gauthey, Le Meix Bataille, Les Riottes, Sur la Velle, La Taupine, Les Vignes Rondes, Le Village de Monthélie.

RED Monthélie's *premiers crus* are hard to find, but worth the effort.

🍇 Pinot Noir, Pinot Gris, Pinot Liébault

🍷 8–20 years

WHITE Paul Garaudet's delicately perfumed Champs-Fulliot *blanc* is the only white *premier cru* I have come across.

✓ *Eric Boigelot* • *Denis Boussey* (Les Champs Fulliots) • *Jehan Changarnier* • *Gérard Doreau* • *Paul Garaudet* • *Château de Monthélie* ❽ • *Annick Parent*

MONTHÉLIE-CÔTE DE BEAUNE AOC

Alternative appellation for red wines only. *See* Monthélie AOC.

LE MONTRACHET AOC
See Montrachet AOC

MONTRACHET AOC
Grand Cru

Many consider Montrachet to be the greatest dry white wine in the world. On the other hand, I do remember reading somewhere that its flavours can be so intense that it is difficult to know whether it is a joy to drink or whether you are giving your palate an end-of-term exam. It definitely is a joy to drink, but I know what the writer means.

WHITE When it is fully mature, Montrachet has the most glorious and expressive character of all dry white wines. Its honeyed, toasty, floral, nutty, creamy, and spicy aromas are simply stunning.

🍇 Pinot Chardonnay (*sic*)

🍷 10–30 years

✓ *Guy Amiot & Fils* • *Amiot-Bonfils* • *Bouchard Père & Fils* • *Chartron et Trebuchet* • *Marc Colin* • *Louis Jadot* • *Comte Lafon* ❽ • *Leflaive* ❽ • *Marquis de Laguiche* (made and sold by Joseph Drouhin) • *Pierre Morey* ❽ • *Jacques Prieur* • *de la Romanée-Conti*

PERNAND-VERGELESSES AOC

This village, near Aloxe-Corton, is the most northerly appellation of the Côte de Beaune.

RED With the exception of the silky wines recommended below, too many of these are rustic and overrated and would be better off in a *négociant* Côte de Beaune-Villages blend.

🍇 Pinot Noir, Pinot Gris, Pinot Liébault

🍷 7–15 years

WHITE Although this village is famous for its Aligoté, growers such as Jacques Germain produce smooth, deliciously balanced wines that deserve more recognition.

🍇 Chardonnay, Pinot Blanc

🍷 4–8 years

✓ *Denis Père & Fils* • *P Dubreuil-Fontaine* • *Jacques Germain* • *Olivier Leflaive*

PERNAND-VERGELESSES-CÔTE DE BEAUNE AOC

Alternative appellation for red wines only. *See* Pernand-Vergelesses AOC.

PERNAND-VERGELESSES PREMIER CRU AOC

Premiers crus: En Caradeux, Creux de la Net, Les Fichots, Île des Hautes Vergelesses, Les Basses Vergelesses.

RED These wines repay keeping until the fruit develops a silkiness that hangs gracefully on the wine's structure and gives Pernand's *premiers crus* the class its village wines lack.

🍇 Pinot Noir, Pinot Gris, Pinot Liébault

🍷 10–20 years

WHITE The Beaune firm of Chanson Père & Fils produces a consistent wine of medium body, which is dry but mellow. However, Pavelot is the best white *premier cru* from this village I have tasted.

🍇 Chardonnay, Pinot Blanc

🍷 4–8 years

✓ *Delarche* • *P Dubreuil-Fontaine* • *Roger Jaffelin & Fils* (Creux de la Net) • *Pavelot* • *Rapet Père & Fils* • *Rollin Père & Fils*

POMMARD AOC

A very famous village with a "reborn" image built up by a group of dedicated and skilful winemakers.

RED The "famous" dark, alcoholic, and soupy wines of Pommard are now mostly a thing of the past, having been replaced by exciting fine wines.

🍇 Pinot Noir, Pinot Gris, Pinot Liébault

🍷 8–16 years

✓ *Robert Ampeau* • *Comte Armand* • *Billard-Gonnet* • *Jean-Marc Boillot* • *Bernard & Louis Glantenay* • *Leroy* ❽ • *Aleth Leroyer-Girardin* • *Hubert de Montille* • *F Parent* • *Château de Pommard* • *Vaudoisey-Creusefond* (Croix Blanche)

POMMARD PREMIER CRU AOC

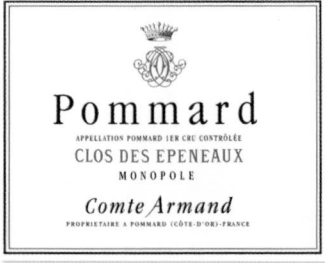

Premiers crus: Les Arvelets, Les Bertins, Clos Blanc, Les Boucherottes, La Chanière, Les Chanlins-Bas, Les Chaponnières, Les Charmots, Les Combes-Dessus, Clos de la Commaraine, Les Croix Noires, Derrière St-Jean, Clos des Epeneaux, Les Fremiers, Les Grands Epenots, Les Jarolières, En Largillière (or Les Argillières), Clos Micot, Les Petits Epenots, Les Pézerolles, La Platière, Les Poutures, La Refène, Les Rugiens-Bas, Les Rugiens-Hauts, Les Saussilles, Clos de Verger, Village.

RED The best *crus* are the various *climats* of Les Rugiens (deep and voluptuous) and Les Epenots (soft, fragrant, and rich).

Pinot Noir, Pinot Gris, Pinot Liébault

10–20 years

Comte Armand (Les Petits Epenots ❸) • Denis Carré • Billard-Gonnet • Jean-Marc Boillot • de Courcel (Les Vaumuriens) • Vincent Dancer • Lejeune • Leroy ❸ • Olivier Leflaive • Catherine et Claude Maréchal • Moissenet-Bonnard (Les Epenots) • Hubert de Montille • Pierre Morey ❸ • Parent • Nicolas Potel • Pothier-Rieusset • de la Pousse d'Or • de la Vougeraie ❸

PULIGNY-MONTRACHET AOC

One of two Montrachet villages producing some of the greatest dry whites in the world.

RED Although some fine wines are made, Puligny-Montrachet *rouge* demands a premium for its scarcity.

Pinot Noir, Pinot Gris, Pinot Liébault

10–20 years

WHITE Basic Puligny-Montrachet from a top grower is a very high-quality wine: full bodied, fine, and steely, requiring a few years to develop a nutty honey-and-toast flavour.

Chardonnay, Pinot Blanc

5–12 years

Robert Ampeau • Jean-Marc Boillot • Louis Carillon & Fils • des Lambrays (Clos du Cailleret) • Leflaive ❸ • Olivier Leflaive • Étienne Sauzet

PULIGNY-MONTRACHET PREMIER CRU AOC

Premiers crus: Le Cailleret (or Demoiselles), Les Chalumeaux, Champ Canet, Champ Gain, Au Chaniot, Clavaillon, Les Combettes, Ez Folatières, Les Folatières, La Garenne (or Sur la Garenne), Clos de la Garenne, Hameau de Blagny, La Jaquelotte, Clos des Meix, Clos de la Mouchère (or Les Perrières), Peux Bois, Les Pucelles, Les Referts, En la Richarde, Sous le Courthil, Sous le Puits, La Truffière.

RED I have never encountered any.

Pinot Noir, Pinot Gris, Pinot Liébault

WHITE A *premier cru* Puligny by a top grower such as Étienne Sauzet is one of the most flavour-packed taste experiences imaginable.

Chardonnay, Pinot Blanc

7–15 years

Guy Amiot & Fils • Robert Ampeau • d'Auvenay ❸ • Jean-Marc Boillot • Jean-Claude Boisset • Michel Bouzereau & Fils (Les Champs Gains) • Louis Carillon & Fils • Joseph Drouhin • Louis Jadot (La Garenne) • Leflaive ❸ • Lucien Lemoine • Olivier Merlin ◉ • Martelet de Cherisey • Hubert de Montille • Marc Morey • Jacques Prieur • Étienne Sauzet

PULIGNY-MONTRACHET-CÔTE DE BEAUNE AOC

Alternative appellation for red wines only.
See Puligny-Montrachet AOC.

ST-AUBIN AOC

This underrated village has many talented winemakers and is an excellent source for good-value wines.

RED Delicious, ripe but light, fragrant, and fruity red wines that quickly develop a taste of wild strawberries.

Pinot Noir, Pinot Gris, Pinot Liébault

4–8 years

WHITE Super-value white wines – a sort of "Hautes-Côtes Montrachet"!

Chardonnay, Pinot Blanc

3–8 years

Jean-Claude Bachelet • Françoise & Denis Clair • Clerget • Marc Colin • Hubert Lamy & Fils

ST-AUBIN-CÔTE DE BEAUNE AOC

Alternative appellation for red wines only.
See St-Aubin AOC.

ST-AUBIN PREMIER CRU AOC

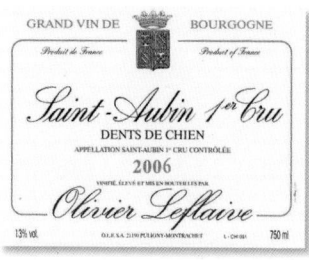

Premiers crus: Le Bas de Gamay à l'Est, Bas de Vermarain à l'Est, Les Castets, Les Champlots, Es Champs, Le Charmois, La Chatenière, Les Combes au Sud, Les Cortons, En Créot, Derrière chez Edouard, Derrière la Tour, Echaille, Les Frionnes, Sur Gamay, Marinot, En Montceau, Les Murgers des Dents de Chien, Les Perrières, Pitangeret, Le Puits, En la Ranché, En Remilly, Sous Roche Dumay, Sur le Sentier du Clou, Les Travers de Marinot, Vignes Moingeon, Le Village, En Vollon à l'Est.

The best of these *premiers crus* are Les Frionnes and Les Murgers des Dents de Chien, followed by La Chatenière, Les Castets, En Remilly, and Le Charmois.

RED Very appealing strawberry and oaky-vanilla wines that are delicious young, yet improve further with age.

Pinot Noir, Pinot Gris, Pinot Liébault

5–15 years

WHITE These dry wines are often superior to the village wines of Puligny-Montrachet and always much cheaper.

Chardonnay, Pinot Blanc

4–10 years

Guy Amiot & Fils • Jean-Claude Bachelet • Clerget • Marc Colin • Vincent Girardin • Hubert Lamy • Olivier Lamy • Patrick Miolane • Bernard Morey • Marc Morey • Henri Prudhon & Fils • Gérard Thomas

ST-ROMAIN AOC

A little village amid picturesque surroundings in the hills above Auxey-Duresses.

RED Good-value, medium-bodied, rustic reds that have a good, characterful flavour.

Pinot Noir, Pinot Gris, Pinot Liébault

4–8 years

WHITE Fresh and lively, light- to medium-bodied dry white wines of an honest Chardonnay style.

Chardonnay, Pinot Blanc

3–7 years

Ambroise Bertrand • de Chassorney • Joseph Drouhin • Alain Gras • Thévenin-Monthélie

ST-ROMAIN-CÔTE DE BEAUNE AOC

Alternative appellation for red wines only.
See St-Romain AOC.

SANTENAY AOC

This most southerly village appellation of the Côte d'Or (but not of the Côte de Beaune) is a source of good-value Burgundy.

RED These wines are fresh and frank, with a clean rendition of Pinot Noir fruit supported by a firm structure.

Pinot Noir, Pinot Gris, Pinot Liébault

7–15 years

WHITE Only 2 per cent of Santenay is white, but some good buys can be found among the top growers.

Chardonnay, Pinot Blanc

4–8 years

Bernard Bachelet & Fils • Roger Belland • Françoise & Denis Clair • Vincent Girardin • Alain Gras • Prieur-Brunet

SANTENAY PREMIER CRU AOC

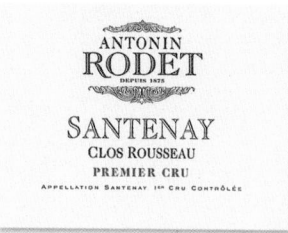

Premiers crus: Beauregard, Le Chainey, La Comme, La Comme Dessus, Clos Faubard, Les Fourneaux, Grand Clos Rousseau, Les Gravières, La Maladière, Clos des Mouches, Passetemps, Petit Clos Rousseau, Clos de Tavannes.

The best are Clos de Tavannes, Les Gravières, La Maladière, and La Comme Dessus.

RED In the pure and frank mould of Pinot Noir wines, but with an added expression of *terroir*.

Pinot Noir, Pinot Gris, Pinot Liébault

6–15 years

WHITE Rarely encountered.

Chardonnay, Pinot Blanc

5–10 years

Roger Belland • Françoise & Denis Clair • Vincent Girardin • Alain Gras (also sold as René Gras-Boisson) • Lecquin-Colin (Vieilles Vignes) • Bernard Morey • Lucien Muzard & Fils • de la Pousse d'Or • Jean-Marc Vincent (Beaurepaire, Passetemps)

SANTENAY-CÔTE DE BEAUNE AOC

Alternative appellation for red wines only.
See Santenay AOC.

SAVIGNY AOC

See **Savigny-lès-Beaune AOC**

SAVIGNY PREMIER CRU AOC

See **Savigny-lès-Beaune Premier Cru AOC**

SAVIGNY-CÔTE DE BEAUNE AOC

Alternative appellation for red wine only.
See Savigny-lès-Beaune AOC.

SAVIGNY-LÈS-BEAUNE AOC

This village has gifted winemakers producing very underrated and undervalued wines.

RED Delicious, easy-to-drink, medium-bodied wines that are very soft and Beaune-like in style.

🍇 Pinot Noir, Pinot Gris, Pinot Liébault

🍷— 7–15 years

WHITE Some excellent dry wines with good concentration of flavour, a smooth texture and some finesse, but they are difficult to find.

🍇 Chardonnay, Pinot Blanc

🍷— 4–10 years

✓ *Robert Ampeau • Simon Bize & Fils • Bouchard Père & Fils • Camus-Brochon • Philippe Delagrange* (blanc) *• Maurice Giboulot • Girard-Vollot • Pierre Guillemot • Lucien Jacob • Maréchal-Caillot • Parent • Jean-Marc Pavelot • du Prieuré • Rollin Père & Fils • Tollot-Beaut*

SAVIGNY-LÈS-BEAUNE PREMIER CRU AOC

Premiers crus: Aux Clous, Aux Fournaux, Aux Gravains, Aux Guettes, Aux Serpentières, Bas Marconnets, Basses Vergelesses, Clos la Bataillères (*or* Aux *or* Les Vergelesses), Champ Chevrey (*or* Aux Fournaux), Les Charnières, Hauts Jarrons, Les Hauts Marconnets, Les Jarrons (*or* La Dominode), Les Lavières, Les Narbantons, Petits Godeaux, Les Peuillets, Redrescut, Les Rouvrettes, Les Talmettes

RED These wines have a very elegant, soft, and stylish Pinot flavour that hints of strawberries, cherries, and violets. The best are: Les Lavières, La Dominode, Aux Vergelesses, Les Marconnets, and Aux Guettes.

🍇 Pinot Noir, Pinot Gris, Pinot Liébault

🍷— 7–20 years

WHITE Domaine des Terregelesses produces a splendidly rich, dry Les Vergelesses.

🍇 Chardonnay, Pinot Blanc

🍷— 5–15 years

✓ *Simon Bize & Fils • Bouchard Père & Fils • Camus-Brochon • Chandon de Briailles •*

Chanson Père & Fils • Bruno Clair • Maurice Ecard • François Gay & Fils • Machard de Gramont • A-F Gros (Clos des Guettes) *• Louis Jadot • Leroy* Ⓑ *• Albert Morot* (La Bataillère aux Vergelesses) *• Olivier Père & Fils (Les Peuillets) • Pavelot • des Terregelesses* (Les Vergelesses) *• Tollot-Beaut*

SAVIGNY-LÈS-BEAUNE-CÔTE DE BEAUNE AOC

Alternative appellation for red wines only.
See Savigny-lès-Beaune AOC.

VOLNAY AOC

Volnay ranks in performance with such great *crus* as Gevrey-Chambertin and Chambolle-Musigny. It is the most southerly red-wine-only appellation in the Côte d'Or, and the only great wine village located above its vineyards.

RED These wines are not cheap, but they are firm and well coloured with more silky finesse than should be expected from a village appellation.

🍇 Pinot Noir, Pinot Gris, Pinot Liébault

🍷— 6–15 years

✓ Marquis d'Angerville • Michel Lafarge • Régis Rossignol

VOLNAY PREMIER CRU AOC

Premiers crus: Les Angles, Les Aussy, La Barre, Bousse d'Or (or Clos de la Bousse d'Or), Les Brouillards, En Cailleret, Les Caillerets, Cailleret Dessus (part of which may be called Clos des 60 Ouvrées), Carelles Dessous, Carelle sous la Chapelle, Clos de la Caves de Ducs, En Champans, Chanlin, En Chevret, Clos de la Chapelle, Clos des Chênes (or Clos des Chânes), Clos de Ducs, Clos du Château des Ducs, Frémiets (or Clos de la Rougeotte), La Gigotte, Les Grands Champs, Lassolle, Les Lurets, Les Mitans, En l'Ormeau, Pitures Dessus, Pointes d'Angles, Robardelle, Le Ronceret, Taille Pieds, En Verseuil (or Clos du Verseuil), Le Village.

RED No *grands crus*, but its silky-smooth and fragrant *premiers crus* are great wines, showing tremendous finesse. The best are: Clos des Chêne,

Taille Pieds, Bousse d'Or, Clos de Ducs, the various *climats* of Cailleret, Clos des 60 Ouvrées, and En Champans.

🍇 Pinot Noir, Pinot Gris, Pinot Liébault

🍷— 8–20 years

✓ *Marquis d'Angerville • Jean-Marc Boillot • Jean-Marc Bouley* (Les Carelles) *• Antonin Guyon • Louis Jadot • Michel Lafarge • Comte Lafon* Ⓑ *• Olivier Leflaive • Leroy* Ⓑ *• Hubert de Montille • Nicolas Potel • de la Pousse d'Or • Régis Rossignol*

VOLNAY-SANTENOTS PREMIER CRU AOC

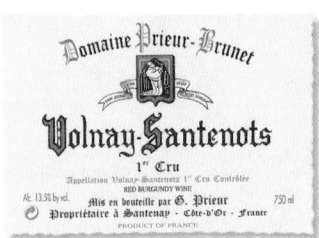

This confusing appellation is in Meursault, not Volnay, although it does run up to the boundary of that village. It dates back to the 19th century, when the Meursault *lieu-dit* of Les Santenots du Milieu became famous for its red wines. White wines cannot be called Volnay-Santenots and must be sold as Meursault or, if produced from the two-thirds of this vineyard furthest from the Volnay border, they may be sold as Meursault Premier Cru AOC or Meursault-Santenots. The right to the Volnay-Santenots appellation was accorded by Tribunal at Beaune in 1924.

RED These wines, which are not often found, are similar to Volnay with good colour and weight, but can lack its silky elegance.

🍇 Pinot Noir, Pinot Gris, Pinot Liébault

🍷— 8–20 years

✓ *Robert Ampeau • Comte Lafon* Ⓑ *• Leroy* Ⓑ *• Matrot • François Mikulski • Jacques Prieur • Prieur-Brunet*

GRAND CRU VINEYARD CORTON CLOS DES VERGENNES
The tiny vineyard of Corton Clos des Vergennes is under single ownership and the wines are distributed by Moillard-Grivot.

THE CÔTE CHALONNAISE

This is a simple district in wine terms, with just five appellations, two exclusively white and three red or white. Despite the fact that many of the wines are little known, their quality in all appellations is very good, and the value for money is even better.

THE CÔTE CHALONNAISE, or Région de Mercurey, as it is sometimes called, was once the forgotten area of Burgundy, perceived as too serious for its own good. Because its flavoursome reds and buttery whites have more in common with the wines of the Côte de Beaune than elsewhere, merchants categorized them as inferior or pretentious. Perhaps the Côte Chalonnaise would not have been forgotten had merchants thought of it more as a superior Mâconnais than as an inferior Côte de Beaune. However, over the past 20 years, as merchants across the world have become more willing to seek out lesser-known wines, the area has built up a reputation as one of Burgundy's best sources of quality wines.

EXCELLENT NÉGOCIANTS
The Burgundy drinker is blessed with a fine choice of *négociants* in the Côte Chalonnaise, including Chandesais, Delorme, and

Faiveley. There is a good *coopérative* at Buxy, and an increasing number of talented growers. This area produces fine Crémant de Bourgogne and, in Bouzeron, has the only single-village appellation of Aligoté wine.

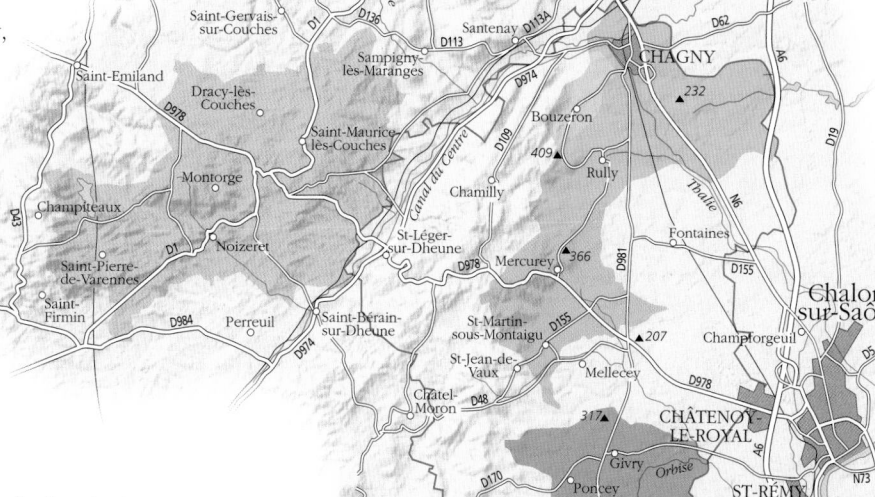

THE CÔTE CHALONNAISE, *see also p182*
The vine-growing zones form three separate "islands" west of Chalon, between the Côte de Beaune to the north and the Mâconnais to the south.

FACTORS AFFECTING TASTE AND QUALITY

LOCATION
These three islands of vines are situated to the west of Châlon-sur-Saône, 350 kilometres (217 miles) southeast of Paris, between the Côte de Beaune in the north and the Mâconnais in the south.

CLIMATE
Slightly drier than that of the Côte d'Or, with many of the best slopes protected from the worst ravages of frost and hail.

ASPECT
This is a disjointed district in which the great plateau of the Côte d'Or peters out into a complex chain of small hills with vines clinging to the most favourable slopes, at an altitude of between 230 and 320 metres (750 to 1,050 feet), in a far more sporadic fashion than those in the Côte d'Or.

SOIL
Limestone subsoil with clay-sand topsoils that are sometimes enriched with iron deposits. At Mercurey there are limestone ooliths mixed with iron-enriched marl.

VITICULTURE AND VINIFICATION
The wines are produced in an identical way to those of the Côte de Beaune, with no exceptional viticultural or vinification techniques involved, *see p198*.

GRAPE VARIETIES
Primary varieties: Chardonnay, Pinot Noir
Secondary varieties: Aligoté, Pinot Blanc, Pinot Liébault

THE APPELLATIONS OF
THE CÔTE CHALONNAISE

BOURGOGNE CÔTE CHALONNAISE AOC
As from the 1990 vintage, basic Bourgogne made exclusively from grapes harvested in the region may bear this specific appellation.

RED A & P de Villaine's Digoine has outstanding fruit and finesse for such a modest appellation. Only Michel Goubard's Mont-Avril comes close in richness, and can be truly excellent, but is not in the same class. Both are terrific value.

🍇 Pinot Noir, Pinot Liébault, Pinot Gris

🍷 1–3 years

WHITE Normally softer and fuller than a Mâcon, but not particularly rich in fruit, except for A & P de Villaine's Clous, which is the best white wine in the appellation, and Venot's La Corvée, the number two.

🍇 Chardonnay, Pinot Blanc

┠⇢ Upon purchase

ROSÉ Seldom encountered, and not special, although no reason why it should not be successful.

▒ Pinot Noir, Pinot Liébault, Pinot Gris

┠⇢ Upon purchase

✓ *René Bourgeon • Caves de Buxy • André Delorme • Michel Derain • Michel Goubard (Mont Avril) • Guy Narjoux • Venot (La Corvée) • A & P de Villaine* ◉

BOURGOGNE CÔTES DU COUCHOIS, *or* BOURGOGNE COUCHOIS, AOC

Although the Côtes du Couchois extends across five communes (Dracy-Lès-Couches, Saint-Jean-de-Trézy, Saint-Maurice-Lès-Couches, Saint-Pierre-de-Varennes, and Saint-Cernin-du-Plain) in addition to Couches itself, at just 20 hectares (50 acres) this appellation is nowhere near as large as the Côte Chalonnaise, which comprises 665 hectares (1,643 acres) of vines. The wines I have tasted (Domaine des Trois Monts, Bichot's Château de Dracy, and Serge Prost), although restricted in number and style (red only, although white and rosé are also permitted), have not been special.

BOUZERON AOC

In 1979 Bouzeron became the only *cru* to have its own appellation specifically for the Aligoté grape, as Bourgogne Aligoté Bouzeron AOC, and in 1998 achieved full village status.

WHITE This excellent and interesting dry wine is much the fullest version of Aligoté available. In weight, fruit, and spice, its style is nearer to Pinot Gris than to Chardonnay. The Bouzeron produced by A & P de Villaine is a class apart.

▒ Aligoté

┠⇢ 1–5 years

✓ *Bougeot • Ancien Carnot (sold by Bouchard Père & Fils) • Chanzy Frères • André Delorme • A & P de Villaine* ◉

GIVRY AOC

Underrated wines from just south of Mercurey.

RED Light- to medium-bodied, soft, and fruity wine with delightful nuances of cherry and redcurrant.

▒ Pinot Noir, Pinot Gris, Pinot Liébault

┠⇢ 5–12 years

WHITE Just 10 per cent of Givry is white – a deliciously clean, dry Chardonnay that can have an attractive spicy-buttery hint on the aftertaste.

▒ Chardonnay, Pinot Blanc

┠⇢ 3–8 years

✓ *René Bourgeon • Chofflet-Vaudenaire • Michel Derain • Didier Erker (En Chenèvre) • Mme du Jardin • Joblot • Louis Latour • François Lumpp • Parize Père & Fils (Champ Nalot) • Jean-Paul Ragot • R Remoissenet & Fils • Baron Thénard*

GIVRY PREMIER CRU AOC

Premiers crus: Clos de la Barraude, Les Berges, Bois Chevaux, Bois Gauthier, Clos de Cellier aux Moines, Clos Charlé, Clos du Cras Long, Les Grandes Vignes, Grand Prétants, Clos Jus, Clos Marceaux, Marole, Petit Marole, Petit Prétants, Clos St-Paul, Clos St-Pierre, Clos Salomon, Clos de la Servoisine, Vaux, Clos du Vernoy, En Vignes Rouge, Le Vigron.

RED Best examples are medium bodied, soft, rich, and fruity with delightful nuances of cherry and redcurrant.

▒ Pinot Noir, Pinot Gris, Pinot Liébault

┠⇢ 5–12 years

WHITE Similar in character to Givry AOC, the deliciously clean, dry Chardonnay can have an attractive spicy-buttery hint on the aftertaste.

▒ Chardonnay, Pinot Blanc

┠⇢ 3–8 years

✓ *René Bourgeon • Chofflet-Vaudenaire • Michel Derain • Mme du Jardin • Joblot • Louis Latour • François Lumpp • Parize & Fils • Jean-Paul Ragot • R Remoissenet & Fils • Baron Thénard*

MERCUREY AOC

The wines of Mercurey, including the *premiers crus*, account for two-thirds of the production of the entire Côte Chalonnaise.

RED Medium-bodied wines with excellent colour and fine varietal character that have an exceptional quality-for-price ratio.

▒ Pinot Noir, Pinot Gris, Pinot Liébault

┠⇢ 5–12 years

WHITE Dry wines that combine the lightness and freshness of the Mâconnais with some of the fatness and butteriness of the Côte de Beaune.

▒ Pinot Chardonnay (*sic*)

┠⇢ 3–8 years

✓ *Brintet (white Vieilles Vignes) • Château de Chamilly • Louis Desfontaine • Lorenzon • Antonin Rodet*

MERCUREY PREMIER CRU AOC

Premiers crus: La Bondue, Les Byots, La Cailloute, Champs Martins, La Chassière, Le Clos, Clos des Barraults, Clos Château de Montaigu, Clos l'Evêque, Clos des Myglands, Clos du Roi, Clos Tonnerre, Clos Voyens (or Les Voyens), Les Combins, Les Crêts, Les Croichots, Les Fourneaux (or Clos des Fourneaux), Grand Clos Fortoul, Les Grands Voyens, Griffères, Le Levrière, Le Marcilly (or Clos Marcilly), La Mission, Les Montaigus (or Clos des Montaigus), Les Naugues, Les Petits Voyens, Les Ruelles, Sazenay, Les Vasées, Les Velley.

RED These *premiers crus* have increased in number from 5 to 27 and in area from 15 to over 100 hectares (37 to 250 acres).

▒ Pinot Noir, Pinot Gris, Pinot Liébault

┠⇢ 5–15 years

WHITE I have encountered white Mercurey only at the basic village level.

✓ *Brintet • Faiveley • Jeannin-Nastet • Émile Juillot • Michel Juillot • Lorenzon • Guy Narjoux • François Raquillet • Antonin Rodet (Château de Chamirey)*

MONTAGNY AOC

As all the vineyards in this AOC are *premiers crus*, the only wines that appear under the basic village appellation are those that fail to meet the technical requirement of 11.5 per cent alcohol before chaptalization.

WHITE These dry white wines are good-value, fuller versions of the white Mâcon type.

▒ Chardonnay

┠⇢ 3–10 years

✓ *Maurice Bertrand & François Juillot • Caves de Buxy • Faiveley • Louis Latour • Antonin Rodet*

MONTAGNY PREMIER CRU AOC

Premiers crus: Les Bassets, Les Beaux Champs, Les Bonnevaux, Les Bordes, Les Bouchots, Le Breuil, Les Burnins, Les Carlins, Les Champs-Toiseau, Les Charmelottes, Les Chandits, Les Chazelles, Clos Chaudron, Le Choux, Les Clouzeaux, Les Coères, Les Combes, La Condemine, Cornevent, La Corvée, Les Coudrettes, Les Craboulettes, Les Crets, Creux des Beaux Champs, L'Epaule, Les Garchères, Les Gouresses, La Grand Pièce, Les Jardins, Les Las, Les Males, Les Marais, Les Marocs, Les Monts Cuchots, Le Mont Laurent, La Mouillère, Moulin l'Echenaud, Les Pandars, Les Pasquiers, Les Pidans, Les Platières, Les Resses, Les St-Mortille, Les St-Ytages, Sous les Roches, Les Thilles, La Tillonne, Les Treufferes, Les Varignys, Le Vieux Château, Vignes Blanches, Vignes sur le Clou, Les Vignes Couland, Les Vignes Derrière, Les Vignes Dessous, La Vigne Devant, Vignes Longues, Vignes du Puits, Les Vignes St-Pierre, Les Vignes du Soleil.

With every one of its 60 vineyards classified as *premier cru*, Montagny is unique among the villages of Burgundy.

WHITE These delicious dry wines have a Chardonnay flavour that is more akin to that of the Côte de Beaune than it is to Mâconnais.

▒ Chardonnay

┠⇢ 4–12 years

✓ *Stéphane Aladame • Arnoux Père & Fils • Caves de Buxy • Château de Davenay (blanc) • Maurice Bertrand & François Juillot • Château de la Saule • Jean Vachet*

RULLY AOC

The Côte Chalonnaise's northernmost appellation produces wines that are closest in character to those from the southern Côte de Beaune.

RED These delightfully fresh and fruity wines of light to medium body and some finesse are uncomplicated when young but develop well.

▒ Pinot Noir, Pinot Gris, Pinot Liébault

┠⇢ 5–12 years

WHITE Serious dry wines that tend to have a crisper balance than wines made further south in Montagny, although a few can be quite fat.

▒ Chardonnay

┠⇢ 3–8 years

✓ *Chanzy Frères • André Delorme • Joseph Drouhin • Raymond Dureuil-Janthial • de Folie • des Fromanges • H et P Jacqueson • de la Renard • Antonin Rodet (Château de Rully)*

RULLY PREMIER CRU AOC

Premiers crus: Agneux, Bas de Vauvry, La Bressaude, Champ-Clou, Chapitre, Clos du Chaigne, Clos St-Jacques, Les Cloux (or Cloux), Ecloseaux, La Fosse, Grésigny, Margotey (or Margoté), Marissou, Meix-Caillet, Mont-Palais, Moulesne (or Molesme), Phillot, Les Pieres, Pillot, Préau, La Pucelle, Raboursay (or Rabourcé), Raclot, La Renarde, Vauvry.

RED Fine-quality, medium-bodied wines with a silky texture added to the summer-fruit flavour.

▒ Pinot Noir, Pinot Gris, Pinot Liébault

┠⇢ 5–15 years

WHITE Generally finer, fuller, and richer dry wines, many with excellent finesse.

▒ Chardonnay

┠⇢ 4–12 years

✓ *Belleville • Jean-Claude Brelière • Michel Briday • André Delorme • de Folie • Vincent Girardin • H et P Jacqueson • Laborde-Juillot • Albert Sounit*

THE MÂCONNAIS

The Mâconnais produces three times more white wine than the rest of Burgundy put together and, although it never quite matches the high quality achieved in the Côte d'Or, its best producers make the world's greatest-value pure Chardonnay wines.

THE MÂCONNAIS IS AN ANCIENT viticultural area that was renowned as long as 1,600 years ago when Ausonius, the Roman poet of St-Émilion, mentioned its wines. Today, it makes sense to couple it with the Beaujolais because, while Chardonnay is the dominant white grape in both districts (as it is in the rest of Burgundy), the Gamay is the dominant black grape, which it is not elsewhere; this forms a link between the two. The Mâconnais can be seen as essentially a white-wine producing area, while the Beaujolais is almost entirely red.

MÂCON ROUGE – A RELIC OF THE PAST?

Although the Mâconnais is a white-wine district in essence, some 25 per cent of the vines planted here are in fact Gamay; and a further 7.5 per cent are Pinot Noir. The Gamay does not, however, perform very well on the limestone soils of the Mâconnais, and despite the smoothing effect of modern vinification techniques,

FACTORS AFFECTING TASTE AND QUALITY

LOCATION
Situated halfway between Lyon and Beaune, the vineyards of the Mâconnais adjoin those of the Côte Chalonnaise to the north and overlap with those of Beaujolais to the south.

CLIMATE
The climate is similar to that of the Côte Chalonnaise, but with a Mediterranean influence gradually creeping in towards the south, so occasional storms are more likely.

ASPECT
The soft, rolling hills in the north of the Mâconnais, which are a continuation of those in the Côte Chalonnaise, give way to a more closely knit topography with steeper slopes and sharper contours becoming increasingly prominent as one travels further south into the area that overlaps the Beaujolais.

SOIL
The topsoil consists of scree and alluvium, or clay and clay-sand, and covers a limestone subsoil.

VITICULTURE AND VINIFICATION
Some exceptional wines (eg, the Vieilles Vignes Château de Fuissé made in Pouilly Fuissé) can stand a very heavy oak influence, but most of the whites are fermented in stainless steel and bottled very early to retain as much freshness as possible. The reds are vinified by carbonic maceration, either fully or in part.

GRAPE VARIETIES
Primary varieties: Chardonnay, Gamay
Secondary varieties: Aligoté, Melon de Bourgogne, Pinot Beurot (Pinot Gris), Pinot Blanc, Pinot Liébault, Pinot Noir (restricted to generic Bourgogne AOC)

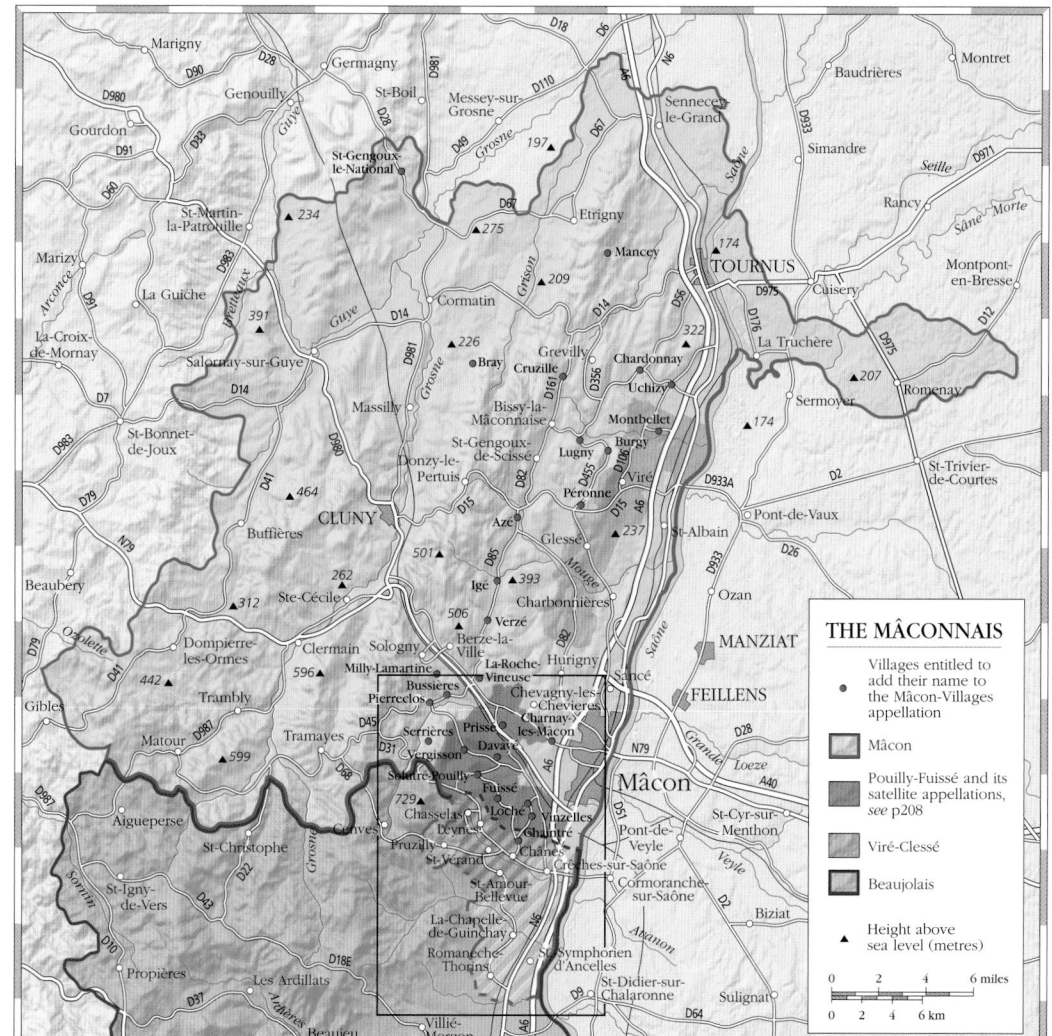

THE MÂCONNAIS
- Villages entitled to add their name to the Mâcon-Villages appellation
- Mâcon
- Pouilly-Fuissé and its satellite appellations, *see p208*
- Viré-Clessé
- Beaujolais
- ▲ Height above sea level (metres)

0   2   4   6 miles
0   2   4   6 km

THE ROCK OF SOLUTRÉ
The dramatic shape of the Rock of Solutré towers over the village's vineyard. Solutré is one of the 42 villages of the Mâcon-Villages appellation, and a commune of Pouilly-Fuissé.

THE MÂCONNAIS, *see also p182*
Concentrated to the west of the river Saône, the famous appellations of the Mâconnais spread out over the area to the northwest and interlace with those of Beaujolais to the south.

these wines will always be of rustic quality with a characteristic hard edge. I well remember a blind tasting I once organized as editor of *The Sunday Telegraph Good Wine Guide*. All that the tasters knew was that the wines were produced from the Gamay grape and were thus most probably Beaujolais. British Master of Wine Christopher Tatham simply wrote "Limestone's the trouble!" about one wine. It turned out to be the only non-Beaujolais wine; it was Mâcon Rouge, which meant that limestone was indeed the problem. Such an accurate observation under blind conditions highlights how inappropriate the Gamay is in the Mâconnais.

It is no longer possible to make a pure Pinot Noir Mâcon *rouge*. Because the market assumed that this appellation was pure Gamay, there was little incentive for producers to plant the more noble grape. The Mâcon Rouge appellation was therefore changed to reflect these expectations and must now be 100 per cent Gamay, as indeed must all red-wine appellations in this district. There are a few areas of granite in the very south of the district where good Gamay can be produced with some consistency, and a few villages are even beginning to make something drinkable on limestone, albeit usually only where there is clay or other soils to affect the pH. Gone, too, is the Mâcon Supérieur AOC, which had almost dropped into total disuse.

BERZÉ-LE-CHÂTEL, SAÔNE-ET-LOIRE, MÂCONNAIS
The massive fortifications of Berzé-le-Châtel, the seat of the first feudal barony of Mâcon, boast 13 medieval towers.

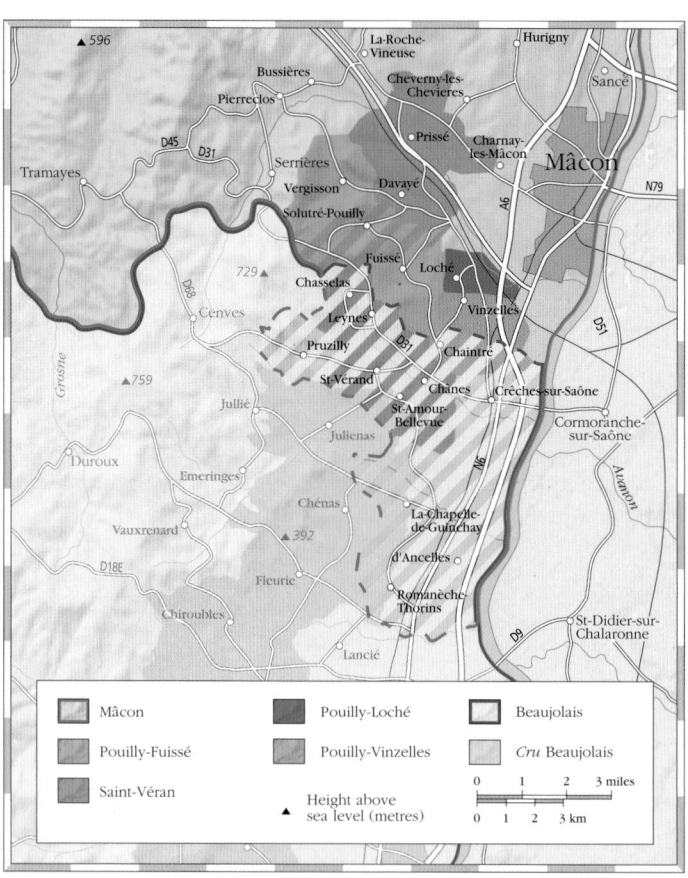

MÂCONNAIS OR BEAUJOLAIS
The Mâcon and Beaujolais appellations overlap, with parts of Mâcon, Saint-Véran, and Pouilly-Fuissé creeping into red-wine country. Almost half of Saint-Véran is in Beaujolais, going as far as the famous Beaujolais cru *of Saint-Amour, where the lacework of vineyards dictate whether a grower can produce one or more of Beaujolais, Beaujolais Villages, Saint-Amour, Mâcon, and Saint-Véran appellations.*

THE APPELLATIONS OF
THE MÂCONNAIS

MÂCON AOC

Most wines from this district-wide appellation are produced in the area north of the Mâcon-Villages area.

RED Better vinification techniques have improved these essentially Gamay wines, but Gamay is still a grape that does not like limestone.

🍇 Gamay, Pinot Noir

⌛ 2–6 years

WHITE These are basic-quality Chardonnay wines that are also fresh, frank, tasty, and dry; they are easy to quaff and superb value. They may be sold as *primeur* or *nouveau* from the third Thursday of November following the harvest.

🍇 Chardonnay

⌛ 1–4 years

ROSÉ These lightweight wines have an attractive, pale raspberry colour and light fruit flavour, and are more successful than their counterparts. They may be sold as *primeur* or *nouveau* from the third Thursday of November after the harvest.

🍇 Gamay, Pinot Noir

⌛ 1–3 years

✓ *Bénas Frères • E Brocard* (rouge) *• Desvignes • Maurice Gonon* (rouge) *• Guffens-Heynen • Héritiers du Comte Lafon* ❽ *• Jean Thévenet*

(Bongran ◉) *• Gauthier Thévenet* (De Roally) *• Saumaize-Michelin* (Les Bruyères rouge) *• Valette*

MÂCON-VILLAGES AOC

Of 96 villages within the 90 communes in the basic Mâcon appellation, this superior white-only appellation encompasses no fewer than 84 villages, of which 11 overlap the Beaujolais appellation (Ancelle, Chaintré, Chânes, Chasselas, Crêches-sur-Saône, La Chapelle-de-Guinchay, Leynes, Pruzilly, Romanèche-Thorins, St-Amour-Bellevue, and St-Vérand). For individual Mâcon village denominations, *see* the following appellation.

WHITE These are some of the world's most delicious, thirst-quenching, easy-drinking, dry Chardonnay wines. They also represent tremendous value. These wines may be sold as *primeur* or *nouveau* commencing from the third Thursday of November following the harvest.

🍇 Chardonnay

⌛ 1–4 years

✓ **Mâcon-Villages** (without a named village) *Cave des Vignerons de Buxy* (Clos de Mont-Rachet) *• Gonon • Héritiers du Comte Lafon* ❽ *• René Michel* (Vieilles Vignes) *• Jean Thévenet* (Emilian Gillet) *• Vignerons des Terres Secrètes*

MÂCON WITH VILLAGE DENOMINATIONS

These AOCs have been consolidated from 41 white-only denominations to just 27, and most of these appellations now allow red and rosé wines, as well as white. The white wines can now be made only from Chardonnay (with Pinot Blanc no longer allowed), while the red and rosé wines must be pure Gamay (no Pinot Noir or Pinot Gris). All recommendations are for white wines only, unless specifically stated otherwise.

MÂCON AZÉ AOC

Red, white, and rosé wines exclusively from the village of Azé, which has a good *coopérative*. Azé has a reputation for fatness and consistency.

✓ *Cave d'Azé* (Cuvée Jules Ricard) *• Georges Blanc* (d'Azenay) *• des Grand Bruyères • Duvergey-Taboureau* (de la Garonne)

MÂCON BRAY AOC

Red, white, and rosé wines grown in the villages of Blanot, Bray, Chissey-lès-Mâcon, and Cortambert. Reds have occasionally done well here.

✓ *de Thalie*

MÂCON BURGY AOC

Red, white, and rosé wines exclusively from the village of Burgy. The whites from Domaine de Chervin can show stunning elegance.

✓ *de Chervin* • *Verget*

MÂCON BUSSIÈRES AOC

Red, white, and rosé wines exclusively from the village of Bussières, where Domaine de la Sarazinière manages to craft reds of extraordinary elegance for Gamay (especially Les Devants) but truly excels with brilliantly pure whites (Le Pavillon and Cuvée Claude Seigneuret).

✓ *Héritiers du Comte Lafon* ❽ • *de la Sarazinière* • *du Terroir de Jocelyn*

MÂCON CHAINTRÉ AOC

Red, white, and rosé wines grown in the villages of Chaintré, Chânes, and Crêches-sur-Saône, which all overlap the Beaujolais district. Indeed, Chaintré is home to Georges Duboeuf's older brother Roger, but he produces strictly white wines. This village is also one of four that form the appellation of Pouilly-Fuissé.

✓ *CCV de Chaintré* • *Roger Duboeuf* • *des Granges* • *Valette*

MÂCON CHARDONNAY AOC

Red, white, and rosé wines grown in the villages of Chardonnay, Ozenay, Plottes, and in part of Tournus. These wines have a certain following due to some extent, no doubt, to the novelty of their name. Nevertheless, the *coopérative* does produce fine wines.

✓ *Cave de Lugny* (L'Originel)

MÂCON CHARNAY-LÈS-MÂCON AOC

Excellent red, white, and rosé wines exclusively from the village of Charnay-lès-Mâcon, east of Pouilly-Fuissé, where even Gamay can show well in some hands (Jean-Paul Brun).

✓ *Jean-Paul Brun* (Terres Dorées) • *Chevalier & Fils* • *Jean Manciat* • *Manciat-Poncet* • *Didier Tripoz* (Clos des Tournons)

MÂCON CRUZILLE AOC

Red, white, and rosé wines grown in the villages of Grevilly, Martailly-lès-Brancion, and in part of Cruzille. This village denomination is in the extreme north of the appellation area.

✓ *Bret Brothers* ❽ • *Demessy* (Château de Messy) • *Guillot-Broux*

MÂCON DAVAYÉ AOC

Red, white, and rosé wines exclusively from the village of Davayé. Some excellent whites are made in this village, which is also part of Saint-Véran AOC.

✓ *des Deux Roches* • *Lycée Viticole de Davayé*

MÂCON FUISSÉ AOC

These top-quality white wines are grown exclusively in the village of Fuissé, which unsurprisingly is also one of four communes that form the Pouilly-Fuissé AOC.

✓ *Bret Brothers* • *Christophe Cordier* • *de Fussiacus* • *Yves Giroux* • *Le Moulin du Pont* • *Robert-Denogent* • *Jean-Paul Thibert*

MÂCON IGÈ AOC

Red, white, and rosé wines exclusively from the village of Igè, a village denomination that is seldom seen, but has a good reputation.

✓ *Fichet* • *Les Vignerons d'Igé*

MÂCON LOCHÉ AOC

White wines only, grown exclusively in the village of Loché, an associated commune of Mâcon itself, which also has the right to the Pouilly-Loché and Pouilly-Vinzelles AOCs.

✓ *Caves des Grands Crus Blancs* • *Marcel Couturier* • *Château de Loché*

MÂCON LUGNY AOC

Red, white, and rosé wines grown in the villages of Bissy-la-Mâconnaise, Lugny, Saint-Gengoux-de-Scissé, and in part of Cruzille. The white wines of Mâcon Lugny are probably the most ubiquitous of all Mâcon village wines that have a right to their own appellation.

✓ *Louis Latour* • *Cave de Lugny* • *du Prieuré* • *Jean Rijckaert*

MÂCON MANCEY AOC

Red, white, and rosé wines grown in the villages of Boyer, La Chapelle-sous-Brancion, Etrigny, Jugy, Laives, Mancey, Montceaux-Ragny, Nanton, Royer, Sennecey-le-Grand, and Vers et Tournus. Mancey itself has something of a reputation for red wine, and the local cooperative's Les Essentielles Vieilles Vignes is probably the most consistent.

✓ *Cave des Vignerons de Mancey* (Les Essentielles)

MÂCON MILLY-LAMARTINE AOC

Red, white, and rosé wines grown in the villages of Berzé-la-Ville, Berzé-le-Châtel, Milly-Lamartine, and Sologny. The white wines from this top Mâcon appellation enjoy the best reputation, particularly those by Cordier and Lafon from the Clos du Four. The red wines from the local *coopérative* Vignerons des Terres Secrètes, can be good, despite its limestone soil, but their white Mâcon Milly-Lamartine is far better.

✓ *Christophe Cordier* (Clos du Four) • *Héritiers du Comte Lafon* (Clos du Four) ❽ • *Vignerons des Terres Secrètes*

MÂCON MONTBELLET AOC

These white wines are grown exclusively in the village of Montbellet and develop well after a couple of years in bottle.

✓ *Jean Rijckaert* (En Pottes Vieilles Vignes) • *Gauthier Thévenet* (de Roally)

MÂCON PÉRONNE AOC

Red, white, and rosé wines grown in the villages of Péronne, Saint-Maurice-de-Satonnay, and in part of Mâcon Clessé. These wines seem to be fuller on the nose and stronger on the palate than those of most villages, but with less initial charm.

✓ *Maurice Josserand* • *de Lanques* (Les Berthelots) • *des Légères* • *Cave de Lugny* • *du Mortier* • *Daniel Rousset*

MÂCON PIERRECLOS AOC

Red, white, and rosé wines exclusively from the village of Pierreclos. Although there are some good reds produced on granitic soils in this village, the white wines truly excel, and Guffens-Heynen is by far the best producer.

✓ *Des Deux Roches* (rouge) • *Guffens-Heynen* • *Henri de Villamont* • *Vignerons des Terres Secrètes* (rouge) • *Thierry Morot* (Rouge Vieilles Vignes) • *Jean-Claude Thévenet*

MÂCON PRISSÉ AOC

Red, white, and rosé wines exclusively from the village of Prissé, which is also part of the Saint-Véran appellation. Excellent minerality in the whites.

✓ *Vignerons des Terres Secrètes* • *de Thibert Père & Fils*

MÂCON LA ROCHE-VINEUSE AOC

Red, white, and rosé wines grown in the villages of Chevagny-lès-Chevrières, Hurigny, and La Roche-Vineuse. These under-rated wines are produced on west- and south-facing slopes north of Pouilly-Fuissé, the potential of which is pushed to the very limits by Olivier Merlin, one of Mâcon's greatest winemakers.

✓ *Olivier Merlin* ◉ • *Vignerons des Terres Secrètes* • *Verget*

MÂCON SOLUTRÉ-POUILLY AOC

White wines only, grown exclusively in the village of Solutré-Pouilly, which is one of the four communes of Pouilly-Fuissé and also forms part of the Saint-Véran area. Its wines, therefore, have a choice of three appellations. Robert-Denogent is outstanding.

✓ *André Depardon* • *Jean-Michel & Béatrice Drouhin* • *Robert-Denogent* • *des Gerbeaux* • *Chantal & Dominique Vaupré*

MÂCON SAINT-GENGOUX AOC

Far from the madding crowd in the northwestern corner of the Mâconnais, the red, white, and rosé wines from this very large village appellation are made from vines grown in the villages of Ameugny, Bissy-sous-Uxelles, Bonnay, Bresse-sur-Grosne, Burnand, Champagny-sous-Uxelles, Chapaize, Cortevaix, Curtil-sous-Burnand, Lournand, Malay, Massy, Saint-Gengoux-le-National, Saint-Ythaire, Salornay-sur-Guye, Savigny-sur-Grosne, Sigy-le-Châtel, and La Vineuse. Rarely encountered up to now, but the excellent *coopérative* at Buxy produces a good white from Saint-Gengoux-le-National itself, where their members have vines on Mont Goubot, which is one of the highest points in the village.

✓ *Cave des Vignerons de Buxy* (Buxynoise)

MÂCON SERRIÈRES AOC

Only red and rosé wines, grown exclusively in the village of Serrières. Only red wines encountered so far, and nothing has stood out.

MÂCON UCHIZY AOC

Red, white, and rosé wines exclusively from the village of Uchizy, which is adjacent to Chardonnay and usually produces good-quality, thirst-quenching white wines.

✓ *Bret Brothers* ❽ • *Héritiers du Comte Lafon* ❽ • *Raphaël et Gard Sallet* (Clos des Ravières) • *Paul & Philebert Talmard* • *Vignerons des Terres Secrètes*

MÂCON VERGISSON AOC

White wines only, grown exclusively in the village of Vergisson, which is one of the four villages with the right to the Pouilly-Fuissé AOC. These wines are richer than most and can be aged a few years in bottle without losing their freshness and appeal.

✓ *Daniel Barraut* • *Michel Forest* • *Verget*

MÂCON VERZÉ AOC

Red, white, and rosé wines exclusively from the village of Verzé, where it is the white wines that truly excel, exhibiting some of the purest minerality in the Mâconnais.

✓ *du Clos Gandin* • *Leflaive* • *Nicolas Maillet* • *Vignerons des Terres Secrètes*

MÂCON VINZELLES AOC

White wines only, grown exclusively in the village of Vinzelles, which also has the right to the Pouilly-Vinzelles AOC. These are excellent, fresh, vibrant wines.

✓ *Bret Brothers* (Domaine Soufrandiere) **❸**

POUILLY-FUISSÉ AOC

This pure Chardonnay wine should not be confused with Pouilly-Fumé, the Sauvignon Blanc wine from the Loire. This appellation covers a wide area of prime vineyards spread over four villages (Chaintré, Fuissé, Solutré-Pouilly, and Vergisson), but there is considerable variation. The following *climats* (*lieux-dits*) may be attached to the Pouilly-Fuissé AOC: Les Chevrières, Les Vignes Blanches, Aux Chailloux, and Les Crays.

WHITE These dry wines range from typical Mâcon *blanc* style, through slightly firmer versions, to the power-packed, rich oaky flavours of Michel Forest and Vincent's Château Fuissé Vieilles Vignes. Although these last two are widely regarded as the finest in Pouilly-Fuissé, they are by no means typical of Mâcon, leaning more towards the Côte Chalonnaise, sometimes even the Côte de Beaune, and ardent admirers of the more traditional, light, and fluffy Mâcon will not even touch them. On the other hand, wines from producers such as Guffens-Heynen can be just as rich and intense as either Forest or Château Fuissé, but without any oak whatsoever.

🍇 Chardonnay

🍷 3–8 years

✓ *Daniel et Martine Barraud* • *Christophe Cordier* • *Nadine Ferrand* (Prestige) • *Des Gerbeaux* (Cuvée Jacques Charvet) • *Guffens-Heynen* • *Jeandeau* (Terre Jeanduc) • *Dominique Lafon* • *Roger Lassarat* • *Olivier Merlin* **◉** • *Pascal Rollet* (Clos de la Chapelle) • *Jean Rijckaert* • *Thibert Père & Fils* (Vignes de la Côte) • *Pierre Vessigaud* (Vieilles Vignes) • *Robert-Denogent* • *Valette* • *Verget* • *Vincent & Fils* (Château de Fuissé Vieilles Vignes)

POUILLY-LOCHÉ AOC

One of Pouilly-Fuissé's two satellite appellations. Good value. Two *climats* (*lieux-dits*) may be attached to the Pouilly-Loché AOC: Les Mûres and Aux Barres.

WHITE This village may produce Mâcon-Loché AOC, Pouilly-Loché AOC, or Pouilly-Vinzelles AOC. The dry wines of this village are more of the Mâcon style, whatever the AOC.

🍇 Chardonnay

VILLAGE OF FUISSÉ SURROUNDED BY ITS VINEYARDS
Fuissé, which dates back to Neanderthal settlements, sits at the centre of an amphitheatre of vineyards.

🍷 1–4 years

✓ *Bret Brothers* • *Christophe Cordier* • *Louis Jadot* (Château de Loché) • *Tripoz* (Clos des Rocs)

POUILLY-VINZELLES AOC

One of Pouilly-Fuissé's two satellite appellations. Some of these wines have the potential to challenge Pouilly-Fuissé. Two *climats* (*lieux-dits*) may be attached the Pouilly-Vinzelles AOC: Les Quarts and Les Longeays.

WHITE More the Mâcon-type of Pouilly-Fuissé, for similar reasons to those of Pouilly-Loché.

🍇 Chardonnay

🍷 1–4 years

✓ *Bret Brothers* • *Thibert Père & Fils* (aka Thibert-Parisse) • *Valette* • *Verget*

SAINT-VÉRAN AOC

This appellation overlaps the Mâconnais and Beaujolais districts, and is itself bisected by the Pouilly-Fuissé AOC, with two villages to the north (Davayé and Prissé) and five to the south (Chânes, Chasselas, Leynes, Saint-Amour, and Saint-Vérand). Saint-Véran was named after Saint-Vérand, but the "d" was dropped in deference to the growers in certain other villages, who it was feared would not support the new appellation if they felt their wines were being sold under the name of another village.

This appellation was introduced in 1971 to provide a more suitable outlet for white wines produced in Beaujolais than the Beaujolais Blanc appellation.

WHITE Excellent value, fresh, dry, and fruity Chardonnay wines that are very much in the Mâcon-Villages style. Vincent, the proprietor of Château Fuissé, produces an amazingly rich wine that is far closer to Pouilly-Fuissé than to Macon-Villages, with hints of oak and honey.

🍇 Chardonnay

🍷 1–4 years

✓ *Daniel et Martine Barraud* • *Christophe Cordier* • *Pierre Janny* • *Roger Lassarat* • *Olivier Merlin* **◉** • *Michel Paquet* (Cuvée Hors Classe) • *Jean Rijckaert* • *Verget* • *Vignerons des Terres Secrètes*

VIRÉ-CLESSÉ AOC

This appellation was created in February 1999, by combining the Mâcon-Viré and Mâcon-Clessé sub-appellations, and recognizing the wines from Viré-Clessé in their own right, above and beyond those of Mâcon-Villages. The appellation was retrospectively applied to the 1998 vintage, but producers could continue using either of the original two AOCs up to and including the 2002 vintage. Viré was always the most ubiquitous of the Mâcon-Villages wines, but it was also the most consistent and one of the best, while Clessé showed the most finesse. The regulations are slightly stricter in terms of yield, with an increased minimum natural sugar content for wines bearing one of the following *climats* (*lieux-dits*): La Montagne, La Bussière, En Collonge, and Quintaine.

🍇 Chardonnay

🍷 1–4 years

✓ All those recommended under Mâcon-Viré and Mâcon-Clessé are potential recommendations here, but those that have actually excelled are: *André Bonhomme* • *Bret Brothers* (Sous Les Plantes) • *Héritiers du Comte Lafon* **❸** • *Jean Rijckaert* (L'Epinet) • *Gauthier Thévenet* (De Roally) • *Jean Thévenet* (Emilian Gillet) • *Verget* (Vieilles Vignes) • *Cave de Viré* (Cuvée Spéciale)

THE BEAUJOLAIS

After the self-made vin de merde *debacle (see p212) in 2001, sales of cheap Beaujolais crashed, forcing growers to reduce yields and increase quality. This coincided with a string of exceptional vintages, including the stunning 2009, resulting in the best-quality Beaujolais in living memory.*

AT LONG LAST, Beaujolais is again producing the only classic quality Gamay in the world. Most of its production will always be unpretentious – a purple-coloured, fresh, light, easy-to-quaff wine – but hopefully, as well as ditching the really bad stuff, producers will consign the worst excesses of the Beaujolais Nouveau style to the dustbin of history. The aroma of bubblegum, bananas, or nail varnish and the taste of "peardrop" boiled sweets are all too often passed off as the varietal character of Gamay, but they are nothing to do with the grape. What we are smelling is the production process, carbonic maceration – or, as Beaujolais producer Jean-Marie Guffens once famously described it, "carbonic masturbation".

HARVESTING IN FLEURIE
To encourage semi-carbonic maceration, the Gamay grapes must arrive at the cuverie in whole bunches, on their stalks, and as uncrushed as possible.

There is nothing wrong with carbonic maceration, just the degree to which it is used. Just 10–15 per cent can, for example, give a freshness, fragrance, and fruitiness to hot-climate-grown Pinot Noir, while excessive use of carbonic maceration will produce a preponderance of amyl acetate ester (commonly known as "banana oil" or "pear oil") and ethyl acetate (used in nail varnish). These chemical compounds will do you no harm. On a one-to-one basis, ethyl acetate is 20 per cent less toxic than alcohol, and amyl acetate ester is more than 50 per cent less toxic. Furthermore, of course, alcohol represents a significant proportion of any wine, while amyl acetate ester and ethyl acetate combined barely rise above what can be effectively described as trace level.

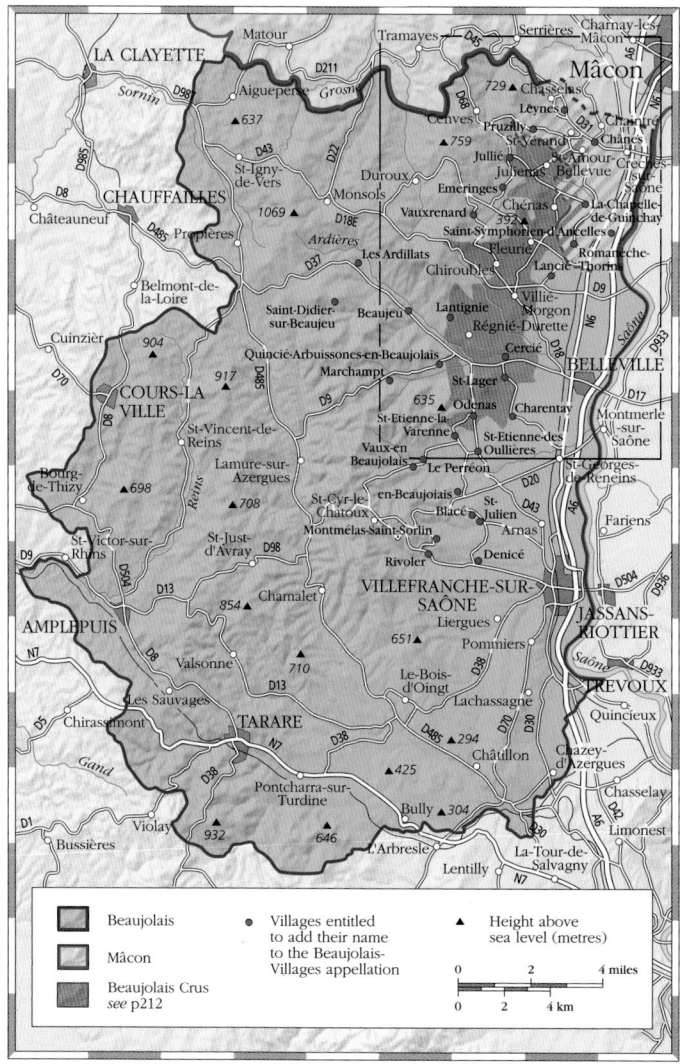

THE BEAUJOLAIS, *see also p182*
Forming the southernmost part of the Burgundy region, the Beaujolais area is planted almost entirely with Gamay vines, the best vineyards being on granite soil.

Map legend:
- Beaujolais
- Mâcon
- Beaujolais Crus *see p212*
- Villages entitled to add their name to the Beaujolais-Villages appellation
- ▲ Height above sea level (metres)

0 ─── 2 ─── 4 miles
0 ─── 2 ─── 4 km

FACTORS AFFECTING TASTE AND QUALITY

LOCATION
Beaujolais, the most southerly of Burgundy's districts, is located in the Rhône *département*, which is 400 kilometres (250 miles) southeast of Paris.

CLIMATE
Beaujolais has an essentially sunny climate tempered by the Atlantic and Mediterranean, as well as by continental influences. Although the annual rainfall and temperature averages are ideal for winegrowing, they are subject to sudden stormy changes due to the influence of the Mediterranean.

ASPECT
A hilly district where vines grow at between 150 and 550 metres (500 to 2,000 feet) on slopes facing all points of the compass.

SOIL
The northern Beaujolais, which encompasses the famous *crus* and those communes entitled to the Beaujolais-Villages AOC, is an area renowned for its granite-based soil, the only type on which the Gamay has so far excelled. The topsoils are often schistous or comprised of decomposed granite mixed with sand and clay. The southern section is essentially limestone-based and this is a problem for the Gamay grape, which accordingly produces much lighter wines, which lack the class of those in the north.

VITICULTURE AND VINIFICATION
The vines are trained and pruned to the Gobelet system (*see p21*), which gives them a totally different appearance from those in the rest of Burgundy. Grapes are hand-harvested and undergo whole-bunch fermentation by semi-carbonic maceration, which encourages the accumulation of carbon dioxide in the top half of the vat, although *cru* Beaujolais are more traditionally produced, have greater skin contact (around seven days as opposed to just two days for Beaujolais Nouveau), and may be matured with some new oak.

GRAPE VARIETIES
Primary variety: Gamay
Secondary varieties: Aligoté, Chardonnay, Melon de Bourgogne, Pinot Beurot (Pinot Gris), Pinot Blanc, Pinot Liébault, Pinot Noir (restricted to generic Bourgogne and Bouguignons AOCs)

NEW BEAUJOLAIS NOUVEAU?

As in every French AOC, not all wines produced in the 10 *crus* Beaujolais deserve their classic status, while many basic Beaujolais, Beaujolais Supérieur, and Beaujolais Villages can be superior to lacklustre *cru* Beaujolais. However, the focus has shifted upwards, where the quality has generally soared, and the very best *crus* Beaujolais are now wines to die for. This process now needs to

filter down to Beaujolais Nouveau, to make this entry-level Beaujolais a wine to be proud of, and this is not as difficult as it sounds. Tackling the problem of Beaujolais Nouveau has always been avoided because it has been such a cash cow, and French politicians are always wary of stepping between a farmer and his income. Of all the problems that the French wine industry faces today, though, this is probably the easiest to resolve and the solution the most obvious to imagine. By restricting the proportion of carbonic maceration allowed for all wines bearing the Beaujolais name – not just Nouveau – producers not only get to keep their cash cow but should also enjoy increased sales. After all, if you had a choice between a glass of bubblegum and a juicy-fruity red wine teeming with crunchy Gamay flavour, which would you make a repeat purchase of? Furthermore, by using carbonic maceration to show off the true Gamay character rather than hide it, there would be a reason for consumers to explore the higher-quality, more *terroir*-specific Gamay that are Beaujolais's true forte. Seems like a win/win solution to me.

THE INTRODUCTION OF COTEAUX BOURGUIGNONS

In the wake of the *vin de merde* case (*see below*), cheap Beaujolais became almost impossible to sell, so much of it was offloaded, quite legally, under the Bourgogne AOC. This was not popular with the rest of Burgundy, where Pinot Noir is synonymous with Burgundy, thus even good Gamay could give consumers the wrong impression. The thought that the public would be drinking Gamay *vin de merde* – as Beaujolais's local *Lyon Mag* had called it – believing it to be Pinot Noir Burgundy was the final straw. It is now no longer possible to sell any Beaujolais Gamay as Bourgogne, other than Gamay grown in one of the 10 *cru* Beaujolais, and that must be sold as Bourgogne Gamay AOC (*see p184*). All other Gamay grown in the Beaujolais district must be sold as Coteaux Bourguignons AOC, although if the focus on quality continues and can be seen to encompass Beaujolais Nouveau, there should be no reason why all Beaujolais should not be proudly sold under a Beaujolais appellation – in which case, Coteaux Bourguignons should become surplus to requirements.

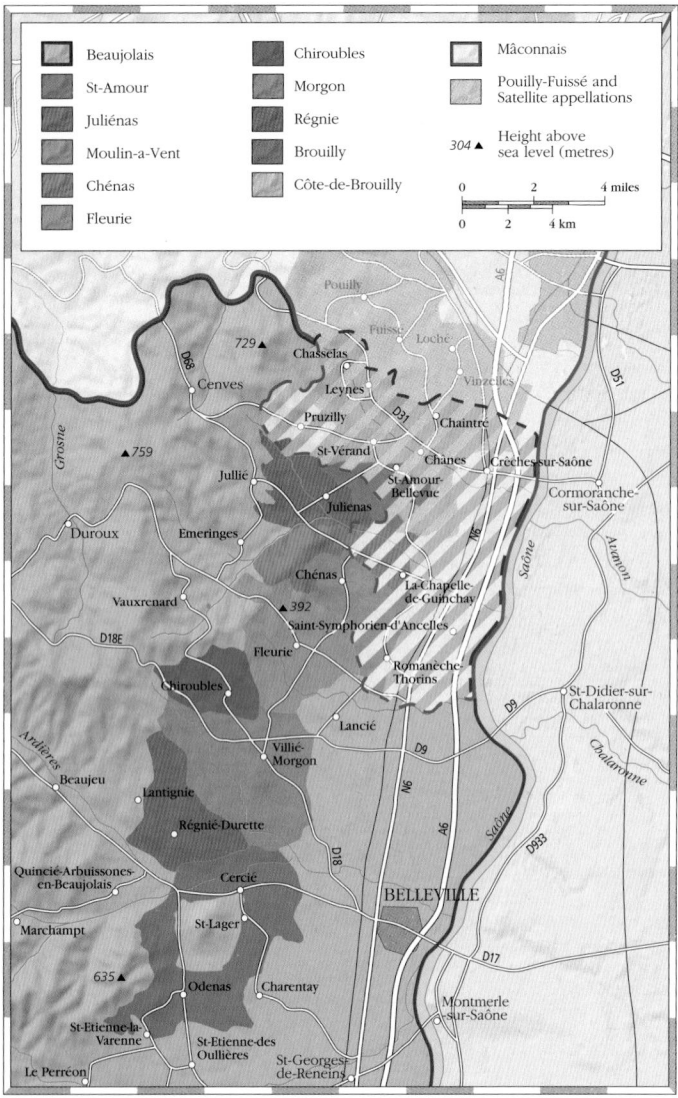

CRUS BEAUJOLAIS
All the best growths of Beaujolais are found in the northeastern corner of the region, where they overlap with some of the finest wines of Mâcon.

THE LEGEND OF "PISSE VIEILLE"

The vineyard of Pisse Vieille in Brouilly amuses English-speaking consumers, who are dismayed by those writers who dare only to print the vineyard's story in French. It goes like this:

One day, an old woman called Mariette went to confession. The priest was new to the village and unaware of its dialect. He also did not know that Mariette was hard of hearing. When he heard her confession, he merely said "Allez! Et ne péchez plus!" ("Go! And do not sin again!"). Mariette misheard this as "Allez! Et ne piché plus!", which in the dialect meant "Go! And do not piss again!", *piché* being the local form of *pisser*. Being a devout Catholic, Mariette did exactly as she was told. When her husband asked what terrible sin she had committed she refused to tell and, after several days, he went to ask the new priest. When he found out the truth he hurried home, and as soon as he was within shouting distance, began yelling "Pisse, vieille!" ("Piss, old woman!").

THE VIN DE MERDE CASE

After 100,000 hectolitres of Beaujolais had to be distilled in 2001, a French wine critic by the name of François Mauss claimed in *Lyon Mag*, a small French magazine, that poor-quality Beaujolais of this ilk was "not proper wine, but rather a sort of lightly fermented and alcoholic fruit juice". No wonder they could not sell it. Mauss blamed the need for distillation on the craze for Beaujolais Nouveau, which is rushed to market barely two months after the harvest. Beaujolais producers, he claimed, had ignored all warning signs that consumers were no longer willing to buy such wine, which he branded as *vin de merde* or "shit wine", and the proverbial hit the fan.

Even though this description was not the assessment of *Lyon Mag per se*, but a quote from someone being interviewed, and despite the fact that the publication balanced these comments with those of a Beaujolais representative defending the wine, an association of 56 Beaujolais cooperative producers decided to sue the magazine, not for libel, but under a rarely used French law that protects products from being denigrated. A cynic might ask why these producers did not feel able to sue for libel, but even more disturbing is the fact that a modern-day court in a supposedly civilized society could actually find what this magazine published to be illegal in any way. But it did, and more disturbingly, the court (in Villefranche-sur-Saône, the heart of Beaujolais country) considered this quote to be so serious a wrongdoing that it ordered *Lyon Mag* to pay €350,000, which for such a small, employee-owned publication would have put it out of business. On appeal, this was reduced to €113,000 and, after a backlash of bad publicity around the world, the Beaujolais cooperatives decided not to pursue any damages, just their costs, which amounted to €2,800.

At the time of writing, *Lyon Mag* was planning to appeal on a point of principle, and was intent on taking it all the way to the European Court of Human Rights if necessary. If the association of 56 cooperative producers started this case to protect the reputation of Beaujolais Nouveau, it clearly achieved the opposite result, since its reputation has been dealt a more severe blow by the worldwide coverage of "The Shit Wine Case". If the cooperatives don't like wine critics describing Beaujolais Nouveau as crap, they should make it delicious and fruity to drink. Is that too much to ask?

THE APPELLATIONS OF
THE BEAUJOLAIS

BEAUJOLAIS AOC

This generic Beaujolais appellation accounts for half the wine produced in the district and more than half of this is sold as Beaujolais "Primeur". The basic quality of these wines means that they cannot be bought from the great *négociants* of the Côte d'Or, although *cru* Beaujolais can be.

RED Due to their method of vinification, most of these wines have a "peardrop" character to their fruitiness. The best also have a delightful freshness and frankness that beg for the wine to be consumed in large draughts.

🏵 Gamay, Pinot Noir, Pinot Gris

⌛ 1–3 years

WHITE Less than half of 1 per cent of the production of this basic appellation consists of dry white wine, and the specialist producers of this usually make very fine wines. Pierre Charmet's Beaujolais *blanc* is aromatic and peachy.

🏵 Chardonnay, Aligoté

⌛ 1–3 years

ROSÉ Fresh, "pretty", and fruity.

🏵 Gamay, Pinot Noir, Pinot Gris

⌛ 1–3 years

✓ *Jean-Paul Brun* (Terres Dorées) • *Jean-Jacques Martin* (blanc) • *Cave Sain-Bel* (Les Bruyères) • *Cave Saint-Vérand* (Vieilles Vignes) • *Terres Morel* • *Vissoux* (Traditionnelle)

BEAUJOLAIS NOUVEAU AOC
See Beaujolais Primeur AOC

BEAUJOLAIS PRIMEUR AOC

At its height, more than half of all the Beaujolais produced was sold as *vin de primeur*, but production has dropped to one-third following the *vin de merde* saga. Swinging from the vine one moment, this wine is subjected to intensive carbonic maceration in order to hit the shelf just a few weeks later (usually the third Thursday of November). Sold mostly as Beaujolais Primeur in France but better known on export markets as Beaujolais Nouveau, this is supposed to be a fun wine, but the merrymaking has worn a bit thin. Even the official governing body, the Union Interprofessionnelle des Vins du Beaujolais (UIVB) is unable to name one good Beaujolais Nouveau. While organizing tastings for the preparation of the previous major revision of this book (2005), I asked the UIVB to include as many good-quality Beaujolais Nouveau wines as possible, and although they put on a splendid tasting of Beaujolais, Beaujolais Supérieur, Beaujolais Villages, and all 10 *cru* Beaujolais, the UIVB were unable to source a single good Beaujolais Nouveau. Actions speak louder than words, but I am still waiting to see what action will be taken to tighten up the regulations for this appellation before its fun wines turn into a seriously bad joke.

BEAUJOLAIS SUPÉRIEUR AOC

Only 1 per cent of all Beaujolais wines carry this appellation. It is very rare to find a Beaujolais Supérieur that is superior in anything other than strength to basic Beaujolais AOC, since this appellation merely indicates that the wines contain an extra 1 per cent alcohol. Red and rosé Beaujolais Supérieur may be sold as *primeur* or *nouveau* from the third Thursday of November following the harvest.

RED By no means superior to Beaujolais AOC – buy basic Beaujolais for fun or *cru* Beaujolais for more serious drinking.

🏵 Gamay, Pinot Noir, Pinot Gris

⌛ 3–8 years

WHITE Barely 5 per cent of this tiny appellation produces white wine. Fine as it may be, it has no intrinsic superiority over the quaffing quality of basic Beaujolais *blanc*.

🏵 Chardonnay, Aligoté

⌛ 1–3 years

ROSÉ I have not encountered any pink versions of this appellation.

✓ *Cave Beaujolais du Bois-d'Oingt* • *Cave Saint-Vérand*

BEAUJOLAIS-VILLAGES AOC

The 38 villages that may add their names to the Beaujolais AOC (*see* Beaujolais [village name] AOC) also have the right to this appellation and must use it if the wine is a blend of wines from two or more villages.

RED If you find a good example, these wines are well coloured with a rich Gamay flavour and should have all the superiority that Beaujolais Supérieur wines mysteriously lack.

🏵 Gamay, Pinot Noir, Pinot Gris

⌛ 3–8 years

WHITE Very little encountered, but more Villages *blanc* is produced than Beaujolais *blanc*. These wines may be sold as *primeur* or *nouveau* from the third Thursday of November following the harvest.

🏵 Chardonnay, Aligoté

⌛ 1–3 years

ROSÉ Seldom encountered, but the Cave Beaujolais du Bois-d'Oingt makes an attractive wine. These wines may be sold as *primeur* or *nouveau* from the third Thursday of November following the harvest.

🏵 Gamay, Pinot Noir, Pinot Gris

⌛ 1–3 years

✓ *Aucoeur* • *Philippe Deschamps* • *des Duc* • *Stephane Gardette* • *Jean-Claude Lapalu* (Vieilles Vignes) • *Manoir du Pavé* • *Sermezy* • *Michel Tête* (Clos du Fief)

BEAUJOLAIS
(VILLAGE NAME) AOC

Of the 38 villages that may add their names to this appellation, very few do. One reason is that all or part of 15 of these villages (asterisked below) qualify for one of the superior *cru* Beaujolais appellations and it makes no sense to use a less famous name to market the wines. Another is that eight of the villages are entitled to the Mâcon-Villages AOC (marked "M") and four of these are also within the St-Véran AOC (*see also* p210), marked "S-V", which overlaps with Mâconnais and Beaujolais; some of these villages, of course, produce more white wine than red. These village names are also under-exploited because, apart from a few that are famous (the best wines of which will claim *cru* Beaujolais status), the rest are either unknown or more suggestive of Mâcon than Beaujolais, thus it is easier to sell them as nothing more specific than Beaujolais-Villages. The wines may be sold as *primeur* or *nouveau* from the third Thursday of November following the harvest.

The following is a complete list of villages that may use the appellation: Arbuisonnas; Les Ardillats; Beaujeu; Blacé; Cercié*; Chânes (M, S-V); La Chapelle-de-Guinchay* (M); Charentay; Chénas; Chiroubles*; Denicé; Durette; Emeringes*; Fleurie*; Jullié*; Juliénas*; Lancié; Lantignié; Leynes (M, S-V); Marchampt; Montmelas; Odenas; Le Perréon; Pruzilly* (M); Quincié*; Régnié*; Rivolet; Romanèche-Thorins* (M); St-Amour-Bellevue* (M, S-V); St-Étienne-des-Ouillères; St-Étienne-la Varenne*; St-Julien; St-Lager; St-Symphorien-d'Ancelles (M); St-Vérand (M, S-V); Salles; Vaux; Vauxrenard; Villié-Morgon*

RED Good examples should be richly flavoured Gamay wines of similar quality to non-specific Beaujolais-Villages but with more personality.

🏵 Gamay, Pinot Noir, Pinot Gris

⌛ 3–8 years

WHITE I have rarely encountered these wines.

🏵 Chardonnay, Aligoté

⌛ 1–3 years

ROSÉ Rarely encountered, and uninspiring when they are.

🏵 Gamay, Pinot Noir, Pinot Gris

⌛ 1–3 years

BROUILLY AOC
Cru Beaujolais

The largest and most southerly of the ten *cru* villages, this is the only one, with Côte de Brouilly, to permit grapes other than Gamay.

RED Most Brouilly are serious wines, even if they do not rank among the best *cru* Beaujolais. They are not quite as intense as Côte de Brouilly wines, but they are full, fruity, and supple, if a little earthy. They should be rich and can be quite tannic.

🏵 Gamay, Chardonnay, Aligoté, Melon de Bourgogne

⌛ 2–7 years (4–12 years for *vin de garde* styles produced in the very best vintages)

✓ *de la Chanaise* (Château du Prieuré) • *Daniel Guillet* • *Jean-Claude Lapalu* (Vieilles Vignes) • *Joseph Pellerin* • *Château Thivin*

CHÉNAS AOC
Cru Beaujolais

The smallest of the *cru* Beaujolais, situated on the slopes above Moulin-à-Vent. These slopes used to be occupied by oak trees, and so its name derives from *chêne*, the French for oak.

RED Although most Chénas cannot match the power of the wines from neighbouring Moulin-à-Vent, they are nevertheless in the full and generous mould, and wines made by gifted growers such as Jean Benon and Champagnon are seductively rich and powerful, the former oaked, the latter not.

🏵 Gamay

⌛ 3–8 years (5–15 years for *vin de garde* styles produced in the very best vintages)

✓ *Jean Benon* (especially Vieillis en Fût de Chêne) • *Champagnon* • *des Duc* (Chante Grilles) • *Hubert Lapierre* (Vieilles Vignes)

CHIROUBLES AOC
Cru Beaujolais

Situated high in the hills above the Beaujolais plain, the terrace of Chiroubles produces the most fragrant of all the *cru* Beaujolais.

RED These light-bodied wines have a perfumed bouquet and a deliciously delicate, crushed-grape flavour. They are charming to drink when young, but exceptional examples can improve with age.

🍇 Gamay

🍷 1–8 years (5–15 years for *vin de garde* styles produced in the very best vintages)

✓ *Alain Passot • Bernard Métrat • Céline & Gilles Méziat* (Petit Puits) • *Maison des Vignerons de Chiroubles* (Cuvée Vidame de Rocsain) • *Château de Raousset*

CÔTE DE BROUILLY AOC
Cru Beaujolais

If there were such things as *grands crus* in Beaujolais, Côte de Brouilly would undoubtedly be classified as the *grand cru* of Brouilly (the vineyards of which practically surround those of this appellation).

RED A fine Côte de Brouilly is full, rich, and flavoursome. Its fruit should be vivid and intense, with none of the earthiness that may be found in a Brouilly.

🍇 Gamay, Pinot Noir, Pinot Gris

🍷 3–8 years (5–15 years for *vin de garde* styles produced in the very best vintages)

✓ *Jean-Paul Brun* (Terres Dorées) • *Georges Duboeuf • Franchet • Griffon • Château Thivin* (especially Cuvée Zacharie) • *Bernadette et Gilles Vincent*

COTEAUX DU LYONNAIS AOC

This is not part of the true Beaujolais district, but it falls within its sphere of influence and certainly utilizes classic Beaujolais grapes. In May 1984, this wine was upgraded from VDQS to full AOC status.

RED Light-bodied wines with fresh Gamay fruit and a soft balance. These wines may be sold as *primeur* or *nouveau* from the third Thursday of November following the harvest.

🍇 Gamay

🍷 2–5 years

WHITE Fresh and dry Chardonnay wine that is softer than a Mâcon and lacks the definition of a Beaujolais *blanc*. These wines may be sold as *primeur* or *nouveau* from the third Thursday of November following the harvest.

🍇 Chardonnay, Aligoté

🍷 1–3 years

ROSÉ I have not encountered these wines.

✓ *Ris Descotes* (blanc) • *de Prapin* (blanc) • *Clos du Saint-Marc*

FLEURIE AOC
Cru Beaujolais

The evocatively-named Fleurie is the most expensive of the *crus* and its finest wines are the quintessence of classic Beaujolais.

RED The wines of Fleurie quickly develop a fresh, floral, and fragrant style. Not as light and delicate as some writers suggest, their initial charm belies a positive structure and a depth of fruit that can sustain the wines for many years.

🍇 Gamay

🍷 2–8 years (4–16 years for *vin de garde* styles produced in the very best vintages)

✓ *Christian Bernard • Michel Chignard • Jean-Marc Despres* (Cuvée Spéciale Vieilles Vignes) • *Georges Duboeuf* (Château des Bachelards, Prestige) • *de la Madone • Bernard Métrat • Alain Passot • Vissoux* (Garants)

JULIÉNAS AOC
Cru Beaujolais

Situated in the hills above St-Amour, Juliénas is named after Julius Caesar and, according to local legend, was the first Beaujolais village to be planted. It is probably the most underrated of the 10 Beaujolais *crus*.

RED The spicy-rich, chunky-textured fruit of a youthful Juliénas will develop a classy, satin-smooth appeal if given time to develop in bottle.

🍇 Gamay

🍷 3–8 years (5–15 years for *vin de garde* styles produced in the very best vintages)

✓ *Mme Ernest Aujas • Jean Benon • François Condemine • J M Coquenlorge • Georges Duboeuf* (La Trinquée) • *Château de Juliénas • Henri Lespinasse • Cellier de la Vieille Église* (Cuvée fût de chêne)

MORGON AOC
Cru Beaujolais

Just as the Côte de Brouilly is a finer and more concentrated form of Brouilly, so the wines of Mont du Py in the centre of Morgon are far more powerful than those of the surrounding vineyards in this commune.

RED Although these wines are variable in character and quality, the best of them rank with those of Moulin-à-Vent as the most sturdy of all Beaujolais. They have a singularly penetrating bouquet and very compact fruit.

🍇 Gamay

🍷 4–9 years (6–20 years for *vin de garde* styles produced in the very best vintages)

✓ *Aucoeur • Daniel Bouland • Jean-Marc Burgaud • de la Chanaise • de la Chaponne • François Condemine • Louis-Claude Desvignes • Donzel* (Cuvée Prestige) • *Foillard • J Gonard & Fils • Marcel Lapierre • Jacques Lespinasse* (Maupas) • *Michel Tête* (Clos du Fief)

MOULIN-À-VENT AOC
Cru Beaujolais

Because of its sheer size, power, and reputation for longevity, Moulin-à-Vent is known as the "King of Beaujolais". The exceptionally powerful character of Moulin-à-Vent has been attributed to the high manganese content of its soil. The availability of manganese to the vine's metabolic system depends on the pH of the soil, and in the acid, granite soil of Beaujolais, manganese is all too readily available. For a healthy metabolism, however, the vine requires only the tiniest trace of manganese, so its abundance at Moulin-à-Vent could be toxic (to the vine that is, not the consumer!), may well cause chlorosis, and would certainly affect the vine's metabolism. This naturally restricts yields and could alter the composition of the grapes produced.

RED These well-coloured wines have intense fruit, excellent tannic structure, and, in many cases, a spicy-rich oak flavour.

🍇 Gamay

🍷 4–9 years (6–20 years for *vin de garde* styles produced in the very best vintages)

✓ *Christian Bernard • de la Chanaise • Château de Chénas • Desperrier Père & Fils* (Clos de la Pierre) • *Georges Duboeuf* (Carquelin, Prestige, Rosiers) • *Gay-Coperet • Château des Jacques* (lieu-dit cuvées only) • *Paul Janin* (Clos du Tremblay) • *Olivier Merlin* ⊙ • *Château du Moulin-à-Vent* (Cuvée Exceptionnelle) • *du Vissoux* (Rochegès, Rochelles)

RÉGNIÉ AOC
Cru Beaujolais

The growers claim this village was the first to be planted with vines in Beaujolais, but so do the growers of Juliénas. Régnié was upgraded to full *cru* Beaujolais status in December 1988. Too many half-hearted efforts nearly sank the ship while it was being launched, but the best growers are gradually carving a reputation for this fledgling *cru*.

RED There are two distinct styles of red wine here: one is light and fragrant, the other much fuller and more meaty, but all the best examples are fruity and supple, showing a fresh, invigorating aroma.

🍇 Gamay

🍷 2–7 years (4–12 years for *vin de garde* styles produced in the very best vintages)

✓ *Lydie et Lucien Grandjean • Jacky Gauthier • Les Petit Pierres • Michel Rampon & Fils*

ST-AMOUR AOC
Cru Beaujolais

This is the most northerly of the ten *crus*, and is more famous for its Mâcon wines than for its *cru* Beaujolais. Despite its modern-day connotations, St-Amour has nothing to do with love, but derives from St-Amateur, a Roman soldier who was converted to Christianity and founded a monastery in the locality.

RED Charming wines of fine colour, seductive bouquet, and soft, fragrant, fruity flavour. They will also repay a little ageing.

🍇 Gamay

🍷 2–8 years (4–12 years for *vin de garde* styles produced in the very best vintages)

✓ *des Duc* (especially Cuvée Saint Valentin) • *Jean-Marc Monnet* (Chataignier Durand) • *André Poitevin • Michel Tête • Georges Trichard*

BARRELS AND FLOWERS AT ST-AMOUR, BEAUJOLAIS
Just five cru *Beaujolais were originally classified in 1936 (Chénas, Chiroubles, Fleurie, Morgon, and Moulin-à-Vent), a further three (Brouilly, Côte de Brouilly, and Juliénas) in 1938, while St-Amour became the ninth* cru *in 1946 and Régnié the tenth in 1988.*

CHAMPAGNE

Never has the quality of Champagne been more inconsistent or its potential longevity so debatable, as a number of low- and no-dosage cuvées flood the market. Disgorge a great Champagne in the cellar where it was made, and it will be a delight and a privilege to taste or drink without any dosage whatsoever. Once it has been exposed to the oxidative effects of the open air, though, it would be folly to reseal it without adequate sulphur and at least 6 grams of residual sugar – yet that is precisely what is happening.

IF YOU HAVE BECOME ACCUSTOMED to the quality and character of good Champagne, there really are few other sparkling wines that will satisfy you – and when you do find one to rival Champagne, the cost required to achieve that level of quality in a less-than-ideal growing environment will make it just as expensive as the real thing.

No other vine-growing region can challenge Champagne's claim to produce the world's greatest sparkling wine, because no other area resembles this viticultural twilight zone where the vine struggles to ripen grapes each year. In order to produce a truly great sparkling wine in the classic *brut* sense, the grapes must be harvested with a certain balance of richness, extract, and acidity, which can be achieved only through the long-drawn-out ripening process that occurs when the vine is grown on a knife-edge between success and failure. The Champagne *terroir*, which includes a cold, sometimes mean, northern climate and lime-rich chalk soil, is the key to the wine's intrinsic superiority, yet if such an area were to be discovered today, modern wine experts would quickly dismiss it as unsuitable for viticulture, thus economically unsound for winemaking.

The closest competitor would be the southeast of England, where the climate is just as bad and the soil is geologically the same, but it is also one of the most densely populated areas in

AUTUMNAL VIEW OF VILLEDOMMANGE
The premier cru vineyards of Villedommange completely surround the village, which is located in the Petite Montagne, a few kilometres southwest of Reims. Pinot Meunier reigns supreme, although the Pinot Noir, shown above, accounts for 30 per cent of the vines grown.

Europe so has no hope of developing into a true region as such, let alone competing with Champagne on a region-to-region basis. Its individual producers might, though, just as a few individual producers of top-quality sparkling wine spread all over the world might compete. But what effect could they have on the reputation of the entire Champagne region? Not much, one would imagine, unless they had some help from within the Champagne industry

THE FIVE MAJOR DISTRICTS

There are five major districts in Champagne, and each produces numerous base wines that differ distinctly within a region, as well as between regions. When these wines are blended in various proportions, many contrasting styles are produced. The best way to appreciate regional influences is to seek out grower-producer Champagnes.

MONTAGNE DE REIMS
The vineyards of the northern *montagne* face north and would not ripen grapes but for the fact that the *montagne* itself is a free-standing formation, which allows the chilled night air to slip down the slopes on to the plain, to be replaced by warmer air from a thermal zone that builds up above the *montagne* during the day. The vines here

generally produce darker-coloured, bigger-bodied wines than those from the southern *montagne*, which often have a deeper flavour, more aromatic character, and greater finesse.
Primary grape variety Pinot Noir
Best villages Ambonnay, Aÿ-Champagne, Bouzy, Verzenay, Verzy

CÔTE DES BLANCS
The name of this area is derived from its almost exclusive cultivation of white Chardonnay grapes. The wines produced from these grapes have become the most sought-after in all Champagne. They contribute great finesse and delicacy yet mature to an absolutely unequalled intensity of flavour.
Primary grape variety Chardonnay
Best villages Cramant, Avize, le Mesnil-sur-Oger

VALLÉE DE LA MARNE
Essentially easy-drinking, fruity, and forward wines produced from an extremely high proportion of Pinot Meunier, which is cultivated in the frost-prone valley vineyards due to its late bud-break and early ripening.
Primary grape variety Pinot Meunier
Best villages Mareuil-sur-Aÿ (for Pinot Noir), Dizy and Hautvillers (for both Pinot Noir and Pinot Meunier), Cumières, Leuvrigny, and Ste-Gemme (for Pinot Meunier)

THE AUBE
Ripe, fruity wines are produced in this southern part of Champagne, which is closer to Chablis than to the classic vineyards of the Marne. The wines are better in quality than those of the outer areas of the Vallée de la Marne around Château-Thierry.

Primary grape variety Pinot Noir
Best village les Riceys, Avirey-Lingey

CÔTE DE SÉZANNE
The Sézannais is a rapidly developing area 16 kilometres (10 miles) southwest of the Côte des Blancs. Like its neighbour, the Sézannais favours Chardonnay, but its wines are fruitier, with less finesse, than those of the Côte des Blancs, and can be quite exotic and musky. These wines are ideal for people who enjoy New World sparkling wines but may have difficulty coming to terms with the more classic style of Champagne.
Primary grape variety Chardonnay
Best villages Bethon, Villenauxe-la-Grande

CHAMPAGNE, *see also p101*
*The green AOC boundary
on this map reflects the latest
regional limits set down
by INAO.*

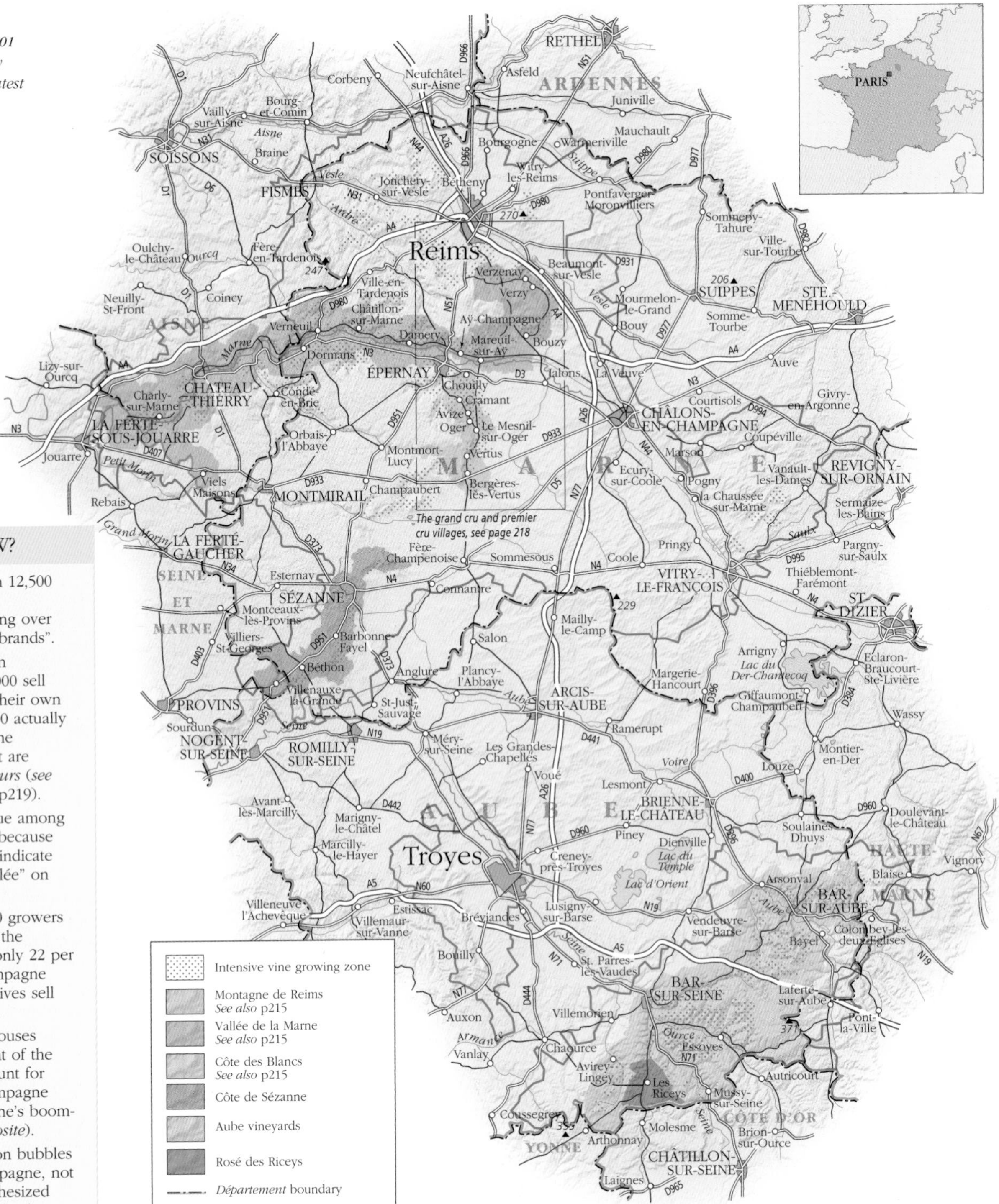

PARIS

DID YOU KNOW?

- There are more than 12,500 different brands of Champagne, including over 3,000 "buyer's own-brands".

- Of 15,000 growers in Champagne, just 5,000 sell Champagne under their own name, but only 3,750 actually make the Champagne themselves. The rest are *récoltants-coopérateurs* (*see* Types of Producer, p219).

- Champagne is unique among French AOC wines because it does not have to indicate "Appellation Contrôlée" on the label.

- Champagne's 15,000 growers own 88 per cent of the vineyards, but sell only 22 per cent of all the Champagne produced (cooperatives sell another 7 per cent).

- Champagne's 264 houses own just 12 per cent of the vineyards, but account for 71 per cent of Champagne sales (*see* Champagne's boom-bust economy, *opposite*).

- There are 250 million bubbles in a bottle of Champagne, not 49 million as hypothesized by scientist Bill Lembeck.

- The pressure inside a Champagne bottle is equal to that inside a double-decker bus tyre.

- As the wine ages, minuscule amounts of oxygen enter a Champagne bottle through the cork, against the internal pressure, due to a principle known as exchange of gases.

- The chalk bed that surfaces in Champagne's Côte des Blancs is contiguous with the seam of chalk that extends westward, beneath Paris, to emerge as the White Cliffs of Dover in the UK.

Legend

- Intensive vine growing zone
- Montagne de Reims *See also p215*
- Vallée de la Marne *See also p215*
- Côte des Blancs *See also p215*
- Côte de Sézanne
- Aube vineyards
- Rosé des Riceys
- *Département* boundary
- Proposed AOC Champagne Zone d'Elaboration
- ▲ Height above sea level (metres)

0   5   10   15   20 miles
0 5 10 15 20 25 30 35km

The grand cru and premier cru villages, see page 218

CHAMPAGNE'S CHALK SUBSOIL

This subsoil is part of a seabed that dried up 65 million years ago and is part of the same bed of chalk as the White Cliffs of Dover. It was formed by the slow accumulation of coccoliths, a calcareous matter secreted by sea organisms. It took 1,000 billion coccoliths to produce each cubic inch of this pure-white chalk.

FACTORS AFFECTING TASTE AND QUALITY

LOCATION
This most northerly of the AOC wine regions of France lies some 145 kilometres (90 miles) northeast of Paris, and is separated from Belgium by the forested hills of the Ardennes. Four-fifths of the region is in the Marne, and the balance is spread over the Aube, Aisne, Seine-et-Marne, and the Haute-Marne.

CLIMATE
This cold and wet northern climate is greatly influenced by the Atlantic, which has a cooling effect on its summer and makes the seasons generally more variable. Its position at the northern edge of the winemaking belt stretches the duration of the vine's growth cycle to the limit, making frost a major problem during spring and autumn.

ASPECT
Vineyards are planted on the gently rolling east- and southeast-facing slopes of the Côte des Blancs at altitudes of 120 to 200 metres (380 to 640 feet). On the slopes of the Montagne de Reims (a plateau) the vines grow at altitudes similar to those on the Côte. The best valley vineyards lie in sheltered situations on the right bank of the Marne.

SOIL
The vineyards of the Côte des Blancs, Montagne de Reims, Marne Valley, and Côte de Sézanne are all situated on a porous chalk subsoil up to 300 metres (960 feet) thick, which is covered by a thin layer of drift derived in various proportions from sand, lignite, marl, loam, clay, and chalk rubble. The pure-white chalk in Champagne's soil drains well, yet retains enough water for the vines to survive a drought. The chalk's high active lime content encourages the vines to produce grapes that have relatively high acid when they become ripe.

VITICULTURE AND VINIFICATION
Jacquesson is leading the way to improve quality from the ground up, operating a very expensive form of viticulture, from cover-cropping to ploughing, leaving off herbicides, short pruning, double-debudding, and so on. This house is the first Champagne grower to train Pinot Noir and Meunier on a permanent cordon, as opposed to employing a replacement branch, and growing the vines much closer together to restrict the branch length. This means fewer fruiting canes, but entails a lot more work to improve exposure and ventilation. The resultant grapes actually looked like grapes even in the obscenely huge, largely rotten, and under-ripe 2001 vintage, something that not many others managed to achieve. No mechanical harvesting is allowed, hence the entire Champagne crop is gathered by hand. Picking usually starts around mid-October. Contrary to popular belief, the grapes are not early-picked, but are on average picked two weeks later than Bordeaux. In exceptional years the harvest has commenced as early as August and as late as November. Rain invariably interrupts the flowering, resulting in at least two crops, although the second, known in *champenois* as the *bouvreux*, rarely ripens and is traditionally left for the birds. The once-traditional sorting into shallow trays called *osiers* is rarely carried out today. Roederer and Bollinger both sort their grapes on occasions, but not so thoroughly as in the past, and most houses do not use any form of selection, although some small growers have started. With rot being a regular problem, intensive sorting should be a legal requirement. If a minimum percentage of grapes must be discarded for Châteauneuf-du-Pape in the sunny south of France, logic dictates that a similar law would be even more beneficial in rainy Reims. Most grapes are still pressed using the traditional, vertical Champagne press or *pressoir coquard*, although pneumatic presses are fairly common, and even Coquard has introduced an innovative inclined stainless-steel press (PAI). Increasing use is being made of stainless-steel vats with temperature-controlled conditions for the first fermentation, but a few houses and many growers still ferment part or all of their wines in cask, with the younger generation employing only a percentage of new oak. The second fermentation gives the wine its sparkle, and this always takes place in the bottle in which it is sold. A non-vintage Champagne must not be sold until at least 15 months after 1 January following the harvest (of the youngest wines in the blend), although most non-vintage Champagnes now spend 24 months on yeast. A vintaged Champagne must not be sold for at least 36 months but most are aged for much longer. Ageing improves Champagne because the sediment contains dead yeast cells that break down through autolysis, which contributes to the wine's inimitable "champagny" character.

GRAPE VARIETIES
Primary varieties: Chardonnay, Pinot Meunier, Pinot Noir
Secondary varieties: Arbanne, Petit Meslier, Pinot Blanc Vrai (Pinot Blanc)

itself, and that might just be happening, as the inconsistent quality and poor longevity of low- and no-*dosage* Champagnes start to chip away at the reputation from the inside.

A SPECIFIC WINE, NOT A STYLE
Champagne is not a generic term for any sparkling wine but is the protected name of a sparkling wine produced from grapes grown within a specific, legally defined area of northern France.

In Europe and various countries throughout the world, strict laws ensure that only true Champagne may be sold under the name "Champagne", but this principle is not respected everywhere. The most blatant misuse in the developed world is in the US, although the Americans are not entirely to blame since the *Champenois* have stubbornly refused even to consider a compromise, such as "Champagne-style". Considering this intransigence and the fact that for many years some of the most powerful Champagne houses have sold the sparkling wines they produce in South America under the name "Champaña", which is Spanish for Champagne, the *Champenois* deserve the treatment they get in the US. In 1985, the term *méthode champenoise* was banned for all wines produced or sold in the European Economic Community (now the EU). The term, while not a guarantee, had proved useful for sorting the wheat from the chaff, since the quality of the product must warrant the cost of fermenting in bottle. Now consumers have to look for linguistic variations along the *méthode traditionnelle* or *classique* theme. In addition, there are Crémant AOCs in France, Cava DO in Spain, as well as new terms (for example, Talento in Italy), which crop up all the time.

CHAMPAGNE'S BOOM-BUST ECONOMY
Champagne sales are notoriously cyclical, going from boom to bust and back to boom again. This is due partly to achieving worldwide fame at a time when the Industrial Revolution created new money, and partly because of the intrinsic imbalance of vineyard ownership. For centuries the fashionability of Champagne had vied with that of Burgundy, so it was only by chance that Champagne happened to be in vogue in the 1870s, when the *nouveau riche* were on the rise. The pop of the cork and liveliness of the bubbles captured the imagination and suited the celebratory lives of the *nouveau riche*, who quickly made Champagne the most chic drink in London, Paris, and New York, doubling its sales in the process. That is why Champagne is inextricably linked to celebration and happiness. Champagne sales are thus extremely sensitive to the mood of consumers, making fluctuations unavoidable. Any well-organized industry should be able to cope with such fluctuations, but the disparity in vineyard ownership creates tensions in supply and demand that convert what would otherwise be relatively harmless fluctuations into damaging booms and busts. Just 12 per cent of the vineyards are owned by the houses, which are responsible for over 70 per cent of Champagne

CHAMPAGNE PRESS
The design of the pressoir coquard *is basically the same as it was in the 17th century, when Dom Pérignon devised several winemaking methods still practised in Champagne today.*

sales. When Champagne sales boom, the houses are desperate for grapes, which the growers withhold, selling only a fraction of what they normally would, demanding as much as they can in the process. The pressure created by disproportionate vineyard ownership causes an artificially high demand, which is inevitably followed by a crash. When the bubble bursts, the houses do not want to buy grapes, and will ignore all but those growers with whom they have long-term relationships, especially those who have speculated at their expense.

This boom-bust recipe for commercial disaster could be consigned to history, but the system is rigged to keep vineyards under the control of small growers, preserving the imbalance in vineyard ownership that is at the root of Champagne's boom-bust woes. It would be an equal travesty if growers were forced to sell any vineyards to the *négoce*, but it should at least be possible for houses to buy or rent vineyards. In theory they can, but only in theory. Ostensibly, there is nothing stopping anyone buying any land in France, but in practice, Champagne's strict adherence to certain controls ensures that the growers maintain ownership of the vineyards. The only realistic way for a house to acquire more vineyards is to take over ailing companies that owned land prior to

SEDIMENT
The Champagne's second fermentation creates a sediment that falls in separate sticky layers; it must be worked down the bottle by an operation called remuage.

the Contrôlée des Structures, a law that forbids any firm from farming more than 15 hectares (37 acres), whether owned or rented. This law applies throughout France, but Champagne is very stringent in its application, which has not only maintained an artificial imbalance in vineyard ownership, but has encouraged the industry's polarization.

CLASSIFICATION OF CHAMPAGNE VINEYARDS
Champagne's vineyards are quality-rated on a village-by-village basis using a percentile system known as the *Échelle des Crus*, which constitutes a pro-rata basis for grape prices. Villages with

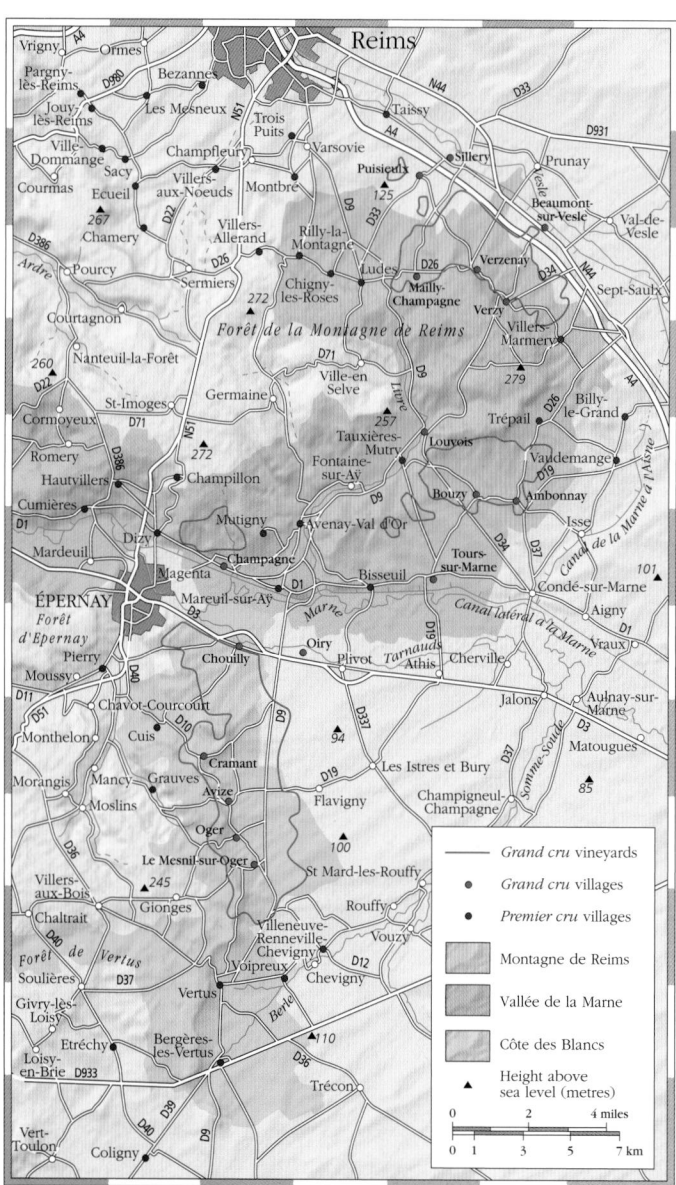

THE GRAND CRU AND PREMIER CRU VILLAGES
Within the three important districts surrounding Épernay, 17 villages have grand cru *status and 44 the status of* premier cru.

WHO OWNS THE BRANDS?

GROUP	TOTAL PRODUCTION	BRANDS
LVMH	58 million bottles	Krug, Mercier, Moët & Chandon, Ruinart, Veuve Clicquot
Lanson-BCC	24 million bottles	Besserat de Bellefon, Boizel (including Camuset, Kremer, Montoy, Veuve Borodin, Veuve Delaroy), Alexandre Bonnet, Brossault, Maison Burtin, Chanoine, Lanson, Philipponnat, De Venoge [plus 200 low-profile brands]
Vranken Monopole	15 million bottles	Barancourt, Charbaut, Collin, Demoiselle, Germain, Heidsieck & Co Monopole, Charles Lafitte, Pommery, Vranken
Laurent-Perrier	14 million	Beaumet, De Castellane (including Chaurey, Freminet, Ettore Bugatti, Jacques Cattier, A Mérand), Delamotte, Jeanmaire, Laurent-Perrier (including Lemoine), Oudinot, Salon
Pernod-Ricard	10 million bottles	Mumm, Perrier-Jouët
Rapeneau	10 million bottles	Château de Bligny, De Cazenove (including Baudry, J Lanvin, Magenta, Marguerite Christel), Mansard-Baillet, G H Martel (including De Noiron, Rapeneau, Charles du Roy, Charles Oban, P L Martin, Balahu, Mortas, Comte de Lamotte, Marcel Pierre)
Rémy-Cointreau	9 million bottles	Heidsieck, Charles Heidsieck, Piper-Heidsieck
CV de Chouilly	8 million bottles	Nicolas Feuillatte
Duval-Leroy	6 million bottles	Duval-Leroy (including Baron de Beaupré, E Michel, Henri de Varlane, Paul Vertay)
Thienot	6 million bottles	Canard-Duchêne, Joseph-Perrier, Malard (including Georges Goulet, Gobillard), Marie Stuart, Alain Thienot (including Billiard, Castille, Petitjean)
Taittinger	5 million bottles	Taittinger (including Irroy, Saint-Eyremond)
Roederer	4 million bottles	Deutz, Louis Roederer, Théophile Roederer

The figures above are based on a five-year average (2005–2009) of declared, reported, and estimated production, the last year of which sales fell by 21%.

the maximum *échelle* of 100 per cent are *grands crus*, while those rated between 90 and 99 per cent are *premiers crus* and receive a correspondingly lower price for their grapes. The lowest-rated villages are currently classified at 80 per cent, but the *Échelle des Crus* was originally a true percentile system, starting at just 22.5 per cent. It would be unrealistic for any such system to commence at 1 per cent, since no village with merely one-hundredth the potential of a *grand cru* should even be part of the Champagne appellation, but when first conceived, the *Échelle des Crus* had a comprehensive structure of *crus* covering the middle ground, which is something that it lacks today. Due to various *ad hoc* reclassifications and political posturing, the minimum *échelle* has gradually increased from 22.5 per cent to 80 per cent, and in truth the present system is nothing more than a 20-point scale. There are 17 villages possessing official *grand cru* status. Until 1985 there were only 12. The 5 villages elevated to *grand cru* in 1985 were Chouilly, le Mesnil-sur-Oger, Oger, Oiry, and Verzy.

THE DANGER OF CURRENT TRENDS

Although I am a sceptic about various aspects of climate change, if there is one region that has nothing to gain from manipulating global-warming data, then that region has to be Champagne. Without wishing to diminish the huge role that chalk soil plays in making Champagne the world's greatest sparkling wine, the one factor above all else that determines Champagne's success is being at the coldest edge of where viticulture is possible on a commercial scale. This is the primary reason why its grapes ripen at an exceptionally low potential alcohol, a relatively high acidity, and a low pH. Nowhere else is it possible to harvest such grapes on such a large scale. Since it follows that the very last thing the *Champenois* want to admit is that their growing season is

TYPES OF PRODUCER

The label on a bottle of Champagne will include some initials, usually found at the bottom and preceding a small code or number. These initials are the key to the type of producer who has made the Champagne.

NM = Négociant-Manipulant
Traditionally referred to as a "house", a *négociant-manipulant* is a producer that is allowed to purchase grapes and *vins clairs* in large volumes from growers, cooperatives, and other houses. A few houses, such as Bollinger and Louis Roederer, own sufficient vineyards to supply as much as two-thirds of their own needs, whereas some own none or hardly any at all (Alfred Gratien).

RM = Récoltant-Manipulant
Otherwise known as a grower-producer, or grower for short. In principle, a grower is not allowed to buy grapes or *vins clairs*, as the Champagne sold under their label is supposed to be 100 per cent from their own vineyards. However, growers are legally permitted to purchase grapes or wines from each other, up to a maximum of 5 per cent of their total production. The reasoning behind this is to enable

those with exclusively Chardonnay vines to buy Pinot Noir for the production of rosé.

CM = Coopérative-Manipulant
A cooperative of growers that makes and sells Champagne under one or more brands that it owns.

RC = Récoltant-Coopérateur
A grower who delivers grapes to a cooperative and, in part or full payment, receives back ready-made Champagne, which they sell under their own name. Although more than 4,000 RC brands are registered, they are seldom encountered even in France, and many of these cooperative clones are still sold with RM numbers. Moves to rectify this are ongoing.

SR = Société de Récoltants
A publicly registered firm set up by two or more growers – often related – who share premises to make and market their Champagne under more than one brand.

ND = Négociant-Distributeur
A company that sells Champagne it did not make to others, who then retail it.

MA = Marque d'Acheteur
A brand name owned by the purchaser, such as a restaurant, supermarket, or wine merchant.

RECENT CHAMPAGNE VINTAGES

2010 Yet another Chardonnay year. Harvesting ripe Pinot Noir in pristine health does not happen very often in Champagne, so when anyone over there tells you that it is a Chardonnay year, you can be sure that it is not going to be an exceptional vintage. Problems started in the summer, which was so dry that the vine's metabolism closed down, halting the ripening process, with the *véraison* of black grapes most affected, particularly the Meunier. Then, over a period of just three days at the start of the harvest, three months of rain dropped out of the sky. This was both good and bad: good because the ripening process restarted; and bad because there was a threat of rot, and it became a race against time to get the grapes harvested. Fortunately, the yield had been artificially set at 10,500 kg/ha for economic reasons (the previous year's sales had dropped by more than one-fifth, and ironically the harvest coincided with the release of the equivalent of over 48 million bottles of reserves from the 2009 harvest), and with as much as 14,000 kg/ha on the vines, it was relatively easy to select only the healthiest grapes. It became even easier when Champagne enjoyed a full week of dry, cool, windy weather, stopping the rot dead in its tracks. Very little good Meunier was harvested, but there were some good Pinot Noir plots, albeit very patchy, and the Chardonnay was splendid, especially on the Côte des Blancs. For the houses, this is a vintage to test the blending skills of

the *chefs de caves*, while for the growers it is the Côte des Blancs that will be the winners.

2009 This is a Pinot Noir year, so it must be good! In fact, this is an excellent to great year, with no rot, healthy grapes of well above vintage ripeness, great concentration, and fine acid levels. Certainly the greatest vintage since 2002 and possibly even better.

2008 A potentially excellent year, although less so for Meunier. Although the summer was cool and cloudy, slow ripening will never be a problem for the potential quality of Champagne if – and it's a big if – the weather warms up and stays dry and the harvest can be carried out under ideal conditions. The big if happened, and the vines enjoyed two weeks of dry, warm, breezy weather for the second half of September. This vintage was marked by classic vintage ripeness and beautifully crisp acidity, thanks to the open night skies that provided a 16°C (61°F) diurnal difference.

2007 A curious year, with the first buds appearing as early as 5 April, and a very hot spring encouraging some observers to think that picking could commence on 14 August, seven days earlier than 2003, which is the earliest harvest on record. July, however, saw strange weather: dark and brooding one moment, followed by an expected heavy downpour, then completely unexpected bright sunshine, and it seemed to rain all night,

every night. Even while it was sunny, there was an almost electric tension in the air. Spring frost is usually Champagne's most dangerous meteorological threat, but in 2007 it was summer hail. On 4 July, hail destroyed 10–40% of the potential crop in Chigny, Rilly, Ludes, Taissy, Cormontreuil, and Montbré. The summer was relatively cold, dragging out the *véraison* and putting back the harvest to 28 August. Tasting the *vins clairs*, the biggest problem was a reductive tendency in some of the Chardonnay. This is generally a non-vintage year that turned out better than hoped, with Mesnil, Avize, and Villers-Marmery among the most successful villages for Chardonnay; Aÿ, Mareuil-sur-Aÿ, Bouzy, and Verzy showing well for Pinot Noir; and Cumières and Villedommange for Meunier. Some producers declared a vintage, and Roederer was among the best of those.

2006 Definitely a "Chardonnay vintage", with some excellent base wines produced on the Côte des Blancs, but the Pinot Noir suffered rather more rot in 2006 than most producers were inclined to admit, and the Meunier was even worse. With nearly 16 per cent affected, the normally hardy Meunier was exceptionally rot-prone for the second year running. This does not mean that some fine-quality Champagnes won't be produced from black grapes; it's just that selection will very much be the key to this vintage. The Aube produced the most interesting Pinot Noir, although some were over-ripe.

warming up, we can believe them when they say it is. Therefore, there is no reason for the *Champenois* to lie when they tell us that, while the 40-year average for their growing-season temperature was 14.3ºC (57.7°F) between the 1950s and 1980s, this crept up to 15.0ºC (59°F) in the 1990s and increased alarmingly to as high as 16.6ºC (61.9°F) in the first 10 year of the new millennium. These temperatures do not (yet) spell disaster for Champagne, which, even with a growing-season average of 16.6ºC (61.9°F), is still the envy of sparkling-wine producers worldwide. Champagne producers have so far managed to contend with gradually riper grapes, but if the warming up continues, they will have to learn from their New World cousins how to acidify. (Jean-Baptiste Lecaillon at Roederer is one of the few in Champagne who is highly skilled at this procedure.) We shall also probably see a reversal in the attitude to stopping malolactic conversion. All Champagnes used to be non-malolactic in the 19th and early 20th centuries, but very few producers have maintained this style – the most notable exceptions are Bollinger, Gratien, Krug, and Lanson – while some, including Roederer, use partial-malolactic techniques, where Jean-Baptiste Lecaillon is famous for his *à la carte* use of non-malolactic for Chardonnay and *tailles*. Should the growing-season temperature continue to increase, it is likely that the pendulum will swing back the other way, as more and more producers start to block the malolactic, either fully or partly.

The knee-jerk reaction to riper grapes was to lower the *dosage*, and many have done that without either acidifying or tweaking the malolactic. A subtle combination of all three options would have had the least obvious effect on any individual Champagne style, but *dosage* levels alone have been slashed over the past 10 years. There is a widespread belief that the lower the *dosage*, the better; but the lower the *dosage*, the more oxidative Champagne becomes, particularly if little or no sulphur is added with the *dosage*, as often happens with the low- or no-*dosage* style. In my experience, cellaring Champagnes with less than 6 grams of residual sugar per litre is very risky, and 6 grams itself should be reserved for recently disgorged Champagnes of mature age (15 years or more). Over the past 10 years or so, I have seen relatively few Champagnes that will age as well as the great vintages of the past. The Champagnes with the least potential longevity have all received low or no *dosage*, and worryingly, most have come from producers whose Champagnes used to have exemplary longevity (not Pol Roger, thank goodness). I can walk into houses today

CHAMPAGNE CORKS

1 A crown-cap to seal the wine during second fermentation.
2 The plastic pot in which the deposit is collected during *remuage*.
3 A cork before insertion. Note its cylindrical shape.
4 A cork from a youthful Champagne. The mushroom head is achieved when ramming it into the bottle.
5 The cork of a more mature Champagne. Note that it has shrunk and straightened through age.

1   2   3   4   5

COMBATING FROST
Vines are protected from frost, the most harmful of Champagne's natural hazards, by aspersion. Aspersion (water-sprinkling) is performed by a system that operates automatically whenever the vineyard temperature drops below freezing. The frost expends its energy in freezing the water, leaving the delicate shoots and buds safely cocooned in ice.

where I know that I can still taste great Champagnes that are still in prime condition, even though they have been historically disgorged and traditionally "dosaged" more than 50 years ago. Will Champagne writers be equally sure and privileged in 50 years' time? Somehow I doubt it, unless the trend for low-*dosage* Champagne has run its course.

HOMEGROWN
Is it better for a Champagne producer to grow its own grapes? Does this guarantee a better quality and greater consistency of style? As the table opposite demonstrates, the answer is "maybe" to the first question and "no" to the second. Own grapes do not guarantee a better quality or a greater consistency of style. They make it easier to achieve these ends, but there are more than enough cooperatives and growers making poor Champagne exclusively from their own vineyards to realize that own grapes do not guarantee quality, whereas the likes of Alfred Gratien and Gosset, neither of whom own a single vine, demonstrate that the highest levels of quality and consistency can be achieved exclusively from purchased grapes. Economically, it is cheaper to grow grapes than to buy them, unless yields are deliberately reduced, and other quality-enhancing viticultural techniques are practised.

CHAMPAGNE'S SO-CALLED EXPANSION
Just before the global recession hit in 2008, sales of Champagne had increased for an unprecedented eighth year in a row, creating the largest and most lucrative boom in Champagne's history. With almost every square inch of AOC land cultivated, and with unrivalled pressure on stocks from record sales, it seemed as if they really would run out of Champagne. As from 2003, the Champagne industry tried to curb demand by increasing prices, but the demand kept rising. The producers obviously did not mind fattening their profit margins, but equally obviously they knew that sales could not continue at such a high rate. The only solution, they concluded, was to expand the vineyards, which, from both a moral and PR viewpoint, was the worst possible decision that the guardians of any strictly delimited wine region could make. If no other solution could be found, then the only honest option would have been simply to run out of product every year, something that most manufacturers can only dream about.

But to want to sell even more? No wonder the Champagne industry was vilified by the news media for unmitigated greed. However, this was one foot the *Champenois* did not have to shoot themselves in. Had the proposal been conceived in 2003 expressly to fuel runaway sales, then Champagne producers could legitimately be accused not only of greed but also of showing as much contempt for their own appellation as for the consumers they were trying to hoodwink. The fact is that the proposal had been under consideration for more than 30 years to my own knowledge, and as you will shortly discover, it was not an expansion at all. They only had to put the announcement into historical context, and it probably would not even have been reported.

DIFFERENT ZONES

Before we look at the historical context, we have to understand the geographical framework by which the Champagne (and indeed every French wine) appellation is constructed. There are three zones: the Zone de l'Élaboration, the Zone de Production, and the Zone Parcellaire de Production de Raisins. The Zone de l'Élaboration is the outer limits of the region, where grapes, bulk wines, and bottled wines may be freely transported. It is also that part of the region where – and only where – it is legal to vinify the wines of that specific appellation. The Zone de Production is located within the Zone de l'Élaboration and consists of the communes where vines may be cultivated, but only within a lacework of delimited areas representing a fraction of the surface area. The Zone Parcellaire de Production de Raisins is that lacework of delimited areas. To provide real-life examples, the appellations mapped in this book are primarily the Zones de l'Élaboration, since they usually represent just one contiguous block or perhaps a few blocks at most and thus are visually easy to grasp.

Prior to the proposed expansion, Champagne's Zone de l'Élaboration comprised of 637 communes. Although this has been extended to 675 communes, it was not a straightforward enlargement, since it entailed the removal of 117 villages, as well as the addition of 157 villages. The reasoning behind most of these changes had nothing to do with increasing vineyards and everything to do with the logistics of moving grapes to *pressoirs* and wine to *cuveries*. Within the Zone de l'Élaboration, the Zone de Production consisted of 319 communes prior to the expansion, covering approximately 300,000 hectares (740,000 acres), only 35,200 hectares (87,000 acres) of which was classified as AOC Champagne. The expansion saw the number of communes increase to 357 by removing 2 villages and adding 40 villages, but the land classified as AOC Champagne within these villages remains at 35,200 hectares because the committee of experts is not due to release its first report on any parcel-by-parcel classification of potential new vineyards until 2017. If it does, the earliest that any new vines can be planted will be 2019; therefore, it will not be until at least 2023 before the first Champagne from any new vineyards will be on the shelf.

The historical aspect that seems to have been forgotten in all this is that the appellation law of 1927 recognized 46,000 hectares (113,670 acres) of AOC Champagne in 407 villages; and by 1951, following a serious slump in the market, Champagne had requested, and had been granted, a contraction in the delimited area to 34,000 hectares (84,000 acres) spread over just 302 villages (the area has increased slightly since). From an idealistically ethical point of view, this might not be the right way to run any strictly delimited appellation – but in practice, this is the way that most French appellations work. Had the authorities put the expansion in context of the 1951 reduction, at least one process would be some sort of justification for the other, and had the news media been made aware of the original boundaries of AOC Champagne, there would have been very little talk of expansion.

VINEYARDS BELONGING TO THE HOUSES

PRODUCER	VINEYARDS OWNED	PROPORTION OF PRODUCTION[1]	CHAMPAGNES MADE FROM OWN GRAPES[2]
Billecart-Salmon[3]	11 hectares	5%	Entire range (?%)
Bollinger	163 hectares	67%	Vieilles Vignes Françaises (100%) Grande Année (80–90%) Grande Année Rosé (80–90%)
Deutz	37 hectares	30%	Entire range (30%)
Gosset	None	Zero	None
Alfred Gratien	1 hectare	Zero	None
Henriot	28 hectares	20%	Entire range (20%)
Jacquesson	33 hectares	60%	Avize Grand Cru (100%) Grand Vin Signature (67%) NV cuvées (40–60%) In the pipeline: Aÿ Grand Cru (100%) Dizy Premier Cru (100%) Forthcoming Grand Vin Signature (75%)
Krug	21 hectares	40%	Clos du Mesnil (100%) Rest of range (40%)
Lanson	1 hectare	0.08%	Clos du Lanson (100%) Rest of range (none)
Moët & Chandon	576 hectares[4]	up to 25%	Dom Pérignon (100%) Vintage cuvées (50–75%)
Mumm	218 hectares	25%	Entire range (25%)
Perrier-Jouët	65 hectares	25%	Entire range (25%)
Bruno Paillard	24 hectares	14%	Most used in Brut Première Cuvée, but sometimes part in Chardonnay Réserve Privée or Vintage or NPU.
Philipponnat	20 hectares	33%	Clos des Goisses (100%) Réserve Millésimée (75%) Cuvée 1522 (65%)
Pol Roger	85 hectares	over 50%	Chardonnay ("largely") Rest of the range (over 50%)
Pommery	230 hectares[5]	14%[5]	
Roederer	214 hectares	67%	Vintage cuvées (100%) NV cuvées (50%)
Taittinger	288 hectares	50%	Entire range (50%)
Veuve Clicquot	515 hectares	up to 30%	Grande Dame (up to 100%) Grande Dame Rosé (up to 100%) vintage cuvées (predominantly)

Notes
[1] Represented by own grapes. An average figure that very much depends on the harvest.
[2] An average figure that very much depends on the harvest (especially when no vintage wines are produced) and, of course, the ultimate freedom to construct each cuvée according to the judgement of the house rather than any set formula that dictates a certain percentage.
[3] There are also 90 hectares belonging to Frey, a major, but not majority, shareholder in Billecart-Salmon, which has first refusal on all grapes grown as of October 2004.
[4] Includes Mercier.
[5] Vranken Group.

SWEETNESS CHART

The sweetness of a Champagne can be accurately indicated by its residual sugar level, measured in grams per litre. The percentage *dosage*, which some books refer to, is not an accurate indicator because the *liqueur* added in the *dosage* itself can and does vary in sweetness. The legal levels changed in 2009 and are as follows.

BRUT NATURE: 0–<3 grams per litre Absolutely bone dry!

EXTRA BRUT: 0–<6 grams per litre Bone dry

BRUT: 0–<12 grams per litre Dry to very dry, but should never be austere*

EXTRA SEC OR EXTRA DRY: 12–17 grams per litre A misnomer – dry to medium-dry

SEC OR DRY: 17–32 grams per litre A bigger misnomer – medium to medium-sweet

DEMI SEC: 33–<50 grams per litre Definitely sweet, but not true dessert sweetness

DOUX: 50+ grams per litre Very sweet; this style was favoured by the tsars but is no longer commercially produced

* Although it appears as if the top end of the *brut dosage* has decreased from 15 to 12 grams, the regulations permit a 3-gram variation. Officially, this allows for the odd bottle that might still have a little residual sugar after the second fermentation, but in practice, nothing has changed: the top end of *brut* is still 15 g, as it should be.

WHO INVENTED CHAMPAGNE?

Originally Champagne was a still wine (a "faintly reddish" *vin gris*); any incidental fizziness would have been considered a fault back then, as it would be in, say, a *cru classé* claret today. To find the first sparkling wine, we must ignore accidents and faults, and look for the earliest deliberate rendering of a wine in the sparkling format: the precursor to the evolutionary process we know as the *méthode champenoise*.

PÉRIGNON THE PRETENDER
The French would have us believe that Dom Pérignon invented Champagne in the late 1690s, but there is no evidence that he made a single bottle of sparkling wine, and every suggestion that he regarded fizziness as a fault. If anything, the legendary Benedictine monk spent his life trying to rid Champagne of bubbles. So what do the French traditionalists base their belief on? They rely on a French document, *Mémoire sur le Manière de cultiver la Vigne et de faire le Vin de en Champagne*, written in 1718 by an anonymous author (believed to be Jean Godinot), which contains the first use of the term "vin mousseux" and refers to its popularity having been established "more than 20 years earlier". This is not proof, of course, but if we accept it as an accurate account, sparkling wines became mainstream in France circa 1697.

LACK OF TECHNOLOGY
It could not possibly have been much earlier than this because the French did not have the technology. They did not have a strong enough glass bottle to withstand the internal pressure of a sparkling wine, or an effective seal to maintain it. French glass was wood-fired, and thus too weak, while cork-stoppers had been "lost" during decline of the Roman Empire, and replaced by wooden bungs wrapped in hemp, which would hardly keep the draught out, let alone the fizz in.

INVENTION OF INVENTOR
There is no mention in Godinot's *mémoire* of Dom Pérignon. Incredible though it may seem, the first documented claim that Dom Pérignon made sparkling Champagne was made in 1821, more than a century after his death, by Dom Grossard, who wrote "As you know, it was the celebrated Dom Pérignon who found the secret of making white sparkling wine". But there was

DOM PÉRIGNON
How could Dom Pérignon have invented Champagne when "sparkling Champaign" was mentioned in English literature six years before the famous monk arrived in the region?

no secret process. The manifestation of effervescence in wine was a capricious and ephemeral effect that Godinot attributed to the phases of the moon! However, despite his claim of sparkling Champagne's popularity in France from the late 1690s, the 1721 edition of *Dictionnaire Universel* did not refer to any wine as "mousseux", an adjective that would not appear in this context until the 1724 edition.

ENGLISH CHAMPAGNE
Yet sparkling Champagne was not only available in England much earlier than this; it had become so popular that dramatists were mentioning it by 1676, when Sir George Etherege wrote in *The Man of Mode*:

To the Mall and the Park
Where we love till 'tis dark,
Then sparkling Champaign
Puts an end to their reign;
It quickly recovers
Poor languishing lovers,
Makes us frolic and gay,
And drowns all sorrow;
But, Alas,
We relapse again on the morrow.

ENGLISH PARADOX
How could sparkling Champagne be recorded in English literature two decades before even the French admit the first sparkling Champagne was made? Because whereas the French did not have the technology, the English did, and being inveterate meddlers, they used it to make still French wines fizzy. Although the French did not rediscover cork until 1685 at the earliest (almost a decade after Etherege's "sparkling Champaign"), the English, who also lost the cork after the Romans had left, came across it more than 130 years before the French. All wines in Shakespeare's time were shipped to England in casks, but the English habitually bottled their wines, sealing them with corks, from the late 16th century onwards. And whereas French glass was wood-fired and intrinsically weak, English glass was coal-fired at a much higher temperature, making it a vastly stronger product.

It is clear that the English had the means to preserve the effervescence of a sparkling Champagne long before its first recorded mention by Sir George Etherege, but how and why did still wine from Champagne end up sparkling?

IRRELEVANCE OF NATURAL FIZZ
Obviously there were many occurrences of accidental refermentation causing a wine to become fizzy. The most common cause for such faulty wines was the cold northerly situation of Champagne, where we can be sure that fermentation would have prematurely stopped at the first snap of winter, only for it to recommence once bottled and stored in the warmth of an English tavern. However,

accidentally sparkling wines have been a fact of life since Biblical times, and such incidents are an irrelevance to historians searching for the first intentionally sparkling wine.

MÉTHODE MERRET
Conclusive proof can only be demonstrated by documentary evidence describing the most rudimentary element of the *méthode champenoise* – the addition of sugar to a finished wine to induce a second fermentation with the specific intention of making it not just "gay", "brisk", or "lively" (words often thought to imply effervescence), but unequivocally sparkling. Such a document exists, not in Reims or Épernay, but in London, where an eight-page paper entitled "Some observations concerning the ordering of wines" was presented on 17 December 1662 to the newly formed Royal Society by Christopher Merret, who stated "our wine-coopers of recent times use vast quantities of sugar and molasses to all sorts of wines to make them drink brisk and sparkling".

PROOF POSITIVE
Merret goes on to state that this process was also "… to give them spirit as also to mend their bad tastes, all which raisins and cure and stum perform". His use of "spirit" denotes increased alcohol content, while his "stum perform" describes precisely in 17th-century English a new fermentation. Although Merret does not mention Champagne specifically, he does state "all wines" and this would surely have included Champagne. Furthermore, we can deduce that of "all wines" it was Champagne that suited the process better than any other because, within a very short while, all efforts were concentrated on that wine. If not, then "sparkling Champaign" could not have achieved the level of fame required for Etherege to wax lyrical about it just 14 years later.

Thus the English invented the Champagne process, and did so at least six years before Dom Pérignon set foot in Champagne, more than 30 years before the French made their first sparkling Champagne, over 60 years before *mousseux* was first mentioned in a French dictionary, and almost 80 years before the first Champagne house was established.

THE WINE STYLES OF
CHAMPAGNE

NON-VINTAGE BRUT

No wine depends upon the winemaker's blending skills more than non-vintage Champagne, which accounts for more than 75 per cent of all Champagne sold. Although non-vintage Champagnes are not usually the finest Champagnes, they are capable of being so. Their base wine, to which reserve wines may be added, will always be from the last harvest. Most producers make up between 10 and 15 per cent of their blends from reserves from the previous two or three years, but some utilize as much as 40 per cent, while a few will add much less reserve wine in volume, but from a greater number of much older vintages. Many growers have no reserve wines, thus their non-vintage will in fact be from one year, but of a lesser quality than the *cuvée* selected for their vintage Champagne. All but the most dynamic *coopératives* typically make up just 5 per cent of their blends from reserves from the year immediately preceding that of the base wine – and they seldom excel.

Billecart-Salmon • Chanoine (Tsarine Premium) • *Deutz* (Classic) • *Charles Heidsieck • Lanson* Extra Age • *Bruno Paillard • Piper-Heidsieck* (Florens Louis) • *Louis Roederer • Taittinger* • *Vilmart & Cie* (Grand Cellier d'Or)

VINTAGE BRUT

Not more than 80 per cent of any year's harvest may be sold as vintage Champagne, so at least 20 per cent of the best years' harvests are conserved for the future blending of non-vintage wines. Some houses stick rigidly to declaring a vintage in only the greatest years, but many, sadly, do not, which is why we have seen vintage Champagnes from less than ideal years. Most *coopératives* and a large number of grower-producers produce a vintage virtually every year, which is possible, of course, but rather defeats the object and debases the value of the product. However, even in great years, a vintage Champagne is more the result of tightly controlled selection of base wines than a reflection of the year in question, and this makes these wines exceptionally good value. The character of a vintage Champagne is more autolytic, giving it an acacia-like floweriness, than that of a non-vintage of the same age because it has no reserve-wine mellowness. If you like those biscuity or toasty bottle-aromas, you should keep vintage for a few years.

Billecart-Salmon (Cuvée Nicolas-François Billecart) • *Deutz • Alfred Gratien • Charles Heidsieck • Krug • Lanson • Piper-Heidsieck* • *Pol Roger • Louis Roederer • Veuve Clicquot*

BLANC DE BLANCS
Non-vintage, vintage, and prestige

Literally meaning "white of whites", this wine is produced entirely from white Chardonnay grapes and possesses the greatest ageing potential of all Champagnes. *Blanc de blancs* may be made in any district of Champagne, but the best examples come from a small part of the Côte des Blancs between Cramant and Le Mesnil-sur-Oger. If consumed too early, a classic *blanc de blancs* can be austere and seem to lack fruit and generosity, yet with proper maturity this style of Champagne can be very succulent. Given a few years' bottle ageing after purchase, most *blanc de blancs* develop a toasty-lemony bouquet together with intense, beautifully focused fruit.

Non-vintage Billecart-Salmon • Boizel • *Bonnaire • Gaston Chicquet • Delamotte* • *Pierre Gimonnet • Alfred Gratien • Bruno Paillard • Joseph Perrier • Piper-Heidsieck* (Divin) • *Vilmart & Cie* • **Vintage** *Billecart-Salmon • Deutz • Duval-Leroy • Pierre Gimonnet* (Collection *en magnum*) • *Jacquesson* (Avize) • *Henri Mandois* (Chardonnay Brut) • *Le Mesnil* (Vigne Sélectionnée) • *Pol Roger • Louis Roederer* • **Prestige cuvée** *Boizel* (Joyeau) • *Deutz* (Amour de Deutz) • *Charles Heidsieck* (Cuvée de Millénaires) • *Krug* (Clos du Mesnil) • *Ruinart* (Dom Ruinart) • *Salon* ("S") • *Taittinger* (Comtes de Champagne)

BLANC DE NOIRS
Non-vintage, vintage, and prestige

Literally translated as "white of blacks", these Champagnes are made entirely from black grapes, either Pinot Noir or Pinot Meunier, or a blend of the two. The most famous and most expensive is Bollinger's Vieilles Vignes Françaises, which is a unique example of pure Pinot Noir Champagne made from two tiny plots of ungrafted vines, which between them cannot produce more than 3,000 bottles, hence the hefty price tag. Apart from Bollinger, few producers have traditionally used the term *blanc de noirs*, but the Vieilles Vignes Françaises has given it a certain cachet and a few commercially minded houses have begun to cash in on the term (Beaumet, Jeanmaire, Mailly Grand Cru, Oudinot, and De Venoge, for example). Many supermarkets now sell their own-label brand of *blanc de noirs*. Bollinger inadvertently created the myth that a *blanc de noirs* is intrinsically a big, full, and muscular Champagne, but it is generally little different in style from the other *cuvées* a house may produce. The Bollinger *blanc de noirs* myth was completely accidental. Because the ungrafted vines are planted in super-high density, each plant bears relatively little fruit and this naturally ripens one week earlier than the vines in surrounding vineyards. At first, Bollinger applied for special dispensation to harvest one week earlier, but they were refused; consequently, the grapes have always been over-ripe, making a uniquely rich and concentrated Champagne. If you try Serge Mathieu's Champagne, you will discover a wine so elegant that you would never guess it is made only from Pinot Noir, let alone that it is grown in the Aube. Pommery's Wintertime and the Mailly cooperative's basic non-vintage Blanc de Noirs Grand Cru just miss the cut, but deserve an honorary mention. Another cooperative, Veuve A Devaux, has just come back on stream with its non-vintage Blanc de Noirs, which should make the list next time around if standards are maintained.

Non-vintage Devaux • Serge Mathieu (Cuvée Tradition) • *De Venoge* • **Vintage** *Serge Mathieu* • **Prestige cuvée** *Billecart-Salmon* (Le Clos Saint-Hilaire) • *Bollinger* (Vieilles Vignes Françaises) • *Canard-Duchêne* (Charles VII) • *Krug* (Clos d'Ambonnay)

EXTRA SEC

Rarely encountered except on supermarket Champagne, fooling all those who like to "talk dry but drink sweet" with the "extra dry" misnomer on a Champagne with 12–17 grams of residual sugar per litre.

EXTRA BRUT

The best Champagnes in this category can be wonderfully bracing, but with just 0–6 grams of residual sugar, cellaring is not advised unless you know and enjoy the oxidative manner in which they evolve. If at the top end of the scale (6 grams), this represents a good *dosage* for mature vintages.

Non-vintage Doyard (Vendémaire) • *Ployez-Jacquemart • De Sousa* (3A) • **Vintage** *Bollinger* (RD) • *Duval Leroy • Pierre Gimonnet* (Cuvée Oenophile Extra-Brut) • *Jacquesson* (Grand Vin Signature) • *Pannier* (Exact) • *Union Champagne de Saint Gall* (Blanc de Blancs)

SEC

With a residual sugar greater than 17 grams per litre but less than 32 grams, the lower end of this style (say, 17–24 grams) can make a fabulous gastronomic experience when accompanying dishes with a distinct hint of sweetness, such as *foie gras* or indeed any savoury dish with a fruit content or garnish.

Non-vintage De Venoge (Vin du Paradis) • *Louis Roederer* (Carte Blanche) • *Jacques Selosse* (Cuvée Exquise Sec) • *Taittinger* (Nocturne) • **Vintage** *Veuve Clicquot* (Rich)

RICH OR RICHE

Under the old Champagne laws, these terms were strictly used as an official alternative designation for *demi-sec*, but they are currently used for anything between Sec and Demi Sec. *See* Sec and Demi Sec.

DEMI SEC

Although this style of Champagne may contain between 33 and 50 grams of residual sugar per litre, most are closer to the minimum these days and, as such, fall between two stools: too sweet for conventional use at 33 grams, while even at 50 grams, a *demi-sec* Champagne would struggle with many desserts. Much *demi-sec*, therefore, is used to dispose of inferior-quality Champagne, hidden beneath a veneer of sugar and sold to consumers who do not know better and could not care less as it is quaffed at Christmas or the New Year. However, if you are a consumer who does know better and has found a good use for *demi-sec* Champagne, the following are seriously produced with high-quality wines.

Non-vintage Billecart-Salmon (Demi-Sec Réserve) • *Mumm • Pol Roger* (Rich) • *Louis Roederer* (Carte Blanche) • **Vintage** *Deutz*

DOUX

According to André Simon, Doux represented as much as 60 per cent of all Champagne shipments until 1960, and half of that had 100 grams of residual sugar, but Brut caught on, and by the late 1980s this style had disappeared. Only in recent years has it started to make something of a comeback. With this level of sweetness, Champagne Doux is a match for any dessert wine and makes an ideal candidate for restaurant sales by the glass, the effervescence bringing a refreshing lift to the end of a meal. From Courteron, the same Aubois village as Fleury, Schreiber also produces a *doux*, but I have not yet tasted it.

🏆 **Non-vintage** *Doyard* (Libértine) • **Vintage** *Fleury*

ROSÉ
Non-vintage, vintage, and prestige

The first record of a commercially produced rosé Champagne is by Clicquot in 1777 and this style has enjoyed ephemeral bursts of popularity ever since. It is the only European rosé that may be made by blending white wine with a little red; all other rosé, whether still or sparkling, must be produced by macerating the skins and juice to extract pigments. More pink Champagne is produced by blending than through skin contact, and in blind tasting it has been impossible to tell the difference. Both methods produce good and bad wine that can be light or dark in colour and rich or delicate in flavour. A good pink Champagne will have an attractive colour, perfect limpidity, and a snow-white mousse. Why no Krug Rosé? Intrinsically it would come very close to the top of my list of "multi-vintage" rosés, but Krug either makes too much or it does not sell quickly enough – or they don't make it often enough. It is the only wine in the Krug range that does not repay keeping, and there have been too many occasions when a tired Krug Rosé was the only Krug Rosé available. Laurent-Perrier's Cuvée Grand Siècle Alexandra, the first couple of vintages of which were to die for, is edged out of the top ten prestige *cuvée* rosés for having no track record between the 1990 and 1997 vintages. On the other hand, Chanoine's 1999 Tsarine Rosé was not only a beautifully elegant start for this new vintaged wine, it was also exceptionally fine for a 1999, but will Chanoine maintain this standard?

🏆 **Non-vintage** *Billecart-Salmon* • *Château de Boursault* • *Gosset* (Grand Rosé) • *Charles Heidsieck* • *Henriot* • *Henri Mandois* • *Serge Mathieu* • *Piper-Heidsieck* (Rosé Sauvage) • **Vintage** *Bollinger* • *Deutz* • *Charles Heidsieck* • *Jacquesson* (Signature) • *Pol Roger* • *Louis Roederer* • *Veuve Clicquot* • **Prestige cuvée** *Billecart-Salmon* (Cuvée Elisabeth) • *Deutz* (Cuvée William Deutz) • *Lanson* (Noble Cuvée) • *Moët & Chandon* (Dom Pérignon) • *Perrier-Jouët* (Belle Epoque) • *Pommery* (Cuvée Louise Pommery) • *Louis Roederer* (Cristal) • *Ruinart* (Dom Ruinart) • *Taittinger* (Comtes de Champagne) • *Veuve Clicquot* (Grande Dame)

BRUT NATURE
Non-vintage and vintage

The first non-*dosage* Champagne to be sold was Laurent-Perrier's Grand Vin Sans Sucre in 1889. Officially Brut Extra, but commercially labelled variously as Brut Zéro, Brut Sauvage, Ultra Brut, or Sans Sucre, these wines became fashionable in the early 1980s, when consumers began seeking lighter, drier wines. This trend was driven by critics who had been privileged to taste wonderful old vintages straight off their lees, which led them to believe that

a Champagne without any *dosage* was somehow intrinsically superior to a Champagne with a *dosage*. It is, of course, if it is of superior quality, at least 10 years old before disgorgement and is consumed on the spot as soon as it is disgorged, without any oxidative effect being allowed to develop. It is not superior, however, if the Champagne is of normal commercial age, when it can only be austere, tart, and unpleasant to drink, which is why the fashion was so short-lived. Sometimes, even I think that I have discovered a great non-*dosage* Champagne, only to discover most of the follow-up releases disappointing. These include De Bruyne, Mailly (Cassiopee), and Philipponnat (Cuvée 1522 Extra Brut). I could have died for the first release of André et Michel Drappier NV Pinot Noir Zero Dosage, but later shipments fell a long way short. Even Billecart-Salmon reduced a great Champagne to merely a very good one when launching its single-vineyard Les Clos St-Hilaire with no *dosage* in the inaugural 1995 vintage. (Later vintages mercifully benefited from a *dosage*, albeit a very minor one.) Pol Roger is shaping up to be, possibly, the only regular aged exception to the rule. Jacquesson's 1988 Dégorgement Tardif Brut (with no *dosage*) drew an extraordinarily rare 98 points from me at *The World of Fine Wine* magazine's low- and no-*dosage* tasting in 2009.

🏆 **Non-vintage** *Pol Roger* (Pure) • **Vintage** *Pommery* (Flacon d'Excellence Nature en magnum) • *Roses de Jeanne* (La Bolorée)

CUVÉE DE PRESTIGE
Brut style – Non-vintage and vintage

Also known as special or deluxe *cuvées*, Cuvées de Prestige should be the best that Champagne has to offer, regardless of the price. Dom Pérignon was the first commercial example of these Champagnes, launched in 1936, although Louis Roederer's Cristal has a far longer history, having first been produced in 1876, but that was made exclusively for Tsar Alexander II. The first commercially available Cristal *cuvée* was not produced until 1945.

A typical prestige *cuvée* may be made entirely of wines from a firm's own vineyards, and the blend is often restricted to grapes from *grand cru* villages. Most of these are vintage Champagnes, and many are produced by the most traditional methods (fermented in wood, sealed with a cork and *agrafe*, rather than a crown-cap, then hand-disgorged), aged for longer than normal, and sold in special bottles at very high prices. Some are clearly over-priced; others are over-refined, having so much mellowness that all the excitement has been squeezed out of them; but a good number are truly exceptional Champagnes and worth every penny.

Mumm's Cuvée R Lalou has taken over the mantle of the greatest prestige *cuvée* of modern times from Pol Roger's Cuvée Sir Winston Churchill, although the latter remains as great as ever. Mumm's Cuvée R Lalou also represents the most serious and painfully precise project ever conducted to create a new Champagne from the ground up. Having selected and ring-fenced 18 parcels in 12 *lieux-dits* located within eight *grand cru* villages, Mumm still puts these wines through a rigorous selection and *assemblage* process. Every stage of production – from the pruning, to the composition and *élevage* of the base wine used for the *dosage* – has been dissected and re-evaluated, and the result is a Champagne of great minerality and exquisite finesse.

🏆 **Non-vintage** *Jacquart* (Cuvée Katarina) • *Krug* (Grande Cuvée) • *Laurent-Perrier* (Grand Siècle La Cuvée) • *Piper-Heidsieck* (Cuvée Rare) • *Taittinger* (Prélude) • **Vintage** *Billecart-Salmon* (Grande Cuvée) • *Deutz* (Cuvée William Deutz

– since 1995) • *Moët & Chandon* (Dom Pérignon) • *Mumm* (R Lalou) • *Perrier-Jouët* (Belle Epoque) • *Pol Roger* (Cuvée Sir Winston Churchill) • *Pommery* (Cuvée Louise Pommery) • *Louis Roederer* (Cristal) • *Veuve Clicquot* (Grande Dame) • *Vilmart* (Coeur de Cuvée)

Note Top-performing prestige *cuvées* that are *blanc de blancs*, *blanc de noirs*, *rosé*, or single-vineyard Champagnes are not included above, but are recommended under their respective headings. For those who might wonder about the absence of Krug Vintage, it was a matter of juggling the top 10 selections, so I have included that under Vintage Brut.

SINGLE VINEYARD
Non-vintage and vintage

Although the winemakers of Champagne are gradually becoming aware of the concept of single-vineyard sparkling wines, it is only a handful of houses that are doing this and not the growers, who are those best equipped to take advantage of and promote the concept of wines that are expressive of *terroir*. The trio of non-vintage single-vineyard Champagnes sold under Leclerc-Briant's Les Authentiques label have not lived up to their initial promise, and only one of Moët's three single-vineyard *grand cru* Champagnes stands out, but keep your eye out for Lenoble's non-vintage Cuvée Les Aventures, which might, if the initial 1990/5/6 blend is anything to go by. Billecart-Salmon's Les Clos St-Hilaire is very good, but needs a *dosage* to achieve a listing below.

🏆 **Non-vintage** *Cattier* (Clos du Moulin) • *Taittinger* (Les Folies de la Marquetterie) • **Vintage** *Billecart-Salmon* (Clos Saint Hilaire) • *Drappier* (Grande Sendrée Brut and Rosé) • *Krug* (Clos d'Ambonnay, Clos du Mesnil) • *Philipponnat* (Clos des Goisses, Clos des Goisses Juste Rosé)

COTEAUX CHAMPENOIS AOC
Non-vintage and vintage

The still wines (red, white, and rosé) that are produced in Champagne are low in quality and high in price. The white and rosé are the least interesting, although with modern technology they should be more successful in a fresh, easy-to-drink style. Château Saran from Moët & Chandon is a Coteaux Champenois *blanc* that has to achieve a certain minimum standard, since it comes from some of the vines reserved for Dom Pérignon, which is a 50/50 blend; thus, for every bottle of Château Saran produced, two bottles of Dom Pérignon must be sacrificed! Regrettably, the minimum standard is not that special, and, although it is a nice enough, smooth, dry white wine when released, it does not improve after a year in bottle.

Although Champagne's notorious climate is very punishing on those who try to make a red wine every year, it is the Coteaux Champenois rouge that can be the most fascinating of all. Black grapes rarely ripen sufficiently to obtain a good colour without over-extraction, which merely brings out the harsh, unripe tannins. Most reds are, therefore, light- to medium-bodied wines that barely hint at the flush of fruit found in a good Burgundy at the most basic level.

However, the all-too-rare exceptions can be singly impressive in their deep colour and rich fruit. Such wines often have a slightly smoky style distinctly reminiscent of Pinot Noir. Bouzy is the most famous of these wines, but a good vintage rarely occurs in the same village more than once in 10 years and various other growths can be just as good. The best reds from a successful vintage in

Ambonnay, Aÿ, or any other winegrowing village in Champagne can certainly be compared to Bouzy.

Because of this intrinsic unreliability, it is impossible to recommend any Coteaux Champenois on a regular basis. However, virtually all the famous houses have a bottle or two of an amazing rouge – usually Bouzy from venerable vintages such as 1929, 1947, or 1959 – but their current commercial bottlings are usually pretty mediocre. Bollinger is the exception, with a *barrique*-matured Aÿ rouge from the *lieu-dit* La Côte aux Enfants, which consistently tries hard, even if it is more successful in some years than others. Joseph Perrier's Cumières Rouge is also worth keeping an eye on. I cannot in all honesty list a top 10 of such a variable product, but to give readers a starting point, in addition to La Côte aux Enfants listed below and Joseph Perrier's Cumières Rouge already mentioned, the Coteaux Champenois I have had most joy from over the years include Paul Bara (Bouzy), Edmond Barnault (Bouzy), André Clouet (Bouzy), Denois (Cumières), Paul Déthune (Ambonnay), Egly-Ouriet (Bouzy), Fresnet-Baudot (Sillery), Gatinois (Aÿ), René Geoffroy (Cumières), Gosset-Brabant (Aÿ), Patrick Soutiran (Ambonnay), and Emmanuel Tassin (Celles-sur-Ource). The largest producer of Coteaux Champenois in all three denominations is Laurent Perrier, but the quality is seldom more exciting than acceptable.

🍷 *Bollinger* (La Côte aux Enfants)

RATAFIA AOC

This *vin de liqueur* is made in the same fashion as Pineau des Charentes AOC (*see* p249), by adding neutral spirit to unfermented grape juice. The only Ratafia I have found outstanding in 30 years of tasting has been Janisson Baradon 2005 Single-Cask, which, although brown in colour and not particularly limpid, possessed an incredible taste of pure chocolate and was a delight to drink.

ROSÉ DES RICEYS AOC

This is not part of the Coteaux Champenois AOC, but is a totally separate appellation. This pure Pinot Noir, still, pink wine is made in the commune of Les Riceys in the Aube *département* and is something of a legend locally, its fame dating back to the 17th century and Louis XIV, who is said to have served it as often as he could. It should be dark pink, medium bodied, and aromatic. The best are often reminiscent of chocolate, herbs, and even mint, and can possess a penetrating, fruity flavour with a long, smooth finish. Production has greatly increased in recent years, with even Vranken, the most commercial of commercial houses, producing one, but quality is erratic, and I have never tasted an example anywhere near Horiot's 1971. Also try Veuve A Devaux, Gallimard, and Morel – but be prepared for more disappointments than successes.

🍷 *Horiot*

THE WINE PRODUCERS OF

CHAMPAGNE

Notes

GM Former *grande marque*
NV Non-vintage
V Vintage
PC Prestige *cuvée* (*see* p224)
SV Single vineyard

Where "entire range" is recommended, this applies to Champagne only, not to Coteaux Champenois.

ACE OF SPADES

See Armand de Brignac

ALLIANCE CHAMPAGNE

Created in 1998, Alliance Champagne today consists of associated *coopératives* with a combined ownership of 2,400 hectares (6,000 acres): Coopérative Générale des Vignerons in Aÿ-Champagne (aka COGEVI, the primary brand of which is Champagne Collet); Coopérative de la Vallée de la Marne in Château-Thierry (aka COVAMA, the primary brand of which is Champagne Pannier); and Union Auboise (the primary brand of which is Champagne Vve Devaux). The purpose of this alliance is to assure grape supplies from all major districts in the region for the shared Alliance brand of Champagne Jacquart and for any BOB order that might otherwise be difficult for one cooperative to fulfil.

ANGEL

8 rue Piper
51100 Reims

This is promoted by singer Mariah Carey, who is also a minor shareholder in Champagne Angel, which was established by Stefano Zagni, the creative mind behind the brand. Three *cuvées* are sold: NV Brut ($980), NV Rosé ($1,019), and Vintage ($1,764). I'm not sure how much the leather tubes with diamond-encrusted screw heads and silver bases and tops are worth, but with a magnum of "12-year-old vintage" inside, it will knock you back a cool quarter of a million US dollars. These Champagnes are produced mostly from grapes grown at Bouzy, Cramant, and Mesnil-sur-Oger and vinified at CRVC (the *coopérative* that produces Champagne De Castelnau) in Reims. The non-vintage at the time of writing is a blend of 15% 1996, 15% 1998, 60% 2002, and 10% 2004.

ANGEL DUST

A non-vintage *blanc de blancs* from Michel Gonet, with no connection to the Champagne Angel associated with Mariah Carey.

AGRAPART

57 avenue Jean Jaures
51190 Avize
☆

Malolactic can show through at times, but there is no doubting the creamy-walnut complexity of Agrapart's single vineyard Vénus, although its Mineral and L'Avizoise *cuvées* consistently outperform it, due perhaps to its slightly higher *dosage*.

✓ *L'Avizoise* (**V**) • *Mineral* (**V**)

ARLAUX

20 rue de la Vigne du Roi
51390 Vrigny
☆Ⓥ

A good value non-vintage, but the vintage is more hit-and-miss.

✓ *Brut* (**NV**)

MICHEL ARNOULD

28 rue de Mailly
51360 Verzenay
★Ⓥ

A specialist in pure Verzenay Champagne, including a very rich but exquisitely balanced *blanc de noirs* Grand Cru Brut Réserve.

✓ *Grand Cru Brut* (**NV**) • *Grand Cru Brut Rosé* (**NV**) • *Grand Cru Brut Réserve* (**NV**) • *Memoire des Vignes* (**V**)

AYALA & CO (GM)

Château d'Aÿ
51160 Aÿ-Champagne
★☆Ⓥ

Now owned by Bollinger, Ayala is under the direct control of Hervé Augustin, former head of De Castellane, who has successfully raised the profile of this house by specializing in the low-/no-*dosage* style, although *brut* still represents the majority of sales. The 2001 Perle d'Ayala has a stunning intensity of fruit for such a dilute year.

✓ *Brut Millésime* (**V**) • *Perle d'Ayala* (**V**) • *Perle d'Ayala Brut Nature* (**V**)

PAUL BARA

4 rue Yvonnet
51150 Bouzy
★

Grower Champagnes that are always made with the pure expression of the richness of Bouzy.

✓ *Millésimé* (**V**) • *Spécial Club* (**V**)

BARONS DE ROTHSCHILD

2 rue Camille Lenoir
51100 Reims
☆

These well-made Champagnes are sold with the heavy premium of the Rothschild imprimatur. All three wine branches of the Rothschild dynasty put their historical differences to one side to form this joint venture in 2005 in collaboration with the Goutte d'Or *coopérative* in Vertus, where the wines are made. There are currently three non-vintage styles: Brut (50% Chardonnay, 50% Pinot Noir); Blanc de Blancs, and a rosé (85% Chardonnay, 15% Pinot Noir).

✓ *Entire range*

LOUIS BARTHELEMY

1 rue des Côtelles
51200 Epernay
★

This promising new Champagne producer is under the same Chancel family ownership as Domaine Val-Joannis in the Côtes du Lubéron.

✓ *Brut Améthyste* (**NV**) • *Pink Brut* (**NV**)

BCC

See Lanson-BCC

ANDRÉ & JACQUES BEAUFORT

1 rue de Vaudemanges
51150 Ambonnay
☆Ⓑ

This grower specializes in offering many different mature vintages for all of his vintaged *cuvées*. I've tasted some weird older vintages from here, but I have not tasted comprehensively through all the years on offer, so do not let me put you off. All bottles (not just mature vintages) carry the date of disgorgement. This is also one of the few to produce a true *doux* Champagne.

✓ *Brut Millésimé* (**V**) • *Ambonnay Doux* (**V**)

BEAUMONT DES CRAYÈRES

64 rue de la Liberté
51318 Mardeuil
☆Ⓥ

The vineyards of this cooperative are mostly of modest origin, but they are tended like gardens, without resort to machines or chemical treatments to produce richly flavoured Champagne with a light *dosage*.

✓ *Fleur de Rosé* (**V**) • *Fleur de Prestige* (**V**)

BÉRÊCHE
La Craon de Ludes
51500 Ludes
⭐

Highly rated by some, young Raphael and Vincent Bérêche have produced several stunning *cuvées*, but like many of Champagne's younger generation, there is a tendency to use low *dosage*, and whether as a result or not, the results are not always consistent when tasting the same wine at a later date. The Reflet d'Antan also has *solera*-based construction, which is not a process I find works well in Champagne. I have enjoyed the Brut Réserve most of all.

✓ *Brut Réserve* (**NV**)

BESSERAT DE BELLEFON
19 avenue de Champagne
51200 Epernay
⭐ 🅥

Although this was a favourite of mine in the 1980s, the quality began to decline in the 1990s, after it was taken over by Marne et Champagne, even though that company was capable of producing some excellent Champagnes. (I can still remember the taste of the brilliant Alfred Rothschild 1981 in magnum.) The quality pendulum has swung back the other way over the past few years, as the BCC group has begun to rationalize the stocks and production inherited from the takeover of Lanson International, which included Marne et Champagne. Now all that needs to be done is to drop the pressure of the *mousse* by 1–1.5 atmospheres to reinstate the *crémant* style this brand was built on. The term *crémant* might be illegal in Champagne, but the style certainly is not.

✓ *Cuvée des Moines Brut* (**NV**) • *Cuvée des Moines Blanc de Blancs* (**NV**) • *Cuvée des Moines Rosé* (**NV**)

BILLECART-SALMON (GM)
40 rue Carnot
51160 Mareuil-sur-Aÿ
⭐⭐

This is a small, family-owned (55% family, 45% Frey Group), *grande marque* of exceptionally high quality, but I must confess that, due to the lower *dosage* levels of these Champagnes, I enjoy them less than I used to five years ago, and I am definitely reluctant to cellar them very long.

✓ *Entire range*

BILLIOT
1 place de la Fontaine
51150 Ambonnay

Non-malolactic Champagnes that can sometimes suffer from elevated pineapple fruit.

H BLIN
5 rue de Verdun
51700 Vincelles
⭐

A good-value small cooperative.

✓ *Brut* (**NV**) • *Rosé* (**NV**)

LE BILLIONAIRE
Leon Verres Luxury Group
Sheikh Road
43630 Dubai

This was all over the Internet in 2009, when the so-called Leon Verres Luxury Group claimed to have sold four out of just five Salmanazars produced of Le Billionaire Champagne for a cool $2.75 million each, making these large-format bottles clad in diamond-studded fake fur the world's most expensive "Champagne". For those with insufficiently deep pockets for a Salmanazar, Leon Verres later offered a regular 75cl bottle for $2,750, with a choice of red, green, turquoise, or purple fake fur – all diamond-studded, of course. It was announced that Leon Verres had teamed up with The Billionaire Exchange to sell these "cheaper" bottles, and by July 2010 Leon Verres claimed to have sold out, but the Billionaire Exchange passed on only "a few enquiries". The CIVC stated that Le Billionaire Champagne trademark was "registered in 2008, crossed out a year after, and has not been used for Champagne", and there has been an uninformative response from Leon Verres's website, which appears to sell only T-shirts. Is it all a sophisticated fabrication?

BOËRL & KROFF
26 place de la Madeleine
75008 Paris

The world's most expensive buyer's-own-brand Champagne! Produced exclusively in magnums by Drappier for the owners of Boërl & Kroff, the non-vintage would set you back $5,500, and you would have to cough up $7,500 for the 1996 at the time of writing. I've tasted each wine only once. The non-vintage (70% Pinot Noir, 30% Chardonnay from Urville in the Aube) was okay but nothing special. Just fresh, light, soft, and easy-going, with no real depth or persistence. I would pay a standard big-brand non-vintage price for this wine, but no more. The 1996 (90% Pinot Noir, 7% Meunier, 3% Chardonnay, also from Urville) was a deepish colour – not browning, but with a definite butter-yellow hue – with a nose and palate that were distinctly oxidizing – not oxidative as a style, or completely oxidized – with toffee aromas dominating. The structure and depth of the vintage demonstrated that it was obviously a very interesting wine once, but tasted the very same week, Drappier's sublime 1982 and 1985 in magnum both seemed 30 years younger than Boërl & Kroff's 1996. I was told that there must have been something wrong with these samples, but I can only report on the

Champagne I tasted. Part of the cost is the presentation. Admittedly, these magnums come in beautifully lacquered boxes with exquisite hinges, and the magnums themselves sport 22-carat gold plaques, but if Boërl & Kroff is supposed to be a serious Champagne that should be cellared and consumed, not displayed as an *objet-d'art* in a warm apartment, then what are Boërl & Kroff customers expected to do with so many gold plaques and lacquered boxes?

BOIZEL
14 rue de Bernon
51200 Epernay
⭐ 🅥

Good-value Champagnes with the occasional *blanc de blancs cuvée* of amazing quality. This house is part of Lanson-BCC, in which the Roques-Boizel family are major shareholders.

✓ *Brut* (**NV**) • *Blanc de Blancs* (**NV**) • *Rosé* (**V**) • *Joyau de France* (**PC**) • *Joyau de Chardonnay* (**V**)

BOLLINGER (GM)
rue Jules Lobet
51160 Aÿ-Champagne
⭐⭐⭐

This house has always produced gems, but across the board Bollinger has become more fruit-friendly and focused in recent years. For non-vintage drinkers, Special Cuvée in magnum is the insider's secret here, while for vintage drinkers who worship post-disgorgement aromas, it will be the Grande Année, which, when cellared, rewards the buyer not only with superior quality to the RD but also far better value. However, the true jewel in Bollinger's crown is its Vieilles Vignes Françaises (*see* Blanc de Noirs, p223), the jaw-dropping quality of which often makes it the greatest Champagne of the vintage. Its price was once considered equally jaw-dropping, but although it has steadily edged upwards, it is dirt cheap compared to Krug Clos d'Ambonnay, let alone all the obscenely priced new "bling" Champagnes that have started to appear on the market. Vieilles Vignes Françaises used to be made from three tiny plots of ungrafted wines: Chaudes Terres (actually in Maison Bollinger's back garden in Aÿ), Clos St-Jacques (a walled garden, also in Aÿ, just along the road from Maison Bollinger), and Croix Rouge (on a corner just outside Bouzy). In 2004, however, the vines in Croix Rouge were decimated by phylloxera, so since 2005, Vieilles

Vignes Françaises has been made from just two plots and will therefore be pure Aÿ.

✓ *Entire range*

BONNAIRE
120 rue d'Epernay
51530 Cramant
⭐⭐ 🅥

Although occasionally spoiled by dominant malolactic or the whisper of lifted fruit, most wines are a pure joy, with beautifully focused fruit, and a luxuriantly creamy finish.

✓ *Blanc de Blancs Non-Dosé* (**NV**) • *Brut Blanc de Blancs* (**NV**) • *Cuvée Prestige* (**V**) • *Cramant Grand Cru* (**V**)

CÉDRIC BOUCHARD
See Roses de Jeanne

RAYMOND BOULARD
Route Nationale 44
51220 Cauroy-les-Hermonville
◉⭐⭐ 🅥

Run by Francis Boulard, whose style tends to be lifted fruit with oxidative complexity. Avoid the Brut Nature; these Champagnes need a *dosage*.

✓ *Cuvée Rosé Brut* (**NV**) • *Brut Tradition* (**NV**)

CHÂTEAU DE BOURSAULT
Boursault
51480 prés Epernay
⭐ 🅥

Made by owner Harald Fringhian, these Champagnes are now outperforming the château's modest 84 per cent *échelle*, which is probably helped by the fact that the vineyards are a genuine *clos* (an enclosed plot of land).

✓ *Rosé* (**NV**)

ARMAND DE BRIGNAC
6 et 11 rue Dom Pérignon
51500 Chigny-les-Roses
⭐

This brand is associated with Shawn Carter, aka Jay-Z, but belongs to Champagne Cattier. The conception process began in 2002, when Cattier was looking to break into the US market and began discussions with the Berish family, who own Sovereign Brands, the sole importer of Armand de Brignac in the USA. Four years later, Champagne Armand de Brignac was promoted by Jay-Z in the video of "Show Me What You Got", a single from his 2006 "comeback" album *Kingdom Come*. This was released just after his very public tiff with Roederer, when Jay-Z took exception to comments allegedly made by Frédéric Rouzaud, the chief executive of Louis Roederer. Jay-Z publicly dropped his beloved Cristal just weeks before his video came out showcasing Armand de Brignac, aka "Ace of Spades", and the conspiracy theorists pounced. The timing was just too much of a coincidence, they thought, and as the Berish family had already launched a vodka brand, 3Vodka, with the involvement of another rap star, Jermaine Dupri, surely Jay-Z must have some financial involvement or endorsement deal going? Well, I'm sorry to spoil a good story with the truth, but the deal with Jermaine Dupri had not even been conceived in 2002 and came to an amicable end the year before the launch of Armand de Brignac because Dupri had too many other commitments. The final nail in the conspiracy theory's coffin, according to Brett Berish, is that he would chop off a limb to have Jay-Z's formal involvement. It would be something he could use, not hide. I have tasted all three non-vintage Armand de Brignac *cuvées*, including the first two releases of the primary Brut blend. They all have a capacity to age, but they are not in the same class as Cattier's Clos du Moulin. A 30-litre bottle of Armand de Brignac fetched $100,000 when it was sold in the aptly named XS nightspot in Las Vegas in 2010.

✓ *Entire range*
(but age 1–3 years first)

BRICE
22 rue Gambetta
51150 Bouzy
★

These are stylishly presented, non-malolactic *monocru* Champagnes that can range from bizarre to brilliant. The bizarre releases can have unpleasantly odd aromas, but the brilliant releases are so exciting that they cannot be ignored. With more consistency, Brice could be a two-star Champagne.

✓ *Entire range* (with caution)

EMMANUEL BROCHET
7 Impasse Brochet
51500 Villers-aux-Noeuds
●★✰

With just 2.5 hectares (6 acres) and the same *cuvées* not necessarily produced every year, the tiny production from this highly regarded grower is much sought after. I have only tasted the Non-Dosé Le Mont Benoit, which was very pure and precise, with great minerality of fruit, but would have been so much better with a light *dosage*.

CANARD DUCHÊNE (GM)
1 rue Edmond Canard
51500 Ludes
★✰✓

Owned by Veuve Clicquot from 1978 until 2003, when it was sold to the Alain Thienot group. The Blanc

de Noirs version of Charles VII prestige *cuvée* can be serious quality, but it is inconsistent.

✓ *Brut* (**NV**) • *Rosé* (**NV**) • *Charles VII Blanc de Noirs* (**NV**)

DE CASTELLANE
57 rue Verdun
51200 Epernay
★✰

Part of the Laurent-Perrier group, this is an excellent source of under-valued, ripe, exotic *blanc de blancs*, as are the more expensive Cuvée Commodore and Cuvée Florens de Castellane.

✓ *Chardonnay* (**NV**) • *Cuvée Royale Chardonnay* (**V**) • *Cuvée Commodore* (**PC**) • *Cuvée Florens de Castellane* (**PC**)

DE CASTELNAU
5 rue Gosset
51066 Reims
★✰✓

Produced by CRVC (Coopérative Régionale des Vins de Champagne), which was the original creative force behind the Jacquart brand prior to the formation of Alliance Champagne. CRVC severed all ties with Jacquart in 2006, since when De Castelnau has become its primary focus. The 1998 vintage was very good, but the non-vintage Brut is both good value and improving.

✓ *Brut* (**NV**) • *Vintage* (**V**)

CATTIER
6 et 11 rue Dom Pérignon
51500 Chigny-les-Roses
★✰✓

The star here is Clos du Moulin, Cattier's great single-vineyard Champagne. A two-star Champagne in its own right, Clos du Moulin is a blend of three vintage years (indicated on the back label). *See also* Armand de Brignac.

✓ *Brut* (**V**) • *Clos du Moulin* (**SV**)

CHANOINE
avenue de Champagne
51100 Reims
★✰✓

This marque was established in 1730 (just one year after Ruinart, the oldest house in Champagne) but was relaunched by Philippe Baijot in 1991 and formed, with Bruno Paillard's Champenoise des Grands Vins, the fledgling beginnings of what quickly became BCC, now Lanson-BCC. The vintaged Tsarine *cuvées* are top quality, and the exquisite Tsarina, launched in 2010, is even more exciting.

✓ *Tsarina* (**NV**) • *Tsarine* (**NV**) • *Tsarine* (**V**)

CHAPUY
rue de Champagne
51190 Oger
★

The presentation might be disappointingly 1950s, but there is nothing disappointing about the rich, yeast-complexed Champagne inside

the bottle. Chapuy consistently makes outstanding Brut Réserve Blanc de Blancs Grand Cru, and, particularly, Livrée Noire.

✓ *Brut Réserve Grand Cru* (**V**) • *Livrée Noire* (**V**)

GUY CHARLEMAGNE
4 rue de la Brèche d'Oger
51190 Le Mesnil-sur-Oger
★

The top-of-the-range Mesnillésime is the one to go for here. Typically rich and exuberant in its youth before tightening up in bottle, this Champagne emerges with even greater intensity after several years of cellaring under ideal conditions.

✓ *Mesnillésime*

CHARTOGNE-TAILLET
37-39 Grande Rue
51220 Merfy
★✓

While Merfy is very modest *terroir*, it should not be forgotten that most New World sparkling-wine producers would love to grow grapes anywhere in Champagne, and Elisabeth and Philippe Chartogne work hard to squeeze every morsel of potential from their vines. The Fiacre Tête de Cuvée has bold flavours, high acids, and typically goes toasty-walnutty, while the vintage stands out for its value, complexity, and finesse.

✓ *Brut* (**V**) • *Fiacre Tête de Cuvée* (**NV**)

CHAUVET
41 avenue de Champagne
51150 Tours-sur-Marne
★★✰✓

A small, quality-conscious house situated opposite Laurent Perrier, Chauvet is possibly the most unknown or under-rated producer in Champagne.

✓ *Entire range*

GASTON CHIQUET
890-912 avenue du Général-Leclerc
51310 Dizy
★★✓

Antoine and Nicolas Chiquet are grower cousins of *négociants* Jean-Hervé and Laurent Chiquet of Jacquesson, which is also in Dizy. The style here is succulent and creamy, with moreish juicy fruit.

✓ *Entire range*

ANDRÉ CLOUET
8 rue Gambetta
51150 Bouzy
★

André Clouet, a small, quality-conscious grower, produces a very large range of attractive, rich, and beautifully made Champagnes.

✓ *Brut Grande Réserve* (**NV**) • *Brut Millésime* (**V**)

COLLET
14 boulevard Pasteur
51160 Aÿ-Champagne

Capable of producing premium-quality, classic non-vintage Champagne.

✓ *Blanc de Blancs* (**NV**) • *Brut Grand Art* (**NV**)

COMTE AUDOIN DE DAMPIERRE
5 Grande Rue
51140 Chenay
★✓

This Anglophile, lovingly eccentric, classic car fanatic of an aristocrat is one of those larger-than-life characters who are simply too charming and polite to ignore. Elegant and fruity, most *cuvées* are nicely made for current drinking, but the best vintages age well.

✓ *Entire range*

DEHOURS
1-2 rue de la Chapelle
51700 Cerseuil
★

It is almost impossible to imagine, but Jérôme Dehours once sold one million bottles a year under his family brand until it was half-subsumed by the Frey Group. Now this boutique Champagne house specializes in low- and no-*dosage lieu-dit* Champagne. The Brisefer Collection Extra Brut is perhaps the most successful, although it, along with the others, would age far more gracefully with a good *brut dosage*. Check out the large range of *lieu-dit* Coteaux Champenois.

DEHU
3 rue Saint George
02650 Fossoy
★

This environmentally friendly, family-owned concern produces Champagnes that are worth keeping an eye on. I am surprised why I have been impressed by the Extra Brut Tradition but not the Tradition Brut.

✓ *Cuvée Léon L'Hermitte* (**NV**) • *Extra Brut Tradition* (**NV**) • *Rosé Prestige* (**NV**)

DELAMOTTE PÈRE & FILS
5 rue de la Brèche
51190 Le Mesnil-sur-Oger
★✓

Part of the Laurent-Perrier group and situated next door to Champagne Salon, which also belongs to Laurent-Perrier, Delamotte is a small, under-rated, high-quality, good-value house that has been privately owned by the

Nonancourt family (the owners of Laurent-Perrier) since the end of World War I, when it was purchased by Marie Louise de Nonancourt, the sister of Victor and Henri Lanson.

✓ *Brut* (**NV**) • *Blanc de Blancs* (**NV**) • *Blanc de Blancs* (**V**) • *Nicolas Louis Delamotte* (**PC**)

PAUL DÉTHUNE

2 rue du Moulin
51150 Ambonnay
★★✪✪

As one of the more consistent growers, Paul Déthune always makes good vintage and rosé, but is best known for his prestige *cuvée*, the luxuriously rich, big, deliciously creamy Princesse des Thunes, which is made from an assemblage of mature vintages.

✓ *Grand Cru Rosé* (**NV**) • *Millésimé* (**V**) • *Trilogy* (**V**) • *Princesse des Thunes* (**PC**)

DEUTZ (GM)

16 rue Jeanson
51160 Aÿ-Champagne
★★★✪✪

On stunning form for two decades, Deutz produces Champagnes of sleek and stylish proportions that are totally different in style from those of Roederer, its parent company, yet very much equal in quality.

✓ *Entire range*

DOSNON

4 *bis* rue du Bas de Lingey
10340 Avirey-Lingey
★★

Although some *cuvées* can be under-dosaged, all the Champagnes from this recently established, small *négociant* are impeccably produced. The Récolte Noire, a pure Pinot Noir *blanc de noirs*, is the standout, but the Rosé can be gorgeous. Often referred to as Dosnon & Lepage.

✓ *Récolte Noir* (**NV**) • *Récolte Rosé* (**NV**)

DOYARD

39 avenue du Général Leclerc
51130 Vertus
★

Richly styled wines with a partial and well-integrated use of oak. Yannick Doyard's Vendémaire Extra Brut is one of those rare Champagnes that is perfectly balanced with a low *dosage* when released. Well, more times than not. The Brut Vendémaire is, however, superior for cellaring. His La Libertine is also one of the very few true *doux* Champagnes currently made.

✓ *Cuvée Vendémaire Brut* (**NV**) • *Cuvée Vendémaire Extra Brut* (**NV**) • *La Libertine Doux* (**V**)

DOYARD-MAHÉ

Le Moulin d'Argensole
51130 Vertus
★

An exceptional 2004-based Carte d'Or Blanc de Blancs Extra Brut in 2010.

DRAPPIER

Grande Rue
10200 Urville
★★✪✪

Drappier's Champagnes are brilliantly consistent, ultra-fruity, and rapidly acquire mellow biscuity complexity. Drappier came equal second in *The World of Fine Wine*'s 1982 vs. 1985 tasting in 2010, and I personally rated its 1982 and 1985 equal first, but with 40 wines (20 pairs of these two vintages) from the good and the great – including names such as Billecart-Salmon, Bollinger, Comtes de Champagne, Salon, *et al* – to get both vintages anywhere near the top would be an amazing achievement.

✓ *Entire range*

J DUMANGIN

3 rue de Rilly
51500 Chigny-les-Roses
★✪✪

Run by Gilles Dumangin, who makes soft, fruit-driven Champagnes that tend to go biscuity rather than, or as well as, toasty. The vintage *cuvée* has gained in finesse from 1998 on, but I'm not so keen on the range of older vintages on offer.

✓ *Brut* (**V**) • *Brut Grande Réserve* (**NV**) • *Extra Brut* (**NV**)

DUVAL-LEROY

65 avenue de Bammental
51130 Vertus
★★✪✪

Duval-Leroy has achieved a great consistency of quality for its fresh, light, and elegant house style. With single vineyard *cuvées*, dabbling with oak, and a seriously high-class prestige *cuvée* (Femme), there is an interesting choice from this forward-thinking producer. Although the production is not exclusively organic, Duval-Leroy's collaboration with organic and biodynamic growers makes this one of the 10 largest organic producers in Champagne.

✓ *Entire range*

EGLY-OURIET

9-15 rue de Trépail
51150 Ambonnay

The very rich, theoretically top-drawer quality of the raw material here is let down by a low *dosage* regime that results in far too many oxidative notes. Some *cuvées* can look quite dark.

NICOLAS FEUILLATTE

CV de Chouilly
51206 Chouilly
★✪✪

Some of this giant cooperative's customers seem to be under the impression that Nicolas Feuillatte is a small, lone grower. The guy exists, but he just represents this super-cooperative brand. As readers will know, I'm not the greatest fan of low- or no-*dosage cuvées* or the use of new oak in Champagne, but in 2010 I was blown away by Nicolas Feuillatte's Brut Extrem and Cuvée 225. Fingers crossed that the quality of those two *cuvées* can be maintained.

✓ *Cuvée Speciale* (**V**) • *Palmes d'Or* (**V**) • *Palmes d'Or Rosé* (**V**)

FLEURY

43 Grande Rue
10250 Courteron
Ⓑ★✪✪

One of the more readily available biodynamic Champagnes on export markets, Fleury was nothing more than acceptable until the 1996 vintage, when this grower produced a classic *barrique*-fermented Champagne with a mind-blowing barrage of aromas and flavours.

✓ *Brut* (**V**) • *Blanc de Blancs Doux* (**V**) • *Fleur de l'Europe Brut* (**NV**)

FLUTEAU

5 rue de la Nation
10250 Gyé-sur-Seine
★✪✪

Thierry Fluteau and his American wife Jennifer tend to release their Champagnes one year ahead of most others, when they are very fruity and easy to drink. Vintaged *cuvées* are worth keeping and should be purchased in magnums, which are at their beautiful best in their seventh or eighth year.

✓ *Entire range*

GARDET & CIE

13 rue Georges Legros
51500 Chigny-les-Roses
★✪✪

This Champagne used to be sold as Georges Gardet in the UK and Charles Gardet in France, but the emphasis is now on Gardet plain and simple. Gardet has always prided itself on the longevity of its wines, but I prefer the vintage almost before it is even released.

✓ *Brut Spécial* (**NV**) • *Brut* (**V**) • *Blanc de Blancs* (**V**)

GATINOIS

7 rue Marcel Mailly
51160 Aÿ-Champagne
★

Pierre Cheval's pure Pinot Noir Grand Cru Réserve is the non-vintage to go for here, as the Grand Cru Tradition is invariably sold too young. Even so, it pays to age even the Réserve. Classic vintage.

✓ *Grand Cru Réserve* (**NV**) • *Grand Cru Brut Millésimé* (**V**)

RENÉ GEOFFROY

150 rue du Bois-des-Jots
51480 Cumières
★✪✪

These Champagnes do not go through malolactic fermentation and may be matured in oak *foudres*, are classic in style, long-lived, and capable of great complexity.

✓ *Brut Rosé* (**NV**) • *Cuvée Prestige* (**NV**) • *Cuvée de Réserve Brut* (**NV**) • *Cuvée Sélectionnée Brut* (**V**) • *Millésime Extra Brut* (**V**)

PIERRE GIMONNET

1 rue de la République
51530 Cuis
★★✪✪

This excellent grower's vineyards are all planted with Chardonnay, hence every wine is a *blanc de blancs*, which is a very rare phenomenon, even among growers on the Côte des Blancs. Quality is exceptionally high and prices very reasonable.

✓ *Entire range*

HENRI GIRAUD

71 boulevard Charles de Gaulle
51160 Aÿ-Champagne

Having been one of the first to acknowledge the extraordinary quality of Henri Giraud's 1993 Grand Cru Fût de Chêne Brut, I am as disappointed as anyone that he has not been able to replicate that quality. The Esprit Brut and Rosé failed to achieve even a "commended" at the *Decanter* World Wine Awards.

✓ *Code Noir* (*blanc* only)

PAUL GOERG

4 place du Mont Chenil
51130 Vertus
★✪✪

This small but superior *coopérative* produces very fine and elegant, yet rich, concentrated Champagnes.

✓ *Blanc de Blancs* (**NV**) • *Brut* (**V**) • *Cuvée Lady C* (**V**)

PHILIPPE GONET

1 rue de la Brèche d'Oger
51190 Le-Mesnil-sur-Oger

Fewer highlights among the vintages since the 1990s, but the non-vintaged Roy Soleil Grand Cru is consistently excellent.

✓ *Roy Soleil Grand Cru* (**NV**)

GONET-MÉDEVILLE

1 chemin de la Cavotte
51150 Bisseuil
★

A marriage between two artisanal families, the Gonets of Champagne and the Médevilles of Sauternes (Château Gilette *et al*). The most consistent performer here is the non-vintage Blanc de Noirs, which is very good and a significant step up from the Tradition, but it could be even better with another 2–3 grams of residual sugar. If the 2000 vintage is anything to go by, the Cuvée Théophile has the potential to be a truly great Champagne, but it is held back by its minuscule *dosage*. This is, however, a very young estate, and it will be interesting to see how it develops.

✓ *Blanc de Noirs* (**NV**)

GOSSET (GM)
69 rue Jules Blondeau
51160 Aÿ-Champagne
★★★✫ **V**

Established in 1584, Gosset is the oldest house in the region, but for still wines, not sparkling. At just 3.5 grams per litre, the *dosage* for the top-of-the-range Celebris Brut, Rosé, and Blanc de Blancs is precariously low, which is a pity, because the quality is so high that they really should be cellared. The one that works best, particularly at the table, is the non-vintage Celebris Blanc de Blancs, probably because it is a blend of several mature vintages (1999, 1998, 1996, and 1995 at the time of writing), but I have stopped cellaring it.

✓ *Entire range* (except Brut Excellence)

HENRI GOUTORBE
11 rue Jeanson
51160 Aÿ-Champagne
★★ **V**

With 15 hectares (37 acres) of vineyards and half a million bottles in stock, this is one of the larger wine growers. Henri Goutorbe produces some rich, classic, and well-structured Champagnes that become very satisfying with age.

✓ *Entire range*

ALFRED GRATIEN
30 rue Maurice-Cerveaux
51201 Epernay
★★★

This house is part of Gratien, Meyer, Seydoux & Cie, who also sell a range of Loire traditional method wines under the Gratien & Meyer brand. Alfred Gratien is one of the most traditionally produced Champagnes available. The old vintages never fail to amaze, as they are brilliant in quality and retain a remarkable freshness for decades. The non-vintage wine is beautifully fresh with mature reserves coming through on the palate, making it a wine to drink now, yet one that will improve with age.

✓ *Vintage Brut*

HEIDSIECK & CO MONOPOLE (GM)
17 avenue de Champagne
51205 Epernay
★✫ **V**

Part of the Vranken empire, this was to be his jewel in the crown until the Belgian financial wizard got his hands on Pommery, so now it plays a definite second fiddle, but that can be to our advantage in terms of value.

✓ *Silver Top* (**V**) • *Gold Top* (**V**) • *Prestige Top* (**V**)

CHARLES HEIDSIECK (GM)
12 allée du Vignoble
51061 Reims
★★★ **V**

At the time of writing, Rémy-Cointreau had put its Champagne group (Charles Heidsieck and Piper-Heidsieck) up for sale. The beginning of the new millennium is a crucial juncture in the commercial development of Champagne that could see the new owners either make or break both brands. Hopefully they won't be absorbed by another larger group – or, worse, have their vineyards asset-stripped and the brands sold on – because both are poised on the threshold of exceptional success. The superb quality reputation of Charles Heidsieck was masterminded by the late Daniel Thibault, one of Champagne's greatest winemakers, and the legacy he left has been ably maintained by his successor, Regis Camus. If you ask the heads of other houses which competitor's Champagne they would order if their own brand was not on a wine list, many of them would say Charles Heidsieck. When these Champagnes go head to head with the rising stars of the younger generation of grower Champagnes under blind conditions in competitions such as the *Decanter* World Wine Awards and the International Wine & Spirit Competition, the Champagnes of Charles Heidsieck put them in their place every time.

✓ *Entire range*

HENRIOT
3 place des Droits-de-l'Homme
51100 Reims
★

Under family ownership since 1994, when Joseph Henriot left Clicquot, the house he had famously performed a reverse-takeover on

prior to the formation of LVMH. Apart from the fact that the Enchanteleurs is more often than not released far too late, there is not much to criticize here.

✓ *Cuvée des Enchanteleurs* (**V**) • *Brut Millésime* (**V**) • *Blanc de Blancs Brut* (**NV**)

HORIOT PÈRE & FILS
10340 Les Riceys Bas

The 1971 Rosé des Riceys was the only truly great example of this AOC I have ever tasted.

OLIVIER HORIOT
25 rue de Bise
10340 Les Riceys Bas
★ **V**

A member of the local cooperative, whose blended Champagne Olivier sells under the Serge Horiot brand, while his own Champagnes and the increasingly more refined Rosé des Riceys, made exclusively from and by this small estate, are all sold under the Olivier Horiot label, which has become sought after.

✓ *Esquisse de Rosé des Riceys*

SERGE HORIOT
See Olivier Horiot

JACQUART
34 boulevard Lundy
51100 Reims
★★✫ **V**

A *coopérative* that cleverly converted its primary brand into a *négociant-manipulant* Champagne by making its members shareholders. The Jacquart brand is now fully owned by Alliance Champagne, a commercial grouping of three cooperatives: COGEVI (aka Collet), which produces the vintage, *blanc de blancs* and premium Jacquart styles; COVAMA (aka Pannier), which contributes to the blend of Nominée and some Mosaïque and Tradition *cuvées*; and Union Auboise (aka Vve Devaux), which primarily produces Jacquart rosé *cuvées* but also contributes to it Mosaïque and Tradition blends. The quality of Jacquart is under-rated; it is always acceptable at the very least, and some *cuvées* can be outstanding. These Champagnes should not be under-estimated just because they are cooperative-produced. When Jacquart submits its Champagnes to the *Decanter* World Wine Awards, they usually win several gold medals.

✓ *Allegra* (**V**) • *Brut de Nominée* (**NV**) • *Cuvée Katarina* (**NV**) • *Cuvée Mosaïque Brut* (**V**) • *Cuvée Mosaïque Blanc de Blancs* (**V**) • *Cuvée Mosaïque Rosé* (**V**) • *Cuvée Onctueuse Rosé* (**NV**) • *Rosé Grand Millésime* (**V**)

ANDRÉ JACQUART
63 avenue de Bammental
51130 Vertus
★★

Since launching the new highly-focused range, the Doyard-Jacquart family has become one of the very

best producers of low-*dosage* Champagnes, with results that are as precise and pure as the sleek presentation of their bottles suggests. If I have any criticism, it is purely constructive: to produce at least one traditional *brut dosage* (preferably a version of Mesnil Experience), so that consumers like me might have the confidence to cellar the wine for 20 years or more. This level of quality deserves that level of respect.

✓ *Entire range*

JACQUESSON & FILS
68 rue du Colonel Fabien
51310 Dizy
★★

This small, family-owned house is run by the Chiquet brothers, two of the most charming people you are likely to meet. Jacquesson has pioneered various quality-enhancing practices in the vineyards, while in the winery it has turned Champagne's traditional non-vintage concept on its head by not attempting any consistency in style. Rather than smooth out the differences presented by each harvest, the new concept is to produce the best possible non-vintage Champagne each year. It is something that no large *grande marque* would dare contemplate, but it is a very clever move for a small house, as it effectively creates a second vintage wine and one that is easier to make, given the flexibility of blending in wine from other years.

✓ *Entire range*

JACQUINOT
34-36 rue Maurice Cerveaux
51202 Epernay

Jean-Manuel Jacquinot's biggest claim to fame is his association with Nyetimber in England, which is essentially why he was hired as the official "mentor" to English sparkling-wine producers in preference to world-class sparkling-wine consultants. I have not tasted a memorable Champagne Jacquinot since the 1990 Symphony Brut Grande Réserve, and that was just good, not exceptional.

ANDRÉ JARRY
Rue Principale
51260 Bethon
★ **V**

Excellent Champagne in a style that is midway between the classic character of Champagnes from the Marne *département* and the exotic character of Sézannais Champagnes, full of biscuity richness yet with an aftertaste of vanilla and peaches.

✓ *Cuvée Special* (**NV**)

KRUG & CO (GM)
5 rue Coquebert
51051 Reims
★★★

Krug puts quality first and makes Champagne in its own individual style, regardless of popular taste or

production costs. This sort of quality is not equalled by any other Champagne house, although it could be if they were willing to sell tiny quantities at very high prices. However, if everyone did this, it would be a disaster – Champagne has to be affordable – but that at least one house does is not just laudable, it is very important for Champagne. Up to a point, that is, and that point was reached in May 2008, when Krug released its Clos d'Ambonnay at a suggested retail price of $3,500 per bottle. At the same time, Krug's 1995 Clos du Mesnil was selling for $725, while just three vintages earlier, the 1989 had sold for $210 and it vied with Bollinger's Vieilles Vignes Françaises as the world's most expensive Champagne. Is it Krug's fault that Champagne is now littered with "bling" that commands prices that make these true artisanal masterpieces look cheap by comparison? Clos d'Ambonnay is great Champagne, but it is not as good as Clos du Mesnil, and only some vintages of Clos du Mesnil have come close to challenging the quality of Krug Vintage. Krug goes to pains to explain that it prices its Champagnes not according to quality but to quantity: the less available, the more it costs. Well, if I purchased according to quantity, and was offered one bottle of Clos d'Ambonnay, two bottles of Clos du Mesnil, or 10 bottles of Krug Vintage, I know which I would pick: 10 bottles of the best Champagne!

✓ *Entire range*

BENOÎT LAHAYE
33 rue Jeanne d'Arc
51150 Bouzy
Ⓞ

I have found strangely exotic aromas on a number of these well-reputed Champagnes, but I have also enjoyed the Rosé de Macération and Bouzy Rouge.

LAHERTE
3 rue des Jardins
51530 Chavot

After a run of fairly disappointingly oxidative Champagnes from this producer, I was impressed by the richness of the 2004 Prestige Brut and the intensity and minerality of the 2004 Les Vignes d'Autrefois.

LANSON-BCC

Formerly known as BCC, the Lanson-BCC group is one of the industry's youngest and most dynamic companies, comprising Lanson, Boizel, Chanoine (including

Tsarine), Philipponnat, De Venoge, Besserat de Bellefon, Alexander Bonnet (including Ferdinand Bonnet), and Maison Burtin (including hundreds of *sous marques*). Bruno Paillard is the chairman of BCC, and the Paillard family are, directly and indirectly, the largest shareholders in this publicly quoted company, although Champagne Bruno Paillard is not part of the Lanson-BCC group itself. Philippe Baijot (chairman of Lanson) and the Roques-Boizel family (*see* Boizel) are the two other major shareholders, each owning more than the total combined public shareholding.

LANSON PÈRE & FILS (GM)
12 boulevard Lundy
51056 Reims
★★Ⓥ

Purchased in 1991 by Marne et Champagne and now owned by Lanson-BCC, this house famously eschews malolactic, excelling at classic, slow-maturing, biscuity vintage Champagnes. Indeed, Lanson is the only large-volume *grande marque* to have remained true to Champagne's historic non-malolactic style. However, if this region's growing season continues to warm up, non-malolactic could once again be the norm instead of the exception in Champagne. A new addition to the range and already one of my all-time favourite Champagnes is Extra Age. Launched in 2010 to celebrate Lanson's 250th anniversary, Extra Age is a stylishly presented blend (60% Pinot Noir, 40% Chardonnay) from five *grands crus*, one *premier cru*, and three vintages (1999, 2000, and 2003 for the first release).

✓ *Entire range*

GUY LARMANDIER
30 rue du Général Koenig
51130 Vertus
★

Guy and François Larmandier have a well-earned reputation for finely balanced wines of surprising depth and obvious finesse.

✓ *Blanc de Blancs Cramant* (NV)

LARMANDIER-BERNIER
43 rue du 28 août
51130 Vertus
Ⓑ★

These high-quality *blanc de blancs* Champagnes are made by Pierre Larmandier, who is proving to be one of the better producers of *extra brut*.

✓ *Entire range*

JACQUES LASSAIGNE
7 chemin du Coteaux
10300 Montgueux

The stylishly presented Champagnes from this highly regarded producer are enjoyable on purchase but require a more effective *dosage* if you are thinking of cellaring.

LAURENT-PERRIER (GM)
Avenue de Champagne
51150 Tours-sur-Marne
★★Ⓥ

With the sad loss in 2010 of Bernard de Nonancourt, one of the great figures of the Champagne industry, ownership of this *grande marque* passed to his daughters Alexandra and Stéphanie. The greatest wines here are the Grand Siècle Brut and Grand Siècle Alexandra (named after one of the daughters), but the cash cow is Cuvée Rosé Brut, with its famous "*Financial Times*" pink" label. The Cuvée Rosé Brut is okay, especially in magnums and given a couple of years' additional ageing, but it is not special. Not that anyone's opinion of the quality matters for a Champagne that flies off the shelf. With focus of attention on Grand Siècle and Cuvée Rosé Brut, the vintage is consistently overlooked and under-rated, and when the Brut L-P is on form, it can be very good (as in 2006 and 2010, for example).

✓ *Entire range* (except Ultra Brut)

DAVID LECLAPART
10 rue de la Mairie
51380 Trépail
Ⓑ

With no or low *dosage* and a minimal sulphur regime, these Champagnes can show great minerality when released, but they age too oxidatively for me.

LECLERC BRIANT
67 rue de la Chaude-Ruelle
51204 Epernay
ⒷⓋ

Pascal Leclerc-Briant sadly passed away in 2010, just as the quality of his Champagnes was beginning to turn the corner. Although he was the first to produce an entire range of single-vineyard Champagnes, the concept was always far better than the content. Quality has often been variable. His Rubis Noir, for example, was always so dark it should have been described as red, not rosé, and most *cuvées* were as clumsy as they looked. Yet in some years, the fruit could be so pure Pinot that it was irresistible (the *cuvée* sold in 2005 being the last, as far as I can remember). Sometimes the malolactic was just too heavy-handed – the 2002 Divine, for example, only for the 2004 Divine to be, well, divine. Just before Pascal's death at 60 years of age, I got the impression that, having made such an effort converting all of his vineyards to biodynamic agriculture, he was acutely aware that he needed to refine his winemaking style and was in the process of doing just that. If so, we won't be sure until more Champagnes are released, but hopefully they will be an apt tribute to one of Champagne's larger-than-life characters.

✓ *Divine* (PC)

MARIE-NOËLLE LEDRU
5 place de la Croix
51150 Ambonnay
★

Although the Ambonnay Brut Nature and Extra Brut are very good, they are wasted at these levels of *dosage*, as they have the

---

MORE GREEN CHAMPAGNES

In addition to the few Champagnes listed in this directory that are biodynamic or organic, there are also the following. No negative inference of quality should be taken from the fact that they are not featured among the recommended Champagne producers. The truth is that there are over 12,500 brands, and I have no experience of the Champagnes produced by many of the following.

Biodynamic
Champagne Barbichon (Gýe-sur-Seine)
Champagne Françoise Bedel (Crouttes-sur-Marne)
Champagne Vincent Bliard (Hautvillers)
Champagne Thierry Demarne (Villé-sur-Arce)
Champagne Réaut-Noirot (Courteron)
Champagne Ruffin (Avenay)

Organic
Champagne José Ardinat (Vandières)
Champagne Bénard-Pitois (Mareuil-sur-Aÿ)
Champagne Jean Bliard (Hautvillers)

Champagne Bruno Michel (Pierry)
Champagne Couche (Buxeuil)
Champagne Doquet (Vertus)
Champagne Dufour (Landreville)
Champagne Serge Faust (Vandières)
Champagne Roger Fransoret (Mancy)
Champagne Frison de Marne (Villé-sur-Arce)
Champagne Vincent Laval (Cumières)
Champagne Lefèvre (Bonneil)
Champagne Régis Poirrier (Venteuil)
Champagne Ruffin (Avenay-Val d'Or)

structure to develop into great Champagnes of potentially impressive complexity and finesse.

LILBERT FILS
223 rue du Moutier
51200 Cramant
★

This house is a consistent producer of firm *blancs de blancs* that show finesse and age gracefully.

✓ *Entire range*

LUXOR
La Boisson en Or
11 boulevard Clémenceau
21200 Beaune

Although this is sold by some French retailers as Champagne, and the wine in the bottle is indeed Champagne, the disgorgement is carried out in Beaune by Boisson en Or, who add the 24-carat gold flakes (I'm not kidding), which is why it is labelled simply "Product of France", without any mention of Champagne.

MAILLY GRAND CRU
28 rue de la Liberation
51500 Mailly-Champagne
★☆ⓥ

The quality and innovation have been on a roll for a few years.

✓ *Cassiopée* (**NV**) • *Brut Millésime* (**V**) • *Cuvée des Echansons* (**V**) • *Cuvée l'Intemporelle* (**V**) • *Cuvée du 60e Anniversaire* (**V**)

HENRI MANDOIS
66 rue du Gal-de-Gaulle
51200 Pierry
★☆ⓥ

The house style of Henri Mandois is for elegant Champagnes that have a very satisfying length of attractive, creamy fruit and a fine balance.

✓ *Entire range*

MARGAINE
3 avenue de Champagne
51380 Villers-Marmery

Although I'm not keen on the basic non-vintage *brut*, the rich yet crisp and vintaged *blanc de blancs* is a classy Champagne that repays cellaring, demonstrating that the eastern *crus* of the Montagne de Reims can, in their own way, compete with the very best villages of the Côte des Blancs.

MARGUET
1 place Barancourt
51150 Ambonnay

Benoît Marguet has all the right ideals, but I simply cannot get to grips with his wine, which has unusual, often bizarre aromas. Look out for a new *cuvée* in collaboration with Hervé Jestin. The vines are located just above Krug's Clos d'Ambonnay and look to be in a superior position. The *vins clairs* from barrel were sensational, so if this ends up weird, I'll be looking very closely at Marguet's second fermentation and *dosage* techniques. Fingers crossed!

SERGE MATHIEU
Les Riceys
10340 Avirey-Lingey
★★ⓥ

Mathieu, a small grower in the Aube, consistently produces excellent Champagnes that are beautifully focused, have much finesse, and a real richness of fruit for such light and elegantly balanced wines.

✓ *Entire range*

MERCIER (GM)
75 avenue de Champagne
51200 Epernay
ⓥ

Mercier, established by Eugène Mercier in 1858, was the original owner of the Dom Pérignon brand, although this house never utilized it and sold it to Moët & Chandon in 1930. Moët bought Mercier some 40 years later. Mercier is still the best-selling brand in France, no matter how hard the parent company tries to make Moët number one, although Moët is way ahead in global sales.

✓ *Brut* (**V**)

LE MESNIL
Union des Propriétaires Récoltants
51390 Le Mesnil-sur-Oger
★★ⓥ

If only this cooperative's basic Champagnes were as stunning as the strict selections recommended below.

✓ *Vigne Sélectionnée Blanc de Blancs* (**V**) • *Réserve Sélection, Blanc de Blancs* (**V**) • *Sublime* (**V**)

MOËT & CHANDON (GM)
20 avenue de Champagne
54120 Epernay
★★

The largest Champagne house by a mile, Moët is also the leading company in the LVMH group, which also includes Mercier, Krug, Ruinart, Pommery, and Veuve Clicquot. In December 2008, Montaudon was sucked into the group, stripped of its 42 hectares (104 acres) of vineyards, and spat out as little more than a brand with some stocks for Jacquart to purchase. When first released, the soft style of Brut Impérial makes it amenable to everyone and offensive to no one, but after a further 12 months bottle-age, it mellows into a much fuller, toasty-rich Champagne that has won many a competitive tasting. Between the unfairly criticized non-vintage and the universally praised Dom Pérignon, the vintage Brut Impérial and Brut Impérial Rosé is often ignored. These vintaged *cuvées* have always been under-rated, but since the 2000 vintage, there has been a sea change in both quality and winemaking philosophy. Gone is the need to make the Moët house style every year. Now every vintage is made as an ultimate expression of the year in question, and some of these vintages are of an

extraordinary quality. The 2003 was released before the superb, classic 2002, and the old regime would never have thought of, let alone permitted, the production of a Champagne like 2003, which fluttered beautifully for a short while but soon declined, but that was part of the magic of 2003 – even the 2003 By Bollinger was an ephemeral delight. All of this coincides with Benoît Gouez taking over as *chef de cave* and Richard Geoffroy, the *chef de cave* of Dom Pérignon, assuming full control of all winemaking and vineyard activities.

✓ *Brut Impérial* (**V**) • *Dom Pérignon* (**PC**) • *Dom Pérignon Rosé* (**PC**)

MONCUIT
11 rue Persault-Maheu
51190 Le Mesnil-sur-Oger

Some years (or disgorgements of apparently the same wine) can have overly dominant buttery-malo aromas, while others are fresh and crisp, with lively-rich fruit that is tasty and satisfying. Usually matures into a creamy-biscuity style.

✓ *Cuvée Nicole Moncuit Vieille Vigne* (**V**)

MOUTARD
rue des Ponts
10110 Buxeuil

This very inconsistent but pioneering producer almost single-handedly preserved the tradition of making Champagne with ancient varieties such as Arbanne (called Arbane here). But except for the occasional *cuvée*, they have been resinous, with an unpleasant aftertaste that catches at the back of the throat. The latest exception was the Vieilles Vignes Cépage Arbane, which was on the market in 2005 and had fresh orchard fruits, with a fatter mouthfeel than Chardonnay, the typical white *champenois* variety. The very first Cuvée aux 6 Cépages was the first drinkable Champagne I had encountered from Moutard. Although a pure 2000 vintage, this was initially released as a non-vintage after just two years on yeast. It inspired ill-fated hope that Moutard had moved up a gear in quality and consistency, but it was at least a taste of history, having been made in equal parts from Chardonnay, Pinot Noir, Pinot Meunier, and Champagne's lesser-known Pinot Blanc, Petit Meslier, and Arbane, fermented in two-year-old Burgundian *barriques*, sealed with corks rather than crown-caps for the second fermentation and lightly dosaged (6 grams). The oak was not noticeable unless tasted blind with other non-*barrique* Champagnes, and the fruit on the palate had a tantalizing richness yet a lightness and freshness. Some of the later *cuvées*, all released as vintage Champagnes, have been okay, but they have all failed to live up to the early promise of the 2000.

Several of his other Champagnes have had some pretty weird and unclean aromas, with only the non-vintaged Cuvée Prestige and Grande Cuvée having any consistency. Tasting back over the vintages to test Moutard's consistency, the 1998 was best, and I would happily drink the 1991, 1992, and 1995, but the 1993 was unclean, while the 1996 and 1985 stank of mercaptans. Hopefully, this historically important producer will be able to instil some quality control in the future.

MOUTARDIER
route d'Orbais
51210 Le Breuil

Englishman Jonathan Saxby has married into this rural Champagne-producing family and generally fares best with the vintage *cuvée*, although his Cuvée Pure Meunier Brut Nature has the greatest potential, if only he produced this as a vintage with a *brut dosage*.

G H MUMM & CO (GM)
29 et 34 rue du Champ-de-Mars
51053 Reims
★★ⓥ

With Perrier-Jouët, this house is part of the Pernod-Ricard group, which masterfully hired a young Dominique Demarville to clean up the quality of Mumm Champagne. Demarville was so successful that he was headhunted by Veuve Clicquot, and his assistant, Didier Mariotti, took over. If there was any doubt about whether he was up to the task, Mariotti's impeccable handling of the *dosage* (not just the residual sugar, but the choice of base wine for the liqueur, when to disgorge, and the amount of post-disgorgement ageing prior to release) of the 1999 Cuvée R Lalou should earn him a lifetime-guaranteed job at Mumm. The 1998 was simply sensational, but the 1999, from a supposedly lesser vintage, is even better. Textbook stuff!

✓ *Demi-Sec* (**NV**) • *Mumm de Cramant* (**NV**) • *Millésimé* (**V**) • *Cuvée R Lalou* (**V**)

BRUNO PAILLARD
avenue du Champagne
51100 Reims
★★ⓥ

Bruno Paillard opts for elegance rather than body or character, and his Première Cuvée is not just elegant, but one of the most consistent non-vintage Champagnes on the market. This house belongs personally to Bruno Paillard and is not part of the Lanson-BCC group, which he also heads.

✓ *Entire range*

PALMER & CO
67 rue Jacquart
51100 Reims
★★ⓥ

A great source of vintage, particularly vintage *blanc de blancs* in magnum, which age gracefully for 30 years or more. The *blanc de blancs* is often pure Montagne de Reims.

✓ *Millésime* (**V**) • *Blanc de Blancs* (**V**)

PANNIER
23 rue Roger Catillon
02400 Château-Thierry
★**⒱**

The past 10 years have seen a slow but steady increase in quality here, yet a decrease in consistency. Some *cuvées* and vintages can slug it out with the best, but others cannot. Not only that, some releases of apparently the same competition-winning *cuvée* or vintage can disappoint so badly that you could be forgiven for wondering whether it is an entirely different Champagne. Frankly, I prefer the chance of encountering the odd, occasional superstar to a life of boredom, hence the increased star rating.

✓ *Brut Tradition* (**NV**) • *Brut Vintage* (**V**) • *Egérie de Pannier* (**V**)

FRANCK PASCAL
1 bis rue Valentine Régnier
51700 Baslieux-sous-Châtillon
Ⓑ

Another biodynamic producer highly regarded for his low- and no-*dosage* Champagnes.

JOSEPH PERRIER (GM)
69 avenue de Paris
51005 Châlons-sur-Marne
★**⒱**

The non-vintage has been disappointingly amylic of late, and the last exceptional vintage was 1998. But Cuvée Joséphine has gained in length and potential longevity since the 2002 vintage, when it went from a 40/60 Chardonnay/Pinot Noir to 60/40.

✓ *Cuvée Joséphine* (**V**)

PERRIER-JOUËT (GM)
26/28 avenue de Champagne
51200 Epernay
★★✬

The Belle Époque (or Flower Bottle as it's known in the USA) might be the headline-grabber here, but it is the potentially long-lived vintaged Grand Brut that is the wisest buy.

✓ *Grand Brut* (**V**) • *Belle Époque Brut* (**PC**) • *Belle Époque Rosé* (**PC**) • *Belle Époque Blanc de Blancs* (**PC**)

PHILIPPONNAT
13 rue du Pont
51160 Mareuil-sur-Aÿ
★✬

Under the day-to-day control of Charles Philipponnat, a direct descendant of the oldest (not necessarily sparkling) wine family in Champagne, this house is a key player in the Lanson-BCC group. During Charles's tenure, the house style here has moved quite dramatically from a classic Champagne to a more powerfully structured, Pinot Noir-influenced food wine, and having tasted these Champagnes under both blind and open conditions, and consumed them with food for many years, I am firmly convinced that the Philipponnat style today is not one that necessarily shines under clinically blind conditions but inevitably impresses with the label showing, preferably at the table, being consumed rather than sniffed and spat. However, above all else, Clos des Goisses (individually rated three stars) remains Philipponnat's jewel in the crown. This is a very special vineyard that could – and should – be produced every year.

✓ *Grand Blanc* (**V**) • *Clos des Goisses* (**PC**) • *Abel Lepitre* (Cuvée No. 134, Brut Millésime)

PIPER-HEIDSIECK (GM)
51 boulevard Henri Vasnier
51100 Reims
★★⒱

This was and is the volume-selling *grande marque* sibling of Charles Heidsieck, but Piper-Heidsieck has never been just about volume, and its quality has soared in recent years. The vintage and vintaged Rare *cuvées* are both equal to the quality of Charles Heidsieck, while the non-vintage Florens-Louis (usually restricted to the duty-free market) is much better than just an aged version of Piper-Heidsieck's house non-vintage. At times, Florens-Louis tastes totally different from the NV Piper-Heidsieck; indeed, at times, Florens-Louis tastes like Charles Heidsieck Brut Reserve.

✓ *Entire range*

PLOYEZ-JACQUEMART
51500 Ludes
★⒱

The potential longevity of these Champagnes has reduced as the *dosage* has dropped, but they are still elegantly rich and well made.

✓ *Entire range*

POL ROGER & CO (GM)
1 rue Henri Lelarge
51206 Epernay
★★★⒱

What would we do without Pol Roger vintage? It's still potentially one of the longest-lived Champagnes produced, and providing this house keeps its no-*dosage* to its new Pure *cuvée*, it should remain so. The Pure was such a breakthrough in this category

when first released that I felt compelled to write to Patrice Noyelle, the CEO of Pol Roger, telling him so, but I started off by slagging-off zero-*dosage* Champagnes, and poor Patrice, suffering from a cold and feeling miserable, thought I was complaining and felt like going back to bed until he got to the end of my rant, which then made him feel very pleased. Take a look on the Pol Roger website; the letter should still be there. The Cuvée Sir Winston Churchill is as superb as ever but quite lonely, and as Pol Roger makes such a wonderful *blanc de blancs* for a Pinot-dominated house, it deserves to be partnered by a Cuvée Sir Winston Churchill Blanc de Blancs. "But Winnie never drank the stuff," complains Patrice. "Don't you think he would have, if he had been born a couple of generations later?" I respond. "And whose *blanc de blancs* would he drink?"

✓ *Entire range*

POMMERY (GM)
5 place Général-Gouraud
51053 Reims
★★

One of the few *grande marque* houses that claim 100% *grand cru* for its standard vintage Champagne, and *chef de cave* Thierry Gasco has maintained its quality under the Vranken regime. Cuvée Louise can be sublime. I am the wrong age and possibly the wrong sex to comment sensibly on sucking Champagne through a straw from a quarter-bottle of Pommery POP, but whenever I have tasted this *cuvée*, the quality has not been bad at all.

✓ *Grand Cru Millésimé* (**V**) • *Cuvée Louise* (**V**)

POUILLON
3 rue de la Couple
51160 Mareuil-sur-Aÿ
★

Young Fabrice Pouillon has spoken some of the best theory when it comes to the restrained use of oak *barriques* for Champagne, but his Fleur de Mareuil has been very oaky indeed, and I have yet to see a lighter hand applied for that *cuvée*. His 2000 Millésime Grand Cru is labelled Extra Brut but receives no *dosage* and yet has great finesse.

✓ *Millésime Grand Cru Extra Brut* (**V**)

JÉRÔME PRÉVOST
2 rue de la Petite Montagne
51390 Gueux

Jérôme Prévost might be highly regarded, but his Champagnes are as variable as any low- or no-*dosage* Champagne; thus, in 2009 I found La Closerie Les Beguines 2006 unpleasantly high-toned, while La Closerie Les Beguines 2004 had a lovely toasty-lemony oak and a creamy-smooth mousse.

LOUIS ROEDERER (GM)
21 boulevard Lundy
51100 Reims
★★★⒱

This family-owned *grande marque* has always been one of the most consistent, greatest-quality Champagne houses, but ever since Jean-Baptiste Lecaillon took over as director of the cellars and vineyards, the quality has soared even higher. Roederer also owns Deutz.

✓ *Entire range*

ROSES DE JEANNE
13 rue du Vivier
10110 Celles-sur-Ource
Ⓞ★★

This is one artisanal producer that manages to get away with no *dosage* every time and with no oxidative aromas to get me riled, although I have not tried to age any of these Champagnes. Not that there is any need, as they are ready to go when released. With very few vines and pruned to reduce yields, the production is tiny and prices are high. All the wines are from single vineyards, with a style that is seductively soft and vibrantly fruity, but that description does no justice to the nuanced complexity and finesse of each *cuvée*. These wines benefit from decanting and not being served too chilled. All these *cuvées* are beautifully presented.

✓ *Entire range*

RUINART (GM)
4 rue de Crayères
51053 Reims
★★

The 2002 Dom Ruinart is the best vintage ever produced, but with Frédéric Panaiotis (Fred to his friends) – one of Champagne's young bright stars, and the *chef de cave* since 2007 – I would not want to bet on how long that record will stand! The *crayères* in Ruinart's cellars are uniquely registered as a National Monument. Part of the LVMH group.

✓ *Entire range*

LOUIS DE SACY
6 rue Verzenay
51380 Verzy

I have been following these Champagnes for 30 years, and over that time they have gone from fine fruitiness through amylic to VA-lifted, but have, for the past decade or so, stayed firmly in the fine fruity spectrum. The rosé is always easy to drink. Probably the best kosher Champagne producer of recent times.

SALON (GM)
5 rue de la Brèche
51190 Le Mesnil-sur-Oger
★★

Have I been looking at Salon with rose-tinted spectacles? Since its acquisition by Laurent-Perrier in 1989, I have tasted some very good vintages here, but nothing like the

1982, let alone a vintage that will have the longevity of extraordinarily great years like 1971, 1947, or 1928.

✓ *"S"* (**V**)

SCHREIBER
1 rue du Pont
10250 Courteron
Ⓑ

Erick Schreiber used to be the vineyard manager for Fleury, also located in Courteron. One of the very few producers of a true *doux* Champagne, although I have yet to taste it.

JACQUES SÉLOSSE
22 rue Ernest Vallée
51190 Avize
★

Generally far too much raw oak for my liking, but there is no denying the quality of the wine underneath, and rated for those who like the style.

✓ *Millésime*

DE SOUSA
12 place Léon Bourgeois
51190 Avize
Ⓑ

Erick de Sousa has always been a very dedicated grower, but until recently he has shone more in the vineyard than the winery, making Champagnes that have too often been high-toned, estery, and volatile. Over the past couple of years, however, the quality has perked up, and I predict great moments for the future, particularly from his vintaged Cuvée des Caudalies, if he could craft the fruit from these 50-year-old Chardonnay vines in a more reductive style. The 3A (for Avize, Aÿ, and Ambonnay) is one of the few *extra brut* Champagnes that tastes perfectly balanced without any additional *dosage*. This *récoltant-manipulant* also markets Champagne under the Zoémie de Sousa *négociant* label, which I first tasted in 2005 but have not yet been impressed by.

TAITTINGER (GM)
9 place Saint-Nicaise
51061 Reims
★★☆

Those who criticize *grandes marques* like Taittinger for their mediocrity should reflect on the fact that in 2008 and 2010 Taittinger entered eight Champagnes for the *Decanter* World Wine Awards. These were not selected *cuvées* but included everything from the basic house non-vintage to the Comtes de Champagne. On both occasions, Taittinger came away with five golds and three silvers, winning the Non-Vintage Trophy with different blends of its Les Folies de la Marquetterie. How many other producers can match that? None – not even Charles Heidsieck, which has won more gold medals and trophies at the same competition than any other Champagne producer.

✓ *Entire range*

TARLANT
51480 Oeuilly near Epernay
★

This grower has lots of ambition and a heart in the right place. The 100% Meunier Vigne d'Or can excel with its excellent richness, demonstrating that this grape does not always have to play second fiddle to the more famous Pinot Noir. Cuvée Luis is sometimes over-oaked, but the blend of 1998 and 1997 tasted at *The World of Fine Wine*'s low-*dosage* tasting in 2009 was absolutely gorgeous, and this *cuvée* has a brilliant back label, telling customers everything they could possibly want to know. In fact, three out of the four Champagnes submitted by Tarlant for that tasting excelled. Although the 2004-based Tarlant Zéro Brut Nature was simplistic, the 2005-based *cuvée* of the same wine was very good. Certainly one to watch.

ALAIN THIENOT
14 rue des Moissons
51100 Reims
★Ⓥ

A very savvy financier who has quietly built up a significant group (including Joseph Perrier, Canard-Duchêne, George Goulet, and Marie Stuart), Alain Thienot also produces good-value, fruit-driven Champagnes under his own label, ranging from a successful pouring quality non-vintage, through good-quality vintage *brut* and rosé, to an excellent Cuvée Stanislas.

✓ *Brut Rosé* (**V**) • *Grand Cuvée Brut* (**V**) • *Cuvée Stanislas* (**V**)

UNION CHAMPAGNE
7 rue Pasteur
51190 Avize
★Ⓥ

Champagne de St-Gall is this cooperative's primary brand, with Cuvée Orpale its prestige *cuvée*. There are two ranges, Grands Crus and Premiers Crus, and wines in the former range are not always superior.

✓ *Grands Crus Millésime* (**N**) • *Cuvée Orpale* (**PC**)

DE VENOGE
30 avenue de Champagne
51200 Epernay
★Ⓥ

Part of the Lanson-BCC group, this remains a good-value, well-made brand, but its prestige Champagne, the often truly excellent Cuvée des Princes, looks ridiculous in its novelty tear-shaped bottle.

✓ *Blanc de Noirs* (**V**) • *Brut* (**V**) • *Cuvée des Princes* (**PC**)

VERGNON
1 Grande Rue
51190 Le Mesnil-sur-Oger

I have found a touch of VA in some of these wines, ranging from sweet and sour to a pleasing lift to the fruit. The 2000 Confidence Brut Nature was a potentially excellent

Champagne that had gone aldehydic because of the absence of *dosage*, yet the 2003 was one of the best interpretations of that difficult year, demonstrating that if you are going to make this style, you cannot rely on it working every year. The Grand Cru Extra Brut is turning into a lovely, rich, satisfying food wine.

VEUVE CLICQUOT-PONSARDIN (GM)
12 rue du Temple
51054 Reims
★★☆

Dominique Demarville is now in charge of vineyards and winemaking here. He's the guy who cleaned up Mumm and was so successful that he was promoted from *chef de cave* (indeed, at 31, he had been the youngest ever cellar master of a large *grande marque* house) to director of vineyards and winemaking for both Mumm and Perrier-Jouët – a position that included a seat on the board. Demarville was soon headhunted by Veuve Clicquot to take over from the legendary Jacques Peters, but initially to serve as merely an assistant *chef de cave* for three years. So why would this rising star leave the top job at two *grandes marques* to take a lower position at just one house? It was not a surprise to anyone who knew that Jacques Peters was Demarville's winemaking idol. Such was Demarville's humility that, despite holding a top job at such a young age, he knew he still had much to learn. And such is his wisdom and honesty to himself that he gave up the status of one of the most powerful winemaking positions in Champagne to study under Peters for three years. He told me that it was a very hard decision to leave Mumm but extremely simple to accept Veuve Clicquot's offer: "Jacques Peters was going to retire. It was literally a once-in-a-lifetime opportunity. It would never be repeated. How could I refuse?" What a wise head on such young shoulders. This house is in safe hands.

✓ *Entire range*

VEUVE A DEVAUX
Domaine de Villeneuve
10110 Bar-sur-Seine
★Ⓥ

The quality here took a dip at the turn of the millennium but is now back on track.

✓ *Grande Réserve Brut* (**NV**) • *Cuvée D Brut* (**NV**) • *Blanc de Noirs* (**NV**) • *Cuvée Distinction Rosé* (**V**) • *D de Devaux* (**V**)

VEUVE FOURNY
12-5 rue du Mesnil
51130 Vertus
★Ⓥ

I have found the Cuvée R distressingly amylic, but vintaged Blanc de Blancs Vertus is excellent. Even the non-vintaged Brut Nature version of Blanc de Blancs Vertus can be compelling. At *The World of Fine Wine*'s low-*dosage* tasting in 2009, I scored the Blanc de Blancs Vertus Brut Nature 90 points, even though this blend of 2005, 2004, and 2003 has 40% *solera*-based reserve wine, which is not my favourite practice in Champagne. Yet any self-respecting taster must be true to the wine on the day, whatever preconceived ideas we might have, and on the day I described it as "Meursault with bubbles! Gorgeous! Delicious citrus fruits underpinned by the effect of oak rather than its unwelcome aromas."

✓ *Blanc de Blancs Vertus Brut Nature* (**NV**) • *Blanc de Blancs Vertus Brut* (**V**)

VILMART
4 rue de la République
51500 Rilly-la-Montagne
◉★★

Occasionally some high-toned aromas have pervaded these Champagnes in recent years, just as too much oak dominated in the early 1990s, but this is still one of the finest hand-crafted Champagnes.

✓ *Entire range*

VOUETTE ET SORBÉE
8 rue de Vaux
10110 Buxières-sur-Arce

I have found the Fidele (100% Pinot Noir) oxidatively rustic.

VRANKEN-POMMERY
42 avenue de Champagne
51200 Epernay
❷

Owned by Belgian Paul Vranken, who undoubtedly has one of the cleverest commercial brains in the region, the Vranken-Pommery group includes lacklustre brands such as Barancourt, Diamant, Demoiselle, Charles Lafitte, René Lallement, and Vranken. Heidsieck & Co Monopole rises above this level, as does Pommery. Notice the difference between the naming of this group – where the personal emphasis is on Vranken, the owner, which takes precedence over the famous Pommery brand name – and Lanson-BCC, where the group owners are under no illusion which name will outlive the other. Vranken-Pommery also owns subsidiaries in Portugal (Port: Quinta do Convento, Quinta do Paco, and São Pedro) and Spain (Cava: Senora and Vranken).

ALSACE

Welcome to Alsace, the world's only medium-sweet wine region. Are you fed up of drinking crisp, dry whites? Then try these increasingly sweeter wines. Do you find dry wines difficult to drink with food? How about a good dollop of sugar in an Alsace wine to wash down that delicate white-fish dish? This might sound a bit harsh on those who still produce dry Alsace wines, but that is the direction in which a growing number of producers are taking the reputation of this region.

SETTING THE SCENE

A fascinating mixture of French and German characteristics pervades this northeastern fragment of France, cut off from the rest of the country by the barrier of the Vosges mountains, and separated from neighbouring Germany by the mighty Rhine. The colourful combination of cultures is the result of wars and border squabbles that have plagued the ancient province since the Treaty of Westphalia put an end to the Thirty Years' War in 1648. This gave the French sovereignty over Alsace, and royal edicts issued in 1662, 1682, and 1687 proffered free land to anyone willing to restore it to full productivity. As a result of this, Swiss, Germans, Tyroleans, and Lorrainers poured into the region. In 1871, at the end of the Franco-Prussian War, the region once again came under German control, and remained so until the end of World War I, when it once again became French. At this juncture, Alsace began to reorganize the administration of its vineyards in line with the new French AOC system, but in 1940 Germany reclaimed the province from France before this process was complete. Only after World War II, when Alsace reverted to France, was the quest for AOC status resumed, finally being realized in 1962.

The vineyards of Alsace are dotted with medieval towns of cobbled streets and timbered buildings, reflecting – as do the wines – the region's myriad Gallic and Prussian influences. The grapes are a mixture of German, French, and the exotic, with the German Riesling and Gewurztraminer (written without an umlaut in Alsace), the French Pinot Gris, and the decidedly exotic Muscat comprising the four principal varieties. Sylvaner, another German grape, also features to some extent, while other French varieties include Pinot Noir, Pinot Blanc, Auxerrois, and Chasselas. While

Gewurztraminer is definitely German (and fine examples are still to be found in the Pfalz, its area of origin), only in Alsace is it quite so spicy. And only in Alsace do you find spicy Pinot Gris, a grape that is neutral elsewhere. Even the Pinot Blanc may produce spicy wines in Alsace, although this is normally due to the inclusion of the fat-spicy Auxerrois grape.

Very little red wine is made in Alsace. What is produced is intended principally for local restaurants and *Weinstuben*. Ninety per cent of the wine in Alsace is white. Traditionally, the style of these very fruity wines is dry, although some varieties, such as the Gewurztraminer, have always been made less dry than others. With the introduction of Vendange Tardive and Sélection de Grains Nobles wines, growers have deliberately reduced yields to chase high sugar levels. This practice has resulted in even the most basic *cuvées* being too rich for a truly dry style, so the tendency to produce less dry wine has now spread to other grape varieties.

RECENT ALSACE VINTAGES

2010 Significantly lower yields than 2009 (which itself was low-yielding), a long, cool ripening season, and typically dry and sunny harvesting weather in September and October produced beautiful, precise fruit highlighted by fine, ripe acidity. A classic Alsace vintage.

2009 The well-delineated seasons helped make this a sublime year for all varieties and styles. As André Ostertag exclaimed, "A real vintage with real seasons, like in the old days!" A dry, cold winter, followed by a mild spring, a hot and occasionally stormy summer for both heat and precipitation, and yet another typically Alsace Indian summer for picking produced great Alsace wines across the board.

2008 Very hard acids mar the fruit in many wines from this year. The 2008s are not heavily malic, like the awful, smelly 1996s, but the less successful 2008s have an awkward, hard, angular acidity that will never attain finesse, while the best will require longer cellaring than usual.

2007 As in Champagne, a fantastically hot spring pushed the vines on one month in advance of their normal growth, but the weather started to fall apart in June. April and May were exceptionally hot and sunny, but on 15 June a hailstorm devastated up to 150 hectares (370 acres) in the villages of Ammerschwihr, Sigolsheim, Kientzheim, Bennwihr, and Kaysersberg. Mid-August rains encouraged the most meticulous growers to remove the leaves above bunches to help avoid a repeat of the rampant rot of 2006. Despite these climatic difficulties, the harvest took place under ideal conditions throughout a typically sunny Alsatian September, with many great white wines produced in both dry and sweet styles. Riesling and Gewurztraminer, two diametrically opposite varieties as far as viticultural requirements are concerned, were far and away the most successful. Pinot Blanc and Pinot Gris also excelled. Most varieties performed consistently well, with the primary exception of Pinot Noir, which was the most inconsistent variety of the vintage.

2006 The year of the mushroom! Over the past 20 years, only 2003 and 1996 yielded worse wines, but unlike those two years, this was neither an unpleasant nor a difficult year to taste. While the dead fruit and lack of acidity made the 2003s hard-going, and the malic (not malolactic) stink of the 1996s is still repulsive, the mushroom aroma pervading most 2006s has never been offensive, even though it comes from the high incidence of rot. One enterprising American importer put a positive spin on the mushroom aroma, selling the 2006s as "risotto wine", and they flew off the shelf! The worst varietal performance was *blanc de noirs* from Pinot Noir that was not fit for red wine. Many did not bother with red wine, including some top names, yet some, like René Muré, made the best red wine of their lives. This is not a vintage to buy on spec. Every producer was affected. You must taste, and you must be very picky, because some wines that were seemingly pristine one year after the harvest have since developed a mushroom aroma.

HEADQUARTERS OF HUGEL & FILS
The small wine shop, cellars, and offices of the merchants Hugel & Fils in Riquewihr are marked by a typically Alsatian sign.

PINOT GRIS, ROTENBERG
*A view of Turckheim from the steep slopes of Rotenberg vineyard in
Wintzenheim, where Domaine Zind Humbrecht produces fabulously
fat Pinot Gris wines with powerful aromatic qualities.*

DISAPPEARING DRY WINES

Although there has been an explosion in the numbers of
producers making and selling VT and SGN wines – from just two
or three prior to the decree to literally hundreds – the production
of these late-harvest wines remains minute at just 2 per cent of
Alsace wines as a whole. The vast bulk of Alsace wines have
traditionally been dry, but these so-called dry wines have become
increasingly sweet over the last 10 years or so, and some are very
sweet indeed. So much so that it has become almost impossible
for the wine-drinking public to tell whether the wine they are
buying is dry or sweet. This is not because Alsace producers
deliberately chose to create sweeter wines; it is merely the
regrettable by-product of good intentions and worshipping the
false concept of "physiological ripeness".

Grammatically, "physiological ripeness" is a nonsense because
the ripening process is, in any case, intrinsically a physiological
one, but a lot of winemakers (particularly, but not exclusively,
biodynamic growers) have been brainwashed into believing that
"physiological ripeness" involves a certain skin colour, stem
maturity, tannin ripeness, aroma development, berry shrivel, pulp
texture, and seed ripeness. The truth is that these factors, with
the conventional parameters of sugar, acidity, and pH, are all
indicators of the progress of grape ripeness, not of grape ripeness
per se. The only ripeness that matters is flavour ripeness, and that
usually begins when tartaric acid starts to dominate. The decision
when to pick after this point is a quality judgment that, subject to
weather considerations, is based purely on the style of wine to be
produced. If winemakers want to delay harvesting, that is their
prerogative, but they cannot claim that earlier-picked grapes are
not ripe – yet they do. There are some very famous winemakers in
Alsace who maintain that Riesling grapes grown on limestone or
calcareous clay are far too sugar-rich to make a dry wine by the
time they are "physiologically ripe". Well, Trimbach's Clos Ste-
Hune and Cuvée Frédéric-Émile are both grown on calcareous
clay, and both are beautifully dry. If they are made from unripe
grapes, then all wines should be made from unripe grapes!

No one is saying no sweet wine in Alsace. No one should dictate
the style of wine any producer makes. If a specific producer wants
to make wine with lots of alcohol and residual sugar, they are
perfectly entitled to do so, but they should not pretend they have
to because of so-called physiological ripeness, as if what they are
doing is more noble or more natural. If they have plenty of

customers with a sweet enough tooth to buy those wines, then it is
not only the right thing to do, it also makes good business sense.
However, not every Alsace producer has a cult following, let alone
one with a sweet tooth, so before others follow these Pied Pipers
down this route, they should ask themselves just how many
medium-sweet-wine drinkers there are. Sometimes the purveyors
of physiological ripeness are also non-interventionists, allowing the
yeasts literally to do their own thing, and in some of the less
overripe batches there can be very healthy and energetic yeasts
that will ferment the wine completely or almost completely dry.
The initial reaction of most dry-wine drinkers might be, "I want
to taste a dry wine from this cult producer" – but with a few truly
tremendous exceptions, the wines are not balanced. And even
those truly tremendous exceptions can be 15.8 or even 16.2 per
cent alcohol. Who wants to drink that every day?

The abundance of sweeter, highly alcoholic Alsace wines has
had a negative impact on the reputation of this region for those
who have, until the past 10 years, seen it as a wonderful source
of dry wines, even if some "dry" Gewurztraminer and, to a lesser
extent, "dry" Pinot Gris were always less dry than other dry wines.

Throughout Alsace, Gewurztraminer and Pinot Gris now
frequently contain residual sugar of 30 to 40 grams per litre, with
50 to 70 grams per litre not unusual. More often than not, these
wines do not carry any indication of sweetness, which comes as

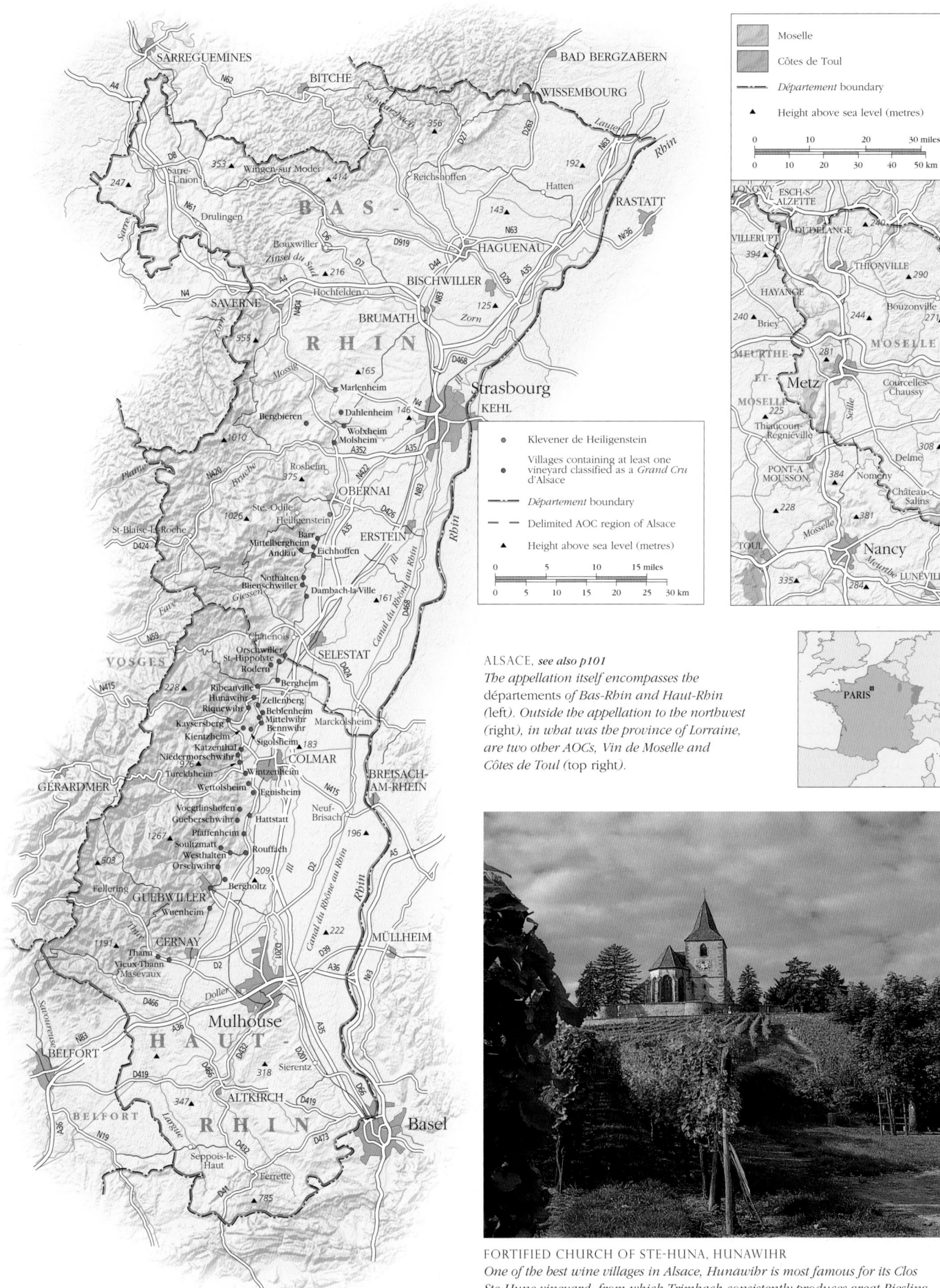

Legend (top right):
- Moselle
- Côtes de Toul
- *Département* boundary
- ▲ Height above sea level (metres)

0 10 20 30 miles
0 10 20 30 40 50 km

Map labels (left, main map):

SARREGUEMINES
BITCHE
BAD BERGZABERN
WISSEMBOURG
RASTATT
N62
356 ▲
D27
D263
Lauter
Rhin
247 ▲
353 ▲
Wingen-sur-Moder
414 ▲
Reichshoffen
Hatten
192 ▲
D8
Sare-Union
N61
Drulingen
143 ▲
N63
B A S -
Bouxwiller
216 ▲
Zinsel du Sud
HAGUENAU
Hochfelden
BISCHWILLER
D29
125 ▲
N83
SAVERNE
BRUMATH
Zorn
N4
Zorn
555 ▲
R H I N
165 ▲
Mossig
Marlenheim
Strasbourg
KEHL
D468
Bergbieren
Dahlenheim
146 ▲
N4
1010 ▲
Wolxheim
Molsheim
A352
A35
Bruche
Rosheim
375 ▲
N422
N83
Plane
OBERNAI
Ste.-Odile
1026 ▲
Heiligenstein
D426
ERSTEIN
St-Blaise-la-Roche
Barr
Mittelbergheim
Andlau
Eichhoffen
Ill
D424
Nothalten
Blienschwiller
Giessen
161 ▲
Dambach-la-Ville
Canal du Rhône au Rhin
D468
Châtenois
Orschwiller
St-Hippolyte
Rodern
SELESTAT
D424
V O S G E S
Bergheim
N59
Ribeauvillé
Zellenberg
Hunawihr
Riquewihr
Beblenheim
Mittelwihr
Marckolsheim
228 ▲
Kaysersberg
Bennwihr
Kientzheim
Sigolsheim
183 ▲
Katzenthal
COLMAR
Niedermorschwihr
976 ▲
Wintzenheim
Turckheim
Wettolsheim
BREISACH-AM-RHEIN
GÉRARDMER
Eguisheim
N415
Voegtlinshofen
Neuf-Brisach
Gueberschwihr
Hattstatt
1267 ▲
Pfaffenheim
196 ▲
Soultzmatt
Rouffach
Westhalten
Orschwihr
209 ▲
503 ▲
Ill
D2
Fellering
Bergholtz
A5
GUEBWILLER
Wuenheim
Thur
222 ▲
MÜLLHEIM
CERNAY
1191 ▲
Thann
Vieux-Thann
Masevaux
D2
Canal du Rhône au Rhin
Rhin
D39
A36
N3
Doller
D466
H A U T -
Mulhouse
A35
BELFORT
318 ▲
Sierentz
BELFORT
D419
D466
D201
R H I N
347 ▲
ALTKIRCH
D419
D96
Basel
N19
Largue
D432
D473
Seppois-le-Haut
Ferrette
785 ▲

Legend (center box):
- ● Klevener de Heiligenstein
- ● Villages containing at least one vineyard classified as a *Grand Cru d'Alsace*
- — *Département* boundary
- – – Delimited AOC region of Alsace
- ▲ Height above sea level (metres)

0 5 10 15 miles
0 5 10 15 20 25 30 km

ALSACE, *see also p101*
The appellation itself encompasses the départements of Bas-Rhin and Haut-Rhin (left). Outside the appellation to the northwest (right), in what was the province of Lorraine, are two other AOCs, Vin de Moselle and Côtes de Toul (top right).

Inset map (top right, Lorraine):
LONGWY
ESCH-S-ALZETTE
240 ▲
VILLERUPT
DUDELANGE
394 ▲
THIONVILLE
290 ▲
HAYANGE
Bouzonville
240 ▲
Briey
244 ▲
271 ▲
MEURTHE-
ET-
MOSELLE
281 ▲
Metz
M O S E L L E
MOSELLE
225 ▲
Courcelles-Chaussy
Thiaucourt-Regniéville
308 ▲
Delme
PONT-A-MOUSSON
384 ▲
Nomeny
Château-Salins
228 ▲
381 ▲
TOUL
Moselle
Nancy
Meurthe
335 ▲
284 ▲
LUNÉVILLE
Seille

PARIS

FORTIFIED CHURCH OF STE-HUNA, HUNAWIHR
One of the best wine villages in Alsace, Hunawihr is most famous for its Clos Ste-Hune vineyard, from which Trimbach consistently produces great Riesling.

a bit of shock when pouring a glass. For Riesling, it is much less, but at 20 to 30 grams it is still very sweet for a dry-wine drinker, especially if he's expecting something crisp. The situation is not quite as bad as it appears in restaurants and on the best export markets. This is because the phenomenon applies primarily to the best producers and vineyards, particularly *grands crus*. These are the wines that make the headlines, are reviewed and entered into competitions. It might seem odd to argue for less sugar in Alsace and more sugar in Champagne, but of course neither argument is about sugar *per se*. Both arguments are based on what is necessary for their respective styles of wine. For Champagne, it is just a few grams for the smooth, non-oxidative evolution of the wine, while for Alsace it is to preserve a dry wine style, which is the type of wine the majority of people drink most of the time. What is far more bizarre is the mirror image of this position, where many of the critics who are happy to see a proliferation of sugar levels of up to 60 grams per litre in Alsace wines are also apt to describe the relatively minuscule residual sugar in a *brut* Champagne (just 6 to 12 grams plus much higher acidity, the perception of which is further enhanced by the effervescence) as a sweet cosmetic masking the true quality of a Champagne.

The sweetness issue would not be a problem in Alsace if those wines were sold under one of the region's two sweet-wine designations: Vendanges Tardives or Sélection de Grains Nobles. These are speciality wines and, as such, are expected to be rarities, prized and expensive, so why are producers not using them? Or to be more accurate, why do producers who use these designations not use them for all the sweet wines they sell? Because they do not want to advertise their sweetness? Because they want to produce sweet wines that do not have to adhere to the strict quality controls required for Vendanges Tardives or Sélection de Grains Nobles?

Let's look at this from the opposite angle: why not have an obligatory dry-wine designation to help consumers make an informed choice? Not to force producers to make wines that are exclusively dry, but to force producers to label dry wines as dry. Or is that too sensible? They have recently ruled that as from August 2008, all generic Riesling and Pinot Noir (vinified red or rosé) must be dry (maximum of 9 grams for unchaptalized Riesling, 6 grams for chaptalized Riesling, 5 grams for rosé Pinot Noir, and 2 grams for red Pinot Noir). Hopefully this is just a stepping stone, because making the dry style compulsory was unnecessary, and restricting these limits to generic wines does not tackle the worst excesses of residual sugar (if you are trying to find a dry wine), which are produced in the warmer *grand cru* and *lieu-dit* sites. When will they understand that there is no need for any stick or carrot, just transparency and honesty? Will someone see sense and replace this compulsory but far too narrow dry-wine regulation with a complete freedom to make wines of any degree of sweetness, providing that all wines from every permitted grape variety that fall within agreed dry-wine parameters must be labelled dry? Then dry-wine drinkers who have deserted Alsace will at long last have the confidence to return to these wines, while those with a sweet tooth can choose between Vendanges Tardives, Sélection de Grains Nobles, and the balance of Alsace wine without any of these three designations.

THE GRANDS CRUS OF ALSACE

The original *grand cru* legislation was introduced in 1975, but it was not until 1983 that the first list of 25 *grand cru* sites appeared. Three years later, a further 23 were added, and by 2001 there were 50. The rapid deployment of such a large number of so-called *grands crus* attracted much criticism, not least because it excluded what was acknowledged as one of the most famous, truly great *crus* of Alsace: Kaefferkopf in Ammerschwihr. The contention over the exclusion of Kaefferkopf was part of all that was wrong with the declared strategy of the *grand cru* system in Alsace: the decision to limit this status to pure varietal wines of just four grapes. While it might have been true that Muscat, Riesling, Pinot Gris, and Gewurztraminer were and still are the finest wines that Alsace can produce, restricting *grand cru* vineyards to these four varieties robbed us of the chance to buy the finest-quality Pinot Noir, Pinot Blanc, Sylvaner, and Chasselas. Furthermore – and this is where Kaefferkopf comes in – restricting *grand cru* status to pure varietal wines, whether from the famous four grapes or more, robbed us of the opportunity to experience classic blended wines from the greatest vineyards of Alsace.

Even if it is accepted (and for some it is not) that other varietal wines are not in the same league as the big four, why prevent their cultivation for AOC Alsace Grand Cru, when market forces will dictate that most growers would plant the four classic varieties in their most prized *grand cru* sites because they fetch the highest prices? If a producer is determined to grow any of the less lucrative varieties on *grand cru* sites and is willing to accept the drop in income, why prevent him from doing so and us from benefitting from the experience?

Common sense prevailed, and in 2004 Zotzenberg became the first *grand cru* for a variety other than the original four, when this village was recognized as being special for Sylvaner. This was followed by Altenberg de Bergheim for a blend of grapes, and having cleared that hurdle, INAO was forced to award Kaefferkopf *grand cru* status for its blended wines in 2006. It will not stop there. The ball will just keep rolling for other varieties and blends in those *grands crus* that have a history and a passion.

Under the same law that permits local *syndicats* of growers to press for different wine styles under their own particular *grand cru*, they are also permitted to impose more stringent quality criteria on a growth-by-growth basis. Where the *syndicats* have actually done this, you will find the new specifications listed below. Where there are no new specifications, the criteria laid down in the *grand cru* decree applies, and that is as follows. **Riesling and Muscat**: maximum yield of 66 hl/ha (basic limit of 55 hl/ha plus 11 hl/ha PLC); minimum ripeness equivalent to 11% at time of harvest, and chaptalization up to 1.5% allowed. **Pinot Gris and Gewurztraminer**: maximum yield of 66 hl/ha (basic limit of 55 hl/ha plus 11 hl/ha PLC); minimum ripeness equivalent to 12.5% at time of harvest, and chaptalization up to 1.5% allowed. Note that all ripeness levels are expressed as % ABV.

ALTENBERG DE BERGBIETEN

Bergbieten

An exceptional growth, but not a truly great one. Its gypsum-permeated, clayey-marl soil is best for Gewurztraminer, which has a very floral character with immediate appeal, yet can improve for several years in bottle. The wines are allowed to be blended from different varieties. The local *syndicat* has renounced the PLC, limiting the yield to a maximum of 55hl/ha. It has also outlawed all chaptalization, and has increased the minimum ripeness of Riesling and Muscat from 11% to 12%, and that of Pinot Gris and Gewurztraminer from 12.5% to 14%.

🍷 *Etienne Lowe • Frédéric Mochel*

ALTENBERG DE BERGHEIM

Bergheim

This Altenberg has been a true *grand cru* since the 12th century. Its calcareous clay soil is best suited to Gewurztraminer, which is tight and austere in youth, but gains in depth and bouquet with ageing. This *cru* now permits wines made from a blend of grapes.

🏆 *Marcel Deiss* ❽ • *Georges et Claude Freyburger*
• *Louis Freyburger* ❽ • *Charles Koehly* •
Gustave Lorentz

ALTENBERG DE WOLXHEIM
Wolxheim

Although appreciated by Napoleon, this calcareous
clay *cru* cannot honestly be described as one of
the greatest growths of Alsace, but it does have
a certain reputation for its Riesling.

🏆 *Zoeller*

BRAND
Turckheim

This *cru* might legitimately be called Brand New,
the original Brand being a tiny *cru* of little more
than three hectares. In 1924 it was expanded to
include surrounding sites: Steinglitz, Kirchthal,
Schneckenberg, Weingarten, and Jebsal, each with
its own fine reputation. By 1980 it had grown to 30
hectares (74 acres) and it is now almost double that.
This confederation of *lieux-dits* is one of the most
magnificent sites in the entire region, and the
quality of the wines consistently excites me – great
Riesling, Pinot Gris, and Gewurztraminer. The local
syndicat has reduced chaptalization of Riesling and
Muscat from the allowable 1.5% to 1%, and that of
Pinot Gris and Gewurztraminer from 1.5% to 0.5%.
It has also increased the minimum ripeness of
Riesling and Muscat from 11% to 11.5%, and that of
Pinot Gris and Gewurztraminer from 12.5% to 13.5%.

🏆 *Albert Boxler* • *Dopff Au Moulin* • *JosMeyer* ❽
• *Preiss-Zimmer* • *Zind Humbrecht* ❽

BRUDERTHAL
Molsheim

Riesling and Gewurztraminer – reputedly the best
varieties – occupy most of this calcareous clay *cru*.
I have tasted good, fruity Riesling from Bernard
Weber, which was elegant, but not really top stuff.
Gérard Neumeyer used not to impress me at all,
but his genuinely dry 2001 Pinot Gris was one of
the best Bruderthal I have tasted. The local *syndicat*
has renounced all chaptalization. It has also
increased the minimum ripeness of Riesling and
Muscat from 11% to 12%, and that of Pinot Gris
and Gewurztraminer from 12.5% to 13%.

🏆 *Alain Klingenfus* • *Gérard Neumeyer*

EICHBERG
Eguisheim

This calcareous clay *cru* has the lowest rainfall in
Colmar and produces very aromatic wines of
exceptional delicacy, yet great longevity. Famous
for Gewurztraminer, which is potentially the finest
in Alsace, Eichberg is also capable of making
superb long-lived Riesling and Pinot Gris. The local
syndicat has reduced chaptalization of Riesling from
1.5% to 1%, and outlawed it completely for Pinot

Gris and Gewurztraminer. It has also increased the
minimum ripeness of Riesling from 11% to 11.5%,
and Pinot Gris and Gewurztraminer from 12.5% to
13%. The chaptalization and minimum ripeness of
Muscat remain the same.

🏆 *Charles Baur* ❽ • *Emile Beyer* • *Léon Beyer*
(not sold as such, Beyer's Cuvée des Comtes
d'Eguisheim is 100% pure Eichberg) • *Paul
Ginglinger* ◉ • *Gruss* • *Albert Hertz* ❽

ENGELBERG
Dahlenheim and Scharrachbergheim

One of the least-encountered *grands crus*, this
vineyard gets long hours of sunshine and is supposed
to favour Gewurztraminer and Riesling, but few of
the wines I have tasted suggest anything special.

🏆 *Jean-Pierre Bechtold* • *Pfister*

FLORIMONT
Ingersheim and Katzenthal

Mediterranean flora abounds on the sun-blessed,
calcareous clay slopes of this *cru* – hence its
name, meaning "hill of flowers" – the excellent
microclimate producing some stunning Riesling
and Gewurztraminer.

🏆 *François Bohn* • *Jean Geiler* • *René Meyer*
• *Bruno Sorg*

FRANKSTEIN
Dambach-la-Ville

Not so much one vineyard as four separate spurs,
the warm, well-drained, granite soil of this *cru* is
best suited to the production of delicate, racy
Riesling, and elegant Gewurztraminer. J Hauller
used to be by far and away the best producer of
Frankstein, for both the Riesling and Gewurztraminer.

🏆 *Charles & Dominique Frey* ❽ • *Ruhlman* •
Schaeffer-Woerly

FROEHN
Zellenberg

This *cru* sweeps up and around the southern half
of the hill upon which Zellenberg is situated. The
marly-clay soil suits Muscat, Gewurztraminer, and
Pinot Gris, in that order, and the wines are typically
rich and long lived. The local *syndicat* has outlawed
all chaptalization, and increased the minimum
ripeness of Riesling and Muscat from 11% to 12%,
and that of Pinot Gris and Gewurztraminer from
12.5% to 13.5%.

🏆 *J P & J F Becker* ❽

FURSTENTUM
Kientzheim and Sigolsheim

This estate is best for Riesling, although the vines
have to be well established to take full advantage
of the calcareous soil. Gewurztraminer can also be
fabulous – in an elegant, more floral, less spicy style
– and Pinot Gris excels even when the vines are
very young. The local *syndicat* has reduced all
chaptalization from the allowable 1.5% to 0.5%. It
has also increased the minimum ripeness of Riesling
and Muscat from 11% to 11.5%, and Pinot Gris and
Gewurztraminer from 12.5% to 13%.

🏆 *Paul Blanck* ◉ • *Bott-Geyl* ❽ • *Albert Mann* ◉
• *Weinbach/Faller*

GEISBERG
Ribeauvillé

Geisberg has been well documented since as long
ago as 1308 as Riesling country *par excellence*. The
calcareous, stony-and-clayey sandstone soil

produces fragrant, powerful, and long-lived wines
of great finesse. Trimbach owns vines here, and
in a contiguous plot with vines in Osterberg, the
whole of which produces the superb Riesling
Cuvée Frédéric Émile. The local *syndicat* has
reduced the chaptalization of Riesling, Pinot Gris,
and Gewurztraminer from 1.5% to 0.5%. It has
also increased the minimum ripeness of Riesling
from 11% to 11.5%, and that of Pinot Gris
and Gewurztraminer from 12.5% to 13%.
The chaptalization and minimum ripeness of
Muscat remain the same.

🏆 *Robert Faller* • *André Kientzler*

GLOECKELBERG
Rodern and St-Hippolyte

This clay-granite *cru* is known for its light,
elegant, and yet persistent style of wine, with
Gewurztraminer and Pinot Gris the most successful
varieties. The local *syndicat* has halved the PLC,
thereby reducing the absolute maximum yield
allowed to 60.5hl/ha.

🏆 *Koberlé-Kreyer*

GOLDERT
Gueberschwihr

Dating back to the year 750, and recognized on
export markets as long ago as 1728, Goldert derives
its name from the colour of its wines, the most
famous of which is the golden Gewurztraminer. The
Muscat grape variety also excels on the calcareous
clay soil, and whatever the varietal, the style of
wine is rich and spicy, with a luscious creaminess.

🏆 *Ernest Burn* (Clos St-Imer) • *Zind
Humbrecht* ❽

HATSCHBOURG
Hattstatt and Voegtlinshoffen

Gewurztraminer from this south-facing, calcareous
marl soil slope excels, but Pinot Gris and Riesling
are also excellent.

🏆 *Buecher-Fix* • *Joseph Cattin* • *André Hartmann*
• *Lucien Meyer*

HENGST
Wintzenheim

Hengst Gewurztraminer is a very special, complex
wine, seeming to combine the classic qualities of
this variety with the orange zest and rose-petal
aromas more characteristic of the Muscat grape
variety. But Hengst is a very flexible *cru*. Besides
Gewurztraminer, its calcareous marl soil also
produces top-quality Muscat, Riesling, and Pinot Gris.
The local *syndicat* has renounced all chaptalization.
It has also increased the minimum ripeness of
Riesling and Muscat from 11% to 12%, and that of
Pinot Gris and Gewurztraminer from 12.5% to 13%.

🏆 *JosMeyer* ❽ • *Albert Mann* ◉ • *Zind
Humbrecht* ❽

KAEFFERKOPF
Ammerschwihr

The saga of Kaefferkopf's classification finally ended in 2006, when it became the 51st *grand cru*. The first list of potential *grands crus* was published in 1975, and although Kaefferkopf had been the very first named site in Alsace to have its boundaries delimited (in 1932 by a Colmar tribunal) and was also the only named site to be recognized in the original AOC Alsace of 1962, it was not included in the 50 *grands crus* delimited between 1983 and 1992. Kaefferkopf's traditional practice of blending two or more grape varieties was in direct conflict with the pure varietal connotation of AOC Alsace Grand Cru. Furthermore, it was claimed that the original 1932 delimitation covered an area of geologically diverse soils. However, the concept of *grand cru* wine consisting of more than one variety was accepted in principle by 2005, following the changes to Altenberg de Bergheim, and the question of geological uniformity, so often spouted by pedants of the *grand cru* system, can only be true to the subsoil, not the topsoil, and the subsoil across the entire area originally classifed by the tribunal is pure granite. All in all, some 70ha have been delimited, compared to the 67.81ha delimited in 1932. This not only includes vineyards that were not previously classified as Kaefferkopf; it also excludes some vineyards that were. (However, their owners have the right to use the Kaefferkopf name for the next 25 years!) Authorized grape varieties are Gewurztraminer, Riesling, and Pinot Gris (each of which may be either a single variety or part of a blend) plus Muscat (only as part of a blend).

⚆ *J B Adam* (Jean-Baptiste) ◉ • *Audrey & Christian Binner* ◉ • *Marcel Freyburger* ❸ • *Keuhn* • *Meyer-Fonné* (Nicolas) • *Martin Schaetzel* ❸ • *Maurice Schoech*

KANZLERBERG
Bergheim

Although this tiny cru adjoins the western edge of Altenberg de Bergheim, the wines of its gypsum-permeated, clayey-marl *terroir* are so different from those of the Altenberg growth that the vinification of the two sites has always been kept separate. The wines have the same potential longevity, but the Kanzlerbergs are fuller and fatter. Kanzlerberg has a reputation for both Riesling and Gewurztraminer, but their ample weight can be at odds with their varietal aromas when young, and both wines require plenty of bottle age to achieve their true finesse. The local *syndicat* has renounced the PLC, limiting the yield to an absolute maximum of 55hl/ha. It has also outlawed all chaptalization, and increased the minimum ripeness of Riesling and Muscat from 11% to 12%, and that of Pinot Gris and Gewurztraminer from 12.5% to 14%.

⚆ *Louis Freyburger* ❸ • *Sylvie Spielmann* ❸

KASTELBERG
Andlau

One of the oldest vineyards in Alsace, Kastelberg has been planted with vines since the Roman occupation. Situated on a small hill next to Wiebelsberg, Andlau's other *grand cru*, the very steep, schistous *terroir* has long proved to be an excellent site for racy and delicate Riesling, although the wines can be very closed when young and require a few years to develop their lovely bottle aromas. Kastelberg wines remain youthful for 20 years or more, and even show true *grand cru* quality in so-called "off" years.

⚆ *Guy Wach*

KESSLER
Guebwiller

Though a *cru* more *premier* than *grand* (the truly famous sites of Guebwiller being Kitterlé and Wanne, the latter not classified), the central part of Kessler is certainly deserving of *grand cru* status. Here, the vines grow in a well-protected, valley-like depression, one side of which has a very steep, south-southeast facing slope. Kessler is renowned for its full, spicy, and mellow Gewurztraminer, but Riesling can be much the greater wine. The local *syndicat* has renounced the PLC, limiting the yield to an absolute maximum of 55hl/ha. It has also outlawed all chaptalization, and increased the minimum ripeness of Riesling and Muscat from 11% to 11.5%, and that of Pinot Gris and Gewurztraminer from 12.5% to 13.5%.

⚆ *Dirler-Cadé* ❸ • *Schlumberger*

KIRCHBERG DE BARR
Barr

The true *grands crus* of Barr are Gaensbroennel and Zisser, but these have been incorporated into the calcareous marl *terroir* of Kirchberg, which is known for its full-bodied yet delicate wines that exhibit exotic spicy fruit, a characteristic that applies not only to Pinot Gris and Gewurztraminer but also to Riesling.

⚆ *Stoeffler* ◉

KIRCHBERG DE RIBEAUVILLÉ
Ribeauvillé

One of the few *lieux-dits* that has regularly been used to market Alsace wine over the centuries. It is famous for Riesling, which typically is firm, totally dry, and long lived, developing intense petrolly characteristics with age. Kirchberg de Ribeauvillé also produces great Muscat with a discreet, yet very specific, orange-and-musk aroma, excellent acidity, and lots of finesse. The local *syndicat* has reduced the chaptalization of Riesling, Pinot Gris and Gewurztraminer from 1.5% to 0.5%. It has also increased the minimum ripeness of Riesling from 11% to 11.5%, and that of Pinot Gris and Gewurztraminer from 12.5% to 13%. The chaptalization and minimum ripeness of Muscat remain the same.

⚆ *André Kientzler* • *Jean Sipp* • *Louis Sipp* ◉

KITTERLÉ
Guebwiller

ALSACE
DOMAINES
SCHLUMBERGER

GRAND CRU
KITTERLÉ 2001
GEWURZTRAMINER

Of all the grape varieties that are grown on this volcanic sandstone *terroir*, it is the crisp, petrolly Riesling that shows greatest finesse. Gewurztraminer and Pinot Gris are also very

good in a gently rich, supple, and smoky-mellow style. The local *syndicat* has renounced the PLC, limiting the yield to an absolute maximum of 55hl/ha. It has also outlawed all chaptalization, and has increased the minimum ripeness of Riesling and Muscat from 11% to 11.5%, and that of Pinot Gris and Gewurztraminer from 12.5% to 13.5%.

⚆ *Schlumberger*

MAMBOURG
Sigolsheim

The reputation of this *cru* has been documented since 783, when it was known as the "Sigolttesberg". A limestone *coteau*, with calcareous clay topsoil, Mambourg stretches for well over 1 kilometre (¾ mile), penetrating further into the plain than any other spur of the Vosges foothills. Its vineyards, supposed to be the warmest in Alsace, produce wines that tend to be rich and warm, mellow and liquorous. Both the Gewurztraminer and the Pinot Gris have plenty of smoky-rich spice in them. The local *syndicat* has reduced chaptalization of Riesling, Pinot Gris and Gewurztraminer from 1.5% to 0.5%. It has also increased the minimum ripeness of Riesling from 11% to 12%, and that of Pinot Gris and Gewurztraminer from 12.5% to 13%.

⚆ *J-M & F Bernhard* • *Marcel Deiss* ❸ • *Daniel Fritz* • *Pierre Sparr* • *Marc Tempé* ❸

MANDELBERG
Mittelwihr and Beblenheim

Mandelberg – "almond tree hill" – has been planted with vines since Gallo-Roman times, and used as an appellation since 1925. Its reputation has been built on Riesling, although today more Gewurztraminer is planted; high-quality Pinot Gris and Muscat is also produced. The local *syndicat* has renounced the PLC, limiting the yield to an absolute maximum of 55hl/ha. It has also outlawed chaptalization for Pinot Gris and Gewurztraminer, increasing the minimum ripeness for these two grapes from 12.5% to 13%. The minimum ripeness for Riesling and Muscat remains at 11%, and the possibility of chaptalization is retained exclusively for these two varieties.

⚆ *Bott-Geyl* ❸ • *Hartweg* • *Frédéric Mallo* • *André Stentz* ◉

MARCKRAIN
Bennwihr and Sigolsheim

Markrain is the east-facing slope of the Mambourg, which overlooks Sigolsheim. The soil is a limestone-marl with oolite pebbles interlayering the marl beds. It is mostly planted with Gewurztraminer, with some Pinot Gris and a few Muscat vines. The Bennewihr *coopérative* usually makes a decent Pinot Gris under the Bestheim label. The local *syndicat* has reduced the chaptalization of Pinot Gris and Gewurztraminer from an allowable 1.5% to 1%, and increased the minimum ripeness of these grapes from 12.5% to 13%. The chaptalization and minimum ripeness of Riesling and Muscat remain the same.

⚆ *Bestheim* • *Stirn*

MOENCHBERG
Andlau and Eichhoffen

Moenchberg – "monk's hill"– was owned by a Benedictine order until 1097, when it was taken over by the inhabitants of Eichhoffen. With its clayey-marl soil, excellent exposure to the sun, and very hot, dry microclimate, this *cru* has built up a reputation for firm, intensely fruity, and very racy Riesling. Excellent though it is, however, the finest

Moenchberg wines I have tasted have been Pinot Gris. Not to be confused with the equally excellent *grand cru* Muenchberg of Nothalten.

♟ *André & Rémy Gresser*

MUENCHBERG
Nothalten

This sunny vineyard belonging to the abbey of Baumgarten, whose monks tended vines in the 12th century, nestles under the protection of the Undersberg, a 900-metre (2,950-feet) peak in the Vosges mountains. The striking style of Muenchberg's wines is due in part to the special microclimate it enjoys, and also to the ancient, unique, and pebbly volcanic sandstone soil. The wines are now allowed to be blended from different varieties. The local *syndicat* has renounced the PLC, limiting the yield to an absolute maximum of 55hl/ha. It has also outlawed all chaptalization and has increased the minimum ripeness of Riesling and Muscat from 11% to 12%, and that of Pinot Gris and Gewurztraminer from 12.5% to 14%.

♟ *André Ostertag ❸ • Jean-Luc Schwartz*

OLLWILLER
Wuenheim

Ollwiller's annual rainfall is one of the lowest in France, with Riesling and Gewurztraminer faring best on its clayey-sand soil – although it is not one of the greatest *grands crus*, and the recommended wines are rated in that context.

♟ *Château Ollwiller • CV Vieil Armand*

OSTERBERG
Ribeauvillé

This stony-clay growth abuts Geisberg, another Ribeauvillé *grand cru*, and makes equally superb Riesling country. The wines age very well, developing the petrolly nose of a fine Riesling. Trimbach owns vines here, and in a contiguous plot with vines in Geisberg, the whole of which produces the superb Riesling Cuvée Frédéric Émile. Gewurztraminer and Pinot Gris also fare well.

♟ *André Kientzler • CV de Ribeauvillé • Louis Sipp ◉*

PFERSIGBERG *also spelled* PFERSICHBERG & PFIRSIGBERG
Eguisheim and Wettolsheim

A calcareous sandstone soil well known for its full, aromatic, and long-lived Gewurztraminer – although Pinot Gris, Riesling, and Muscat also fare well here. The wines all share a common succulence of fruit acidity, and possess exceptional aromas. The local *syndicat* has reduced chaptalization of Riesling from 1.5% to 1% and outlawed it completely for Pinot Gris and Gewurztraminer. It has also increased the minimum ripeness of Riesling from 11% to 11.5%, and that of Pinot Gris and Gewurztraminer from 12.5% to 13%. The chaptalization and minimum ripeness of Muscat remain the same.

♟ *Charles Baur ❸ • Emile Beyer • Léon Beyer* (not

sold as such, but Beyer's Cuvée Particulière is 100% pure Pfersigberg) • *Pierre Freudenreich • Bruno Sorg*

PFINGSTBERG
Orschwihr

All four *grand cru* varieties grow well on the calcareous-marl and clayey-sandstone of this *cru*, producing wines of typically floral aroma, combined with rich, honeyed fruit. The local *syndicat* has renounced all chaptalization. It has also increased the minimum ripeness of Riesling and Muscat from 11% to 12%, and that of Pinot Gris and Gewurztraminer from 12.5% to 13.5%.

♟ *Lucien Albrecht • François Braun • François Schmitt • Albert Ziegler*

PRAELATENBERG
Kintzheim and Orschwiller

Although Praelatenberg dominates the north side of the village of Orschwiller, virtually all the *cru* actually falls within the boundary of Kintzheim, 1.5 kilometres (1 mile) away. The locals say that all four varieties grow to perfection here, but Pinot Gris has been best in my experience, followed by Riesling, and then Gewurztraminer. The local *syndicat* has reduced all chaptalization from an allowable 1.5% to 1%. It has also increased the minimum ripeness of Riesling and Muscat from 11% to 11.5%, and that of Pinot Gris and Gewurztraminer from 12.5% to 13%.

♟ *Allimant-Laugner • Jean Becker • Engel Frères • Siffert*

RANGEN
Thann and Vieux-Thann

The 15th-century satirist Sebastian Brant, writing about the little-known travels of Hercules through Alsace, reveals that the mythical strongman once drank so much Rangen that he fell asleep. So ashamed was he on waking that he ran away, leaving behind his bludgeon – the club which today appears on Colmar's coat of arms.

So steep that it can be cultivated only when terraced, Rangen's volcanic soil is very poor organically, but extremely fertile minerally. It also drains very quickly, and its dark colour makes it almost too efficient in retaining the immense heat that pours into this sweltering suntrap. However, this fierce heat and rapid drainage are essentially responsible for the regular stressing of the vine, which is what gives the wines their famed power and pungency. Rangen produces great wines even in the poorest years, making it a true *grand cru* in every sense.

♟ *Schoffit • Wolfberger • Zind Humbrecht ❸*

ROSACKER
Hunawihr

First mentioned in the 15th century, this *cru* has built up a fine reputation for Riesling, but one wine – Trimbach's Clos Ste-Hune – is almost every year far and away the finest Riesling in Alsace. Occasionally other producers make an exceptional vintage that may challenge it, but none has consistently matched Clos Ste-Hune's excellence. Trimbach makes no mention of Rosacker on its label because the family believes, as do a small number of internationally known producers, who avoid using the term, that much of Rosacker should not be classified as *grand cru* (although Trimbach used to sell Clos Ste-Hune *grand cru* in the 1940s). Rosacker's calcareous and marly-clay soil is rich in magnesium and makes fine Gewurztraminer

as well as top Riesling. The local *syndicat* has reduced chaptalization of Riesling, Pinot Gris, and Gewurztraminer from 1.5% to 1%. It has also increased the minimum ripeness of Riesling from 11% to 11.5%, and that of Pinot Gris and Gewurztraminer from 12.5% to 13%. The chaptalization and minimum ripeness of Muscat remain the same.

♟ *Mader • CV de Hunawihr • Roger Jung • F E Trimbach* (Clos Ste-Hune)

SAERING
Guebwiller

This vineyard, first documented in 1250 and marketed since 1830, is situated below Kessler and Kitterlé, Guebwiller's other two *grands crus*. Like Kessler, this *cru* is more *premier* than *grand* (yet still better than many of the *grands crus*). The floral, fruity, and elegant Riesling is best, especially in hot years, when it becomes exotically peachy, but Muscat and Gewurztraminer can also be fine.

♟ *Dirler-Cadé ❸ • Loberger • Schlumberger*

SCHLOSSBERG
Kientzheim and Kaysersberg

The production of Schlossberg was controlled by charter in 1928, and in 1975 it became the first Alsace *grand cru*. Although its granite *terroir* looks equally shared by the two sites, less than half a hectare (1.25 acres) belongs to Kaysersberg. Schlossberg is best for Riesling, but Gewurztraminer can be successful in so-called "off" vintages. The wine is full of elegance and finesse, whether produced in a classic, restrained style, as Blanck often is, or with the more exuberant fruit that typifies Weinbach/Faller. The local *syndicat* has reduced the chaptalization of Pinot Gris and Gewurztraminer from an allowable 1.5% to 0.5%, and increased the minimum ripeness of these grapes from 12.5% to 13%. The chaptalization and minimum ripeness of Riesling and Muscat remain the same.

♟ *Paul Blanck ◉ • Joseph Fritsch • Albert Mann ◉ • Weinbach/Faller • Ziegler-Mauler*

SCHOENENBOURG
Riquewihr

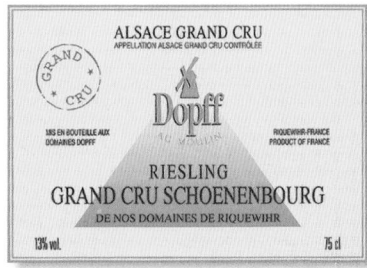

This vineyard has always had a reputation for producing great Riesling and Muscat, although modern wines show Riesling to be supreme, with Pinot Gris vying with Muscat for the number two spot. Schoenenbourg's gypsum-permeated, marly-and-sandy soil produces very rich, aromatic wines in a *terroir* that has potential for VT and SGN.

♟ *J P & J F Becker ❸ • Marcel Deiss ❸ • Roger Jung*

SOMMERBERG
Niedermorschwihr and Katzenthal

Known since 1214, the fame of this *cru* was such that a strict delimitation was in force by the 17th century. Situated in the foothills leading up to Trois-Épis, its granite soil is supposed to be equally excellent for all four classic varieties, although

Riesling stands out in my experience. Sommerberg wines are typically aromatic, with an elegant succulence of fruit.

🏆 *Albert Boxler*

SONNENGLANZ
Beblenheim

In 1935, two years after Kaefferkopf was defined by tribunal at Colmar, Sonnenglanz received a similar certification. Unlike at Kaefferkopf, however, its producers failed to exploit the appellation until 1952, when the local cooperative was formed. But Sonnenglanz is a *grand cru* and Kaefferkopf technically is not. Once renowned for its Sylvaner, the calcareous clay soil of Sonnenglanz is best suited to Gewurztraminer and Pinot Gris, which can be very ripe and golden in colour.

🏆 *J P & J F Becker* ❽ • *Bott-Geyl* • *Hartweg*

SPIEGEL
Bergholtz and Guebwiller

Known for only 50 years or so, this is not one of the great *grands crus* of Alsace. However, its sandstone and marl *terroir* can produce fine, racy Riesling with a delicate bouquet and good, though not great, Gewurztraminer and Muscat. The local *syndicat* has renounced all chaptalization of Pinot Gris and Gewurztraminer, but permissible chaptalization of Riesling and Muscat remains at 1.5%. It has also increased the minimum ripeness of Pinot Gris and Gewurztraminer from 12.5% to

13.5%, but that of Riesling and Muscat remains 11%.

🏆 *Dirler-Cadé* • *Loberger* • *Eugène Meyer* ❽ • *Wolfberger*

SPOREN
Riquewihr

Sporen is one of the truly great *grands crus*, its stony, clayey-marl soil producing wines of remarkable finesse. Historically, this *terroir* is famous for Gewurztraminer and Pinot Gris, which occupy virtually all of its vineyard today, but it was also traditional to grow a mix of varieties and vinify them together to produce a classic non-varietal wine, such as Hugel's Sporen Gentil, which was capable of ageing 30 years or more (and in a totally different class from that firm's own Gentil, which does not come from Sporen and is a blend of separately vinified wines).

🏆 *Dopff Au Moulin* • *Roger Jung* • *Mittnacht-Klack*

STEINERT
Pfaffenheim and Westhalten

Pinot Gris is the king of this stony, calcareous *cru*, although historically Schneckenberg (now part of Steinert) was always renowned for producing a Pinot Blanc that tasted more like Pinot Gris. The Pfaffenheim cooperative still produces a Pinot Blanc Schneckenberg (although not a *grand cru*, of course), and its stunning Pinot Gris steals the show. Steinert's Pinot Blanc-cum-Gris reputation illustrates the exceptional concentration of these wines. Gewurztraminer fares best on the lower slopes, Riesling on the higher, more sandy slopes. The local *syndicat* has reduced chaptalization of Riesling and Muscat from the allowable 1.5% to 1%, and that of Pinot Gris and Gewurztraminer from 1.5% to 0.5%.

It has also increased the minimum ripeness of Riesling and Muscat from 11% to 12%, and that of Pinot Gris and Gewurztraminer from 12.5% to 13.5%.

🏆 *CV Pfaffenheim* • *Rieflé* • *François Runner* • *Pierre Paul Zink*

STEINGRUBLER
Wettolsheim

Although this calcareous-marl and sandstone *cru* is not one of the great names of Alsace, I have enjoyed some excellent Steingrubler wines, particularly Pinot Gris. This can be very rich, yet show great finesse. Certainly Steingrubler is one of the better lesser-known *grands crus*, and it could well be a great growth of the future. The local *syndicat* has reduced all chaptalization from an allowable 1.5% to 1%. It has also increased the minimum ripeness of Riesling and Muscat from 11% to 11.5%, and that of Pinot Gris and Gewurztraminer from 12.5% to 13%.

🏆 *Barmès-Buecher* ❽ • *Robert Dietrich* • *Albert Mann* ◉ • *Wolfberger* • *Wunsch & Mann* (Collection Joseph Mann)

STEINKLOTZ
Marlenheim

Steinklotz ("block of stone") was part of the estate of the Merovingian king Childebert II, from which Marlenheim derives its reputation for Pinot Noir, but since it has flown the *grand cru* flag, Steinklotz is supposed to be good for Pinot Gris, Riesling, and Gewurztraminer. However, local growers are determined to have their Pinot Noir recognized and will be applying for *grand cru* status for these wines.

🏆 *Romain Fritsch* • *Helfrich*

VORBOURG
Rouffach and Westhalten

All four varieties excel in this calcareous sand-stone *terroir*, whose wines are said to develop a bouquet of peaches, apricots, mint, and hazelnut – but Riesling and Pinot Gris fare best. Muscat favours warmer vintages, when its wines positively explode with flavour, and Gewurztraminer excels in some years but not in others. Vorbourg catches the full glare of the sun from dawn to dusk and so is also well suited to Pinot Noir, which is consequently heavy with pigment. The local *syndicat* has renounced all chaptalization. It has also increased the minimum ripeness of Riesling and Muscat from 11% to 12%, and that of Pinot Gris and Gewurztraminer from 12.5% to 13.5%.

🏆 *de l'École* (Fleuron de Vorbourg) • *Muré* ◉ (Clos St-Landelin)

WIEBELSBERG
Andlau

This vineyard has very good sun exposure, and its siliceous soil retains heat and drains well. Riesling does well, producing wines that can be very fine

THE VILLAGE OF RIQUEWIHR
Alsace is full of beautiful villages, but Riquewihr is one of the most delightful, having avoided much of the commercial exploitation that has made nearby Ribeauvillé a more thriving yet less intimate place.

and floral, slowly developing a delicate, ripe-peachy fruit on the palate.

🏆 *André & Rémy Gresser • André Rieffel*

WINECK-SCHLOSSBERG
Katzenthal and Ammerschwihr

Wineck-Schlossberg's granite vineyards enjoy a sheltered microclimate that primarily favours Riesling, followed by Gewurztraminer. The wines are light and delicate, with a fragrant aroma.

🏆 *J B Adam* (Jean-Baptiste) ⊚ • *Bernhard • Clément-Klur • Meyer-Fonné*

WINZENBERG
Blienschwiller

Locals claim that this *cru* is cited in "old documents" and that Riesling and Gewurztraminer fare best in its granite vineyards. The Riesling I have encountered has been light and charming, but not special. Gewurztraminer has definitely been much the superior wine, showing fine, fresh aromas with a refined spiciness of some complexity.

🏆 *Auther*

ZINNKOEPFLÉ
Soultzmatt and Westhalten

Zinnkoepflé's hot, dry microclimate gives rise to a rare concentration of Mediterranean and Caspian fauna and flora near its exposed summit. The heat and the arid, calcareous sandstone soil are what gives it its reputation for strong, spicy, and fiery styles of Pinot Gris and Gewurztraminer. The Riesling is a delicate and most discreet wine, but this is deceptive and it can, given decent bottle-age, be just as powerful. Mention should be made of Seppi Landmann, who has produced some stunning Zinnkoepflé, but also far too many ordinary wines, and a few absolute bummers, thus does not get a wholehearted recommendation below.

🏆 *Léon Boesch* ⊚ • *Agathe Bursin • Jean-Marie Haag • Schlegel-Boeglin*

ZOTZENBERG
Mittelbergheim

First mentioned in 1364, when it was known as Zoczenberg, the wines of this calcareous clay *terroir* have been sold under its own *lieu-dit* since the beginning of the 20th century. It is historically the finest site in Alsace for Sylvaner, and in 2004 became the first *grand cru* to be officially recognized for this supposedly lowly grape variety. Gewurztraminer and Riesling show a creamy richness of fruit.

🏆 *Agathe Bursin • André Rieffel*

THE APPELLATIONS OF
ALSACE AND LORRAINE

ALSACE AOC

This appellation covers all the wines of Alsace (with the exception of Alsace Grand Cru and Crémant d'Alsace), but 95 per cent of the wines are often sold according to grape variety. These are: Pinot (which may also be labelled Pinot Blanc, Clevner, or Klevner), Pinot Gris, Pinot Noir, Riesling, Gewurztraminer, Muscat, Sylvaner, Chasselas (which may also be labelled Gutedel), and Auxerrois. This practice effectively creates nine "varietal" AOCs under the one umbrella appellation, and these are listed separately.

ALSACE GRAND CRU AOC

The current production of *grand cru* wine is approximately 4 per cent of the total volume of AOC Alsace. Because every *cru*, or growth, makes a wine of a specific character, it is impossible to give a generalized description.

🍷 WHITE *See* The Grands Crus of Alsace, p237

🍇 Muscat, Riesling, Gewurztraminer, Pinot Gris, Sylvaner (Zotzenberg only)

ALSACE SÉLECTION DE GRAINS NOBLES AOC

This is not an AOC in itself, but a subordinate designation that may be appended either to the basic appellation or to Alsace Grand Cru AOC. Its production is strictly controlled, and the regulations are far tougher than for any AOC elsewhere. In theory, these wines are harvested after VT, but in practice they are picked in several *tries* prior to the best VT, which will be produced from what remains on the vine after a further period of ripening.

These rare and sought-after wines are made from botrytis-affected grapes. Unlike Sauternes, however, Alsace is no haven for "noble rot", which occurs haphazardly and in much reduced concentrations. The wines are, therefore, produced in tiny quantities and sold at very high prices. The *sauternais* are often amazed not only by the high sugar levels (while chaptalization is not permitted in Alsace, it has become almost mandatory in Sauternes), but also by how little sulphur is used, highlighting why SGN has become one of the world's greatest dessert wines.

🍷 WHITE Now made with less alcohol and higher sugar than when first introduced, these wines possess even more finesse than before. While Gewurztraminer is almost too easy to make, Pinot Gris offers the ideal balance between quality and price; just a couple of Muscat have been produced, and Riesling SGN is in a class of its own. Check the appropriate varietal entry for the best producers.

🍇 Gewurztraminer, Pinot Gris, Riesling, Muscat

🍂 5–30 years

ALSACE VENDANGE TARDIVE AOC

This is not an AOC in itself, but a subordinate designation that may be appended either to the basic appellation or to Alsace Grand Cru AOC. Its production is controlled, and the regulations are far stricter than for any AOC elsewhere in France. VT is far less consistent in quality and character than SGN. This is because some producers make these wines from grapes that have the correct minimum sugar content, but that were picked with the rest of the crop, not late-harvested. Such VT lacks the true character of a late-harvested wine, which is only brought about by the complex changes that occur inside a grape that has remained on the vine until November or December. As the leaves begin to fall and the sap retreats to the protection of the root system, the grapes, cut off from the vine's metabolic system, start dehydrating. The compounds that this process (known as *passerillage*) produces are in turn affected by the prevailing climatic conditions. *Passerillé* grapes that have endured progressively colder temperatures (the norm) and those that have enjoyed a late Indian summer (not uncommon) will produce entirely different wines.

Until the regulations are changed to ensure that VT is always harvested after a certain specified date, choose recommended wines and look for a date of harvest on the back label.

Another aspect that requires regulating is the relative sweetness of the wine, as VT can be anything from almost dry to sweeter than some SGN. Refer to the appropriate varietal entry for the best producers.

🍷 WHITE Whether dry, medium-sweet, or sweet, this relatively full-bodied wine should always have the true character of *passerillage* – although sometimes this will be overwhelmed by botrytis. Gewurztraminer is the most commonly encountered variety, but only the best have the right balance; Pinot Gris and Riesling both offer an ideal balance between quality, availability, and price. Muscat is almost as rare for VT as it is for SGN, as it tends to go very flabby when overripe.

🍇 Gewurztraminer, Pinot Gris, Riesling, Muscat

🍂 5–20 years

AUXERROIS AOC

Theoretically this designation does not exist, but Auxerrois is one of the varieties permitted for the production of Pinot wine and makes such a distinctly different product that it has often been labelled separately. This practice, currently on the increase, is "officially tolerated".

WHITE Fatter than Pinot Blanc, with a more buttery, honeyed, and spicy character to the fruit, the greatest asset of Auxerrois is its natural richness and immediate appeal. Inclined to low acidity, it can easily become flabby and so musky it tastes almost foxy, but the best Auxerrois can give Pinot Gris a run for its money.

🍇 Auxerrois

⌛ Up to 5 years

✓ *Emile Beyer • Rolly Gassmann • JosMeyer* ❽ *• André Kientzler • Julien Rieffel* (the Klevner Vieilles Vignes is pure Auxerrois despite the Pinot Blanc synonym) *• Bruno Sorg • Marc Tempé* ❽ (Vieilles Vignes)

CHASSELAS AOC

Rarely seen, but enjoying something of a revival among a few specialist growers.

WHITE The best Chasselas wines are not actually bottled, but sit in vats waiting to be blended into anonymous *cuvées* of Edelzwicker. They are neither profound nor complex, but teem with fresh, fragrant fruit and are an absolute joy to drink; they taste better, however, before they are bottled than after. The fruit is so delicate that it needs a lift to survive the shock of being bottled, and the wine would probably benefit from being left on lees and bottled very cold to retain a bit of tongue-tingling carbonic gas.

🍇 Chasselas

⌛ Upon purchase

✓ *Paul Blanck • JosMeyer* ❽ *• André Kientzler • Schoffit*

CLASSIC ALSACE BLENDS

Despite the varietal wine hype, Alsace is more than capable of producing the finest-quality classic blends, but their number is small and dwindles every year because so few consumers realize their true quality. It is difficult for producers to make potential customers appreciate why their blends are more expensive than ordinary Edelzwicker, but classic Alsace blends should no more be categorized with Edelzwicker than *crus classés* compared with generic Bordeaux. This category focuses attention on the region's top-performing blends which, whether or not they fetch them, deserve *grand cru* prices. Unlike the blending of Edelzwicker, for which various wines are mixed together – and where there is always the temptation to get rid of unwanted wines – the different varieties in most classic Alsace blends always come from the same vineyard and are traditionally harvested and vinified together. *See also* Kaefferkopf, p239.

WHITE Most of these wines improve with age, but go through phases when one or other grape variety dominates, which is interesting to observe and should help you to understand why you prefer to drink a particular blend. Depending on the amounts involved, Gewurztraminer typically dominates in the young wine, followed by Pinot Gris then, many years later, Riesling, but other varieties may also be involved when overripe.

🍇 Chasselas, Sylvaner, Pinot Blanc, Pinot Gris, Pinot Noir, Auxerrois, Gewurztraminer, Muscat Blanc à Petits Grains, Muscat Rosé à Petits Grains, Muscat Ottonel, Riesling

✓ *Marcel Deiss* ❽ (Grand Vin de Schoenbourg, Altenberg de Bergheim Assemblage, Burg, Engelgarten) *• CV Ribeauvillé* (Clos du Zahnacker equal parts Gewurztraminer, Pinot Gris, and Riesling) *• Rominger* ◉ (Le Zinn) •

Jean Sipp (Clos du Schlossberg 50% Riesling, 20% Gewurztraminer, 20% Pinot Gris, 10% Muscat) *• Louis Sipp* ◉ (Côtes de Ribeauvillé 40% Pinot Blanc plus 60% Sylvaner, Riesling, and Gewurztraminer)

CLEVNER AOC

Commonly used synonym under which Pinot is marketed, sometimes spelled Klevner, but not to be confused with Klevener. *See* Pinot AOC.

CÔTES DE TOUL AOC

Part of the once-flourishing vineyards of Lorraine, these *côtes* are located in eight communes west of Toul, in the *département* of Meurthe-et-Moselle, and were elevated to AOC status in 2003. Although the best are merely ready-drinking country wines, Laroppe easily outclasses the competition.

RED The Pinot Noir is the most successful, and the wine is usually sold as a pure varietal. It can have surprisingly good colour for wine from such a northerly region, and good cherry-Pinot character.

🍇 Pinot Meunier, Pinot Noir

⌛ 1–4 years

WHITE These wines represent less than two per cent of the appellation, just 76 hectolitres (844 cases). Nevertheless, the Auxerrois is the best grape, its fatness making it ideal for such a northerly area with a calcareous soil.

🍇 Aligoté, Aubin, Auxerrois

⌛ 1–3 years

ROSÉ Most Côtes de Toul is made and sold as *vin gris*. This pale rosé is delicious when it is still youthful.

🍇 Gamay, Pinot Meunier, Pinot Noir, plus a maximum of 15% Aligoté, Aubin, and Auxerrois

⌛ Upon purchase

✓ *Vincent Gorny • Michel & Marcel Laroppe • de la Linotte • Isabelle et Jean-Michel Mangeot • CV du Toulouis*

CRÉMANT D'ALSACE AOC

Although small growers like Dirler had made Vin Mousseux d'Alsace as early as 1880, it was not until 1900 that Dopff Au Moulin created a sparkling wine industry on a commercial scale, and 1976 before an AOC was established. The quality is good, and is improving. Good to see the Hartenberg Pinot Gris back on form.

SPARKLING WHITE Although the Pinot Blanc has perfect acidity for this sort of wine, it can lack sufficient richness, and after intensive tastings I have come to the conclusion that the Pinot Gris has the right acidity and richness.

🍇 Pinot Blanc, Pinot Gris, Pinot Noir, Auxerrois, Chardonnay, Riesling

⌛ 5–8 years

SPARKING ROSÉ These delightful wines can have a finer purity of perfume and flavour than many pink Champagnes.

🍇 Pinot Noir

⌛ 3–5 years

✓ *René Barth • Bernard Becht • Joseph Gruss • Klein-Brand • CV Pfaffenheim* (Hartenberg Pinot Gris) *• Rieflé • Wolfberger*

EDELZWICKER AOC

This appellation – its name means "noble blend" – is reserved for wines blended from two or more of the authorized grape varieties, and it was indeed

once noble. However, since the banning of AOC Zwicker, which was never meant to be noble, and due to the fact that there has never been a legal definition of which varieties are noble, producers simply renamed their Zwicker blends Edelzwicker. Consequently, this appellation has become so tarnished that many producers prefer to sell their cheaper AOC Alsace wines under brand names or simply AOC Alsace, rather than put the debased Edelzwicker name on the label. *See also* Classic Alsace Blends.

WHITE Essentially dry, light-bodied wines that have a clean flavour and are best drunk young. Most Edelzwickers are either Sylvaner or Pinot Blanc-based. Better or slightly more expensive products have a generous touch of Gewurztraminer to fatten up the blend, but most of these have forsaken the Edelzwicker designation, and there are now no examples that can be recommended with confidence.

🍇 Chasselas, Sylvaner, Pinot Blanc, Pinot Gris, Pinot Noir, Auxerrois, Gewurztraminer, Muscat Blanc à Petits Grains, Muscat Rosé à Petits Grains, Muscat Ottonel, Riesling

⌛ Upon purchase

GEWURZTRAMINER AOC

No other wine region in the world has managed to produce Gewurztraminer with any real spice, which is probably why this is usually the first Alsace wine people taste. Its voluptuous, up-front style is always immediately appealing.

WHITE The fattest and most full-bodied of Alsace wines. Classic renditions of this grape typically have the aroma of banana when young and take 3 to 4 years in bottle to build up a pungent spiciness of terpene-laden aromas, often achieving a rich gingerbread character when mature.

🍇 Gewurztraminer

⌛ 3–10 years (20–30 years for great examples)

✓ *Barmès-Buecher* ❽ *• Laurent Barth • Charles Baur* ❽ *• Léon Beyer • Paul Blanck* ◉ *• Bott-Geyl • Albert Boxler • Camille Braun* ◉ (Cuvée Annabelle) *• Brobecker* (Cuvée Spéciale) *• Gruss • Helfrich* (Steinklotz) *• Hugel & Fils* (Jubilée) *• Jean Geiler* (Florimont) *• JosMeyer* ❽ *• André Kientzler • Meyer-Fonné* (Réserve Particulière) *• Muré* ◉ (Clos St-Landelin) *• Rolly Gassmann • Georges et Claude Humbrecht* (Vieilles Vignes) *• Martin Schaetzel* ❽ *• A Scherer • Schlumberger* (Kitterlé) *• François Schmitt* (Pfingstberg) *• Schoffit* (Harth Cuvée Caroline) *• Jean Sipp • Bruno Sorg* (Pfersigberg) *• Sylvie Spielmann* ❽ *• Antoine Stoffel • F E Trimbach • Weinbach/Faller • Zeyssolff* (Cuvée Z) *• Zind Humbrecht* ❽

VT *J B Adam • Léon Beyer • Léon Boesch ◉ • Joseph Cattin • René Fleith-Eschard ◉ • Louis Freyburger ❸* (Kanzlerberg) *• Geschikt ❸ • Hugel & Fils • Jean Huttard* (Burgreben) *• Roger Jung • André Kientzler • Ostertag ❸ • Pierre Meyer • Maurice Schoech • André Thomas ❸ • Weinbach/Faller • Zind Humbrecht ❸*

SGN *Léon Beyer* (especially Quintessence) *• Paul Blanck ◉ • Léon Boesch ◉ • Albert Boxler • Dirler-Cadé ❸ • Hugel & Fils • JosMeyer ❸ • André Kleinknecht ❸ • Albert Mann ◉ • Muré ◉* (Clos St-Landelin) *• Rolly Gassmann • Seppi Landmann • Damien Schlegel • Schlumberger* (Cuvée Anne) *• Sick-Dreyer • Pierre Sparr • F E Trimbach • Weinbach/Faller • Zind Humbrecht ❸*

GUTEDEL AOC

Synonym under which Chasselas may be marketed. *See* Chasselas AOC.

KLEVENER DE HEILIGENSTEIN AOC

An oddity in Alsace for three reasons: firstly, the wine is made from a grape variety that is native to the Jura further south and not found anywhere else in Alsace; secondly, of all the famous village appellations (Rouge d'Ottrott, Rouge de Rodern, etc), it is the only one specifically defined in the regulations; thirdly, it is the only grape confined by law to a fixed area within Alsace (the village of Heiligenstein). It is not to be confused with Klevner, a common synonym for the Pinot Blanc.

WHITE Dry, light-bodied wines of a subdued, spicy aroma, and delicate, fruity flavour. Sadly, no wines worth recommending.

🍇 Savagnin Rosé

🍷 2–4 years

✓ *Zeyssolf* (L'Opaline)

KLEVNER AOC

See Pinot Blanc AOC

MOSELLE AOC

Although many restaurants list German Mosel as "Moselle", the river and the wine it produces are called Mosel in Germany, only becoming Moselle when crossing the border into France (and Luxembourg). Gamay is limited by law to a maximum of 30 per cent of the surface area of this appellation. A maximum of 12.5 per cent alcohol is applied to prevent producers from over-chaptalizing.

RED Château de Vaux produces a surprisingly good Pinot Noir.

🍇 Gamay, Pinot Meunier, Pinot Noir

🍷 Upon purchase

WHITE There has been an improvement in these wines, particularly the Pinot Gris.

🍇 Auxerrois, Müller-Thurgau, Pinot Blanc, Pinot Gris, Riesling, Gewurztraminer

🍷 Upon purchase

✓ *Michel Maurice* (Pinot Gris) *• Oury-Schreiber • Château de Vaux* (Pinot Noir Les Hautes Bassières)

MUSCAT AOC

The best Muscat wine, some growers believe, is made from the Muscat d'Alsace, a synonym for both the white and pink strains of the rich, full Muscat à Petits Grains. Others are convinced that the lighter, more floral Muscat Ottonel is best. A blend of the two is probably preferable. These wines are better

in average years, or at least in fine years that have good acidity, rather than in truly great vintages.

WHITE Dry, aromatic wines with fine floral characteristics that often smell of orange-flower water and taste of peaches. A top-quality Muscat that is expressive of its *terroir* is a great wine.

🍇 Muscat Blanc à Petits Grains, Muscat Rosé à Petits Grains, Muscat Ottonel

🍷 Upon purchase

✓ *Jean Becker • J-M & F Bernhard* (Tradition) *• Emile Beyer • Bott Frères • Paul Buecher* (Réserve) *• Ernest Burn* (Clos St-Imer) *• Rolly Gassmann • Pierre Henri Ginglinger ❸ • Sylvain Hertzog • JosMeyer ❸ • Roger Jung • André Kientzler • Frédéric Mochel • Muré ◉* (Clos St-Landelin) *• Bruno Sorg • Pierre Sparr • Sylvie Spielmann ❸ • Weinbach/Faller • Wolfberger* (Cuvée de la Comtesse) *• Zind Humbrecht ◉* (Goldert) **VT** *Jean-Marc et Frédéric Bernhard • Barmès-Buecher ❸* **SGN** *Claude Bleger • Fernand Engel ◉ • Romain Fritsch • Albert Mann ◉* (Le Tri)

PINOT AOC

Not necessarily pure Pinot Blanc, this white wine may be made from any of the Pinot grape varieties, including Auxerrois (often confused with Pinot Blanc but in fact a totally separate variety). Most Pinot wines are a blend of Pinot Blanc and Auxerrois; the further north the vines are cultivated, the more Auxerrois is used to plump out the Pinot Blanc. Zind is included under Zind Humbrecht below because this luscious, effectively dry blend of 50 per cent Auxerrois, 35 per cent Chardonnay, and 15 per cent Pinot Blanc used to be sold under the Pinot designation. When the authorities enforced the regulations that state Chardonnay may only be used in Crémant d'Alsace, not a still wine under the AOC, Zind Humbrecht was forced to sell the wine as *vin de table*. Since it is not allowed to indicate a vintage on a *vin de table* (the European Union wine regime obviously does not believe in greater transparency), Olivier Humbrecht used a code, and it does not take a genius to figure out Z001 stands for 2001, or that the next NV will be numbered Z002, and so on. The funny thing is that the maximum permitted yield for *vin de table* is 90 hectolitres per hectare as opposed to 100 hectolitres per hectare for the Alsace appellation, and chaptalization is banned. Silly us for thinking that an AOC is supposed to be superior to a *vin de table*!

WHITE Some Pinot wines are occasionally spineless, but lacklustre examples are not as common as they used to be, as it is the plump and juicy *cuvées* that have made this the fastest-growing category of Alsace wine.

🍇 Pinot Blanc, Auxerrois, Pinot Noir (vinified white), Pinot Gris

🍷 2–4 years

✓ *J B Adam • Camille Braun ◉ • CV Cléebourg • Pierre Frick ◉* (Précieuse) *• Rolly Gassmann • JosMeyer ❸ • Koeberlé-Kreyer • Albert Mann ◉ • CV Pfaffenheim • Sylvie Spielmann ❸ • Weinbach/Faller • Zind Humbrecht B* (including Zin *vin de table*)

PINOT BLANC AOC

This designation should only be used if the wine is made from 100 per cent Pinot Blanc. *See also* Pinot AOC.

PINOT GRIS AOC

This designation is now the most common way of marketing wine from the rich Pinot Gris grape. For hundreds of years, it has been known locally as Tokay d'Alsace. Legend had it that the Pinot Gris was brought back to Alsace from Hungary by Baron Lazare de Schwendi in the 1560s, and as Tokay or Tokaji was the only famous Hungarian wine, it was assumed that this was the grape Tokay was made from, and the name stuck. But they got it all wrong: this grape came to Alsace from Burgundy; Schwendi had nothing to do with it, and Pinot Gris has nothing to do with Tokay/Tokaji. In the 1980s, the Hungarians wanted their name back, and initially the French agreed, but after counter arguments from Alsace producers, alleging over 400 years' use of the name, the French reneged, and agreed instead to change the name from Tokay d'Alsace to Tokay-Pinot Gris, with vague promises that they might drop the Tokay bit at some time in the future. That did not happen, but the fall of communism did, and with Hungary's entry to the European Union, the French were forced to honour their partner's historic appellation, so all bottles will have to be labelled Pinot Gris, with no reference to Tokay, no later than the end of 2006.

WHITE This full-bodied, off-dry wine is decadently rich, but has excellent acidity, and its fullness of flavour never tires the palate. A young Pinot Gris can taste or smell of banana, sometimes be smoky, with little or no spice, but as it matures it increasingly develops a smoky-spice, toasty-creamy richness, finally achieving a big, honeyed walnut-brazil complexity with good bottle age. Top Alsace Riesling can be much finer, but the variety is so sensitive to soil conditions and handling that the quality is nowhere near as consistent as Pinot Gris across the board.

🍇 Pinot Gris

🍷 5–10 years

✓ *Lucien Albrecht • Barmès-Buecher ❸ • J P & J F Becker ❸* (Froehn) *• Paul Blanck ◉* (Furstentum) *• Albert Boxler • CV Cléebourg • Robert Faller* (Bénédicte) *• CV de Hunawihr* (Rosacker) *• JosMeyer ❸ • André Kientzler • Henri Klée • Albert Mann ◉ • Mittnacht-Klack • Muller-Koeberle • André Ostertag ❸ • Antoine Stoffel • Bernard Weber* (Finkenberg) *• Weinbach/Faller • Zind Humbrecht ❸* **VT** *Lucien Albrecht • Joseph Cattin • Jean-Marie*

Koehly • Marc Kreydenweiss ⓑ • Hugel & Fils • Vignobles Reinhart • Zind Humbrecht ⓑ

SGN J B Adam • Léon Beyer (Quintessence) • Albert Boxler • Marcel Deiss ⓑ • Louis Freyburger ⓑ (Altenberg de Bergheim) • Hugel & Fils • Marc Kreydenweiss ⓑ • Koberlé-Kreyer • Kuentz-Bas ⓑ • Albert Mann ⓞ (Altenbourg Le Tri) • F E Trimbach • Weinbach/Faller • Zind Humbrecht ⓑ • Pierre Paul Zink (Barrique)

PINOT NOIR AOC

Not so long ago, Pinot Noir d'Alsace was synonymous in style with rosé, but the trend has swung hard over towards a true red wine. After a steep learning curve, during which many wines were overextracted, lacked elegance, were prone to rapid oxidation, and bore the most ungainly caramelized characteristics, Alsace winemakers have now managed to master the handling of oak and red-wine techniques. Alsace producers are now allowed to use a fatter bottle of almost Burgundian proportions for Pinot Noir instead of the Flûte d'Alsace, the use of which has been enshrined in law since 1959. This is a positive move, and although strictly confined to Pinot Noir, I hear rumours that it will be used for other Pinot varieties, which would also be good.

RED Most are unsatisfactory (overextracted, too tannic, or too oaky – sometimes all three), but Marcel Deiss's Burlenberg is in a different class and is comparable to a good Burgundy. A step down, but still good, is Domaine Weinbach Réserve in a good year, and the most commercial of all, Hugel Jubilée Pinot Noir, with its special selection Le Neveaux, is a serious contender for Deiss's crown, as is Paul Blanck. And that is about it. You can find perhaps another four or five wines each year that are delightful on the nose, but do not live up to the promise on the palate. Why is it that although both Alsace and Germany started at the same time (mid-1980s) to develop Pinot Noir as a serious red

wine style (as opposed to rosé), only Germany has succeeded? The cadre of top-performing German Pinot Noir producers includes the likes of Deutzerhof, Kreuzberg, Huber, Johner, Knipser, Philipp Kuhn, Bernhart, Fürst, August Kesseler, and Aldinger, yet the only Alsace producer who would not be shown up in such company is Deiss, and the very best of Hugel's wines.

🍇 Pinot Noir

🍷 2–6 years (12 years for exceptional cuvées)

ROSÉ At its best, this dry, light-bodied wine has a deliciously fragrant aroma and flavour, which is reminiscent of strawberries, raspberries, or cherries. Seldom seen on export markets, but still commonly encountered by the pichet in local winstubs.

🍇 Pinot Noir

🍷 1–2 years

☑ Paul Blanck ⓞ ("F") • Marcel Deiss ⓑ (Burlenberg) • Hugel & Fils (Jubilée Le Neveux) • Muré ⓑ (Clos St-Landelin, "V") • Weinbach/Faller (Réserve)

RIESLING AOC

Of all Alsace grape varieties, Riesling is the most susceptible to differences in soil: clay soils give fatness and richness; granite Riesling is also rich, but with more finesse; limestone adds obvious

finesse but less richness; and volcanic soil gives a well-flavoured, spicy style.

WHITE In youth, fine Rieslings can show hints of apple, fennel, citrus, and peach, but can be so firm and austere that they give no hint of the beautiful wines into which they can evolve.

🍇 Riesling

🍷 4–20 years

☑ J B Adam • Lucien Albrecht (Clos Schild) • J-M & F Bernhard (Wineck-Sclossberg) • Barmès-Buecher ⓑ • Léon Baur ⓑ • Léon Beyer • Paul Blanck ⓞ (Furstentum, Schlossberg) • Bott Frères (Réserve Personnelle) Bott-Geyl ⓑ (Mandelberg) • Albert Boxler (Sommerberg Vieilles Vignes) • Rolly Gassmann • Greiner-Schleret • Albert Hertz ⓑ • CV de Hunawihr (Rosacker) • JosMeyer ⓑ (Hengst) • Gustave Lorentz (Altenberg de Bergheim) • Mader • Albert Mann ⓞ (Cuvée Albert, Schlossberg) • Frédéric Mochel • Muré ⓞ (Clos St-Landelin) • André Ostertag ⓑ (Muechberg) • Pfister (Engelberg) • CV de Ribeauvillé (Osterberg) • Martin Schaetzel ⓑ • Schlumberger (Kessler, Kitterlé, Saering) • Roland Schmitt ⓞ • Schoffit • Jean Sipp • Louis Sipp ⓞ • Sipp-Mack • Bruno Sorg • Sylvie Spielmann B • Bernard Schwach • F E Trimbach (Cuvée Frédéric Emile, Clos Ste-Hune, Réserve) • Weinbach/Faller • Wunsch & Mann • Zind Humbrecht ⓑ

VT Jean Becker • Hugel & Fils • JosMeyer ⓑ • André Kientzler • Lichtlé • Weinbach/Faller • Zind Humbrecht ⓑ

SGN Hugel & Fils • Fernand Engel ⓞ • André Kientzler • F E Trimbach • Weinbach/Faller • Zind Humbrecht ⓑ

SYLVANER AOC

Hugh Johnson once described the Sylvaner as "local tap-wine", and this is how it should be served – direct from the stainless-steel vat, with all the zip and zing of natural carbonic gas (normally filtered out during the bottling process). Like the Muscat, it does not suit heat, and is a wine to buy in cooler years. Most attempts at late-harvest or botrytized styles (which cannot legally be sold as either VT or SGN) are diabolical. This does not mean that people should give up, just that they should not try to palm off these failures on the public. Better to add their tiny quantity to a much larger volume of an Edelzwicker – or whatever they like to call it – and sell more bottles of a turbo-charged basic appellation at a much smaller premium, as this might result in better reviews and a better profit. Alsace producers should take a lesson from Angelo Publisi of Ballandean winery (see p660), who replicates the VT style by cutting the fruit-bearing canes just after véraison. This cuts the grape off from the vine's metabolism and the effect is much the same as when the leaves drop and sap returns to the roots after the first snap of winter. The resulting wine is consistently fabulous.

WHITE Sylvaner is an unpretentious, dry, light- to medium-bodied wine, with fragrance rather than fruitiness. It is generally best drunk young, but, like the Muscat, exceptionally long-living examples can always be found.

🍇 Sylvaner

🍷 Upon purchase

☑ Agathe Bursin • Rolly Gassmann • JosMeyer ⓑ (Rouge – sic) • Weinbach/Faller • Zind Humbrecht ⓑ

VIN D'ALSACE AOC

Alternative designation for Alsace AOC.

MORE GREEN ALSACE

In addition to the Alsace producers recommended above, and which are either biodynamic or organic, there are also the following. No negative inference of quality should be taken from the fact that they are not featured among my recommended Alsace producers. There are a number that have been recommended in other editions, and still make some fine wines, but have been culled out to make room for others.

Biodynamic
Yves Amberg (Epfig)
Pierre-Paul Humbrecht (Pfaffenheim)
Patrick & Mireille Meyer (Notholten)
Trapet (Beblenheim)
Valentin Zusslin Fils (Orschwihr)

Organic
Yves Amberg (Epfig)
Yannick et Jean Baltenweck (Ribeauvillé)
Laurent Bannwarth (Obermorschwihr)
Maurice Barthelme (Wettolsheim)
François Baur (Turckheim)
Rémy Biwand (Mackenheim)
Buecher-Fix (Wettolsheim)
Burckel-Jung (Gertwiller)
Lucien et Théo Dietrich (Sigolsheim)
Yves Dietrich (Sigolsheim)
André Durrmann (Andlau)
Eblin-Fuchs (Zellenberg)
Fernand Engel (Rorschwihr)
Luc Faller (Itterswiller)
Frey (Dambach-la-Ville)
Gilg (Wettolsheim)
Pierre-Henri Ginglinger (Eguisheim)

Michel Goujot (Lucey – Moselle AOC)
Haegelin (Orschwihr)
Hausherr (Eguisheim)
Philippe & Fernand Heitz (Molsheim)
Léon Heitzmann (Ammerschwihr)
Pierre-Paul Humbrecht (Pfaffenheim)
Annick Hummel (St-Léonard Boersch)
Bernard Hummel (St-Léonard Boersch)
Martin Jund (Colmar)
Clément Klur (Katzenthal)
Mathieu Knecht (Dambach la Ville)
Pierre Martin (Scherwiller)
Mersiol (Dambach-la-Ville)
Mischler (Bennwihr)
Mittnacht Frères (Hunawihr)
Charles Muller & Fils (Traenheim)
François-Joseph Munsch (Jungholtz)
François Otter (Hattstatt)
François Platz (Bergheim)
André Rohrer (Mittelbergheim)
Rominger (Westhalten)
Jean-Paul Schmitt (Scherwiller)
Albert Staehle (Wintzenheim)
Philippe Vorburger (Voegtlinshoffen)
Odile & Danielle Weber (Eguisheim)

THE LOIRE VALLEY

In winemaking terms, the Loire Valley is best imagined as a long ribbon with crisp white wines at either end and fuller wines of all types in the middle. It is the home of Sauvignon Blanc, the only wine area in the world that specializes in Cabernet Franc and, in truly great vintages, makes some of the most sublime and sumptuous botrytized Chenin Blanc wines.

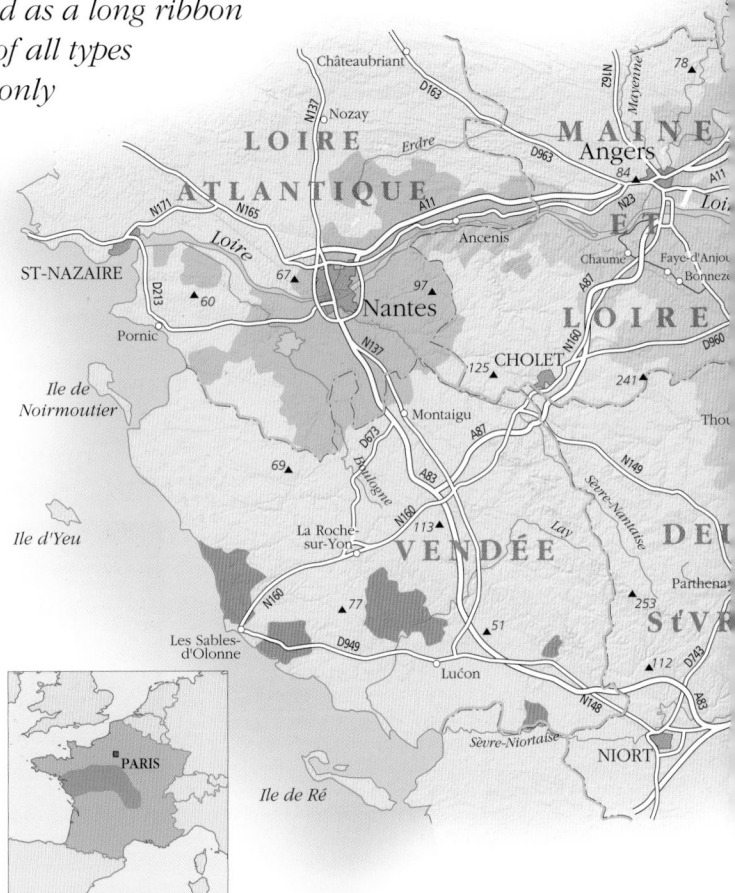

THE LOIRE IS THE LONGEST RIVER in France. From its source in the Cévennes Mountains, it flows 1,000 kilometres (620 miles) through 12 *départements*. The variations in soil, climate, and grape varieties found along its banks and those of its tributaries are reflected in the wide range of wines grown in the four major wine-producing districts. Red, white, and rosé; still, *pétillant*, and fully sparkling wines are produced in 87 different appellations ranging in style from bone dry to intensely sweet.

THE LOIRE'S MOST IMPORTANT GRAPE

The Chenin Blanc grape produces four distinctly different styles of wine – dry, semi-sweet, sweet, and sparkling. This is due to traditional practices that have been forced on growers by the vagaries of climate. This grape has abundant natural acidity and, if it receives enough sun, a high sugar content. But the Loire is considered a northern area in viticultural terms, and growers must contend with late frosts, cold winds, and variable summers. Given a sunny year, the grower's natural inclination is to make the richest wine possible with this sweet and tangy grape; but in many vintages, only a medium or a dry style can be achieved. This variation in style is the root of the Loire's problems because it is difficult to build a reputation on uncertainty. If you take into account overproduction, the all too often debilitating effect of ignoble rot, and the lack of almost any selection criteria for picking

VINEYARDS AT VOUVRAY
In sunny years the area just to the east of Tours produces sweet, slow-maturing wines, valued for their longevity.

RECENT LOIRE VINTAGES

2010 Widespread rot made for variable quality throughout the different districts and styles, but those who kept yields low, maintained their vineyards by best practices, and picked late have produced wines that probably are at least as good as the 2009s. Some amazing Coteaux du Layon bearing unheard of levels of botrytis concentration were produced.

2009 Excellent, homogenous quality, with bright fruit and ripe acidity in all styles.

2008 An extremely variable year – in terms of both weather and wine – with crops reduced almost everywhere (by as much as 50 per cent in Muscadet). A cool August led to a late harvest that produced some crisp, fresh fruity wines at best.

2007 A cool summer and some of the highest incidences of rot for decades led to a small and variable harvest, with excellent minerality in Muscadet, some prayers answered and some not for Sauvignon and reds (fresh and fruity at best), and very good sweet wines from the Coteaux du Layon, yet mostly miserable in Vouvray.

2006 As with the rest of France, the July heat wave pushed vine growth on at a tremendous rate, but unlike most other regions, the August cold spell had minimal effect. The harvest in September was good, although the tail end of tropical storms dumped a lot of water, particularly on Muscadet. The result was not bad for every wine style, particularly for those who decrease yields from the outset by rubbing off buds, and those who grass between the vines, with Sancerre and, amazingly, Muscadet faring best. Crispness, freshness, and good fruit will be the hallmark of most 2006s.

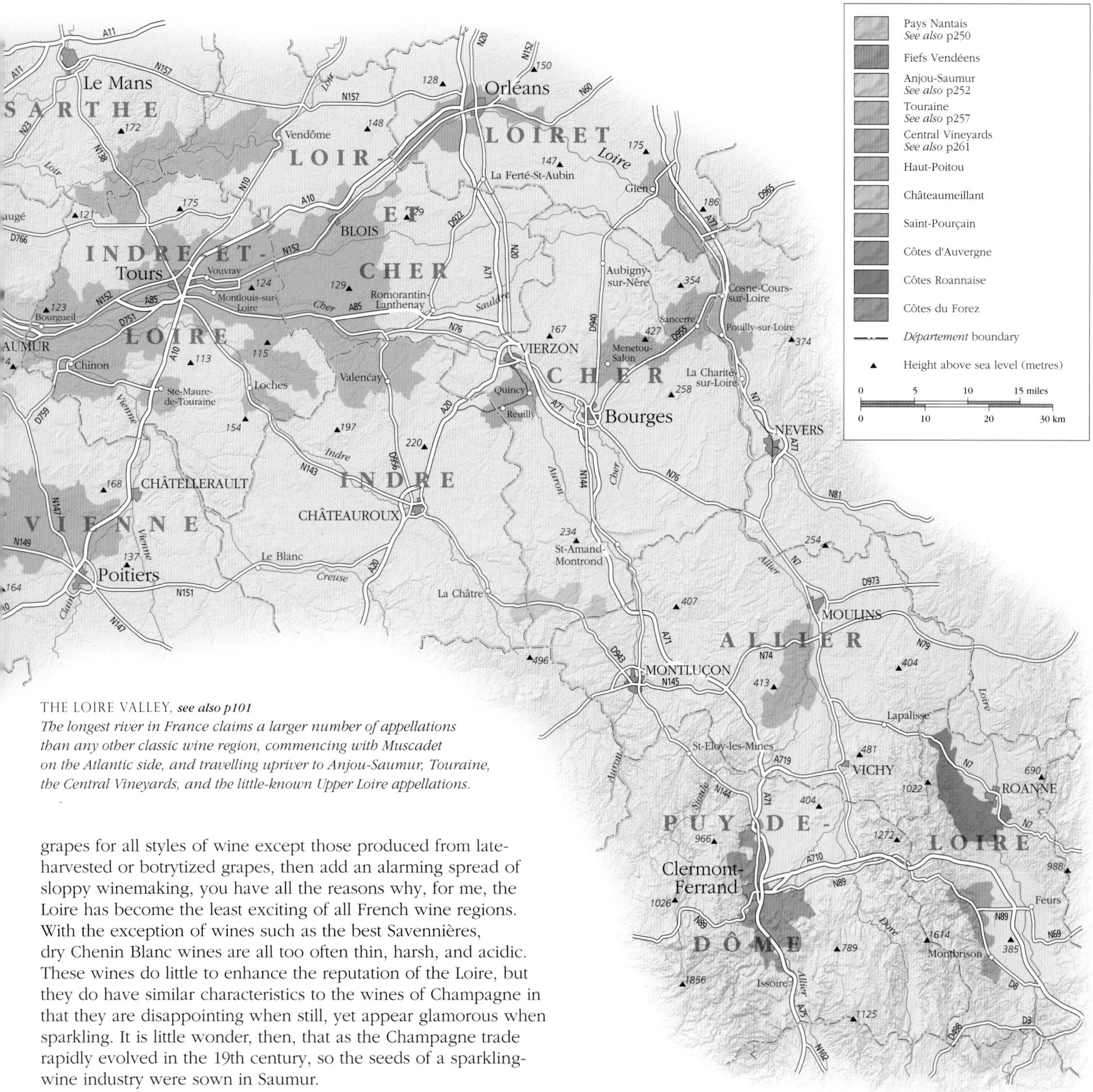

Map legend:

Pays Nantais *See also p250*
Fiefs Vendéens
Anjou-Saumur *See also p252*
Touraine *See also p257*
Central Vineyards *See also p261*
Haut-Poitou
Châteaumeillant
Saint-Pourçain
Côtes d'Auvergne
Côtes Roannaise
Côtes du Forez

— *Département* boundary
▲ Height above sea level (metres)

0 5 10 15 miles
0 10 20 30 km

THE LOIRE VALLEY, *see also p101*
The longest river in France claims a larger number of appellations than any other classic wine region, commencing with Muscadet on the Atlantic side, and travelling upriver to Anjou-Saumur, Touraine, the Central Vineyards, and the little-known Upper Loire appellations.

grapes for all styles of wine except those produced from late-harvested or botrytized grapes, then add an alarming spread of sloppy winemaking, you have all the reasons why, for me, the Loire has become the least exciting of all French wine regions. With the exception of wines such as the best Savennières, dry Chenin Blanc wines are all too often thin, harsh, and acidic. These wines do little to enhance the reputation of the Loire, but they do have similar characteristics to the wines of Champagne in that they are disappointing when still, yet appear glamorous when sparkling. It is little wonder, then, that as the Champagne trade rapidly evolved in the 19th century, so the seeds of a sparkling-wine industry were sown in Saumur.

THE LOIRE NEAR SANCERRE
In this area the ground rises well above the river and the neighbouring vineyards.

DID YOU KNOW?

- The Loire is the last wild river in Europe and was designated a World Heritage Site by the United Nations Educational, Scientific, and Cultural Organization (UNESCO).
- As a wild river, the water level can vary by several metres within a few days, and its islands slowly move from year to year.
- The Loire Valley is known as the "Garden of France".
- The Loire Valley is the second-largest sparkling wine region in France (although Crémant d'Alsace is the second-largest individual appellation).

To suggest that the Chenin Blanc is fit only for fizzing up is to do the grape a great injustice. Firstly, it is not in fact suited to the classic *brut* style of sparkling wine, as its aromatic qualities tend to fight rather than absorb the subtle effects of second fermentation. Secondly, it is this very character that makes Chenin Blanc one of the world's great wine grapes when botrytized. However, it is not the grape that is intrinsically disappointing when vinified as a still wine, but merely the methods employed by the grower and winemaker.

Chenin Blanc has been given pride of place in the Anjou-Saumur district, but unfortunately its cultivation has spread to unsuitable areas over the past 25 years. Producers more interested in making money than building a fine reputation have taken advantage of the Chenin Blanc's natural inclination to over-crop. It is a grape that should be harshly pruned, but most growers lack the courage to do this, and when the weather is unsettled, these same growers are the first to harvest. The heavier the crop, the less ripe the grapes, and the less ripe the grapes, the more washed out the flavours.

However, there are quality-conscious growers in the Loire, who restrict their yield and allow the grapes to ripen, yet still agonize over whether to risk the weather for one more day's maturity. It is from such top-performing growers as Domaine Baumard in the Coteaux du Layon, Clos Naudin and Huet in Vouvray, and Dominique Moyer in Montlouis that we get Chenin Blanc wines that dazzle our palates.

FROM SOURCE TO SEA

For some inexplicable reason, most references restrict the Loire to its four major districts of Pays Nantais, Anjou-Saumur, Touraine, and Central Vineyards. Although some books incorporate the outlying areas of Fiefs Vendéens and Haut-Poitou, few mention the appellations of the Upper Loire, yet the wines of Côtes du Forez, Côte Roannaise, Côtes d'Auvergne, St-Pourçain, and Châteaumeillant are equally legitimate members of the Loire's family of wines. And whereas the most famous appellations could and should rank among the most exciting wines of the world, there are so many underachievers that the major districts have become a minefield for wine lovers, while growers in the lesser-known areas of the Upper Loire have everything to prove.

THE GENERIC AND OUTLYING APPELLATIONS OF
THE LOIRE VALLEY

CHÂTEAUMEILLANT AOC

This appellation, which borders the Cher and Indre, around Bourges, was upgraded from the defunct VDQS to AOC in 2010. Although only red-wine grapes are grown, white wine of some standing used to be made here, and its production is still permitted.

RED The Gamay grape usually dominates the red wines, which should be drunk as young as possible.

🍇 Gamay, Pinot Gris, Pinot Noir

🍷 6–12 months

ROSÉ The best Châteaumeillant wines. They are fresh, grapey, and delicately balanced.

🍇 Gamay, Pinot Gris, Pinot Noir

🍷 6–12 months

✓ *Du Chaillot* • *CV Châteaumeillant* • *Valérie et Frédéric Dallot* • *De Pavillon*

CÔTES D'AUVERGNE AOC

Upgraded from VDQS to AOC in 2010, Côtes d'Auvergne is located south of Saint-Pourçain and west of Côtes du Forez on the edge of the Massif Central. This is the most remotely situated of all the outer areas that fall officially within the Loire region. The wines from certain villages are superior and have therefore been given the right to use the following communal appellations: Côtes d'Auvergne-Boudes (villages of Boudes, Chalus, and St-Hérant); Côtes d'Auvergne-Chanturgues (villages of Clermont-Ferrand and Cézabat [part]); Côtes d'Auvergne-Châteaugay (villages of Châteaugay and Cézabat [part]); Côtes d'Auvergne-Corent (villages of Corent, Les Martres-de-Veyre, La Sauvetat, and Veyre-Monton); and Côtes d'Auvergne-Madargues (village of Riom).

RED The best of these dry, light-bodied, and fruity wines carry the Chanturgues appellation. Most are made from Gamay, a grape that has traditionally been grown in the area, and are very much in the style of Beaujolais.

🍇 Gamay, Pinot Noir

🍷 1–2 years

WHITE These dry, light-bodied wines made from Chardonnay have been overlooked but can be more accessible than the same variety grown in more classic areas of the Loire, thus they are surely a marketable commodity in view of Chardonnay's upmarket status.

🍇 Chardonnay

🍷 1–2 years

ROSÉ These are dry, light-bodied wines with an attractive cherry flavour. They are made in the village of Clermont-Ferrand, and carry the Chanturgues appellation.

🍇 Gamay, Pinot Noir

🍷 Within 1 year

✓ *Vignoble de l'Arbe Blanc* ◉ • *Pradier* • *Gilles Persilier*

CÔTES DU FOREZ AOC

Similar to Beaujolais, this wine is produced in the Loire *département* adjacent to Lyon, and was upgraded from VDQS to AOC in 2000. The wines are improving through the efforts of the *coopérative* and a few quality-conscious growers, but they could be better.

RED These are dry, light-bodied wines with some fruit. They are best drunk young and at a cool temperature.

🍇 Gamay

🍷 Upon purchase

ROSÉ Simple, light-bodied, dry rosés that make attractive, unpretentious picnic wines.

🍇 Gamay

🍷 Upon purchase

✓ *Gilles Bonnefoy* (La Madone) ◉ • *Les Vignerons Foreziens* • *Odile Verdier et Jacky Logel* ◉

CÔTE ROANNAISE AOC

Red and rosé wines made from a localized Gamay clone called Gamay Saint-Romain. Grown on south- and southwest-facing slopes of volcanic soil on the left bank of the Loire some 40 kilometres (25 miles) west of the Mâconnais district of Burgundy. This appellation was promoted from VDQS to full AOC status in 1994.

RED Some of these dry, medium- to full-bodied wines are produced using a form of carbonic maceration, and a few are given a little maturation in cask. The result can vary between well-coloured wines that are firm and distinctive, and oaky and fruity Beaujolais-type versions for quaffing when young.

🍇 Gamay

🍷 1–5 years

ROSÉ Dry, medium-bodied, well-made wines that are crisp and fruity.

🍇 Gamay

🍷 2–3 years

✓ *Alain Baillon* (Cuvée Monplaisir) • *Paul et Jean-Pierre Benetère* (Vieilles Vignes) • *Des Pothiers* ◉ • *De la Rochette* (Vieilles Vignes) • *Robert Serol* ◉

CRÉMANT DE LOIRE AOC

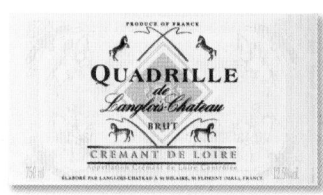

Of all the Loire's sparkling wines, this is probably the most underrated, yet it has the greatest potential because it can be blended from the wines of Anjou-Saumur and Touraine and from the widest range of grape varieties.

SPARKLING WHITE The better-balanced *cuvées* of these dry to semi-sweet, light- to medium-bodied wines are normally a blend of Chenin Blanc in the main, with a good dash of Cabernet Franc and Chardonnay. The best Chardonnay clones are yet to be established in the Loire, but at least Chardonnay is widely utilized for sparkling wines, whereas Pinot Noir is not – this is a mystery, as it is a proven variety in the region.

🍇 Chenin Blanc, Cabernet Franc, Cabernet Sauvignon, Pineau d'Aunis, Pinot Noir, Chardonnay, Arbois, Grolleau Noir, and Grolleau Gris

🍶 1–3 years

SPARKLING ROSÉ The best of these light- to medium-bodied wines are *brut*, and usually contain a high proportion of Cabernet Franc and Grolleau Noir grapes. Cabernet Franc makes the most distinctive wine. A pure Pinot Noir *crémant* rosé would be interesting to taste.

🍇 Chenin Blanc, Cabernet Franc, Cabernet Sauvignon, Pineau d'Aunis, Pinot Noir, Chardonnay, Arbois, Grolleau Noir and Gris

🍶 Most are best consumed upon purchase, although some benefit if kept 1–2 years.

✓ *Baumard • Yves Lambert • Château de l'Aulée • Château de Montgueret • De Nerleux • Château de Putille • CV de Saumur*

HAUT-POITOU AOC

Haut-Poitou became an AOC in 2010, after the VDQS designation was dropped. Situated 80 kilometres (50 miles) southwest of Tours, the Poitiers district produces wines that have achieved a remarkable reputation despite its hot, dry climate, and flat land that is more suited to arable farming than to viticulture.

RED This is a wine to watch: although the really successful reds have until now been in short supply and confined mainly to Cabernet, there is a feeling that a general breakthrough is imminent. The quality of the entire appellation is likely to rise significantly, and there is promise of some exciting, pure varietal reds.

🍇 Pinot Noir, Gamay, Merlot, Malbec, Cabernet Franc, Cabernet Sauvignon, and a maximum of 20% each of Gamay de Chaudenay and Grolleau

🍶 Within 3 years

WHITE Dry, light- to medium-bodied, varietal wines. Those made from pure Sauvignon are softer and more floral than most of their northern counterparts, yet retain the freshness and vitality that is so important to this grape variety.

🍇 Sauvignon Blanc, Chardonnay, Pinot Blanc, and up to a maximum of 20% Chenin Blanc

🍶 Within 1 year

ROSÉ These dry, light- to medium-bodied wines are fresh and fruity.

🍇 Pinot Noir, Gamay, Merlot, Malbec, Cabernet Franc, Cabernet Sauvignon, and a maximum of 20% each of Gamay de Chaudenay and Grolleau

🍶 Within 3 years

✓ *Ampelidae ◉ • Du Centaure • CV Haut-Poitou*

ORLÉANS AOC

Although recognized as a VDQS appellation in its own right in 2000, this area has been growing vines since the 10th century. Legend has it that vines were originally brought from the Auvergne, hence the local synonyms of Auvernat Rouge for Pinot Noir and Auvernat Blanc for Chardonnay. Upgraded to AOC in 2006, the delimited area consists of 200 hectares (494 acres) in scattered parcels, of which 160 hectares (395 acres) are currently planted, encompassing the outskirts of Orléans, where the soil is silty, and 11 neighbouring villages, stretching from the chalky soils of Saint Hilaire, and red, sandy-stony soils of Sologne, near Mézières, to clayey soils elsewhere.

RED Successful wines have good colour and just about enough fruit to balance the tannins, affording a more supple finish. Montigny-Piel's Clos Saint-Fiacre stands out as the best wine of this appellation in all its colour formats.

🍇 Minimum of 60% Pinot Meunier, plus Pinot Noir and Pinot Gris

🍶 Within 3 years

WHITE The least exciting wines so far, although it is very early days for these dry white wines, which must possess no more than 4 grams per litre of residual sugar.

🍇 Minimum of 60% Chardonnay, plus Pinot Gris

🍶 Within 1 year

ROSÉ The few encountered have been fresh, easy drinking with Meunier-cum-Pinot character, expressed more as red summer fruits than cherries.

🍇 Minimum of 60% Pinot Meunier, plus Pinot Noir and Pinot Gris

🍶 Within 3 years

✓ *Montigny-Piel (Clos Saint-Fiacre)*

ORLÉANS-CLÉRY AOC

This sub-appellation was granted in 2002, and is restricted to red wines produced in Cléry-Saint-André and four neighbouring villages southwest of Orléans, but confusingly from entirely different grapes from the main appellation.

RED The local *coopérative* (Grand Maison) makes a good wine from 25-year-old vines, which is old for this rediscovered part of the Loire, but most Cabernet-based wines from this area suffer too much from a herbaceous character.

🍇 Minimum of 75% Cabernet Franc, plus Cabernet Sauvignon planted before October 2002

🍶 Within 3 years

✓ *Jacky Legroux • CV de la Grand Maison*

PINEAU DES CHARENTES AOC

A *vin de liqueur* produced in the Cognac region, which is between the Loire and Bordeaux (thus not really the Loire Valley, but it has to go somewhere!).

WHITE Few manage to rise above the typically dull, oxidative *vin de liqueur* style that goes *rancio* with age.

🍇 Cabernet Franc, Cabernet Sauvignon, Colombard, Folle Blanche, Jurançon Blanc, Meslier Saint-François, Merlot, Merlot Blanc, Montils, Sauvignon Blanc, Sémillon, Ugni Blanc

🍶 Upon opening

ROSÉ Few manage to rise above the typically dull, oxidative *vin de liqueur* style that goes *rancio* with age.

🍇 Cabernet Franc, Cabernet Sauvignon, Malbec, Merlot

🍶 Upon opening

✓ *Barbeau & Fils (Tres Vieux Rosé Grand Réserve)*

• *Chais du Rouissoir* (Rosé) • *Vinet* (Félix-Marie de la Villière Blanc)

ROSÉ DE LOIRE AOC

A dry rosé wine introduced in 1974 to exploit the international marketing success of Rosé d'Anjou and to take advantage of the trend for drier styles. The result has been very disappointing on the whole, although the few producers (recommended below) who have really tried demonstrate that very good-quality dry rosé can be made throughout the Loire.

ROSÉ Dry, light- to medium-bodied rosé from the Loire that could (and should) be the most attractive wine of its type – a few growers try, but most do not. These wines may be sold from 1 December following the harvest without any mention of *primeur* or *nouveau*.

🍇 Pineau d'Aunis, Pinot Noir, Gamay, Grolleau, and at least 30% Cabernet Franc and Cabernet Sauvignon

🍶 Upon purchase

✓ *De Chanteloup • Lecheteau • De Montgilet • Château de Passavant*

ST-POURÇAIN AOC

The wines of Saint-Pourçain have a long and impressive history for what was, after all, an obscure VDQS until as recently as 2009, with vineyards first planted not by the Romans, as elsewhere in the Loire Valley, but by the Phoenicians. The Saint-Pourçain area covers 19 communes southeast of the Bourges appellations of the Central Vineyards in the Allier *département*. The growers are quite ambitious, and many people think that these wines have a particularly promising future. There are 500 hectares (1,235 acres) of vineyards.

RED Dry, light- to medium-bodied wines, but they can vary from very light Beaujolais lookalikes to imitations of Bourgogne Passetoutgrains, depending on the grape varieties in the blend.

🍇 Gamay, Pinot Noir, and up to a maximum of 10% Gamay Teinturier

🍶 1–2 years

WHITE Dry, light- to medium-bodied wines. The Tresallier grape (which is known as the Sacy in Chablis), when blended with Chardonnay and Sauvignon, produces a crisp, toasty, full-flavoured wine that does have some merit. Very little is known about the Saint-Pierre-Doré, except that locals say it makes a "filthy wine", according to Master of Wine Rosemary George in *French Country Wines*.

🍇 A maximum of 50% Tresallier and 10% Saint-Pierre-Doré, plus Aligoté, Chardonnay, and Sauvignon Blanc

🍶 1–2 years

ROSÉ Crisp, dry, light- to medium-bodied wines that have a fragrance that is reminiscent of soft summer fruits. The rosés are generally more successful than the red wines of the area, but both styles are particularly refreshing and thirst-quenching.

🍇 Gamay, Pinot Noir, and up to a maximum of 10% Gamay Teinturier

🍶 1–2 years

✓ *De Bellevue • Jallet (Les Ceps Centenaires) • CV de Saint-Pourçain (Cuvée Réserve) • Cave Touzain*

PAYS NANTAIS

Nantais is Muscadet country. The Sèvre-et-Maine district produces the richest Muscadet, while Côtes de Grandlieu, granted its own appellation in 1994, and the Coteaux de la Loire to the north produce wines with extra acidity.

SOUTHEAST OF NANTES are the vineyards of Muscadet. The best are those of the Sèvre-et-Maine district, named after two rivers, which is much hillier than the surrounding countryside and protected from northwesterly winds by Nantes itself. Sèvre-et-Maine accounts for one-quarter of the general appellation area, yet 85 per cent of all Muscadet produced. Only in unusually hot or dry years, when they contain extra natural acidity, can Muscadet grapes grown further north in the Coteaux de la Loire sometimes surpass those of Sèvre-et-Maine.

THE MUSCADET GRAPE AND ITS WINES

It is uncertain when the Muscadet grape, also known as the Melon de Bourgogne and the Gamay Blanc, was first planted in the area. There is a plaque at Château de la Cassemichère that claims that the first Muscadet vine was transplanted there from Burgundy in 1740. But Pierre Galet, the famous ampelographer (vine botanist), tells us that "following the terrible winter of 1709, Louis XIV ordered that the replanting of the frozen vineyards of Loire-Atlantique be with Muscadet blanc".

The wine produced from the Muscadet grape is neutral in flavour and bears no hint of the muskiness that some believe its name implies. Traditionally, it is harvested early to preserve acidity, and yet, in doing so, the grower risks making a wine that lacks fruit. But if the wine is left in contact with its sediment and bottled *sur lie*, this enhances the fruit, adds a yeasty-roundness, and, by retaining more of the carbonic gas created during fermentation, imparts a certain liveliness and freshness.

There have always been rare examples of exceptionally ripe Muscadet, which tend to age like a modest Burgundy after a few years in bottle. More recently, however, there has been a trend among quality-conscious growers to pick riper grapes (which is a significant risk, given the weather), in order to produce fuller, richer wines. This practice has come under attack from more conservative growers, who believe that there should not only be a maximum alcoholic strength for the finished wine (currently 12 per cent after any chaptalization), but also a high minimum total acidity.

I have some sympathy with these traditionalists, since the Melon de Bourgogne grape is intrinsically incapable of competing with Chardonnay at even modest levels, thus most of the wines produced in this manner, while being extraordinary for Muscadet, make disappointing "Burgundy". Furthermore, I like the way that a correctly lean structure and naturally high acidity yield a certain nervosity of fruit in good Muscadet. However, good Muscadet represents perhaps one out of every 10 bottles, and it is a lack – sometimes a total absence – of fruit that is the pitfall of the rest. The *sur lie* process cannot magic fruit out of thin air. But, despite their initial concentration on richness rather than fruit, the new winemakers should be encouraged, as they need to experiment in every direction if they are to find a reliable way to impart a feather-light fruit and freshness to these wines. There is no need for traditionalists to worry about the classic Muscadet style being perverted by a few; they have already done much worse by allowing the majority to all but destroy its classic quality. They should give the rebels the chance to do better; they will not want a reputation for poor man's Burgundy, but rather for rich man's Muscadet.

FACTORS AFFECTING TASTE AND QUALITY

LOCATION
The Pays Nantais lies in the coastal area and the westernmost district of the Loire Valley, with vineyards occupying parts of the Loire-Atlantique and the Maine-et-Loire *départements*.

CLIMATE
Mild and damp, but winters can be harsh and spring frosts troublesome. Summers are generally warm and sunny, although they are also rainy.

ASPECT
Some of the vineyards are found on the flat land around the mouth of the Loire southwest of Nantes. There are rolling hills in the Sèvre-et-Maine and Coteaux de la Loire, with the best vineyards on gentle riverside slopes. Some of the smaller valleys are actually too steep for viticulture, and the vines in these areas occupy the hilltops.

SOIL
The best vineyards of the Sèvre-et-Maine are light and stony, with varying proportions of sand, clay, and gravel above a granitic, schistous, and volcanic subsoil that is rich in potassium and magnesium. The Coteaux de la Loire is more schistous, while the Côtes de Grandlieu is schistous and granitic, and vineyards in the generic Muscadet appellation have sand with silt. These soils provide good drainage, essential here.

VITICULTURE AND VINIFICATION
The Muscadet is a frost-resistant, early-ripening grape that adapts well to the damp conditions of the Pays Nantais. It is harvested early (mid- to late September) to preserve its acidity, although a number of growers have started to reduce yields and pick riper. The best Muscadet is left in vat or barrel on its sediment – *sur lie* – until it is bottled. This imparts a greater depth and fruitiness, and a faint prickle of natural carbonic gas.

GRAPE VARIETIES
Primary varieties: Gros Plant (Folle Blanche), Muscadet (Melon de Bourgogne)
Secondary varieties: Cabernet Franc, Cabernet Sauvignon, Chardonnay, Chenin Blanc, Gamay, Gamay de Bouze, Gamay de Chaudenay, Groslot Gris (Grolleau Gris), Négrette, Pinot Noir

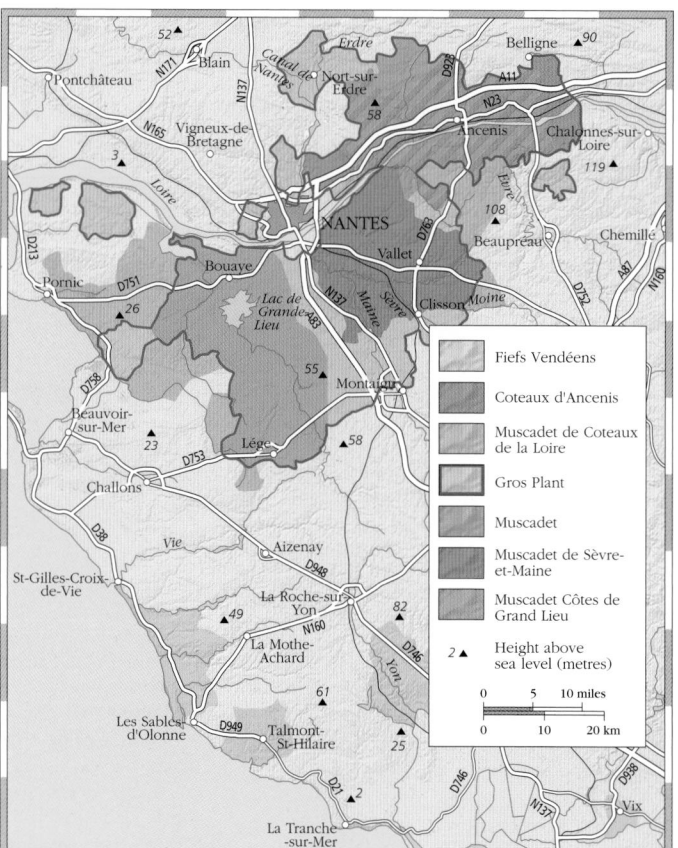

PAYS NANTAIS, *see also p246*
The finest wines in the Pays Nantais are produced to the east of Nantes in Sèvre-et-Maine and Coteaux de la Loire.

THE APPELLATIONS OF
PAYS NANTAIS

COTEAUX D'ANCENIS AOC

These varietal wines, which come from the same area as Muscadet Coteaux de la Loire, were promoted to full AOC status in 2009.

RED Bone-dry to dry, and light- to medium-bodied wines that include Cabernets, made from both Cabernet Franc and Cabernet Sauvignon grapes. Surprisingly, they are not as successful as the juicy Gamay wines that represent no less than 80 per cent of the total production of this appellation.

🍇 Cabernet Sauvignon, Cabernet Franc, Gamay, and up to a combined total of 5% Gamay de Chaudenay and Gamay de Bouze

⌛ 2 years

WHITE Dry to medium-dry, light-bodied wines. The Pinot Gris, also sold as "Malvoisie", is not as alcoholic as its Alsatian cousin, yet can possess a light richness that will linger in the mouth. The Chenin Blanc, known locally as "Pineau de la Loire", is rarely very special.

🍇 Chenin Blanc, Pinot Gris

⌛ 12–18 months

ROSÉ Bone-dry to dry, light- to medium-bodied wines, some of which are fresh, firm, and lively. Gamay is the most popular grape variety.

🍇 Cabernet Sauvignon, Cabernet Franc, Gamay, and up to a combined total of 5% Gamay de Chaudenay and Gamay de Bouze

⌛ 2 years

✓ *CV des Terroirs de la Noëlle* • *Guindon* • *Du Haut Fresne*

FIEFS VENDÉENS AOC

Fiefs Vendéens was a *vin de pays* until 1984, and VDQS until 2009, when it was upgraded to full AOC status. The regulations controlling the grape varieties permitted for this appellation are unique. They determine the proportion of each variety that must be cultivated in the vineyard, yet they do not limit the percentages of grapes contained in the final blend; thus blends and pure varietals are allowed.

RED The communes of Vix and Mareuil-sur-Lay-Disais produce the best wines. They are dry, medium-bodied, and firm, but not long-lived. They can have a grassy character, derived from the Cabernet Franc, which is the predominant grape grown in both these villages.

🍇 A minimum of 50% Gamay and Pinot Noir plus Cabernet Franc, Cabernet Sauvignon, Négrette, and up to a maximum of 15% Gamay de Chaudenay

⌛ Within 18 months

WHITE Bone-dry to dry, light-bodied wines that, apart from those of Vix and Pissotte, are of limited quality. This could be because the Chenin Blanc rarely ripens properly in a northerly coastal area. If some of the other permitted grape varieties were grown over a much wider area, quality might improve.

🍇 A minimum of 50% Chenin Blanc, plus Sauvignon Blanc and Chardonnay. A maximum of 20% Melon de Bourgogne in the communes of Vix and Pissotte and a maximum of 30% Groslot Gris in the coastal vineyards around Les Sables d'Olonne.

⌛ Upon purchase

ROSÉ Dry, light- to medium-bodied wines. The best wines of Vix and Mareuil-sur-Lay-Disais are soft, delicate, and underrated.

🍇 A minimum of 50% Gamay and Pinot Noir plus Cabernet Franc, Cabernet Sauvignon, Négrette, and a maximum of 15% Gamay de Chaudenay. A maximum of 30% (was as high as 30% until 1994) Groslot Gris in the coastal vineyards around Les Sables d'Olonne.

⌛ Within 18 months

✓ *Coirer* (Pissotte Sélection) • *Des Dames* (Les Aigues Marines) • *Saint Nicolas* (Brem Reflets) ❸

GROS PLANT NANTAIS AOC

Gros Plant is the local synonym for the Folle Blanche – one of the grapes used to make Cognac. At one time, it was thought that Gros Plant Nantais would be the only VDQS to opt for IGT (Vin de Pays) rather than AOC, but a change of heart in 2010 led to its application for, and receipt of, full AOC status.

WHITE Gros Plant is normally so dry, tart, and devoid of fruit and body that it seems tough and sinewy to taste. I would rather drink lemon juice than 99 per cent of the Gros Plant that I have had, but if yields are limited and the wine bottled *sur lie*, it can have sufficient depth to match its inherent bite.

🍇 Gros Plant, Montils, and a maximum of 20% Colombard

⌛ Usually upon purchase

✓ *De la Boitaudière* (Sur Lie) • *Guy Bossard* ❸ (De l'Ecu) • *La Haut-Vrignais* (Sur Lie)

MUSCADET AOC

This basic appellation covers the whole Muscadet area, yet the wines produced under it account for only 10 per cent of the total production.

WHITE Bone-dry, light-bodied wines that, with very few exceptions, are ordinary at best, and often lack balance. Not one basic Muscadet has impressed me in recent years. These wines may be sold as *primeur* or *nouveau* as from the third Thursday of November following the harvest.

🍇 Muscadet

⌛ Upon purchase

✓ *de la Chauvinière*

MUSCADET DES COTEAUX DE LA LOIRE AOC

The Coteaux de la Loire is the most northerly wine area on the French coast, above which it is almost impossible to grow grapes of sufficient ripeness for winemaking.

WHITE Bone-dry, light-bodied wines of variable quality, usually lacking in fruit, but can be the best balanced of all Muscadets in very hot years.

🍇 Muscadet

⌛ Upon purchase

✓ *Guindon* • *Du Moulin Giron* • *De la Varenne*

MUSCADET CÔTES DE GRANDLIEU AOC

Delimited in 1994, this area west of Sèvre-et-Maine once represented 73 per cent of the basic Muscadet appellation. The wines now fetch a nice premium above that received when they were merely perceived as generic Muscadets and, while some deserve elevated price and status, many plainly do not.

WHITE Bone-dry, light-bodied wines that initially displayed considerable variation in quality, but the best are now showing a fine, floral-minerality of fruit.

🍇 Muscadet

⌛ Upon purchase

✓ *Du Fief Guerin* • *Gandais Père & Fils* • *Les Hautes Noëlles* ⊙ • *Château des Herbauges*

MUSCADET DE SÈVRE-ET-MAINE AOC

Classic Muscadet from a small area containing most of the best wines. Some 45 per cent of this appellation is bottled and sold as *sur lie*, having remained in contact with its sediment for at least one winter before bottling. There are so many groupings of Muscadet estates that I have decided to list them separately where I can.

WHITE Bone-dry to dry, light-bodied wines. The best should have fruit, acidity, and elegance, but although they can be reminiscent of a modest white Burgundy and exceptional wines can survive considerable ageing, they seldom improve and always trade off finesse for depth.

🍇 Muscadet

⌛ 2 years, although some may last 3–4 years

✓ *Guy Bossard* ❸ (De l'Ecu) • *De la Braudière* • *Michel Bregeon* • *De la Chauvinière* • *Chasseloir* • *Coing de Saint-Fiacre* • *Comte Leloup de Chasseloir* • *Jean Douillard* • *les Frères Couillaud* • *Gandais Père & Fils* • *Grand Fief de la Cormeraie* • *La Haute Févrie* • *De la Louvetrie* • *Des Petites Cossardières* • *De la Quilla* • *Château des Roi* • *Abbaye de Ste Radegonde* • *Sauvion* ⊙ • *Château la Tarcière*

MUSCADET SUR LIE AOC

Until recently, there were no controls and unscrupulous producers would simply describe an ordinary filtered wine as *sur lie* and thereby demand a higher price. Since 1994, however, this term may be applied to only one of the three sub-appellations (Coteaux du Loire, Côtes de Grandlieu, and Sèvre-et-Maine) and may not be used on any wines bearing the generic Muscadet AOC. Quite what the logic is to this is uncertain, since Gros Plant VDQS is permitted to use *sur lie* and it is even more inferior than the generic Muscadet appellation. The lesser the wine, the more need for a *sur lie* boost, thus rather than limiting its use, more emphasis should be placed on stricter controls.

At the moment Muscadet *sur lie* must remain in contact with its sediment for one winter, and may not be bottled before the third week of March following the harvest, with a second bottling period of mid-October to mid-November for fuller styles. The wine must also be bottled directly off its lees, and must not be racked or filtered, but there is still no regulation on the size and type of vessel in which the wine should be kept *sur lie*. Some growers would like the term applied only to wines kept in wooden barrels, arguing that the effect of keeping a wine in contact with its lees in huge vats is negligible, but at the very least vats over a certain size should be equipped with paddles to circulate the lees.

ANJOU-SAUMUR

Anjou-Saumur is a microcosm of the entire Loire Valley, with almost every grape available in the Loire producing virtually every style of wine imaginable – from dry to sweet, red through rosé to white, and still wines to sparkling.

SAUMUR IS THE LOIRE'S SPARKLING-WINE CENTRE, where tourists flock in the summer, visiting the numerous cellars hewn out of the solid tufa subsoil. The magnificent white tufa-stone castle that overlooks the town was built in the 14th century. It is regarded as one of the finest of the Loire châteaux, and is used by the Confrérie des Chevaliers du Sacavins (one of Anjou's several wine fraternities) for various inaugural ceremonies and celebrations.

THE WINES OF ANJOU
Rosé still represents as much as 45 per cent of Anjou's total wine output, even though it is on the decline. The figure was 55 per cent in the late 1980s. However, although rosé remains this district's

VINEYARDS, COTEAUX DU LAYON
In favourable sites, the vines are sometimes attacked by "noble rot". The area is famous for its sweet white wines.

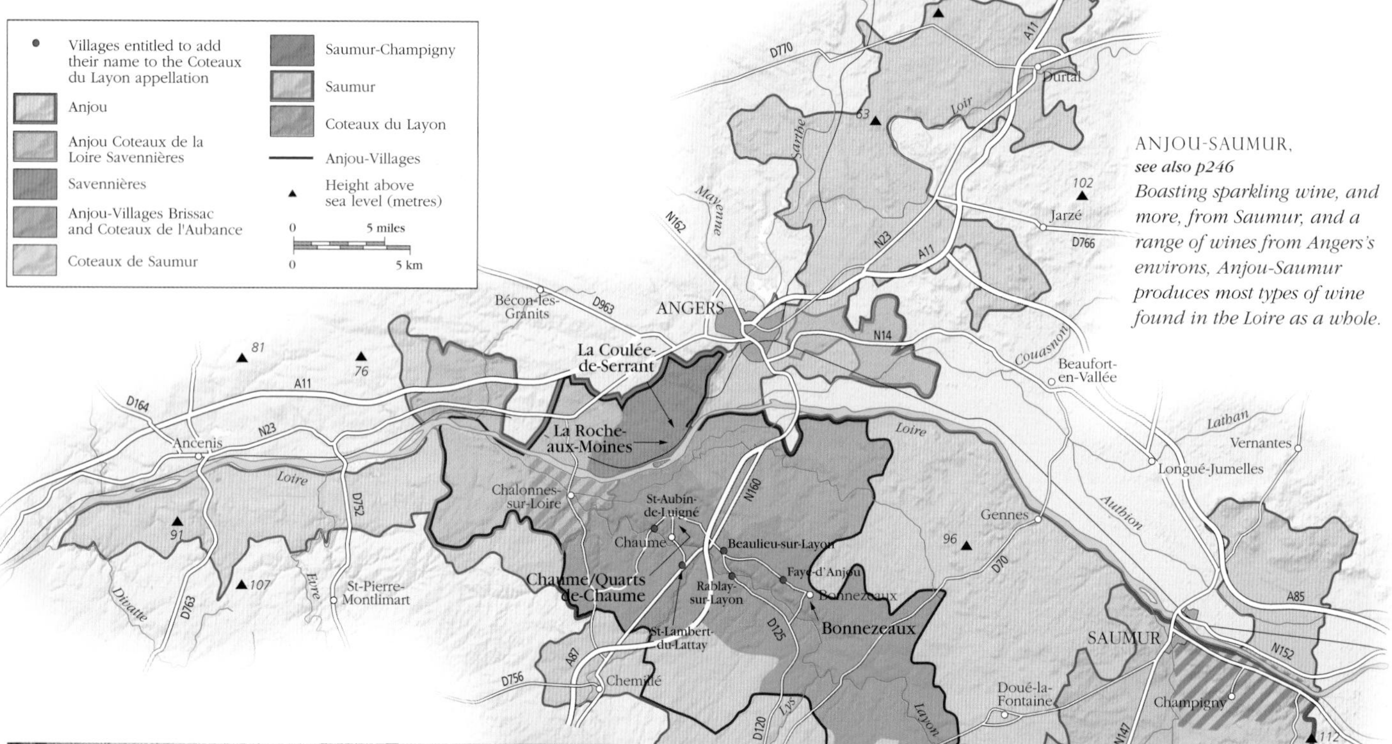

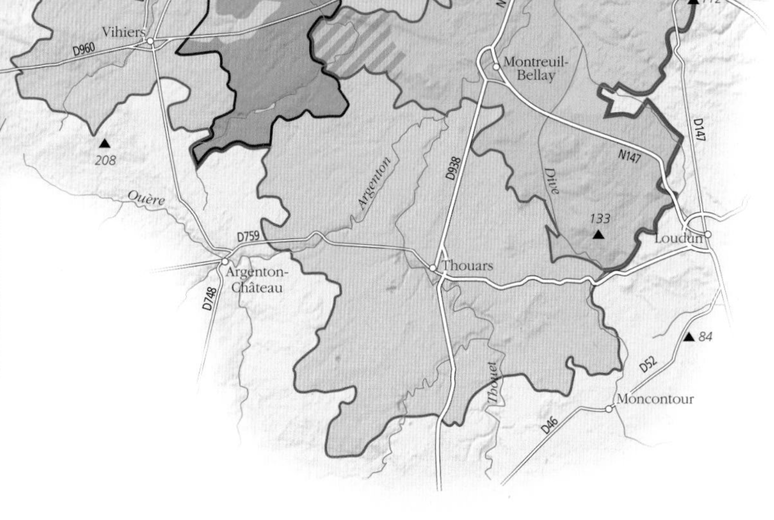

ANJOU-SAUMUR,
see also p246
Boasting sparkling wine, and more, from Saumur, and a range of wines from Angers's environs, Anjou-Saumur produces most types of wine found in the Loire as a whole.

Legend:
- ● Villages entitled to add their name to the Coteaux du Layon appellation
- Anjou
- Anjou Coteaux de la Loire Savennières
- Savennières
- Anjou-Villages Brissac and Coteaux de l'Aubance
- Coteaux de Saumur
- Saumur-Champigny
- Saumur
- Coteaux du Layon
- Anjou-Villages
- ▲ Height above sea level (metres)

0   5 miles
0   5 km

TUFA SUBSOIL CELLARS
The tufa-stone not only dominates the architecture; the subsoil is ideal for the sparkling-wine cellars.

most popular wine, it has a down-market image and is essentially a blend of minor grapes; thus, its commercial success has not propelled a specific variety to fame. Anjou's most celebrated grape is the Chenin Blanc used to make white wines. This vine has been cultivated in the area for well over a thousand years. It has many synonyms, from "Pineau de la Loire" to "Franc-blanc", but its principal name, Chenin Blanc, stems from Mont-Chenin in 15th-century Touraine. Under other names it can be traced as far back as the year 845, to the abbey of Glanfeuil (south of the river in the Anjou district). The distinctive tang of the Chenin Blanc grape comes from its inherently high tartaric acid content and this, combined with a naturally high extract, makes for unacceptably tart and often bitter styles of dry and medium-dry white. Exceptions to this rule are few and mostly confined to the four sun-blessed, southeast-facing slopes of Savennières. Anjou growers go by the rule rather than the exception, and the common practice has always been to leave the harvest of this variety until as late as possible. This invites the risk of rain, but by going over the vines several times in the time-honoured tradition of *tries*, picking only the ripest and healthiest grapes on each and every sweep of the vineyard, a miraculous wine may be made. Although this is a time-consuming, labour-intensive operation, the unique quality of overripe grapes produced can result in the most succulent and immaculately balanced of sweet wines. Unlike poor and boring dry Chenin Blanc wines that only deteriorate with age, these treasures are vinous investments that are capable of great maturity and can achieve wonderfully complex honeyed characteristics.

THE SPARKLING SAUMUR INDUSTRY

With the rapid growth of the Champagne market in the 19th century, producers in the Loire began to copy effervescent winemaking practices, believing that here, at last, was a potential outlet for the surplus of thin, tart Chenin Blanc wines with which even the most quality-conscious growers were often lumbered. Saumur eventually turned into the largest French sparkling-wine industry outside Champagne. In many parts of the Loire the Chenin Blanc grape has the perfect acidity required for a quality sparkling wine, although devotees of the true yeasty character of Champagne can find its bouquet sweet and aromatic, maintaining that its flavour is too assertive to be properly transmuted by the traditional method. However, the wines are hugely popular, and the mixture of Chardonnay and other neutral varieties can greatly improve the overall blend. The most ardent admirer of Champagne has been known to fall prey to the charms of a superior pure Chenin Blanc bubbly from this region, and even I have been known to be besotted by Bouvet-Ladubay's luxuriously ripe, oak-fermented Trésor.

THE REGION'S RED WINES

It is in Anjou, especially south of Saumur, that the Cabernet Franc emerges as the Loire's best red-wine grape. However, beyond neighbouring Touraine, its cultivation rapidly diminishes. The Loire is the largest wine region in France, yet surprisingly it boasts just three classic red wines – Saumur-Champigny, Bourgueil, and Chinon – to which we might now add Anjou-Villages. It is no coincidence that most of the vineyards producing these wines are clustered together in a compact area around the confluence of the Vienne and the Loire – two rivers that long ago established the gravel terraces so prized for growing Cabernet Franc today.

FACTORS AFFECTING TASTE AND QUALITY

LOCATION
West-central district with mostly left-bank vineyards situated between Angers and Saumur.

CLIMATE
A gentle Atlantic-influenced climate with light rainfall, warm summers, and mild autumns, but frost is a problem in Savennières.

ASPECT
Soft, rolling hills which hold back the westerly winds. The best sites are the south-facing rocky hillsides of Savennières and the steep-sided valley of the River Layon.

SOIL
In the west and around Layon, the soil is schist with a dark, shallow topsoil that stores heat well and helps ripen the grapes, but some colder clay-soil areas produce heavier wines. The chalk-tufa soil in the east of the district around Saumur produces lighter wines, while the shale and gravel in Saumur-Champigny favours Cabernet Franc.

VITICULTURE AND VINIFICATION
The Chenin Blanc is a particularly slow-ripening grape that is often left on the vine until November, especially in the Coteaux du Layon. The effect of the autumn sun on the dew-drenched, overripe grapes can encourage "noble rot", particularly in Bonnezeaux and Quarts-de-Chaume. In good years, pickers go through the vineyards several times, selecting only the ripest or most rotten grapes – a tradition known as *tries*. Most wines are bottled in the spring following the vintage, but wines produced from such richly sweet grapes take at least three months to ferment and, for this reason, might not be bottled until the following autumn.

GRAPE VARIETIES
Primary varieties: Cabernet Franc, Chenin Blanc, Gamay, Grolleau (Grolleau Noir)
Secondary varieties: Cabernet Sauvignon, Chardonnay, Cot (Malbec), Pineau d'Aunis, Sauvignon Blanc

THE APPELLATIONS OF
ANJOU-SAUMUR

ANJOU AOC

DOMAINE
JO PITHON

ANJOU
LES BONNES BLANCHES
2002

The Anjou district encompasses the vineyards of Saumur; thus Saumur may be sold as Anjou, but not vice versa. The red wines are by far the best, the whites the worst, and the rosé wines, although waning in popularity, remain the most famous. Because "mousseux" has "cheap fizz" connotations, the wines officially designated as Anjou Mousseux appellation are often marketed simply as "Anjou".

RED Dry, medium- to full-bodied wines, made mostly from pure Cabernet Franc or with a touch of Cabernet Sauvignon. These delightful wines are best drunk young, although the odd oak-aged wine of surprising complexity can be found.

⊞ Cabernet Franc, Cabernet Sauvignon, Pineau d'Aunis

⌇ 1–3 years

✓ *Des Baumard* • *Bouvet-Ladubay* (Non Pareils) • *Château de Fesles* • *Richard Leroy* ◉ • *Le Logis du Prieuré* • *D'Orgigné* • *Des Sablonnettes* (Genêts) ◉ • *Saint Arnoul* • *De la Sansonnière* ⑬ • *Château Soucherie* (Champ aux Loups) • *De Terrebrune*

WHITE Although these wines vary from dry to sweet and from light- to full-bodied types, there are too many aggressively acid-dry or simply mediocre medium-sweet Chenin Blanc wines in the appellation. Some improvement has been made by growers maximizing the 20 per cent Chardonnay and Sauvignon allowance, while Jacques Beaujeu and a few others use oak to smooth out Chenin's jagged edges, and Ogereau even ferments *en barrique*. These wines may be sold from 1 December following the harvest without any mention of *primeur* or *nouveau*.

⊞ A minimum of 80% Chenin Blanc and a maximum of 20% Chardonnay and Sauvignon Blanc

⌇ Upon purchase

✓ *Philippe Delesvaux* ◉ • *Les Grandes Vignes* (Varenne de Combre) ◉ • *Ogereau* • *Château de Passavant* ◉ • *Château Pierre-Bise* • *Des Sablonnettes* ◉ • *Pithon-Paillé* ◉ • *Du Regain* • *Du Roy René* (Les Pierres) • *Richou* • *Château La Varière*

ROSÉ Once a marketing miracle, Anjou Rosé or Rosé d'Anjou sells less well in today's increasingly sophisticated markets. There is nothing intrinsically wrong with a wine that happens to be pink with some sweetness, although you would be forgiven for thinking this is exactly why some critics turn up their noses at these wines. I prefer dry

rosés, but I enjoy medium-sweet rosés when they are very fresh and fruity. The trouble with so many of these medium-sweet, light- to medium-bodied, coral-pink wines is that, while they can be delicious in the early spring following the vintage, an alarming number quickly tire in the bottle. The moral is, therefore, that even when you have found an Anjou rosé you like, never buy it by the case. These wines may be sold as *primeur* or *nouveau* from the third Thursday of November following the harvest or from 1 December without any mention of *primeur* or *nouveau*.

⊞ Predominantly Grolleau, with varying proportions of Cabernet Franc, Cabernet Sauvignon, Pineau d'Aunis, Gamay, Malbec

⌇ Upon purchase

✓ *CV de la Loire* (Elysis) • *Château La Varière*

ANJOU COTEAUX DE LA LOIRE AOC

This rare, white-only appellation is situated southwest of Angers. Production is small and will dwindle even further as vineyards are replanted with Cabernet for the increasingly popular Anjou Rouge appellation. The minimum natural richness of the grapes at harvest is 221 grams per litre (the same as Sauternes), with a minimum residual sugar in the finished wine of 17 grams per litre.

WHITE Although currently produced in dry through to medium styles, this was originally legally defined in 1946 as a traditionally sweet wine. Today, producers following the trend for drier styles are hampered by out-of-date regulations that set the alcoholic strength too high and the yield too low.

⊞ Chenin Blanc

⌇ Within 1 year

✓ *Musset Roullier*

ANJOU GAMAY AOC

Gamay is only allowed in Anjou AOC wines if the name of the grape is added to the appellation on the label.

RED Dry to medium-dry, light-bodied wines that are rarely of great interest. These wines may be sold as *primeur* or *nouveau* as from the third Thursday of November following the harvest.

⊞ Gamay

⌇ Upon purchase

✓ *De la Charmoise* • *Roy René* (La Creusette)

ANJOU MOUSSEUX AOC

This traditional method wine is softer, but less popular than its Saumur equivalent, although it may come from the communes within Saumur itself.

SPARKLING WHITE These dry to sweet, light- to medium-bodied wines desperately need a change of regulation to allow a little Chardonnay in the blend. Its fatter, more neutral character would enable producers to make a more classic, less frivolous style of sparkling wine.

⊞ A minimum of 60% Chenin Blanc plus Cabernet Sauvignon, Cabernet Franc, Malbec, Gamay, Grolleau, Pineau d'Aunis

⌇ 1–2 years

SPARKLING ROSÉ If you want to know what Anjou Rosé tastes like with bubbles, try this

light- to medium-bodied wine, which is mostly sold as *demi-sec*.

⊞ Cabernet Sauvignon, Cabernet Franc, Malbec, Gamay, Grolleau, Pineau d'Aunis

⌇ Upon purchase

ANJOU PÉTILLANT AOC

A little-used appellation for gently sparkling traditional method wines with a minimum of nine months' bottle age, which must be sold in ordinary still-wine bottles with regular corks.

SEMI-SPARKLING WHITE These are dry to *demi-sec*, light-bodied sparkling wines. Considering the variable quality of Anjou Blanc, many producers might be better advised to fizz it up and sell it under this appellation.

⊞ A minimum of 80% Chenin Blanc and a maximum of 20% Chardonnay and Sauvignon Blanc

⌇ Upon purchase

SEMI-SPARKLING ROSÉ Dry to medium, light-bodied wines which are rarely encountered outside the area and may be labelled "Anjou Pétillant", "Anjou Rosé Pétillant", or "Rosé d'Anjou Pétillant".

⊞ Grolleau, Cabernet Franc, Cabernet Sauvignon, Pineau d'Aunis, Gamay, Malbec

⌇ Upon purchase

ANJOU ROSÉ AOC

See Anjou AOC

ANJOU-VILLAGES AOC

This superior, red-wine-only appellation was first delimited in 1986, but it did not come into effect until 1991. If you buy from the best growers, you will get some of the finest red wines that the Loire has to offer.

RED The very best wines can be deeply coloured with a creamy-raspberry aroma and flavour.

⊞ Cabernet Franc, Cabernet Sauvignon

⌇ 2–6 years

✓ *Patrick Baudouin* ◉ • *De la Bergerie* • *Château Pierre-Bise* • *Des Griottes* ◉ • *L & F Martin* • *De la Motte* • *Ogereau* • *De la Poterie* • *De Putille* • *Des Quatre Quarres* • *Michel Robineau* • *Des Saulaies* • *Château La Varière*

ANJOU–VILLAGES BRISSAC AOC

This village was singled out under the Anjou-Villages appellation in 1998 and backdated for wines from 1996 onwards. It covers the area of Brissac-Quincé and nine surrounding communes.

✓ *Davieu* (Château de Brissac) • *De Haute-Perche* • *Du Prieuré* • *Richou* • *Des Rochelles* (La Croix de Mission) • *Château La Varière*

BONNEZEAUX AOC

Grown on three south-facing river slopes of the commune of Thouarcé in the Coteaux du Layon, this is one of the undisputed great sweet wines of France. The grapes must be harvested in *tries* with the pickers collecting only the ripest, often botrytis-affected fruit, which can take up to two weeks. In 2003 the minimum natural richness of the grapes at harvest was increased from 204 to 238 grams per litre (compared to 221 grams per litre for Sauternes), and the minimum residual sugar increased from 17 to 34 grams per litre and finally to 51 grams in 2009.

WHITE Intensely sweet, richer, and more full-bodied than Quarts-de-Chaume, the other great growth of the Layon Valley, this wine can have pineapple and liquorice fruit when young, often achieving a beautiful honeyed-vanilla complexity with age.

🍇 Chenin Blanc

🍷 Up to 20 years or more

✓ *de la Petite-Croix* • *Philippe Delesvaux* ◉ • *Château de Fesles* • *Godineau/Des Petit Quarts* • *Claude Robin* (Floriane) • *De la Sansonnière* ⑧ • *De Terrebrune* • *Château La Varière*

CABERNET D'ANJOU AOC

This appellation includes Saumur, and it was a *saumurois* named Taveau who, in 1905, was the first person to make an Anjou Rosé from Cabernet grapes. Despite its classic Cabernet content and an extra degree of natural alcohol, this is not as superior to Anjou Rosé as it should be because bulk sales at cheap prices have devalued its reputation.

ROSÉ Good examples of these medium to medium-sweet, medium-bodied wines produced by the best domaines have a clean and fruity character with aromas of raspberries. These wines may be sold as *primeur* or *nouveau* from the third Thursday of November following the harvest or from 1 December without any mention of *primeur* or *nouveau*.

🍇 Cabernet Franc, Cabernet Sauvignon

🍷 Upon purchase

✓ *La Croix des Loges* • *CV de la Loire* (Elysis) • *Des Petite Grouas* • *De Preville*

CABERNET DE SAUMUR AOC

All Cabernet de Saumur wines have the right to claim the appellation Cabernet d'Anjou, but those sold as Saumur are usually finer in quality.

ROSÉ A delicate, medium-sweet, light- to medium-bodied wine with a hint of straw to its pink colour and a distinctive raspberry aroma. These wines may be sold as *primeur* or *nouveau* from the third Thursday of November following the harvest or from 1 December without any mention of *primeur* or *nouveau*.

🍇 Cabernet Franc, Cabernet Sauvignon

🍷 Upon purchase

✓ *Du Val Brun* ◉

CHAUME AOC

After much legal wrangling, there are now only two Chaume appellations: this one and Quarts-de-Chaume. Coteaux du Layon-Chaume and Chaume 1er Cru des Coteaux du Layon have both been rescinded, replaced in 2009 with Chaume, plain and simple. The geographical difference between Chaume and Quarts-de-Chaume is that the latter is restricted to just three *lieux-dits*: Les Quarts, Les Roueres, and Le Veau in the commune of Rochefort-sur-Loire, whereas Chaume may come from selected parcels all over the commune of Rochefort-sur-Loire. The technical requirements are more stringent than they were for Chaume 1er Cru des Coteaux du Layon, as the minimum natural sugar of grapes destined for this new Chaume appellation is 272 grams per litre, rather than 238 grams, while the minimum residual sugar in the finished wine is 68 grams per litre, compared to just 34 grams for Chaume 1er Cru des Coteaux du Layon (and

indeed for Quarts-de-Chaume). There are plans for this appellation to be classified once more as *premier cru* (but without mention of Coteaux du Layon) when Quarts de Chaume itself is awarded *grand cru* status.

WHITE Big, rich, lusciously sweet wines that will make their mark in years to come.

🍇 Chenin Blanc

🍷 5–15 years

✓ *Château Pierre-Bise* • *Michel Blouin* • *Cady* • *Château de Fesles* (Château de la Roulerie Aunis) • *Des Forges* (Les Onnis) • *Château de la Guimonière* • *L & F Martin* • *Du Petit Metris* • *Du Rocher* • *De la Soucherie*

COTEAUX DE L'AUBANCE AOC

These wines are made from old vines grown on the schistous banks of the River Aubance. To be entitled to this appellation growers must use grapes that are well ripened and harvested by *tries*, a labour-intensive system that is not cost-effective, thus until recently most growers produced Cabernet d'Anjou. A new generation of growers has transformed this appellation such that in 2003 the minimum natural sugar of the grapes at harvest was increased from 204 to 230 grams per litre (compared with 221 grams per litre for Sauternes) or 294 grams per litre for Coteaux l'Aubance "Sélection de Grains Nobles", as indicated on the label. The minimum residual sugar was also increased from 17 to 34 grams per litre.

WHITE A few growers still make this rich and semi-sweet, medium- to full-bodied wine of excellent longevity and exceptional quality.

🍇 Chenin Blanc

🍷 5–10 years

✓ *De Bablut* ◉ • *Davieu* • *De Montgilet* (Clos Prieur) • *Richou*

COTEAUX DU LAYON AOC

This appellation, which overlaps Anjou Coteaux de la Loire in the northwest and Saumur in the southeast, has been famous for its sweet white wines since the 4th century. In favourable sites the vines are sometimes attacked by "noble rot", but in all cases the grapes must be extremely ripe and harvested by *tries* to a minimum of 12 per cent alcohol from a maximum 30 hectolitres per hectare. Due to the relatively low price this appellation commands, harvesting by *tries* is viable only for the top domaines. In 2003 the minimum natural richness of the grapes at harvest was increased from 204 to 221 grams per litre (the same as Sauternes) or 294 grams per litre (323 grams since 2009) for Coteaux du Layon "Sélection de Grains Nobles". The minimum residual sugar was also increased from 17 to 34 grams per litre.

WHITE Green-gold- to yellow-gold-coloured, soft-textured, sweet, medium- to full-bodied wines, rich in fruit, and potentially long lived.

🍇 Chenin Blanc

🍷 5–15 years

✓ *Patrick Baudouin* ◉ • *Baumard* (le Paon) • *Château Pierre-Bise* • *Château Pierre-Bise des Forges* • *Philippe Delesvaux* ◉ • *Dhomme* • *Château de Fesles* (Château de la Roulerie) • *De la Gerfauderie* (Les Hauts de la Gerfauderie) • *Ogereau* (Prestige) • *Du Petit Val* (Simon) • *Du Portaille* (Planche Mallet) • *Du Regain* (Le Paradis) • *Des Sablonnettes* (La Bohème) ◉

COTEAUX DU LAYON VILLAGES AOC

Historically, these six villages have consistently produced the cream of all the wines in the Coteaux du Layon, and thus have the right to add their names to the basic appellation. In 2003 the minimum natural sugar of the grapes at harvest was increased from 204 to 238 grams per litre (compared to 221 grams per litre for Sauternes) or 294 grams per litre (323 grams since 2009) for Coteaux du Layon Villages "Sélection de Grains Nobles". The minimum residual sugar was also increased from 17 to 34 grams per litre.

WHITE Sweet wines that are medium- to full-bodied. According to the "Club des Layon Villages", Beaulieu has a soft, light aroma; Faye has a scent reminiscent of brushwood; Rablay is big, bold, and round; Rochefort is full-bodied, tannic, and matures well; St-Aubin has a delicate aroma that develops; and St-Lambert is robust yet round.

🍇 Chenin Blanc

🍷 5–15 years

✓ **Beaulieu** *Château de Breuil* • *Château Pierre-Bise* • **Faye** *Château de Fresne* (Clos de Cocus), *Richard Leroy* • **Rablay** *Des Sablonnettes* ◉ • **Rochefort** *De la Motte* • **St-Aubin** *Des Barres, Philippe Delesvaux* ◉, *Jo Pithon, De la Roche Moreau* • **St-Lambert** *Ogereau, Pithon-Paillé* ◉, *Du Roy René* (Les Cartelles), *Michel Robineau*

COTEAUX DE SAUMUR AOC

After the ban in 1985 on the use of the term *méthode champenoise* for wines produced or sold in the European Union (see p215), there were moves to develop this little-used appellation as the principal still wine of the Saumur district in order to promote Saumur AOC as an exclusively sparkling wine. That idea has, it seems, ground to a halt.

WHITE Relatively rare, semi-sweet, medium- to full-bodied wines that are richly flavoured and worth seeking out.

🍇 Chenin Blanc

🍷 5–10 years

✓ *Champs Fleuris* (Sarah) • *De Nerleux* • *De Saint Just* (La Valboisière)

QUARTS-DE-CHAUME AOC

These wines are grown on the plateau behind the village of Chaume in the Coteaux-du-Layon commune of Rochefort-sur-Loire. The vineyards of Quarts-de-Chaume used to be run by the abbey of Ronceray, whose landlord drew a quarter of the vintage as rent. In 2003 the minimum natural sugar of the grapes at harvest was increased from 204 to 238 grams per litre (298 grams since 2009), and the minimum residual sugar increased from 17 to 34 grams per litre. *See also* Chaume AOC.

WHITE These are semi-sweet to sweet, medium- to full-bodied wines. Although harvested by *tries* and produced in the same manner as Bonnezeaux, Quarts-de-Chaume comes from a more northerly area and as a result is slightly lighter in body. It also tends to have a touch less sweetness.

🍇 Chenin Blanc

🍷 Up to 15 years or more

✓ *Des Baumard* • *Château de Bellerive* • *De Laffourcade* • *Château de la Roche Moreau* • *Château Pierre-Bise* • *Château La Varière*

ROSÉ D'ANJOU AOC
See Anjou AOC

ROSÉ D'ANJOU PÉTILLANT AOC
See Anjou Pétillant AOC

SAUMUR AOC

Saumur, situated within the borders of the Anjou appellation, is regarded as the pearl of Anjou. Its wine may be sold as Anjou, but Anjou does not automatically qualify as Saumur. Unless made from Cabernet grapes, all rosé wines must adopt the Anjou Rosé appellation. Like Anjou, its white wines are variable, yet its red wines are excellent.

RED These fine, bone-dry to dry, medium- to full-bodied wines are often similar to the red wines of Anjou, although they can vary from light and fruity to deep-coloured and tannic.

🍇 Cabernet Franc, Cabernet Sauvignon, Pineau d'Aunis

🍷 1–10 years according to style

✓ *Du Bois Mignon* (La Belle Cave) • *Du Collier* • *De Fiervaux* • *De Château-Gaillard* ❽ • *Filliatreau* ◉ • *Guiberteau* ◉ • *Des Hautes Vignes* • *Langlois-Château* (Vieilles Vignes) • *Des Nerleux* • *De la Paleine* • *Château de Passavant* ◉ • *Des Raynières* • *CV de Saumur* (Reserve) • *Château Yvonne* ◉

WHITE Varying from bone-dry to sweet and from light- to full-bodied, these wines have a style more akin to Vouvray than Anjou, due to the limestone and the tufa soil. In poor-to-average years, however, a Saumur is easily distinguished by its lighter body, leaner fruit, and a tartness of flavour that can sometimes have a metallic edge on the aftertaste. These wines may be sold as from 1 December following the harvest without any mention of *primeur* or *nouveau*.

🍇 A minimum of 80% Chenin Blanc and up to 20% Chardonnay and Sauvignon Blanc

🍷 Upon purchase

✓ *Du Collier* • *Guiberteau* (Le Clos) ◉ • *Château de Hureau* • *Langlois-Château* (Vieilles Vignes) • *De la Paleine* • *Des Roches Neuves* • *Clos Rougeard* ◉ • *CV de Saumur* • *Château de Villeneuve*

SPARKLING WHITE Although the production per hectare of this wine is one-third more than for its Anjou equivalent, Saumur is – or at least should be – better in quality and style due to its Chardonnay content and the tufa-limestone soil. Most wines are made in a true, bone-dry, *brut* style, although the full gamut is allowed and wines up to *demi-sec*

sweetness are relatively common. The vast majority of these wines have a tart greengage character, lack finesse, and do not pick up bottle aromas. The wines indicated below have an elegance sadly lacking in most Saumur, and possess gentler, more neutral fruit, which will benefit from a little extra time in bottle, although after a while all these wines tend to age rather than mature gracefully. The creamy-rich *barrique*-fermented Bouvet Trésor is the one significant exception as not only is it just the best sparkling wine in the Loire, it can be compared to very good-quality Champagne, although it is in a very different style.

🍇 Chenin Blanc plus a maximum of 20% Chardonnay and Sauvignon Blanc, and up to 60% Cabernet Sauvignon, Cabernet Franc, Malbec, Gamay, Grolleau, Pineau d'Aunis, and Pinot Noir

🍷 3–5 years

✓ *De Beauregard* • *De la Bessière* • *Bouvet-Ladubay* (Mlle Ladubay, Trésor) • *De Brizé* • *Gratien & Meyer* (Flamme) • *CV de Saumur* (Spéciale)

SPARKLING ROSÉ An increasing number of pink Saumurs are pure Cabernet Franc and an increasing number are showing very well. However, the aggressive potential of this grape can quickly turn a thrilling raspberry-flavoured fizz into something hideous. Pure Cabernet Sauvignon rosés can be much smoother, less overt, and not as intrinsically Saumur as a Cabernet Franc *cuvée*.

🍇 Cabernet Sauvignon, Cabernet Franc, Malbec, Gamay, Grolleau, Pineau d'Aunis, Pinot Noir

🍷 Upon purchase

✓ *Bouvet-Ladubay* (Trésor) • *Gratien & Meyer* (Flamme)

SAUMUR-CHAMPIGNY AOC

Many people believe that the vineyards southeast of Saumur entitled to add the village name of Champigny to their appellation produce the best red wines in the Loire.

RED Bone-dry to dry, full-bodied wines with a distinctive deep colour and full and fragrant raspberry aromas, often tannic and long-lived.

🍇 Cabernet Franc, Cabernet Sauvignon, Pineau d'Aunis

🍷 5–10 years

✓ *Du Bois Moze Pasquier* • *La Bonnelière* ◉ • *Des Champs Fleuris* • *Filliatreau* ◉ • *Château du Hureau* • *René-Noël Legrand* • *Petit Saint Vincent* • *De Rocfontaine* (Vieilles Vignes) • *Des Roches Neuves* ❽ • *Clos Rougeard* ◉ • *De Saint Just* • *Château de Villeneuve* • *Château Yvonne* ◉

SAUMUR MOUSSEUX AOC

This is the technically correct appellation for all fully sparkling white and rosé Saumur wines made by the traditional method, but producers have shied away from the down-market term *mousseux*, selling the wines simply as Appellation Saumur Contrôlée.

There is no allowance for this in the regulations, but it is a widespread practice. A significant amount of red traditional method wine is also produced, but this cannot claim AOC status. *See also* Saumur AOC.

SAUMUR D'ORIGINE AOC

When the European Union banned the term *méthode champenoise*, this marketing term was developed by the producers of sparkling Saumur to promote and advertise their wines. *See also* Saumur AOC.

SAUMUR PÉTILLANT AOC

Little-used appellation for gently sparkling, traditional method wines with a minimum of nine months' bottle age, which must be sold in ordinary still-wine bottles with regular corks.

SEMI-SPARKLING WHITE These dry to *demi-sec*, light-bodied, and fruity wines are not dissimilar to the fine wines of the Montlouis Pétillant appellation and should be revived.

🍇 A minimum of 80% Chenin Blanc and a maximum of 20% Chardonnay and Sauvignon Blanc

🍷 Upon purchase

SAVENNIÈRES AOC

When this small portion of Anjou Coteaux de la Loire produced only sweet wines, the AOC regulations set a correspondingly low maximum yield. This concentrates the wines on four southeast-facing slopes of volcanic debris that produce the world's greatest dry Chenin Blanc.

WHITE Bone-dry to dry wines of great mineral intensity, Savennières can be some of the longest-lived dry white wines in the world. Most critics believe that the single greatest Savennières is Nicolas Joly's Clos de la Coulée de Serrant and, while I agree that it is one of the greatest wines of the Loire, I think that Baumard's Clos du Papillon (not to be confused with Clos du Papillon from other growers) consistently displays greater elegance and finesse. Over the past 15 years or so, a few producers have resurrected the semi-sweet style that used to be more popular in Savennières in the first half of the 20th century.

🍇 Chenin Blanc

🍷 5–8 years (10–15 years for Clos de la Coulée de Serrant)

✓ *Des Baumard* • *Du Closel* (Clos du Papillon) • *Château de Fesles* (Château de Varennes) • *De Forges* • *Nicolas Joly* (Clos de la Coulée de Serrant) ❽ • *De la Monnaie* • *Château Pierre-Bise* • *Pierre Soulez*

SAVENNIÈRES COULÉE-DE-SERRANT AOC

One of just two single-vineyard designations authorized for Savennières, Coulée-de-Serrant is 7 hectares (17 acres) and a mono-*cru*, solely owned by Nicolas Joly of Château de la Roche-aux-Moines. Many consider this to be the single-greatest Loire dry white wine. *See also* Savennières AOC.

SAVENNIÈRES ROCHE-AUX-MOINES AOC

The second and largest of the two single-vineyard designations authorized for Savennières, Roche-aux-Moines is 17 hectares (42 acres) and owned by three producers: Nicolas Joly of Château de la Roche-aux-Moines, Pierre and Yves Soulez of Château de Chamboureau, and Madame Laroche of au Moines. *See also* Savennières AOC.

TOURAINE

Wines bearing Touraine appellations are prolific and capable of giving good value, but for the most part they are not great. However, there are notable exceptions, such as the wines from Vouvray and the less well-known but equally elite wines of Montlouis, Bourgueil, and Chinon.

THE WINE-GROWING DISTRICT around Tours dates back to Roman times, as does the town itself. The Cabernet Franc, known locally as Breton, was flourishing in the vineyards of the abbey of Bourgueil 1,000 years ago and, as recently as 500 years ago, the Chenin Blanc – today's predominant Touraine grape – acquired its name from Mont Chenin in the south of the district.

TOURAINE'S WINE REGIONS

With the possible exception of Saumur-Champigny, the best red wines in the Loire come from the appellations of Chinon and Bourgueil, which face each other across the Loire River, just west of Tours. Made predominantly from Cabernet Franc, good vintages aged in oak may be complex and comparable to claret, while the more everyday wines have the aromas of fresh-picked raspberries and can be drunk young and cool. To the east, Vouvray and Montlouis produce rich, sweet, long-lived *moelleux* wines from overripe Chenin Blanc grapes in sunny years. North of Tours, the wines produced in Jasnières are from the same grape, but the dry style is distinctly different. Jasnières is a singular white sub-appellation within a wider red, white, and rosé AOC called the Coteaux du Loir. The "Loir" is not a typographical error for "Loire", but a tributary of the great river. Also grown on the banks of the Loir, Coteaux du Vendômois produces the full spectrum of still-wine styles, as does Cheverny to the east, including a distinctive dry white wine from the obscure Romorantin grape. Touraine Sauvignon Blanc makes an attractively priced, unassuming alternative to Sancerre, while the fruity Gamay makes easy-drinking reds and rosés. Chenin Blanc is still the dominant variety here and, as in Anjou-Saumur, the

tradition has been to produce naturally sweet wines in great years when these grapes are full of sugar, although lighter, not completely dry styles are more usual. The surplus of less-than-overripe grapes, like that in Anjou-Saumur, is traditionally utilized for sparkling wines.

TOURAINE, *see also p246*
Surrounded by different appellations, the ancient city of Tours is the focal point of an area rich in the variety of its wines.

FACTORS AFFECTING TASTE AND QUALITY

LOCATION
East-central district with most of its vineyards in the *département* of Indre-et-Loire, but they extend into Loir-et-Cher, Indre, and Sarthe.

CLIMATE
Touraine falls under some Atlantic influence, but the climate is less maritime than in the Nantes district and Anjou-Saumur. Protected from northerly winds by the Coteaux du Loir. Warm summer, low October rainfall.

ASPECT
Attractively rolling land, flatter around Tours itself, hillier in the hinterland. Vines are planted on gently undulating slopes, which are often south-facing, at between 40 and 100 metres (130 to 330 feet) above sea level.

SOIL
Clay and limestone over tufa subsoil east of Tours around Vouvray and Montlouis. Tufa is chalk boiled by volcanic action.

It is full of minerals, retains water, and can be tunnelled out to make large, cool cellars for storing wine. Sandy-gravel soils in low-lying Bourgueil and Chinon vineyards produce fruity, supple wines; the slopes or *coteaux* of sandy-clay produce firmer wines.

VITICULTURE AND VINIFICATION
White-wine fermentation takes place at low temperatures and lasts for several weeks for dry wines, several months for sweet wines. The reds undergo malolactic fermentation. Some Bourgueil and Chinon is aged for up to 18 months in oak casks before bottling.

GRAPE VARIETIES
Primary varieties: Cabernet Franc, Chenin Blanc, Grolleau (Grolleau Noir), Sauvignon Blanc **Secondary varieties:** Arbois, Cabernet Sauvignon, Chardonnay, Gamay, Gamay Teinturier, Cot (Malbec), Meslier, Pineau d'Aunis, Pinot Noir, Romorantin

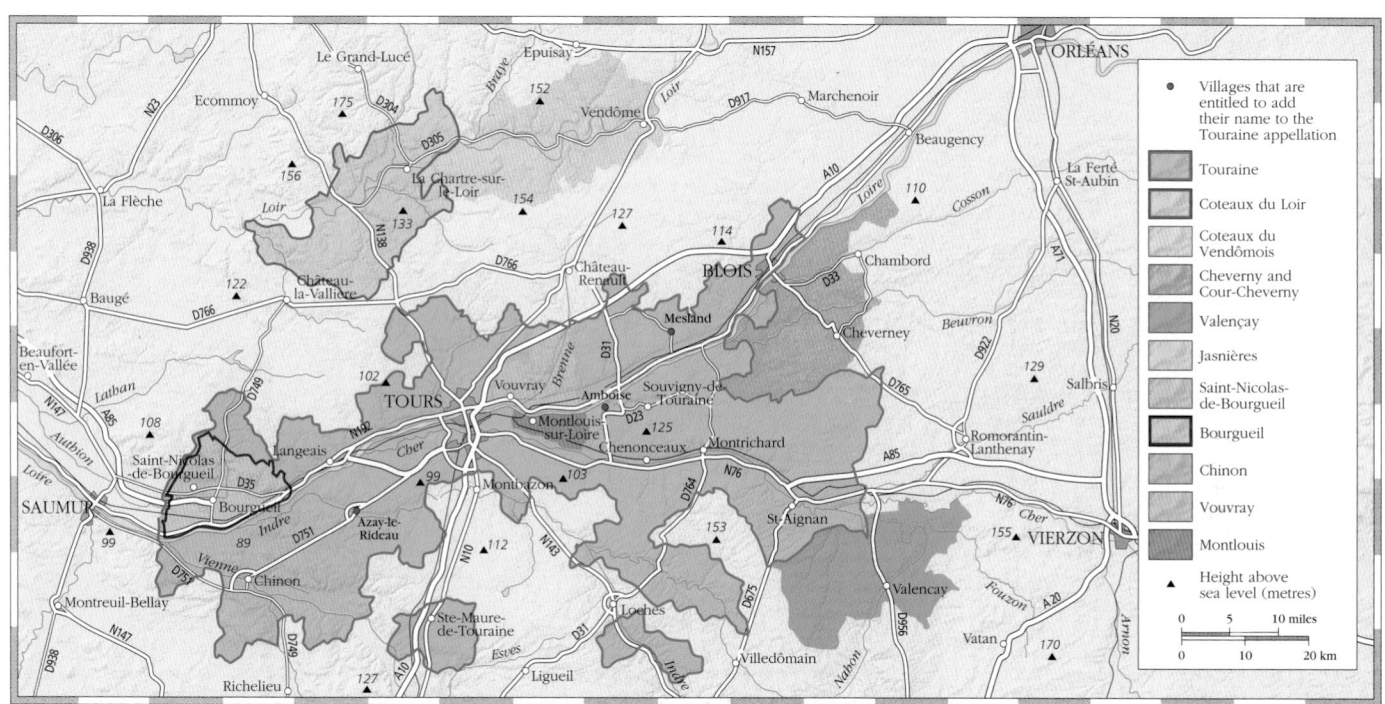

Map legend:
- Villages that are entitled to add their name to the Touraine appellation
- Touraine
- Coteaux du Loir
- Coteaux du Vendômois
- Cheverny and Cour-Cheverny
- Valençay
- Jasnières
- Saint-Nicolas-de-Bourgueil
- Bourgueil
- Chinon
- Vouvray
- Montlouis
- ▲ Height above sea level (metres)

0   5   10 miles
0   10   20 km

THE APPELLATIONS OF
TOURAINE

BOURGUEIL AOC

Most of the vines are grown on a sand-and-gravel plateau, or *terrasse*, by the river. The wines have a pronounced fruity character and are delicious to drink when less than six months old. Those grown on the south-facing clay and tufa slopes, or *coteaux*, ripen up to 10 days earlier and produce more full-bodied, longer-lived wines.

RED Bone-dry to dry, medium-bodied, lively wines, full of soft-fruit flavours, which are often aged in cask. They are very easy to quaff when less than six months old; many close up when in bottle and need time to soften. Wines from the *terrasse* vineyards are best drunk young, while those from the *coteaux* repay keeping.

🍇 Cabernet Franc with up to 10% Cabernet Sauvignon

🍷 Within 6 months or after 6 years

ROSÉ Bone-dry to dry, light- to medium-bodied wines that are very fruity with aromas of raspberries and blackberries and good depth of flavour. They deserve to be better known.

🍇 Cabernet Franc with up to 10% Cabernet Sauvignon

🍷 2–3 years

✔ *Yannick Amirault* (Les Quartier Vieilles Vignes) • *De la Butte* • *Breton* ◉ • *Des Chesnaies* (Prestige) ◉ • *De la Chevalerie* (Busardières) ◉ • *De la Cotelleraie* • *Delaunay Père & Fils* • *Vignoble de la Grioche* (Santenay) • *Frédéric Mabileau* ◉ • *Des Ouches* • *Du Petit Bondiau* (Le Petit Mont) • *Guy Saget* (L'Echallerie) • *De la Taille au Loups*

CHEVERNY AOC

Upgraded from VDQS to full AOC status in 1993. These good-value, crisp, and fruity wines deserve their promotion and should be better known. Cheverny is usually made and marketed as a pure varietal wine, the most interesting of which, Romorantin, has been awarded its own AOC for the best vineyards around Cour-Cheverny itself. *See also* Cour-Cheverny AOC.

RED Dry, light- to medium-bodied wines. The smaller growers mostly produce pure Gamay wines of very acceptable quality, although the addition of 10 per cent or more Pinot Noir gives a smoother wine. Gamay Teinturier de Chaudenay, which has coloured juice, is no longer permitted.

🍇 Between 40 and 65% Gamay, plus Pinot Noir, Cabernet Franc, Malbec. Cabernet Sauvignon is no longer permitted.

🍷 1–2 years

WHITE Dry, light-bodied, modest wines with a fine, flowery nose, delicate flavour, and crisp balance. Now primarily a Sauvignon Blanc wine, as Romorantin may not be used and the amount of Sauvignon in these wines has been regulated since 1993.

🍇 Between 65 and 80% Sauvignon Blanc, plus Chardonnay, Chenin Blanc, and Arbois

🍷 1–2 years

ROSÉ Only small quantities are produced, but the wines are agreeably dry and light-bodied and very consistent in quality. Since acquiring full AOC status, Cabernet Franc, Cabernet Sauvignon, and Malbec have been allowed for the production of these wines, which has boosted the quantity even further.

🍇 At least 50% Gamay, plus Cabernet Franc, Cabernet Sauvignon, Malbec, Pineau d'Aunis, and Pinot Gris

🍷 1–2 years

✔ *De la Desoucherie* • *De la Gaudronnière* (Tradition) • *Du Moulin* ◉ • *Sauger & Fils*

CHINON AOC

The appellations of Chinon and Bourgueil produce the best red wine in Touraine using the Cabernet Franc grape, known locally as Breton. Chinon wines are generally lighter and more delicate than those of Bourgueil, but those from the tufa hill slopes have greater depth and flavour and age well.

RED Bone-dry to dry, light- to medium-bodied wines that are lively, soft, and delicate. Most growers use small oak casks for ageing and produce wines of very good quality.

🍇 Cabernet Franc with up to 10% Cabernet Sauvignon

🍷 2–3 years

WHITE A tiny production of clean, dry, light- to medium-bodied wines that are strangely aromatic for Chenin Blanc with an intriguing perfumed aftertaste.

🍇 Chenin Blanc

🍷 1–2 years

ROSÉ These are dry, fairly light-bodied, smooth, and fruity wines which, like Bourgueil rosés, are very easy to drink and deserve to be better known.

🍇 Cabernet Franc with up to 10% Cabernet Sauvignon

🍷 2–3 years

✔ *Philippe Alliet* • *Château de l'Aulée* (Artissimo) • *Bernard Baudry* • *Guy Saget* (Marie de Beauregard) • *Breton* ◉ • *Château de Coulaine* ◉ • *Couly-Dutheil* (Clos de l'Echo) • *Charles Joguet* • *J L Page* (Sélection Clément Martin) • *Philippe Pichard* • *Jean-Marie Raffault* (Le Puy) • *De Saint-Louand* (Réserve de Trompegueux) • *Serge et Bruno Sourdais*

COTEAUX DU LOIR AOC

This is an area that had extensive vineyards in the 19th century. Production has since declined and these generally unexciting wines come from the Loir, which is a tributary of, and not to be confused with, the Loire.

RED These are dry, medium-bodied wines that can have a lively character and good extract in sunny years.

🍇 Minimum of 30% Pineau d'Aunis with Gamay, Pinot Noir, Cabernet Franc, and Cabernet Sauvignon

🍷 1–2 years

WHITE Bone-dry to dry, light-bodied wines that are high in acidity that can be mean and astringent.

🍇 Chenin Blanc

🍷 As early as possible

ROSÉ Dry, fairly light-bodied wines, a few of which are fruity and well balanced.

🍇 Pineau d'Aunis, Cabernet Franc, Gamay, and Malbec with up to 25% Grolleau

🍷 Within 1 year

✔ *De Bellivière* ◉ • *Jean-François Maillet* (Réserve d'Automme)

COTEAUX DU VENDÔMOIS AOC

Situated on both banks of the Loir, upstream from Jasnières, this steadily improving wine was upgraded to full AOC status in 2001, when the *encépagement* changed.

RED Dry, fairly light-bodied wines that are full of soft-fruit flavours and very easy to drink.

🍇 Minimum of 40% Pineau d'Aunis plus 10–40% Gamay, Pinot Noir, and Cabernet Franc, with a maximum of 20% Gamay reducing to 10% in 2016 (Cabernet Sauvignon is no longer permitted)

🍷 1–2 years

WHITE Dry, fairly light-bodied wines which, when made from pure Chenin Blanc, have a tendency to be very astringent. Growers who blend Chardonnay with Chenin Blanc produce better-balanced wines.

🍇 Primarily Chenin Blanc with up to 20% Chardonnay

🍷 Within 1 year

ROSÉ Fresh and fragrant, Coteaux du Vendômois is one of the most appealing, yet little seen, of the Loire's dry rosés.

🍇 Pineau d'Aunis (Gamay is no longer permitted)

🍷 1–2 years

✔ *Patrice Colin* • *Du Four à Chaux* • *CV de Villiers-sur-Loir*

COUR-CHEVERNY AOC

Cheverny gained this special single-village appellation exclusively for Romorantin when it was upgraded in 1993 from a VDQS to an AOC, but it lost its right to produce sparkling wine. Romorantin is grown in the best sites around Cour-Cheverny. *See also* Cheverny AOC.

WHITE These are dry, light-bodied, modest wines, which have a fine, flowery nose, delicate flavour, and crisp balance.

🍇 Romorantin

🍷 1–2 years

✔ *De la Desoucherie* • *De la Gaudronnière* (Le Mur de Gaudronnière) • *Du Moulin* ◉

JASNIÈRES AOC

This is the best area of the Coteaux du Loir – the wines produced here can, in hot years, achieve a richness that compares well with those of Savennières in Anjou (*see* p256).

WHITE Medium-bodied wines that can be dry or sweet. They are elegant and age well in good years, but they can be unripe in poor years.

🍇 Chenin Blanc

🍷 2–4 years

✔ *De Bellivière* ◉ • *J Martellière* (Poète)

MONTLOUIS-SUR-LOIRE AOC

All Montlouis appellations were renamed Montlouis-sur-Loire AOC from November 2003. Like Vouvray, Montlouis produces wines that can be dry, medium-dry, or sweet depending on the vintage, and, like those of its more famous neighbour, the greatest wines of Montlouis are the sweetest, most botrytis-rich wines, often sold as *moelleux*. The wines are very similar in style to those of Vouvray, but Montlouis is terribly underrated, whereas Vouvray is often overrated. I would rank Moyer's 1959 and the 1947 Montlouis alongside even the greatest vintages of Château d'Yquem Sauternes.

WHITE Light- to medium-bodied wines that can be dry or sweet. They are softer and more forward than the wines of Vouvray but can have the same honeyed flavour in fine years. Sweet Montlouis is aged in cask, but the best medium-dry styles are clean-fermented in stainless steel.

🍇 Chenin Blanc

🍷 1–3 years for medium-dry, up to 10 years for sweeter wines

✓ *Laurent Chatenay* ⊙ • *François Chidaine* ⑱ • *Cossais* (Le Volagre) • *De la Croix Melier* • *Alex Mathur* (Dionys) • *Dominique Moyer* • *De la Taille au Loups*

MONTLOUIS-SUR-LOIRE MOUSSEUX AOC

In poor vintages the grapes are used to make traditional method sparkling versions of Montlouis. The medium-dry (*demi-sec*) styles of the AOC are very popular in France.

SPARKLING WHITE These light- to medium-bodied wines can be *brut, sec, demi-sec,* or *moelleux.* The last two styles are made only in years that are particularly sunny.

🍇 Chenin Blanc

🍷 Upon purchase

✓ *Alain Joulin* • *Thierry et Daniel Mosny*

MONTLOUIS-SUR-LOIRE PÉTILLANT AOC

Gently effervescent, Montlouis Pétillant is one of the most successful, yet least encountered and under-rated, slightly sparkling French white wines.

SEMI-SPARKLING WHITE Light- to medium-bodied wines that can be dry or sweet. Very consistent in quality, with a rich, fruity flavour balanced by a delicate *mousse* of fine bubbles.

🍇 Chenin Blanc

🍷 Upon purchase

✓ *Levasseur* • *Dominique Moyer*

ST-NICOLAS-DE-BOURGUEIL AOC

This is a commune with its own appellation in the northwest corner of Bourgueil. The soil is sandier than that of surrounding Bourgueil and the wines are lighter but certainly equal in terms of quality. These are some of the finest red wines in the Loire.

RED Bone-dry to dry, medium-bodied wines that age well and have greater finesse than the wines of Bourgueil.

🍇 Cabernet Franc with up to 10% Cabernet Sauvignon

🍷 After 5–6 years

ROSÉ A small amount of dry, medium-bodied rosé with firm, fruity flavour is produced.

🍇 Cabernet Franc with up to 10% Cabernet Sauvignon

🍷 Upon purchase

✓ *Yannick Amirault* • *Max Cognard* (Estelle, Malagnes) • *De la Cotelleraie* • *Sebastian David* • *Frédéric Malibeau* (Coutures, Eclipse) • *Jacques et Vincent Malibeau* (La Gardière Vieilles Vignes) • *Clos des Quarterons* (Vieilles Vignes) • *Du Rochouard* (Pierre du Lane)

TOURAINE AOC

A prolific appellation with sparkling wines in dry and medium-dry styles, plus sweet white, red, and rosé still wines from all over Touraine. Most are pure varietal wines and the label should indicate which grape they have been made from. *See also* Touraine Mousseux AOC and Touraine Pétillant AOC.

RED Dry, light- to medium-bodied wines of little interest, which cannot be enhanced by the fact that the lacklustre Grolleau grape has been used in Touraine *rouge* since 1994. Those made from Gamay are fresh and fruity, and may be sold as *primeur* or *nouveau* from the third Thursday of November following the harvest.

🍇 Gamay, Cabernet Franc, Cabernet Sauvignon, Malbec, Pinot Noir, Pinot Meunier, Pinot Gris, Pineau d'Aunis, and Grolleau

🍷 Within 3 years

WHITE These are bone-dry to dry, medium-bodied wines; when made from pure Sauvignon, they are fresh, aromatic, and fruity. Good Touraine Sauvignon is better than average Sancerre. Chardonnay has been restricted in Touraine *blanc* since 1994. These wines may be sold from 1 December following the harvest without any mention of *primeur* or *nouveau.*

🍇 Chenin Blanc, Sauvignon Blanc, Arbois, and a maximum of 20% Chardonnay

🍷 1–2 years

ROSÉ Dry, light- to medium-bodied wines, while those made from Pineau d'Aunis are drier and more subtle than Anjou rosé. They may be sold as *primeur* or *nouveau* from the third Thursday of November following the harvest.

🍇 Cabernet Franc, Gamay, Grolleau, and Pineau d'Aunis with up to 10% Gamay Teinturier de Chaudenay or Gamay de Bouze

🍷 1–2 years

✓ *De la Charmoise* (also those simply labelled Henry Marionnet) • *Des Corbillères* • *Grange Tiphaine* ⊙ • *De la Garrelière* ⑱ • *Henri Marionnet* • *Jacky Marteau* • *Michaud* • *Dominique Percereau* • *De la Puannerie* ⊙ • *Du Pre Baron* • *Clos Roche Blanche* ⊙ • *Les Vaucorneilles* (Gamay)

TOURAINE AMBOISE AOC

Modest white wines and light reds and rosés are produced by a cluster of eight villages surrounding, and including, Amboise. The vines are grown on both sides of the Loire adjacent to the Vouvray and Montlouis areas.

RED Dry, light-bodied wines that are mostly blended. Those containing a high proportion of Malbec are the best.

🍇 A minimum of 60% Gamay, plus 10–30% Cabernet Franc and Malbec, with an optional maximum of 10% Cabernet Sauvignon until 2010, when it will no longer be allowed

🍷 2–3 years

WHITE These bone-dry to dry, light-bodied Chenin Blancs are usually uninspiring; the rosés are superior.

🍇 A minimum of 60% Chenin Blanc, plus a maximum of 30% Sauvignon Blanc, and a maxiumum of 15% Chardonnay

🍷 Upon purchase

ROSÉ These dry, light-bodied, well-made wines are mouth-watering.

🍇 A minimum of 80% Gamay, plus Cabernet Franc and Malbec

🍷 Within 1 year

✓ *Dutertre* • *Guy Saget* • *Lionel Truet* (Grande Foucaudière)

TOURAINE AZAY-LE-RIDEAU AOC

Good-quality wines from eight villages on either side of the Indre River, a tributary of the Loire.

WHITE Delicate, light-bodied wines that are usually dry but may be *demi-sec.*

🍇 Chenin Blanc

🍷 1–2 years

ROSÉ Attractive, refreshing, truly dry (maximum of 3 grams per litre residual sugar) wines that are coral-pink and often have a strawberry aroma.

🍇 A minimum of 60% Grolleau, plus Malbec, Gamay, Cabernet Franc, and Cabernet Sauvignon (the last two must not total more than 10% of the entire blend)

🍷 1–2 years

✓ *Château de l'Aulée* • *J L Page* • *Pibaleau Père & Fils* ⊙

TOURAINE MESLAND AOC

Wines from the vineyards of Mesland and the five surrounding villages on the right bank of the Loire. The reds and rosés of this appellation are definitely well worth looking out for.

RED These dry, medium- to full-bodied wines are the best of the AOC and can be as good as those of Chinon or Bourgueil.

🍇 A minimum of 60% Gamay, plus 10–30% Cabernet Franc and Malbec, with an optional maximum of 10% Cabernet Sauvignon until 2010, when it will no longer be allowed

🍷 1–3 years

WHITE Dry, light-bodied wines with a high acidity that is only tamed in the best and sunniest years.

🍇 A minimum of 60% Chenin Blanc, plus a maximum of 30% Sauvignon Blanc, and a maximum of 15% Chardonnay

🍷 1–2 years

ROSÉ These dry, medium-bodied wines have more depth and character than those of Touraine Amboise.

🍇 A minimum of 80% Gamay, plus Cabernet Franc and Malbec

🍷 1–3 years

✓ *De la Briderie* ⑱ • *Château Gaillard* ⑱

TOURAINE MOUSSEUX AOC

Very good-value traditional method red, white, and rosé wines. While the grapes for the white and rosé can come from the entire Touraine AOC area, those for red Touraine Mousseux may come from only the following areas: Bourgueil, St-Nicolas-de-Bourgueil, or Chinon.

SPARKLING RED Dry, light- to medium-bodied wines that are fruity and refreshing.

🍇 Cabernet Franc

⏳ Upon purchase

SPARKLING WHITE These light- to medium-bodied wines are made in dry and sweet styles, and the quality is consistent due to the large production area, which allows for complex blending.

🍇 Primarily Chenin Blanc but may also include Arbois and up to 20% Chardonnay and a combined maximum of 30% Cabernet, Pinot Noir, Pinot Gris, Pinot Meunier, Pineau d'Aunis, Malbec, and Grolleau

⏳ Upon purchase

SPARKLING ROSÉ Light- to medium-bodied wines that are attractive when *brut*, though a bit cloying if sweeter.

🍇 Cabernet Franc, Malbec, Noble, Gamay, and Grolleau

⏳ 1–2 years

✓ *Blanc Foussy* (Robert de Schlumberger, Veuve Oudinot) • *Jean-Pierre Laissement* (Rosé) • *Monmousseau* (JM)

TOURAINE NOBLE-JOUÉ AOC

A rosé-only appellation, this AOC was created in 2001 in recognition of the *vin gris* produced that was modestly famous in the 19th century, but its vineyards were gradually swallowed by the creeping urbanization southwest of Tours.

ROSÉ Yet to re-establish a reputation, the best of these wines so far have been fresh, light-bodied, elegantly fruity wines with smoky-floral minerality.

🍇 A minimum of 40% Pinot Gris, plus at least 20% Pinot Gris and a minimum of 10% Pinot Noir

⏳ Upon purchase

✓ *Bernard Blondeau*

TOURAINE PÉTILLANT AOC

Refreshing, slightly effervescent white and rosé wines made from the same grape varieties as Touraine Mousseux. None are exported.

SEMI-SPARKLING RED Medium-dry, light-bodied wines that are not very popular.

🍇 Cabernet Franc

⏳ Upon purchase

SEMI-SPARKLING WHITE Well-made, refreshing, light-bodied wines, in dry and sweet styles.

🍇 Chenin Blanc, Arbois, Sauvignon Blanc, and up to 20% Chardonnay

⏳ Upon purchase

SEMI-SPARKLING ROSÉ Attractive, light, quaffing wines that are made in dry and sweet styles.

🍇 Cabernet Franc, Malbec, Noble, Gamay, and Grolleau

⏳ Upon purchase

VALENÇAY AOC

Situated in the southeast of Touraine around the River Cher, these vineyards produce well-made, attractive wines. Promoted from VDQS to AOC in 2003, when the *encépagement* changed. Rarely seen outside France.

RED Dry, light-bodied, fragrant wines that can be very smooth and full of character. The Malbec, known locally as Cot, is particularly successful.

🍇 30–60% Gamay, with at least 30% in total of Pinot Noir and Malbec, plus optional Cabernet Franc and Cabernet Sauvignon, which together must not exceed 10% of the entire blend (20% up to the 2003 vintage)

⏳ 1–2 years

WHITE Simple, dry, light-bodied wines that are improved by the addition of Chardonnay.

🍇 A minimum of 70% Sauvignon Blanc, plus Arbois and Chardonnay

⏳ 1–2 years

ROSÉ Dry to medium-dry, light-bodied wines that can be full of ripe soft-fruit flavours.

🍇 30–60% Gamay, with at least 30% in total of Pinot Noir and Malbec, plus an optional maximum of 30% Pinot d'Aunis, with or without Cabernet Franc and Cabernet Sauvignon, which together must not exceed 20% of the entire blend

⏳ Upon purchase

✓ *Chantal et Patrick Gibault* • *Jean-François Roy* ⊙

VOUVRAY AOC

These white wines may be dry, medium-dry, or sweet depending on the vintage. In sunny years, the classic Vouvray that is made from overripe grapes affected by the "noble rot" is still produced by some growers. In cooler years, the wines are correspondingly drier and more acidic, and greater quantities of sparkling wine are produced.

WHITE At its best, sweet Vouvray can be the richest of all the Loire sweet wines. In good years, the wines are very full bodied, rich in texture, and have the honeyed taste of ripe Chenin Blanc grapes.

🍇 Chenin Blanc but may also contain Arbois

⏳ Usually 2–3 years; the sweeter wines can last up to 50 years

✓ *Des Aubuisières* (Giraudières) • *Champalou* (Le Clos du Portail Sec) • *Philippe Foreau* (Clos Naudin) • *De la Haute Borne* (Tendre) • *Huet* Ⓑ • *Clos de Nouys* • *Pichot* • *De la Taille au Loups* • *Vigneau Chevreau* ⊙ • *Alain Robert* (La Sablonnière)

VOUVRAY MOUSSEUX AOC

These sparkling wines are made from overripe grapes. In years when the grapes do not ripen properly they are converted into sparkling wines using the traditional method and blended with reserve wines from better years.

SPARKLING WHITE Medium- to full-bodied wines made in both dry and sweet styles. They are richer and softer than sparkling Saumur but have more edge than sparkling Montlouis.

🍇 Chenin Blanc and Arbois

⏳ Non-vintage 2–3 years, vintage *brut* and *sec* 3–5 years, vintage *demi-sec* 5–7 years

✓ *Marc Brédif* • *Champalou* • *Champion* • *Clos de l'Epinay* (Tête de Cuvée) • *Philippe Foreau* • *Domaine de la Galinière* (Cuvée Clément) • *Sylvain Gaudron* • *Huet* Ⓑ • *Laurent et Fabrice Maillet* • *Château de Moncontour* (Cuvée Prédilection)

VOUVRAY PÉTILLANT AOC

These are stylish and consistent semi-sparkling versions of Vouvray, but very little is produced.

SEMI-SPARKLING WHITE Medium- to full-bodied wines made in dry and sweet styles. They should be drunk young.

🍇 Chenin Blanc and Arbois

⏳ Upon purchase

✓ *Gilles Champion* • *Jean-Charles Cathelineau* • *Huet* Ⓑ

MORE GREEN WINES

In addition to the Loire producers recommended in this book that are either biodynamic or organic, there are also the following. They include a number that have been recommended in other editions, and still make some fine wines, but have been culled out to make room for others.

PAYS NANTAIS
Biodynamic
St Nicolas (Brem sur Mer)
Organic
Chevolleau-Goulpeau (Aubigny), *De la Louvetrie* (La Haye-Fouassière), *De la Parentière* (Vallet), *Bruno Dejardin* (Rosnay)

ANJOU-SAUMUR
Biodynamic
De la Charmeres se (Faye d'Anjou), *De la Sansonnière* (Thouarcé), *Château La Tour Grise* (Le Pûy Notre Dame)
Organic
Laurent Charrier (Doué la Fontaine), *Collegiale des de Loire* (Le Puy Notre Dame), *Cousin Leduc* (Martigne Briand), *De Dreuillé* (Champ-sur-Layon), *De l'Echalier* (Rablay-sur-Layon), *Elliau* (Vaudelany), *Foucault* (Chacé), *Château Fouquet* (Dampierre-sur-Loire), *Des Frogères* (Chacé), *I & J Godineau Pithon* (St-Lambert du Lattay), *Anne Hacquet* (Beaulieu-sur-Layon), *Hauret* (Martigné Briand), *Henquinet-Pilbon* (Champ-sur-Layon), *Michel Joseph* (Chacé), *Du Layon* (St-Georges du Layon), *Gérard Leroux* (Les Verchers-sur-Layon), *Manoir de la Tête Rouge* (Le Puy Notre Dame), *De Mosse* (St-Lambert du Lattay), *Nouteau-Cerisier Père & Fils* (Faye d'Anjou), *Du Pas St Martin* (Doué la Fontaine), *Régnier-David* (Meigné), *Rochais* (Rochefort-sur-Loire), *De Rochambeau* (Soulaines-sur-Aubance), *Rochard* (Chanzeaux), *Ste-Barbe* (Saumur), *Patric Thomas* (St-Georges-sur-Layon), *Val Brun* (Parnay), *Du Vieux Tuffeau* (Le Puy Notre Dame), *Vintrou* (St Jean des Mauvrets)

TOURAINE
Biodynamic
De Pontcher (Thesée)
Organic
Clos Roches Blanches (Mareuil-sur-Cher), *Philippe Tessier* (Cheverny), *Michelle Thibault* (Bourgueil), *Du Clos Tue Boeuf* (Les Montils), *Breton* (Restigné), *Yves Lecocq* (Bourgueil), *Loquineau (Cheverny), De la Mabillière (Vernou*-sur-Brenne), *Joseph Moreau* (Vallères), *Du Mortier* (St Nicolas de Bourgueil), *Château de la Roche* (Cheillé), *Les Cailloux du Paradis* (Soings en Sologne), *Alain Courtault* (Thésée), *Joël Courtault* (Thésée – in conversion to biodynamic), *Denis Père et Fils* (Civray de Touraine), *Des Deux Saintes* (St Aubin le Dépeint), *Georget* (La Brosse-Touvois), *Guion* (Le Pontarin)

CENTRAL VINEYARDS
Organic
Claude Prugnard (Orcet), *Clos St Jean Clos de la Chapelle* (St Jean St Maurice), *Carroget Gautier* (Anetz), *Christian Chaput* (Prompsat), *Joël Lapalue* (St Jean St Maurice)

CENTRAL VINEYARDS

In this district of scattered vineyards, all the classic wines are dry variations of the Sauvignon Blanc, but there are some discernible differences between the best of them – the concentration of Sancerre, the elegance of Pouilly Fumé, the fresh-floral character of Menetou-Salon, the lightness of Reuilly, and the purity of Quincy.

THE CENTRAL VINEYARDS are so called because they are in the centre of France, not the centre of the Loire Valley. This is a graphic indication of how far the Loire Valley extends and, while it might not be a surprise to discover the vineyards of Sancerre are quite close to Chablis, it does take a leap of the imagination to accept that they are nearer to the Champagne region than to Tours. And who could discern by taste alone that Sancerre is equidistant between the production areas of such diverse wines as Hermitage and Muscadet?

Best known of all the towns in this district is Orléans, famous for its liberation by Joan of Arc from the English in 1429. The other important town is Bourges, which is situated in the south between the wine villages of Reuilly, Quincy, and Menetou-Salon, and was once the capital of the Duchy of Berry.

THE REGION'S SAUVIGNON BLANC WINES

The Sauvignon Blanc is to the Central Vineyards what Muscadet is to the Pays Nantais. It produces the classic wine of the district, which, like Muscadet, also happens to be both white and dry. But two dry white wines could not be more different in style and taste. In the best Muscadet *sur lie* there should be a yeasty fullness, which can sometimes be misread as the Chardonnay character of a modest Mâcon. In Central Vineyard Sauvignons, however, whether they come from Sancerre or Pouilly – or even from one of the lesser-known, but certainly not lesser-quality, villages around Bourges – the aroma is so striking it sometimes startles. The rasping dryness of the wine's flavour catches the breath and can come from only one grape variety.

CHÂTEAU DU NOZET, POUILLY-SUR-LOIRE
This 19th-century château at Pouilly-sur-Loire is the home of Patrick de Ladoucette, the baron of Pouilly.

A BURGUNDIAN INFLUENCE

Historically, this district was part of the Duchy of Burgundy, which explains the presence of Pinot Noir vines. After the scourge of phylloxera, the area under vine shrank. That brought back into production was mostly replanted with Sauvignon Blanc, which began to dominate the vineyards, although isolated spots of Pinot Noir were maintained. Some of the wines these produce today can be good, although they are extremely delicate in style; and however fine the quality, they are but a shadow of great Burgundian Pinot.

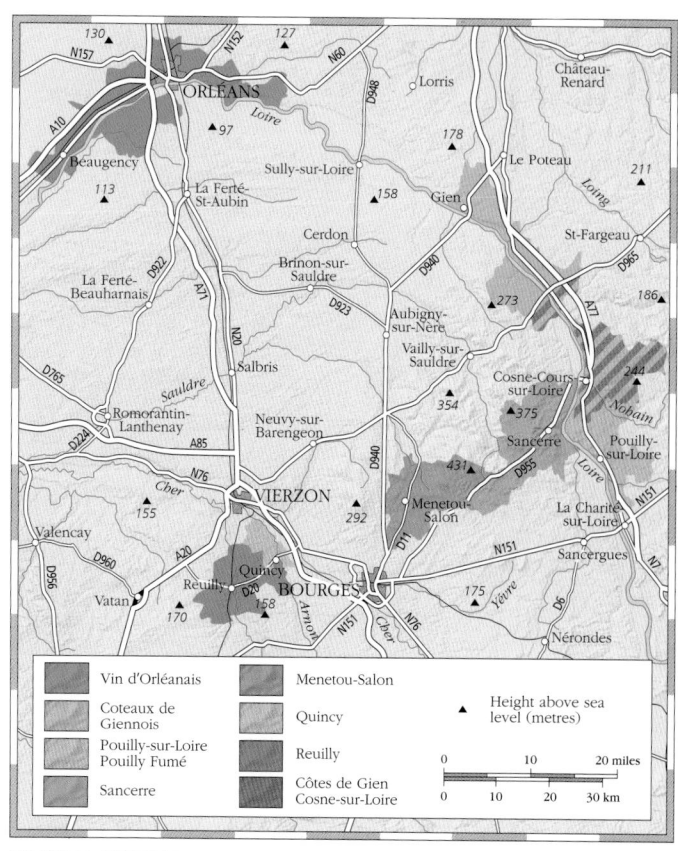
CENTRAL VINEYARDS, *see also p246*
The most easterly of the Loire's vineyards, and the most central of France, the Central Vineyards are famous for wines made from the Sauvignon Blanc grape.

FACTORS AFFECTING TASTE AND QUALITY

LOCATION
The most easterly vineyards of the Loire are situated in the centre of France, chiefly in the *départements* of Cher, Nièvre, and Indre.

CLIMATE
More continental than areas closer to the sea. The summers are shorter and hotter, and the winters are longer and colder. Spring frosts and hail are particular hazards in Pouilly. Harvests are irregular.

ASPECT
Chalk hills in a quiet, green landscape. Vines occupy the best sites on hills and plateaux. At Sancerre they are planted on steep, sunny, sheltered slopes at an altitude of 200 metres (660 feet).

SOIL
The soils are dominated by clay or limestone, topped with gravel and flinty pebbles. When mixed with chalk-tufa, gravelly soils produce lighter, finer styles of Sauvignon wines; when combined with Kimmeridgian clay, the result is firmer and more strongly flavoured.

VITICULTURE AND VINIFICATION
Some of the vineyard slopes in Sancerre are very steep, so cultivation and picking are done by hand. Most properties are small and use the traditional wooden vats for fermentation, but some growers have stainless-steel tanks.

GRAPE VARIETIES
Primary varieties: Pinot Noir, Sauvignon Blanc
Secondary varieties: Cabernet Franc, Chasselas, Gamay, Pinot Blanc, Pinot Gris

THE APPELLATIONS OF
CENTRAL VINEYARDS

CÔTES DU GIEN COSNE-SUR-LOIRE AOC

Of the 16 communes that produce Coteaux du Giennois, only eight are entitled to add Cosne-sur-Loire to the appellation. It was promoted from VDQS to AOC in 1998.

RED Dry, bright ruby-coloured wines. Often full-tasting, but rarely with the body to match and sometimes quite tannic.

🍇 Gamay, Pinot Noir – since 1992, neither variety may exceed 80% of the total blend

🍷 1–2 years

WHITE These are dry, medium-bodied, curiously aromatic white wines that develop a full, toasty flavour with a little bottle age.

🍇 Sauvignon Blanc

🍷 1–2 years

ROSÉ Light-salmon-coloured wines, slightly fuller bodied than the Coteaux du Giennois made a little further to the north, but equally capable of the same citrous fragrance.

🍇 Gamay, Pinot Noir – since 1992, neither variety may exceed 80% of the total blend

🍷 1–4 years

✓ *Alain Paulat* ◉

COTEAUX DU GIENNOIS AOC

This appellation could boast nearly a thousand growers at the turn of the 20th century when it was 40 times its current size. Promoted from VDQS to AOC in 1998.

RED Dry, light-bodied red wines that often have less colour than many rosés.

🍇 Gamay, Pinot Noir – since 1992, neither variety may exceed 80% of the total blend

🍷 1–2 years

WHITE These very basic, dry, light-bodied wines lack interest. Chenin Blanc can no longer be used to make this wine.

🍇 Sauvignon Blanc

🍷 1–2 years

ROSÉ Light-salmon-coloured, light-bodied wines that can have a fragrant citrous character.

🍇 Gamay, Pinot Noir – since 1992, neither variety may exceed 80% of the total blend

🍷 1 year

✓ *Emile Balland* • *De Beaurois* • *De Villegeai*

MENETOU-SALON AOC

This underrated appellation covers Menetou-Salon and the nine surrounding villages.

RED These are dry, light-bodied, crisp, and fruity wines with fine varietal aroma. They are best drunk young, although some oak-matured examples can age well.

🍇 Pinot Noir

🍷 2–5 years

WHITE Bone-dry to dry wines. They are definitely Sauvignon in character, but the flavour can have an unexpected fragrance.

🍇 Sauvignon Blanc

🍷 1–2 years

ROSÉ Extremely good-quality, dry, light-bodied aromatic wines, full of straightforward fruit.

🍇 Pinot Noir

🍷 Within 1 year

✓ *Georges Chavet & Fils* • *De Loye* • *Henry Pellé*

POUILLY BLANC FUMÉ AOC

See Pouilly Fumé AOC

POUILLY FUMÉ AOC

This used to be the world's most elegant Sauvignon Blanc wine, but too many wines of ordinary and often quite dire quality have debased this once-great appellation. In Pouilly-sur-Loire and its six surrounding communes, only pure Sauvignon wines have the right to use "Fumé" in the appellation name, a term that evokes the grape's gunsmoke character.

WHITE Great Pouilly Fumé is rare but when found, its crisp, gooseberry flavour will retain its finesse and delicacy in even the hottest years.

🍇 Sauvignon Blanc

🍷 2–5 years

✓ *Bouchié-Chatellier* • *Jean-Claude Châtelain* • *Didier Dagueneau* • *André & Edmond Figeat* • *Michel Redde* • *Château Tracy*

POUILLY-SUR-LOIRE AOC

This wine comes from the same area as Pouilly Fumé, but it is made from the Chasselas grape, although Sauvignon Blanc is allowed for blending. Chasselas is a good dessert grape but makes very ordinary wine.

WHITE Dry, light-bodied wines. Most are neutral, tired, or downright poor.

🍇 Chasselas, Sauvignon Blanc

🍷 Upon purchase

✓ *Guy Saget*

QUINCY AOC

These vineyards, on the left bank of the Cher, are situated on a gravelly plateau. Although located between two areas producing red, white, and rosé wines, Quincy produces only white wine, from Sauvignon Blanc.

WHITE Bone-dry to dry, quite full-bodied wines in which the varietal character of the Sauvignon Blanc is evident. There is a purity that rounds out the flavour and seems to remove the rasping finish usually expected in this type of wine.

🍇 Sauvignon Blanc

🍷 1–2 years

✓ *Bailly* • *De Ballandors* • *Mardon* • *De Puy-Ferrand* • *Philippe Portier* • *Silice de Quincy*

REUILLY AOC

Due to the high lime content in the soil, Reuilly produces wines of higher acidity than those of neighbouring Quincy.

RED These are dry, medium-bodied wines. Some are surprisingly good, although often tasting more of strawberries or raspberries than the more characteristic redcurrant flavour associated with Pinot Noir.

🍇 Pinot Noir, Pinot Gris

🍷 2–5 years

WHITE These are bone-dry to dry, medium-bodied wines of good quality with more of a grassy than a gooseberry flavour, yet possessing a typically austere dry finish.

🍇 Sauvignon Blanc

🍷 1–2 years

ROSÉ This bone-dry to dry, light-bodied wine is a pure Pinot Gris wine, although it is simply labelled Pinot.

🍇 Pinot Gris

🍷 2–5 years

✓ *Aujard*[1] • *Pascal Desroches* (Clos des Varennes) • *Claude Lafond* • *Valéry Renaudat* • *De Seresnes*[1] • *Jean-Michel Sorbe*[1]

[1]Also particularly recommended for red or rosé

SANCERRE AOC

This appellation is famous for its white wines, but originally its reds were better known. Recently the reds and rosés have developed greater style.

RED These wines have been more variable in quality than the whites, but the consistency is improving rapidly. They are dry, light- to medium-bodied wines, with a pretty floral aroma and a delicate flavour.

🍇 Pinot Noir

🍷 2–3 years

WHITE Classic Sancerre should be bone dry, highly aromatic, and have an intense flavour, sometimes tasting of gooseberries or even peaches in a great year. However, too many growers overproduce, never get the correct ripeness, and make the most miserable wines.

🍇 Sauvignon Blanc

🍷 1–3 years

ROSÉ Attractive, dry, light-bodied rosés with strawberry and raspberry flavours.

🍇 Pinot Noir

🍷 Within 18 months

✓ *Henri Bourgeois* • *François Cotat* • *Pascal Cotat* • *Dominique Crochet*[1] • *Lucien Crochet*[1] • *Vignoble Dauny* ◉ • *André Dezat*[1] • *Fouassier* (Clos Paradis, Les Grands Groux) ◉ • *Fournier* (La Chaudouillonne Grande Cuvée) • *Gitton* • *Alphonse Mellot* ⓑ • *Henry Natter* • *Vincent Pinard* • *Claude Riffault* • *Christian Thirot* (Des Vieux Pruniers)

[1]Also particularly recommended for red or rosé

VINS DE L'ORLÉANAIS AOC

These wines have been made for centuries, but only one-third of the appellation is worked now.

RED Dry, medium-bodied, fresh, and fruity wines that are given a short maceration, producing a surprisingly soft texture. They are usually sold as pure varietal wines: the Pinot can be delicate; the Cabernet Franc is fuller.

🍇 Pinot Noir, Pinot Meunier, Cabernet Franc

🍷 1–2 years

WHITE Very small quantities of interesting wines are made from Chardonnay, known locally as Auvernat Blanc. Dry, medium-bodied, and surprisingly smooth and fruity.

🍇 Chardonnay (Auvernat Blanc), Pinot Gris (Auvernat Gris)

🍷 1–2 years

ROSÉ The local speciality is a dry, light- to medium-bodied rosé known as Meunier Gris – an aromatic *vin gris* with a crisp, dry finish.

🍇 Pinot Noir, Pinot Meunier, Cabernet Franc

🍷 Within 1 year

✓ *Clos St-Fiacre* • *Vignerons de la Grand'Maison*

THE RHÔNE VALLEY

Famous for its full, fiery, and spicy-rich red wines, the Rhône Valley also produces small quantities of rosé and white, and even some sparkling and fortified wines. Although essentially red-wine country, and great red-wine country at that, the Rhône has experienced a kind of revolution in white-wine production. There has been a growing number of exotic, world-class white wines in various appellations since the late 1980s, when just a few began to emerge in Châteauneuf-du-Pape.

STRETCHING FROM VIENNE TO AVIGNON, the Côtes-du-Rhône appellation occupies a 200-kilometre (125-mile) length of the Rhône River. Beyond this great region other Rhône wines exist, and some are not even French. The banks of this mighty European river are clad with vines all the way from the Valais vineyards of Visp in Switzerland, just 50 kilometres (30 miles) from the Rhône's glacial origins in the Alps, to the *vin de pays* vineyards of the Bouches-du-Rhône, set amid the Rhône delta just west of Marseille, where the river finally and sluggishly runs into the Mediterranean.

Only a tiny patch of vineyards in the very north of this region is, in fact, located within the Rhône *département* (which is a geographic misnomer, as it actually accounts for 70 per cent of Burgundy's output). Comparing the contrasting characters of

LA LANDONNE VINEYARD, CÔTE RÔTIE
Syrah grapes are harvested on the steep slopes of Guigal's top-performing La Landonne vineyard in the Côte Brune area of Côte Rôtie, above Ampuis.

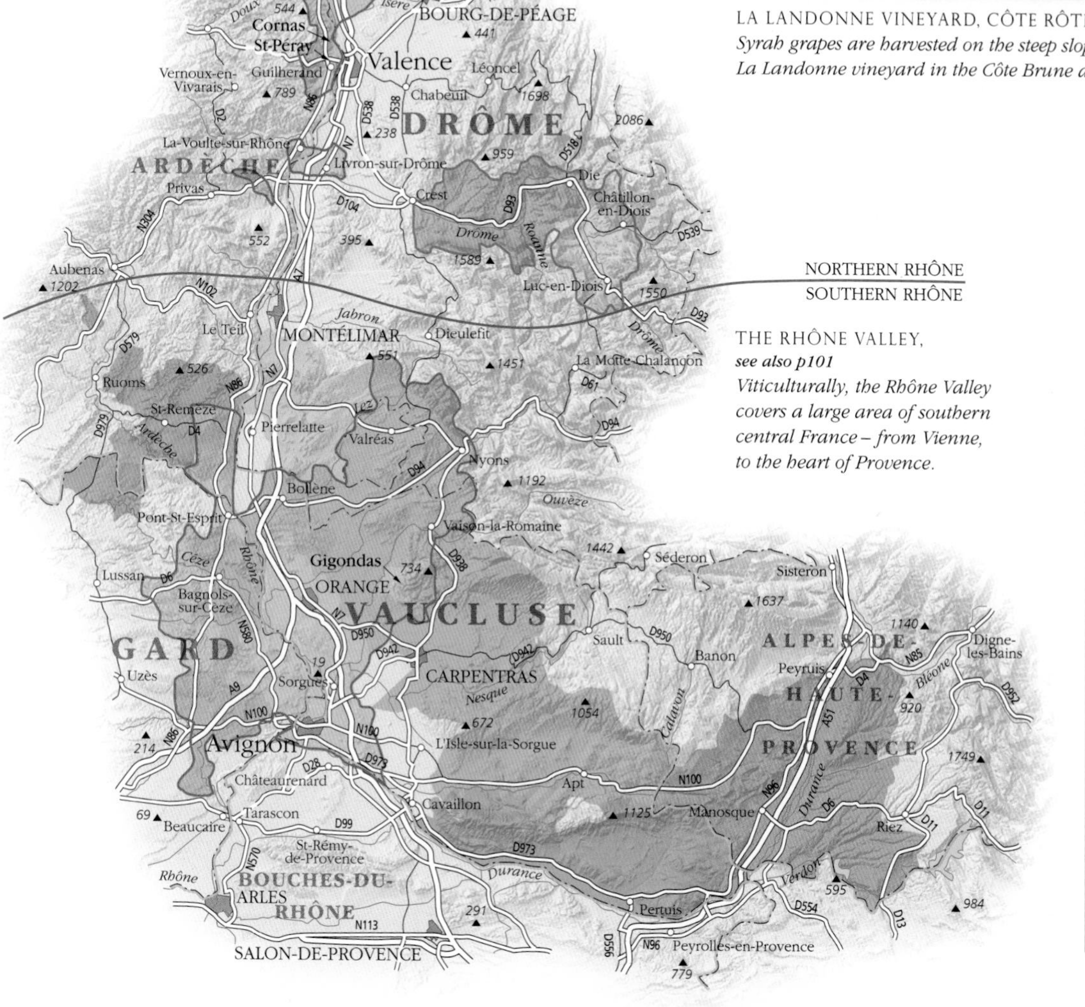

NORTHERN RHÔNE
SOUTHERN RHÔNE

THE RHÔNE VALLEY,
see also p101
Viticulturally, the Rhône Valley covers a large area of southern central France – from Vienne, to the heart of Provence.

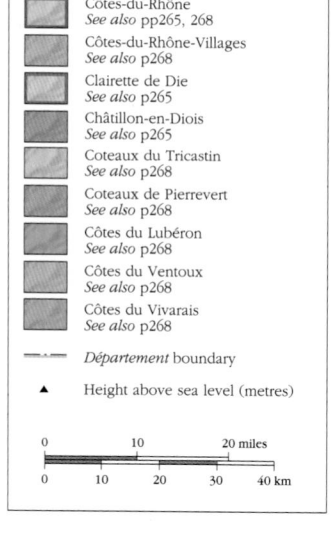

	Côtes-du-Rhône *See also pp265, 268*
	Côtes-du-Rhône-Villages *See also p268*
	Clairette de Die *See also p265*
	Châtillon-en-Diois *See also p265*
	Coteaux du Tricastin *See also p268*
	Coteaux de Pierrevert *See also p268*
	Côtes du Lubéron *See also p268*
	Côtes du Ventoux *See also p268*
	Côtes du Vivarais *See also p268*

- - - *Département* boundary

▲ Height above sea level (metres)

0   10   20 miles

0 10 20 30 40 km

RECENT RHÔNE VINTAGES

2010 Very low yields of great intensity, freshness, and elegance in both northern and southern Rhône, including the best Grenache in memory. Even more homogenous than 2009. Some outstanding white wines were also made.

2009 Fabulous northern Syrah; excellent reds in the south. Very good white wines, too.

2008 This was a very difficult year, but it was better in the southern Rhône than in the north.

2007 Fabulous southern Rhône reds, and although it was more difficult in the north, some excellent Hermitage and Crozes-Hermitage were produced.

2006 Hermitage and Côte Rôtie are the standouts, but this year is an excellent vintage for all styles in both northern and southern Rhône. The reds have a lace of fine acidity threading through all the wines.

CÔTE BRUNE ON THE CÔTE RÔTIE, NORTHERN RHÔNE
The Côte Brune is an area of the Côte Rôtie where the rust colour of the earth is visible evidence of iron-rich elements in its granitic sandy soil.

Rhône and Burgundy wines produced within the one *département* can have a humbling effect on all those who glibly talk about regional styles. For example, what could be further apart than a rich, classic Condrieu and a fresh, light Mâcon, or an intense, ink-black Côte Rôtie and a quaffing, cherry-coloured Beaujolais? Yet all of these wines are produced in the same *département* and could thus be described as coming from the same region.

BEAUMES-DE-VENISE, SOUTHERN RHÔNE
Home to one of the most elegant and consistent fortified Muscat wines in the world, Beaumes-de-Venise also produces a soft, peppery red wine under the Côtes-du-Rhône-Villages appellation.

A REGION DIVIDED

In terms of grape varieties, the Rhône divides neatly into two – the Syrah-dominated north and the Grenache-influenced south – although there are those who confuse the issue by separating the southernmost section of the northern district and calling it the Middle Rhône. The north and south differ not only in terrain and climate, but also contrast socially, culturally, and gastronomically.

THE NORTHERN RHÔNE

The Northern Rhône is dominated by the ink-black wines of Syrah, the Rhône's only truly classic black grape. A small amount of white wine is also produced and, in the south of the district, at St-Péray and Die, sparkling wines are made.

THE NORTHERN RHÔNE might be the gateway to the south, but it has more in common with its northern neighbour, Burgundy, than it does with the rest of the Rhône, even though its wines cannot be compared with those from any other area. Indeed, it would be perfectly valid to isolate the north as a totally separate region called the Rhône, which would, therefore, allow the Southern Rhône to be more accurately defined as a high-quality extension of the Midi.

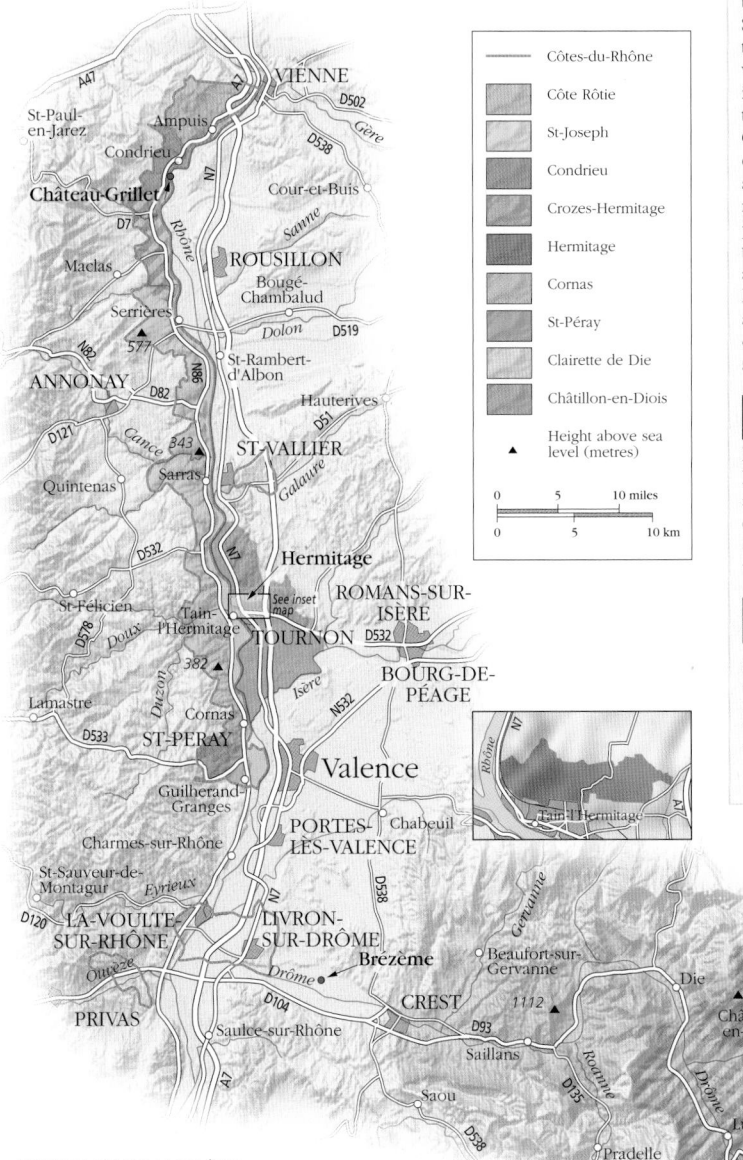

THE NORTHERN RHÔNE,
see also p263
At the heart of this region, the towns of Tain and Tournon face each other across the river.

FACTORS AFFECTING TASTE AND QUALITY

LOCATION
The narrow strip of vineyards that belong to the Northern Rhône commences at Vienne, just south of Lyon, and extends southwards to Valence.

CLIMATE
The general effect of the Mediterranean is certainly felt in the Northern Rhône, but its climate has a distinctly continental influence. This results in the pattern of warmer summers and colder winters, which is closer to the climate of southern Burgundy, to the north, than to that of the Southern Rhône. The climatic factor that the area does have in common with the southern half of the Rhône is the mistral, a bitterly cold wind that can reach up to 145 kilometres (90 miles) per hour and is capable of denuding a vine of its leaves, shoots, and fruit. As a result, many mistral-prone vineyards are protected by poplar and cypress trees. The wind can, however, have a welcome drying effect in humid harvest conditions. The average summertime temperature is just one degree Celsius lower than in the south.

ASPECT
The countryside is generally less harsh than that of the southern Rhône, with cherry, peach, chestnut, and other deciduous trees in evidence. The valley vineyards are cut far more steeply into the hillsides than they are in areas further south.

SOIL
The Northern Rhône's soil is generally light and dry, granitic and schistous. More specifically, it is made up of: granitic-sandy soil on the Côte-Rôtie (calcareous-sandy on the Côte Blonde and ruddy, iron-rich sand on the Côte Brune); granitic-sandy soil at Hermitage and Condrieu with a fine overlay of decomposed flint, chalk, and mica, known locally as *arzelle*; heavier soil in Crozes-Hermitage with patches of clay; granitic sand with some clay between St-Joseph and St-Péray, getting stonier towards the southern end of the region, with occasional outcrops of limestone; and limestone and clay over a solid rock base in the area that surrounds Die.

VITICULTURE AND VINIFICATION
Unlike the Southern Rhône, most Northern Rhône wines are produced entirely or predominantly from a single grape variety, the Syrah, despite the long list of grapes that are occasionally used (*see* Secondary varieties, *below*). Viticultural operations are labour-intensive in the northern stretch of the district and, owing to the cost, the vineyards were once under the threat of total abandonment. Since that threat, we pay much more for Côte Rôtie, but at least it has remained available. Vinification techniques are very traditional and, when wines are aged in wood, there is less emphasis on new oak than is given in Bordeaux or Burgundy, although chestnut casks are sometimes used.

GRAPE VARIETIES
Primary varieties: Syrah, Viognier
Secondary varieties: Aligoté, Bourboulenc, Calitor, Camarèse (Brun Argenté), Carignan, Chardonnay, Cinsault, Clairette, Counoise, Gamay, Grenache, Marsanne, Mauzac, Mourvèdre, Muscardin, Muscat Blanc à Petits Grains, Pascal Blanc, Picardan, Picpoul , Pinot Blanc, Pinot Noir, Roussanne, Terret Noir, Ugni Blanc, Vaccarèse (Brun Argenté)

THE QUALITY OF THE NORTHERN RHÔNE
The ink-black classic wines of Hermitage and Côte Rôtie stand shoulder to shoulder with the *crus classés* of Bordeaux in terms of pure quality, and the greatest Hermitage and Côte Rôtie deserve the respect given to *premiers crus* such as Latour, Mouton, or Lafite. Cornas can be even bigger and blacker than Hermitage or Côte Rôtie, and the top growers can rival the best of wines from its better-known neighbours. While the fine, dry white wines of Condrieu and (potentially) Château Grillet are unique in character, the presence of such a style in this part of France is not as surprising as that of the sparkling white wines of St-Péray and Die, particularly the latter, which Francophiles would describe as a superior sort of Asti!

THE NORTHERN RHÔNE

BRÉZÈME CÔTES DU RHÔNE AOC

A regulatory curiosity, Brézème is not one of the 16 Côtes du Rhône Villages that may attach their name only to the end of that appellation but is an anomalous village that through a peculiarity in the AOC laws is allowed to put its name before the basic Côtes du Rhône appellation (although some prefer to place Brézème after, in much larger letters). The story dates back to the mid-1800s, when the wines from Brézème almost rivalled those of Hermitage, and sold for nearly as much. In 1943, when Brézème was first allowed to add its own name to the Côtes du Rhône AOC, the vineyards amounted to a mere 10 hectares (25 acres). Shortly afterwards, most of the vineyards were abandoned and the village was all but forgotten. By 1961 there was barely 1 hectare (2.47 acres) under cultivation, yet remarkably a few producers continued to make Brézème. According to Eric Texier, one of the most respected growers was a Monsieur Pouchoulin, who was known as the "Grandfather of Brézème". Texier, a former nuclear engineer, took over Pouchoulin's vines, which are all Syrah and range from 60 to 100 years old. Thanks to Pouchoulin and others like him, the Brézème AOC was extended to include 84 hectares (208 acres) and, with renewed interest in the wine, plantings have increased by a further 22 hectares (55 acres), with more vines going in each year.

RED This pure Syrah wine has been likened to a Crozes-Hermitage, but some *cuvées* (Lombard's Grand Chêne and Eugène, for example) are aged in a percentage of new oak and are not at all like a Northern Rhône wine.

🍇 The full spectrum of Côtes du Rhône grapes is allowed, but Syrah is the only red wine grape grown

⌜∼ 3–10 years

WHITE Texier produces a pure Viognier and a pure Roussanne.

🍇 The full spectrum of Côtes du Rhône grapes is allowed, but only Marsanne, Roussanne, and Viognier are grown

⌜∼ 3–10 years

✓ *Jean-Marie Lombard* • *Eric Texier* (Syrah, Viognier)

CHÂTEAU GRILLET AOC

Château Grillet has remained under the same family ownership (Neyret-Gachet) since 1830, and is one of only two single-estate appellations in France, the other being Romanée-Conti. Although it is often described as one of the world's great white wines, this is a legacy from more than a century ago. Château Grillet has not achieved anything like its full potential for at least the last few decades. There is no doubt that its sun-blessed terraces could produce Viognier of a singularly outstanding quality, but there is no inkling the proprietors can be bothered to pursue such a course. Who could blame them when Château Grillet could charge two or three times the price of Condrieu? But the price of some of the best Condrieu are now snapping at its heels, and unless there is a dramatic increase in quality, Château Grillet will drop in price. In today's more transparent market, fine wine consumers are no longer willing to drink labels.

WHITE This is, potentially, a wine of great finesse and complex character, but regularly fails to achieve its potential. Recent vintages have been fresher,

with better acidity, but lack the varietal intensity of the best Condrieu and are sometimes spoilt by VA-lift on the finish.

🍇 Viognier

⌜∼ 3–7 years

CHÂTILLON-EN-DIOIS AOC

This wine was raised to full AOC status in 1974, although it is hard to comprehend what merited such an elevation then or now.

RED Light in colour and body, thin in fruit, with little discernible character.

🍇 Gamay, plus up to 25% Syrah and Pinot Noir

WHITE Sold as pure varietal wines, the light and fresh, gently aromatic Aligoté is as good as the richer, fuller, and rather angular Chardonnay.

🍇 Aligoté, Chardonnay

ROSÉ I have not encountered any.

🍇 Gamay, plus up to 25% Syrah and Pinot Noir

✓ *Didier Cornillon* (Clos de Beylière)

CLAIRETTE DE DIE AOC

This dry sparkling wine is being phased out in favour of Crémant de Die from 1999 in what must be a classic example of Gallic logic – removing the name Clairette from an appellation of a wine that must be made from 100 per cent Clairette grapes, yet retaining it for one (*see below*) that does not have to contain any! *See also* Crémant de Die AOC.

CLAIRETTE DE DIE MÉTHODE DIOISE ANCESTRALE AOC

Formerly sold as Clairette de Die Tradition, this wine may contain Clairette, but it is not the primary grape. What makes it so different, however, is that it is produced from one fermentation only, as opposed to the two required by Crémant de Die, the old Clairette de Die Mousseux, and most other sparkling wines.

In the *méthode dioise ancestrale*, the wine first undergoes a long, cold part-fermentation in bulk and when bottled must contain a minimum of 55 grams of residual sugar per litre and no *liqueur de tirage*. Fermentation continues inside the bottle, but when disgorged the wine must still retain at least 35 grams of residual sugar per litre. The wine undergoes *transvasage* (meaning it is filtered into a fresh bottle) and is corked without any addition of a *liqueur d'expédition*.

SPARKLING WHITE A very fresh, deliciously fruity, gently sparkling wine of at least *demi-sec* sweetness, with a ripe, peachy flavour.

🍇 At least 75% Muscat à Petits Grains (this went up in 1993 from a minimum of 50%), plus Clairette

⌜∼ Upon purchase

✓ *Buffardel Frères* • *CV du Diois* (Clairdie, Clairdissime)

CONDRIEU AOC

This is the greatest white-wine appellation in the entire Rhône Valley, with more up-and-coming young talent among its producers than anywhere else in the world. Initially the trend was to produce sweet and medium-sweet wines, but Condrieu has tended to be a distinctly dry wine for a couple of decades now. When the vintage permits, late-harvested sweeter wines are produced, and these styles are

very much part of Condrieu's recent revival as one of the undisputed great white wines of the world.

WHITE These pale-gold-coloured wines were once essentially dry, but had such an exotic perfume that you thought they were sweet when you first breathed in their heavenly aroma, but now so many of them have a real touch of sweetness. A great Condrieu has a beguiling balance of fatness, freshness, and finesse that produces an elegant, peachy-apricoty coolness of fruit on the finish. Do not be fooled into cellaring these wines – the dry ones in any case – as their greatest asset is the freshness and purity of fruit, which can only be lost over the years. Most of the top Condrieu are spoilt by too much new oak. Even those recommended below are too oaky from a classic point of view.

🍇 Viognier

⌜∼ 4–8 years

✓ *Cuilleron* (Les Ayguets, Les Chaillets, Vertige) • *Delas* (Clos Boucher) • *Stéphane Montez* (Les Grandes Chaillées, Domaine du Monteillet) • *Alain Paret* (Lys de Volan) • *Georges Vernay* • *François Villard* (Le Grand Vallon)

CORNAS AOC

The sun-trap vineyards of Cornas produce the best value of all the Rhône's quality red wines, but you have to buy it as soon as it is released as it is always sold far too young, so there is none left when it starts to show its true potential.

RED Ink-black, full-bodied, strong-flavoured, pure Syrah wines with lots of blackcurrant and blackberry fruit, lacking only a little finesse if compared to a great Hermitage or Côte Rôtie.

🍇 Syrah

⌜∼ 7–20 years

✓ *Thierry Allemand* • *Auguste Clape* • *Jean-Luc Colombo* • *Du Coulet* ❽ • *Courbis* (Les Eygats) • *Yves Cuilleron* • *Eric & Joël Durand* • *Paul Jaboulet Aîné* • *Patrick Lesec* • *Johann Michel* • *Vincent Paris* • *Tardieu-Laurent* (Vieilles Vignes) • *Du Tunnel*

CÔTE RÔTIE AOC

The terraces and low walls of the "burnt" or "roasted" slopes of Côte Rôtie must be tended by hand, but the reward is a wine of great class that vies with Hermitage as the world's finest example of Syrah.

RED A garnet-coloured wine of full body, fire, and power, made fragrant by the addition of Viognier grapes. The result is a long-living and complex wine with nuances of violets and spices, and great finesse.

🍇 Syrah, plus up to 20% Viognier

⌜∼ 10–25 years

✓ *Patrick & Christophe Bonnefond* • *Clusel-Roch* ◉ • *Yves Cuilleron* • *Delas* (Seigneur de Maugiron) • *Duclaux* • *Des Entrefeaux* • *Jean-Michel Gerin* (Champin le Seigneur) • *E Guigal* • *Paul Jaboulet Aîné* • *Joseph Jamet* • *Patrick Jasmin* • *Stéphane Montez* • *Michel Ogier* • *Stéphane Pichat* • *René Rostaing* • *Jean-Michel Stéphan* • *Vidal-Fleury* (La Chatilonne) • *François Villard* (La Brocarde)

COTEAUX DE DIE AOC

This new appellation was created in 1993 to soak up wines from excess Clairette grape production that were formerly sold under previous sparkling-wine appellations.

WHITE Perhaps it is unfair to prejudge a wine that has had so little time to establish itself, but it is hard to imagine a quality wine made from this grape. In effect, Coteaux de Die is the still-wine version of Crémant de Die. It is easy to see why such a bland dry wine needs bubbles to lift it, yet so few make the transition successfully.

🜲 Clairette

🍷 Upon purchase

✓ *Jean-Claude Raspail*

CÔTES DU RHÔNE AOC

Although generic to the entire region, relatively little Côtes du Rhône (CDR) is made in this district, where the only difference in technical criteria is that Syrah may replace Grenache as the principal red wine variety.

CRÉMANT DE DIE AOC

This dry sparkling wine was introduced in 1993 to replace Clairette de Die Mousseux, which was phased out by January 1999. Like the old Clairette de Die Mousseux appellation, Crémant de Die must be made by the traditional method, but whereas the former could include up to 25 per cent Muscat à Petit Grains, the latter must be made entirely from Clairette.

SPARKLING WHITE It is too early to make a definitive pronouncement, but it looks as if Crémant de Die will be every bit as neutral and lacklustre as Clairette de Die.

🜲 Clairette

🍷 1–3 years

✓ *Carod*

CROZES-ERMITAGE AOC
See Crozes-Hermitage AOC

CROZES-HERMITAGE AOC

Crozes-Hermitage is made from a relatively large area surrounding Tain, so the quality is very variable. But good Crozes-Hermitage will always be a great bargain.

RED These well-coloured, full-bodied wines are similar to Hermitage, but they are generally less intense and have a certain smoky-rustic-raspberry flavour that only deepens into blackcurrant in the hottest years. The finest wines do, however, have surprising finesse, and make fabulous bargains.

🜲 Syrah, plus up to 15% Roussanne and Marsanne

🍷 6–12 years
  8–20 years for top wines and great years

WHITE These dry white wines are improving and gradually acquiring more freshness, fruit, and acidity.

🜲 Roussanne, Marsanne

🍷 1–3 years

✓ *Aléofane* • *Chapoutier* ❽ (Les Varonnières) • *Yann Cha*ve (Tête de Cuvée) ◉ • *Les Chenets* • *CV des Clairmonts* (Pionniers) • *du Colombier* (Gaby) • *Combier* ◉ (Clos des Grives) • *Emmanuel Darnaud* • *Fayolle* • *Alain Graillot* • *Hauts-Chassis* • *Paul Jaboulet Aîné* (Thalabert) • *des Remizières* (Emilie) • *David Reynaud* ◉

ERMITAGE AOC
See Hermitage AOC

HERMITAGE AOC

One of the great classic French red wines, produced entirely from Syrah grapes in virtually all cases, although a small amount of Marsanne and Roussanne may be added. The vines are grown on a magnificent south-facing slope overlooking Tain.

RED These wines have a deep and sustained colour, a very full body, and lovely, plummy, lip-smacking, spicy, silky, violety, blackcurrant fruit. A truly great Hermitage has boundless finesse, despite the weighty flavour.

🜲 Syrah, plus up to 15% Roussanne and Marsanne

🍷 12–30 years

WHITE These big, rich, dry white wines have a full, round, hazelnut and dried-apricot flavour. The wines have improved recently but are generally no more than curiosities.

🜲 Roussanne, Marsanne

🍷 6–12 years

✓ *M Chapoutier*[1] ❽ (Ermite, Méal, L'Orée, Pavillon) • *Jean-Louis Chave*[1] • *Yann Chave* ◉ • *Emmanuel Darnaud* • *Delas* (Les Bassards) • *Alain Graillot* • *E Guigal* (Ex Voto) • *Paul Jaboulet Aîné* (La Chapelle) • *des Remizières*[1] (Emilie) • *Marc Sorrel* (Gréal) • *Tardieu-Laurent* (Vieilles Vignes)

[1]Particularly recommended for white as well as red.

HERMITAGE
VIN DE PAILLE AOC

In 1974, Gérard Chave made a *vin de paille* for "amusement". Chapoutier has since made several vintages of Hermitage *vin de paille* on a commercial basis – or as near commercial as you can get with this style of wine – and other producers include Michel Ferraton, Jean-Louis Grippat, and Guigal. Even the local *coopérative* has churned some out. At one time all Hermitage *blanc* was, in effect, *vin de paille*, a style that dates back in this locality to at least 1760. (Marc Chapoutier apparently drank the last wine of that vintage in 1964 when it was 204 years old.) The traditional *vin de paille* method in Hermitage is not as intensive as the one revived relatively recently in Alsace, in which the grapes are dried out over straw beds until more than 90 per cent of the original juice has evaporated before they are pressed, as even Chave's legendary 1974 was made from grapes bearing as much as a third of their original juice, but some of the results have been equally stunning.

WHITE Some *vins de paille* are rich and raisiny, while others – the best – have a crisp, vivid freshness about them, with intense floral-citrous aromas and a huge, long, honeyed aftertaste. After his famed 1974 vintage, Chave made a 1986 and at least a couple more vintages since. His *vin de paille* is reputed to be the greatest, but is practically unobtainable. This wine is made in the most commercial quantity, yet this still amounts to hardly anything, since the wine is hard to find and very expensive. Jean-Louis Grippat made a *vin de paille* in 1985 and 1986, neither of which I have had the privilege to taste, but John Livingstone-Learmonth describes them as "not quite like late-harvest Gewurztraminer" in his seminal work *The Wines of the Rhône*.

🜲 Roussanne, Marsanne

🍷 Up to 30 years

✓ *Chapoutier* ❽

L'ERMITAGE AOC
See Hermitage AOC

L'HERMITAGE AOC
See Hermitage AOC

ST-JOSEPH AOC

At last, some truly exciting wines are being produced under this appellation. St-Joseph has now replaced Cornas as the bargain-seeker's treasure trove.

MORE GREEN
NORTHERN RHÔNE

In addition to the producers in this directory that are either biodynamic or organic, there are also the following. No negative inference of quality should be taken from the fact that they are not featured among the other producers. There are a number that have been recommended in other editions, and still make some fine wines, but have been culled out to make room for others.

Biodynamic
Ferme des Sept Lunes (Bogy)
Monier (St-Desirat)

Organic
Achard-Vincent (Sainte-Croix)
Barou (Charnas)
Bégot (Serves-sur-Rhône)
du Coulet (Cornas)
CV de Die Jaillance (Die)
Giniès (Piégon)
Lattard (Autichamp)
des Treilles (Montbrison-sur-Lez)

RED The best wines are dark, medium- to full-bodied, with intense blackberry and blackcurrant fruit aromas and plenty of soft fruit, whereas mediocre St-Joseph remains much lighter-bodied with a pepperiness more reminiscent of the Southern Rhône.

🜲 Syrah, plus up to 10% Marsanne and Roussanne

🍷 3–8 years

WHITE At their best, clean, rich, and citrous-resinous dry wines.

🜲 Marsanne, Roussanne

🍷 1–3 years

✓ *Aléofane* • *De Champal* • *Chapoutier* ❽ (Les Granits) • *Chave* • *Courbis*[1] (Les Roys) • *Pierre Coursodon* (Le Paradis Saint-Pierre) • *Yves Cuilleron* • *Pierre Finon* • *Pierre Gaillard* • *Gonan*[1] (Les Oliviers) • *E Guigal* (Vignes de la Hospices) • *Stéphane Montez* • *Vincent Paris* • *Tardieu-Laurent* (Vieilles Vignes) • *Du Tunnel* • *François Villard* (Reflet)

[1]Particularly recommended for white as well as red

ST-PÉRAY AOC

This white-wine-only village appellation is curiously out of step with the rest of the area.

WHITE Firm and fruity, with good acidity for a wine from the south of the region, but unfortunately it usually lacks charm. Even the best growers within this region, recommended below, struggle to produce anything of interest.

🜲 Marsanne, Roussanne

🍷 1–3 years

✓ *J-F Chaboud* • *Bernard Gripa* • *Jean Lionnet* • *Alain Voge*

ST-PÉRAY MOUSSEUX AOC

This traditional-method sparkler is made from the wrong grapes grown on the wrong soil. The growers would be advised to rip the whole lot up and replant with black grapes for a red Côtes du Rhône.

SPARKLING WHITE An overrated, dry sparkling wine with a coarse *mousse*.

🜲 Marsanne, Roussanne

✓ *Du Tunnel*

THE SOUTHERN RHÔNE

While the mellow warmth of the Grenache is found in most Southern Rhône wines, this region is in fact a blender's paradise, with a choice of up to 23 different grape varieties.

THE SOUTHERN RHÔNE is a district dominated by herbal scrubland, across which blows a sweet, spice-laden breeze. This is a far larger district than the slender northern *côtes*, and its production is, not unnaturally, much higher. Allowing the north a generous 10 per cent of the generic Côtes du Rhône appellation, the southern Rhône still accounts for a staggering 95 per cent of all the wines produced in the region.

WINES OF THE MIDI OR PROVENCE?

At least half of the Southern Rhône is in what was once called the Midi, an area generally conceded to cover the *départements* of the Aude, Hérault, and Gard. This is never mentioned by those intent on marketing the Rhône's image of quality, because the Midi was infamous for its huge production of *vin ordinaire*. The Rhône River marks the eastern border of the Midi and its most famous appellations are geographically part of Provence. But, viticulturally, these areas do not possess the quasi-Italian varieties that dominate the vineyards of Provence and may, therefore, be more rationally defined as a high-quality extension of the Midi.

THE SOUTHERN RHÔNE, *see also p263*
The wider southern part of the Rhône Valley area stretches its fingers down towards Provence and eastwards to the Alps.

FACTORS AFFECTING TASTE AND QUALITY

LOCATION
The Southern Rhône starts at Viviers, south of Valence, and runs south to Avignon.

CLIMATE
The Southern Rhône's climate is unmistakably Mediterranean and its vineyards are far more susceptible to sudden change and abrupt, violent storms than are those of the Northern Rhône.

ASPECT
The terrain in the south is noticeably Mediterranean, with olive groves, lavender fields, and herbal scrub amid rocky outcrops.

SOIL
The limestone outcrops that begin to appear in the south of the Northern Rhône become more prolific and are often peppered with clay deposits, while the topsoil is noticeably stonier. Châteauneuf-du-Pape is famous for its creamy-coloured drift boulders, which vary according to location. Stone-marl soils persist at Gigondas and weathered-grey sand in Lirac, Tavel, and Chusclan. The soils also incorporate limestone rubble, clay-sand, stone-clay, calcareous clay, and pebbles.

VITICULTURE AND VINIFICATION
The vines are traditionally planted at an angle leaning into the wind so the mistral may blow them upright when they mature. The south is a district where blends reign supreme, but pure varietals are gaining ground. Traditional vinification methods are used on some estates, but modern techniques are common.

GRAPE VARIETIES
Primary varieties: Carignan, Cinsault, Grenache, Mourvèdre, Muscat Blanc à Petits Grains, Muscat Rosé à Petits Grains
Secondary varieties: Aubun, Bourboulenc, Calitor, Camarèse (Brun Argenté), Clairette, Clairette Rosé, Counoise, Gamay, Grenache Blanc, Grenache Gris, Macabéo, Marsanne, Mauzac, Muscardin, Oeillade, Picpoul Blanche, Picpoul Noir, Pinot Blanc, Pinot Noir, Rolle (Vermentino), Roussanne, Syrah, Terret Noir, Ugni Blanc, Vaccarèse (Brun Argenté), Viognier

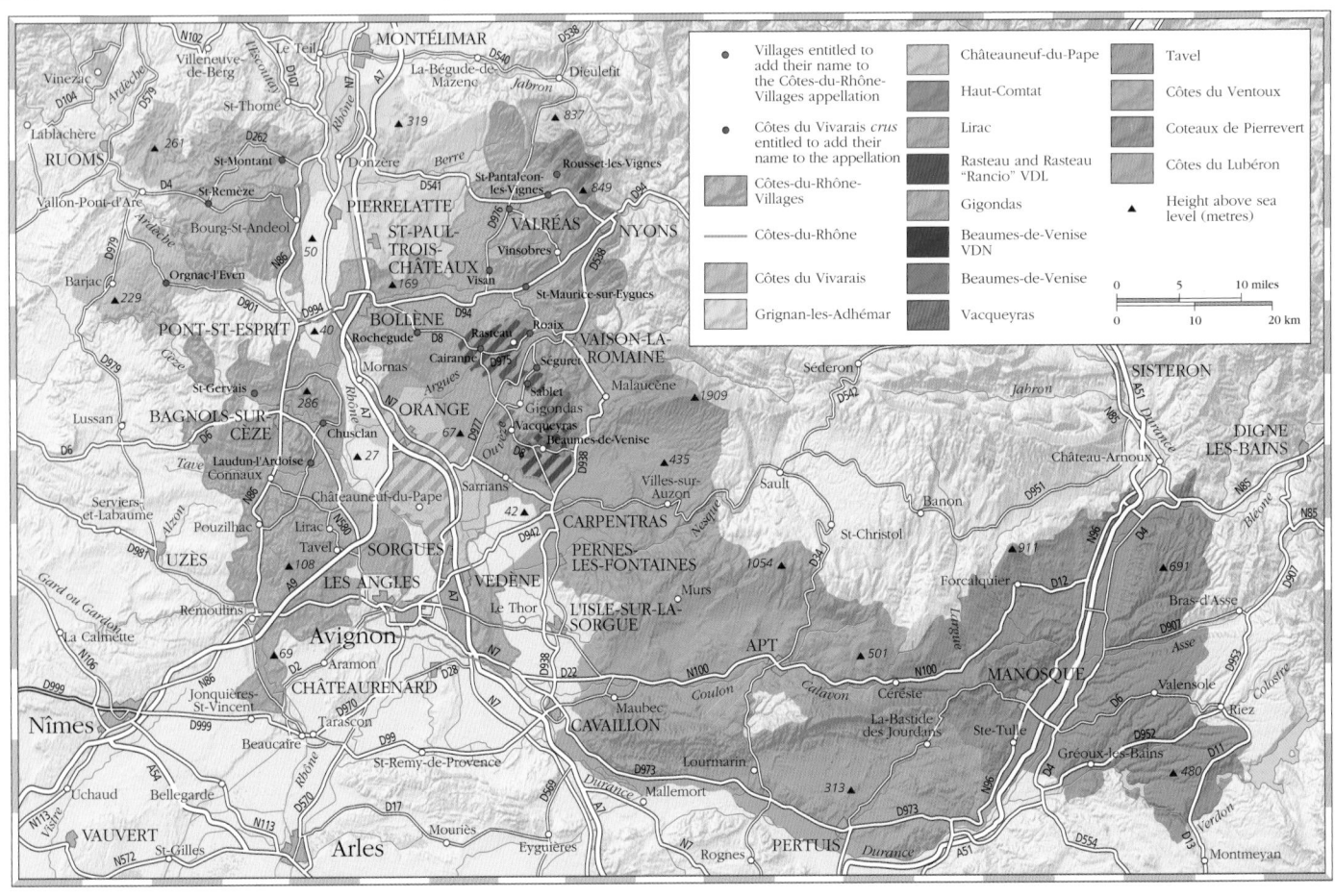

THE APPELLATIONS OF
THE SOUTHERN RHÔNE

BEAUMES-DE-VENISE AOC

Although primarily famous for its delectable, sweet Muscat wine, Beaumes-de-Venise also produces pleasant red wines, which were sold as Beaumes-de-Venise Côtes du Rhône until achieving single *cru* status in 2005. Dry white and rosé wines are produced under the generic AOC.

RED Good peppery-raspberry fruit flavour; the best have a certain plumpness and a touch of oak.

🍇 At least 50% Grenache, plus 25–50% Syrah, with an optional choice of any other CDR grape varieties (maximum of 10% white grapes)

🍷 2–7 years

✓ *Cassan • CV de Beaumes-de-Venise* (Chapelle Notre Dame d'Aubune, Les Garrigues d'Eric Beaumard) • *Durban*

CAIRANNE AOC

When Vacqueyras was promoted single *cru* status in 1990, Cairanne was clearly the top-performing village remaining in the Côtes du Rhône Villages appellation but had to wait almost 20 years and see another three villages receive individual recognition before being awarded its own appellation in 2009.

RED An excellent source of rich, warm, and spicy red wines that seem to integrate better with oak than other Côtes du Rhône.

🍇 At least 50% Grenache, plus 25–50% Syrah, with an optional choice of any other CDR grape varieties (maximum of 10% white grapes)

🍷 2–7 years.

✓ *d'Aeria • De l'Ameillaud • Daniel et Denis Alary • Brusset • Des Escaravailles • Les Grand Bois* (Mireille) • *Les Hautes Cances • de l'Oratoire St-Martin • Marcel Richaud* (L'Ebrescade)

CHÂTEAUNEUF-DU-PAPE AOC

The name Châteauneuf-du-Pape dates from the time of the dual papacy in the 14th century. The appellation is well known for its amazingly stony soil, which at night reflects the heat stored during the day, but the size, type, depth, and distribution of the stones varies enormously, as does the aspect of the vineyards. These variations, plus the innumerable permutations of the 13 grape varieties that may be used, account for the diversity of its styles. In the early 1980s, some growers began to question the hitherto accepted concepts of *encépagement* and vinification; winemaking in Châteauneuf-du-Pape is still in an evolutionary state. The steady decline of the traditionally dominant Grenache has speeded up as more growers are convinced of the worth of the Syrah and Mourvèdre. The Cinsault and Terret Noir are still well appreciated, and the Counoise is beginning to be appreciated for its useful combination of fruit

and firmness. The use of new oak is under experimentation and it already seems clear that it is better suited to white wine than red.

The regulations for this appellation have a unique safeguard designed to ensure that only fully ripe grapes in the healthiest condition are utilized: between 5 and 20 per cent of the grapes harvested within the maximum yield for this AOC are rejected and may be used to make only *vin de table*. This process of exclusion is known as *le rapé*.

RED Due to the variations of *terroir* and almost limitless permutations of *encépagement*, it is impossible to describe a typical Châteauneuf-du-Pape, but there are two categories – the traditional, full, dark, spicy, long-lived style and the modern, easy-drinking Châteauneuf-du-Pape, the best of which are unashamedly upfront and brimming with lip-smacking, juicy fruit. Both are warmer and spicier than the greatest wines of Hermitage and Côte Rôtie.

🍇 Grenache, Syrah, Mourvèdre, Picpoul, Terret Noir, Counoise, Muscardin, Vaccarèse, Picardan, Cinsault, Clairette, Roussanne, Bourboulenc

🍷 6–25 years

WHITE Early harvesting has reduced sugar levels and increased acidity, while modern vinification techniques have encouraged a drop in fermentation temperatures, so these wines are not as full as those produced previously. They can still be very rich, albeit in a more opulent, exotic fruit style, with a much fresher, crisper finish. The very best white Châteauneuf-du-Pape is generally agreed to be Château de Beaucastel Vieilles Vignes.

🍇 Grenache, Syrah, Mourvèdre, Picpoul, Terret Noir, Counoise, Muscardin, Vaccarèse, Picardan, Cinsault, Clairette, Roussanne, Bourboulenc

🍷 1–3 years (4–6 years in exceptional cases)

✓ *Paul Autard* (Côte Ronde) • *Barville • Château de Beaucastel*[1] ⑧ • *de Beaurenard* (Boisrenard) • *Benedetti*[1] • *Bois de Boursan* (Felix) • *Bousquet des Papes • La Boutinière • Clos du Caillou • Les Cailloux* (Centenaire) • *Réserve des Célestins • Chapoutier* ⑧ (Barbe Rac, Croix de Bois) • *de la Charbonnière • Gérard Charvin • de Cristia • Font de Michelle • Château de la Gardine • Grand Veneur • de la Janasse • Mark Kreydenweiss* ⑧ • *Lafond Roc-Epine • Patrick Lesec • de Marcoux* ⑧ • *Font de Michelle* (Etienne Gonet) • *Monpertuis* • *Château Mont-Redon • de la Mordorée* (Reine des Bois) • *de Nalys • Château la Nerthe*[1] ⑧ • *de Panisse • Clos des Papes • du Pegaü • Château Rayas*[1] • *Roger Sabon • Clos St-Jean • Clos St Michel* (Grand Clos) • *de la Solitude • Tardieu-Laurent* (Vieilles Vignes) • *Pierre Usseglio • de la Vieille Julienne • du Vieux Télégraphe • de Villeneuve* ⑧

[1]Particularly recommended for white as well as red

COTEAUX DE PIERREVERT AOC

This appellation consists of some 400 hectares (990 acres) and was upgraded from VDQS to full AOC status in 1998.

RED Dull, uninspiring wines with little original character to commend them.

🍇 Carignan, Cinsault, Grenache, Mourvèdre, Oeillade, Syrah, Terret Noir

🍷 2–5 years

WHITE Unspectacular, light, dry white wines with more body than fruit.

🍇 Clairette, Marsanne, Picpoul, Roussanne, Ugni Blanc

🍷 1–3 years

ROSÉ Well-made wines with a blue-pink colour and a crisp, light, fine flavour.

🍇 Carignan, Cinsault, Grenache, Mourvèdre, Oeillade, Syrah, Terret Noir

🍷 1–3 years

✓ *La Blaque* (Réserve) • *Vignobles de Régusse* (Bastide des Oliviers)

CÔTES DU LUBÉRON AOC

The wine of Côtes du Lubéron was promoted to full AOC status in February 1988. Much of the credit must go to Jean-Louis Chancel: his vineyards at Château Val-Joanis are still young, but the promise is such that this property has been described as the jewel in Lubéron's crown.

RED These are bright, well-coloured wines, with plenty of fruit and character, improving with every vintage. The Val-Joannis Syrah Reserve Les Griottes has the quality and density of a fine Hermitage. I'm not suggesting that it can be compared to the very best Hermitage, but it can stand shoulder to shoulder with many good Hermitage in elegant rather than weightier styles.

🍇 A blend of two or more varieties to include a minimum of 60% Grenache and Syrah (in total) – of which Syrah must represent at least 10%; a maximum of 40% Mourvèdre; 20% (each) of Cinsault and Carignan; and 10% (either singly or in total) of Counoise, Pinot Noir, Gamay, and Picpoul

🍷 3–7 years

WHITE As white Lubéron has no established style or reputation, it seems bureaucratic nonsense to be so precise about the percentage of each grape variety that may or may not be included in its production. There was a feeling that some sort of quality and style was about to emerge in these wines in the late 1980s when Lubéron was merely a VDQS. Even then the regulation concerning grape varieties was unnecessarily complicated. Since its upgrade to full AOC status, the regulations have become even more confusing, and I doubt if it is a coincidence that Lubéron *blanc* has completely lost its way over the same period.

🍇 A blend of two or more varieties, which can include Grenache Blanc, Clairette, Bourboulenc, Vermentino, a maximum of 50% Ugni Blanc, and up to 20% (of the blend) of Roussanne and/or Marsanne

🍷— 1–3 years

ROSÉ These attractively coloured, fresh, fruity wines are much better quality than most Provence rosé.

🍇 A blend of two or more varieties to include a minimum of 60% Grenache and Syrah (in total) – of which Syrah must represent at least 10%); a maximum of 40% Mourvèdre; 20% (each) of Cinsault and Carignan; 20% (in total) of Grenache Blanc, Clairette, Bourboulenc, Vermentino, Ugni Blanc, Roussanne, and Marsanne; plus 10% (either singly or in total) of Counoise, Pinot Noir, Gamay, and Picpoul

🍷— Upon purchase

✓ *de la Bastide de Rhodarès • Château la Canorgue • de la Citadelle • Château Constantin-Chevalier* (Fondateurs) • *de Fontenille* (Prestige) • *Cellier de Marrenon* (Grand Lubéron) • *de Mayol • de la Royere • Château Thouramme* ◉ • *Château Val Joanis*

CÔTES DU RHÔNE AOC

A generic appellation that covers the entire Rhône region, although the vast majority of wines are actually produced in the Southern Rhône. There are some superb Côtes du Rhônes, but there are also some disgusting wines. The quality and character varies to such an extent that it would be unrealistic to attempt any generalized description. The red and rosé may be sold as *primeur* or *nouveau* from the third Thursday of November following the harvest, although the reds can be sold only unbottled as *vin de café*. Red, white, and rosé wines can go on sale from 1 December without mention of *primeur* or *nouveau*.

RED The red wines are the most successful of this basic appellation, and often represent the best choice when dining in a modest French restaurant with a restricted wine list. Top *négociants* like Guigal consistently produce great-value Côtes du Rhône, but those below are all capable of very special quality.

🍇 A minimum of 40% Grenache (except in the Northern Rhône, where Syrah may be considered the principal variety), plus Syrah

and/or Mourvèdre, with up to 30% in total of any of the following: Camarèse, Carignan, Cinsault, Clairette Rosé, Counoise, Grenache Gris, Muscardin, Vaccarèse, Picpoul Noir, Terret Noir, and no more than 5% in total of any of the following white varieties: Clairette, Grenache Blanc, Marsanne, Picpoul, Roussanne, Bourboulenc, Ugni Blanc, Viognier

🍷— 3–10 years

WHITE These wines have improved tremendously in the past 5–10 years and continue to do so in encouraging fashion.

🍇 Bourboulenc, Clairette, Grenache Blanc, Marsanne, Roussanne, Viognier and up to 20% Ugni Blanc and/or Picpoul

🍷— 1–3 years

ROSÉ Many of the best rosés are superior in quality to those from more expensive Rhône appellations.

🍇 A minimum of 40% Grenache (except in the Northern Rhône, where Syrah may be considered the principal variety), plus Syrah and/or Mourvèdre, with up to 30% in total of any of the following: Camarèse, Carignan, Cinsault, Clairette Rosé, Counoise, Grenache Gris, Muscardin, Vaccarèse, Picpoul Noir, Terret Noir, and no more than 5% in total of any of the following white varieties: Clairette, Grenache Blanc, Marsanne, Picpoul, Roussanne, Bourboulenc, Ugni Blanc, Viognier

🍷— 1–3 years

✓ *Max Aubert* (de la Présidente) • *Castan • Coudoulet de Beaucastel • Cuilleron-Gaillard-Villard • Fond Croze • Château de Fontsegune • Grand Veneur • Clos de l'Hermitage • Paul Jaboulet Aîné • Clos des Magnaneraie • Clos Martin • Château de Montfaucon • Château Mont-Redon • Rigot • des Roches Fortes* (Prestige) • *Xavier Vignon*

CÔTES DU RHÔNE VILLAGES AOC

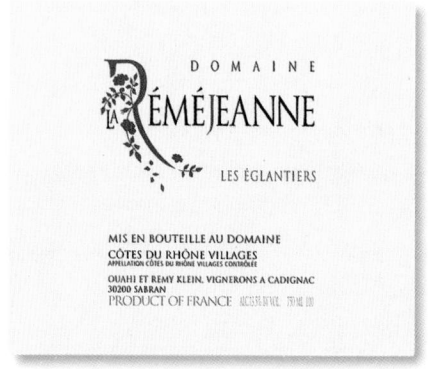

Compared with the generic Côtes du Rhône, these wines generally have greater depth, character, and quality. The area covered by the appellation is

entirely within the Southern Rhône. If the wine comes from one commune only, then it has the right to append that name to the appellation.

Gigondas, Cairanne, Chusclan, and Laudun were the original Côtes du Rhône Villages (CDRV), an appellation that has waxed and waned over the years as some villages attained their own AOCs (Gigondas in 1971, Vacqueyras in 1990, Beaumes-de-Venise and Vinsobres in 2005, and Cairanne in 2009) and others were added (the latest being Massif d'Uchaux, Plan de Dieu, Puymeras, and Sinargues in 2005).

The wines recommended below are for the Côtes du Rhône Villages appellation without any specified village, followed by separate entries for each of the 16 villages that are currently allowed to add their name to this AOC.

RED These wines are mostly excellent.

🍇 A minimum of 50% Grenache, plus a minimum of 20% Syrah and/or Mourvèdre, with up to 20% in total of Camarèse, Carignan, Cinsault, Clairette Rosé, Counoise, Grenache Gris, Muscardin, Vaccarèse, Picpoul Noir, Terret Noir

🍷— 3–10 years

WHITE These wines are improving – Vieux Manoir du Frigoulas is the best.

🍇 Bourboulenc, Clairette, Grenache Blanc, Marsanne, Picpoul, Roussanne, Viognier

🍷— 1–3 years

ROSÉ These wines can be very good.

🍇 A minimum of 50% Grenache, plus a minimum of 20% Syrah and/or Mourvèdre; up to 20% in total of Camarèse, Carignan, Cinsault, Clairette Rosé, Counoise, Grenache Gris, Muscardin, Vaccarèse, Picpoul Noir, Terret Noir; no more than 20% in total of any of the following white varieties: Bourboulenc, Clairette, Grenache Blanc, Marsanne, Picpoul, Roussanne, Viognier; and a maximum of 20% Ugni Blanc and/or Picpoul

🍷— 1–3 years

✓ *Les Aphillanthes* ◉ • *Bouche • Le Clos du Caillou • Château la Gardine • Château d'Hugues* (L'Orée des Collines) • *de la Janasse* (Terre Argile) • *Mas de Libian* ◉ • *du Petit-Barbras* (Le Chemin de Barbras Sélection) • *La Réméjeanne* (Eglantiers) • *Dominique Rocher* (Monsieur Paul) • *St-Anne • Saint Estève d'Uchaux* (Vieilles Vignes) • *CV de St-Hilaire d'Ozilhan* (Saveur du Temps) • *Viret* (Emergence)

THE 16 VILLAGES OF THE CÔTES DU RHÔNE VILLAGES

These single-villages versions of the above appellation wines can add their village name to the AOC Côtes du Rhône Villages.

CHUSCLAN CÔTES DU RHÔNE VILLAGES AOC
Red and rosé only

Chusclan may also be made from vines growing in Bagnols-sur-Cèze, Cadolet, Orsan, and St-Etienne-des-Sorts. These villages are situated just north of Lirac and Tavel, two famous rosé appellations, and make an excellent rosé. However, most of the wines are red, and produced in a good, quaffing style.

✓ *CV de Chusclan* (Esprit de Terroir) • *Château Signac*

LAUDUN CÔTES DU RHÔNE VILLAGES AOC

Red, white, and rosé

Laudun can be made from vines grown outside the village in St-Victor-Lacoste and Tresques. Excelling in fine, fresh, and spicy red wines, Laudun also makes the best white wines in the CDRV appellation, and a small amount of quite delightful rosé wines.

✓ *Château St-Maurice*

MASSIF D'UCHAUX CÔTES DU RHÔNE VILLAGES AOC

Red only

New CDRV-named village since 2005, for vines growing on sandstone hillsides at 100–280 metres (330–920 feet) at Massif d'Uchaux and five surrounding communes, including Mondragon, the first wines of which were recorded in 1290.

✓ *Château de Fonsalette • Château du Grand Moulas*

PLAN DE DIEU CÔTES DU RHÔNE VILLAGES AOC

Red only

New CDRV-named village since 2005, Plan de Dieu extends over four communes, where grapes grow on gravelly terraces under the shadow of Mont Ventoux, an area that was originally planted with vines by the Knights Templar.

✓ *Bernard Latour*

PUYMERAS CÔTES DU RHÔNE VILLAGES AOC

Red only

New CDRV-named village since 2005. The wines are made from grapes grown in Puymeras and four surrounding communes, including two in the neighbouring *département* of Drôme.

ROAIX CÔTES DU RHÔNE VILLAGES AOC

Red, white, and rosé

Neighbouring the vineyards of Séguret, Roaix produces a similar dark-coloured red wine that requires two or three years in bottle to mellow. A little rosé is also produced.

✓ *CV de Roaix-Séguret*

ROCHEGUDE CÔTES DU RHÔNE VILLAGES AOC

Red, white, and rosé

Only the red wine of Rochegude may claim the CDRV appellation. The local *coopérative* wine is good quality, well coloured, soft, and plummy. The white and rosé are sold as generic Côtes du Rhône.

✓ *CV de Rochegude*

ROUSSET-LES-VIGNES CÔTES DU RHÔNE VILLAGES AOC

Red, white, and rosé

The neighbouring villages of Rousset-les-Vignes and St-Pantaléon-les-Vignes possess the most northerly vineyards of this appellation, close to the verdant Alpine foothills. With the coolest climate of all the Côtes du Rhône villages, the wines are light, but soft and quaffable.

✓ *La Bouvade*

SABLET CÔTES DU RHÔNE VILLAGES AOC

Red, white, and rosé

This village's soft, fruity, and quick-maturing red and rosé wines are consistent in quality, and are always good value.

✓ *de Piaugier* (Montmartel)

ST-GERVAIS CÔTES DU RHÔNE VILLAGES AOC

Red, white, and rosé

The valley vineyards of St-Gervais are not those of the great river itself, but belong to the Cèze, one of its many tributaries. The red wines are deliciously deep and fruity, and the whites are fresh and aromatic with an excellent, crisp balance for wines from such a southerly location.

✓ *Clavel* (L'Étoile du Berger) • *CV de St-Gervais* (Prestige) • *Sainte-Anne*

ST-MAURICE CÔTES DU RHÔNE VILLAGES AOC OR ST-MAURICE-SUR-EYGUES CÔTES DU RHÔNE VILLAGES AOC

Red, white, and rosé

Light, easy-drinking red and rosé wines. Production is dominated by the local *coopérative*.

✓ *CV des Coteaux St-Maurice*

ST-PANTALÉON-LES-VIGNES CÔTES DU RHÔNE VILLAGES AOC

Red, white, and rosé

The neighbouring villages of St-Pantaléon-les-Vignes and Rousset-les-Vignes possess the most northerly vineyards of this appellation. With the coolest climate of all the CDRV, the wines are light, but soft and quaffable. Production is monopolized by the local *coopérative*, which has yet to make anything special.

SÉGURET CÔTES DU RHÔNE VILLAGES AOC

Red, white, and rosé

Séguret produces red wine that is firm and fruity with a good, bright, deep colour. A little quantity of white and rosé is also made, but they seldom excel.

✓ *de l'Amauve • de Mourchon* (Grande Réserve) • *Eric Texier*

SINARGUES CÔTES DU RHÔNE VILLAGES AOC

Red only

New CDRV-named village since 2005, for the most southerly named village in this appellation, encompassing vines grown in Domazan, Estézargues, Rochefort du Gard, and Saze to the east of Avignon.

VALREAS CÔTES DU RHÔNE VILLAGES AOC

Red, white, and rosé

These are fine red wines with plenty of fruit flavour. A little rosé is also made.

✓ *Clos Petite Bellane • Comte Louis de Clermont-Tonnerre • des Grands Devers • Le Val des Rois*

VISAN CÔTES DU RHÔNE VILLAGES AOC

Red, white, and rosé

These red wines have good colour and true *vin de garde* character. Fresh, quaffing white wines are also made.

✓ *de la Coste Chaude • Olivier Cuilleras*

CÔTES DU VENTOUX AOC

The limestone subsoil of this AOC produces a relatively lighter wine.

RED These fresh and fruity, easy-to-drink reds are the best wines in this AOC. The wines may be sold as *primeur* or *nouveau* from the third Thursday of November following the harvest.

🍇 Grenache, Syrah, Cinsault, and Mourvèdre, plus up to 30% Carignan, and a maximum of 20% (in total) of Picpoul Noir, Counoise, Clairette, Bourboulenc, Grenache Blanc, Roussane, and – until the 2014 vintage – Ugni Blanc, Picpoul Blanc, and Pascal Blanc

🍷 2–5 years

WHITE A little white is produced, but it is seldom anything of interest. These wines may be sold as *primeur* or *nouveau* from the third Thursday of November following the harvest.

🍇 Clairette, Bourboulenc, plus up to 30% (in total) of Grenache Blanc, Roussanne, and – until the 2014 vintage – Ugni Blanc, Picpoul Blanc, and Pascal Blanc

ROSÉ Fresh character and deliciously delicate fruit. They may be sold as *primeur* or *nouveau* from the third Thursday of November following the harvest.

🍇 Same as red-wine grape varieties

🍷 Upon purchase

✓ *La Ferme Saint Pierre* (Roi Fainéant) • *Le Murmurium • Château Talaud • Les Terrasses d'Eole* (Lou Mistrau) • *Château Valcombe • Vindémio • de la Verrière • Xavier Vignon* (Xavier)

CÔTES DU VIVARAIS AOC

The *côtes* of Vivarais look across the Rhône River to the *coteaux* of Tricastin. Its best cru villages (Orgnac, St-Montant, and St-Remèze) may add their names to the Côtes du Vivarais. Promoted from VDQS to AOC in 1999.

RED These light, quaffing reds are by far the best wines in the district.

🍇 A minimum of 90% in total of Syrah (minimum 40%) and Grenache (minimum 30%), with Cinsault and Carignan optional

🍷 1–3 years

WHITE These wines were always rather dull and disappointing but have improved in recent years.

🐝 At least two varieties from Clairette, Grenache Blanc, and Marsanne, with no variety accounting for more than 75%

🍷 1–3 years

ROSÉ Pretty pink, dry wines that can have a ripe, fruity flavour.

🐝 At least two varieties from Syrah, Grenache, and Cinsault, with no variety accounting for more than 80%

🍷 1–3 years

✓ *Les Chais du Vivarais*

GIGONDAS AOC

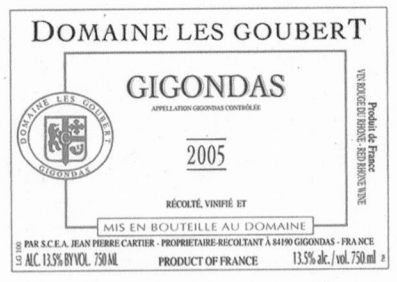

Gigondas produces some of the most underrated red wines in the Rhône Valley.

RED The best have an intense black-red colour with a full, plummy flavour.

🐝 A maximum of 80% Grenache, plus at least 15% Syrah and Mourvèdre, and a maximum of 10% (in total) of Clairette, Picpoul, Terret Noir, Picardan, Cinsault, Roussanne, Marsanne, Bourboulenc, Viognier, Counoise, Muscardin, Vaccarèse, Pinot Blanc, Mauzac, Pascal Blanc, Ugni Blanc, Calitor, Gamay, and Camarèse

🍷 7–20 years

ROSÉ Good-quality, dry rosé wines.

🐝 A maximum of 80% Grenache and a maximum of 25% (in total) of Clairette, Picpoul, Terret Noir, Picardan, Cinsault, Roussanne, Marsanne, Bourboulenc, Viognier, Counoise, Muscardin, Vaccarèse, Pinot Blanc, Mauzac, Pascal Blanc, Ugni Blanc, Calitor, Gamay, and Camarèse

🍷 2–5 years

✓ *Des Bosquets* • *La Bouissière* • *Brusset* (Le Grand Montmirail, Les Hauts des Montmirail) • *du Cayron* • *de la Gardette* • *Les Goubert* (Florence) • *Grapillon d'Or* (Elevé en Vieux Foudres) • *de Longue-Toque* • *Gabriel Meffre* (Château Raspail) • *De Montvac* • *Moulin de la Gardette* • *L'Oustau Fauquet* (Secret de la Barrique) • *Les Paillières* • *La Roubine* • *Saint Cosme* • *Saint-Damien* (Les Souteyrades) • *de St-Gayan* (Fontmaria) • *Sainte Anne* • *Santa Duc* • *La Tourade*

GRIGNAN-LES-ADHÉMAR AOC

This was Coteaux du Tricastin until 2010, when producers changed the name for fear of bad publicity following a uranium leak from the Tricastin nuclear facility. Most English-speaking consumers probably did not even know there was a nuclear facility at Tricastin. Well, now they do! And what a great new name! The Comte de Grignan might be a locally well-known 17th-century aristocrat, but Grignan-les-Adhémar hardly trips off the Anglo-Saxon tongue, does it? Furthermore, it means nothing on export markets until its previous identity is revealed, and that can only lead to questions about the name change – not a well

thought-out strategy. Hopefully, sales on the French market are healthy, because the producers of these wines are waving goodbye to more than 40 years of establishing the Coteaux du Tricastin name abroad.

RED Very good wines, especially the deeply coloured, peppery Syrah wines that are a delight after a few years in bottle. These wines may be sold as *primeur* or *nouveau* from the third Thursday of November following the harvest.

🐝 A maximum combined or individually of 80% Grenache and Syrah, plus Carignan, Cinsault, Marsanne, Marselan, Mourvèdre, Roussanne, or Viognier

🍷 2–7 years

WHITE Although I was unable to recommend Tricastin *blanc* in the first edition of this book (1988), the variety of grapes permitted has since been expanded to include Roussanne, Marsanne, and Viognier, which has enabled some producers to make richer, crisper, more interesting wines.

🐝 Grenache Blanc, Clairette, Bourboulenc, Marsanne, Roussanne, Viognier

ROSÉ A small production of fresh and fruity dry rosé that occasionally yields an outstandingly good wine. These wines may be sold as *primeur* or *nouveau* as from the third Thursday of November following the harvest.

🐝 A maximum combined or individually of 80% Grenache and Syrah, plus Carignan, Cinsault, Marsanne, Marselan, Mourvèdre, Roussanne, or Viognier

🍷 Upon purchase

✓ *Bour* • *des Estubiers* • *de Grangeneuve* • *de Montine* • *Saint-Luc*

LIRAC AOC

This appellation was once the preserve of rosé, but the production of red is now on the increase.

RED In really great years, the Syrah and Mourvèdre can dominate despite the quite small quantities used, which produces a more plummy wine with silky-spicy finesse.

🐝 A minimum of 40% Grenache and 25% (in total) of Syrah and Mourvèdre, plus up to 10% Carignan and no limit on the amount of Cinsault (although this used to be restricted to 20%, and I suspect this relaxation is due to a clerical error when the regulations were rewritten in 1992)

🍷 4–10 years

WHITE A fragrant, dry white wine, the best of which has improved since 1992, when Marsanne, Roussanne, and Viognier were permitted for use in this appellation. The cheapest wines have declined in quality because the amount of Clairette allowed has been doubled. Macabéo and Calitor are no longer permitted.

🐝 Up to 60% (each) of Bourboulenc, Clairette, and Grenache Blanc; plus up to 25% (each) of Ugni Blanc, Picpoul, Marsanne, Roussanne, and

Viognier (but these secondary varieties must not represent more than 30% of the blend in total)

🍷 1–3 years

ROSÉ Production is declining in favour of red wine, but these dry rosés can have a delightful summer-fruit flavour that is fresher than either Tavel or Provence.

🐝 A minimum of 40% Grenache and 25% (in total) of Syrah and Mourvèdre, plus up to 10% Carignan, no limit on the amount of Cinsault (but *see* red wine grapes, *above*), and up to 20% (in total) of Bourboulenc, Clairette, Grenache Blanc, Ugni Blanc, Picpoul, Marsanne, Roussanne, and Viognier

🍷 1–3 years

✓ *Château d'Aquéria* • *Lafond Roc-Epine* • *Maby* (La Fermade) • *de la Mordorée*

MUSCAT DE BEAUMES-DE-VENISE AOC

These wines from Muscat de Beaumes-de-Venise are the most elegant of the world's sweet fortified Muscat wines. Very little sweet Muscat was made before World War II. When the AOC was granted in 1945, the wine was classified as a *vin doux naturel*. The process by which this is made entails the addition of pure grape spirit, in an operation called *mutage*, after the must has achieved 5 per cent alcohol by natural fermentation. The final wine must contain at least 15 per cent alcohol, plus a minimum of 110 grams per litre of residual sugar. The Coopérative des Vins & Muscats, which was established in 1956, accounts for a formidable 90 per cent of the wine produced. It is often said that this wine is always non-vintage, but in fact 10 per cent is sold with a vintage on the label.

WHITE/ROSÉ The colour varies between the rare pale gold and the common light apricot-gold, with an aromatic bouquet more akin to the perfume of dried flowers than fruit. You should expect Muscat de Beaumes-de-Venise to have hardly any acidity, which surprisingly does not make it cloying, despite its intense sweetness, but does enable it to be one of the very few wines to partner ice cream successfully.

🐝 Muscat Blanc à Petits Grains, Muscat Rosé à Petits Grains

🍷 1–2 years

✓ *de Coyeux* • *de Durban* • *Paul Jaboulet Aîné* • *Gabriel Meffre* (Laurus) • *Pigeade* • *de St-Saveur* • *Vidal-Fleury*

RASTEAU AOC

This village is best known for its *vin doux natural*, particularly its *rancio* style (*see below*), yet it produces nearly four times as much natural, unfortified dry red (in particular), white, and rosé as it does Rasteau of CDRV-level quality. The primarily

Grenache-based *vin doux natural* appellation was created in the early 1930s and was promoted to full AOC status in 1944; as such, it was the first of the Rhône's two *vin doux naturel* appellations.

RED (NOT FORTIFIED) Deep-coloured, full, and rich, with a spicy warmth.

A minimum of 50% Grenache, plus a minimum of 20% Mourvèdre and Syrah, with an optional choice of any other CDR grape varieties (maximum of 5% white grapes)

2–10 years

√ *de Beaurenard* (Argiles Bleus) • *Bressy-Masson* • *Des Coteaux des Travers* (Cuvée Prestige) • *La Couránçonne* (Magnificat) • *des Escaravailles* (La Ponce) • *La Soumade* (Confiance) • *Tardieu-Laurent*

RED (FORTIFIED) Most are rich, sweet, coarse, grapey-flavoured concoctions with plenty of grip, a rather awkward spirity aroma, and a pithy, apricot-skin aftertaste. Some are not even that sweet. Domaine de Beaurenard is in a different league in terms of sweetness and quality, being smooth, rich, and truly sweet, but beautifully balanced and not in the slightest cloying, making it more like a vintage Port. The term *grenat* might be seen on some Rasteau Vin Doux Naturel, indicating a more reductive-style red that must not be bottled any later than 1 March of the second year, whereas *tuilé* (literally "tile-coloured") is an oxidative style that is orange-red in colour.

A minimum of 90% Grenache, plus up to 10% (in total) of any CDR-permitted grape varieties

1–5 years

√ *de Beaurenard*

WHITE/TAWNY/ROSÉ (FORTIFIED) This wine can be white, tawny, or rosé depending on the technique used and on the degree of ageing. It does not have the grip of the red, but has a mellower sweetness. Wines labelled *ambré* will be oxidative in style and tawny coloured.

A minimum of 90% Grenache Gris or Blanc, plus up to 10% (in total) of any CDR-permitted grape varieties

1–5 years

RANCIO (FORTIFIED) These fortified wines are similar to those above, except they must be stored in oak casks "according to local custom", which effectively means exposing the barrels to sunlight for a minimum of two years. This allows the wines to develop their distinctive *rancio* character.

A minimum of 90% Grenache (Noir, Gris, or Blanc), plus up to 10% (in total) of any CDR-permitted grape varieties

TAVEL AOC

Tavel is the most famous of all French dry rosé wines, but only the very best domaines live up to its reputation. In order to retain its

---

MORE GREEN SOUTHERN RHÔNE

In addition to the producers recommended in this directory that are either biodynamic or organic, there are also the following. No negative inference of quality should be taken from the fact that they are not featured among the other recommended producers. There are a number that have been recommended in other editions, and still make some fine wines, but have been culled out to make room for others.

Biodynamic
Pierre André (Courthézon), *Château de Bastet* (Sabran), *des Estubiers* (Les Granges Gontardes), *Grande Bellane* (Domaine de la Grande Bellane), *Gaïa* (Saint-Marcellin), *Patrick Pélisson* (Goult), *Eric Saurel* (Sarrians), *St Apollinaire* (Vaison-La-Romaine)

Organic
des Adrès (Villedieu), *Arbre aux Soleils* (Faucon), *des Auzières* (Roaix), *de Balazut* (St Paulet de Caisson), *des Carabiniers* (Roquemaure), *Catherine Le Goeuil* (Cairanne), *des Cèdres* (St Nazaire), *Le Clos de Caveau* (Vacqueyras), *Clos du Joncuas* (Gigondas), *des Coccinelles* (Domazan), *Château de la Croix* *des Pins* (Mazan), *Jean David* (Séguret), *Michel Delacroix* (Theziers), *Duseigneur* (St Laurent des Arbres), *de la Gautière* (La Penne-sur-Ouvèze), *Goisbault* (Saze), *Grange de Louiset* (Flassans), *Herbouze* (St Alexandre), *de la Jasse* (Violès), *de Lumian* (Valreas), *Monastère de Solan* (La Bastide d'Engras), *CV du Nyonsais* (Nyons), *de la Roche Buissière* (Faucon St Honorat) (Domazan), *St Pons* (Villars), *Terres de Solence* (Mazan), *CV des Vignerons de Vacqueyras* (Vacqueyras), *Val de Morcasse* (Montfrin), *Le Van* (Bedoin), *du Vieux Chêne* (Camaret-sur-Aigues), *La Vigneronne* (Vaison la Romaine)

---

characteristic freshness, Tavel's alcoholic level is restricted to a maximum of 13 per cent.

ROSÉ Some properties still cling to the old-style vinification methods and, frankly, this means the wines are too old before they are sold. The top domaines in the appellation make clean-cut wines with freshly scented aromas and fine fruit flavours, which are invariably good food wines.

Grenache, Cinsault, Clairette, Clairette Rosé, Picpoul, Calitor, Bourboulenc, Mourvèdre, and Syrah (none of which may account for more than 60% of the blend), plus a maximum of 10% Carignan

1–3 years

√ *Château d'Aquéria* • *Mireille Petit-Roudil* • *de la Mireille Petit-Roudil* (Dame Rousse)

VACQUEYRAS AOC

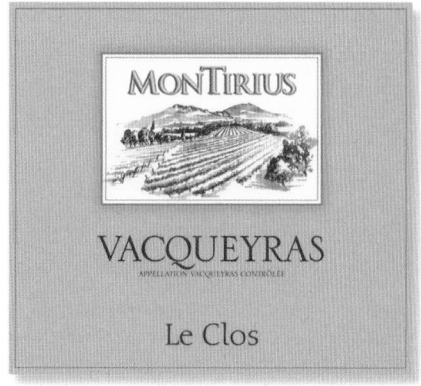

Formerly one of the single-village wines under the AOC Côtes du Rhône-Villages, Vacqueyras was elevated to full AOC status in 1990, without any mention of Côtes du Rhône or Côtes du Rhône-Villages, and is now theoretically on a par with Gigondas. The vines are spread over two communes, Vacqueyras and Sarrians, growing in the foothills of the Dentelles de Montmirail.

RED The best are dark, rich, and robust, with a warm, black-pepper spiciness.

At least 50% Grenache, plus up to 20% in total of Syrah and/or Mourvèdre, plus no more than 10% in total of any of the following: Camarèse, Carignan, Cinsault, Clairette Rosé, Counoise, Grenache Gris, Muscardin, Vaccarèse, Picpoul Noir, Terret Noir

4–12 years

WHITE This is the least successful style of the appellation; most tend to be either flabby or so dominated by modern, cool vinification methods that they are simply fresh and could come from anywhere.

Grenache Blanc, Clairette, and Bourboulenc, plus up to 50% in total of Marsanne, Roussanne, and Viognier

2–3 years

ROSÉ Can be lovely, fresh, and fruity.

At least 60% of Grenache, plus a minimum of Mourvèdre and/or Cinsault, with an optional maximum 10% of any of the following: Camarèse, Carignan, Cinsault, Clairette Rosé, Counoise, Grenache Gris, Muscardin, Vaccarèse, Picpoul Noir, Terret Noir

2–3 years

√ *des Amouriers* • *de la Brunely* (Elevé en Fût de Chêne) • *de la Charbonnière* • *La Fourmone* • *Les Grands Cypres* • *de la Monardière* (Vieilles Vignes) • *De Montvac* • *Le Sang des Cailloux* (Lopy) • *Tardieu-Laurent* (Vieilles Vignes) • *Xavier Vignon* (Povidis)

VINSOBRES AOC

Formerly a Côtes du Rhône Villages, Vinsobres has been an appellation in its own right since 2005. The vineyards are primarily devoted to Grenache (72%) and Syrah (18%), although there are small amounts of Carignan, Cinsault, and Mourvèdre.

RED Deep ruby in colour, with full, rich, spicy fruit. The quality has improved over the past few years.

A minimum of 50% Grenache, plus a minimum of 20% Mourvèdre and Syrah, with an optional choice of any other CDR grape varieties (maximum of 5% white grapes)

3-10 years

√ *L'Ancienne École* • *Des Ausellons* • *du Coriançon* • *du Moulin* (Charles Joseph) • *Perrin*

THE JURA, BUGEY, AND SAVOIE

White wines dominate the production from these picturesque vineyards set amid the ski slopes of the French Alps. Sparkling wines are the speciality of Savoie, while Jura can boast the rare, sweet vins de paille *and the amazingly long-lived* vins jaunes.

THE JURA IS DOMINATED by the town of Arbois, a little alpine community reigned over by Henri Maire, which owns no fewer than 300 of the region's 1,900 hectares (740 of 4,700 acres). Henri Maire's famous sparkling "Vin Fou", or "Mad Wine", has no appellation and comes in various different *cuvées*, of which some are better than others, but many taste the same. Despite the light-hearted approach to its consumption, "Vin Fou" has performed one admirable function: it has introduced wine drinkers to the district of Jura and Savoie and its many better wines. This could not have been achieved by the *vins de paille* and *vins jaunes*, due to their scarcity and high price. The very sweet *vin de paille*, or "straw

wine", is so called because the grapes were traditionally dried on straw mats to concentrate the juice into a syrup. The *vin jaune*, or "yellow wine", derives its name from the colour that results from its deliberate oxidation under a yeast *flor* when matured in casks that are not topped up for six years. This region also produces a number of more ordinary wines, often pure varietals, that are seldom exciting. The Jura's other claim to fame is, of course, as the birthplace of Louis Pasteur (1822–1895), who for all intents and purposes invented oenology, having been requested by Napoléon III to investigate the changes already observed during the maturation of wine. Born in the Arbois, where a small museum dedicated to him exists today, Pasteur's discoveries included the vital role of yeast during fermentation – totally unsuspected in his day, but without the knowledge of which the branch of chemistry called oenology would not exist. His vineyard, just outside Arbois, is now owned by the firm of Henri Maire.

THE SAVAGNIN CONSPIRACY
The Savagnin grape is none other than the Traminer or, to be more precise, the non-spicy Traminer as found in Tramin, Italy, and Heiligenstein in Alsace, where it is sold as Klevener de Heiligenstein. At best it has very delicate aromatics, but more often than not it is quite bland. In the Jura, however, it has always had a

CHÂTEAU-CHALON VINEYARDS
This commune produces the most famous of all the vins jaunes from 100 per cent Savagnin. Best drunk very old, the wine takes its name from its deep honey-gold colour.

THE JURA, BUGEY, AND SAVOIE,
see also p101
This region lies parallel to Burgundy, between Beaune and the southern limits of the Beaujolais. There are two mountain ranges.

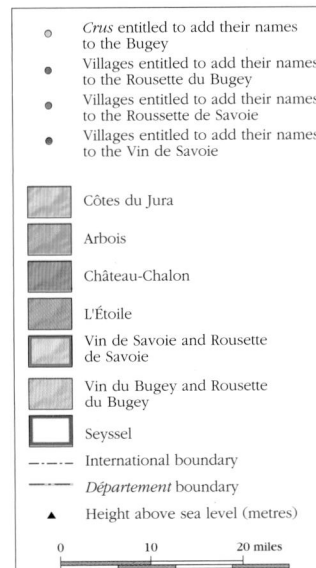

PARIS

○	*Crus* entitled to add their names to the Bugey
●	Villages entitled to add their names to the Rousette du Bugey
●	Villages entitled to add their names to the Roussette de Savoie
●	Villages entitled to add their names to the Vin de Savoie

	Côtes du Jura
	Arbois
	Château-Chalon
	L'Étoile
	Vin de Savoie and Roussette de Savoie
	Vin du Bugey and Roussette du Bugey
	Seyssel
–·–·–	International boundary
––––	*Département* boundary
▲	Height above sea level (metres)

0   10   20 miles
0   10   20   30   40 km

RECENT JURA, BUGEY, AND SAVOIE VINTAGES

2010 Another exceptional year, especially in Bugey. Reds excelled.

2009 An excellent vintage all round.

2008 This was an inconsistent year, particularly for red wines. Savoie whites fared best.

2007 Late-ripening varieties such as Chardonnay, Poulsard, Savagnin, and Trousseau fared best in the Jura, but only for those growers who were brave enough to pick late. Despite rampant mildew in the summer, this is an excellent vintage in the Savoie.

2006 Consumers will have to be very selective in this generally poor and extremely mixed vintage.

FACTORS AFFECTING TASTE AND QUALITY

LOCATION
Running down the mountainous eastern border of France, the Jura and Savoie are parallel to the Burgundy region.

CLIMATE
The climate is continental, with hot summers and cold winters. The close proximity of the Jura and the Savoie mountain ranges can provoke sudden changes, although these may sometimes be mitigated by the calming effect of lakes Geneva and Bourget.

ASPECT
The vineyards of the Jura are situated on the lower slopes of the Jura mountains. The vines grow at an altitude of 250 to 500 metres (820 to 1,640 feet). The Savoie vineyards lie lower than those of the Jura.

SOIL
The limestone of the Jura is generally mixed with clay over a subsoil of compacted marl. There are limestone and marl topsoils over a base of sandy and gravelly marls at Arbois and Château-Chalon and a limestone scree, calcareous sand, and clay-like sand with alluvial deposits at Bugey and Seyssel.

VITICULTURE AND VINIFICATION
The Jura is famous for two special techniques: the viticultural practice responsible for *vin de paille* and the vinification procedure required to make *vin jaune*. For *vin de paille*, wicker trays or wire mesh may be used, but in most cases bunches of grapes are hung from the rafters of heated huts, after which the shrivelled-up, highly concentrated, raisin-like grapes produce an amber-coloured sweet wine of great potential longevity. *Vin jaune* is produced entirely from the Savagnin grape, which, after a normal fermentation, is left to age in wooden barrels for six years with no topping up. A yeast *flor* develops similar to that generated during the production of *fino* Sherry and the results are not dissimilar. Light dry Jura white wines made from the traditional Savagnin grape used to be distinctly oxidized due to the common practice of blending in any *vin jaune* that failed to make the grade, but some producers have begun to make at least a few of these wines without any declassified *vin jaune*, thus in a totally fresh, non-oxidative style.

GRAPE VARIETIES
Aligoté, Altesse, Cabernet Franc, Cabernet Sauvignon, Chasselas, Chasselas Roux, Chasselas Vert, Etraire de la Dui, Gamay, Gringet, Gros Noiren (Pinot Noir), Jacquère, Joubertin, Malvoisie Rosé (Frühroter Veltliner), Marsanne, Melon d'Arbois (Chardonnay), Molette, Mondeuse, Mondeuse Blanche, Naturé (Savagnin), Persan, Pinot Blanc, Ploussard (Poulsard), Roussette, Roussette d'Ayze, Serène (Syrah), Trousseau, Verdesse

tendency to oxidize. Or so we were told. Every time I tasted a pure Savagnin produced in a light table wine style, it always had at least a niggling oxidative hint. And every time I asked the producer, whether in the Jura or at tastings in London, why this should be so in a grape variety that is not oxidative elsewhere, I was always told "*C'est le Savagnin, il est un vin typé*". And now I know that each time, every producer I spoke to lied. It is not the Savagnin. It is the *vin jaune* that fails to receive certification, or has been weeded out somewhere along its six year route to certification, and that they have disposed of by blending it into their dry white table wines.

While I fully support a certification process that prevents inferior wines from bearing the *vin jaune* designation, and I understand the dilemma of producers faced with stocks of yellow, oxidized wine they are unable to sell as *vin jaune*, the answer is not to spoil fresh, light table wines. The only rational solution is to create a *vin de pays* for the *vin jaune* style. Consumers will understand that the *vin de pays* version is not supposed to be of the same standard and, indeed, this would be reflected in the price. However, although cheaper than *vin jaune* proper, a *vin de pays* "*vin jaune*" would probably attract a premium over the price of the Jura's light table wines, and without the rejected *vin jaune*, the light table wines would be fresher, crisper, cleaner, and fruitier, the sales and price of which could only increase. Better profits for producers, and better wines for consumers. A result all round, I would have thought. And no need to tell lies.

DID YOU KNOW?

In 2011, a bottle of 1774 *vin jaune* was sold for €57,000.

CAVE DE LA REINE JEANNE
These 14th-century vaulted cellars belong to the négociant business of Domaine André et Mireille Tissot, an artisanal venture run by Stéphane Tissot. Stéphane is a committed biodynamic practitioner and one of the very best of producers in Arbois.

THE ARBOIS APPELLATION
Arbois is the Jura's most famous appellation, and some of its finest wines come from the hillside vineyards surrounding the old town itself. Arbois was once part of the Duchy of Burgundy, so Pinot Noir and Chardonnay have always grown there.

THE APPELLATIONS OF
THE JURA, BUGEY, AND SAVOIE

ARBOIS AOC

This is the best-known appellation of the Jura, from in and around the town of Arbois.

Pupillin is a single-commune appellation for red, white, rosé, *vin jaune*, and *vin de paille* made to the same specification as Arbois AOC.

RED Trousseau wines are rich, and sometimes coarse, and Pinot wines are light and rustic.

🍇 Trousseau, Poulsard, Pinot Noir

⌛ 2–8 years

WHITE Light, fresh Chardonnays are best; pure Savagnin can be delicately aromatic when not blended with declassified *vin jaune*, good examples of which are world renowned.

🍇 Savagnin, Chardonnay, Pinot Blanc

⌛ 1–3 years

ROSÉ Famous for its firm and distinctive dry rosé wines made in the pale *vin gris* style.

🍇 Poulsard, Trousseau, Pinot Noir

⌛ 1–3 years

✓ *Daniel Dugois • Raphaël Fumey & Adeline Chatelain • Michel Gahir* (Trousseau Grands Vergers) *• Labet Père & Fils • Désiré Petit & Fils* (Vin de Paille) *• De la Pinte* (Terre Rouge) ◉ *• Jacques Puffeney • Cave de la Reine Jeanne • De la Renardière • Jean Rijckaert • André & Mireille Tissot • Jacques Tissot • De la Tournelle* ◉

MOUSSEUX This is a traditional method sparkling white wine seldom seen outside Arbois. These fresh, dry sparkling wines show more potential than quality.

🍇 Savagnin, Chardonnay, Pinot Blanc

⌛ 1–3 years

✓ *Foret • Fruitière Vinicole d'Arbois* (Montboise)

VIN JAUNE This regional speciality wine is not fortified but is deliberately oxidized and has a Sherry-like aroma. Château-Chalon is the most famous *vin jaune*, but Arbois comes closest in quality of all the other *vin jaune* produced in the Jura. For a full description of *vin jaune*, see Château-Chalon.

⌛ 10–50 years

✓ *De la Pinte* ◉ *• Jacques Puffeney • Rolet • André & Mireille Tissot* ◉ *• Jacques Tissot*

VAN DE PAILLE Arbois *vin de paille* is made from grapes that are dried to concentrate the juice, followed by a long fermentation and up to four years in wood. These are very sweet wines with an old-gold colour, complex bouquet, and a rich, nutty flavour.

🍇 Poulsard, Trousseau, Savagnin, Chardonnay

⌛ 10–50 (or more) years

✓ *Rolet • André & Mireille Tissot* ◉

BUGEY AOC

Formerly called Vin de Bugey, this wine has had its criteria changed substantially since the decree of January 2004, particularly the *encépagement* and the villages that may add their name to this appellation: Cerdon (sweet sparkling rosé only), Manicle (red and white wines only), and Montagnieu (red and sparkling or *pétillant* white wines only). The villages of Machuraz and Virieu-le-Grand no longer have the right to add their name to this appellation.

RED Fresh wines that range from the fruity Pinot to the rich Mondeuse. Manicle must be made exclusively from Pinot Noir, while Montagnieu must be Mondeuse.

🍇 Gamay, Mondeuse, Pinot Noir

⌛ 2–8 years

✓ *Monin* (Mondeuse: Les Griots, Les Perrailles)

WHITE Off-dry, fresh, light, and gently fruity. Manicle must be made exclusively from Chardonnay.

🍇 At least 70% Chardonnay, plus optional Aligoté, Altesse, Jacquère, Mondeuse Blanche, and Pinot Gris

⌛ 1–3 years

ROSÉ Light and refreshing dry wines.

🍇 At least 70% in total or separately of Gamay and Pinot Noir, plus optional Mondeuse, Pinot Gris, and Poulsard

⌛ 1–3 years

SPARKLING WHITE These wines may be anything from *pétillant* to fully *mousseux*.

🍇 At least 70% Chardonnay, Jacquère, and Molette, plus optional Aligoté, Altesse, Gamay, Mondeuse (Noir and Blanche), Pinot Gris, and Poulsard

⌛ 1–2 years

SPARKLING ROSÉ These wines may be anything from *pétillant* to fully *mousseux*. Cerdon – which must be made from only Gamay or Poulsard by the *méthode ancestrale*, with a minimum of 40 grams of residual sugar per litre – is a fresh, rich, grapey-aromatic sparkling wine with a soft mousse.

🍇 At least 70% in total or separately of Gamay and Pinot Noir, plus optional Mondeuse, Pinot Gris, and Poulsard

⌛ 1–2 years

✓ *Daniel Boccard • Christian Bolliet*

CHÂTEAU-CHALON AOC

The Jura's *vins jaunes* possess a unique style and Château-Chalon (which is the name of a commune) is its most legendary exponent. It is normally fermented, then left to age in sealed wooden barrels for six years with no topping up. During this time, a *flor* develops – a skin of yeast that floats on top of the wine. The changes induced by the *flor* give the acetaldehyde-dominated *vin jaune* a resemblance to a *fino* Sherry, but the fact that it is not fortified (whereas Sherry is) and is made from a different grape produces its unique character.

VIN JAUNE This is something of an acquired taste and should be drunk when very old. The vast array of complex nuances of bouquet eventually subdue and transmute the Sherry-like smell of acetaldehyde.

It has a dry flavour.

🍇 Savagnin

⌛ 10–100 years

✓ *Baud Père & Fils • Berthet-Bondet • Philippe Butin • Durand-Perron • Jean Macle*

CÔTES DU JURA AOC

This generic appellation contains some of the most widely encountered Jura wines. Its larger area of production gives it an edge over Arbois, the better-known AOC within its boundaries.

RED Usually light in colour and body, with elegant fruit and a little finesse.

🍇 Poulsard, Trousseau, Pinot Noir

⌛ 2–8 years

WHITE Simple dry whites that make an ideal accompaniment to the local *raclette* cheese dish.

🍇 Savagnin, Chardonnay

⌛ 1–3 years

ROSÉ These dry rosés have a fine and fragrant *vin gris* style, with solid fruit.

🍇 Poulsard, Trousseau, Pinot Noir, Pinot Gris, Savagnin, Chardonnay

⌛ 1–3 years

✓ *Château d'Arlay • Daniel & Pascal Chalandard* (Cuvée Siloé) *• Charbonnier • Ganevat* (Florine Ganevat Chardonnay, Julien Ganevat Pinot Noir) ◉ *• Grand Frères* (Tradition) *• Labet • Jean Macle • Pignier* ◉ (Trousseau) *• Jean Rijckaert • Rolet* (Chardonnay) *• André & Mireille Tissot* ◉

SPARKLING WHITE This is probably Jura's best sparkling-wine appellation. The wines have a persistent *mousse* of tiny bubbles, excellent balance, surprising finesse, and great potential.

🍇 Savagnin, Chardonnay, Pinot Blanc

⌛ 1–3 years

✓ *Château Gréa*

VIN JAUNE Deliberately oxidized, unfortified wines with a Sherry-like aroma. For a full description of *vin jaune*, see Château-Chalon.

⌛ 10-20 years

✓ *Château d'Arlay • Philippe Butin*

VIN DE PAILLE Labelled *vin de paille*, these very sweet wines have old-gold, honey-gold, and amber-gold colours; a full, distinctive, and complex bouquet; a powerfully rich and nutty flavour; and a surprisingly crisp finish, with a raisiny, apricot-skin aftertaste.

🍇 Poulsard, Trousseau, Savagnin, Chardonnay

⌛ 10–50 (or more) years

✓ *Berthet-Bondet • Denis & Marie Chevassu • Richard Delay • Château Gréa • Labet • Morel-Thibaut • Désiré Petit & Fils • Pignier Père & Fils* ⓑ *• Philippe Vandelle*

CRÉMANT DU JURA AOC

This appellation was introduced in 1995. It can be used for any wine conforming to *vin mousseux* AOCs of the Côtes du Jura, Arbois, and L'Étoile, and may be applied retrospectively to any of these wines from 1991 onwards. Part of the "crémantization" of French traditional method appellations, once most sparkling wines in the region are marketed as Crémant du Jura, the unwieldy bunch of *mousseux* appellations will be quietly dropped.

✓ *Richard Delay* • *Grand Frères* (Prestige)
• *De Montebourgeau* • *Désiré Petit & Fils*
(Cuvée Désiré) • *Rolet Père & Fils* (Coeur
de Chardonnay) • *Jacques Tissot*

L'ÉTOILE AOC

These wines are named after the star-shaped fossils
found in the local limestone.

WHITE Light, dry white wines whose aromas reveal
the scents of alpine herbs and bracken.

🥂 At least 80% Chardonnay or Savagnin, plus
optional Poulsard

🍷 1–3 years

✓ *Baud Père & Fils*

SPARKLING WHITE Not quite up to the standard
of Côtes du Jura Mousseux, but this traditional-
method wine has more potential than Arbois
Mousseux. De Montbourgeau makes a fine-quality,
dry, sparkling wine.

🥂 At least 80% Chardonnay or Savagnin, plus
optional Poulsard

🍷 1–3 years

✓ *Château de l'Étoile*

VIN JAUNE Deliberately oxidized, unfortified wines
with a Sherry-like aroma. For a full description of
vin jaune, see Château-Chalon.

🥂 Savagnin

🍷 10–100 years

✓ *Château de l'Étoile* • *Claude & Cédric Joly*

MACVIN AOC *or*
MACVIN DU JURA AOC

Macvin, a *vin de liqueur*, is made by adding marc
(local brandy distilled from the residue of skins)
to grape juice, preventing fermentation.

RED Typical dull *vin de liqueur* aroma; sweet, grapey.

🥂 Poulsard, Trousseau, Pinot Noir

🍷 Upon purchase or never

WHITE This has a typical dull *vin de liqueur* aroma,
and is sweet and grapey. This is the most oxidative
Macvin style.

🥂 Chardonnay, Poulsard, Savagnin

🍷 Never!

ROSÉ Typical dull *vin de liqueur* aroma, sweet and
grapey.

🥂 Poulsard, Trousseau, Pinot Noir

🍷 Upon purchase or never

✓ *Labet*

ROUSSETTE DU BUGEY AOC

Roussette is a local misnomer for the Altesse grape.
The following villages may add their name to this
appellation if harvested with a lower yield:
Montagnieu and Virieu-le-Grand. Alglefort,
Arbignieu, Chanay, and Lagnieu are no longer
permitted to add their names to this appellation.

WHITE Light, fresh, and agreeable off-dry wines
with few pretensions.

🥂 Altesse

🍷 1–3 years

✓ *Jean Peillot*

ROUSSETTE DE SAVOIE AOC

The following villages have the right to add their
name to this appellation, if the wine is 100 per
cent Roussette: Frangy, Marestel, Monterminod,
and Monthoux.

WHITE Drier than Roussette de Bugey, these wines
have fine, tangy fruit.

🥂 Altesse

🍷 1–3 years

✓ *Dupasquier* • *Château de Monterminod* •
André & Michel Quenard • *De Saint-Germain*

SEYSSEL AOC

The still white Seyssel is a favourite après-ski wine.
It was Varichon & Clerc that first carved a niche for
Seyssel *mousseux* in the export market.

WHITE These are fragrant, dry, refreshing wines.

🥂 Altesse

🍷 1–3 years

✓ *Maison Mollex*

SPARKLING WHITE With a full, yeasty nose, fine
mousse, and elegant flavour, the Royal Seyssel
Private Cuvée is a yardstick for other producers.

🥂 Altesse, Chasselas, Molette

🍷 1–3 years

✓ *Maison Mollex* • *Royal Seyssel*

VIN DE SAVOIE AOC

The wines in this generic appellation are
produced to a high standard. The following
villages have the right to add their name to the
appellation: Abymes (white wines only), Apremont
(white), Arbin (red), Ayze (white or sparkling white,
sometimes spelled Ayse), Chautagne (red and
white), Chignin (red and white), Chignin-Bergeron
(white), Crépy (white), Cruet (white), Jongieux (red
and white), Marignan (white), Marin (white),
Montmélian (white), Ripaille (white), Saint-Jean-de-
la-Porte (red), and Saint-Jeoire-Prieuré (white). The
villages of Bergeron (except as Chignin-Bergeron),
Charpignat, and Sainte-Marie d'Alloix are no longer
permitted to add their names to this appellation.

RED Blends and single-variety wines; the blended
wines are usually better.

🥂 Gamay, Mondeuse, Pinot Noir, plus
a maximum of 30% (in the Haute-Savoie
département) of Cabernet Franc, and Cabernet
Sauvignon, Persan, and (in the Isère
département) Etraire de la Dui, Joubertin,
Persan, and Servanin. Arbin and Saint-Jean
de la Porte must be 100% Mondeuse; while
Chautagne, Chignin, and Jongieux must be at
least 70% Gamay, Mondeuse, or Pinot Noir.

🍷 2–8 years

WHITE These dry wines are the best of the AOC,
with Abymes, Apremont, and Chignin the best
villages. All are fine, rich, and complex.

🥂 Aligoté, Altesse, Chardonnay, Jacquère,
Mondeuse Blanche, Roussette, Veltliner Rouge
Précoce, plus a maximum of 30% (in the
Haute-Savoie *département*) of Chasselas,
Gringet, Roussette d'Ayze, and (in the Isère

---

département) Marsanne and Verdesse. Ayze
must be at least 70% Gringet; Abymes,
Apremont, Ayze, Chautagne, Chignin, Cruet,
Jongieux, Montmélian, and Saint-Jeoire-Prieuré
must contain at least 70% Jacquère; Chignin-
Bergeron must be 100% Roussanne; Crépy,
Marignan, Marin, and Ripaille must all contain
at least 70% Chasselas.

🍷 1–3 years

ROSÉ Attractive, light, and fruity, dry to off-dry
rosés made for early drinking.

🥂 Gamay, Mondeuse, Pinot Noir, plus a maximum
of 30% (in the Haute-Savoie *département*)
Cabernet Franc and Cabernet Sauvignon,
Persan, and (in the Isère *département*) Etraire de
la Dui, Joubertin, Persan, and Servanin

🍷 1–3 years

✓ *Pierre Boniface, Dupasquier, De L'Idylle*
(Mondeuse), *Louis Magnin* (Jacquère, Rousette),
Jean Perrier & Fils (Mondeuse Vieilles Vignes),
De Rouzan (Gamay), *De Saint-Germain*
(Chardonnay) • **Best single-cru wines:**
Abymes *Frédéric Giachino* ✪; **Apremont**
Philippe Betemps; **Arbin** *Genoux, Louis
Magnin, Charles Trosset* (Mondeuse);
Chignin *André & Michel Quénard, Raymond
Quénard* (Mondeuse); **Chignin-Bergeron**
Gilles Berlioz ✪, *Louis Magnin, André &
Michel Quénard, Philippe Ravier, Viallet,
Jean Vullien*; **Crépy** *Goutte d'Or* (Tête de
Cuvée); **Jongieux** *Edmond Jacquin & Fils*;
Montmélian *Louis Magnin*

SPARKLING & SEMI-SPARKLING WHITE
Wispy-light wines with an Alpine-fresh, clean taste.
The best can have a fragrant aroma and fine acidity.

🥂 Aligoté, Altesse, Chardonnay, Gamay, Jacquère,
Mondeuse (Blanche and Noir), Pinot Noir, and
Veltliner Rouge Précoce, plus (in the Haute-
Savoie *département*) Chasselas, Gringet, Molette,
and Roussette d'Ayze, and (in the Isère
département) Marsanne and Verdesse. Wines
with the Ayze village denomination must be
made from at least 70% Gringet, plus optional
Altesse and Roussette d'Ayze.

🍷 Within 1–2 years

✓ *Belluard* ✪ (Ayse) • *Les Rocailles*

SPARKLING & SEMI-SPARKLING ROSÉ Attractive,
early-drinking wines, with a soft mousse and
delicate fruit.

🥂 Aligoté, Altesse, Chardonnay, Gamay, Jacquère,
Mondeuse (Blanche and Noir), Pinot Noir, and
Veltliner Rouge Précoce, plus (in the Haute-
Savoie *département*) Chasselas, Gringet, Molette,
and Roussette d'Ayze, and (in the Isère
département) Marsanne and Verdesse

🍷 Within 1 year

SOUTHWEST FRANCE

*This region encompasses numerous small,
scattered areas that combine to produce an
impressively wide range of excellent-value wines
with diverse, but quite discernible, stylistic
influences from Bordeaux, Spain, Languedoc-
Roussillon, and the Rhône.*

AT THE HEART OF THE REGION lies Gascony, the great brandy
district of Armagnac. It was from here that d'Artagnan set out in
around 1630 to seek fame and fortune in the King's Musketeers. The
narrow tracks upon which his eventful journey began still wind their
lonely way around wooded hills and across bubbling brooks. Apart
from brightly coloured fields of cultivated sunflowers, surprisingly
little has changed since Alexandre Dumas painted such a vivid and
colourful picture of these parts, for they remain sparsely populated
to this day. Time passes slowly even in the towns, where the main

square is usually deserted all day long, except during the five
o'clock rush hour, which lasts for all of 10 minutes.

THE DIVERSITY OF THE APPELLATIONS

The Southwest does not have a single wine of truly classic status,
yet it probably offers more value for money and is a greater
source of hidden bargains than any other French region. From
the succulent, sweet Jurançon *moelleux* and Monbazillac to the
fine wines of Bergerac, Buzet, and Marmandais, the revitalized
"black wines" of Cahors, the up-and-coming Frontonnais, the
tannic Madiran, and the highly individual Irouléguy of the Basque
Country, this part of France represents tremendous potential for
knowing wine drinkers.

Perhaps because it is a collection of diverse areas, rather than
one natural region, the appellations of the Southwest seem at first
numerous and confusing – even within one area there appear to be
needless duplications. In Bergerac, for example, the dry white wines
and red wines are reasonably easy to understand, since there are

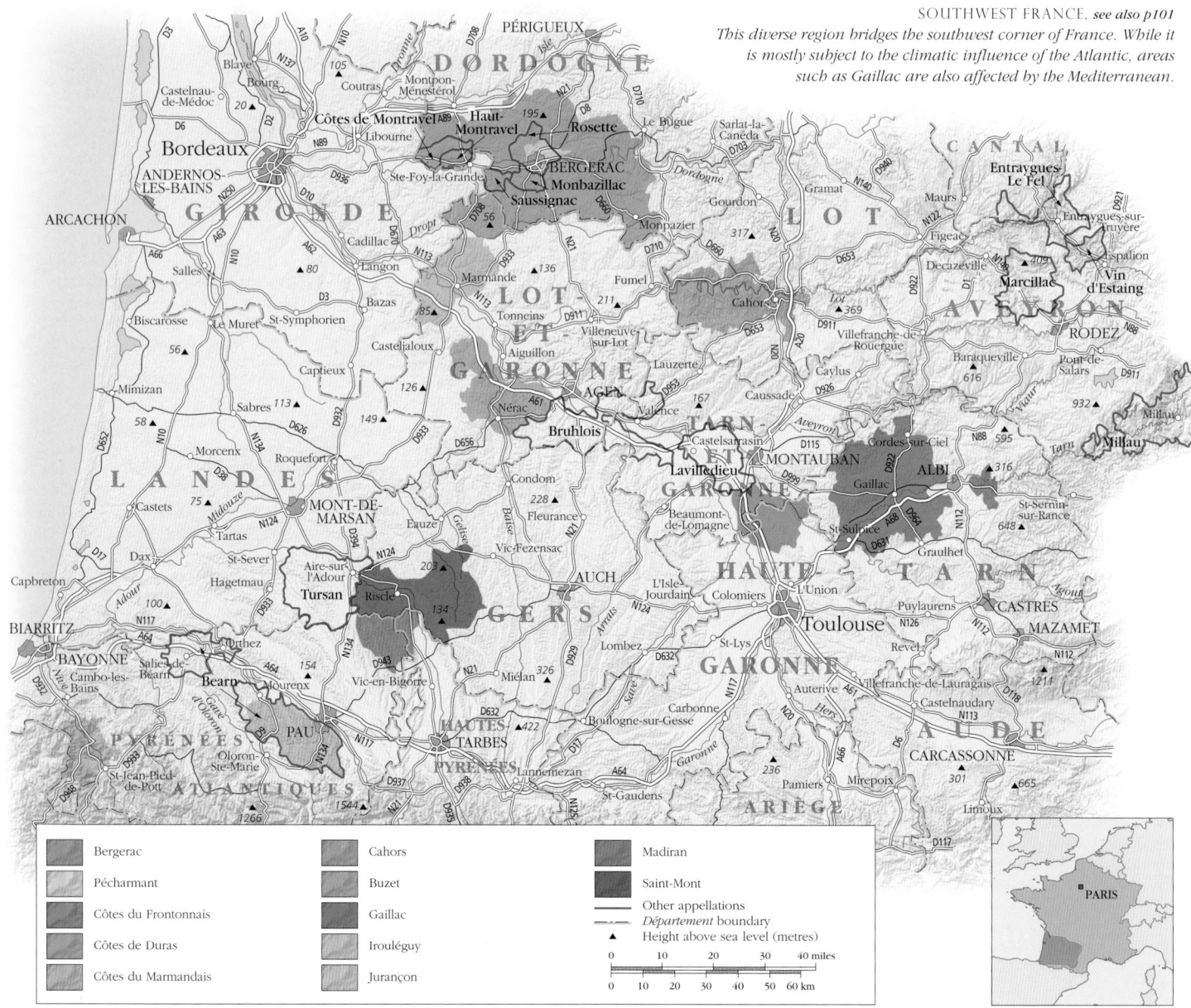

SOUTHWEST FRANCE, *see also p101*
*This diverse region bridges the southwest corner of France. While it
is mostly subject to the climatic influence of the Atlantic, areas
such as Gaillac are also affected by the Mediterranean.*

Bergerac	Cahors	Madiran	
Pécharmant	Buzet	Saint-Mont	
Côtes du Frontonnais	Gaillac	Other appellations	
Côtes de Duras	Irouléguy	*Département* boundary	
Côtes du Marmandais	Jurançon	▲ Height above sea level (metres)	

CÔTES DE BUZET VINEYARDS
*This good-value Bordeaux satellite is barely 15 kilometres
(9 miles) from the Gironde* département.

three dry appellations (Bergerac, Bergerac sec, and Montravel)
and three red-wine appellations (Bergerac, Côtes de Bergerac, and
Pécharmant), but there is a veritable galaxy of sweet and semi-sweet
appellations (Bergerac, Bergerac Moelleux, Montbazillac, Côtes de
Montravel, Haut-Montravel, Rosette, and Saussignac). When such a
small and relatively minor area as Bergerac can develop so many
different appellations, it is little wonder that a large and famous
region such as Bordeaux has evolved into 50-odd appellations. It
would surely be simpler to have a single Bergerac appellation to
which certain villages might be allowed to add a communal name;
if the same logic were applied throughout this region, more of its
wines could achieve marketing success, rather than attracting only
occasional attention as hidden bargains. With a more cohesive
image and some enterprising wineries straddling the many different
appellations, Southwest France should be at least as exciting as
Languedoc-Roussillon has become. Flying winemakers have
occasionally come to roost here in the past few years, but it will
take a permanent New World winery for the exciting potential
of Southwest France to be fully recognized.

RECENT SOUTHWEST FRANCE VINTAGES

2010 A great vintage of deep-coloured, concentrated reds and rich
and powerful sweet whites.

2009 Some of the greatest red wines ever produced.

2008 An inconsistent year with a few surprisingly high-quality
standouts surrounded by a sea of mediocrity. Good but not exceptional
dry white wines.

2007 The reds are very patchy, but there are some excellent dry and
sweet white wines.

2006 Extremely variable, from poor to excellent, according to the
weather and when growers decided to harvest.

FACTORS AFFECTING TASTE AND QUALITY

LOCATION
The southwest corner of
France, bordered by Bordeaux, the
Atlantic, the Pyrenees, and the
vineyards of Languedoc-Roussillon.

CLIMATE
The climate of southwestern
France is Atlantic-influenced, with
wet winters and springs, warm
summers, and long, sunny autumns.
The vineyards of Cahors, Fronton,
and Gaillac are subject to the
greater heat but more changeable
characteristics of the Mediterranean.

ASPECT
Mostly east- and east-through-
to-south-facing slopes, affording
protection from the Atlantic, in a
varied countryside that can range
from rolling and gently undulating
to steep and heavily terraced.

SOIL
This collection of diverse areas
has, not unexpectedly, a number of
different soils: sandy-and-calcareous
clay over gravel in the best
vineyards of Bergerac; sandy soils
on the Côte de Duras; calcareous
and alluvial soils in the *côtes* of
Buzet and Marmandais; gravel-clay
and gravel crests over marly
bedrock in the hilly hinterland of
Cahors, and alluvial soils peppered
with pebbly quartz, limestone, and
gravel over a calcareous bedrock in
the Lot Valley; limestone, clay-and-
limestone, and gravel at Gaillac;
sandy soils in Madiran, Tursan, and
Irouléguy; and stony and sandy
soils in Jurançon.

VITICULTURE AND VINIFICATION
The viticultural traditions and
vinification techniques of Bergerac,
Buzet, Marmandais, and, to some
extent, Cahors, are similar to those
of Bordeaux. Other districts of this
composite region have very much
their own distinctive, individual
practices: Béarn, Gaillac, and
Jurançon produce almost every
style of wine imaginable by many
vinification techniques, among
them the *méthode rurale* (known
locally as the *méthode gaillaçoise*).
Although the winemaking technique
in these areas is generally very
modern, the Basque district of
Irouléguy remains stoutly
traditional, allowing only the
introduction of Cabernet Sauvignon
and Cabernet Franc to intrude
upon its set ways.

GRAPE VARIETIES
Abouriou, Arrufiac, Auxerrois
(Malbec), Baroque, Cabernet
Franc, Cabernet Sauvignon,
Camaralet, Castets, Chardonnay,
Chenin Blanc, Cinsault, Clairette,
Colombard, Courbu Blanc, Courbu
Noir, Duras, Fer, Folle Blanche,
Fuella, Gamay, Gros Manseng,
Jurançon Noir, Lauzet, Len de
l'El, Manseng Noir, Mauzac,
Mauzac Rosé, Mérille, Merlot,
Milgranet, Mouyssagues,
Muscadelle, Négrette, Ondenc,
Petit Manseng, Picpoul, Pinot
Noir, Raffiat, Rousselou,
Sauvignon Blanc, Sémillon,
Syrah, Tannat, Ugni Blanc,
Valdiguié

THE APPELLATIONS OF
SOUTHWEST FRANCE

BÉARN AOC

This modest AOC shines in the local Basque area. Wines made in Bellocq, Lahontan, Orthez, and Saliès are allowed to add the communal designation Bellocq to the appellation.

RED Fresh, light, and fruity wines with a good balance, but lacking depth.

🍇 A maximum of 60% Tannat, plus Cabernet Franc, Cabernet Sauvignon, Fer, Manseng Noir, Courbu Noir

🍷 1–4 years

WHITE Light, dry, and aromatic wines.

🍇 Petit Manseng, Gros Manseng, Courbu Blanc, Lauzet, Camaralet, Raffiat, Sauvignon Blanc

🍷 1–2 years

ROSÉ Simple, fruity, dry rosés with a fresh floral aroma.

🍇 Tannat, Cabernet Franc, Cabernet Sauvignon, Fer, Manseng Noir, Courbu Noir

🍷 1–2 years

✓ *Bouscassé* ◉ (Rosé) • *CV de Jurançon* (Larribère)

BÉARN-BELLOCQ AOC

See Béarn AOC

BERGERAC AOC

Adjoining Bordeaux, Bergerac produces wines that are sometimes mistaken for the modest appellations of its more famous neighbour. Its wines were shipped to London as early as 1250. Supplies dried up after the Hundred Years' War, which ended with the Battle of Castillon, and Castillon-la-Bataille marks the ancient English-French boundary between Bergerac and Bordeaux.

RED The best reds have a good garnet or ruby colour, fine fruit, and an elegant balance.

🍇 Cabernet Sauvignon, Cabernet Franc, Merlot, Malbec, Fer, Mérille

🍷 2–8 years

WHITE Mostly dry Bordeaux-style wines, but semi-sweet wines with up to 54 grams per litre of residual sugar are permitted. Until 1993, such wines had to be described as *moelleux*; however, as this is no longer compulsory, we will not know whether some of these wines are *moelleux* or not. Bergerac Blanc may be sold from 1 December following the harvest without any mention of *primeur* or *nouveau*.

🍇 Sémillon, Sauvignon Blanc, Muscadelle, Ondenc, Chenin Blanc, and up to 25% Ugni Blanc (on the proviso that the quantity of Sauvignon Blanc used is at least equal)

🍷 1–3 years

ROSÉ These are light, easy, and attractive dry wines. They may be sold from 1 December following the harvest without mention of *primeur* or *nouveau*.

🍇 Cabernet Sauvignon, Cabernet Franc, Merlot, Malbec, Fer, Mérille

🍷 1–3 years

✓ *de l'Ancienne Cure* • *Julienne* (Casnova des Conti) • *Château Les Justices* • *Château Laulerie* • *Château Miaudoux* (Inspiration) • *Château Le Payral* (Héritage) • *Château Pion* • *Julien de Savignac* (Rosé) • *Château Thénac* • *Château Tour des Gendres* • *Les Verdots* (Les Verdots selon David Fourtout)

BERGERAC SEC AOC

These white wines are distinguished from Bergerac Blanc by having to be dry, with no more than 4 grams per litre of residual sugar.

WHITE Dry Bordeaux-style wines. They may be sold from 1 December following the harvest without any mention of *primeur* or *nouveau*.

🍇 Sémillon, Sauvignon Blanc, Muscadelle, Ondenc, Chenin Blanc, and up to 25% Ugni Blanc (on the proviso that the quantity of Sauvignon Blanc used is at least equal)

🍷 1–3 years

✓ *de l'Ancienne Cure* • *Château Cailevet* (Accent) • *Château Miaudoux* • Château de Panisseau (Divin) • *Michel Roche* (Le Top de Mazière) • *Julien de Savignac* (Les Jardins de Cyrano) • *Château Tour des Gendres* ◉ • *Château Tourmentine* (Barrique) • *Les Verdots* (Les Verdots selon David Fourtout)

BUZET AOC

Formerly known as Côtes de Buzet, this super-value Bordeaux satellite is located on the northern edge of the Armagnac region.

RED The best are always very good, with considerable finesse and charm.

🍇 Merlot, Cabernet Sauvignon, Cabernet Franc, Malbec

🍷 3–10 years (15 in exceptional cases)

WHITE These dry whites are the least interesting wines in this appellation. They may be sold from 1 December following the harvest without any mention of *primeur* or *nouveau*.

🍇 Sémillon, Sauvignon Blanc, Muscadelle

🍷 1–3 years

ROSÉ Ripe, fruity, dry rosés. They may be sold from 1 December following the harvest without any mention of *primeur* or *nouveau*.

🍇 Merlot, Cabernet Sauvignon, Cabernet Franc, Malbec

🍷 1–4 years

✓ *Baron d'Albret* • *CV de Buzet* • *Château Sauvagnères*

CAHORS AOC

The once-famous "black wine" of Cahors got its name from the Malbec grape, which, prior to phylloxera, produced dark, inky-coloured wines. But the vines did not graft well to the earliest American rootstocks and Cahors fell into decline. Compatible rootstocks were developed, and with the introduction of the Merlot and Tannat, Cahors has started to improve. The sheer number of good producers now makes Cahors one of the most reliable red-wine appellations in France. Vieux Cahors must be aged in oak for at least three years.

RED Most Cahors wines have a deep colour with a blackcurrant tinge. They are full of fruit and have a good, plummy, Bordeaux-like taste, with a silky texture and a distinctive violet-perfumed aftertaste.

🍇 A minimum of 70% Malbec, plus up to 30% (in total) of Merlot and Tannat – Jurançon Noir has not been permitted since 1996

🍷 3–12 years (20 in exceptional cases)

✓ *Château de Clasou* • *Château la Caminade* (Commandery, Esprit) • *Château du Cèdre* • *Château de Chambert* • *Cosse-Maisonneuve* ◉ • *de la Coustarelle* • *Croix du Mayne* (Elevé en Fûts de Chêne) • *CV Côtes d'Olt* • *Clos de Gamot* • *Château Gautoul* • *des Grauzils* • *Château Haut Monplaisir* (Pur Plaisir) • *Clos d'Un Jour* • *Château Lacapell Cabanac* ◉ (Prestige Elevé en Fûts de Chêne) • *Château Lagrezette* • *Château Lamartine* (Expression, Particulière) • *Primo Palatum* • *du Prince* • *Château La Reyne* (Vente d'Ange) • *des Saverines* • *Clos Triguedina*

COTEAUX DU QUERCY AOC

Located just south of the Cahors area, and a *vin de pays* since 1976, Coteaux du Quercy was promoted to VDQS in 1999, when its *encépagement* changed (formerly Gamay- and Merlot-dominated wines). In 2011, this appellation received full AOC status.

RED Richly coloured, full-bodied wines, the best of which have plenty of morello cherry and black-berry fruit.

🍇 A minimum of 40% Cabernet Franc, plus optional Malbec, Merlot, and Tannat

🍷 1–4 years

ROSÉ Soft, easy-drinking, fresh, and fruity rosé, with a maximum of 3 grams per litre residual sugar, thus truly dry.

🍇 A minimum of 40% Cabernet Franc, plus optional Malbec, Merlot, and Tannat

🍷 Upon purchase

✓ *de Merchien*

CÔTES DE BERGERAC AOC

Geographically, there are no *côtes*; the only difference between this appellation and Bergerac is an extra degree of alcohol. The appellation Côtes de Bergerac Moelleux was withdrawn in 1993

(wines from this appellation must now be sold as Bergerac or Bergerac Moelleux); thus, any wine bearing Côtes de Bergerac must now be red.

RED Should be richer than Bergerac AOC.

🍇 Cabernet Sauvignon, Cabernet Franc, Merlot, Malbec, Fer, Mérille

⏳ 3–10 years

✓ *Château La Bard Les Tendoux* (Elevé en Fûts de Chêne) • *Château Les Mailleries* (Dany Moelleux) • *Château Masburel* • *Marlene & Alain Mayet* (Révelation du Bois de Pourquie) • *Château Tour des Verdots*

CÔTES DU BRULHOIS AOC

Elevated to VDQS from *vin de pays* in November 1984 and to AOC in 2011, this appellation encompasses vineyards along the Garonne immediately west of Buzet.

RED Decent, if unexciting, Bordeaux-like wine, though more rustic in style.

🍇 Cabernet Franc, Cabernet Sauvignon, Fer, Merlot, Malbec, Tannat

⏳ 2–4 years

ROSÉ This fresh, easy-to-drink dry wine must be produced by the *saignée* method.

🍇 Cabernet Franc, Cabernet Sauvignon, Fer, Merlot, Malbec, Tannat

⏳ 1–3 years

✓ *Château Grand Chêne* (Elevé en Fûts de Chêne)

CÔTES DE DURAS AOC

An appellation of increasing interest.

RED Light Bordeaux-style wines.

🍇 Cabernet Sauvignon and Franc, Merlot, Malbec

⏳ 2–3 years

WHITE Clean, crisp, and dry wines, except for those designated *moelleux*, which must have a minimum of 4 grams per litre of residual sugar, although most good *moelleux*, such as Château Lafon, contain much more than this and are definitely sweet. With the exception of *moelleux*, these wines may be sold from 1 December following the harvest without any mention of *primeur* or *nouveau*.

🍇 Sauvignon Blanc, Sémillon, Muscadelle, Mauzac, Chenin Blanc, Ondenc, and up to 25% Ugni Blanc (provided that the quantity of Sauvignon Blanc used is at least equal)

⏳ 1–3 years

ROSÉ These attractively coloured, dry, crisp, fruity rosés are firm and fresh. They may be sold from 1 December following the harvest without any mention of *primeur* or *nouveau*.

🍇 Cabernet Sauvignon, Cabernet Franc, Merlot, Malbec

⏳ 1–3 years

✓ *des Allergrets* (Elevé en Fûts de Chêne) • *Duc de Berticot* (Elevé en Fûts de Chêne) • *Château la Grave Bechade* (Alexandre Elevé en Fûts de Chêne) • *Château Laplace* • *Château Moulière* • *Château La Petite Bertrande* (Elevé en Fûts de Chêne) • *du Petit Malromé* (Sarah Elevé en Fûts de Chêne)

CÔTES DU FRONTONNAIS AOC

Situated just west of Gaillac. The wines of two villages, Fronton and Villaudric, are allowed to add their own names to the appellation.

RED These medium- to full-bodied wines have excellent colour and violet-perfumed fruit.

🍇 50–70% Négrette, up to 25% (in total) of Malbec, Mérille, Fer, Syrah, Cabernet Franc, and Cabernet Sauvignon, plus a maximum of 15% Gamay, Cinsault, and Mauzac

⏳ 2–8 years

ROSÉ Overtly fruity wines.

🍇 50–70% Négrette, up to 25% (in total) of Malbec, Mérille, Fer, Syrah, Cabernet Franc, and Cabernet Sauvignon, plus a maximum of 15% Gamay, Cinsault, and Mauzac

⏳ 1–3 years

✓ *Château Baudare* • *Château Bellevue la Forêt* • *Château Bouissel* • *Château Devès* (Allegro) • *Château Laurou* (Elevé en Fûts de Chêne) • *Château Plaisance* ◉ • *Château le Roc*

CÔTES DU FRONTONNAIS FRONTON AOC

See Côtes du Frontonnais AOC

CÔTES DU FRONTONNAIS VILLAUDRIC AOC

See Côtes du Frontonnais AOC

CÔTES DU MARMANDAIS AOC

This successful Bordeaux imitation, upgraded from VDQS to AOC in 1990, is situated on the border of Bordeaux itself; its vines grow either side of the Garonne, on the left-bank Côtes de Cocumont and the right-bank Côtes de Beaupuy. Few French people outside the region know anything about these wines, but the English have shipped them since the 14th century.

RED Fresh, clean, and impeccably made wines.

🍇 A maximum of 75% (in total) of Cabernet Franc, Cabernet Sauvignon, and Merlot, plus up to 50% (in total) of Abouriou, Malbec, Fer, Gamay, and Syrah

⏳ 2–5 years

WHITE These dry white wines are soft and delicious. They may be sold from 1 December following the harvest without any mention of *primeur* or *nouveau*.

🍇 At least 70% Sauvignon Blanc, plus Ugni Blanc and Sémillon

⏳ 1–2 years

ROSÉ Ripe and dry wines. They may be sold from 1 December following the harvest without any mention of *primeur* or *nouveau*.

🍇 A maximum of 75% (in total) of Cabernet Franc, Cabernet Sauvignon, and Merlot, plus up to 50% (in total) of Abouriou, Malbec, Fer, Gamay, and Syrah

⏳ 1–2 years

✓ *CV de Cocumont* (Beroy) • *Château La Gravette* (Elevé en Fûts de Chêne) • *Elian da Ros*

CÔTES DE MONTRAVEL AOC

This wine must have a minimum of 8 grams and a maximum of 54 grams per litre of residual sugar in order to meet the requirements of the appellation. Any red wines produced here are sold as Bergerac AOC.

WHITE These fat, fruity wines are usually produced in a *moelleux* style.

🍇 Sémillon, Sauvignon Blanc, Muscadelle

⏳ 3–8 years

✓ *Château du Bloy* • *Château Lespinassat* (Vieilles Vignes) • *Château Masburel*

ENTRAYGUES – LE FEL AOC

This area overlaps the Aveyron and Cantal *départements* in the northeast of the region, but only a tiny amount is made. The wines are rarely encountered and never exported. Promoted from VDQS to AOC in 2010.

RED Light, rustic wines that are best consumed locally because they need all the local ambience they can get.

🍇 At least 40% Fer, plus optional Cabernet Franc, Cabernet Sauvignon, Mouyssaguès, and Négret de Banhars

⏳ 1–2 years

WHITE Light, dry, and crisp wines for unpretentious quaffing.

🍇 At least 90% Chenin Blanc, plus optional Fel, Mauzac, and Saint-Côme

⏳ Upon purchase

ROSÉ Light, fresh, and very fruity, with an off-dry finish.

🍇 At least 40% Fer, plus optional Cabernet Franc, Cabernet Sauvignon, Mouyssaguès, and Négret de Banhars

⏳ 1–2 years

✓ *Jean-Marc Viguer*

ESTAING AOC

This area is contiguous with the southern tip of Entraygues – Le Fel AOC, and production is even more minuscule.

RED These wines are light bodied, attractive, and fruity.

🍇 At least three varieties, including a minimum of 50% Fer and Gamay, plus one or more of Abouriou, Cabernet Franc, Cabernet Sauvignon, Castet, Duras, Merlot, Mouyssaguès, and Pinot Noir

⏳ 1–3 years

WHITE These are unpretentious, dry white wines with a crisp flavour and a rustic, tangy style.

🍇 At least two varieties, including a minimum of 90% Chenin Blanc, plus optional Fel, Mauzac, and Rousselou (Saint-Côme)

⏳ 1–2 years

ROSÉ These pleasant dry wines are probably the most interesting in the appellation.

🍇 At least three varieties, including a minimum of 50% Fer and Gamay, plus one or more of Abouriou, Cabernet Franc, Cabernet Sauvignon, Castet, Duras, Merlot, Mouyssaguès, and Pinot Noir

⏳ Upon purchase

✓ *CV d'Olt* (Prestige)

FLOC DE GASCOGNE AOC

This *vin de liqueur* is produced in the Armagnac region.

WHITE Few manage to rise above the typically dull, oxidative *vin de liqueur* style that goes *rancio* with age.

A minimum of 70% Colombard, Gros Manseng, and Ugni Blanc, plus Baroque, Folle Blanche, Petit Manseng, Mauzac, Sauvignon Blanc, and Sémillon

⌐ Upon opening

ROSÉ Few manage to rise above the typically dull, oxidative *vin de liqueur* style that goes *rancio* with age.

A minimum of 50% Tannat, plus Cabernet Franc, Cabernet Sauvignon, Fer Servadou, Malbec, and Merlot

⌐ Upon opening

✓ *CV du Muscat de Lunel* (Prestige) • *Saint Pierre de Paradis* (Vendange d'Automne)

GAILLAC AOC

These vineyards, among the oldest in France, have only recently begun to make their mark. In order to emphasize local styles, there has been a concerted move away from classic grapes towards different native varieties. Gaillac Liquoreux and Gaillac Moelleux are no longer permitted appellations, but such wines are still available under the Gaillac Doux appellation. The Gaillac Sec Perlé denomination for slightly *pétillant* dry white wines has been dropped (although Gaillac Perlé still seems to flourish), and the sparkling wines of Gaillac are now segregated by their method of production (*see* Gaillac Mousseux AOC and Gaillac Mousseux Méthode Gaillaçoise AOC). The required *encépagement* has always been confusingly complex, but became even more so with the new regulations introduced in 2001.

RED Wines made mostly in the fresh, soft but light carbonic-maceration style. They may be sold as *primeur* or *nouveau* from the third Thursday of November following the harvest.

At least 60% Duras, Fer, Gamay, and Syrah, of which Duras, Fer, and Syrah (or any two of these) must represent at least 30% of the entire blend; furthermore, there must be at least 10% each of Duras and Fer, plus optional Cabernet Franc, Cabernet Sauvignon, and Merlot

⌐ 1–3 years

WHITE Dry and fresh, these wines may be sold as *primeur* or *nouveau* as from the third Thursday of November following the harvest.

At least 15% of Len de l'El or Sauvignon Blanc (or a blend of the two), plus Mauzac, Mauzac Rosé, Muscadelle, Ondenc, and Sémillon

⌐ Upon purchase

ROSÉ Easy to drink, light, fresh, and dry rosés.

At least 60% Duras, Fer, Gamay, and Syrah, of which Duras, Fer, and Syrah (or any two of these) must represent at least 30% of the entire blend; furthermore, there must be at least 10% each of Duras and Fer, plus optional Cabernet Franc, Cabernet Sauvignon, and Merlot

⌐ 1–2 years

✓ *Causse Marines* (Délires d'Automne) • *Manoir de l'Émeille* (Tradition) • *d'Escausses* (La Vigne l'Oubli) • *de Gineste* (Aurore, Grand Cuvée) • *de Larroque* (Privilège d'Autan) • *Château de Lastours* • *Château Lecusse* (Spéciale) • *Château Montels* • *Paysels* (Tradition) • *Robert Plageoles* • *René Rieux* (Concerto) • *Rotier* • *des Terrisses* (Saint-Laurent) • *Château La Tour Plantade*

GAILLAC DOUX AOC

These are naturally sweet wines that must contain a minimum of 70 grams per litre of residual sugar.

WHITE Sweet to very-sweet wines of ripe-peach, or richer, character.

At least 15% (each or in total) of Len de l'El and Sauvignon Blanc, plus Mauzac, Mauzac Rosé, Muscadelle, Ondenc, and Sémillon

⌐ 5–15 years

✓ *Barreau* (Caprice d'Automne) • *Château Palvie* (Les Secrets) • *Peyres-Combe* (Flaveurs d'Automne) • *Robert Plageoles* • *Rotier* (Renaissance) • *Sanbatan* (Muscadelle) • *de Vayssette* (Maxime) • *Les Vergnades*

GAILLAC MOUSSEUX AOC

This is a sparkling wine made by the traditional method. Expect to see a phasing out of the term *mousseux* on these and other Gaillac sparkling-wine appellations.

SPARKLING WHITE These wines are fresh and fragrant with a fine sparkle.

At least 15% (each or in total) of Len de l'El and Sauvignon Blanc, plus Mauzac, Mauzac Rosé, Muscadelle, Ondenc, and Sémillon

⌐ 1–3 years

SPARKLING ROSÉ Attractive, fresh, fruity wines.

At least 60% Duras, Fer, Gamay, and Syrah, of which Duras, Fer, and Syrah (or any two of these) must represent at least 30% of the entire blend; furthermore, there must be at least 10% each of Duras and Fer, plus optional Cabernet Franc, Cabernet Sauvignon, and Merlot

⌐ 1–2 years

✓ *Manoir de l'Emeille* • *René Rieux*

GAILLAC MOUSSEUX MÉTHODE GAILLAÇOISE AOC

Sparkling wines made by the *méthode rurale*, involving just one fermentation, with no addition of a *liqueur de tirage*. The wine is bottled before the fermentation stops and no *liqueur d'expédition* is added prior to distribution, thus any residual sweetness is entirely from the original grape sugars. Styles include *brut* and *demi-sec*. A *doux* is also available, but is governed by stricter rules and is given its own appellation (*see below*).

SPARKLING WHITE These very fresh, fragrant, and grapey wines have a fine natural sparkle.

At least 15% (each or in total) of Len de l'El and Sauvignon Blanc, plus Mauzac, Mauzac Rosé, Muscadelle, Ondenc, and Sémillon

⌐ 1–3 years

SPARKLING ROSÉ These wines are attractive, fresh, and deliciously fruity.

At least 60% Duras, plus Fer, Gamay, Syrah, Cabernet Sauvignon, Cabernet Franc, Merlot

⌐ 1–2 years

GAILLAC MOUSSEUX MÉTHODE GAILLAÇOISE DOUX AOC

This is a sparkling wine made by the *méthode rurale* (*see* Gaillac Mousseux Méthode Gaillaçoise AOC) from riper grapes (minimum of 11 per cent) than those of any other Gaillac sparkling-wine appellation, and with at least 45 grams of residual natural sugar per litre.

SPARKLING WHITE Not as exotic as, say, Clairette de Die Méthode Dioise Ancestrale, but delicious, grapey, and fragrant all the same.

At least 15% (each or in total) of Len de l'El and Sauvignon Blanc, plus Mauzac, Mauzac Rosé, Muscadelle, Ondenc, and Sémillon

⌐ 1–3 years

SPARKLING ROSÉ I have never come across a Gaillac Doux rosé, but if the white is anything to go by, it would be an interesting wine.

At least 60% Duras, Fer, Gamay, and Syrah, of which Duras, Fer, and Syrah (or any two of these) must represent at least 30% of the entire blend; furthermore, there must be at least 10% Cabernet Franc, Cabernet Sauvignon, and Merlot

⌐ 1–2 years

GAILLAC PREMIÈRES CÔTES AOC

These are dry white wines that come from 11 communes. The grapes must be riper than for ordinary Gaillac AOC and the wine must conform to the technical requirements of Gaillac Doux in all but sweetness.

✓ *Robert Plageoles* • *Château de Salettes*

HAUT-MONTRAVEL AOC

This wine must have minimum residual sugar of 8 grams per litre and a maximum of 54 grams per litre to meet the requirements of the appellation. Any red wines produced here are sold as Bergerac AOC.

WHITE Fat, fruity, and *moelleux* wines.

Sémillon, Sauvignon Blanc, Muscadelle

⌐ 3–8 years

✓ *Château Puy-Servain*

IROULÉGUY AOC

The local *coopérative* dominates this Basque appellation, which makes some of the most distinctive red wines in Southwest France. Surprisingly, however, the production of rosé outweighs that of red.

RED These deep, dark, tannic wines have a rich and mellow flavour, with a distinctive earthy-and-spicy aftertaste.

Tannat, plus at least 50% (in total) of Cabernet Sauvignon and Cabernet Franc

⌐ 4–10 years

WHITE These modest dry whites are the least interesting of this appellation.

Courbu, Manseng

ROSÉ This salmon-coloured, very fruity dry rosé is best drunk very young and fresh.

Tannat plus at least 50% (in total) of Cabernet Sauvignon and Cabernet Franc

🍷 Upon purchase

✓ *Arretxa* ⊙ • *Etxegaraya* • *Henri Mina*

JURANÇON AOC

The sweet version of this wine from the Pyrénées-Atlantiques was used at Henri de Navarre's christening in 1553 and is often sold today as *vendanges tardives* or *moelleux*. Most production is, however, tart, dry, and nervy, and sold as Jurançon Sec (*see below*).

WHITE The best wines have a fine, spicy, and tangy bouquet and flavour, and can hint of pineapples and peaches, candied peel, and cinnamon.

🍇 Petit Manseng, Gros Manseng, Courbu, plus up to 15% (in total) of Camaralet and Lauzet

🍷 5–20 years

✓ *Bru-Baché* • *Cauhapé* • *Clos Lapeyre* ⊙ • *Primo Palatum* • *Clos Thou* ⊙ • *Clos Uroulat*

JURANÇON SEC AOC

This wine has to meet the same requirements as Jurançon AOC, but less residual sugar is allowed, and the grapes may be less ripe. It is best drunk young. These wines may be sold from 1 December

following the harvest without any mention of *primeur* or *nouveau*.

WHITE If any wine in the world habitually has a certain nervousness, it has to be Jurançon Sec. Most lack any individual character that would make them stand out from other dry whites, and none has the complexity and richness of Jurançon's late-harvest wines, but the best can have an intensity that hints of grapefruit.

🍇 Petit Manseng, Gros Manseng, Courbu, plus up to 15% (in total) of Camaralet and Lauzet

🍷 2–5 years

✓ *Capdevieille* (Brise Océane) • *Cauhape* (Sève d'Automne) • *du Cinquau* • *CV de Jurançon* (Grain Sauvage) • *Lapeyre* ⊙ • *Larredya* • *Nigri* • *Primo Palatum*

LAVILLEDIEU AOC

Situated south of Cahors, this appellation is a northern extension of the Frontonnais, with vines growing on a *boulbènes* soil that is similar to that of Bordeaux's Entre-Deux-Mers district. Production is dominated by the local *coopérative*, and the wines are seldom seen outside the locality.

RED Nicely coloured, medium-bodied wines with a fresh, fruity flavour.

🍇 A blend of at least four of the following varieties: Cabernet Franc, Gamay, Négrette, Syrah, Tannat, plus optional Fer and Milgranet

🍷 3–6 years

ROSÉ Fresh, dry, and crisp, with delicately rich fruit.

🍇 A blend of at least four of the following varieties: Cabernet Franc, Gamay, Négrette, Syrah, Tannat, plus optional Fer and Milgranet

✓ *CV de Lavilledieu du Temple*

MADIRAN AOC

One of the most individually expressive appellations in Southwest France, but there are as many disappointments as successes. Many domaines are trying new oak, and there is a trend towards more Cabernet Franc.

RED You literally have to chew your way through the tannin in these dark, rich, and meaty wines when young.

🍇 40–60% Tannat, plus Cabernet Franc, Cabernet Sauvignon, and Fer

🍷 5–15 years

✓ *Berthoumieu* • *Château Bouscassé* • *Château Labranche-Laffont* • *Château Laffitte-Teston* • *Laffont* • *Château Montus* • *Plaimont* (Arte Benedicte) • *Primo Palatum* • *Château de Viela*

MARCILLAC AOC

This rarely encountered wine from the northeastern borderlands was upgraded from Vin de Marcillac VDQS to Marcillac AOC in 1990, when greater focus was placed on the local Fer and Gamay, while Jurançon Noir, Mouyssaguès, and Valdiguié were disallowed.

RED Rough and rustic when young, these wines soften with age.

🍇 At least 90% Fer, plus Cabernet Franc, Cabernet Sauvignon, and Merlot

🍷 3–6 years

ROSÉ Full, ripe, and attractive dry rosés that have expressed more individual style since the minimum Fer content has tripled.

🍇 At least 90% Fer, plus Cabernet Franc, Cabernet Sauvignon, and Merlot

🍷 1–3 years

✓ *CV de Ladrecht*

MILLAU AOC

Upgraded to VDQS in 1994 from *vin de pays* status (Gorges et Côtes de Millau), this appellation gained full AOC status in 2010.

RED The best *cuvées* usually contain a significant proportion of Syrah. *Vin primeur* is a speciality.

🍇 A blend of at least two varieties, including a minimum of 30% Gamay and Syrah, plus optional Fer, Duras, and up to 20% Cabernet Sauvignon

THE DORDOGNE RIVER, SEEN FROM THE TOWN OF DOMME
This part of Southwest France includes appellations lying just east of Bordeaux, such as Côtes de Duras and Bergerac on the Dordogne, as well as areas of vineyard close to the Spanish border.

WHITE Cannot be compared to the acidity found in the best Loire Chenin Blanc, but most are fresh and good for quaffing.

🍇 At least 50% Chenin Blanc, plus optional Mauzac

ROSÉ Fresh and delicately fruity.

🍇 At least 50% Gamay, plus optional Syrah, Cabernet Sauvignon, Fer, and Duras

✓ *CV des Gorges du Tarn* (Maitre des Sampettes) • *du Vieux Noyer*

MONBAZILLAC AOC

An excellent value Sauternes-style appellation at the heart of Bergerac, these wines date back to 1080, when vines were planted by the abbey of St-Martin on a hill called Mont Bazailhac.

WHITE These intensely sweet, rich wines are of a very high quality.

🍇 Sémillon, Sauvignon Blanc, Muscadelle

🍷 7–20 years

✓ *de l'Ancienne Cure* (Abbaye, L'Extase) • *Château Caillavel* • *Château Fonmorgues* • *Grande Maison* ◉ (Cuvée du Château) • *Château Tirecul La Gravière*

MONTRAVEL AOC

The largest of the three Montravel appellations and the only one where the white wine can (and must) be dry.

RED Elegant, ruby-coloured reds that are very much in the Bergerac style. These wines may be sold from 1 December following the harvest without any mention of *primeur* or *nouveau*.

🍇 A minimum of 50% Merlot, plus Cabernet Franc, Cabernet Sauvignon, and Malbec

🍷 2–8 years

WHITE Dry, crisp, and aromatic Sauvignon-dominated wines. These wines may be sold from 1 December following the harvest without any mention of *primeur* or *nouveau*.

🍇 A minimum 25% each of Sémillon and Sauvignon Blanc, plus optional Muscadelle (Chenin Blanc, Ondenc, and Ugni Blanc are no longer allowed)

🍷 1–2 years

✓ *Château du Bloy* (Le Bloy) • *Château Laulerie* • *Moulin Caresse* (Cent pour 100) • *Château Pagnon* • *Château Pique-Sègue* • *Portes du Bondieu* • *Château Puy-Servain* (Marjolaine)

PACHERENC DU VIC-BILH AOC

New oak is being used increasingly in this white-only appellation, which covers the same area as Madiran.

WHITE Exotic floral aromas, a fruit salad of flavours, Pacherenc du Vic-Bilh is made in off-dry (sold as *sec*), medium-sweet (*moelleux*), and sweet (*doux*) styles.

🍇 A minimum of 30% Arrufiac, which with Courbu and Petit Manseng must represent at least 60%

of the entire blend, plus Gros Manseng and a maximum of 10% in total of Sauvignon Blanc and Sémillon

🍷 3–7 years

✓ *Château Bouscassé* • *Berthoumieu* • *Château Labranche-Laffont* • *Château de Viela*

PÉCHARMANT AOC

These are the finest red wines of Bergerac; all but one (Saint-Saveur) of the communes in this appellation are also within the Rosette AOC.

RED All the characteristics of the Bergerac, but with a greater concentration of colour, flavour, and tannin.

🍇 Cabernet Franc, Cabernet Sauvignon, Merlot, Malbec

🍷 4–12 years

✓ *Château Beauportail* • *Château de Biran* (Prestige de Bacchus) • *Château Champarel* • *Château Hugon* (Elevé en Fûts de Chêne)

ROSETTE AOC

A white-wine-only appellation. The wines must contain 8 to 54 grams per litre of residual sugar. Any red wines are sold as Bergerac AOC.

WHITE Soft and delicately fruity with a sweet, waxy flavour.

🍇 Sémillon, Sauvignon Blanc, Muscadelle

🍷 4–8 years

✓ *Château de Contancie*

SAINT-MONT AOC

Situated within the Armagnac region, the vineyards of this appellation, which achieved AOC status in 2011, extend northwards from Madiran. Wine production is dominated by the local *coopérative*.

RED Well-coloured wines of good flavour and medium body. They are not dissimilar to a lightweight Madiran, although they could become deeper, darker, and more expressive if the *coopérative* were prepared to reduce yields and produce better-quality wine.

🍇 At least 50% Tannat, plus optional Cabernet Franc, Cabernet Sauvignon, Fer, Merlot, and a maximum of 10% white varieties

🍷 2–5 years

WHITE Fruity, dry wines with a tangy finish.

🍇 An elaboration of three varieties: Arrufiac, Petit Courbu, and at least 50% Gros Manseng

🍷 1–2 years

ROSÉ Dry wines with a clean, fruity flavour.

🍇 At least 20% Tannat, plus optional Cabernet Franc, Cabernet Sauvignon, Fer, Merlot, and a maximum of 10% white varieties

🍷 1–3 years

✓ *Producteurs Plaimont* • *Château Saint-Go* (Elevé en Fûts de Chêne)

SAUSSIGNAC AOC

The wines of this sweet-wine appellation must have a minimum of 18 grams of residual sugar per litre. Any red wines are sold as Bergerac AOC.

WHITE The best can be very rich, fat, and full.

🍇 Sémillon, Sauvignon Blanc, Muscadelle, Chenin Blanc

🍷 5–15 years

✓ *Château Le Chabrier* ◉ • *Château Eyssards* (Flavie) • *Château Grinou* ◉ (Elevé en Fûts de Chêne) • *Château La Maurigne* (La Maurigne) • *Château Miaudoux*

TURSAN AOC

The reds rely on the Tannat, the same primary grape used in Madiran; the whites are essentially Baroque, a variety more at home in Tursan. There was a change of *encépagement* as from 2003. Promoted from VDQS to AOC in 2009.

RED Rich and chewy, or finer-flavoured and aromatic, depending on the dominant grape.

🍇 Cabernet Franc and Tannat, plus optional Cabernet Sauvignon and Fer

WHITE The *coopérative* traditionally makes a full-bodied white with a solid, somewhat rustic, rich flavour, but it is gradually being influenced by the growing reputation of the wine made under the relatively new Château de Bachen label, baron de Bachen, which is far more aromatic and elegant.

🍇 Baroque and Gros Manseng, plus optional Chenin Blanc, Petit Manseng, Sauvignon Blanc, and Sauvignon Gris

🍷 2–5 years

ROSÉ An unpretentious dry wine with good, juicy, fruit flavour.

🍇 Cabernet Franc and Tannat, plus optional Cabernet Sauvignon and Fer

🍷 1–3 years

✓ *Michel Guérard* (Baron de Bachen) • *CV de Landais* (Haute Carte)

LANGUEDOC-ROUSSILLON

Dollar for dollar, the swelling numbers of top-quality red wines from Languedoc-Roussillon provide more value and excitement than any of the famous wine regions of France.

THE WIZARDS OF OZ

The 1990s saw an influx of Australian winemakers, who have since played a not insignificant role in the raising of standards; but the sale in 2003 of the Australian-owned Domaine de la Baume could signal a swing back to a more home-grown stimulus. Domaine de la Baume is not significant in terms of the total production of this region, but there is no denying that its purchase by BRL Hardy in 1990, at the beginning of Australia's inexorable success on export markets, gave local wine producers a psychological boost.

In a strange way, the presence of a top Australian group was viewed as a seal of approval for local winemakers, just as the presence of Moët & Chandon in Australia had been seen by that country's sparkling winemakers. It was all a matter of timing: Australian wines were surging, French wines were slowing down, and the south was all potential, with very few wineries taking advantage of it. And *vins de pays* were not, as yet,

VINEYARDS AT BAGES
The Mediterranean coastal vineyards of the Côtes du Roussillon, around Perpignan, are reputed to be some of the hottest in France.

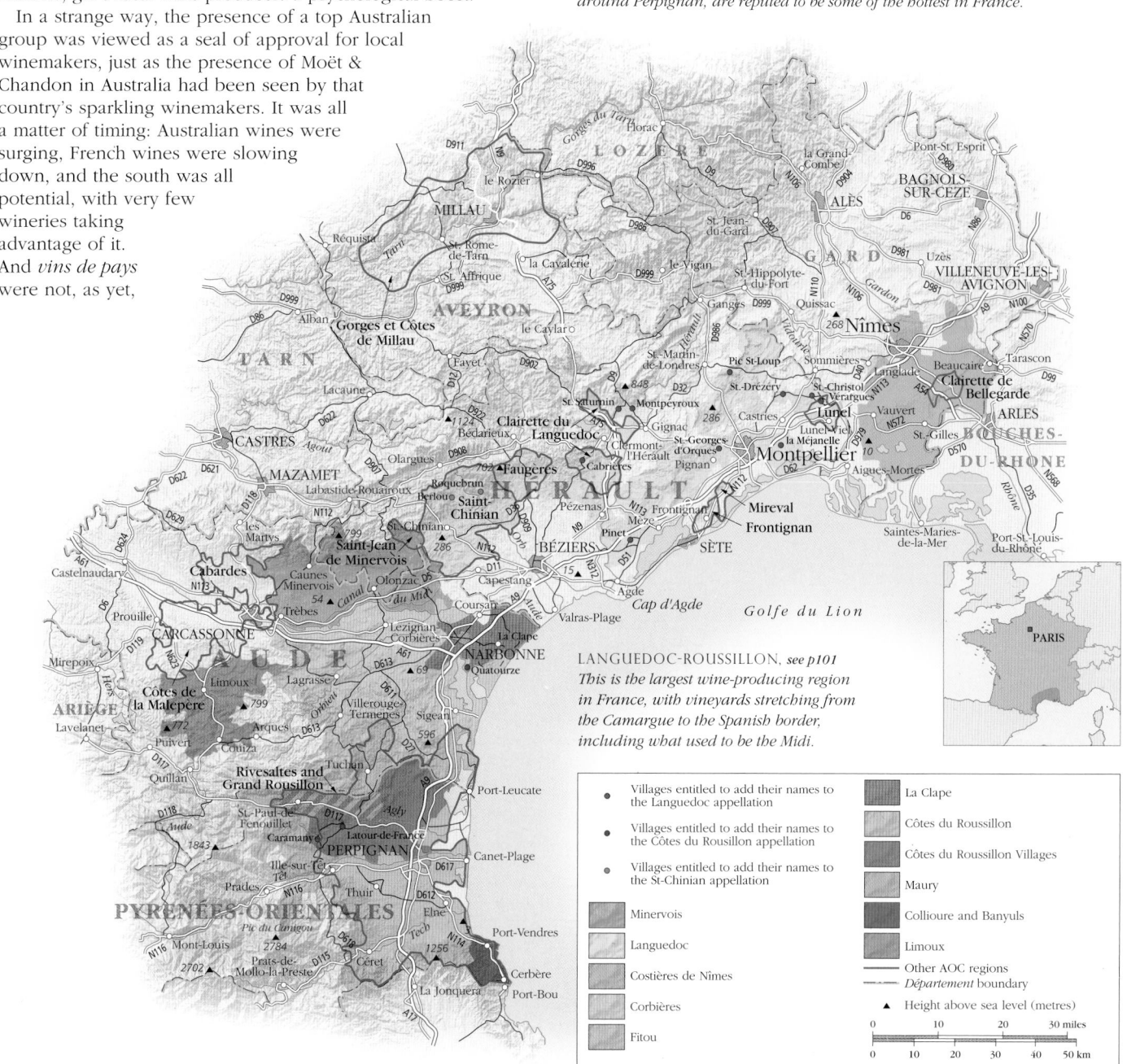

LANGUEDOC-ROUSSILLON, see p101
This is the largest wine-producing region in France, with vineyards stretching from the Camargue to the Spanish border, including what used to be the Midi.

- • Villages entitled to add their names to the Languedoc appellation
- • Villages entitled to add their names to the Côtes du Rousillon appellation
- • Villages entitled to add their names to the St-Chinian appellation

Minervois	La Clape
Languedoc	Côtes du Roussillon
Costières de Nîmes	Côtes du Roussillon Villages
Corbières	Maury
Fitou	Collioure and Banyuls
	Limoux

Other AOC regions
Département boundary
▲ Height above sea level (metres)

0   10   20   30 miles
0 10 20 30 40 50 km

a force to be reckoned with. BRL Hardy, or Hardy's as it was known then, was leading the Australian charge on global exports, and yet it saw sufficient promise in a small domaine in an unknown part of France to be sidetracked into purchasing it outright. The next few years saw the rise of *vins de pays*, particularly Vin de Pays d'Oc, including those of Domaine de la Baume, which became a commercial success on the UK market, against the tide for most other inexpensive French wines. During this time, there was an internationalization of grape varieties and wine styles in the south of France, and, barring some unfortunate experiments in the late 1970s and the 1980s, this development was far from regrettable.

Some French producers had started putting their own houses in order long before the BRL Hardy purchased Domaine de la Baume. Indeed, a number of domaines began bottling their own wines in the late 1970s, when the government's *vins de pays* scheme was encouraging quality-conscious growers to reduce yields. The problem was that there were never enough "quality-conscious" growers. But those who were formed a new generation of elite winemakers. They combined modern technology with the best traditional practices, including the use of some ageing with new oak, to create exciting new wines in the early 1980s. As other growers observed the vastly increased prices that their pioneering neighbours were attracting, more of them switched from selling in bulk to domaine-bottling, and it was this potential that attracted the Australians.

It was thus the French who created the new-found pride in this region, but it was the Australians who grabbed the limelight, focusing international attention on the fabulous potential. It is almost possible to give consumers an iron-clad guarantee that if they buy ultra-premium *cuvées* from Languedoc-Roussillon, they will not only be delighted with the wines, but they will be cheaper than and far superior to medium-priced wines bearing the most famous French appellations.

RECENT LANGUEDOC-ROUSSILLON VINTAGES

2010 Lack of rain and a hot summer produced a low yield of tiny, very concentrated berries, which result in a "dead fruit" character, but there will also be exceptional wines, particularly reds. Expect some sensational sweet wines, VDN, and Banyuls.

2009 Another vintage marked by concentrated fruit, richer in Roussillon, more mineral in Languedoc.

2008 Lack of water produced very rich and concentrated wines.

2007 A good year in Languedoc, a great year in Roussillon, where the yields were dramatically reduced and the *véraison* stretched to a long cool, but sunny finish, preserving acidity, purity of fruit, and minerality.

2006 Ripe but soft, making for easy drinking. Moderately good quality. Better in Languedoc than Roussillon.

FACTORS AFFECTING TASTE AND QUALITY

LOCATION
A crescent of vineyards situated in southern France between the Rhône to the east and the Pyrenees to the southwest.

CLIMATE
The Mediterranean-influenced climate is generally well suited to the cultivation of the vine, although it is subject to occasional stormy weather. Two winds dominate: the cold and parching mistral, which blows down from the heights of the Alpine glaciers, and the wet and warm marin, which comes in from the sea and can cause rot at harvest time. There are many microclimates in this collection of isolated vine-growing areas.

ASPECT
Famous for its unending tracts of flat, *vin ordinaire* vineyards that stretch across the vast plains; the best sites of Languedoc-Roussillon, however, mostly occupy south-, southeast-, and east-facing *garrigues* and hillsides, or nestle beneath protective overhanging cliffs.

SOIL
In general terms, the plains and valleys have rich alluvial soils, while the hillsides are schist or limestone and the *garrigues*, or former moorlands, are comprised of stony, carbonaceous soils over fissured limestone. However, specific situations vary enormously.

VITICULTURE AND VINIFICATION
This remains the great *vin ordinaire* region of France, where everything is mechanized and the vines of the plain are farmed like wheat or corn. There is a trend towards developing single-domaine vineyards that have potentially expressive *terroirs*, growing classic varieties and combining various traditional methods with modern techniques. Limoux still practises the ancient *méthode rurale* – in Blanquette Méthode Ancestrale AOC (*see opposite*) – although the majority of the wines are pure traditional method and sold under the new *crémant* appellation.

GRAPE VARIETIES
Aspiran Gris, Aspiran Noir, Aubun, Bouboulenc (known erroneously as Malvoisie in Clape), Cabernet Franc, Cabernet Sauvignon, Carignan, Carignan Blanc, Cinsault, Clairette, Duras, Fer, Grenache, Grenache Blanc, Grenache Gris, Listan Negra (the black version of Spain's Palomino), Lladoner Pelut, Macabéo, Malbec, Marsanne, Merlot, Mourvèdre, Muscat d'Alexandrie, Muscat Blanc à Petits Grains (*see individual appellations for local synonyms*), Muscat Rosé à Petits Grains, Négrette, Oeillade, Picpoul, Picpoul Noir, Rolle (Vermentino), Roussanne, Syrah, Terret, Terret Noir, Ugni Blanc

THE APPELLATIONS OF

LANGUEDOC-ROUSSILLON

Note In the following entries, a wine described as a *vin doux naturel* (or VDN) is made from very ripe grapes and fortified with pure grape spirit after its fermentation has reached 5 or 6 per cent. It has the natural sweetness of the grape. To be labelled "Rancio", a VDN must be stored in oak casks "according to local custom", which often means exposing the barrels to direct sunlight for a minimum of two years. This imparts the distinctive *rancio* flavour that is so prized in Roussillon. Depending on the colour of the original wine, the wine technique used, and how long it has been aged, the style of the wine produced varies; it can be red, white, rosé, or tawny.

BANYULS AOC
The most southerly appellation in France, the vineyards of this *vin doux naturel* are literally

a stone's throw from those of Spain. The vines are grown on precipitous slopes of schist where man and mule have great difficulty in maintaining a foothold, mechanization is out of the question, yields are extremely low, and ripeness very high. You will often see "rimage" on labels; this word is derived from the Catalan *rime*, or "grape", and refers to the vintage.

RED This is the deepest and darkest of all VDNs. A rich, sweet, red Banyuls (without too much barrel-age) has a chocolaty, bottled-fruitiness, which is the nearest France gets to the great wines of Portugal's Douro region. It lacks the fire of a great port, but has its own immense charm. After 15 to 20 years in bottle, a great Banyuls develops a curious but wonderful complexity that falls somewhere between the porty-plummy, dried-fruit spice of a mature

vintage port and the coffee-caramel, nutty-raisiny smoothness of a fine old tawny.

⌛ 10–40 years

WHITE/ROSÉ/TAWNY Like all VDNs that may be made in red, white, and rosé style, they can all turn tawny with time, particularly *rancio* wines.

🍇 All wines: a minimum of 50% Grenache, plus Grenache Gris, Grenache Blanc, Macabéo, Tourbat, Muscat Blanc à Petits Grains, Muscat d'Alexandrie, and a maximum 10% (in total) of Carignan, Cinsault, and Syrah

⌛ 10–20 years

✓ *Le Dominican* (Hanicotte) • *CV l'Étoile* (Extra Vieux) • *Du Mas Blanc* • *De la Rectorie* • *De la Tour Vieille* • *Du Traginer* ◉ (Rimage Mis Tardive)

BANYULS GRAND CRU AOC

The requirements are the same as for Banyuls AOC, but a minimum of 75 per cent Grenache is required. The grapes must be destemmed and macerated for a minimum of five days and the wine matured in oak for at least 30 months. The wines are similar in character to those of the basic, although not at all ordinary, Banyuls appellation, but in terms of classic port styles, they veer more towards the tawny than vintage.

√ *L'Abbé Rous* (Christian Reynal) • *L'Étoile* (Réserve) • *Cellier des Templiers*

BANYULS GRAND CRU "RANCIO" AOC
See Banyuls Grand Cru AOC

BANYULS "RANCIO" AOC
See Banyuls AOC

BERLOU ST-CHINIAN AOC
See St-Chinian (Villages) AOC

BLANQUETTE DE LIMOUX AOC

The best Blanquette de Limoux have improved, but many are still somewhat rustic and must adopt a more refined style if they are to compete internationally.

SPARKLING WHITE These wines used to have the distinctive aroma of fresh-cut grass, but they are slowly developing finer aromas.

🍇 Mauzac, Chardonnay, Chenin Blanc

🕰 1–3 years (up to 12 for vintages)

√ *Antech* (Flascon des Maïstre) • *Robert* (Dame Robert, Maistre Blanquetiers) • *Sieur d'Arques* (Aimery Princesse)

BLANQUETTE MÉTHODE ANCESTRALE AOC

Formerly called Vin de Blanquette, but still produced by the ancient *méthode rurale*.

SPARKLING WHITE These succulently sweet sparkling wines are a hedonist's dream and should be far more commercially available. The ancient *méthode rurale* should be perfected so that prestige *cuvées* can be sold at a premium, allowing Limoux to capitalize on its historical value and individual wines' reputation.

🍇 Mauzac

√ *Sieur d'Arques* (Dame d'Arques)

CABARDÈS AOC

An obscure appellation north of Carcassonne, these wines were once sold as Côtes du Cabardès et de l'Orbiel VDQS, but this hardly tripped off the tongue, thus the shortened form was in common usage long before the appellation was promoted to full AOC status in 1999, when the *encépagement* changed.

RED The best wines have elegant fruit and a leaner, more Bordeaux-like balance than most of the warmer, spicy-ripe southern French reds.

🍇 At least 40% Grenache and Syrah, plus a minimum of 40% Cabernet Franc, Cabernet Sauvignon, and Merlot (Aubun and Carignan are no longer allowed)

🕰 3–8 years

ROSÉ A rich, fruity, well-coloured rosé.

🍇 At least 40% Grenache and Syrah, plus a minimum of 40% Cabernet Franc, Cabernet Sauvignon, and Merlot (Aubun and Carignan are no longer allowed)

🕰 Between 2–3 years

√ *Château de La Bastide* (L'Esprit) • *Claude et Michelle Carayol* (Cabrol Vent d'Est) • *Château de Pennautier* (L'Esprit) • *Château Ventenac* (Le Carla)

CLAIRETTE DE BELLEGARDE AOC

When compared with all the best *vins de pays*, this appellation, which is dedicated to the lowly, intrinsically flabby Clairette grape, does not deserve to be an AOC.

WHITE Unimpressive dry white wines.

🍇 Clairette

🕰 Before Christmas of the year of production

CLAIRETTE DU LANGUEDOC AOC

The appellation of Clairette du Languedoc covers three basic wine types. These are natural, fortified, and *rancio*. The *rancio* must be aged in sealed casks for at least three years, and can be produced in both natural and fortified styles.

WHITE The natural wine is fuller and richer than Bellegarde, but has more alcohol and less sweetness in its *rancio* form. The fortified version is off-dry to medium-sweet, with a resinous flavour that is stronger in *rancio* character than the natural white.

🍇 Clairette

🕰 1–3 years for naturally fermented wines, 8–20 years for fortified wines and *rancio* wines

√ *Saint Rome* (Moelleux)

CLAIRETTE DU LANGUEDOC "RANCIO" AOC
See Clairette du Languedoc AOC

LA CLAPE AOC

These red, white, and rosé wines come from vineyards on a limestone outcrop extending across five communes of the Aude *département* where the appellations of Coteaux du Languedoc and Corbières overlap. One of only two whites allowed under the Coteaux du Languedoc Villages appellation, it must be made from at least 60 per cent Bourboulenc and Grenache Blanc. White La Clape can be full, fine, and golden or firm, with an attractive Mediterranean spice, and is generally more expensive than the red. But the latter is easily best, with its full, rich flavour and *vin de garde* style. The rosé is refreshing, light, and well worth seeking out.

√ *Château de l'Anglès* • *Ferri Arnaud* (Romain Elevé en Fûts de Chêne) • *Château de Camplazens* • *Château l'Hospitalet* • *Château de la Négly* (La Falaise) • *Château Pech Redon* • *Château Rouquette-sur-Mer* (Henry Lapierre) • *Mas du Soleilla*

COLLIOURE AOC

An obscure but exciting appellation for unfortified wines from normally harvested grapes grown in Banyuls.

RED These deep, dark, and powerful wines have a full and concentrated fruit flavour, with a soft, spicy aftertaste.

🍇 At least 60% (in total) of Grenache, Mourvèdre, and Syrah (no variety may exceed 90%), plus

Cinsault and no more than 30% Carignan (Grenache Gris is no longer allowed)

🕰 2–10 years

WHITE These wines had to be sold as Vin de Pays de la Côte Vermeille until 2002, when white Collioure was first allowed.

🍇 Minimum of 70% in total of Grenache Blanc and/or Grenache Gris, plus a maximum of 30% in total (and individually a maximum of 15%) of Malvoisie, Macabéo, Marsanne, Rousanne, and Vermentino

🕰 1–3 years

ROSÉ I have not encountered these wines.

🍇 Same as for red

🕰 Upon purchase

√ *Château des Abelles* • *Du Mas Blanc* (Les Junquets) • *Mas Cornet* • *Celliers des Templiers* (Abbaye de Valbonne) • *Madeloc* (Magenca) • *De la Rectorie* • *De la Tour Vieille* (Puig Oriol) • *Du Traginer* (Octobre)

CORBIÈRES AOC

When this appellation was elevated to full AOC status in December 1985, its area of production was practically halved to its current realm of 23,000 hectares (57,000 acres). The top estates often use carbonic maceration, followed by 12 months or so in new oak and the results can be stunning. There is such a great diversity of *terroirs* in the appellation. This has led to the unofficial formation of 11 internal zones, only one of which, Boutenac, has achieved its own AOC status (*see* Corbières-Boutenac). The other 10 are: **Durban** (wedged between the two hilly halves of Fitou, this zone is cut off from any Mediterranean influence); **Fontfroide** (extending from the northern tip of Durban to the western outskirts of Narbonne, this zone has a very low rainfall and is well suited to Mourvèdre); **Lagrasse** (protected limestone valley vineyards immediately west of Boutenac); **Lézignan** (a low plateau of gravelly vineyards in the most northerly zone of Corbières); **Montagne d'Alaric** (northerly zone just west of Lézignan, with vines growing on well-drained slopes of gravel over limestone); **Quéribus** (most southerly zone, with vineyards on high, stony slopes); **St-Victor** (the very heart of Corbières); **Serviès** (the northwestern perimeter, the wettest zone, with calcareous-clay soils particularly well suited to Syrah); **Sigean** (the coastal strip of Corbières, where Syrah performs best); **Termenès** (the western perimeter, between Serviès and Quéribus, with the highest vineyards in the appellation).

RED These wines have an excellent colour, a full, spicy-fruity nose, and a creamy-clean, soft palate that often hints of cherries, raspberries, and vanilla.

🍇 A minimum of 50% of Grenache, Lladoner Pelut, Mourvèdre, and Syrah, plus Carignan, Picpoul Noir, Terret, and a maximum of 20% Cinsault (Macabéo and Bourboulenc are no longer allowed)

🍷 2–5 years (3–8 years in exceptional cases)

WHITE Soft, almost clinically clean, dry wines that have acquired a more aromatic character in recent vintages – Château Meunier St-Louis is probably the best example – but many of the wines should be more expressive. There have been some successful experiments with oak fermentation. These wines may be sold from 1 December following the harvest without any mention of *primeur* or *nouveau*.

🍇 Bourboulenc, Grenache Blanc, Macabéo, Marsanne, Roussanne, and Vermentino, plus a maximum of 10% Clairette, Muscat Blanc à Petit Grains, Picpoul, and Terret

🍷 1–3 years

ROSÉ The best of these dry wines have an attractive colour and a pleasant, floral aroma, but are nothing special.

🍇 A minimum of 50% of Grenache, Lladoner Pelut, Mourvèdre, and Syrah, plus Carignan, Picpoul Noir, Terret Noir, a maximum of 20% Cinsault, and no more than 10% Bourboulenc, Grenache Blanc, Macabéo, Marsanne, Roussanne, and Vermentino, plus a maximum of 10% Clairette, Muscat Blanc à Petit Grains, Picpoul, and Terret

🍷 1–3 years

✓ *Clos de L'Anhel* • *Des Chandelles* • *Clos Canos* (Les Cocobirous) • *Desmoiselles* (Blanc de Blancs) • *Château des Erles* (La Recaoufa) • *CV de Gruissan* (Elevé en Fûts de Chêne) • *Château de Mansenoble* (Marie-Annick, Réserve) • *CV du Mont Ténarel d'Octaviana* (Sextant) • *Les Clos Perdus* ❷ • *Château de Romilhac* (Privilège) • *Rouire-Ségur* (Vieilles Vignes) • *Château la Voulte-Gasparets* (Romain Pauc)

CORBIÈRES-BOUTENAC AOC

This appellation in the central-northern district of Corbières is the first internal zone to achieve its own AOC status, and it encompasses nine villages in addition to Boutenac itself (Fabrezan, Ferrals-les-Corbières, Lézignan-Corbières, Luc-sur-Orbieu, Montséret, Ornaisons, Saint-André-de-Roquelongue, Saint-Laurent-de-la-Cabrerisse, and Thézan-des-Corbières). All the grapes must be manually harvested.

RED More black fruits than most Corbières.

🍇 At least 70% Carignan, Grenache, and Mourvèdre (but no one variety may represent more than 80% of the blend), plus optional Syrah

🍷 3–10 years

✓ *Château la Voulte-Gasparets*

COSTIÈRES DE NÎMES AOC

ARMONIÓ 2002

Upgraded from a VDQS called Costières du Gard in 1986.

RED Simple, light, fruity wines are the norm, yet the best are round, aromatic, and spicy.

🍇 A maximum of 40% (each) Carignan and Cinsault, a minimum of 25% Grenache, and at least 20% (in total or each) of Mourvèdre and Syrah

🍷 2–3 years (average wines), 3–8 years (better *cuvées*)

WHITE Fresh, soft, but uninspiring. These wines may be sold from 1 December following the harvest without any mention of *primeur* or *nouveau*.

🍇 A blend of at least two varieties including Bourboulenc, Clairette, Grenache, Macabéo, Marsanne, Roussanne, a maximum of 30% Ugni Blanc (not permitted as from 2010), Vermentino, and a maximum of 10% Viognier

🍷 1–2 years

ROSÉ Good-value dry wine with a delightful colour and ripe fruit. These wines may be sold from 1 December following the harvest without any mention of *primeur* or *nouveau*.

🍇 A maximum of 40% (each) of Carignan and Cinsault, a minimum of 25% Grenache, at least 20% (in total or each) of Mourvèdre and Syrah, plus up to 10% (in total) of Clairette, Grenache Blanc, Bourboulenc, Ugni Blanc, Marsanne, Roussanne, Macabéo, Vermentino, and Viognier

🍷 Within 1–2 years

✓ *Château Amphoux* (Les Galion des Crêtes Elevé en Fûts de Chêne) • *Barbe-Caillette* (Haut Jovis) • *Château Grande Cassagne* • *Marc Kreydenweiss* ◉ • *Château Lamargue* (Aegidiane) • *Mas Neuf* • *Château d'Or et de Gueles* • *Château La Tour de Beraud* • *Château Tuilerie* (Carte Blanche) • *Château de Valcombe* (Garence)

CÔTES DU ROUSSILLON AOC

Situated south of Corbières, this appellation began to shrug off the reputation that typified the wines of the Midi long before Languedoc.

RED The best of these wines have a good colour and a generosity of southern fruit, with the tiniest hint of vanilla and spice. They may be sold as *primeur* or *nouveau* from the third Thursday of November following the harvest.

🍇 A blend of at least three of the following varieties, no two of which may exceed 90% of the total: Carignan (60% maximum), Cinsault, Grenache, Lladoner Pelut, Macabéo (10% maximum), Mourvèdre, and Syrah (there must be at least 20% of Syrah and/or Mourvèdre)

🍷 3–8 years

WHITE The best of these floral wines were fat, and all too often lacked acidity, prior to the change of *encépagement* in 2002. (So was 2003, but that was the vintage, rather than the varietal mix.) They may be sold as *primeur* or *nouveau* from the third Thursday of November following the harvest.

🍇 At least 50% of Grenache, Macabéo, and Tourbat, plus a minimum of 20% Marsanne, Roussanne, and Vermentino (all varieties obligatory)

🍷 1–2 years

ROSÉ Fresh and attractive dry wines, these rosés may be sold as *primeur* or *nouveau* from the third Thursday of November following the harvest.

🍇 As for red

🍷 1–2 years

✓ *Alquier* (Des Filles) • *Mas Amiel* • *Mas des Baux* (Soleil) • *De Casenove* • *CV Catalans* • *Mas Crémat* (Dédicace, La Llose) • *Cazes Frères* • *Clos des Fées* • *Jaubert-Noury* (Château Planères) • *Joliette* (André Mercier) • *Lafage* (Le Vignon) • *Du Mas Rous* (Elevé en Fûts de Chêne) • *Mosse* (Tradition) • *CV de Passa* (Mas d'en Badie) • *Piquemal* • *Primo Palatum* • *Pujols* (La Montadella) • *Château de Rey* (Les Galets Roulés) • *Sarda-Malet* • *Sol-Payre* (Scelerata Ame Noire)

CÔTES DU ROUSSILLON LES ASPRES AOC

New red-wine-only designation for Côtes du Roussillon (not Villages), Les Aspres must be produced from at least three varieties, with a minimum of 50 per cent Grenache, Mourvèdre, and Syrah (the latter two representing at least 20 per cent of the entire blend), plus a maximum of 20 per cent Carignan. Too early to critique.

CÔTES DU ROUSSILLON VILLAGES AOC

This appellation encompasses exclusively red wines from 25 villages along the Agly River and its hinterland in the best area of the Côtes du Roussillon. The *encépagement* changed in 2003.

RED Just as good value as basic Côtes du Roussillon, the best can have even more character and finesse.

🍇 A blend of at least three of the following varieties, no two of which may exceed 90% of the total: Carignan (60% maximum), Cinsault, Grenache, Lladoner Pelut, Macabéo (10% maximum), Mourvèdre, and Syrah (furthermore, there must be at least 30% of Syrah and/or Mourvèdre)

🍷 3–10 years

✓ *Château Aymerich* (Général Joseph Aymerich) • *Château de Caladroy* (La Juliane) • *Clot de L'Oum* (Saint Bart Vieilles Vignes) • *Clos des Fées* • *Força Real* (Hauts de Força) • *Gardiés* • *Haute Coutume* (Schistes de Trémoine) • *Mas de Lavail* (Tradition) • *Château Planezes* (Elevé en Fûts de Chêne) • *Des Schistes* (Tradition)

CÔTES DU ROUSSILLON VILLAGES CARAMANY AOC

This super-value red wine conforms to the requirements of Côtes du Roussillon Villages, except for a minimum Syrah content and the stipulation that the Carignan must be vinified by carbonic maceration. (This seemingly strange criterion stems from the fact that, in 1964, the local *coopérative* claimed to be the first in France to use this technique.)

RED Simply the fullest, richest, and longest-living wines of Roussillon, despite the carbonic maceration, which just goes to prove how useful that process can be when used to lift the natural fruit of a wine instead of dominating it with peardrop aromas.

🍇 As for Côtes du Roussillon Villages except that there must be at least 25% Syrah

🍷 3–15 years

✓ *CV Catalans*

CÔTES DU ROUSSILLON VILLAGES LATOUR-DE-FRANCE AOC

This is a fine-value red wine that conforms to the requirements of Côtes du Roussillon Villages. Virtually the entire production of Latour-de-France used to be sold to, and through, the national French wine-shop group Nicolas, which was a great advantage when this village obtained its own appellation, as its seemingly cheeky name was already known the length and breadth of the country.

RED Full in colour and body, these fine-value wines have a fruity flavour.

⌇— 3–15 years

✓ *De L'Ausseil* (La Capitelle)

CÔTES DU ROUSSILLON VILLAGES LESQUERDE AOC

Restricted to vines growing in the villages of Lansac, Lesquerde, and Rasiguères. It conforms to the requirements of Côtes du Roussillon Villages, except for some of the *encépagement* and the stipulation that the Carignan must be vinified by carbonic maceration (*see* Côtes du Roussillon Caramany for explanation).

RED Rich, well-coloured wines that deserve their own village designation.

🍇 As for Côtes du Roussillon Villages except that Macabéo is not allowed, and there must be at least 30% Syrah and Mourvèdre

⌇— 3–15 years

✓ *Semper* (Voluptas) • *CV de Tautavel* (Tradition)

CÔTES DU ROUSSILLON VILLAGES TAUTAVEL AOC

Restricted to vines growing in the villages of Tautavel and Vingrau. It conforms to the requirements of Côtes du Roussillon Villages, except for some of the *encépagement*, the stipulation that at least 50 per cent of the Carignan content must be vinified by carbonic maceration (*see* Côtes du Roussillon Caramany for explanation), and the fact that the wines may not be released for sale prior to 1 October following the year of harvest.

RED Rich, well-coloured wines that deserve their own village designation.

🍇 As for Côtes du Roussillon Villages except that Macabéo is not allowed, and there must be at least 20% Grenache and Lladoner Pelut, and no more than 50% Carignan

⌇— 3–15 years

✓ *Des Chênes* (La Carissa) • *Fontanel* (Prieuré Elevé en Fûts de Chêne)

CRÉMANT DE LIMOUX AOC

This sparkling wine was introduced in 1989 to allow producers to decide the future name of their appellation: Blanquette de Limoux or Crémant de Limoux. The former relied primarily on the Mauzac grape and Crémant de Limoux on Chardonnay and Chenin Blanc. The choice was not merely about a name, but what direction and style the wine should follow. It was thought that Mauzac-based Blanquette de Limoux would take the slow lane while Chardonnay-influenced Crémant would be in the fast lane. By law, they should have made this decision by the end of 1994, but Crémant de Limoux did not take off as anticipated. Both styles deserve to exist.

SPARKLING WHITE Chardonnay tends to be the main base, with just enough Mauzac retained to assure a certain style, and Chenin Blanc is used as a natural form of acid adjustment. The wines are generally more refined than Blanquette de Limoux, and the best have a finesse that the more traditional products cannot match.

🍇 A maximum of 90% in total of Chardonnay and Chenin Blanc, including at least 20% of the latter, plus a maximum of 20% in total of Mauzac and Pinot Noir, with the latter restricted to no more than 10%

✓ *De l'Aigle* • *Sieur d'Arques* • *Veuve Tailhan*

FAUGÈRES AOC

Although fair-sized, Faugères is an obscure and overlooked appellation, probably due to the fact that it was formerly known for *eau-de-vie* and fortified Muscat, with red wine a post-war development. Despite the similarity between the schistous, hillside vineyards and grape varieties here and in neighbouring St-Chinian, the two appellations make distinctly different wines.

RED These rustic wines have a deep colour and are heavy with the spicy, warm flavours of Cinsault and Carignan.

⌇— 3–10 years

WHITE Fresh, exotic fruits with a touch of zest.

🍇 A minimum of two grape varieties, including at least 30% Roussanne, plus Grenache Blanc, Marsanne, and Vermentino. Also permitted up to a maximum of 10% each are Clairette and (if planted before 2005) Bourboulenc, and (if planted before 1998) Carignan or Macabéo

⌇— 1–3 years

ROSÉ Small production of attractively coloured, ripe, and fruity dry rosés. These wines may be sold as from 1 December following the harvest without any mention of *primeur* or *nouveau*.

🍇 A maximum of 40% Carignan, and no more than 20% Cinsault, plus at least 20% Grenache and/or Lladoner Pelut, a minimum of 15% Syrah, and at least 5% Mourvèdre (furthermore Grenache, Lladoner Pelut, Mourvèdre, and Syrah represent at least 50% of the entire blend)

⌇— 1–2 years

✓ *Alquier* • *Château des Estanilles* • *Abbaye de Sylva Plana*

FITOU AOC

When it was made an AOC in 1948, Fitou was fast asleep. But wine buyers beat a path to its desolate door in the early 1980s, making it the fastest-rising star in the Mediterranean firmament. It seems to have returned to its dozing state. The *encépagement* changed in 2001.

RED Even at the lowest level, these wines have a fine colour and a spicy warmth of Grenache that curbs and softens the concentrated fruit and tannin of low-yielding Carignan.

🍇 A minimum of 30% Carignan, plus Mourvèdre, Syrah, and at least 30% Grenache and Lladoner Pelut; within this Carignan, Grenache, and Lladoner Pelut must account for at least 70% of the entire blend; and until 2007 there must be at least 10% Cinsault, while as from 2008 there must be at least 10% Mourvèdre (Macabéo and Terret Noir are no longer allowed)

⌇— 3–6 years (4–10 years in exceptional cases)

✓ *Bertrand Bergé* • *Château des Erles* • *CV de Mont Tauch* (Seigneur de Don Neuve) • *Château de Nouvelles* • *De la Rochelière* (Noblesse du Temps) • *De Roland*

FRONTIGNAN AOC
See Muscat de Frontignan AOC

GRAND ROUSSILLON AOC

The largest appellation producing the smallest amount of wine, Grand Roussillon is a VDN that encompasses 100 communes, yet produces as little as 30 hectolitres (330 cases) of wine per year. This has nothing to do with low yields or a strict selection process – the appellation is apparently used as a sort of *sous marque* or dumping ground for the inferior wines produced by the better VDNs within its boundaries.

🍇 Muscat d'Alexandrie, Muscat Petits Grains, Grenache (Gris, Blanc, and Noir), Macabéo, Tourbat, plus up to 10% (in total) of Carignan, Cinsault, Syrah, and Listan

GRAND ROUSSILLON "RANCIO" AOC
See Grand Roussillon AOC

LANGUEDOC AOC

This appellation consists of a collection of areas strung out across three *départements*, which gives rise to a variation in style, but the quality is remarkably consistent.

RED Full and honest red wines that make excellent everyday drinking. These wines may be sold as *primeur* or *nouveau* from the third Thursday of November following the harvest.

🍇 A minimum of 50% Grenache (itself limited to maximum of 40%), Lladoner Pelut, Mourvèdre, and Syrah (these last two must represent at least 10% of the entire blend), no more than 40% of either Carignan or Cinsault, plus a maximum of 10% (in total) Counoise, Grenache Gris, Terret, and Picpoul Noir

⌇— 1–4 years

WHITE Getting better by the day, some wonderfully fresh, aromatic, dry white wines are being made by the appellation's younger *vignerons*, often with a little new oak and not infrequently from very old vines. These wines may be sold from 1 December of the vintage indicated without any mention of *primeur* or *nouveau*.

🍇 Bourboulenc, Clairette, Grenache Blanc, Picpoul, Marsanne, Roussanne, Vermentino, plus a maximum of 30% Macabéo, Terret Blanc, Carignan Blanc, and Ugni Blanc (growers may no longer plant Carignan Blanc, Macabéo, or Ugni Blanc)

ROSÉ These dry wines have good fruit and are far more enjoyable than many a pricey Provence rosé. These wines may be sold as *primeur* or *nouveau* from the third Thursday of November following the harvest.

🍇 As for red, plus the following may be included with the optional maximum 10%: Bourboulenc, Carignan Blanc, Clairette, Grenache, Macabéo, Marsanne, Roussanne, Ugni Blanc, and Vermentino

⌇— 1–2 years

✓ *De l'Aiguelière* • *Des Aires Hautes* • *Mas Bayle* (Grande Cuvée) • *Mas Beles Eaux* • *Borie de la Vitarèle* • *Château Chenaie* (Le Douves Blanches) • *Château La Clotte-Fontaine* (Mouton) • *Château des Crès Ricards* (Les Hauts de Milési) • *Dupéré-Barrera* (Chien de Prairie) • *Château Daurion* (Prestige Elevé en Fûts de Chêne) • *CV La Fontesole* (Prieuré Saint-Hippolyte) • *De Ganoupiac* (Les Cresses) • *Château Grès Saint Paul* (Antonin) • *Mas Haut-Buis* (Costa Caoude) • *De l'Hortus* • *Virgile Joly* (Virgile) • *Château de Lascaux* (Les Secrets) • *Mas Lumen* (La Sylve) • *Paul Mas* • *Château de Montpezat* (La Pharaonne) • *Château de la Négly* (L'Ancely) • *Peyre Rose* ⦿ • *Prieuré St-Jean de Bébian* • *De Roquemale* • *CV de Saint-Saturnin* • *Château de Sérame* • *Mas de la Seranne* (Les Griottiers) • *Le Clos du*

Serres (Le Florilège) • *De Serres Cabanis* (Bos de Canna) • *Mas du Soleilla* • *Les Souls* • *Château Le Thou* (Georges et Clem)

LANGUEDOC (VILLAGE NAME) AOC

Except where stated, the wines bearing the names of the following villages conform to the requirements of Coteaux du Languedoc AOC.

CABRIÈRES AOC

This is a single commune of steep schistous slopes in the centre of the Clairette du Languedoc sub-appellation. Cabrières's production is dominated by the local *coopérative*. This village produces mostly rosé: a fine, firm, and racy wine that contains more Cinsault than other Languedoc rosés. A little red is also produced, and its *vin vermeil*, so-called because of its vivid vermilion colour, is best known.

✓ *Du Temple* (Jacques de Molay)

COTEAUX DE LA MÉJANELLE AOC
See La Méjanelle AOC

COTEAUX DE ST-CHRISTOL AOC
See St-Christol AOC

COTEAUX DE VÉRARGUES AOC
See Vérargues AOC

GRÈS DE MONTPELLIER AOC

New red-wine-only appellation as from the 2002 vintage, Grès de Montpellier effectively encompasses the Coteaux du Languedoc Villages designations of St-Christol, St-Drézéry, St-Georges-d'Orques, and Vérargues. It must be produced from at least 70 per cent in total of Grenache (itself a minimum of 20 per cent), Mourvèdre, Syrah, and up to 30 per cent Carignan.

✓ *Château Peuch Haut*

LA MÉJANELLE AOC

This appellation, which may also be sold as Coteaux de la Méjanelle, covers four communes in an area once part of the Rhône delta – river-smoothed boulders litter the vineyards. Rosé is permitted, but La Méjanelle produces mostly red wines of a dark, rich, and well-structured *vin de garde* style. Château de Flaugergues consistently ranks as the best.

✓ *Château de Flaugergues* (Sommelière)

MONTPEYROUX AOC

This village is located on schistous hills next to St-Saturnin, just north of the Clairette du Languedoc sub-appellation. The style of all but the best of these red and rosé wines is firm and somewhat rustic, but they are honest and pleasing, and those recommended below rank among the finest in Languedoc.

✓ *D'Aupilhac* • *Des Grecaux* (Hêméra) • *Château de Lancyre* (Vieilles Vignes)

PÉZENAS AOC

Prieuré de Saint-Jean-de-Bébian, owned by Chantal Lecouty and Jean-Claude Le Brun, former editors of the *Revue du Vin*, demonstrate the potential here (although still sold as a straight Coteaux du Languedoc AOC).

✓ *Prieuré de Saint-Jean-de-Bébian*

PICPOUL-DE-PINET AOC

Covering six communes, this white-wine-only appellation must be made, as the name suggests, from 100 per cent Picpoul, which in Pinet produces a lively young wine that quickly tires, and thus must be drunk as young as possible. Gaujal is undoubtedly the best.

✓ *Château Font-Mars* • *CV de Florensac* (Ressac Prestige) • *Des Lauriers*

PIC-ST-LOUP AOC

Red and rosé wines from 12 communes in Hérault and one in Gard, all in the vicinity of the *pic*, or peak, of Pic St-Loup, including some high-altitude locations that must rank among the coolest vineyards in southern France. Permitted grape varieties for Pic-St-Loup break from the norm – red wines must be made from a blend of at least two of the following: Grenache, Mourvèdre, and Syrah (no minimum or maximum restrictions), plus up to 10 per cent Carignan and Cinsault (Counoise, Grenache Gris, Terret Noir, Picpoul Noir, and Lladoner Pelut are not allowed). The grapes for rosé are the same, except that Carignan is excluded and as much as 30 per cent Cinsault may be used.

✓ *Devois du Claus* (Elevé en Fûts de Chêne) • *Foulaquier* (Les Chalades) • *Mas Gourdou* (Les Roches Blanches) • *De l'Hortus* • *Clos Marie* • *Morties* (Que Sera Sera) • *Château Taurus-Montel* (Prestige Elevé en Fûts de Chêne)

QUATOURZE AOC

These sandy-soil vineyards just south of Narbonne overlap the Corbières appellation, but the wines, mostly red with some rosé, are rather stern and four-square, although the best can fill out and soften up with a few years in bottle. I have tasted nothing recommendable from this village since the last edition.

ST-CHRISTOL AOC

Just north of Lunel, the calcareous-clay soil of St-Christol produces ripe, spicy, well-balanced red and rosé wines that may also be sold as Coteaux de St-Christol AOC. The local *coopérative* dominates production.

✓ *De la Coste* (Sélectionné) • *Guinand* (Elevé en Fûts de Chêne) • *Gabriel Martin* • *CV de St-Christol*

ST-DRÉZÉRY AOC

Both red and rosé wines are allowed under this village appellation north of Montpellier, but I have encountered only reds, and those have been of a very modest quality.

ST-GEORGES-D'ORQUES AOC

Just west of Montpellier, the St-Georges-d'Orques appellation extends over five communes and produces mostly red wines of very good colour, plenty of fruit, and no little finesse for this unpretentious Languedoc appellation. A small quantity of rosé is also made, the best having a bouquet of dried flowers and some summer fruits on the palate.

✓ *Château de l'Engarran* (Quetton Saint-Georges) • *Château Icard* (Elevé en Fûts de Chêne) • *Les Quatre Pilas*

ST-SATURNIN AOC

Named after the first bishop of Toulouse, these red and rosé wines come from three communes in the foothills of the Cévennes Mountains, just west of Montpeyroux, where deep-coloured, fine, and full-flavoured red wines are possible, if not always evident. Production is dominated by the *coopératives* of St-Félix-de-Lodez and St-Saturnin, the former specializing in a pleasant, slightly *pétillant* rosé, while the latter makes a *vin d'une nuit*, a light-bodied red that has been macerated for only one night.

✓ *Lucian* • *Virgile Joly*

TERRASSES DE BÉZIERS AOC

Although the *syndicat* representing this appellation has existed since 1990, the wines have yet to appear on the shelf.

TERRASSES DU LARZAC AOC

Terrasses du Larzac is another *coteaux* appellation that still has to put wines on the shelf bearing its own individual name. However, Le Mas de l'Ecriture already produces some of the most exciting wines in the south of France from these vineyards, albeit under the straight Coteaux du Languedoc AOC.

✓ *Mas Cal Demoura* • *Le Mas de l'Ecriture* • *Mas Jullien* • *La Sauvageonne*

TERRES DE SOMMIÈRES AOC

This is still something of a work in progress!

VÉRARGUES AOC

Vérargues produces large quantities of quaffing, but otherwise unexceptional red and rosé wines from nine communes, four of which also constitute the Muscat de Lunel appellation. They are also sold as Coteaux de Vérargues AOC.

✓ *Château du Grès-St-Paul*

LIMOUX AOC

In 1993, Limoux became the first French AOC to insist upon barrel fermentation and some fabulous successes quickly established an enviable reputation for the Chardonnay-dominated wines of this appellation. The only question now is will Limoux have equal success with Chenin Blanc? A new red Limoux was introduced in 2004.

RED Too early to tell. We need to see more wines made by different producers, since the cooperative Cave Anne de Joyeuse currently churns out some 70% of the total production.

🐝 Minimum of 50% Merlot, plus Cabernet Franc, Cabernet Sauvignon, Carignan, Grenache, Malbec and Syrah. Carignan must not exceed 10% and is due to be phased out by 2010. There must be at least three varieties, no two of which may exceed 90% of the blend.

🍷— 3–6 years

WHITE Although every wine must contain at least 15 per cent Mauzac, you will encounter supposedly pure Chardonnay and Chenin Blanc varietal wines (and Mauzac, of course). This is explained by the European Union law that requires that a pure varietal wine must contain at least 85 per cent of the grape named. Chardonnay varietals are sherbetty-fresh with a zesty style at minimum; the best are beautifully rich, with succulent, lemony-oaky fruit and mouth-watering acidity. The pure Mauzac from Rives-Blanques makes me wonder whether it would not be better for producers to focus on this, their local grape, rather than resign themselves to making yet another Chardonnay in a world awash with that variety. This was not initially my view. Tasted when first released, the Chardonnay clearly outshines the

Mauzac, thus it is little wonder that the Cuvée Occitania hoovers up so many medals for Rives-Blanques. However, follow them in bottle for just 12 months, and the Mauzac evolves into the more expressive wine.

🐝 A minimum of 15% Mauzac, plus Chardonnay and Chenin Blanc

🍷 1–2 years

✓ *D'Antugnac* (Gravas) • *Rives-Blanques* (Dédicace) • *Sieur d'Arques* (Toques et Clochers)

MALEPÈRE AOC

Between the Razès *coopérative* and Domaines Virginie (Des Bruyère), this is becoming one of the fastest-rising, value-for-money, superb-quality appellations in Languedoc-Roussillon. Upgraded from Côtes de la Malepère VDQS to Malepère AOC in 2007.

RED Well-coloured wines of medium to full body, with elegant, deliciously spicy fruit.

🐝 A minimum of 50% Merlot, at least 20% Cabernet Franc and Malbec, plus optional Cabernet Sauvignon, Cinsault, Grenache, and Lladoner Pelut (Syrah is no longer allowed)

🍷 3–7 years

ROSÉ These attractive dry wines are totally different from the reds, due to the greater use and mellow effect of Grenache.

🐝 A minimum of 70% Cabernet Franc, Cinsault, and Grenache, plus optional Cabernet Sauvignon, Malbec, Merlot, and Syrah (Lladoner Pelut is no longer allowed, and growers must not plant any more Syrah)

🍷 1–3 years

✓ *Château de Barthe* • *Girard* (Neri) • *Château Guilhem* (Prestige) • *Château Guiraud*

MAURY AOC

Despite the long list of possibilities, these fortified wines are mostly pure Grenache, a fact that is recognized by the gradual increase in the compulsory percentage of this grape – the minimum was just 50 per cent 15 years ago.

RED/WHITE/ROSÉ/TAWNY Pale and intricate wines, they have a combination of tangy, toasty, berry flavours and nutty-raisiny richness.

🐝 At least 75% Grenache (a minimum of 70% for pre-2000 vintages), a maximum of 10% Macabéo (15% for pre-2000 vintages), plus Grenache Gris, Grenache Blanc, Muscat à Petits Grains, Muscat d'Alexandrie, Tourbat, and a combined maximum of 10% of Carignan, Cinsault, Syrah, and Listan Negra

🍷 10–30 years

✓ *Mas Amiel* • *Jean-Louis Lafage* (Prestige Vieilli en Fûts de Chêne) • *CV de Maury* (Solera 1928 Cask No.886) • *Pouderoux* • *La Preceptorie de Centernach*

MAURY "RANCIO" AOC

See Maury AOC

MINERVOIS AOC

North of Corbières and adjoining the western extremity of the Coteaux du Languedoc, the rocky Minervois area has the typically hot and arid air of southern France. Elevated to full AOC status in February 1985, its vineyards are divided into zones. As in Corbières, these are not official, but one day they may in part or whole join La Livinière, which was recognized as a cru in its own

right in 1999. The zones are: L'Argent Double (rough, rugged vineyards amid rocky outcrops in the arid heart of Minervois); La Clamoux (a cooler western area with a touch more rainfall than most Minervois zones, with Grenache and Syrah doing well, particularly on the higher-altitude vineyards); La Clause (rugged, mountain climate and stony, *terra rosa* soil combine to produce rather rustic *vins de garde* in the north of Minervois); Les Côtes Noires (under a harsh mountain climate, these high-altitude vineyards situated in the northwestern corner of Minervois are better suited to the production of white wine rather than of red); Le Petit Causse (when it can get enough moisture, Mourvèdre does well on these baking-hot, sheltered, limestone slopes in the arid heart of Minervois – La Livinière is located at the heart of Le Petit Causse); Les Serres (very dry, stony vineyards over limestone subsoil, mostly planted with Carignan). The *encépagement* for red and rosé changed in 2003.

RED At worst, these wines are rough and ready for an AOC, but some of the best domaines also produce *vins de pays* that are better than the Minervois of other properties, thus their Minervois can be very good indeed.

🐝 A minimum of 40% Grenache, Lladoner Pelut, Mourvèdre, and Syrah (these last two must represent at least 10% of the entire blend, and at least 20% as from 2006), plus optional Aspiran Noir, Carignan, Cinsault, Picpoul Noir, and Terret Noir

🍷 1–5 years

WHITE Less than one per cent of Minervois is white. A simple, dry, and fruity wine fermented at cooler temperatures than was once standard, it is now fresher and more aromatic.

🐝 Bourboulenc, Grenache Blanc, Macabéo, Marsanne, Roussanne, Vermentino, plus not more than 20% Clairette, Muscat à Petits Grains (itself limited to a maximum of 10%), Picpoul, and Terret Blanc

🍷 Within 1 year

ROSÉ Most of these are good-value wines with a pretty pink colour and a dry, fruity flavour.

🐝 A minimum of 40% Grenache, Lladoner Pelut, Mourvèdre, and Syrah (these last two must represent at least 10% of the entire blend, and at least 20% as from 2006), plus optional Aspiran Noir, Carignan, Cinsault, Picpoul Noir, and Terret Noir, with no more than 10% Bourboulenc, Clairette, Grenache Blanc, Macabéo, Marsanne, Roussanne, Muscat à Petits Grains, Picpoul, Terret Blanc, and Vermentino

🍷 Within 1 year

✓ *Des Aires Hautes* • *Borie de Maurel* (Sylla) • *Le Cazal* (Le Paps de Zarat) • *Hegarty Chamans* • *Château Maris* • *Château d'Oupia* (Oppius) • *Primo Palatum* • *Du Roc* (Passion) • *Saint-Jacques d'Albas* • *La Tour Buisse*

MINERVOIS LA LIVINIÈRE AOC

Located in Le Petit Causse, the central-northern zone of Minervois, La Livinière was in 1999 the first *cru* in this appellation to be recognized in its own right. The vines grow on the best areas of the Petit Causse, the sheltered, limestone cliffs that skirt the foot of the Montagne Noir at a height of 140 metres (460 feet).

RED Where there is sufficient finesse to match the structure of these wines, they represent some of Minervois's best *vins de garde*.

🐝 A minimum of 40% Grenache, Lladoner Pelut,

Mourvèdre, and Syrah (these last two must represent at least 10% of the entire blend, and at least 20% as from 2006), plus optional Aspiran Noir, Carignan, Cinsault, Picpoul Noir, and Terret Noir

🍷 2–10 years

✓ *Clos de L'Escandil* • *CV des Crus de Haut-Minervois* (Gaïa) • *Château Faiteau*

MUSCAT DE FRONTIGNAN AOC

It is claimed that the Marquis de Lur-Saluces visited Frontignan in 1700 and it inspired him to make sweet wines at Château d'Yquem in Sauternes, but Muscat de Frontignan is no longer botrytized – it is a fortified wine. Muscat de Frontignan may either be a *vin doux naturel* (VDN) or a *vin de liqueur* (VDL). In the latter, the spirit is added to the grape juice before any fermentation whatsoever can take place. If the label does not differentiate between the two, the small green tax mark on the cap should bear the letters VDN or VDL.

WHITE The VDNs are delightful, golden-coloured, raisiny-rich, sweet, and delicious wines that have a succulent, honeyed aftertaste with a somewhat fatter style than those of Beaumes, although many lack its finesse. The VDLs are much sweeter.

🐝 Muscat Doré de Frontignan

🍷 1–3 years

✓ *Château des Aresquiers* • *Château de la Peyrade*

MUSCAT DE LUNEL AOC

Situated on limestone terraces northeast of Montpellier, this undervalued VDN approaches Frontignan in terms of pure quality.

WHITE/ROSÉ Lighter than Frontignan, these wines nevertheless have fine, fragrant Muscat aromas of great delicacy and length.

🐝 Muscat Blanc & Rosé à Petits Grains

🍷 1–3 years

✓ *Lacoste* (Clos Bellevue, Passerillé) • *CV du Muscat de Lunel* (Prestige)

MUSCAT DE MIREVAL AOC

This is a little-seen VDN appellation.

WHITE Light and sweet wines that can have a better balance and (relatively) more acidity than those from neighbouring Frontignan.

🐝 Muscat Blanc à Petits Grains

🍷 1–3 years

✓ *Château d'Exindre* (Vent d'Anges) • *Du Mas Neuf*

MUSCAT DE RIVESALTES AOC

This appellation should not be confused with the blended Rivesaltes VDNs that bear no mention of the Muscat grape.

WHITE/ROSÉ Rich, ripe, grapey-raisiny wines that are very consistent in quality.

🍇 Muscat Blanc à Petits Grains, Muscat d'Alexandrie

⏳ 1–3 years

✓ *Cazes Frères* ❸ • *Des Chênes* • *Cornelianum* • *Jean Estavel* (Prestige) • *Lafage* • *Laporte* • *Château de Nouvelles* • *Sarda-Malet* • *Des Schistes* • *Arnaud de Villeneuve*

MUSCAT DE ST-JEAN-DE-MINERVOIS AOC

This tiny sub-appellation of Minervois produces a little *vin doux naturel* that used to be grossly underrated but can be excellent.

WHITE/ROSÉ These golden wines have a balanced sweetness and an apricot flavour.

🍇 Muscat Blanc & Rosé à Petits Grains

⏳ 1–3 years

✓ *De Barroubio* • *La Muscat* (Petit Grain)

RIVESALTES AOC

This appellation represents half of the *vin doux naturel* produced in France. Optional legally defined terms include *ambré* for an oxidative style of tawny coloured Rivesaltes; *tuilé* for an oxidative red; and *grenat* for a reductive-style red that must not be bottled any later than 1 March of the second year. *Hors d'age* requires a minimum of five years' ageing.

RED/ROSÉ The warm, brick-red glow of these wines belies their astringent-sweet, chocolate, and cherry-liqueur flavour and drying, tannic finish.

🍇 A minimum of 50% (for oxidative style) or 75% (for reductive style) Grenache, plus Grenache Blanc, Grenache Gris, Tourbat, with a maximum of 10% Carignan, Cinsault, Palomino, and Syrah

⏳ 10–40 years

WHITE/TAWNY Because much of the red version can be lightened after lengthy maturation in wood, all Rivesaltes eventually merge into one tawny style with time. The whites do not, of course, have any tannic astringency and are more oxidative and raisiny, with a resinous, candied-peel character.

🍇 Grenache Blanc, Grenache Gris, Macabéo, Muscat Blanc à Petits Grains, Muscat d'Alexandrie, Muscat Romain, Tourbat (the Muscat varieties must not exceed 20% of the entire blend in total or separately)

⏳ 10–20 years

✓ *Du Mas Alart* (Ambré Hors d'Age) • *Des Chênes* • *Cazes Frères* ❸ • *Gardies* • *Château de Nouvelles* (Tuilé) • *Sarda-Malet* (La Carbasse) • *Château de Sau* (Ambré Hors d'Age) • *Terrassous* (Ambré Vinifié en Fûts de Chêne) • *Arnaud de Villeneuve* (Ambré Hors d'Age)

RIVESALTES "RANCIO" AOC

See Rivesaltes AOC

ROQUEBRUN ST-CHINIAN AOC

See St-Chinian (Villages) AOC

ST-CHINIAN AOC

This excellent-value appellation is the nearest that native southern French grapes come to Bordeaux.

Similar varieties from comparable schistous hillsides in neighbouring Faugères make an entirely different, far more rustic wine.

RED Relatively light in colour and weight, these wines have an elegance that belies their Mediterranean origin.

🍇 At least 50% in total of Grenache, Lladoner Pelut, Mourvèdre, and Syrah, plus a maximum of 40% Carignan and no more than 30% Cinsault

⏳ 2–6 years

WHITE Crisp, grassy fruits with more minerality than most whites made in Languedoc-Roussillon.

🍇 A minimum of two grape varieties, including at least 30% Grenache Blanc, plus Marsanne, Roussanne, and Vermentino. Bourboulenc, Carignan, Clairette, and Macabéo are allowed, but new plantations are not authorized.

⏳ 1–2 years

ROSÉ Dry and delicately fruity rosés with an attractive, fragrant bouquet and flavour. May be sold from 1 December following the harvest without any mention of *primeur* or *nouveau*.

🍇 Same as red

⏳ 1–3 years

✓ *Clos Bagatelle* • *Berloup* (Vignes Royales) • *Mas Canet Valette* • *De Canimals Le Haut* • *Mas Champart* • *Château de Combebelle* • *Château La Dournie* • *Fontaine Marcousse* • *Des Jougla* (Vieihs Arrasics) • *Navare* (Olivier)

ST-CHINIAN (VILLAGES) AOC

These two multi-communal village red-wine only appellations were created in 2005 and backdated to the 2004 vintage, but those wines did not appear on the shelf until 2006. The local *coopératives* dominate production under both village appellations, particularly Roquebrun, but that's no bad thing as both *coopératives* are excellent producers of very good-value wine.

BERLOU ST-CHINIAN AOC

The emphasis here is Carignan – which is not surprising, since there are some interesting old Carignan vineyards in this area – but the wines may also include Grenache, Syrah, and Mourvèdre. The vines for all varieties must be at least 10 years old (compared to being in their third year for AOCs in general).

✓ *CV de Berlou*

ROQUEBRUN ST-CHINIAN AOC

With the terrain comprised mainly of schistous hillsides, this is a distinctly Syrah-influenced wine, although Grenache and Mourvèdre may also be included.

✓ *CV de Roquebrun*

VIN DE FRONTIGNAN AOC

See Muscat de Frontignan AOC

MORE GREEN WINES

In addition to the producers recommended in this directory that are either biodynamic or organic, there are also the following. No negative inference of quality should be taken from the fact that they are not featured among the other recommended producers. There are a number that have been recommended in other editions, and still make some fine wines, but have been culled out to make room for others.

Biodynamic

Beau-Thorey (Corconne), *De Bila-Haut* (Latour de France), *De Combebelle* (Villespassans), *Jean-Claude Daumond* (Vendargues), *De Fontedicto* (Caux), *De Malaïgue* (Uzés), *Des Perrières* (Manduel), *Le Petit Domaine de Gimios* (St Jean de Minervois), *St Julien* (Azille), *Sylvain Saux* (Lauraguel)

Organic

Cabanis (Beauvoisin), *De Caillan* (Bessan), *De Camplazens* (Combaillaux), *Château de Caraguilhes* (St Laurent de la Cabrerisse), *De Clairac* (Cazouls lès Béziers), *Combes-Giraud* (Valros), *Costeplane* (Cannes et Clairan), *CV les Côteaux de Creissan* (Creissan), *Jean Bigou* (Rouvenac), *Blanquette Beirieu* (Roquetaillade), *Bourguet* (Béziers), *Alain Bousquet* (St Etienne de Gourgas), *Couderc* (Neffies), *Mas Coutelou* (Puimisson), *Du Farlet* (Meze), *La Fon de Lacan* (St Pargoire), *Jacques Frélin Vignobles* (Villeneuve lès Béziers), *Grand Bourry* (Le Cailar), *La Grangette* (Castelnau de Guers), *De Gressac* (Verfeuil), *Mas de Janiny* (St Bauzille de la Sylve), *Mas Jullien* (Jonquières), *CV La Clairette* (Bellegarde), *La Tour* (Beaucaire), *Du Lac* (Montescot), *CV Languedoc Roussillon* (Montpellier), *Bernard Legoy* (Condat-en-Combrailles), *CV Les Gres* (Vendargues), *De Litenis* (St Jean de Fos), *Lou Pas d'Estrech* (St Christol de Rodières), *Loupia* (Pennautier), *Louvet/Cellier du Languedoc Vins Distribution* (Narbonne), *Château Maris* (La Livinière), *Maurel Vedeau* (Servian), *Antoine Maurel* (Conques-sur-Orbiel), De Mayrac (Couiza),

De Montahuc (St Jean de Minervois), *Croix de Bel-Air* (Marseillan), *De Montjouy* (Florensac), *CV de Montpeyroux* (Montpeyroux), *Ochre Rouge* (Dions), *Château du Parc* (Pezenas), *Pastouret* (Bellegarde), *Château Pech-Latt* (Lagrasse), *De Petit Roubié* (Pinet), *Château des Auzines* (Auzines), *Bannières* (Castries), *Du Mas Barjac* (Monteils), *Bassac* (Puissalicon), *De Malavieille* (Merifons), *Peyre-Rose* (St Pargoire), *De Picheral* (Mus), *Château Roubia* (Roubia), *La Solana* (Festes), *Des Soulié* (Assignan), *St Alban* (Neffies), *Château St Auriol* (Lézignan-Corbières), *De St Blaise* (Cessenon), *Ste Marie des Pins* (Verzeille), *Des Syles* (Béziers) *La Triballe* (Guzargues), *De Valescure* (Aimargues), *Abbaye de Valmagne* (Villeveyrac), *Château Ventaiolle* (Ventenac-Cabardes), *Château Veredus* (Cruscades), *Zumbaum-Tomasi* (Claret), *De l'Ametlier* (Pézenas), *Anthéa* (Sallès d'Aude), *La Batteuse* (Antugnac), *Château Bel Air La Côte* (Beauvoisin), *Château Belaussel* (Lagrasse), *Belles Croix Robin* (Guzargues), *Château Bousquette* (Cessenon-sur-Orb), *De Brau* (Villemoustaussou), *De Buzarens* (Assas), *Arnaudiés* (Ceret), *Batlle-Jacquet* (Fourques), *Carle-Courty* (Millas), *Henri-Albert Foxonet* (Toulouges), *Joliette* (Espira de l'Agly), *Franck Jorel* (St Paul de Fenouillet), *Château de L'Ou* (Montescot), *Laguerre* (St Martin de Fenouillet), *Le Casot de Mailloles* (Banyuls-sur-Mer), *Lenan* (Trouillas), *Nivet-Galinier* (Toulouges), *Jean-Michel Paraire* (Fourques), *Olivier Pithon* (Calce), *De la Rourède* (Fourques), *Du Soula* (St Martin de Fenouillet), *Clos St Martin* (Bompas)

PROVENCE AND CORSICA

It is the fascinating Italian twist to these wines that makes both Provence and Corsica unique among the wine regions of France. Numerous Italian varieties entered Provence via the Alps, while Corsica's link is a more direct one, the island having been purchased by France from the Republic of Genoa in 1764. Italian remained the lingua di coltura *for Corsicans until the late 19th century, and the cultivation of Italian grape varieties has never stopped.*

Take off those rose-tinted spectacles! If any wine fulfils the overworked cliché of a wine that does not travel, it has to be Provence rosé, but it is the romantic location, not the wine, that does not travel. Provence rosé is probably the world's most

CHÂTEAU D'ESCLANS
Home to Sacha Lichine – son of the late, great Alexis Lichine – Château d'Esclans in La Motte-en-Provence is the focal point for revolutionary progress in the bold attempt to raise the quality of Provence rosé to that of a truly fine wine.

overrated wine, but when you're on holiday and the sun is blazing, you are drinking in the atmosphere, not the ice-cold rosé. Take the same bottle home, and all you are guaranteed is disappointment. It may come in an exotically shaped bottle, but exotic is the last word that could be used to describe its dull, flabby contents. They have been making wine here for more than 2,600 years, and by the time the Romans arrived, in 125 BC, it was already so good that they immediately exported it back to Rome. But ask yourself this question: do you think that wine was a rosé? Of course not; Provence rosé is a relatively recent phenomenon and, some would cynically say, one that was deliberately designed to swindle the gold-draped *nouveau riche* who flock here.

Rosé still represents more than half of all Provençal production, although sales have declined in recent years, as the once-exclusive resorts become more accessible to the sophisticated middle classes, who recognize how dull these wines are. Quality improved in the 1980s, but has reached a plateau and, without resorting to actually acidifying the wines, modern vinification techniques will never be

FACTORS AFFECTING TASTE AND QUALITY

LOCATION
Provence is situated in the southeast of France, between the Rhône delta and the Italian border. A further 110 kilometres (68 miles) southeast lies Corsica.

CLIMATE
Winters are mild, as are springs, which can also be humid. Summers are hot and stretch into long, sunny autumns. A vine requires 1,300 hours of sunshine in one growing season – 1,500 hours is preferable, but in Provence, it luxuriates in an average of 3,000 hours. The close proximity of the Mediterranean, however, is also capable of inducing sharp fluctuations in the weather. Rain is spread over a limited number of days in autumn and winter.

ASPECT
The vineyards run down hillsides and on to the plains.

SOIL
The geology of Provence is complex. Many ancient soils have undergone chemical changes and numerous new soils have been created. Sand, red sandstone, and granite are, however, the most regular common denominators, with limestone outcrops that often determine the extent of superior *terroirs*: the Var *département* has mica-schist, chalky scree, and chalky tufa as well as granite hillsides; there are excellent flinty-limestone soils at Bandol; and pudding stones (conglomerate pebbles) that are rich in flint at Bellet. The south of Corsica is mostly granite, while the north is schistous, with a few limestone outcrops and deposits of sandy and alluvial soils in between.

VITICULTURE AND VINIFICATION
All the vines used to be planted in *gobelet* fashion, but most are now trained on wires. The recent trend towards Cabernet Sauvignon has stopped, although many excellent wines are still made from this grape. The current vogue is to re-establish a true Provençal identity by relying exclusively (where possible) on local varieties, and the laws have been changed to encourage this particular evolution. Much of the rosé has been improved by modern cool-vinification techniques, although most remains tired and flabby.

GRAPE VARIETIES

Aragnan, Aramon, Aramon Gris, Barbarossa, Barbaroux, Barbaroux Rosé, Braquet, Brun-Fourcat, Cabernet Sauvignon, Carignan, Castets, Chardonnay, Clairette, Clairette à Gros Grains, Clairette à Petits Grains, Clairette de Trans, Colombard, Counoise, Doucillon (Bourboulenc), Durif, Fuella, Grenache, Grenache Blanc, Manosquin (Téoulier), Marsanne, Mayorquin, Muscat Blanc à Petits Grains (*see* individual appellations for local synonyms), Muscat Rosé à Petits Grains, Nielluccio, Pascal Blanc, Pecoui-Touar (Calitor), Petit-Brun, Picardan, Picpoul, Pignerol, Plant d'Arles (Cinsault), Rolle (Vermentino), Rossola Nera (Mourvèdre), Sauvignon Blanc, Sémillon, Sciacarello, Syrah, Terret Blanc, Terret-Bourret (Terret Gris), Terret Noir, Terret Ramenée, Tibourenc (Tibouren), Ugni Blanc, Ugni Rosé

RECENT PROVENÇAL AND CORSICAN VINTAGES

2010 The news-grabbing floods affected less than 1 per cent of the vineyards, and although rain and hail delayed picking for two weeks, the mistral performed its usual blow-dry, preventing rot. Some good wines with fresh acidity were produced.

2009 Good to very good wines produced in all styles.

2008 Excellent quality, particularly for red-wine styles.

2007 A good-quality vintage.

2006 No excessive heat, and no drought, resulted in an excellent vintage that is at least the equal of 2005, particularly for reds and rosés.

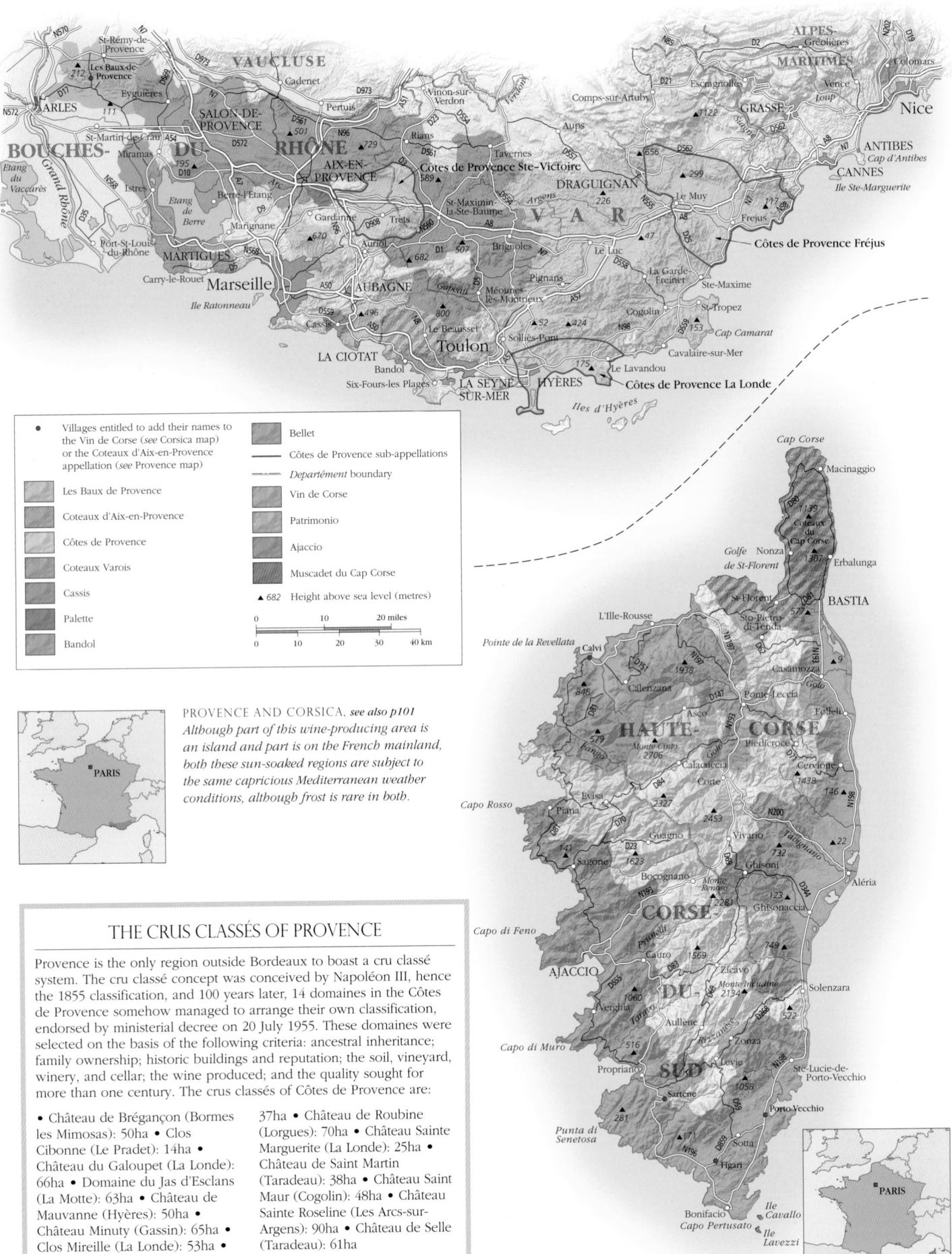

PROVENCE AND CORSICA, *see also p101*
Although part of this wine-producing area is an island and part is on the French mainland, both these sun-soaked regions are subject to the same capricious Mediterranean weather conditions, although frost is rare in both.

THE CRUS CLASSÉS OF PROVENCE

Provence is the only region outside Bordeaux to boast a cru classé system. The cru classé concept was conceived by Napoléon III, hence the 1855 classification, and 100 years later, 14 domaines in the Côtes de Provence somehow managed to arrange their own classification, endorsed by ministerial decree on 20 July 1955. These domaines were selected on the basis of the following criteria: ancestral inheritance; family ownership; historic buildings and reputation; the soil, vineyard, winery, and cellar; the wine produced; and the quality sought for more than one century. The crus classés of Côtes de Provence are:

• Château de Brégançon (Bormes les Mimosas): 50ha • Clos Cibonne (Le Pradet): 14ha • Château du Galoupet (La Londe): 66ha • Domaine du Jas d'Esclans (La Motte): 63ha • Château de Mauvanne (Hyères): 50ha • Château Minuty (Gassin): 65ha • Clos Mireille (La Londe): 53ha • Domaine de Rimauresq (Pignans): 37ha • Château de Roubine (Lorgues): 70ha • Château Sainte Marguerite (La Londe): 25ha • Château de Saint Martin (Taradeau): 38ha • Château Saint Maur (Cogolin): 48ha • Château Sainte Roseline (Les Arcs-sur-Argens): 90ha • Château de Selle (Taradeau): 61ha

able to rid them of the flabbiness that is their sunny southern heritage. Until very recently, there were only about half a dozen Provence rosés that could be recommended with any confidence, and those recommendations are relative to the wine's generally lacklustre quality. I had never come across a Provence rosé that I could, hand on heart, describe as a truly fine wine. Until, that is, Sacha Lichine, son of the famous Alexis Lichine, purchased Château d'Esclans at La Motte-en-Provence in 2006. With the help of Michel Rolland, Sacha set about perfecting that most elusive of Provençal wines: a truly fine rosé. The result is a range of beautifully refined, ultra-premium rosés. Top of the range is Garrus, which retails for £50–100 ($80–160) depending on the store. Is it worth it? I confess that I was very dubious at the thought of any Provence rosé being worth that sort of money and must confess that I have seldom approached any tasting with the lack of objectivity that was lurking at the back of my mind when I first encountered Garrus. Yet I was blown away, particularly by the 2009 Garrus, the exquisite finesse of which not only sets it apart from anything that has gone before, but also elevates the potential greatness of the rosé genre to that of a classic red or white wine. And why not? This must have been the question that Sacha Lichine asked himself before purchasing Château d'Esclans, and it is now up to the rest of Provence to respond.

THE TRUE CLASSIC WINES OF PROVENCE

For most people, Provence evokes the beaches of St-Tropez or the rich, *bouillabaisse*-laden aromas of backstreet Marseille, but there are other experiences to be had in this sun-blessed corner of southern France. For while the wines of Provence may not have the classic status of Burgundy or Bordeaux, the reds, such as the magnificent Bandol, the darkly promising Bellet, and the aptly named Cassis, have an abundance of spice-charged flavours that show more than a touch of class. Silly-shaped bottles are being discarded by the more serious winemakers who find the classic, understated lines of Bordeaux- and Burgundy-style bottles better reflect the quality of their wines.

The top estates of the Riviera produce red wines of a far more serious calibre than might be expected from an area better known for its play than its work. Maximum yields are low, however, and the potential for quality can be high. The smaller AOCs of Bandol, Bellet, and Palette are restricted to a maximum of 40 hectolitres per hectare (180 cases per acre), which is very modest for a region that could easily average more than double this amount. Even the all-embracing AOCs of Côtes de Provence and Coteaux d'Aix-en-Provence are absolutely full of fine vineyards capable of producing the exciting red wine that must surely be Provence's future.

CORSICA – "THE ISLE OF BEAUTY"

In Corsica, the advent of France's *vin de pays* system meant that around one-third of the island's vineyards were uprooted and put to better use. If the *vin de pays* system was intended to encourage the production of superior-quality wines from the bottom of the market upwards, then here at least it has been successful, for this island is no longer the generous contributor to Europe's "wine-lake" it used to be.

The days when Corsica's wines were fit only for turning into industrial spirit are long gone, but nor is this a potentially fine wine region. Just 15 per cent of its vineyards are AOC, and these yield barely more than 5 per cent of Corsica's total wine production. Although this is a fair and accurate reflection of its true potential, most critics agree that even within the modest limits of *vin de pays* production there should be many more individually expressive domaines. What has restricted their numbers is, however, something few are willing to talk about – intimidation and extortion by the local Mafia, which has caused more than one brave new Corsican venture to founder.

THE APPELLATIONS OF

PROVENCE AND CORSICA

Note * denotes producers who are particularly recommended for rosé.

AJACCIO AOC

This is a predominantly red-wine appellation on the west coast of Corsica.

RED When successful, this will inevitably be a medium-bodied Sciacarello wine with a good bouquet.

🍇 At least 60% (in total) of Barbarossa, Nielluccio, Vermentino, and Sciacarello (the last of which must account for at least 40%), plus a maximum of 40% (in total) of Grenache, Cinsault, and Carignan (the last of which must not exceed 15%)

WHITE Decently dry and fruity, the best have a good edge of Ugni Blanc acidity.

ROSÉ Average to good-quality dry rosé with a typical southern roundness.

🍇 As for the red

🍷 All wines: 1–3 years

☑ *Comte Abbatucci* (Faustine Abbatucci) • *Comte Peraldi*

BANDOL AOC

The red wine of this Provence appellation is a true *vin de garde* and deserves recognition. The white wine *encépagement* changed in 2003.

RED The best of these wines have a dark purple-black colour, a deep and dense bouquet, masses of spicy-plummy Mourvèdre fruit, and complex after-aromas that include vanilla, cassis, cinnamon, violets, and sweet herbs.

🍇 A blend of at least two of the following: Mourvèdre, Grenache, and Cinsault, of which a minimum of 50% Mourvèdre is obligatory, plus no more than 15% in total or 10% individually of Syrah and Carignan

🍷 3–12 years

WHITE These dry wines are now fresher and more fragrant than they were, but they are nothing special compared with the reds.

🍇 A minimum of 20% (50% as from 2011) Clairette, plus 40% (60% as from 2011) of Bourboulenc and/or Ugni Blanc (Sauvignon Blanc is no longer allowed)

🍷 Within 1 year

ROSÉ Well-made, attractive dry rosés, with body, structure, and a fine individual character.

🍇 As for red but no minimum Mourvèdre content

🍷 1–2 years

☑ *Château des Baumelles* • *Bunan* (Moulin des Costes Charriage, Château la Rouvière, Mas de la Rouvière) • *Dupéré-Barrera* (India) • *du Gros'Noré* • *de l'Hermitage* • *de la Laidière* • *Lafran-Veyrolles* • *Château de Pibarnon* • *Château Pradeaux* • *Château Ste-Anne* 🏵 • *des Salettes* • *La Suffrene* (Les Lauves) • *Tempier* • *Terrebrune* • *Vannières*

LES BAUX DE PROVENCE AOC

Excellent red and rosé wines, sold under the sub-appellation of Coteaux d'Aix-en-Provence Les Baux until 1995, when they were given their own AOC and the requirements changed.

RED Deep, dark, and rich, with creamy-spicy cherry and plum flavours.

🍇 A minimum of 60% Grenache, Mourvèdre and Syrah, no two varieties of which must account for more than 90% of the entire blend, plus a maximum 30% in total of one or more of the following: Carignan, Cinsault and Counoise, with a maximum of 20% Cabernet Sauvignon

🍷 4–10 years

ROSÉ De la Vallongue is rich and ripe.

🍇 A minimum of 60% Cinsault, Grenache, and Syrah, no two varieties of which must account for more than 90% of the entire blend, plus a maximum of 30% in total of one or more of the following: Carignan, Counoise, and Mourvèdre, with a maximum of 10% Cabernet Sauvignon

🍷 1–2 years

☑ *Hauvette* 🏵 • *Mas Sainte-Berthe* (Louis David) • *de la Vallongue** 🏵

BELLET AOC

This tiny Provence appellation is cooled by Alpine winds and produces exceptionally fragrant wines for such a southerly location.

ROSÉ Fine, floral, dry rosés that are exceptionally fresh and easy to drink.

🐝 Braquet, Fuella, Cinsault, plus up to 40% (in total) of Grenache, Rolle, Ugni Blanc, Mayorquin, Clairette, Bourboulenc, Chardonnay, Pignerol, and Muscat à Petits Grains

⌛ 1–2 years

RED These wines have a good colour and structure, with a well-perfumed bouquet.

🐝 Braquet, Fuella, Cinsault, plus up to 40% (in total) of Grenache, Rolle, Ugni Blanc, Mayorquin, Clairette, Bourboulenc, Chardonnay, Pignerol, and Muscat à Petits Grains

⌛ 4–10 years

WHITE Fine, firm yet fragrant, and highly aromatic, dry white wines of unbelievable class and finesse.

🐝 Rolle, Ugni Blanc, Mayorquin, plus up to 40% Clairette, Bourboulenc, Chardonnay, Pignerol, and Muscat à Petits Grains

⌛ 3–7 years

✓ *Château de Bellet* • *Clos Saint-Vincent* (Clos)

CASSIS AOC

This is a decent but overpriced Provence appellation located around a beautiful rocky bay, a few kilometres east of Marseille. In all but a few enterprising estates, these vineyards are on the decline.

RED These solid, well-coloured red wines can age, but most do not improve.

🐝 Grenache, Carignan, Mourvèdre, Cinsault, Barbaroux, plus up to 10% (in total) of Terret Noir, Terret Gris, Terret Blanc, Terret Ramenée, Aramon, and Aramon Gris

WHITE These dry white wines have an interesting bouquet of herby aromas of gorse and bracken, but are usually flabby and unbalanced on the palate. However, Bagnol and St-Magdeleine produce excellent, racy whites for such southerly vineyards, and Ferme Blanche can be almost as good.

🐝 Ugni Blanc, Sauvignon Blanc, Doucillon, Clairette, Marsanne, Pascal Blanc

ROSÉ Pleasantly fresh, dry rosés of moderately interesting quality.

🐝 Grenache, Carignan, Mourvèdre, Cinsault, Barbaroux, plus up to 10% (in total) of Terret Noir, Terret Gris, Terret Blanc, Terret Ramenée, Aramon, and Aramon Gris

⌛ All wines: 1–3 years

✓ *du Bagnol* • *Clos Val Bruyère*

CORSE AOC

See Vin de Corse AOC

COTEAUX D'AIX-EN-PROVENCE AOC

This large appellation has many fine estates, several of which have been replanted and re-equipped.

RED The best are deeply coloured *vins de garde* with lots of creamy-cassis, spicy-vanilla, and cherry flavours of some complexity.

🐝 Grenache, plus a maximum of 40% of Cinsault, Counoise, Mourvèdre, Syrah, Cabernet Sauvignon, and Carignan (the last two of which must not exceed 30%)

⌛ 3–12 years

WHITE Dry and fruity white wines that are of moderate quality, and are certainly improving. These wines may be sold from 1 December following the harvest without any mention of *primeur* or *nouveau*.

🐝 A maximum of 70% (each) of Bourboulenc, Clairette, Grenache Blanc, Vermentino, up to 40% Ugni Blanc and no more than 30% (each) of Sauvignon Blanc and Sémillon

⌛ Upon purchase

ROSÉ Fine-quality dry rosés that are light in body, but bursting with deliciously fresh and ripe fruit. These wines may be sold from 1 December following the harvest without any mention of *primeur* or *nouveau*.

🐝 As for red, plus up to 10% (in total) of Bourboulenc, Clairette, Grenache Blanc, Vermentino, Ugni Blanc, Sauvignon Blanc, and Sémillon

⌛ 1–2 years

✓ *des Béates* ❸ (Terra d'Or) • *Château de Beaupré* • *Château de Calissanne* • *de Camaissette* (Amadeus) • *Jean-Luc Colombo* (Pin Couchés) • *Château la Coste** • *Hauvette* ◉ • *Château Pigoudet* (La Chapelle) • *Château St-Jean**

COTEAUX VAROIS AOC

Upgraded from *vin de pays* to VDQS in 1985 and to AOC in 1993, this appellation covers an area of pleasant country wines in the centre of Provence. The *encépagement* changed in 2001.

RED The best have good colour, a deep fruity flavour, and some finesse.

🐝 At least two of the following must represent 80 to 90% of the entire blend: Cinsault, Grenache, Mourvèdre, and Syrah, plus optional Cabernet Sauvignon, Carignan, and Tibouren (permitted since 2001)

WHITE Soft and fresh at best.

🐝 A minimum of 30% Vermentino, plus Clairette, Grenache Blanc, a maximum of 30% Sémillon, and no more than 25% Ugni Blanc

ROSÉ These attractive, easy-to-drink, dry rosés offer better value than some of the more famous, pretentious wines of Provence.

🐝 At least two of the following must represent 80 to 90% of the entire blend: Cinsault, Grenache, Mourvèdre, and Syrah, plus optional Cabernet Sauvignon, Carignan, and Tibouren (permitted since 2001), and no more than 10% Clairette, Grenache Blanc, Sémillon, Ugni Blanc, and Vermentino

⌛ All wines: 1–3 years

✓ *des Chaberts* (Prestige) • *de Garbelle* (Les Barriques de Barbelle) • *Château Lafoux* • *de Ramatuelle* • *Château Thuerry* (Les Abeillons) • *Château Trians*

CÔTES DE PROVENCE AOC

While this AOC is famous for its rosés, it is the red wines of Côtes de Provence that have real potential, and they seem blessed with good vintages, fine estates, and talented winemakers. Inferior wines are made, but drink the best and you will rarely be disappointed. The major drawback of this all-embracing appellation is its very size. There are, however, several areas with peculiarities of soil and specific microclimates that have long made it obvious that such a large and wide-ranging AOC could support more defined internal zones, and in 2009 three sub-appellations were introduced for red and rosé wines only.

Fréjus At the opposite end of the Côtes de Provence to Sainte-Victoire, Fréjus is as sunny as anywhere else in the region, but its maritime influence provides the highest amount of beneficial rainfall, which drains through its sandy-clay soils from west to east into the Argens River.

La Londe This sub-appellation is at the very centre-south of the Côtes de Provence, where the foothills of the Massif des Maures meet those of La Londe les Maures. The schist and quartz soils provide a superior distinctive *terroir*.

Sainte-Victoire This is on the deep, dry, stony lower slopes of Mont Sainte-Victoire, on the western periphery of the Côtes de Provence.

RED There are too many exciting styles to generalize, but the best have a deep colour and many show an exuberance of silky Syrah fruit and plummy Mourvèdre. Some have great finesse; others are more tannic and chewy. The southern spicy-cassis of Cabernet Sauvignon is often present and the Cinsault, Grenache, and Tibouren grapes also play important roles.

🐝 The following must represent at least 70% (80% as from 2015) of the entire blend: Cinsault, Grenache, Mourvèdre, Syrah, and Tibouren, but no two varieties may account for more than 90%; plus optional Barbaroux Rosé, Cabernet Sauvignon, Calitor, and Carignan, with no more than 10% of Clairette, Sémillon, Ugni Blanc, and Vermentino

⌛ 3–10 years

WHITE Moderate but improving soft, dry, fragrant, and aromatic wines. These wines may be sold from 1 December following the harvest without any mention of *primeur* or *nouveau*.

🐝 Clairette, Sémillon, Ugni Blanc, and Vermentino

⌛ 1–2 years

ROSÉ Mediterranean sun is integral to the enjoyment of these wines, even the best of which fail to perform against other rosés under blind conditions; their low acidity makes them seem flat and dull. Château d'Esclans is, so far, the only exception. Its purity of fruit, so beautifully integrated with oak in three of four rosés (the "bottom" of the range is exclusively fruit-driven), demonstrates to other producers the heights to which this previously boring wine can aspire. The acidity is so perfectly balanced that the rosés of Château d'Esclans never lose site of their expression of *terroir*. These wines may be sold from 1 December following the harvest without any mention of *primeur* or *nouveau*.

🐝 The following must represent at least 70% (80% as from 2015) of the entire blend: Cinsault, Grenache, Mourvèdre, Syrah, and Tibouren, but no two varieties may account for more than 90%; plus optional Barbaroux Rosé, Cabernet Sauvignon, Calitor, and Carignan, with no more than 10% of Clairette, Sémillon, Ugni Blanc, and Vermentino

⌛ 1–2 years

✓ *Clos d'Alari* (Manon) • *Château des Anglades* (Collection Privée) • *Château de l'Aumerade* (Louis Fabre) • *Château Barbeyrolles* • *de la Bastide Neuve* (d'Antan) • *Ludovic de Beauséjour* (Bacarras) • *de la Courtade* • *Château Coussin Sainte-Victoire* (César) • *Château d'Esclans** • *Dupéré-Barrera* (En Caractère) • *Domaines Gavoty* • *du Grand Cros* (Nectar) • *de Jalle* (La Bouïsse) • *de La Lauzade* • *de la Malherbe** • *Château Maravenne* • *Château Minuty* (Prestige) • *Commanderie de Peyrassol** • *Château Requier** (Tête de Cuvée) • *de Rimauresq* • *La Rouvade* (Prestige) • *Saint-André de Figuière* • *de St-Baillon* • *Château Sainte-Roseline* • *Château Sarrins** • *Château de Selles** (also Clos Mireille) • *Château de la Tour*

MORE GREEN WINES

In addition to the producers recommended in this directory that are either biodynamic or organic, there are also the following. No negative inference of quality should be taken from the fact that they are not featured among the other recommended producers. There are a number that have been recommended in other editions, and still make some fine wines, but have been removed to make room for others

Biodynamic

Château la Canorgue (Bonnieux), *Les Fouques* (Hyères), *Château Romanin* (St Rémy de Provence), *St Estève* (Lambesc)

Organic

des Terres Blanches (St Rémy-de-Provence), *du Thouar* (Le Muy), *de l'Adret des Salettes* (Lorgues), *des Alysses* (Pontèves), *des Annibals* (Brignoles), *L'Attilon* (Mas Thibert), *Les Bastides* (Le Puy Ste Réparade), *de Beaujeu* (Arles), *Château de Beaulieu* (Rognes), *Château La Calisse* (Pontevès), *CV des Vignerons de Correns et du Val* (Correns), *de Costebonne* (Eygalières), *Mas de la Dame* (Les Baux de Provence), *Chateau du Duvivier* (Pontevès),

Château d'Esclans (La Motte), *Château Les Eydins* (Bonnieux), *Mas de Gourgonnier* (Mouriès), *Hauvette* (St Rémy de Provence), *de l'Isle des Sables* (Fourques), *du Jas d'Esclans* (La Motte), *La Bastide du Puy* (St Saturnin Lès Apt), *de Landue* (Solliés-Pont), *Mas de Longchamp* (St Rémy de Provence), *Château Miraval* (Correns), *de Pierrascas* (La Garde), *de Pinchinat* (Pourrières), *Rabiega* (Draguignan), *de Révaou* (La Londes les Maures), *Richeaume* (Puyloubier), *Robert* (Rognes), *de la Sanglière* (Bormes Les Mimosas), *SCIEV* (Molleges), *de Séoule* (St Saturnin Lès Apt), *St André de Figuière* (La Londe des Maures), *de St-Jean-de-Villecroze* (Villecroze)

---

l'Evéque • *Vignerons Presqu'Ile St-Tropez* (Château de Pampelonne, Carte Noire) • *Vannières* • *Vitis Alba* (Elevé en Fûts de Chêne)

MUSCAT DU CAP CORSE AOC

When I first wrote this book in 1988, Corsica's only truly classic wine, the succulent sweet Muscat of Cap Corse, was not even recognized, let alone awarded the AOC status it deserved, and it took five more years to get it on the statute books. The Muscat du Cap Corse appellation overlaps Vin de Corse Coteaux du Cap Corse and five of the seven communes that comprise the Patrimonio AOC.

WHITE The wines of Clos Nicrosi (in particular) demonstrate that Corsica has the ability to produce one of the most fabulous Muscats in the world. These wines are so pure and succulent, with wonderful fresh aromas, that they have very little to gain through age.

🍇 Muscat Blanc à Petits Grains

🍷 Upon purchase

✓ *Clos Nicrosi* • *Leccia* • *Orenga de Gaffory*

PALETTE AOC

The ridiculously long list of permissible grapes here illustrates one of the worst excesses of the AOC system. What is the point of such a large number of diverse grape varieties? Ignoring the fact that it includes some low-quality ones that should, if anything, be banned, it is obvious that no specific style could possibly result from the infinite permutation of varieties and percentages this AOC permits. Why not simply have an appellation that guarantees that Palette is from Palette? Despite this farce, Palette is one of the best in Provence. It can be considered the equivalent of a *grand cru* of Coteaux d'Aix-en-Provence, standing out from surrounding vineyards by virtue of its calcareous soil. Three-quarters of this appellation is occupied by just one property – Château Simone.

RED Though not in the blockbusting style, this is a high-quality wine with good colour and firm structure, and can achieve finesse.

🍇 At least 50% (in total) of Mourvèdre, Grenache, and Cinsault, plus Téoulier, Durif, and Muscat (any variety planted), Carignan, Syrah, Castets,

Brun-Fourcat, Terret Gris, Petit-Brun, Tibouren, Cabernet Sauvignon, and up to 15% (in total) of Clairette (any variety planted), Picardan, Ugni Blanc, Ugni Rosé, Grenache Blanc, Muscat (any variety planted), Picpoul, Pascal, Aragnan, Colombard, and Terret-Bourret

🍷 7–20 years

WHITE Firm but nervy dry wine with a pleasantly curious aromatic character.

🍇 At least 55% (in total) of Clairette (any variety planted), plus Picardan, Ugni Blanc, Ugni Rosé, Grenache Blanc, Muscat (any variety planted), Picpoul, Pascal, Aragnan, Colombard, and a maximum of 20% Terret-Bourret

🍷 Upon purchase

ROSÉ A well-made but unexceptional wine that is perhaps made too seriously for its level of quality.

🍇 At least 50% (in total) of Mourvèdre, Grenache, and Cinsault, plus Téoulier, Durif, and Muscat (any variety planted), Carignan, Syrah, Castets, Brun-Fourcat, Terret Gris, Petit-Brun, Tibouren, Cabernet Sauvignon, and up to 15% (in total) of Clairette (any variety planted), Picardan, Ugni Blanc, Ugni Rosé, Grenache Blanc, Muscat (any variety planted), Picpoul, Pascal, Aragnan, Colombard, and Terret-Bourret

🍷 1–3 years

✓ *Château Crémade* • *Château Simone*

PATRIMONIO AOC

This is a small appellation situated west of Bastia in the north of Corsica. The *encépagement* changed in 2002.

RED Some fine-quality red wines of good colour, body, and fruit are made.

🍇 At least 90% Nielluccio, plus Grenache, Sciacarello, and Vermentino

WHITE Light and dry wines of a remarkably fragrant and floral character for Corsica.

🍇 Vermentino

ROSÉ Good-value dry rosés that have a coral-pink colour and an elegant flavour.

🍇 At least 75% Nielluccio, plus Grenache, Sciacarello, and Vermentino

🍷 All wines: 1–3 years

✓ *Aliso-Rossi* • *Clos Benardi* • *de Catarelli* • *Gentile* (Sélection Noble) • *Giacomett* (Cru des Agrigates) • *Leccia* • *Orenga de Gaffory* • *Pastricciola* • *Clos Teddi*

VIN DE BANDOL AOC
See Bandol AOC

VIN DE BELLET AOC
See Bellet AOC

VIN DE CORSE AOC

Vin de Corse is a generic appellation covering the entire island. The *encépagement* changed in 2003.

RED These honest wines are full of fruit, round, and clean, with rustic charm.

🍇 At least 50% Grenache, Nielluccio, Sciacarello, and Grenache Noir, plus a maximum of 50% Barbarossa, Carignan, Cinsault, Mourvèdre, Syrah, and Vermentino (Carignan and/or Vermentino must not exceed 20% of the entire blend)

WHITE The best are well made, clean, and fresh, but not of true AOC quality.

🍇 At least 75% Vermentino, plus optional Ugni Blanc

ROSÉ Attractive, dry, fruity, easy-to-drink wines.

🍇 At least 50% Grenache, Nielluccio, Sciacarello, and Grenache Noir, plus a maximum of 50% Barbarossa, Carignan, Cinsault, Mourvèdre, Syrah, and Vermentino (Carignan and/or Vermentino must not exceed 20% of the entire blend)

🍷 All wines: 1–3 years

✓ *Andriella* • *Casabianca* • *Clos Colombu* • *CV de L'Ile de Beauté* (Réserve du Président) • *Maestracci* • *Musoleu* (Monte Cristo) • *Clos de L'Orlea* • *Clos Poggiale*

VIN DE CORSE CALVI AOC

Lying north of Ajaccio, this sub-appellation of Vin de Corse AOC requires the same grape varieties and meets the same technical level.

✓ *Colombu* • *Maestracci* • *Renucci*

VIN DE CORSE COTEAUX DU CAP CORSE AOC

A sub-appellation of Vin de Corse, this requires the same varieties, except that Codivarta may be used with Ugni Blanc in support of Vermentino.

✓ *Clos Nicrosi* • *Pieretti*

VIN DE CORSE FIGARI AOC

Situated between Sartène and Porto Vecchio, Vin de Corse Figari is a sub-appellation of Vin de Corse AOC and requires the same grape varieties and technical level.

✓ *de Petra Bianca* (Vinti Legna)

VIN DE CORSE PORTO VECCHIO AOC

The southeastern edge of Corsica, around Porto Vecchio, is a sub-appellation of Vin de Corse AOC and requires the same grape varieties and technical level.

✓ *De Torraccia*

VIN DE CORSE SARTENE AOC

South of Ajaccio, this sub-appellation of Vin de Corse AOC requires the same grape varieties and conforms to the same technical level.

✓ *Clos d'Alzeto* • *Saparale*

VINS DE FRANCE AND VINS DE PAYS

Vin de France is a revamped vin de table that permits, for the first time, the vintage and grape variety to be shown on the label. Vins de pays *have not disappeared or been replaced by IGP (Indication Géographique Protégée), as some reports suggest. All* vins de pays *will all carry the EU's IGP certification, just as all AOCs once carried the EU's VQPRD stamp and now carry its AOP certification. Many* vins de pays *are switching entirely to IGP, but technically there is no difference in their status.*

THIS CATEGORY OF WINE includes some of the most innovative and exciting wines being produced in the world today, yet most of the 154 *vin de pays* denominations are superfluous and confusing. The success of the *vin de pays* system lies not in creating more appellations, but in freeing producers from them, which allows the most talented individuals to carve out their own reputations.

Vins de pays, or "country wines", are supposed to be unpretentious, but many are better than average-quality AOC wines and the best rank as some of the finest wines that France can produce. This was never the intention; a *vin de pays* was merely meant to be a quaffing wine that should display, in a very rudimentary sense, the broadest characteristics of its region's greatest wines. However, because of this modest aim, *vin de pays* had fewer restrictions than higher appellations. This encouraged the more creative winemakers to produce wines that best expressed their *terroir* without being hampered by an over-regulated AOC system, and in so doing, they managed to equal and occasionally surpass the quality of the more famous local appellations. As news of these exciting *vins de pays* hit the headlines of the international wine press, so the thought of shedding the shackles of AOC restrictions attracted a new generation of winemakers, including a number of Australians. The combination of French and foreign winemakers opened up the *vin de pays* system, turning it into something its creators had never imagined.

COUNTRY ORIGINS

The expression "Vin de Pays" first appeared in the statute books in a decree dated 8 February 1930. The law in question merely allowed wines to refer to their canton of origin provided they attained a certain alcoholic degree; for example "Vin de Pays de Canton X". These cantons were not controlled appellations as such: there was no way of enforcing a minimum standard of quality, and the relatively small amounts of these so-called *vins de pays* were often the product of inferior hybrid grapes. It was not until 1973 that the concept was officially born of *vins de pays* that were a superior breed of *vins de table*, originating from a defined area and subject to strict controls. By 1976, a total of 75 *vins de pays* had been established, but all the formalities were not worked out until 1979, and between 1981 and 1982 every single existing *vin de pays* was redefined and another 20 created. Currently there are 154, although the number fluctuates as *vins de pays* are upgraded to VDQS, when new *vins de pays* are created, or, as has happened recently, when some *départements* are denied the right to produce a *vin de pays* (*see* Vins de Pays at a Glance, p300).

Officially, a *vin de pays* was originally a *vin de table* from a specified area that conforms to quality-control laws that were and are very similar to those regulating AOC wines, although obviously not quite as strict. *Vin de pays* came of age in 1989, when *Vin de Table Français* was dropped from the label.

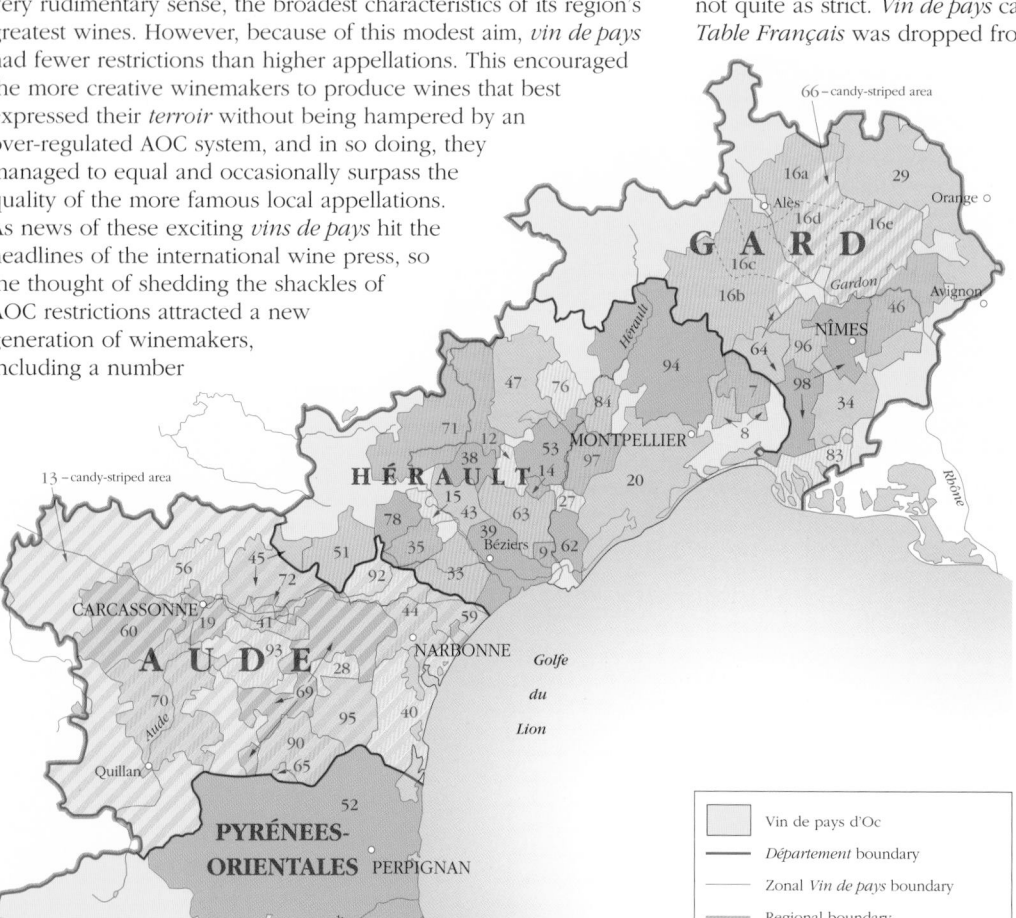

DOMAINE DE LA BAUME
This property was made famous by BRL Hardy, one of Australia's largest wine companies. Believing the French had not exploited varietal wines and seeing an opening in the market for Australian-made French wines, Hardy puchased Domaine de la Baume on the outskirts of Béziers just in time for the 1990 harvest.

	Vin de pays d'Oc
	Département boundary
	Zonal *Vin de pays* boundary
	Regional boundary

VIN DE PAYS, MAP A,
see also opposite
Languedoc-Roussillon encompasses the greatest concentration of zonal vins de pays *and is dominated by the regional Vin de Pays d'Oc, by far the most successful* vin de pays.

VARIETY IS THE SPICE OF LIFE FOR VIN DE PAYS

While the universally recognized great wines produced in the most famous regions of France remain, very much, in a cosy market of their own, their volume in global terms is minute, and the average-quality AOC wines have been losing the export battle against the New World, particularly "Brand Australia". It was left to the up-and-coming *vins de pays* to fight a rearguard action, while the AOC regions sort out their problems of perennial mediocrity (if indeed they can). However, even with fewer restrictions than AOCs, *vins de pays* have had to fight with one

hand behind their back. The first and most important disadvantage was that *vins de pays* were marketing wines under names such as Coteaux du Littoral Audois or Comté Tolosan, while the opposition was simply selling Chardonnay or Cabernet Sauvignon. While the varietal concept might cause a "sense of place" crisis for the New World's finer wines, when they try to ride the export surf into Europe, it matters not a jot in the USA, and the *vins de pays* are not up against such wines. At the

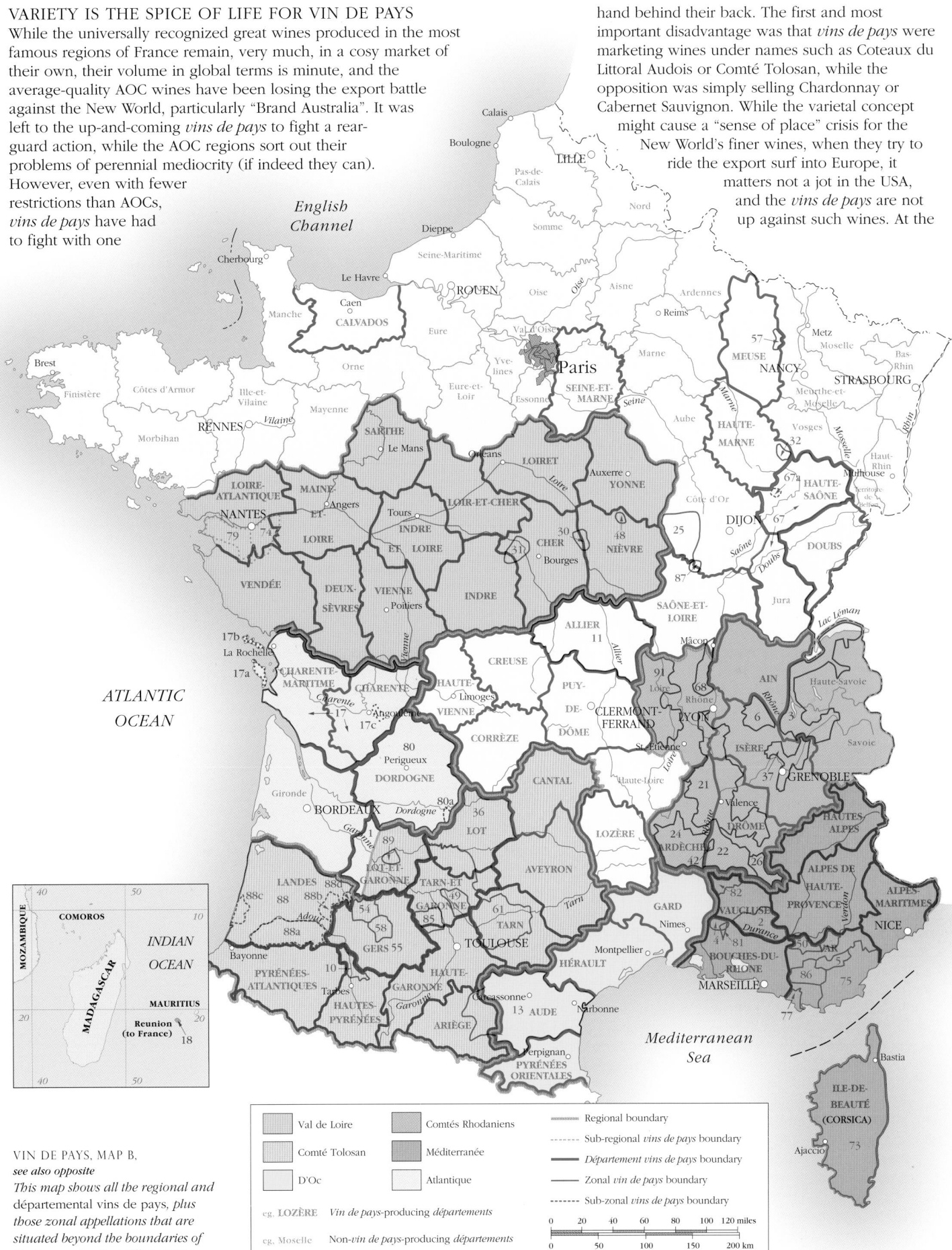

VIN DE PAYS, MAP B,
see also opposite
This map shows all the regional and départemental vins de pays, plus those zonal appellations that are situated beyond the boundaries of the Languedoc-Roussillon region.

Val de Loire	Comtés Rhodaniens	Regional boundary
Comté Tolosan	Méditerranée	Sub-regional *vins de pays* boundary
D'Oc	Atlantique	*Département vins de pays* boundary

eg. **LOZÈRE**   *Vin de pays-producing départements*

eg. Moselle   *Non-vin de pays-producing départements*

Zonal *vin de pays* boundary

Sub-zonal *vins de pays* boundary

VINS DE PAYS AT A GLANCE

154 VIN DE PAYS DENOMINATIONS IN TOTAL
Or 168 if the sub-regional and sub-zonal *vins de pays* are included. From virtually zero production in 1973 to an annual average of almost 15 million hectolitres (166 million cases), *vins de pays* now represent over 30 per cent of the total French wine production, and this expansion is continuing.

TYPES OF VINS DE PAYS
There are three basic categories of *vins de pays*: regional, *départementale*, and zonal. Although no official quality differences exist between these, it is not an unreasonable assumption that the zonal *vins de pays* may sometimes show more individual character than the much larger *vins de pays départementaux* or all-encompassing regional *vins de pays*, but this is not always so.

A grower within a specific zone may find it easier to sell wine under a more generic *vin de pays*, which explains why so many individual wines are to be found under the vast Vin de Pays d'Oc denomination. Also, the geographical size of a *vin de pays* can be deceptive, with many *départements* producing relatively little wine compared with some more prolific, relatively minute, zonal *vins de pays*. In the Loire few producers bother with the *départementale* denominations.

REGIONAL VINS DE PAYS (49 per cent of total *vin de pays* output)
There are now six of these wide-ranging appellations: Atlantique; Comté Tolosan; Comtés Rhodaniens; Val de Loire (which includes a further two sub-regional denominations); Oc; and Méditerranée. Each encompasses two or more *départements*. They represented only 12 per cent of *vin de pays* production in 1990, yet Vin de Pays d'Oc alone accounts for 33 per cent today.

DÉPARTEMENTALE VINS DE PAYS (24 per cent of total *vin de pays* output)
These cover entire *départements*, and although 55 are officially in use, some are effectively redundant as producers have opted for one of the more widely supported regional appellations, which are often easier to promote. In theory every *département* in France can claim a *vin de pays* under its own *départementale* denomination, but to avoid

confusion with AOC wines the following were in 1995 expressly forbidden from exercising this right: the Marne and Aube (in Champagne), the Bas-Rhin and Haut-Rhin (in Alsace), the Côte-d'Or (in Burgundy), and the Rhône (which encompasses Beaujolais but is likely to cause confusion with the Côtes du Rhône AOC). Jura, Savoie, and Haut-Savoie have also been disenfranchised.

ZONAL VINS DE PAYS (27 per cent of total *vin de pays* production)
There are now 93 zonal *vins de pays*, plus 14 sub-zonal denominations, although many of the former and some of the latter are seldom encountered.

VINS DE CÉPAGE
After a widespread authorization of pure varietal *vins de pays* in 2000, regulations for which lagged well behind the actual production, this category has taken off to such an extent that it now accounts for half of all the *vins de pays* produced each year, with 80 per cent sold under one of six regional *vins de pays*, of which 70 per cent is Vin de Pays d'Oc.

VINS DE PAYS PRIMEUR
Since 1990, all *vin de pays* denominations have been permitted to produce these wines, which may be marketed from the third Thursday of October following the harvest (much earlier than Beaujolais Nouveau). The regulations allow for red and white wines to be made as *vins primeurs*, but strangely not rosé, although by the very nature of their production, many reds are lighter than some rosés, so it is a somewhat moot point. White wines are vinified by cool-fermentation techniques and red wines by one of three methods: carbonic maceration (*see* Micropedia), part-carbonic maceration (some of the grapes are crushed and mixed with the whole bunches), and "short-classic" (traditional vinification with minimum skin contact). Cool-fermented whites and carbonic maceration reds are dominated by amylic aromas (pear drops, banana, nail varnish). "Short-classic" rarely provides enough fruit, depth, or colour, whereas part-carbonic maceration can be very successful in enhancing the fruitiness of a wine without drowning it in amylic aromas, but it has to be expertly applied.

Percentages of red, white, and rosé vins de pays

73.6%

10.4%

16%

---

price point of most *vins de pays* and their New World opponents, the appellation *per se* is irrelevant. All readers of this encyclopedia will drink such wines, and delight in searching out those that are the best and most interesting, but the vast majority of consumers do not know or even care about appellations. They see Chardonnay on two or three bottles and grab one. Why? Probably because they have had it before, and it was okay, or for no other reason than the label looks smarter than the others – but the reason is immaterial. What is important is that in making their choice, they – that is, the vast majority – have gone straight past the Coteaux du Littoral Audois *et al*.

This is the old story of customers proclaiming, "I don't want Chablis, I want Chardonnay", and the French authorities have agonized about how to get around the problem. The French being French could not bring themselves to allow *vins de pays* to be sold as pure varietal wines. Instead, in 1996, they tried to divert consumer attention from single-varietal names with the twin-varietal concept, enabling producers to market wines as Cabernet-Merlot, Chardonnay-Sémillon, and so on. Although some very good wines were produced, the idea never really took off. It is fine in a New World country, where the varietal-wine concept is all, and a twin-varietal is simply seen as a logical move, but for the *vins de pays*, it was like learning to run before they could walk.

The French realized this, and in 2000 issued wide-sweeping decrees authorizing varietal wines for almost all *vins de pays*. It was still an unfair fight because the regulations insisted that such wines be made from 100 per cent of the variety indicated, whereas New World imports merely had to comply with the European Union minimum of 85 per cent. At the price point of most *vins de pays* and New World varietals, the flexibility to strengthen or soften a variety to one degree or another in a given year is a major advantage. Another advantage the opposition had was to use oak chips. It is one thing to expect a *cru classé* château to use casks

rather than chips (although I cannot see why it actually has to be illegal), but it is impossible for *vins de pays* to compete at the same price as the New World wines if the French have to use oak casks or nothing. With casks, they cannot even get the wine on the shelf at the same time, let alone the same price. Fortunately, Hervé Gaymard, the French Minister of Agriculture, finally agreed that it was unfair, and in July 2004 authorized producers to use oak chips and to blend up to 15 per cent of another variety and vintage into a single-varietal *vin de pays*.

VIN DE FRANCE

These wines were formerly known as Vin de Table, but rather than a bottomless pit of anonymous wines, it is now possible to find a *vin de France* labelled with a vintage and one or more grape varieties. There is no geographic origin for these wines other than France itself, the idea being to allow vintaged varietal wines to be blended across two or more regions in the hope of providing a consistency of quality at a good-value price. It is not obligatory for a *vin de France* to be a blend of two or more regions, but that has been the prime locomotive for change in this category of wine: to enable France to compete with entry-level vintaged varietal wines from the New World.

☑ *Auriol* (So Light Terret-Sauvignon) • *Badet Clément* (Séraphine Carignan-Syrah) • *Cuvée des Bouquets* (Pinot Gris Récolte Tardive, Pinot Noir, Sauvignon Blanc) • *Brise de France* (Cinsault, Merlot) • *Lacheteau* (Kiwi Cuvée Sauvignon Blanc) • *French Connection* (Reserve Chardonnay, Reserve Merlot, Grande Reserve Shiraz) • *LGI* (La Campagne Sauvignon Blanc, Montgravet Chardonnay) • *Lurton* (L'Herré Chardonnay – Gros Manseng, Fumées Blanches Sauvignon Blanc, Fumées Blanches Rosé) • *Montgravet* (Chardonnay) • *Rémy Pannier* (Dames de la Vallée Merlot) • *Guy Saget* (La Petite Perrière Pinot Noir)

THE VINS DE PAYS OF
FRANCE

AGENAIS
Zonal *vin de pays* Map B, No.1

These red, white, and rosé wines are produced from a combination of classic *bordelais* grapes and some rustic regional varieties, including the Tannat and Fer. Although more than three-quarters of the output is red, it is the rosé made primarily from Abouriou that is best known.

✓ *de Cazeaux* (Tradition)

AIGUES
Zonal *vin de pays* Map B, No.2

Created in 1993, this *vin de pays* roughly corresponds to the Coteaux du Lubéron, and has a similar range of grape varieties.

AIN
Départementale *vin de pays* Map B

This *départementale vin de pays* encompasses unclassified vineyards in southern Burgundy, and has relatively recently come into usage, but the level of production remains insignificant. Pure varietal wines have been allowed since 2000.

✓ *Jean-Christophe Pellerin* (Chardonnay Cép d'Argent)

ALLIER
Départementale *vin de pays* Map B

Relatively recent *départementale vin de pays* for red and rosé wines, primarily from Cabernet Franc, Cabernet Sauvignon, Gamay, and Grolleau, but also Abouriou, Pinot d'Aunis, and Pinot Noir. Whites primarily from Chardonnay, Chenin Blanc, and Sauvignon Blanc, but also Arbois, Folle Blanche, Grolleau Gris, Melon de Bourgogne, and Pinot Blanc. Pure varietal wines have been allowed since 2000.

ALLOBROGIE
Zonal *vin de pays* Map B, No.3

This is the *vin de pays* equivalent of the Vin de Savoie, although it extends beyond the borders of that AOC into cattle country where the existence of vines is very sporadic. The wines are similar to Vin de Savoie, if somewhat lighter and more rustic in style. Almost 90 per cent of production is white, made primarily from Jacquère, Chardonnay, and Chasselas, although Altesse, Mondeuse Blanche, Roussanne, and Molette can also be used. The balance of the production is essentially red and may be made from Gamay, Mondeuse, and Pinot Noir, with rosé accounting for less than 1 per cent. Pure varietal wines have been allowed since 2000.

✓ *Demeure-Penet* (Jacquère)

ALPES DE HAUTE-PROVENCE
Départementale *vin de pays* Map B

Most of these wines come from the Durance Valley in the east of the *département*. Production is mostly red, made from Carignan, Grenache, Cinsault, Cabernet Sauvignon, Merlot, and Syrah. Rosé accounts for 15 per cent and white made from Ugni Blanc, Clairette, Chardonnay, and Muscat for just 7 per cent. Pure varietal wines have been allowed since 2000.

✓ *La Madeleine* (Cabernet Sauvignon) • *CV de Pierrevert* (Cuvée 42 Blanc) • *de Réguisse* (Aligoté, Muscat Moelleux, Pinot Noir, Merlot)

ALPES-MARITIMES
Départementale *vin de pays* Map B

Some 70 per cent of production is red and 30 per cent rosé, made from Carignan, Cinsault, Grenache, Ugni Blanc, and Vermentino grapes, mostly from the communes of Carros, Mandelieu, and Mougins. White wines may also be produced. Pure varietal wines have been allowed since 2000.

✓ *de Toasc* (Lou Vin d'Aqui)

ALPILLES
Zonal *vin de pays* Map B, No.4

Geographically, this is the *vin de pays* equivalent of Les Baux de Provence.

✓ *Mas de la Béruguette*

ARDÈCHE
Départementale *vin de pays* Map B

VIOGNIER
Vin de Pays de l'Ardèche

MOMMESSIN
ÉLÉGANCE

Red and white wines, from a range of Rhône and *bordelais* grapes. Pure varietal wines allowed.

✓ *de Champal* (Viognier Arzelle) • *Vignerons Ardéchois* (Cuvée Orélie)

ARGENS
Zonal *vin de pays* Map B, No.5

Almost 50/50 rosé and red are made from Carignan, Cinsault, Syrah, Roussanne du Var, Mourvèdre, and Cabernet Sauvignon. A little white is also produced.

ARIÈGE
Départementale *vin de pays* Map B

A small production of red, white, and rosé, Ariège is from the foot of the Pyrenees, overlapping the notional borders of Southwest France and Languedoc-Roussillon. Pure varietals allowed.

ATLANTIQUE
Regional *vin de pays* Map B

Encompassing the *départements* of Charente, Charente-Maritime, Dordogne, Gironde, and the northwestern corner of Lot-et-Garonne. Red, white, and rosé wines made from varieties permitted for each respective *département*.

AUDE
Départementale *vin de pays* Map B

Although still the second or third largest *vin de pays*, this used to boast almost exactly the same output as Vin de Pays d'Oc in 1993, but while the production of the latter appellation has more than trebled, Vin de Pays de L'Aude has virtually stood still. Nevertheless, a lot of fresh and fruity wine is made here, most of which is red, with just 5 per cent each of rosé and white. Mediterranean grape varieties dominate. Pure varietal wines have been allowed since 2000.

✓ *Boutinot* (Le Fou Pinot Noir) • *de La Bouysse* ⑬ (Merlot) • *de Fontannelles* (Poête Renaissance) • *Pradines d'Amont* (Cuvée Demi Lune) • *De la Souterranne* (Cuvée Christophe Old Vine Carignan)

AVEYRON
Départementale *vin de pays* Map B

Since most of the wines produced in this *département*, which is situated between Cahors and Hérault, used to claim the Vin de Pays des Gorges et Côtes de Millau (now Millau AOC) appellation, it will be interesting to see how many *vin de pays* producers utilize this denomination or prefer to use the wider Comté Tolosan appellation. Pure varietal wines have been allowed since 2000.

BALMES DAUPHINOISES
Zonal *vin de pays* Map B, No.6

In the denomination of Balmes Dauphinoises, dry white, made from Jacquère and Chardonnay, accounts for 60 per cent of production, and red, made from Gamay and Pinot Noir, accounts for 40 per cent. Rosé may also be produced.

BÉNOVIE
Zonal *vin de pays* Map A, No.7

This denomination is located at the eastern extremity of the Coteaux du Languedoc and overlaps part of the Muscat-de-Lunel area. Almost 80 per cent of the production is a light, fruity red, made predominantly from Carignan, Grenache, Cinsault, and Syrah, although Merlot and Cabernet Sauvignon may also be used. A fair amount of attractive rosé is made, mostly by the *saignée* method, plus a small quantity of Ugni Blanc-based dry white. Pure varietal wines have been allowed since 2000.

✓ *des Hospitaliers* (Merlot)

BÉRANGE
Zonal *vin de pays* Map A, No.8

Production in Bérange is 75 per cent red, 20 per cent rosé, and 5 per cent white, made from a range of grape varieties very similar to those used in the Coteaux du Languedoc and neighbouring Bénvoie.

BESSAN
Zonal *vin de pays* Map A, No.9

This tiny, single-village denomination just east of Béziers is best known for its dry, aromatic rosé, which now accounts for 65 per cent of production. Just 10 per cent red is made, with simple Ugni Blanc-based white accounting for the balance.

✓ *Le Rose de Bessan* (Cuvée Spéciale)

BIGORRE
Zonal *vin de pays* Map B, No.10

Mostly full, rich, Madiran-type red wine is made here, plus a little good crisp, dry white. Rosé may also be produced.

BOUCHES-DU-RHÔNE
Départementale *vin de pays* Map B

This denomination has one of the largest *vin de pays* productions in the country, some 80 per cent of which is red and most of that comes from the Coteaux d'Aix-en-Provence area. These wines are warm, spicy, and often quite powerfully structured from Carignan, Grenache, Cinsault, Cabernet Sauvignon, Merlot, and Syrah. The production of rosé is just 12 per cent, which is a reasonable proportion for the style, and also in view of the absence of the mystique of a name (it cannot have Provence on the label). The quality is invariably much better than most of the AOC rosé from this area. A little white is also made from Ugni Blanc, Clairette, Bourboulenc, Vermentino, Chardonnay, and Chasan (a slightly aromatic Listan and Chardonnay cross). Domaine de Trévallon is not only the finest wine of the appellation, but one of the greatest *vins de pays*, producing a quality easily equal to some of the best *crus classés* of Bordeaux. Pure varietal wines have been allowed since 2000.

✓ *Hauvette* ◉ • *de l'Île St-Pierre* (Chardonnay) • *La Michelle* (Rouge) • *Jean-Paul Luc* (Minna Vineyard Rouge) • *de Trévallon*

BOURBONNAIS
Zonal *vin de pays* Map B, No.11

This is a rarely seen *vin de pays* from a white-only area of unclassified vines in the Loire Valley.

CALVADOS
Départementale vin de pays Map B

Growers are legally entitled to produce a *vin de pays* named after the *département* in which the vines are located, but after all the fuss about *départementale* names that could be construed to come from a classic wine region, it is surprising to see Calvados approved. Although a *départementale vin de pays*, the area of vines is very small, located at Grisy, west of St Pierre-sur-Dives. The wines are varietal (Auxerrois, Pinot Gris, Melon, and Müller-Thurgau) made by Gérard Samson under the Arpents du Soleil label. Pure varietal wines have been allowed since 2000.

CANTAL
Départementale vin de pays Map B

Better known for its excellent mountain cheese, Cantal has few vines, mostly in the southwestern corner. Never encountered.

CASSAN
Zonal *vin de pays* Map A, No.12

This area is in the Coteaux du Languedoc north of Béziers and overlaps part of Faugères. Almost three-quarters of the wine is red and full bodied, from Carignan, Cinsault, Grenache, Cabernet Sauvignon, Merlot, and Syrah. The balance is split between a well-flavoured rosé and a crisp, dry white made primarily from Ugni Blanc, although Clairette and Terret may also be used. Since 2000, however, it has been permissible to market wines as pure varietals, without any specification in the new regulation as to what those varieties may be, hence the Tempranillo below.

✓ *de La Tour Penedesses* (Tempranillo Mas de Couy Elevé en Fûts de Chêne)

CATHARE
Zonal *vin de pays* Maps A & B, No.13

This area overlapping the Aude and Ariège *départements* was made a *vin de pays* in 2001. Red wines are made from the following: Merlot, Cabernet Franc, Cabernet Sauvignon, and Merlot, one or more of which must represent 50 to 70 per cent of the entire blend, plus at least two of the following must account for 30 to 50 per cent: Arinarnoa, Caladoc, Carignan, Cinsaut, Chenanson, Eiodola, Grenache, Malbec, Marselan, Pinot Noir, Pinot Gris, Pinot

Blanc, Portan, and Syrah. For white wine, there should be 60 to 80 per cent of Chardonnay and/or Sauvignon Blanc, plus 20 to 40 per cent Bourboulenc, Chasan, Chenin Blanc, Grenache, Grenache Blanc, Macabéo, Marsanne, Mauzac, Roussanne, Sémillon, Ugni Blanc, Vermentino, and Viognier. Rosé is made from Merlot, Cabernet Franc, Cabernet Sauvignon, and Syrah, one or more of which must represent 50 to 70 per cent of the entire blend, plus one or more of the following, which must account for 30 to 50 per cent: Caladoc, Cinsaut, Chanson, Grenache, and Portan.

✓ *de Sautes* (Signature Cathare)

CAUX
Zonal *vin de pays* Map A, No.14

This *vin de pays* produces a good, typical dry and fruity rosé in a Languedoc style from vines growing north of Béziers. Some 40 per cent of the output is red, and a little white and rosé are also made. Pure varietal wines have been allowed since 2000.

✓ *Caves Molière* (Barbier Gely Rouge, Cuvée des Comédiens Rouge) • *De Nizas* (Carignan Vieilles Vignes) • *Pech Rome* (Tempranillo)

CESSENON
Zonal *vin de pays* Map A, No.15

This appellation produces red wines of a rustic St-Chinian style, plus a little rosé.

CÉVENNES
Zonal *vin de pays* Map A, No.16

This new appellation is an amalgamation of four former *vins de pays*, now sub-zones: Coteaux Cévenols (16a), Coteaux du Salavès (16b), Côtes du Libac (16c – originally Serre du Coiran), Mont Bouquet (16d), and Uzège (16e), each of which may add its sub-zonal name to the Vin de Pays des Cévennes. Most of the wines are red; 15 per cent are rosé, with *saignée* rosé a speciality. Pure varietal wines have been allowed since 2000. Very small quantities of white *vin primeur* are also produced. Production is mostly of an honest, fruity Languedoc style. Pure varietal wines have been allowed since 2000.

✓ *Clos de La Roque* (Pinot Noir) • *Les Terrasses* (Roche Fourcade) • *Vindivin* (Domaine Fonce Grives Rouge)

CHARENTAIS
Zonal *vin de pays* Map B, No.17

The dry white wines are really good, even though 50 per cent of the grapes used are Ugni Blanc. It seems that this lowly variety and, indeed, the Colombard make light but very fresh, crisp, and tangy wine in the Charente, which is not only well suited to distilling Cognac, but makes a cheap, cheerful, quaffable wine. Some red and rosé wines from Gamay and *bordelais* grapes are also made. The following sub-zonal areas are allowed to add their names to Vin de Pays Charentais: Île d'Oléron (17a), Île de Ré (17b), and Saint Sornin (17c). Pure varietal wines have been allowed since 2000.

✓ *de La Chauvillière* (Chardonnay) • *Gardrat* (Colombard) • *Chai du Roussoir* (Cabernet Terroir de Fossiles) • *Terra Sana*

CHARENTE
Départementale vin de pays Map B

Hardly used *départementale vin de pays*, most producers preferring the wider-known Vin de Pays Charentais. Pure varietal wines have been allowed since 2000.

CHARENTE-MARITIMES
Départementale vin de pays Map B

Hardly used *départementale vin de pays*, most producers preferring the wider-known Vin de Pays Charentais. Pure varietal wines have been allowed since 2000.

CHER
Départementale vin de pays Map B

Mostly Touraine-like, Gamay-based red wine, plus a small amount of dry rosé in a light *vin gris* style. Since 1997, an increasing amount of dry white Sauvignon Blanc has been made by the cooperative at Venesmes, which makes a wine comparable to a rustic Sancerre or Menetou-Salon. Pure varietal wines have been allowed since 2000.

CILAOS
Zonal *vin de pays* Map B, No.18

The most remote of all French wines, the Vin de Pays de Cilaos was created in January 2004 for vines growing on the island of Réunion, a French protectorate in the Indian Ocean, 680 kilometres (420 miles) east of Madagascar. Grape varieties already grown include Chenin Blanc, Pinot Noir, and Malbec, with plans to plant Gros Manseng, Pinotage, Syrah, and Verdelho. The styles produced are red, white, rosé and, because the tendency is for grapes to overripen rather too easily, *moelleux*. The only wine producer currently is the local cooperative, which in January 2004 enjoyed its first harvest of 28 tons of grapes and now averages 50,000 bottles a year. *Cilaos* means "the place you never leave".

CITÉ DE CARCASSONNE
Zonal *vin de pays* Map A, No.19

Red wines account for over 90 per cent of production, rosé 5 per cent, and white wine barely 1 per cent. The wines come from 11 communes around Carcassonne. Pure varietal wines have been allowed since 2000. If blended, red and rosé wines must include at least 20 per cent of one or more of the following: Cabernet Franc, Cabernet Sauvignon, Malbec, Merlot, Pinot Noir, and Syrah, plus a maximum of 40 per cent Alicante Bouschet, Arinarnoa, Caladoc, Carignan, Chenanson, Cinsault, Eiodola, Grenache, Marselan, and Portan. Red *vin de primeur* is restricted to Chenanson, Cinsault, Merlot, Portan, and Syrah. White wine blends may be made from any of the following: Bourboulenc, Carignan Blanc, Chardonnay, Chasan, Chenin Blanc, Clairette, Colombard, Grenache Blanc, Macabéo, Marsanne, Mauzac, Muscat d'Alexandrie, Muscat à Petits Grains Blanc, Picpoul, Roussanne, Sauvignon Blanc, Sémillon, Terret, Turbat, Ugni Blanc, and Viognier.

✓ *Auzias* • *Sarrail* (Pech l'Estagnère)

COLLINES DE LA MOURE
Zonal *vin de pays* Map A, No.20

More than 80 per cent of production is basic red, made from a choice of Carignan, Cinsault, Grenache, Syrah, Cabernet Sauvignon, and Merlot, the last two of which are often vinified separately. A light, dry rosé accounts for about 15 per cent of production, but very little white is made and it is mostly from Ugni Blanc. Although late-harvest rather than a *vin doux naturel*, it should still come as no surprise that this *vin de pays* denomination roughly corresponds to the AOCs Muscat de Mireval and Muscat de Frontignan.

✓ *Du Chapitre-Montpellier* (Les Délices Rouge) • *Montlobre* (La Chapelle) • *de Mujolan* (Mas de Mante Vertige)

COLLINES RHODANIENNES
Zonal *vin de pays* Map B, No.21

A large denomination at the centre of Comtés Rhodaniens, this *vin de pays* straddles five *départements* (Rhône, Isère, Drôme, Ardèche, and Loire) and produces primarily red wines from Gamay, Syrah, Merlot, and Pinot Noir. Some extremely small quantities are made of rosé and white, the latter coming from an interesting choice of Chardonnay, Marsanne, Roussanne, Viognier, Jacquère, Aligoté, and Clairette. With the range of body, fatness, aromatic complexity, and acidity that a successful blend of these varieties could bring, there is ample scope for Collines Rhodaniennes to develop a first-rate reputation for white wines. Pure varietal wines have been allowed since 2000.

✓ *Cuilleron-Gaillard-Villard* (Sotanum) • *François Villard* (Syrah)

COMTÉ DE GRIGNAN
Zonal *vin de pays* Map B, No.22

Virtually all the production of Comté de Grignan is red and most of that Grenache-dominated, although Syrah, Cinsault, Gamay, Carignan, Merlot, and Cabernet Sauvignon are also allowed. Rosé accounts for just 1 per cent, and white is virtually non-existent.

COMTÉ TOLOSAN
Regional *vin de pays* Map B

Modest quantities of mostly red wines are produced, with some rosé and a tiny amount of white (of which Daubert and Ribonnet stand out). The white wines should be made from the same grape varieties permitted for Armagnac (Blanc Dame, Colombard, Folle Blanche, Graisse, Jurançon Blanc, Mauzac, Mauzac Rosé, Meslier St-François, Ugni Blanc, and until 2010 Baco Blanc). Red wine grapes are not specified beyond "what is growing"! Certainly the white wines are the most successful. Domaine de Ribonnet makes a very good stab at the Australian Chardonnay-Sauvignon Blanc style. Pure varietal wines have been allowed since 2004.

✓ *Baudave* (Rouge) • *François Daubert* (Madrigal sur le Mauzac) • *Claude Nicolas* (Les Castellanes Blanc) *Plaimont* (Rive Haute Sauvignon Blanc) • *de Ribonnet* • *Tarani* (Malbec, Sauvignon) • *Terréo* (Negrette Rosé) • *Clos Triguedina* (Vin de Lune le Molleux du Clos)

COMTÉS RHODANIENS
Regional *vin de pays* Map B

Created in 1989, Comtés Rhodaniens encompasses eight *départements* and its name can be given only to wines that have already qualified as a zonal *vin de pays*. It is the smallest of the five regional *vins de pays*, with just one-tenth of the production of the second-smallest regional *vin de pays* (Comté Tolosan), and a mere one-thousandth of the largest (Oc).

✓ *CV Ardechois*

CORRÈZE
Départementale vin de pays Map B

Mostly reds from Cabernet Franc, Merlot, and Gamay, grown on the stony, limestone *coteaux* of Branceilles, the vineyards of which flourished in the 19th century, but were restored in the 1990s. Pure varietal wines have been allowed since 2000.

✓ *Mille et Une Pierre* (Elevé en Fûts de Chêne)

CÔTE VERMEILLE
Zonal *vin de pays* Map A, No.23

Mostly red and rosé, these wines are the *vin de pays* equivalent of Collioure, which in turn is the table-wine equivalent of Banyuls.

✓ *Vial Magnères*

COTEAUX DE L'ARDÈCHE
Zonal *vin de pays* Map B, No.24

This large denomination has a very significant output and is particularly well known for its dark, spicy red wine, which accounts for 80 per cent of the total production. Often Syrah-dominated, this wine may also include Cabernet Sauvignon, Carignan, Cinsault, Grenache, Gamay, and Merlot. Louis Latour's Chardonnay put this *vin de pays* on the map during the 1990s, and the same firm's stunning Pinot Noir is proving to be an even greater success. Just over 10 per cent of this denomination's total output is rosé, and just under 10 per cent is white, the latter made from Bourboulenc, Marsanne, Viognier, Roussanne, Marsanne, Sauvignon Blanc, and Ugni Blanc. About 30 per cent of all wines produced are sold as pure varietal.

✓ *CV Ardèchois* • *de Bournet* (Chris) • *Mas d'Intras* • *Louis Latour* • *des Louanes* (L'Encre de Sy)

COTEAUX AUXOIS
Zonal *vin de pays* Map B, No.25

This zonal *vin de pays* has replaced the *départementale* denomination Côte d'Or (which some growers want to utilize for a new AOC), and may produce red and rosé wines from one or more of Gamay, Pinot Gris, and Pinot Noir; while white wines are made from one or more of Aligoté, Auxerrois, Chardonnay, Pinot Gris, Melon de Bourgogne, Sauvignon Blanc, and Sauvignon Gris.

✓ *CV de Flavigny* (Chardonnay Fûts de Chêne)

COTEAUX DES BARONNIES
Zonal *vin de pays* Map B, No.26

Almost 90 per cent of Coteaux des Baronnies wines are red and almost 10 per cent rosé, made from Cabernet Sauvignon, Cinsault, Syrah, Grenache, Pinot Noir, Gamay, and Merlot. Less than 2 per cent is white, with varietal wines generally increasing. Pure varietal wines have been allowed since 2000.

✓ *du Rieu Frais* (Cabernet Sauvignon) • *La Rosière* (Merlot)

COTEAUX DE BESSILLES
Zonal *vin de pays* Map A, No.27

Fresh, light, rustic-style wines from the Coteaux du Languedoc immediately north of Pinet. Production is two-thirds red, one-quarter rosé, and the balance white. Pure varietal wines have been allowed since 2000.

✓ *Les Grands Chais de France* (François Dulac Rouge) • *St-Hilaire* (Vermentino)

COTEAUX DE LA CABRERISSE
Zonal *vin de pays* Map A, No.28

Mostly red wine, as might be expected from what is after all the heart of Corbières, with 10 per cent rosé and just 3 per cent white, including some *vins primeurs*. There is a wide range of grape varieties permitted, particularly for the red, which may be made from Carignan, Grenache, Cinsault, Syrah, Mourvèdre, Terret Noir, Cabernet Sauvignon, Cabernet Franc, Merlot, and the Teinturier grape Alicante Bouschet. White grapes include Terret, Grenache Blanc, Clairette, Ugni Blanc, and Macabéo.

COTEAUX DE CEZE
Zonal *vin de pays* Map A, No.29

This is a large denomination with a modest output of roughly 80 per cent red and 20 per cent rosé, with a minuscule amount of white.

✓ *Armand et Roger Maby*

COTEAUX CHARITOIS
Zonal *vin de pays* Map B, No.30

Basic white wines and light reds (Pinot Noir) from the Loire Valley.

✓ *de la Vernière* (Pinot Noir)

COTEAUX DU CHER ET DE L'ARNON
Zonal *vin de pays* Map B, No.31

The reds and *vin gris* are made from Gamay, and dry white from Sauvignon Blanc.

COTEAUX DE COIFFY
Zonal *vin de pays* Map B, No.32

A relatively new and as yet untested *vin de pays* from way up north, between Champagne and Alsace, in the southeastern corner of the Haute-Marne *département*. Red and rosé from Gamay and Pinot Noir; whites from Aligoté, Arbane, Auxerrois, Chardonnay, Pinot Blanc, Pinot Gris, and Petit Meslier. Pure varietal wines have been allowed since 2001.

✓ *CV les Coteaux de Coiffy* (Auxerrois)

COTEAUX D'ENSÉRUNE
Zonal *vin de pays* Map A, No.33

This *vin de pays* west of Béziers used to produce two-thirds red and one-third rosé, but red wines now account for almost 90 per cent of the output, made from a typical range of Languedoc grapes. Just 10 per cent rosé is produced, but hardly any white. However, Jeanjean makes a nice, soft, fruity dry white from Ugni Blanc, Marsanne, and Chardonnay.

✓ *Foncalieu* (Enseduna) • *Jeanjean*

COTEAUX FLAVIENS
Zonal *vin de pays* Map A, No.34

From hills named after the Roman Emperor Flavius, this *vin de pays* just south of Nîmes in the Costières de Nîmes produces a full, warm-hearted red which accounts for 85 per cent of the output. Most of the rest is rosé, and just a small amount of white is made. Carignan, Grenache, Cinsault, Cabernet Sauvignon, Merlot, and Syrah are the main grape varieties used.

✓ *Marc Kreydenweiss* ⑬

COTEAUX DE FONTCAUDE
Zonal *vin de pays* Map A, No.35

This area overlaps much of Saint-Chinian in the

eastern section of the Coteaux du Languedoc. Almost 80 per cent of the wines are red, and these are made in a light, fresh but interesting style from Carignan, Cinsault, Grenache, Cabernet Sauvignon, and Syrah. Rosé and a little white are also to be found.

COTEAUX DE GLANES
Zonal *vin de pays* Map B, No.36

This appellation produces mainly red wines, which are Gamay or Merlot dominated, plus a little rosé.

COTEAUX DU GRÉSIVAUDAN
Zonal *vin de pays* Map B, No.37

Red and rosé Savoie-style wines made from Gamay, Pinot, and Etraire de la Dui (a local grape variety), and Jacquère-based dry whites.

COTEAUX DE LAURENS
Zonal *vin de pays* Map A, No.38

Some 85 per cent of these wines are a red *vin de pays* equivalent of Faugères, made mostly from Carignan, Cinsault, Syrah, and Grenache, but some of the better wines also include Cabernet Sauvignon and Merlot. A small amount of rosé and even less white is made.

✓ *de la Commanderie de St-Jean*

COTEAUX DU LIBRON
Zonal *vin de pays* Map A, No.39

Situated around Béziers itself, this *vin de pays* produces mainly red wines, made from Carignan, Grenache, Cinsault, Cabernet Sauvignon, Merlot, and Syrah. Some 12 per cent of the output is rosé, and less than 7 per cent white, the latter being made mainly from Ugni Blanc, with a touch of Terret and Clairette. Pure varietal wines have been allowed since 2000.

✓ *de la Colombette* • *de Pierre-Belle* (Réserve) • *Preignes le Vieux* (Alicante par Preignes) • *Terroirs en Garrigues* (Fou de Bassan Rouge)

COTEAUX DU LITTORAL AUDOIS
Zonal *vin de pays* Map A, No.40

This area corresponds geographically to the unofficial Sigean zone of Corbières, where Syrah performs best and is used, not surprisingly, in many of these *vins de pays*, of which red wine accounts for no less than 98 per cent of the total output. Other black grape varieties permitted include Carignan, Grenache, Cinsault, Merlot, and Cabernet Sauvignon. Minuscule amounts of rosé and white are produced; the latter is made mainly from Grenache Blanc and Macabéo, but can also include Ugni Blanc, Terret, and Clairette.

COTEAUX DE MIRAMONT
Zonal *vin de pays* Map A, No.41

Red wines from a typically Mediterranean range of *bordelais* and southern-Rhône grapes dominate this denomination, which bridges the Côtes de La Malepère and Corbières. Rosé and white together account for less than 5 per cent of output, including some *vins primeurs*.

✓ *Foncalieu* • *Py*

COTEAUX DE MONTÉLIMAR
Zonal *vin de pays* Map B, No.42

This *vin de pays* was established in September 2004, and encompasses vineyards between Montélimar and Dieulefit in the Drôme *département*, just north of the Coteaux de Tricastin AOC. Pure varietal

wines are allowed. Red and rosé must be made from one or more of the following: Cabernet Sauvignon, Carignan, Cinsault, Gamay, Grenache, Marselan, Merlot, Pinot Noir, and Syrah. White wines from one or more of Chardonnay, Clairette, Grenache Blanc, Marsanne, Muscat à Petits Grains, Roussanne, Sauvignon Blanc, and Viognier.

COTEAUX DE MURVIEL
Zonal *vin de pays* Map A, No.43

Just next to the Saint-Chinian area, this *vin de pays* produces some very good reds, which account for 85 per cent of the output, made from Carignan, Cinsault, Grenache, Cabernet Sauvignon, Merlot, and Syrah. There are a number of rosés, but very few whites.

✓ *de Ciffre* (Val Taurou) • *de Ravanès* (Les Gravières du Taurou Grande Réserve)

COTEAUX DE NARBONNE
Zonal *vin de pays* Map A, No.44

Mostly soft red wines, and just 4 per cent in total of white and rosé, come from this coastal edge of Corbières where the vines overlap with those of Coteaux du Languedoc.

✓ *Hospitalet*

COTEAUX DE PEYRIAC
Zonal *vin de pays* Map A, No.45

Full and rustic red wines, made from local grape varieties augmented by the Syrah, Cabernet, and Merlot, account for more than 80 per cent of the production of this *vin de pays* in the heart of Minervois. The remainder is mostly rosé, with less than 1 per cent white.

✓ *La Bouscade* (Old Vine Carignan)

COTEAUX DU PONT DU GARD
Zonal *vin de pays* Map A, No.46

The Pont du Gard is a stunningly beautiful, three-tier Roman aqueduct from the 1st century BCE. Its bottom tier is still strong enough to support modern traffic 2,000 years later, but the wines of Coteaux du Pont du Gard, though mostly rich and powerful reds, are built for a considerably shorter life-span. A small amount of white and rosé is also produced, with *vins primeurs* a local speciality.

✓ *Mas de Forton* • *Leyris Mazière*

COTEAUX DU SALAGOU
Zonal *vin de pays* Map A, No.47

Production is 80 per cent red and 20 per cent rosé, from a range of typical Languedoc grapes.

✓ *Mas d'Agalis*

COTEAUX DE TANNAY
Zonal *vin de pays* Map B, No.48

This relatively new *vin de pays* area east of Sancerre was created in 2001. White wines are made from Chardonnay or Melon de Bourgogne. Red and rosé come from Gamay and Pinot Noir, plus up to 20 per cent of Gamay Teinturier de Bouze and Gamay de Chaudenay. Pure varietal wines are allowed.

✓ *Cyrille Raty* (Chardonnay)

COTEAUX ET TERRASSES DE MONTAUBAN
Zonal *vin de pays* Map B, No.49

Red and rosé wines from the Pays de La Garonne.

✓ *de Montels* (Louise)

COTEAUX DU VERDON
Zonal *vin de pays* Map B, No.50

This *vin de pays* in the northern hinterland of Côtes de Provence and Coteaux Varois was created in 1992 and has no restriction on the grape varieties that may be used.

✓ *La Colline de Vignoble* (Merlot-Cabernet Sauvignon)

CÔTES DU BRIAN
Zonal *vin de pays* Map A, No.51

An area in Minervois, Côtes du Brian produces 90 per cent red, from Carignan for the most part, although Grenache, Cinsault, Cabernet Sauvignon, Merlot, and Syrah may also be used. The balance of the production is principally rosé, with very few white wines. Pure varietal wines have been allowed since 2000.

✓ *Alliance Minervois* (Augustin Florent Rouge) • *la Combe Blanche* (Le Dessous de l'Enfer)

CÔTES CATALANES
Zonal *vin de pays* Map A, No.52

Much enlarged following the absorption of and merger with the former *vins de pays* of Catalan, Coteaux de Fenouillèdes, and Vals d'Agly. This nonsensical exercise of bureaucratic expediency has angered many, not least those in the Coteaux de Fenouillèdes, who were just beginning to make a name for themselves when their *vin de pays* was suppressed in September 2003. Furthermore, the inhabitants of the Fenouillèdes are not Catalan, nor do they speak Catalan. Pure varietal wines have been allowed since 2000.

✓ *Boudau* (Le Petit Clos Rosé, Muscat Sec) • *Calvet-Thunevin* (Cuvée Constance) • *Caves de Baixas* (Rozy) • *Cazes Frères* ❸ • *La Différence* (Carignan, Grenache Noir, Viognier Muscat) • *Galhaud* (Oenoalliance) • *Gauby* ❸ (La Soula) • *Lauriga* • *Mas Baux* (Velours Rouge) • *Mas Karolina* (Blanc Sec) • *Mas de Lavail* (Ballade) • *Matassa* ❸ • *de Pézilla* • *Salvat* (Fenouil Rouge) • *Arnaud de Villeneuve* (Muscat Moelleux, Prieuré de la Garrigue Chardonnay)

CÔTES DU CÉRESSOU
Zonal *vin de pays* Map A, No.53

Typically light and fruity Languedoc wines are produced in fairly large amounts; 60 per cent is red, 15 per cent white, and 25 per cent rosé.

CÔTES DU CONDOMOIS
Zonal *vin de pays* Map B, No.54

Production includes 60 per cent red, dominated by the Tannat grape, and 40 per cent white, from the Colombard or Ugni Blanc. A little rosé is also produced.

✓ *Plaimont* (Prestige du Condomois)

CÔTES DE GASCOGNE
Zonal *vin de pays* Map B, No.55

These deliciously tangy, dry white wines are the undistilled produce of Armagnac. Those made from the Colombard grape are the lightest, while those from the Ugni Blanc are fatter and more interesting. Manseng and Sauvignon Blanc are also used to good aromatic effect in some blends. Less than 20 per cent of production is red and barely 1 per cent rosé. Pure varietal wines have been allowed since 2000.

✓ *Les Acacias* (Petit Manseng) • *Alain Brumont* (Les Menhirs) • *des Cassagnoles* (Gros Manseng Sélection) • *Chiroulet* (Soleil Automne, Terres

Blanche) • *Famille Laplace* (Aramis) • *de Joy* (Sauvignon Gros Manseng) • *de Lartigue* • *De Pellehaut* (Ampelomeryx) • *Plaimont* • *Répertoire* (Hidden Treasures) • *SDU* (Domus Gascogne Rosé) • *Sovino Cox* • *du Tariquet* • *UBY* (Sauvignon-Chardonnay-Muscadelle) • *Vignoble de Gascogne* (Face à Face)

CÔTES DE LASTOURS
Zonal *vin de pays* Map A, No.56

This area roughly corresponds to the Cabardès VDQS and produces mostly red wines from a similar range of grapes. Just 4 per cent rosé and 3 per cent white (Mauzac, Chenin, Chardonnay, and Ugni Blanc) is made, with *vins primeurs* a local speciality.

✓ *Baron d'Ambres*

CÔTES DE MEUSE
Zonal *vin de pays* Map B, No.57

Until 1974, this was just 40 hectares (100 acres) of vineyards halfway between Champagne and Alsace, in an area that fell into neglect following phylloxera at the end of the 19th century. But then Roland Pierson of Domaine Montgrignon replanted it and led an effort to restore wine culture to these parts. The grape varieties are Gamay, Pinot Meunier, and Pinot Noir for reds, and Aligoté, Auxerrois, Chardonnay, Pinot Blanc, and Pinot Gris for whites.

CÔTES DE MONTESTRUC
Zonal *vin de pays* Map B, No.58

Production includes reds, made from Alicante Bouschet, Cabernets, Malbec, Merlot, and Jurançon Noir, and white wines, made from the Colombard, Mauzac, and Ugni Blanc.

CÔTES DE PÉRIGNAN
Zonal *vin de pays* Map A, No.59

This area is within the southern extremity of the Coteaux du Languedoc, just north of La Clape AOC and incorporating some of La Clape's northern slopes. Almost 90 per cent is red wine that is similar, if more rustic, in style to the wines of La Clape and made from a similar range of grape varieties, but with Grenache, Syrah, and Cinsault dominating. The fresh, dry rosé can be good quality and flavoursome too. Just 1 per cent of white wine is made, mainly from Clairette and Ugni Blanc, but Terret and Macabéo are also permitted. *Vin primeur* is also made.

✓ *Christophe Barbier* (Les Terres Salées) • *de La Negly* (Palazy Rosé)

CÔTES DE PROUILLE
Zonal *vin de pays* Map A, No.60

These red, white, and rosé wines produced by the Côtes de Prouille appellation come from the Aude *département*.

CÔTES DU TARN
Zonal *vin de pays* Map B, No.61

Côtes du Tarn is the *vin de pays* equivalent of Gaillac: some 60 per cent is red, 30 per cent white, and the rest rosé. These wines are made from *bordelais* and southwestern grape varieties, plus, uniquely for France, the Portugais Bleu. Gamay is often used for Côtes du Tarn Primeur, while together with Syrah it makes an appealing, delicate *saignée* rosé. Pure varietal wines have been allowed since 2000.

✓ *Chaumet Lagrange* (Braucol) • *Guy Fontaine* (Les Vignes des Garbasses Syrah) • *Sabrelle* (Chardonnay)

CÔTES DE THAU
Zonal *vin de pays* Map A, No.62

A small denomination west of Béziers, producing almost equal quantities of red, white, and rosé from all the usual Languedoc varieties. These wines used to be used for vermouth until the upswing in *vin de pays*.

✓ *Caves Richemer* (L'Ephèbe Rouge) • *de Marie-Anais* (Syrano) • *Hugues de Beauvignac* (Syrah)

CÔTES DE THONGUE
Zonal *vin de pays* Map A, No.63

Mostly red wine, from grapes including Grenache, Cinsault, Cabernet Sauvignon, Merlot, Syrah, and Carignan, with *vins primeurs* of the last three varieties a speciality. Emphasis is placed on pure varietal wines of all styles. Some 15 per cent rosé and 10 per cent white.

✓ *Chemins de Bessac* • *de Brescou* (Syrah) • *Coste Rousse* • *CV d'Alignan du Vent* (Icare, Montarels) • *Clos de l'Arjolle* • *de la Croix Belle* (Cascaïllou, No.7 Rouge) • *Deshenrys* (Lissac) • *Les Filles de Septembre* • *Mont d'Hortes* (Sauvignon) • *de Montmarin* • *Montplézy* (Félicité) • *Saint Rose* (Roussanne) • *Les 3 Poules* (La Coquine) • *Vignerons de l'Occitane* (Clamery Réserve Rouge)

CÔTES DU VIDOURLE
Zonal *vin de pays* Map A, No.64

Wedged between the Coteaux du Languedoc and Costières de Nîmes, more than 80 per cent of the wines produced are red, from Carignan, Grenache, Cinsault, Cabernet Sauvignon, Merlot, Cabernet Franc, and Syrah. About 15 per cent rosé is made, but white is seldom seen.

CREUSE
Départementale *vin de pays* Map B

Little-used *départementale vin de pays* right in the centre of France. Red and rosé wines are made primarily from Cabernet Sauvignon, Cabernet Franc, Merlot and Tannat. White wines are primarily from Chenin Blanc, Sauvignon Blanc, and Sémillon. Pure varietal wines are allowed.

CUCUGNAN
Zonal *vin de pays* Map A, No.65

A tiny denomination of essentially red wines in the midst of the Côtes du Roussillon Villages district, produced from Rhône varieties boosted by Cabernet Sauvignon and Merlot. Rosé may be made, but it seldom is, although there is an average of 1 per cent dry white from Mauzac, Chenin Blanc, Chardonnay, and Ugni Blanc.

DEUX-SÈVRES
Départementale *vin de pays* Map B

Simple wines of a frank nature, from the vineyards with the richest soil (and thus the poorest for wine production) in the Nantais. Pure varietal wines have been allowed since 2000.

✓ *Bouvet-Ladubay* (Non Pareils)

DORDOGNE
Départementale *vin de pays* Map B

The *département* is named after one of the two great rivers of Bordeaux and includes AOCs such as Bergerac and Monbazillac, thus should have plenty of potential for aspiring *vin de pays* producers. Grape varieties include Cabernet Franc, Cabernet Sauvignon, Gamay, Malbec, Merlot, and Pinot Noir for reds or rosés, and Chardonnay, Chenin Blanc, Colombard, Folle Blanche, Sémillon, and Ugni Blanc for whites.

DOUBS
Départementale *vin de pays* Map B

Recent *départementale vin de pays* with minute production, Doubs is in the very east of France, between the Jura and Alsace. Pure varietal wines have been allowed since 2000.

DRÔME
Départementale *vin de pays* Map B

Red, white, and rosé wines are produced from typical Rhône varieties augmented by Gamay, Cabernet Sauvignon, and Merlot. More than 90 per cent of the output is red and similar in style to Coteaux du Tricastin AOC. A small amount of decent rosé is made. Pure varietal wines have been allowed since 2000.

✓ *Le Plan* (Rouge) • *Sud-Est Appellations* (Syrah)

DUCHÉ D'UZÈS
Zonal *vin de pays* Map A, No.66

This area overlaps all but 10 of the 131 villages in Vin de Pays des Cévennes.

✓ *les Collines du Bourdic* (La Rabassières) • *Philippe Nusswitz* (Orénia Réserve)

FRANCHE COMTÉ
Zonal *vin de pays* Map B, No.67

A vast area overlapping the Jura and Savoie, Franche Comté produces fresh, clean, crisp, but otherwise unremarkable red and rosé wines. Only the white, made from Chardonnay, Pinot Gris, and Pinot Blanc, is of any note. Wines produced in the village of Champlitte have the right to add the sub-zonal name Coteaux de Champlitte (67a) to the Franche Comté *vin de pays*.

✓ *Vignoble Guillaume* (Pinot Noir Collection Réservée, Chardonnay Collection Réservée)

GARD
Départementale *vin de pays* Map B

A large production of mostly red wines made from Carignan, Grenache, Cinsault, Cabernet Sauvignon, Merlot, and Syrah. Some clean, fruity rosé and mainly Ugni Blanc-based white wines (with Viognier a growing niche within this small percentage). Pure varietal wines have been allowed since 2000.

✓ *Nathalie Estribeau* (Syrah-Carignan) • *Mas Aveylands* • *Mas de Bressades* • *de Campuget* (Viognier Prestige) • *des Cantarelles* • *de Guiot* • *Saint-Antoine*

GAULES
Zonal *vin de pays* Map B, No.68

This covers "just" 95 villages in the Beaujolais district Revillages, and not the larger area that was originally envisaged. Red, white, and rosé wines made from Aligoté, Chardonnay, Gamay, Pinot Noir, Syrah, and Viognier. A minimum cellarage of three months prevents any *vin de primeur*, thereby protecting Beaujolais Nouveau.

✓ *Marcel Lapierre*

GERS

Départementale vin de pays Map B

Mostly white wines, similar in style to Côtes de Gascogne. Pure varietal wines have been allowed since 2000.

✓ *Patrick Azcué* • *Château Bouscassé* • *Plaimont* (Rive Haute)

GIRONDE

Départementale vin de pays Map B

Red and white wines made in isolated areas not classified for the production of Bordeaux. Pure varietal wines have been allowed since 2000.

HAUTE GARONNE

Départementale vin de pays Map B

Robust red and rosé wines made from Jurançon Noir, Négrette, and Tannat grapes grown in old vineyards south of Toulouse, with a little Merlot, Cabernet, and Syrah. A minuscule amount of dry white is made, and total production of all styles is very small, but De Ribonnet has put this denomination on the viticultural map and is in a class apart from all the other producers. Pure varietal wines have been allowed since 2000.

✓ *de Ribonnet*

HAUTE MARNE

Départementale vin de pays

Located adjacent to Champagne's Aube and Burgundy's Côte d'Or, it is not surprising that Le Muid Montsaugeonnais has made some pretty good Pinot Noir. Pure varietal wines have been allowed since 2000.

✓ *Le Muid Montsaugeonnais* (Pinot Noir Elevé en Fûts de Chêne)

HAUTERIVE

Zonal vin de pays Map A, No.69

Formerly called Vin de Pays d'Hauterive en Pays d'Aude, this appellation was renamed in 2004, when it was merged with the former *vins de pays* of Coteaux de Termenès, Côtes de Lézignan, and Val d'Orbieu. Production is primarily red, made from a range of typical Languedoc and southwestern grapes in the Corbières. A little *vin primeur* is made, as well as small amounts of white and rosé.

✓ *Du Cerbier*

HAUTES-ALPES

Départementale vin de pays Map B

Very little wine is produced under this denomination, which is the *département* just south of the Savoie. Pure varietal wines have been allowed since 2000.

✓ *Allemond* (Blanc) • *de Trésbaudon* (Rouge)

HAUTE-SAÔNE

Départementale vin de pays Map B

Rarely used, this is a minor *départementale vin de pays* for red, white, and rosé wines from unclassified vineyards in the south of Burgundy. Pure varietal wines have been allowed since 2000.

HAUTES-PYRÉNÉES

Départementale vin de pays Map B

Better known for Lourdes, ski resorts, and trekking, Haut-Pyrénées boasts very few vineyards, although authorized varieties include Abouriou, Cabernet Franc, Cabernet Sauvignon, Cot, Duras, Fer, Jurançon Noir, Merlot, Négrette, Tannat, and Fer Servadou for reds, and Colombard, Gros

Manseng, Len de l'El, Muscadelle, Sauvignon, and Sémillon for whites.

HAUTE-VALLÉE DE L'AUDE

Zonal vin de pays Map A, No.70

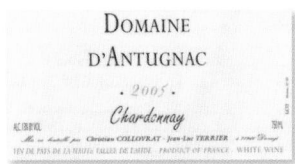

Mostly dry whites, from Chardonnay, Chenin, Mauzac, and Terret grapes grown in the Limoux district. A quarter of the output is red, from *bordelais* grapes, with just 3 per cent rosé. Pure varietal wines have been allowed since 2000.

✓ *de l'Aigle* (Chardonnay Les Aigles, Pinot Noir Terres Rouges) • *Marc Ramires* (Prieuré d'Antugnac)

HAUTE-VALLÉE DE L'ORB

Zonal vin de pays Map A, No.71

A limited amount of red, white, and rosé, primarily from Pinot Noir, Chardonnay, and Viognier. Pure varietal wines have been allowed since 2000.

✓ *Marc Ramires* (Prieuré d'Antugnac) • *de Roquebrun* (Terres d'Orb)

HAUTE-VIENNE

Départementale vin de pays Map B

Rarely used, minor *départementale vin de pays* for red, white, and rosé wines east of the Cognac region. Pure varietal wines have been allowed since 2000.

HAUTS DE BADENS

Zonal vin de pays Map A, No.72

These red and rosé wines are produced in a rustic Minervois style.

HÉRAULT

Départementale vin de pays Map B

Red wine accounts for 85 per cent of production and is increasing. The choice of grapes is quite wide, but most blends are based on Carignan, Cinsault, Grenache, and Syrah, boosted by a small proportion of *bordelais* varieties. About 10 per cent rosé and 5 per cent white wine is produced, the latter made from Clairette, Macabéo, Grenache Blanc, and Ugni Blanc. Production is vast, over one million hectolitres (11 million cases), making it the second or third largest *vin de pays*, together with Vin de Pays de l'Aude. Improved viticultural techniques have transformed what was once the heart of Midi mediocrity into delicious, brilliant-value wine in some cases. Pure varietal wines are allowed.

The most famous wine bearing this modest *vin de pays* denomination is, of course, Mas de Daumas Gassac. Situated northwest of Montpellier at Aniane, this property has been dubbed "the Lafite of the Languedoc", but when Aimé and Véronique Guibert

purchased it, wine was the last thing on their minds. That was, however, before the visit of Professor Enjalbert, the Bordeaux geologist and author, who discovered Daumas Gassac had a rare, fine, powdery volcanic soil that is an incredible 20 metres (65 feet) deep. Enjalbert predicted that it would yield a world-class wine if cultivated as a *grand cru*, and that is exactly what Aimé Guibert set out to do. I am not convinced about the rosé, and the white has been far too flabby in recent vintages, but the red is the equivalent of a Bordeaux *cru classé*. Even in lighter vintages, when Guibert gets slated by the critics, I think his red has a rare elegance that is missed just because it is not as big as people expect.

✓ *Château d'Agel* • *Alchemy* (Sandpiper Carignan-Shiraz) • *Mas de Daumas Gassac* (Rouge) • *de la Fadèze* • *Foncalieu* (Carignan-Merlot) • *CV Frontignan* (Abeillon) • *La Grange des Pères* • *Mas de Janiny* (Cabernet Sauvignon) • *Moulin de Gassac* (Guilhem, Villeveyrac) • *Les Quatre Pilas* (Mouchère) • *Valjulius*

ÎLE DE BEAUTÉ

Zonal vin de pays Map B, No.73

With AOC wines accounting for just 15 per cent of Corsica's wine output, its one all-encompassing (though technically not *départementale*) vin de pays has a huge impact on the perceived quality of this island's wine. Almost 60 per cent of this *vin de pays* is red and 25 per cent rosé, both made from a wide range of grapes, including many indigenous Corsican varieties, some of which may be related to certain Italian grapes. Grape varieties used include: Aleatico (red Muscat-like variety), Cabernet Sauvignon, Carignan, Cinsault, Grenache, Merlot, Syrah, Barbarossa, Nielluccio (the widest-planted on the island and said to be related to Sangiovese), Sciacarello (echoes of Provence's Tibouren), and Pinot Noir. A lot of effort is made to promote Corsican Pinot Noir, but at the time of writing this seems to be totally misguided. The best show decent varietal aroma, but lack an elegance of fruit and do not possess the essence of Pinot on the palate. Maybe someone will make good Corsican Pinot Noir, but it is a variety that requires a lot more care and attention in the vineyard and winery than is evident in any example I have tasted so far. Nielluccio has a reputation for good rosé, but as Orenga de Gaffory of Patrimonio in Corsica has shown, it also has the ability to produce a very fine red wine.

White wines from Chardonnay, Ugni Blanc, Muscat, and Vermentino are usually more demonstrative of clean, anaerobic handling and very cool fermentation than they are of any expression of *terroir*. Pure varietal wines have been allowed since 2000.

✓ *Casabianca* (Moderato, Nectar d'Automne) • *du Mont Saint-Jean* (Aleatico, Pinot Noir) • *de Patrapiana* (Nielluciu) • *de Saline* • *Skalli* (Terra Vecchia Rouge) • *Union des Vignerons* (Marestagno, Réserve du Président Muscat)

INDRE

Départementale vin de pays Map B

Red, white, and rosé wines, including a pale *vin gris* style, from traditional Loire grape varieties are produced under this appellation. Pure varietal wines have been allowed since 2000.

INDRE-ET-LOIRE

Départementale vin de pays Map B

From vineyards east of Tours, this *vin de pays* is 80 per cent red, made primarily from Gamay, although

Cabernet Franc and Grolleau are also used. A little white, but even less rosé, is made. Pure varietal wines are allowed.

ISÈRE
Départementale vin de pays Map B

Hardly used *départementale vin de pays*, most producers preferring one of a number of zonal appellations for the unclassified vineyards in this part of the northern Rhône Valley. Mostly red wine, a smattering of white, but no rosé. Pure varietal wines have been allowed since 2000.

LANDES
Départementale vin de pays Map B

Red, white, and rosé wines are produced under this appellation. Approximately 80 per cent is red, and the grapes used are traditional southwestern varieties. Pure varietal wines have been allowed since 2000.

✓ *Duprat Frères* (Cabernet-Tannat)

LOIRE-ATLANTIQUE
Départementale vin de pays Map B

Red and rosé wines, including a pale *vin gris*, are made from Gamay and Grolleau, while Folle Blanche and Melon are used for white, with some interesting developments using Chardonnay. Pure varietal wines are allowed.

✓ *Jean Douillard* (Melon)

LOIRET
Départementale vin de pays Map B

A small amount of red and rosé, including a pale *vin gris* style, made from Gamay. A Sauvignon Blanc white is also made. Pure varietal wines have been allowed since 2000.

LOIR-ET-CHER
Départementale vin de pays Map B

Red, white, and rosé wines, including a pale *vin gris*, are made from traditional Loire grape varieties, mostly from around Blois in the Cheverny area. Almost half the production is red and the rest white, but a touch more of the former is made, with very little rosé. Pure varietal wines have been allowed since 2000.

LOT
Départementale vin de pays Map B

Most wines are red, and claim either the regional Comté Tolosan denomination or Vin de Pays des Coteaux de Glanes. Pure varietal wines have been allowed since 2000.

✓ *des Ardailloux* (Chardonnay Tradition) • *Côtes d'Olt* (Terreo Malbec Réserve)

LOT-ET-GARONNE
Départementale vin de pays Map B

This denomination is seldom seen, as the wines in this *département* are mostly red and sold as Vin de Pays du Comté Tolosan, but a tiny amount of white wine is produced under the Vin de Pays du Lot-et-Garonne label. Pure varietal wines have been allowed since 2000.

✓ *CV des Coteaux du Mézinais* (Gros Manseng Moelleux)

LOZÈRE
Départementale vin de pays Map B

Noted for its wild, mountainous beauty, Lozère is the least populated *département* in France, with very few vineyards. However, authorized grape varieties include Cabernet Franc, Cabernet Sauvignon, Carignan, Grenache, Mourvèdre, and Syrah for reds, and Chardonnay, Grenache Blanc, Muscat, and Viognier for whites.

MAINE-ET-LOIRE
Départementale vin de pays Map B

Production is 85 per cent red, and white and rosé account for the rest, made from traditional Loire grape varieties in the Anjou-Saumur district. Substantial quantities are produced, but most are sold from the back door. Pure varietal wines have been allowed since 2000.

✓ *Gaillard* ❸

MARCHES DE BRETAGNE
Sub-regional *vin de pays* Map B, No.74

Wines from the Marches de Bretagne sub-region have the right to add this name to the Vin de Pays du Val de Loire. Production includes red and rosé wines, made predominantly from Abouriou, Gamay, and Cabernet Franc, plus a little white from Muscadet and Gros Plant.

MAURES
Zonal *vin de pays* Map B, No.75

This denomination has a very large production and covers most of the southern part of the Côtes de Provence. Almost half the wines are rosé of a similar style and quality to those of the Vin de Pays du Var. The rest is red, which is rich, warm, and spicy, while white wine accounts for just 5 per cent of total output. Pure varietal wines have been allowed since 2000.

✓ *Borrely-Martin* (Le Carre de Laure) • *Dupéré-Barrera* (Nowat Syrah) • *Marouine* (Carignan Vieilles Vignes)

MEUSE
Départementale vin de pays Map B

This *vin de pays* produces red and rosé wines, including a pale *vin gris*, from Pinot Noir and Gamay. Some white wine from Chardonnay, Aligoté, and Auxerrois is also made. Pure varietal wines have been allowed since 2000.

✓ *de Coustille* (Pinot Gris) • *Laurent Degenève* (Auxerrois)

MONT BAUDILE
Zonal *vin de pays* Map A, No.76

Production is mostly red wine, from a typical Languedoc range of grapes grown in the foothills of the Causses de Larzac. Rosé and white account for less than 15 per cent of the total output, although crisp, dry whites are on the increase.

✓ *d'Aupilhac* • *Le Carignan de la Bastide* • *De Familongue* (Mas des Vignals) • *Cave de Mont Peyroux* (Ethnik)

MONT-CAUME
Zonal *vin de pays* Map B, No.77

Effectively the *vin de pays* of Bandol – it is indeed the red wines that are the best here, including some truly outstanding wines, such as Bunan's classic Cabernet Sauvignon. However, the main varieties for most red and rosé wines (which account for 45 per cent of the total production) are Carignan, Grenache, Cinsault, Syrah, and Mourvèdre. A little white is produced, but it is of little interest. Pure varietal wines have been allowed since 2000.

✓ *Bunan* (Cabernet Sauvignon, Mourvèdre) • *Gauby* (Ginestre)

MONTS DE LA GRAGE
Zonal *vin de pays* Map A, No.78

These red and rosé wines are produced in a basic Languedoc style, often beefed up with Syrah grapes. White wines must be truly dry (less than 2.5 grams per litre residual sugar). Pure varietal wines have been allowed since 2000.

✓ *de la Bergerie d'Amilhac* (Syrah) • *Le Bosc* (Syrah) • *Condamine Bertrand* (Petit Verdot Gourmandise) • *de la Fadèze* (Merlot Elevé en Fûts de Chêne) • *Grange des Rouquette* (Agrippa) • *de Malleport* (Alexandre) • *Mas Montelle* (Jéricho) • *de Montlobre* (Tête de Cuvée) • *de Saint-Louis* • *du Soleil* (Solstice Merlot Réserve Barrique) • *des Soulie* (Merlot) • *de Terre Mégère* (Cabernet Sauvignon) • *Vigne Blanche* (Cabernet Sauvignon)

NIÈVRE
Départementale vin de pays Map B

Red, white, and rosé wines, production of which is mostly confined to the areas of Charité-sur-Loire, La Celle-sur-Nièvre, and Tannay. Pure varietal wines have been allowed since 2000.

OC
Regional *vin de pays* Map B

This vast appellation is the most successful of all *vins de pays*, commercially and qualitatively. It sells well because of the simplicity of its name, which even Anglo-Saxons have no difficulty pronouncing, and it encompasses most of the best *vins de pays* produced in France. The "Oc" of this regional *vin de pays* is southern dialect for "yes", it being "oui" elsewhere in France, thus Languedoc, the "tongue of Oc". Some 70 per cent of production is red, with the balance split equally between white and rosé. Even though most of the finest *vins de pays* are produced here, the volume of output is so vast that the quality will inevitably be variable. What has enabled so many truly fine wines to emerge in this denomination is the role of the so-called *cépages améliorateurs*. These grapes, such as Cabernet Sauvignon, Merlot, Syrah, Chardonnay, and Sauvignon Blanc, are not traditional in the region, but add greatly to the quality and finesse of more rustic local varieties. They also make excellent varietal wines. Viognier is on the increase as a varietal wine and makes a good-value, juicy-fruity, more exotic alternative to Chardonnay. Marselan (Cabernet Sauvignon x Grenache) has been authorized since December 2005.

✓ *de l'Aigle* (Chardonnay Les Aigles) • *des Aires Hautes* • *Astruc* (Chardonnay Réserve) • *Auriol* (Merlot, Le Jour et la Nuit) • *Barton & Guestier* (Cabernet Sauvignon) • *de la Baume* • *De Bellemare* (Le Délice de la Trouffière Rouge) • *Condamine Bertrand* (Cigalus, Elixir Rouge) • *Gérard Bertrand* • *Jean-Marc Boillot* (de la Truffière) • *des Bons Auspices* (Emparitz Cabernet Sauvignon) • *Du Bosc* (Petit Verdot) • *Camplazens* (Syrah) • *CV de Cers Portiragnes* (Cabernet Sauvignon Sensation) • *Chantovent* (Chardonnay Dolmen des Fées) • *Crescendo Vignobles* (La Bouscade Chardonnay) • *Jean-Louis Denois* • *La Différence* • *De Familongue* • *Le Fort* (Blanche Chardonnay) • *Foncalieu* (Bouquet d'Oriane, Enseduna Réserve Syrah) • *de Gourgazaud* • *La Grange des Quatre Sous* • *de Granoupiac* (Merlot) • *Jeanjean* (L'Incompris) • *Lalande* (Pinot Noir) • *Michel Laroche* (La Croix Chevalière) • *Lorgeril* (Viognier de Pennautier) • *Paul Mas* • *Mas Carlot* (Syrah-Grenache) • *Mas Neuf* • *Gabriel Meffre* • *Laurent Miquel* • *Montlobre* (Tête de

Cuvée Rouge) • *Philippe Nusswitz* (Miratus)
• *Château d'Or et de Guelles* (La Syrah de
Charlotte) • *L'Ormarine* (Haut de Sénaux Syrah)
• *de l'Orviel* (Chardonnay) • *Primo Palatum*
(Chardonnay) • *Pavillon Blanc* (Les Collines du
Bourdic) • *Peirière* (Elevé en Fûts de Chêne:
Cabernet Sauvignon, Merlot, Syrah) • *Michel
Picard* (Chardonnay) • *Preignes le Vieux* (Petit
Verdot) • *Antonin Rodet* (Syrah) • *Saint Marc*
(Sauvignon) • *St-Hilaire* • *de Sérame* (Muscat
Réserve) • *Skalli* (Réserve F, Cabernet
Sauvignon, Merlot) • *du Soleil* (La Chasse du
Pape: Chardonnay, Viognier, or Syrah) • *de
Terre Mégère* • *CV des Trois Terroirs* (L'Esprit du
Midi Viognier, XL Les Grès) • *Val d'Orbieu*
(Mythique, Duo Mythique) • *Vedeau*
(Chardonnay Terre d'Amandiers) • *Arnaud de
Villeneuve* (Grenache, Syrah) • *Vindivin*
(Grenache Blanc) • *Virginie* (Castel Chardonnay
Réservée, Gold Label Cabernet Merlot Réserve)
• *Les Yeuses* (Cuvée La Soure, Les Épices Syrah)

PAYS DE RETZ
Sub-regional *vin de pays* Map B, No.79

This denomination may be added to the Vin de
Pays du Val de Loire. Best known for its rosé made
from the Grolleau Gris (typified by Domaine du
Parc), although red wines are also made from
Grolleau, Gamay, and Cabernet Franc and account
for as much as 70 per cent of production. A tiny
amount of white from Grolleau Gris can be found.
Pure varietal wines have been allowed since 2000.

✓ *du Parc* (Grolleau)

PÉRIGORD
Zonal *vin de pays* Map B, No.80

This name replaced the *départementale* Vin de Pays
of Dordogne for vines growing on the *causse* or
limestone region of Périgord, where vineyards
flourished in the 19th century. Now there are just
18 hectares (45 acres), producing 35 per cent
rosé, 10 per cent Périgord Noir, and 50 per cent
Tradition (an oak-matured red wine). The balance is
sold as *vin primeur*. The sub-zonal Vin de Domme
(80a) is allowed to add its name to this *vin de pays*.

✓ *CV des Coteaux du Céou* (Vin de
Domme Tradition) • *Grand Gaillard*
(Sauvignon Blanc)

PETITE CRAU
Zonal *vin de pays* Map B, No.81

A small *vin de pays* just south of Avignon,
production is almost 80 per cent red and 20
per cent rosé from mostly Carignan, Grenache,
Cinsault, and Syrah. Most rosé wines are made
from, or dominated by, the Cinsault using the
saignée method. Insignificant amounts of white
from Ugni Blanc and Clairette are also produced.
Pure varietal wines are allowed.

✓ *CV de Laure* (Cabernet Pétrarque et Laure)

PORTES DE MÉDITERRANÉE
Regional *vin de pays* Map B

A vast regional *vin de pays*, but merely a modest
production.

✓ *CV de Beaumes-de-Venise* (Balma Venitia) • *La
Blaque* (Pinot Noir) • *Mas Bleu* (Blue Touch
Rosé) • *de Régusse* (Muscat Moelleux) • *Roy
René* (Florie Rouge, Massilia Rosé)

PRINCIPAUTÉ D'ORANGE
Zonal *vin de pays* Map B, No.82

This is a full red wine, made predominantly from
Rhône grape varieties grown around Orange, north
of Avignon, in an area that bridges Châteauneuf-du-
Pape and Côtes-du-Rhône Villages. Just 4 per cent
rosé and barely 1 per cent white is made.

✓ *de l'Ameillaud* • *Font Simian*
• *Les Pialons* (Rosé)

PUY-DE-DÔME
Départementale *vin de pays* Map B

Red, white, and rosé wines of simple, rustic
quality are made under this appellation. A *puy*
is a volcano stack, a number of which are found
in the Puy-de-Dôme *département*. Pure varietal
wines have been allowed since 2000.

PYRÉNÉES-ATLANTIQUES
Départementale *vin de pays* Map B

Two-thirds red and one-third white wine from
traditional southwestern grape varieties is produced
under this appellation. Pure varietal wines have
been allowed since 2000.

PYRÉNÉES-ORIENTALES
Départementale *vin de pays* Map B

From the most southerly French *département*,
bordering Spain's Andorra region, much of the
vin de pays in the Pyrénées-Orientales comes from
the same area as the AOC Côtes-du-Roussillon and
Vin de Pays Catalan. Most of the production consists
of full, fruity reds, with just 10 per cent rosé and
5 per cent white. Pure varietal wines have been
allowed since 2000.

✓ *The Fifteen* (Grenache) • *Le Roc des Anges* (Les
Vieilles Vignes)

SABLES DU GOLFE DU LION
Zonal *vin de pays* Map A, No.83

A very go-ahead *vin de pays* situated along the
Mediterranean coast of Gard, Hérault, and
Bouches-du-Rhône, where the vines are mostly
ungrafted and grown on an amazing sandbar with
seawater on both sides. Production is, unusually,
two-thirds rosé, including a large proportion in pale
vin gris style, plus 30 per cent red and a small
amount of white wine. Pure varietal wines have
been allowed since 2000.

✓ *Jean Berteau* • *Bosquet-Canet* (Cabernet
Sauvignon) • *Jeanjean* (Le Pive Blanc) • *Listel*
(Jarras Gris de Gris) • *du Petit Chaumont*
(Chardonnay)

SAINT-GUILHEM-LE-DÉSERT
Zonal *vin de pays* Map A, No.84

Formerly called Vin de Pays des Gorges de
L'Héraut, this denomination is in Coteaux du
Languedoc and overlaps most of the Clairette du
Languedoc appellation, yet less than 10 per cent of
its wines are white, with Ugni Blanc and Terret
supporting Clairette. They are, however, better
known than the reds, which account for over 80 per

cent of output. Some rosés are also made.

✓ *d'Aupilhac* (Plos des Baumes)

SAINT-SARDOS
Zonal *vin de pays* Map B, No.85

This *vin de pays* produces wines from a typical
jumble of grape varieties, with reds and rosés from
Cabernet Franc, Cabernet Sauvignon, Gamay, Syrah,
and Tannat, plus a maximum of 30 per cent in total
of Gamay Teinturier de Bouze and Teinturier de
Chaudenay, both of which have coloured juice;
while whites are made from Chardonnay, Mauzac,
Muscadelle, Sauvignon Blanc, and Sémillon.

✓ *CV de Saint-Sardos* (Gilles de Morban Rouge)

SAINTE BAUME
Zonal *vin de pays* Map B, No.86

This *vin de pays* was established in September
2004, and encompasses vineyards in the villages
of Bras, Brignoles, La Celle, Mazaugues, Méounes-
lès-Montrieux, Nans-les-Pins, Néoules, Ollières,
Plan-d'Aups, Riboux, La Roquebrussanne, Rougiers,
Saint-Maximin, Saint-Zacharie, Signes, and Tourves
in the Var *département*. No grape varieties are
specified, but pure varietal wines are allowed.

SAINTE-MARIE-LE-BLANCHE
Zonal *vin de pays* Map B, No.87

This *vin de pays* area straddles the border between
Côte d'Or and Saône-et-Loire. Those in the Côte
d'Or are just a few kilometres east of Beaune, and
used to have the right to the Vin de Pays de la Côte
d'Or until it was suppressed in 1998. Pure varietal
wines are allowed. Red wines are made from one
or more of Gamay, Pinot Gris, and Pinot Noir, while
white wines are made from one of the following:
Aligoté, Auxerrois, Chardonnay, Melon de
Bourgogne, Pinot Blanc, and Pinot Gris.

✓ *Vincent Sauvestre* (Chardonnay)

SAÔNE-ET-LOIRE
Départementale *vin de pays* Map B

Rarely exported *départementale vin de pays* for
mostly red and white wines from unclassified
vineyards in the Burgundy region. Pure varietal
wines have been allowed since 2000.

SARTHE
Départementale *vin de pays* Map B

Red, white, and rosé wines may be made, although
production of this *départementale vin de pays* is
minuscule and, as far as I am aware, limited to just
one grower in Marçon. Pure varietal wines have
been allowed since 2000.

SEINE-ET-MARNE
Départementale *vin de pays* Map B

Recently created, rarely used, minor *départementale
vin de pays* for red, white, and rosé wines from
unclassified vineyards in between Champagne and
Paris. Red and rosé wines from Gamay and Pinot
Noir, white wines from Aligoté, Auxerrois,
Chardonnay, and Sauvignon Blanc. Pure varietal
wines have been allowed since 2000.

TARN
Départementale *vin de pays* Map B

Relatively minor *départementale vin de pays* for
red, white, and rosé wines produced outside the
well-known Côtes du Tarn *vin de pays*. Pure
varietal wines have been allowed since 2000.

✓ *Champ d'Orphée* • *Chaumet Lagrange* (Les

Marguerites Braucol) • *CV de Labastide de Lévis* (Les Trois Bastides) • *David* (Maître Vigneron Rouge) • *Verdier* (Domaine des 3 Moineaux Braucol) • *Vigne-Lourac* (Prestige Sauvignon, Duras-Cabernet)

TARN-ET-GARONNE
Départementale vin de pays Map B

Red wine accounts for 90 per cent of the tiny production of this appellation, although some rosé and a minuscule amount of white is also made. Most of these vines are west of Montauban, in an area that can also claim the Vin de Pays Saint-Sardos, which overlaps part of a southwest VDQS called Vins de Lavilledieu. The grape varieties are similar to those for Lavilledieu, except for the fact that they can also include Merlot, Cabernet, and Tannat. Pure varietal wines have been allowed since 2000.

TERROIRS LANDAIS
Zonal *vin de pays* Map B, No.88

These are red, white, and rosé wines from four separate sub-zonal areas in Aquitaine, each of which may be appended to this *vin de pays* denomination: **Les Coteaux de Chalosse** (88a – the largest area in the south of the Landes *département*, where vines grow in and around Dax and Murgon); **Les Côtes de l'Adour** (88b – from vines around Aire-sur-Adour and Geaune); **Les Sables de l'Océan** (88c – the romantic-sounding "Sands of the Ocean" refers to vines growing in the sand dunes around Messanges); and **Les Sables Fauves** (88d – the "Wild Sands" is a tiny enclave of vines west of Eauze). Reds and rosés are made from Tannat supported by *bordelais* varieties, while whites are primarily Ugni Blanc plus Colombard, Gros Manseng, and Baroque.

✓ *Michel Guérard* (Rouge de Bachen)

THÉZAC-PERRICARD
Zonal *vin de pays* Map A, No.89

This is a small *vin de pays* adjoining the western extremity of Coteaux du Quercy, producing Cahors-like reds from Cabernet Franc, Cabernet Sauvignon, Gamay, Malbec, Merlot, and Tannat.

✓ *CV de Thézac-Perricard* (Vin du Tsar Le Bouquet)

TORGAN
Zonal *vin de pays* Map A, No.90

As this is geographically the *vin de pays* equivalent of Fitou AOC, it is no surprise to discover that 98 per cent of its wines are red. They are in fact made from a very similar range of grapes as that used to make Fitou, but certain other grapes are also permitted, including *bordelais* varieties and the Teinturier Alicante Bouschet. Rosé may be made, but seldom is, and the minuscule amount of aromatic dry white may be made from Clairette, Macabéo, and Marsanne. This *vin de pays* used to be known as Coteaux Cathares.

✓ *Bertrand-Bergé* (Le Méconnu Blanc) • *CV du Mont Tauch* (de Gardie, l'If Merlot-Carignan)

URFÉ
Zonal *vin de pays* Map B, No.91

Red wine is made in modest quantities. White and rosé may also be produced.

VAL-DE-CESSE
Zonal *vin de pays* Map A, No.92

These are mostly red wines, plus 10 per cent rosé, and 5 per cent white from local grape varieties in the Minervois area.

VAL-DE-DAGNE
Zonal *vin de pays* Map A, No.93

This area overlaps part of the Côtes de Malepère and produces almost entirely red wines from a choice of Carignan, Grenache, Terret Noir, Merlot, Cabernet Sauvignon, Cabernet Franc, and the Teinturier Alicante Bouschet. Very little rosé and white is made.

VAL DE LOIRE
Regional *vin de pays* Map B

This *vin de pays* produces red, white, and rosé wines from 14 *départements* covering most of the Loire Valley. It would seem, from the wines most commonly encountered, that the majority of this vast output must be dry white, dominated by either Chenin Blanc or Sauvignon Blanc, but, according to the statistics, 60 per cent is red. Generally a disappointing appellation, with the thin, acid Chardonnays being the most depressing, but the Cabernet Sauvignon from Pierre & Paul Freuchet is surprisingly soft and perfumed for this northerly denomination. Pure varietal wines have been allowed since 2000.

✓ *Ampelidae* (Marigny-Neuf) • *L'Aujardière* (Fié Gris) • *Paul Boutinot* (Signature Chardonnay) • *De la Coche* • *Adéa Consules* (Ligeria) • *Bruno Cormerais* (Elevé en Fûts de Chêne) • *de la Couperie* (Clyan Elevé en Fûts de Chêne) • *Marquis de Goulaine* (Chardonnay) • *De la Houssais* • *Levin* (Sauvignon Blanc) • *Manoir La Perrière* (Chardonnay) • *Henry Marionnet* (Provinage) • *du Petit Château* (Chardonnay) • *Petiteau-Gaubert* (Domaine de la Tourlaudière Cabernet Sauvignon Rosé) • *Château de La Ragotière* • *de la Saulze* (Gamay Rosé)

VAL DE MONTFERRAND
Zonal *vin de pays* Map A, No.94

Mostly red wines, but rosé accounts for 25 per cent of production, and white for 15 per cent in this denomination, which encompasses the *garrigues* below the Cévennes. The usual Languedoc grapes are used. *Vin primeur* and *vin d'une nuit* are local specialities produced in relatively large quantities.

✓ *L'Hortus* • *Mas de Martin* (Roi Patriote)

VALLÉE DU PARADIS
Zonal *vin de pays* Map A, No.95

Mostly red wines from an area that overlaps Corbières and Fitou, made from Carignan, Syrah, Grenache, Cinsault, Cabernet Sauvignon, and Merlot. Very little white wine is made (usually as *vin primeur*) and even less rosé. A heavenly name, even to Anglo-Saxon ears, which no doubt helps it on export markets, which account for almost half its sales.

✓ *de Garrigotes* (Rouge) • *Jeanjean* • *Mont Tauch*

VAR
Départementale vin de pays Map B

This denomination is one of the largest producers of *vins de pays*. Covering the vast majority of the Côtes de Provence AOC, it not surprisingly produces a large quantity of rosé: no less than 45 per cent, in fact. The wines are usually made by the *saignée* method and range from a very pale *vin gris* style, through orange to almost cherry-red. The quality is equally as variable. The big, rich, spicy reds are much better and of a more consistent quality, often using Syrah, Mourvèdre, and

Cabernet Sauvignon to boost the Grenache, Cinsault, Carignan, and Roussanne du Var, on which the rosés mainly rely. Some white wines are also made, but represent just 5 per cent of production. They are not usually very exciting, and are mostly made from Ugni Blanc, Clairette, Bourboulenc, and Vermentino. The white from Rabiega is one of the exceptions, relying on Chardonnay for body and Viognier and Sauvignon Blanc to lift the Ugni Blanc base. Pure varietal wines have been allowed since 2000.

✓ *les Caves du Commandeur* (Rolle, Syrah) • *de Garbelle* (Vermentino) • *le Saint André* • *Château Sarrins* • *Château Thuerry* (L'Exception)

VAUCLUSE
Départementale vin de pays Map B

Three-quarters of output of this *vin de pays* is red, similar to basic Côtes-du-Rhone. Rosé can be fresh, and accounts for just 10 per cent of output; white is generally the least interesting. Pure varietal wines are allowed.

✓ *Boutinot* (Floria) • *de la Citadelle* (Cabernet Sauvignon) • *Fondacci* (Chasan) • *Fontaine du Clos* (Chardonnay) • *Léonce Amouroux* (Collection Privée) • *de Marotte* • *Mas Saint-Victor*

VAUNAGE
Zonal *vin de pays* Map A, No.96

Light red wines made in typical Languedoc style.

VENDÉE
Départementale vin de pays Map B

Red, white, and rosé wines are produced in small quantities, in a similar style to Fiefs Vendéens (which was a *vin de pays* until it was promoted to VDQS status in December 1984). Pure varietal wines are allowed.

VICOMTÉ D'AUMELAS
Zonal *vin de pays* Map A, No.97

Overlapping part of Cabrières, this *vin de pays* produces mostly red wines of a simple, fresh, fruity style, from traditional southwestern grape varieties, such as the typical Languedoc grape. Just over 10 per cent of wines are rosé, and a tiny amount of crisp, dry white is produced.

✓ *d'Aubaret* (Sauvignon)

VIENNE
Départementale vin de pays Map B

This appellation produces red, white, and rosé wines, most of which are grown in and around the Haut-Poitou district. Pure varietal wines have been allowed since 2000.

✓ *Ampelidae*

VISTRENQUE
Zonal *vin de pays* Map A, No.98

This appellation produces red and rosé wines, which are made in very small quantities. White wine may also be produced.

YONNE
Départementale vin de pays Map B

The Yonne is a white-only appellation, and its production of wines is quite small. Pure varietal wines have been allowed since 2000.

The WINES of
ITALY

THE WINES OF ITALY ARE RICH IN POTENTIAL but lack focus; consequently, the country's image is muddled when it should really be no more complicated than diverse. In Italy, vines are so easy to grow that one even expects them to shoot up from cracks in the pavement after a Mediterranean squall. Furthermore, the number of interesting indigenous grape varieties is greater than can be found in any other major winemaking country of the world, including France. The greatest Italian wines should be as famous as, and considered equal to, the greatest French wines, but there are no wine regions, great or otherwise, in Italy. Instead, there is just one province after another, all abutting each other, and all growing vines and making wines of every imaginable style and quality. How confusing is that? Consumers cannot visualize Italian wines in the maps of their minds as they can French wines. Vine varieties and the types of wine they make not only merge within provinces but overlap their boundaries, blurring the already bewildering picture. Despite this, Italy, like France, makes a quarter of the world's wines, and Italian exports are healthy. If and when Italy manages to project a coherent image of distinct regional styles, France will have a rival to worry about.

TUSCANY
In this typical Tuscan scene, a sun-blessed vineyard is set against the backdrop of a hilltop town with characteristic poplar trees lining the horizon.

ITALY

This country has an extraordinary and exceptional potential to make some of the greatest wines in the world, yet seems even more inept than France at running its wine industry. Italy churns out new appellations as if there is no tomorrow, with far too many that are much too obscure. The trend also continues to promote ordinary DOCs to even-less-than-ordinary DOCGs.

It is staggering to think that a quarter of the world's wine is Italian yet, despite 4,000 years of Italian winemaking history, the Italian wine industry remains in a state of flux. Italy's enormous wine production has given many discerning wine drinkers a misleading impression of the country's true quality potential. Italy can, and does, make many fine wines, but they have always been surrounded by so much *vin ordinaire* that finding them is a

hit-and-miss affair. Like Italy, France churns out a huge volume of wine and its production can include a fair amount of dross, but the names of great French wines roll off the tongue of even the uninitiated, and, rightly or wrongly, France has managed to get away with it, whereas Italy never has. Yet Italy has at least as much potential in terms of the diversity of its *terroir* and a plethora of native grape varieties. The key problem is identity: in Italy vines grow in every corner, whereas in France they are mostly confined to half a dozen major regions and each of these has its own recognizable style and reputation.

ITALY'S LAW OF MEDIOCRITY

Italy's DOC legislation was introduced in 1963, but this law was fundamentally flawed because it failed to establish a small number of easily identifiable regions, each bearing an umbrella name and style. It also actively encouraged increased volume by officially recognizing the most productive grape varieties and classifying the highest-yielding areas on the edges of famous appellations. The late 1950s and early 1960s were crucial in the development of the modern wine industry in Europe, and Italy's DOC system encouraged its largest bottlers to move out of the low-yielding, hilly, *classico* areas, which make better wines than the higher-yielding plains but are the more difficult and expensive to maintain. From this point, the Italian wine industry became

MONTALCINO
With its famous Brunello vines in the foreground, Montalcino basks in Tuscan sunshine. Viticulturally, the surrounding area is highly prestigious; its tannic red wines generally need at least 10 years' maturation.

increasingly dominated by mass production; most wineries became passionless factories and the quality of Italy's most famous wines sank as fast as the volume of production increased.

At first, out of respect for Senator Paolo Desana, who fathered the DOC concept, Italy ignored foreign criticism of its new wine regime. But by the early 1980s, its greatest wine names were so devalued that many of its best wines were being sold as *vini da tavola*, which made a mockery of the DOC system. In the end, even the most conservative Italians had to admit something must be done. Over the next 10 years, successive agricultural ministers tried to overhaul Italy's wine laws, but failed owing to the political clout of the industrial bottlers, who had a lot to gain by flooding the market with cheap wines. When agricultural minister Giovanni Goria declared his intention of pressing for even more radical changes than any of his predecessors had, few took him seriously. No one would have

bet a single lira on Goria's success, yet within 10 weeks of his appointment, a "New Disciplinary Code for Denomination of Wines of Origin" had been ratified by the Senate.

GORIA'S LAW

In February 1992 Law 164, now known simply as Goria's Law or the Goria Law, replaced Desana's wine regime. When the law first came into force, much attention was focused on the introduction of a brand new category called IGT (*Indicazioni Geografiche Tipiche*). The equivalent of French *vins de pays*, IGTs were supposed to form a buffer between the DOCs and *vini da tavola*, Goria having denied the latter the right to bear any geographical provenance other than Italy itself. Each IGT would come from an officially recognized zone of production, but could not claim to be anything more specific, such as the product of a village, microzone, estate, or single vineyard. Under Law 164 all such specific origins were restricted to DOC or DOCG wines.

ITALY
As might be expected of a nation so geographically and culturally diverse, Italy produces a vast array of different types of wine. Away from the mainland, the islands of Sicily and Sardinia both have thriving wine industries.

	Northwest Italy *see also pp316, 317*
	Northeast Italy *see also p326*
	West Central Italy *see also pp334, 335*
	East Central Italy *see also p342*
	Southern Italy and the Islands *see also pp347, 348*

—— Regional boundary

▲ Height above sea level (metres)

In the euphoric first few months of this new law, it was predicted that there would be 150 to 200 IGTs, accounting for some 12 million hectolitres (130 million cases) of wine, which should – according to Goria's own plans – rise to 40 per cent of the total Italian wine output, representing 10 per cent of world production. For almost five years, no applications were received for IGT status. Without the right to mention the specific origins of these wines, yet being obliged to meet similar criteria to a DOC, why would producers bother, when they might as well opt for DOC or simply make *vino da tavola*? This is why the major thrust of Goria's ground-breaking law was considered, even in Italy, to have been stillborn. Then, with the 1996 harvest, the applications poured in, and there are now no fewer than 118 classified IGTs, in addition to the 315 DOCs and 36 DOCGs.

NEW RESPECT FOR THE DOCS?

Did the Goria Law successfully reconfigure the fundamentally flawed DOCs and DOCGs? The answer is yes and no. "No" because Italy's wines will never achieve their true potential until, like those of France, they can be encapsulated within half a dozen major regions of recognizable style (*see* DOC's Lack of Specificity, *right*) and reputation. Goria did not even attempt to tackle this problem. Furthermore, Italy's greatest wines will never receive the international acclaim they deserve until their delimited areas are reduced to the original hilly *classico* districts, about which Goria also did nothing.

Until Goria's Law, many wines were denied the *vini da tavola* status because Italy's appellation system defined the characteristics of each DOC and, in so doing, did not take into account the foreign grapes and non-traditional vinification methods that most premium *vini da tavola* came to employ. Giovanni Goria had the sense to realize that any system that did not recognize some of the country's finest wines is a discredited system. He thus made it easier for such wines to be accepted within established DOCs. To qualify for DOC status, the wine or wines must have a history of at least five years' production. Any DOC with a further five years of recorded production can apply for a DOCG, providing it has acquired a "reputation and commercial impact both at home and at an international level".

DOC'S LACK OF SPECIFICITY

Part of the problem of Italian wines being unable to project a readily discernible image is the number of ways in which a single DOC wine may be interpreted. An appellation system should project and protect a recognizable style (and, one hopes, quality) through detailed regulations, or it should simply make sure the provenance of a wine is as stated – guaranteeing where it comes from, even if it is a blend of different areas. The very last thing that any wine regime should do is insist on an intricate recipe of grape-variety percentages and precise geographical limitation, then say it can be dry, off-dry, medium sweet, sweet, still, *passito*, *frizzantino* (slightly sparkling), *frizzante* (semi-sparkling), or *spumante* (fully sparkling). All this does is foster the uncertain image with which Italian wines have long been lumbered.

ALL THAT SPARKLES

No country has as many sparkling wine appellations as Italy, with its optional "may be *spumante*" clauses littering over 100 of its DOCs, including some of its truly greatest red wines. However, despite so many possibilities, Italy had no specific appellation for dry sparkling wine until 1995, when Franciacorta was given DOCG status. The only other traditional-method sparkling-wine appellation created since is Trento DOC. The rest of Italy's little-known, half-forgotten sparkling wine appellations are all *cuve* close. Bottle-fermentation does not guarantee quality, but it does encourage producers in the right direction, which is why it is a mistake for any dry sparkling DOC wine to be produced by any other process. Until all DOC *cuve close* is outlawed, no Italian dry sparkling wine will be taken seriously and Franciacorta's efforts to establish the country's first classic *brut* appellation will be frustrated.

FUTURE SIMPLICITY

The solution to Italy's wine worries is very simple. Map out no more than half-a-dozen truly classic Italian wine regions, reduce the number of DOCs within these regions to a maximum of 100, all limited to historically authentic areas, and the most famous styles (no more multiple choice appellations!), with tough regulations and qualifying tastings performed by an independent body with no vested interests. Set up a panel of experts to determine the 12 truly greatest wines to receive DOCG status, and set that in stone, so that no expansion can ever dilute the DOCG reputation. Within each DOCG, an Italian equivalent of *grand cru* and *premier cru* classification should be made. Then dispose of all the 118 IGTs except for the 12 regional IGTs (Basilicata, Toscana,

RIONERO, BASILICATA
This 17th-century farm building stands on the Conca d'Oro estate in Vulture, where Fratelli d'Angelo produces a great red wine called Aglianico del Vulture.

ITALIAN LABEL LANGUAGE

Abboccato Slightly sweet

Amabile Sweeter than *abboccato*

Amaro Bitter or very dry

Annata This means "year" and often precedes or follows the vintage date. At least 85 per cent of the wine must be from the vintage indicated. *See also Vendemmia*

Appassimento Includes the partial use of semi-dried grapes

Asciutto Bone dry

Auslese German term used in the Alto Adige for wines from selected grapes

Azienda, Azienda agricola, Azienda agraria, or Azienda vitivinicola Estate winery

Bianco White

Cantina Winery

Cantina sociale or **Cooperativa** A cooperative winery

Cascina North Italian term for a farm or estate

Casa vinicola A commercial winery

Cerasuolo Cherry red, used for vividly coloured *rosato* wines

Chiaretto Wines falling between very light red and genuine *rosato*

Classico The best, oldest, or most famous part of a DOC zone

Consorzio A group of producers who control and promote wine, usually insisting on higher standards than DOC regulations enforce

Denominazione di Origine Controllata, or **DOC** There are more than 250 DOCs, but some are multiple-varietal appellations covering as many as 12 different wines, resulting in more than 600 DOC names. This is similar, and just as worthless as, the French AOC system, as both merely guarantee mediocrity. The producer's name is still the best assurance of quality.

Denominazione di Origine Controllata e Garantita, or **DOCG** Theoretically the highest-quality official denomination, but encompasses a lot of very ordinary wine, as well as isolated pockets of truly fine wine. Again, the producer's name is the best assurance of quality.

Dolce Very sweet

Fattoria Large wine estate

Fermentazione naturale Method of producing sparkling wine by natural refermentation in a tank or bottle

Fiore Term meaning "flower". Often part of a name, it indicates quality, as it implies that the first grape pressing has been used. Frizzante Semi-sparkling, the equivalent of *pétillant*

Frizzantino Very lightly sparkling

Imbottigliato all'origine Estate-bottled

Incrocio Literally meaning a cross (as in cross-bred), and the name following *incrocio* is the name of that cross

Indicazione Geografica Tipica, or **IGT** The Italian equivalent of a French *vin de pays*

Liquoroso Usually fortified and sweet, but may also be dry wine that is simply high in alcohol

Località, Ronco, or **Vigneto** Indicates a single-vineyard wine

Messo in bottiglia nell'origine Estate-bottled

Metodo classico or **Metodo tradizionale** The Italian for traditional method

Occhio di pernice Literally "partridge's eye", this term is traditionally applied to a sweet red *vin santo*.

Pas dosé Used for sparking wine that has not received any *dosage*, this term is the equivalent of *brut nature* in Champagne.

Passito Strong, often sweet wine made from semi-dried grapes

Passito annoso Aged *passito*

Pastoso Medium-sweet

Produttore all'origine Estate-bottled

Ramato Copper-coloured wine made from Pinot Grigio grapes that are briefly macerated on their skins.

Recioto Strong, sweet wine made from semi-dried grapes

Ripassa, Ripassato, or **Ripasso** Wine refermented on the lees of a *recioto* wine

Riserva or **Riserva speciale DOC** or **DOCG**

wines that have been matured for a statutory number of years (the *speciale* is older)

Ronco Hillside vineyard or estate

Rosato Rosé

Rosso Red

Secco Dry

Semi-secco Medium-sweet

Spumante Fully sparkling

Stravecchio Very old wines aged according to DOC or DOCG rules

Superiore When part of the appellation, this usually refers to a longer minimum ageing period before the wine can be sold

Talento A registered trademark signifying a sparkling wine made by the traditional method

Tenuta Estate

Uva Grape variety

Uvaggio Wine blended from various grape varieties

Vecchio Old

Vendemmia This means "harvest" and often precedes or follows the vintage date. At least 85 per cent of the wine must be from the vintage indicated. *See also Annata*

Vendemmia tardiva Late-harvest sweet wine

Vigna or **Vigneto** Vineyard

Vin santo or **Vino santo** Traditionally sweet, occasionally dry, white wine made from *passito* grapes stored in sealed casks, and not topped up for several years

Vino Wine

Vino novello Italian equivalent of Vin Primeur or Vin Nouveau

Vino da pasto Ordinary wine

Vino da tavola Literally "table wine", this is Italy's most basic category, but as well as including most of the country's plonk, it also includes some of its greatest wines. However, although many of the latter are gradually developing their own appellations.

Sicilia etc), and increase their number to 20, which would cover the entire country. There should be no other type of IGT. The French can afford a more complex IGP (French equivalent of IGT) or *vin de pays* sector because they have long since registered the name, location, and relative styles of their greatest wine regions in the psyches of wine drinkers worldwide, yet even France is struggling with this sector, selling no less than 65 per cent of all *vins de pays* under just five of its 154 denominations. With no route map to wines of Italy hard-wired into the minds of consumers, the Italian wine industry simply cannot afford to get bogged down in such a plethora of IGTs. That is why there should be a maximum of 20 IGTs, all regional. To balance the restriction in IGTs, I would encourage the greatest flexibility in their regulations, including the use of single-village, single-estate, and individual site names. I would even allow the use of obsolete DOCs and IGTs (providing they are not classified as such, and their names are printed at no more than one-third the size of the regional IGT), so that no producer could claim that he had been prevented from selling his wine under the appellation for which it had become known, however obscure or meaningless that might have been to the outside world. The bureaucrats might squeal at the thought of such a thing, but it really does not matter. What

matters is that these IGTs would have a recognizable name and therefore offer some sense of place for drinkers in other countries. Just as important, a flexible IGT could be used both to preserve traditional values and promote innovation. And, finally, the clever part: the Italians should steal the late René Renou's concept of *Site et Terroir d'Excellence* (STE – see p104). If the French authorities are too stupid to adopt such an ingenious idea, then the Italians should demonstrate what an opportunity they have missed. With the number of regional IGTs and DOCGs fixed, there must be another means of rewarding true standout quality, if any new system is to avoid the current wine regime's guarantee of mediocrity, and a nice big STE stamp on the label of an IGT or DOC wine would provide that. Imagine the difference it would make. A cluster of STE-awarded IGT wineries might one day elect to form a new DOC, but the flexibility of IGT and premium attracted by STE status should be sufficient to keep most wineries in the IGT system, thereby reducing any threat of a major expansion of the number of DOCs. And while the highest-flying STE-awarded DOCs should never be allowed to join the ranks of the DOCGs (all the best systems have something intrinsically unfair, yet inherently stable, built into them), they might well fetch the price of a top DOCG.

NORTHWEST ITALY

This area includes the great wine region of Piedmont, as well as the regions of Liguria, Lombardy, and Valle d'Aosta. Generally, the wines are fuller and richer than those of northeastern Italy, which is a more mountainous area.

FEW AREAS ENCOMPASS such contrasting topographies as northwest Italy, from the alpine *pistes* of the Valle d'Aosta and the Apennines of Liguria to the alluvial plains of the River Po. Contrast is also evident in the character of its two most famous wines – the big, black, and tannic Barolo DOCG and the light, water-white, effervescent, and grapey-sweet Asti DOCG.

PIEDMONT (PIEMONTE)

Piedmont is dominated by two black grapes (Nebbiolo and Barbera) and one white (Moscato). Nebbiolo makes the magnificently rich and smoky Barolo and the elegant, more feminine, yet sometimes just as powerful, Barbaresco. The Barbera has a much greater yield than Nebbiolo but is potentially almost as fine. It is softer in tannin, at least as high in acidity, and excels around Alba and, to a slightly lesser extent, around Asti. White Asti, made from Moscato, is Italy's most popular fine wine. Whether still, *frizzantino*, or *spumante*, Asti is light and succulently sweet, with a mesmerizing grapey character. Fully sparkling Asti is no longer

Trino
Barbera d'Asti
Asti
ALESSANDRIA
Bra
Alba
Acqui Terme
Dolcetto d'Alba
Cairo-Montenotte
Mondovi
Savona
Appellation named on map: eg, Dolcetto d'Alba
1 Freisa d'Asti
2 Malvasia di Casorzo d'Asti
3 Grignolino d'Asti
4 Dolcetto d'Asti
5 Cisterna d'Asti
6 Asti & Moscato d'Asti
7 Barbera d'Alba
8 Nebbiolo d'Alba
9 Dolcetto di Diano d'Alba
Provincia boundary
0 10 20 30 miles
0 20 40 60 km

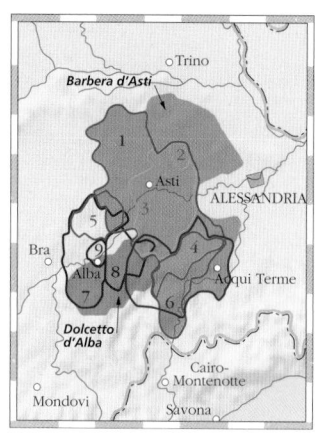

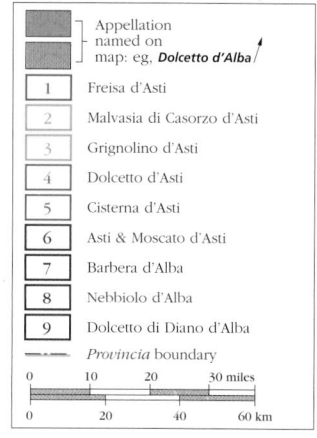

ASTI AND ALBA, *see also below*
The complexity of appellation upon appellation in the Asti-Alba area is such that they have to be divided between the main map (below) and this additional map.

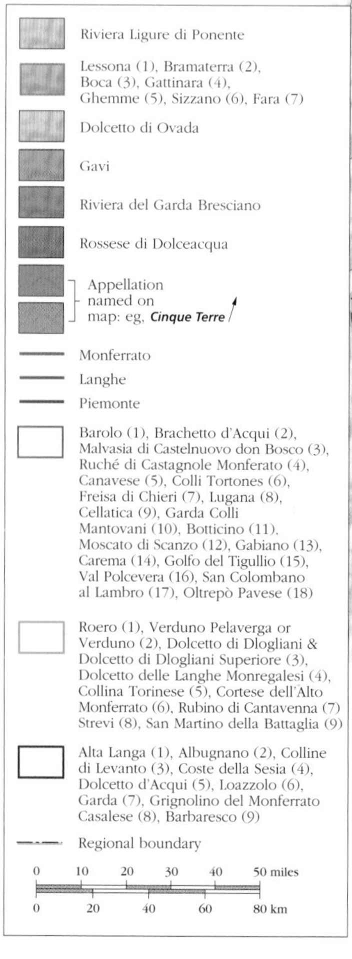

Riviera Ligure di Ponente
Lessona (1), Bramaterra (2), Boca (3), Gattinara (4), Ghemme (5), Sizzano (6), Fara (7)
Dolcetto di Ovada
Gavi
Riviera del Garda Bresciano
Rossese di Dolceacqua
Appellation named on map: eg, Cinque Terre
Monferrato
Langhe
Piemonte
Barolo (1), Brachetto d'Acqui (2), Malvasia di Castelnuovo don Bosco (3), Ruché di Castagnole Monferrato (4), Canavese (5), Colli Tortones (6), Freisa di Chieri (7), Lugana (8), Cellatica (9), Garda Colli Mantovani (10), Botticino (11), Moscato di Scanzo (12), Gabiano (13), Carema (14), Golfo del Tigullio (15), Val Polcevera (16), San Colombano al Lambro (17), Oltrepò Pavese (18)
Roero (1), Verduno Pelaverga or Verduno (2), Dolcetto di Dlogliani & Dolcetto di Dlogliani Superiore (3), Dolcetto delle Langhe Monregalesi (4), Collina Torinese (5), Cortese dell'Alto Monferrato (6), Rubino di Cantavenna (7) Strevi (8), San Martino della Battaglia (9)
Alta Langa (1), Albugnano (2), Colline di Levanto (3), Coste della Sesia (4), Dolcetto d'Acqui (5), Loazzolo (6), Garda (7), Grignolino del Monferrato Casalese (8), Barbaresco (9)
Regional boundary
0 10 20 30 40 50 miles
0 20 40 60 80 km

Hinterrhein
St. Moritz
Brig
Sierre
Martigny
Chamonix
For detail, see next page
VALLE D'AOSTA
Aosta
Val d'Isère
Locarno
Bellinzona
Sondrio
Tirano
Valtellina & Valtellina Superiore
Sforzato or Sfursat di Valtellina
Dimaro
TRENTINO-ALTO ADIGE
Tione di Trento
Trento
Riva del Garda
Rovereto
Menaggio
Laveno
Lecco
Valcalepio
Lovere
Arona
Colline Novaresi
COMO
BERGAMO
MONZA
BRESCIA
Salò
Peschiera
VERONA
VENETO
Gattinara
Biella
Legnano
Franciacorta
Ivrea
Erbaluce di Caluso & Caluso Passito
NOVARA
Milano
LOMBARDIA
Vercelli
Ciriè
Vigevano
Pavia
Canneto
Nogara
Susa
Valsusa
Torino
Cremona
Ostiglia
PIEMONTE
Stradella
PIACENZA
Casalmaggiore
Guastalla
Lambrusco Mantovano
ALESSANDRIA
Asti
Tortona
Colli Piacentini
Pinerolo
Pinerolese
Crissolo
Bra
Alba
Acqui Terme
Bobbio
PARMA
ROMAGNA
EMILIA
Fornovo di Taro
Saluzzo
Colline Saluzzesi
Acceglio
Bardi
Colli di Parma
Cuneo
LIGURIA
For further Asti and Alba detail, see above
Genova
Chiavari
Pontremoli
TOSCANA
Isola 2000
Garessio
Finale Ligure
Golfo di Genova
Cinque Terre
Sarzana
LA SPEZIA
Massa
Ormeasco di Pornassio
Colli di Luni
Villars sur Var
Imperia
San Remo
Monaco
NICE
ROME

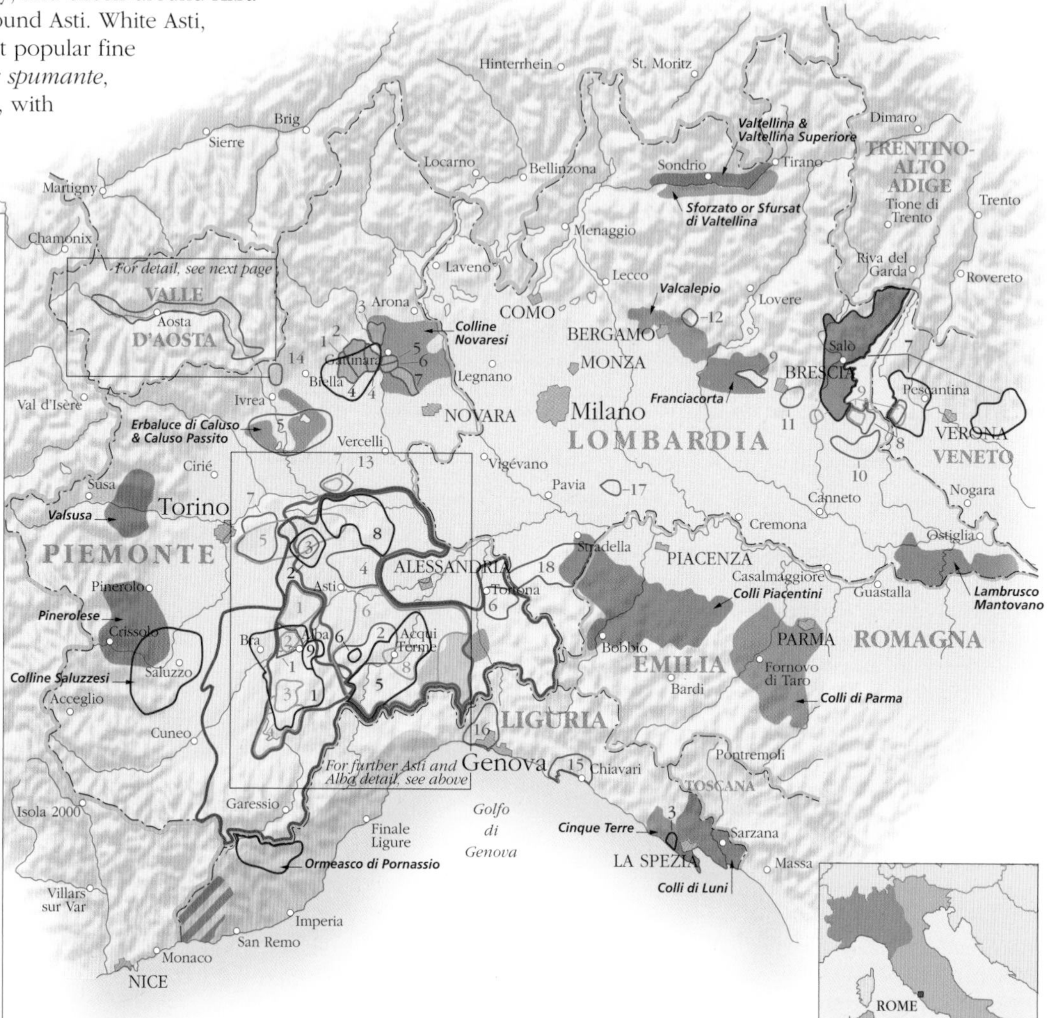

NORTHWEST ITALY, *see also p313*
The presence of the Alps gives this largely hilly region a hot growing season and a long autumn. The finest wines come from the foothills of Piedmont, which provide ideal growing conditions for the late-ripening Nebbiolo grape.

PERGOLA-TRAINED VINES
These Nebbiolo vines, grown near Carema in Piedmont, are trained on a Pergola Piemontese. They are made into a fragrant, medium-bodied wine.

called Asti Spumante because *spumante*, like *mousseux*, has a cheap, low-quality connotation and Asti is undeniably the world's greatest dessert-style sparkling wine.

LOMBARDY (LOMBARDIA)

Northeast of Piedmont, Lombardy stretches from the flat plains of the Po Valley to snow-clad Alpine peaks. The region's finest wines include Franciacorta's full reds and its new DOCG for classic *brut* sparkling wines, plus the best of Valtellina's red Sassella. These wines are still relatively unknown compared with Piedmont's Barolo and Barbaresco and are good value.

LIGURIA

One of Italy's smallest regions, Liguria is more famous for its Riviera, which is set against the dramatic and beautiful backdrop of the Maritime Alps, than it is for its wines. Cinque Terre, which is the best-known Ligurian wine, is named after the *Cinque Terre*, or five villages, which are perched along the Ligurian coast, above which the steep, intricately terraced vineyards tower like some great Aztec pyramid. Other than the Cinque Terre, interesting wines include the soft, spicy Rossese di Dolceacqua and the vividly coloured Albenga *rosato* of the Riviera Ligure di Ponente DOC. The Colli di Luni is almost Tuscan, and part of this DOC even overlaps that region, so it is not surprising that it is capable of producing a decent Sangiovese. However, most Ligurian wines belong to the category of pleasant holiday drinking, and some of the best potential vineyards have been grubbed up to accommodate the tourists who drink them.

FACTORS AFFECTING TASTE AND QUALITY

LOCATION
Flanked to the north and west by the Alps and by the Ligurian Sea to the south, northwest Italy contains the provinces of Piedmont, Lombardy, Liguria, and Valle d'Aosta.

CLIMATE
The winters are severe with frequent inversion fogs rising out of the valleys. Summers are hot, though not excessively so, but hail can damage the grapes at this time of year. Long autumns enable the late-ripening Nebbiolo grape to be grown very successfully.

ASPECT
This area covers mountains, foothills (*piedmont* means "foothill"), and the valley of Italy's longest river, the Po. Grapes are grown on hillsides that provide good drainage and exposure to the sun. In classic areas such as Barolo, every south-facing hillside is covered with vines, while in Lombardy many vineyards extend down to the rich, alluvial plains of the Po Valley.

SOIL
A wide range of soils with many local variations, the predominant type is calcareous marl (*see* p19), which may be interlayered or intermingled with sand and clay.

VITICULTURE AND VINIFICATION
The great red wines of the region have suffered in the past from long ageing in large wooden vats, as many growers bottled their wine only when they sold it. This practice dried up the fruit and oxidized the wine. However, many wines are bottled at the optimum time although there is still no consensus about the best ageing vessels. The use of *cuve close* for sweet, grapey styles of wine from Asti has been very successful and these wines sell well internationally. Some of the same *spumante* houses have developed dry *spumante* from Pinot and Chardonnay grapes, using the traditional method, to produce fine-quality sparkling wines.

GRAPE VARIETIES
Primary varieties: Barbera, Chiavennasca (Nebbiolo), Moscato (Muscat Blanc à Petits Grains)
Secondary varieties: Arneis, Blanc de Morgex, Bonarda, Bonarda in Lombardy but not the true Bonarda of Piedmont (Croatina), Brachetto, Brugnola, Buzetto (Trebbiano), Cabernet Franc, Cabernet Sauvignon, Chardonnay, Cortese, Erbaluce, Favorita, Freisa, Fumin, Gamay, Grenache, Grignolino, Gropello, Incrocio Terzi (Barbera x Cabernet Franc), Lambrusco, Malvasia, Marzemino, Mayolet, Merlot, Neyret, Oriou (Petit Rouge), Ormeasco in Liguria (Dolcetto), Petite Arvine, Pigato, Pignola Valtellina, Pinot Bianco (Pinot Blanc), Pinot Grigio (Pinot Gris), Pinot Nero (Pinot Noir), Premetta, Riesling Italico (Welschriesling), Riesling Renano (Riesling), Rossese, Rossola, Ruché, Sauvignonasse (Friulano), Schiava Gentile, Syrah, Timorasso, Uva Rara, Vermentino, Vespolina, Vien de Nus

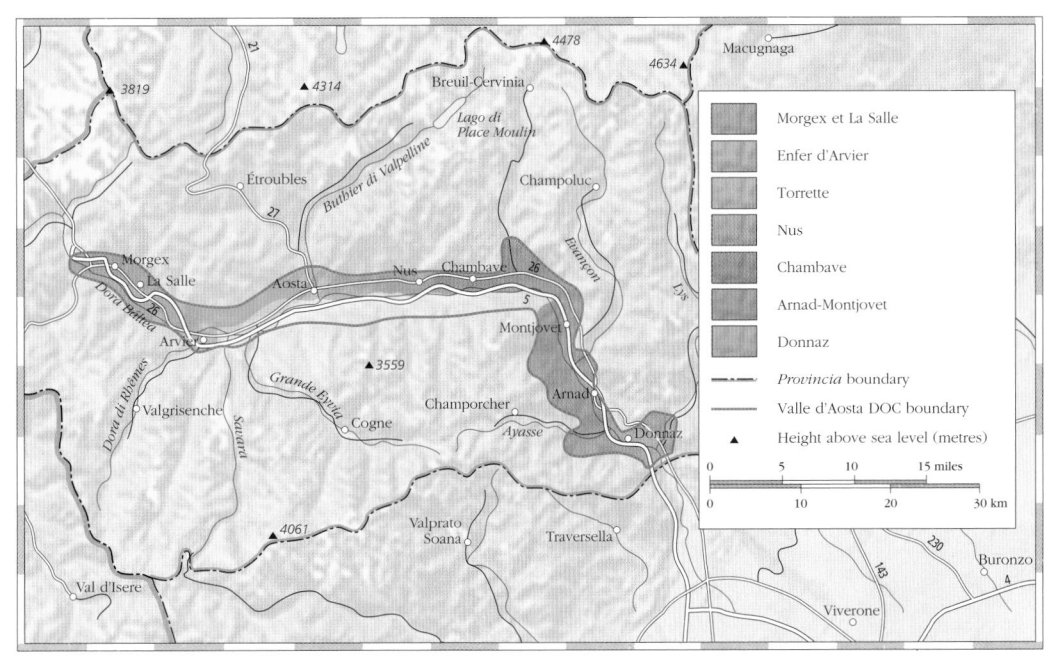

Morgex et La Salle

Enfer d'Arvier

Torrette

Nus

Chambave

Arnad-Montjovet

Donnaz

– – – *Provincia* boundary

—— Valle d'Aosta DOC boundary

▲ Height above sea level (metres)

0   5   10   15 miles

0   10   20   30 km

VALLE D'AOSTA, *see also opposite*
The winters here are cold and snowy, but summers in the valley can be very hot with contrastingly cold nights, which should make for some exciting wines.

VALLE D'AOSTA

If Liguria is a marginal wine region, then Valle d'Aosta is almost subliminal. High in the Alps, overlooked by Mont Blanc and the Matterhorn, the Valle d'Aosta looks at first as if it could be a part of France or Switzerland, but the only easy, natural access is from Piedmont along the Dora Baltea River. Italy's smallest and most mountainous wine region, the Valle d'Aosta has picturesque vineyards that produce some enjoyable wines, particularly Chambave, Nus, and Torrette. However, most are tourist wines; the best are easy-drinking and unpretentious.

REGIONS AT A GLANCE

REGION	TOTAL AREA UNDER VINE	DOC/DOCG AREA UNDER VINE	DOC/DOCG PRODUCTION	TOTAL PRODUCTION
Piedmont	70,000 ha (173,000 acres)	35,900 ha (89,000 acres)	1.2 million hl (50/50 red/white)	3.27 million hl (36.33 million cases)
Lombardy	30,000 ha (74,000 acres)	16,700 ha (41,000 acres)	450,000 hl (51/49 red/white)	1.7 million hl (18.88 million cases)
Liguria	60,000 ha (148,000 acres)	504 ha (1,245 acres)	13,000 hl (25/75 red/white)	280,000 hl (3.11 million cases)
Valle d'Aosta	925 ha (2,285 acres)	66 ha (163 acres)	2,400 hl (67/33 red/white)	29,000 hl (322,190 cases)

THE APPELLATIONS OF
NORTHWEST ITALY

ALBENGA DOC
Liguria

Vividly coloured, dry, and characterful, Liguria's best-known *rosati* are now part of the Riviera Ligure di Ponente DOC. *See* Riviera Ligure di Ponente DOC.

ACQUI DOCG
See Brachetto d'Acqui DOCG

ALBUGNANO DOC
Piedmont

Nebbiolo-based red and *rosato* wines produced at Albugnano and four surrounding villages in a small, hilly area to the north of Asti, where the vineyards climb to 520 metres (1,700 feet) in altitude.

ALTA LANGA DOC
Piedmont

These red, white, and *rosato* sparkling wines from the southern half of the Langa district must be made from at least 90% Chardonnay or Pinot Noir.

✓ *Enrico Serafino*

ALTO MINCIO IGT
Lombardy

Geographically, this IGT is roughly equivalent to the Colli Mantovani DOC. Anything goes, but most utilized for Pinot Grigio at the moment.

✓ *Prendina*

ARNAD-MONTJOVAT DOC
Valle d'Aosta

A red-only sub-appellation of the regional Valle d'Aosta DOC producing Nebbiolo-based red wines, with up to 30 per cent Dolcetto, Freisa, Neyret, Pinot Noir, and Vien de Nus. *See* Valle d'Aosta DOC.

ARNEIS DI ROERO DOC
Piedmont

These wines are produced from the ancient Arneis grape grown in the hills north of Alba. Formerly a *vino da tavola*, the high price and reputation of these wines ensured they would eventually become part of the Roero DOC. The best are amazingly rich and full-flavoured white wines, yet soft and deftly balanced with a fine *frizzantino*. Essentially dry wines, some renditions are, however, less dry than others and Deltetto's Bric Tupin has started a trend for a lusciously sweet style. *See* Roero DOC.

⏲— 3–5 years

✓ *Ceretto* (Blangé) • *Carlo Deltetto* • *Bruno Giacosa* • *Castello di Neive* • *Vietti*

ASTI DOCG
Piedmont

Formerly sold as Asti Spumante, the *spumante* (which means "sparkling") has been removed because it has become tarnished by cheap products that also use the term. It is now known simply as Asti and has been promoted to full DOCG status, which the best wines deserve, but an increasing number of under-performers do not. One of the most famous sparkling wines in the world, Asti is made by *cuve close*, which is far superior to the traditional method when producing an aromatic, sweet sparkling wine. The grapes used are grown in 52 communes throughout the provinces of Asti, Cuneo, and Alessandria.

The best Asti has a fine *mousse* of tiny bubbles, a fresh and grapey aroma, a luscious sweetness, and a light, delicately rich flowery-fruitiness that hints at peaches. Asti should be consumed as young as possible primarily because one of the most important compounds contributing to the Moscato aroma is geraniol, which is wonderful when fresh, but with bottle-age assumes a pungent geranium odour. Gancia's special selection *cuvée* called Camilo Gancia (no longer produced) was the best Asti I ever tasted. *See also* Moscato d'Asti DOCG.

⏲— Upon purchase

✓ *Barbero* (Conte di Cavour) • *Walter Barbero* (Acini Dolce) • *Batasiolo* • *Bersano* • *Capetta* • *Villa Carlotta* • *Cerutti* (Cesare) • *Conte di Cavour* • *Giuseppe Contratto* • *Romano Dogliotti* (La Selvatica) • *Fontanafredda* (Millesimato) • *Marenco* ◉ • *De Miranda* • *Mondoro* • *Perlino* • *Sperone* • *Tosti* • *Cantina Sociale Vallebelbo*

BARBARESCO DOCG
Piedmont

Generally more feminine and elegant than Barolo, Barbaresco has a greater suppleness, softer fruit, and a more obvious charm, although some producers overlap the weightier Barolo style. Produced from Italy's greatest indigenous grape variety, Nebbiolo, these wines must be aged for a minimum of two years, one of which must be in oak or chestnut casks.

⏲— 5–20 years

✓ *Adriano Marco & Vittorio* • *Brema* • *Ca' del Baio* • *Burlotto* • *Piero Busso* • *Cascina Luisin* • *Ceretto* • *Pio Cesare* • *Fontanabianca* • *Fratelli Cigliuti* • *Giuseppe Cortese* • *Angelo Gaja* • *Bruno Giacosa* • *Piero Busso* • *Cantina del Glicine* • *Ugo Lequio* • *Marchesi di Gresy* • *Moccagatta* • *Fiorenzo Nada* • *Castello di Neive* • *Paitin* • *Piazzo Armando* • *Pelissero* (Vanotu) • *Produttori di Barbaresco* • *Alfredo Prunotto* • *Albino Rocca* • *Bruno Rocca* • *Scarpa* • *Scottimano* • *La Spinetta*

BARBERA D'ALBA DOC
Piedmont

The most prolific Piedmont vine, Barbera has suffered unfairly from a somewhat lowly image. In fact, it is one of Italy's great grapes, and the best Barbera from Alba are magnificently rich and full of flavour, and quite capable of challenging Barolo and Barbaresco very closely in intrinsic quality. The production of Barbera d'Alba is very small, in fact often minute, in comparison with that of Barbera d'Asti.

⏲— 5–12 years

✓ *Marziano Abbona* • *Pio Cesare* • *Fratelli Cigliuti* • *Clerico* • *Aldo Conterno* • *Giacomo Conterno* • *Conterno Fantino* • *Damilano* • *Damonte* • *Franco Fiorina* • *Gepin* • *Elio Grasso* • *Manzone* • *Giuseppe Mascarello* • *Prunotto* • *Renato Ratti* • *Bruno Rocca* • *Vajra* • *Vietti* • *Roberto Voerzio*

BARBERA D'ALBA COLLINE NICESI DOC
Piedmont

The lower yield of this proposed sub-zone of Barbara d'Alba is intended to lead the way to full DOCG status for part or all of the current Barbera d'Alba DOC classified wines.

BARBERA D'ASTI DOC
Piedmont

Similar in character to Barbera d'Alba, but softer and more supple, with simpler generic wines, but equally profound single-vineyard wines.

⏲— 3–8 years

✓ *Marchesi Alfieri* • *Paolo Avezza* • *Cascina la Barbatella* • *Bava* (Stradivario) • *Alfiero Boffa* • *Braida* (Bricco della Figotta) • *Brema* • *Cascina Castelet* (Passum) • *Chiarlo* (Valle del Sole) • *Coppo* • *Cossetti* (Cascina Salomone) • *Franco Martinetti* • *Neirano* (Le Croci) • *Olim Bauda* • *Antica Casa Vinicola Scarpa* • *Scrimaglio* • *Zonin* (Castello del Poggio)

BARBERA DEL MONFERRATO DOC
Piedmont

Most of the wines produced by Barbera Del Monferrato are lesser versions of Barbera d'Asti. Semi-sweet or *frizzante* styles may also be made.

✓ *Accornero & Figli* • *CS di Castagnole Monferrato* (Barbera Vivace) • *Montaldo* • *Pico Gonzaga*

BAROLO DOCG
Piedmont

Barolo is unquestionably Italy's greatest wine appellation and its finest wines are the ultimate expression of the Nebbiolo grape. All the best vineyards of Barolo are located on a small, raised area of mostly gentle, but occasionally steep, slopes surrounded by the hills of the Langhe. The soil is essentially calcareous marl (*see* p19), the northwestern half high in magnesium and manganese, the southeastern half more iron-rich.

This small difference is deemed to be the reason why Barolo wines from the northwest have more elegance, while those from the southeast are fuller in body.

The biggest factor in the quality of Barolo has, however, been due more to man than to soil, especially with the trend over the past 10 years to isolate the very best Barolo and market them under single-vineyard names. A vineyard name will not necessarily guarantee excellence, but hardly any of the very top Barolo are blended these days, and quality should continue to rise under the Goria Law (*see* p313), which requires significantly lower yields from any wine claiming single-vineyard status.

Great Barolo is incomparable, but there are still poor Barolo wines, although not as many as in the late 1980s. But even then the emergence of a new wave of fruit-driven Barolo was fairly evident. Initially, this split Barolo; the modern-style wines had more fruit, riper and more supple tannins, and were aged in small *barriques* of new oak, while the worst of the so-called traditionalists carried on producing thick, tannic, dried-out wines.

The popular belief that so many traditional Barolo are dried out because they are bottled late is only half right. The truth is that they are – or were – bottled to order. This meant that some of the shipments of the same vintage would be more dried-out than others. There is still a large number of producers who perceive themselves to be traditional, but this simply means that they eschew *barriques* and new oak. Most traditionalists now bottle their Barolo when the wines – not the orders – require it, which, in effect, is earlier than before. They also tend to pick later and began to drop their yields even before the Goria Law of 1992. Today, both the modern and traditional schools of producers make stunning Barolo.

Modern styles are riper and more creamy than traditional ones, supported by the vanilla of new oak, whereas the traditional styles are arguably more complex, with tobacco, tar, and smoky aromas replacing the clean-cut vanilla. The best of both, however, are deep, sometimes inky-deep, in colour and share lashings of fruit. All Barolo should be powerfully built, even the more elegant, earlier-drinking styles, and the best have surprising finesse for such weighty wines.

⌛ 8–25 years

✓ *Marziano Abbona* • *Accomasso* • *Elio Altare* • *Abbazia dell'Annunziata* • *Ascheri* • *Azelia* • *Fratelli Barale* • *Enzo Boglietti* • *Giacomo Borgogno* • *Gianfranco Bovio* • *Brezza* • *Bricco Asili* • *Bricco Roche* • *Fratelli Brovia* • *Burlotto* • *Giuseppe Cappellano* • *Castello di Verduno* • *Cavalotto* • *Ceretto* • *Michele Chiarlo* • *Clerico* • *Elvio Cogno* • *Aldo Conterno* • *Giacomo Conterno* • *Paolo Conterno* • *Conterno-Fantino* • *Corino* • *Franco-Fiorina* • *Fratelli Alessandria* • *Fratelli Oddero* • *Gagliasso* • *Bruno Giacosa* • *Elio Grasso* • *Manzone* • *Marcarini* • *Marchesi di Barolo* • *Mario Marengo* • *Bartolo Mascarello* • *Giuseppe Mascarello* • *Pianpolvere Soprano* • *Piazzo Armando* • *Pio Cesare* • *Luigi Pira* • *Alfredo Prunotto* • *Renato Ratti* • *Michele Reverdito* • *Rinaldi Giuseppe* • *Giovanni Rosso* • *Luciano Sandrone* • *Antica Casa Vinicola Scarpa* • *Paolo Scavino* • *Schiavenza* • *Edoardo Sobrino* • *Vietti* • *Vigna Rionda-Massolino* • *Roberto Voerzio*

BAROLO CHINATO DOCG
Piedmont

This Barolo, aromatized with quinine, is a DOCG, which is a bit like classifying Bordeaux's aperitif "Lillet" as a *cru classé*.

BENACO BRESCIANO IGT
Lombardy

Red, white, and *rosato* wines produced in the foothills west of Lake Garda, where the best so far appear to be red-wine blends of three or four varieties, including Cabernet Franc, Cabernet Sauvignon, Marzemino, Massimo, Merlot, and Sangiovese.

✓ *Terra Lunari* • *Ca' dei Frati* (Ronchedone)

BERGAMASCA IGT
Lombardy

From the hillside vineyards just outside of Bergamo, where all styles are permitted and the most successful grape varieties include Manzoni Bianco,

Moscato, and Pinot Bianco for whites, and Cabernet Sauvignon, Merlot, and Schiava for red and *rosato* wines. Mostly produced by the local cooperative.

BOCA DOC
Piedmont

These are medium- to full-bodied, spicy red Nebbiolo wines. They are hard to find, but wines have been made here since Roman times and when found can be good value.

⌛ 3–6 years

✓ *Antonio Vallana* • *Le Piane* • *Podere ai Valloni*

BOTTICINO DOC
Lombardy

Full-bodied, Barbera-based red wines with a good level of alcohol and a light tannic structure.

⌛ 3–5 years

✓ *Miro Bonetti* • *Benedetto Tognazzi*

BRACHETTO D'ACQUI DOCG
Piedmont

A sort of red Asti, Brachetto d'Acqui is as sweet as Australian sparkling Shiraz but without the weight, tannin, or oak. Totally fruit-driven fizz, the best of which have lovely, fresh, aromatic grapey fruit with a lush, soft *mousse* and impressive raspberry acidity underpinning the sweetness. Must be 100 per cent Brachetto grape and may be sold simply as Acqui.

✓ *Batasiolo* • *Contero* • *Duchessa Lia*

BRAMATERRA DOC
Piedmont

Good value, full-bodied red wines produced primarily from Nebbiolo, but which may include Bonarda, Croatina, and Vespolina grapes.

⌛ 3–6 years

✓ *Luigi Perazzi* • *Fabrizio Sella*

BUTTAFUOCO DOC
See Oltrepò Pavese DOC

CALUSO DOC
Piedmont

These are fresh, dry, light-bodied white wines made from the Erbaluce, which is a rather undistinguished grape. A far more interesting *passito* version exists and it is probably this that gave Erbaluce its overrated, albeit localized, reputation. *See also* Caluso Passito DOC.

⌛ 1–3 years

✓ *Luigi Ferrando* • *Orsolani*

CALUSO PASSITO DOC
Piedmont

Fragrant yet full-bodied, sweet white wines made from *passito* Erbaluce grapes.

⌛ 3–5 years

✓ *Vittorio Boratto*

CANAVESE DOC
Piedmont

The best-known wine produced from these vineyards in the hills surrounding Lake Viverone is Erbaluce, but reds and *rosato* wines are also made with Barbera, Bonarda, Freisa, Nebbiolo, and Negroamaro. The reds are best.

✓ *CV del Canavese* (Rosso) • *Ferrando* (Rosso)

CAPRIANO DEL COLLE DOC
Lombardy

Rarely encountered red wines made from the Sangiovese, which are blended with Marzemino, Barbera, and Merlot, and tart white wines made from the Trebbiano.

CAREMA DOC
Piedmont

Soft, medium-bodied Nebbiolo wines that are grown on the mountainous slopes close to the border with the Valle d'Aosta. They are good and reliable but rarely exciting.

⌁ 2–5 years

☑ *Luigi Ferrando*

CELLATICA DOC
Lombardy

This aromatic and flavoursome red wine has been made in the hills overlooking Brescia for 400 years. Permitted grapes are Barbera, Marzemino, Schiava Gentile, and Incrocio Terzi.

⌁ 2–6 years

☑ *Barbi*

CHAMBAVE DOC
Valle d'Aosta

A sub-appellation of the regional Valle d'Aosta DOC, Chambave produces attractively scented, crisp red wines primarily from Petit Rouge grapes, plus up to 40 per cent Dolcetto, Gamay, and Pinot Noir. Two white wines are also permitted; one sweet, long-lived, and *passito* in style, the other a highly perfumed, early-drinking, dry- to off-dry white – both from the Moscato grape. *See* Valle d'Aosta DOC.

⌁ 2–3 years (red and *passito*) • upon purchase (white)

☑ *La Crotta di Vegneron • Ezio Voyat*

CINQUE TERRE *or* CINQUETERRE DOC
Liguria

Spectacular coastal vineyards producing good, though not exactly spectacular, delicately fruity, dry white wines, primarily from Bosco, Albarola, and Vermentino grapes (plus a maximum of 20% optional other local varieties) and the more exciting Cinque Terre Sciacchetrà, a medium-sweet *passito* wine. The permitted sub-appellations of Costa da Posa, Costa de Campu, and Costa de Sera are all named sites that overlook the pretty coastal town of Riomaggiore.

⌁ 1–3 years

☑ *Walter de Batté • Buranco • Forlini Cappellini*

CINQUE TERRE SCIACCHETRÀ DOC
See Cinque Terre DOC

CISTERNA D'ASTI DOC
Piedmont

Named after the Cisterna fortress, built where Saint Paul supposedly stopped while attempting to convert the local population. Red still or *frizzante* wines made from at least 80% Croatina.

COLLI DI LUNI DOC
Liguria

Sangiovese-based reds and Vermentino whites from the eastern extremity of Liguria, bordering and even overlapping part of Tuscany.

⌁ 2–5 years (red) and 1–2 years (white)

☑ *Bosoni • La Colombiera • Lambruschi*

COLLI TORTONESI DOC
Piedmont

Most are robust and rather rustic, full-bodied Barbera reds, and crisp, dry, rather lightweight, and sometimes *frizzante* Cortese whites. In recent years, however, a few committed producers have started to craft some beautiful reds that walk the tightrope between fine minerality and sensational softness.

☑ *Luigi Boveri • La Colombera • Claudio Mariotto • Vignetti Massa*

COLLINA DEL MILANESE IGT
Lombardy

The geographical equivalent of San Colobano DOC, this IGT allows all styles of wine from many different grape varieties, but much of the production is in the form of a rustic *frizzante* from one or more of the following varieties: Bonarda, Cabernet Sauvignon, Chardonnay, Cortese, Malvasia, Merlot, Trebbiano, and Verdea.

☑ *Poderi San Pietro* (Solarò Vino Bianco Fermo Passito)

COLLINA TORINESE DOC
Piedmont

From vineyards just outside of Turin, on foothills overlooking the city, these red wines are primarily made from Barbera or Freisa in dry, sweet, *novello*, and *frizzante* styles, although pure Barbera, Bonarda, and Malvasia di Schierano varietal red wines in dry or *passito* styles are also produced, but not *frizzante*.

COLLINE DI LEVANTO DOC
Liguria

This DOC consists of vineyards clinging precariously to the cliffs and hills in the eastern extremity of the spectacular Cinque Terre vineyards; thus it enjoys the same combination of soil, climate, and grape varieties, in addition to which red wines are also produced (primarily from Sangiovese and Ciliegiolo grapes).

COLLINE NOVARESI DOC
Piedmont

A new DOC for red and white wines from the Novarese province northwest of Milan; the white is dry and made exclusively from the Erbaluce grape, whereas the red is a blend of at least 40 per cent Uva Rara and 30 per cent Nebbiolo, plus up to 30 per cent Vespolina and Croatina.

COLLINE SALUZZESI DOC
Piedmont

These red wines may be either blended from Pelaverga, Nebbiolo, and Barbera, or pure varietal for Pelaverga. A still or sparkling red wine varietal is also allowed for Quagliano, an ancient local variety that might have become extinct had the growers in this DOC not planted well-known varieties such as Nebbiolo and Barbera, which enabled their businesses to survive.

COLLINE SAVONESI IGT
Liguria

Freed of any DOC restrictions, the hills overlooking the Ligurian Riviera make a fascinating source of long-forgotten grape varieties, including Corvino (sic), Lumassina, Mataòssu, Pigato, and even the local Granaccia, which is an assertively independent localized clone of the better-known Grenache.

☑ *Bruna* (Pulin) • *Punta Crena*

CORONATA DOC
See Val Polcevera DOC

CORTESE DELL'ALTO MONFERRATO DOC
Piedmont

Dry, crisp, still, frizzante, and fully sparkling white wines that often incline to a coarser style than expected for the Cortese grape.

CORTESE DI GAVI DOCG
See Gavi DOCG

COSTE DELLA SESIA DOC
Piedmont

Red wines produced from Vespolina, Croatina, and Nebbiolo grapes growing in a hilly area overlapping Lessona, Bramaterra, and Gattinara.

☑ *Antoniolo*

DIANO D'ALBA DOC
See Dolcetto di Diano d'Alba DOC

DOLCEACQUA DOC
Liguria

This appellation is located at the extreme western edge of the Ligurian Riviera, bordering Provence, where red wine is produced from the so-called Rossese di Ventimiglia, which is probably the Tibouren grape. The best wines are light, easy-drinking reds that are capable of rich, lush fruit, a soft texture, and a spicy aromatic aftertaste. If qualified by Superiore, this wine must be aged for a minimum of 12 months prior to release.

⌁ 1–4 years

☑ *Terre Bianche* (Bricco Arcagna) • *Maccario Dringenberg* (Posau) • *Giobatta Cane • Lupi • Antonio Perrino*

DOLCETTO D'ACQUI DOC
Piedmont

Dolcetto is a plump grape with a low acid content that is traditionally used to make cheerful, Beaujolais-type wines that are deep purple in colour and best enjoyed young.

⌁ 1–3 years

☑ *Viticoltori dell'Acquese • Villa Banficut*

DOLCETTO D'ALBA DOC
Piedmont

Dolcetto d'Alba DOC produces some soft, smooth, juicy wines that should be drunk while they are young, fresh, and fruity.

🍷 1–3 years

✓ *Elio Altare • Azelia • Batasiolo • Fratelli Brovia • Ca' Viola • Ceretto • Pio Cesare • Fratelli Cigliuti • Aldo Conterno • Cascina Drago • Franco Fiorina • Elio Grasso • Bartolo Mascarello • Pira • Roberto Voerzio*

DOLCETTO D'ASTI DOC
Piedmont

These wines are lighter than Dolcetto d'Alba.

DOLCETTO DELLE LANGHE MONREGALESI DOC
Piedmont

Rare wines produced in tiny quantities, reputed to have an exceptionally fine aroma.

DOLCETTO DI DIANO D'ALBA *or* DIANO D'ALBA DOC
Piedmont

Diano is a hilltop village just south of Alba, which produces wines that are slightly fuller and more grapey than most other Dolcetto wines.

🍷 3–5 years

✓ *Alario • Casavecchia • Colué • Fontanafredda • Giuseppe Mascarello • Cantina della Porta Rossa • Mario Savigliano • Veglio & Figlio*

DOLCETTO DI DOGLIANI DOC
Piedmont

Most Dolcetto from Dogliani used to be made to drink young and fruity, but more is now being made in a *vin de garde* style, the best of which now claim Dolcetto di Dogliano Superiore DOCG status, although Abbona's DOC offerings give them a run for their money.

✓ *Abbona • Chionetti • Luigi Einaudi*

DOLCETTO DI DOGLIANI SUPERIORE DOCG
Piedmont

With more perfumed finesse than the basic Dolcetto di Dogliani DOC, these wines must be aged for at least 18 months prior to release.

✓ *Cascina Corta (Pirochetta) • Luigi Einaudi • Pecchenino*

DOLCETTO DI OVADA DOC
Piedmont

These are the fullest and firmest of Dolcettos.

🍷 3–6 years (up to 10 for the very best)

✓ *Cascina Scarsi Olivi*

ERBALUCE DI CALUSO DOC
See Caluso DOC

FARA DOC
Piedmont

In the hands of someone like Dessilani, Fara DOC proves to be an underrated, enjoyable, Nebbiolo-based wine with lots of fruit combined with a spicy-scented character.

✓ *Luigi Dessilani (Caramino)*

FRANCIACORTA DOCG
Lombardy

The sparkling white and *rosato* wines made by Franciacorta were promoted to DOCG status in September 1995. Produced by the traditional method with 25 months' ageing on the lees (or 37 if *riserva*), Franciacorta had already shown its potential for producing fine, biscuity, *brut*, and lightly rich *rosato* sparkling wines when this book was first published. It not only deserves its prestigious classification, it is an object lesson for the rest of the Italian wine industry for two reasons. Firstly, the still wines have retained their former DOC status (*see* Terre di Franciacorta DOC), making it one of Italy's more prestigious appellations. Meanwhile, the selection of only sparkling wines for DOCG enhances this new classification, whereas promoting an entire DOC devalues it. Not every region has a super-category to promote as Franciacorta has, but others could, for example, restrict production to the original *classico* area and a reduced yield. This would result in both a DOC and DOCG for the same region and, in the mind of the consumer, it would ensure that the "G" did guarantee an elevated quality equivalent to *grand cru*, for example. The second lesson is that as the first Italian wine to insist on bottle-fermentation, Franciacorta is currently the only Italian dry sparkling-wine appellation that can demand respect from the rest of the world. *See* Terre di Franciacorta DOC for still wines.

🍷 2–5 years

✓ *Banfi • Bellavista • Fratelli Berlucchi • Bersi Serlini • Ca'del Bosco • Bredasole • Castelfaglia • Tenuta Castellino • Casteveder • Cavalleri • Cola • Ricci Curbastro • Faccoli • Lantieri de Paratico • Majolini • La Montina • Barone Pizzini • Lo Sparviere • Villa*

FREISA D'ASTI DOC
Piedmont

Known for centuries, and a favourite of King Victor Emmanuel, this is the original and most famous Freisa. These fruity red wines may be made fully sparkling, *frizzante*, or still, and in both dry and sweet styles.

🍷 3–6 years (up to 10 for the very best)

✓ *Gilli*

FREISA DI CHIERI DOC
Piedmont

Freisa di Chieri produces the same styles of wine as Freisa d'Asti from just outside Turin.

GABIANO DOC
Piedmont

The full-bodied, red Barbera wines of Castello di Gabiano seemed to make this a promising DOC, but the appellation has not taken off and these wines are seldom encountered.

GARDA DOC
Lombardy

A wide-ranging appellation encompassing 18 grape varieties and innumerable other local non-aromatic varieties grown over three separate areas of hillsides around Lake Garda, including two that are in Veneto. In addition to blended red, *rosato*, *chiaretto*, white, and *frizzante* wines, there are seven varietal red wines: Barbera (still and *frizzante*), Cabernet Franc, Cabernet Sauvignon, Cortese, Groppello Classico (including a Riserva for

wines that are aged at least 24 months before release), Merlot, and Pinot Nero; and eight varietal white wines: Chardonnay (still and *spumante*), Corvina, Garganega, Pinot Grigio, Riesling (still and *spumante*), Riesling Italico, Sauvignon, and Sauvignonasse.

✓ *Cavalchina • Costaripa • Delai (Vigna Nobile) • La Guarda (Gropello, Rosso Sabbioso) • Monte Cicogna (Don Lisander, Rubinere)*

GARDA COLLI MANTOVANI DOC
Lombardy

Although vines have been cultivated since ancient times in Lake Garda, today viticulture is one of the least important crops. The wines are dry, light-bodied, red, white, and *rosato*, produced from a wide variety of grapes.

GATTINARA DOCG
Piedmont

From Nebbiolo and up to 10 per cent Bonarda grown on the right bank of the Sesia River in northern Piedmont, Gattinara can be a fine, though not a great, wine, especially now that overcropping problems have been reduced since Gattinara attained DOCG status. When young, the fruit can be chunky and rustic when compared with Barbaresco or Barolo, but the best Gattinara wines develop a fine, silky-textured flavour and a graceful, violet-perfumed finesse when mature. Gattinara earned its DOC and then full DOCG status through the almost single-handed efforts of Mario Antoniolo, whose wines have always been among the greatest produced in the area. Others have followed his example, but have been too few and too slow to give Gattinara the sort of reputation that a world-class wine appellation ought to have.

🍷 6–15 years

✓ *Mario Antoniolo • Le Colline • Torraccia di Piantavigna • Travaglini*

GAVI *or* CORTESE DI GAVI DOCG
Piedmont

BROGLIA
2009
GAVI
DENOMINAZIONE DI ORIGINE CONTROLLATA E GARANTITA
DEL COMUNE DI
GAVI
LA MEIRANA

The quality and character of these highly fashionable wines is very uneven, although prices are uniformly high. At best, they are soft-textured, dry white wines with a slight *frizzantino* when young, and can develop a honey-rich flavour after a couple of years in bottle. Too many examples have all their character fermented out at low temperatures, which gives them an amylic peardrop aroma, and some are definitely *frizzante*.

🍷 2–3 years

✓ *Nicola Bergaglio • Gian Piero Broglia • Chiarlo (Fior di Rovere) • Carlo Deltetto • La Scolca • Villa Sparina*

GHEMME DOCG
Piedmont

A Nebbiolo-based wine produced on the bank opposite Gattinara, Ghemme is usually seen as the inferior of the two appellations, but it has never been as persistently overcropped and is generally more consistent. Although not capable of reaching the heights of Antoniolo's Gattinara, for example, most Ghemme has just as much colour, body, and flavour as Gattinara in general, and starts off with a much finer bouquet and more elegant fruit. In addition to Nebbiolo, Vespolina and Bonarda may be used.

🍷⤙ 4–15 years

☑ *Antichi Vigneti di Cantelupo • Le Colline • Luigi Dessilani • Torraccia de Piantavigna*

GOLFO DEL TIGULLIO DOC
Liguria

This DOC covers a number of different wines, primarily varietals from Vermentino, Bianchetta Genovese, and Moscato for whites and Ciliegiolo (including *novello*) for reds. Except for Moscato, which must be sweet and may be *passito*, all of these grapes may be made into either dry still wine or *frizzante*. Still and *frizzante* blends are also permitted in both red and white. A dry white blended *spumante* is also allowed.

GRIGNOLINO D'ASTI DOC
Piedmont

Grignolino d'Asti DOC produces lightly tannic red wines with a slightly bitter aftertaste.

GRIGNOLINO DEL MONFERRATO CASALESE DOC
Piedmont

These are light, crisp, fresh red wines made from Grignolino around the Casalese Monferrato.

GRUMELLO DOCG
See Valtellina Superiore DOCG

INFERNO DOC
See Valtellina Superiore DOC

LAMBRUSCO MANTOVANO DOC
Lombardy

Not all Lambrusco comes from Emilia-Romagna. This one is produced just across the border on the plains of Mantua (Mantova). Formerly a *vino da tavola*, Mantovano is red and *frizzante* with a pink foam and may be dry or sweet.

🍷⤙ Upon purchase

☑ *CS di Quistello*

LANGHE DOC
Piedmont

This area overlaps the DOCGs of Barolo and Barbaresco and, among others, the DOCs of Nebbiolo d'Alba, Dolcetto d'Alba, and Barbera d'Alba. As such, it always had the potential to raise the quality of those other famous wines if only the Langhe DOC would not merely siphon off the dregs but include good and very good wines; this would enhance the reputation of this appellation and

ensure that only the very greatest wines would be reserved for truly iconic bottles, such as Barolo and Barbaresco. Then along came Angelo Gaja, a man whose wines have become more iconic than the famous appellations from which they come. And what did Gaja do? He turned Langhe and Barolo on their heads by bottling his very best Barolo vineyards – Sperss, Conteisa, and Dagromis – under the Langhe DOC. White, red, and six varietal wines are permitted: Dolcetto, Freisa, and Nebbiolo for red, and Arneis, Favorita, and Chardonnay for white.

☑ *Elio Altare • Ca' Viola • Chionetti • Aldo Conterno • Angelo Gaja • Ettore Germano • Giuseppe Mascarello*

LESSONA DOC
Piedmont

These are red wines that can be delightfully scented, with rich fruit and some finesse.

☑ *Sella*

LOAZZOLO DOC
Piedmont

From the village of Loazzolo, south of Canelli, this Moscato *passito* is aged for two years, including six months in *barriques*, to produce a golden-hued, richly flavoured, lusciously textured, exotically sweet wine. A wine that can age, but which is best drunk young.

🍷⤙ 2–4 years

☑ *Borgo Maragliano • Borgo Sambui • Bricchi Mej • Giancarlo Scaglione*

LUGANA DOC
Lombardy

These are soft, smooth, dry white wines made from Trebbiano grown on the shores of Lake Garda, slightly overlapping Veneto in northeast Italy. There are many dullards, but the very best Lugana manage to transcend the lacklustre level normally expected from this grape variety and almost always come from the Lombardian side.

🍷⤙ 1–2 years

☑ *Ca' dei Frati • Provenza • Visconti*

MALVASIA DI CASORZO D'ASTI DOC
Piedmont

These are lightly aromatic, sweet, red, and *rosato* wines that may also be sparkling.

🍷⤙ 1–2 years

☑ *Bricco Mondalino*

MALVASIA DI CASTELNUOVO DON BOSCO DOC
Piedmont

The DOC of Malvasia di Castelnuovo Don Bosco produces attractive, lightly aromatic, sweet, red, still, and sparkling wines.

🍷⤙ 1–2 years

☑ *Bava*

MANTOVA *or* PROVINCIA DI MANTOVA IGT
Lombardy

This southeastern corner of Lombardy is close to Emilia-Romagna and is both better known for and far better suited to the production of wonderfully aged Parmigiano Reggiano cheese than for any of its wines. However, of its wines, Lambrusco is by far the best known, and most is sold under the Lambrusco Mantovano DOC, although this IGT does allow *frizzante* Lambrusco, and some is indeed produced. All grape varieties and wine styles are allowed for this IGT, but apart from Lambrusco, the only Mantova I have encountered have been either Trebbiano or Merlot-Cabernet blends.

MAROGGIA DOCG
See Valtellina Superiore DOCG

MONFERRATO DOC
Piedmont

This is a relatively new DOC, which was introduced in 1995 for red, white, and *ciaret* or *chiaretto* (rosé) Dolcetto, Casalese, and Freisa from a wide area overlapping the Asti region.

☑ *La Barbatella • Martinetti • Villa Sparina • Luigi Spertino* (La Mandorla) • *La Spinetta*

MONTENETTO DI BRESCIA IGT
Lombardy

These wines are made from vineyards in Brescia and half a dozen surrounding villages from Barbera, Cabernet Franc, Cabernet Sauvignon, Marzemino, Merlot, or Sangiovese for reds, and Chardonnay, Pinot Bianco, or Trebbiano for whites. *Novello*-style reds are allowed, provided that one or more of the following grapes represents at least 70%: Marzemino, Merlot, Sangiovese.

MORGEX ET LA SALLE DOC
Valle d'Aosta

A sub-appellation of the regional Valle d'Aosta DOC, the vineyards of these two communes reach as high as 1,300 metres (4,265 feet), which makes it one of the highest wine-growing areas in Europe. However, most vines in these two villages are grown between 900 and 1,000 metres (2,952 and 3,280 feet), although even this is remarkable as, in theory, grapes do not ripen above 800 metres (2,625 feet) in the Valle d'Aosta. However, in practice they ripen, and produce a fine, dry, *frizzantino* white. Brut, Extra Brut, and Demi Sec *spumante* versions are also made. *See also* Valle d'Aosta DOC.

🍷— 1–3 years

☑️ *Alberto Vevey*

MOSCATO D'ASTI DOCG
Piedmont

Wines similar in flavour to Asti, but with a minimum pressure of three atmospheres, as opposed to five. Still, slightly *frizzantino*, and positively *frizzante* examples of Moscato d'Asti exist. Those with some degree of effervescence are bottled without any *dosage*, while the first fermentation is still underway, as opposed to Asti plain and simple, which is made by the *cuve close* method. Compared with Asti, Moscato d'Asti is generally, though not necessarily, less alcoholic (5.5 to 8 per cent instead of 7.5 to 9 per cent) and almost always much sweeter. If there is any criticism of this luscious, heavenly nectar, it is the unfortunate trend to make these wines fizzier, as there is often little difference between modern Moscato d'Asti and Asti itself. Rarely does one find a still Moscato d'Asti with the barest prickle, as in the past. That said, this is the Asti DOC to pick. As there are fewer than 3 million bottles, as opposed to 85 million Asti, it is more expensive, and the best, such as Borgo Maragliano's La Caliera, which is in a completely different class from the rest, are definitely fine.

🍷— Upon purchase

☑️ *Araldica • Castello Banfi • Alfiero Boffa • Borgo Maragliano • Redento Dogliotti • Tenuta il Falchetto • Gatti • Marchesi di Gresy • Villa Lanata • Luciana Rivella • La Spinetta-Rivetti*

MOSCATO DI SCANZO DOC
Lombardy

This red Moscato wine is made from the Moscato di Scanzo grape (aka Muscat Noir à Petits Grains) grown in the vineyards of Scanzorosciate in the province of Bergamo. It must be sweet and may be *passito* but must not be *frizzante*.

☑️ *Monzio Compagoni • Il Cipresso (Serafino)*

NEBBIOLO D'ALBA DOC
Piedmont

Pure Nebbiolo wines come from between Barolo and Barbaresco. Most are fine, full, rich, and fruity. Sweet and sparkling versions are allowed.

🍷— 4–10 years

☑️ *Ascheri • Fabrizio Battaglino • Tenuta Carretta • Ceretto • Pio Cesare • Aldo Conterno • Giacomo Conterno • Franco Fiorina • Bruno Giacosa • Hilberg-Pasquero • Giuseppe Mascarello • Val de Prete • Vietti*

NUS DOC
Valle d'Aosta

A sub-appellation of the Valle d'Aosta DOC, Nus makes an interesting red from Vien de Nus, Petit Rouge, and Pinot Noir grapes. Dry and *passito* styles of white wine are made from Pinot Gris or Malvoisie de Nus. *See also* Valle d'Aosta DOC.

🍷— 2–4 years

☑️ *La Crotta di Vegneron*

OLTREPÒ PAVESE DOC
Lombardy

The Oltrepò Pavese covers 42 communes south of the Po River, although much of the production is not marketed under this DOC, but sold to specialist wineries in Piedmont. These wineries turn it into non-DOC *spumante* by the *cuve close* process or the traditional method. There used to be three geographical sub-appellations, but Barbacarlo has since been recognized as the exclusive product of Lino Maga, reverting to *vino da tavola* status. The two remaining sub-appellations are **Oltrepò Pavese Buttafuoco** ("sparks of fire"), a deep-coloured, fruity, dry or semi-sweet *frizzante* red; and **Oltrepò Pavese Sangue di Giuda** (charmingly named "blood of Judas"), a soft, sweet, red *spumante*. Both wines are restricted to vineyards around the villages of Broni, Canetto Pavese, Castana, Cigognola, Montescano, Pietra de Giorgi, and Stradella. Apart from blended red, white, and *rosato* wines, Oltrepò Pavese permits 11 varietal wines: Barbera, Bonarda (made from Croatina), Cabernet Sauvignon, and Pinot Noir (still and *spumante*) for red; and Chardonnay, Cortese, Malvasia, Moscato (still, *spumante*, and *liquoroso*), Pinot Grigio, Riesling Italico, and Riesling Renano for white.

🍷— 1–3 years (white, *rosato*, and sparkling)
2–5 years (red)

☑️ *Giacomo Agnes • Angelo Ballabio • Bianchina Alberici • Castello di Cigognola (Barbera Poggio della Maga) • Doria (Pinot Nero) • Frecciarossa (Pinot Nero Giorgio Odero) • Lino Maga (see also Barbacarlo) • Tenuta Mazzolino • Monsupello • Piccolo Bacco dei Quaroni • Tronconero (Bonarda) • Zonin (Moscato spumante)*

ORMEASCO DI PORNASSIO DOC
See Pornassio DOC

PAVIA *or* PROVINCIA DI PAVIA IGT
Lombardy

The IGT equivalent of the Oltrepò Pavese DOC, in foothills that rise south of the Po Valley, where Pinot Grigio is most commonly used for this IGT, although any locally grown variety is permitted, and Cortese, Pinot Nero, and Riesling Italico are also often used.

☑️ *Picchioni (Arfena Pinot Nero)*

PIEMONTE DOC
Piedmont

Introduced in 1995, this DOC embraces all the other DOC areas in the Piedmont and, with the exception of Piemonte Moscato and Piemonte Moscato Passito, which must be made from 100 per cent Moscato grapes, all wines claiming this appellation are required to contain at least 85 per cent of the variety indicated. Permitted red wine varietals are Barbera, Bonarda, Brachetto, Dolcetto, and Pinot Noir, while in addition to the Moscato wines already mentioned above, white varietals include Cortese, Pinot Blanc, and Pinot Gris. The creation of this regional DOC probably explains why no IGT wines have been declared in Piedmont, and it is doubtful whether any IGT will be in the future.

☑️ *Coppo • Paolo Saracco (Moscato)*

PINEROLESE DOC
Piedmont

This appellation includes varietal wines (Barbera, dry or sweet Bonarda, Dolcetto, the rare Doux d'Henry, and a *frizzante* Freisa), a blended red called Ramie (produced from Avanà, Avarengo, and Neretto, plus a maximum of 35% other local non-aromatic red varieties), and unnamed red and *rosato* blends (from Barbera, Bonarda, Nebbiolo, and Neretto, plus a maximum of 50%; other local non-aromatic red varieties).

☑️ *Le Marie (Barbera Colombè, Debàrges)*

PORNASSIO DOC
Liguria

A dry red or sweet *passito* wine made from the Ormeasco grape, a localized clone of Dolcetto that has been growing in the Riviera di Ponente area since the 14th century. The dry red wine may be labelled Superiore if aged 12 months prior to release. Sciac-tra or Sciacchetrà is a red *passito* wine that has been made in a dry or relatively dry style.

☑️ *Fontanacota • Nirasca (Superiore) • Lorenzo Ramò (Rosso)*

PROVINCIA DI MANTOVA IGT
See Mantova IGT

PROVINCIA DI PAVIA IGT
See Pavia IGT

QUISTELLO IGT
Lombardy

Mostly produced by the Quistello cooperative, whose wines include *frizzante* red (Lambrusco) and *frizzante* white (Chardonnay, Trebbiano, Moscato) from grapes grown in the same general area as the Mantova IGT in the southeastern corner of Lombardy, close to Emilia-Romagna.

RIVIERA DEL GARDA BRESCIANO *or* GARDA BRESCIANO DOC
Lombardy

This area makes light, fruity, slightly bitter red wines that are no more interesting than the bulk of Valpolicella, produced on the opposite bank of Lake Garda. Most are blended from Gropello, Sangiovese, Marzemino, and Barbera, but some are pure varietal wines from the Gropello grape and these tend to be superior. Although the whites may be pure Riesling, this is taken to mean either Riesling Renano, which is true Riesling, or Riesling Italico, which is not. Furthermore, as up to 20 per cent of other local grape varieties may be used, Garda Bresciano *bianco* has not been of much interest so far. The most successful wine here has been the *rosato*, or *chiaretto*, which, although it is made from exactly the same varieties as the *rosso*, can be much softer and easier to drink.

🍷— Upon purchase

☑️ *Costaripa*

RIVIERA LIGURE DI PONENTE DOC
Liguria

Four former *vini da tavola* are grouped together under this appellation, which covers the western Riviera of Liguria. These are: *Ormeasco*, bright, cherry-red wines with juicy, raspberry, Dolcetto fruit; *Pigato*, full-flavoured yet somewhat precocious red wines; *Rossese*, well-scented, characterful reds; and *Vermentino*, rich, full, and characterful dry white wines.

☑️ *Maria Donata Bianchi • Bruna • Lupi (Le Serre) • Poggio dei Gorleri*

ROERO DOCG
Piedmont

This DOC covers light-bodied, easy-drinking, inexpensive Nebbiolo reds and the highly regarded, highly priced Arneis whites from the Roeri hills north of Alba. *See* Arneis di Roero.

🍷 1–2 years

✓ *Cascina Ca' Rossa • Carlo Deltetto • Giovanni Almondo • Matteo Correggia • Monchiero Carbone • Filippo Gallino • Malvirà*

RONCHI DI BRESCIA IGT
Lombardy

This IGT encompasses red (which may be *novello*) and white (still, *frizzante*, or *passito*) wines from the villages of Bovezzo, Caino, Cellatica, Concesio, Collebeato, Naivo, and Villa Carcina to the north of the city of Brescia, and Botticino, Nuvolento, Nuvolera, and Rezzato to the east of the city, exclusively from Chardonnay, Invernenga, Pinot Bianco, Trebbiano di Soave, and Trebbiano Toscano for whites, and Barbera, Cabernet Franc, Cabernet Sauvignon, Incrocio Terzi No.1, Marzemino, Merlot, Sangiovese, and Schiava for reds.

ROSSESE DI DOLCEACQUA DOC
See Dolceacqua DOC

ROSSO DI VALTELLINA DOC
See Valtellina Rosso DOC

RUBINO DI CANTAVENNA DOC
Piedmont

A full-bodied red wine blend of mostly Barbera, Grignolino, and sometimes Freisa. It is made by a *cooperativa* called Rubino, which was solely responsible for creating this appellation, but failed to interest other producers. As a result, the DOC has not taken off.

RUCHÉ DI CASTAGNOLE MONFERRATO DOC
Piedmont

When grown on the vineyards overlooking Castagnole Monferrato, the Ruché grape is supposed to produce an aromatic red wine that ages like Nebbiolo. Up to 10 per cent Barbera and Brachetto may be used in production.

🍷 3–5 years

✓ *Piero Bruno • Ruché del Parrocco*

SABBIONETA IGT
Lombardy

Although white, red, *rosato*, and *frizzante* styles are allowed from any grapes grown in this area of lush, fertile, sandy meadows on the north bank of the

River Po, Lambrusco dominates and the most interesting wines are the *passito*-style sweet red wines made from late-picked grapes, almost all of which are consumed locally.

SAN COLOMBANO AL LAMBRO *or* SAN COLOMBANO DOC
Lombardy

Rich, robust, if somewhat rustic red wines made from Croatina, Barbera, and Uva Rara are produced by this DOC. San Colombano is the only DOC in the Milan province.

🍷 2–5 years

✓ *Carlo Pietrasanta*

SAN MARTINO DELLA BATTAGLIA DOC
Lombardy

From Friulano (aka Sauvignonasse) grapes grown in one of three separated areas overlooking the southern shores of Lake Garda, one of which is in Veneto, this is a dry, full-flavoured white wine with a flowery aroma and a slightly bitter aftertaste. A sweet *liquoroso* version is also produced.

SANGUE DI GIUDA DOC
See Oltrepò Pavese DOC

SASSELLA DOCG
See Valtellina Superiore DOCG

SEBINO IGT
Lombardy

Effectively the IGT equivalent of Franciacorta, where, freed of the DOC restrictions of Terre di Franciacorta, several top-quality Chardonnay, Pinot Nero, and Bordeaux-blends are produced.

✓ *Maurizo Zanella*

SFORZATO DI VALTELLINA *or* SFURSAT DI VALTELLINA DOCG
Piedmont

Sforzato, or *sfursat*, literally means "strained", and this wine is made from grapes that have been left to shrivel on the vine and have been vinified dry, with a minimum of 14.5 per cent alcohol, making this highly concentrated red wine the equivalent of an *amarone*. All wines must be aged for a minimum of 18 months prior to release. *See also* Valtellina Superiore DOCG.

✓ *Nino Negri • Mamete Prevostini*

SIZZANO DOC
Piedmont

These are good, full-bodied red wines that are produced from a Gattinara-like blend on a bank of the River Sesia, just south of Ghemme.

STÄGAFÄSSLI DOCG
See Valtellina Superiore DOCG

STREVI DOC
Piedmont

A sweet *passito* wine made from Moscato grapes grown in the vineyards surrounding Acqui Terme.

TERRAZZE RETICHE DI SONDRIO IGT
Lombardy

An excellent source of dry red and white wines (although *frizzante* is also permitted) from approximately the same area as Valtellina.

✓ *Nino Negri*

TERRE DI FRANCIACORTA DOC
Lombardy

Part of the original Franciacorta appellation since 1967, the still wines were renamed Terre di Franciacorta in 1995 when the name in its singular form, Terra di Franciacorta, was reserved for the new DOCG. Produced northeast of Milan, on hilly slopes near Lake Iseo, the red wines are typically well coloured, medium- to full-bodied, made from Cabernet Franc and Cabernet Sauvignon, with the possible addition of Barbera, Nebbiolo, and Merlot. Many are richly flavoured and show some finesse. The dry whites, primarily from Chardonnay with a little Pinot Blanc allowed, have improved greatly.

🍷 3–8 years (red), 1–3 years (white)

✓ *Ca'del Bosco • Enrico Gatti • Ragnoli*

TORRETTE DOC
Valle d'Aosta

A red-only sub-appellation of the regional Valle d'Aosta DOC, Torrette produces deep-coloured wines of good bouquet and body from the Petit Rouge, plus up to 30 per cent Dolcetto, Fumin, Gamay, Mayolet, Pinot Noir, Premetta, and Vien de Nus. *See also* Valle d'Aosta DOC.

✓ *Elio Cassol • Grosjean*

VAL POLCEVERA *or* CORONATA DOC
Liguria

Genoa's very own wine, Val Polcevera encompasses a wide range of wine styles: white (which can be still, *frizzante*, *spumante*, or *passito* and must be at least 60% Vermentino, Bianchetta Genovese, or Albarola, plus optional Pigato, Rolle, and Bosco), red, or *rosato* (which can be still or *frizzante* and must contain a minimum of 60% Ciliegiolo, Dolcetto, or Sangiovese, plus optional Barbera). Vermentino is the only pure varietal wine allowed. The use of Coronata on the label is reserved for white wines coming from this ancient village, which is perched high above the sea at the southernmost tip of Genoa, where very few vines survive today.

VALCALEPIO DOC
Lombardy

An up-and-coming appellation for well-coloured, deeply flavoured red wines made from a blend of Merlot and Cabernet Sauvignon, and for light, delicately dry white wines made from Pinot Blanc and Pinot Gris.

🍷 1–3 years (white), 3–7 years (red)

✓ *Tenuta Castello*

VALCAMONICA IGT
Lombardy

The Camonica Valley is best known as a UNESCO site, boasting the greatest complex of ancient rock drawings in Europe, but the area also contains some of the world's most spectacular, stunningly steep, terraced vineyards. All grapes and wine styles are allowed, but the most widely planted varieties are

SPRINGTIME AT MORGEX, VALLE D'AOSTA
Grown at more than 900 metres (3,000 feet), these vines annually disprove the theory that grapes should not ripen above 800 metres (2,600 feet) in the Valle d'Aosta.

Chardonnay, Incrocio Manzoni, Müller-Thurgau, Pinot Bianco, Riesling Renano, and Trebbiano for white wines, and Barbera, Ciliegiolo, Incrocio Terzi, Marzemino, Merlot Sebina, and Valcamonec for red. Unfortunately, many rare local varieties such as Valcamonec, Erbanno, and Sebina are disappearing.

VALGELLA DOCG
See Valtellina Superiore DOCG

VALLE D'AOSTA *or* VALLÉE D'AOSTE DOC
Valle d'Aosta

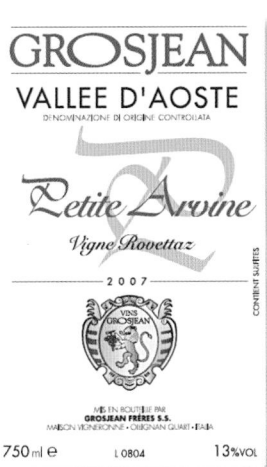

A regional DOC encompassing 20 different styles of wine, Valle d'Aosta took under its wings the only two DOCs formerly recognized in the region: Donnaz and Enfer d'Arvier. These are now two of the seven sub-appellations within this DOC, the other five being Arnad-Montjovat, Chambave, Morgex et La Salle, Nus, and Torrette (*see* individual entries). The Valle d'Aosta DOC has revitalized this region's tiny production of somewhat low-key wines. Apart from blended red, white, and *rosato*, the following varietal wines are permitted: Fumin, Gamay, Nebbiolo, Petit Rouge, Pinot Noir, and Premetta for reds; and Chardonnay, Müller-Thurgau, Petit Arvine, and Pinot Gris for whites. There is also a Bianco di Pinot Nero, which you might see labelled as a Blanc de Noir de Pinot Noir, as all Valle d'Aosta wines have official alternative French designations.

🍷— 1–3 years

✓ *Anselmet • Brégy & Gillioz • Les Crêtes • La Crotta di Vegneron • CV de Donnas • Les Granges • Grosjean • Lo Triolet*

VALSUSA DOC
Piedmont

Situated just south of the Valle d'Aosta and close to the French border, the Valle di Susa is where this red wine is blended from at least 60% Avanà, Barbera, or Dolcetto, plus optional Beretta Cuneese and other local non-aromatic varieties.

✓ *Carlotta*

VALTELLINA ROSSO DOC
Lombardy

Encompasses 19 communes of the province of Sondrio. Most are light-scented, medium-bodied red wines of simple, but pleasing, character. Many critics believe Valtellina to be very overrated, and the basic appellation certainly is, but the fine wines are virtually all classed as Valtellina Superiore. *See also* Valtellina Superiore DOC.

VALTELLINA SFORZATO *or* VALTELLINA SFURSAT DOCG
See Sforzato di Valtellina DOCG

VALTELLINA SUPERIORE DOCG
Lombardy

The best wines of Valtellina are produced from a narrow strip of vineyards on the north bank of the Adda River near the Swiss border, and must contain a minimum of 12 per cent alcohol, as opposed to the 11 per cent required for Valtellina. Most of the wines come from six sub-districts: **Grumello** (the lightest), **Inferno** (supposedly the hottest, rockiest part of the valley), **Maroggia** (the smallest subregion at just 24 hectares [60 acres]), **Sassella** (the best), **Stägafässli** (reserved for Valtellina Superiore bottled over the border in Switzerland), and **Valgella** (the most productive but least interesting). Essentially produced from Chiavennasca, the local synonym for Nebbiolo, to which up to 5 per cent Brugnola, Pinot Noir, Merlot, Pignola Valtellina, and Rossola may be added. All wines must be aged for a minimum of 24 months prior to release, or 36 months if the term Riserva is used. The richness of the best of these wines is belied by their elegance. They have good colour and are capable of developing exquisite finesse after several years in bottle. *See also* Sforzato di Valtellina DOCG.

🍷— 5–15 years

✓ *Enologica Valtellinese • Sandro Fay • Fondazione Fojanini • Nino Negri • Conti Sertoli-Salis • Fratelli Triacca • Mamete Prevostini • Aldo Rainoldi*

VERDUNO *or* VERDUNO PELAVERGA DOC
Piedmont

Apparently the Pelaverga of Verduna, known locally as the Pelaverga Piccolo, is a distinctly different variety from the Pelaverga grown in the Colline Saluzzesi and elsewhere. The red wine it produces is quite fragrant, verging on spicy, with good acidity and minerality.

✓ *Fratelli Alessandria • Ascheri • Burlotto • Michele Reverdito • Castello di Verduno*

NORTHEAST ITALY

Freshness, crisp acidity, and purity of varietal character personify the wines of the northeastern regions of Trentino-Alto Adige, Friuli-Venezia Giulia, and the Veneto. However, beware the mass-produced wines, which are so clean and pure that they lack any fruit.

THIS IS A MORE MOUNTAINOUS AREA than the northwest (with the exception of that region's Valle d'Aosta), as just over half the land is occupied by the Dolomites and their precipitous foothills. Some of the finest wines are grown in the lush, verdant vineyards of the South Tyrol (Alto Adige), just over the border from Austria. A great deal of wine is exported; the bulk of it is unexciting Soave and Valpolicella. Locally there is much greater variety and value to be had – a number of French and German grapes are grown in addition to fascinating local varieties, and dedicated producers continue to experiment. Austria to the north and Slovenia to the east have influenced the styles produced.

TERMENO VINEYARDS, ALTO ADIGE
The town of Termeno, or Tramin as it is also called, is situated between Bolzano and Trento, in the Alto Adige region. This is where the Traminer Aromatico, or Gewürztraminer, is supposed to have originated, but the local clone is far more restrained than the classic Alsace version, with hardly any spice to its character.

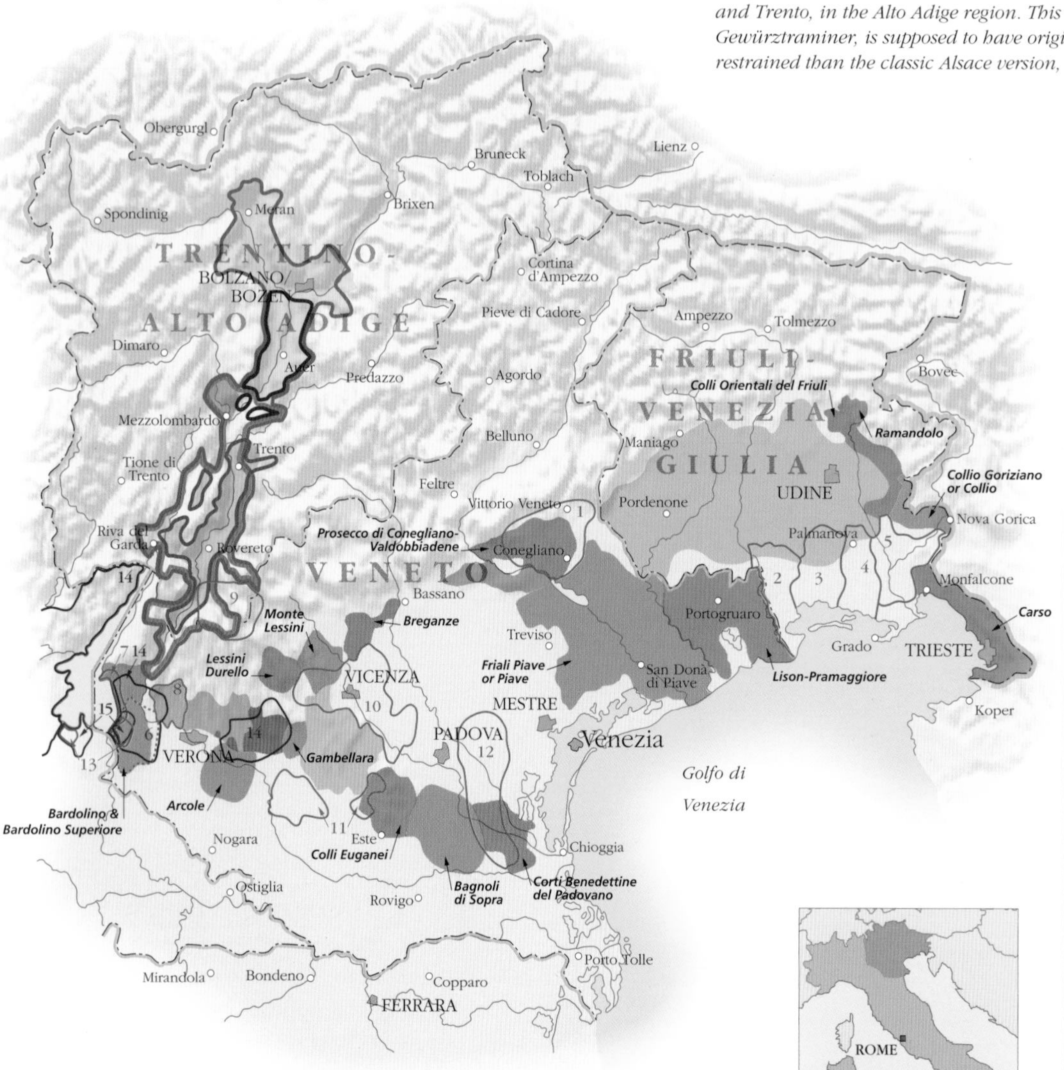

NORTHEAST ITALY, *see also p313*
The variety of sites offered by the mountains and the hills of this area enables many grape varieties to be grown in addition to local ones. The most exciting wines come from the high vineyards of the South Tyrol, the hills of Friuli, and around Vicenza in the Veneto.

Map legend

- Trento
- Caldaro or Lago di Caldaro
- Valdadige
- Casteller
- Teroldego Rotaliano
- Alto Adige
- Trentino, Casteller, Sorni
- Valpolicella
- Soave & Soave Superiore
- Colli Berici
- Montello e Colli Asolani
- Friuli-Grave
- Appellation named on map: eg, *Arcole*

1. Colli di Conegliano
2. Friuli Latisana
3. Friuli Annia
4. Friuli Aquileia
5. Friuli Isonzo or Isonzo
6. Bianco di Custoza
7. Bardolino Classico
8. Valpolecella Classico
9. Valdadige Terradeiforte
10. Vicenza
11. Merlana
12. Riviera del Brenta
13. San Martino della Battaglia
14. Garda
15. Lugana

Regional boundary

0   10   20   30   40 miles
0   20   40   60 km

Map labels

Obergurgl, Bruneck, Lienz, Spondinig, Meran, Brixen, Toblach, TRENTINO-ALTO ADIGE, BOLZANO/BOZEN, Cortina d'Ampezzo, Dimaro, Pieve di Cadore, Ampezzo, Tolmezzo, Bovec, FRIULI-VENEZIA GIULIA, Predazzo, Agordo, Ramandolo, Mezzolombardo, Colli Orientali del Friuli, Tione di Trento, Trento, Belluno, Maniago, UDINE, Feltre, Collio Goriziano or Collio, Riva del Garda, Vittorio Veneto, Pordenone, Palmanova, Nova Gorica, Rovereto, Prosecco di Conegliano-Valdobbiadene, Conegliano, Monfalcone, VENETO, Bassano, Carso, Monte Lessini, Breganze, Treviso, Portogruaro, Grado, TRIESTE, Lessini Durello, VICENZA, San Donà di Piave, Lison-Pramaggiore, Koper, MESTRE, Friali Piave or Piave, Gambellara, PADOVA, Venezia, Golfo di Venezia, Bardolino & Bardolino Superiore, Arcole, VERONA, Nogara, Este, Colli Euganei, Chioggia, Ostiglia, Bagnoli di Sopra, Corti Benedettine del Padovano, Rovigo, Mirandola, Bondeno, Copparo, Porto Tolle, FERRARA, ROME

REGIONS AT A GLANCE

REGION	TOTAL AREA UNDER VINE	DOC/DOCG AREA UNDER VINE	DOC/DOCG PRODUCTION	TOTAL PRODUCTION
Veneto	90,000 ha (222,400 acres)	35,400 ha (87,500 acres)	1.7 million hl (45/55 red/white)	8.5 million hl (94.4 million cases)
Trentino-Alto Adige	13,500 ha (33,350 acres)	11,100 ha (27,400 acres)	730,000 hl (70/30 red/white)	1.2 million hl (13.3 million cases)
Friuli-Venezia Giulia	21,000 ha (51,900 acres)	12,300 ha (30,400 acres)	430,000 hl (40/60 red/white)	1.1 million hl (12.2 million cases)

TRENTINO-ALTO ADIGE

This is the most westerly and spectacular of the northeast's three regions, and more than 90 per cent of its area is covered by mountainous countryside. It is made up of two autonomous provinces, the Italian-speaking Trento in the south and the German-speaking Bolzano, or South Tyrol, in the north. In Bolzano the wines may possess alternative German names and can carry a QbA (*Qualitätswein bestimmter Anbaugebiete*) designation. The generic Alto Adige DOC (*Südtiroler QbA*) is remarkably good and accounts for one-third of the region's total DOC output. There are also numerous fine wines produced in these cool, high vineyards.

THE VENETO

The Veneto stretches from the Po River to the Austrian border, between Trentino-Alto Adige to the west and Friuli-Venezia Giulia to the east, and most of the wines are grown on alluvial plains in the south. Once famous, but more recently infamous, for its Valpolicella and Soave, the Veneto is also one of the most exciting hunting grounds for some of Italy's best Bordeaux-type blends, and there are signs that even the aforementioned abused wine names are beginning to regain a little of their former respectability.

FRIULI-VENEZIA GIULIA

Situated in the northeastern corner of Italy, this predominantly mountainous region has grown many non-Italian varieties since phylloxera wiped out its vineyards in the late 19th century. The naturally innovative Friulians (and South Tyroleans) used the opportunity to replant their vineyards with several better-quality foreign grape varieties, starting with the Merlot, which was brought to this region by Senator Pecile and Count Savorgnan in 1880. Over the past 100 years, the northeast has consistently demonstrated that the use of superior grape varieties and relatively lower yields can produce wines of dramatically improved quality. Friuli is the home of some of the country's finest wines, including many of its most complex Cabernet blends. Girolamo Dorigo's Montsclapade, which

is the best of an exceptionally fine group of wines, is a typically Friulian blend of both Cabernets, Merlot, and Malbec. It is rare to find the Malbec variety on this side of the Alps, but it fares well in Friuli and might well be the key to the complexity of these wines. A few rather unconventional blends are found, the most unusual being Abbazia di Rosazzo's multi-national Ronco dei Roseti, which mixes the four Bordeaux varieties with the German Limberger, the Italian Refosco, and the obscure Tazzelenghe. Another Abbazia di Rosazzo wine, Ronco delle Acacie, is a rare masterpiece in the new Italian school of "super-deluxe" *vini da tavola* white wines – a category of dry white Italian wine that is expensive but mostly disappointing.

The largest volume of fine wines produced in the northeast comes from Colli Orientali del Friuli, one of Friuli's two *colli*, or "hilly", areas. This one is situated close to the former Yugoslav border and encompasses many varietal wines. These wines are well worth looking out for – with the exception of the Picolit, which is a grossly overrated and horrendously overpriced sweet wine wherever it comes from. The Picolit produced in Colli Orientali del Friuli is the only one in Italy to have DOC status, but, in fact, the wine is no better than other examples to be found throughout the country.

FACTORS AFFECTING TASTE AND QUALITY

LOCATION
The northeast is bounded by the Dolomites to the north and the Adriatic Sea to the south.

CLIMATE
Similar to the northwest in that summers are hot and winters cold and harsh, but fog is less of a problem and hail more frequent. There are unpredictable variations in the weather from year to year so vintages are important, particularly for red wines.

ASPECT
Vineyards are found on a variety of sites ranging from the steep, mountainous slopes of Trentino-Alto Adige to the flat, alluvial plains of the Veneto and Friuli-Venezia Giulia. The best vineyards are always sited in hilly countryside.

SOIL
Most vineyards are on glacial moraine – a gritty mixture of sand, gravel, and sediment deposited during the Ice Age. Most are clayey or sandy clay and the best sites are often marly and rich in calcium. The light, stony soil in the South Tyrol is rapidly leached by weathering and fertilizers have to be added annually.

VITICULTURE AND VINIFICATION
The northeast has led Italy's move towards more modern vinification

techniques and experimentation with foreign grape varieties. It was the first area to use cold fermentation and, initially, the wines produced were so clean that they lacked natural character. There is now much experimentation into how to increase intensity of flavour through the use of new oak.

GRAPE VARIETIES
Bianca Fernanda (Cortese), Cabernet Franc, Cabernet Sauvignon, Chardonnay, Corvinone (Corvina), Cruina (Corvina), Durello, Friulano, Friularo (Raboso), Garganega, Gewürztraminer, Incrocio Manzoni 215 (Glera x Cabernet Sauvignon), Incrocio Manzoni 6013 (Riesling x Pinot Blanc), Kerner, Lagrein, Lambrusco a Foglia Frastagliata, Limberger (Franconia), Malbec, Malvasia, Marzemino, Merlot, Moscato (Muscat Blanc à Petit Grains), Nosiola, Petit Verdot, Picolit, Pinello (Pinella), Pinot Bianco (Pinot Blanc), Pinot Grigio (Pinot Gris), Pinot Nero (Pinot Noir), Portoghese (Blauer Portugieser), Refosco (Mondeuse), Ribolla, Riesling, Rossara/Rossanella (Molinara), Sauvignon Blanc, Sauvignonasse (Friulano), Schioppettino, Serprina/Serprino (Glera), Tazzelenghe, Teroldego, Terrano (Mondeuse), Trebbiano (Ugni Blanc), Veltliner (Rossola), Verduzzo, Vernatsch (Schiava), Vespaiolo

BARDOLINO VINEYARDS
Ripening grapes adorn rows of vines in the Veneto's Bardolino area, which has a good reputation for light, dry red, and rosato wines.

THE APPELLATIONS OF
NORTHEAST ITALY

ALTO ADIGE *or* SÜDTIROLER DOC
Trentino-Alto Adige

This generic appellation covers the entire Alto Adige, or South Tyrol, which is the northern half of the Valdadige DOC.

There are seven red-wine varietals: Cabernet covers either Cabernet Sauvignon or Cabernet Franc, or both, and ranges from simple, but delightful, everyday wines to deeper-coloured, fuller-bodied, richer wines that become warm, mellow, and spicy after five to 10 years; Lagrein Scuro, or *Lagrein Dunkel*, is made from an underrated, indigenous grape and can have a fine, distinctive character and good colour; Malvasia, or *Malvasier*, is produced here as a red wine, although it would be better made into white or *rosato*; Merlot can be simply light and fruity or can attain greater heights, with a good spicy, sweet-pepper aroma and a fine, silky texture; Pinot Noir, or *Blauburgunder*, is a difficult varietal to perfect, but those from Mazzon are good and a speciality of this region (they will have Mazzoner on the label); Schiava, or *Vernatsch*, accounts for one in five bottles produced under this appellation and is the most popular tavern wine; Schiava Grigia, or *Grauervernatsch*, has recently been added to the list, as have two red-wine blends of Cabernet-Lagrein and Cabernet-Merlot.

There are no fewer than 10 different white-wine varietals: Chardonnay can range from light and neutral to delicately fruity, and even *frizzantino* or verging upon *spumante* – the fuller versions can have recognizable varietal characteristics, but still lack the weight and intensity of flavour of even basic Burgundy; Moscato Giallo, or *Goldenmuskateller*, is made into delicious dessert wines; Pinot Bianco, or *Weissburgunder*, is the most widely planted of all the white grape varieties and produces most of Alto Adige's finest white wines; Pinot Grigio, or *Ruländer*, is potentially as successful as Pinot Blanc, but does not always occupy the best sites; Riesling Italico, or *Welschriesling*, is insignificant in both quantity and quality; Riesling Renano, or Rheinriesling, is fine, delicate, and attractive at the lowest level, but can be extraordinarily good in exceptional vintages; Riesling x Silvaner, or *Müller-Thurgau*, is relatively rare, which is a pity because it achieves a lively spiciness in this region; Sauvignon was very scarce in the early 1980s, but as the vogue for this grape spread so its cultivation increased and the crisp, dry, varietally pure Sauvignon is now one of the most successful wines of the Alto Adige; Silvaner is made mostly to be drunk young and fresh; Traminer Aromatico, or *Gewürztraminer*, is far more restrained than the classic Alsace version, even if, as some claim, the variety originated in the village of Tramin or Termeno, between Bolzano and Trento. If you can forget the full-blown spicy wine of Alsace, the delicate aroma and understated flavour of this wine can have a certain charm of its own.

Only three dry varietal *rosato*, or *Kretzer*, wines are allowed: Lagrein Rosato, or *Lagrein Kretzer*, is overtly fruity in a very round and smooth style; Merlot Rosato, or *Merlot Kretzer*, is a relatively recent addition and makes a curiously grassy or bell-pepper *rosato*; Pinot Nero Rosato, or *Blauburgunder Kretzer*, is more successful as a *rosato* than as a red.

Moscato Rosa, or *Rosenmuskateller*, are very flamboyant, deep-pink to scarlet-red, semi-sweet to sweet wines with an unusually high natural acidity, intense floral perfume, and an exaggerated Muscat flavour.

There is one sparkling-wine denomination for pure or blended Pinot Blanc and/or Chardonnay with up to 30 per cent Pinot Gris and Pinot Noir, with both *cuve close* and the traditional method permissible.

In 1994 five former DOCs were incorporated into the Alto Adige, or Südtiroler, DOC as geographical sub-appellations. **Colli di Bolzano DOC**, or *Bozner Leiten*, for soft, fruity, early-drinking, Schiava-based red wines from the left bank of the Adige River, and both banks of the Isarco near Bolzano; **Meranese**, or **Meranese di Collina DOC**, or *Meraner Hügel*, from the hills around Merano, north of Bolzano, where the Schiava grape produces a light, delicately scented red wine, which may be labelled as Burgravito, or *Burggräfler*, if it comes from the part of the Meranese that was formerly part of the Contea di Tirol; **Santa Maddalena DOC**, or *Sankt Magdalener*, in the heart of the Colli di Bolzano (*see above*), where the Schiava-based red wines are just as soft and fruity, but fuller in body and smoother in texture – few Italian references today boast that Santa Maddalena was ranked by Mussolini (over-optimistically) as one of Italy's greatest wines; **Terlano DOC**, or *Terlaner*, which overlaps most of Caldaro DOC on the right bank of the Adige, running some 16 kilometres (10 miles) northwest of Bolzano to 24 kilometres (15 miles) south, and covers one blended, one *spumante*, and the following eight varietal white wines: Pinot Bianco (*Weissburgunder*), Chardonnay, Riesling Italico (*Welschriesling*), Riesling Renano (*Rheinriesling*), Silvaner, Müller-Thurgau, and Sauvignon; and, finally, **Valle Isarco DOC**, or *Eisacktaler*, which takes in both banks of the Isarco River from a few miles north of Bolzano to just north of Bressanone, where the vineyards are high in altitude and the vines trained low to absorb ground heat. Six white-wine varietals are produced: Kerner, Müller-Thurgau, Pinot Grigio, or *Ruländer*, Sylvaner, Traminer Aromatico, or *Gewürztraminer*, and Veltliner. Valle Isarco also includes a geographical blend called *Klausner Leitacher* for red wines from the villages of Chiusa (also known as *Klausen*), Barbiano, Velturno, and Villandro, which must be made from at least 60 per cent Schiava plus up to 40 per cent Portoghese and Lagrein. Furthermore, any Valle Isarco wine produced in Bressanone or Varna can be labelled "di Bressanone" or "*Brixner*".

🍷— 2–10 years (red and *rosato*), 2–5 years (white), 1–3 years (sparkling)

✓ *Abbazia di Novacella • Cantina Caldaro • Cantina Gries-Bolzano • Cantina Terlano • Castel Juval • Colterenzio • Cortaccia • Anton Gojer • Giorgio Grai • Franz Haas • Haderburg • Hofstätter • Kettmeir • Günther Kershbaumer • Klosterkellerei Eisacktaler • Klosterkellerei Schreckbichl • Alois Lageder • Josephus Mayr • Mazo Foradori • Muri-Gries • Nalles Niclara Magre • Nals Margreid • Stiftskellerei Neustift • Niedermayr • Manfred Nössing • Peter Pliger • Plattner-Waldgries • Gumphof Markus Prackwieser • Franz Pratzner • Prima & Nuova • Heinrich Rottensteiner • San Michele (Sanct Valentin) • Santa Margherita • Schloss Rametz • Schloss Sallegg • Schloss Schwanburg • Termeno • Tiefenbrunner • Elena Walch • Baron Georg von Widmann*

ALTO LIVENZA IGT
Friuli-Venezia Giulia and Veneto

All grapes and styles are possible from this IGT, which straddles the Friuli-Veneto border between the Colli di Conegliano and the Friuli-Grave DOCs, but I have not encountered anything so far.

AMARONE DELLA VALPOLICELLA *or* RECIOTO DELLA VALPOLICELLA AMARONE DOC
See Valpolicella DOC

AQUILEA DOC
See Friuli-Aquilea DOC

ARCOLE DOC
Veneto

This DOC abuts the southeastern corner of Valpolicella and covers a wide range of wine styles: white (which can be still, *frizzante*, *spumante*, or *passito* and must be at least 50% Garganega), red or *rosato* (which can be *frizzante* or still, including *novello* and *riserva*, and must contain a minimum of 50% Merlot), and the following varietal wines: Cabernet Sauvignon, Carmenère, Chardonnay (can be *frizzante*), Garganega, Merlot, Pinot Bianco, Pinot Grigio, and Sauvignon.

✓ *Sartori*

ATESINO DELLE VENEZIE IGT
Trentino-Alto Adige

This IGT just north of Bolzano has seldom been used since the 1990s. *See* Delle Venezie DOC.

BAGNOLI *or* BAGNOLI DI SOPRA DOC
Veneto

This typically Italian all-purpose appellation covers still, *passito*, *frizzante*, and *spumante* wines from a wide range of grapes grown southwest of Venice in a large area sandwiched between the Colli Euganei and Corti Benedettine del Padovano. The most important grape varieties are Cabernet Franc, Cabernet Sauvignon, Carmenère, Merlot, Raboso Piave, and Raboso Veronese for reds, and Chardonnay, Sauvignon, and Sauvignonasse for whites, while the *rosato* must be at least 50% Raboso Piave or Raboso Veronese. Varietal wines are red only and restricted to Merlot and, perhaps potentially the most interesting, Friularo (aka Raboso Piave), which may be produced in a *vendemmia tardiva* style.

BARDOLINO DOC
Veneto

From the hills surrounding the eastern shore of Lake Garda, these wines are made from 35–65% Corvina, 10–40% Rondinella plus a maximum of 20% optional varieties (Barbera, Cabernet Sauvignon, Marzemino, Merlot, Molinara, Rossignola, Sangiovese), no single variety of which must exceed 10% of the total blend. They may be dry, still, *spumante*, red, *chiaretto*, or *novello*. Most Bardolino DOC is light and bland, but *see* Bardolino Superiore DOCG.

✓ *Corte Gardoni* • *Le Fraghe* • *Guerrieri-Rizzardi*

BARDOLINO SUPERIORE DOCG
Veneto

The geographical area and grape-variety requirements are precisely the same as for Bardolino DOC. The only differences are in vine density, which is higher; grape yield, which is lower; and style, which may only be a dry red wine. This is where Bardolino starts to get interesting.

✓ *La Prendina* (San Lucia) • *Corte Gardoni* (Le Fontane)

BIANCO DI CUSTOZA DOC
Veneto

Effectively the white wines of Bardolino, they can be scented with a smooth aftertaste and may sometimes be sparkling. Some critics compare Bianco di Custoza to Soave, which neatly sums up the quality. The grapes are Trebbiano, Garganega, Friulano, Cortese, and Malvasia.

✓ *Corte Gardoni* (Mael)

BOZNER LEITEN *or* COLLI DI BOLZANO DOC
See Alto Adige DOC

BREGANZE DOC
Veneto

This is one of Italy's unsung DOC heroes, largely due to the excellence of Maculan. As a generic red, Breganze is an excellent Merlot-based wine with the possible addition of Pinot Noir, Freisa, Marzemino, Gropello Gentile, Cabernet Franc, and Cabernet Sauvignon. As a white, it is fresh, zesty, and dry and made from Friulano, with the possible addition of Pinot Blanc, Pinot Gris, Welschriesling, and Vespaiolo. But it is mostly sold as a varietal, of which there are two red (Cabernet and Pinot Nero) and three white (Pinot Bianco, Pinot Grigio, and Vespaiolo).

🍷 2–5 years (red), 1–2 years (white)

✓ *Bartolomeo da Breganze* • *Maculan* • *Vigneto Due Santi*

CALDARO *or* LAGO DI CALDARO DOC
Trentino-Alto Adige

As this overlaps the heart of the Terlano area, Caldaro might as well be yet another sub-appellation of the Alto Adige DOC, along with Terlano and the other former DOCs that have now been absorbed. These Schiava-based red wines have the possibility of adding up to 15% in total of Pinot Nero or Lagrein and are mostly soft and fruity, hinting of almond, and easy to drink. Later-harvested wines may be labelled Auslese, Klassisch Auslese, or Scelto. The Caldaro or Lago di Caldaro DOC may also be labelled in German as Kalterer or Kaltereresee DOC.

✓ *Cantina di Caldaro* • *Erste & Neue* • *Manincor* • *Thomas Pichler* (Alte Reben)

CARSO DOC
Friuli-Venezia Giulia

Carso Terrano must consist of at least 85 per cent Terrano (also known as Mondeuse or Refosco), which makes a deep, dark, and full red wine that can be fat and juicy. Carso Malvasia is a rich and gently spicy, dry white wine.

🍷 1–3 years

✓ *Edi Kante* • *Skerk* • *Zidarich*

CASTELLER DOC
Trentino-Alto Adige

The thin strip of hilly vineyards that produces these wines is virtually identical to the Trentino DOC. Dry or semi-sweet, red and *rosato* wines for everyday drinking from Schiava, Merlot, and Lambrusco a Foglia Frastagliata grapes.

COLLI BERICI DOC
Veneto

In addition to a sparkling Garganega-based white wine, this DOC includes three red varietals (Merlot, the so-called Tocai Rosso, and Cabernet) and five white (Garganega, Friulano, Pinot Bianco, Sauvignon, and Chardonnay). The Cabernet can be rich and grassy with chocolaty fruit, and the Merlot, in the right hands, is plump and juicy; the "Tocai Rosso" is unusual and interesting, and the Chardonnay suffices as usual. However, the other wines from this area immediately south of Vicenza are less exciting.

🍷 2–5 years (red), 1–2 years (white)

✓ *Castello di Belvedere* • *Portogodi* (Pozzare) • *Villa dal Ferro*

COLLI DI BOLZANO *or* BOZNER LEITEN DOC
See Alto Adige DOC

COLLI DI CONEGLIANO DOC
Veneto

Still red- and white-wine DOC from a large chunk of Prosecco-land for Glera-based whites and, by far the best, Bordeaux-blend reds.

✓ *Sorelle Bronca* (Ser Bele)

COLLI EUGANEI DOC
Veneto

Bordering Colli Berici to the southeast, this area produces soft, full-bodied, dry or semi-sweet red-wine blends (from Merlot plus Cabernet Franc, Cabernet Sauvignon, Barbera, and Raboso) and four red varietals: Cabernet, Cabernet Franc, Cabernet Sauvignon, and Merlot. There are dry or semi-sweet white-wine blends (from Garganega, Glera, and Friulano with the possible addition of Chardonnay, Pinot Blanc, Pinella, and Welschriesling) and seven white varietals: Chardonnay, Fior d'Arancio (from the Moscato Giallo grape in sweet *frizzantino*, *spumante*, and *liquoroso* styles), Moscato (sweet *frizzantino* and *spumante* styles), Pinella or Pinello, Pinot Bianco, Serprina or Serprino (dry or sweet in still, *frizzantino*, *frizzante*, or *spumante* styles), and Friulano.

🍷 2–5 years (red), 1–2 years (white)

✓ *Cavalchina* (Amedeo) • *Monte de Frà* (Ca' del Magro) • *Villa Sceriman* ◉ • *Vignalta*

COLLI ORIENTALI DEL FRIULI DOC
Friuli-Venezia Giulia

Larger than neighbouring Collio and initially more prestigious, both DOCs have now shown their excellent potential. In addition to a generic *rosato* blend, there are seven red varietals (Cabernet, Cabernet Franc, Cabernet Sauvignon, Merlot, Pinot Noir, Refosco, and Schioppettino); and 12 white (Chardonnay, Malvasia, Picolit, Pinot Bianco, Pinot Grigio, Ramandolo (dessert-style Verduzzo), Ribolla, Riesling Renano, Sauvignon Blanc, Friulano, Traminer Aromatico, and Verduzzo Friulano).

🍷 3–8 years (red), 1–3 years (white)

✓ *Borgo del Tiglio* • *Girolamo Dorigo* • *Le Due Terre* • *Livio Felluga* • *Dorino Livon* • *Miani* • *Ronc di Vico* • *Ronchi di Manzano* • *Scubla* • *Giordano Sirch* • *La Tunella* • *Le Vigne di Zamò* • *Volpe Pasini*

COLLI ORIENTALI DEL FRIULI PICOLIT DOCG
Friuli-Venezia Giulia

This sweet white wine has always been over-rated and over-priced. These wines must be aged for at least 12 months prior to release, unless qualified by "Cialla" on the label, in which case it must be aged for at least 24 months.

✓ *Ronco delle Betulle*

COLLI TREVIGIANI IGT
Veneto

This area overlaps Treviso and the classic Conegliano-Valdobbiadene region, so understandably a fair amount of passable Prosecco, both *spumante* and *frizzante*, has always been produced under this IGT. However, as from the 2009 vintage, the name Prosecco is allowed only for DOC and DOCG wines. Exactly the same wines continue to be made but using the name Glera for what was formerly known as the Prosecco grape. Apart from an absence of the Prosecco name, anything goes in this IGT, as it does in most others, and the most popular varieties found include Cabernet Sauvignon, Chardonnay, and Pinot Nero.

COLLIO *or* COLLIO GORIZIANO DOC
Friuli-Venezia Giulia

A large range of mostly white wines from a hilly area close to the Slovenian border, Collio now encompasses 19 different wines. With some top producers making very high-quality wines, this appellation is clearly in line for full DOCG status in the near future. As well as a blended dry white (primarily from Ribolla, Malvasia, and Friulano), which can be slightly *frizzantino*, and blended red (Merlot, Cabernet Sauvignon, and Cabernet Franc, plus Pinot Noir and possibly one or two others), there are five red varietals (Cabernet, Cabernet Franc, Cabernet Sauvignon, Merlot, and Pinot Nero); and 12 white (Chardonnay, Malvasia, Müller-Thurgau, Picolit, Pinot Bianco, Pinot Grigio, Riesling Italico, Riesling Renano, Friulano, Ribolla, Sauvignon, and Traminer Aromatico). Jerman makes some of the very greatest wines, but now markets his wines under the IGT Delle Venezie. They are included below for completeness.

⌐ 1–4 years (red), 1–3 years (white)

√ • *Borgo del Tiglio* • *Branko* • *Castello di Spessa* • *Eugenio Collavini* • *Colle Duga* • *Josko Gravner* • *Jermann* • *Edi Keber* • *Dorino Livon* • *Isidoro Polencic* • *Doro Princic* • *Dario Raccaro* • *Ronco dei Tassi* • *Russiz Superiore* • *Schioppetto* • *Franco Toros* • *Venicia & Venicia* • *Villa Russiz*

CONSELVANO IGT
Veneto

This large IGT west of the Venetian lagoon encompasses most of the DOCs of Colli Euganei, Bagnoli di Sopra, Corti Benedettine del Padovano, and the Riviera del Brenta. Consequently, it offers lots of potential but is seldom used.

CORTI BENEDETTINE DEL PADOVANO DOC
Veneto

This typically wide-ranging Italian appellation allows so many different wines that it should be used as a textbook example of how not to create a DOC. The basic red or *rosato* must be a blend of 60–70% Merlot, 10–40%, Raboso, and up to 30% other local red varieties. Why? The basic white must be a blend of at least 50% Chardonnay and/or Pinot Bianco and/or Pinot Grigio and/or Sauvignon and/or Sauvignonasse. How could such a confused concoction ever project a wine for which this region could be recognized? But it does not stop there. The red may be sold as a *novello*; the white cannot. A *passito* style is permitted, as long as it consists of at least 70% Moscato Giallo (optional varieties are Chardonnay, Pinot Bianco, Pinot Grigio, and Sauvignon); a blend of Cabernet Franc and Cabernet Sauvignon may be sold as Cabernet, and Cabernet Sauvignon may be produced as a pure varietal wine, although Cabernet Franc cannot. In addition to the Cabernet Sauvignon, which may be sold as a *riserva* if aged 24 months prior to release, there are numerous varietal wines, which for red wine include Merlot (which cannot be sold as a *riserva*), Raboso (which can be sold as a *riserva* and, indeed, as a *passito* wine, either sweet or dry), and Refosco dal Peduncolo (which cannot be produced as a *passito* but can be sold as a *riserva*). The white varietals are Chardonnay (which can be *frizzante* or *spumante*), Moscato (which must be sweet and *spumante*), Pinot Bianco, Pinot Grigio, and Sauvignon (none of which may be either *frizzante* or *spumante* or, for that matter, *passito*). Are we to believe that all these very different and somewhat specific wines have made this area so famous in the minds of wine consumers across the globe that the name Corti Benedettine del Padovano trips so easily from our tongues? Of course not, but it does illustrate perfectly why only very specific, truly famous wines should be DOC or DOCG and how all other wines would benefit from being sold under one IGT for an entire region – in this case, Veneto – with absolutely no restrictions on grape variety or wine style.

DELLE VENEZIE IGT
Friuli-Venezia Giulia and Veneto

Considering this vast appellation covers all grape varieties and styles of wine produced in either Friuli-Venezia Giulia or Veneto, it has a remarkably reliable reputation, especially in the gifted hands of Jermann. And unlike with most IGTs, customers can immediately identify its area of origin.

√ *Albino Armani* • *Jermann*

EISACKTALER *or* VALLE ISARCO DOC
See Alto Adige DOC

ETSCHTALER DOC
See Valdadige DOC

FRIULI ANNIA DOC
Friuli-Venezia Giulia

Named after the Via Annia, an ancient Roman road built by Titus Annius Rufus in 131 BC, this DOC has a relatively small production that is focused on the Friulano (formerly Tocai Friulano), although the combination of wines allowed is typically large, with blended red, white, and *rosato* wines, *passito*, *frizzante*, *spumante*, and plenty of varietal wines (Cabernet Franc, Cabernet Sauvignon, Chardonnay, Friulano, Malvasia, Merlot, Pinot Bianco, Pinot Grigio, Refosco dal Peduncolo Rosso, Sauvignon, and Verduzzo Friulano).

√ *Emiro Bortolusso*

FRIULI-AQUILEA DOC
Friuli-Venezia Giulia

Formerly know simply as Aquilea, this is a wide-ranging appellation that covers five varietal red wines (Merlot, Cabernet, Cabernet Franc, Cabernet Sauvignon, and Refosco); eight white varietals (Chardonnay, Friulano, Pinot Bianco, Pinot Grigio, Riesling Renano, Sauvignon, Traminer, and Verduzzo Friulano); and a generic *rosato* of at least 70 per cent Merlot plus Cabernet Franc, Cabernet Sauvignon, and Refosco. There is also a Chardonnay *spumante*. All are generally light, crisply balanced wines, although some producers excel in better years.

⌐ 1–4 years (red), 1–3 years (white, *rosato*, and sparkling)

√ *Ca' Bolani*

FRIULI-GRAVE *or* GRAVE DEL FRIULI DOC
Friuli-Venezia Giulia

Formerly called Grave del Friuli, this massive appellation spreads out on either side of the Tagliamento River between Sacile in the west and Cividale di Friuli in the east, and accounts for over half of the region's total production. It is a huge and complicated, but rapidly improving, multi-varietal DOC in which several winemakers regularly produce fine wines. In addition to generic red and white blends, there are six red varietals (Cabernet, Cabernet Franc, Cabernet Sauvignon, Merlot, Refosco, and Pinot Noir); and eight white varietals (Chardonnay, Pinot Bianco, Pinot Gris, Riesling Renano, Sauvignon, Friulano, Traminer Aromatico, and Verduzzo Friulano). There is a Chardonnay *frizzante*, Verduzzo *frizzante*, Chardonnay *spumante*, and a blended generic *spumante*.

⌐ 1–4 years (red), 1–3 years (white, *rosato*, and sparkling)

√ *Borgo Magredo* • *Pighin* • *Vigneti le Monde* • *Vigneti Pittaro*

FRIULI ISONZO *or* ISONZO *or* ISONZO DEL FRIULI DOC
Friuli-Venezia Giulia

Just south of the Collio, nestling close to the border with Slovenia, Friuli Isonzo encompasses red, white, *rosato*, *frizzante*, *spumante*, and *vendemmia tardiva*, the inevitable Cabernet for a blend of Cabernet Franc and Cabernet Sauvignon, Pinot Spumante for a blend of Pinot Bianco, Pinot Grigio, Pinot Nero, and a whole raft of varietal wines (Cabernet Franc, Cabernet Sauvignon, Chardonnay, Franconia, Friulano, Malvasia, Merlot, Moscato Giallo, Moscato Rosa, Pinot Bianco, Pinot Grigio, Pinot Nero, Refosco dal Peduncolo Rosso, Riesling, Riesling Italico, Sauvignon, Schioppettino, Traminer Aromatico, and Verduzzo Friulano), often of good quality and value.

⌐ 1–4 years (red), 1–3 years (white)

√ *Borgo Conventi* • *Borgo San Daniele* (Friulano) • *Mauro Drius* (Pinot Bianco) • *Lis Neris-Pecorari* • *Ronco del Gelso* • *Vie di Romans* (Sauvignon) • *Tenuta Villanova* (Malvasia Saccoline)

FRIULI LATISANA DOC
Friuli-Venezia Giulia

An area that stretches from the central section of the Friuli-Grave to the Adriatic coast at Lignano Sabbiadoro. In addition to a generic, blended *rosato* (Bordeaux varieties) and *spumante* (Chardonnay and Pinot varieties) there are five red varietal wines (Merlot, Cabernet Sauvignon, Franconia (Limberger), Pinot Nero, and Refosco); and nine white varietals (Chardonnay, Malvasia, Pinot Bianco, Pinot Grigio, Riesling Renano, Sauvignon, Friulano, Traminer Aromatico, and Verduzzo Friulano). Chardonnay, Malvasia, and Pinot Nero may also be produced in a *frizzante* style.

GAMBELLARA DOC
Veneto

Produces scented, dry, or sometimes semi-sweet white wines and fruity, semi-sweet, still, *frizzante* or fully sparkling white *recioto*. A smooth, sweet *vin santo* is also produced here.

⌐ 2–5 years

√ *La Biancara* • *Luigino del Masso* (Riva del Molino)

GARDA DOC
Veneto

A wide-ranging appellation encompassing 18 grape varieties and innumerable other local non-aromatic varieties grown over three separate areas of hillsides around Lake Garda, the largest of which is in neighbouring Lombardy. In addition to blended red, *rosato*, *chiaretto*, white, and *frizzante* wines, there are seven varietal red wines: Barbera (still and *frizzante*), Cabernet Franc, Cabernet Sauvignon, Cortese, Groppello Classico (including a *riserva* for wines that are aged at least 24 months before release), Merlot, and Pinot Nero, and eight varietal white wines: Chardonnay (still and *spumante*), Corvina, Garganega, Pinot Grigio, Riesling (still and *spumante*), Riesling Italico, Sauvignon, and Sauvignonasse.

√ *Cavalchina* • *Costaripa* • *Delai* (Vigna Nobile) • *La Guarda* (Gropello, Rosso Sabbioso) • *Monte Cicogna* (Don Lisander, Rubinere)

GRAVE DEL FRIULI DOC
See Friuli Grave DOC

ISONZO *or* ISONZO DEL FRIULI DOC
See Friuli Isonzo DOC

KALTERER *or* KALTERERSEE DOC
See Caldaro DOC

LAGO DI CALDARO DOC
See Caldaro DOC

LATISANA DOC
See Friuli Latisana DOC

LESSINI *or* MONTI LESSINI DOC
Veneto

This appellation is found just northeast of Soave, in the high hills between the provinces of Verona and Vicenza. Formerly a white-wine-only DOC called Lessini Durello, this area remains best known for still, *frizzantino*, and *spumante* wines from the Durello grape, but the DOC has been opened up to other wines, including a generic white (50% Chardonnay, plus a choice of Pinot Bianco, Pinot Grigio, Pinot Nero, and Sauvignon Blanc), which must rate as an object lesson in how to throw away what small reputation Lessini has. There is also a generic white or *passito spumante* (50% Chardonnay, plus a choice of Pinot Bianco, Pinot Grigio, or Pinot Nero), a generic red (50% Merlot plus a choice of Cabernet Sauvignon, Carmenère, Corvina, and Pinot Nero). Thankfully, Durello remains the only permissible varietal wine but may now be made as a *passito* wine, as well as dry white, but no longer *frizzantino*.

✓ *Marcato*

LISON-PRAMAGGIORE DOC
Veneto and Friuli-Venezia Giulia

This DOC, which is in the very east of the Veneto, and overlaps a small part of Friuli, originally combined three former DOCs (Cabernet di Pramaggiore, Merlot di Pramaggiore, and Tocai di Lison) into one. However, it has since been expanded to encompass a total of seven white varietal wines (Chardonnay, Pinot Bianco, Pinot Grigio, Riesling Italico, Sauvignon, Friulano, and Verduzzo); and four reds (Cabernet, Cabernet Franc, Cabernet Sauvignon, and Refosco dal Peduncolo Rosso). Cabernet and Merlot are still the best in a rich, delicious, chocolaty style.

⌛ 3–8 years (red), 1–3 years (white)

✓ *Santa Margherita* • *Russola* • *Tenuta Sant'Anna* • *Villa Castalda* (Cabernet Franc)

LUGANA DOC
Veneto

This DOC is split into two sections, both at the southern end of Lake Garda, with one part in Veneto and the other in Lombardy. It is the Lombardian part that tends to fare best. *See Lugana DOC (Lombardy) under Northwest Italy.*

✓ *Ottella* (Molceo)

MARCA TREVIGIANA IGT
Veneto

This area overlaps Treviso and the classic Conegliano-Valdobbiadene region, so understandably a fair amount of passable Prosecco, both *spumante* and *frizzante*, has always been produced under this IGT. However, as from the 2009 vintage, the name Prosecco is allowed only for DOC and DOCG wines. Exactly the same wines continue to be made but using the name Glera for what was formerly known as the Prosecco grape. Apart from an absence of the Prosecco name, anything goes in this IGT, as it does in most others, and a wide range of varieties can be found, including Cabernet Franc, Chardonnay, Sauvignon, Manzoni Bianco, Pinot Bianco, Pinot Nero, Raboso, Refosco dal Peduncolo, and Verduzzo.

✓ *Sachetto* • *Villa Sandi* (Corpore)

MERANESE *or* MERANESE DI COLLINA *or* MERANER HÜGEL DOC
See Alto Adige DOC

MERLARA DOC
Veneto

Established as recently as 2000, this DOC is split in two, with one part in the province of Verona, the other in the province of Padua. The wines include a Friulano-based generic white that may be *frizzante* and a Merlot-based generic red that may be *novello*. There is a blended generic white (Cabernet Sauvignon, Marzemino (which must be *frizzante*) and Merlot for reds, and Friulano and Malvasia for whites.

MITTERBERG IGT
Trentino-Alto Adige

This IGT is centred on Merano at the northern end of the Valdadige. Although all grape varieties and types of wine are allowed, Schiava and Lagrein seem to make the most expressive reds, while Pinot Bianco is probably the most consistent for whites.

✓ *Cantina Vini Merano*

MONTELLO E COLLI ASOLANI DOC
Veneto

From vineyards at the foot of the aptly named Mount Grappa, most of wines are varietals, comprising two reds (Merlot and Cabernet); four whites (Prosecco, Chardonnay, Pinot Bianco, and Pinot Grigio); and three *spumante* (Chardonnay, Pinot Bianco, and Prosecco). Any red wines that do not carry a varietal name will be primarily Cabernet-Merlot blends.

⌛ 1–3 years

✓ *Fernando Berta* • *Abbazia di Nervesa*

MONTI LESSINI DOC
See Lessini DOC

PIAVE *or* VINI DEL PIAVE DOC
Veneto

A large area to the west of Lison-Pramaggiore producing five red varietals (Merlot, Cabernet, Cabernet Sauvignon, Pinot Nero, and Raboso); and five whites (Chardonnay, Friulano, Pinot Bianco, Pinot Grigio, and Verduzzo). The Cabernet and Raboso can be particularly good.

⌛ 1–3 years

✓ *Reichsteiner*

PICOLIT DOC
See Colli Orientali del Friuli DOC

PROSECCO DOC
Veneto

This DOC covers both *spumante* and *frizzante* styles of Prosecco produced and bottled in the provinces of Treviso, Vicenza, Venice, Padua, and Belluno in Veneto, and Pordenone, Udine, Gorizia, and Trieste in Friuli-Venezia Giulia. This DOC was formed when Prosecco di Conegliano-Valdobbiadene was promoted to DOCG status and Prosecco IGT was banned (last vintage permissible being 2008).

PROSECCO DI CONEGLIANO-VALDOBBIADENE *or* PROSECCO DI CONEGLIANO *or* PROSECCO DI VALDOBBIADENE DOCG
Veneto

Since the previous edition, I have come to respect Prosecco – or, at least, the best Prosecco – and the best Prosecco invariably come from the hilly Conegliano-Valdobbiadene region. I see Prosecco as more of a bar drink than a sparkling wine I would drink with food. What impresses me is that the producers of Conegliano-Valdobbiadene have long accepted that Prosecco gains nothing from fermentation in bottle, time on yeast, or post-disgorgement ageing, a process that merely blurs the fruit of this grape. So, what do Prosecco producers do? They go to such lengths to preserve as many of Prosecco's primary aromas as possible. They ferment their wine in large, shiny, stainless-steel cans and get it off the lees and into bottle as quickly as possible. They even use unfermented Prosecco juice as a sugar source for both the second fermentation (which is effectively part of the first fermentation) and *dosage*. This not only preserves freshness but adds grapiness to the primary aromas. Prosecco is all about maintaining freshness. It should never be aged. Most Prosecco is made in the extra-dry style, but with an average of just 16 grams of residual sugar, it is not one of the sweeter extra-dry sparkling wines on the market. The strategy is to enhance the primary aromas and grapiness, rather than project any sweetness as such. One Prosecco that definitely has a sweetness about it is Cartizze, the so-called *grand cru* of Prosecco. A recent addition is **Rive**, which in the local dialect refers to high hillsides, where the slopes are so steep that they can be very difficult to work. A Prosecco with a Rive denomination will come from a specific locality within the Conegliano-Valdobbiadene region. Rive is therefore an extension of the Cartizze concept but for a drier style. Of all Prosecco, I reckon that Bisol Crede is the best base for a Bellini (freshly squeezed peach juice and Prosecco, never Champagne), and the best Bellini in the world is served in the Bar Dandalo of the Hotel Danieli in Venice. By all means, taste one at Harry's Bar, where it was invented, if only out of a sense of history, but then take a short stroll along the promenade of Saint Mark's Square to the Hotel Danieli, where you can taste the difference for yourself. It was only while chatting to the barman, Solindo Soncin, that I saw the wall behind the bar adorned with diplomas certifying that he had won the Best Barman in Italy title since the year dot. No wonder he makes a great Bellini. Bisol is also ahead of the game, selling vintaged single-vineyard Prosecco before Rive was conceived. Most Prosecco is not vintaged, but for a wine that you should consume as fresh as possible, knowing the year of production is vital.

⌛ Upon purchase

✓ *Andreola* (especially Dirupo) • *Astoria* (Cuvee Tenuta Val de Brun) • *Bisol* (especially Garnei) • *Fratelli Bortolin* (Cartizze) • *Sorelle Bronca* (Particella 68) • *Carpenè Malvolti* • *Le Colture* • *Nino Franco* (Grave di Stecca, Primo Franco) • *Terre di San Venanzio* (Fortunato) • *La Tordera* (Cru Dry) • *Col Vetoraz* (Cartizze)

PROVINCIA DI VERONA IGT
See Veronese IGT

RAMANDOLO DOCG
Friuli-Venezia Giulia

A sweet late-picked wine that is almost, but not quite, a *passito* from a local clone of Verduzzo Friulano called Ramandolo. This variety is grown in the foothills of the Alps above Nimis, where the vineyards are so steep that the vines are trained, pruned, and harvested by the same methods as those used at the time of Pope Gregory XII, when Ramandolo was served at the Council of 1409.

✓ *Anna Berra* • *Dario Coos*

RECIOTO DELLA VALPOLICELLA *or* RECIOTO DELLA VALPOLICELLA AMARONE DOC
See Valpolicella DOC

RECIOTO DI SOAVE DOCG
Veneto

Naturally sweet Soave made from *passito* grapes, to produce wines that are either *liquoroso* or *spumante*. Most are too oxidative, but Pieropan is as pure as driven snow.

✓ *Pieropan* (Le Colombare Vendemmia Tardiva)

RIVIERA DEL BRENTA DOC
Veneto

From a large appellation inland from the Venetian lagoon, this DOC centres primarily on vineyards along the banks of the Brenta River, where the wines include a Friulano-based generic white that may be *frizzante* and a Merlot-based generic red and *passito* that may be *novello*. There is a blended Cabernet and various varietal wines: Merlot, Raboso, and Refosco dal Penduncolo, with white varietals of Chardonnay (which must be *frizzante* or *spumante*), Pinot Bianco (which must be *frizzante* or *spumante*), Pinot Grigio, and Friulano.

SANTA MADDALENA *or* SANKT MAGDALENER DOC
See Alto Adige DOC

SAN MARTINO DELLA BATTAGLIA DOC
Veneto

From Friulano (aka Sauvignonasse) grapes grown in one of three separated areas overlooking the southern shores of Lake Garda, two of which are located in Lombardy, this is a dry, full-flavoured white wine with a flowery aroma and a slightly bitter aftertaste. A sweet *liquoroso* version is also produced.

SOAVE DOC
Veneto

PIEROPAN
VITICOLTORI IN SOAVE
Soave Classico

Most Soave is still over-cropped, thin, and bland, but Cantina del Castello defies the odds as it continues to make immensely enjoyable wines from Garganega and Trebbiano from this basic DOC. However, there are other better Soave appellations, and virtually all the top Soave wines are made in the Classico area (*see* Soave Classico DOC). Soave DOC may be produced and sold as *spumante*, even when labelled Classico, although a classic Soave is definitely a dry still wine. As with all Soave appellations, the wine must be at least 70% Garganega, to which Chardonnay, Pinot Bianco, Trebbiano, and up to 5% other local varieties may be added. In addition to the Soave appellations below, *see* Recioto di Soave DOC.

🍷 1–4 years

✓ *Cantina del Castello* (Monte Pressoni)

SOAVE CLASSICO DOC
Veneto

These wines are restricted to the central, hilly Classico area in the communes of Monteforte and Soave itself, just two of the 13 communes that comprise the entire Soave DOC area. Soave Classico is officially superior to Soave DOC but inferior to Soave Superiore DOCG. However, of the few top-quality Soave produced, most of the best are Soave Classico DOC, not Soave Superiore DOCG.

🍷 1–4 years

✓ *Ca' Rugat* (Monte Alto, Monte Fiorentine) • *Campi* (Campo Vulcano) • *Inama* (Vigneto du Lot) • *Pieropan* (Vigneto Calvarino, Vigneto la Rocca) • *Prà* (Staforte) • *Suavia* (Le Rive, Monte Carbonare) • *Fratelli Tedeschi* (Capitel Tenda)

SOAVE COLLI SCALIGERI DOC
Veneto

This denomination is reserved for Soave made from grapes grown on hillsides outside of the Classico area.

🍷 1–4 years

✓ *Filippi* (Castelcerino)

SOAVE SUPERIORE DOCG
Veneto

Geographically, this DOC is second in size to the basic Soave DOC only, encompassing 11 of that appellation's 13 communes (Buon Albergo, Caldiero, Cazzano di Tramigna, Colognola ai Colli, Illasi, Lavagno, Monteforte d'Alpone, Roncà, San Martino Buon Albergo, San Giovanni Ilarione, and last but not least, Soave). Other varieties in both instances are a maximum of 30% Chardonnay and/

or Pinot Bianco plus no more than 5% other local non-aromatic white varieties. Other differences include the style, which for Soave Superiore DOCG must be dry and aged for a minimum of 10 months (24 months if sold as a *riserva*).

🍷 1–4 years

✓ *Cantina del Castello* (Acini Soavi [sic] Late Harvest) • *Agustino Vicentini* (Il Casale)

SÜDTIROLER DOC
See Alto Adige DOC

TERLANO *or* TERLANER DOC
See Alto Adige DOC

TEROLDEGO ROTALIANO DOC
Trentino-Alto Adige

Full-bodied red wines made from the Teroldego in the Rotaliano area, where the grape is said to have originated. There is also a fuller *Superiore* version and an attractive *rosato*.

🍷 1–4 years

✓ *Bolognani* • *Cavit* (Maso Cervara) • *Foradori* (Vigneto Morei) • *Conti Martini* • *Mezza Corona*

TRENTINO DOC
Trentino-Alto Adige

This appellation represents the southern half of the Valdadige DOC and its wines are generally softer and less racy than those from Alto Adige to the north, although there is an equally bewildering number of varietal wines. If no variety is shown, white wines will be Chardonnay- Pinot Blanc blends and reds Cabernet-Merlot. There are seven red-wine varietals (Cabernet, Cabernet Franc, Cabernet Sauvignon, Lagrein, Marzemino, Merlot, and Pinot Nero); and nine white (Chardonnay, Moscato Giallo, Müller-Thurgau, Nosiola, Pinot Bianco, Pinot Grigio, Riesling Italico, Riesling Renano, and Traminer Aromatico). Furthermore, the Nosiola can be made in *vin santo* style, while all Pinot (Blanc, Gris, and Noir) may be fully sparkling. There is also a bright scarlet, lusciously sweet Moscato Rosa, and both Moscato Rosa and Moscato Giallo may be made in *liquoroso* style.

Sorni is a sub-appellation for wines just south of Mezzolombardo at the confluence of the rivers Avisio and Adige. Here we find soft Schiava-based reds are often improved by the addition of Teroldego and Lagrein. Light, fresh, delicate Nosiola-based white wines are usually charged with a dollop of Müller-Thurgau, Silvaner, and Pinot Blanc.

✓ *Barone de Cles* • *Càvit* • *Cesconi* • *LaVis* • *Longariva* • *Madonna del Vittoria* • *Conti Martini* • *Maso Poli* • *Pojer & Sandri* • *Giovanni Poli* • *Tenuta San Leonardo* • *Armando Simoncelli* • *Sorini* • *de Tarczal* • *Vallarom* • *Roberto Zeni*

TRENTO DOC
Trentino-Alto Adige

The only traditional-method sparkling-wine appellation to be created since Franciacorta DOCG, Trento must be made solely with Chardonnay, Pinot Bianco, Pinot Meunier, or Pinot Nero grapes, with at least 15 months on lees for non-vintage, 24 months for vintage, and 36 months for *riserva*.

✓ *Cavit* (Graal Brut Riserva) • *Balta* (Riserva) • *Dorigati* (Methius Brut Riserva) • *Ferrari* • *Letrari* (Riserva) • *Abate Nero* (Brut Domini)

VALDADIGE *or* ETSCHTALER DOC
Trentino-Alto Adige and Veneto

This huge generic denomination encompasses both the Alto Adige and Trentino DOCs, myriad sub-appellations, and extends well into the Veneto. Few producers bother to use what is generally considered to be Trentino-Alto Adige's lowest quality DOC. If the IGTs proposed by the Goria Law actually existed and worked, the size and location of Valdadige would make it an ideal candidate, as producers could select their best wines to go out under Alto Adige, Trentino, or another label, selling off the balance as an unpretentious Valdadige country wine. As it is already a DOC, nobody would dare suggest downgrading it to IGT, so the result is that hardly anyone uses it anyway. And, of the few who do, the dry and semi-sweet white and red wines that they sell inevitably attract a poor reputation as DOCs, whereas underselling the same products as IGTs would make them honest, good-value introductions to the finer wines of Trentino-Alto Adige.

VALDADIGE TERRADEIFORTI DOC
Trentino-Alto Adige and Veneto

Four varietal wines from vines growing on the southeastern corner of the Valdadige, where it overlaps the Veneto region: Enantio (local synonym for Lambrusca a Foglia Frastagliata, which may be vinified as a dry red, with fuller, softer, spicier fruit than might otherwise be expected from any Lambrusca, or a red *passito*), Casetta (aka Foja Tonda, an obscure black-skinned grape rescued from possible extinction by Albino Armani; an interesting variety, but it can have too much of a tannic bite for its weight), Pinot Grigio, and Chardonnay.

✔ *Albino Armani* (Foja Tonda) • *Roeno* (Enantio)

VALLAGARINA IGT
Trentino-Alto Adige and Veneto

This IGT covers the extreme southern tip of the Valdadige, where *bordelais* varieties come into their own.

✔ *Tenuta San Leonardo*

VALLE ISARCO *or* EISACKTALER DOC
See Alto Adige DOC

VALPANTENA DOC
Veneto

Sub-appellation for Valpolicella, in *recioto, amarone, spumante*, and regular *rosso* styles. *See* Valpolicella DOC.

VALPOLICELLA DOC
Veneto

Made from at least 80 per cent Corvina with the possible addition of Rossignola, Negrara, Trentina, Barbera, and Sangiovese, most Valpolicella are simply light-red and light-bodied, with lacklustre, attenuated fruit hinting of cherries, and a dry, slightly bitter finish. There are an increasing number of wines that are full of juicy cherry-fruit flavours, but they are still in a minority and for truly fine wines bearing the Valpolicella DOC you have to seek out exceptional wines from the tiny number of producers recommended below.

Valpantena is a sub-appellation for the vineyards around Quinto in the centre of the Valpolicella district.

Valpolicella *recioto* is a bittersweet, yet very smooth, deep-coloured, Port-like wine made from *passito* grapes, although it may also be produced in a *frizzante* or *spumante* style. *Amarone* is a derivative of recioto, with a similar deep colour, but in a dry or off-dry style, which seems to make the flavours more powerful and chocolaty-spicy with a distinctly bitter finish. There is also something very specific that marks the fruit in *amarone* wines, which wine writer Oz Clarke once described – perfectly to my mind – as a "bruised sourness". This is an oxidative character that will not appeal to lovers of clean, precise, well-focused flavours, but its complexity is undeniable and such wines age wonderfully. Quintarelli is the most outstanding producer, with Allegrini hard on his heels.

🕰 Upon purchase for most, 2–5 years for recommendations

✔ **Valpolicella** and **Valpolicella Superiore** *Allegrini* (La Grola) • *Bolla* (Vigneti di Jago) • *Corta Sant'Alda* (Mithas) • *Grassi* (Superiore) • *Guerrieri-Rizzardi* (Villa Rizzardi Poiega) • *Marion* (Superiore) • *Quintarelli* • *Le Ragose* • *Romano dal Forno* (Lodoletta) • *Serègo Alighieri* • *Fratelli Tedeschi* (Capitel delle Lucchine, Capitel dei Nicalò) • *Tommasi* (Vigneto del Campo Rafael) • *Viviani* (Campo Morar)
Recioto della Valpolicella *Stefano Accordini* (Acinatico) • *Allegrini* (Gardane) • *Lorenzo Begali* • *Tommaso Bussola* (TB) • *Masi* (Mazzanella) • *Quintarelli* • *Serègo Alighieri* (Casel dei Ronchi) • *Fratelli Tedeschi* (Capitel Monte Fontana)
Amarone della Valpolicella *Allegrini* • *Begali* (Monte Ca' Bianca) • *Cecilia Beretta* • *Bertani* • *Brigaldara* • *Tommaso Bussola* • *Giuseppe Campagnola* • *Garbole* • *Marion* • *Masi* • *Fratelli Pasqua* (Vigneti Casterna) • *Quintarelli* • *Rizzardi* (Calcarole) • *Romano Dal Forno* (Vigneto di Monte Lodoletta) • *Sant'Alda* • *Sant'Antonio* (Campo de Gigli) • *Santi* (Proemio) • *Speri* (Vigneto Monte Sant'Urbano) • *Fratelli Tedeschi* (Capitel Monte Olmi) • *Tommasi* • *Trabucchi* (Marchetto) • *Venturini* (Campmasua) • *Viviani* (Casa de Bepi) • *Zenato* (Sergio Zenato)

VALPOLICELLA "RIPASSO" DOC
Veneto

Ripasso ("re-passed") wine has long been traditional in the Veneto. The best young Valpolicella is put into tanks or barrels that still contain the lees of the recioto for which they were previously used. When mixed with the young wine, active yeast cells in this sediment precipitate a second fermentation. This increases the alcohol content and gives it some recioto character. After having undergone this process, the wines usually cannot carry the Valpolicella appellation and are therefore sold as *vino da tavola* under various brand names, although some Valpolicella wines are turbocharged by ripasso without any mention of it on the label.

🕰 6–15 years

✔ *Allegrini* (Palazzo alla Torre) • *Boscaini* (Le Cane) • *Fratelli Tedeschi* (Capitel San Rocco) • *Masi* (Campo Fiorin)

VENETO IGT
Veneto

This area encompasses all Veneto, including the classic Conegliano-Valdobbiadene region, so understandably a fair amount of passable Prosecco,

both *spumante* and *frizzante*, has always been produced under this IGT. However, as from the 2009 vintage, the name Prosecco is allowed only for DOC and DOCG wines. Exactly the same wines continue to be made, but using the name Glera for what was formerly known as the Prosecco grape. Apart from an absence of the Prosecco name, anything goes in this IGT, as it does in most others, and a wide range of varieties can be found, including Cabernet Franc, Cabernet Sauvignon, Chardonnay, Corvina, Garganega, Merlot, Moscato, Pinot Grigio, Pinot Nero, Sangiovese, Sauvignon Blanc, and Teroldego. This IGT is full of terrific-value wines, both red and white, and the fact that Roberto Anselmi sells all of his top wines under this IGT, rather than Soave DOCG, illustrates that Veneto IGT is not entirely about value but also boasts some of the greatest-quality wines.

✔ *Anselme* • *Bortolomiol* • *Bosco del Merlo* • *Coffele* • *Costadoro* • *Inama* • *Maculan* • *Sachetto* • *Villa Sandi* • *Zenato*

VENETO ORIENTALE IGT
Veneto

This IGT covers the eastern corner of Veneto, roughly equivalent to Lison-Prammagiore DOC, overlapping into Piave DOC. Chardonnay, Lagrein, and Bordeaux varieties do well.

✔ *Santa Margherita*

VENEZIA GIULIA IGT
Friuli-Venezia Giulia

All locally grown grape varieties and styles apply. Exceptionally fresh and vividly fruity styles from the best producers.

✔ *Jermann* • *San Simon* • *Schiopetto* • *Zidarich*

VERONESE IGT
Veneto

All varieties and styles abound, but some of the best varietals include Cabernet Sauvignon, Corvina, Garganega, Merlot, Rondinella, and Sangiovese.

✔ *Allegrini* • *Musella* • *Sartori*

VICENZA DOC
Veneto

The wines include a Garganega-based generic white that may be normal, *frizzante*, or *spumante* and dry or sweet, and a Merlot-based generic red and *passito* that may be *novello* for reds and normal or *spumante*, dry or sweet for *passito*. There is a blended Cabernet and various varietal wines: Cabernet Sauvignon, Marzemino (which must be *frizzante*), Merlot, Pinot Nero, and Raboso for reds, and Chardonnay (may be *spumante*), Garganega (may be *spumante*), Manzoni, Moscato (may be normal or *spumante*, dry or sweet), Pinot Bianco (may be *spumante*), Riesling, and Sauvignon whites.

✔ *La Berolà*

VIGNETI DELLE DOLOMITI IGT
Trentino-Alto Adige and Veneto

This IGT covers the foothills of the Dolomites, either side of the border between Trentino-Alto Adige and Veneto.

✔ *Endrizzi* • *Foradori* • *MezzaCorona* • *Pojer & Sandri* • *Tenuta San Leonardo*

VINI DEL PIAVE DOC
See Piave DOC

WEST CENTRAL ITALY

*The heart of Italy is also the centre of the country's
most important quality-wine exports, which are
dominated by famous red Sangiovese wines from
the tiny Tuscan hills and valleys between Florence
and the Umbria-Latium border.*

TUSCANY (TOSCANA)

The home of traditional winemaking, Tuscany has also been the
main focus of experimentation. Its powerful red Vino Nobile di
Montepulciano was Italy's first DOCG, and has been followed
by Brunello di Montalcino, Chianti, Carmignano, and Vernaccia
di San Gimignano. But not all of its finest wines bear these
famous appellations, a fact recognized by the Tuscan producers
themselves, who, on the one hand, sought the ideal DOCG
solution for Chianti, while on the other began to invest in
premium wines that were not restricted by the DOC. It was
the uncompromising quality of their Super-Tuscan wines that
encouraged premium *vini da tavola* throughout the rest of Italy.
Unfortunately, they were less successful with the DOCG of Chianti.

The Tuscans had two sensible, forward-thinking approaches: one
was to apply DOCG to the Chianti Classico area and other isolated
areas, such as parts of Rufina and the Colli Fiorentini, where most
of the finest wines have traditionally been made, and to leave the
rest as DOC Chianti; the other was to grant DOCG status to the
best 10 per cent, regardless of origin. Either would have made
Chianti a success. But the biggest Chianti producers had more
political clout than the best producers, and the new regulations
gave DOCG status to the whole area and all Chianti wines,
regardless of their origin or quality.

It is true that the Trebbiano Toscano, a localized clone, is
an intrinsically high-class Trebbiano and, indeed, it can make
some charming wines, but it is not a fine-wine grape. Currently,
Tuscany has no white-wine sister for its red Sangiovese grape.
Unfortunately, its best dry white-wine grape so far has been
Chardonnay, a variety that excels in almost every half-decent wine
area. Vermentino might be Tuscany's white-wine grape of the
future, although it is really a Sardinian grape and currently mostly
restricted to Tuscany's coastal
areas. It is time someone
managed to rekindle an

WEST CENTRAL ITALY,

see also p313
*The hills of this area provide the
best sites for vineyards, tempering
the summer's heat and providing
a variety of microclimates suitable
for classic French grape varieties, as
well as traditional Italian ones.*

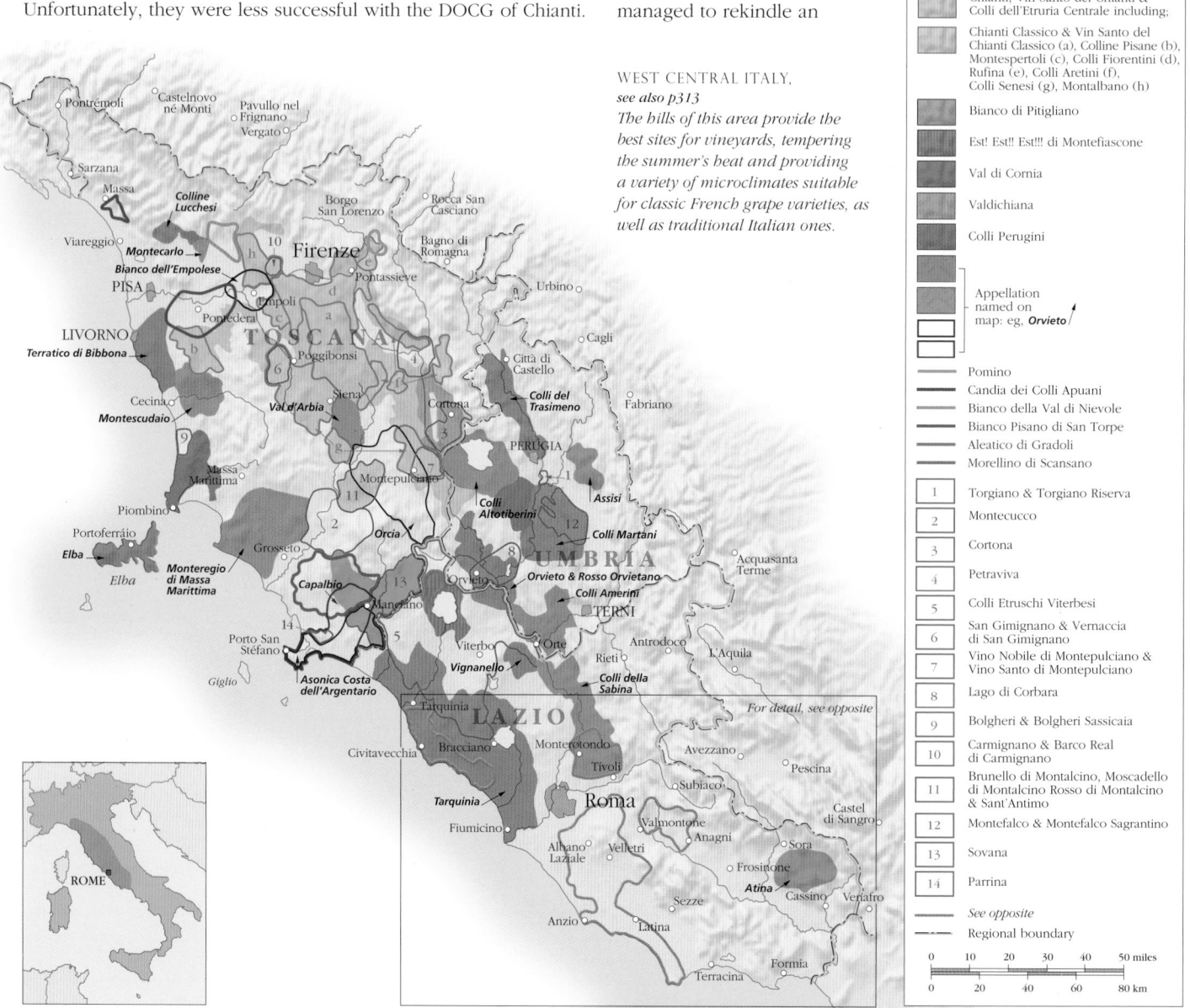

FACTORS AFFECTING TASTE AND QUALITY

LOCATION
Located between the Apennines to the north and east, and the Tyrrhenian Sea to the west.

CLIMATE
Summers are long and fairly dry and winters are less severe than in northern Italy. Heat and lack of rain can be a problem throughout the area during the growing season.

ASPECT
Vineyards are usually sited on hillsides for good drainage and exposure to the sun. Deliberate use is made of altitude to offset the heat, and black grapes grow at up to 550 metres (1,800 feet) and white grapes at up to 700 metres (2,275 feet). The higher the vines, the longer the ripening season and the greater the acidity of the grapes.

SOIL
These are very complex soils with gravel, limestone, and clay outcrops predominating. In Tuscany a rocky, schistose soil, known in some localities as *galestro*, covers most of the best vineyards.

VITICULTURE AND VINIFICATION
After much experimentation, particularly in Tuscany, with classic French grapes, the trend recently has been to develop the full potential of native varieties.

Many stunning Cabernet-influenced, super-Tuscan wines still exist, and always will, but top-performing producers are seeking clones, *terroirs*, and techniques to maximize the fruit and accessibility of their own noble grapes.

A traditional speciality is the sweet, white *vin santo*, which is made from *passito* grapes dried on straw mats in attics. It is aged for up to six years, often in a type of *solera* system.

GRAPE VARIETIES
Primary varieties: Brunello (Sangiovese), Malvasia, Morellino (Sangiovese), Procanico (Ugni Blanc), Prugnolo (Sangiovese), Sangioveto (Sangiovese), Tignolo (Sangiovese), Uva Canina (Sangiovese)
Secondary varieties: Abbuoto, Aglianico, Albarola, Aleatico, Ansonica (Inzolia), Barbera, Bombino, Cabernet Franc, Cabernet Sauvignon, Cesanese, Chardonnay, Ciliegiolo, Colorino, Drupeggio in Umbria (Canaiolo), Gamay, Greco (Grechetto), Greco but not Grechetto (Albana), Mammolo, Merlot, Montepulciano, Moscadello/Moscato (Muscat Blanc à Petits Grains), Pinot Bianco (Pinot Blanc), Pinot Grigio (Pinot Gris), Pulciano (Grechetto), Roussanne, Sagrantino, Sauvignon Blanc, Sémillon, Syrah, Uva di Spagna (Carignan), Verdello, Vermentino, Vernaccia, Welschriesling

TRADITION AND INNOVATION
This tranquil landscape appears to have remained unchanged for many centuries, but, while Tuscan winemaking is steeped in tradition, the area is now also experimenting with different grape varieties and barrique *ageing.*

ROME AND ITS ENVIRONS, *see also opposite*
The recent proliferation of appellations in the hills surrounding Italy's capital are evidence of a wine regime gone mad – this country's wines need cohesion, not further diversity.

ancient, all-but-extinct Tuscan white grape and rescue it with commercial success, much as the *piemontesi* did with Arneis and, as I suspect, they will next try with Timorasso.

BIRTH OF THE SUPER-TUSCANS
Most of the exceptional Tuscan wines 20 years ago were the then relatively new *barrique*-aged Super-Tuscans. Their story began in 1948 when the now famous Sassicaia wine was made for the first time by Incisa della Rochetta using Cabernet Sauvignon vines reputedly from Château Lafite-Rothschild. This was an unashamed attempt to produce a top-quality Italian wine from Bordeaux's greatest grape variety, decades before the idea became old hat in the wine world. It became so successful that in the wake of the 1971 vintage, a new red called Tignanello was introduced by Piero Antinori with a Sangiovese base and 20 per cent Cabernet Sauvignon, as a compromise between Tuscany and Bordeaux. Although Frescobaldi had used Cabernet Sauvignon in its Nipozzano Chianti for over a century and it grew

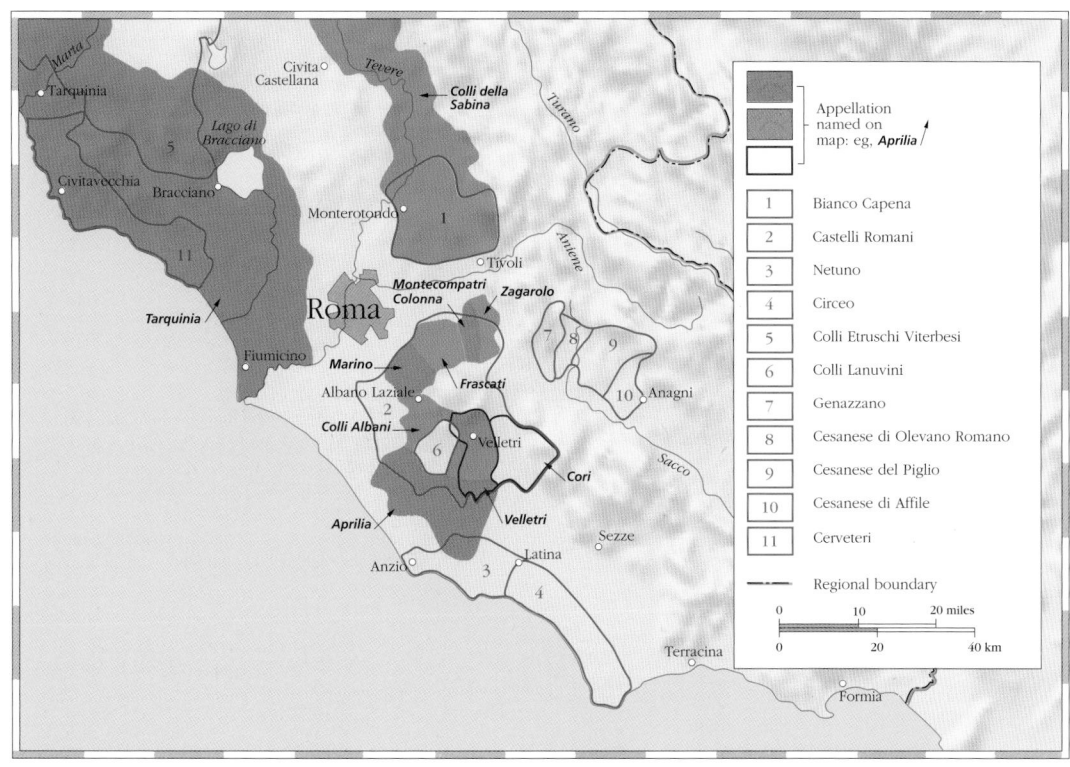

VERNACCIA VINES IN AUTUMN
These vines grow exclusively around the medieval Tuscan town of San Gimignano, whose impressive towers can be seen here in the distance. When it comes from good producers, the white Vernaccia can be a deliciously crisp, fruity dry wine.

Map legend:
Appellation named on map: eg, *Aprilia*

1	Bianco Capena
2	Castelli Romani
3	Netuno
4	Circeo
5	Colli Etruschi Viterbesi
6	Colli Lanuvini
7	Genazzano
8	Cesanese di Olevano Romano
9	Cesanese del Piglio
10	Cesanese di Affile
11	Cerveteri

Regional boundary

0   10   20 miles
0   20   40 km

REGIONS AT A GLANCE

REGION	TOTAL AREA UNDER VINE	DOC/DOCG AREA UNDER VINE	DOC/DOCG PRODUCTION	TOTAL PRODUCTION
Tuscany	86,000 ha (212,500 acres)	30,500 ha (75,350 acres)	1.2 million hl (86/14 red/white)	3.6 million hl (40 million cases)
Latium	65,600 ha (162,100 acres)	17,400 ha (43,000 acres)	535,000 hl (5/95 red/white)	5 million hl (55.5 million cases)
Umbria	22,000 ha (54,350 acres)	5,600 ha (13,800 acres)	165,000 hl (20/80 red/white)	1.1 million hl (12.2 million cases)

in the Carmignano area in the 18th century, nobody had truly appreciated the harmony that could be achieved between the two grapes until Tignanello appeared. The blend was akin to the natural balance of Cabernet and Merlot, only the Cabernet added weight to the Sangiovese and provided balance through a more satisfying flavour. Tignanello thus sparked off a new wave of Super-Tuscan *vini da tavola*. However, as the numbers grew, so they became an embarrassment, as observers realized that very few of the region's greatest wines actually qualified for DOC. But at the same time, many of the winemakers responsible for these French-influenced Super-Tuscans were also working hard to make the Sangiovese stand alone. After extensive clonal and site selection, reduced yields, improved viticultural practices and vinification techniques, a new breed of Super-Tuscan emerged; first as Sangiovese-dominated blends, such as Tignanello, then as pure Sangiovese wines. Now that the Goria Law has opened the door for Italy's greatest *vini da tavola*, many who had resorted to making wines outside the DOC system are using their experience in remoulding the Sangiovese to re-establish the great old names of the past (Chianti, Brunello di Montalcino, Vino Nobile di Montepulciano) by making wines that are complete without the help of foreign varieties.

UMBRIA

Orvieto is Umbria's best-known and best-forgotten wine. Next to Frascati and Soave, it is the most used and abused name in the world's Italian restaurants. While there are a few good Orvieto wines, and tiny amounts of truly exciting *muffato* (a lusciously sweet botrytized version), they are in a lamentable minority. One of Umbria's few deservedly famous names is Lungarotti Rubesco Torgiano, whose reputation led to the Torgiano DOC and, more recently, to DOCG status for Torgiano Riserva. Lungarotti also leads in the production of Umbria's excellent new-wave wines. These use various grapes, both native and French, and are made in various styles, although nearly always aged in new-oak *barriques*.

LATIUM (LAZIO)

One of Italy's largest regions, Latium appropriately boasts one of its largest-selling wines, Frascati, the Latin Liebfraumilch, and Est! Est!! Est!!!, probably the blandest tourist wine in existence. For a region responsible for Falernum, a classic wine of antiquity, it can now boast only two truly fine wines, Boncompagni Ludovisi's Fiorano Rosso and Cantina Colacicchi's Torre Ercolana, both innovative Cabernet-Merlot blends, which are very good.

THE APPELLATIONS OF

WEST CENTRAL ITALY

ALEATICO DI GRADOLI DOC
Latium
Sweet, aromatic red from Aleatico grapes growing on the northern shore of the crater lake of Bolsena.

ALLERONA IGT
Umbria
Mostly Grechetto from an area encompassing Orvieto.

ALTA VALLE DELLA GREVE IGT
Tuscany
This IGT is centred on the vineyard's around Greve in the Chianti district, and Poggio Scalette's dark, dense, and imposing *barrique*-aged Sangiovese called Il Carbonaione is a wine that some rank as high as the very best Chianti itself.
✓ *Poggio Scalette*

ANSONICA COSTA DELL'ARGENTARIO DOC
Tuscany
Theoretically the same variety as Marsala's insipid Inzolia, but in southern Tuscany, bordering Latium, the localized version of this grape produces a more distinctive wine, albeit with little finesse.

APRILIA DOC
Latium
This DOC has two red varietals, Merlot and Sangiovese, and one white, Trebbiano, which is uninspiring. The washed-out flavours indicate that official yields are far too high.

ASSISI DOC
Umbria
In the hills surrounding Assisi, birth place of St Francis of Assisi, this DOC encompasses a Trebbiano-based generic white, a Sangiovese-based generic red and *passito*, a blended Cabernet, and four varietal red wines (Cabernet Sauvignon, Grechetto, Merlot, and Pinot Nero).
✓ *Sportoletti*

ATINA DOC
Latium
A red-wine-only DOC located in the hills between Sora (which famously fought off Hannibal) and Cassino (where the Germans fiercely defended the Monte Cassino during World War II). Just two wines are allowed: a generic red (a minimum of 50% Cabernet Sauvignon, 10% Cabernet Franc, 10% Merlot, 10% Syrah, and a maximum of 20% other local non-aromatic varieties) and a blended Cabernet that must contain at least 85% Cabernet Sauvignon and Cabernet Franc.

BARCO REALE DI CARMIGNANO DOC
Tuscany
After Carmignano became a DOCG, this appellation was adopted for easy-drinking, Sangiovese-dominated (with a touch of Cabernet) red wines in order to retain simple DOC status. This acted as a selection instrument to increase and maintain quality for the superior denomination. *See also* Carmignano DOC and Carmignano DOCG.

BETTONA IGT
Umbria
A seldom-used IGT in the Orvieto region.

BIANCO CAPENA DOC
Latium
This blended white wine is produced between Monterotondo and Tivoli, northeast of Rome, from at least 55% Malvasia, 25% Trebbiano, Romagnolo, or Giallo, and up to 20% Bellone and Bombino.

BIANCO DELL'EMPOLESE DOC
Tuscany
This is an over-rated, over-priced, and uninspiring dry white Trebbiano from the Empoli hills, west of Florence. A *passito* may be sold as *vin santo* under the same denomination.

BIANCO DELLA VAL DI NIEVOLE *or* BIANCO DELLA VALDINIEVOLE DOC
Tuscany
Dry white wines and soft, white *vin santo*, made primarily from Trebbiano grapes.

BIANCO DI PITIGLIANO DOC
Tuscany
Delicate, refreshing, dry, and easy-drinking Trebbiano-based white wines, which are improved by the possible inclusion of Malvasia, Grechetto,

Verdello, Chardonnay, Sauvignon, Pinot Blanc, and Welschriesling. A *spumante* version is also allowed.

🍷 1–2 years

✓ *La Stellata*

BIANCO PISANO DI SAN TORPÈ DOC
Tuscany

These dry white wines and dry or semi-sweet *vin santo* are made from Trebbiano grown in a large area southeast of Pisa.

BOLGHERI & BOLGHERI SASSICAIA DOC
Tuscany

This was once a relatively anonymous, pleasant, but hardly exciting DOC, producing delicate, dry whites and dry, slightly scented, Sangiovese *rosato*. Reds were ignored, even though it was home to Sassicaia, one of Italy's greatest wines. Now that reds are allowed, Sassicaia has its own sub-appellation, and two varietal whites (Sauvignon and Vermentino) and a pink *vin santo*, Occhio di Pernice, have been added.

🍷 1–3 years (white), 3–7 years (most reds), 8–25 years (Sassicaia and vin santo)

✓ *Antinori* (Guado al Tasso) • *Castello di Bolgheri* • *Angelo Gaja* (Ca' Marcanda Camarcanda) • *Le Macchiole* (Paleo) • *Colle Massari* (Grattamacco) • *Podere Sapaio* • *Enrico Santini* • *Michele Satta* • *Tenuta dell'Ornellaia* • *Tenuta San Guido* (especially Sassicaia)

BRUNELLO DI MONTALCINO DOCG
Tuscany

One of Italy's most prestigious wines, made from Brunello, a localized clone of Sangiovese. Many relatively unknown producers offer classic wines. The idea is that the wines should be so thick with harsh tannins that they must be left for at least 20 years. If they are ripe skin tannins and there is enough fruit, this can be a formula for a wine of classic stature. But too many are macerated for too long and are not destemmed, leaving the tannins in even the most expensive wines incapable of softening. The producers below make wines requiring at least 10 years' maturation, but packed with fruit that develops into layers of complex, smoky-spicy, plummy-fruit flavours.

🍷 10–25 years

✓ *Altesino, Tenuta di Argiano* • *Villa Banfi* (especially Poggio all'Oro) • *Fattoria dei Barbi* (Vigna del Fiore) • *Biondi Santi* • *Campogiovanni* • *Canalicchio di Sopra* • *Capanna* • *Tenuta Caparzo* • *Caprili* • *Tenuta Carlina* (La Torgata) • *Casanova di Neri* • *Case Basse* • *Castelgiocondo* • *Castello di Argiano* • *Castello Romitorio* • *Cerbaiona* • *Col d'Orcia* • *Conti Costanti Frescobaldi* • *Eredi Fuligni* • *Fanti-San Filippo* • *Lisini* • *Mastrojanni* • *La Palazzetta* • *Pertimali* • *Podere Salicutti* • *La Poderina* (Poggio Banale) • *Poggio Antico* • *Salvioni-La Cerbaiola* • *Tenementi Ruffino* • *Tenuta Il Poggione* • *Tenuta Silvio Nardi* (Manachiara) • *Tenuta Vitanza* • *Siro Pacenti* • *Solaria-Cencioni* • *Talenti* • *Uccelliera*

CANDIA DEI COLLI APUANI DOC
Tuscany

Delicate, slightly aromatic, dry or semi-sweet whites from Vermentino and Albarola grapes.

CANNARA IGT
Umbria

This IGT covers the floodplain of Perugia, celebrated more for its onions than wines.

CAPALBIO DOC
Tuscany

This appellation covers the rolling hillsides of southern Grosseto, encompassing Parrina and large parts of four other DOCs (Ansonica Costa dell'Argentario, Bianco di Pitigliano, Morellino di Scansano, and Sovana). The wines include a generic Trebbiano-based white, a generic Sangiovese-based red and *passito*, a *vin santo* (which may be dry or sweet), one varietal white (Vermentino), and two varietal reds (Cabernet Sauvignon and Sangiovese). A *riserva* must be red and aged for a minimum of 32 months prior to release.

CARMIGNANO DOC
Tuscany

Since Carmignano achieved DOCG status, the DOC has been used for *rosato*, *vin santo*, and *vin santo rosato*, called Occhio di Pernice (even though these styles were not allowed before the upgrading). The declassified Carmignano reds can now be sold as Barco Reale di Carmignano.

CARMIGNANO DOCG
Tuscany

Only traditional red Carmignano from this tiny appellation west of Florence may claim DOCG status. Other wines are classified as either Carmignano DOC or Barco Reale di Carmignano DOC. This DOCG is made from 45 to 65 per cent Sangiovese, 10 to 20 per cent Canaiolo Nero, 6 to 10 per cent Cabernet Sauvignon, 10 to 20 per cent Trebbiano, Canaiolo Bianco or Malvasia, and up to 5 per cent Mammolo or Colorino. The result is similar to medium-bodied Chianti, but with less acidity, which, with its Cabernet content, gives a chocolaty-finesse to the fruit. *See also* Carmignano DOC and Barco Reale di Carmignano DOC.

🍷 4–10 years

✓ *Fattoria di Ambra* • *di Artimino* • *Fattoria di Bacchereto* • *Contini Bonacossi* (Villa di Capezzana, Villa di Trefiano) • *Fattoria Il Poggiolo* • *Piaggia*

CASTELLI ROMANI DOC
Latium

Covering a vast area of volcanic hillsides south and southeast of Rome, Castelli Romani encompasses no fewer than nine other DOCs, including Frascati. Dry, sweet, or *frizzante* whites may be produced from at least 70% Malvasia and/or Trebbiano; dry, sweet, or *frizzante* red and *passito* from at least 85% of one or more of Cesanese, Merlot, Montepulciano, Nero Buono, and Sangiovese. Dry, sweet, and *frizzante* styles are also allowed for red *novello* wines.

✓ *Gotto d'Oro*

CERVETERI DOC
Latium

Rustic Sangiovese-based reds, dry and semi-sweet Trebbiano-Malvasia whites of decent, everyday quality.

CESANESE DEL PIGLIO *or* PIGLIO DOC
Latium

This DOC covers a complicated range of basically simple red wines, from Cesanese grapes grown in a hilly area southeast of Rome. The styles include bone-dry, off-dry, medium-dry, semi-sweet, and sweet, and may be still, *frizzantino*, *frizzante*, or *spumante*.

CESANESE DI AFFILE *or* AFFILE DOC
Latium

This DOC produces the same styles as Cesanese del Piglio from a neighbouring area.

CESANESE DI OLEVANO ROMANO *or* OLEVANO ROMANO DOC
Latium

Much smaller than the previous two nearby Cesanese DOCs, but covering the same styles.

CHIANTI & CHIANTI CLASSICO DOCG
Tuscany

When Chianti was granted DOCG status, its yields were reduced, the amount of white grapes allowed in Chianti Classico was cut, and up to 10 per cent Cabernet Sauvignon was permitted in the blend. However, the DOCG was applied to the entire Chianti production area and thus has failed to be a guarantee of quality. Most Chianti is still garbage, albeit in a cleaner, more sanitized form than it used to be. The best basic Chianti, however, is full of juicy cherry, raspberry, and plummy fruit flavours, which makes an enjoyable quaffer, although it is not what DOCG should be about. Only the finest wines of Chianti deserve DOCG status and they are usually sold as *classico* (the original, hilly Chianti area), although Rufina (from a small area northeast of Florence, which should not be confused with Ruffino, the brand name) and Colli Fiorentini (which bridges the Classico and Rufina areas), which are both outside the Classico district, also produce *classico*-like quality. Both also have lower yields than the rest of Chianti, with the exception of Classico, which demands the lowest yield of all. Whatever the industrial bottlers do to continue debasing Chianti's reputation, readers must not forget that the best wines from these three areas rank among the greatest in the world. Rufina and Colli Fiorentini are, however, just two of six sub-appellations collectively known as the Chianti Putto, which covers the peripheral areas surrounding Chianti Classico itself. The other four are Colli Senesi (the largest and most varied, and so inconsistent that few wines claim this provenance, two portions of which are better known for Brunello di Montalcino and Vino Nobile di Montepulciano); Colli Pisani (lightest of all Chianti); Colli Aretini (young, lively Chianti); and Montalbano (in effect the second wine of Carmignano, although there are two of those, so maybe it is the third wine?).

All Chianti other than *classico* must contain between 75 and 90 per cent Sangiovese plus the possibility of 5 to 10 per cent Canaiolo Nero, 5 to 10 per cent Trebbiano or Malvasia, and up to a maximum of 10 per cent Cabernet or any other specified black grape varieties. This recipe applied to Chianti Classico until 1995, when it was changed to allow up to 100 per cent Sangiovese, which should be a good move for those dedicated growers who are striving to get this difficult variety right. With the amount of Cabernet and other black grapes increased to 15 per cent, this DOC is wide open to many of the so-called Super-Tuscans to be classified as Chianti Classico and thereby greatly enhance the reputation of this once great appellation.

🍷 3–5 years (inexpensive, everyday drinking), 4–8 years (more serious Chianti), 6–20 years (finest *classico*)

✓ *Antinori* (Peppoli) • *Badia a Coltibuono* • *Barone Ricasoli* (Castello di Brolio) • *Carobbio* (Riserva) • *Caparsa* (Doccio a Matteo Riserva) • *Castellare di Castellina* (Vigna Il Poggiale) • *Castellini Villa* • *Castello di Ama* • *Castello di Cacchiano* • *Castello di Fonterutoli* • *Castello Querceto* • *Castello di Radda* • *Castello di Rampolla* • *Castello di San Polo in Rosso* • *Castello di Volpaia* • *Chianti Geografico* • *Corzano e Paterno* • *Felsina* (Rancia) • *Fontodi* • *Isole e Olena* • *La Massa* (Giorgio Primo) • *Monsanto* • *Podere Il Palazzino* (Grosso Sanese) • *Poggerino* • *Poggio al Sole* (Casasilia) • *Querciabella* • *Riecine* (Riserva) • *Rocca di Castagnoli* • *Rocca della Macie* (Roccato) • *Rocca di Montegrossi* • *San Fabiano Calcinaia* (Cellole Riserva) • *San Felice* (Poggio Rosso Riserva) • *San Giusto* (Gaio) • *San Vicente* (Riserva) • *Spadaio e Piecorto* • *Terrabianca* • *Uggiano* • *Vecchie Terre di Montefili* • *Villa Vignamaggio* (Mona Lisa Riserva)

CIRCEO DOC
Latium

The most southerly DOC in Latium, Circeo is where the sorceress Circe once lived, according to Homer's *Odyssey*. Dry, sweet, or *frizzante* whites may be produced from at least 60% Trebbiano, up to 30% Malvasia, and up to 30% other local varieties; dry, sweet, or *frizzante* red and *passito* from at least 85% Merlot (dry, sweet, and *frizzante novello* are also allowed for red wines); and two varietals: Sangiovese (for red and dry *passito*, either still or *frizzante*) and Trebbiano (dry white only).

✓ *Sant'Andrea* (Il Sogno)

CIVITELLA D'AGLIANO IGT
Latium

This IGT covers the southern half of the Orvieto region and is starting to produce some exciting wines, particularly for the white Grechetto and red Violone, but also for Merlot and Cabernet Sauvignon.

✓ *Isabella Mottura* • *Sergio Mottura*

COLLI ALBANI DOC
Latium

A white-only appellation, Colli Albani DOC is southeast of Rome and must contain 5–45% Malvasia del Lazio, 25–50% Trebbiano, up to 60% Malvasia di Candia, plus a maximum of 10% other local, non-aromatic varieties. The wine must be dry or sweet, still or *spumante*. *Novello* is permitted for dry or sweet styles, but they must be still, not *spumante*.

COLLI ALTOTIBERINI DOC
Umbria

An interesting DOC in the hilly upper Tiber Valley area, which produces dry white wines from Trebbiano and Malvasia, and firm, fruity reds from Sangiovese and Merlot. However, it is the crisp, fragrant *rosato* wines that most people prefer.

COLLI AMERINI DOC
Umbria

This appellation is found in the southwestern corner of Umbria, in a hilly area far more famous for olive oil than for wine. The wines include a generic Trebbiano-based white, a generic Sangiovese-based red and *passito*, a *vin santo* (which may be dry or sweet), one varietal white (Malvasia), and one varietal red (Merlot). A *riserva* must be red and aged for a minimum of 24 months prior to release. A *novello* red is allowed.

✓ *Cantina dei Colli Amerini* (Ameroe, Carbio)

COLLI CIMINI IGT
Latium

Southwest of Vignanello DOC; the most widely used grapes are Ciliegiolo and Sangiovese for reds, and Trebbiano and Malvasia for whites. The reds are often produced by carbonic maceration.

COLLI DELL'ETRURIA CENTRALE DOC
Tuscany

The idea was fine, to provide an alternative appellation for lesser red, white, and *rosato* wines produced in the Chianti area and thus improve the DOCG through selection. But the name hardly trips off the tongue for consumers, and very few producers have been attracted by the typically Italian raft of wine styles, all of which are constrained by impossible grape-variety percentages. The wines include a generic dry white (at least 50% Trebbiano plus a maximum of 50% Chardonnay and/or Trebbiano and/or Pinot Bianco and/or Sauvignon Blanc and/or Vernaccia di San Gimignano, with an optional maximum of 25% other local white varieties), a generic red and dry *passito* (at least 50% Sangiovese plus a maximum of 50% Cabernet Franc and/or Cabernet Sauvignon and/or Canaiolo Nero and/or Merlot and/or Pinot Nero, with an optional maximum of 25% other local black varieties), a *novello* red (at least 50% Sangiovese plus a maximum of 50% Canaiolo Nero and/or Ciliegiolo and/or Gamay and/or Merlot, with an optional maximum of 25% other local black varieties), a *vin santo*, which may be dry or sweet (at least 70% Malvasia and/or Trebbiano, with an optional maximum of 30% other local white varieties), and a sweet red or *rosato vin santo* Occhio di Pernice (at least 50% Sangiovese, with an optional maximum of 50% other local varieties, black or white). The white *vin santo* must be aged at least 36 months prior to release, or 48 months if labelled *riserva*. The red *vin santo* Occhio di Pernice must also be aged at least 36 months prior to release but may not be classified *riserva*. When the free-thinking, innovative winemakers who had to bypass the constraints of DOC regulations to create the super-Tuscan category and had to sell those wines initially as *vino da tavola* saw this heap of pointless regulation, they must have asked, "Why bother?" and subsequently never did.

✓ *Bindella* (Dolce Sinfonia Vin Santo Occhio di Pernice)

COLLI ETRUSCHI VITERBESI DOC
Latium

This massive appellation encompasses a large swathe of northern Latium and a wide variety of wines. The wines include a generic Trebbiano-Malvasia-based white, a generic Sangiovese-Montepulciano-based red and *passito*, four varietal white wines (Grechetto, Moscatello, Procanico, and Rossetto), four varietal reds (Canaiolo, Greghetto, Merlot, and Violone), and one varietal *passito* (Sangiovese). The generic white may be dry or sweet, still or *frizzante*; the generic red, dry or sweet, still or *frizzante*, and may be sold as *novello*, while the generic *passito* may be dry or sweet, still or *frizzante*. For the varietal whites, Grechetto may be still or *frizzante* but must be dry; Moscatello may be dry or sweet, still, *frizzante*, *passito*, or *novello*; and Procanico and Rossetto are both distinctively different localized clones of Trebbiano. (The Grechetto must be dry and may be still, *frizzante*, or novello, while Rossetto may be dry or sweet but can only be produced in a normal still-wine style.) All the varietal reds must be produced in a classic dry still-wine style. Greghetto

is in fact a black-skinned variant of Grechetto, and Violone is none other than the Montepulciano. The Sangiovese *passito* may be dry or sweet, still or *frizzante*. A *vin santo* is also allowed and may be dry or sweet.

COLLI DI LUNI DOC
See Colli di Luni DOC (Liguria, Northwest Italy)

COLLI LANUVINI DOC
Latium

Smooth, white wines, either dry or semi-sweet.

COLLI MARTANI DOC
Umbria

This covers four varietal wines from a large but promising area encompassing the Montefalco DOC: Sangiovese, Trebbiano, Grechetto, and the single-commune Grechetto di Todi.

COLLI PERUGINI DOC
Umbria

Dry, slightly fruity, Trebbiano-based white wines, full-bodied red wines, and dry, fresh *rosato* wines, primarily from Sangiovese grapes. Produced in a large area between Colli del Trasimeno and the Tiber, covering six communes in the province of Perugia and one in the province of Terni.

COLLI DELLA SABINA DOC
Latium

Named after the Sabinium, an ancient neighbour and enemy of Rome, this appellation is located along the banks of the Tiber River to the northeast of the city. The wines include a generic Trebbiano-based white and a generic Sangiovese-based red and *passito*. The white must be dry but can be *frizzante*, *spumante*, or still. *Rosato* must be dry and may be either *frizzante* or still. The red must be dry and may be *frizzante*, *spumante*, or still. A dry *novello* red may also be *frizzante*, *spumante*, or still.

COLLI DELLA TOSCANA CENTRALE IGT
Tuscany

A superstar IGT for super-Tuscan wines, this appellation comes from hilly areas of central Tuscany and, consequently, has the potential to produce some of the finest wines in Italy. This IGT fulfils this potential with some very exciting wines, yet Colli dell'Etruria Centrale, a DOC that was conceived to cater for exactly the same super-Tuscan wines, has failed miserably by comparison, which just goes to prove that flexibility trumps the DOC's supposed status when quality truly matters and ludicrous legal grape-variety percentages do not. Expect Sangiovese with or without backing from Bordeaux varieties for reds, and Chardonnay for the much rarer whites, as well as some quirky stuff such as Pinot Nero.

✓ *Fontodi* • *Gagliole* • *Castellare di Castellina* (I Sodi di San Niccolò) • *Folonari* (Il Pareto) • *Castello di Querceto* • *Piazzano* • *Rocca delle Macie* • *Tenuta di Lilliano* • *Torraccia di Presura* • *Vecchie Terre di Montefili*

COLLI DEL TRASIMENO DOC
Umbria

A very large DOC on the Tuscan border. The dry and off-dry whites are ordinary, but the reds, in which the bitter edge of Sangiovese is softened with

Gamay, Ciliegiolo, Malvasia, and Trebbiano, are more interesting.

🕰 2–5 years

☑ *La Fiorita*

COLLINE LUCCHESI DOC
Tuscany

This DOC produces light, soft, Chianti-like reds and bland, dry, Trebbiano-based whites.

CORI DOC
Latium

Little-seen and rarely exciting, dry, semi-sweet, or sweet white wines and smooth, vinous reds.

CORTONA DOC
Tuscany

Located on the southern border close to Umbria, this is primarily an all-varietal DOC, with six red-wine varietals (Cabernet Sauvignon, Gamay, Merlot, Pinot Nero, Sangiovese, and Syrah), all made in a classic dry still-wine style, and five white-wine varietals (Chardonnay, Grechetto, Pinot Bianco, Riesling Italico, and Sauvignon Blanc), all made in a classic dry still-wine style. There is just one generic blend, a *passito* (40–60% Sangiovese and 10–30%; Canaiolo Nero, with up to 30% from other optional local varieties), which again must be made in a classic dry still-wine style. There is also a *vin santo*, which must be at least 80% Trebbiano, Grechetto, or Malvasia Bianca Lunga, and a sweet red or *rosato vin santo* Occhio di Pernice (at least 80% Sangiovese or Malvasia Nera, with an optional maximum of 20% other local non-aromatic black varieties).

☑ *Tenementi Luigi d'Alessandro* (Migliari Syrah)

ELBA DOC
Tuscany

The range of wines from the holiday isle of Elba have been expanded to include ten types: Trebbiano-based dry white; Sangiovese-based red, and *riserva* red; *rosato*; Ansonica dell'Elba (dry white from the Ansonica, better known as the Inzolia grape of Sicily); Ansonica Passito dell'Elba; Aleatico dell'Elba; Vin Santo dell'Elba, Vin Santo dell'Elba Occhio di Pernice; and a white *spumante*. However, these wines are mostly made for tourists.

🕰 In situ only

☑ *Acquabona*

EST! EST!! EST!!! DI MONTEFIASCONE DOC
Latium

The name is the most memorable thing about these dry or semi-sweet white wines made from Trebbiano and Malvasia grapes grown around Lake Bolsena, adjacent to the Orvieto district. Traditionally, the name dates to the 12th century, when a fat German bishop called Johann Fugger had to go to Rome for the coronation of Henry V. In order to drink well on his journey, he sent his *majordomo* ahead to visit the inns along the route and mark those with the best wine with the word "Est", short for "*Vinum est bonum*". When he arrived at Montefiascone, the *majordomo* so liked the local wine that he chalked "Est! Est!! Est!!!". Fugger must have agreed with him, because once he had tasted the wine, he cancelled his trip and stayed in Montefiascone until his death. The truth of the story is uncertain, for, although a tomb in the village church bears Fugger's name, whether it contains his 800-year-old body or not is unknown.

FRASCATI DOC
Latium

Most Frascati used to be flabby or oxidized, but with recent improvements in vinification techniques they are now invariably fresh and clean, although many still have a bland, peardrop aroma and taste. The few exceptions come from virtually the same group of top-performing producers as they did a decade or so ago and these wines stand out for their noticeably full flavour, albeit in a fresh, zippy-zingy style. Frascati is made from Trebbiano and Malvasia grapes, primarily dry, but semi-sweet, sweet, and *spumante* styles are also made.

🕰 1–2 years

☑ *Colli di Catone* (especially Colle Gaio – other labels include Villa Catone and Villa Porziana) • Fontana Candida (Vigneti Santa Teresa) • *Poggio Le Volpi* (Epos) • *Villa Simone*

FRUSINATE IGT
Latium

This appellation is located in the rugged hillside country of Latium's Piglio area and is thus the IGT equivalent of Cesanese del Piglio DOC. Indeed, some of the red and *rosato* wines produced under this IGT are from the Cesanese grape, but there are also wines from Sangiovese, Cabernet, Merlot Olivella (aka Sciascinoso), and Syrah grapes, plus whites from the Albana (known locally as the Passerina), Bellone, Bombino, Malvasia, Moscato, and Pinot Bianco.

☑ *Giovanni Terenzi*

GENAZZANO DOC
Latium

Located in the rolling foothills of Monti Prenestini to the east of Rome, where just two wines are produced: a red from 70–90% Sangiovese, 10–30% Cesanese, and an optional maximum of 20% other local black varieties; and a white from 50–70% Malvasia, 10–30% Bellone and Bombino grapes, and an optional maximum of 40% other local white varieties

LAGO DI CORBARA DOC
Umbria

This DOC is for red wines from the Orvieto region, but without being lumbered by the Orvieto name (*see* Orvieto Rosso), which most of us think of in terms of white wine and, for some, a not very inspiring white wine. The wines from this DOC include a generic blend from at least 70% Cabernet Sauvignon, Merlot, Pinot Nero, or Sangiovese, and up to 30% from a choice of Aleatico, Barbera, Cabernet Franc, Canaiolo, Cesanese, Ciliegiolo, Colorino, Dolcetto, and Montepulciano.

☑ *Castello di Corbara*

LAZIO IGT
Latium

With a few top producers turning out some really exciting red and white wines under this regional IGT, who needs a DOC?

☑ *Falesco* (Montiano) • *Casale del Giglio* • *Falesco* • *Sant'Isidoro* (Soremidio)

MAREMMA TOSCANA IGT
Tuscany

This IGT covers the coastal Maremma west of Grosseto – an area that has traditionally been famous for its long-horned Maremma cattle but, over the past 20 years or so, has also built up an extraordinary reputation for its typically super-Tuscan wines

☑ *Ampeleia* • *Belguardo* • *Brancaia* • *Elisabetta Gepetti* • *Loacker* • *Magliano* • *Poggio Argentiera* • *Querciabella* (Mongrana) • *Castello del Terriccio* • *Verrano*

MARINO DOC
Latium

A typically light and unexciting Trebbiano and Malvasia blend that may be dry, semi-sweet, or *spumante*. Paola di Mauro's deliciously rich and caramelized Colle Picchioni Oro stands out due to its relatively high proportion of Malvasia grapes, and the fact that it receives a pre-fermentation maceration on its skins and is matured in *barriques*.

🕰 1–4 years

☑ *Colle Picchioni* (Oro)

MONTECARLO DOC
Tuscany

Some interesting dry white wines are starting to appear in this area situated between Carmignano and the coast. Although based on the bland Trebbiano, supplementary varieties (Roussanne, Sémillon, Pinot Grigio, Pinot Bianco, Sauvignon Blanc, and Vermentino) may account for 30 to 40 per cent of the blend, thus allowing growers to express individual styles, from light and delicate to full and rich, either with or without *barrique*-ageing. Red wines may be made from Sangiovese, Canaiolo, Ciliegiolo, Colorino, Syrah, Malvasia, Cabernet Franc, Cabernet Sauvignon, and Merlot. A white *vin santo* and a pink Occhio di Pernice *vin santo* are also allowed.

🕰 4–10 years

☑ *Fattoria dell Buonamico* • *Carmignani* • *Fattoria Michi* • *Vigna del Greppo*

MONTECOMPATRI COLONNA DOC
Latium

These dry or semi-sweet, Malvasia-based white wines may bear the name of one or both of the above towns on the label.

MONTECUCCO DOC
Tuscany

Abutting Brunello di Montalcino to the southwest, this DOC consists of a Sangiovese-based generic red, a Trebbiano-based generic white, and two varietals (Sangiovese and Vermentino).

☑ *Colle Massari* (Lombrone) • *Salustri* (Grotte Rosse)

MONTEFALCO DOC
Umbria

There is a significant difference in quality between these basic reds and whites and the more interesting, characterful DOCG Sagrantino of Montefalco.

MONTEFALCO SAGRANTINO DOCG
Umbria

Upgraded to DOCG in 1992 and detached from the basic Montefalco denomination, these distinctive red wines in dry and sweet *passito* styles are made exclusively from Sagrantino, which has the advantage of being grown on the best-exposed hillside vineyards southwest of Perugia. The *passito* wines are the most authentic in style, dating back to the 1400s, but the dry table-wine style, hinting of ripe, fresh-picked blackberries, is the best and most consistent.

🕰 3–12 years

✓ *Fratelli Adanti* • *Antonelli* • *Villa Antico* • *Arnaldo Caprai* • *Colpetrone* • *Villa Mongalli* (Della Cima) • *Perticaia* • *Tabarrini* (Colli Grimaldesco)

MONTEREGIO DI MASSA MARITTIMA DOC
Tuscany

These are red, white, *rosato*, *novello*, and *vin santo* from the northern part of the province of Grosseto. A dry white Vermentino varietal wine and a pink *passito* called Occhio di Pernice are also included within Monteregio di Massa Marittima DOC.

MONTESCUDAIO DOC
Tuscany

A Trebbiano-based dry white wine, a soft, slightly fruity, Sangiovese-based red, and a *vin santo* from the Cecina Valley.

🍷 1–3 years

✓ *Poggio Gagliardo* • *Sorbaiano*

MORELLINO DI SCANSANO DOC
Tuscany

This DOC produces some good Brunello-like wines from 100 per cent Sangiovese, which are thick with tasty, ripe fruit and can age well.

🍷 4–8 years

✓ *Erik Banti* • *Poggio Argentiera* (Capa Tosta) • *Motta* • *Fattoria Le Pupille*

MOSCADELLO DI MONTALCINO DOC
Tuscany

An ancient style of aromatic, sweet Muscat that was famous long before Brunello. Fortified versions and sweet *frizzante* are also possible.

🍷 Upon purchase

✓ *Villa Banfi* (Vendemmia Tardiva) • *Col d'Orcia* • *Tenuta Il Poggione*

NARNI IGT
Umbria

This is the IGT equivalent of Colli Amerini DOC. The best producers here manage to tease a bit more Sangiovese out of the heritage of the Ciliegiolo grape than anywhere else.

✓ *Cantina dei Colli Amerini* (Ciliegiolo, Ciliegiolo Ani)

NETTUNO DOC
Latium

Abutting Circeo on the Tyrrhenian coast south of Rome, further inland this DOC also overlaps the southern tip of Aprilia. Nettuno includes a generic Merlot-Sangiovese red, a generic Sangiovese-Trebbiano dry *passito*, and a generic Bellone-Trebbiano dry white, plus a varietal Bellone, which may be labelled Cacchione and is thought to be indigenous to the area. The red may be sold as *novello*, and the white and rose may be *frizzante*.

OCCHIO DI PERNICE DOC
Tuscany

A sweet red or *rosato vin santo* traditionally produced in Bolgheri and permitted in the Colli dell'Etruria Centrale DOC. *See* Bolgheri & Bolgheri Sassicaia DOC, Colli dell'Etruria Centrale DOC, Cortona DOC, and Sant'Antimo DOC.

ORCIA DOC
Tuscany

Dry Trebbiano-based white, Trebbiano or Malvasia *vin santo*, and a Sangiovese-based red (which may be sold as *novello*) from a large area overlapping much of Montalcino and Montepulciano, encompassing the Val d'Orcia.

ORVIETANO ROSSO *or* ROSSO ORVIETANO DOC
Umbria

This DOC allows a Cabernet blend, as well as a generic red blend, at least 70% of which must consist of two or more of the following: Aleatico, Cabernet Franc, Cabernet Sauvignon, Canaiolo, Ciliegiolo, Merlot, Montepulciano, Pinot Nero, and Sangiovese, plus an optional choice of Aleatico, Barbera, Cesanese, Colorino or Dolcetto. However, Orvietano is primarily a varietal appellation for Aleatico, Cabernet Franc, Cabernet Sauvignon, Canaiolo, Ciliegiolo, Merlot, Pinot Nero, and Sangiovese, all of which must be produced in a classic, dry still style.

ORVIETO DOC
Umbria and Latium

The vineyards for this popular, widely exported, dry or semi-sweet, Trebbiano-based white wine are primarily located in Umbria. In general, Orvieto is still disappointing, although Bigi's Vigneto Torricella remains outstanding and the number of wines aspiring to a similar quality is growing. The best semi-sweet, or *abboccato*, style will include a small proportion of botrytized grapes. Fully botrytized, or *muffato*, Orvieto are extremely rare, but well worth tracking down as they offer a fabulous combination of elegance, concentration, and youthful succulence.

🍷 Upon purchase

✓ *Antinori* (Campogrande) • *Barberani* (Castagnolo) • *Bigi* (Torricella) • *Decugnano dei Barbi* • *Lungarotti* • *Palazzone* (Terre Vineate)

PARRINA DOC
Tuscany

The dry whites of Parrina, the most southerly of Tuscany's DOCs, are the least interesting. The Sangiovese-based reds used to be merely soft, light, and attractive, but of late have become much darker, fuller, and richer, like an oaky Chianti, with just a touch of vanillin sweetness on the finish, and even an occasional wisp of mint on the aftertaste.

🍷 3–7 years

✓ *Franca Spinola*

PIETRAVIVA DOC
Tuscany

Located in the Chianti region, west of Arezzo, Pietraviva was Michelangelo's favourite wine. This DOC produces a generic Sangiovese-based red and *passito*, a generic Chardonnay-Trebbiano-based white, and a number of varietal wines: Cabernet Sauvignon, Canaiolo, Ciliegiolo, Merlot, and Sangiovese for reds, and Chardonnay or Malvasia for whites.

POMINO DOC
Tuscany

This wine dates back to 1716, and a Pomino was marketed as a single-vineyard Chianti by Marchesi de' Frescobaldi long before it was resurrected as its own DOC in 1983. The white is a blend of Pinot Blanc, Chardonnay, and Trebbiano, although Frescobaldi's Il Benefizio is pure Chardonnay. The red is a blend of Sangiovese, Canaiolo, Merlot, Cabernet Franc, and Cabernet Sauvignon. A semi-sweet *vin santo* is also made in both red and white styles.

🍷 1–3 years (blended white) 3–7 years (red and Il Benefizio)

✓ *Frescobaldi* • *Fattoria Petrognano*

ROSSO DI MONTALCINO DOC
Tuscany

This appellation is for lesser or declassified wines of Brunello di Montalcino or for wines made from young vines. Although there has been a tendency in recent years to produce deeper, darker, more concentrated wines, as a rule the biggest Rosso di Montalcino wines are much more accessible in their youth than Brunello, which some readers may prefer.

🍷 5–15 years

✓ *Altesino* • *Castelgiocondo* • *Cerbaiona* • *Conti Costanti* • *Lisini* • *Poggio di Sotto* • *Tenuta Il Poggione* • *Val di Suga*

ROSSO DI MONTEPULCIANO DOC
Tuscany

This DOC is for the so-called lesser wines of Vino Nobile di Montepulciano and, like Rosso di Montalcino DOC, its wines are softer and more approachable when young.

🍷 5–15 years

✓ *Avignonesi* • *Bindella* • *Podere Boscarelli* • *Le Casalte* • *Contucci* • *Fattoria del Cerro* • *Poliziano* • *Tenuta Trerose*

ROSSO ORVIETANO DOC
See Orvietano Rosso DOC

SANT'ANTIMO DOC
Tuscany

This DOC in Montalcino includes a generic red and white from 100% unnamed local varieties, four red varietals (Cabernet Sauvignon, Merlot, Pinot Grigio, and Pinot Nero), two white varietals (Chardonnay and Sauvignon Blanc), a dry or sweet Trebbiano-Malvasia-based *vin santo*, and a sweet red Sangiovese-Malvasia Nero-based *vin santo* Occhio di Pernice.

✓ *Castello Banfi* (Cum Laude, Tavernelle) • *Casanova di Neri* • *Ciacci Piccolomini d'Aragona* • *Fanti* • *San Polo*

SAN GIMIGNANO DOC
Tuscany

When Vernaccia was promoted to DOCG status, all other white varieties remained DOC only, together with red and *rosato* wines.

SASSICAIA DOC
See Bolgheri & Bolgheri Sassicaia DOC

SOVANA DOC
Tuscany

This DOC in the south of Tuscany includes a generic Sangiovese-based red and dry *passito*, as well as four red varietals: Aleatico, Cabernet Sauvignon, Merlot, and Sangiovese.

✓ *San Lorenzo*

SPELLO IGT
Umbria

Sportoletti produces delicious wines from Merlot, Cabernet Franc, and Cabernet Sauvignon for reds, and from Grechetto and Chardonnay for whites, from vines growing around Spello and Assisi to the southeast of Perugia.

✓ *Sportoletti*

TARQUINIA DOC
Latium

This vast appellation produces a generic Sangiovese-based red and *passito*, a generic Chardonnay-Trebbiano-based white, and a number of varietal wines: Cabernet Sauvignon, Canaiolo, Ciliegiolo, Merlot, and Sangiovese for reds, and Chardonnay and Malvasia for whites.

✓ *Sant'Isidoro* (Corithus)

TERRATICO DI BIBBONA DOC
Tuscany

East and south of Livorno, this large DOC allows a generic Sangiovese-Merlot-based red, a Vermentino-based generic dry white, four red varietal wines (Cabernet Sauvignon, Merlot, Sangiovese, and Syrah), and two generic dry white varietal wines (Trebbiano and Vermentino).

TORGIANO DOC
Umbria

This DOC was built on the back of the reputation of one producer, Lungarotti (*see also* Torgiano Riserva DOCG). As before, Torgiano DOC covers generic blends for red and *rosato* (Sangiovese, Canaiolo, Trebbiano, Ciliegiolo, and Montepulciano) and white (Trebbiano, Grechetto, Malvasia, and Verdello), but also sparkling (Pinot Noir and Chardonnay) and five varietals: Chardonnay, Pinot Grigio, Riesling Italico, Cabernet Sauvignon, and Pinot Noir.

🍷— 3–8 years (red), 1–5 years (white and *rosato*)

✓ *Lungarotti*

TORGIANO RISERVA DOCG
Umbria

Lungarotti's best *rosso*, the *riserva* is a model of how all DOCG denominations should work, and has deservedly been upgraded from DOC.

🍷— 4–20 years

✓ *Lungarotti*

TOSCANA *or* TOSCANO IGT
Tuscany

Anything goes for this region-wide IGT, and the freedom it allows has encouraged the best producers to let rip with the entire gamut of local and international grape varieties. There are ways to include almost any variety grape in Tuscany, but the specifically authorized varieties are Chardonnay, Malvasia, Pinot Grigio, Sauvignon, Traminer, Trebbiano, Verdello, and Vermentino for whites, and Aleatico, Alicante, Cabernet Franc, Cabernet Sauvignon, Canaiolo, Ciliegiolo, Merlot, Pinot Nero, Sangiovese, and Syrah for reds.

✓ *Avignonesi & Capanelle* (50 & 50) • *Badia di Morrona* • *Barone Ricasoli* • *Bindella* (Sifonia de Vallocaia) • *Biondi Santi* (Il Tosco) • *Bonelli* (Poggiassai) • *Boscarelli* • *Buonamico* (Montecarlo Rosso) • *Tenuta di Capezzana* •

Carpinetta (Do Ut Des, Dofana) • *Casa Emma* (Soloìo) • *Castellare di Castellina* • *Il Colombaio di Cencio* • *Dievole* (Broccato) • *Felsina* (Fontalloro) • *Folonari* • *La Fonti* (Fontissimo) • *Tenuta di Ghizzano* • *Angelo Gaja* (Ca' Marcanda) • *Isole e Olena* • *Loacker* • *Lornano* (Commendator Enrico) • *Marchesi Antinori* • *Le Macchiole* (Messorio) • *Montevertine* • *Montenidole* (Sono Montenidole) • *Petrola* (Galatrona) • *Podere Ormo* • *Poggio Argentiera* • *Querciabella* (Camartina, Palafreno) • *Rocca di Castagnoli* • *Ruffino* (Modus, Romitoro di Santedame) • *Michele Satta* • *San Fabiano* • *Tenuta dell'Ornellaia* • *San Felice* • *San Guido* (Guidaberto) • *Tua Rita* (Redigaffi)

UMBRIA IGT
Umbria

A region-wide IGT that allows all varieties of grape and every style of wine, including one of the world's very few examples of a dry Aleatico (Alea Viva, produced by Andrea Occhipinti).

✓ *Antinoro* (Cevaro della Sala) • *Occhipinti*

VAL D'ARBIA DOC
Tuscany

A large area south of the Chianti Classico district, producing a dry, fruity, Trebbiano-based white wine boosted by Malvasia and Chardonnay, which may be dried prior to fermentation for dry, semi-sweet, or sweet *vin santo*.

VAL DI CHIANA *or* VALDICHIANA DOC
Tuscany

This hugely fertile plain was once swampland but has long since been turned to agricultural use. However, it is better known for Chiana, one of the oldest breeds of cattle, than for wine.

VAL DI CORNIA DOC
Tuscany

A large area of scattered vineyards in hills east of Piombino and south of Bolgheri. Rarely seen Trebbiano dry whites and Sangiovese reds and *rosato*, with the sub-appellations of Campiglia Marittima, Piombino, San Vincenzo, and Surveto.

✓ *Russo* (Barbicone)

VAL DI MAGRA IGT
Tuscany

A vast appellation covering the province of Massa e Carrara at the very northern tip of Tuscany, where the following varieties are permitted: Ciliegiolo, Groppello, Merlot, and Pollera for red and *passito* wines, and Albarola, Durella, Trebbiano, Verdello, and Vermentino for whites.

VELLETRI DOC
Latium

Rather uninspiring, dry or semi-sweet white wines and reds from the Castelli Romani area.

VERNACCIA DI SAN GIMIGNANO DOCG
Tuscany

This dry white wine was Italy's first-ever DOC, so DOCG status was inevitable, even if most are bland. The best have always been deliciously crisp and full of vibrant fruit, which makes them well worth seeking out, but not seriously worthy of DOCG status if this is supposed to signify one of the world's finest wines.

🍷— 1–3 years

✓ *Falchini* • *Panizzi* • *Teruzzi & Puthod*

VIGNANELLO DOC
Latium

This is a new and untested DOC for red, white, and *rosato* blends, plus pure Grechetto dry white wine in still and fully sparkling formats.

VIN SANTO DEL CHIANTI DOC
Tuscany

Inexplicably the *vin santo* remained a DOC when Chianti was elevated to DOCG. When it comes to *vin santo*, there is no evidence in the bottle that Chianti is inferior to Chianti Classico.

✓ *Cantagallo* • *Frascole* • *Grignano* • *Lanciola* • *Castello di Monastero* (Lunanuova) • *Castello della Panneretta* • *Torre a Cona* (Merlaia) • *Travignoli* (Rufina) • *Villa Petriolo* • *Villa Pillo* • *Villa Vignamaggio*

VIN SANTO DEL CHIANTI CLASSICO DOC
Tuscany

Inexplicably the *vin santo* remained a DOC when Chianti Classico was elevated to DOCG.

✓ *Avignonesi* • *Folonari* • *Isole e Olena* • *Rocca di Montegrossi* • *La Ripa* • *La Sala* • *San Felice* • *Borgo Scopeto* • *Villa Vignamaggio* • *Vistarenni*

VIN SANTO DI MONTEPULCIANO DOC
Tuscany

Inexplicably the *vin santo* remained a DOC when Vino Nobile di Montepulciano was elevated to DOCG.

✓ *Poliziano*

VIN SANTO OCCHIO DI PERNICE DOC
Tuscany

This sweet red or *rosato vin santo* is traditionally produced in Bolgheri and permitted in the Colli dell'Etruria Centrale DOC. *See* Bolgheri & Bolgheri Sassicaia DOC, Colli dell'Etruria Centrale DOC, Cortona DOC, and Sant'Antimo DOC.

VINO NOBILE DI MONTEPULCIANO DOCG
Tuscany

Made largely from the Sangiovese clone Prugnolo Gentile plus Canaiolo and other local grapes, including white varieties, these wines from Montepulciano used to be over-rated and over-priced, and some still are, but a growing number of producers make wines that deserve DOCG status. The best resemble a fine *riserva* Chianti Classico, but have a more exuberant character, with generous ripe-fruit flavours hinting of cherry and plum.

🍷— 6–25 years

✓ *Avignonesi* • *Bindella* • *Podere Boscarelli* • *Le Casalte* • *Contucci* • *Fattoria de Cerro* • *Poliziano* • *Tenuta Trerose*

ZAGAROLO DOC
Latium

This DOC has a tiny production of dry or semi-sweet white from Malvasia and Trebbiano grapes, which are grown east of Frascati in an area more famed for its wines half a millennium ago than it is now.

EAST CENTRAL ITALY

This area comprises the regions of Emilia-Romagna, the Marches, the Abruzzi, and Molise. The best-quality wines come from the Marches and the Abruzzi, but the best-known is Emilia-Romagna's lollipop wine, Lambrusco, which is exported in vast quantities.

IF THIS REGION, which extends across almost the entire width of northern Italy into Piedmont, appears geographically to wander off its central-east designation, it certainly does not do so topographically, for every hectare lies east of the Apennines on initially hilly ground that flattens out into alluvial plains stretching towards the Adriatic.

EMILIA-ROMAGNA
Emilia-Romagna is protected on its western flank by the Apennines, the source of seven major, and many minor, rivers. The rich soil

results in abundant grape production, the most prolific varieties being Lambrusco, Trebbiano, and Albana, which produce rustic white wines that, unaccountably, have been given Italy's first DOCG for a white wine. Emilia-Romagna does, however, have some genuinely outstanding *vini da tavola*, such as Fattoria Paradiso's Vigna del Dosso, a red from the Barbarossa, and, especially, a classy Sangiovese-Cabernet blend from Fattoria Zerbina, called Marzeno di Marzeno.

THE ABRUZZI (ABRUZZO)
Although its hills have a variety of soils and microclimates, and should be capable of producing many fine wines, the Abruzzi offers only one – Montepulciano d'Abruzzo. But winemakers are conservative here and only one producer, Santoro Corella, is experimenting with different grape varieties.

EAST CENTRAL ITALY, *see also p313*
With the Apennines forming the region's western border, the eastern part of central Italy is dominated by their foothills and the plains.

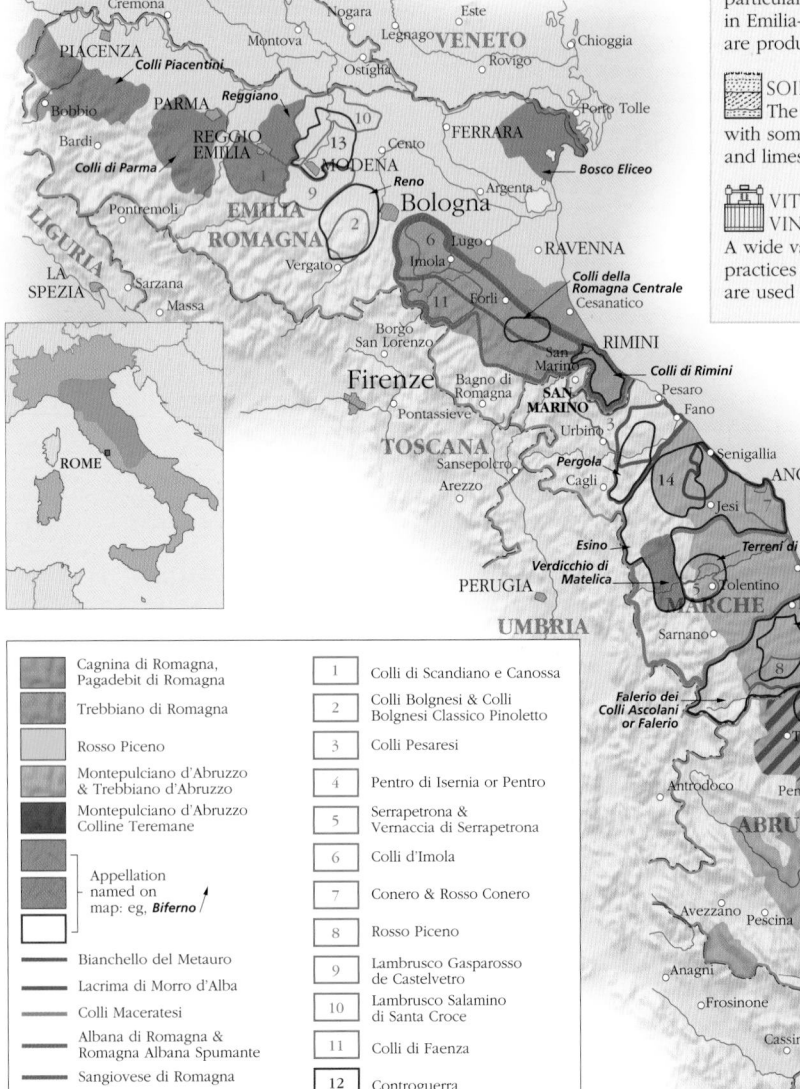

Legend
- Cagnina di Romagna, Pagadebit di Romagna
- Trebbiano di Romagna
- Rosso Piceno
- Montepulciano d'Abruzzo & Trebbiano d'Abruzzo
- Montepulciano d'Abruzzo Colline Teramane
- Appellation named on map: eg, *Biferno*
- Bianchello del Metauro
- Lacrima di Morro d'Alba
- Colli Maceratesi
- Albana di Romagna & Romagna Albana Spumante
- Sangiovese di Romagna
- Regional boundary

0 10 20 30 40 50 60 miles
0 20 40 60 80 100 km

1 | Colli di Scandiano e Canossa
2 | Colli Bolgnesi & Colli Bolgnesi Classico Pinoletto
3 | Colli Pesaresi
4 | Pentro di Isernia or Pentro
5 | Serrapetrona & Vernaccia di Serrapetrona
6 | Colli d'Imola
7 | Conero & Rosso Conero
8 | Rosso Piceno
9 | Lambrusco Gasparosso de Castelvetro
10 | Lambrusco Salamino di Santa Croce
11 | Colli di Faenza
12 | Controguerra
13 | Lambrusco di Sobara
14 | Verdicchio dei Castelli di Jesi

THE MARCHES (MARCHE)

This region has a beautiful coastline where holidaymakers quench their thirst with the local white – the dry Verdicchio. But there are more exciting wines to be found in the exceptionally fine DOCs of Rosso Conero and Rosso Piceno and, in a few circumstances, Sangiovese dei Colli Pesaresi, together with excellent *vini da tavola*, such as Rosso di Corinaldo and Tristo di Montesecco.

MOLISE

This poor region with high unemployment has a badly equipped wine industry. Until 1963, it was combined with the Abruzzi and only gained its first DOC in 1983. Italian-wine expert Burton Anderson believes that it may one day provide wines of real class.

VERNACCIA DI SERRAPETRONA GRAPE HARVEST
The most commonly encountered Vernaccia is the Vernaccia di Oristano, a white grape, but the Vernaccia di Serrapetrona seen here is black-skinned.

REGIONS AT A GLANCE

REGION	TOTAL AREA UNDER VINE	DOC/DOCG AREA UNDER VINE	DOC/DOCG PRODUCTION	TOTAL PRODUCTION
Emilia-Romagna	76,000 ha (187,800 acres)	26,700 ha (66,000 acres)	700,000 hl (75/25 red/white)	7.6 million hl (84.4 million cases)
Molise	9,350 ha (23,104 acres)	157 ha (388 acres)	2,000 hl (80/20 red/white)	550,000 hl (6.1 million cases)
Marches	31,000 ha (76,600 acres)	10,000 ha (24,700 acres)	282,000 hl (25/75 red/white)	2.1 million hl (23.33 million cases)
Abruzzi	30,000 ha (74,100 acres)	9,800 ha (24,200 acres)	320,000 hl (90/10 red/white)	3.8 million hl (42.2 million cases)

THE APPELLATIONS OF
EAST CENTRAL ITALY

ALBANA DI ROMAGNA DOCG
Emilia-Romagna

These straightforward, fruity, sometimes dry, occasionally semi-sweet white wines are still or sparkling and may be in a very sweet style, either by regular vinification or from *passito* grapes. This is the precise style, reputation, and quality that in 1987 became the first Italian white wine to receive DOCG status. From any angle, this occurred as a result of a political fudge. It's a bit like the French setting up a super-AOC and making Muscadet the first white to receive elite status. On the bright side, the producers of Albana di Romagna have had so much stick that they have had to work hard at improving their product, to good effect.

⌀ In situ only

✓ *Montecino Rosso* (Secco Codronchio) • *Paradiso* • *Zerbina* (Passito)

ALTO TIRINO IGT
Abruzzi

Under this IGT, Cataldi Madonna have taken the Pecorino, a white grape that has previously been viewed as little more than blending fodder to soften some red wines, and started to craft a truly fine wine of good acidity and surprising minerality.

✓ *Cataldi Madonna*

BERTINORO DOC
See Pagadebit di Romagna DOC

BIANCHELLO DEL METAURO DOC
Marches

Dry, delicate white wines are made from the Bianchello grape (possibly with some Malvasia) which is grown in the lower Metauro Valley.

BIANCO DI CASTELFRANCO EMILIA IGT
Emilia-Romagna

This IGT is for generic Montù- (aka Montini-) based white wines from the provinces of Bologna and Modena.

BIANCO DEL SILLARO *or* SILLARO IGT
Emilia-Romagna

A vast IGT covering generic Albana-based white wines from the provinces of Bologna, Ravenna, Forlì-Cesena, and Rimini.

BIFERNO DOC
Molise

Smooth, slightly tannic, red and fruity *rosato* wines from Montepulciano, Trebbiano, and Aglianico grapes; and dry, lightly aromatic, white wines from Trebbiano, Bombino, and Malvasia.

BOSCO ELICEO DOC
Emilia-Romagna

A large coastal region, separated from the major Emilia-Romagna viticultural areas in the northeast. There is a rustic red varietal from the mysterious Fortana grape, also called the Uva d'Oro, although I know nothing of it. Bosco Eliceo Fortan can be dry or sweet, has a slightly bitter tannic bite, is *frizzante*, and not dissimilar to Lambrusco. There is also a generic blended white (Trebbiano, Sauvignon, and Malvasia – may be *frizzante*); two pure varietals, a Merlot (sometimes *frizzantino*) and a Sauvignon (may also be *frizzantino*).

CAGNINA DI ROMAGNA DOC
Emilia-Romagna

Tannic but sweet and fruity red wines, with balancing high acidity.

COLLI APRUTINI IGT
Abruzzi

This IGT allows white (still, *frizzante*, or *passito*), red (still, *novello*, *frizzante*, or *passito*) and *passito* (still, *novello*, or *frizzante*) from a vast range of grapes growing in the province of Teramo.

✓ *Cvetic* (Iskra)

COLLI BOLOGNESI DOC
Emilia-Romagna

Also known as Colli Bolognesi dei Castelli Medioevali or Colli Bolognesi di Monte San Pietro, this appellation covers an Albana- and Trebbiano-based generic white; three red varietals, Barbera, Cabernet Sauvignon, and Merlot; and five whites, Riesling Italico, Sauvignon (may be *frizzantino*), Pinot Bianco, Pignoletto, and Chardonnay. The last three are made still, *frizzante*, and *spumante*.

⌀ 1–3 years

✓ *Terre Rosse*

COLLI BOLOGNESI CLASSICO PIGNOLETTO DOC
Emilia-Romagna

From the same geographic area as Colli Bolognesi DOC, this wine is however restricted to the Perricone grape (known locally as Pignoletto), produced in a classic dry white style only.

COLLI DI FAENZA DOC
Emilia-Romagna

A Chardonnay-based dry generic white, a Cabernet Sauvignon-based generic red, two varietal whites (Pinot Bianco and Trebbiano), and one varietal red (Sangiovese).

✓ *Il Pratello*

COLLI D'IMOLA DOC
Emilia-Romagna

This DOC includes a varietally non-specific generic white, which must be dry and may be *frizzante*; a varietally non-specific generic red, which may be frizzante; three varietal whites (Chardonnay, Pignoletto, and Trebbiano); and three varietal reds (Barbera, Cabernet Sauvignon, and Sangiovese).

COLLI MACERATESI DOC
Marches

This huge area produces a dry, white-wine blend that used to be Trebbiano-based, but now must contain at least 80 per cent Maceratino, and Verdicchio, Malvasia, and Chardonnay if possible.

COLLI DI PARMA DOC
Emilia-Romagna

Solid, slightly *frizzantino* red wines and two white varietals, Malvasia and Sauvignon, in dry, sweet, still, *frizzante*, or *spumante* styles.

COLLI PESARESI DOC
Marches

Originally a Sangiovese DOC, Colli Pesaresi now includes four different wines, although the deeply flavoured Sangiovese-based red still stands out, with the best showing real class. Focara may contain up to 15 per cent Pinot Noir, but displays Sangiovese-like characteristics. There is also a Trebbiano-based dry white and a very similar wine called Roncaglia.

⌐— 3–8 years

✓ *Tattà* • *Umani Ronchi* • *Vallone* • *Villa Pigna*

COLLI PIACENTINI DOC
Emilia-Romagna

Fourteen wines produced in the Piacenza hills, where Julius Caesar's father-in-law made a wine that was traditionally drunk from a vessel called a *gutturnium*. This is the origin of Gutturnio, the DOC's most famous wine, a Barbera-Bonarda blend. A red, it is usually dry and still, although a semi-sweet *frizzantino* or *frizzante* version is often made. There are two blended whites: an aromatic wine called Monterosso Val d'Arda (Malvasia, Moscato, Trebbiano, and Ortrugo, possibly with Beverdino and Sauvignon) in dry, sweet, still, *frizzantino*, or *frizzante* styles; and wine called Val Nur (Malvasia, Moscato, Trebbiano, and Ortrugo), which may be dry or sweet, still, *frizzante*, or *spumante*. The following whites may be *frizzantino*, *frizzante*, or *spumante*: Chardonnay, Trebbiano Val Trebba, Malvasia,

Ortrugo, Pinot Grigio, and Sauvignon. The Chardonnay, Pinot Grigio, and Sauvignon must be dry, but the others may be dry or sweet. Three red varietals: Barbera, Cabernet Sauvignon, and Pinot Nero can be dry or sweet, still, *frizzantino*, *frizzante*, or *spumante*.

COLLI DI RIMINI DOC
Emilia-Romagna

A Trebbiano-based dry generic white, a Sangiovese-based generic red, two varietal whites (Biancame [aka Albana] and Rebola), and one varietal red (Cabernet Sauvignon).

COLLI DELLA ROMAGNA CENTRALE DOC
Emilia-Romagna

Chardonnay-based dry generic white, a Cabernet Sauvignon-based generic red, two varietal whites (Chardonnay and Trebbiano), and two varietal reds (Cabernet Sauvignon and Sangiovese).

COLLI DEL SANGRO IGT
Abruzzi

This IGT allows white (still, *frizzante*, or *passito*), red (still, *novello*, *frizzante*, or *passito*), and *passito* (still, *novello*, or *frizzante*) from a wide range of grapes growing in Torino di Sangro and surrounding villages in the province of Chieti.

COLLI DI SCANDIANO E CANOSSA DOC
Emilia-Romagna

Formerly Bianco di Scandiano, this DOC has been considerably widened both geographically and in the scope of wines that may be produced, which now include a Sauvignon-based dry generic white, a Marzemino-based generic red, four varietal whites (Chardonnay, Malvasia, Pinot Bianco, and Sauvignon Blanc, the latter of which may be labelled Spergola, the local synonym for Sauvignon), four varietal reds (Cabernet Sauvignon, Lambrusco Gasparosa, Malbo Gentile, and Marzemino), and one varietal that may be either red or *passito*: Lambrusco Monterico. All wines except for the Sauvignon Blanc must be dry and can be either still or *frizzante*. Sauvignon Blanc may be dry or sweet *passito*. All white wines may also be made in a fully *spumante* style, with the exception of Sauvignon Blanc.

COLLINE FRENTANE IGT
Abruzzi

This appellation allows white (still, *frizzante*, or *passito*), red (still, *novello*, *frizzante*, or *passito*), and passito (still, *novello*, or *frizzante*) from a wide range of grapes growing in Castel Frentano and surrounding villages in the province of Chieti.

COLLINE PESCARESI IGT
Abruzzi

This IGT allows white (still, *frizzante*, or *passito*), red (still, *novello*, *frizzante*, or *passito*), and passito (still, *novello*, or *frizzante*) from a vast range of grapes growing in the province of Pescara.

✓ *Pasetti*

COLLINE TEATINE IGT
Abruzzi

This IGT allows white (still, *frizzante*, or *passito*), red (still, *novello*, *frizzante*, or *passito*), and passito (still, *novello*, or *frizzante*) from a wide range of

grapes growing in Ripa Teatina, San Giovanni Teatino, and surrounding villages in the province of Chieti.

✓ *Masciarelli*

CONERO DOCG
Marches

As from the 2004 vintage, the *riserva* category of Rosso Conero DOC was renamed simply as Conero and elevated to DOCG status. Conero DOCG comes from the same area of production as Rosso Conero DOC, but it is restricted to lower yields and fractionally riper grapes, and the wines must be aged at least 24 months prior to release. *See also* Rosso Conero DOC.

⌐— 6–25 years

✓ *Moroder* (Dorico) • *Piantate Lunghe* (Rossini) • *Silvano Strologo* (Decebalo) • *Umani Ronchi* (Cùmaro)

CONTROGUERRA DOC
Abruzzi

A Trebbiano-based generic white that may be dry or sweet (*passito* or *passito annoso*), *frizzante* or *spumante*; a Montepulciano-based generic red that may be dry or sweet (*passito* or *passito annoso*), *frizzante*, *spumante*, or *novello*; five varietal whites (Chardonnay, Malvasia, Passerina [aka Albana], and Riesling); three red varietals (Ciliegiolo, Merlot, and Pinot Nero); and a blended Cabernet.

DEL VASTESE IGT
See Histonium IGT

EMILIA IGT
Emilia-Romagna

This IGT allows white (still, *frizzante*, or *passito*), red (still, *novello*, *frizzante*, or *passito*), and *passito* (still, *novello*, or *frizzante*) from a vast range of grapes growing in the provinces of Ferrara, Modena, Parma, Piacenza, Reggio Emilia, and part of Bologna.

✓ *Bassi* (Barbera, Pinot Bianco) • *La Stoppa* (Ageno, Barbera, Macchiona)

ESINO DOC
Marches

This very large DOC encompasses four other DOCs, including Verdicchio dei Castelli Jesi and Verdicchio di Matelica, yet Esino's generic dry white is Verdicchio-based. Go figure. Just two wines are made under this DOC, the other being a generic Sangiovese-based red.

FALERIO *or* FALERIO DEI COLLI ASCOLANI DOC
Marches

Dry, lightly scented white wines made from a blend of Trebbiano, Passerina, Verdicchio, Malvasia, Pinot Blanc, and Pecorino.

⌐— 1–3 years

✓ *Cocci Grifoni* (Vigneti San Basso)

FOCARA DOC
See Colli Pesaresi DOC

FORLÌ IGT
Emilia-Romagna

This IGT allows white (still, *frizzante*, or *passito*), red (still, *novello*, *frizzante*, or *passito*), and *passito* (still, *novello*, or *frizzante*) from a large range of grapes growing in the province of Forlì-Cesena.

FORTANA DEL TARO IGT
Emilia-Romagna

This varietal IGT is restricted to Brugnola (known locally as Fortana) grown in the province of Parma. It can be made still or *frizzante* and may be sold as *novello*.

GUTTURNIO or GUTTURNIO DEI COLLI PIACENTINI DOC
See Colli Piacentini DOC

HISTONIUM or VASTESE IGT
Abruzzi

This IGT allows white (still, *frizzante*, or *passito*), red (still, *novello*, *frizzante*, or *passito*), and *passito* (still, *novello*, or *frizzante*) from a wide range of grapes growing in Vasto (Historium in Latin) and surrounding villages in the province of Chieti.

LACRIMA DI MORRO D'ALBA DOC
Marches

Nothing to do with the wine Lacryma Christi or the town of Alba in Piedmont, this is a soft, medium-bodied red from the mysterious Lacrima grape grown in and around Morro d'Alba, in the province of Ancona. A seemingly single-village wine, this DOC has the largest appellation of the Marches region. Montepulciano and Verdicchio may also be used.

LACRYMA (*or* LACRIMA) CHRISTI DOC
See Vesuvio DOC (Southern Italy and the Islands)

LAMBRUSCO GRASPAROSSA DI CASTELVETRO DOC
Emilia-Romagna

Dry or semi-sweet, vinous, *frizzantino* reds and *rosati*, usually better than non-DOC versions, but not quite matching the Lambrusco di Sorbara.

LAMBRUSCO REGGIANO DOC
See Reggiano

LAMBRUSCO SALAMINO DI SANTA CROCE DOC
Emilia-Romagna

These dry or semi-sweet, vinous, semi-*spumante* red and *rosato* wines are the most aromatic of the Lambruscos and can come up to the standard of the Lambrusco di Sorbara.

LAMBRUSCO DI SORBARA DOC
Emilia-Romagna

Mostly dry, although sometimes semi-sweet, these are medium-bodied, *frizzantino* reds or *rosati* with more body and depth of flavour than most.

✓ *Chiarli* (Fondatore)

MARCHE IGT
Marches

This regional IGT allows white (still, *frizzante*, or *passito*), red (still, *novello*, *frizzante*, or *passito*), and *passito* (still, *novello*, or *frizzante*) from Barbera, Cabernet Franc, Cabernet Sauvignon, Chardonnay, Grechetto, Merlot, Passerina, Pinot Bianco, Pinot Grigio, Pinot Nero, Sangiovese, Sauvignon Blanc, and Trebbiano growing anywhere in the Marches region.

✓ *Il Pollenza* • *Oasi degli Angeli* (Kurni) • *Valturio*

MODENA or PROVINCIA DI MODENA IGT
Emilia-Romagna

This IGT is restricted to red, white, and *passito frizzante* wines from a large range of grapes growing throughout the province of Modena.

MOLISE DOC
Molise

This DOC does not cover the entire Molise region, but it does cover a huge portion, including the entire eastern half and a chunk out of the western half. The wines allowed include a generic Montepulciano red, a generic Chardonnay-based *spumante*, four varietal reds (Aglianico, Cabernet Sauvignon, Sangiovese, and Tintilia), and six varietal whites (Chardonnay, Greco, Moscato, Pinot Bianco, Sauvignon, and Trebbiano). All wines may be produced in either still or *frizzante* styles. Chardonnay, Moscato, and Pinot Bianco may also be produced as a *spumante*.

✓ *Di Majo Norante* (Don Luigi, Contago)

MONTEPULCIANO D'ABRUZZO DOC
Abruzzi

Produced in the provinces of Chieti, L'Aquila, Pescara, and Teramo, two distinct styles are made from Montepulciano with up to 15 per cent Sangiovese. Both are very deep in colour, but one is full of soft, luscious fruit, the other firmer and more tannic. A lighter style called *cerasuolo* exists for cherry-pink wine with fresh fruit but is only occasionally as exciting. The sub-zones Casauria and Terre dei Vestini must be 100% Montepulciano.

🍷 4–8 or 8–20 years (red), 1–3 years

✓ *Agriverde* (Solàrea) • *Barba* (Vigna Franca) • *Luigi Cataldi Madonna* (Malandrino) • *Illuminati* (Ilico) • *Masciarelli* • *Emidio Pepe* ◉ • *Tenuta del Priore* • *Torre dei Beati* • *La Valentina* (Bellovedere) • *Valentini* • *Valle Reale* (San Calisto) • *Villa Medoro*

MONTEPULCIANO D'ABRUZZO COLLINE TERAMANE DOCG
Abruzzi

The hilly terrain of Colline Teramane in the province of Teramo has always been considered superior, which is why it was originally declared a sub-zone of Montepulciano d'Abruzzo that could be indicated with the appellation on the label. The wines from these hillsides have now been upgraded to DOCG and must be at least 90% Montepulciano (as opposed to 85% for the DOC, although the DOC's two sub-zones are strictly 100%), with lower yields and aged a minimum of 24 months prior to release. Wines claiming *riserva* status must be aged at least 36 months.

✓ *Illuminati* (Pieluni, Zanna) • *Valentini* • *Villa Medoro* (Adrano)

MONTEROSSO VAL D'ARDA DOC
See Colli Piacentini DOC

OFFIDA DOC
Marches

At the southern end of the Marches region, just to the north of Montepulciano d'Abruzzo, this DOC includes a generic Montepulciano-Cabernet red, a Pecorino varietal dry white, and a varietal Passerina white that may be dry in either still or *spumante* styles, dry or sweet *vin santo*, or sweet *passito*.

OSCO IGT
See Terre degli Osci IGT

PAGADEBIT DI ROMAGNA DOC
Emilia-Romagna

Dry and semi-sweet, still or *frizzante* white wines from the Bombino Bianco grape, known locally as "Pagadebit". This DOC includes a single-village wine called Bertinoro, the characteristics of which are the same, although potentially finer.

PENTRO or PENTRO DI ISERNIA DOC
Molise

Smooth, slightly tannic reds and dry, fruity *rosati* from Montepulciano and Sangiovese; and dry, fresh whites from Trebbiano and Bombino.

PERGOLA DOC
Marches

Dry or sweet *passito* Aleatico-based wines overlapping Rosso Piceno.

PROVINCIA DI MODENA IGT
See Modena IGT

RAVENNA IGT
Emilia-Romagna

This IGT allows white (still, *frizzante*, or *passito*), red (still, *novello*, *frizzante*, or *passito*), and *passito* (still, *novello*, or *frizzante*) from a large range of grapes growing in the province of Ravenna.

✓ *Zerbina*

REGGIANO DOC
Emilia-Romagna

Although formerly known as Lambrusco Regiano, this remains an exclusively Lambrusco appellation, which may be dry or sweet, and still or *frizzante*, with *novello* allowed for all styles.

✓ *Ermete Medici & Figli* (Secco Concerto)

RENO DOC
Emilia-Romagna

This white-wine-only DOC includes an Albana- or Trebbiano-based generic blend and two varietals: Montù (aka Montini) and Pignoletto. All wines may be produced either dry or sweet, still or *frizzante*.

ROMAGNA ALBANA SPUMANTE DOC
Emilia-Romagna

The sparkling version of Albana di Romagna, the very first white DOCG.

RONCAGLIA DOC
See Colli Pesaresi DOC

ROSSO CONERO DOC
Marches

Fine Montepulciano-based wines that improve with *barrique*-ageing. Deep-coloured and rich.

⌛ 6–15 years

✓ *Conte Leopardi Dittajuti* • *Garofoli* (Agontano) • *Piantate Lunghe* • *Umani Ronchi* (San Lorenzo) • *Marchetti* • *Mecvini* • *Moroder* (Aión) • *Silvano Strologo* (Julius, Traiano) • *Fattoria Le Terrazze* (Sassi Neri, Vision of J)

ROSSO PICENO DOC
Marches

Small amounts of Trebbiano and Passerina may now be added to this excellent Sangiovese and Montepulciano wine. The best are firm and ruby-coloured with smooth fruit. Often *barrique*-aged.

⌛ 4–10 years

✓ *Saladini Pilastri* ◉

ROTAE IGT
Molise

This IGT allows white (still, *frizzante*, or *passito*), red (still, *novello*, *frizzante*, or *passito*), and *passito* (still, *novello*, or *frizzante*) from any authorized grapes growing in the province of Isernia.

RUBICONE IGT
Emilia-Romagna

This IGT allows white (still, *frizzante*, or *passito*), red (still, *novello*, *frizzante*, or *passito*), and *passito* (still, *novello*, or *frizzante*) from a wide range of grapes growing in the provinces of Ravenna, Forlì-Cesena, and Rimini.

✓ *Umberto Cesari* (Liano, Moma Rosso, Tauleto) • *San Patrignano* • *San Valentino*

SANGIOVESE DI ROMAGNA DOC
Emilia-Romagna

These solid red wines rarely excite, unless from exceptional vineyards.

⌛ 3–7 years

✓ *Calonga* (Michelangiolo) • *Poderi dal Nespoli* • *Fattoria Paradiso* (Vigneti delle *Lepri*) • *San Patrignano* (Avi Riserva) • *Stefano Berti* (Calisto) • *Tre Monti* (Petrignone) • *Villa Venti* (Primo Segno)

SERRAPETRONA DOC
Marches

The only difference between this dry, red, sparkling Vernaccia DOC and Vernaccia di Serrapetrona DOCG is a slightly higher minimum alcoholic strength and the fact that it need only be aged for 8 months prior to release rather than 12 months for the DOCG.

SILLARO IGT
See Bianco del Sillaro IGT

TERRE DEGLI OSCI IGT
Molise

This IGT allows white (still, *frizzante*, or *passito*), red (still, *novello*, *frizzante*, or *passito*), and *passito* (still, *novello*, or *frizzante*) from a wide range of grapes growing in the province of Campobasso.

✓ *Di Majo Norante*

TERRE DI CHIETI IGT
Abruzzi

This IGT allows white (still, *frizzante*, or *passito*), red (still, *novello*, *frizzante*, or *passito*), and *passito* (still, *novello* or *frizzante*) from a vast range of grapes and encompasses the entire province of Chieti.

✓ *Collefrisio*

TERRE DI VELEJA IGT
Emilia-Romagna

This IGT is restricted to a Malvasia-Trebbiano generic white, a Barbera-Bonarda generic red and *passito*, and five varietal wines (Berverdino, Fortana, Marsanne, Moscato, and Trebbiano) produced in the following styles: white (still, *frizzante*, or *passito*), red (still, *novello*, *frizzante*, or *passito*), and *passito* (still, *novello*, or *frizzante*) from grapes growing in part of the province of Piacenza.

TERRENI DI SAN SEVERINO DOC
Marches

This red-wine-only DOC includes a Vernaccia-based dry red generic, a sweet red Vernaccia-based *passito*, and "Moro", a Montepulciano-based dry red.

TREBBIANO D'ABRUZZO DOC
Abruzzi

These are usually dry, neutral, and mediocre white wines, although they can sometimes be delicately scented and velvety in texture.

⌛ 1–3 years

✓ *Emidio Pepe* ◉ • *Masciarelli* • *Tenuta del Priore* • *Valentini* • *Valle Reale*

TREBBIANO DI ROMAGNA DOC
Emilia-Romagna

This producer makes dry, neutral white wines that are also made in dry, sweet, and semi-sweet *spumante* versions.

VAL NUR *or* VAL NUR DEI COLLI PIACENTINI DOC
See Colli Piacentini DOC

VAL TIDONE IGT
Emilia-Romagna

This IGT is restricted to a generic still or sparkling red blend (based on Barbera and/or Bonarda), a generic still or sparkling white blend (based on Malvasia, Moscato, and/or Trebbiano), and six varietal wines (Barbera, Bonarda, Riesling, Fortana, Marsanne, and Müller-Thurgau) produced in part of the province of Piacenza.

VALLE PELIGNA IGT
Abruzzi

This IGT allows white (still, *frizzante*, or *passito*), red (still, *novello*, *frizzante*, or *passito*), and *passito* (still, *novello* or *frizzante*) from a wide range of grapes growing in Pratola Peligna and surrounding villages in the province of L'Aquila.

VERDICCHIO DEI CASTELLI DI JESI DOC
Marches

These are popular, lean, fresh, and mostly uninteresting dry white wines. *Spumante, frizzante*, and *frizzantino* versions are also produced. Majestic wines such as Umani Ronchi's Casal di Serra elevate themselves well beyond the norm of this appellation.

⌛ 1–4 years

✓ *Brunori* • *Bucci* • *Cortese Moncaro* • *Fazi Battaglia* • *Garofoli* • *Marotti Campi* • *Monte Schiavo* • *Montecappone* • *Pievalta* • *Umani Ronchi* • *Vecchi Vigne* • *Zaccagnini*

VERDICCHIO DI MATELICA DOC
Marches

Made in a hilly area in the centre of Macerata, these wines are slightly fatter than those of Castelli di Jesi, but most are just as uninteresting to drink.

⌛ 1–4 years

✓ *Belisario* (Meridia) • *Fratelli Bisci* • *La Monacesca*

VERNACCIA DI SERRAPETRONA DOCG
Marches

Made from Vernaccia grapes, Sangiovese, Montepulciano, and Ciliegiolo may be added to these semi-sweet to sweet *spumante* reds.

SOUTHERN ITALY AND THE ISLANDS

Hot and largely hilly, with volcanic soils, southern Italy is an ancient and prolific wine-growing area. Overproduction continues to be a problem, but well-made wines were starting to clean up Italy's southern-plonk image over a decade ago, since when a host of flying winemakers have made some remarkably expressive wines utilizing local varieties.

JUTTING OUT INTO THE BLUE WATERS of the Mediterranean, the vineyards of southern Italy receive very little natural moisture and bake rather than bask in unrelenting sunshine. This explains the deep-coloured wines with strong flavours and high alcoholic levels. Although these heavy wines do not suit modern tastes and southern Italy continues to produce a glut of these almost unsaleable wines, the region is subtly changing course. Its small

but growing volume of cleaner, finer, more expressive wines may enable it to establish an identity capable of thriving in ever more sophisticated world-wine markets. In this respect, it is being helped by foreign investment and flying winemakers, but the biggest obstacle to consolidating these isolated successes is the poverty that has for so long blighted southern Italy.

APULIA (PUGLIA)

Apulia's exceptionally fertile plains make it one of Italy's largest wine-producing regions, but until the 1970s most of its wines were seen as fit only for blending or for making Vermouth. Because of this, most Apulian producers chose to try to rid themselves of this lowly reputation, bringing about a radical transformation of their industry. A great number of very ordinary wines are still produced, but various changes have greatly improved the situation. Irrigation schemes, the introduction of lower-yielding, higher-quality grape varieties (including many classic French ones), and a move away from the single-bush cultivation, known as *alberello*, to modern wire-trained systems, have led to both new wines gaining favour and some traditional ones showing renewed promise. The two most important grape varieties are now the Primitivo, which has been identified as the Zinfandel of California and is the earliest-ripening grape grown in Italy, and the Uva di Troia, which has no connection with the town of Troia in Apulia's northern province of Foggia, but refers to ancient Troy, whence the grape originates. It was brought to the region by the first Greeks to settle in the Taranto area.

SOUTHERN ITALY, **see also p313**
Southern Italy produces huge quantities of wine. Apulia makes distinguished wines, but apart from the Aglianico wines of Basilicata and Campania, the quality is patchy.

ROME

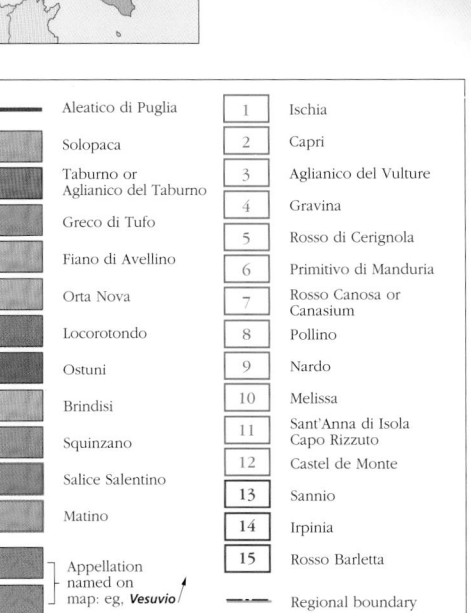

Legend

Aleatico di Puglia		1	Ischia
Solopaca		2	Capri
Taburno or Aglianico del Taburno		3	Aglianico del Vulture
Greco di Tufo		4	Gravina
Fiano di Avellino		5	Rosso di Cerignola
Orta Nova		6	Primitivo di Manduria
Locorotondo		7	Rosso Canosa or Canasium
Ostuni		8	Pollino
Brindisi		9	Nardo
Squinzano		10	Melissa
Salice Salentino		11	Sant'Anna di Isola Capo Rizzuto
Matino		12	Castel de Monte
		13	Sannio
Appellation named on map: eg, **Vesuvio**		14	Irpinia
		15	Rosso Barletta
			Regional boundary

0   20   40   60   80 miles
0   40   80   120 km

THE AMALFI COAST
These vines and citrus trees are terraced on cliffs typical to this area.

REGIONS AT A GLANCE

REGION	TOTAL AREA UNDER VINE	DOC/DOCG AREA UNDER VINE	DOC/DOCG PRODUCTION	TOTAL PRODUCTION
Sicily	164,500 ha (406,500 acres)	21,000 ha (51,900 acres)	277,000 hl (5/95 red/white)	11 million hl (122 million cases)
Sardinia	65,900 ha (162,850 acres)	7,400 ha (18,300 acres)	104,000 hl (35/65 red/white)	2.18 million hl (24 million cases)
Apulia	107,715 ha (266,170 acres)	20,000 ha (49,400 acres)	275,000 hl (70/30 red/white)	7.24 million hl (80 million cases)
Calabria	31,600 ha (78,100 acres)	3,400 ha (8,400 acres)	40,000 hl (90/10 red/white)	1.1 million hl (12.2 million cases)
Campania	46,800 ha (115,650 acres)	1,550 ha (3,830 acres)	25,000 hl (33/67 red/white)	2.5 million hl (27.8 million cases)
Basilicata	16,300 ha (40,300 acres)	1,470 ha (3,630 acres)	6,500 hl (all red)	400,000 hl (4.44 million cases)

CAMPANIA

The best-known wine of Campania Felix, as the Romans called this area, is Lacryma Christi (Tears of Christ), but the best quality is the lesser-known Taurasi DOCG made from the underrated Aglianico grape. Falerno del Massico is an up-and-coming Aglianico-based DOC, but apart from wines made by individual producers such as Mastroberardino and Antica Masseria Venditti, there is little else of interest produced here.

THE ISLANDS, *see also p313*
Sicily and Sardinia are usually included with southern Italy because they are on the same latitude, but they had to be separated for mapping purposes in this edition because of the proliferation of new appellations, including the contentious DOCG status of Vermentino di Gallura in Sardinia.

BASILICATA

Basilicata is a dramatic and wild region dominated by the extinct volcano Mount Vulture. Manufacturing industry is scarce here, accounting for less than one per cent of the region's output, and the mountainous terrain makes mechanized agriculture extremely difficult. Lacking investment finance and with two in every three inhabitants unemployed, Basilicata has not had the means nor the incentive to modernize its wine industry. Consequently, with the exception of the first-class, if idiosyncratic, Aglianico del Vulture, (Basilicata's solitary DOC), a wonderful non-DOC Aglianico called Canneto from Fratelli d'Angelo, and delicious Moscato and Malvasia from Fratelli d'Angelo and Paternosta, the fine-wine scene in Basilicata is as barren as the landscape, although it should make fertile pastures for flying winemakers.

CALABRIA

The decline in Calabria's viticultural output since the 1960s has been for the better in terms of quality. Since then, the most unsuitable land has been abandoned, and the 10 current DOCs, located in hilly and mountainous terrain, may eventually prove to be a source of quality wine. At the moment, however, improvement in wine technology is slow and, with the exception of Umberto Ceratti's succulent Greco di Bianco, a world-class dessert wine that is a relic of the past, Odoardi's Vigna Vecchia, a fruity red from the obscure Gaglioppo variety, and a luscious Moscato *vino da tavola* from Guido Lojelo, this region also has little in the way of interesting wine.

SICILY (SICILIA)

Sicily is the largest island in the Mediterranean and, in terms of quantity, is one of Italy's most important wine regions, annually producing a quantity roughly equal to the Veneto or Emilia-Romagna. Much of this is produced at high yields deliberately to take advantage of the EU's intervention scheme, which takes the wine off the market and distills it. The ancient port of Marsah-el-Allah, built under Arab rule, gives its name to Sicily's once popular classic wine, Marsala. By the mid-19th century, Marsala had evolved into a style between that of Madeira and sherry, but now finds itself as popular as bread and dripping, and just as likely to come back into fashion. Indeed, until recently, Sicilian wines were generally unfashionable. Then in 1995, the Planeta family established their winery, the wines started to attract attention and growing respect in the early 2000s, and Planeta is now not only the island's top producer, but also one of Italy's greatest.

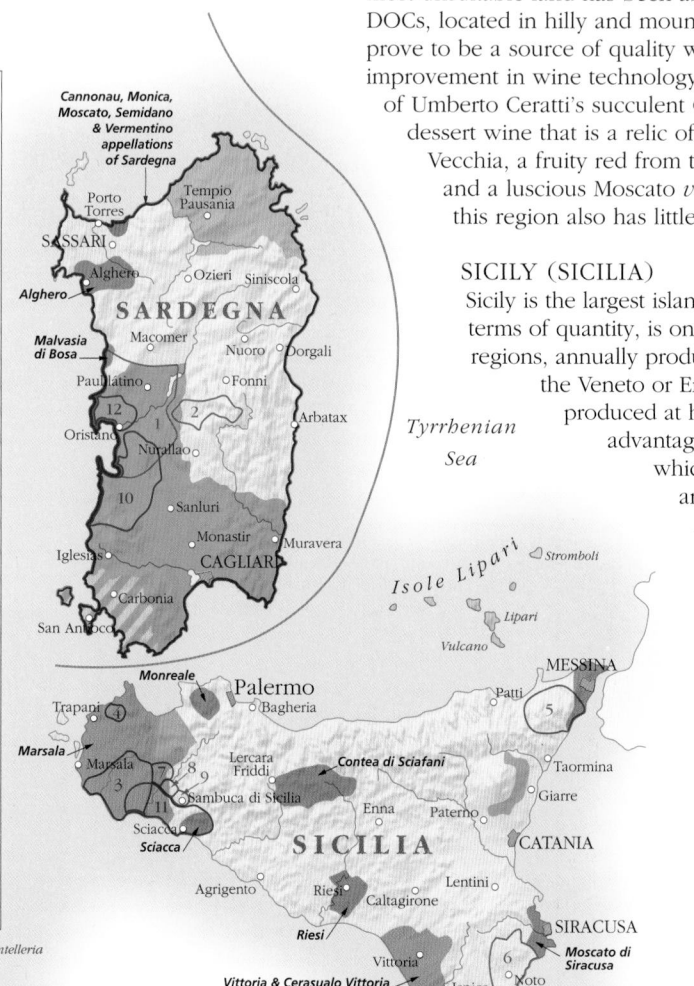

Moscato di Sorso-Sennori

Cagliari appellations of Girò, Malvasia, Monica, Moscato, Nasco & Nuragus

Vermentino di Gallura

Carignano del Sulcis

Etna

Alcamo

Faro

Moscato di Pantelleria & Moscato Passito di Pantelleria

Malvasia delle Lipari

Appellation named on map: eg, **Alghero**

1 Arborea
2 Mandrolisai
3 Delia Nivolelli
4 Erice
5 Mamerino di Milazzo
6 Moscato di Noto
7 Salaparuta
8 Santa Margherita de Belice
9 Sambuca di Sicilia
10 Campidano di Terralba
11 Menfi
12 Vernaccia di Oristano

0   20   40   60 miles
0   40   80   120 km

THE POLLINO MOUNTAINS, CALABRIA
Spring flowers carpet the slopes above Frascineto, in the foothills of the Pollino Mountains. This small mountain range gives its name to the fruity chiaretto-style wine made from Gaglioppo, Greco Nero, Malvasia, and Guarnaccia.

The stunning quality of these wines encouraged some long-established wineries (such as Tasca d'Almerita and, when it was bought by Illva Saronno, Corvo) to raise standards, as well as investment from big mainland producers, such as Zonin, which established Feuda Principi di Butera.

SARDINIA (SARDEGNA)

Sardinia is the second-largest island in the Mediterranean and, while it produces virtually all styles of wine, the modernization its wine industry has undergone since the late 1970s has had a more radical effect on its white wines than on any other style. Although Sardinia produces no "fine" wines in the classic sense, the wines are generally well made and easy to enjoy, and a small number of top-performing wineries make interesting wines under the

Carignano del Sulcis and Cagliari DOCs, while exceptional Malvasia *vini da tavola* are made by Gian Vittorio Naitana. Vermentino di Gallura was another enjoyable DOC, but its controversial promotion was the most ludicrous abuse of DOCG status since Albana di Romagna. Gallura does offer potential for fine wines, but more for reds than whites. Indeed, much of the hilly terrain on this island is naturally suited to lower-yielding, black grape varieties, which if harvested fully ripe could produce intensely flavoured, age-worthy reds, such as Turriga from Antonio Argiolas, an excellent Cannonau-based blend.

FACTORS AFFECTING TASTE AND QUALITY

LOCATION
This area includes the southern mainland regions of Apulia, Campania, Basilicata, Calabria, the islands of Sicily further south, and Sardinia, across the Tyrrhenian Sea to the west.

CLIMATE
The south is by far the hottest and driest region of Italy, although the coastal areas and islands are tempered by maritime winds.

ASPECT
Most of the region is either mountainous or hilly, although vineyards are to be found on the flat land and gentle slopes of Apulia. The best sites are always found on the north-facing, higher slopes of hillsides where the vines receive less sun and benefit from the tempering effect of altitude, thus ensuring a longer growing season.

SOIL
Soil is predominantly volcanic and granitic, but there are some isolated outcrops of clay and chalk.

VITICULTURE AND VINIFICATION
This area, together with the Midi in France, is the principal source of Europe's infamous "wine lake". Nevertheless, producers using better-quality grape varieties grown on higher sites are making wines of a standard and style that deserve wider recognition. Flying winemakers have helped enormously by showing what can be done.

GRAPE VARIETIES
Abbondosa (Nuragus), Aglianico, Aleatico, Alicante Bouschet, Ansolia (Inzolia), Ansonica (Inzolia), Arvino (Gaglioppo), Asprino (Asprinio), Axina de Margiai (Nuragus), Axina de Poporu (Nuragus), Barbera, Bianco d'Alessano, Biancolelle (Biancolella), Bombino, Bombino Nero, Bovale (Monastrell), Cabernet Franc, Cannamelu (Guarnaccia), Cannonadu (Grenache), Cannonao (Grenache), Cannonatu (Grenache), Cannonau (Grenache), Canonau (Grenache), Caprettone (Coda del Volpe), Carignano (Carignan), Carricante, Cataratto, Chardonnay, Coda di Pecora (Coda del Volpe), Damaschino, Falanghina, Fiano, Francavilla (Francavidda), Frappato (Nerello), Gaioppo (Gaglioppo), Grecanico (Garganega), Girò, Grechetto, Greco Nero, Grillo, Ianculella (Biancolella), Ianculillo (Biancolella), Impigno, Incrocio Manzoni 6013 (Riesling x Pinot Blanc), Lacrima Nera (Gaglioppo), Magliocc (Gaglioppo), Malbec, Malvasia, Malvasia Nero, Mantonico Nero (Gaglioppo), Marsigliana, Meragus (Nuragus), Monaca (Monica), Montepulciano, Montonico Nero (Gaglioppo), Moscato (Muscat Blanc à Petits Grains), Munica (Monica), Muristrellu (Monastrell), Nascu (Nasco), Negroamaro, Nero d'Avola (Calabrese), Niedda (Monica), Niura d'Avola (Calabrese), Nocera, Notar Domenico, Nusco (Nasco), Nuragus Trebbiana (Nuragus), Nzolia (Inzolia), Olivella (Sciascinoso), Olivese (Asprinio), Ottavianello (Cinsault), Pacali (Monica), Pallagrello Bianco (Coda del Volpe), Palombina Nera (Piedirosso), Pampanino (Pampanuto), Passale (Monica), Pedepalumb (Piedirosso), Per'e Palumme (Piedirosso), Per'e Palummo (Piedirosso), Petit Blanche (Biancolella), Pied di Colombo (Piedirosso), Pignatello (Perricone), Pinot Bianco (Pinot Blanc), Pinot Grigio (Pinot Gris), Pinot Nero (Pinot Noir), Primitivo (Zinfandel), Ragusan (Asprinio), Sangiovese, Sauvignon, Susumaniello, Teneddu (Biancolella), Tintilla (Monica), Trebbiano (Ugni Blanc), Uarnaccia (Guarnaccia), Uva Asprina (Asprinio), Uva di Spagna (Carignan), Uva di Troia, Verdeca, Vermentino, Vernaccia, Zagarese (Zinfandel), Zibibbo (Moscato variant)

AGLIANICO DEL TABURNO DOC

See Taburno DOC

AGLIANICO DEL VULTURE DOC

Basilicata

This is the only DOC in Basilicata to encompass the volcanic slopes of Mount Vulture and its surrounding hills, which make the best growing areas for the Aglianico grape. A big but balanced red wine of warm colour, rich, chocolate-cherry fruit, and firm tannin structure, Aglianico del Vulture can be slightly rustic in youth, yet develops a true silky finesse with age.

Some would argue that it is the greatest Aglianico and will doubtless achieve DOCG status. If described as *vecchio* (old), Aglianico del Vulture will have been aged for a minimum of three years, while *riserva* will have had five; both will have been aged for two years in wood. Aglianico del Vulture may also be sold as semi-sweet and *spumante*.

⌛— 6–20 years

✓ *D'Angelo • Basilisco • Elena Fucci* (Titolo) • *Maccarico • Paternosta • Terre degli Svevi* (Manfredi)

ALCAMO *or* BIANCO D'ALCAMO DOC

Sicily

Dry, slightly fruity white wines from the Catarratto grape with the possible addition of Damaschino, Garganega, and Trebbiano. The soil is too fertile and yields far too high to produce wines of any real quality or character.

ALEATICO DI PUGLIA DOC

Apulia

Produced in tiny quantities throughout the region, this wine is rarely exported. Opulent and aromatic wines with a full, warming, smooth, and exotic flavour, ranging from very sweet and fortified (*liquoroso* or *liquoroso dolce naturel*) to medium-sweet and unfortified (*dolce naturel*). A *riserva* must be aged for at least three years from the date of harvest or, in the case of *liquoroso*, the date of fortification.

⌛— Upon purchase

✓ *Francesco Candido*

ALEZIO DOC

Apulia

A DOC since 1983 for red and *rosato* wines made from Negroamaro, with the possible addition of Sangiovese, Montepulciano, and Malvasia Nera. The red is alcoholic, slightly tannic, and not very interesting, but the dry *rosato* can be soft and flavourful with delicate fruit.

⌛— Upon purchase (*rosato*)

✓ *Michele Calò* (Mjère)

ALGHERO DOC

Sardinia

From vineyards surrounding the ancient city of Alghero in the northwest of the island, this DOC includes a varietally non-specific generic red that may be still or sparkling, dry or sweet (*liquoroso* must be aged for at least 36 months prior to release,

and *liquoroso riserva* for at least 60 months); a varietally non-specific generic white; a varietally non-specific generic dry *passito* that may be still or *frizzante*; a Cabernet blend; and the following varietal wines: Cagnulari (or Cagniulari), Chardonnay (may be *spumante*), Sangiovese, Sauvignon, Torbato (may be *spumante*), Trebbiano (may be *frizzante*), and Vermentino (may be *frizzante*).

✓ *Sella & Mosca* (Marchese di Villamarina)

ARBOREA DOC

Sardinia

Three varietal wines: Sangiovese red, Sangiovese *rosato*, and a dry or semi-sweet Trebbiano white.

ARGHILLÀ IGT

Calabria

This IGT is restricted to red and *rosato* wines (may be *novello*) from any locally authorized varieties found in the foothills behind Villa San Giuseppe, north of Régio di Calabria.

ASPRINIO DI AVERSA *or* AVERSA DOC

Campania

Asprinio is an ancient variety that was known by the Etruscans, who commonly grew vines in trees. Their practice perseveres here, where the vine is trained up poplar trees to a height of 13 metres (45 feet) to produce fresh, crisp, dry white wines that may be still or *spumante*.

BARBAGIA IGT

Sardinia

White, red, *passito*, *frizzante*, and *novello* wines made in and around the villages of Fonni, Gavoi, Lodine, Mamoiada, Nuoro, Oliena, Ollolai, Olzai, Oniferi, Orani, Orgosolo, Orotelli, Ortine, Ottana, and Sarule.

BASILICATA IGT

Basilicata

Geographically and stylistically, this IGT is extremely wide-ranging, covering white (still, *frizzante*, or *passito*), red (still, *novello*, *frizzante*, or *passito*), and *passito* (still, *novello*, or *frizzante*) from the entire Basilicata region. D'Angelo's Canneto is one of Italy's finest wines.

✓ *D'Angelo* (Canneto)

BENEVENTANO IGT

Campania

This IGT encompasses vineyards growing around the hilltop town of Beneventano.

✓ *Feudi di San Gregorio*

BIANCO D'ALCAMO DOC

See Alcamo DOC

BIVONGI DOC

Calabria

A generic dry white blend (Greco and/or Guardavelle, plus Montonico, Malvasia, or Asonica), red (including *novello*), and dry *passito* generic blend (Gaglippo and/or Greco Nero, plus Nocera, Calabrese, or Castiglione) from vineyards around Bivongi in the Stilaro Valley on the slopes of Monte Consolino.

BRINDISI DOC

Apulia

Smooth, vinous red wines and dry, light, fruity *rosati*, both primarily from Negroamaro grapes, although Montepulciano, Malvasia Nera, Sangiovese, and Susumaniello may also be used.

⌛— 3–6 years (red)

✓ *Cosimo Taurino* (Patriglione)

CACC'E MMITTE DI LUCERA DOC

Apulia

The name of this full-bodied red *uvaggio*, which is made from seven grape varieties, loosely means "knock it back" (*cacc'e* means "drink" and *mmitte* means "pour"), which aptly applies to this simple, easy-drinking red wine.

CAGLIARI DOC

Sardinia

Six varietals: Girò (classic red, *liquoroso secco*, *liquoroso dolce naturale*); Malvasia (a smooth, delicately scented red wine in dry, sweet, and *liquoroso* styles); Monica (*liquoroso* only, may be *secco* or *dolce naturale*); Moscato (rich, succulently sweet white wines that may be fortified); Nasco (finely scented, delicate, dry and sweet white wines that can also be *liquoroso*); and Nuragus (a large production of dry, semi-sweet, and *frizzante* white wines from the Nuragus grape).

⌛— 1–2 years

✓ *Fratelli Porcu • Meloni* ◉ • *Pala* (Nuragus)

CALABRIA IGT

Calabria

This regional IGT allows white (still, *frizzante*, or *passito*), red (still, *novello*, *frizzante*, or *passito*), and *passito* (still, *novello*, or *frizzante*) from a wide range of grape varieties grown in the Calabria region.

✓ *Viola* (Moscato di Saracena, Moscato Passito)

CAMARRO IGT

Sicily

Permitted are white (still, *frizzante*, or *passito*), red (still, *novello*, *frizzante*, or *passito*), and *passito* (still, *novello*, or *frizzante*) from a wide range of grapes growing in and around Partanna, in Trapani.

✓ *Tasca d'Almerita*

CAMPANIA IGT

Campania

This regional IGT allows white (still, *frizzante*, *aamabile*, or *passito*), red (still, *novello*, *frizzante*, *liquoroso*, *aamabile*, or *passito*), and *passito* (still, *novello*, *liquoroso*, *aamabile*, or *frizzante*) from a wide range of grape varieties growing anywhere in the Campania region.

✓ *Villa Matilde • Feudi di San Gregorio • La Guardiense • Mastroberardino • Pietracupa* (Cupo)

CAMPI FLEGREI DOC

Campania

Two generic blends: red (Piedirosso, Aglianico, and Sciascinoso) and white (Falanghina, Biancolella, and Coda del Volpe); plus one red-wine varietal:

Piedirosso (dry or *passito* dry-to-sweet); and one dry white varietal Falanghina (still or *spumante*).

CAMPIDANO DI TERRALBA DOC
See Terralba DOC

CANASIUM *or* ROSSO CANOSA DOC
Apulia

Canasium is Latin for Canosa di Puglia, around which this DOC is centred. The wines are primarily based on Uva di Troia, plus Montepulciano or Sangiovese.

CANNONAU DI SARDEGNA DOC
See Sardegna DOC

CAPRI DOC
Campania

Easy-to-drink, dry white wines seldom seen beyond the Isle of Capri. The island's soil and climate suggests that these wines should be much finer, but the land for vines is scarce and expensive, encouraging growers to extract far too much from those vineyards that do exist.

CARIGNANO DEL SULCIS DOC
Sardinia

Promising red and *rosato* wines from the Carignan grape, to which a little Monica, Pascale, and Alicante Bouschet may be added.

🖟— 1–4 years

✓ *CS di Santadi* (Riserva Rocca Rubia, Terre Brune) • *Sar Dus Pater* (Arenas)

CASTEL DEL MONTE DOC
Apulia

The region's best-known wine is named after the 13th-century castle built by Emperor Frederick von Hohenstaufen. With the exception of a red *riserva* made by Rivera and called Il Falcone (The Falcon), the wines are less lofty than the name of this DOC suggests. In addition to the generic red and *rosato*, which are made from Uva di Troia and Aglianico grapes, and the basic dry white from Pampanuto and Chardonnay, there are two red varietals, Pinot Nero and Aglianico; four white varietals, Chardonnay, Pinot Bianco, Pinot Bianco da Pinot Nero, and Sauvignon; plus a rose, Aglianico.

🖟— 2–6 years (red, but 8–20 years for Il Falcone)

✓ *Rivera* (especially Il Falcone and Terre al Monte) • *Tormaresca* (Bocca di Lupo) • *Torre Vento* (Vigna Pedale)

CASTEL SAN LORENZO DOC
Campania

A relatively new DOC covering several communes in the province of Salerno, Castel San Lorenzo encompasses generic red and *rosato* (Barbera and Sangiovese), white (Trebbiano and Malvasia), one red wine varietal (Barbera) and one sweet white varietal (Moscato, still or *spumante*).

CERASUOLO DI VITTORIA DOCG
Sicily

Cherry-coloured wines made from 50% Nero

d'Avola plus a maximum of 50% Nerello in the southeastern corner of Sicily.

✓ *Poggio di Bortolone • Cos • Planeta • Valle dell'Acate*

CILENTO DOC
Campania

Vines struggle in the rocky vineyards of Cilento, where generic red and *rosato* are made from Aglianico, Piedirosso, and Barbera, and generic white from Fiano, Trebbiano, Greco, and Malvasia. An Aglianico varietal exists but has yet to prove itself.

✓ *Viticoltori di Conciliis* (Donnaluna Fiano, Donnaluna Aglianico) • *Librandi* (Duca Sanfelice) • *Luigi Maffini* (Cenito)

CIRÒ DOC
Calabria

Strong, alcoholic Gaglioppo-based red and *rosato*, and Greco-based dry white wines that rely too heavily on the Cirò name, which was famous in ancient times.

COLLI DEL LIMBARA IGT
Sardinia

This IGT allows red, white, and *passito* in still and *frizzante* styles (also *novello* for red wines) from a wide range of grapes growing on the slopes of Mount Limbara in the province Budoni e San Teodoro and Nuoro in the very north end of the island.

COLLI ERICINI IGT
Sicily

This IGT is restricted to hillside vineyards around Buseto Palizzolo in Marsala-land of western Sicily, where generic dry whites may be made from primarily Cararratto Bianco, and red and *passito* may be blended or pure Nerello Mascalese, Perricone (known locally as Pignatello), and Frappato. Wines are either dry or sparkling.

COLLI DI SALERNO IGT
Campania

This IGT is restricted to hillside vineyards in the province of Salerno. It allows white (still, *frizzante*, *aamabile*, or *passito*), red (still, *novello*, *frizzante*, *liquoroso*, *aamabile*, or *passito*), and *passito* (still, *novello*, *liquoroso*, *aamabile*, or *frizzante*), with blended wines from any locally authorized variety, but varietal wines are restricted to Aglianico, Barbera, Coda di Volpe, Falanghina, Fiano, Greco, Moscato, Piedirosso, Primitivo, and Sciascinoso.

✓ *Montevetrano*

CONDOLEO IGT
Calabria

Generic red and *passito* wines may be made in classic dry or *novello* styles from any locally authorized grape varieties found in and around Mondatoriccio in the province of Cosenza.

CONTEA DI SCLAFANI DOC
Sicily

Generic Nero d'Avola-based red; Catarratto or Grecanico (aka Garganega) white; and Nerello Mascalese-based *passito*, plus numerous varietal wines (Ansonica, Cabernet Sauvignon, Calabrese, Catarratto, Chardonnay, Grecanico [aka Garganega], Grillo, Merlot, Nerello Mascalese, Nero d'Avola, Perricone, Pinot Bianco, Pinot Nero, Sangiovese, Sauvignon, and Syrah). All reds must be dry but may also be *novello*. Whites may be dry or sweet,

still or *spumante*. *Rosato* must be dry but may be still or *spumante*.

✓ *Tasca d'Almerita* (Rosso del Conte)

CONTESSA ENTELLINA DOC
Sicily

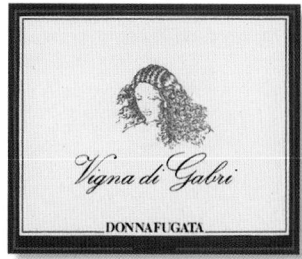

This new DOC encompasses vineyards in the commune of Contessa Entellina in the province of Palermo for a delicate dry white blend of Inzolia, Catarratto, Garganega, Chardonnay, Sauvignon, and Müller-Thurgau; and three dry white-wine varietals, Chardonnay, Grecanico (Garganega), and Sauvignon.

✓ *Donnafugata* (Mille e Una Notte)

COPERTINO DOC
Apulia

This appellation is named after the town of Copertino, although the wines that qualify for this DOC can also come from five other villages. These smooth, rich red wines and dry, finely scented *rosato* wines are made primarily from the Negroamaro grape with the possible addition of Malvasia Nera, Montepulciano, and Sangiovese.

🖟— 2–5 years

✓ *CS di Copertino* (*riserva*)

COSTA D'AMALFI DOC
Campania

For traditional wines made from local grape varieties grown in the province of Salerno, with three sub-zones that may be indicated on the label: Furore, Ravello, and Tramonti. The white must be dry and primarily Falanghina and/or Biancolella; the red and *passito*, also dry, must be primarily Piedirosso, plus Sciascinoso and/or Aglianico.

COSTA VIOLA IGT
Calabria

Generic red and *passito* wines may be made in classic dry or *novello* styles from any locally authorized grape varieties growing in the coastal hills of Bagnara, Calabra, Palmi, Scilla, and Seminara in the province of Reggio Calabria.

CREMOVO ZABAIONE VINO *or* CREMOVO ZABAIONE VINO AROMATIZZATO DOC
See Marsala DOC

DAUNIA IGT
Apulia

Red (dry or sweet *passito*, still or *frizzante*, and *novello*), white (dry or sweet *passito*, still or *frizzante*), and *passito* (still or *frizzante*) wines produced in the province of Foggia.

DELIA NIVOLELLI DOC
Sicily

From vineyards in the province of Trapani, this DOC includes a generic white (which must be dry, may be still or *frizzante*, and can be a blend of any two or more of the following: Grecanico [aka Garganega], Grillo, and Inzolia), a generic red (can be a blend of any two or more of the following: Cabernet Sauvignon, Merlot, Nero d'Avola, Perricone, Sangiovese, and Syrah), and a generic *spumante* (can be a blend of any two or more of the following: Chardonnay, Damaschino, Grecanico [aka Garganega], Grillo, and Inzolia), plus seven white varietals (Chardonnay, Damaschino, Grecanico [aka Garganega], Grillo, Inzolia, Müller-Thurgau, and Sauvignon) and five red varietals (Nero d'Avola, Merlot, Pignatello [aka Perricone], Sangiovese, and Syrah).

DONNICI DOC
Calabria

Fruity, cherry-coloured red and *rosato* wines (traditionally *chiaretto*) from Gaglioppo and Greco Nero grapes grown in the province of Cosenza. They are best drunk young.

DUGENTA IGT
Campania

Red, *novello* red, and dry *passito* from vineyards around the town of Dugenta.

ELORO DOC
Sicily

This appellation straddles the provinces of Ragusa and Siracusa, where a generic red and *rosato* (Calabrese, Frappato, and Pignatello) are produced and, if the blend contains at least 80 per cent Calabrese, it may be called Pachino. These grapes are also vinified separately to produce three varietal wines, the Calabrese being sold under its local synonym Nero d'Avola.

EPOMEO IGT
Campania

This regional IGT allows white (still, *frizzante*, *aamabile*, or *passito*), red (still, *novello*, *frizzante*, *liquoroso*, *aamabile*, or *passito*), and *passito* (still, *novello*, *liquoroso*, *aamabile*, or *frizzante*) from any authorized variety growing on the island of Ischia.

ERICE DOC
Sicily

This typically Italian wide-ranging DOC east of Trapani in Marsala-land allows a Catarratto-based generic dry white, a Calabrese-based generic red, nine white varietals (Ansonica [aka Inzolia], Catarratto, Chardonnay [may be *spumante*], Grecanico [aka Garganega], Grillo, Moscato [may be *passito*], Müller-Thurgau, Sauvignon [may be *vendemmia tardiva*], and Zibibbo [may be *vendemmia tardiva* or *passito*]), and six red varietals (Cabernet Sauvignon, Calabrese [aka Nero d'Avola], Frappato, Merlot, Perricone [aka Pignatello], and Syrah).

ESARO IGT
Calabria

Blended or varietal wines produced in red (including *novello*), white, and *passito* (may also be *novello*) styles from any varieties authorized to grow in the province of Consenza.

ETNA DOC
Sicily

According to Homer, this is the wine that Ulysses used to intoxicate the Cyclops. There are three basic styles: a full red and fruity *rosato* from the Nerello grape, and a soft but bland dry white

from Carricante and Catarratto with the possible addition of Trebbiano.

✓ *Benanti* (Pietramarina, Serra della Contessa) • *Biondi* (Outis) • *Cottanera* (Rosso) • *Destro* (Skiarakè) • *Pietradolce* (Archineri) • *Tenuta delle Terre Nere* (Santo Spirito)

FALERNO DEL MASSICO DOC
Campania

This appellation celebrates Falernum, the wine so enjoyed in ancient Rome, which was made in the northwest of Campania and Latium. The deep-coloured, full-bodied, and rustically robust red generic is a blend of Aglianico and Piedirosso with the possible addition of Primitivo and Barbera. The round, fruity dry white generic is, in fact, pure Falanghina. A red varietal Primitivo is also produced.

🍷 3–7 years (red), upon purchase (white, *rosato*)

✓ *Villa Matilde* • *Michele Moio* (Primitivo)

FARO DOC
Sicily

Ruby-coloured, medium-bodied but firmly flavoured red wines from Nerello and Nocera grapes grown around Messina. Calabrese, Gaglioppo, and Sangiovese may also be used.

🍷 2–5 years

✓ *Bagni* • *Palari*

FIANO DI AVELLINO DOCG
Campania

Mastroberardino's Vignadora is the best wine in this unusual, but well above average, dry white wine DOCG, made from Fiano grapes grown in the hilly hinterland of Avellino.

🍷 1–3 years

✓ *Colli di Lapio* • *Mastroberardino* • *Ciro Picariello* • *Villa Diamante* (Congregazione)

FONTANAROSSA DI CERDA IGT
Sicily

This IGT is restricted to Cerda in the province of Palermo and includes a generic red (from one or more of the following: Cabernet Sauvignon, Mascalese, Nero d'Avola, and Perricone; this wine may also be *frizzante* or *novello*), a generic white (from one or more of the following: Catarratto, Chardonnay, Inzolia, and Trebbiano; this wine may also be *frizzante*), and a generic blended *passito* (same varieties as for red; may also be *frizzante*), plus just three varietals: one red (Cabernet Sauvignon) and two white (Ansonica and Chardonnay).

GALATINA DOC
Apulia

This DOC in the "heel" of Italy covers generic Chardonnay-based dry whites, generic Negroamaro-based red (may be *novello*) and *passito* wines (may be *frizzante*), and two varietals (Chardonnay and Negroamaro).

GALLUCCIO DOC
Campania

A Falanghina-based white and Aglianico-based red grown around the extinct volcano Roccamonfina.

GIOIA DEL COLLE DOC
Apulia

For this large DOC in the province of Bari, there are generic red and *rosato* blends (Primitivo,

Montepulciano, Sangiovese, Negroamaro, and Malvasia Nera); a dry white (Trebbiano and anything else that moves); and two varietals, a sweetish Primitivo and an intensely sweet Aleatico (which can be fortified).

✓ *Chiaromonte* • *Polvanera*

GIRÒ DI CAGLIARI DOC
See Cagliari DOC

GRAGNANO DOC
See Penisola Sorrentina DOC

GRAVINA DOC
Apulia

Dry or semi-sweet, blended white wines that may be still or *spumante*, made from Malvasia, Greco, and Bianco d'Alessano, with the possible addition of Bombino, Trebbiano, and Verdeca.

GRECO DI BIANCO DOC
Calabria

Made on the very tip of Calabria, around Bianco, from the Grechetto grape, known locally as Greco Bianco. With the exception of Umberto Ceratti's exceptional rendition, Greco di Bianco is a simple *passito* wine. Ceratti harvests tiny, already shrivelled grapes and, apparently, plunges them into boiling water immediately after picking (to flash pasteurize the wine, which removes or reduces the need to use sulphur). His Greco di Bianco is deceptively strong, succulently sweet and smooth, with a vivacious bouquet, exuberant fruit, and a luscious silk finish.

🍷 3–5 years

✓ *Umberto Ceratti* • *Benito Ferrara* • *Feudi di San Gregorio* (Cutizzi) • *Pietracupa* • *Vadiaperti* (Tornante)

GRECO DI TUFO DOCG
Campania

Delicate, dry, and soft white wines that may sometimes be *spumante*, from the true Greco grown north of Avellino.

🍷 Upon purchase

✓ *Cantine dell'Angelo* • *Mastroberardino* (Vignadangelo)

GROTTINO DI ROCCANOVA DOC
Basilicata

Formerly known as Rosso di Roccanova, these wines became Grottino di Roccanova in 2000, when it was recognized as an IGT and both red and white wines were allowed. In 2009, Grottino di Roccanova was promoted to DOC, and this appellation now encompasses red (which may be *novello*), white (may be *frizzante* or *aamabile*), and passito (may be *frizzante*, *aamabile*, or *passito*) wines from any authorized varieties growing in Roccanova, Castronuovo di Sant'Andrea, and Sant'Arcangelo in the province of Potenza.

GUARDIA SANFRAMONDI *or* GUARDIOLO DOC
Campania

Located in the hilly terrain of the Benveneto, this DOC consists of a generic dry white (Malvasia and Falanghina plus up to 30 per cent pick-and-mix), generic Sangiovese-based red and *rosato*, one dry white varietal (Falanghina), which may be *spumante*, and one red varietal (Aglianico).

IRPINIA DOC
Campania

This appellation was promoted from IGT to DOC in 2005 and is best known for its deeply coloured Aglianico. However, it covers many different wines: generic Greco-Fiano-based dry white; generic Aglianico based red, *novello* red, and generic dry *passito*; four varietal whites (Coda di Volpe, Falanghina [may be *spumante*], Fiano [may be *passito* or *spumante*], Greco [may be *passito* or *spumante*]); and three varietal reds: (Aglianico [may be *passito* or *liquoroso*], Piedirosso, and Sciascinoso). Wines bearing the sub-zonal denomination of Campi Taurasini must be at least 85% Aglianico.

✓ *Cantine Antonio Caggiano* • *Feudi di San Gregorio* (Patrimo, Serpico) • *Tenuta del Cavalier Pepe* (Coda di Volpe, Sanserino)

ISCHIA DOC
Campania

Vinous, medium-bodied generic red (Guarnaccia and Piedirosso, plus 20 per cent pick-and-mix); a lightly aromatic, generic dry white (Forastera and Biancolella), which may be *spumante*; two dry white varietal wines (Biancolella and Forastera); and one red varietal (Piedirosso), which can be either dry or *passito*.

⌾ 2–4 years (red), upon purchase (white and *rosato*)

✓ *D'Ambra*

ISOLA DEI NURAGHI IGT
Sardinia

Still or *frizzante* red (may also be *novello*), white, and *passito* wines from any authorized varieties growing in the provinces of Cagliari, Nuoro, Oristano, and Sassari. Vermentino works best for dry whites, and Barbera and Cannonau for reds, although Montepulciano and Mourvèdre (known locally as Bovale) can also excel.

✓ *Antonio Argiolas* (Turriga) • *Cantine di Dolianova* (Falconaro, Montesicci, Terresicci) • *Ferruccio Deiana* (Ajana) • *Masone Mannu* (Entu, Mannu) • *Feudi della Medusa* (Gerione) • *Pala* (Essentija, S'Arai, Silenzi) • *Punica* (Barrua)

LAMEZIA DOC
Calabria

Originally a one-wine DOC for a light, delicately fruity, but otherwise unexceptional blended red wine (Nerello, Gaglioppo, Greco Nero, and Marsigliana), Lamezia has now been expanded to include a generic, full dry white (Grechetto, Trebbiano, and Malvasia) and a white varietal called Greco, the local name for Grechetto. The light red has been split into red and *rosato*.

LETTERE DOC
See Penisola Sorrentina DOC

LEVERANO DOC
Apulia

Alcoholic red wines and fresh, fruity *rosato* wines (Negroamaro with the possible addition of Sangiovese, Montepulciano, and Malvasia Nera), and soft, dry white wines (Malvasia plus Bombino and Trebbiano). Conti Zecca's elegant red Vigna del Sareceno stands out.

⌾ 3–7 years (red)

✓ *Conti Zecca* (Vigna del Saraceno)

LIPUDA IGT
Calabria

Still or *frizzante* red (may also be *novello*), white, and *passito* wines from any authorized varieties growing in Carfizzi, Casabona Cirò, Cirò Marina, Crucoli, Melissa, Strangoli, and Umbriatico in the province of Crotone.

LIZZANO DOC
Apulia

Negroamaro-based red and *rosato*, still or *frizzante* generic wines, which may be boosted by the addition of Montepulciano, Sangiovese, Bombino Nero, Pinot Noir, and Malvasia Nera. The *rosato* can also be fully *spumante*, as can the generic white blend of Trebbiano and Chardonnay (with the possible addition of Malvasia, Sauvignon, and Bianco d'Alessano), which also comes in still or *frizzante* styles. There are two red varietal wines, Negroamaro and Malvasia Nera; and one *rosato* varietal, Negroamaro – in straightforward, dry still-wine styles.

LOCOROTONDO DOC
Apulia

Fresh, lightly fruity, dry white wines of improving quality from Verdeca and Bianco d'Alessano, with the possible addition of Fiano, Malvasia, and Bombino, made in still and *spumante* styles.

⌾ Upon purchase

✓ *CS di Locorotondo*

LOCRIDE IGT
Calabria

Red, *novello* red, white, and *passito* wines from locally authorized varieties growing in Locri and its surrounding towns in the Province of Reggio Calabria.

MALVASIA DI BOSA DOC
Sardinia

Rich, sweet and dry white wines, and sweet and dry *liquoroso* wines. Generally fuller-bodied than Malvasia di Cagliari.

MALVASIA DI CAGLIARI DOC
See Cagliari DOC

MALVASIA DELLE LIPARI DOC
Sicily

Sweet, aromatic, *passito* white wines.

⌾ 2–5 years

✓ *Carlo Hauner*

MAMERTINO DI MILAZZO DOC
Sicily

This DOC includes a Grillo-Inzolia- or Inzolia-Grillo-based generic dry white, a Calabrese-based generic red, and a varietal Calabrese (aka Nero d'Avola).

MANDROLISAI DOC
Sardinia

Red and *rosato* wines with a bitter aftertaste blended from Bovale (Monastrell), Cannonau (Grenache), and Monica.

MARMILLA IGT
Sardinia

Still or *frizzante* red, white, and *passito* wines produced in the towns of Collinas, Furtei, Morgongiori, Pabillonis, Pompu, Samassi, Sanluri, Sardara, Serrenti, Simala, Siris, Villamar, and Villanovaforru in the province of Cagliari and in Baressa, Gonnoscodina, Gonnostramatza, Masullas, and Mogoro in province of Oristano. With the specific exception of Cannonau, Carignano, Girò, Malvasia, Monica, Moscato, Nasco, Nuragus, Semidano, Vermentino, and Vernaccia, all other locally authorized grapes are allowed.

MARSALA DOC
Sicily

This wine was conceived by John Woodhouse, who began shipping it in 1773. Its name is Arabic, deriving from *Marsah-el-Allah*, the old name of the port of Marsala. The grapes used include Grillo (the original Marsala variety and still considered the best), Catarratto, Pignatello, Garganega, Calabrese, Damaschino, Nerello, and Inzolia. The wine is fortified by the adding of neutral spirit and, where appropriate, sweetened with grape concentrate made locally. Marsala can be dry (*secco*), semi-sweet (*semi-secco*), or sweet (*dolce*); is further defined by colour, gold (*oro*), amber (*ambra*), and red (*rubino*); and is made in four basic styles, *Fine, Superiore, Vergine*, and *Solera*.

Marsala Fine, the lowest category, is aged for just a year (not necessarily in wood) with at least 17 per cent ABV. As Italian-wine expert David Gleave MW has put it, Marsala Fine is "usually anything but fine, being a cheap and rather nasty travesty of the name". Marsala Superiore is aged for at least two years in wood (four years if *riserva*), with a minimum 18 per cent ABV. Marsala Vergine is aged for at least five years in wood, or 10 if *stravecchio* or *riserva*, is only *secco* (thus no grape concentrate allowed), and must have a minimum 18 per cent ABV. Marsala Solera is also aged for at least five years in wood, or 10 years if *stravecchio* or *riserva*, is only *secco* (thus no grape concentrate allowed), and must have a minimum of 18 per cent ABV. Some historical abbreviations are still found on labels: IP (stands for Italy Particular – Marsala Fine), LP (London Particular – Marsala Superiore), SOM (Superior Old Marsala – Marsala Superiore), GD (Garibaldi Dolce – Marsala Superiore). Flavoured Marsala may be sold as Cremovo Zabaione Vino or Cremovo Zabaione Vino Aromatizzato (sickly sweet egg nog containing at least 80 per cent Marsala wine, eggs, and a minimum of 200 grams of residual sugar per litre), "*preparato con l'impiego di Vino Marsala*" (for other Marsala-based products containing not less than 60 per cent Marsala wine), and you will find non-DOC Marsala-based concoctions with all sorts of flavourings (banana, chocolate, orange, etc). I must confess that, except for rare old bottlings of Vergine or Solera, most Marsala leaves me cold and the flavoured versions horrify me, but the best producers are well known.

🍷— Upon purchase

✓ *Cantina de Bartoli* • *Florio* • *Carlo Pellegrino*

MARTINA *or* MARTINA FRANCA DOC
Apulia

These dry white wines in still or *spumante* styles are very similar to those of Locorotondo.

MATERA DOC
Basilicata

This city is more famous for its Sassi di Matera (prehistoric cave dwellings) than for wine. The DOC allows styles that include a Malvasia-based generic dry white (which may be *spumante*), a Sangiovese-Aglianico-based generic red, and two red varietals (Moro and Primitivo).

MATINO DOC
Apulia

Dry, robust red and slightly vinous *rosato* wines made from Negroamaro with the possible addition of Malvasia Nera.

MELISSA DOC
Calabria

An appellation of full-bodied reds (Gaglioppo, Greco Nero, Grechetto, Trebbiano, and Malvasia) and crisp, dry whites (Grechetto, Trebbiano, and Malvasia).

MENFI DOC
Sicily

Made in and around Menfi at the western end of the south coast, these wines include a generic red (at least 70% from one or more of the following: Cabernet Sauvignon, Merlot, Nero d'Avola, Sangiovese, and Syrah), a generic white (at least 75% from one or more of the following: Catarratto, Chardonnay, Inzolia, and Grecanico), a generic *vendemmia tardiva* (from one or more of the following: Catarratto, Chardonnay, Inzolia, and Sauvignon), two sub-zones (Bonera [at least 85% from one or more of the following: Cabernet Sauvignon, Merlot, Nero d'Avola, Sangiovese, and Syrah] and Feudo dei Fiori [at least 85% Chardonnay and/or Inzolia]), five varietals (Cabernet Sauvignon, Merlot, Nero d'Avola, Sangiovese, and Syrah), and three white varietals (Chardonnay, Grecanico [aka Garganega], and Inzolia).

MONICA DI CAGLIARI DOC
See Cagliari DOC

MONICA DI SARDEGNA DOC
See Sardegna DOC

MONREALE DOC
Sicily

Another typically Italian wide-ranging DOC, Montreale includes a Catarratto- and/or Inzolia-based generic white (which may be dry or, if *vendemmia tardive*, sweet), a Calabrese-Perricone-based generic red dry *passito*, five white varietals (Ansonica [aka Inzolia], Catarratto, Chardonnay, Grillo, and Pinot Bianco), and six red varietals (Cabernet Sauvignon, Calabrese [aka Nero d'Avola], Merlot, Perricone [aka Pignatello], Sangiovese, and Syrah).

✓ *Spadafora* (Syrah)

MOSCATO DI CAGLIARI DOC
See Cagliari DOC

MOSCATO DI NOTO DOC
Sicily

Still, *spumante*, or fortified semi-sweet and sweet Moscato wines.

✓ *Marabino*

MOSCATO DI PANTELLERIA DOC
Sicily

Sicily's best still, *spumante*, and fortified semi-sweet and sweet *passito* Moscato are made on the island of Pantelleria, closer to Tunisia than to Sicily.

✓ *De Bartoli* (Passito Bukkuram) • *Cantine Florio* (Morsi di Luce) • *Donnafugata* (Passito) • *Salvatore Murana*

MOSCATO PASSITO DI PANTELLERIA DOC
See Moscato di Pantelleria DOC

MOSCATO DI SARDEGNA DOC
See Sardegna DOC

MOSCATO DI SIRACUSA DOC
Sicily

These sweet, smooth white wines are made from semi-*passito* grapes.

✓ *Pupillo*

MOSCATO DI SORSO-SENNORI DOC
Sardinia

Sweet, rich, white Moscato and sweet, aromatic *liquoroso*. The wines are fuller than either Moscato di Cagliari or Moscato di Sardegna.

MOSCATO DI TRANI DOC
Apulia

Tiny production of luscious, ultra-smooth, sweet white Moscato wines, which may be fortified. These wines are high quality and distinctive.

🍷— Upon purchase

✓ *Fratelli Nugnes*

MURGIA IGT
Apulia

From the province of Bari, still and *frizzante* red wines produced from one or more of the following varieties: Aglianico, Aleatico, Cabernet Franc, Cabernet Sauvignon, Lambrusco, Pinot Nero, Primitivo, Sangiovese, and Uva di Troia; dry, *frizzante*, and *passito* white wines from one or more of the following varieties: Bianco d'Alessano, Bombino, Chardonnay, Fiano, Garganega, Greco, Malvasia, Moscatello Selvatico, Moscato, Pampanuto, Pinot Bianco, Sauvignon, and Verdeca; and still or *frizzante passito* from one or more of the following: Aglianico, Bombino Nero, Pinot Nero, Sangiovese, and Uva di Troia.

NARDO DOC
Apulia

Cherry-red *rosato* wines from Negroamaro, with Malvasia Nera and Montepulciano permitted.

NASCO DI CAGLIARI DOC
See Cagliari DOC

NUORO *or* PROVINCIA DI NUORO IGT
Sardinia

This regional IGT allows still or *frizzante* red (may also be *novello*), white, and *passito* wines from any authorized varieties growing in the Nuoro province.

NURAGUS DI CAGLIARI DOC
See Cagliari DOC

NURRA *or* NURRA ALGHERESE IGT
Sardinia

Still and *frizzante* white; still, *frizzante*, and *novello* red; still and *frizzante passito* from authorized varieties growing in and around Alghero.

OGLIASTRA IGT
Sardinia

Still and *frizzante* white; still, *frizzante*, and *novello* red; and still and *frizzante passito* from authorized varieties growing in Arzana, Barisardo, Baunei, Cardedu, Elini, Gairloch, Girasole, Ierzu, Ilbono, Lanusei, Loceri, Lotzorai, Osini, Perdasdefogu, Seui, Talana, Tertenia, Tortoli, Triei, Ulassai, Urzulei, Ussassai, and Villagrande in Nuoro, and in Villaputzu and San Vito in Cagliari.

✓ *Jerzu* (Akratos, Radames)

ORTA NOVA DOC
Apulia

These are full-bodied red and dry *rosato* Sangiovese-based wines from the villages of Orta Nova and Ordona in the province of Foggia.

OSTUNI DOC
Apulia

A delicate, dry white made from Impigno and Francavidda and a light-bodied red from the Cinsault grape, known locally as Ottavianello, with the possible addition of Negroamaro, Notar Domenico, Malvasia Nera, and Susumaniello.

PAESTUM IGT
Campania

This IGT extends throughout most of the province

of Salerno, encompassing white (still, *frizzante*, *aamabile*, or *passito*), red (still, *novello*, *frizzante*, *aamabile*, or *passito*), and *passito* (still, *aamabile*, or *frizzante*) wines blended from any locally authorized variety, but varietal wines are restricted to the following: Aglianico, Barbera, Coda di Volpe, Fiano, Greco, Moscato, Piedirosso, Primitivo, and Sciascinoso.

✓ *De Conciliis* (Naima) • *Luigi Maffini* (Pietraincatenata) • *Montevetrano*

PALIZZI IGT
Calabria

Red, *novello* red, and dry *passito* wines from locally authorized varieties growing in Palizzi Staiti and its surrounding towns in the province of Reggio Calabria.

PARTEOLLA IGT
Sardinia

Still and *frizzante* red, white, and *passito* wine from locally authorized varieties growing in Dolianova, Donovan, Monastir, Serdiana, and Soleminis Ussana, in the province of Cagliari.

PELLARO IGT
Calabria

Red, *novello* red, and dry *passito* wines from locally authorized varieties growing in Pellaro and its surrounding towns in the province of Reggio Calabria.

PENISOLA SORRENTINA DOC
Campania

This is a relatively new DOC for former *vini da tavola* from the Sorrento peninsula, including a generic red (Piedirosso with the possible addition of Sciascinoso, Aglianico, and other unspecified non-aromatic varieties), which can also be made in a purple-coloured *frizzante* style, and a dry white generic (Falanghina with the possible addition of Biancolella, Greco, and other non-aromatic varieties). If the subzones Sorrento (for white and still red), Gragnano, or Lettere (red *frizzante*) appear on the label, the wines must conform to higher standards, including extra-ripe grapes.

PLANARGIA IGT
Sardinia

Still and *frizzante* red, white, and *passito* wine from locally authorized varieties growing in Bosa, Flussio, Magomadas, Modolo, Sagama, Suni, and Tinnura in the province of Nuoro and in Tresnuraghes in the province of Oristano.

POLLINO DOC
Calabria

Full, fruity, *chiaretto* wines from Gaglioppo, Greco Nero, Malvasia, and Guarnaccia.

POMPEIANO IGT
Campania

Obviously alluding to the ancient city of Pompeii, this IGT allows white (still, *frizzante*, *aamabile*, or *passito*), red (still, *novello*, frizzante, *liquoroso*, *aamabile*, or *passito*), and *passito* (still, *novello*, *liquoroso*, *aamabile*, or *frizzante*) from a wide range of grape varieties growing anywhere on the mainland in the province of Naples, but varietal wines are restricted to the following: Aglianico, Coda di Volpe, Falanghina, Piedirosso, and Sciascinoso.

✓ *Mastroberardino*

PRIMITIVO DI MANDURIA DOC
Apulia

Dry to semi-sweet, full-bodied red wines which may also be fortified and naturally sweet, and fortified and dry. Until I tasted Giordano's 1993 vintage in 1996, no Primitivo had shown any class.

🍷— 3–10 years

✓ *Cantolio Manduria* • *Fino* (ES) • *Gianfranco Giordano* • *Pervino* (Archidamo) • *Vinicola Savese* • *Soloperto* (CentoFuochi) • *Vigne & Vini* (Moi)

PROVINCIA DI NUORO IGT
See Nuoro IGT

PUGLIA IGT
Apulia

This region-wide IGT covers still and *frizzante* red (may also be *novello* or *passito*), white (may also be *passito*), and *passito* wine from locally authorized varieties growing anywhere in the Apulia region, plus a great many specified varietal wines: Aglianico, Aleatico, Bianco d'Alessano, Bombino, Bombino Nero, Cabernet Franc, Cabernet Sauvignon, Chardonnay, Falanghina, Fiano, Greco, Lambrusco, Malvasia, Malvasia Nera, Moscatello Selvatico, Moscato, Negroamaro, Pampanuto, Pinot Bianco, Pinot Nero, Primitivo, Riesling, Sangiovese, Sauvignon, Trebbiano, Uva di Troia, and Verdeca.

✓ *Rasciatano* • *TorreVento* (Kebir, MaterVitae Aglianico) • *Vigne & Vini* (Primadonna Chardonnay)

RIESI DOC
Sicily

This DOC covers just three wines: a Calabrese- and/or Cabernet Sauvignon-based dry red, which may be *novello*, aged 24 months, or, if labelled *riserva*, aged 36 months; an Ansonica- and/or Chardonnay-based white, which may be dry and still, *spumante*, or sweet *vendemmia tardiva*; and a Calabrese-based dry *passito*.

ROCCAMONFINA IGT
Campania

This IGT includes white (still, *frizzante*, *aamabile*, or *passito*), red (still, *novello*, *frizzante*, *aamabile*, or *passito*), and *passito* (still, *aamabile*, or *frizzante*) from a wide range of varieties growing in Roccaromana and surrounding villages in the province of Caserta, but varietal wines are restricted to Aglianico, Coda di Volpe, Falanghina, Fiano, Greco, Piedirosso, Primitivo, and Sciascinoso.

✓ *Galardi* (Terra di Lavoro) • *Villa Matilde* (Cecubo, Eleusi)

ROMANGIA IGT
Sardinia

Still and *frizzante* white; still, *frizzante*, and *novello* red; still and *frizzante passito* from authorized varieties growing in Castelsardo, Osilo, Sennori, Sorso, and Valledoria in the province Sassari, with the following specific varietal exceptions: Cannonau, Carignano, Girò, Malvasia, Monica, Moscato, Nasco, Nuragus, Semidano, Vermentino, and Vernaccia.

✓ *Tenute Dettori* (Bianco, Rosso, Tenores)

ROSSO BARLETTA DOC
Apulia

Medium-bodied, ruby-coloured, everyday-quality red wines made from Uva di Troia with the possible addition of Montepulciano, Sangiovese, and a small amount of Malbec. Most Rosso Barletta is consumed locally when very young.

ROSSO CANOSA DOC
See Canasium DOC

ROSSO DI CERIGNOLA DOC
Apulia

Rare, rustic reds from Negroamaro and Uva di Troia with the possible addition of Sangiovese, Barbera, Montepulciano, Malbec, and Trebbiano.

SALAPARUTA DOC
Sicily

This DOC on the eastern fringe of the Marsala region allows a Catarratto-based generic dry white, a Nero d'Avola-based generic red, a Nero d'Avola-Merlot based generic dry *passito*, four white varietals (Catarratto, Chardonnay, Grillo, and Inzolia), and four red varietals (Cabernet Sauvignon, Merlot, Nero d'Avola, and Syrah).

SALEMI IGT
Sicily

This IGT is restricted to still and *frizzante* white; still, *frizzante*, and *novello* red; and still and *frizzante passito* from Ansonica, Catarratto, Grecanico (aka Garganega), and Damaschino grapes only. The wines may be blended or pure varietal.

SALENTO IGT
Apulia

This IGT includes white (still, *frizzante*, or *passito*), red (still, *novello*, *frizzante*, or *passito*), and *passito* (still or *frizzante*) from a wide range of grape varieties growing in the provinces of Brindisi, Lecce, and Taranto, but varietal wines are restricted to the following: Aglianico, Cabernet Franc, Cabernet Sauvignon, Lambrusco, Negroamaro and Primitivo for reds; and Bombino, Chardonnay, Fiano, Garganega, Greco, Malvasia, Moscato, Pinot Bianco, Sauvignon, Trebbiano, Verdeca, and Vermentino for whites.

✓ *Conti Zecca* (Cantaloupe Riserva, Fiano, Negroamaro, Nero, Primitivo, Sole) • *Vinicola Mediterranea* (Don Vito, Il Nobile) • *Morella* (La Signora) • *Vigne & Vini* (Schiaccianoci) • *Tenute Rubino* (Negroamaro, TorreTesta, Visellio) • *Tormaresca* (Masseria Màime, Torcicoda) • *Vallone* (Gratticciaia) • *Vetrere* (Barone Pazzo, Taranto Rosato, Tempio di Giano)

SALICE SALENTINO DOC
Apulia

Full-bodied reds and smooth, alcoholic *rosati* from Negroamaro with the possible addition of Malvasia Nera, and more recently two dry whites: a Chardonnay, which may be *frizzante*, and a Pinot Bianco, which may be *spumante*; plus a sweet red Aleatico, which can be fortified. The Negroamaro-based reds are still the best wines in this DOC.

🍷— 3–7 years

✓ *Francesco Candido* • *Due Palmi* • *Leone de Castris* • *Vinicola Mediterranea* (Granduca, Sirio) • *Cosimo Taurino* • *Vallone*

SALINA IGT
Sicily

This IGT includes white (still, *frizzante*, or *passito*), red (still, *novello*, or *frizzante*), and *passito* (still or *frizzante*) from the island of Lipari. All grapes authorized for the province of Messina are allowed, but local resources are limited, and the most likely varieties in any blend will probably be Alicante, Calabrese, Corinto, Nerello, Nero d'Avola, Nocera, or Sangiovese for reds, and Catarratto, Grecanico (aka Garganega), Grillo, or, mostly, Malvasia for whites.

✓ *Hauner* (Hierà, Malvasia Passito)

SAMBUCA DI SICILIA DOC
Sicily

An Asonica-based white that may be either dry or *passito*; a Nero d'Avola dry red and *passito*, plus five red varietals (Cabernet Sauvignon, Merlot, Nero d'Avola, Sangiovese, and Syrah); and three white varietals (Ansonica, Chardonnay, and Greciano).

SANNIO DOC
Campania

This is the modern equivalent of Samnium – a famous ancient Roman wine described by Pliny, Columella, Cato, and Horace – but rather than focusing on one style to resurrect that reputation, this is yet another typically wide-ranging DOC, allowing Trebbiano-based generic white, which may be still and dry, or *frizzante*; a Sangiovese-based red and *passito*, which must be dry and may be still but could also be *frizzante* or *novello*; a generic *spumante* that must contain Aglianico, Greco, or Falanghina to the exclusion of all other varieties and must be aged at least 14 months before release; five red varietals (Aglianico, Barbera, Piedirosso, Primitivo, and Sciascinoso); and five white varietals (Coda di Volpe, Falanghina, Fiano, Greco, and Moscato).

✓ *Mastroberardino* • *Feudi di San Gregorio* (Falanghina)

SANT'AGATA DEI GOTI DOC
Campania

Relatively new DOC for generic red, dry white, and *rosato* from Aglianico and Piedirosso (thus the white is a *blanc de noirs*); two red wine varietals, Aglianico and Piedirosso; and two white varietals, Greco and Falanghina.

SANT'ANNA DI ISOLA CAPO RIZZUTO DOC
Calabria

Vinous reds and *rosati* from Gaglioppo, Greco Nero, and Guarnaccia grapes from the Ionian hills.

SANTA MARGHERITA DI BELICE DOC
Sicily

An Asonica-, Grecanico-, or Catarratto-based white; a Nero d'Avola-, Sangiovese-, or Cabernet Sauvignon-based red; plus two red varietals (Nero d'Avola and Sangiovese) and three white varietals (Ansonica, Cataratto, and Greciano).

SAN SEVERO DOC
Apulia

Dry, vinous red and *rosato* wines made from Montepulciano and Sangiovese, and dry, fresh whites from Bombino and Trebbiano, with the possible addition of Malvasia and Verdeca.

SAN VITO DI LUZZI DOC
Calabria

A new DOC covering generic red, *rosato* (Gaglioppo and Malvasia with the possible addition of Greco Nero and Sangiovese), and dry white (Malvasia,

Grechetto, and Trebbiano) wines produced in and near the village of Luzzi in the province of Conseza.

SARDEGNA SEMIDANO DOC
Sardinia

This DOC is for wines made from grapes grown throughout the island, although in practice they are generally restricted to traditional areas. For Moscato, vines must not be grown above 450 metres (1,476 feet). Moscato di Sardegna is sweet and surprisingly delicate, usually in a natural still-wine style, although *spumante* is produced and the sub-appellations Tempio Pausania, Tempio, and Gallura are reserved for sparkling wines in the Gallura area. Monica di Sardegna is a fragrant red wine that may be dry or sweet, still or *frizzante*, but unlike Monica di Cagliari, is never fortified. Vermentino di Sardegna is a light-bodied, soft, clean, unexciting dry white wine that all too often has its flavours washed out by cool fermentation techniques. Cannonau (aka Grenache), is this DOC's most successful varietal, especially as a dry red, although it may also be produced as semi-sweet or sweet red, *rosato*, and *liquoroso*.

✓ *Antonio Argiolas* • *Carpante* (Vermentino Frinas, Vermentino Longhera) • *Pala* (Monica, Vermentino) • *Pedres* (Moscato) • *CS di Santadi* (Vermentino Cala Silente)
Cannonau *Carpante* • *Contini* (Inu Reserva, Tonaghe) • *Ferruccio Deiana* (Síleno) • *Cantine Dolinova* (Azenas) • *Dorgali* • *Feudi della Medusa* • *Giuseppe Gabbas* • *Giorgantinu* • *Jerzu* • *Alberto Loi* • *Piero Mancini* • *Giuseppe Sedilesu* (Mamuthone) • *Tenute Soletta*

SAVUTO DOC
Calabria

Fresh, fruity red or *rosato* wines from Gaglioppo, Greco Nero, Nerello, Sangiovese, Malvasia, and Pecorino grapes grown in Catanzaro province.

🍷 1–3 years

✓ *Odoardi* (Vigna Vecchia)

SCAVIGNA DOC
Calabria

Generic red, *rosato* (Gaglioppo, Nerello, and Aglianico) and a fruity dry white (Trebbiano, Chardonnay, Grechetto, and Malvasia) from the communes of Nocera Terinese and Falerna.

🍷 1–3 years

✓ *Abbazia Sant'Anastasia* (Passomaggio)

SCIACCA DOC
Sicily

An Inzolia-, Grecanico-, or Chardonnay-based white; a Merlot-, Nero d'Avola-, Sangiovese-, or Cabernet Sauvignon-based red and dry *passito*; plus four red varietals (Cabernet Sauvignon, Merlot, Nero d'Avola, and Sangiovese) and three white varietals (Ansonica, Cataratto, and Greciano). Riserva Rayna is a sub-zonal denomination for a Catarratto- and/or Inzolia-based dry white that must be aged for at least 24 months.

SCILLA IGT
Calabria

Red, *novello* red, and dry *passito* from any locally authorized variety growing in Scilla in the province of Reggio Calabria.

SIBIOLA IGT
Sardinia

Still or *frizzante* red, white, and *passito* from Serdiana and Soleminis in the province of Sassari

from any locally authorized grape variety, with the specific exclusion of Cannonau, Carignano, Girò, Malvasia, Monica, Moscato, Nasco, Nuragus, Semidano, Vermentino, and Vernaccia. Reds may also be sold as *novello*.

SICILIA IGT
Sicily

All – not just most – of the very best wines produced on this island are sold under this IGT, and considering Sicily's reputation up to now, the prices that some of these wines achieve should be an object lesson to all the odd, obscure IGTs on the mainland.

✓ *Benanti* (Il Drappo, Lamorèmio, Majora) • *Cottanera* (Sole di Sesta) • *Cusumano* (Noà, Sàgana) • *Duca di Salaparuta* (Bianca di Valguarnera, Duca Enric, Kados, Lavico) • *Fatascià* (Almanera) • *Feuda Principi di Butera* (Deliella) • *Feudi del Pisciotto* (Versace) • *Feudo Maccari* (Saia) • *Firriato* (Camalot, Harmonium) • *Gulfi* (Nerosanlore', Neromaccarj) • *MandraRossa* (especially Cartagho) • *Morgante* (Don Antonio) • *Passo Pisciaro* • *Planeta* (Burdese, Cometa, Merlot, Santa Cecilia, Syrah) • *Santa Anastasia* (Litra) • *Spadafore* (Sole dei Padri) • *Tasca d'Almerita* (Contea di Sciafani, Cabernet Sauvignon) • *Tenute Rapitala* (Hugonis, Nuhair, Solinero) • *Trapani* (Forti Terre Cabernet Sauvignon) • *Valle dell'Acate* (Bidis, Il Moro, Rusciano, Tanè)

SOLOPACA DOC
Campania

Smooth generic red and *rosato* (Sangiovese and Aglianico with the possible addition of Piedirosso, Sciascinoso, and up to 30 per cent pick-and-mix), generic dry white (Trebbiano, Falanghina, Malvasia, and Coda di Volpe), one red wine varietal (Aglianico) and one white varietal (Falanghina – still or *spumante*). Solopaca comes from the Calore Valley.

🍷 1–4 years

✓ *Antica Masseria Venditti*

SORRENTO DOC
See Penisola Sorrentina DOC

SQUINZANO DOC
Apulia

Full-bodied red wines and lightly scented *rosato* wines from Negroamaro with the possible addition of Sangiovese and Malvasia Nera, grown in Squinzano and the surrounding communes.

🍷 2–4 years (red), upon purchase (*rosato*)

✓ *Villa Valletta*

TABURNO DOC
Campania

This DOC started out life as Aglianico del Taburno in red and *rosato*, but it is one of those DOCs that just grows. It now includes a generic red (Sangiovese and Aglianico); white (Trebbiano and Falanghina, plus 30 per cent pick-and-mix); a *spumante* (Coda di Volpe and Falanghina, plus 40 per cent pick-and-mix); three white wine varietals (Falanghina, Greco, and Coda di Volpe); and one red (Piedirosso).

✓ *Cantina del Taburno* (Blue Apis)

TARANTINO IGT
Apulia

Still and *frizzante* red (may also be *novello* or *passito*), white (may also be *passito*), and *passito* wine from locally authorized varieties (with the specific exception of either Montepulciano or Ottavianello) growing in the province of Taranto. Only two varietal wines are allowed: Negroamaro and Malvasia Nera.

✓ *Vigne & Vini*

TAURASI DOCG
Campania

Red wines made primarily from Aglianico grapes (up to 15 per cent in total of Barbera, Piedirosso, and Sangiovese may be added) that are grown in Taurasi and 16 nearby villages. It was elevated to DOCG status in 1993. Along with Basilicata's thicker tasting Aglianico del Vulture, it is one of the country's greatest wines from this underrated grape variety, in an equally age-worthy style. Mastroberardino's *riserva* excels.

⌛ 5–10 years (some may last for as long as 20)

✓ *Antonio Caggiano* • *Di Prisco* • *Mastroberardino* • *Perillo* • *Giovanni Struzziero* • *Urciuolo*

TERRALBA DOC
See Campidano di Terralba DOC

TERRE DEL VOLTURNO IGT
Campania

This IGT covers most of the province of Casera, plus the towns of Giugliano, Qualiano, and Sant'Antimo in the province of Naples. The wines include a white (still, *frizzante*, *aamabile*, or *passito*), red (still, *novello*, *frizzante*, *aamabile*, or *passito*), and passito (still, *aamabile*, or *frizzante*) from a wide range of grape varieties growing in Roccaromana and surrounding villages in the province of Caserta, but varietal wines are restricted to the following: Aglianico, Asprinio, Cassavecchia, Coda di Volpe, Falanghina, Fiano, Greco, Pallagrello Nero, Primitivo, and Sciascinoso.

✓ *Vestini* (Cavavecchia, Kaja Nero) • *Terre del Principe* (Centomoggio)

TERRE DELL'ALTA VAL D'AGRI DOC
Basilicata

A relatively small DOC in the hills of Viggiano, Moliterno, and Grumento Nova, approaching the southeastern border of Campania, where a red and dry *passito* Merlot-Cabernet can be made.

THARROS IGT
Sardinia

Still or *frizzante* red, white, and *passito* produced in the province of Oristano from any locally authorized grape variety, with the specific exclusion of Cannonau, Carignano, Girò, Malvasia, Monica, Moscato, Nasco, Nuragus, Semidano, Vermentino, and Vernaccia. Reds may also be sold as *novello*.

TREXENTA IGT
Sardinia

Still or *frizzante* red, white, and *passito* produced in part of the province of Cagliari from any locally authorized grape variety, with the specific exclusion of Cannonau, Carignano, Girò, Malvasia, Monica, Moscato, Nasco, Nuragus, Semidano, Vermentino, and Vernaccia. Reds may also be sold as *novello*.

✓ *Cantina Trexenta*

VALLE BELICE IGT
Sicily

This IGT includes white (still, *frizzante*, or *passito*), red (still, *novello*, or *frizzante*), and *passito* (still or *frizzante*) from locally authorized grape varieties growing in the Belice Valley as it passes through Menfi, Montevago, and Santa Margherita Belice in the province of Agrigento and in Contessa Entellina in the province of Palermo.

VALLE DEL CRATI IGT
Calabria

This IGT includes white (still, *frizzante*, or *passito*), red (still, *novello*, or *frizzante*), and *passito* (still or *frizzante*) from locally authorized grape varieties growing throughout the Crati Valley in the province of Cosenza.

VALLE D'ITRIA IGT
Apulia

This IGT includes white (still, *frizzante*, or *passito*), red (still, *passito*, *novello*, or *frizzante*), and *passito* (still or *frizzante*) from locally authorized grape varieties growing in the Itria Valley throughout the provinces of Bari, Brindisi, and Taranto. Varietal wines are restricted to the following: Aleatico, Cabernet Franc, Cabernet Sauvignon, Malvasia Nera, Negroamaro, Pinot Nero, Primitivo, and Sangiovese for red and *passito* wines; and Bianco d'Alessano, Bombino, Chardonnay, Fiano, Impigno, Malvasia, Moscatello Selvatico, Moscato, Pinot Bianco, Sauvignon, Trebbiano, and Verdeca for whites.

VAL DI NETO IGT
Calabria

This IGT includes white (still, *frizzante*, or *passito*), red (still, *novello*, or *frizzante*), and *passito* (still or *frizzante*) from locally authorized grape varieties in the Neto Valley in the province of Crotone.

✓ *Librandi* (Gravello, Magno Megonio, Le Passule)

VALLI DI PORTO PINO IGT
Sardinia

Still or *frizzante* red, white, and *passito* produced in Giba, Masainas Narcao, Nuxis, Perdaxius, Piscinas, Santadi, Sant'Anna Arresi, Teulada, Tratalias, and Villaperuccio in the province of Cagliari from any locally authorized grape variety, with the specific exclusion of Cannonau, Carignano, Girò, Malvasia, Monica, Moscato, Nasco, Nuragus, Semidano, Vermentino, and Vernaccia. Reds may also be sold as *novello*.

VALLE DEL TIRSO IGT
Sardinia

Still or *frizzante* red, white, and *passito* produced in the Tirso Valley in the province of Oristano from any locally authorized grape variety, with the specific exclusion of Cannonau, Carignano, Girò, Malvasia, Monica, Moscato, Nasco, Nuragus, Semidano, and Vermentino. Reds may also be sold as *novello*.

✓ *Antilio Contini* (Barrile, Nieddera Rosso)

VALDAMATO IGT
Calabria

This IGT includes white (still, *frizzante*, or *passito*), red (still, *novello*, or *frizzante*), and *passito* (still or *frizzante*) from locally authorized grape varieties growing in Curinga, Feroleto, Gizzeria, Lamezia Terme, Maida, and Maida Pianopoli San Pietro in the province of Catanzaro.

VERBICARO DOC
Calabria

A large but fairly focused DOC encompassing just three wines: a dry white based on Greco, Malvasia, or Guarnaccia Bianca (aka Grenache Blanc) and a red or dry *passito* based Gaglioppo (the local name for the Grenache) or Greco Nero.

VERMENTINO DI GALLURA DOCG
Sardinia

Despite cool fermentation, this is the best Vermentino Sardinia offers, the hilly *terroir* of Gallura producing intense flavours. Although this wine was elevated to DOCG status in 1997, it could be much better quality and cheaper to make if fermented at slightly higher temperatures.

⌛ 1–2 years

✓ *Tenuta di Capichera* • *CS di Gallura* • *Giorgantinu* • *Piero Mancini* • *Masone Mannu* • *Pedres* • *CS del Vermentino*

VERMENTINO DI SARDEGNA DOC
See Sardegna DOC

VERNACCIA DI ORISTANO DOC
Sardinia

The DOC of Vernaccia di Oristano makes dry and lightly bitter white wines, which are sherry-like in style. Also produced are *liquoroso* sweet and dry wines.

⌛ Upon purchase

✓ *Contini* • *Fratelli Serra*

VESUVIO DOC
Campania

Restricted to vines on the volcanic slopes of Mount Vesuvius, a generic dry white (Coda di Volpe and Verdeca grapes, with the possible addition of Falanghina and Greco), and a generic *rosato* (Piedirosso and Sciascinoso with the possible addition of Aglianico) are produced by Vesuvio DOC. Those that are labelled Lacryma (or Lacrima) Christi del Vesuvio are usually dry white wines, but less commonly they may also be *spumante* or sweet and fortified.

VITTORIA DOC
Sicily

When Cerasuolo di Vittoria gained its DOCG status in 2005, this DOC was created for red wines that are also produced from Nero d'Avola and Nerello grapes but with slightly more Nero d'Avola. The wines may be sold as *novello*, so they can be a tad softer. There are also three varietal wines, all red: Ansonica (aka Inzolia and may be labelled Inzolia or Insolia), Calabrese (aka Nero d'Avola and may be labelled Nero d'Avola), and Frappato (aka Nerello).

The WINES of
SPAIN

Spain continues to overperform, providing more wines of real interest and quality than the most optimistic critic could reasonably hope for. Why do I say that? For a start, as indigenous grape varieties go, Tempranillo is Spain's only class act. Furthermore, although most Spanish vineyards are not totally lacking in potential (otherwise we would not have witnessed the revolution in Spanish wines that we have), there are no really world-class *terroirs* to be found beyond parts of Rioja, Penedès, and the Ribera del Duero. Yet the number of truly fine Spanish wines continues to increase, with at least as much excitement at the lower end of the quality scale as at the higher end. As recently as the 1980s, with the general exception of Rioja, most Spanish wines were either oxidized or over-sulphured. Never has an established, traditional winemaking nation got its act together as quickly or as thoroughly as Spain.

BODEGAS YSIOS, RIOJA
Set at the foot of Sierra de Cantabria, this ultra-modern winery was designed by the Spanish architect Santiago Calatrava, whose many other works include Dublin's Samuel Beckett Bridge.

SPAIN

In the early 1970s, Spanish wines had such a bad reputation that, by comparison, Italian wines seemed preferable. By the late 1980s, however, the wines of Spain were being taken seriously, whereas those of Italy generally were not.

THAT SPAIN COULD ACHIEVE such a swift turn-around in the quality of its wines can be put down to its efforts to get out of the bulk wine market. The Spanish did not stop selling bulk wine altogether, but prevented this low-quality product from dominating exports. By its very volume, bulk wine dilutes and downgrades a country's winemaking reputation, and in the 1970s Spanish bulk wine was so bad that the country's worsening image threatened to undermine its share of global markets just as the culture of wine drinking was developing in the USA, UK, and other potentially lucrative markets. It was not as if there was a meeting at which the entire Spanish wine industry took a vote

to change things, but there must have been some sort of industry-wide determination to improve quality because the situation was reversed so quickly. Spain's reputation leap-frogged Italy's, despite having much less going for it in terms of native grape varieties and *terroirs*, establishing the country as one of the best-value sources in Europe.

ANCIENT ORIGINS
Vines were first planted in Spain *c.*1100 BC around Cádiz by, it is believed, the Phoenicians. The earliest wines were by all accounts rich, sweet, and heavy, the precursors of modern-day sherry. However, from the start of the 8th century until the end of the 15th, southern Spain was under the rule of the Moors, and being Mohammedans, wine production was not a priority. This is not to say that the Moors never drank wine; indeed, Al-Motamid, the last Moorish king of Seville, enjoyed wine so much that he publicly mocked anyone who drank water. The Moors also enjoyed the grape as a fruit and for its fresh, unfermented juice, but under a theoretically abstemious rule, winemaking stagnated. So, while

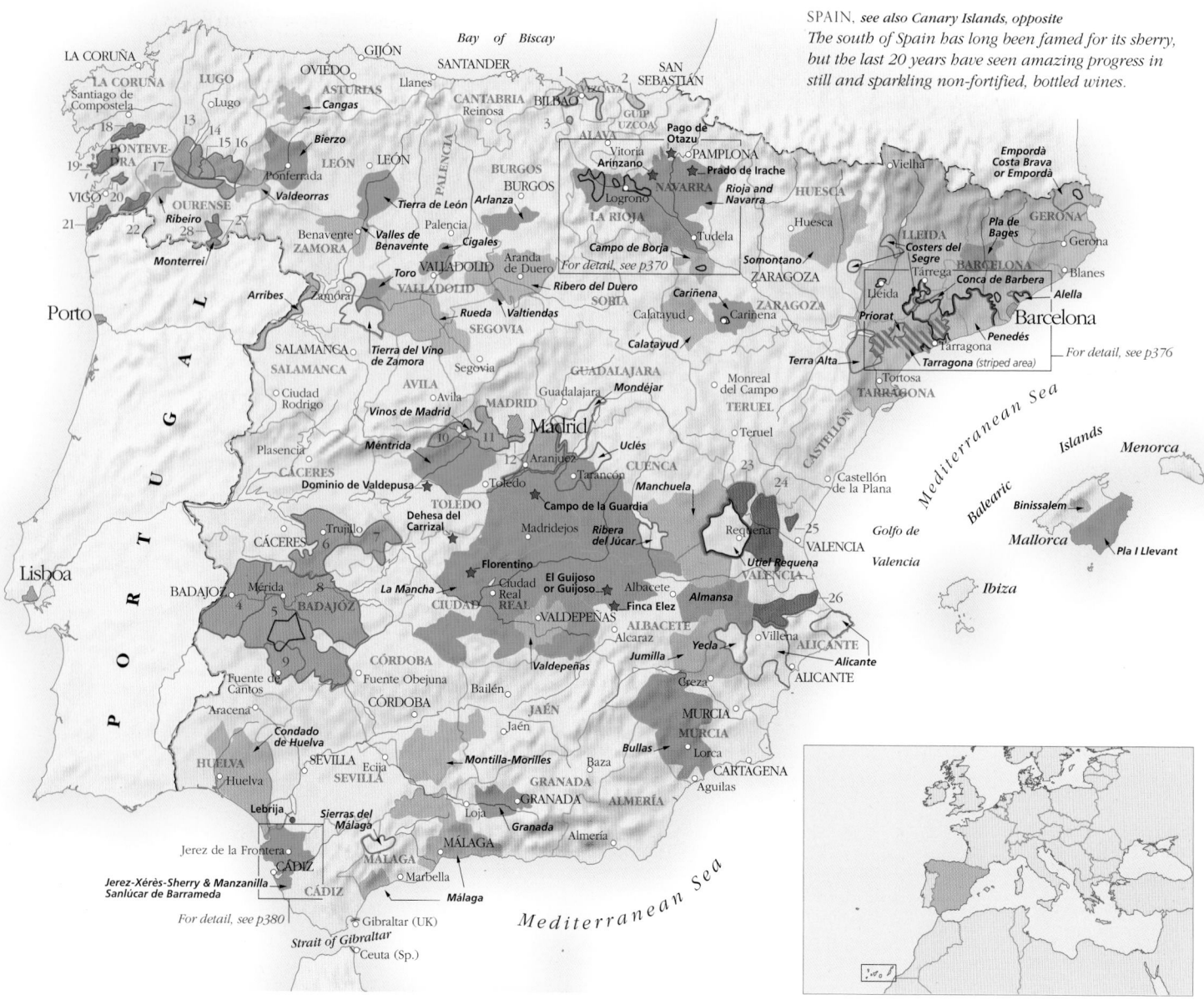

SPAIN, *see also Canary Islands, opposite*
The south of Spain has long been famed for its sherry, but the last 20 years have seen amazing progress in still and sparkling non-fortified, bottled wines.

RECENT SPANISH VINTAGES

2010 The cool but dry summer and autumn allowed the crop to ripen slowly, preserving better acidity levels than usual and resulting in a potentially excellent vintage the length and breadth of Spain.

2009 Potentially excellent in Rioja, Catalunya, and northwestern Spain; good to very good elsewhere, though less consistent.

2008 A relatively cool year with too much rain in places. This is an inconsistent vintage, with the best wines found in Navarra and northwestern Spain. Catalunya and Rueda are not bad, but they require selection.

2007 A mixed, and in some places very difficult, vintage. The standouts were Navarra and Catalunya.

2006 Some great wines, but generally good to very good. Whites are less successful, except around Bilbao and in northwestern Spain.

TRADITIONAL VERSUS MODERN STYLES

It used to be possible to speak of new-wave Spanish wines, as the tradition had been to leave wines in oak for longer than most modern winemakers consider wise and a younger generation of winemakers reacted by producing wines that were as fresh, clean, and unoaked as possible. However, although the old style for reds was dried-out and that for whites oxidized, the new style was so clean, it was clinical, and was no great improvement as such. The tendency now is to talk of modern style rather than new-wave, as the wines are much fruitier and the use of oak is not so much avoided, as restrained, with French casks more likely than American, and fermented rather than aged.

Spain can claim a 3,000-year history of wine, the diversity of its wine areas and styles did not commence until the 1490s, just 30 years before the Spanish planted the first vines in the Americas. Some parts of the Old and New Worlds are much closer in age, in terms of winemaking, than these terms imply.

SPAIN'S BEST WINES AND ITS APPELLATION SYSTEM

Vega Sicilia in the Ribera del Duero was once definitively Spain's most expensive wine, leading many to believe that it must be Spain's greatest. Others can now lay equal claim to be the most

THE HILLTOP TOWN OF LAGUARDIA
Set against the majestic backdrop of the Sierra de Cantabria is the hilltop town of Laguardia, which boasts some of the finest vineyards of the Rioja Alava.

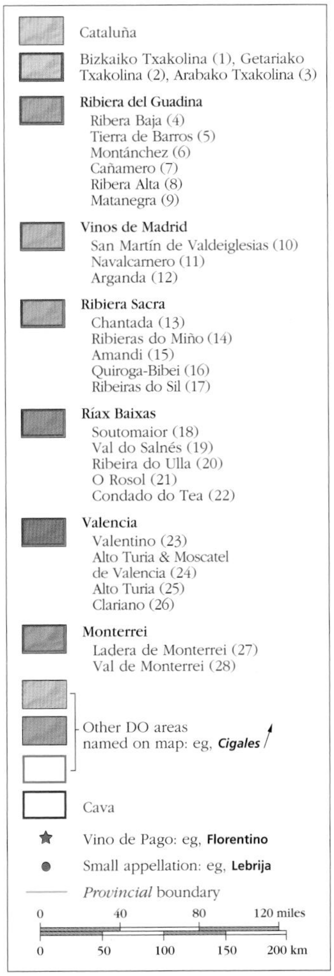

CANARY ISLANDS (BELOW)
The first of these appellations was established in 1992, but "Canary sack" was famous in Shakespeare's time.

Map legend (left column):

- Cataluña
- Bizkaiko Txakolina (1), Getariako Txakolina (2), Arabako Txakolina (3)
- Ribiera del Guadina
  - Ribera Baja (4)
  - Tierra de Barros (5)
  - Montánchez (6)
  - Cañamero (7)
  - Ribera Alta (8)
  - Matanegra (9)
- Vinos de Madrid
  - San Martín de Valdeiglesias (10)
  - Navalcarnero (11)
  - Arganda (12)
- Ribiera Sacra
  - Chantada (13)
  - Ribieras do Miño (14)
  - Amandi (15)
  - Quiroga-Bibei (16)
  - Ribeiras do Sil (17)
- Ríax Baixas
  - Soutomaior (18)
  - Val do Salnés (19)
  - Ribeira do Ulla (20)
  - O Rosol (21)
  - Condado do Tea (22)
- Valencia
  - Valentino (23)
  - Alto Turia & Moscatel de Valencia (24)
  - Alto Turia (25)
  - Clariano (26)
- Monterrei
  - Ladera de Monterrei (27)
  - Val de Monterrei (28)
- Other DO areas named on map: eg, *Cigales*
- Cava
- ★ Vino de Pago: eg, **Florentino**
- ● Small appellation: eg, **Lebrija**
- —— *Provincial* boundary

0   40   80   120 miles
0 50 100 150 200 km

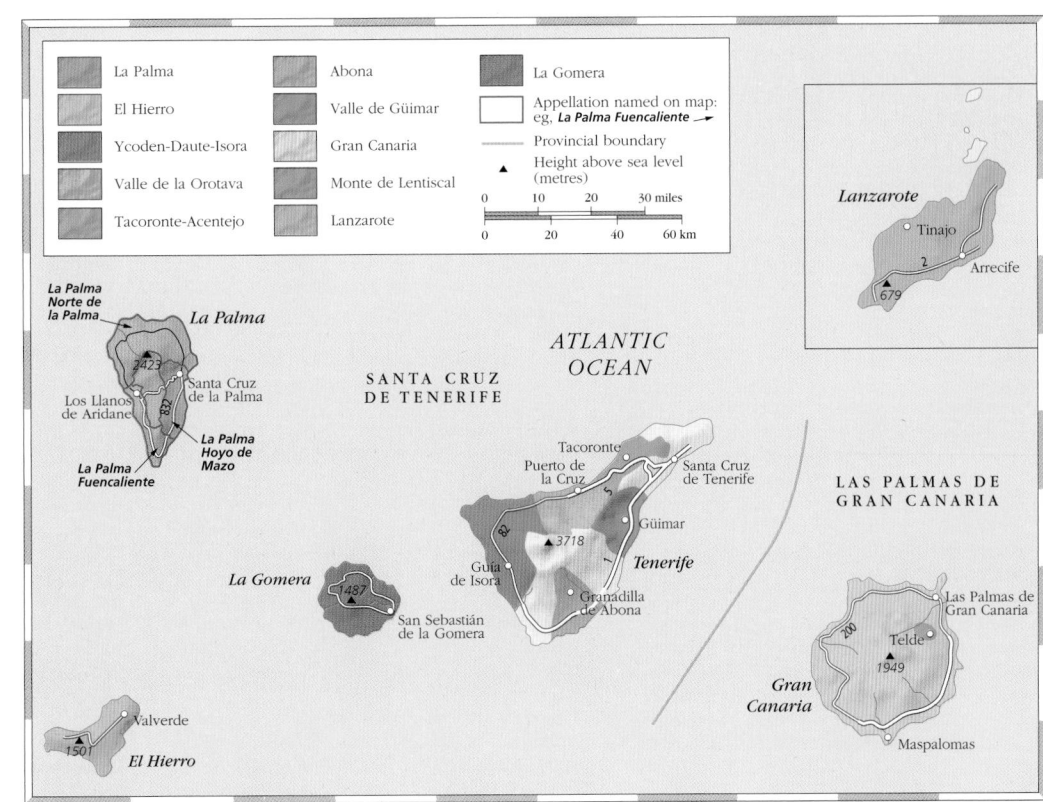

Canary Islands map legend:

- La Palma
- El Hierro
- Ycoden-Daute-Isora
- Valle de la Orotava
- Tacoronte-Acentejo
- Abona
- Valle de Güimar
- Gran Canaria
- Monte de Lentiscal
- Lanzarote
- La Gomera
- Appellation named on map: eg, *La Palma Fuencaliente* →
- —— Provincial boundary
- ▲ Height above sea level (metres)

0   10   20   30 miles
0   20   40   60 km

expensive and greatest of Spanish wines (Clos l'Ermita, Dominio de Pingus, and Cirsión are likely candidates), and many more are equal in quality if not quite as ridiculously priced, including Pesquera, Rioja (Contino, Barón de Ley, Muga Prado Enea, Murrieta Castillo Ygay Gran Reserva), Penedès (Torres and Jean Léon), and even some non-appellation wines such as Marqués de Griñón.

The *Denominación de Origen* (DO) system is Spain's equivalent of the French *Appellation d'Origine Contrôlée* (AOC) or Italian *Denominazione di Origine Controllata* (DOC) systems. The only higher Spanish classification is *Denominación de Origen Calificada* (DOCa), and Rioja remains the only recipient of this superior status since its inception in 1981, although other high-quality wines may be promoted to DOCa in the future. Ribera del Duero, Navarra, Penedès, and Cava all spring to mind as candidates for such promotion. If there is a lesson the Spanish could learn from Italy, it is not to overlook outstanding non-appellation wines such as Marqués de Griñón's Cabernet Sauvignon and Syrah from south of Madrid. Indisputably two of Spain's great wines, they should jump from DO straight to DOCa status, if Spain's regime is to avoid the same fate as Italy's, whose best *vini da tavola* were forced to build up reputations at the expense of the official system.

SPANISH LABEL LANGUAGE

Adega Winery

Añada Wine from a single vintage

Añejo Aged for 12 months in cask or bottle

Blanco White

Bodega Literally a "wine cellar", commonly used as part of the name of a wine firm

Cava A sparkling DO wine produced using the traditional method

Clarete Mid-way between light red and dark *rosado*, synonymous with *tintillo*

Cosecha Means vintage, and indicates that a minimum of 85 per cent of a wine thus labelled is produced in the year marked

Cosechero A fresh, fruity, "new" or nouveau style wine, synonymous with *nuevo* and *vino joven*, and usually a *Viñedos de España* (or *vino de mesa* in those regions that have not adopted this denomination)

Criado y embotellado por Blended and bottled by

Crianza A red *crianza* must be aged for a minimum of 2 years (of which at least 6 months must be in oak); a white or *rosado crianza* requires 1 year of ageing (with at least 6 months in oak)

Crianza corta Wines that have less than the legal minimum cask-age for any cask-age designation. Synonymous with *sin crianza*

Denominación de Origen (DO) Wine that originates from a controlled-quality wine region

Denominación de Origen Calificada (DOCa) The highest official classification, above *Denominación de Origen*

Doble pasta This term refers to red wines that have been macerated with double the normal proportion of grape skins to juice during fermentation. Such wines are opaque, with an intense colour, and may be sold in the bottle or for blending.

Dulce Sweet

Embotellado por Bottled by

Espumoso A sparkling wine made by any method

Generoso A fortified or dessert wine

Gran Reserva Red wines must be at least 5 years old, with a minimum of 18 months in oak. White and *rosado gran reservas* must be at least 4 years old, with a minimum of 6 months in oak

Noble Aged for 2 years in cask or bottle

Nuevo A fresh, fruity, "new" or nouveau style wine, synonymous with *cosechero* and *vino joven*, and usually a *Viñedos de España* (or *vino de mesa* in those regions that have not adopted this denomination)

Pago A wine from a single vineyard, which may or may not be a *pago* denomination (effectively a single-vineyard DO, which is a sort of "*grand cru*" appellation)

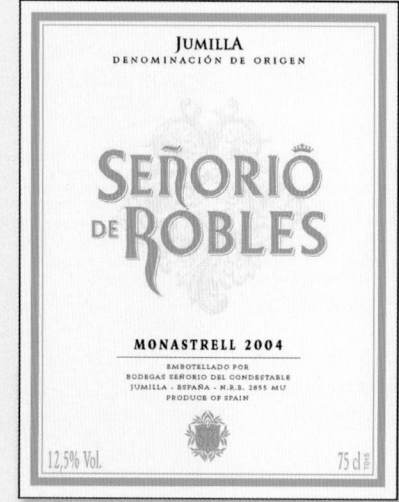

JUMILLA
DENOMINACIÓN DE ORIGEN

SEÑORIO DE ROBLES

MONASTRELL 2004

EMBOTELLADO POR
BODEGAS SEÑORIO DEL CONDESTABLE
JUMILLA · ESPAÑA · N.R.E. 2855 MU
PRODUCE OF SPAIN

12,5% Vol. 75 d℮

ROMERAL

CRIANZA

RIOJA
Denominación de Origen Calificada

Reserva Red wines must be at least 3 years old, with a minimum of 12 months in oak. White and *rosado reservas* must be at least 18 months old, with a minimum of 6 months in oak.

Rosado Rosé

Seco Dry

Semidulce Medium-sweet

Semiseco Medium-dry (which is as "dry" as *demi-sec* in France)

Sin crianza A wine without wood-ageing, including all cool-fermented, early-bottled white and most *rosado* wines. The term *sin crianza* is falling out of use, in favour of *vino joven*

Tintillo Mid-way between light red and dark *rosado*, synonymous with *clarete*

Tinto Red

Viejo A term that literally means "old". Use of this term was not controlled by law until 2005; since then, a *viejo* wine must be aged for at least 3 years.

Viña or **viñedo** Literally "vineyard", but often merely part of a brand name, and nothing to do with a specific vineyard

Viñedos de España The equivalent of *Vin de France*, this new denomination takes advantage of EU laws that have dispensed with all national forms of *vin de table* (formerly *vino de mesa* in Spain) and now permit such wines to be labelled with the vintage and grape variety. Various regions have opted out of this new denomination (at the time of writing, these included the Canaries, Balearics, Asturias, and Cantabria), so *vino de mesa* will be around for the time being at least.

Vino añejo A wine that has been aged in oak or in bottle for at least 24 months

Vino comarcal A regional wine, above *Viñedos de España* (or *vino de mesa* in those regions that have not adopted this denomination) and below *vino de la tierra*

Vino de aguja A semi-sparkling, or *pétillant*, wine

Vino de calidad con indicación geográfica A stepping stone between *Vino de la tierra* and *Denominación de Origen*

Vino de crianza Red wines must be at least 2 years old, with a minimum of 6 months in oak. White wines must be at least 18 months old, but with no oak-ageing requirement

Vino de la tierra Literally "country wine"

Vino de licór A sweet, possibly fortified wine

Vino de mesa Literally "table wine"; likely to be seen on the labels of very ordinary, inexpensive wines

Vino de pasto An ordinary, inexpensive, and often light style of wine

Vino joven Wine made to be drunk within the year. There are moves to replace the term *sin crianza* with *vino joven*, but while wines in both categories must be without any wood-ageing, some *sin crianza* wines are made to age well in bottle, unlike *vino joven*.

Vino noble A wine that has been aged in oak or in bottle for at least 18 months

Vino viejo A wine that has been aged in oak or in bottle for at least 36 months

Vinum Optimum Rare Signatum or **Very Old Rare Sherry (VORS)** Minimum age of 30 years

Vinum Optimum Signatum or **Very Old Sherry (VOS)** Minimum age of 20 years

THE APPELLATIONS OF
SPAIN

Note DO is short for *Denominación de Origen*. DOCa is for *Denominación de Origen Calificada*. VC is for *Vino de Calidad con Indicación Geográfica* – the equivalent of the recently redundant French VDQS and likely to follow the same fate (ie, with the wines quietly upgraded to DO and the classification dispensed with). VP is for *Vino de Pago*, a single-vineyard appellation that is very similar to the revolutionary STE appellation proposed by the late René Renou when he was director of INAO but foolishly spurned by his colleagues in the French wine industry (*see* p104). A synonym for a particular grape variety is indicated by "*syn*".

ABONA DO
Canary Islands

This appellation was established in 1996 for white wines made in the south of Tenerife, where the vines are grown on terraces that are also planted with potatoes. Before they gained DO status, these wines were sold under the names of Granadilla, San Miguel, and Vilaflor.

🍇 Listán, Malvasia

🍷 *Viña Peraza*

ALELLA DO
Catalunya

This is a tiny, predominantly white appellation just north of Barcelona, where grapes are traditionally grown on windy granite hills, but due to urban development, the DO was extended in 1989 into the colder, limestone *vallès* of the Cordillera Catalana. The red wines of Alella have good colour, medium body, and a soft, fruity flavour. White and *rosado* are pale-coloured, fresh, and delicate, with good acidity when made with grapes from the best north-facing slopes.

🍇 Chardonnay, Chenin Blanc, Garnacha, Garnacha Blanca, Garnacha Peluda, Pansá Rosada, Tempranillo, Xarel-lo

🍷 1–5 years (red), 1–2 years (white and *rosado*), 1–4 years (sweet)

🍷 *Alta Alella Chardonnay* • *Alellasol* • *Marfil* • *Marqués de Alella*

ALICANTE DO
Valencia

These mild-climate red, white, and *rosado* wines are grown on dark, limey soil in the hills behind Alicante. The red wines are naturally deep in colour and, when made in a *doble pasta* style, they can be ink-black and astringent, but younger, fruitier styles are emerging, as indeed they are among *rosados* and whites. Fortified Moscatels from this region are light and refreshing. A fortified wine of local repute called Fondillón is made from Monastrell grapes in a tawny port style.

🍇 Airén, Bobal, Garnacha, Garnacha Tinta, Meseguera, Moscatel Romano, Monastrell, Planta Fina, Tempranillo, Viura

🍷 6–12 years (reds)

🍷 *Enrique Mendoza* • *Hijo de Luís García Poveda* (Costa Blanca) • *Artadi Landeras* (El Sequé)

ALMANSA DO
Castille-La Mancha

This red and *rosado* appellation, which lies north of Jumilla and Yecla, bridges the heights of the central plains of La Mancha and the lowlands of Valencia. The red wines produced here are full-bodied and richly coloured, with the best examples being quite smooth and fruity. Good examples of *rosado* can be fruity and clean.

🍇 Airén, Garnacha, Meseguera, Monastrell, Tempranillo

🍷 3–10 years (red), 1–3 years (*rosado*)

🍷 *Alfonso Abellan* • *Carrion* • *Piqueras*

ARABAKO TXAKOLINA *or* TXAKOLI DE ÁLAVA *or* CHACOLI DE ÁLAVA DO
Basque Country

The smallest and youngest of Txakolina's three geographical appellations, Arabako Txakolina is also the most southerly, being located almost halfway between Bilbao and the outer limits of the Rioja region. The main varieties here, as in the other two Txakolina appellations, are Ondarrabi Zuri (or Hondarrabi Zuri, aka Courbu Blanc) and Ondarribi Beltza (or Hondarrabi Beltza), plus Ondarribi Zuri Zerratia (or Hondarrabi Zuri Zerratia, aka Petit Courbu), Izkiriota (aka Gros Manseng), and Izkiriota Ttippia (aka Petit Manseng). The climate is the warmest of the three Txakolina areas, but the wine is often kept crisp by deliberately bottling with a small amount of residual carbonic gas. Reds are rare, and *rosados* are nice and zippy.

🍷 *Xarment*

ARINZANO VP
Navarra

In 2009, Chivite's Gran Vino de Arínzano (a blend of Tempranillo, Merlot, and Cabernet Sauvignon) became the first *Pago* appellation in northern Spain, Pago de Arínzano, and this single-vineyard estate-bottled red is indeed one of Spain's finest wines.

ARLANZA DO
Castille-León

This DO in the Burgos province was finalized as recently as 2008. It's high-altitude Tempranillo vineyards show the most potential, but other varieties are Tinta del País, Garnacha, Mencía, Cabernet Sauvignon, Merlot, and Petit Verdot for reds; and Albillo and Viura for whites. The red is special and well deserves its exalted status.

ARRIBES DO
Castille-León

This is another DO finalized as recently as 2008, and the vineyards of Arribes currently cover just 750 hectares (1,850 acres) but used to be prolific, stretching from Zamora south through Salamanca, along the border with Portugal. What used to be a secondary grape in Arribes, Juan García, is now a primary variety, and this could lead to some interesting results. Juan García is a synonym for Tempranillo in some areas, but not here, where this grape is authorized in addition to the Tempranillo. Other varieties allowed are Rufete, Tempranillo, Mencía, and Garnacha for reds; and Malvasia, Verdejo, Albillo, and Puesto en Cruz for whites.

🍷 *Hacienda Durius* (Magister)

BIERZO DO
Castille-León

One of the more exciting of Spain's less traditional DOs, Bierzo includes red, white, and *rosado* wines. Young reds stand out, being made from a minimum of 70 per cent Mencía, an underrated variety capable of attractively aromatic wines.

🍇 Doña Blanca, Garnacha, Godello, Malvasía, Mencía, Palomino

🍷 1–4 years (red), 9–18 months (white and *rosado*)

🍷 *Agribergidum* (Spanish Steps) • *Bodegas CA del Bierzo* • *Bodegas Palacio de Arganza* (non-DO wines) • *Bodegas Peique* (Tinto Mencía) • *Descendientes de J Palacios* • *Luna Beberide* (M Mencía) • *Pérez Caramés* • *Casa Valdaiga*

BINISSALEM DO
Balearic Islands

This appellation owes its existence primarily to just one man, José Ferrer, but there are at least two other producers of Majorca's best-known wine who are worth searching out. The white and *rosado* are simple, but the reds are slightly more serious and show some potential.

🍇 A minimum of 50% Manto Negro (for reds) or 70% Moll for whites, plus Callet, Monastrell, Parellada, Tempranillo, and Viura

🍷 Upon purchase

🍷 *José L Ferrer* • *Jaume Mesquida* • *Miguel Oliver*

BIZKAIKO TXAKOLINA *or* TXAKOLI DE BIZKAIA *or* CHACOLI DE VIZCAYA DO
Basque Country

Of Txakolina's three geographical appellations, Bizkaiko Txakolina is the largest, and its vineyards are located west and east of Bilbao. New regulations in 2008 permitted the use of barrel-fermentation and added Folle Blanche, Manseng, Gros Manseng, and a number of other varieties, but their plantation is restricted in order to maintain the dominance of traditional varieties: Ondarrabi Zuri (or Hondarrabi Zuri, aka Courbu Blanc) for whites and Ondarrabi Beltza (or Hondarrabi Beltza) for reds. Almost 90 per cent of the wines are white, and in this Atlantic-influenced climate, they can be wonderfully fresh and crisp, though a tad rounder and fuller than those of Getaria Txakolina. Doniene even produces an eminently palatable red in what really should be white-wine-only country.

🍷 *Doniene* • *Gurrutxaga*

BULLAS DO
Murcia

This is a large region just south of Jumilla where the soil is so poor that, apart from vines, only olives and almonds can survive. The young red wines here are made primarily from Monastrell grapes and seem to have the best potential, but white and *rosado* wines are also allowed.

🍇 Airén, Garnacha, Monastrell, Tempranillo

🍷 *Rosario* (3000)

CALATAYUD DO
Aragón

A patchwork of vineyards, mostly planted with Garnacha vines, tussle with fruit trees for meagre sustenance from the poor, buff-coloured rocky soil. Increasing the amount of Tempranillo vines and temperature-controlled stainless-steel vats will eventually improve the potential here, but the best wines are still simple, fresh, fruity *rosados*.

🍇 Garnacha, Garnacha Blanca, Juan Ibáñez, Malvasía, Mazuelo, Miguel de Arco, Moscatel Romano, Monastrell, Tempranillo, Viura

🍷 Upon purchase

✓ *Jalón* • *Langa* • *Las Rocas* (Garnacha Viñas Viejas)

CAMPO DE BORJA DO
Aragón

This name derives from the notorious Borgia family, who used to run things here at the height of their power in the late 15th century. The whites are fresh, but somewhat neutral. The reds and *rosados* are full, robust, and can be alcoholic, but they are improving. Their character is sometimes compared with that Navarra once had, and Campo de Borja is now experimenting with Cabernet Sauvignon in the same way as Navarra once did. This is a wine area to watch.

🍇 Garnacha, Garnacha Blanca, Viura

🍷 3–8 years (red), 9–15 months (white and *rosado*)

✓ *Bordeje* • *Agrícola de Borja* (Borsao) • *Aragonesas* (Garnacha) • *CA del Campo Union* • *Agraria del Santo Cristo* • *CA del Campo San Juan Bautista*

CAMPO DE LA GUARDIA VP
Castille-La Mancha

The wines of this single-vineyard appellation south of Madrid come from Bodegas Martúe, which is owned by Fausto Gonzalez, who also owns Viñedos de Nieva (Pie Franco wines) in Rueda and Seis Quintas in Portugal's Douro Valley. Like all *Pago* wines, Campo de la Guardia must be estate-bottled, and the styles claiming this single-vineyard appellation currently include Martúe (Tempranillo, Cabernet Sauvignon, Syrah, Merlot, and Petit Verdot), Martúe Especial (Cabernet Sauvignon, Syrah, and Merlot), Martúe Syrah, and Martúe Chardonnay.

CANGAS VC
Asturias

Mostly red *joven*-style blends of Verdejo Negro and Mencía, but white and *rosado* are allowed, and other recommended grapes are Albariño, Albillo, Garnacha, and Picapoll (aka Picpoul), plus the following authorized varieties: Alvarín Negro, Carraquín, Godello, Gewürztraminer, Merlot, Moscatel, Pinot Noir, and Syrah.

CARIÑENA DO
Aragón

Cariñena's low rainfall accounted for the traditionally high alcohol content of these wines, but modern vinification now makes a fresher, lighter, fruitier, more aromatic style. Reds are the best of this appellation, especially from parcels of old Garnacha. Some deliberately maderized *rancio* wines are still produced.

🍇 Cabernet Sauvignon, Cariñena, Garnacha, Garnacha Blanca, Juan Ibáñez, Moscatel Romano, Monastrell, Parellada, Tempranillo, Viura

🍷 1–5 years (red), 9–18 months (white and *rosado*)

✓ *Añadas* • *Covinca* • *Gran Ducay* • *Bodegas Terra* (G, Pléyades)

CATALUNYA DO
Catalunya

With all styles of red, white, *rosado*, and fortified wine allowed, this basic, regional appellation offers innovative winemakers more flexibility than the supposedly superior, smaller, more specific DOs.

🍇 Bobal, Cabernet Franc, Cabernet Sauvignon, Cariñena, Chardonnay, Chenin Blanc, Garnatxa Blanca, Garnatxa Negra, Garnatxa Tintorera, Gewürztraminer, Macabeu, Malvasia, Malvasia de Sitges, Mazuela, Merlot, Monastrell, Muscat d'Alexandrie, Parellada, Pedro Ximénez, Peluda, Picapoll, Pinot Blanc, Pinot Noir, Riesling, Sauvignon Blanc, Syrah, Tempranillo, Ull de Llebre, Xarel-lo

✓ *Mas Gil* (Clos d'Agon) • *Torres*

CAVA DO
See Penedès: Cava Country, p376

CHACOLI *or* TXAKOLINA DO
Basque Country

This is Basque Country, and inevitably the Basque name Txakolina is preferred for labelling. *See* Arabako Txakolina DO, Bizkaiko Txakolina DO, and Getariako Txakolina DO.

CIGALES DO
Castille-Léon

This appellation is best known for fresh, fruity, light reds and *rosados*.

🍇 Albillo, Garnacha, Palomino, Tempranillo, Verdejo, Viura

✓ *CA de Cigales* (Escogido del Año, Viña Torondos) • *Emeterio Fernández* (La Legua Capricho) • *Frutos Villa* (Conde Ansurez, Viña Calderona) • *González Lara* (Fuente del Conde Rosado)

CONCA DE BARBERÁ DO
Catalunya

This once little-known appellation for red, white, and *rosado* wines from the hilly hinterland of Penedès promises to be one of Spain's most exciting areas. Chardonnay is outstanding here, as the rich, potentially complex Torres Milmanda demonstrates. Merlot is the most up-and-coming variety in the red department, but Trepat could mount a few surprises for fresh, easy-drinking styles of both red and *rosado*.

🍇 Cabernet Sauvignon, Garnacha, Merlot, Parellada, Tempranillo, Trepat, Viura

🍷 1–5 years

✓ *Torres* (Milmanda Chardonnay)

CONDADO DE HUELVA DO
Andalucía

The sweet dessert wines of this area, which is sandwiched between the Sherry district of southwest Spain and the Algarve of Portugal were mentioned by Chaucer in *The Canterbury Tales*. They ended up, however, as blending fodder for Sherry. There are two basic types of fortified wine here: *pálido*

(young, pale-straw colour, dry, austere wines, of 14–17 per cent alcohol) and *viejo* (solera-matured, mahogany-hued, in both dry and sweet styles that are deliberately oxidized, of 15–23 per cent alcohol).

🍇 Garrido Fino, Palomino, Zalema

🍷 Upon purchase

COSTERS DEL SEGRE DO
Catalunya

This is a top-performing appellation taking in four areas of different viticultural character in the province of Lérida: Les Garrigues and Valls de Riu Corb (primarily white-grape districts); Artesa (planted almost entirely with black grapes); and Raimat (dominated by foreign grape varieties and has quickly assumed classic status through Codorníu's innovative Raimat Estate).

🍇 Cabernet Sauvignon, Cariñena, Chardonnay, Garnacha, Garnacha Blanca, Merlot, Monastrell, Parellada, Trepat, Ull de Llebre, Viura, Xarel-lo

🍷 2–6 years (red), 1–4 years (white)

✓ *Castell d'Encus* (Ekam, Thalarn) • *Cuisiné* (Geol, Finca Racons, Macabeu) • *Raïmat* • *Castell del Remei*

DEHESA DEL CARRIZAL VP
Castille-La Mancha

In 2006 this became Spain's third *Pago*, or single-estate, appellation. Legend has it that Marcial Gómez Sequeira planted this semi-desert area with Cabernet Sauvignon some 20 years ago as part of a bet, but it was so successful that he enlarged the vineyard to 22 hectares (54 acres) with Chardonnay, Merlot, Syrah, and Tempranillo.

DOMINIO DE VALDEPUSA VP
Castille-La Mancha

Owned by Carlos Falcó of Marqués de Griñón fame, Dominio de Valdepusa became Spain's first *Pago* appellation in 2001. It was Spain's first vineyard to use a new trellis system and drip-irrigation, both in 1973. More recently, Dominio de Valdepusa became the first vineyard in Europe to adopt the Australian PRD technique, and one of the first in the world to deploy dendrometers (*see* Micropedia). Over the years, Falcó has employed a veritable gaggle of gurus (Lichine, Peynaud), with Rolland and Smart his current advisors. According to Smart, the red clay over limestone at Dominio de Valdepusa is identical to the famous *terra rossa* soil of Coonawarra.

🍇 Cabernet Sauvignon, Petit Verdot, Syrah

✓ *Marqués de Griñón* (Dominio de Valdepusa)

EMPORDA *or* EMPORDA–COSTA BRAVA DO
Catalunya

Lying at the foot of the narrowest section of the Pyrenees, this is the closest Spanish wine appellation to France. Most of the production is *rosado* and aimed at tourists, but the reds are much better, having a fairly deep, cherry-red colour, medium to full body, and a crisp, plummy flavour. Whites are fruity and may be off-dry or slightly sweet, with a pale, often greenish-tinged colour, and are sometimes *pétillant* (lightly sparkling). Despite opening up this appellation to other grapes, the most widely planted varieties are still Carignan and Grenache (known locally as Samsó and Lledoner, respectively).

🍇 Cariñena, Garnacha, Garnacha Blanca, Viura, Cabernet Sauvignon, Chardonnay, Gewürztraminer, Macabeo, Merlot, Muscat, Sauvignon Blanc, Tempranillo, Syrah, Xarel-lo

🍷 2–5 years (red), 9–18 months (white and *rosado*)

✓ *Castillo Perelada* (ROC Tinto Crianza) •
Convinosa • *Marti Fabra* (Verd Albera) •
Oliveda • *Vinya Ivo* (S'Alqueria)

FINCA ELEZ VP
Castille-La Mancha

Located near the village of El Bonillo, in the heart of
the Sierra de Alcaraz, this single-estate appellation
was established in 2002 and is owned by Manuel
Manzaneque, a theatre director and producer.

🍇 Cabernet Sauvignon, Chardonnay, Merlot, Syrah,
Tempanillo

✓ *Finca Elez*

FLORENTINO VP
Castille-La Mancha

This is an estate-bottled Tempranillo of delicious
proportions, produced by Bodegas La Solana at
Malagón in the province of Ciudad Real, towards
the western extremity of La Mancha. La Mancha DO
once had a bulk-wine image but now includes no
fewer than four *Pago* superstar appellations. La
Solana is under the same ownership as Bodegas
Arzuaga in Ribera del Duero.

GETARIAKO TXAKOLINA *or*
TXAKOLI DE GETARIA *or*
CHACOLI DE GETARIA DO
Basque Country

Even though these wines first saw the light of day
in DO terms as recently as 1990, Getariako
Txakolina is the oldest of Txakoli's three
geographical appellations; consequently, its wines,
which are the crispest and most *pétillant* of all
three, have come to represent the style of wine that
foreign markets expect from this part of northern
Spain. The vineyards here are often steep and
narrowly terraced and, set among the verdant
landscape surrounding the towns of Getaria and
Zarautz, are closer to San Sebastián than Bilbao.
The primary grapes used are Ondarrabi Zuri (or
Hondarrabi Zuri, aka Courbu Blanc) for whites and
Ondarrabi Beltza (or Hondarrabi Beltza) for rare
reds, but other varieties are also authorized,
including Ondarrabi Zuri Zerratia (or Hondarrabi
Zuri Zerratia, aka Petit Courbu), Izkiriota (aka Gros
Manseng), Chardonnay, and Riesling. Mune Mahatsa
and Txori Mahatsa may also be encountered. More
than 90 per cent of the wines are white, and in this
Atlantic-influenced climate, they can be wonderfully
fresh and crisp, often with a touch of *pétillance*,
and some of the local stuff can be really quite fizzy,
although *espumoso* is specifically prohibited. Reds
are rare and *rosados* nice and zippy. The local
custom is to pour this wine from a height to create
a head and dispense with much of the fizziness.

✓ *Ameztoi* • *Txomin*

LA GOMERA DO
Canary Islands

This island just southwest of Tenerife has 120
hectares (300 acres) of vineyards, which mainly
grow Listan Negra and Negramoll for reds and
Forastera, Gomera Blanca, Listán Blanca, and
Marmajuelo for whites. All are ungrafted. La
Gomera produces some of the more interesting
Canary Islands wines.

GRAN CANARIA DO
Canary Islands

There are 220 hectares (545 acres) of vineyards,
planted mostly with five black varieties (Listan

Negro, Negramoll, Tintilla, Malvasia Rosada, and
Moscatel Negra) and 11 white (Malvasia, Güal,
Pedro Ximénez, Marmajuelo, Vijariego, Albillo,
Listán Blanco, Burrablanca, Torrontés, Breval, and
Moscatel). All are ungrafted. Wines are produced by
a dozen commercial *bodegas*.

GRANADA VC
Andalucía

This area used to make little more than rustic
fortified wines that were called Costa-Albondón, but
its growers have made efforts to upgrade the quality
of their wines in recent years, producing full-bodied
reds from Tempranillo supported by various
international grape varieties, including Cabernet
Sauvignon, Merlot, and Syrah. Whites have
improved, using cooler fermentation for mostly
Macabéo or Moscatel.

GUIJOSO VP
Castille-La Mancha

Pago Guijoso encompasses the estate of Bodegas
Sanchez Multiterno, which currently produces
Divinus (Chardonnay, partly *barrica*-fermented),
Vega Guijoso (Merlot-dominated, plus Cabernet
Sauvignon, Tempranillo, and Syrah), Viña
Consolación (Cabernet Sauvignon), and
Magnificus (Syrah).

EL HIERRO DO
Canary Islands

El Hierro is the smallest and most westerly island in
the archipelago, yet the local cooperative is one of
the most advanced in the Canary Islands. Before
gaining DO status, these wines were sold under
the local names of Frontera and Valverde. The
Negramoll grape is best for reds and *rosados*,
while the Verijadiego is best for whites.

🍇 Listán, Malvasía, Moscatel, Negramoll, Pedro
Ximénez, Verdello, Verijadiego

✓ *Fontera*

JEREZ *or*
JEREZ-XÉRÈS-SHERRY DO
See Sherry Country, p379

JUMILLA DO
Murcia

The high, hilly vineyards of Jumilla have never been
affected by phylloxera, and most of the vines are
still ungrafted. Almost all the wines produced here
are red, and until recently were lacklustre, unless
made in a *doble pasta* style, which produces wines
so thick and intense that they are in great demand
for blending purposes throughout Spain and also
abroad. The best reds carry the Jumilla Monastrell
varietal appellation and can be very smooth, fruity,
and aromatic, tending to improve with age. With
earlier picking and temperature-controlled
fermentation, lighter, more accessible wines are

now being made that are best drunk when young
and juicy, including some soft, fruity whites as well
as some *rosados*.

🍇 Airén, Garnacha, Meseguera, Monastrell, Pedro
Ximénez, Tempranillo

🍷 1–3 years (red, but up to 6 years for wines
made in *doble pasta* style), 9–15 months (white
and *rosado*)

✓ *Bleda* (Castillo Jumilla) • *Bodegas Silvano
Garcia* (Rosado Monastrell, Dulce Monastrell) •
Julia Roch e Hijos • *Jumilla Union Vitivinícola*
(Cerrillares, Incunable) • *Señorío del
Condestable*

LANZAROTE DO
Canary Islands

This appellation was established in 1995 for the
island of Lanzarote, where the lunar landscape is
dotted with vines in crater-like depressions,
protected by low stone walls. The most spectacular
example of this weirdly beautiful form of viticulture
can be viewed at La Geria, an area west of Arrecife
where no fewer than 2,000 hectares (5,000 acres) of
such vineyards are to be found.

🍇 include: Caleta, Diego, Listán, Malvasia

MÁLAGA DO
Andalucía

Just northeast of Jerez in southern Spain, the coastal
vineyards of Málaga produce one of the most
underrated classic dessert wines in the world. Most of
this is matured by the *solera* system, involving some
six scales (*see* Sherry Country, p379) and may be
blended in a Sherry-like manner using various
grape-based colouring and sweetening agents, such as
arrope, *vino de color*, *vino tierno*, and *vino maestro*.
The colour of these fortified wines can range from
gold through tawny to brown and red, depending on
the style of Málaga, its age, and method of maturation,
its degree of sweetness, and the grape variety used.

Málaga may be any one of the following. Dulce
Color is a dark, medium-bodied Málaga that has
been sweetened with *arrope*. Lágrima is made from
free-run juice only, and is the most luscious of all
Málaga styles. Moscatel is a sweet, rich, raisiny,
medium- to full-bodied wine that is similar to the
Jerez version, only more luscious. Old Solera has
the most finesse, depth, and length of all Málagas
and is capable of complexity rather than
lusciousness. It is medium to full bodied, still sweet
yet with a dry finish. Oscuro is a dark, sweet
Málaga that has been sweetened with *arrope* and
coloured by *vino de color*. Pajarette or Paxarete is
darkish in colour, and less sweet, but more
alcoholic, than other Málagas. Pedro Ximénez is a
smooth, sweet, deliciously rich varietal wine with
an intense flavour, which is similar in character to
the Jerez version. Seco is a pale, dry, tangy wine
with a distinctive creamy hazelnut character.

🍇 Moscatel, Pedro Ximénez

🍷 Upon purchase (although it can last, but not
improve, for several years)

✓ *Jesús del Perdón* (Gran Lopez Tempanillo
Rosado) • *Jorge Ordoñez* (No.1 Selección
Especial) • *Finca Perico* (Tempanillo-Syrah)
• *Scholtz Hermanos* • *Pérez Texeira* • *Larios*

LA MANCHA DO
Castille-La Mancha

Although its output remains enormous, accounting
for some 40 per cent of all Spanish wines produced,
the wine-land of Don Quixote has improved
tremendously since the 1980s. Many producers now
harvest much earlier than previously and ferment at

cooler temperatures (sometimes too cool), achieving fresher, lighter, more aromatic wines. The best wines of La Mancha used to be made in Valdepeñas DO, and that appellation still boasts most of the best, but the arrival of Alejandro Fernández (El Vinculo) in 1999 has raised the stakes. Who would have thought that any wine bearing "La Mancha" could be considered up-and-coming?

🍇 Airén, Cabernet Sauvignon, Garnacha, Merlot, Moravia, Pardina, Tempranillo, Viura

🍷 1–4 years (red), 9–15 months (white and *rosado*)

✓ *Ayuso* (Estola Gran Reserva) • *Vinícola de Castilla* (Castillo de Alhambra, Señorío de Guadianeja) • *Jesús Díaz e Hijos* • *El Vinculo* •*C Españolas* (Fuente del Ritmo) • *Hermanos Morales* (Gran Créacion) • *CA del Campo Nuestra Señora de Manjavacas* (Zagarrón) • *CA del Campo Nuestra Padre Jesús de Perdon* (Casa la Teja, Gran Lopez Airén-Sauvignon Blanc, Lazarillo, Yuntero) • *Rama Corta* • *Rodriguez y Berger* (Viña Santa Elena) • *Julián Santos* • *Torres Filoso* (Arboles de Castollejo)

MANCHUELA DO
Castille-La Mancha

This is a very large region, encompassing La Mancha, Ribera del Júcar, Utiel-Requena, and Almansa, with cooperatives accounting for two-thirds of the *bodegas*, and a quality that is seldom better than an acceptable quaff. Much is a lot worse. The delicious red wines of Finca Sandova are, however, a class apart, and the improving Gualberto may one day reach a similar level.

🍇 Albillo, Bobal, Cabernet Sauvignon, Cencibel, Chardonnay, Garnacha, Macabéo, Merlot, Monastrell, Moravia Dulce, Sauvignon Blanc, Syrah, Verdejo

✓ *Finca Sandoval* • *Gualberto*

MANZANILLA *or* MANZANILLA SANLÚCAR DE BARRAMEDA DO
See Sherry Country, p379

MÉNTRIDA DO
Castille-La Mancha

Wines from this DO were once cheap and mostly consumed locally, but yields have dropped, and several *bodegas* have improved their facilities. The improvement in quality has turned these one-time rustic reds into well-structured *vins de garde*.

🍇 Garnacha, Tempranillo

✓ *Jiménez-Landi* (Piélago)

MONDÉJAR DO
Castille-La Mancha

Although fewer bulk wines are being produced here

since Mondéjar achieved DO status, the wines are still mostly uninspiring, with Mariscal the solitary producer that seems interested in improving quality.

🍇 Airén, Cabernet Sauvignon, Garnacha, Jaén, Macabéo, Malvar, Tempranillo, Torrontés

✓ *Mariscal*

MONTE DE LENTISCAL DO
Canary Islands

This subzonal DO is located on the island of Gran Canaria, south of Las Palmas de Gran Canaria, where 200 hectares (500 acres) are planted mostly with six black grapes (Listán Negra, Negra Común, Negramoll, Malvasia, Tintilla, and Moscatel Negra) and 10 white grapes (Albillo, Breval, Güal, Malvasia, Marmajuelo, Pedro Ximénez, Vijariego, Burrablanca, Torrontés, and Listán Blanco). All ungrafted.

MONTERREI DO
Galicia

This area was first awarded a provisional DO in the early 1980s, but this was revoked when too few of its growers showed any interest in modernizing their estates. However, some progress was made in the late 1980s, and this appellation has now been granted full DO status.

🍇 Alicante, Doña Blanca, Godello, Gran Negro, Mencía, Mouratón, Palomino

✓ *Pazo Pondal* (Lenda Pondal)

MONTILLA-MORILES DO
Andalucía

The Sherry-like wines of Montilla fall into three categories: *generosos* (fortified *finos*, *amontillados*, *olorosos*, and magnificent PX); unfortified traditional wines (cream, medium, and dry at 14.5 per cent alcohol); and *jóvenes afrutados* (ghastly).

🍇 Airén, Baladí, Moscatel, Pedro Ximénez, Torrontés

🍷 Can be kept, but consume upon opening

✓ *Marqués de la Sierra* • *Alvear* • *Mora Chacon* • *Gracia Hermanos* • *Perez Barquero* • *Rodriguez Chiachio* • *Toro Albalá* (Don PX)

MONTSANT DO
Catalunya

A potentially exciting appellation clasping the eastern, western, and southern edges of Priorat.

🍇 Cabernet Sauvignon, Cariñena, Garnacha, Merlot, Monastrell, Syrah, Tempranillo

✓ *Can Blau* • *Celler de Capéanes* (Mas Picosa) • *Fra Guerau* • *Laurona*

NAVARRA DO
See Rioja and Navarra, p370

OTAZU VP
Navarra

The single-vineyard, estate-bottled appellation Pago de Otazu is located just 8 kilometres (5 miles) from Pamplona. At the time of writing, most Otazu wines are sold under the Navarra DO, with just two wines (released in 2010) claiming full Pago de Otazu status: a *barrica*-fermented Chardonnay and a Tempranillo blend supported by Merlot and Cabernet Sauvignon. This represents a very promising start, especially the labelling, which offers the transparency missing from so many of even the greatest wines, certifying not only the *lieux-dits* from which the grapes came but also the type of oak used to produce the barrels in which the wines were aged.

LA PALMA DO
Canary Islands

This appellation was established in 1995 for the island of La Palma. It was in Fuencaliente, in the south of the island, that the famed "Canary Sack" of Shakespeare's time was produced, and the grape responsible, Malvasia, still grows here, amid four smoking volcanoes, in the same sort of crater-like depressions that abound on Lanzarote. An oddity aged in pine casks and curiously called Vino del Tea ("Tea" being the local name for a particular species of pine) is available in the north of the island, but only the most ardent admirers of Retsina should search it out.

🍇 Bujariego, Gual, Listán, Malvasia, Negramoll

✓ *Hoyo de Mazo*

PENEDÈS DO
See Penedès: Cava Country, p376

PLA DE BAGES DO
Catalunya

Winemaking is an old tradition in Bages, and yet this is an up-and-coming DO, with many newly planted vineyards and a small but growing band of modern *bodegas*, of which Massies d'Avinyó clearly leads the way. "Bages" is a derivative of Bacchus, the name of the Roman god of wine.

🍇 Chardonnay, Garnatxa, Macabéo, Malbec, Merlot, Picapoll, Pinot Noir, Sauvignon Blanc, Sumoll, Tempranillo

✓ *Massies d'Avinyó*

PLA I LEVANT DO
Mallorca

The island's newest appellation produces some of its best wines.

🍇 Cabernet Sauvignon, Callet, Chardonnay, Frogoneu, Manto Negro, Macabéo, Merlot, Moscatel, Parellada, Pinot Noir, Prensal Blanc, Syrah, Tempranillo

✓ *Miquel Geabert* • *Miquel Oliver*

PRADO DE IRACHE VP
Navarra

This single-vineyard appellation is for estate-bottled wines from a vineyard belonging to Bodegas Irache called Prago de Irache, located in Ayegui, at the foot of the forest-clad Montejurra in the Navarra region. Prior to its *Pago* status, Prado Irache earned its reputation because it was made only in truly vintage years from a severely restricted selection of grapes and sold in numbered bottles. Pago de Prado de Irache is a blend of Tempranillo, Cabernet Sauvignon, and Merlot.

PRIORAT DOCa
Catalunya

This area has a dry climate and poor soil, in which the vines' roots spread everywhere in search of moisture, the local saying being that Priorat vines can suck water out of stone. The best wines are currently being made around the hilltop town of Gratallops, by a group of young winemakers led by Bordeaux-trained Riojan oenologist Alvaro Palacios, who brought with him a wealth of experience from Château Pétrus to the Napa Valley. New-style reds are huge, serious, and stunningly rich, but those of the old style tend to be heavy, over-alcoholic, and oxidized, although the best traditional wines fall somewhere in between. One of the country's oldest appellations, Priorat is one of the Spanish wine industry's super-stars. The use of the spelling "Priorato" has been dropped on bottles in favour of the Catalan version "Priorat", and DOQ, the Catalan equivalent of DOCa, is now prevalent.

🍇 Cabernet Sauvignon, Cariñena, Garnacha, Garnacha Blanca, Merlot, Monastrell, Pedro Ximénez, Syrah, Viura

🍷 5–15 years (red)

✓ *Mas Alta* (Artigas, Le Creu) • *René Barbier* (Clos Mogador) • *Clos Erasmus* • *Costers del Siurana* (Clos de l'Obac, Miserere) • *Masia Barril* • *De Muller* • *Alvaro Palacios* ❸ (Finca Dofi, Clos l'Ermita, Las Terrasses) • *Pasanau* (Ceps Nous) • *Pinord* (+7) • *Joan Sangenís* (Mas d'En Compte) • *Sangenís i Vaqué* (Clos Monlleó) • *Scala Dei* (Cartoixa, El Cipres, Novell) • *Torres* (Perpetual, Salmos) • *Vinicola del Priorato* (Mas d'Alba, Onix)

RÍAS BAIXAS DO
Galicia

Spain's fastest-rising star in the DO firmament, the Rías Baixas appellation covers various red, white, and *rosado* wines, but the best-known and most enjoyable wines are the softly perfumed, zippy whites made from low-yielding Albariño grapes, which can have real depth and fruit, and a fresh, lively acidity. Although I have always admired the best of these wines, I did wonder whether they are worth what appeared to be an increasingly high price. At the table, however, they accompany fine food beautifully, which in my book makes even the most expensive Rías Baixas well worth the price demanded for it.

🍇 Albariño, Brancellao, Caiño Blanco, Caiño Tinto, Espadeiro, Loureira Blanca, Loureira Tinta, Mencía, Sousón, Torrontés, Treixadura

🍷 1–3 years

✓ *Albariño do Salnes* • *Pazo de Barrantes* • *Cardallal* • *Adega Castrocelta* (Albariño) • *Lagar de Cevera* • *del Palacio de Fefiñanes* • *Granxa Fillaboa* • *Major de Mendoza* (Fulget) • *Morgadio-Agromiño* • *Pazo Pondal* • *Pazo de Señorans* (Selección de Añada) • *Bodegas Valamor* (Albariño) • *de Vilariño Cambados* (Martín Códax, Organistrum) • *Santiago Ruíz*

RIBEIRA SACRA DO
Galicia

The most widely planted grape variety here is Palomino, but on the steep, terraced vineyards of Ribeira Sacra, Albariño is far more exciting, and the Mencía variety also shows promise for red wines.

🍇 Albariño, Brancellao, Caiño, Doña Blanca, Espadeiro, Ferrón, Godello, Garnacha, Loureira, Loureira Tinta, Mencía, Merenzao, Negrada, Palomino, Sousón, Torrontés

🍷 1–3 years

✓ *Adegas Moure* (Albariño Abadia da Cova)

RIBEIRO DO
Galicia

Due to the Atlantic-influenced climate of northwest Spain, the styles of Ribeiro's red and white wines reflect that of Portugal's Vinhos Verdes, except that they are somewhat more fruity and aromatic. The very best examples possess a wonderfully fresh, pure, vibrancy of fruit.

🍇 Albariño, Albillo, Brancellao, Caiño, Ferrón, Garnacha, Godello, Jerez, Loureira, Mencía, Sousón, Tempranillo, Torrontés, Treixadura, Viura

🍷 9–18 months

✓ *Alanis* • *Arsenio Paz* • *Rivera* • *CA del Ribeiro*

RIBERA DEL DUERO DO
Castille-León

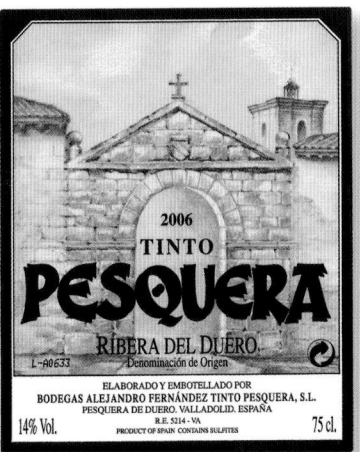

From the upper reaches of the Duero River (which becomes the Douro, once it crosses the Portuguese border), the *rosados* are fresh, dry, fruity wines of a *clarete* or *claro* style, but are nowhere near the class of the best reds, which have a truly dense, black colour and are packed solid with rich, oaky-sweet, plummy-blackcurrant fruit flavours.

Ribera del Duero DO built its reputation on Vega Sicilia, formerly Spain's most expensive wine. In the first edition of this book, I categorically stated that contrary to the informed opinion of many other wine critics, this was not Spain's greatest red wine, although it was potentially the best. The problem was that 10 or more years in wood took its toll on the fruit in a way that would destroy many of the greatest wines of Bordeaux. There was also no logic to the duration and mode of ageing at Vega Sicilia, which occurred in different sizes and ages of wooden cask, the various vintages being transferred from one vessel to another simply to fulfil the logistical necessity of moving the wines around in order to accommodate the incoming harvest. Since the first edition, however, Vega Sicilia has given its wines no more than six years in wood and now has a more disciplined approach to how long wines spend in various types and ages of cask, including new oak *barriques*. It is once again one of Spain's greatest wines, but not necessarily the greatest Ribera del Duero, with a handful of *bodegas* capable of matching, sometimes surpassing, the quality of Vega Sicilia. These include Aalto, Vega Sicilia's own Alion, Alejándro Fernández's Pesquera, Condado de Haza (also owned by Fernández), Dominio de Pingus, and Pago de los Capellanes, with a few others waiting in the wings.

🍇 Cabernet Sauvignon, Garnacha, Malbec, Merlot, Pardina, Tinto del País

🍷 3–8 years (modern red), 5–25 years (traditional red), 1–2 years (*rosado*)

✓ *Aalto* • *Abadía Retuerta* • *Alión* • *Cillar & Silos* (Torresilo) • *Arzuaga Condado de Haza* • *Dominio de Pingus* ❸ • *Emelio Moro* • *Ismael Arroyo* • *Julio Cesar Conde Delgado y Otros* (Neo) • *Bodegas García Figuero* (especially Tinus) • *O Fournier* (Alfa Spiga) • *Legaris* • *Mauro* • *Pago de Carraovejas* • *Pago de los Capellanes* • *Pagos del Rey* • *Pérez Pascuas* (Viña Pedrosa) • *Pesquera* • *Pomar Vinédos* • *Real Sitio de Ventosilla* (Prado Rey) • *Reyes* • *Sastre* • *Uvaguilera Aguilera* • *Vega Sicilia* (including Valbuena)

RIBERA DEL GUADIANA DO
Extramadura

A group of six *vinos de la tierra* (Cañamero, Matanegra, Montanchez, Ribera Alta, Ribera Baja, and Tierra de Barros), which retain this classification, but also form subzones of the Ribera del Guadiana DO, entitling them to make wines under two different origins of quality.

✓ *La de Barros* • *Santa Mariña*

RIBERA DEL JÚCAR DO
Castille-La Mancha

This red-wine DO since the 2003 vintage encompasses some of La Mancha's best vineyards. Although the grapes authorized include Cabernet Sauvignon, Merlot, Pinot Noir, and Syrah, most wines released so far are cheap Tempranillo or Tempranillo-based blends.

RIOJA DOCa
See Rioja and Navarra, p370

RUEDA DO
Castille-León

This small district down-river from Ribeiro del Duero is known primarily for fresh, crisp, dry white wines made almost entirely from the Verdejo grape. Traditionally, though, the wines were fortified in *fino* (Palido Rueda) and *rancio* (Dorado Rueda)

styles, and they can still be found today. A *méthode champenoise* Rueda Espumoso is also allowed.

🍇 Palomino, Sauvignon Blanc, Verdejo, Viura (Macabéo)

⏳ 1–2 years

✓ *Agricola Castellana* • *Frutos Villar* (María de Molina) • *Marqués de Griñon* • *Marqués de Riscal* • *Bodegas Naia* (Naiades) • *Vinedos de Nieva* (Pie Franco)

SHERRY *or* JEREZ-XÉRÈS-SHERRY DO
See Sherry Country, p379

SIERRAS DE MÁLAGA DO
Andalucía

Although Málaga is one of Spain's oldest DOs, this appellation was granted in 2001, for an area that is higher in altitude than Málaga, and for red, white, and *rosado* wines that cannot be fortified.

🍇 Airén, Cabernet Franc, Cabernet Sauvignon, Chardonnay, Colombard, Doradilla, Garnacha, Macabeo, Merlot, Moscatel d'Alejandrie, Moscatel Morisco, Pedro Ximénez, Petit Verdot, Pinot Noir, Romé, Sauvignon Blanc, Syrah, Tempranillo

✓ *Cortijo Los Aguilares* (Pinot Noir, Rosado) • *F Schatz* ◉

SITGES
Catalunya

This is a famous, but rare, non-DO fortified Malvasia and Moscatel wine that is made just south of the outskirts of Barcelona, from grapes that are allowed to shrivel on the vine.

✓ *Cellers Robert*

SOMONTANO DO
Aragón

Set at the foot of the Pyrenees mountains, between the regions of Penedès and Navarra, Somontano is destined to become one of Spain's greatest wine regions. Chardonnay is by far the best grape grown here for serious, barrel-fermented white wines, but both Tempranillo and Cabernet Sauvignon show superb potential for making fragrant reds with a lively richness of fruit.

🍇 Alcañón, Cabernet Sauvignon, Chardonnay, Garnacha, Garnacha Blanca, Moristel, Parreleta, Tempranillo, Viura

⏳ 2–5 years (red), 1–3 years (white)

✓ *Aragonesa* • *Otto Bestué* • *Viñas del Vero* • *Enate* • *Lalanne* • *Pirineos* (especially Pico de Aneto)

TACORONTE-ACENTEJO DO
Canary Islands

Established in 1992, this is the oldest Canary Islands appellation and, so far, it has proved to be the best, although it is too early to tell how the others will fare.

🍇 Castellano, Gual, Listán, Listán Negro, Malvasía, Marmajuelo, Moscatel, Negra Común, Negramoll, Pedro Ximénez, Tintillo, Torrontés, Verdello

✓ *El Lomo* • *Monje* • *Viña Norte*

TARRAGONA DO
Catalunya

This is the largest appellation in Catalunya, but its potential quality is modest compared with that of neighbouring Penedès. Having said that, Australian winemakers Nick Butler and Mark Nairn have been quietly raising standards at Pedro Rovira, using hands-off methods to retain as much natural character in the wine as possible. The best red, white, and *rosado* from this region can all be fresh, fruity, and rewarding. Even the local fortified wine, which is sold as Tarragona Classico, can be worth looking out for.

🍇 Cariñena, Garnacha, Garnacha Blanca, Parellada, Tempranillo, Viura, Xarel-lo

⏳ 1–5 years (red), 1–2 years (white and *rosado*)

✓ *CA de Valls* • *Fustel* (Monasterio de Santa Cruz) • *José Lopez Beltrán* (Don Beltrán) • *Pedro Masana* (non-DO wines) • *De Müller* (Moscatel Seco, Parxete) • *Pedro Rovira*

TERRA ALTA DO
Catalunya

This slowly improving appellation lies in the highlands well away from the coast. It produces some good, everyday-drinking red and white wines, but the best sites are not always planted with the most suitable varieties and have to compete with Cava growers. It is advisable to avoid the local sweet, fortified *mistela*.

🍇 Cabernet Sauvignon, Cariñena, Garnacha, Garnacha Blanca, Merlot, Moscatel, Parellada, Tempranillo, Viura

⏳ 1–2 years

✓ *Fuster Dardell* (Catalan Eagle) • *CA Gandesa* • *CA la Hermandad* • *Pedro Rovira* (Alta Mar, Viña d'Irto) • *Vinalba dels Arcs* (Vall de Berrús)

TIERRA DE LÉON DO
Castille-Léon

It is no coincidence that after endless fields of wheat and grain, this outcrop of vineyards is located where two pilgrim roads, the Via de la Plata and Camino de Santiago, cross. Traditionally, the wines here were *rosado* or *clarete* and produced from a blend of black and white grape varieties. However, although all styles – red, white, and *rosado* – can be produced under this DO, the current focus is firmly fixed on fuller-bodied reds. The most important varieties for such wines are Prieto Picudo and Mencía, but Garnacha and Tempranillo are also recommended for red (and *rosado*) wines, with Albarín, Verdejo, Godello, Palomino, and Malvasia for whites.

✓ *Villacezán* (Molendores Rosado)

TIERRA DEL VINO DE ZAMORA DO
Castille-Léon

Abutting the western fringes of Rueda and Toro, this area is traditionally known for its Tempranillo-based reds, but other varieties include Garnacha and Cabernet Sauvignon for red and *rosado* wines, and Malvasia, Moscatel, Verdejo, Albillo, Palomino, and Godello for whites.

✓ *Alizán* • *Alter Ego* • *Brochero* • *Viñas del Cenit*

TORO DO
Castille-León

The exciting quality of Toro wines today is a very recent phenomenon, built on a sudden influx of high-profile names, which has tripled the number of *bodegas* since 2000. When this DO was established in 1987, there were just four *bodegas*, the decrepit local cooperative dominated production, and the quality was really quite dire. By 2000, the number of *bodegas* had increased to 18, but, more importantly, the Álvarez family of Vega Sicilia fame had been purchasing land under an assumed name since 1997, and after this was announced in 2002, the floodgates opened, so that at the last count there were 40 *bodegas*. Consequently, land prices have soared, and the battle for Toro's true quality has only just begun. Vega Sicilia's rival, Alejándro Fernández of Pesquera, followed suit in 1998, but his great Dehesa La Granja wine is made from vines growing just outside this DO, near Zamora. I suspect this may be a single-estate DO in waiting.

🍇 Garnacha, Malvasía, Tinta de Toro, Verdejo Blanco

⏳ 2–8 years (red), 1–3 years (white)

✓ *Alquiriz* • *Bajoz* • *Covitoro* (Cañus Verus Viñas Viejas) • *Fariña* (Celeste Gran Colegiata, Gran Colegiata Campus) • *Jacques & François Lurton* (El Albar Excelencia, Campo Eliseo) • *Maurodós* • *Numanthia* • *Bodega del Palacio de los Frontaura y Victoria* (Dominio de Valdelacasa) • *Pesquera* • *Protos* • *Yllera* (Garcilaso)

TXAKOLI DE ÁLAVA DO
See Arabako Txakolina DO

TXAKOLI DE BIZKAIA DO
See Bizkaiko Txakolina DO

TXAKOLI DE GETARIA DO
See Getariako Txakolina DO

UCLÉS DO
Castille-La Mancha

The first vintage allowed for this red-wine DO was 2005. This DO encompasses some of La Mancha's best high-altitude vineyards, located either side of the Altomira Mountains. Authorized grapes include Cabernet Sauvignon, Garnacha, Merlot, Syrah, and Tempranillo, with a sliding scale of maximum yield ranging from 8,000 kg/ha for 6-year-old vines, down to 5,000 kg/ha for vines that are 40 years or older.

UTIEL-REQUENA DO
Valencia

This large and important, essentially red-wine district is situated in the extreme west of the province of Valencia. Although distilling wine and the *doble pasta* process were once the area's forte, softer, more palatable reds are now being made, and the best dry *rosados* are fresh and delicate for such sunny climes.

🍇 Bobal, Garnacha, Meseguera, Tardana, Tempranillo, Viura

🍷 2–5 years (red), 9–18 months (*rosados*)

✓ *Augusto Egli* (Casa Lo Alto)

VALDEORRAS DO
Galicia

Until Rías Baixas came on the scene, this was Galicia's most promising district. With vines planted on terraced, slaty hillsides flanking the River Sil and Valdeorras's northern, wet, Atlantic-influenced climate, these wines have never been overburdened with alcohol, as so much Spanish wine was once upon a time, and refreshing acidity is part of their charm. The best wineries have now been modernized and are even better than they used to be, particularly for white wines made from the Godello grape.

🍇 Doña Blanca, Garnacha, Godello, Gran Negro, Lado, María Ardoña, Mencía, Merenzao, Palomino

🍷 1–4 years (red), 1 year (white and *rosado*)

✓ *Godeval • Guitián • Jesus Nazareno • Joaquín Rebolledo • Valdesil* (Godello Sobre Lías)

VALDEPEÑAS DO
Castille-La Mancha

This was once Castille-La Mancha's solitary fine-wine area. Despite the torrid heat (the climate has been described as nine months of winter, three months of hell) and an apathetic attitude held by far too many producers, some terrific wines are being made here by a minority of wineries, and they represent very good value. The rich, red, stony soil hides a water-retentive limestone base that helps offset the lack of rainfall. The best reds are medium to full bodied, pure Tempranillo, with a wonderfully rich yet well-balanced flavour, and more and more new-oak influence. The *rosados* can be smooth and fruity, but it would take a complete overhaul of the vineyards, replanting them with something decent, to make the white wines appealing, although there is really no excuse for their not being fresh.

🍇 Airén, Tempranillo

🍷 2–6 years (red), 9–18 months (*rosado*)

✓ *Miguel Calatayud • J A Megía • Los Llanos • Luis Megía* (Marqués de Gastañaga) *• Felix Solis* (Viña Albali Reserva) *• Casa de la Viña* (Vega de Moriz)

VALENCIA DO
Valencia

This area was once renowned for its heavy, alcoholic, and low-quality *vino de mesa*. However, most modern wineries produce much lighter wines than before, and they are at least fresh and drinkable. There are some good reds from the Monastrell grape, which are smooth and medium bodied, and these wines may sometimes be aged in oak, but it is Tempranillo with international varietal back-up from Cabernet Sauvignon and Syrah that are making the fastest progress. The deliciously sweet and raisiny Moscatel is consistently excellent value, often performing well under blind conditions against French Muscat de Beaumes de Venise that sells for twice the price.

🍇 Forcayat, Garnacha, Malvasía, Meseguera, Monastrell, Moscatel, Pedro Ximénez, Planta Fina, Tempranillo, Tortosí, Viura

🍷 1–4 years (red), 9–18 months (white and *rosado*), upon opening (Moscatel)

✓ *Rafael Cambra* (Uno, Minimum) *• CA de Villar • Vícente Gandía • Augusto Egli* (particularly good-value Moscatel) *• Enguerro* (Distinto) *• Schenk* (Cavas Murviedro) *• Tierra Hernández • La Viña* (El Prado)

VALLE DE GÜÍMAR DO
Canary Islands

This appellation was established in 1996 for wines from the eastern side of Tenerife, just south of downtown Santa Cruz. The vineyards here abut cultivated fields, which are irrigated and thus indirectly feed these vines. Before gaining DO status, these wines were not even sold locally, but consumed by the people who produced them.

🍇 Listán, Listán Negro, Negramoll

VALLE DE LA OROTAVA DO
Canary Islands

Established in 1996, this appellation covers wines produced on the lush, northern side of Tenerife, between the appellations of Tacoronte-Acentejo and Ycoden-Daute-Isora. Before they were granted DO status, these wines were sold under the *vino de la tierra* (literally "country wine") of La Orotava-Los Realos.

🍇 Listán, Listán Negro

VALLES DE BENAVENTE VC
Castille-Léon

Immediately south of Tierra de Léon DO, across the provincial border in Zamora, the vineyards of Benavente were once famous for producing inexpensive *pétillant rosado*. Pago de Valleoscuro, a blend of Tempranillo and Prieto Picudo, is not a *Pago* denomination, but it is the region's best wine.

✓ *Bodegas Otero* (Pago de Valleoscuro)

VALTIENDAS VC
Castille-Léon

To all intents and purposes, this could be a little chunk of Ribera del Duero in the province of Segovia, where only the following grape varieties are allowed: Albillo, Cabernet Sauvignon, Garnacha, Merlot, Syrah, and Tempranillo.

VINOS DE MADRID DO
Madrid

Much admired by Casanova, who sought refuge in Madrid at a time when the capital was rapidly expanding at the expense of its vineyards, these wines probably assumed a rarity value that outshone their intrinsic quality. By extending the appellation well beyond its fast-disappearing 18th-century boundaries, Vinos de Madrid was resurrected in 1990, although you would have to be a greater lover of these wines than Casanova to declare your open admiration for them. There are, however, a couple of exceptions to the rule, and one of these, Jesús Díaz e Hijos, is exceptional by any standards.

🍇 Airén, Albillo, Garnacha, Malvar, Tinto Fino

🍷 Upon purchase (2–3 years for recommended wines)

✓ *Jesús Díaz e Hijos • Francisco Figuero • Jeromín* (Manu)

XÉRÈS *or* JEREZ-XÉRÈS-SHERRY DO
See Sherry Country, p379

YCODEN-DAUTE-ISORA DO
Canary Islands

This DO was established in 1995 for the wines that are produced on the northwestern corner of the island of Tenerife. In this area, the grapes are usually grown on terraces, which are often irrigated. Before they gained DO status, these wines were sold under the *vino de la tierra* of Icod de Los Vinos, a name that recalls their long-lost fame. After the Battle of Trafalgar, the Canaries were a favourite watering hole with the British Royal Navy, and the orange-tinged white wines of this area were apparently enjoyed by all ranks.

🍇 Listán, Listán Negro

YECLA DO
Murcia

You might think that these stony-limestone vineyards between Alicante and Jumilla should do rather well in terms of quality, but although some decent wines can be found, nothing special stands out.

The reds produced here are either ink-black, *doble pasta*-style wines, or are cherry-coloured, generally with good body and fruit. Wines from the Campo Arriba zone in the north of this appellation are permitted to add this name to the Yecla DO if they are either red or *rosado*, and are made from 100 per cent Monastrell grapes harvested at almost half the yield required elsewhere in Yecla. The white wines produced in Yecla are at their best fresh, clean, and pleasantly fruity, but, again, tend not to be remarkable.

🍇 Garnacha, Meseguera, Monastrell, Verdil

🍷 2–5 years (red, but 3–6 years for Yecla Campo Arriba), 1–2 years (white and *rosado*)

✓ *Castaño* (Monastrell, Pozuelo, Las Gruesas) *• Bodegas Juan Gil* (Pedrera) *• Ochoa Palao* (Cuvée Prestige)

YECLA CAMPO ARRIBA DO
See Yecla DO

RIOJA AND NAVARRA

The first wine to receive DOCa status, Spain's highest classification, Rioja still produces more fine wine than any other region in this country. Neighbouring Navarra, which was once regarded as the country's best source of rosado *but little else, has upgraded its vineyards and wineries and now boasts three* Pago *appellations, making it one of the most exciting sources of new-wave Spanish wines.*

ONLY A SHORT DRIVE from the shabby suburbs of the commercial city of Bilbao, the dramatic beauty of an upland valley becomes apparent, rich with architectural treasures of the 12th century, isolated hilltop *pueblos*, a philanthropic people, a generous tradition, and a hearty cuisine.

RIOJA

Rioja is oaky, and all attempts to rid the wine of oak are doomed to failure. Oak is the basis of its fame and the reason it became Spain's first and greatest red-wine success, and while critics who suggest that these wines are too oaky for today's more sophisticated

consumers may have a point, there is precious little left in most Rioja once you take away the oak.

It was the French who originally blessed the wines of this region with their unmistakable sweet-vanilla oak identity. As early as the 18th century, a few enlightened *Riojanos* had looked to France – Bordeaux particularly – to improve their winemaking skills. The transformation that resulted was subtle compared to the radical changes that occurred in Rioja in the 1840s and 1860s, after phylloxera, a louse that attacks vine roots, had wreaked havoc on French vineyards. A number of *vignerons*, mostly *Bordelais* but some Burgundian too, gave up hope of reviving their own vineyards and descended upon Rioja to set up new wineries. Their methods dramatically improved the quality and style of Rioja, while other Frenchmen, mostly merchants from Bordeaux, opened up an instantly lucrative trade for the wine, as they desperately sought to top up the dwindling produce of their own devastated vineyards.

Origins

Wine has been made in Rioja since at least the 2nd century BC, when the Romans conquered the area. Rioja was sufficiently well respected by 1560 that its producers forbade the use of grapes from outside the region, guaranteeing the authenticity of their

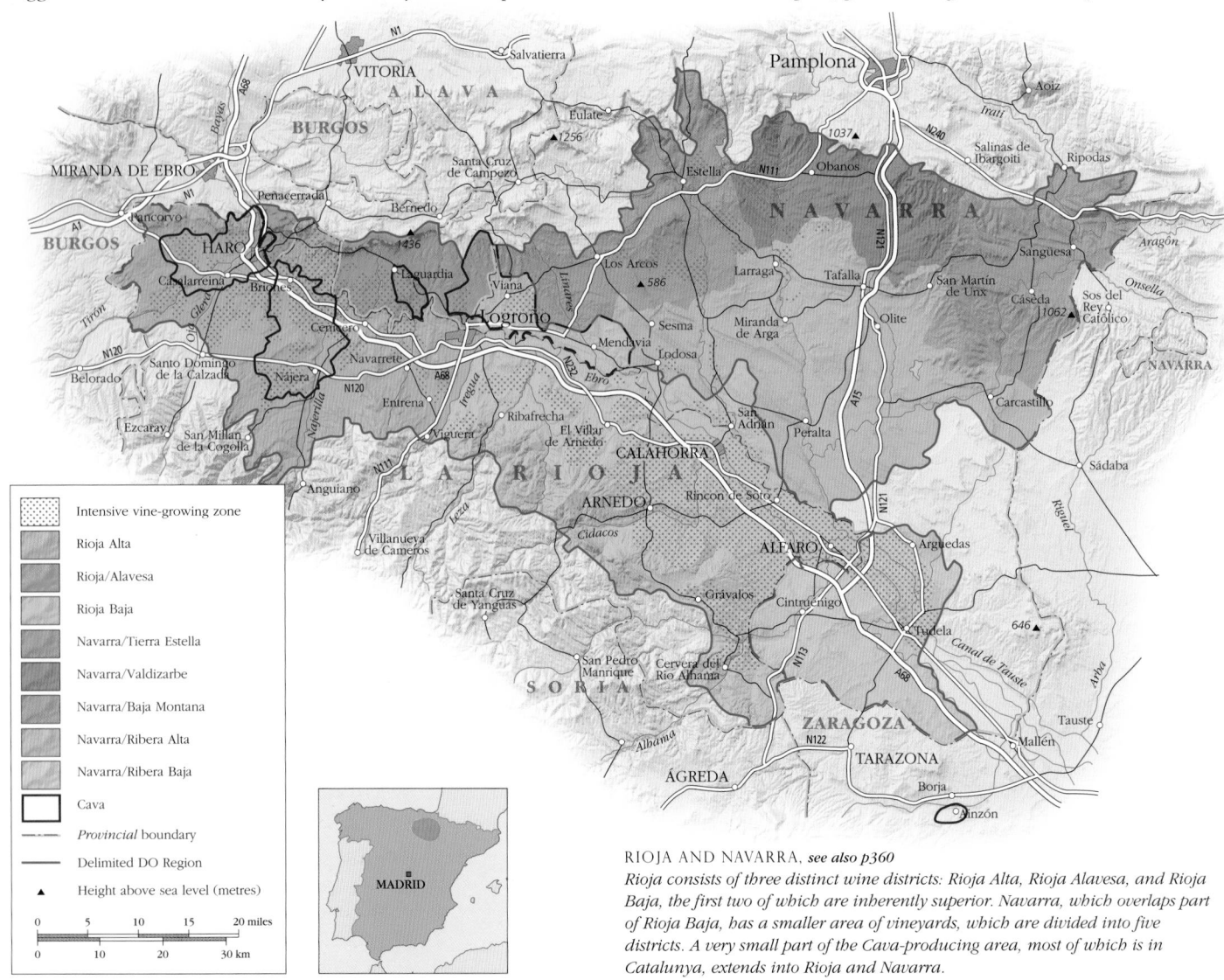

RIOJA AND NAVARRA, *see also p360*
Rioja consists of three distinct wine districts: Rioja Alta, Rioja Alavesa, and Rioja Baja, the first two of which are inherently superior. Navarra, which overlaps part of Rioja Baja, has a smaller area of vineyards, which are divided into five districts. A very small part of the Cava-producing area, most of which is in Catalunya, extends into Rioja and Navarra.

Intensive vine-growing zone
Rioja Alta
Rioja/Alavesa
Rioja Baja
Navarra/Tierra Estella
Navarra/Valdizarbe
Navarra/Baja Montana
Navarra/Ribera Alta
Navarra/Ribera Baja
Cava
Provincial boundary
Delimited DO Region
▲ Height above sea level (metres)

0   5   10   15   20 miles
0   10   20   30 km

FACTORS AFFECTING TASTE AND QUALITY

LOCATION
Situated in northern Spain in the upper valley of the River Ebro, Rioja and Navarra are bounded to the northeast by the Pyrenees and to the southwest by the Sierra de la Demanda. Navarra has the second-most northerly vineyards in Spain.

CLIMATE
The Cantabrian Mountains, a range that is modest in elevation yet impressive in structure, provide a major key to the quality of Rioja, protecting the region from the devastating winds whipped up over the Bay of Biscay and holding in precarious check the influence of the Atlantic and Mediterranean. That of the former is at its strongest in Navarra, and of the latter in the Rioja Baja. Temperature rises and rainfall decreases as one moves east towards the Mediterranean. The Pyrenees also provide shelter from the north, but winters can be cold and foggy, particularly in Navarra. Rioja can suffer from hailstorms and the hot, dry *solano* wind.

ASPECT
Vineyards are variously located, from the highest in the foothills of the Pyrenees in Navarra to those on the flatter lands of the Rioja Baja in the southeast. Generally, the best vineyards are in the central hill country of the Rioja Alta and the Alavesa.

SOIL
Although soils do vary, the common denominator is limestone. In Navarra, limestone contains between 25 and 45 per cent "active" lime, and is coated by a layer of silty-alluvium near the Ebro or by weathered limestone and sandstone topsoil in drier areas. Limestone with either sandstone or calcareous clay and slaty deposits dominate the Rioja Alavesa and Alta, while a ferruginous-clay and a silty-loam of alluvial origin cover a limestone base in the Rioja Baja.

VITICULTURE AND VINIFICATION
Most wines are a blend of at least three grapes from different areas within a single appellation; very few are 100 per cent pure varietal or single-estate wines. The traditional vinification process, which is still used to produce the local *vino nuevo*, is a crude form of carbonic maceration carried out in open vats; the grapes are trodden after the first few days of inter-cellular fermentation. This is much as Beaujolais wines used to be made, but the result here is much coarser, with a dark-damson colour and lots of youthful tannin. Most wines are, however, vinified in the normal manner, but aged longer than other commercial wines. Although recent trends favour shorter oak-ageing and longer bottle-maturation, the unique character of Rioja still relies heavily on oak, and it is essential for its future that it should remain so.

GRAPE VARIETIES
Primary varieties: Tempranillo, Viura (Macabéo)
Secondary varieties: Cabernet Sauvignon, Chardonnay, Cinsault, Garnacha (Grenache), Garnacha Blanca (Grenache Blanc), Graciano, Malvasia, Mazuelo (Carignan), Monastrell (Mourvèdre), Moscatel Grano Menudo (Muscat Blanc à Petits Grains)

---

wines with a brand on the *pellejos* (goat-skins) in which they were transported. Wooden barrels came into use in the 18th century, but were five times the size of casks today and it was not until 1860 at Marqués de Riscal that the first Bordeaux *barriques* were used (although there seems to be evidence that Manuel Quintano was the first, *c.*1800). One particularly influential Frenchman, Jean Pineau, was employed to teach French methods to local growers. In 1868, upon completion of his contract, Pineau was employed by Don Camilo Hurtado de Amezaga, the Marqués de Riscal, who was an admirer of Médoc wines and had lived in Bordeaux for 15 years. He had planted Cabernet Sauvignon on his estate in 1863 and wanted Pineau to develop his new *bodega* in the manner of the most advanced wine châteaux in the Médoc.

RIOJA'S CLASSIC WINE DISTRICTS
Rioja's vineyards are located along the Ebro Valley, between Haro and Alfaro, and throughout its hinterland, with vines clustered around many of the Ebro's tributaries, one of which, the Oja River, has given its name to the region. Most Rioja is red and blended from wines or grapes (primarily Tempranillo and Garnacha) originating from the region's three districts (Rioja Alta, Rioja Alavesa, and Rioja Baja), although many of the best-quality are single-district wines and a handful of single-estate Rioja have also emerged in recent years.

Rioja Alta
Logroño and Haro, the principal towns of Rioja, are both in the Rioja Alta. Logroño is a very big town by Spanish standards, but Haro, at the western edge of the region, is an enclosed hilltop community and a much smaller, far more charming, older, and traditional place. The area's wine is Rioja's fullest in terms of fruit and concentration, and can be velvety smooth. Bodegas Muga makes fine examples of pure Rioja Alta, as do CVNE (Compañía Vinícola del Norte de España) – in the form of their Imperial range – in nine years out of every ten.

Rioja Alavesa
There are no large towns in the Alavesa, a district that is similar in climate to the Alta. Wines produced here are Rioja's fullest in body and reveal a much firmer character than those of the Alta and the Baja, with greater acidity. It was to the Alavesa that Pedro Domecq came, after years of intensive research, to plant a vast estate of 400 hectares (985 acres), cultivating his vines on wires as opposed to using the bush method traditional to the region. Apart from Bodegas Domecq, which produces mainly pure Alavesa wines, Remelluri and Contino, two single-estate Alavesas, are both typical of the district.

Rioja Baja
Baja is a semi-arid area influenced by the Mediterranean, and is hotter, sunnier, and drier than the Alta and the Alavesa, with rainfall averaging between 38 and 43 centimetres (15 and 17 inches) per year, but falling as low as 25 centimetres (10 inches) at Alfaro in the

GRAPE VARIETIES IN RIOJA

Although there has been a recent trend towards pure varietal wines (particularly Tempranillo for *tinto* and Viura for *blanco*), most Rioja is still blended, thus its character and quality depend to a large extent upon the producer's own house style. In addition to blending the strengths and weaknesses of different terroirs, there is usually an attempt to balance the various varietal characteristics of one or more of the seven grapes that are permitted in Rioja. These grape varieties are: Tempranillo, Garnacha, Graciano, Mazuelo, Viura, Malvasia, and the little-utilized Garnacha Blanca.

A TYPICAL RED RIOJA BLEND

Tempranillo 70 per cent for its bouquet, acidity, and ageing qualities. It ripens some two weeks before the Garnacha (*temprano* means "early") and is also known in Spain as the Cencibel, Tinto Fino, or Ull de Llebre. Tempranillo has a naturally low oxidizing enzyme content, giving its wines exceptional longevity.

Garnacha 15 per cent for body and alcohol – too much can make the wine coarse. This is the Grenache of the Rhône, also known as the Lladoner and Aragonés. It is the major variety of the Rioja Baja, where it can produce wines of 16 per cent alcohol.

Graciano 7.5 per cent for freshness, flavour, and aroma. A singular variety with the unusual property of thin, yet tough black skin.

Mazuelo 7.5 per cent for colour, tannin, and good ageing characteristics. This is the Carignan of southern France and is also known in Spain by the alternative name of the Cariñena.

To the above a small proportion of white grapes, perhaps 5–10 per cent of Viura, may sometimes be added, but this tradition is fading. Cabernet Sauvignon is not an authorized variety in Rioja, but is permitted by special dispensation for *bodegas* that have historically used the variety (such as Marqués de Riscal, which uses 15 to 60 per cent) and those who are growing it on a trial basis. Although a number of *bodegas* have experimental plantations, Cabernet Sauvignon is not of any great significance for the vast majority of Rioja wines.

A TYPICAL WHITE RIOJA BLEND

Viura 95 per cent for freshness and fragrance. This grape has reasonable acidity and a good resistance to oxidation. It is also known as the Macabéo and Alcañón in other parts of Spain, and is one of three major Cava varieties.

Malvasia 5 per cent for richness, fragrance, acidity, and complexity. Also known as the Rojal Blanco and Subirat, this grape has a tendency to colour a patchy red when ripe, so pressing must be quick to avoid tainting the juice.

Most white wines are pure Viura, although some contain up to 50 per cent Malvasia. Some *bodegas* use a tiny amount of Garnacha Blanca, particularly in lesser years, to increase alcohol levels, but they do so at the expense of a certain amount of freshness and aroma.

south. Some 20 per cent of the vines growing here come within, and can claim, the Navarra appellation. The wines are deep-coloured and very alcoholic, some as strong as 18 per cent, but lack acidity, aroma, and finesse, and are best used for blending.

NAVARRA

The wine-growing region of Navarra overlaps part of the Rioja Baja, but although not quite in the same league as Rioja in general, it is capable of producing some fine wines of exceptional value.

Recent marketing successes have halted the decline in Navarra's vineyards and encouraged various ambitious trials with foreign grapes such as Merlot, while previous experimental varieties such as Cabernet Sauvignon are now fully recommended. According to the Estación de Viticultura y Enología de Navarra (EVENA), Spain's most advanced viticultural and oenological research station, these Bordeaux varieties are ideally suited to Navarra's soil and climate.

A rosy past

Navarra was once virtually synonymous with *rosado* and this style still accounts for almost half of total production, but what has really held back the reputation of this area has been the high-yielding clones of the Garnacha (*syn* Grenache) grape. This grape variety can make good *rosado*, but except as part of a blend, rarely excels in red wines when cropped at high levels. Garnacha took up more than 65 per cent of Navarra's vines, so the region was ill equipped to develop beyond its *rosado* horizon. Furthermore, Tempranillo, the grape upon which Rioja's success has been built and indubitably Spain's finest red-wine variety, represents just 15 per cent of Navarra's vines. This proportion has, however, doubled since 1990, and with Tempranillo and Cabernet Sauvignon making up 60 per cent and 20 per cent respectively of all new vines currently being planted, Navarra is set to achieve a tremendous boost in quality.

According to Javier Ochoa, former chief oenologist at EVENA,

TIERRA ESTELLA, NAVARRA
The picturesque village of Maneru is situated near Estella, southwest of Pamplona. Tempranillo is the main variety grown in the area's vineyards.

the perfect Navarra blend should be something in the order of 50 per cent Tempranillo, 30 per cent Garnacha, and 20 per cent Cabernet Sauvignon, but I wonder if even this is tempered by the large amount of Garnacha that will still exist when the replanting programme has concluded. Reminiscent of Australia's decision to rip out its oldest Riesling vineyards just before its top-quality Riesling wines started to receive the recognition they long deserved, so Navarra has pulled up some of its oldest Garnacha vineyards just as wine lovers the world over began to appreciate just how stunning Garnacha could be from low-yielding old vines.

NAVARRA'S DISTRICTS

The region is divided into five districts:

Baja Montaña

Situated in the Montaña foothills, Baja Montaña is the highest and wettest area of Navarra and the vintage is considerably later here than in the south of the region, hence the greater importance placed on early-ripening Tempranillo. Extra rain causes the grape yield to be between 50 and 100 per cent higher than that of any of the other four areas. The district produces some of Navarra's best *rosados*, fresh and fruity in aroma and flavour.

Ribera Alta

With twice the number of vineyards as Baja Montaña and Tierra Estella, this is one of the two most important of Navarra's districts. Ribera Alta borders the Rioja Alta and produces some of the region's finest wines. The *rosados* are smooth and aromatic, and the reds soft and fruity, but with as much as 40 per cent Viura planted, this is a major white-wine player and the style is soft, dry, and fresh.

Ribera Baja

One of the two most important wine districts of Navarra, Ribera Baja is very hot and dry and includes approximately 20 per cent of what is effectively the Rioja Baja district. The wines produced are mostly red, made principally from the Garnacha (Grenache) grape, and typically deep-coloured, full, and robust. Muscat à Petits Grains accounts for 10 per cent of the vines planted and produces a sweet Moscatel-style wine.

Tierra Estella

Viticulturally as important as Baja Montaña and climatically similar to Valdizarbe in the north, though gradually getting drier further south, the Tierra Estella makes pleasant, fruity reds and *rosados* from the Tempranillo, which is heavily planted here. The Garnacha variety is less important since its wines tend to oxidize. Some crisp white wines from the Viura grape are also produced.

Valdizarbe

The smallest of Navarra's five districts, Valdizarbe has a slightly drier climate than the Baja Montaña and is an excellent source of good-value red and *rosado* wines, although some of these have an unfortunate tendency to oxidize.

THE WINE PRODUCERS OF
RIOJA AND NAVARRA

Note Unless specifically stated otherwise, all recommendations (including "Entire range") are for red wine only. Reds from both regions are generally drinking well in their third year, but top *cuvées* often improve for up to ten years,

and exceptional ones can age gracefully for decades, while most white and *rosado* wines are best fresh and should thus be consumed when purchased. *See* p362 for details of the wine styles mentioned.

BODEGAS AGE
Rioja
***See also* Campo Viejo and Marqués del Puerto**

Part of Bebidas (formerly Savin), this *bodega* is now better known as Bodegas & Bebidas or ByB, and is

under the same ownership as Campo Viejo and Marqués del Puerto. The basic quality is rather uninspiring, but top of the range wines are usually very good value indeed. Labels include Agessimo, Azpilicueta Martínez, Credencial, Don Ernesto, Marqués del Romeral (traditional style and the best), and Siglo (modern style).

✓ *Reserva • Gran Reserva*

FINCA ALLENDE
Rioja
★★

One of the fastest-rising stars on the Riojan firmament.

✓ *Entire range*

AMÉZOLA DE LA MORA
Rioja
★

I have encountered a couple of interesting wines from this Rioja Alta estate. One to watch.

✓ *Viña Amézola • Señorío de Amézola*

ARTADI
Rioja
★★

The finest modern-style, fruit-driven Rioja from the very expensive top of the range (the awesome El Pison), right down to the juicy *joven*. Artadi also produces wines in Navarra (*see* Artazuri) and Alicante (Artadi Landeras).

✓ *Entire range*

BAIGORRI
Rioja
★★

Sleek, beautifully crafted wines by super-gifted Simon Arina.

✓ *Entire range* (especially Reserva)

BARÓN DE LEY
Rioja
★★★☆ Ⓥ

See also El Coto

An exciting single-estate Rioja, produced by Barón de Ley using exclusively French, rather than American, oak. It is currently one of the two greatest Riojas in production (the other being Contino).

✓ *Entire range*

BODEGAS BERBERANA
Rioja
★☆ Ⓥ

This producer can be disappointing at the lower end, but makes good to very good *reserva* and *gran reserva* wines that are full, fat, and sometimes even blowsy, with soft, oaky fruit. Berberana is also good value for older vintages. Labels include Preferido (*joven* style), Carta de Plata (younger style), Carta de Oro (bigger, richer), and Berberana *reserva* and *gran reserva* (best).

✓ *Reserva • Gran Reserva • Tempranillo • Dragon Tempranillo*

BODEGAS BERONIA
Rioja

This is an old firm on the up, with some truly exciting wines, including fascinating pure varietals.

✓ *Gran Reserva • Ill A C • Reserva •*

Reserva Mazuelo • Selección de 198 Barricas

BODEGAS BILBAÍNAS
Rioja
★☆

Major vineyard owners, Bilbaínas are producers of traditionally styled Rioja. Labels include Viña Pomal (deep, dark, and well-oaked with plummy fruit), Viña Zaco (oakier), Vendimia Especial (excellent older vintages) and Royal Carlton (one of Rioja's Cava brands).

✓ *Reserva • Gran Reserva*

LA CALANDRIA
Navarra
★

This boutique *bodega* was established by Javier Continente and Luis Fernández, two friends since childhood. Javier studied fine arts and, to this day, runs a touring miniature mechanical theatre. Luis went to Bordeaux to study oenology. They both have a passion for pure Garnacha and are on a mission to save some of the oldest Garnacha vineyards in Spain, which are in danger of being lost just as the world wakes up to the potential of this grape. Tierga is the most exciting pure Garnacha I have tasted in years. It comes from 60-year-old Garnacha vines in the Moncayo Valley, an unclassified area in the wilds to the west of Zaragoza in a *Vino de la Tierra* area called Bajo Aragón. It is midway between Campo de Borja DO and Cariñena DO, both areas that were traditionally viewed as Garnacha country. The old vines in Tierga produce a Garnacha vastly superior to any such wine from Navarra – or, for that matter, any other Spanish DO. I have been following this wine since before it was released and found its Grenache fruit to be so fresh, beguiling, and utterly delicious that when I first saw a bottle of the 2008 with a label, I was shocked to read it claimed a strength of 16%. It did not taste or smell alcoholic. It could have been 14% or a very clever 14.5%, but never 16%, so I sought confirmation and was assured of its accuracy. The 2009 Cientruenos was a mere 14.5%. A *calandria* is a type of lark, and the ambition of this winery is to nest in as many old Garnacha vineyards as possible.

✓ *Tierga • Cientruenos*

BODEGAS CAMPILLO
Rioja
★ Ⓥ

See also Faustino Martínez

Touted by many as a new Rioja, Campillo has been around for some years, initially as a second label of Faustino Martínez. Even at the time of the first edition of this encyclopedia in 1988, Campillo was "often better than the principal label". This was because these wines were used to break in Faustino's new barrels, a strategy that caused Campillo to outshine

Faustino's flagship wines.

✓ *Entire range*

BODEGAS CAMPO VIEJO
Rioja
★ Ⓥ

See also Bodegas AGE and Marqués del Puerto

A large producer with major vineyard holdings under the same ownership as Bodegas AGE and Marqués del Puerto, Campo Viejo has a well-earned reputation for good-quality wines of exceptional value. Its *tinto* wines are typically full-bodied and marked by a fatness of ripe fruit and rich vanilla-oak. Labels include Albor (*joven* style), Viña Alcorta (wood-aged pure varietals), San Asensio (exuberantly fruity) and Marqués de Villamagna (created for bottle-ageing, classic and fine rather than fat).

✓ *Reserva • Gran Reserva • Marqués de Villamagna Gran Reserva*

LUIS CAÑAS
Rioja
★★★☆

Wine growers for more than two centuries and winemakers since 1928 – but winemakers of great class since the late 1990s, when the effect of their new winery (1994) began to kick in. A tendency for high alcohol levels, especially in its horrendously expensive flagship wine Hiru 3 Racimos, but the fruit is so pure and the tannins so soft, ripe, and elegantly structured that they are not big.

✓ *Entire range* (especially Hiru 3 Racimos, Amaren Tempranillo Reserva)

BODEGAS CARLOS SERRES
Rioja

Carlos Serres was founded by Charles (later known as Carlos) Serres in 1869, one year after his fellow Frenchman Jean Pineau went to Marqués de Riscal. The house style tends to be on the light side, but the *reserva* and *gran reserva* wines often have an elegant richness.

✓ *Carlomagno* (Reserva) • *Carlos Serres* (Gran Reserva)

BODEGAS CASTILLO DE MONJARDÍN
Navarra
★

An up-and-coming new *bodega* growing a high proportion of Tempranillo and French varieties. Fresh, creamy-rich red and white wines, both with and without oak. Exciting potential.

✓ *Chardonnay • Tinto Crianza*

CONTINO
Rioja
★★★☆

Owned by CVNE and a group of growers (whose combined holdings comprise the vineyards of this

single-estate Rioja), Contino was not the first single-vineyard Rioja, but its great success encouraged other boutique wineries to follow. It also stimulated interest in French oak as opposed to American.

✓ *Contino Rioja Reserva • Viña del Olivo*

BODEGAS CORRÁL
Rioja

This improving *bodega* has relatively few vineyards and is best-known for its Don Jácobo range, although the underrated Corral Gran Reserva is by far its best wine.

✓ *Corral Gran Reserva*

COSECHEROS ALAVESES
Rioja
★☆ Ⓥ

Perhaps one reason why this is one of Rioja's better cooperatives is that it is so small that it is hardly a cooperative in the commonly accepted definition of the term. The other reason is the excellent location of their vines around Laguardia in Rioja Alavesa. The style is always bright and fruity.

✓ *Artadi* (including *blanco*) • *Orobio • Valdepomares*

BODEGAS EL COTO
Rioja
★★☆

See also Barón de Ley

These are wines of immaculate style, grace, and finesse, particularly the Coto de Imaz and, more recently, the single-vineyard Barón de Ley.

✓ *El Coto • Coto de Imaz Reserva*

CVNE
Compañía Vinícola del Norte de España Rioja
★

See also Contino

Also known as Cune (pronounced "coonay"), Compañía Vinícola del Norte de España Rioja was once the most old-fashioned and traditional of Rioja producers and its vintages were legendary, easily lasting 30 years or more. Ironically these wines went through a dicey patch following the installation of a £12 million state-of-the-art winery, but CVNE is coming to terms with this new technology, and recent vintages are picking up.

✓ *Imperial* (Reserva, Gran Reserva) • *Viña Real* (Gran Reserva, Pagos de Viña Real)

BODEGAS DOMECQ
Rioja
★ Ⓥ

Part of Pernod Ricard since 2005, this is just one of 11 Domecq wineries scattered over nine Spanish appellations. José Ignacio Domecq's original concept to create the largest contiguous vineyard in Rioja was daring, but one-time second brand Marqués de Arienzo has come out on top. It was impossible to establish Domecq Domaine (sold as Privilegio Rey Sancho on the Spanish market itself) as a super-sized, single-vineyard Rioja. Marqués de Arienzo is effectively the wine that Domecq Domaine once was, with Viña Eguia taking over as the cheaper brand.

✓ *Gran Reserva* • *Reserva*

DOMINIO DE MONTALVO
Rioja
★

This is an innovative barrel-fermented, pure Viura *blanco*.

✓ *Dominio de Montalvo Viura*

BODEGAS FAUSTINO MARTÍNEZ
Rioja
★

If given sufficient bottle-age (keeping five years will do no harm) Faustino *reserva* and *gran reserva* can attain exceptional finesse, but are often outshone by Campillo, which started out as a second brand tasked with soaking up the unwanted oakiness from the *bodega's* new barrels.

✓ *Faustino V* (Reserva) • *Faustino I* (Gran Reserva)

FEDERICO PATERNINA
Rioja

These wines are generally light and lacking, especially Banda Azul, its best-known label. You must go up to *reserva* level to find real richness, although the *gran reserva* (Conde de Los Andes) is unpredictable, ranging from pure brilliance to absolute volatility.

✓ *Viña Vial* (Reserva)

BODEGAS GUELBENZU
Non-DO Navarra
★★ ⓥ

Taken out of the DO in order to increase quality and consistency through less restrictive regulations, these wines are sold as *Vino de la Tierra* (Ribera de Queiles). The ridiculously cheap Guelbenzu Jardín is a delicious, easy-drinking wine made from 30–40 year-old Garnacha vines, superior to 90 per cent of "authentic" DO Navarra. Guelbenzu Azul (mainly Tempranillo-Cabernet Sauvignon with 10–20 per cent Merlot) is where the class starts. Evo (Cabernet Sauvignon-Tempranillo reverses the emphasis, plus 10–20 per cent Merlot) was once the top-of-the-line, but Guelbenzu has topped this with the magnificent Lautus (50 per cent Tempranillo, 30 per cent Merlot, 10 per cent Cabernet Sauvignon, 10 per cent Garnacha).

✓ *Entire range*

BODEGA INURRIETA
Navarra
★

With vines in the ground as recently as 1999 and the winery opened two years later, this up-and-coming producer has quickly impressed with a varied range of Navarra wines, including some really nice highlights.

✓ *Altos* • *Mediodía* • *Norte* • *Orchídea*

BODEGAS IRACHE
Navarra
★

This *bodega* includes the Prado de Irache vineyard, one of only nine such denominations in the entire country.

✓ *Gran Irache* • *Pago de Prado de Irache* • *Viña Irache*

BODEGAS JULIÁN CHIVITE
Navarra
★★☆

Bodegas Julián Chivite typically produces soft, mellow, smooth, oaky wines with plenty of creamy-coconutty fruit flavour. In 2009, Chivite's Gran Vino de Arínzano (a blend of Tempranillo, Merlot, and Cabernet Sauvignon) became the first *Pago* appellation in Northern Spain.

✓ *Blanco Colección 125* • *Blanco Colección 125 Vendimia Tardía* • *Chivite Reserva* • *Gran Feudo* • *Pago de Arínzano* • *Viña Marcos*

LAR DE PAULA
Rioja
★

Pure Tempranillo specialist Toni Meruelo buys his grapes only from top-quality Alavesa vineyards. He produces ultra-modern wines brimming with juicy fruit and supported by silky tannins.

✓ *Entire range*

LEALTANZA
Rioja
★★

High-tech winery blending the best of tradition to produce top-class, exclusively Tempranillo wines.

✓ *Entire range*

BODEGAS MAGAÑA
Navarra
★

Juan Magaña is best-known for varietal wines, particularly the excellent Merlot, but his Merlot-Tempranillo blend called Eventum has more finesse.

✓ *Eventum* • *Merlot*

MANZANOS
Rioja
★★

High-tech winery blending the best of tradition to produce a range of top-class, exclusively Tempranillo wines.

✓ *Entire range*

MARQUÉS DE ARIENZO
See Bodegas Domecq

MARQUÉS DE CÁCERES
Rioja
★

Marqués de Cáceres is often quoted as part of the modern school of Rioja winemaking, but is more accurately described as a traditional Bordeaux style, and its wines benefit from bottle-ageing.

Antea is an excellent barrel-fermented white.

✓ *Antea* • *Reserva* • *Gran Reserva*

MARQUÉS DE GRIÑÓN
Rioja
★★ ⓥ

Marqués de Griñón is perhaps better known for its outstanding Dominio de Valdepusa, Spain's first *Pago* DO, from south of Madrid, but it also produces excellent modern-style Rioja, including some wines that incorporate "experimental" Syrah, Merlot and Cabernet Sauvignon. Wines also sold under the Marqués de Concordia label.

✓ *Entire range*

MARQUÉS DE MURRIETA
Rioja
★★★☆

The wines from this *bodega* have undergone a transformation over the past decade, leaning towards a much fresher, more modern style, but Marqués de Murrieta has had the wisdom to retain its remarkable range of old vintages under the Castillo Ygay label, even if they are a pale reflection of how they used to make this wine. Castillo Ygay is a *gran reserva*, which today requires just five years' ageing before release, including at least 18 months in oak. Although the Castillo Ygay at the time of writing – the 2001 – was well over these legal limits, having spent 31 months in oak, the oldest vintage commercially available at the same time – the 1978 – spent no less than 216 months in oak. Yet even that is a shadow of Castillo Ygay's former self. For a start, the oldest vintage available is less than 30 years old, whereas I can remember the oldest vintage changing in 1983 from 1934 to a sprightly 1942, and the time in oak moving from 560 months to a mere 470 months. Were these wines refreshed? Of course they were probably well within the 85% EU minimum.

✓ *Entire range*

MARQUÉS DE RISCAL
Rioja
★★★☆

When the first edition of this book came out, Riscal's Swiss importer faxed Francisco Hurtado de Amezaga a copy of this page claiming "the red wines from Rioja's most famous *bodega* have an unpleasant musty-mushroom character", upon receipt of which Hurtado de Amezaga recalled his top winemaker from Riscal's Rueda outpost to investigate. These wines had gradually acquired a musty character since the 1960s, prior to which they were always among the top three Riojas produced, but since they had the oldest and greatest reputation in Rioja, no one had dared mention this. Every one of Riscal's 20,000 barrels was tasted and 2,000 were immediately destroyed, with the equivalent of 600,000 bottles of

wine poured away. Another 2,000 borderline barrels were earmarked for replacement the next year and a programme instigated to renew all 20,000 over 10 years. In turning around the situation so quickly and with no expense spared, Hurtado de Amezaga ensured that Riscal would regain its position among the world's finest wines.

✓ *Reserva* • *Gran Reserva* • *Barón de Chirel*

BODEGAS DE LA MARQUESA
Rioja
★

This range includes fascinating pure varietal versions of Graciano and Mazuelo.

✓ *Entire range*

BODEGAS MARTÍNEZ BUJANDA
Rioja
★

This high-tech winery consistently produces pure, fresh *blanco* and fine, firm, fruit-driven *tinto*.

✓ *Conde de Valdemar*

BODEGAS MONTECILLO
Rioja
★

Owned by Osborne of Jerez, Montecillo covers the spread of styles, from fruity *crianza* reds, through zippy *blanco*, to great *gran reserva* reds.

✓ *Viña Cumbrero* (*blanco*) • *Reserva* • *Gran Reserva*

BODEGAS MUGA
Rioja
★★★☆

Lovely *rosado* here, but the reds are really top-class, especially Prado Enea. The basic Muga crianza is much younger and fresher, but can be bottle-aged to obtain a similar elegance and seductive, silky finish to those found in the Prado Enea.

✓ *Entire range*

BODEGAS MURUA
Rioja
★

This is a small winery dedicated to producing pure Rioja Alta Tempranillo of some finesse.

✓ *Reserva* • *Gran Reserva*

BODEGAS NEKEAS
Navarra
★★

The amazing discovery of the 1996 International Wine Challenge, Nekeas defeated some of the greatest Chardonnays from Burgundy and the New World to win the coveted Chardonnay Trophy. Made by Spain's former agricultural minister, Francisco San Martin, who certainly knows his vines, and probably his onions too.

✓ *Entire range*

BODEGAS OCHOA
Navarra
❷

After an off-period in the 1990s, this old-established Navarra producer has not put a foot wrong of late.

✓ *Entire range* (especially Graciano and Garnacha)

BODEGAS OLARRA
Rioja
★

This ultra-modern winery always used to produce a good Rioja across the range, but vintages became erratic in the mid-1980s, then decidedly poor. Improvements were first noticed with the 1990 vintage in the mid-1990s. Since then, the quality has been consistent. Labels include La Catedral.

✓ *Añares and Cerro Añón ranges*

OTAZU
Navarra
★★

This winery has earned a *Pago* denomination, effectively a *grand cru* – one of just nine in the entire country, though there are three in the Navarra region.

✓ *Entire range*

BODEGAS PALACIO
Rioja
★★

An old *bodega* that has truly excelled since the early 1990s, Palacio uses French and American oak. Wines range from the pure Tempranillo Cosme Palacio y Hermanos, a very traditional Rioja that is consistently Palacio's best wine, and Milflores, which gushes with delicious, juicy fruit, making it one of the better *joven* wines produced.

✓ *Cosme Palacio y Hermanos • Glorioso • Milflores*

PALACIO DE EZA
See Tandem

BODEGAS PALACIO REMONDO
Rioja
★★

Class Rioja from the gifted hands of Alvaro Palacio.

✓ *Entire range*

PALACIO DE LA VEGA
Navarra
★★

José María Nieves produces beautifully packaged, stylish wines that are brimming with fruit and finesse, made exclusively from vines grown on this excellent estate.

✓ *Cabernet Sauvignon* (Reserva)

BODEGAS PIEDEMONTE
Navarra
★

This up-and-coming *bodega* produces excellent Cabernet Sauvignon with a silky texture and a spicy finesse.

✓ *Oligitum Cabernet Sauvignon*

BODEGAS PRÍNCIPE DE VIANA
Navarra
★❤

Formerly known as Agronavarra Cenal and having devoured and dispensed with Bodegas Canalsa, Príncipe de Viana, (the firm's premium product), has been adopted as the name of the high-tech *bodega*. Bodegas Príncipe de Viana wines have become something of a bargain compared to those of other top Navarra *bodegas*, which have gained in price as they have achieved greater quality. Príncipe de Viana does not have the finesse of the best Navarra wines, but they are much cheaper and have oodles of rich, coconutty fruit, with which I associate American oak – although some of the wines claim to use French barrels. Labels include Agramont and Campo Nuevo.

✓ *Cabernet Sauvignon • Chardonnay*

BODEGAS RAMÓN BILBAO
Rioja
★

With few of its own vineyards and a small production from mostly bought-in grapes, Ramón Bilbao's best wine is Viña Turzaballa. Its blend contains 90 per cent Tempranillo, and the wine is given plenty of time in oak. Viña Turzaballa also benefits from up to six years further ageing in bottle.

✓ *Viña Turzaballa Gran Reserva*

REAL COMPAÑÍA DE VINOS
Rioja
★

Good-value, high-quality wines exclusively from the Alavesa district.

✓ *Entire range*

REMELLURI
La Granja Nuestra Señora de Remelluri
Rioja
★★

These single-vineyard Riojas that are of consistently high quality from Labastida de Alava possess exquisite balance, elegance, and finesse, great richness of ripe fruit, and a long creamy-vanilla oak finish.

✓ *Labastida de Alava*

LA RIOJA ALTA
Rioja
★★

The Viña Alberdi *crianza* is an excellent introduction to these wines, but the serious business begins with the elegant Viña Arana and Viña Ardanza *reservas*, which are remarkably complex wines considering that they account for more than half of the firm's production. The Gran Reserva 904 is an exceptionally concentrated and classy wine, while the Gran Reserva 890 is a rare product indeed.

✓ *Barón de Oña • Finca San Martín • Gran Reserva 890 • Gran Reserva 904 • Marqués de Horo • Viña Alberdi • Viña Ardanza* (Reserva)

BODEGAS RIOJANAS
Rioja
★★

This *bodega* has built its reputation on red wines, particularly the *reserva* and *gran reserva* versions of its rich-oaky Viña Albina and the dark, plummy Monte Real with its vanilla-spice aftertaste.

✓ *Canchales* (Vino Nuevo) • *Viña Albina* (Reserva) • *Monte Real* (Reserva)

SAN VICENTE
Rioja
★★

Top quality Rioja from the makers of Numanthia in Toro.

✓ *Entire range*

BODEGA DE SARRÍA
Navarra
★

A large, well-established estate with a modern winery, producing clean, fruity wines that are constantly improving despite the death of Francisco Morriones, the oenologist responsible for establishing this *bodega's* current reputation. Labels include Viña del Portillo, Viña Ecoyen, and Viña del Perdón.

✓ *Gran Vino del Señorío de Sarría • Viña del Perdon • Viña Ecoyen • Blanco seco • Rosado*

TANDEM
Navarra
★

A new, small estate in the Valle de Yerri, with 22 hectares (55 acres) of Tempranillo, Cabernet Sauvignon, and Merlot. The presentation is very minimalist. They currently produce three wines, all of which are impressively clean and pure. My favourite is Tandem's entry-level wine Ars In Vitro, a 50/50 blend of Tempranillo and Merlot. Exactly the same wine can be found under the Palacio de Eza label.

✓ *Entire range*

TENERO
Rioja
★

The 95% Tempranillo Picea 650 is the standout at this small, estate-bottled Rioja winery.

✓ *Entire range*

BODEGAS TOBIA
Rioja
★★

Beautifully balanced wines from old vineyards.

✓ *Entire range*

VALSCARO
Rioja
★

Estate-bottled, quality-minded Rioja Baja, Valscaro is good now but has much greater potential and the ambition, ability, and strategy to make this a wine to watch.

✓ *Entire range*

VIÑA IJALBA
Rioja
★

One of the smallest and potentially most exciting of Rioja *bodegas* makes startling wines in weird bottles, including a rare pure Graciano.

✓ *Ijalba* (Graciano) • *Solferino* (Tempranillo)

VIÑA SALCEDA
Rioja
★

Fresh, gluggy *crianza* reds, huge, rich, and serious *gran reservas*.

✓ *Gran Reserva*

VIÑA TONDONIA
López de Heredia Viña Tondonia
Rioja
★★

Just up the hill from the very traditional Bodegas Muga is Tondonia, a firm that makes Muga look high-tech. It is impossible to find a more old-fashioned *bodega*, from the huge cobwebs in the tasting room to the religious dipping into wax of all bottle ends as if they contained port. The wines are rich and oaky, and capable of great age. Tondonia is the finest, Bosconia the fattest, and Cubillo the youngest.

✓ *Viña Bosconia • Viña Cubillo • Viña Tondonia* (including *blanco*)

VINÍCOLA DE LABASTIDA
Rioja
★

Probably the best Rioja cooperative.

✓ *Gastrijo* (Reserva) • *Castillo Labastida* (Gran Reserva)

VINÍCOLA NAVARRA
Navarra
❤

Richly coloured and flavoured wines, sometimes a touch porty, but always cheap and good value, Vinicola Navarra is part of the sprawling ByB empire.

✓ *Las Campanas • Castillo de Tiebas* (Reserva)

BODEGAS YSIOS
Rioja
★★

Established as recently as 1998, but after building this architectural design statement of a winery, the quality has to be exceptional, otherwise it simply becomes an insanely expensive joke. Fortunately, the wines, which start at *reserva* level, are very classy indeed.

✓ *Entire range*

PENEDÈS: CAVA COUNTRY

The worldwide popularity of Cava – Spain's only traditional method sparkling DO wine – together with the success of winemaking genius Miguel Torres, have made Penedès the most famous district in Catalunya, opening up the entire region's wine to export markets.

PRIOR TO PHYLLOXERA, which struck Penedès in 1876, more than 80 per cent of the vineyards here were planted with black grapes. When the vines were grafted on to American rootstock, white varieties were given priority due to the growing popularity of sparkling white wines. It is easy to recognize the classic imported varieties in the vineyards because they are trained along wires, whereas traditional Spanish vines grow in little bushes.

THE DISTRICTS OF PENEDÈS

Penedès can be divided into three wine districts: Bajo Penedès, Medio Penedès, and Alta Penedès (also called Penedès Superior).

Bajo (or Baix) Penedès

The following grape varieties are grown in the Bajo Penedès: Monastrell, Malvasía, Grenache (*syn* Garnacha), Cariñena, and various other, mostly black, grape varieties.

This area occupies the coastal strip and is the warmest of all three areas. The land of the Bajo Penedès is low and flat, with vines growing on limestone, clay, and sandy soil. This area produces more and more full-bodied red wines such as Torres's Sangre de Toro.

Medio (or Mitja) Penedès

The grapes grown are mostly Xarel-lo and Macabéo, but this is also the best area for Tempranillo, Cabernet Sauvignon, Merlot, and Monastrell.

The middle section of the Penedès is slightly hilly, occasionally flat land at an altitude of some 200 metres (660 feet) in the foothills west of Barcelona, on a soil of mostly limestone and clay. It has a cooler climate than the Bajo, with most areas equivalent to Regions II and III of the California heat-summation system (*see* p538). This is essentially Cava country, but it also produces the best of the new-style reds, including Torres's various Coronas wines.

Alta (or Alt) Penedès

Grape varieties grown in this district are almost exclusively white, being mostly Parellada, plus Riesling, Gewürztraminer, and Muscat. A little Pinot Noir is also grown.

This area is the furthest inland, and the grapes are grown on chalky foothills at an altitude of between 500 and 800 metres (1,640 and 2,620 feet). Climatic conditions are the coolest in Penedès, equivalent to Regions I and II. It is so cool that Cabernet Sauvignon will not ripen here and almost all wines produced are white, although Pinot Noir for Torres's Mas Borras is grown at San Marti. Most pure Alta Penedès wines are fresh, of the cool-fermented type, and can show remarkably fine aroma and acidity.

CAVA: SPAIN'S SPARKLING WINE

The first Spanish sparkling wine was made by Antoni Gali Comas some time prior to 1851, when he entered it in a competition in Madrid. He did not persevere, and the next milestone was with

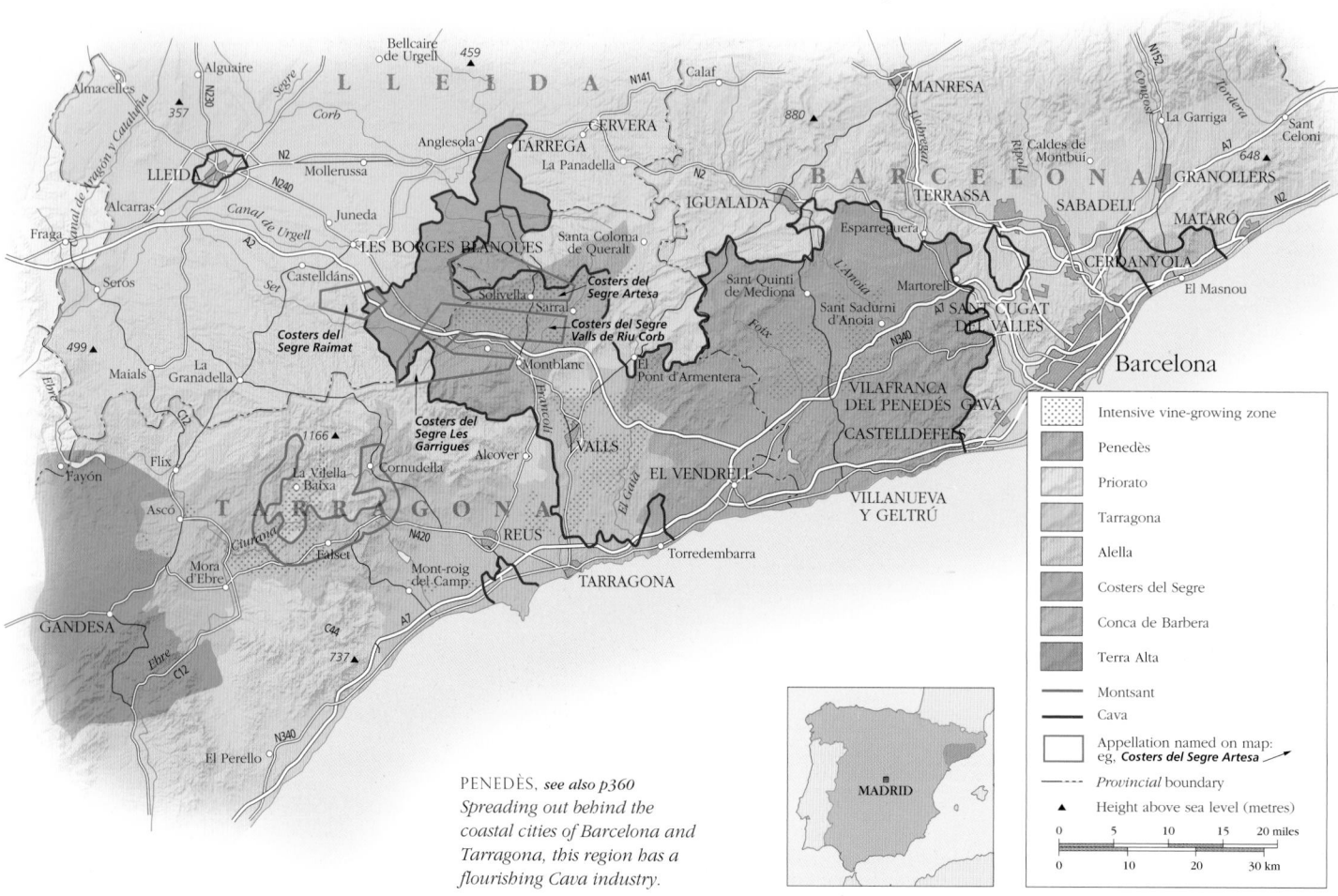

PENEDÈS, *see also p360*
Spreading out behind the coastal cities of Barcelona and Tarragona, this region has a flourishing Cava industry.

Intensive vine-growing zone
Penedès
Priorato
Tarragona
Alella
Costers del Segre
Conca de Barbera
Terra Alta
Montsant
Cava
Appellation named on map: eg, **Costers del Segre Artesa**
Provincial boundary
▲ Height above sea level (metres)

0   5   10   15   20 miles
0   10   20   30 km

FACTORS AFFECTING TASTE AND QUALITY

LOCATION
Lying in the northeast corner of Spain, where Rioja's River Ebro enters the Mediterranean, Penedès is part of Catalunya, which also includes Alella, Tarragona, Priorat, and Terra Alta.

CLIMATE
A mild Mediterranean climate prevails in Penedès, becoming more continental (hotter summers and colder winters) moving westwards and inland towards Terra Alta. In the same way, problems with fog in the northeast are gradually replaced by the hazard of frost towards the southwestern inland areas. In the high vineyards of Alta Penedès, white and aromatic grape varieties are cultivated at greater altitudes than traditional ones; since they benefit from cooler temperatures.

ASPECT
Vines are grown on all types of land, ranging from the flat plains of the Campo de Tarragona, through the 400-metre- (1,300-foot-) high plateaux of Terra Alta, to the highest vineyards in the Alta Penedès, which reach an altitude of 800 metres (2,620 feet). For every 100-metre (330-foot) rise in altitude, the temperature drops 1°C (1.8°F).

SOIL
There is a wide variety of soils, ranging from granite in Alella, through limestone-dominated clay, chalk, and sand in Penedès, to a mixture of mainly limestone and chalk with granite and alluvial deposits in Tarragona. The soil in Priorat is an unusual reddish slate with particles of reflective mica in the north, and schistose rock in the south.

VITICULTURE AND VINIFICATION
Catalunya is a hot-bed of experimentation. Ultra-modern winemaking techniques have been pioneered by Cava companies such as Codorníu and fine-wine specialists like Torres. Viticultural and vinification practices are generally quite modern throughout Catalunya. This is especially so at the Raimat Estate in Lérida, where the technology ranges from the latest and most efficient "Sernagiotto" continuous press for bulk production to the "Potter gravity crusher". Described as the simplest press ever designed, this extracts no more than 50–60 per cent of the grape's potential juice.

GRAPE VARIETIES
Primary varieties:
Alcayata (Mourvèdre), Aragonés (Grenache), Cabernet Sauvignon, Cariñena (Carignan), Lladoner (Grenache), Mazuelo (Carignan), Monastrell (Mourvèdre), Pansá Bianca (Xarel-lo), Ull de Llebre (Tempranillo), Viura (Macabéo)
Secondary varieties: Cabernet Franc, Chardonnay, Chenin Blanc, Gewürztraminer, Merlot, Moscatel Grano Menudo (Muscat Blanc à Petits Grains), Parellada, Pinot Noir, Riesling, Sauvignon, Malvasia Riojana (Subirat-Parent)

France and, of course, Spain has its own indigenous varieties, thus internationally renowned grapes like Chardonnay can only dilute the wine's identity. However, as Codorníu has shown, blending with Chardonnay can fill out a Cava in a way that the traditional varieties (Macabéo, Parellada, and Xarel-lo) cannot.

At a Cava shippers' dinner in 1991, when Manuel Duran, the chairman of Freixenet, admitted that they were still undecided as to whether Cava's varieties were ideally suited to sparkling wine, he was challenged not simply to find an indigenous substitute for Chardonnay, but to try to experiment with black Spanish varieties. Cava's traditionalists have, for some bizarre reason, always considered black grapes in a white Cava to be sacrilegious, yet Duran picked up the gauntlet, producing a Monastrell-Xarel-lo *cuvée* (the first release was too flabby, but the second release in 1997 was much better – the Catalunyans are not used to handling black grapes for white wines, and I expect this Cava to continue improving). Prior to Freixenet's project, Codorníu was the only house to try black grapes in white Cava and succeeded in producing one of the most sumptuous Spanish sparkling wines ever using Pinot Noir.

Whether it is Monastrell, Grenache (*syn* Garnacha), Trepat, Tempranillo, or some other Spanish grape, I believe that Cava will one day benefit from the use of indigenous black varieties and when that happens, Codorníu will, I am sure, use them, just as they will use any Spanish white variety that is discovered to be as useful in plumping up a *cuvée* as Chardonnay.

CAVA AND PENEDÈS
Although many Cava producers are either manual or computer-controlled girasols, *which enable* remuage *to be performed by the pallet-load, some of the more traditional houses, such as the family-owned firm of Juvé y Camps, still use* pupitres.

Luis Justo i Villanueva, the Laboratory Director at the Agricultural Institute of Sant Isidre in Catalunya. It was under Villanueva that all the earliest commercial producers of Spanish sparkling wine learned the Champagne process. In 1872, three of his former students, Domenec Soberano, Francesc Gil, and Augusti Vilaret, entered their sparkling wines in a Barcelona competition. All used classic Champagne grapes grown in Catalunya. Soberano and Gil were awarded gold medals, while Vilaret, who used raspberry liqueur in the dosage, received a bronze. Vilaret's firm, Caves Mont-Ferrant, is the only one of these enterprises to have survived.

The above facts are fully documented and thus contradict Codorníu's claim that it was first to produce Spanish sparkling wine in 1872. Codorníu did not, in fact, sell its first sparkling wines until 1879, and it would not be until 1893 that its production hit 10,000 bottles, a level that the three original firms achieved in the 1870s. What everyone seems to agree on, however, is that José Raventós i Fatjó of Codorníu was the first to make bottle-fermented sparkling wine out of Parellada, Macabéo, and Xarel-lo and that these grapes came to form the basis of the entire Cava industry.

CAVA'S SPANISH CHARACTER
The production of Cava is dominated by two firms: Codorníu and Freixenet. The latter has always been violently opposed to the invasion of Cava vineyards by foreign grape varieties. Freixenet's argument is certainly valid – that the introduction of foreign varieties could erode Cava's Spanish character. Cava is, after all, the only dry sparkling-wine appellation of any repute outside

THE WINE PRODUCERS OF
CAVA AND PENEDÈS

Note For recommended wines of all other Catalunyan appellations, see the relevant DO under "The Appellations of Spain" on p363. Included below are only those wines that come under Cava DO and Penedès DO. Reds from Penedès generally drink well in their third year, but top *cuvées* often improve for up to 10 years, and exceptional ones can age gracefully for decades. Penedès white and *rosado* wines and sparkling Cava are best fresh and should thus be consumed when purchased.

ALBET I NOYA
★

Established as recently as 1981, Josep Albet i Noya soon became a respected producer of fresh, lively Cava and well-made white Penedès, but is now turning out some spectacular reds.

 Cava (Vintage) • *Blanc Novell* • *Cabernet Sauvignon* • *Tempranillo*

CAN RAFOLS DELS CAUS
★

This is an up-and-coming small estate producing excellent Cabernet (Franc and Sauvignon), and a Merlot blend called Gran Caus. Other labels include Petit Caus.

 Gran Caus

CASTELL DE VILARNAU
★

This producer is not as consistent as it should be, but has always been capable of richer, more complex Cava, even before the general improvement that lifted the industry in the mid-1990s.

 Cava (Vintage)

CASTELLBLANCH
★ ❶

Castellblanch is a firm owned by Freixenet, and it produces a remarkably consistent Cava wine.

 Cava (Brut Zero)

CODORNÍU
★

The largest and most innovative Cava firm, its production dwarfs even that of Moët & Chandon in Champagne. Codorníu started the foreign grape controversy by introducing Chardonnay, first through Raïmat Cava in Conca de Barberà, then in its own range. When grown in the right area, Chardonnay does plump-up the quality, depth, and finesse of Cava, but there is opposition to non-traditional Spanish grape varieties from those who fear they will erode the intrinsically Spanish character of the wine.

 Cava (Anna de Codorníu Chardonnay, Jaume de Codorníu, Brut Rose)

CONDE DE CARALT
★

This is a reliable Cava from part of the Freixenet group.

 Cava (Brut)

COVIDES
★

This cooperative produces a surprisingly rich style of Cava.

 Cava (Duc de Foix Brut, Duc de Foix Vintage, Xenius)

FREIXENET
★

Freixenet is the second-largest Cava firm, and produces probably the best known of all Cavas. Other labels include Castellblanch, Conde de Caralt, Paul Cheneau, and Segura Viudas.

 Cava (Carta Nevada, Cuvée DS, Elyssia)

GRAMONA
★

Of its tangy Cavas, Celler Battle shows rare vanilla-finesse on finish.

 Celler Battle • *Imperial III Lustros*

CAVAS HILL
★

This old-established, family-owned estate produces elegant Cavas and some very good still wines.

 Cava (Reserva Oro Brut) • *Blanc Cru* • *Gran Civet* • *Gran Toc*

JAUME SERRA
★

Jaume Serra produces good Cava, but even better Penedès still wines, made in modern, fruit-driven style in collaboration with Chilean winemaker Ignacio Recabarren.

 Cava (Cristalino) • *Viña de Mar*

JEAN LÉON
★★

Following the death of Jean Léon, these wines are now made and marketed by Torres. These big, rich, oaky wines are stunning, but some vintages can disappoint. By no means infallible.

 Cabernet Sauvignon • *Chardonnay*

JUVÉ Y CAMPS

I have failed to discern any of the intrinsically superior qualities in these wines that some Cava-infatuated critics have found. However, I do hasten to add that there is nothing wrong with the wines of this respected, traditional, family firm. They are just not special.

MARQUÉS DE MONISTROL
★

This competent Cava firm, owned by Martini & Rossi, also makes a fine Reserva red Penedès wine and a fresh, youthful Merlot.

 Cava • *Penedès Reserva* • *Merlot*

MAS RABASSA
★

Mas Rabassa makes fresh and quite delicious, new-style wines.

 Xarel-lo • *Macabéo*

CAVAS MASCARÓ
★

A small family-owned producer founded in the immediate post-war era, Mascaró is best known for its Don Narciso brandy, but also makes an underrated range of wines.

 Cava (Brut) • *Anima Cabernet Sauvignon*

MASÍA BACH
★

Renowned more for its sweet, oak-aged white Extrísimo Bach, than for its reds, which have always been merely soft and acceptable, this Codorníu-owned firm began to take its red winemaking seriously when it released a stunning 1985, simply labelled Masía Bach.

 Masía Bach (Reserva) • *Viña Extrísima* (Reserva)

MESTRES
★

Mestres is a small, traditional, family-owned Cava business, which produces numerous wines of fine autolytic character.

 Cava • *Clos Nostre Senyor* • *Mas-Via*

MONT MARÇAL
★

This is a well-made Cava produced by a private family firm.

 Cava (Nature, Chardonnay)

PARXET
★

Under the same ownership as Marqués de Alella, Parxet is capable of producing refined sparkling wines. Its pink-hued "Cuvée Dessert" is sweeter than a *demi-sec* and needs to be cellared for a couple of years. This firm is not afraid to go out on a limb.

 Cava (Brut Nature, Brut Reserva)

CELLARS PUIG I ROCA
★★

Cellars Puig and Roca are exciting, estate-bottled wines from ex-Torres trouble-shooter Josep Puig. The

entrepreneurial Puig even produces a varietal vinegar from Cabernet Sauvignon, which is aged in chestnut casks for flavour.

 Augustus (Cabernet Sauvignon, Cabernet Sauvignon Rosado, Chardonnay, Merlot)

RAÏMAT
★★ ❶

In the Conca de Barberà, the Raïmat estate is owned by Codorníu and utilizes innovative equipment to make an excellent range of fine wines (Abadia, Tempranillo, Cabernet Sauvignon, and Merlot), using classic grape varieties, in addition to its Cava, which was Spain's first pure Chardonnay sparkling wine.

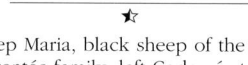 *Abadia Reserva Cabernet Sauvignon* (Mas Castell) • *Chardonnay* (Seleccion Especial) • *Sparkling wine* (Chardonnay)

RAVENTÓS I BLANC
★

Josep Maria, black sheep of the Raventós family, left Codorníu to set up his own Cava house, producing, fresh, lively *cuvées*, sometimes of excellent quality.

 Cava (Brut)

RENÉ BARBIER FILL
★★

Not the old-established firm of René Barbier, which belongs to Freixenet, but René Barbier Fill (*fill* being Catalan for "son") – a relatively new company that has been founded in Gratallops in Priorat.

 Priorat (Clos Mogador)

SEGURA VIUDAS
★ ❶

The best Cava house in the huge Freixenet group, the wines produced by Segura Viudas seem to have extra richness and relatively greater ageing potential.

 Cava (Aria, Heredad, Vintage Brut)

TORRES
★★

The Torres name conjures up French grape varieties and limited editions of world-class wines, but it is actually one of the largest family-owned wine producers in Spain, with 800 hectares (2,000 acres) of vineyard and annual sales of 1.4 million cases of wine. Considering that Sangre de Toro accounts for some 300,000 cases, which is almost a quarter of Torres' total production, this modest, hearty red wine is of a remarkable quality.

 Entire range (but especially Atrium Fransola, Viña Esmeralda, Mas la Plana Cabernet Sauvignon)

SHERRY COUNTRY

On 1 January 1996, Sherry regained exclusive use in Europe of its own name, which had suffered decades of abuse by producers of so-called "sherry" in other countries, especially Great Britain and Ireland. The governments of these countries had shamelessly vetoed the protection of Sherry's name when Spain joined the Common Market in 1986.

SUCH ARE THE BLOCKS and checks of the European Union (EU) that it took 10 years for this legislation allowing the abuse of Sherry's name to be reversed, ensuring that the name Sherry (also known as Jerez or Xérès) may now be used only for the famous fortified wines made around Cádiz and Jerez de la Frontera in the south of Spain. Due to the Sherry industry's own folly in trying to compete with these cheaper, fortified rip-offs, the vineyards of Jerez got into massive over-production problems, but this was recognized in the early 1990s, when lesser-quality vineyards were uprooted, reducing the viticultural area from 17,500 hectares (43,000 acres) to the current 10,600 hectares (26,000 acres).

SHERRY'S ANCIENT ORIGINS
The vinous roots of Sherry penetrate three millennia of history, back to the Phoenicians who founded Gadir (today called Cádiz), in 1100 BC. They quickly deserted Gadir because of the hot, howling *levante* wind that is said to drive men mad, and they established a town further inland called Xera, which some historians believe may be the Xérès or Jerez of today. It was probably the Phoenicians who introduced viticulture to the region. If they did not, then the Greeks certainly did, and it was the

JEREZ DE LA FRONTERA
Palomino vines amid the brilliant white albariza soil of Montigillilo, Emilio Lustau's superb 120-hectare (300-acre) vineyard, just north of Jerez.

Greeks who brought with them their *hepsema*, the precursor of the *arropes* and *vinos de color* that add sweetness, substance, and colour to modern-day sweet or cream sherries. In the Middle Ages, the Moors introduced to Spain the *alembic*, a simple pot-still with which the people of Jerez were able to turn their excess wine production into grape spirit, which they added, along with *arrope* and *vino de color*, to their new wines each year to produce the first crude but true Sherry. The repute of these wines gradually spread throughout the Western world, helped by the English merchants who had established wine-shipping businesses in Andalucía at the end of the 13th century. After Henry VIII broke with Rome, Englishmen in Spain were under constant threat from the Inquisition. The English merchants were rugged individualists and they survived, as they also did, remarkably, when Francis Drake set fire to the Spanish fleet in the Bay of Cádiz in 1587. Described as the day he singed the King of Spain's beard, it was the most outrageous of all Drake's raids, and when he returned home, he took with him a booty of 2,900 casks of Sherry. The exact size of these casks is not known, but the total volume is estimated to be in excess of 150,000 cases, which makes it a vast shipment of one wine for that period in history. It was, however, eagerly consumed by a relatively small population that had been denied its normal quota of Spanish wines during the war. England has been by far the largest market for Sherry ever since.

THE UNIQUENESS OF JEREZ SHERRY
It is the combination of Jerez de la Frontera's soil and climate that makes this region uniquely equipped to produce Sherry, a style of wine attempted in many countries around the world but never truly accomplished outside Spain. Sherry has much in common with Champagne, as both regions are inherently superior to all others in their potential to produce a specific style of wine. The parallel can be taken further: both Sherry and Champagne are made from neutral, unbalanced base wines that are uninspiring to drink before they undergo the elaborate process that turns them into high-quality, perfectly balanced, finished products.

The famous albariza soil
Jerez's *albariza* soil, which derives its name from its brilliant white surface, is not chalk but a soft marl of organic origin formed by the sedimentation of diatom algae during the Triassic period. The *albariza* begins to turn yellow at a depth of about 1 metre (3 feet)

FACTORS AFFECTING TASTE AND QUALITY

LOCATION
This winemaking region is situated in the province of Cádiz, around Jerez de la Frontera in the southwest of Spain.

CLIMATE
This is the hottest wine region in Spain. Generally, the climate is Mediterranean, but towards the Portuguese border, the Atlantic influence comes into play and, further inland, around Montilla-Moriles, it becomes more continental. It is the Atlantic-driven *poniente* wind that produces the *flor* yeast of *fino* Sherry.

ASPECT
Vines are grown on all types of land, from the virtually flat coastal plains producing *manzanilla*, through the slightly hillier Sherry vineyards rising to 100 metres (330 feet), to the higher gentle inland slopes of Montilla-Moriles and the undulating Antequera plateau of Málaga at some 500 metres (1,640 feet).

SOIL
The predominant soil in Jerez is a deep lime-rich variety known as *albariza*, which soaks up and retains moisture. Its brilliant white colour also reflects sun on to the lower parts of the vines. Sand and clay soils also occur but, although suitable for vine-growing, they produce second-rate sherries. The equally bright soil to the east of Jerez is not *albariza*, but a schisto-calcareous clay.

VITICULTURE AND VINIFICATION
Vinification is the key to the production of the great fortified wines for which this area is justly famous. Development of a *flor* yeast and oxidation by deliberately underfilling casks are vital components of the vinification, as, of course, is the *solera* system that ensures a consistent product over the years. The larger the *solera*, the more efficient it is, because there are more butts. Montilla is vinified using the same methods as for Sherry, but is naturally strong in alcohol, and so less often fortified.

GRAPE VARIETIES
Moscatel Gordo Blanco (Muscat d'Alexandrie), Palomino, Pedro Ximénez

and turns bluish after 5 metres (16 feet). It crumbles and is super-absorbent when wet, but extremely hard when dry. This is the key to the exceptional success of *albariza* as a vine-growing soil. Jerez is a region of baking heat and drought; there are about 70 days of rain each year, with a total precipitation of some 50 centimetres (20 inches). The *albariza* soaks up the rain like a sponge and, with the return of the drought, the soil surface is smoothed and hardened into a shell that is impermeable to evaporation. The winter and spring rains are imprisoned under this protective cap, and remain at the disposal of the vines, the roots of which penetrate some 4 metres (13 feet) beneath the surface. The *albariza* supplies just enough moisture to the vines, without making them too lazy or over-productive. Its high active-lime content encourages the ripening of grapes with a higher acidity level than would otherwise be the norm for such a hot climate. This acidity safeguards against unwanted oxidation prior to fortification.

The levante and poniente winds

The hot, dry *levante* is one of Jerez de la Frontera's two alternating prevailing winds. This easterly wind blow-dries and vacuum-cooks the grapes on their stalks during the critical ripening stage. This results in a dramatically different metabolization of fruit sugars, acids, and aldehydes, which produces a wine with an unusual balance peculiar to Jerez. Alternating with the *levante* is the wet Atlantic *poniente* wind. This is of fundamental importance, as it allows the growth of several *Saccharomyces* strains in the microflora of the Palomino grape. This is the poetically named Sherry *flor* (*see opposite*), without which there would be no *fino* in Jerez.

SHERRY'S CLASSIC GRAPE VARIETIES

British Sherry expert Julian Jeffs believes that as many as 100 different grape varieties were once traditionally used to make Sherry and, in 1868, Diego Parada y Barreto listed

42 then in use. Today only three varieties are authorized: Palomino, Pedro Ximénez, and Moscatel Fino. The Palomino is considered the classic Sherry grape and most Sherries are, in fact, 100 per cent Palomino, though they may be sweetened with Pedro Ximénez for export markets.

HOW GREAT SHERRY IS MADE
The harvest

Twenty or more years ago, it was traditional to begin the grape harvest in the first week of September. After picking, Palomino grapes were left in the sun for 12–24 hours; Pedro Ximénez and Moscatel, for 10–21 days. Older vines were picked before younger ones, and Pedro Ximénez and Moscatel were picked first of all because they required longer sunning than Palomino. At night, the grapes were covered with *esparto* grass mats as a protection against dew. This sunning is called the *soleo*, and its primary purpose is to increase sugar content, while reducing the

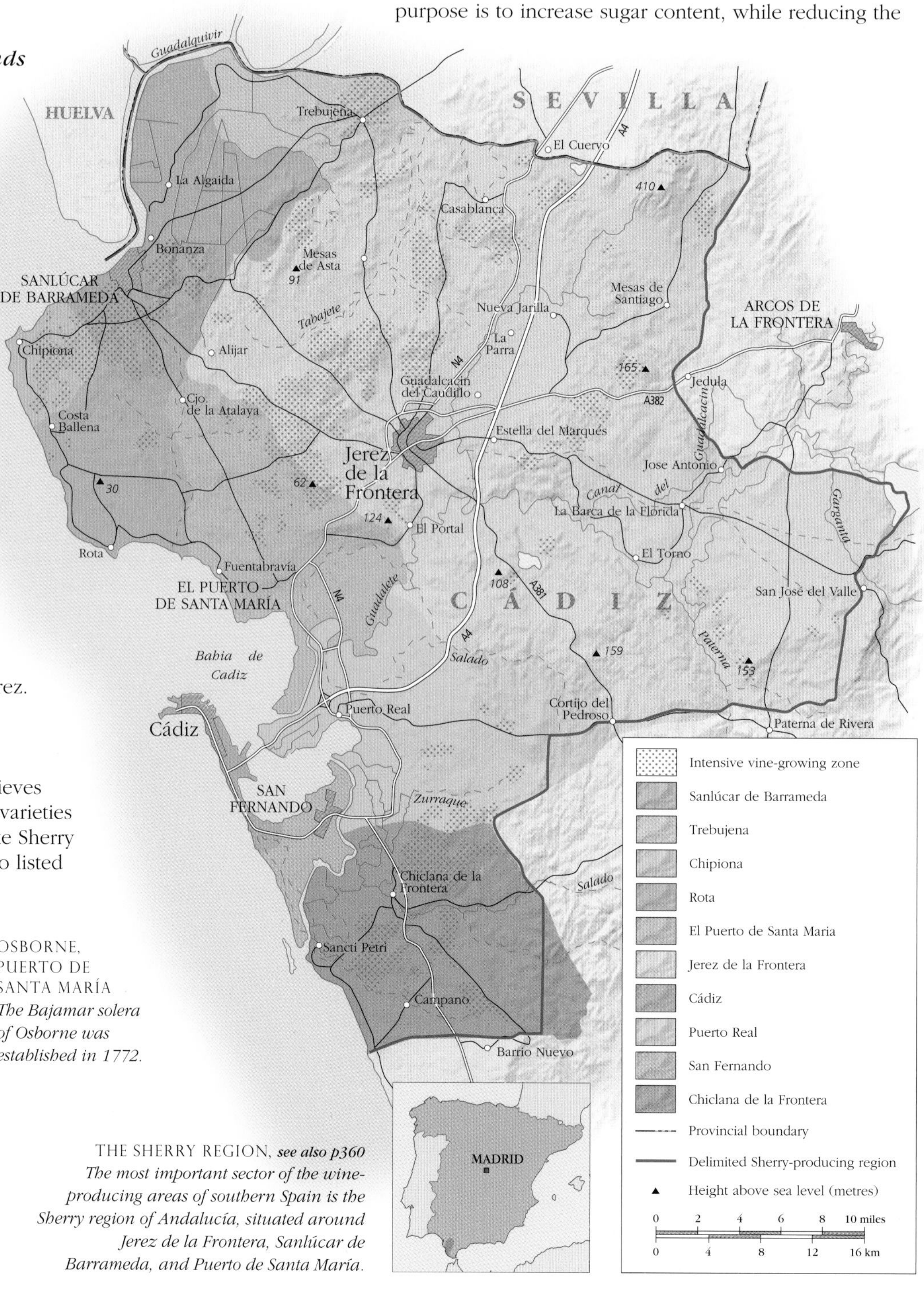

OSBORNE,
PUERTO DE
SANTA MARÍA
*The Bajamar solera
of Osborne was
established in 1772.*

THE SHERRY REGION, *see also p360*
*The most important sector of the wine-
producing areas of southern Spain is the
Sherry region of Andalucía, situated around
Jerez de la Frontera, Sanlúcar de
Barrameda, and Puerto de Santa María.*

Map labels:

Guadalquivir
HUELVA
SEVILLA
Trebujena
El Cuervo
A4
La Algaida
410
Casablanca
Bonanza
Mesas de Asta
91
SANLÚCAR DE BARRAMEDA
Mesas de Santiago
Nueva Jarilla
ARCOS DE LA FRONTERA
Tabajete
Chipiona
Alijar
La Parra
765
Jedula
A382
Cjo. de la Atalaya
Guadalcacín del Caudillo
Costa Ballena
Estella del Marqués
Jose Antonio
30
Jerez de la Frontera
62
Canal del
124
El Portal
La Barca de la Flórida
Rota
El Torno
Fuentabravía
Guadalete
108
San José del Valle
EL PUERTO DE SANTA MARÍA
A381
159
Paterna
153
CÁDIZ
Bahía de Cadiz
Salado
Paterna de Rivera
Cádiz
Puerto Real
Cortijo del Pedroso
SAN FERNANDO
Zurraque
Chiclana de la Frontera
Salado
Sancti Petri
Campano
Barrio Nuevo

Legend:

- Intensive vine-growing zone
- Sanlúcar de Barrameda
- Trebujena
- Chipiona
- Rota
- El Puerto de Santa María
- Jerez de la Frontera
- Cádiz
- Puerto Real
- San Fernando
- Chiclana de la Frontera
- --- Provincial boundary
- — Delimited Sherry-producing region
- ▲ Height above sea level (metres)

0 2 4 6 8 10 miles
0 4 8 12 16 km

MADRID

malic acid and tannin content. Although some producers still carry out the *soleo*, most harvest in the second week of September and forgo the *soleo* for all grapes but Pedro Ximénez and Moscatel, used in the sweetest Sherry. The grapes are now left in the sun for far fewer than the traditional 10–21 days.

The yeso

Traditionally, prior to pressing the grapes, the stalks are removed and a small proportion of *yeso* (gypsum) is added to precipitate tartrate crystals. This practice, which is dying out, may have evolved when growers noticed that grapes covered by *albariza* dust produced better wine than clean ones. *Albariza* has a high calcium carbonate content that would crudely accomplish the task.

The pressing

Traditionally, four labourers called *pisadores* were placed in each *lagar* (open receptacle) to tread the grapes, not barefoot but wearing *zapatos de pisar*, heavily nailed cow-hide boots to trap the pips and stalks undamaged between the nails. Each man tramped 58 kilometres (36 miles) on the spot during a typical session lasting from midnight to noon. Automatic horizontal, usually pneumatic, presses are now in common use.

Fermentation

Some Sherry houses still ferment their wine in small oak casks purposely filled to only 90 per cent capacity. After 12 hours, the fermentation starts and continues for between 36 and 50 hours at 25–30°C (77–86°F), by which time as much as 99 per cent of available sugar is converted to alcohol; after a further 40 or 50 days, the process is complete. Current methods often use stainless-steel fermentation vats, and yield wines that are approximately 1 per cent higher in alcohol than those fermented in casks due to an absence of absorption and evaporation.

THE MAGICAL FLOR

For the majority of Sherry drinkers, *fino* is the quintessential Sherry style. It is a natural phenomenon called *flor* that determines whether or not a Sherry will become a *fino*. *Flor* is a strain of *Saccharomyces* yeast that appears as a grey-white film floating on a wine's surface, and it occurs naturally in the microflora of the Palomino grape grown in the Jerez district. It is found to one degree or another in every butt or vat of Sherry and *manzanilla*, but whether or not it can dominate the wine and develop as a *flor* depends upon the strength of the *Saccharomyces* and the biochemical conditions. The effect of *flor* on Sherry is to absorb remaining traces of sugar, diminish glycerine and volatile acids, and greatly increase esters and aldehydes. To flourish, *flor* requires:
- An alcoholic strength of between 13.5 and 17.5 per cent. The optimum is 15.3 per cent, the level at which vinegar-producing acetobacter is killed.
- A temperature of between 15 and 30°C (59 and 86°F).
- A sulphur dioxide content of less than 0.018 per cent.
- A tannin content of less than 0.01 per cent.
- A virtual absence of fermentable sugars.

CASK CLASSIFICATION AND FORTIFICATION

The cellarmaster's job is to sniff all the casks of Sherry and mark on each one in chalk how he believes it is developing, according to a recognized cask-classification system. At this stage, lower-grade wines (those with little or no *flor*) are fortified to 18 per cent to kill any *flor*, thus determining their character once and for all and thereafter protecting the wine from the dangers of acetification. The *flor* itself is a protection against the acetobacter that threaten to turn the wine into vinegar, but it is by no means invincible and will be at great risk until it is fortified to 15.3 per cent, or above, the norm for *fino*, and is not truly safe until it is

GRAPE-BASED SWEETENING AND COLOURING AGENTS

The most traditional and most important sweetening agent in the production of Sherry, although gradually giving way to other less expensive ones, is that made from pure, overripe, sun-dried Pedro Ximénez grapes, also known as PX. After the *soleo*, or sunning, of the grapes (*see opposite*), the sugar content of the PX increases from around 23 per cent to between 43 and 54 per cent. The PX is pressed and run into casks containing pure grape spirit. This process, known as muting, produces a mixture with an alcohol level of about 9 per cent and some 430 grams of sugar per litre. This mixture is tightly bunged and left for four months, during which time it undergoes a slight fermentation, increasing the alcohol by about one degree and reducing the sugar by some 18 grams per litre. Finally, the wine undergoes a second muting, raising the alcoholic strength to a final 13 per cent but reducing the sugar content to about 380 grams per litre. Other sweetening agents are:

MOSCATEL
This is prepared in exactly the same way as PX, but the result is not as rich and its use, which has always been less widespread than PX, is technically not permitted under DO regulations.

DULCE PASA
Preparation is as for PX and Moscatel, but using Palomino, which achieves up to a 50 per cent sugar concentration prior to muting. Its use is on the increase. This must not be confused with *dulce racimo* or *dulce apagado*, sweetening agents that were once brought in from outside the region and are now illegal.

DULCE DE ALMIBAR *OR* DULCE BLANCO
A combination of glucose and laevulose blended with fino and matured, this agent is used to sweeten pale-coloured Sherries.

SANCOCHO
A dark-coloured, sweet, and sticky non-alcoholic syrup that is made by reducing unfermented local grape juice to one-fifth of its original volume by simmering over a low heat. It is used in the production of *vino de color* – a "colouring wine".

ARROPE
This dark-coloured, sweet, and sticky non-alcoholic syrup, made by reducing unfermented local grape juice to one-fifth of its original volume, is also used in the production of *vino de color*.

COLOR DE MACETILLA
This is the finest *vino de color* and is produced by blending two-parts *arrope* or *sancocho* with one-part unfermented local grape juice. This results in a violent fermentation and, when the wine falls bright, it has an alcoholic strength of 9 per cent and a sugar content of 235 grams per litre. Prized stocks are often matured by *solera*.

COLOR REMENDADO
This is a cheap, commonly used *vino de color*, which is made by blending *arrope* or *sancocho* with local wine.

HOW THE FERMENTED SHERRY DEVELOPS

The larger *bodegas* like to make something of a mystery of the *flor*, declaring that they have no idea whether or not it will develop in a specific cask. There is some justification for this – one cask may have a fabulous froth of *flor* (looking like dirty soapsuds), while the cask next to it may have none. Any cask with good signs of dominant *flor* will invariably end up as *fino*, but others with either no *flor* or ranging degrees of it may develop into one of many different styles. There is no way of guaranteeing the evolution of the wines, but it is well known that certain zones can generally be relied upon to produce particular styles.

ZONE	STYLE	ZONE	STYLE
Añina	*Fino*	Madroñales	Moscatel/sweet
Balbaina	*Fino*	Miraflores	*Fino/manzanilla*
Carrascal	*Oloroso*	Rota	Moscatel/sweet
Chipiona	Moscatel/sweet	Sanlúcar	*Fino/manzanilla*
Los Tercios	*Fino*	Tehigo	Colouring wines
Macharnudo	*Amontillado*	Torrebreba	*Manzanilla*

bottled. A 50/50 mixture known as *mitad y mitad*, *miteado*, or *combinado* (half pure alcohol, half grape juice) is usually used for fortification. However, some producers prefer to use mature Sherry for fortification instead of grape juice.

Further cask-classification

The wines are often racked prior to fortification, and always after. A fortnight later, they undergo a second, more precise classification, but no further fortification, or other action, will take place until nine months have elapsed, after which they will be classified regularly over a period of two years to determine their final style.

CASK CLASSIFICATION IN THE CELLAR

FIRST CASK CLASSIFICATION

CHALK MARK		CHARACTER OF WINE	PROBABLE STYLE OF SHERRY	ACTION TO TAKE
/	*una raya*	Light and good	*Fino/amontillado*	Fortify up to 15.5%
/'	*raya y punto*	Slightly less promising	Undecided	Fortify up to 15.5%
//	*dos rayas*	Less promising	*Oloroso*	Fortify up to 18%
///	*tres rayas*	Coarse or acid	–	Usually distil
Ve	*vinegar*	–	–	Immediately remove to avoid infection

SECOND CASK CLASSIFICATION

CHALK MARK		CHARACTER OF WINE	PROBABLE STYLE OF SHERRY	ACTION TO TAKE
Y	*palma*	A wine with breeding	Has *flor*	–
/	*raya*	Fuller	No *flor*	–
//	*dos rayas*	Tending to be coarse	No *flor*	–
#	gridiron	No good at all	No *flor*	–

FURTHER CASK CLASSIFICATION

CHALK MARK		CHARACTER OF WINE	PROBABLE STYLE OF SHERRY	ACTION TO TAKE
Y	*palma*	Light and delicate	*Fino* Sherry	–
✗	*palma cortada*	Fuller than a *fino*	*Fino-amontillado* or *amontillado*	–
+	*palo cortado*	No *flor*, but, exceptional full-bodied, and delicate	*Palo cortado*	–
/	*raya*	Darker, fuller, not breeding *flor*	Medium-quality *oloroso*	–
//	*dos rayas*	Darker and fuller, but coarser	Low-quality *oloroso*, for blending cheap Sherries that are usually sweetened	–
✓	*pata de gallina*	A *raya* that has developed the true fragrance of a fine *oloroso*	Top-quality *oloroso*, to be aged and kept dry	–

The solera blending system

Once the style of the Sherry has been established, the wines are fed into fractional-blending systems called *soleras*. A *solera* consists of a stock of wine in cask, split into units of equal volume but different maturation. The oldest stage is called the *solera*; each of the younger stages that feed it is a *criadera*, or nursery. There are up to seven *criaderas* in a Sherry *solera*, and up to 14 in a *manzanilla solera*. Up to one-third (the legal maximum) of the *solera* may be drawn off for blending and bottling, although some *bodegas* may restrict their very high-quality, old *soleras* to one-fifth. The amount drawn off from the mature *solera* is replaced by an equal volume from the first *criadera*, which is topped up by the second *criadera*, and so on. When the last *criadera* is emptied of its one-third, it is refreshed by an identical quantity of *añada*, or new wine. This comprises like-classified Sherries from the current year's production, aged up to 36 months, depending on the style and exactly when they are finally classified.

THE EVOLUTION OF SHERRY STYLES

The tree shows the course taken by each Sherry to become one of the well-known styles by which it is sold.

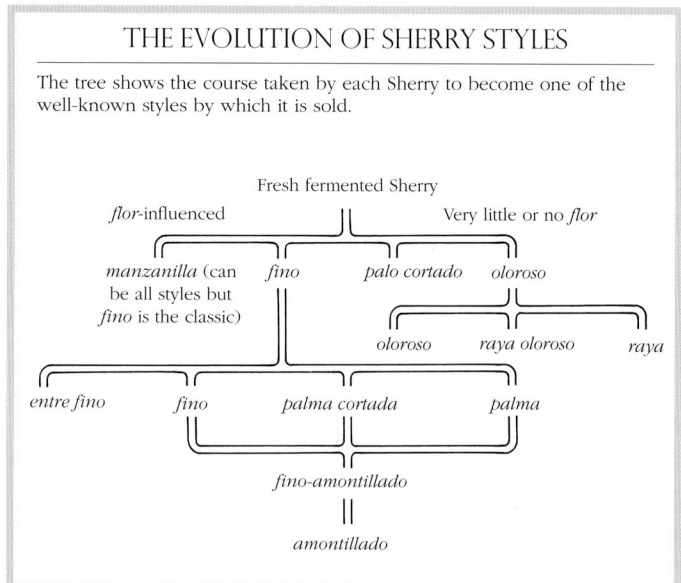

THE STYLES OF
SHERRY

The development of a Sherry can be natural, so that a *fino* can, without the help of increased fortification, turn into an *oloroso* (thus a natural *oloroso* may have developed with the aid of *flor*, whereas the increased fortification usually used to turn a *fino* into an *oloroso* would prevent the development of *flor*). A *palo cortado* can develop from either an *amontillado* or an *oloroso*. A genuine old *fino* Sherry can surprise everyone and turn into an *oloroso*.

ALMACENISTA OR BODEGAS DE ALMACENADO

This is not a style, but a category of increasing interest among Sherry enthusiasts. An *almacenista* is a private stockholder whose pure, unblended Sherries are held as an investment for 30 years or more, after which they are in great demand by large *bodegas*, who use them to improve their commercial blends. Lustau, itself an *almacenista* until the 1950s (and now part of the Caballero group), was the first firm to market the concept,

making these purest of sherries available to consumers (and they registered "Almacenista" as a trademark in the process). All styles of Sherry and *manzanilla* exist in *almacenista* form and are, almost by definition, guaranteed to be of extraordinary quality. Fractions on the label such as ⅛, ½, or 1/40 indicate the number of barrels in the *solera* from which it was drawn, therefore the lower the denominator (the number below the line), the greater the rarity of the wine and consequently the more expensive it will be.

✓ *Lustau*

AMONTILLADO

With age, a *fino* develops an amber colour in cask and becomes a *fino-amontillado*, then, after at least eight years, a full *amontillado*, when it takes on a nutty character and acquires more body. A true *amontillado* is completely dry, with between 16 and 18 per cent alcohol, but will often be sweetened to a medium style for export markets.

The term *amontillado* means "Montilla style"; it was originally used to distinguish a Sherry with characteristics similar to those of Montilla (then part of the Jerez region – *see* p379). Ironically, it was illegal for producers of Montilla to use the term *amontillado* under the Spanish republic, thus Sherry could be made in a Montilla-style, but not Montilla! Under the EU, however, this has changed and once again Montilla houses are shipping Montilla *amontillado*.

✓ *Domecq* (Botaina) • *Gonzalez Byass* (Duque) • *Harveys* • *Sandeman* (Bone Dry Old Amontillado) • *Valdespino* (Coliseo, Don Tomás) • *Wisdom & Warter* (Very Rare Solera Muy Viejo)

BROWN

This sweetened *oloroso* is usually, but not always, of lesser quality than *oloroso*. High-quality Brown Sherries used to be very popular in Scotland.

✓ *Williams & Humbert* (Walnut Brown)

CREAM *or* DARK CREAM

An *oloroso* style that is usually sweetened with Pedro Ximénez, the quality of which can range from the commercial to extremely good.

✓ *Diego Romero* (Jerezana) • *Lustau* (Premium Solera, Vendimia)

EAST INDIA

Some sources believe that this rich, sweet, Madeira-like style of Sherry dates back to as early as 1617, but the practice of shipping Sherry to the Orient and back gradually disappeared during the 19th century with the advent of steam-driven ships. It was revived in 1958 by the owners of the Ben Line and Alastair Campbell, an Edinburgh wine merchant, when they sent a hogshead of Valdespino Oloroso on a 32,000-kilometre (20,000-mile) round trip to the Far East, but although the style survives, the effects of the sea voyage, as with Madeira, are now replicated in the cellar.

✓ *Lustau* (Old East India) • *Osborne* (India Rare Solera Oloroso)

FINO

A *palma* is the highest quality of *fino* Sherry and may be graded in a rising scale of quality: *dos palmas, tres palmas, cuatro palmas*. A *palma cortada* is a *fino* that has developed more body, has a very dry, but smooth, almondy flavour, and is veering towards *amontillado*. An *entre fino* has little merit. Few *finos* remain *fino* with age in cask, which is why genuine Old Fino Sherry is rare. A *fino* is light, dry, and delicate; its *flor* nose should overpower any acetaldehyde.

This style is best appreciated straight from the cask, when it is crisp and vital, as it quickly tires once bottled and further declines rapidly as soon as it is opened. Until producers are required to declare the bottling date on the label (fat chance), the only sensible advice is not to buy *fino* until the day you want to drink it and, once opened, consume the entire contents: don't keep it. The wines are invariably 100 per cent Palomino with an alcoholic strength of between 15.5 and 17 per cent.

✓ *Tomás Abad* • *Domecq* (La Ina) • *Gonzalez Byass* (Tio Pepe) • *La Riva* (Tres Palmas) • *Williams & Humbert* (Pando)

MANZANILLA

Sea winds in the Sanlúcar de Barrameda area create a more even temperature and higher humidity than those found in Jerez itself, which with the tradition of allowing more ullage (empty volume) in *manzanilla* casks, encourages the thickest, whitest, and most vigorous growth of *flor* in the region. *Fino* is therefore the most classic style, but *manzanilla*, too, has its *fino-amontillado* (called *pasada*) and *amontillado*. *Oloroso* and various intermediary styles are also produced, but these are invariably sold as Sherry, rather than *manzanilla*, even when they are exclusively composed of the latter.

MANZANILLA AMONTILLADA

Fuller than a *pasada*, but lighter and more fragrant than Jerez *amontillado*, this is less common than the previous two, but can be excellent.

✓ *Barbadillo* (Principe) • *Lustau* (Manuel Cuevas Jurado)

MANZANILLA FINA

Manzanilla (Sherry made in Sanlúcar de Barrameda) is a relatively modern, early-picked, *fino*. Its production differs from that of a traditional *fino* in that its fortification is lower and the *solera* system more complex. A true *manzanilla fina* is pale, light-bodied, dry, and delicate with a definite *flor* nose, a touch of bitterness on the palate, and sometimes even a slightly saline tang. *See* general *fino* style (*left*) about freshness and when to consume. These wines are usually 100 per cent Palomino with an alcoholic strength of 15.5 to 17 per cent.

✓ *Barbadillo* (Eva) • *Diez-Mérito* (Don Zoilo) • *Duff Gordon* (Cabrera)

MANZANILLA PASADA

When a *manzanilla* begins to age, it loses its *flor*, gains alcoholic strength, and becomes the equivalent of a *fino-amontillado*, known in Sanlúcar de Barrameda as a *pasada*. These wines are invariably 100 per cent Palomino with an alcoholic strength of up to 20.5 per cent.

✓ *Barbadillo* (Solear) • *Delgado Zuleta* (Amontillado Fino, La Goya) • *Hidalgo* (Pasada)

MILK

Sweetened *amontillado*, usually of lesser quality.

MOSCATEL

Occasionally, releases of this wine can be rich, raisiny delights.

✓ *Lustau* (Las Cruzes, Solera Reserva Emelin)

OLOROSO

Oloroso means fragrant, and when it is genuinely dry, rich, and complex from age, I find it certainly has the greatest finesse and is the most rewarding wine in Jerez. Much of its character is due to the relatively high fortification it receives and the generous glycerine content that develops without the aid of *flor*. The alcoholic strength of these wines usually ranges between 18 and 20 per cent. Some high-quality, sweeter, dessert-style *oloroso* wines are also produced.

✓ **Dry** *Barbadillo* (Oloroso Seco) • *Diez-Mérito* (Victoria Regina) • *Domecq* (Río Viejo) • *Gonzalez Byass* (Alfonso, Apostles) • *Hidalgo* (Oloroso Seco) • *Lustau* (Don Nuno, Emperatríz Eugenia, Principe Rio, Tonel) • *Osborne* (Bailén, Alonso el Sabio) • *Diego Romero* (Jerezana) • *Sandeman* (Dry Old Oloroso) • *Valdespino* (Don Gonzalo)

Dessert style *Gonzalez Byass* (Matúsalem) • *Sandeman* (Royal Corregedor) • *Valdespino* (Solera 1842)

PALE CREAM

Pale cream is sweetened, usually lesser-quality, *fino* Sherry.

PALE DRY

This style is synonymous with *fino*.

PALO CORTADO

This wine cannot be deliberately made, nor even encouraged (a *palo cortado solera* is very difficult to operate); only one butt in a thousand turns into a true *palo cortado*. A law unto itself, it is a naturally dry wine with a style somewhere between *amontillado* (on the nose) and *oloroso* (on the palate), but this description does not by any means convey the stunning richness, nutty complexity, and fabulous finesse, which really must be experienced to be believed.

It should be totally dry, but some sweeter dessert-style *palo cortado* wines are produced and can be wonderful. Like *palma*, *palo cortado* may be graded: *dos cortados, tres cortados, cuatro cortados*.

✓ *Fernando de Castilla* (Antique) • *Domecq* (Sibarita) • *Hidalgo* (Wellington VORS) • *Lustau* (Peninsula) • *Rosario Fantante* (Dos Cortados) • *Sandeman* (Dry Old) • *Valdespino* (Cardenal) • *Williams & Humbert* (Dos Cortados)

Dessert style *Osborne* (Abocado Solera) • *Sandeman* (Royal Ambrosante) • *Wisdom & Warter* (Tizón)

PEDRO XIMÉNEZ

Although it is primarily produced as a sweetening agent, Pedro Ximénez is occasionally released in limited bottlings that are invariably very old and utterly stunning. These are huge, dark, deep, powerfully rich wines piled high with complex yet succulent, raisiny, Muscovado flavours. These bottlings of Pedro Ximénez can be compared in quality, weight, and intensity – though not in character – with only some of the oldest and rarest Australian liqueur Muscats.

✓ *Gonzalez Byass* (Noe) • *Lustau* (Murillo, San Emilio) • *Sanchez Romate* (Superior) • *Valdespino* (Solera Superior) • *Williams & Humbert* (20 Years) • *Wisdom & Warter* (Viale Viejisimo)

PUERTO FINO

This is a *manzanilla*-type Sherry that is produced in El Puerto de Santa Maria, where the winds are almost as legendary as those of Sanlúcar de Barrameda.

✓ *Burdon* (Puerto Fino Superior Dry) • *Osborne* (Coquinera Amontillado)

The WINES of
PORTUGAL

THIS COUNTRY IS SLOWLY BUT SURELY
shaking off its image of tired white wines and
dusty-dry reds. Thanks to a bonanza of grants
during Portugal's honeymoon period of
European Union membership, its wine industry
underwent a massive technological upgrade in
the 1990s, and we are now reaping the rewards.
First came fresh, fruity, inexpensive red wines,
then a whole raft of classy, up-market reds hit
the shelves. Over the next few years, we shall
see similar improvements in Portugal's white
wines. International varieties still have a role to
play, but it will be this country's indigenous
grapes that will establish its reputation in the
third millennium. And while Madeira suffers the
same woes as most other fortified wines, Port
remains by-and-large resistant to the modern
trend of ignoring this style of wine.

QUINTA DE VARGELLAS
The first ever single-quinta Port to be released, Vargellas is the
heart of Taylor's Vintage Port in declared years.

PORTUGAL

As recently as the early 1990s, Dão typified the sort of dried-out, fruitless reds and dull, oxidized whites we had come to expect from Portugal. But following a decade of technological investment, this country now makes bold, ripe, accessible reds and a growing range of fresh, crisp whites.

PORTUGAL HAS COME A LONG WAY in a short time. Indeed, it has had to come a long way. Not so long ago, it was illegal for large wine producers to buy grapes, so they were forced to buy wines from growers who barely had a grasp of how to cultivate their vines, let alone ferment wines. It's been a huge learning curve, from grape to glass, across the entire country, but thanks to the huge investment of EU funds in the 1990s, the infrastructure of the Portuguese wine industry has been transformed. Producers large and small have used modern technology to craft reds of previously unimaginable elegance and finesse and have looked

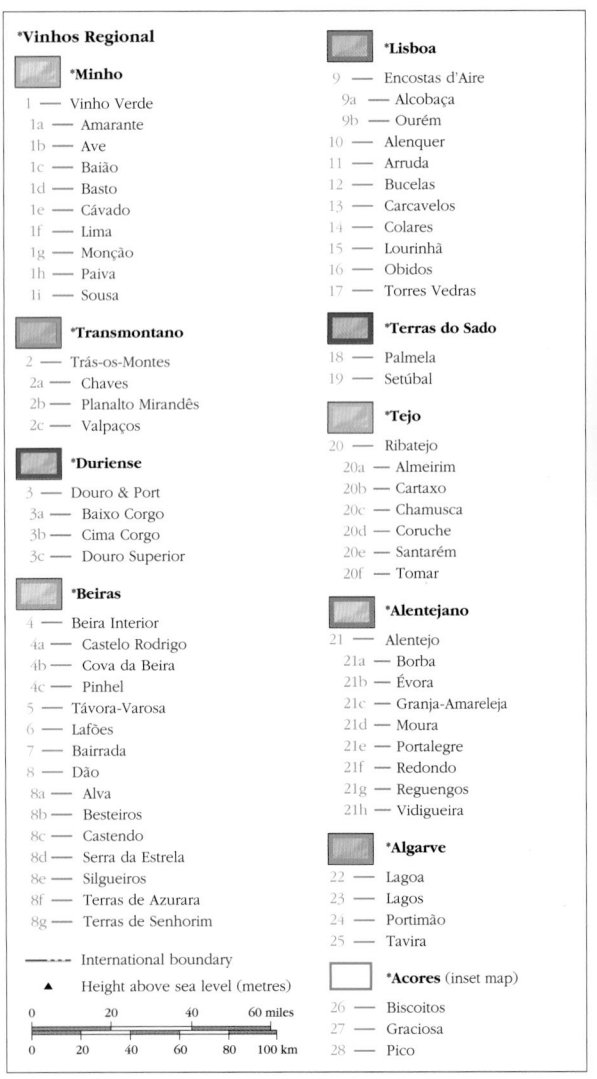

*Vinhos Regional

*Minho
1 — Vinho Verde
1a — Amarante
1b — Ave
1c — Baião
1d — Basto
1e — Cávado
1f — Lima
1g — Monção
1h — Paiva
1i — Sousa

*Transmontano
2 — Trás-os-Montes
2a — Chaves
2b — Planalto Mirandês
2c — Valpaços

*Duriense
3 — Douro & Port
3a — Baixo Corgo
3b — Cima Corgo
3c — Douro Superior

*Beiras
4 — Beira Interior
4a — Castelo Rodrigo
4b — Cova da Beira
4c — Pinhel
5 — Távora-Varosa
6 — Lafões
7 — Bairrada
8 — Dão
8a — Alva
8b — Besteiros
8c — Castendo
8d — Serra da Estrela
8e — Silgueiros
8f — Terras de Azurara
8g — Terras de Senhorim

- - - - International boundary
▲ Height above sea level (metres)

0   20   40   60 miles
0 20 40 60 80 100 km

*Lisboa
9 — Encostas d'Aire
9a — Alcobaça
9b — Ourém
10 — Alenquer
11 — Arruda
12 — Bucelas
13 — Carcavelos
14 — Colares
15 — Lourinhã
16 — Óbidos
17 — Torres Vedras

*Terras do Sado
18 — Palmela
19 — Setúbal

*Tejo
20 — Ribatejo
20a — Almeirim
20b — Cartaxo
20c — Chamusca
20d — Coruche
20e — Santarém
20f — Tomar

*Alentejano
21 — Alentejo
21a — Borba
21b — Évora
21c — Granja-Amareleja
21d — Moura
21e — Portalegre
21f — Redondo
21g — Reguengos
21h — Vidigueira

*Algarve
22 — Lagoa
23 — Lagos
24 — Portimão
25 — Tavira

*Açores (inset map)
26 — Biscoitos
27 — Graciosa
28 — Pico

PORTUGAL
It is in the north of the country that the most famous wines – Port and Vinho Verde – are produced, along with the most upwardly mobile, those from Bairrada and Dão.

to the *terroir* for an expression of minerality in some of Portugal's finest white wines. So-called international varieties have played an intermediate role in boosting the quality of Portugal's indigenous varieties, but it has been a much smaller role than in Spain, and there are now renewed efforts to explore these native varieties, some of which are turning out to be Spanish grapes under a different name and vice versa.

The Duriense or Duoro region leads the way – not just for Port but also for unfortified red and white wines, which is understandable given the reputation and performance of Ribera del Duero just across the border in Spain. The Tejo and Alentejano regions are now firmly in second place, while traditional appellations such as Dão and Bairrada are noticeably lagging behind.

Improvements usually commence at the top end of the wine-quality pyramid, where price can pay for the investments necessary to achieve the desired aims and then takes time to filter down to cheaper, larger-volume products. But Portugal's makeover started at the bottom and quickly worked its way up. It is even possible to pinpoint where and when this revolution began to materialize in 1995, when deliciously fruity upfront reds and fresh, crisp whites came on-stream with wines such as Alta Mesa and Ramada from (the then) Estremadura. There were many top-quality reds produced in the late 1990s, but the defining moment for me was the release of Charme Douro 2002 by Niepoort. If a producer

in the sweltering hot Douro can produce a wine of such beautifully soft and silky fruit with velvety tannins, then Portugal must surely be one of the most potentially diverse winemaking countries in the world.

RECENT PORTUGUESE VINTAGES

2010 The third hot year in a row in the north, this is more of a single-*quinta* year than a classic vintage for Port.

2009 A very hot year in the Douro, where the harvest was difficult and the quality varied. Not a vintage Port year, but some unfortified wines in the Douro performed well.

2008 Very good quality across the board. This was the first of three consecutive hot summers in the Douro, but 2008 turned out to be a good to very good year, rather than a great Port vintage.

2007 A great year all over Portugal, especially in the Douro, where the cool summer stretched out the *véraison*, ending with perfect harvest conditions and a superb vintage Port year.

2006 Some excellent white wines, with Setúbal Moscatels standing out, but patchy for red wines due to ripening problems.

PORTUGUESE LABEL LANGUAGE

Adamado Sweet
Adega Literally "cellar", and commonly used as part of the name of a company or cooperative, similar to the Spanish term *bodega*.
Aperitivo Apéritif
Branco White
Bruto Portuguese adaptation of the French *brut*, used to describe a dry sparkling wine.
Carvalho Oak
Casa Refers to the property or estate and may also indicate a single-vineyard wine.
Casta Grape variety
Casta predominante Refers to the major grape variety used in a wine.
Colheita This means vintage and is followed by the year of harvest.
Clarete Bordeaux-style or deep rosé
Claro New, or "nouveau", wine
Doce Sweet
Denominacão de origem cóntrolada (doc) Roughly equivalent to a French AOC.
Engarrafado por Bottled by
Engarrafado na origem Estate-bottled
Escolha Choice or selection
Espumante A sparkling wine that may be

made by any method unless qualified by another term.
Garrafa Bottle
Garrafeira This term may be used only for a vintage-dated wine that possesses an extra 0.5 per cent of alcohol above the minimum requirement. Red wines must have a minimum of three years' maturation, including one year in bottle; white wines must have one year, with six months in bottle. The wine may come from a demarcated region, or be blended from various areas.
Generoso An apéritif or dessert wine rich in alcohol and usually sweet.
Indicação de Proveniência Regulamentada (IPR) Roughly equivalent to a French VDQS
Licoroso A fortified wine
Maduro Literally "matured" – it often refers to a wine that has been aged in a vat.
Palácio Refers to the property or estate and may also indicate a single-vineyard wine.
Produzido e engarrafado por Produced and bottled at or by
Quinado Tonic wine
Quinta Farm or estate

Rosado Rosé
Reserva A term that can be used only to qualify a vintage year of "outstanding quality", where the wine has an alcoholic strength of at least 0.5 per cent above the minimum requirement. Wine may come from a demarcated region, but does not have to; it could be blended from different areas.
Seco Dry
Solar Refers to the property or estate and may also indicate a single-vineyard wine.
Tinto Red
Velho Literally means "old" and, in the past, this term used not to have any legal definition. Now it can only be applied to wines with a strict minimum age: three years for red wines and two years for whites.
Vinha Vineyard
Vinho Regional (VR) Similar to a large-sized *vin de pays* and may also be labelled IGP.
Vinho de mesa The table wine equivalent to French *vin de table*. If the label does not state a specific DOC or Garrafeira, the wine will be a cheap blend.

THE APPELLATIONS OF
PORTUGAL

Note DOC stands for *Denominação de Origem Controlada*, Portugal's equivalent of France's AOC, Spain's DO, etc.

IPR stands for *Indicação de Proveniência Regulamentada*, roughly equivalent to VDQS or a "DOC in waiting", a number having been promoted to DOC status in recent years.

VR stands for *Vinho Regional*, a sort of large-sized *vin de pays*, the equivalent to *Indicações Geográficas Protegidas*, or IGP, which you may well see on the label of some of these wines in the future.

ACORES VR *or* IGP
Inset map, all islands of the Azores

This regional appellation covers the entire Azores. As in Spain's Canary Islands, the vines here are usually grown in depressions in the lava-strewn volcanic soil, protected by windbreaks built from the blocks of lava that had to be removed to plant each vine. These depressions are called *currais* and are rectangular, rather than circular as in the Canary Islands. The most impressive *currais* are

found on the island of Pico, where UNESCO has declared the vineyards a World Heritage site. Traditionally, the wines of the Azores are fortified, but natural unfortified red, white, and *rosado* wines are made under the regional Acores denomination. *See also* Biscoitos IPR, Graciosa IPR, and Pico IPR.

🍇 Arinto, Fernão Pires, Generosa, Rio Grande, and Seara Nova for white wines; and Cabernet Franc, Cabernet Sauvignon, Merlot, Saborinho, and Syrah for reds

ALENQUER DOC
Map (no.10)

The valley-side vineyards of Alenquer are well-suited to viticulture, ripening grapes easily and producing full, ripe-flavoured reds, with peppery-spicy aromas and soft, easy-going, creamy-dry whites.

🍇 Arinto, Camarate, Fernão Pires, Jampal, Mortágua, Periquita, Preto Martinho, Tinta Miuda, Vital

🍷 1–3 years (new-wave, fruity style) 2–5 years (others)

✓ *Quinta de Abrigada • Quinta de Plantos • Quinta do Carneiro*

ALENTEJANO VR *or* IGP
Map (nos.21 & 21a–21h and surrounding region)

Stretching up from the Algarve, the plains of Alto and Baixo Alentejo cover about one-third of Portugal. A sparsely populated area with large estates and a scattering of vines, Alentejo was once better known for cork than vineyards, even though it has produced some of the country's most outstanding one-off wines and has achieved this with both indigenous and imported grape varieties. This denomination covers the entire region, including the best areas upgraded to DO, and many of the most talented producers have opted to label their wines as Alentejano rather than Alentejo.

🍇 Abundante, Alfrocheiro Preto, Alicante Bouschet, Antão Vaz, Aragonez, Arinto, Cabernet Sauvignon, Carignan, Chardonnay, Diagalves, Fernão Pires, Grand Noir, Manteudo, Moreto, Periquita, Perrum, Rabo de Ovelha, Trincadeira

🍷 1–3 years (new-wave, fruity style), 2–5 years (others)

✓ *Cortes de Cima • Esporão • Fitapreta • Herdade de Mouchão • J B (Júlio B Bastos Alicante Bouschet, Dona Maria Reserva) • José de Sousa • Paolo Laureano (Vinea Julieta Talhão 24) • A C de Reguengos • Quinta do Mouro (Rótulo Dourado) • Tapada do Chaves*

ALENTEJO DOC
Map (no.21)

Politically, Alentejo encompasses the entire Alentejano region, but as a DOC it covers only the delimited areas of Borba, Évora, Granja-Amareleja,

CELLARS AT QUINTA DO CENTRO
Owned by Richard Mayson and Rui Reguinga, Quinta do Centro is on the mid-slopes of the Serra de São Mamede at Reguengo in the Alentejo region.

Moura, Portalegre, Redondo, Reguengos, and Vidigueira within the Alentejano region. Alentejo literally means "beyond the Tagus", referring to the river that separates the entire region from the rest of Portugal. This is a good source for some of Portugal's groundbreaking modern reds.

🍇 Abundante, Alfrocheiro Preto, Alicante Bouschet, Antão Vaz, Aragonez, Arinto, Cabernet Sauvignon, Carignan, Chardonnay, Diagalves, Fernão Pires, Grand Noir, Manteudo, Moreto, Periquita, Perrum, Rabo de Ovelha, Trincadeira

🍷 1–3 years (fruity style), 2–5 years (others)

✓ *Tapada do Chaves • Esporão • Herdade da Malhadinha* (Matilde) *• Pêra Manca • Quinta do Centro • A C de Reguengos • Sogrape* (Vinha do Monte) *• António Saramago* (Dúvida) *• José de Sousa • Terra d'Alter* (Outeiro do Mouro)

ALENTEJO BORBA DOC
Map (no.21a)

The first sub-appellation of the Alentejo region to gain recognition outside of Portugal itself, especially for its inexpensive, juicy red wines.

🍇 Aragonez, Periquita, Perrum, Rabo de Ovelha, Roupeiro, Tamarêz, Trincadeira

🍷 1–3 years (new-wave, fruity style), 2–5 years (others)

✓ *AC de Borba* (Reserva)

ALENTEJO ÉVORA DOC
Map (no.21b)

Spread out to the north, south, and west of Évora, the capital of Alentejo, this area is destined to be one of Portugal's most exciting appellations, especially for full-bodied, creamy-rich red.

🍇 Aragonez, Arinto, Periquita, Rabo de Ovelha, Roupeiro, Tamarêz, Tinta Caida, Trincadeira

🍷 2–5 years

✓ *Herdade da Cartuxa • Pêra Manca* (branco)

ALENTEJO GRANJA AMARELEJA DOC
Map (no.21c)

The harsh climate and schistous soils of this sub-appellation of the Alentejo region can produce powerful, spicy reds, but it has yet to establish itself on export markets.

🍇 Manteudo, Moreto, Periquita, Rabo de Ovelha, Roupeiro, Trincadeira

ALENTEJO MOURA DOC
Map (no.21d)

Cool, red clay soil stretches out the grape's ripening period in this hot patch of the Alentejo, adding a certain finesse to the lush, plump fruit in these wines, which promise great things, but the appellation has not yet established itself.

🍇 Alfrocheiro, Antão Vaz, Fernão Pires, Moreto, Periquita, Rabo de Ovelha, Roupeiro, Trincadeira

ALENTEJO PORTALEGRE DOC
Map (no.21e)

Powerful, yet elegant, spicy reds, and rather heavy, alcoholic whites produced in the Alentejo region, adjacent to the Spanish frontier.

🍇 Aragonez, Arinto, Assário, Fernão Pires, Galego, Grand Noir, Manteudo, Periquita, Roupeiro, Trincadeira

ALENTEJO REDONDO DOC
Map (no.21f)

A sub-appellation within the progressive Alentejo region, Redondo shows promise for the sort of gushy, upfront, fruity reds that are popping up all over Portugal at a grassroots level.

🍇 Aragonez, Fernão Pires, Manteudo, Moreto, Periquita, Rabo de Ovelha, Roupeiro, Tamarez, Trincadeira

🍷 1–3 years

✓ *A C de Redondo*

ALENTEJO REGUENGOS DOC
Map (no.21g)

An up-and-coming DOC in the Alentejo, Reguengos is already producing both gluggy and much finer reds, plus increasingly good whites, making it an appellation to watch.

🍇 Aragonez, Manteudo, Moreto, Periquita, Perrum, Rabo de Ovelha, Roupeiro, Trincadeira

🍷 1–3 years (new-wave, fruity style), 2–5 years (others)

✓ *A C de Reguengos* (tinto) *• J P Vinhos* (Quinta da Anfora)

ALENTEJO VIDIGUEIRA DOC
Map (no.21h)

This appellation takes its name from one of three towns around which vineyards flourish on volcanic soils, while the name of the town itself is derived from the word *videira*, meaning "wine", illustrating how long vines have been growing in this part of the Alentejo.

🍇 Alfrocheiro, Antão Vaz, Manteudo, Moreto, Periquita, Perrum, Rabo de Ovelha, Roupeiro, Trincadeira

ALGARVE VR *or* IGP
Map (nos.22–25 and surrounding region)

The downgrading of Algarve to Vinho Regional was just a smoke-screen to gain acceptance for its four new internal DOCs: Lagos, Portimão, Lagoa, and Tavira. Lagoa used to have a reputation for fortified whites, which is not surprising considering its proximity to Jerez, but although wine is still produced, none of any interest, fortified or not, is made in the Algarve these days. It is wise to remember that the tourist economy, not quality, regulates wine appellations in the Algarve.

🍇 Arinto, Bastardo, Diagalves, Moreto, Negra Mole, Periquita, Perrum, Rabo de Ovelha, Tamarêz d'Algarve

✓ *Adega do Cantor*

ARRUDA DOC
Map (no.11)

From intensively cultivated hillsides surrounding the town of Arruda in the Lisboa region, come some of Portugal's cheapest, yet reliable, fruity reds.

🍇 Camarate (possibly the same as Castelão Nacional), Fernão Pires, Graciano (*syn* Tinta Miuda), Jampal, Trincadeira, Vital

🍷 1–3 years (new-wave, fruity style), 2–5 years (others)

✓ *AC de Arruda*

BAIRRADA DOC
Map (no.7)

This area produces one of Portugal's two most important red wines and the best have a deep colour with good tannin and fine, capsicum-blackcurranty fruit. However, it is only just beginning to demonstrate its potential for white wines. Sogrape's Nobilis exemplifies Bairrada's fast-emerging rosé style, which really hits the spot with its freshness and depth of fruit.

🍇 Baga, Bical, Castelão Francês, Maria Gomes, Rabo de Ovelha, Tinta Pinheira

🍷 3–12 years (reds) 1–3 years (rosés and whites)

✓ *José Maria da Fonseca* • *Gonçalves Faria* (Reserva) • *Luis Pato* (especially Quinta do Ribeirinho Vinhos Velhos) • *Quinta de Pedralvites* • *Casa de Saima* • *Caves São João* • *Sogrape* (Reserva, Nobilis Rosé) • *Terra Franca* (tinto)

BEIRA INTERIOR DOC
Map (no.4)

Created within the Beiras region as recently as 2005, this DOC comprises three sub-regional DOCs: Beira Interior Castelo Rodrigo, Beira Interior Cova da Beira, and Beira Interior Pinhel.

🍇 Arinto, Baga, Bastardo, Bical, Camarate, Cerceal, Esgana Cão, Fernão Pires, Jaen, Malvasia, Marufo, Monvedro, Periquita, Rabo de Ovelha, Rufete, Touriga Nacional, Trincadeira Preta, Verdelho, Vital

🍷 1–3 years (new-wave, fruity style), 2–5 years (others)

✓ *Quinta do Cardo* • *Quinta dos Currais* (Colheita Selecionada) • *A C do Fundão* (Fundanus Prestige)

BEIRA INTERIOR CASTELO RODRIGO DOC
Map (no.4a)

These full, spicy reds on the border with Spain, south of the Douro, in the Beiras region, show excellent potential, but have yet to establish an international reputation.

🍇 Arinto, Arinto do Dão, Bastardo, Codo, Fonte Cal, Marufo, Rufete, Touriga Nacional

🍷 1–3 years (new-wave, fruity style), 2–5 years (others)

✓ *Quinta do Cardo*

BEIRA INTERIOR COVA DE BEIRA DOC
Map (no.4b)

Located in the Beira Alta, between the Vinho Verde and Dão districts, Cova de Beira is the largest of Portugal's IPRs. As with the Beiras VR, every style of wine is produced in varying quality, but the area is best-known for its lightweight reds.

🍇 Arinto, Arinto do Dão, Jaen, Marufo, Periquita, Pérola, Rabo de Ovelha, Rufete, Trincadeira Preta

BEIRA INTERIOR PINHEL DOC
Map (no.4c)

In the Beiras region, just south of the Douro, Pinhel makes dry, full, and earthy-tasting white wines, mostly sold to sparkling-wine producers.

🍇 Arinto, Arinto do Dão, Bastardo, Codo, Fonte Cal, Marufo, Rufete, Touriga Nacional

BEIRAS VR *or* IGP
Map (nos.4 & 4a–4c and surrounding regions)

Located in the north of Portugal, the Beiras region encompasses not only the three sub-regions of Rodrigo, Cova de Beira, and Pinhel, but also the surrounding DOCs of Dão, Bairrada, and Távora-Varosa, plus the IPR of Lafões. Understandably, therefore, the Beiras region produces virtually every imaginable style of wine, and standards can vary enormously. There is some super-value modern winemaking going on, though, not to mention some super-quality standouts such as Luis Pato's Quinta do Ribeirinho Pré Franco from ungrafted Baga vines.

🍇 Arinto, Baga, Bastardo, Bical, Camarate, Cerceal, Esgana Cão, Fernão Pires, Jaen, Malvasia, Marufo, Monvedro, Periquita, Rabo de Ovelha, Rufete, Touriga Nacional, Trincadeira Preta, Verdelho, Vital

🍷 1–3 years (new-wave, fruity style) 2–5 years (others)

✓ *Bright Brothers* (Baga) • *Buçaco* • *Conde de Santar* (Reserva) • *Entre Serras* • *Filipa Pato* • *João Pato* • *Quinta dos Cozinheiros* • *Quinta de Foz de Arouce*

BISCOITOS IPR
Map (no.26)

Fortified wines produced on the Azores island of Terceira, where viticulture has flourished since the 16th century. Winemaking was halted by phylloxera but quickly re-established by Francisco Maria Blum in the 1890s. A Flemish winemaker (it was the Flemish who settled much of the Azores), Blum was known locally as Chico Maria, under which name his old winery operates to this day. Named after a village on the island, Biscoitos literally means "biscuits" in English. Unfortified wines are usually sold under the regional Acores VR. Biscoitos is rarely encountered beyond the Azores.

🍇 Arinto, Terrantez, Verdelho

BUCELAS DOC
Map (no.12)

The Arinto grape grows particularly well on the loam soil of this small district, but the antiquated winemaking methods are still holding back what is obviously a potentially fine white-wine appellation. Cool fermentation, early bottling, and a delicate touch of new oak would make this wine an international superstar, but so many wines are dried-out and over-acidic. Quinta da Romeira is the most consistent Bucelas, and is recommended in this context, but has failed to live up to its promise.

🍇 Arinto, Esgana Cão

🍷 Upon purchase

✓ *Quinta da Romeira* (Prova Régia)

CARCAVELOS DOC
Map (no.13)

Famous in Portugal itself since the late 18th century when the Marquis of Pombal owned a large vineyard and winery here. This area's oldest surviving vineyard, Quinta do Barão, stopped production in 1991, but a relatively new one, Quinta dos Pesos, is trying desperately to rekindle interest in Carcavelos. Rarely seen on export markets, it is a topaz-coloured, off-dry fortified wine with a nutty aroma, delicate almondy flavour, and a velvety texture.

🍇 Arinto, Boal, Galego Dourado, Negra Mole, Trincadeira, Torneiro

🍷 5–20 years

✓ *Quinta dos Pesos*

COLARES DOC
Map (no.14)

This small wine area is famous for its ungrafted Ramisco vines planted in trenches dug out of the sandy dunes of Sintra, which not only protects them from salt-blighting Atlantic winds, but also from the dreaded phylloxera louse. This is a historic wine, but should not be vinified in such an antiquated fashion if it is going to appeal to modern consumers. If the greatest Bordeaux châteaux have moved with the times, why not Colares? The reds are well-coloured and full-bodied, but have so much tannin that they are mouth-puckeringly astringent, smoothing out to a silky finish only with great age, when there is no fruit left. If the grapes could be picked according to tannin-ripeness, rather than fruit-ripeness, and more careful fermentation techniques employed, Colares could be world class. The dry whites are traditional *maduro*-style and not recommended.

🍇 Arinto, Jampal, Galego Dourado, Malvasia, Ramisco

🍷 15–30 years (red)

✓ *Antonio Bernardino Paulo da Silva* (Chitas)

DÃO DOC
Map (nos.8 & 8a–8g)

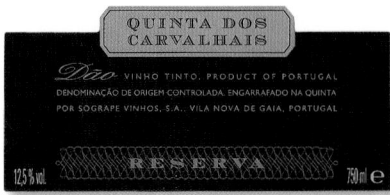

For 25 years there have been rumours that Dão wines have more fruit and less tannin, but only in recent times have we seen this promise fulfilled in the glass, as fruit-filled Dão have begun to emerge.

They have sufficient fruit to drink much earlier than the old-style Dão wines, but have a certain structure and dry, spicy-finesse that expresses their Portuguese origins. The best whites can be clean and fresh, but not yet truly special, although the Quinta de Saes branco is surprisingly good, especially when consumed with food.

🍇 Alfrocheiro Preto, Arinto do Dão, Barcelo, Bastardo, Borrado das Moscas, Cercial, Encruzado, Jaen, Tinta Pinheira, Tinta Roriz, Touriga Nacional, Verdelho

🍷 3–8 years (reds), 1–3 years (whites)

✓ *Campos da Silva Oliveira* • *Casa da Insua* • *Duque de Viseu* • *José Maria da Fonseca* (Garrafeira P) • *Paço das Cunhas* • *Quinta de Cabriz* (Four C) • *Quinta dos Carvalhais* (Encruzado) • *Quinta da Falorca* (Garafeira) • *Quinta dos Roques* (Reserva) • *Quinta de Saes* (Reserva Branco) • *Sogrape* (Callabriga Reserva)

DÃO ALVA DOC
Map (no.8a)

Named after the Alva River, which forms the southern border of the sub-region in the Coimbra district.

DÃO BESTEIROS DOC
Map (no.8b)

With a warmer, more Mediterranean climate than the rest of Dão, Besteiros is located southwest of Viseu but still in the Viseu district, where the soils are composed of a more fertile, slightly acid, granitic-based loam.

DÃO CASTENDO DOC
Map (no.8c)

This sub-regional DOC encompasses three valleys – the Dão, Vouga, and Caja – towards the northeastern corner of the region.

DÃO SERRA DA ESTRELA DOC
Map (no.8c)

Located in the higher-altitude foothills of the Serra da Estrela, in the Guarda district, to the east of the Dão region, this DOC has many vineyards at 700–750 metres (2,300–2,450 feet) above sea level. Due to the height, its vineyards are more exposed to the maritime effects of the Atlantic than elsewhere in the region, much of which is protected by the Serra do Caramulo to the west. With this exposure comes increased rainfall (although it occurs mostly in the winter), the reserves of which can be tapped during the growing season by vines that are well established with deep roots.

✓ *Quinta das Maias*

DÃO SILGUEIROS DOC
Map (no.8e)

Centred around Viseu, the capital of the Dão, in the northwestern corner of the region.

✓ *Quinta da Falorca* • *Quinta do Perdigão*

DÃO TERRAS DE AZURARA DOC
Map (no.8f)

As with both *terras* sub-regions, these vineyards are located between the two rivers, the Dão and Modego, at the very heart of the Dão region. The Terras de Azurara is farther upstream, where the vines grow mostly on red granitic sand, with some schist and clay, at heights of up to 450 metres (1,475 feet) above sea level.

DÃO TERRAS DE SENHORIM DOC
Map (no.8g)

Terras de Senhorim is farther upstream than Terras de Azurara, but as with both *terras* sub-regions, these vineyards are located between the two rivers, the Dão and Modego, at the very heart of the Dão region.

DOURO DOC
Map (nos.3 & 3a-3c)

Known principally for its Port, the Douro Valley in fact makes as much table wine as fortified wine. Because the finest Port is produced on schist soils, most table wines are relegated to areas of the region's other dominant soil, granite. I remain surprised that the Syrah, which thrives in the Northern Rhône's hot, granite soil, has not been tried here, even though it has been experimented with in the Alentejo, where there is much less potential for this variety. The Douro's table wine quality potential is highlighted by Barca Velha, Portugal's most expensive table wine, made by Ferreira at Quinta do Vale de Meão, although its second wine, Reserva Especial, is often just as good, if not better. Is it a coincidence that across the Spanish frontier, where the Douro becomes the Duero, Vega Sicilia, Spain's most expensive wine, grows on its banks? There is nothing porty about these table wines, which range from the lighter, claret types to the fuller, richer Burgundian style. New oak is almost *de rigueur* for premium quality wines.

🍇 Bastardo, Donzelinho Branco, Gouveio, Malvasia Fina, Rabigato, Mourisco Tinto, Tinta Amarela, Tinta Barroca, Tinta Cão, Tinta Roriz, Touriga Nacional, Touriga Francesa, Viosinho

🍷 2–10 years (red, but up to 25 for Barca Velha), 1–4 years (white)

✓ *Apegadas* (Quinta Velha Grande Reserva) • *Bright Brothers* • *CARM* (Reserva, Quinta do Côa, Quinta do Côa Reserva) • *Casa Ferreirinha* (Vértice Tinto, Vinha Grande) • *Churchill* (Touriga Nacional, Quinta da Gricha) • *Domingos Alves de Souza* (Abandonado) • *Duorum* (Reserva Vinhas Velhas) • *Encostas do Douro* (Palestra) • *Ferreirinha* (especially Barca Velha, Reserva Especial) • *J & F Lurton* (Quinta do Malhô) • *Niepoort* (Redoma and especially Charme Douro) • *Jorge Nobre Moreira* (Poeira) • *Prats & Symington* (Chryseia, Post Scriptum de Chryseia) • *Quanta Terra* • *Quinta do Côtto* (Grande Escholha) • *Quinta do Crasto* • *Quinta da Foz* • *Quinta do Noval* • *Quinta da Padrela* (Grande Reserva) • *Quinta de Passadouro* • *Quinta de Pellada* • *Quinta do Portal* (Auru) • *Quinta da Romaneira* • *Quinta de la Rosa* • *Quinta do Vale Meão* • *Quinta do Vale Dona Maria* • *Quinta do Vale da Raposa* • *Quinta de Vallado* • *Quinta de Ventozelo* (Touriga Nacional) • *Quinta do Vesuvio* • *Ramos-Pinto* (Duas Quintas) • *Secret Spot* (Moscatel) • *Sogrape* (Reserva) • *Vale do Bomfim* (Reserva) • *Vinhas de Ciderma* (Reserva) • *Vinilourenço* (D Graça Grande Reserva, D Graça Reserva Especial) • *Wine & Soul* (Pintas Character)

DOURO BAIXO CORGO DOC
Map (no.3a)

The Baixo (or Lower) Corgo extends from Barqueiros on the north bank of the Douro to just east of Régua, where the Corgo River and the Ribeiro de Temilobos form a confluence with the Douro. This area is the smallest of the Douro's three sub-regions geographically, but with more than 14,500 hectares (35,800 acres) of vines, it is the second most important area viticulturally speaking. The Baixo Corgo has the wettest climate, but it is winter rain. The summers are as dry and hot as you imagine the Douro to be.

DOURO CIMA CORGO DOC
Map (no.3b)

The Cima (or Upper) Corgo extends upstream from the confluence of the Corgo River and the Ribeiro de Temilobos to the Cachão de Valeira, encompassing just under 21,000 hectares (51,900 acres) of vines. Virtually all of the very best *quintas* are to be found in the Cima Corgo.

DOURO SUPERIOR DOC
Map (no.3c)

The Douro Superior, or Very Upper Douro, is exclusively applied to the area from the Cachão de Valeira to the Spanish border, which makes it the largest of the three sub-regions, but with just over 10,000 hectares (25,000 acres), it is viticulturally the least important. The Douro Superior has the driest climate.

DURIENSE VR *or* IGP
Map (nos.3 & 3a-3c and surrounding region)

Effectively the same boundary as Douro DOC, but its level IGP Vinho Regional designation allows its winegrowers and winemakers to benefit from far greater regulatory flexibility.

🍇 Alvarelhão, Arinto, Avesso, Bastardo, Boal, Branco Sem Nome, Cabernet Franc, Cabernet Sauvignon, Casculho, Castela, Cercial, Chardonnay, Códega, Cornifesto, Coucieira, Donzelinho (Branco and Tinto), Esganacão, Fernão Pires, Folgosão, Gewürztraminer, Gouveio, Malvasia (Corada, Fina, Parda, Preta, and Rei), Merlot, Moreto, Moscatel Galego, Mourisco (aka Palomino), Mourisco (de Semente and Tinto), Pederna, Periquita, Pinot Noir, Praça, Rabigato, Rufete, Samarrinho, Sauvignon Blanc, Sémillon, Sousão, Syrah, Tinta Amarela, Tinta Bairrada, Tinta Barroca, Tinta Cão, Tinta Carvalha, Tinta da Barca, Tinta Francisca, Tinta Roriz, Tinto Martins, Touriga Branca, Touriga Brasileira, Touriga Francesa, Touriga Naçional, Viosinho

🍷 Reds 1–5 years (up to 10 years for some ultra-serious quality red), whites 1–3 years (1–2 years for Sauvignon Blanc)

✓ *Carla Ferreira* (Unipessoal Bastardo Duriense) • *Conceito Bastardo* • *Casa de Vila Verde* (Alvarinho) • *Quinta do Noval* (Cedro, Labrador Syrah)

ENCOSTAS D'AIRE DOC
Map (nos.9 & 9a-9b)

Taking up almost all of the northern half of the Lisboa region, the limestone hills of this appellation should produce some excellent wines, but most have so far been light and rather dried-out.

🍇 Primary red or *rosado* varieties (minimum 65%): Aragonêz, Baga, Castelão, Tinta Miúda, Touriga Nacional, Trincadeira; secondary red or *rosado* varieties (maximum 35%): Alicante Bouchet, Caladoc, Grand Noir, Syrah; tertiary red and *rosado* varieties (maximum 15%): Alfrocheiro, Amostrinha, Bastardo, Cabernet Sauvignon, Rufete, Touriga Franca. Primary white varieties (minimum 65%): Arinto, Fernão Pires, Ratinho, Seara Nova, Tamarez, Vital; secondary white varieties (maximum 35%): Alicante Branco, Bical, Boal Branco, Cercial, Chardonnay, Rabo de Ovelha, Trincadeira Branca

ENCOSTAS D'AIRE ALCOBAÇA DOC
Map (no.9a)

These wines from the hills surrounding the old monastic town of Alcobaça are predominantly white. Yields are unfavourably high, producing thin reds and light whites significantly lower in alcohol than wines from surrounding areas.

🍇 Primary red or *rosado* varieties (minimum 65%): Aragonêz, Castelão, Tinta Miúda, Touriga Nacional; secondary red or *rosado* varieties (maximum 35%): Alicante Bouchet, Syrah; tertiary red and *rosado* varieties (maximum 15%): Amostrinha, Rufete, Touriga Franca. Primary white varieties (minimum 65%): Fernão Pires, Ratinho, Tamarez, Vital; secondary white varieties (maximum 35%): Bical, Cercial, Chardonnay, Rabo de Ovelha, Trincadeira Branca

ENCOSTAS D'AIRE OURÉM DOC
Map (no.9b)

From the northern section of the Encostas d'Aire, this sub-regional DOC is focused on pure varietal wines and restricted to two traditional varieties.

🍇 Trincadeira (reds), Fernão Pires (whites)

GRACIOSA IPR
Map (no.27)

Rarely encountered light table wines produced on the island of Graciosa in the Azores.

🍇 Arinto, Fernão Pires, Malvasia Fina
• Terrantez, Verdelho

LAFÕES IPR
Map (no.6)

Light, acidic, red and white wines produced in a small area between the Vinho Verde and Dão regions, where veal is more famous than wine.

🍇 Amaral, Arinto, Cerceal, Jaen

LAGOA DOC
Map (no.22)

Formerly known for fortified white wines, which are still made, but are not of interest, this sub-appellation of the Algarve does not deserve its DOC classification.

🍇 Crato Branco, Negra Mole, Periquita

LAGOS DOC
Map (no.23)

These Algarve wines do not deserve their DOC classification.

🍇 Boal Branco, Negra Mole, Periquita

LISBOA VR *or* IGP
Map (nos.9, 9a–9b & 10–17 and surrounding region)

From Lisbon, this region (formerly called Estremadura) stretches north to the Bairrada region. This is Portugal's largest wine-producing region in terms of volume (although Beiras and Alentejo are much larger geographically), and as such, Lisboa is often perceived as a source of cheap, uninteresting wine. While there are indeed cheap wines made here, they are good guzzlers and far from uninteresting, with a few *quintas* making much finer, more serious wines that are not remotely expensive.

🍇 Alfrocheiro Preto, Antão Vaz, Arinto, Baga, Bastardo, Bical, Cabernet Sauvignon, Camarate, Chardonnay, Esgana Cão, Fernão Pires, Jampal, Malvasia, Moreto, Periquita, Rabo de Ovelha, Ramisco, Tália, Tamarêz, Tamarêz d'Azeitão, Tinta Miuda, Trincadeira Preta, Vital

🍷 2–4 years (reds, 4–8 years for better wines), 1–3 years (whites)

✓ *A C do Arruda* (selected *cuvées*) • *A C de São Mamede da Ventosa* • *A C do Torres Vedras* (selected *cuvées*) • *Baron Bruemmer* (Senhor d'Adraga) • *Espiga* • *Palha Canas* • *Quinta do Chocapalha* (Arinto) • *Quinta da Folgorosa* • *Quinta do Monte d'Oiro* (Ex Aequo) • *Quinta de Pancas*

LOURINHÃ DOC
Map (no.15)

This is traditionally brandy country, but it also produces fresh, low-alcohol, easy-drinking white wines.

🍇 Alicante Branco, Alvadurão, Boal Espinho, Cabinda, Malvasia Rei, Marquinhas, Thalia.

MADEIRA DOC
See Madeira, p400

MINHO VR *or* IGP
Map (nos.1 & 1a–1i and surrounding region)

A sort of *vin de pays* Vinhos Verdes, except that this appellation also allows for still table wines from foreign varieties. Predictably lightweight. The Minho region falls almost entirely between the River Douro to the south and the Minho River to the north.

🍇 Alvarelho, Alvarinho, Avesso, Azal Branco, Azal Tinto, Batoca, Borracal, Cabernet Sauvignon, Chardonnay, Espadeiro, Loureiro, Merlot, Paderna, Padreiro de Basto, Pedral, Rabo de Ovelha, Riesling, Trajadura, Vinhão

✓ *Covela Escolha*

OBIDOS DOC
Map (no.16)

The white wines from this area have traditionally been distilled, but the firm, cedary-oaky reds might have potential.

🍇 Arinto, Bastardo, Camarate, Fernão Pires, Periquita, Rabo de Ovelha, Tinta Miuda, Vital

PALMELA DOC
Map (no.18)

The Palmela area was first made famous by the João Pires off-dry white made from early-picked Muscat grapes, but it is equally good for full-bodied reds and the inspired, high-volume João Pires now claims the much larger Terras do Sado appellation, as have others, hence there are no recommendations, despite the excellent wines made here.

🍇 Alfrocheiro, Arinto, Espadeiro, Fernão Pires, Moscatel de Setúbal, Periquita, Rabo de Ovelha

PICO IPR
Map (no.28)

Fortified wines produced on the Azores island of Pico, where the vineyards were declared a UNESCO World Heritage site in 2004. Vines cover almost one-third of the total island and are planted in lava-strewn depressions called *currais*, which are rectangular rather than crater-like, as on some Canary Islands, such as Lanzarote. The most (locally) famous wine is a fortified wine not dissimilar to a white Port, and although the most commonly found fortified Pico is produced by the local cooperative under Lajido, it is rarely encountered beyond the Azores.

🍇 Arinto, Terrantez, Verdelho

PORT *or* PORTO DOC
Map (nos.3 & 3a–3c)
See The Douro and the Minho, p394

PORTIMÃO DOC
Map (no.24)

These Algarve wines do not deserve their DOC classification.

🍇 Crato Branco, Negra Mole, Periquita

PORTO BAIXO CORGO DOC
Map (no.3a)

The Baixo (or Lower) Corgo extends from Barqueiros on the north bank of the Douro to just east of Régua, where the Corgo River and the Ribeiro de Temilobos form a confluence with the Douro. This area is the smallest of the Douro's three sub-regions geographically, but with more than 14,500 hectares (35,800 acres) of vines, it is the second most important area viticulturally speaking. The Baixo Corgo has the wettest climate, but it is winter rain. The summers are as dry and hot as you imagine the Douro to be.

PORTO CIMA CORGO DOC
Map (no.3b)

The Cima (or Upper) Corgo extends upstream from the confluence of the Corgo River and the Ribeiro de Temilobos to the Cachão de Valeira, encompassing just under 21,000 hectares (51,900 acres) of vines. Virtually all the very best *quintas* are found here.

PORTO DOURO SUPERIOR DOC
Map (no.3c)

The Douro Superior, or Very Upper Douro, is exclusively applied to the area from the Cachão de Valeira to the Spanish border, which makes it the largest of the three sub-regions, but with just over 10,000 hectares (25,000 acres), it is viticulturally the least important. The Douro Superior has the driest climate.

RIBATEJO DOC
Map (nos.20 & 20a–20f)

When the former Ribatejo VR was renamed Tejo VR, much of the region was elevated to Ribatejo DOC in recognition of the fresh, modern, soft, fruity reds from the best producers.

🍇 Arinto, Cabernet Sauvignon, Camarate, Carignan, Chardonnay, Esgana Cão, Fernão Pires, Jampal, Malvasia Fina, Malvasia Rei, Merlot, Periquita, Pinot Noir, Rabo de Ovelha, Sauvignon Blanc, Syrah, Tália, Tamarêz, Tamarêz d'Azeitâo, Tinta Muida, Touriga Nacional, Trincadeira Preta, Vital

🍷 1–5 years (reds), 1–3 years (whites)

✓ *Bright Brothers* • *Falua* • *Fuiza* • *Terra de Lobos*

RIBATEJO ALMEIRIM DOC
Map (no.20a)

An up-and-coming area in the Ribatejo region, rapidly becoming known as a source for cheap, fruity red and white wines, often from the plains, known locally as *lezíria* and simply sold as *vinho de mesa*. Terraced vines on the left bank of the Tagus apparently have more potential.

🍇 Arinto, Castelão Nacional, Fernão Pires, Periquita, Poeirinha, Rabo de Ovelha, Tália, Tamarêz d'Azeitão, Trincadeira Preta, Vital

🍷 6–18 months

✓ *AC de Almeirim* (including wines under Falcoaria and Quinta das Verandas labels)

RIBATEJO CARTAXO DOC
Map (no.20b)

This flat, fertile area produces good, fruity, value-for-money reds and whites.

🍇 Arinto, Castelão Nacional, Fernão Pires, Periquita, Preto Martinho, Tália, Tamarêz d'Azeitão, Trincadeira Preta, Vital

🍷 1–3 years

✓ *Almeida*

RIBATEJO CHAMUSCA DOC
Map (no.20c)

This sub-appellation of the Ribatejo region is adjacent to Almeirim and produces similar wines, but not quite of the same potential.

🍇 Arinto, Castelão Nacional, Fernão Pires, Periquita, Tália, Tamarêz d'Azeitão, Trincadeira Preta, Vital

RIBATEJO CORUCHE DOC
Map (no.20d)

This appellation covers wines made from sandy, well-irrigated plains covering the southern half of the Ribatejo region, but Coruche is seldom encountered and has yet to make its mark.

🍇 Fernão Pires, Periquita, Preto Martinho, Tália, Tamarêz d'Azeitão, Trincadeira Preta, Vital

RIBATEJO SANTARÉM DOC
Map (no.20e)

A new appellation for the area around the capital of the Ribatejo region, Santarém should begin to establish itself over the next few years.

🍇 Arinto, Castelão Nacional, Fernão Pires, Periquita, Preto Martinho, Rabo de Ovelha, Tália, Tamarêz d'Azeitão, Trincadeira Preta, Vital

RIBATEJO TOMAR DOC
Map (no.20f)

Red and white wines grown on limestone slopes of the right bank of the River Tagus in the Ribatejo region.

🍇 Arinto, Baga, Castelão Nacional, Fernão Pires, Malvasia, Periquita, Rabo de Ovelha, Tália

SETÚBAL DOC
Moscatel de Setúbal
Map (no.19)

This style of fortified Muscat wine is believed to have been created by José-Maria da Fonseca, the old-established company that still has a quasi-monopoly over its production today. There are various wood-aged styles (5- or 6-Year-Old is best for freshness and the grapey-apricoty varietal character, while 20- or 25-Year-Old is darker and far more complex with a raisiny-nutty-caramel-apricoty intensity), but single-vintage Setúbal is top of the range.

🍇 Moscatel de Setúbal), Moscatel do Douro, Moscatel Roxo plus up to 30 per cent Arinto,

Boais, Diagalves, Fernão Pires, Malvasia, Olho de Lebre, Rabo de Ovelha, Roupeiro, Tália, Tamarêz, Vital

🍶 Upon purchase (but will last many years)

✓ J M Fonseca

TAVIRA DOC
Map (no.25)

These Algarve wines do not deserve their DOC classification.

🍇 Crato Branco, Negra Mole, Periquita

TÁVORA-VAROSA DOC
Map (no.5)

Located in the foothills of the Serra da Nave, between the rivers Paiva and Tavora, where red and white wines, both still and sparkling, are produced.

🍇 **RED:** Alvarelhão, Aragonez, Bastardo, Malvasia Preta, Marufo, Castelão, Rufete, Tinta Barroca, Barca, Touriga Franca, Touriga Nacional, Trincadeira Preta, Vinhão
WHITE: Arinto, Bical, Chardonnay, Dona Branca, Fernão Pires, Folgasão, Gouveio, Malvasia Fina, Malvasia Rei, Rabo de Ovelha, Síria, Viosinho
SPARKLING RED: Alvarelhão, Aragonez, Pinot Noir, Barca, Tinta Barroca, Touriga Franca, Touriga Nacional;
SPARKLING WHITE: Arinto, Bical, Chardonnay, Dona Branca, Fernão Pires, Folgasão, Gouveio, Malvasia Fina, Malvasia Rei, Pinot Blanc

TEJO VR or IGP
Map (nos.20 & 20a-20f and surrounding region)

This large province is sandwiched between Lisboa and Alentejano, northeast of Lisbon, where the temperate climate and rich alluvial plains of the River Tagus encourage high yields, making this the second most important wine region in Portugal. However, some very good wines are made here by those who restrict yields and use modern techniques to vinify soft fruity reds at extremely reasonable prices.

🍇 Arinto, Cabernet Sauvignon, Camarate, Carignan, Chardonnay, Esgana Cão, Fernão Pires, Jampal, Malvasia Fina, Malvasia Rei, Merlot, Periquita, Pinot Noir, Rabo de Ovelha, Sauvignon Blanc, Syrah, Tália, Tamarêz, Tamarêz d'Azeitão, Tinta Muida, Touriga Nacional, Trincadeira Preta, Vital

🍶 1–5 years (reds), 1–3 years (whites)

VINEYARDS, SETÚBAL
The area's Moscatel vines (Muscat d'Alexandrie) produce a celebrated fortified wine that has its own Denominação de Origem Controlada.

✓ *Quinta da Alorna* (Marquesa de Alorna Reserva) • *Bright Brothers* • *Companhia das Lezírias* (Reserva) • *Falua* • *Fuiza* • *Rui Reguinga* (Tributo) • *Terra de Lobos* • *Vale D'Algares* (D)

TERRAS DO SADO VR or IGP
Map (nos.18 & 19 and surrounding region)

Probably the most clever appellation the Portuguese could conjure up, Terras do Sado covers a fairly large area fanning out from the Sado estuary far beyond the Setúbal peninsula, where a good many innovative wines originated, but their development had been threatened by the urban sprawl south of Lisbon. If such wines take up the Terras do Sado appellation, they can be sourced from a much wider area. João Pires, Periquita, Quinta de Camarate, and Quinta da Bacalhôa have all claimed this humble VR status without it affecting the prices they command, which has made Terras do Sado an attractive appellation for future new wines.

🍇 **RED** At least 50 per cent Aragonez, Cabernet Sauvignon, Castelão Francês, Merlot, Moscatel Roxo, Trincadeira Preta, and Touriga Nacional, plus up to 50 per cent Alfrocheiro Preto, Alicante Bouschet, Bastardo, Carignan, Grand Noir, Monvedro, Moreto, Tinto Miuda
WHITE At least 50 per cent Arinto, Chardonnay, Fernão Pires, Malvasia Fina, Moscatel de Setúbal, and Roupeiro, plus up to 50 per cent Antão Vaz, Esgana Cão, Rabo de Ovelha, Sauvignon, Tália, Tamarêz d'Azeitão

🍶 1–3 years (new-wave style), 2–5 years (others)

✓ *J M Fonseca* (João Pires, Periquita, Quinta de Camarate Tinto) • *J P Vinhos* (Quinta da Bacalhôa, Cova da Ursa)

TORRES VEDRAS DOC
Map (no.17)

Originally called simply "Torres" until Miguel Torres objected, these high-yielding vineyards in the Lisboa region of Portugal have traditionally supplied the largest producers with bulk wines for their high-volume branded *vinho de mesa*.

🍇 Arinto, Camarate, Fernão Pires, Jampal, Mortágua, Periquita, Rabo de Ovelha, Seara Nova, Tinta Miuda, Vital

TRANSMONTANO VR or IGP
Map (nos.2 & 2a-2c and surrounding region)

A large area north of the Douro and west of Rios do Minho, Transmontano encompasses the Trás-os-Montes DOC and its three sub-zones.

TRÁS-OS-MONTES DOC
Map (nos.2 & 2a-2c)

The province of Trás-os-Montes is situated in northeastern Portugal, and encompasses the IPRs of Chaves, Valpaços, and Planalto-Mirandês. The style of wine ranges from light-bodied in the higher altitude vineyards to full-bodied and alcoholic in the south. But the most important wine made in terms of volume is semi-sweet, semi-sparkling *rosado*.

🍇 Bastardo, Cabernet Franc, Cabernet Sauvignon, Chardonnay, Donzelinho, Gewürztraminer, Gouveio, Malvasia Fina, Merlot, Mourisco Tinto, Pinot Noir, Rabigato, Sauvignon Blanc, Sémillon, Tinta Amarela, Tinta Barroca, Tinta Cão, Tinta Roriz, Touriga Francesa, Touriga Nacional, Viosinho

🍶 1–3 years (new-wave style), 2–5 years (others)

✓ *Casal de Valle Pradinhos* • *Quintas dos Bons Ares*

TRÁS-OS-MONTES CHAVES DOC
Map (no.2a)

From the upper reaches of the River Tâmega in the Trás-os-Montes VR, this appellation tends to produce a similar but lighter style to that of the Douro DOC.

🍇 Bastardo, Boal, Codega, Gouveio, Malvasia Fina, Tinta Carvalha, Tinta Amarela

TRÁS-OS-MONTES PLANALTO MIRANDÊS DOC
Map (no.2b)

In the Trás-os-Montes region, in the very northeastern corner of Portugal, Planalto Mirandês borders Spain, producing full-bodied reds and heavy whites.

🍇 Bastardo, Gouveio, Malvasia Fina, Mourisco Tinto, Rabigato, Tinta Amarela, Touriga Francesa, Touriga Nacional, Viosinho

TRÁS-OS-MONTES VALPAÇOS DOC
Map (no.2c)

Firm reds and slightly *pétillant* rosés from the upper reaches of the Tua, a tributary of the Douro, in the Trás-os-Montes region.

🍇 Bastardo, Boal, Codega, Cornifesto, Fernão Pires, Gouveio, Malvasia Fina, Mourisco Tinto, Rabigato, Tinta Amarela, Tinta Carvalha, Tinta Roriz, Touriga Francesa, Touriga Nacional

VINHO VERDE DOC
Map (nos.1 & 1a–1i)

The vines literally grow on trees, up telegraph poles, and along fences – on anything that takes them above the ground. Training the vine in such a way enables the smallholders – and there are more than 30,000 of them in the Minho – to grow the cabbages, corn, and beans that the families survive on, and to produce grapes, which are either sold to large wineries or made into wine locally and sold to tourists. Genuine Vinho Verde is sharp, may be slightly fizzy, but should always be totally dry, either delicately or raspingly dry, depending primarily on the grape varieties used. The best two grape varieties are Alvarinho and Loureiro. The Alvarinho is a low-cropping variety that is more at home in the northern part of the Minho, between the Lima Valley and the Spanish border. It produces the most substantial Vinhos Verdes, with alcohol levels of 12.5 per cent ABV, compared to the norm of 9.5–10 per cent. Palácio da Brejoeira is the yardstick for this grape, and widely considered to be a class apart from any other Vinho Verde. The Loureiro is a heavier-cropping variety, producing aromatic wines. Vinhão is the most successful grape for red Vinho Verde, followed by Azal Tinto and Espadeiro, and the best examples of these deep-purple wines have a peppery smack to them, even if it is quickly washed down the throat in a fizzy rush. The most widely planted varieties throughout the region are Arinto, Batoca, Loureiro, and Trajadura for white Vinho Verde, and Borraçal for red Vinho Verde. Grapes that favour one or more sub-regions are indicated under their relevant entries below. The soil in all sub-regions is granitic, although there are patches of schist, most notably in Monção and, to a lesser degree, Cávado.

🍇 Alvarelho, Alvarinho, Avesso, Azal, Azal Tinto, Batoca, Borraçal, Espadeiro, Loureiro, Paderna, Pedral, Rabo de Anho, Trajadura, Vinhão

🍷 Upon purchase (9–18 months maximum)

✔ **Red single-quintas** *Afros • Casa do Valle • Ponte de Lima*

White single-quintas *Casa de Sezim • Anselmo Mendes • Morgadio de Torre • Palácio da Brejoeira • Ponte de Lima • Quinta de Azevedo • Quinta do Convento da Franqueira • Quinta de Gomariz* (Grande Escolha) *• Quinta da Tamariz • Soalheiro Primeiras • Solar de Bouças*

White commercial blends *Cepa Velha (Alvarinho) • Chello • Gazela • Grinalda*

VINHO VERDE AMARANTE DOC
Map (no.1a)

As one of the interior sub-regions, Amarante is protected from much of the Atlantic's maritime influence. Consequently, it favours later-ripening varieties and tends to produce wines with a higher alcoholic degree than the regional norm. The red Vinho Verde is particularly deep coloured. Azal is one of the dominant varieties in interior sub-regions such as Amarante, where it has a citrus and green-apple aroma. Its black-skinned sibling, the Azal Tinto, is grown here for red Vinho Verde.

VINHO VERDE AVE DOC
Map (no.1b)

Vineyards are located on an irregular topography around the Ave River basin, where the vines are exposed to the Atlantic influence. Consequently, this sub-region favours earlier-ripening varieties and tends to produce crisp wines with lower alcohol. Loureiro tends to grow in the coastal area to the west of this sub-region.

VINHO VERDE BAIÃO DOC
Map (no.1c)

As one of the interior sub-regions, Baião is protected from much of the Atlantic's maritime influence. Consequently, it favours later-ripening varieties and tends to produce wines with a higher alcoholic degree than the regional norm. Azal is one of the dominant varieties in interior sub-regions such as Baião, where it has a citrus and green-apple aroma. Its black-skinned sibling, the Azal Tinto, is grown here for red Vinho Verde. Baião is renowned for a lingering floral-almond aroma and a lively acidity of wines from the Avesso grape.

VINHO VERDE BASTO DOC
Map (no.1d)

As one of the most interior sub-regions, Basto is particularly protected from the Atlantic, although with the Lima sub-region, it has one of the highest levels of rain (mostly in the winter). Azal is one of the dominant varieties in interior sub-regions such as Basto, where it has a citrus and green-apple aroma. Batoca is another important grape, and it brings smoothness to the mid-palate. Basto produces a high proportion of red Vinho Verde, and the black-skinned Azal Tinto, Padeiro, and Rabo de Anho grapes all grow well here.

✔ *Casa do Valle*

VINHO VERDE CÁVADO DOC
Map (no.1e)

Vineyards are located on an irregular topography around the Cávado River basin, where the vines are low in altitude and exposed to the Atlantic influence. Consequently, this sub-region favours earlier-ripening varieties, but the wines are not as crisp as in other coastal sub-regions. Loureiro tends to grow in the coastal area to the west of this sub-region, but this sub-region is best known for its red Vinhos Verdes made from Vinhão and Borraçal grapes.

VINHO VERDE LIMA DOC
Map (no.1f)

The vineyards here are not as exposed to the effects of the Atlantic as other coastal sub-regions, despite its combination of proximity and northerly location. Loureiro tends to grow in the coastal area to the west of this sub-region, and its wines are locally considered the best, although Lima also has a reputation for red Vinhos Verdes made from Vinhão and Borraçal grapes.

✔ *Afros • Quinta do Ameal • Ponte de Lima* (Loureiro Seleccionada)

VINHO VERDE MONÇÃO DOC
Map (no.1g)

This is the "*grand cru*" of Vinho Verde, and its success is built on a series of exceptions. The only white variety growing in Monção is the Alvarinho, which is the best Vino Verde grape, and relatively little Alvarinho is grown elsewhere in the Minho. Monção is also the only Vinho Verde sub-region with vineyards that are actually on the banks of the Minho River. Even red Vinho Verde is special, as the black-skinned Alvarelhão and Pedral grapes are the only other varieties grown here, yet they are rarely encountered elsewhere in the Minho.

✔ *Palácio da Brejoeira • Anselmo Mendes* (Contacto Alvarinho) *• Palácio da Brejoeira*

VINHO VERDE PAIVA DOC
Map (no.1h)

A small, high-altitude area close to the Douro, Paiva is a semi-interior sub-region of the Minho and can be scorching hot, which makes its vineyards better suited to black-skinned varieties. Azal Tinto is grown here, but Paiva is most famous for red Vinhos Verdes from Amaral and, particularly, Vinhão.

VINHO VERDE SOUSA DOC
Map (no.1i)

Another semi-interior sub-region of the Minho, but with a far more temperate climate than neighbouring Paiva. Azal is one of the dominant varieties in Sousa, where it has a citrus and green-apple aroma. Its black-skinned sibling, the Azal Tinto, is grown here for red Vinho Verde, although Borraçal and Vinhão are more common.

PORT: THE DOURO VALLEY

"It should feel like liquid fire in the stomach... it should burn like inflamed gunpowder... should have the tint of ink... it should be like the sugar of Brazil in sweetness and the spices of India in aromatic flavour."

THESE WORDS WERE WRITTEN in 1754 by the agents for the Association of Port Wine Shippers, and such vivid accounts of Port remain a fair description of the great after-dinner wine we know today. Yet no two neighbouring districts could produce wines of more contrasting styles than the deep-coloured, rich, sweet, warm, and spicy fortified Port of Portugal's Douro Valley, and the light, water-white, sharply dry, semi-sparkling Vinho Verde of the Minho region.

THE ORIGIN OF PORT

It is hard to imagine how such a wonderful winter-warming drink as Port could ever have been conceived in such a hot and sunny country as Portugal. Popular belief has it that that it was not the Portuguese but the British who were responsible for Port; however, this is not entirely accurate. We can thank the Portuguese for dreaming up this most classic of fortified wines; the British merely capitalized on their original idea.

In 1678, two Englishmen were sent by a Liverpool wine merchant to Viana do Castello, north of Oporto, to learn the wine trade. Holidaying up the River Douro, they were regally entertained by the Abbot of Lamego. Finding his wine "very agreeable, sweetish, and extremely

smooth", they asked what made it exceptional among all others tasted on their journey. The Abbot confessed to doctoring the wine with brandy, but the Englishmen were so pleased with the result this had that they purchased the entire stock and shipped it home.

THE ORIGIN OF THE PORT TRADE

The ancient house of C N Kopke & Co had been trading in Douro wines for nearly 40 years by the time the above encounter took place. Eight years before they stumbled upon the Abbot of Lamego, another Englishman named John Clark was busy building up a business that would become Warre & Co. In 1678, the same year as the encounter, Croft & Co was established, and this was followed by Quarles Harris in 1680 and Taylor's in 1692. By the time the Methuen Treaty of 1703 gave Portuguese wines preferential rates of duty in Britain, many British firms had set up trade in Oporto. Other nationalities followed, but it was the British shippers who virtually monopolized the trade, frequently abusing their power. In 1755, the Marquis of Pombal, who had assumed almost dictatorial powers over Portugal, put a curb on their activities through the Board of Trade. The privileges enjoyed by the British under two 100-year-old treaties were restricted. He also established the Oporto Wine Company, endowing it with the sort of powers to which the British had been accustomed.

GRAPE PICKERS NEAR AMARANTE, SOUTHERN MINHO
Grape pickers use ladders with buckets fixed to them to harvest the overhead bunches.

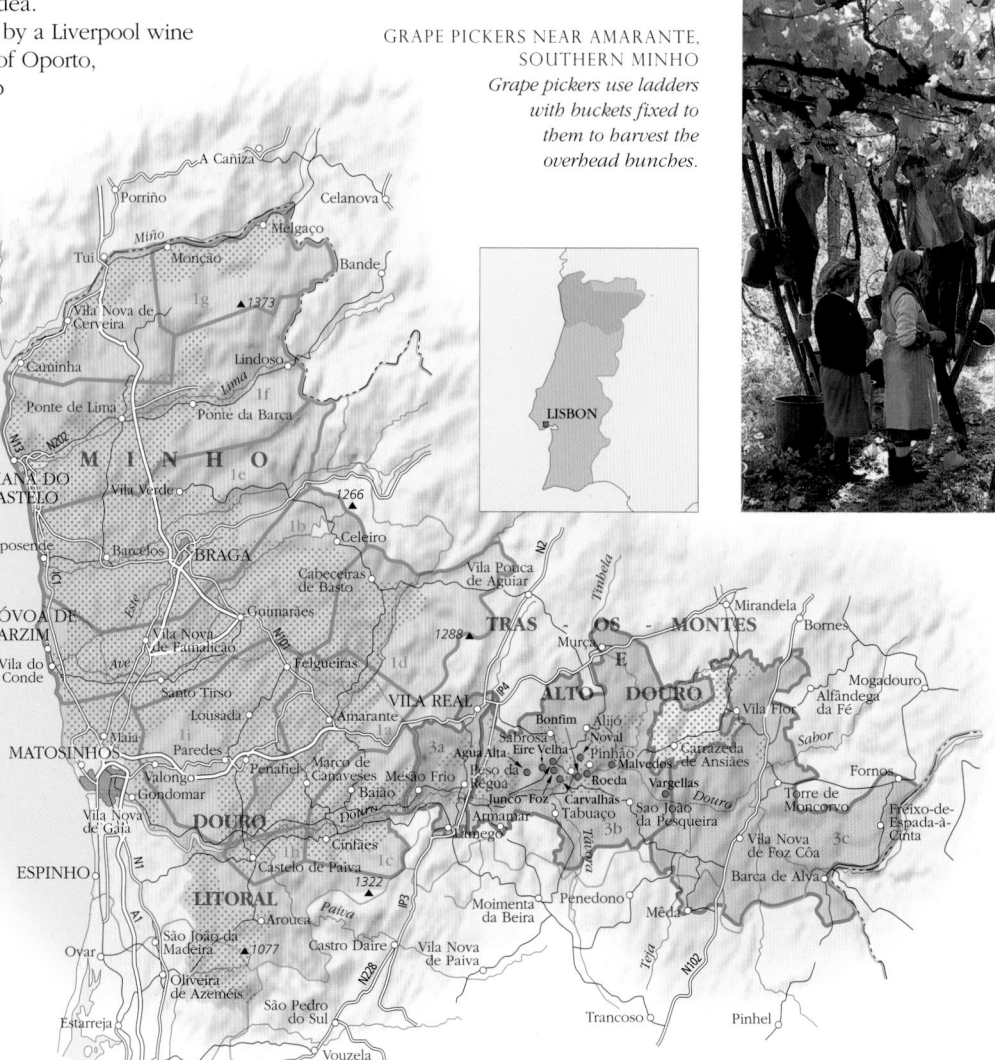

Legend

- • Quintas
- Intensive vine-growing zone
- **Vinho Verde**
- 1a — Amarante
- 1b — Ave
- 1c — Baião
- 1d — Basto
- 1e — Cávado
- 1f — Lima
- 1g — Monção e Melgaço
- 1h — Paiva
- 1i — Sousa
- **Port**
- 3a — Baixo Corgo
- 3b — Cima Corgo
- 3c — Douro Superior
- ---- International boundary
- — Provincial boundary
- ▲ Height above sea level (metres)

0   10   20   30 miles
0 10 20 30 40 50 km

THE DOURO AND THE MINHO,
see also p386
These two northern areas produce the celebrated Port and Vinho Verde. The River Douro has long been crucial to the Port trade.

LISBON

PORT GRAPE VARIETIES

There are 48 grape varieties permitted in the production of Port. This simple fact goes a long way to explaining the great variation in quality and character of Ports within the same basic style. The official classification of the grapes is as follows:

VERY GOOD BLACK GRAPES
Bastardo, Donzelinho Tinto, Mourisco, Tinta Cão, Touriga Franca (Touriga Francesa), Tinta Francisca, Tinta Roriz (Tempranillo), Touriga Nacional

GOOD BLACK GRAPES
Cornifesto, Malvasia Preta, Mourisco de Semente, Periquita, Rufete, Samarrinho, Sousão, Tinta Amarela, Tinta da Barca, Tinta Barroca, Tinta Carvalha, Touriga Brasileira

AVERAGE BLACK GRAPES
Alvarelhão, Avesso, Casculho, Castela, Coucieira, Moreto, Tinta Bairrada, Tinto Martins

VERY GOOD WHITE GRAPES
Boal (Malvasia Fina), Donzelinho, Esgana Cão (Sercial), Folgosão, Gouveio (Verdelho), Malvaisia Rei, Rabigato, Viosinho

GOOD WHITE GRAPES
Arinto, Boal (Malvasia Fina), Cercial, Códega, Malvasia Corada, Moscatel Galego

AVERAGE WHITE GRAPES
Branco sem Nome, Fernão Pires, Malvasia Parda, Perdernã, Praça, Touriga Branca

THE SIX BEST PORT GRAPE VARIETIES
The six Port grape varieties currently considered by growers and winemakers to be the best are:

Touriga Nacional
Almost universally agreed to be the very best of all Port grapes, this has tiny berries and produces pitch-black wine with intense aromatic properties, great extract, and high tannin content. It prefers hotter situations, but is a poor pollinator and does not yield a large crop. Cloning is underway to increase production by 15 per cent and sugar content by 10 per cent, the most successful clone so far being R110.

Tinta Cão
This variety can add finesse and complexity to a blend, but it enjoys a cooler environment and requires training on wires to produce a decent crop. As traditional cultivation methods make it a poor producer, growers are not overly eager to cultivate it; the grape's survival will depend upon the willingness of Port shippers to maintain the variety on their large, managed estates.

Tinta Roriz
Not really a member of the Tinta family, this grape is sometimes simply called the Roriz. It is, in fact, the well-known Spanish variety, Tempranillo, the mainstay of Rioja. In the Douro it likes heat and fares best on the sunniest front rows of terraces cut into south- or west-facing slopes. Its dark grapes have thick skins, high sugar content, and low acidity, providing great colour, tannin, and succulence in a blend. Some believe this to be better than the Touriga Nacional.

Tinta Barroca
The wine produced by this grape variety is quite precocious and is therefore useful in younger-drinking Ports, or to dilute wines that are too tannic and distinctive. Like Tinta Cão, this grape variety prefers cooler situations and particularly enjoys north-facing slopes.

Touriga Francesa
A member of the Touriga family, this grape has no connection with the similarly named Tinta Francisca, a member of the Tinta family. According to the late Bruce Guimaraens of Fonseca and Taylor's, this high-quality variety is useful for "filling in the gaps" in vineyards between those areas occupied by vines that like either hot or cool situations. It gives fruit and aroma to a blend.

Tinta Amarela
This grape variety is dark-coloured and very productive. Its importance has been on the increase in recent years. As this high-quality vine is susceptible to rot, it performs best in the hottest, driest areas.

FACTORS AFFECTING TASTE AND QUALITY

LOCATION
Port is made in the Cima Corgo, Baixo Corgo, and Douro Superior districts of the Douro Valley in the north of Portugal.

CLIMATE
The summers are dry and hot, the winters mild and wet, becoming more continental in the upper Douro Valley, where the summers are extremely hot, rainfall is high – 52 centimetres (20.5 inches) – and winters can be very cold.

ASPECT
Vines are planted on generally hilly land that becomes very steep in some parts.

SOIL
The Douro is a patchwork of hard, sun-baked, granite, and schist soils, with the finest Ports originating from the schist vineyards that dominate upriver. Because of the importance of schist to Port production, Douro table wines are relegated to granite soils.

VITICULTURE AND VINIFICATION
Terracing in the Douro is widespread to maximize the use of the land, although the current trend is to make wider terraces, thus enabling mechanization. Some of the less precipitous slopes are now cultivated in vertical rows. Steep terraces mean labour-intensive viticulture, and the hard Douro soil often requires blasting to enable planting. Port wines are made and fortified in the Douro, but most are blended and bottled at lodges in Vila Nova de Gaia.

GRAPE VARIETIES
See Port Grape Varieties, *left*

because he had added the brandy during, and not after, the fermentation, thus interrupting, or "muting", the process with the natural sweetness that had so attracted the two Englishmen. Even after several centuries, the Port trade is still dominated by the British. It is even possible to generalize about the stylistic difference between the wines of British- and Portuguese-owned Port houses. The British tend to go for bigger, darker, sweeter, fruit-driven wines and have made vintage Port their particular niche, while the Portuguese opt for lighter, elegant, more mellow styles, the best of which are exquisitely aged tawnies. At one time, some Portuguese houses rarely even declared a vintage, as they majored on tawny. When they did, the wines were so much lighter in style that export countries often dismissed them as inferior. Although a few were indeed inferior, many were just different. Now, of course, world markets demand that if they are to survive, the Portuguese houses must declare vintages as often as British-owned houses.

When considering stylistic differences between vintage Port and the lighter, tawny styles, it is probably more accurate to categorize the fuller, fatter vintage Port as North European, not simply British, because this style is also preferred by Dutch, German, and French Port houses.

THE HISTORIC BARCO RABELO
Based on the Viking warship, these flat-bottomed boats, loaded with pipes of Port, would sail for Oporto on the hazardous journey from the upper Douro.

This infuriated the British, but their protests were to no avail and Pombal went on to instigate many worthy, if unpopular, reforms, including limiting the Douro's production area to the finest vineyards, the banning of elderberries for colouring the wine, and the outlawing of manure, which reduced yields but greatly improved quality.

The production of Port had not been perfected at this time. Fifty years after the encounter with the Abbot of Lamego, the trade had widely accepted the practice of brandying, but the importance of when, and in what quantity, to administer the brandy had not been recognized. Ironically, the Abbot's wine was superior

HOW PORT IS MADE

If any wine is perceived as having been "trodden", then it is Port. This is perhaps because the pressing and winemaking traditionally takes place in the vineyards where, until relatively recently, affairs

THE QUINTA CLASSIFICATION

A *quinta* is a wine-producing estate or vineyard. The Douro Valley covers 243,000 hectares (600,000 acres), of which 33,000 hectares (82,000 acres) are cultivated. Within this area, there are approximately 80,000 individual vineyards or *quintas* owned by 29,620 growers. Each vineyard is classified according to a points system allocated for the categories listed below. The better the classification, the higher official price a vineyard receives for its grapes and the greater its permitted production.

CATEGORY	MINIMUM	MAXIMUM
Location	-50	+600
Aspect	1,000	+250
Altitude; lowest is best	(-900)	(+150)
Gradient; steepest is best	(-100)	(+100)
Soil	(-350)	(+100)
Schist	(N/A)	(+100)
Granite	(-350)	(N/A)
Mixture	(-150)	(N/A)
Microclimate; sheltered is best	0+	60
Vine varieties; official classification	-300	+150
Age of vines; oldest is best	0	+60
Vine density; lowest is best	-50	+50
Productivity; lowest is best	-900	+120
Vineyard maintenance	-500	+100
Total	-3,150	+1,490

Vineyards are classified from **A**, for best, to **F**, for worst, as follows: • **Class A** (1,200 points or more); **Class B** (1,001–1,199 points); **Class C** (801–1,000 points); **Class D** (601–800 points); **Class E** (400–600 points); **Class F** (400 points or below).

CLASS A
Aciprestes (Royal Oporto), *Atayde* (Cockburn), *Bomfim* (Dow), *Bom-Retiro* (Ramos-Pinto), *Carvalhas* (Royal Oporto), *Carvalheira* (Calem & Filho), *Boa vista* (Offley Forrester), *Corte* (privately owned, managed by Delaforce), *Corval* (Royal Oporto), *Cruzeiro St. Antonio* (Guimaraens), *Cavadinha* (Warre), *Eira Velha* (Taylor's), *Ervamoira* (Ramos-Pinto), *Fontela* (Cockburn), *Fonte Santa* (Kopke), *Foz* (Calem & Filho), *La Rosa* (privately owned), *Lobata* (Barros, Almeida), *Madalena* (Warre), *Malvedos* (Graham), *Mesquita* (Barroa, Almeida), *Monte Bravo* (privately owned, managed by Dow), *Nova* (privately owned, managed by Warre), *Panascal* (Guimaraens), *Passa Douro* (Sandeman), *Sagrado* (Càlem & Filho), *Santo Antonio* (Càlem & Filho), *Sibio* (Royal Oporto), *St Luiz* (Kopke), *Terra Feita* (Taylor's), *Tua* (Cockburn), *Vale de Mendiz* (Sandeman), *Vale Dona Maria* (Smith Woodhouse), *Vargellas* (Taylor's), *Vedial* (Càlem & Filho), *Zimbro* (privately owned, managed by Dow)

CLASS A–B
Aradas (Noval), *Avidagos* (Da Silva), *Casa Nova* (Borges & Irmao), *Ferra dosa* (Borges & Irmao), *Hortos* (Borges & Irmao), *Junco* (Borges & Irmao), *Leda* (Ferreira), *Marco* (Noval), *Meao* (Ferreira family), *Noval* (Noval), *Porto* (Ferreira),

Roeda (Croft), *Seixo* (Ferreira), *Silho* (Borges & Irmao), *Silval* (Noval), *Soalheira* (Borges & Irmao), *Urqueiras* (Noval), *Velho* Roncao (Pocas), *Vezuvio* (Symington family)

CLASS B
Carvoeira (Barros, Almeida), *Dona Matilde* (Barros, Almeida), *Laranjeira* (Sandeman), San Domingos (Ramos-Pinto), *Urtiga* (Ramos-Pinto)

CLASS B–C
Sta Barbara (Pocas)

CLASS C
Porrais (Ferreira family), *Quartas* (Pocas), *Valado* (Ferreira family)

CLASS C AND D
Sidro (Royal Oporto)

CLASS C, D, AND E
Granja (Royal Oporto)

CLASS D
Casal (Sandeman), *Confradeiro* (Sandeman)

CLASS NOT DISCLOSED
Agua Alta (Churchill), *Alegria* (Santos), *Cachão* (Messias), *Côtto* (Champalimaud), *Crasto* (privately owned), *Fojo* (privately owned), *Forte* (Delaforce), *Infantado* (privately owned), *Rosa* (privately owned), *Val de Figueria* (Càlem & Filho), *Vau* (Sandeman)

were conducted on farms in a rather rustic style. Nowadays, few Ports are trodden, although several houses have showpiece *lagares* – troughs used for crushing grapes – for tourists. Many houses have "autovinificators" – rather antiquated devices that rely on the build-up of carbonic gas pressure given off during fermentation to force the juice up and over the *manta* (cap) of grape skins. The object is to extract the maximum amount of colouring matter from the skins, because so much is lost by fortification. It is possible also to achieve this using special vats and several have been installed throughout the Port industry.

FERMENTATION AND FORTIFICATION

The initial fermentation phase of Port differs little from that in the rest of the world, except that vinification temperatures are often as high as 32°C (90°F). This has no detrimental effect on Port, and in fact probably accounts for its chocolaty, high pH complexity. When a level of about 6 to 8 per cent alcohol has been achieved, the wine is fortified, unlike Sherry, for which the fermentation process is allowed to complete its natural course. Port derives its sweetness from unfermented sugars, whereas sweet Sherries are totally dry wines to which a syrupy concentrate is added. The timing of the addition of brandy is dependent upon the sugar reading, not the alcohol level. When the sweetness of the fermenting juice has dropped to approximately 90 grams per litre of sugar, the alcoholic strength will normally be between 6 and 8 per cent, but this varies according to the richness of the juice, which in turn is dependent upon the grape variety, where it is grown, and the year.

The use of the word "brandy" is somewhat misleading. It is not, in fact, brandy in the true sense, but a clear, flavourless, grape-distilled spirit of 77 per cent alcohol, known in Portugal as *aguardente*. It adds alcoholic strength to a Port, but not aroma or flavour. *Aguardente* is produced either from wines made in southern Portugal, or from excess production in the Douro itself. Its price and distribution to each shipper are strictly rationed. On average 110 litres (24 gallons) is added for every 440 litres (97 gallons) of wine, making a total of 550 litres (121 gallons) – the capacity of a Douro pipe, a specific size of cask used for shipping wine from the valley to the lodges at Vila Nova de Gaia. A drier Port has a slightly longer fermentation and requires less than 100 litres (22 gallons) of *aguardente*, while a particularly sweet (or *geropiga*) Port is muted with as much as 135 litres (30 gallons). If gauged correctly, the brandy which has been added to arrest the fermentation will eventually harmonize with the fruit and the natural sweetness of the wine. Our conception of balance between fruit, alcohol, and sweetness is, of course, greatly affected by what we are used to drinking. In deepest Douro a local farmer is likely to use a far higher proportion of alcohol for Port he intends to drink himself than for the Port he makes for export. Generally, British shippers prefer more fruit and less brandy, but all commercial shippers, British or Portuguese, would consider the domestic Port of a Douro farmer to lack sufficient body to match the brandy.

MATURATION AND BLENDING

Until 1986, by law, all Port had to be matured and bottled at Vila Nova de Gaia on the left bank of the Douro estuary opposite Oporto. At some 75 kilometres (47 miles) from the region of production, this was like insisting that all Champagne be blended, bottled, and disgorged at Le Havre. This law was made in 1756, and it was ostensibly created by and for the big shippers, since it effectively prevented small growers from exporting their wine, as they could not possibly afford the expense of a lodge at Vila Nova de Gaia. By the late 18th century, most of the famous Port names were already established, and this restrictive law enabled them to maintain the status quo, especially on the lucrative international markets. All this has changed, and though most Ports still come from the big shippers' lodges, many new Ports now find their way on to the market direct from privately owned Douro *quintas*.

THE STYLES OF
PORT OR PORTO

Note With the exception of white Port, there are just two basic styles from which all variants stem: ruby and tawny. What distinguishes these two styles is bottle-ageing for rubies and cask-ageing for tawnies.

AGED TAWNY PORT

These 10-, 20-, 30-Year-Old and Over 40 Years Old Ports are traditionally known as "Fine Old Tawnies", but like fine old rubies, there are no legal requirements. By constant racking over a period of 10, 20, or more years, Port fades to a tawny colour, falls bright, and will throw no further deposit. It assumes a smooth, silky texture, a voluptuous, mellow, nutty flavour, and complex after-aromas that can include freshly ground coffee, caramel, chocolate, raisins, nutmeg, and cinnamon. The years are merely an indication of age; in theory, a 20-Year-Old tawny could be just a year old, if it could fool the Port Wine Institute. In practice, most blends probably have an age close to that indicated. Most tawny Port experts find 20-Year-Old the ideal tawny, but 30- and Over 40 Years Old tawnies are not necessarily past it. The only relatively negative aspect of a good 30- or Over 40 Years Old is that it will be more like a liqueur than a Port.

🍷 Upon purchase

✓ **10-Year-Old** *Cálem • Churchill's • Cockburn's • Croft • Dow's • Ferreira* (Quinta do Porto) *• Fonseca • Graham's • Niepoort • Offley* (Baron Forrester) *• Ramos-Pinto • Robertson's* (Pyramid) *• Smith Woodhouse • Taylor's • Warre's* (Optima, Sir William)

20-Year-Old *Barros Almeida • Burmester • Cálem • Cockburn's • Croft* (Director's Reserve) *• Dow's • Ferreira* (Duque de Bragança) *• Fonseca • Graham's • Niepoort • Noval • Offley* (Baron Forrester) *• Ramos-Pinto* (Quinta do Bom) *• Robertson's* (Private Reserve) *• Sandeman* (Imperial) *• Taylor's*

30-Year-Old *Cálem • Croft • Dow's • Fonseca • Niepoort • Ramos-Pinto*

Over 40 Years Old *Cálem • Fonseca • Graham's • Noval • Sandeman • Taylor's*

CRUSTED PORT *or* CRUSTING PORT

The greatest non-vintage ruby Port, this is a blend of very high-quality wines from two or more years, given up to four years in cask and, ideally, at least three years in bottle. Like vintage, it throws a deposit in bottle, hence the name. Ready to drink when purchased, providing it is carefully decanted.

🍷 1–10 years

✓ *Churchill's • Graham's • Martinez • Smith Woodhouse*

LATE-BOTTLED VINTAGE PORT (LBV)

A late-bottled vintage is a pure vintage Port from a good, but not necessarily great year. LBVs are usually made in lighter, generally undeclared years. Lighter, more precocious vintages are usually chosen for this less expensive category, and the wines are given between four and six years in cask to bring them on even quicker. LBVs are thus ready for drinking when sold, but will continue to improve in bottle for another five or six years.

🍷 5–10 years

✓ *Burmester • Churchill's • Graham's • Quinta de la Rosa • Ramos-Pinto • Smith Woodhouse • Warre's*

PINK PORT

Croft created and launched the first Pink Port in 2008, to entice women and generally younger customers who might otherwise think of Port as old-fashioned. The production method is similar to a non-oxidative white port, which is then back-blended with pressed skins to tease out a little colour. It's a very fresh, in-your-face, fruit-driven style that is meant to be drunk young and, because of its fortified structure, can be served on the rocks. I was initially doubtful, but it works, certainly as a bar drink.

🍷 Upon purchase

✓ *Croft • Porto Cruz • Quinta & Vineyard*

RUBY PORT

The cheapest red Ports are rubies with less than a year in cask and often no time at all. Sold soon after bottling, they do not improve if kept. Inexpensive rubies have a basic, pepper-grapey flavour that can be quite fiery. Superior-quality wines are blended from various vintages with up to four years in cask, giving a more homogenous taste, though they should still have the fruity-spice and warmth of a young ruby.

🍷 Upon purchase

✓ *Cálem • Churchill's • Cockburn's* (Special Reserve) *• Ferreira* (Bin 27, Terra Prima Organic Reserve) *• Graham's* (Six Grapes) *• Quinta de la Rosa* (Finest Reserve) *• Sandeman* (Signature) *• Warre's* (Warrior)

SINGLE-QUINTA PORT

A wine from a single vineyard, this may be a classic vintage Port from an established house or a special release from an undeclared vintage. With interest in these Ports increasing, the change in the law allowing Port to be matured at the *quintas*, and the fact that individual domaine wines are seen as more prestigious, this category has become as esteemed as vintage Port itself.

🍷 8–25 years

✓ *Quinta de Agua Alta* (Churchill's) *• Quinta do Bom • Quinta da Cavadinha* (Warre's) *• Quinta do Côtto* (Champalimaud) *• Quinta de Foz* (Cálem) *• Quinta Nova • Quinta do Noval • Quinta do Panascal* (Fonseca) *• Quinta Passadouro • Quinta do Passadouro* (Niepoort) *• Quinta Portal • Quinta Prelada • Quinta da Roeda* (Croft) *• Quinta de Roriz • Quinta de la Rosa • Quinta do Sagrado • Quinta do Seixo* (Ferreira) *• Quinta Senhora da Ribeira* (Dow's) *• Quinta do Tedo • Quinta da Urtiga* (Ramos-Pinto) *• Quinta Vale Dona Maria • Quinta do Vallado • Quinta de Vargellas* (Taylor's) *• Quinta Ventozelo • Quinta de Vesuvio*

SINGLE-QUINTA TAWNY PORT

Although most single-vineyard Ports are vintage and ruby in style, some are made as tawny, either with an indicated age or vintage-dated.

🍷 Upon purchase

✓ **10-Year-Old:** Quinta do Sagrado • Ramos-Pinto (Quinta da Ervamoira)

20-Year-Old: Ramos-Pinto (Quinta do Bom-Retiro)

Vintage-Dated: Borges' Quinta do Junco

TAWNY PORT

These are often a blend of red and white Ports. Some skilful blends can be very good and have even the most experienced Port-tasters guessing whether they are tawny by definition or blending. On the whole it is wise to pay more to ensure you are buying an authentically aged product. The best tawnies are usually eight years old, although this is seldom indicated.

🍷 Upon purchase

✓ *Delaforce* (His Eminence's Choice) *• Dow's* (Boardroom) *• Warre's* (Nimrod)

VINTAGE CHARACTER PORT

This misleading term was banned in 2002, although it took some time for stocks to clear the global distribution systems. Most producers have rebranded these wines as wines as Reserve.

VINTAGE-DATED TAWNY *or* COLHEITA PORT

These excellent-value, often sublime, cask-aged wines are from a single vintage, and may have 20 or 50 years in cask. They must not be confused with the plumper, fruitier vintage Ports. There should be an indication of when the wine was bottled or a term such as "Matured in Wood". Some vintage Ports are simply labelled "vintage" and tawnies "Colheita". Other clues are "Reserve", "Reserva", or "Bottled in" dates.

🍷 Upon purchase

✓ *Barros Almeida • Burmester • Cálem • Delaforce • Offley* (Baron Forrester) *• Niepoort • Noval*

VINTAGE PORT

By law, a vintage Port must be bottled within two years. Maturation in bottle is more reductive than cask-ageing and the wine that results has a certain fruitiness that will not be found in any Fine old tawny. When mature, a fine vintage Port is a unique taste experience with a heady bouquet and a sultry flavour. A warming feeling seems to follow the wine down the throat – more an "afterglow" than an aftertaste. The grape and spirit are totally integrated and the palate is near to bursting with warm, spicy-fruit flavours.

🍷 12–30 years (but *see* individual producers)

✓ *Churchill's • Champalimaud* (Quinta do Côtto) *• Dow's • Ferreira • Fonseca • Fonseca Guimaraens • Gould Campbell • Graham's • Niepoort • Pintas • Quinta do Noval* (especially Nacional) *• Smith Woodhouse • Taylor's • Warre's*

WHITE PORT

Most dry white Ports taste like flabby Sherry, but there are some interesting sweet ones such as Ferreira's Superior White, which is creamy-soft and delicious. Truly sweet white Port is often labelled Lagrima. Niepoort pure Moscatel can make an nice alternative to Moscatel de Setúbal.

🍷 Upon purchase

✓ *Andresen 10-Year-Old Dry White • Ferreira's Superior White*

THE WINE PRODUCERS OF
THE DOURO VALLEY

Note The age range for "when to drink" refers to the optimal enjoyment of vintage Ports and appears only when this style is recommended. When the entire range is recommended, this includes all wines with the exception of the most basic ruby and tawny or any white Port, unless otherwise stated.

BARROS
Barros Almeida
★

Manuel de Barros started work as an office boy at Almeida & Co, ending up not only owning the company, but also building a Port empire, as he and his descendants took over Douro Wine Shippers and Growers, Feist, Feuerheerd, Hutcheson, Kopke, Santos Junior, and Viera de Sousa. Only Kopke and Barros Almeida itself retain any form of independence. In 2006, Barros Almeida was taken over by Sogevinus, the drinks arm of the Spanish Caixanova bank and owners of Port houses Burmester, Cálem, and Gilberts.

✓ *20-Year-Old Tawny • Vintage-Dated Tawny • Colheitas*

BORGES & IRMÃO
✗

Established in 1884, the Portuguese-owned house of Borges & Irmão is best known for its Soalheira 10-Year-Old and Ronção 20-Year-Old Tawnies, but the quality of their Port has suffered under a lack of direction from Portuguese government ownership.

BURMESTER
★

Of Anglo-German origin, Burmester is an underrated house that is best for mature tawny styles, but also makes good vintage. *See* Cálem.

✓ *Late-Bottled • Vintage • 20-Year-Old Tawny • Colheitas • Vintage*

CÁLEM
★

Cálem was established in 1859 and today is owned by Sogevinus. Consistently elegant tawny, single-*quinta*, and vintage Port. Also owns Barros, Burmester, and Gilberts.

🍷 15–25 years

✓ *10-, 20-, 30-, and 40-Year-Old Tawny • Vintage Character • Quinta de Foz • Vintage*

CHAMPALIMAUD
Quinta do Côtto
★★✫

Although Miguel Montez Champalimaud can trace his family's viticultural roots in the Douro Valley back to the 13th century, he did not produce his first Port until 1982, when it became the world's first

estate-bottled single-*quinta* Port, making him the fastest-rising star among the new wave of privately owned grower Ports.

🍷 12–25 years

✓ *Quinta do Côtto*

CHURCHILL'S
★★✫

Established in 1981 by Johnny Graham, a member of the Graham's Port family who was married to Caroline (*née* Churchill), this was the first Port shipper to be established in recent times, and it has quickly risen to the top.

🍷 12–25 years

✓ *Entire range*

COCKBURN'S
★★

Founded in 1815 by Robert Cockburn, who married Mary Duff, a lady much admired by Lord Byron. The Cockburn's brand was owned by Jim Beam Global but was sold to the Symington Group in 2010. Cockburn's best-selling Special Reserve and Fine Old Ruby are surprisingly good despite being produced in vast quantities. The vintage Ports are consistently excellent in quality.

🍷 15–30 years

✓ *Entire range*

CROFT
★✫

To many people, Croft is best known for its Sherries, yet it is one of the oldest Port houses, having started production in 1678. Croft's elegant style best suits Fine Old Tawnies. In all but a few years, its vintage Ports are among the lightest. Now part of Taylor's.

✓ *10-, 20-, and 30-Year-Old Tawny*

CRUZ
✗

The lacklustre quality of Cruz says a lot about the average Frenchman's appreciation of the world's greatest fortified wine. France takes nearly half of all the Port currently exported and this is the best-selling brand. The French could be forgiven if they cooked with it, but they actually drink the stuff. Now under the same ownership as C da Silva. Pink Port seems to be the limit of Porto Cruz's capabilities.

DELAFORCE
★

The style of Delaforce is very much on the lighter-bodied side, which particularly suits His Eminence's Choice, an exquisite old tawny with a succulent balance as well as a lingering fragrance.

✓ *His Eminence's Choice Superb Old Tawny*

DIEZ
Diez Hermanos
❷

Interesting recent vintages make this low-key producer one to watch.

DOURO WINE SHIPPERS
AND GROWERS
See Barros

DOW'S
Silva & Cosens
★★

Although the brand is Dow's, this firm is actually called Silva & Cosens. It was established in 1862 and James Ramsay Dow was made a partner in 1877, when his firm, Dow & Co, which had been shipping Port since 1798, was merged with Silva & Cosens. Dow's is now one of the many brands belonging to the Symington family, and consistently makes one of the very greatest vintage Ports. *See also* Cockburn's, Gould Campbell, Graham's, Quarles Harris, Smith Woodhouse, Warre's.

🍷 18–35 years

✓ *Entire range*

FEIST
See Barros

FERREIRA
★★

This house was established in 1761 and was family-owned until 1988, when it was taken over by Sogrape, the largest wine-shipper in Portugal. The brand leader in Portugal itself, Ferreira did not establish its present reputation until the mid-19th century, when it was under the control of Dona Antonia Adelaide Ferreira, who was so successful that when she died she left an estate of £3.4 million, valued at 1896 rates. Ever mindful of its Portuguese roots, it is not surprising that elegantly rich tawny Port is Ferreira's forte. Equally consistent is the style of its vintage Port. While this wine is typically light, smooth, and mellow, it does age beautifully.

🍷 12–30 years

✓ *Entire range*

FEUERHEERD
See Barros

FONSECA
Fonseca Guimaraens
★★★✫

This house was originally called Fonseca, Monteiro & Co, but changed its name when it was purchased by Manuel Pedro Guimaraens in 1822. Although it has been part of Taylor, Fladgate & Yeatman since 1948, it operates in a totally independent fashion, utilizing its own *quintas* and contracted suppliers. Fonseca has always been the top-quality brand, but even its

second wine, Fonseca Guimaraens, puts many Port houses to shame.

🍷 15–30 years

✓ *Entire range*

GOULD CAMPBELL
★

Although at the cheaper end of the Symington Group, Gould Campbell, which was established in about 1797, produces fine, sometimes stunningly fine, vintage Ports. *See also* Cockburn's, Dow's, Graham's, Smith Woodhouse, Quarles Harris, Warre's.

🍷 12–25 years

✓ *vintage*

GRAHAM'S
W & J Graham & Co
★★★

Graham's was founded as a textile business and only entered the Port trade when, in 1826, its Oporto office accepted wine in payment of a debt. Along the way, Graham's took over the firm of Smith Woodhouse and both of them became part of the Symington Port empire in 1970. It is the vintage Port that earned Graham's its reputation, but the entire range is of an equally high quality, category for category. *See also* Cockburn's, Dow's, Gould Campbell, Quarles Harris, Smith Woodhouse, Warre's.

🍷 18–40 years

✓ *Entire range, including basic Six Grapes Ruby*

GUIMARAENS
See Fonseca

HUTCHESON
See Barros

KOPKE
See Barros

MARTINEZ
Martinez Gassiot
★★✫

Martinez was founded in 1797 by Sebastian González Martinez, a Spaniard, but became affiliated to Cockburn in the early 1960s. Rather underrated, it produces small quantities of high-quality vintage and great value crusted, and is also a source of extraordinarily good own-label Port. *See also* Cockburn's.

🍷 12–20 years

✓ *Entire range*

MORGAN
★✫

One of the oldest Port houses, Morgan was acquired by Croft in 1952, but Croft itself was sold by Diageo to Taylor's in 2001. The Morgan brand was retained by Diageo (owners of Captain Morgan Rum), but its production has stopped and its future remains uncertain. A number of excellent own-label Ports have filtered on to the market bearing the Morgan Brothers name in small type, and Taylor's sold off a large cache of excellent Morgan vintages at auction in 2007.

NIEPOORT
★★

This small Dutch-owned firm is best known for its elegantly rich tawnies, especially the colheitas, but also makes fine, underrated vintage Port.

🍷 12–25 years

☑ *Entire range*

NOVAL
Quinta do Noval
★★
Nacional ★★★

Originally a Portuguese house, having been founded in 1813 by Antonio José da Silva, Quinta do Noval was controlled by the Dutch van Zeller family for four generations until it was purchased by the French AXA group. Although officially known as Quinta do Noval, it carefully markets most products under the Noval brand, reserving the *quinta* name for those Ports made exclusively from the property itself.

🍷 15–35 years (25–70 years for Nacional)

☑ *Vintage • Nacional • 20- and 40-Year-Old Tawny*

OFFLEY
Offley Forrester
★★

Established in 1737, this firm once belonged to the famous Baron Forrester, but is now owned by Sogrape. Offley makes excellent quality colheitas, elegant vintage Ports, and a deeper-coloured single-*quinta* Boa Vista.

🍷 12–25 years

☑ *Vintage • Boa Vista • Colheita • 10- and 20-Year-Old Tawny*

POÇAS
Poças Junior

Established in 1918, like many Portuguese-owned firms, Poças Junior started declaring vintage Ports relatively recently (1960s) and is primarily known for its tawnies and colheitas. Second labels include Lopes, Pousada, and Seguro.

QUARLES HARRIS

Established in 1680 and the second-largest Port house in the 18th century, when it was taken over by Warre's, Quarles Harris is now one of the smallest Port brands under the control of the progressive Symington Group. *See also* Cockburn's, Dow's, Gould Campbell, Graham's, Quarles Harris, Smith Woodhouse, Warre's.

QUINTA DE LA ROSA
★

Promising new estate-bottled, Single-Quinta Port. Look out for the new 10-Year-Old tawny.

🍷 8–25 years

☑ *Finest Reserve • Late Bottled Vintage • Vintage*

QUINTA DO CÔTTO
See Champalimaud

QUINTA DO INFANTADO
★ V

The vintage Port from this estate-bottled single-*quinta* have been rather lightweight, but the 1991 late-bottled vintage was a real gem, so it might be worth keeping an eye on future releases from this independent producer.

QUINTA DO NOVAL
See Noval

QUINTA DO VESUVIO

This massive, 400-hectare (990-acre), former Ferreira property was considered to be the greatest *quinta* in the Douro when planted in the 19th century. Owned since 1989 by the Symington group, which has already established its vintage Port as exceptional, but how exceptional remains to be seen.

🍷 12–30 years

☑ *Vintage*

RAMOS-PINTO
★★

Established in 1880 by Adriano Ramos-Pinto, when he was 20 years old, this firm remained in family ownership until 1990, when it was purchased by Champagne Louis Roederer. Ramos-Pinto always has produced excellent tawnies, particularly the single-*quintas* 10- and 20-Year-Old and its colheitas, but if the 1994 is anything to go by, vintage Port could be its future *forte*.

🍷 12–25 years

☑ *Late-Bottled Vintage • Single-Quinta (Quinta da Ervamoira 10-Year-Old, Quinta do Bom-Retiro 20-Year-Old) • Colheitas • Vintage (from 1994)*

REBELLO VALENTE
See Robertson Brothers and Co

ROBERTSON BROTHERS AND CO
★

Established in 1881, this small Port house is now a subsidiary of Sandeman and thus owned by Sogrape. Best known for its tawnies and, under the famous Rebello Valente label, very traditional vintage Ports.

🍷 12–25 years

☑ *10- and 20-Year-Old Tawnies • Vintage*

ROYAL OPORTO
Real Companhia Velha
★ V

Founded in 1756 by the Marquis de Pombal to regulate the Port trade. Its reputation as a good source of inexpensive tawny and vintage

character Ports has ensured its survival, but it is focusing its greatest efforts on non-fortified Douro wines.

☑ *Vintage Character* (The Navigator's)

ROZES
★

Part of the giant Moët-Hennessy group, Rozes has yet to establish a reputation beyond France.

SANDEMAN
★

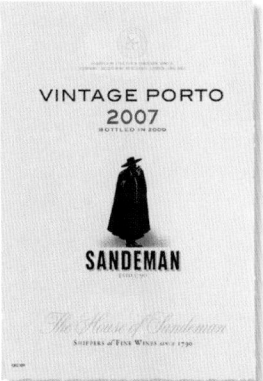

Also known for its sherry and Madeira, Sandeman was established in 1790 and took over Robertson's and Rebello Valente in 1881, after which it acquired Diez and Offley, and is itself owned by Sogrape. The quality of Sandeman's vintage Port is variable and seldom blockbusting, but its tawnies are reliable, especially Imperial 20-Year-Old.

☑ *20-Year-Old Tawny* (Imperial) • *Vintage Character* (Signature)

SANTOS JUNIOR
See Barros

SILVA & COSENS
See Dow's

SILVA, C DA

Now under the same ownership as Cruz.

SMITH WOODHOUSE
★★ V

The products of this famous British Port house are not as well known in Portugal as they are on export markets, where they are much appreciated for tremendous value across the entire range, and also for some of the very greatest vintage Ports ever made. *See also* Cockburn's, Dow's, Gould Campbell, Graham's, Smith Woodhouse, Warre's.

🍷 12–25 years

☑ *Entire range*

SYMINGTON GROUP

The Symingtons are one of the most well-known and successful of all Port families, owning seven brands, yet not one of these boasts the family name. *See also* Cockburn's, Dow's, Gould Campbell, Graham's, Quarles Harris, Smith Woodhouse, and Warre's.

TAYLOR'S
Taylor, Fladgate & Yeatman
★★★

Founded in 1692 by Job Bearsley, this house underwent no fewer than 21 changes of title before adopting its present one, which derives from the names of various partners: Joseph Taylor in 1816, John Fladgate in 1837, and Morgan Yeatman in 1844. At one time the firm was known as Webb, Campbell, Gray & Cano (Joseph Cano was, as it happens, the only American ever to be admitted into the partnership of a Port house). In 1744, Taylor's became the first shipper to buy a property in the Douro, but its most famous acquisition was Quinta de Vargellas in 1890, a prestigious property that provides the heart and soul of every Taylor's vintage Port.

🍷 20–40 years

☑ *Entire range*

VIERA DE SOUSA
See Barros

WARRE'S
★★★

Only the German-founded house of Kopke can claim to be older than Warre's, which was established in 1670, although it only assumed its present name in 1729 when William Warre entered the business. This house, which now belongs to the entrepreneurial Symington family, normally vies with Graham's, another Symington brand, as the darkest and most concentrated vintage Port after that of Taylor's. *See also* Cockburn's, Dow's, Gould Campbell, Graham's, Quarles Harris, Smith Woodhouse.

🍷 18–35 years

☑ *Entire range*

WEISE & KROHN

Weise & Krohn Port house was originally founded in 1865 by two Norwegians of German extraction, Theodore Weise and Dankert Krohn. It has been owned by the Portuguese Carneiro family since the 1930s. It makes rather insubstantial vintage Port, and is best known for its tawnies.

☑ *Colheitas*

MADEIRA

The island of Madeira gives its name to the only wine in the world that must be baked in an oven! This fortified wine is deliberately heated to replicate the voyages of old during which the wine accidentally underwent maderization at equatorial temperatures.

PRINCE HENRY THE NAVIGATOR sent Captain João Gonçalves in search of new lands in the 15th century. The Captain's nickname was Zarco, or "squinter", as he had been wounded in one eye while fighting the Moors. Although "squinter" seems an odd name for someone whose job it is to keep his eyes peeled for events on the horizon, particularly at that time, when every sailor was worried about falling off the edge of the world, this nickname is fact not fiction. Indeed, he was so proud of being called the "squinter" that he adopted it as a surname, becoming João Gonçalves Zarco. Despite this impediment to his sight, Zarco not only navigated his ship safely but actually managed to discover places. In 1418, for example, he found Madeira, although it must be admitted that he was searching for Guinea at the time. Zarco actually thought it was a cloud, but the more he squinted, the more suspicious he became: it was always in the same

position. One day he chased the cloud, sailed through it and bumped into an island. It was entirely covered in dense forest and the cloud was merely the mist of transpiration given off in the morning sun. The forest was impenetrable (Madeira means "island of woods"), so Zarco lit fires to denude areas of the island, sat back, and waited. By all accounts he had a long wait, as the fires raged for seven years and consumed every bit of vegetation, infusing the permeable volcanic soil with potash, which by chance rendered it particularly suitable for vine-growing.

THE ORIGIN OF MADEIRA'S DISTINCTIVE WINE

As a source of fresh food and water, the island soon became a regular port of call for east-bound ships, which would often transport barrels of Madeira wine for sale in the Far East or Australia. As the ships journeyed through the tropics, the wine was heated to a maximum of 45°C (113°F) and cooled again during the six-month voyage, giving it a very distinctive character. The winemakers of Madeira were totally unaware of this until one unsold shipment returned to the island. Since then, special ovens, called *estufas*, have evolved in order that this heating and cooling can be replicated in the *estufagem* process (cheaper wines do this in large concrete vats, while the casks of better-quality wines experience a much longer, gentler process in warm rooms). All Madeiras undergo a normal fermentation prior to the *estufagem* process. Drier wines are fortified prior to *estufagem*, the sweeter styles afterwards.

THE FUTURE OF MADEIRA

Although sales of Madeira are growing, they are doing so from a relatively low base. Madeira has fallen a long way from its height of fame in the 19th century, when Russia was its greatest market and one Grand Duke alone purchased the equivalent of 76,000 cases a year. Far too much Madeira today is cheap, made from the lowly Tinta Negra Mole grape, and sold in bulk to France, Germany, and Belgium, where the natural impulse is to cook with it. If Madeira is to survive, it must concentrate on quality by replanting with classic varieties, encouraging a new wave of independent producers, banning bulk wines, and updating the concept of Vintage Madeira. Pushing Madeira upmarket is not merely required to re-establish its reputation, it is simple logic – viticulture on this precipitous island is so labour-intensive that cheap wine makes no economic sense.

COASTAL VIEW, MADEIRA
Terraced vineyards cling to Madeira's rocky terrain, where irrigation is accomplished via a network of aqueducts.

MADEIRA, *see also p386*
The island of Madeira, in the Atlantic Ocean west of Morocco, is famed for its fortified wine. Funchal is the capital of the island, where many wine lodges are found.

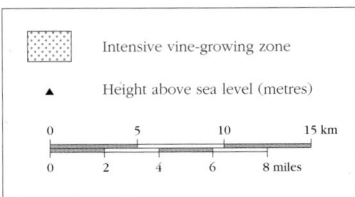

Intensive vine-growing zone

▲ Height above sea level (metres)

0   5   10   15 km

0   2   4   6   8 miles

LISBON

MADEIRA

Porto do Moniz
Achadas da Cruz
Ponta do Pargo
Ponta do Pargo
Seixal
Janela
Seixal
São Vicente
Arco de São Jorge
Ponta de São Jorge
Santana
Fajã da Ovelha
1310 ▲
Porto da Cruz
Jardim do Mar
Achada
1619 ▲
Serra d'Agua
São Roque
1362 ▲
1759 ▲
Machico
Caniçal
Machico
Calheta
Ponta do Sol
Brava
Curral das Freiras
Santo da Serra
Santa Cruz
Santa Cruz
Ponta do Sol
Ribeira Brava
Socorridos
Santo António
Monte
Porto Novo
Camacha
São Gonçalo
Campanário
Câmara de Lobos
FUNCHAL
Ponta da Cruz

THE STYLES OF
MADEIRA

There have traditionally been four basic styles of Madeira, named after the following grape varieties: Sercial, Verdelho, Bual, and Malmsey. During the 20th century, however, the majority of Madeira produced was blended with a high proportion of Tinta Negra Mole (or its variant Complexa) or of American hybrids. Since 1990, however, no hybrids have been allowed, and since 1993, those wines made from Tinta Negra Mole may use only generic terms of sweetness (and not the stylistic terms listed below), such as *seco* (dry), *meio seco* (medium dry), *meio doce* (medium sweet), and *doce* (sweet), accompanied by descriptors such as pale, dark, full, or rich, while at least 85 per cent of a varietal wine must be made from the grape indicated.

Note Madeira should be ready to drink when sold and good Madeira will keep indefinitely, so no optimal drinking periods are given below.

BASTARDO

Another rarity from Madeira's once glittering past, there is some question as to whether this black grape variety is related to the Douro variety of the same name, but there is no doubting its great potential quality, making it yet another golden oldie that is long overdue a revival.

✓ *D'Oliveira's* (1927)

BOAL *or* BUAL

Definitely sweeter and darker than the styles above, Bual can often be recognized under blind conditions by its khaki-coloured meniscus. This style has soft, gentle fruit with noticeable fatness and ripeness, underscored by a baked, smoky complexity. The legal limit for residual sugar is 78–96 grams per litre.

✓ *Blandy's* (1977, 1968, 1920) • *H M Borges* (1977) • *Cossart* (Colheita 1995) • *D'Oliveira's* (1933) • *Henriques & Henriques* (Grand Old Boal, 15-Year-Old Boal)

COLHEITA

Relatively rare, cask-aged, pure vintage Madeira; it may be pure varietal but does not have to be.

✓ *Barbeito* (Cask 8a & d) • *Blandy's* (Malmsey: 2000, 1992, 1990) • *Cossart* (Bual 1995, Sercial 1988)

EXTRA RESERVE *or*
OVER-15-YEAR-OLD MADEIRA

This style is rarely encountered, but is always significantly richer and more complex than 10-Year-Old Madeira. The 15 years reference is excluded from some wines that are much older.

✓ *Barbeito* (25-Year-Old Bual) • *Cossart* (Malmsey 15-Year-Old Malmsey, Very Old Duo Centenary Celebration Bual, Very Old Duo Centenary Celebration Sercial) • *Henriques & Henriques* (Verdelho, Boal)

FINEST *or*
3-YEAR-OLD MADEIRA

This, the lowest level of Madeira, will be the style of any Madeira whose age is not given. It consists primarily of Tinta Negra Mole, and some Moscatel. Three years is too short a time for any decent wine to evolve into a true Madeira and much is sold in bulk for cooking, and cannot be recommended.

MALMSEY

Made from both white and black varieties of Malvasia grown on the island's lowest and warmest regions, Malmsey is the ultimate Madeira and my own favourite. It is the most luscious, the sweetest, and most honeyed of all Madeira styles. Potentially the most complex and long-lived Madeira, Malmsey matures to an ultra-smooth, coffee-caramel succulence, which lasts forever in the mouth. The legal limit for residual sugar is 96–135 grams per litre.

✓ *Blandy's* (1985, Colheitas: 2000, 1992, 1990) • *Justino's* (1933) • *Quinta & Vineyard* (2001)

MOSCATEL

Madeira has made some interesting Moscatel, but only a few remain available for tasting today. However, with so many fortified Muscats of superb quality made throughout the world, Madeira's Moscatel should perhaps be reserved for blending purposes only.

RAINWATER

This is effectively a paler, softer version of a medium-dry Verdelho but, because varietal names are never used, making Rainwater with Verdelho would be a waste of this good-quality classic grape. Rainwater is more likely to be a paler, softer version of Tinta Negra Mole trying to emulate Verdelho. There are two theories about the origin of this curiously named Madeira style. One is that it came from the vines, which were grown on hillsides where it was impossible to irrigate, thus growers had to rely on rainwater. The other theory concerns a shipment that was bound for Boston in the US: even though the wine was accidentally diluted by rain en route, the Madeira house in question had hoped to get away with it and was shocked when the Americans loved it so much they wanted more!

RESERVE *or*
5-YEAR-OLD MADEIRA

This is the youngest age at which the noble varieties (Sercial, Verdelho, Bual, Malmsey, Bastardo, and Terrantez) may be used, so if no single variety is claimed, you can be sure that it is mostly, if not entirely, Tinta Negra Mole. Five years was once far too young for a classic Madeira from noble grapes, but they are much better than they used to be and some bargain five-year-old varietals can be found.

✓ *Barbeito* (Malmsey) • *Blandy's* (Sercial, Bual, Malmsey) • *Cossart* (Sercial)

SERCIAL

This grape is known on the Portuguese mainland as Esgana Cão, or "dog strangler", and is grown in the island's coolest vineyards. Sercial is the palest, lightest, and driest Madeira, but matures to a rich, yet crisp, savoury flavour with the sharp tang of acidic spices and citrus fruits. The legal limit for residual sugar is 18–65 grams per litre (the bottom end of this range tastes bone dry when balanced against an alcohol level of 17 per cent in such an intensely flavoured wine, and even 40 grams per litre can seem dry).

✓ *Cossart* (Colheita 1988)

SOLERA MADEIRA

Although an old *solera* will contain barely a few molecules from the year on which it was based and which it boasts on the label, the best examples of authentic Madeira *soleras* (there have been several frauds) are soft, sensuous, and delicious.

✓ *Blandy's Solera 1863 Malmsey* • *Blandy's Solera 1880 Verdelho* • *Cossart Solera 1845 Bual*

SPECIAL RESERVE *or*
10-YEAR-OLD MADEIRA

This is where serious Madeira begins, and even non-varietals may be worthy of consideration, since, while some wines in this style may be made with Tinta Negra Mole, producers will risk only superior wines from this grape for such extended ageing.

✓ *Blandy's* (Sercial, Malmsey) • *Cossart* (Verdelho, Malmsey) • *Henriques & Henriques* (Sercial, Malmsey) • *Power Drury* (Malmsey) • *Rutherford & Miles* (Bual, Malmsey)

TERRANTEZ

This white grape variety is virtually extinct on the island, but the highly perfumed, rich, powerfully flavoured, and tangy-sweet Madeira wine it produced is so highly regarded that old vintages can still attract top prices at auction. If and when the Young Turks ever reach Madeira, this is one variety they will be replanting in earnest.

✓ *Blandy's* (1976) • *D'Oliveira's* (1977)

20-YEAR-OLD

Although 20-year-old Madeira is not specified in the regulations in the same way as 3- (Finest), 5- (Reserve), 10- (Special Reserve) or 15- (Extra Reserve) Year-Old Madeiras are, there is nothing in the regulations that prohibits its use.

✓ *Henriques & Henriques* (Malmsey)

VERDELHO

Some modern renditions of this style are almost as pale as Sercial, but Verdelho, both white and black varieties of which are grown on the island, traditionally produces a golden Madeira whose colour deepens with age. It is, however, always made in a medium-dry to medium-sweet style, which gives it somewhat more body than Sercial, and this can make it seem softer and riper than it actually is, although its true astringency is revealed on the finish. The legal limit for residual sugar in these wines is 49–78 grams per litre.

✓ *Blandy's* (1968, Colheita 2000) • *Henriques & Henriques* (15-Year-Old Verdelho)

VINTAGE MADEIRA

All Madeira wines at one time bore a vintage, but this practice is unusual today, since most are blends or products of *solera* systems. Current regulations stipulate that vintage Madeira must spend at least 20 years in cask, but if Madeira is to prosper, this outdated approach must be discarded and a system similar to that used for vintage port must be adopted. This is not to suggest that vintage Madeira should not spend 20 years in cask, just that this rather lengthy process ought not to be mandatory. Consumers worldwide perceive vintage wines to be superior to non-vintage ones, and it does not seem to matter that the opposite is sometimes true. If Madeira is to reclaim the world stage and capture international imaginations, producers simply must put the spotlight on vintage Madeira, and the world is unlikely to wait 20 years for this to happen. Madeira must therefore release some of its vintages when they are much younger and put the onus on consumers to age the wines themselves. This would have the added advantage of feeding the auction circuit with a new investment and, as the different vintages are successively tasted and retasted, reported and discussed by critics, this would raise consumer awareness of these wines, thus very usefully enhancing the reputation of Madeira in general.

The WINES of
GERMANY, AUSTRIA, AND SWITZERLAND

CLASSIC GERMAN RIESLING IS INCOMPARABLE. No other wine can offer in a single sip as much finesse, purity of fruit, intensity of flavour, and thrilling acidity as a fine Riesling, yet it remains underrated. German Pinot Noir (Spätburgunder) is even more underrated. Few people have even heard of it. Yet, almost 40 per cent of Germany's vineyards are planted with black grapes and, of that, one-third is Pinot Noir. Top Spätburgunder from the Ahr, Baden, and the Pfalz can be compared in quality with some of the best *premiers crus* in Burgundy. The only question is whether such wines can be produced at prices that do not make good Burgundy seem cheap by comparison! Austria also makes beautiful, under-appreciated Riesling and Pinot Noir, in addition to which, top quality examples of one of its indigenous varieties, the highly distinctive Grüner Veltliner, are at last being taken seriously. And if German red wine is a surprise, nearly half of all Swiss wine is red, with smooth Pinot Noir and dense-yet-velvety Merlot the up-and-coming stars. These three countries will offer consumers some of the most exciting and diverse wine experiences of the new millennium.

BURGRUINE LANDSHUT, BERNKASTEL-KUES
The ruins of this 13th-century castle overlook the Schlossberg vineyard on the banks of the River Mosel. The castle once belonged to the archbishops of Trier.

GERMANY

Qualitatively, Germany has turned itself around literally at root level, with Riesling and Spätburgunder (Pinot Noir) now representing one-third of the total area under vine, compared to 1995, when Müller-Thurgau was still the widest-cultivated variety in the country and Pinot Noir accounted for less than 7 per cent, even though that figure was double what it had been another 15 years earlier.

ALTHOUGH THE BEST GERMAN WINES (Riesling and Pinot Noir) are better than ever, the worst have never been as bad, and the German wine law passed in 1994 to replace the flawed law of 1971 has unfortunately not improved matters. On top of this, we now have a befuddled *Grosses Gewächs* classification muddying the water at the very top end of the market, and wine labels with Anglicized fantasy names at the bottom end of the market. The latter are supposed to simplify labelling, yet make the wines look as if they were made in Eastern Europe.

Every German wine is graded by the natural sugar content of its grapes: the more sugar, the higher the quality. Therefore, the greatest German wines are inevitably the sweetest. Although the philosophy that equates ripeness with greatness is misguided and has proved harmful to Germany's reputation, it is not an unreasonable one, for ripe grapes are required to make fine wine, and in Germany's northerly climate it is usually only the best sites that can fully ripen grapes. Nonetheless, taken to its ultimate conclusion, the German ideal implies, nonsensically, that a drier wine is inherently inferior to a sweeter wine. In the quest for sweetness and greater volume, the Riesling was gradually discarded in favour of German crosses such as Müller-Thurgau and Kerner, which easily ripened at much higher sugar levels and yielded far larger crops.

A GERMAN ESTATE-WINE REVIVAL?

In the 18th and 19th centuries, German wines from the Rhine were as famous and as expensive as the wines of Bordeaux, and Germany's system of aristocratic wine estates was on a par with

SCHLOSS JOHANNISBERG
This historic, mansion-style schloss, which dominates the Rheingau slope between Winkel and Geisenheim, was built in 1563.

the great wine châteaux of France. Today, almost every wine critic agrees that Germany's best estates must reassert their position if this country wants to regain its reputation for quality. But this is not currently possible because each estate makes far too many wines to project any sort of unified image, let alone reputation. In Bordeaux one can speak of the style and quality of, say, Château Margaux *vis-à-vis* Château Latour, but what can be said about any top German estate, when the wines range from QbA, through *Kabinett, Spätlese, Auslese, Beerenauslese,* and

THE WINE REGIONS OF GERMANY

Viticulturally, Germany is made up of four large *Deutscher Tafelwein* regions encompassing eight *Tafelwein* sub-regions, within which there are separate infrastructures for 13 *Qualitätswein* and 20 *Landwein* regions. (The two *Qualitätswein* and two *Landwein* regions in former Eastern Germany fall outside the *Tafelwein* structure.) The *Qualitätswein* regions encompass 39 *Bereiche* (districts), containing 160 *Grosslagen* (collective sites), which in turn encapsulate 2,632 *Einzellagen* (single sites).

DEUTSCHER TAFELWEIN REGIONS	DEUTSCHER TAFELWEIN SUB-REGIONS	LANDWEIN REGIONS	QUALITÄTSWEIN REGIONS
Rhein-Mosel	Rhein	Ahrtaler Landwein	Ahr
		Starkenburger Landwein	Hessische Bergstrasse
		Rheinburgen Landwein	Mittelrhein
		Nahegauer Landwein	Nahe
		Altrheingauer Landwein	Rheingau
		Rheinischer Landwein	Rheinhessen
		Pfälzer Landwein	Pfalz
	Mosel	Landwein der Mosel	
	Saar	Saarländischer Landwein	Mosel
		Landwein der Ruwer	
Bayern	Main	Fränkischer Landwein	Franken
	Donau	Regensburger Landwein	
	Lindau	Bayerischer Bodensee Landwein	Württemberg
Neckar	-	Schwäbischer Landwein	
Oberrhein	Römertor	Südbadischer Landwein	Baden
	Burgengau	Unterbadischer Landwein	
		Taubertäler Landwein	
		Mitteldeutscher Landwein	Saale-Unstrut
		Sächsischer Landwein	Sachsen
Stargarder Land		Mecklenburger Landwein	

QUALITY STRUCTURE OVERVIEW

This is a simplistic overview because each category varies according to the grape variety and its area of origin. More detailed analyses are given under each region (*see* Quality Requirements and Harvest Percentages box, p406).

QUALITY CATEGORY	MINIMUM OECHSLE	MINIMUM POTENTIAL ALCOHOL
Deutscher Tafelwein*	44–50°	5.0–5.9%
Landwein*	47–55°	5.6–6.7%
Qualitätswein bestimmter Anbaugebiete (QbA)*	50–72°	5.9–9.4%
QUALITÄTSWEIN MIT PRÄDIKAT (QmP):		
Kabinett	67–85°	8.6–11.4%
Spätlese	76–95°	10.0–13.0%
Auslese	83–105°	11.1–14.5%
Beerenauslese	110–128°	15.3–18.1%
Eiswein	110–128°	15.3–18.1%
Trockenbeerenauslese (TBA)	150–154°	21.5–22.1%

Chaptalization is allowed, and will be necessary if the wine has a potential alcoholic strength of less than 8.5 per cent.

Trockenbeerenauslese to *Eiswein* for each grape variety grown? At one time Germany's top wine estates did not market a vast number of *Prädikat* wines. Instead, they built their reputations on a single, flagship *cuvée*, which was invariably pure Riesling and, no matter how many times the vineyards were combed for grapes, just one wine was produced. It would be like combining

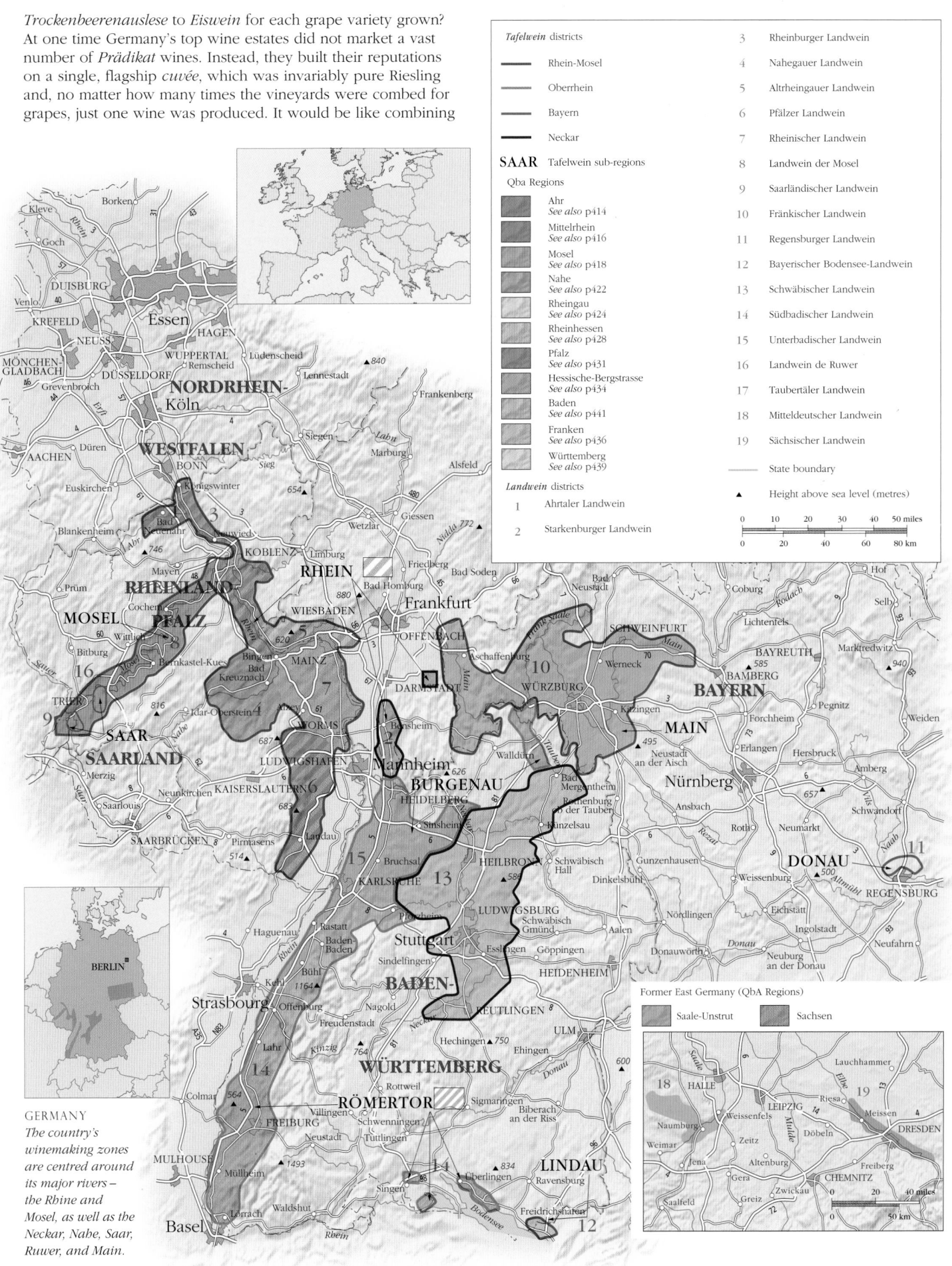

GERMANY
The country's winemaking zones are centred around its major rivers – the Rhine and Mosel, as well as the Neckar, Nahe, Saar, Ruwer, and Main.

Tafelwein districts	
———	Rhein-Mosel
———	Oberrhein
———	Bayern
———	Neckar

SAAR Tafelwein sub-regions

Qba Regions

	Ahr *See also p414*
	Mittelrhein *See also p416*
	Mosel *See also p418*
	Nahe *See also p422*
	Rheingau *See also p424*
	Rheinhessen *See also p428*
	Pfalz *See also p431*
	Hessische-Bergstrasse *See also p434*
	Baden *See also p441*
	Franken *See also p436*
	Württemberg *See also p439*

Landwein districts

1   Ahrtaler Landwein
2   Starkenburger Landwein

3   Rheinburger Landwein
4   Nahegauer Landwein
5   Altrheingauer Landwein
6   Pfälzer Landwein
7   Rheinischer Landwein
8   Landwein der Mosel
9   Saarländischer Landwein
10 Fränkischer Landwein
11 Regensburger Landwein
12 Bayerischer Bodensee-Landwein
13 Schwäbischer Landwein
14 Südbadischer Landwein
15 Unterbadischer Landwein
16 Landwein de Ruwer
17 Taubertäler Landwein
18 Mitteldeutscher Landwein
19 Sächsischer Landwein

——— State boundary
▲   Height above sea level (metres)

Former East Germany (QbA Regions)

	Saale-Unstrut
	Sachsen

QUALITY REQUIREMENTS AND HARVEST PERCENTAGES

Germany is notorious for the variation of its vintages. Therefore as a form of insurance, most of the crop is harvested early. This secures a minimum income from Deutscher Tafelwein and QbA wines, with those grapes that remain on the vine providing a possibility of higher-quality wines from late harvests. If, when, and how much these grapes ripen is the most basic indication of the nature of any vintage. The degree of ripeness attained is expressed in degrees *Oechsle* and the minimum level for each QmP can vary according to the region and grape variety in question. Each degree of *Oechsle* is the equivalent of 2–2.5 grams per litre of sugar. The exact amount of sugar varies according to the level of unfermentable extract also present. (For a survey of each region, see the individual charts in the regional sections.)

all the different *Prädikat* wines into one super-rich blend today. In the days of Germany's illustrious wine estates, the wines were fermented more fully, rather than being arrested at artificially low alcohol levels in order to retain sweetness. Thus these flagship *cuvées* were not just richer than today's wines, but drier, fuller-bodied, and more alcoholic. It was this sort of wine that made Germany's finest wine estates famous throughout the world, and only when they return to the same basic philosophy will they be able to rebuild their reputations.

THE 1971 GERMAN WINE LAW

In 1971, a wine law was established to take account of EEC legislation regulating wine production. The main aspect of the law was to reduce 30,000 *Einzellagen* (individually named vineyards) to 2,600. The law allowed the boundaries of each of the original *Einzellagen* to be extended in order to cover a minimum area of five hectares. The solution appeared efficient, but missed the point of why any plot of land evolves a name or reputation to distinguish it from neighbouring vineyards: *terroir*. The enshrining of these amalgamated vineyards in law has duped the public into believing that highly priced wines come from specific, historical sites when, in fact, they may originate from the surrounding areas that, on average, are more than 10 times the size.

This was nothing less than legalized fraud, but the bureaucratic bungling did not end there. The lawmakers went on to create an entirely new geographical appellation called the "*Grosslage*", which has turned out to be an even greater deception. In fact, once this law's capacity to deceive was fully understood, it became known on English-speaking markets as the "Gross lie". A *Grosslage*, or "collective site", is a very large area, not merely encompassing several *Einzellagen* (single sites as the term literally means) but many villages, each of which comprises a

COMPARISON OF GERMAN HARVESTS 2006–2009

Production varies enormously in Germany – from as much as 15.4 million hectolitres (171 million cases) in 1982 to as little as 5.2 million hectolitres (58 million cases) in 1985 – as does the spread of wines across the range of quality categories, shown by the table below.

	2006	2007	2008	2009
QUALITY CATEGORY				
Tafelwein to Landwein	4.4%	5.8%	6.0%	3.5%
QbA	52.3%	49.7%	57.0%	43.4%
QmP	43.3%	44.5%	37.0%	53.1%
SIZE OF HARVEST				
Millions of hectolitres	8.9	10.3	10.0	9.2
Millions of cases	98.9	114.4	111.1	102.2
Hectares under vine	99,172	99,702	99,744	100,101
(Acres)	(245,059)	(246,369)	(246,472)	(247,355)
Hectolitres per hectare	91.4	104.0	100.3	91.3

DECODING THE AP NUMBER

All QbAs and QmPs, including *Deutscher Sekt*, must carry an AP number (*Amtliche Prüfnummer*). This proves that a wine has undergone and passed various tasting and analytical tests and its origin has been established to the board's satisfaction. Each time a producer applies for an AP number, specially sealed samples of the approved wine are kept by both the board and the producer. Should there be a fault or a fraud enquiry, these samples are analysed and checked against a sample of the product on the market that has given rise to complaint or investigation. This sounds foolproof, and it is indeed more stringent than the EU's Lot Number, which has been in operation since 1989. But like all systems it can be abused, which in this case would simply mean printing fictitious AP numbers on the label, although if noticed the penalty for this would be imprisonment, plus a ban from operating for the company, and a large fine. Understanding the AP number can be very useful. If the wine is a non-vintage QbA, it can give you some idea of how long it has been in bottle.

2002 "Weingut Müller-Catoir" Riesling Spätlese Qualitätswein mit Prädikat (QmP)

5 = Examination Board number

174 = number of the commune where the wine was bottled

079 = the bottler's registered number

16 = the bottler's application number

03 = the year in which the bottler made the application

The communes' and bottlers' numbers run into thousands and are of the least significance to the consumer. It is the last two sets of numbers that provide the most useful information. In this instance, the 16 and 03 reveal that this is Weingut Müller-Catoir's 16th application made in 2003. The application numbers are sequential, but do not necessarily apply to the same wine, ie none of the 15 previous applications made by Weingut Müller-Catoir in 2003 need necessarily apply to its 2002 Riesling Spätlese QmP. You will find that some references state that the application number actually refers to a specific cask the wine came from (which in this case would be *fuder* 16), but although this is so in some cases (Fritz Haag, and Von Schubert's Maximin Grünhaus, for example), this is only because the producer in question will number his cask to coincide with the application number. What the last two sets of digits tell us is that if they are the same, then the wine is *exactly* the same. If you find two bottles of 2002 Weingut Müller-Catoir Riesling Spätlese QmP both bearing the AP number 5 174 079 16 03, then you know beyond any doubt that the contents of both bottles swam with each other before being bottled together. If you find two bottles of 2002 Weingut Müller-Catoir Riesling Spätlese QmP both bearing the AP number where either or both of the last two sets of digits are different, then you know that the contents are, at the very least, subtly different. They might simply be bottled on a different date, or from a different cask, but when the designation is as broad as Riesling Spätlese QmP, the grapes could have been grown miles apart, picked on different days, vinified in different tanks, with radically different sugar, alcohol, and acidity readings.

large number of *Einzellagen*. On average, each *Grosslage* consists of 17 post-1971 *Einzellagen* or 197 pre-1971 *Einzellagen*. Such wines are widely blended and of modest quality, but this in itself would not have been a problem had it been obligatory for the term "*Grosslage*" to appear on the label before the name of the *Grosslage* itself, as "*Bereich*" (district) has to. Not only does the term *Grosslage* not have to appear anywhere on the label, but the name of the *Grosslage* appears after that of the village, in precisely the same way as the name of an *Einzellage* does, constantly leading consumers to believe that a *Grosslage* wine is from a single *Einzellage*. The criteria that originally established Germany as one of the great wine-producing countries of the world – the pre-eminence and defining quality of the Riesling grape, the famous villages or estates where it was grown, and the legendary quality of the individually named vineyards, or true *Einzellagen* – no longer applied after 1971.

GERMANY LABEL LANGUAGE

Abfüllung Bottling.

Auslese A category of German QmP wine that is very sweet, made from late-picked grapes, and which may also contain some botrytized grapes, *Auslese* is one step of sweetness above *Spätlese* but one below *Beerenauslese*, and most of the best lean upwards rather than downwards.

Badisch Rotgold A speciality rosé wine made from a blend of Ruländer and Spätburgunder, Badischer Rotgold must be of at least QbA level, and can be produced only in Baden.

Bariquewein Fermented or matured in new oak casks.

Beerenauslese A category of German QmP wine that comes above *Auslese* in sweetness, but beneath *Trockenbeerenauslese* and is made from botrytized grapes. It has more finesse and elegance than any other intensely sweet wine, with the possible exception of *Eiswein*.

Bereich If the wine carries the appellation of a *Bereich*, it will simply state this – "Bereich Burg Cochem", for example.

Deutscher German.

Deutscher Qualitäts-schaumwein or **Deutscher Sekt bestimmter Anbaugebiete** A sparkling wine made by any method (but probably *cuve close*), from 100 per cent German grapes grown in one specified region, although it may indicate an even smaller area of origin if at least 85 per cent of the grapes come from that named area.

Deutscher Sekt or **Deutscher Qualitätsschaumwein** A sparkling wine made by any method (but probably *cuve close*), from 100 per cent German grapes. It may indicate a maximum of two grape names and should be at least 10 months old when sold.

Deutscher Weinsiegel An official seal of quality awarded to wines that receive a higher score than the minimum required for an AP number, Deutscher Weinsiegels use a colour-coding system: *trocken* wines bear a bright yellow seal; *halbtrocken* a lime green seal, and sweeter wines a red seal.

Edelfäule The German term for noble rot.

Einzellage A single-vineyard wine area; the smallest geographical unit allowed under German wine law.

Eiswein A rare wine resulting from the tradition of leaving grapes on the vine in the hope of attracting *Botrytis cinerea*. The grapes are frozen by frost or snow, then harvested, and pressed while frozen. This is done because only the ice freezes and, as this rises to the top of the vat, it can be scraped off to leave a concentrated juice that produces a wine with a unique balance of sweetness, acidity, and extract.

Erstes Gewächs *See* Grosses Gewächs

Erste Lage *See* Grosses Gewächs

Erzeugerabfüllung At one time this was considered to mean estate-bottled, but so many cooperatives use it (because, they claim, their members' estates are the cooperative's estates) that it now means no more than producer-bottled, thus some estates now use *Gutsabfüllung*.

Flaschengärung A bottle-fermented *Sekt* that is not necessarily made by the traditional method.

Flaschengärung nach dem traditionellen Verfahren A *Sekt* made by the traditional method, although it is not likely to show much autolytic character.

Füder A large oval cask with a capacity of 1,000 litres, more prevalent in the Mosel than the Rhine.

Für Diabetiker Geeignet Suitable for diabetics, the wines must be *trocken* (dry), contain less than 1.5 grams per litre of sulphur dioxide (as opposed to the legal maximum of 2.25 grams per litre) and no more than 12 per cent alcohol.

Grosses Gewächs (Great Growth), **Erstes Gewächs** (First Growth – Rheingau only), and **Erste Lage** (First Site – Mosel only) are reserved for wines from the most highly rated vineyards. Only *Auslese, Beerenauslese, Trockenbeerenauslese,* or *Eiswein prädikate* are allowed, except in Mosel, where *Kabinett* and *Spätlese prädikate* and various other designations may also be used. When not qualified by any *prädikat, Grosses Gewächs* must be a dry wine made from grapes with a minimum *Spätlese* must weight. In the Ahr, only dry Pinot Noir or Frühburgunder of a minimum *Auslese* must weight qualify for *Grosses Gewächs*. All *Grosses/Erstes Gewächs* and *Erste Lage* wines must be hand harvested to a maximum yield of 50 hl/ha, subjected to a VDP taste test, and cannot be released until September of the year following that of the harvest (two years for red wines).

Grosslage A *Grosslage*, or "collective site", is a large area under which name cheap, bulk-blended wines are sold.

Gutsabfüllung This term literally means "bottled on the property" and has been taken up by those who feel that *Erzeugerabfüllung* has been so debased by the cooperatives that it no longer stands for a wine that is truly estate-bottled. *Gutsabfüllung* can only be used by a winemaker who holds a diploma in oenology. This means any naturally gifted winemaker who has not sat the examination, but owns an estate and makes brilliant wines, has no legal way of indicating his or her wine is an authentic product that has been grown on, fermented at, and bottled on a individual wine estate.

Gutswein and **Ortswein** (estate wine and commune wine) is applicable to wines observing the VDP's general standards, which include viticultural methods adhering to strict controls, regular inspection of vineyards, higher must weights than those prescribed by law, and a maximum yield of 75 hl/ha.

Halbtrocken Literally "half-dry", although practically semi-sweet on most occasions, this wine does not contain more than 18 grams per litre of residual sugar and 10 grams per litre of acid.

Jahrgang Vintage year.

Klassifizierter Lagenwein (wine from a classified site) is restricted to wines from classified vineyards that impart site-specific traits, with a maximum yield of 65 hl/ha.

Kabinett The predicate at the end of this wine's name (it can come either before or after the grape variety) reveals that it is the lightest and driest of the QmP wines.

Landwein This Teutonic version of the French *vin de pays* is not only a failure in commercial terms (unlike its Gallic compatriot), but is also rather strange in that it may be produced in only *trocken* and *halbtrocken* styles.

Lieblich Technically medium-sweet, although nearer to the French *moelleux*, this wine may have up to 45 grams per litre of residual sugar.

Ortswein *See* Gutswein

Qualitätswein mit Prädikat (QmP) The wine comes from the highest quality category of German wine and will carry one of the predicates that range from *Kabinett* up to *Trockenbeerenauslese*.

Perlwein Cheap, semi-sparkling wines made by carbonating a still wine. Mostly white, but may be red or rosé.

QbA *Qualitätswein bestimmter Anbaugebiete*, this is the theoretical equivalent of the French AOC.

QmP *Qualitätswein mit Prädikat*, this literally means a "quality wine with predication", and is a term used for any German wine above QbA, from *Kabinett* upwards. The predication carried by a QmP wine depends upon the level of ripeness of the grapes used in the wine.

Qualitätsschaumwein A "quality sparkling wine" can be produced by any member state of the EU, but the term should be qualified by the country of origin (of the wine). Only *Deutscher Qualitätsschaumwein* will necessarily be from Germany.

Rebe Grape variety.

Restusse Residual sugar.

Rosewein or **Roseewein** Rosé.

Rotling A rosé wine that may be made from black grapes or a mixture of black and white. This designation must be indicated on the label of any category of *Tafelwein* up to and including *Landwein*, and must also be featured on the label of QbA wine, although it is optional for QmP.

Rotwein Red wine. This designation must be indicated on the label of any category of *Tafelwein* up to and including *Landwein*, and must also be featured on the label of QbA wine, although it is optional for QmP.

Schaumwein With no further qualification, such as *Qualitätsschaumwein*, this indicates the cheapest form of sparkling wine, probably a carbonated blend of wines from various EU countries.

Schillerwein A style of wine produced in Württemberg that is the same as a *Rotling*.

Sekt Sparkling wine.

Spätlese A QmP wine that is one step of sweetness above *Kabinett*, but one below *Auslese*. It is fairly sweet and made from late-picked grapes.

Süss A sweet wine with in excess of 45 grams per litre of residual sugar.

Tafelwein A lowly table wine or *vin de table*.

Trocken Literally "dry", a *trocken* wine must not contain more than 4 grams per litre of residual sugar, although up to 9 grams per litre is permitted if the acidity is 2 grams per litre or more.

Trockenbeerenauslese A wine produced from individually picked, botrytized grapes that have been left on the vine to shrivel, it is typically golden-amber to amber in colour, intensely sweet, viscous, very complex and as different from *Beerenauslese* as that wine is from *Kabinett*.

VDP *Verband Deutscher Prädikats-und Qualitätsweingüter*, an association of top wine estates.

Weissherbst A single-variety rosé produced from black grapes only, the variety of which must be indicated.

Weisswein White wine. This designation must be indicated on the label of any category of *Tafelwein* up to and including *Landwein*. It may also be featured on the label of QbA and higher-quality wines, but this is not mandatory.

SÜSSRESERVE

Süssreserve is sterilized grape juice that may have just one or two degrees of alcohol, but has none if processed before fermentation can commence. It not only contributes the grapey freshness and sweetness for which German wines are famous, but also provides the winemaker with a convenient last-minute ingredient with which he can correct the balance of a wine. The origin of *Süssreserve* must, in essence, be the same as the wine to which it is added. Its quality, or degree of ripeness, should by law be at least the equivalent of the wine itself. The quantity added is not in itself restricted, but is indirectly controlled by the overall ratio of sugar to alcohol.

QUALITY	GRAMS OF ALCOHOL FOR EVERY GRAM OF RESIDUAL SUGAR PER LITRE	EXECEPTIONS
Tafelwein	3g	Franconian red 5g
Qualitätswein	3g	Franconian red 5g
		Franconian white and rosé 3.5g
		Württemberg red 4g
		Rheingau white
Kabinett	no controls	Franconian red 5g
		Franconian white and rosé 3g

THE 1994 WINE LAW

In 1994, when Germany was required to bring its wine law into line with those of other EU member states, it had a chance to remedy the flaws in the 1971 wine law. Those who cared about quality bravely attempted reforms, but the large private and cooperative bottlers of inferior wine were too powerful, thus the bad law of 1971 was replaced by the even worse law of 1994. *Grosslagen* and *Bereiche* could and should have been disposed of because they are unnecessary appellations that do not enhance the reputation of German wines. But if such a simple yet radical move was too difficult to accomplish, then a temporary and perfectly adequate means of stopping the rot would have been to focus on reforming the *Grosslagen*, which are a deception as well as a distraction. This would have been easy to achieve simply by making it mandatory to print the term *Grosslage* on the label, in the same way that *Bereich* must appear. Until there is a consensus on the reform or eradication of the *Grosslagen*, there is no hope of reinstating the authentic names and boundaries of the *Einzellagen*, yet this is the only hope Germany has of reclaiming equal fine-wine status with France. Only a hierarchical classification of

WEINGUT MAX FERD RICHTER, MÜLHEIM
A producer of great Riesling, particularly from Juffer Sonnenuhr in Braunberg, Dr Richter is justly famous for his superb Eiswein.

Germany's greatest vineyards will put this country back among the elite winemaking nations of the world, but it would be pointless to build one on the current tissue of lies. The number of *Einzellagen* was reduced to 2,600 in 1971 because, it was claimed, 30,000 was too confusing to contemplate; but this claim was without justification. It does not matter whether there are 30,000 or 300,000 – there are as many *Einzellagen* as there are; they all have the same right to exist, but only the outstanding ones will ever earn a reputation, so where is the potential for confusion? No one has suggested that all 30,000 should be classified. If the Germans ever conduct an official classification, and it is done properly, it would probably consist of no more than the best 250 *Einzellagen* and only the top 10 per cent of these would need to create the sort of international reputation that Bordeaux's *premiers crus* have so effectively achieved.

VDP CLASSIFICATION

Without the will or authority to impose a legally recognized nationwide classification, this task has been left to voluntary, quality-conscious organizations. The earliest response was in 1983 in the Rheingau, where the late George Breuer pushed through the now famous Charta (pronounced "karta"), whereby vineyards were classified as *Erstes Gewächs* (First Growths), a designation that could only be used for wines that are essentially dry in style and comply with strict quality criteria. The most important aspect of the Charta, however, was its reclassification of the *Einzellagen*. It demonstrated that some famous sites had been inflated by as much as 806 per cent under the 1971 wine law. It was hoped this example would be copied on a pan-regional basis by the largest organization of wine estates, the

RECENT GERMAN VINTAGES

2010 A difficult year, with low volumes and high – sometimes extraordinarily high – acidity, produced some outstanding late-harvest wines, thanks to a sunny October. But some dry Rieslings are awkward.

2009 A fabulous Spätburgunder vintage, producing rich, plump, impressive reds, and an excellent year for all other varieties and styles, although they will not be as long-lived as the 2008s.

2008 There is a refreshing streak of piquant acidity winding its way through this vintage, making it an outstanding year for sweet Riesling and enhancing the minerality in dry Rieslings. Some great Spätburgunder, too.

2007 A spectacular vintage for top-end reds and late-harvest wines almost everywhere, as well as for dry Riesling in the Mosel and Nahe. The Pfalz was disappointing.

2006 Erratic weather kept growers on their toes, and an Indian summer raised hopes, only to be dashed by floods. Some fabulous exceptions everywhere, particularly in the Mosel, but generally this is a vintage to avoid, except in the Ahr and Mittelrhein, which excelled for both reds and Riesling, and to a lesser extent the Saale-Unstrut and Sachsen areas around Berlin, where the quality was good.

A LITTLE GERMAN

Those who don't speak German may find it helpful to know that the plural of German words ending in "e" is achieved by adding an "n", thus one *Grosslage*, two or more *Grosslagen*. For the plural of words ending with a consonant, an "e" is added, thus one *Bereich*, two or more *Bereiche*.

BOPPARD
All the vineyards in Boppard are steep and slate-strewn, but the best face due south thanks to the loop in the river.

Verband Deutscher Prädikatsweingüter (VDP). Unfortunately, the VDP did not pick up the gauntlet until June 2002, when it announced its *Grosses Gewächs* (Great Growths) classification for all regions, except the Ahr and Mosel (the Mosel joined the scheme in March 2003, and the Ahr in August 2003).

The delay was much less of a worry than what had prompted the VDP into action in the first place. It was not so much vineyard classification, as the new dry wine designations of Classic and Selection. The VDP agreed with most of the criteria for the top Selection designation, which is restricted to *Einzellage* wines, but objected to the lack of any vineyard classification, other than the mostly bloated and meaningless *Einzellage* created by the 1971 wine law. It therefore withdrew its support of Classic and Selection designations, and launched instead its *Grosses Gewächs* concept. Thus the whole *Grosses Gewächs* concept has become irrevocably and unnecessarily entangled in stylistic issues, instead of setting out with blinding simplicity the true boundaries of Germany's greatest vineyards.

By not concentrating on a sense of place, the VDP became engrossed in ridiculous arguments as to what wine styles should be permitted to use the *Grosses Gewächs* classification, with definitions differing from region to region, not to mention the designation itself, which now accommodates the already established *Erstes Gewächs* in the Rheingau and *Erstes Lage* (First Site) in the Mosel, plus, of course, *Grosses Gewächs*.

CHANGING IDEAS ABOUT GERMAN WINES

The modern idea of which German wines to drink, and how and when to drink them, is based on a tradition that is over a hundred years old. Outside Germany itself, the predilection for Rhine and Mosel is essentially a British one. Historically, this has always been so. Even two world wars failed to diminish the British fondness for these wines, and despite a 25 per cent drop in exports in the early 1990s, Britain remains Germany's biggest customer.

At one time, the British, whose tastes influenced the rest of the world, drank only Hock, a name that originally applied only to the wines of Hochheim in Rheingau, but soon became generic for all white Rhine wines. Unlike the light, grapey Rhine wines

we know today, the passion in the 19th century was for mature, full-flavoured, amber-coloured wines. In fact, Hock glasses traditionally have brown stems because they were deliberately made to reflect the desired amber hue of age into the wine. The Christie's auction of May 1777 listed "Excellent Genuine Old Hock" of the 1719 vintage, and another London sale offered "Hock Hocheim" 1726 in August of 1792. How a modern Hock might taste in 60 years or so is anyone's guess, but mine is that it would not be very pleasant by today's standards – unless it happened to be a *Trockenbeerenauslese*.

FROM HOCK TO MOSEL

By the time Mosel wines became popular, the trend was for lighter, younger wines, hence traditional green-stemmed Mosel glasses were manufactured. The green stem reflected the verdancy of youth from the glass into the wine. (Incidentally, "Moselle" is the name of the river in France's most northerly wine area, producing VDQS Vins de Moselle, and as soon as the river crosses the border it becomes "Mosel". Surprisingly, too many English-labelled German wines mistakenly use the spelling "Moselle".) The brown- or amber-stemmed "Hock" glass was introduced in the 18th century, when it had become fashionable to drink Rhine of great maturity; the coloured glass was intended to reflect the desired hues of honeyed-richness and maturity in the wine.

LIEBFRAUMILCH – NOT A WINE THE GERMANS DRINK OR EVEN KNOW!

More than one-third of all German wine exports are sold as Liebfraumilch, an inexpensive, bulk-blended product that few Germans have even heard of, let alone tasted. Less than 0.01 per cent of the 1.1 million hectolitres (12 million cases) produced each year is consumed in Germany itself, and most of that is sold to foreign tourists and servicemen. Virtually 100 per cent of all Liebfraumilch is consumed by non-Germans and, although it is no longer fashionable among the new generation of drinkers in the UK, it nevertheless remains the number one best-selling wine in Britain's largest supermarket groups. While the two largest markets, the UK and US, continue to consume such vast quantities of Liebfraumilch, I am duty-bound to tell the full story.

Myriad theories surround the origin of the name Liebfraumilch (or Liebfrauenmilch), but many agree that it means "milk of Our Lady" and refers to the wine produced from one small and fairly indifferent vineyard in the suburbs of Worms that was once called Liebfrauenkirche, or "Church of Our Lady". This is now part of Liebfrauenstift-Kirchenstück, which in turn is part of the 1,000-hectare (2,470-acre) *Grosslage* Liebfrauenmorgen. The single-vineyard wine that gave birth to the name of Liebfraumilch has no bearing whatsoever on the bulk-blended wine of today, nor, for that matter, any connection with the Liebfraumilch that was sold more than 100 years ago. What is interesting, however, is the nature of those early Liebfraumilch wines that gave the blended product of today its worldwide reputation and huge sales. The blurred and non-specific character of this wine was officially classified by the Worms Chamber of Commerce in 1910, when it stated that Liebfraumilch was merely "a fancy name" that merchants "have made use of", applying it to "Rhine wines of good quality and character". The ill-defined use of this "fancy name" widened during the following 20 years. Even between 1945 and the advent of the new German wine laws in 1971, one-third of the wines blended into Liebfraumilch came from German regions other than the Rhine.

This should have ended when Liebfraumilch was granted *Qualitätswein* status under the 1971 German wine law because the law further stated that a *Qualitätswein* could come only from one specified region. However, the regulations also specified that Liebfraumilch could be made only from Rheinhessen, Pfalz, Rheingau, and Nahe grapes and, although few people doubted the spirit of the law, many producers interpreted this quite literally.

BERNKASTEL-KUES, MOSEL
Looking across the Mosel to Bernkastel-Kues, above which is the famous Doctor vineyard, from which some of Germany's greatest wines come.

They considered Liebfraumilch to be an umbrella designation that entitled the wine to come from any one or more of the four specified regions. Now, however, at least 85 per cent of every Liebfraumilch has to come from just one region, which must be indicated on the label.

There have been many moves to reclassify Liebfraumilch as a *Tafelwein*, which would permit it to be blended with grape varieties from the much wider *Tafelwein* regions and this would be more in keeping with its quality, which is not poor or bad *per se*, simply unpretentious and of non-specific character. However, Liebfraumilch producers disliked the idea of the *Tafelwein* classification – a misguided view in my opinion, not least because Liebfraumilch sells on its brand name. Although not intrinsically poor quality, far too many Liebfraumilch are bad wines, just as far too many cheap German wines in general are. Taken at its best, a decent Liebfraumilch should possess a fresh, flowery aroma and sweet, grapey taste. It has proved to be a good stepping-stone, with statistics showing that the vast majority of seasoned wine drinkers originally "cut their teeth" on this accessible wine, but there will always be some Liebfraumilch drinkers who never stray beyond it. Those drinkers, if honest, dislike the taste of alcohol, but enjoy the effect it has and most of them are not too keen on tannin, acidity, and the assertively dry taste found in most "real" wines. There is no reason why they should – it is all a matter of taste.

WHAT IS LIEBFRAUMILCH?

Ironically, Germany's most criticized wine is the only one to be defined by taste and sweetness in its wine laws. According to the regulations, the minimum residual sugar allowed is 18 grams per litre, equivalent to the maximum allowed for a *halbtrocken*, although few are actually this low, and some are twice as high. Producers have their own idea of what level of sweetness is right for the market and make their wines accordingly. Many buyers insist on a certain ratio of sugar to acidity; most brands contain between 22–35 grams per litre of sugar, with 27–28 grams per litre of sugar as a good average. Liebfraumilch labels must now show one of the four permitted regions; at least 85 per cent of the wine must come from the region stated. On average, the Rheinhessen and the Pfalz produce more than nine out of every 10 bottles of Liebfraumilch, while the Nahe makes very little and the Rheingau virtually none. Any grape permitted for German QbA wine may be used for the production of Liebfraumilch, the only control being that at least 51 per cent of the blend must be composed of one or more of the following varieties: Riesling, Silvaner, Müller-Thurgau, and Kerner. According to the present regulations, the wine should taste of these grapes, although I have so far met no expert who can either describe or detect a definitive blend of four such different varieties in the wine. What I have discovered, however, is that some of the best blends have actually been denied their AP numbers because they have received a beneficial Süssreserve of aromatic Morio-Muskat. The examining board for Liebfraumilch apparently believes these eminently more attractive wines to be atypical of the appellation.

SEKT – GERMANY'S SPARKLING WINE

Germany's *Sekt* or sparkling wine industry is very important, producing almost half a billion bottles a year, more than twice that of Champagne. This is almost entirely made by *cuve close* and over 85 per cent is not *Deutscher Sekt* at all, but *Sekt* plain and simple, made from imported wines. Despite a fourfold increase in exports over the past 15 years, foreign markets still represent barely 8 per cent of sales. In general, Germans make *Sekt* for themselves and its bland, off-dry style with a very young tartness to it has a peculiarly domestic appeal that sparkling wine drinkers in most international markets cannot comprehend, whether they are used to Champagne or New World fizz. *Deutscher Sekt* is little better, and the best *Deutscher Sekt* is seldom encountered. On those rare occasions when bottle-fermented wines are produced, *Sekt* will not appeal to most sparkling-wine drinkers outside Germany itself because the grapes are too aromatic for the expected mellow biscuity character to develop. However, there are Pinot Noir-based *Sekt* rosés that cross the barrier, and the best mature Riesling *Sekt* can appeal to a niche market, just as Australia's sparkling Shiraz does.

HOW TO USE THE "APPELLATIONS OF..." SECTIONS

The entries that follow for each of Germany's wine regions are set out in a logical order. In each of these regions, or *Anbaugebiete*, every *Bereich* is listed and the wine styles are described; this is followed by the *Grosslagen* within that particular *Bereich*. Under each *Grosslage*, the best villages are listed where applicable and, within each of these, the finest *Einzellagen*, or vineyards, are named.

In Germany, vineyards are rarely owned only by one estate – as they are in Bordeaux, for example. It is therefore important to be aware of not only which are the top vineyards, but also who makes the best wines there, which is why I recommend growers and estates within each of the finest vineyards. The term "village" covers both *Gemeinden* – communes, which may be anything from a tiny village to a large, bustling town – and *Ortsteile*, which are villages absorbed within the suburbs of a larger *Gemeinde*. The term "*Grosslagenfrei*" refers to villages and *Einzellagen* within one *Bereich* that are not part of any of its *Grosslagen*.

Where it is stated that there are no outstanding villages, vineyards, estates, or growers in a particular *Grosslage*, excellent estates and growers might well own vineyards there, but the wine produced in these vineyards may not actually be of the highest standard.

All styles and descriptions of wines refer to Riesling, unless otherwise stated. The following sample entry is given from the Franken region.

BEREICH	# BEREICH STEIGERWALD
GROSSLAGE	## GROSSLAGE SCHLOSSBERG
BEST VILLAGE	**RÖDELSEE**
BEST VINEYARD AND/OR .... **BEST GROWERS**	☑ **Vineyard** *Küchenmeister* **Grower** *Juliusspital Würzburg* • **Vineyard** *Schwanleite* **Grower** *Johann Ruck*

THE WINE STYLES OF
GERMANY

Note From *Wein* to *Trockenbeerenauslese*, the categories below are in ascending order of quality, and not in alphabetical order, after which different styles are listed. Only the broadest character can be given for each category, since so much depends upon the grape variety. The grape variety can even determine the colour of a wine, although some 90 per cent of the production is white. Most grape varieties likely to be encountered, including all the most important crosses, are included in the ABC of Grape Varieties (*see* pp46–67).

The area of origin also has a strong influence on the type of wine a particular grape variety will produce. A winemaker can either make the most of what nature brings, or fail. For full details on these two aspects, see the regional chapters in which styles are described and growers recommended.

WEIN

The existence of this term without the qualification "Tafel-", indicates a cheap, blended wine made from grapes grown outside the EU.

TAFELWEIN

Table wine may be a blend from different EU countries or wine made in one member country from grapes harvested in another. Known as "Euroblends", these products are sometimes dressed up to look like German wines, but the wine beneath the Gothic writing and German language usually turns out to be an Italian or multi-state blend. This practice, once prolific, now less so, is tantamount to deception and contrary to EU regulations. To be sure of drinking a genuine German product, check that "Tafelwein" is qualified by the all-important "Deutscher". The more successful of these wines are made in years when Germany is overburdened by such a huge yield of basic-quality wines that the wineries turn back the convoy of tankers from Italy and dump the excess production in their bulk-selling Euroblends. The best have a good dose of fresh and flowery Morio-Muskat *Süssreserve*.

🍷 Upon purchase

DEUTSCHER TAFELWEIN

This is the lowest grade of pure German wine, which about 10 years ago represented between 3 and 5 per cent of the country's total production, but now, when added to *Landwein*, it accounts for between 1 and 2 per cent. The quality of production has not dramatically improved at the bottom end of the German wine market and the cheapest QbAs have actually deteriorated in quality – now you know why.

This wine must be 100 per cent German and, if at least 75 per cent comes from any one of the *Tafelwein* regions or sub-regions indicated earlier in the table, the label is allowed to show that name. These regional names are the most specific geographic location permitted, although, prior to the introduction of *Landwein* legislation, it was permissible sometimes to include the name of a *Bereich*.

A *Deutscher Tafelwein* should convey the basic characteristics of the region from which it comes, so a Rhein, for example, might be expected to have a more flowery aroma, but less acidity than a Mosel. In practice, however, the wines are blended from such a hotchpotch of grape varieties, mostly crosses, that all one can hope for is something fresh and fruity in a medium-dry "Germanic" style!

🍷 Upon purchase

LANDWEIN

Landwein is a *Deutscher Tafelwein* from a specific region and the label must contain both terms. The major difference is that the former must be made either as *trocken*, with up to 9 grams per litre residual sugar, or as *halbtrocken*, with a maximum of 18 grams per litre.

Landwein was introduced in 1982 to parallel the French *vin de pays* system, although there are significant differences. The 153 or so *vins de pays* represent a group of wines that aspire to VDQS and, theoretically, AOC status, and it has become one of the most exciting categories of wine in the world (*see* p298). The German category is not a transitional one, it consists of 20 fixed areas that have no hope of achieving anything more illustrious than a "dressed-up" *Tafelwein* status.

Although *Landwein* can never be the same as a *vin de pays*, it could and should serve a very useful, one might even say essential, purpose: to improve the quality of German wines in the QbA (primarily) and QmP categories through selection. By siphoning off the lesser elements of these wines of superior status, it could have improved not only their quality, but the quality of *Landwein* itself. It would be great to think that the biggest producers had taken this category to heart and, through a genuine desire to raise standards all round, reduced yields and used *Landwein* to mop up 15 or 20 per cent of total German production. However, the authorities have instead opted to use this category to increase yields, which is why the country's best winemakers have not been attracted to the notion of *Landwein* as a legitimate means to increase the quality of their other wines, thus there have been no special *Landweins* to attract critics and consumers. The wines have not taken off and, together with *Deutscher Tafelwein*, account for less than 2 per cent of Germany's total production, which has not helped this country's wine reputation one iota.

🍷 Upon purchase

QUALITÄTSWEIN BESTIMMTER ANBAUGEBIETE *or* QBA

A QbA is literally a quality wine from one of the 13 specified regions. These wines may be (and invariably are) chaptalized to increase the alcohol content, and sweetened with *Süssreserve*. The legal minimum potential alcoholic strength of a QbA is merely 5.9 per cent, so it can be understood why the alcohol level is not increased for its own sake, but to give the wine a reasonable shelf-life. The category includes Liebfraumilch and the vast majority of Niersteiner Gutes Domtal, Piesporter Michelsberg, and other generic wines. Most *Grosslage* and *Bereich* wines are sold as QbAs. There is no technical or legal reason why this is so, but it makes marketing sense if more specific wines, such as *Einzellagen* or estate-bottled wines, are sold as prestigious QmPs, as they can demand higher prices. Although a QbA has a lower *Oechsle* than a *Kabinett*, it is a more commercial product and therefore often distinctly sweeter.

🍷 1–3 years (up to 10 years for exceptional wines)

QUALITÄTSWEIN GARANTIERTEN URSPRUNGS *or* QGU

Qualitätswein garantierten Ursprungs is a QbA from a specific district, vineyard or village that has a consistent taste profile associated with its appellation of origin. Such wines are subject to more stringent sensory and analytical requirements than QbAs generally. Some Mosel vintners near the Luxembourg border were the first to make use of QgU status with an Obermosel Elbling Trocken.

🍷 1–3 years

QUALITÄTSWEIN MIT PRÄDIKAT *or* QMP

This means "a quality wine affirmed (predicated) by ripeness" and covers the categories *Kabinett*, *Spätlese*, *Auslese*, *Beerenauslese*, *Eiswein*, and *Trockenbeerenauslese*. The grower must give the authorities prior notice of his intention to harvest for any QmP wine and, whereas a QbA can be blended from grapes gathered from all four corners of an *Anbaugebiet*, providing it carries only the name of that region, the origin of a QmP must be a geographical unit of no greater size than a *Bereich*. A QbA can be chaptalized, but a QmP can not. A certain very highly respected estate owner who believes he could make much better QmP wines if he were allowed to chaptalize them, once made the interesting observation that the French chaptalize their best wines, while Germans chaptalize only their poorest! It is, however, permissible to add *Süssreserve*, although many growers maintain that it is not the traditional method and claim that sweetness is best achieved by stopping the fermentation before all the natural grape sugars have been converted to alcohol. (*See* the various QmP entries.)

KABINETT QMP

The term *Kabinett* once referred to wines that were stored for their rare and exceptional qualities, much as "Reserve" is commonly used today. In this context, it originated at Kloster Eberbach in the Rheingau in the early 18th century. The first documented existence of this word appeared as "Cabernedt" on an invoice from the Elville master cooper Ferdinand Ritter to the Abbot of Eberbach in 1730. Just six years later, another bill in Ritter's hand refers to the "Cabinet-Keller". (The meaning of "Cabinet" as a treasured store found its way into the French language as early as 1547, and is found in German literature in 1677.) *Kabinett* is the first of the predicates in the *Oechsle* scale. Its grapes must reach an *Oechsle* level of 67–85°, the exact minimum varying according to the grape variety concerned and its geographical origin. With no chaptalization, this means that the wine has a minimum potential alcoholic strength of between 8.6 and 11.4 per cent by volume.

Although made from riper (thus sweeter) grapes

than a QbA, a *Kabinett* is usually, though not necessarily, made in a slightly drier style. Some producers resolutely refuse to bolster the wine with *Süssreserve*. This makes *Kabinett* the lightest and, for some, the purest of German wine styles.

🍷 2–5 years (up to 10 years in exceptional cases)

🏆 **Riesling** Mittelrhein: *Didinger* • Rheingau: *Leitz, Künstler* • Mosel: *Dr Loosen, Vollenweider* • Nahe: *Göttelmann, Kruger-Rumpf* • Pfalz: *Koehler-Ruprecht, Mosbacher* • Rheinhessen: *Kühling-Gillot, Manz* • Baden: *Bercher*

SPÄTLESE QMP

Technically, "*Spätlese*" implies that a wine is made from late-harvested grapes, but it is important to remember that "late" is relative to the normal (early) occurrence of a harvest in Germany. As both QbA and *Kabinett* are produced from grapes that have not fully ripened, *Spätlese* can more accurately be seen as the first level of German wine to be produced from ripe grapes. The minimum *Oechsle* level of 76–95°, which would give a minimum potential strength of between 10 and 13 per cent by volume, is hardly an indication of overripe grapes. Although a *Spätlese* is made from grapes that merely have a modest degree of ripeness, the style of wine produced is traditionally sweet, with excellent balancing acidity.

🍷 3–8 years (up to 15 in exceptional cases)

🏆 Mittelrhein: *Didinger, Weingart* • Mosel: *J J Prüm, Fritz Haag, Grans-Fassian, Molitor* • Nahe: *Dr Crusius, Dönnhoff, Emrich-Schönleber* • Rheingau: *Künstler, Leitz* • Rheinhessen: *Gunderloch, Keller, Wittmann* • Pfalz: *A Christmann, Müller-Catoir* • Baden: *Andreas Laible* • Württemberg: *Graf Adelmann, Karl Haidle*

AUSLESE QMP

This predicated wine is made from bunches of grapes left on the vines after the *Spätlese* harvest and as such is truly late-harvested. The regulations state that bunches of fully ripe to very ripe grapes free from disease or damage must be selected for this wine – how this can be achieved by machine-harvesting, which has been permitted

for *Auslese* since the new German wine laws of 1994, is beyond the imagination of every quality-conscious German winemaker I have spoken to.

Auslese must also possess an *Oechsle* reading of 83–105°, the exact minimum varying according to the grape variety concerned and its geographical origin. With no chaptalization, this means that the wine has a minimum potential strength of between 11.1 and 14.5 per cent by volume.

Traditionally this rich and sweet wine is made in exceptional vintages only. There may be some hint of *Edelfäule* (botrytis), especially if the wine comes from a top estate that has a policy of under-declaring its wines, and thus an *Auslese* might be borderline *Beerenauslese*, but even without *Edelfäule*, an *Auslese* is capable of some considerable complexity. It is possible to find totally dry *Auslese* wine and this may or may not be labelled *Auslese trocken*, depending on the whim of the winemaker. *Auslese* is the perfect ripeness level for *trocken* wines, but ideally a different designation should be found for these wines to distinguish them from their sweet counterparts.

🍷 5–20 years

🏆 **Sweet style** Franken: *Horst Sauer* • Rheingau: *Leitz, Dr Weil* • Mittelrhein: *Weingart* • Mosel: *Dr Loosen, Fritz Haag, J J Prüm, Egon Müller, Molitor, Grans Fassian, Knebel* • Nahe: *Dönnhoff, Emrich-Schönleber* • Pfalz: *Bassermann-Jordan, Bürklin-Wolf, A Christmann, Müller-Catoir* • Rheinhessen: *Gunderloch, Keller, Wittmann*

BEERENAUSLESE QMP

A very rare wine made only in truly exceptional circumstances from overripe grapes that have been affected by *Edelfäule*. According to the regulations, each berry should be shrivelled, and be individually selected on a grape-by-grape basis. They must achieve an *Oechsle* level of 110–128°, the exact minimum varying according to the grape variety concerned and its geographical origin. With no chaptalization, this means that the wine has a minimum potential strength of between 15.3 and 18.1 per cent by volume, but only 5.5 per cent need actually

be alcohol, with residual sugar accounting for the rest.

These intensely sweet, full-bodied wines are remarkably complex and elegant. Personally I actually prefer *Beerenauslese* to the technically superior *Trockenbeerenauslese* – it is much easier to drink and be delighted by the former, whereas the *Trockenbeerenauslese* requires concentration and appraisal.

🍷 10–35 years (up to 50 years in exceptional cases)

🏆 Baden: *Andreas Laible* • Mosel: *Molitor, Fritz Haag, J J Prüm, Dr Loosen* • Nahe: *Dönnhoff, Emrich-Schönleber* • Rheingau: *Fritz Allendorf, August Kesseler, Dr Weil* • Rheinhessen: *Keller* • Pfalz: *Müller-Catoir*

EISWEIN QMP

Until 1982 this was a qualification used in conjunction with one of the other predicates. It was previously possible to obtain *Spätlese Eiswein, Auslese Eiswein*, and so on; but *Eiswein* is now a predicate in its own right, with a minimum *Oechsle* level for its grapes equivalent to *Beerenauslese*. An *Eiswein* occurs through extremely unusual circumstances whereby grapes left on the vine to be affected by *Edelfäule* are frozen by frost or snow. They are harvested, rushed to the winery and pressed in their frozen state. Only the water inside the grape actually freezes; this either remains caked inside the press or rises to the top of the vat in the form of ice, which is then skimmed off. What remains available for fermentation is a freeze-condensed juice that is rich, concentrated, and capable of producing wines that are the equivalent of, but totally different from, *Beerenauslese* or *Trockenbeerenauslese*.

This icy harvest can be very late. It seldom occurs before December and often takes place in January of the following year (although it must carry the previous year's vintage). The *Oechsle* level of an *Eiswein*, which must be at least the equivalent of a *Beerenauslese*, can be every bit as high as a *Trockenbeerenauslese*. Its quality is also comparable, although of an entirely different character, due essentially to its far higher acidity

IMMACULATE VINEYARDS, BADEN
Baden's greatest wines are produced around the extinct volcano of Kaiserstuhl, in neat vineyards that are perfect examples of Flurbereinigung.

balance. For me, it is the zippy, racy, tangy vitality of this acidity that makes it superior. The finest *Eiswein* has a finesse unequalled by other botrytis wine. The quality-minded wanted the new law to demand hand-picking for *Eiswein*, which would bring it in line with *Auslese*, *Beerenauslese*, and *Trockenbeerenauslese*, but the industrial bottlers fended this off, making it legal for it to be machine-harvested, although it is impossible to collect authentic *Eiswein* grapes this way.

🍾⏤ 0–50 years

🍷 **Ahr:** *Deutzerhof* • **Mittelrhein:** *Didinger* • **Mosel:** *Molitor, Max Ferd Richter, Karthäuserhof (Ruwer), Egon Müller (Saar)* • **Nahe:** *Schlossgut Diel, Dönnhoff, Emrich-Schönleber, Schäfer-Fröhlich* • **Rheingau:** *Weil* • **Rheinhessen:** *Keller, Manz* • **Franken:** *Fürstlich Castellsches Domäneamt, Horst Sauer* • **Württemberg:** *Aldinger*

TROCKENBEERENAUSLESE QMP *or* TBA

Germany's legendary TBA is produced from heavily botrytized grapes, left on the vine to shrivel into raisin-like berries that must be individually picked. These grapes must reach an *Oechsle* level of 150–154°. With no chaptalization, the wine will have a minimum potential strength of between 21.5 and 22.1 per cent by volume, although only 5.5 per cent need be alcohol, the rest being residual sugar.

Consulting charts, however, does little to highlight the difference in style that exists between a *Beerenauslese* and a TBA, which is every bit as great as that between a *Kabinett* and a *Beerenauslese*. The first noticeable difference is often the colour. Going from *Auslese* to *Beerenauslese* is merely to progress from a light to a rich gold or buttercup yellow. The TBA colour range extends from a raisin khaki through various shades of brown, to dark iodine, with some distinctly odd orange-tawny hues in between. The texture is very viscous and its liqueur-like consistency is just one of many reasons why it is impossible to drink TBA. Taking a good mouthful of TBA is about as easy as swigging cough mixture – one can merely sip it. Its intensity and complexity, and the profundity of its aromas and flavours really must be experienced. It demands attention and provokes discussion, but is not really a wine to enjoy, and is difficult to relax with.

🍾⏤ 12–50 years

🍷 **Mittelrhein:** *Weingart* • **Mosel:** *Fritz Haag, Egon Müller (Saar), Heymann-Löwenstein, Molitor* • **Nahe:** *Dönnhoff, Emrich-Schönleber* • **Rheingau:** *Weil* • **Franken:** *Horst Sauer, Staatlicher Hofkeller Würzburg* • **Rheinhessen:** *Gunderloch, Keller* • **Pfalz:** *A Christmann, Ökonomierat Rebholz, Müller-Catoir*

RED WINE

Even members of the wine trade find it surprising that almost 37 per cent of German vineyards are planted with black grape varieties. The most commonly encountered German red wines are Spätburgunder (Pinot Noir), Dornfelder, and Regent, and many of the best are sold simply as *Qualitätswein* or even *Tafelwein* to allow producers a greater freedom of expression. Dornfelder is grown mostly in the Pfalz, Rheinhessen, and Württemberg, and producers have developed three basic styles: *barrique*-aged for serious drinking; early-drinking Beaujolais-style; and an off-dry grapey style. Regent is a relatively new hybrid ([Silvaner x Müller-Thurgau] x Chambourcin), grown for its resistance to rot and mildew, and though mainly produced in a quaffing style, it can also yield wines with serious quality aspirations. Spätburgunder (Pinot Noir) is

the widest-planted black grape variety in the country, and over the past 15–20 years some talented winemakers have produced truly beautiful, silky-smooth, well-coloured red wines from it. A few growers have been almost as successful with with Frühburgunder, a lighter mutation of Pinot Noir that has evolved in and around the village of Bürgstadt in the Franken, where it has been grown for at least 150 years. The Frühburgunder nearly became extinct in the 1970s because it was considered uneconomical due to its low and variable yields, but dedicated growers such as Rudolf Fürst have coaxed exquisitely elegant wines from it by lowering yields. Contrary to some international misconceptions, Germany has clearly demonstrated that it is a world-class producer of quality Pinot Noir. The only question that remains is whether German producers can put them on the shelf at generally affordable prices.

🍾⏤ 2–8 years

🍷 **Spätburgunder Ahr:** *Meyer-Näkel, Deutzerhof, Stodden* • **Pfalz:** *Friedrich Becker, Bernhart, A Christmann, Philip Kuhn* (including Sangiovese but especially Frühburgunder) • **Baden:** *Huber, Duijn, Johner* • **Rheingau:** *August Kesseler*

Frühburgunder Franken: *Fürst*

Dornfelder Pfalz: *Knipser*

SEKT *or* SPARKLING WINE

The common method of production for this anonymous sparkling wine is *cuve close*, although when the industry was born in the 1820s, all *Sekt* was bottle-fermented. Today, not only is it an industrialized product, but most is made from grapes grown outside Germany, usually from Italy or the Loire Valley in France. Furthermore, until 1986, this Euro-fizz could be called *Deutscher Sekt*. This was because *Sekt* was considered to be a method of production and, so it was argued, if production took place in Germany, it must logically be German or *Deutscher Sekt*. As the vast majority of Germany's huge *Sekt* industry used imported grapes, juice, or wine (and still does), this was more a matter of lobbying by those with vested interests, than logic. However, much of the effort to dispose of this false logic came from honourable sectors within the German wine industry itself. Common sense finally won through on 1 September 1986, when an EU directive brought this appellation into line with the general philosophy of the EU's wine regime. There has been a noticeable upsurge in the numbers of what are now genuine German *Deutscher Sekt*, although *Sekt* plain and simple still dominates the market.

DEUTSCHER SEKT

SEKT SWEETNESS CHART	
SWEETNESS RATING	RESIDUAL SUGAR (GRAMS PER LITRE)
Naturherb or Brut Nature	0–<3
Extra Herb or Extra Brut	0–<6
Herb or Brut	0–<12
Extra Trocken or Extra Dry	12–<17
Trocken*	17–<32
Halbtrocken*	32–<50
Mild, Süss, Drux, Doux, or Sweet	50>

*Not to be confused with still-wine limits, which are no more than 9 grams per litre for trocken *and 18 grams per litre for* halbtrocken.

Deutscher Sekt must be made from 100 per cent German grapes. The best are usually Riesling-based and do not allow autolysis (the enzymatic

breakdown of yeast) to interfere with the pure varietal aroma and flavour of the wine, characteristics that are held in the greatest esteem by its producers and the vast majority of its German consumers. Try Max Ferdinand. The best *Sekt* I have ever tasted was Wegeler-Deinhard Bernkasteler Doctor, but it is rarely produced and very expensive. *See also* Deutscher Qualitätsschaumwein bestimmter Anbaugebiete.

🍾⏤ 3–8 years

DEUTSCHER SEKT BESTIMMTER ANBAUGEBIETE *or* DEUTSCHER SEKT BA

See Deutscher Qualitätsschaumwein bestimmter Anbaugebiete

DEUTSCHER QUALITÄTSSCHAUMWEIN BESTIMMTER ANBAUGEBIETE *or* DEUTSCHER QUALITÄTSSCHAUMWEIN BA

This *Deutscher Sekt* must be made entirely from grapes grown within one specified wine region and may come from a smaller geographical unit, such as a *Bereich, Grosslage*, or *Einzellage*, providing that at least 85 per cent of the grapes used come from the area indicated. An alternative appellation is *Deutscher Sekt bestimmter Anbaugebiete*.

🍾⏤ 3–8 years

TROCKEN/ HALBTROCKEN WINES

Wines of the *trocken* category must not contain more than 9 grams per litre of residual sugar, or 18 grams for the off-dry *halbtrocken* category. National demand for drier style wines really started to take off in the early 1990s and now accounts for more than 50 per cent of all German wines produced, but some of these can be thin, weak, and disappointing. There are some terrific *trocken* wines, but to be any good, *trocken* really has to be made from grapes of Auslese ripeness. Only then does it have the body, structure, and weight that most dry wine drinkers are used to. The VDP's *Grosses Gewächs* classification considers *Spätlese trocken* ripe enough, but some of the wines released under this banner do not really meet the standard expected from a *grand cru* designation. The former practice of quality-conscious growers to make and sell trocken offerings as Deutscher Tafelwein has more or less ceased except for one or two producers of red wines.

🍾⏤ 2–6 years

🍷 **Riesling Trocken Baden:** *Dr Heger, Bercher* • **Nahe:** *Emrich-Schönleber, Schlossgut Diel* • **Pfalz:** *Bürklin-Wolf, A Christmann* • **Rheingau:** *August Eser, Breuer* • **Rheinhessen:** *Keller, Wittmann*

Riesling Halbtrocken Mittelrhein: *Matthias Müller, Weingart* • **Mosel:** *Knebel, Molitor* • **Nahe:** *Emrich-Schönleber, Kruger-Rumpf* • **Rheingau:** *Leitz, Künstler*

Grau- and Weissburgunder Trocken Baden: *Bercher, Huber, Johner, R u C Schneider* • **Franken:** *Fürst* • **Pfalz:** *Münzberg, Dr Wehrheim, Ökonomierat Rebholz*

Gewürztraminer Trocken Pfalz: *Bernhart*

Silvaner Trocken Franken: *Horst Sauer*

THE AHR

The Ahr is red-wine country. It may be surprising that black grapes can grow here at all, considering how northerly the Ahr is. Yet the Spätburgunder accounts for more than 60 per cent of this region's vines, and its best growers consistently produce some of Germany's greatest reds.

SPÄTBURGUNDER CAN GROW HERE because the Ahr is a deep valley – protected by the Hohe Eifel hills – that captures sunlight in its rocky, slaty soil. The cumulative effect of the heat allows black grapes to ripen, but until recently few growers took advantage of these favourable conditions. Consequently the Ahr became known for mild, dilute red wines, popular with social clubs on weekend outings.

A change in winemaking philosophy, however, has propelled a good number of the region's Spätburgunders into contention for Germany's red wine crown. Unfortunately quantities will always be too small to quench the international wine

THE REGION AT A GLANCE

Area under vine
558 ha or 1,379 acres (increasing)

Average yield
80 hl/ha (decreasing)

Red wine
71%

White wine
13% (decreasing)

Rotling
16%

Most important grape varieties
61% Spätburgunder, 8% Portugieser, 8% Riesling, 23% others

Infrastructure
Bereich 1; *Grosslage* 1; *Einzellagen* 43

Note: The vineyards of the Ahr straddle 11 *Gemeinden* (communes), the names of which may appear on the label.

FACTORS AFFECTING TASTE AND QUALITY

LOCATION
The Ahr is one of Germany's northernmost wine regions, with vineyards extending only 24 km (15 miles) along the lower reaches of the Ahr River, 10 kilometres (6 miles) south of Bonn.

CLIMATE
Despite its northerly position, the deep Ahr valley is sheltered by the surrounding Hohe Eifel hills and maintains temperatures that are favourable for viticulture, with a greenhouse-like climate on some of the steeper sites.

ASPECT
The best vineyards of the Ahr are sited on steeply terraced rocky valley sides, with higher yielding vineyards on gentler slopes in the broader, eastern end of the valley.

SOIL
Deep, rich, loess soils in the lower Ahr valley (eastern); slate, volcanic stone, and rocky soils in the middle Ahr; and basalt and slaty stone soils with some tufa in the upper Ahr valley (western).

VITICULTURE AND VINIFICATION
Three-quarters of vineyards are worked by part-time farmers, whose wines are sold by cooperatives. Most vines are cultivated under labour-intensive conditions, hence the wines are expensive to produce. Nearly all of the region's wine is consumed locally or sold to tourists. Pure varietal Weissherbst, usually Spätburgunder, is a speciality, but in terms of pure quality, this easy-drinking rosé has given way to fully red styles. As Riesling vines diminish, the Spätburgunder is taking over as the classic Ahr variety.

GRAPE VARIETIES
Primary variety: Spätburgunder
Secondary varieties: Dornfelder, Frühburgunder, Kerner, Müller-Thurgau, Portugieser, Riesling

community's thirst, thus readers are unlikely to find the Ahr's best reds in their local wine shop. These remain the preserve of knowledgeable consumers willing to put on walking boots and take a trip to the Ahr to buy them direct. Not that the wines are cheap. The likes of Meyer-Näkel, Deutzerhof, and Kreuzberg produce some of Germany's greatest Pinot Noirs, and the wines are priced accordingly. The region takes the name of the river that flows parallel to, and north of, the lower Mosel and joins the Rhine just south of Bonn. It is one of the

THE AHR, *see also p405*
The most northerly of Germany's wine-producing regions prior to reunification, the Ahr is made up of districts close to the Ahr River, a tributary of the Rhine.

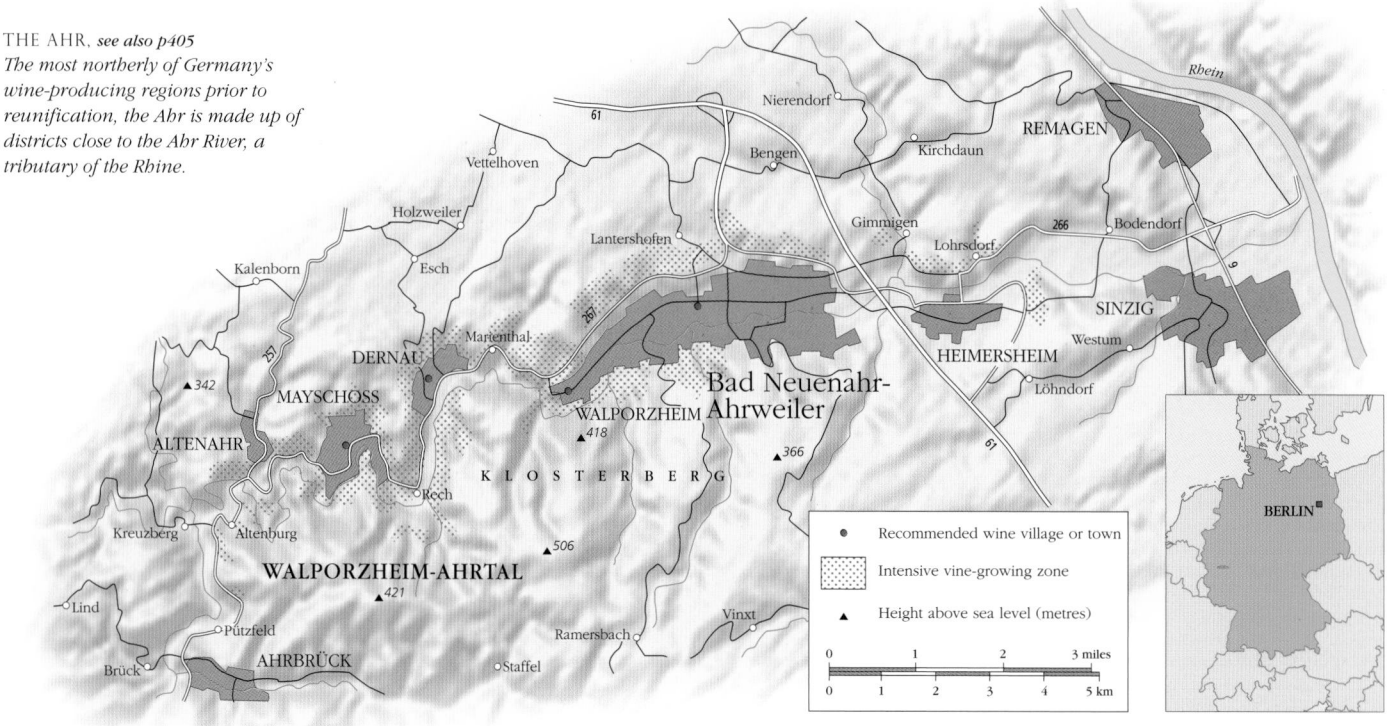

Recommended wine village or town

Intensive vine-growing zone

▲ Height above sea level (metres)

0   1   2   3 miles

0 1 2 3 4 5 km

world's most beautiful and serene viticultural landscapes, as anyone who has ever travelled along the *Rotweinwanderweg*, the Ahr's red-wine route, will verify.

RIESLING

Riesling grapes can produce fresh, racy, aromatic wines here, but over the years have given way to black grapes and now comprise just under 8 per cent of the region's vines. Given the healthy prices that Ahr reds command, Riesling is unlikely to regain its share.

HARVESTING IN THE AHR
These steeply sloping vineyards at Marienthal are planted with the black grape varieties Spätburgunder and a little Portugieser, and 80 per cent of the region's wines are, in fact, red.

QUALITY REQUIREMENTS AND AVERAGE QMP PRODUCTION

AHR'S MINIMUM OECHSLE	QUALITY CATEGORY	HARVEST BREAKDOWN
44°	Deutscher Tafelwein	0.5%
47°	Landwein	0.5%
50–60°	* QbA	80%
67–73°	* Kabinett	12.5%
76–85°	* Spätlese	6%
83–88°	* Auslese	0.5%
110°	Beerenauslese	–
110°	Eiswein	–
150°	Trockenbeerenauslese	–

* Minimum Oechsle levels vary according to grape variety; those that have a naturally lower sugar content may qualify at a correspondingly lower level.

THE APPELLATIONS OF
THE AHR

BEREICH WALPORZHEIM-AHRTAL

This is the only *Bereich* in the Ahr region. Walporzheim-Ahrtal produces many kinds of wines, from light, ruby-coloured Portugiesers to Dornfelders with great intensity, but the real class is provided by some of Germany's finest Spätburgunders. Those areas in the *Bereich* with slaty soil give a vigorous wine, while those situated on rich loess soil produce a softer style.

At one time, the wines used to be fairly sweet, but the trend nowadays is for drier wines. The Weissherbst is a soft and fruity wine, and the

CERTIFIED ORGANIC PRODUCERS

Christoph Bäcker (Mayschoss)
Ursula & Christoph Richter (Ahrweiler)

Riesling fresh and racy. Try the Rotwein with *Rauchfleisch* (smoked meats), the Weissherbst with *Schinken* (ham), and the Riesling with trout or with the salmon that has recently been reintroduced and is now thriving in the river.

GROSSLAGE KLOSTERBERG

The only *Grosslage* in the *Bereich*, the area of Klosterberg is thus identical to that of Walporzheim-Ahrtal.

AHRWEILER

⋀✓ **Vineyard** *Silberberg* **Grower** *Kreuzberg* (red) • **Vineyard** *Rosealnth* **Growers** *J J Adeneur* (red), *Jean Stodden* (red)

ALTENAHR

⋀✓ **Vineyard** *Eck* **Grower** *Deutzerhof* (red and white)

DERNAU

⋀✓ **Vineyard** *Pfarrwingert* **Growers** *Kreuzberg* (red), *Meyer-Näkel* (red)

HEIMERSHEIM

⋀✓ **Vineyard** *Landskrone* **Growers** *Deutzerhof* (red), *Nelles* (red) • **Vineyard** *Burggarten*

Grower *Weingut Burggarten* (red)

MAYSCHOSS

⋀✓ **Vineyard** *Moenchberg* **Grower** *Deutzerhof* (red)

NEUENAHR

⋀✓ **Vineyard** *Schieferlay* **Grower** *Kreuzberg* (red) • **Vineyard** *Sonnenberg* **Growers** *J J Adeneuer* (red), *Kreuzberg* (red), *Meyer-Näkel* (red), *Jean Stodden* (red)

RECH

⋀✓ **Vineyard** *Herrenberg* **Grower** *Jean Stodden* (red)

WALPORZHEIM

⋀✓ **Vineyard** *Gärkammer* **Grower** *J J Adeneuer* (red) • **Vineyard** *Kräuterberg* **Grower** *Meyer-Näkel* (red) • **Premium red wine blends Growers** *J J Adeneuer* (No.1), *Deutzerhof* (Melchior, Grand Duc), *H J Kreuzberg* (Devonschiefer), *Peter Kriechel* (Jubilus Goldkapsel), *Meyer-Näkel* (S, Goldkapsel), *Nelles* (B48, B52, B59), *Jean Stodden* (Alte Reben), *Winzergenossenschaft Mayschoss-Altenahr* (Ponsart, Pinot Noir "R")

THE MITTELRHEIN

Possessing precariously perched vineyards that have declined by almost 50 per cent since 1965, the Mittelrhein is a region that is all too often overlooked by serious wine drinkers. Yet it offers some of Germany's finest and most underrated wines.

IT WAS FROM THE MITTELRHEIN that the Celts spread out across Europe. With such ancient roots, it is not surprising that this region is so steeped in Germany's mythical history. It was at the Drachenfels in Königswinter, for instance, that Siegfried slew the dragon, and, in fact, the vineyards in this area produce a red Spätburgunder wine known as Drachenblut, or "Dragon's blood". The Rhine River, associated with many myths and fables, flows past numerous medieval castles and towers, and rushes through the Rhine Gorge, past the famous "Loreley" rock on to which the siren lured many ships to their final and fatal destination.

SHRINKING VINEYARDS, GROWING TOURISM

The difficulty of working the steepest of the Mittelrhein's vineyard slopes has encouraged many of the workforce to forsake them and seek higher wages for easier work in Germany's industrial cities. This has led to a decline in the number of vineyards, but the Mittelrhein is by no means deserted, as its dramatic beauty makes it one of Germany's favourite tourist spots. In this region, where many tiny tributaries provide valley vineyards of a superior natural aspect for

QUALITY REQUIREMENTS AND AVERAGE QMP PRODUCTION

MITTELRHEIN'S MINIMUM	QUALITY CATEGORY	HARVEST OECHSLE
44°	Deutscher Tafelwein	1%
47°	Landwein	1%
50–60°	* QbA	68%
67–73°	* Kabinett	18%
76–85°	* Spätlese	4%
83–88°	* Auslese	2%
110°	Beerenauslese	2%
110°	Eiswein	2%
150°	Trockenbeerenauslese	2%

* Minimum Oechsle levels vary according to grape variety; those that have a naturally lower sugar content may quality at a correspondingly lower level.

THE MITTELRHEIN, *see also p405*
North and south of Koblenz, the Mittelrhein's vineyards run up towards the steep, rocky escarpments that closely border this stretch of the Rhine.

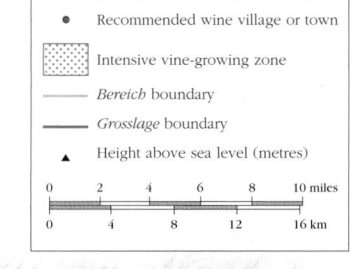

- ● Recommended wine village or town
- ▦ Intensive vine-growing zone
- — *Bereich* boundary
- ━ *Grosslage* boundary
- ▲ Height above sea level (metres)

0   2   4   6   8   10 miles
0   4   8   12   16 km

FACTORS AFFECTING TASTE AND QUALITY

LOCATION
A 160-kilometre (100-mile) stretch of the Rhine Valley between Bonn and Bingen.

CLIMATE
The benefits of the sun are maximized by the steep valley sides that afford protection from cold winds. The river acts as a heat-reservoir, tempering the low night and winter temperatures.

ASPECT
Vines on the steep valley sides benefit from any available sunshine. North of Koblenz the vineyards are on the east bank, while to the south most are on the west bank.

SOIL
Primarily clayish slaty soil and greywacke. There are also small, scattered deposits of loess and,

towards the north, some vineyards are of volcanic origin.

VITICULTURE AND VINIFICATION
Virtually all remaining vineyards have been *flurbereinigt* (modernized by abolishing terraces) and many slopes are a patchwork of steep vineyards. With a high proportion of Riesling giving an average yield that is very low by German standards, quality is generally high. About 80 per cent of growers are part-time and a quarter of the harvest is processed by the coops using normal white-wine techniques.

GRAPE VARIETIES
Primary variety: Riesling
Secondary varieties: Bacchus, Kerner, Müller-Thurgau, Optima, Portugieser, Scheurebe, Silvaner, Spätburgunder

THE REGION AT A GLANCE

Area under vine
461 ha or 1,139 acres (decreasing)

Average yield
71 hl/ha (increasing)

Red wine
10%

White wine
84% (decreasing)

Rotling
6%

Most important grape varieties
67% Riesling (decreasing), 9% Spätburgunder, 6% Müller-Thurgau (decreasing), 18% others

Infrastructure
Bereiche 2; *Grosslagen* 11; *Einzellagen* 111

Note The vineyards of the Mittelrhein straddle 59 *Gemeinden* (communes), the names of which may appear on the label.

MITTELRHEIN VINEYARDS
The region's weekend winegrowers have plenty to do to maintain these slopes, which include some of the steepest vineyards in Germany.

viticulture than most others on the Rhine, there is much potential for producing high-quality Riesling on its slaty soil. There are a few excellent estates making exciting wines that display a vigorous varietal character, intense flavour, and splendid acidity. The acidity, so prized that *Sekt* houses try to buy as much of the lesser quality and surplus wines as possible, makes the rare occurrence of *Auslese* and higher QmP wines something special.

THE APPELLATIONS OF

THE MITTELRHEIN

BEREICH LORELEY

This new *Bereich* is formed from the two former *Bereiche* of Bacharach (the very small but heavily cultivated southern end of the Mittelrhein, restricted to the west bank and named after the beautiful old market town of Bacharach) and Rheinburgengau (a very large, successful area bordering the Rheingau).

GROSSLAGE BURG HAMMERSTEIN

Starting south of Königswinter and stretching along the right bank, almost as far as Koblenz, this long, scenic *Grosslage* comprises scattered vineyards, with the only unbroken stretch of fine Riesling vines at Hammerstein itself.

GROSSLAGE BURG RHEINFELS

A village-sized *Grosslage* on the west bank, with its best vineyards situated on the southeast-facing banks of a small tributary at Werlau, an *Ortsteil* of Sankt Goar.

GROSSLAGE GEDEONSECK

A top-performing *Grosslage* where a bend in the river allows for good east- and south-facing vineyards, the best of which are situated within an *Ortsteil* of Boppard.

BOPPARD HAMM

✓ **Vineyard** *Engelstein* **Growers** *Matthias Müller, Weingart* • **Vineyard** *Feuerlay* **Growers** *Didinger* (Oberspay), *Matthias Müller, Weingart* (Spay) • **Vineyard** *Mandelstein* **Growers** *Matthias Müller, Weingart* (Spay) • **Vineyard** *Ohlenberg* **Growers** *Weingart* (Spay), *Matthias Müller*

GROSSLAGE HERRENBERG

The southeastern end of this *Grosslage* abuts the western edge of the Rheingau, but all of the *Einzellagen* are located in the north, between

Dörscheid and Kaub, just downstream from Bacharach on the opposite bank.

GROSSLAGE LAHNTAL

There are no outstanding villages, vineyards, estates, or growers in this *Grosslage*, which has been in a state of decline for years.

GROSSLAGE LORELEYFELSEN

Some fine Riesling vineyards set amid dramatic scenery that includes the famous "Loreley" rock.

GROSSLAGE MARKSBURG

The vineyards on the Mittelrhein side of Koblenz have mostly been overtaken by urban sprawl, but one of the best remains in the *Ortsteil* of Ehrenbreitstein. The others in this *Grosslage* are located to the north and south of the city. There is a natural similarity between these wines and those of the lower Mosel.

GROSSLAGE PETERSBERG

The same area as *Bereich* Siebengebirge. There are no outstanding villages, vineyards, estates, or growers, although good wines are made in the Drachenfels vineyard of Königswinter.

GROSSLAGE SCHLOSS REICHENSTEIN

There are no outstanding villages, vineyards, estates, or growers in this *Grosslage* that faces the Rheingau across the river and neighbours the Nahe to the south, but good wines are made in the village of Niederheimbach, especially the vineyard of Froher Weingarten.

GROSSLAGE SCHLOSS SCHÖNBURG

The reputation of the fine Riesling vineyards in this *Grosslage* has been laid to rest.

GROSSLAGE SCHLOSS STAHLECK

There is perhaps more potential here, in the south-facing vineyards that belong to tributaries of

the Rhine, than in the east-facing vineyards on the great river itself. Yet it is wines from Hahn and Posten at Bacharach, with both easterly and southerly aspects, that excel.

BACHARACH

✓ **Vineyard** *Hahn* **Grower** *Toni Jost-Hahnenhof* • **Vineyard** *Kloster Fürstental* **Grower** *Ratzenberger* • **Vineyard** *Wolfshöhle* **Grower** *Ratzenberger*

SIEBENGEBIRG

A single-*Grosslage Bereich* covering the vineyards of Königswinter Siebengebirge.

CERTIFIED ORGANIC PRODUCERS

Dr Randolph Kauer (Bacharach-Steeg)
Edelfaul (Manubach); Gerd Lang (Rodenbach)
Hof Wildeck (Urbar); Joachim Scherer (Manubach)

MOSEL

The greatest Rieslings grown along the Mosel River have a legendary acidity that can only be relieved through a knife-edge balance of sweetness. Unlike in the warmer Rhine regions, the Riesling grape is at its best here in hot vintages.

IF ANY GRAPE IS INTRINSICALLY RACY, it is the vigorous Riesling; and if any region can be singled out for emphasizing this raciness, it must be Mosel. Grown on the steepest, slaty slopes, Riesling combines a relatively high acidity with an irrefutable suggestion of lightness and elegance. But a fine Mosel is never thin, as these wines have surprisingly high extract levels that, together with the acidity, intensify the characteristics of flavour.

In even the hottest vintages, the best *Auslesen* and *Beerenauslesen* remain racy, while those from the other regions appear fat and overblown by contrast. Even the most modest wines retain a freshness and vitality in sunblessed years that will be lacking in those from the warmer regions.

THE GOOD DOCTOR

There are many great vineyards in this region, but none so famous as the legendary Bernkasteler Doctor, which produces Germany's most expensive wine. The story is that Boemund II, the Archbishop of Trier in the 14th century, was so ill that his doctors could do nothing for him. A winegrower from Bernkastel recommended the restorative powers of the wine produced from his vineyard. Boemund drank some, made a miraculous recovery, and declared "The best doctor grows in this vineyard in Bernkastel". More recently, the Doctor vineyard has been the subject of a lengthy court case. The original vineyard comprised 1.35 hectares (3.33 acres), but in 1971 the new German wine law proscribed a ban on all vineyards of less than 5 hectares (12.33 acres). The authorities planned to expand the Doctor almost equally to the west (into the *Einzellage* Graben) and to the east

(into an area classified merely as Grosslage Badstube). This enabled 13 different producers to make and sell Bernkasteler Doctor, whereas only three owners of the true Doctor vineyards had existed before. It is not surprising that the owners of the original Doctor vineyard felt strong enough to take their objections to court. The case continued until finally, in 1984, after an

THE BERNKASTELER DOCTOR VINEYARD TODAY
The red outline encloses the area of the original vineyard (yellow) and those areas finally adopted in 1984 (light and mid-green). The area excluded in 1984 is pink.

FACTORS AFFECTING TASTE AND QUALITY

LOCATION
This region follows the Mosel river, as it meanders for 250 km (150 miles) from Koblenz south to the border with France. It includes the vineyards of two major tributaries, the Saar and the Ruwer, which flow into the Mosel from the south.

CLIMATE
The moderate rainfall and rapid warming of the steep and protective valley sides provide ideal conditions for vines to flourish and produce grapes with high acidity, even when late harvested.

ASPECT
The Mosel has more loops and bends than any other German river, and most of the vines grow at an altitude of between 100 and 350 metres (330 and 1,150 feet). This valley provides slopes of every aspect, with many that are spectacularly steep, boasting gradients as high as 70 degrees.

SOIL
Soils in this region vary from sandstone, shell-limestone, and red marl in the upper Mosel, to Devon slate in the middle Mosel, Saar, and Ruwer, and clay slate and grey stony soil in the lower Mosel. Alluvial sand and gravel soils are also found in lower sites. Classic Riesling sites are slaty; the Elbling prefers limestone.

VITICULTURE AND VINIFICATION
Many of the greatest German wines come from the highest and steepest vineyards in this area, most of which are situated in the upper reaches of the valleys. In these notoriously difficult sites, each vine has to be tied to its own eight-foot wooden stake, and the slate soil that is washed down to the bottom of the slope by the winter rains has to be carried back up every year. Tending the vines is thus unavoidably labour-intensive and this, combined with a longer winter than experienced elsewhere in Germany, accounts for the higher prices asked for fine Mosel wines. The early onset of winter causes fermentation to take place at cool temperatures, and when the wines are bottled early they retain more carbonic gas, which emphasizes the crisp, steely character of the Riesling grape. There are about 13,750 growers owning very small plots of land. The regional cooperative in Bernkastel-Kues alone processes one-fifth of the entire crop, but much is sold on to the commercial wineries, which sell 60 per cent of the total wine produced, whereas the cooperatives sell just 13 per cent and this figure is declining. On the other hand, growers and estates account for 28 per cent of sales, and are increasing their share.

GRAPE VARIETIES
Primary variety: Riesling
Secondary varieties: Auxerrois, Bacchus, Elbling, Kerner, Müller-Thurgau, Optima, Ortega, Spätburgunder

BERNKASTEL FROM THE DOCTOR VINEYARD
Bernkasteler Doctor wines are some of Germany's most prestigious and expensive. Bernkastel lies in the Badstube Grosslage.

QUALITY REQUIREMENTS AND AVERAGE QMP PRODUCTION

MOSEL'S MINIMUM OECHSLE	QUALITY CATEGORY	HARVEST BREAKDOWN
44°	Deutscher Tafelwein	1%
47°	Landwein	1%
50–60°	* QbA	72%
67–73°	* Kabinett	18%
76–85°	* Spätlese	4%
83–88°	* Auslese	1%
110°	Beerenauslese	1%
110°	Eiswein	1%
150°	Trockenbeerenauslese	1%

* Minimum Oechsle levels vary according to grape variety; those that have a naturally lower sugar content may qualify at a correspondingly lower level.

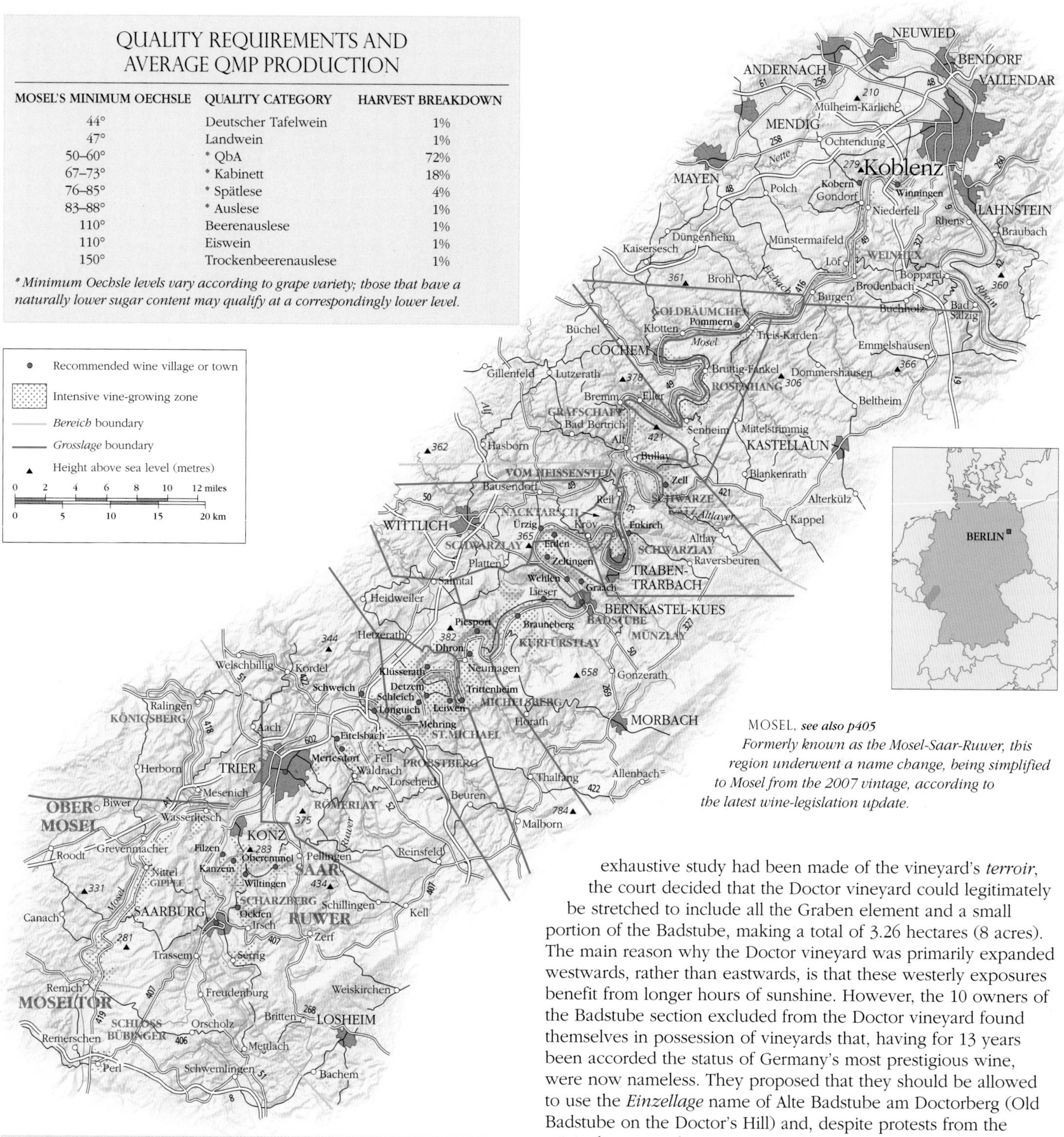

Legend

- ● Recommended wine village or town
- ▦ Intensive vine-growing zone
- ─ Bereich boundary
- ━ Grosslage boundary
- ▲ Height above sea level (metres)

0 2 4 6 8 10 12 miles
0 5 10 15 20 km

MOSEL, *see also p405*

Formerly known as the Mosel-Saar-Ruwer, this region underwent a name change, being simplified to Mosel from the 2007 vintage, according to the latest wine-legislation update.

exhaustive study had been made of the vineyard's *terroir*, the court decided that the Doctor vineyard could legitimately be stretched to include all the Graben element and a small portion of the Badstube, making a total of 3.26 hectares (8 acres). The main reason why the Doctor vineyard was primarily expanded westwards, rather than eastwards, is that these westerly exposures benefit from longer hours of sunshine. However, the 10 owners of the Badstube section excluded from the Doctor vineyard found themselves in possession of vineyards that, having for 13 years been accorded the status of Germany's most prestigious wine, were now nameless. They proposed that they should be allowed to use the *Einzellage* name of Alte Badstube am Doctorberg (Old Badstube on the Doctor's Hill) and, despite protests from the original owners, this was accepted by officials.

Not only was the expansion of the *terroir* open to question in this case, but the general directive that a single vineyard should be of a stipulated minimum size was sheer folly and illustrative of one of the fundamental flaws in the 1971 German wine law (*see also* p406). It would have been much more effective to have amended the law to allow any genuine vineyard name the right to appear in small print on a label, and to establish a register of perhaps 100 or more (but certainly not 2,600) truly great vineyards that would have the right to appear on the label in a dominant size of print with an appropriate designation of elevated status. If the greatest German wines could trade on a reputation similar to that of the finest wines of France, the Mosel would probably have more "grands crus" than any other region, although the Rheingau would give it a good fight.

THE REGION AT A GLANCE

Area under vine
9,034 ha or 22,323 acres (decreasing)

Average yield
99.5 hl/ha (increasing)

Red wine
6%

White wine
91% (decreasing)

Rotling
3%

Most important grape varieties
60% Riesling (increasing), 14% Müller-Thurgau (decreasing), 6% Elbling (decreasing), 4% Kerner (decreasing), 16% others

Infrastructure
Bereiche 6; *Grosslagen* 19; *Einzellagen* 523

Note The vineyards of Mosel straddle 192 *Gemeinden* (communes), the names of which may appear on the label.

THE APPELLATIONS OF

MOSEL

BEREICH BERNKASTEL

This covers the entire Mittelmosel, encompassing all of the river's most famous villages and towns, and most of its best vineyards. Much wine is sold under this *Bereich* appellation, but unfortunately most of it is disappointing.

GROSSLAGE BADSTUBE

Badstube must be the grandest *Grosslage* in Germany encompassing as it does the most famous of all *Einzellagen*, the Doctor vineyard, as well as the almost equally well-known Lay, the superb Graben, and six other good sites. The quality of even the surplus wine from such great vineyards is so high that it is practically impossible to find poor Badstube, and the *Grosslage* wines are especially good in relatively poor years when grapes from the Doctor vineyard fail to achieve *Kabinett* level and are included in these blends.

GROSSLAGE BLEND

✓ **Grower** *Wwe Dr H Thanisch-Erben Thanisch*

BERNKASTEL

✓ **Vineyard** *Doctor* **Growers** *Wwe Dr H Thanisch-Erben Thanisch, Wegeler-Gutshaus Bernkastel* • **Vineyard** *Alte Badstube am Doctorberg* **Grower** *Dr Pauly-Bergweiler/ Peter Nicolay*

GROSSLAGE KURFÜRSTLAY

This includes the lesser wines of Bernkastel and the superior wines of Brauneberg, the best of which come from the fabulous vineyards on the south-southeast-facing Juffer hill that rises from the river opposite the village of Brauneberg. Its wines are remarkably racy considering their exceptional fullness of body and some prefer them to those of the Doctor, although I find it impossible to choose, and delight in their differences.

BRAUNEBERG

✓ **Vineyard** *Juffer* **Growers** *Fritz Haag-Dusemonder Hof, Max Ferd Richter* • **Vineyard** *Juffer Sonnenuhr* **Growers** *Fritz Haag, Reichsgraf von Kesselstatt, Schloss Lieser, Max Ferd Richter, Paulinshof* • **Vineyard** *Kammer* **Grower** *Paulinshof* • **Vineyard** *Klostergarten* **Grower** *Markus Molitor* (red) • **Vineyard** *Mandelgraben* **Grower** *Markus Molitor*

LIESER

✓ **Vineyard** *Niederberg Helden* **Growers** *Sybille Kuntz, Schloss Lieser*

GROSSLAGE MICHELSBERG

There are some great wines made in the village of Piesport in the Michelsberg *Grosslage*, but the thin, characterless Piesporter Michelsberg is not one of them. It is a *Grosslage* wine that comes not from steep, slaty slopes such as Goldtröpfchen or Domherr, but from very high-yielding, flat, alluvial land. No great grower would contemplate cultivating such fertile soil, the low-quality wines of which have unfairly debased the Piesporter village name to such a degree that its wine in the trade has become known as Piss-pot. The great wines of Trittenheim have not had to suffer from such great indignities, and the village of Dhron especially should not be forgotten for its produce.

PIESPORT

✓ **Vineyard** *Domherr* **Growers** *Kurt Hain, Reinhold Haart* • **Vineyard** *Goldtröpfchen* **Growers** *Reinhold Haart, Kurt Hain, Grans-Fassian, St Urbans-Hof, Reichsgraf von Kesselstatt*

TRITTENHEIM

✓ **Vineyard** *Apotheke* **Growers** *Ernst Clüsserath, Ansgar Clüsserath, Clüsserath-Eifel, Clüsserath-Weiler, Grans-Fassian, Josef Rosch* • **Vineyard** *Altärchen* **Grower** *Franz-Josef Eifel*

GROSSLAGE MÜNZLAY

The three villages in this *Grosslage* may lack the fame of Bernkastel and the popularity of Piesport, but they possess truly superb Mosel vineyards and boast an incomparable number of great growers and estates.

GRAACH

✓ **Vineyard** *Domprobst* **Growers** *Kees-Kieren, S A Prüm, Willi Schaefer* • **Vineyard** *Himmelreich* **Growers** *Kees-Kieren, Markus Molitor* (red), *J J Prüm, Max Ferd Richter, Willi Schaefer* • **Vineyard** *Josephshof* **Grower** *Reichsgraf von Kesselstatt* • **Vineyard** *Josephshof* **Grower** *Reichsgraf von Kesselstatt*

WEHLEN

✓ **Vineyard** *Sonnenuhr* **Growers** *Dr Loosen, J J Prüm, Wegeler-Gutshaus Bernkastel, Markus Molitor*

ZELTINGEN

✓ **Vineyard** *Himmelreich* **Grower** *Selbach-Oster* • **Vineyard** *Sonnenuhr* **Growers** *Markus Molitor, Selbach-Oster*

GROSSLAGE NACKTARSCH

The labels of this *Grosslage* are collectors' items because of the naked bottoms featured on many of them – reflecting not only the name but also the quality of most of the wine.

GROSSLAGE PROBSTBERG

There are no outstanding villages or vineyards, except at Longuic and Sweich, which face each other at the confluence with the Ruwer at Eitelsbach.

GROSSLAGE ST MICHAEL

Popular but generally overrated wines come from Klüsserath these days, although the wonderful wines of Kirsten and Franz-Josef Regnery are bringing back the glory days. Detzem, Mehring, and Schleich all have good potential, but it is Leiwen that truly excels, especially in its steepest and sunniest vineyards of Laurentiuslay and Klostergarten, which stretch up above the village, exposing their superb southwesterly aspect.

LEIWEN

✓ **Vineyard** *Laurentiuslay* **Growers** *Carl Loewen, Grans-Fassian*

GROSSLAGE SCHWARZLAY

Erden and Urzig are two of the Mittelmosel's most underrated villages. Their spectacular vineyards cling to cliff-like slopes in defiance of gravity and are capable of producing rich, racy wines of rapier-like acidity, stunning intensity, and immaculate style.

BURG

✓ **Vineyard** *Wendelstück* **Grower** *Steffens-Keß*

ENKIRCH

✓ **Vineyard** *Ellergrub* **Grower** *Weiser-Künstler* • **Vineyard** *Zeppwingert* **Grower** *Weiser-Künstler*

ERDEN

✓ **Vineyard** *Treppchen* **Growers** *Karl Erbes, Jos Christoffel Jun, Joh Jos Christoffel Erben, Dr Loosen, Mönchhof-Robert Eymael, Kees-Kieren* • **Vineyard** *Prälat* **Growers** *Dr Loosen, Mönchhof-Robert Eymael, Dr Pauly Bergweiler/ Peter Nicolay, Andreas Schmitges*

TRARBACH

✓ **Vineyard** *Schlossberg* (red) **Grower** *Markus Molitor*

ÜRZIG

✓ **Vineyard** *Würzgarten* **Growers** *Jos Christoffel Jun, Dr Loosen*

WOLF

✓ **Vineyard** *Goldgrube* **Grower** *Vollenweider*

GROSSLAGE VOM HEISSEN STEIN

There are two growers who excel in this otherwise modest *Grosslage*.

PÜNDERICH

✓ **Vineyard** *Marienburg* **Grower** *Clemens Busch* ◉

REIL

✓ **Vineyard** *Goldlay* **Grower** *Steffens-Keß* •
Vineyard *Mullay-Hofberg* **Grower** *Melsheimer*

BEREICH BURG COCHEM

Formerly Bereich Zell, this covers the lower Mosel, and is generally regarded as an area of unexciting wines, yet there are some good ones to be found.

GROSSLAGE GOLDBÄUMCHEN

There are few outstanding villages, vineyards, or growers in this *Grosslage*, although good wines are made in the village of Eller at Pommern.

POMMERN

Vineyard *Zeisel* **Grower** *Leo Fuchs*

GROSSLAGE GRAFSCHAFT

Good wines are made in the villages of Alf and Bullay, but the best come from the Bremmer Calmont, Europe's steepest vineyard.

BREMM

Vineyard *Calmont* **Growers** *Franzen, Uli Stein*

GROSSLAGE ROSENHANG

This is a promising *Grosslage* which winds along the right bank of the Mosel downstream from *Grosslage* Schwarze Katz.

GROSSLAGE SCHWARZE KATZ

The village of Zell has some good *Einzellagen* with officially classified slopes that can make fine and aromatic Riesling, but it is best known for its *Grosslage* label that carries the famous Schwarze Katz "Black Cat" logo. In 1863, three merchants from Aachen were selecting wines in cellar in Zell, but could not decide which of three casks to buy. When the grower tried to take a second sample of one of the wines, his black cat leapt on to the barrel, arched its back, and hissed. The merchants thought that the cat was perhaps defending the best wine, thus purchased it, returning each year for what they dubbed the "Schwarze Katz" wine. As this story spread, so it became customary for other producers in Zell to label their best wines with the insignia of the black cat, but since Merl and Kaimt have been merged with Zell, it has become merely a blended *Grosslage* wine.

GROSSLAGE WEINHEX

This *Grosslage* extends over both banks of the Mosel and into the suburbs of Koblenz, encompassing some very steep slopes planted entirely with Riesling. Three growers coax some world-class Riesling from this tourist-unfashionable end of the river.

WINNINGEN

✓ **Vineyard** *Brückstück* **Grower** *Richard Richter* • **Vineyard** *Uhlen* **Growers** *Heymann-Löwenstein, Knebel* • **Vineyard** *Röttgen* **Growers** *Knebel, Heymann-Löwenstein*

PREMIUM WHITES WITHOUT VINEYARD DESIGNATION

✓ **Growers** *Heymann-Löwenstein* (Schieferterrassen, von blauem Schiefer)

BEREICH MOSELTOR

This is the most southerly *Bereich* on the Mosel. It encompasses the upper reaches of the river that flows from its source in the Vosges mountains of France through Luxembourg and into Germany, hence the name Moseltor or "Mosel gate". Its wines are very light and acidic, and of little significance except to the *Sekt* houses.

GROSSLAGE SCHLOSS BÜBINGER

Haven of the less than heavenly Elbling. While colleagues across the river in Luxembourg earn a good living out of wine and tourism, the acidic Elbling wines of this *Grosslage* do not make it easy for its growers to survive.

BEREICH OBERMOSEL

The Obermosel, or Upper Mosel, runs parallel to the Luxembourg border and is planted mostly with Elbling. The wines are thin, acidic, and mostly made into *Sekt*.

GROSSLAGE GIPFEL

No outstanding villages, vineyards, or growers, although respectable wines are made in the village of Nittel.

GROSSLAGE KÖNIGSBERG

No outstanding villages, vineyards, or growers.

BEREICH RUWERTAL

The northern half of the former Bereich Saar-Ruwer.

GROSSLAGE RÖMERLAY

This covers the vineyards of the Ruwer and incorporates the ancient Roman city of Trier, as well as a few scattered plots on the Mosel, including one on the left bank facing Trier. The Ruwer is much the smaller of the two tributaries, yet it has its share of exceptional vineyards owned by gifted growers who make very aromatic, vital wines that are as racy as any on the Mosel, but not quite as biting as those of the Saar. The quality is high and few wines are seen under the *Grosslage* appellation.

EITELSBACH

✓ **Vineyard** *Karthäuserhofberg* **Grower** *Karthäuserhof*

KASEL

✓ **Vineyard** *Nieschen* **Growers** *Erben von Beulwitz, Reichsgraf von Kesselstatt*

MERTESDORF

✓ **Vineyard** *Maximin Grünhäuser Abtsberg* **Grower** *Gutsverwaltung von Schubert-Maximin Grünhaus*

BEREICH SAAR

The southern half of the former Bereich Saar-Ruwer.

GROSSLAGE SCHARZBERG

This covers the Saar and a small section of the Mosel between Konz and Trier to the north. These wines are so racy that they are positively biting and steely in their youth, but they age gracefully, harmonizing into exquisitely piquant flavours. Very modest Saar wines can be too thin and unripe to enjoy, but *Kabinett* and higher predicates from great growers are almost sure to please. Unlike the Ruwer's Römerlay, this *Grosslage* appellation is often used.

KANZEM

✓ **Vineyard** *Altenberg* **Grower** *Von Othegraven*

OBEREMMEL

✓ **Vineyard** *Hütte* **Grower** *Von Hövel*

OCKFEN

✓ **Vineyard** *Bockstein* **Growers** *Weinhof Herrenberg* (Schoden) ◉, *St Urbans-Hof* (Leiwen)

SAARBURG

✓ **Vineyard** *Rausch* **Grower** *Forstmeister Geltz Zilliken*

SCHARZHOFBERG

✓ **Vineyard** *Scharzhofberger* **Growers** *Reichsgraf von Kesselstatt, von Hövel, Egon Müller, Van Volxem*

SCHODEN

✓ **Vineyard** *Herrenberg* **Grower** *Weinhof Herrenberg* • **Vineyard** *Saarfeilser* **Growers** *St Urbans-Hof, Peter Lauer*

SERRIG

✓ **Vineyard** *Schloss Saarstein* **Grower** *Schloss Saarstein*

WILTINGEN

✓ **Vineyard** *Gottesfuß* **Grower** *Van Volxem* • **Vineyard** *Braune Kupp* **Grower** *Egon Müller*

OTHER CERTIFIED ORGANIC PRODUCERS

Biodynamic
Öko-Rita & Rudolf Trossen (Kinheim-Kindel)
Ulrich Treitz (Traben-Trarbach)

Organic
Ferienhof Josef Luy (Konz)
Alfred Cuy (Zell-Merl)
Artur Mentges (Kröv)
Christoph Rimmele (Zell/Kaimt)
Dr Renate Wilkomm (Bernkastel-Kues)
Frank Brohl (Pünderich)

Gerhard Lönnartz (Ernst)
Günther (Wincheringen)
Hugo Schorn (Burg)
Joachim Deis (Senheim)
Johannes Schneider (Maring-Noviand)
Klaus Schweisel (Osann-Monzel)
Klaus Stülb (Zell/Kaimt)
Laurentiushof (Bremm)
Paul Schwarz (Neumagen)
Peter IG Frommer (Traben-Trabach)

Peter Mentges (Bullay)
Rudolf Holbach (Wincheringen)
Sekt und Karl Weber (Wincheringen)
Steffens-Keß (Steffens-Keß (Reil)
Udo Wick (Kröv)
Volker Manz (Konz Kommlingen)
Weingut-Sektkellerei Uwe Kreuter (Alf)
zur Römerkelter (Maring-Noviand)

THE NAHE

In the Nahe region, a sunny microclimate and varied soils combine to produce wines that have the elegance of a Rheingau, the body of a light Rheinhessen, and the acidity of a Mosel. The perfumed aroma of a Nahe wine is unique, as are its extremely fragrant flavour and soft, smooth style.

DESPITE AN ABUNDANCE of Roman roads and villas, viticulture came relatively late to the Nahe, in the 8th century. As in the rest of Germany, the vineyards underwent expansion in the 12th and 13th centuries, and by the 19th century the Nahe was universally considered to be on a par with the Rheingau. Strangely, by World War II it had become Germany's least-known region. This had nothing to do with a loss of either quantity or quality: excellent vineyards such as Kupfergrube at Schlossböckelheim, today widely acclaimed as the greatest of all Nahe vineyards, did not even exist before 1900. The decline was probably due instead to the fact that the region was a relatively small area of scattered vineyards, and as such it was difficult to compete with larger, more compact ones. When those larger competitors also became industrialized, they prospered and developed sophisticated transport systems, edging the Nahe further into the cold. As a region with an essentially rural, non-industrialized, mixed-agricultural economy,

it looked inwards. Its own population could consume most of its production with little trouble and so the Nahe's wines adopted a lower profile on national and international markets.

SMALL COULD BE SO BEAUTIFUL

If the majority of the grape varieties cultivated in the Nahe were Riesling, the region would be able to capitalize on its limited size, and market the exclusive quality of its fine-wine production.

THE REGION AT A GLANCE

Area under vine
4,155 ha or 10,267 acres (decreasing)

Average yield
85 hl/ha (increasing)

Red wine
25%

White wine
71% (decreasing)

Rotling
4%

Most important grape varieties
27% Riesling (increasing), 13% Müller-Thurgau (decreasing), 11% Dornfelder, 49% others

Infrastructure
Bereich 1; Grosslagen 7; Einzellagen 328

Note The vineyards straddle 80 Gemeinden (communes), the names of which may appear on the label.

QUALITY REQUIREMENTS AND AVERAGE QMP PRODUCTION

NAHE'S MINIMUM OECHSLE	QUALITY CATEGORY	HARVEST BREAKDOWN
44°	Deutscher Tafelwein	1%
47°	Landwein	1%
50–60°	* QbA	76%
67–73°	* Kabinett	17%
76–85°	* Spätlese	1%
83–88°	* Auslese	1%
110°	Beerenauslese	1%
110°	Eiswein	1%
150°	Trockenbeerenauslese	1%

* Minimum Oechsle levels vary according to grape variety; those that have a naturally lower sugar content may qualify at a correspondingly lower level.

THE NAHE, *see also p405*
Between Rheinhessen and the Mittelrhein nestles the self-contained wine-producing region of the Nahe. Its namesake river has many tributaries running between spectacular overhanging cliffs.

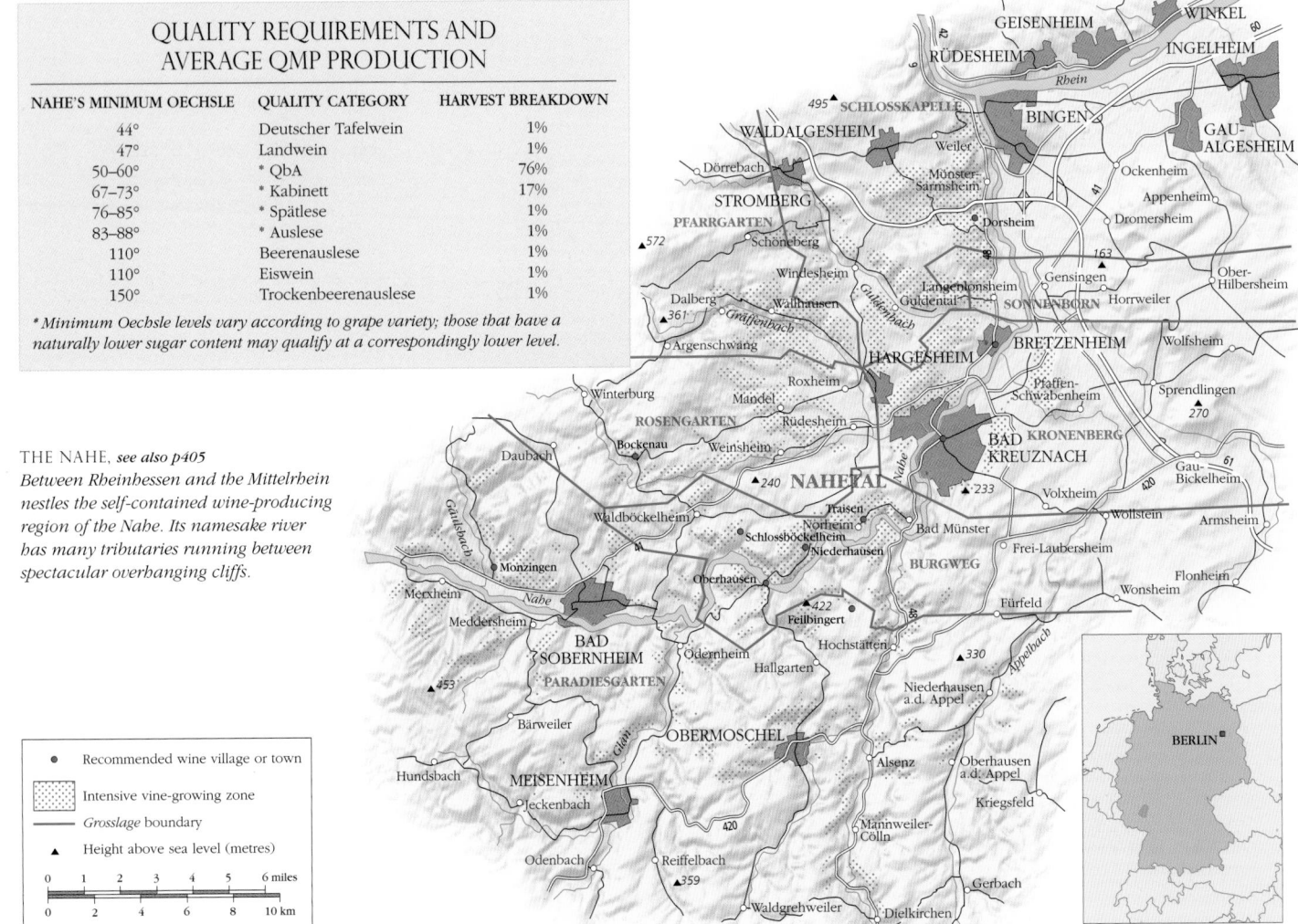

- ●   Recommended wine village or town
- ▦   Intensive vine-growing zone
- ——   *Grosslage* boundary
- ▲   Height above sea level (metres)

| 0 | 1 | 2 | 3 | 4 | 5 | 6 miles |
| 0 | 2 | 4 | 6 | 8 | 10 km |

FACTORS AFFECTING TASTE AND QUALITY

LOCATION
The region balloons out from between Rheinhessen and Mittelrhein around the Nahe River, which runs parallel to, and 40 kilometres (25 miles) southeast of, the Mosel.

CLIMATE
A temperate, sunny climate with adequate rainfall and no frosts. Local conditions are influenced by the Soonwald forest to the northeast and heat-retaining, rocky hills to the east. Protected south-facing vineyards enjoy microclimates that are almost Mediterranean.

ASPECT
Vineyards are found on both the gentle and steep slopes of the Nahe and its hinterland of many small tributary river valleys. Vines grow at altitudes of between 100 and 300 metres (330 and 985 feet).

SOIL
Diverse soils ranging from quartzite and slate along the lower reaches to porphyry (hard rock poor in lime), melaphyry (hard rock rich in lime), and coloured sandstone in the middle and upper reaches. Near Bad Kreuznach, weathered clay, sandstone,

limestone, loess, and loam soil may also be found. The greatest Riesling wines grow on sandstone.

VITICULTURE AND VINIFICATION
Since the mid-1960s, cultivation of Riesling and Silvaner has declined by 20 and 15 per cent respectively, yet Riesling is still the most widely planted variety, accounting for some 26 per cent of the Nahe's vineyards. This is due to the increased cultivation of crosses such as Kerner, Scheurebe, and Bacchus. In the cellar, methods remain traditional but very

efficient, with technically up-to-date cooperatives processing just 20 per cent of the crop. As much as 40 per cent of all Nahe wine is processed by small growers who sell direct to passing customers, with the remaining 40 per cent belonging to the traditional trade and export houses.

GRAPE VARIETIES
Primary variety: Riesling
Secondary varieties: Bacchus, Faberrebe, Kerner, Müller-Thurgau, Ruländer, Scheurebe, Silvaner, Weissburgunder

THE APPELLATIONS OF
THE NAHE

BEREICH NAHETAL

This region-wide *Bereich* replaces the former *Bereich* of Kreuznach, which covered the area once called Untere Nahe, or Lower Nahe, and Schlossböckelheim, which is the most famous.

GROSSLAGE BURGWEG

Not to be confused with the Grosslagen of the same name in the Rheingau and Franken, this Burgweg produces the Nahe's greatest range of fine Riesling wines. For many years Schlossböckelheimer Kupfergrube was regarded as the best of all, but today the Oberhäuser Brücke gets most of the rave reviews.

NIEDERHAUSEN

✓ **Vineyard** *Hermannshöhle* **Growers** *Hermann Dönnhoff, Jakob Schneider*

NORHEIM

✓ **Vineyard** *Kirschheck* **Grower** *Hermann Dönnhoff* • **Vineyard** *Dellchen* **Grower** *Dönnhoff*

OBERHAUSEN

✓ **Vineyard** *Brücke* **Grower** *Hermann Dönnhof*

SCHLOSSBÖCKELHEIM

✓ **Vineyard** *Kupfergrube* **Growers** *Hermann Dönnhoff, Schäfer-Fröhlich* • **Vineyard** *Felsenberg* **Growers** *Dr Crusius, Hermann Dönnhoff, Schäfer-Fröhlich*

TRAISEN

✓ **Vineyard** *Bastei* **Grower** *Dr Crusius* • **Vineyard** *Rotenfels* **Grower** *Dr Crusius*

GROSSLAGE KRONENBERG

This is not a branded beer, but one of the best *Grosslagen* in the Nahe, although all its finest

wines, invariably Rieslings with a magical blend of perfumed fragrance and soft yet racy acidity, carry *Einzellage* names.

BAD KREUZNACH

✓ **Vineyard** *Paradies* **Grower** *Korrell-Johanneshof*

GROSSLAGE PARADIESGARTEN

This *Grosslage* consists of many scattered vineyards of very variable quality. Apart from Oberndorf, all its finest wines come from the very eastern edge of the Nahe. One grower, Emrich-Schönleber, has raised the Rieslings of Monzingen from relative obscurity to cult status.

MEDDERSHEIM

✓ **Vineyard** *Rheingrafenberg* **Growers** *Bamberger, Hexamer*

MONZINGEN

✓ **Vineyard** *Frühlingsplätzchen* **Grower** *Emrich-Schönleber* • **Vineyard** *Halenberg* **Growers** *Emrich-Schönleber, Schäfer-Fröhlich*

SOBERNHEIM

✓ **Vineyard** *Marbach* **Grower** *Hexamer*

GROSSLAGE PFARRGARTEN

Although the *Grosslage* of Pfarrgarten is relatively small, it is intensively cultivated. Grosslage Pfarrgarten lies west and slightly north of Bad Kreuznach. Wallhausen wines are the best.

GROSSLAGE ROSENGARTEN

The true, original, and famous Rüdesheimer Rosengarten is a great Rheingau Riesling from an *Einzellage* called Rosengarten. The Nahe version may be honest enough, but it is not particularly special, being merely a modest *Grosslage* wine and, in all probability, a blend of Müller-Thurgau and Silvaner.

BOCKENAU

✓ **Vineyard** *Felseneck* **Grower** *Schäfer-Fröhlich*

GROSSLAGE SCHLOSSKAPELLE

In this *Grosslage* there are a number of attractive, good-quality wines from Münster-Sarmsheim and Dorsheim, which are excellent value. In addition to some full and rich Riesling, the Weisser and Grauer Burgunder are also making a name for themselves.

BURG LAYEN

✓ **Vineyard** *Schlossberg* **Grower** *Schlossgut Diel*

DORSHEIM

✓ **Vineyard** *Burgberg* **Grower** *Schlossgut Diel* • **Vineyard** *Goldloch* **Growers** *Schlossgut Diel, J B Schäfer* • **Vineyard** *Pittermännchen* **Grower** *Schlossgut Diel*

LAUBENHEIM

✓ **Vineyard** *Karthäuser* **Grower** *Tesch* • **Vineyard** *St Remigiusberg* **Grower** *Tesch*

WINDESHEIM

✓ **Non-Einzellagewein Grower** *Lindenhof* (red)

MÜNSTER (-SARMSHEIM)

✓ **Vineyard** *Dautenpflänzer* **Growers** *Göttelmann, Kruger-Rumpf* • **Vineyard** *Rheinberg* **Grower** *Göttelmann* • **Vineyard** *Pittersberg* **Grower** *Kruger-Rumpf* • **Non-Einzellagen** wine *Kruger-Rumpf* (red)

GROSSLAGE SONNENBORN

Sonnenborn is a one-village *Grosslage* and at least one grower in Langenlonsheim produces some interesting and fulsome wines.

LANGENLONSHEIM

✓ **Vineyard** *Löhrer Berg* **Grower** *Tesch*

CERTIFIED ORGANIC PRODUCERS

Biodynamic
Fuchs Jacobus (Waldaubersheim)
Im Zwölberich (Langenlonsheim)
Klaus Krost (Waldlaubersheim)
Wolfgang Hermes/Hermeshof (Bretzenheim)

Organic
Aloys Müller (Pfaffen-Schwabenheim)
Anke Eckes (Windesheim)
Anni & Hermann Steitz (Dielkirchen)
Brühler Hof (Volxheim)
Georg Forster (Rümmelsheim)
Gutshöfe FVA Ernst Anhauser (Bad Kreuznach)
Hans-Gerhard Hamann (Guldental-Heddenheim)
Hanmühle (Mannweiler-Cölln)
Häussling (Laubenheim)
Konrad Knodel (Windesheim)
Rheinhold Grossmann (Windesheim)
Schillingshof (Waldlaubersheim)

THE RHEINGAU

There can be no doubt that Riesling, the king of Germany's grapes, is more at home in and around the village of Johannisberg in the Rheingau than anywhere else in the world. Nowhere else can it produce such lush, juicy-ripe wines with distinctive, silky-smooth peach fruit.

MANY COUNTRIES OF THE WORLD use the synonym "Johannisberg Riesling" to distinguish the true Riesling grape variety from the many false and inferior Rieslings that claim the name. There can be no doubt that the Riesling grape luxuriates on this single sun-blessed slope of the Johannisberg vineyard in a most unique way.

Even at QbA level, the relaxed and confident style of a good Rheingau wine will leave a soft, satisfying, and elegant taste of peaches in the mouth. This gradually merges into a youthful, honeyed character that has nothing to do with *Edelfäule* (botrytis, or noble rot), over-ripeness, or bottle-ageing. One can prefer

VITICULTURE IN THE RHEINGAU
Just under 80 per cent of the vines are Riesling, and it is here that Riesling has historically ripened to such perfection that the wines have a juicy peachiness.

other stylistic renditions of the Riesling grape, but it is impossible to find finer, more graceful examples.

THE RHEINGAU'S INITIAL CHARTA FOR QUALITY
In the midst of the excitement generated by Germany's new *trocken* wines, it became evident to various top Rheingau estates that most of the wines exported were bulk blended and of low commercial quality. Since these properties had traditionally produced naturally drier wines, they believed that a continuance of poor *trocken* wines could damage their own image, so they banded together to protect it. In 1983, the Association of Charta- (pronounced "karta") Estates was launched to "further the classic

THE REGION AT A GLANCE

Area under vine
3,125 ha or 7,722 acres (decreasing)

Average yield
81 hl/ha (increasing)

Red wine
9%

White wine
87% (decreasing)

Rotling
4%

Most important grape varieties
79% Riesling, 12% Spätburgunder, 2% Müller-Thurgau, 7% others

Infrastructure
Bereich 1; *Grosslagen* 10; *Einzellagen* 118

Note The vineyards of Rheingau straddle 28 *Gemeinden* (communes), the names of which may appear on the label.

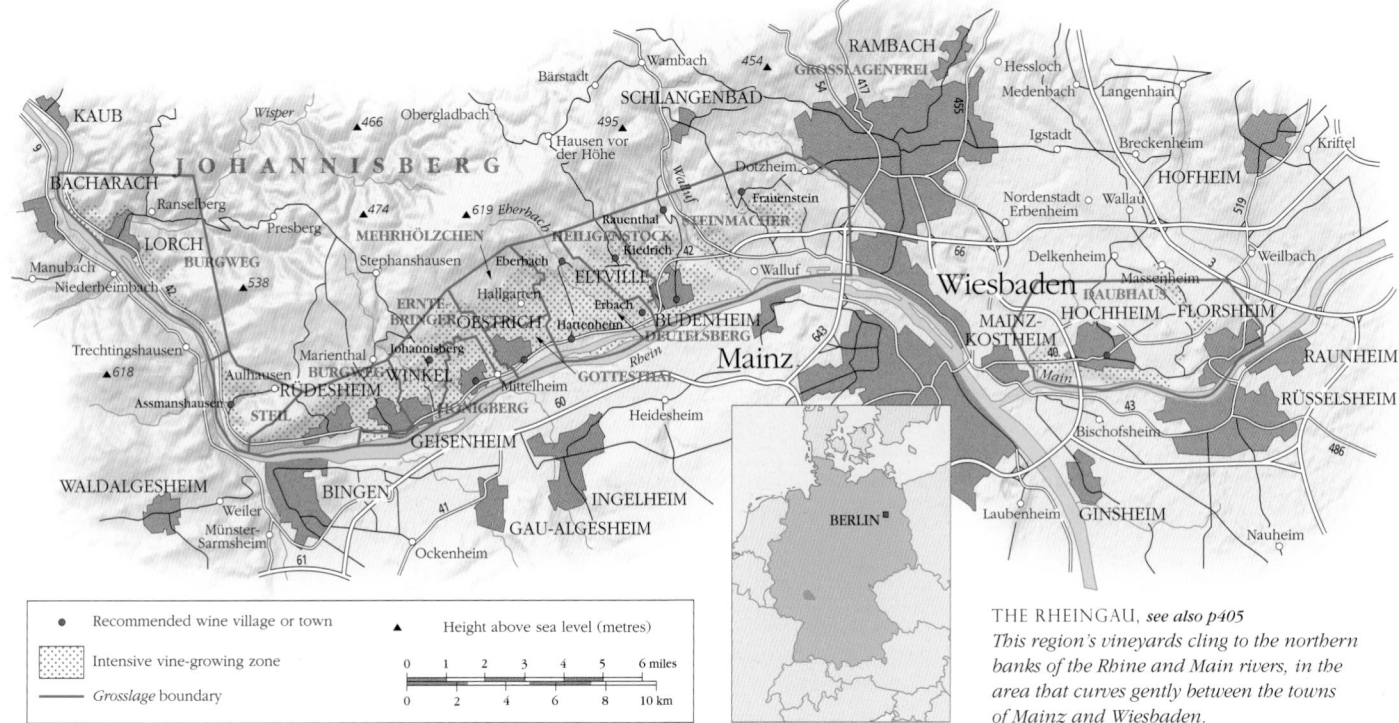

●	Recommended wine village or town	▲	Height above sea level (metres)
	Intensive vine-growing zone		
	Grosslage boundary		

0 1 2 3 4 5 6 miles
0 2 4 6 8 10 km

THE RHEINGAU, *see also p405*
This region's vineyards cling to the northern banks of the Rhine and Main rivers, in the area that curves gently between the towns of Mainz and Wiesbaden.

QUALITY REQUIREMENTS AND AVERAGE QMP PRODUCTION

RHEINGAU'S MINIMUM OECHSLE	QUALITY CATEGORY	HARVEST BREAKDOWN
44°	Deutscher Tafelwein	0.5%
53°	Landwein	0.5%
57–60°	* QbA	70%
73–80°	* Kabinett	20%
85–95°	* Spätlese	5%
95–105°	* Auslese	1%
125°	Beerenauslese	1%
125°	Eiswein	1%
150°	Trockenbeerenauslese	1%

* Minimum Oechsle levels vary according to grape variety; those that have a naturally lower sugar content may qualify at a correspondingly lower level.

Rheingau Riesling style, to upgrade the quality of Rheingau wines, and to make them unique among wines from other growing areas". Although this could not have succeeded without the active support of almost all the best Rheingau producers, the engine that relentlessly drove the Charta organization was, until his untimely death, Georg Breuer. Under his direction, Charta became the antithesis of any official quality-control system, as it aspired to the highest possible quality, rather than succumbing to the lowest common denominator. When first drawn up, the Charta's rules were uncommonly stiff, yet every few years, Breuer would tighten the ratchet a bit more by issuing even tougher rules.

TROCKEN WINES

One in every five bottles of German wine is *trocken* or dry, but many of these are thin and short. The intrinsically riper grapes grown by the Rheingau's Charta estates produce a fatter, fuller style of wine that adapts naturally to the *trocken* style, especially with food, but *trocken* wines produced in other regions have come on in leaps and bounds since the early 1990s. They are now well balanced, with an elegance that was missing from even the best of the best in the late 1980s. Due to the botrytis found in *Spätlese* and *Auslese* grapes used, they also possess a level of youthful complexity that is seldom encountered in other wines. They are very accessible when young, but rarely improve after their first flush of youth.

SCHLOSS VOLLRADS
This famous wine schloss was built circa 1300 by the Knights of Greiffenclau.

THE CHARTA RULES.

I have tasted many Charta wines and am convinced that they are indeed superior to other Rheingau wines. It must be emphasized, however, that it is only dry styles that are subject to the Charta organization's regulations – great QmP Rheingau wines of sweet styles from *Auslese* upwards are not affected. A Charta wine may be recognized by the traditional tall, slim, brown bottle typical of the Rheingau region and by the distinctive "Charta capsule" consisting of a Romanesque double-arch on a white background. There is also a label on the back with the same insignia.

Charta wines are examined organoleptically (using only the senses of taste, smell, and sight) before and after bottling. There is a second examination to check the authenticity of the original sample. Wines destined to receive the Charta imprimatur must be accompanied by official analysis documents and must also satisfy certain criteria laid down by the Association of Charta Estates, as follows:

The wines that are submitted for examination must be made in a "dry" style and conform to the following:

- 100 per cent own-estate production
- 100 per cent Riesling grapes
- Grapes hand-picked by *tries*
- Minimum of 12 per cent potential alcohol
- Maximum production of 50 hl/ha
- No *Prädikat* may be mentioned*

The wines must have the true characteristics of a Riesling, of the specific vintage, and of the vineyard where the grapes were grown.

Registration has to be made four weeks prior to the date of examination, indicating the vintage and category.

*Older vintages of Prädikat wines may be encountered. These will not have been produced according to the above rules if only for the simple reason that they have not been made in a dry style, but they will have undergone the same exhaustive tasting and, if selected, become "Charta Designated", rather than "Charta Approved".

As a control, normal wines of comparable location and category are tasted blind alongside wines submitted for examination. Charta wines have to surpass the quality of these standard wines in each of the required aspects. The wines provided for the second tasting, as well as being a control, have to be accompanied by the analysis of the AP number (*see* p406). The results of these tests are lodged with the association and can be used in the eventuality of any subsequent claim that a member is passing off an inferior wine as a Charta wine.

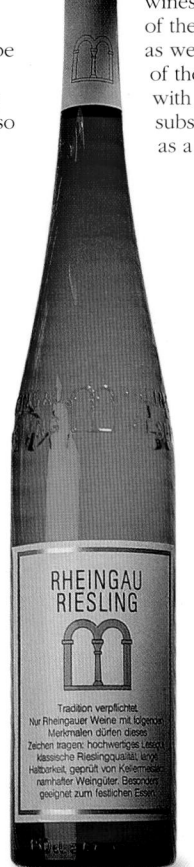

Charta bottle

Charta capsule

RHEINGAU RIESLING

CHARTA

Nur Rheingauer Rieslinge, die den strengen Anforderungen der Vereinigung der CHARTA-Weingüter entsprechen, tragen das Zeichen CHARTA® auf dem Etikett. Dieser klassisch herbe Riesling eignet sich besonders als Essenbegleiter.

Back label

CAPSULE AND BACK LABEL

All wines that have passed the Charta examination are sealed with a capsule bearing the organization's logo consisting of a Romanesque double-arch that also appears on the back label.

CHARTA BOTTLE

Originally all bottles were embossed with the Charta logo similar to the example here. However, the cost of embossing proved prohibitive for some of the smaller producers, and it is now optional.

BERG SCHLOSSBERG VINEYARDS, RÜDESHEIM
*These south-facing vineyards on the slopes of Berg Schlossberg
are blessed with perfect exposure to the sun's rays.*

FACTORS AFFECTING TASTE AND QUALITY

LOCATION
The Rheingau is a compact region only 36 kilometres (22 miles) long, situated on the northern banks of the Rhine and Main rivers between Bingen and Mainz.

CLIMATE
Vines are protected from cold by the tempering effect of the rivers and the shelter provided by the Taunus Mountains. The region receives above-average hours of sunshine during the growth period of May to October.

ASPECT
The vines grow at an altitude of 100 to 300 metres (330 to 985 feet) on a superb, fully south-facing slope.

SOIL
Quartzite and weathered slate-stone in the higher situated sites produce the greatest Riesling, while loam, loess, various types of clay, and sandy gravel soils of the lower vineyards give a fuller, more robust style. The blue phyllite-slate

around Assmannshausen is traditionally thought to favour the Spätburgunder.

VITICULTURE AND VINIFICATION
In contrast to other German regions, the Rheingau consists of a large number of independent wine estates (500 odd) in a relatively compact area. There are approximately 2,600 private growers, many of whom make and market their own wines, while others supply the region's 10 cooperatives. The Riesling grape variety represents almost 80 per cent of the vines cultivated and it is traditional in this region to vinify all but the sweetest wines in a drier style than would be used in other regions. Assmannshausen is famous for its red wine, one of Germany's best.

GRAPE VARIETIES
Primary variety: Riesling
Secondary varieties: Ehrenfelser, Kerner, Müller-Thurgau, Silvaner, Spätburgunder, Weissburgunder

THE CHARTA'S NEW CLASSIFIED VINEYARD WINES

Look out for Charta *Einzellage* wines with a black bottom border bearing not one but three Romanesque double-arches on the front label. This is verification that the wine comes not from the grossly inflated official *Einzellagen*, but from the original, authentic site, which Charta has called *Erstes Gewächs* or First Growths. They must conform to the same rules

(ie, dry style with no mention of *Prädikat*), although new regulations to cover botrytis and even Spätburgunder *Erstes Gewächs* are under study. The difference between official and authentic *Einzellage* size can be, as you can see, quite enormous. In fact, the 1971 German wine law is nothing less than the promotion of legalized fraud on a massive and widespread scale.

VILLAGE	EINZELLAGE	VINEYARD SIZE		1971 EXPANSION
		Official	Charta	
Lorch	Bodenthal-Steinberg	28.1	12.3	128%
Lorch	Kapellenberg	56.9	17.9	218%
Lorch	Krone	14.5	7.5	93%
Assmannshausen	Höllenberg	43.4	20	117%
Rüdesheim	Berg Schlossberg	25.5	23.2	10%
Rüdesheim	Berg Roseneck	26.7	16.2	65%
Rüdesheim	Berg Rottland	36.2	32.3	12%
Geisenheim	Fuchsberg	44.4	5.6	693%
Geisenheim	Rothenberg	26.8	9	198%
Geisenheim	Kläuserweg	57.6	14.3	303%
Geisenheim	Mäuerchen	32.6	3.6	8.60%
Johannisberg	Schloss Johannisberg	21.9	16.6	32%
Johannisberg	Klaus	2	2	0%
Johannisberg	Hölle	20.9	6.2	237%
Johannisberg	Mittelhölle	6.5	6.5	0%
Winkel	Jesuitengarten	31.2	26	20%
Winkel	Hasensprung	103.8	19.9	421%
Winkel	Schloss Vollrads	37.7	15	151%
Mittelheim	St Nikolaus	44.8	6.7	569%
Oestrich	Lenchen	130.6	35.8	265%
Oestrich	Doosberg	137.9	38.4	259%
Hattenheim	Engelmannsberg	14.1	10.5	34%
Hattenheim	Mannberg	8.1	8.1	0%
Hattenheim	Pfaffenberg	6.6	6.6	0%
Hattenheim	Nussbrunnen	10.8	10.8	0%
Hattenheim	Wisselbrunnen	16.9	9.7	74%
Hattenheim	Steinberg	36.7	26.9	36%
Hallgarten	Schönhell	52.1	18.9	176%
Erbach	Marcobrunn	5.2	5.2	0%
Erbach	Steinmorgen	28.2	8.6	228%
Erbach	Siegelsberg	15.1	13.7	10%
Erbach	Hohenrain	17.1	5.8	195%

VILLAGE	EINZELLAGE	VINEYARD SIZE		1971 EXPANSION
		Official	Charta	
Erbach	Schlossberg	28.1	12.3	128%
Kiedrich	Gräfenberg	56.9	17.9	218%
Kiedrich	Wasseros	14.5	7.5	93%
Eltville	Sonnenberg	43.4	20	117%
Rauenthal	Baiken	25.5	16.2	10%
Rauenthal	Gehrn	26.7	16.2	65%
Rauenthal	Rothenberg	36.2	32.3	12%
Rauenthal	Nonnenberg	44.4	5.6	693%
Rauenthal	Wülfen	26.8	9	198%
Rauenthal	Wildsau	57.6	14.3	303%
Martinsthal	Langenberg	32.6	3.6	806%
Walluf	Walkenberg	21.9	16.6	32%
Wiesbaden	Neroberg	2	2	0%
Hochheim	Domdechaney	20.9	6.2	237%
Hochheim	Kirchenstück	6.5	6.5	0%
Hochheim	Hölle	31.2	26	20%
Hochheim	Königin Victoria Ber	103.8	19.9	421%

GEORG BREUER
RÜDESHEIM
BERG SCHLOSSBERG
RHEINGAU

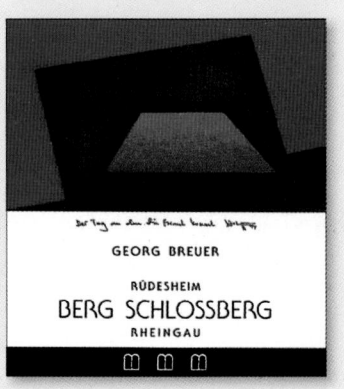

GEORG BREUER
RÜDESHEIM
BERG SCHLOSSBERG
RHEINGAU

THE APPELLATIONS OF
THE RHEINGAU

BEREICH JOHANNISBERG

This *Bereich* covers the entire Rheingau. Trading off the famous village of Johannisberg, situated behind Schloss Johannisberg, lesser wines sell well under it. However, some producers have started using *Grosslage* names on labels and because they do not use the word "*Grosslage*", this implies the wine might be from one specific site, and perhaps of better quality.

GROSSLAGE BURGWEG

This is the westernmost *Grosslage*. If a wine bears its name on the label and clearly shows "Riesling", it may well be good, but it will not in any way compare with Burgweg's superb *Einzellage* wines that are produced by the great estates or small growers.

GEISENHEIM

✓ **Vineyard** *Rothenberg* **Grower** *Wegeler-Gutshaus Oestrich*

RÜDESHEIM

✓ **Vineyard** *Berg Roseneck* **Growers** *Georg Breuer, Josef Leitz, August Kesseler* • **Vineyard** *Berg Rottland* **Growers** *Georg Breuer, Johannishof, Josef Leitz, Wegeler-Gutshaus Oestrich* • **Vineyard** *Berg Schlossberg* **Growers** *Georg Breuer, August Kesseler* (red and white), *Josef Leitz, Hessische Staatsweingüter Kloster Eberbach, Wegeler-Gutshaus Oestrich* • **Premium red wine blends Growers** *Breuer* (Spätburgunder "S"), *Kesseler* (Cuveé Max)

GROSSLAGE DAUBHAUS

The best vines of Daubhaus, which is the most easterly *Grosslage* in *Bereich* Johannisberg, grow in just one tiny, isolated, but excellent strip at Hochheim. The wines are firm and full, but do not quite match the elegance of the Rheingau's very best.

HOCHHEIM

✓ **Vineyard** *Domdechaney* **Grower** *Domdechant Werner'sches Weingut* • **Vineyard** *Kirchenstück* **Grower** *Franz Künstler* • **Vineyard** *Hölle* **Grower** *Franz Künstler* • **Vineyard** *Reichestal* **Grower** *Franz Künstler* (red) • **Vineyard** *Weiß Erd* **Grower** *Franz Künstler*

WICKER

✓ **Vineyard** *Mönchsgewann* **Grower** *Joachim Flick* • **Vineyard** *Nonnberg* **Grower** *Joachim Flick*

GROSSLAGE DEUTELSBERG

Grosslage Deutelsberg encompasses the great Erbach vineyards as well as the rather under-rated wines of Hattenheim that have great strength and longevity. It also includes the famous Kloster Eberbach and Mariannenau Island vineyard, where there is a little Chardonnay grown.

HATTENHEIM

✓ **Vineyard** *Pfaffenberg* **Grower** *Domäne Schloss Schönborn* • **Vineyard** *Wisselbrunnen* **Grower** *Josef Spreitzer*

GROSSLAGE ERNTEBRINGER

The most often-seen of the Rheingau's *Grosslagen*, Erntebringer is also its best, although not

comparable to the *Einzellagen*, particularly the legendary Schloss Johannisberg and the grossly under-rated Klaus.

GEISENHEIM

✓ **Vineyard** *Klaus* **Grower** *Prinz von Hessen*

JOHANNISBERG

✓ **Vineyard** *Hölle* **Grower** *Johannishof* • **Vineyard** *Schloss Johannisberg* **Grower** *Domäne Schloss Johannisberg*

MITTELHEIM

✓ **Vineyard** *St Nikolaus* **Growers** *Peter Jakob Kühn, F B Schönleber*

WINKEL

✓ **Vineyard** *Schloss Vollrads* **Grower** *Schloss Vollrads*

GROSSLAGE GOTTESTHAL

It is strange that this *Grosslage*, sandwiched between the superb Deutelsberg and Honigberg, should be disappointing in the wines it produces. However, some excellent, long-lived Riesling can be found.

OESTRICH

✓ **Vineyard** *Lenchen* **Growers** *Peter Jakob Kühn, Josef Spreitzer, Querbach* • **Vineyard** *Doosberg* **Growers** *Josef Spreitzer, Querbach*

GROSSLAGE HEILIGENSTOCK

The best product of this small *Grosslage* is the fabulous, peach-and-honey Riesling of Kiedrich, often culminating in some of the world's most noble sweet wines. The *Grosslage* wine can also be good.

KIEDRICH

✓ **Vineyard** *Gräfenberg* **Grower** *Robert Weil* • **Vineyard** *Turmberg* **Grower** *Robert Weil*

GROSSLAGE HONIGBERG

Wines of great vitality, finesse; all the elegant, mouthwatering, peachy fruit and youthful honey you could expect from top Rheingau wines.

ERBACH

✓ **Vineyard** *Marcobrunn* **Growers** *Schloss Schönborn, Schloss Reinhartshausen* ◉ • **Vineyard** *Michelmark* **Grower** *Jakob Jung* • **Vineyard** *Steinmorgen* **Grower** *Heinz Nikolai* • **Vineyard** *Schlossberg* **Grower** *Schloss Reinhartshausen* ◉

GROSSLAGE MEHRHÖLZCHEN

The *Grosslage* of Mehrhölzchen, on higher, steeper slopes than the rest of the Rheingau, is tucked up beneath the Taunus hills. The area is planted almost entirely with Riesling, and the wine is typically fat, almost heavy. It is sometimes full of fruit, displaying a unique spicy aroma.

HALLGARTEN

✓ **Vineyard** *Jungfer* **Grower** *Prinz*

GROSSLAGE STEIL

The tiny *Grosslage* of Steil divides the *Grosslage* of Burgweg. Steil is famous for the red wines of Assmannshausen. The majority of the vineyards in Grosslage Steil are situated on steep, southwest-facing slopes, but those of Höllenberg, which notably produce the best wine, are situated on a tiny, south-facing tributary.

ASSMANNSHAUSEN

✓ **Vineyard** *Höllenberg* **Growers** *August Kesseler* (red), *Hessische Staatsweingüter Domaine Assmannshausen* (red), *Hessische Staatsweingüter Kloster Eberbach* (red), *Weingut Krone* (red)

GROSSLAGE STEINMÄCHER

The vineyards of Grosslage Steinmächer are less intensively cultivated than those situated in the main body of the Rheingau's vine-growing area, but this does not mean that the wines they produce are in any way less impressive.

ELTVILLE

✓ **Vineyard** *Sonnenberg* **Grower** *J Koegler* (red and white)

RAUENTHAL

✓ **Vineyard** *Baiken* **Grower** *Hessische Staatsweingüter Kloster Eberbach* • **Vineyard** *Nonnenberg* **Grower** *Georg Breuer*

WALLUF

✓ **Vineyard** *Walkenberg* **Grower** *J B Becker*

OTHER CERTIFIED ORGANIC PRODUCERS

Organic
Altenkirch & Schmidt (Lorch im Rheingau)
Asbach-Kretschmar (Rüdesheim)
Bernd J Richter (Hochheim)
Graf von Kanitz (Lorch im Rheingau)
Hans-Josef Engelmann (Kiedrich)
Hirt-Albrecht (Eltville)
Jakob Hamm (Oestrich-Winkel)
Rheinhard Glassner (Lorch im Rheingau)
Stefan Muskat (Geisenheim)
Troitzsch-Pusinelli (Lorch)

RHEINHESSEN

Rheinhessen is the most heavily cultivated of all Germany's Qualitätswein regions. The diversity of its soils and grape varieties makes it impossible to convey a uniform impression of its wines. Riesling is planted in just eight per cent of its vineyards. Most vineyards produce cheap, unpretentious wines, ranging from mild Silvaner to aromatic Müller-Thurgau, but some truly fine wines are to be found.

RHEINHESSEN IS INDISPUTABLY LINKED with the ubiquitous Liebfraumilch. This is partly because the area is responsible for producing one in every two bottles, partly because of the famous Liebfraumilch-Kirchenstück in Worms, where the Liebfraumilch story began, and partly because Sichel & Co brews up perhaps the most famous Liebfraumilch ("Blue Nun") in sleepy Alzey. Nierstein carries a similar stigma to that of Liebfraumilch in the minds of many experienced drinkers,

FACTORS AFFECTING TASTE AND QUALITY

LOCATION
This region is situated between the towns of Bingen, Mainz, and Worms, immediately south of the Rheingau.

CLIMATE
Rheinhessen enjoys a temperate climate and is protected from cold winds by the Taunus hills to the north and the Odenwald forest to the east. Vineyards that slope down to the river are protected by the Rhine terrace itself.

ASPECT
Vines on the river slopes of the Rhine Terrace grow on east- and southeast-facing slopes at an altitude of between 100 and 200 metres (330 and 660 feet), while those in Rheinhessen's hinterland are found at various heights and with every possible aspect.

SOIL
Mainly loess deposited during inter-glacial sandstorms, but also limestone, sandy-marl, quartzite, porphyry-sand, and silty-clay. Riesling growers favour heavier marl soil, except near Bingen, where there is an outcropping of quartzite-slate. A red, slaty-sandy clay soil known as rotliegendes is found on the best, steep riverfront vineyards of Nackenheim and Nierstein.

VITICULTURE AND VINIFICATION
Due to the large number of part-time growers, much of the wine is made from vast vineyard yields, and bulk-blended into cheap generic wines such as Bereich Nierstein, and, of course, Liebfraumilch. At the other extreme, small quantities of some fine wines are produced on the best estates.

GRAPE VARIETIES
Primary varieties: Müller-Thurgau, Riesling, Silvaner
Secondary varieties: Bacchus, Faberrebe, Huxelrebe, Kerner, Morio-Muskat, Portugieser, Scheurebe

due to the huge quantities of the cheap Bereich Nierstein and Niersteiner Gutes Domtal that flood the market and which downgrade the reputation of the high-quality Niersteiner *Einzellagen*.

THE RHINE TERRACE
Despite the high volume of indifferent wines, there are many great growers and estates producing good wine in this region. If you are looking for an initial

RHINE TERRACE
VINEYARDS AT NIERSTEIN
Nierstein is one of the nine member villages of the "Rhein Terrasse" group, which offers good-value, quality wines. New grape crosses are a feature of this area.

RHEINHESSEN, *see also p405*
One of Germany's largest regions in terms of hectares under vine, this is an area of great variety where several different grapes are grown.

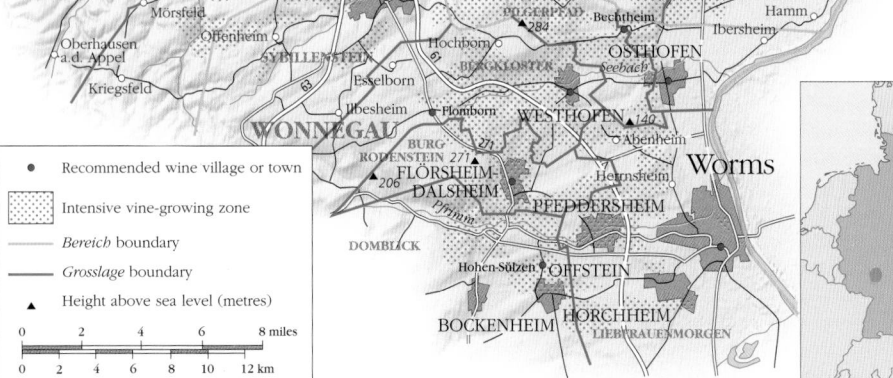

Recommended wine village or town

Intensive vine-growing zone

Bereich boundary

Grosslage boundary

▲ Height above sea level (metres)

0   2   4   6   8 miles

0   2   4   6   8   10   12 km

increase in quality for a modest price, look out for the "Rhein Terrasse" sticker on bottles of Rheinhessen wine.

The Rhine Terrace comprises nine villages on the slopes that descend from Rheinhessen's plateau to the Rhine River. These villages and their *Grosslagen* are as follows: Bodenheim in the St Alban *Grosslage*; Nackenheim in the Gutes Domtal *Grosslage*; Nierstein, which is shared by the *Grosslagen* of Gutes Domtal, Spiegelberg, Rehbach, and Auflangen; Oppenheim in the *Grosslagen* of Güldenmorgen and Krötenbrunnen; Dienheim, also in the Krötenbrunnen *Grosslage*; Guntersblum and Ludwigshöhe, both of which are in the Krötenbrunnen and Vogelsgarten *Grosslagen*; and Alsheim and Mattenheim, in the *Grosslage* of Rheinblick.

LIEBFRAUMILCH COUNTRY IN THE SPRING
The village of Grau-Heppenheim, near Alzey, the home of Blue Nun, in the large Petersberg Grosslage.

QUALITY REQUIREMENTS AND AVERAGE QMP PRODUCTION

RHEINHESSEN'S MINIMUM OECHSLE	QUALITY CATEGORY	HARVEST BREAKDOWN
44°	Deutscher Tafelwein	0.5%
53°	Landwein	0.5%
60–62°	* QbA	69%
73–76°	* Kabinett	17%
85–90°	* Spätlese	8%
92–100°	* Auslese	1%
125°	Beerenauslese	2%
125°	Eiswein	1%
150°	Trockenbeerenauslese	1%

* Minimum Oechsle levels vary according to grape variety; those that have a naturally lower sugar content may qualify at a correspondingly lower level.

THE REGION AT A GLANCE

Area under vine
26,444 ha or 65,344 acres (increasing)

Average yield
103 hl/ha (increasing)

Red wine
31%

White wine
59% (decreasing)

Rotling
10%

Most important grape varieties
16% Müller-Thurgau (decreasing), 14% Riesling (increasing), 13% Dornfelder (increasing), 9% Silvaner (decreasing), 6% Portugieser (decreasing), 5% Kerner (decreasing), 5% Spätburgunder, 4% Scheurebe (decreasing), 4% Grauburgunder, 24% others

Infrastructure
Bereiche 3; *Grosslagen* 24; *Einzellagen* 434

Note The vineyards of Rheinhessen straddle 167 *Gemeinden* (communes), the names of which may appear on the label.

THE APPELLATIONS OF
RHEINHESSEN

BEREICH BINGEN

Abutting the Nahe region to the west and separated by the Rhine from the Rheingau to the north, Bereich Bingen is the smallest of Rheinhessen's three *Bereiche* and the least important in terms of both the quantity and quality of the wine produced.

GROSSLAGE ABTEY

The *Grosslage* of Abtey does not have any outstanding villages, vineyards, or growers, although good-quality wines are produced in the village of St Johann.

GROSSLAGE ADELBERG

Some good value wines can be found in the small town of Wörrstadt, but in terms of quality no vineyards or growers stand out.

GROSSLAGE KAISERPFALZ

Kaiserpfalz is a *Grosslage* consisting mainly of Bingen and Mainz, with vineyards facing to both the east and west. This *Grosslage* produces some of the region's most promising red wines from the Portugieser and Spätburgunder grapes. The village of Ingelheim is one of the places that claim to be the birthplace of the emperor Charlemagne.

INGELHEIM
☑ **Vineyard** *Steinacker* **Grower** *Arndt F Werner* ◉ (red)

GROSSLAGE KURFÜRSTENSTÜCK

Gau-Bickelheim is the home of Rheinhessen's huge central cooperative, but it has been the good growers or excellent *Staatsdomäne* from the *Einzellage* of Kapelle that have produced superior wines in the past.

GROSSLAGE RHEINGRAFENSTEIN

Some exciting efforts from a new shooting star demonstrate the potential of this *Grosslage*.

SIEFERSHEIM
☑ **Vineyard** *Heerkretz* **Grower** *Wagner-Stempel* •
Vineyard *Höllberg* **Grower** *Wagner-Stempel* •
Premium red wine blend Grower *Wagner-Stempel* (Spaetburgunder "R")

GROSSLAGE SANKT ROCHUSKAPELLE

Bingen is often thought to belong more to the Nahe region than to Rheinhessen, but 14 of its 18 *Einzellagen* belong to this Rheinhessen *Grosslage*, which is among the best in *Bereich* Bingen.

BEREICH NIERSTEIN

Although this is a famous *Bereich* with many superb sites and great growers, most wines sold under its label include some of the most dull, characterless, and lacklustre in all Germany. Wine enthusiasts will find it best to choose the great *Einzellagen* and leave these *Grosslage* products alone.

GROSSLAGE AUFLANGEN

This is the best of the three *Grosslagen* that encompass some parts of Nierstein (the other two are Rehbach and Spiegelberg). Its vineyard area actually begins in the centre of the town, then stretches west to include the south and southeast facing vineyards of the tiny tributary of the Rhine that flows through Schwabsburg, and then north to the Kranzberg, which overlooks the Rhine itself.

NIERSTEIN
☑ **Vineyard** *Oelberg* **Growers** *Heyl zu Herrnsheim* ◉, *St Antony, Kühling-Gillot*

GROSSLAGE DOMHERR

Once forming ecclesiastical vineyards (Domherr means "Canon of the Cathedral"), this *Grosslage* has good vineyards on steep slopes, but there are few outstanding growers.

GROSSLAGE GÜLDENMORGEN

Güldenmorgen was once a fine-quality *Einzellage* belonging to Oppenheim, but now encompasses three villages. The best wines come from the Sackträger site. Please note that although the village of Uelversheim is clearly situated in the *Grosslage* of Krotenbrunnen, the eastern tail-end of its vineyards actually overlaps Güldenmorgen.

OPPENHEIM

✓ **Vineyard** *Sackträger* **Growers** *Manz, Kübling-Gillot*

GROSSLAGE GUTES DOMTAL

This district covers a vast area of Rhine hinterland behind the better *Grosslagen* of Nierstein. Although it encompasses 15 villages, most is sold under the ubiquitous Niersteiner Gutes Domtal (sometimes Domthal) name. Much is decidedly inferior and cheapens the reputation of Nierstein's truly great wines. The most famous village is Dexheim, because of its so-called Doktor, named after the old spelling of the great Bernkasteler Doctor vineyard. But neither Dexheim generally, nor Dexheimer Doktor specifically, warrant the attention.

WEINOLSHEIM

✓ **Vineyard** *Kehr* **Grower** *Manz*

GROSSLAGE KRÖTENBRUNNEN

This district encompasses those parts of Oppenheim's vineyards that are not included in the *Grosslage* Güldenmorgen, and the wide-ranging vineyards of Guntersblum.

GROSSLAGE PETERSBERG

This *Grosslage* lies behind Gutes Domtal and is wedged between the *Bereiche* of Bingen and Wonnegau. Although large, this *Grosslage* has few if any exciting sites or growers.

GROSSLAGE REHBACH

Rehbach is one of the greatest *Grosslagen* in Rheinhessen, consisting of a long, thin strip of very steep terraced slopes overlooking the Rhine, just north of Nierstein. Riesling wines produced by these vineyards are aromatic, intense, and delightfully mellow, yet have a definite raciness on the finish.

NIERSTEIN

✓ **Vineyard** *Hipping* **Growers** *Georg Albrecht Schneider, St Antony* • **Vineyard** *Pettenthal* **Growers** *Heyl zu Herrnsheim* ◉, *St Antony, Kübling-Gillot*

GROSSLAGE RHEINBLICK

This district produces better-than-average *Grosslage* wines.

GROSSLAGE ST ALBAN

Named after the St Alban monastery, which once owned most of the land in this under-rated *Grosslage* situated between Mainz and Nierstein. The *Einzellage* wines have fine, positive character and usually represent excellent value for money.

GROSSLAGE SPIEGELBERG

The largest of Nierstein's riverside districts, its vineyards stretch to the north and south of both the famous town and the Grosslage Auflangen. Ignore the ubiquitous, mild, and neutral-flavoured *Grosslagen* wines and choose the wines of the finer *Einzellagen* that are situated between Nierstein and Oppenheim.

NACKENHEIM

✓ **Vineyard** *Rothenberg* **Grower** *Gunderloch*

GROSSLAGE VOGELSGARTEN

This is not, in fact, one of the best Rheinhessen districts, although Weingut Ohnacker makes fine, rich, sometimes powerful wines that are well worth seeking out.

BEREICH WONNEGAU

The least-known of Rheinhessen's three *Bereiche*, Wonnegau contains the world-famous (although not world-class) Liebfrauenstift *Einzellage*, which had the rather dubious honour of giving birth to Liebfraumilch. Wonnegau means "province of great joy".

GROSSLAGE BERGKLOSTER

Some of Germany's top dry Riesling comes from Westhofen.

WESTHOFEN

✓ **Vineyard** *Abtserde* **Grower** *Keller* • **Vineyard** *Aulerde* **Growers** *Wittmann* ◉, *K F Groebe* • **Vineyard** *Brunnenhäuschen* **Grower** *Wittmann* • **Vineyard** *Morstein* **Growers** *Wittmann, Gerhard Gutzler* (red), *Keller, Seehof-Ernst Fauth* • **Vineyard** *Kirchspiel* **Growers** *Wittmann, K F Groebe, Keller* • **Premium red wine blend Growers** *Gerhard Gutzler* ("GS" *barrique*), *Keller* (Spätburgunder "FR")

GROSSLAGE BURG RODENSTEIN

A large proportion of the wines made in the Grosslage Burg Rodenstein district are sold under its *Grosslage* name. Most of it is well above average quality, although not in the same class as its best *Einzellage* wines. Since the mid-1990s, Keller has been considered by many critics to be Germany's top wine estate.

DAHLSHEIM (an *Ortsteil* of Flörsheim-Dalsheim)

✓ **Vineyard** *Hubacker* **Grower** *Keller* • **Vineyard**

Bürgel (red) **Grower** *Keller* • **Non-Einzellage premium white Grower** *Keller* (G-Max, varietals)

NIEDERFLÖRSHEIM (an *Ortsteil* of Flörsheim-Dalsheim)

✓ **Vineyard** *Frauenberg* **Grower** *Battenfeld-Spanier*

GROSSLAGE DOMBLICK

There are few outstanding growers here, although good wines are made in the village of Monsheim, and the *Grosslage* label usually offers sound value.

HOHEN-SÜLZEN

✓ **Vineyard** *Kirchenstück* **Grower** *Battenfeld-Spanier*

MONSHEIM

✓ **Vineyard** *Silberberg* **Grower** *Keller* (Flörsheim-Dalsheim)

GROSSLAGE GOTTESHILFE

A tiny district encompassing the excellent wine village of Bechtheim. Very little wine is seen on export markets under the *Grosslage* label.

BECHTHEIM

✓ **Vineyard** *Geyersberg* **Grower** *Dreißigacker*

GROSSLAGE LIEBFRAUENMORGEN

This familiar sounding *Grosslage* includes the famous Liebfrauenstift-Kirchenstück vineyard in Worms, the birthplace of Liebfraumilch.

WORMS

✓ **Vineyard** *Liebfrauenstift-Kirchenstück* **Growers** *Gerhard Gutzler, Schembs*

GROSSLAGE PILGERPFAD

This *Grosslage* stretches from the lesser vineyards of Bechtheim to the large Petersberg district in Bereich Nierstein.

DITTELSHEIM

✓ **Vineyard** *Geyersberg* **Grower** *Winter*

GROSSLAGE SYBILLENSTEIN

There are no outstanding villages, vineyards, or growers in this *Grosslage*, although some valid efforts with Silvaner can be reported from the Kappellenberg vineyard. Alzey is the location of Sichel & Co, master-blenders of "Blue Nun" Liebfraumilch.

OTHER CERTIFIED ORGANIC PRODUCERS

Biodynamic
Armin Ackermann (Mettenheim)
Helmut and Walfried Sander (Gau-Odernheim)
Volker Feth (Flörsheim-Dalsheim (Ortsteil Dalsheim)

Organic
Adam Schmitt (Mommenheim)
Albrecht Schütte (Alsheim)
Axel (Ober-Hilbersheim)
Bardo Kneib (Zornheim)
Berthold Ferstl (Zwingenberg)
Birkenhof (Armsheim)
Brüder Dr Becker (Ludwigshöhe)
Dieter Klein (Offstein)
Dr Helmut Scholl (Bornheim)

Dr Schnell (Guntersblum)
E Weidenbach (Ingelheim)
Eckhard (Ingelheim)
Eckhard Weitzel (Ingelheim)
Eugen Schönhals (Bieblenheim)
Gerhard Huf (Ingelheim)
Gerhard Sander (Mettenheim)
Goldberg (Osthofen)
Hans L Spanier (Hohen-Sülzen)
Harald Scholl (Gau-Heppenheim)
Haxthäuser Hof (Ingelheim (Wackernheim)
Heinz-Walter Metzler (Bermersheim)
Helmut Kloos (Worms-Horchheim)
Hirschof (Westhofen)
Hollerhof (Fürfeld)

Jakob Neumer (Uelversheim)
Jutta & Raimund Huster (Ingelheim-Grosswinternheim)
Klaus Knobloch (Ober-Flörsheim)
Lehnerhof (Mettenhein)
Lunkenheimer (Ingelheim-Groswinternheim)
Marienhof (Dienheim)
Reh Kendermann (Bingen am Rhein)
Rösch-Spies (Guntersblum)
Rothes (Aspisheim)
Schäfer (Armsheim)
Villa Sachsen (Bingen)
Villa Waldorf Schulz (Biebelsheim)
Wambolderhof (Stadecken-Elsheim)

THE PFALZ

Germany's rising star, the Pfalz, or Rheinpfalz as it was called until recently, has always been capable of producing world-class wines, but it has only just started doing so on any widespread scale. The best winemakers of the Pfalz now tend to make rich, powerful, spicy wines that are more reminiscent of Alsace than those of Alsace's mirror-image, Baden.

RARE PHYSICAL EVIDENCE of ancient German wines exists in the Pfalz at the wine museum at Speyer. Here a glass amphora contains genuine, golden 1,600-year-old wine, made by the Romans. By the 12th century, the Bishop of Speyer owned the best vineyards in the Pfalz and they remained the property of the Church until acquired by Napoleon.

After the great Corsican emperor somewhat reluctantly left the region, the socio-economic composition of the Pfalz changed dramatically and irrevocably. With the restructuring came a considerably less monopolistic form of land ownership.

THE PFALZ TODAY

Sometimes referred to as the Palatinate, the Pfalz covers 80 kilometres (50 miles) of the sun-blessed vineyards of the Haardt Mountains and the Pfalz forest. It has some 25,000 smallholders, each of whom works less than 1 hectare (about 2.5 acres) on average; most are part-time. Many sell their grapes to cooperatives, who process

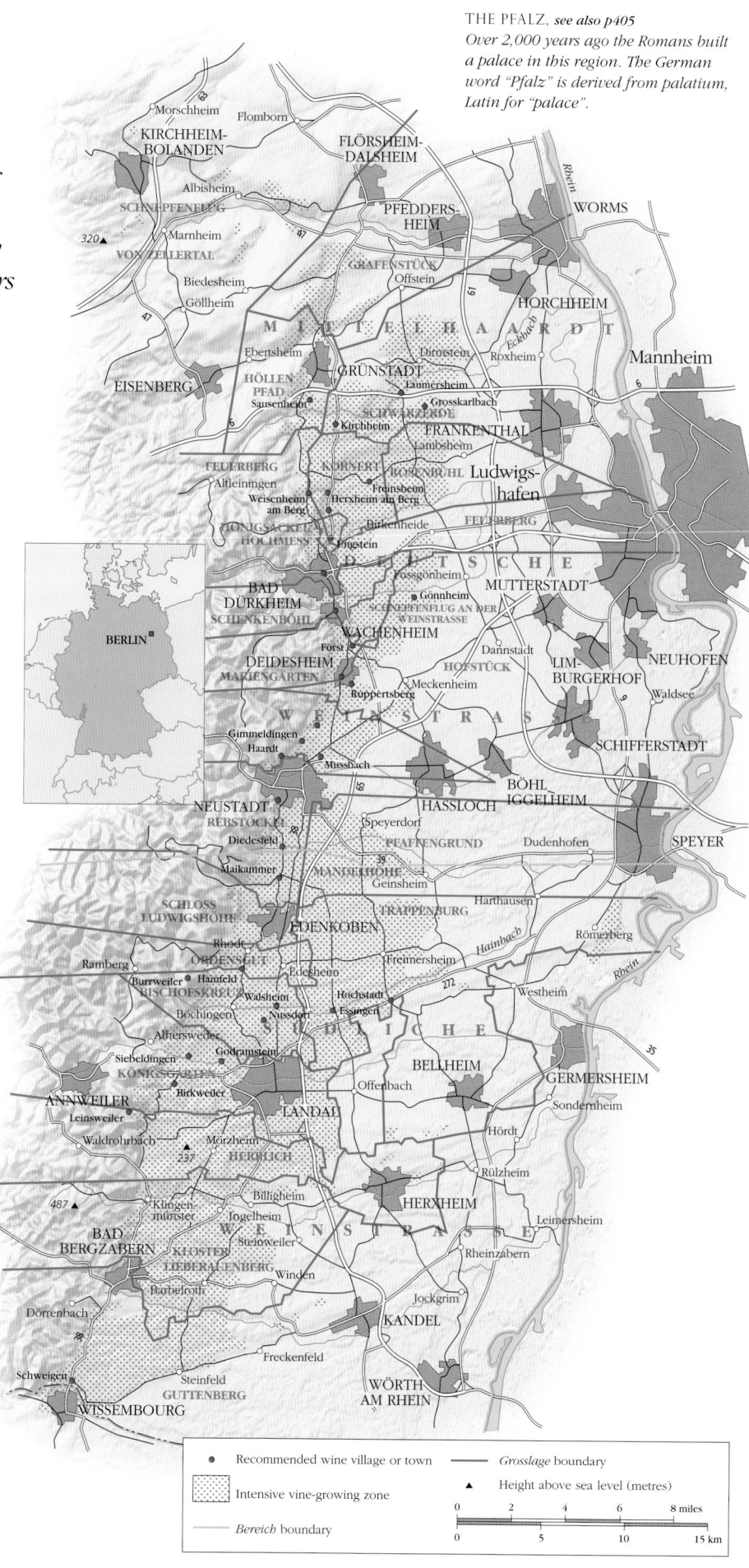

THE PFALZ, *see also p405*
Over 2,000 years ago the Romans built a palace in this region. The German word "Pfalz" is derived from palatium, Latin for "palace".

THE REGION AT A GLANCE

Area under vine
23,461 ha or 57,973 acres (increasing)

Average yield
104 hl/ha (increasing)

Red wine
38%

White wine
49% (decreasing)

Rotling
13%

Most important grape varieties
23% Riesling (increasing), 14%

Dornfelder (increasing), 10% Müller-Thurgau (decreasing), 9% Portugieser (decreasing), 7% Spätburgunder (increasing), 5% Kerner (decreasing), 5% Grauburgunder, 4% Weissburgunder, 23% others

Infrastructure
Bereiche 2; *Grosslagen* 25; *Einzellagen* 335

Note: The vineyards straddle 170 communities, the names of which may appear on the label.

Map legend

- ● Recommended wine village or town
- ▦ Intensive vine-growing zone
- Bereich boundary
- Grosslage boundary
- ▲ Height above sea level (metres)

0 2 4 6 8 miles
0 5 10 15 km

about 25 per cent of the Pfalz's output. There is, however, still a minority of estates that have larger land-holdings. The vast numbers of growers, grapes, soil types, and microclimates combine to create a diversity of wine styles, from close to half of all Liebfraumilch produced (Rheinhessen accounts for most of the other half) to a wealth of expressive pure varietals. This region yields more wine than any other in Germany, and it is the smallest growers who make it such a great one.

QUALITY REQUIREMENTS AND AVERAGE QMP PRODUCTION

PFALZ'S MINIMUM OECHSLE	QUALITY CATEGORY	HARVEST BREAKDOWN
44°	Deutscher Tafelwein	1%
50–53°	Landwein	0.5%
60–62°	* QbA	70%
73—76°	* Kabinett	19.5%
85–90°	* Spätlese	5%
92–100°	* Auslese	1%
120°	Beerenauslese	1%
120°	Eiswein	1%
150°	Trockenbeerenauslese	1%

* Minimum Oechsle levels vary according to grape variety; those that have a naturally lower sugar content may qualify at a correspondingly lower level.

FACTORS AFFECTING TASTE AND QUALITY

LOCATION
The second-largest German wine region, stretching 80 kilometres (50 miles) from Rheinhessen to Alsace, bounded by the Rhine on the east and Haardt Mountains on the west.

CLIMATE
The Pfalz is the sunniest and driest wine-producing region in Germany, sheltered by the Haardt Mountains and Donnersberg hills.

ASPECT
Vineyards are sited mainly on flat land or gentle slopes, at an altitude of between 100 and 250 metres (330 and 820 feet).

SOIL
Although loam is prevalent, it is often interspersed with a wide range of other soils, from loess, sand, and weathered sandstone to widely dispersed "islands" of limestone, granite, porphyry, and clayish slate.

VITICULTURE AND VINIFICATION
The Pfalz vies with Rheinhessen as the largest wine producer among Germany's wine regions. The leading estates have a relatively high proportion of Riesling in their vineyards, and produce wines of the very highest quality, although speciality Gewürztraminers and Muskatellers can be extraordinarily good when vinified dry. One-third of Pfalz wine is sold directly to consumers and half is marketed through large commercial wineries and two dozen or so cooperatives.

GRAPE VARIETIES
Primary varieties: Müller-Thurgau, Riesling
Secondary varieties: Bacchus, Dornfelder, Gewürztraminer, Huxelrebe, Kerner, Morio-Muskat, Muskateller, Portugieser, Ruländer, Scheurebe, Silvaner, Spätburgunder

---

THE APPELLATIONS OF
THE PFALZ

Note In the Pfalz wine region, each *Grosslage* can be prefixed only by a specified village name. The village name has been listed here under the name of the *Grosslage*.

BEREICH MITTELHAARDT-DEUTSCHE WEINSTRASSE

The quality of wines from this *Bereich* is so high, few are sold as anything less than *Einzellagen*.

GROSSLAGE FEUERBERG
Bad Dürkheim

A versatile *Grosslage*, producing a wide range of wines from full, spicy Gewürztraminers to soft, velvety Spätburgunders.

ELLERSTADT
☑ **Vineyard** *Kirchenstück* **Grower** *Klaus Schneider* (also red and white *cuvées*)

GROSSLAGE GRAFENSTÜCK

Producer Ludi Neiss stands out with some excellent Spätburgunder and Frühburgunder.

KINDENHEIM
☑ **Non-Einzellagen red wines Grower** *Ludi Neiss*
MÜHLHEIM
☑ **Vineyard** *Sonnenburg* **Grower** *Matthias Gaul*

GROSSLAGE HOCHMESS
Bad Dürkheim

This is a small, but high-performance *Grosslage*. It includes the best vineyards of Bad Dürkheim, although some fine wines are also produced within the boundaries of the two neighbouring *Grosslagen* of Feuerberg and Schenkenböhl. The attractive wines of Grosslage Hochmess display a perfect harmony of full flavour and flowery fragrance.

BAD DÜRKHEIM
☑ **Vineyard** *Michelsberg* **Grower** *Karl Schaefer* •
Vineyard *Spielberg* **Grower** *Karl Schaefer*

GROSSLAGE HOFSTÜCK
Deidesheim

Grosslage Hofstück produces homogeneous, noble, and elegant wines. The outstanding quality of these wines owes a great deal to the vineyard's favourable soil conditions.

DEIDESHEIM
☑ **Vineyard** *Nonnenstück* **Growers** *Bürklin-Wolf, Reichsrat von Buhl*
RUPPERTSBERG
☑ **Vineyard** *Gaisböhl* **Grower** *Bürklin-Wolf* •
Vineyard *Reiterpfad* **Growers** *Bassermann-Jordan, Bergdolt, A Christmann*

GROSSLAGE HÖLLENPFAD
Grünstadt

Produces a range of wines that are full and substantial in body but lack finesse.

GROSSLAGE HONIGSÄCKEL
Ungstein

This is a small *Grosslage* composed of varied soil and making full-bodied wines of intense flavour, especially Scheurebe.

UNGSTEIN
☑ **Vineyard** *Herrenberg* **Grower** *Pfeffingen-Fuhrmann-Eymael* • **Vineyard** *Weilberg* **Grower** *Pfeffingen-Fuhrmann-Eymael*

GROSSLAGE KOBNERT
Kallstadt

A single vineyard prior to the 1971 wine law, this is now a *Grosslage*, but a very good one.

HERXHEIM AM BERG
☑ **Vineyard** *Berg Honigsack* **Grower** *Pfleger* •

Vineyard *Himmelreich* **Grower** *Schumacher* (red and white) • **Premium non-Einzellagen red Grower** *Pfleger* (Edition Curator)
KALLSTADT
☑ **Vineyard** *Saumagen* **Grower** *Koehler-Ruprecht* • **Premium non-Einzellagen red Grower** *Koehler-Ruprecht* (Philippi Trocken),

GROSSLAGE MARIENGARTEN
Forst an der Weinstrasse

Nowhere in the Pfalz can Riesling wines of such incomparable finesse and intensity be found.

DEIDESHEIM
☑ **Vineyard** *Kalkofen* **Growers** *Weingut von Winning Dr Deinhard, Bürklin-Wolf* • **Vineyard** *Kieselberg* **Growers** *Josef Biffar, Georg Mosbacher* • **Vineyard** *Herrgottsacker* **Grower** *Weingut von Winning Dr Deinhard* • **Vineyard** *Hohenmorgen* **Growers** *Bassermann-Jordan, Bürklin-Wolf, A Christmann* • **Vineyard** *Langenmorgen* **Grower** *Dr Deinhard*
FORST
☑ **Vineyard** *Freundstück* **Grower** *Georg Mosbacher* • **Vineyard** *Jesuitengarten* **Growers** *Bassermann-Jordan, von Buhl, Bürklin-Wolf, Weingut von Winning Dr Deinhard* • **Vineyard** *Kirchenstück* **Growers** *Bassermann-Jordan, Bürklin-Wolf, Heinrich Spindler* • **Vineyard** *Pechstein* **Growers** *Bassermann-Jordan, von Buhl, J L Wolf, Heinrich Spindler* • **Vineyard** *Ungeheuer* **Growers** *Bassermann-Jordan, J L Wolf, Lucashof, Bürklin-Wolf, Von Buhl, Georg Mosbacher, Weingut von Winning Dr Deinhard*
WACHENHEIM
☑ **Vineyard** *Rechbächel* **Grower** *Bürklin-Wolf*

GROSSLAGE MEERSPINNE
Neustadt-Gimmeldingen

These climatically pampered vineyards, on the sheltered slopes of the Haardt Mountains, produce some of the very finest Pfalz wines.

GIMMELDINGEN

✓ **Vineyard** *Mandelgarten* **Growers** *A Christmann, Müller-Catoir* • **Vineyard** *Schlössel* **Grower** *Müller-Catoir*

HAARDT

✓ **Vineyard** *Bürgergarten* **Grower** *Müller-Catoir* • **Vineyard** *Herrenletten* **Growers** *Müller-Catoir, Weegmüller* • **Vineyard** *Mandelring* **Growers** *Müller-Catoir, Weegmüller*

KÖNIGSBACH

✓ **Vineyard** *Idig* **Grower** *A Christmann* (red and white)

GROSSLAGE PFAFFENGRUND
Neustadt-Diedesfeld

This is not an exceptional *Grosslage*.

DUTTWEILER

✓ **Vineyard** *Kalkberg* **Grower** *Bergdolt* (red and white)

GROSSLAGE REBSTÖCKEL
Neustadt-Diedesfeld

No outstanding villages, vineyards, or growers.

GROSSLAGE ROSENBÜHL
Freinsheim

No outstanding villages, vineyards, or growers.

GROSSLAGE SCHENKENBÖHL
Wachenheim

The third *Grosslage* to share the vineyards of Bad Dürkheim.

GROSSLAGE SCHNEPFENFLUG AN DER WEINSTRASSE
Forst an der Weinstrasse

Except for a small part of Forst's vineyards (the rest belong to Grosslage Mariengarten), few outstanding growers are to be found here.

GROSSLAGE SCHNEPFENFLUG VOM ZELLERTAL
Zell

No outstanding villages, vineyards, or growers.

GROSSLAGE SCHWARZERDE
Kirchheim

Mediocre Silvaner-based wines are standard here, but there are a couple of excellent growers in obscure villages that offer good value.

DIRMSTEIN

✓ **Vineyard** *Mandelpfad* **Grower** *Knipser*

GROSSKARLBACH

✓ **Vineyard** *Burgweg "im grossen Garten"* (red and white) **Growers** *Knipser, Philipp Kuhn* (white)

LAUMERSHEIM

✓ **Vineyard** *Kirschgarten* (red) **Growers** *Knipser, Philipp Kuhn* • **Vineyard** *Mandelberg* (Steinbuckel and Himmelsrech) **Grower** *Knipser* • **Premium non-Einzellagen red Growers** *Knipser* (Syrah *barrique*, Dornfelder*** *barrique*), *Philipp Kuhn* (Frühburgunder *barrique*)

BEREICH SÜDLICHE WEINSTRASSE

Dominated by rather dull and neutral Müller-Thurgau, but the younger winemakers are beginning to excel.

GROSSLAGE BISCHOFSKREUZ
Walsheim

Improving quality.

BURRWEILER

✓ **Vineyard** *Schlossgarten* **Grower** *Theo Minges* • **Premium non-Einzellagen white Grower** *Herbert Messmer* (Chardonnay *trocken barrique*)

GLEISWEILER

✓ **Vineyard** *Hölle* **Grower** *Theo Minges*

WALSHEIM

✓ **Vineyard** *Silberberg* **Grower** *Karl Pfaffmann*

GROSSLAGE GUTTENBERG
Schweigen

When is a German wine not German? When it's grown in France, of course, where 130 hectares (321 acres) of Schweigen's "sovereign" vineyards are located. Every year the growers pick their grapes in France and trundle across the border to vinify them. Weird as it might sound, the grapes are German if pressed in Germany, but French if pressed in France! The *terroir* of this *Grosslage* is most suited to the Burgunder varietals and Gewürztraminer, reflecting the area's northern extension of the Alsace vineyards.

SCHWEIGEN

✓ **Vineyard** *Sonnenberg Sankt Paul* **Grower** *Friedrich Becker* (red) • **Vineyard** *Sonnenberg Rädling* **Grower** *Bernhart* (red) • **Vineyard** *Kammerberg* **Grower** *Friedrich Becker* (red) • **Premium non-Einzellagen red wines Grower** *Friedrich Becker* (Pinot Noir Trocken, "Only Sansibar", "die verbotenen Früchte")

GROSSLAGE HERRLICH
Eschbach

An area easily capable of producing good QmP wines. The *Auslese* can be astonishingly cheap.

ILBESHEIM

✓ **Vineyard** *Kalmit* **Grower** *Kranz*

LEINSWEILER

✓ **Vineyard** *Sonnenberg* **Grower** *Siegrist* (red and white) • **Non-Einzellagen red and white wines Grower** *Siegrist* (Pinot Noir**** Trocken)

GROSSLAGE KLOSTER LIEBFRAUENBERG
Bad Bergzabern

Not renowned for outstanding villages or vineyards.

GROSSLAGE KÖNIGSGARTEN
Godramstein

This *Grosslage* consists of some excellent wine villages and several talented winemakers.

ALBERSWEILER

✓ **Vineyard** *Latt* **Grower** *Ökonomierat Rebholz*

BIRKWEILER

✓ **Vineyard** *Kastanienbusch* **Growers** *Ökonomierat Rebholz, Dr Wehrheim* (red and white), *Gies-Düppel, Siener, Ökonomierat Johannes Kleinmann* • **Vineyard** *Mandelberg* **Growers** *Dr Wehrheim, Gies-Düppel* • **Premium non-Einzellagen white Grower** *Dr Wehrheim* (Chardonnay "Keuper" Trocken "R")

GODRAMSTEIN

✓ **Vineyard** *Münzberg "Schlangenpfiff"* **Grower** *Münzberg*

SIEBELDINGEN

✓ **Vineyard** *Im Sonnenschein* **Growers** *Ökonomierat Rebholz* (red and white), *Wilhelmshof* (red and white) • **Premium red wine blend Grower** *Ökonomierat Rebholz* (Tradition)

GROSSLAGE MANDELHÖHE
Maikammer

Some pleasant, attractive Rieslings.

KIRRWEILER

✓ **Vineyard** *Mandelberg* **Grower** *Bergdolt*

MAIKAMMER

✓ **Vineyard** *Kapellenberg* **Grower** *Faubel* • **Vineyard** *Kirchenstück* **Grower** *Faubel*

GROSSLAGE ORDENSGUT
Edesheim

Grosslage Ordensgut is currently improving the quality of its produce, and some sound Burgunder varietal wines can be found at bargain prices.

GROSSLAGE SCHLOSS LUDWIGSHÖHE
Edenkoben

No outstanding villages, vineyards, or growers in this *Grosslage*, although good wines are produced in the village of St Martin.

GROSSLAGE TRAPPENBERG
Hochstadt

Apart from Essingener Rossberg, there are few outstanding vineyards in this *Grosslage*, although there are some good wines made in the village of Hochstadt.

ESSINGEN

Vineyard *Rossberg* **Grower** *Weingut Winfried Frey & Soehne* (noble sweet wines only) • **Vineyard** *Sonnenberg* **Grower** *Weingut Winfried Frey & Soehne* (noble sweet wines only)

CERTIFIED ORGANIC PRODUCERS

Organic

Andreas Kopf (Landau)
Brigitte Hohl (Freinsheim)
Dr Helmut Scholl (Bornheim)
Feitig-Richter (Siebeldingen)
Fippinger-Wick (Zell)
Franz Braun (Ranschbach)
Franz Krahl (Heinfeld)
Friedrich Graf (Edesheim)
G Schwarztrauber (Mußbach)
Georg Siben Erben (Deidesheim)
Hans Clödy (Niederotterbach)
Hans Manck (Freinsheim)
Hans Pflüger (Bad Dürkheim)

Hartmut Risser (Kerzenheim)
Hartmut Stauch (Kallstadt)
Heiner Sauer (Böchingen)
Helmut Krauss (Zellertal/Zell)
Hoffmann (Göcklingen)
Isegrim-Hof, Klaus Wolf (Bad Dürkheim-Ungstein)
Janson Bernhard (Zellertal-Harxheim)
Karin Deutscher (Klein-Bockenheim)
Klaus Hohlreiter (Göcklingen)
Kurt Weber (Böchingen)
Lebenshilfe (Bad Dürkheim)

Ludwig Seiler (Weyher)
Martinshof (Böbingen)
Marzolph (Landau-Wollmesh)
Rudolf Eymann (Gönnheim)
Rummel (Landau-Nussdorf)
Schneider-Beiwinkel (Edenkoben)
Spinnrädel (Kaiserslautern)
Stefan Kuntz (Landau)
Stephanshof (St Martin)
Walhbacherhof (Contwig)
Walter Merk (Ellerstadt)
Winfried Seeber (St Martin)
Wöhrle (Bockenheim)

THE HESSISCHE BERGSTRASSE

Situated between the Rheinhessen and Franken, the northern tip of Baden's vineyards is the Hessische Bergstrasse. This is the smallest and least-known of Germany's Qualitätswein regions, and its fruity wines are marked by a pronounced earthy acidity, with almost 60 per cent made in a dry style.

THIS REGION CORRESPONDS to the northern section of the old Roman *strata montana*, or "mountain road", hence Bergstrasse. This ancient trade route ran from Darmstadt to Wiesloch, which is south of Heidelberg in what is now the Baden region. The Romans brought viticulture to this area, but without the monasteries, which developed, spread, and maintained the vineyards throughout the medieval period, the tradition of winemaking would have ceased long ago.

The vineyards of the Hessische Bergstrasse are dotted among orchards in a strip of foothills along the western edge of Odenwald. Protected by the Odenwald, the fragrance of fruit trees in full bloom noticeably hangs over these hills in springtime. Indeed, Odenwald's forested mountains offer such effective protection that the sun-trap vineyards of Bensheim boast the highest annual mean temperatures in Germany. This exceptional heat is, of course, relative to Germany's cool northern climate, and the wines produced here have an excellent level of acidity, but there is a definite peachiness to the finest Rieslings, which is an indication of their ripeness. The Hessische Bergstrasse is planted with a relatively high proportion of Riesling, particularly in the *Bereich* Starkenburg where the best wines are grown.

The vines, which grow on relatively rich soils, produce very fruity wines that have a typical and easily recognized, earthy

UNTERHAMBACH
A vineyard above Unterhambach, where small-scale winemaking is the norm. The cooperative at nearby Heppenheim receives 70 per cent of the region's grapes.

THE HESSISCHE BERGSTRASSE, *see also p405*
This area is called the "spring garden", because of the early flowering of its fruit and almond orchards, between which vineyards are planted.

Map legend:
- ● Recommended wine village or town
- ▦ Intensive vine-growing zone
- Bereich boundary
- Grosslage boundary
- ▲ Height above sea level (metres)

0   2   4   6   8 miles
0   2   4   6   8   10   12 km

THE REGION AT A GLANCE

Area under vine
439 ha or 1,085 acres (decreasing)

Average yield
81 hl/ha (increasing)

Red wine
22w%

White wine
74% (decreasing)

Rotling
4%

Most important grape varieties
48% Riesling (decreasing),
10% Spätburgunder,
9% Grauburgunder (increasing),
33% others

Infrastructure
Bereiche 2; *Grosslagen* 3;
Einzellagen 22

Note The vineyards of the Hessische Bergstrasse straddle 10 *Gemeinden* (communes), the names of which may appear on the label.

acidity, with a style that is richer than most Rheinhessen wines and more reminiscent of a somewhat rustic Rheingau. The Müller-Thurgau is not Germany's best, but it can be fragrant; the Silvaner lacks the assertive character found in Franken to the east; but the Gewürztraminer can have a fine, subdued style.

The vineyards are farmed by more than 1,000 individual growers with the average-sized plot being barely more than one-third of a hectare (four-fifths of an acre). Most of these growers are part-timers who tend their plots at weekends. This helps to explain the anonymity of the area's wines, and this will remain until a number of large, quality-minded estates are established.

GRONAU, HESSISCHE BERGSTRASSE
Looking down the south-facing slopes of the Hemsburg vineyard towards Gronau, an Ortsteil of Bensheim.

FACTORS AFFECTING TASTE AND QUALITY

⊕ LOCATION
Between Darmstadt and Heppenheim, beside the Odenwald Mountains, with the Rhine to the west and the Main to the north.

CLIMATE
The vineyards on the southern slopes of the valleys flanking the Bergstrasse benefit from an average temperature of over 9°C (48°F). Combined with an annual rainfall of 75.5 centimetres (30 inches), this produces ideal conditions. Bensheim is supposed to be the hottest place in Germany.

ASPECT
The best vineyards are generally on southwest-facing slopes in the grosslagen of Schlossberg and Wolfsmagen (particularly Kalkgasse in Bensheim and Centrericht in Heppenheim). The terrain is more one of hilly hinterland than steep valleys.

SOIL
Most of the soil consists of varying amounts of light, finely structured loess and basalt.

VITICULTURE AND VINIFICATION
The vineyards are not contiguous, but are planted rather haphazardly, sometimes on old-established terraces among orchards. Although a great many individuals grow grapes, more than half the crop is processed by the regional cooperative in Heppenheim. Müller-Thurgau is giving way to Grauburgunder, and almost 60 per cent of the total wines produced in this region are technically dry (*trocken*). The State Wine Domain in Bensheim is the region's largest vineyard owner, but given the small size of this region, almost all of its wines are consumed locally.

🍇 GRAPE VARIETIES
Primary varieties: Müller-Thurgau, Riesling
Secondary varieties: Ehrenfelser, Gewürztraminer, Grauburgunder, Kerner, Ruländer, Scheurebe, Silvaner, Weissburgunder

QUALITY REQUIREMENTS AND AVERAGE QMP PRODUCTION

NAHE'S MINIMUM OECHSLE	QUALITY CATEGORY	HARVEST BREAKDOWN
44°	Deutscher Tafelwein	1%
47°	Landwein	1%
50–60°	* QbA	76%
67–73°	* Kabinett	17%
76–85°	* Spätlese	1%
83–88°	* Auslese	1%
110°	Beerenauslese	1%
110°	Eiswein	1%
150°	Trockenbeerenauslese	1%

* Minimum Oechsle levels vary according to grape variety; those that have a naturally lower sugar content may qualify at a correspondingly lower level.

THE APPELLATIONS OF
THE HESSISCHE BERGSTRASSE

BEREICH STARKENBURG

This is the larger of this region's *Bereiche*, and the best in terms of quality. Riesling is planted in most of its vineyards.

GROSSLAGE ROTT

The largest of Starkenburg's three *Grosslagen*, this includes the northern section of Bensheim, one of the region's best communes. Historically, the finest wine came from Bensheim's south-facing Herrnwingert vineyard, but while *terroir* always holds the potential, it is up to the winemaker to exploit it, and today the best wines come from Auerbach's Höllberg vineyard.

AUERBACH
✓ **Vineyard** *Höllberg* **Grower** *Simon-Bürkle*

GROSSLAGE SCHLOSSBERG

This *Grosslage* covers part of Bensheim and three villages to the south, with Heppenheim the most

highly rated. A unique peachiness is associated with the sun-drenched Stemmler and Centgericht vineyards.

HEPPENHEIM
✓ **Vineyard** *Centgericht* **Grower** *Staatsweingut Bergstrasse*

GROSSLAGE WOLFSMAGEN

This includes the southern section of Bensheim with the two *Ortsteile* of Zell and Gronau.

BENSHEIM
✓ **Vineyard** *Kalkgasse* **Grower** *Weingut der Stadt Bensheim*

BEREICH UMSTADT

There are no remarkable villages, vineyards, or *Grosslagen* in this *Bereich*, as its six *Einzellagen* are *Grosslagenfrei*. The grape varieties Müller-Thurgau, Ruländer, and Silvaner dominate.

ZELL VINEYARD
Vineyard in the Streichling Einzellage at Zell, near Bensheim, Hessen.

FRANKEN

Classic Franconian Silvaner wine is distinctly dry with an earthy or smoky aroma and is bottled in the traditional flask-shaped Bocksbeutel. *In this region, the Silvaner grape variety has, to a certain extent, given way to Müller-Thurgau, among others, although this trend is now being reversed.*

THERE IS ALMOST TWICE AS MUCH land under vine in Franken as there is in the Rheingau, for instance, but the vineyards are scattered over a far greater area and they are interspersed with meadows and forests. Franken is also a beer-producing region, and many say that more pleasure can be had from a stein of

INTERIOR OF THE RESIDENZ, WÜRZBURG
The Residency at Würzburg, with its Baroque grand staircase, is now part of the Bavarian State Domain.

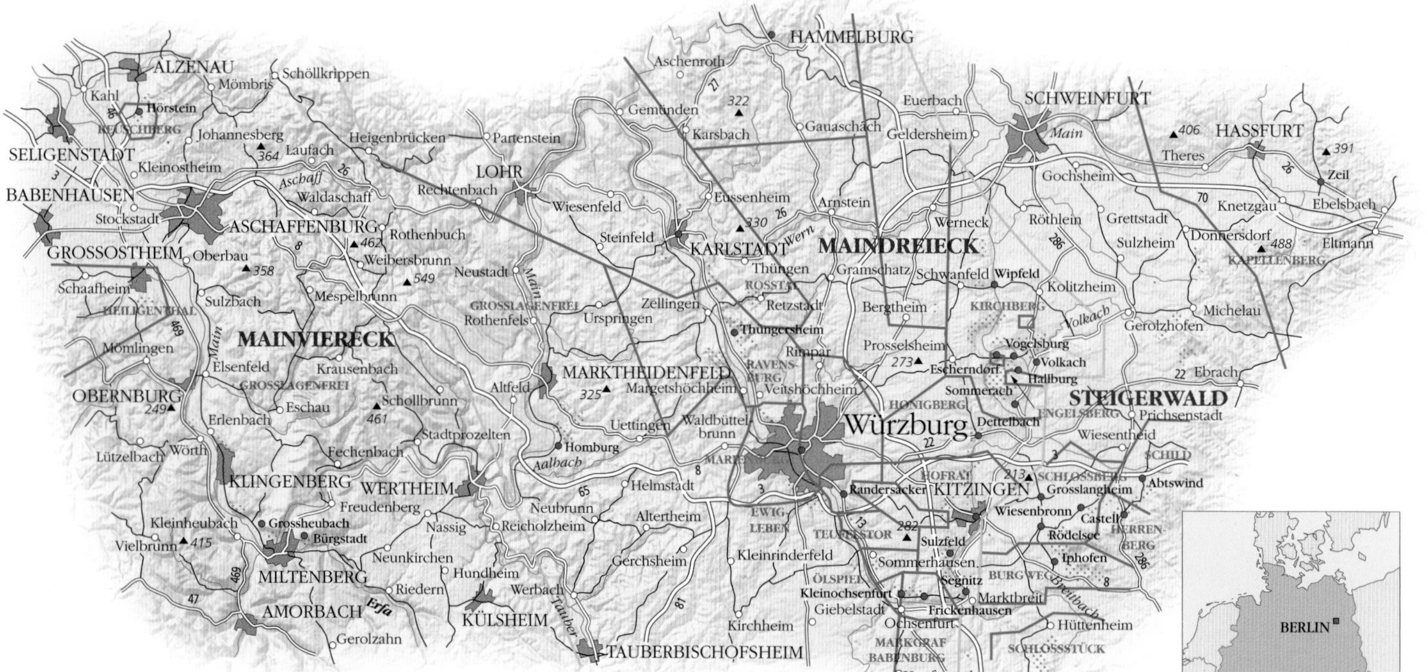

QUALITY REQUIREMENTS AND AVERAGE QMP PRODUCTION

FRANKEN'S MINIMUM OECHSLE	QUALITY CATEGORY	HARVEST BREAKDOWN
44°	Deutscher Tafelwein	1%
50°	Landwein	1%
60°	* QbA	69%
76–80°	* Kabinett	21%
85–90°	* Spätlese	4%
100°	* Auslese	1%
125°	Beerenauslese	1%
125°	Eiswein	1%
150°	Trockenbeerenauslese	1%

* Minimum Oechsle levels vary according to grape variety; those that have a naturally lower sugar content may qualify at a correspondingly lower level.

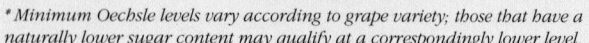

Map labels

HAMMELBURG

ALZENAU · Schöllkrippen
Kahl · Hörstein · Mömbris
Aschenroth
Gemünden · 322 · Euerbach · SCHWEINFURT
Johannesberg · Heigenbrücken · Partenstein · Karsbach · Gauaschach · Geldersheim · Main · ▲406 · HASSFURT
SELIGENSTADT · 364 · Laufach · LOHR · Eussenheim · Arnstein · Werneck · Theres · ▲391
Kleinostheim · Rechtenbach · Wiesenfeld · 330 · 26 · Röthlein · Gochsheim · Zeil
BABENHAUSEN · Aschaff · Waldaschaff · Steinfeld · Thüngen · KARLSTADT · Wern · MAINDREIECK · Grettstadt · 70 · Knetzgau · Ebelsbach
Stockstadt · ASCHAFFENBURG · Rothenbuch · ▲462 · Gramschatz · Schwanfeld · Wipfeld · Sulzheim · Donnersdorf · ▲488 · Eltmann
GROSSOSTHEIM · Oberbau · ▲358 · Weibersbrunn · Neustadt · ROSSTAL · Retzstadt · Bergtheim · KAPELLENBERG
Schaafheim · Sulzbach · Mespelbrunn · ▲549 · GROSSLAGENFREI · Zellingen · Thüngersheim · Prosselsheim · KIRCHBERG · Volkach · Michelau
HEILIGENTHAL · Rothenfels · Ursprungen · Rimpar · Vogelsburg · Gerolzhofen
Mömlingen · MAINVIERECK · Elsenfeld · Krausenbach · Altfeld · MARKTHEIDENFELD · RAVENS · Escherndorf · Volkach · 22 · Ebrach
OBERNBURG · ▲249 · GROSSLAGENFREI · Eschau · Schöllbrunn · 325 · Margetshöchheim · BURG · Sommerach · STEIGERWALD
Erlenbach · 461 · Stadtprozelten · Uettingen · Veitshöchheim · HONIGBERG · Dettelbach · ENGELSBERG · Prichsenstadt
Lützelbach · Wörth · Fechenbach · Homburg · Waldbüttelbrunn · Würzburg · Wiesentheid · SCHILD
KLINGENBERG · WERTHEIM · Aalbach · Helmstadt · MARK · HOFRAT · 213 · SCHLOSSBERG · Abtswind
Kleinheubach · Freudenberg · Neubrunn · EWIG · Randersacker · KITZINGEN · Grosslangheim
Vielbrunn · ▲415 · Grossheubach · Bürgstadt · Nassig · Reicholzheim · LEBEN · TELTERSTOR · Wiesenbronn · Castell · HERREN
▲462 · MILTENBERG · Neunkirchen · Hundheim · Gerchsheim · Sulzfeld · Rödelsee · Iphofen · BERG
47 · AMORBACH · Riedern · Werbach · Kleinrinderfeld · Sommerhausen · ÖLSPIEL · BURGWEG
Gerolzahn · KÜLSHEIM · Kirchheim · Kleinochsenfurt · Segnitz · Marktbreit
TAUBERBISCHOFSHEIM · Giebelstadt · Frickenhausen · Hüttenheim
MARKGRAF · Ochsenfurt · SCHLOSSSTÜCK
Hopferstadt

BERLIN

Legend

●   Recommended wine village or town

▒   Intensive vine-growing zone

—   Bereich boundary

—   Grosslage boundary

▲   Height above sea level (metres)

0   4   8   12   16 miles
0   5   10   15   20   25 km

FRANKEN, *see also p405*
This region is in the very heart of Germany. At the centre of Franken lies Würzburg, which is actually famous for its beer, although most of the region's vineyards are not far away.

THE REGION AT A GLANCE

Area under vine
6,063 ha or 14,982 acres
(increasing)

Average yield
80 hl/ha (decreasing)

Red wine
15%

White wine
77% (decreasing)

Rotling
8%

**Most important
grape varieties**
30% Müller-Thurgau (decreasing),
21% Silvaner (static),
12% Bacchus (static),
37% others

Infrastructure
Bereiche 3; *Grosslagen* 20;
Einzellagen 171

Note: The vineyards of
Franken straddle 125 *Gemeinden*
(communes), the names
of which may appear on labels.

THE CELLAR AT THE RESIDENZ, WÜRZBURG
*The magnificent cellar under the Baroque Residency at Würzburg has been
state run since 1803.*

Würzburger beer than from a glass of Würzburger Stein, Franken's
most famous wine. Exported wine invariably comes from the
better estates and it is relatively expensive, particularly if bottled
in the traditional *Bocksbeutel*.

Wines made from this region's Silvaner grape have a full taste
and an earthy bite, sometimes attaining smoky complexity, making
it far more interesting than most examples of this variety. However,
my favourite Franconian wine is Riesling because, although it

accounts for less than 3 per cent of the vines grown and often
fails to ripen here, it can be made into exceptional wines in sunny
years. Rieslaner (Riesling x Silvaner cross), Bacchus, and Kerner
are all successful, particularly as QmP, although it is rare to find
a wine above *Auslese* level.

FACTORS AFFECTING TASTE AND QUALITY

LOCATION
Situated in Bavaria, Franken
was the most northerly of Germany's
wine regions until reunification.

CLIMATE
The most continental climate
of Germany's wine regions, with
dry warm summers and cold
winters. Severe frosts affect yields.

ASPECT
Many vineyards face south
and are located on the slopes of
the valleys of the Main and its

tributaries, as well as on sheltered
sites of the Steigerwald.

SOIL
Franken's three *Bereiche* have
different soil structures: Mainviereck
has predominantly weathered
coloured sandstone; Maindreieck
limestone with clay and loess; and
Steigerwald, weathered red marl.

**VITICULTURE AND
VINIFICATION**
The classic Franconian vine, the
Silvaner, has become less widely

planted than the Müller-Thurgau,
although the pendulum has started
to swing back the other way.
Rieslaner is something of a local
speciality. Franken wines generally
are usually drier than most in
Germany and accompany food
well. There are 6,000 growers,
allowing for a great range of
styles, although 40 per cent of the
wines are processed by the regional
cooperative in Kitzingen and
smaller cooperatives. Exports are
insignificant, with four out of every
five bottles of Franken wine

consumed within a 250-km radius
of where they were produced.

GRAPE VARIETIES
Primary varieties: Müller-
Thurgau, Silvaner
Secondary varieties: Bacchus,
Kerner, Ortega, Perle, Rieslaner,
Riesling, Scheurebe, Spätburgunder,
Traminer (Savagnin Blanc)

THE APPELLATIONS OF

FRANKEN

Note In Franken, certain *Grosslagen* can be prefixed
only by a specified village name, which is listed
immediately beneath the relevant *Grosslage* name.

BEREICH MAINDREIECK

Most of the vineyards in this *Bereich* are in the
vicinity of Würzburg. Grapes grown on the
limestone soils can produce exceptional wines.

GROSSLAGE BURG
Hammelburg

Robust, earthy Silvaners and the lighter, fragrant
Müller-Thurgaus are the main attractions.

GROSSLAGE ENGELSBERG

This *Grosslage* encompasses part of two *Einzellagen*
formerly in the *Grosslage* Kirchberg, the Sommeracher
vineyards of Katzenkopf and Rosenberg.

SOMMERACH

✓ **Vineyard** *Katzenkopf* **Grower** *Glaser-Himmelstoss*

GROSSLAGE
EWIG LEBEN

This *Grosslage* contains the greatest concentration
of fine vineyards in Franken and some fine wines
are available under its generic designation. Ewig
Leben has the advantage of a particularly favourable
microclimate, which helps create wines of a rare
harmony. Rieslings from this area possess an
original natural charm complemented by a
bouquet often reminiscent of peaches.

RANDERSACKER

✓ **Vineyard** *Pfülben* **Growers** *Juliusspital,
Schmitt's Kinder* • **Vineyard** *Sonnenstuhl*
Growers *Schmitt's Kinder, Schloss
Sommerhausen, Störrlein* • **Vineyard** *Marsberg*
Grower *Schmitt's Kinder*

GROSSLAGE HOFRAT
Kintzingen

This is one of Franken's few relatively large
Grosslagen, where the *Einzellagen* seldom excel,

except for the vineyards on the lazy bend of the
Main River north and south of Sulzfeld.

SULZFELD

✓ **Vineyard** *Cyriakusberg* **Grower** *Zehnthof Theo
Luckert* • **Vineyard** *Maustal* **Grower** *Brennfleck*

GROSSLAGE HONIGBERG

In this *Grosslage* there are no particularly outstanding
villages, vineyards, or growers, although a few good
wines are made in the village of Dettelbach.

GROSSLAGE KIRCHBERG
Volkach

Grosslage Kirchberg contains some of the finest vineyards in all of Franken. After years of mediocrity the full potential offered by the land is now being realized by a number of growers.

ESCHERNDORF

✓ **Vineyard** *Fürstenberg* **Grower** *Horst Sauer* •
Vineyard *Lump* **Growers** *Michael Fröhlich, Juliusspital, Max Müller I, Horst Sauer, Rainer Sauer*

NORDHEIM

✓ **Vineyard** *Vögelein* **Growers** *Divino Nordheim Winzergenossenschaft, Waldemar Braun, Glaser-Himmelstoss*

SOMMERACH

✓ **Vineyard** *Katzenkopf* **Grower** *Winzer Sommerach Der Winzerkeller*

VOLKACH

✓ **Vineyard** *Karthäuser* **Growers** *Rudolf Fürst* (red), *Juliusspital*

GROSSLAGE MARIENBERG

This has been created as a new Grosslage for the previously *Grosslagenfrei* vineyards north and west of Würzburg.

WÜRZBURG

✓ **Vineyard** *Stein* **Growers** *Bürgerspital zum Heiligen Geist, Juliusspital Würzburg, Am Stein-Ludwig Knoll* • **Vineyard** *Stein Harfe* **Grower** *Bürgerspital zum Heiligen Geist* • **Vineyard** *Innere Leiste* **Growers** *Juliusspital, Am Stein-Ludwig Knoll* • **Vineyard** *Abtsleite* **Grower** *Juliusspital Würzburg*

GROSSLAGE MARKGRAF BABENBERG

Some very good wines are made in Frickenhausen.

FRICKENHAUSEN

✓ **Vineyard** *Kapellenberg* **Grower** *Bickel-Stumpf*

GROSSLAGE OELSPIEL

This *Grosslage's* main feature is a fine strip of vineyards on the right bank of the Main, southeast of Würzburg. Schloss Sommerhausen has emerged as the district's leading producer.

SOMMERHAUSEN

✓ **Vineyard** *Steinbach* **Grower** *Schloss Sommerhausen*

GROSSLAGE RAVENSBURG
Thüngersheim

Grosslage Ravensburg is situated downstream from Franken's best vineyards, but some of the wines here can still be quite attractive.

GROSSLAGE ROSSTAL
Karlstadt

One grower who has shown promise in this otherwise lacklustre *Grosslage* is the Weingut Am Stein in Stetten.

STETTEN

✓ **Vineyard** *Stein* **Grower** *Am Stein-Ludwig Knoll*

GROSSLAGE TEUFELSTOR

The *Grosslage* of Teufelstor is a continuation of Ewig Leben, but the quality of the wines it produces is not as good.

EIBELSTADT

✓ **Vineyard** *Kapellenberg* **Grower** *Schloss Sommerhausen*

GROSSLAGENFREI

Many vineyards in this *Bereich* are *Grosslagenfrei* (composed of individual *Einzellagen* that are not grouped under any *Grosslagen*).

HALLBURG

✓ **Vineyard** *Schlossberg* **Grower** *Graf von Schönborn Schloss Hallburg*

HOMBURG

✓ **Vineyard** *Kallmuth* **Grower** *Fürst Löwenstein*

RÖTTINGEN

✓ **Vineyard** *Feuerstein* **Grower** *Hofmann*

BEREICH MAINVIERECK

Mainviereck is the smallest of the *Bereiche*, as well as being the most westerly, and the wines it produces are modest.

GROSSLAGE HEILIGENTHAL

This *Grosslage* comprises one village, Grossostheim, with just two *Einzellagen*, most vineyards in the area being *Grosslagenfrei*.

GROSSLAGE REUSCHBERG

This *Grosslage* comprises one village, Hörstein, and just two *Einzellagen*, most vineyards in the area being *Grosslagenfrei*.

GROSSLAGENFREI

Most of Mainviereck's vineyards are *Grosslagenfrei* (individual *Einzellagen* not grouped under any *Grosslage*). Standards have been rising over the last two decades and there is potential for excellent red wines on sites featuring red sandstone soils.

BÜRGSTADT

✓ **Vineyard** *Centgrafenberg* **Growers** *Rudolf Fürst, Hunsrück*

KLINGENBERG

✓ **Vineyard** *Schlossberg* **Grower** *Rudolf Fürst*

MICHELBACH

✓ **Vineyard** *Apostelgarten* **Grower** *Heilmann*

BEREICH STEIGERWALD

The distinctive, earthy character of Franconian wine is evident in *Bereich* Steigerwald, where heavier soils result in fuller-bodied wines.

GROSSLAGE BURGWEG

This *Grosslage* contains one of Franken's greatest wine villages, Iphofen.

IPHOFEN

✓ **Vineyard** *Julius-Echter Berg* **Growers** *Johann Ruck, Hans Wirsching, Juliusspital Würzburg* • **Vineyard** *Kalb* **Grower** *Hans Wirsching* • **Vineyard** *Kronsberg* **Grower** *Hans Wirsching*

GROSSLAGE HERRENBERG

There are a number of south-facing vineyards in Herrenberg, yet it is the northwest-facing ones in Castell that yield the exceptional wines.

CASTELL

✓ **Vineyard** *Kugelspiel* **Grower** *Castellsches Dömänenamt* • **Vineyard** *Schlossberg* **Grower** *Castellsches Dömänenamt* ◉

GROSSLAGE KAPELLENBERG

There are no outstanding villages, vineyards, or growers in Grosslage Kapellenberg, although a number of good wines are often produced in the village of Zeil.

ZEIL

✓ **Vineyard** *Mönchshang* **Grower** *Dr Heigel*

GROSSLAGE SCHILD

This *Grosslage* has no outstanding villages, vineyards, or growers, although good wines are made in the villages of Abtswind and Greuth.

GREUTH

✓ **Vineyard** *Bastel* **Grower** *Brügel*

GROSSLAGE SCHLOSSBERG

Underrated, with excellent, sheltered vineyards.

RÖDELSEE

✓ **Vineyard** *Küchenmeister* **Grower** *Weltner* • **Vineyard** *Schwanleite* **Grower** *Johann Ruck*

WIESENBRONN

✓ **Vineyard** *Geißberg* **Grower** *Roth* (red and white)

GROSSLAGE SCHLOSSTÜCK

No outstanding villages, vineyards, or growers, although good wines are made in Ippesheim.

OTHER CERTIFIED ORGANIC PRODUCERS

Organic		
Anton Hell (Wiesenbronn)	Geier (Königheim)	Manfred Schwab (Iphofen)
Bausewein (Iphofen)	Gerhard Roth (Wiesenbronn)	Rainer Zang (Nordheim am Main)
Erwin Christ (Nordheim)	Helmut Christ (Nordheim)	Roland Hemberger (Rödelsee)
Fred Ruppert (Prichstenstadt-Kirch)	Hermann Kramer (Simmershofen)	Wille Gebrüder (Esselbach)
	Lauerbach (TBB-Impfingen)	Willert-Eckert (Müdersheim)
	Mainstockheim (Mainstockheim)	

WÜRTTEMBERG

Württemberg is not well known as a wine region, principally because the wines produced in the area (a light red wine and a rosé called "Schillerwein") are not styles that are much in demand outside the region itself.

WÜRTTEMBERG IS GERMANY'S red-wine-producing region, but this is not red wine as most non-German wine drinkers would perceive it. Black grape varieties grow in over half the vineyards in Württemberg, and half of these are planted with Trollinger, a grape that produces a light, fresh, and grapey wine with none of the body, tannin, or other characteristics associated with a true red wine. The most concentrated Trollinger wines are made between Heilbronn and Winnenden, just northeast of Stuttgart, but they do not compare with reds produced in nearby Baden.

Red Lemberger is enjoyed locally, but until recently it produced unimpressive neutral-flavoured wines. A few growers have begun to get more out of this variety, but it is never going to make waves.

The rosé Schillerwein is a speciality and usually has more character than red wines made from other black grapes grown here, such as Schwarzriesling (Pinot Meunier), which makes a better white wine than red or rosé.

WHITE WINES

White Württemberg wines are usually of modest quality, although there are exceptions, such as robust, intensely flavoured Riesling, with pronounced acidity. The region's other white grape varieties make very ordinary wines, unless harvested at one of the higher QmP categories. One of these white grapes – Kerner – deserves a mention as this Trollinger x Riesling cross was created at the Württemberg Weinsberg viticultural institute and named after the local 19th-century doctor and poet Justinus Kerner.

WÜRTTEMBERG, *see also p405*
Most of the region's vineyards, in fertile districts near the Neckar River, are interspersed with farmland.

- ● Recommended wine village or town
- ▦ Intensive vine-growing zone
- — *Bereich* boundary
- — *Grosslage* boundary
- ▲ Height above sea level (metres)

0   4   8   12   16 miles

0   5   10   15   20   25 km

THE REGION AT A GLANCE

Area under vine
11,511 ha or 28,444 acres (increasing)

Average yield
105 hl/ha (static)

Red wine
67%

White wine
22% (decreasing)

Rotling
11%

Most important grape varieties
21% Trollinger (decreasing),
18% Riesling (decreasing),
15% Schwarzriesling (decreasing),
14% Lemberger (increasing),
11% Spätburgunder (increasing),
3% Müller-Thurgau, 18% others

Infrastructure
Bereiche 6; *Grosslagen* 17;
Einzellagen 206

Note The vineyards of Württemberg straddle 230 communes, the names of which may appear on the label.

QUALITY REQUIREMENTS AND AVERAGE QMP PRODUCTION

WÜRTTEMBERG'S MINIMUM OECHSLE	QUALITY CATEGORY	HARVEST BREAKDOWN
40°	Deutscher Tafelwein	1%
50°	Landwein	1%
57–63°	* QbA	84%
72–78°	* Kabinett	9%
85–88°	* Spätlese	3%
95°	* Auslese	0.5%
124°	Beerenauslese	0.5%
124°	Eiswein	0.5%
150°	Trockenbeerenauslese	0.5%

* Minimum Oechsle levels vary according to grape variety; those that have a naturally lower sugar content may qualify at a correspondingly lower level.

FACTORS AFFECTING TASTE AND QUALITY

LOCATION
Württemberg is situated between Frankfurt to the north and Lake Constance to the south.

CLIMATE
Sheltered by the Black Forest to the west and the hilly Swabian Alb to the east, this area has an especially warm growing season.

ASPECT
Vineyards are widely scattered either side of the Neckar River.

SOIL
Soils vary, but red marl, clay, loess, keuper and loam dominate, with scatterings of shell-limestone in the Neckar Valley area. Topsoils are deep and well drained, producing full wines with a firm acidity.

VITICULTURE AND VINIFICATION
Most of Württemberg's 16,500 growers own tiny plots and tend them part-time, taking their grapes to the cooperatives for processing. Most of the production is consumed locally. Trollinger has overtaken Riesling as the leading grape, while Lemberger and Spätburgunder are the fastest expanding. Another

major variety, Schwarzriesling, is the same as Pinot Meunier. Over half the wine is made in *halbtrocken* style.

GRAPE VARIETIES
Primary varieties: Lemberger, Riesling, Schwartzriesling (Pinot Meunier), Trollinger (Schaiva)
Secondary varieties: Kerner, Müller-Thurgau, Portugieser, Ruländer, Silvaner, Spätburgunder

---

THE APPELLATIONS OF

WÜRTTEMBERG

BEREICH BAYERISCHER BODENSEE

This has one *Grosslage* with four *Einzellagen*. Climatic conditions are not favourable enough for Reisling, and the small production consists mainly of Müller-Thurgau whites, Spätburgunder reds, and Spätburgunder *Weissherbst*.

GROSSLAGE LINDAUER SEEGARTEN

Although closest to the Baden *Grosslage* of Sonnenufer and politically part of Bavaria, which encompasses the QbA Franken, this outpost of vines is classified as part of Württemberg in German wine law.

BEREICH KOCHER-JAGST-TAUBER

White wines that rarely excel.

GROSSLAGE KOCHERBERG

Modest wines are made in Criesbach.

GROSSLAGE TAUBERBERG

Some good Rieslings, Traminers, and Muscats.

BEREICH OBERER NECKAR

A tiny *Bereich* with no outstanding vineyards.

BEREICH REMSTAL-STUTTGART

The second-largest *Bereich*.

GROSSLAGE HOHENNEUFFEN

Good wines are made in Metzingen.

GROSSLAGE KOPF

Improvements in a once uninspiring *Grosslage*.

WINTERBACH
✓ **Vineyard** *Hungerberg* **Grower** *Ellwanger*
✓ **Non-Einzellagen premium blends Growers** *Ellwanger* ("Hades", red and white), *Albrecht Schwegler* ("Saphir", "Granat", both red)

GROSSLAGE SONNENBÜHL

No outstanding villages, vineyards, or growers.

GROSSLAGE WARTBÜHL

Superior wines from between the unremarkable *Grosslagen* of Kopf and Sonnenbühl.

STETTEN
✓ **Vineyard** *Pulvermächer* **Growers** *Karl Haidle, Beurer* • **Premium red blends Grower** *Karl Haidle* ("Ypsilon", and *trocken barrique* wines)

GROSSLAGE WEINSTEIGE

Over the years, the cooperative of Untertürkheim has produced consistently reliable wines in this *Grosslage*, but they have recently been eclipsed by some truly fine Rieslings from rising stars.

FELLBACH
✓ **Vineyard** *Goldberg* **Grower** *Heid* (red)
Vineyard *Lämmler* **Growers** *Aldinger* (red and white), *Schnaitmann*

UNTERTÜRKHEIM
✓ **Vineyard** *Herzogenberg* (red and white) **Grower** *Wöhrwag* • **Non-Einzellagen premium red blends Growers** *Aldinger* (cuvées "C" and "M"), *Schnaitmann* (Simonroth), *Weinmanufaktur Untertürkheim, Wöhrwag* (cuvées "X" and "Philipp")

BEREICH WÜRTTEMBERGISCH BODENSEE

A one-*Einzellage Bereich* on Lake Constance.

BEREICH WÜRTTEMBERGISCH UNTERLAND

This *Bereich* encompasses more than 70 per cent of Württemberg's vineyards.

GROSSLAGE HEUCHELBERG

Some of Württemberg's finest wines.

NEIPPERG
✓ **Vineyard** *Schlossberg* **Grower** *Graf zu Neipperg*
PFAFFENHOFEN
✓ **Vineyard** *Hohenberg* **Grower** *Wachtstetter* (also Cuvée Ernst Combe premium red and white wines) • **Non-Einzellagen premium red Grower** *Wachtstetter* (Junges Schwaben Lemberger)

SCHWAIGERN
✓ **Vineyard** *Ruthe* **Grower** *Graf zu Neipperg*

GROSSLAGE KIRCHENWEINBERG

Pinot Meunier dominates in this area.

GROSSLAGE LINDELBERG

A small, scattered area east of Heilbronn, where *barrique*-matured Lemberger red is making a name for itself in an area that is better suited to Riesling.

VERRENBERG
✓ **Vineyard** *Verrenberg* **Grower** *Fürst zu Hohenlohe Öhringen* (red and white)

GROSSLAGE SALZBERG

Sandwiched between Heilbronn and Lindelberg; fine Rieslings could be produced on its steepest vineyards.

GROSSLAGE SCHALKSTEIN

Käsberg vineyard is the finest in this *Grosslage*. It specializes in full, dark red wines.

GROSSLAGE SCHOZACHTAL

Mostly white wines, including fine Riesling, but also some encouraging *barrique*-matured Lemberger and Spätburgunder.

GROSSLAGE STAUFENBERG

This covers the town of Heilbronn, its *Ortsteile*, and several outlying villages.

HEILBRONN
✓ **Non-Einzellagen premium red Grower** *Kistenmacher-Hengerer* (Junges Schwaben, Cuvée Maximilian) • **Non-Einzellagen wines Grower** *Drautz-Able* (red and white varietals)
WEINSBERG
✓ **Non-Einzellagen wines Grower** *Staatsweingut Weinsberg* ⊙ (red and white varietals and *cuvées*)

GROSSLAGE STROMBERG

A predominantly black-grape area.

BÖNNIGHEIM
✓ **Vineyard** *Sonnenberg* **Grower** *Ernst Dautel* • **Premium red wine blend Grower** *Ernst Dautel* (Kreation)

GROSSLAGE WUNNENSTEIN

For many years now, Graf Adelmann has carried the torch for an area that could otherwise be regarded as vinous hinterland.

KLEINBOTTWAR
✓ **Vineyard** *Süssmund* **Grower** *Graf Adelmann*

BADEN

Often described as Germany's southernmost wine-producing region, Baden is not so much one region as a hotchpotch of politically diverse districts that once produced wine in the now defunct Grand Duchy of Baden.

THE MOST NORTHERLY SECTION of Baden is parallel with the Mosel, bridging Franconia and Württemberg, while south from Baden-Baden, the vineyards are the mirror-image of Alsace across the border, and three pockets of vines on the shores of Bodensee are almost the most southerly in Germany; that dubious honour goes to Württemberg's nearby *Grosslage* of Lindauer Seegarten.

This variation of geographical, geological, and climatic conditions produces a wide range of wines, from mild Silvaner, through light, spicy Gutedel, to the full-bodied Ruländer, the attractive pink-coloured Weissherbst, a speciality of the region, and a good deal of Germany's best red wines. If, however, anything

QUALITY REQUIREMENTS AND AVERAGE QMP PRODUCTION

BADEN'S MINIMUM OECHSLE	QUALITY CATEGORY	HARVEST BREAKDOWN
50–55°	Deutscher Tafelwein	0.5%
55°	Landwein	0.5%
60–72°	* QbA	81%
76–85°	* Kabinett	10%
86–92°	* Spätlese	5%
100–105°	* Auslese	1%
128°	Beerenauslese	1%
128°	Eiswein	–
154°	Trockenbeerenauslese	1%

* Minimum Oechsle levels vary according to grape variety; those that have a naturally lower sugar content may qualify at a correspondingly lower level.

THE REGION AT A GLANCE

Area under vine
15,906 ha or 39,304 acres (increasing)

Average yield
82 hl/ha (increasing)

Red wine
32%

White wine
56% (decreasing)

Rotling
12%

Most important grape varieties
37% Spätburgunder (increasing), 17% Müller-Thurgau (decreasing), 11% Grauerburgunder (increasing), 7% Riesling (decreasing), 7% Gutedel (decreasing), 7% Weissburgunder, 14% others

Infrastructure
Bereiche 8; *Grosslagen* 16; *Einzellagen* 306

Note The vineyards of Baden straddle 315 *Gemeinden* (communes). Their names may appear on the label.

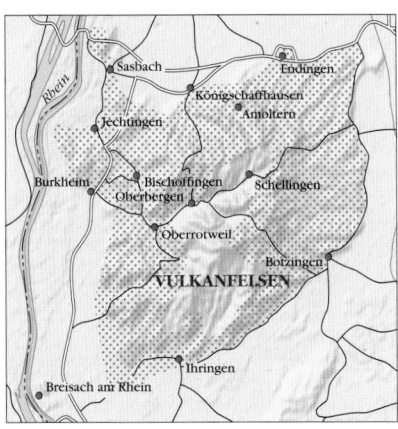

BADEN, *see also p405*
The vineyards of this huge wine-producing region are mostly spread along a strip extending beside the western boundary of the Black Forest, between it and the border with France. Inset right is the northerly area of the Bereich of Tauberfranken, while inset above is the Grosslage of Vulkanfelsen, which has been magnified to reveal all the recommended wine villages of this first-class wine district.

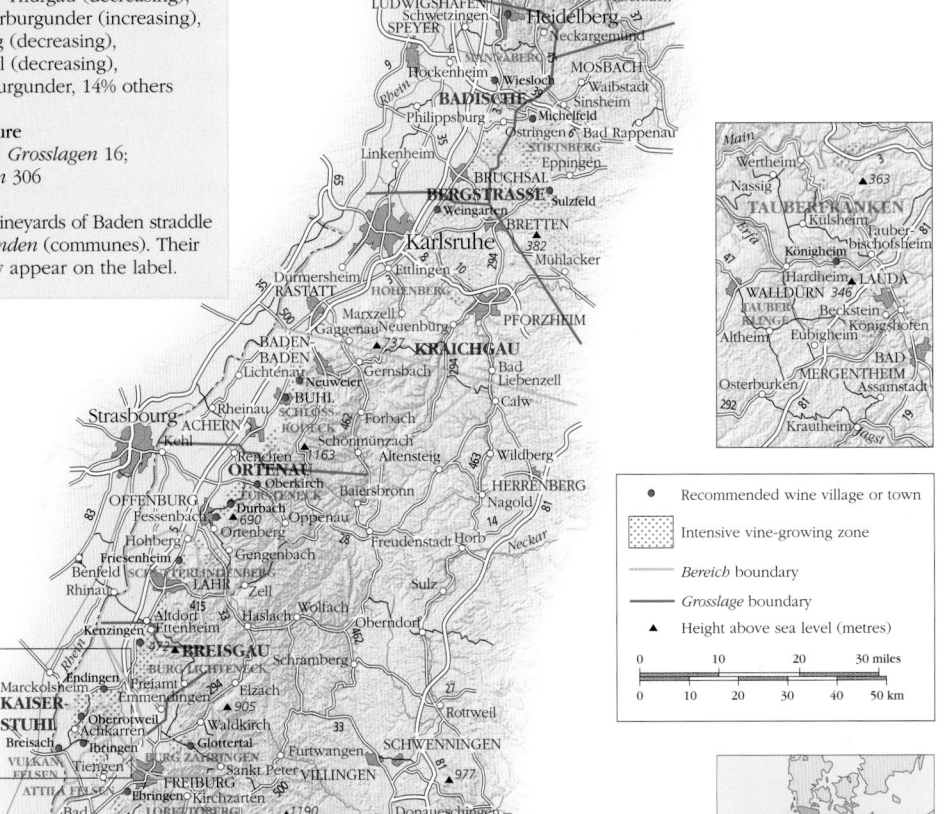

●	Recommended wine village or town
▦	Intensive vine-growing zone
----	*Bereich* boundary
—	*Grosslage* boundary
▲	Height above sea level (metres)

RIESCHEN VINEYARD
The old and new castles above the Rieschen vineyard,
on the north shore of the Bodensee at Meersburg.

can be said to be the mark of a Baden wine, it must be a certain warmth, roundness, and mellowness.

Baden is considered to be one of Germany's newest wine regions, yet by 1800 it had become its largest, possessing more than 27,000 hectares (66,700 acres) of vines, almost twice the amount grown today. Ironically, it was when Germany acquired a wealthy and viticulturally prolific Alsace in 1871, as one of the spoils of the Franco-Prussian War, that Baden's vineyards began to decline. The downward trend continued, despite the formation of the Baden Wine Growers' Association founded by the priest and winemaker Heinrich Hansjakob at Hagnau in 1881. Even after the return of Alsace to French sovereignty in 1918, Baden's wine production continued to decline, primarily through lack of investment. In the 1920s, wine production was adversely affected by inheritance laws that split Baden's vineyards into smaller and smaller units. By 1950, with barely 6,000 hectares (14,800 acres) of vines, Baden's wine industry was at its lowest ebb.

The eventual resurgence of Baden's wine industry began in 1952 with the formation of the Zentralkellerei Kaiserstuhler Winzergenossenschaften (Central Winery of Kaiserstuhl), which two years later expanded into the Zentralkellerei Badischer Winzergenossenschaften (Central Winery of Baden), or ZBW for short. ZBW built a £25-million ($40.5-million) vinification and storage plant at Breisach that helped to raise quality standards throughout the region and adopted an aggressive marketing

policy on the domestic scene. Baden established itself as Germany's third-largest wine producing region, yet its wines were virtually unknown outside the country until ZBW made a serious effort to export its products in the early 1980s. Sadly, Baden is now a victim of its own success, for ZBW, which accounts for some 90 per cent of the region's output, has established such a clear-cut identity for its wines that Baden is generally perceived to produce one style of well-made, but rather basic, characterless wine. The truth is that while this one style represents the bulk of ZBW's and thus Baden's production, both ZBW and the region's independent producers have a wealth of other wines that are seldom seen or spoken about outside their locality. It is now time for ZBW to turn its marketing expertise to the relatively small number of very high-quality wines within its region, and promote them as independent wine estates for the benefit of all.

FACTORS AFFECTING TASTE AND QUALITY

LOCATION
The longest *Anbaugebiete*, Baden stretches for approximately 400 km (250 miles), from Franken in the north, past Württemberg and the Badische Bergstrasse to Bodensee, or Lake Constance, some of Germany's most southerly vineyards.

CLIMATE
Compared with the rest of Germany, the bulk of Baden's vineyards have a sunny and warm climate, due in part to the shelter afforded by the Black Forest and the Odenwald Mountains.

ASPECT
Most vineyards are on level or gently sloping ground. Some, however, are to be found higher up the hillsides, and these avoid the frosts of the valley floors.

SOIL
Baden's soils are rich and fertile, varying from heat-retaining gravel near Lake Constance, through limestone, clay, marl, loam, granite, and loess deposits to limestone and keuper, a sandy-marl, in the Kraichgau and Taubergrund. Volcanic bedrock forms the main subsoil structure throughout most of the region.

VITICULTURE AND VINIFICATION
The relatively flat and fertile vineyards of this region are easily mechanized. Although the geographical spread and variety of soils has led to a large number of different, traditional styles of wine, they are over-shadowed by the mild and neutrally fruity, bulk-produced Baden QbA marketed by ZBW. More than 90 per cent of the winemaking in Baden is conducted by its 54 cooperatives, but there are several independent and top-quality estates among the region's 26,000 growers. Spätburgunder has now officially taken over from Müller-Thurgau as Baden's most important grape, and more than half the wines produced from all varieties in this region are made in a dry or *trocken* style. A speciality that is unique to Baden is Badisch Rotgold, a soft, delicately-flavoured rosé made from pressing Ruländer and Spätburgunder grapes together.

GRAPE VARIETIES
Primary varieties: Müller-Thurgau, Ruländer, Spätburgunder
Secondary varieties: Gutedel (Chasselas), Kerner, Nobling, Riesling, Silvaner, Traminer (Savagnin Blanc), Weissburgunder

BODENSEE (LAKE CONSTANCE)
These vines are in the south of Baden, at Meersburg, the best village of the
Sonnenufer Grosslage, with some of the most southerly vineyards in Germany.

THE APPELLATIONS OF

BADEN

BEREICH BADISCHE BERGSTRASSE-KRAICHGAU

This *Bereich* has four *Grosslagen*, two in the Badische Bergstrasse, north and south of Heidelberg, and two in the Kraichgau, a larger but sparsely cultivated area further south. Only one *Grosslage*, Stiftsberg, in the Kraichgau, has any reputation at all. Half the *Bereich* is planted with Müller-Thurgau grapes, but it makes mostly dull and lacklustre wine. When successful, the best wines are Ruländer and Riesling.

GROSSLAGE HOHENBERG

In this *Grosslage* there are no outstanding villages, vineyards, or growers, although good wines are made in the village of Weingarten.

GROSSLAGE MANNABERG

This *Grosslage* is situated just southeast of Mannheim and it encompasses the historic university town of Heidelberg, which has some fine steep vineyard slopes overlooking the Neckar River.

HEIDELBERG

✓ **Vineyard** *Herrenberg* (red and white) **Grower** *Seeger* (Leimen)

UNTERÖWISHEIM

✓ **Vineyard** *Kirchberg* **Grower** *Klumpp* • **Premium non-Einzellagen wines Growers** *Seeger* (Spätburgunder – "R","S", "RR"), *Klumpp* (Alte Reben)

GROSSLAGE RITTERSBERG

There are no outstanding villages, vineyards, or growers here although good wines are made in the villages of Leutershausen, Lützelsachen, Schriesheim, and Weinheim.

GROSSLAGE STIFTSBERG

Situated in the Kraichgau, this is the *Bereich*'s most successful *Grosslage*. Nearly half of its vineyards are classified as "steep", which officially means sloping at more than 20 degrees, and this contributes to the extreme fruitiness of the Ruländer and the relatively racy character of the Riesling.

SULZFELD

✓ **Non-Einzellagen premium red Grower** *Burg Ravensburg* (Corvus, Dicker Franz)

BEREICH BODENSEE

In the Hochrhein of Bodensee, or the Upper Rhine of Bodensee (known in English as Lake Constance), the wines are not great, but can be very acceptable. They range from the fruity and lively Müller-Thurgau to Rotwein and Weissherbst, both produced from Spätburgunder.

GROSSLAGE SONNENUFER

The steep sides of Lake Constance around Meersburg are the most spectacular vineyards here. The brothers Aufricht have brought a new dimension to the wines of this district, taking over the lead from Winzerverein Meersburg, Germany's first state domain (since 1802).

MEERSBURG

✓ **Vineyard** *Sängerhalde* **Grower** *Aufricht*

BEREICH BREISGAU

Strangely, the old city of Breisach is not part of the *Bereich* that takes its name; it is, in fact, situated in the *Bereich* of Kaiserstuhl-Tuniberg to the south. The wines of Bereich Breisgau have narrowed the gap on the better-known Kaiserstuhl-Tuniberg, with fruity, off-dry Müller-Thurgau balanced by some excellent Weissburgunder, Grauburgunder, and Spätburgunder.

GROSSLAGE BURG LICHTENECK

Besides those of the villages recommended below, good wines are also made in Altdorf.

BOMBACH

✓ **Vineyard** *Sommerhalde* **Grower** *Bernhard Huber* (red)

HECKLINGEN

✓ **Vineyard** *Schlossberg* **Grower** *Bernhard Huber* (red and white)

MALTERDINGEN

✓ **Vineyard** *Bienenberg* **Grower** *Bernhard Huber* (red and white) • **Non-Einzellagen premium wines Growers** *Bernhard Huber* (red: Wildenstein, Alte Reben), *Fritz Waßmer* (single varietal reds: Barrique and Alte Reben)

GROSSLAGE BURG ZÄHRINGEN

There are no outstanding villages, vineyards, or growers in this *Grosslage*, although good wines are made in the village of Glottertal.

GROSSLAGE SCHUTTER-LINDENBERG

There are no outstanding villages, vineyards, or growers in this *Grosslage*, although good wines are made in the villages of Friesenheim and Lahr.

LAHR

✓ **Vineyard** *Kronenbühl* **Grower** *Stadt Lahr – Familie Wöhrle* (red and white)

BEREICH KAISERSTUHL

Formerly part of Kaiserstuhl-Tuniberg, this *Bereich* is dominated by the extinct volcano of Kaiserstuhl, whose immaculate slopes are copybook examples of *Flurbereinigung* (growing vines in rows up and down slopes).

In this, Germany's warmest and driest *Bereich*, there are microclimates that favour certain sites protected by the volcano. Some of Baden's best wines come from these *Einzellagen*, although most of the wine is sold under the *Bereich* name, usually with the grape name attached; Bereich Kaiserstuhl Müller-Thurgau dominates. But it is the very full white Ruländer and the assertive Weissherbst Ruländer that made the reputation of the *Bereich*. Some fine, rich Spätburgunder wines enhance this reputation.

GROSSLAGE VULKANFELSEN

Vulkanfelsen is the largest and most successful of the two *Grosslagen* that belonged to the now defunct Kaiserstuhl-Tuniberg. As its name implies (Vulkanfelsen means volcano rock), it covers the superior, high volcanic vineyards of the Kaiserstuhl mound itself. Above all else, it is the full, fiery intensity of Ruländer wines from the Kaiserstuhl that give this district its reputation.

ACHKARREN

✓ **Vineyard** *Schlossberg* **Growers** *Dr Heger* (red and white), *Michel* (red and white), *Winzergenossenschaft Achkarren* • **Non-Einzellagen premium red and white wines Grower** *Johner* (SJ)

BICKENSOHL

✓ **Vineyard** *Herrenstück* **Grower** *Holger Koch* • **Non-Einzellagen premium red and white wines Grower** *Holger Koch* (Selection***)

BLANKENHORNSBERG

✓ **Vineyard** *Doktorgarten* **Grower** *Staatsweingut Freiburg und Blankenhornsberg* (red and white)

BURKHEIM

✓ **Vineyard** *Feuerberg* **Grower** *Bercher* (red and white) • **Vineyard** *Schlossgarten* **Grower** *Bercher*

ENDINGEN

✓ **Vineyard** *Engelsberg* **Grower** *Knab* (red and white) • **Non-Einzellagen premium red and white varietals Grower** *Reinhold und Cornelia Schneider*

IHRINGEN

✓ **Vineyard** *Winklerberg* **Growers** *Dr Heger* (red and white), *Stigler*

OBERBERGEN

✓ **Vineyard** *Bassgeige* **Grower** *Franz Keller-Schwarzer Adler* (red and white)

• **Premium red and white blends Grower** *Franz Keller-Schwarzer Adler* (Selection A and S)

OBERROTTWEIL

✓ **Vineyard** *Eichberg* **Growers** *Freiherr von Gleichenstein, Salwey* (red and white) • **Vineyard** *Kirchberg* **Grower** *Salwey* (red and white)

SASBACH

✓ **Vineyard** *Limburg* **Grower** *Bercher* (red and white) • **Vineyard** *Rote Halde* **Grower** *Winzergenossenschaft Sasbach*

SCHELINGEN

✓ **Vineyard** *Kirchberg* **Grower** *Schätzle* (red and white)

BEREICH MARKGRÄFLERLAND

This is the second-most important *Bereich* in Baden. The principal grape variety is, unusually, Gutedel, which makes a light, dryish, and neutral wine that benefits from a slight spritz and can be most attractive when very youthful. Other prominent varieties include Nobling, an up-and-coming cross between Gutedel and Silvaner that makes a more characterful wine than the light Müller-Thurgau. The latter can be attractive nevertheless. Spätburgunder can be full and successful, and Gewürztraminer also fares well.

GROSSLAGE ATTILAFELSEN

Not enough is made of the potential for good wines at this small volcanic outcrop of the Tuniberg.

GROSSLAGE BURG NEUENFELS

The vast majority of vineyards in this *Grosslage* are on steep ground. These vineyards make some of Germany's most delicious Gutedel, although the greatest potential lies in the Burgunder varietals.

BADENWEILER

✓ **Vineyard** *Römerberg* **Grower** *Dörflinger* (red and white)

BRITZINGEN

✓ **Vineyard** *Sonnhole* **Grower** *Winzergenossenschaft Britzingen*

LAUFEN

✓ **Non-Einzellagen wines Grower** *Hartmut Schlumberger* (red and white)

MAUCHEN

✓ **Vineyard** *Sonnenstück* **Grower** *Lämmlin-Schindler* ⊙ • **Vineyard** *Frauenberg* **Grower** *Lämmlin-Schindler*

GROSSLAGE LORETTOBERG

A part-time asparagus grower and a Chardonnay specialist have brought some credibility to a long-underestimated *Grosslage*.

SCHERZINGEN

✓ **Vineyard** *Batzenberg* **Grower** *Heinemann* (red and white)

SCHLATT

✓ **Non-Einzellagen wines Grower** *Martin Wassmer* (red and white)

GROSSLAGE VOGTEI RÖTTELN

Although much wine is sold under this *Grosslage*, its exceptional vineyards are known for Gutedel and, to a lesser extent, Spätburgunder.

EFRINGEN-KIRCHEN

✓ **Non-Einzellagen premium red and white wines Grower** *Ziereisen* (all Pinots and Syrah)

WEIL

✓ **Vineyard** *Schlipf* **Grower** *Claus Schneider* (red and white)

BEREICH ORTENAU

Sheltered by the Black Forest, the two *Grosslagen* in this *Bereich* produce some of Baden's greatest wines. They are generally full, fruity, and often very spicy. The Riesling, known locally as Klingelberger, is extremely fine for such a powerful and spicy variation of this normally racy variety. Müller-Thurgau is particularly good and full, and a successful Ruländer-Spätburgunder blend called Badisch Rotgold is also produced. Confusingly, the Gewürztraminer is often called Clevner, which is usually a synonym for Pinot Blanc.

GROSSLAGE FÜRSTENECK

This *Grosslage* sports some of Baden's finest estates.

The range of grape varieties is greater here than anywhere else within Baden and the wines include Rieslings that range from firm and spicy to fine and delicate; powerful Gewürztraminer; some of Germany's best Müller-Thurgau; and some extraordinary Gutedel. Many of the wines are made in increasingly drier styles, although some estates are famous for their sweeter, late-harvested products.

DURBACH

✓ **Vineyard** *Kochberg* **Grower** *Heinrich Männle* (red and white) • **Vineyard** *Plauelrain* **Grower** *Andreas Laible* • **Vineyard** *Schloss Grohl* **Grower** *Gräflich Wolff Metternich'sches Weingut* • **Vineyard** *Schlossberg* **Grower** *Gräflich Wolff Metternich'sches Weingut* (red and white)

ORTENBERG

✓ **Non-Einzellagen wines Grower** *Schloss Ortenberg*

GROSSLAGE SCHLOSS RODECK

For many years Schloss Neuweier was the undisputed number one in this *Grosslage*, but a Dutch newcomer has propelled himself to the forefront of developments with Spätburgunder in *barriques*.

BÜHL

✓ **Non-Einzellagen premium red wines Grower** *Duijn*

NEUWEIER

✓ **Vineyard** *Altenberg* **Grower** *Holger Dütsch* • **Vineyard** *Mauerberg* **Grower** *Schloss Neuweier* • **Vineyard** *Schlossberg* **Grower** *Holger Dütsch, Schloss Neuweier*

SINZHEIM

✓ **Non-Einzellagen premium wines Grower** *Ewald Kopp*

BEREICH TAUBERFRANKEN

The most northerly of Baden's vineyards, Bereich Tauberfranken bridges Franken and Württemberg. The wines have a similar style to those produced in both regions. If anything, the crisp, dry, aromatic, and slightly earthy Müller-Thurgau and Silvaner wines bear more resemblance to Franken wines rather than to Württemberg wines. Only that part of the *Bereich* outside Franken itself is allowed to use Franken's famous *Bocksbeutel* bottle.

GROSSLAGE TAUBERKLINGE

As well as at Reicholzheim, good wines are also made in the villages of Beckstein, Königshofen, and Tauberbischofsheim.

REICHHOLZHEIM

✓ **Vineyard** *First* **Grower** *Konrad Schlör* (red and white)

BEREICH TUNIBERG

Formerly part of Kaiserstuhl-Tuniberg, this *Bereich* is to the south of the mighty Kaiserstuhl and it is the far less awesome sight of the Tuniberg, another volcanic outcrop, that provides the only other topographical and viticultural relief. The Tuniberg's steeper, west-facing slopes are cultivated, but neither its reputation nor its bulk can match those of Kaiserstuhl's fabulous recommendations above.

OTHER CERTIFIED ORGANIC PRODUCERS

Biodynamic
Alfons Schüber (Sasbach-Jechtingen)
Breitehof Hubert Schies (Vogtsburg-Burkheim a Kaiserstuhl)
Christoph Brenneisen (Sulburg-Laufen)
Guido Friderich (Sasbach)
Josef u Klara Vögtle (Sasbach-Jechtingen a Kaiserstuhl)
Josef Wörner (Durbach)
Markus Bürgin (Fischingen)
Max und Alice Schneider (Sasbach)

Organic
Andrea und Heiner Renn (Hagnau)
Andreas Fritz (Bühlertal)
Bettina Beck (Bahlingen)
Daniel Feuerstein (Heitersheim)
Edmund Eisele/Schelb (Ehrenkirchen)
Eduard Mannsperger (Sinsheim-Dühren)
Erwin Mick (Nimburg)
Freiburg (Heiliggeist Freiburg im Breisgau)
Friedhelm Rinklin (Eichstetten)
Friedrich & Bärbel Ruesch (Buggingen)
Fritz Lampp (Heitersheim)
Gallushof/Hügle (Teningen-Heimbach)
Geier (Königheim)
Gerd Köpfer (Staufen-Grunern)
Gerhard Aenis (Binzen)

Gretzmeier (Merdingen)
Gudrun Lauerbach (Tauberbischofsheim-Impfingen)
Günther Kaufmann (Efringen-Kirchen)
H & J Sprich (Weil-Haltingen)
Hans Hardt (Herbolzheim)
Harald Süssle (Merdingen)
Harteneck (Schliengen)
Hermann Helde & Sohne (Jechtingen)
Hermann Neuner-Jehle (Immenstaad)
HP & Helmut Grether (Laufen-Sulzburg)
Hubert Lay (Ihringen)
Jette Krumm (Auggen)
Joachim Netzhammer (Klettgau-Erzingen)
Johannes Haug (Nonnenhorn)
Kirchberghof (Kenzingen-Bombach)
Klaus Benz (Ballrechten-Dottingen)
Klaus Bischoff (Kelltern)
Klaus Vorgrimmler (Freiburg-Munzingen)
Koehly-Harteneck (Bad Bellingen)
Kuckuckshof (Karlsbad-Ittersbach)
Kurt Breisacher (Riegel)
Langwerth Öko-Wein (Esselbach)
Ludwig Missbach (Ebringen)
Manfred & Eva Maria Schmidt (Vogtsburg-Bischoffingen)
Manfred Dannmeyer (Bamlach)

Markgräfler Wyhus (Efringen-Kirchen)
Martin Hämmerlin (Buggingen)
Martin Küchlin (Buggingen-Betberg)
Martina Heitzmann (Bahlingen)
Matthias Höfflin/Schambachhof (Bötzingen)
Matthias Seywald (Ballrechten-Dottingen)
Matthias Wolff (Riedlingen)
Peter Kaiser (Bahnbrücken)
Philip Isele (Achkarren)
Pix (Ihringen A K)
Rabenhof (Vogtsburg-Bischofingen)
Reblandhof (Sulzfeld)
Reinhard Burs (March)
Richard G Schmidt (Eichstetten)
Siegfried Frei (Wasenweiler)
Sonnenbrunnen (Freiburg-Opfingen)
Stadt Lahr (Lahr/Schwarzwald)
Stränglehof (Leiselheim)
Thomas Schaffner (Bötzingen am Kaiserstuhl)
Thomas Selinger (Merdingen)
Tobias Kehnel (Broggingen)
Trautwein (Bahlingen)
Ulrich Klumpp (Bruchsal)
Walter J Schür (Vogtsburg-Oberrotweil)
Wendelin Brugger (Laufen)
Wilhelm Zähringer (Heitersheim)
Willi Frey (Freiburg-Tiengen)
Winzerhof Leber (Vogtsburg-Schelingen)
Wolfgang Ibert (Wallburg)

SAALE-UNSTRUT AND SACHSEN

These two eastern outposts of viticulture are the most northerly in Germany and even though their terraced vineyards are being renovated and replanted, and modern vinification facilities installed, their wines can never be more than a tourist curiosity.

PARADOXICALLY THIS LIMITATION may be the saving grace for the wines of Saale-Unstrut and Sachsen because they are far too small and rustically structured to stand any chance of competing with the large volumes of cheap dross churned out by cooperatives in Germany's more intensively cultivated wine regions. Furthermore, as Meissen and Dresden are lucrative tourist areas, thus the wines must adhere to a certain standard if they are to satisfy tourists with far more sophisticated palates than those who consumed them under former GDR mismanagement. Most of the vineyards are between Dresden and Diesbar-Scusslitz, with a few vineyards that have been restored on the southern outskirts of Dresden itself. The state-owned cellars in historic Schloss Wackerbarth in Radebeul and the region's oldest (and privately owned) estate at Schloss Proschwitz are Sachsen's largest estates. The largest estate in Saale-Unstrut is Kloster Pforta, which was named after the 12th-century monastery between Bad Kösen and Naumburg.

THE FUTURE – VARIETAL EVOLUTION

When Germany was reunified in 1989, the most commonly cultivated grape variety in the former GDR's rundown vineyards was Müller-Thurgau, and although it remains an important grape,

it is on the decline, and its days must be numbered. Riesling has increased from five to seven per cent of the vines grown, but it is Germany's greatest variety, thus more will be planted, if only for the sake of national pride. The area is, however, more suited to the full, rich, and distinctively earthy wine produced by Silvaner and, perhaps surprisingly for such a northerly, frost-prone region, also to red wine grape varieties. But of all the varieties to choose from, who would have predicted the rise of Weissburgunder when the Berlin Wall came down? Very few, I think, but it is the best placed to succeed Müller-Thurgau as this region's more important variety, although it will take a few years yet.

THE REGION AT A GLANCE

Area under vine
1,147 ha or 2,834 acres (increasing)

Average yield
54 hl/ha (increasing)

Red wine
20%

White wine
76% (decreasing)

Rotling
4%

Most important grape varieties
18% Riesling (increasing), 11% Müller-Thurgau (decreasing), 7% Weissburgunder (decreasing), 5% Silvaner (decreasing), 4% Spätburgunder, 3% Grauburgunder, 52% others

Infrastructure
Bereiche 5; *Grosslagen* 8;
Einzellagen 35

Note The vineyards of Saale-Unstrut and Sachsen straddle 63 *Gemeinden* (communes), the names of which may appear on the label.

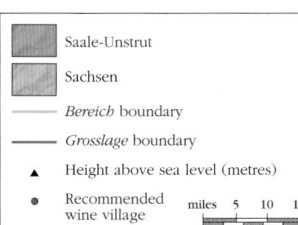

Saale-Unstrut

Sachsen

Bereich boundary

Grosslage boundary

▲ Height above sea level (metres)

● Recommended wine village or town

miles 5 10 15
km 5 10 15 20 25

SAALE-UNSTRUT AND SACHSEN,
see also p405
Almost 700 hectares (1,700 acres) of vines grow in these areas, formerly part of East Germany. Production is centred at Bad Kösen, Freyburg, and near the confluence of the Saale and Unstrut rivers at Naumberg.

FACTORS AFFECTING TASTE AND QUALITY

LOCATION
The most northerly wine regions in Germany, Saale-Unstrut is equidistant between Berlin and the Franken region, while Sachsen is about 128 kilometres (80 miles) east, around Dresden, close to the border with the Czech Republic.

CLIMATE
Despite their northerly position, the continental climate ensures high summer temperatures. However, winters are long and very cold, resulting in a short and dry growing season compared with other German regions. Spring and autumn frosts are a particular danger, often cutting yields by 20–70 per cent in Saale-Unstrut and as much as 90 per cent in Sachsen.

ASPECT
Vineyards are on south and southeast facing valley slopes, but much of the terracing has deteriorated under Communist rule and the current reconstruction will take some time to complete.

SOIL
Limestone and a tiny amount of sandstone in Saale-Unstrut, with loam and loess over granite and volcanic subsoils in most of Sachsen, and weathered granite and gneiss on its steepest slopes.

VITICULTURE AND VINIFICATION
Many of the small parcels are planted on steep, labour-intensive stone terraces, most of which are cultivated by part-time growers who deliver their crop to Saale-Unstrut's regional cooperative in Freyburg or Sachsen's regional cooperative in Meissen. Yields were very low prior to reunification, but although production has since increased, yields remain very low due to the northerly situation. There are problems such as decimation of production by fierce attacks of frost, decaying terracing, dead vines, and rustic production methods, but it would be a pity if old vines were replaced and if the hardy but highest-yielding characterless crosses were introduced in place of classic varieties. Weissburgunder and Riesling are the fastest expanding grape varieties. Mostly dry wines are produced, with only 4 per cent of the production sweeter than *halbtrocken*, and as much as 86 per cent sold as *trocken*.

GRAPE VARIETIES
Primary varieties: Müller-Thurgau, Weissburgunder
Secondary varieties: Bacchus, Dornfelder, Elbling, Gewürztraminer, Grauburgunder, Gutedel (Chasselas), Kerner, Morio-Muskat, Portugieser

THE APPELLATIONS OF

SAALE-UNSTRUT AND SACHSEN

ANBAUGEBIET SAALE-UNSTRUT

Wines have been produced in this area for nearly 1,000 years, but it took the GDR less than 50 years to erase these once-well-known names from the memory of wine drinkers. This region comprises two *Bereiche*, and Müller-Thurgau is the most important grape variety. It accounts for some 35 per cent of the vines planted and black grapes account for some 10 per cent.

BEREICH SCHLOSSNEUENBURG

By far the largest of Saale-Unstrut's two *Bereiche*, Schloss Neuenburg encompasses all but a tiny section in the very south of the Saale-Unstrut region, plus the island of vines just west of Halle.

GROSSLAGE BLÜTENGRUND

Some respectable wines have appeared on the market under the designation of this *Grosslage*.

GROSSLAGE GÖTTERSITZ

Previous expectations in this *Grosslage* have not been quite fulfilled.

NAUMBURG

✓ **Vineyard** *Steinmeister* **Grower** *Gussek*

GROSSLAGE KELTERBERG

No outstanding villages, vineyards, or growers.

GROSSLAGE SCHWEIGENBERG

One grower stands out in this, the most respected *Grosslage* of the Saale-Unstrut region.

FREYBURG

✓ **Vineyard** *Edelacker* **Grower** *Pawis*

BEREICH THÜRINGEN

The southern tip of the Saale-Unstrut region does not contain any *Grosslagen*, just two *Einzellagen*, one in Grossheringen, the other in Bad Sulza.

BEREICHEFREI AND GROSSLAGENFREI MARK BRANDENBURG

Mark Brandenburg covers the vineyards around Werder, from which no outstanding wines have so far been made.

ANBAUGEBIET SACHSEN

Incorporating Dresden and Meissen, this *Aubaugebiet* produces wines that are grown along the River Elbe (Sachsen was formerly known as Elbethal). The area is even more prone to frost damage than Saale-Unstrut, with Riesling relatively more important (13 per cent as opposed to Saale-Unstrut's 5 per cent). The quantity of black grapes is minuscule.

BEREICH DRESDEN

This *Bereich* covers most of the southern half of Sachsen.

GROSSLAGE ELBHÄNGE

Continuous efforts have finally paid off for one grower in this otherwise unremarkable *Grosslage*.

PILLNITZ

✓ **Vineyard** *Königlicher Weinberg* **Grower** *Klaus Zimmerling*

GROSSLAGE LÖSSNITZ

There are no outstanding villages or vineyards, and no remarkable growers to be recommended in this *Grosslage*.

BEREICH ELSTERTAL

This is a *Bereich* consisting of three villages at the southern end of Sachsen. There are relatively few vines and, so far, no village has produced any outstanding wines.

BEREICH MEISSEN

The northern end of the Sachsen region, Meissen itself will always be more well known for the porcelain it once produced than its wine. This area, however, did have something of a name for producing fine wine at the beginning of the 19th century. Wine drinkers can only wait and see if there is sufficient potential for that reputation to be recaptured sometime in the future.

GROSSLAGE SCHLOSS-WEINBERG

North of Meissen, some decent wines can come from a bend in the Elbe at Diesbar-Seusslitz where the vineyards face south.

GROSSLAGE SPAARGEBIRGE

Substantial investments have helped to bring at least one estate's shine back to this *Grosslage*.

PROSCHWITZ

✓ **Vineyard** *Schloss Proschwitz* **Grower** *Schloss Proschwitz*

CERTIFIED ORGANIC PRODUCER

Organic
Hof Loessnitz (Dresden)

AUSTRIA

Austrian wine in the 21st century has changed. The Wachau still produces some of the world's greatest Riesling, but Grüner Veltliner has grabbed media attention and is proving to be a far more versatile variety than imagined 20 years ago.

IN THE LATE 1970s, Austrian wine production increased as domestic consumption declined, resulting in the largest wine lake outside the then EC. Austria's wine industry was designed chiefly for exports to Germany, traditionally its only significant customer. After a succession of bumper harvests in both Germany and Austria, sales to Germany dried up, but overproduction in Austria continued. With hindsight, the so-called "anti-freeze" scandal which took place in 1985 can be seen as a godsend for Austrian wine. Call it a scam or a scandal, but it was not the health scare it was made out

to be. It did, however, have the effect of putting the Austrian government under enormous pressure to tighten up controls, with the result that Austria now has the most strictly controlled, safest wine industry in the world.

WHAT WAS THE ANTI-FREEZE SCANDAL?
In 1985, a handful of Austria's 40,000 wine producers used diethylene glycol to sweeten their wines artificially. The media throughout the world claimed that Austrian wines had been poisoned with anti-freeze, but it was not actually anti-freeze, of course. (Ethylene glycol is anti-freeze.) Diethylene glycol is in fact less toxic than alcohol, so adding it actually made the wines less poisonous.

THE MODERN WINE TRADE
Enthusiasts have always known that Austria produces some of the greatest botrytized wines in the world, yet just how

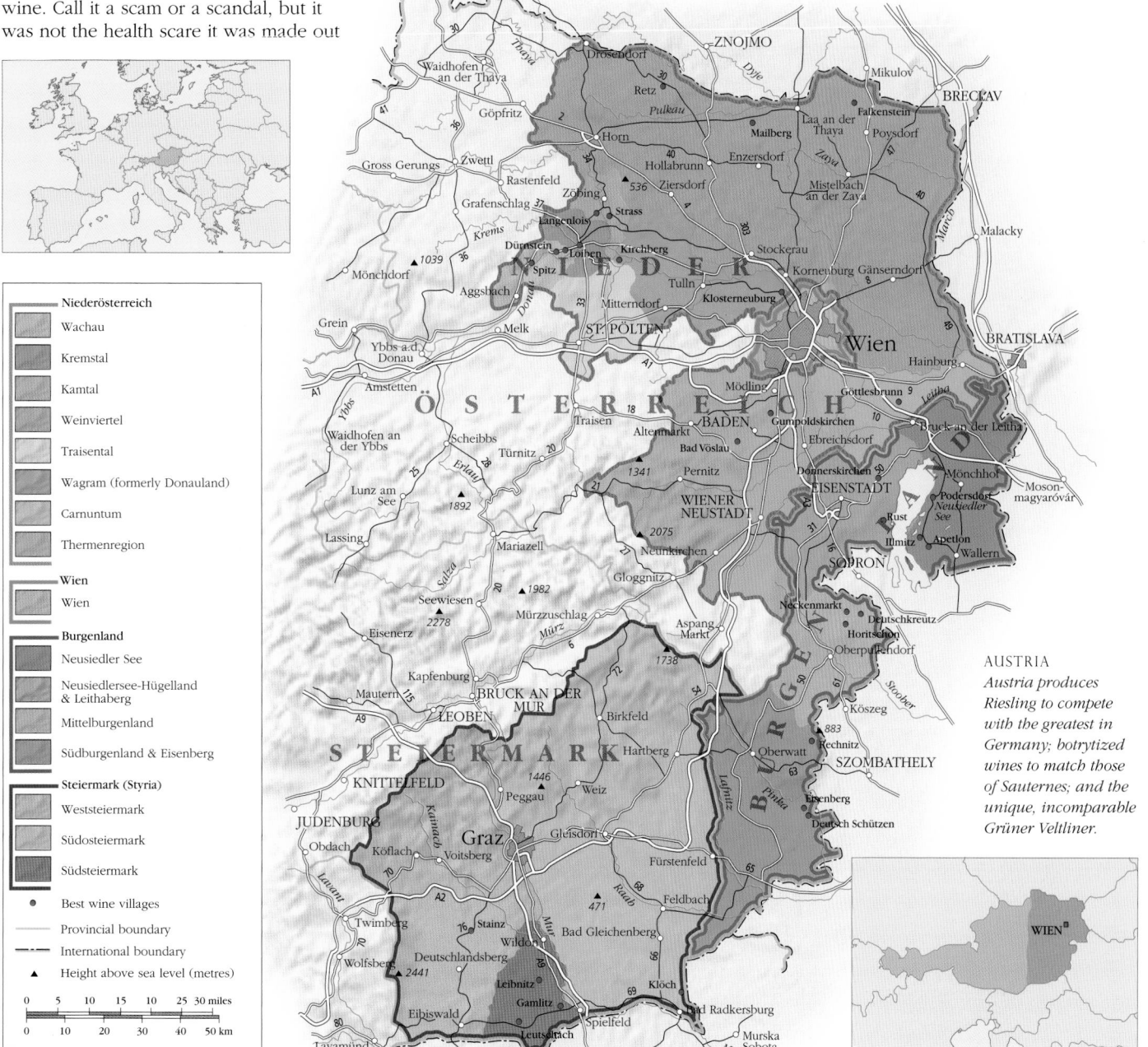

Niederösterreich
- Wachau
- Kremstal
- Kamtal
- Weinviertel
- Traisental
- Wagram (formerly Donauland)
- Carnuntum
- Thermenregion

Wien
- Wien

Burgenland
- Neusiedler See
- Neusiedlersee-Hügelland & Leithaberg
- Mittelburgenland
- Südburgenland & Eisenberg

Steiermark (Styria)
- Weststeiermark
- Südosteiermark
- Südsteiermark

- ● Best wine villages
- — Provincial boundary
- --- International boundary
- ▲ Height above sea level (metres)

| 0 | 5 | 10 | 15 | 10 | 25 | 30 miles |
| 0 | 10 | 20 | 30 | 40 | 50 km |

AUSTRIA
Austria produces Riesling to compete with the greatest in Germany; botrytized wines to match those of Sauternes; and the unique, incomparable Grüner Veltliner.

electrifying these wines can be became clear when Willi Opitz, one of the smallest, but truly greatest, dessert wine producers, took the trouble to tour world markets and speak to people about his products.

Over the past few years, Austria has produced Cabernet Sauvignon and Chardonnay to a very high standard, and even St Laurent, an obscure local variety of grape, has proved to be quite stunning. What Austria must do now is to promote its greatest Riesling wines, which can compare with the best from Germany, and export its top Grüner Veltliner, and keep pushing these wines onto the international markets.

THE WACHAU
Much of Austria is very picturesque, making it a popular tourist destination; here the lush vineyards complement this typical Lower Austrian landscape.

FACTORS AFFECTING TASTE AND QUALITY

LOCATION
The vineyards are in the east of the country, north and south of Vienna, bordering the Czech Republic, Hungary, and Yugoslavia.

CLIMATE
The climate is warm, dry, and continental, with annual rainfall between 57 and 77 centimetres (23 to 31 inches). The hottest and driest area is Burgenland, where in the warm autumns, mists rising from the Neusiedler See help promote *Botrytis cinerea* (the "noble rot" beloved by winegrowers).

ASPECT
Vines are grown on all types of land, from the plains of the Danube to its valley sides – which are often very steep and terraced – and from the hilly Burgenland to the slopes of mountainous Styria.

SOIL
Soils vary from generally stony schist, limestone, and gravel (though occasionally loamy) in the north, through predominantly sandy soils on the shores of the Neusiedler See in Burgenland, to mainly clay with some volcanic soils in Styria.

VITICULTURE AND VINIFICATION
Not surprisingly, Austria's methods are similar to those of Germany, but,

although modern techniques have been introduced here, far more Austrian wine is produced by traditional methods than is the case in Germany. More than 85 per cent of the country's vines are cultivated by the Lenz Moser system. This is a method of training vines to twice their normal height, thereby achieving a comparatively higher ratio of quality to cost, by enabling the use of mechanized harvesting. This system brought fame to its Austrian inventor, Lenz Moser, and has been adopted by at least one grower in most winemaking countries. Harvesting is traditionally accomplished in *tries*, particularly on steeper slopes and for sweeter styles.

GRAPE VARIETIES
Blauer Portugieser, Blauer Wildbacher, Blaufränkisch (Limberger), Bouviertraube (Bouvier), Cabernet Franc, Cabernet Sauvignon, Chardonnay, Frühroter Veltliner (Malvoisie Rosé), Furmint, Gewürztraminer, Goldburger, Grauer Burgunder, Grüner Veltliner, Pinot Blanc, Pinot Noir, Merlot, Müller-Thurgau, Muscat Ottonel, Muskateller, Neuburger, Riesling, Roter Veltliner, Rotgipfler, St-Laurent, Sauvignon Blanc, Scheurebe, Silvaner, Trollinger (Schiava), Welschriesling, Zierfandler, Zweigelt

RECENT AUSTRIAN VINTAGES

2010 A cool, wet spring delayed the flowering and made for difficult fruit set. July was warm, dry, and sunny, but the rain returned in August and stayed until the end of October. A difficult year. Customers must be as picky as they hope the best growers were. Low volume, higher prices.

2009 A damp summer slowed maturation, but a long dry harvest into early November yielded healthy ripe grapes with lovely acidity.

2008 Humidity was a problem, and only those who timed the harvest just right and strictly selected only the healthiest grapes are successful. Those exceptions are rich. Generally, however, it is a difficult year, particularly for Blaufränkisch, but this vintage excels for botrytized wines, which were made in large volumes of exceedingly high quality.

2007 After a beautiful flowering and a hot summer, some early-ripening varieties were picked as early as August, but September was wet, thus only those who waited benefited, and some had to wait for November.

2006 Variable quantity and quality, but some good to excellent reds (particularly Blaufränkisch, but also Cabernet Sauvignon and Pinot Noir) and sweet and dry whites (Riesling and Grüner Veltliner). A very good year for Styrian Sauvignon Blanc.

AUSTRIA VERSUS GERMANY

Both countries operate wine regimes that base levels of quality on degrees of ripeness by measuring the amount of sugar found in the grapes at the time of harvest. As in Germany, Austrian wines range from *Tafelwein*, through *Qualitätswein*, to *Trockenbeerenauslese*. The overview below shows that most Austrian wines conform to higher minimum standards than their German counterparts. More significant, however, is the fact that the minimum level for each category is rigid, so it has a distinctive style. This gives the consumer a clear idea of what to expect, whereas a German category varies according to the variety of grape and its area of origin. In Germany, only experience can reveal that a Mosel *Auslese*, for example, tastes no sweeter than a *Spätlese* from other regions. Also, *Süssreserve* is not allowed for any *Prädikat* wines, whereas in Germany this is permitted for *Kabinett*.

MINIMUM OECHSLE LEVELS

QUALITY CATEGORY	AUSTRIA	GERMANY
Tafelwein	63°	44–50°
Landwein	63°	47–55°
Qualitätswein (*Steinfeder**)	73°	50–72°
Kabinett (*Federspiel**)	83.5°	67–85°
Spätlese	94°	76–95°
Auslese (*Smaragd**)	105°	83–105°
Beerenauslese	127°	110–128°
Eiswein	127°	110–128°
Ausbruch	138°	N/A
Trockenbeerenauslese	156°	150–154°

* Special terms in the Wachau

AUSBRUCH – A RELIC OF THE AUSTRO-HUNGARIAN EMPIRE

Ausbruch is a still-popular style of wine that harks back to the days of the Austro-Hungarian Empire (and is also still produced in Hungary). At 138° *Oechsle* (*see above*), *Ausbruch* falls between the sweetness levels of *Beerenauslese* (127°) and *Trockenbeerenauslese* (156°). In terms of character, however, *Ausbruch* should be totally different from either a *Beerenauslese* or *Trockenbeerenauslese*. The name means "to break up"; the wine is made traditionally from the richest and sweetest botrytized grapes that are so shrivelled and dried-out that to press them is virtually impossible without first moistening the mass (breaking it up) with a more liquescent juice (the regulation stipulates *Spätlese* quality). A true *Ausbruch* is overwhelmed by an intensely raisiny aroma and flavour that may be even more botrytized than a *Trockenbeerenauslese*, yet the wine itself need not necessarily be as rich.

THE WINE STYLES OF
AUSTRIA

BLAUBURGER

RED A Blauer Portugieser/Blaufränkisch cross that produces a well-coloured wine of little distinction, but tends to improve in bottle.

⏳ 1–3 years

🏆 *Schützenhof Fam Faulhammer-Körper • Willi Opitz*

BLAUER PORTUGIESER

RED Once Austria's most widely planted black grape variety, this is still commonly found in Lower Austria, particularly Paulkautal, Retz, and the Thermen region, where it makes a light-bodied but well-coloured red wine with a mild flavour, hinting of violets.

⏳ 1–2 years

🏆 *Johann Gipsberg*

BLAUER WILDBACHER

RED/ROSÉ Otherwise known as Schilcher, this variety traditionally produces a light, dry, crisp, and fruity, pale rosé wine.

⏳ 1–2 years

🏆 *E & M Müller*

BLAUFRÄNKISCH

RED Called Lemberger in Germany and Kékfrankos in Hungary, this variety is popular in Neusiedlersee-Hügelland Burgenland, where it produces tart, fruity wine with good tannin and an underlying hint of cherries and spice. The best Blaufränkisch examples are fat and sometimes given time in oak.

⏳ 2–4 years

🏆 *Feiler-Artinger • Fam Igler • Gessellmann (Creitzer) • K + K Kirnbauer • H und M Krutzler • Moric • Muhr-Van de Niepoort • Pichler-Krutzler • Pittnaur • Prieler • Schiefer • Wohlmuth*

BOUVIER

WHITE An early-ripening table grape that has a low natural acidity and is often used for high-quality *Prädikatswein*.

⏳ 1–3 year (*Qualitätswein*), 2–8 years (*Prädikatswein*)

🏆 *Willi Opitz*

CABERNET SAUVIGNON

RED Very little of this variety used to be grown in Austria. Until 1982 the only commercial cultivation of Cabernet Sauvignon was by Schlumberger at Bad Vöslau. Then Lenz Moser received special permission to cultivate 2.5 hectares (6 acres) at Mailberg, and the first Cabernet Sauvignon was grown in 1986 in Lower Austria. Nowadays, everyone seems to be growing Cabernet Sauvignon.

⏳ 5–6 years (*Qualitätswein*), 10–15 years (*Prädikatswein*)

🏆 *Lenz Moser* (Siegendorf Prestige) • *Fam Igler • Gessellmann*

CHARDONNAY

WHITE Also known in Austria as Feinburgunder, this grape variety has been grown for decades in Styria, where it is known as Morillon. Cultivation of this grape has risen rapidly since the early 1990s, producing some fat, rich wines.

⏳ 2–5 years

🏆 *Bründlmayer • Juris-Stiegelmar • Andreas Schafler • Gottfried Schellmann • Tement*

FRÜHROTER VELTLINER

WHITE Sometimes labelled Malvasia, this dry wine has more alcohol and body than Austria's most widely grown white wine, Grüner Veltliner.

⏳ 1–2 years

🏆 *Leth*

FURMINT

WHITE This is a rarely encountered Hungarian dry, medium- to full-bodied, rich, and fruity varietal that does well at Rust in Burgenland.

⏳ 3–5 years

🏆 *Weinbau Ladislaus und Robert Wenzel*

GEWÜRZTRAMINER

WHITE Usually labelled Traminer or Roter Traminer, the wines from this variety range from light and floral to intensely aromatic. They may be dry or have one of various shades of sweetness. They are the fullest, richest, and most pungent of *Trockenbeerenauslesen*.

⏳ 3–6 years

🏆 *Rheinhold Polz • Andreas Schafler • Herbert Zillinger*

GOLDBURGER

WHITE This is a Welschriesling/Orangetraube cross that produces white wines that are used for blending.

⏳ 1–3 years

GRÜNER VELTLINER

WHITE This grape has reinvented itself following the much-publicized thrashing it gave Burgundy in the tasting organized by Jancis Robinson MW and Tim Atkin MW in 2002. The new-found respect for Grüner Veltliner could be just as quickly lost, however, if the current trend for bigger, fatter, and less varietal wines continues. It won the contest not because the Burgundies chosen were inferior or too young – they included *grands crus* with good bottle-age from top growers, not to mention a number of top-quality international Chardonnay wines. (Burgundy should be thankful that Grüner Veltliner stole the limelight; being trounced by Chardonnays from Australia, Austria, California, Italy, and South Africa might have had an even greater negative effect.) No, it won because of its intrinsic minerality – the distinctive hint of fiery, freshly ground pepper that comes through on the finish; yet many producers have forgotten these roots and pushed ripeness levels so high that some of the wines they make have become parodies of the Chardonnay they so roundly defeated. Instead of mimicking Chardonnay, growers of Grüner Veltliner should concentrate on exploiting their *terroir* to express the truly diverse range of varietal styles that can be achieved – from the rich but distinctive *barrique*-fermented wines that can beat the greatest Chardonnay without being bigger or heavier, to the leanest and raciest Veltliners, which can have such fantastically fine minerality that they may be compared to the best Rieslings.

⏳ 1–4 years (*Qualitätswein*), 3–10 years (*Prädikatswein*)

🏆 *Anton Bauer • Bründlmayer • Ebner Ebenauer*

• *Brigit Eichinger • Freie Weingärtner Wachau • Geyerhof • Graf Hardegg • Gritsch Mauritiushof • Heidler • Hirtzberger* (Spitzer) • *Huber • Jurtschitsch-Sonnof • Knoll • Laurenz V • Loimer • Metternich-Sandor • Nikolaihof • F X Pichler • Franz Prager • Rabl • Schloss Gobelsburg • Steininger • Salomon Undhof • Petra Unger • Wieninger*

JUBLINÄ UMSREBE

WHITE A Blauer Portugieser/Blaufränkisch cross, this is allowed for *Prädikatswein* only, as its mild character is transformed by botrytis.

⏳ 3–7 years

MERLOT

RED Small amounts are grown in Krems, Mailberg, and Furth in Lower Austria, plus in a few scattered plots in Burgenland. This variety has potential in Austria, as it can produce richly coloured red wines with soft, spicy-juicy fruit, but has been under-exploited until quite recently.

⏳ 1–3 years (*Qualitätswein*), 3–5 years (*Prädikatswein*)

🏆 *Hofkellerei des Fürsten von Liechtenstein* (Herrenbaumgärtner Spätlese)

MÜLLER-THURGAU

WHITE Often labelled as Riesling x Silvaner, this is Austria's second most prolific grape variety. The best of Austria's pure varietal Müller-Thurgaus have a fine, spicy character that is superior to the average German version.

⏳ 1–2 years

🏆 *Hirtzberger • Schützenhof Fam Korper*

MUSKATELLER

WHITE This is an under-exploited variety that makes some of Burgenland's best *Prädikatswein* and excels in the sheltered sites of Styria.

⏳ 1–3 years (*Qualitätswein*), 2–10 years (*Prädikatswein*)

🏆 *Leth • Weinhof Platzer • Weinbau Ladislaus und Robert Wenzel*

MUSKAT-OTTONEL

WHITE Less weighty than the Muskateller, the Muskat-Ottonel variety has more immediate aromatic appeal and is best drunk when young.

⏳ 2–4 years

🏆 *Willi Opitz*

NEUBURGER

WHITE An Austrian variety that excels on chalky soil, making full-bodied wines with a typically nutty flavour in all categories of sweetness.

⏳ 2–4 years (*Qualitätswein*), 3–8 years (*Prädikatswein*)

🏆 *Dipl Ing Karl Alphart*

PINOT BLANC

WHITE Often called Klevner or Weisser Burgunder, this produces a fresh, light-bodied, easy-to-drink wine at lower quality levels. In exceptional years, it can develop a fine spicy-richness in the upper *Prädikatswein* categories.

🍷 2–4 years (*Qualitätswein*), 3–8 years (*Prädikatswein*)

🏆 *Skoff*

PINOT GRIS

WHITE Sold in Austria as Ruländer or Grauer Burgunder, this is a fuller, spicier version of Pinot Blanc, but it has a typical nutty richness.

🍷 2–4 years (*Qualitätswein*), 3–8 years (*Prädikatswein*)

🏆 *Tement*

PINOT NOIR

RED Labelled Blauer Burgunder, Blauer Spätburgunder, or Blauburgunder in different parts of Austria, the wines are often disappointing, although there are a few growers that excel.

🍷 1–3 years

🏆 *Bründlmayer • Johann Gipsberg • Juris-Stiegelmar • Jurtschitsch-Sonnof*

RIESLING

WHITE In Austria, wine from this grape should be sold as Weisser Riesling or Rheinriesling, to distinguish it from Welschriesling. Wachau and Kremser Riesling can be compared with fine German examples.

🍷 2–6 years (*Qualitätswein*), 4–12 years (*Prädikatswein*)

🏆 *Bründlmayer* (Spätlese) • *Freie Weingärtner Wachau* (Weissenkirchner Achleiten "Federspiel" and "Smaragd") • *Hirtzberger* (Spitzer Steinterrassen "Federspiel") • *Hofkellerei des Fürsten von Liechtenstein* (Spätlese) • *Thiery-Weber* (Kremser Sandgrube)

ROTER VELTLINER

WHITE This grape makes a rather neutral white wine that is usually blended in light, dry styles.

🍷 1–3 years

ROTGIPFLER

WHITE This makes a robust, full-bodied, spicy wine of not dissimilar character to the Zierfandler, which is often made into a dry style, although the semi-sweet Rotgipfler of Gumpoldskirchen may be the most famous rendition of this grape.

🍷 3–7 years

🏆 *Heinrich Harti • Hoffer • Weinbau Franz Kurz • Gottfried Schellmann*

ST-LAURENT

RED This variety typically produces a light, mild-flavoured wine of quaffing character. St-Laurent is thought to be related to Pinot Noir, and it has to be said that some producers can craft lovely, velvety wines of Pinot-like quality and style.

🍷 1–3 years

🏆 *Gessellmann • Johann Gipsberg • Johanneshof Reinisch • Pittnauer • Schloss Halbturn • Umathum*

SAUVIGNON BLANC

WHITE Called Muskat-Silvaner (or occasionally Weisser Sauvignon), this variety grown in Styria normally makes an austere, dry style, but can excel at the higher levels of *Prädikatswein*.

🍷 2–4 years (*Qualitätswein*), 4–10 years (*Pradikätswein*)

🏆 *Fam Kollwentz* (Römerhof) • *Rheinhold Polz* • *Walter Skoff* (Gamlitz Eckberg Edel Kabinett) • *Tement*

SCHEUREBE

WHITE This is not very pleasant at *Qualitätswein* level, but develops a beautiful aromatic character at higher levels of *Prädikatswein*.

🍷 2–4 years

🏆 *Gessellmann • Willi Opitz*

SILVANER

WHITE Seldom seen, tomato-tasting varietal.

🍷 1–2 years

🏆 *Sonnhof Josef Jurtschitsch*

WELSCHRIESLING

WHITE Austria's third most prolific variety, making very ordinary dry wines, but can be rich and stylish at upper levels of *Prädikatswein*.

🍷 1–3 years (*Qualitätswein*), 2–8 years (*Pradikätswein*)

🏆 *Bründlmayer • Willi Opitz • Weinhof Platzer • Tement*

ZIERFANDLER

WHITE Also known as Spätrot, this variety makes full-bodied and well-flavoured dry wine.

🍷 2–6 years

🏆 *Hoffer • Weinbau Franz Kurz • Gottfried Schellmann*

ZWEIGELT

RED Another mild red wine variety, Zweigelt is sometimes given the name Blauer Zweigelt or Rotburger. The best examples have a structure that is suited to food, with big, peppery fruit, but the norm is rather light and lacklustre.

🍷 1–3 years

🏆 *Johann Gipsberg • Walter Glatzer* (Dornenvoge) • *K+K Kirnbauer • Leth • Maria Magdalena Romer* (Schweizerreid) • *Schloss Halbturn*

BLENDED RED

The finest of these blended reds are usually oak-aged in new *barriques* and Cabernet-Sauvignon-based for backbone, with Blaufränkisch, St-Laurent, and sometimes Zweigelt added for fruit and softness.

🍷 2–8 years

🏆 *Gessellmann* (Opus Eximium) • *Igler* (Cuvée Vulcano) • *Josef Pöckl* (Admiral) • *Schlossweingut Malteser Ritterorden* (Cabernet Sauvignon-Merlot) • *Ernst Triebaumer* (Blaufränkisch-Cabernet) • *Umathum* (Ried Hallebühl Cuvée Rot)

BLENDED WHITE

Cheap, commercial white wine blends are commonly found in Austria, whereas finer examples of the blender's art are thin on the ground. However, Franz Mayer produces an intriguing blend of Grüner Veltliner, Müller-Thurgau, Riesling, Silvaner, and Zierfandler.

🏆 *Franz Mayer* (Grinzinger Reisenberg)

BOTTLE-FERMENTED SPARKLING

Austria's best-known sparkling wine is the bottle-fermented Schlumberge, produced in Vienna, but it seldom excels in quality.

🏆 *Weinhof Platzer* (Pinot Cuvée)

THE APPELLATIONS OF
AUSTRIA

Note Austria's quality designation DAC (*Districtus Austriae Controllatus*) was introduced in 2001, when Weinviertel was the first to receive this status. It dictates the style of wine and how its is made. All wines undergo a tasting to qualify.

BURGENLAND

Austria's easternmost region is also its warmest. It consistently provides overripe grapes, almost guaranteeing a substantial production of Prädikatswein each year. The Mittelburgenland and Südburgenland are Austria's most important red wine areas, with black varieties accounting for some 75 per cent of the vines cultivated.

MITTELBURGENLAND DAC

Mittelburgenland was originally part of the old Rust-Neusiedlersee, but it is physically separated from the Neusiedler See by the Sopron wine area of Hungary. Mittelburgenland wines are more *passerillage* than botrytized in character. This is a red-wine district, with some 75 per cent of the production coming from varieties such as Blaufränkisch and Zweigelt. The wines from this region do not have the body, tannin, and acidity balance that is associated with even the most modest red wines.

☑ **Villages** *Deutschkreuz • Horitschon • Neckenmarkt*

  Growers *Johann Heinrich • K+K Kirnbauer • Igler • Moric • Weninger • Wohlmuth*

NEUSIEDLER SEE

These vineyards and those of Neusiedlersee-Hügelland are within the area of influence of Neusiedler See, a vast, shallow pan of water barely 2 metres (6.5 feet) deep. Its microclimate produces more botrytized grapes than any other wine area in the world.

☑ **Villages** *Apetlon • Frauenkirchen • Gols • Halbturn • Illmitz • Podersdorf • Schützen*

  Growers *Juris • Heinrich • Alois Kracher • Willi Opitz • Pittnauer • Prieler • Schloss Halbturn • Umathum • Velich*

NEUSIEDLERSEE-HÜGELLAND & LEITHABERG DAC

The western side of Neusiedler See produces a similar range of wines to those on the eastern side, although more red wine is produced here, and this is also the home of *Ausbruch* wines.

☑ **Villages** *Donnerskirchen • Grosshöflein • Rust*

  Growers *Feiler-Artinger • Kollwentz • Schandl • Schröck • Triebaumer • Wenzel*

SÜDBURGENLAND & EISENBERG DAC

The red wines, mainly Blaufränkisch, are generally uninspiring. Some surprisingly fine *Prädikatswein* from the modest Welschriesling are also made.

✓ **Villages** *Deutsch Schützen • Eisenberg • Rechnitz • Weinberg • Welgersdorf*

Growers *Krutzler • Pichler-Krutzler • Schiefer*

KÄRNTEN

The wines of Kärnten are confined to a small area 50 kilometres (30 miles) west of Weststeiermark (thus off the map), comprising a few vineyards scattered between the towns of Klagenfurt and St Andrä (not the St Andrä in Südsteiermark). Red, white, Schilcher, and Bergwein wines of modest quality are produced and sold by one or two small firms.

NIEDERÖSTERREICH

This is Austria's premier dry wine region. It is famous for its peppery Grüner Veltliners and the elegance of its Rieslings. Top Rieslings can be light and airy in their youth, but they attain a richness after a few years in bottle and they can achieve a fine, racy balance comparable to that of some of the best German Rieslings. *Kabinett* is the style that dominates the classic wines of this region, although *Spätlese* and, occasionally, *Auslese* wines are made in the hottest years.

CARNUNTUM

Part of Donauland-Carnuntum until 1994, this appellation consists of vineyards on the banks of the Danube, and its hinterland, between Vienna and the Slovakian border. Although white grapes dominate (with Chardonnay and Grüner Veltliner standing out), red wines have proved most successful, resulting in more black varieties being planted.

✓ **Villages** *Göttlesbrunn • Rohrau*

Growers *Glatzer • Markowitsch • Muhr-Van de Niepoort • Pittnauer*

KAMTAL DAC

North of Kremstal, this region produces some of Austria's finest Riesling and Grüner Veltliner and is home to some of the country's most gifted, innovative, and expressive winemakers.

✓ **Villages** *Gobelsburg • Langenlois • Strass*

Growers *Brandl • Bründlmayer • Brigit Eichinger • Heidler • Jurtschitsch Sonnhof • Laurenz V • Rabl • Schloss Gobelsburg • Steininger*

KREMSTAL DAC

Part of the old Kamtal-Donauland region, this relatively small area north and south of a short stretch of the Danube was singled out in 1994, due to the fame of Krems, renowned for its high-quality Grüner Veltliner. Some good Rieslings are also produced. Zweigelt can do well, and there are occasional international varietal highlights from Chardonnay, Cabernet Sauvignon, and even Pinot Noir.

✓ **Villages** *Krems • Stein*

Growers *Angerer • Buchegger • Geyerhof • Mantler • Nigl • Salomon Undhof • Petra Unger*

THERMENREGION

Named after the hot springs, Thermenregion is also, coincidentally, one of Austria's warmest regions. Wines produced are both red and white, with the Blauer Portugieser and Neuburger grape varieties dominating. Zierfandler and Rotgipfler are specialities of Gumpoldskirchen.

✓ **Villages** *Bad Vöslau • Gumpoldskirchen*

Growers *Alphart • Hartl • Johanneshof Reinisch • Andreas Schafler • Gottfried Schellmann*

TRAISENTAL DAC

Formerly the southwestern half of Donauland, Traisental achieved independence as a regional appellation in 1994.

✓ **Villages** *Herzogenburg • Reichersdorf*

Growers *Huber • Neumayer*

WACHAU

Lower Austria's top-performing district, Wachau makes many fine varietals, including Grüner Veltliner, the most important, and Riesling, definitely the best.

✓ **Villages** *Durnstein • Loiben • Spitz*

Growers *Alzinger • Donabaum • Gritsch-Mauritiushof • Hirtzberger • Höllmüller • Knoll • Jamek • Lagler • Nikolaihof • F X Pichler • Franz Prager • Wess*

WAGRAM

Formerly Donauland, or land of the Danube, the Wagram region houses the world's oldest viticultural college at Klosterneuburg. Best for Grüner Veltliner.

✓ **Villages** *Kirchberg • Klosterneuburg • Wagram*

Growers *Anton Bauer • Josef Bauer • Leth • Ott • Söllner*

WEINVIERTEL DAC

This large area combines two former districts of Retz (the hinterland of Kamtal and Donauland) and Falkenstein, which is a totally separate area north of Vienna. Both extend northwards to the border with the Czech Republic. Some reds but mostly white wines are made here. Although few could be said to have any class, they are well made, drinkable, and represent great value for money.

✓ **Villages** *Ebenthal • Falkenstein • Mailberg • Poysdorf • Retz*

Growers *Ebner-Ebenauer • Graf Hardegg • Pfaffl • Malteser Ritterorden • Herbert Zillinger*

OBERÖSTERREICH

This is a large region to the west of the Wachau, but with just 85 hectares (210 acres) of vineyards in the vicinity of Linz (80 kilometres [50 miles] to the west and thus off the map). To my knowledge, all the wines are sold under the Weinbauer brand in a *gasthof* at Hofkirchen.

STEIERMARK *or* STYRIA

Situated in the southeastern corner of Austria, this region has a high level of rainfall interspersed with exceptional levels of sunshine and warmth. The region makes red and very dry white wines and, although few particularly fine-quality wines are encountered, there are many interesting local specialities. The most famous is Schilcher. Made from the obscure Blauer Wildbacher grape, Schilcher is a sort of blush-wine that results from the briefest maceration on the grape skins. There are three wine districts in this region.

SÜDOSTSTEIERMARK

The Müller-Thurgau and Welschriesling are surprisingly successful in the Südoststeiermark, and the Gewürztraminer can be the most expressive in Austria. Gräflich Stürgkh'sches is the oldest, best-known, and most traditional producer, but the wines of Manfred Platzer are more expressive.

✓ **Village** *Kloch*

Growers *Neumeister • Platzer • Winkler-Hermaden*

SÜDSTEIERMARK

The very best wines of this area have Styria's naturally high acidity, but this is combined with delicate and pure fruit flavours, making for exceptional finesse, particularly in varieties such as Gewürztraminer, Chardonnay (known locally as Morillon), and Riesling.

✓ **Villages** *Gamlitz • Leibnitz • Leutschach*

Growers *Gross • Maitz • Polz • Sattler • Skoff • Tement*

WESTSTEIERMARK

Made of some 70 per cent Schilcherwein, Zwiebelschilcher is an onion-skin-coloured Schilcher, which is grown on the slopes above Stainz. Another speciality is Sauvignon Blanc, known locally as Muskat-Silvaner, a somewhat mystifying synonym since the searingly dry wines it produces in these vineyards (and elsewhere for that matter) have absolutely no hint of either Muskat or Silvaner, and the parentage of the Sauvignon Blanc vine has, of course, no connection with either of these grape varieties.

✓ **Village** *Stainz*

Growers *Müller*

TIROL

The Zirler Weinhof (300 kilometres [185 miles] southwest of Weststeiermark and thus off the map) produces some 135 hectolitres (1,500 cases) of very ordinary wine from just 1.5 hectares (less than 4 acres) of Müller-Thurgau, Blauer Portugieser, and Zweigelt at Zirl. This might seem an unlikely place to plant a vineyard, if not for the fact that it is conveniently placed on the tourist route to the popular resort of Seefeld.

VIENNA *or* WIEN

Until Madrid recently revived its ancient appellation, Vienna was the only capital city in Europe to have its own wine-growing region. Most of the wines are sold by the pitcher as Wiener Heuriger, in the city's many bars called *Heurigen* (also known as *Buschenschanken*). The wine is less than one year old when sold. As much as 28 per cent is blended, but pure varietals of classic grapes are on the increase. There are no inner districts, but there are several wine villages within the city limits, of which the most famous is Grinzing.

✓ **Growers** *Franz Mayer • Wieninger*

VORARLBERG

Vorarlberg is the westernmost region of Austria (thus off the map). It used to boast 100 hectares (247 acres) of vines, but only 6 hectares (15 acres) exist today, strung out between Bregenz, on Lake Constance (Bodensee), and Frastanz, which is close to Liechtenstein. The quality of the wine produced here is unremarkably ordinary, and there are only about half a dozen growers who sell their wines commercially.

SWITZERLAND

The increasing emphasis of Swiss wines, as far as international recognition is concerned, is on its improving reds, with Pinot Noir on the increase but Merlot from Ticino in the south the most consistent top performer.

AT THEIR BEST, Swiss wines are as fresh and clean as the Alpine air. Although many grape varieties are cultivated in Switzerland, the most famous grape grown here is the Chasselas. In France, this variety is perceived as a table grape, yet the Swiss make it into a light, dry, spritzy, and delicately delicious wine that is the perfect partner to the Swiss cheese fondue. The Chasselas can be found under the guise of the Dorin in the Vaud region, the Perlan in Geneva, and, most famous of all, the Fendant in the Valais. However, although this country's most popular grape variety represents 27 per cent of the vines cultivated, almost 60 per cent of all Swiss vines produced are, rather surprisingly, black varieties.

There is, in fact, as much as 30 per cent Pinot Noir, 10 per cent Gamay, and, nowhere near as important, but very much on the increase, Merlot, which currently accounts for 7 per cent, leaving all the other varieties just 13 per cent of the vineyards.

The quality of Swiss wines has certainly improved over the past decade, but yields have always been much too high in general (80 hectolitres per hectare on average, with some cantons producing as much as 120 hectolitres per hectare) for Switzerland to achieve a serious international reputation as a quality wine-producing country.

Producers who keep their yields low make some splendid wines, but unfortunately they are at present too few to change the reputation of the

country as a whole. The accepted wisdom on this issue is that the value of the Swiss franc and the high cost of living inevitably makes these wines expensive in international terms, especially the very best wines. Since the Swiss drink twice as much wine as they can produce and are conditioned to high prices, there is no need to export and little incentive, therefore, to develop better-value wines. Price aside, the finest Swiss whites can be delightful, and the best reds are getting deeper and more velvety by the vintage.

RECENT SWISS VINTAGES

2010 Another excellent vintage anticipated.

2009 A great vintage for both reds and whites.

2008 This was a difficult year for both reds and whites.

2007 After an early start, a cool end to the spring delayed the growing season, but a hot July got the vines back on track, while blue skies throughout September and October provided a perfect harvest. Very good quality, particularly for whites, which are highlighted by their ripe yet crisp acidity.

2006 An excellent red-wine vintage, but not quite so good for the whites.

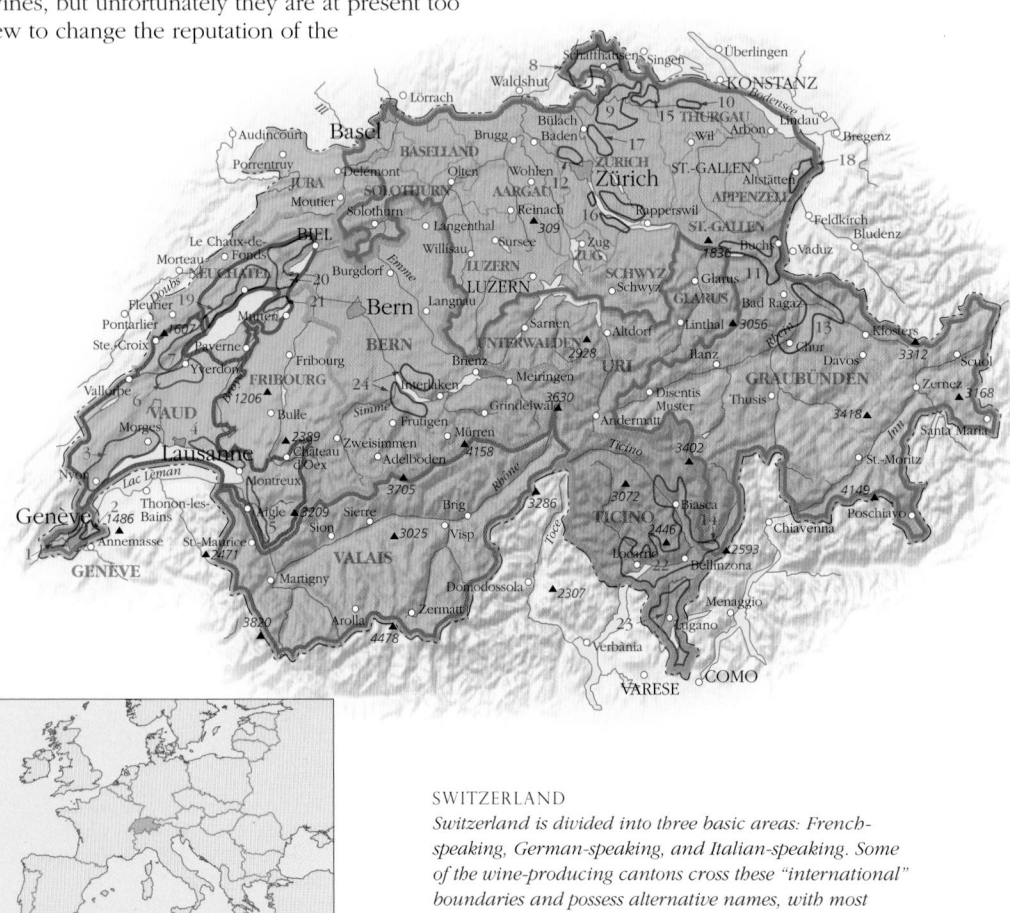

SWITZERLAND
Switzerland is divided into three basic areas: French-speaking, German-speaking, and Italian-speaking. Some of the wine-producing cantons cross these "international" boundaries and possess alternative names, with most vineyards concentrated around the country's lakes and rivers.

Romansch-speaking Switzerland
French-speaking Switzerland
German-speaking Switzerland
Italian-speaking Switzerland

Valais

Genève
1 — Mandement
2 — Arve-et-Lac

Vaud
3 — Überland
4 — Lavaux
5 — Chablais
6 — Côtes de l'Orbe
7 — Bonvillars

Eastern Switzerland
8 — Klettgau
9 — Weinland
10 — Thurtal
11 — Oberland
12 — Limmattal
13 — Bündner Herrschaft
14 — Misox
15 — Untersee
16 — Zürichsee
17 — Züricher Unterland
18 — Rheinthal

Neufchatel & Trois Lacs
19 — Neuchâtel
20 — Bielersee
21 — La Côte

Ticino
22 — Sopraceneri
23 — Sottoceneri

Bern
24 — Vully

—— Canton boundary
––– International boundary
▲ Height above sea level (metres)

0   10   20   30   40   50 miles
0   20   40   60   80 km

FACTORS AFFECTING TASTE AND QUALITY

LOCATION
Situated between the south of Germany, north of Italy, and the central-east French border.

CLIMATE
Continental Alpine conditions prevail, with local variations due to altitude, the tempering influence of lakes, and the sheltering effects of the various mountain ranges. An Alpine wind called the Foehn raises, rather than lowers, temperatures in some valleys. Rainfall is relatively low, and a number of areas, such as the Valais in the south, are very dry indeed. Spring frosts are a perennial threat in most areas.

ASPECT
Vines are grown in areas ranging from valley floors and lake shores to the steep Alpine foothill sites, which have an average altitude of 750 metres (2,460 feet), although just south of Visp, they reach nearly 1,200 metres (3,940 feet) and are reputedly the highest vineyards in Europe. The best sites are found on south-facing slopes, which maximize exposure to sun, and where the incline is too steep to encourage high yields.

SOIL
Mostly a glacial moraine (scree) of decomposed slate and schist, often with limestone over sedimented bedrock of limestone, clay, and sand. In the Vaud, Dézaley is famous for its "pudding stones", Chablais has limestone and marl, and Ollon and Bex both benefit from gypsum deposits.

VITICULTURE AND VINIFICATION
Terracing is required on the steeper sites, and so too is irrigation (with mountain water) in dry areas such as the Valais. Most vineyard work is labour-intensive, except in a few more gently sloping vineyards such as those around Lake Geneva (Lac Léman), where mechanical harvesting is practical. Careful vinification produces remarkably high yields. The last three decades have seen a growth in the production of red wine in what is generally a white-wine-dominated region.

GRAPE VARIETIES
Aligoté, Amigne, Ancellota, Bacchus, Blauburgunder, Bonarda, Bondola, Cabernet Franc, Cabernet Sauvignon, Chardonnay, Charmont, Chenin Blanc, Completer, Ermitage (Marsanne), Fendant (Chasselas), Freisa, Gamaret, Gamay, Gwäss (Gouais), Heida (Savagnin Blanc), Humagne Blanc, Humagne Rouge (Cornalin), Kerner, Lafnetscha (possibly same variety as Completer), Landroter (Cornalin), Malbec, Malvoisie, Merlot, Muscat à Petits Grains, Paien (Savagnin Blanc), Petit Arvine (Arvine), Pinot Blanc, Pinot Gris, Räuschling (Elbling), Riesling, Riesling x Sylvaner (Müller-Thurgau), Sauvignon Blanc, Sémillon, Seyval Blanc, Silvaner, Syrah, Traminer (Savagnin Blanc)

THE WINE STYLES OF
SWITZERLAND

AMIGNE
WHITE Old Valais variety mostly grown at Vétroz, the Amigne usually makes a full, rustic, smooth, dry white, although Germanier-Balavaud makes a sweet, luscious, late-harvest style.

1–2 years

André Fontannaz • Germanier-Balavaud (Mitis)

ARVINE or PETIT (PETITE) ARVINE
WHITE Another old Valais variety that makes an even richer, dry white, with a distinctive grapefruit character and good acidity. The Petite Arvine (to distinguish it from the lesser-quality Grosse Arvine) adapts well to late-harvest styles and is highly regarded by Swiss wine lovers in both dry and sweet styles.

1–3 years

Chappaz (especially Grain Noble) • Jean-Yves Crettenand • René Favre • François et Dominique Giroud • Simon Maye

BONDOLA
RED An indigenous grape producing rustic reds on its own, Bondola is at its best in a wine called Nostrano, in which it is blended with Bonarda, Freisa, and other local varieties.

BONVILLARS
WHITE Restricted to Chasselas grown around Lac de Neuchâtel in the villages of Côtes de l'Orbe and Vully, Bonvillars is lighter and more delicate and lively than Vaud wines of this variety grown farther south.

CV Bonvillars (Vin des Croisés)

CABERNET SAUVIGNON
RED A relatively new variety that does well in the Chablais district and Ticino, both pure and blended.

2–6 years

Christine & Stéphanie Delarze-Baud • Les Hutins • Pierre-Alain Meylan

CHARDONNAY
WHITE Just what the world needs, another Chardonnay, and at Swiss prices! However, the very best are worth a try.

1–4 years

Caves Cidis • Gilles & Joell Cina • Fromm • Peter Graf • Johanniterkeller • Kuntzer & Fils

CHASSELAS
WHITE Called Fendant in the Valais, Dorin in the Vaud, and Perlan in Geneva, this is the most important Swiss grape variety and can be nicely flavoured, often having a charming *pétillance*. When grown on light, sandy soils it may have a lime-tree blossom aroma. The grape is sensitive to soil, with different characteristics depending on whether the soil is limestone, flint, gypsum, marl, schist, or whatever. Although it is possible to find relatively full, potentially long-lived wines from this variety, it is a wine best enjoyed young.

1–3 years

Henri Badoux (Cuvée Prestige) • Louis Bovard • La Colombe • Dé Zaley • Blaise Duboux • Paccot

CLASSIC RED BLEND
RED Although Ticino grows Switzerland's best Merlot and up-and-coming Cabernet Sauvignon, it also makes the best Bordeaux-style blends.

3–10 years

Huber Vini (Montagna Magica)

COMPLETER
WHITE The Completer is rare grape variety of ancient origin that makes a fascinating, rich, *Auslese*-style of wine from scattered plots found in Graubünden.

3–7 years

Adolf Boner • Peter & Rosi Hermann • Malans

CORNALIN
RED Most vines of this indigenous Swiss variety are very old, and restricted to the Valais, where they make dark, powerful red wines that are rich and concentrated, with a full, spicy complexity.

3–7 years

Jean-René Germanier • Denis Mercier • Maurice Zufferey

LA CÔTE
RED & WHITE Grown exclusively at La Côte (which encompasses the villages of Aubonne, Begnins, Bursinel, Coteau de Vincy, Féchy, Luins, Mont-sur-Rolle, Morges, Nyon, Perroy, and Vinze, as well as La Côte itself), where the Chasselas grape is at its most floral and aromatic, and fruity reds are often blended from two or more varieties, including Gamay, Gamaret, and Garanoir.

1–2 years

Caves Cidis (Gamaret/Garanoir/Gamay, Garanoir) • Philippe Rossier (Aubonne Merlot)

DÔLE
RED A light red comprised of at least 50 per cent Pinot Noir plus up to 50 per cent Gamay, Dôle is the Swiss (Valais) equivalent of Burgundy's Passetoutgrains.

1–3 years

Simon Maye • Dubuis et Rudaz

DÔLE BLANCHE
WHITE The *blanc de noirs* version is popular, but does not carry its own appellation.

ERMITAGE
WHITE A synonym for the Marsanne used in the Valais, where it makes a delicately rich, dry white wine that is often aged too long in bottle by its aficionados.

1–4 years

⒰ *Marie-Thérèse Chappaz • Dom Cornulus •
Adrian Mathier • Philippoz Frères*

FENDANT

WHITE This Chasselas synonym is used in the
Valais, where it produces a fleshy-styled, dry white
wine, the best of which can have a flinty,
lime-tree-blossom aroma and a crisp, minerality of
fruit. Ideal with cheese fondue.

‰ 1–3 years

⒰ *Frédéric Dumoulin* (L'Orpailleur) • *Adrian
Mathier • Simon Maye • Dubuis et Rudaz •
Raphaël Vergère • Zufferey*

GAMAY

RED Until recently, this Beaujolais grape rarely
made red wines of distinction in its pure varietal
form, and was much more successful when blended
with Pinot Noir (*see* Dôle).

‰ 1–3 years

⒰ *Gérald Besse • Jean-René Germanier • Les
Hutins • Madeleine et Jean-Yves Mabillard-Fuchs*

GEWÜRZTRAMINER

WHITE Rarely encountered.

‰ 1–5 years

⒰ *Dominique Passaquay* (Passerillé) • *Maurice
Dupraz*

HEIDA

WHITE Fresh, lightly aromatic, dry and off-dry wine
made from the Savagnin (Traminer) grape.

‰ 1–2 years

⒰ *Chanton • Simon Maye* (Païen)

HUMAGNE BLANC

WHITE The Humagne Blanc is a wine with a
relatively high iron content, which could be the
reason it used to be given to babies, although it is
probable that the dear little things cried when
allowed to suck on Humagne Blanc. It has a green
bean or capsicum aroma, hints of exotic fruit on the
palate, and a touch of bitterness on the finish.

HUMAGNE ROUGE

RED An old Valais variety, this dark-skinned grape
hails from Italy's Valle d'Aosta and makes big, rich,
rustic reds that go well with feathered game.

‰ 1–4 years

⒰ *Jean-René Germanier*

JOHANNISBERG

WHITE This is not the Johannisberg Riesling, but
the official synonym for Sylvaner in the Valais,
where it is supposedly musky, although they are
usually sappy and savoury with some sweetness.

‰ Upon purchase

⒰ *Adrian Mathier • Albert Mathier & Söhne
• Claudy Clavien • Domaine du Mont d'Or •
François et Dominique Giroud*

LAFNETSCHA

This Completer x Humagne Blanc cross has long
grown in the Haut Valais, where it produces dry
whites with a leafy aroma.

⒰ *Chanton*

LAVAUX

WHITE Grown exclusively at Lavaux (which
encompasses the villages of Calamin, Chardonne,
Dézaley, Epesses, Lutry, Saint-Saphorin, Vevey-
Montreux, and Villette, as well as Lavaux itself), the
Chasselas is at its softest yet fullest.

‰ 1–2 years

MERLOT
DEL TICINO

RED The Merlot grape accounts for more than 80
per cent of the vines planted in Italian-speaking
Switzerland, where it produces red wines that range
from young and light-bodied to fuller, better-coloured
wines that have a nice varietal perfume and are often
aged in *barriques*. The VITI classification on a bottle
of Merlot del Ticino used to be seen as a guarantee of
superior quality, but now merely indicates the wine
has had one year's ageing before being bottled.

‰ 2–4 years (lighter styles), 3–10 years
(*barrique* wines)

⒰ *Adriano Kaufmann • Werner Stucky • Carlo
Tamborini • Huber Vini • Luigi Zanini •
Christian Zündel*

MÜLLER-THURGAU

WHITE This most prolific (supposedly) Riesling x
Sylvaner cross was created in 1882 by Dr Hermann
Müller, who hailed from the canton of Thurgau,
hence the name, which makes it rather ironic that
the Swiss should call this grape Riesling x Sylvaner
(particularly as it has now been established that
Müller-Thurgau is a Riesling x Madeleine Royale
cross!), rather than by the name that honours its
Swiss origins. However, the mild, grapey wine this
variety produces even in its home canton is no more
exciting than it is elsewhere, although relatively
superior examples are produced in Aargau.

‰ 1–2 years

⒰ *Schlossgut Bachtobel • Baumann • Andrea
Davaz • Daniel Marugg*

MUSCAT

WHITE The Muscat à Petits Grains is traditionally
grown in the Valais, in small quantities. It makes
wines of very light body, with the grape's
unmistakable varietal flowery aroma. Some interesting
late-harvest styles are beginning to emerge.

‰ 2–4 years

⒰ *Cave Emery* (Grains Nobles de la Saint Nicolas
– Séduction) • *Domaine des Muses • Stéphane
Clavien* (Coteaux de Sierre)

NOSTRANO

RED This used to be an inexpensive blend of *vin
ordinaire* quality, produced from grapes that failed
to reach appellation standard, but now it has its
own official classification and the quality has
certainly improved. Nostrano means "our" and
literally refers to the local varieties used, as opposed
to American hybrids.

OEIL DE PERDRIX

ROSÉ Oeil de Perdrix, which literally means
"partridge eye", is a French term for pale, dry rosé
wines made from free-run Pinot Noir.

‰ Upon purchase

⒰ *Alain Gerber • Cave de Champ de Clos*

PAÏEN

This is the local synonym for the Heida, aka
Savagnin. *See* Heida.

PERLAN

WHITE In the canton of Geneva the Chasselas
makes a slightly spritzy flowery wine that is sold as
Perlan. Geneva must be mentioned on the label, or
a village name: L'Allondon, Bardonnex, Dardagny,
Jussy, Lully, Peissy, Russin, or Satigny.

PINOT BLANC

WHITE Recently planted, fashionable variety, but
few wines stand out.

‰ 1–3 years

⒰ *Bad Osterfingen • Domaine des Abeilles d'Or •
Domaine Saint-Raphaël*

PINOT GRIS

WHITE This famous Alsace grape is becoming quite
fashionable in Switzerland, where it makes more of
a Pinot Grigio style, with some very successful
vendange tardive emerging.

‰ 1–3 years

⒰ *Cave Saint-Pierre • Caves du Château
d'Auvernier* (Vendange Tardive) • *La Colombe •
Domaine E de Montmollin Fils* (Vendange
Tardive) • *Schlossgut Bachtobel/Hans Ulrich
Kesselring • Urs Pircher Stadtberg* (Egfisauer
Stadtberger)

PINOT NOIR

RED In a country like Switzerland, which adores
Burgundy, it is not surprising that top producers make
some of Switzerland's most serious wines with this
grape variety – well coloured, velvety, with soft, cherry
fruit and a touch of oak. Although this wine is sold as
Blauburgunder in German-speaking Switzerland, and
Pinot Nero in Italian-speaking Switzerland, there are
moves towards harmonizing under the internationally
recognizable Pinot Noir name.

‰ 3–6 years (up to 10 years in exceptional cases)

⒰ *Agriloro • Bündner Herrschaft • Caves Fernand
Cina • Eichholz • Fromm • Daniel & Martha
Gantenbein • Christian Hermann • Mattmann
• Simon Maye • Schlossgut Bachtobel • Peter
Wegelin • Weingut am Worrenberg*

RÄUSCHLING

WHITE This rare variety is in decline and is now
found only along the shore of Lake Zurich, where it
is prized for its very fresh scents and fine acidity.

‰ Upon purchase

⒰ *Weingut Picher • Schwarzenbach*

RIESLING

WHITE Apart from exceptional botrytized wines,
Swiss Riesling does not have the quality or varietal
intensity of Germany or Austria.

⒰ *Schlossgut Bachtobel*

SALVAGNIN

WHITE A light, supple red-wine blend of Pinot

Noir and Gamay, this is the Vaud's equivalent of the more famous Dôle.

◐⤳ 1–3 years

⚗ *Jean-Pierre Walther*

SAUVIGNON BLANC

Although this grape represents less than 1 per cent of Switzerland's vineyards, a few interesting interpretations are beginning to emerge.

⚗ *Mattmann • Schlossgut Bachtobel*

SÜSSDRUCK

ROSÉ A soft, fresh, dry rosé produced in eastern Switzerland from free-run Pinot Noir.

SYRAH

RED This grape is at home in the heat and exposure of the northern Côtes du Rhône, and in Valais the Rhône River is as northerly as it gets. Peppery black fruits distinguish these fast-improving, increasingly fashionable wines.

◐⤳ 3–10 years

⚗ *Antoine et Christophe Bétrisey • Roger Burgdorfer* (Diable) *• Caves Fernand Cina • Domaine des Graves • Dubuis et Rudaz • Jean-René Germanier • François et Dominique Giroud • Simon Maye • Romain Papilloud • J & P Testuz* (Les Oenocrates) *• Zufferey*

VIN DU GLACIER
Valais

Although Switzerland's equivalent of Germany's Eiswein tends to be oxidative, this rare product does have its enthusiastic followers.

CERTIFIED ORGANIC PRODUCERS

Biodynamic
Ca di Ciser (Mergoscia)
Domaine de Beaudon (Fully)
Liesch-Hiestand (Malans)

THE APPELLATIONS OF
SWITZERLAND

Note Under the federal appellation system, all cantons have the right to their own appellation and each winemaking village within each canton can register its own appellation. Geneva was the first canton to comply in 1988, followed by Valais in 1991, Neuchâtel in 1993, and Vaud in 1995. Along with these village appellations, each canton may also designate generic district and stylistic appellations, the number of which is increasing all the time.

FRENCH-SPEAKING SWITZERLAND

Cantons *Fribourg, Gea, Jura, Neuchâtel, Valais, Vaud*

District appellations *Vully* (part in Fribourg, part in Neuchâtel); *Arve-et-Lac, Arve-et-Rhône, Mandement* (Geneva); *Bonvillars, Chablais, La Côte, Côtes de l'Orbe, Lavaux* (Vaud)

French-speaking Switzerland represents only 16 per cent of the country by area, yet manages to boast more than 80 per cent of its vineyards. Two-thirds of the wines are white, with Chasselas accounting for 90 per cent, while the Pinot Noir and Gamay together represent 99 per cent of the black grapes planted. Valais is the longest-established, most famous, and by far the most intensively cultivated of Switzerland's cantons, with vineyards stretching along 50 kilometres (30 miles) of the Rhône, from Lac Léman (Lake Geneva) to Brig (in the German-speaking sector). The Valais canton accounts for more than one-third of the country's wines, and even its lowliest wine villages are at least as good as the best villages of other Swiss cantons. The Vaud canton encompasses almost one-quarter of Switzerland's vineyards, which makes it the second most intensively cultivated canton in the country. The village of Salgesch is a fast-rising star for red wines – everything from elegant Pinot Noir to muscular Syrah.

☑ **Villages** *Auvernier, Cortaillod* (Neuchâtel) *• Salgesch • St-Léonard, Vétroz* (Valais) *• Calamin • Dézaley* (Vaud)

Growers *Adrian Mathier • Alain Gerber, Albert Mathier & Söhne • Alphonse Orsat • André Ruedin • Antoine et Christophe Bétrisey • Cave de Champ de Clos • Cave de la Madelaine/ André Fontannaz • Cave Emery • Cave Saint-Pierre • Caves Cidis • Caves de Riondaz • Caves du Château d'Auvernier • Caves Fernand Cina • Chanton • Charles Bonvin • Charles Favre • Château d'Allaman • Château de Vaumarcus • Château de Vinzel • Château*

Lichten • Château Maison Blanche • Christine & Stéphanie Delarze-Baud • Claudy Clavien • Clos de la George • CV Bonvillars • Denis Mercier • Didier Joris • Domaine de la Lance • Domaine E de Montmollin Fils • Domaine de Riencourt • Domaine des Abeilles d'Or • Domaine des Graves • Domaine des Muses • Domaine du Martheray • Domaine du Mont d'Or • Domaine Saint-Raphaël • Dominique Passaquay • Dubuis et Rudaz • François et Dominique Giroud • Frédéric Dumoulin • Gérald Besse • Gérard Pinget • Germanier-Balavaud • Gilles & Joell Cina • Hammel • Henri Badoux • J & P Testuz • Jean-René Germanier • Jean-Michel Novelle • Jean-Pierre Walther • Jean-Yves Crettenand • Kuntzer & Fils • Louis Bovard • Louis Vuignier • Madeleine et Jean-Yves Mabillard-Fuchs • Marie-Thérèse Chappaz • Maurice Dupraz • Maurice Gay • Maurice Zufferey • Pierre-Alain Meylan • Philippe Rossier • Raphaël Vergère • René Favre • Robert Isoz • Roger Burgdorfer • Romain Papilloud • Rouvinez • Stéphane Clavien • Vincent Favre

GERMAN-SPEAKING SWITZERLAND

Cantons *Aargau, Basel, Bern, Graubünden* (part), *St-Gallen, Schwyz, Schaffhausen, Thurgau*

District appellations *Bielersee, Uberland* (Bern); *Bündner Herrschaft* (Graubünden); *Oberland, Rheinthal* (St-Gallen); *Klettgau* (Schaffhausen); *Thurtal, Untersee* (Thurgau); *Flaachtal, Limmattal, Rafzerfelder, Züricher Unterland, Weinland* (Zürich)

By far the largest of the three cultural divisions, German-speaking Switzerland (eastern Switzerland) covers almost two-thirds of the country, yet encompasses only one-sixth of its total viticultural area. Aargau is best known for its red wines, but also produces off-dry, light, fragrant white wines of low alcohol content. Basel is a producer of white wine only. Although some rather thin and mean red wines are produced in Bern, the majority of grapes grown are white and produce wines that are fragrant and lively, with refreshing acidity. In Graubünden vineyards on the upper reaches of the Rhine, the Pinot Noir ripens well and provides wines made from it with comparatively good colour and body. Saint-Gallen also encompasses the upper reaches of the Rhine and produces mostly red wine. The southern

fringes of Graubünden fall within the Italian-speaking sector of Switzerland, where the canton is referred to locally as Grigioni. The vines of Schaffhausen grow within sight of the famous falls of the Rhine. Thurgau is, of course, home of the famous Dr Müller, who left his mark on world viticulture with his prolific Müller-Thurgau cross, and inevitably the grape grows there, although more than 50 per cent of the vines are Pinot Noir and the fruity wine that grape produces is far superior. Zürich is the most important canton in German-speaking Switzerland, but it produces some of the most expensive, least impressive wines in the entire country, although Pinot Noir grown on sheltered slopes with a good exposure to the sun can produce attractive fruity wines.

☑ **Villages** *Brestenberger • Goldwand • Netteler* (Aargau) *• Schafis* (Bern) *• Fläsch, Jenins, Maenfeld • Malans* (Graubünden) *• Leutschen* (Schwyz) *• Hallau • Schaffhausen* (Schaffhausen)

Growers *Adelheid von Randenburg • Adolf Boner • Daniel & Martha Gantenbein • Georg & Ruth Fromm • Christian Hermann • Graaf von Spiegelberg • Hans Schlatter • Schlossgut Bachtobel/Hans Ulrich Kesselring • Peter & Rosi Hermann • Peter Graf, Peter Wegelin • Urs Pircher Stadtberg • Weingut am Worrenberg • Weingut Picher*

ITALIAN-SPEAKING SWITZERLAND

Cantons *Ticino, Grigioni* (part)

District appellations *Misox* (Grigioni); *Sopraceneri, Sottoceneri* (Ticino)

Italian-speaking Switzerland consists of the cantons of Ticino (also known as Tessin) and the southern fringes of Graubünden (known in Italian as Grigioni) and more than 80 per cent of the vineyards are planted with the Merlot grape variety. Merlot del Ticino is consistently one of the best wines produced in Switzerland. Labour costs are nowhere near as high as they are in the rest of the country, which also makes Merlot del Ticino the least expensive of Switzerland's finest wines.

☑ **Village** *Misox* (Grigioni)

Growers *Adriano Kaufmann • Agriloro, Carlo Tamborini • Christian Zündel • Huber Vini • Johanniterkeller • Luigi Zanini • Tamborini • Werner Stucky*

The WINES of
NORTHWESTERN EUROPE

IF ENGLISH WINE COMES AS A SURPRISE TO SOME, then the thought of commercial vineyards in Belgium, the Netherlands, and even on a Danish island north of Poland will beggar belief – yet they exist. Their scope will always be limited because of the combination of northerly latitude and the uncertain climatic effect of the northern Atlantic. However, sparkling wines produced by Nyetimber and Ridgeview demonstrate that world-class quality can be achieved in England. The success enjoyed by these producers has encouraged the English wine industry to focus its efforts on perfecting sparkling wines, and other countries in northwestern Europe would be well advised to follow this lead.

DENBIES, DORKING, ENGLAND
At the foot of Box Hill in the chalky North Downs of Surrey, Denbies cultivates 107 hectares (265 acres) of vines in an area where the Atrebates, a local pre-Roman Celtic tribe, minted gold coins bearing a vine leaf.

THE BRITISH ISLES

On 17 December 2012, England will celebrate the 350th Anniversary of OEM, the Original English Method, the earliest documented description of adding sugar to a wine to create a second fermentation, six years before Dom Pérignon even set foot in Champagne. The account was written by Christopher Merret, a founding member of The Royal Society, who spoke of "sparkling" wine 60 years before the equivalent French term mousseux *was first recorded in any French document.*

ANY ENGLISH OR WELSH VINEYARD OWNERS who do not have the courage to replace their hybrids and crosses with classic grape varieties and follow the fizz trailblazers will become marginalized. Although this country's winemaking efforts are destined to remain a cottage industry, this is not because England and Wales lack serious or successful producers; it is due to two simple facts: British vineyards are a very recent phenomenon, and Great Britain is a densely populated island. If any *grand cru* sites ever existed, they would be under concrete or asphalt today. It will always be difficult to find suitable land for vineyards; therefore, the potential growth of English and Welsh wine will always be severely limited. It would be impossible to start up the French wine industry from scratch in a country that is half the size and twice as densely populated, particularly if it were burdened with a less favourable climate.

ANCIENT BRITONS

Winemaking in Britain is not new, but dates back to AD 43, when every important villa had a garden of vines. It was not until 1995, however, when a 8-hectare (20-acre) Roman vineyard was excavated at Wollaston in Northamptonshire, that the true scale of this early viticulture was realized. The Domesday Book reveals the existence of some 40 vineyards of significance during the reign of William the Conqueror; by medieval times the number had risen to 300, most of which were run by monks. The Black Death took its toll in the mid-14th century and, almost 200 years later, the dissolution of the monasteries virtually brought an end to English winemaking. Apart from a couple of vineyards in the mid-18th century and two more in the late 19th century, winemaking on a commercial scale was almost non-existent until Hambledon was established in 1951. English vineyards began to boom in the late 1960s and peaked in the early

THE DELL ON DENBIES, DORKING, SURREY
Set amid Surrey countryside, Denbies Estate is the largest winery in Great Britain, surrounded by more than 107 hectares (265 acres) of vineyards.

FACTORS AFFECTING TASTE AND QUALITY

LOCATION
Most of the vineyards are located in England and Wales, south of a line drawn through Birmingham and the Wash.

CLIMATE
Great Britain is at the northerly extreme of climates suitable for the vine, but the warm Gulf Stream tempers the weather sufficiently to make viticulture possible. Rainfall is relatively high and conditions vary greatly from year to year, making harvests somewhat unreliable. High winds can be a problem, but winter frosts are less troublesome than in many wine regions.

ASPECT
Vines are planted on all types of land, but the best sites are usually sheltered, south-facing slopes with the consequent microclimate advantages that can be crucial for wine production in this marginal viticultural region.

SOIL
Vines are grown on a wide variety of different soils ranging from granite through limestone, chalk, and gravel to clay.

VITICULTURE AND VINIFICATION
The commonly encountered high-trained vine systems indicate that many vineyards are poorly sited in frost-prone areas. Vigour is also a problem, as sap bypasses the fruit to produce an excessively luxuriant canopy of leaves, resulting in unnecessarily small grape clusters, delayed ripening, and overly herbaceous flavours. This problem is exacerbated by the use of rootstocks that actually promote vigour, but the New World influence that has already had its effect on English winemaking techniques will hopefully encourage the introduction of low-vigour rootstock. Although the British climate is least favourable for growing black grapes, an increasing amount of red and rosé has been produced since the early 1990s, but bottle-fermented sparkling wine is clearly the most up-and-coming of all the English wine styles.

GRAPE VARIETIES
Primary varieties: Bacchus, Chardonnay, Dornfelder, Pinot Noir, Regent, Rondo, Seyval Blanc
Secondary varieties: Auxerrois, Cabernet Sauvignon, Cascade, Chasselas, Dunkelfelder, Ehrenfelser, Faber (Faberebe), Gutenborner, Huxelrebe, Kanzler, Kerner, Léon Millot, Madeleine Angevine, Müller-Thurgau, Optima, Orion, Ortega, Perle, Phoenix, Pinot Blanc, Pinot Gris, Pinot Noir Précoce (Frühburgunder), Regner, Scheurebe, Schönberger, Siegerrebe, Triomphe d'Alsace, Wrotham Pinot (Pinot Meunier), Würtzer, Zweigeltrebe

1970s. Since then almost 500 have been planted, although just over 300 survive today, and only 109 of these have their own winery.

Few vineyards in the UK can reasonably expect more than an average of 800 degree-days Celsius (1,440 degree-days Fahrenheit) – well below the accepted winemaking minimum of 1,000 degree-days Celsius (1,800 degree-days Fahrenheit), so even the best-situated vineyards risked failure when first established. Some vineyards were unsuccessful, but those in existence today have proved the theoretical conditions to be just that – theoretical.

FUTURE TRENDS

Although English wine will remain forever a cottage industry, this does not mean it cannot earn a reputation for quality. High duty rates do mean, however, that it is difficult for the smallest vineyards, which have the highest overheads, to establish sales of a new product. Initially, this problem was overcome by contract winemaking, with virtually all the oldest and largest vineyards providing a service. Since the early 1990s, however, cooperative groups have formed to produce large volumes of relatively inexpensive wines by blending wines from their members, all of whom also make and market their own single-vineyard products.

The next step in the development of English wine is to rid the country of most of its crosses and hybrids. The reason these funny grapes with funny names must go is because they have a negative impact on most serious consumers. Wine drinkers are attracted to classic varieties and even willing to dabble with more obscure

NETHERLAND VINEYARDS, NYETIMBER
One of Nyetimber's recent acquisitions, Netherland (sic) is located near Tillington in West Sussex and shows exceptional potential. The name is genuinely historical and has nothing to do with its new owner Eric Heerema being Dutch.

vinifera grapes, particularly when indigenous to the wine-producing area of origin, but they either do not understand hybrids or find them a turn-off. As for German crosses, how can producers expect to establish an English or Welsh wine reputation with names like Reichensteiner or Siegerrebe? It is not that these varieties cannot produce fine wines; it is just that their fine wines are the exception rather than the rule, and the vast majority of the wines produced are the ones that will ultimately decide this country's reputation as no good. I shall continue to recommend good, sometimes excellent exceptions, but if English (and Welsh) sparkling wines are to make any sort of lasting international impact, then this country's non-sparkling wines must become as marginalized and as focused as Coteaux Champenois wines are in Champagne.

HERE COMES THE CAVALRY!

It took two Americans, Stuart and Sandy Moss, the original owners of Nyetimber, to shake the English out of their lethargy. The pioneering Mosses had a crazy ambition to make a top-quality English fizz from classic Champagne varieties, but when they sought so-called expert advice, they were told that Chardonnay would not ripen and Pinot Noir would just rot. Believing most English experts might be prejudiced by their training (most went to Geisenheim, where many of the crosses occupying most English vineyards originated), they did something nobody had bothered to do: they asked the *champenois* for help. They arrived, examined the soil, and advised what clones should be planted and how they should be trained. They even helped make the wine. Consequently, the Mosses created this country's first world-class wine, kick-started the English sparkling-wine industry, and, in the process, demonstrated that bottle-fermented sparkling wine is the only way forward for all English and Welsh vineyards with any ambition of a reputation. They have since retired, but Nyetimber continued to be the UK's flagship wine, first under songwriter Andy Hill and more recently Dutchman Eric Hereema. Mike Roberts at Ridgeview was the first to snap at Nyetimber's heels with his aptly named Cuvée Merret. Bob Lindo's multi-award-winning Camel Valley was next in line, with his sublime Pinot Noir, particularly as a rosé, which can be compared to the finest and most delicate Champagne rosé, but also Camel Valley's rose-hued *blanc de noirs*. There are, however, plenty of potential stars waiting in the wings, such as Henners and Herbert Hall, both built from the vineyard up to be sparkling-wine

operations and whose trial disgorgements have already demonstrated their superiority. Plus the promise of other sparkling-wine producers of the future whose wines have not yet been made, such as Steven Spurrier's Bride Valley, Jody Scheckter's Laverstoke Park, Coates & Seely, and even the royal family, with a vineyard planted at Windsor Castle in 2011 – all exciting ventures that are determined to excel. The future for English wine is truly sparkling.

THE END GAME

Ideally the UK will end up with a reduced number of commercial vineyards growing sparkling-wine clones of Chardonnay, Pinot Noir, and Pinot Meunier, with all those who are serious at making their own sparkling wine (rather than the indispensable task of supplying others) equipped with modern, on-site wineries and storage facilities. Some of these vineyards might also want to grow suitable clones of Auxerrois, Pinot Blanc, Pinot Gris, and Gamay. On a very limited scale, still wines would, in my opinion, be best focused on Bacchus for crisp dry white (because it makes the most "English" of wines), Auxerrois for *barrique*-fermented dry whites, and Pinot Noir (including Pinot Noir Précoce) and Pinot Meunier for rosé. It is inevitable that some Seyval Blanc will remain, due to its relative indestructibility in this country's wet climate, and from recent performances by Avalon, Hendred, and especially Three Choirs, why not? The UK is heading for something like this scenario. There were fewer than 50 hectares (125 acres) of Chardonnay and Pinot Noir in the country in 1990, out of 929 hectares (2,296 acres) planted, whereas today these are the two most widely planted varieties, accounting for 516 hectares (1,275 acres), including Pinot Noir Précoce, or 40% of the 1,324 hectares (3,272 acres) planted. Bacchus and Seyval Blanc are the third and fourth most widely planted varieties. However, there are still a lot of individual vineyards, including many with good potential and high standards of production, that are bursting at the seams with far too many varieties, the majority of which still hark to the 1980s, when no one outside these shores had any respect for English wine. These vineyards should not be lulled into a false sense of security by awards received at local wine competitions, even if they sell out every year, as the demand for 1980s wine styles will dwindle. They need to rationalize their varieties and replant or bud-graft the existing rootstock if they want to be part of the UK's emerging world-class sparkling-wine scene and attract 21st-century custom.

THE WINE REGIONS OF
THE BRITISH ISLES

Regional characteristics have not yet been established in the wine regions of the British Isles, and I am not sure that they ever will be, but it is very difficult to build up a proper spatial awareness of where English vineyards are located without first breaking them down into a small number of workable areas.

The following regions are all officially recognized by the United Kingdom Vineyard Association (UKVA), which took over from the English Vineyard Association in 1996, and it would help if more vineyard owners were to utilize these regions on their labels in addition to a more specific location. Until they do, British consumers will be less informed about their own wines than they are about those of France or Australia.

EAST ANGLIA

Bedfordshire, Cambridgeshire, Essex, Hertfordshire, Norfolk, Suffolk

The flattest and most exposed of all the regions, East Anglia is subject to bitterly cold easterly and northeasterly winds, but has fertile soils, which can encourage significantly higher yields than in some areas of England. Quite often this has the effect of trading off quality for an attempt to preserve consistency.

MERCIA

Cheshire, Derbyshire, Lancashire, Leicestershire, Lincolnshire, Northamptonshire, Nottinghamshire, Rutland, Shropshire, Staffordshire, Warwickshire, West Midlands, West Yorkshire

This is a very large and naturally diverse region, with vineyards planted both on flat ground and slopes, with soils ranging from light sand to heavy clay. About the only common factor is Madeleine Angevine, which seems to be the most reliable variety.

SOUTHEAST

East and West Sussex, Kent, Surrey

This region covers the "Garden of England", which probably says it all. It is not as wet as the West Country, and milder than East Anglia, but not as warm as Thames and Chiltern. Soils range from clay to chalk. The latter forms the same basin that creates the chalk cliffs at Dover and goes under the Channel to rise in Champagne.

SOUTHWEST

Bristol, Cornwall, Devon, Gloucestershire, Herefordshire, Isles of Scilly, Republic of Ireland, Somerset, South Wales, Worcestershire

Geographically the largest region, with vineyards as far apart as Cornwall, where the Gulf Stream has its greatest effect but there is also a tendency to wet weather, and North Wales, which takes the brunt of weather systems from the Atlantic. Although prevailing westerly winds make conditions difficult in the west of Cornwall and Wales, the region is generally milder than the east coast. The topography of the region ranges from mountainous to flat, with some areas below sea level. Soils vary tremendously from limestone through shale, clay, and peat to granite.

THAMES AND CHILTERN

Berkshire, Buckinghamshire, Oxfordshire

This large area is the warmest of all the regions, and most vineyards are located on slopes of moisture-retaining soils. There are also many aquifers in the area, which prevent stress during drought conditions.

WESSEX

Channel Islands, Dorset, Hampshire, Isle of Wight, Wiltshire

The major factor linking these counties together is the interesting pattern of isotherms that form south of the Isle of Wight and provide a more temperate climate than the surrounding regions.

THE WINE PRODUCERS OF
THE BRITISH ISLES

1 A'BECKETT'S VINEYARD

Devizes, Wiltshire (Wessex)

★

A commercial orchard growing just under 4 hectares (10 acres) of wines on chalk soil in the village of Littleton Panell.

✓ *Estate Reserve Red* • *Pinot Noir*

2 ADGESTONE

Adgestone, Isle of Wight (Wessex)

Estate-bottled wines from a south-facing chalk slope that was first planted in 1962.

ARDEONAIG

Ardeonaig, Stirling, Scotland

After a trial of 48 vines planted in 2006 had demonstrated that they could survive the winter at the Ardeonaig Hotel and Restaurant on Loch Tay, a further 800 vines were planted in 2010. The fatalistic ambition was to produce a wine to serve in the restaurant only when a summer is hot enough and to turn it into vinegar to use on dishes if the wine is not good, but the hotel closed due to insolvency in October 2010. What the new owners will do is anybody's guess.

3 ASTLEY

Stourport on Severn, Worcestershire (Southwest)

★ ⓥ

This award-winning vineyard was established in 1979 by Jonty Daniels and Janet Baldwin. Sparkling could be better.

✓ *Classic white blend* (Dry Reserve) • *Late Harvest*

AVALON VINEYARD

East Pennard, Somerset (Southwest)

★ ◉

I tasted the sparkling wine from this vineyard too late to include it on the map, but at the time of tasting, its clean fruit and developing biscuity complexity was "as good as Seyval Blanc fizz gets". Since then, the 2010 release from Three Choirs has blown that judgment out of the water, but it does not diminish the intrinsic quality of Avalon's Pennard Brut, which demands inclusion.

✓ *Sparkling wine* (Pennard Brut)

BALFOUR

See Hush Heath

BART'S BUBBLY

See Bookers

4 BEARSTED

Bearsted, Kent (Southeast)

Small boutique winery with 1.6 hectares (4 acres) planted in the late 1980s by former research chemist John Gibson.

✓ *Sparkling* (Brut Vintage)

5 BEAULIEU

Nr Brockenhurst, Hampshire (Wessex)

This enthusiastic, aristocratic venture has been running since 1958.

6 BEECHES HILL

Upton Bishop, Herefordshire (Southwest)

Established in 1991, Beeches Hill grows Madeleine Angevine and Seyval Blanc grapes, but the wines are made by Three Choirs.

7 BIDDENDEN

Biddenden, Kent (Southeast)

A former orchard on a gentle south-facing slope in a shallow, sheltered valley, Biddenden is principally known for its Ortega. Wines produced in part or whole from grapes grown elsewhere are sold under the Gribble Bridge label.

✓ *Ortega* • *Rosé* (Gribble Bridge)

8 BINFIELD

Wokingham, Berkshire (Thames and Chiltern)

A dry white wine and a light red are produced here, but the emphasis is on a fizz under the Champion label, which is linked to the Bob Champion Cancer Fund, a charity that receives a percentage of the price of every bottle sold.

9 BLUEBELL VINEYARD ESTATES

Furners Green, East Sussex (Southeast)

Planted with Chardonnay, Pinot Meunier, and Pinot Noir in 2005 and 2006 exclusively for sparkling-wine production under the Hindleap label, with the Blanc de Blancs proving to be the most successful *cuvée* so far.

BOLNEY WINE ESTATE

See Bookers

10 BOOKERS

Bolney, Sussex (Southeast)

★ ⓥ

The first vines were planted in 1973, but initially the Pratt family sold their grapes, and only started making their own wine in 1983. The wines are sold under the Bolney Wine Estate label. Although Bookers currently produces four different sparkling wines and most of my experience of this range has been confined to Bart's Bubbly and the Blanc de Blancs, I have been able to recommend only one of these wines in the past 12 years and that was 12 years ago! This very professional operation should seek advice from a sparkling-wine consultant of the calibre of Michel Salgues or Tony Jordan.

✓ *Classic red blend* (Dark Harvest)

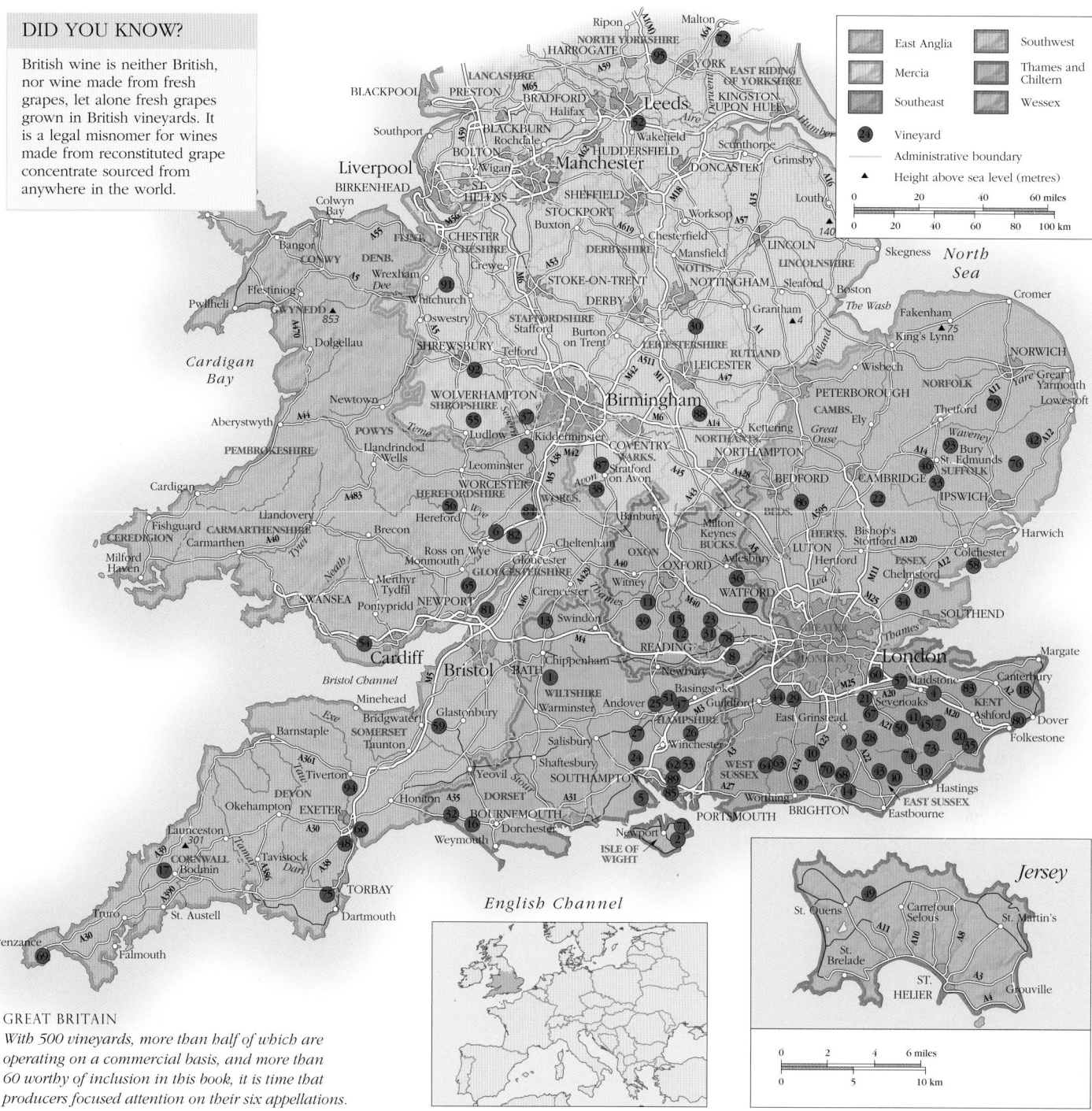

GREAT BRITAIN
With 500 vineyards, more than half of which are operating on a commercial basis, and more than 60 worthy of inclusion in this book, it is time that producers focused attention on their six appellations.

11 BOTHY
Frilford Heath, Oxfordshire (Thames and Chiltern)

★☉

The most successful wine produced by new owners Sian and Richard Liwicki is their Oxford Dry. Although from a typically English hotchpotch of grape varieties, it is a refreshing dry white that anyone partial to Sauvignon Blanc would enjoy. The sparkling wine cannot be recommended, and I'm surprised that it was even contemplated, with this combination of grapes (Ortega, Findling, Huxelrebe, Albalonga, and Bacchus).

✎ *Oxford Dry*

12 BOZE DOWN
Whitchurch-on-Thames, Oxfordshire (Thames and Chiltern)

Established in 1985 by Dick and Sandra Conn, Boze Down Vineyard lies on the sheltered southern slopes of the Chiltern Hills overlooking the River Thames between Reading and Oxford.

✎ *Classic white blend* (Skippetts)

13 BOW-IN-THE-CLOUD
Malmesbury, Wiltshire (Wessex)

Bow-in-the-Cloud vineyard was planted in 1992 and has been producing wine since 1995. Pure varietal wines are sold under the

Arkadian label, while blends are sold under the Cloud Nine label.

14 BREAKY BOTTOM
Northease, Sussex (Southeast)

★☉

Peter Hall used to release his Seyval-based fizz far too young, but now he is running the risk of holding on to them for too long. The two *cuvées* below are best to buy and drink when Hall offers them at 5–6 years of age.

✎ *Müller-Thurgau • Seyval Blanc • Sparkling* (Cuvée Maman Mercier, Cuvée Remy Alexandre)

15 BRIGHTWELL VINEYARD
Wallingford, Oxfordshire (Thames & Chiltern)

Steadily improving sparkling Chardonnay from the driest area in Oxfordshire.

16 BRIDE VALLEY
Litton Cheyney, Dorset (Wessex)

Owned by Steven and Bella Spurrier, who planted 3.2 hectares (8 acres) for this exclusively sparkling-wine venture in 2009, these vineyards will reach 10 hectares (25 acres) by 2012. Steven Spurrier is, among many things, consultant editor for *Decanter* magazine, chair of chairs at *Decanter*'s World Wine Awards, and the architect of The Judgment of Paris, the events of which were immortalized and, Spurrier claims, fictionalized in the film *Bottle Shock*, starring Alan Rickman as Spurrier himself. With such a profile, the wines are bound to come under severe scrutiny when released, but knowing Spurrier, they should be worth the wait. The initial 3.2-hectare block should provide a small first crop in 2012, when the vines will be on their "third leaf", and whatever the weather or condition of the grapes, Spurrier will harvest grapes on 5 October 2011, his 70th birthday! The wine will be made by Ian Edwards at Furleigh. The plan is to have a non-vintage blend, using Pol Roger White Foil, one of Spurrier's favourite Champagnes, as a sort of stylistic blueprint. There will also be a vintage *blanc de blancs*.

17 CAMEL VALLEY
Nanstallon, Cornwall (Southwest)
★★Ⓥ

Bob and Sam Lindo's Pinot Noir sparkling wines (the *blanc de noirs* and, particularly, the rosé) are right up there with the very best that Nyetimber and Ridgeview have produced. The only reason Camel Valley is half a star shy of its rivals' rating is because there are no other sparkling wines of this ilk. No one is suggesting that the Lindos should stop making their Seyval Blanc-and-Reichensteiner-based Cornwall Brut. It's a cash cow and an eminently drinkable one. But Camel Valley fans deserve to see what the Lindos can do with Chardonnay and a classic Chardonnay-Pinot blend. The recent

introduction of a 100% Rondo sparkling red was just a hair's breadth away from being a real success and only needs to pick up a trick or two from the Aussies to come right.

✓ *Bacchus • Seyval Blanc • Sparkling* (Cornwall Brut, Pinot Noir Blanc de Noirs, Pinot Noir Rosé)

18 CANTERBURY CHOICE
Ash, Kent (Southeast)
★Ⓥ

The label under which the wines from Barnsole Vineyard are sold.

✓ *Dry Reserve • Pilgrim's Harvest*

19 CARR TAYLOR
Westfield, Sussex (Southeast)

The Carr Taylor family has been making bottle-fermented sparkling wine for nearly 30 years, and the varietal mix used (Reichensteiner and Schönburger) remains firmly fixed in that past. The Medium Dry has always been the best fizz from Carr Taylor, due no doubt to the grapes used, and the vintage on sale (2006) at the time of writing is as fresh, clean, and delicious as ever and not at all cloying. The sparkling rosé is the only concession to demands of the modern-day market, being a blend of 75% Pinot Noir and 25% Pinot Meunier, but the 2006 was spoiled by dominant malolactic aromas. If they have used the proper low-diacetyl-producing malolactic bacteria, then they really do have problems that need sorting before moving over to classic Champagne varieties (for all but the Medium Dry).

✓ *Reichensteiner* (Alexis) • *Sparkling* (Medium Dry)

CASTERBRIDGE
See Furleigh

20 CHAPEL DOWN
Tenterden, Kent (Southeast)
★Ⓥ

One of the country's largest wine producers, this company was formed in early 2001, when Chapel Down Wines at Tenterden Vineyard merged with Lamberhurst Vineyard. Also referred to as English Wines Plc, the multi-award-winning Chapel Down still has the feel of a large and expanding winery that is finding its way, which indeed it is, but the quality and consistency has greatly improved since the merger. The rosé is perhaps Chapel Down's most celebrated sparkling wine, and although it can be good, fresh, and easy to slurp when initially released, sometimes it is kept on its lees too long (even if that is not necessarily very long in chronological terms) and matures rather too rapidly. On the other hand, the 2004 Pinot Reserve was as fresh as a daisy in 2010, with excellent high English acids focusing the fruit on the palate and a lovely Pinot Noir perfume on the finish. The non-vintage Chapel Down Brut is the market leader in the UK but does nothing for me.

✓ *Sparkling* (Pinot Reserve), *Bacchus*

21 CHIDDINGSTONE
Chiddingstone, Kent (Southeast)

This vineyard was established by the late Dudley Quirk, whose two sons run Chiddingstone today.

22 CHILFORD HUNDRED
Linton, Cambridgeshire (East Anglia)
★Ⓥ

This large vineyard was established in 1972, but it did not produce its first sparkling wine until 1994.

✓ *Sparkling* (Aluric de Norsehide)

23 CHILTERN VALLEY
Hambledon, Oxfordshire (Thames and Chiltern)

Also known as Luxters, because owner David Ealand established his winery on the site of Old Luxters pig farm. Has produced some interesting wines in the past, although they have a lower profile these days.

24 COACH HOUSE
Romsey, Hampshire (Wessex)

This vineyard is owned by Roger Marchbank, who is better known as the chairman of UKVA, and cannot be accused of using his position to promote his wine, as I have never tasted Coach House wine, and seldom heard mention of it!

25 COATES & SEELY
Whitchurch, Hampshire (Wessex)

A new joint venture between financial wizard Nicholas Coates and Christian Seely, who runs Château Pichon-Longueville-Baron and Quinta do Noval, among others, for AXA. Coates and Seely have taken over Wooldings Vineyard near Whitchurch, which they have converted exclusively to Chardonnay, Pinot Noir, and a little Pinot Meunier. They have a state-of-the-art winery that includes a Bucher Vaslin Inertys, which presses in a controlled inert-gas atmosphere. The first wines are due to be released in 2011.

26 COURT LANE
Alresford, Hampshire (Wessex)

Stephen Flook must have broken a record when he took 12 years to plant just over one acre of vines.

27 DANEBURY
Stockbridge, Hampshire (Wessex)

Anne Bishop named her fizz Cossack after the controversial winner of the 1847 Derby.

28 DAVENPORT
Rotherfield, East Sussex & Horsmonden, Kent (Southeast)
❂★Ⓥ

Will Davenport is a graduate of Roseworthy College in Australia, and has worked for wineries in Alsace, California and South Australia before setting up in England in 1990. He has a still wine vineyard at Horsmonden in Kent, but his Rotherfield vineyard is primarily for sparkling wine. The exciting potential expressed by the 1999 and 2000 vintages of Limney Brut has not been repeated, but the Blanc de Blancs can still be fresh and crisp.

✓ *Sparkling* (Blanc de Blancs)

29 DENBIES WINE ESTATE
Dorking, Surrey (Southeast)
★Ⓥ

With 107 hectares (265 acres) of vines, Denbies Wine Estate is the largest English vineyard. Its winery

ANNIE'S SEYVAL, CAMEL VALLEY
This block of Seyval Blanc was the first Camel Valley vineyard planted. It has always been pruned by Annie Lindo, hence Annie's Seyval. In 2009, Annie made her millionth pruning cut; to celebrate, a 20th-anniversary sparkling wine was made.

looks like a generic commercial building and is designed and equipped to receive tourists by the bus-load; consequently Denbies is also the most visited of English vineyards. Capable of producing award-winning wines, but has not been consistent throughout the range. With the recent appointment of John Worontschak of Litmus Wines to make operational improvements, hopefully the consistency will improve. There are two particularly big problems: some of the sites on this massive estate should not have been planted in the first place (because of "wet feet" and other site problems); and there are so many varieties that are either unsuitable or not in tune with modern trends growing over such a vast expanse that even bud-grafting these vines would be a long-term, multiphase project. On a more positive note, Denbies has planted 3 hectares (7.4 acres) of Sauvignon Blanc, which is a risk but potentially a very interesting one. Denbies Greenfield is a sparkling wine of great intensity and acidity that is made in a deliberate oxidative style, with sufficient class to attract Bollinger drinkers looking for a sparkling wine closer to home. The Cubitt is a crisper wine with no oxidative tendencies and will repay ageing in a cool cellar for a few years. Denbies sparkling rosé is spoiled by malolactic, which is also present on the Whitelands but is held back by the cigarette ash on the main palate!

✓ *Rosé* (Rose Hill) • *Sparkling* (Cubitt Reserve Blanc de Noirs, Greenfields)

30 EGLANTINE

Costock, Nottinghamshire (Mercia)

Readers might think that Tony Skuriat's vineyard is northerly enough, without deliberately freezing his grapes, but this is how he produces his award-winning wine North Star.

✓ *Dessert wine* (North Star)

31 FAWLEY

Henley-on-Thames, Oxfordshire (Thames and Chiltern)

Nick and Wendy Sargent are just beginning to establish a reputation for Bacchus.

✓ *Bacchus*

32 FURLEIGH

Bridport, Dorset (Wessex)

These sparkling wines, sold under the Casterbridge label, are made by Ian Edwards, who will be producing Steven amd Bella Spurrier's Bride Valley sparkling wine.

33 GIFFORD'S HALL

Hartest, Suffolk (East Anglia)

John and Jeanie Kemp claim to tread their grapes, and they also produce a variety of homemade liqueurs, but Gifford's Hall was up for sale in 2004.

34 GREAT STOCKS

Stock, Essex (East Anglia)

This vineyard was established between 1993 and 1999 by Brian and Gillian Barnard, who are hoping that Rondo will provide good red wine.

GRIBBLE BRIDGE

See Biddenden

35 GUSBOURNE ESTATE

Appledore, Ashford, Kent (Southeast)

This vineyard has been described by English wine guru Stephen Skelton MW as "one of the most impressive and exciting new vineyards I have seen". Skelton also describes owner Andrew Weeber as "a man who leaves no stone unturned in his quest for the answer – whatever the question. The first vintage won medals at the UKVA Competition: a gold for the Classic Blend and silver for the Blanc de Blancs.

36 HALE VALLEY

Boddington, Buckinghamshire (Thames and Chiltern)

Sparkling wine has been Antony and Carol Chapman's most successful wine so far.

✓ *Sparkling* (Brut Vintage)

37 HALFPENNY GREEN

Halfpenny Green, Staffordshire (Mercia)

★ⓥ

Just over 9 hectares (22 acres) were planted between 1983 and 1991, then a winery was built in 1994. As with most northerly English vineyards, Madeleine Angevine has proved the most reliable variety.

✓ *Classic white blend* (Penny Black) • *Huxelrebe* • *Madeleine Angevine*

38 HEART OF ENGLAND

Welford-on-Avon, Warwickshire (Mercia)

This 6-hectare (15-acre) vineyard on southwest-facing slopes overlooking the Vale of Evesham in Shakespeare Country was planted by David Stanley in 1995 but did not achieve its first commercial harvest until 2000.

✓ *Classic red blend* (Oberon)

39 HENDRED VINEYARD

East Hendred, Wantage, Oxfordshire (Thames & Chiltern)

★ⓥ

Planted back in 1971 by the late Mac Mackinnon, whose first wines were vinified by the legendary Jack Ward, this is today under the ownership of Steve and Viviane Callaghan. The wine to buy here is definitely the Hendred Brut, one of the best sparkling renditions of the Seyval Blanc, with ripe acidity and a hint of pineapple on the finish.

✓ *Sparkling wine* (Hendred Brut)

40 HENNERS

Herstmonceux, East Sussex (Southeast)

★★⯪

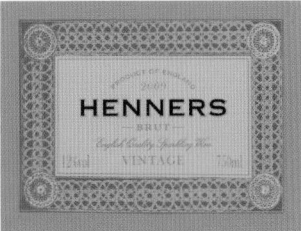

These south-facing chalk slopes are in just the right place for top-quality sparkling wine. Planted with an ideal match of Chardonnay, Pinot Noir, and Pinot Meunier clones, and with a sensibly equipped winery in place to process the very first crop, Henners has the making of one of England's best sparkling wines. With the first wines from that crop not due to be released until 2012, I have tasted only trial disgorgements, but the potential quality of the 2009 Brut Reserve is easy to see, with its lovely true English acidity and great elegance and finesse. Such a high rating at this stage of the game is unusual, but when Lawrence Henners's wines are ready for sale, I expect to raise the rating to two full stars.

41 HERBERT HALL

Marden, Tonbridge, Kent (Southeast)

◉★

Another exciting venture, the first wines from which are not due to be released until 2012 – hence I have tasted only trial disgorgements of the 2009 and this, too, is going to be an excellent sparkling wine. I love the fruit and the structure. And the *mousse* – which must never be forgotten – is exceptional. There is a big chunk of Meunier (30%), which is interesting for an English sparkling wine, and a hint of oxidative character. Absolutely no oak aroma, just the oxidative effect of fermentation in a wooden vessel. Truly masterful. With further development and the right *dosage*, this should not be noticeable as anything other than a certain *je ne sais quoi* of complexity. The difficulty will be in getting the *dosage* right, because it is one of the few sparkling wines I feel does not need more than 6 grams, and definitely should not have less! Serious trial will be required to work on the perfect-*dosage* base wine to carry those 6 grams.

42 HEVENINGHAM HALL

Near Halesworth, Suffolk (East Anglia)

Pronounced "Henningum" Hall, this massive Palladian pile is owned by Jon Hunt, who founded Foxtons estate agency and sold it at just the right time to rake in £390 million ($574 million). There is a 1-hectare (2.47-acre) vineyard planted with 14 trial varieties and an ambition for sufficient expansion and a state-of-

the-art winery to produce an iconic English sparkling wine that has seen at least one of the world's top sparkling-wine consultants tread this earth. However, there could be an immovable obstacle in the form of Capability Brown, because to fit in with the landscape he designed, the vineyards would not just be in the wrong place but would have "wet feet". There are good vineyard sites here, but so far it appears that the property tycoon prefers the advice of the 18th century's greatest gardener to any viticultural experts. And why not? Heveningham Hall does not need a vineyard, and if Jon Hunt has a real passion for English sparkling wine, he has the money to buy a much better site somewhere else.

43 HIDDEN SPRINGS

Horsham, Sussex (Southeast)

★ⓥ

Although Martyn Doubleday and Chris Cammel make some trophy-winning wines, devotees would kill for Hidden Springs Art Deco labels, even if they put nothing inside the bottles!

✓ *Classic red blend* (Dark Fields) • *Classic white blend* (Decadence) • *Rosé* (Sussex Sunset) • *Sparkling wine* (Vintage Brut)

44 HIGH CLANDON VINEYARD

High Clandon, Surrey (Southeast)

This tiny half-hectare (1.2-acre) vineyard is owned by Sibylla and Bruce Tindale, whose first wine, a sparkler bearing the 2008 vintage called Grand Anniversary, was vinified by Bookers. It has great acids and very good extract, and although it is a bit early to predict anything from a solitary wine, this is certainly worth keeping an eye on.

45 HUSH HEATH VINEYARD

Cranbrook, Kent (Southeast)

★

A beautiful Tudor timber-framed manor set in impeccably maintained Italianate gardens, Hush Heath is owned by Richard Balfour-Lynn, hence the name of its sparkling wine. Since the first release of Balfour Rosé, the 2004, 2005, and 2006 have all been persistent award winners, and although I thoroughly endorse those plaudits, I think they could be even better. With a brand-new winery built on-site for the 2010 vintage, perhaps we will see an improvement. Until 2010, Balfour Rosé has been produced by Chapel Down, and with all those awards that winery obviously cannot be faulted. But whenever a winery is built in situ, there is always an opportunity to tighten up the process. With English wines' hopes firmly pinned on sparkling wine, an all-rosé sparkling-wine specialist is a smart move.

✓ *Sparkling* (Rosé)

46 ICKWORTH

Horringer, Suffolk (East Anglia)

This National Trust property is well worth a visit, even if only to learn about the aristocratic Hervey family that built Ickworth and ranged from a licentious bishop of Derry to a jewel thief. The vineyard is planted in a beautiful Victorian walled garden, and the Walled Garden White is usually the best bet here. But with better vine varieties and an on-site winery, this *clos* could do so much better.

47 JENKYN PLACE

Bentley, Hampshire (Wessex)

I have only tasted the first vintage (2006), and although its peppery fruit with ripe overtones is fresh and crisp, there is obviously a lot to be done to increase the finesse. However, it's no worse than the first vintage of Roederer Estate, and the second vintage turned out to be the first sparkling wine produced outside of Champagne itself that could be compared to a good-quality Champagne, so maybe the finessing has already been accomplished in the vintages already in the pipeline of this exclusively sparkling-wine venture.

48 KENTON VINEYARD

Exeter, Devon (Southwest)

Established by Matthew Bernstein in 2003, this vineyard is currently planted with Auxerrois, Bacchus, Dornfelder, Pinot Noir Précoce, Ortega, Rondo, Seyval Blanc, and Solaris, with a dedicated winery built on-site for the 2006 vintage. The first vintage was well received, and in the 2010 UKVA competition, Bernstein scooped up two golds, one silver, and two bronzes. With some rationalizing in the vineyard and more focus on few wines (not necessarily those that are currently the most successful), Kenton Vineyards could do even better.

√ Estate Red, Estate Rose

49 LA MARE

Jersey, Channel Islands (Wessex)

The Channel Islands' first and now only vineyard also produces a Norman-style cider and has installed a small Calvados pot still for apple brandy. It is clear to see that there is a passion here for the *barrique*-aged apple brandy, but I'm not even sure there is any understanding of wine, let alone a comparable passion. The vineyards are being extended, but they are on the wrong (unprotected) side of the island. I will reserve final judgment until I have tasted the wines from the newly equipped winery, but the chocolate and "black butter" are highly recommended!

50 LAMBERHURST

Lamberhurst, Kent (Southeast)

★ⓥ

Merged with Chapel Down in 2001 to form English Wines Plc.

√ Classic white blend (Fumé)

51 LAVERSTOKE PARK

Laverstoke, Hampshire (Wessex)

ⓑ

Great things are expected from owner Jody Scheckter, the former Formula 1 world-champion racing driver, if the rest of Laverstoke Park is anything to go by. This 1,000-hectare (2,470-acre) polycultural enterprise has sometimes been referred to as "the world's largest smallholding" and "the University of Organics", because of the diversity of its breeds and crops and the fact that Laverstoke Park has taken organic and biodynamic farming to new levels. Laverstoke Park does not need to seek advice from the Soil Association; the Soil Association consults Laverstoke Park, which must have more doctorates per hectare than any other comparable enterprise. Laverstoke Park boasts all the oldest, pure native breeds of almost every sort of farm animal imaginable, including one-third of all the pure native Aberdeen Angus in the UK and a herd of 800 water buffalo. If Jody cannot find a pure native breed, he reverse-breeds the best available breed back to its authentic format. Everything is sustainable to the ultimate degree, and if Jody can make sparkling wine half as good as his mozzarella cheese or coffee-flavoured buffalo-milk ice cream, it will be special indeed. In 2010, Laverstoke Park enjoyed its first tiny harvest.

52 LEVENTHORPE VINEYARD

Woodlesford, West Yorkshire (Mercia)

Established by chemist-turned-winemaker George Bowden in 1986, Leventhorpe vineyard is just a stone's throw away from the historic stately home of Temple Newsome. This is one of the country's most northerly vineyards, and it crops ripe grapes every year and has its own winery.

53 LITTLE WEST END FARM

Chidden, Hampshire (Wessex)

This 4-hectare (10-acre) vineyard on a chalk hilltop is owned and run by Didier Pierson and his British-born wife Imogen Whitaker. The couple also run Le Vieux Cèdre, a small B&B mansion in Avize. Didier Pierson is a winemaker for a cooperative on the Côte des Blancs and has his own brand, Champagne Pierson Whitaker.

54 LLANERCH VINEYARD

Hensol, Vale of Glamorgan, Wales (Southwest)

★ⓥ

Wines are sold under the Cariad label. The fizz is improving.

√ Classic white blend (Cariad Celtic Dry) • Sparkling (Cariad Blush)

55 LUDLOW VINEYARD

Clee St Margaret, Shropshire (Mercia)

★ⓥ

An up-and-coming new vineyard, Ludlow might have struck it lucky with 2003 as its inaugural vintage, but it was an impressive start nonetheless. Clee Moonlight is a blend of Madeleine Angevine, Seyval, and Phoenix with a slight hint of oak. Only 200 bottles were made.

√ Clee Moonlight

56 LULHAM COURT VINEYARD

Hereford, Herefordshire (Southwest)

This vineyard in the Wye Valley, close to the village of Madley, was planted back in 1984, and the Müller-Thurgau, Reichensteiner, and Seyval Blanc grown here today are definitely stuck in that era.

57 MEOPHAM

Wrotham, Kent (Southeast)

Part organic production, including an organic medium-sweet Pinot Noir.

58 MERSEA

Mersea Island, Essex (East Anglia)

On an island 15 kilometres (9 miles) south of Colchester, halfway between West Mersea and East Mersea, this vineyard and winery also boasts a micro-brewery.

59 MOORLYNCH

Bridgwater, Somerset (Southwest)

This vineyard is situated on a sunny south-facing hillside that has, surprisingly for England, a somewhat dry microclimate. Owner-winemaker Peter Farmer's most successful wine so far has been his 1996 Vintage Reserve Brut sparkling wine.

60 MOUNT VINEYARD

Shoreham, Kent (Southeast)

Former financial commentator Jim Moulton planted this vineyard in 2004 and 2006 with a typically 1980s selection of grapes (Müller-Thurgau, Reichensteiner, and Seyval Blanc). There is also Pinot Noir, but it is not a sparkling-wine clone, although there is a sparkling wine in the pipeline.

61 NEW HALL

Purleigh, Essex (East Anglia)

Established by the Greenwood family in 1969, this 37-hectare (91-acre) vineyard is one of the oldest and largest English wine producers, and the first to be planted in Essex.

62 NORTHBROOK SPRINGS

Bishop Waltham, Hampshire (Wessex)

Owner-winemaker Brian Cable Young has made some good-value fizz and noble rot dessert wines in the past.

63 NUTBOURNE VINEYARD

Pulborough, West Sussex (Southeast)

This vineyard of just over 7 hectares

(17 acres) of gentle slopes was planted in 1980 and today consists of Bacchus, Chardonnay, Huxelrebe, Müller-Thurgau, Pinot Noir, Reichensteiner, and Schönburger. Until recently, the wine was made at Chapel Down. Of the wines produced, it has normally been the Nutty Brut sparkling that has stood out, and the last time I tasted this wine (2010), it was clean and fruity with a red fruit-gum finish but not as special as I suspect it could be. After all, Nutbourne Vineyard is virtually opposite Nyetimber, so it should only be a matter of the right grape varieties and a little application. Dropping Reichensteiner from the Nutty's blend is the obvious first move, but that would involve planting more Chardonnay and Pinot Noir or grafting the Reichensteiner over. The owners have recently made a serious investment in a new winery as a joint venture with Redfold Farm Vineyard, a facility that will be operated by former Chapel Down winemaker Owen Elias, who must know the potential of Nutbourne Vineyard. However, that potential is affected by the vineyard, and to maximize the return on the winery investment, a hard-headed rationalization of the vineyard is required.

64 NYETIMBER

Pulborough, Sussex (Southeast)

★★

I have never been more confident about the future of Nyetimber since the heydays of Stuart and Sandy Moss, who established this ground-breaking vineyard – and that comes after expressing concerns in the 2007 edition about how the quality and style of Nyetimber might be affected when it is no longer made from its original 14 acres (35 acres) but from half a dozen or more sites spread over two counties and totalling 105 hectares (260 acres), under the expansion plans of Dutchman Eric Heerema, the owner since 2006. But 105 hectares was an under-estimate, as Heerema has ended up with 143 hectares (353 acres) over eight locations. I have tasted not only forward through all vintages and *cuvées* that will not be released for quite a while, but also current and previous vintages and *cuvées*. Even though it was difficult to match the last pure Nyetimber (2007) with the first two broader-spectrum Nyetimber vintages (2008 and 2009) because of the exceptionally high acidity of the first and the very early phase of the second (barely six months on yeast), I cannot help but be hugely impressed by the quality and direction of these sparkling wines. In fact, I have never been more impressed by any of Nyetimber's winemakers than by Canadian-born Cherie Spriggs. Her 2007 rosé was the first wine she made and released, and it is pure magic – so good that I ordered a case. The services of French consultant Jacquinot were terminated in 2009, and it was a good thing, too. His usefulness began and ended with the planting of the vineyard. I always thought the previous owners had all made world-class sparkling wines despite Jacquinot's involvement, not because of it. Certainly, I cannot remember a single outstanding Champagne Jacquinot of the past 30 years or more.

✓ *Entire range*

65 PARVA FARM
Tintern, Monmouthshire, Wales (Southwest)
★✓

Emerging Pinot Noir potential from steep vineyards set within a working farm environment.

✓ *Pinot Noir*

66 PEBBLEBED
Topsham, Devon (Southwest)

Established in 2000, Pebblebed has won a number of medals for its wines, including the sparkling rosé, which is a blend of Seyval Blanc and Rondo. These crazy guys even have Cabernet Sauvignon and Merlot! Pebblebed underwent a six-month biodynamic trial with Edward Templeman, a mature student at Plumpton Viticulture College.

PENNARD BRUT
See Avalon Vineyard

67 PENSHURST
Penshurst, Kent (Southeast)

First planted in 1972 on a south-facing slope, the first crop was promising, and some excellent wines have been produced here. The picturesque label is charming

and very English, except for the hidden kangaroo!

68 PLUMPTON COLLEGE
Plumpton, East Sussex (Southeast)

The only educational facility in the UK to provide courses in all aspects of wine, Plumpton College also possesses a well-equipped, commercial winery.

✓ *Sparkling* (The Dean Brut)

69 POLGOON VINEYARD
Penzance, Cornwall (Southwest)
★✓

John and Kim Coulson had no intention of becoming winemakers; they were just looking for a larger property, but it came with 10 hectares (25 acres), and they have gone from fish merchants to award-winning cider and wine producers within just six years!

✓ *Rosé*

70 RIDGEVIEW ESTATE
Ditchling, Sussex (Southeast)
★★✓

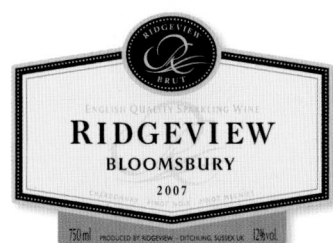

Mike Roberts's Ridgeview Estate did not come into full production until 1997, five years after Nyetimber, yet its wines were immediately snapping at the latter's heels. In those early days, the difference between the two brands was more distinct than today, with Nyetimber going the aged, yeast-complexed route, and Ridgeview the younger, fresher, more fruit-driven style. Since then, however, Nyetimber has sold some younger *cuvées* and Ridgeview

has gradually increased its time on lees and released the occasional older vintage. Although there remains a clear difference between the two today, it is more stylistic than chronological. Ridgeview wines are marketed as Cuvée Merret, a registered name that honours the first person to describe the second-fermentation process (*see* p222). Each wine in the Cuvée Merret range is named after an area of London, the most important being **Bloomsbury** (Chardonnay-dominated blend of all three varieties in which Pinot Meunier plays a minor role), **Cavendish** (most recent vintages have been Pinot Meunier-dominated blends of all three varieties), **Fitzrovia** (Chardonnay-dominated rosé blend of all three varieties), **Grosvenor** (100% Chardonnay), and **Knightsbridge** (only two vintages of this *blanc de noirs* of Pinot Noir and Pinot Meunier have been produced: 1999 and 2006).

✓ *Entire range*

71 ROSEMARY VINEYARD
Ryde, Isle of Wight (Wessex)

This sheltered spot was planted back in 1986, and today Rosemary Vineyard grows Bacchus, Madeleine Angevine, Orion, Pinot Gris, Reichensteiner, Rondo, Schönburger, and Triomphe d'Alsace. Most of these varieties should be pulled up or grafted over, and the range of wines needs to be simplified, with styles brought into line with 21st-century expectations.

72 RYEDALE VINEYARDS
Westow, North Yorkshire (Mercia)

This is the country's most northerly vineyard. Wolds View – a blend of Solaris, Phoenix, and Seyval Blanc – is a refreshing light, crisp, and citrussy dry white that beats 70 per cent of Loire whites, and it comes from grapes grown north of York!

73 SANDHURST VINEYARDS
Sandhurst, Kent (Southeast)

A 10-hectare (25-acre) vineyard established in 1988 by the Nicholas family on Hoads Farm.

74 SEDLESCOMBE
Robertsbridge, Sussex (Southeast)
ⓑ

In 1994 Sedlescombe became Britain's first organic vineyard, and in this rain-swept country, there have not been many brave enough to follow. In 2010 Sedlescombe produced the first biodynamic English wines.

✓ *Classic white blend* (Dry White)

75 SHARPHAM
Asprington, Devon (Southwest)
★✓

Sharpham makes and markets wine from Beenleigh Manor Vineyard in Harbertonford, which was Britain's first "real" red wine in the 1980s. The sparkling wine here has become really impressive of late.

✓ *Classic red blend* (Beenleigh) • *Classic white blend* (Dart Valley Reserve) • *Madeleine Angevine* (Barrel Fermented Dry) • *Pinot Noir* • *Sparkling* • *Dornfelder* (Rosé)

76 SHAWSGATE
Framlingham, Suffolk (East Anglia)
★✓

Established in 1973, this vineyard offers the chance to rent a row of vines, from which wine will be made for you – because they are "your" vines, the wine will be tax-free!

✓ *Rosé*

77 SHARDELOES FARM
Amersham, Buckinghamshire (Thames and Chiltern)

Tony and Cindy Williams have planted 4 hectares (10 acres) of their equestrian farm with Dornfelder, Dunkelfelder, Léon Millot, Reichensteiner, and Triomphe d'Alsace. I'm not sure why they would go for these varieties in the 21st century, but the Shardeloes Brut isn't bad considering it is a Reichensteiner and Triomphe d'Alsace blend. The *mousse* could be softer, but I doubt that has anything to do with the grapes.

78 STANLAKE PARK
Stanlake Park, Berkshire (Thames and Chiltern)
★✓

This vineyard was established by Jon Leighton in 1979. Originally called Thames Valley Vineyards, then simply Valley Vineyards, the name changed again when Leighton sold up and returned to the warmer climes of Australia. The sparkling wines can no longer be recommended.

✓ *Classic white blend* (Fumé) • *Rosé* (Pinot Blush) • *Schönburger* (Hinton Grove)

RIDGEVIEW ESTATE FROST PREVENTION
These frost-prevention candles are burning in the Chardonnay vineyard adjacent to the Ridgeview Estate winery. The grapes from this vineyard are mostly used for the Grosvenor Blanc de Blanc and Chardonnay-dominated Bloomsbury blend.

79 TAS VALLEY

Foncett St Peter, Norfolk (East Anglia)

If malolactic Reichensteiner is your idea of bliss, then Tas Valley offers you heaven. It's not mine.

80 TERLINGHAM VINEYARD

Hawkinge, Kent (Southeast)

Steve and Penny Riley planted this vineyard in 2006 and built an on-site winery. Their 100% Seyval Blanc Terlingham Brut is nice, clean, and dry in a typically tangy English style, with very good acids.

THEALE VINEYARD

Theale, Berkshire (Thames and Chiltern)

Oxidative-style, multi-award-winning sparkling wines from a tiny artificial south-facing slope created by Laithwaite's wine merchant when building their new offices.

81 THORNBURY CASTLE

Thornbury, Gloucestershire (Southwest)

A former Michelin-starred restaurant, Thornbury Castle is now part of the von Essen private collection of hotels. Having moved to nearby Berkeley, this is now my local English vineyard, so I wish I could be more generous in my praise, but these wines do no good to the reputation of the hotel and restaurant, where, of course, they are served. If anyone with any knowledge of wine in the von Hessen group has actually tasted these wines, they will agree that there are only two options: grub up the vineyard, or do the job properly. Since the vineyard is reputed to be on the site of a vineyard that was planted within the castle walls 500 years ago, grubbing it up would be sacrilege. However, to do the job properly would require not only bud-grafting the current vineyard over to sparkling-wine clones of Chardonnay, Pinot Noir, and Pinot Meunier, but also expanding it with the same varieties, as it currently covers just one-fifth of a hectare (half an acre). If indeed there was a walled vineyard here 500 years ago, then it is most likely that it would have covered the entire *clos*, which at a glance I would estimate to be about 1 hectare (2.47 acres). This would make it smaller than Krug's Clos du Mesnil but larger than Krug's Clos d'Ambonnay, thus an ideal size for a truly iconic, barrel-fermented English sparkling wine, sold no doubt at an equally iconic price!

82 THREE CHOIRS

Newent, Gloucestershire (Southwest)

★❤

One of the country's four largest wine producers, Three Choirs has always had the potential, but had been disappointing until the 2002/2003 vintages. Three Choirs has upped its game in recent years, particularly with its sparkling wines, which now have true finesse. The fresh, sleek, classy non-vintage Classic Cuvée on sale in 2010 was the greatest Seyval Blanc sparkling wine I had tasted up to that point.

✓ *Bacchus* (Estate Reserve) • *Dessert* (Estate Reserve Noble Rot) • *Siegerrebe* (Estate Reserve) • *Sparkling* (Classic Cuvée, Pinot Blanc de Noir)

83 THROWLEY

Throwley, Kent (Southeast)

★❤

A southwest-facing slope of the North Downs that is developing a reputation for Ortega, but the sparkling wine cannot be recommended.

✓ *Ortega* (Reserve)

84 TILTRIDGE

Upton-on-Severn, Worcestershire (Southwest)

★❤

Peter and Sandy Barker have not been very successful with their Elgar sparkling wine, the grapes for which obviously have more potential for still wines.

✓ *Schönburger* (Cello) • *Seyval* (Oaked)

85 TITCHFIELD VINEYARD

Titchfield, Hampshire (Wessex)

The microclimate of this sheltered vineyard is mediated by the warm waters of the Solent. The first vines went in the ground in 1991, and the first crop was 1996. Currently the vines include Auxerrois, Bacchus, Dunkelfelder, Faber, Faberebe, Regent, Reichensteiner, Madeleine Angevine, and Pinot Noir. This is too many. When most of the varieties cultivated are not suitable for the 21st century, the existing customer base will eventually dwindle; better to rationalize the vineyard and wines produced sooner rather than later.

THE URBAN WINE COMPANY

Tooting, London

Established by Richard Sharp in 2007, when he invited people locally to bring grapes from the odd few vines grown in back gardens, from which he made just 20 bottles of so-called Chateau Tooting Furzedown Blush, which hit the headlines in all the UK's national newspapers. Within just two years, he was receiving in excess of 1.5 tonnes of grapes from around the country. Members of this collective contribute 3–100 kilograms (6.6–220 pounds), and receive a bottle for every 2 kilos (4.4 pounds).

86 WARDEN ABBEY

Biggleswade, Bedfordshire (East Anglia)

Established in 1986 by Jane Whitbread at the Abbey of Warden, founded by Cistercian monks in 1135 as the "daughter abbey" to Rievaulx Abbey in Yorkshire.

✓ *Bacchus*

87 WELCOMBE HILLS

Snitterfield, Warwickshire (Mercia)

A tiny vineyard less than three-quarters of a hectare (1.8 acres), Welcombe Hills is more than three times the size it was when originally planted in 2001. Although owners Chris and Jane Gallimore have won a number of awards for their wines, they could do even better if they rationalized their vineyard and range of (currently) nine wines, which is far too many for less than 1 hectare. A sparkling Bacchus and a Blanc de Noirs (Pinot Noir) have just been released.

88 WELLAND VALLEY

Market Harborough, Leicestershire (Mercia)

With up to seven different wines produced each year from less than 1 hectare (2.47 acres), this vineyard would benefit from a rationalization of varieties to focus on fewer wines. Welland Valley won a couple of bronze medals with its 2002 and 2003 sparkling wines, but although the Steeplechase Brut (60% Reichensteiner, 40% Seyval Blanc) was acceptable, the 2007 Tickled Pink (50% Reichensteiner, 50% Seyval Blanc) I tasted had a geranium aroma.

89 WICKHAM VINEYARD

Shedfield, Hampshire (Wessex)

This large vineyard has changed hands three times since 2000, with the latest owners investing heavily on the vinification side since 2006. They also opened Vatika, an on-site, fine-dining restaurant, in 2008. This is a successful, award-winning operation, but with ten grape varieties (Bacchus, Dornfelder, Faber, Kerner, Pinot Noir, Reichensteiner, Rondo, Schönburger, Triomphe d'Alsace, and Würzer), all but one of which belonging more to the 1980s than the 21st century, a rationalization of its vineyards would give Wickham an even better focus for the future.

90 WISTON ESTATE

Findon, West Sussex (Southeast)

Owned by Harry and Pip Goring, who were approached in 2004 by Champagne Duval-Leroy about establishing a sparkling-wine venture on their property. After Duval-Leroy pulled out of the negotiations, the Gorings found themselves bitten by the viticultural bug and proposed to Nyetimber that they should continue with plans to plant a vineyard as additional supplies for the growing Nyetimber brand. Nyetimber's then owner Andy Hill and his winemaker Dermot Sugrue visited the Wiston Estate and were blown away by the 2,600 hectares (6,425 acres) of chalk Downland – especially an amphitheatre-shaped site where Sugrue suggested they should start planting. Everything was agreed in principle, but Hill sold Nyetimber the following year, and six months later Sugrue left. Meanwhile, the Gorings continued with the plan to plant the amphitheatre site, and Sugrue worked the 2006 harvest in Champagne, returning in October 2006 to manage Wiston Estate and set up its winery. By the first harvest in 2008, Sugrue had acquired a traditional Coquard press, and the first sparkling wines were produced: just 2,000 bottles and 200 magnums of a classic blend of 60% Chardonnay, 30% Pinot Noir, and 10% Pinot Meunier, three-quarters of which was fermented in used Burgundian *barriques*; and an even smaller experimental *blanc de blancs cuvée* of merely 50 bottles and 50 magnums.

91 WORTHENBURY

Worthenbury, Wrexham, Wales (Southwest)

The most northerly cultivation of Chardonnay, Pinot Noir, and Sauvignon Blanc, the grapes have to be trucked 272 to 420 kilometres (170 to 260 miles) (depending on the destination winery) to be vinified.

✓ *Classic white blend* (Chardonnay/ Sauvignon)

92 WROXETER ROMAN VINEYARD

Wroxeter, Shropshire (Mercia)

This is not an ancient vineyard; the name refers to the village of Wroxeter's past as the Roman city Uriconium. The first vines were planted here in 1991 by David and Christine Millington, whose son Martin is the current winemaker.

93 WYKEN

Stanton, Suffolk (East Anglia)

Interesting still wines from a typically English jumble of grapes, and a more than passable sparkling wine, Wyken Moonshine, from Auxerrois and Pinot Noir. You should also try the Good Dog Ale (apparently makes you want to "sit and stay"). Wyken's on-site Leaping Hare restaurant has a Bib Gourmand recommendation in the Michelin Guide.

94 YEARLSTONE

Bickleigh, Devon (Southwest)

Originally established by the late, lamented Gillian Pearkes, who planted her first vineyard in 1963 at the age of 18, and whose pioneering book *Growing Grapes in Britain* (1969) was used as a blueprint by many of today's vineyards. Yearlstone vineyard in the Exe Valley was taken over by Roger White, a BBC radio presenter, when Pearkes died in 1993.

✓ *Classic white blend* (Number 5) • *Sparkling* (Brut Rosé)

95 YORKSHIRE HEART VINEYARD

Green Hammerton, York (Mercia)

North of York, and only a few miles short of being the most northerly vineyard in England, Yorkshire Heart Vineyard is the brave venture of Chris and Gillian Spakouskas, who started planting this vineyard as recently as 2005.

THE WINE STYLES OF
THE BRITISH ISLES

AUXERROIS

This grape variety is capable of producing fresh, creamy-rich wine that adapts well to oak and can also be a useful blending component for classic bottle-fermented sparkling wine.

BACCHUS

Fat and grapey with rich, Muscat-like fruit when ripe, this grape provides high sugar levels even in cool climates, making it one of Great Britain's more successful German crosses. It does, however, develop an intensely herbaceous, elderflower style in cooler years and is downright catty when unripe.

 *Camel Valley*

CABERNET

Grown with Merlot in plastic tunnels at Beenleigh, this has promised deep, plummy fruit but has always been ruined during vinification.

CHARDONNAY

Mostly planted for sparkling wine, but some still wine versions are beginning to emerge. Winemakers need to look to Champagne for the best clones (95, 96, 75, and 121) and to New Zealand for advice on how to handle this variety in a maritime-influenced growing environment.

Nyetimber (Premier Cuvée)

EHRENFELSER

Penshurst specializes in this grape, which is the darling of British Columbia in Canada, but to my mind it performs much better in Kent, where in warm years it is soft and ripe with a Riesling-like peach-stone intensity that develops well.

GAMAY

The climate in Great Britain might not have the warmth to make good red wine from this grape, but if Thames Valley's effort in 1992 (Clocktower Gamay) was not an anomaly, it could well be one of the most useful grapes for bottle-fermented sparkling wine.

HUXELREBE

Easy-going fruit that sometimes has a herbaceous-grapefruit bite and can become elderflower-tasting or catty in poor years.

KERNER

More aromatic in Great Britain than in Germany, where it was developed, Kerner is unsuitable for oak and is often grown for its late budding (thus frost avoidance) and high sugar level.

MADELEINE ANGEVINE

This grape has a light, floral aroma and after-perfume, and can have apricoty fruit, but often fights against an elderflower pungency.

Halfpenny Green • *Sharpham* (Barrel Fermented Dry)

MÜLLER-THURGAU

Müller-Thurgau is a typically German style that can become elderflower-tasting or catty, although wines of real flavour are possible.

Breaky Bottom

ORTEGA

Fat and jammy when ripe, becoming herbaceous in cooler years, with an elderflower, white currant character when unripe.

Biddenden • *Throwley*

PINOT BLANC

Can be delicious, easy-drinking, and reminiscent of what Alsace does with this variety.

PINOT GRIS

England's Pinot Gris is not the spiciest in the world, but it does offer richer fruit per gram of acidity than either Pinot Blanc or Chardonnay. It can be successfully oaked, although the best- known example, Denbies 1995 Special Release, was over-oaked and would have been better if blended with another variety.

PINOT NOIR

Some vineyard owners fear that English weather and this variety's susceptibility to rot will not mix, but those growers who have chosen the right clone (115, 114, 779, and 927) have been successful. In a good year, this grape is capable of making an elegant English red with a very attractive cherry and raspberry flavour. In less ripe years, colour extraction can be a problem, and a school of thought reckons that such grapes should be used for sparkling wine, but Pinot Noir that cannot produce a light red will not make good fizz, and would be better used making off-dry, New World-style *blanc de noirs*.

Hidden Springs (Dark Fields) • *Parva Farm* (Rosé)

REICHENSTEINER

Appreciated by growers for its resistance to rot and by winemakers for its high sugar levels, but its neutral character is seldom enjoyed by wine enthusiasts, although exceptions exist.

SCHÖNBURGER

Soft and peachy when ripe, good examples should have at least a light spiciness. There is nothing worse than a dry Schönburger from a cool year, when it smells like a tom-cat's spray.

Stanlake Park (Hinton Grove)

SEYVAL BLANC

Relatively neutral and capable of oak-ageing, but classic English style is crisp and unoaked, with a grassy-elderflowery intensity that is very tangy and almost Sauvignon-like, although unlike Sauvignon, good Seyval ages well in bottle. However, it can be catty with less ripeness.

Breaky Bottom • *Camel Blanc* • *Sparkling* (Avalon, Hendred, and especially Three Choirs)

SIEGERREBE

A Madeleine Angevine/Gewürztraminer cross that can produce fat wines with tangy fruit.

Three Choirs (Estate Reserve)

TRIOMPHE

Triomphe is a red-wine hybrid with a hint of foxiness on the aftertaste, but this can be hidden in a clever blend.

OTHER STYLES

BOTRYTIS *or* LATE-HARVEST

There's no doubt that the UK can guarantee sufficiently damp mornings to encourage rot, but it requires a strong burn-off from mid-morning sun for two weeks to encourage noble rot, which is not that common. When it occurs, however, these wines can have a stunning piquance of mouthwatering fruit and acidity.

Three Choirs (Estate Reserve Noble Rot)

BOTTLE-FERMENTED SPARKLING WINE

The best wines use non-aromatic varieties, preferably classic Champagne grapes. Nyetimber has shown that these varieties can succeed.

Nyetimber • *Ridgeview* • *Camel Valley* • *Henners*

CLASSIC RED BLENDS

Most English red wines are light and insubstantial, but New World influence has encouraged softer, more upfront, fruity styles.

Sharpham (Beenleigh) • *Hidden Springs* (Dark Fields)

CLASSIC WHITE BLENDS

One way to ignore the funny-sounding grape names of hybrids and crosses is to blend them into a wine sold under a proprietary label.

Hidden Springs (Decadence) • *Sharpham* (Dart Valley Reserve) • *Stanlake Park* (Fumé)

OAKED WHITES

As in the US, some producers have adopted the term *fumé* to indicate oak-ageing. Marginal climatic conditions produce wines of leaner structure than those of Europe or the New World, thus oak can easily overwhelm, and winemakers tend to restrain its use. Normally only non-aromatic varieties such as Seyval Blanc are oaked.

Sharpham (Madeleine Angevine Barrel Fermented Dry) • *Stanlake Park* (Fumé)

ROSÉ

Although the British climate makes it difficult to produce a true red wine year in and year out, the viticultural fringe should be ideal for making crisp, ultra-fresh, off-dry rosés and a few vineyards are beginning to realize the potential.

Denbies (Rose Hill) • *Hidden Springs* (Sussex Sunset) • *Stanlake Park* (Pinot Blush)

LUXEMBOURG

A small but varietally diverse wine-producing country on the northern cusp of commercially viable viticulture, Luxembourg's best vineyards consistently produce wonderfully fresh and pure dry white wines that are delicious to drink with food or without, and they fit conveniently into the niche vacated by so many Alsace producers as they make sweeter and sweeter wines.

LUXEMBOURG DERIVES ITS NAME from Lucilinburhuc, or "Little Fortress", which is the Saxon name for a defensive position originally built by the Romans on a rocky promontory around which the city of Luxembourg was destined to grow. Under the Romans, this area held no geopolitical identity, but was part of the Trier region, where vines were grown 2,000 years ago. Today, the vineyards are scattered around and between 28 towns and villages, stretching from Wasserbillig in the north to Schengen in the south. This viticultural area is the mirror image across the Moselle River of the German *Bereiche* of Obermosel and Moseltor, which are situated on the right bank, and generally produce less exciting wines than those from Luxembourg's vineyards opposite. It is from the German side of the river that the topography of Luxembourg's vineyards can best be observed, especially when the river bends north and south. This strip of the Moselle's left bank is officially designated *Appellation Moselle Luxembourgoise Contrôlée*, and vines are not allowed to be planted anywhere else in Luxembourg.

TERROIR?

These vineyards are at their narrowest in the northern half of Luxembourg's Moselle valley, where the dolomite limestone subsoil has resisted erosion, leaving a narrower valley with steeper slopes. This pinkish-brown bedrock can be seen overhanging the old Caves St Martin – now owned by the firm of Gales – which were carved out of the dolomite in 1919–21. Going south from Remich, much softer marly and clayey soils dominate; consequently the area has been

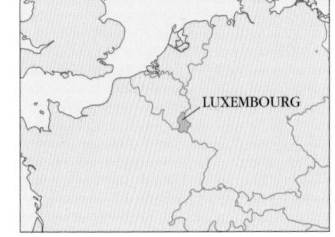

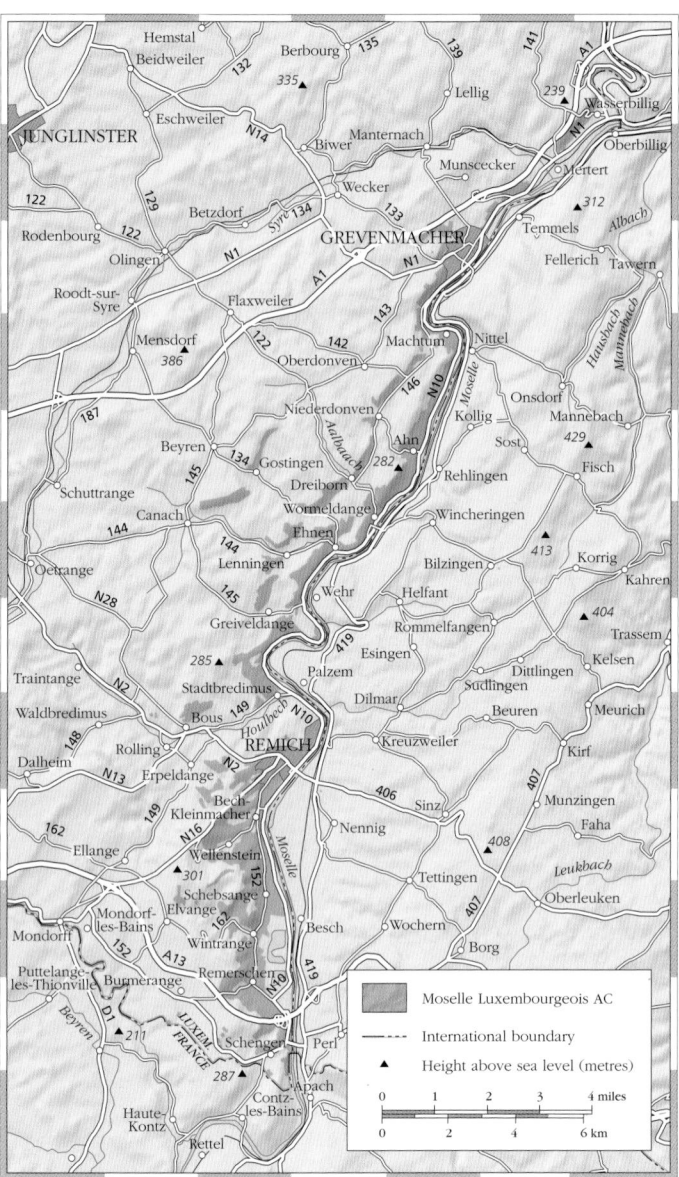

LUXEMBOURG
A country united by other tongues: French is used by its government and courts, with most newspapers published in German, leaving the national dialect with no official role.

Map legend:
- Moselle Luxembourgeois AC
- International boundary
- ▲ Height above sea level (metres)

THE LIEUX-DITS – LUXEMBOURG'S BEST-KEPT SECRET

The *lieux-dits* represent Luxembourg's richest source of fine, expressive wines, and a joint project between the Institut Viti-Vinicole (IVV) and the German Weather Institute could be this country's key to international success. This project is identifying the best areas in each *lieu-dit* according to meteorological criteria (rain, sunshine, heat, etc), which some believe could be the basis of a future *grand cru*-type classification. Weather is an infinitely better way of discerning which parts of a vineyard (rather than vineyards *per se*) should be classified than the French system. The French claim to isolate an individual *terroir* by its geological homogeneity compared with the surrounding area within a historically established

named site. As the relatively recent classification of Alsace's *grands crus* illustrates, not only does the geological homogeneity fly out of the window in the process, but so does the extent of the historically established named site. As growers on the periphery of a historically established named site realize the premium that can be demanded by a wine with *grand cru* on the label, they ask "If his plot is going to be classified *grand cru*, why not mine?". And, of course, once they are allowed, their own neighbours – who were previously separated by unclassified land – want in. Thus it was that *grands crus* like Brand in Turckheim grew from less than 3 hectares to almost 58! Such corrupt behaviour would kill Luxembourg's

fledgling reputation. This is the one area where the IVV needs a firm hand. Its hardest task will be to establish in law the true historical boundary of every *lieu-dit*, after which the meteorological data cannot be argued with – growers cannot claim to have more or less rain, sunshine, or heat than the records show. So it should be possible, not merely to use this data to classify *grands crus*, but also to subdivide each *lieu-dit* so that, for example, parts of the *lieu-dit* of Greiveldange Fels are officially designated Greiveldange Fels *grand cru* and Greiveldange Fels *premier cru*, while the rest remains Greiveldange Fels *lieu-dit* plain and simple, albeit a single-vineyard wine in its own right.

RECENT LUXEMBOURG VINTAGES

2010 A typical fresh and fruity vintage in which the Riesling stand out due to a sunny ripening period in October.

2009 This is a truly great vintage, with all varieties showing aromatic freshness and minerality of fruit. There are exceptional *vendanges tardives*, *vins de glace*, and *vins de paille*.

2008 Ideal harvest conditions produced a lovely, ripe, elegant year.

2007 A ripe year with a good slow finish to the *véraison* process made a good vintage for both reds and whites. Age-worthy Rieslings are the standouts.

2006 One of the earliest and shortest harvests on record, and one that was blighted by a lot of rot, this is a vintage in which the growers had to be very strict in selecting only the cleanest fruit. Consumers should also be very strict in what they select.

LUXEMBOURG'S GRAPE VARIETIES

Based on 2002 statistics

Growers not to exceed a maximum yield of 140 hl/ha for Elbling and Rivaner, 120hl/ha for all the other varieties, but since average yields for four varieties exceed these parameters, the law is obviously being flouted on a wide scale.

VARIETY	HECTARES	% OF VINES	HL/HA	HECTOLITRES	% OF WINES
Rivaner	411.62	31.4%	139.51	57,425	37.32%
Auxerrois	171.31	13.1%	113.23	19,397	12.61%
Riesling	169.08	12.9%	96.85	16,375	10.64%
Pinot Gris	166.68	12.7%	94.11	15,686	10.19%
Elbling	143.03	10.9%	145.66	20,834	13.54%
Pinot Blanc	136.96	10.5%	114.95	15,744	10.23%
Pinot Noir	81.67	6.2%	79.98	6,532	4.25%
Gewürztraminer	14.35	1.1%	64.46	925	0.60%
Chardonnay	11.77	0.9%	78.33	922	0.60%
Others (Gamay, Muscat)	2.62	0.2%	12.21	32	0.02%
TOTAL	1,309.09	100.0%	117.55*	153,872	100.00%

* Average yield

prone to erosion, which has widened the valley, leaving a softer landscape of gently rolling hills. It is said in Luxembourg itself that the wines in the south are soft, mellow, and best drunk young, whereas those in the north are crisper and finer, requiring more time in bottle, but I have found little evidence of this in the wines. If yields averaged 40 hectolitres per hectare rather than the current greedy 120, provenance might become a factor in determining two contrasting styles of wine, but the differences that exist at the moment are more likely to be due to the stylistic preference of individual growers.

LUXEMBOURG: THE NEW ALSACE?

Although this country has a tiny, emerging production of *vendange tardive*, *vin de glace*, and *vin de paille*, it will take a decade or more for any producer to establish a lasting reputation like that of Hugel's Riesling Vendange Tardive. Luxembourg certainly has nothing to compare with great dry wines like those of Trimbach's Clos Ste-Hûne, or any producers with reputations that come near those of Zind-Humbrecht, Weinbach, or Deiss. And there are wines such as Gewürztraminer and Pinot Noir at which Luxembourg will never be successful in anything other than heat-wave years like 2003. But what Luxembourg does have is what Alsace no longer offers, and that is a large range of uncomplicated, refreshing, easy-drinking, fine-quality varietal wines that consumers know to be dry without asking. This country's wines were boring in the 1980s, but underwent a quiet revolution in the 1990s, and have been attracting disenfranchised Alsace consumers since the turn of the century. The consistency in quality is already remarkable.

FACTORS AFFECTING TASTE AND QUALITY

LOCATION
A 42-kilometre (26-mile) strip of land along the country's southeastern flank, where 1,300 hectares (3,200 acres) of vines grow on the left bank of the Moselle River, overlooking the southernmost section of Germany's Mosel region.

CLIMATE
A modified continental climate with mild winters and cool summers, the rainiest months coinciding with ripening and harvest. Frost can be dangerous, reducing yields by 80 per cent on rare occasions, but rain and cold temperatures at flowering more commonly reduce yields.

ASPECT
Going south from Remich, the valley widens, facilitating the growth of vines. Going north from Remich, it narrows and the slopes become steeper. More than 400 hectares (1,000 acres) of vines are grown on slopes of above 30 per cent incline.

SOIL
Marly and clayey in the south, with pinkish-brown dolomite limestone in the north.

VITICULTURE AND VINIFICATION
Luxembourg's vineyards have undergone a restructuring, replacing traditional terracing with wider-spaced, vertically sloping rows. Called *remembrement*, this started in Wormeldange in 1970 and is nearly complete. Most vines are trained using a single Guyot system, though some are trained using the Trierer Rebenrad. Average yields are much too high (120 hl/ha), but individual producers prune for smaller yields. There is a closed-shop system of 60 wine producers, including 6 commercial shippers and 6 cooperatives. Some *barriques* are used, and a number of traditional producers have large old oak *fûdres*, but stainless-steel predominates, and the new *crémant* facility of Caves Gales at Ellange-Gare is state of the art.

GRAPE VARIETIES
Primary varieties: Auxerrois, Elbling, Pinot Blanc, Pinot Gris, Riesling, Rivaner (Müller-Thurgau)
Secondary varieties: Chardonnay, Gamay, Gewürztraminer, Muscat, Pinot Noir

APPELLATION MOSELLE LUXEMBOURGOISE CONTRÔLÉE

There is just one appellation, and all *Appellation Contrôlée* wines must carry a state-controlled Marque Nationale mini-label. To get the Marque Nationale, wines are submitted to the Institut Viti-Vinicole (IVV) for chemical analysis and a blind-tasting test. The basic Marque Nationale is open to all varieties and styles, and is awarded to any wine scoring 12–13.9 points (out of 20) from the IVV tasting panel. For most grape varieties, a wine scoring 16–17.9 points is classified as a *premier cru*, while a wine scoring 18–20 points is deemed a *grand premier cru*. Any wine achieving fewer than 12 points is declassified into *vin de table*. This is a significant selection process, with as many as 32 per cent of the wines submitted declassified.

Classifying a wine as a *cru* (growth) of any sort on the basis of tasting, regardless of whether the wine comes from a single site, is irrational and contrary to the spirit of the European Union's wine regime. There are only two logical options: either all wines submitted must be the product of a *lieu-dit* (named site) or the designation should be altered to something like *premier vin* and *grand premier vin*. The latter would make it possible to reserve the terms *premier cru* and *grand cru* for future classifications for existing *lieux-dits* (*see box, opposite*).

If a Rivaner scores 14–15.9 points, it is designated as a *vin classé*, the highest classification any wine from this grape can achieve. The Elbling, Pinot Noir, and Crémant de Luxembourg may aspire to no more than the basic appellation. This is more nonsense, although it should be noted that, as with the *premier cru* and *grand premier cru* misnomers, these practices date from times when even French wine regions like Alsace were blending

grands crus and unfairly discriminating against wines because of the varietal content, rather than intrinsic quality. Things moved on in the world of wine, and the IVV's tasting panel needs to recalibrate its palate to modern standards. Many *premier cru* wines are no more than basic in quality, and even some of *grand premier cru* are little better. They might have stood out against other Luxembourg wines in the 1980s, but such standards do not apply today. I have tasted some groundbreaking wines that have failed to pass even the basic appellation, being rejected on stylistic grounds. The IVV is repeating the mistakes made by French and German official tasting panels, which denied the appellation to many of the most forward-thinking winemakers, resulting in an annihilation of their exports by New World rivals. Luxembourg cannot afford to follow suit.

THE WINE STYLES OF
LUXEMBOURG

ÄISWÄIN
See Vin de Glace

AUXERROIS
Minimum natural ripeness (2003):
63° Oechsle (8% ABV)
Maximum yield:120 hl/ha

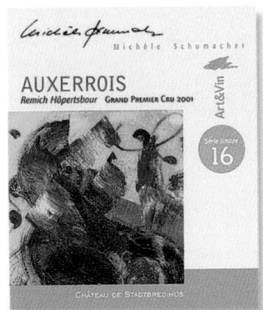

One of Luxembourg's most successful grape
varieties, which is amazing considering that its
yield is second only to the rampant Rivaner. Yet
Auxerrois ranks with the best you can find in the
Haut-Rhin. Some producers leave a little residual
sugar in these wines, but essentially they are light,
dry, and delicious to drink.

⏳ 1–2 years

🍷 *Aly Duhr* (Wormeldange Koeppchen)
• *Max-Lahr et Fils* (Wormeldange
Heiligenhäuschen) • *Pundel-Hoffeld*
(Machtum Alwengert) • *R Kohll-Leuck*
(Ehnen Ehnerberg) • *Vinsmoselle Caves de
Stadtbredimus* (Stadtbredimus Primerberg)

CHARDONNAY
Minimum natural ripeness (2003):
63° Oechsle (8% ABV)
Maximum yield:120 hl/ha

The clones planted are 95 and 96, which are good
for both still and sparkling wines, although 96 fares
better at the latter, and this far north growers should
really be trying 75 and 121. Everyone who had
this variety told me that their Chardonnay had
been planted for sparkling wine, yet they all just
happened to be making a still wine from it, none of
which was any better than a Belgian Chardonnay
(Clermont, Genoels-Elderen, and others). A certain
warmth is required to make premium-quality
Chardonnay, and Luxembourg just does not have
this on any regular basis. If decent-quality, still
Chardonnay is extremely rare in Champagne,
what chance has Luxembourg?

⏳ 1–2 years

🍷 *Gales* (Coteaux de Stadtbredimus)

ELBLING
Minimum natural ripeness (2003):
57° Oechsle (7% ABV)
Maximum yield:140 hl/ha

Traditionally grown as low-quality, low-tax fodder
for Germany's *Sekt* industry, Elbling typically
provides a neutral-flavoured, high-acid wine. I
once thought that it might be interesting to look
out for the odd wine made from low-yield Elbling,
but gave up when it became patently clear that
no such thing exists.

GEWÜRZTRAMINER
Minimum natural ripeness (2003):
63° Oechsle (8% ABV)
Maximum yield:120 hl/ha

This grape is not as abundant as it is in Alsace,
and it lacks the gravitas and broader notes found
in the latter region's truly classic examples. The
significantly lower level of ripeness reduces the
availability of spice-laden terpenes, while its lower
alcohol content (3–4 per cent lower) gives an
entirely different, much lighter, less viscous,
mouthfeel. If anyone in Luxembourg is really
serious about this grape, it must be grown on the
very best, south-facing sites that have been
traditionally reserved for Riesling, with yields
halved, and harvested as late as possible.

⏳ 1–2 years

🍷 *A Gloden* (Schengen Markusberg) • *Charles
Decker* (Remerschen Kreitzberg) • *Domaine
Mathis Bastian* ◉ (Domaine et Tradition)•
Schmit-Fohl (Ahn Goellebour)

PINOT BLANC
Minimum natural ripeness (2003):
63° Oechsle (8% ABV)
Maximum yield:120 hl/ha

The crystal-clear, refreshing, light, dry and fruity
entry-level wine for any half-serious Luxembourg
wine drinker. The sooner that plantings of
Rivaner and Elbling are reduced to a statistical
insignificance, the sooner that Auxerrois will be
the entry-level wine for all consumers, with Pinot
Blanc the flagship, and the better Luxembourg's
wine reputation will be.

⏳ 1–2 years

🍷 *Cep d'Or* (Stadtbredimus Goldberg)
• *Domaine Gales* (Domaine et Tradition)
• *Domaine Gales* (Bech-Macher Rétschelt)
• *Häremillen* (Wormeldange Weinbour) •
Mathes (Wormeldange Mohrberg) • *Mathis
Bastian* (Coteau de Remich) • *Pundel-Hoffeld*
(Machtum Gëllebour) • *R Kohll-Leuck* (Ehnen
Rousemen) • *Schram & Fils* (Bech-Kleinmacher
Falkenberg) • *Schumacher-Lethal*
(Wormeldange Heiligenhäuschen)

PINOT GRIS
Minimum natural ripeness (2003):
63° Oechsle (8% ABV)
Maximum yield:120 hl/ha

Luxembourg's Pinot Gris has none of the spice
found in Alsace, and is simply a slightly richer,
equally delicious version of Pinot Blanc –
everything Italy's Pinot Grigio should be, yet
seldom is. It is probably impossible for Pinot Gris
to ripen sufficiently in Luxembourg's climate to
create enough terpenes in the grape's skin for
these to develop into spicy bottle-aromas.

⏳ 1–4 years

🍷 *A Gloden & Fils* (Wellenstein Foulschette)
• *Cep d'Or* (Stadtbredimus Primerberg Signature
Terroir et Cépage) • *Häremillen* (Mertert
Herrenberg) • *Jean Schlink-Hoffeld* (Machtum
Ongkâf "Arômes et Couleurs") • *Krier Welbes*
(Bech-Kleinmacher Naumberg) • *Pundel-
Hoffeld* (Machtum Widdem) • *Mathes*
(Wormeldange Woûsselt) • *R Kohll-Leuck*
(Ehnen Kelterberg) • *Schmit-Fohl* (Ahn
Goellebour)

PINOT NOIR
Minimum natural ripeness (2003):
63° Oechsle (8% ABV)
Maximum yield:120 hl/ha

The clones planted are 115 and 114, which are
good, but also 375, which is not (overcropper,
low quality, poor varietal character), and this
far north growers should be trying 779 and 927.
I tasted nothing interesting from 2002, which
was a riper than normal vintage. The wines
have a certain sour-cherry varietal character,
but lack fruit, structure, finesse, and complexity.
If nothing special is produced from the 2003
vintage, then they should give up on Pinot Noir
as a red varietal wine (although it would make
a useful sparkling wine component).

🍷 *Cep d'Or* (Stadtbredimus Goldberg)

RIESLING
Minimum natural ripeness (2003):
63° Oechsle (8% ABV)
Maximum yield:120 hl/ha

This is Luxembourg's finest potential wine, but most
Riesling growers are not realizing this potential. In
such a northern, Atlantic-influenced area, it is
madness to average almost 100 hectolitres per
hectare. It is widely understood that Riesling can be
successfully cultivated only on fully south-facing
sites in Luxembourg, yet the growers throw away
the potential of the country's greatest sites by
squeezing every last drop from the vines. They
should be aiming for 12–13 per cent alcohol without
chaptalization, but they are averaging barely 9 per
cent. Luxembourg Riesling is dry, and if some are
surprisingly good, it should not be taken as
vindication of such ridiculously high yields. If all
Riesling vines grown on the best slopes of
Luxembourg's finest *lieux-dits* were cropped at a
maximum of 35 hectolitres per hectare, this country's
wines would have an international reputation.
Riesling is tailor-made for Luxembourg: it adores
cold October nights and is the only grape that can
keep ripening at 12°C (Pinot and Gewürztraminer
stop at 18°C). A few specialists produce excellent
wines at reduced yields, but even they need to crop
lower; unlike in Alsace, there is no danger inducing
overripe grapes that the wines will become sweet.

⏳ 1–8 years

🍷 *Aly Duhr* (Domaine et Tradition) • *Cep d'Or
Riesling* (Stadtbredimus Fels "Signature Terroir
et Cépage") • *Domaine Alice Hartmann*
(Wormeldange Koeppchen and Les Terrasses de
la Koeppchen la Chapelle) • *Domaine Gales*
(Wellenstein Kurschells) • *Pundel-Hoffeld
Riesling* (Wormeldange Elterberg "Cuvée
Spéciale") • *Schumacher-Knepper* (Wintrage
Felsberg) • *Steinmetz-Jungers* (Grevenmacher
Fels) • *Vinsmoselle* (Coteaux de Schengen) •
Vinsmoselle Caves de Grevenmacher (Mertert
Herrenberg)

RIVANER
Minimum natural ripeness (2003):
57° Oechsle (7% ABV)
Maximum yield:140 hl/ha

Also known as Müller-Thurgau. Although this
ubiquitous grape accounts for almost one-third of
all the vines growing in Luxembourg today, it is
definitely on the decline. Twenty-five years ago
every other bottle of wine produced in the Grand

Duchy was made from Rivaner. This grape is grown at very high yields and turned into a sweetish, Liebfraumilch-type wine, making it Luxembourg's least interesting variety, but one that enjoys high-volume sales. Rivaner prices are low, and the popularity of this style of wine extends beyond the domestic market to Belgium, where it accounts for more than half of global exports of Vins Moselle Luxembourgoise. As long as the cultivated area of this variety continues to decline, there seems little point in getting high-minded about its yield. It will eventually bottom-out, and lowering yield will hardly produce a noticeably finer quality of wine.

🍷— Upon purchase

🏆 *Aly Duhr* (Sélection Ahn Hohfels) • *Cep d'Or* (Stadtbredimus Goldberg) • *Domaine Viticole Kox* (Remich Primerberg) • *Krier-Welbes* (Bech-Kleinmacher Naumberg)

OTHER GRAPE VARIETIES
Minimum natural ripeness (2003):
63° Oechsle (8% ABV)
Maximum yield:120 hl/ha

Gamay did not impress me, although the three Muscats demonstrated that it might be worth persevering with this variety, especially Charles Decker's Muscat Ottonel (deliciously creamy 2001, and evocatively strawberry 1997).

🍷— 1–4 years

🏆 *Charles Decker* (Muscat Ottonel, Remerschen Kreitzberg)

OTHER STYLES

CRÉMANT DE LUXEMBOURG
Maximum yield:120 hl/ha

Champagne – real Champagne – was in fact produced in Luxembourg by Mercier from 1886 up to almost the beginning of World War II. During this time, Mercier was known as "Champagne Mercier, Epernay-Luxembourg", and both establishments were famous for being completely powered by 19th-century electricity. Today, of course, Champagne is a prohibited term, and the Crémant de Luxembourg appellation was created as part of the deal with Champagne not to use the term *méthode champenoise*. Curiously, it gets lumped in with French Crémant appellations (Alsace, Bordeaux, Bourgogne, Die, Jura, Limoux, Loire, and Luxembourg) at the annual Concours des Crémants. Most Crémant de Luxembourg encountered outside the country is boring, but the general standard is much higher, primarily because it is much fresher, and these sparkling wines are a delight to drink young. The style is fresh, soft, and elegant, with good acids providing a crisp, fruity finish. The only exception is Domaine Alice Hartmann Brut, which is chock-a-block full of flavour and character, perhaps at the expense of finesse, and could be criticized for being too big and too oaky, but has to be admired, and is currently Luxembourg's greatest sparkling wine. However, it's a style that I would not like to see more than two or three other producers emulate, as Luxembourg is more naturally attuned to the Gales style of freshness and finesse. Whereas Crémant de Luxembourg must be made exclusively from grapes grown within the appellation Moselle Luxembourgoise, readers should be aware that any Luxembourg wines labelled Vin Mousseux, Vin Pétillant, Perlwein, or sold as "boissons effervescents à base de vin" may be blended from imported grapes, juice, or wine.

🍷— 1–2 years

🏆 *Domaine Alice Hartmann* (Brut) • *Gales* (Heritage) • *Gales* (Jubilée) • *Gales* (Cuvée Premier Rosé) • *Vinsmoselle* (Poll-Fabaire Cuvée Art Collection)

VENDANGE TARDIVE

Only Auxerrois, Pinot Blanc, Pinot Gris, Riesling, and Gewürztraminer are authorized. The minimum ripeness level of 243 grams per litres (220 for Riesling) of natural sugar content is as tough as the *vendange tardive* law introduced in Alsace in 1984, and raising ripeness levels is more difficult in Luxembourg's colder, more northerly climate. Alsace raised the bar in 2001 (to 235–257 grams per litre), and Luxembourg should do likewise, confident in the knowledge that its vineyards are nothing like the suntraps in Alsace, thus the Grand Duchy will never be in danger of losing its primary crop of dry wine grapes. Vendange Tardive is a new, emerging category of wine, and too many of the wines are noticeably high VA, with a bitter finish. This will change, as producers get used to the style – some, like Domaine Thill Frères, already are.

🍷— 1–8 years

🏆 *Domaine Thill* (Château de Shengen Riesling)

VIN DE GLACE *or* ÄISWÄIN

Only Pinot Blanc, Pinot Gris, and Riesling are authorized. The minimum ripeness level is 292 grams of natural sugar per litre. Luxembourg seems to be more climatically adept at *vin de glace* than *vendange tardive*, but it is a style that generally attracts a high VA level, and the Grand Duchy is no exception.

🍷— 1–8 years

🏆 *Charles Decker* • *Domaine Gales*

VIN DE PAILLE

Only Auxerrois, Pinot Blanc, Pinot Gris, and Gewürztraminer are authorized. The minimum ripeness level is 317 grams per litre of natural sugar. Only one outstanding example so far.

🍷— 1–8 years

🏆 *Caves Sunnen-Hoffmann* ◉ ⑬ (Auxerrois)

THE APPELLATIONS OF
LUXEMBOURG

Note Due to the varying usage of all three languages (Luxembourgish, German, French, and sometimes Dutch/Low German), spellings of some villages and *lieux-dits* can vary. The most common variations are shown below. To list all the villages and all the *lieux-dits* in use today in all languages, not to mention the odd variant in each language, would confuse more than it would inform. It is obvious that Luxembourg must clean up its labelling act, obliging everyone to use the same nomenclature, and most observers would agree that Luxembourgish should be the dialect of choice.

AHN
Lieux-dits *Palmberg, Vogelsang, Elterberg, Hohfels/ Houfels, Göllebour, Pietert, Nussbaum*

Warmer vineyards enable Gewürztraminer to succeed in exceptionally hot years. It is said that Luxembourg's first Traminer and Muscat vines were grown here at the beginning of the 20th century. Also good for Pinot Gris, Auxerrois, Riesling, and occasionally Crémant de Luxembourg. Domaine Viticole Mme Aly Duhr & Fils is the most famous producer here, but I have been at least as pleased by Schmit-Fohl, followed by Steinmetz-Duhr. Other Ahn wines that have impressed me on occasions have been Clos du Rochers (Bernard-Massard) and Jean Ley-Schartz.

BECH-KLEINMACHER
Lieux-dits *Enschberg, Jongeberg, Falkenberg, Naumberg, Fuusslach, Gaalgeberg, Brauneberg, Gottesgôf, Kurschels, Rëtschelt*

Two villages, Bech and Macher, merged 100 years or so ago, when they built a communal church. Just two producers resident in the town (Krier-Bisenius and Schram et Fils), but growers sell most grapes to the cooperative at Wellenstein and Caves Gales for their sparkling wine (they also grow their own grapes here). Naumberg has been the most successful *lieu-dit* in my tasting, with fine Pinot Gris from Krier Welbes and the cooperative at Wellenstein. Schram makes a very good Pinot Blanc on both Falkenberg and Kurschells.

BOUS
Lieux-dits *Johannisberg, Fels*

Just one local producer (Caves Beissel) and nothing outstanding so far.

EHNEN
Lieux-dits *Kelterberg, Mesteschberg, Ehnerberg/ Einerberg, Rousemen, Bromelt, Wousselt*

Ehnen is one of the prettiest villages on the Luxembourg wine route. I have enjoyed wines from Jean Linden-Heinisch and M Kohll-Reuland. Pinot Gris and Auxerrois fare well, with Mesteschberg and Kelterberg among the most successful *lieux-dits*.

ELLINGEN/ELLANGE
Lieux-dits *None*

Two very good producers are located here, Caves Gales and Krier Welbes, but no mono-*cru* wines produced. Growers either deliver their grapes to the cooperative or sell them to one of the six commercial wineries.

ELVANGE/ELVINGEN
Lieux-dits *None*

No producers are located here. Although there is one grower who owns three plots within this village that are delimited for the production of *Appellation Moselle Luxembourgoise Contrôlée*, and have been exploited in the recent past, there are no vines growing here at the moment.

ERPELDINGEN
Lieux-dits *None*

No producers are located here. Growers either deliver to the cooperative or sell to one of the six commercial wineries.

GOSTINGEN

Lieux-dits Bocksberg, Häreberg

Just one local producer (Caves Fernand Rhein) and nothing outstanding so far.

GREIVELDANGE/ GREIWELDIGEN

Lieux-dits Hutte/Hëtt, Dieffert, Herrenberg/ Häreberg, Hëttermillen

The village is two kilometres from the Moselle, but the vineyards extend down to the river's banks. Of the two local producers, Beck-Franck and Stronck-Pinnel, the latter makes one of Greiveldange's best Rieslings from the Hëtt *lieu-dit*, while the former makes better wines from other villages. However, most of the growers belong to the village cooperative, and Vinsmoselle makes most of the best wines here, especially Dieffert Pinot Gris and Herrenberg Auxerrois.

GREVENMACHER

Lieux-dits Fels, Rosenberg/Rouseberg, Leitschberg/ Leiteschberg, Pietert, Groaerd/Groärd

The best-known producer here is Bernard Massard, one of Luxembourg's truly international exporters. The Fels *lieu-dit* is for Riesling, Leitschberg, and Pietert for Pinot Blanc. Steinmetz-Jungers, Vinsmoselle's Caves de Grevenmacher, and Fédération Viticole make the finest local wines.

LENNINGEN

Lieux-dits Häreberg

Just one local producer (Caves Fernand Rhein) and nothing outstanding so far.

MACHTUM

Lieux-dits Alwengert, Hohenfels, Ongkâf, Goellebour/Göllebour, Widdem

Matchum is supposedly known for its Ongkâf Riesling, but it produces better Pinot Gris, and to be truthful, Göllebour vies with Ongkâf as the top *lieu-dit* in the village. Matchum also makes good Pinot Blanc. The Riesling is good, but no better than Auxerrois and, in hotter years, Gewürztraminer. The two local producers, Jean Schlink-Hoffeld and Pundel-Hoffeld, are both very good, with Vinsmoselle and Cep d'Or the best producers from outside the village.

MERTERT

Lieux-dits Bocksberg, Herrenberg/Häreberg

The best *lieu-dit* in this ugly, industrial port is Herrenberg, which thankfully is closer to Wasserbillig. Pinot Gris is Herrenberg's most successful variety, with Häremillen and the local Vinsmoselle Caves de Grevenmacher the top-performing producers.

MONDORF

Lieux-dits None

No producers are located here. Growers either deliver to the cooperative or sell to one of the six commercial wineries.

NIEDERDONVEN

Lieux-dits Fels, Gölleberg, Diedenacker

No producers are located here. Growers either deliver to the cooperative or sell to one of the six commercial wineries.

OBER-WORMELDINGEN

Lieux-dits None

No producers are located here. Growers either deliver to the cooperative or sell to one of the six commercial wineries.

OBERDONVEN

Lieux-dits None

No producers are located here. Growers either deliver to the cooperative or sell to one of the six commercial wineries.

REMERSCHEN

Lieux-dits Jongeberg, Kräitchen, Kreitzberg, Rodernberg/Roudeberg, Reidt

Charles Decker is the award-winning producer here; many of his medals are for wines that were denied the most lowly appellation, having been rejected by the IVV. In the best years, Decker can produce good Muscat Ottonel and Gewürztraminer on the Kreitzberg *lieu-dit*, while Krier Frères has made good Riesling on Jongeberg.

REMICH

Lieux-dits Fels, Goldberg, Gaalgeberg, Hélwéngert, Hôpertsbour, Primerberg, Scheuerberg

Primerberg is the most important *lieu-dit* here, and Riesling its best variety, with Krier Frères and Mathis Bastian the top producers, but this vineyard also makes fine Pinot Blanc and Auxerrois (St Remy Desom), and Pinot Gris (Gales). Overall Remich is most successful for Pinot Blanc, with Mathis Bastian (Coteau de Remich) and Krier Frères (Hôpertsbour) both vying with St Remy Desom.

ROLLING

Lieux-dits None

No producers are located here. Growers either deliver to the cooperative or sell to one of the six commercial wineries.

ROSPORT

Lieux-dits None

Everyone in the Luxembourg wine trade will tell you that Wasserbillig is the very northern limit of *Appellation Moselle Luxembourgoise Controlée*, yet I found these vines 14 kilometres (8.5 miles) farther north, and they are officially within the delimited region, even though they are not on the Moselle or even in its hinterland, but located on a tributary called the Sauer.

SCHENGEN

Lieux-dits Fels, Markusberg

Although Fels Riesling is supposed to be best known, this most southerly of Luxembourg's wine villages is definitely Pinot country (Blanc and Gris), with Vinsmoselle dominating, though A Gloden & Fils also makes some fine wines.

SCHWEBSINGEN/ SCHWEBSANGE

Lieux-dits Letscheberg, Steilberg, Hehberg, Kolteschberg

Supposedly good for Gewürztraminer, but I have yet to confirm that. The best *lieu-dit* is Kolteschberg, where Vinsmoselle Caves de Wellenstein and Laurent & Benoît Kox produce some good Pinot Gris and Riesling.

STADTBREDIMUS

Lieux-dits Primerberg, Goldberg, Dieffert, Fels

Only Wormeldingen produces more top-quality Luxembourg wines than Stadtbredimus. Most of the best come from Vinsmoselle Caves de Stadtbredimus and Cep d'Or, but some also from Gales and Laurent & Benoît Kox. The largest *lieu-dit* is the Primerberg, but Dieffert and Fels are the best, producing some of the finest Rieslings in the country. Pinot Gris is the second best variety in Stadbredimus, and Primerberg, Goldberg and Fels the most successful *lieu-dit* for this grape.

WASSERBILLIG

Lieux-dits Bocksberg, Häreberg

Supposedly the most northerly of Luxembourg's main drag of vineyards, but not strictly so (*see* Rosport).

WELLENSTEIN

Lieux-dits Foulschette, Kurschels, Veilchenberg, Roetchelt, Brauneberg, Knipp, St Annaberg

Kurschels stands out as the best *lieu-dit*, and the best *lieu-dit* for Riesling. Foulschette is the second-best *lieu-dit*, and the best *lieu-dit* for Pinot Gris. Krier Welbes and Gales are the top producers in this region, followed closely by Mathis Bastian and Vinsmoselle (Série Limitée Art).

WINTRANGE/WINTRINGEN

Lieux-dits Hommelsberg, Felsberg

Felsberg is the best-known *lieu-dit*, with its statue of St Donatus crowning the hill, where Pinot Gris and Riesling are supposed to be among the best in Luxemboug, although I have tasted only one wine that matches up to that sort of reputation (and that is Vinsmoselle Caves de Remerschen Riesling Grand Premier Cru Wintrange Felsberg).

WORMELDANGE/ WORMELDINGEN

Lieux-dits Elterberg, Heiligenhäuschen, Koeppchen/Köppchen, Moorberg, Nidert, Nussbaum, Péiteschwengert, Pietert, Weinbour, Wousselt

Wormeldingen is the superstar of Luxembourg's wine villages, Koeppchen its greatest *lieu-dit*, Domaine Alice Hartmann its best producer, and Riesling its king of grapes. Domaine Alice Hartmann is by no means the only top producer making wines from this village. I have also been impressed by Wormeldingen wines from Aly Duhr, Fédération Viticole, Häremillen, Jean Schlink-Hoffeld, Mathes, Pundel-Hoffeld, Schumacher-Lethal, St Remy Desom, Steinmetz-Jungers, and Vinsmoselle Caves de Wormeldange. I have tasted some good Pinot Gris, Pinot Blanc, and Auxerrois from these producers, but with one exception (Aly Duhr), they have all been from other *lieux-dits*. If I have learned anything about the wines of Luxembourg, it is that the best parts of Koeppchen produce the country's finest Riesling, and it would be a great shame to plant this *terroir* with any other variety.

OTHER WINEMAKING COUNTRIES OF NORTHWESTERN EUROPE

In the northern hemisphere, the farther north a vine grows, the fewer hours of daylight it receives and the greater the angle at which the sunlight is spread out, thus the longer it takes to ripen grapes. Factor in the wet, windy, and uncertain climes of the Atlantic, and it may seem surprising that these countries produce any wine.

BELGIUM
In Belgium, winegrowing dates back to Roman times. Today, more than 100 hectares (250 acres) of vineyards are cultivated by over 100 growers. Most of these growers are part-time or hobbyists, although there are around 20 who could be described as commercial to one extent or another.

✓ *Genoels-Elderen* (Chardonnay Goud, Zwarte Parel, Maastricht Riesling)
• *Peter Colemont* (Chardonnay Clos d Opleeuw)

DENMARK
There are 25 hectares (62 acres) of vines in this country. Even more amazingly, the EU has limited growth to no more than 99 hectares (245 acres). There are nine commercial producers, the oldest of which is Domain Aalsgaard, which was established in 1975. Chateau Lille Gadegard produced its first vintage in 2003 on Bornholm, a Danish island in Eastsee, to the north of Poland.

IRELAND
Better suited to stout and whiskey, Ireland had absolutely no winemaking history when, in 1972, Michael O'Callaghan planted Müller-Thurgau vines at Mallow in County Cork. O'Callaghan has just over 1 hectare (2.5 acres) of exclusively Reichensteiner vines nowadays, and his wine is sold exclusively in the restaurant of his country house hotel, Longueville House. Just 5 kilometres (3 miles) away from Mallow is another Irish vineyard, called Blackwater Valley, where owner Dr Christopher has 5 hectares (12 acres), growing Reichensteiner, Madeleine Angevine, and Seyval Blanc. Another venture, West Waterford Vineyards at Cappoquin, has 2,000 vines growing in the Blackwater River Valley.

LATVIA
Jukka Huttunen tends 160 wine-producing vines planted in 2001 on ground warmed by buried coolant pipes from Olkiluoto nuclear power station. At 61° 13′ latitude, this is the most northerly vineyard in the world.

LIECHTENSTEIN
Situated between Germany and Switzerland, this tiny principality grows just 15 hectares (37 acres) of planted vines. They are primarily Pinot Noir and Chardonnay and are mostly owned by the Crown Prince through his private winery, the Hofkellerei Fürsten von Liechtenstein.

NETHERLANDS
Although the Netherlands is north of Belgium, and therefore would seem an even more unlikely location for growing vines, almost all its vines grow east of Maastricht, so they are actually situated farther south than the vineyards in the Belgian part of Brabant. There are over 100 growers farming 50 hectares (124 acres) of

CLOS D'OPLEEUW, BELGIUM
A true clos *in the Haspengouw AOC, the Clos d'Opleeuw is owned by Peter Colemont, who learned viticulture from Burgundy's Bernard Dugat-Py.*

vines, primarily consisting of Riesling, Müller-Thurgau, Auxerrois, and the inevitable German crosses.

✓ *Apostelhoeve* (Auxerrois, Riesling)

NORWAY
The wine-producing Hallingstad vineyard was planted close to Harten (59° 24′) in 1992 by Sveier Hansen, who exports to the United States.

POLAND
Vines have been grown in Poland since at least the 14th century but ceased production during the Communist era. However, a few isolated areas were replanted a few years before Solidarity changed the face of Europe forever in 1989. These vineyards were confined to the Carpathian Mountains in the very south of the country, but when Poland became a member of the EU in 2003, the Polish Wine Institute was established, and hundreds of vineyards were created in six Polish wine regions (Zielona Góra-Wielkopolskie, Central and Northern Poland, Lower Silesia, Malopolska-Vistula-Lubelskie, Malopolska-Vistula-Świętokrzyskie, and Carpathia), where no fewer than 87 wineries officially exist, although most of these are not commercial enterprises by international standards. Four of the more important wineries are Winnica Golesz, Winnica Jasiel, Winnice Jaworek, and Winnica Pałac Mierzęcin.

SWEDEN
Although Akessons have produced sparkling wine since 1985, the grapes were not grown in Sweden. The first three vineyards to be established in this country are Blaxta Vingård (planted in 2000, first wines in 2002) southwest of Stockholm near Flen (59° 03′), and two in the Skåne region farther south: Kullabygden Vingård (planted in 2000, first wines in 2002) near Helsingborg, and the Nangijala Vingård (planted in 2001, first wines in 2003) near Malmö.

The WINES of
SOUTHEASTERN
EUROPE

ALMOST ALL THE COUNTRIES IN Southeastern Europe have the capacity to become major players in the global wine market, but Hungary has the lead and, probably, the most potential of all. It leads because Tokaji is already regarded as one of the world's greatest classic wines and because its government had been dabbling in a mixed-market economy long before the collapse of Communism, whereas the other countries in the Eastern Bloc and former USSR were – and still are – struggling. Tokaji gives Hungary instant status in the wine world, and this attracts international investors, but the role of a botrytized wine is very small in the scheme of things. Red wine is Hungary's future, and it has a long way to go in honing regional styles and developing markets for this wine. Indeed, all the countries in this region should be exploiting their red wine potential, as their various *terroirs* are better suited to it than to white wine, whatever they happen to be making at the moment.

DISZNÓKŐ DŰLŐ, TOKAJ, HUNGARY
This is the Disznókő dűlő (vineyard), from which the Disznókő Tokaji estate took its name. The grapes from these Furmint vines are destined for Disznókő's best aszú wines. The building visible here is a tractor garage designed by Ybl-prize winning architect Dezső Ekler.

BULGARIA

Bulgarian wines, particularly Cabernet Sauvignon, were affordably fashionable in the West between the late 1970s and early 1990s, but the wine industry lost its way after the collapse of Communism and has taken a long time to find its feet in a free-market economy.

IT WAS NOT UNTIL THE 1970s that the Bulgarians made any real effort to export their wines. Cabernet Sauvignon was the most fashionable wine grape, and Bordeaux reigned supreme, but an economic depression put wine drinkers on the lookout for cheaper alternatives, and Cabernet Sauvignon from Bulgaria's Suhindol region was not just cheap, it was also a darn sight better than a lot of unclassified claret at twice the price. Indeed, it was almost a pastiche of the ideal red wine as far as Western wine drinkers were concerned, and Pepsi cola was the reason. Pepsi wanted to sell cola behind the iron curtain, but Bulgaria had no hard currency, so Pepsi provided the Suhindol winery with expertise from UC Davis, whose formularized Cabernet Sauvignon opened the door for sales of Pepsi!

Domaine Boyar was the very first private wine company to be formed under democracy. This put it one step ahead in terms of sourcing by enabling the company to forge links with the best vineyards and wineries around the country, resulting in some of Bulgaria's finest wines, but Domaine Boyar was also one of the producers whose misguided international marketing strategy could have ruined the Bulgarian wine image when it launched its Blueridge export brand in 1999. There are still several Bulgarian brands that are too Anglicized but none that are quite as blatantly dressed up as New World fodder.

There is a difference between international input and internationalization, and this distinction now appears to be fully appreciated. With 40 years' experience of classic grape varieties, it would be wrong to impose any sort of ABC restriction, but now is

FACTORS AFFECTING TASTE AND QUALITY

LOCATION
Situated in the centre of the Balkan Peninsula, Bulgaria's eastern border is formed by the Black Sea, while its neighbours to the north, west, and south are respectively Romania, Serbia/Macedonia, and Greece/Turkey.

CLIMATE
The climate is warm continental, although it is cooler in the north and more temperate towards the east due to the influence of the Black Sea. Annual rainfall averages between 47 and 95 centimetres (19 and 38 inches).

ASPECT
Vines are grown largely on the flat valley floors and coastal plains.

SOIL
Predominantly fertile alluvium in the valleys, with dark-grey and brown forest soils in the northern region, and rich, black carbonate soils in the southern region, becoming sandy in the vineyards of the southeast coastal area.

VITICULTURE AND VINIFICATION
Most vineyards are concentrated in the valleys of the Rivers Danube and Maritsa. The disruption of privatization has not been a positive factor for Bulgaria, whose vineyards are highly fractured, with many that are poorly maintained. The wineries are comparatively well equipped, and vinification methods have been updated; there is a state-of-the-art facility at Sliven (Blueridge).

GRAPE VARIETIES
Primary varieties: Cabernet Sauvignon, Gamza (Kadarka), Mavrud, Merlot, Pamid, Red Misket, Rkatsiteli, Ugni Blanc, Welschriesling
Secondary varieties: Aligoté, Cabernet Franc, Chardonnay, Dimiat, Fetjaska, Gamay, Melnik, Muskat Ottonel, Pinot Gris, Pinot Noir, Riesling, Rubin (Nebbiolo x Syrah), Sauvignon Blanc, Sylvaner, Syrah, Tamianka (Muscat Blanc à Petits Grains)

the time for its winemakers to look also to their viticultural roots. The obvious strategy would be to obtain the best clones of Gamza (a Hungarian variety, aka Kadarka, that has a long history in Bulgaria), Mavrud (potentially the most expressive), and Melnik – each easy enough to pronounce on export markets – and grow them in the best, most specific *terroirs*. To forge truly iconic

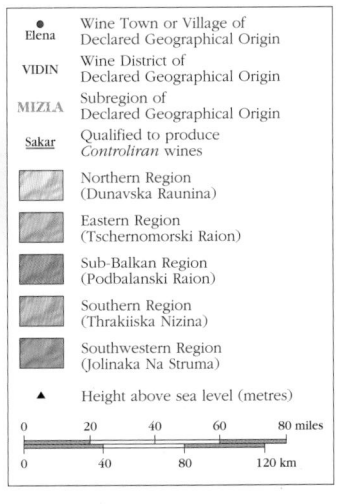

BULGARIA
Situated in the centre of the Balkan Peninsula, Bulgaria has an extremely varied landscape, many different soil types, and an attractive climate.

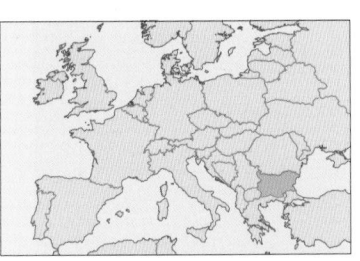

Elena	Wine Town or Village of Declared Geographical Origin
VIDIN	Wine District of Declared Geographical Origin
MIZIA	Subregion of Declared Geographical Origin
Sakar	Qualified to produce *Controliran* wines
	Northern Region (Dunavska Raunina)
	Eastern Region (Tschernomorski Raion)
	Sub-Balkan Region (Podbalanski Raion)
	Southern Region (Thrakiiska Nizina)
	Southwestern Region (Jolinaka Na Struma)
▲	Height above sea level (metres)

RECENT BULGARIAN VINTAGES

2010 Very fresh, fruity, and typical wines.

2009 Great aromatic freshness and minerality of fruit.

2008 A lovely, ripe, elegant year.

2007 Another potentially great vintage for both red and white wines, but it was spoiled by some who picked late and made heavy wines.

2006 Possibly the best vintage of the 2000s but some of the wines are over-ripe.

Bulgarian varietals would require planting in sufficiently high densities, pruning the vines to achieve ultra-low yields (being careful to maintain elegance without going the over-ripe, "dead fruit" route). Once these varieties provide Bulgaria with its own native flagship wines, the same practices could be applied to other less highly rated indigenous varieties to see if they could rise above their current reputation. For example, is Pamid the simple, light-bodied variety we imagine it to be, or is this merely the result of high-yield production? Too many Bulgarian vineyards are still being cropped at very high yields, so why not? Why couldn't Pamid be something special? In a country where the people elect former King Simeon II as prime minister, and only six months later elect a former Communist as president, anything can happen!

BULGARIAN LABEL LANGUAGE

Bjalo vino White wine
Butiliram To bottle
Cherveno vino Red wine
Controliran These wines constitute just 2 per cent of the total production of quality wines, and are made from grapes that originate from strictly defined and controlled micro-regional vineyards, with a limited maximum yield of grapes per hectare and defined minimum sugar content.
Country wine Inexpensive blended wine on a par with French *vins de pays*.
Desertno Dessert or sweet wine

Iskriashto vino Sparkling wine
Kolektziono Reserve
Lozia Vineyard
Lozova prachka Vine or vine variety
Naturalno Natural
Sladko vino Sweet wine
Reserve This term is restricted to DGO and *Controliran* wines, and indicates ageing in oak of at least three years for white and four for red, although after an intitial, indeterminate period the wines may be transferred from small *barriques* to large wooden vats.

Sostatachna zakar Semi-dry or medium wine
Suho vino Dry wine
Traditzioni Regionalni Vino Country Wine
Vino Kontrolirano Naimenovanie za Proizhod *Controliran* wine (*see Controliran*)
Vino ot Deklariran Geografski or **DGO** Wine of Declared Geographical Origin. This category constitutes 70 per cent of all Bulgarian quality wines, those made from selected grapes originating from a particular geographical region.
Vinoproizuoditel Wine producer

THE APPELLATIONS OF
BULGARIA

Note Bulgaria's quality wines are divided into two categories: wines of Declared Geographical Origin, or DGOs, which carry sub-regional, district, town, or village appellations, and *Controliran* wines, the highest-quality category, which have to be made from specified grape varieties grown in certain DGOs.

EASTERN REGION

This region accounts for 30 per cent of Bulgaria's vineyards and includes four regional DGOs. The Schumen district has long been noted for white wines, particularly those from Khan Krum, but it was only recently that they rose to international standards, thanks to Australian expertise. Other well-known Schumen Chardonnays come from Novi Pazar and Preslav. Preslav now makes good, gluggy Chardonnay-Sauvignon blends. Khan Krum is also known for its Riesling and Dimiat, which has become very fresh and tangy. South Coast Rosé is an off-dry Cabernet Sauvignon blush wine from Burgas, an under-rated district that produces many inexpensive yet very drinkable Country Wines.

🍇 Aligoté, Bolgar, Cabernet Sauvignon, Chardonnay, Dimiat, Gewürztraminer (Traminer), Pamid, Rkatsiteli, Red Misket, Riesling (Rheinriesling), Sauvignon Blanc, Tamianka, Ugni Blanc, Varneski Misket, Welschriesling (Italian Riesling)

✓ *Domaine Boyar* • *Pomorie* • *Shumen* • *Targovischte*

NORTHERN REGION

This region accounts for 35 per cent of Bulgaria's vineyards, encompassing two sub-regional DGOs. Suhindol's reputation is based on Bulgaria's best-selling Cabernet Sauvignon, but two others from the district are worth trying: the grapey-oaky Gamza, which is a *Controliran* wine, and the interesting, soft-textured Merlot-Gamza blend, equally good but only a DGO. Russe has produced gorgeously fruity, so-called "unvatted" reds and, under the guidance of winemaker Kym Milne, Lyaskovetz is now making easy-drinking, inexpensive blended whites.

🍇 Cabernet Sauvignon, Chardonnay, Gamay, Gamza, Muskat Ottonel, Pinot Noir, Red Misket, Rkatsiteli, Sauvignon Blanc, Traminer, Vrachanski Misket

✓ *Borovitza* • *Château de Val* • *Maxxima* • *Tellish* (Merlot)

SOUTHERN REGION

This region accounts for 22 per cent of Bulgaria's vineyards and encompasses eight regional DGOs. Assenovgrad is justly famous for its dark, dry, plummy-spicy Mavrud wine, which can age well for 10 or more years. Plovdiv makes fine, firm, blackcurranty Cabernet Sauvignon, as does Stara Zagora, a district that boasts a superb Cabernet Sauvignon-Merlot *Controliran* wine from Oriachovitza. Oriachovitza also makes a classy Cabernet Sauvignon Reserve. From the Strandja region comes Sakar Mountain Cabernet, one of the first wines to establish a reputation on export markets, although it is the Merlot from this area that has *Controliran* status. East of Stara Zagora is Iambol, which produces a very rich Cabernet Sauvignon Reserve in which the oak can take on a spicy-caramel complexity, while in the southeast, Elhovo churns out a much cheaper Cabernet with obvious coconutty aromas that should suit budget-conscious oak-lovers. Bessa Valley is an exciting joint venture between the Damianitza Winery, Count von Neipperg of Pomerol fame, French oenologist Mark Dworkin, and a couple of investors, who are building a Bordeaux-type wine estate with over 100 hectares (250 acres) of grapes (Malbec, Merlot, Petit Verdot, and Syrah).

🍇 Aligoté, Cabernet Sauvignon, Dimiat, Gamay, Malbec, Mavrud, Merlot, Pamid, Petit Vardot, Pinot Noir, Red Misket, Sauvignon Blanc, Syrah

✓ *Bessa Valley* • *Castra Ruba* • *Katarzyna Estate* • *Maxxima* • *Miroglio* • *Oriachovitza* • *Rumella* • *Terre Tangra* • *Todoroff* (Terres)

SOUTHWESTERN REGION

This region accounts for 6 per cent of Bulgaria's vineyards and includes four regional DGOs. The most famous wine is Melnik, which is generally well-coloured, rich, and warm, and may be tannic or soft, depending on how it is made. Damianitza Melnik is very smooth and rich. No Man's Land is pure Cabernet Sauvignon. Re Dark is a dense-coloured, super-premium wine made from Merlot. Uniquato is made from a unique early-ripening clone of Melnik known locally as Shiroka Melnishka Loza.

🍇 Cabernet Sauvignon, Chardonnay, Melnik, Merlot, Shiroka Melnishka Loza, Tamianka

✓ *Bessa Valley* • *Damianitza* (No Man's Land, Re Dark, Uniquato) • *Logodaj* • *Santa Sarah Estate*

SUB-BALKAN REGION

This region accounts for 7 per cent of vineyards and has one regional DGO. The Rozova Dolina Misket is made in the Karlovo district, and Sungurlare Misket in Slaviantzi. Both are light-golden, floral-scented, musky wines. Sliven makes one of the world's cheapest Merlot blends, using Pinot Noir to add a touch of elegance to what is a very gluggy wine indeed.

🍇 Cabernet Sauvignon, Chardonnay, Merlot, Red Misket, Riesling, Ugni Blanc

✓ *Blueridge* • *Slaviantzi* • *VINI*

HUNGARY

For Hungarian wine to prosper in the 21st century, it needs to find a flagship red. There is no denying the greatness of Tokaji. It is one of the world's truly classic wines, but it is as unreasonable to expect this country to make any global impact through Tokaji as it would be to imagine that the French wine industry could build an international reputation off the back of Sauternes. From Hungary's continental location, customers might be forgiven for thinking that it should be at least as famous for red wine as it is for sweet wine – and with a little work, Kadarka could be that wine.

THERE ARE MORE THAN 100 ancient Carpathian varieties currently catalogued, with many more in the pipeline waiting to be identified. Any of these might make Hungary's greatest red and white wines at some time in the future, but for the moment Kadarka is its best-known indigenous grape. Furthermore, it is a variety that has the potential to make a world-class wine, and it is easy for Anglo-Saxon tongues on export markets to pronounce. Kadarka could certainly produce something special in Villány and renewed efforts should be made in Eger, where "Bull's Blood" used to be 100 per cent Kadarka. All it would take is for a national- or EU-funded project to seek out potential *"grand cru"* Kadarka sites in both these regions, where trials should be held to find the best clones. When the best sites are established, they

FACTORS AFFECTING TASTE AND QUALITY

LOCATION
Hungary is sandwiched between Austria and Romania, north of Yugoslavia, in the Carpathian basin south of Slovakia.

CLIMATE
Generally a continental climate, with some Mediterranean influence in the southern wine districts. The annual mean temperature is 10.5°C (51°F), with an average rainfall of 60 centimetres (23 inches). In the Carpathian foothills of Tokaj, in northeastern Hungary, long misty autumns encourage botrytis.

ASPECT
Almost half of the country's vines are grown on the Great Plain, where the land is flat or gently undulating river plains. The rest of the country is hilly.

SOIL
Slate, basalt, clay, and loess in the west, through the sandy soils of

the Great Plain, to the clay, loess, and volcanic rock in the northeast, and volcanic, slate, and sandy soils in the south.

VITICULTURE AND VINIFICATION
Tokaji necessitates the harvesting and sorting of botrytized grapes. Otherwise, all Hungarian red and white wines are produced using standard vinification techniques, with no exceptional practices. However, a steady modernization of winemaking facilities has taken place since the 1990s.

GRAPE VARIETIES
Cabernet Franc, Cabernet Sauvignon, Chardonnay, Ezerjó, Furmint, Hárslevelü, Irsai Olivér, Kadarka, Kékfrankos (Limberger), Kékporto (Portugieser), Leányka (Fetjaska), Olaszrizling (Welschriesling), Pinot Blanc, Pinot Gris, Sauvignon Blanc, Tramini (Gewürztraminer), Zweigelt

DID YOU KNOW?

• The most famous Tokaji is Imperial Tokaji, an elixir so prized by the tsars of Russia that they maintained a detachment of Cossacks solely for the purpose of escorting convoys of the precious liquid from Hungary to the royal cellars at St Petersburg.

HUNGARY
A country that has great potential for red wine, although this is overshadowed by the history and fame of Tokaji, one of the world's classic botrytized wines.

Balaton
Badascony
Appellation named on map: eg, *Sopron*

1 ⭐ Debrői Hárslevelü
2 ⭐ Izsaki Arany Sárfehér

--- International boundary

0   20   40   60   80 miles
0   50   100 km

could be classified for a bit of media attention, then the best Kadarka clones could be farmed out to selected sites throughout other Hungarian regions to broaden the reputation of this grape variety. When Hungary can claim to produce a truly iconic red wine, then it will be the time to explore its rich patrimony of other indigenous varieties to give breadth and depth to its wine reputation. For the moment, though, its producers must focus on finding that flagship red.

When democracy arrived in 1989, Hungary had a clear advantage over other former Eastern Bloc countries because even under Communist rule it had long been dabbling with a mixed economy. Exploiting this to the full, the transition from a centrally planned economy to a market-driven one has been relatively smooth. This has provided most Hungarian industries with the economic success and stability required to attract further investment to expand and improve, but although the wine industry has enjoyed some foreign investment, it has not expanded and improved across the board. Why? Because finance alone cannot create a range of fine wines. It takes quality-conscious growers and inspirational winemakers, something that Hungary does not appear to have in any great number. There is a handful of talented producers, and that number is growing, albeit at a painfully slow pace, and there is certainly no one who comes within a mile of István Szepsy for pure genius in winemaking.

INVESTMENT IN TOKAJ
The first area that received investment was Tokaj. This is understandable, as Tokaji is the only classic wine of authentic historical reputation in all Eastern Europe. Hugh Johnson and the Australian-trained, Anglo-Danish maestro winemaker Peter Vinding-Diers (no longer involved) purchased the Royal Tokaji Wine Company in Mád and 63 hectares (156 acres) of vineyards. Interestingly, the Royal Tokaji vineyards have never been state-owned. After this dynamic duo came a number of others, including Jean-Louis Laborde of Château Clinet (Château Pajzos & Château Megyer); Ludovico Antinori (Baron Bornemisza); the D'Aulan family, formerly owners of Piper-Heidsieck (Dereszla); AXA (Disznókő); Grandes Millésimes de France (Hétszőlő); Philippines-born American Anthony Hwang (Királyudvar); and Vega Sicilia (Oremus), with the likes of Michel Rolland and Noël Pinguet consulting in some instances.

The one thing these investors have in common is a change in the methods used to produce Tokaji. It was suggested that the French were intent on making Sauternes in Hungary, and this rankled local pride, with some critics wondering "whether Tokaji should not legitimately remain an oxidative wine". Old-style Tokaji (including all the greatest Communist-era vintages that still come up at auction) was not, however, merely oxidative;

it was intentionally oxidized. Like Sherry and *vin jaune*, they were deliberately left in part-filled barrels to oxidize. However, Sherry and *vin jaune* casks are part-filled for a purpose: the ullage allows for the growth of *flor*, a froth of rare yeast that is responsible for the particular character and style of those wines. In the Tokaji process, there is no guarantee of *flor* and thus no justification for exposing the wine to the air – in which it merely oxidizes.

Tokaji old and new
It would be wrong to divide old and new style between Hungarian and foreign producers. Firstly, old style is only as old as the Communist era. There is no evidence of half-filled casks in the 19th century; this practice is not mentioned in the meticulously detailed *Tokaj-Hegyaljai Album* (1867). Secondly, not all foreign-funded ventures are successful at the new style. Some have not gone the full distance – or they have old-style stocks they are gradually disposing of by fractional blending. And it is wrong to suggest that only foreign winemakers pioneered new-wave Tokaji. The first and the best by a long chalk was István Szepsy. No one has ever made Tokaji with the purity, precision, and finesse that Szepsy can manage.

RECENT HUNGARIAN VINTAGES

2010 This year produced a small crop of very good quality.

2009 A good year for reds and dry whites.

2008 Early-drinking whites are the only rays of sunshine in this very wet year.

2007 With a perfect growing year and just the right amount of rain during the harvest to wash the grapes without causing rot, this was an excellent vintage for both red and white wines.

2006 Excellent quality for red, white, and Tokaji styles. The extreme diurnal differences resulted in exceptionally good acids and aromatics.

DID YOU KNOW?
- Tokaj is the place, Tokaji is the wine, and Tokay is the old, Anglicized spelling, which is no longer used.
- *Szamorodni* is Polish, not Hungarian, for "the way it comes" and indicates a wine to which *aszú* (over-ripe grapes for sweetening) has not been added.

HUNGARIAN LABEL LANGUAGE

Asztali bor Table wine, the lowest quality of wine.
Aszú Over-ripe grapes for sweetening Tokaji, equivalent of German *Auslese*
Bor Wine
Borkülönlegessége szölögazdaságának A speciality from the vineyards of the region named
Borvidék Wine region
Dűlő Vineyard
Édes Sweet
Fehér White
Fordítás A sweet Tokaji produced from re-used *aszúpaste*, drained from a *gönc* of *aszú* wine, re-kneaded and macerated in fresh must. The result is comparable to a 4 or 5 *puttonyos* in

sweetness, but more tannic. They say that a Fordítás from a very good year is often better than an *aszú* from a poor vintage, but I have yet to see this difference demonstrated by the same Tokaji producer.
Habzó Sparkling
Hordó Cask or barrel
Jegbor Ice wine, or *Eiswein*
Késői Szüretelésű Late harvest
Kímert bor Ordinary wine
Kötnyéki bor Country wine
Különleges minőségű Official denomination denoting "special quality", placing it above Minősegi bor.
Máslás A dry version of Fordítás (*see*

Fordítás), but fermented on the unpressed lees of an *aszú* wine, with much less lees to wine ratio. Máslás literally means "copy".
Minösegi bor Quality wine, equivalent to French AOC.
Országos Borminősitő Bizottság or **OBB** National Wine Qualification Board
Országos Borminősitő Intézet or **OBI** State Wine Qualification Institute
Palack Bottle
Palackzás Bottling
Palackozott Bottled
Pezsgo Sparkling
Pince Cellar
Siller A dark rosé or light red

Szamorodni Literally "as it comes", the term often refers to Tokaji that has not been specially treated with *aszú* and is therefore usually dry, though it can be used for other wines.
Száraz Dry
Szőlő Grapes
Szőlőbirtok Wine estate
Szőlőskert Vineyard
Tájbor Country wine, equivalent to a French *vin de pays*
Termelő Production
Tőke Vine
Töppedt szőlőből készült Botrytis selection
Vörös Red

THE APPELLATIONS OF
HUNGARY

Note DHC stands for *Districtus Hungaricus Controllatus*, the Hungarian equivalent of the French AOC system.

ASZÁR-NESZMÉLY DHC

Winemaking traditions date back to the Middle Ages. Vineyards were cultivated along the lines of large estates as from the 18th century, with the famous Esterházi Csákvári estate considered to be a model vineyard and cellars in the 19th century. Most soils are loess-based. The climate is milder than the surrounding Great Plains area, with less risk of spring and autumn frost. Mostly fresh, fragrant, lively white wines. The internationally known Hilltops winery produces over 50 different wines every year in Neszmély.

🏵 Chardonnay, Cserszegi Fûszeres, Királylányka, Irsai Olivér, Olaszrizling, Pinot Gris, Sauvignon Blanc, Szürkebarát

✓ *Hilltops* (Cserszegi Fûszeres, Riverview Cabernet Sauvignon, Virgin Vintage Chardonnay, Virgin Vintage Sauvignon Blanc)

BADACSONY DHC

With its south-facing volcanic slopes on the northerly shores of Lake Balaton, Europe's largest lake, Badacsony is noted for its own indigenous grape called Kéknyelú. This increasingly rare white variety has excellent potential for full-bodied white wines, with a fiery palate, fine acids, and an intensive, aromatic bouquet, but often produces a disappointing quality.

🏵 Kékfrankos, Kéknyelu, Olaszrizling, Szürkebarát

✓ *Szent Orbán Pince* (Szőlősgyöröki Olaszrizling) • *Szeremley* (Kéknyelu, Szürkebarát, Tihanyi Kékfrankos)

BALATONBOGLÁR DHC

The winemaking potential of Lake Balaton's south shore was seldom fulfilled until the early 1990s, when Australian flying winemaker Kym Milne started producing extremely rich, oak-aged Chardonnay at the Balatonboglár Winery under the Chapel Hill label. With Master of Wine Milne still in charge, ably assisted by Kiwi Clive Hartnell, and fellow Australian Richard Smart advising in the vineyard, the quality at Chapel Hill has strengthened in the 2000s. Other products from the Balatonboglár Winery are far less exciting, and some producers churn out a lot of very second-rate wines, particularly in the semi-sweet Olaszrizling category.

🏵 Chardonnay, Cserszegi Fûszeres, Kékfrankos, Királyleányka, Merlot, Olaszrizling, Rizlingszilváni, Szürkebarát, Sauvignon Blanc

✓ *Ottó Légli* (Szőlőskislaki Barrique Chardonnay)

BALATONFELVIDÉK DHC

With its hot, sunny, Mediterranean climate, and the extraordinary beauty of this area, it is no surprise that so many artists have set up home here. The best wines are full-bodied, with a fine fragrance and crisp acidity.

🏵 Chardonnay, Olaszrizling, Szürkebarát

BALATONFÜRED-CSOPAK DHC

On the northern shore of Lake Balaton, viticulture and winemaking have prospered here since Roman times. The wines are full-bodied yet fragrant, with fine acidity.

🏵 Cabernet Sauvignon, Chardonnay, Merlot, Olaszrizling, Rizlingszilváni, Tramini

✓ *Isván Jásdi* (Csopaki Olaszrizling)

BÜKK DHC

Grown on the southern and southwestern slopes of the Bükk Mountains, where Kékfrankos and Leányka are the major varieties, but produce wines that are lighter than those of neighbouring Eger. As in Eger and Tokaj farther east, cellars have long been hewn out of rhyolite-tuffa rock, with more than 1,000 such cellars carved out of the slopes of Avas.

🏵 Cserszegi Fûszeres, Kékfrankos, Olaszrizling, Leányka

CSONGRÁD DHC

This Great Plain wine region is the warmest and sunniest part of the country during the vegetation period of the vine. Principally, the red and rosé wines are renowned. The white wines of the region contain moderate acids and are rich in fragrance and aroma. The red wines are characterized by richness in colouring agents, pleasant acerbity, and excellent aroma.

🏵 Kadarka, Kékfrankos, Olaszrizling, Zweigelt

DEBRŐI HÁRSLEVELŰ DHC

A single-commune, pure varietal appellation for the famed Hárslevelű growing in Debrői and surrounding villages in the Eger region.

EGER DHC

Located halfway between Budapest and Tokaj is Eger, a region famous for the legend of Egri Bikavér, or "Bull's Blood of Eger". The story dates from 1552, when the fortress of Eger, fiercely defended by István Dobó and his Magyars, was besieged by the numerically superior force of the Turkish army, led by Ali Pasha. It is said that, throughout the battle, the Magyars drank copious quantities of the local wine and that when the Turks saw the beards of their ferocious enemies stained red with wine, they ran in terror, thinking that all Magyars gained their strength by drinking the blood of bulls. Hence the name of this wine was born. Other regions produce Bikavér, but Egri Bikavér is the Bull's Blood that is most famously associated with the legend. It was never a pretentious wine, but it was traditionally a robust, Kadarka-based red of firm structure and fiery flavour.

🏵 Cabernet Franc, Cabernet Sauvignon, Kadarka, Kékfrankos, Kékoportó, Leányka, Merlot, Olaszrizling

✓ *GIA* (Bikavér, Cabernet Sauvignon, Chardonnay) • *István Balla* (Barrique Olaszrizling) • *József Hagymási* (Cabernet Sauvignon) • *Thummerer* (Bikavér, Kékfrankos, Vili Papa Cuvee) • *Tibor Gál* (Bikavér) • *Béla Vincze* (Cabernet Franc)

ETYEK-BUDA DHC

Etyek-Buda is supposedly Hungary's sparkling wine region, but the quality of its largest producer, Törley, leaves much to be desired, and more vineyards are moving over to still, dry white wines from individual estates, but since this region overlaps the prettier, hilly half of Budapest, it receives a lot of attention. The vines grow on a black loess soil over a limestone base, in a dry, sunny, but windy climate.

🏵 Chardonnay, Királyleányka, Olaszrizling, Pinot Blanc, Pinot Gris, Sauvignon Blanc

✓ *Nyakashegy* (Budai Chardonnay)

HAJÓS-BAJA DHC

The white wines of this Great Plains region are rich in fragrance and aroma, while the reds rival the highly ranked wines produced in hilly regions.

🏵 Cabernet Franc, Cabernet Sauvignon, Kadarka, Kékfrankos, Merlot, Olaszrizling, Riesling

IZSAKI ARANY SÁRFEHÉR DHC

A single-commune, pure-varietal appellation for Arany Sárfehér growing in Izsaki and surrounding villages in the Kunság region. Arany Sárfehér typically yields a pale-coloured wine with green hues, with excellent acidity and minerality.

KUNSÁG DHC

This Great Plain wine region is the largest wine region in Hungary. The wines of this region can be rich in fragrance and flavours.

🏵 Ezerjó, Cserszegi Fûszeres, Kékfrankos, Olaszrizling

MÁTRA DHC

At Gyöngyös the first truly excellent Hungarian dry white wine was produced in the early 1980s, and no prizes for guessing that it was made from Chardonnay. But it was essential to demonstrate what could be done with grapes of a certain quality and the right technology. That particular Chardonnay steadily improved until 1995, when it jumped up another notch in quality, and Sauvignon Blanc can be almost as successful, but nowadays winemakers are looking at achieving at least the same general quality with local varieties, such as Chardonnay, Hárslevelű, and Muskotály.

🏵 Chardonnay, Hárslevelű, Kékfrankos, Müller-Thurgau, Muscat Ottonel, Muskotály, Olaszrizling, Tramini, Rizlingszilváni, Sauvignon Blanc, Zweigelt

MÓR DHC

Ezerjó is the best grape variety suited to this region, where it makes one of Hungary's most distinctive dry white wines.

🏵 Ezerjó, Leanyka, Olaszrizling, Rizlingszilvani, Tramini

NAGU-SOMLÓ DHC

This is the smallest wine region of Hungary. Its wines are fiery, with a heavy, masculine character, and they have high acid and alcohol content. The long ageing in wooden barrels produces a fine, elegant harmony of fragrance, taste, and aroma. According to popular memory, in the imperial court of Vienna, the newlyweds drank Somló wines on their wedding night to promote the birth of a male heir to the throne.

🍇 Chardonnay, Furmint, Hárslevelű, Juhfark, Olaszrizling, Tramini

✓ *Béla Fekete* (Chardonnay) • *Joózsef Laposa* (Bazalt Borhaz Olaszrizling)

PANNONHALMA DHC

Viticulture dates back to 996, when Benedictines settled on St Martin Mountain, and established Hungary's first monastery at Pannonhalma. The first document mentioning vinegrowing is the deed of foundation of this monastery. The fresh, crisp, varietally pure Pannonhalmi Sauvignon Blanc from Szőllősi Mihály Pricészette winery is the best dry Hungarian white wine I have tasted.

🍇 Chardonnay, Cserszegi Fûszeres, Irsai Olivér, Királyleányka, Müller-Thurgau, Olaszrizling, Riesling, Tramini

✓ *Szőllősi Mihály Pricészette* (Sauvignon Blanc)

PECS DHC

Vineyards here scattered over more than 80 kilometres (50 miles) of warm slopes around the historic city of Pécs, which has long been noted for Olaszrizling, although the traditional Furmint and Cirfandli vines are giving way to international varieties.

🍇 Cabernet Franc, Cabernet Sauvignon, Chardonnay, Cirfandli, Furmint, Merlot, Olaszrizling, Pinot Noir, Riesling, Rizlingszilváni, Sauvignon Blanc

✓ *Ebner Andreas* (Cosmo Cuvée)

SOPRON DHC

One of the most ancient wine regions of Hungary, the Sopron lies on the foothills of the Alps in the northwestern corner of the country. For centuries, the city of Sopron itself enjoyed thriving trade and, surprisingly, until the 18th century Sopron was reputedly the largest wine-trading centre in central Europe. Sopron is a potentially fine wine region, where the Kékfrankos grape is most famous, although the quality in the vineyard and the bottle could and should be significantly superior to the light, everyday-drinking wines that are commonplace in this region. Although essentially a red wine region, Sopron does also produce some interesting whites.

🍇 Cabernet Franc, Kékfrankos, Leányka, Sauvignon Blanc, Zöld Veltelini, Zweigelt

✓ *Franz Weninger* (Kékfrankos, Merlot, Rosé, Syrah) • *Hilltop* (Soproni Sauvignon Blanc)

SZEKSZÁRD DHC

The Szekszárd vineyards have been noted for their wines since Roman times and for red wines since the 15th century. In this sunny wine region with its greater Mediterranean influence, excellent red wines can be produced, which are known for their velvety texture, and often show more elegance than the red wines of Villány. The Szekszárdi Bikavér (Bull's Blood of Szekszárd) is ranked outstandingly high. The indigenous Kadarka variety gives excellent flavoured, deep red wine, plus a local speciality,

Nemes Kadar, made from botrytized grapes. Very good Kékfrankos, Cabernet Sauvignon, and some stunning Merlot are also produced.

🍇 Cabernet Sauvignon, Kadarka, Kékfrankos, Merlot, Olaszrizling, Rizlingszilváni

✓ *Dúzsi Tamás* (Kékfrankos Rozé) • *Péter Vida* (Cabernet Franc-Merlot) • *Szent Gaál Kastély* (Merlot) • *Takler Pince* (Cabernet Sauvignon Selection, Primarius Merlot, Regnum Monarchia Gold Selection) • *Vesztergombi* (Cabernet Sauvignon)

TOKAJ-HEGYALJA DHC

As with all great sweet wines, Tokaji owes its quality and character to over-ripe, semi-dried grapes (Furmint and Hárslevelű), some of which have been affected by *Botrytis cinerea*, or noble rot. The essential difference today is that this selection is now made in the vineyard rather than the winery. The origin of the Aszú Puttonyos name that is used to predicate the sweetness of Tokaji is a wooden hod called a *putton*. Traditionally, the shrivelled (*aszú*) grapes (that is, botrytized) were collected in these *puttonyos* (plural) and left for six to eight days. This allowed time for highly concentrated juice to collect at the bottom of the container (and this also started the oxidative process). This juice, known as *essencia*, was used for sweetening purposes. Each *putton* held 25 kilograms (50 pounds) of *aszú* grapes, yet yielded only a quarter of a pint of pure *essencia*. After the *essencia* was removed for the legendary Tokaji Essencia, the *putton* of *aszú* grapes would be kneaded into paste and added to a cask of dry base wine made from a blend of non-botrytized Furmint and Hárslevelű grapes. In the Communist era, these casks were deliberately not filled up, to encourage the oxidized side of Tokaji's character. The sweetness of the Tokaji depended on how many *puttonyos* were added to the dry base wine. Today the process is far more like that for Sauternes, and the grapes are not left hanging around in a wooden bucket for a week or so, although the *puttonyos* grading is still used. The wines with their modern-day sweetness measured in grams of residual sugar per litre are: Száraz (dry, 0–4g); Edes (sweet, 20–50g); Aszú 2 Puttonyos (allowed but not made since 1938, 50–60g); Aszú 3 Puttonyos (60–90g); Aszú 4 Puttonyos (90–120g); Aszú 5 Puttonyos (120–

150g); Aszú 6 Puttonyos (150–180g); Aszú Essencia or Aszúéssencia (180–450g); and Essencia or Natúressencia (pure *aszú*, 450–850g).

🍇 Furmint, Hárslevelű, Sárga Muskotály, Zeta (formerly Oremus)

✓ *Arvay és Társa* • *Borok Úri* • *Disznókő* • *Dobogó* • *István Szepsy* • *Királyudvar* • *Oremus* • *Pajzos* • *Patricus* • *Pendits*

TOLNA DHC

Although Tolna became a wine region in its own right in 1998, winemaking traditions go back centuries, and were strengthened in the 16th century, when the area was settled by Germans.

🍇 Chardonnay, Grüner Veltliner, Kadarka, Kékfrankos, Müller-Thurgau, Olaszrizling

VILLÁNY DHC

In Villány, the more Mediterranean climate produces some of Hungary's best red wines, including dark, spicy Kadarka and more velvety Bordeaux varietals. The red wine potential of Villány is probably the greatest of all of the 22 Hungarian wine regions. The wines of Siklós are white and fiery, including those that have been produced from late-harvested grapes, although they are more *passerillé* in style than botrytized.

🍇 Cabernet Sauvignon, Cabernet Franc, Hárslevelű, Kékporto, Olaszrizling, Pinot Noir, Zweigelt

✓ *Attila Gere* (Kopár Villanyi Cuvée, Merlot Solus) • *Gere Tamás Pincészet* • *Malatinszky* • *Tiffán* (Villányi Cuvée) • *Vylyan Pincészet*

ZALA DHC

On the eastern and northeastern flank of Lake Balaton. The Zala hills are known for their so-called harrow-cellars, made in the 19th century from timbers and plastered inside and out with clay. The Balatonmelléke, with its brown forest soils and mild, wet climate, was revived as a wine region in 1998.

🍇 Chardonnay, Kékfrankos, Müller-Thurgau, Olaszrizling, Oportó, Rizlingszilváni, Tramini, Zöld Veltelini (Veltliner), Zweigelt

✓ *László Bussay* (Csörnyeföldi Szürkebarát)

THE VILLAGE OF TOLSCVA, TOKAJ
The south- and southwest-facing hillside vineyards overlooking Tolscva (or Tolcsva) are among the 23 most highly prized vineyards in the Tokaj region, as the Bodrog River creates optimal conditions for noble rot.

ROMANIA

Romania has at least as much potential as any other Eastern European winemaking country. It has been growing French varieties since its recovery from phylloxera and has an increasing reputation for Pinot Noir, particularly from the Dealul Mare region. However, Romania has received a fraction of the foreign investment that Hungary has enjoyed, and not only needs both financial and technical expertise to compete internationally, but has the potential to repay any such investments.

THE BIGGEST PROBLEM IN ROMANIA has been a lack of consistency. Since the early 1990s, we have seen flashes of promise – from exciting Gewürztraminer from Transilvania to deep, dark, brooding Cabernet Sauvignon from Dealul Mare, only to see some of these wines followed up by vintages of barely *vin de table* quality. Only a handful of wineries have received significant foreign investment and expertise, and it is no coincidence that they generally make the best wines in Romania today.

MORE IMPORTANT THAN RUSSIA

Viticulture and winemaking is an old tradition in Romania, dating back 4,000 years. In Europe, only France, Italy, Spain, and Germany are bigger wine-producing countries. Romania is significantly more important than Hungary or Russia in winemaking terms. As in Bulgaria, there was a massive planting programme in the 1960s, when the country was geared up to

LOW-TECH VINEYARDS
Rickety pergolas providing support for vines and old thatched-roofed buildings reflect the conditions that most of Romania's agricultural industry has survived on since medieval times.

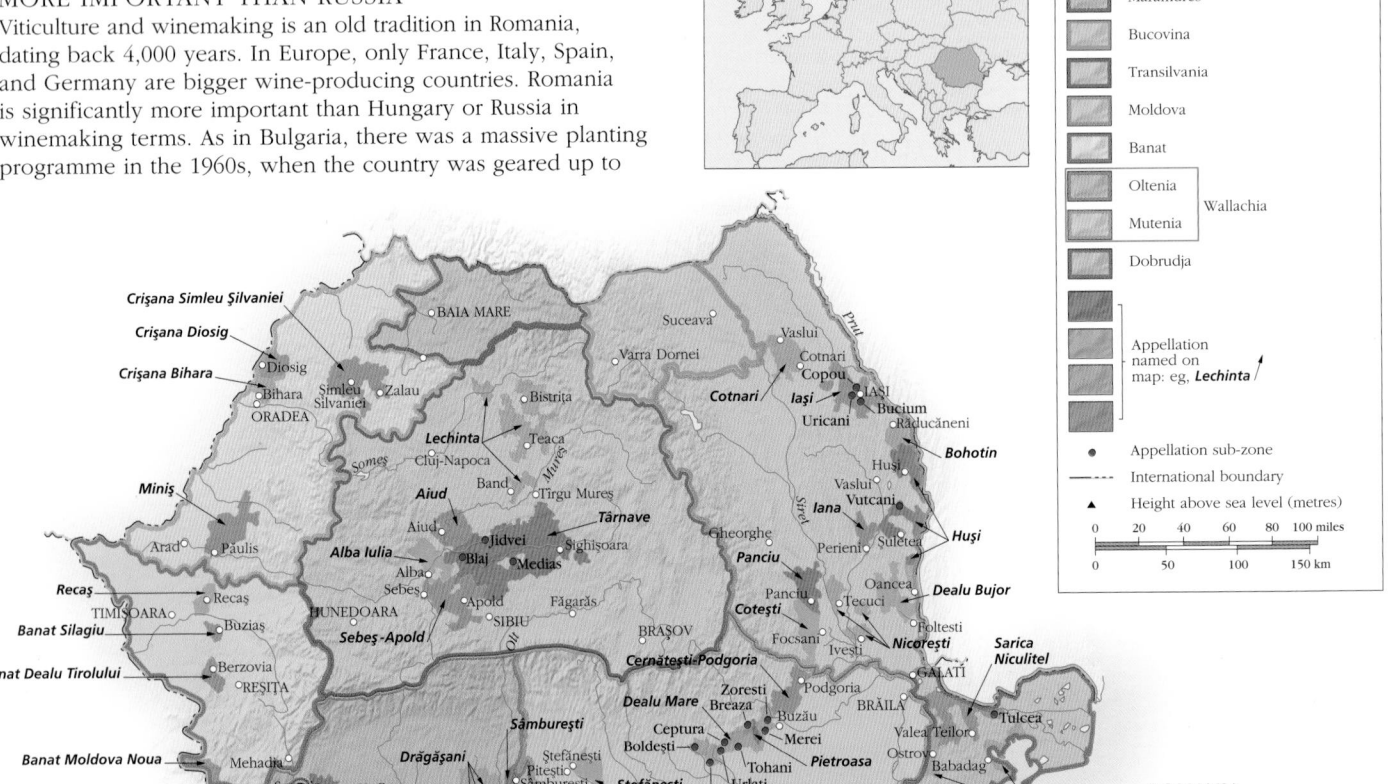

Legend:
- Crisana
- Maramures
- Bucovina
- Transilvania
- Moldova
- Banat
- Oltenia — Wallachia
- Mutenia — Wallachia
- Dobrudja
- Appellation named on map: eg, *Lechinta*
- • Appellation sub-zone
- - - International boundary
- ▲ Height above sea level (metres)

0 20 40 60 80 100 miles
0   50   100   150 km

ROMANIA
The main winemaking areas in Romania are scattered throughout the country: in the Carpathian foothills, on the plateau lands of Dobrudja, and on the plains.

RECENT ROMANIAN VINTAGES

2010 An excellent all-round vintage.

2009 Large harvest of above-average quality.

2008 This is a good white-wine vintage.

2007 Very good red-wine vintage from those producers who avoided the rot.

2006 A good, solid vintage.

supply Comecon states with bulk-blending fodder, but most wine today is purchased and consumed on the home market. After the fall of Ceausescu in December 1989, the area under vine increased, going against the trend of other Eastern Bloc wine-producing countries. However, much of the replanting saw *vinifera* varieties being replaced with hybrids, as the new private owners did not know how to look after their vineyards – or if they did, they could not care less – and hybrids are much hardier, yielding the highest volumes for the least effort. This expansion continued until 1995, when it started to decline. Both new planting and the replanting of old vineyards now represent less than two per cent of the total area under vine, with a staggering amount of land planted with hybrids (estimates vary wildly between the official 30,000 hectares and external observers' 119,000 hectares). Furthermore, despite privatization, almost 23 per cent of the vineyards still belong to the Romanian state. There are now eight wine regions encompassing 37 winegrowing districts, and vineyard registration is slowly coming into operation in preparation for Romania's EU membership in 2007–2010. The two largest wine-producing regions, Moldova and Mutenia, together account for more than 60 per cent of all Romanian wines.

THE FUTURE

Despite the difficulties of the past and accession to the EU, which will present the growers with as many problems as solutions, Romania has an excellent future – if it can be grasped. According to pre-membership agreements between Romania and the EU, all hybrids must be removed by 2014; although, on past experience, this will no doubt be extended. And extended. And extended. Far more

FACTORS AFFECTING TASTE AND QUALITY

LOCATION
The main wine-producing areas in Romania spread from Iaşi in the northeast of the country down through the Carpathian foothills to the Danube River.

CLIMATE
A continental climate, with hot summers and cold winters, which are tempered only in the southeast by the Black Sea.

ASPECT
Romanian vines are grown on all types of land – from the plains through the plateau land of Dobrudja to the slopes of the Carpathian foothills.

SOIL
A wide variety of soil types, including the generally sandy-alluvial plains and the stony, hillside soils of Banat; the limestone of Dobrudja; the oolitic limestone of Mutenia's Pietroasele vineyards; and the stony fringes of the Carpathian Mountains.

VITICULTURE AND VINIFICATION
Although some modernization of facilities has taken place since the 1990s, and a few new wineries have been established, at least half the wines are produced in antiquated conditions, and almost two-thirds must be made from hybrids, whatever the official statistics state.

GRAPE VARIETIES
Băbeaskă, Băbeaskă Neagră, Cabernet Sauvignon, Fetească Regălă, Galbenă Uriasa (Galbena), Galbenă Ourata (Galbena), Grasă, Merlot, Pinot Gris, Pinot Noir, Riesling, Tămaioasă (Muscat Blanc à Petits Grains), Welschriesling

important than replanting hybrid vines with *vinifera* is to ensure that only the best vineyards are replanted and that an emphasis is put on growing the best indigenous varieties, such as those of the Fetească family: Fetească Albă, Fetească Neagră, and Fetească Regălă. Other potentially interesting local varieties include Băbeaskă, Busuioaca, Francusa, Galbenă, Grasă, and Tămaîoasă. Most wines currently produced from these grapes are a bit rustic, but they do show promise. Once the clones are sorted out; the vines are grown in the best-suited sites, at low yields; and skilful winemakers are employed to hone the style of the wines they produce, there will be no stopping Romania taking its rightful place in the world of wine.

NEW VINEYARDS IN DEALUL MARE
A vineyard is staked out, waiting to support new vine growth in the Dealul Mare district of Mutenia.

ROMANIAN LABEL LANGUAGE

Cules la Innobilarea Boabelor (CIB) Equivalent to *Beerenauslese* or above (a minimum of 112° *Oechsle*)

Cules la Maturiate Deplina (CMD) Similar to a high *Spätlese* (a minimum of 95° *Oechsle*)

Cules la Maturiate Innobilarea (CMI) Similar to a high *Auslese* (a minimum of 100° *Oechsle*)

Dulce Sweet

Edelbeerenlese Equivalent to *Beerenauslese* or above (a minimum of 112° *Oechsle*)

Edelreiflese Equivalent to *Auslese* or above (a minimum of 100° *Oechsle*)

Imbuteliat Bottled

IVV This stands for cooperative and should be followed by its name or location.

Pivnită Cellar

Recolta Vintage

Sec Dry

Spumos Sparkling

Strugure Grape

Vie Vine

Viile Vineyard

Vin alb White wine

Vin de masă Table wine

Vin rose Rosé wine

Vin rosu Red wine

Vin superior Superior wine

Vin usor Light wine

Vollreiflese Similar to a high *Spätlese* (a minimum of 95° *Oechsle*)

VSO Basic quality-wine designation

VSOC Categorized-quality wine designation similar to Germany's QmP and covering *Edelbeerenlese* (CIB), *Edelreiflese* (CMI), and *Vollreiflese* (CMD)

THE APPELLATIONS OF
ROMANIA

BANAT

Although Banat is one of the better known wine regions in Romania – and has been since the 1980s – it is the smallest by a large margin, representing less than two per cent of the country's vineyards. The sandy plain of the Teremia district is best known for its large production of eminently drinkable white wines, while the mountain slopes of Recaş-Tirol produce Valea Lunga, a pleasant, light-bodied red wine.

🍇 Cabernet Sauvignon, Cadarca, Fetească Regală, Merlot, Mustoasă, Pinot Noir, Riesling

✓ *Recaş*

BUCOVINA

Despite the name, there is no connotation of wine, since Bucovina means "beech land" and refers to a forested area between the Carpathian Mountains and the Prut River.

CRIŞANA

Formerly part of the Banat region, the hilly Minis-Maderat area provides excellent, inexpensive reds from Cadarca, Pinot Noir, Cabernet Sauvignon, and Merlot grapes grown on stony terraces. Diosig produces acidic wines that are ideal for brandy distillation.

🍇 Cabernet Sauvignon, Cadarca, Fetească Regală, Merlot, Mustoasă, Pinot Noir, Riesling

DOBRUDJA

Murfatlar is the most important and oldest winemaking district in Dobrudja (or Dobrogea), with well-organized vineyards on hills close to the Black Sea and an experimental state research station that has introduced many classic Western varieties. Once reliant on the region's prestigious past, the wines used to be too old, oxidized, and heavy, but they are beginning to receive the attention they deserve now that they are clean and well balanced; the lovely, late-picked, softly sweet, and stylish Gewürztraminer is a good example of this style.

🍇 Cabernet Sauvignon, Chardonnay, Gewürztraminer, Muscat Ottonel, Pinot Gris, Pinot Noir, Riesling

✓ *The Carpathian Winery* • *Murfatlar* (Ferma Noua, Trei Hectare)

MARAMURES

A breathtakingly wild and beautiful mountainous area full of rather strange but friendly people living a folksy, arts-and-crafts life in a place that time forgot. Maramures is a white-wine-only region.

🍇 Burgund Mare, Cabernet Sauvignon, Cadarca, Fetească Regală, Merlot, Muscat Ottonel, Pinot Noir, Welschrieling

MOLDOVA

The vineyards of Odobesti surrounding the industrial town of Focsani produce quantities of rather ordinary red and white wine. There are, however, exceptions: Cotesti, for example, has a good reputation for Pinot Noir and Merlot, while Nicoresti is known for its full-coloured, spicy red wine produced from the Băbească grape. The vineyards of Cotnari are the most famous in Romania; their reputation dates back to the

15th century. The wine is a rich dessert wine, not unlike Tokaji but not as complex. The Bucium hills of Visan and Doi Peri overlook the city of Iaşi and the cool conditions are reflected in Cabernet Sauvignon wines that have crisp, leafy characteristics.

🍇 Băbească, Cabernet Sauvignon, Fetească Albă, Fetească Neagră, Grasă, Merlot, Pinot Noir, Welschriesling

MUTENIA

Dealul Mare is located to the north of Bucharest, stretching across the lower, southeast-facing slopes of the Carpathian Mountains. It is famous for Pinot Noir, Cabernet Sauvignon, and Merlot. There is a small area of chalky soil within this district that has a special microclimate best suited to the production of sweet white wines with fine, balancing acidity. It is here that the vineyards of Pietroasele are situated. The area's Tămâioasă or "Frankincense" grape is a Muscat-related variety that makes a lusciously sweet, gold-coloured wine of very expressive quality. One of the most remarkable Romanian wines I have tasted was a beautiful, botrytized rosé *Edelbeerenlese* version of the normally lacklustre Fetească Neagră grape.

🍇 Băbească Neagră, Cabernet Sauvignon, Fetească Neagră, Fetească Regală, Galbenă, Merlot, Pinot Gris, Pinot Noir, Riesling, Tămâioasă

✓ *Casa Davino* • *Prahova Valley* (Cabernet

Sauvignon, Merlot) • *SERVE* (Cuvée Charlotte, Terra Romana) • *Vinarte* (Castel Bolovanu, Villa Zorilor)

OLTENIA

Simburesti in the Drăgasăni district produces Oltenia's best reds. It is also known for a full, dry red wine from the Fetească Neagră grape, as well as for Cabernet Sauvignon. The Segarcea district also produces red wines. The Pinot Noir produced here is good, although it is not as well known as the Cabernet Sauvignon. Interesting sweet wines are found on the west side of the River Oltul.

🍇 Cabernet Sauvignon, Fetească Neagră, Fetească Regală, Muscat Ottonel, Pinot Noir, Riesling, Sauvignon Blanc, Tămâioasă

✓ *Domeiul Coroanei* • *Stirbey*

TRANSILVANIA

Of all the winegrowing regions of Romania, Transilvania is perhaps the most exciting. The crisp fruit and good acidity of its white wines lies somewhere between the styles of Alsace and South Tyrol. The steep Tirnave vineyards produce good-quality white wines with more than just a hint of Germanic style and delicacy. Not surprisingly, German settlers in Transilvania introduced many of their own grape varieties to the region. The native Fetească grape is also successful.

🍇 Fetească Albă, Fetească Regală, Muscat Ottonel, Pinot Gris, Riesling, Sauvignon Blanc, Traminer, Welschriesling

✓ *Carl Reh* • *Vinarte* (Terasse Danubiane)

SLOVAKIA AND THE CZECH REPUBLIC

Slovakia has twice as much area under vine as the Czech Republic, even though it is a smaller country. However, Slovakia's vineyards are in a state of decline, and the Czech Republic is rightly better known for its beer than its wine.

ALTHOUGH THE FIRST VINES were planted in Moravia (now part of the Czech Republic) by the Romans as early as the third century AD, and winemaking in Slovakia is supposed to date back 3,000 years, none of the wines from anywhere encompassed by the borders of these countries today has ever gained sufficient repute to warrant significant exports, let alone worldwide fame. And, as with the rest of the former Eastern Bloc wine-producing countries, the period of centralized processing under Communist rule obscured whatever local reputations there were and cast a grey shadow over any individual efforts, as the vineyards were replanted high and wide for mass production.

SLOVAKIA

Most Slovakian wine is classified as lowly table wine, which would be a good thing if this were the result of a quality-conscious culling of the total production to produce stunning quality top wines, but that is not the case – the wines are naturally of a dismal quality. Potentially the quality of Slovakian wine is greater than that of the Czech Republic, but the decline in the state of the Slovakian wine industry is greater, so it will be an even tougher job to turn around. More than 85 per cent of Slovakian wine is white, with Müller-Thurgau, Ryzlink Vlašsky (Welschriesling), and Veltlinske Zelene (Grüner Veltliner) together accounting for over 60 per cent of all the vines growing in this country. Sparkling wines have been made since 1825 at Sered and are still marketed under the Hubert brand, but quality is not high.

The most intriguing wine from this country is Slovakian Tokaji, produced in the small part of the world-famous district that falls within Slovak borders. The same grapes are grown as in the rest of the Tokaji-producing region (Furmint, Hárslevelű, and Muscat), and the wine is supposedly made in a very similar style to the great Hungarian version. In truth they do not compare, but there

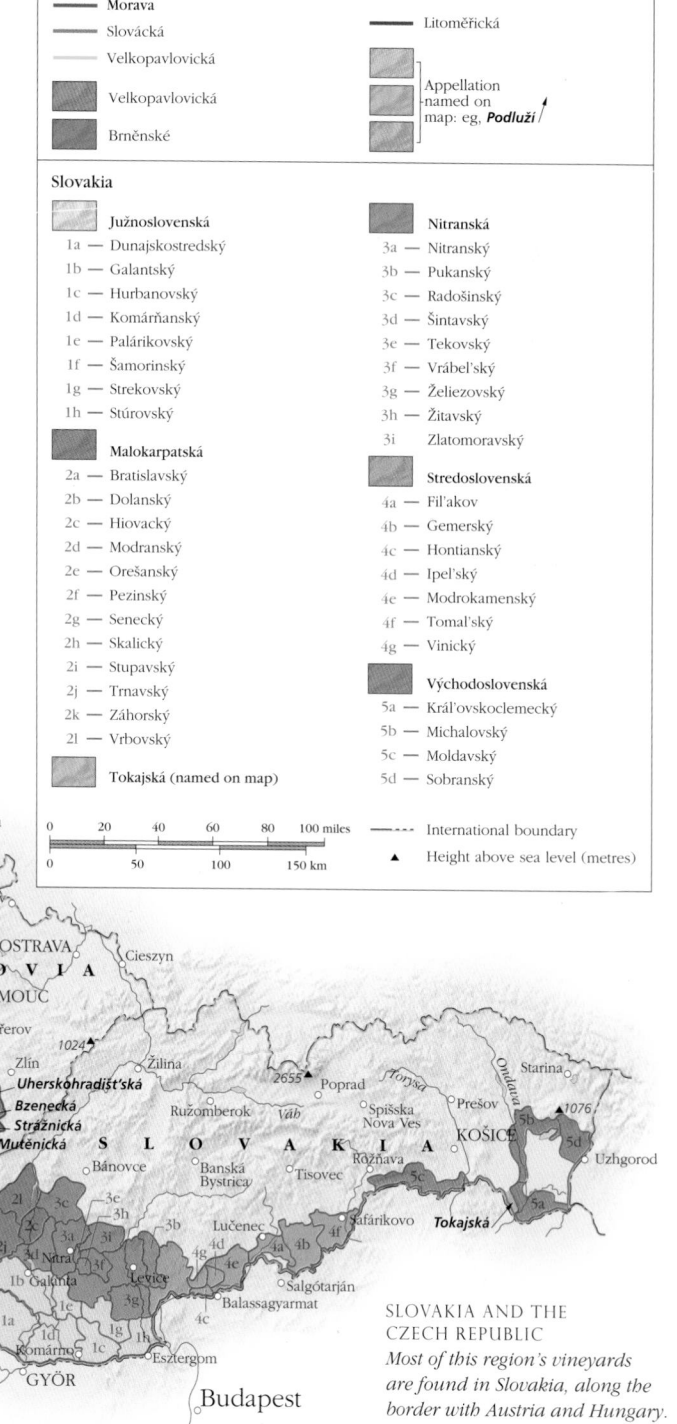

Czech Republic

Morava		
Slovácká		Litoměřická
Velkopavlovická		
Velkopavlovická		Appellation named on map: eg, *Podluží*
Brněnské		

Slovakia

Južnoslovenská		Nitranská
1a – Dunajskostredský		3a – Nitranský
1b – Galantský		3b – Pukanský
1c – Hurbanovský		3c – Radošinský
1d – Komárňanský		3d – Šintavský
1e – Palárikovský		3e – Tekovský
1f – Šamorínsky		3f – Vrábel'ský
1g – Strekovský		3g – Želiezovský
1h – Stúrovský		3h – Žitavský
		3i – Zlatomoravský
Malokarpatská		
2a – Bratislavský		**Stredoslovenská**
2b – Dolanský		4a – Fil'akov
2c – Hiovacký		4b – Gemerský
2d – Modranský		4c – Hontiansky
2e – Orešanský		4d – Ipel'ský
2f – Pezinský		4e – Modrokamenský
2g – Senecký		4f – Tomal'ský
2h – Skalický		4g – Vinický
2i – Stupavský		
2j – Trnavský		**Východoslovenská**
2k – Záhorský		5a – Král'ovskoclemecký
2l – Vrbovský		5b – Michalovský
		5c – Moldavský
Tokajská (named on map)		5d – Sobranský

0 20 40 60 80 100 miles		International boundary
0 50 100 150 km		▲ Height above sea level (metres)

SLOVAKIA AND THE CZECH REPUBLIC

Most of this region's vineyards are found in Slovakia, along the border with Austria and Hungary.

SLOVAK AND CZECH LABEL LANGUAGE

Biele víno White wine

Červené víno Red wine

Dezertné korenené víno Aromatized dessert wine

Dezertné víno Dessert wine

Dia Suitable for diabetics (in other words, sugar-free)

Jakostní víno The equivalent of a *vin de pays*; must have a natural alcoholic potential of 8–11%

Kabinet Equivalent to the German term *Kabinett*; must have a natural alcoholic potential of 11–12%

Ledové víno The equivalent of *Eiswein*, which not only must have a natural alcoholic potential of at least 16%, but the grapes must be picked at below -6°C (21°F) and must remain frozen throughout pressing

Odrodové vína Grape variety

Obsah cukru Sugar content

Polosladké Semi-sweet

Pozdní sběr Literally "late harvest"; must have a natural alcoholic potential of 12–14%

Ružové víno Rosé wine

Sladké Sweet

Slámové víno Literally a "straw wine", which not only must have a natural alcoholic potential of at least 16%, but, for 3 months prior to being pressed, must also be stored on straw or reeds or hung in a well-aired place

Stolní víno Table wine, the lowest quality; must have a natural alcoholic potential of 5.5–8%

Suché Dry

Šumivé víno Sparkling wine

Vína s přívlastkem A wine of appellation, thus the equivalent of a French AOC

Vinárskych závodov Wine producer

Víno Wine

Výběr A wine predicated by selection; must have a natural alcoholic potential of at least 14%

Výběr z hroznů A wine predicated by selection of individual grapes; must have a natural alcoholic potential of at least 16%

Zvyškovym cukrom Residual sugar

FACTORS AFFECTING TASTE AND QUALITY

LOCATION
The Czech Republic is an inland central European country north of Austria and its vines are mostly located in Moravia. There are also vineyards in Bohemia, mainly to the north and northeast of Prague. Slovakia is located south of Moravia.

CLIMATE
Generally a continental climate with occasional maritime influences from the Atlantic. In the Czech Republic, Moravia is significantly sunnier (1,760 hours) than Bohemia (1,450 hours), but Slovakia is even more favourable (2,000 hours), with less precipitation.

ASPECT
In the Czech Republic, vines are grown on rolling hills in Bohemia, and on mountain foothills in Moravia. Generally steeper and hillier in Slovakia.

SOIL
The primarily loess topsoils found in most Czech vineyards cover the acidic crystalline slate of the Bohemian Massive, the exception being in the Bohemian limestone basin around Prague. Sandy or rocky soils, with scattered alluvial deposits, dominate Slovakia.

VITICULTURE AND VINIFICATION
Although some modernization of facilities has taken place in the Czech Republic since the 1990s, and a few new wineries have been set up, at least half the production occurs under antiquated conditions, and far too much wine is made from hybrids for the country to be able to build a reputation. While the situation in Slovakia is worse, the potential quality is greater.

GRAPE VARIETIES
Slovakian primary varieties:
Chardonnay, Devin, Frankovka Modrá (Limberger), Ryzlink Vlašsky (Welschriesling), Sauvignon Blanc, Svätovavrinecké (St-Laurent), Veltlinske Zelene (Grüner Veltliner)

Slovakian secondary varieties:
Cabernet Sauvignon, Dievčie Hrozno, Furmint, Lipovina (Hárslevelů), Rulandské Bílé, Ryzlink Rýnský (Riesling), Sylvánske Zelené

Czech primary varieties:
Frankova (Limberger), Müller-Thurgau, Rulandské Bílé, Ryzlink Rýnský (Riesling), Ryzlink Vlašsky (Welschriesling), Veltlínské Červené Roter Veltliner), Svatovav'rinecke (St-Laurent)

Czech secondary varieties:
André, Chardonnay, Modrý Portugal (Portugieser), Muskat Moravské, Neuburské (Neuburger), Rulandské Modrý, Rulandské Šedé, Sauvignon Blanc, Tramin (Savagnin Blanc), Zweigeltrebe

is no reason why, with properly maintained vineyards, adequately equipped producers of Slovakian Tokaji should not compete with their famous neighbours. With a little imagination, this wine has the potential to be so lucrative that it must surely be the door-opener for that much-needed foreign investment.

THE CZECH REPUBLIC

Most Czech wines are produced in Moravia, where the majority of the vineyards are located. The two major areas of production are Hustopěce-Hodonin on the Morava River and Znojmo-Mikulov on the Dyje River. Around 80 per cent of all the wine produced is white, with a good level of winemaking expertise for light, elegant, and aromatically fresh whites. Although the climate does not generally suit red-wine production, some interesting reds (such as the Cabernet Sauvignon from Pavlovice) are produced. Sparkling wines are made in the towns of Mikulov and Bzenec by *cuve close* and continuous methods. Since the 1995 Czech Wine Law was introduced, wines are categorized according to the grapes' sugar contents: effectively table wine, *vin de pays*, and AOC equivalents, followed by German-style predicated wines: Kabinet, Pozdní sběr, Výběr z hroznů, Výběr z bobulí, Ledová vína, and Slámová vína (see Label Language, *above*).

RECENT SLOVAKIAN AND CZECH VINTAGES

2010 Good quality all round.

2009 Another very good year for rare reds and richer whites, especially late-harvest styles.

2008 Typically fresh, fruity styles produced.

2007 A very good year for rare reds and richer whites, especially late-harvest styles.

2006 A great vintage all round, in Slovakia and the Czech Republic.

THE APPELLATIONS OF

SLOVAKIA AND THE CZECH REPUBLIC

SLOVAKIA

JUŽNOSLOVENSKÁ

Internal regions: *Dunajskostredský, Galantský, Hurbanovský, Komárňanský, Palárikovský, Šamorinský, Strekovský, Stúrovský*

The Južnoslovenská or Southern Slovak region is warm and sunny; rich clay soils encourage late-harvest whites and well-coloured reds.

Cabernet Franc, Cabernet Sauvignon, Frankovka Modrá, Muškat Moravský, Ryzlink Rýnsky, Rulandské, Rulandské Bílé, Rulandské Modré, Tramín Červný (Red Traminer)

✓ *Château Belá* • *Karpatská Perla* • *Vino-Masaryk*

MALOKARPATSKÁ

Internal regions: *Bratislavský, Dolanský, Hlovecký, Modranský, Orešanský, Pezinský, Senecký, Skalický, Stupavský, Trnavský, Vrbovský, Záhorský*

The Malokarpatská or "Little Carpathian" region has a winemaking tradition of almost 3,000 years. Riesling from Limbach has the greatest reputation, followed by Modrý Portugal (Blauer Portugieser) from Oresany.

Chardonnay, Modrý Portugal, Veltlinske Zelene, Ryzlink Rýnsky, Ryzlink Vlašsky

✓ *Karpatská Perla* • *Mrva & Stanko* • *Pomfy-Mavín*

NITRANSKÁ

Internal regions: *Nitranský, Pukanský, Radošinský, Šintavský, Tekovský, Vrábel'ský, Želiezovský, Žitavský, Zlatomoravský*

This region produces a mixed bag of red and white, dry and sweet, still and sparkling wines.

🍇 Cabernet Sauvignon, Frankovka Modrá, Müller-Thurgau, Pálava, Ryzlink Vlassky, Rulandské Modré, Svätovavřinecké, Veltlinske Zelene

✓ *Mrva & Stanko • Vinanza*

STREDOSLOVENSKÁ

Internal regions: *Fil'akovský, Gemerský, Hotiansky, Ipel'ský, Modrokamenský, Tornal'ský, Vinícky*

In the Stredoslovenská, otherwise known simply as the Central Slovakian wine region, Tramín is considered to be the best variety.

🍇 Cabernet Sauvignon, Chardonnay, Ryzling Vlassky, Svätovavřinecké, Tramín, Veltlinske Zelene

✓ *Mrva & Stanko*

TOKAJSKÁ

This tiny region is surrounded on three sides by the Východoslovenská region, and on one by the Tokaj region in Hungary. Slovakian Tokajské is made from the same varieties as Hungarian Tokaji (Furmint, Lipovina or Hárslevelű, and Muškát Žltý or Sárga Muskotály). Wines made from other varieties are not sold as Tokajské.

🍇 Devín, Furmint, Lipovina, Muškát Žltý, Rulandské Bílé, Tramín Červený (Red Traminer)

✓ *J & J Ostrožovič*

VÝCHODOSLOVENSKÁ

Internal regions: *Král'ovskochlmecký, Michalovský, Moldavský, Sobranský*

The heavy clay soils of the Východoslovenská, or Eastern Slovakian, wine region are mostly thought to be suited to white grapes, although red wines are made.

🍇 Frankovka Modrá, Müller-Thurgau, Ryzling Vlassky, Svätovavřinecké, Tramín, Veltlinske Zelene

THE CZECH REPUBLIC

BRNĚNSKÁ

With two basic soil types, white grapes are mostly grown on lighter sandy soils, with black grapes grown on gravelly soils. Dolní Kounice is the most important wine town.

🍇 Frankovka, Modrý Portugal, Müller-Thurgau, Muskat Moravské, Palava, Svätovavřinecké, Tramín, Veltlinske Zelene

BZENECKÁ

Orechov, Bzenec, Polesovice, and Vracov are the most important wine villages in Bzenecká, the Czech Republic's smallest wine region. Clayey, sandy, and gravelly soils predominate. The local speciality is Bzenecká Lipká, made from Ryzlink Rýnsky. Olsava and Vitra are new varieties created by Cultivation Station at Polesovice.

🍇 Frankovka, Muskat Moravské, Olsava, Rulandské Bílé, Ryzlink Rýnsky, Svätovavřinecké, Veltlinske Zelene, Vitra

CÁSLAVSKÁ

A small enclave of vines growing at the foot of the Kutna Hora Mountain.

🍇 Modrý Portugal, Müller-Thurgau, Svätovavřinecké, Sylvanske Zelene

KYJOVSKÁ

The best wines are made from vines grown at Vresovice, on south-facing slopes, at 550 metres (1,640 feet) in altitude; the grapes produced in this region have a pronounced acidity.

🍇 Müller-Thurgau, Svatovavřinecké, Veltlinske Zelene

MĚLNICKÁ

The largest wine region in Bohemia, Mělnická has a certain reputation for oak-aged reds, but produces better Chardonnay.

🍇 Chardonnay, Rulandské Bílé, Rulandské Modré, Rulandské Šedé, Ryzlink Rýnsky, Svatovavřinecké, Zweigeltrebe

MIKULOVSKÁ

With 2,500 hectares (6,180 acres) under vine, Mikulovská is the largest wine region in the country. Most wines produced are white, with the best coming from limestone soils, although sandy and marly soils are also quite common. The new Palava variety (Tramin x Müller-Thurgau) was developed here.

🍇 Chardonnay, Müller-Thurgau, Neuburské, Palava, Ryzlink Vlassky, Silvánske Zelené, Tramin, Veltlinske Zelenc

✓ *Sklepy • Tanzberg*

MOSTECKÁ

This region has an extremely dry climate and volcanic (basalt) soils. A significant portion of the wine is traditionally produced under strictly Kosher conditions.

🍇 Müller-Thurgau, Ryzlink Rýnsky, Svatovavřinecké, Zweigeltrebe

MUTĚNICKÁ

The vines grow on various clayey, sandy soils, with the best on calcareous clay. Although Mutěnická encompasses 14 communes, almost 90 per cent of the vineyards are located in Cejkovice, where the wines have pronounced acidity. Most of the rest of the vines are located in Mutěnice, the location of Moravia's premier viticultural research station.

🍇 Frankovka, Müller-Thurgau, Ryzlink Vlassky, Svatovavřinecké, Veltlinske Zelene

PODLUŽÍ

The vines grow in mineral-deficient clayey, sandy, and gravelly soils on frost-prone sites in this small region bordering Austria and Slovakia. The best

wines are made from Veltlinske Zelene and originate in the clayey soils of Prušánsky.

🍇 Frankovka, Rulandské Bílé, Rulandské Šedé, Ryzlink Rýnsky, Ryzlink Vlassky, Svatovavřinecké, Veltlinske Zelene, Zweigeltrebe

✓ *Nové Vinařstvi*

PRAŽSKÁ (PRAGUE)

Although this is the smallest region in the Czech Republic, Prague used to be the largest wine-producing town in Bohemia in centuries past. Modrý Portugal is the most widely planted variety, but the best wines are made from Riesling and Pinot Blanc, while colder, less-suitable sites are planted with Kerner and Müller-Thurgau.

🍇 Chardonnay, Modrý Portugal, Müller-Thurgau, Muskat Moravské, Rulandské Šedé, Ryzlink Rýnsky, Tramín, Svatovavřinecké, Zweigeltrebe

ROUDNICKÁ

Once famous for Sylvaner, Roudnická now grows a considerable amount of Müller-Thurgau and has had some success with red wines made on the valley slopes, with gold-medal Rulandské Modré (Pinot Noir) giving short-lived hope in the mid-1990s. Most vines are grown on a marly limestone and chalk plateau, covered by loess and gravelly sand, near the Elbe River.

🍇 Modrý Portugal, Müller-Thurgau, Rulandské Modré, Svatovavřinecké

STRÁZNICKÁ

The vineyards in this region are located on the heavy clay slopes of the Bílé Karpaty, where red wines can be hard. Growers therefore mainly grow white-wine varieties.

🍇 Müller-Thurgau, Rulandské Šedé, Veltlinske Zelene

USHERSKOHRADIŠTSKÁ

Vines grow on the banks of the Morava River and in its hinterland, on sandy and gravelly sand slopes of Chirby and Bílé Karpaty. Primarily white wines.

🍇 Müller-Thurgau, Rulandské Šedé

VELKOPAVLOVICKÁ

The best wines are made from Neuburské and Veltlinske Zelene grown in the north of Velkopavlovická, the Czech Republic's second-largest wine region (2,350 hectares [5,810 acres]).

🍇 Frankovka, Modrý Portugal, Müller-Thurgau, Neuburské, Ryzlink Vlassky, Veltlinske Zelene

✓ *Stapleton & Springer* (Pinot Noir) • *Vinařstvi Sonberk • Vinum*

ZERNOSECKÁ

Typical of Bohemia's sporadic viticultural character today, Zernosecká has just 16 wine producers (owning in total just 70 hectares [170 acres] of vineyards spread over five wine villages), whereas the village of Litoměřice alone was once surrounded by more than 500 hectares (1,235 acres) of vines.

🍇 Müller-Thurgau, Rulandské Bílé, Rulandské Modré, Ryzlink Rýnsky, Svatovavřinecké

ZNOJEMSKÁ

This region's best wines come from Znojmo, which is not so much a city as two cities in one. Znojmo resides above its own underground city, comprising 30 kilometres (18 miles) of interconnecting catacombs.

🍇 Müller-Thurgau, Ryzlink Rýnsky, Sauvignon Blanc, Veltlinske Zelene

✓ *Znovín Znojmo*

THE WESTERN BALKANS

Few regions in the world have undergone so much political turmoil and human tragedy over such a relatively short period as the Western Balkans. Until the early 1990s, the entire region was supposedly just one country – Yugoslavia. However, Yugoslavia comprised at least seven one-time sovereign nations and was populated by five ethnic groups.

FOLLOWING THE DEATH OF TITO, and the general collapse of Communism, it was inevitable that this artificial edifice would start to unravel, and the powder-keg of centuries of resentment would one day explode into bloody conflict. In these more peaceful times, newly independent countries at least have a chance to establish their own wine reputations.

ALBANIA

Although vineyards have been cultivated in Albania since pre-Roman times, most Albanians became Muslim, so wine production has not been of much importance in recent historical terms. Furthermore, under a xenophobic Communist government, for 46 years there were no exports, meaning the potential for this country's wine industry has been severely restricted. Since democracy was established between 1990 and 1992, successive governments have sought viticultural expert advice from the West, but the area under vine in Albania is now less than 6,000 hectares (14,800 acres), which is actually less than one-fifth of the area that was planted under Communist rule.

There are three regions: the Plain Bregdetare, Rajon Kodrinor, and Ragion Nën-malore. The Plain Bregdetare, or coastal plain, is mainly flat but rises to about 300 metres (985 feet) above sea level in places. Rajon Kodrinor is the hilly region at the centre of the country. Ragion Nën-malore covers the foothills and some mountain slopes of the Pindus Mountains up to 1,000 metres (3,300 feet) in altitude. Everywhere you go in this rugged country it is like one endless farm, with sheep, cows, pigs, turkeys, and chickens roaming among crops of corn, fruit, and cabbages, with no distinction of ownership that any outsider can discern. Donkeys and horses are everywhere, and here and there among the smallholdings you will find a patch of vines, with the occasional garage-sized building where wines are made. The term winery would be much too grand, although there is at least one commercial-sized winery (Boukas at Gjirokaster, in the south of Plain Bregdetare). Some well-known varieties such as Cabernet Franc, Mavrud, Merlot, and Welschriesling are grown in Albania, but indigenous varieties such as Shesh i Zi, Shesh i Barhe, and Kalmet (aka Kadarka) represent almost 60 per cent of all Albanian vines, and three other local grapes (Vlosh, Serine, and Debine) account for most of the rest.

BOSNIA-HERZEGOVINA

Although most vines are confined to the Brotnjo hills around Mostar, where the climate and rocky soil favour two indigenous varieties – Zilavka for white wine and Blatina for red – other viticultural regions are Kozar, Ukrina, Majevica, Rama, Jablanica, Srednja Neretva, Listica, and Trebišnjica. There are currently 1,400 hectares (3,460 acres) planted. Other significant varieties grown are Bena, Dobrogostina, Krkoshia, Podbil, and Rkaciteli for white wines, and Alicante Bouschet, Cabernet Sauvignon, Gamay, Merlot, Plavka, Trnjak, and Vranac for reds.

KOSOVO

Despite Kosovo having declared its independence in 2008, this is still contested by Serbia. Even the UN asked the International Court of Justice for an advisory opinion on the issue upon the express request of Serbia, and in 2010 the court ruled that Kosovo's declaration of independence did not violate international law.

There are seven winegrowing districts in Kosovo: Djakovica, Istok, Mališevo, Orahovac, Pec, Prizren, and Suva Reka. Until the conflict, the Rahovic winery had a lucrative contract to supply the German Racke group with 20–30 million litres of light red Kosovar wine, which was sold under the Amselfelder brand, but due to the uncertain political situation, production was transferred elsewhere. In these more peaceful times, Kosovo finds itself with a substantial wine industry, but no ready market.

MACEDONIA

Following the secession of Slovenia and Croatia in 1991, Macedonia received full international recognition in 1993. The official regions are Pcinja-Osogovo, or Eastern Region (which includes the districts of Kocanski, Kratovo, Kumanovo, and Pijanecko); Povardarje, or Central Region (which includes the districts of Gevgelija Valandovo, Ovce Pole, Skopje, Strumica-Radovište, Titov Veles, and Tikves or Tikves Krater); and Pelagonija-Polog, or Western Region (which includes the districts of Bitola, Kicevo, Ohrid, Prespa, Prilep, and Tetovo). The grape varieties grown in this country include Grenache, Kadarka, Kratošija, Plovdina, Prokupac, Temjanika, and Vranac. Phylloxera, which devastated European vineyards in the late 19th century, did not reach Macedonia until 1912.

The most popular Macedonian wine is Kratošija, which is a deep-coloured red made from native Vranac and Kratošija varieties. It has a distinctive taste and aroma, full body, and a smooth flavour. It is bottled in its second year, when the bouquet is at its fullest, and is best drunk when very young. Prokupac and Kadarka make interesting reds, Belan produces a neutral white Grenache wine, and Temjanika an aromatic white.

MONTENEGRO

There are three winegrowing districts in Montenegro: Primorje, Lake Skadar, and Podgorica. The best-known vineyards of this region are those that are located on the terraced southern slopes of Lake Skadar. There are approximately 4,000 hectares (10,000 acres) of vines, with Vranac the primary grape cultivated. Other varieties grown include Kratosija, Krstac, and Merlot. The Vranac and Merlot wines can be good, but Montenegro is better known for its grape brandy than for its wine.

SERBIA

Although the Federal Army made abortive attempts to put down independence in Slovenia and Croatia, and supported the Bosnian Serbs, it did not fight any battles on its home ground until the Kosovo conflict. Most Serbian vineyards thus remain unaffected.

There are eight major wine regions in Serbia: Suboticka Pešcara (including the districts of Cocka, Palic-Horgos, and Potisje); Srem (including the district of Fruška Gora); Banat (including the districts of Bela Crkva-Deliblato, Pešcara, and Vršac); Pocerina-Podgora; Šumadija Velika Morava (including the districts of Beograd, Jagodina, Mlav, and Oplenac); Zapadna Morava (including the districts of Cacak and Kruševac); Nišava Juzna Morava (including the districts of Aleksinac, Nišava, Toplica, Leskovac, Niš, and Vranje); and Timok (including the districts of Krajina and Knjazevac). Serbia is better known for its excellent fruit brandies (particularly peach, pear, and plum) than for its wines, but it definitely has the potential to become a serious wine-producing country.

The vines grown include Ezerjó, Graševina (Welschriesling), Kadarka, Merlot, Riesling, Sauvignon Blanc, Sémillon, and Traminer. The Traminer is a more interesting alternative and the soft, fruity Merlot a good buy for red-wine drinkers. I think that the best potential here is for Cabernet Sauvignon and Merlot when grown in Južna Morava and, possibly, Timok, but the best level of quality currently being achieved is by producers of the snappy, fresh Sauvignon Blanc from Kruševac in Zapadna Morava.

✔ *Podrum Vina Aleksandroć* • *Rubin* (Sauvignon Blanc) • *Wow Winery*

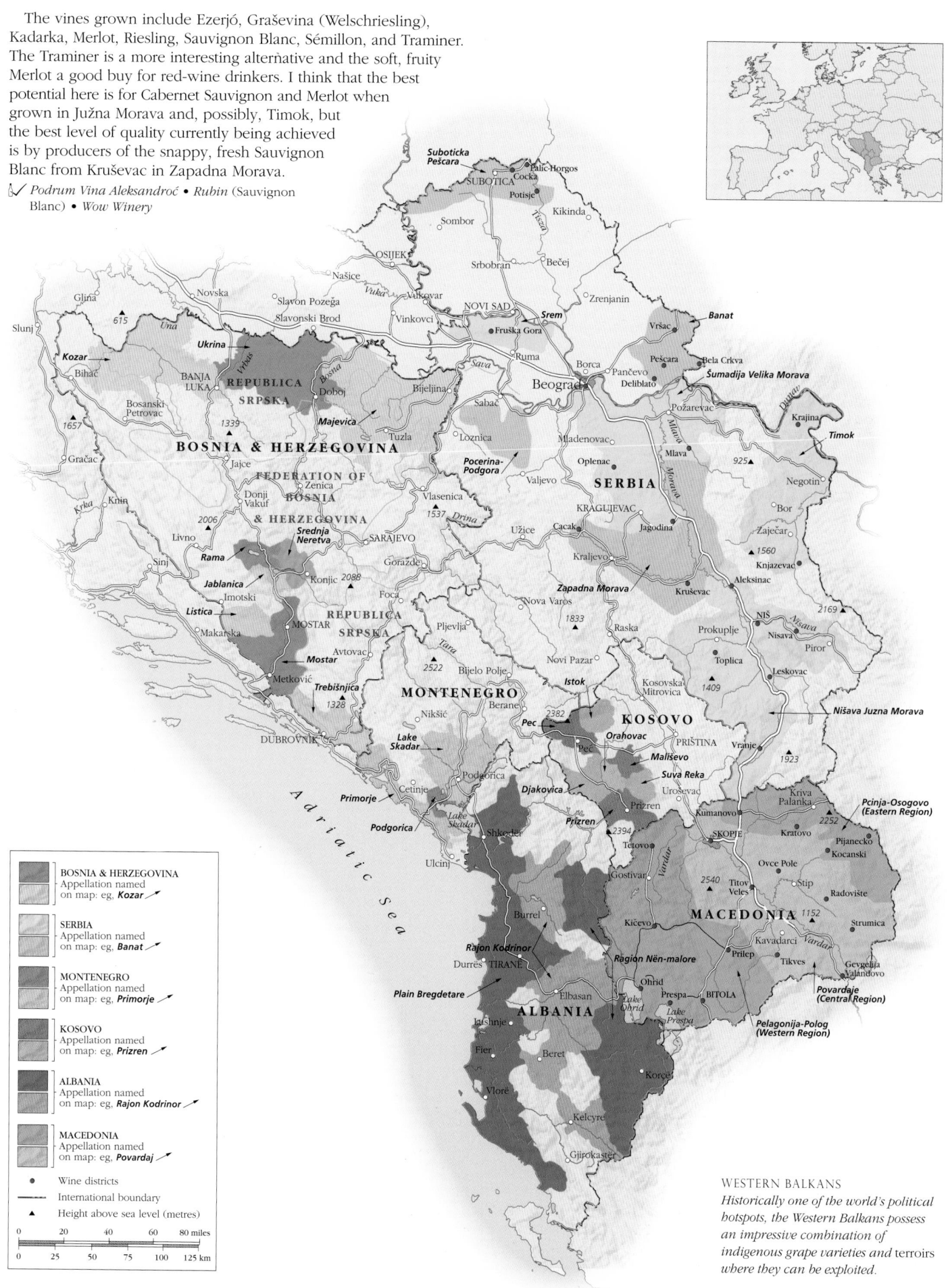

WESTERN BALKANS
Historically one of the world's political hotspots, the Western Balkans possess an impressive combination of indigenous grape varieties and terroirs where they can be exploited.

Legend:

BOSNIA & HERZEGOVINA
Appellation named on map: eg, *Kozar*

SERBIA
Appellation named on map: eg, *Banat*

MONTENEGRO
Appellation named on map: eg, *Primorje*

KOSOVO
Appellation named on map: eg, *Prizren*

ALBANIA
Appellation named on map: eg, *Rajon Kodrinor*

MACEDONIA
Appellation named on map: eg, *Povardaj*

● Wine districts
— International boundary
▲ Height above sea level (metres)

0 20 40 60 80 miles
0 25 50 75 100 125 km

CROATIA

Nobody knew that the Crljenak Kastelanski was California's famous Zinfandel until 2001, when it was identified at Kastel Novi, near Split. This discovery has radically changed how the world views the potential of this wine country and how Croatian winemakers see their own destiny.

FROM CROATIA, the Crljenak Kastelanski was transplanted to Apulia, where it became known as Primitivo, and the rest, as they say, is history – albeit fairly recent history. Since the Zinfandel story broke, thanks to the combined efforts of Dr Jasenka Piljac Zegarac and Professor Carole Meredith, Croatia has become a hot spot for every budding ampelographer seeking to make a name for himself. This is a country that had at least 300 indigenous grape varieties prior to phylloxera, although that number has dramatically declined since. There are still well over 100 that are known to exist, however, and who knows how many waiting to be discovered on Croatia's most remote islands, where small pockets of vines are likely to have escaped the ravages of phylloxera?

KONTINENTALNA HRVATSKA OR CONTINENTAL CROATIA

Situated mostly between the Slovenian and Hungarian borders, Kontinentalna Hrvatska encompasses seven winegrowing districts: Moslavina, Pleśivica, Podunavlje, Pokuplje, Prigorje-Bilogora, Slavonija, and Zagorje-Medimurje. More than 90 per cent of the production is white wine, with over half of the vineyards planted with Grasevina (Welschriesling). Of the few black varieties, Frankova (Lemberger) is the most important. Other grapes include Chardonnay, Gewürztraminer, Muscat Ottonel, Riesling, Traminer, and Sauvignon Blanc.

✓ *Bodren • Krauthaker • Kutjevo*

PRIMORSKA HRVATSKA OR COASTAL CROATIA

The Dalmatian coast and its islands contain five winegrowing districts: Dalmatinska Zagora, Istria, Hrvatsko Primorje, Sjeverna Dalmacija, and Srednja i Južna Dacija. White wine is also important here, accounting for no less than 70 per cent of total production. The grape varieties grown are more diverse, with Malvasia the most widely planted yet accounting for less than 10 per cent of the vineyards. Other varieties include Debit, Grk, Marastina, Plavac Mali, Posip, Vugava, and Zlahtina. New plantations include Cabernet Sauvignon, Merlot, and serious attempts to revive Crljenak Kastelanski (Zinfandel).

✓ *Arman • Vina Bibich • Dubrovački • Grigic Vina • Korak • Korta Katarina • Zlatan Otok • Tomic (aka Bastijana)*

CROATIA

This country not only has its own viticultural heritage but also established the New Zealand wine industry via the likes of Babich, Brajkovich, Delegat, Fistonich, Nobilo, Selaks, et al.

Continental Croatia (Kontinentalna Hrvatska)	
	Moslavina
	Plešivica
	Podunavlje
	Pokuplje
	Prigorje-Bilogora
	Slavonija
	Zagorje-Medimurje
Coastal Croatia (Primorska Hrvatska)	
	Dalmatinska zagora
	Hrvatsko primorje
	Istra
	Sjeverna Dalmacija
	Srednja i Južna Dalmacija
- - -	International boundary
▲ 1534	Height above sea level (metres)

0   20   40   60 miles

0   20   40   60   80   100 km

SLOVENIA

This country is emerging as a serious world-class contender for all styles of white wine, but it still has a long way to go as far as red wines are concerned.

Perhaps the most illuminating experience when tasting around any former Communist state is how young, up-and-coming winemakers talk about their grandfathers, never their fathers. This is due not to any disrespect – far from it – but because their father's era was the Communist era, when large cooperatives processed everything down to the lowest common denominator. It is little wonder that there are some lost souls in the Slovenian wine industry, but the latest generation is getting there.

Movia makes an interesting sparkling rosé wine from 100 per cent Pinot Noir, but the grapes ripen at too high an alcoholic potential and would make better red wine. To overcome this, owner Ales Simčič uses grape must for the second fermentation, which does not increase the alcohol. However, he is still left with a sparkling wine that does not have the acidity to take a *dosage* and has come up with another novel idea to avoid the oxidative route that would inevitably result if he sold the wine as a *brut zero*: he sells the wine on its lees and encourages sommeliers to partake in a little theatre by disgorging the wines submerged in a special glass bowl, so that customers can see the pink cloud of the underwater "explosion"!

The vineyards of Slovenia are divided into one coastal region, Primorska, and two inland regions, Posavje and Podravje.

PRIMORSKA

The smallest region, the coastal Primorska, is located in the southwest of the country, stretching from Koper, south of Trieste, around the city, to Goriška, north of Trieste, on the border with Italy. Primorska consists of four districts: Goriška Brda, Koper, Kras, and Vipavska Dolina. The climate is of mild Mediterranean type, except in Goriška Brda, which is an extension of Italy's Collio

region and comes under the moderating influence of the Alps. Brda means "Collio" in Slovenian, and Goriška Brda is for my mind every bit as exciting as Italy's Collio just over the border. Vipavska Dolina is one of the least likely districts to produce some of Slovenia's best red wines, yet one producer, TILIA, is particularly talented. Indeed, the TILIA 2006 Pinot Noir is still the greatest Slovenian red wine I have ever tasted, even if it cannot be replicated every year. Grapes grown in the Primorska region include Barbera, Cabernet Franc, Cabernet Sauvignon, Chardonnay, Merlot, Picolit, Pinot Blanc, Pinot Gris, Ribolla, Sauvignon Blanc, Teran (Refosco), Tocai Friulano, and Zelen (Rotgipfler).

✓ *Fornazarič* (Chardonnay) • *Guerila* • *Aljoša Jakončič* (Rdeča Carolina) • *Vinska Klet* (Goriška Brda A + Belo) • *Marko Kristančič* (reds) • *Movia* • *Edi Simčič* (Duet Lex) • *Marjan Simčič* (sweet) • *Sutor* (Chardonnay) • *TILIA*

POSAVJE AND PODRAVJE

These two inland regions are squeezed among Austria, Hungary, and Croatia. Podravje is the largest and most northerly, comprising six districts: Haloze, Ljutomer-Ormož, Maribor, Prekmurje, Radgona-Kapela, and Srednje Slovensk Gorice. The grapes grown include Cabernet Sauvignon, Sipon, Traminer, Pinot Blanc, Riesling, Sauvignon Blanc, and Welschriesling. If any part of the Ljutomer-Ormož region is managing to enhance the reputation of Laški Riesling, it has to be Podravje, where late-harvest and, particularly, Ledeno (Icewine) styles of this grape are simply stunning.

The other inland region, Posavje, encompasses four districts: Bela Krajna, Bizeljsko-Sremič, Dolenjska, and Šmarje Virštanj.

✓ *Bračko* (sweet) • *Juri Brumec* (sweet Laški Riesling) • *Marof* (Breg Chardonnay) • *PRA-vinO* (sweet wines, especially Laški Riesling Ledeno) • *Ptujkska Klet* (sweet Laški Riesling) • *Prus* (sweet) • *Sturm* (late-harvest, especially Runeni Muškat) • *Versus*

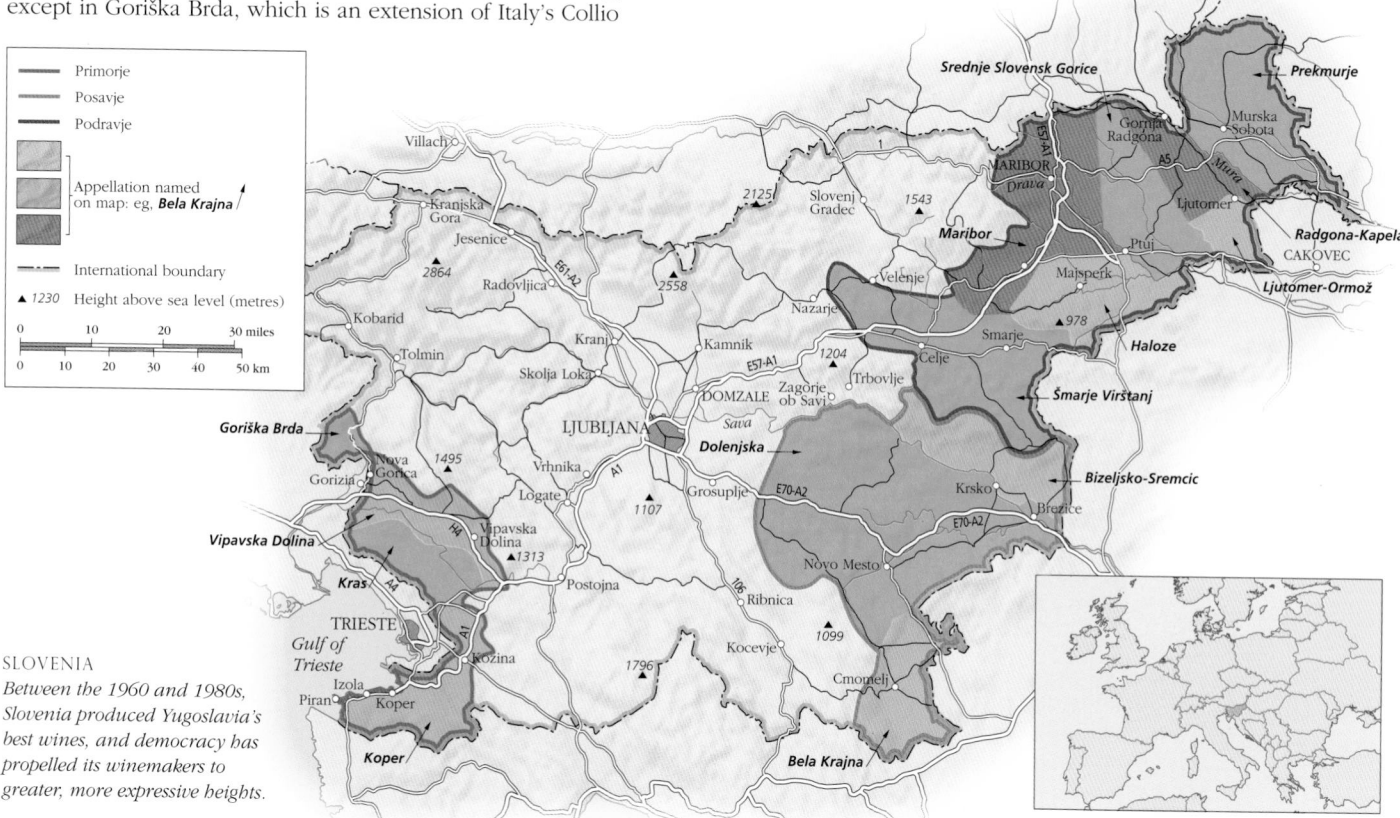

SLOVENIA
Between the 1960 and 1980s, Slovenia produced Yugoslavia's best wines, and democracy has propelled its winemakers to greater, more expressive heights.

THE BLACK AND CASPIAN SEAS

Although Russia is the largest wine-producing country in this region, the wines of Moldova are better known internationally. And while Armenia and Georgia can claim the world's earliest attempts at viticulture and winemaking, it is the legendary wines of Krym in Ukraine that boast the most illustrious more recent history.

ARMENIA

At the height of the Soviet Union's hegemony, Armenia's vineyards covered 36,500 hectares (90,150 acres), but this declined following the collapse of Communism, and by 2003 amounted to just 12,000 hectares (29,650 acres), although investments and expansions have seen this increase to 35,600 hectares (87,970 acres), matching the Communist era's level but with better-quality vineyards. More than 200 grape varieties are grown here, many of them indigenous, but only 30 are wine grapes, and these include Adisi, Anait, Areni, Azateni, Dmak, Garan, Kahet, Karmrayut, Megrabuir, Mskhali, Muscat (various), Nerkeni, Rkatsiteli, Tokun, and Voskeat. The Ararat Valley is the most important winegrowing region, claiming up to 60 per cent of the country's vineyards, but as with Armenian wine in general, most of the production is distilled. Currently, high-strength table wines and strong dessert wines are made, with grape brandy this country's most important alcoholic product. This could well change, however, following the discovery in 2011 of the world's oldest winery at Areni in the Vayots Dzor province (*see* A Chronology of Wine, p84). Now that Armenia shares the history of the birthplace of viticulture and winemaking with Georgia, it should feel obliged to set its sights on building a world-class wine industry.

AZERBAIJAN

Official statistics for the area under vine are notoriously inaccurate, having gone from 181,000 hectares (447,000 acres) in 1990 to less than 12,000 hectares (29,650 acres) in 2001 and back up to 22,000 hectares (54,360 acres) in 2009. In 2004, the French Castel Group was hired to consult on expanding these vineyards, in the hope of exporting an improved quality of Azerbaijan wine to Russia. Azerbaijan has yet to resolve its conflict with Armenia over the largely Armenian-populated Azerbaijani Nagorno-Karabakh enclave, where vines are also planted.

GEORGIA

Georgia has one of the oldest winemaking traditions in the world. There is evidence that the first vines could have spread from here or, at least, been preserved in this area during the last major ice age (*see* A Chronology of Wine, p84). Georgia has numerous valleys, each with its own favourable microclimate, and it is said that they contain 1,000 indigenous grape varieties. A handful of producers are making some excellent wines, but this is only the beginning. There is no doubt that both Georgia and Armenia will be bursting at the seams with high-class boutique wineries in 50 years' time. The only question is how long it will take to reach that level of sophistication.

✓ *Chandrebi Estate • Metekhi • Schuchmann • Tamada* (Napareuli) • *Tblivino • Telavi*

BLACK AND CASPIAN SEAS
This region in general, and Georgia in particular, is thought to have provided a safe haven for the vine during the last ice age.

KAZAKHSTAN

This is the country made famous by Borat, a character played by comic genius Sacha Baron Cohen, who claims that in Kazakhstan wine is made from horses' urine! The wine is not, in fact, that bad, but if any Kazakh entrepreneur decided to sell a wine labelled "Horses' Urine" (not too far away from the New Zealand "Cat's Pee"), they would probably double their country's exports overnight. The largest concentration of Kazakhstan's vineyards is in the extreme east, between Chimkent and Alma-Ata, in the foothills of the Tien Shan Mountains.

MOLDOVA

A small country the size of Belgium, Moldova is, in fact, an extension of Romania's Moldova.

Pucari is 160 kilometres (100 miles) south of the capital in the heart of red-wine country. Negru de Pucari is a deep-coloured and firm-structured red wine blended from Cabernet Sauvignon and Saperavi; Purpuruiu de Pucari is a softer Pinot-Merlot blend; and Rosu de Pucari is a dark rosé made from Cabernet Sauvignon, Merlot, and Malbec. Romanesti's vineyards lie 50 kilometres (30 miles) farther north. Romanesti was named after the Romanov Czar Alexander I, who restarted the Moldovan wine industry by establishing his own winery here. Vines include Aligoté, Cabernet Sauvignon, Malbec, Merlot, Pinot Noir, and Rkatsiteli, but it is the Bordeaux varieties that tend to fare best.

Halfway between Kishinev and Romanesti is Cricova, where unremarkable and often faulty sparkling wines are made in the most remarkable and elaborate underground city. Its entrance is a massive pair of steel doors in a rock face, through which the largest articulated lorries can drive, winding their way 80 metres (262 feet) below the surface, where a city has been hewn out of solid rock. Its size corresponds to the area covered by 25 villages on the surface and it is serviced by 65 kilometres (40 miles) of underground roads, complete with traffic lights and road signs. In addition to these roads, there are 120 kilometres (75 miles) of galleries, which almost equals the entire storage capacity of the Champagne region of France. Why, I asked myself, is this workplace equipped with opulent reception halls, a dining room the like of which I have not seen anywhere else during the Eastern Bloc era, and a cellar containing priceless old vintages of Mouton Rothschild, Latour, Romanée-Conti, and so on? I had absolutely no doubts that this was where the Politburo would head in a nuclear exchange.

✓ *Acorex* • *Albastrele* (especially Sauvignon Blanc) • *AurVin* (Firebird) • *Château Vartely* • *Cricova* • *Dioysis Mereni* • *Vinaria Purcari* (especially the Pinot Noir in magnum)

RUSSIA

Climate is something of an obstacle to vinegrowing in Russia, as winters are generally very cold indeed, often -30°C (-22°F), and the vines in many regions have to be buried in the earth to survive the bitterly cold months. Summers are very hot and dry and, but for the tempering effect of the Black and Caspian Seas, climatic conditions would probably be impossible for viticulture. There are five major winegrowing districts in Russia: Checheno-Ingush, Dagestan, Krasnodar, Rostov-na-Donu, and Stavropol, with grape varieties that include Aligoté, Cabernet, Muscatel, Pinot Gris, Pinot Noir, Plechistik, Pukhljakovsky, Rizling, Rkatsiteli, Sylvaner, and Tsimlyansky. In general, Russian producers concentrate on white and sparkling wines in the north and west, and red in the south and east.

In the mid-1950s, a system that has become known as the "Russian Continuous Flow Method" was developed for producing sparkling wine cheaply, easily, and quickly by a natural second fermentation. Krasnodar's most reputable vineyards are on southwest-facing coastal slopes overlooking the Black Sea. Abrau is known for its dry Rizling (Riesling), Cabernet, and Durso sparkling wine. Anapa, just along the coast to the north, also makes Rizling, while down the coast at Gelendzhik, Aligoté is the local speciality. To the east of Krasnodar and north of the Caucasus, Stavropol is known for its dry Rizling and Silvaner, as well as the Muscatel Praskoveiski dessert wines. Other dessert wines include the spicy Mountain Flower; and Rostov-na-Donu, located around the confluence of the rivers Don and Kan and the Taganrogskiy Zaliv estuary, is famous for its rich Ruby of the Don dessert wines. Plechistik is a grape variety that is used to lend backbone to Tsimlyansky and, throughout the state, it also makes decent, dry red wines.

On the east-facing slopes of the Caucasus Mountains, overlooking the Caspian Sea, are the vineyards of the Republic of Dagestan. This is a black grape area that is known for the full body and flavour of its dry red wines; the best come from Derbent in the south. Checheno-Ingush is another republic with vineyards on the Caucasus, but these are found inland, along its northern slopes, to the southeast of Stavropol. Most of the wines produced in this area are of the port type.

✓ *Château le Grand Vostock* • *Fanagoria*

UKRAINE

As viticulture represents one-fifth of this recently re-established nation's agricultural economy, it will be instrumental in building up overseas trade. This is necessary to replace Ukraine's trade with Russia, upon which it is still dependent. The state's wine industry is mainly concerned with producing still white wines, although red wines and white sparkling wines are also produced in the Crimea, and dessert wines are a local speciality. Crimea (Krym) is the peninsula that encloses the Sea of Azov. Sparkling "Krim" is a traditional method wine made in five styles, from Brut through to Sweet, and in a semi-sweet red version. The grapes used include Chardonnay, Pinot Noir, Rizling, Aligoté, and Cabernet. The wines are coarse, and the traditional addition of brandy does not help, but the Brut and Demi-Sec Red are widely available on export markets and sell on novelty value. The Ruby of Crimea, which is a blend of Saperavi, Matrassa, Aleatika, Cabernet, and Malbec, is a robust, rustic, full-bodied red that is quite commonly encountered in various countries.

Nikolayev-Kherson, just northeast of Crimea, and Odessa, near the Moldova state border, produce various white, sparkling, and dessert wines. The best known local wines are dry white wines such as Perlina Stepu, Tropjanda Zakarpatja, and Oksamit Ukrainy.

That this region is capable of not merely good but great wines of exceptional longevity is beyond doubt. In 1990 David Molyneux-Berry MW brought back some extraordinary wines for auction at Sotheby's in London. These came from the famous Massandra cellars, which were built on the outskirts of Yalta in the Crimea for the Russian imperial court at the end of the 19th century. This was not a winery, merely an ageing facility acting as the central hub to a complex of 25 satellite wineries. The wineries were in the surrounding hills of Krymskiye Gory, where the vineyards were situated, thus the grapes did not have to be transported, and almost every ounce of their potential quality was retained. This would be an ambitious project even by today's standards. The wines Molyneux-Berry showed at a pre-auction tasting dated back to the first few decades of the 20th century and were nothing less than sensational.

✓ *Guliev* • *Massandria* • *Veles*

The WINES of
THE EASTERN
MEDITERRANEAN

WHEN THIS ENCYCLOPEDIA WAS FIRST
published in 1988, you could count the
recommended wine producers in Greece on
the fingers of one hand. There was general
despair at how the first civilization to develop
viticulture and winemaking could be reduced to
such a pathetic state. Now it is one of Europe's
most exciting wine-producing countries and,
with thousands of unidentified ancient grape
varieties preserved in its nurseries, it should be
able to delight and surprise wine lovers for
centuries to come. Turkey has the potential to
rival Greece, but its political and religious
constraints will not allow that to happen in our
lifetime. The two most up-and-coming wine-
producing countries are Lebanon and Israel;
wines from here have flourished since the new
millennium, as new boutique wineries have
started to blossom – quite miraculously, all
things considered. There is even improvement
in the quality of Egyptian wine, not that it
could have become much worse!

NEMEA, PELOPONNESE, GREECE
Vines growing near the ancient Temple of Zeus in Korinthos,
where the Nemean games were held from 573 BC onwards
as part of the four panhellenic festivals.

GREECE

The new generation of Greek wineries are at long last bringing respect to the people who taught the Romans all they knew about viticulture and winemaking. Now they can start looking at all the indigenous varieties that exist in this country. Yet no one, not even the Greeks, has any idea what they might make in terms of truly fine wine.

OVER 20 YEARS AGO, in the first edition of this encyclopedia, I told a story about the occasion on which I asked Yannis Boutaris, then one of the country's few decent wine producers, why Greek wines were invariably oxidized, maderized, or sometimes just plain bad. Boutaris stretched, raised a gentle smile, and replied that most Greeks actually liked oxidized wines – and that if most Greek producers made fresh, clean wines, they would not be able to sell

DOMAINE PORTO CARRAS
Looking out across the blue waters of the Aegean to the fishing village of Maramas from the vineyards of Domaine Porto Carras, which also consists of a luxurious leisure and sporting complex.

them on the domestic market and would have to export them. He doubted this would work because most foreigners considered Greek wines to be either dross or Retsina, so no-one would buy them.

He was probably right, but the speed with which the best boutique wineries in this country have turned around the reputation of Greek wines is nothing less than breathtaking. And the future promises to be even better as they start experimenting with more than 300 untested, but possibly very exciting, indigenous grapes.

RECENT GREEK VINTAGES

2010 Potentially good to very good.

2009 More drought and heat stress. Early-picked whites fared best. Drama was surprisingly successful.

2008 A difficult year of mixed quality due to drought and heat stress.

2007 The year of the fires, although thankfully only one winery, the up-and-coming Tetramythos winery in the Peloponnese, was actually burned down. The outstanding success of Xinomavro was the key to this vintage, which saw Naoussa, Amyndeo, Goumenissa, and Raspani excel.

2006 The quality is very good, but not as special and not as consistent as 2005.

FACTORS AFFECTING TASTE AND QUALITY

LOCATION
Greece is located halfway between southern Italy and Turkey. Vines grow throughout the mainland and its many islands, but most are in Macedonia and Peloponnisos.

CLIMATE
Mild winters followed by sub-tropical summers, during which the heat in many vineyards is tempered by sea breezes called *meltemi* and they are bathed in around 3,000 hours of sunshine. Extremes are mountain vineyards in Macedonia, where grapes sometimes fail to ripen, and on Crete, where the summer brings 5 months of intense heat and drought.

ASPECT
Vines grow on all types of land, from flat coastal sites on the mainland, through rolling hills and river valleys, to mountain slopes. The best sites are north-facing (to avoid the sun) slopes up to 610 metres (2,000 feet) above sea level.

SOIL
Mainland soils are mostly limestone, while those on the islands are rocky and volcanic.

VITICULTURE AND VINIFICATION
The Greek cooperatives have long been in possession of thermostatically controlled stainless-steel vats as well as other modern equipment, but they have only started to take advantage of this technology since the mid-1990s. The majority of the best Greek wines on the market today are made by small, high-tech, boutique wineries.

GRAPE VARIETIES
Primary varieties: Agiorgitiko, Assyrtiko, Liatiko, Limnio, Malvasia, Mandelaria, Mavrodaphne, Muscat (various sub-varieties), Rhoditis, Robola, Xinomavro
Secondary varieties: Cabernet Franc, Cabernet Sauvignon, Chardonnay, Syrah

HARVEST TIME
Harvesting the vineyards of Domaine Porto Carras, which were bulldozed out of the slopes of Sithonia, the middle prong of Halkidiki's three peninsulas.

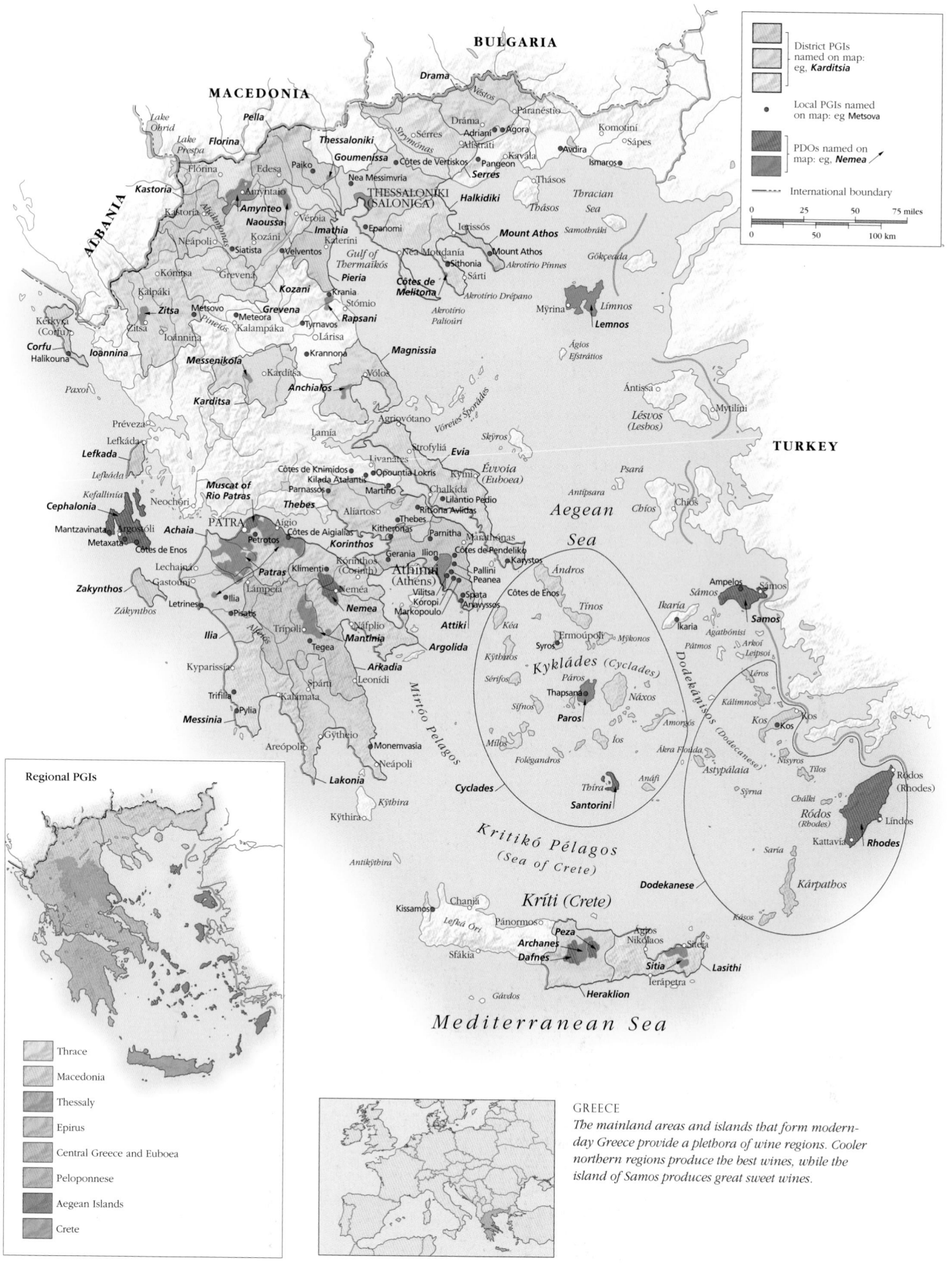

District PGIs
named on map:
eg, *Karditsia*

• Local PGIs named
on map: eg Metsova

PDOs named on
map: eg, *Nemea*

International boundary

0   25   50   75 miles
0   50   100 km

BULGARIA

MACEDONIA

ALBANIA

TURKEY

Aegean
Sea

Thracian
Sea

Kykládes (Cyclades)

Dodekánisos (Dodecanese)

Kritikó Pélagos
(Sea of Crete)

Kríti (Crete)

Mediterranean Sea

Drama
Dráma
Adriani
Agora
Komotíni
Sápes
Sérres
Alistráti
Pangeon
Kavála
Avdira
Ismaros
Serres
Pella
Thessaloniki
Goumenissa
Côtes de Vertiskos
Nea Messimvria
THESSALONIKI
(SALONICA)
Halkidiki
Florina
Edesa
Paiko
Flórina
Amynteo
Kastoria
Kastoria
Neápoli
Amynteo
Naoussa
Veroia
Imathia
Katerini
Siatista
Velventos
Kozáni
Kozani
Pieria
Epanomi
Nea Moudania
Sithonia
Sárti
Mount Athos
Mount Athos
Akrotírio Pínnes
Ierissós
Thásos
Thásos
Samothráki
Gökçeada
**Côtes de
Melitona**
Akrotírio Drépano
Mýrina
Límnos
Lemnos
Ágios
Efstrátios
Kalpáki
Kómsa
Grevena
Kránia
Stómio
Zitsa
Zitsa
Metsovo
Meteora
Kalampáka
Grevena
Tyrnavos
Rapsani
Ioánnina
Ioánnina
Lárisa
Magnissia
Corfu
Kérkyra
(Corfu)
Halikouna
Messenikóla
Kardítsa
Krannóna
Vólos
Ántissa
Lésvos
(Lesbos)
Mytilíni
Paxoí
Préveza
Karditsa
Anchialos
Agriovótano
Vóreies Sporádes
Skýros
Psará
Antípsara
Chíos
Chios
Lefkada
Lefkáda
Lamía
Strofyliá
Evia
Évvoia
(Euboea)
Lefkáda
Livanátes
Opountia Lokris
Kými
Cephalonia
Kefallinia
Neochóri
Côtes de Knimidos
Kilada Atalantis
Parnassós
Martino
Chalkída
Lilàntio Pedio
Thebes
Aliartoso
Thebes
Ritsóna Avlidas
Kárystos
Achaia
Mantzavinata
Metaxata
PÁTRA
Aígio
Petrotos
Côtes de Aigialias
Klimenti
Kitherónas
Parnitha
Marathónas
Côtes de Pendeliko
Karystos
Andros
Côtes de Enos
Samos
Ampelos
Sámos
Samos
Ikaría
Ikaria
Agathónisi
Arkoí
Leipsoí
Côtes de Enos
Zakynthos
Zákynthos
Letrines
Pisatis
Lechainó
Gastoúni
Patras
Ilia
Ilia
Nemea
Neméa
Geranía
Ilion
Pallini
Peanea
Spata
Anavyssos
Attiki
Argolida
Korinthos
Korinthos
(Corinth)
Athína
(Athens)
Vilitsa
Kóropi
Markopoulo
Náfplio
Trípoli
Mantinia
Tegea
Arkadia
Leonídi
Kyparissía
Spárti
Kalamáta
Trifilia
Pylia
Messinia
Gýtheio
Areópoli
Monemvasia
Neápoli
Lakonia
Kýthira
Antikýthira
Léros
Kálymnos
Kos
Kos
Nísyros
Tílos
Dodekanisos
Ródos
(Rhodes)
Ródos
(Rhodes)
Líndos
Kattavia
Rhodes
Chálki
Sými
Astypálaia
Ákra Floúda
Saría
Kárpathos
Kásos
Kýthnos
Cyclades
Kéa
Sérifos
Sífnos
Mílos
Folégandros
Syros
Ermoúpoli
Mýkonos
Tínos
Páros
Thapsaná
Paros
Náxos
Amorgós
Íos
Anáfi
Thíra
Santorini
Dodecanese
Peza
Archanes
Dafnes
Ágios
Nikólaos
Siteia
Sitia
Lasithi
Ierápetra
Heraklion
Kissamos
Chania
Lefká Óri
Pánormos
Sfákia
Gávdos

Gulf of
Thermaikós

Pindos

Mirtóo Pélagos

Regional PGIs

Thrace
Macedonia
Thessaly
Epirus
Central Greece and Euboea
Peloponnese
Aegean Islands
Crete

GREECE
The mainland areas and islands that form modern-day Greece provide a plethora of wine regions. Cooler northern regions produce the best wines, while the island of Samos produces great sweet wines.

GREEK LABEL LANGUAGE

ΑΦΡΩΔΗΣ ΟΙΝΟΣ, ΗΜΙΑΦΡΩΔΗΣ
Αφρώδης Οίνος, Ημιαφρώδης
Sparkling wine, semi-sparkling
ΕΛΛΗΝΙΚΟ ΠΡΟΙΟΝ Ελληνικό Προϊόν
Produce of Greece
ΕΠΙΤΡΑΠΕΖΙΟΣ ΟΙΝΟΣ Επιτραπέζιος Οίνος
Table wine
ΕΡΥΘΡΟΣ, Ερυθρός
Red
ΗΜΙΓΛΥΚΟΣ Ημίγλυκος
Sweet, semi-sweet
ΗΜΙΞΗΡΟΣ Ημίξηρος
Dry, semi-dry
ΛΕΥΚΟΣ Λεύκος
White
ΞΗΡΟΣ Ξήρος
Dry

ΟΙΝΟΣ Οίνος or **ΚΡΑΣΙ Κρασί**
Wine
ΟΙΝΟΠΟΙΕΙΟΝ Οινοποιείον
Winery
ΟΝΟΜΑΣΙΑ ΚΑΤΑ ΠΑΡΑΔΟΣΗ Ονομασία κατα παράδοση
Traditional appellation (reserved for Retsina only)
ΠΑΡΑΓΩΓΗ ΚΑΙ ΕΜΦΙΑΛΩΣΕΙΣ Παραγωγή και Εμφιαλώσεις
Produced and bottled by
ΠΡΟΣΤΑΤΕΥΟΜΕΝΗ ΟΝΟΜΑΣΙΑ ΠΡΟΕΛΕΥΣΗΣ Προστατευόμενη Ονομασία Προέλευσης (ΠΟΠ)
Protected Designation of Origin (PDO)
ΠΡΟΣΤΑΤΕΥΟΜΕΝΗ ΟΝΟΜΑΣΙΑ ΠΡΟΕΛΕΥΣΗΣ
Προστατευόμενη Γεωγραφική Ένδειξη (ΠΓΕ)
Protected Geographical Indication (PGI)

ΡΕΤΣΙΝΑ Ρετσίνα
Retsina. May carry no appellation of origin and may therefore be blended
ΡΕΤΣΙΝΑ ΑΤΤΙΚΗΣ Ρετσίνα Αττικής
Retsina with appellation of origin from Attica
ΡΕΤΣΙΝΑ ΕΥΒΟΙΑΣ Ρετσίνα Ευβοίας
Retsina with appellation of origin from Evia
ΡΟΖΕ Ροζέ
Rosé

VINTAGE As Greece belongs to the European Union, the vintage on the label should mean that at least 85 per cent of the wine comes from the year indicated.

CELLARS AT DOMAINE GEROVASSILIOU
These cellars contain not only barrels of the best wines from this top-performing domaine, but also a museum of viticulture, winemaking, bottling, and cooperage tools. The museum includes the world's second most highly valued collection of antique corkscrews, with many unique pieces, dating back to the 18th century.

THE APPELLATIONS OF
GREECE

Note The spellings of the following appellations are from the latest official list but may differ slightly from what you see on the labels of some wines because the transliteration of the Greek alphabet is not a precise science, and individual producers have different ideas. Hopefully, with time, the official Latinized names will be adopted by all producers.

PDO (Protected Designation of Origin)
PGI (Protected Geographical Indication)
TA (Traditional Appellation)
Only existing primary grape varieties grown are provided for PGI wines because the inherent flexibility of PGI regulations permits an almost endless list, unless restrictions are imposed locally. This is the first attempt by any reference work to list all of the PGIs, most of which are in their earliest formative years and many have not yet been produced, thus it is possible only to provide the briefest of styles permitted.

ACHAIA *or* ACHAIKOS PGI
Peloponnese

White (dry or semi-dry), semi-sweet or sweet rosé (dry or semi-dry), or red (dry) from Achia.

🍇 Athiri, Assyrtiko, Malagousia, Muscat Blanc, Rhoditis, Robola, Chardonnay, Riesling, Sauvignon Blanc, Trebbiano, Kalavrytino Black, Mavrodaphne, Cabernet Sauvignon, Cabernet Franc, Grenache, Merlot, Syrah

✓ *Antonopoulos* (Cabernet Nea-Dris, Chardonnay) • *Mega Spileo*

ADRIANI PGI
Macedonia

White (dry), rosé (dry), red (dry) from Drama.

🍇 Viognier, Chardonnay, Sémillon, Trebbiano, Cabernet Sauvignon, Cabernet Franc, Merlot, Syrah

AEGEAN SEA PGI
Aegean

White (dry or semi-dry), rosé (dry or semi-dry), red (dry) wines from grapes authorized for any of the PDOs in the region indicated.

AGORA PGI
Macedonia

White (dry), rosé (dry), and red (dry) from the Drama region.

🍇 Rhoditis, Muscat d'Alexandrie, Chardonnay, Sauvignon Blanc, Trebbiano, Cabernet Sauvignon, Cabernet Franc, Merlot

AMYNTEO PDO
Macedonia

The brilliant *terroir*-driven Alpha Estate has demonstrated this northerly appellation to be one of the most exciting places in the country to make wine, with potential for high ripe acids that no other Greek region can match.

🐝 Xinomavro

ANAVYSSOS PGI
Central Greece

White (dry) from Attica.

🐝 Assyrtiko, Rhoditis, Savatiano, Trebbiano

ANCHIALOS PDO
Thessaly

Medium-bodied dry white wines from the Nea Anchialos area on the Gulf of Pegassitikos near Volos.

🐝 A minimum of 80% Rhoditis plus Savatiano

ARCADIA PGI
Peloponnese

White (dry or sweet), rosé (dry), red (dry), white (semi-sparkling, dry, or semi-dry), and rosé (semi-sparkling, dry, or semi-dry) from Arcadia.

🐝 Asproudes, Moschofilero, Rhoditis, Robola, Savatiano, Gewürztraminer, Riesling, Chardonnay, Sauvignon Blanc, Agiorgitiko, Kolliniatiko, Mavroudi, Skylopnichtis, Cabernet Sauvignon, Cabernet Franc, Merlot, Syrah

ARCHANES PDO
Crete

This red-wine-only appellation has six sub-zones: Ano and Kato Archanes, Ayios Síllas, Profítis Ilías, Skalani, and Vasilíes.

🐝 Kotsifali, Mandelaria

ARGOLIDA PGI
Peloponnese

White (dry, semi-dry, semi-sweet, sweet), rosé (dry, semi-dry, semi-sweet, sweet), and red (dry, semi-dry, semi-sweet, sweet) from Argolida.

🐝 Asproudes, Assyrtiko, Malagousia, Moschofilero, Rokaniaris, Savatiano, Chardonnay, Viognier Agiorgitiko, Voidomatis, Mavroudi, Cabernet Sauvignon, Cabernet Franc, Merlot, Syrah

🍷 *Ktima Pirgakis* (Merlot)

ATTICA or ATTIKOS PGI
Central Greece

White (dry or semi-dry) and red (dry) from Attica.

🐝 Savatiano, Cabernet Sauvignon

🍷 *Costa Lazaridi* (Oenotria Land Syrah - Agiorgitiko)

AVDIRA PGI
Thrace

White (dry, semi-dry, semi-sweet), rosé (dry, semi-dry, semi-sweet), and red (dry, semi-dry, semi-sweet) from Xanthi.

🐝 Athiri, Assyrtiko, Zoumiatiko, Malagousia, Muscat d'Alexandrie, Rhoditis, Chardonnay, Sauvignon Blanc, Trebbiano, Limnio, Mavroudi, Pamidi, Cabernet Sauvignon, Grenache, Merlot, Syrah

CENTRAL GREECE or STEREA ELLADA PGI
Central Greece

White (dry), rosé (dry), and red (dry) wines from grapes authorized for any of the PDOs in the region indicated.

🍷 *Sabani* (White) • *Thivaiki* (Hoolen Stone)

CEPHALONIA or KEFALONIA PGI
Ionian Islands

Gentilini's non-appellation Syrah is probably the best single wine produced here.

CORFU PGI
Ionian Islands

White (dry) from Corfu.

🐝 A minimum of 60% Kakotrygis plus Petrokoritho

CORINTH or CORINTHIAKOS PGI
Peloponnese

White (dry), rosé (dry), and red (dry) from Corinth.

🐝 Asproudes, Assyrtiko, Lagorthi, Malagousia, Moschofilero, Rhoditis, Savatiano, Chardonnay, Sauvignon Blanc, Agiorgitiko, Mavroudi, Cabernet Sauvignon, Merlot, Syrah

🍷 *Boutari* (Ode) • *Oinotechniki* (Erythros Zacharia)

CÔTES DE AMBELOS PGI
Aegean

This PGI on the island of Samos is allowed but not yet activated.

CÔTES DE AIGION or CÔTES DE EGIALIA PGI
Peloponnese

White (dry), rosé (dry), and red (dry) from costal hills overlooking Aigion in the Achaia province.

🐝 **WHITES:** Volitsa, Lagorthi
REDS: Cabernet Sauvignon

🍷 *Oenoforos* (Ianos Syrah)

CÔTES DE ENOS PGI
Ionian Islands

White (dry) and red (dry) from Cephalonia.

🐝 Goustolidi, Tsaoussi Mavrodaphne

CÔTES DE KITHERONA PGI
Central Greece

White (dry, semi-dry, semi-sweet), rosé (dry, semi-dry, semi-sweet), and red (dry, semi-dry, semi-sweet) from Attica & Viotia.

🐝 Athiri, Assyrtiko, Rhoditis, Savatiano, Chardonnay, Sauvignon Blanc, Grenache, Cabernet Sauvignon, Carignan, Merlot, Syrah

CÔTES DE KNIMIDA PGI
Central Greece

White (dry) and red (dry) from Fthiotida.

🐝 Athiri, Assyrtiko, Kontokladi, Malagousia, Rhoditis, Robola, Savatiano, Chardonnay, Sauvignon Blanc, Trebbiano, Vradiano, Limnio, Mavroudi, Grenache, Cabernet Franc, Cabernet Sauvignon, Merlot, Refosco, Syrah

CÔTES DE MELITON PDO
Macedonia

This appellation covers the red and dry white wines on the central-western coast of Sithonia, the middle of Halkidiki's three peninsulas. The entire Porto Carras complex of hotels, fishing village, vineyard, and winery was created by the late John Carras. Although secondary to the tourist resort itself, the Porto Carras vineyard and winery were profitable from the start, but the resort swallowed all the

money, eventually bankrupting both ventures. The winery and vineyards were sold to Technical Olympic group in 2000. The Greek wine industry owes John Carras a debt of gratitude because, in the early 1980s, Domaine Porto Carras and, in particular, its flagship wine Château Carras were the first Greek wines of modern times to establish a truly international reputation. John Carras hired Bordeaux consultant Professor Émile Peynaud, and it was Peynaud's choice of his ex-pupil Evanglos Gerovassiliou to be winemaker that sealed the success of this venture, because it was Vangelis (as he is known to his friends), as much as Peynaud, who made Château Carras the legend it became. Vangelis went on to establish Domaine Gerovassiliou (see Epanomi PGI) and can be regarded as the father of modern winemaking in northern Greece.

🐝 **WHITES:** Athiri, Assyrtiko, Rhoditis
REDS: Limnio, Cabernet Franc, Cabernet Sauvignon

🍷 *Porto Carras* (Château Carras, Porto Carras Syrah)

CÔTES DE PAIKO PGI
Macedonia

White (dry, semi-dry, semi-sweet, sweet), rosé (dry, semi-dry, semi-sweet, sweet), and red (dry, semi-dry, semi-sweet, sweet) from Kilkis.

🐝 Assyrtiko, Malagousia, Rhoditis, Chardonnay, Sauvignon Blanc, Limnio, Negoska, Xinomavro, Cabernet Sauvignon, Merlot, Syrah

CÔTES DE PARNITHA PGI
Central Greece

This PGI covering Attica and Viotia is allowed, but not yet activated.

CÔTES DE PENDELIKO PGI
Central Greece

White (dry) from Attica.

🐝 Chardonnay

CÔTES DE PETROTO PGI
Peloponnese

Red (dry) from Achaia.

🐝 A minimum of 60% Mavrodaphne plus Cabernet Sauvignon

CÔTES DE VERTISKOS PGI
Macedonia

White (dry), rosé (dry), and red (dry) from Thessaloniki.

🐝 Athiri, Assyrtiko, Malagousia, Rhoditis, Chardonnay, Xinomavro, Pamidi, Cabernet Sauvignon, Merlot, Syrah

CRETE or KRITIKOS PGI
Crete

White (dry, semi-dry, semi-sweet), rosé (dry, semi-dry, semi-sweet), and red (dry, semi-dry, semi-sweet) wines from grapes authorized for any of the PDOs in the region indicated.

🍷 *Idaia* (Syrah) • *Lyrakisa* (Symbolo Grande Cuvée) • *Estate Michalakis* (Gold Cuvee red) • *Minas Tamiolakis* (Syrah-Kotsifali)

CYCLADES PGI
Aegean

White (dry, semi-dry, semi-sweet, sweet), rosé (dry, semi-dry, semi-sweet, sweet), and red (dry, semi-dry, semi-sweet, sweet) from Cyclades.

🍇 Athiri, Aidani, Asprouda of Santorini, Assyrtiko, Gaidouria, Katsano, Kritiko, Maloukaro, Muscat Blanc, Savatiano, Athiri Black, Aidani Blank, Avgoustiatis, Vaftra, Voidomatis, Kotsifali, Mandelaria, Mavrotragano, Fokiano

DAFNES PDO
Crete

Douloufakis is the best-known producer of these red wines, which may dry or sweet, from the Liatiko grape.

DODECANNESE *or* DODECANNESIAKOS PGI
Aegean

White (dry, semi-dry, semi-sweet), rosé (dry, semi-dry, semi-sweet), and red (dry, semi-dry, sweet) from Dodecannese.

🍇 Athiri, Assyrtiko, Malagousia, Muscat Blanc, Muscat Trani, Chardonnay, Sauvignon Blanc, Trebbiano, Mandelaria, Grenache, Cabernet Sauvignon, Merlot, Mourvèdre, Cinsault, Syrah, Tempranillo

DRAMA PGI
Macedonia

A potentially exciting region huddled among the Falakro, Menekio, and Peggio mountains, in the far northeast of the country.

🍇 Assyrtiko, Rhoditis, Malagousia, Muscat d'Alexandrie, Robola, Chardonnay, Sauvignon Blanc, Sémillon, Trebbiano, Viognier, Agiorgitiko, Limnio, Cabernet Sauvignon, Cabernet Franc, Merlot, Nebbiolo, Refosco, Syrah, Tempranillo

✓ *Domain Michaelidi* (Anthaleia) • *Ktima Pavlidis* (Syrah, Tempranillo, Thema) • *Wine Art* (Idisma Drios Assyritiko, Techni Alipias)

EMATHIA PGI
Macedonia

White (dry) and red (dry) from Emathia.

🍇 Xinomavro (maximum of 60% for reds), Rhoditis, Prikadi

EPANOMI PGI
Macedonia

This regional wine area has been put on the map single-handedly by Evanglos Gerovassiliou, the winemaker who made the first great Greek wine of modern times: Château Carras. Gerovassiliou planted experimental vines on his family's property in 1981, while still working for Domaine Porto Carras and has had no formal relationship with that winery since the Carras family relinquished ownership (*see* Côtes de Meliton PDO) in 1999. The low, hilly land of Epanomi might not be the greatest place in Greece to grow wine grapes, but under Gerovassiliou it definitely produces some of the country's greatest wines, both red and – particularly – white.

🍇 Assyrtiko, Malagousia, Viognier, Chardonnay, Sauvignon Blanc, Limnio, Xinomavro, Grenache, Cabernet Sauvignon, Merlot, Syrah

✓ *Domaine Gerovassiliou*

EPIRUS *or* EPIROTIKOS PGI
Epirus

White (dry, semi-dry, semi-sweet), rosé (dry, semi-dry), and red (dry). The whites and the rosés may be semi-sparkling. The whites may be sparkling.

EVIA PGI
Central Greece

White (dry, semi-dry, semi-sweet, sweet), rosé (dry, semi-dry, semi-sweet, sweet), and red (dry, semi-dry, semi-sweet, sweet) from Evia, otherwise known as Euboea.

🍇 Aidani, Athiri, Assyrtiko, Malagousia, Monemvassia, Moschofilero, Rhoditis, Savatiano, Grenache Blanc, Sauvignon Blanc, Agiorgitiko, Karabraimis, Liatiko, Mandelaria, Grenache, Cabernet Sauvignon, Merlot, Syrah

✓ *Avantis* (Agios Chronos)

FLORINA PGI
Macedonia

White (dry, semi-dry, semi-sweet, sweet), rosé (dry, semi-dry, semi-sweet, sweet), and red (dry, semi-dry, semi-sweet, sweet). The white may be sparkling. This is the appellation that top-performing Alpha Estate uses for wines outside of the Amyndeon PDO, and the wines are at least as exciting.

🍇 Assyrtiko, Malagousia, Rhoditis, Gewürztraminer, Riesling, Chardonnay, Sauvignon Blanc, Limnio, Mavrodaphne, Xinomavro, Cabernet Franc, Cabernet Sauvignon, Merlot, Montepulciano, Barbera, Negro Amaro, Pinot Noir, Syrah, Tannat

✓ *Alpha Estate*

GERANIA PGI
Central Greece

White (dry), rosé (dry), and red (dry) from Attica.

🍇 Rhoditis, Savatiano, Agiorgitiko, Grenache, Carignan, Merlot, Syrah

GOUMENISSA PDO
Macedonia

A light-bodied red wine from the Goumenissa district, northeast of Naoussa, usually of good fruit and a certain elegance. The best undergo a light maturation in cask and can be relatively rich in flavour.

🍇 A minimum of 20% Negoska plus Xinomavro

GREVENA PGI
Macedonia

Rosé (dry, semi-dry, semi-sweet) and red (dry, semi-dry, semi-sweet) from Grevena.

🍇 Rhoditis, Xinomavro, Mosvomavro, Merlot, Cabernet Sauvignon, Syrah

HALIKOUNA PGI
Ionian Islands

White (dry) from Corfu.

🍇 Kakotrygis

HALKIDIKI PGI
Macedonia

White (dry, semi-dry, semi-sweet), rosé (dry, semi-dry, semi-sweet), and red (dry, semi-dry, semi-sweet) from Halkidiki.

🍇 Athiri, Assyrtiko, Malagousia, Rhoditis, Muscat d'Alexandrie, Sauvignon Blanc, Trebbiano, Limnio, Xinomavro, Grenache, Cabernet Sauvignon, Merlot, Syrah

✓ *Claudia Papayianni*

HERAKLION *or* HERAKLIOTIKOS PGI
Crete

White (dry, semi-dry, semi-sweet), rosé (dry, semi-dry, semi-sweet), and red (dry, semi-dry, semi-sweet) from Heraklion.

🍇 Athiri, Vilana, Vidiano, Dafni, Thrapsathiri, Muscat Blanc, Plyto, Chardonnay, Sauvignon Blanc, Sylvaner, Kotsifali, Kotsifoliatiko, Liatiko, Ladikino, Mandelaria, Grenache, Cabernet Sauvignon, Carignan, Merlot, Mourvèdre, Syrah

✓ *Boutari* (Skalani)

IKARIA PGI
Aegean

White (dry, semi-dry, semi-sweet), rosé (dry, semi-dry, semi-sweet), and red (dry, semi-

VINEYARDS AT DOMAINE GEROVASSILIOU
Having cut his viticultural teeth establishing the vineyards of Château Carras under the guiding hand of the legendary Professor Peynaud of Bordeaux University, Evanglos Gerovassiliou put all his hard-earned experience to work establishing his own domaine in Epanomi.

dry, semi-sweet) from Samos.

🐝 Athiri, Assyrtiko, Begleri, Vaftra, Mandelaria, Fokiano

ILIA PGI
Peloponnese

White (dry), rosé (dry), and red (dry) from Ilia.

🐝 Asproudes, Assyrtiko, Rhoditis, Robola, Skiadopoulo, Fileri, Viognier, Chardonnay, Sauvignon Blanc, Trebbiano, Agiorgitiko, Avgoustiatis, Kolliniatiko, Mandelaria, Mavrodaphne, Mavroudi, Grenache, Cabernet Sauvignon, Carignan, Merlot, Mourvèdre, Refosco, Syrah

ILION PGI
Central Greece

White (dry) from Attica.

🐝 Malagousia, Rhoditis, Savatiano, Chardonnay, Sauvignon Blanc

IOANNINA PGI
Epirus

White (dry, semi-dry), rosé (dry, semi-dry), and red (dry). The white and the rosé may be sparkling.

🐝 Debina (maximum of 60% for whites), Vlachiko (minimum of 50% for reds), Bekiari, Cabernet Sauvignon

ISMAROS *or* ISMARIKOS PGI
Thrace

White (dry, semi-dry, semi-sweet), rosé (dry, semi-dry, semi-sweet), and red (dry, semi-dry, semi-sweet) from Rodopi.

🐝 Muscat d'Alexandrie, Rhoditis, Chardonnay, Sauvignon Blanc, Limnio, Mavroudi, Grenache, Cabernet Sauvignon, Merlot, Mourvèdre, Syrah

KARDITSA PGI
Thessaly

White (dry, semi-dry, semi-sweet), rosé (dry, semi-dry, semi-sweet), and red (dry, semi-dry, semi-sweet) wines.

🐝 Assyrtiko, Malagousia, Batiki, Debina, Rhoditis, Chardonnay, Limniona, Messenikola, Cabernet Sauvignon, Carignan, Cinsault, Merlot, Syrah

KARYSTOS PGI
Central Greece

White (dry, semi-dry, semi-sweet, sweet), rosé (dry, semi-dry, semi-sweet, sweet), and red (dry, semi-dry, semi-sweet, sweet) from Evia.

🐝 Aidani, Athiri, Assyrtiko, Malagousia, Monemvassia, Rhoditis, Savatiano, Grenache Blanc, Sauvignon Blanc, Agiorgitiko, Liatiko, Mandelaria, Grenache, Cabernet Sauvignon, Merlot, Syrah

KASTORIA PGI
Macedonia

White (dry) and red (dry) wines.

🐝 Rhoditis, Sauvignon Blanc, Xinomavro, Sefka, Cabernet Sauvignon, Cinsault, Merlot, Syrah

KEFALONIA PGI
See Cephalonia PGI

KISSAMOS PGI
Crete

White (dry), rosé (dry), and red (dry) from Chania.

🐝 Athiri, Thrapsathiri, Vilana, Romeiko, Ugni Blanc (maximum of 20%), Cabernet Sauvignon, Grenache, Carignan, Syrah

KLIMENTI PGI
Peloponnese

White (dry), rosé (dry), and red (dry) from Corintos.

🐝 Malagousia, Moschofilero, Chardonnay, Agiorgitiko, Cabernet Sauvignon, Merlot, Syrah

KORINTH
See Corinth PGI

KOROPI PGI
Central Greece

White (dry) from Attica.

🐝 A minimum of 80% Savatiano

KOS PGI
Aegean

White (dry, semi-dry, semi-sweet), rosé (dry, semi-dry, semi-sweet), and red (dry, semi-dry, semi-sweet) from Dodecannese.

🐝 Athiri, Assyrtiko, Malagousia, Chardonnay, Sauvignon Blanc, Grenache, Cabernet Sauvignon, Merlot, Mourvèdre, Cinsault, Syrah, Tempranillo

KOZANI PGI
Macedonia

White (dry, semi-dry, semi-sweet), rosé (dry, semi-dry, semi-sweet), and red (dry, semi-dry, semi-sweet) wines.

🐝 Malagousia, Batiki, Rhoditis, Gewürztraminer, Chardonnay, Trebbiano, Limnio, Moschomavro, Xinomavro, Cabernet Sauvignon, Cinsault, Syrah

KRANIA PGI
Thessaly

White (dry) and red (dry) from Larissa.

🐝 Chardonnay, Cabernet Sauvignon, Merlot

KRANNONA PGI
Thessaly

White (dry) and red (dry) from Larissa.

🐝 Sauvignon Blanc, Cabernet Sauvignon, Merlot, Syrah

KRITIKOS
See Crete PGI

LACONIA *or* LACONIKOS PGI
Peloponnese

White (dry, semi-dry, semi-sweet, sweet), rosé (dry, semi-dry, semi-sweet), and red (dry, semi-dry, semi-sweet, sweet) wines.

🐝 Athiri, Assyrtiko, Aidani, Kydonitsa, Malagousia, Monemvassia, Rhoditis, Petroulianos, Agiorgitiko, Thrapsa, Mandelaria, Mavroudi, Cabernet Sauvignon, Merlot

LASSITHI *or* LASSITHIOTIKOS PGI
Crete

White (dry, semi-dry, semi-sweet), rosé (dry, semi-dry, semi-sweet), and red (dry, semi-dry, semi-sweet) wines.

🐝 Athiri, Assyrtiko, Vilana, Thrapsathiri, Muscat Blanc, Plyto, Viognier, Chardonnay, Trebbiano,

Kotsifali, Ladikino, Liatiko, Mandelaria, Grenache, Cabernet Sauvignon, Carignan, Merlot, Syrah

LEFKADA PGI
Ionian Islands

White (dry), rosé (dry, semi-dry, semi-sweet), red (dry, semi-dry, semi-sweet) from Lefkada.

🐝 Vardea, Vertzami, Merlot

LEMNOS *or* LIMNOS PDO
Aegean

This unfortified Muscat wine may be made in dry, off-dry, and semi-sweet styles and is usually soft and flowery, with an attractive Muscat aroma, followed by clean fruit.

🐝 Muscat d'Alexandrie

LETRINES PGI
Peloponnese

Red (dry) from Ilia.

🐝 Agiorgitiko, Mavrodaphne, Merlot, Refosco, Syrah

LILANTIO PEDIO PGI
Central Greece

White (dry, semi-dry, semi-sweet, sweet), rosé (dry, semi-dry, semi-sweet), and red (dry, semi-dry, semi-sweet, sweet) from Evia.

🐝 Athiri, Assyrtiko, Malagousia, Moschofilero, Rhoditis, Savatiano, Sauvignon Blanc, Agiorgitiko, Vradiano, Karabaimis, Mandelaria, Ritino, Grenache, Cabernet Sauvignon, Merlot, Syrah

MACEDONIA *or* MACEDONIKOS PGI
Macedonia

White (dry, semi-dry, semi-sweet), rosé (dry, semi-dry, semi-sweet), and red (dry, semi-dry, semi-sweet) wines from grapes authorized for any of the PDOs in the region indicated.

MAGNISSIA PGI
Thessaly

White (dry, semi-dry, semi-sweet), rosé (dry, semi-dry, semi-sweet), and red (dry, semi-dry, semi-sweet) wines.

🐝 Asproudes, Assyrtiko, Rhoditis, Savatiano, Trebbiano, Vradiano, Limnio, Mavroudi, Xinomavro, Sykiotis, Grenache, Cabernet Sauvignon, Merlot, Syrah

MANTINIA PDO
Peloponnese

This is a dry white wine from mountain vineyards in the centre of the Peloponnese, where the vines grow at an altitude of 650 metres (2,130 feet) and produce some very fresh, young wines with nice lively fruit.

🐝 A minimum of 20% Moschofilero plus Asproudes

✓ *Antonopoulos • Spiropoulos*

MANZAVINATA PGI
Ionian Islands

White (dry), rosé (dry), and red (dry) wines from Cephalonia.

🐝 Goustolidi (Vostilidi), Tsaoussi, Araklino, Theako

MARKOPOULO PGI
Central Greece

White (dry) from Attica.

🍇 A minimum of 80% Savatiano

MARTINO PGI
Central Greece

White (dry), rosé (dry), and red (dry) from Fthiotida.

🍇 Athiri, Malagousia, Rhoditis, Robola, Chardonnay, Sauvignon Blanc, Trebbiano, Cabernet Sauvignon, Cabernet Franc, Merlot, Syrah

MAVRODAPHNE OF CEPHALONIA PDO
Ionian Islands

The Mavrodaphne of Kefalonia is a sweet red liqueur wine, similar in character to the Mavrodaphne of Patras but not quite in the same class.

🍇 Mavrodaphne

MAVRODAPHNE OF PATRAS PDO
Peloponnese

A rich, sweet, red liqueur wine with a velvety smooth, sweet-oak finish. Often compared to a Recioto della Valpolicella, the best Mavrodaphne are, I think, far better, but they have a similar oxidative, raisiny-Sherry aroma. One delightful aspect is that this wine can be drunk with equal pleasure either young and fruity or smooth and mature.

🍇 Mavrodaphne, Corinthiaki

✓ *Achaia Clauss* (Grand Reserve) • *Parparoussis* (Reserve)

MESSENIKOLA PDO
Thessaly

This appellation was introduced in 1994 but has not exactly taken off. The primary variety, Mavro Messenikola, is grown at an altitude of 250–300 metres (825–990 feet).

🍇 70% Mavro Messenikola, 30% Carignan and Syrah

MESSINIA *or* MESSINIAKOS PGI
Peloponnese

White (dry) and red (dry) from Messinia.

🍇 Assyrtiko, Lagorthi, Rhoditis, Fileri, Arintho, Chardonnay, Sauvignon Blanc, Trebbiano, Fokiano Black, Grenache, Cabernet Sauvignon, Carignan, Merlot

METAXATA PGI
Ionian Islands

This PGI on the island of Cephalonia is allowed but not yet activated.

METEORA PGI
Thessaly

White (dry, semi-dry, semi-sweet), rosé (dry, semi-dry, semi-sweet), and red (dry) from Trikala.

🍇 Assyrtiko, Malagousia, Batiki, Debina, Rodits, Zalovitiko, Xinomavro, Cabernet Sauvignon, Cinsault, Syrah

METSOVO *or* METSOVITIKOS PGI
Epirus

Red (dry) from Ioannina.

🍇 A minimum of 60% Cabernet Sauvignon

MONEMVASSIA *or* MONEMVASSIOS PGI
Peloponnese

White (dry) and red (dry) from Laconia.

🍇 Aidani, Athiri, Asproudes, Assyrtiko, Kydonitsa, Malagousia, Rhoditis, Petrouliano, Monemvassia, Fileri, Agiorgitiko, Thrapsa, Mandelaria, Mavroudi, Cabernet Sauvignon, Merlot

MOUNT ATHOS *or* HOLLY MOUNTAIN PGI
Macedonia

White (dry, semi-dry, sweet), sweet rosé (dry, semi-dry), and red (dry, semi-dry, sweet) wines from Halkidiki.

🍇 Athiri, Assyrtiko, Rhoditis, Chardonnay, Sauvignon Blanc, Limnio, Xinomavro, Cabernet Sauvignon, Grenache, Syrah

MUSCAT OF CEPHALONIA *or* KEFALONIA PDO
Ionian Islands

Muscat of Kefalonia is one of the lesser-known, sweet liqueur wines from the Muscat grape.

🍇 Muscat Blanc

MUSCAT OF LEMNOS *or* LIMNOS PDO
Aegean

A superior liqueur Muscat wine that is richer and sweeter than Patras, though not in the class of Samos. So-called Muscat of Limnos Grand Cru is the sweetest style.

🍇 Muscat Blanc

MUSCAT OF PATRAS PDO
Peloponnese

A gold-coloured, sweet liqueur Muscat that can be delicious in its typically raisiny way.

🍇 Muscat Blanc

✓ *Achaia Clauss* (Collector Series)

MUSCAT OF RHODES PDO
Aegean

White (sweet) wine.

🍇 Muscat Blanc, Muscat Trani

MUSCAT OF RIO (*or* RION) PATRAS PDO
Peloponnese

From a defined area around Rio, this gold-coloured sweet Muscat is often less raisiny than Muscat of Patras due to a shorter drying time, although there is no legal requirement for this.

🍇 Muscat Blanc

✓ *Parparousis*

NAOUSSA PDO
Macedonia

Generally reliable wines are grown west of Thessalonika at a height of 350 metres (1,150 feet) on the southeastern slopes of Mount Velia. Good Naousa is well-coloured, rich, and aromatic, with heaps of spicy fruit and a long finish. Great Naousa is world-class. Semi-dry and semi-sweet reds are also allowed.

🍇 Xinomavro

✓ *Boutari* (Grande Reserve) • *Chrisohoou* • *Thimiopoulos*

NEA MESSIMVRIA PGI
Macedonia

White (dry, semi-dry) and red (dry, semi-dry) from Thessaloniki.

🍇 Zoumiatiko, Malagousia, Rhoditis, Chardonnay, Rhoditis, Sauvignon Blanc, Limnio, Grenache, Cabernet Sauvignon, Merlot, Cinsault, Syrah

NEMEA PDO
Peloponnese

Grown in the Corinth district at an altitude of 250–800 metres (820–2,620 feet), the Agiorgitiko grape comes into its own, producing a deep-coloured, spicy red wine that is fuller-bodied than this grape manages elsewhere but can sometimes be spoiled by dried-out or "dead" fruit. Known locally as the Blood of Hercules, because his blood was shed when he killed the Nemean lion, Nemea's Agiorgitiko wine has been produced for 2,500 years. Semi-dry and semi-sweet reds are also permitted.

🍇 Agiorgitiko

✓ *Gaia* • *Lykos* (Kratistos) • *Mitravelas Estate* • *Papaïoannou* (Microclima, Old Vines, Terroir) • *Pavilos Estate* (Noema, Ammos Reserve Terra Leone) • *Nicolas Repanis* (Golden Angel Moschofilero Sur Lies) • *Tselepos* (Agiorgitiko Driopi)

OPOUNTIA LOKRIDOS PGI
Central Greece

White (dry), rosé (dry), and red (dry) wines from Fthiotida.

🍇 Athiri, Assyrtiko, Robola, Chardonnay, Sauvignon Blanc, Limnio, Xinomavro, Cabernet Sauvignon, Merlot, Syrah

PALLINI *or* PALLINIOTIKOS PGI
Central Greece

White (dry) wine from Attica.

🍇 Savatiano

PANGEON PGI
Macedonia

An exciting regional wine area south of Drama in an ocean-influenced, mountainous microclimate, the elevation and weather of which result in a significantly longer growing season.

🍇 Assyrtiko, Rhoditis, Muscat d'Alexandrie, Chardonnay, Sauvignon Blanc, Trebbiano, Limnio, Pamidi, Cabernet Franc, Cabernet Sauvignon, Merlot, Syrah

✓ Biblia Chora

PARNASSOS PGI
Central Greece

White (dry), rosé (dry), and red (dry) from Thebes.

🍇 Athiri, Assyrtiko, Malagousia, Rhoditis, Robola, Savatiano, Chardonnay, Sauvignon Blanc, Mavroudi, Cabernet Franc, Cabernet Sauvignon, Merlot, Syrah

PAROS PDO
Aegean

The red is a deep-coloured wine that is strangely light-bodied with an underlying aromatic character, which is due to its mix of one-third black

Mandilaria grape and two-thirds white aromatic Monemvassia grape. Pure white Monemvassia wines are also produced.

PATRAS PDO
Peloponnese

Patras plain and simple is a light, dry, semi-dry, or semi-sweet white wine made exclusively from the Rhoditis grape. These wines were once dull and flabby but are now clean and crisp, although they seldom excite.

🍇 Rhoditis

✔ *Oenoforos* (Asprolithi)

PEANEA PGI
Central Greece

White (dry) from Attica.

🍇 Savatiano plus up to 20% Assyrtiko

PELLA PGI
Macedonia

White (dry, semi-dry), rosé (dry, semi-dry), and red (dry, semi-dry) wines.

🍇 Rhoditis, Chardonnay, Sauvignon Blanc, Trebbiano, Agiorgitiko, Limnio, Moschomavro, Xinomavro, Negoska, Cabernet Sauvignon, Merlot, Cinsault, Syrah

PELOPONNESE *or* PELOPONNESIAKOS PGI
Peloponnese

White (dry), rosé (dry), and red (dry) wines from grapes authorized for any of the PDOs in the region indicated.

✔ *Palivos Estate* (Terra Leone Syrah) • *Skouras* (Mega Oenos, Merlot) • *Ktima Tselepos* (Kokkinomilos)

PEZA PDO
Crete

The white wines lack crispness, whereas the red wines are often dried out and could be fresher.

🍇 **WHITES:** Vilana
REDS: 75% Kotsifali, 25% Mandelaria

PIERIA PGI
Macedonia

White (dry, semi-dry, semi-sweet, sweet), rosé (dry, semi-dry, semi-sweet, sweet), and red (dry, semi-dry, semi-sweet, sweet) from Pieria.

🍇 Assyrtiko, Malagousia, Rhoditis, Savatiano, Chardonnay, Sauvignon Blanc, Trebbiano, Agiorgitiko, Limniona, Xinomavro, Pamidi, Grenache, Cabernet Sauvignon, Merlot, Cinsault, Syrah

PISATIS PGI
Peloponnese

White (dry) wine from Ilia.

🍇 Rhoditis, Chardonnay, Sauvignon Blanc

PLAGIES *or* PLAYIES

Synonymous with *côtes*. See "Côtes de" appellations.

PYLIA PGI
Peloponnese

White (dry) from Messinia.

🍇 Assyrtiko, Rhoditis, Chardonnay, Trebbiano

RAPSANI PDO
Thessaly

Uninspiring dry red wines from flat, uninspiring vineyards in the vicinity of Mount Olympus.

🍇 Xinomavro, Krassato, Stavroto

RETSINA *or* RITINITIS OENOS TA
Greece

Although rosé is not unknown, most Retsina is white, with 85 per cent of the blend coming from the Savatiano grape. Production is mostly Central Greece, and most of that is from Attica, but it may be produced anywhere in the country. There are 12 specific Retsina Traditional Appellations (Attica, Evia, Kropias or Koropi, Markopoulo, Megara, Messogia, Peanea or Liopesi, Pallini, Pikermi, Spata, Theva, and Viotia), and the best Retsina is said to come from three of these areas: Attica, Evia, and Viota. However, the best Retsinas I have tasted have all been labelled under the basic Retsina TA. To make Retsina, pine resin is added during fermentation – a practice that dates back to antiquity, when wine was stored in jars and amphorae. As these vessels were not air-tight, the wines rapidly deteriorated. Over the course of time, people learned to seal the jars with a mixture of plaster and resin, and the wines naturally lasted longer. This increased longevity was attributed to the antiseptic effect of resin, the aroma and flavour of which was very noticeable in the best-preserved wines. It was, of course, a false assumption, but in the absence of Pasteur's discoveries (then some 25 centuries in the future), it appeared to be supported by the fact that the more resinous the wine, the less it deteriorated. Within a short time, resin was being added directly to the wine, and the only difference between modern and ancient Retsina is that the resin is now added directly to the wine during fermentation, rather than after. Strictly speaking, Retsina is not wine, it is an aromatized wine just like Vermouth, but it has been uniquely recognized as a wine by the EU. There are degrees of resination, ranging from relatively light to heavy, and the quality of the pine resin itself can range from poor to fine; the best is said to come from the Alep or Aleppo pine trees of Attica. Despite its penetrating aroma and flavour, pine resin cannot hide a tired, flabby, oxidized, or simply bad wine, which is the sort of stuff that most tourists encounter. Personally, I do not want to drink even the best pine-resinated wine, but there is such a thing as fine-quality Retsina, and if you taste around enough, it is easy to discern the difference between the bottles of pine disinfectant and the subtle aromas of a *barrique*-fermented Retsina.

🍇 Primarily Rhoditis and/or Savatiano, but numerous other grape varieties are permitted outside Central Greece

✔ *Gaia* (Ritinitis Nobilis) • *Kechris* (The Pine's Tear)

RODOS *or* RHODES PDO
Aegean

Reds are pure Mandilaria (known locally as Amoryano), and whites are pure Athiri, which can be surprisingly fresh and crisp for such a sunny Mediterranean isle. The non-appellation sparkling wines of CAIR, the local cooperative, are rather coarse by today's more sophisticated market demands.

✔ *Emery*

RITSONA OF AVLIDA PGI
Central Greece

White (dry, semi-dry, semi-sweet), rosé (dry, semi-dry), and red (dry, semi-dry), from Evia.

🍇 Aidani, Athiri, Assyrtiko, Malagousia, Monemvassia, Moschofilero, Savatiano, Grenache Blanc, Sauvignon Blanc, Agiorgitiko,

MANOLATES, SAMOS, GREECE
One of 22 villages growing grapes for the legendary sweet Muscat wines of Samos, famous throughout Greek literature since 1200 BC.

Vradiano, Karabraimis, Liatiko, Mandelaria, Ritino, Grenache, Cabernet Sauvignon, Merlot, Syrah

ROBOLA PDO
Ionian Islands

White (dry) wine.

🍇 Robola

SAMOS PDO
Aegean

One of the great sweet wines of the world, the local cooperative's Samos, Samos Grand Cru, Samos Nectar, and Samos Anthemis are, in order of increasing complexity and sweetness, all superb, perfectly balanced, rich, and mellifluous wines. It also produces a deliciously dry and fresh, non-appellation version called Doryssa, as well as two that are off-dry: Samena and Samena Gold, which are both as clean as a whistle, with a delightful orange flower-water aroma and delicate fruit.

🍇 Muscat à Petits Grains

✓ *Samos Cooperative*

SANTORINI PDO
Aegean

If you want to know what *terroir* is, then taste a full-bodied dry white Assyrtiko from Santorini, with its intriguing combination of high alcohol and acidity, which only seems to amplify the excruciating *goût de terroir* from the volcanic soil. It's not to everybody's taste – in fact, it's not to most people's taste – but it is fascinating, and it is instructive. However, to my mind, it is the sweet wines that excel here. These may be a *vin de liqueur* or *vin doux naturel*, but almost always they will be made as a *vin de paille* – the famous *vinsanto* of Santinori.

🍇 **WHITES:** Assyrtiko, Aidani, Athiri
SWEET WHITES: Assyrtiko, Aidani

✓ *Argyros* (Assytriko, Vinsanto) • *Boutari* (Vinsanto) • *Hatzidakis* (Vinsanto) • *Volcan* (Vinsanto)

SERRES PGI
Macedonia

White (dry, semi-dry, semi-sweet), rosé (dry, semi-dry, semi-sweet), and red (dry, semi-dry, semi-sweet) wines.

🍇 Zoumiatiko, Muscat Blanc, Batiki, Rhoditis, Chardonnay, Limnio, Pamidi, Cabernet Sauvignon, Merlot, Cinsault

SIATISTA PGI
Macedonia

White (dry, sweet), rosé (dry), and red (dry) from Kozani.

🍇 Batiki, Priknadi, Gewürztraminer, Moschomavro, Xinomavro, Hondromavro, Cabernet Sauvignon, Merlot, Cinsault

SITHONIA PGI
Macedonia

White (dry) and red (dry) from Halkidiki.

🍇 Malagousia (minimum of 60% for whites), Syrah (minimum of 60% for reds), and others

SITIA PDO
Crete

The red wines can be dry or sweet, fortified or not. White wines must be dry and cannot be fortified. These have traditionally been somewhat rustic in

character, but the cooperative has improved out of all recognition, and Yannis Economou has been working hard since the mid-1990s to bring some elegance and finesse to wines.

🍇 **WHITES:** Vilana (minimum of 70%), Thrapsathiri
REDS: Liatiko (minimum of 80%), Mandelaria

✓ *Economou*

SPATA PGI
Central Greece

White (dry) from Attica.

🍇 A minimum of 85% Savatiano

STEREA ELLADA PGI
See Central Greece PGI

SYROS *or* SYRIANOS PGI
Aegean

This PGI for the island of Syros is allowed but not yet activated.

TEGEA PGI
Peloponnese

Red (dry) and white (dry, semi-dry, semi-sweet) from Arcadia.

🍇 Cabernet Sauvignon, Cabernet Franc, Merlot, Rhoditis, Fileri, Grenache Blanc, Chardonnay, Trebbiano

THAPSANA OF PAROS PGI
Aegean

This PGI is inactive.

THEBES *or* THIVAIKOS PGI
Central Greece

White (dry, semi-dry, semi-sweet), rosé (dry, semi-dry, semi-sweet), and red (dry, semi-dry, semi-sweet) from Viotia.

🍇 Athiri, Assyrtiko, Rhoditis, Savatiano, Chardonnay, Sauvignon Blanc, Agiorgitiko, Grenache, Cabernet Franc, Cabernet Sauvignon, Carignan, Merlot, Syrah

THESSALONIKI PGI
Macedonia

White (dry), rosé (dry), and red (dry) wines from Thessaloniki.

🍇 Athiri, Assyrtiko, Zoumiatiko, Malagousia, Rhoditis, Savatiano, Viognier, Chardonnay, Sauvignon Blanc, Trebbiano, Limnio, Xinomavro, Pamidi, Grenache, Cabernet Sauvignon, Cinsault, Syrah

THESSALY *or* THESSALIKOS PGI
Thessaly

White (dry, semi-dry, semi-sweet), rosé (dry, semi-dry, semi-sweet), and red (dry, semi-dry, semi-sweet) wines from grapes authorized for any of the PDOs in the region indicated.

✓ *Dougos* (Meth'Imon Opsimo, Rhoditis-Assyrtiko)

THRACE PGI
Thrace

White (dry, semi-dry, semi-sweet), rosé (dry, semi-dry, semi-sweet), and red (dry, semi-dry,

semi-sweet) wines from grapes authorized for any of the PDOs in the region indicated.

✓ *Tsantali* (Organic Cabernet Sauvignon)

TRIFILIA PGI
Peloponnese

Rosé (dry, semi-dry, semi-sweet) and red (dry, semi-dry, semi-sweet) from Messinia.

🍇 Agiorgitiko, Grenache, Cabernet Franc, Cabernet Sauvignon, Carignan, Merlot, Syrah, Tempranillo

TYRNAVOS PGI
Thessaly

White (dry, semi-dry, semi-sweet), rosé (dry, semi-dry, semi-sweet), and semi-sparkling red (dry, semi-dry, semi-sweet) from Larissa.

🍇 Debina, Rhoditis, Savatiano, Chardonnay, Sauvignon Blanc, Batiki, Maccabeu, Trebbiano (maximum 30%), Limnio, Limniona, Muscat de Hamburg, Grenache, Cabernet Sauvignon, Merlot, Syrah

✓ *Migas Dimitrios* (Syrah, Paleos Ampelos Merlot-Syrah)

VALLEY OF ATALANTI PGI
Central Greece

White (dry), rosé (dry), and red (dry) wines from Fthiotida.

🍇 Athiri, Assyrtiko, Malagousia, Rhoditis, Robola, Savatiano, Chardonnay, Sauvignon Blanc, Trebbiano, Vradiano, Limnio, Mavroudi, Cabernet Franc, Cabernet Sauvignon, Merlot, Refosco, Syrah

VELVENTOS PGI
Macedonia

White (dry), rosé (dry), and red (dry) from Kozani.

🍇 Batiki, Rhoditis, Chardonnay, Xinomavro, Moschomavro, Cabernet Sauvignon, Merlot

VERDEA TA
Ionian Islands

White (dry) wine from Zakynthos.

🍇 A minimum of 50% Skiadopoulo plus Gourstolidi and Pavlos

VILITSA PGI
Central Greece

Red (dry) from Attica.

🍇 Cabernet Sauvignon

ZITSA PDO
Epirus

White wines only, Zitsa may be dry, dry semi-sparkling or sparkling, semi-dry semi-sparkling or sparkling, or semi-sweet sparkling, but most are dry and semi-dry and slightly spritzy. These wines are invariably clean, and the best have a delicate fruitiness. The vineyards are located around Zitsa and six neighbouring villages, where the vines grow at an altitude of 600 metres (1,970 feet). Most of the production is processed by the cooperative at Ioannina.

🍇 Debina

✓ *Ioanninan cooperative* (Orion)

THE LEVANT

Lebanon and Israel have the most extensive boutique-winery industries; Cyprus is just beginning to show the world that there is more to this island's wines than Commandria, as wonderfully complex as that dessert wine can be; and there are the first shoots of growth in Turkey's wine industry.

THE WINE INDUSTRY IN TURKEY might be embryonic, but compared to that of Syria or Jordan, it's serious business indeed. There are wines being produced in Egypt, but it will be a long time before this country can live up to the rich winemaking history that is painted on the walls of its pyramids.

CYPRUS

Wine districts: *Akama, Commandaria, Laona, Krasohoria Lemesou, Krasohoria Lemesou-Afames, Krasohoria Lemesou-Laona, Pitsilia, Vouni Panayia-Ampelitis*

Wines have been made on this beautiful island for at least 4,000 years, and Cyprus's historically famous wine, Commanderie St John, is one of a handful that claim to be the world's oldest wine. It can be traced back to 1191, when Richard the Lionheart, King of England, acquired the island during the Crusades. He subsequently sold it to the Order of the Knights of the Temple, who established themselves as Commanderies and later became known as the Knights of the Order of St John. Commanderie St John is a *solera*-matured, sweet dessert wine, which is made from a blend of black and white grapes that have been left in the sun for between 10 and 15 days after the harvest to shrivel and concentrate the grape sugars. It used to be rich and luscious with a fine, toasty fullness, but there is nothing special about the wine produced today. Those privileged enough to taste rarities dating back to the turn of the 20th century will recognize just how great these wines once were.

In recent years, early harvesting, temperature-controlled stainless-steel vats, and various modern vinification techniques have revolutionized Cypriot winemaking, producing much lighter, cleaner, and crisper wines. The large cooperative producers are cutting down the time taken to get the harvest to the winery, delays which were detrimental to the quality of their wines at one time. The emergence of small, independent wineries since the early 1990s is beginning to offer consumers real choice. It is these new wineries that are leading the way with non-fortified wines, particularly Syrah, which is often labelled Shiraz on this island. The best Syrah are extremely polished wines. Cypriot winemakers must hone their

CYPRIOT VINEYARDS
One of the island's thriving winemaking areas is situated in the foothills of the Troödos Mountains.

FACTORS AFFECTING TASTE AND QUALITY

LOCATION
Technically, the Levant comprises the countries along the eastern Mediterranean shores, which for practical reasons this encyclopedia has extended northwest to Turkey, southwest to Egypt, east to Jordan, and this necessitates that Cyprus is also included.

CLIMATE
Hot and dry for the most part, with a minority of cooler microclimates due to their proximity to the Mediterranean, or high altitude. Vines in Lebanon's Bekaa Valley receive an amazing 300 days of sunshine per year and no rain during the harvest.

ASPECT
Vines grow on all types of land from coastal plains to higher mountain slopes.

SOIL
Soils vary greatly from volcanic origin on Cyprus, through the alluvial river and sandy coastal plains to the Bekaa Valley's gravel over limestone.

VITICULTURE AND VINIFICATION
Better-quality vineyards are being planted on higher mountain slopes, grapes are being harvested at lower sugar levels, and the resulting wines are being fermented at cooler temperatures, with increasing use of new French oak for top-of-the-range wines.

GRAPE VARIETIES
Cypriot varieties: Cabernet Sauvignon, Chardonnay, Grenache, Maratheftiko, Mavro, Xinisteri
Israeli varieties: Cabernet Franc, Cabernet Sauvignon, Carignan, Chardonnay, Colombard, Merlot, Riesling, Sauvignon Blanc
Lebanese varieties: Cabernet Sauvignon, Carignan, Chardonnay, Chasselas, Cinsault, Clairette, Gamay, Grenache, Muscat (various), Pinot Noir, Riesling, Sémillon, Syrah, Ugni Blanc
Turkish varieties: Adakarasi, Ak Dimrit, Alicante Bouschet, Boğazkere, Cabernet Sauvignon, Carignan, Clairette, Emir, Gamay, Moskhatos (Misket), Narince, Sémillon, Sultaniye

skills on well-known international varieties before turning their full attention towards the island's indigenous grapes, otherwise we will never know if poor quality is intrinsic to the grape or its producers. The black-skinned Maratheftiko, for example, definitely has potential when grown at reduced yields in the right area, whereas Xinisteri, the most widely planted white variety on the island, appears to be very ordinary indeed. But this is an emerging wine region where, in general, the producers are better at red wine than white. We will not know the true potential of Xinisteri until Cyprus has produced world-class white wines from recognizable grape varieties and the producers of those wines, if they are so inclined, start to grow Xinisteri at reduced yields in the best-suited *terroirs*.

☑ *Aes Ambelis* (Liastos, Shiraz) • *Ayia Mavri* (Mosxatos) • *Domaine Hadjantonas* (Shiraz) • *Ezousa* • *Fikardos* (Shiraz) • *K & K Vasilikon* (Ayios Onoufrios, Xynisteri) • *KEO* (St John Commandria) • *Sodap* (Commandria St Barnabus) • *Vlassides* • *Zambartas* •

EGYPT

Wine districts: *Dr Armanios Vineyard, Karm El Nada, Minya, Sahara Vineyards (Khatatba), Sahara Vineyards (Luxor), Soos Vineyard, Taba*

Sometime between 3000 BC and 2890 BC, the world's earliest "wine labels" were stamped into clay on sealed wine jars later found in the tomb of King Den at Abydos, certifying that the wine they contained was produced at a vineyard dedicated to Horus. Tomb paintings from the same era show vines grown in raised troughs to avoid wasting precious irrigation resources, and trained into arbours for easy harvesting, demonstrating that Egyptian viticulture was already extraordinarily sophisticated almost 1,700 years before Greece reached its peak. Paintings in the tomb of Parennefer (1330 BC), illustrate that the Egyptians had even invented a primitive but effective form of air-conditioning, burying fermentation jars in sand that is kept wet and fanned, so that the jar and its contents were cooled as the water evaporated. However, winemaking in this country came to an abrupt end in AD 641, when it was conquered by Muslim Arabs. The first winery in more recent terms was established in 1882 by Nestor Gianaclis, a Greek-born Egyptian cigarette manufacturer. The Gianaclis (pronounced "jaana-cleesse") winery was nationalized in 1963, but the government maintained production for the lucrative tourist industry before privatizing business in 1999 for a swift and healthy return on its investment. The buyer, Al-Ahram Beverages Company (ABC), thought it was purchasing a monopoly on both wine and (financially far more rewarding) beer and believed, quite rationally, that there would be far too much pressure on the government of a Muslim country to allow any other purveyors of alcohol to set up business. Although the wine produced by Gianaclis was not of sufficient quality to export and was taxed at 100 per cent on the domestic market, foreign imports faced a 300 per cent tax,

so monopolized sales to Egypt's growing tourist industry would be a licence to print money. How wrong they were. The very year that ABC purchased Gianaclis, its monopoly was brushed aside by El Gouna Beverages Company, which immediately undercut ABC's prices, marketing its Obelisk brand so aggressively that it soon captured no less than 40 per cent of domestic wine sales. ABC could not compete, so it bought out El Gouna in 2001, following which ABC was itself taken over by Heineken in 2002. El Gouna's former managing director, André Hadji-Thomas, then formed another company, the Egyptian International Beverage Company (formerly shortened to EIBCO but now known as EgyBev), which launched the Shahrazade and Jardin du Nil brands at the end of 2005. As recently as 2007, white Egyptian wines were best, although you

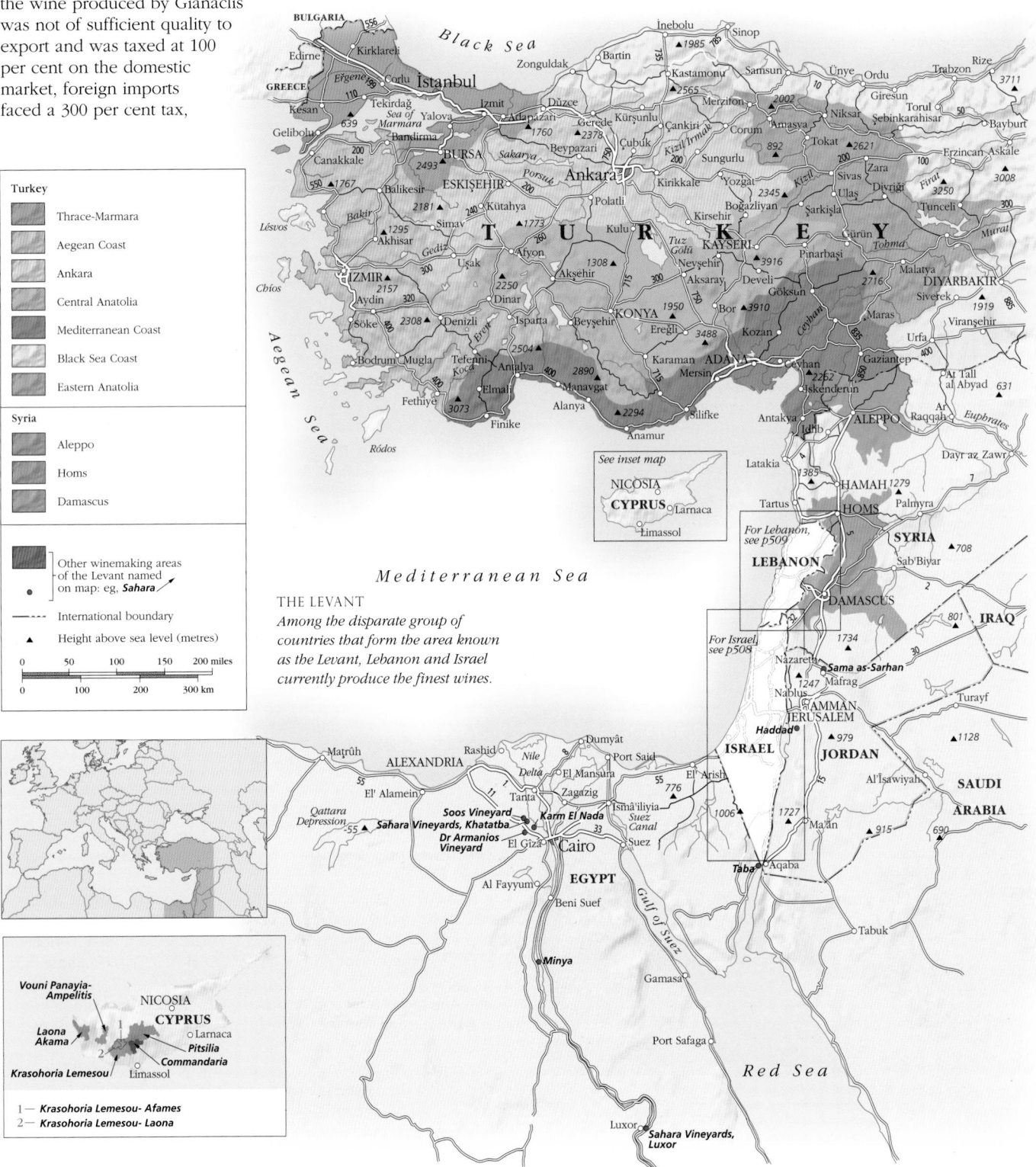

THE LEVANT
Among the disparate group of countries that form the area known as the Levant, Lebanon and Israel currently produce the finest wines.

EGYPT'S EXTREME VITICULTURE
Extending the vineyards at Karm El Nada requires one man, one bulldozer, lots of water, and a harvest that starts in mid-July!

never knew exactly what you were drinking (Gianaclis Pinot Blanc was Thompson Seedless, and EIBCO's Chardonnay was Vermentino-Chardonnay), but with lots of better varieties coming on-stream, it is now quite clear that red Egyptian wine is best, and it makes more sense. The biggest problem for tourists and, indeed, local non-Muslim drinkers is storage and age of stocks, because what you taste in a hotel or on a Nile boat seldom tastes as fresh as it does at the winery. Sahara Vineyards and EgyBev's brands (Shahrazade, Jardin du Nil, and Beausoleil) are generally the most reliable, and although Domaine Gianaclis 2007 Syrah is one of the best Egyptian wines I have tasted, this winery's range is not one you can trust. (I would not touch Giancalis Leila Rosé with a bargepole, and Gianaclis Ayan is much worse!) Equal to Domaine de Gianaclis 2007 Syrah is the red Jardin du Nile from 2007 (blend of Cabernet Sauvignon, Merlot, Petit Verdot, and Syrah), while the very best Egyptian wine I have tasted so far has been a special Jardin du Nile 2008 blend of 50% Syrah, 25% Petit Verdot, and 25% Cabernet Sauvignon. Sahara Vineyards may not be reach the same heights, but it's all perfectly drinkable, and owner Karim Hwaidak is a man with the commitment, passion, and money to achieve that sort of quality across the range. Sahara Vineyards is therefore the one to watch.

✓ *Giancalis* (Domaine de Gianaclis Syrah) • *Jardin du Nile* (red and special blends)

JORDAN

Wine district: *Amman-Zarqua*

Jordan is a country where the vine once flourished, but its fast-diminishing vineyards now cover barely more than one-quarter of the area they did in the late 1990s, and only a small percentage of these vines produce wine. Jordanians are not wine drinkers, preferring Arrack, the aniseed-flavoured spirit that is ubiquitous in the Levant; but one person is determined to put this country back on the wine map: Omar Zumot. In the mid-1990s, Zumot began planting his first three vineyards. His best wines today come from Sama as-Sarhan, 80 kilometres (50 miles) north of Amman. Everything is organic, right down to the irrigation. Rather than rely on nitrate fertilizers, he constructed an industrial-sized fishpond, fed by an aquifer, and stocked it with 150,000 fish to provide natural nitrate-rich irrigation water. The choice of fish was his only problem. First he tried tilapia, which thrived in the summer but died in the winter; then trout, which loved the winter but died in the summer. Finally, he chose carp, and that worked. Zumot successfully grows Chardonnay, Gewürztraminer, Sauvignon Blanc, and Viognier for white wines, and Cabernet Sauvignon, Merlot,

Pinot Noir, Sangiovese, and Syrah for reds. The wines are sold under the Saint-George label. Other Jordanian wines are produced from the East Bank by the Haddad Group under the brands of Chateau de Mouab, Chateau St Catherine, Domaine Jordan, Mount Nebo, and Vin de Chateau. These wines are extremely variable, ranging from decent, sometimes good quality, to undrinkable.

SYRIA

Wine districts: *Aleppo, Homs, Damascus*

In ancient times, wine was second only to olives in terms of agricultural production in Syria. However, since Muslims now account for 90 per cent of the country's population, the vines planted are mostly used for table grapes, sultanas, and currants, with wine production rarely exceeding 8,000 hectolitres (90,000 cases) a year. The above-mentioned vinegrowing districts are situated on lower mountain slopes.

It was, apparently, French troops stationed in the country during World War II who were the catalyst for the wine industry that does exist today – because the French, being French, demanded wine. In 2008, Saadé Wineries in Lebanon announced that they will produce a high-end Syrian wine. If, in the meantime, you want to taste Syrian wines, visit France, where an increasing number of Syrian-made "Lebanese" wines are finding their way on to Lebanese and North African restaurant wine lists!

TURKEY

Wine districts: *Thrace-Marmara, Ankara, Mediterranean Coast, Black Sea Coast, Central Anatolia, Central-South Anatolia, East Anatolia*

This country has the fourth-largest area under vine in the world (after Spain, Italy, and France), but because its population is predominantly Muslim, most vines produce table grapes, sultanas, or currants. Just 2.5 per cent of Turkish vineyards produce wine. Perhaps surprisingly, there are over 100 wineries in Turkey, but their wines are generally flabby, too alcoholic, heavy, over-sulphured, and all too often oxidized. The best known are Trakya (dry white Sémillon from Thrace), Trakya Kirmisi (a red blend of native grapes that also comes from Thrace), and the amusingly named Duo Hosbag (red Gamay, from Thrace) and Buzbag (red wine made from native grapes grown in southeast Anatolia), but despite local fame these wines should be avoided.

There are reportedly more indigenous varieties in Turkey than any other country can boast, maybe as many as 1,200, or four times that of neighbouring Greece. This is one of the oldest known origins of *vinifera* varieties, with innumerable areas that are cut off from the rest of the country, where individual varieties might have remained unchanged for centuries, possibly millennia. Who is to say what viticultural treasure there might be? This is why Turkey needs to build up a critical mass of wine producers to push each other with international varieties, so that there will be a viable production base of sufficient expertise and quality to try out these grapes as and when the scientists catalogue them.

It is worth noting that Villa Doluca was founded in 1926 by Nihat Kutman, a Muslim. Obviously, the religious dimension is not the brick wall that some might think. Kutman's son, Davis-trained Ahmet Kutman, teamed up with his old school buddy Güven Nil to establish Sarafin, a project involving the establishment of Sauvignon Blanc, Chardonnay, Cabernet Sauvignon, and Merlot vineyards at Saroz Bay on the Gallipoli Peninsula. Kavaklıdere is the country's largest winery, and it can produce some good wines, too. New small producers are starting to emerge, and with consultant Michel Salgues now involved both financially and on the production side in this industry, the future looks bright.

✓ *Doluca* (Kav, Villa Doluca) • *Kavaklıdere* (Egeo Cabernet Sauvignon, Prestige Bogazkere, Tatli Sert Narince) • *Likya* (Podalia) • *Mey Içki San & Tic* (Terra Shiraz) • *Sarafin* (Chardonnay, Merlot) • *Turasan* (Seneler Cabernet Sauvignon-Merlot-Syrah)

ISRAEL

Israel has reached the stage where a combination of large companies producing fine, terroir-*specific wines and an increasing number of small, quality-focused boutique wineries has achieved the critical mass required to push the overall quality to a higher level. In the process, the country's entire wine industry has gained global recognition.*

SINCE THE OPENING of the Golan Heights winery in 1983, Israeli wine has evolved from being mostly unremarkable and frequently undrinkable to world-class. Or some wines are world-class, while most of the rest are at least drinkable. The initial driving force behind this change was the Carmel winery, which was established in 1882 by Baron Edmond de Rothschild of Château Lafite, long before a nation state existed. In the 1960s, Carmel produced 90 per cent of all Israeli wines, and it was impossible to find any other brand on most export markets. By the 1980s, its market share had dropped to 75 per cent. Faced with unprecedented international plaudits for the newly released Golan Heights, Carmel had to improve to survive – and improve it did, although this took time for such a massive winery. In the lull that followed, there was an opportunity for others to get their foot in the door, and this led to the boom in boutique wineries that started in the early 1990s. These new ventures started to come on-stream at the turn of the millennium, and it was the huge explosion they provided in choice – not simply the number of brands but also the different grape varieties that became available – that has influenced our perception of Israeli wines over the past five years or so.

Carmel started pulling its weight at about the same time, and the fact that it was capable of producing world-beating wines was confirmed in 2010, when its 2006 Kayoumi Single Vineyard Shiraz from Upper Galilee won the International Rhône Varietal Trophy against everything that Australia, the Rhône Valley, and everywhere else could sling at it. Carmel might produce only 35 per cent of all Israeli wines these days, but the market, both domestic and export, is much larger. Carmel still produces a staggering 10 million bottles, including some very good wines indeed. If peace could be guaranteed in the Middle East, the wine industries of both Israel and Lebanon could be guaranteed a bright future.

☑️ *Domaine de Baal* • Carmel (Limited Edition, Single Vineyard) • *Castel* • Barkan (Cabernet Sauvignon Altitude, Shiraz Superieur) • *Domaine de Baal* • Flam (Cabernet Sauvignon Reserve) • *Galil Mountain* • Clos de Gat • Chateau Golan (Eliad, Merlot, Syrah) • *Golan Heights* (especially Yarden, Golan and Katzrin) • *Margalit* • *Pelter* • *Yatir* (especially Yatir Forest)

ISRAEL
While helping on this map, my Israeli colleague said, "We are a very young country, so forgive us if we are not sure of some of the boundaries." I responded: "If Israel did not keep changing its borders, perhaps you might know where they are…" The map was resolved within 24 hours!

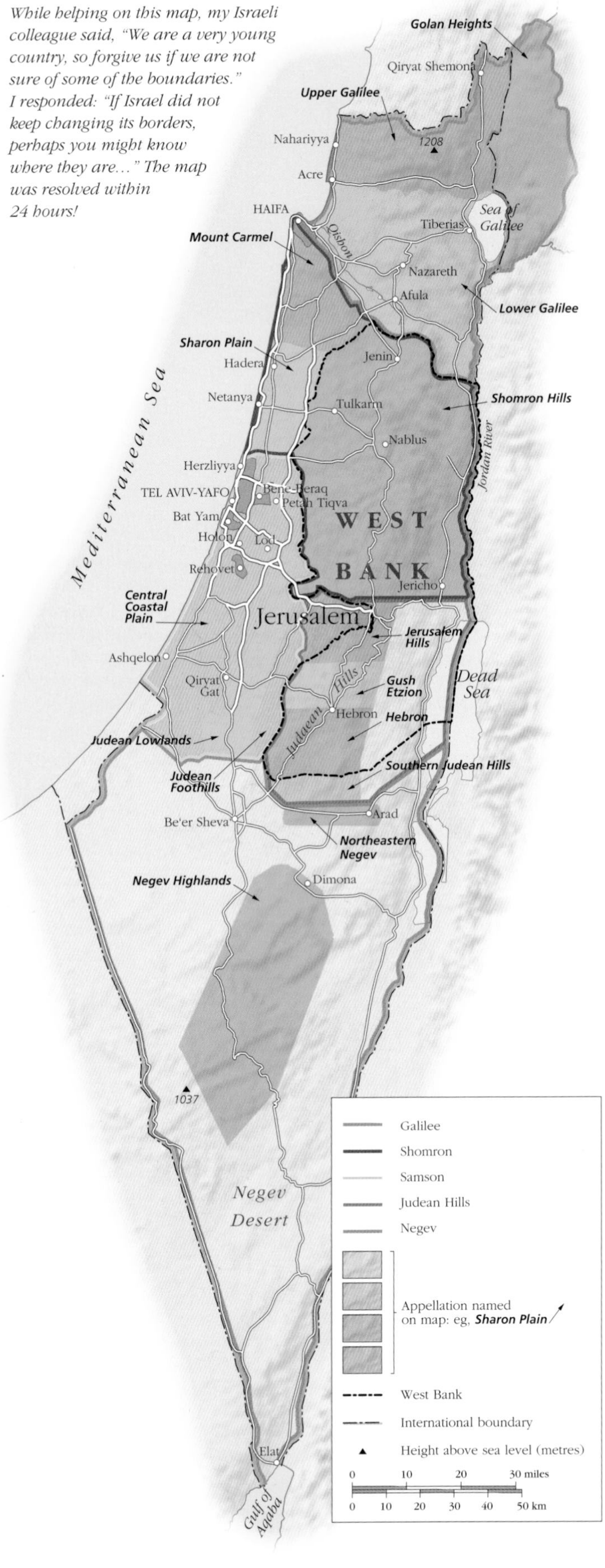

KAYOUMI VINEYARD, UPPER GALILEE
Shiraz from this, Carmel's top-performing vineyard, picked up the International Red Rhône Varietal Trophy at the 2010 Decanter *World Wine Awards.*

Golan Heights
Qiryat Shemona
Upper Galilee
Nahariyya
1208
Acre
HAIFA
Sea of Galilee
Mount Carmel
Tiberias
Qishon
Nazareth
Afula
Lower Galilee
Sharon Plain
Hadera
Jenin
Netanya
Tulkarm
Shomron Hills
Nablus
Jordan River
Herzliyya
Bene-Beraq
Petah Tiqva
TEL AVIV-YAFO
Bat Yam
W E S T
Holon
Lod
B A N K
Rehovot
Jericho
Central Coastal Plain
Jerusalem
Jerusalem Hills
Ashqelon
Judean Hills
Gush Etzion
Qiryat Gat
Hebron
Hebron
Dead Sea
Judean Lowlands
Southern Judean Hills
Judean Foothills
Arad
Be'er Sheva
Northeastern Negev
Negev Highlands
Dimona
1037
Negev Desert
Elat
Gulf of Aqaba
Mediterranean Sea

Galilee
Shomron
Samson
Judean Hills
Negev
Appellation named on map: eg, **Sharon Plain**
West Bank
International boundary
▲ Height above sea level (metres)
0   10   20   30 miles
0   10   20   30   40   50 km

LEBANON

This land is part of ancient Canaan, the vital link between Mesopotamia, where the vine was first cultivated as a crop, and Egypt, the first civilization to master winemaking. Miraculously, Lebanese wine is beginning its seventh millennium, and even more miraculously, it is on the rise again.

I SAY "EVEN MORE MIRACULOUSLY" because Lebanon's modern-day boutique wineries have had to suffer Syrian tanks, Israeli jets, Hezbollah, and all sorts of other militia ploughing through its vineyards, particularly in the war-torn Bekaa Valley, where most of this country's wine grapes grow. Jean-Pierre Sara of Château Ksara was kidnapped twice and endured a mock execution in the Lebanese Civil War.

Château Ksara, founded in 1857, is the country's oldest winery (of the past few hundred years, that is), but it was Château Musar, established in 1930, that put Lebanon on the map, and it was Serge Hochar who achieved this as recently as 1979. Hochar took a small stand at Bristol's World Wine Fair, and Michael Broadbent MW was so taken by Hochar's wines that he declared Château Musar "the find of the fair" in the *London Evening Standard*. Hochar's international reputation, and that of the Bekaa Valley, was sealed in 1984 when he was named *Decanter*'s first ever "Man of the Year" for transporting grapes across half of Lebanon to avoid militia minefields, roadblocks, and Syrian tanks, to reach his winery north of Beirut. A quarter of a century later, Hochar's wines are out of kilter with modern tastes, which do not care for such high levels of volatile acidity, but it is all part of the deliberate style, and he has enough fans devoted to Château Musar and other Hochar Père & Fils wines to sell as much as he wants.

That quarter of a century has not been kind to Lebanon, which had just rebuilt Beirut only to see it and much of the country's infrastructure taken apart by the Israeli air force in 2006. Yet life in the vineyards has continued, and prior to those hostilities, an amazing number of small, hopeful, quality-minded wineries sprang up. Most, but not all, are located in the Bekaa Valley, where grapes are grown at a cool climatic height of 1,000 metres (3,300 feet) on hillside slopes of gravelly soil over limestone bedrock, receiving no fewer than 300 days of sunshine per year and no rain during the harvest.

✓ *Chateau Belle-Vue* (La Renaissance) • *Cave Kouroum* (Syrah/Cabernet Sauvignon) • *Chateau Kefraya* (Chateau Kefraya, Comte de M) • *Chateau Ksara* (Chardonnay, Cuvée de Printemps, Vin Gris) • *Massaya* (Gold Reserve, Selection) • *Clos St Thomas* (Chateau St Thomas, Les Emirs) • *Domaine des Tourelles* (Red, Syrah du Liban) • *Wardy* (Private Selection)

CHÂTEAU KEFRAYA, BEKAA VALLEY
The second-largest wine producer in Lebanon, Château Kefraya has its vineyards located at an altitude of 1,000 metres (3,280 feet), at the foot of the Chouf mountain range.

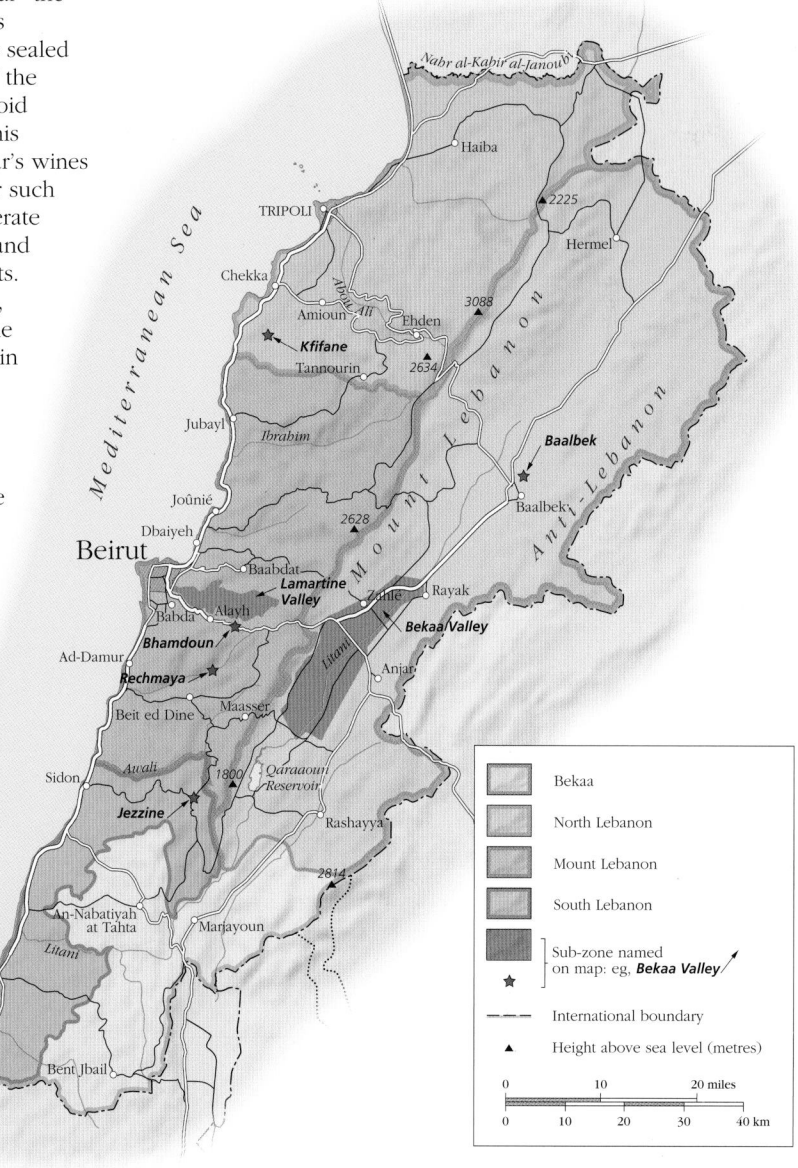

LEBANON
Although the vast majority of Lebanese wines still comes from the Bekaa Valley, the emergence of new wineries has seen viticulture spread west and north towards more Mediterranean-influenced areas.

	Bekaa
	North Lebanon
	Mount Lebanon
	South Lebanon
★	Sub-zone named on map: eg, **Bekaa Valley**
– – –	International boundary
▲	Height above sea level (metres)

The WINES of
THE AFRICAS

THE OLD WORLD MEETS THE NEW WORLD
on the African continent, although they are
thousands of kilometres apart. There is no
interest, let alone excitement, in the former
French colonies of Algeria, Morocco, or Tunisia.
The wine industries in these increasingly
fundamentalist Islamic countries face difficult
times, but if they can survive, there is certainly
potential and it is only a matter of time before a
flock of flying winemakers arrives to exploit it.
If and when this happens, our perception of
North African wine could change profoundly.
There are a number of commercial wineries on
Madagascar and a few curiosities found in
Ethiopia, Kenya, Namibia, and Tanzania. The
French even have a *vin de pays* on the island of
Réunion. But the class act in Africa is, of course,
South African wine. We saw its exports soar in
the Mandela years, but that was merely filling
the void created by its isolation under apartheid.
Sales of South African wine in the second half
of the 1990s were little more than an
international expression of solidarity with the
new Rainbow State. Since 2000, however, a
technological revolution has transformed the
quality and diversity of Cape wine, putting this
country on a firm footing as a New World
player that is second to none.

FRANSCHOEK VALLEY IN THE PAARL REGION, SOUTH AFRICA
*An aerial view of vineyards that are higher and steeper than most
of the Paarl region, and well suited to red wines.*

SOUTH AFRICA

New vineyards, new vine stock, and – thanks to the deregulation of this country's wine-estate system – new terroir-driven wineries have given the new South Africa a new sense of pride in its wines.

IN 1995, SOUTH AFRICAN WINE ESTATES were allowed, for the first time, to buy grapes from outside their own domain to produce non-estate wines, and in 2005 all wineries could offer single-vineyard wines from other locations. This has led to a search for those areas in which each variety fares best. The cool, ocean-tempered southern and western coastal regions in the Cape are exciting white-wine areas in general, just as the hotter inland areas make the fuller red styles. But that is rather simplistic, as there are some excellent coastal *terroirs* that are ideal for red wines, and the higher the vineyards climb inland, the better suited they become to white wines or tempering the excesses of some red varietals. Quite what the future holds for South African wine can only be appreciated in the long term, but there is such a diversity of topographical, climatical, and geological possibilities that there must be top-class *terroirs* in South Africa for virtually every variety known. However, it will take time to perfect some varieties. After all, there is still a lot of work to be done on Pinotage. And what about Sauvignon Blanc? After putting the 2007 revision of this book to bed, it became apparent that there were some very interesting Sauvignon Blanc wines emerging, although I was not as enamoured as some of my colleagues. At the time, I considered Flagstone's Berrio to be the equal of a good Marlborough Sauvignon Blanc, but some critics thought that this variety not only reached higher levels of quality in South Africa than New Zealand, but that there was a broader range of styles available. I did not agree but decided to put this to the test on my next trip to the Cape and asked the South African Sauvignon Blanc Interest Group to put together a tasting of what they considered to be the best.

Stellenbosch and Paarl were traditionally viewed as the country's two greatest wine districts, but since the establishment of Hamilton Russell's top-performing vineyard at Hermanus, many other areas are now considered to be potentially as fine for winemaking. Elgin has developed into another startlingly good wine area. Elgin is the Cape's apple-growing capital, and, as Washington in the United States quickly learned, wherever apple growers choose to go, fine-quality wine grapes will follow. Even further east, there is great hope for Plettenberg Bay, which was first planted in 2000.

THELEMA MOUNTAIN VINEYARDS
These beautifully tended vineyards on the Simonsberg in Stellenbosch belong to Thelema Mountain, one of South Africa's most exciting wineries.

This mountainous terrain some 20 kilometres (12 miles) east of Plettenberg Bay itself is thought to be a premium Sauvignon Blanc area. Other promising new areas include: Cape Agulhas (which

FACTORS AFFECTING TASTE AND QUALITY

LOCATION
South Africa is on the southernmost tip of the African continent.

CLIMATE
The climate is generally mild Mediterranean, but coastal areas have a much higher rainfall and are cooler than inland parts in spring and autumn. All coastal areas are cooled by sea breezes chilled by the icy Benguela current from Antarctica. The coolest, Constantia, like Stellenbosch, rates as low Region III. Klein Karoo, Tulbagh, Olifants River, and parts of Paarl (Dal Josaphat) are the hottest, falling between high Region IV and low Region V (*see* p538).

ASPECT
Most vines are cultivated flat on gently undulating valley floors. More recently, higher slopes have been increasingly cultivated and Klein Constantia, Thelema Mountain Vineyard, Bellingham, and Boschendal all have very steep vineyards.

SOIL
Soils range from gravel and heavy loams of sandstone, shale, and granitic origin on the coastal plain, to the deep alluvial, sandy, and lime-rich, red-shale soils of Klein Karoo and other river valleys.

VITICULTURE AND VINIFICATION
Contrary to popular belief, Cape vineyards sometimes fail even to ripen their grapes, although there are, of course, many hot areas where vines may suffer from heat-stress and grapes can quickly overripen. Irrigation is often necessary in Robertson, Worcester, and Vredendal,

where successful cultivation depends on the availability of water. Where the heat factor is critical, some estates may conduct the harvest at night, under floodlight. South Africa has a history of overproduction, due to having too great an area under vine, too little emphasis on high-quality varieties, poor clones, and undesirably high yields, but is quickly upgrading its vineyards, and is now at the forefront of research on new clones and rootstock. Yields are also being lowered to appeal to export markets. Until the early 1990s, estates were slow to cultivate higher, cooler slopes, but this has changed, especially with emergence of a new breed of winery that buys in from single vineyards, often over a large area. There is a trend for each estate or winery to develop one "flagship" wine, usually a classic red blend.

GRAPE VARIETIES
Primary varieties: Cabernet Franc, Cabernet Sauvignon, Cape Riesling* (Crouchen), Chardonnay, Cinsault, Colombard, Hanepoot (Muscat d'Alexandrie), Merlot, Pinot Noir, Pinotage, Rhine Riesling (Riesling), Ruby Cabernet, Sauvignon Blanc, Sémillon, Shiraz (Syrah), Steen (Chenin Blanc), White Muscadel (Muscat à Petits Grains)
Secondary varieties: Barbera, Carignan, Chenel (Chenin Blanc x Ugni Blanc), Emerald Riesling, Fernão Pires, Gamay, Gewürztraminer, Hárslevelű , Malbec, Mourvèdre, Nebbiolo, Petit Verdot, Pinot Gris, Red Muscadel (Muscat Rosé à Petits Grains), Rooi Grenache (Grenache), Sangiovese, Souzào, Tinta Barroca, Touriga Nacional, Ugni Blanc, Viognier, Zinfandel

* Still commonly referred to in South Africa as Cape Riesling

encompasses Elgin, with Sauvignon Blanc, Sémillon, and Shiraz the most successful contenders); Philadelphia (a new ward north of Durbanville, where vines on hilly terrain up to 260 metres/850 feet in altitude benefit from cooling Atlantic influences and high diurnal differences, currently noted for Cabernet Sauvignon, Merlots, and red blends); Bamboes Bay (Olifants River area on the west coast, with exciting Sauvignon Blanc potential); Outeniqua (hopes for Pinot Noir in Little Karoo Region); and Langeberg-Garcia (the most recently demarcated ward). There is even a KwaZulu-Natal WO, planted in 2000 and demarcated in 2005, with the first certified WO wines released in 2006; this area in the province of KwaZulu-Natal north of Durban stretches from Greytown to Oribi Flats and the Midlands, where vines grow at altitudes of up to 1,500 metres (4,920 feet).

THREE CENTURIES OF WINEMAKING

Most of South Africa's vineyards are found within 220 kilometres (138 miles) of Cape Town. The first vines were planted in 1655 and the wines were not, by all accounts, particularly successful. Simon van der Stel, who arrived in 1679, complained about the "revolting sourness" of the local wines. He proceeded to remedy the situation by founding Constantia, the most illustrious wine farm in the country's history (this has

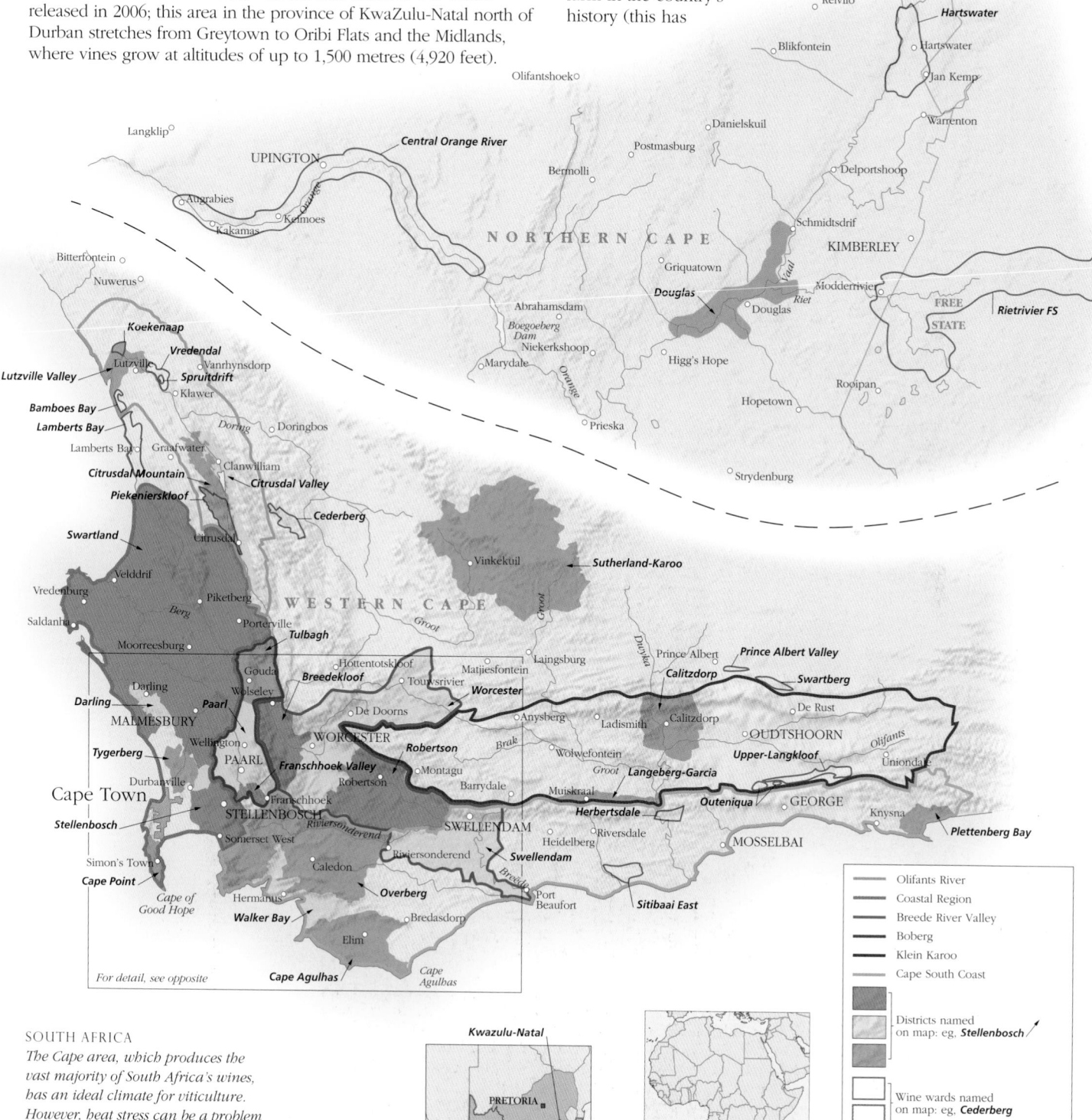

SOUTH AFRICA

The Cape area, which produces the vast majority of South Africa's wines, has an ideal climate for viticulture. However, heat stress can be a problem in some areas, and irrigation may be crucial. Most quality wine areas lie in the Coastal and Breede River Valley Wine of Origin regions, but other outlying districts are also interesting.

Olifants River
Coastal Region
Breede River Valley
Boberg
Klein Karoo
Cape South Coast

Districts named on map: eg, *Stellenbosch*

Wine wards named on map: eg, *Cederberg*

Cape (on small map showing all of Africa)

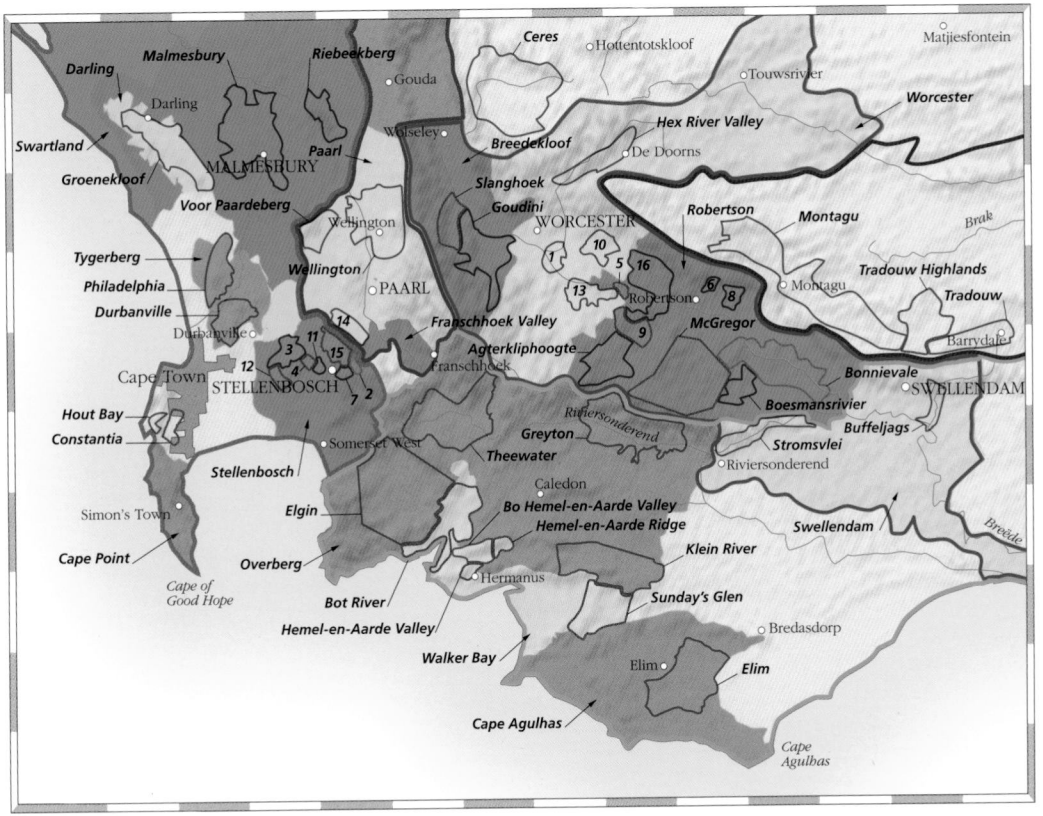

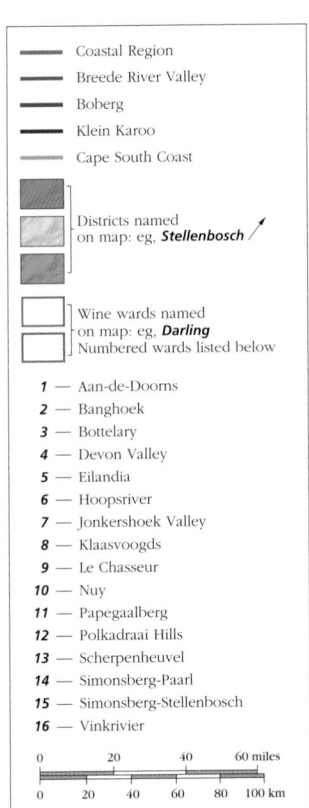

Coastal Region
Breede River Valley
Boberg
Klein Karoo
Cape South Coast

Districts named
on map: eg, *Stellenbosch*

Wine wards named
on map: eg, *Darling*
Numbered wards listed below

1 — Aan-de-Doorns
2 — Banghoek
3 — Bottelary
4 — Devon Valley
5 — Eilandia
6 — Hoopsriver
7 — Jonkershoek Valley
8 — Klaasvoogds
9 — Le Chasseur
10 — Nuy
11 — Papegaalberg
12 — Polkadraai Hills
13 — Scherpenheuvel
14 — Simonsberg-Paarl
15 — Simonsberg-Stellenbosch
16 — Vinkrivier

SOUTH AFRICAN LABEL LANGUAGE

Although an increasing number of South African wine labels are in English or in English and Afrikaans, Afrikaans-only terms may be found on labels.

Cape Dated Tawny Port Wine of a single year which must have the character of a tawny Port, and the label must include the year of vintage, the words "matured in wood" and the words "Tawny Port".

Cape Late Bottled Vintage (LBV) Port Should be a Port-style of a single year of quality, be dark and full-bodied with signs of going tawny in colour. The main label could indicate the year of bottling as well as the vintage, and the description "Late Bottled Vintage" or "LBV" must appear on the label. The port will be aged for three to six years, of which at least two are spent in oak, before bottling.

Cape Ruby Port A blend of young, full-bodied, round, and fruity Port-style wine. Components could be aged in wood for up to three years, depending on the size of wood used, but no components should be aged for less than six months. The average age should not be less than one year.

Cape Tawny Port A blend of wine that has been wood matured, this Port-style wine must be amber/orange (tawny) in colour and must have acquired a smooth, light, slightly nutty flavour. Blending of white and red port for tawny port is not allowed.

Cape Vintage Port A Port-style wine from one harvest, dark and full bodied, aged in wood of any size. The words "Vintage Port" and date of vintage may appear on the label.

Cape Vintage Reserve Port A Port-style wine from one harvest, produced in a year of recognized quality, with exceptional organoleptic characteristics, dark and full-bodied, with very fine aroma and palate. The producer can be assisted by a tasting panel set up by the Association. The wine must preferably be aged for an average of at least one year or more in wood of any size. The wine must be sold exclusively in glass. The words "Vintage Reserve Port" and date of vintage must appear on the label.

Cape White Port Made from a non-Muscat white cultivar, aged in wood of any size for a minimum period of six months.

Cultivar Cultivar derives from a shortened form of "cultivated variety" and is the South African term for grape variety.

Edel laat-oes Noble late harvest. Botrytized grapes must be used for this style, which must have a minimum of 50 grams of residual sugar per litre.

Edelkeur This literally means "noble rot".

Fortified wine, liqueur wine This style of wine must have an alcoholic strength of no less than 16.5 per cent by volume and no more than 22 per cent. This category includes port and sherry, plus such uniquely South African wines as Jerepigo or Jerepiko.

Gebottel in... Bottled in...

Gekweek en gemaak op... Grown and made on... (ie, but not bottled on)

Gekweek, gemaak en gebottel op... Grown, made, and bottled on... (ie, estate-bottled)

Geproduser en gebottel in... Produced and bottled in...

Geproduser en gebottel in die Republiek van Sud-Afrika Produced and bottled in the Republic of South Africa.

Grape variety Since 2005, wine must contain at least 85 per cent of the grape variety or varieties indicated.

Jerepigo or **Jerepiko** A very sweet liqueur wine with at least 220 grams per litre of residual sugar. All Muscadels are Jerepigos, but not all Jerepigos are Muscadels, since some are made from varieties other than Muscat de Frontignan.

Koöperatiewe, köperatieve, koöperasie, or **koöperatief** Cooperative.

Laat-oes Late harvest, with natural alcoholic strength of at least 10 per cent and 20 grams of residual sugar per litre.

Landgoedwyn Estate wine.

Méthode Cap Classique A general term that is used to describe a bottle-fermented sparkling wine.

Moskonfyt Concentrated grape paste.

Oesjaar Vintage.

Origin of the wine (WO) The Wine of Origin (or *Wyn van Oorsprong*) is South Africa's equivalent of *Appellation d'Origine Contrôlée*. WO wines must be 100 per cent from the appellation area indicated.

Semi-soet The Afrikaans term for "semi-sweet".

Spesiale laat-oes Special late harvest. This usually, but not necessarily, implies that some botrytized grapes have been used; there is a minimum natural alcoholic strength of 11 per cent by volume, and no restrictions on residual sugar.

Stein A semi-sweet style of wine that is normally Chenin-based.

Vintage A vintage must contain at least 75 per cent of the year indicated or 85 per cent for exported wines (the balance must come from either the preceding or succeeding vintage).

Wyn van Oorsprong (WO) Dutch for Wine of Origin, South Africa's equivalent of *Appellation d'Origine Contrôlée*. WO wines must be 100 per cent from the appellation area indicated.

since split into three properties: Groot Constantia, Klein Constantia, and Buitenverwachting).

The arrival of French Huguenots, with their viticultural and winemaking expertise, greatly improved the quality of Cape wines, and by the early 1700s they were beginning to be held in high esteem. When French Revolutionary forces entered Holland in 1806, the British occupied the Cape and, cut off from supplies of French wines, began exporting South African wines to the many corners of their empire, enhancing the wines' growing reputation there.

By 1859, the export of Cape wines to Britain alone had reached 45,000 hectolitres (1 million gallons) per year. However, in Britain, Richard Cobden (the "apostle of the free market") and William Gladstone secretly negotiated a commercial treaty with the French that had a devastating effect on this wine trade. In 1860, Cape wine exports fell to 22,000 hectolitres; the next year this dropped to 5,700 hectolitres; and by 1865 just 4,200 hectolitres were being exported.

Despite this setback to the wine trade, production was not checked. In fact, the large influx of immigrants, attracted by the discovery of gold and diamonds in the late 19th century, prompted a rapid expansion of vineyards in anticipation of a vastly increased demand. This increase in demand was realized, but the sudden wealth of these immigrants sparked off the Boer War, and sales of wine decreased at home and abroad.

PINOTAGE AND THE "CAPE BLEND"

There are those who think that a "Cape Blend" with an obligatory Pinotage component should become the flagship of South Africa's export drive in the 21st century. And then there are those who are less than enamoured with the Cape's own grape. It might be possible

RECENT SOUTH AFRICAN VINTAGES

2011 An early, small harvest. Good quality anticipated.

2010 A very difficult year climatically, with ripening patterns gone astray. Some dilute wines, so choose carefully.

2009 A great vintage for both red and white wines from both early- and late-ripening varieties.

2008 A cool and challenging year, rather than a difficult one, with a long *véraison*, a late start to the harvest, and an unusually simultaneous ripening of different varieties creating logistical problems. Even so, some elegant red and white wines have been produced.

2007 The heat wave at the end of January was balanced by cool nights and a cooler February, resulting in fresh, fruity whites and intense, well-structured reds.

to play down this grape's typically high-toned, estery character and, in particular, iron out its high acetate (often incorrectly referred to as acetone) content with appropriate vinification techniques. And if it is cultivated on the Cape's higher slopes, it should be possible to utilize extended hang-time to harvest Pinotage on tannin ripeness without running the risk of producing wines that are big and cumbersome, with too much alcohol. In this way, Pinotage does not have to have its rough edges, green tannins, or the banana and nail-varnish aroma of acetate-laden fruit. But, as its detractors inside South Africa point out, they will still be left with a rustic 1920s cross.

THE APPELLATIONS OF
SOUTH AFRICA

Note Although estates and single vineyards are the smallest demarcated WO (Wine of Origin), wine wards are the most specific type of WO appellation listed here and can be found italicized in the text, following their respective districts in bold. The largest WO appellations are the four "geographical units" mapped above and included in the following text.

BOBERG WO

Wine districts Paarl WO, Tulbagh WO

This regional WO is restricted to fortified wine made within the Franschhoek, Paarl, and Tulbagh districts. Non-fortified wines from these districts come under the Coastal Region WO.

BREEDE RIVER VALLEY WO

Wine districts Breedekloof WO, Robertson WO, Worcester WO

This region's vineyards, east of the Drakenstein Mountains and mostly dependent on irrigation, tend towards white or fortified wines. **Breedekloof** (including the wine wards of *Goudini* and *Slanghoek*) covers a large proportion of the Breede River Valley and its tributaries, where vineyards are found on alluvial valley soils over well-drained gravel beds. The vines can be highly productive: inexpensive Sauvignon Blanc and Cabernet Sauvignon but some stylish, high-quality Shiraz. **Robertson** (including the wine wards of *Agterkliphoogte*, *Bonnievale*, *Boesmansrivier*, *Eilandia*, *Hoopsrivier*, *Klaasvoogds*, *Le Chasseur*, *McGregor*, and *Vinkrivier*) is known as "the valley of vines and roses", but its hot climate relegated this region to largely bulk-produced wine until the emergence of fine-wine hot spots on its lime-rich soils. It now has several top-performing

estates with well-established reputations for white wines, particularly Chardonnay and sparkling, and an emerging one for reds, including several up-and-coming Syrahs. **Worcester** (including the wine wards of *Aan-de-Doorns*, *Hex River Valley*, *Nuy*, and *Scherpenheuvel*) is on the western edge of Little Karoo, adjoining the eastern border of Paarl, in the Breede River catchment area, which is intensively cultivated with vines. The hot climate is tempered in the west by high rainfall, while in the east, rainfall is very low, with soils derived from Table Mountain sandstone and the fertile red shale of Little Karoo. Although there are some good-value red wines made here, Worcester is best known for its exceptionally fine white and fortified wines. Top producers include Bergsig, Goudini, Nuy, and Du Toitskloof.

CAPE SOUTH COAST WO

Wine districts Cape Agulhas WO, Overberg WO, Plettenberg WO, Swellendam WO, Walker Bay WO

This new region neatly tidies up the frontier wine areas on the south coast, but it is debatable whether Cape Agulhas, Overberg, and Walker Bay are south or west coast. They might better have formed their own southwest coast. Most of the vineyards are in **Cape Agulhas** (including its solitary wine ward of *Elim*), where cool summer winds preserve the acidity and aromas of late-ripening varieties such as Sauvignon Blanc, Sémillon, and Syrah. The **Overberg** (including the wine wards of *Elgin*, *Greyton*, *Klein River*, and *Theewater*) replaced the original Caledon WO and used to encompass Walker Bay until it was upgraded to district status. This region has some high-altitude vineyards, the daytime temperatures of which are tempered, even at the height of the summer, by a cold wind known as the Black Southeaster. That's the

upside. The downside is that the Black Southeaster is caused by a deep low-pressure system over the Cape, and this often brings rain, which can increase the pressure of rot and other fungal diseases. It is probably the extremes of Overberg that make it one of South Africa's most exciting wine districts for Pinot Noir, Chardonnay, Sauvignon Blanc, and perhaps Riesling. The Raka winery in Klein River also excels with Merlot and Shiraz. The first vines in **Plettenberg** went in the ground in 2000 and were mostly Sauvignon Blanc, a grape this district excels in, even to the point of making a pure Sauvignon Cap Classic. Pinot Noir is also showing potential. The major part of **Swellendam** (including the wine wards of *Buffeljags*, *Malgas*, and *Stormsvlei*) has a Mediterranean-type climate and is better suited to Chardonnay and Cabernet Sauvignon. It had been patently obvious that **Walker Bay** (including the wine wards of *Bot River*, *Hemel-en-Aarde Ridge*, *Hemel-en-Aarde Valley*, *Sunday's Glen*, and *Upper* [or *Bo*] *Hemel-en-Aarde Valley*) would be one of the hottest cool-climate spots on South Africa's wine map for Chardonnay and Pinot Noir since Hamilton Russell was established in 1975, but the industry was quite different back then. It was a very conservative (with both a lower- and upper-case C) industry, and many of Hamilton Russell's colleagues considered growing vines in such a cool coastal location to be too much of a gamble. It took a couple of decades and democracy for others to start following in numbers, but there are now quite a few highly reputed wineries, the highest flyers of which include Ataraxia, Beaumont, Bartho Eksteen, Bouchard Finlayson, Newton Johnson, Sumaridge, and Whalehaven. Others such as Creation and Luddite are also starting to impress. Cape South Coast also includes two wine wards outside any district wines of origin: *Herbertsdale* and *Stilbaai East*.

COASTAL REGION WO

Wine districts Cape Point WO, Darling WO, Franschhoek or Franschhoek Valley WO, Paarl WO, Stellenbosch WO, Swartland WO, Tulbagh WO, Tygerberg WO

The most frequently encountered appellation, the Coastal Region comprises two external wine wards (*Constantia* and *Hout Bay*) in addition to the above six districts and their wards, stretching up the western side of the Cape from just south of Cape Town. At the southern tip, **Cape Point** is a challenging new cool-climate district on the western and southern slopes of the Cape Peninsula, its vineyards having quickly demonstrated great potential for white wines, although the jury is still out for its red. Chardonnay and Sauvignon Blanc stand out, with the eponymous, stellar-performing Cape Point Vineyards as this district's only producer. **Darling** (including the wine ward of *Groenekloof*) was once part of Swartland, but its vineyards, particularly those in the higher Groenekloof area, were too good not to have their own appellation. Groenekloof occupies a large part of Darling, where a series of red, decomposed granite hills running parallel to the ocean makes attractively aromatic Sauvignon Blanc. Pinotage is the best red wine performer, although Merlot and Shiraz also fare well. The French Huguenot-influenced **Franschhoek** (Afrikaans for "French Corner") is known as the gourmet capital of South Africa, thanks to its famous restaurants and wineries. Not before time, these valley vineyards have been promoted from a wine ward of Paarl to its own fully fledged district. Surrounded on three sides by towering mountains, Franschhoek makes many excellent wine styles, including Cabernet Sauvignon, Shiraz, and Cap Classique and boasts more top-performing wineries than you can shake a stick at. The **Paarl** (including the wine wards of *Simonsberg-Paarl*, *Voor Paardeberg*, and *Wellington*) embraces the fertile Berg River valley and vineyards surrounding the towns of Franschhoek, Wellington, and Paarl itself. The vineyards of this district are located on three main types of soil: granite in the Paarl district, Table Mountain sandstone along the Berg River, and Malmesbury slate to the north. The climate is Mediterranean, and although this once used to be a white-wine area, it is definitely more red-wine country than white, even if both excel, and naturally enough it is Mediterranean varieties that stand out. Cabernet Sauvignon is currently the top performer, but that could change as vineyards are planted with less obviously international varieties. The **Stellenbosch** district (including the wine wards of *Banghoek*, *Bottelary*, *Devon Valley*, *Jonkershoek Valley*, *Papegaaiberg*, *Polkadraai Hills*, and *Simonsberg-Stellenbosch*) is located between False Bay to the south and Paarl to the north and is centred around the leafy university town of Stellenbosch itself. This is where the greatest concentration of South Africa's finest wine estates have traditionally been situated. There are three types of soil: granite-based in the east (considered best for red wines), Table Mountain sandstone in the west (favoured for white wines), and alluvial soils around the Eerste River. With warm, dry summers, and cool and moist winters, irrigation is often unnecessary. Helderberg is the current hot spot. **Swartland** (including the wine wards of *Malmesbury* and *Riebeekberg*) replaced Malmesbury WO. Of the vast area covered by this district, most is arable land, with viticulture confined to the southern section around Darling, Malmesbury, and Riebeek. The soils are Table Mountain sandstone and Malmesbury slate, with a rainfall that is light enough to make irrigation generally necessary. This is blossoming into a fine-wine district, especially for Rhône blends. **Tulbagh** is bordered to the south by the Riversonderend Mountains and to the north by Langeberg Range. Soil, climate, and topography are,

for the most part, similar to those of the Karoo, although somewhat more temperate. It is associated with Cap Classique, but all styles are produced. While many non-South Africans might not have heard of **Tygerberg** (including the wine wards of *Durbanville* and *Philadelphia*), most wine lovers will know Meerendal Estate and need only understand that its vineyards sit on the southeastern slopes of the Tygerberg to put this district into perspective. Rich, red soils combine with moderated temperatures and airflow from the cool summer winds to provide Tygerberg with an excellent growing environment, especially in Philadelphia, one of the latest, most exciting wine wards to emerge, with the reds from Havana Hills grabbing the headlines. Durbanville is located in the lowlands of the Tygerberg hills, close to Cape Town, where the deep, well-weathered, red, granite-based soils have a particularly good water retention, and the vines are cooled and dried by the sea breezes coming in from Table Bay. De Grendel Koetshuis wet-pebble Sauvignon Blanc is the stand-out in Durbanville. As mentioned above, the Coastal Region also includes two wine wards that are unattached to any district Wine of Origin: *Constantia* and *Hout Bay*. The vineyards of Constantia are situated on the eastern, red-granitic slopes of Constantia Mountain, south of Cape Town. Bordered by sea on two sides, the climate is very moderate, of Mediterranean character, but it is quite wet, with up to 120 centimetres (47 inches) annual rainfall. Constantia is, of course, the most historic and thus most famous of South Africa's winelands, being the location of Simon van der Stel's original Constantia Estate (*see* p513).

EASTERN CAPE WO

This vast area is a geographical unit Wine of Origin between the Western Cape and Kwazulu-Natal, which includes the wine ward of *St Francis Bay* but contains very few vineyards.

KLEIN KAROO WO

Wine districts Calitzdorp WO, Langeberg-Garcia WO

This appellation is a long, narrow strip that stretches from Montagu in the west to De Rust in the east. The vineyards require irrigation to survive the hot and arid climate. The famous red, shale-based Karoo soil and the deep alluvium closer to the various rivers are very fertile and well suited to the Jerepigo, Muscadel, and other dessert wines for which this area is known. The **Calitzdorp** is a semi-arid desert region, with summer temperatures of up to 40°C (104°F) moderated by afternoon sea breezes, and cool nights providing a beneficial diurnal effect of ensuring better acidity levels than would otherwise be found in such a hot climate. Port varieties such as Tinta Barroca and Touriga Nacional grow here, and the local Boplaas Estate is famous for its Port-style fortified wines, arguably the finest of their kind in South Africa. **Langeberg-Garcia** is the latest new district to emerge in the Klein Karoo. Located north of the Langeberg mountain range, between the Gourits and Brand rivers, Langeberg-Garcia produces everyday red, white, and sparkling wines under the Virgin Earth label. The Klein Karoo includes a number of wine wards unattached to any district Wine of Origin: *Montagu*, *Outeniqua*, *Tradouw*, *Tradouw Highlands*, and *Upper Langkloof*. Joubert-Tradouw in the Tradouw Highlands is probably faring best with beefy Cabernet, Merlot and Shiraz.

KWAZULU-NATAL WO

This very large area is a geographical unit Wine of Origin northeast of the Eastern Cape. There are no wine wards with WO status and very few vineyards.

NORTHERN CAPE

Wine districts Douglas WO, Sutherland-Karoo WO

Formerly Orange River, this region now encompasses everything from Sutherland-Karoo, the newest district, in the south to the wine ward of *Hartswater*, South Africa's northernmost viticultural area, 80 kilometres (50 miles) north of Kimberley. No fine wines as such are made here, but good fortified wines and an improving quality of good-value, fruity varietals are made by Hartswater Wine Cellar, Landzicht, Oranjerivier Wine Cellars, and Douglas Winery. As well as Hartswater, the Northern Cape includes the wine wards of *Central Orange River* (previously called Lower Orange) and *Rietrivier* (the vast majority of which is technically in the Free State and may be called Rietrivier FS or Rietrivier Free State).

OLIFANTS RIVER

Wine districts Citrusdal Mountain WO, Citrusdal Valley WO, Lutzville Valley WO

The Olifants River is good-value Chenin country, especially **Citrusdal Mountain** (including the wine ward of *Piekenierskloof*) and **Citrusdal Valley**, although Sauvignon Blanc and Chardonnay also fare well, as do some black varieties such as Cabernet Sauvignon, Shiraz, and Pinotage. **Lutzville Valley** (including the wine ward of *Koekenaap*) is the most northerly wine district in the Western Cape, producing large volumes of everyday red and white wines from several varieties, including Chardonnay, Sauvignon Blanc, Sémillon, Chenin Blanc, and Colombard for whites, and Cabernet Sauvignon, Merlot, Pinotage, and Shiraz for reds. The Olifants River region also includes a number of wine wards unattached to any district Wine of Origin. The tiny Sauvignon Blanc hopeful wine ward of *Bamboes Bay* is located between Lutzville to the north and Lamberts Bay to the south. *Vredendal* is not much larger and encompasses the much tinier wine ward of *Spruitdrift*, but this area in intensively cultivated with vines, producing huge volumes of good, everyday-quality red and white wines from many different varieties. Reds fare best, particularly Cabernet Sauvignon, Merlot, and Shiraz.

WESTERN CAPE WO

This geographical unit Wine of Origin encompasses Boberg, Breede River Valley, Coastal Region, Klein Karoo and Olifants River regions of origin and a number of unattached wine wards. *Cederberg* is an up-and-coming wine ward that consists of the Cederberg Wilderness Area, which lies within the Cape's famous "fynbos" region, one of the world's six floral kingdoms. Cederberg Cellars (formerly a cooperative but now owned by the Nieuwoudt family) is one of the South African wine industry's fastest-rising superstars. With vineyards planted an altitude of 1,000 metres (3,280 feet), the highest in the country, Cederberg Cellars is producing a raft of award-winning wines, including a coveted Veritas Double Gold. *Ceres* is a very large, unattached, wine ward between the Tulbagh and Worcester districts. *Lamberts Bay* is a long, Atlantic-influenced coastal wine ward that favours Sauvignon Blanc and is located high up on the west coast in no-man's-land between the Olifants River and Swartland. *Prince Albert Valley* is a 20-kilometre (12-mile) valley at the foot of the Swartberg Mountain Nature Reserve, north of Klein Karoo, in an area better known for its olives than for wine, although it has attracted considerable investments recently, including the Dutch-funded Bergwater Winery, which is irrigated by pure mountain water. *Swartberg* is a promising wine ward that overlooks Prince Albert Valley.

THE WINE PRODUCERS OF
SOUTH AFRICA

Note Wines listed under Late Harvest may be either Late Harvest or Noble Late Harvest.

ADORO
Stellenbosch
★ ✩

Elegant, refined style. Part-owned by malt-whisky producer Ben Riach.

✓ *Entire range*

ALLESVERLOREN
Swartland
★ ✩

Traditionally one of the Cape's greatest port producers, the latest generation owner-winemaker Danie Malan has stepped up a gear over the last few years.

✓ *Cabernet Sauvignon • Fortified* (Port) • *Syrah* (Shiraz) • *Tinta Barocca*

ALTO
Stellenbosch
★ ✩

This estate has improved greatly in the 2000s, thanks to a new winemaker and new viticultural and winemaking consultants.

✓ *Cabernet Sauvignon • Classic red blend* (Alto Estate) • *Syrah* (Shiraz)

ANWILKA
Stellenbosch
★ ★

A collaboration of Bruno Prats (former owner of Château Cos-d'Estournel), Hubert de Bouard de Laforest (co-owner of Château Angélus), and Lowell Jooste (Klein Constantia Estate), the 40-hectare (100-acre) Anwilka vineyard on the Heldeberg was extensively replanted with Cabernet Sauvignon, Merlot, and Syrah in 1998. The first vintage was not produced until 2005.

✓ *Classic red blend* (Anwilka)

ASARA
Stellenbosch
★

Formerly sold under the Verdun estate label, Asara is a luxury hotel that has produced some fine wines, including Avalon, a quirky Amarone-inspired blend of Pinotage and Shiraz.

✓ *Cabernet Sauvignon • Chardonnay • Classic red blend* (Bell Tower, Avalon) • *Late Harvest* (Noble Late Harvest Chenin Blanc) • *Petit Verdot • Syrah* (Shiraz)

ASHBOURNE
Walker Bay
★ ★ ✩

By a long, stretched-out *véraison* under true, cool-climate conditions, Hamilton Russell demonstrates the delicacy, fragrance, and finesse that Pinotage can achieve. Restricted production, with no varietal name mentioned on the label. Ashbourne Sandstone is a fine, mineral-driven Sauvignon-dominated blend.

✓ *Entire range*

ATARAXIA
Walker Bay
★ ✩

Owner Kevin Grant used to be the winemaker at Hamilton Russell, so it's no surprise that he produces masterful Chardonnay here, but his award-winning Sauvignon Blanc can be a touch green.

L'AVENIR
Stellenbosch
★ ✩ ✓

L'Avenir shot to fame when François Naudé became winemaker in 1992. In 2005 it was taken over by Michel Laroche (Chablis), which is now part of Advini, a group that is dominated by Jeanjean and includes various others, such as Ogier, Antoine Moueix and Cazes.

✓ *Cabernet Sauvignon • Chardonnay • Chenin Blanc • Classic red blend* (Black Label Reserve) • *Fortified* (Cape Port) • *Pinotage*

AVONDALE
Paarl
◉ ★ ★

The wines here have shown that organic wines from this country have double-gold potential. Avondale is now dabbling in biodynamics (Cyclus & La Luna).

✓ *Chenin Blanc* (Amina) • *Classic red blend* (Navitas) • *Sauvignon Blanc • Syrah* (Samsara)

AXE HILL
Calitzdorp
★ ✩

Bought in 1993 by the late and much-loved Tony Mossop, who quickly established Axe Hill as one of South Africa's iconic Port-style wines. Wines are made by Miles Mossop, Tony's youngest son and winemaker at both Tokara and his own Miles Mossop winery.

✓ *Entire range*

BACKSBERG
Paarl
★ ★

This estate is owned by Michael Back and it produces some of South Africa's most consistent and classy wines, combining richness, finesse, and complexity with great success.

✓ *Chardonnay* (Babylons Toren) • *Classic red blend* (Babylons Toren Cabernet Sauvignon Merlot, Klein Babylons Toren) • *Viognier* (Babylons Toren)

BADENHORST
Swartland
★ ★

Brilliant red and white blends. The red is 80 per cent Syrah plus Mourvèdre, Grenache, and Cinsault; the white, an eclectic, hedonistic brew of 30 per cent Chenin Blanc plus Chardonnay, Grenache Blanc, Roussanne, Verdelho, and Viognier. Production of a sleek botrytized Sémillon has just started.

✓ *Entire range*

GRAHAM BECK
Robertson
★ ★ ✓

Graham Beck's senior winemaker is Pieter Ferreira, one of South Africa's top sparkling winemakers, but he's a genius with other styles too.

✓ *Classic red blend* (The Joshua, The William) • *Pinotage* (The Old Road) • *Sparkling wine* (Blanc de Blancs, Brut Rosé) • *Syrah* (Shiraz, The Ridge Syrah)

BEIN
Stellenbosch
★

Swiss couple Luca and Ingrid Bein produce five wines, all Merlot!

✓ *Merlot* (Merlot, Little Merlot, Merlot Reserve)

BELLEVUE ESTATE
Stellenbosch
★

Long-time grape farmers, the Morkel family released the first wines under their own label with the 1999 vintage, to resounding success.

✓ *Classic red blend* (Tumara) • *Malbec* (Limited Release) • *Pinotage* (PK Morkel) • *Sauvignon Blanc* (Morkel)

BELLINGHAM
Franschhoek
★ ★ ✓

Owned by Douglas Green, Bellingham is a totally separate, standalone operation that makes some pretty remarkable wines.

✓ *Cabernet Franc* (Spitz) • *Cabernet Sauvignon* (Maverick) • *Chardonnay* (Spitz) • *Chenin Blanc* (Maverick) • *Merlot* (Spitz) • *Syrah* (Founder's Shiraz, Maverick Syrah) • *Viognier* (Maverick)

BEAUMONT
Walker Bay
★ ✩

This rising star was established in 1993 by Raoul and Jane Beaumont, whose son Sebastian crafts top-quality Chenin and a fabulous blended red.

✓ *Chenin Blanc* (Hope Marguerite) • *Classic red blend* (Ariane)

THE BERRIO
Cape Agulhas
★ ★

These premises used to belong to Bruce Jack's Flagstone winery, but that business was taken over by Constellation, who made Jack their frontman in South Africa. Jack retained the premises and one of his old brands, The Berrio, relaunching the winery, which has always been a joint venture with vineyard owner Francis Pratt, to yet another success. The Sauvignon Blanc continues to be The Berrio's flagship wine, although The Weather Girl is looking pretty tasty, too!

✓ *Classic white blend* (The Weather Girl) • *Sauvignon Blanc*

BEYERSKLOOF
Stellenbosch
★ ★

Part-owned by Beyers Truter, who earned his reputation for Pinotage at Kanonkop.

✓ *Classic red blend* (Field Blend, Synergy) • *Pinotage* (Diesel, Reserve)

BILTON
Stellenbosch
★ ✩

Another name to watch, Mark Bilton established this operation on the Helderberg with his first vintage in 1998.

✓ *Cabernet Sauvignon • Merlot • Syrah* (Shiraz)

BIZOE
Franschhoek
★★

Although the first release was as recent as 2008, Rikus Neethling hit the ground running so fast with these classy wines that Bizoe must be rated two stars. The white is a 70/30 Sauvignon-Semillon blend from Franschhoek; the red is practically a straight Shiraz, with the barest hint of Cabernet Sauvignon and Malbec. This nicely focused strategy is far more preferable to churning out a large range of wines. How can any winery be famous for a dozen different wines? That's not how Margaux, Lafite, *et al* became famous. Neethling's strategy is as impeccable as his wines.

✓ *Entire range*

BLACK OYSTERCATCHER
Elim
★

A fascinating collection of wines, including a standout Sauvignon Blanc, with classic wet-pebble finesse.

✓ *Sauvignon Blanc*

BOEKENHOUTSKLOOF
Franschhoek
★★

This rapidly risen star continues to make good. Entry-level wines are also sold under the Porcupine Ridge

CABRIÈRE
At Cabrière – or as it is now more commonly known, Haute Cabrière – these old Pinot Noir vines are trained in the Cordon de Royat style, which is traditionally employed in Champagne's grand cru vineyards.

label, with the Syrah punching well above its weight.

✓ *Cabernet Sauvignon* • *Classic red blend* (The Chocolate Block) • *Late Harvest* (Noble Late Harvest Sémillon) • *Syrah* • *Sémillon*

BOPLAAS
Calitzdorp
★★✓

Lurking in a large range of commercially acceptable products are a number of extremely fine fortified wines, including one, the Vintage Reserve Port, one of South Africa's very greatest "ports".

✓ *Fortified* (Cape Tawny Port, Red Muscadel, Vintage Reserve Port)

BOSCHENDAL
Paarl
★★

Although this large producer is best known as one of the Cape's pioneering traditional method producer, Boschendal Estate also makes a large range of still wines, many of which, particularly the reds, are more exciting than the fizz, although that is rapidly improving.

✓ *Cabernet Sauvignon* • *Chardonnay* (1685) • *Sauvignon Blanc* (Cecile John Reserve, Reserve Collection) • *Syrah* (Cecile John Reserve Shiraz)

BOUCHARD-FINLAYSON
Walker Bay
★★★⯪

This small, deluxe enterprise was started by Hamilton Russell's winemaker Peter Finlayson, who was joined by Paul Bouchard from Burgundy. In 2001, however, controlling interest in the winery was taken over by Bea and Stanley Tollman. Bouchard remains a partner and Finlayson continues as winemaker. Finlayson is a bit of a gentle giant, and his wines reflect that, building quietly in the mouth to a remarkable elegance and depth of flavour. Galpin Peak Pinot Noir and Galpin Peak Tête de Cuvée Pinot Noir are the standouts here.

✓ *Chardonnay* (Kaaimansgat, Missionvale, Sans Barrique) • *Classic red blend* (Hannibal) • *Pinot Noir*

BUITENVERWACHTING
Constantia
★★

Outstanding since the 1990s, and the highest standards have been maintained since winemaker Brad Paton joined cellar master Hermann Kirschbaum at the winemaking helm in 2004, but it's a pity the Riesling was grubbed up in 2010. Hussey's Vlei Sauvignon Blanc is hugely admired inside South Africa.

✓ *Cabernet Sauvignon* • *Chardonnay* • *Classic red blend* (Christine, Rough Diamond) • *Merlot* • *Muscat* (1769) • *Sauvignon Blanc*

CABRIÈRE
Franschhoek
★⯪

This estate belongs to Achim von Arnim, formerly the winemaker at Boschendal, and, not surprisingly, he has carved out his initial reputation by specializing in Cap Classique, but also produces a very good Pinot Noir.

✓ *Sparkling wine* (Pierre Jourdan: Blanc de Blancs, Brut, Cuvée Belle Rose, Cuvée Reserve) • *Pinot Noir* (Haut Cabrière)

CAPE POINT VINEYARDS
Cape Point

Uniquely located between two oceans – Atlantic and Pacific – Cape Point Vineyards produces some of South Africa's most thrilling Sauvignon Blanc, as well as many other splendid wines.

DEL CAPO
See Anthonij Rupert

CEDERBERG
Cederberg
★★

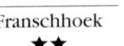

South Africa's highest-altitude vineyards produce wines of great length and finesse, rather than heavy in weight and alcohol.

✓ *Cabernet Sauvignon* • *Chenin Blanc* • *Classic red blend* (Cederberger) • *Sauvignon Blanc*

CHAMONIX
Franschhoek
★★

This winery started to up its game in the 2001 or 2002 vintage, and again in 2008.

✓ *Cabernet Sauvignon* • *Chardonnay* (especially Reserve) • *Classic red blend* (Troika) • *Pinotage* (Greywacke) • *Pinot Noir* • *Sauvignon Blanc* (Reserve) • *Sparkling wines* (Blanc de Blancs, Reserve)

CLOOF
Darling
★★✓

Too big for me, but these massively structured, high-alcohol wines are highly regarded award-winners within South Africa.

✓ *Pinotage* • *Syrah* (Crucible Shiraz)

CLOS MALVERNE
Stellenbosch
★★⯪

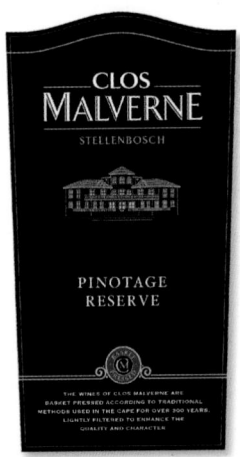

Noted for its deep-coloured, powerful, slow-developing wines.

Cabernet Sauvignon • Classic red blend (Auret Cape Blend, Cabernet Sauvignon Pinotage Cape Blend, Cabernet Sauvignon Shiraz) • *Pinotage* (Reserve)

PAUL CLUVER
Elgin
★★

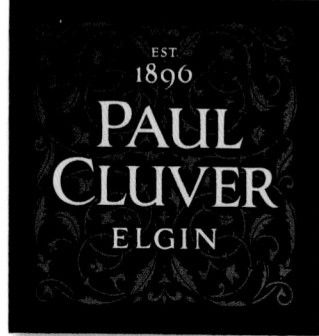

Pioneering Elgin wines from the first vintage in 1997, Dr Paul Cluver now produces some of South Africa's greatest wines, particularly Pinot Noir, the only red in the range.

Chardonnay • Late Harvest (Weisser Riesling Noble Late Harvest) • *Pinot Noir* (especially Seven Flags) • *Riesling* (Weisser Riesling)

THE COMPANY OF WINE PEOPLE
Stellenbosch
★ⓥ

This is the latest reinvention of what was formerly known as Omnia and, before that, Stellenbosch Vineyards. In 1996 the cooperatives of Helderberg, Welmoed, Bottelary, and Eersterivier amalgamated into a commercial entity called the Stellenbosch Exchange. The 150 growers who originally owned these three cooperatives converted their memberships into shareholdings and relaunched themselves in 1997 as Stellenbosch Vineyards. In October 2004, Stellenbosch Vineyards merged with Vinfruco, of which they already owned 34 per cent. This new venture was called Omnia, and its purpose was to focus on brand marketing to those customers, mostly on export markets, that they had jointly been supplying. The most important of these brands was and still is Arniston Bay, followed by Thandi, Kumkani, Shamwari, Versus, Welmoed, and Inglewood (a joint venture with Neil Ellis). Omnia changed to the quirky but rather splendid name of The Company of Wine People in 2006. Used to make some excellent-value reds under the old Genesis label, but now excels at white.

Classic white blend (Arniston Bay Chenin-Chardonnay, Kumkani Chardonnay-Viognier, Kumkani VVS, Thandi Sauvignon-Sémillon) • *Pinotage* (Kumkani) • *Syrah* (Kumkani Shiraz) • *Sauvignon Blanc* (Kumkani, Kumkani Lanner Hill) • *Viognier* (Kumkani)

CONSTANTIA GLEN
Constantia
★★

Classy wines from a magnificent location overlooking False Bay.

Entire range

CONSTANTIA UITSIG
Constantia
★☆

Since David and Marlene McCay purchased this estate, which was part of Simon van der Stel's original property, they have not only replanted its magnificent vineyards but also built a luxury boutique hotel and spa, with three award-winning restaurants and its own cricket ground. With such an investment, it is little wonder that the McCays needed to sell half the ownership in 2006 (to Mvelaphanda Holdings, a consortium led by Tokyo Sexwales, a former ANC politician turned millionaire businessman). Constantia Uitsig makes one of South Africa's most lush red wines.

Chardonnay (Reserve) • *Classic red blend* (Cabernet Sauvignon-Merlot) • *Classic white blend* (Sémillon-Sauvignon Blanc) • *Sémillon* (Reserve)

CRYSTALLUM
Walker Bay
★★

Peter-Allan and Andrew Finlayson, sons of Peter Finlayson of Bouchard-Finlayson fame, are only doing what comes naturally to the Finlaysons – making brilliant Pinot Noir and Chardonnay.

Entire range

DALLA CIA
Stellenbosch
★

Not as compelling as in his heyday at Meerlust, Giorgio Dalla Cia can still pull out the odd stunner.

Cabernet Sauvignon • Classic red blend (Giorgio)

JEAN DANEEL
Napier
★★

Former Morgenhof winemaker, Jean Daneel produces small volumes of exceptionally expressive wines from his own winery.

Chenin Blanc (Signature) • *Classic red blend* (Cabernet Sauvignon-Merlot)

DARLING CELLARS
Darling
★☆ⓥ

Abé Beukes produces increasingly fine wines at this former cooperative, although the alcohol levels can be alarmingly high.

Late Harvest (Onyx Noble Late Harvest) • *Merlot • Pinotage* (Onyx)

DELAIRE GRAFF
Stellenbosch
★★

Established as Delaire by John Platter, South Africa's best-known wine writer, but has since changed hands a couple of times and now belongs to international jeweller Laurance Graff, who has revamped the range and taken the quality a step higher since the 2008 vintage. Winemaker Morne Very honed his knowledge of international palates at the world-famous Summertown Wine Café in Oxford.

Chardonnay • Classic red blend (Delaire Red, Botmaskop)

DELHEIM
Stellenbosch
★☆ⓥ

Always good value, but until recently the quality is more good than great, and more consistent than outstanding. In recent years, however, Delheim has shown a dramatic improvement in quality.

Cabernet Sauvignon (Grand Reserve) • *Merlot • Late Harvest* (Edelspatz) • *Syrah* (Vera Cruz Estate Shiraz)

DEMORGENZON
Stellenbosch
★★

From the mountain-slope vineyards of this estate, it is possible to see Cape Town, Table Mountain, Cape Point, Cape Hangklip, the Hottentots Holland Mountains, Helderberg, Simonsberg, and the Atlantic and Pacific oceans. Outstanding Chenin Blanc and a Syrah-dominated red that's not too heavy or alcoholic.

Chenin Blanc • Classic red blend (Concerto)

DIEMERSDAL
Durbanville
★★ⓥ

Although the 14 per cent plus alcoholic strength of these wines is not unusual for a premium South African producer, the surprisingly elegant style is. Winemaker Thys Louw is acquiring a reputation for fine-quality Sauvignon Blanc.

Cabernet Sauvignon • Chardonnay • Classic red blend (Private Collection) • *Pinotage • Sauvignon Blanc*

DIEMERSFONTEIN
Wellington
★☆ⓥ

Full-throttle Pinotage in the "coffee" style adored by South Africans.

Pinotage (Carpe Diem)

DORNIER
Stellenbosch
★☆

Dornier shows astonishing quality and consistency for a winery whose first vintage was 2002.

Cabernet Sauvignon • Classic red

blend (Donatus) • *Classic white blend* (Donatus White) • *Pinotage*

DURBANVILLE HILLS
Durbanville
★★☆

Apparently, it is so cold during the harvest that the Durbanville Hills pickers have to wear thick woollen sweaters. No doubt this is the explanation for the excellent, bracing quality of the white wines at this up-and-coming joint venture between Distell and seven leading Durbanville growers.

Chardonnay (Rhinofields) • *Classic red blend* (Caapmans Cabernet Sauvignon-Merlot) • *Sauvignon Blanc*

EAGLES' NEST
Constantia
★★

If this vineyard focused exclusively on its Shiraz, its rating would be two and a half stars. Lovers of low-acid Viognier might like to try Eagles' Nest's opulent offering.

Classic red blend (Verreaux) • *Syrah* (Shiraz)

EDGEBASTON
Stellenbosch
★☆

This is owned and run by Walter and David Finlayson, brother and nephew respectively of Peter Finlayson. Winemaking is obviously in the Finlayson genes, although this side of the family leans more towards Bordeaux and Rhône.

Cabernet Sauvignon (especially GS) • *Chardonnay • Syrah* (Shiraz)

EIKENDAL
Stellenbosch
★★☆

This Swiss-owned producer is perhaps best known on export markets for its blockbuster Chardonnay, but it actually produces finer reds.

Cabernet Sauvignon (Reserve) • *Chardonnay • Classic red blend* (Classique, Rossini) • *Merlot • Sauvignon Blanc • Sémillon*

NEIL ELLIS
Stellenbosch
★★

The Cape's first and foremost winemaker-négociant, Ellis's uncanny skill in sourcing grapes from cutting-edge viticultural areas, and equal expertise in crafting some of South Africa's classiest wines from them, has sparked off a whole raft of wineries that buy in from selected vineyards.

Cabernet Sauvignon (Stellenbosch, Jonkershoek) • *Classic red blend* (Cabernet Sauvignon-Merlot) • *Chardonnay* (Aenigma, Elgin) • *Pinotage* (Stellenbosch) • *Sauvignon Blanc* (Groenekloof) • *Syrah* (Jonkershoek Shiraz)

ERNIE ELS
Stellenbosch
★★

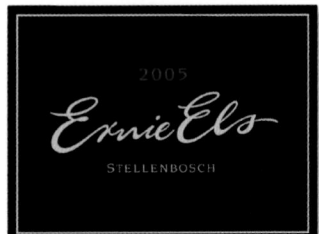

South African golfer Ernie Els owns possibly the most serious of the so-called celebrity wineries, because although the two classic blends (Ernie Els "signature" Bordeaux-type blend and the Proprietors, which is a similar blend but with the added dimension of Shiraz) are the best wines made here, the entire range is consistently excellent.

✓ *Entire range*

FAIRVIEW
Paarl
★★

This estate is run by Charles Back, one of the most innovative wine producers in South Africa, offering a large and constantly expanding range of wine styles. The poorest wines here are good, and the best are sensational.

✓ *Cagignan* (Pegleg) • *Chardonnay* (Akkerbos) • *Classic red blend* (Caldera) • *Dessert* (La Beryl Blanc) • *Pinotage* (Primo) • *Sauvignon Blanc* • *Sémillon* (Oom Pagel) • *Shiraz* (Cyril Back, Solitude) • *Viognier*

FLAGSTONE
Stellenbosch
★★

This winery used to belong to Bruce Jack but was taken over by Constellation. However, Jack is still very much the front here and, indeed, for all of Constellation's activities in South Africa, and Flagstone wines continue to win awards.

✓ *Classic red blend* (Mary Le Bow) • *Pinotage* (Writer's Block) • *Pinot Noir* (Fiona) • *Sauvignon Blanc* (Free Run) • *Syrah* (The Dark Horse Shiraz)

FLEUR DU CAP
Stellenbosch
★★ⓥ

Made and marketed by the Bergkelder at Stellenbosch, Fleur du Cap has established a high standard of quality for its basic wines, but has reinvented itself with spectacular success with its "Unfiltered" range.

✓ *Cabernet Sauvignon* (Unfiltered) • *Chardonnay* (Unfiltered) • *Chenin Blanc* • *Classic white blend* (Unfiltered Viognier-Chardonnay-Sauvignon Blanc-Sémillon) • *Late Harvest* (Noble Riesling) • *Merlot* (Unfiltered) • *Sauvignon* (Unfiltered Limited Release) • *Sémillon* (Unfiltered)

KEN FORRESTER
Stellenbosch
★★☆

This property dates back to 1689, when the farm was called Zandberg, and by 1692 some 12,000 vines had been planted. But the first wine in modern times was produced in 1994, when owners Ken and Teresa Forrester pressed a small quantity of Sauvignon Blanc grapes to produce a Blanc Fumé. Forrester and his winemaker Martin Meinert are recognized as South Africa's most passionate champions of Chenin Blanc. They also part-own the wonderful restaurant opposite the vineyard called 96 Winery Road.

✓ *Chenin Blanc* (FMC, Petit Chenin) • *Classic red blend* (Gypsy) • *Late Harvest* (T Noble)

FORT SIMON
Stellenbosch
★★☆

Since its first vintage in 1998, Fort Simon Estate has impressed with the elegance of its wines.

✓ *Chardonnay* • *Chenin Blanc* (Barrel Fermented)

THE FOUNDRY
Voor Paardeberg
★★

Although originally made at Meerlust, this is the private label of Chris Williams and his business partner James Reid of Kumala fame. In 2004 Chris Williams took over from the legendary Giorgio Dalla Cia, as Meerlust's winemaker, and brought The Foundry label with him. The Foundry has moved to the Voor Paardeberg area, where it will eventually carry out all of its winemaking activities. This will involve expanding the range to include single-vineyard wines from Voor Paardeberg, neighbouring Swartland, and other *terroirs* around the Cape, but there are no plans to stop producing the single-vineyard Syrah and Viognier from Stellenbosch that created the reputation of this label. Lovers of fat, blowsy Viognier will not like The Foundry's lean version, which favours more minerality than this variety usually offers.

✓ *Grenache Blanc* • *Syrah* • *Viognier* (Double Barrel)

GLEN CARLOU
Paarl
★★☆

Donald Hess of The Hess Collection in Napa was the co-owner, until he bought out David Finlayson. While Finlayson remained as winemaker, he produced some of South Africa's finest Chardonnay, but the wines have lost class and finesse since his departure.

✓ *Chardonnay* (Quartz Stone) • *Pinot Noir* • *Syrah*

GLENELLY
Stellenbosch
★★☆

Owned by May-Eliane de Lencquesaing, the proprietor of Château Pichon Longueville Comtesse de Lalande until 2006, when she sold it to Champagne Roederer. She has been very diplomatic, insisting that Glenelly be seen as truly South African, not a *Bordelais*-owned and influenced property. However, it would do no harm to reflect on how châteaux such as Pichon Longueville Comtesse built up the reputations that have lasted centuries. It was not through a range of wines, just the *grand vin*. The concept of a "second wine" is a relatively new one, but it performs the same function that selling off the lesser wines did for centuries before: to ensure the quality and thus the reputation of the *grand vin* is maintained. The range of wines at Glenelly is not as large as at other South African wineries, and although the recent introduction of an unoaked Chardonnay shows promise, the Merlot and Shiraz varietal wines have not exactly grabbed the headlines. What has, however, are the blends: Glenelly, a Syrah-based blend, and Lady May, a Bordeaux-type blend. These are both acknowledged as supremely elegant wines that are made to improve in the bottle. It would be easier to build the reputation of Glenelly on just the Chardonnay and these two blends (which might get even better without the varietals to worry about). Maybe there has been too much effort to avoid the Bordeaux influence, when there is much that South Africa could learn from it – not so much the winemaking, as the centuries-old marketing.

GLENWOOD
Franschhoek
★

A small production that regularly sells out long before the next vintage is ready.

✓ *Chardonnay* (Vigneron's Selection)

GRANDE PROVENCE
Franschhoek
★★☆

These wines were once marketed as Augusta, but they have since reverted to the original name of the restaurant that makes them. Top-class wines.

✓ *Cabernet Sauvignon* • *Chardonnay*

GRANGEHURST
Stellenbosch
★★

One of the new breed of winemakers who source grapes from various other growers, Grangehurst makes exciting, well-crafted, elegant yet substantive wines.

✓ *Cabernet Sauvignon* (Chairman's Reserve) • *Classic red blend* (Cabernet Sauvignon-Merlot, Nikela) • *Pinotage*

DE GRENDEL
Tygerberg
★★☆

De Grendel's Koetshuis is one of the country's very best Sauvignon Blancs.

✓ *Classic red blend* (Rubaiyat) • *Classic white blend* (Winifred) • *Sauvignon Blanc* (especially Koetshuis) • *Syrah* (Shiraz)

GROOT CONSTANTIA
Constantia
★★☆

This property is part of the original Constantia farm, the oldest and most

GROOT CONSTANTIA
The first owner, Simon van der Stel, would have walked this very piece of earth in 1685, when he received title to this land, then 763 hectares (1,885 acres). By 1709, he had planted 70,000 vines and was producing 56 hectolitres of wine per year.

famous of Cape estates, and is currently being run with passion and great skill.

✓ *Classic red blend* (Gouverneurs Reserve) • *Merlot* (Gouverneurs) • *Syrah* (Gouverneurs Shiraz)

HAMILTON RUSSELL
Walker Bay
★★★

Established by Tim Hamilton Russell, this was once Africa's most southerly vineyard. Now there are many this far south and some further still. No expense was spared to ensure that this would become one of the finest wineries in the Cape, and winemaker Peter Finlayson helped make that dream come true. Finlayson left to establish his own winery, Bouchard-Finlayson (which is just next door), but his replacement, Kevin Grant, continued to make some of the Cape's most spellbinding Burgundian varietals. Hannes Storm became the new winemaker at the Hamilton Russell vineyard in 2004.

✓ *Entire range*

HARTENBERG
Stellenbosch
★★

Some stunning wines, but what a pity they ripped out the Zinfandel!

✓ *Cabernet Sauvignon* • *Chardonnay* • *Merlot* • *Syrah* (Shiraz)

HASKELL
Stellenbosch
★★

Recent and fast-rising star Rianie Strydom produces highly regarded wines in the Helderberg foothills.

✓ *Entire range*

HERMANUSPIETERS-FONTEIN VINEYARDS
Walker Bay
★★

One of the fast-rising Sauvignon Blanc stars of the up-and-coming Walker Bay district. Owner and viticulturist-winemaker Bartho Eksteen also produces superbly sleek reds.

✓ *Classic red blend* (Die Arnoldus, Die Martha) • *Sauvignon Blanc*

HILLCREST
Durbanville
★✫Ⓥ

This estate's first vintage was in 2002, yet the deftly sculpted wines scream out for attention.

✓ *Classic red blend* (Merlot-Cabernet Sauvignon) • *Sauvignon Blanc*

IONA
Overberg

Reputation built on Sauvignon Blanc.

JORDAN
Stellenbosch
★★

This property is now a Cape front-ranker, especially for Cobblers Hill classic red wine blend, but its primary reputation is for rich and vibrant white wines.

✓ *Chardonnay* (Nine Yards) • *Classic red blend* (Cobblers Hill) • *Sauvignon Blanc* • *Merlot*

KAAPZICHT
Stellenbosch
★★Ⓥ

Established in 1984, Kaapzicht Estate has only just awoken to provide a number of exciting wines in recent years. Although the Pinotage is usually a big wine, it is so well balanced that it belies its 15 point something of alcohol.

✓ *Cabernet Sauvignon* • *Classic red blend* (Steytler Vision) • *Pinotage* (Steytler) • *Shiraz*

KANONKOP
Stellenbosch
★★✫

Widely regarded within South Africa as its leading "First Growth". Kanonkop's reputation grows year after year, which is highly unusual for old-established producers.

✓ *Entire range*

KANU
Stellenbosch
★✫Ⓥ

Delightful, easy-drinking, good-value standard range, and serious to stunning Limited Release wines from this winery that has captured much attention since it was established in 1998.

✓ *Cabernet Sauvignon* (Limited Release) • *Chardonnay* (Limited

Release) • *Chenin Blanc* (Wooded) • *Classic red blend* (Keystone) • *Merlot* (Limited Release)

KLEIN CONSTANTIA
Constantia
★★

This property was part of Simon van der Stel's original Constantia Estate, but after centuries of neglect it was replanted in 1982. Note that Vin de Constance is not a botrytis wine, nor is it fortified; it is supposedly a faithful replication of the famous Constantia of old.

✓ *Cabernet Sauvignon* (Reserve) • *Dessert* (Vin de Constance) • *Late Harvest* (Noble Late Harvest Sauvignon Blanc) • *Riesling* (Rhine Riesling) • *Sauvignon Blanc*

KLEINE ZALZE
Stellenbosch
★★Ⓥ

This former Gilbeys property was purchased by Kobus Basson and Jan Malan in 1996, since when its wines have been put on the map and its reputation continues to rise.

✓ *Cabernet Sauvignon* (Barrel Matured) • *Chardonnay* (Barrel Fermented) • *Merlot* (Barrel Matured, Cellar Selection)

KWV
Paarl
★★Ⓥ

The privatized former super-sized cooperative can still turn out great-value wines, with a few gems along the way, and new cellar master Richard Rowe is determined to upgrade the quality.

✓ *Chenin Blanc* (The Mentors) • *Petit Verdot* (The Mentors) • *Syrah* (The Mentor Shiraz)

LAIBACH
Stellenbosch
Ⓞ★

This farm was called Good Success until it was purchased by Swiss-based German businessman Friedrich Laibach, who built a new cellar and bottled these wines for the first time in 1997. Almost 15 per cent of the Laibach vineyard is farmed organically.

✓ *Classic red blend* (Friedrich Laibach, The Ladybird) Ⓞ • *Pinotage*

LAMMERSHOEK
Malmesbury
Ⓞ★★

Top-performing organic producer intent on reducing alcohol levels.

✓ *Chenin Blanc* • *Classic red blend* (Roulette, Zinfandel-Syrah) • *Classic white blend* (Roulette) • *Dessert wine* (Straw Wine) • *Syrah*

LAND OF HOPE
Somerset West
★

This joint venture between Land of Hope Trust (chaired by John Platter) and The Winery of Good Hope (later in this list) is currently producing excellent Chenin Blanc and Cabernet Sauvignon.

LUDDITE
Bot River
★★✫

Shiraz is the standout in this excellent range of wines grown on the slopes of the Houw Hoek Mountains.

✓ *Entire region*

MAISON
Franschhoek
★★✫

An excellent Shiraz, with a Cap Classique waiting in the wings. Classy minimalist labelling.

MEERLUST
Stellenbosch
★★★✫

For more than 35 years, this has been one of the Cape's most consistent wine estates. Meerlust is owned by the Myburgh family, who have been assisted from the very start by the visionary winemaker Giorgio Dalla Cia. Dalla Cia retired in 2004, handing over to Chris Williams, who worked with Michel Rolland, and was Dalla Cia's assistant winemaker between 1995 and 2000, when he set up The Foundry. All wines produced are among the very best in the country for their particular styles, but with eighth generation Hannes Myburgh in overall charge, and such a talented, inquisitive new winemaker at the helm, Meerlust has gone from top gear into overdrive.

✓ *Entire range*

MEINERT
Stellenbosch
★☆

Since 1997, Ken Forrester's winemaking partner Martin Meinert has made some splendid wines under his own label.

✓ *Classic red blend* (Devon Crest, Synchronicity) • *Merlot*

MIDDELVLEI
Stellenbosch
★

This estate made its reputation with Pinotage, but has recently been producing stunning Syrah.

✓ *Classic red blend* (Momberg) • *Pinotage* • *Syrah* (Shiraz)

MONIS
Paarl
★☆♥

This famous old Cape fortified brand belongs to Distell (*see* separate entry).

✓ *Fortified* (Cream Sherry, Muscadel, Very Old Tawny Port)

MOOIPLAAS
Stellenbosch
★☆♥

After making and selling wine in bulk for 30 years, the owners started selling wines under their Mooiplaas label in 1995.

✓ *Cabernet Sauvignon* • *Pinotage* • *Syrah* (Shiraz)

MÔRESON
Franschhoek
★★☆

Acquired by Richard Friedmann in 1985, this estate initially developed a reputation for its white wines, although it is its reds that have shone out in recent vintages.

✓ *Cabernet Sauvignon* • *Chardonnay* (Premium) • *Classic red blend* (Magia) • *Pinotage* • *Sauvignon Blanc*

MORGENHOF
Stellenbosch
★★☆♥

This historic wine estate is owned by Anne Cointreau. Morgenhof makes some truly stylish wines, with excellent-value entry-level wines sold under the Fantail label.

✓ *Cabernet Sauvignon* (Reserve) • *Chardonnay* • *Classic red blend* (Première Sélection) • *Merlot* (Reserve) • *Pinotage* • *Sauvignon Blanc*

MORGENSTER
Stellenbosch
★★

Morgenster originally grew just four Bordeaux varieties (Merlot, Cabernet Sauvignon, Cabernet Franc, and Petit Verdot), but has recently planted a relatively small amount of Sangiovese and Nebbiolo. The Tosca is a super-Tuscan inspired blend of Sangiovese, Merlot, and Cabernet Sauvignon.

✓ *Classic red blend* (Lourens, Morgenster, Tosca) • *Nebbiolo* (Nabusco)

MILES MOSSOP
Stellenbosch
★★

The youngest son of the late Tony Mossop, Miles is also the winemaker at Tokara and excels at all three.

✓ *Entire range*

LA MOTTE
Franschhoek
★★

Owned by Hanneli Koegelenberg, the daughter of Anton Rupert, the second richest man in South Africa, La Motte's wines have been made by Edmund Terblanche since 2001. La Motte also sources grapes from its own vineyards in the Bot River area.

✓ *Chardonnay* • *Classic red blend* (Shiraz-Grenache, Shiraz-Viognier, and especially Pierneef Shiraz-Viognier) • *Sauvignon Blanc* • *Syrah* (Shiraz)

MULDERBOSCH
Stellenbosch
★★

These are top-flight wines from superbly sited mountain vineyards, with moves towards organic viticulture, and crafted by skilful winemaking. Purchased in 2010 by Charles Banks, co-owner of Screaming Eagle.

✓ *Chardonnay* • *Chenin Blanc* (Steen-op-Hout) • *Classic red blend* (Beta Centauri, Faithful Hound) • *Sauvignon Blanc*

MULLINEUX
Swartland
★★

Chris Mullineux made his name at Tulbagh Mountain Vineyards, where he met Andrea Kozlowski, an assistant winemaker. They left, got married, and started up their own highly successful venture.

✓ *Entire range*

MURATIE
Stellenbosch
★☆

Owned by the Melck family, who have made some brilliant wines since 2000. Guillaume Nell has been winemaker since 2003. Improving.

✓ *Cabernet Sauvignon* • *Classic red blend* (Ansela) • *Fortified* (Cape Vintage) • *Syrah* (Shiraz)

NEDERBURG
Paarl
★★♥

Owned by Distell. As with Fleur du Cap, the consistency is remarkable for such a commercial range. Under Razvan Macici, the quality improved with each year over the past decade. The Private Bin wines sold exclusively at the annual Nederburg Auction is recommended, but they become available only should a retailer successfully bid for a lot, and later decide to market them.

✓ *Cabernet Sauvignon* (Private Bin) • *Classic red blend* (Edelrood) • *Classic red blend* (Prelude) • *Late Harvest* (Noble Late Harvest) • *Sauvignon Blanc* (Private Bin) • *Shiraz* (Private Bin)

NELSON
Paarl
★★☆

Established in 1993 by the Nelson family, this estate has moved up a gear since the new millennium.

✓ *Classic red blend* (Cabernet Sauvignon-Merlot) • *Chardonnay* • *Syrah* (Shiraz)

NEWTON JOHNSON
Walker Bay
★★♥

One of the brightest new stars in the exciting Walker Bay wine scene.

✓ *Cabernet Sauvignon* • *Chardonnay* • *Classic red blend* (Shiraz-Mourvèdre) • *Pinot Noir* • *Sauvignon Blanc*

NITIDA CELLARS
Durbanville
★★☆♥

Small, up-and-coming boutique in the Durbanville Kloof, where there is a distinct intensity to the wines. Due to launch a Cap Classique in 2011.

✓ *Cabernet Sauvignon* • *Sémillon*

OAK VALLEY
Elgin
◉★★♥

A massive 1,786-hectare (4,413-acre) mountainside polycultural farm, where super-value, great-quality wine competes with beef and cut flowers for attention.

✓ *Entire range*

OLD VINES
Rosebank
★☆♥

South Africa's only women's empowerment winery, Old Vines was established in 1995 by mother and daughter, Irina von Holdt and Françoise Botha, whose primary aim is to raise awareness of Chenin Blanc as the Cape's white wine flagbearer.

✓ *Chenin Blanc*

L'ORMARINS
See Anthonij Rupert

PLAISIR DE MERLE
Simonsberg-Paarl
★★

Grapes from Plaisir de Merle formed the heart of many Nederburg wines until 1993, when with the help of consultant Paul Pontallier of Château Margaux, owner-winemaker Niel Bester launched a range of estate-bottled wines that are worthy of Distell's flagship domaine.

✓ *Classic red blend* (Grand Plaisir) • *Merlot* • *Sauvignon Blanc*

QUOIN ROCK
Stellenbosch
◉★★

Sauvignon Blanc is probably the most rewarding wine here, but with vineyards in both Stellenbosch and Cape Agulhas, the entire range is truly excellent.

✓ *Entire range*

RAATS
Stellenbosch
★★

Highly regarded, award-winning Chenin Blanc and Cabernet Franc specialist Bruwer Raats, whose Mvemve Raats de Compostella is world-class.

✓ *Entire range*

RADFORD DALE
Stellenbosch
★★

Having crossed paths in Burgundy and South Africa, Barossa-born Ben Radford and British-born Alex Dale discovered they shared the same wine philosophy – "answer only to yourself and to your glass; no compromise and no pressure to achieve margins" – and decided they were destined to work together. Produced and marketed in partnership with The Winery of Good Hope, of which Alex Dale is the majority partner.

✓ *Chardonnay* • *Classic red blend* (Gravity) • *Pinot Noir* (Freedom) • *Viognier* (Vine Dried)

REYNEKE
Stellenbosch
⑧★☆

An excellent range of focused wines from environmental ethics graduate Johan Reyneke. Standouts are the organic Cornerstone and the biodynamic Reyneke Reserve (Syrah).

✓ *Entire range*

LE RICHE
Stellenbosch
★★☆

After 20 years at the Rustenberg estate, Etienne Le Riche struck out on his own in a rented house and unused cellar at Leef-op-Hoop (which aptly means "Living on Hope") in the Jonkershoek Valley. Essentially a red-wine specialist (although he does release tiny amounts of delicious Chardonnay), Le Riche makes two of the very greatest South African red wines almost every year in the form of Cabernet Sauvignon Reserve and Cabernet Sauvignon-Merlot. He also produces a Bergerac, Domaine de Garrou, from the same varieties, same equipment, and same winemaking philosophy, yet strangely it has never stood out.

✓ *Entire range*

RIETVALLEI
Robertson
★

Classic Muscadel.

✓ *Chardonnay* • *Fortified* (Muscadel 1908, Red Muscadel) • *Syrah* (Shiraz)

RIJK'S PRIVATE CELLAR
Tulbagh
★★

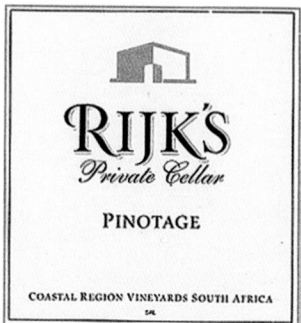

Whereas I might think that the Bravado classic red blend, Cabernet Sauvignon, Chenin Blanc (especially Touch of Oak), Pinotage, Shiraz, and Syrah are the standouts here, others might legitimately consider other wines to be at the top. Frankly, there is seldom anything produced here that would not stand out to one degree or another in a blind tasting of Cape wines, hence the entire range must be recommended – and that is saying something when there is (or was at the last count) no fewer than 18 wines in the range.

✓ *Entire range*

ROBERTSON WINERY
Robertson
★✰Ⓥ

For a cooperative that could be relied upon for little more than fortified wine, the Robertson Winery has developed an exciting range of modern, finely honed table wines, and these have been on a roll since the early 2000s.

✓ *Chardonnay* (Kings River) • *Classic red blend* (No.1 Constitution Road) • *Late Harvest* (Wide River Reserve) • *Syrah* (Wolfkloof Shiraz)

RUDERA
Stellenbosch
★★

Established with the 2001 vintage by Teddy Hall, former financial whiz kid of the 1990s turned winemaker and widely acclaimed Chenin Blanc specialist. Hall moved on in 2008, following the breakdown of his marriage, and now produces, among other wines, a fine bubbly under his new eponymous brand. His former wife, Riana Hall, remains and the extraordinarily high quality of Rudera wines has not wavered, if the award-winning 2009s are anything to go by.

✓ *Cabernet Sauvignon* • *Chenin Blanc* • *Late Harvest* (Noble Late Harvest Chenin Blanc) • *Syrah*

ANTHONIJ RUPERT
Franschhoek
★

Based at L'Ormarins and named in honour of the late Toni Rupert, who quickly established this estate at the very top of Cape winemaking. As the son of Anton Rupert, then the second-richest person in South Africa, Toni might have had unlimited finances at his disposal, but it was not just money that made the reputation of L'Ormarins. Toni Rupert had the pick of almost any wine estate he wanted, and he chose L'Ormarins. However, the quality of the wines has not matched the exceptional potential of these vineyards in recent years, and L'Ormarins is now just one of several brands: Terra del Capo, Protea, Leopard Creek, and Anthonij Rupert itself.

✓ *Cabernet Franc* (Anthonij Rupert) • *Cabernet Sauvignon* (Anthonij Rupert) • *Merlot* (Anthonij Rupert) • *Classic red blend* (L'Ormarins Optima)

RUPERT & ROTHSCHILD
Franschhoek
★★

A mega-rich partnership delivering world-class wines of various origin, both pure and blended, from Barrydale, Bot River, Darling, Elgin Robertson, Simonsberg-Paarl, and Stellenbosch. The two top wines are Baron Edmond (a Cabernet-Merlot blend) and Baroness Nadine (a *barrique*-fermented Chardonnay).

✓ *Entire range*

RUST EN VREDE
Stellenbosch
★★

Owned by Jean Engelbrecht, who produces wines that are just as big and as dense as his father, Jannie Engelbrecht, a former Springbok, used to make but in a much more approachable style. Jannie produced only wines he liked to drink, whereas Jean produces wines his American buyers like to drink, and he does it with considerable style.

✓ *Entire range*

RUSTENBERG
Stellenbosch
★★✰

Once heralded as the very best of South Africa's top growths, the quality at Rustenberg faltered in the early 1990s, only for it to be picked up as from the 1996 vintage, and pushed higher than it has ever been. Rustenberg Estate is now under the direct control of Simon Barlow, who installed a brand new winery and has done everything necessary to ensure that Rustenberg's reputation remains

impeccable, despite the occasional rumour to the contrary.

✓ *Cabernet Sauvignon* (Peter Barlow) • *Chardonnay* (Five Soldiers, Stellenbosch) • *Classic red blend* (John X Merriman) • *Late Harvest* (QF)

THE SADIE FAMILY WINES
Swartland
◉★★

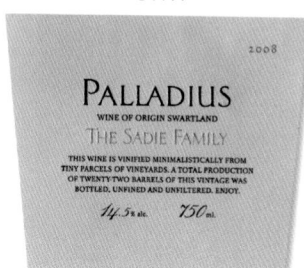

Eben Sadie is one of the true pioneers of fine wine from Swartland. I remember tasting a Syrah out of the barrel with him at Charles Back's Spice Route, which he headed up. Jabulani Ntshangase had taken me to Spice Route in its start-up days, but rather than talk about the Spice Route blend, Eben was more interested in showing me this single barrel, which he reckoned was the direction that Swartland should be going. From the finesse of that Syrah, which was quite remarkable from any part of South Africa in the late 1990s, it was impossible to disagree, and from 2000 on, Eben has proved his point time and again with Columella, an 80/20 blend of Syrah and Mourvèdre.

✓ *Classic red blend* (Columella) • *Classic white blend* (Palladius)

SAXENBURG
Stellenbosch
★★

This Swiss-owned winery has been a rising star for wines of increasingly high quality and complexity since the late 1990s.

✓ *Cabernet Sauvignon* (Private Collection) • *Chardonnay* (Private Collection) • *Classic red blend* (Gwendolyn, Manuel) • *Merlot* (Private Collection) • *Pinotage* (Private Collection) • *Sauvignon Blanc* (Private Collection) • *Syrah* (Shiraz Select)

SEQUILLO
Malmesbury
★★

More classics from Eben Sadie (*see* The Sadie Family Wines) in the form of Rhône blends, both red and white.

✓ *Entire range*

SHANNON
Elgin
★★

Stunning Merlot and beautiful Pinot Noir.

✓ *Entire range*

SIGNAL HILL WINES
Cape Town
★★

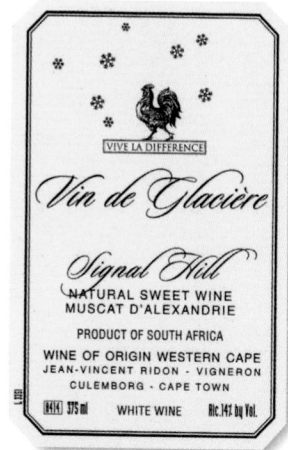

The boutique of boutique wineries. Jean-Vincent Ridon and Kyle Zulch produce "inner-city wines" from three urban vineyards, the first of which was planted with ungrafted Syrah on Signal Hill, next to Table Mountain, and is known as Clos d'Oranje. The second, Kalk Bay Vineyard, is located behind the Olympia Bakery, which is not just inner city but is the closest any South African vineyard gets to the ocean. The first Kalk Bay wine, a Cabernet Franc-based classic red blend, was produced in 2006. The third is Camps Bay, a Mourvèdre vineyard first cropped in 2009. Until these vines came on-stream, Signal Hill bought in grapes to produce a splendid range of wines that have been so well received that they continue to this day.

✓ *Dessert* (Empereur Rouge, Eszenzia, Straw Wine) • *Grenache Blanc* • *Grenache Noir* (Piekenierskloof) • *Late Harvest* (Muscat d'Alexandrie Crème de Tête Noble Late Harvest) • *Malbec* • *Mourvèdre* (Camps Bay) • *Petit Verdot* • *Sparkling* (Pinot Noir) • *Syrah* (Clos d'Oranje, Merindol)

SIJNN
See De Trafford

SIMONSIG
Stellenbosch
★✰

This winery has a huge production, and its wines range from the sensational down to pretty standard stuff, with an increasing proportion of the former.

✓ *Classic red blend* (Frans Malan, Tiara) • *Late Harvest* (Vin de Liza) • *Petit Verdot* (Auction Reserve) • *Sparkling* (Kaapse Vonkel) • *Syrah* (Merindol)

SOLMS DELTA
Groot Drakenstein
★

Three farms have been integrated to form this venture, which is one-third

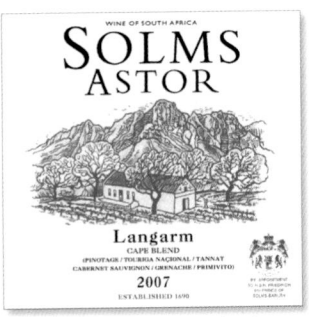

empowerment-owned under the direction of Mark Solms.

✓ *Entire range*

SPICE ROUTE
Swartland
★★

This estate was originally owned by a consortium of Charles Back, Jabulani Ntshangase, John Platter, and Gyles Webb, but it is now solely owned by Back. Spice Route excels at red wines, and its signature style is typically deep, dark, rich, and spicy, with masses of black fruit. Its Flagship Syrah is still one of the best I have tasted from South Africa.

✓ *Chenin Blanc • Classic red blend* (Malabar) • *Merlot* (Flagship) • *Syrah* (Flagship)

SPIER
Stellenbosch
★★

A winery has been added to this deluxe, classy hotel complex, which now belongs to Winecorp. The first vintage produced here was in 1996. The very best wines are sold under Spier's Private Collection label (which is a considerable step up in quality).

✓ *Cabernet Sauvignon* (Private Collection) • *Chenin Blanc* (Private Collection) • *Late Harvest* (Noble Late Harvest) • *Merlot* (Private Collection) • *Pinotage • Sauvignon Blanc* (Private Collection) • *Viognier* (Private Collection)

SPRINGFIELD
Robertson
◉★☆

Owner-winemaker Abrie Bruwer is considered a bit of an eccentric in his own country, but virtually all of his practices merely represent an organic approach.

✓ *Cabernet Sauvignon* (Méthode Ancienne, Whole Berry) • *Chardonnay* (Méthode Ancienne, Wild Yeast) • *Classic red blend* (The Work of Time) • *Sauvignon Blanc* (Life From Stone)

STARK-CONDÉ
Stellenbosch
◉★★

This artisanal boutique winery in the Jonkershoek Valley belongs to Jose Condé and his father-in-law, Hans Schroder, owner of Neil Ellis Wines. The Three Pines wines come from the highest vineyards, whereas Pepin Condé wines are sourced from areas outside of the valley. Excellent Chenin and Sauvignon in the Pepin Condé range, but red wines stand out nevertheless.

✓ *Cabernet Sauvignon* (especially Twin Peak) • *Chenin Blanc* (Pepin Condé) • *Sauvignon Blanc* (Pepin Condé) • *Syrah* (especially Twin Peak)

STEENBERG
Constantia
★★☆

From small quantities of gorgeously fresh Sauvignon Blanc to a fabulous range of stunning wines in a myriad of styles, including the country's best Sémillon.

✓ *Classic red blend* (Catharina) • *Classic white blend* (Magna Carta) • *Nebbiolo • Sauvignon Blanc • Sémillon*

STELLENZICHT
Stellenbosch
★

Not as consistent as it once used to be, the Shiraz still stands out for some in South Africa, but on this side of the hemisphere, it can be a bit too weighty, and the once-classic Sémillon is not as pure as it used to be. For me, however, the classic red blend still demonstrates the potential of these vineyards, and that Pinotage makes a fine blending component.

✓ *Classic red blend* (Stellenzicht)

STRANDVELD
Elim
★★☆ Ⓥ

This small but expanding operation in cool-climate Elim excels with both Sauvignon Blanc and Syrah.

✓ *Classic white blend* (Adamastor) • *Sauvignon Blanc • Syrah* (Shiraz)

THELEMA MOUNTAIN
Stellenbosch
★★☆

Under the steady hand of owner-winemaker Gyles Webb, ably assisted by Rudi Schultz since 2000, Thelema Mountain has become one of the country's most exciting producers, producing stunningly rich, refined, and complex wines.

✓ *Cabernet Sauvignon* (especially Auction Reserve and The Mint) • *Chardonnay* (especially Ed's Reserve) • *Merlot* (Reserve) • *Pinotage • Sauvignon Blanc • Syrah* (Auction Reserve)

TOKARA
Stellenbosch
★★

Winemaker Miles Mossop also produces his own label (*see* Miles Mossop) and those of Axe Hill, which belonged to his late father Tony Mossop.

✓ *Entire range*

TOPIARY WINES
Franschhoek
★★

Roy Andrews purchased the topiary bedecked La Tramontane wine farm in 2005, and winemaker Chris Albrecht produced the first wines the following year. The reds are excellent but totally overshadowed by a stunning *blanc de blancs*.

✓ *Cabernet Sauvignon • Syrah* (Shiraz) • *Sparkling wine* (Blanc de Blancs)

DE TOREN
Stellenbosch
★★

This winery's first vintage was 1999, after which it achieved an almost immediate cult following for its stunningly successful Fusion V, a classic blend of five varieties (Cabernet Sauvignon, Cabernet Franc, Merlot, Malbec, and Petit Verdot).

✓ *Classic red blend* (Diversity Beta, Fusion V)

DE TRAFFORD
Stellenbosch
★★☆

This ultra-small boutique winery has established a reputation for beautifully crafted Cabernet, and it still rates as one of De Trafford's greatest wines, alongside the classic red blend Elevation 393. But the production and range have grown over the years, and all the wines here are pure joy. There has been a promising start from new vineyards on the lower Breede River in the far eastern limb of the Swellendam, 40 kilometres (25 miles) from any other vineyards. (The wines are sold under the Sijnn label.)

✓ *Entire range* (De Trafford label only)

WINE-TASTING LODGE, VERGELEGEN
Vergelegen is a beautiful estate to visit, and every one of its wines is worth buying – but don't tell the tasting-room staff that until you've gone through the list from top to bottom.

TULBAGH MOUNTAIN VINEYARDS
Tulbagh
☉★☆

The eco-warrior winemaking at this polycultural is highly regarded for Rhône-style wines.

✓ *Classic red blend* (Syrah-Mourvèdre, Victoria) • *Classic white blend* (White) • *Dessert wine* (Vin Pi One) • *Syrah* (Swartland)

TWEE JONGEGEZELLEN
Tulbagh
★ⓥ

Also known as the House of Krone, because Nicky Krone's family have farmed this estate for 300 years. The sparkling wines are back on form now that they are given greater bottle age.

✓ *Sparkling wines* (entire range)

UVA MIRA
Stellenbosch
☉★★

Dramatic quality from a dramatic setting, especially the compelling Chardonnay and classy red blend.

✓ *Entire range*

VEENWOUDEN
Paarl
★★ⓥ

This boutique winery enjoyed its first vintage in 1993. Since then it has built up a compact range of increasingly fine quality.

✓ *Chardonnay* (Special Reserve) • *Classic red blend* (Classic, Vivat Bacchus) • *Merlot* • *Veenwouden* (Cabernet blend)

VERGELEGEN
Stellenbosch
★★★

This immaculately restored, historic wine estate must be everyone's choice as the leading South African wine producer, thanks to the meticulous efforts of its winemaker André van Rensburg. Most of these vineyards have been replanted to counter virus, making Vergelegen probably the most virus-free property in the Cape. The sleek and profound Vergelegen classic red blend remains the core quality of an estate that is more famous for its red wines than whites, yet this could all be eclipsed by the performance of its classic white blend, which has been on awesome form since the 2005 vintage.

VERGENOEGD
Stellenbosch
★☆ⓥ

Owner-winemaker John Faure has gradually focused the quality of these wines since the 1990s.

✓ *Cabernet Sauvignon* • *Classic red blend* (Vergenoegd) • *Fortified* (Old Cape Colony Vintage Port) • *Merlot* • *Syrah* (Shiraz)

VILAFONTÉ
Simonsberg-Paarl
★★ⓥ

This is a joint venture between winemaking guru Zelma Long, viticulturist Phillip Freese, Warwick Estate's Mike Ratcliffe, and Bartholomew Broadbent, the American wine merchant son of Michael Broadbent. Vilafonté is taken from the name *vilafontes*, the grey, sandy soil on the property, which its owners believe to have a significant impact on the flavour profile and development of their wines. The vineyards are in Simonsberg-Paarl district, on the northern side of the Simonsberg Mountains, and planted in high density with four Bordeaux varieties (Cabernet Franc, Cabernet Sauvignon, Malbec, and Merlot). All of the farming is carried out with four-wheel-drive motor bikes to reduce soil compaction. Series C is Cabernet Sauvignon-based, whereas Series M is Merlot-based.

✓ *Classic red blend* (Series C, Series M)

VILLIERA
Paarl
★★ⓥ

VILLIERA

INSPIRATION

Villiera Estate was a rapidly rising star when the first edition of this encyclopedia was published in 1988, and it is now a well-established producer by current Cape wine standards.

✓ *Chenin Blanc* • *Classic red blend* (Monro) • *Classic white blend* (Down to Earth) • *Late Harvest* (Chenin Blanc Noble Late Harvest) • *Sparkling* (Brut Natural Chardonnay, Monro Brut, Tradition Brut, Tradition Rosé) • *Sauvignon Blanc* (Traditional Bush Vine)

VINUM AFRICA
See The Winery of Good Hope

WARWICK
Stellenbosch
★★

Michael Ratcliffe is doing a masterly job of filling his father's shoes, following Stan Ratcliffe's untimely death. Innovations include moving away from some varietals into the classic red "flagship" blend, and holding back five cases of every wine for re-release five years later. I can't help wondering why other wineries around the world do not hold back limited quantities like this, particularly for those wines in the range that tend to sell out well before their prime.

✓ *Cabernet Franc* • *Chardonnay* • *Classic red blend* (Three Cape Ladies, Trilogy)

WATERKLOOF
Stellenbosch
★☆

Owned by British wine merchant Paul Boutinot, Waterkloof produces increasingly expressive wines.

✓ *Chardonnay* • *Classic red blend* (Circle of Life) • *Merlot* • *Sauvignon Blanc* • *Syrah* (Shiraz)

WATERFORD
Stellenbosch
★★

After nine years at Delheim and ten at Rust en Vrede, Kevin Arnold struck out on his own, basing his choice of land and what varieties to grow on more than 20 years' experience on the slopes of the Helderberg. He's still happy to learn, having recently planted Tempranillo and Grenache to see what those varieties might bring.

✓ *Entire range*

WELTEVREDE
Robertson
★

Weltevrede means "well satisfied". The Travelling Stone Sauvignon Blanc and most of the Chardonnay wines are still excellent (although I am not sure that Vanilla Chardonnay is a wise choice of label), and the Bedrock Black Syrah was a pleasant surprise. However, the Riesling is disappointing, and the range of other wines is not as consistent as it used to be.

✓ *Chardonnay* (Place of the Rocks, Poet's Prayer, Rusted Soil) • *Sauvignon Blanc* (The Travelling Stone) • *Syrah* (Bedrock Black)

DE WETSHOF
Robertson
★★☆

Quite how Danie de Wet can make such exquisite Chardonnay wines when you can cook an egg on the rocks in his vineyard is a mystery; such mysteries are part of the eternal fascination that wine holds for enthusiasts.

✓ *Riesling* (Rhine Riesling) • *Chardonnay* • *Fortified* (Muscadel) • *Edeloes* (botrytis)

THE WINERY OF GOOD HOPE
Stellenbosch
★

The origin of this business is exactly the same as it is for Radford Dale, one of the wine ranges produced and marketed by The Winery of Good Hope. Both start with Alex Dale, who is the majority shareholder in the whole show. Alex was born into a British wine-merchant family but escaped in his mid-teens to read French literature at Dijon University, where he became fascinated by the great wines of Burgundy. Eleven years later, after a successful career in marketing the wines of Jacques Prieur, Joseph Drouhin, and others, Alex Dale was lured to South Africa by vineyard-owning friends during the late 1980s. He visited the country every year for six years and settled here in 1994, after Nelson Mandela became the first democratically elected president of South Africa, realizing that a new wine frontier had to emerge and that he wanted to be part of it. In 1998, Alex and Ben Radford formed The Winery (later to become The Winery of Good Hope) and started selling wines under the Radford Dale label, followed by Vinum Africa and The Winery of Good Hope (TWGH) itself. The Chenin Blanc is improving, but Radford Dale remains a class apart. *See also* Radford Dale.

✓ *Cabernet Sauvignon* (Vinum Africa) • *Chenin Blanc* (Vinum Africa) • *Classic red blend* (TWGH Oceanside Cabernet Sauvignon-Merlot) • *Pinot Noir* (TWGH Reserve)

ZANDVLIET
Robertson
★

Zandvliet is famous for its Syrah, and its new Hill of Eon wine is certainly the best yet. Astonvale is its second label.

✓ *Shiraz*

ZEVENWACHT
Stellenbosch
★ⓥ

Zevenwacht grew rapidly in the 1980s, making wines that were fresh, frank, and aromatic, but perhaps not all that exciting. Recently, however, there have been considerable improvements in quality, and these wines can represent great value.

✓ *Classic white blend* (Tin Mine White) • *Merlot* • *Sauvignon Blanc* • *Syrah*

OTHER CERTIFIED ORGANIC WINE PRODUCERS

Rozendal (Stellenbosch)
Stellar Winery (Olifants River)

NORTH AFRICA

The recent wind of change that has swept through north Africa's political regimes has not so far had any effect, negative or positive, on the dwindling importance of wine in these Muslim states, and it is not likely to until we know whether future governments will continue their previous increasingly fundamentalist course.

THE WINE INDUSTRIES of Algeria, Morocco, and Tunisia, and the appellation systems within which they work, are all based on the structure left behind by the colonial French. Although some good wines can be found, and a trickle of foreign investment exists, the development of wine industries in these countries has been held back by their governments, which do not promote alcohol in Islamic states. Furthermore, their laws do not allow direct sales by wineries to the public, making wine tourism impossible.

Cultivation of the vine flourished in Algeria, Morocco, and Tunisia as far back as 1000 BC, and winemaking was firmly established by at least the 6th century BC. Under French rule, North Africa was one of

BERBER WOMEN WORKING IN A TUNISIAN VINEYARD
The best and most reliable AOC wines in Tunisia are Muscats, although rosé enjoyed an ephemeral fashion just after World War II.

AVERAGE ANNUAL PRODUCTION

COUNTRY	VINEYARDS TOTAL	VINEYARDS WINE GRAPES	WINE PRODUCTION Hectolitres	Cases	MAJOR GRAPE VARIETIES
Algeria	185,000 ha (457,000 acres)	74,000 ha (183,000 acres)	800,000	5.0m	Alicante Bouschet, Carignan, Cinsault, Grenache, Muscat d'Alexandria
Morocco	114,000 ha (282,000 acres)	12,000 ha (29,600 acres)	350,000	3.3m	Alicante Bouschet, Cabernet Sauvignon, Carignan, Cinsault, Grenache
Tunisia	71,600 ha (177,000 acres)	11,000 ha (27,000 acres)	300,000	4.6m	Alicante Bouschet, Carignan, Cinsault, Grenache, Sangiovese

NORTH AFRICA
Morocco, Algeria, and Tunisia are all wine-producing countries. Most vineyards are concentrated along the coastal belts.

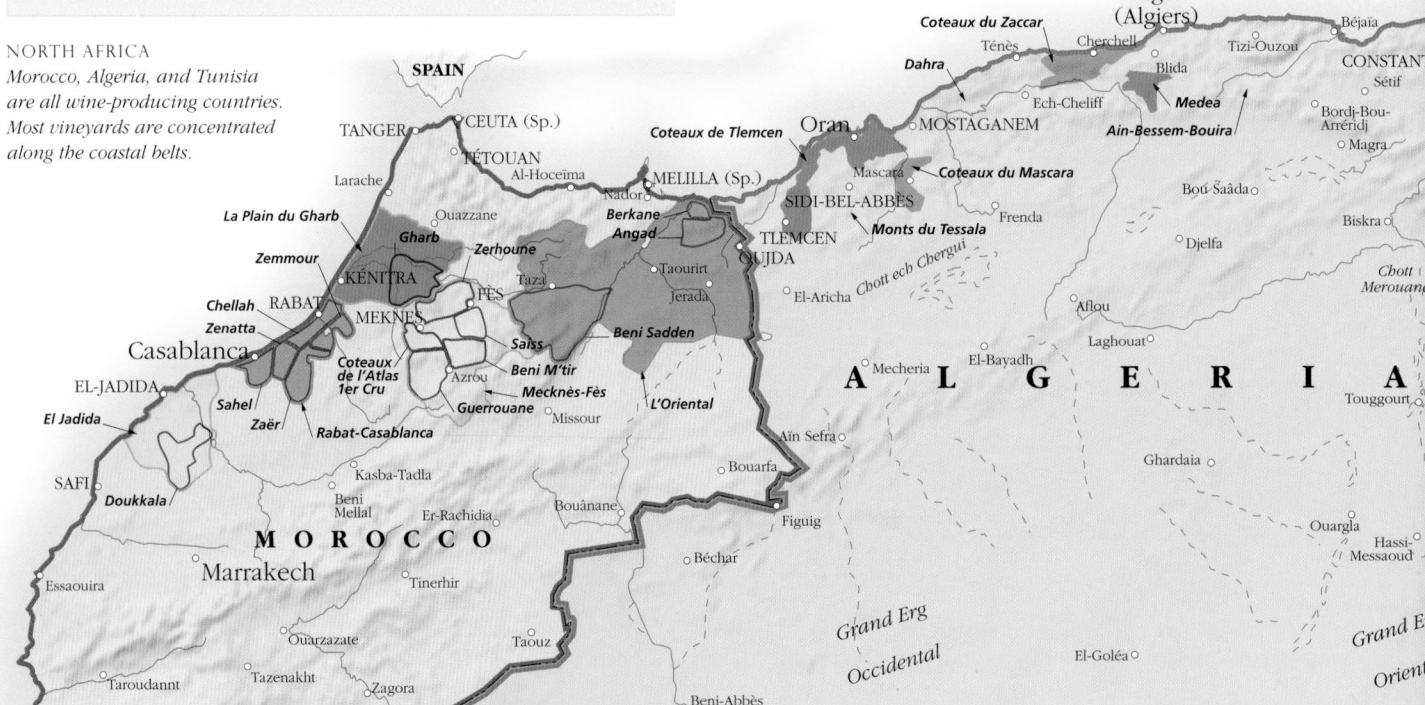

the most important winemaking regions in the world. Yet today it is difficult to see how the quality of wine can progress in any of these countries, where wine production is at best tolerated, and even that level of forbearance is often undermined by government officials who would personally like to see a total ban.

ALGERIA

Wine districts *Aïn-Bessem-Bouïra, Coteaux du Mascara, Coteaux de Tlemcen, Coteaux du Zaccar, Dahra, Médéa, Monts du Tessala*
In 1830, Algeria became the first North African country to be colonized by the French, which gave it a head start in viticulture over other North African countries. Algeria has always dominated North African viticulture in terms of quantity, if not quality. The French desperately planted vines in Algeria in the second half of the 19th century to offset the loss of their own vineyards to phylloxera. Viticulturally, it was to be the "second France", and for a while it was not only the second-largest wine producer in the world but also the largest exporter of wine. Most of it went to France, where no doubt it was blended into some of the most famous red wines in the world! The demise of the country's wine industry after it gained independence in 1962 made it clear that cynical remarks about the use of its wine in bolstering Burgundies were true, but the ironic fact is that both the Algerian and the Burgundian wines benefited from being blended together. It was not the best Burgundies that were enhanced with dark Algerian red, but the poorest, thinnest, and least attractive wines. After the blending, they were not Burgundian in character, but were superior to the original thin, low-quality Burgundy. By 1938 the Algerian wine industry had reached a peak of 400,000 hectares (988,000 acres) and 22 million hectolitres (244 million cases). Since independence, these vineyards have shrunk, and the number of wineries has plummeted from more than 3,000 to fewer than 50. Algeria has never known phylloxera, thus its varieties retain their own rootstock. Of the few reds that can honestly be recommended, the best are from Château Tellagh in Coteaux de Médéa and Cave de Bourkika in Coteaux de Mascara. Other wineries that produce reasonably good wine include: Coteaux de

KHEMIS MILIANA, ALGERIA
Gently undulating vineyards south of Cherchell in the Alger region, just west of Haut-Dahra district.

Mascara (Domaine El Bordj, Domaine Mamounia, Domaine Beni Chougrane); Coteaux de Tlemcen (Domaine de Sebra); Coteaux du Zaccar (Chateau Romain); and Dahra (Domaine de Khadra). Algeria has dropped further behind its wine-producing neighbours, but with the recent involvement of Jabulani Ntshangase, South Africa's only black winery owner (Thabani), and a real mover and shaker, it could be a sign that the future might be brighter than anticipated.

√ (with care) *Domaine de St Augustin • Vins d'Algerie*

MOROCCO

Wine districts L'Oriental: *Beni Sadden AOG, Berkane AOG, Angad AOG;* Meknès-Fès: *Guerrouane AOG, Beni M'tir AOG, Saiss AOG, Zerhoune AOG, Coteaux de l'Atlas 1er Cru;* La Plain du Gharb: *Gharb AOG;* Rabat-Casablanca: *Chellah AOG, Zemmour AOG, Zaër AOG, Zenatta AOG, Sahel AOG;* El-Jadida: *Doukkala AOG*
Wines were made here during Roman times, but after more than 1,000 years of Muslim rule, viticulture died out. In 1912, however, most of Morocco came under either French or Spanish control (with an international zone encompassing Tangiers) and it once more became an active winemaking country. When Morocco gained independence in 1956, the new government introduced a quality-control regime similar to the French AOC (*Appellation d'Origine Contrôlée*) system and, in 1973, it nationalized the wine industry. However, few wines carry the official *Appellation d'Origine Garantie* designation. In 1998, the first *Appellation d'Origine Contrôlée* was created, Les Coteaux de l'Atlas, encompassing the districts of Sidi-Slimane, Mjat, and Boufekrane, on the cool slopes of the Atlas Mountains, where the lime-rich clayey soils over dry, siliceous subsoil is particularly suitable for viticulture. Here we find Cabernet Sauvignon, Chardonnay, Merlot, and Syrah growing, and the wines

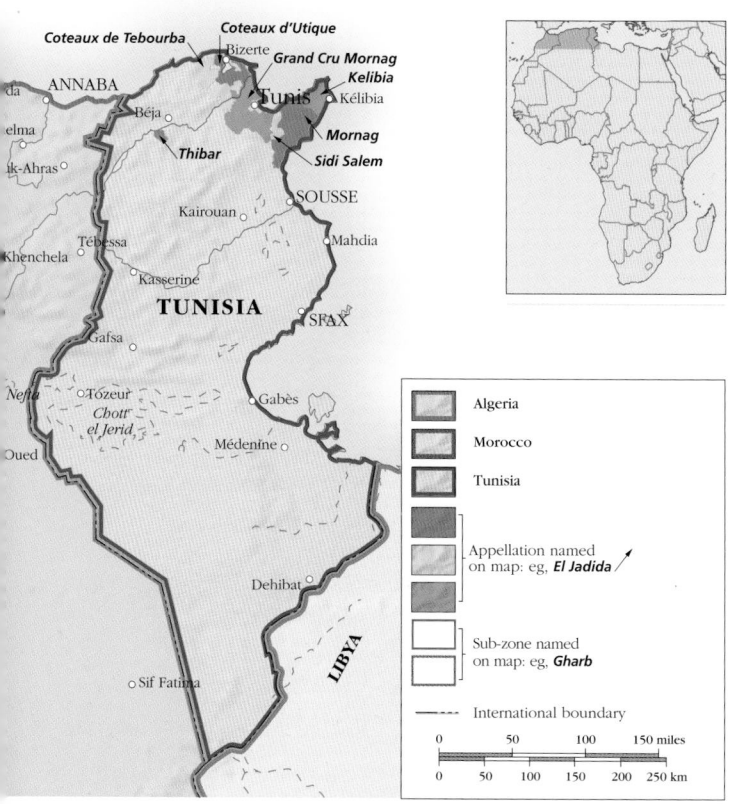

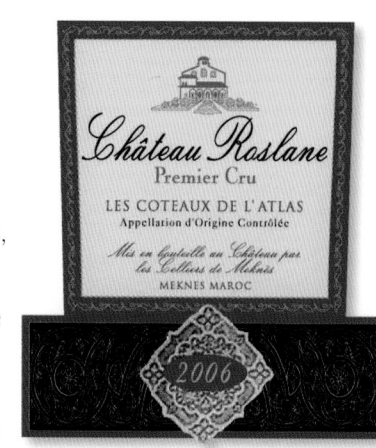

Château Roslane
Premier Cru
LES COTEAUX DE L'ATLAS
Appellation d'Origine Contrôlée
Mis en bouteille au Château par les Celliers de Meknès
MEKNES MAROC

2006

OLD MUSCAT VINES
Vineyards at Bizerte in the Bizerte-Mateur-Tébourba region at the northern tip of Tunisia.

produced by Les Celliers de Meknès, particularly the classic red blend, are the finest that Morocco currently has to offer. The country's more tradtional wines are made from Carignan, Cinsault, and Grenache, usually in a pale rosé style, and often sold as *vin gris*. These can be pleasant when served chilled, but the best of even the traditional wines are red, and the most successful of these are also produced by Les Celliers de Meknès, but sold under the Les Trois Domaines label. Owned by Reda Zniber, who is regarded as something of a "godfather" in Morocco, Les Celliers de Meknès produces 90 per cent of the country's wine, and most of it is at least drinkable. Or it is when it leaves the cellars. Most is sold on the home market, and much of this is at undeservedly high prices to tourists who are not willing to pay the even more exorbitant prices demanded for heavily taxed imported wines. Poor storage conditions inevitably spoil both Moroccan and imported wines. Moroccans themselves do drink wine, although there is a notable discrepancy between international per capita consumption figures (one litre) and Morocco's own religiously sensitive official estimation (zero!).

✔ (with care) *Cave Viticole de Bou-Argoub • Castel Frères • Les Deux Domaines • Ksar Babia • Celliers de Meknes • Château Roslane • Thalvin • Val d'Argan • Volubilia*

TUNISIA

Wine districts *Coteaux de Tebourba, Coteaux d'Utique, Grand Cru Mornag, Kelibia, Mornag, Sidi Salem, Thibar*

Wines were first made around the Carthage area in Punic times, but production was forbidden for 1,000 years under Muslim rule. After French colonization in 1881, viticulture resumed, and by Tunisian independence in 1955, the foundations of a thriving wine industry had been laid. At this time two basic appellations had been established – *Vin Supérieur de Tunisie*, for table wines, and *Appellation Contrôlée Vin Muscat de Tunisie*, for liqueur Muscat. These designations did not, however, incorporate any controls to safeguard origin, and in 1957 the government introduced a classification system that established four levels as follows: *Vins de Consommation Courante, Vins Supérieurs, Vins de Qualité Supérieure*, and *Appellation d'Origine Contrôlée*.

The best traditional Tunisian wines are those made from the Muscat grape, ranging from the lusciously sweet, rich, and viscous Vin de Muscat de Tunisie, to fresh, delicate, dry Muscats such as the Muscat de Kelibia. There are also a small number of good red wines, such as Château Feriani, Domaine Karim, and Royal Tardi, with Carignan and Cinsault the most important black grape varieties. The finest new-wave wines are made by the partly German-owned Domaine Magon, which is working proficiently with Cabernet Sauvignon, Merlot, Pinot Noir, and Syrah. There is also encouraging news of progress from research scientist Amor Jaziri, who produces organic wines under the Almory label, from his 14-hectare (35-acre) vineyard near Jedeida.

✔ (with care) *Ceptunes • Dom Neferis • Kurubis • Vignerons de Carthage*

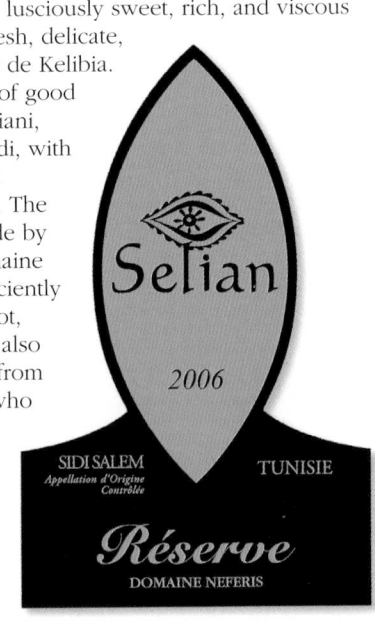

OTHER WINEMAKING COUNTRIES OF

AFRICA

ETHIOPIA

Grape-growing in Ethiopia? In fact, viticulture has existed here for many centuries. This country converted to Christianity in the 4th century, and locally grown Communion wine has been used by the Ethiopian Orthodox Church since at least the 12th century. So entrenched is grape-growing in Ethiopian history that it has entered the language as a specific term. Ethiopians distinguish three altitude-defined climatic zones: dega, wayna-dega, and kola. Dega means "cold" and indicates areas that are higher than 2,500 metres (8,200 feet) above sea level. Kola means "hot place", and applies to areas below 1,800 metres (5,900 feet). Wayna-dega literally means "grape elevation", or "place where you grow grapes", and refers to areas between 1,800 and 2,500 metres in height.

Ethiopia's largest vineyard is located at Awash, 160 kilometres (100 miles) east of Addis Ababa, in the Harar province, where some 30 hectares (74 acres) of Aleatico, Barbera, Chenin Blanc,

Grenache, Petit Sirah, and Ugni Blanc are grown. There are also 75 hectares (185 acres) of so-called "local" varieties, including Debulbul Attere, Key Dubbi, Nech Debulbul, and Tiku Weyn. There are two harvests each year, and the grapes are trucked to the Awash Winery in the outskirts of Addis Ababa, where reasonable-quality red and white wines are produced. The most commonly encountered wines are Axumite (sweetish white), Crystals (dry white), Dukam (red), and Gouder (Ethiopia's best red, from the Gouder vineyard, 135 kilometres (84 miles) west of Addis Ababa). However, the Awash Winery is located next to the Awash River, which irrigates the Awash vineyards 160 kilometres (100 miles) downstream, and in 1998 researchers from the University of Turku found the Awash River to be polluted downstream from the winery's own effluent discharge, but not upstream. This situation will have to be rectified before any serious thoughts of export can be entertained, as will its practice of using rehydrated imported raisins in some of the wines.

Currently, the most exported wine is made from honey, not grapes. Called Tej, it is made all over the country, and is much more famous than its grape-based counterparts. The Awash Winery exports Tej to Sweden and the USA, but Ethiopia is not really wine country, whether from honey or grapes. It is coffee country, to the point of giving the world the name itself – the province of Kaffa was the etymological origin of the word "coffee".

KENYA

Lake Naivasha Vineyards are located on volcanic soils beside Lake Naivasha, situated 1,900 metres (6,200 feet) above sea level in the Rift Valley. The Rift Valley is the Flower Garden of Africa, the blooms of which are flown to florists all over the world. In fact, you can grow absolutely anything here, and grow it twice a year, too. You can certainly grow grapes, as John and Elli D'Olier did between 1982 and 1992, with cuttings they brought back from California. They ripped out most of the vines in 1992 when overnight hikes in local taxes made Kenyan wine economically unviable, making just the odd wine for home consumption, only to replant in earnest in 2002. The economics are not much better now than they were in 1992, but the d'Oliers just cannot give up on the idea of Kenyan wine.

Richard Leakey is famous for finding a 2.5-million-year-old human skull in Kenya, but he is also one of this country's newest winemakers. He might have lost both legs below the knee in a plane crash, and have only one kidney (and that the gift of Philip Leakey, his younger brother and sometime political foe), but this anthropologist, palaeontologist, bruised politician, great African patriot, and tireless warrior against the ivory trade is still game for a new challenge. Leakey is not the sort of person to settle for Kenyan Carignan or Cardinal, but who would have thought that he, or anyone else in this country, could set their sights on Pinot Noir, the Holy Grail of winemaking? Well Leakey has, and by 2001 he had succeeded in cropping Pinot Noir at his Ol Choro Onyore vineyard in Ngong, and putting it (and Sauvignon Blanc) in bottle.

MADAGASCAR

Affectionately known as "Mad" to Anglo-Saxon inhabitants of the African continent, Madagascans have been growing grapes and making wine since the 19th century. Most of the vines growing on the island today are hybrids. With not a little tongue in cheek, John and Erica Platter write in *Africa Uncorked* (2002) that Stéphane Chan Foa Tong's sparkling Grand Cru d'Antsirabe is "Unquestionably the best sparkling wine in all Madagascar. Probably the finest Couderc Blanc *méthode champenoise* in the world!", and certainly it seems better than his still wines. The clean and decent, but hardly exciting, wines of Clos Malaza in the Ambatomena area are generally agreed by the locals to be the best that Madagascar currently produces, from 30 hectares (74 acres) of well-trained Chambourcin, Couderc Blanc, Petit Bouchet, Villardin, Varousset, and Villard Noir vines. However, from an outsider's point of view, the Chan brothers in Ambalavao produce more promising wine under the Côte de Fiana appellation (their best wine is sold as an exclusivity under the Tsara be label). Domaine Manomisoa is also known as Soavita Estate, and even more confusingly, its best wine is sold as Château Verger. Other wines are produced under the following labels: Clos de la Maromby (from the Masina Maria monastery, near Fiana) and Lazan'i Betsileo (a small cooperative in Fiana). Nothing really stands out among these wines, but with better grape varieties growing at altitude on the drier, eastern side of the island, which are pruned to yield less than half the current average crop, Madagascar does have the potential to produce some very much more interesting wines.

MAURITIUS

Beware Mauritian-looking wine sold under the Oxenham label, which is made from imported grape concentrate. While there is nothing wrong with that, the fact should be made clear.

NAMIBIA

Commercial Namibian wine is a relatively recent phenomenon, dating back to 1994, when Helmuth Kluge established Kristall Kellerei at Omaruru, on the periphery of the Namib desert. All wines are clean and well made, with fresh, zesty Colombard the best.

RÉUNION

This African island is, believe it or not, the most far-flung of all French wines areas: Vin de Pays de Cilaos. Created in 2004, the *vin de pays* regulations forced the removal of the hybrids that used to grow here. Hybrids are still the mainstay of viticulture on Madagascar, which arguably offers greater potential, but the performance of the classic *vinifera* varieties growing on Réunion (Chenin Blanc, Pinot Noir, and Malbec) could well change the mind of those "Mad" people. There are plans to plant Gros Manseng, Pinotage, Syrah, and Verdelho. The styles produced are red, white, rosé, and, because the tendency is for grapes to overripen rather too easily, Moelleux. The only wine producer currently is the local cooperative, Chais du Cilaos, which harvested just 28 tons of grapes in 2004. The vines grow at an altitude of 1,200 metres (3,930 feet) on volcanic soil, cropping in January. The wines are fresh, crisp, and well made, fermented in new, temperature-controlled, stainless-steel vats.

TANZANIA

There is only one winery, Tanganyika Vineyards, in Tanzania but two harvests a year, producing a decent, but not exciting, Chenin Blanc, and a Makutupora red and white.

ZIMBABWE

Although the first production of wine began in the early 1950s under the labels of Worringham and Lorraine, these semi-sweet wines were made from table grapes. It was not until UDI that this most beautiful country in Africa gave birth to a truly

commercial wine industry. During the mid-1960s, when sanctions bit deep, and anything that could be produced locally was produced locally, Rhodesian farmers grew the grapes to make the wines they could no longer import. In the 1990s, many low-quality grape varieties were ripped up, and replaced by classic *vinifera*, with drip irrigation. The grape varieties grown in Zimbabwe today include Cabernet Sauvignon, Cinsault, Clairette Blanche, Colombard, Chenin Blanc, Cruchen, Gewürztraminer, Merlot, Pinotage, Pinot Noir, Riesling, Ruby Cabernet, Sauvignon Blanc, and Seneca (*Lignan Blanc* x *Ontario* hybrid), but many wine farms have been occupied by "war vets". Worringham still exists, both as a wine farm (45 hectares; 111 acres) and as a brand, and is owned by African Distillers (also known as Stapleford Wines), but other familiar wine names from the early days, such as Philips and Monis, no longer exist, having been absorbed by the Mukuyu Winery. Export brands such as Flame Lily, which made an ephemeral appearance on the UK market, have also fallen by the wayside. Meadows Estate used to be a shining example of cutting-edge viticulture in the 1980s, growing Gewürztraminer, Riesling, Chardonnay, and Pinot Noir, but it is a rose farm now, although Mukuyu still sell wines under the Meadows Estate brand. The 1990s also saw the installation of cool-fermentation technology, and internationally trained winemakers deployed on flying visits, with New Zealander Clive Hartnell (of Hungary's Chapel Hill renown) currently winging his way around the wineries of African Distillers. The late Peter Raynor and his son Humphrey established Zimbabwe's largest private vineyard near Wedza, but its once impeccably trained vines have been unattended since the Raynor family were evicted by Minister of Youth Brigadier Ambrose Mutinhiri in December 2004. They had been forcibly removed in July of that year, only to be herded back three weeks later and told to produce a crop. They are trying to get back in, but the current situation seems ominously more permanent. In addition to the human tragedy, this sadly marks the end of the brief promise shown by Zimbabwe's first and, now, only single-vineyard, pure varietal wines – Fighill 2002 Chardonnay and Fighill 2003 Shiraz, which the Raynors made from a super-selected five per cent of their own production. Most of their crop used to be split 50/50 between African Distillers (which bottled their domain wines) and Mukuyu (which is 65 per cent Government owned, thus escaped its threatened compulsory acquisition in December 2001). Private farms have been so vulnerable to compulsory acquisition (ie, occupation by "war vets") that African Distillers and Mukuyu are now the only producers here.

The WINES *of*
THE AMERICAS

ALL OF THE MOST FAMOUS WINE REGIONS — California, Washington, Oregon, and Chile – are found on or inland from the western coast. This is because eastern seaboards are generally too humid and prone to severely cold winters. Of the famous regions in the Americas, California is, of course, the most important. It is staggering to think that the 25 largest wineries in this state on their own produce twice the output of Argentina (which itself is the fifth-largest winemaking country in the world), but California is actually more about quality than quantity. It produces some of the world's greatest Cabernet Sauvignon, Merlot, Zinfandel, Pinot Noir, and Chardonnay wines. Although Washington has always been a considerably larger wine-producing state than Oregon, from an international perspective it used to live in the shadow of the latter's excellent but over-hyped Pinot Noir. Well, no more. Washington is now justly famous for powerful *bordelais* varietals, not to mention its up-and-coming Syrah. British Columbia has far more in common with Washington State than it does with Ontario, and is creating at least as much of a buzz in the wine world. Chile still rules in South America, but a small number of quality-conscious Argentinian producers are giving their old rival a good run for its money.

CABERNET SAUVIGNON VINES IN THE NAPA VALLEY
Mustard planted near vines provides a habitat for predators of vine pests and also prevents the evaporation of moisture.

NORTH AMERICA

The USA is the fourth-largest wine-producing country in the world, and the output of California alone is more than that of the sixth-largest wine-producing country (Australia), yet almost every state in this vast country produces wine. And, of course, North America does not consist of just the USA; it also encompasses the viticultural areas of Ontario and British Columbia in Canada (see also pp600–5), and the Baja California and Sierra Madre in Mexico (see also pp606–7).

IN 1521, WITHIN ONE YEAR of invading Mexico, the Spanish planted vines and set about making the first North American wines. Fourteen years later, when French explorer Jacques Cartier sailed down the St Lawrence to New France, he discovered a large island overrun by wild vines and decided to call it the Île de Bacchus. He had second thoughts, however, and later renamed it the Île d'Orléans, a calculated move in view of the fact that the then Duke of Orléans was the son of King Francis I of France. It is assumed that, circa 1564, the Jesuit settlers who followed in the wake of Cartier's explorations were the first winemakers in what was to become Canada. The earliest wines made in what is now the United States of America came from Florida. In 1564, French Huguenot settlers produced wines from native Scuppernong grapes on a site that would become Jacksonville.

JEKEL VINEYARDS, CALIFORNIA
An irrigation pipe skirts rows of vines in one of the drier parts of Monterey County. Conditions are a far cry from those around the Finger Lakes, New York.

NATIVE NORTH AMERICAN GRAPE VARIETIES

All classic grape varieties belong to one species, *Vitis vinifera*, but North America's native varieties belong to several different species, not one of which happens to be *Vitis vinifera*. There were plenty of native vines growing wild wherever the early settlers travelled, and so they came to rely on them for their initial wine production. Settlers in Australia, on the other hand, were forced to wait for precious shipments of classic European vines before they could plant vineyards. Although various European varieties were taken across the Atlantic in the 19th century, nearly all North American wines apart from Californian ones remained products of native varieties until relatively recently.

The most common native North American species, *Vitis labrusca*, has such a distinctive aroma and flavour that it seems truly amazing that those pioneers who were also winemakers did not pester their home countries for supplies of more acceptable vines. The *labrusca* character, commonly referred to as "foxy", is so exotic, it cloys at the back of the throat, and is generally not appreciated by European and antipodean palates.

PROHIBITION IN THE UNITED STATES

Although total Prohibition in the United States was confined to 1920–1933, the first "dry legislation" was passed as early as 1816, and the first state to go completely dry was Maine, in 1846. By the time the 18th Amendment to the Constitution was put into effect in 1920, forbidding "the manufacture, sale, or transport of intoxicating liquors", more than 30 states were already totally dry.

The result of Prohibition was chaos. It denied the government legitimate revenue and encouraged bootleggers to amass fortunes. The number of illicit stills multiplied quicker than the authorities could find and dismantle them, and the speakeasy became a way of life in the cities. Not only did the authorities often realize that it was much easier to turn a blind eye to what was going on, the federal government actually found it useful to open its own speakeasy in New York! Many vineyards were uprooted, but those grapes that were produced were often concentrated, pressed, and sold as "grape bricks". These came complete with a yeast capsule and instructions to dissolve the brick in one gallon of water, but warned against adding the yeast because it would start a fermentation! This would turn the grape juice into wine "and that would be illegal", the warning pointed out.

Prohibition and the wine industry

By the mid- to late 19th century, the Californian wine industry had such a reputation that great French wine areas, such as Champagne, began to form syndicates to protect themselves, in part, from the potential of California's marketing threat. However, the 13 years of Prohibition coincided with a vital point in the evolution of wine, and set the Californian wine industry back a hundred years, as other wine regions had just recovered from the effects of phylloxera (*see* p539), and were busily re-establishing their reputations and carving out future markets. In Europe, World War I had robbed every industry of its young, up-and-coming generation, but the rich tradition of the wine industry enabled it to survive until the arrival of a new generation. The early 1900s were also the era of the foundation of the French *Appellation Contrôlée* laws, a quality-control system that many other serious winemaking countries would eventually copy.

The United States also lost much of one generation in World War I, but it had less of a winemaking tradition to fall back on and, by 1920, there was virtually no wine industry whatsoever to preserve. After Prohibition came one of the worst economic depressions in history, followed by World War II, which took yet another

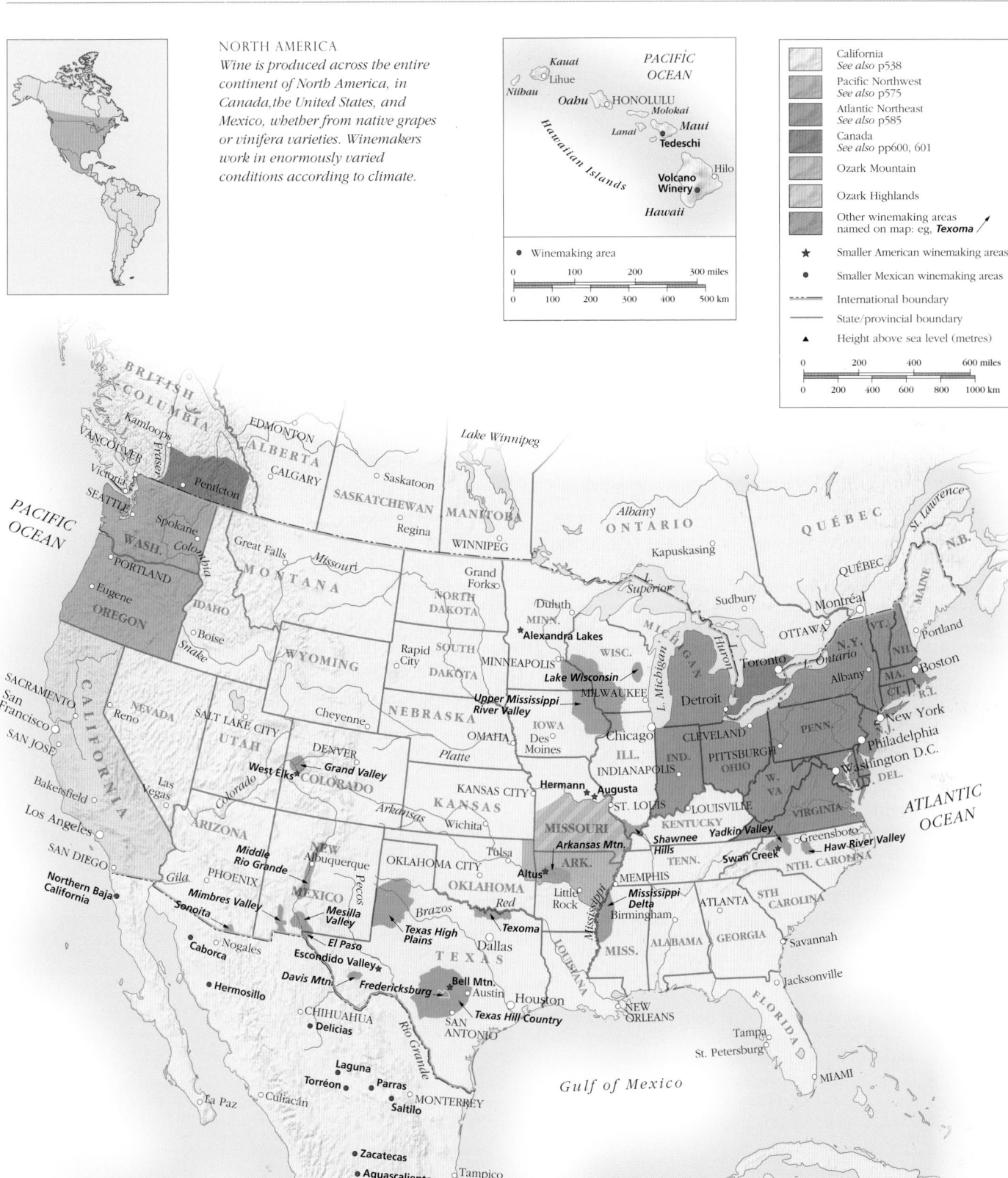

NORTH AMERICA
Wine is produced across the entire continent of North America, in Canada, the United States, and Mexico, whether from native grapes or vinifera varieties. Winemakers work in enormously varied conditions according to climate.

PACIFIC OCEAN

Kauai
Lihue
Niihau
Oahu HONOLULU
Molokai
Lanai Maui
Tedeschi
Hilo
Volcano Winery
Hawaii
Hawaiian Islands

● Winemaking area

| 0 | 100 | 200 | 300 miles |
| 0 | 100 | 200 | 300 | 400 | 500 km |

California
See also p538

Pacific Northwest
See also p575

Atlantic Northeast
See also p585

Canada
See also pp600, 601

Ozark Mountain

Ozark Highlands

Other winemaking areas named on map: eg, **Texoma**

★ Smaller American winemaking areas

● Smaller Mexican winemaking areas

–·–·– International boundary

——— State/provincial boundary

▲ Height above sea level (metres)

| 0 | 200 | 400 | 600 miles |
| 0 | 200 | 400 | 600 | 800 | 1000 km |

PACIFIC OCEAN

ATLANTIC OCEAN

Gulf of Mexico

PACIFIC OCEAN

MOUNT PLEASANT VINEYARDS
These vineyards in Augusta, Missouri were America's first Approved Viticultural Area.

generation of bright young minds. It was, therefore, little wonder that by the late 1940s the wine industry of the United States was so out of date. It had lost touch with European progress and resorted to the production of awful *labrusca* wines that had been the wine drinker's staple diet in pre-Prohibition days. California produced relatively little *labrusca* compared to the eastern states, but its winemakers also resorted to old-fashioned styles, making heavy, sweet, fortified wines.

The fact that Californian wine today is a match for the best of its European counterparts and that its industry is healthy, growing fast, and looking to compete on foreign markets, clearly proves that in the United States opportunity is boundless.

THE APPELLATION SYSTEM OF THE UNITED STATES
The older generation of appellations of the United States is based on political boundaries such as counties or states, and still exists. However, during the mid-1970s, the Department of Treasury's Bureau of Alcohol, Tobacco, and Firearms (BATF) considered the concept of specific controlled appellations based on geography and climate, and in September 1978 BATF published its first laws and regulations designed to introduce a system of Approved Viticultural Areas (AVAs), to supplement the old system, which is now run by the Alcohol and Tobacco Tax and Trade Bureau (TTB). Every state, from Hawaii to Alaska, and the counties they contain, are recognized in law as their own individual appellations of origin, but other generic appellations are also recognized:

American or United States This appellation classifies blended and varietal wines from anywhere in the US, including the District of Columbia and the Commonwealth of Puerto Rico. These wines, like *vins de tables* in France, are not allowed to carry a vintage, which is, in my opinion, irrational. It is the only appellation allowed for wines shipped in bulk to other countries.

Multi-State Appellation This appellation is used to classify a wine from any two or three contiguous states. The percentage of wine from each state must be clearly indicated on the label.

State Appellation A wine from any state may use this appellation; at least 75 per cent of grapes must come from grapes grown within the one state indicated (except for Texas, which is 85 per cent, and California 100 per cent). Thus wine claiming the appellation of Oregon may contain up to 25 per cent produce of other states. The grapes can be shipped to a neighbouring state and still be given the originating state name, but not to any state that does not share a border. Grapes can therefore be shipped from California to Oregon, where they are turned into wine, and may be called California wine (as long as the wine is at least 75 per cent from those grapes), but the same grapes cannot be shipped to Washington State and be called California wine (although such a wine could be labelled California-Oregon-Washington, if it contained grapes from all three states, *see* Multi-State Appellation). The same principles apply to County Appellations and Multi-County Appellations.

Multi-County Appellation This appellation classifies a wine from any two or three contiguous counties. The percentage of wine from each county must be clearly indicated on the label.

County Appellation A wine from any county within any state may use this appellation: at least 75 per cent of the wine must come from grapes grown within the one county indicated.

THE SEMI-GENERIC SAGA

It is not only easy to understand how the misuse of famous European wine names started in America, it is perfectly understandable. As European immigrants poured into this land, some brought vines with them and when they made different styles of wine, it was inevitable that they would use the only wine names they knew to distinguish between them. Names like Burgundy, Chablis, Champagne *et al*. There is nothing to forgive. Until now, that is. Ever since the California wine industry became a significant exporter, opening the door for other wine-producing states, it was incumbent upon the USA to respect all other legitimate geographical appellations, however well entrenched the usage might have become within the USA itself. However, in 1978, well after California wines had stepped onto the international stage, the director of the Department of Treasury's Bureau of Alcohol, Tobacco, and Firearms (BATF) legally enshrined the concept of semi-generic wine names within Federal Regulations, citing, but not restricting itself to, 14 such examples: "Burgundy, Claret, Chablis, Champagne, Chianti, Madeira, Malaga, Marsala, Moselle, Port, Rhine Wine, Sauterne, Sherry, Tokay". The regulations state that these so-called semi-generic names must be qualified by their true place of origin: American Chablis, California Champagne, and so on. However, American regulations are not only unfair, they are decidedly quirky. While it is perfectly legal for US wineries to sell wines labelled as Champagne or Chablis, the name Liebfraumilch is protected by the full might of Federal Law. And whereas Burgundy is permitted, Bordeaux or Rhône are not. Where is the logic? As the most abused wine names were French, it was left initially to that country to redress the situation, but they got nowhere and, frankly, were not helped by their own antics in South America, where the *champenois* were abusing the Champagne appellation. The French were also chronically short-sighted when turning down an under-the-table deal that would have seen "Champagne" dropped in favour of "Champagne Style". Since then, the production of American wine sold under famous Italian appellations has become a substantial industry in itself, which with the use of other European wine names has seen the European Union take up the fight. Its negotiators have been hammering away at the USA through the World Trade Organization, but they have not been any more successful than the French. What they have failed to understand is that they have nothing to bring to the negotiating table that the USA is in the slightest bit bothered about, but when they recognize this, it should provide the European authorities with the obvious solution. If the French, Italians, Spanish, Portuguese, and Hungarians officially created a few new appellations, like Napa Valley, Sonoma County Green Valley, and, to catch the attention of the East Coast elite, North Fork of Long Island and Northern Neck George Washington Birthplace, the EU would soon find that it had something to bargain with, and the USA might at least understand why Europeans are so protective of their appellations. The irony is that should such appellations be formally adopted and the wines put into distribution in their country of origin, they would be automatically eligible for sale in the USA, where the law defines an acceptable foreign appellation on an imported wine to be "a delimited place or region the boundaries of which have been recognized and defined by the country of origin for use on labels of wine available for consumption within the country of origin". Perhaps the wine-producing countries who feel that they have been treated unfairly by the USA will realize that sometimes it does take a wrong to right another wrong. Virtually all self-respecting, quality wine producers in the USA will be on their side because they are proud of their own products, which do not need any famous European names as a crutch.

DID YOU KNOW?

- America's third president, Thomas Jefferson, was the country's greatest wine connoisseur, and even tried to grow vines at Monticello.
- There is a winery in every state of the USA, even Alaska (although the grapes have to be trucked in, of course).
- Although almost every state in the USA grows wine grapes, California accounts for more than 90 per cent of the wines produced.
- It is legal to produce and sell American Champagne or Burgundy, but not American Bordeaux or Rhône.
- There are still "dry" counties in some US states.
- The oldest winery in the USA is the Brotherhood Winery (1839) at Washingtonville in the foothills of the Catskills of New York State.

AMERICAN LABEL LANGUAGE

Alcohol It is obligatory to indicate the alcoholic strength of a US wine, and this is expressed as a percentage by volume.

Angelica An authentic American fortified wine style of 17–24 per cent, traditionally made from Mission grapes, typically blended 50/50 wine and brandy, with the spirit added after fermentation has achieved just 5 per cent alcohol, resulting in excess of 100 g/l of residual sugar. If the strength is less than 18 per cent, the wine must be labelled "Light Angelica". Other grapes that are sometimes used include Grenache, Muscat, and Palomino. The quality can be extremely high. Angelica was named after Los Angeles by Spanish Missionary winemakers in the 18th century, when the city was just a town and its name in full was El Pueblo de Nuestra Señora Reina de los Ángeles de la Porciuncula.

Bottle fermented A sparkling wine derived through a second fermentation in "glass containers of not greater than one (US) gallon capacity". Usually refers to a wine that, after second fermentation, is decanted and filtered under pressure before rebottling.

Burgundy A semi-generic name allowed under US Federal Law for a red wine of legally undefined "Burgundy-style", such products today are inevitably of basic quality and made from almost anything, although high-yielding Carignane, Grenache, and Zinfandel are traditional. American Burgundy is typically dark in colour, and full in body, but with some residual sweetness to give an impression of softness.

Carbonated wine Still wine made bubbly through the addition of carbon dioxide from a bottle of gas, the method used to produce fizzy drinks such as lemonade or cola.

Champagne A semi-generic name allowed under US Federal Law for a wine rendered sparkling through a second fermentation in "glass containers of not greater than one (US) gallon capacity".

Chianti A semi-generic name allowed under US Federal Law for a red wine of legally undefined style, American Chianti is generally medium-bodied, falling somewhere between American claret and American Burgundy in colour, character, and residual sweetness, with a more pronounced fruitiness, but is equally basic in quality.

Claret A semi-generic name allowed under US Federal Law for a red wine of legally undefined style, American claret is a basic wine that is generally drier than American Burgundy, as well as being lighter in colour and body.

Crackling wine A sparkling wine derived through a second fermentation in "glass containers of not greater than one (US) gallon capacity", thus the same as for American "Champagne", although with a lesser degree of effervescence. It may also be called *pétillant*, *frizzante*, or *crémant*.

Crackling wine – bulk method I have not actually seen "Bulk Method" on a wine label, but it does exist, and it means the same as for "Crackling Wine" but made by the *cuve close* method.

Dessert wine A wine with an alcohol content of 14–24 per cent that is usually fortified. If less than 18 per cent, the wine must be labelled "Light Dessert Wine".

Fermented in the bottle A simple and clever way of describing a wine that has been made by the traditional *méthode champenoise*.

Fumé blanc Widely used term for oak-aged Sauvignon Blanc.

Grape variety If a single grape variety is mentioned on a label, the wine must contain at least 75 per cent of the grape variety indicated (90 per cent in Oregon). Although the potential of varietal labelling was recognized in Alsace in the 1920s, the international marketing phenomenon these wines represent today was brought about by the widespread application of the concept by California wineries.

Haute Sauterne (*sic*) Rarely encountered, highly questionable, semi-generic name allowed and misspelled under US Federal Law for medium-sweet and sweet variants of Sauterne (*sic*).

Health warning Health warnings are required by federal law, yet none of the proven health advantages are permitted on the label (*see* Micropedia).

Hock A semi-generic name allowed under US Federal Law for an undefined style of wine that, curiously, is light and dry, rather than vaguely approximating some sort of German Rhine wine. The grapes used are often the same as for American Chablis, but are blended to produce something lighter (which is correct) and drier (which is not).

Light Wine A wine with an alcohol level not in excess of 14 per cent (synonymous with Table Wine).

Madeira A semi-generic name allowed under US Federal Law for any fortified wine of 17–24 per cent, made in a legally undefined "Madeira-style" that is usually sweet to some degree. If it contains less than 18 per cent alcohol, the wine must be labelled "Light Madeira". This slowly diminishing style of wine is primarily Californian and is traditionally produced by blending American sherry with Angelica.

Malaga A semi-generic name allowed under US Federal Law for any fortified wine of 17–24 per cent, made in a legally undefined "Malaga-style" that is usually sweet to some degree. If it contains less than 18 per cent alcohol, the wine must be labelled "Light Malaga". Made primarily from Concord grapes, American Malaga is often a kosher product and is used for sacramental rites.

Marsala A semi-generic name allowed under US Federal Law for any fortified wine of 17–24 per cent, made in a legally undefined "Marsala-style" that is amber or brown in colour, usually sweet to some degree, and sometimes flavoured with herbs. If it contains less than 18 per cent alcohol, the wine must be labelled "Light Marsala".

Moselle A semi-generic name allowed under US Federal Law for an undefined style of wine that is traditionally made from Chenin Blanc and Riesling grapes.

American Moselle is light in body, pale in colour, medium sweet to taste, and sometimes very lightly *pétillant*. It is softer and lighter than American hock.

Muscatel Generally a more basic quality version of sweet Muscat wine (which is usually sold varietally as Muscat Frontignan or Muscat Canelli), Muscatel is usually a blend of two or more of the following: Aleatico, Malvasia Bianca, and Muscat (Alexandria, Canelli, and Frontignan). Black Muscatel is a blend of Aleatico and Black Muscat (also known as Muscat Hamburg).

Natural wine A wine may be called "natural" only if it has not been fortified with grape brandy or alcohol.

Port A semi-generic name allowed under US Federal Law for any fortified wine of 17–24 per cent that has been made in a legally undefined "Port style". If it contains less than 18 per cent alcohol, the wine must be labelled "Light Port". Zinfandel, Petite Sirah, and Cabernet Sauvignon are the most common grapes to be declared on a label, but others widely used include Alicante Bouschet, Carignane, Grenache, and Mission. Additionally, there is a small but growing category of quality ports, blended and varietal, that are made from various Portuguese varieties such as Tinta Madeira, Tinta Cão, Alvarelhão, Touriga, and Bastardo or Trousseau. When blended from different Portuguese varieties, the wine is often sold as a Tinta port. Whichever grapes are used, the wines are usually sweet to some degree, and often qualified by traditional Port terminology such as Ruby, Tawny, and Vintage. Some examples can be very good, particularly from port specialists.

Rhine wine Synonymous with American hock.

Sauterne (*sic*) A semi-generic name allowed and misspelled under US Federal Law for a wine that is usually of basic quality, less sweet than genuine Sauternes, and with no hint of botrytis. A few better-quality Sauterne wines are made, usually from Sémillon and Sauvignon Blanc, but most Sauterne are nothing more than bland blends of Palomino, Sauvignon Vert, Thompson Seedless, and other even less respectable varieties. Amazingly for a semi-generic wine that should by definition be intensely sweet, Sauterne wines range from dry to very sweet, and are often qualified by "Dry" or "Sweet", with "Chateau" weirdly used for the sweetest styles. The cheapest dry Sauterne wines are not dissimilar to American Chablis. Some California producers spell Sauternes correctly, but it is difficult to work out which spelling constitutes the worst insult.

Semi-generic A semi-generic name is a geographical designation that has, in the opinion of the Director of the Department of Treasury's Alcohol and Tobacco Tax and Trade Bureau (TTB), become at least as well known for a specific style of wine, wherever it might happen to be produced, and is thus allowed under US Federal Law to

be used by any wine producer in the USA. Thus it is entirely legal within the borders of the USA to abuse the appellations of Burgundy, Chablis, Champagne, Chianti, and many others.

Sherry A semi-generic name allowed under US Federal Law for any fortified wine of 17–24 per cent that has been made in a legally undefined "Sherry style", usually sweet to some degree. If the alcohol content is less than 18 per cent, the wine must be labelled "Light Sherry". Palomino is the favoured variety for high-class sherries, and is also known in California as the Golden Chasselas or Napa Golden Chasselas. Palomino is the only varietally labelled sherry that is likely to be encountered, since the other grapes used (Mission, Thompson Seedless, and *labrusca*) are hardly worth shouting about. Although legally undefined by Federal Law, the best sherries will often involve the use of *flor* and will be blended under a *solera* system. However, the most common production method is to heat the wines for several months in order to replicate Sherry's oxidative style, and some efforts are worse than others. Whatever method of production used, there are numerous sub-styles produced. Some sherries are actually labelled Dry, Medium, or Sweet, in addition to which there are Pale Dry (closer to *fino* or Cocktail sherries, which are dry; Golden or Amber sherries, which are medium sweet; and Cream, which is sweet.

Sparkling wine This term may be used to describe "carbonated", *cuve close*, "bottle-fermented", or *méthode champenoise* wine. If the label bears no other information, the consumer should fear the worst (carbonated or *cuve close*). However, the label may indicate any of the following terms: Champagne, Bottle Fermented, Fermented in this Bottle, Crackling Wine (including Crackling Wine – Bulk Method), and Carbonated Wine.

Sulfites It is obligatory for all American wines to state "Contains sulfites" or "Contains sulfiting agent/s" when sulphur dioxide or a sulphuring agent can be detected at a level of 10 or more parts per million.

Table wine A wine with an alcohol level not in excess of 14 per cent (synonymous with Light Wine).

Tokay All-American blend of Angelica, Dry Sherry (to reduce the sweetness), and a dash of port to provide its tawny-pink colour, Tokay is a medium-sweet dessert wine with a slightly nutty flavour, and 17–24 per cent in strength. If less than 18 per cent, the wine must be labelled "Light Tokay".

Vintage At least 95 per cent of the wine must be from the vintage indicated. Until the 1970s, the law demanded that the figure was 100 per cent, but wine-makers, particularly those producing higher-quality wines aged in small oak barrels, petitioned for a small margin to enable topping-up, and this was granted.

Volume This must be stated somewhere on the bottle by law.

Approved Viticultural Areas There are no AVA rules governing the varieties grown, the methods of vine-training employed, the yields allowed, or the style of wines produced, and AVAs are all the better for it. Although some have evolved to a point where they can be said to favour certain grape varieties and produce identifiable styles, many have not and probably never will. America's AVAs are much maligned by various American critics, yet they are the healthy product of New World free enterprise. The *raison d'être* of the AVA system is truthful labelling: a wine comes from where it says it comes from (or, at least, a minimum of 85 per cent has to). The AVA process merely establishes the boundary of what must be demonstrated to be a fairly homogenous growing zone, whether small or large. Unfortunately, the law does not insist that the AVA name should be immediately followed by the term "Approved Viticultural Area". As a result, who is to know if a geographical area (or a seemingly geographical area) on a wine label has any official connotation whatsoever?

HEALTH WARNINGS ON AMERICAN WINE LABELS

The following "Government Warning" must appear on every bottle of wine sold in the United States: 1 According to the Surgeon General, "women should not drink alcoholic beverages during pregnancy because of the risk of birth defects"; 2 "Consumption of alcoholic beverages impairs your ability to drive a car or operate machinery and may cause health problems". In my opinion, however, the warning is grossly misleading and contains half-truths and unsubstantiated claims, while proven health benefits are not included on the label. As to the first part of the warning, women alcoholics can give birth to children deformed by "foetal alcohol syndrome", but a study of 2,000 Australian women concluded (in line with other reports) that "there is no significant relationship between light and moderate maternal alcohol intake and foetal growth effect". There can be no argument with the first part of the second warning because the "consumption of alcoholic beverages" does "impair" the ability to "drive a car or operate machinery", but while the second part is true – that alcohol may cause health problems – it is grossly misleading because it does not put into context the word "may". The US government was forced to use this word because only excessive alcohol consumption is a potential health hazard, whereas global tests and studies, many carried out by America's most respected institutions, have shown various benefits to health of drinking alcohol in moderation (*see* Health Benefits of Wine in the Micropedia). The more studies that are conducted, the more confirmation there is, as in "New Data on the Effects of Alcohol During Pregnancy" (*Medical News Today*, 18 October 2010).

What truly amazes me is that a country regarded by the rest of the world as litigation-mad has a wine industry that does not have the conviction to stand up for itself. I am informed that it would be impossible to prove the Surgeon General's

VINEYARDS, UPSTATE NEW YORK
Rows of vines combine to form an emerald-green patchwork on the gently sloping countryside near Hammondsport. In the distance is Keuka Lake, one of the finger-shaped lakes that have a moderating influence on the area's climate.

unsubstantiated claim about birth defects in a court of law, so why not hire the largest firm of first-rate lawyers in the country and sue the Surgeon General for $50 billion lost revenue? Instead, they welcomed with open arms the right (won in 1999) to put the following message on a bottle of wine: "The proud people who made this wine encourage you to consult your family doctor about the health effects of wine consumption". Such is the unempowered state of the US wine industry that some of its members have been absolutely euphoric about this statement, declaring it a small victory in the quest to redress the negative effect of the health warning, but what does it actually say? Wine is so good for you that you should consult your doctor before drinking it? That sounds more like a warning than a benefit to me. No wonder the Surgeon General approved it.

FAR NIENTE, OAKVILLE, NAPA VALLEY
Some may think electricity and water should never mix, but Far Niente has floated 1,000 solar panels on pontoons in its irrigation pond. This produces enough electricity to power the winery and also prevents precious irrigation water from evaporating.

CALIFORNIA

California's finest wines have become a victim of their own success. Ignoring the ridiculously priced iconic wines, the vast majority of California's greatest wines can stand shoulder-to-shoulder with equivalently priced wines from the classic regions of France, yet while the international market is willing to pay such prices for famous names from Bordeaux, Burgundy, and the Rhône, it is either unwilling or lacks the knowledge to pay the same price for the California wines. This has resulted in mid-priced California wines filling the top end of the available range on even the most open-minded export markets. Thus, what is perceived to be the best that California has to offer is not really its best at all.

CALIFORNIA WAS FIRST SETTLED by the Spanish in 1769 and formed part of Mexico until 1848, when it was ceded to the United States, becoming a State of the Union in 1850. The first California wine was made in 1782 at San Juan Capistrano, by Fathers Pablo de Mugártegui and Gregorio Amurrió. Mission grapes, from vines brought to California by Don José Camacho on the *San Antonio*, which docked at San Diego on 16 May 1778, were used to make the wine. However, it was not until 1833 that *Bordelais* Jean-Louis Vignes established California's first commercial winery. He was the first Californian winemaker to import European vines and, in 1840, he also became the first to export Californian wines.

THE AMAZING HARASZTHY
Eight years before California passed from Mexican to American sovereignty, a certain Hungarian political exile named Agoston Haraszthy de Mokesa settled in Wisconsin. Haraszthy was a colourful, flamboyant entrepreneur in the mould of Barnum or

NAPA VALLEY VINEYARDS
Of all California's winemaking regions, the Napa Valley is perhaps the best known, and its wines are the most sought after. The first vines were planted here in 1838, and today the valley boasts a vast area under vine, with a bewildering array of grape varieties.

RECENT CALIFORNIA VINTAGES

2010 A cool growing season yielded what Europeans see as an elegant vintage but some Americans might view as light. Lower alcohol and higher acids produced refreshing whites and reds that have good colour but are more restrained than usual.

2009 Rain at harvest time caused rot, particularly in late-ripening varieties, but excellent quality for those who picked before the rain, particularly for Chardonnay and Pinot Noir.

2008 Severe spring frosts, summer heat spikes, drought, and forest fires made this a difficult year, but some very good wines have been produced. Cabernet Sauvignon and Rhône varieties performed best.

2007 Very good to excellent everywhere, with Napa the standout, and the only negative was a logistical one: that of coping with different varieties ripening at the same time, which made for difficult choices in some areas.

2006 In a strangely similar pattern to much of Europe, California wilted under a sweltering July, causing the vines' metabolism to shut down, and a cool, wet August. Consequently the harvest was late and irregular, but it produced great quality across the board, with exceptional aromatics, focused fruit, and exceptional natural acid levels.

Champagne Charlie. Among other things, he founded a town in Wisconsin and modestly called it Haraszthy (it was later renamed Sauk City), ran a Mississippi steamboat, and cultivated the first vineyard in Wisconsin – all within two years of beginning a new life in a strange country.

In 1849, Haraszthy moved to San Diego, leaving his business interests in the hands of a partner, who promptly took advantage of a rumour that he had perished during his transcontinental trek, sold all the business and properties, and vanished with the money. Haraszthy was broke, yet within six months he was farming his own 65-hectare (160-acre) fruit and vegetable ranch. Such rapid success followed by disaster then an even greater triumph was to become Haraszthy's trademark. Within a few months of acquiring his ranch, he also became the owner of a butcher's shop and a livery stable in Middleton, a part of San Diego that still boasts a Haraszthy Street. In addition, he ran an omnibus company, started a construction business, was elected the first sheriff of San Diego, was made a judge, and became a lieutenant in the volunteer militia. He also began importing cuttings of numerous European vine varieties.

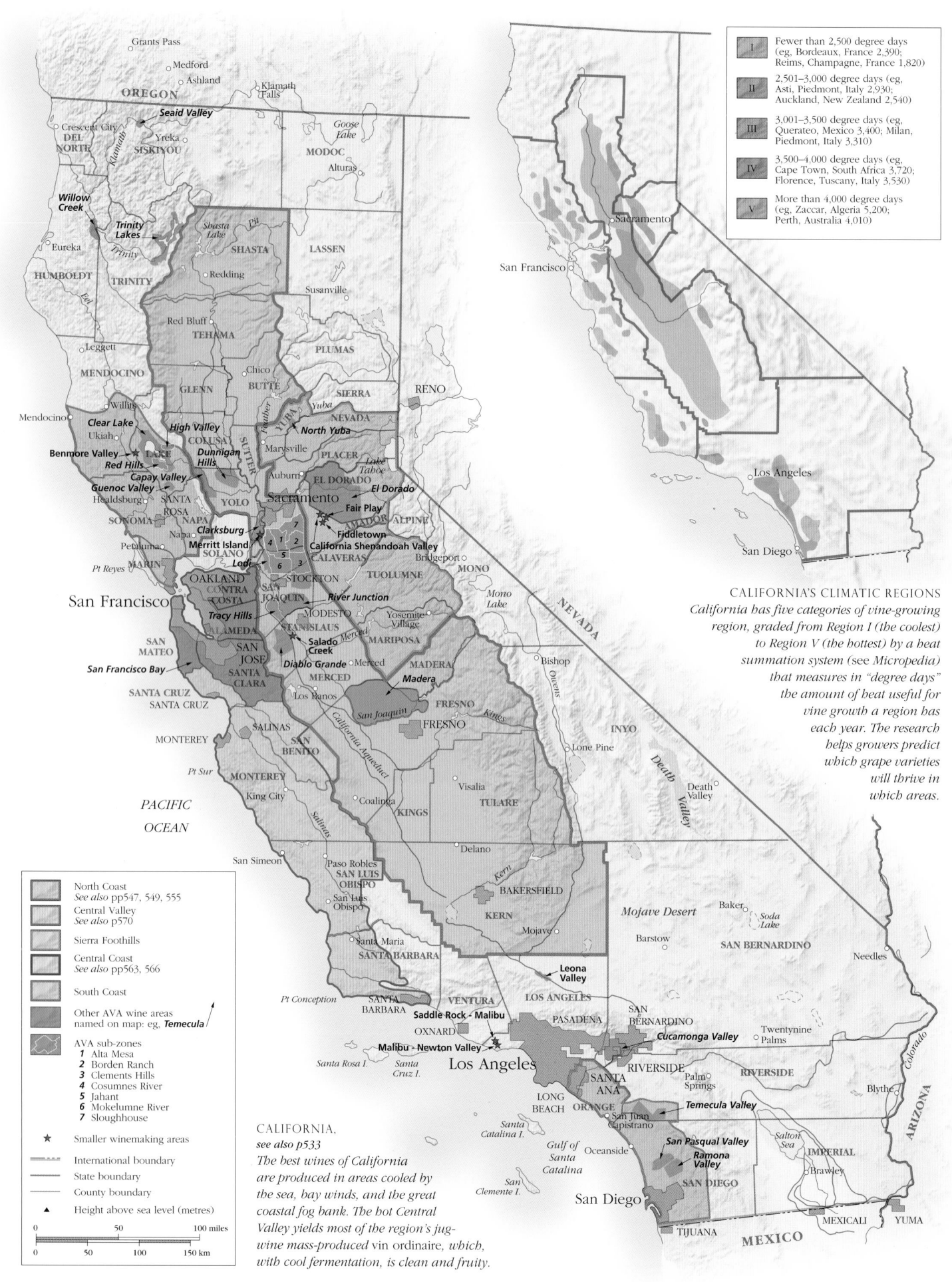

CALIFORNIA'S CLIMATIC REGIONS
California has five categories of vine-growing region, graded from Region I (the coolest) to Region V (the hottest) by a heat summation system (see Micropedia) that measures in "degree days" the amount of heat useful for vine growth a region has each year. The research helps growers predict which grape varieties will thrive in which areas.

I	Fewer than 2,500 degree days (eg, Bordeaux, France 2,390; Reims, Champagne, France 1,820)
II	2,501–3,000 degree days (eg, Asti, Piedmont, Italy 2,930; Auckland, New Zealand 2,540)
III	3,001–3,500 degree days (eg, Quereteo, Mexico 3,400; Milan, Piedmont, Italy 3,310)
IV	3,500–4,000 degree days (eg, Cape Town, South Africa 3,720; Florence, Tuscany, Italy 3,530)
V	More than 4,000 degree days (eg, Zaccar, Algeria 5,200; Perth, Australia 4,010)

CALIFORNIA,
see also p533
The best wines of California are produced in areas cooled by the sea, bay winds, and the great coastal fog bank. The hot Central Valley yields most of the region's jug-wine mass-produced vin ordinaire, which, with cool fermentation, is clean and fruity.

North Coast *See also pp547, 549, 555*
Central Valley *See also p570*
Sierra Foothills
Central Coast *See also pp563, 566*
South Coast
Other AVA wine areas named on map: eg, *Temecula*

AVA sub-zones
1 Alta Mesa
2 Borden Ranch
3 Clements Hills
4 Cosumnes River
5 Jahant
6 Mokelumne River
7 Sloughhouse

★ Smaller winemaking areas
International boundary
State boundary
County boundary
▲ Height above sea level (metres)

THE SECOND COMING

Because phylloxera, a root-feeding insect, came from the USA to destroy European vineyards, which were saved only when the vines were grafted on to phylloxera-resistant native American varieties, there is a widespread belief that California's vineyards have always been safe. Nothing could be further from the truth. Phylloxera's home was east of the Rockies, where over aeons native vines, such as *Vitis berlandieri* and *V riparia*, developed a natural resistance to phylloxera. When European *vinifera* vines were introduced to California, phylloxera was bound to follow, via the wagon trains across the Rockies or on the vines themselves, and *vinifera* varieties proved to be as vulnerable in California as anywhere else.

THE ANTI-BEAST

Phylloxera was first identified at Sonoma in 1873, coincidentally at the same time as another native American bug, *Tyroglyphus*, was deliberately being shipped to France. The idea of using *Tyroglyphus*, which was harmless to the vine but a deadly enemy of phylloxera, to infect phylloxera-infested vineyards was an imaginative one. Unfortunately, unlike phylloxera, *Tyroglyphus* did not care for the European climate and failed to settle.

In California, the effect of phylloxera was devastating. By 1891, Napa could boast 7,200 hectares (18,000 acres) of vines, but phylloxera multiplies at a terrifying rate (one female bug can be responsible for one billion offspring in twelve 30-day generation cycles every year) that this had been reduced to a mere 1,200 hectares (3,000 acres). Under the auspices of Professor Hilgard, Head of Agriculture at the Department of Viticulture and Enology in the University of California at Berkeley (established in 1880, moved to Davis in 1906), California's growers eventually adopted the same method as the Europeans to control the pest, grafting *vinifera* vines on to phylloxera-resistant varieties. Ironically, it was some time before Californians realized these wonder vines originated from eastern American states and initially imported them from France! Only half the vineyards had been grafted when they were hit by another, even more lethal, plague – Prohibition. By the late 1940s, UC Davis had assembled one of the most formidable teams of viticultural and oenological experts in the world. Headed by such legendary figures as Amerine, Olmo, and Winkler, the university was primarily responsible for making California the wine force it is today. Along the way, however, they made some errors, such as placing too much emphasis on volume and technical correctness, but the biggest mistake of all was to recommend the widespread use of AxR#1 rootstock.

ROOT CAUSE

Despite warnings from various European sources about its susceptibility to phylloxera (all acknowledged but brushed aside by numerous university textbooks), UC Davis recommended AxR's use on fertile valley floors, such as Napa, because of its ability to increase yields. As Winkler *et al* put it in *General Viticulture*: "This is a case where the choice of (root) stock cannot be based entirely on its resistance to phylloxera".

These words came back to haunt the faculty at Davis in the 1980s, when, slowly but inexorably, vineyards grafted on to AxR failed and the culprit, phylloxera, was identified. Three out of every four vines in California will have to be replaced, which will bring financial ruin to many, although for the California wine industry as a whole, it will ultimately be recognized as a blessing in disguise as undesirable grapes will not only be replaced by selected clones of better-quality varieties, but will also be grafted on to less productive rootstocks and planted at higher densities. Most of California's AxR#1 vineyards were replanted by the turn of the millennium, at an estimated cost of billions. The Napa and Sonoma districts alone cost in excess of $1.5 billion.

SHARPSHOOTERS

Just as California's growers were counting the cost of dealing with phylloxera, so their vineyards were being invaded by another, possibly more dangerous, bug – *Homalodisca coagulata*, or the Glassy-Winged Sharpshooter. This leaf-hopper is not harmful in itself, but it carries the bacterium that infects vines with Pierce's disease. This disease is considerably faster-acting than phylloxera, killing vines in just one to five years, but what really frightens the industry is that there is no known cure. With no way to defeat Pierce's disease, most efforts have been focused on trying to control its vector, the Glassy-Winged Sharpshooter. In August 2000, David Morgan, a post-doctoral research scientist at the Riverside campus of the University of California, began a programme to control the spread of Sharpshooters by releasing their natural enemy, *Gonatocerus triguttatus*. This tiny, stingless wasp had been effective in reducing populations in Texas and Mexico, but has yet to turn the tide in the Golden State, the southern and central counties of which are already infected. Despite Morgan's efforts, it is still predicted that the Glassy-Winged Sharpshooter will probably become a "permanent part of various habitats throughout northern California".

The Buena Vista Winery

Having imported no fewer than 165 different vine varieties from Europe, in 1856 Haraszthy purchased 230 hectares (560 acres) of land near the town of Sonoma, in an area called the Valley of the Moon. Here, he built a winery, which he named Buena Vista, and dug six cellars out of the sandstone hill. With north California's first significant wine estate, Haraszthy won several awards, and he attracted much publicity for both his vineyard and his wine. This venture drew so much attention that, in 1861, the governor of California commissioned Haraszthy to visit Europe and report on its winegrowing areas. Haraszthy's trip took him to every wine region in France, Germany, Italy, Spain, and Switzerland, where he interviewed thousands of winegrowers, took notes, consulted foreign literature, and so accumulated a library of reference material. He returned to the USA with a staggering 100,000 cuttings of 300 different vine varieties, only to have the state Senate plead poverty when he presented them with a bill for $12,000 for his trip, although the cuttings alone were worth three times that amount. He was never reimbursed for his trouble and many of the cuttings, which he had expected to be distributed among the state's other winegrowers, simply rotted away.

Haraszthy was not deterred: within seven years he managed to expand Buena Vista to 2,430 hectares (6,000 acres). In doing so, he totally changed the course of Californian viticulture, transferring the focus of attention from the south of the state to the north. At the height of its fame Buena Vista had offices in San Francisco, Philadelphia, Chicago, New York, and London. However, this success was purely superficial, for the vineyard was described in 1864 as "the largest wine-growing estate in the world and the most unprofitable". Haraszthy also suffered a number of losses on the stock exchange and was faced with a new tax on brandy, which resulted in further loss of income. A fire at the winery then destroyed much of his stock and the bank proceeded to cut off his credit.

Enough was enough, even for Agoston Haraszthy de Mokesa. He left California for Nicaragua, where he was successful in obtaining a government contract to distil rum from sugar. An enigmatic character to the end, Haraszthy disappeared altogether in 1869, presumed drowned while trying to cross an alligator-infested stream on his plantation.

LEARNING CURVE

With California's natural abundance of sun and what to most Europeans seems like America's preoccupation with size, it was perhaps inevitable that the 1950s and early 1960s saw a series of massive, ink-black, tannic Cabernet Sauvignon blockbusters hitting the shelves. The late 1960s witnessed the introduction of high-tech wineries and the use of 100 per cent new oak, and the precision of style and focus of fruit that resulted were welcomed at the time, as were the supple tannins that replaced harsh ones. The mid-1970s saw the irresistible rise of Chardonnay, but the wines were blatantly too rich and oaky. Sidetracked by the quest for finesse, the wines went too far in the wishy-washy vintages of 1982 and 1983, when over-acidified, tart, and downright stingy wines were made. Some winemakers wanted to sacrifice the voluptuousness that is inherent in this sunny state in a fruitless bid to fabricate some sort of European-styled, slower-developing, longer-lived wine (a number still pursue this misguided idea), but the truly magnificent 1985 vintage, the best year since 1974, was a turning point for California's wine industry. Virtually everyone got it right. Since then, the wines of all those who sought elegance without stripping away their natural expression have deliciously demonstrated that the original quest for finesse was no folly.

This learning curve has established in California, as it has elsewhere, that the secret of fine wine is merely a matter of balance. The difficulty is in achieving it, for perfect balance is by definition a natural state that can be achieved only in the vineyard, not in the winery.

LONGEVITY

Now that most of California's makers of fine wines have found their direction, the only obstacle to prevent them from achieving their full potential (apart from the vagaries of vintage and occasional over-zealousness), is the problem of cellarage temperature. Air conditioning is vital in California, but few people seem to realize that at 14°C (57°F), which seems to be the norm here, potentially fine white wines will fall over after two or three years and the longevity of even the best-quality red wines will be halved. The additional cost of maintaining a temperature just a few degrees lower can be considerable, but once the bottle maturation process has set in, it can only be speeded up, not slowed down, so it is a cost that cannot be cut. The *champenois* know this more than anyone else, as even their cheapest products must spend years in their cellars prior to distribution, which is why they are stored at between 10 and 11°C (50 and 52°F). Once most California cellars are kept at no more than 12°C (53.5°F), the notion that these wines rapidly mature will be shown to be a myth.

TOO MUCH OF A GOOD THING?

Investors overestimated public demand for sparkling wines in the 1980s, when they copied Domaine Chandon in a number of new dedicated sparkling wine operations (Piper-Sonoma in 1980, Maison Deutz in 1981, Freixenet's Gloria Ferrar in 1982, Roederer Estate in 1982, Mumm Napa in 1985, Taittinger's Domaine Carneros in 1987, and Codorníu in 1991), only to release their products onto a market plateau, sparking off a fizz war, as they tried to grab a slice of the shrinking cake. The only real winner was Domaine Chandon, which had already recouped its capital outlay and was the only one that could afford to play the discount game and still make a profit. Also Roederer Estate, which refused to participate, and has subsequently built up a reputation as one of the greatest sparkling wine producers outside of Champagne itself. Domaine Carneros and Mumm Napa have both survived by discounting their entry-level wines, while creating awareness for some of their higher-quality *cuvées*, but Piper-Sonoma is just a label operating out of a small corner of what was once its own proud winery, but was purchased by Judy Jordan for the production of her premium-quality "J" sparkling wine. Maison Deutz has been defunct since 1997, and Codorníu was renamed Artesa and now specializes in up-market still wines.

History repeated itself on a grander scale at the turn of the 21st century. In the mid-1990s, California was riding on the crest of the French Paradox wave, which started with the *60 Minutes* television programme in 1991 and increased per capita wine consumption in the USA by almost one third. In 1995, California experienced the largest growth in its wine sales for 20 years, when the industry was hit by a small crop. Sales continued to soar in 1996, and that year's crop was also down. Faced with the prospect of increasing sales and diminishing crops, growers commenced planting new vineyards at such a rate that by 2001 the acreage under vine had increased by more than 60 per cent – then global economic decline was heightened by September 11. Wine drinking did not slow down, but consumers became more sensitive to price points. This resulted in $10 wines being discounted to $6, and cheaper wines being sold off anonymously. The ripple effect caused tens of thousands of acres to be grubbed up. This may not have been such a bad thing, as they were mostly fit for little more than blending, but it did seem a bit back to front that while vines were being planted at the fastest rate ever in marginal areas like the Atlantic Northeast, vineyards were actually disappearing in sunny California. There was even talk that California's wine glut was affecting sales of its ultra-premium products, but although their prices have dropped, this was not the result of a general sensitivity to price points. The minuscule tip of the California wine market had become overcrowded with $100-plus wines, and their primary patrons, California's new money, eventually realized the value of scarcity.

SPRING MUSTARD FLOWERS IN THE NAPA VALLEY
This bright yellow carpet of mustard seed in full bloom will soon be ploughed in as a "green manure" to feed the vines.

CALIFORNIA'S GRAPE VARIETIES

The area under vine in California has decreased by 40,000 acres since 2003, but this is due to the increasingly rapid decline of raisin farming. The breakdown of vines in 2010 was as follows:

VINE TYPE	2003 ACRES	2010 ACRES	INCREASED ACREAGE	PERCENTAGE GROWTH
Wine grape varieties	529,000	535,000	6,000	1.13%
Raisin grape varieties	260,000	213,000	-47,000	-18.08%
Table grape varieties	93,000	94,000	1,000	1.07%
TOTAL	882,000	842,000	-40,000	-4.53%

From the breakdown below of wine grape varieties by colour, the swing from white to red wine varieties has slowed almost to a complete halt compared to the eight years to 2003, which saw an increase of no less than 101 per cent. As reported in the previous edition, this was almost double the 58 per cent increase in white grape varieties. That period of expansion saw the focus of growth shifting from white wines, which accounted for 57 per cent of production during the 1980s, thanks to the so-called "French paradox" (see Micropedia), which was publicized on American CBS television's 60 Minutes programme. If you look at the grand totals for black and white grape varieties, very little appears to have changed between 2003 and 2010, but this has been a period of consolidation, involving a huge upheaval on a variety-by-variety basis as the vineyards are tweaked to suit the demands of the market.

GRAPE COLOUR	2003 ACRES	%	2010 ACRES	%	INCREASED ACREAGE	PERCENTAGE GROWTH
Black	287,075	61%	294,528	62%	7,453	2.59%
White	185,373	39%	181,849	38%	-3,524	-1.90%
TOTAL	472,448	100%	476,377	100%	3,929	0.83%

CALIFORNIA'S WHITE GRAPE VARIETIES

In 2010, there were 181,849 acres of white grapes growing in California, with just 12 varieties accounting for almost 95 per cent of this total. The increased interest in Pinot Gris commented on in the previous edition has continued, and this time around it has seen the greatest increase in white acreage and is the third fastest growing white variety percentage-wise. The crown for greatest proportional increase goes to the Albariño, which has risen by 920 per cent.

LE5	FG5	GRAPE VARIETY	2003 ACREAGE	2010 ACREAGE	INCREASED ACREAGE	PERCENTAGE GROWTH
		Chardonnay	97,680	95,271	-2,409	-2.47%
		French Colombard	31,865	24,824	-7,041	-22.09%
		Sauvignon Blanc	15,308	15,407	99	0.65%
1.	5.	Pinot Gris	5,908	12,907	6,999	118.47%
		Chenin Blanc	13,416	7,223	-6,193	-46.16%
2.		Riesling	1,844	3,831	1,987	107.75%
		Muscat of Alexandria	3,775	3,391	-384	-10.17%
4.		Viognier	2,089	2,993	904	43.27%
3.		Muscat Canelli	970	1,908	938	96.70%
		Gewürztraminer	1,358	1,735	377	27.76%
		Malvasia Bianca	1,857	1,317	-540	-29.08%
		Burger	1,500	1,222	-278	-18.53%
		Symphony	612	940	328	53.59%
		Sémillon	1,255	890	-365	-29.08%
5.		Triplett Blanc	0	856	856	N/A
		Pinot Blanc	627	456	-171	-27.27%
		Roussanne	176	362	186	105.68%
		Palomino	623	315	-308	-49.44%
		Muscat Orange	163	272	109	66.87%
	2.	Grenache Blanc	64	266	202	315.62%
		Sauvignon Musque	184	220	36	19.56%
		Ugni Blanc	275	197	-78	-28.36%
	4.	Catarratto	70	187	117	167.14%
	1.	Albariño	15	153	138	920.00%
		Emerald Riesling	267	149	-118	-44.19%
		Tocai Friulano	128	121	-7	-5.47%
		Marsanne	68	115	47	69.12%
	3.	Verdelho	24	94	70	291.66%
		Grüner Veltliner	0	61	61	N/A
		Other	3,252	4,166	914	28.11%
		WHITE WINE TOTAL	185,373	181,849	-3,524	-1.9%

CALIFORNIA'S BLACK GRAPE VARIETIES

In 2010, there were 294,528 acres of black grapes growing in California, with just 16 varieties accounting for almost 96 per cent of this total. The big drop in Merlot and even larger increase in Pinot Noir can be safely attributed to the film Sideways, in which the wine-snob character worshipped West Coast Pinot Noir but would not be seen dead drinking Merlot – or more colourful words to that effect.

LE5	FG5	GRAPE VARIETY	2003 ACREAGE	2010 ACREAGE	INCREASED ACREAGE	PERCENTAGE GROWTH
3.		Cabernet Sauvignon	75,154	77,602	2,448	3.26%
		Zinfandel	50,199	49,136	-1,063	-2.18%
		Merlot	51,973	46,762	-5,211	-10.03%
1.		Pinot Noir	23,950	37,290	13,340	55.70%
4.		Syrah	17,140	19,283	2,143	12.50%
		Rubired	12,467	11,844	-623	-5.00%
2.		Petite Sirah	5,166	7,999	2,833	54.84%
		Barbera	8,851	6,936	-1,915	-21.63%
		Grenache	8,668	6,170	-2,498	-28.82%
		Ruby Cabernet	7,472	5,761	-1,711	-22.90%
		Cabernet Franc	3,547	3,480	-67	-1.89%
		Carignane	5,132	3,393	-1,739	-33.89%
		Sangiovese	2,603	1,950	-653	-25.09%
5.		Petit Verdot	1,096	1,927	831	75.82%
		Malbec	1,065	1,616	551	51.74%
		Alicante Bouschet	1,074	1,065	-9	-0.84%
		Tempranillo	767	957	190	24.77%
		Mataro (Mourvèdre)	644	939	295	45.81%
		Carnelian	1,637	782	-855	-52.23%
		Mission	656	639	-17	-2.59%
5.		Muscat Hamburg	173	345	172	99.42%
		Gamay	539	309	-230	-42.67%
		Tannat	140	248	108	77.14%
		Royalty	480	240	-240	-50.00%
3.		Touriga Nacional	81	227	146	180.25%
		Primitivo	240	206	-34	-14.16%
		Nebbiolo	177	185	8	4.52%
		Meunier	207	163	-44	-21.25%
		Dolcetto	89	123	34	38.20%
		Cinsaut	144	118	-26	-18.05%
		Salvador	555	106	-449	-80.90%
		Montepulciano	58	90	32	55.17%
		Lagrein	86	87	1	1.16%
		Charbono	81	86	5	6.17%
		Centurian	305	84	-221	-72.46%
	2.	Teroldego	18	81	63	350.00%
		Souzão	51	68	17	33.33%
	1.	Carmenère	10	57	47	470.00%
	4.	Pinotage	21	55	34	161.90%
		Counoise	51	52	1	1.96%
		Aglianico	27	51	24	88.89%
		Other	4,281	6,016	1,735	40.53%
		RED WINE TOTAL	287,075	294,528	7,453	2.60%

Notes
LE5 = Five largest-expanding varieties by increased acreage.
FG5 = Five fastest-growing varieties by percentage difference.

THE WINE STYLES OF
CALIFORNIA

BARBERA

This Italian grape is mostly cultivated in the Central Valley, where its high natural acidity makes it useful for blending purposes. This said, it is cultivated on a much smaller scale in fine-wine areas, particularly Sonoma, Mendocino, and Sierra Foothills, where a number of wineries produce a pure varietal Barbera in one form or another. Although L'Uvaggio di Giacomo's best Barbera is La Pantera, its Il Gufo is extraordinarily good for a Central Valley wine.

⌇— 3–6 years (up to 10 in exceptional cases)

♟ *Eberle • Kunde Estate • L'Uvaggio di Giacomo* (La Pantera) • *Palmina • Preston • Renwood* (Sierra Series) • *Thornton* (Curran Ranch)

BOTRYTIZED AND LATE-HARVEST STYLES

Some of the world's most succulent botrytized and late-harvest wines are made in California. The "sunshine state" brings a wonderfully ripe peachiness to Riesling and mouthwatering tropical fruit freshness to Chenin and Muscat. Several excellent Icewines have been made, including one from Bonny Doon's irrepressible Randall Grahm, even though he openly admits to storing the grapes in his freezer before pressing them! I cannot write this section without mentioning the legendary wines of Sine Qua Non in the Edna Valley, which I have never visited because it is between Pinot Noir wineries, and I have always feared that a stop there could very well kill my dry wine palate for a couple of days. However, it would be unfair to suggest anything other than that its wines should be included on this page.

⌇— Ready when released (but last well in bottle)

♟ *Arrowood* (Riesling Owl Hoot) • *Beringer* (Nightingale) • *Bonny Doon* (Muscat Vin de Glaciere) • *Dolce • Domaine de la Terre Rouge* (Muscat à Petits Grains) • *Château St Jean* (Special Late Harvest Johannisberg Riesling) • *J C Cellars* (Ripken Late Harvest Viognier) • *Martinelli* (Jackass Hill) • *The Ojai Vineyard* (Late Harvest Viognier)

BOTTLE-FERMENTED SPARKLING WINES

California used to be notorious for its cheap sparkling wine until Schramsberg and Domaine Chandon led the way in the early 1970s. Then in 1991, by dint of tasting back, it could be discerned that a number of houses had come of age with the wines that were made only four years earlier. Roederer Estate, in particular, was in a class of its own, and still is, but so many other producers dramatically improved the style and finesse of their wines that the quality of California sparkling wine in general had quadrupled by 1995. Michel Salgues, who put Roederer Estate on the map, now consults for Caraccioli in the Santa Lucia highlands.

⌇— 2–5 years (up to 10 in very exceptional cases)

♟ *Caraccioli • Domaine Carneros* (Le Rêve) • *Gloria Ferrer* (Royal Cuvée) • *Handley* (Vintage Blanc de Blancs, Vintage Brut, Vintage Rosé) • *Robert Hunter* (Vintage Brut de Noirs) • *Iron Horse* (Classic Vintage Brut) • *J* (magnums) • *Mumm* (DVX) • *Roederer Estate*

CABERNET FRANC

California's cultivation of this Bordeaux variety tripled between 1983 and 1988. At that time, it was primarily used for effecting better-balanced Cabernet Sauvignon blends, and the only pure varietal versions readers were likely to encounter were rosés from the North Coast area. Since then, the area occupied by Cabernet Franc vines has doubled and pure varietals will shortly become commonplace. Top California Cabernet Franc seems to have a fragrance and finesse not dissimilar to the way it performs in the best St-Émilion vineyards.

⌇— 1–4 years

♟ *Detert Family Vineyards • Nevada City Winery • Peju • Pride • Rancho Sisquoc • Raymond Burr Vineyards • Reverie • Gainey Vineyard* (Limited Selection) • *Titus*

CABERNET SAUVIGNON

California's most widely planted, and probably potentially its finest, black grape variety. In areas that are too cool, Cabernet Sauvignon wines can have capsicum character, or even green bean, but in most other areas they tend to produce saturated, purple-hued wines with a smooth texture, deliciously ripe blackcurrant fruit, and oak-derived notes of vanilla, mocha, cedar, and spice. Oak is now used intelligently and some of the most exciting Cabernet wines are blended with Merlot, Cabernet Franc, and/or Petit Verdot, although not to the extent of a classic blend (*see* Classic Red Blends and Meritage). At their best, these wines are a match for all but the very greatest vintages of Bordeaux *premiers crus*. Indeed, California is so blessed with Cabernet Sauvignon that it is impossible to come up with a definitive top ten, just ten of the best, and in compiling the list below I have tried not to go overboard on too many fabulously expensive, virtually unobtainable iconic wines.

⌇— 3–5 years (inexpensive), 5–12 years (top wineries), 8–25 (or more) years (exceptional wines)

♟ *Abreu • Atalon • Behrens and Hitchcock • Caymus* (Special Selection) • *Colgin* (Tychson Hill) • *Duckhorn* (Estate Grown) • *Dunn • Lewelling Vineyards • Lokoya • Robert Mondavi* (Reserve)

CARIGNANE

Surprisingly, this rarely sighted varietal is the 11th most widely grown black grape in California, well ahead of more prestigious varieties such as Cabernet Franc. Carignan, or Carignane as it is spelled in the USA, provides a high yield of well-coloured, strongly flavoured wine that can be quite coarse and tannic. It is useful for blending both in California and in its native south of France, where it is one of the 13 grapes permitted in Châteauneuf-du-Pape. It has a less harsh character in California's coastal districts, where some wineries produce a pure varietal version, and very old vines can lose the coarse character, yielding wines of extraordinary depth and quality.

⌇— 3–6 years (up to 10 years in exceptional cases)

♟ *Cline* (Ancient Vines) • *Jessie's Grove* (Ancient Vine) • *Ravenswood • Ridge • Windsor* (Oat Valley Vineyards)

CHARBONO

This variety is the Corbeau, an almost extinct French variety that is also known as the Charbonneau. It produces a wine with vibrant cherry fruit and tingling ripe acidity, in a not dissimilar style to Barbera. Indeed, Inglenook Vineyards, which was the first winery to make a pure varietal wine from this grape, labelled it Barbera until Dr Winkler of the UC-Davis nursery identified it properly as Charbono.

⌇— 2–4 years

♟ *Duxoup • Robert Foley • Turley* (Tofanelli)

CHARDONNAY

California might be awash with dross Chardonnay, but it also boasts more great-quality and/or great-value Chardonnay than ever. Although massive, blockbusting Chardonnays still abound, the best have improved and there have never been so many Chardonnay wines showing as much finesse as they do today. It is at the bottom end of the market where much of the dross exists. Unlike the readers of this and other wine books, most consumers are no more interested in learning about wine than most drivers are in understanding cars. There is no reason why they should be, but this has resulted in most consumers budgeting for

Chardonnay as they would baked beans, and within this price-banding they have come to think of Chardonnay as a brand with recognizable characteristics like butter and vanilla. They do not realize that butter is diacetyl produced by malolactic or that the vanilla is vanillin from oak. Because Chardonnay was the first, biggest, and, for a long time, practically the only wine that most American consumers drank, the signature notes of methods used at that time have become mistaken in consumer psyche as Chardonnay's varietal character. This misconception has prevented Chardonnay as a whole from progressing, particularly at the bottom end of the market. This phenomenon is not unique to the USA, but it does seem to be stronger and longer lasting. If the country could only go through a trend for zippy, zingy, unoaked Chardonnay, then it would help raise standards from the basement upwards, and this would percolate through to even the most expensive Chardonnay wines, in which it would then become commercially acceptable to allow more fruit to show through. It has to be said that far too many of the most widely acclaimed California Chardonnay wines betray their production techniques on the nose long before they express their fruit or origin. Beware, also, the residual sugar level in some of these wines. There could be dozens of top ten best California Chardonnays, all of them arguably correct, thus when I have had to make a choice, I have opted for the wine with the most harmonious acidity balance, which provides the longest, most beautifully focused, and graceful finish.

🍷— 2–8 years (15 or more years in very exceptional cases)

🏆 *Au Bon Climat* (Harmony Nuits-Blanches au Bouge) • *Beringer* (Sbragia) • *Blackjack Ranch* • *Brewer-Clifton* (Sweeney Canyon) • *Cuvaison* (Carneros Estate) • *Du Mol* (Chloe) • *Hartford* Court (Three Jacks) • *Kistler* (Vine Hill Road) • *Martinelli* (Three Sisters Vineyard) • *Walter Hansel* (Cahill Lane)

CHENIN BLANC

This Loire Valley grape is famous for wines such as the sweet, honey-rich Vouvray and the very dry, searingly flavoured Savennières. In California it is the fourth most widely planted white wine grape, yet it is seldom spoken of. Although the recent trend to improve the acidity balance has raised the standard of California Chenin Blanc, it fares less well in this state than it does in France. Since I am not a fan of any but the greatest Chenin Blancs, it is hard for me to work up much enthusiasm for the Chenin Blanc in California. I have long wondered about the veracity of all those books that carry the same spiel – that Clarksburg is the only area to produce a regionally identifiable Chenin Blanc, especially as finding wines with any Central Valley AVA is something of a quest. The now defunct R & J Cook winery used to be the most prolific producer of wines bearing the Clarksburg appellation, but produced better Petite Sirah than Chenin. Dry Creek Vineyard is considered by some to produce the best Chenin Blanc, but it used to blend Clarksburg with Sonoma fruit until relatively recently, thus it was never possible to assess Dry Creek Clarksburg Chenin Blanc in its own right. Now we can, of course, and the quality is at least as good as it ever was, so almost 30 years after the Clarksburg AVA was established, we are finally seeing this appellation make a name for itself. However, although Dry Creek is one of California's best

Chenin Blanc wines, collecting more awards for this variety than any other winery in the USA, it is not always that special, and others can make much finer wines on occasions. Furthermore, because of the lack of consistency for this varietal and, indeed, the small number of producers, it is sometimes worth checking out the following: Callaway Coastal, Chappellet, Foxen Vineyard, Meador Estate, Sutter Home. All the best wines below are dry or off-dry. *See* Botrytized and Late-Harvest Wines for sweeter styles.

🍷— 1–4 years

🏆 *Baron Herzog* (Clarksburg) • *Beringer* • *Casa Nuestra* • *Chalone* • *Dry Creek* (Clarksburg) • Husch (La Ribera) • *Windsor Vineyards*

CINSAUT

Until the Rhône-style wine revolution in California, this variety was better known as the Black Malvoisie. There is precious little Cinsault or Cinsaut in the state, even though plantings have increased by more than 150 per cent since 1995, and what does exist is mostly used in blends, although Frick continues to make a statement with 30-year-old Cinsaut vines in Sonoma's Dry Creek. There are very few pure Cinsaut wines produced in California; the only others I have come across are Castle (Sonoma), Domaine de la Terre Rouge, and Preston.

🍷— 2–5 years

🏆 *Frick*

CLASSIC RED BLENDS

On balance I would say that Bordeaux-style blends are more successful in California than pure Cabernet Sauvignon varietals. However, it has proved very difficult to persuade California wine drinkers that they should pay the same price, let alone a premium, for such wines. For this reason the Meritage Association was formed (*see* Meritage), but not all wineries are members and some of the greatest Bordeaux-style blends do not actually use the *portmanteau*. Therefore many of the best Bordeaux-style blends recommended here and under the producer profiles do not necessarily carry the Meritage designation. Furthermore, this encyclopedia's definition of a Classic Red Blend is not restricted to Bordeaux varieties, and California has experienced a substantial growth in Rhône-style blends since the mid-1990s. In American usage, this encyclopedia's Classic Red Blend can be taken as synonymous with a "Proprietary" red blend, but only from a certain classic quality and upwards.

🍷— 3–5 years (inexpensive), 5–12 years (top wineries), 8–25 (or more) years (exceptional wines)

🏆 *Beringer* (Alluvium) • *Blackjack Ranch* (Harmonie) • *Colgin* (Cariad) • *Dalla Vale* (Maya) • *Harlan* • *L'Aventure* (Cuvée) • *Lewis* (Cuvée L) • *Peter Michael* (Les Pavots) • *Niebaum-Coppola* (Rubicon) • *Pride Mountain Vineyards* (Reserve Claret)

CLASSIC WHITE BLEND

The combination of Sauvignon and Sémillon is a good one, the traditional view being that the Sauvignon provides the aromatics, freshness, acidity, and crispness, while the Sémillon adds the necessary fat, weight, depth, and complexity. In some New World areas, however, including

California, the Sauvignon is too soft and neutral for this philosophy to work successfully and is much better used to play the Sémillon's role, whereas a small quantity of that grape can, if harvested early enough, provide a grassy herbaceousness that is more like Sauvignon than Sauvignon. The effect is similar, but the reasoning somewhat back to front. This category includes all high-quality white wine blends, not just Bordeaux-style (*see* Meritage). Having found it difficult to whittle down the Classic Red Blends below 30-odd wines, all arguably top-ten material, it is clear that California is far better blessed for its red blends than its whites, as I have failed to find 10 worthy inclusions!

🍷— 2–4 years

🏆 *Andrew Murray* (Enchanté) • *Beringer* (Alluvium) • *Luna Vineyards* (Bianco) • *Ojai* (Vin du Soleil) • *Signorello* (Seta) • *St Supéry* (Virtú)

COLOMBARD

Amazingly, this is the second most widely planted white grape in California, and it is not even shrinking, having seen another 200 hectares (540 acres) planted since 1995. Colombard, also known as French Colombard, has always been more than adequate, but its true potential was realized only with the advent of cool fermentation techniques. A pure-varietal Colombard is not a fine-quality wine, but it can be superb value in a totally unpretentious and absolutely delicious way, if it is consumed young and fresh.

🍷— Upon purchase

🏆 *De Loach*

FORTIFIED STYLES

A small number of California wineries are fast catching up with Australia in the fortified wine category. Port is the most successful style. Long before its demise, Inglenook used to be the yardstick for California Palomino Sherry.

🍷— Ready when released (but last well in bottle)

🏆 *Bellow Wine Company* (Touriga Nacional Vintage Reserve Port) • *Cedar Mountain* (Chardonnay del Sol) • *Ficklin* (Vintage Port) • *Geyser Peak Winery* (Henry's Reserve Shiraz Vintage Port) • *Guenoc* (Vintage Port) • *Joseph Filippi* (Angelica Elena) • *Joseph Filippi* (Oloroso Sherry Library Reserve) • *V Sattui* (Madeira) • *Windsor* (Distinguished Cream Sherry)

FUMÉ BLANC

This term was first coined by Mondavi in the 1970s, who stole and transposed two words from the French appellation Pouilly Blanc Fumé. It was very simple, yet very clever, and by fermenting the wines in oak *barriques*, he was able to sell what was then a very unfashionable grape variety under a new and catchy name. Fumé Blanc is now used as a generic name for a Sauvignon Blanc wine that has been fermented and/or aged in oak, with the results ranging from a subtle, *barrique*-fermented influence to a heavily oaked character. *See also* Sauvignon Blanc.

🍷— 1–3 years

🏆 *Château St Jean* (La Petite Étoile) • *De Loach* (Russian River Valley) • *Grgich Hills Cellar* (Estate Grown) • *Robert Mondavi* (To Kalon I Block) • *Murphy-Goode* (Reserve)

GEWÜRZTRAMINER

Although by no means one of California's commonly encountered varietal wines, Gewürztraminer must be one of its most overrated. The hype surrounding California's Gewürztraminers baffles me – most of them lack not only the varietal definition I expect of any classic grape, but their winemakers will insist on acidifying what is an intrinsically low-acid variety. The only way to extract the true pungency of spice that admirers of this varietal expect is through a pre-fermentation maceration. The spice will not be immediately apparent when bottled, but requires additional ageing for the terpene-laden bottle-aromas to develop. The phenolics picked up from the skins during the pre-fermentation maceration are essential to the balance and length of such low-acid wines, providing a tactile impression that literally sears the spice on to the palate in its later life. It also gives such wines surprising longevity. The problem is that virtually every winemaker in California has been brainwashed into avoiding phenolics in white wine as if they were the plague. In case American readers should think I am taking an unreasonably European viewpoint, I quote Robert Parker: "Anyone who has tasted fine French Gewürztraminer must be appalled by what is sold under this name in California". About the only thing most California Gewürztraminer has in common with its French counterparts is that classic dry renditions are equally rare.

⌛ 1–3 years

🏆 *Claiborne & Churchill* (Dry Alsatian Style) • *Fetzer* (Echo Ridge) • *Navarro* • *Windsor Vineyards*

GRENACHE

Although cultivation of this variety has been in decline in recent years, it still accounts for some 10 per cent of California's black grapes and, despite being traditionally associated in this state with medium-dry rosé and tawny-port-type dessert wines, some truly delicious, high-quality pure varietals have surfaced.

⌛ 1–3 years

🏆 *Alban Vineyards* • *Bonny Doon* (Clos de Gilroy) • *Epiphany* (Revelation Rodney's Vineyard) • *Holly's Hill* (El Dorado) • *Wild Horse* (Equus James Berry Vineyard)

MALBEC

Although a few wineries are now making good pure varietals from this grape, it has never really caught on in California, where, if it is not ignored entirely, Malbec is merely regarded as a blending component, much as it is in Bordeaux. Perhaps California's winemakers should look more to the 19th-century Black Wines of Cahors than to Bordeaux when considering this variety. When grown ungrafted or on low-yield rootstock, Malbec can produce excellent deep-coloured red wines with soft, chewy fruit and has demonstrated the capability of developing much individuality and complexity in most warm climes, particularly when grown on gravelly-clay and marly-clay soils.

⌛ 2–5 years

🏆 *Arrowood* • *Benzinger* • *Clos du Bois* (L'Étranger) • *Rancho Sisquoc* (Flood Family Vineyard) • *River Run* (Mannstand Vineyard)

MERITAGE

Concocted from "merit" and "heritage", the term "Meritage" was devised as a designation for upmarket Bordeaux-style blends in 1988, and trademarked the following year. Meritage was first coined by Neil Edgar, who was one of 6,000 entrants in an international contest to come up with a name. There are no rules or regulations governing wines that use this trademark, other than that the wineries must be paid-up members of the Meritage Association, and the blends conform to very simple rules of varietal content. Such blends must consist of two or more of the following varieties: Cabernet Sauvignon, Merlot, Cabernet Franc, Petit Verdot, St Macaire, Gros Verdot, Carmenère, and Malbec for reds; and Sauvignon Blanc, Sémillon, Muscadelle, Sauvignon Vert, and Sauvignon Musque for whites; with no single variety making up more than 90 per cent of the blend. Certainly not the most inspired of American marketing terms, it has nevertheless been adopted by a wide range of wineries and restaurants, which often list these wines separately. The most outstanding, plus the many first-class blends that are not marketed as Meritage, are recommended under the Classic Red Blend and Classic White Blend categories.

MERLOT

It has always been obvious that Merlot possessed everything required to make it one of California's most fashionable and sought-after varietals, and that is exactly what it became in the early 1990s. Its lush fruit and velvety texture are tailor-made for this sunshine state, although up to 25 per cent Cabernet Sauvignon may be blended into supposedly pure varietals in order to give the wines added structure (25 per cent if exported to EU countries).

⌛ 3–8 years

🏆 *Beringer* (Founders' Estate) • *Blackjack Ranch* (Billy Goat Hill) • *Cosentino* (Reserve) • *Gainey Vineyards* (Limited Edition) • *Hartwell* • *Havens Wine Cellar* (Reserve) • *Napa Cellars* • *Newton* (Epic) • *Paloma* • *Pride* (Mountaintop Vineyard)

MOURVÈDRE

Sometimes known as Mataro, this is one of the most underrated Rhône varieties, and can produce dark, silky-soft, smooth wines that compare to the Syrah, but are not as rich or dense. In California, Mourvèdre can easily acquire a raspberry-jam flavour, which is fine for inexpensive wines and even better as a blending component, although it is possible to find some exciting pure varietals.

⌛ 2–5 years

🏆 *Bonny Doon* (Old Telegram) • *Cline Cellars* (Ancient Vines) • *Jade Mountain* (Evangelho Vineyard) • *Joseph Filippi* (Library Reserve) • *Ridge* (Mataro) • *Rosenblum Cellars* (Continente Vineyard) • *Sean Thackrey* (Taurus)

MUSCAT BLANC
See Muscat Canelli

MUSCAT CANELLI

Also known as Muscat de Frontignan, Muscat Blanc, and Moscato Canelli, this grape is in fact the Muscat Blanc à Petits Grains, and it is surprisingly successful in California, producing some delightfully perfumed, flowery-flavoured wines in off-dry through to very sweet and dessert styles. *See* Botrytized and Late-Harvest Wines for even sweeter styles.

⌛ Upon purchase

🏆 *Bonny Doon* (Vin de Glaciere) • *Eberle* • *Fresno State Winery* (John Diener Vineyard) • *Maurice Car'rie* • *Rosenblum* (Muscat de Glacier) • *Robert Pecota* (Muscato di Andrea) • *St Supéry* (Moscato)

PETITE SIRAH

In the first edition I suggested that ignorance was perhaps bliss in the case of California's Petite Sirah. Although California's growers had referred to this grape as Petite Sirah since the 19th century, it was unknown to consumers until the 1960s, when varietal wines began to take off. Petite Sirah quickly gained in popularity on the back of the Rhône's Syrah, only for prices to plummet ridiculously in the 1970s, when it was identified as the Durif, a lowly French variety. It was the same wine, but its humble origins obviously lacked cachet for budding new wine consumers of that era. In 1997, Dr Carole Meredith used DNA "fingerprinting" to determine that only four of the seven Petite Sirahs in the UC Davis collection were in fact Durif, and that one was identified as true Syrah. As consumers began to wonder if their favourite Petite Sirah might not in fact be Syrah, the prestige and price of this varietal began to soar. But while 10 per cent of Petite Sirah is indeed Syrah, the mix is found on a vine-by-vine basis. Rather than find one vineyard of Syrah for every nine vineyards of Durif, growers find they have 10 per cent Syrah in their Petite Sirah vineyards. And not just Syrah. Petite Sirah vines are mostly found in old vineyards, planted with perhaps the odd Peloursin, Carignane, Grenache, Barbera, or Alicante Bouschet, in what is known as a "field blend". Despite increased prices, the purple-coloured wine made by Petite Sirah, with its floral, blackfruit aromas, is not considered the equal of a true Syrah (although Switchback Ridge and Turley Cellars Petite Syrah [sic] definitely are), thus it remains one of California's most underrated varietals.

🍷 4–8 years

🏆 *Biale* (Thomann Station) • *Delectus* • *Girard Winery* • *J C Cellars* (Frediani Vineyard) • *Jeff Runquist* ("R" Enver Salmon Vineyard) • *La Jota* • *Lava Cap* • *Rosenblum* (Rockpile) • *Switchback Ridge* • *Turley Cellars* (Petite Syrah)

PINOT BLANC

When grown with care and barrel-fermented, it is virtually impossible to tell Pinot Blanc from a Chardonnay, particularly the examples from Napa, Monterey, and Sonoma. There are some excellent, very serious makers of pure varietal Pinot Blancs, but essentially this is one of California's most under-exploited varieties.

🍷 1–3 years

🏆 *Arrowood* (Saralee's Vineyard) • *Chalone* • *Etude* (Carneros) • *Michel-Schlumberger* (Dry Creek Valley) • *Navarro* • *Steele* (Santa Barbara)

PINOT GRIS

Even at its best, California Pinot Gris is not at all the spicy heavyweight of Alsace fame, but more like a superior Pinot Grigio, with riper, purer fruit. Many of these wines are, in fact, sold as Pinot Grigio, which is preferable, as Pinot Gris implies a definite spicy element to the fruit and that is almost impossible to find outside of Alsace.

🍷 Upon purchase

🏆 *Etude* (Carneros Pinot Gris) • *Gallo of Sonoma* (Sonoma Coast Pinot Gris) • *Luna* (Pinot Grigio) • *Monteviña* (Pinot Grigio) • *Navarro* (Pinot Gris) • *Palmina* (Alisos Vineyard Pinot Grigio)

PINOT NOIR

Beyond all expectations, this Burgundian grape has found a natural home in parts of California, most notably in Sonoma's Russian River Valley, the Carneros area straddling Sonoma and Napa, and the Santa Ynez Valley in Santa Barbara. Santa Barbara does, I think, have the greatest potential of all; equally fine Pinot Noir will be made elsewhere, but the largest number of Pinot Noir producers will eventually be seen to come from this southerly district. Other areas also show promise, particularly San Benito, Monterey, and the Arroyo Grande.

🍷 2–5 years

🏆 *Au Bon Climat* (La Bauge Au-dessus) • *Brewer-Clifton* (Melville) • *Gary Farrell* (Rochioli-Allen Vineyards) • *Gainey Vineyards* (Limited Edition) • *Kistler* (Occidental Vineyard Cuvée Elizabeth) • *Martinelli* (Blue Slide Ridge) • *J Rochioli* (West Block) • *Siduri* (Pisoni Vineyard) • *Talley Vineyards* (Rosemary's Vineyard) • *Williams Selyem* (Rochioli Riverblock Vineyard)

RIESLING

Also known as Johannisberg Riesling and White Riesling, this grape covers more than 10 per cent of California's white-grape vineyards. Apart from a small, but increasing number of sensational, tangy-dry exceptions, most wines are made in a slightly sweet, commercial style to placate consumer demand. I have tried, wherever possible, to shortlist only the drier styles below, as the sweeter ones are found elsewhere. *See* Botrytized and Late-Harvest Wines for sweeter styles.

🍷 1–3 years

🏆 *Château Montelena* (Potter Valley) • *Claiborne & Churchill* (Dry Alsatian Style) • *Fetzer* (Echo Ridge) • *Kendall-Jackson* (Vintner's Reserve) • *Navarro* • *Rancho Sisquoc* (Flood Family Vineyard) • *Robert Mondavi* (Private Selection) • *Sanford Winery* (Vin Gris Santa Rita Hills) • *Windsor Vineyards* (California)

ROSÉ *or* BLANC DE NOIRS

One of the most overlooked wine styles in California, its well-made, unpretentious rosés can be delicious. All the wines recommended below are dry or off-dry.

🍷 Upon purchase

🏆 *Bonny Doon* (Vin Gris de Cigare) • *Eberle* (Syrah Rosé) • *Heitz* (Grignolino Rosé) • *Thornton* (Grenache Rosé) • *V Sattui* (Gamay Rouge – sic) • *Verdad*

SANGIOVESE

Cultivation of this variety has increased over 20-fold since the late 1980s, and much of this is due to the number of winemakers and grape-growers who are of Italian descent. Its success will depend on the choice of site, where the vine should struggle, so there is no need to employ labour-intensive methods to reduce yields through green pruning.

🍷 3–7 years (15 years or more in exceptional cases)

🏆 *Atlas Peak* • *Beringer* (Knights Valley) • *Coturri* (Jessandre Vineyard) • *Luna* (Riserva) • *Pride Mountain Vineyards* • *Saddleback* (Penny Lane Vineyard) • *Seghesio* • *Silverado Vineyards*

SAUVIGNON BLANC

Also known as the Fumé Blanc, a synonym now adopted for an oaked style that is dealt with separately. Many wines labelled Sauvignon Blanc rather than Fumé Blanc are also oaked, but it would be too confusing to list them in this category, so all recommended wines are listed according to their labels, whether they adhere to that style or not. A straight California Sauvignon Blanc should have a crisp style, with the vibrancy of its varietal fruit picked up by, and highlighted with, abundant ripe acidity. California Sauvignon Blanc has, however, an identity problem, as most are soft and neutral, and some are downright wishy-washy. Although there has been a move towards better, more racy acidity by California's best winemakers, the greatest wines from this grape definitely lean more towards a Graves style than varietal purity. There is none of the turbo-charged vibrancy of fruit found in New Zealand's Marlborough Sauvignon Blanc, let alone any gooseberry or passion-fruit intensity, yet that country built its reputation on the UCD1 clone imported from the USA, and until recently, UCD1 was the only clone available for planting in the USA. It is about time that Davis re-imported UCD1 back from New Zealand, performed comparative trials with the UCD1 motherstock, and made available the Kiwi-evolved UCD1 to growers in the USA.

🍷 Upon purchase

🏆 *Araujo Estate* (Eisele Vineyard) • *Artesa* (Napa Valley Reserve) • *Atalon* • *Gary Farrell* (Redwood Ranch) • *Geyser Peak Winery* (Block Collection) • *Lail* (Georgia) • *Peter Michael* (L'Après-Midi) • *Peju Province* • *J Rochioli* • *Spottswoode*

SYRAH

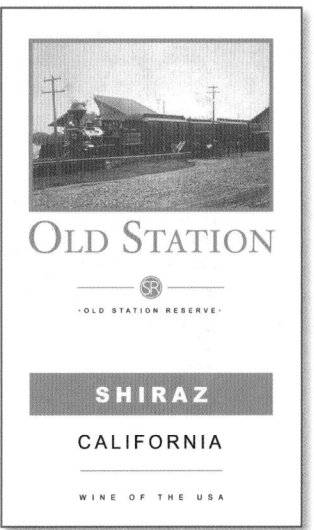

This classic Rhône grape illustrates how quickly things move in California. In the first edition I mentioned how surprised I was that the Syrah was not more widely planted. Since then it has increased from 45 hectares (110 acres) to a massive

6,403 hectares (14,934 acres), making it the fourth most widely planted variety in California. There is a sumptuousness about California Syrah that makes it a totally different wine from either French Syrah or Australian Shiraz, although when full and ripe all three versions share the silky *cassis* fruit and have the potential to develop a fine smoky-spicy complexity. From the top Syrahs listed below, it is obvious that this grape can be successfully grown in several areas of California, but the warmer areas of Santa Barbara do stand out.

🍷 3–10 years

🏆 *Alban* (Lorraine Vineyard) • *Araujo* (Eisel Vineyards) • *Arrowood* (Saralee's Vineyard) • *Blackjack* (Maximus) • *Du Mol* (Eddie's Patch) • *J C Cellars* • *Kongsgaard* (Hudson Vineyard) • *Martinelli* • *The Ojai Vineyard* (Thompson Vineyard) • *Pax* (Adler Springs The Terraces)

VIOGNIER

This great Rhône white-wine grape was non-existent in California until 1985, when the first vines were planted by Joseph Phelps, thus when the first edition of this book was published in 1988 they were not even bearing fruit. At that time, just 4.5 hectares (11 acres) of these vines existed. Now there are more than 800 hectares (2,000 acres), and it is the fourth largest-expanding white varietal in the state. While the vine really seems to thrive in California, the wines seldom capture its elusive character. The same could be said about Château Grillet, of course, but if Condrieu has been able to overcome Viognier's inherent difficulties, there was no reason why more California winemakers could not follow suit. And in a way they have, as it is one of California's most successful white wines. What does bother me, however, is that the notoriously difficult Viognier should thrive so well in the golden state: not only is there no problem with flowered vines failing to fruit, but the yield is exceptionally high even by the greediest French grower's standard. This leads me to suspect the authenticity of the vines being sold as Viognier in California. Or, if indeed they are genuine, to wonder what else might have been eradicated during the eight years it took UC Davis to remove the virus from its Viognier bud stock before release. Perhaps the exquisiteness that makes the best Viognier wines great can be achieved only through debilitated vines? Because, although very successful, far too many are overtly floral, instead of being peachy-floral or, at least, fruity-floral, with too much residual sweetness (apart from those that are made in a Late-Harvest style, and should be sweet), and too little acidity, making them flabby. Authentic Viognier is not over-blessed with acidity, but when it is grown at low yields, and harvested physiologically ripe, rather than sugar-ripe, there is a certain acid balance that, together with the proper fruit structure, will provide sufficient grip and length to avoid any connotation of flabbiness.

🍷 Upon purchase

🏆 *Alban* (Alban Estate Vineyard) • *Alan Murray* (Calzada Vineyard) • *Arrowood* (Saralee's Vineyard) • *Calera* • *Cold Heaven* • *Eberle* (Mill Road Vineyard) • *Failla* (Alban Vineyard) • *Foxen* (Rothberg Vineyard) • *J C Cellars* (Ripken Vineyard) • *Pride Mountain Vineyards*

ZINFANDEL

This was once thought to be America's only indigenous *Vitis vinifera* grape, but was later positively identified by Dr Carole Meredith as the Primitivo grape of southern Italy by Isozyme "finger printing", a method of recording the unique pattern created by the molecular structure of enzymes found within specific varieties. However, this led to a conundrum because the earliest records of Primitivo in Italy date from the late 19th century, whereas the Zinfandel name appears in the nursery catalogue of William Prince of Long Island, dated 1830. One clue was that Italian growers often referred to their Primitivo as a foreign variety. This led Meredith further afield and, with the help of Croatian researchers, she was able to announce in 2002 that the Zinfandel and Primitivo are in fact an obscure variety called Crljenak Kastelanski (pronounced Sirl-YEN-ak Kastel-ARN-ski). Referred to as Crljenak, for short, this grape was once widely planted throughout Dalmatia and on more than 1,000 islands, but has mostly been replaced by Croatia's best-known variety, Plavac Mali (the result of a cross-pollination of Crljenak and Dobricic). Nothing special has been produced so far by Crljenak in its homeland, but there will no doubt be efforts to see what can be achieved with it in the future. In the meantime, UC Davis has imported Crljenak and are growing it side by side with Primitivo and Zinfandel, to see which local characteristics these "localized clones" of the same variety might possess. Since the Crljenak gave way to Plavak Mali in Croatia because its tight grape clusters attracted rot, it would seem to be much closer to the tight-clustered Zinfandel than Primitivo, which has much looser fruit clusters. It is not unreasonable to surmise that the Primitivo clone probably adapted to the much hotter, drier local conditions in southern Italy by developing looser-hung berries.

Some growers have already started to vinify Primitivo separately from Zinfandel, and one day we shall probably see the emergence of California Crljenak. When this happens, it would make sense also to develop a blend of all three, and it strikes me that the new UC Davis classication for these grapes – ZPC – would be the ideal name for such *cuvées*. Depending on the way it is vinified, Zinfandel produces many different styles of wine, from rich and dark to light and fruity, or *nouveau* style, from dry to sweet, white to rosé, dessert wine or sparkling. The reason for such a variation in styles is that it is virtually impossible to harvest Zinfandel when all the grapes have an even ripeness. When most of the bunch achieves perfect ripeness, some grapes are green, but if the grower waits for these to ripen, the shoulder clusters quickly raisin. There are several ways to overcome this, but they are all labour-intensive, seemingly wasteful, and inevitably costly, which is why great Zinfandel is never cheap. Great Zinfandel is as rich and deep-coloured as only California could produce, with ripe, peppery-spicy fruit, liquorice intensity, and a chocolate-herb complexity. When young, such wines are chewy and have classic berry-fruit flavours, which can swing towards black-cherry or simply have a gluggy jamminess. It is the only varietal that positively demands the coconutty aromas of American oak, and it is often improved when blended with Petite Sirah for increased backbone. This is a wine that requires a certain amount of bottle-ageing to bring out the dried-fruit spiciness.

Zinfandel is not one of California's longest-lived wines, but without sufficient time in bottle, the wine will merely have a richness of oak and berry fruits, and lack complexity. Massive, black, opaque Zinfandels with 16.5 per cent plus of alcohol are on the increase, but they are grotesque abominations, and certainly do not stir my soul as they obviously do those of numerous American critics. I don't

know what difference in style Crljenak might possess on California's soil, but when Primitivo is vinified by the same winemaker, it is usually less alcoholic (just a 0.5 per cent reduction), and a little softer, with less berry fruit and less "sweet and sour" flavour.

🍷 2–5 years (good but inexpensive wines), 5–15 years (expensive, more serious styles)

🏆 *DeLoach* (OFS) • *Edmeades* (Zeni Vineyard) • *Gary Farrell* (Maple Vineyard) • *Hartford Court* (Hartford Vineyard) • *Martinelli* • *Nalle* (Reserve) • *Rosenblum* • *Storybook Mountain* (Estate Reserve) • *Turley Cellars* (Hayne Vineyard) • *Williams-Selyem* (Forchini Vineyard)

OTHER VARIETALS

This section lists the best examples found of California's rarely encountered varietals, some of which will no doubt become more widely established one day.

🏆 **Albariño** *Havens* • *Verdad*
Alicante Bouschet *Topolos*
Dolcetto *Mosby*
Grignolino *Emilio Guglielmo* (Santa Clara Valley Reserve)*
Nebbiolo *Palmina* • *Santa Barbara Winery* (Stolpman Vineyard) • *Thornton* (Curran Ranch)
Negrette *De Rose* (Cienega Valley)*
Orange Muscat *Quady* (Electra) • *Renwood*
Pinot Meunier *Domaine Chandon*
Sémillon *St Supéry* (Dollarhide Ranch)
Sylvaner *Rancho Sisquoc*
Symphony *Ironstone*
Teroldego *Mosby*
Tempranillo *Clos du Bois* (Alexander Valley Reserve) • *Gundlach-Bundschu* (Rhinefarm Vineyard) • *Verdad* (Santa Ynez Valley)
Trousseau *Fanucchi Vineyards* (Wood Road Vineyard Gris)*

* Wineries not featured in the following pages.

MENDOCINO COUNTY

The best vineyards here are located on the fork of the Navarro and Russian rivers in the south of Mendocino, a district that has become a buzz-word for top-quality California sparkling wine since the emergence of Roederer Estate. Such is the climatic variation here that some excellent Zinfandel is made, and aromatic varieties may also do very well.

IN THE EARLY 1980S, Champagne Louis Roederer sunk some $15 million into a 200-hectare (500-acre) vineyard and winery in the Anderson Valley, where the climate is far cooler than in surrounding areas. A non-vintage wine in the *champenois* tradition, the first, 1986-based release was nothing special, yet the 1987-based release was the best non-Champagne sparkling wine – a quality maintained ever since. The diversity of *terroir* within the sparkling-wine growing areas of Mendocino provides a fascinating contrast of styles, for Scharffenberger, just around the corner from Roederer, could hardly make a wine more different from Roederer. Whereas Roederer is rich, well-structured, and potentially complex in a style that leans decidedly towards Champagne, Scharffenberger is all lightness and elegance with a purity of fruit that gains in finesse every year.

GROWTH OF THE WINE INDUSTRY

Parts of Mendocino are too hot for classic wine production, so there has been a tendency in the past to plant highly productive vines for jug-wine blends. But the county has a complex climate, and in some areas coastal influences dominate and cooler Region I and II climates (*see* p538) prevail. This has been recognized by a rise in the number of wineries in the area: from 16 in 1981, to 92 in 2010.

FACTORS AFFECTING TASTE AND QUALITY

LOCATION
160km (100 miles) northwest of San Francisco, Mendocino is the most northerly of the major viticultural coastal counties.

CLIMATE
The mountain ridges surrounding the Upper Russian and Navarro rivers climb as high as 1,070m (3,500ft) and form a natural boundary that creates the reputed transitional climate of Mendocino. This climate is unusual in that either coastal or inland influences can dominate for long or short periods, although it generally has relatively warm winters and cool summers. This provides for a growing season with many warm, dry days and cool nights. The Ukiah Valley has the shortest, warmest growing season north of San Francisco.

ASPECT
Mainly flat ground on valley bottoms or gentle, lower slopes at a height of 76 to 445m (250 to 1,460ft), with some rising to 490m (1,600ft). The vines generally face east, though just south of Ukiah they face west.

SOIL
Deep, diverse alluvial soils in the flat riverside vineyards, gravelly-loam in parts of the Russian River Valley, and a thin scree on the surrounding slopes.

VITICULTURE AND VINIFICATION
The average growing season is 268 days, compared with 308 in Sonoma (bud-break is 10 days earlier here), and 223 days in Lake County.

GRAPE VARIETIES
Primary varieties: Cabernet Sauvignon, Carignan, Chardonnay, Chenin Blanc, Colombard, Sauvignon Blanc, Zinfandel
Secondary varieties: Barbera, Early Burgundy (Abouriou), Flora, Folle Blanche, Gamay, Gamay Beaujolais, Gewürztraminer, Grenache, Grey Riesling (Trousseau Gris), Green Hungarian, Malvasia Bianca, Merlot, Muscat Blanc, Palomino, Petite Sirah (Durif), Pinot Blanc, Pinot Noir, Ruby Cabernet, Sauvignon Vert (Muscadelle), Sémillon, Sylvaner, Syrah, White Riesling (Riesling)

Mendocino extended area

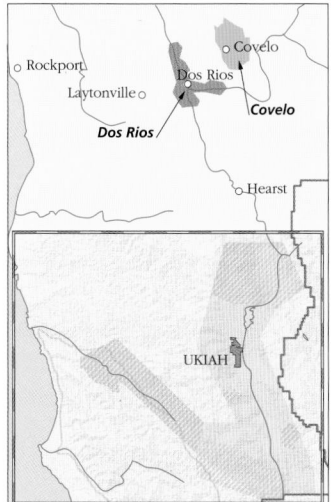

MENDOCINO, *see also p538*
This area's northerly location need not mean harsher microclimates. Inland regions are protected by the mountains, although the Anderson Valley is cooler.

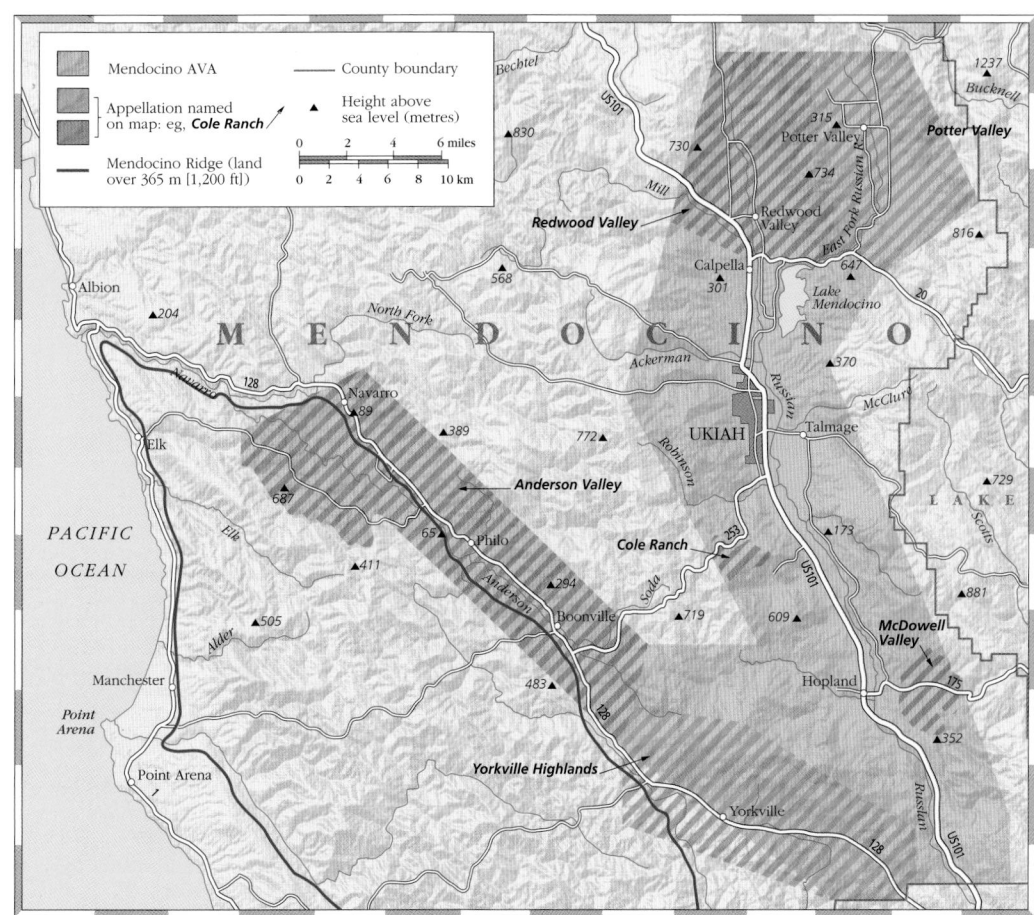

Mendocino AVA
Appellation named on map: eg, **Cole Ranch**
Mendocino Ridge (land over 365 m [1,200 ft])
County boundary
▲ Height above sea level (metres)

0   2   4   6 miles
0   2   4   6   8   10 km

THE APPELLATIONS OF
MENDOCINO COUNTY

ANDERSON VALLEY AVA

Of some 23,300 hectares (57,600 acres) in this area, a mere 240 hectares (600 acres) have been planted with vines. Anderson Valley's coastal-influenced microclimate is cooler than in the rest of Mendocino. This is seen as one of California's coolest wine-growing areas, but temperatures do rise the farther southwest that vines are grown. The valley's soil consists of more than 20 alluvial soils, providing the diversity required for wineries such as Roederer Estate and Scharffenberger to produce a variety of base wines, the building blocks of any fine-quality sparkling wine. This area is also suitable for aromatic varieties such as Gewürztraminer and Pinot Gris, and farther inland Cabernet Sauvignon and Zinfandel are possible.

COLE RANCH AVA

Situated in a small, narrow valley, this appellation consists of just 25 hectares (62 acres) of Cabernet Sauvignon, Chardonnay, and Johannisberg Riesling vineyards, all owned by the Cole family. Soils range from gravelly-clay loam to gravelly-silty clay.

MCDOWELL VALLEY AVA

The McDowell Valley enjoys the natural protection of the mountains encircling it. All its vineyards are restricted to the gravelly-loam soils at around 300 metres (1,000 feet), other soils being unsuitable for vines. The microclimate here warms up when other areas are experiencing spring frosts. It is, however, slightly cooler in the growing season.

MENDOCINO AVA

This may only be used for wines produced from grapes that are grown in the southernmost third of the county. It encompasses four other smaller AVAs plus surrounding vineyards.

MENDOCINO COUNTY AO

This appellation (not an AVA) covers the wines from anywhere within the county of Mendocino.

POTTER VALLEY AVA

This appellation consists of 11,130 hectares (27,500 acres) situated northwest of Clear Lake, some 4,450 hectares (11,000 acres) of which are under vine. Vines grow on the valley floor and are protected by the surrounding hills.

REDWOOD VALLEY AVA

This area is where the first Mendocino vines were planted. It has been known as Redwood Valley since it was settled in the mid-1850s and covers 90 square kilometres (35 square miles), with some 930 hectares (2,300 acres) of area under vine already in existence. The grapes ripen later than in the hotter and drier Ukiah area, providing higher acidity, colour, and tannin.

YORKVILLE HIGHLANDS AVA

Geographically, but not topographically, this appears to be an extension of the Anderson Valley AVA. Yorkville Highlands has a rocky soil with high gravel content, and a cool climate that is comparable to the middle of the Anderson Valley. Sauvignon Blanc does well here, and this AVA could also favour red Bordeaux varieties.

THE WINE PRODUCERS OF
MENDOCINO COUNTY

BONTERRA
Ukiah
⊙★✦Ⓥ

Part of the Brown-Forman group, but its organic philosophy proves that big business can be good guys, too.

✓ *Chardonnay • Merlot*

EDMEADES VINEYARDS
Philo
★★

Part of the Kendall-Jackson group.

✓ *Zinfandel*

FETZER VINEYARDS
Redwood Valley
★Ⓥ

Owned by Brown-Forman, Fetzer produces value-for-money wines.

✓ *Cabernet Sauvignon • Gewürztraminer • Merlot • Pinot Noir* (Ben Nacido Vineyard Reserve, Five Rivers Ranch) • *Syrah • Zinfandel*

FREY
Redwood Valley
★Ⓥ

The oldest and largest fully organic winery in the USA, Frey was set up in 1980 and was the first US winery to make biodynamic wines. Just over 10 per cent of its wine is biodynamic.

✓ *Petite Sirah Ⓑ • Sangiovese • Syrah*

GREENWOOD RIDGE VINEYARDS
Philo
★✦Ⓥ

An underrated winery best-known for its Riesling, particularly its Late Harvest, although other varieties are well worth a look.

✓ *Cabernet Sauvignon • Classic red blend* (Home Run Red) • *Pinot Noir • White Riesling* (Late Harvest)

HANDLEY
Philo
★Ⓥ

An excellent, underrated *méthode champenoise* specialist. Handley's crisp Vintage Brut has creamy-vanilla richness, but he also makes flavourful Pinot Noir and Sauvignon Blanc of increasing elegance.

✓ *Pinot Noir* (Estate Reserve) • *Sauvignon Blanc* (Handley Vineyard) • *Sparkling wine* (Vintage Brut) • *Syrah*

HUSCH VINEYARDS
Philo
★✦Ⓥ

Founded by Tony Husch, this winery was sold in 1979 to Hugo Oswald, the current owner and winemaker, who also has large vineyard holdings in the Anderson and Ukiah Valleys, from which his unpretentious white-wine varietals always stand out.

✓ *Chardonnay • Chenin Blanc* (La Ribera) • *Muscat Canelli* (La Ribera) • *Sauvignon Blanc* (La Ribera)

NAVARRO VINEYARDS
Philo
★Ⓥ

Some critics believe these vineyards produce some of California's best Gewürztraminer, although I think they have the potential to do much better. If I had to name the worst varietal for a sparkling wine, it would probably be Gewürztraminer, and I've only come across four producers stupid enough to try. Yet Navarro is the exception that proves the rule. It has nothing to do with classic sparkling wine as we generally perceive it, but there are far more spicy bottle-aromas in Navarro's fizzy Gewürztraminer than there are in its regular still wine. If you can appreciate the finest Riesling Sekt and sparkling Shiraz, then you really should try Navarro Sparkling Gewürztraminer. Otherwise, it's the purity of fruit found in the Pinot wines that most attracts me to this producer at the moment.

✓ *Pinot Blanc • Pinot Gris • Pinot Noir • Riesling* (Riesling Cluster Select) • *Sparkling wine* (Gewürztraminer)

PARDUCCI WINE CELLARS
Ukiah
★Ⓥ

Parducci is a large winery, with over 142 hectares (351 acres), which was founded in Sonoma in 1918 and moved to Ukiah in 1931, where a new winery was built in preparation for the end of Prohibition. The wines are clean and fruity, and possess a good depth of flavour for their price.

✓ *Petite Sirah • Zinfandel* (Zingaro)

ROEDERER ESTATE
Philo
★★✦Ⓥ

The first New World venture to achieve a quality of sparkling wine comparable not just to Champagne, but to very good Champagne, Roederer Estate (or Quartet as it is known on export markets) ages like no other California sparkling wine. L'Ermitage is the greatest wine here, but the standard non-vintage Brut can be almost as stunning. A bottle of the 1994-based non-vintage, which was disgorged in February 1997 and matured in my own cellar until 2002, still displayed beautifully pristine fruit of great finesse, when most California sparkling wines of a similar age would be as dead as a dodo.

✓ *Entire range*

SCHARFFENBERGER CELLARS
Ukiah
★✦Ⓥ

Founded by John Scharffenberger in 1981 and part-owned by Pommery until it was transferred to Veuve Clicquot. After it was decided to change the name to Pacific Echo, a soulless name with no sense of place, the writing was on the wall. Veuve Clicquot did nothing to encourage exports and even thwarted efforts to promote the brand abroad. It came as no surprise when Pacific Echo was purchased in July 2004 by the Roederer-owned Maisons Marques & Domaines USA, and announced that they would drop Pacific Echo in favour of a return to the original Scharffenberger name. They have retained Tex Sawyer, who has been the winemaker from the start; he has slowly and consistently increased the elegance and finesse of these sparkling wines.

✓ *Sparkling wine* (Blanc de Blancs, Rosé)

SONOMA COUNTY

Six fertile valleys combine to make Sonoma County California's most prolific wine-producing area, with an output comprising equal quantities of red and white wine, and a reputation for quality now fast approaching that of Napa County.

BECAUSE OF THE VOLUME of its production, Sonoma County was classed as little more than a source of blending wine until the late 1960s. It produced better-quality blending wine than the Central Valley, admittedly, but that wine was still nothing more than pep-up fodder for the bulk-produced anonymous generics. Then, in 1969, Russell Green, a former oil mogul and owner of a fast-growing vineyard in the Alexander Valley, purchased Simi, a once-famous winery founded in 1876, but at the time in decline. Green had great plans for Simi, many of which he successfully carried out, but soaring costs forced him to sell up in 1973. During those four brief years, however, he managed to restore the pre-Prohibition reputation of the old winery by creating a new genre of high-quality varietal Sonoma wines. With this achievement, he made other winemakers in the district ambitious to improve the quality of their own wines.

Not only did this result in a very pleasing plethora of interesting vinous delights, but Green's activity also attracted new blood to the area. By 1985 there was a remarkable total of 93 wineries, and since then the number has increased to a staggering 350.

FACTORS AFFECTING TASTE AND QUALITY

LOCATION
North of San Francisco, between Napa and the Pacific.

CLIMATE
Extremes of climate range from warm (Region III, *see* p538) in the north of the county to cool (Region I, *see* p538) in the south, mainly due to ocean breezes. Fog is prevalent around Petaluma.

ASPECT
Sonoma Valley creek drains into the San Francisco Bay, and the Russian River flows directly into the Pacific. The vines grow at an altitude of approximately 120 metres (400 feet) on flatland, or on the gentle lower slopes. Steeper slopes are being cultivated in the Sonoma Valley.

SOIL
The soil situation varies greatly, from low-fertile loams in the Sonoma Valley and Santa Rosa areas, to highly fertile alluvial soils in the Russian River Valley, with limestone at Cazadera, a gravelly soil in Dry Creek, and vent-based volcanic soils within the fall-out vicinity of Mount St Helena.

VITICULTURE AND VINIFICATION
Bulk winemaking is no longer important in the Russian River Valley; boutique wineries specializing in premium varietals have taken over.

GRAPE VARIETIES
Primary varieties: Cabernet Sauvignon, Chardonnay, Chenin Blanc, Colombard, Gewürztraminer, Merlot, Petite Sirah (Durif), Pinot Blanc, Pinot Noir, Sauvignon Blanc, White Riesling (Riesling), Zinfandel
Secondary varieties: Aleatico, Alicante Bouschet, Barbera, Cabernet Franc, Carignan, Chasselas Doré, Folle Blanche, Gamay, Gamay Beaujolais, Grenache, Malbec, Malvasia, Muscat Blanc, Palomino, Pinot St George (Négrette), Ruby Cabernet, Sauvignon Vert (Muscadelle), Sémillon, Sylvaner, Syrah

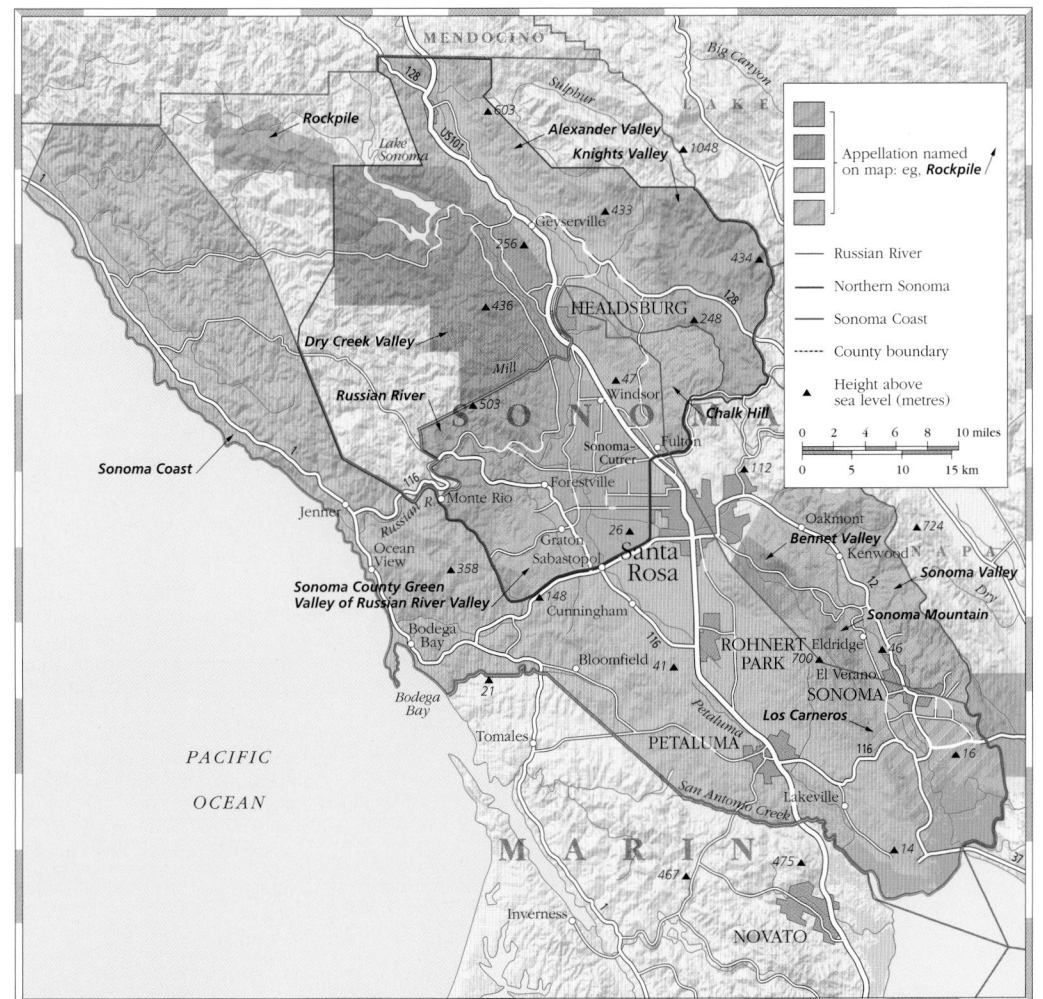

DRY CREEK VALLEY
Sonoma's Dry Creek lies close to the Russian River, of which Dry Creek is a tributary. Moist and fertile, the valley has a gravelly soil unique to the area, enabling it to claim AVA status.

SONOMA COUNTY, *see also p538*
One of California's most important wine regions, Sonoma has a varied climate with different soils, which produce a broad spectrum of wines. It is perhaps aptly named, as Sonoma is derived from the local Wintun Native American word for "nose".

THE APPELLATIONS OF
SONOMA COUNTY

ALEXANDER VALLEY AVA

Located in the northeast of the county, this appellation extends from the banks of the Russian River into the foothills of the Mayacamas Mountains. In 1986 its boundaries were extended so that it overlapped the Russian River AVA, and were extended farther in 1990 to incorporate Sir Peter Michael's Gauer Ranch and Ellis Alden's Chestnut Springs vineyards in the foothills east of Geyserville. Cabernet Sauvignon and Merlot are ideally suited to this area, where very fine Nebbiolo, Sangiovese, and Chardonnay can also be produced. Formerly part of Dry Creek AVA, the Gill Creek watershed area was reclassified as Alexander Valley AVA in 2001.

CHALK HILL AVA

This appellation covers 85 square kilometres (33 square miles) and encompasses 650 hectares (1,600 acres) of vineyards rising in altitude from 60 to 400 metres (200 to 1,300 feet). There is no chalk here; the soil's whiteness is in fact derived from volcanic ash with a high quartzite content. Emitted by Mount St Helena over many centuries, the ash has mixed with local sandy and silty loams to provide a deep soil that is not particularly fertile. This area is protected by a thermal belt that promotes a September harvest, compared with October in surrounding areas.

DRY CREEK VALLEY AVA

This appellation faces that of the Alexander Valley across the Russian River. Its climate is generally wetter and warmer than surrounding areas, with a longer growing season than the Russian River appellation to the south, and varietal suitability is very flexible, stretching from Sauvignon Blanc to Zinfandel. The Gill Creek watershed area was declassified as Dry Creek in 2001, and reclassified under the Alexander Valley AVA.

KNIGHTS VALLEY AVA

Knight's valley covers an area of approximately 140 square kilometres (55 square miles) containing 400 hectares (1,000 acres) of vineyards. The vines grow on rocky and gravelly soil of low fertility at altitudes that are generally higher than those in the adjacent AVAs, making it ideal Cabernet country.

LOS CARNEROS AVA

The Los Carneros, or simply Carneros, appellation covers an area of low, rolling hills that straddle the counties of Sonoma and Napa. This was originally sheep country, but the cool sea breezes that come off San Pablo Bay to the south provide an excellent fine-wine growing climate, especially for Chardonnay, Pinot Noir, and sparkling-wine varieties.

NORTHERN SONOMA AVA

The large appellation of Northern Sonoma completely encapsulates six other AVAs, those of Alexander Valley, Chalk Hill, Dry Creek Valley, Knights Valley, Russian River Valley, and Sonoma County Green Valley, and is separated from the Sonoma Valley appellation to the south by the city of Santa Rosa.

RUSSIAN RIVER VALLEY AVA

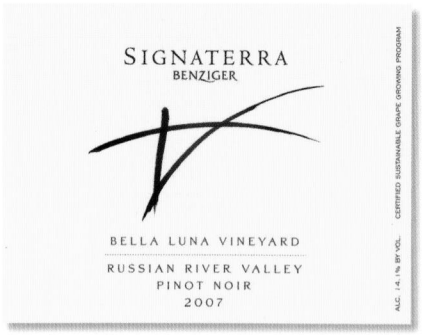

SIGNATERRA
BENZIGER

BELLA LUNA VINEYARD
RUSSIAN RIVER VALLEY
PINOT NOIR
2007

ALC. 14.1% BY VOL.   CERTIFIED SUSTAINABLE GRAPE GROWING PROGRAM

The name Russian River began appearing on wine labels in 1970, although vineyards in this region date from the 19th century. The early-morning coastal fog provides a cooler growing season than that of neighbouring areas, making the Russian River Valley very well suited to Pinot Noir – and indeed it produces some of California's finest Pinot Noir wines. In September 2003, this AVA was expanded to include 307 hectares (767 acres) south of Fulton.

SONOMA COAST AVA

An appellation covering 1,940 square kilometres (750 square miles), Sonoma Coast AVA is made up of the area directly inland from the length of Sonoma's Pacific coastline – the AVA's western boundary. It is significantly cooler than other areas owing to the persistent fog that envelops the Coast Ranges, the mountains that are within sight of the Pacific Ocean.

SONOMA COUNTY GREEN VALLEY OF RUSSIAN RIVER VALLEY AVA

Originally it was proposed that this area within the Russian River Valley AVA be called, simply, Green Valley, but to avoid confusion with Solano County's Green Valley appellation, it was decided to add "Sonoma County". The climate here is one of the coolest in the Russian River Valley and the soil is mostly fine sandy loam, well suited to sparkling wine.

SONOMA MOUNTAIN AVA

This tiny appellation is within the Sonoma Valley AVA. Sonoma Mountain AVA has a thermal belt phenomenon that drains cold air and fog from its steep terrain to the slopes below, creating a climate that is characterized by more moderate temperatures than the surrounding areas.

SONOMA VALLEY AVA

The first vines were planted here in 1825 by the Mission San Francisco de Sonoma. Rainfall is lower than elsewhere in the county and fog rarely penetrates the Sonoma Mountains. It is red-wine country; particularly for Cabernet Sauvignon and Zinfandel.

THE WINE PRODUCERS OF
SONOMA COUNTY

A RAFANELLI
Healdsburg
★

It was always said that Americo Rafanelli, who died in 1987, made wine "as they used to in the olden days". Well, he would be proud of the blockbusters made by his son David from this small, unirrigated, hillside vineyard.

☘✓ *Zinfandel*

ALEXANDER VALLEY VINEYARDS
Healdsburg
★♥

An underrated winery built on the original homestead of Cyrus Alexander, who gave his name to the Alexander Valley, now a famed AVA. Most products are well worth buying as value-for-money, everyday drinking wines, but some are much finer than that, despite their modest prices, and the Cyrus comes precariously close to making the top ten classic red blends in California.

☘✓ *Cabernet Sauvignon* • *Chardonnay* (Wetzel Family Estate) • *Classic red blend* (Cyrus) • *Merlot* • *Pinot Noir*

ARROWOOD VINEYARDS
Glen Ellen
★♥

Richard Arrowood makes very stylish wines and the quality gets better each year, as he hones down his varietals. Excellent-value second label (Grand Archer). Now part of Jackson Family Wine Estates.

☘✓ *Cabernet Sauvignon* (Grand Archer, Réserve Spéciale) • *Chardonnay* (Cuvée Michel Berthod) • *Merlot* (Grand Archer, Réserve Spéciale) • *Pinot Blanc* • *Riesling* (Special Select Late Harvest Riesling Hoot Owl) • *Syrah* • *Viognier*

B R COHN
Glen Ellen
☆

Sometimes you have to spit the splinters out of these wines, but you cannot deny the quality and have to admire the enthusiasm.

☘✓ *Cabernet Sauvignon* (Olive Hill) • *Merlot* (Sonoma Valley)

BELVEDERE
Healdsburg
★♥

Large vineyards enable owner Bill Hambrecht to make a wide range of wines. He used to excel at Chardonnay, but his best and most consistent wines are now Merlot and Zinfandel.

☘✓ *Merlot* (Healdsburg Ranches) • *Zinfandel* (Healdsburg Ranches)

BENZIGER
Glen Ellen
⓼★☆♥

Since selling its Glen Ellen and MG Vallejo high-volume brands to Heublein, Mike Benziger now concentrates on producing more focused, quality wines under the family name. His highly successful Imagery series now has its own winery off Highway 12.

✓ *Cabernet Sauvignon* (Sonoma Coast) • *Chardonnay* (Carneros) • *Pinot Noir* (Sonoma Coast) • *Syrah* (California)

BUENA VISTA WINERY
Sonoma
★ ♥

Haraszthy's original winery (*see* p537) is now owned by Allied-Domecq. Buena Vista's Carneros Estate wines are usually good value, particularly the Cabernet Sauvignon and Pinot Noir.

✓ *Cabernet Sauvignon* (Carneros Estate, Grand Reserve)

CARMENET VINEYARD
Sonoma
★ ♥

Owned by Chalone Vineyards of Monterey, Carmenet offers some excellent-value wines.

✓ *Cabernet Sauvignon* (North Coast Dynamite) • *Merlot* • *Sauvignon Blanc* (Reserve)

CHALK HILL WINERY
Healdsburg
★

This excellent operation was known as Donna Maria Vineyards when the owner only grew and sold grapes, but became Chalk Hill Winery when it first began to make and sell wines in 1981. Chardonnay has always been a major focus, and in the 2000 vintage Chalk Hill released a fascinating collection of six single-clone versions of this varietal.

✓ *Cabernet Sauvignon* (Estate Bottled) • *Chardonnay* (Estate Bottled)

CHÂTEAU SOUVERAIN
Geyserville
★ ♥

Good-value basic range, but the Winemaker's Reserve is seldom any better.

✓ *Merlot* (Alexander Valley) • *Sauvignon Blanc* (Alexander Valley) • *Zinfandel* (Dry Creek Valley)

CHATEAU ST JEAN
Kenwood
★ ♥

Prior to former Japanese owners (Suntory) selling this prestigious winery to Beringer, the style of some of these wines had already swung from overt richness to elegance. The quality remains, but

some American critics are less appreciative of the change.

✓ *Cabernet Sauvigno*n (Sonoma Coast, Sonoma Coast Reserve) • *Chardonnay* (Robert Young Vineyard Reserve) • *Classic red blend* (Cinq Cépages) • *Merlot* (Sonoma Coast) • *Riesling* (Special Late-Harvest) • *Sauvignon Blanc* (Fumé Blanc La Petite Étoile)

CHRISTOPHER CREEK
Healdsburg
★ ½

Formerly known as the Sotoyme Winery, Christopher Creek was snapped up by Englishman John Mitchell, who makes a wonderfully deep, rich, smoky Petite Sirah and, even better, a silky, stylish Syrah.

✓ *Petite Sirah* (Russian River Estate Bottled) • *Syrah* (Reserve, Russian River Estate Bottled) • *Zinfandel* (Dry Creek Valley)

CLINE CELLARS
Sonoma
★ ½ ♥

These excellent Rhône-style wines range from the jammy Côtes d'Oakly to the serious, oaky Mourvèdre, but it is the superb range of full-throttle, all-American Zinfandel wines that Cline is truly famous for.

✓ *Carignane* (Ancient Vines) • *Mourvèdre* (Ancient Vines, Late Harvest) • *Syrah* (Los Carneros) • *Zinfandel* (Ancient Vines)

CLOS DU BOIS
Healdsburg
★ ★ ♥

Owned by Allied-Domecq, Clos du Bois has made fleshy, well-textured, medal-winning wines from its impressive 370 hectares (925 acres) of vineyards under a variety of highly talented winemakers.

✓ *Cabernet Sauvignon* (Alexander Valley Reserve, Winemaker's Reserve) • *Chardonnay* (Flintwood) • *Classic red blend* (Marlstone) • *Malbec* (Winemaker's Reserve) • *Merlot* (Winemaker's Reserve) • *Pinot Noir* (Sonoma Coast) • *Syrah* (Shiraz) • *Tempranillo* (Alexander Valley Reserve) • *Zinfandel* (Dry Creek Valley Reserve, Russian River)

H COTURRI & SONS LTD
Glen Ellen
☉ ★ ♥

A wide range of sometimes excellent varietals, but as is often the case with organic winemaking, the quality ranges between rustic and brilliant. If they are drunk on release, the best examples of the following can be mind-blowing. The Albarello is essentially Zinfandel and Petite Sirah field-blend that includes a mishmash of other varieties.

✓ *Carignane* • *Charbono* • *Classic red blend* (Albarello) • *Sangiovese* • *Zinfandel* (Chauvet, Freiberg, Workingman's)

DE LOACH VINEYARDS
Santa Rosa
★ ½ ♥

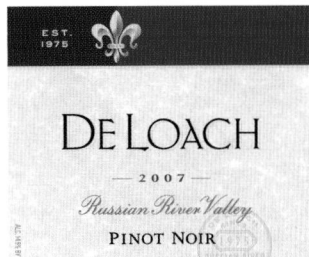

This winery's signature wine used to be Chardonnay, but the reputation of De Loach is now firmly embedded in its exceptional range of Zinfandel wines. Anyone who does not like Zinfandel or is hard to please should really try De Loach, as these wines are the smoothest you are ever likely to encounter. Top of the range wines are sold as OFS (Our Finest Selection). De Loach was acquired by Burgundy's Jean-Claude Boisset in 2003.

✓ *French Colombard* • *Pinot Noir* (OFS) • *Sauvignon Blanc* (Russian River Valley Fumé Blanc) • *Zinfandel*

DRY CREEK VINEYARD
Healdsburg
★ ½ ♥

Not all of David Stare's elegant Dry Creek Vineyard wines actually come from the Dry Creek Valley AVA.

✓ *Cabernet Sauvignon* • *Chenin Blanc* (Clarksburg) • *Fumé Blanc* • *Zinfandel* (Heritage, Old Vines)

DU MOL
Orinda
★ ★

Although based in Orinda, this small operation produces some of the classiest Chardonnay and Pinot Noir in the Russian River Valley, not to mention one of California's finest Syrahs.

✓ *Chardonnay* • *Pinot Noir* • *Syrah*

DUXOUP
Healdsburg
★ ½

The first time I visited Duxoup, I managed to get lost and started to express my apologies for being two hours late, but Andy Cutter waved away my apology with "Don't worry. When your colleagues Robert Joseph and Charles Metcalfe paid a visit, they were two days late," and I am very happy to say the delicious wines are equally laid-back.

✓ *Charbono* • *Sangiovese* (Gennaio) • *Syrah*

FERRARI-CARANO
Healdsburg
★ ½ ♥

Don and Rhonda Carano sold up their Reno casino and hotel to buy 200 hectares (500 acres) of Sonoma vineyards in 1981, and their Italian-styled wines have always been a special feature.

✓ *Classic red blend* (Sienna, Tresor) • *Dessert style* (Eldorado Noir) • *Fumé Blanc*

FISHER VINEYARDS
Santa Rosa
★ ½ ♥

With two hillside vineyards situated in the Mayacamas Mountains and another one on the Napa Valley floor, Fred Fisher has always crafted some high-quality wines, but in particular from his Cabernet Sauvignon grapes.

✓ *Cabernet Sauvignon* (Lamb Vineyard, Wedding Vineyard) • *Chardonnay* (Unity, Whitney's Vineyard) • *Merlot* (RCF Vineyard)

FRITZ CELLARS
Cloverdale
★ ♥

This winery is best known for Chardonnay and Sauvignon, but it is the intense, extraordinarily long-lived Zinfandel that excites most. Particularly the Old Vine, made from a combination of 50-, 60-, and 80-year-old vines, and Rogers Reserve, from 100-year-old vines.

✓ *Cabernet Sauvignon* • *Zinfandel* (Old Vines)

GARY FARRELL
Healdsburg
★ ★

Gary Farrell makes truly special Russian River Pinot Noir, full of style, and rich in fruit, with amazing finesse and complexity.

✓ *Chardonnay* (Redwood Ranch) • *Classic red blend* (Encounter) • *Pinot Noir* • *Sauvignon Blanc* (Redwood Ranch) • *Zinfandel* (Maple Vineyard)

GALLO OF SONOMA
Healdsburg
◉✩★ 🅥

Gina and Matt Gallo literally moved hillsides to create this estate, but they have been unable to bulldoze away the prejudice that exists in some quarters against anything remotely connected with the Gallo empire, while true enthusiasts just let the wine do the talking.

✓ *Barbera* (Barrelli Creek) • *Cabernet Sauvignon* • *Chardonnay* • *Pinot Gris* (Sonoma Coast) • *Zinfandel* (Frei Ranch Vineyard)

GEYSER PEAK WINERY
Geyserville
★★ 🅥

Hugely underrated because of low price points, but the Block Collection range is a stunning success, and Australian winemaker Daryl Groom is a magician with even the least expensive, most modest of wines.

✓ *Cabernet Sauvignon* (Block Collection) • *Chardonnay* (Alexander Valley Reserve, Block Collection, Ricci Vineyard, Sonoma County) • *Classic red blend* (Reserve Alexandre Meritage) • *Fortified* (Henry's Reserve Shiraz Vintage Port, Tawny Port) • *Merlot* (Sonoma County) • *Riesling* (Late Harvest Reserve) • *Sauvignon Blanc* (Block Collection, California, Russian River Valley) • *Shiraz* (Sonoma County Reserve) • *Viognier* (Block Collection) • *Zinfandel* (Sonoma County)

GLORIA FERRER
Sonoma
★ 🅥

Established by Cava-giant Freixenet in 1982 and named after the wife of José Ferrer, the Spanish firm's president, Gloria Ferrer. Bob Iantosca, Gloria Ferrer's ponytailed winemaker might look as if he was left behind when the hippies trekked north to Oregon, but he is very much at home in the new millennium California, as his outstanding Royal Cuvée testifies. Royal Cuvée might not be the most expensive wine in the range, but it is certainly the best.

✓ *Sparkling wine* (Blanc de Noirs, Carneros Rosé, Royal Cuvée, Sonoma Brut)

GUNDLACH-BUNDSCHU WINERY
Sonoma
★

High-quality Cabernet and Zinfandel from the fifth generation of the family of the founder, Jacob Gundlach, this winery also shows promising signs for other varietals.

✓ *Cabernet Sauvignon* (Rhinefarm Vineyard) • *Tempranillo* (Rhinefarm Vineyard) • *Zinfandel* (Rhinefarm Vineyard)

HACIENDA WINE CELLARS
Sonoma
★ 🅥

This operation used to encompass part of Haraszthy's original Buena Vista vineyard, but the brand was sold in 1993 to the Bronco Wine Company. Although little more than a label for pan-California wine blends, there are some amazing bargains.

✓ *Chardonnay* (Claire de Lune) • *Dry Chenin Blanc*

HANZELL VINEYARDS
Sonoma
★✩

James Zellerbach, the founder of Hanzell Vineyards, revolutionized the California wine industry in 1957 by ageing a Chardonnay wine in imported Burgundian *barriques*. The emphasis today of the 100 per cent estate-bottled wines is *terroir*, rather than oak.

✓ *Chardonnay* • *Pinot Noir*

HARTFORD COURT
Sonoma
★★✩

Owned by Don Hartford, who is married to the daughter of Jess Jackson of Kendall-Jackson fame, Hartford Court makes extremely classy Pinot Noir and Chardonnay, and a huge, oaky Zinfandel that is definitely out to grab attention.

✓ *Chardonnay* (Arrendell Vineyard) • *Pinot Noir* (Arrendell Vineyard) • *Zinfandel* (Hartford Vineyard)

HOP KILN
Healdsburg
★ 🅥

The hop-drying barn that houses Hop Kiln winery was built in 1905, and has been declared a national historic landmark. A Thousand Flowers is a very inexpensive, unpretentious, soft, flowery, off-dry blend of Riesling, Chardonnay, and Gewürztraminer.

✓ *Classic white blend* (A Thousand Flowers) • *Zinfandel* (Old Windmill Vineyard, Primitivo Vineyard)

IMAGERY ESTATE
Glen Ellen
★✩ 🅥

Mike Benziger's Imagery series now has its own dedicated winery, and has branched out into single-vineyard varietals.

✓ *Cabernet Franc* (BlueRock Vineyard) • *Cabernet Sauvignon* (Ash Creek Vineyard) • *Merlot* (Sunny Slope Vineyard)

IRON HORSE VINEYARDS
Sebastopol
★★✩

Once the only railway stop in Sonoma Green Valley, hence the name (it also gave rise to its second label, Tin Pony), Iron Horse is famous for its textbook *méthode champenoise*, but also makes some elegant Pinot Noir wines that only reveal their hidden depth with food.

✓ *Pinot Noir* • *Sparkling wine* (Blanc de Blancs, Blanc de Blancs LD, Classic Vintage Brut, Rosé, Russian Cuvée)

J ROCHIOLI VINEYARDS
Healdsburg
★★

The Rochioli family has been growing grapes at this long-established vineyard since the 1930s, but did not build a winery until 1984, making their first wine the following year. They now offer a large range of all too drinkable estate-bottled wines, including some of the most velvet-textured, varietally pure Pinot Noirs in all of California.

✓ *Pinot Noir* • *Sauvignon Blanc*

J WINE COMPANY
Healdsburg
★✩

Established in 1986 by Judy Jordan, who rented space in her father's Jordan Winery until 1997, when she purchased Piper Sonoma's specialist sparkling wine facility, renaming it the J Wine Company. J sparkling wine was fundamentally perfected by the 1990/1991 vintage, and magnums have a particularly noticeable effect on these wines, thus well worth the investment. Like all sparkling wine ventures that diversify into still wines, the crossover was not entirely smooth, as such wineries are designed for something entirely different. However, following extensions to the winery, including new equipment and a barrel room, the still wines have become more polished in recent years.

✓ *Pinot Gris* (Russian River Valley) • *Pinot Noir* (Nicole's Vineyard, Russian River Valley) • *Sparkling wine* (Brut)

JORDAN
Healdsburg
★✩

This winery majors on rich, complex Cabernet Sauvignon, and is gradually honing its Chardonnay into a much finer wine than it used to be.

✓ *Cabernet Sauvignon* • *Chardonnay*

JOSEPH SWAN VINEYARDS
Forestville
✩

For the son of teetotal parents, the late Joe Swan was an extraordinary winemaker in many senses, and his son-in-law, Rod Berglund, has continued his tradition of producing very small batches of high-quality wines, with Zinfandel his most consistent style.

✓ *Zinfandel*

KENWOOD VINEYARDS
Kenwood
★ 🅥

Concentrated wines with good attack are consistently produced at these vineyards.

✓ *Cabernet Sauvignon* (Art Series, Jack London Vineyard) • *Chardonnay* (Russian River Reserve) • *Pinot Noir* (Olivet Reserve, Russian River Reserve) • *Sauvignon Blanc* (Sonoma County)

KISTLER VINEYARDS
Trenton
★★✩ 🅥

Mark Bixler and Steve Kistler are outstanding single-vineyard Chardonnay specialists, who also turn out masterly Pinot Noir. No apologies for the value rating. Put these Sonoma Coast wines side by side with Burgundies of the same price, and Kistler wins more often than not.

✓ *Chardonnay* • *Pinot Noir*

KORBEL CHAMPAGNE CELLARS
Guerneville
❓

No wine encyclopedia would be complete without mention of California's leading sparkling-wine specialist in the popular sector, even though I have been able to recommend only one of its wines on a consistent basis. While the odd blend of this and that *cuvée* might rise above the norm, only Korbel Rouge is worthy of recommending year in, year out. The irony is, of course, that this medium-sweet red fizz is usually the one that most critics turn their noses up at, yet its bold colour and equally bold flavours, enhanced with some sweetness, would not fare too badly in a blind tasting of highly respected Australian sparkling reds. Owned by Brown-Forman.

✓ *Sparkling red* (Rouge)

KUNDE ESTATE
Kenwood
★✩

Kunde Estate winery was set up by a well-established group of Sonoma growers who started selling their own wines in 1990, and have rapidly made a huge impact with critics and consumers alike.

✓ *Cabernet Sauvignon* (Drummond) • *Chardonnay* (Kinneybrook Wildwood) • *Sauvignon Blanc* (Magnolia Lane) • *Zinfandel* (Robusto)

LA CREMA
Geyserville
★✩ 🅥

With a well-deserved reputation for reasonably priced, high-quality Chardonnay and Pinot Noir from the Russian River (9 Barrel being top of the range), La Crema also produces less expensive wines of reliable quality from the Sonoma Coast AVA.

✓ *Chardonnay* (9 Barrel, Russian River) • *Pinot Noir* (9 Barrel, Anderson Valley, Carneros, Russian River)

LANDMARK VINEYARDS
Windsor
★

These vineyards are best known for Chardonnay of a much fatter, richer, more complex style than they used to be, and are now developing a growing reputation for Pinot Noir.

✓ *Chardonnay* (Lorenzo) • *Pinot Noir* (Kastania Vineyard)

LAUREL GLEN VINEYARD
Glen Ellen
★☆

Laurel Glen offers a succulent Sonoma Mountain Cabernet Sauvignon, with Counterpoint as a half-price version. Reds is a seriously underrated classic red sold for under $10 a bottle. The 2002, for example, contained 60 per cent Zinfandel from 80-year-old vines, 30 per cent Carignane from 117-year-old vines, plus 10 per cent Petite Sirah.

✓ *Cabernet Sauvignon* • *Classic red blend* (Reds)

LAURIER
Forestville
★ⓥ

Formerly called Domaine Laurier, with production restricted to a 12-hectare (30-acre) vineyard, this is now a brand belonging to the Bronco Wine Company.

✓ *Cabernet Sauvignon* (Dry Creek Valley) • *Chardonnay* (Los Carneros) • *Merlot* (Dry Creek Valley)

LYETH WINERY
Geyserville
☆

Pronounced "Leeth", this was an exciting new winery in the 1980s, but when the founder died in a plane crash in 1988, it was sold off and is now owned by Burgundian *négociant* Boisset. Their second label is Christophe.

✓ *Classic red blend* (Lyeth) • *Classic white blend* (Lyeth)

MARIETTA CELLARS
Healdsburg
★

Owner-winemaker Chris Bilbro started up this operation in 1980, after selling off his share in the Bandeira Winery, which he had established while still working as an administrator for Sonoma State Hospital. He built his reputation on lush Merlot and great-value wines.

✓ *Classic red blend* (Old Vine Red) • *Petite Sirah* • *Zinfandel* (Cuvée Angeli)

MARIMAR ESTATE
Sebastopol
★★☆

Miguel Torres planted his sister's vineyard with Chardonnay and Pinot Noir, at three to four times the normal density for California. These high-density vines work best for Pinot Noir, which has a combination of silky fruit, finesse, and age-worthiness that is uncommon in California.

✓ *Chardonnay* (Dobles Lias) • *Pinot Noir*

MARTINELLI VINEYARDS
Fulton
★★

Experienced grape growers, who turned winemakers in the early 1990s, the Martinelli family turns out limited quantities of lush, stylish wines under the guidance of Helen Turley. The range includes wonderfully classy Pinot Noir, stunning Syrah and Zinfandel, and sumptuous late-harvest Muscat Alexandria.

✓ *Entire range*

MATANZAS CREEK WINERY
Santa Rosa
★★☆

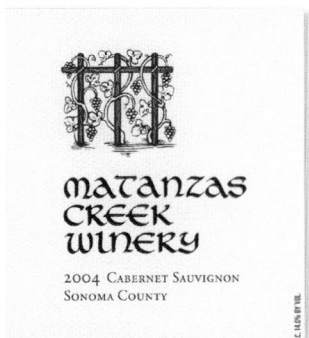

MATANZAS CREEK WINERY

2004 CABERNET SAUVIGNON
SONOMA COUNTY

This small, highly reputed winery has been owned by Jess Jackson and Barbara Banke of Kendall-Jackson since 2000, when the founding McIver family retired and sold up. The style is fine, rich, and elegant, with a signature of good fruit-acidity, probably better suited to European palates than American.

✓ *Cabernet Sauvignon* • *Chardonnay* • *Sauvignon Blanc*

MICHEL-SCHLUMBERGER
Healdsburg
☆

Formerly known as Domaine Michel Winery, under the ownership of Swiss-born Jean-Jacques Michel, but it is now in collaboration with Jacques Schlumberger, whose family comes from Alsace.

✓ *Cabernet Sauvignon* • *Chardonnay* (La Brume) • *Merlot* (Dry Creek Valley) • *Pinot Blanc* (Dry Creek Valley)

NALLE
Healdsburg
★★

Doug Nalle was winemaker at Quivira, when he started making Zinfandel under his own label in 1984. His Zinfandel wines are usually augmented with 6–12 per cent of Petite Sirah, Syrah, Carignane, Alicante Bouchet, and Gamay, and aged exclusively in French oak. They are not the massive monsters that win gold after gold or make national headlines, but the Brits appreciate them.

✓ *Zinfandel*

PAX
Santa Rosa
★★☆

Former Dean and Deluca wine-buyer Pax Mahle established California's fastest-rising Syrah superstar in 2000, and the mesmerizing quality of his low-yield, hands-off, single-vineyard wines has charmed the critics off their perch.

✓ *Entire range*

PELLEGRINI FAMILY VINEYARDS
South San Francisco
★ⓥ

These vineyards produce delicious, vividly flavoured red wines, with oodles of fresh fruit.

✓ *Cabernet Sauvignon* (Cloverdale Ranch) • *Merlot* (Cloverdale Ranch) • *Pinot Noir* (Olivet Lane Estate) • *Zinfandel* (Eight Cousins)

PETER MICHAEL WINERY
Calistoga
★★

With no expense spared, Englishman Sir Peter Michael has applied New World technology to the very best of traditional methods to produce some of the classiest wines in California. Air conditioning is vital in California, but this winery has computer-controlled steam jets to maintain sufficient humidity to reduce evaporation through the staves of new oak to virtually zero. The aim is for the wines not to overwhelm when served with food, but to build in finesse and complexity in the glass, and this is achieved most of the time. Some of the Chardonnays can be far too soft, flabby even, but when this varietal has a good acidity balance (such as the 2001 and 2002 Point Rouge, or the 2002 Cuvée Indigène), they are a match for the greatest Chardonnays from California and the Côte d'Or.

✓ *Chardonnay* (Cuvée Indigène, Pointe Rouge for power) • *Classic red blend* (Les Pavots) • *Sauvignon Blanc* (L'Après-Midi)

PIPER SONOMA
Windsor
★☆ⓥ

When will someone give Raphael Brisbois the home he deserves? For years he has had to make do with a corner of the winery that was once Piper Sonoma's own facility. Since 1997, however, it has been the J Wine Company, owned by Judy Jordan. If I were Oded Shakked, J's winemaker, I would not want a lodger in my winery, and if I were Brisbois, I would be pretty miffed about being the master of my own premises. Not only does Brisbois not have a proper home for his wine, but he is subject to one of the most miserly budgets for grape supplies and time on yeast I have seen at any half-decent *méthode champenoise* producer, yet Piper Sonoma is better than many California sparkling wines that sell for two or three times the price. If Rémy-Cointreau (owners of Piper-Heidsieck, the Reims-based *grande marque* Champagne house) cannot afford or be bothered to do this operation justice, they should sell the brand to someone who can and will.

✓ *Sparkling wine* (Blanc de Noirs, Brut)

PRESTON VINEYARDS
Healdsburg
★☆ⓥ

These Dry Creek vineyards are planted with an amazing and successful mix of varieties and are capable of making high-quality wines. Carignane, Cinsault, and Mourvèdre are worth keeping an eye on.

✓ *Barbera* • *Classic red blend* (L Preston Red) • *Syrah* • *Viognier* • *Zinfandel*

PRIDE MOUNTAIN VINEYARDS
Santa Rosa
★★

Established in 1990 by the late Jim Pride, who transformed a rundown, under-performing vineyard into the current immaculate wine estate, which produces equally immaculate red wines and one of California's finest Viogniers under the skilful guidance of winemaker Bob Foley.

✓ *Cabernet Franc* • *Cabernet Sauvignon* • *Classic red blend* (Reserve Claret) • *Merlot* • *Sangiovese* • *Viognier*

QUIVIRA
Healdsburg
★☆ⓥ

Quivira was named after a legendary American kingdom that Europeans spent 200 years searching for. Not able to locate Quivira, the earliest settlers apparently used the name for this part of northern California before it was called Sonoma.

✓ *Classic red blend* (Dry Creek Cuvée) • *Zinfandel*

RAVENSWOOD
Sonoma
★★

Joel Peterson is the master when it comes to monstrous Zinfandel. Some growers of tiny mountainside plots produce such low yields that their wines would be too intense to drink on their own, which is why even Ravenswood's Zinfandel blends can be quite sensational. Peterson's other first-class varietals should not be overlooked.

✓ *Cabernet Sauvignon* (Gregory) • *Carignane* • *Classic red blend* (Pickberry) • *Merlot* (Sangiacomo) • *Zinfandel* (Belloni, Cooke, Dickerson, Old Hill)

RAYMOND BURR VINEYARDS
Geyserville
★ Ⓥ

Named after the late actor, who was a partner, but he died three years before the first wines were released. Best known for Cabernet Sauvignon, yet makes one of California's best Cabernet Francs.

✓ *Cabernet Franc* • *Cabernet Sauvignon*

ROBERT STEMMLER
Sonoma
★

This winery formerly produced a full range of wines at Robert Stemmler's own winery in Healdsburg, when Pinot Noir was its biggest seller, and that variety is still its best wine, even though Robert Stemmler is now produced at and marketed by Buena Vista.

✓ *Chardonnay* (Three Clone) • *Pinot Noir*

RODNEY STRONG VINEYARDS
Windsor
★ Ⓥ

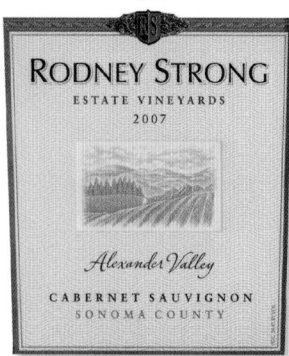

Rodney Strong Vineyards produces rich Cabernet Sauvignon and soft-styled Chardonnay, but the fresh, easy-drinking Sauvignon is now emerging as his best wine. Constantly improving.

✓ *Cabernet Sauvignon* (Alden Vineyards) • *Chardonnay* (Chalk Hill) • *Sauvignon Blanc* (Charlotte's Home Vineyard) • *Zinfandel* (Knotty Vines Estate)

SEBASTIANI
Sonoma
★ Ⓥ

Even Sebastiani's top-of-the-range wines are inexpensive, and although this winery has unfortunately suffered from an inconsistent performance in the past, the quality is improving and levelling, with some real bargains to be found. Other labels include Pepperwood Grove, Talus, August Sebastiani, Vendange, and Richard Cuneo. *See also* Richard Cuneo.

✓ *Barbera* • *Cabernet Sauvignon* (Alexander Valley) • *Chardonnay* (Dutton Ranch) • *Classic red blend* (Cherryblock) • *Pinot Noir* (Russian River Valley) • *Zinfandel* (Domenici Vineyard, Sonoma County)

SEGHESIO
Healdsburg
★★ Ⓥ

This family-owned and -operated winery owns a considerable spread of well-established vineyards, the oldest of which date back to 1895, when Edoardo Seghesio planted his first vineyard in the Alexander Valley. Although he made and sold wine in bulk, it was not until 1983 that his grandchildren were persuaded by their own children to sell wines under the Seghesio label.

✓ *Sangiovese* • *Zinfandel*

SIDURI
Santa Rosa
★★

Named after the Babylonian goddess of wine by Adam and Diana Lee, a couple of Pinot Noir fanatics who source their wines from as far north as Oregon's Willamette Valley to as far south as Santa Barbara's Santa Rita Hills.

✓ *Pinot Noir*

SIMI WINERY
Healdsburg
★

Simi's one-time dependability seems to have disappeared, with extreme variability playing havoc with what was once a power-packed range of ultra-California character. Some wines are still first class, such as the 1999 Alexander Valley Cabernet Sauvignon, but no one line has shown consistency of late. The only wine that stands out annually is the Goldfields Vineyard Chardonnay.

✓ *Chardonnay* (Goldfields Vineyard Reserve)

SONOMA-CUTRER VINEYARDS
Windsor
★

Now owned by Brown-Forman, Sonoma-Cutrer continues to specialize in producing high-quality, single-vineyard Chardonnays.

✓ *Chardonnay* (Les Pierres, Founder's Reserve)

SONOMA-LOEB
Geyserville
★

This producer is owned by John Loeb, a former American Ambassador to Denmark, who has grown grapes here since the early 1970s. However, he did not start making and selling wine under his own label until 1988.

✓ *Chardonnay* (Private Reserve)

ST FRANCIS VINEYARD
Kenwood
★ Ⓥ

Situated just across the road from Château St Jean, this was an underrated winery, but is not producing as many cellar wines as it used to.

✓ *Cabernet Sauvignon* (Reserve Nuns Canyon) • *Chardonnay* (Reserve Behler) • *Zinfandel* (Reserve Pagani Vineyard)

STARRY NIGHT WINERY
Novato
★

This could be one to watch, having started in 1999, yet achieving some very polished wines almost immediately. The bulk of the production is Zinfandel, and the Russian River Old Vine stands out, but my favourite wine of all is a Rhône-style blend of Carignane, Grenache, and Syrah called Adara.

✓ *Classic red wine blend* (Adara) • *Zinfandel* (Russian River Valley Old Vine)

STONESTREET
Healdsburg
★★

One of the wineries in Kendal-Jackson's "Artisans & Estates" group, Stonestreet produces good Chardonnay, brilliant Sauvignon, and gorgeously sumptuous Cabernet and Merlot, but truly excels with its classy Legacy blend.

✓ *Cabernet Sauvignon* (Christopher's) • *Chardonnay* (Upper Barn Vineyard) • *Classic red blend* (Legacy) • *Merlot* (Sonoma County) • *Sauvignon Blanc* (Upper Barn Vineyard)

TOPOLOS AT RUSSIAN RIVER VINEYARDS
North Forestville
Ⓞ Ⓥ Ⓐ

From good vineyards around the winery and on Sonoma Mountain, Topolos sometimes comes up with a gem in what can be an alarmingly wayward (hence rating) bunch of wines, including a bewildering array of Zinfandel.

✓ *Alicante Bouschet* • *Petite Sirah* • *Zinfandel*

TRENTADUE WINERY
Geyserville
★ Ⓥ

The fast-improving Trentadue Winery produces a characterful selection of good-value varietal wines that are rarely, if ever, filtered.

✓ *Classic red blend* (Old Patch) • *Petite Sirah* • *Zinfandel* (La Storia)

WALTER HANSEL
Santa Rosa
★★

A Burgundian specialist who uses wild yeast and does not fine or filter, resulting in some of California's finest Chardonnay and Pinot Noir wines.

✓ *Chardonnay* • *Pinot Noir*

WILLIAMS SELYEM
Fulton
★★★

Established in 1981 by Burt Williams and Ed Selyem (since retired), William Selyem has carefully carved out a reputation for tiny quantities of some of the most sought-after Pinot Noir in California. The signature note of these wines is their beautiful balance and finesse.

✓ *Chardonnay* • *Pinot Noir* • *Zinfandel*

WINDSOR VINEYARDS
Asti
★ ★ Ⓥ

This producer is grossly underrated because it is corporate-owned and offers so many wines at such inexpensive prices that many think there cannot possibly be anything worth drinking. Yet on the competition circuit, Windsor Vineyards is very well known and highly respected, ranking as one of the three most award-winning wineries in the USA every year for the last two decades. One reason to take a look at these wines is that Toni Stockhausen has been chief winemaker since 1999. Not only is she the daughter of Karl Stockhausen, who was quite probably Lindemans' (Australia) greatest ever winemaker, but Toni started as an oenologist at Lindemans and went on to win awards at Australia's top wine shows before being sent to the USA to head this operation. So, if you rate Australian wines, you should at least try some of these California wines made with an Aussie touch.

✓ *Cabernet Sauvignon* (Private Reserve, Signature Series, Simoneau Ranch) • *Carignane* • *Chenin Blanc* • *Classic red blend* (Signature Series Meritage) • *Gewürztraminer* • *Merlot* (Signature Series) • *Petite Sirah* (Mendocino County) • *Pinot Noir* (Private Reserve, Russian River Valley - Signature Series) • *Sauvignon Blanc* (Middle Ridge Vineyard) • *Syrah* • *Zinfandel* (North Coast, Signature Series)

NAPA COUNTY

Napa is the heart and soul of the California wine industry. Its vineyards are the most concentrated in the state, it has more wineries than any other county, and they produce the greatest number and variety of fine wines in all of North American.

IT IS HARD TO BELIEVE that Napa was planted after Sonoma, but it was, by some 13 years; in 1838 a trapper from North Carolina, George Yount, acquired a few Mission vines from General Mariano Vallejo's Sonoma vineyard and planted them outside his log cabin, 3 kilometres (2 miles) north of present-day Yountville, to make a little wine for himself. Within six years he was harvesting an annual average of 900 litres (200 gallons); by the turn of the decade, other vineyards had sprung up, and in 1859, Samuel Brannan, an ex-Mormon millionaire, bought 8 square kilometres (3 square miles) of valley land and planted cuttings of various European vine varieties. Within another 20 years there would be 7,300 hectares (18,000 acres) of vines in the county, more than half the amount currently cultivated and almost twice the area now covering Mendocino. Today, Napa's wines, particularly Chardonnay and Cabernet Sauvignon, are the most sought-after and highly prized in the Americas and will continue to be so for the foreseeable future.

FACTORS AFFECTING TASTE AND QUALITY

LOCATION
Starting alongside San Francisco Bay, Napa runs 54 kilometres (34 miles) north and west to the foothills of Mount St Helena. Flanking it are the Sonoma Valley to the west and Lake Berryessa to the east.

CLIMATE
This ranges from cool (Region I, *see* p538) near the Bay, in the often foggy Carneros District, to warm (Region III, *see* p538) in the northern section of the Napa Valley and in Pope Valley.

ASPECT
Vines are mostly planted on the valley floors but some are cultivated on slopes. The altitude of the valley floors ranges from barely 5 metres (17 feet) above sea level at Napa itself, to 70 metres (230 feet) at St Helena, and 122 metres (400 feet) at Calistoga in the north. The wooded western slopes provide afternoon shade, which adds to the tempering effect of altitude and so favours white grapes, whereas the eastern slopes favour red varieties.

SOIL
Fertile clay and silt loams in the south of the region, and gravel loams of better drainage and lower fertility in the north.

VITICULTURE AND VINIFICATION
There is a vast range of wineries here, from a small number of large firms employing the latest high-tech methods, to an increasing number of small boutique wineries. The latter have limited production, based on traditional methods, although often with judicious use of modern techniques.

GRAPE VARIETIES
Primary varieties: Cabernet Sauvignon, Chardonnay, Chenin Blanc, Merlot, Pinot Noir, Sauvignon Blanc, White Riesling (Riesling), Zinfandel
Secondary varieties: Aleatico, Alicante Bouschet, Barbera, Black Malvoisie, Cabernet Franc, Carignane (Carignan), Colombard, Early Burgundy (Abouriou), Flora, Folle Blanche, Gamay, Gamay Beaujolais, Gewürztraminer, Grey Riesling (Trousseau Gris), Green Hungarian, Grenache, Malbec, Malvasia Bianca, Mourvèdre, Mission, Muscat Blanc, Palomino, Petite Sirah (Durif), Pinot Blanc, Pinot St George (Négrette), Ruby Cabernet, Sauvignon Vert (Muscadelle), Sémillon, Sylvaner, Syrah

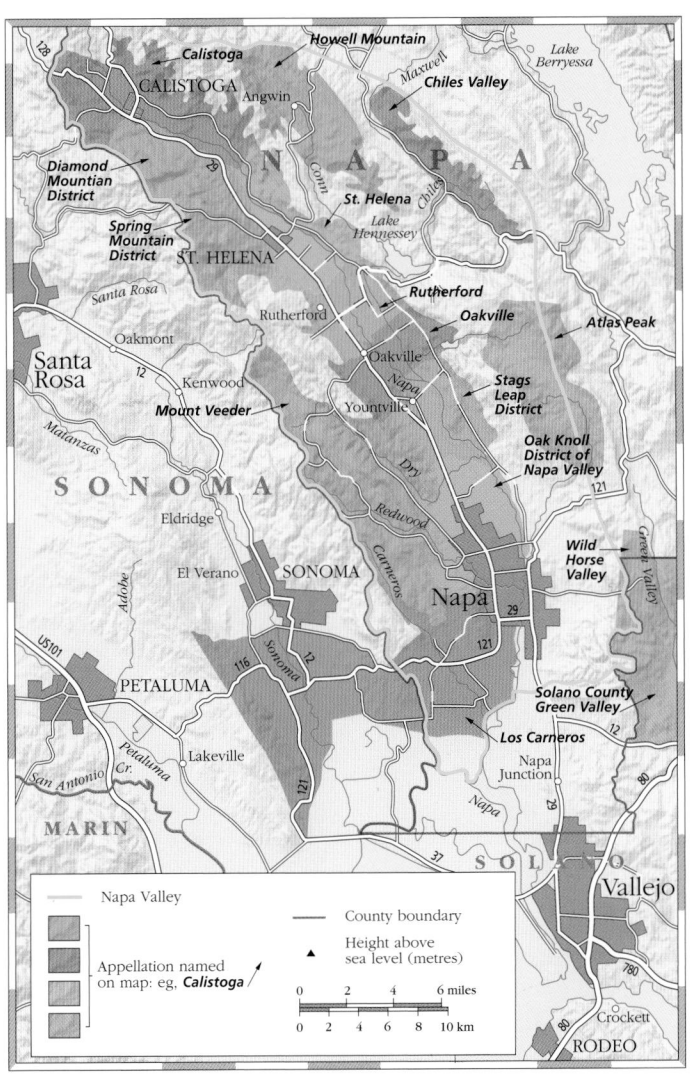

NAPA VINEYARDS
In this, the most famous of all California wine regions, vines grow mostly on the fertile valley floors, although more and more vineyards are being established in the wooded foothills, where the earliest settlers first planted vines.

NAPA COUNTY, *see also p538*
The intensive winegrowing areas of this illustrious California district occupy a long, narrow strip running roughly parallel to those of Sonoma County. Many famous names are crowded around Route 29.

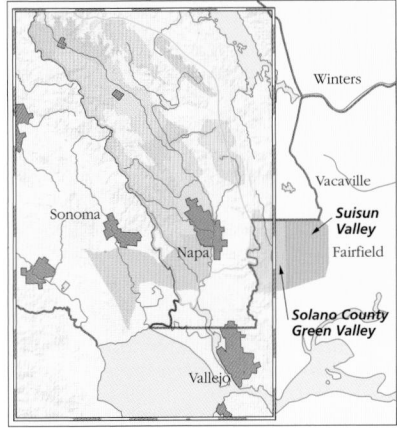

Napa Valley extended area

THE APPELLATIONS OF
NAPA COUNTY

ATLAS PEAK AVA

The Atlas Peak appellation consists of 4,600 hectares (11,400 acres) on and around Atlas Peak mountain, where more than a quarter of California's Sangiovese vines are planted.

CARNEROS AVA

Also known as Los Carneros, this AVA overlaps Napa and Sonoma counties. *See also* Los Carneros, Sonoma.

CHILES VALLEY AVA

A narrow area of vines in the Vaca Mountains overlapping the northeast edge of the Napa Valley, the Chiles Valley was named after Joseph Ballinger Chiles, who was given a land grant for this area from the Mexican government in the middle of the 19th century. The cooling bay breezes that moderate the Napa Valley do not reach Chiles Valley, but its altitude of 240 to 300 metres (800 to 1,000 feet) and the prevailing northwesterly winds that funnel dry air through the valley, in combination with the airflow from the Vaca Mountains, tend to cool the grapes down more quickly than in the main areas of the Napa Valley itself. The vines growing here are primarily Zinfandel, Cabernet Sauvignon, Chardonnay, and Sauvignon Blanc.

DIAMOND MOUNTAIN AVA

Just one-tenth of this appellation's 2,000 hectares (5,000 acres) are planted. Diamond Mountain AVA can be found in the Mayacamas Range on the northeastern corner of Napa Valley, where porous volcanic soils and extended exposure to the sun are the key to its legendary success for Cabernet Sauvignon. Other varieties, such as Cabernet Franc and Zinfandel, are almost as successful, and this is also the home of Schramsberg sparkling wine.

HOWELL MOUNTAIN AVA

The relatively flat table-top of Howell Mountain is a sub-appellation of the Napa Valley, covering 57 square kilometres (22 square miles) and encompassing some 81 hectares (200 acres) of vineyards at an altitude of between 420 and 890 metres (1,400 and 2,200 feet). Vines were first planted here in 1880. It is best for Cabernet Sauvignon but also capable of top-flight Zinfandel and Chardonnay.

MOUNT VEEDER AVA

Situated on the east-facing slopes of the Mayacamas Mountains and named after the volcanic peak that dominates this AVA, Mount Veeder is one of the hilly areas where winemakers went to escape the Napa Valley's fertile valley floor. Cool sea breezes from San Pablo Bay and occasional marine fogs temper the climate, while air-drainage prevents frost. Chardonnay and Cabernet Sauvignon are the two dominant varieties, the latter being quite exceptional in its varietal intensity and completely different in structure from the lush valley-floor Cabernets.

NAPA COUNTY AO

This is an appellation that covers grapes grown anywhere in the entire county.

NAPA VALLEY AVA

This AVA includes all of the county with the exception of the area around Putah Creek and Lake Berryessa. The Napa Valley appellation is 40 kilometres (25 miles) long and between 12 and 16 kilometres (8 and 10 miles) wide, and is sheltered by two parallel mountain ranges. The majority of vineyards occupy the flat valley floor in a continuous strip from Napa to Calistoga, although the slopes are also beginning to be cultivated.

OAKVILLE AVA

If Rutherford has the greatest concentration of famous Cabernet Sauvignon vineyards, then neighbouring Oakville, which is equally Napa's heartland, excels by its very diversity. Great Cabernet Sauvignon, Merlot, and Chardonnay are made here, and even the Sauvignon Blanc from these vineyards can be extraordinary.

RUTHERFORD AVA

One of the most famous names in Napa, yet one of the last to gain AVA status because many growers feared that dividing the Napa Valley's heartland into smaller, possibly more prestigious sub-appellations would gradually have the effect of diluting the reputation of Napa itself. This AVA encompasses more than 30 wineries, including some of California's most famous, and contains many of Napa's greatest Cabernet Sauvignon vineyards.

SPRING MOUNTAIN DISTRICT AVA

Originally proposed as Spring Mountain, but as this was already a brand name, the AVA was changed to Spring Mountain District to prevent confusion. This appellation is located within the Napa Valley AVA, just west of St Helena, on the eastern flank of the Mayacamas Mountains, and comprises 3,480 hectares (8,600 acres), of which approximately 800 hectares (1,980 acres) are planted with vines.

ST HELENA AVA

The latest AVA to be established in a bid to carve up the Napa Valley into communal districts in a similar manner to the Médoc, St Helena is immediately north of Rutherford.

STAGS LEAP DISTRICT AVA

Confusingly, Stags Leap is spelled in three slightly different ways: with an apostrophe before the "s" in the famous Stag's Leap Wine Cellar, with an apostrophe after the "s" in the lesser-known Stags' Leap Winery, and without an apostrophe in the AVA name. Stag's Leap Wine Cellar shot to fame in 1976 when its Cabernet Sauvignon trumped top Bordeaux wines at a blind tasting in Paris. Stags Leap District vies with Rutherford as the crème of Napa Valley Cabernet Sauvignon, but also makes good Petite Sirah, excellent Merlot, and stunning red Bordeaux-style blends.

WILD HORSE VALLEY AVA

Technically attached to Napa, Wild Horse Valley actually straddles the county line, occupying more of Solano than Napa.

YOUNTVILLE AVA

Although less famous than Rutherford or Oakville, this AVA does have one of the Napa Valley's coolest vineyard exposures, which is why some people rate its Cabernet Sauvignon above those of its neighbours.

THE WINE PRODUCERS OF
NAPA COUNTY

ABREU
Napa
★★★☆

I often wondered what would happen when an immovable object (such as the density of the fruit used to make these wines) met an irresistible force like David Abreu's passion for great class and finesse, and here we have it in the form of Cabernet Sauvignon taken to another dimension (for where else could it go?). If you like massive, you must try Abreu.

✓ *Cabernet Sauvignon*

ACACIA WINERY
Napa
★★

Acacia Winery produces wines of increasing finesse, from a fine Chardonnay, which has a touch of spice, to a lovely Pinot Noir that is silky textured and all cherries and vanilla.

✓ *Chardonnay* (Sangiacomo Vineyard) • *Pinot Noir* (Beckstoffer Vineyard, Carneros, Field Blend)

ARAUJO ESTATE
Calistoga
🅑★★

Bart and Daphne Araujo now own the highly regarded Eisele vineyard, which is located north of Cuvaison and makes Cabernet Sauvignon of outstanding quality.

✓ *Cabernet Sauvignon* (Eisele Vineyard) • *Sauvignon Blanc* (Eisele Vineyard) • *Syrah* (Eisele Vineyard)

ARTESA
Napa
★☆

Formerly called Codorníu Napa, this is the Californian arm of the famous Catalan Cava producer, and originally opened in 1991. Although the quality increased as the years went by, Codorníu found it difficult to sell a sparkling wine at California prices, as consumers obviously wondered why they should pay twice the price for Codorníu with California on the label. It did not help that Codorníu was always synonymous with Cava, one of the cheapest sparkling wines on the US market. The decision to pull the plug was taken in 1996, the winery was totally transformed into one suited for the production of classic varietal wines, and Artesa was born.

✓ *Cabernet Sauvignon • Sauvignon Blanc* (Napa Valley Reserve)

ATALON
Oakville
★★❶

Even the entry-level Cabernet Sauvignon is a stunning, classic structured wine of great class and supreme elegance. And relatively inexpensive for such quality – but for how long? Also fine Merlot.

✓ *Cabernet Sauvignon • Merlot*

ATLAS PEAK
Atlas Peak
★★☆

This exciting venture is backed with big bucks from Allied-Domecq (which also owns Clos du Bois and William Hill) with expertise provided by Champagne Bollinger and the famous Chianti house of Antinori. Sangiovese is the star here, and invariably the standard bottling that excels above that of the Sangiovese Reserve.

✓ *Cabernet Sauvignon* (Consenso) • *Sangiovese*

BARNETT VINEYARDS
St Helena
★★

These mountain vineyards make intense yet delicious, very elegant Cabernet Sauvignon, among other wines.

✓ *Cabernet Sauvignon* (Rattlesnake Hill)

BEAULIEU VINEYARD
Rutherford
★

This was the centre of innovation in California under the legendary winemaker André Tchelistcheff, but has long since passed into corporate hands, and is currently owned by the UK-based Diageo group. Not the force it was, although on its own, the legendary Georges de Latour would easily rate as a two-star entry. Other wines have their day (such as the 2000 Pinot Noir Carneros Reserve), but lack consistency.

✓ *Cabernet Sauvignon* (Georges de Latour)

BEHRENS AND HITCHCOCK
Oakville
★★

Born in the back-of-beyond, viticulturally speaking, of Arcata, Humboldt County, not far from the Oregon border, where they made 175 cases a year from trucked-in grapes in 1991, Behrens and Hitchcock moved to a rented winery in Napa in 1997, before building their own winery in 1999. When I first nosed around Humboldt and Siskiou counties in 1994, this was just one of a handful of such producers, none of whom were taken very seriously, yet they now craft some of California's finest Cabernet Sauvignon.

✓ *Cabernet Sauvignon • Petite Sirah*

BELO WINE COMPANY
St Helena
★❶

This fortified wine specialist grows traditional Portuguese grape varieties, and makes great vintage port, both blended and varietal.

✓ *Fortified* (Vintage Port)

BERINGER VINEYARDS
St Helena
★★❶

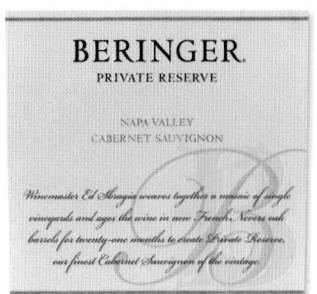

Although all the products from Beringer Vineyards are among the finest in California, you do get proportionately more for your money if you pay extra for the better wines, with the singular exception of the Founders' Estate Merlot, which can offer extraordinary finesse for so few dollars. Indeed, if all vintages were as brilliant as the 2000, I would not hestitate to claim it to be one of California's 10 greatest Merlots. However, I must take issue with the name of this entry-level range. Beringer might be open about its diverse origins, hence the California AVA, but Founders' Estate does imply that the vineyards in question are part of a single estate of historic origins, and I'm not so sure that Jacob and Frederick Beringer owned vineyards stretching from Santa Barbara to Mendocino!

✓ *Botrytized* (Nightingale) • *Cabernet Sauvignon • Chardonnay* (Sbragia) • *Chenin Blanc • Classic red blend* (Alluvium) • *Classic white blend* (Alluvium) • *Merlot* (Bancroft Ranch, Founders' Reserve)

BIALE VINEYARDS
Napa
★★

Amazing, huge, rich, and gorgeously ripe, single-vineyard Zinfandel, and one of California's greatest Petite Sirah.

✓ *Zinfandel* (Aldo's Vineyard)

BOUCHAINE VINEYARDS
Napa
★

Noticeable by its absence from most American critics' thoughts, Bouchaine's Pinot Noir and Chardonnay are probably too light and elegant to stir up much opinion in the USA, but have a purity and finesse much appreciated by European palates.

✓ *Pinot Noir*

BRYANT FAMILY VINEYARD
Calistoga
❓

This relatively new boutique winery is reputedly turning out masterly Cabernet Sauvignon.

BUEHLER VINEYARDS
St Helena
★★

This estate is again producing Cabernet Sauvignon reminiscent of the size and quality that once made it legendary.

✓ *Cabernet Sauvignon*

BURGESS CELLARS
St Helena
★❶

Owner Tom Burgess and winemaker Bill Sorenson often produce well-weighted, oaky wines of fine quality.

✓ *Syrah • Zinfandel*

CAIN CELLARS
St Helena
★★☆

These are interesting, innovative, and well-made wines.

✓ *Classic red blend* (Cain Concept, Cain Five) • *Sauvignon Blanc* (Cain Musqué Ventana Vineyard)

CAKEBREAD CELLARS
Rutherford
★★☆

Bruce Cakebread has a well-deserved reputation for producing one of the most delicious Sauvignon Blanc wines in California.

✓ *Cabernet Sauvignon* (Three Sisters, Vine Hill Ranch) • *Sauvignon Blanc • Syrah*

CASA NUESTRA
St Helena
★★☆❶

A tiny, high-quality winery that is up and coming, although it has been in existence since 1979. This makes its wines great value now, but demand could change all that

by a future edition, so best to taste them while you can still afford to. Casa Nuestra produces classic styles such as Merlot and Meritage, but some quirky ones, too, such as one of California's finest Chenin Blanc and a classic red blend (Tinto) made from nine varieties, including Cabernet Pfeffer. Cabernet what? That's right: Cabernet Pfeffer (*see* ABC of Grape Varieties).

✓ *Chenin Blanc • Classic red blend* (Tinto)

CAYMUS VINEYARDS
Rutherford
★★☆

This extraordinary winery now focuses exclusively on deep, dark brooding Cabernet Sauvignon of superb quality. The classic white wine blend Conundrum is now sold under that name alone and, since 2007, has had its own dedicated winery in Monterey. (See Conundrum in the Central Coast [North] section)

✓ *Cabernet Sauvignon* (Napa Valley, Special Selection)

CHAPPELLET VINEYARDS
St Helena
★★☆

Chappellet is an excellent winery with a range of skilfully produced wines that show great finesse.

✓ *Cabernet Sauvignon • Chardonnay • Chenin Blanc • Johannisberg Riesling • Merlot* (Napa Valley)

CHARLES KRUG
St Helena
★☆❶

Purchased by the Mondavi family in 1943 and run by Bob Mondavi's less prominent brother Peter, this winery used to be known for its Cabernet Sauvignon, but Krug's reputation is diluted by its production of jug wine and generics sold under a second label – C K Mondavi.

✓ *Cabernet Sauvignon • Merlot* (Reserve)

CHÂTEAU MONTELENA WINERY
Calistoga
★★☆

The style of this small, prestigious winery has changed over the years, but the quality has always been high, especially for Cabernet Sauvignon, although the Chardonnay has been almost as good in recent years.

✓ *Cabernet Sauvignon • Chardonnay*

CHÂTEAU POTELLE
Mount Veeder
★

This winery was established in 1985 by a *bordelais* couple, who ironically were best known in their early days for their slow-evolving Chardonnay, but have since developed a reputation for other age-worthy varietals.

✓ *Cabernet Sauvignon* (VGS) •
Chardonnay (VGS) • *Zinfandel*
(VGS)

CHIMNEY ROCK
Napa
★

Part of the Terlato Wine Group
(which includes Sandford,
Rutherford Hill, and Alder Brook),
this was originally Chimney Rock
Golf Club, until its nine holes were
bulldozed and a vineyard planted.

✓ *Cabernet Sauvignon* • *Classic red
blend* (Elevage)

CLIFF LEDE VINEYARD
Napa
★

Cliff Lede took over S Anderson
in 2002, and uses that label
exclusively for the traditional
method wines that Carol Anderson
had garnered such a reputation
for. The style is as elegant as the
labelling, with layers of intense,
finely poised fruit.

✓ *Cabernet Sauvignon* • *Sauvignon
Blanc* • *Sparkling wine* (Blanc de
Blancs, Brut, Rosé)

CLOS DU VAL
Napa
★ ⓥ

Bernard Portet still makes some fine
wines, but there is less of a buzz
about these wines.

✓ *Cabernet Sauvignon* (Stags Leap
District) • *Chardonnay*
(Carneros) • *Zinfandel* (Stags
Leap District Reserve)

CLOS PEGASE
Calistoga
★

A welcome, understated use of oak
coupled with lush fruit produces
wines of some elegance.

✓ *Cabernet Sauvignon* •
Chardonnay • *Classic red blend*
(Hommage) • *Merlot*

COLGIN
Napa
★★★

Tiny production of huge-priced,
high-class Cabernet Sauvignon,
with sufficient structure to support
the weight.

✓ *Cabernet Sauvignon* • *Classic red
blend* (Cariad)

CONN CREEK WINERY
St Helena
☆

Owned by Stimson Lane (which
also owns Château Ste Michelle,
Columbia Crest, and Villa Mount
Eden), Conn Creek is best known
for its supple, fruity Cabernet
Sauvignon, but does not have the
cachet it once had.

✓ *Cabernet Sauvignon* • *Classic red
blend* (Anthology) • *Merlot*

CORISON
St Helena
★★☆

After 10 years as Chappellet's
winemaker, Cathy Corison struck
out on her own, and has not looked
back since, purchasing small parcels
of the finest Napa Valley grapes to
produce lush, supple Cabernet
wines of surprising longevity.

✓ *Cabernet Sauvignon*

CORNERSTONE CELLARS
Oakville
★★★ ⓥ

Owned by two Memphis doctors,
Michael Dragutsky and David Sloas.
In 1991, Sloas happened to be
tasting on Howell Mountain with
Randy Dunn, who mentioned that
he had received almost 5 tons of
grapes more than he needed from
one of his farmers. Sloas telephoned
his friend Dragutsky in Memphis,
they agreed they had both lost their
minds and purchased the grapes,
thus going from wine consumers to
wine producers in a few minutes.

✓ *Cabernet Sauvignon* • *Merlot*

COSENTINO
Yountville
★★

Mitch Cosentino has more wines on
his list than there are dishes on a
Chinese menu. The once hit-you-
between-the-eyes styles have been
toned down and, although the wines
are still exuberant in their fruit, they
now have much more finesse. Some
brilliant Merlot of late (2000 Reserve
is simply stunning). CE2V is an ultra-
premium brand, while Crystal Valley
is Cosentino's second label.

✓ *Classic red blend* (CE2V Meritage,
M Coz, The Poet Meritage) •
Dessert (Viognier Vin Doux Kay)
• *Dolcetto* (Celle Vineyard) •
Merlot (Reserve) • *Petite Sirah*
(Knoll Vineyard) • *Sangiovese*
(CE2V Napa Valley, Il Chiaretto) •
Zinfandel (Cigarzin, The Zin)

CUVAISON
Calistoga
★ ⓥ

This Swiss-owned winery is making
better reds than whites.

✓ *Chardonnay* (Carneros Estate
Selection) • *Pinot Noir* (Carneros
Estate Selection) • *Syrah* (Carneros)

DALLA VALLE
Oakville
★★

Dalla Valle produces great Cabernet
in addition to a truly heroic
Cabernet-based blend.

✓ *Cabernet Sauvignon* • *Classic red
blend* (Maya)

DELECTUS
Oakville
★★☆

Small, ultra-high-quality operation
established in 1989 by Austrian-born
Gerhard Reisacher and his wife Linda.

✓ *Classic red blend* (Cuvée Julia) •
Petite Sirah

DETERT FAMILY VINEYARDS
Oakville
★★★ ⓥ

Former Opus One Cabernet
Franc vines produce this relatively
new winery's best and cheapest
wine, but don't let that put you
off Detert's beautifully focused
Cabernet Sauvignon.

✓ *Cabernet Franc* • *Cabernet
Sauvignon*

DIAMOND CREEK VINEYARDS
Calistoga
★★☆

This small winery specializes in
awesomely long-lived, awesomely
priced Cabernet Sauvignon.

✓ *Cabernet Sauvignon* (Red Rock
Terrace, Gravelly Meadow,
Volcanic Hill)

DOLCE
Oakville
★★★

Established by Far Niente as the
only winery in the USA solely
devoted to producing a single late-
harvest wine, Dolce is a lusciously
sweet, heavily botrytized, Sauternes-
styled dessert wine made from
approximately 90 per cent Sémillon
and 10 per cent Sauvignon Blanc.
The only pity is that they went
for such a kitsch, *nouveau riche*
presentation, instead of the
understated elegance that such
a classy, unique wine deserves.

✓ *Botrytized* (Dolce)

DOMAINE CARNEROS
Napa
★★

This winery has the pristine façade
of Taittinger's 17th-century Château
de la Marquetterie in Champagne,
and Le Rêve is one of the greatest
21st-century sparkling wines
produced outside Champagne.

✓ *Pinot Noir* (Avant-Garde) •
Sparkling wine (Brut, Brut Rosé,
Le Rêve)

DOMAINE CHANDON
Yountville
★ ⓥ

Moët & Chandon's seal of approval
kick-started California's sparkling
wine industry, which until then had
consisted of just one producer,
Schramsberg. Although the style of
its sparkling wine has lacked finesse
in the past, there has been a
noticeably lighter hand in recent
years. The same could be said for
its Pinot Noir, but that all changed
with the 2000 vintage, which was
impressive by any yardstick, while
the Pinot Meunier has always
been a delight.

✓ *Chardonnay* (Carneros) • *Pinot
Meunier* • *Pinot Noir* (Carneros)

• *Sparkling wine* (Mt Veeder,
Riche, Vintage)

DOMINUS
Yountville
★★

Christian Moueix of Château Pétrus
joined forces with the daughters of
John Daniel to produce Dominus, a
massively structured Bordeaux-like
blend from the historic Napanook
vineyard. The best vintages are from
1990 onwards, with the most recent
being the most impressive.

✓ *Classic red blend* (Dominus)

DUCKHORN VINEYARDS
St Helena
★★☆

These superb, dark, rich, and tannic
wines have a cult following. Also
owns the Goldeneye winery in
Mendocino. Other labels include
Paraduxx (Zinfandel-Cabernet
Sauvignon blend), Decoy
(Bordeaux-style blend) and
Migration (Pinot Noir).

✓ *Cabernet Sauvignon* • *Merlot*
(Three Palms) • *Sauvignon Blanc*

DUNN VINEYARDS
Angwin
★★

Randy Dunn makes a very small
quantity of majestic Cabernet
Sauvignon from his Howell
Mountain vineyard.

✓ *Cabernet Sauvignon*

ELYSE
Napa
★★☆

These wines have always had
richness of fruit and expressive style,
but increasingly show greater finesse.

✓ *Cabernet Sauvignon* (Morisoli
Vineyard, Tietjen Vineyard) •
Zinfandel (Howell Mountain,
Morisoli Vineyard)

ETUDE
Oakville
★★

Tony Soter has eased back on his
consultancy work to spend more
time crafting some beautifully
proportioned, silky-smooth,
succulent, and stylish wines at the
venture he established, and Beringer
Blass now owns.

✓ *Cabernet Sauvignon* (Napa
Valley) • *Merlot* (Napa Valley) •
Pinot Blanc (Carneros) • *Pinot
Gris* (Carneros) • *Pinot Noir*
(Heirloom)

FAILLA
Calistoga
★★

In the short history of this winery, which was established in 1998, husband and wife team Ehren Jordan and Anne-Marie Failla have found themselves in hot water, as the original name for their winery – Failla Jordan – came under heavy legal barrage from the Jordan winery for infringement of its trademark. They had no option but to drop their own family name in favour of what is, I think, a much better, more elegant label.

✓ *Chardonnay* (Keefer Ranch) • *Pinot Noir* (Hirsch, Keefer Ranch) • *Syrah* • *Viognier* (Alban Vineyard)

FAR NIENTE
Oakville
★

A revitalized pre-Prohibition winery that made its mark with fine Chardonnay in the 1980s, but that wine can sometimes be overblown, and Cabernet Sauvignon is the more consistent and classier bet.

✓ *Cabernet Sauvignon* • *Chardonnay*

FLORA SPRINGS
St Helena
★★ Ⓥ

This winery produces an exciting Trilogy, a blend of Merlot with two Cabernets, and a Soliloquy, a barrel-fermented Sauvignon Blanc bottled *sur lie*.

✓ *Cabernet Sauvignon* (Rutherford Hillside Reserve, Wild Boar Vineyard) • *Classic red blend* (Poggio del Papa, Trilogy) • *Merlot* (Napa Valley) • *Sauvignon Blanc* (Soliloquy)

FORMAN VINEYARDS
St Helena
★

Rick Forman, formerly of Sterling Vineyard, set up this small winery in 1983. He has a following for classic yet opulent wines from his own vineyard, which sits on a gravel bed as deep as 17 metres (56 feet).

✓ *Cabernet Sauvignon* • *Chardonnay*

FRANCISCAN VINEYARDS
Rutherford
★★☆ Ⓥ

A consistent producer since the mid-1980s of smooth, stylish, premium-quality wines.

✓ *Chardonnay* (Cuvée Sauvage) • *Classic red blend* (Magnificat Meritage)

FREEMARK ABBEY
St Helena
★★☆ Ⓥ

When it comes to its Cabernet Bosché and Chardonnay in general, Freemark Abbey consistently combines high quality and good value. Now part of Jackson Family Wine Estates.

✓ *Cabernet Sauvignon* (Bosché) • *Chardonnay*

FROG'S LEAP WINERY
St Helena
Ⓞ★

One of California's best-known organic producers, Frog's Leap was established in 1981 by John Williams, who had taken inspiration from his first Napa Valley winemaking post at Stag's Leap Cellars as the name for his new venture.

✓ *Chardonnay* • *Merlot* • *Sauvignon Blanc* • *Zinfandel*

GIRARD WINERY
Oakville
★★☆

Top-quality, smooth, and stylish Napa Valley Red boasts seamlessly integrated oak, and is the top wine here, although Girard's Petite Sirah is one of California's finest.

✓ *Chardonnay* (Russian River) • *Classic red blend* (Napa Valley Red) • *Petite Sirah*

GRACE FAMILY VINEYARDS
St Helena
★★

Produces minuscule amounts of huge, dark, extremely expensive Cabernet Sauvignon wine, with wonderfully multi-layered fruit, oak, and *terroir* flavours.

✓ *Cabernet Sauvignon*

GRGICH HILLS CELLAR
Rutherford
★☆ Ⓥ

Owned and run by Mike Grgich, once winemaker at Château Montelena, this winery produces intense, rich, and vibrant styles of high-quality wine.

✓ *Cabernet Sauvignon* (Napa Valley) • *Merlot* (Napa Valley) • *Sauvignon Blanc* (Estate Grown Fumé Blanc) • *Zinfandel* (Miljenko's Old Vine)

GROTH VINEYARDS
Oakville
★★

Although these wines are not as consistent as they used to be, Groth's Cabernet Sauvignon can still hack it with the finest in California.

✓ *Cabernet Sauvignon* (Oakville)

HARLAN ESTATE
Napa
★★★☆

Classic quality from the hills above Oakville, but you have to pay for it!

✓ *Bordeaux-style red* (Napa Valley)

HARTWELL VINEYARDS
Napa
★★

From a one-acre harvest in 1990, Bob and Blanca Hartwell's vineyard has become one of the fastest-rising stars in the Stags Leap District, and is now known for immaculate grapes and the deep, full, lush style of the wines produced.

✓ *Cabernet Sauvignon* • *Merlot*

HAVENS
Napa
★★ Ⓥ

For 25 years, Mike Havens has attracted an enviable reputation for his supremely rich Merlot Reserve, which is certainly one of California's finest, but he also makes Syrah that is in a class of its own and a masterly Bordeaux-style red wine blend called Bourriquot. There is also an interesting, authentically dry Albariño.

✓ *Albariño* • *Classic red blend* (Bourriquot) • *Merlot* • *Syrah*

HEITZ WINE CELLARS
St Helena
★★

The TCA of the 1990s (or bacterial infection as some have claimed) appears to have been overcome, although too few American critics dared tell the late king that he had no clothes on at the time. It will be a surprise to some, but Heitz is a master of Grignolino, making a delightful, quaffing red and a gorgeous rosé, not to mention a very appealing port-style fortified wine, which leans closer to the lighter, traditional Portuguese style than the Ink Grade Vineyard.

✓ *Cabernet Sauvignon* (Martha's Vineyard, Trailside Vineyard) • *Fortified* (Grignolino Port, Ink Grade Vineyard Port) • *Grignolino* (Rosé)

JADE MOUNTAIN
Angwin
★★☆

These high-quality Rhône-style wines are achieving increasingly well integrated oak in recent years. The Mourvèdre Ancient Vines from the Evangelho Vineyard were planted in 1890.

✓ *Classic red blend* (La Provençale) • *Mourvèdre* (Ancient Vines Evangelho Vineyard) • *Syrah* (Paras Vineyard, Paras Vineyard Block P-10)

JOSEPH PHELPS VINEYARDS
St Helena
★★

This prestigious winery continues to make a large range of top-quality wines, with an increasing emphasis on exciting Rhône-style wines, including the excellent Le Mistral blend, although Insignia remains its very greatest product.

✓ *Cabernet Sauvignon* (Backus) • *Chardonnay* (Ovation) • *Classic red blend* (Insignia, Le Mistral) • *Merlot* (Napa Valley) • *Syrah* (Napa Valley)

KENT RASMUSSEN
Napa
★★

As a librarian, Kent Rasmussen loved wine and yearned, so he took a BSc in oenology at UC Davis in 1983, picked up some useful experience at Robert Mondavi Winery and Domaine Chandon, took a *stage* at Stellenbosch Farmers' Winery in South Africa, then at Saltram's Wine Estate in Australia, before setting up his own winery in 1986. Since then he has created a reputation for producing Carneros Pinot Noir at its most luscious.

✓ *Chardonnay* (Napa Valley) • *Pinot Noir* (Carneros)

KONGSGAARD
Oakville
★★★☆

Many small wineries claim to make hand-crafted wines, but John and Maggy Kongsgaard's is one of the few that actually does, as they limit their production – literally – to the wine they can make with their own hands. This and their nigh-fanatical minimalist approach yield wines of exceptional richness, balance, and finesse.

✓ *Entire range*

LA JOTA
Angwin
★★☆

La Jota is best known for lavishly flavoured Cabernet Sauvignon, but produces a much smaller quantity of equally fine Petite Sirah.

✓ *Cabernet Sauvignon* • *Petite Sirah*

ROBERT KEENAN WINERY
St Helena
★

This Spring Mountain hillside winery produces admirably restrained Cabernet Sauvignon and Merlot.

✓ *Cabernet Sauvignon* • *Merlot*

LAIL
Napa
★★

Established in 1995 by Robin Lail, the daughter of John Daniel, the great-nephew of the legendary Gustave Niebaum. Lail trained at Mondavi, and was the co-founder of Dominus and Merryvale, before selling her share in those businesses to set up on her own.

✓ *Classic red blend* (Blueprint, J Daniel Cuvée) • *Sauvignon Blanc* (Georgia)

LARKIN
St Helena
★★

After representing a number of small, high-quality wineries, Sean Larkin made his first wine in 1999 and achieved instant critical success from all the biggest names in the business.

✓ *Cabernet Franc*

LEWELLING VINEYARDS
St Helena
★★ Ⓥ

The Lewelling family established these vineyards in 1864 and, after the usual Prohibition hiatus, developed a reputation for supplying some of Napa's greatest wineries with grapes. The wines, however, only date from 1992, when the Wright family, descendants of the Lewellings, decided to produce wine under their own vineyard designation, and now produce some of California's greatest Cabernet Sauvignon.

✓ *Cabernet Sauvignon*

LEWIS CELLARS
Napa
★★

A small, hands-on winery run by ex-racing car driver Randy Lewis and his wife Debbie. The Merlot could be called a California version of top-class Pomerol.

✓ *Chardonnay* • *Classic red blend* (Alec's Blend, Cuvée L) • *Merlot* • *Syrah*

LOKOYA
Oakville
★★★⯪

Named after a Native American tribe that lived on Mount Veeder, Lokoya is a Napa Cabernet Sauvignon specialist *par excellence*. All three styles are outstanding, from the Howell Mountain, which is the most lush, through the Mount Veeder, which packs the most complex fruit, to Diamond Mountain, which is probably the closest to Bordeaux in style.

✓ *Cabernet Sauvignon*

LONG VINEYARDS
St Helena
★★⯪

This operation was established in the 1970s by Robert and Zelma Long, who have since divorced but are still joint owners. Amazingly, they not only continue to run this winery together but they also do so with their respective new partners. The wines are equally smooth, stylish, and sophisticated.

✓ *Botrytis* (Johannisberg Riesling Estate Grown) • *Cabernet Sauvignon* (Estate Grown) • *Chardonnay* (Old Vines)

LOUIS M MARTINI
St Helena
★⯪ Ⓥ

The quality of this winery had been slowly turning around for the better when it was purchased by E & J Gallo in 2002, although its reputation is still very patchy from vintage to vintage, even for its most successful wines.

✓ *Cabernet Sauvignon* (Monte Rosso) • *Chardonnay* (RVS) • *Fortified* (Cream Sherry, *Dry* Sherry) • *Sangiovese* (Dunnigan Hills) • *Zinfandel* (Monte Rosso)

LUNA VINEYARDS
Napa
★Ⓥ

An artisanal winery with an Italian bent, located at the southern tip of the Silverado Trail.

✓ *Classic red blend* (Canto) • *Classic white blend* (Bianco) • *Pinot Grigio* • *Sangiovese* (Riserva)

MARCASSIN
Calistoga
★★

This small operation belongs to Helen Turley, who made her name at B R Cohn and the Peter Michael Winery, and is one of California's most sought-after consultants. Marcassin produces highly desirable, nigh-unobtainable, extraordinarily lavish, yet extremely stylish wines.

✓ *Chardonnay* • *Pinot Noir*

MARKHAM VINEYARDS
St Helena
★⯪ Ⓥ

This under-rated Japanese-owned (Mercian Corporation) winery is best known for Merlot and Cabernet from its Napa Valley vineyards situated at Calistoga, Yountville, and Oakville, but other varietals are beginning to emerge. Good-value wines are also produced under Markham's second label, Glass Mountain.

✓ *Cabernet Sauvignon* • *Merlot* • *Petite Sirah* • *Zinfandel*

MAYACAMAS VINEYARDS
Napa

This prestigious small winery is renowned for its tannic, long-lived Cabernet, but actually produces much better, more user-friendly Chardonnay as well.

✓ *Chardonnay*

MERRYVALE VINEYARDS
St Helena
★★⯪

These are classy, stylish wines, particularly the Bordeaux-style blends.

✓ *Cabernet Sauvignon* (Beckstoffer Vineyard X) • *Chardonnay* (Silhouette) • *Classic red blend* (Profile)

MONTICELLO CELLARS
Napa
⯪

This producer used to be better for whites than reds, but although Monticello still receives many plaudits for its Chardonnay, it is the red wines that are now established as its most exciting.

✓ *Cabernet Sauvignon* (Corley Reserve, Jefferson Cuvée) • *Classic red blend* (Corley Proprietary Red) • *Merlot* (Estate Grown)

MUMM NAPA WINERY
Rutherford
★⯪ Ⓥ

This impeccably run sparkling-wine operation is under the helm of Greg Fowler, who was the winemaker at Schramsberg for seven years. Fowler really lets his winemaking skills fly with his Sparkling Pinot Noir, which has an outrageous deep cerise colour, an aroma of strawberries, and intensely perfumed Pinot fruit.

✓ *Sparkling wine* (Blanc de Blancs, DVX, Sparkling Pinot Noir, Winery Lake)

MURPHY-GOODE
Geyserville
★Ⓥ

The top wines are all rich, oaky blockbusters, but I get the most pleasure from Murphy-Goode's Fumé Blanc.

✓ *Fumé Blanc* (Alexander Valley Reserve)

NAPA CELLARS
Oakville
★⯪ Ⓥ

A brilliant source of great-value, great-quality wines that hit well above their weight, often outclassing famous brands at two or three times the price.

✓ *Cabernet Sauvignon* • *Chardonnay* • *Merlot*

NEYERS
Rutherford
★★ Ⓥ

Bruce and Barbara Neyers have been producing classy wines since 1992, but seem to have stepped up a gear since moving to their current renovated winery in 2000. Part of the production is from the Neyers' own 20-hectare (50-acre) Conn Ranch vineyard, but most is bought in from selected growers.

✓ *Chardonnay* • *Grenache* • *Merlot* • *Syrah*

NEWTON VINEYARDS
St Helena
★★ Ⓥ

This top-notch estate has a track record for wines with impeccable oak integration, silky smooth fruit, and supple-tannin structure.

✓ *Cabernet Sauvignon* • *Chardonnay* • *Classic red blend* (Claret) • *Merlot*

NIEBAUM-COPPOLA
Rutherford
◉★★

Hollywood movie director Francis Ford Coppola purchased the old Gustave Niebaum homestead and half of the original Inglenook vineyards in 1975, producing his first wine, a classic red Bordeaux-style blend called Rubicon, in 1978. He bought almost all of the remaining Inglenook vineyards in 1995, plus the Inglenook winery, but not the brand (now the property of Mission Bell Winery, which belongs to Constellation Brands), and in 2002 Coppola paid out a record $31.5 million for the 24-hectare (60-acre) J J Cohn vineyard (no connection with B R Cohn in Sonoma, which adjoined the southern section of his own property). The Cabernet and Merlot grapes from this Rutherford vineyard should not only allow for increased production of Rubicon, but should also plug some holes that occasionally appeared in the quality of wines made in whole or part with bought-in fruit. Note that only pure estate wines are made exclusively from organically grown grapes.

✓ *Cabernet Sauvignon* (Cask Cabernet) • *Classic red blend* (Rubicon) • *Merlot* (Estate) • *Zinfandel* (Edizione Pennino)

OPUS ONE
Oakville
★⯪

The product of collaboration between Robert Mondavi and the late Baron Philippe de Rothschild, Opus One was the first Bordeaux–California joint venture and there is no denying the quality of this Cabernet-Merlot blend, just as there is no getting away from its outlandish price.

✓ *Opus One*

PAHLMEYER
Napa
★★

Typical of the boutique wineries established by America's affluent professional class, this operation was founded in 1985 by lawyer Jayson Pahlmeyer, who has hired various consultants, such as Randy Dunn, Helen Turley, and David Abreu, in his pursuit of varietal concentration allied to an expression of *terroir*. The Jayson is a blend of the wines that did not make the cut for Pahlmeyer's Proprietary Red.

✓ *Chardonnay* • *Classic red blend* (Jayson, Proprietary Red) • *Merlot*

PALOMA
Spring Mountain District
★★

This reclaimed 19th-century vineyard is located at an altitude of between 618 and 672 metres (2,060 and 2,240 feet) on Spring Mountain, and the difference between these wines and valley floor wines is that you get more complexity and length for the same weight of wine.

✓ *Cabernet Sauvignon • Merlot • Syrah*

PATZ AND HALL
Napa
★★☆

This winery specializes in rich, lush, single-vineyard Burgundian-style varietals.

✓ *Chardonnay • Pinot Noir* (Alder Springs, Pisioni Vineyard)

PEJU PROVINCE
Rutherford
★★

Established by Tony and Herta Peju in 1982, but with 90 per cent of sales going through its tasting room, it has only been in the past 10 years or so that Peju Province has really started to grab wider attention.

✓ *Cabernet Franc • Merlot* (Napa Valley Estate) • *Sauvignon Blanc*

PHILIP TOGNI VINEYARD
St Helena
★★☆

Philip Togni earned great respect at Chalone, Chappellet, Cuvaison, Mayacamus, and Chimney Rock, before establishing this vineyard.

✓ *Cabernet Sauvignon*

PINE RIDGE WINERY
Napa
★★☆ Ⓥ

These are interesting wines of exciting quality that are in the mid-price range.

✓ *Cabernet Sauvignon* (Stags Leap District) • *Classic red blend* (Andrus Reserve) • *Classic white blend* (Chenin-Viognier) • *Merlot* (Crimson Creek)

PLUMPJACK
Napa
★★☆

Owned by the Getty family and Gavin Newsom, Plumpjack is named after the roguish spirit of Shakespeare's Sir John Falstaff, dubbed "Plump Jack" by Queen Elizabeth. There's a whole Plumpjack empire out there, starting with shops and cafés before the Plumpjack winery was established in 1997. Plumpjack made headlines in 2000, when it sold its 1997 Reserve Cabernet Sauvignon under screwcap at $135 a bottle, while the regular cork-sealed version retailed for $125. Not only was Newsom making a statement, but he was also years ahead of his time in making it as far as red wines are concerned.

✓ *Cabernet Sauvignon*

RAYMOND
St Helena
☆ Ⓥ

The Raymond family remain true to their reputation for vividly fruity Chardonnay and stylish Bordeaux-style reds. The cheaper Amberhill label is not to be overlooked.

✓ *Cabernet Sauvignon* (Amberhill, Napa Valley Reserve, Raymond Estates) • *Chardonnay* (Amberhill, Napa Valley Reserve) • *Merlot* (Amberhill, Raymond Estates)

ROBERT CRAIG
Mount Veeder
★★★ Ⓥ

Capable of classy, purple-hearted Cabernet Sauvignon.

✓ *Cabernet Sauvignon • Chardonnay*

ROBERT FOLEY
Angwin
★★★ Ⓥ

This red wine specialist makes just two wines, a classic blend (essentially Cabernet Sauvignon, plus a little Merlot and Petit Verdot) from his own vineyard on Candlestick Ridge, and Charbono grown by Gary Heitz.

✓ *Charbono • Red wine blend* (Claret)

ROBERT MONDAVI
Oakville
★★☆

Established in 1966 by Bob Mondavi, who hoped to build a wine dynasty, and appeared to have succeeded beyond his wildest dreams by the 1980s. However, the Mondavi brand struggled to maintain its value in the new millennium, when profits plunged by 40 per cent, and the company was sold to Constellation Brands in November 2004. The irony is that the top Robert Mondavi wines remain as great as they have ever been. Cabernet Sauvignon is Mondavi's greatest strength, even at the basic Napa Valley appellation, which can be very special in years such as 2000 and 2002. This winery has been rightly accused of turning out large volumes of very ordinary wine, yet it would be rated two and a half stars if judged on Cabernet Sauvignon alone, as its Stags Leap District *cuvée*, and single-vineyard wines from To Kalon, Vine Hill, and Moffet are all on the same top quality level as the Reserve. The Io is not sold under the Mondavi name and its Santa Barbara mix (Syrah, Grenache, Mourvèdre) often contains more Syrah than some supposedly pure Syrah varietals.

✓ *Cabernet Sauvignon • Classic red blend* (Boomerang! Io) • *Riesling* (Private Selection) • *Sauvignon Blanc* (To Kalon I Block Fumé Blanc)

ROBERT PECOTA WINERY
Calistoga
★☆ Ⓥ

This under-rated winery always made ravishing white wines, and now has an excellent Cabernet.

✓ *Cabernet Sauvignon* (Kara's Vineyard) • *Muscat Canelli* (Moscato di Andrea)

ROBERT PEPI WINERY
Oakville
★☆ Ⓥ

This winery is still excellent value for Sauvignon Blanc, but is developing a reputation for interesting Italian-based blends.

✓ *Barbera • Classic red blend* (Colline di Sassi) • *Sangiovese • Sauvignon Blanc*

ROBERT SINSKEY VINEYARDS
Napa
Ⓑ★☆

These vineyards produce vividly flavoured Pinot, classy Vineyard Reserve, luscious Vin Gris, and crisp, age-worthy Chardonnay.

✓ *Chardonnay • Classic red blend* (Vineyard Reserve) • *Pinot Noir • Rosé* (Vin Gris of Pinot Noir)

SADDLEBACK
Oakville
★★☆

Nils Venge, formerly at Groth, is a master of the massive, old-fashioned, port-like style of Zinfandel.

✓ *Sangiovese* (Penny Lane Vineyard) • *Zinfandel*

SAINTSBURY
Napa
★★☆

David Graves and Dick Ward make plump, juicy Pinot Noir at this increasingly impressive winery.

✓ *Chardonnay • Pinot Noir*

SCHRAMSBERG VINEYARDS
Calistoga
★

This prestigious winery started the modern California sparkling-wine industry rolling in 1965 and, until Domaine Chandon was set up a few years later, was the only producer of serious-quality bottle-fermented sparkling wine in the US. The head winemakers at Codorníu, Franciscan, Kristone, Mumm Napa Valley, and Piper-Sonoma all cut their teeth here.

✓ *Sparkling wine* (Blanc de Noirs, Crémant, J Schram)

SCREAMING EAGLE
Oakville
★★☆

Tiny quantities of cult Cabernet Sauvignon, always excruciatingly expensive, and mostly of exceptional quality, although I have found the odd under-performer at blind tastings.

✓ *Cabernet Sauvignon*

SEAVEY
St Helena
★

Small quantities of beautifully crafted Cabernet Sauvignon wines are produced here. The Merlot is good, but less intense.

✓ *Cabernet Sauvignon • Merlot*

SEQUOIA GROVE
Napa
★

Jim and Steve Allen have been producing great Cabernet Sauvignon since 1978, and are now sourcing fine Chardonnay from Carneros.

✓ *Cabernet Sauvignon • Chardonnay*

SHAFER VINEYARDS
Napa
★★☆

Although the Cabernet Sauvignon Hillside Select is definitely the best wine, Shafer also makes very stylish Merlot and Chardonnay. The deliciously smooth Firebreak is a sort of Californian Super-Tuscan, while Relentless is a powerful blend of Syrah and Petite Sirah.

✓ *Cabernet Sauvignon* (Hillside Select) • *Chardonnay • Classic red blend* (Firebreak, Relentless) • *Merlot*

SIGNORELLO VINEYARDS
Napa
★★☆ Ⓥ

The late Ray "Padrone" Signorello bought a vineyard on the Silverado Trail as long ago as 1970s, but only came to the fore with a bewildering display of fruity yet complex wines in the 1990s. If anything, the quality and consistency have stepped up a gear under Ray Signorello, Jr.

✓ *Cabernet Sauvignon* (Estate) • *Chardonnay* (Hope's Cuvée, Vieilles Vignes) • *Classic red blend* (Padrone) • *Classic white blend* (Seta) • *Zinfandel* (Luvisi Vineyard)

SILVER OAK CELLARS
Oakville
★

Concentrates solely on one variety, Cabernet Sauvignon, but there are three – Napa Valley, Bonny's Vineyard (also Napa Valley AVA), and Alexander Valley. I prefer the latter because it has the least oak and the most finesse.

✓ *Cabernet Sauvignon* (Alexander Valley)

SILVERADO VINEYARDS
Napa
★★☆

Silverado is owned by the widow of the late Walt Disney, but it has never produced a Mickey Mouse wine.

✓ *Cabernet Sauvignon* (Limited Reserve, Stags Leap Vineyard) • *Sangiovese • Sauvignon Blanc*

SMITH-MADRONE
St Helena
★★☆

This winery consists of some 16 hectares (40 acres) of high-altitude vines producing a small, high-quality range of wines.

✓ *Cabernet Sauvignon •
Chardonnay • Riesling*

SPOTTSWOODE
St Helena
◉★★

On benchland in the Mayacamas
Mountains, the Novak family
produce just two wines – tiny
amounts of powerful but stylish
Cabernet Sauvignon, and a
deliciously fresh Sauvignon Blanc.

✓ *Cabernet Sauvignon •
Sauvignon Blanc*

SPRING MOUNTAIN
VINEYARDS
St Helena
★★

Known to millions as "Falcon Crest",
this winery can produce wines that
require ageing and develop finesse.

✓ *Classic red blend* (Elivette –
formerly sold as Reserve) •
Sauvignon Blanc • Syrah

ST CLEMENT VINEYARDS
St Helena
★★

One of the best-performing California
wineries in the Beringer-Blass group.

✓ *Cabernet Sauvignon •
Chardonnay • Classic red blend*
(Oroppas) • *Merlot*

ST SUPÉRY
Rutherford
★★ⓥ

Capable of producing Cabernet
of a rare level of finesse, and a
deliciously tangy, yet inexpensive
Sauvignon Blanc. Owned by Robert
Skalli of South of France fame.

✓ *Cabernet Sauvignon* (Dollarhide
Ranch, Napa Valley) • *Classic red
blend* (Elú Meritage, Rutherford
Limited Edition) • *Merlot •
Muscat Canelli* (Moscato) •
Sauvignon Blanc • Sémillon
(Dollarhide Ranch)

STAG'S LEAP
WINE CELLARS
Napa
★★

This is the famous Stag's Leap, with
the apostrophe before the "s" and its
legendary, ultra-expensive Cabernet
Sauvignon Cask 23, although its Fay
Vineyard and SLV can sometimes
rival it in quality. Artemis is a lighter,
easier-drinking, highly recommended,
less expensive blend of the Stag's
Leap Arcadia vineyard with the
leftovers from the selection of the
three top Cabernet Sauvignons. Its
second label is Hawk Crest.

✓ *Cabernet Sauvignon •
Chardonnay* (Arcadia)

STAGS' LEAP WINERY
Napa
★

This is the other Stags' Leap winery,
with the apostrophe after the "s"

and less well known, although,
ironically, the first to be established,
as long ago as 1893. Stags' Leap
Winery makes good Cabernet
Sauvignon, particularly the Reserve,
but it is not in the same class as the
better-known Stag's Leap, whereas
it does make one of California's
finest Petite Sirah wines.

✓ *Cabernet Sauvignon • Petite Sirah*
(Petite Syrah)

STERLING VINEYARDS
Calistoga
★

Astonishingly high quality in the
mid-1970s, Sterling's standards
dropped after Coca-Cola purchased
it in 1978, but started a revival
when Seagram took over in 1983
and has continued to improve.

✓ *Cabernet Sauvignon* (Napa Valley
Reserve) • *Chardonnay* (Napa
Valley Reserve, Carneros Winery
Lake) • *Merlot* (Three Palms,
Napa Vy Reservealle)

STONY HILL
VINEYARD
St Helena
★

The Chardonnays here are still
world-class, but fatter than before.

✓ *Chardonnay*

STORYBOOK MOUNTAIN
VINEYARDS
Calistoga
★★

Jerry Seps, a former university
professor, has created a reputation
for one of California's finest
Zinfandels on this mountain
vineyard, originally established by
Adam and Jacob Grimm in 1880.

✓ *Zinfandel*

SUTTER HOME
WINERY
St Helena
★ⓥ

Zinfandel of one style or another
accounts for the majority of this
winery's vast production under the
state-wide California AVA. Some
wines are brilliant one year, but
nothing special the next, making
recommendations difficult, but
when the wines are good, the
value is always great.

✓ *Chenin Blanc • Sauvignon Blanc*

SWITCHBACK RIDGE
Calistoga
★★

This converted orchard on the
Peterson Ranch at the northern end
of the Silverado Trail makes some
of Napa's best and biggest reds.

✓ *Cabernet Sauvignon • Merlot •
Petite Sirah*

THE HESS COLLECTION
Napa
★★

Swiss-born art collector David Hess
makes wines to be consumed not

collected, although they do last
well. Readers should note that Hess
Select is a second label, not a
premium *cuvée*.

✓ *Cabernet Sauvignon* (Mount
Veeder)

TITUS
St Helena
★★

Lee Titus brought his family from
Minnesota to Napa, where he
purchased this vineyard in separate
lots in 1967. He replanted with
classic varieties, and began to
supply some of the top Napa Valley
brands until the next generation
decided to make and sell their
own wine. With Phillip Titus as
winemaker, and his brother Eric
running both the business and the
vineyard, Titus now threatens to
become "the most fashionable new
name in California winedom",
according to Robert Parker.

✓ *Cabernet Franc*

TREFETHEN VINEYARDS
Napa
★

This winery combines quality and
consistency with good value.

✓ *Cabernet Sauvignon •
Chardonnay* (Library Selection)
• *Riesling*

TRINCHERO WINERY
Napa
★ⓥ

Although Sutter Home is the bigger
brand and gets all the press, it has
been owned by the Trinchero family
since 1947, and they make sure that
some pretty good wines go out
under their own label.

✓ *Cabernet Sauvignon* (Mario's
Vineyard) • *Classic red blend*
(Mario's Reserve Meritage) •
Sauvignon Blanc (Family
Reserve)

TURLEY
Napa
★★★

Talented brother and sister
winemakers Larry and Helen Turley
produce a raft of spectacular
Zinfandel, with Petite Syrah (*sic*)
and other interesting odds and ends.

✓ *Charbono* (Tofanelli Vineyard) •
Petite Syrah (sic) • *Zinfandel*

V SATTUI
St Helena
★★ⓥ

This under-rated winery boasts a
large range of relatively inexpensive,
award-winning wines, but is let
down by its rustic, 1950s labelling
and presentation. Understated livery
would do wonders.

✓ *Cabernet Sauvignon* (Morisoli
Vineyard, Suzanne's Vineyard) •
Chardonnay (Napa Valley) •
Classic red blend (Family Red) •
Fortified (Madeira) • *Merlot*
(Napa Valley) • *Riesling* (Dry

Johannisberg, Off-Dry
Johannisberg) • *Rosé* (Gamay
Rouge) • *Zinfandel* (Duarte
Vineyard "Old Vine")

VIADER
St Helena
◉★★

Tiny quantities of deeply coloured,
concentrated, red Bordeaux-style
wine blended from vines grown on
the slopes of Howell Mountain.
Viader is a blend of 55–70 per cent
Cabernet Sauvignon with Cabernet
Franc, while the firmer V is typically
58 per cent Petit Verdot, 34 per cent
Cabernet Sauvignon, 8 per cent
Cabernet Franc.

✓ *Classic red blend* (V, Viader)

VILLA MT EDEN WINERY
Oakville
★ⓥ

Owned by Stimson Lane, Villa Mt
Eden established a high reputation
in the 1980s, but has become less
exciting since branching into a wider
range of wines, although the wines
that do excel are always great value.

✓ *Cabernet Sauvignon* (Grand
Reserve, Signature) • *Chardonnay*
(Grand Reserve, Signature)

WHITEHALL LANE
WINERY
St Helena
★★

Despite various owners, Whitehall
Lane consistently produces inspired
wines, as endorsed by the *Decanter*
World Wine Awards, when its 2001
Reserve Cabernet Sauvignon swept
the boards to carry off the North
American Bordeaux Varietal Trophy.

✓ *Cabernet Sauvignon • Merlot*

WILLIAM HILL WINERY
Napa
★★

An improving winery in the Allied-
Domecq stable.

✓ *Cabernet Sauvignon •
Chardonnay • Merlot*

ZD WINES
Napa
★★

Pronounced "Zee Dee", this winery
used to make variable Cabernet
Sauvignons, but is now very
consistent; this wine now challenges
Chardonnay's position as ZD's best
varietal, and ZD sometimes comes
out with a killer Pinot Noir (the
2000 Carneros Reserve).

✓ *Cabernet Sauvignon •
Chardonnay • Pinot Noir*
(Carneros Reserve)

THE CENTRAL COAST (NORTH)

Originally a district where a few big companies produced a vast quantity of inexpensive wines, the northern Central Coast can now boast a large number of top-quality, highly individual wineries.

WINEMAKING IN THE northern Central Coast district dates from the 1830s, when virtually all the vineyards were in and around Santa Clara County; this remained so until the late 1950s and early 1960s, when the growing urban sprawl of San Jose forced the industry to search out new areas for vine-growing. This search coincided with the publication of a climatic report based on heat summation (*see* p538) by the University of California, pinpointing cooler areas farther south, particularly in Monterey, that should support fine-wine vineyards.

THE MOVE TO MONTEREY

In 1957, Mirassou and Paul Masson were the first companies to make the move, buying some 530 hectares (1,300 acres) in the Salinas Valley. Some areas, however, were too cool or exposed to excessive coastal winds. These failures were due to producers who could not conceive that grapes would not ripen in California.

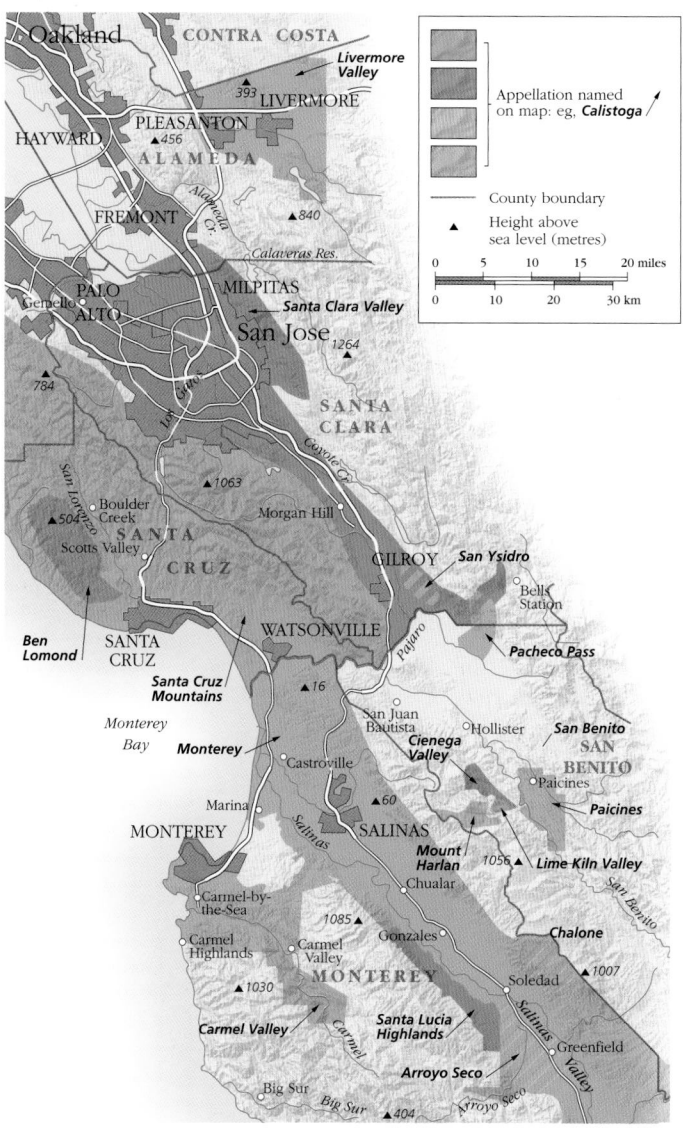

FACTORS AFFECTING TASTE AND QUALITY

LOCATION
The Central Coast's northern sector stretches from the San Francisco Bay area to Monterey.

CLIMATE
Generally warm (Region III, *see* p538), but with variations such as the cooler (Region I, *see* p538) areas of the Santa Cruz Mountains and the northern part of the Salinas Valley. Low rainfall in the south necessitates much irrigation, but there are micro-climates with higher rainfall.

ASPECT
Vines are planted mainly on the flat and sloping lands of the various valleys. Variations are found: on the steep slopes of the Santa Cruz Mountains and the high benchland of the Pinnacles above Soledad, for example.

SOIL
A wide variety of gravel loams, often high in stone content and rich in limestone, in the Livermore Valley; clay and gravel loams in Santa Clara; sandy and gravelly loams over granite or limestone in San Benito; and gravelly, well-drained, low-fertility soils in Monterey.

VITICULTURE AND VINIFICATION
A small number of big wine companies produce a vast quantity of inexpensive wines utilizing high-tech, production-line methods. The number of small wineries is growing. Many of these are quality-conscious and some are justifiably famous.

GRAPE VARIETIES
Barbera, Cabernet Sauvignon, Carignane (Carignan), Chardonnay, Chenin Blanc, Colombard, Gamay, Gewürztraminer, Grenache, Grey Riesling (Trousseau Gris), Mourvèdre, Muscat, Petite Sirah (Durif), Pinot Blanc, Pinot Gris, Pinot Noir, Sauvignon Blanc, Sémillon, Syrah, Trebbiano (Ugni Blanc), Viognier, White Riesling (Riesling), Zinfandel

In October 1966, the two authors of the heat-summation study, professors Winkler and Amerine, were honoured at a special luncheon where a toast was made to "the world's first fine-wine district established as the direct result of scientific temperature research". Although this might have seemed premature, it has been substantiated by Monterey's viticultural growth. Bill Jekel first brought the quality potential of this area to international fame, but this winery has been eclipsed by an eclectic bunch such as Bonny Doon, David Bruce, Calera, Chalone, Edmunds St John, Frick, Morgan, Mount Eden, Ridge, Rosenblum, and Tamas.

JEKEL VINEYARDS
Oak barrels wait to be filled at one of the Central Coast's pioneering wineries. Intensive irrigation systems have made the hot, dry Salinas Valley more synonymous with crisp salad vegetables than with wines, and the new pioneering wineries have moved into the hills.

THE CENTRAL COAST (NORTH), *see also p538*
Although Santa Clara County is still the Central Coast's northern heartland, it has long been in a slow decline, while Monterey and Santa Cruz are the area's fastest-growing counties.

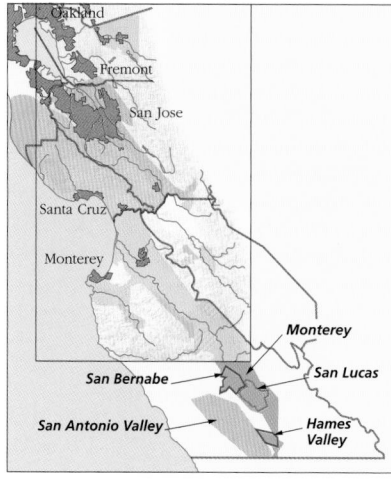

The Central Coast (North) extended area

THE APPELLATIONS OF
THE CENTRAL COAST (NORTH)

ALAMEDA COUNTY AO

This appellation covers grapes grown anywhere within Alameda County.

ARROYO SECO AVA
Monterey County

Triangular-shaped, sloping benchland, with frost-free vineyards of coarse sandy loam.

BEN LOMOND MOUNTAIN AVA
Santa Cruz County

This AVA covers 155 square kilometres (60 square miles) on Ben Lomond Mountain, encompassing just 28 hectares (70 acres) of vines.

CARMEL VALLEY AVA
Monterey County

This appellation covers 78 square kilometres (30 square miles) around the Carmel River and Cachagua Creek. A distinctive microclimate is created by the valley's elevation and the north-eastern Tularcitos Ridge, which curbs the marine fog and provides more sunny days.

CHALONE AVA
Monterey County

Benchland vineyards at 500 metres (1,650 feet) above sea level, with volcanic and granitic soils of high limestone content. The soil combines with an arid climate to stress the vines. Suited to Chardonnay, Pinot Noir, and Pinot Blanc.

CIENEGA VALLEY AVA
San Benito County

The Cienega valley is located at the base of the Gabilan (or Gavilan) Mountain Range where the Pescadero Creek is used artificially to augment the area's rainfall. The soil is loamy, well-drained, and often lies over weathered granite.

CONTRA COSTA COUNTY AO

An appellation covering grape varieties grown anywhere within Contra Costa County.

HAMES VALLEY AVA
Monterey County

North of Lake Nacimiento, where more than 250 hectares (600 acres) of vineyards already exist.

LIME KILN VALLEY AVA
San Benito County

Annual rainfall ranges from 41 centimetres (16 inches) on the valley floor to 102 centimetres (40 inches) in the mountainous west. Soils are sandy and gravelly loams over limestone, with a high magnesium carbonate content.

LIVERMORE VALLEY AVA
Alameda County

One of the coastal inter-mountain valleys surrounding San Francisco, the Livermore Valley has a moderate climate, cooled by sea breezes and morning fog, with very little spring frost.

MONTEREY AVA
Monterey County

This AVA is distinguished by a very dry climate, although the watersheds of the Santa Lucia, Gabilan, and Diablo Mountain Ranges provide sufficient water, through the presence of underground aquifers, to irrigate the vineyards.

MONTEREY COUNTY AO

An appellation covering grapes that are grown anywhere within Monterey County.

MOUNT HARLAN AVA
San Benito County

Like Chalone, Mount Harlan is, for all intents and purposes, a single-winery AVA (Calera in this instance), and is situated on rare limestone outcrops in the same range of hills (the San Benito Range), albeit at the other end and on the opposite-facing flank, and higher – 670 metres (2,200 feet).

PACHECO PASS AVA
Santa Clara and San Benito Counties

The terrain sets this area apart from its neighbours. It is a small valley, with a flat or gently sloping topography that contrasts with the rugged hills of the Diablo Range to the east and west. The climate is moderate and wetter than that of the Hollister Basin to the south.

PAICINES AVA
San Benito County

Here the days are warm and the nights cool, and the annual rainfall ranges between 30 and 38 centimetres (12 and 15 inches). This AVA has fallen into disuse since Almadén, the winery that proposed it, moved to Santa Clara.

SAN BENITO AVA
San Benito County

Not to be confused with San Benito County, this AVA encapsulates the smaller AVAs of Paicines, Cienega Valley, and Lime Kiln Valley.

SAN BENITO COUNTY AO

This is an appellation covering grapes grown anywhere within San Benito County.

SAN FRANCISCO BAY AVA

This appellation encompasses more than 1.5 million acres that are, to some degree, affected by coastal fog and winds from San Francisco Bay. It also includes the city of San Francisco, apparently to justify the appellation name, but this could lead to the emergence of Moraga-like vineyards (*see* p574).

SAN LUCAS AVA
Monterey County

This AVA consists of a 16-kilometre (10-mile) segment of the Salinas Valley between King City and San Ardo, in the southern section of Monterey County. The soils in this area are mostly alluvial loams.

SAN MATEO COUNTY AO

This is an appellation covering grapes grown anywhere within San Mateo County.

SAN YSIDRO AVA
Santa Clara County

The appellation covers a small enclave of vineyards at the southeastern end of the Santa Clara AVA. San Ysidro sits between two hills that channel the sea breezes coming up the Pajaro River, and is particularly noted for Chardonnay.

SANTA CLARA COUNTY AO

This is an appellation covering grapes grown anywhere within Santa Clara County.

SANTA CLARA VALLEY AVA
Santa Clara County

Encompassing the entire municipality of San Jose to the north and better known as Silicon Valley in the south, this AVA must qualify as the most built-up wine appellation in the world.

SANTA CRUZ MOUNTAINS AVA
Santa Clara County

The name "Santa Cruz Mountains" was first recorded in 1838. Its climate is influenced in the west by ocean breezes and maritime fog, while the east is moderated by San Francisco Bay. Cool air coming down from the mountains forces warmer air up, lengthening the growing season to a full 300 days. The soils are forms of shale that are peculiar to the area.

THE WINE PRODUCERS OF
THE CENTRAL COAST (NORTH)

BONNY DOON VINEYARD
Santa Cruz County
★★ⓥ

This is one of California's brightest, most bizarre, and most innovative stars, with wines that are electrifying in their brilliance and style, often showing surprising finesse. I have got lost trying to find Bonny Doon on two occasions, but it was worth the effort just to meet the whacky winemaker, Randall Grahm. In 2001, Grahm officially declared himself "off his rocker" when he macerated three wines on ground-up rocks from three different parcels of his Cigare Volant red wine. This led to an extremely limited run of "The Rock Quartet". In 2006, Grahm sold off his bestselling Cardinal Zin and Big House brands to The Wine Group – "Doonsizing", as he termed it, from 400,000 cases to just 40,000. And in that same year, he also separated out his Pacific Rim label, which was located in Washington State; this was sold to Italy's Castello Banfi in 2010. Bonny Doon still holds the power to fascinate, however.

√ *Entire range*

DAVID BRUCE
Santa Cruz County
★ ❤

Having gone through a learning curve, David Bruce now produces far more elegant wines than he used to. Pinot Noir has emerged as his consistently finest style.

✓ *Merlot* (Central Coast) • *Petite Syrah* (sic) (Central Coast, Shell Creek Vineyard) • *Pinot Noir* • *Zinfandel* (Paso Robles)

CALERA WINE COMPANY
San Benito County
★★

One of California's premier pioneers in the continuing quest for perfect Pinot Noir, Calera continues to produce some of the state's greatest examples of this wine, although the focus on varietal purity can sometimes result in overly pretty fruit.

✓ *Pinot Noir* • *Viognier*

CARACCIOLI
Monterey County

This small family-owned enterprise has cleverly secured the services of Michel Salgues, who established the reputation of Roederer Estate and is now one of just a few truly world-class sparkling-wine consultants. Some would say he is the best. Certainly these *cuvées* demonstrate a degree of class rarely seen in California sparkling wines.

✓ *Sparkling wine* (Brut, Brut Rosé)

CEDAR MOUNTAIN
Alameda County
★ ❤

This boutique winery was established in 1990 and early vintages are promising, if a little too correct and in need of a personal signature.

✓ *Cabernet Sauvignon* • *Fortified* (Chardonnay del Sol) • *Zinfandel*

CHALONE VINEYARD
Monterey County
★★

This winery's 63-hectare (155-acre) vineyard has its own AVA. The Chenin Blanc is from the Gavilan Mountain ridge, 540 metres (1800 feet) above the Salinas Valley, where the vines were planted as long ago as 1919. These venerable vines have the capacity to make California's finest Chenin Blanc, and in some years they succeed in doing so, although there is variation in quality.

✓ *Chardonnay* • *Chenin Blanc* • *Pinot Blanc* • *Pinot Noir*

CONCANNON VINEYARD
Alameda County
☆

This winery continues to make fine Petite Sirah wines, but is also getting a name for its Merlot.

✓ *Merlot* (Selected Vineyard) *Petite Sirah* (Heritage)

CONUNDRUM
Monterey County
★★

Under the same ownership as Caymus Vineyard, where Conundrum started out as a new addition to the range in 1989. Conundrum was created by Jon Bolta, who had assisted in the making of Caymus wines, and who has made every vintage to date. The idea behind Conundrum was to make a blended white wine to suit the new Pacific cuisine of coastal California. Jon originally experimented with 11 white grapes before deciding on the five that have been used ever since: Sauvignon Blanc, Chardonnay, Muscat Canelli, Sémillon, and Viognier.

✓ *Classic white blend* (Conundrum)

EDMUNDS ST JOHN
Alameda County
★☆

Steven Edmunds and Cornelia St John established this exciting winery in 1985 in what used to be the East Bay Wine Works, where they have honed some of California's most beautifully balanced wines, with a particular penchant for classy Syrah.

✓ *Syrah* • *Viognier* (Rozet Vineyard)

FRICK WINERY
Santa Cruz County
★

This winery is an up-and-coming Rhône-style specialist with a hands-off approach to winemaking.

✓ *Cinsaut* • *Classic red blend* (C2) • *Syrah*

HAHN ESTATES
Monterey County
★☆ ❤

Nicky Hahn of Smith & Hook launched this label in 1991, and his flavour-packed, bargain wines now have their own dedicated winery.

✓ *Cabernet Franc* • *Classic red blend* (Meritage) • *Merlot* (Central Coast, Cycles Gladiator) • *Syrah*

HELLER ESTATE VINEYARDS
Monterey County
◉★☆

Although under new ownership since the death of Bill Durney, this winery continues to produce heroically dark, rich, densely flavoured Cabernet Sauvignon, and splendidly long-lived Chardonnay, with Celebration the standout wine.

✓ *Cabernet Sauvignon* • *Chardonnay* • *Classic red blend* (Celebration Meritage) • *Merlot*

J C CELLARS
Alameda County
★★

The personal label of Jeff "Rhône-in-his-Bones" Cohn specializes in single-vineyard, hillside-grown Syrah, Petite Syrah (one of California's best), Viognier, and Zinfandel.

✓ *Petite Sirah* • *Syrah* • *Viognier*

JEKEL VINEYARD
Monterey County
★ ❤

Once known for its fascinating range of Riesling, this winery owned by Brown-Forman was closed in February 2004, but the vineyards have been retained and production of wines under this label continues. Even before the closure, this was no longer the force it used to be in Bill Jekel's heyday, although some wines still excite.

✓ *Classic red blend* (Sanctuary) • *Syrah* (Monterey County)

J LOHR
Santa Clara County
★ ❤

The Valdigué used to be labelled Gamay until correctly identified by UC Davis. It is made in a fruity Gamay style that is not just a good quaffer, but really quite elegant and well perfumed with plenty of refreshing acidity.

✓ *Cabernet Sauvignon* (Crosspoint) • *Chardonnay* (Arroyo Vista Vineyard) • *Classic red blend* (Cuvée Pom Meritage) • *Valdigué* (Wildflower)

MORGAN WINERY
Monterey County
★★ ❤

Possibly California's most underrated, age-worthy Pinot Noir and Chardonnay are produced here. Although plenty of Americans love good Burgundy, such consumers are by and large not avid fans of West Coast wines, and regular California wine drinkers are often put off by Morgan's Burgundian-like character. Those of you who fall between these two stools should give these wines a try. The fresh, zesty Sauvignon Blanc is consistently good, but the Rhône-style wines need some work.

✓ *Chardonnay* • *Pinot Noir* • *Sauvignon Blanc*

MOUNT EDEN VINEYARDS
Santa Clara County
★

This winery produces just three varietals. The range of Chardonnay excels, but the deep, dark, chocolaty Old Vines Cabernet comes a close second.

✓ *Cabernet Sauvignon* (Cuvée Saratoga, Old Vine Reserve) • *Chardonnay*

MURRIETA'S WELL
Alameda County

Run by Phil Wente, whose blends are significantly better than his pure varietal wines. His style is generally understated, but finer than that of his more prominent brother, Eric of Wente Bros. The red Vendimia is a classic Bordeaux-style blend, while Zarzuela is Tempranillo-based.

✓ *Classic red blend* (Vendimia, Zarzuela) • *Classic white blend* (Vendimia)

RIDGE VINEYARDS
Santa Clara County
★★

Those who wonder about the long-term maturation potential of California wines should taste these stunning ones, some of which need between 10 and 20 years in bottle before they are even approachable.

✓ *Cabernet Sauvignon* (Monte Bello) • *Chardonnay* (Howell Mountain, Santa Cruz Mountains) • *Classic red blend* (Geyserville) • *Mourvèdre* (Mataro) • *Petite Sirah* (York Creek) • *Zinfandel*

ROSENBLUM CELLARS
Alameda County
★★ ❤

Established in 1978 by Kent Rosenblum, a Minnesotan who came to California to set up a veterinary practice but got sidetracked by the local wines. He produces over 100,000 cases of over 40 different wines from more than 75 vineyards throughout California, plus a few in Australia, and still finds time to run his veterinary practice. Excellent-value wines also sold under the Chateau La Paws and Cote de Bone labels.

✓ *Cabernet Sauvignon* • *Classic red blend* (Holbrook Mitchell Trio) • *Dessert style* (Rosie Rabbit Zinfandel) • *Marsanne* (Dry Creek) • *Merlot* (Mountain Selection) • *Mourvèdre* (Continente Vineyard) • *Muscat Canelli* (Muscat de Glacier) • *Petite Sirah* (Rockpile) • *Syrah* (England Shaw, Hillside Vineyards) • *Viognier* (Ripken Ranch Late Harvest) • *Zinfandel*

ROBERT TALBOTT VINEYARDS
Monterey County
★

Run by the son of the late founder, the Talbott family is best known for the internationally renowned Monterey-based Talbott Tie Company.

✓ *Chardonnay*

WENTE BROS
Alameda County
★ ❤

Established for more than a century, Wente's wines used to range from overtly fruity to distinctly dull, but have improved in recent years.

✓ *Chardonnay* (Riva Ranch Reserve) • *Sauvignon Blanc* (Livermore Valley)

THE CENTRAL COAST (SOUTH)

An up-and-coming wine district in general, the southern Central Coast has very rapidly become one of the very best areas in the world, outside of Burgundy itself, for Pinot Noir. Chardonnay is equally exciting, and Italian varietals could well be the most prized wines of the new millennium.

PASO ROBLES IN SAN LUIS OBISPO COUNTY was originally planted with vines in the late 18th century; the Santa Ynez Valley, in Santa Barbara County, had a flourishing wine industry in pre-Prohibition times, and Santa Barbara town was once dotted with vineyards. Yet both counties were virtually devoid of vines in the early 1960s; it was not until Estrella, in Paso Robles, and Firestone, in Santa Ynez Valley, established vineyards in 1972 that others followed.

Quite why Santa Barbara of all areas in the southern Central Coast has suddenly become the mecca for Pinot Noir specialists is difficult to unravel. In the late 1980s, California seemed the least likely place to be in a position to challenge Burgundy for the Holy Grail of winemaking. Oregon and New Zealand looked much more likely, but they have both since proved too small and prone to inconsistency. If it was going to be California, 15 years ago no one would have put their money on Santa Barbara, way down south, just a stone's throw from Los Angeles; Carneros or Russian River seemed a more likely bet. The foundations for Santa Barbara's sudden surge of wonderful Pinot Noir wines were laid

innocently in the 1970s, when the land was relatively cheap and planted with this variety in order to supply the sparkling-wine industry in the north of the state. It is impossible to pinpoint exactly when local winemakers realized the potential of making their own still wine, but much of California's finest, purest, and most consistent Pinot Noir wines now come from this valley.

The Santa Ynez Valley makes the best Santa Barbara Pinot, yet the area where it excels is restricted: 14 kilometres (9 miles) from the ocean and the valley is too cool to ripen grapes; 26 kilometres (16 miles) and it is ideal for Pinot Noir; but for every 1.5 kilometres (1 mile) farther from the ocean the grapes gain an extra degree (ABV) of ripeness, and by 32 kilometres (20 miles) from the coast, this is Cabernet country. The best Pinot Noir vineyard in the Santa Ynez Valley is Sanford & Benedict. In the Santa Maria Valley, also well suited to Pinot Noir, the best vineyard is Bien Nacido.

FACTORS AFFECTING TASTE AND QUALITY

LOCATION
This stretches southwards along the coast from Monterey, and includes the counties of San Luis Obispo and Santa Barbara.

CLIMATE
Generally warm (Region III, *see* p538), except for areas near the sea, particularly around Santa Maria in the middle of the region where Regions I and II (*see* p538) prevail because of the regular incursion of the tail of the great coastal fog bank. Annual rainfall ranges from 25 centimetres (10 inches) to 114 centimetres (45 inches).

ASPECT
Most vines grow on hillsides in San Luis Obispo and southern-facing benchland in Santa Barbara County, at altitudes from 37 to 180 metres (120 to 600 feet) in the Edna Valley, to 180 to 305 metres (600 to 1,000 feet) in Paso Robles, and 460 metres (1,500 feet) on York Mountain.

SOIL
Mostly sandy, silty, or clay loams, but soil can be more alkaline, as in the gravelly lime soils on the Santa Lucia Mountains foothills.

VITICULTURE AND VINIFICATION
By the mid-1980s, the cooler areas

had invited experimentation with the Burgundian varieties planted in the early 1970s to supply sparkling-wine producers in the north of the state, and by the late 1980s a number of world-class Pinot Noirs had been produced. This variety is the region's main claim to fame, although viticultural methods are still developing, as indeed are vinification processes. Open-top fermenters are commonly used, the cap being punched down frequently. Some producers have incorporated 15–30 per cent whole-cluster, but most have shied away from this. A cold maceration is followed by natural yeast fermentation, the temperatures of which run nice and high. After a gentle pressing, the wines are matured in *barriques* with 25–50 per cent new oak. The oak is all French, and nearly everyone prefers tight-grain, with many going for a heavy toast.

GRAPE VARIETIES
Barbera, Cabernet Franc, Cabernet Sauvignon, Chardonnay, Chenin Blanc, Gewürztraminer, Malvasia, Muscat, Pinot Blanc, Pinot Noir, Sangiovese, Sauvignon Blanc, Sauvignonasse (Friulano), Sémillon, Sylvaner, Syrah, White Riesling (Riesling), Zinfandel

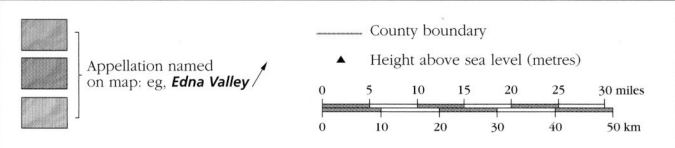

THE CENTRAL COAST (SOUTH), *see also p538*
Based on San Luis Obispo and Santa Barbara counties, this area has a fine reputation for top-quality Pinot Noir.

THE APPELLATIONS OF
THE CENTRAL COAST (SOUTH)

ARROYO GRANDE VALLEY AVA
San Luis Obispo County

An area of 173 square kilometres (67 square miles) some 19 kilometres (12 miles) southeast of the town of San Luis Obispo, the Arroyo Grande Valley enjoys a Region I to II climate (see p538), thanks primarily to its proximity to the ocean and the frequent fog produced by marine air in the mornings and evenings. Planted at an altitude of between 90 and 300 metres (300 and 1,000 feet), vines grow at much higher altitudes than those in the neighbouring Edna Valley AVA, and also receive slightly more rain. The hillsides cultivated range from moderate to very steep slopes, with deep, well-drained, sandy-clay and silty-clay loam soils. With a 17°C (30°F) drop in night-time temperatures, relatively high acidity levels are maintained throughout ripening. The potential for sparkling wine is considerable, so it is perhaps not surprising that Maison Deutz is the best-known winery here,

with the largest vineyards in the appellation. Deutz has also produced some still Chardonnay and Pinot Noir, and although rather strange, disjointed, and hardly indicative of any potential for such wines, Au Bon Climat has had stunning success with these varieties.

EDNA VALLEY AVA
San Luis Obispo County

This elongated valley is located just south of Paso Robles, and is well defined by the Santa Lucia Mountains to the northeast, the San Luis Range to the southwest, and a low hilly complex to the southeast. In the northwest, the Edna Valley merges with the Los Osos Valley, forming what is, in effect, a wide-mouthed funnel that sucks in ocean air from Morro Bay. This marine air flows unobstructed into the valley, where it is captured by the pocket of mountains and hills, providing a moderate summer climate that differentiates it from surrounding areas. The vines grow on the valley floor, rising to 120 metres (600 feet) in the Santa Lucia Mountains, on soils that are mostly sandy-clay loam, clay loam, and clay.

PASO ROBLES AVA
San Luis Obispo County

This area was given its name in the 18th century, when travellers passed through it on their way from the San Miguel to the San Luis Obispo missions. It is one of California's oldest winegrowing regions: grapes have been harvested in this area of rolling hills and valleys since c.1797. There is no penetration by coastal winds or marine fog and, consequently, there is the equivalent of an additional 500 to 1,000

degree-days here compared to viticultural areas to the west and east. This obviously has a considerable effect on grape-ripening patterns, making Paso Robles red-wine country, particularly for Zinfandel and Rhône varieties.

SAN LUIS OBISPO AO

An appellation covering grapes grown anywhere within the entire county of San Luis Obispo.

SANTA BARBARA AO

An appellation covering grapes grown anywhere within the entire county of Santa Barbara.

SANTA MARIA VALLEY AVA
Santa Barbara County

The Pacific winds blow along this funnel-shaped valley, causing cooler summers and winters and warmer autumns than in the surrounding areas. The terrain climbs from 60 to 240 metres (200 to 800 feet), with most of the vineyards concentrated at 90 metres (300 feet). The soil is sandy and clay loam, and is free from the adverse effects of salts. This is top-quality Pinot Noir country and Bien Nacido (to

RUGGED MOUNTAINS IN THE VAST LOS PADRES NATIONAL FOREST, CALIFORNIA
California's best wines are produced in areas cooled by the sea, bay winds, and the great coastal fog bank.
The Central Coast (South) has rapidly acquired a good reputation for its Pinot Noir.

which many winemakers have access) in the Tepesquet Bench area is far and away its best vineyard. Noises about Bien Nacido in the 1990s are reminiscent of the fuss made a decade earlier about the Sanford & Benedict vineyard in the Santa Ynez Valley. The Santa Maria Valley also grows top-quality Chardonnay and even one of California's best Syrahs.

SANTA RITA HILLS AVA
Santa Barbara County

This appellation is located almost entirely within the pre-existing Santa Ynez Valley AVA, and includes all the latter's coolest areas. The Santa Rita Hills is primarily planted with Chardonnay and Pinot Noir, although Syrah and Riesling are on the increase.

SANTA YNEZ VALLEY AVA
Santa Barbara County

The Santa Ynez Valley is bounded by mountains to the north and south, by Lake Cachuma to the east, and by a series of low hills to the west. The valley's close proximity to the ocean serves to moderate the weather with maritime fog, and this tends to lower the temperatures. The Santa Rita Hills block penetration of the coldest of the sea winds, however, so the middle and eastern end of the valley do not have the coolest of coastal climates (2,680 degree-days), while Lompoc, which is just 3 kilometres (2 miles) outside the appellation's western boundary, has just 1,970 degree days. The vineyards are located at an altitude of between 60 and 120 metres (200 and 400 feet) in the foothills of the San Rafael Mountains, and the vines are grown on soils that are mostly well drained, sandy, silty, clay, and shale loam. Santa Barbara's finest Pinot Noir wines come from the Sanford & Benedict vineyard (to which a number of winemakers have access) in the west, yet just a few miles farther up the valley it is Cabernet and Zinfandel country. The Santa Ynez Valley also grows top-quality Chardonnay.

TEMPLETON
San Luis Obispo County

Templeton is situated within Paso Robles. It is not an AVA, but I have included it for the purposes of clarification, because various sources have stated that it is. Even official publications from California's Wine Institute have made the same error.

YORK MOUNTAIN AVA
San Luis Obispo County

This small appellation is just 11 kilometres (7 miles) from the sea, situated at an altitude of 450 metres (1,500 feet) in the Santa Lucia Mountains, close to the western border of Paso Robles. Its Region I (*see* p538) climatic classification, and 114 centimetres (45 inches) of rain per year, set it apart from the warmer, and considerably drier, surrounding areas.

THE WINE PRODUCERS OF
THE CENTRAL COAST (SOUTH)

ALBAN VINEYARDS
San Luis Obispo County
★★

John Alban claims that his family-owned vineyard, founded in 1989, was "the first American winery and vineyard established exclusively for Rhône varieties". He certainly produces some of the best California Rhône varietals.

 Classic red blend (Pandora) • *Grenache* • *Syrah* • *Viognier*

ANDREW MURRAY
Santa Barbara County
★★

Up-and-coming, Rhône-style specialist, producing immaculately crafted wines from hillside vineyards.

 Classic white blend (Enchanté) • *Syrah* • *Viognier*

AU BON CLIMAT
Santa Barbara County
★★

It was Jim Clendenen's wines of the 1980s that convinced me of Santa Barbara's suitability to Pinot Noir, since when, of course, this area of the Central Coast has established a soaring reputation for Rhône grape varieties as well as Burgundian varieties.

 Chardonnay (especially Sanford & Benedict) • *Pinot Noir*

BABCOCK VINEYARDS
Santa Barbara County
★☆

Babcock vineyards best wines are the succulent Pinot Noir and, the deep, dark, rewarding Syrah.

 Chardonnay (Grand Cuvee) • *Pinot Noir* • *Sauvignon Blanc* • *Syrah*

BARON HERZOG
Santa Barbara County
★Ⓥ

A story of riches to rags and back to riches again. Eugene Herzog was born into an aristocratic family, who were renowned as suppliers of wine since the days of the Austro-Hungarian Empire. Having survived the Nazis only to see his property confiscated by the Communists, he fled Czechoslovakia in 1948, taking his family to New York, where he came down to earth with a bump, working as a driver and salesman for the Royal Wine Company. The company was short of cashflow, and paid part of his salary in shares, but Herzog's selling acumen was such that he became the majority shareholder, purchasing the rest of the company within 10 years of setting foot in the USA. The Baron Herzog winery was established in 1986, since when it has not been one of the flashy high-flyers, but has steadily produced a number of modestly priced, award-winning wines.

 Chenin Blanc (Clarksburg) • *Sauvignon Blanc* (California) • *Zinfandel* (Lodi Old Vines)

BLACKJACK RANCH
Santa Barbara County
★★☆

In 1989, Roger Wisted invented, patented, copyrighted, and trademarked "California Blackjack", the proceeds of which enabled him to indulge in his lifelong fantasy to plant his own vineyard. His first vintage was 1997, since when his wines have displayed a structure and acidity balance that sets them apart.

 Chardonnay • *Classic red blend* (Harmonie) • *Merlot* • *Syrah*

BONACCORSI
Santa Barbara County
★★

Master Sommelier Michael Bonaccorsi is formerly of Spago Restaurant in Beverly Hills, which has won the Wine Spectator's Best of Award of Excellence each year since 1995. In 1999, Bonaccorsi set up his own winery, which has swiftly achieved an enviable reputation for the highly polished style of its wines.

 Chardonnay • *Pinot Noir* • *Syrah*

BREWER-CLIFTON
Santa Barbara County
★★

Specialists in sourcing top-class Burgundian varietals from single-vineyards in the best areas of Santa Rita Hills AVA.

 Chardonnay • *Pinot Noir*

BYRON
Santa Barbara County
★★☆

Under Mondavi ownership since 1990, and now part of Jackson Family Wine Estates, these wines are still made by founder Byron Ken Brown, whose white wines are even better than his Pinot Noir.

 Chardonnay • *Pinot Blanc* • *Pinot Gris* • *Pinot Noir*

CAMBRIA
Santa Barbara County
★★☆

Personally owned by Jess Jackson's wife, Barbara Banke, rather than the Kendall-Jackson company, Cambria's strength is its extraordinary range of high-quality Chardonnay. Also produces interesting single-clone Pinot Noir wines from the same vineyard and vintage.

 Chardonnay • *Pinot Noir* (Rae's)

CLAIBORNE & CHURCHILL
San Luis Obispo County
★★☆Ⓥ

Alsatian specialists, with 25 years' experience, Claiborne Thompson and Fredericka Churchill are particularly enthusiastic about genuinely dry, classically structured Gewürztraminer. When I first heard of these wines I was sceptical, but as soon as I tasted them, I was convinced. Drink on purchase.

 Gewürztraminer (Dry Alsatian Style) • *Riesling* (Dry Alsatian Style)

COLD HEAVEN
Santa Barbara County
★★☆

Made by Jim Clendenen's wife, Morgan, whose main focus is on Viognier, but also produces an increasingly silky-stylish Pinot Noir.

 Pinot Noir (Le Bon Climat Vineyard) • *Viognier*

EBERLE WINERY
San Luis Obispo County
★★☆

Look no further if you want massively built Zinfandel, but the Cabernet is the better-balanced, much classier wine, while the Steinbeck Syrah is the best of both worlds.

 Barbera • *Cabernet Sauvignon* • *Muscat Canelli* • *Sangiovese* (Fillipponi & Thompson Vineyard) & *Syrah* (Steinbeck) • *Viognier* (Glenrose Vineyard)

EDNA VALLEY VINEYARD
San Luis Obispo County
★★☆

A joint venture between Chalone and the Niven family, who own the Paragon Vineyard, Edna Valley

Vineyard still produces rich, toasty Chardonnay and very good Pinot Noir, but now also turns out a refreshing Pinot Gris that has a certain spicy potential if given a couple of years' ageing. The Syrah has yet to find its feet, but other varieties are beginning to show promise.

✓ *Chardonnay* (Paragon Vineyard) • *Pinot Gris* (Paragon Vineyard) • *Pinot Noir* (Paragon Vineyard)

EPIPHANY VINEYARDS
Santa Barbara County
★ ✓

The personal winery of Eli Parker, son of Fess (*see below*).

✓ *Grenache* (Revelation Rodney's Vineyard) • *Pinot Gris*

FESS PARKER WINERY
Santa Barbara County
★ ✰ ✓

Unless you enjoyed a 1950s childhood, the name of actor Fess Parker is not likely to mean anything to you, but for me it will always be synonymous with his role as Davy Crockett, so it was quite amusing to see a fat American lady at least twice my age swoon in front of this still imposing figure. Unfortunately, she found all the wines too dry, even the excellent off-dry Riesling failed to please, but she did buy a poster of Mr Crockett taking a bath wearing just his coonskin hat. These wines get better with each vintage.

✓ *Chardonnay* (Marcella's Vineyard) • *Pinot Noir* • *Syrah* • *Viognier*

FIRESTONE VINEYARD
Santa Barbara County
★ ✓

Although Firestone can occasionally lapse, the wines are usually rich and ripe, and are gradually assuming more finesse.

✓ *Johannisberg Riesling* • *Merlot* • *Sauvignon Blanc* • *Syrah*

FOXEN VINEYARD
Santa Barbara County
★ ✰ ✓

I am not as enamoured as some by this winery's Pinot Noir, but have great respect for virtually everything else produced here.

✓ *Classic red blend* (Foothills Reserve) • *Pinot Noir* • *Syrah* • *Viognier*

GAINEY VINEYARDS
Santa Barbara County
★ ★ ✓

This winery still makes one of Santa Barbara's best Pinots, but is now best known for its Merlot, and turns out a number of amazing bargains.

✓ *Chardonnay* (Limited Selection) • *Merlot* (Limited Selection) • *Pinot Noir* (Limited Selection Santa Rita Hills) • *Riesling* (Santa Ynez Valley) • *Sauvignon Blanc* (Limited Selection) • *Syrah* (Limited Selection)

THE HITCHING POST
Santa Barbara County
★ ✰ ✓

Frank Ostini is the soft-spoken, friendly, fun-loving chef-owner of the Hitching Post restaurant in Santa Maria, which serves tasteful, unpretentious American barbecue food at its best. Frank also enjoys making wines with his fisherman friend, Gray Hartley. They started out in a corner of Jim Clendenen's Au Bon Climat winery, but in 2001 moved to Central Coast Wine Services in Santa Maria, and continue to make a number of excellent wines, particularly the polished Pinot Noirs.

✓ *Pinot Noir* • *Syrah* (Purisima Mountain)

L'AVENTURE
San Luis Obispo County
★ ★ ✰

Monstrous wines from *bordelais* Stephan Asseo, whose vision of Bordeaux meets Rhône in Pas Robles has attracted rave reviews. Second label: Stephan Ridge.

✓ *Classic red blend* (Côte-à-Côte, Cuvée) • *Syrah*

LANE TANNER
Santa Barbara County
★ ✰ ✓

The eponymous Lane Tanner established this small winery in 1989, since when she has honed a deliciously deep style of ripe, pure-flavoured Pinot Noir.

✓ *Pinot Noir* • *Syrah*

LONGORIA
Santa Barbara County
★ ★

Rick Longoria started making tiny quantities under his own label while he was at Gainey Vineyard, which he put on the map as winemaker there for 12 years. Now that he has his own winery, he still produces small batches of wine (ranging between 70 and 850 cases), but the quantities are massive by comparison with his early years. The quality is, however, even better – especially the Pinot Noir.

✓ *Chardonnay* • *Pinot Noir* • *Syrah* (Alisos Vineyard)

MOSBY WINERY
Santa Barbara County
★ ✰ ✓

Bill and Jeri Mosby run this interesting, sometimes provocative, Italian-style specialist operation.

✓ *Dolcetto* • *Pinot Grigio* • *Teroldego*

PALMINA
Santa Barbara County
★ ★ ❷

Some of California's greatest Italian style wines, especially the single-vineyard offerings, from the owners of Brewer-Clifton.

✓ *Barbera* • *Classic red blend* (Savoia) • *Nebbiolo* • *Pinot Grigio*

QUPÉ
Santa Barbara County
★ ✰ ❷

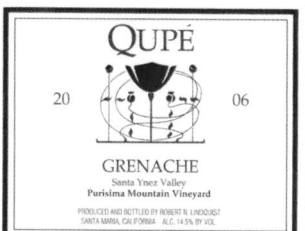

Owned by Bob Lindquist, who operates out of the Au Bon Climat winery. Great for Rhône-style reds, particularly the various single-vineyard Syrahs. Lindquist also owns Verdad with his wife Louisa.

✓ *Classic red blend* (Los Olivos) • *Grenache* (Purisma Mountain Vineyard) • *Syrah*

RANCHO SISQUOC
Santa Barbara County
★ ★ ✓

These vividly fruity wines come from one of Santa Barbara's first vineyards. Rancho Sisquoc covers 80 hectares (200 acres) of the massive 14,500-hectare (36,000-acre) Flood Ranch.

✓ *Cabernet Franc* • *Classic red blend* (Sisquoc River Red Meritage) • *Chardonnay* (Flood Vineyard) *Malbec* (Flood Family Vineyard) • *Riesling* (Flood Family Vineyard) • *Sylvaner*

RIVER RUN
Santa Clara County
★ ✓

After more than 30 years of continuous production, River Run has finally grabbed attention with an exciting-quality, well-priced Malbec.

✓ *Malbec* (Mannstand Vineyard)

SANFORD WINERY
Santa Barbara County
◉ ★ ★ ✓

One of the twin founders of the eponymous Sanford & Benedict vineyard, and modern-day pioneer of Santa Barbara winemaking in general, Richard Sanford released his first wine in 1976, and it is now hard to imagine why that should be Riesling. However, he quickly gained a stellar reputation for Pinot Noir, attracting dozens of crusading wineries to open up around him.

✓ *Pinot Noir* (La Riconada, Sanford & Benedict, Vin Gris Santa Rita Hills) • *Sauvignon Blanc*

SANTA BARBARA WINERY
Santa Barbara County
★ ✰ ✓

Although this is the oldest Santa Barbara winery, dating back to the early 1960s, it did not get interested in premium-quality wines until a decade later, after the Sanford & Benedict revolution. It soon began producing a number of great-value Burgundian varietals, and has since moved into Rhône-style wines, making some of the region's most impressive Syrah.

✓ *Chardonnay* (Lafond Vineyard, SRH) • *Nebbiolo* (Stolpman Vineyard) • *Pinot Noir* (Lafond Vineyard, SRH) • *Sauvignon Blanc* (Lafond Vineyard Late Harvest) • *Syrah* • *Zinfandel* (Beaujour, Essence)

TALLEY VINEYARDS
Santa Clara County
★ ✓

Burgundian-style specialists with 100 per cent estate-bottled production.

✓ *Chardonnay* • *Pinot Noir*

VERDAD
Santa Barbara County
★ ✰ ✓

Owned by Bob and Louisa Lindquist of Qupé, Verdad is, however, very much Louisa's baby, and she is starting to make waves with these Spanish-style wines.

✓ *Albariño* • *Rosé* • *Tempranillo* (Santa Ynez Valley)

WILD HORSE
San Luis Obispo County
★ ✓

Established in 1982 by Ken Volk, Wild Horse was acquired in 2003 by Fortune Brands, the owners of Geyser Peak. Wild Horse crushes some 30-odd grape varieties, and has something of a reputation for coming up with lesser-known varieties such as Arneis, Lagrein, Negrette, Tocai Friulano, Trousseau Gris, and Verdelho. There is a tendency to diversify into different brands, rather than create various ranges under the same label, Equus being the latest and most successful of such ventures.

✓ *Blaufränkisch* • *Grenache* (Equus James Berry Vineyard) • *Zinfandel*

ZACA MESA WINERY
Santa Barbara County
★ ✓

Best for inexpensive, refreshing Chardonnay, and exciting, low-yield Syrah.

✓ *Chardonnay* (Zaca Vineyard) • *Grenache* (Late Bottled) • *Roussanne* (Estate Bottled) • *Syrah* (Black Bear Block, Eight Barrel, The Mesa O & N)

THE CENTRAL VALLEY

While California's coastal areas are its most famous wine districts and those most capable of producing fine wines, they are not as significant in terms of quantity as the baking-hot, flat, and dry Central Valley, which accounts for three-quarters of all of California's wine; one company, Gallo, produces half of that.

IF I HAD ANY PLANS at all for the California section of this new edition, it was to shine a light on the Central Valley, which has always been brushed to one side by authors because of its jug-wine reputation. Looking through the first edition of this book, I was nagged by the same question – "Surely the source of three out of every four bottles of California wine is worthy of some attention?". To find an answer, I made two visits specifically to look for the wines of the Central Valley. I wanted to establish whether any areas or wines truly stood out and the reasons why.

Why do AVAs such as Clarksburg, Merritt Island, and Lodi exist, if they do not mean something? Clarksburg is supposed to be good for Chenin Blanc, and Lodi has an even greater, older reputation for Zinfandel, but if this is true, why aren't the UK and other price-conscious, value-minded markets flooded with such wines? Perhaps in this valley of giant producers there are a number of small wineries making some stunning wines for the price, but lacking the money or marketing muscle to get them noticed?

To find some answers, I asked a local expert to set up a tasting of the best Central Valley AVA wines. I imagined there would be well over a hundred different wines, but he was able to assemble only 36, and a number of those were old vintages from wineries that no longer exist. After discounting those that were supposedly produced from pure or mostly Central Valley grapes but did not make any such claims on the bottle and were not very interesting in any case, there were just eight wines currently available that proudly proclaimed their origins. Maybe more will be available by the time this book is published, but it was evident that there were few individually expressive wines waiting to be discovered in the Central Valley. I tasted some passable Chenin from

FRANZIA WINERY AT RIPON, NEAR MODESTO
Looking more like oil refineries than wineries, firms such as Franzia have perfected the art of industrialized winemaking.

Clarksburg, but nothing special, and the best were only supposedly from Clarksburg, as they did not claim the AVA.

The wines from Bogle Vineyards on Merritt Island, at the heart of Clarksburg, were not particularly impressive at the tasting but, having had the opportunity to taste younger vintages at the winery itself, it was obviously one of the few independent Central Valley producers likely to succeed. I came away feeling that Bogle makes much better red than white wine, particularly Merlot, but it blends in up to 60 per cent bought-in grapes, using the generic California appellation. As for the Lodi Zinfandel, the few examples claiming the AVA were big, old-fashioned, tasted maderized, and sometimes stank quite foully.

Although I failed to find any outstanding wines, the experience taught me that the Central Valley AVAs are an irrelevance because the state's largest wineries (particularly Gallo, but also Mondavi at Woodbridge, in the heart of Lodi) have ignored them. When they select exceptional wines to bear and show off these AVAs, perhaps consumers will no longer be dismissive of the Central Valley?

HARVESTED CABERNET SAUVIGNON GRAPES
Despite its huge output, premium-quality wines can be produced in Central Valley.

FACTORS AFFECTING TASTE AND QUALITY

LOCATION
The viticultural area of this huge fertile valley stretches 640 kilometres (400 miles) from Redding in the north to Bakersfield in the south, running between the Coastal Ranges to the west and the Sierra Nevada to the east.

CLIMATE
Generally homogenous from end to end, warming steadily from Region IV (*see* p538) in the north to Region V (*see* p538) in the south. The area around Lodi is the only exception, being cooled by sea air sweeping up the Sacramento River.

ASPECT
The vines are grown on the vast flat area of the valley floors, intersected and irrigated by a network of levees.

SOIL
Very fertile sandy loam dominates the length and breadth of the valley.

VITICULTURE AND VINIFICATION
Production of vast quantities of reliable-quality jug wine, using the latest techniques of mechanization and irrigation, and a virtually continuous fermentation and bottling process. Somewhat higher-quality Zinfandel and sweet dessert wines are produced around Lodi.

GRAPE VARIETIES
Barbera, Cabernet Sauvignon, Carnelian, Carignane (Carignan), Chenin Blanc, Colombard, Grenache, Merlot, Mourvèdre, Muscat, Petite Sirah (Durif), Ruby Cabernet, Sauvignon Blanc, Sémillon, Zinfandel.

THE APPELLATIONS OF
THE CENTRAL VALLEY

CAPAY VALLEY AVA
Yolo County

Established in 2003, this appellation is located 130 kilometres (80 miles) northeast of San Francisco, just east of Napa over the Blue Ridge Mountains, bordering Napa, Lake, and Colusa counties. Currently, the grapes grown are Tempranillo, Syrah, and Viognier.

CLARKSBURG AVA
Sacramento County

A large area south of Sacramento encompassing the AVA of Merritt Island, Clarksburg is cooled by the breezes that roll in off Suisun Bay. The average annual rainfall is 41 centimetres (16 inches), which is greater than the precipitation experienced in areas to the south and west, but less than that which occurs north and east. The area is crisscrossed by more than 1,600 kilometres (1,000 miles) of river and irrigation channels.

DIABLO GRANDE AVA
Sacramento County

This AVA, which is owned entirely by the Diablo Grande Resort Community, encompasses 12,000 hectares (30,000 acres), although only 15 (36 acres) are planted with vines. The Diablo Grande AVA is named after Mount Diablo, the highest peak in the Pacific Coast Range; the appellation is in its western foothills where, due to the elevation of 300 to 540 metres (1,000 to 1,800 feet), there is greater rainfall and lower average temperatures than in surrounding areas.

DUNNIGAN HILLS AVA
Yolo County

This is a new AVA located northwest of Sacramento in the rolling Dunnigan Hills. Much of the 445 hectares (1,100 acres) of vineyards cultivated in this area belongs to R H Phillips, a go-ahead winery that has led the Dunnigan Hills reputation for easy-drinking varietals.

LODI AVA
Sacramento and San Joaquin counties

An inland area that comprises alluvial fan, plains that are prone to flood, and terrace lands both above and below the levees. This AVA expanded its southern and western boundaries in August 2002, increasing the viticultural area by 17 per cent.

MADERA AVA
Madera and Fresno Counties

A viticultural area not to be confused with Madera County, Madera AVA is located in both the Madera and Fresno counties and contains more than 14,500 hectares (36,000 acres) of wine grapes, plus substantial areas of raisin and table grapes.

MERRITT ISLAND AVA
San Joaquin County

An island bounded on the west and north by Elk Slough, by Sutter Slough on the south, and the Sacramento River on the east. Its climate is tempered by cooling southwesterly breezes from the Carquinez Straits, near San Francisco, which reduce the temperature substantially compared with that of the city of Sacramento, located just 10 kilometres (6 miles) north. The soil is primarily sandy loam, while areas to the west have clay-type soil, and to the south, an organically structured, moderately fertile peat dirt.

RIVER JUNCTION AVA
San Joaquin County

As the name suggests, River Junction AVA is located at the confluence of two rivers: the San Joaquin and Stanislaus rivers. It is an area where cool maritime air collects, causing land surrounding the river junction to be significantly cooler than other Central Valley areas, and it is the only place in which a substantial amount of Grangeville fine sandy loam can be found. River Junction AVA is entirely owned by McManis Family Vineyards, which has already planted three-quarters of the appellation's 520 hectares (1,300 acres), with Chardonnay accounting for 90 per cent of the planting.

SUISUN VALLEY AVA
Solano County

Adjacent to Solano County Green Valley, and a stone's throw from the Central Valley, Suisun Valley AVA enjoys the same cool, moist winds that blow from spring until autumn in both of these areas. The soils consist of various forms of clay, and silty and sandy loams.

THE WINE PRODUCERS OF
THE CENTRAL VALLEY

BOGLE VINEYARDS
Sacramento County

Chris Smith, a former assistant winemaker at Kendall-Jackson in Lake County, is improving the quality at this winery, which has large vineyards on Merritt Island.

✓ *Merlot • Petite Sirah*

DELICATO
San Joaquin County
★ ♥

From penny-pinching jug wines to real quality bargains, with pure fruit and focus presented in smart blue livery. How this Central Valley winery has come up in the world!

✓ *Merlot • Syrah* (Shiraz)

E & J GALLO WINERY
Stanislaus County
❓

From the air, Gallo's Modesto premises might look like an oil refinery, but from the ground you see peacocks roaming freely over well-manicured lawns and inside the building there is a marble-bedecked reception, with waterfalls cascading into large pools surrounded by lush tropical vegetation, and containing carp the size of submarines. Gallo not only makes a lot of cheap plonk, but it also produces inexpensive yet drinkable varietal wines. The plonk comes under a variety of labels (such as Totts, André, Bartles & James, Carlo Rossi), which encompass coolers, sweet wines from foxy-flavoured native grapes such as Concord, and most of the generics (Burgundy, Chablis, Rhine), while the varietals bear the Gallo name itself (the non-vintage Cabernet Sauvignon is a real penny-saver). Some generics such as Hearty Burgundy and Chablis Blanc can cross the divide into the reasonably drinkable (sometimes amazingly drinkable) category, and the better generics also carry the Gallo name; there is a big difference between Gallo Hearty Burgundy or Chablis Blanc and Carlo Rossi Burgundy or Chablis. This is how the brothers Ernest and Julio Gallo, two struggling grape-growers who had to borrow money to buy a crusher when Prohibition ended, built up their business to become the most powerful wine producers in the world. This commercial success was not enough, however, as both brothers also wanted the critical acclaim of making some of California's finest wines, which is why they literally moved mountains to terraform their prized Sonoma estate. But if the Gallo family is satisfied, it should not be. To create Gallo Sonoma with the money it threw at a single project was no challenge at all. If the Gallo family really does want respect and critical acclaim, then I repeat my challenge: give your winemakers at Modesto a free rein to do two things: bottle off small batches of anything exceptional, and allow them to develop pet projects.

I have never been one to condemn the huge wineries because of size. The bigger they are, then the more likely it is that they will come across an outstanding batch of grapes or wine. The choice of losing these little gems in some mega-blend or of giving them due recognition is what separates the best large wineries from the worst. That Gallo has an army of highly qualified oenologists is beyond question, but it is obvious that those with any creativity will want to express that talent. If Gallo allowed its winemakers to propose and carry out their own projects (such as working with Lodi growers to make the best local Zinfandel possible), this would induce them to stay.

By following these two strategies, Gallo could very quickly attract rave reviews from the most hardened critics for limited bottlings of truly exciting wines. It would reveal the best that can be expected from California's Central Valley vineyards, verify whether the AVAs that exist deserve to be recognized, and pinpoint any other potential appellations that might exist. That would be a fitting achievement for a company that has benefited more than any other from the Central Valley, and an ideal legacy for which Gallo would always be remembered.

✓ *Cabernet Sauvignon* (Turning Leaf Coastal Reserve) • *Sauvignon Blanc* (Turning Leaf California)

FICKLIN VINEYARDS
Madera County
★✰🅥

Ficklin is California's leading estate-bottled port-style specialist. The vineyards are planted with authentic Douro varieties such as Touriga Nacional and Tinta Cão, plus Sousão, which is used for Dão.

✔ *Fortified* (Old Vine Tinta Port, Touriga Nacional Vintage Reserve, Vintage Port)

FRESNO STATE WINERY
Fresno County
★🅥

While Davis has the best-known university wine course in the USA, Fresno is the only one with a commercial winery on its campus, and a very successful one it is, too, having amassed a large number of medals since its inception in 1997. However, presentation is of fundamental importance to any wine venture its students might be running in the future, and the Fresno Winery label launched in 2004 wins no medals!

✔ *Barbera* (California, Duarte Linden Hills Vineyard) • *Muscat Canelli* • *Syrah* • *Viognier* (John Berghold Vineyard)

JEFF RUNQUIST
Amador County
★✰🅥

Standout wines from an under-rated producer that majors in Zinfandel from the Shenandoah Valley but also makes stunning Central Valley wines.

✔ *Barbera* ("R" Nostro Vino Vineyard) • *Cabernet Sauvignon* ("R" Colina Poca Vineyard) • *Petite Sirah* ("R" Enver Salmon Vineyard) • *Pinot Noir* ("R" Sisters Vineyard) • *Primitivo* ("R" Nostro Vino Vineyard) • *Sangiovese* • *Syrah* ("R" Paso Robles) • *Zinfandel* ("Z" Masoni Rach)

JESSIE'S GROVE
San Joaquin County
★✰🅥

Tiny production of high-quality Lodi varietals, with especially noteworthy Zinfandel and a tip-top Carignane, made from vines over 120 years old.

✔ *Carignane* (Ancient Vines) • *Zinfandel*

KLINKER BRICK WINERY
Lodi
★🅥

I came across Steve and Lori Felten's sleek, elegant, beautiful Zinfandel at the IEC wine competition in 2006. These fifth-generation growers and their 100-year-old Zinfandel vines should be treasured.

✔ *Zinfandel* (Old Vines) • *Syrah* (Farah)

QUADY WINERY
Madera County
★

Quady is an eclectic fortified wine specialist par excellence, although I am not so fond of the Vya vermouth-style offerings. By contrast, Electra is a low-alcohol (4 per cent) Moscato d'Asti-style light wine.

✔ *Fortified* (Muscat – Elysium, Essensia; Port – Starboard) • *Muscat* (Electra)

R H PHILLIPS
Sacramento County
★✰🅥

A spotless, hard-to-find winery on the Diamond G Ranch in the rolling Dunnigan Hills, R H Phillips is well worth searching out for supreme-value wines that are wickedly easy to drink.

✔ *Cabernet Sauvignon* (Dunnigan Hills) • *Alliance* (red Rhône style) • *Diamond G* (Sémillon-Sauvignon) • *Mourvèdre* (EXP) • *Night Harvest Cuvée Rouge*

OTHER APPELLATIONS OF
CALIFORNIA

Note This section contains a round-up of the various California wine areas that are not dealt with in the preceding pages. Each of the AVAs listed below can be found on the regional California map (*see* p538).

SIERRA FOOTHILLS AVA

In the 1850s, this land of majestic vistas was California's gold-rush country, but since the 1970s scores of new wineries have opened up, mostly of the one-man "boutique" ilk. The Sierra Foothills is a quality-wine area that is definitely not part of the Central Valley. It attracts rugged specialists who, not content with the safe option of farming fertile valley floors, want the challenge of making expressive wine in limited quantities in one of the few areas of California where, owing to the altitude, cultivating grapes is not always possible. In the 19th century, Zinfandel was the king of these mountain vineyards, and quickly re-established itself as the big, blockbusting, spicy star of the 1980s. However, Sauvignon Blanc and Riesling were quick to take up the challenge, with Barbera and, predictably, Cabernet Sauvignon and Merlot not far behind.

CALIFORNIA SHENANDOAH VALLEY AVA
Amador County

The famous Shenandoah Valley is, of course, in Virginia and, like this AVA, received its status in 1983. The California Shenandoah Valley AVA, which is set amid the Sierra Foothills, was named by Virginian settlers who migrated to California during the gold rush. Vines were first grown here in 1881 when the diggers ran out of gold, and, as a result, turned to making wine instead. The soil is well drained, moderately deep, and consists mostly of coarse sandy loams formed from weathered granitic rock over heavy, often clayey, loam.

EL DORADO AVA
El Dorado County

The soil is mostly decomposed granite, except on Apple Hill, east of Placerville, where an old lava flow exists (*see* Lava Cap winery). Apple Hill is one of two main winegrowing areas and, as the name suggests, the area is covered with orchards. Orchards invariably predate vineyards in the USA and vines always do extremely well wherever apples have grown best. The other main vineyard is located in the southeast of the AVA, between Quitingdale and Fairplay. Go any farther east and not only is it too cold for grapes, but grizzly bears become a real pest.

FIDDLETOWN AVA
Amador County

The Fiddletown viticultural area is located in the eastern Sierra Foothills of Amador County. It differs from the neighbouring Shenandoah Valley of California area because of its higher elevations, colder temperatures at night, and greater rainfall. Grapes are grown without any irrigation and the vineyards are located on deep, moderately well-drained, sandy loams.

NORTHERN CALIFORNIA

SEIAD VALLEY
Siskiyou County

Located just 21 kilometres (15 miles) south of the Oregon border, the Seiad Valley AVA is comprised of 877 hectares (2,165 acres), of which just over one (2.5 acres) is planted with vines.

WILLOW CREEK AVA
Humboldt County

The Willow Creek area is influenced primarily by two major climatic forces - namely the Pacific Ocean and the warmer climate of the Sacramento Valley, 160 kilometres (100 miles) to the east. These create easterly winds that give Willow Creek fairly cool temperatures in the summer and infrequent freezes in the winter. The area to the east of Willow Creek experiences colder temperatures in the winter and hotter temperatures in the summer.

SOUTHERN CALIFORNIA

CUCAMONGA VALLEY AVA
Los Angeles and San Bernardino Counties

An area of more than 40,500 hectares (100,000 acres), some 72 kilometres (45 miles) from Los Angeles, the Cucamonga Valley was first planted with Mission grapes in about 1840. Despite Prohibition, the vineyards reached their peak in the 1950s, when more than 14,000 hectares (35,000 acres) of land were under vine. As the viticultural emphasis in California moved northwards, these vineyards declined, but there are still five operational wineries and some 800 hectares (2,000 acres) of vine in this AVA today.

MALIBU-NEWTON CANYON AVA
Los Angeles County

This is a one-vineyard appellation on the south-facing slopes of the Santa Monica Mountains.

SAN PASQUAL AVA
San Diego County

A natural valley located in the Santa Ysabel watershed, the San Pasqual Valley is fed by natural streams that feed the San Diequito River, and is substantially affected by coastal influences. Temperatures are warm in the summer, but seldom very hot, and ocean breezes cool the area, especially during the night-time. The surrounding areas have a variety of very different climates ranging from tropical, through desert-like, to mountainous.

TEMECULA AVA
Riverside County

Temecula is located in Riverside County, southern California, and includes Murrieta and Rancho California. Marine breezes entering the area through the Deluz and Rainbow Gaps cool the area to moderate temperatures. Sauvignon Blanc and Chardonnay are the most widely planted varieties, and Chenin Blanc and Cabernet Sauvignon the least successful.

LAKE, MARIN, AND SOLANO COUNTIES

The only other counties of significance are Lake, Marin, and Solano, all of which are part of the North Coast AVA. Of these, Lake is the only area of real repute.

BENMORE VALLEY AVA
Lake County

Surrounded by the 1,000-metre (2,900-foot) peaks of the Mayacamas Mountains, this AVA encompasses 50 hectares (125 acres) of vines, but no wineries.

CLEAR LAKE AVA
Lake County

Located between the Mayacamas Mountains and the Mendocino National Forest, Clear Lake's large water mass moderates the AVA's climate. Although this area is best for Chardonnay and Sauvignon Blanc, well-textured Cabernet Sauvignon is also produced.

FAIR PLAY AVA
Amador County

Named after an old gold-mining camp, Fair Play is located in rolling hills at an altitude of 600 to 900 metres (2,000 to 3,000 feet), which, averaged, makes it the highest elevation of any California AVA. Low annual rainfall and loam soils favour Zinfandel, followed by Rhône and Italian varietals.

GUENOC VALLEY AVA
Lake County

This appellation lies south of McCreary Lake and east of Detert Reservoir. Situated within the North Coast AVA, the valley has a more extreme climate, lower rainfall, and less severe fog than the nearby Middletown area.

NORTH YUBA AVA
Yuba County

North Yuba is located in the middle and upper foothills of Yuba County, immediately west of the Sierra Nevada and north of the Yuba River. This area escapes both the early frosts and the snow of higher elevations in the Sierra Nevada and the heat, humidity, and fog common to the Sacramento Valley lowlands, and the climate is therefore relatively temperate compared with the rest of the AVA.

SOLANO COUNTY GREEN VALLEY AVA
Solano County

Green Valley is sandwiched between the Napa Valley to the west and the Suisun Valley to the east. The soil here is a clay loam and the climate is influenced by the cool, moist winds that blow inland from the Pacific and San Francisco Bay almost continuously from spring through to autumn.

OTHER WINE PRODUCERS OF

CALIFORNIA

SIERRA FOOTHILLS

AMADOR FOOTHILL WINERY
Amador County

The wines from this winery, with its small Shenandoah Valley vineyards, are made by owner and ex-NASA chemist Ben Zeitman.

✓ *Zinfandel*

BOEGER WINERY
El Dorado County
★

The first winery to re-open the pre-Prohibition Sierra Foothill vineyards, Boeger has established itself as a producer of understated fine wines that take time to flesh out in bottle, more appealing perhaps to European palates than to those in California.

✓ *Barbera • Classic red blend* (Mourvèdre/Syrah, Reserve El Dorado Meritage) • *Zinfandel*

DOMAINE DE LA TERRE ROUGE
Amador County
★★

Billed as the winery where the Rhône Valley meets the Sierra Nevada, Domaine de la Terre Rouge produces elegant, stylish Syrah and an exotically sweet late-harvest Muscat à Petits Grains.

✓ *Muscat à Petits Grains • Syrah* (Ascent) • *Zinfandel*

HOLLY'S HILL
El Dorado County
★ Ⓥ

A boutique winery concentrating to a large degree on Rhône-style wines, Holly's Hill is planted with the latest French clones from Beaucastel and Rayas.

✓ *Grenache* (El Dorado) • *Syrah* (Wylie-Fenaughty) • *Zinfandel* (Sierra Foothills)

IRONSTONE
Calaveras County
★ Ⓥ

Opened in 1994, John Kautz's winery in gold-rush country has already shown a capability for smooth, lush Cabernet Franc and rich, oaky Syrah (labelled Shiraz, as in Australia).

✓ *Cabernet Franc* (Reserve) • *Cabernet Sauvignon* (Reserve) • *Syrah* (California Shiraz – sic) • *Zinfandel* (Reserve)

LAVA CAP
Placerville
★★ Ⓥ

This under-rated producer just gets better and better. Brilliant-value wines, including one of California's finest Petite Sirahs, grown on the volcanic soils, some 760 metres (2,500 feet) up Apple Hill in the El Dorado AVA.

✓ *Cabernet Franc • Mourvèdre • Petite Sirah • Syrah* (Reserve) • *Viognier • Zinfandel*

MONTEVINA
Amador County
★ Ⓥ

Part of Trinchero Family Estates, together with Sutter Home, Monteviña is best known for Zinfandel, but has also helped the Latino trend with its Italian varieties planted in the Shenandoah Valley.

✓ *Barbera* (Amador) • *Pinot Grigio • Sauvignon Blanc* (California) • *Zinfandel*

NEVADA CITY WINERY
Nevada County

The ultimate garage winery, Nevada City Winery is located in the historic Miners Foundry Garage, on Spring Street in downtown Nevada City. It was founded in the early 1980s and has gone from strength to strength, winning several awards. Red, white, rosé, and dessert wines are produced.

✓ *Cabernet Franc • Zinfandel*

RENAISSANCE
Yuba County
★

Founded by the Fellowship of Friends, Renaissance is a self-sufficient community of like-minded people dedicated to the fine arts, whose wines are made in a clever, circular winery surrounded by an amphitheatre of vines in one of the most idyllic spots on earth. Although the quality at Renaissance has always been patchy, due to its reliance on *terroir* and a relatively hands-off approach to winemaking, it has to be said that the high-quality peaks seem to be getting fewer and the best wines today fall a long way short of the world-class 1985 Riesling Special Select Late Harvest.

✓ *Late Harvest* (Riesling, Sauvignon Blanc Select, Sémillon) • *Pinot Noir • Riesling • Syrah*

RENWOOD
Amador County
★ Ⓥ

These well-made, good-value wines have just started to appear on my radar. The hillside location has produced some fine results.

✓ *Barbera* (Sierra Series) • *Viognier* (Sierra Series) • *Zinfandel* (Fiddletown, Jack Rabbit Flat

SOUTHERN CALIFORNIA

Southern California, site of the state's first vineyard, has even less land under vine than the Sierra Foothills. Since 1977 it has undergone a revival, particularly in Riverside and, to a lesser extent, San Diego counties.

CALLAWAY
Riverside County
★☆ Ⓥ

One of the first wineries to prove that parts of southern California have, in fact, excellent microclimates for producing fine-wine grapes.

✓ *Dolcetto* (Temecula Special Selection) • *Merlot* (Coastal)

JOSEPH FILIPPI
San Bernadino County
★★ Ⓥ

This 35-year-old winery has moved from Fontana to Ranch Cucamonga, where it continues to produce a wide range of wines, including a number of very successful fortified styles.

✓ *Fortified* (Alicante Bouschet Port, Ciello Port Reserve, Oloroso Sherry Library Reserve) • *Mourvèdre* (Library Reserve) • *Muscat Canelli* (Library Reserve)

MAURICE CAR'RIE WINERY
Riverside County
★☆ Ⓥ

The Van Roekels came to Temecula to retire in 1984, but were sidetracked into just "one more venture" and haven't stopped since.

✓ *Muscat Canelli* • *Sauvignon Blanc*

MORAGA
Los Angeles County
★★

This winery is owned by Tom Jones. Not the singer, but the one who made his millions through Stealth technology. Six acres of Bel-Air real estate worth $3 million seems an odd place to grow vines when each bottle would have to retail at $50 for 22 years in order to gross – not cover – the original investment. Viticulturally, however, this tiny sandstone and limestone canyon is a good choice. It has a discernible microclimate with 61 centimetres (24 inches) of rain each year, compared with 38 centimetres (15 inches) on nearby properties, and the wines are also truly fine by any standards. Bel Air is a soft, deep-coloured red Bordeaux-style blend with seamless oak integration and beautifully layered fruit, the flavour building in the mouth. He also makes a tiny amount of fresh, soft, delicately rich Sauvignon Blanc.

✓ *Moraga* (Bel Air) • *Sauvignon Blanc*

THE OJAI VINEYARD
Ventura County
★★★☆

Adam Tolmach, a former partner in Au Bon Climat, teamed up with Helen Hardenbergh to create this boutique winery. Stylish, smoky-blackcurrant Syrah stands out, but some great Pinot Noir too, all wines of all designations can be top-notch. The white Vin du Soleil is a non-malolactic Roussanne-Viognier blend.

✓ *Chardonnay* • *Classic white blend* (Vin du Soleil) • *Pinot Noir* • *Sauvignon Blanc* • *Syrah* • *Viognier* (Late Harvest)

THORNTON
San Diego County
★☆ Ⓥ

Best known for its sparkling wine, particularly its Cuvée Rouge (although not my favourite), but these wines would be much better if sold younger and fresher. In recent years, however, the quality of Thornton's table wines has far exceeded that of its fizz, and its Nebbiolo can rival the best that California has to offer.

✓ *Classic red blend* (Côte Red) • *Muscat Canelli* • *Nebbiolo* (Curran Ranch) • *Rosé* (Grenache) • *Sémillon* (Miramonte Vineyard) • *Sparkling wine* (Brut Rosé, Cuvée de Frontignan) • *Zinfandel* (Lopez Vineyard, Old Vine)

LAKE, MARIN, AND SOLANO COUNTIES

GUENOC WINERY
Lake County
★☆ Ⓥ

This was once the property of Lillie Langtry (a mistress of Edward VII, when he was the Prince of Wales), and her picture is used to market one of these excellent-value wines.

✓ *Cabernet Sauvignon* • *Chardonnay* • *Classic red blend* (Langtry Meritage, Victorian Claret) • *Classic white blend* (Langtry Meritage) • *Petite Sirah* (North Coast, Serpentine Meadow) • *Zinfandel*

KALIN CELLARS
Marin County
❓

After waiting for four years before selling his 1990 Chardonnay, only to attract great acclaim, microbiologist Terry Leighton has stretched his late-release philosophy to bizarre lengths. In October 2004, for example, Leighton decided the time was right to release his 1996 Potter Valley Sauvignon Blanc! On average, he puts his whites on the market when they are six years old, and his reds when they are eight years old. This works better for some styles than others. While Leighton was initially to be applauded, it is always best to err on the side of youth, as the wine-buying public can always cellar a wine, but cannot turn back the clock.

KENDALL-JACKSON
Lake County
★★ Ⓥ

It's amazing to think that when I started researching the first edition of this encyclopedia, the Kendall-Jackson brand was barely 12 months old. Since then, K-J has become one of California's best-selling brands, although its impact on export markets has been minimal. In the USA this company has become so successful that some critics now love to bash the brand they helped to create, when really it is only the obviousness of the entry-level Vintner's Reserve and cheaper subsidiary brands they object to. Yet it is the obviousness of these wines that make them so popular, and the people who buy Vintner's Reserve seldom read a wine critic's column, so what's the point of putting question marks in the minds of those who do? Better instead to point out the plus points, and K-J has plenty of those, not least in its higher level ranges, where the wines pack in one hell of a lot of quality at what are relatively inexpensive prices. K-J is a private company belonging to Jess Jackson, who also owns Cambria (which is run by his wife, Barbara Banke), La Crema, Edmeades, and Stonestreet. Other brands include Camelot, and Pepi.

✓ *Cabernet Sauvignon* (Great Estates, Hawkeye Mountain, Napa Mountain, Stature) • *Chardonnay* (Camelot, Clark, Durell, Stature, Grand Reserve) • *Classic red blend* (Stature Meritage) • *Muscat Canelli* (Vintner's Reserve) • *Pinot Noir* (Great Estates, Stature) • *Riesling* (Vintner's Reserve) • *Zinfandel* (Great Estates)

ORFILA VINEYARDS & WINERY
San Diego County
★★ Ⓥ

Good value wines, including the odd gem that punches well above its weight, from the winery of Argentinian Alejandro Orfila, who was twice elected Secretary General of the Organization of American States.

✓ *Muscat Canelli* • *Sangiovese* (Collina Estate) • *Syrah* (San Pasqual Valley) • *Viognier* (Lotus)

SEAN THACKREY AND COMPANY
Marin County
★★☆

San Francisco art dealer Sean Thackrey loved Burgundy, which led him to establish this winery in 1980 and, naturally enough, try his hand at sculpting Pinot Noir. It was not until the late 1980s that his big, thick, richly flavoured wines began to appear and quickly attracted attention. Since then Thackrey's obsession for fermenting under the stars, along with several other artisanal quirks of ancient winemaking, have intrigued critics and consumers alike.

✓ *Petite Sirah* (Sirius) • *Syrah* (Orion)

STEELE
Lake County
★★

This is the personal label of Jed Steele, who is a former Kendall-Jackson winemaker and a highly regarded wine consultant. His debut vintage was 1991, and his brightly flavoured, brilliantly stylish wines made an instant impact. Excellent all round, but truly excels in his single-vineyard Pinot Noir range. The second label is Jed Steele's Shooting Star.

✓ *Chardonnay* • *Pinot Blanc* (Santa Barbara) • *Pinot Noir* • *Zinfandel* (Catfish Vineyard)

THE PACIFIC NORTHWEST

Oregon has a wet, maritime climate and has long been noted for its Pinot Noir, whereas Washington is a dry, semi-desert wine area that has relatively recently become known for its muscular Bordeaux and Rhône varieties. After decades of needing to ride the Pacific Northwest denomination, both states are now emerging with their own clear identity.

FOR MOST OF ITS WINEGROWING HISTORY, Washington has not had a reputation for any specific style, which is probably why its wines have taken so long to register with wine drinkers, even though it has always produced vastly larger volumes of wine than Oregon. The contrary is true for Oregon, which has had a disproportionately high profile for such a small output of wine, due no doubt to its focus on one variety: Pinot Noir.

WASHINGTON STATE

In 1775 the Spanish declared the land now known as Washington State to be theirs, but 17 years later, Robert Gray, captain of the first US ship to circumnavigate the globe, claimed it for the Americans. To further confuse the issue of sovereignty, George Vancouver had actually claimed it for the British a month before Gray had even reached the area. However, it remained Spanish until 1819, although it was effectively controlled by America through its domination of the fur trade, and American authority was irrevocably recognized in 1889, when Washington became the 42nd state.

The early wine trade

The first planting of vines in Washington was in about 1825, at Fort Vancouver on the Columbia River, by traders working for the Hudson's Bay Company, though it is not known whether wine was actually produced. Washington's earliest winery was established at Walla Walla in the 1860s, and the first *vinifera* vines were planted at Yakima in 1871, although the production

THE PACIFIC NORTHWEST,
see also p533
Encompassing thousands of square kilometres, the Pacific Northwest is a collection of well-dispersed winemaking areas. The ocean defines its western border from northern California in the south to the Canadian border in the north. The sea moderates the climate, although it has little effect on inland Idaho.

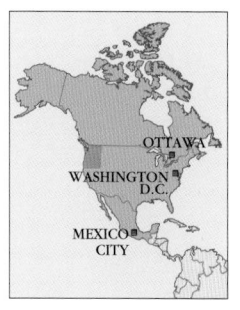

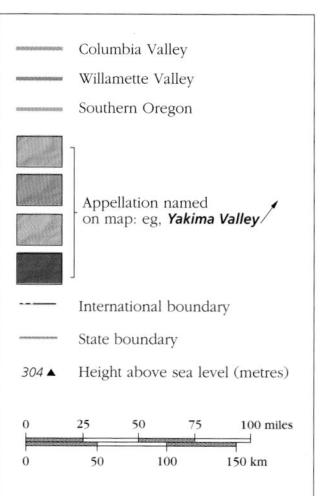

	Columbia Valley
	Willamette Valley
	Southern Oregon

Appellation named on map: eg, *Yakima Valley*

- - - International boundary

——— State boundary

304 ▲ Height above sea level (metres)

0   25   50   75   100 miles
0   50   100   150 km

of wine on a truly commercial scale was not effected until the post-Prohibition New Deal era allowed funding of the Columbia River irrigation project, which transformed an arid desert into an agricultural paradise.

Washington's wine industry grew rapidly, and 42 wineries were in operation by 1937, but the vineyards, like those in the rest of North America, were essentially *Vitis labrusca*-based. In addition to supplying California wineries with base wines for their abysmal "Cold Duck" blends (*see also* Andrés Wines, Canada), the industry produced its own cheap, sweet, and often fortified wines from Concord, Island Belle, and other cloyingly foxy-tasting grapes. *Vitis vinifera* did exist: William Bridgman's Upland Winery in Yakima was making Muscat, Riesling, and Sémillon wines as early

as 1934. It was not until 1951 that the first commercial plantings of *vinifera* vines of the post-Prohibition period took place, but the example was not followed. Trial studies of *vinifera* varieties were conducted in the late 1950s at the Washington State University by Dr Walter Clore. Clore's enthusiasm for these grapes earned him the nickname "Grandpa Grape" and encouraged the American Wine Growers (now called Chateau Ste Michelle) to start the *vinifera* ball rolling with the first of several considerable plantings in the early 1960s. By 1978, 1,000 hectares (2,500 acres) of *vinifera* vines were being grown in Washington. Today, there are more than 16,400 hectares (40,500 acres), producing almost 12 million cases of wine, making Washington the second-largest producer of premium wines in the USA.

FACTORS AFFECTING TASTE AND QUALITY

LOCATION
An arbitrary grouping of three northwestern states: Washington, Oregon, and Idaho. The Yakima Valley, running through Washington, is at roughly the same latitude as northern Bordeaux and southern Burgundy. Washington is more logically a southern extension of British Columbia's inland, desert-based vineyards than a northern extension of Oregon's coastal, rainswept hills.

CLIMATE
The temperatures generated by continental air masses are moderated in Washington and Oregon by westerly winds from the Pacific Ocean. Oregon is the coolest state, and Washington the wettest, but with the exception of Puget Sound, all the viticultural areas of Washington are not only hotter but also much drier than those of Oregon, with plentiful sunshine (averaging over 17 hours per day in June) and crisp, cool nights during the critical ripening period. Climatic conditions are generally more continental towards Idaho.

ASPECT
The vines are located in valleys, usually planted on low-lying slopes, but also on the valley floors and, in Oregon, in the hilly hinterland.

SOIL
The soils are deep, fertile, light-textured, silty, sandy, or clay loams over volcanic bedrock, and sometimes more clayey in Oregon.

VITICULTURE AND VINIFICATION
Washington vines are ungrafted, irrigation is widely practised, with the oldest vines protected by cutting off the water supply prior to winter, thus allowing them to become dormant before the cold sets in. According to various surveys, Washington's viticultural areas are almost phylloxera-free, but some growers say it is rife in the state's Concord vines, which are resistant to the pest, yet for some mysterious reason it has not

attacked *vinifera* vines growing on the same soil in adjacent vineyards. There is a general belief that Washington will have to graft over its vines, but it is difficult from a survival point of view in areas where the winters are so cold. Oregon is also looking at clonal and rootstock selection, but with much of Domaine Drouhin Oregon's success put down to the tight spacing of its vines, the big issue is whether to go for high-density vineyards. More than 50 per cent of Oregon's Pinot Noir is planted at a density of less than 2,000 vines per hectare, and 30 per cent are between 2,000 and 3,000. A small number have tried increasing the density to between 3,000 and 4,500 vines per hectare, but claim there is no discernible advantage. However, the benefits do not kick in until vine density gets above 4,500, and Drouhin's vines are planted at 7,450 per hectare. A good proportion of Oregon wine producers who are not certified organic manage both their vineyards and winery using sustainable and environmentally friendly practices.

GRAPE VARIETIES
Oregon
Primary varieties: Chardonnay, Pinot Gris, Pinot Noir
Secondary varieties: Cabernet Franc, Cabernet Sauvignon, Gewürztraminer, Merlot, Müller-Thurgau, Pinot Blanc, Riesling, Sauvignon Blanc, Sémillon, Syrah, Zinfandel

Washington
Primary varieties: Chardonnay, Cabernet Sauvignon, Merlot, Riesling, Syrah
Secondary varieties: Cabernet Franc, Sangiovese, Sauvignon Blanc, Sémillon, Viognier

Idaho
Primary varieties: Chardonnay, Cabernet Sauvignon, Riesling
Secondary varieties: Cabernet Franc, Chenin Blanc, Sauvignon Blanc, Gewürztraminer, Lemberger, Merlot, Pinot Gris, Pinot Noir, Sémillon, Syrah

RECENT PACIFIC NORTHWEST VINTAGES

2010 After an awkward year, during which the weather was so cool that fruit had to be cut to ensure the balance remaining would ripen, Oregon enjoyed a harvest under perfect conditions and made some excellent Pinot Noir and whites. A good but not great-quality harvest following an even more unusually cool growing season in Washington.

2009 A difficult drought year in Washington, but a cool growing season and dry harvest conditions produced lovely fruit-forward Pinot Noir in Oregon.

2008 One of the greatest vintages on record for all varieties in both Washington and Oregon.

2007 This year reflected the climactic differences either side of the Cascade Mountains, bringing rain to the Oregon harvest, while the crop in Washington was picked under blue skies. This resulted in tip-top quality for all styles in Washington, while it was the earlier-picked whites that excelled in Oregon. However, there are also some very good Oregon Pinot Noirs, though you have to be very picky and prepared to pay a premium.

2006 Excellent to great for all varieties in Oregon and Washington.

IRRIGATION IN WASHINGTON
Although some parts have a notoriously wet climate, much of eastern Washington, where most of the vineyards are located, relies on irrigation.

More recent developments

It is amazing to think that when I visited Washington State to research the first edition of this book, Alex Golitzen's Quilceda Creek was the only red wine of consistently great quality that I could find, and that was produced in minuscule amounts with rickety equipment that he kept stashed away in the back of a garage. Now there are more than 700 wineries, with every one of them producing red wines.

The proportion of black grapes to white has swung from just 30 per cent in 1996, to nearly 60 per cent by 2002, and back to 48 per cent by 2010. Despite the slight trend back to white, which is due to the resurgence of Riesling, Washington remains quintessentially a red-wine region. From a quality-wine perspective, Washington stands shoulder to shoulder with California.

OREGON

The first *vinifera* vines were planted in Oregon's Rogue River Valley as early as 1854. These and other *vinifera* vineyards were still in existence at the time of Prohibition, but, as in Washington, the wine industry in Oregon relied almost entirely on *labrusca* grapes of the Concord variety until the 1970s. Change began in a small way in the 1960s and 1970s, when wineries were established by California drop-outs such as Richard Sommer (Hill Crest, 1961), David Lett (The Eyrie Vineyards, 1965), and Bill Fuller (Tualatin, 1973).

Oregon's overnight fame came in 1979, when Lett entered his 1975 Pinot Noir in a blind wine-tasting competition organized by Robert Drouhin. Drouhin's Chambolle-Musigny 1959 had won, but Lett's The Eyrie Vineyards 1975 Pinot Noir came second, trouncing Drouhin's fabulous 1961 Clos-de-Bèze and many other prestigious Burgundies in the process. Since that eventful day, most critics have believed that it would only be a matter of time before the Pinot Noirs of Oregon would rival those of Burgundy.

By the mid-1980s, such success seemed imminent, and the Oregon wine industry, with more than one eye on hyping up the publicity, declared McMinnville host to an annual World Pinot Noir Conference, thereby endorsing the perception that Oregon is Pinot country. This state's vineyards have increased from a total of 2,407 hectares (5,950 acres) in 1992 to 8,296 hectares (20,500 acres) in 2010. Most of the expansion has been due to Pinot Noir – which has grown by more than 520 per cent over the same period and, by 2010, was in excess of 5,020 hectares (12,400 acres) – and Pinot Gris – which has grown by over 530 per cent, though from a much lower base, to 1,112 hectares (2,747 acres) by 2010. After a period of decline just before and after the turn of the millennium, Riesling and Chardonnay have both doubled.

Oregon's reputation for patchy quality is being left behind as producers learn how to cope with the wet climate, and stop making wines for short-term success at competitions. At one time, almost all the production was consumed locally, but half of the wines are now being sold to other US states. There is room for improvement in exports, which are less than 4 per cent, and should be at least half the total production if consumers around the world are to find these wines. Oregon Pinot Noir needs to be exported, not only to raise its international standing, but also because its producers need to spread their risk over as many markets as possible, enabling them to focus sales on the healthiest economies when others are in decline.

IDAHO

At the Chicago World's Fair in 1898, a prize was awarded to a wine produced by Robert Schleiser, from his vineyard near Lewiston in Idaho's Clearwater River Valley. In more modern times, grape-growing spread from Washington and Oregon to Idaho in 1969. This state's vineyards today are effectively an extension of Washington State's Snake River, and the altitude of these volcanic-soil vineyards – up to 1,050 metres (3,500 feet) – is the highest in the Pacific Northwest. Such extreme elevation ensures that the vines enjoy sunny days but extremely cold nights, and it is this extreme diurnal difference that produces wines with an unusually high acidity and alcohol balance.

THE WINEMAKING STATES AND APPELLATIONS OF

THE PACIFIC NORTHWEST

IDAHO

There are a couple of wineries well north of the Snake River region, in Idaho's Panhandle area, around Coeur d'Alene, the state's largest, deepest, and quite possibly most beautiful lake, just a stone's throw from Spokane in Washington. There are now almost 20 wineries in Idaho, but its wine industry remains embryonic, and since Ste Chapelle is one of the largest wineries in the entire northwest, there is no real competition. However, there are much smaller, even more embryonic winemaking states in the USA, so it is quite surprising that not one AVA has been proposed for Idaho, especially as there are locally defined areas, and the growing environment is such that the wines are renowned for their distinctive style of vivid fruit flavours heightened by intrinsically high acidity.

OREGON

APPLEGATE VALLEY AVA

Completely encased within the Rogue Valley AVA, this appellation has higher elevations than surrounding areas, and is largely protected from cooling coastal influences, resulting in a warmer, drier climate that encourages growers to cultivate Chardonnay, Syrah, and black Bordeaux varieties, in addition to Oregon's ubiquitous Pinot Noir.

COLUMBIA VALLEY AVA
Oregon and Washington

See Washington.

ROGUE VALLEY AVA

Within a short distance of California, this is the most southerly and warmest of Oregon's wine regions. With a mixture of elevations and exposures, and soil types ranging from loam to clay and some decomposed granite, it has been difficult for growers to decide what grape to focus on, hence the mishmash of varieties planted. Not surprisingly, Chardonnay is the most consistent, after which Cabernet Sauvignon and Pinot Noir are the most widely cultivated, which illustrates how undecided everyone is. Even though the elevation of the Rogue Valley AVA is very high, it is the only area in Oregon where Bordeaux varieties ripen regularly.

UMPQUA VALLEY AVA

A great variation in altitude, exposure, and other topographical factors has led to a much greater range of varieties than are grown elsewhere, with such diverse grapes as Riesling and Cabernet every bit as popular as both Pinot Noir and Chardonnay.

WALLA WALLA VALLEY AVA
Washington and Oregon

See Washington.

WILLAMETTE VALLEY AVA

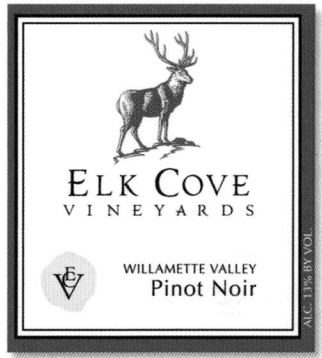

The Willamette Valley is well known for Pinot Noir, although this reputation was founded in 1970, when David Lett planted The Eyrie Vineyards in the Red Hills of Dundee. After Lett's 1975 Pinot

Noir embarrassed Drouhin's 1961 Clos-de-Bèze, and Drouhin became serious about founding a winery in Oregon, it was no surprise that the Burgundian chose the Red Hills for the location. The Eola Hills, also in the Willamette Valley, which share the same volcanic soil as the hills of Dundee and straddle Yamhill and Polk counties, is an up-and-coming area within the Willamette Valley.

WASHINGTON

COLUMBIA VALLEY AVA
Oregon and Washington

Columbia Valley is Washington's largest appellation, encompassing two other AVAs, the Yakima Valley and Walla Walla Valley, and no fewer than 99 per cent of the state's *vinifera* vines. At approximately 46,500 square kilometres (18,000 square miles), it is one-and-a-half times the size of Belgium, and consists of a large, treeless basin surrounding the Columbia, Yakima, and Snake rivers. There is a vast, undulating, semi-arid plateau of between 300 and 600 metres (1,000 and 2,000 feet) in altitude, through which these three rivers cut many dramatic gorges, particularly just south of their confluence, where the Columbia makes a 180-degree turn to follow the Oregon border, creating some of America's most vivid, striking, and contrasting scenery.

The Columbia Valley encompasses numerous microclimates, but they mostly fall between 1,240 and 1,440 degree-days Celsius (2,232 and 2,592 degree-days Fahrenheit), which overlaps regions I and II on the California heat summation system (*see* p538). Due to its northerly latitude and cloudless climate, the Columbia Valley averages two hours' more sunlight during midsummer than the Napa Valley, a state and a half farther south. Astonishingly, there are more than 300 cloud-free days every year, and, although Washington as a whole is the wettest state in the nation, annual rainfall in the Columbia Valley is usually no more than 38 centimetres (15 inches).

Apart from the two sub-appellations of Yakima and Walla Walla, dealt with later, there are a number of other recognized areas within the Columbia Valley AVA. Without doubt, the most exciting of these is Canoe Ridge, which some people seem to think is in Walla Walla because that is where the Canoe Ridge winery is, but it is, in fact, 80 kilometres (50 miles) to the west, just beyond Paterson. The vines grow on the right bank of the Columbia, where there are great hopes for world-class Merlot, Cabernet, and Chardonnay, although some of its vineyards are prone to winds in excess of 40 kilometres per hour (25 mph), the point at which viticulturists have recently discovered the vine temporarily shuts down its metabolism, hindering the ripening process. Other areas of note within the vast Columbia Valley AVA include Northern Columbia Valley (a convenient umbrella appellation for a collection of disparate wine regions, including Saddle Mountain, Wahluke Slope, Royal Slope, and Skookumchuck Creek, where the scenery is often breathtaking, but the wine seldom is) and Snake River (located between Red Mountain – *see* Yakima – and the Walla Walla, in the broad hills either side of the lower reaches of the Snake River, just a few kilometres east of Pasco, where it would seem that Cabernet and Merlot fare best).

PUGET SOUND AVA

Seattle has a reputation as one of the world's wettest cities ("They don't tan in Seattle," Californians claim, "they rust!"), and rainfall initially put severe restrictions on what was grown. Bainbridge Island Winery boasts the nearest vines to downtown Seattle, with Müller-Thurgau and Siegerrebe growing just a couple of kilometres away by ferry, while farther south on the mainland, Johnson Creek Winery grows Müller-Thurgau. Bainbridge Island was the first vineyard in Puget Sound to grow Pinot Noir.

This AVA is a climatic contradiction since it is significantly drier than Burgundy and sunnier than Bordeaux, yet as cool as the Loire. And, in a state of such homogenous soil, the basin drained by rivers and streams that flow into the Sound is marked by a glacial moraine not seen anywhere else in the Pacific Northwest. However, these statistics are a bit like those used by Atlanta to secure the 100th Anniversary Olympics in 1996, as the annual rainfall within Puget Sound ranges between 43 and 114 centimetres (17 and 45 inches), so many areas are a lot wetter than Burgundy, even if the average is drier. Recognized areas within Puget Sound include Mount Baker and Lopez Island.

RED MOUNTAIN AVA

Washington's smallest appellation, Red Mountain, overlaps Yakima AVA, encompassing 1,616 hectares (4,040 acres), of which more than 280 (700 acres) are under vine. This AVA has a full southern exposure, with gentle slopes that are protected from frost by excellent air-drainage. The sandy loam soil has a high calcium content, which with the diurnal inflence of warm summer days and cool nights, encourages increased acidity levels in the grapes grown (Cabernet Franc, Cabernet Sauvignon, Sangiovese, and Syrah).

WALLA WALLA VALLEY AVA

This area has been called the Walla Walla Valley since it was settled in the 1850s, before the creation of either Oregon or Washington. With less than half of one per cent of the state's vineyards, Walla Walla would not perhaps seem to warrant its own AVA, but it can receive up to 50 centimetres (20 inches) of rain, which is more than twice as much as the rest of the Columbia Valley, and this makes Walla Walla a truly distinctive viticultural area with the potential to produce outstanding non-irrigated wine. For every kilometre you travel east from Walla Walla towards the Blue Mountains, you get another 1.6 centimetres of rain.

Although viticulture is growing fast in Walla Walla – from just a dozen wineries cultivating 69 hectares (170 acres) of vines in 1998, to nearly 100 wineries and more than 648 hectares (1,600 acres) of vineyards in 2010 – wine remains very much small potatoes compared to Walla Walla's wheat country, which still runs to almost 100,000 hectares (250,000 acres). But Walla Walla wine punches well above its weight when it comes to the excitement factor. At one time, Mountain Dome was one of the few outsiders to buy grapes from this AVA, traditionally sourcing a third of its Chardonnay and almost all of its Pinot Noir from Whisky Creek vineyard. Nowadays, Walla Walla is all the rage, with wineries from all over the state lining up to get their hands on some of its production. A novel experience for local producers who until recently relied heavily on fruit purchased from outside the area. The Walla Walla AVA also encompasses a small chunk of Oregon.

YAKIMA VALLEY AVA

One of the Columbia Valley's two sub-appellations, the Yakima Valley contains the greatest concentration of Washington's wineries and 40 per cent of the state's vineyards. It is in every sense the home and historical centre of the Washington wine industry. Most vineyards are on the southeast-facing slopes of the Rattlesnake Hills, especially in the mid-valley area from Sunnyside to Prosser, and intermingle with the apple, cherry, and peach orchards that are found between two old irrigation canals, the Roza and the Sunnyside. The Roza is higher up the slopes and sometimes an odd plot of vines, a windbreak of trees, or an orchard can be seen above this canal, where the deep, lush green of irrigated vegetation stands out in contrast to the yellow-ochre starkness of semi-arid desert. In this way, the Yakima is representative of the agricultural success brought to eastern Washington by irrigation projects dating back to the turn of the century, although real prosperity occurred under the great Columbia irrigation scheme funded by the New Deal. Everything grows here: apples, apricots, asparagus, cherries, hops, pears, lentils, mint, peas, plums, potatoes, and raspberries. The apple farmers arrived first and took all the best vineyard sites (apple trees and vines prefer a similar growing environment). In recent years, vineyards have slowly encroached on prime apple orchards. Old cherry orchards have also proved quite favourable for the vine, but former apple sites have proven superior and those chosen for Red Delicious the best of all (because this variety needs a warm site and is susceptible to frost). Other recognized areas that are located within the Yakima Valley AVA are Red Mountain, Red Willow, and Cold Creek. Red Mountain is just northeast of Benton City, where the wild west is at its wildest and reminiscent of the Australian outback. Despite this, Red Mountain Cabernet Sauvignon has been an ingredient in such award-winning wines as Quilceda Creek and Woodward Canyon and it is therefore an area for future viticultural development. Red Willow is located 24 kilometres (15 miles) southwest of Yakima itself, on Ahtanum Ridge, which is on the opposite side of the valley to the Roza and Sunnyside canals. It has a steep slope, particularly on the west side, where there is little topsoil, most of it having been dispersed by the winds that blow across the ridge. The west side produces small, thick-skinned berries, whereas the east side, which has less of a slope and a deep topsoil, produces larger berries and softer, less tannic wines. Mike Sauer, who first planted Red Willow in 1973, claims that the complexity of the east-slope soils and the different air movements that occur over the various blocks of the vineyard create eight distinctly different microclimates. Red Willow is the source of Columbia Winery's best Cabernet Sauvignon, its top-class Syrah, and Milestone Merlot, and at least one winery is trying Nebbiolo there. Cold Creek is close to being the driest, warmest spot in the state and one of the first vineyards to start harvest, yet when the vineyards around Prosser are covered in an autumnal carpet of leaves, just over the low Rattlesnake Hills, the vines of Cold Ridge are still verdant. The reason for this is that it has one of the longest growing seasons in Washington, so it is not only the first to start harvesting, but the last to finish, whereas the explanation for its name is that it is one of the most bitterly cold places in the state in winter. Originally noted for Chardonnay, Cold Creek Vineyard has matured into the consistent source for most of Chateau Ste Michelle's premium varietal.

THE WINE PRODUCERS OF
THE PACIFIC NORTHWEST

IDAHO

HELLS CANYON
Caldwell
★☆Ⓥ

One of the older boutique wineries, Hells Canyon Winery was founded in 1980 by Steve and Leslie Robertson, whose longer experience makes their wines stand out from most of the rest in this state.

☑ *Merlot* (Reserve) • *Syrah* (Deer Slayer, Falcons Fall Vineyard)

INDIAN CREEK
Kuna
★☆Ⓥ

The owner of Indian Creek, Bill Stowe, is a Pinot Noir fanatic stuck in Riesling country!

☑ *Pinot Noir* • *White Riesling*

KOENIG
Caldwell
★☆Ⓥ

Andy and Greg Koenig run an award-winning distillery and are beginning to get noticed for their wines.

☑ *Cabernet Sauvignon* (Bitner Vineyard) • *Riesling* (Ice Wine, Late Harvest) • *Syrah* (Three Vineyard Cuvée)

PARMA RIDGE VINEYARDS
Parma
★☆Ⓥ

Dick and Shirley Dickstein grow Chardonnay, Gewürztraminer, Merlot, Syrah, Viognier, and even Zinfandel at an altitude of 720 metres (2,400 feet) on his 4-hectare (9.5-acre) vineyard overlooking the Boise River.

☑ *Chardonnay* (Reserve)

PEND D'OREILLE WINERY
Sandpoint
★☆Ⓥ

Julie and Stephen Meyer have a good reputation for their Vickers Vineyard Chardonnay and were judged "Idaho Winery of the Year" in 2003.

☑ *Chardonnay* (Vickers Vineyard)

ROSE CREEK VINEYARDS
Hagerman
★☆Ⓥ

Former Ste Chapelle employee Jamie Martin makes some very creditable wine at Rose Creek Vineyards, from both Idaho and Washington fruit, pure and mixed.

☑ *Chardonnay* • *Riesling*

STE CHAPELLE
Caldwell
★☆Ⓥ

Let's face it, these wines are not cheap. No, they're practically given away! Established in 1976 and named after the Gothic Ste Chapelle in Paris, Idaho's largest and oldest winery has set a particularly fine standard for others to follow. Ste Chapelle is, in fact, the fourth-largest winery in the Northwest, and part of Constellation Brands, the largest wine group in the world.

☑ *Cabernet Sauvignon* • *Riesling* (Ice Wine)

SAWTOOTH WINERY
Nampa
★☆Ⓥ

Part of Corus Vineyards, Sawtooth draws on a south-facing vineyard on their large ranch just west of Boise.

☑ *Cabernet Sauvignon* • *Merlot* • *Roussanne* • *Syrah* • *Viognier*

SNAKE RIVER WINERY
Parma
★☆Ⓥ

Improvised canopy management has yielded positive results since 1999.

☑ *Cabernet Sauvignon* (Arena Valley Vineyard) • *Merlot*

OREGON

A TO Z
Dundee
★Ⓥ

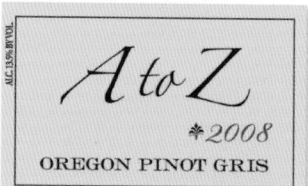

If A to Z has any address, it is a post office box in Dundee, but if you wanted to find its winemakers, Sam Tannahill (former Archery Summit winemaker) or his wife Cheryl Francis (former Chehalem winemaker), you would have to search a number of wineries in Yamhill county. Together with their partners William Hatcher, who developed and managed Domaine Drouhin, and his wife Debra, these two families have established a *négociant*-style business to mop up any excess production from the wineries they work with. Although the individual wines purchased by A to Z are theoretically inferior or, at best, unwanted, Tannahill and Francis should be able to blend them into a harmonious product that is greater than the sum of its parts, if they are gifted at this particular oenological discipline. And it seems that they are. *Food & Wine* magazine named their 2001 Pinot Noir Willamette Valley "the best American Pinot Noir

under $20", and since then A to Z has been set to become Oregon's fastest-growing brand.

☑ *Pinot Noir* (Willamette Valley)

ABACELA VINEYARDS
Roseburg
★★☆

A small, family-owned and -operated winery, with an interesting gaggle of grapes, including Tempranillo, Syrah, Merlot, Dolcetto, Malbec, Cabernet Franc, Grenache, Viognier, and Albariño, growing on sunny south-sloping rocky hillsides.

☑ *Albariño* • *Tempranillo* (South East Block Reserve) • *Syrah* • *Viognier*

ADEA
Gaston
★★☆

Known as Fisher Family Vineyards until this name was subject to a trademark conflict, when ADEA was adopted. It is always written in capital letters, as it was formed from the first letter of the Christian names of the Fisher family members Ann, Dean, Erica, and Adam, who together produce delightful, velvety-textured Pinot Noir wines that are brimming with juicy fruit.

☑ *Pinot Noir*

ADELSHEIM VINEYARD
Newberg
★★★☆

Fine wines across the range, and most successful for Pinot Noir, which is consistently among the best half-dozen in Oregon.

☑ *Chardonnay* • *Pinot Gris* • *Merlot* (Layne Vineyards Grant's Pass) • *Pinot Noir* • *Sauvignon Blanc*

AMITY VINEYARDS
Amity
★★☆

Most famous for Pinot Noir, yet this can be Myron Redford's least consistent varietal, as it is always well structured and can sometimes lack the fruit to support the tannin. However, when there is plenty of

fruit, Amity makes one of the best-value Pinot Noirs in Oregon. Produces some sulphite-free wines.

☑ *Pinot Blanc* • *Pinot Noir* • *Riesling*

ARCHERY SUMMIT
Dundee
★★☆

Californian Gary Andrus put Archery Summit on the map with his gorgeously plump, infinitely classy Pinot Noir, but lost ownership of this winery following a very public divorce (*see also* Gypsy Dancer). Biodynamic experimentation under way.

☑ *Pinot Noir*

ARGYLE WINERY
Dundee
★★★Ⓥ

Part of the Australian Lion Nathan group, Argyle's exceptional sparkling wine performance is solely due to three people: Allen Holstein, who runs Domaine Drouhin's vineyards as well as Argyle's; Rollin Sole, who is this winery's gifted, laid-back winemaker; and Brian Croser, who was one of the original partners and whose intellectual curiosity into the hows and whys of everything that sparkles was the very catalyst of Argyle's success. Some excellent still wines are made, even though the Pinot Noir was once dire.

☑ *Chardonnay* (Nuthouse) • *Pinot Noir* • *Riesling* • *Sparkling wine* • *Syrah* (Nuthouse)

BEAUX FRÈRES
Dundee
★★★☆

Wine critic Robert Parker owns a share of this vineyard and winery, which is run by his partner Mike Etzel. At approximately 6,000 vines per hectare (2,430 vines per acre), only Domaine Drouhin is planted at a higher density. These wines were very good when I wrote the previous revision of this book, but now they are sensational. The Renegade Vineyard is farmed biodynamically.

☑ *Pinot Noir*

BENTON-LANE
Sunnymount Ranch
★☆

A joint venture between Stephen Girard of Girard Winery and Carl Doumani of Stag's Leap, whose vineyard has been certified for its sustainable viticulture by LIVE (Low Input Viticulture and Enology).

✓ *Pinot Noir* (Reserve, Sunnymount Cuvee)

BERGSTRÖM
Dundee
Ⓑ★★☆

Established in 1997 by the Bergström family, who sent son Josh to France for a post-graduate course in Viticulture and Oenology at Beaune. The standard has been nothing less than exemplary since the first vintage in 1999. Their own winery was built in 2001.

✓ *Pinot Noir*

BETHEL HEIGHTS VINEYARD
Salem
★★Ⓥ

One of the best half-dozen wineries in the state, Bethel Heights' basic Pinot Noir (not the cheaper First Release) is often as good as the individual block bottlings and sometimes can even be better balanced, so it not only ranks as one of Oregon's best-quality Pinot Noirs, it also ranks as one of the best value.

✓ *Pinot Noir*

BRICK HOUSE VINEYARD
Newburg
Ⓞ★★

These organic wines have shown a dramatic increase in elegance and finesse in recent years. Biodynamic experimentation under way.

✓ *Gamay* • *Pinot Noir*

BRIDGEVIEW
Cave Junction
★Ⓥ

Located in the Illinois Valley in the Cascades, where Chardonnay benefits from a fairly dense cultivation of just over 4,450 vines per hectare.

✓ *Chardonnay* • *Pinot Noir* (since 1994)

BROADLEY VINEYARDS
Monroe
★★★

Established by Craig and Claudia in 1982, this winery made a big splash with its 1994 Claudia's Choice Pinot Noir, but it was not until the mid-2000s that this level of extraordinary quality could be found consistently in all the wines.

✓ *Entire range*

CAMERON WINERY
Dundee
★☆Ⓥ

An underrated winery with a good, easy-drinking, if sometimes bizarre, style.

✓ *Chardonnay* • *Pinot Blanc* • *Pinot Noir*

CHÂTEAU LORANE
Lorane
Ⓞ★☆Ⓥ

Linde and Sharon Kester produce a wide range of varietals that is eclectic, bordering on bizarre, with crosses and hybrids mingling with classic to obscure *vinifera*. The Marechal Foch is highly regarded by lovers of that hybrid.

✓ *Chardonnay* • *Pinot Gris*

CHEHALAM
Newburg
★★

One of Oregon's most exciting, up-and-coming wineries, Chehalam draws its fruit from three vineyards, two of which belong to Harry Peterson-Nedry, the major shareholder, while his partners Bill and Cathy Stoller own the other one.

✓ *Chardonnay* (Ian's Reserve) • *Pinot Noir*

COOPER MOUNTAIN
Beaverton
Ⓑ☆

This winery produces fine-quality, barrel-fermented Chardonnay from an extinct volcano overlooking the Tualatin Valley. Cooper Mountain was certified organic in 1995, and biodynamic in 1999. Some wines are sulphite free.

✓ *Chardonnay* • *Pinot Gris* • *Pinot Noir*

CRISTOM
Salem
★★

Native yeast fermentations produce some of Oregon's most gluggy Pinot Noirs.

✓ *Pinot Noir* • *Viognier*

DROUHIN ESTATE
Dundee
★★★

Joseph Drouhin was intrigued by this state's potential after David Lett's The Eyrie Vineyard 1975 Pinot Noir came second to Drouhin's 1959 Chambolle-Musigny in a tasting organized in France in 1979. Although Lett's wine came second, it trounced Drouhin's Clos-de-Bèze 1961 and many other Burgundies. Drouhin purchased a property close to The Eyrie Vineyard in the Dundee Hills, planted his own vineyard, and built a winery – and just nine years after that eventful tasting, he produced his first vintage of Oregon Pinot Noir. When it was released, locals and critics alike marvelled at how Drouhin's wine instantly possessed more colour, depth, and complexity than any other Oregon Pinot Noir yet still maintained the grape's varietal purity and finesse. The secret, it was assumed, was the

density of Drouhin's vines, which he planted three and a half times closer than the average in Oregon, but that first vintage (1988) did not contain a single grape from his own vineyard, as it was too young. The real secret lay in the way that Drouhin had handled the grapes, which itself was ironic, because the only reason he made a wine in 1988 with bought-in grapes was because he wanted hands-on experience of Oregon fruit. Even the stunning 1991 was not a pure Drouhin estate wine, as two-thirds of the blend came from Bethel Heights, Canary Hill, Durant, Knudsen, Hyland, and Seven Springs. The first pure Domaine Drouhin was 1992, and all *cuvées* of every Domaine Drouhin vintage has been exceptional since then.

✓ *Entire range*

DOMAINE SERENE
Carlton
★★

This winery made an excellent debut with the 1992 vintage, but a shaky period followed. It is now finding its feet again.

✓ *Pinot Noir*

ELK COVE VINEYARDS
Gaston
★☆

Joe and Pat Campbell can produce easy-going, varietally pure Pinot Noir, but the quality is still a little erratic.

✓ *Pinot Noir* • *Riesling* (Ultima)

EOLA HILLS
Rickreall
★☆

Founded in 1986 by Tom Huggins, Eola Hills has made great improvements over the last 10 years, and is now at least as good for Chardonnay as for Pinot Noir.

✓ *Chardonnay* • *Pinot Noir* • *Sauvignon Blanc* (Vin d'Or Late Harvest)

ERATH WINERY
Dundee
★☆

Formerly Knudsen Erath, this is sometimes one of the best wineries in Oregon for Pinot Noir, but vintages can lurch between firm-tannic and soft, creamy, and voluptuous.

✓ *Chardonnay* • *Pinot Gris* • *Pinot Noir*

EVESHAM WOOD
Salem
Ⓞ★☆

Evesham Wood is a small but expanding winery and is one of Oregon's rising stars.

✓ *Pinot Gris* • *Pinot Noir*

FIRESTEED
Rickreall
★★Ⓥ

This soft, delicious, easy-drinking wine offers excellent value and is

sourced from Oregon vineyards by Washington-based *négociant* Howard Rossbach. Originally devised to satisfy the demands of his mother, Eleanor, whose drinking prowess once featured in *Vogue* magazine, Firesteed is now a brand, and Rossbach also produces barrel-fermented Pinot Noir from his own estate.

✓ *Pinot Noir*

GYPSY DANCER
Hillsboro
★★

Get in on the ground floor of these great Pinot Noir wines from Californian Gary Andrus, who made some stunning vintages at Archery Summit before losing the winery in a divorce settlement.

✓ *Pinot Noir*

HENRY ESTATE
Umpqua
★☆Ⓥ

The Henry Estate is not the most consistent of producers, but at its best it can produce one of Oregon's top Pinot Noir wines.

✓ *Classic red blend* (Henry V) • *Riesling* (Select Clusters)

KEN WRIGHT CELLARS
McMinnville
★★★

High-performance winery founded by the former Panther Creek owner Ken Wright, who has established a reputation for sumptuous, stylish, expressive Pinot Noir sold under single-vineyard names.

✓ *Chardonnay* (Celio Vineyard) • *Pinot Noir*

KING ESTATE
Eugene
Ⓞ★Ⓥ

This vast and still-expanding vineyard surrounds a high-tech, hilltop winery that promises to put Oregon on the commercial map with a 200,000-case capacity.

✓ *Pinot Gris* (Vin Glacé) • *Pinot Noir*

LA BÊTE
McMinnville
★

Unfiltered wines made in an uncompromising style.

✓ *Aligoté* • *Pinot Noir*

LEMELSON
Carlton
Ⓞ★★

The Lemelson family are as organic-minded as certified organic producers, but do it out of respect for the land, rather than to parade an organically produced sticker on their bottles. They make vividly expressive Pinot Noir wines that brim with bright fruit flavour.

Lemelson was certified organic just before the 2004 harvest.

 Pinot Noir

MONTINORE VINEYARDS
Forest Grove
◉✫

A large project by Oregon standards, with all wines 100 per cent estate grown, Montinore is at long last beginning to reflect its true potential.

 Pinot Gris (Entre Deux) • *Pinot Noir* (Parson's Ridge, Winemaker's Reserve)

OAK KNOLL WINERY
Hillsboro
✫

This winery used to produce one of Oregon's finest Pinot Noirs, and has been trying very hard since the late 1990s to reclaim that reputation. And if you ever want a pure *labrusca* Oregon wine, this winery has not lost its reputation for that outdated varietal since the 1970s!

 Pinot Noir

OWEN ROE
Newberg
★★

This winery is the result of a collaboration between Jerry Owen, who looks after the vineyards, and David O'Reilly, who makes and sells these Oregon and Washington wines. The top-of-the-range wines have beautiful photogravure labels bearing the inspired photography of fellow Irishman David Brunn. Entry-level wines are sold under the O'Reilly label. For other David O'Reilly wines, *see* Sineann.

 Cabernet Sauvignon (DuBrul Vineyard) • *Chardonnay* (Casa Blanca Vineyard) • *Merlot* (DuBrul Vineyard) • *Pinot Noir* • *Syrah* (DuBrul Vineyard)

PANTHER CREEK
McMinnville
★★

This tiny winery specializes in opulent Pinot Noir wines that rank among the very finest in Oregon. It also makes a delicious white wine from the Muscadet grape, sold under its synonym of Melon.

 Melon • *Pinot Noir*

PATRICIA GREEN
Newberg
★★Ⓥ

Green is a long-time Oregon winemaker who launched her own operation in 2000, and makes remarkably consistent, delicious, elegant Pinot Noir.

 Pinot Noir

PENNER-ASH
Newberg
★★

Established by former CEO of Rex Hill winery, Lynn Penner-Ash, who has quickly established a reputation for stylish Pinot Noir.

 Pinot Noir • *Syrah*

PONZI VINEYARDS
Beaverton
★★

One of Oregon's top-performing Pinot Noirs for more than a decade.

 Pinot Noir

RAPTOR RIDGE
Cheshire
★Ⓥ

"Raptor" is synonymous with bird of prey, and the name was chosen because of the large number of hawks, kestrels, and owls that hunt within the vicinity of this winery and vineyards. The bright, fruity wines produced here are also worth chasing down.

 Pinot Noir

REDHAWK VINEYARD
Salem
★Ⓥ

Proud winner of *Decanter* magazine's Worst Wine Label Awards, Redhawk has an uncanny knack with Bordeaux varieties, and is now moving into Italian and Rhône styles. The most expensive wines here cost less than the cheapest wines at some other wineries.

 Cabernet Franc • *Cabernet Sauvignon* (Safari Vineyard)

REX HILL VINEYARDS
Newberg
Ⓑ★★

Best known for its range of fine, stylish Pinot Noir wines, which consistently rank in the top half-dozen in Oregon. The Estate wines are biodynamic, but some bought-in grapes used in non-Estate wines may not be organic.

 Pinot Gris • *Pinot Noir*

ST INNOCENT
Salem
★★

Vineyard-designated wines made from purchased grapes grown in the Eola Hills that rank as some of Oregon's greatest Pinot Noirs.

 Chardonnay • *Pinot Noir*

SHEA WINE CELLARS
Yamhill
★★★

You could not get two more diametrically opposed worlds than Wall Street and farming in Oregon, but Dick Shea made the transition with ease in 1996, and quickly achieved huge respect from local winemakers for his long, classy, complex Pinot Noir.

 Cabernet Sauvignon • *Merlot*

SIDURI
Santa Rosa
★★

Named after the Babylonian goddess of wine by Adam and Diana Lee, a couple of Pinot Noir fanatics who are based as far south as Santa Barbara's Santa Rita hills, but source their wines from as far north as Oregon's Willamette Valley. The Oregon Pinot Noir is grown at their Archery Summit vineyard, where they reduce yields, yet still end up rejecting up to 85 per cent of the barrels made.

 Pinot Noir

SINEANN
Santa Rosa
★★

Winemaker Peter Rosback and his business partner David O'Reilly source wines for their own label from all over the northwest: Pinot Noir and Pinot Gris from the Willamette and the Hood River valleys; Cabernet Sauvignon, Merlot, and Zinfandel from the Columbia Valley; and Gewürztraminer from the Willamette Valley and the Columbia Gorge. For other David O'Reilly wines, *see* Owen Roe.

 Cabernet Sauvignon ("Block One" Champoux Vineyard, Baby Poux Vineyard) • *Fortified* (CJ Port) • *Merlot* (Columbia Valley) • *Pinot Noir* (all Oregon wines) • *Zinfandel* (Old Vine Columbia Valley)

SILVAN RIDGE
Eugene
★

Erratic Pinot Noir lurches between bizarre and brilliant, but surprisingly good Cabernet Sauvignon. Early Muscat Semi-Sparkling is always gorgeously peachy, and occasionally there are some extraordinary late-harvest styles.

 Cabernet Sauvignon • *Muscat* (Early Muscat Semi-Sparkling) • *Merlot*

SOKOL BLOSSER WINERY
Dundee
◉★✫

This winery produces some lush, seductive, early-drinking Pinot Noirs that regularly rank among some of Oregon's finest. Biodynamic experimentation continues.

 Chardonnay • *Pinot Noir*

SOTER
Yamhill
★★

Tony Soter's Oregon venture was established in 1997, and abuts properties such as Beaux Frères and Brick House. In 2003, this vineyard was awarded a LIVE Farming Certificate, which is not organic as such, but recognizes the "sustainable farming practices" that have been employed since the Soter's purchase of the land.

 Chardonnay • *Pinot Noir*

THE EYRIE VINEYARDS
McMinnville
★✫

The man who started it all, the late David Lett, also made Pinot Noir to age, Chardonnay for medium-term storage, and Pinot Gris that is best drunk young. His son Jason continues in the same style.

 Chardonnay • *Pinot Gris* • *Pinot Noir* (Reserve)

TORII MOR
Dundee
★★

One of the best producers of nicely oaked, fat, juicy Pinot Noir.

 Pinot Gris • *Pinot Noir*

TUALATIN VINEYARDS
Forest Grove
★✫

Classically structured, yet elegant Pinot Noir.

 Pinot Noir

VALLEY VIEW VINEYARD
Jacksonville
★

This is one of the few consistent producers of Cabernet Sauvignon in Oregon. Jacksonville in the Rogue Valley is one of those idyllic towns everyone should visit. The Anna Maria *cuvée* is a reserve produced only in the best years, and is therefore not available for all varietals in every year.

 Chardonnay (Anna Maria) • *Cabernet Sauvignon* (Anna Maria) • *Reserve* (Anna Maria) • *Sauvignon Blanc* (Anna Maria)

VAN DUZER
Dallas
★★✫

This vineyard is located in the foothills of the Van Duzer corridor, where the vines are affected by the cool Pacific air that flows inward to the Willamette Valley, and the ripening process benefits from the diurnal effect of warm days chased by cool nights. Van Duzer's sustainable farming practices have been given the seal of approval; they have been endorsed by the LIVE (Low Input Viticulture and Enology) program.

 Pinot Noir

WILLAKENZIE ESTATE
Turner
★★

Located on the rolling hillsides on the Chehalem Mountains, this winery was named after the Willakenzie soil, on which the vineyards are planted, and these vineyards are maintained today by sustainable viticulture.

 Pinot Noir

WITNESS TREE
Salem
★☆

This vineyard takes its name from an ancient oak tree used as a surveyor's landmark as far back as 1854, during the Oregon Trail era. All wines produced are 100 per cent estate grown.

✓ *Pinot Noir*

WASHINGTON

ANDREW WILL
Vachon
★★☆

Andrew Will as a person does not actually exist, as Chris and Annie Camarda, owners of this winery, named it after their nephew Andrew and son Will. These wines are superb, especially the range of beautifully crafted classic red blends.

✓ *Cabernet Franc* (Sheridan) • *Cabernet Sauvignon* (Klipsun) • *Classic red blend* (Champoux, Ciel du Cheval, Seven Hills, Sheridan, Sorella) • *Merlot* (Klipsun) • *Sangiovese* (Ciel du Cheval)

APEX CELLARS
Sunnyside
★★

Also known as Washington Hills, this venture was established in the 1980s by Harry Alhadeff, who owned a chain of wine shops and restaurants, and Brian Carter, whose winemaking skills brought the Paul Thomas winery to international attention when there were only 16 wineries in the entire state. Since 1990, Carter has produced a string of superb wines, particularly under the Apex label, which has put this winery among the very elite of Washington's producers.

✓ *Cabernet Franc* (Bridgman) • *Cabernet Sauvignon* (Apex) • *Chardonnay* (Apex) • *Gewurztraminer* (Apex Ice Wine) • *Merlot* (Apex) • *Riesling* (Apex Late Harvest) • *Syrah* (Apex)

ARBOR CREST
Spokane
★ⓥ

Formerly a cherry winery, Arbor Crest is owned by the Mielke family, with Kristina Mielke van Lvben Sels the winemaker since 1999. The vines growing around the Cliff House winery, with its spectacular view, are the only ones you are likely to see in or around Spokane, although there are a number of other wineries in the locality. Spokane is not the best place in the world to grow vines. All the best wines from Arbor Crest and its neighbouring wineries are made from grapes sourced elsewhere.

✓ *Cabernet Sauvignon* (Columbia Valley) • *Chardonnay* (Conner Lee Vineyard) • *Classic red blend* (Dionysus)

BADGER MOUNTAIN
Kennewick
◉☆ⓥ

Established in 1983 by Greg and Bill Powers, Badger Mountain became Washington's first certified organic vineyard in 1990. One of the more consistent organic producers, especially in recent years, this winery uses its Powers label to produce wines from grapes that are not grown in its own 100 per cent organic farmed vineyards. All Vintners Estate Series wines are organic, and heartily recommended, but those with "No Sulfites Added" are not as consistent.

✓ *Syrah* (Vintners Estate Series)

BARNARD GRIFFIN
Kennewick
★ⓥ

Owners Deborah Barnard and Rob Griffin have a track record for Merlot, but have made some splendid Cabernets since the early 1990s and some stunning Syrahs since the late 1990s.

✓ *Merlot* (Red Mountain Ciel du Cheval) • *Sauvignon Blanc* (Fumé Blanc) • *Syrah* (Handcrafted Selection)

BETZ FAMILY VINEYARDS
Woodinville
★★

When I first met Bob Betz, he was a director at Chateau Ste Michelle. I thought that here was someone who was good at connecting with visitors, but also a person who, I realized, would be happier with his hands in the soil, getting back to his winemaking roots. Over the years he has become the second only Master of Wine in the Pacific Northwest, and in 1997 he began releasing wine under his own label, while still at Chateau Ste Michelle. At that first meeting, Betz was full of enthusiasm for Red Mountain, and that was long before any Washington wine drinkers had heard of it. He left Chateau Ste Michelle in 2003, and it is no surprise to find that he now sources many of his wines from Red Mountain. Production is tiny, just 200 cases or so of each wine.

✓ *Cabernet Sauvignon* (Père de Famille) • *Classic red blend* (Clos de Betz) • *Syrah* (La Côte Rousse, La Serenne)

BOOKWALTER
Pasco
★☆

Jerry Bookwalter graduated from UC Davis in 1962, but did not start up on his own until 1983, after 20 years' experience with Sagemoor Farms and other vineyards in Washington and Oregon. The winery is now run by his son, John.

✓ *Cabernet Sauvignon* • *Merlot*

BUTY
Walla Walla
★☆

Artisanal winery established in 2000 by Nina Buty Foster and Caleb Foster, whose Chardonnay and Syrah reflect Caleb's years at Woodward Canyon Winery, followed by overseas winemaking experience in New Zealand and South Africa. This should be one to keep an eye on.

✓ *Chardonnay* • *Syrah* (Rediviva of the Stones)

CADENCE
Seattle
★★

Gaye McNutt and Ben Smith produce small lots of classy red blends: Bel Canto (Merlot-based), Coda (Cabernet Franc-based), Ciel du Cheval (Cabernet Sauvignon-based), Klipsun (Merlot-based), and Tapteil (Cabernet Sauvignon-based). I like all five of these wines, but four are a class apart, and of those, Ciel du Cheval and Tapteil stand out.

✓ *Classic red blend* (Bel Canto, Ciel du Cheval, Klipsun, Tapteil)

CANOE RIDGE
Walla Walla
★☆

Owned by Chalone Vineyards of California, Canoe Ridge used Woodward Canyon and Hyatt Vineyards to make wines before setting up this winery to the east of its Canoe Ridge vineyards.

✓ *Merlot* (Reserve)

CAYUSE
Walla Walla
Ⓑ★★☆

This exciting boutique winery is owned by Christophe Baron of Champagne Baron Albert. Baron has always been a very enthusiastic Champagne producer, but due to the far too westerly location of his vineyards, he has not been the most consistent. Now he has gone as far west as he can without doubling back on himself, and his wines are extremely consistent. He has planted five vineyards totalling 16 hectares (41 acres), all on stony ground, which prompted Baron to name his venture after one of three local Native American tribes, as a play on the French word for stony: *cailloux*. Mostly planted with Syrah, plus a few other Rhône varieties. Look out for a future release of Tempranillo. Most of Baron's wines

have single-vineyard designations, while those that don't are usually of a humorous ilk; this is a Frenchman who does not mind gently mocking himself, as his top-performing "Bionic Frog" Syrah demonstrates.

✓ *Syrah*

CHATEAU STE MICHELLE
Woodinville
★★ⓥ

If rated on the top-of-the-range wines alone, Chateau Ste Michelle would deserve two and a half stars. However, to increase its overall rating to two full stars since 1997 indicates that this Stimson Lane-owned winery has made huge strides even at entry level. Col Solare is a Cabernet-Merlot blend with a dash of Syrah and Malbec, made in partnership with Piero Antinori. Eroica is the result of a collaboration with Ernest Loosen, and it has caused such a renaissance for this grape in Washington that growers are having to replant it as quickly as they can.

✓ *Cabernet Sauvignon* (Canoe Ridge Estate, Cold Creek) • *Chardonnay* (Canoe Ridge Estate, Indian Wells) • *Classic red blend* (Artist Series Meritage, Col Solare) • *Merlot* (Cold Creek) • *Riesling* (Eroica, Ice Wine, Single Berry Select) • *Syrah* (Reserve)

COLUMBIA CREST
Prosser
★☆ⓥ

Owned by Stimson Lane, this winery continues to impress, but is in the middle of nowhere, and will never realize its tourist potential. As tourism not only provides profit, but also increases the reputation of a wine area, it seems odd that Stimson Lane did not build its wine wonder-palace in the Yakima Valley, which has the greatest concentration of wineries and almost half the state's vineyards.

✓ *Cabernet Sauvignon* (Reserve) • *Classic red blend* (Walter Clore Reserve) • *Merlot* (Grand Estates, Reserve) • *Syrah* (Shiraz, Two Vines Shiraz)

COLUMBIA WINERY
Bellevue
★ⓥ

Formerly Associated Vintners, these wines are made by Master of Wine David Lake, who makes some of Washington's best-value red wines.

✓ *Cabernet Sauvignon* (Red Willow Vineyard) • *Merlot* (Milestone) • *Syrah* (Red Willow Vineyard)

COUGAR CREST
Walla Walla
★☆ⓥ

Deborah and David Hansen own 20 hectares (50 acres) of vineyards in the Walla Walla AVA, and had sold their grapes to other wineries for many years when, in 2001, they established this winery at Walla

Walla airport. Very strong in red wine generally, with Cabernet Sauvignon the very best performer.

✔ *Cabernet Franc* • *Cabernet Sauvignon* • *Merlot* • *Syrah*

COVEY RUN
Zillah
⭐

This winery started as a partnership between several Yakima farmers as an outlet for their grapes using the Quail Run label, but they soon fell foul of Quail Ridge in California, and changed the name to Covey Run. Capable of good value, rather than special quality.

✔ *Cabernet Sauvignon* • *Chardonnay* • *Classic red blend* (Cabernet-Merlot) • *Riesling* (Ice Wine) • *Syrah* (Barrel Select)

DE LILLE CELLARS
Woodinville
⭐⭐⯪

If anything is proof of the strength of Washington's classic red wine blends, it is Chris Upchurch, a self-confessed inveterate blender, who has swiftly realized the potential of this state's vineyards with his range of top-performing blends. Even its second wine, D2, is so good that he had to name it twice (the D stands for Deuxième!), as if to emphasize its modest aspirations, yet it regularly knocks seven bells out of most other proprietary reds. All percentages vary from vintage to vintage, of course, but the D2 is usually around 50 per cent Merlot, 35 per cent Cabernet Sauvignon, 10 per cent Cabernet Franc, and 5 per cent Petit Verdot, while both Harrison Hill and Chaleur Estate are effectively 65 per cent Cabernet Sauvignon, 25 per cent Merlot, and 10 per cent Cabernet Franc, the difference being that Harrison Hill is a single vineyard, whereas Chaleur Estate is an *assemblage* of half a dozen different vineyards.

✔ *Classic red blend* (D2, Harrison Hill, Chaleur Estate) • *Syrah* (Doyenne)

DISTEFANO
Woodinville
⭐⯪ⓥ

Owner-winemaker Mark Newton was a mechanical and nuclear engineer, who first turned his hand to sparkling winemaking in the 1980s, under the Newton & Newton label, but has really begun to shine since 1990, when he started making still wines to honour a wedding vow to his bride, Donna DiStefano.

✔ *Cabernet Franc* (Sogno) • *Cabernet Sauvignon* • *Classic red blend* (Ottimo) • *Merlot*

DUNHAM CELLARS
Walla Walla
⭐⭐

Established in 1995 by Eric Dunham, who was born and brought up in

Walla Walla, and served his winemaking apprenticeship under Marty Clubb at L'Ecole No. 41.

✔ *Cabernet Sauvignon* (Columbia Valley, Roman numeral series) • *Classic red blend* (Trutina) • *Syrah* (Columbia Valley, Lewis Vineyard)

FIDELITAS
Kennewick
⭐ⓥ

When flight test engineer Charlie Hoppes gave up his job to set up this winery, his life really took off. Sleek, minimalist presentation for far-from-minimalist wines.

✔ *Classic red blend* (Columbia Valley Meritage) • *Syrah* (Yakima Valley)

FIELDING HILLS
Wenatchee
⭐ⓥ

Although this is only a small boutique winery established in 2000, co-owner/winemaker Mike Wade has quickly made a big splash with the serious quality of these wines, which are ready to drink as soon as released, yet can easily age a decade or so.

✔ *Classic red blend* (Riverben Red) • *Cabernet Sauvignon* (Columbia Valley)

FIVE STARS CELLARS
Walla Walla
⭐⯪ⓥ

Another top-producing Walla Walla boutique winery.

✔ *Cabernet Sauvignon* (Walla Walla Valley) • *Merlot* (Walla Walla Valley)

GORDON BROTHERS
Pasco
⭐⯪ⓥ

One of the more mature Washington wineries, with a large range of exclusively estate-produced wines. Bill Gordon retired in 1998, the same year that a new winery was built on the vineyard. In 2003, Jeff Gordon hired David Harvey as winemaker.

✔ *Chardonnay* • *Classic red blend* (Tradition) • *Syrah*

HEDGES CELLARS
Benton City
⭐⭐ⓥ

I have never tasted a Hedges wine I would not want to drink. Tom

Hedges has the amazing knack of being able to produce premium-quality Bordeaux-style reds that are lush, drinkable, and not lacking complexity and finesse within less than a year of the grapes being picked.

✔ *Classic red blend* (CMS, Red Mountain Reserve) • *Classic white blend* (Fumé Chardonnay)

HOGUE CELLARS
Prosser
⭐⯪ⓥ

Part of the Canadian-based Vincor group since 2001, Hogue Cellars has reinvented itself in recent years and the image today is one of a higher, more focused quality than before.

✔ *Cabernet Sauvignon* (Reserve) • *Chardonnay* (Reserve) • *Fumé Blanc* • *Merlot* (Reserve) • *Viognier* (Genesis)

ISENHOWER CELLARS
Walla Walla
⭐

Former pharmacists Brett and Denise Isenhower made their first wine in 2000, but began to build their reputation for great Syrah in 2001, and constructed their own winery in 2002.

✔ *Cabernet Sauvignon* (Batchelor's Button) • *Syrah* (River Beauty, Wild Alfalfa)

JANUIK
Woodinville
⭐⭐

Owned and run by Mike Januik, former Head Winemaker at Château Ste Michelle. Both "basic" and single-vineyard wines of each varietal are of equally fabulous quality.

✔ *Cabernet Sauvignon* • *Merlot*

K VINTNERS
Walla Walla
⭐⭐

A raunchy range of silky, sensuous, saturated Syrah at prices that must surely double, so buy while you can. Some wonderfully eclectic classic red blends emerging too. Second wines sold under The Magnificent Wine Co label.

✔ *Syrah*

KESTREL
Prosser
⭐⯪ⓥ

Established in 1999, Kestrel has rapidly created a reputation for good-value, flavourful wines that are ripe and easy to drink.

✔ *Chardonnay* • *Syrah*

KIONA VINEYARDS
Benton City
⭐

The arid backdrop to this lush vineyard illustrates how irrigation can transform a desert. Kiona is the most important vineyard on Red Mountain and, although it might

not always hit the bull's eye in the Kiona wines themselves, the same fruit has consistently shown its potential in the wines of Woodward Canyon and has been one of three main ingredients of Quilceda Creek.

✔ *Cabernet Sauvignon* (Red Mountain) • *Chenin Blanc* • *Gewürztraminer* (Late Harvest) • *Merlot* (Red Mountain Reserve) • *Riesling* • *Sangiovese*

L'ECOLE NO 41
Lowden
⭐⭐ⓥ

Marty Clubb has carved out quite a reputation from the wines made at this old school house. L'Ecole No. 41 is primarily known for its Sémillon, but, although this is very good (particularly the Fries Vineyard), Marty's red wines are a class apart.

✔ *Cabernet Sauvignon* (Walla Walla Valley) • *Classic red blend* (Pepperbridge Vineyard Apogee) • *Merlot* (Columbia Valley, Walla Walla Valley) • *Sémillon* • *Syrah* (Seven Hills Vineyard)

LEONETTI CELLAR
Walla Walla
⭐⭐⭐

Owner-winemaker Gary Figgins has a cult following that is matched only by Quilceda Creek, and asking devotees of either wine which is best is a bit like asking a young kid in the 1960s to choose between the Beatles and the Rolling Stones. Figgins has never swayed from his convictions, but it is clear to see that over time he has perfected his handling of oak to match the distinctive style of his wines. While some of the earlier vintages could be criticized for showing too much oak, any objective observer must acknowledge that for some time now they have been beautifully balanced, highly polished, finely focused wines of great complexity, finesse, and longevity.

✔ *Entire range*

LONG SHADOW VINTNERS
Walla Walla
❓

The rating is undecided because this is such a new venture that only one wine from the inaugural 2003 vintage had been released at the time of writing, but if this ambitious project is only half successful, it should produce truly exciting results. Long Shadow is the culmination of all the dreams and fantasies Allen Shoup had during the 20 years he ran Stimson Lane (Chateau Ste Michelle, Columbia Crest, *et al*). It was his collaboration with Piero Antinori and, particularly, Ernst Loosen (which led to Eroica), that convinced Shoup his idea could work. After retiring from Stimson Lane in 2000, he invited several of the world's most iconic winemakers to the sunny slopes where the

Snake River and the Yakima River flow into the mighty Columbia, and explained his vision. He wanted them to tour the region, run the soil through their fingers, survey the leafy trellises that spill down the hillsides of the Columbia Valley appellation, and decide where ideally they would grow those varieties they had had a lifetime's experience with. The objective is to create seven or eight stand-alone, ultra-premium wineries, producing no more than 5,000 cases or so, with a focus on a single varietal or blend, made under the supervision of world-famous winemakers, comparable in stature to those they crafted in their native wine regions. Long Shadow Vintners is so named in tribute to the reputation of Shoup's select group of winemakers. So far, only Armin Diel's Poet's Leap Riesling has been released. Watch out for forthcoming wines: Randy Dunn's Feather Cabernet, John Duval's Sequel Syrah, Augustin Huneeus and Philippe Melka's Pirouette (Cabernet-Merlot blend), Allen Shoup and Gilles Nicault's Chester-Kidder (Merlot-Cabernet blend with a classic Washington twist of Syrah), and Michel Rolland's Pedestal (Merlot-Cabernet blend).

✓ *Riesling* (Poet's Leap)

MATTHEWS
Woodinville
★☆Ⓥ

Very young, exclusively Yakima Valley operation, Matthews demonstrates an innate sense of class in the quality of wine produced and its presentation in bottle.

✓ *Cabernet Sauvignon* (Elerding Vineyard) • *Syrah* (Hedges Estate)

MCCREA
Rainier
★Ⓥ

Promoted as "Washington State's first winery dedicated to Rhône varietals", McCrea's efforts were rather patchy initially, as he tried to understand a number of varieties, some of which might never have the potential in this state, but he was one of the first to perfect Syrah.

✓ *Classic red blend* (Sirocco) • *Syrah*

MOUNTAIN DOME
Spokane
★Ⓥ

The Manz family live in a dome that is cut into the side of a mountain. This is one of half a dozen producers dotted around the world who have the potential to make truly exceptional sparkling wine.

✓ *Entire range*

NORTHSTAR
Walla Walla
★★Ⓥ

Consistently one of the finest Merlots in the Pacific Northwest.

✓ *Classic red blend* (Stella Maris) • *Merlot*

OWEN SULLIVAN
Tukwilla
★★Ⓥ

From a first vintage of a paltry 80 cases in 1997, Bill Owen and Rob Sullivan have quickly built up their sales on a reputation for Bordeaux-style reds full of sultry fruit and a long, lingering finish.

✓ *Cabernet Franc* (Champoux Vineyard) • *Classic red blend* (R3, Ulysses)

PAUL THOMAS
Bellevue
★☆Ⓥ

Underrated because it began with fruit wines, Paul Thomas now makes excellent-value, vividly fruity wines.

✓ *Classic red blend* (Cabernet-Merlot) • *Chardonnay*

PEPPER BRIDGE
Walla Walla
★★Ⓥ

Having supplied grapes for some of Washington's greatest wines from its Pepper Bridge and Seven Hills vineyards, Norm McKibben built a classic gravity-fed winery on his property just in time for the 2000 harvest.

✓ *Cabernet Sauvignon* • *Merlot*

PRECEPT BRANDS
Seattle
☆Ⓥ

Established in 2003, Precept Brands is headed by Andrew Browne, who was the CEO of Corus until it was sold for $52 million to Canandaigua in 2001. Browne is attempting to repeat the success of Corus, but without the overheads and on an even larger scale. Whereas Corus owned wineries such as Covey Run, Columbia Winery, and Paul Thomas, Precept Brands has no winery as such. Browne is taking advantage of excess production, producing *négociant*-style wines under seven Washington labels (Avery Lane, Barrelstone, Painted Stone, Pavin & Riley, Pine & Post, Sockeye, and Washington Hills) in the wineries where he buys the wine. At the same time, Precept Brands launched four Australian labels (Outback Chase, Red Knot, Shingleback, and The Gate) and one Spanish brand (El Paseo).

✓ *Cabernet Sauvignon* (Sockeye) • *Merlot* (Avery Lane, Pavin & Riley) • *Riesling* (Avery Lane, Washington Hills) • *Sauvignon Blanc* (Avery Lane) • *Syrah* (Barrelstone, Washington Hills)

PRESTON WINE CELLARS
Pasco
☆Ⓥ

Bill Preston turned his retirement home into what was, in the 1970s, the largest privately owned winery in the Pacific Northwest.

✓ *Cabernet Sauvignon* (Reserve) • *Syrah* (Preston Vineyards)

QUILCEDA CREEK
Seattle
★★★☆

Washington's first truly great red wine, Quilceda Creek is still produced in tiny quantities and remains one of this state's very elite. After 25 years of authentic garage winemaking, Alex Golitzen and his son Paul built a state-of-the-art winery in time for the 2004 vintage.

✓ *Entire range*

REININGER
Walla Walla
★★☆

Since Chuck Reininger established this up-and-coming Walla Walla boutique winery in 1997, he has hardly put a foot wrong.

✓ *Cabernet Sauvignon* • *Merlot* • *Syrah*

RUSSELL CREEK
Walla Walla
★Ⓥ

Larry Krivoshein made smooth progress from five-gallon jars of homemade wine in 1988 to fine and sophisticated red wines from a fully bonded winery in 1998.

✓ *Cabernet Sauvignon* (Winemaker's Select) • *Classic red blend* (Tributary) • *Syrah* (Walla Walla)

SAGELANDS VINEYARDS
Wapato
★☆Ⓥ

Formerly known as Staton Hills, this winery and its vineyards were taken over by the Chalone Group in 1999, and relaunched as Sagelands in 2000.

✓ *Cabernet Sauvignon* (Four Corners) • *Merlot* (Four Corners)

SEVEN HILLS WINERY
Walla Walla
★★Ⓥ

Grapegrowers since 1980, Casey McClellan has some of Washington's best vineyards at his fingertips, and it shows in the wonderfully expressive wines he produces.

✓ *Cabernet Sauvignon* (Klipsun, Seven Hills, Walla Walla Reserve) • *Merlot* (Seven Hills)

SPRING VALLEY
Walla Walla
★★Ⓥ

These wines are made exclusively from Spring's own 16 hectares (40 acres) of vineyards, situated in the midst of over 240 hectares (600 acres) of wheat land that the Derby family has been farming for over a century.

✓ *Cabernet Sauvignon* (Derby) • *Classic red blend* (Frederick, Uriah) • *Merlot* (Muleskinner) • *Syrah* (Nina Lee)

TAMARACK CELLARS
Walla Walla
★☆Ⓥ

Another highly regarded Walla Walla boutique winery, Tamarack Cellars was established in 1998 by Ron and Jamie Coleman, whose rich, ripe, opulent Cabernet Sauvignon has quickly earned them a reputation.

✓ *Cabernet Sauvigno*n (Columbia Valley) • *Classic red blend* (Firehouse Red)

THREE RIVERS
Walla Walla
★

Established in 1999 by Steve Ahler, Bud Stocking, and Duane Wollmuth, Three Rivers has produced a raft of brilliant, award-winning wines in a very short time.

✓ *Cabernet Sauvignon* (Champoux Vineyard) • *Classic red blend* (Meritage) • *Classic white blend* (Meritage) • *Merlot* • *Sangiovese* (Pepper Bridge) • *Syrah* (Boushey Vineyard)

WALLA WALLA VINTNERS
Walla Walla
★★

Owner-winemakers Myles Anderson and Gordon Venneri have built a thriving business yet still hang on to their day jobs, as an insurance agent and a psychology teacher.

✓ *Cabernet Sauvignon* (Columbia Valley, Walla Walla Valley) • *Merlot* (Columbia Valley, Walla Walla Valley)

WATERBROOK
Walla Walla
★★☆Ⓥ

Founded in 1984 by Eric and Janet Rindal, who named this winery to reflect that of Walla Walla itself, which means "running water".

✓ *Cabernet Sauvignon* (Columbia Valley) • *Classic red blend* (Mélange, Red Mountain Meritage) • *Merlot* (Columbia Valley) • *Viognier* (Columbia Valley)

WOODWARD CANYON WINERY
Lowden
★★

This Walla Walla winery has hardly put a foot wrong since it was set up in 1981, making some of the state's most consistent and most elegant, award-winning red wines, showing great finesse and focus.

✓ *Cabernet Sauvignon* • *Classic red blend* (Charbonneau) • *Classic white blend* (Charbonneau) • *Chardonnay* (Celilo Vineyard, Conner Lee Vineyard) • *Merlot* (Columbia Valley)

THE ATLANTIC NORTHEAST

Michigan continues to outclass New York, despite having only 112 wineries compared with the latter's 349, and nothing like its financial resources. The general consensus is that New York has the greatest potential of all northeastern states, but only a handful of its wineries are working hard to achieve that potential. Virginia promises to be the East Coast's Washington State, while Pennsylvania and Ohio are the dark horses.

LONG ISLAND, NEW YORK
These rows of vines are widely spaced to accommodate vineyard machinery, and are a far cry from the mid-17th century, when Long Island was one of the first places in the Atlantic Northeast to be planted.

ALL THAT HOLDS the Atlantic Northeast back is its harsh winters. Although this does not prevent the cultivation of classic grape varieties, it does make grafting wounds highly vulnerable, and this dictates where such grafted vines are planted. If vineyards could be chosen for their ripening potential, rather than for winter survival, the eastern seaboard could rival California, as it has a much greater variation of soils and microclimates. Since the first transgenic vines were produced, only the identity of two genes has stood in the way of the Atlantic Northeast achieving its full potential – the gene that makes *Vitis amurensis* immune to Siberian winters, together with the one that enables native American vines to resist phylloxera.

AMERICA'S OLDEST WINE INDUSTRY
Wines have been made in America's Northeast since the middle of the 17th century, when vineyards were first established on Manhattan and Long Island. The emphasis, however, has always

been on the notoriously "foxy" *labrusca* varieties. *Vinifera* vines were not cultivated until 1957, although the series of events that culminated in this most important development in the Atlantic Northeast's quest for quality wines began in 1934.

Immediately after Prohibition, Edwin Underhill, the president of Gold Seal Vineyards, went to Champagne and persuaded Charles Fournier, the *chef de cave* at Veuve Clicquot, to return with him to the United States. But Fournier found the *labrusca* grape varieties planted in New York State's Finger Lake vineyards far too aromatic. Persuaded by local wine growers that *vinifera* vines could not

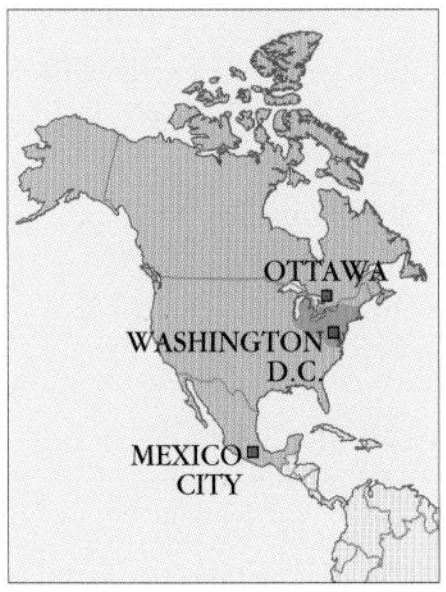

THE ATLANTIC NORTHEAST,
see also p533
The most prominent state in the Atlantic Northeast, New York has established this area's reputation for vinifera *wines, but Virginia and Michigan are now rivalling this supremacy. The wine industries of many of the other states are dominated almost entirely by native* labrusca.

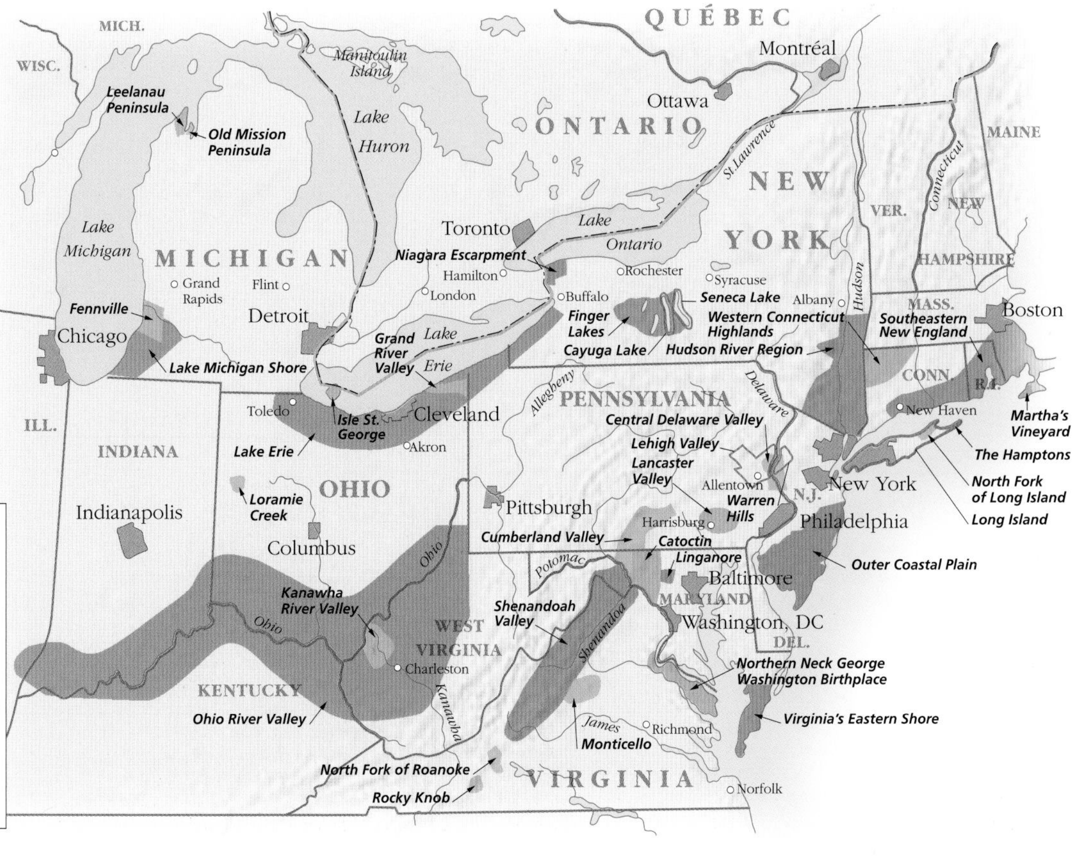

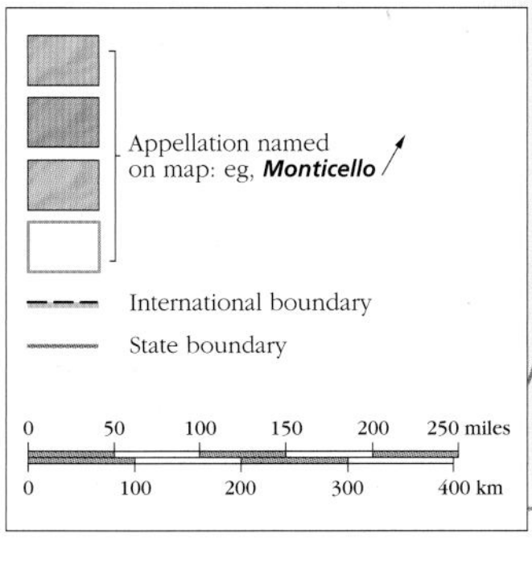

Appellation named on map: eg, **Monticello**

– – – International boundary
——— State boundary

| 0 | 50 | 100 | 150 | 200 | 250 miles |
| 0 | 100 | 200 | 300 | 400 km |

survive the harsh winters, he began planting hybrid vines (crosses between French and native American varieties). These were initially shipped from France, and then acquired from a winemaker by the name of Philip Wagner, who had already established a considerable collection of hybrids at his Boordy Vineyard in Maryland.

In 1953 Fournier heard that one Konstantin Frank, a Ukrainian viticulturist who had arrived in the US in 1951, had been criticizing the industry for not planting European *vinifera* vines. On his arrival in the US, Frank, who spoke no English and had no money, had washed dishes to support his wife and three children. However, as soon as he had learned enough English to get by, he applied for a job at the New York State viticultural research station at Geneva, informing his prospective employers of his studies in viticulture at Odessa, and his experience in organizing collective farms in the Ukraine, teaching viticulture and oenology at an agricultural institute, and managing farms in Austria and Bavaria. When told that the winters were too harsh for European vines, he dismissed the idea as absurd. Two years later, when Fournier heard Frank's claims, he employed him, taking the chance that his theory would prove correct. Frank's claims were justified, particularly after the great freeze of February 1957. Later that year, some of the hardiest *labrusca* vines failed to bear a single grape, yet fewer than 10 per cent of the buds on Frank's Riesling and Chardonnay vines were damaged and they produced a bumper crop of fully ripe grapes.

In the 1980s Frank was still battling with the Geneva viticultural station. *Vinifera* had not taken off in New York State, despite Frank's success. He blamed this on the "Genevians", who maintained that *vinifera* was too risky to be cultivated by anyone other than an expert. Frank had, however, become articulate in his new language: "The poor Italian and Russian peasants with their shovels can do it, but the American farmer with his push-button tools cannot".

MECHANICAL HARVESTING
Grapes are picked by machine at vineyards belonging to the Taylor Wine Company. Based at Hammondsport, the winery is one of New York State's most successful.

FACTORS AFFECTING TASTE AND QUALITY

LOCATION
An arbitrary grouping of states situated between the Great Lakes and the Atlantic Ocean.

CLIMATE
Despite severe winters, the moderating effect of large masses of inland water, such as the Great Lakes or the Finger Lakes, creates microclimates that make cultivation of *vinifera* vines possible. Harsh winter temperatures represent the most prevalent factor holding back the wine industry in the Atlantic Northeast. There are other more localized drawbacks, such as Virginia's heat and humidity at harvest time, which can cause rapid acidity drop and encourage cryptogamic diseases, but these problems can and will be overcome by viticultural practices.

ASPECT
Many of the vineyards are planted on flat ground around the various lake shores, and on the nearby lower slopes of the various mountain ranges.

SOIL
New York: shale, slate, schist, and limestone in the Hudson River Region. **Virginia**: silty loam and gravel at Rocky Knob, limestone and sandstone at North Fork of Roanoke. **Michigan**: glacial scree in Fennville. **Ohio**: shallow drift soil over fissured limestone bedrock on Isle St George. **Pennsylvania**: deep limestone-derived soils in the Lancaster Valley.

VITICULTURE AND VINIFICATION
In many areas, despite some advantageous microclimates, *vinifera* vines can survive the harsh winters only by being buried under several feet of earth before the winter arrives. Sparkling wines are a speciality of New York State and of the Finger Lakes area in particular. Through very careful vineyard practices, the use of the latest sprays, and the aid of new technology in vinification, the number of *vinifera* varietals produced is increasing and their reputation growing.

GRAPE VARIETIES
Native grapes such as Catawba, Delaware, Muscadine, and Norton predominate; French-American hybrids such as Aurore, Baco Noir (Baco I), Maréchal Foch, Seyval Blanc, and Vidal Blanc are important, but the acreage of *vinifera* varieties such as Cabernet Franc, Cabernet Sauvignon, Chardonnay, Gewürztraminer, Pinot Blanc, Pinot Gris, Pinot Noir, Riesling, Sauvignon Blanc, Syrah, and Viognier continues to increase.

RECENT ATLANTIC NORTHEAST VINTAGES

2010 Low volumes of a potentially excellent red-wine vintage in New York and Michigan, with whites that are ripe and plush. Cabernet Sauvignon did exceptionally well in Virginia.

2009 Some Michigan growers believed this was the worst vintage in living memory, but the long hang-time in good autumnal weather suited the Riesling. Similar in New York, although better for reds on Long Island.

2008 A difficult year, with rainstorms spoiling quality in much of New York, although some Finger Lake Rieslings have turned out well.

2007 A great red-wine vintage throughout the northeast, but some of the whites have grown heavy in bottle.

2006 Much better whites than reds, with some Rieslings that could age well.

THE APPELLATIONS OF
THE ATLANTIC NORTHEAST

CONNECTICUT

No documented evidence exists of the first vineyard in this state, but from the great seal of Connecticut it seems certain that its earliest settlers at least attempted to plant vines. The great seal today depicts three grapevines bearing fruit, but the original seal, carried over from England in 1639, had 15 grapevines and the motto *Sustinet Qui Transtulit* ("who transplants sustains"). It soon became clear, however, that tobacco was the farm crop of choice. The first Connecticut wines of modern times were made by Ciro Buonocore, who planted various French hybrid varieties at North Haven.

SOUTHEASTERN NEW ENGLAND AVA
Connecticut, Rhode Island, and Massachusetts

An area distinguished in New England by the moderate climate, caused by its proximity to various coastal bodies of water.

WESTERN CONNECTICUT HIGHLANDS AVA

A vast 3,900-square-kilometre (1,500-square-mile) area of rolling hills that rise to 150 metres (500 feet) above sea level, and the Western Connecticut Highlands, small mountains that reach to 460 metres (1,500 feet).

DELAWARE

The Swedes encouraged their settlers to plant vines and make wine in 1638, as did the Dutch, after they conquered the Swedes in 1655, but they found it easier to grow apples. Nassau Valley Vineyards was the first winery in this state, but it has not shown any distinction so far.

DISTRICT OF COLUMBIA

John Adlum, the author of America's first book on winemaking, tried unsuccessfully to persuade the federal government in the 1820s to support a national experimental vineyard with every variety of native vine in existence "to ascertain their growth, soil, and produce".

INDIANA

The first vines were planted by Jean-Jacques Dufour in 1804, at what would be Vevay in Switzerland county, 12 years before Indiana became a state. Dufour was a Swiss immigrant who had been sent by his family from war-torn Europe to search the newly opened lands of America for a location where they could establish a Swiss colony dedicated to winemaking. He landed in 1796, and by 1799 had already planted a vineyard at Big Bend, near Lexington, in Kentucky, but it was not a success, so he purchased land north of the Ohio River, in the newly surveyed Indiana Territory. The wines made by this Swiss colony achieved two firsts: they were made from the first American hybrid (commonly known as Alexander or Cape), and they were the very first American-grown wines sold to the public. However, this state was also the first to introduce a Prohibition law, which went on the books in Indiana in 1816, forbidding the sale of any alcohol on Sunday (still enforced to this day). By the 1840s numerous towns and whole counties throughout Indiana had gone totally "dry", as indeed they had in Georgia, Iowa, Michigan, New Hampshire, New York, and Ohio. Currently contemplating introducing IQ (Indiana Quality alliance) to elevate the quality and reputation of these wines.

OHIO RIVER VALLEY AVA
Indiana, Ohio, West Virginia, and Kentucky

This is a vast AVA. Until 1859, Ohio was the leading wine-producing state. However, during the Civil War, black rot and powdery mildew took hold and destroyed nearly all its vineyards.

MAINE

With vintners relying on *vinifera* grapes shipped in from as far afield as Washington, and only just steeling themselves to make the transition from fruit wines to own-grown French hybrids, there is hardly even an embryonic wine industry in this most northerly of America's eastern seaboard states. Maine's most important date in wine history was 1851, when it enacted the first state-wide law prohibiting the manufacture and sale of liquor. Within four years, 13 of the then 31 states of the USA had followed suit. In 2010, there were 10 wineries, but although native and hybrid vines are grown, most of the production is fruit wine, and Bartlett Estate Winemaker's Reserve Blueberry is deservedly better known than any grape-based wines.

MARYLAND

In 1662, Lord Baltimore owned Maryland, and he instructed his son, Charles Calvert, the governor, to plant a vineyard and make wine. He planted 96 hectares (240 acres), and another 40 hectares (100 acres) three years later. The vines were native, not European, but the wine was reportedly "as good as the best Burgundy". Taking heart from this success, Lord Baltimore sent his son European vines in 1672, but they all failed to survive their first year. This state now grows no fewer than 140 different grape varieties, although many are French hybrids.

CATOCTIN AVA

Situated west of the town of Frederick, this area's specific *terroir* was well known before the AVA was established, due to the fact that it roughly coincides with the Maryland Land Resource Area. This was determined by the US Soil Conservation Service on the basis of identifiable patterns of soil, climate, water availability, land use, and topography.

CUMBERLAND VALLEY AVA
Maryland and Pennsylvania

The Cumberland Valley is situated between the South Mountains and the Allegheny Mountains and is 120 kilometres (80 miles) long, bending in a northeasterly direction. Although this AVA covers approximately 3,100 square kilometres (1,200 square miles), its vines are confined to small areas where the soil, drainage, rainfall, and protection from lethal winter temperatures permit viticulture. Vineyards are found on high terraces along the north bank of the Potomac River, on the hills and ridges in the basin of the valley, and in the upland areas of the South Mountains.

LINGANORE AVA

Linganore, Maryland's first viticultural area, lies east of Frederick. It is generally warmer and wetter than the areas to the east, and slightly cooler and drier than those to the west.

MASSACHUSETTS

Wines were made from native grapes in the very first summer of the Massachusetts Bay Colony in 1630, but its dubious quality was probably the reason why the settlers immediately petitioned the Massachusetts Bay Company for Frenchmen experienced in planting vines. Two years later, as part of an agreement with the Colonial Legislature, Governor John Winthrop planted a vineyard on Governor's Island, from which he was supposed to supply as annual rent "a hogshead of the best wine". However, there is no evidence that he succeeded and, as his rent was changed to "two bushels of apples" within just a few years, there is every reason to suspect that he had failed. In modern times, the first *vinifera* vines were planted in 1971 by the Mathieson family on, appropriately, Martha's Vineyard.

MARTHA'S VINEYARD AVA

This AVA is an island of Massachusetts, and is surrounded to the north by Vineyard Sound, to the east by Nantucket Sound, and to the south and west by the Atlantic Ocean. The boundaries of the viticultural area include an area known as Chappaquiddick, which is connected to Martha's Vineyard by a sand bar. Ocean winds delay the coming of spring and make for a cooler autumn, extending the growing season to an average of 210 days, compared with 180 days on the mainland.

SOUTHEASTERN NEW ENGLAND AVA
Connecticut, Rhode Island, and Massachusetts

An area distinguished in New England by the moderate climate, caused by its proximity to various coastal bodies of water.

MICHIGAN

Michigan was already a mature winemaking region by 1880, when the first national winegrowing census was taken, but the grapes used were native varieties, and they were grown in the southeast of the state, on the shore of Lake Erie, where virtually no vines exist today. Michigan made the transition to French hybrids in the 1950s and 1960s, although it was not in full swing until the mid-1970s. Meanwhile, the first European varieties were planted at Tabor Hill Vineyard by Len Olsen and Carl Banholzer in 1970, although 20 years later 85–90 per cent of Tabor Hill wines were still being made from hybrids. However, that was in the southwest, in what is now Lake Michigan Shore AVA, and the future as far as quality and diversity of *vinifera* wines was concerned, and a whole raft of new boutique wineries that were about to emerge, lay in the Old Mission Peninsula and Leelanau Peninsula in the northwest of the state. Only one man was crazy enough to plant *vinifera* 225 kilometres (140 miles) north of Canada's Niagara District in 1974, and that was Ed O'Keefe of Château Grand Traverse, where not one single hybrid has ever been planted. O'Keefe is the only person in the entire Michigan wine industry who has been 100 per cent committed to *vinifera* from the very start. His constant arguing of his case did not made him many friends among his fellow winegrowers, particularly those of the old school, who were clinging on to their hybrids, but he was right, and in the end he did everyone in the Michigan wine industry a big favour. Today, Michigan has 5,400 hectares (13,500 acres) of vineyards, making it the fourth-largest grape-growing state, but most of this area is still devoted to juice grapes such as Concord and Niagara. Only 600 hectares (1,500 acres) are devoted to wine grapes, making Michigan the eighth-largest state for wine grape production.

FENNVILLE AVA

Lake Michigan moderates this area's climate, providing slightly warmer winters and cooler summers than other areas within a 48-kilometre (30-mile) radius. Fennville covers 310 square kilometres (120 square miles) and has been cultivating various fruits for well over a century, including grapes for wine production. The soil is mostly scree of glacial origin.

LAKE MICHIGAN SHORE AVA

Located in the southwest corner of Michigan, this AVA is a geographically and climatically uniform region, although it does encapsulate smaller, very specific *terroirs* such as Fennville, which has its own AVA.

LEELANAU PENINSULA AVA

This AVA is on the western shore of Lake Michigan, northwest of Traverse City. The lake delays fruit development beyond the most serious frost period in the spring, and prevents sudden temperature drops in the autumn. Most of Michigan's boutique wineries are located here.

OLD MISSION PENINSULA AVA

This AVA is surrounded on three sides by Grand Traverse Bay, and connected to the mainland at Traverse City. The waters, coupled with warm southwesterly winds, provide a unique climate that makes cultivation of *vinifera* vines possible. The longer established of the two peninsulas, Old Mission houses the smallest number of wineries, but there is renewed interest in the area since Black Star Farms has sourced so many award-winning red wines from here, particularly the Leori Vineyard, and the success of white wines from Peninsula Cellars.

NEW HAMPSHIRE

The first European vines were planted at the mouth of the Piscataqua River by Ambrose Gibbons in 1623, although from his diary we know he suspected that, unlike the native vines that prospered in the wild, they would not survive: "The vines that were planted will come to nothing. They prosper not in the ground where they were set, but them that grow naturally are very good of divers sorts." It would be almost another 250 years before anyone managed to grow wine grapes in this state. In 1965, John J Canepa planted 800 Maréchal Foch vines and, although some died in the severe winter of 1965/66, they yielded a thousand pounds of grapes in 1967, whereupon a photograph of the Canepa vineyard appeared in the *Boston Sunday Globe* with the caption "Soon, Yankee Wine"; the impossibility of this feat drew visitors from far and wide, including baffled university professors. In 1968, Canepa yielded three tons of Maréchal Foch grapes with a potential alcoholic strength of between 18 and 20 per cent. He gave up the day job and built a commercial winery, which was bonded in 1969, but there are still no more than a handful of wine producers in New Hampshire.

NEW JERSEY

Although far more famous for cider than wine, New Jersey does, in fact, boast the first American-grown wine to win an international award. It was as early as 1767 that London's Royal Society of the Arts recognized two New Jersey vintners for producing the first quality wine derived from colonial agriculture, although they were from wild vines, not *vinifera*. This state also gave birth to Dr Thomas Bramwell Welch, the wine-hating dentist who curiously read Pasteur's studies of fermentation, which he turned on their head to sterilize grape juice. It was "Dr Welch's Grape Juice" that established the grape-juice industry, though it was first sold as "Dr Welch's Unfermented Wine". By 2010, there were 32 wineries in this state, where *vinifera* vines are making serious inroads, with more than 100 varieties planted. However, there are still plenty of native and hybrid vines and, indeed, fruit wines.

CENTRAL DELAWARE VALLEY AVA

Pennsylvania and New Jersey

This appellation covers 388 square kilometres (150 square miles), although very little of it is actually planted with vines. The Delaware River modifies the climate.

WARREN HILLS AVA

Wines made in the eastern half of the Central Delaware Valley AVA, which consists of five narrow valleys rather than one broad one, may use this sub-appellation. The narrow valleys provide hillsides that are exposed and funnel the winds, reducing the risk of frost and rot.

NEW YORK

The first vineyard in what is now New York State was cultivated by the Dutch, when it was still New Amsterdam, in 1642. Very little is known about it other than that it failed to survive the winter, so it was probably *vinifera*. Long Island was an important nursery for imported vines in the late 18th and early 19th centuries. At one time, New York was second only to California in terms of acreage of vines, but this peaked in 1975 and had dropped to 12,700 hectares (31,381 acres) by 2010, while the acreage in trailing states has increased significantly since the late 1990s. Furthermore, almost 80 per cent of New York's vineyards is still comprised of nine native varieties (three-quarters being Concord), with only 2,428 hectares (6,000 acres) of *vinifera* and 607 hectares (1,500 acres) of hybrids. Its total, therefore, of 3,035 hectares (7,500 acres) places New York in fourth place, after California's 216,511 hectares (535,000 acres), Washington's 16,421 hectares (40,576 acres), and Oregon's 8,296 hectares (20,500 acres). New York was, until very recently, number two in terms of wine production, but with its production having dropped from 12 million cases to 11 million, while Washington's has increased from 7.4 million cases to 12 million, it is now the third-largest wine-producing state. Since New York has just one-seventh of Washington's *vinifera* acreage yet makes almost as much wine, the bulk of New York's production can only be from native grapes, so it is New York's native-grape wines that are still devaluing the reputation of this state's best *vinifera* wines.

CAYUGA LAKE AVA

This area encompasses vines along the shores of Lake Cayuga, making it part of the Finger Lakes AVA. The soil is predominantly shale and the growing season approximately one month longer than that of most of the Finger Lakes area.

FINGER LAKES AVA

This name is derived from the 11 finger-shaped lakes in west-central New York State. These inland water masses temper the climate, and the topography of the surrounding land creates "air drainage", which moderates extremes of temperature in winter and summer.

HUDSON RIVER REGION AVA

This AVA encompasses all of Columbia, Dutchess, and Putnam Counties, the eastern parts of Ulster and Sullivan Counties, almost all of Orange County, and the northern parts of Rockland and Westchester Counties. This is the Taconic Province, one of the most complex geological divisions where the soil is made up of glacial deposits of shale, slate, schist, and limestone.

LAKE ERIE AVA

New York, Pennsylvania, and Ohio

Overlapping three states, and encompassing the AVAs of Isle St George and Grand River Valley, Lake Erie moderates the climate and is the fundamental factor that permits viticulture.

LONG ISLAND AVA

The Long Island AVA covers the entire island, encompassing the two pre-existing AVAs of North Fork of Long Island and The Hamptons, Long Island.

NORTH FORK OF LONG ISLAND AVA

Although the climate of this AVA is classified as "humid continental", the sea that surrounds it makes it more temperate than many other places of the same latitude in the interior of the US. The growing season is about one to three weeks longer than in the South Fork of the Island and, in general, the sandy soils contain less silt and loam, but are slightly higher in natural fertility.

SENECA LAKE AVA

Because Seneca Lake is the deepest of New York's 11 finger lakes, it is in permanent use by the US Navy's sonar testing platform. With a maximum depth of 203 metres (678 feet), this 56-kilometre-(35-mile-) long body of water in the heart of New York wine country does not freeze, its stored heat warms the surrounding area, and this effect is largely responsible for its success as a wine-growing region. Although best known for Riesling – the steep, slate slopes are ideal for this variety – it is often planted on silty, sandy, or loamy soils, while other varieties such as Pinot Noir are wasted on slate-rich soils, when they would do much better elsewhere.

THE HAMPTONS, LONG ISLAND AVA

The Hamptons has been a productive agricultural area for 300 years. It lies within Suffolk County, next to North Fork of Long Island, with the Peconic River and Peconic Bay its northern boundary. This AVA includes Gardiners Island.

OHIO

When Nicholas Longworth arrived in Cincinnati in the early 1820s, he studied law for a mere six months before setting up in a practice that made him a millionaire. As a hobby, he planted a vineyard in a part of Cincinnati known as Tusculum, but many of the vines he imported from Europe died. Longworth thus turned to native American varieties and quickly discovered Catawba, the so-called "wonder grape", which he planted in 1825. Three years later he made his first Catawba wine and was so impressed that he retired from law to devote his energy to viticulture and winemaking, planting hundreds of acres. At first he produced still wine, but as soon as he made sparkling Catawba, it took off. In 1854, Henry Longfellow even wrote an Ode to Catawba Wine in which he compared it with two of the most famous growths of Champagne, and by 1858 the fame of Catawba had spread as far as Europe, where the *Illustrated London News* reported that "Sparkling Catawba, of the pure, unadulterated juice of the Catawba grape, transcends the

Champagne of France". By 1860, one-third of all the vines in America were planted along the banks of the Ohio, which boasted twice the acreage of California's vineyards, making Ohio the wine centre of the New World prior to the Civil War. Between 1980 and 2000, the number of wineries in this state hardly wavered, moving from 44 to an equally sedate 47, but it has more than doubled since, reaching 108 by 2007, and indicating that some people now think that Ohio could regain its past glories.

GRAND RIVER VALLEY AVA

Located within the Lake Erie AVA, the lake protects these vines from frost damage and forces a longer growing season than vineyards situated in inland areas. The river valley increases "air drainage", giving this AVA a sufficiently different microclimate to warrant its distinction from the Lake Erie AVA.

ISLE ST GEORGE AVA

The northernmost of the Bass Islands, vines have been grown here since 1853. Today they cover over half the island. Although tempered by Lake Erie, the climate is cooler in the spring and summer, and warmer in the winter, than mainland Ohio. The region is frost-free for 206 days a year, which is longer than for any other area in Ohio. The shallow drift soil over fissured limestone bedrock is well suited to viticulture.

LORAMIE CREEK AVA

This small AVA covers only 1,460 hectares (3,600 acres) in Shelby County, west-central Ohio. Moderate-to-poor drainage means vines must be grown on slopes and ridges to prevent "wet feet".

LAKE ERIE AVA

New York, Pennsylvania, and Ohio

Overlapping three states, and encompassing the AVAs of Isle St George and Grand River Valley, Lake Erie moderates the climate and is the fundamental factor that permits viticulture.

OHIO RIVER VALLEY AVA

Indiana, Ohio, West Virginia, and Kentucky

This is a vast AVA. Until 1859, Ohio was the leading wine-producing state. However, during the Civil War, black rot and powdery mildew took hold and destroyed nearly all its vineyards.

PENNSYLVANIA

In 1683, William Penn established a vineyard with French and Spanish varieties he had brought with him, but they failed. However, Conrad Weiser, who arrived at the Penn colony in 1729, and became the greatest Indian interpreter of his time, was spectacularly successful with his vineyard, planted near Womelsdorf in the Tulpehocken Valley. Chambourcin is widely regarded as the most successful variety in this state today, although some good *vinifera* wines are also produced. In 2003, a number of Pennsylvania Limited Wineries established the Pennsylvania's Premium Wine Group, which introduced its PQA (Pennsylvania Quality Assurance) certification system. In order to be awarded a PQA seal, a wine has to be "made to prescribed quality standards as well as be approved by a professional tasting panel". However, this brave effort has declined from 14 member wineries to 10. Despite this, there were 105 wineries in this state by 2010, meaning that the industry as a whole is expanding.

CENTRAL DELAWARE VALLEY AVA

Pennsylvania and New Jersey

This appellation covers 388 square kilometres (150 square miles), although very little of it is actually planted with vines. The Delaware River modifies the climate.

CUMBERLAND VALLEY AVA

Maryland and Pennsylvania

The Cumberland Valley is situated between the South Mountains and the Allegheny Mountains and is 120 kilometres (80 miles) long, bending in a northeasterly direction. Although this AVA covers approximately 3,100 square kilometres (1,200 square miles), its vineyards are confined to the relatively small areas in which the soil, drainage, rainfall, and protection from the lethal winter temperatures permit viticulture. Vineyards are found on high terraces along the north bank of the Potomac River, on the hills and ridges in the basin of the valley, and in the upland areas of the South Mountains.

LAKE ERIE AVA

New York, Pennsylvania, and Ohio

Lake Erie AVA overlaps three US states and encompasses the AVAs of Isle St George and Grand River Valley. Lake Erie itself moderates the climate and is the fundamental factor that permits viticulture here.

LANCASTER VALLEY AVA

Grapes have been grown in Lancaster County since the early 19th century but have only recently provoked any interest from outside. The vines are grown on a virtually level valley floor, at an average altitude of 120 metres (400 feet), where the deep, limestone-derived soils are well drained. Even so, the soils have good moisture retention, are highly productive, and differ sharply from those in the surrounding hills and uplands.

RHODE ISLAND

The smallest and most densely populated US state, Rhode Island is not, of course, an island, but is surrounded on three sides by two other states, Connecticut and Massachusetts. The first vines were planted in Rhode Island in the 1820s by Huguenot settlers who successfully made wine, but these settlers were driven out by legal difficulties, after which viticulture did not continue in the state.

SOUTHEASTERN NEW ENGLAND AVA

Connecticut, Rhode Island, and Massachusetts

An area distinguished in New England by the moderate climate, caused by its proximity to various coastal bodies of water.

VERMONT

Although the home of two native grape varieties, Vergennes and Green Mountain, which were commercially significant in the 19th century, Vermont is now more cider country than wine country, which explains why there were no more than two wineries until 1990. In 2004, there were nine wineries, but they mostly sold fruit wines. By 2010, however, there were 12 wineries, all producing wine from own-grown grapes.

VIRGINIA

This was not the first state to make wine. Strangely enough, that honour goes to Florida, where wine was made from wild grapes *c*.1563; the first settlers in Virginia made wine from "hedge grapes" in 1609. However, Virginia was the first state to attempt the cultivation of *vinifera* grapes for wine, although not by its first governor Lord De La Warre (later corrupted to Delaware), as many sources claim. The first documented attempt to transplant European vines to eastern America was recorded by S M Kingbury of the Virginia Company of London, who reported that French vines and eight French vignerons from Languedoc had been sent out to Virginia in 1619, one year after De La Warre had died at sea. The Virginia Company caused a law to be enacted requiring every householder to plant 10 vines a year "until they have attained the art and experience of dressing a vineyard", but all efforts to cultivate vineyards failed, even though native grapes were rampant in the land. So desperate was Virginia to succeed that an Act of Assembly was passed in 1658 offering 10,000 pounds of tobacco to the first person to make "two tunne of wine raised out of a vineyard made in this colony". No one ever claimed the prize and, almost 30 years later, the offer was quietly dropped. Today, Virginia has the ability to be the Washington State of America's Northeast, but the negative influence of its hot and humid weather during the growing season, particularly towards the end of *véraison* and at harvest time, must first be overcome. There are two main difficulties. First, the sugar-ripeness of the grapes tends to soar away from the rate at which physiological ripeness progresses, resulting in the production of wines bearing green tannins and depleted acidity. Second, the humidity encourages cryptogamic diseases. Various oenological practices are employed to combat the harsh tannins, but the goal must ultimately be to produce grapes with ripe tannins and a good sugar-acidity balance, rather than to sift out unripe seeds (*délestage*). The only way to achieve this is by improving canopy management.

MONTICELLO AVA

Monticello is well known as the home of Thomas Jefferson, who is recorded as having planted wine grapes here. Most of Virginia's best wineries are found in this AVA.

NORTH FORK OF ROANOKE AVA

A valley protected from excessive rainfall in the growing season by mountains to the west and east. The vines are on the limestone southeast-facing slopes and limestone-with-sandstone north-facing slopes. These soils are very different from those in the surrounding hills and ridges.

NORTHERN NECK GEORGE WASHINGTON BIRTHPLACE AVA

This AVA lies on a peninsula 160 kilometres (100 miles) long, between the Potomac and Rappahannock rivers in the tidewater district of Virginia, which runs from Chesapeake Bay in the east to a few kilometres from the town of Fredericksburg to the west. The vines grow in sandy clay soils on the slopes and hills, and in alluvial soils on the river flats. The favourable climate, with excellent air-drainage, is moderated by the surrounding water.

ROCKY KNOB AVA

This AVA is in the Blue Ridge Mountains, and in spring is colder than nearby areas. This means the vines flower later, enabling them to survive the erratic, very cold early spring temperatures. It also causes a late fruit-set, extending the growing season by about a week. The silty-loam and gravel soil provides good drainage.

SHENANDOAH VALLEY AVA

Virginia and West Virginia

The Shenandoah Valley lies between the Blue Ridge Mountains, and the Allegheny Mountains. This AVA extends south beyond the Shenandoah Valley almost as far as Roanoke.

VIRGINIA'S EASTERN SHORE AVA

This is located in Accomack and Northampton counties along the 120-kilometre (75-mile) narrow tip of the Delmarva Peninsula, with the Atlantic to the east and Chesapeake Bay to the west. The climatic influence of these two large bodies of water helps to alleviate the severest winter temperatures, but retards the ripening process and can be problematic at harvest time.

WEST VIRGINIA

Grape-growing began here, along the Ohio River, in the 1830s, when this state was still part of Virginia, and continued after West Virginia had been created during the Civil War. In 2010, there were 17 wineries, mostly producing native, hybrid, and fruit wines, with none standing out as yet.

KANAWHA RIVER VALLEY AVA

This approved viticultural area covers 2,600 square kilometres (1,000 square miles), yet contains just 6 hectares (15 acres) of vines and one bonded winery.

OHIO RIVER VALLEY AVA

Indiana, Ohio, West Virginia, and Kentucky

This is a vast AVA. Until 1859, Ohio was the leading wine-producing state. However, during the Civil War, black rot and powdery mildew took hold and destroyed nearly all its vineyards.

SHENANDOAH VALLEY AVA

Virginia and West Virginia

The Shenandoah Valley lies between the Blue Ridge Mountains, and the Allegheny Mountains. This AVA extends south beyond the Shenandoah Valley almost as far as Roanoke.

THE WINE PRODUCERS OF

THE ATLANTIC NORTHEAST

CONNECTICUT

28 wineries in 2007

CHAMARD

Clinton
★Ⓥ

This is a modern winery just 3 kilometres (2 miles) from Long Island Sound.

☑ *Chardonnay* (Estate Reserve)

STONINGTON VINEYARDS

Stonington
★Ⓥ

This small vineyard and winery was set up in 1986, and produces wines from both hybrid and *vinifera* grapes.

☑ *Chardonnay* (Estate)

INDIANA

40 wineries in 2007

CHÂTEAU THOMAS WINERY

Indianapolis
★Ⓥ

Dr Charles Thomas is so passionate about the wine he drinks, and the cellar of fine European wines that he has built up, that he refuses to grow or buy grapes locally. If these wines seem special, it is because he buys grapes from only the best areas of the Napa Valley.

☑ *Chardonnay • Cabernet Sauvignon • Merlot*

HUBER

Indianapolis
★Ⓥ

One of Indiana's fastest-rising, award-winning wineries.

☑ *Classic red blend* (Heritage) • *Classic white blend* (Lakeside White) • *Vignoles*

MARYLAND

31 wineries in 2007

BASIGNANI

Sparks
★Ⓥ

This small winery makes excellent Cabernet Sauvignon and its Merlot is good enough to attract attention.

☑ *Cabernet Sauvignon • Lorenzino* (red Bordeaux style) • *Merlot*

CATOCTIN VINEYARDS

Brookeville
★Ⓥ

These vineyards are owned by a partnership that includes Bob Lyon.

☑ *Cabernet Sauvignon* (Reserve) • *Chardonnay* (Oak Fermented) • *Johannisberg Riesling*

ELK RUN VINEYARD

Mount Airy
★Ⓥ

The owner-winemaker, Fred Wilson, trained with the legendary Dr Konstantin Frank (*see* p586).

☑ *Cabernet Sauvignon • Chardonnay*

MASSACHUSETTS

17 wineries in 2007

WESTPORT RIVERS

Westport
★Ⓥ

Bob and Carol Russell converted a 17th-century turnip farm into the largest vineyard in New England in 1986, establishing the Westport Rivers winery in 1989.

☑ *Chardonnay*

MICHIGAN

112 wineries in 2007

BEL LAGO

Cedar
★Ⓥ

Charlie Edson has no fewer than 30 different clones of Pinot Noir growing in his vineyard, but it is the Cabernet Franc-Merlot-based Tempesta that is his best wine. Under clinical tasting conditions, the American oak is too dominant, but at Hattie's in Suttons Bay (the best restaurant in the region), I was having dinner with several producers, and numerous bottles were being passed around, yet I consumed an undue amount of Tempesta. In fact, I was accused of hogging the bottle!

☑ *Auxerrois • Chardonnay* (Leelanau Peninsula) • *Classic red blend* (Tempesta) • *Classic white blend* (Crystal) • *Dessert* (Pinot Grigio Ice Wine) • *Pinot Gris • Riesling • Sparkling* (Brut)

BLACK STAR FARMS

Lake Leelanau
★★Ⓥ

Michigan's superstar boutique winery (artisanal creamery and luxury B&B inn) has risen to the top under the skilful guidance of Lee Lutes, this state's most gifted red-winemaker. Lutes even manages to bring a touch of class to hybrids, making a yummy Red House Red from a blend of Maréchal Foch, Dornfelder, Regent, and Cabernet Franc.

☑ *Classic red blend* (Leorie Vineyard Merlot-Cabernet Franc, Red House Red) • *Pinot Gris* (Arcturos) • *Pinot Noir* (Arcturos) • *Riesling* (Arcturos Late Harvest)

BOWERS HARBOR

Traverse City
★

One of those wineries where the dog is the most famous member of the staff, Bowers Harbor has greatly improved over recent years and is within sight of fulfilling its potential as a truly class act.

☑ *Riesling*

CHÂTEAU CHANTAL

Traverse City
★Ⓥ

Owned by a priest who fell in love with a nun and got married. Robert and Nadine Begin gave up their church, but not their beliefs, to live out the ultimate love story. In 1983, they established Château Chantal, with spectacular views of both east and west Grand Traverse Bays, and a guest house so that visitors may enjoy the sun rising and setting over the water.

☑ *Riesling* (Late Harvest)

CHÂTEAU DE LEELANAU

Sutton's Bay
★Ⓥ

The only Michigan winery to be owned by women (Roberta Kurtz and Joanne Smart), Château de Leelanau's Adante is everything German Riesling Sekt should be, but rarely is.

☑ *Sparkling* (Adante Sparkling Riesling) • *Rosé* (Rosé de Cabernet Franc)

CHÂTEAU FONTAINE

Lake Leelanau
★Ⓥ

Dan Matthies came across a potato farm in the 1970s, and saw it as a vineyard in his mind's eye. After selling grapes to Good Harbor for 10 years, he used his wife's middle name (Fontaine) as his own label, which was launched in 2000, with 1998 as the inaugural vintage. Initially, Château Fontaine wines were made at Good Harbor, but the Matthies family now have their own winery.

✓ *Pinot Gris • Classic white blend* (Woodland White)

CHÂTEAU GRAND TRAVERSE
Traverse City
★★ Ⓥ

Château Grand Traverse was established in 1974 by Ed O'Keefe, the first person in Michigan exclusively to plant *vinifera* vines, ruffling many feathers among the locals in the process. And a good job it was, too, for Michigan wine would not be where it is if he had not been as forceful as he was. The first time I had a couple of pints of Guinness with Ed at his local bar, his life story grew wilder the more we drank. I thought it was just blarney, but back at Château Grand Traverse I did indeed find a scrapbook with old, brown clippings of Ed the Olympic gymnast and Ed the Green Beret colonel being decorated. There was nothing about some of his other stories, but it was more than enough to understand that such a man has no need to fabricate anything.

✓ *Classic white blend* (Ship of Fools) • *Riesling* (Botrytized Select Harvest, Dry Icewine, Late Harvest)

CICCONE VINEYARD
Suttons Bay
★★ Ⓥ

Tony Ciccone might be the father of pop star Madonna, but he has eight children, and they are all equal in his eyes. Only one of them, however, has ever attempted to follow in their father's viticultural footsteps, and that is Paula, who has studied oenology at Michigan State University and has done a *stage* at Maison Trimbach in Alsace. However, Paula's commitment remains unknown while she refuses to give up her day job. Rumours of Madonna pumping money into her father's winery are untrue. First, he's too proud. Second, because of an incident I once saw. Tony Ciccone collapsed into an armchair after working a 12-hour day, his blue overalls covered in grape seeds and stained with juice because his one and only pump had broken, and he was trying to move crushed Pinot Noir from the press to a tank with a small bucket. He said, "It's no use, Joan, I'm going to have to buy a new pump," to which his wife replied, "Is that before or after I get the new oven I've needed for the past two years?" That didn't sound to me like they were swimming in Madge's money.

✓ *Chardonnay • Dolcetto • Pinot Gris • Pinot Noir*

DOMAINE BERRIEN
Berrien Creek
★ Ⓥ

It is worth a visit to this southwestern winery in the Lake Michigan Shore AVA, just to run a hand over the glossy wooden counter.

✓ *Viognier*

FENN VALLEY VINEYARDS
Fennville
★ Ⓥ

Established in 1973, this was the first winery to produce wines under the Fennville AVA. The 2002 Late Harvest Vignoles, with its high-voltage acidity, is the best example of that grape I have tasted from any producer anywhere.

✓ *Vignoles* (Late Harvest)

GILL'S PIER VINEYARD
★★✩

Owners Ryan and Kris Sterkenburg employ the talents of Bryan Ulbrich, Michigan's best white-wine maker, to produce their wines, and he's become a dab hand at reds, too.

✓ *Entire range*

GOOD HARBOR
Lake Leelanau
★★ Ⓥ

Owner-winemaker Bruce Simpson is one of Michigan's most prolific medal winners.

✓ *Chardonnay • Riesling • Sparkling* (Moonstruck)

L MAWBY
Suttons Bay
★★ Ⓥ

I have been following Larry Mawby since the mid-1990s, in which time he has gone from erratic (making one decent fizz for every four failures) to remarkably consistent in a surprisingly elegant house style. Not at any time, however, has he had difficulty selling his products. Others saw this and brought out their own bubblies, but in most cases the wines did not sell, so they asked Larry whether he would take the stock off their hands. In the meantime, he had half-jokingly applied for permission to sell a wine called Sex, and when this was approved, he said yes to his colleagues, took back the fizz they couldn't sell, added a little red wine to make it pink, re-labelled it as Sex, and it flew off the shelves quicker than he could stack it. Sex is now made by *cuve close*, thus it comes under his second M Lawrence label. It is not a great-quality fizz, but it is clean, eminently drinkable and the ultimate novelty wine.

✓ *Sparkling* (L Mawby: Blanc de Blancs, Mille, Redd; M Lawrence: Sex)

LEELANAU CELLARS
Omena
★ Ⓥ

Established in 1974 by father and son Michael and Bob Jacobson, this winery had a brisk trade in hybrid wines, and its *vinifera* wines have improved year on year since the late 1990s, although I'm not a fan of their gold-medal-winning Baco Rosé.

✓ *Chardonnay* (Tall Ship) • *Classic red wine* (Meritage) • *Pinot Gris* (Pinot Grigio) • *Riesling* (Late Harvest)

LEFT FOOT CHARLEY
Traverse City
★★

White-wine genius Bryan Ulbrich focuses on Riesling, Pinot Blanc, Pinot Grigio, and Gewürztraminer. Some wines are distinctly better than other, but the others are eminently drinkable!

✓ *Entire range*

LONGVIEW
Leelanau Peninsular

Elegant Cabernet Franc.

OLD SHORE
Lake Michigan Shore

This small vineyard in the southeastern corner of Michigan is capable of good Pinot Gris.

PENINSULA CELLARS
Traverse City
★★✩ Ⓥ

Owned by cherry farmers David and Joan Kroupa, who saw an opportunity to expand the diversity of their 100-hectare (250-acre) farm on Old Mission Peninsula, and planted their first vineyard in 1991. This winery was initially known for its Cabernet-Merlot blend, the first hint that red wines were viable in northern Michigan, and the winemaker, Lee Lutes, was lured away by the new Black Star Farms winery. His assistant, Bryan Ulbrich, took over and produced the first world-class Gewürztraminer outside of Alsace in 2002. Ulbrich is a very talented white-wine maker. His Pinot Blanc is also uncannily Alsace-like. Ulbrich left Peninsula Cellars in 2007 to devote his full attention to his own Left Foot Charley winery in Traverse City.

✓ *Gewürztraminer* (Manigold Vineyard) • *Pinot Blanc*

SHADY LANE
Suttons Bay
★ Ⓥ

Bill Stouten and Joe O'Donnell planted this vineyard in 1989. Initially, Larry Mawby made the wine, but since 2000 the winemaker has been Adam Satchwell, who studied winemaking under his famous uncle, Jed Steele, at Edmeades. The Cabernet Franc is fruity but still needs work to eradicate the herbaceous pyrazines and bring a little plushness. But apart from Black Star's Leorie Vineyard and the other occasional success, that is very much the story for all of Michigan, which is at about the same place

New Zealand reds were in the early 1980s. Riesling does very well here, and Shady Lane's oh-so-pure 2008 Semi-Dry Riesling has one of the most thrilling balances of acidity and sweetness I've come across.

✓ *Chardonnay • Pinot Noir • Riesling*

ST JULIAN WINE COMPANY
Paw Paw
★★ Ⓥ

Founded in 1921 by Mariano Meconi, this winery was established in Canada, where it was called Border City Wine Cellars for a short while, before being renamed Meconi Wine Cellars. It did not become American until 1934, when Meconi moved his business to Detroit. In 1936 he moved the business to its current location, changing its name once again, to the Italian Wine Company. When the US entered World War II, Meconi sought to avoid anti-fascist sentiment by changing his company's name for the third and final time. The St Julian Wine Company is thus the oldest continuously operating winery in Michigan. It is also by far the largest, producing almost as much as all the state's other wineries put together. Although the St Julian Wine Company is rated one star, one of its products would deserve two stars on its own. The perpetually award-winning Solera Cream Sherry is world class, which would be achievement enough for any winery outside of Jerez, but the fact that it is made exclusively from the Niagara grape makes it all the more miraculous. What lets St Julian down is the winery itself, which should be condemned, yet the company actually shows it off to tourists! It's about time that owner David Braganini built an entirely new, state-of-the-art facility.

✓ *Fortified* (Solera Cream Sherry) • *Riesling*

TABOR HILL
Buchanam
★ Ⓥ

Owned by David Upton, son of the founder of Whirlpool (washing machines), this is one of a small handful of wineries in the Fennville AVA of southwestern Michigan. Tabor Hill also boasts an excellent restaurant.

✓ *Cabernet Franc • Riesling*

TABOR HILL BRONTE WINES
Hartford

This winery was originally founded in Detroit as the Bronte Winery, which became the first firm to market the infamous sparkling wine called Cold Duck, a carbonated-Concord concoction that enjoyed an extraordinary vogue in the 1960s. With such an ignominious history, it is little wonder that the firm moved to a different neighbourhood and assumed another identity!

THE ROUND BARN WINERY
Baroda
★ ▼

Established in 1992 by the Moersch family, who were the first to make wines under the Fennville AVA, this winery was known as the Heart of the Vineyard until 2004, when the name was changed to The Round Barn Winery. This was in deference to the historic round barn that was transported 145 kilometres (90 miles) from Rochester, Indiana, by Amish carpenters. They dismantled the barn into a total of just six timbers and then reassembled it, without nails, exactly as it had been originally built. These old barns were round so that the devil could not hide in a corner.

✓ *Muscat* (Muscat Ottonel) • *Pinot Meunier*

2 LADS
★★

The two lads in question are Cornel Oliver, a Stellenbosch-born winemaker, and Chris Baldyga, a local lad. I have tasted only the Pinot Grigio, and it is not only the best I've tasted from Michigan, it is also up there with the best Pinot Grigio (as opposed to full-on Pinot Gris style) I've tasted anywhere. I'm sure the entire range is just as exciting.

✓ *Pinot Grigio*

WILLOW VINEYARDS
Suttons Bay
★ ▼

Just down the road from Ciccone Vineyards, this boutique vineyard and winery was built from scratch (including their home), on a shoestring, by John and Jo Crampton. John undertook occasional carpentry jobs while establishing Willow Vineyards, and Jo waitressed at night to make ends meet. A lovelier couple it would be hard to find, and this comes through in the friendliness of their fruit-filled wines.

✓ *Pinot Gris* • *Pinot Noir*

WYNCROFT
Buchanan
★ ▼

The most southerly of Michigan's wineries, and one of the smallest, Wyncroft is little heard of, even in state. The style is noticeably fatter than most other Michigan wines.

✓ *Chardonnay* • *Pinot Noir*

NEW JERSEY
41 wineries in 2007

ALBA VINEYARD
Milford
★ ▼

This vineyard has occasionally made good Cabernet, but is best for rich, sweet, plummy port-style wines.

✓ *Vintage Port*

TOMASELLO
Hammonton
★ ▼

This winery, which opened up immediately after Prohibition was repealed, has had over 50 years' decent sparkling-wine experience.

✓ *Cabernet Sauvignon* (Atlantic County) • *Chambourcin* (Atlantic County)

UNIONVILLE VINEYARDS
Ringoes
★ ▼

This is one of New Jersey's newest and fastest-rising wineries.

✓ *Classic red blend* (Nielson Proprietary Reserve) • *Riesling*

NEW YORK
349 wineries in 2007

ANTHONY ROAD
Penn Yan
★ ▼

After 15 years of selling their grapes to other wineries, Ann and John Martini established Anthony Road in 1990 with wines made from the 1989 harvest.

✓ *Cabernet Franc* • *Chardonnay* • *Riesling*

BEDELL
Cutchogue
★ ▼

The first harvest of this Long Island winery coincided with Hurricane Gloria in 1985. However, subsequent Bedell vintages have stood the test of time.

✓ *Chardonnay* (Reserve) • *Classic red blend* (Cupola) • *Merlot* (Reserve)

BENMARL WINE COMPANY
Marlboro
★ ▼

One of the state's most successful wineries. *Benmarl* is Gaelic for the vineyard's slate-marl soil, and although hybrids are much less trouble, *vinifera* is grown, including award-winning Zinfandel.

✓ *Baco Noir* • *Zinfandel*

BRIDGEHAMPTON
Bridgehampton
★★ ▼

Long Island's fastest-rising star, Bridgehampton's wines have an intensity of fruit and a fine structure.

✓ *Chardonnay* • *Meritage* (red Bordeaux style) • *Merlot* • *Riesling* • *Sauvignon Blanc*

BROTHERHOOD WINERY
Washingtonville

The oldest winery in continuous operation in the USA, Brotherhood Winery was established by a shoemaker named Jean Jacques, who initially sold wine to the First Presbyterian Church. The wines used to be very much of the old

school, but are now fresher and crisper in character.

CANANDAIGUA WINE COMPANY
Canandaigua

The Seneca Native American word *canandaigua* means "chosen place". Even in the late 1980s, this firm had a huge production, but it is now second only in size to Gallo in terms of American production, and its merger with Australia's BRL Hardy to form Constellation Brands makes it the largest wine producer in the world. Various Atlantic Northeast labels include Richards, J Roget, and Virginia Dare.

CHANNING DAUGHTER
Bridgehampton
★ ★ ▼

This winery has been on the fast track since Walter and Molly Channing, and partner Larry Perrine, launched their first wines with the 1997 vintage.

✓ *Classic white blend* (Silvanus) • *Merlot* (The Sculptor) • *Tocai Friulano*

DR FRANK'S VINIFERA WINE CELLARS
Hammondsport
★ ▼

Run today by Willy Frank, the son of the legendary Konstantin Frank.

✓ *Riesling* (Dry) • *Sparkling* (Blanc de Blancs)

FOX RUN
Hamport

Owner Scott Osborn is one of the movers and shakers in the Finger Lakes wine industry.

✓ *Lemburger* • *Pinot Noir* (Reserve) • *Riesling* (Dry)

GALLUCCIO FAMILY WINERIES
Cutchogue

Vince Galluccio took over Gristina Vineyards in August 2000, since when both brands have been made here.

✓ *Chardonnay* (Galluccio Cru George Allaire) • *Classic red blend* (Galluccio Cru George Allaire) • *Merlot* (Gristina)

GLENORA WINE CELLARS
Dundee
★ ▼

Named after the nearby Glenora waterfall, this winery consistently produces crisp and stylish wines.

✓ *Riesling* • *Seyval Blanc* • *Sparkling Wine* (Vintage Blanc de Blancs)

GOLD SEAL
Hammondsport

Originally called the Imperial Winery, this historic firm built its reputation on "New York Champagne". The quality of this sparkling wine was based on 100 years of Champagne

expertise, in the form of Charles le Breton of Louis Roederer, Jules Crance of Moët & Chandon, Charles Fournier of Veuve Clicquot, and Guy Davaux of Marne & Champagne, who all worked at Gold Seal. Of these, it was Fournier who stood out, and his name lives on as the brand of this firm's quaffing fizz.

GOOSE WATCH WINERY
Romulus
★ ▼

Under the same ownership as Swedish Hill winery, Goose Watch is an up-and-coming departure from the typical Finger Lakes mould, featuring grapes such as Diamond (*labrusca*), Lemberger, Melody, Merlot, Pinot Gris, and Viognier.

✓ *Lemberger* • *Viognier*

GREAT WESTERN WINERY
Hammondsport

Another historic winery, Great Western is now a subsidiary of The Taylor Wine Company. Its wines are less innovative, despite the occasional good *vinifera*.

HARGRAVE VINEYARD
Cutchogue
★ ▼

After looking at wine areas nationwide, Alex and Louisa Hargrave established Long Island's first vineyard in 1973, on what used to be a potato farm.

✓ *Cabernet Franc* (Reserve)

HAZLITT'S 1852 VINEYARDS
Hector
★ ▼

The late Jerry Hazlitt replanted the old family vineyards in 1984.

✓ *Riesling*

HERMANN J WEIMER VINEYARD
Dundee
★ ▼

Est. 1979

Hermann J. Wiemer
Riesling
Dry
2008

Estate Bottled and Grown

FINGER LAKES   ALC. 12.0% BY VOL.

While working for a certain hybrid aficionado, Weimer produced some outstanding *vinifera* wines from his own vineyard. They received rave reviews, and he has not looked back.

✓ *Gewürztraminer* (Dry) • *Riesling* (Dry) • *Sparkling* (Cuvée Brut)

HERON HILL VINEYARDS
Hammondsport
★☆Ⓥ

The name Heron Hill is a flight of fancy on the part of advertising copy writer Peter Johnstone, who so liked Finger Lake on a visit in 1968 that he stayed, set up in business with major shareholder John Ingle, and turned winemaker in 1977.

✓ *Classic red blend* (Eclipse, Game Bird Red) • *Riesling*

HUNT COUNTRY
Branchport
★☆Ⓥ

Owned and operated by Art and Joyce Hunt, the sixth generation to farm this land, but the first to make wine under their own name.

✓ *Vignoles* (Late Harvest)

KEUKA SPRING WINERY
Penn Yan
★☆Ⓥ

After more than 25 years in the business, Len and Judy Wiltberger are producing wines that are getting noticed outside the Finger Lakes district. In 1999, remarkably, they even won the Governor's Cup for their 1998 Cabernet Franc.

✓ *Cayuga* • *Vignoles* • *Riesling*

KNAPP VINEYARD
Romulus
★☆Ⓥ

This producer has always made wines from *vinifera* as well as hybrid varieties, including one of the state's best Seyval Blancs.

✓ *Cabernet Franc* • *Chardonnay* (Barrel Reserve) • *Merlot*

LAKEWOOD VINEYARDS
Watkins Glen
★Ⓥ

Owned and run by the Stamp family, who have farmed this land for four generations.

✓ *Cabernet Franc* • *Dessert* (Glaciavinum) • *Fortified* (Port) • *Pinot Noir* • *Riesling* • *Sparkling* (Brut) • *Vignoles*

LAMOREAUX LANDING
Lodi
★☆Ⓥ

There has always been something about this Finger Lakes winery, its design, and the people who run it that makes it a class act.

✓ *Cabernet Franc* • *Chardonnay* (Reserve) • *Merlot* • *Riesling* • *Sparkling wine* (Blanc de Blanc – sic, Brut)

LENZ
Peconic
★Ⓥ

While running a restaurant, Patricia and Peter Lenz developed a passion for wine, which led them to establish this winery on a potato farm.

✓ *Cabernet Sauvignon* • *Chardonnay* • *Merlot*

MARTHA CLARA
Riverhead
★Ⓥ

Interesting wines from this producer, whose first vintage was 1998.

✓ *Dessert* (Ciel) • *Sémillon*

MCGREGOR VINEYARD WINERY
Dundee
★☆Ⓥ

Established by the McGregor family in 1980, this vineyard began making Chardonnay, Riesling, Gewürztraminer, and Pinot Noir that year, but their heart is obviously in sparkling wine.

✓ *Sparkling* (Blanc de Noirs, Riesling)

PALMER
Aquebogue
★☆Ⓥ

The vineyard was converted from a potato and pumpkin farm in 1983, and the winery, built three years later, quickly started producing attention-grabbing wines. The reds, in particular, simply have more richness than other New York wineries can manage.

✓ *Cabernet Franc* • *Chardonnay* • *Merlot*

PAUMANOK VINEYARDS
Aquebogue
★★☆Ⓥ

Another of Long Island's up-and-coming stars.

✓ *Cabernet Sauvignon* • *Classic red blend* (Assemblage) • *Merlot*

PECONIC BAY WINERY
Cutchogue
★☆Ⓥ

Established in 1979, Peconic Bay was one of the first vineyards on the North Fork, producing its first commercial crop in 1984. The Merlot is particularly outstanding.

✓ *Chardonnay* (La Barrique) • *Merlot*

PELLEGRINI VINEYARDS
Cutchogue
★★☆Ⓥ

A recently established Long Island winery, Pellegrini is one of the most promising North Fork producers.

✓ *Cabernet Sauvignon* • *Chardonnay* • *Merlot*

PINDAR VINEYARDS
Peconic
★Ⓥ

With the intention of growing grapes, Dr Herodotus Damianos converted a potato farm on Long Island into a vineyard. In 1982 he built a winery, named it after the Greek lyric poet, and it is now Long Island's largest producer, and also one of the best.

✓ *Chardonnay* • *Classic red blend* (Mythology) • *Merlot*

RAPHAEL
Peconic
★★☆

Established in 1996, Raphael obviously has the money to make it one of the top two or three East Coast wineries. With Paul Pontallier of Château Margaux consulting, there is no reason why this potential should not be realized.

✓ *Classic red blend* (La Fontana) • *Merlot*

SHELDRAKE POINT VINEYARDS
Ovid
★☆Ⓥ

Some 16 hectares (40 acres) of *vinifera* vines on the shores of Lake Cayuga.

✓ *Riesling* (Ice Wine) • *Cabernet Franc*

SILVER THREAD VINEYARDS
Lodi
◉★☆Ⓥ

One of the first organic producers in the Atlantic Northeast, owner-winemaker Richard Figiel makes one of the Finger Lakes' better Pinot Noirs.

✓ *Pinot Noir*

SWEDISH HILL WINERY
Romulus
★Ⓥ

Founded in 1986 by Dick and Cindy Peterson, Swedish Hill has become one of the largest wineries in the region, producing nearly 40,000 cases of wine a year. *See also* Goose Watch.

✓ *Riesling* • *Sparkling Wine* (R Cuvée, Spumante Blush, Vintage Brut) • *Vidal Blanc*

TRELEAVEN WINES
King Ferry
★Ⓥ

Technically the King Ferry Winery, but owners Peter and Tracie Saltonstall sell their wines under the Treleaven label.

✓ *Riesling* (Semi Dry)

WAGNER VINEYARDS
Lodi
★

Consistently high-quality wines for a quarter of a century.

✓ *Chardonnay* (Barrel Fermented) • *Riesling* (Dry, Icewine) • *Sparkling* (Riesling Champagne)

WARM LAKE ESTATE
Cambria
★☆Ⓥ

With the largest plantation of Dijon Clone Pinot Noir in New York, Michael Von Heckler produces one of this state's better Pinot Noir wines.

✓ *Pinot Noir*

WÖLFFER ESTATE
Cambria
★Ⓥ

Wölffer Estate made history with its 2000 Premier Cru Merlot when it was released as Long Island's first $100 wine.

✓ *Merlot* • *Cabernet Franc*

OHIO
108 wineries in 2007

BUSCH-HARRIS
Mount Victory
★Ⓥ

Exciting new winery making waves with classy, award-winning Cabernet Sauvignon.

✓ *Cabernet Sauvignon*

FERRANTE WINERY
Harpersfield
★

Has made some lovely, rich Riesling that attains a classic petrol aroma after a couple of years.

✓ *Riesling* (Golden Bunchers)

FIRELANDS WINERY
Sandusky
★☆Ⓥ

This winery occupies the original Mantey Vineyard site, which was planted in 1880, and manages to attract 40,000 visitors a year.

✓ *Chardonnay* (Barrel Select) • *Riesling*

MARKKO VINEYARD
Ridge Road, Conneaut
★Ⓥ

This vineyard is owned by Arnulf Esterer, the first of Konstantin Frank's followers to plant *vinifera* grapes in Ohio.

✓ *Cabernet Sauvignon* • *Chardonnay* • *Riesling*

ST JOSEPH
Thompson
★☆

The 2006 Shiraz was classic cracked black pepper over soft fruit.

✓ *Shiraz*

TROUTMAN
Wooster
★☆Ⓥ

Established in 2001, Troutman produces a clutch of guzzlers that should attract wider attention.

✓ *Cabernet Franc* • *Chardonnay* • *Syval Blanc* (White Menagerie) • *Vidal* (Farmer's White)

VALLEY VINEYARDS
Morrow
★

Capable of excellent-quality, creamy Cabernet Franc with classic acidity/tannin balance.

✓ *Cabernet Franc*

PENNSYLVANIA
115 wineries in 2007

ALLEGRO VINEYARDS
Brogue
☆ⓥ

John Crouch is a well-established producer of Cabernet, and is currently on form with Cadenza.

✓ *Cabernet Sauvignon* • *Cadenza* (red Bordeaux-style)

CHADDSFORD WINERY
Chaddsford
★ⓥ

Eric and Lee Miller have established Chaddsford as one of the Atlantic Northeast's most successful wineries.

✓ *Chardonnay* (Barrel Select) • *Merlot*

CLOVER HILL VINEYARDS
Breinigsville
★☆ⓥ

Owner-winemaker John Scrips III is starting to pick up gold medals at his substantial 20,000-case winery.

✓ *Pinot Gris* (Pinot Grigio) • *Vignoles*

RHODE ISLAND
7 wineries in 2007

SAKONNET VINEYARDS
Little Compton
★☆ⓥ

The first winery to open on Rhode Island after Prohibition. New wine called Rhode Island Red not tasted.

✓ *Gewürztraminer* • *Vidal Blanc*

VIRGINIA
140 wineries in 2007

BARBOURSVILLE VINEYARDS
Barboursville
★★☆ⓥ

Once the property of James Barbour, a former governor of Virginia, this estate is now owned by Zonin of Piedmont in Italy. The wines have a remarkable elegance, balance, and finesse. Many seem to think that Virginia's best grape is Cabernet Franc, but Barboursville's Cabernet Sauvignon outperforms its Cabernet Franc most years. The Octagon requires ageing after release.

✓ *Barbera* (Reserve) • *Cabernet Franc* (Reserve) • *Cabernet Sauvignon* (Reserve) • *Classic red blend* (Octagon) • *Nebbiolo* (Reserve) • *Viognier*

BREAUX VINEYARDS
Hillsboro
★☆ⓥ

Created in 1994 by Paul and Alexis Breaux, who bought a 1.2-hectare (3-acre) vineyard planted in 1985 – mature by Virginia standards. The Late Harvest Alexis is a Sauvignon Blanc-Sémillon-Vidal Blanc blend.

✓ *Late Harvest* (Alexis) • *Sauvignon Blanc* • *Seyval Blanc* • *Viognier*

CHÂTEAU MORISETTE
Rocky Mount
☆ⓥ

A relatively well-established (1982), but recently up-and-coming winery.

✓ *Cabernet Sauvignon* • *Merlot* (Reserve)

CHRYSALIS VINEYARDS
Middleburg
★☆ⓥ

Chrysalis produces the most consistent-quality Norton I have found, but don't ask owner Jennifer McCloud about this all-American grape unless you really want to know, because she's probably the world's foremost expert on the subject! The Rubiana is a Tempranillo-Graciano-Fer Servadou-Norton blend.

✓ *Classic red blend* (Rubiana) • *Norton* • *Petit Verdot* (Hollin Reserve) • *Viognier*

HORTON
Charlottesville
★ⓥ

Dennis Horton was once known as Virginia's lone Rhône Ranger, but he now performs best with grapes that are more at home in the southwest of France. Even though there is an inconsistency in Horton's Norton, I have to recommend it because the highlights are minor classics, and everyone just loves the rhyme.

✓ *Cabernet Franc* • *Norton* • *Petit Manseng* • *Tannat*

JEFFERSON VINEYARDS
Charlottesville
★☆ⓥ

Located just outside Charlottesville, a mile from Monticello, on vineyard sites chosen and planted by Thomas Jefferson in 1774, but obviously more successful, as these bear fruit!

✓ *Merlot* (Reserve)

KESWICK VINEYARDS
Keswick
★☆ⓥ

Al and Cindy Schornberg planted a vineyard at the Edgewood Estate, part of the original 1727 Nicholas Meriwether Crown Grant, and produced their first wines in 2002, winning "Best White Wine in the US" at the Atlanta International Wine Summit with their Reserve Viognier.

✓ *Classic red blend* (Trevillian) • *Viognier* (Reserve)

KING FAMILY VINEYARDS
Crozet
★ⓥ

Michael Shaps is considered to be one of Virginia's most talented winemakers, and King Vineyards is one of the most beautiful locations in the scenic state of Virginia. One barrel of 2002 Merlot was by leaps and bounds the greatest red wine component I have ever tasted from any Virginia winery. Pity it was not bottled in its pure format, as it would have acted as a goal for all other wineries. Wines are sold under both King Family Vineyards and Michael Shaps labels.

✓ *Cabernet Franc* • *Merlot* • *Viognier*

KLUGE ESTATE
Charlottesville
☆ⓥ

If any winery is destined to become Virginia's first two-star winery, it's Kluge. Formerly owned by Patricia Kluge, it has benefited from such top international consultants as Michel Rolland (Bordeaux) and Claude Thibaut (sparkling). The estate was purchased by Donald Trump in April 2011. The Cru is a beautifully focused, Vin Doux Naturel style of sweet wine that knocks the spots off most Muscat de Beaumes de Venise. Second wines are sold under the Albemarle label.

✓ *Chardonnay* (Cru) • *Classic red blend* (New World Red) • *Sparkling Wine*

OAKENCROFT
Charlottesville
★☆ⓥ

Felicia Warburg Rogan started this venture in 1983, and is treated with love and respect as a *grande dame* by her younger neighbours.

✓ *Petit Verdot*

OASIS VINEYARD
Hume
★☆ⓥ

When Dirgham Salahi planted this vineyard in 1975, he was warned, like everyone else, against *vinifera* varieties, and the locals thought he was crazy when he not only ignored this advice but also decided to gamble exclusively on premium varieties. He was proved right and has since become one of the state's more consistent producers.

✓ *Chardonnay* (Barrel Select)

PIEDMONT VINEYARDS AND WINERY INC
Middleburg
★★

When Elizabeth Furness planted *vinifera* grapes in 1973, no one advised her otherwise, presumably because anyone who is crazy enough to start a new career at the age of 75 wouldn't listen anyway. She proved to be one of Virginia's best winemakers and revelled in her new job until her death in 1986. Since then her daughter, Elizabeth Worrell, has carried on admirably.

✓ *Cabernet Sauvignon* • *Chardonnay* (Native Yeast) • *Merlot*

PRINCE MICHAEL
Culpeper
★☆ⓥ

Owned by French industrialist Jean Leducq, this is the largest vineyard in Virginia, and its production is supplemented with grapes from the company's own vineyards in Napa. Wines are also sold under the Madison and Rapidan River labels.

✓ *Chardonnay* • *Classic red blend* (Symbius) • *Classic white blend* (Rapidan River Harmony) • *Shiraz* (Madison)

RAPPAHANNOCK CELLARS
Huntly
★☆ⓥ

John Delmare moved from California, and built this winery in 2000.

✓ *Cabernet Sauvignon* • *Classic red blend* (Meritage)

ROCKBRIDGE
Raphine
★☆ⓥ

Owner-winemaker Shepherd Rouse earned a Masters degree in oenology at UC Davis while at Schramsberg, Chateau St Jean, and Carneros Creek. Returning to his native Virginia in 1986, he was the winemaker at Montdomaine Cellars when its 1990 Cabernet Sauvignon won the 1993 Virginia Governor's Cup. Rouse established Rockbridge Vineyard in 1988, winning the Governor's Cup twice (1995 and 2001).

✓ *Chardonnay* (DeChiel Vineyard)

TARARA
Leesburg
★☆ⓥ

Established in 1989, this 16-hectare (40-acre) vineyard and winery started to shine almost immediately.

✓ *Chambourcin* • *Chardonnay* (Reserve) • *Classic red blend* (Meritage) • *Vidal Blanc*

VALHALLA VINEYARDS
Roanoke
★☆ⓥ

Since the Vascick family established Valhalla in 1999, their wines have won over 125 medals in national and international competitions.

✓ *Classic red blend* (Valkyrie)

VERITAS
Afton
★☆ⓥ

British-born neurologist Andrew Hodson is in the process of establishing something special at this ambitious, but stylish and well-considered, family-run winery.

✓ *Merlot* • *Petit Verdot*

WHITE HALL
White Hall
★☆ⓥ

In 1991, Tony Champ planted 2.5 hectares (6 acres) with Chardonnay, Cabernet Sauvignon, Cabernet Franc, and Merlot near the Blue Ridge Mountains. He later added other varieties, and now has 10 hectares (25 acres) of vines and a state-of-the-art winery.

✓ *Classic red blend* (Cuvée des Champs) • *Petit Verdot* • *Viognier*

OTHER WINEMAKING AREAS OF
THE UNITED STATES

ALABAMA

The first commercially cultivated vines were planted here in the 1830s, and the state had a flourishing wine industry prior to Prohibition. However, as many as half its counties remained "dry" until 1975, and legislation licensing farm wineries was not passed until 1978. There are just 11 Alabama wineries (as of 2010), and the wines are made from Muscadine. Other varieties are trucked in from out of state.

ALASKA

How do they do it? Well, not with Alaskan-grown grapes, that's for certain. There are six wineries, mostly making wines from locally grown soft fruits, although the Denali Winery produces a range of *vinifera* wines (Cabernet Sauvignon, Chardonnay, Merlot, Riesling, and the inevitable Alaska Icewine), albeit from trucked-in juice diluted with "crystal clear mountain water".

ARIZONA

Surprisingly, table grapes have long thrived in the irrigated Arizona deserts, but recently classic wine-grape varieties have been cultivated in this state's solitary AVA of Sonoita, which is made possible only through its altitude of between 1,200 and 1,500 metres (4,000 and 5,000 feet). In 2010, there were 48 wineries here.

SONOITA AVA

The Santa Rita, Huachuca, and Whetstone mountain ranges isolate this AVA. Geologically, this appellation is an upland basin rather than a valley, because it comprises the head-waters for three distinct drainages: Sonoita Creek to the south, Cienega Creek to the north, and the Babocamari River to the east. Local growers believe their *terra rosa* soil will determine the potential of this area.

ARKANSAS

More than 100 wineries sprang up in Arkansas after Prohibition, but lack of winemaking skills meant that barely half a dozen survived (nine in 2010). A fortified wine made by Cowie Wine Cellars and called Robert's Port is well respected, as is this winery's Cynthiana.

ALTUS AVA

This plateau lies between the Arkansas River bottom lands and the climatically protective high peaks of the Boston Mountains.

ARKANSAS MOUNTAIN AVA

This covers a huge area in the mountainous region of Arkansas. The Arkansas mountains moderate winter temperatures and provide shelter from violent northerly winds and sudden changes in temperature. Classic European grape varieties are grown here, but cannot survive in the area immediately south because of Pierce's disease, a vine-destroying condition associated with warm climates that attacks *Vitis vinifera*.

OZARK MOUNTAIN AVA

Five major rivers make up this AVA's boundaries: the Mississippi, the Missouri, the Osage, the Neosho, and the Arkansas, and the area includes Mt Magazine, the highest mountain in Arkansas. The Ozark Mountain appellation straddles parts of Missouri and Oklahoma, and is hilly-to-mountainous. The soils are stony, well drained, and contain clay from deeply weathered, well-consolidated sedimentary volcanic rocks.

COLORADO

The growing season in most of Colorado is too short to permit grape-growing, but the number of wineries has grown from just 5 in 1995 to 90 by 2010, and there are more in the pipeline. Chardonnay and Merlot are the most popular *vinifera* varieties.

GRAND VALLEY AVA

Grand Valley is located just west of Grand Junction, and incorporates three localities known as Orchard Mesa, Redlands, and Vinelands.

FLORIDA

The very first wine made in what is now the USA was made by French Huguenots at Fort Caroline in 1564, but the only viticulture of any significance occurred after the Civil War, when Florida was settled by dispossessed Northerners and Southerners alike. The Northerners planted their beloved *labrusca* vines, while the Southerners competed with their even more bizarre Muscadine. Some 200 hectares (500 acres) were cultivated towards the end of the 19th century, and it was the Southerners who won this battle of the grapes, as *labrusca* succumbed to Florida's extreme heat and humidity. Amid this North–South viticultural divide, a Frenchman by the name of Emile Dubois produced Norton and Cynthiana (then believed to be two different varieties) of sufficient quality to win a medal at the Paris Exposition of 1900, but virtually all of Florida's vineyards disappeared shortly thereafter, as it was widely acknowledged that this semi-tropical state was better suited to citrus groves. Not surprisingly, a lot of "orange wine" is made today, not to mention the wines made from Key lime, mango, and passion fruit. Rather odd though these concoctions might be, they are superior to the wine made from the local Muscadine grapes. Florida's growers have tried to grow *vinifera* again and again throughout the 20th century, only to discover that they were being killed by Pierce's disease (PD), for which there is no cure, although Muscadine varieties are unaffected. Since the 1950s, the University of Florida has released a number of complex PD-resistant hybrids created by crossing French hybrids with American ones, with Lake Emerald (developed in 1954), Stover (1968), Conquistador (1983), Suwannee (1983), and Blanc Du Bois (1987) being the most widely planted. Set against this backdrop, it is difficult to understand why there has been an explosion of wineries opening up of late. There were just six in 2000, yet no fewer than 25 by 2010.

GEORGIA

Georgia has cultivated grapes since 1733 and by 1880 was the sixth-largest wine-growing state. Even in modern times, its wines have been based on native Muscadine grapes until fairly recently, and they have been an acquired taste. Since the late 1990s, however, wineries such as Creekstone, Frogtown Cellars, Tiger Mountain, Three Sisters Vineyard, and Wolf Mountain Vineyards have used *vinifera* grapes planted at an altitude of 540 to 600 metres (1,800 to 2,000 feet) in the Northeast Georgia Mountains, where humidity is no problem, and cool nights preserve acidity.

HAWAII

Only Alaska seems a less likely wine-producing state, but vines were first planted here in 1814. The first vines planted in modern times were at Tedeschi Vineyard on Maui in 1974, and the first wines made in 1980. Dozens of experimental varieties were grown, but only Carnelian was chosen for commercial production. The Carnelian is a rather rustic cross developed in the 1930s for use in the hot continental climate of California's Central Valley, but fares less well in Hawaii's tropical climate, where the vine is over-vigorous, producing more leaves than fruit, and tends to crop several times a year. The vineyards have to be sprayed with salt to force the vines into some sort of winter rest. Further problems occurred in 1995, when the Carnelian vines were found to be infected with eutypa, or crown gall, a wasting disease that is difficult to control. In 1987 Volcano Vineyard on Hawaii island was planted with the Symphony cross, which appears to be more successful, and by 2010 the Hawaiian islands boasted five wineries in total, although most are producing tropical fruit wines, and one, Diamond Head Winery, is a do-it-yourself operation utilizing grape juice from the mainland.

ILLINOIS

By 1847, there were over 240 hectares (600 acres) of vineyards on the banks of the Mississippi, supplying no fewer than 40 wineries in Nauvo. In 1851, the oldest Concord vineyard in Illinois was planted in Nauvo State Park, where the vineyard is still producing wine today, as is Baxter's, established in 1857. By 1868, Illinois was producing 852,000 litres (225,000 gallons) a year – very nearly as much as New York. Today, there are 90 wineries in the state.

IOWA

Hiram Barney established 40 hectares (100 acres) of vines at Keokuk in 1869, which he called White Elk Vineyards, and it produced 115,000 litres (30,000 gallons) of wine a year before succumbing to a lethal combination of disease and Prohibition. Most of Iowa's modern-day vineyards were destroyed in 1980 by "2, 4-D" pesticide used on neighbouring crops, forcing wineries to truck in grapes from out of state, or to make fruit wine, although a number of new vineyards have been established since 2001. Norton is the most exciting variety currently grown, and although many of the better-known hybrids are not hardy enough to survive Iowa's winters, Maréchal Foch and La Crosse are two of the more successful ones. However, of the 43 wineries in this state, none has stood out so far.

KANSAS

Kansas has never been a huge winemaking state, but it did produce as much as 110,000 cases of wine a year until it voted to go "dry" in 1880. Although no modern-day wineries existed until 1990, there were 22 wineries by 2010, and Norton is the best grape.

KENTUCKY

In 1799, John James Dufour set up the Kentucky Vineyard Society, which expected to raise $10,000 in capital though the sale of 200 shares of $50 each. Without waiting for the subscriptions certificates to be printed, let alone sold, Dufour had purchased 253 hectares (633 acres) of land at Big Bend on the banks of the Kentucky River, and began planting the optimistically named First Vineyard in 1798. However, almost all the vines had failed by 1802. Like so many early ventures, the cause was probably Pierce's disease, phylloxera, or both. Another more successful early Kentucky venture was planted by Colonel James Taylor at Newport. This vineyard was described by John Melish, an English traveller, as "the finest that I have yet seen in America". In 2010, there were 65 wineries in Kentucky.

LOUISIANA

Jesuit priests made altar wine here as early as 1750, and by 1775 an Englishman we know of only as Colonel Ball produced a wine from the banks of the Mississippi, north of New Orleans, that was considered worthy of sending to George III, but the vineyard died after the colonel and his family were massacred by Indians, according to the August 1822 and December 1826 issues of *American Farmer*. Louisiana's climate is unsuitable for any vine other than Scuppernong, so grapes imported from California, or other fruit such as oranges, were relied upon for winemaking. There are just seven wineries in this state today.

MINNESOTA

Vineyards have to be buried beneath several feet of earth in order to survive Minnesota's winters, which restricts cultivation to native varieties and hybrids, with a heavy dependence on fruit wines, which are preferable more often than not. One exception is Northern Vineyards, which makes some of Minnesota's most exciting, cutting-edge wines from own-grown *vinifera* varieties such as Chardonnay, Pinot Noir, Pinot Gris, Gewürztraminer, and even St Laurent. Of the other 23 wineries in this state, only Carlos Creek, Saint Croix Vineyards, and Whitehaven stand out.

MISSISSIPPI

The pattern here is very similar to that in Kentucky. However, heavy and restrictive taxes were reduced in 1984, when the Mississippi Delta was granted its own AVA. By 2010, there were five wineries, but none are outstanding at the time of writing.

MISSISSIPPI DELTA AVA

A fertile alluvial plain with loess bluffs that abruptly rise 30 metres (100 feet) along the entire eastern side of the delta that also covers parts of Louisiana and Tennessee.

MISSOURI

The first wines were produced in Missouri in the 1830s and the state had a flourishing wine industry in the mid-18th century. The wine industry has almost doubled since the turn of the 21st century, with the number of wineries increasing from 37 in 2000 to 67 in 2010. Norton is the king of Missouri grapes.

AUGUSTA AVA

Grape-growing in Augusta, the country's first established AVA, dates from 1860. The bowl-like ridge of hills from west to east, and the Missouri River on the southern edge of the viticultural area, provide a microclimate that distinguishes Augusta from the surrounding areas.

HERMANN AVA

In 1904, this area furnished 97 per cent of the wine produced in Missouri. The soils are well drained, have a high water capacity, and provide good root development.

OZARK HIGHLANDS AVA

Located within the much larger Ozark Mountain AVA, this area's climate is frost-free and relatively cool during spring and autumn, compared with surrounding areas.

MONTANA

Although the growing season is generally too short for grapes, and most of this state's 11 wineries produce wines from locally grown soft fruits, or grapes trucked in from Washington, Idaho, and California, vines have grown around Flathead Lake and in the Flathead Valley since 1979, when Dr Thomas Campbell established Mission Mountain Winery on Flathead Lake's west shore. Although Mission Mountain remains the only winery to produce pure Montana-grown wines, and has to supplement them with wines made from out-of-state grapes, there are several other growers in this southwestern area of Montana who could start up their own boutique wineries, if the experience of other embryonic wine states is anything to go by. It seems that award-winning Mission Mountain Winery and the other growers all agree that the most successful *vinifera* varieties for Montana so far are Chardonnay, Gewürztraminer, Pinot Noir, and Pinot Gris.

NEBRASKA

The earliest known producer in Nebraska was Peter Pitz, who cultivated 5 hectares (12 acres) of vines near Plattsmouth in the 1890s, and claimed to make red, white, and yellow wine! The first vineyard in modern times was planted at Pierce by Ed Swanson of Cuthills Vineyards, and there are 23 wineries today, although apart from the modest successes of Whiskey Run Creek Vineyard & Winery, and Cuthills itself, no producers stand out. Some wines are made from native varieties, but essentially Nebraska viticulture suits hybrids, of which Edelweiss is most highly regarded, and others found include Cayuga, Chambourcin, DeChaunac, LaCrosse, Marechal Foch, St Croix, and Traminette.

NEVADA

Even though the growing season in Nevada is theoretically too short for growing vines, the first experimental vines were planted here in 1992, and by 1994 there were three vineyards: two in the Carson Valley of southern Nevada, and one in southern Nevada's Pahrump Valley. Instrumental in these ventures were Rick and Kathy Halbardier of Churchill Vineyards, which changed its name to Tahoe Ridge Vineyards & Winery in 1994, and built a research winery in 1996, harvesting its first commercial crop in 2000. There are now five wineries, but as far as I am aware, only Tahoe Ridge Vineyards & Winery and Churchill Vineyards, the latest venture, produce Nevada-grown *vinifera* wines (as well as wines from California grapes), but with eight Nevada vineyards growing various *vinifera* varieties to sell to Tahoe Ridge, the nucleus exists for a small wine industry to blossom in this desert state.

NEW MEXICO

Only Florida can claim an older winemaking industry than New Mexico's, dating from the early 1600s but unknown to Americans until 1821, when the Santa Fe Trail (known then as the Rio del Norte) was opened and reports of its vineyards filtered back to the East Coast. Today, there are 47 wineries.

MESILLA VALLEY AVA

An area that follows the Mesilla Valley along the Rio Grande River from an area just north of Las Cruces, New Mexico (where most of its vineyards are situated) to El Paso, Texas. Soils are alluvial, stratified, deep, and well drained.

MIDDLE RIO GRANDE VALLEY AVA

This narrow valley stretches along the Rio Grande River from Albuquerque to San Antonio. Franciscan missions grew vines here during the 17th century and winemaking existed until Prohibition. At an altitude of between 1,465 and 1,585 metres (4,800 and 5,200 feet), the climate is characterized by low rainfall and hot summers.

MIMBRES VALLEY AVA

An area of the Mimbres River from the north of Mimbres to the south of Columbus.

NORTH CAROLINA

Both the first and second colonies to settle this area were expected to produce wine, and although these hopes are documented, no evidence of any success exists. The hot climate dictates that most wines are produced from the hardy, native Scuppernong vine, which produces the most extraordinary, disturbingly exotic, and unusual wine from large, cherry-like grapes. It was these grapes that made North Carolina the largest wine-producing state in 1840. It was also from Scuppernong grapes that "Captain" Paul Garrett first made his notorious, best-selling Virginia Dare wine from a string of East Coast wineries in the 1900s. After Prohibition, he created the first singing commercial for wine, and Virginia Dare once again became the country's biggest-selling wine. Scuppernong grapes were scarce, however, and despite successfully encouraging many growers in other Southern states to grow this vine, he had to blend in more California wine, and in the process Virginia Dare lost its distinctive (and, by today's standards, not very attractive) character, so sales dropped. There are 51 wineries in North Carolina, but it is still a hostile environment for anything other than Scuppernong.

YADKIN VALLEY AVA

North Carolina's first official appellation, Yadkin Valley was recognized as an AVA in February 2003. This viticultural area comprises 1.4 million acres in the northwestern section of the Piedmont region, where it spans seven counties along the Yadkin River. There were fewer than ten wineries at the time of writing, but more were awaiting approval. Most vines here are *vinifera*, with Chardonnay, Riesling, Cabernet Sauvignon, and Merlot faring best over the long, warm growing season, with mild winters, on the Yadkin Valley's gently rolling hills of well-drained clay and loam soils.

NORTH DAKOTA

According to the TTB, there were 10 wineries in this state by 2010, but the only ones I know of are Maple River Winery in Casselton and Pointe of View in Burlington, both of which make own-grown fruit wines.

OKLAHOMA

The first known Oklahoma wines were made by Edward Fairchild, who in 1890 moved from the viticultural paradise of New York's Finger Lakes to establish a vineyard and orchard near Oklahoma City. Fairchild made commercial quantities of Concord and Delaware wine between 1893 and 1907, when Oklahoma joined the USA as a dry state. In 2010, there were 14 wineries here.

SOUTH CAROLINA

Winemaking began here as long ago as 1748, when Robert Thorpe was paid the handsome prize of £500 by the Commons of South Carolina for being "the first person who shall make the first pipe of good, strong-bodied, merchantable wine of the growth and culture of his own plantation". However, this state has never really recovered from Prohibition, with only 10 wineries in existence in 2010. The grapes used are invariably Muscadine or hybrid varieties, and even these tend to be supplemented with local-grown fruit wines. No wineries really stand out, except for Montmorenci Vineyards, which has won numerous awards for hybrid wines.

SOUTH DAKOTA

Valiant Vineyards was the first ever winery in South Dakota, established in 1993, when Eldon and Sherry Nygaard planted a small vineyard overlooking Turkey Ridge Creek in Turner County. At the time it would have been illegal to build and operate a winery, so the Nygaards drew up a farm winery bill and caused it to be introduced by the South Dakota Legislature, which passed it into law in July 1996. By 2010, there were seven wineries in this state, but none has stood out, although Prairie Berry Winery appears to be the most successful so far.

TENNESSEE

The best-known episode in this state's wine history took place in the 1850s, when a French, German, and Italian Catholic community called Vineland or Vinona established terraced vineyards, and made wine, which was sold to the Scottish Presbyterians in the southern Appalachians. Unfortunately, the Civil War put an end to both the activity and the community. In the 1880s, so-called Victorian Utopians established themselves at Rugby, and German settlers did likewise in the Allardt community of Fentress County. Although Tennessee still has some "dry" counties, the state now has 29 wineries. *Vinifera* vines have been planted here, but they usually perish under severe winter conditions. Most producers purchase grapes (*vinifera*, hybrid, and native varieties such as Scuppernong and Concord) from both in-state and out-of-state sources. Fruit wines are commonly encountered, and some mixed grape and fruit wines are also made. There are even tomato wines! Pure Tennessee grape wines are produced, but authentic is not necessarily superior. The modest wines of Beachhaven Vineyards & Winery are the most successful from this state. I tasted a promising Chambourcin from Beans Creek in 2006.

TEXAS

The Franciscan missions were making wines here at least 130 years before the first vines were grown in California and the first commercial Texan winery, Vel Verde, was established before the first one in California. In 1880, Thomas Volney Munson saved the phylloxera-infected French wine industry by sending Texas rootstock to Charente, and was awarded the French Legion of Honour medal, only the second American recipient at that time (the first being Benjamin Franklin). By 1919 there were 19 wineries in Texas, and a Texas wine won a gold medal at the Paris Exposition that year, but Prohibition destroyed winemaking in Texas as everywhere else. The revival of Texas wine began by accident in the mid-1950s, when Robert Reed, a professor of viticulture at Texas Tech University, took home some discarded vine cuttings. He planted them in his garden and was astonished at how well they grew. Reed and colleague Clinton McPherson planted an experimental vineyard of 75 grape varieties, which led to the founding of Llano Estacado winery in 1975. In 1987, Cordier, the famous Bordeaux *négociant*, invested in a massive 405-hectare (1,000-acre) vineyard called Ste Geneviève, and by 2010 there were no fewer than 80 Texan wineries in existence. In 1983 Texas was the smallest wine-producing state in the USA; today it is the fifth largest. If a wine states "For Sale in Texas Only", it does not have to state its origin.

BELL MOUNTAIN AVA

Located in Gillespie County, north of Fredericksburg (another sub-appellation of the Texas Hill Country AVA), this is a single-winery denomination consisting of some 22 hectares (55 acres) of vines, growing on the southern and southwestern slopes of Bell Mountain. Over a third of the vines are Cabernet Sauvignon, which has so far proved to be significantly better suited to this area than the Pinot Noir, Sémillon, Riesling, and Chardonnay that also grow here. Bell Mountain is drier than the Pedernales Valley to the south and the Llano Valley to the north, and also cooler due to its elevation and its constant breezes. Its soils are sandy-loam, with light, sandy-clay subsoil.

ESCONDIDO VALLEY AVA

Proposed by Cordier, the Escondido Valley AVA in Pecos County encompasses the Ste Geneviève winery. Escondido is an upland valley formed by ranges of mesas to the north and south, the vines growing at an elevation of between 795 and 825 metres (2,600–2,700 feet).

FREDERICKSBURG AVA

This AVA's full title is "Fredericksburg in the Texas Hill Country", but it is usually shortened to distinguish it from the massive Texas Hill Country appellation. Fredericksburg contained eight vineyards when established, but the area is primarily known for its peach orchards. As the peach tree has proved as sensitive to soil and climate as *vinifera* vines, many peach farmers have experimented with grapes, and a number of these are now in commercial production. The soil is sandy loam over a mineral-rich reddish clay.

TEXAS DAVIS MOUNTAIN AVA

Described as a mountain island, this Texas appellation is cooler, twice as wet, and climatically more diverse than the Chihuahua desert that surrounds it. Located in Jeff Davis County, Davis Mountain AVA covers 108,000 hectares (270,000 acres) in the Trans-Pecos region of western Texas that was formed during the glacially slow tectonic and volcanic catastrophe that formed the front range of the Rockies. This viticultural region ranges in height from 1,350 to 2,490 metres (4,500–8,300 feet), with about 20 hectares (50 acres) of vines currently growing on a porous, well-drained soil composed of granitic, porphyritic, and volcanic rocks, as well as limestone.

TEXAS HIGH PLAINS AVA

This massive appellation in the northwest of Texas covers 32,400 square kilometres (12,500 square miles), encompassing 24 counties and 800 hectares (2,000 acres) of vineyards. Soils are generally brown clay loams to the north and fine sandy loam to the south. Rainfall ranges from 36 centimetres (14 inches) in the west to 51 centimetres (20 inches) in the east.

TEXAS HILL COUNTRY AVA

A vast appellation, Texas Hill Country consists of the eastern two-thirds of the Edwards Plateau, encompassing two tiny AVAs (Bell Mountain and Fredericksburg), 40 commercial wineries, and 10 wineries. Most of the hillsides are on limestone, sandstone, or granite, while the valleys contain various sandy or clayey loams.

UTAH

Despite the enormous influence wielded by the powerful Mormon Church based in Salt Lake City, winemaking has a history in this state, ironically originating with the arrival of the seemingly abstemious Latter-Day Saints. Brigham Young, who led the Mormons to Utah in 1847, ordered vineyards to be planted and a winery to be built. He required one of his followers, an experienced German winemaker, to make as much wine as he could, and although he permitted Mormons to drink it for Communion (no longer allowed), he recommended that the bulk should be sold. His advice was not taken by the Dixie Mormons, who ran the winery and kept back their best wines for consumption. Winemaking peaked at the end of the 19th century, declining once the Church clamped down on drinking, and died out during Prohibition. Eight wineries now exist.

WISCONSIN

The present-day Wollersheim Winery is the historic site selected by the famous Agoston Haraszthy to plant his Wisconsin vineyard in the 1840s before moving on to San Diego, after experiencing several years of winter damage on his vines. The Haraszthy vineyard was taken over by Peter Kehl, a German immigrant to the USA, who built the existing winery during the Civil War period. Until relatively recently, this state had a rather more considerable reputation for its cherry, apple, and other fruit wines than for those made from grapes. Fruit wines still dominate in Wisconsin, but grape hybrids are beginning to gain ground, with some *vinifera* varieties, such as Riesling, just starting to emerge. The soils in the region are predominantly clayey loams. There were 42 wineries in the state in 2010.

LAKE WISCONSIN

Wisconsin Lake and River moderate the climate locally, providing winter temperatures that are several degrees higher than those found to the north, south, and west of this region, while the good air circulation helps to prevent both frost and rot.

WYOMING

Established in 1994, Terry Bison Ranch was this state's first winery, and by 2010, there were just four wineries. Most grapes are trucked in from out of state, and Table Mountain Vineyards is the only winery using Wyoming-grown grapes.

OTHER WINE PRODUCERS OF
THE UNITED STATES

ARIZONA
26 wineries in 2007

CALLAGHAN VINEYARDS
Sonoita
★ Ⓥ

Extraordinarily impressive wines have been made here for a number of years, with Syrah a particularly exciting addition to the range.

✓ *Classic red blend* (Back Lot Cuvee) • *Classic white blend* (Lisa's Selection) • *Syrah*

COLORADO
72 wineries in 2007

MOUNTAIN SPIRIT WINERY
Salida
★ Ⓥ

Grapes are trucked in from the Western Slope vineyards of Colorado.

✓ *Rosé* (Angel Blush)

PLUM CREEK CELLARS
Palisade
★ Ⓥ

Founded in 1984, Plum Creek Cellars was one of the pioneers of what was then a fledgling Colorado wine industry, and, having won more than 325 medals, it is one of the most successful.

✓ *Cabernet Franc • Cabernet Sauvignon • Riesling*

GEORGIA
20 wineries in 2007

CREEKSTONE
Helen
★ Ⓥ

Habersham Winery's new premium label reserved for *vinifera* wines grown primarily in its Mossy Creek vineyard.

✓ *Cabernet Sauvignon • Chardonnay* (American Oak) • *Viognier*

THREE SISTERS VINEYARD
Dahlonega
★ Ⓥ

A promising start from Sharon and Doug Paul, whose winery was opened in 2000.

✓ *Cabernet Franc*

TIGER MOUNTAIN VINEYARDS
Tiger

In 1995, John and Martha Ezzard planted the All-American Norton and an eclectic bunch of *vinifera* varieties (Cabernet Franc, Malbec, Mourvèdre, Tannat, Tinta Cão, Touriga Nacional, and Viognier) on mineral-rich, well-drained slopes of their 40-hectare (100-acre) farm, at an altitude of 600 metres (2,000 feet) on the southern Blue Ridge Mountains.

✓ *Cabernet Franc*

HAWAII
4 wineries in 2007

TEDESCHI VINEYARDS
Maui

Still and sparkling wines are made here from Carnelian grapes grown on the Maui's volcanic slopes, although three-quarters of the production is pineapple wine. Blanc de Noirs was the first *méthode champenoise* wine and, although I have visited this winery just twice, the wines have been coarse and uninspiring on both occasions. The easy-going rosé-styled Rose Ranch Cuvée proved to be less ambitious and more successful, although I have not tasted it recently. Tedeschi's grape wines are all made from the same variety, Carnelian, but there are vague plans for growing other varieties, so quality may improve.

VOLCANO WINERY
Hawaii
★

Veterinarian Doc McKinney planted this vineyard between two active volcanoes in preparation for his retirement in 1992, when he "went from working six days a week to seven", as he puts it. He has since sold the winery to Del Bothof. Surrounded by continuous volcanic eruption, the winery is prone to acid rain of such strength that in some years, such as 1993, production can be halved.

✓ *Symphony* (Mele)

ILLINOIS
83 wineries in 2007

ALTO VINEYARDS
Alto Pass
★ Ⓥ

Retired university professor Guy Renzaglia planted Chardonnay and Riesling, as well as hybrids, but the *vinifera* vines did not survive. The Renzaglia family produce a large range of hybrid wines, and have consistently excelled with Chambourcin and Vidal Blanc.

✓ *Chambourcin • Traminette*

MACKINAW VALLEY VINEYARD
Mackinaw
★

Established in 1998 by Paul and Jennie Hahn, whose tasting room did not open until 2003, by which time Mackinaw Valley Vineyard was already the fastest-rising star.

✓ *Classic red blend* (Alexander's Conquest)

KANSAS
16 wineries in 2007

HOLY-FIELD
Basehor
★ Ⓥ

With steadily improving performance over the last 10 years, Holy-Field demonstrates that parts of "fly-over America" are worth a stopover.

✓ *Chambourcin • Fortified* (St Francis Dessert Wine – Port-style) • *Norton* (Cynthiana) • *Seyval Blanc • Vignoles* (Late Harvest)

KENTUCKY
44 wineries in 2007

CHRISMAN MILL
Nicholasville
★ Ⓥ

Kentucky's best own-grown *vinifera* winery. The First Vineyard Reserve is a thoughtful blend of Chambourcin and Cabernet Franc.

✓ *Cabernet Sauvignon • Classic red blend* (First Vineyard Reserve) • *Chambourcin • Vidal Blanc*

MISSOURI
44 wineries in 2007

ADAM PUCHTA
Hermann
★ Ⓥ

Originally established as Adam Puchta & Son Wine Company in 1855, this winery was put out of business during Prohibition, but was resurrected in 1990 by Adam Puchta's great-great-grandson Timothy. Best known for Norton, but probably best at Port-style wines, particularly the Signature Port.

✓ *Fortified* (Signature Port, Vintage Port) • *Norton • Vignoles*

AUGUSTA WINERY
Augusta
★ Ⓥ

Impressive Norton, known in this state as Cynthiana.

✓ *Chambourcin • Norton* (Cynthiana) • *Vignoles*

CROWN VALLEY WINERY
St Genevieve
★ Ⓥ

One of Missouri's fastest-rising stars, this winery was established in 2000 by Joe and Loretta Scott, who planted the first vineyard on their 240-hectare (600-acre) estate in 1998. Crown Valley Winery now has a staggering 66 hectares (165 acres) of vines

(Chambourcin, Chardonel, Concord, Frontenac, Norton, Traminette, and Vignoles) with further expansions planned.

↳✓ *Chambourcin* • *Norton* • *Vignoles*

HEINRICHAUS
St James
★☆♥

Heinrich and Gina Grohe have been making Missouri wine since 1978, prior to which they grew grapes for other wineries.

↳✓ *Norton* (Cynthiana)

HERMANNHOF WINERY
Hermann
★♥

Purchased in 1978 by the Dierberg family, Hermannhof dates back to 1852, and is today one of Missouri's award-winning wineries.

↳✓ *Norton* • *Vignoles*

MONTELLE
Augusta
★☆♥

Clayton Byers was one of Missouri's modern-day viticultural pioneers, establishing Montelle in 1970, when he made his first wines in a converted smokehouse.

↳✓ *Seyval Blanc* • *Vignoles* (Dry)

MOUNT PLEASANT VINEYARDS
Augusta
★♥

A 19th-century winery resurrected in 1967 by Lucien Dressel, who in 1980 successfully proposed Augusta as the USA's first AVA. Produces both Norton and Cynthiana! Wines also sold under the Bethlehem label.

↳✓ *Classic red blend* (Claret) • *Fortified* (Vintage Port) • *Norton* • *Seyval Blanc*

ST JAMES WINERY
St James
★☆♥

Established in 1970 by the late James Hofherr, one of Missouri's viticultural pioneers.

↳✓ *Classic white blend* (School House White) • *Norton* • *Vignoles* (Vintage Select)

STONE HILL WINERY
Hermann
★☆♥

Established in 1847, Stone Hill is the oldest winery in Missouri. Its cellars were used as a mushroom farm during Prohibition but were revived in 1965 by Jim and Betty Held, who flirted briefly with *vinifera* varieties but gave up and are best known for Norton, both as a red wine and a Port style.

↳✓ *Fortified* (Cream Sherry, Port) • *Norton* • *Seyval Blanc* • *Vignoles* (Late Harvest)

NEBRASKA
20 wineries in 2007

CUTHILLS VINEYARDS
Pierce
★☆♥

Ed Swanson chose this location for Nebraska's first winery because of its rolling hills, which he planted with 50-odd varieties of wine grapes, mostly hybrids, in 1985.

↳✓ *Rosé* (Autumn Blush) • *Traminette*

NEW MEXICO
36 wineries in 2007

DOMAINE CHEURLIN
Truth or Consequences
★☆♥

Established in 1981 by Jacques Cheurlin, whose family make Champagne in the Aube district. The wines have a fresh, crisp style.

↳✓ *Sparkling* (New Mexico Brut)

GRUET
Albuquerque
★☆♥

The Gruet family established a cooperative in the Sézanne district of Champagne, but are prone to inconsistency in New Mexico, although some of their best wines have shown extraordinary acidity.

↳✓ *Sparkling* (Blanc de Blancs, Grande Reserve)

MILAGRO VINEYARDS
Corrales
★☆♥

The Milagro family focuses on Chardonnay, Merlot, and Zinfandel, as these varieties have been the most successful since they first planted these vineyards in 1985.

↳✓ *Chardonnay* • *Classic red blend* (Carrales Red) • *Merlot*

NORTH CAROLINA
74 wineries in 2007

BILTMORE ESTATE WINERY
Asheville
★☆♥

French grape varieties were planted in 1979 by the grandson of George Washington Vanderbilt, who built the country's largest mansion (250 rooms) on this 3,200-hectare (8,000-acre) estate. At a height of 1,400 metres (4,500 feet) in the Blue Ridge Mountains, it is not only cool enough for *vinifera* varieties to grow but can sometimes even be too cold for them to ripen. The American appellation on these Biltmore Estate wines is a clue to the grapes that are trucked in from California, and the wines are, I am sure, all the better for it.

↳✓ *Cabernet Sauvignon* (Signature) • *Sparkling*

OKLAHOMA
46 wineries in 2007

STONE BLUFF CELLARS
Haskell
★☆♥

Bob and Sandy McBratney purchased this property in 1994, but did not open their winery until 2000.

↳✓ *Classic white blend* (Cheval Blanc) • *Norton* (Cynthiana)

TEXAS
136 wineries in 2007

CAPROCK
Lubbock
★

Formerly known as Teysha Cellars, but under new ownership since 1992, when its name was changed to CapRock.

↳✓ *Cabernet* (Reserve, Royale) • *Chenin Blanc* • *Sauvignon Blanc*

FALL CREEK VINEYARDS
Austin
★☆♥

Named after the waterfall that feeds Lake Buchanan from an upper ridge of Ed Auler's ranch, Fall Creek is planted on land where he once used to raise prize cattle, and has thus been well fertilized for many years. The wines are fruity and quaffable.

↳✓ *Chenin Blanc*

FLAT CREEK ESTATE
Marble Falls
★☆♥

It was only in 1998 that Rick and Madelyn Naber purchased this property, but they now have 7 hectares (18 acres) under vine in the Texas High Plains AVA and are racking up the awards.

↳✓ *Cabernet Sauvignon* (Travis Peak) • *Classic red blend* (Super Texan) • *Muscat* (Moscato d'Arancia)

LLANO ESTACADO WINERY
Lubbock
★♥

Llano Estacado Winery is the first Texan winery to be established in recent history. It is best for crisp, lively white wines, but the reds are improving.

↳✓ *Cabernet Sauvignon* • *Chardonnay* • *Chenin Blanc* • *Classic white blend* (Signature White)

MESSINA HOF WINE CELLARS
Bryan
★☆♥

Paul Bonnarrigo's family originally came from Messina in Italy, while his wife Merril has a German heritage, hence the name of this winery, the third to be founded in the recent history of Texan wine. Messina Hof can stand shoulder to shoulder with many a West Coast winery in terms of quality.

↳✓ *Cabernet Sauvignon* (Barrel Reserve) • *Chardonnay* • *Chenin Blanc* • *Classic red blend* (Meritage Paulo) • *Merlot* (Private Reserve) • *Muscat Canelli* • *Riesling* (Johannisberg) • *Sauvignon Blanc* • *Sémillon*

PHEASANT RIDGE WINERY
Lubbock
★☆♥

Robert Cox of Pheasant Ridge Winery produces one of the state's best red wines.

↳✓ *Cabernet Sauvignon*

STE GENEVIÈVE
Fort Stockton
★☆♥

The Ste Geneviève winery was originally a Franco-Texan venture to cultivate 400 hectares (1,000 acres) of land that was leased from the University of Texas. However, the partnership dissolved and the French partner, Cordier, took full ownership. Much of the production is sold in bulk.

↳✓ *Cabernet Sauvignon* (Grand Reserve) • *Sauvignon Blanc*

UTAH
7 wineries in 2007

ARCHES VINEYARD
Spanish Fork

The most up-and-coming of Utah's wineries.

↳✓ *Riesling*

WISCONSIN
41 wineries in 2007

CEDAR CREEK WINERY
Cedarburg
★☆♥

An award-winning winery in Wisconsin. And with a winemaker named after a French wine-press, it is little wonder that Philippe Coquard is so successful.

↳✓ *Syrah* • *Vidal Blanc*

WOLLERSHEIM WINERY INC
Prairie du Sac
★☆♥

The Wollersheim Winery was built in 1858 by the Kehl family, from Nierstein in Germany, and then re-established in 1972 by Robert and Joann Wollersheim. Both hybrid and *vinifera* grapes are grown here. Wines are also sold under the Domaine du Sac label.

↳✓ *Classic white blend* (Prairie Fumé) • *Riesling* (Dry) • *Rosé* (Prairie Blush)

CANADA

British Columbia hardly figured in Canada's wine industry when I wrote the first edition of this book, and Ontario was only just beginning to emerge. Now Ontario is old hat, and although it still produces more than 80 per cent of all Canadian wine and thus much of the best, British Columbia is arguably the country's most exciting wine region, and wineries are popping up in Quebec, Saskatchewan, Manitoba, New Brunswick, Nova Scotia… even Newfoundland.

WINE HAS BEEN COMMERCIALLY PRODUCED in Canada since at least 1860. For the first 100 years, Canadian palates preferred the sweet styles produced by the native *labrusca* grape varieties, although from 1913 the Horticultural Research Centre of Ontario at Vineland began its programme to develop hybrids.

ONTARIO

Ask most people, including many Canadians, if they were to trace a finger around a globe at the same latitude as Ontario, where it would point to in Europe, and they would say somewhere in Scandinavia. Some might think Holland or Belgium, but few would imagine Tuscany, which is, in fact, correct. It is only Canada's snowbound winter temperatures that stop Niagara Peninsula, the province's most important viticultural area, from being another California.

At the 1988 launch party of the first edition, I served Inniskillin Pinot Noir and Château des Charmes Cabernet Sauvignon because few knew that Canada even grew vines, let alone any of the classic varieties, and certainly no one imagined this country produced red wines. In fact, on my first visit to Niagara, I could find only three red wines made from *vinifera* grapes. Now there are hundreds. Niagara's flagship wine is Icewine, and it is produced primarily from the Vidal Blanc hybrid, although there are plenty of Riesling Icewines, even Gewürztraminer and, most recently, Cabernet Franc

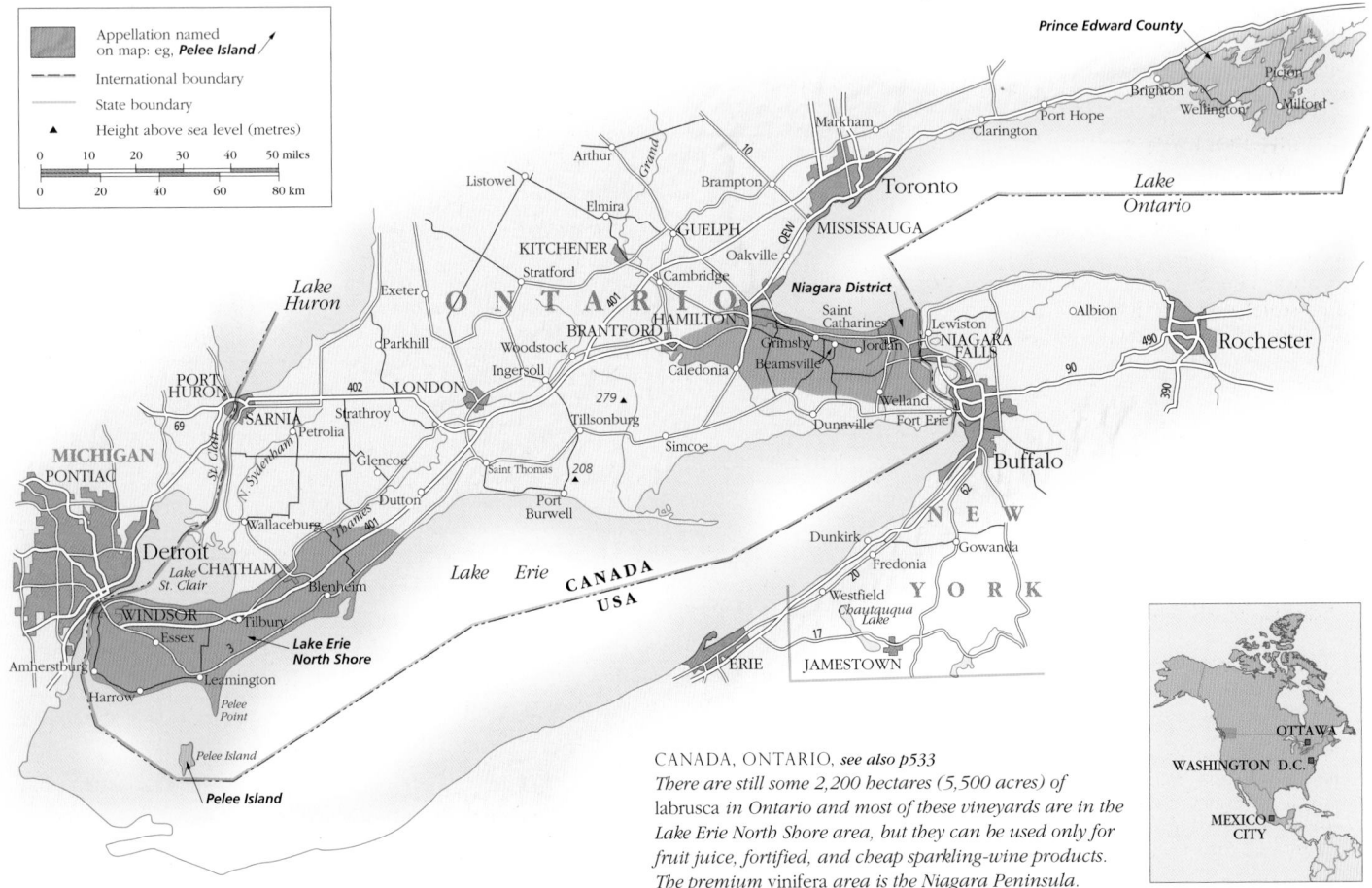

CANADA, ONTARIO, *see also p533*
There are still some 2,200 hectares (5,500 acres) of labrusca in Ontario and most of these vineyards are in the Lake Erie North Shore area, but they can be used only for fruit juice, fortified, and cheap sparkling-wine products. The premium vinifera area is the Niagara Peninsula.

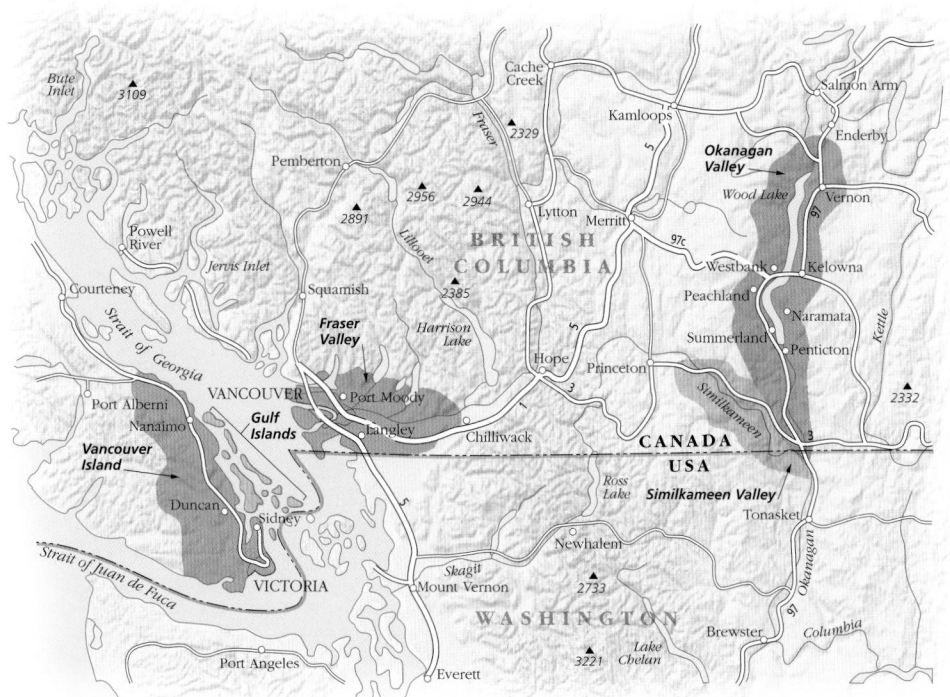

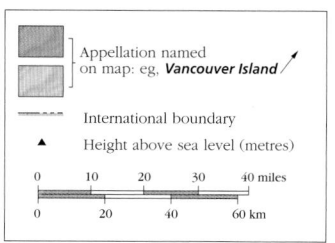

Appellation named on map: eg, *Vancouver Island*

International boundary

▲ Height above sea level (metres)

0 10 20 30 40 miles
0 20 40 60 km

CANADA, BRITISH COLUMBIA,
see also p533

British Columbia is rapidly closing the gap with Ontario. When NAFTA gave cheap California wines free access to the Canadian market, both regions had to upgrade their vineyards to survive. British Columbia's advantage was the smaller size of its vineyards and the tiny amount of labrusca *planted, as this enabled the province rapidly to replace almost all of its hybrids with* vinifera *varieties, while Ontario still has 2,200 hectares (5,500 acres) of labrusca and 2,000 hectares (4,800 acres) of hybrids.*

and even sparkling Icewine. Ontario will always be the world's largest producer of this style of wine because the annual winter lows guarantees the process, but it is hardly everyday drinking and, despite the hype, represents only 5 per cent of Ontario's total wine production. It might be more productive to focus on the juxtaposition of Ontario's seemingly northern vineyards being on the same latitude as Tuscany. It is no coincidence that Merlot and Cabernet Franc have proved to be among Ontario's most outstanding grapes, and wineries need to get the message across before British Columbia steals all its thunder.

BRITISH COLUMBIA

The revolution in Ontario's wine industry over the past 15 years has acted like bait, luring British Columbia along the same premium-quality path. As in Ontario, winemaking here dates back to the 1860s, but the climate is more marginal and so the industry has always been smaller and – until recently – less adventurous. Large-scale plantings of *labrusca* varieties did not commence until the 1930s, and hybrids were not developed until the 1950s. The

RECENT CANADIAN VINTAGES

2010 A great vintage in Ontario, while only those who thinned canes and dropped fruit in British Columbia have produced excellent wine.

2009 Great Ontario whites, including Icewines, and good red and whites in British Columbia.

2008 Ontario whites stand out from an otherwise variable vintage.

2007 An excellent year all round for both Ontario and British Columbia, but particularly so for Ontario Pinot Noir and Cabernet Sauvignon.

2006 The hottest, driest growing season on record, preceded by a devastating frost, produced another great vintage in Ontario, albeit half the normal size and with the added bonus that the Icewines could even be better than in 2005. Great wines were also made across the board in British Columbia.

FACTORS AFFECTING TASTE AND QUALITY

LOCATION
The chief areas are the Niagara Peninsula of Ontario in the east and the Okanagan Valley of British Columbia 3,200 kilometres (2,000 miles) away to the west. Vines also grow in Nova Scotia and Quebec.

CLIMATE
Eighty-five per cent of vines are grown in Ontario at the same latitude as the French vineyards of Provence and the hills of Tuscany. In Ontario, the temperature-moderating influence of Lakes Erie and Ontario, the windbreak effect of the Niagara Escarpment, and the circular airflow from the lakes, protect the vines from winter wind and frost damage.

The Okanagan Valley of British Columbia is on a more northerly latitude, some 49° to 50°N and approximately in line with Champagne and the Rheingau, but the area is technically a desert, with as little as 15 centimetres (6 inches) of rain in the south. The summers have fierce daytime heat that rapidly builds up the grape sugars, followed by cold nights that allow the grapes to retain high acid levels. The glacial Okanagan Lake provides a moderating effect, but winter quickly sets in and grapes do not develop beyond mid-October.

ASPECT
The vines in both Ontario and British Columbia are mostly grown on lakeside slopes. Those in Ontario are sheltered by the Niagara Escarpment, and the better grape varieties are grown on the steep north-facing slopes.

SOIL
Ontario soils cover a wide range from sandy loams to gravel, sand, and clay. Soil is sandy loam to clay on the west bank at the centre of British Columbia's Okanagan Valley, but stony-sandy clay on the east bank, more rocky and gravelly to the south, and much lighter and sandier to the north.

VITICULTURE AND VINIFICATION
The southern, red-wine producing end of the Okanagan Valley is undergoing the most extensive planting in Canada, although Niagara Peninsula's vineyards are still growing rapidly. Ontario's wine industry is mature by Canadian terms, while the smaller British Columbia industry is growing at an even more ferocious rate. The level of technology is high, but as in any young wine industry, methods and practices are changing all the time, as winemakers gain experience. Apart from Icewine production, techniques are in a state of flux.

GRAPE VARIETIES
Auxerrois, Bacchus, Baco Noir (Baco I), Cabernet Franc, Cabernet Sauvignon, Chambourcin, Chardonnay, Ehrenfelser, Gamay, Kerner, L'Acadie, Merlot, Pinot Blanc, Pinot Gris, Pinot Noir, Riesling, Sauvignon Blanc, Sémillon, Seyval Blanc, Shiraz (Syrah), Vidal Blanc, Zweigelt

first *vinifera* varieties were planted in 1974, but they were not a significant presence until 1989, when two-thirds of the vineyards – all *labrusca* and the least fashionable hybrids – were transformed.

My first trip to British Columbia was in 1993, when the state of the industry was similar to that of Ontario in the mid- to late 1980s. There were only seven red wines made from premium varietals, although there were plenty made from hybrids. After seeing how rapidly Ontario changed from hybrid to *vinifera* wines, and how quickly this elevated the province's standing in the international wine community, British Columbia's winemakers managed the same transition even more rapidly.

Such has been the rate of progress in British Columbia that Chardonnay is now the only variety widely acknowledged as consistently better in Ontario, although perhaps its Cabernet Franc and Riesling are often hard to beat, too. In British Columbia, some locals still love their Ehrenfelser, and although I have tasted some nice examples, it usually makes a lacklustre wine, and even the best will mean absolutely nothing to customers outside that province. As for reds, the farther that British Columbia pushes its vineyards into the hotter, southern Okanagan region, the greater the potential becomes. Those big southern reds are all the rage now.

THE APPELLATIONS OF
CANADA

FRASER VALLEY VQA
British Columbia

The Fraser Valley VQA comprises six small farm wineries that harvest hillside vineyards amid country lanes and historic towns, just one hour's drive from Victoria.

LAKE ERIE NORTH SHORE VQA
Ontario

In the southwest of Ontario, along the shoreline of Lake Erie (the shallowest and warmest of the five Great Lakes), the Lake Erie North Shore VQA has the most hours of sunshine in Canada and the grapes are picked weeks ahead of those of other areas. Its *vinifera* vineyards are just 2 per cent of the total vines.

MANITOBA

Manitoba is the easternmost of the three Prairie Provinces. On comparatively level land, plenty of soft fruits grow wild and abundant in Manitoba's rich soil and hot summers, but midwinter daytimes almost always remain well below freezing, making viticulture extremely difficult. However, some people are trying. Tobacco Creek Vineyards started experimenting with 600 vines, involving 20 varieties, in 2000 and has been in harvest for a few years now. Valiant (*Fredonia* x *Wild Montana*) is supposed to be the most likely vine to survive in this province.

NEW BRUNSWICK

This province is more cider and fruit-wine country, with schnapps and liqueurs of every kind produced. There are wines made from berries, apples, honey, and maple syrup, not to mention so-called cider and apple "iced" wines. However, wine from New Brunswick grapes has existed since 2000, when Ferme Maury sold its first own-grown products. There are now seven wineries in this province, but none has stood out so far.

NEWFOUNDLAND

Canada's most easterly province comprises the Island of Newfound and Labrador on the mainland. Viticulture would seem to be impossible in this province, which boasts five wineries, all on Newfoundland itself, and only fruit wines produced.

NIAGARA PENINSULA VQA
Ontario

On the south shore of Lake Ontario, Niagara Peninsula is where the lake-induced airflow is at its greatest, making viticulture most suitable, hence the area encompasses 97 per cent of Ontario's vineyards. Most vines grow at a height of 90 metres (300 feet) above sea level, as the land gently slopes from the foot of the Niagara Escarpment to the lake. The escarpment rises to over 180 metres (600 feet) and contains a number of benches, about which there is increasing interest, especially in the Beamsville area.

NOVA SCOTIA

Although the growing season here is short and cool, with very harsh winters, making vinegrowing more an act of faith than the result of hard work, Nova Scotia has had commercial vineyards since 1982 and today boasts 22 growers, who between them farm 160 hectares (400 acres) of vines. The southern tip is actually below the 45th parallel and its vineyards are to be found there, on the west coast, in the Annapolis Valley. The first varieties to show promise in Nova Scotia were French hybrids, such as Baco Noir, Castel, DeChaunac, Léon Millot, Marechal Foch, and Seyval Blanc. Two Russian hybrids, Mischurnitz and Severnyi, which are *Vitis amurensis* crosses, have also been successful early ripeners, with high sugar content and excellent winter hardiness. Another hybrid, L'Acadie, was specifically created for Nova Scotia at Vineland in Ontario. Grand Pré was the first commercial winery, established by the pioneering Roger Dial, and now owned by Jim Landry and Karen Avery, who added Chardonnay to the varieties grown.

OKANAGAN VALLEY VQA
British Columbia

The largest, oldest, and most important of BC's wine areas, this stretches 160 kilometres (100 miles), with some 970 hectares (2,400 acres) of vines: more than 96 per cent of BC's vineyards. French and German varieties are planted at the northern end, but much activity is focused on the fast-expanding vineyards in the south, which receive less than 152 millimetres (6 inches) of rain and where classic red-wine varieties thrive.

PELEE ISLAND VQA
Ontario

This is the site of Canada's first commercial winery, established in 1866. It is located in Lake Erie, 24 kilometres (15 miles) off the mainland, where its 200 hectares (500 acres) are marginally closer to the equator than Rome is. Picking starts at the end of August and even late-harvested grapes are in by mid-October.

QUEBEC

If Nova Scotia wines seem improbable, then many readers may wonder at the likelihood of vineyards in Quebec, where Arctic-like winters can bring bone-chilling temperatures along with several feet of snow. But it is not the figment of somebody's imagination or a scam to sell wines made from 100 per cent imported grapes. Such vineyards do exist. It was here, after all, that the Jesuits, following in the wake of Jacques Cartier, made Canada's first wines circa 1564. But even if Quebec were at the North Pole, one gets the feeling that its French descendants would make an attempt to grow vines. It's in their blood. There are now 30 wineries in this province, all very small, and most located south of Montréal, near to the border with Vermont.

SASKATCHEWAN

This province covers more than 647,000 square kilometres (250,000 square miles), half of which is covered by forest, and one-eighth with nearly 100,000 freshwater lakes. One-third of Saskatchewan is farmland, but while the hot summers provide numerous berry crops for the three local wineries to make fruit wine from, the long, bitterly cold winters make grape-growing seemingly impossible.

SIMILKAMEEN VALLEY VQA
British Columbia

To the southwest of the Okanagan Valley, in the high desert cattle country of the Similkameen Valley, Crowsnest Vineyards is leading a small band of pioneering wineries. The vines represent just over 2 per cent of BC's vineyards, yet make this the province's second-largest appellation.

VANCOUVER ISLAND VQA
British Columbia

The province's newest wine area, Vancouver Island's wet and windy climate might not seem ideal for viticulture, yet Divino moved here from what some considered to be the finest vineyards in the Okanagan Valley. Vancouver Island is the second most important wine area in BC and shortly promises to overtake the Similkameen Valley as second-largest for vineyards.

THE WINE PRODUCERS OF

CANADA

BRITISH COLUMBIA

ADORA ESTATE

Summerland

⭐✩

Now solely owned by Reid Jenkins, one of the founding partners, Adora Estate started to regain its initial promise in 2008 and opened a brand-new winery in 2010.

ANDRÉS WINES

Port Moody

This is the winery that introduced Canada to the delights of "Baby Duck", a popular and much-imitated sweet pink or red fizzy *labrusca* wine. The original version was known in Germany as "Kalte Ente" or "Cold Duck", and was made from the dregs of both red and white wines, to which some Sekt was added. For anyone not used to foxy-flavoured *labrusca* grapes, Andrés's commercial version was even more disgusting than the original concoction, but it took North America by storm. As *vinifera* wines gave Canada a wine industry to be proud of, even Andrés was forced to sell premium varietals. However, it dawned on Andrés that the sort of discerning customer most likely to buy premium varietals would be the least likely to buy from a firm that was synonymous with "Baby Duck". The Peller Estates label (named after Andrew Peller, the founder of Andrés) was thus launched to market exclusively VQA *vinifera* wines, and is a fast-improving winery today (*see* Peller Estates).

BLUE MOUNTAIN

Okanagan Falls

⭐⭐✩

BLUE MOUNTAIN
Vineyard

Pinot Noir

Ian Mavety's Blue Mountain winery in the Okanagan Valley has come a long way since 1992. Mavety is a master of Pinot in all of its three formats and, under the guidance of Raphael Brisbois (who was formerly at Omar Khayyam in India and Iron Horse in California), he has completely refined the Blue Mountain sparkling wines.

✓ *Pinot Blanc • Pinot Gris • Pinot Noir • Sparkling Wine* (Brut, Brut Rosé)

BURROWING OWL

Oliver

⭐⭐

This is one of British Columbia's most up-and-coming wineries, at the tip of the Sonora Desert, near the north end of Osoyoos Lake, one of Canada's most exciting new wine regions. Improving Cabernet Sauvignon and Syrah should soon join the list of highly recommended wines.

✓ *Cabernet Franc • Chardonnay • Classic red blend* (Meritage) • *Merlot • Pinot Gris*

CALONA

Kelowna

⭐✩ Ⓥ

Calona has been making wine since 1932. Its semi-sweet German-style Schloss Laderheim became Canada's best seller in 1981, but Calona's wines improved, although resting on its relatively modest laurels of late.

✓ *Pinot Blanc* (Artist Series Reserve)

CEDAR CREEK

Kelowna

⭐✩ Ⓥ

This winery has come a long way over the past 10 years, and is now living up to its reputation, yet continues to improve.

✓ *Chardonnay* (Estate Select) • *Classic red blend* (Platinum Reserve) • *Merlot • Pinot Blanc • Pinot Gris • Pinot Noir* (Platinum Reserve) • *Riesling* (Dry)

DOMAINE COMBRET

Osoyoos

⭐✩ Ⓥ

With a reputation for Chardonnay and Cabernet Franc, Combret also produces a very good Gamay.

✓ *Cabernet Franc* (Saint Vincent) • *Chardonnay* (Saint Vincent) • *Gamay* (Reserve)

DOMAINE DE CHABERTON

Langley

⭐✩ Ⓥ

Owner Claude Violet has had winemaking experience in France and Switzerland and was the first to grow grapes in the Fraser Valley.

✓ *Bacchus • Gamay*

GEHRINGER BROTHERS

Oliver

⭐✩ Ⓥ

Gordon and Walter Gehringer's modern winery is tucked into the cleft of a spectacular amphitheatre of immaculate vines.

✓ *Classic red blend* (Cabernet Merlot) • *Pinot Gris* (Private Reserve) • *Pinot Noir* (Private Reserve) • *Sauvignon Blanc*

GRAY MONK CELLARS

Okanagan Centre

⭐ Ⓥ

Gray Monk has a reputation for Gewürztraminer, but it is not this winery's best wine.

✓ *Pinot Blanc • Pinot Auxerrois* (Odyssey) • *Siegerrebe*

HAINLE

Peachland

Ⓞ⭐✩

I cannot fault Tilman Hainle's enthusiasm; he nearly always goes over the top, but can produce wonderfully exciting wines as a result, only to make a complete hash of the same *cuvée* in the following vintage.

✓ *Cabernet Franc • Gewürztraminer • Icewine* (Riesling)

HAWTHORNE MOUNTAIN VINEYARDS

Okanagan Falls

⭐✩ Ⓥ

This winery is owned by Albert and Dixie LeComte, with Dave Carson as winemaker.

✓ *Chardonnay* (Gold Label) • *Classic white blend* (Mountain Select White) • *Icewine* (See Ya Later Ehrenfelser) • *Merlot*

HILLSIDE

Penticton

⭐

Vera Klokocka fled Czechoslovakia when the Soviets invaded in 1968. She has been growing grapes since the mid-1970s, and has been making some wonderfully gluggy wines since 1990.

✓ *Cabernet Franc* (CSPC) • *Pinot Blanc*

INNISKILLIN OKANAGAN

Oliver

⭐

Ontario's premier publicist, Don Ziraldo, started making wines in 1994, when his winery became part of Vincor, but did not have his own premises until 1996, when Inniskillin acquired the former Okanagan Vineyards winery.

✓ *Icewine* (Dark Horse Vineyard Riesling) • *Pinot Noir* (Dark Horse Vineyard)

JACKSON-TRIGGS

Oliver

⭐⭐ Ⓥ

The original Jackson-Triggs winery started out by building a reputation for Icewine, but soon widened its scope, making it one of the country's top, all-round wine producers.

✓ *Classic red blend* (Proprietor's Grand Reserve: Cabernet-Shiraz, Meritage) • *Icewine* (Proprietor's Grand Reserve Riesling) • *Merlot* (Proprietor's Grand Reserve) • *Shiraz* (Proprietor's Grand Reserve) • *Viognier* (Proprietor's Reserve)

LAKE BREEZE VINEYARDS

Naramata

⭐ Ⓥ

Run by a bunch of former bankers and accountants, who now claim to have "dirty fingernails and new calluses". They've certainly got some good wines.

✓ *Chardonnay • Pinot Blanc • Pinot Gris • Sémillon*

LANG VINEYARDS

Naramata

⭐✩ Ⓥ

Owner Guenther Lang left Germany and in 1990 set up Lang Vineyards, the first boutique farm winery in the province, in 1990.

✓ *Maréchal Foch • Pinot Gris • Riesling* (Late Harvest, Reserve)

MISSION HILL VINEYARDS

Westbank

⭐⭐✩

This operation has won more than its fair share of international medals since New Zealander John Simes took over as winemaker in 1992, including North America's only gold medal at the 2001 Chardonnay du Monde Competition, and being named Winery of the Year at the first ever Canadian Wine Awards..

✓ *Chardonnay* (Estate) • *Classic red blend* (Oculus) • *Merlot • Syrah* (Estate, Shiraz)

NICHOL VINEYARD

Naramata

⭐

Alex and Kathleen Nichol have produced one of the Okanagan Valley's fastest-rising star wineries.

✓ *Cabernet Franc • Pinot Noir • Syrah*

QUAILS' GATE

Kelowna

Ⓞ⭐⭐✩ Ⓥ

The Stewart family planted their vineyards in the 1960s, but there was an uncertain feel about these wines even until the early 1990s, when the arrival of Australian-born winemaker Jeff Martin rapidly turned the quality around. The current winemaker, Grant Stanley, hails from New Zealand, has an impressive CV, and since the vintages of the early 2000s he has taken Quails' Gate up to a completely new quality level.

✓ *Cabernet Sauvignon* (Family Reserve) • *Chardonnay* (Family Reserve) • *Chenin Blanc* (Family Reserve) • *Gamay* (Family Reserve) • *Pinot Noir* (Family Reserve)

INNISKILLIN VINEYARD UNDER SNOW
Inniskillin made its first Icewine in 1984, but it was not until 1986 that the technique was perfected and started to attract international interest, which was sealed by the gold medal won at Vinexpo in 1991 for the 1989 Vidal Icewine.

SUMAC RIDGE
Summerland
★✫ⓥ

Now part of Vincor, although still very much run by one of his former partners, Harry McWatters, and continuing to collect a plethora of prizes whenever the wines are entered into competitions.

✓ *Cabernet Sauvignon* (Black Sage Vineyard) • *Classic red blend* (Cabernet Merlot, Meritage) • *Icewine* (Pinot Blanc) • *Merlot* • *Pinot Blanc* (Reserve)

SUMMERHILL ESTATE
Kelowna
◎✫

Whether the pyramid of Cheops on this property actually focuses pyramid-power is open to question, to put it mildly, but there is no doubt whatsoever that owner Stephen Cipes is eccentric. Famed for the world's only Pyramid-Aged "Champagne", Summerhill is appreciated locally for its Gewürztraminer, although far more consistent for its still wines made from Pinot varieties, particularly Meunier.

✓ *Pinot Blanc* • *Pinot Gris* (Platinum Series) • *Pinot Meunier*

TOWNSHIP 7 VINEYARDS
Langley
✫ⓥ

Owners Corey and Gwen Coleman have already grabbed the attention of discerning consumers with their award-winning wines.

✓ *Merlot* (Reserve) • *Syrah*

VINCOR
Oliver

Formerly called Brights-Cartier, this vineyard is the largest wine producer in Canada, owning Le Clos Jordanne, Jackson-Triggs, Inniskillin, Sumac Ridge, and Hawthorne Mountain, with wineries elsewhere, including R H Phillips and Hogue (USA), Goundrey and Amberley Estate (Australia), and Kim Crawford Wines (New Zealand). Part of Constellation since 2006.

NOVA SCOTIA

BENJAMIN BRIDGE
Gaspereau Valley
★✫

With Peter Gamble and fizzmaker extraordinaire Raphaël Brisbois consulting, this specially built sparkling-wine vineyard and winery has quickly produced world-class sparkling wines. The classic *brut* styles made from either purely or predominantly Chardonnay and Pinot Noir (some *cuvées* have also contained L'Acadie and Vidal) are really quite remarkable, drinking well and yet capable of ageing, but the joyful and delicious Nova sparkling Moscato should not to be missed.

✓ *Entire sparkling-wine range*

JOST VINEYARDS
Malagash
✫ⓥ

When Jost Vineyards 1999 Vidal Icewine was named Canada's Wine of the Year 2000, it was the first time in the competition's 20-year history that the winning wine had come from outside Ontario and British Columbia.

✓ *Fortified* (Port) • *Icewine* (Muscat, Vidal) • *Maréchal Foch* • *Michurinetz* (Premium Oak-Aged) • *Muscat* (Eagle Tree)

ONTARIO

13TH STREET
Jordan Station
★★

Established in 1998 by four friends (Ken Douglas, Gunther Funk, Herb Jacobson, and Irv Willms), who make wines from their own vines (Funk Vineyard, and the warmer Sandstone Vineyard), plus bought-in fruit for wines that are not vineyard-designated.

✓ *Gamay* (Unfiltered) • *Pinot Noir* (Reserve)

CAVE SPRING CELLARS
Jordan
★★

A large, ambitious venture founded in 1986 by Leonard Penachetti, whose vineyards are located on the Beamsville Bench, west of St Catharines, and planted at twice the average density for this region. Something of a Chardonnay specialist, producing a rare Chardonnay exclusively from the Musqué clone, althought the CSV is clearly the finest and most consistent of Cave Spring's Chardonnays.

✓ *Chardonnay* (CSV, Musqué, Reserve) • *Gamay* (Reserve) • *Icewine* (Riesling) • *Riesling*

CHÂTEAU DES CHARMES
St Davids
★★

Established by Paul Bosc and run by his son Paul André, Château des Charmes excels with red-wine styles.

✓ *Cabernet Franc* (St David's Bench Vineyard) • *Chardonnay* (St David's Bench Vineyard) • *Classic red blend* (Equuleus, Paul Bosc Estate Vineyard) • *Icewine* (Riesling)

LE CLOS JORDANNE
Jordan
★★★

A joint venture between Vincor (now part of Constellation) and Boisset (Burgundy). The single-vineyard wines from Thomas Bachelder's first vintage (2004) were leaps and bounds better than any Pinot Noir produced in Canada up to that date.

✓ *Entire range* (so far!)

COLIO WINES
Harrow
★✫ⓥ

Colio Wines was founded by a group of Italian businessmen who wanted to import Italian wines from their twin-town of Udine in Friuli-Venezia Giulia, but ultimately found that it was easier to build a winery and make their own.

✓ *Merlot* (CEV) • *Pinot Gris* (HE)

DANIEL LENKO
Vineland
★ⓥ

If you have ever wondered what the same wine tastes like in different oak, Lenko will help you out with its Old Vines Chardonnay, which you can buy in two flavours: American Oak or French Oak.

✓ *Cabernet Franc* • *Chardonnay* • *Merlot* (Old Vines) • *Rosé* (Cabernet Rosé) • *Viognier*

FLAT ROCKS CELLARS
Jordan
★★

A new winery perched on the brink of 75 acres of rolling vineyard located close to the top-performing Clos de Jordanne. South African Marlize Beyers is the winemaker, with Ann Sperling consulting.

✓ *Chardonnay* • *Pinot Noir* • *Riesling* (Nadia's Vineyard)

HENRY OF PELHAM
St Catharines
★

Established in 1988 by the Speck family, who have grown grapes in the area since 1974. After an initial period of inconsistency, this winery has settled to a high standard of quality. Hybrid enthusiasts should taste the Baco Noir, which is one of the best in the world.

✓ *Baco Noir* • *Icewine* (Riesling) • *Riesling* (Botrytis Affected) • *Sauvignon Blanc* • *Vidal* (Special Late Harvest)

HILLEBRAND
Niagara-on-the-Lake
✫

Initially called Newark (the original name for Niagara-on-the-Lake), the title of this winery changed when it was purchased by Scholl & Hillebrand of Rüdesheim in 1983 and sold to Andre Wines in 1998. The best Hillebrand wines are not as outstanding as they used to be.

✓ *Chardonnay* (Trius) • *Classic red blend* (Trius)

INNISKILLIN
Niagara-on-the-Lake
★ⓥ

Founded by Don Ziraldo, an agronomist and one of Canada's greatest wine publicists, and the winemaker Karl Kaiser, a highly respected oenologist. You could not get two more contrasting characters, but the symbiotic relationship between extrovert Ziraldo and introvert Kaiser was essentially responsible for driving the Canadian wine industry from the backwaters to its present position on the international wine stage.

✓ *Cabernet Franc* (Reserve) • *Cabernet Sauvignon* (Klose Vineyard) • *Chardonnay* (Founder's Reserve, Reserve) • *Icewine* (Riesling) • *Pinot Noir* (Montagu Estate Vineyard, Reserve) • *Riesling* (Dry, Select Late Harvest)

JACKSON-TRIGGS
Niagara-on-the-Lake
⭐

Part of Vincor, Jackson-Triggs' new winery opened in Ontario in 2001. Since then, it has set new standards for future wineries, but it has not maintained this promise.

✓ *Chardonnay* (Proprietor's Grand Reserve) • *Classic red blend* (Proprietor's Grand Reserve Meritage) • *Icewine* (Proprietor's Grand Reserve: Gewürztraminer, Riesling) • *Riesling* (Delaine Vineyard)

KONZELMANN
Niagara-on-the Lake
⭐⭐✦

Established in 1984 by Herbert Konzelmann, who introduced the vertical trellising of vines to Canada. Konzelmann is one of the most modest and gifted winemakers in Ontario and his vineyard has always displayed exceptional potential for Gewürztraminer. These wines sell out quickly every year.

✓ *Chardonnay* (Grand Reserve) • *Classic red blend* (Cabernet Merlot Reserve Unfiltered) • *Icewine* (Vidal) • *Merlot* (Barrel Aged) • *Riesling* (Select Late Harvest) • *Riesling Traminer* (Select Late Harvest)

LAILEY VINEYARD
Niagara-on-the-Lake
⭐⭐

English winemaker and part-owner Derrick Barnett has access to some of Canada's oldest *vinifera* vines, planted by the pioneering Donna Lailey more than 40 years ago.

✓ *Cabernet Sauvignon* • *Chardonnay* (Old Vines) • *Classic red blend* (Cabernet) • *Merlot* • *Pinot Noir*

LONG DOG WINERY
Milford
★

The most promising producer in Prince Edward County, Ontario's fastest-rising new wine district.

✓ *Pinot Noir* (The Otto)

MAGNOTTA WINERY
Mississauga
★✦

This winery has vineyards on the Beamsville Bench, where it sources its top-performing Chardonnay and some interesting, often unusual, Icewine.

✓ *Cabernet Sauvignon* • *Carmenère* • *Chardonnay* • *Icewine* (Cabernet Franc, Riesling)

MALIVOIRE
Beamsville
⭐✦★✦

Owned by Martin Malivoire and Moira Saganski, whose choice of Ann Sperling as winemaker paid off in 2004, when she was named Winemaker of the Year at the Ontario Wine Awards (and they had not even entered any wines!). Sperling has since left to start up Southbrook's new winery, leaving her assistant, Shiraz Mottiar, to take over as winemaker.

✓ *Chardonnay* (Moira Vineyard) • *Gewürztraminer* (Moira Vineyard) • *Muscadet* (Estate Melon) • *Pinot Noir* (Estate)

PELEE ISLAND
Kingsville, Pelee Island
★

It takes an hour on a ferry to reach this island in Lake Erie, one of Ontario's VQA areas and the location of Canada's most southerly vineyards. With the longest growing season in the country and the warmest climate, it comes as no surprise that Vin Villa, Canada's first commercial winery, was established here in the 1860s.

✓ *Cabernet Franc* • *Icewine* (Cabernet Franc, Vidal) • *Pinot Gris* (Vendange Tardive) • *Riesling* (Late Harvest) • *Rosé* • *Sauvignon Blanc*

PELLER ESTATES
Niagara-on-the-Lake
⭐✦✦

Large, successful, boutique winery owned by Andrés, the second-largest winery in Canada.

✓ *Icewine* (Founder Series Vidal) • *Merlot* (Signature Series Unfiltered)

PENINSULA RIDGE
Beamsville
⭐★✦✦

Domaine Laroche's former winemaker Jean-Pierre Colas has very quickly established a reputation at Peninsula Ridge estate, not least for the purity of its stellar quality Chardonnays.

✓ *Chardonnay* (Inox) • *Icewine* (Vidal) • *Merlot* (Reserve)

PILLITTERI ESTATES WINERY
Niagara-on-the-Lake
★

The Pillitteri family has been growing grapes on the Niagara Peninsula for more than half a century, and selling wines under their own name since 1993. Although on average Icewine accounts for just 5 per cent of Ontario's wine production, at Pillitteri Estates, it represents no less than one-third of its bottled wine.

✓ *Cabernet Franc* (Family Reserve) • *Merlot* (Family Reserve) • *Icewine* (Riesling) • *Riesling* (Reserve) • *Sparkling* (Riesling Icewine)

REIF ESTATE WINERY
Niagara-on-the-Lake
★

Formerly one of Niagara's top wineries, the wines produced by Klaus Reif, just round the corner from Inniskillin, are 100 per cent estate bottled and are often barrique-influenced.

✓ *Cabernet Sauvignon* (First Growth) • *Classic red blend* (Cabernet Merlot, Meritage) • *Merlot* • *Vidal* (Special Select Late Harvest)

SOUTHBROOK FARMS
Niagara-on-the-Lake
★✦

Established in 1991, under the auspices of Brian Croser (of Petaluma in Australia), who also acted as consultant for the first vintage that year. The grapes came from Reif vineyard, and Klaus Reif was the winemaker initially. Since then owner Bill Redelmeier has hired Colin Campbell, who is obviously just as talented, from the awards he is picking up. In 2006, Southbrook relocated its winery to a 75-acre vineyard at Niagara-on-the-Lake and appointed Ann Sperling as the new winemaker.

✓ *Cabernet Franc* (Watson Vineyard) • *Cabernet Sauvignon* (Lailey Vineyard) • *Chardonnay* (Triomphe) • *Classic red blend* (Triomphe Cabernet-Merlot)

STRATUS VINEYARDS
Niagara-on-the-Lake
★★

Wines produced with "the philosophy of *assemblage*" by Loire-born JL Groux, in a completely pumpless, state-of-the-art, gravity-fed winery.

✓ *Classic red blend* (Stratus Red) • *Classic white blend* (Stratus White)

TAWSE WINERY
Vineland
★★

With a snazzy, six-storey, state-of-the-art, gravity-fed winery powered by natural geo-thermal energy, Deborah Paskus the winemaker, and Pascal Marchand consulting, the strategy of the Tawse family cannot be faulted. This is the one to watch!

✓ *Chardonnay* • *Pinot Noir*

VINELAND ESTATES
Vineland
★

Formerly owned by Herman Weiss, whose family have a winery in the Mosel called St Urban, Vineland Estates is now owned by Allan Schmidt, whose father had been one of the original partners in Sumac Ridge, while Allan's brother Brian is the winemaker.

✓ *Cabernet Franc* • *Icewine* (Vidal) • *Riesling* (Dry)

QUEBEC
CHAPELLE ST AGNÈS
Sutton Mountains

An exquisite amphitheatre of terraced vines, owned by Henrietta Antony and dedicated to dessert wine, Chapelle St Agnès cropped for the first time in 2003. One to watch.

VIGNOBLE DIETRICH-JOOS
Iberville
★✦

This winery has won over 100 medals at international wine competitions since it was founded in 1986.

✓ *Cayuga* (Storikengold) • *Classic white blend* (Cuvée Spéciale) • *Icewine* (Sélection Impérial) • *Rosé* (Rosé d'Iberville)

VIGNOBLE LES CHANTS DE VIGNES
Magog
★✦

One of Quebec's few gold medal winners, even though Vignoble les Chants de Vignes yielded its first crop in 1999.

✓ *Classic red blend* (Le Canon Rouge)

VIGNOBLE LES PERVENCHES
Farnham
★✦

The only producer of Chardonnay in Quebec, in 2004 Vignoble Les Pervenches became one of Quebec's first wineries to be awarded a gold medal, and won two for good measure.

✓ *Classic red blend* (Cuvée de Montmollin) • *Classic white blend* (Seyval-Chardonnay)

VIGNOBLE DE L'ORPAILLEUR
Frelighsburg
★✦

Established in 1982, this vineyard produced its first crop in 1985. Since then Vignoble de L'Orpailleur has produced just 15,000 bottles a year, crafted into 10 artisanal cuvées.

✓ *Icewine* (Vendange de Glace) • *Seyval Blanc* (L'Orpailleur Blanc)

OTHER CERTIFIED ORGANIC PRODUCERS

British Columbia
A Very Fine Winery & Buried Treasure Vineyards (Abbotsford)
Beaumont Estate (Kelowna)
Hollywood & Wine (Summerland)
K & V Vineyards (Kelowna)
Knollvine Farm (Peniction)
Park Hill Vineyards (Oliver)
Stony Paradise (Kelowna)
Vispering Vines (Okanagan Falls)

MEXICO

The biggest obstacle to Mexico's success as a winemaking country is not its hot climate, nor the feared influx of cheaper American wines, let alone even cheaper Chilean imports, but the absence of wine drinking from the culture of its population.

IT WAS THE SPANISH who brought wine to Mexico, the oldest wine-producing country in the Americas. By 1521, just one year after invading Mexico, the conquistadors had planted vines and soon afterwards they began making wine.

In 1524 Hernando Cortez, the governor of New Spain (Mexico), ordered that all Spanish residents who had been granted land and given Indians for forced labour should annually plant "one thousand vines per hundred Indians" for a period of five years. By 1595 the country was almost self-sufficient in wine, and shipments of domestic Spanish wine had dwindled to such an extent that producers in the home country pressured Philip II into forbidding the planting of further vineyards in the New World.

THE ORIGINAL "TEQUILA SUNRISE"

When the Spanish encountered a strange, milky-white Aztec "wine" called *pulque*, they were not impressed. However, in a bid to utilize this popular local product, they tried distilling it – the crystal-clear, colourless spirit that resulted was far more to their taste, and was named *tequila*, after *Agave tequilana*, the species of succulent cactus used to make it (once thought to be part of the lily family). Today, tequila is one of Mexico's most important exports, and vast quantities of *pulque* are still made and consumed by Mexicans.

MODERN MEXICAN WINE

There are 50,000 hectares (125,000 acres) of vines in Mexico, but almost 40 per cent produce table grapes or raisins, and much of the wine produced is distilled into brandy.

It was not long ago that the best Mexican wines tasted little better than *pulque* but, by 1988, when the first edition of this encyclopedia was published, a combination of foreign investment and the demand from tourists for more sophisticated products had already led to significant improvements. At the time, many international oenologists were optimistic about Mexico's future as a producer of good-quality wines, but unfortunately, although the potential remains the same, a lack of sales on the home market has seen more than half of Mexico's wineries close down. Most Mexicans drink beer or *pulque*, not wine. The consumption of wine *per capita* is less than one-thirtieth of that in the USA, and

MEXICAN LABEL LANGUAGE

Many terms found on Mexican wine labels are the same as, or similar to, those seen on Spanish labels (*see Spanish Label Language, p362*). Some common terms are listed below:

VINO TINTO
Red wine
VINO BLANCO
White wine
VARIEDAD
Grape variety
COMBINADOS
Indicates a blend
of different grape
varieties.

CONTENIDO NETO
Contents
COSECHAS
SELECCIONADAS
Special blend
VIÑA
Vineyard
ESPUMOSO
Sparkling
SECO, EXTRA SECO
Dry, Extra Dry

VINO DE MESA
Table wine
BODEGA
Winery
HECHO EN MÉXICO
Made in Mexico

VINE-GROWING AREAS IN MEXICO

STATE	NOTES
Sonora	Abutting Arizona, Sonora is by far the largest grape-growing state in Mexico, but much of the crop is for eating grapes or raisins, and virtually all of the wine grapes harvested go for distillation, although in isolated areas as much as 20–25 per cent of the production is used for wine. L A Cetto owns 1,600 hectares (3,950 acres) of vines in Sonora.
Baja California	Baja California is the largest peninsula in the world, and the northern half, Baja California Norte, produces more than 90 per cent of Mexico's wine, although it grows only 20 per cent of Mexico's grapes. Indeed, just seven wineries in this state produce almost 80 per cent of Mexico's wines. There are main quality districts: Valle de Calafia, Valle de Guadalupe, Ensenada, Tecate, San Antonio de la Minas, Valle de Santó Tomas, San Vincente, and Valle de Mexicali.
Aguascalientes	Just 7 per cent of the vines yield wine grapes.
Zacatecas	Just 7 per cent of the vines yield wine grapes, with vines growing on the Altiplano, at an altitude of 2,000 metres (7,000 feet), the highest wine region in Mexico.
Coahuila	This state and Durango together form La Laguna region, where three-quarters of the grapes grown are distilled, and much of the rest are table grapes, although quality wines are produced in the Valle de Parras.
Chihuahua	More famous for its cheddar-like cheese than wine.
Querétaro	Just 7 per cent of the vines yield wine grapes, mostly sparkling from Finca Freixenet.
Durango	This state and Coahuila together form La Laguna region, where three-quarters of the grapes grown are distilled, and much of the rest are table grapes.

FACTORS AFFECTING TASTE AND QUALITY

LOCATION
Eight of the country's states grow grapes, from Baja California in the north to San Juan del Rio, just north of Mexico City in the south.

CLIMATE
Half of Mexico lies south of the Tropic of Cancer, but altitude moderates the temperature of the vineyards. Most are situated on the high central plateau and some are cooled by the nearby ocean. Principal problems include extreme fluctuation of day and night temperatures, and the fact that most areas have either too little or too much moisture. The dry areas often lack adequate sources of water for irrigation, and the wet districts suffer from too much rain during the growing season.

ASPECT
In the states of Aguascalientes, Querétaro, and Zacatecas, vines are grown on flat plateau lands and the sides of small valleys, at altitudes of 1,600 metres (5,300 feet), rising to nearly 2,100 metres (7,000 feet) in Zacatecas State. In Baja California, vines are located in valley and desert areas at much lower altitudes of between 100 and 335 metres (330 and 1,100 feet).

SOIL
The soils of Mexico can be divided into two wide-ranging categories: slope or valley soils are thin and low in fertility, while plains soils are of variable depth and fertility. In the Baja California, the soils range from a poor, alkaline sandy soil in Mexicali, to a thin spread of volcanic soil, which is intermixed with gravel, sand, and limestone to provide excellent drainage. In Sonora, the soils of Caborca are similar to those found in Hermosillo, but those in Hermosillo are very silty and of alluvial origin. The high plains of Zacatecas have mostly volcanic and silty-clay soils. In the Aguascalientes, the soil in both the valley and the plains is of a scarce depth with a thin covering of calcium. The volcanic, calcareous sandy-clay soil in Querétaro has a good depth and drainage and is slightly alkaline, while in La Laguna the silty-sandy alluvium is very alkaline.

VITICULTURE AND VINIFICATION
Irrigation is widely practised in dry areas such as Baja California and Zacatecas. Most wineries are relatively new and staffed by highly trained oenologists.

GRAPE VARIETIES
Primary varieties: Cabernet Sauvignon, Cariñena (Carignan), Chenin Blanc, Grenache, Mission, Palomino, Riesling, Ruby Cabernet, Sauvignon Blanc, Sémillon, Ugni Blanc, Zinfandel
Secondary varieties: Barbera, Cabernet Franc, Chardonnay, Colombard, Malbec, Merlot, Nebbiolo, Petite Sirah (Durif), Shiraz (Syrah), Tempranillo, Viognier

BAJA CALIFORNIA, MEXICO
Petite Sirah vines basking in the hot midday Mexican sunshine,
with the foothills of the Sierra San Pedro Mártir in the background.

that in turn is less than one-tenth of the European average. The wine industry in the USA is viable only because of the sheer scale of its economy, and the size and affluence of its middle classes, but in Mexico the middle classes are small in number, and do not support the local wine industry. As Christopher Fielden put it in *The Wines of Argentina, Chile and Latin America,* "there is no national pride in the product; those who can afford to drink wine generally prefer to drink imported wine". This has been especially

so since the North American Free Trade Agreement (NAFTA) and the Mexico-EU Free Trade Agreement (MEFTA), which have gradually lowered duty on imported wine. Imports now represent 60 per cent of all the wines sold in Mexico, and this is set to increase. There may, however, be a silver lining in all this foreign infiltration, because Mexico's wineries cannot compete in price with American or Chilean cheap wines; thus, they will have to focus on both quality and exports to survive. This will lead to a whittling down of its vineyards, so that in a decade's time, with only the best areas cultivated with site-specific clones, the full potential of Mexico as a wine producer might finally be realized.

THE WINE PRODUCERS OF
MEXICO

BODEGAS DE SANTO TOMAS
Ensenada
★☆♥

This winery was founded by an Italian goldminer, who sold it to General Rodriguez in 1920. Rodriguez went on to become president of Mexico and the winery passed to Esteban Ferro. The winery now belongs to Elias Pando.

✔ *Cabernet Sauvignon • Classic red blend* (Duetto, Gran Reserva Unico)

CASA DE PIEDRA
San Antonio de las Minas
★

Hugo d'Acosta's expressive Tempranillo-Cabernet Sauvignon blend is a real treasure of a find.

✔ *Classic red blend* (Vino de Piedra Tinto)

CASA MADERO
Monterey
★☆♥

The second-oldest winery on the continent, comprising 400 hectares (1,000 acres) of vineyards in the Valle de Parras. Flying winemaker John Worontschak has produced clean, easy-drinking wine here for Marks & Spencer.

✔ *Cabernet Sauvignon* (Gran Reserva Especial) • *Chardonnay • Chenin Blanc • Classic red blend* (San Lorenzo) • *Merlot*

CAVAS VALMAR
Ensenada
☆

Owners Fernando and Yolanda Martain met when they worked together at Bodegas de Santo Tomás before establishing this boutique winery.

✔ *Cabernet Sauvignon*

CHATEAU CAMOU
Ensenada
★♥

Owner Ernesto Alvarez-Morphy has *bordelais* aspirations, citing Château Margaux as his inspiration, and employing Bordeaux-trained Victor Torres as the winemaker at his state-of-the-art winery in the heart of the Valle de Guadalupe.

✔ *Classic red blend* (Cabernet Franc-Merlot) • *Classic white blend* (Gran Vino Blanco) • *Merlot* (Gran Vino) •

FREIXENET MEXICO
San Juan del Rio
★♥

Freixenet was making a fine, light, fresh sparkling wine that was better than most authentic Spanish Cava as early as 1988. Promising developments with still wines, with young, entry-level wines sold under the Dolores Vivante label, and premium quality under the Viña Doña Dolores label.

✔ *Classic red blend* (Viña Doña Dolores Tinto Gran Reserva) • *Classic white blend* (Dolores Vivante) • *Sparkling* (Sala Vivé)

L A CETTO
Tijuana
★♥

I visited this winery's facility in Mexico City when most of its products were still branded as Domecq and the Cetto wines were unknown internationally. Even back then, the quality here seemed more promising than at other producers.

✔ *Cabernet Sauvignon • Nebbiolo • Petite Sirah • Zinfandel*

MOGOR BADAN
Ensenada
☆

This has been dubbed the "virtual winery" because its wines are produced at other wineries.

✔ *Chasselas*

MONTE XANIC
Ensenada
★☆♥

Pronounced Sha-nic, Xanic is Cora Indian for "the first bloom after the rain" and it certainly is blossoming well as the finest winery in Mexico.

✔ *Cabernet Sauvignon* (Calixa) • *Classic red blend* (Cabernet Sauvignon Y Merlot) • *Chardonnay* (Calixa) • *Classic red blend* (Gran Ricardo) • *Merlot • Syrah*

PEDRO DOMECQ
Mexico City
★♥

This winery's top wine, Château Domecq, produced in Baja California, is still one of Mexico's best Cabernet Sauvignons.

✔ *Chardonnay* (XA) • *Classic red blend* (Château Domecq)

VINAS DE LICEAGA
Ensenada
☆

Production began in 1993, but only now is the wine beginning to show promise.

✔ *Merlot* (Gran Reserva)

Other potentially interesting Mexican wineries include: Bodegas San Antonio, Cavas de Valmar, Casa Martell, and Vergel.

SOUTH AMERICA

The Spanish introduced viticulture to the Americas: first to Mexico in 1521, and then further afield as the conquistadors opened up other areas of the southern continent. Relatively recently, Chile stood out for quality, and Argentina for quantity, but a growing number of ultra-premium

Argentinian wineries are slowly turning around this super-tanker wine-producing country to take on Chile in the quality stakes, while Brazil and Uruguay continue to show some promise.

SOUTH AMERICA'S WINE INDUSTRIES are inextricably linked to Spain's expansionist policies of the 16th century, although the conquistadors were not primarily concerned with the spread of viticulture. They were in South America to plunder gold for Ferdinand of Spain, and when the Indians grew tired of the coloured glass beads traded for their treasures, the conquistadors took what they wanted by more direct and brutal means. In response, the Indians poured molten gold down the throats of captured soldiers, which no doubt quenched the Spanish thirst for the precious metal, but also served as a sardonic retort to the Christian missionaries who had forced them to drink wine as part of the Sacrament.

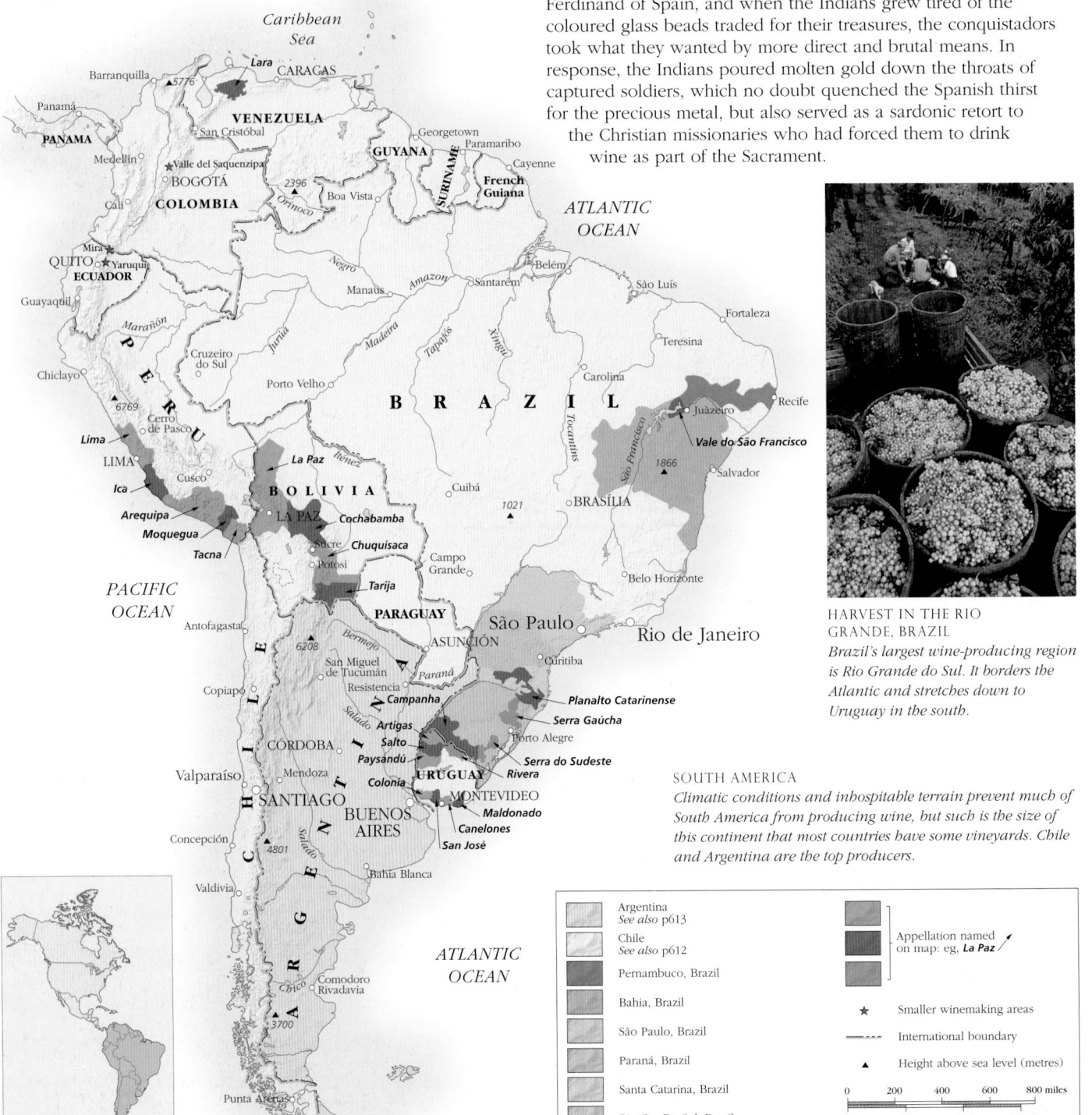

HARVEST IN THE RIO GRANDE, BRAZIL
Brazil's largest wine-producing region is Rio Grande do Sul. It borders the Atlantic and stretches down to Uruguay in the south.

SOUTH AMERICA
Climatic conditions and inhospitable terrain prevent much of South America from producing wine, but such is the size of this continent that most countries have some vineyards. Chile and Argentina are the top producers.

Argentina *See also p613*	Appellation named on map: eg, *La Paz*
Chile *See also p612*	
Pernambuco, Brazil	
Bahia, Brazil	★ Smaller winemaking areas
São Paulo, Brazil	- - - International boundary
Paraná, Brazil	▲ Height above sea level (metres)
Santa Catarina, Brazil	0 200 400 600 800 miles
Rio Gra Do Sul, Brazil	0 400 800 1200 km

In more recent times, it has been the traditional beer-drinking culture of the local populations that has held back the development of South American wines as a whole. This phenomenon has even affected the two major wine-producing countries, Chile and Argentina. Brazil could be leading the way, however, as the switch from beer to wine among the younger generation makes this one of the few countries in the world where wine consumption is actually growing.

SOUTH AMERICAN COUNTRIES: AREA UNDER VINE AND YIELD

COUNTRY	HECTARES	(ACRES)	HECTOLITRES	(CASES)	YIELD
ARGENTINA	207,985	(513,952)	11,200,000	(124,000,000)	54 hl/ha*
CHILE	108,570	(268,287)	5,750,000	(63,900,000)	53 hl/ha
BRAZIL	80,000	(148,260)	4,000,000	(33,000,000)	50 hl/ha
URUGUAY	11,000	(27,181)	710,000	(7,900,000)	65 hl/ha
PERU	10,000	(24,710)	80,000	(900,000)	8 hl/ha**
BOLIVIA	4,000	(9,884)	20,000	(220,000)	5 hl/ha**
COLOMBIA	1,500	(3,706)		N/A	N/A
VENEZUELA	1,000	(2,470)		N/A	N/A
ECUADOR	250	(618)		N/A	N/A
PARAGUAY	negligible			N/A	N/A

*This looks suspiciously low, almost half the expected yield, but the figures come from official statistics for the 2003 harvest.
**These anomalies are because nearly all the wine is distilled into aromatic grape-brandy. Discounting this production, yields can be as high as 160 hl/ha.

VINEYARDS OF SAN PEDRO AT MOLINA, CHILE
Part of the largest single vineyard in Chile, at Molina in the Curicó district, 200 kilometres (124 miles) south of Santiago, with the Andes in the distance.

THE WINE PRODUCERS OF
SOUTH AMERICA

BOLIVIA

LA CONCEPCIÓN
La Concepción
★

This was Bolivia's first modern winery in 1978, and it remains the best.

✓ *Cabernet Sauvignon*

BRAZIL

AMADEU
Bento Gonçalves
★ Ⓥ

An award-winning winery under the guidance of Mario Geisse, formerly of Chandon Brazil.

✓ *Cabernet Sauvignon • Merlot*

CAVE MARSON
Citorpa
★

Fabulous sparkling sweet Moscatel from the Serra Gaúcha region.

✓ *Sparkling* (Marson Espumante Moscatel)

COOPERATIVA VINICOLA AURORA
Bento Gonçalves

This cooperative has more than 1,000 members, who between them account for more than one-third of Brazil's vineyards. There are various labels, including Conde Foucolde and Clos de Nobles. Flying winemaker John

Worontschak has made several wines here for British supermarkets. This might be Brazil's second-largest winery and, in a commercial sense, very successful, but in terms of quality, with the exception of an excellent sweet Moscatel, Vinicola Aurora could do much better.

✓ *Dessert* (Moscatel)

CHANDON DO BRASIL
Rio Grande do Sul
★ Ⓥ

The least impressive of Chandon's far-flung outposts, but at least the sparkling wines are no longer sold shamelessly on the Brazilian market as Champaña.

✓ *Classic red blend* (Grand Philippe) • *Sparkling* (Diamantina)

LOVARA
Rio Grande do Sul
★ Ⓥ

Despite its relatively ancient origins (established by Italian immigrants in the 1870s), Lovara is an up-and-coming winery that has been improving with each year since the 1990s.

✓ *Cabernet Sauvignon • Merlot*

MIOLO
Rio Grande do Sul
★ Ⓥ

Grapegrowers since 1897, the Miolo family built a winery in 1989. Since then their best, medal-winning wines have been some of the most exciting Brazilian wines made.

✓ *Classic red blend* (Lote 43, Quinta do Seival, RAR, Terranova Cabernet Sauvignon-Shiraz)

VINICOLA CAMPO LARGO
Jardim
★

Fabulous sparkling sweet Moscatel from the Serra Gaúcha region.

✓ *Sparkling* (Baccio Espumante Moscatel)

ECUADOR

CHAUPI ESTANCIA WINERY
Yaruqui
★ Ⓥ

A boutique winery with 6 hectares (15 acres) of vineyard 40 kilometres (25 miles) northeast of Quito, Chaupi Estancia Winery was established in 1989 to grow only *vinifera* grapes. Due to the rarefied altitude (2,440 metres; 8,100 feet) and equatorial latitude, viticulturist and winemaker

THE LAW THAT NEVER WAS

In 1993, I asked Yves Bénard, then the head of Moët & Chandon in Champagne, how the *champenois* could justify court actions to prevent the use of the name Champagne or Champaña on any sparkling wine produced outside the officially delimited Champagne region, when Moët had been selling South American sparkling wine as Champaña for more than 30 years.

Bénard told me that they had been trying to get the name Champaña banned, but were required by local laws to use the term, and this raised the question of why any Champagne house would set up business in countries that undermined their own appellation. What prompted my original question was that I had been told no such law existed by Trevor Bell, who was managing director of Piper-Heidsieck. I put it to Bénard that as Piper produced Argentinian sparkling wine, Bell should know what he was talking about, and they could not both be right.

Bénard maintained, "It is the law. I know, because every time the CIVC (Comité Interprofessionnel du Vin de Champagne) takes a case to court, this very question is always raised by the other side and I am called to give evidence in defence of my company's actions."

I asked Bénard to supply the text of the law he was referring to. He offered a translation used as evidence in a Canadian court, but I insisted on a copy of the law itself in original Spanish for Argentina and Portuguese for Brazil, as they would have to be independently translated if there were to be no question about their interpretation.

This was duly promised but did not turn up. Eventually, I received a letter dated 25 June 1993 admitting that "the law in that country requires that sparkling wine should be specified as either champagne, *champaña*, *vino espumoso*, or *vino espumante*. You should be aware that in Argentina to specify a wine as *vino espumoso* or *vino espumante* considerably depreciates the product in the mind of the consumer, and nobody uses these terms." Yet this is precisely the argument used by sparkling-wine producers worldwide, and the *champenois* take them to court to contest it.

No copy of the Brazil law turned up either, and Moët assured me, "production is tiny – less than 200,000 cases. It is not really a problem." Yet when the *champenois* took Thorncroft to court over fewer than 3,000 cases of non-alcoholic Elderflower Champagne, they claimed it was "the thin end of the wedge!"

The idea that sparkling wines in Argentina and Brazil must be labelled Champagne or Champaña by law has now been shattered. It is clear that the *champenois* involved were not legally obliged to use the term "Champaña" and the pity is that the court cases won by the *champenois* can now be challenged and, presumably, reversed. On a positive note, it might have taken a decade, but the shame that this publicity brought on the hypocritical Champagne houses involved has eventually forced them to drop all versions of Champagne and Champaña from the labels of their South American fizz.

Dick Handall has been experimenting with 32 different varieties and many styles and combinations of wine, with Chilean Hector Olivares Madrid consulting.

✓ *Palomino*

PERU

TACAMA
Ica
★ ⓥ

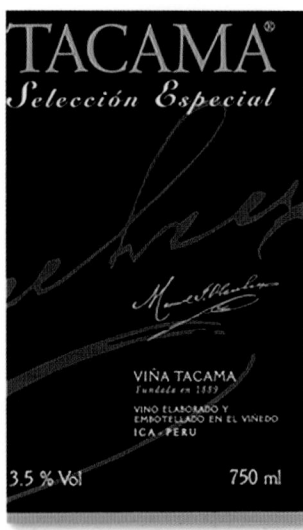

This is the only significant producer in Peru and, although the wine is exported, only the Malbec is up to international standards. Other reds are short or bitter, the whites are fresh but uninteresting, and the sparkling wines unpleasantly explosive. Bordeaux professors Peynaud and Ribéreau-Gayon have consulted here, and flying winemaker John Worontschak has made some quaffing wines (Malbec and Chenin) for British supermarkets. In 2008, another Bordeaux professor, Pierre-Louis Teissedre, discovered a unique clone of Petit Verdot growing in Tacama's vineyard in the Ica Valley.

✓ *Classic red blend* (Selección Especial, Terroir) • *Classic white blend* (Blanco de Blancos) • *Tannat* (Don Manuel)

URUGUAY

ARIANO
Las Piedras
★ ⓥ

Established in 1927 by Adelio and Amilcar Ariano, this winery has begun to shine since the 1990s.

✓ *Tannat*

BODEGAS CARRAU
Montevideo
★ ⓥ

Established in the 1970s by Juan Carrau, this winery is carving a name for itself with well-crafted Tannat.

✓ *Classic red blend* (Gran Tradicion) • *Tannat* (Amat, Tannat de Reserva)

CASTILLO VIEJO
San José
★ ⓥ

The winery of Castillo Viejo makes fresh, crisp whites and sharp, fruity reds from a private estate, which is 100 kilometres (60 miles) northwest of Montevideo. Flying winemaker John Worontschak has made wines here under the Pacific Peak label for British supermarket store Tesco.

✓ *Sauvignon Blanc* • *Tannat* (Reserve, Vieja Parcela)

DE LUCCA
El Colorado
★ ⓥ

De Lucca is an up-and-coming winery, run by passionate winemaker Reinaldo de Lucca. With vineyards situated 30 kilometres (19 miles) inland from the Atlantic coast, De Lucca is able to grow vines that do very well in Uruguay's relatively mild, maritime climate.

✓ *Classic red blend* (Tannat Syrah) • *Sauvignon Blanc*

H STAGNARI
Canelones
★ ⓥ

Exclusively own-grown wines, with no bought-in fruit, the Tannat in particular benefits from the extremely high density of Stagnari's vineyards, which boast 10,000 vines per hectare.

✓ *Tannat* (Castel La Puebla Dayman, Stagnari Viejo)

JUANICO
Canelones
★ ⓥ

One of Uruguay's fastest-rising wineries, Juanico performs to international standards, thanks to a little help in the past from flying winemaker Peter Bright.

✓ *Chardonnay* (Reserve) • *Classic red blend* (Gran Classic Magrez) • *Classic white blend* (Don Pasqual Chardonnay-Viognier) • *Tannat* (Roble)

PISANO
Progreso
★ ⓥ

Established in 1924 by Don Cesare Secundino Pisano, the first generation of his Italian family to be born in Uruguay, the winery is now run by Eduardo Pisano, who has produced some of Uruguay's best wines in recent years. Around half of all the wine produced by this winery is sold abroad.

✓ *Merlot* (RPF) • *Pinot Noir* (RPF) • *Tannat* (RPF)

TRAVERSA
Montevideo
★ ⓥ

Carlos Domingo Traversa started off in 1937 as a grower of Isabela and Moscatel vines, and in 1956 he established a small winery, which has just started to blossom under his grandsons, who have produced some of Uruguay's greatest Tannat.

✓ *Tannat* (Gran Reserva, Roble)

CHILE AND ARGENTINA

Chile has always been the showcase of South America's wine-producing countries, and Argentina its bottomless vat. Yet a growing number of small, artisanal wineries have shown that Argentina can compete with Chile for quality, if its producers will only reduce their yields.

CHILE

The only problem with Chile is that most of its vineyards are in the wrong place. In such a long country, it was natural for the population to live in or near the capital of Santiago, and to plant their vineyards thereabouts, especially as the melting snows of the nearby Andes provided an inexhaustible supply of irrigation. As Chile became South America's best wine region, there was little incentive to search out better viticultural areas in uninhabited, less accessible parts of the country. New areas, such as the Casablanca Valley, are merely the fringe of the country's best wine area, the Secano region, a strip of coastal hills. Here, the cool maritime breezes temper the midday sun and sufficient rainfall permits viticulture without irrigation – if, that is, producers are content with lower yields. Casablanca nudges into the northern end of this future wine area, the greatest potential of which extends as far south as Concepcion. Ironically, the only people with vines here are peasants who cannot afford irrigation (hence its name, Secano, which means "unirrigated") and grow Pais for their own use, but a chain-saw and chip-budding could convert these vineyards overnight, while properly planted ones are laid and, most importantly, roads are built to connect these forgotten areas to the pan-American highway.

From red wines to white

As Chile exported more wine during the 1980s, it became evident that, while it made some really good-value reds, its white wines left much to be desired. In the late 1970s, the quality of Chilean

CABERNET SAUVIGNON, CHILE
This Cabernet Sauvignon vine is more than 100 years old, and grows on ungrafted roots in the Maipo Valley.

FACTORS AFFECTING TASTE AND QUALITY

LOCATION
In Chile, vines are grown along 1,300 kilometres (800 miles) of Pacific coast, and are most concentrated south of Santiago. In Argentina, vines grow mainly in the provinces of Mendoza and San Juan, east of the Andes foothills, west of Buenos Aires.

CLIMATE
Extremely variable conditions prevail in Chile, ranging from arid and extremely hot in the north to very wet in the south. The main wine area around Santiago is dry, with 38 centimetres (15 inches) of rain per year, no spring frosts, and clear, sunny skies. The temperature drops substantially at night due to the proximity of the snow-covered peaks of the Andes, enabling the grapes' acidity levels to remain high. Relatively new areas, such as the Casablanca Valley, are proving far more suitable for winegrowing, particularly for white wines, but inevitably the coastal range of hills will be Chile's fine-wine future, since they receive enough rainfall to allow viticulture at modest yields without irrigation. This is the area most affected by the ice-cold Humboldt Current, which supposedly brings a tempering Arctic chill to all Chilean vineyards, but is effectively blocked from flowing elsewhere in Chile by the coastal hills.

In Argentina's intensively cultivated Mendoza district, the climate is officially described as continental-semi-desertic, and has even less rainfall than Chile, a mere 20–25 centimetres (8–10 inches) per year, although this is mercifully spread over the summer growing months, and temperatures range from 10°C (50°F) at night to 40°C (104°F) during the day.

ASPECT
In both countries, most vines are grown on the flat coastal and valley plains extending into the foothills of the Andes. In Chile, the unirrigated hillside vineyards are found in the Central Zone, although irrigation is widely utilized in other parts of this country. In Argentina, by contrast, the hillside vineyards are usually levelled to a minimal slope in order to allow for more efficient use of water.

SOIL
Vines are grown on a vast variety of soils in these countries. The deeper limestone soils of some parts of Chile are one reason for the generally better quality of wines from this country, but its most famous attribute is a total absence of phylloxera. In Argentina, the soils range from sandy to clay, with a predominance of deep, loose soils of alluvial and aeolian origin.

VITICULTURE AND VINIFICATION
With no climatic challenges, Chile is almost uniquely suited to organic or biodynamic viticulture. While Chile uses traditional methods for most of its wines and often uses Bordeaux techniques, Argentina relies more on bulk-production methods, although high-tech methods are also harnessed in Argentina for its increasing production of higher-grade premium varietals. Modern equipment, stainless-steel vats, and improved technology are standard in most Chilean wineries today. The "native" Pais grape is banned from the label, but is allowed in wines. Wines are often distilled into pisco, which is Chile's local brandy, as well as Peru's.

GRAPE VARIETIES
Chile
Primary varieties: Cabernet Sauvignon, Carmenère, Chardonnay, Merlot, Pinot Noir, Sauvignon Blanc, Syrah
Secondary varieties: Cabernet Franc, Carignan, Gewürztraminer, Malbec, Mourvèdre, Pais, Petit Verdot, Riesling, Sangiovese, Sauvignon Gris, Sauvignonasse (Friulano), Viognier, Zinfandel
Argentina
Primary varieties: Bonarda, Cabernet Sauvignon, Chardonnay, Chenin Blanc, Malbec, Merlot, Petite Sirah (Durif), Sauvignon Blanc, Sémillon, Torrontés Ugni Blanc
Secondary varieties: Barbera, Cabernet Franc, Cereza, Criolla, Greco Nero, Pinot Gris, Pinot Noir, Sangiovese, Sauvignon Gris, Tannat, Tempranillo, Viognier

wines greatly improved with the introduction of temperature-controlled, stainless-steel vats. The early to mid-1980s saw the removal from the winemaking process of *raule* wood, a native variety of beech, which left a taint in the wines that the Chileans had got used to but that international consumers found unpleasant.

With the introduction of new oak *barriques*, mostly of French origin, the 1989 vintage saw a transformation in the quality of Chardonnay, and with this it was widely imagined that Chile had at long last cracked the secret to successful white-wine production. But it soon became evident that even the best producers could not improve their dismal Sauvignon Blanc. Why was this so?

Non-existent Sauvignon

When I confronted producers, most confessed that virtually all the wine sold as Chilean Sauvignon Blanc was, in fact, Sauvignonasse. This "Sauvignon-like" variety is not related to Sauvignon and has no Sauvignon character whatsoever. Whenever I tried to get acreage figures for Sauvignon, the Chileans would lump it together with Sauvignonasse and Sémillon, because they seemed to think it was difficult to distinguish these varieties. When I tried to obtain a breakdown of the three varieties, the best I could squeeze out of any member of the Chilean wine trade was at least 12,500 hectares (31,000 acres) of Sauvignonasse, no more than 2,000 hectares (5,000 acres) of Sauvignon Blanc, and between 2,500 and 4,000 hectares (6,000–10,000 acres) of Sémillon. Therefore, there was on average less than 12 per cent Sauvignon Blanc in virtually every supposed Chilean Sauvignon Blanc wine up until at least the early 1990s. Little wonder, then, that Chilean Sauvignon Blancs possessed little varietal character – they contained very little Sauvignon Blanc!

Doubting these statistics, I returned to Chile to try to locate and identify Sauvignon Blanc in its vineyards. I got my first clue to the true state of affairs while visiting Miguel Torres' vineyard at Curicó. He grinned and said, "So, tell me how you identify Sauvignon Blanc in the field." I launched into the differences between the inferior and superior sinuses of the Sauvignon's leaf when compared with those of Sauvignonasse and Sémillon, and, having agreed with the ampelographic points I had churned out, Miguel Torres then set about pointing these out on the vines in front of us – only they were not there. He did not, in fact, have a pure strain of Sauvignon Blanc. We concluded that he probably had a mutated form of Sauvignon Blanc that was crossed with Sémillon. On that trip, I saw Sauvignonasse – lots of it – and what appeared to be mutations or crosses such as Sémillon with Sauvignon, Sauvignonasse with Sauvignon, and Sauvignonasse with Sémillon, but the only place I saw authentic Sauvignon Blanc was at Viña Canepa, and this was about the only producer engaged in making wine that actually tasted of the variety at that time.

After Chile's non-existent Sauvignon Blanc was exposed in an article in 1991, a number of Chilean wineries commissioned French experts to go through their vineyards with a fine toothcomb. They came to the same conclusion, and since then great swathes of vines have been chip-budded over to true Sauvignon Blanc. In the meantime, however, most wineries tried to make their Sauvignonasse more Sauvignon-like by harvesting early, picking unripe grapes, which resulted in wines that were green and mean. Many such wines still exist, but as the chip-budded vineyards mature, so Chile has begun to produce much better Sauvignon Blanc wines.

And back to red again

Chile always has been red wine country, and over the last decade a concerted effort has been made to project Carmenère as its own unique variety, but at the moment this variety has a better story to tell than wine to make. Carmenère is a Bordeaux variety, but it had virtually died out over there when it was discovered in Chile, masquerading as Merlot. Here was an almost extinct, ancient *bordelais* grape that had been preserved in its pure, ungrafted format. A virtually unique grape variety of impeccable breeding with which to fly the flag for Chilean wines, unchallenged by major plantings anywhere else. So far, so good, but the wine, although rich, is all too often a one-dimensional parody of overripe blackcurrants. Who wants Chile to become known as the Ribena of the wine world? Not me, but Carmenère does deserve investigating – sifting through the natural clones that exist, testing them in different *terroirs*, and applying more thought to their production than the richness and ripeness that extended hang-time brings.

CHILE, *see also p608*
Chile's vineyards are located on the non-humid west coast of South America, stretching 1,300 km (800 miles) from Copiapó Valley in the north, to Malleco Valley in the south.

ARGENTINA

This is the fifth-largest wine country in the world, and could be a major force in the premium-quality sector, if only its excessive yields could be curbed. While Chile has strengthened its position as South America's premier-quality wine-producing country by significantly reducing yields over the past 15 years in order to concentrate on quality, Argentina has done the opposite. On the face of it, Argentina appears to have reduced production by some 10 per cent over the same period, but the fact is it has ripped up a third of its vineyards, thus its yield has actually increased from 66 to 88 hectolitres per hectare (297 to 396 cases per hectare). Scarce rainfall dictates that Argentina's vineyards must depend on irrigation, but it is so cheap and plentiful that growers simply have to turn on the tap to increase the water supply in order to grow more grapes with which to make more wine, and this has killed the passion for quality among almost all the producers. Initially, just a few wineries, such as Catena and Weinert, resolutely refused to go down this route, but as soon as they gave global consumers a glimpse of Argentina's true potential quality, so others saw how much more profitable and prestigious it was to play the international field, and they have followed. However, such is the size of this wine-producing country that it requires an industry-wide change of heart to alter Argentina's image as a bottomless vat. That starts in the vineyards, which will take a generation to bring up to a desirable standard, selecting the right clones of the most appropriate varieties and planting them according to the *terroir* and in much higher densities, trained and pruned for quantity rather than volume. And the entire industry must agree on how to project a coherent, quality image, part of which will be to settle on a flagship variety or style. Malbec appears to be the logical choice. Then they must cooperate on and with major international markets. Until all this happens, even an imperfect Chile will have nothing to fear from Argentina.

High and mighty

Argentina contains the greatest concentration of high-altitude vineyards in the world. Altitude has become such a status symbol for growers in Mendoza that they almost dare each other to plant slightly higher with each new vineyard, with the best wines boasting their altitude as if it were a *grand cru* classification. One advantage of growing grapes at such heights is that they benefit from extended hang-time without producing wines that are too big and alcoholic.

RECENT CHILEAN AND ARGENTINIAN VINTAGES

2011 After a sometimes cool and often rainy growing season in Argentina, a late and large harvest promises good but not exceptional quality. Lower sugars and higher aromatics in Chile.

2010 The year of the earthquake brought Chile a good- but not great-quality vintage, while Argentina enjoyed another relatively cool growing season, which resulted in another truly excellent all-round vintage.

2009 A good to very good red-wine year in both Argentina and Chile.

2008 Unusually, the relative heat situations in both countries flipped, giving Argentina an excellent vintage of vibrant fruit, high aromatics, and crisp acidity, while Chile had to work hard for average quality.

2007 A great vintage in Chile, particularly for reds, but scorching sun and violent storms made for a difficult year in Argentina, even though all closely monitored, well-cared-for vineyards of restricted yield managed to produce good to very good quality.

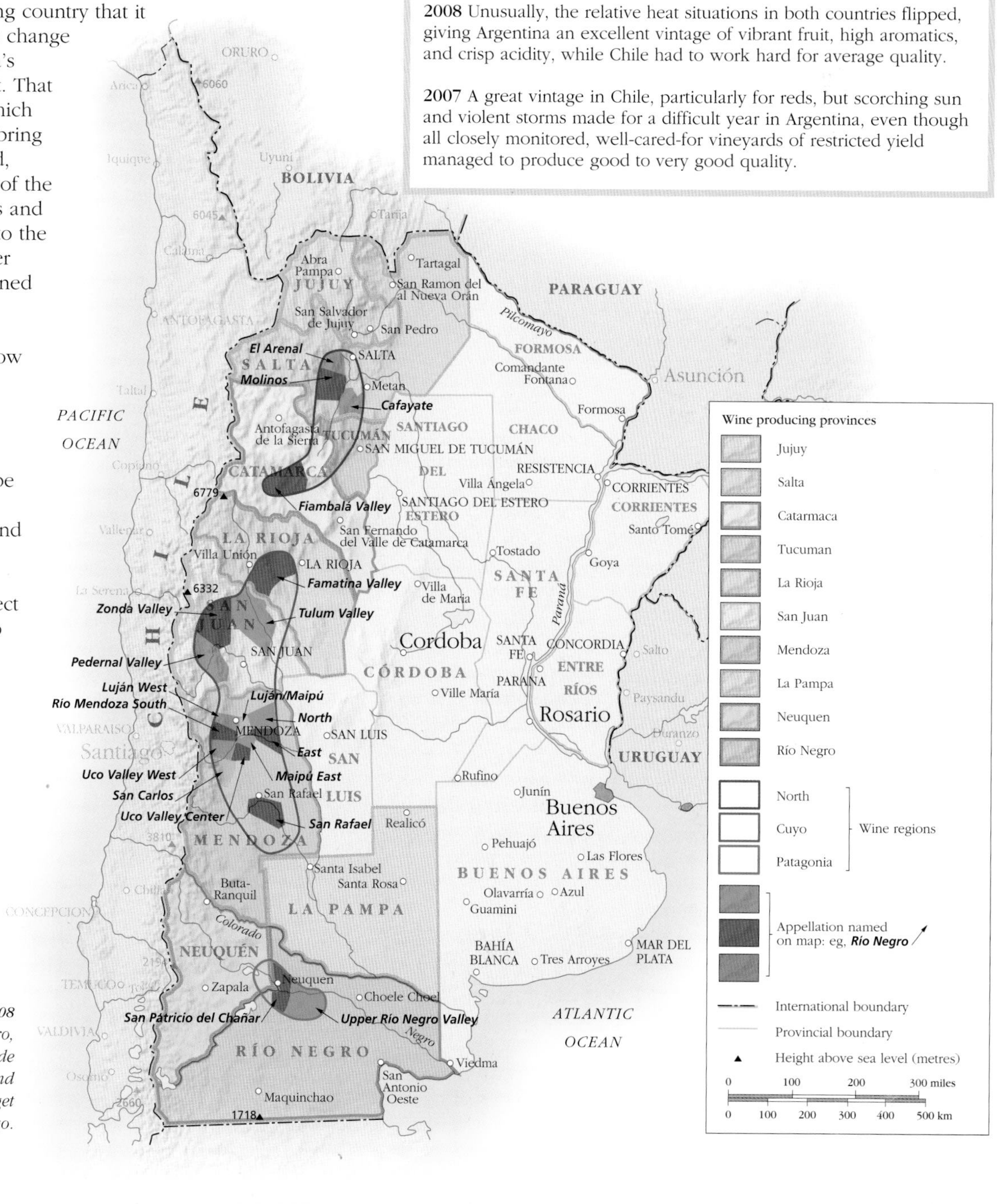

ARGENTINA, *see also p608*
From the low-lying Río Negro, to the seriously high-altitude mountainside sites of Salta and Jujuy, Argentina's vineyards get higher the further north they go.

Wine producing provinces

- Jujuy
- Salta
- Catarmaca
- Tucuman
- La Rioja
- San Juan
- Mendoza
- La Pampa
- Neuquen
- Río Negro

- North
- Cuyo } Wine regions
- Patagonia

Appellation named on map: eg, *Río Negro*

— — — International boundary
——— Provincial boundary
▲ Height above sea level (metres)

0   100   200   300 miles
0   100 200 300 400 500 km

THE APPELLATIONS OF
CHILE AND ARGENTINA

CHILE

ATACAMA VITICULTURAL REGION

Wine districts *Copiapó Valley, Huasco Valley*

The coastal hills are mountainous and join the Andes, with no central valley. Rainfall is virtually non-existent and viticulture is possible only with irrigation. In certain years, when there is rain, plants and insects awaken and what is one of the most arid deserts in the world suddenly bursts into multi-coloured bloom.

CENTRAL VALLEY VITICULTURAL REGION

Wine districts *Curicó Valley (Lontue Valley), Maipo Valley, Maule Valley (Claro Valley, Teno Valley), Rapel Valley (Cachapoal Valley, Colchagua Valley [Apalta Valley])*

The oldest, most central, and most traditional wine region, the Central Valley Viticultural Region contains four wine districts encompassing seven wine areas. The Curicó Valley is situated 200 kilometres (120 miles) south of Santiago, and is home to such brand leaders as Caliterra, Montes, Torres, and Valdivieso. Curicó is known principally for Chardonnay, but also produces fine Cabernet Sauvignon, Merlot, and Pinot Noir. The Maipo Valley around Santiago itself is still the country's most intensively cultivated district and therefore its most famous wine appellation. It is one of the warmest growing districts in the country and, although by no means the best, it is still capable of regularly producing very good wines, particularly reds. Furthest south of all is the Maule Valley, which contains three wine areas and is generally better suited to red wines than whites.

COASTAL VITICULTURAL REGION

Wine districts *Aconcagua Valley, Casablanca Valley, San Antonio Valley (Leyda Valley)*

Also known as the Aconcagua Viticultural Region. Not that long ago, Errázuriz was the only famous winery in the Aconcagua Valley, but it is now one of Chile's best-established, high-quality wine regions, with Panquehue a separately identified internal area. The cooler Casablanca Valley is the country's newest internationally recognized district, and has become famous for the freshness and fruitiness of its wines, particularly Chardonnay and Sauvignon Blanc, but Pinot Noir and other black grape varieties are also showing exciting potential.

COQUIMBO VITICULTURAL REGION

Wine districts *Elquí Valley, Limarí Valley, Choapa Valley*

Like those in the Atacama Viticultural Region, the coastal hills in the Coquimbo Viticultural Region are a mountainous adjunct to the Andes, and viticulture is possible only with irrigation. The Elquí Valley is also known as the Magical Valley, because it lies at the southern end of the spectacular "flowering desert". The vines in all three valleys are found in discrete blocks, rather than in one contiguous section as is the case further south, and the wines are high in alcohol and low in acidity. The Limarí Valley is known for its production of pisco brandy, but since Viña Francisco de Aguire, the country's largest pisco producer, established a winery here in 1993, it has clearly shown excellent potential for the production of fine wine, and more recently Aguatierra and Casa Tamaya.

SOUTHERN VITICULTURAL REGION

Wine districts *Itata Valley, Bio Bio Valley, Malleco Valley*

The Pais is the most commonly cultivated vine here and, apart from the up-and-coming Bio Bio Valley, this region is hardly known.

ARGENTINA

NORTH

Districts: *El Arenal, Cafayete, Fiambalá Valley, Molinos*

Consisting of the provinces of Catamarca, Jujuy, Salta, and Tucumán, this is the least viticulturally developed of this country's three primary regions. Although Jujuy is the smallest of all Argentine wine-producing provinces, its vineyards in the Valles Templados district are surrounded by lake country and close to the international airport of Salvador de Jujuy, making a quick and pleasant in-out visit possible. The vast majority of vines in Argentina's North region are in the larger, more fertile Salta province (*salta* means "very beautiful"), where, at latitudes similar to Egypt, Mozambique, and Alice Springs, the tempering effect of altitude enables the production of fine wines. Here we find three of the Vallees Calchaquies: El Arenal, Cafayete, and Molinos. **El Arenal** is noted for its high-altitude vineyards, reaching 2,700 metres (8,860 feet) along the confluence of rivers between Cachi and Payogasta. **Cafayete** (or Calchaquies) is

geographically the largest and most important of the three local valley appellations, extending south to Aimachá del Valle in the Tucumán province. It is renowned for its Torrontés but also produces excellent Cabernet Sauvignon, Malbec, and Tannat. Etchart (part of Pernod-Ricard) is the most famous producer. **Molinos** is famous for Donald Hess's Bodegas Colomé, where the world's highest-altitude vines creep ever higher (3,111 metres [10,207 feet] at the time of writing). Argentina is a vast country (the eighth largest in the world, just a tad smaller than the entire sub-continent of India), with many out-of-the-way areas and the entire northwest a far-flung outpost; even within that context, Catamarca is remote. With mountains occupying 80 per cent of the province, Catamarca's vineyards in the Fiambalá Valley are well out on a viticultural limb. This is where we find most of Catamarca's relatively few wineries (a dozen perhaps) and they tend to grow Syrah, Bonarda, Cabernet Sauvignon, Malbec, and Torrontés, a variety that has increased dramatically in recent years.

CUYO

Districts: *East, Famatina Valley, Luján West, Luján/Maipú, Maipú East, North, Pedernal Valley, Río Mendoza South, San Carlos, Tulum Valley, Uco Valley Center San Rafael, Uco Valley West, Zonda Valley*

The Cuyo region stretches from Mendoza, where three-quarters of Argentina's vineyards are located, through San Juan, the country's second-largest viticultural province, to La Rioja. Within the above named 13 districts, there are another 40-odd local appellations. At just 650–1,600 metres (2,130–5,250 feet), the altitude of vines is modest by Argentine standards, but the quality is sky-scraping and soaring even higher. The most famous, highest-quality area here is the Uco Valley, just 80 kilometres (50 miles) southwest of Mendoza city. Like most of the New World's greatest wine regions, the Uco Valley was orchard country for the first European settlers. Nicolás Catena was the first to see the winemaking potential, planting his Adrianna vineyard in 1993, since when almost all of Argentina's best producers have put a stake in the ground.

PATAGONIA

Districts: *San Patricio del Chañar, Upper Río Negro Valley*

With low-altitude vineyards at 200–400 metres (650–1,300 feet), the wine-producing provinces of Neuquén and Rio Negro are the polar opposites of the rest of Argentina, but this far-south altitude would be a problem, not part of the solution.

THE WINE PRODUCERS OF
CHILE AND ARGENTINA

CHILE

AGUATIERRA
Punitaqui
◎★Ⓥ

Established in 1999 by James Prior, a Canadian viticulturist, with winemaker Giorgio Flesatti of Viña Falernia. Expect excellent organic wines.

✓ *Rosé* (Organic)

ALMAVIVA
El Monte
★✫Ⓥ

Joint venture between Domaines Baron Philippe de Rothschild and Concha y Toro, Almaviva is a classy single-vineyard, Bordeaux-style red wine.

✓ *Classic red blend* (Almaviva)

ANAKENA
Requínoa
★Ⓥ

Established in the mid-1990s by Jorge Gutíerrez, who excels at finely focused, fruit-driven whites.

✓ *Carmenère* (Single Vineyard) •
Classic white blend (Ona Riesling-Viognier-Chardonnay) •
Riesling (Single Vineyard)

AQUITANIA
Casilla
★★Ⓥ

After a shaky start, this international collaboration between Bruno Prats (ex Château Cos d'Estournel), Ghislain de Montgolfier (Bollinger), Paul Pontallier (Château Margaux), and Felipe de Solminihac (Santa Monica) has become one of Chile's best wineries. The SOLdeSOL is from Solminihac's own property at Traiguén, the most southerly vineyard in Chile, 650 kilometres (400 miles) south of Santiago.

✓ *Cabernet Sauvignon* (Lazuli) • *Chardonnay* (SOLdeSOL)

BALDUZZI
San Javier
★ ✪

Produces fresh, elegant wines with creamy fruit. The Balduzzi family is of Piedmontese extraction. They arrived in Chile at the turn of the 20th century but did not begin exporting wines until 1987.

✓ *Cabernet Sauvignon* • *Chardonnay*

BISQUERTT
Lihueimo
✪

A family-owned venture with large, well-established vineyards in the Colchagua Valley, Viña Bisquertt began bottling its own wines in the early 1990s, and is a rapidly improving producer of soft, easy-drinking, value-for-money wines.

✓ *Cabernet Sauvignon* (Reserve) • *Sauvignon Blanc* (Casa La Joya Reserve)

CALINA
Las Rastras
★ ✫ ✪

Stylish wines, stylishly presented by Kendall-Jackson, which established this winery in 1993. Wines also sold under Alcance and Bravura labels.

✓ *Cabernet Sauvignon* (Alcance) • *Classic red blend* (Alcance Carmenère-Merlot-Cabernet, Bravura)

CALITERRA
Palmilla
★ ✪

Originally a joint venture between Errázuriz and Franciscan Vineyards of California, but when the latter dropped out, the wines became inconsistent (the Sauvignon Blanc was particularly dire) and Caliterra almost assumed the mantle of an Errázuriz second label, but began to turn around after Robert Mondavi became an equal partner, although the reds disappoint.

✓ *Chardonnay* (Reserve) • *Sauvignon Blanc*

CANEPA
Santiago
★ ✫ ✪

This is a high-tech winery producing elegant wines with a perfectly clean line, great clarity of fruit, and excellent finesse. Terrific value wines also sold under Montenuevo, Petroa, and Rowan Brook labels. Part organic.

✓ *Cabernet Sauvignon* (especially Magnificum) • *Chardonnay* (Rancagua) • *Merlot* • *Sauvignon Blanc* • *Zinfandel*

CARMEN
Alto Jahuel
★ ✫

Established in 1850, this is the oldest brand in Chile, now part of the same group as Santa Rita. The winery is overseen by Alvaro Espinoza, one of Chile's best winemakers. Part organic (Nativa range).

✓ *Cabernet Sauvignon* • *Grand Vidure* • *Merlot* • *Petite Sirah* • *Sémillon* (Oak Aged)

CASA LAPOSTOLLE
Las Condes
★ ✫

This is a Franco-Chilean venture between the Marnier-Lapostolle family of Grand Marnier renown (they also own Château de Sancerre) and the Rabats, an old Chilean family whose connections in the wine trade date back to the 1920s, with Michel Rolland consulting. Part organic.

✓ *Merlot* • *Sauvignon Blanc*

CASABLANCA
Casablanca
★ ✫ ✪

Owned by Santa Carolina, Viña Casablanca was put on the map by one of Chile's highest-profile winemakers, Ignacio Recabarren, but the wines became less consistent when he left, and have only just started to return to form in recent years.

✓ *Chardonnay* (Santa Isabel) • *Classic red blend* (Neblus) • *Desert* (Neblus) • *Merlot* (Santa Isabella) • *Sauvignon Blanc* (Santa Isabel)

CASAS DEL BOSQUE
Casilla
★ ★ ✪

In 1993, Juan Cúneo Solari, the son of an Italian immigrant, fulfilled his dream of establishing a vineyard and winery in the Casablanca Valley, where he has become one of Chile's most successful producers of Sauvignon Blanc. Even the entry-level Casa Viva Sauvignon Blanc is an exceptionally fine wine – one of Chile's greatest bargains.

✓ *Cabernet Sauvignon* • *Chardonnay* • *Merlot* (Reserve) • *Sauvignon Blanc*

CHÂTEAU LOS BOLDOS
Requínoa
★ ✫ ✪

This long-established vineyard has been revitalized by its owners, the Massenez family of Alsace (*eaux-de-vie* distillers), who make very good-value wines of richness, finesse, and complexity.

✓ *Cabernet Sauvignon* • *Chardonnay* • *Merlot*

CONCHA Y TORO
Santiago
★ ★ ✪

Some stunningly rich wines, ranging from vibrantly fruity to the complex and age-worthy, Concha y Toro is the largest, yet extremely serious, producer in Chile. Excellent-value wines are produced under the Sunrise and Frontera labels. Concha y Toro also owns Cono Sur and is involved with Domaines Baron Philippe de Rothschild in their Almaviva joint venture. It also owns Trivento in Argentina. Part organic.

✓ *Cabernet Sauvignon* (Don Melchor, Marques de Casa Concha, Terrunyo) • *Carmenère* (Terrunyo) • *Chardonnay* (Amelia) • *Classic red blend* (Trio Cabernet Sauvignon-Shiraz-Cabernet Franc) • *Merlot* (Marques de Casa Concha, Trio) • *Pinot Noir* (Terrunyo) • *Viognier* (Casillero del Diablo)

CONO SUR
Chimbarongo
★ ✫ ✪

This fast-track winery is owned by Concha y Toro, and was put on the map by Californian Ed Flaharty, who made his name with the stunning El Liso Tempranillo in Spain's La Mancha, of all places. Flaharty has since moved on, but Cono Sur continues to make excellent-quality wine, while its Isla Negra label offers brilliant value for money. Good-value wines sold under supermarket own-labels will indicate Tocornal as the producer, rather than Cono Sur (the winery was originally named Viña Tocornal). Part organic.

✓ *Cabernet Sauvignon* (20 Barrels) • *Merlot* (20 Barrels) • *Riesling* (Visíon)

COOPERATIVA AGRÍCOLA VITIVINICOLA DE CURICÓ
Curicó
✫ ✪

This cooperative has been going since 1939, but has shown great improvement under the consultancy of flying winemaker Peter Bright, through wines sold under the Viños Los Robles label.

✓ *Chardonnay* • *Sauvignon-Sémillon*

COUSIÑO MACUL
Bruin
★ ✪

Chile's one-time best winery has been overtaken by other producers who have not had the luxury of Cousiño Macul's established export business. Hungry to break in, others have been receptive to constructive criticism from international markets, and have willingly tailored their wines to suit, while Cousiño Macul maintained its own old-fashioned standards. It has recently relocated to new vineyards, and has started producing fresher, fruitier, better-focused wines since the 2002 vintage.

✓ *Cabernet Sauvignon* (Antigua Reserva) • *Classic red blend* (Finis Terrae) • *Riesling* (Doña Isidora)

ECHEVERRIA
Molina
★ ✪

This small, family-owned venture had long supplied other wineries with its grapes, when in 1992 it began producing wines under its own label.

✓ *Cabernet Sauvignon* (Family Reserva) • *Carmenère* • *Chardonnay* (Reserva) • *Classic red blend* (Syrah Carmenère) • *Sauvignon Blanc*

ERRÁZURIZ
Santiago
★ ★ ✪

Formerly called Errázuriz-Panquehue, this old winery in the Maule Valley has steadily improved under New Zealander Brian Bicknell (now back home), and it should continue to develop under Ed Flaharty, the gifted Californian who established Cono Sur's reputation. Part organic.

✓ *Carmenère* (Single Vineyard) • *Chardonnay* (Arbolleda) • *Classic red blend* (Viñedo Chadwick) • *Cabernet Sauvignon* (Dom Maximiano) • *Sangiovese* (Single Vineyard) • *Syrah* (La Cumbre)

FALERNIA
Vicuña
★ ✪

Founded in 1995 by Aldo Olivier Gramola, Viña Falernia is located in the Elqui Valley, 470 kilometres (290 miles) north of Santiago, making it Chile's most northerly winery.

✓ *Syrah* (Alta Tierra)

LA FORTUNA
Lontue
✫

The Güell family have owned this winery for almost 60 years, but it has been seriously improved in export markets only since the mid-1990s. Winemaker Claudio Barrio has made some appallingly green Sauvignon Blanc (particularly in 1996), but consistently produces lovely, soft, violety-cherry Malbec.

✓ *Malbec*

FRANCISCO DE AGUIRE
Ovalle
★ ✪

This venture is the most northerly of Chile's exporting wineries, and was built on revenue produced by Pisco Capel, the top-selling pisco brand in the country. Viña Francisco de Aguire produces premium varietals just south of the Atacama desert on steep, mineral-rich, drip-irrigated terraces of the Andes foothills. Wines are sold under the Palo Alto, Piedras Atlas, Tierra Arena, and Tierras Atlas labels.

Classic red blend (Tempus Red) • *Late Harvest* (Moscatel de Alejandría Torontel)

GRACIA
Totihue
❓

This is a new winery with 360 hectares (890 acres) of vineyards ranging from the Aconcagua Valley north of Santiago to the Bio Bio Valley in the south. It is too early to make judgement on these wines.

HARAS DE PIRQUE
Pirque
★ Ⓥ

A joint-venture between Chilean entrepreneur Eduardo Matte and Antinori of Tuscany. Located on Matte's stud farm in the Andean foothills, overlooking the Maipo Valley, Haras de Pirque is one of Chile's fastest-rising stars. Unlike some of this country's recently established boutique wineries, which are destined to go bust or be taken over, this operation exudes permanency.

 Chardonnay (Haras Character) • *Syrah* (Haras Character)

LEYDA
Leyda
★ Ⓥ

This up-and-coming winery is proving that the Leyda Valley can produce some of Chile's fruitiest wines, especially Pinot Noir.

 Pinot Noir (Las Brisas Vineyard)

LUIS FELIPE
Colchagua
★★ Ⓥ

These mature vineyards produce stunning-value Cabernet Sauvignon and deliciously ripe, tropical fruit-flavoured Chardonnay. Part organic.

 Cabernet Sauvignon (especially Reserva) • *Chardonnay*

MIGUEL TORRES
Curicó
★★ Ⓥ

The reds produced by Spain's most innovative winemaker are often misunderstood, particularly in Chile itself, where their slow-evolving style is swamped by the immediacy of more flashy, up-front winemaking methods. Part organic.

 Cabernet Sauvignon (Manso de Velasco) • *Carignan* (Cordillera) • *Chardonnay* (Maquehua)

MONTES
Curicó
★ ✩

The brainchild of Aurelio Montes, these wines started out as far too oaky for all but lovers of four-by-two. Their production has now moved from a heavy-handed use of primarily American oak to a more restrained application of French oak. Montes also makes some deliciously fruity unoaked wines. Part organic.

 Cabernet Sauvignon • *Chardonnay* • *Malbec* • *Merlot* • *Syrah* (Folly)

MONTGRAS
Colchagua
★ ✩ Ⓥ

Exciting quality from strict selection of 250 hectares (600 acres) of vineyards, made in a US$15 million winery. Part organic.

 Cabernet Sauvignon (Ninquén Reserva) • *Classic red blend* (Ninquén Cabernet Merlot)

PÉREZ CRUZ
Paine
✩ Ⓥ

Low-yield vineyards and well-ripened fruit are responsible for the intensity of flavour in this winery's Malbec.

 Malbec (Cot Reserva Limited Edition)

LA ROSA
Cachapoal
★ ✩ Ⓥ

A 500-hectare (1,200-acre) vineyard and six-million-dollar winery owned by SOFRUCO, one of Chile's largest fruit producers.

 Cabernet Sauvignon • *Chardonnay* • *Merlot*

SANTA CAROLINA
Santiago

Fresh, crisp, fruity whites are the best value here, although the reds are definitely the best quality. Santa Carolina owns Viña Casablanca.

 Classic red blend (VSC) • *Merlot* • *Sauvignon Blanc* • *Syrah*

SANTA INÉS
Isla de Maipo
◉

This small, quality-minded winery is owned by the De Martino family.

 Carmenère

SANTA MONICA
Rancagua
✩

Owner-winemaker Emilio de Solminihac (a partner in Domaine Paul Bruno) makes wines with a fat, fruity style at his own winery.

 Sauvignon Blanc

SAN PEDRO
Molina
✩ Ⓥ

The wines of San Pedro, one of the pioneers that earned respect for Chilean wines on export markets, went through a patchy period, but are emerging better than before, thanks to an expensive ultra-modern winery and consultancy from flying winemaker Jacques Lurton. Wines are also sold under the penny-saving Gato Blanco and Gato Negro brands. Santa Helena is an export brand.

 Chardonnay (Castillo de Molina Reserva)

SANTA RITA
Santiago
★ ✩ Ⓥ

These wines are fatter and riper than they have been in years, but the "120" range (so-called because Bernardo O'Higgins, the liberator of Chile, and his 120 men hid in these cellars after the battle of Rancagua in 1810) has remained reliable throughout. Santa Rita also owns the Carmen winery, and has a partnership with Lafite-Rothschild in Los Vascos.

 Cabernet Sauvignon ("120", Casa Real) • *Classic red blend* (Triple C) • *Sauvignon Blanc* (Casa Real) • *Merlot* (Medalla Real, Casablanca, Reserve)

SEÑA
Panquehue
★★

A joint-venture between Errázuriz and Robert Mondavi in 1996, Seña had established itself as one of Chile's *grands crus* when Errázuriz purchased Mondavi's share immediately prior to its takeover by Constellation Brands in 2004.

 Classic red blend (Seña)

TERRANOBLE
Talca
★

With Henri Marionnet, one of Touraine's best winemakers, consulting, Terranoble has fashioned an increasingly fine range of red wines.

 Cabernet Sauvignon • *Carmenère* (Reserva)

UNDURRAGA
Santiago
❓

This was the first Chilean winery to export to the USA, and only remains in this encyclopedia for historic reasons, as I have seldom found any exciting wines from Undurraga. Having embarked upon a 1.5-million-dollar renovation and replanting programme in 1997, it was hoped that this might bring about welcome changes for Undurraga's quality, but only the Late-Harvest Sémillon is recommendable, and even that could be an anomaly.

 Sémillon (Late Harvest)

VALDIVIESO
Santiago
★ ✩ Ⓥ

Originally called Champagne Alberto Valdivieso, this company still produces large quantities of ordinary Chilean fizz, but has moved into pure varietal, barrel-fermented table wines in a spectacularly successful fashion. Loco is Valdivieso's top-of-the-range red, a blend of different grape varieties from various vintages. To distinguish which batch is which (and to enable wine enthusiasts to cellar and follow the wines), they are numbered. I have tasted only Caballo Loco Number One, but it is such a masterly wine that I have no hesitation ranking it as one of South America's finest wines. Cheaper wines are sold under the Casa label.

 Caballo Loco • *Cabernet Franc* • *Merlot* • *Pinot Noir*

VILLARD
Casablanca
★

This is a partnership between Thierry Villard (who in 1989 produced what was probably the first truly fine Chilean Chardonnay – Santa Emiliana – which is owned by Concha y Toro) and two growers, one of whom, Pablo Morandé, is Concha y Toro's winemaker.

 Cabernet Sauvignon • *Merlot* • *Pinot Noir*

VIU MANENT
Molina
✩ Ⓥ

An old-established family-owned winery that has moved away from bulk wines to more expressive, high-quality wines under its own label.

 Cabernet Sauvignon (Reserve) • *Malbec* (Single Vineyard)

ARGENTINA

ALTOS LAS HORMIGAS
Ciudad
★ ✩

This vineyard was destroyed by a plague of ants (*hormigas*), hence its name, and had to purchase grapes until a new vineyard came into production.

 Malbec

ARCHÁVAL FERRER
Luján de Cuyo
★★

Established in 1998, its low-yield vineyards and a dedication to quality have made this one of Argentina's fastest-rising, highest-flying wineries.

 Classic red blend (Quimera) • *Malbec* (Finca Altamira)

BODEGAS LOPEZ
Buenos Aires
✩

This family firm produces average-quality wines under the Château Montchenot label (known as Don Federico on some export markets).

BODEGAS LURTON
Buenos Aires
✩

The Lurtons of Bordeaux originally came to Chile as flying winemakers for the British supermarket chain Tesco, but liked the potential so much that, together with the omnipresent Nicolas Catena, they purchased their own winery and are now firmly ensconced.

√ *Malbec*

BODEGAS NACARI
La Rioja

This small cooperative specializes in Torrontes.

CATENA
Córdoba
★★

Argentina's greatest wine visionary, Nicolás Catena, has produced some superb wines with the aid of his Californian winemaker Paul Hobbs, who helped to establish the Opus One winery before going to Argentina. Nicolás Catena Zapata is very much upmarket by local standards, while Caro is produced in conjunction with the Rothschilds of Château Lafite. Catena Alta are fine wines by any standard, and the basic Catena range is stylish, and far from basic. I should recommend the entire range, but have plucked out the very best below. Superb-value fine wines are also sold under the Alamos Ridge, Bodegas Esmerelda, and Libertad labels. Catena also owns Bodegas La Rural, and Cavas de Santa Maria. *See also* Luca and Tikal.

√ *Cabernet Sauvignon* (Catena Alta) • *Chardonnay* (Catena Alta) • *Classic red blend* (Caro, Nicolás Catena Zapata) • *Malbec* (Catena Alta)

CHANDON ARGENTINA
Buenos Aires

This long-established arm of Moët & Chandon makes mostly sparkling wines, which used to be sold shamelessly as *champaña* under the M Chandon and Baron B labels. The quality is fresh, clean, acceptable, and improving, but not special. More interesting is the increasing amount of good and improving still wine now being made with an eye on export markets (*see* Terrazas de Los Andes).

CLOS DE LOS SIETE
Tunuyán
★

Tipped by some as potentially Argentina's greatest winery, Clos de los Siete is an ambitious project headed by Michel Rolland. The venture comprises seven vineyards owned by seven French proprietors, who are expected to produce their own distinct wines within due course (look out for the single vineyard names of Altamira, Lindaflor, Los Dassos, Miraflor, Primaflor, Rocaflor, and Monteviejo). Some critics claim that one investor has already backed out, and the scope of such a project will probably see others jumping ship before long. One partner, the late Jean-Michel Arcaute, tragically

died before the first vintage (2002) was produced.

√ *Classic red blend* (Clos de los Siete)

COLOMÉ
Colomé
Ⓑ ★★

This winery boasts the highest vineyards in the world, and Caifornia owners, Hess Collection, stand every chance of making Argentina's highest-quality wines here. Deliciously fruity, entry-level wines are sold under the Amalaya label.

√ *Classic red blend* (Colme Estate)

DOMINO DEL PLATA
Luján de Cuyo
★ ✪ Ⓥ

One of Argentina's most exciting new wineries, Domino del Plata is owned by husband and wife team Pedro Marchevsky, the viticulturist, and Susana Balbo, the winemaker. The best wines are sold under the Susana Balbo and BenMarco labels, while excellent-value wines are sold in the Crios de Susana Balbo range.

√ *Classic red blend* (Crios de Susana Balbo Syrah-Bonarda, BenMarco VMS) • *Malbec* (BenMarco)

ETCHART
Salta
★ Ⓥ

The very fresh, crisp, and dry Cafayate Torrontes, with its subtle, Muscat-like aromas, is a yardstick for this peculiarly Argentinian variety, but Cabernet Sauvignon is by far the best wine here. Etchart is now fully owned by Pernod-Ricard, with Michel Rolland consulting.

√ *Cabernet Sauvignon* • *Torrontes* (Cafayate)

FINCA LA ANITA
Luján de Cuyo
★ ✪ Ⓥ

Established in 1992 by Antonio Mas, who has attained a very high quality, and continues to improve.

√ *Malbec* • *Sémillon* • *Syrah* • *Tocai Friulano*

FINCA FLICHMAN
Mendoza
✪

After considerable investment in stainless-steel vats and new French oak *barriques*, plus a certain amount of European technical assistance, the quality as well as quantity has increased. Furthermore, emphasis has moved to Latin grape varieties such Barbera, Sangiovese, and Tempranillo, as the choice for blending with local favourites such as Malbec, Cabernet, and Merlot.

√ *Cabernet Sauvignon* (Caballero de la Cepa) • *Sangiovese-Malbec* • *Syrah*

HUMBERTO CANALE
Rio Negro
★ Ⓥ

These are interesting, improving varietal wines from some of the most southerly vineyards in the world.

√ *Malbec* • *Merlot* • *Pinot Noir*

LUCA
Mendoza
★★

Stunning wines produced by Nicolas Catena's daughter Laura at her own winery, from her own vineyard, with typically Catena-like low yields and high altitude.

√ *Cabernet Sauvignon* • *Chardonnay* • *Syrah*

NORTON
Buenos Aires
✪

Although this firm dates back to 1895, it was not until 1989, when Austrian businessman Gernot Langes-Swarovski purchased the winery from its uninspiring English owners, that these wines started to show their true potential. Sangiovese and Barbera are the most interesting but, regrettably, the most variable as well.

√ *Classic red blend* (Privada) • *Malbec*

O FOURNIER
Mendoza
★★

Spanish winery owner Jose Manuel Ortega produces some of Argentina's greatest wines from grapes planted high up in the Valley de Uco.

√ *Entire range*

PEÑAFLOR
Buenos Aires
✪ Ⓥ

The quality here has been greatly improved in recent years by a magnum of flying winemakers in the form of Peter Bright and John Worontschak. The Country Red is a cheap and cheerful blend. Peñaflor also sells wines under the Andean Vineyards, Fond de Cave, Parral, Tio Quinto, and Trapiche labels. *See also* Trapiche.

√ *Classic red blend* (Cabernet-Malbec) • *Torrontes* • *Tempranillo*

PIPER
Buenos Aires

When Englishman Trevor Bell was managing Charles Heidsieck and Piper-Heidsieck in France, he blew the whistle on those Champagne houses – including his own – who claimed they were forced by Argentinian law to use the word *champaña* on their Argentinian sparkling wines. He considered it hypocritical and said that Piper for one would stop the practice. Bell was never heard of again. This is

the only Champagne name that is still prostituting itself. Rémy-Cointreau, the owner of these two Champagne houses, claim that it is not their responsibility, since they do not actually produce the wine. However, they do admit to owning the brand, and licensing it out, which is just as reprehensible.

SAN PEDRO DE YACOCHUYA
Maipú
★ ✪

A joint venture between Michel Rolland and the Etchart family.

√ *Malbec* (Yacochuya)

TERRAZAS DE LOS ANDES
Luján de Cuyo
★ ✪ Ⓥ

These still wines of Chandon Argentina are vastly superior to its sparkling wines.

√ *Cabernet Sauvignon* (Gran Reserva) • *Classic red blend* (Cheval des Andes) • *Malbec* (Gran Reserva)

TIKAL
Mendoza
★★

This winery and vineyard is owned by Ernest Catena, son of the famous Nicolas Catena.

√ *Classic red blend* (Corazon, Júbilo) • *Malbec* (Altos de Mendoza Amorío)

TRAPICHE
Buenos Aires
★ ✪ Ⓥ

Part of Peñaflor, the quality of Trapiche has risen steadily in recent years. Michel Rolland consults. *See also* Peñaflor.

√ *Cabernet Sauvignon* (Medalla) • *Classic red blend* (Iscay) • *Malbec* (Broquel) • *Syrah* (Oak Cask)

VISTALBA
Mendoza
★

This up-and-coming winery makes interesting reds from varieties such as Barbera and Syrah to complement Argentinian faithfuls such as Cabernet and Malbec.

√ *Cabernet Sauvignon* • *Malbec* • *Syrah*

WEINERT
Buenos Aires
★ ✪

Although established as long ago as 1890, this winery emerged as one of Argentina's top two producers only under the present owner, Brazilian-born Bernardo Weinert. He renovated the winery in 1975 and shortly after became the first Argentinian producer to reduce yields in order to raise quality, inspiring others to follow.

√ *Cabernet Sauvignon* • *Classic red blend* (Cavas de Weinert) • *Malbec*

The WINES of
AUSTRALIA,
NEW ZEALAND,
AND ASIA

WE TEND TO THINK OF AUSTRALIA AS THE
older, more traditional winemaking country,
with New Zealand being a much more recent
phenomenon. Yet just a 30-year gap separates
the viticultural origins of these two countries.
Australia's wine industry dates back to 1788, but
New Zealand's started not much later, in 1819.
In modern terms, they are just 10 years apart,
Australia having won its spurs in the 1980s,
with New Zealand assuming classic status in the
1990s. Australia is famous for its big, creamy-
mellow, spicy-cedary Shiraz, while New Zealand
leads with its fresh, crisp, exhilarating Sauvignon
Blanc – but these are just the flagships. Both
countries produce a large and diverse range
of wine styles and are currently discovering
a wealth of *terroirs* and the differences in
expression that they bring. In Asia, Japan and
China continue to dominate; India is treading
water; and we are starting to see wines from
Thailand, Korea, and even Bali.

RIPPON VINEYARD, SOUTH ISLAND, NEW ZEALAND
*One of the most beautiful vineyard settings in the world, the gently
sloping Rippon Vineyard leads down to Lake Wanaka, which has
a moderating effect on the climate enjoyed by these vines.
The nets prevent the grapes from being eaten by birds.*

AUSTRALIA

Having built its name on the consistent quality of its high-volume brands, which have been aggressively marketed through multi-bottle discount deals, "Brand Australia" has grown into the biggest success story in modern wine history. Yet some producers are beginning to wonder whether they will ever sell their wines for what they are really worth – rather than giving them away.

IF ONLY THE AUSTRALIANS were as insecure and indecisive as this on the cricket field! They need not worry, however, as all the evidence suggests that their position will be consolidated over the medium term. The alarms are false, and merely the result of mixed messages generated by the two basic types of wine produced:

brands and site-specific wines. It is no accident that the public perception of Australian wine is so dependent on the concept of branded wine. Australian brands have always been strong, but in 1996 their position was formally promoted by the industry's 30-year plan to become the "world's most influential and profitable supplier of branded wines". Most people reading this for the first time will ask themselves why the word "branded" was inserted, and who could be the author of such a biased quest?

Australian brands have been criticized as overripe, over-alcoholic, formulaic wines that have no soul. Perhaps. However, the fact that so many might taste very similar is in itself an indication of their very consistent quality. They might not exude individuality, and wine lovers might wonder why this commercial category of wine has been singled out for official blessing in the 30-year plan, but Australia's branded wines are made in a soft, rich, consumer-friendly, fruit-driven style. They are nothing more than the equivalent of branded generic wines from, say,

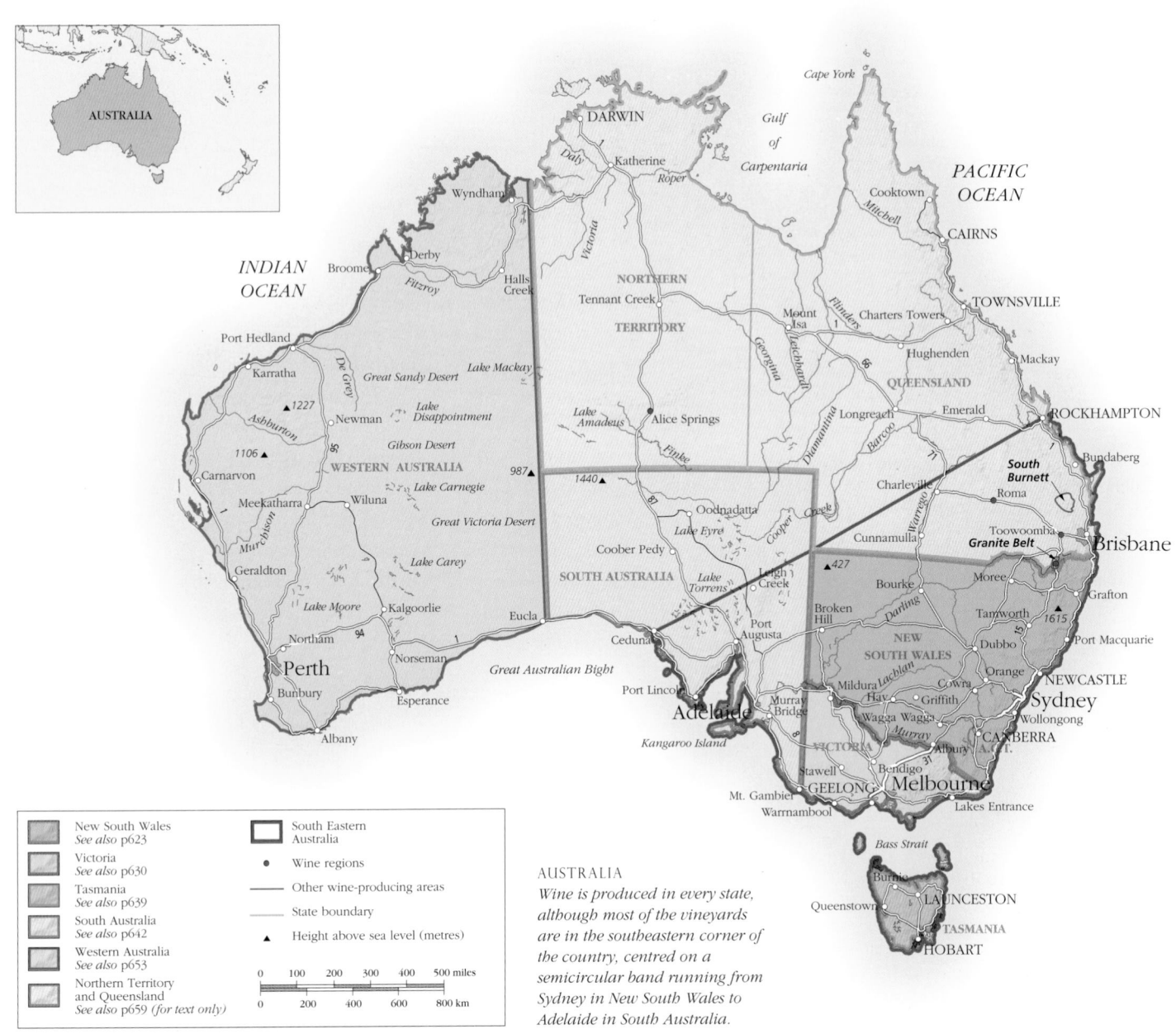

New South Wales
See also p623

Victoria
See also p630

Tasmania
See also p639

South Australia
See also p642

Western Australia
See also p653

Northern Territory
and Queensland
See also p659 (for text only)

South Eastern
Australia

● Wine regions

── Other wine-producing areas

── State boundary

▲ Height above sea level (metres)

0   100   200   300   400   500 miles
0   200   400   600   800 km

AUSTRALIA
Wine is produced in every state, although most of the vineyards are in the southeastern corner of the country, centred on a semicircular band running from Sydney in New South Wales to Adelaide in South Australia.

Bordeaux or Beaujolais, but infinitely more enjoyable. Certainly consumers think so. By 2003 Australia had become the second-largest exporter of wine to the USA, and had even pushed out France from the number one position on the UK market. While it might not seem so surprising that an up-and-coming wine country like Australia should appeal more to consumers, particularly younger ones, than an old and traditional producer such as France, it is an extraordinary feat considering the contrasting size of these two wine industries. France is nothing less than the largest wine producer in the world, responsible for 21 per cent of global production, whereas Australia is a minnow, accounting for less than 4 per cent. How on earth did the Aussies manage to pull this off?

THE EXPORT TRAP

Did Australia achieve its export victories because its brands were sold at economically unsustainable prices, as some now fear? No. How could this be true when the country's largest wine groups have made handsome profits in the process? There has been much talk about falling sales, reduced profit margins, and ailing wine companies, but Australia did not achieve success overnight or, indeed, over just one year, and those ailing companies were all extremely profitable on the way up.

It is evident, therefore, that Australia's brands were not undersold, but if the industry is worried that there is a perception that its wines are too cheap, then it should ask itself a few questions. Should Australia concentrate its exports so heavily on two countries, the UK and USA, which between them take over 70 per cent of all Australian wine exports? And should not the industry change its 30-year plan to become the "world's most influential and profitable supplier of geographically distinct wines"? There is nothing wrong with multi-state blends, such as the all-encompassing Southeastern Australian appellation, which straddles 95 per cent of the country's vineyards. For their own sake, though, brand owners should concentrate less on such wines, and more on expressing some level of individuality.

THE GROWTH OF AUSTRALIA'S WINE TRADE

The first Australian vineyard was planted at Farm Cove in New South Wales in 1788, with vines originating not from France but from Rio de Janeiro and the Cape of Good Hope. These were collected by the first governor, Captain Arthur Phillip, *en route* to Sydney. The rich soil of Farm Cove and its humid climate proved fine for growing vines, but not for making wine. Phillip persevered, however, and planted another vineyard at Parramatta, just north of Sydney. Soil and climate were more suitable and the success of this new venture encouraged Phillip's official requests for technical assistance. England responded by sending out two French prisoners of war, who were offered their freedom in exchange for three years' service in New South Wales, in the belief that all Frenchmen knew something about making wine. This did not prove true: one was so bad at it that he was transported back to England; the other could make only cider, and mistakenly used peaches instead of apples! From these shaky beginnings an industry grew, but with no thanks to the British. At first, Australia's wine trade was monopolized by the needs of the British Empire, later the Commonwealth. It thus gained a reputation for cheap fortified wines – not because these were the only ones it could make, but because Britain wanted them. Unfortunately, Australians also acquired the taste. Although Australia made (and still makes) some of the world's finest dessert wines (botrytized as well as fortified), most wines were heavy, very sweet, and sluggish at a time when the rest of the world was drinking lighter and finer wines. Small quantities of truly fine table wine were produced but, until the 1960s, most of those exported were remarkably uniform in style.

CORIOLE VINEYARDS, MCLAREN VALE
McLaren Vale is currently contesting Coonawarra's reputation as the best red wine region of South Australia, a state that accounts for almost 60 per cent of Australia's total wine output.

THE RENAISSANCE OF AUSTRALIAN WINES

Over the past 40 years or so, the technology used in Australian winemaking has made huge advances, taking with it the quality of the wines. Until the early 1980s, as much as 99 per cent of all Australian wine was consumed domestically. When output dramatically increased, producers had to concentrate on exports, which increased tenfold in the 1980s, and a further tenfold in the 1990s. Today, they represent more than 60 per cent of the country's total production. At the time of writing (2011), there are 2,300 wineries in Australia – two and a half times as many as there were 15 years ago – and a new winery is born every 84 hours.

THE WINE SHOW SYSTEM

Wine shows have been, and remain, a key factor in shaping the Australian wine industry, and, for better or worse, the "Australian style" of wine. The National Wine Show, held in Canberra, is considered to be the grand finale of the Australian wine show circuit, with entries restricted to wines that have previously been awarded a trophy or medal at other shows. Next in the hierarchy are the Australian Capital City Wine Shows (Adelaide, Sydney, etc), followed by regional shows, such as the Australian Inland, Australian Small Winemakers, Ballarat, Barossa, Canberra Regional Wine Show, Clare Valley, Cowra, Griffith, Hunter Valley, Lilydale, Limestone Coast, McLaren Vale, Mount Barker, Mudgee, Riverland, Rutherglen, and Victorian Wines.

Most of these shows are run by Royal Agricultural Societies or are county fair-type shows. As such, wine is just one of the featured competitions. The societies organizing these wine shows are also responsible for other agricultural and horticultural competitions, judging everything from barley to lavender, cattle to goats, and wool to woodchopping. It is understandable how these shows originated, when a crop of grapes was very much like a crop of anything else, but since wine has evolved into such a diverse and sophisticated end product, there are good reasons to bring these competitions under specialist, independent control.

Not that the show system has had a negative effect. Indeed, the reverse has been true, particularly in the final two decades of the last century. The technical correctness demanded by judges raised quality levels across the board, and this was achieved, essentially, by Australian winemakers not being afraid to be very strict in scoring wines of their peers and, sometimes embarrassingly, wines of their own. Compare this with France, where there is reluctance among winemakers to mark down the wines of their peers, unless they are blatantly faulty, for fear of retaliation. In the 1990s, there was a move away from technical correctness, as allowances were made for the contribution of tiny faults to overall complexity.

However, the winners of Australia's wine shows, like the winners of most wine competitions throughout the world, are invariably the biggest wines. The biggest wines are not always the best wines, and almost always never accompany food well. They are just so complete that to partner them with anything else is to detract from their glory. The only Australian wine competition I know of that actually deliberates over the concept of matching the wines to food, and also sets out to reward wine of finesse and elegance, is the Sydney International Wine Competition. In the second round, the judges even taste the wines with a platter of appropriate food. This competition also places a high emphasis on international judges to avoid the "cellar palate" and prejudices of the Australian wine trade and its home-grown commentators.

International judges do take part in the Royal Society shows, particularly the larger ones, but they are in a minority, and can do little against the unwritten rules. Of these, the one that troubles me the most concerns the Riesling class. Depending on the volume of Riesling entries, the trend is to judge the most recent vintage, and, possibly, the previous vintage, as classes on their own. Anything older will be lumped together under some sort of "museum" class, potentially judging a three-year-old wine against one that may be 12 years old or more. One unwritten law among judges is to mark up lime aromas and flavours, and mark down any so-called petrol aromas (*see* Taste and Aroma Chart and Micropedia). This jars with many wine drinkers from northern climes, who enjoy the petrolly bottle-aromas that accompany the honeyed richness of a fine, mature Riesling. However, when it is realized that so many Australian Rieslings, particularly the cheaper ones, develop an overwhelming petrolly character far too rapidly from a simplistic lime fruit base, it is easy to understand how petrol aromas have acquired such a negative connotation in this country. It should be the job of the Australian wine show circuit to promote a better understanding. To recognize that the petrol aroma is not negative *per se*.

VINEYARDS IN MUDGEE
Perhaps atypical of the area, these vineyards occupy flatland rather than the western slopes of the Great Dividing Range.

To mark down a petrolly character that is too dominant for a certain level and simplicity of fruit, but to mark up one that has taken ages to achieve a wonderfully complex nuance. This is particularly relevant now that Australia is making finer and finer Riesling. For these wines to increase will require not only a detailed examination of each new vintage, as is the current practice, but also encouragement of producers to enter Riesling in two distinct classes: 5 to 12 years, and 13 years and older.

GOING GREEN?

Taking the organic route in the vineyard is harder in some countries than others. Essentially, the more rain or humidity there is, the more rot affects the grapes, and the more difficult it becomes to control this by natural means. Some growers are game for the challenge, even in rain-soaked countries like England, whereas hardly any bother in sunny Australia. It should be pointed out that many good growers, and all the best, are "almost" organic the world over, since anyone who is interested in producing the best wine they possibly can will realize that it is in their own interest to ensure that their own viticulture is sustainable for the long term. However, the number of organic producers in a viticultural paradise like Australia is so pathetically small that I feel compelled to list all the wineries I know to be organic, in addition to the few specifically recommended in the following pages.

Certified biodynamic
Jeeleunup Gully Wines
(Mount Barker, Western Australia)
Kiltynane Estate
(Yarra Valley, Victoria)
Robinvale Wines
(Murray Darling, Vicoria)
Rosnay Wines
(Canowindra, New South Wales)
Streamville (Arthurs Creek, Victoria)

Certified organic
Captains Creek
(Macedon Ranges, Victoria)
Glenara Wines
(Adelaide Hills, South Australia)

Mabrook Estate
(Hunter Valley, New South Wales)
Martins Hill Wines
(Mudgee, New South Wales)
Petcheys Bay Vineyard (Tasmania)
Robinvale Wines
(Murray Darling, Victoria)
Temple Breuer
(Langhorne Creek, South Australia)
Serventy Wines
(Margaret River, Western Australia)
Thistle Hill Vineyard
(Mudgee, New South Wales)
Wilkie Estate Wines
(Adelaide, South Australia)

RECENT AUSTRALIAN VINTAGES

2011 This is an exceptionally challenging year, due mainly to rain, with floods not as severe as, but not restricted to, the biblical events in Queensland. That and the cold summer weather make for a potentially difficult vintage.

2010 An excellent vintage for both red and white wines in Southern Australia and Margaret River.

2009 Generally, a very good to excellent year, with great Hunter Valley Sémillon the standout.

2008 Margaret River is the standout region of the vintage, but early-picked varieties in South Australia fared very well.

2007 This was a small, very variable, and disappointing vintage, with the grapes in several areas tainted by smoke from bushfires. Excellent wines, however, can be found from the Margaret River, Hunter Valley, Tasmania, and southern Victoria, particularly Mornington Peninsula.

NEW SOUTH WALES

From the Hunter Valley's weighty Shiraz, through its honeyed, bottle-aged Sémillon, and the easy-drinking Riverina wines, to the fast-rising wines from areas such as Orange, Tumbarumba, and Hilltops – the wines of New South Wales are better in quality and more varied in style than they have ever been.

ALTHOUGH VINES ARRIVED with the British First Fleet, and Australia's first governor, Captain Arthur Phillip, planted the country's first vineyard (at Farm Cove, known by the Aborigines as Woccanmagully, and now the site of Sydney's Royal Botanic Gardens) in 1788, it was Gregory Blaxland who made Australia's first wine. Blaxland planted his vineyard at Ermington, a few miles down river from Phillip's second vineyard at Parramatta. In 1822, Blaxland also became the first person to export Australian wine, when he brandied a quarter pipe (137.5 litres) of red wine so that it might withstand the rigours of being shipped to London, where it won a Silver Medal from the Society for Encouragement of Arts, Manufactures and Commerce (now the Royal Society of Arts).

HUNTER SHIRAZ

The reputation of this state's wine industry will always revolve around the Hunter Valley, particularly the Upper Hunter, however much added value there is to gain from its newer regions. Because Australia has claimed Shiraz as its own, Hunter Shiraz will always play a pivotal role. But our perception of this wine has changed; it is hard to imagine that the Hunter was once famous for a huge, beefy style of Shiraz that gave off a strong, gamey, sweat-and-leather odour and possessed an earthy, almost muddy taste that was "chewed" rather than swallowed. Its "sweaty saddle" smell was supposed to derive from the Hunter Valley's volcanic basalt soil, until it was widely declared to be a defect. For quite some time, it was thought to be a mercaptan fault, but the sweaty saddle odour (also described as "horsey" or "stables") is now known to be ethyl-4-phenol, a specific volatile phenol defect caused by the Brettanomyces yeast.

NEW SOUTH WALES, *see also p620*
North of Sydney, the Lower and Upper Hunter Valley and the Mudgee area excel, while the Murrumbidgee Irrigation Area to the southwest proves that quantity can, to a certain extent, co-exist with quality.

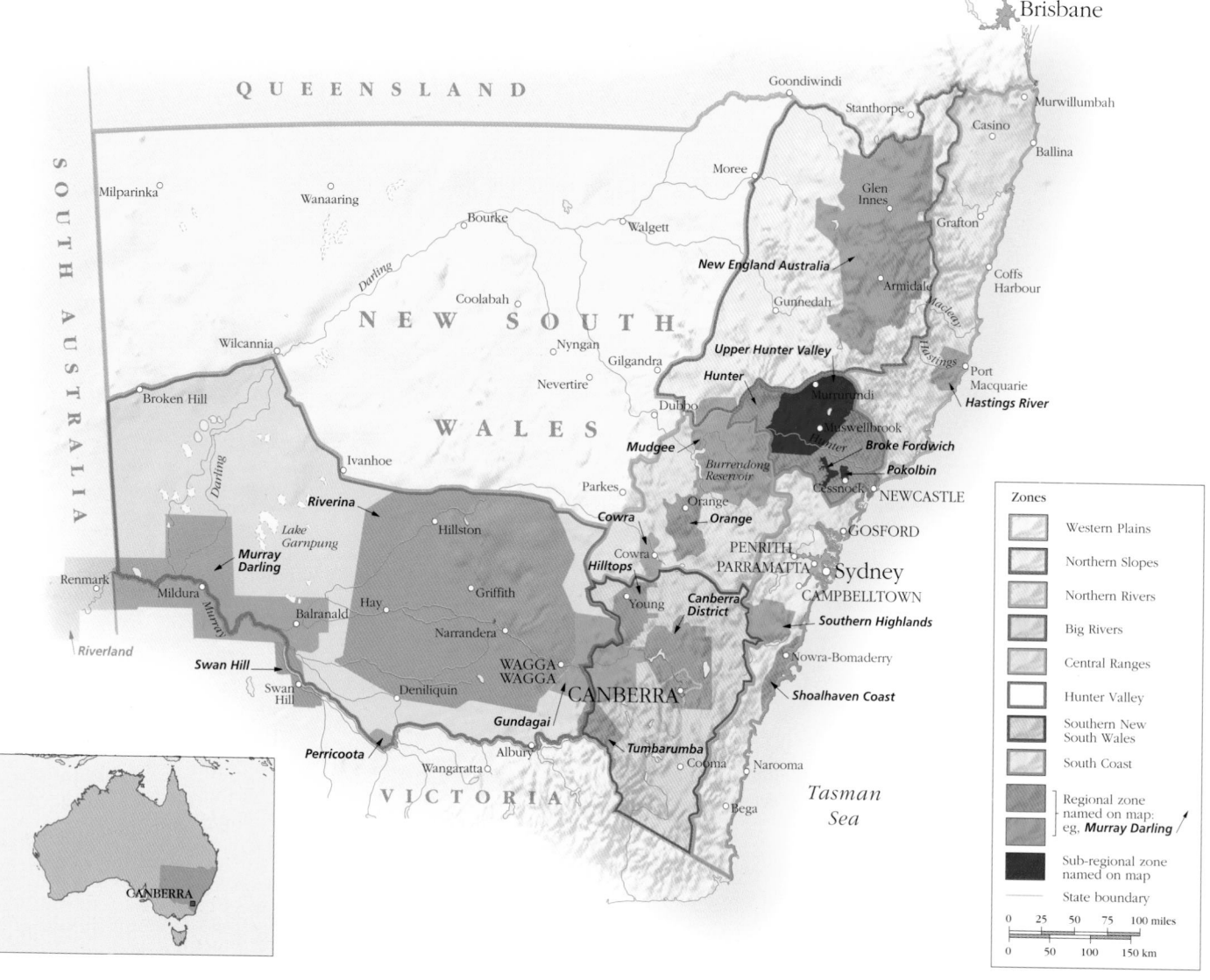

Zones

	Western Plains
	Northern Slopes
	Northern Rivers
	Big Rivers
	Central Ranges
	Hunter Valley
	Southern New South Wales
	South Coast

Regional zone named on map: eg, *Murray Darling*

Sub-regional zone named on map

State boundary

0 25 50 75 100 miles
0 50 100 150 km

FACTORS AFFECTING TASTE AND QUALITY

LOCATION
The southern part of Australia's east coast, between Victoria and Queensland.

CLIMATE
Growing-season temperatures are similar to those of the Languedoc in southern France. Cloud cover can temper the heat in the Hunter Valley, but the accompanying rains often promote rot. The growing season is later, and the climate sunnier, in Mudgee, Orange, and Cowra, while it is hotter and drier in Riverina, and significantly cooler in Tumbarumba.

ASPECT
Vines are grown on generally low-lying, flat, or undulating sites, but also on steeper slopes such as the fringes of the Brokenback Range in the Lower Hunter Valley, where vines are grown at altitudes of up to 500 metres (1,600 feet); on the western slopes of the Great Dividing Range, where some vineyards can be found at an altitude of 800 metres (2,600 feet); and in Canberra at 820 metres (2,706 feet).

SOIL
Soils are varied, with sandy and clay loams of varying fertility found in all areas. Various other types of soil, such as the red-brown volcanic loams, are scattered about the Lower Hunter region and the fertile, but well-drained, alluvial sands and silts of the flat valley floors. Hilltops has a deep, gravelly, red soil, mixed with basalt and sandy granite, while Tumbarumba much further south also has basalt and granite soils.

VITICULTURE AND VINIFICATION
Irrigation is practised throughout the state, particularly in the mainly bulk-wine-producing inland area of Riverina. The range of grape varieties is increasing, and grapes are harvested several days earlier than they used to be, for a crisper style. Temperature-controlled fermentation in stainless-steel vats is common, but new oak is used judiciously.

GRAPE VARIETIES
Primary varieties: Cabernet Sauvignon, Chardonnay, Pinot Noir, Riesling, Sémillon, Shiraz (Syrah)
Secondary varieties: Cabernet Franc, Colombard, Grenache, Malbec, Merlot, Muscat Gordo Blanco (Muscat d'Alexandrie), Petit Verdot, Ruby Cabernet, Sauvignon Blanc, Trebbiano (Ugni Blanc), Verdelho

IRRIGATION CANAL AND DE BORTOLI WINERY
A network of irrigation canals like this one enables Riverina wineries such as De Bortoli to produce vast amounts of modest, easy-drinking wines.

THE APPELLATIONS OF
NEW SOUTH WALES

BIG RIVERS GI

This zonal GI encompasses the regional GIs of Lachlan Valley, Murray Darling, Perricoota, Riverina, and Swan Hill.

BROKE FORDWICH GI

This sub-region of Hunter centres in and around Broke, but also extends south and southwest, encompassing the catchment area of Wollombi Brook, and going north beyond Bulge. Chardonnay and Cabernet Sauvignon seem to be the most successful varieties grown here.

CANBERRA DISTRICT GI

One of the quirkiest GI demarcations must be that of Canberra District, since most of the appellation is not even located within the Australian Capital Territory (ACT), but in New South Wales. In fact, prior to the arrival of BRL Hardy's Kamberra, there were no wineries in ACT, and only 6 hectares (15 acres) of vines. However, the reason for this has nothing to do with any lack of viticultural potential within ACT. The absence of viticulture here was due solely to the fact that the concept of freehold property does not exist within ACT. This hardly makes Canberra an attractive option for anyone in the long-term business of establishing a vineyard, thus no vineyards or smart new boutique wineries are within a stone's throw of the nation's capital. The altitude of most vineyards is 600 to 820 metres (2,000 to 2,700 feet), but most face north or northeast, so the sunshine hours are very high at 7.2 hours per day, enabling grapes to ripen on nearly all aspects. Although the climate is cool in Australian terms, it is not as cool as some local growers might like to boast. Summers are warm and dry, with three out of every four years yielding degree-day equivalents between those of the Médoc and Hermitage. The vineyards are dependent on irrigation, and water is a declining resource. All the usual grape varieties are grown, but snappy Rieslings, elegant Pinot Noir, and Rhône-style Shiraz excel.

CENTRAL RANGES GI

A zonal GI that encompasses the regional GIs of Cowra, Mudgee, and Orange.

COWRA GI

This is a small but growing viticultural area, which is situated some 180 kilometres (120 miles) inland and west from Sydney, and nearly the same distance north of Canberra. As in most of Australia's lesser-known wine areas, viticulture flourished here in the 19th century, and was reignited in the 1970s. But lesser known does not necessarily mean lesser quality, as demonstrated by the earliest vintages of Brian Croser's legendary Petaluma Chardonnay, which were sourced from Cowra.

GUNDAGAI GI

It is surprising how many emerging wine regions in New South Wales happen to be conveniently located for tourist appeal, and Gundagai is no different, since it is touted as a near-perfect stopover between Sydney and Melbourne. Protected by the Snowy Mountains to the southeast, most vineyards are located at 500 to 1,000 metres (1,640 to 3,280 feet) in altitude, with Sémillon providing the most distinctive wines. Other varieties include Chardonnay, Sauvignon Blanc, Cabernet Sauvignon, Merlot, and Shiraz.

HASTINGS RIVER GI

This small region is located on the north coast of New South Wales, where the climate is maritime and subtropical, with high humidity and rainfall. The dominant grape variety is Chambourcin, a French hybrid that survives everything that the local squally weather can throw at it. Chambourcin was pioneered by John Cassegrain, formerly of Tyrrell's, who established a vineyard here in 1980, the first to be planted in the locality since the 1860s. Chardonnay and Sémillon are also supposed to perform well, but it is worth noting that Cassegrain now sources most of his grapes from elsewhere.

HILLTOPS GI

Cool climatic conditions produce an elegant style of Chardonnay, and distinctive Sémillon, with red wines capable of a slow-building complexity, particularly Cabernet Sauvignon and Shiraz. This is essentially cherry orchard country, but the first vines were planted as long ago as the 1860s by Nichole Jaspprizza, a Croatian immigrant who made his money selling the wine he made to diggers in the surrounding goldfields. Peter

Robertson planted the first vines of the modern era at Barwang in 1969. Other varieties growing here include Merlot, Pinot Noir, Riesling, Sauvignon Blanc, and even Zinfandel. Vines grow at an elevation of 450 to 600 metres (1,475 to 2,000 feet) on a deep, gravelly, red soil, mixed with basalt and sandy granite. The climate is continental, cool, and dry with snow in winter and most rainfall occurring from mid-spring to mid-autumn.

HUNTER GI

Sub-region: *Broke Fordwich*

The Hunter sounds as if it should encompass the Hunter Valley, not the other way round. The Hunter covers the areas popularly known as the Lower Hunter Valley and the Upper Hunter Valley. *See* Lower Hunter Valley and Upper Hunter Valley.

HUNTER VALLEY GI

This zonal GI encompasses the regional GI of Hunter.

LOWER HUNTER VALLEY

Not an official GI as yet, but the traditional practice of dividing the Hunter Valley into Lower and Upper regions must be formalized one day, if Australia's Geographical Indications are to be taken seriously. This is the "original" Hunter Valley. Its vineyards were pioneered in the 1820s by such growers as William Kelman of Kirkton and George Wyndham of Dalwood, over 130 years before the Upper Hunter Valley was opened up. The area has long been famous for its rich Sémillons (once sold as Hunter Riesling) and for its forceful Shiraz. The Lower Hunter Valley is not ideal grape country, being too hot and humid, although the nightly air-drainage from the Brokenback Range cools the vines and prevents the acidity of ripening grapes from dropping too rapidly. After a period of slow growth in the 1980s, the Hunter Valley has enjoyed the same rejuvenation as the Barossa Valley in South Australia.

MUDGEE GI

With a continuous history of grape growing since 1856, this is the oldest district on the western side of the Great Dividing Range. Mudgee produces rich and succulent red wines, particularly from Shiraz and Cabernet Sauvignon, and is building a reputation as an excellent source for Sémillon.

MURRAY DARLING GI

The Murray Darling GI straddles New South Wales and Victoria, and is essentially an industrialized wine-growing area. It has a hot and dry continental climate, with little rain, making it ideal for risk-free, large-scale, irrigated production of bag-in-the-box wines, although exceptional wines do exist, such as Tall Poppy's Petit Verdot. Almost every grape variety found in Australia grows here, but the most significant are Chardonnay and Cabernet Sauvignon, with Muscat Gordo Blanco, and clones of Sémillon and Colombard best suited to fortified styles.

NEW ENGLAND AUSTRALIA GI

An upland plateau with cold winters and cool to warm summers, New England Australia is completely contained within the Northern Slopes GI. The main grape varieties are Chardonnay, Riesling, Sauvignon Blanc, and Shiraz.

NORTHERN RIVERS GI

This zonal GI consists of New South Wales' northern coastal strip and encompasses the regional GI of Hastings River.

NORTHERN SLOPES GI

Sandwiched between the Western Plains and the Northern Rivers, and almost as barren as the former.

ORANGE GI

Orange continues to excel. When entering this town, the first thing you see is a huge sign saying "Welcome to Orange" with a large fruit underneath – an apple! That's right, Orange is famous for apples, and only very recently for grapes. As everywhere in the New World, the best potential vineyard areas have invariably turned out to be those that initially became famous for orchards. The vines grow 600 to 900 metres (2,000 to 3,000 feet) above sea level on an extinct volcano called Mount Canobolas, which is itself part of the Great Dividing Range. When I first visited the area in the late 1980s, the only local wine was Bloodwood, grown on a very small vineyard owned by Stephen Doyle, a lecturer at Orange Agricultural College. Now 22 vineyards market their own wine, with many more growers likely to follow suit when the University of Sydney's Orange Campus builds a winery on its Templer's Mill vineyard property, as this is intended to provide contract winemaking services for other vineyard owners. Orange is located between Cowra and Mudgee and, like most famous regions, it has expanded beyond its place of origin. Its most recent and most important plantings are found at Little Boomey, northeast of Molong. This extended region is best known for Cabernet Sauvignon and Chardonnay, but also grows Sauvignon Blanc and increasingly impressive Shiraz, although it could also succeed with Pinot Noir.

PERRICOOTA GI

The Perricoota region is located in the Big Rivers zone on the Victoria border, with most wine production near or around the town of Moama, and only two significant producers. St Anne is owned by the McLean family, whose vines are up to 40 years old, with Chardonnay, Cabernet Sauvignon, Merlot, and Shiraz the main varieties. The other producer is Riverview Estate, which was planted by the Morrison family in 1996 and primarily grows Cabernet Sauvignon, Shiraz, Sauvignon Blanc, and Sémillon. Both also produce fortified wines.

POKOLBIN GI

This GI was established in 2010, but it is one of the most well-established Shiraz, Sémillon, and (later) Cabernet Sauvignon areas of the Hunter Valley, having been exploited long ago by names such as Lindemans, McWilliam's Mount Pleasant, and Tyrrell's.

RIVERINA GI

The centre of this region was formerly known as Murrumbidgee Irrigation Area, which was always a bit of a mouthful, or MIA, which sounded like an American military acronym. Riverina is a much more romantic name to see on a bottle of wine, although Murrumbidgee Irrigation Area accurately described a wine region that was made possible by the flooding and pumping of the Murrumbidgee River. This previously infertile land now cultivates rice and many fruits, including enough grapes to make one-tenth of all the wine in Australia. These wines are not all cheap plonk and include some of Australia's best botrytized wines.

SHOALHAVEN COAST GI

An emerging region on the south coast of New South Wales, where the distinct maritime climate is responsible for Chambourcin being the primary grape, as it is further up the coast at Hastings. Other varieties include Chardonnay, Gewürztraminer, Sauvignon Blanc, Sémillon, Verdelho, Cabernet Sauvignon, Merlot, and Shiraz. The first vines were planted in the 1820s, by Alexander Berry, at Coolangatta Estate, which was revived in 1988, encouraging other vineyards to be established locally, although surprisingly it was not until 1996 that the first Chambourcin was planted (by Humphries Wines). There are now 10 wineries, and a further 5 vineyards owned by growers who supply others for the moment.

SOUTH COAST GI

This zonal GI encompasses the regional GIs of Shoalhaven Coast and the Southern Highlands.

SOUTHERN HIGHLANDS GI

The Southern Highlands is a little further inland than Shoalhaven Coast, but still subject to a maritime climate. With its proximity to both Canberra and Sydney, one eye was obviously on the potential tourist trade when it was decided to plant vineyards in a region that had previously been devoted to sheep, dairy farming, and horse studs. The grapes grown here are primarily Chardonnay, Riesling, Sauvignon Blanc, Cabernet Sauvignon, Pinot Noir, and Shiraz.

SOUTHERN NEW SOUTH WALES GI

This zonal GI encompasses the regional GIs of Canberra District, Gundagai, Hilltops, and Tumbarumba.

SWAN HILL GI

This regional GI overlaps New South Wales and Victoria, with most producers located in the latter.

TUMBARUMBA GI

One of Australia's coolest and most picturesque wine regions, Tumbarumba has an alpine climate that ripens grapes significantly later than in neighbouring Gundagai region (late March to mid-April, as opposed to late February), making it one of the most exciting sources for producers of premium-quality sparkling wine. Still varietal wine successes include Chardonnay, Sauvignon Blanc, Cabernet Sauvignon, and Pinot Noir. The vineyards are in the foothills of the Australian Alps, growing at elevation of 500 to 800 metres (1,640 to 2,600 feet), on basalt or granite soils. Viticulture is relatively new in Tumbarumba, with the very first vines planted in 1983, but in keeping with much New World wine history, it was originally orchard country, and remains known today for its famous Batlow apples.

UPPER HUNTER VALLEY GI

The Upper Hunter Valley was pioneered in the 1960s by Penfolds and put on the map internationally by the sensational performance of Rosemount Estate, whose Show Reserve Chardonnay took export markets by storm in the early 1980s. Although this district is just as hot as the Lower Hunter Valley and the growing season very similar, the climate is drier and the vineyards need irrigation. Despite fertile alluvial soils and high yields – two factors that do not augur well for quality – some very fine wines are made.

WESTERN PLAINS GI

A virtual wilderness as far as wine today is concerned, this zonal GI covers more than one-third of the entire state.

THE WINE PRODUCERS OF
NEW SOUTH WALES

ALLANDALE
Lower Hunter Valley
★★❤

Amazingly good quality. Also uses grapes from Hilltops.

✓ *Cabernet Sauvignon* • *Chardonnay* • *Sémillon* • *Shiraz* • *Verdelho*

ARROWFIELD WINES
Upper Hunter Valley
★❤

This Japanese-owned estate dates back to 1824 when Governor Macquarie granted the land to one George Bowman, who named the huge fields on his property after variations of his family name, hence Arrowfield. Arrowfield primarily sources its grapes from the Hunter Valley and Cowra, tending to blend the wines for maximum effect, but the company has recently launched a regional range, defining the origin as either Hunter Valley or Cowra.

✓ *Chardonnay* (Show Reserve) • *Classic white blend* (Sémillon Chardonnay)

BARWANG VINEYARD
Hilltops
★★❤

Part of the McWilliam's group, Barwang was established in 1969 by Peter Robinson, who planted the vineyards with cuttings that, as chance would have it, came from its future owner.

✓ *Cabernet Sauvignon* • *Merlot* • *Shiraz*

BLOODWOOD
Orange
★★❤

Owned by Stephen Doyle, a pioneer of Orange, Bloodwood's wines are made at the Reynolds Yarraman Estate in the Upper Hunter Valley.

✓ *Cabernet* • *Merlot*

BOTOBOLAR VINEYARD
Mudgee
❤Ⓑ

Good-quality, biodynamically produced wines come from the highest vineyard in the Mudgee district. Botobolar tends to use odd methods such as refermenting two-year-old Shiraz on the skins of freshly picked Shiraz. Low-preservative and preservative-free wines are a feature, but although low sulphur regimes are to be applauded, it has to be said that the preservative-free wines are not among Botobolar's best.

✓ *Marsanne* • *Shiraz*

BRANGAYNE OF ORANGE
Orange
★★❤

Don and Pamela Hoskins make supremely stylish wines, with the ubiquitous dynamic duo of Richard Smart and Simon Gilbert consulting.

✓ *Chardonnay* • *Classic red blend* (The Tristan)

BRIAR RIDGE
Lower Hunter Valley
★★❤

Each year, this winery plays host to guest winemaker Karl Stockhausen, one of the Hunter's legendary Sémillon stylists.

✓ *Chardonnay* (Hand Picked) • *Sémillon* (Signature Stockhausen)

BRINDABELLA HILLS
Canberra District
★

Owner Dr Roger Harris produces some of Canberra District's most elegant wines. The Shiraz is fleshy without being heavy, and a 1994 Riesling tasted in 2001 ranked as the best mature Australian Riesling I had ever tasted, with wonderful zesty-fresh aromas mingling with petrolly mature fruit.

✓ *Chardonnay* • *Cabernet Sauvignon* • *Riesling* • *Shiraz*

BROKENWOOD
Lower Hunter Valley
★★★

This winery was established in 1970 by three partners, one of whom was none other than Australia's very own wine guru, James Halliday, but he has long since moved on. Iain Riggs has been winemaker here since 1983, and he is a driven man when it comes to Sémillon. The basic

release is stunning, but bottle-age puts his ILR Aged Reserve Sémillon in a class of its own, demonstrating the potentially huge longevity and sheer quality of Hunter Sémillon. Brokenwood took over Yarra Valley's Seville Estate in 1997.

✓ *Cabernet Sauvignon* (Graveyard Vineyard) • *Sauvignon Blanc/ Sémillon* (Cricket Pitch) • *Sémillon* • *Shiraz* (Graveyard Vineyard, Rayner Vineyard)

CANOBOLAS-SMITH
Orange
★

These hard-to-find, intensely ripe, complex wines show the great potential of Orange.

✓ *Chardonnay* • *Classic red blend* (Alchemy)

CASELLA WINES
Riverina
★★❤

This winery was founded in 1965 by Filippo and Maria Casella, two Sicilian immigrants who slept through the next three decades. Known primarily for its Yellow Tail brand, which went from zero to 5.9 million cases in just four years, reaching 12 million cases by 2010, Casella is now Australia's third-largest wine producer yet remains family-owned. Casella crushes 10 per cent of Australia's entire harvest every year and accounts for 15 per cent of all Australian wine exports. Its brands include Casella Estate, of course, Crate 31, Mallee Point, Painters Cove, and Yenda Vale, but Yellow Tail is the story here. This brand started with Chardonnay and Shiraz, but the range now extends to six white wines, one rosé, seven reds, two sparkling, and five further reserve wines. The speed of Yellow Tail's success has attracted more than its fair share of adverse comments from various critics, quite often revolving around residual-sugar levels (9 grams per litre in one of the Cabernet Sauvignons, for example), but these wines are unashamedly designed for mass appeal, whereas I have seen the analyses of supposedly higher-quality, medal-winning Australian wines with similar sugar levels – sometimes significantly higher – and they shamefully claim to be something they are not. So, when Yellow Tail wins gold medals from competition judges who have developed a sweet tooth from so-called fine wines with residual sugar, they have only themselves to blame. For Yellow Tail's place in the market, ex-Southcorp winemaker Alan Kennet has done a remarkable job of churning out mega-volumes of soft, clean, fresh, fruit-driven, consumer-friendly wines.

✓ *Merlot* (Carramar Estate, Cottlers Bridge) • *Petit Verdot* (Yenda

Vale) • *Sangiovese* (Yenda Vale) • *Sémillon* (Carramar Estate) • *Tempranillo* (Yenda Vale)

CASSEGRAIN VINEYARDS
Hastings River
★

The Cassegrain family established this winery back in 1980. Some believe the maritime climate is far too marginal for viticulture, but despite the bracing sea breezes and lashing rain – which compelled John Cassegrain to plant the rot-resistant Chambourcin grape – some exciting wines are to be found amid the disappointments. Some of the early vintages of Cassegrain Brut show flashes of promise, but the quality, particularly the finesse, has lacked consistency, and requires considerable input from a top sparkling wine consultant to improve consistency. The Chambourcin is recommended within its class. Cassegrain purchased Hungerford Hill from Southcorp in 1992.

✓ *Chambourcin* • *Fortified* (Old Yarras Tawny Port) • *Fromenteau-Chardonnay* (Reserve) • *Sémillon* (Reserve) • *Verdelho*

CHALKERS CROSSING
Hilltops
★★

Established in 2000, Chalkers Crossing draws on grapes sourced from Tumbarumba and Gundagai to increase the range of wines available from its own 10-hectare (25-acre) vineyard. French-born Céline Rousseau produces regionally defined wines that combine ripe fruit with graceful lines, including a Sémillon to die for.

✓ *Cabernet Sauvignon* (Hilltops) • *Chardonnay* (Tumbarumba) • *Pinot Noir* (Tumbarumba) • *Sémillon* (Hilltops)

CHARLES STURT UNIVERSITY
Wagga Wagga
★

Wagga Wagga is the oenological campus of Charles Sturt University, which has always sold the "students' wines" from its cellar door, but built a brand new commercial-scale winery in 2002.

✓ *Chardonnay* (Orange)

CHATEAU PATO
Lower Hunter Valley
★★

Tiny, family-owned estate producing one of the Hunter Valley's finest Shiraz wines.

✓ *Shiraz*

CLONAKILLA
Canberra District
★★☆

Clonakilla

SHIRAZ
VIOGNIER
2008

14.0% Alc/Vol · WINE OF AUSTRALIA · 750 mL

Since taking over from his father, Tim Kirk has not only put his own stamp on Clonakilla, but has achieved fame above, beyond, and despite Canberra District's low profile. His Shiraz-Viognier has been recognized for more than a decade within Australia itself as one of the country's best reds, and will be known by many Australians who do not realize that Canberra District does, in fact, produce any wine. Any emerging region seeking recognition needs to be famous for something, and if other producers in this region had been quick enough, they might have been able to make Shiraz-Viognier Canberra District's signature wine.

✓ *Chardonnay* • *Classic red blend* (Shiraz-Viognier) • *Riesling* • *Shiraz* • *Viognier*

COWRA ESTATE
Cowra
★☆❶

Owned by South African businessman John Geber, who is obsessed with cricket and has thus introduced the new Classic Bat series of wines. He also magnanimously sells wines from other local wineries from his own cellar door. The wines are made by Simon Gilbert.

✓ *Chardonnay* (Classic Bat) • *Classic red blend* (Classic Bat Cabernet-Merlot) • *Pinot Noir* (Classic Bat)

CRANSWICK ESTATE
Riverina
★❶

Cash-strapped when acquired by Evans and Tate (*see* Western Australia) for A$100 million in March 2003, Cranswick Estate nevertheless increased its new parent company's profits by more than 40 per cent, due to rolling its operations into the fold, and by in excess of 70 per cent the second year. The attraction, however, was the inexpensive Barramundi range, which is Cranswick's top-selling export brand, and should open doors for Evans and Tate.

✓ *Sparkling wine* (Sparkling Shiraz)

DE BORTOLI
Riverina
★★❶

Founded in 1928, De Bortoli has always produced a vast amount of modest wines, as befits the reputation of Riverina. It won international acclaim with its Noble One Botrytis Sémillon, and has gone on to establish a wider reputation for quality with its outpost in Yarra Valley, Victoria. Quality has also risen at Riverina since the acquisition of vineyards in the Hunter Valley, whose wines are sold under the Black Creek label.

✓ *Chardonnay* (Black Creek, Deen De Bortoli Vat 7) • *Classic white blend* (Montage Sémillon-Chardonnay) • *Fortified* (Black Noble, Show Liqueur Muscat, Old Boys Tawny Port) • *Sémillon* (Noble One)

DOONKUNA ESTATE
Canberra District
★

One of the most consistent Canberra District wineries, Doonkuna Estate was founded by the late Sir Brian Murray. It is now owned and run by Barry and Maureen Moran. The winemaker, Malcolm Burdett, likes high, ripe acidity and, although this winery has not produced a Riesling quite as special as Brindabella's 1994, it has been more consistent with this variety than Brindabella or any other Canberra District winery. Shiraz is the best red, but varies too much from year to year to give a blanket recommendation.

✓ *Classic white blend* (Sauvignon Blanc-Sémillon) • *Riesling*

EVANS FAMILY
Lower Hunter Valley
★★

The late indefatigable Len Evans established the famous Rothbury Estate, which is now part of Beringer Blass, leaving him to preside over his own vineyard, the top-quality, ageworthy wines of which are made under contract.

✓ *Chardonnay* • *Sémillon* • *Shiraz*

ANDREW HARRIS
Mudgee
★★☆

One of Mudgee's fastest-rising stars in the 1990s, this winery has significantly increased production and sales. Second wines sold under Twin Beaks label.

✓ *Classic red blend* (Cabernet Merlot The Vision Shiraz Cabernet) • *Sémillon* • *Sparkling* (Double Vision Sparkling Shiraz)

HELM WINES
Canberra District
★

Run by the irrepressible aspiring senator Ken Helms (he ran for the senate in 2001), Helm Wines is a microcosm of Canberra District

itself, hallmarked by inconsistency, yet always capable of shining here and there. Among his best examples is a soft, smooth, easy-drinking Reserve Merlot, but Ken's hobby-horse of the past few years is his Riesling Classic Dry. This is picked at lower ripeness to avoid the typically high alcohol levels of most Australian Rieslings in an attempt to achieve a more European balance, with its light-bodied, refreshingly elegant, lime-free fruit.

✓ *Riesling* (Classic Dry, Premium)

HILLBROOK ESTATE
Canberra District

Hillbrook Estate is a blueprint for any winery wanting to know how to manicure vineyards and set up tourist facilities, but the wines are not so outstanding, although I enjoyed its juicy-fruity 2000 Merlot.

HUNGERFORD HILL
Lower Hunter Valley
★★❶

Hungerford Hill was established in 1969 by John Parker, who quickly expanded his vineyards to more than 200 hectares (500 acres), before shrinking the estate to a fifth of its former size. In 1980, a vineyard in Coonawarra was acquired, and some of the wines were blended from these two regions, which was the geographical equivalent of blending Rioja in Spain with a wine from the Great Hungarian plains! Sales increased to 200,000 cases by the late 1980s, attracting the attention of Seppelt, which took over the company. Seppelt was part of SA Brewing, which acquired Penfolds the same year, thus Hungerford Hill soon became just another Southcorp brand, and wines ended up being sourced from even more diverse regions (Hilltops, Cowra, Gundagai, and Tumbarumba), although the results were equally good. In 2002, the Hungerford Hill brand was sold to the Kirby family, who also retained the services of Phillip John, the winemaker under Southcorp ownership. Members of the Kirby family are major shareholders in Cassegrain, thus the wines were made at that winery for the first year, while the stunning new complex at Pokolbin was being constructed. The wines are still sourced from wide and far, but are primarily pure regional, rather than blended bottlings, and the quality improves with each vintage.

✓ *Chardonnay* (Tumbarumba) • *Merlot* (Orange) • *Pinot Noir* (Tumbarumba) • *Riesling* (Clare Valley)

HUNTINGTON ESTATE
Mudgee
★★☆❶

Bob Roberts entered the business with a law degree and learned winemaking through a British-based correspondence course. Not the

strongest base for success, perhaps, but his clean, fleshy, well-balanced, stylish wines regularly outshine wines made by highly qualified professionals. The same vintage of the same varietal is often released under different bin numbers, prefixed with MB for medium-bodied and FB for full-bodied, and while I might prefer one bin number to another, I have always enjoyed both. Some vintages of the Cabernet Sauvignon and Sémillon possess remarkable longevity.

✓ *Cabernet Sauvignon* (Special Reserve Bin) • *Sémillon* • *Shiraz*

INGLEWOOD WINES
Upper Hunter Valley
★❶

Established as Inglewood Vineyards in 1988, this business initially built its profits selling grapes to Southcorp, an activity that continues under a long-term contract. It gradually moved into wines, eventually purchasing the Tulloch brand (but not winery) from Southcorp in 2002.

✓ *Chardonnay* (Two Rivers Lightning Strike) • *Sémillon* (Two Rivers Stone's Throw)

JEIR CREEK
Canberra District
★

The Pinot Noir shows morello cherries with floral-menthol after-aromas, making an elegant wine, despite sometimes being the colour of a full-bodied Shiraz, while the fresh, luscious Botrytis Sémillon-Sauvignon Blanc was the best dessert wine I encountered in the region on my last visit.

✓ *Botrytis wine* (Sémillon Sauvignon) • *Shiraz*

KAMBERRA
Canberra District
★★☆❶

The decision to name this winery Kamberra is because Canberra itself is a derivation of the Aboriginal word *kamberra*. Australia's capital occupies an area of land that Europeans discovered as recently as 1821, and which was granted to Lieutenant John Moore in 1824. Moore named his property Canberry after hearing local Ngunnawal Aborigines use the word *kamberra* for "meeting place" (which is this winery's second label). For more than 21,000 years the Ngunnawal have congregated at the *kamberra* in late spring to feast on *bogong*, a species of moth otherwise known as *Agrotis infusa*. These moths fly south to escape the coming summer heat, which is ironic for the thousands that end up cooked in sand and hot ashes by the Ngunnawal, who remove wings and legs to eat them straight, or mash and roast them into moth cakes. Except for 6 hectares (15 acres) belonging to Mount Majura,

BRL Hardy's new venture is the only winery to have vineyards that are actually located within the Australian Capital Territory part of the Canberra District GI. BRL Hardy had been purchasing fruit from the Canberra District and surrounds since 1995. This was initially blended into the company's other labels, but the company was sufficiently impressed with the quality to build a winery here, despite the obstacles (*see* Canberra District appellation). In fact, the Chardonnay purchased from Canberra in 1996 made up 30 per cent of the Eileen Hardy label for that vintage, which won the Adelaide trophy for Best Table Wine of Show and a number of other trophies, including the inaugural Max Schubert Trophy. Little wonder that the company decided to invest so heavily in Canberra District! Meeting Place is Kamberra's second label. In March 2007, BRL Hardy agreed to sell Kamberra to the Elvin Group.

✓ *Chardonnay* • *Shiraz* • *Sparkling* (Meeting Place, Pinot Noir Chardonnay)

KYEEMA ESTATE
Canberra District
★

Kyeema has won nearly 30 competition trophies and is renowned for its reds, particularly Shiraz and Merlot. I loved the rich, mellow, and classy reds up to and including 1998, but found a number of the wines from 1999 to be attenuated, with simplistic, capsicum flavours. Only after asking owner Andrew McEwin why there appeared to be a sea-change, did I discover that he had had to change the source of his award-winning grapes, and reckoned his new vines were too young and needed time to settle down. I hoped he was right, and the reds appear to have improved, with Merlot taking over from Shiraz as the very best, so I have rated Kyeema as if he is. Second wines are sold under the Blue Gum label.

✓ *Chardonnay* • *Merlot* • *Shiraz*

LAKE GEORGE
Canberra District
✫

In its original incarnation as Cullarin Vineyard, this was the first winery in Canberra District, and you can still visit the wooden shed where Edgar Rieck made his wines. Rieck not only established this operation in 1971, but was also the driving force behind Canberra's National Wine Show, which is where I once met him and shared one of his remarkably long-lived wines. Lake George is now owned by the Karelas Family Trust, and much has changed since Rieck's days, not just the vineyards and winery, but also the lake that this property is named after and overlooks. Lake George is mostly dry (they even play cricket on it), yet it was once full,

highlighting the dire shortage of water this region faces.

✓ *Merlot* • *Pinot Noir*

LAKE'S FOLLY
Lower Hunter Valley
★★✫

Sydney surgeon Max Lake had no winemaking experience when he founded this property in 1963, hence the name. Yet he introduced the use of new oak to the region and consistently produced vivid, vibrant, and stylish wines. Lake's Folly was sold for A$8 million in 2000 to Peter Fogarty, a Perth businessman, who installed ex-McGuigan's winemaker Rodney Kempe, since when the quality has, if anything, become even better with each vintage.

✓ *Chardonnay* • *Classic red blend* (Cabernet Blend)

LARK HILL
Canberra District
ⓑ★★

The highest vineyard in the Canberra District is one of its best, and where Pinot Noir is concerned, it is the very best. I am also impressed by the richness, complexity, finesse, and length of Lark Hill's Shiraz – not quite in the Clonakilla league, but certainly the best pure Shiraz I have tasted from Canberra District. Readers will realize this is high praise indeed for a winery I first tried to visit in 1991, only to find a note tied to a tree, saying, "Sorry, but we had to go shopping". We had travelled half way around the world, and they had to go shopping … but in the years since, I have really come to like and respect David and Sue Carpenter. And they do make some very good wines.

✓ *Chardonnay* • *Pinot Noir* (Exaltation) • *Riesling* • *Shiraz*

LAMBERT
Canberra District
✫

Owner-winemakers Steve and Ruth Lambert planted their first vines in 1991, and studied winemaking and viticulture at Charles Sturt University in Wagga before they had their first crop. An impressive-looking winery, with a fine restaurant.

✓ *Pinot Noir* • *Shiraz*

LINDEMANS WINES
Lower Hunter Valley

This brand is part of Southcorp, and its historic Hunter Valley home is now no more than a cellar door operation, bizarrely selling Lindemans wines from other areas. It's a shame that Lindemans' once-legendary Hunter Valley Sémillon wine is no longer produced. *See* Lindemans Wines, Victoria.

LITTLE BRIDGE
Canberra District
✫

Owned by four friends, who came up with the idea of planting a vineyard while out drinking a few beers together. The first vines were planted in 1997, and the first wines made in 2001. While passing through in 2006, I found Little Bridge's 2004 Merlot to be the best example of that varietal I had yet tasted from the Canberra District.

✓ *Merlot*

MADEW WINES
Canberra District
✫

On the heels of Doonkuna when it comes to producing the most consistent Riesling. Lettuce-crisp, and limey-floral, it typically goes petrolly within 2 years.

✓ *Riesling*

MARGAN FAMILY
Lower Hunter Valley
★

Although the vineyard was established in 1989, the winery was built in 1998, and the quality is very good.

✓ *Botrytis* (Sémillon) • *Cabernet Sauvignon* • *Merlot* (House of Certain Views)

McGUIGAN WINES
Lower Hunter Valley
★★ⓥ

Now part of McGuigan Simeon, this winery was established by Brian McGuigan in 1992, yet was the precursor to the fifth-largest wine company. A two-star rating might appear controversially high to some critics, but McGuigan produces some superb wines at giveaway prices, performing at least as well as the two-star McWilliam's winery.

✓ *Cabernet Sauvignon* (Genus 4 Old Vine, Hopcroft Estate) • *Chardonnay* (Bin 700, Genus 4 Old Vine) • *Petit Verdot* (Verdot Superior) • *Sémillon* (Bin 9000) • *Shiraz* (Genus 4 Old Vine)

McWILLIAM'S
Riverina
★★ⓥ

The original McWilliam's winery might be based in Riverina, but most of its best wines are sourced from the classic regions.

✓ *Botrytis* (Limited Release Botrytis

Sémillon) • *Chardonnay* (Hanwood) • *Classic white blend* (Margaret River Sémillon-Sauvignon Blanc) • *Fortified* (Amontillado, Family Reserve Tawny Port, Hanwood Fine Tawny, Show Reserve Liqueur Muscat) • *Riesling* (Clare, Eden Valley) • *Sémillon* (Hunter Valley)

McWILLIAM'S MOUNT PLEASANT
Lower Hunter Valley
★★ⓥ

McWilliam's Mount Pleasant Elizabeth bottle-aged Sémillon is one of Australia's finest examples of this unique wine style, and one of its greatest bargains too. Look out for its museum releases.

✓ *Chardonnay* (Maurice O'Shea) • *Classic red blend* ('1877' Cabernet Sauvignon-Shiraz) • *Sémillon* (Elizabeth, Lovedale) • *Riesling* (Collection) • *Shiraz* (Maurice O'Shea, OP & OH) • *Sparkling* (Brut)

MIRAMAR WINES
Mudgee
★ⓥ

Ian McRae used to be seriously underrated, yet – ironically – the greatest of these wines has tapered off in quality since the mid-1990s. At their best, they can still be big and rich, in true Mudgee style.

✓ *Botrytis* (Doux Blanc) • *Cabernet Sauvignon* • *Chardonnay* • *Sémillon* • *Shiraz* (Eljamar)

MOUNT MAJURA
Canberra District
★

The best wine has consistently been Mount Majura's rich, soft, and creamy Chardonnay, but I believe the vineyard will eventually produce greater Pinot Noir. It is also worth keeping an eye on the Cabernet Franc-Merlot blend and the Tempranillo. Second wines sold under the Woolshed Creek label.

✓ *Chardonnay* • *Pinot Noir* • *Riesling* • *Tempranillo* (since 2005)

MOUNT VIEW ESTATE
Lower Hunter Valley
★✫ⓥ

Established in 1971 by Harry and Anne Tulloch, who sold the property in 2000 to John and Polly Burgess. They have hired the talents of Keith Tulloch to maintain family traditions at the 16-hectare (40-acre) terraced estate.

✓ *Cabernet Sauvignon* • *Chardonnay* (Reserve) • *Sémillon* (Reserve) • *Shiraz* (Reserve)

MURRUMBATEMAN WINERY
Canberra District
⭐☆

The creamy-rich, black-pepper fruit in Murrumbateman's Reserve Shiraz just pips the menthol-laden Cabernet-Merlot for this winery's best wine. The juicy, rose-petal infused fruit in the Rose of Australia makes a refreshingly enjoyable picnic wine, but blended from Traminer, Riesling, and Merlot, it should be re-labelled Digger's Hotchpotch.

✓ *Barbera* • *Classic red blend (Cabernet-Merlot)* • *Pinot Noir*

PANKHURST
Canberra District
⭐ⓥ

Since establishing this vineyard in 1986, Allan and Christine Pankhurst have built up a reputation for Pinot Noir. The wines are not made here, but at Lark Hill, where contract winemakers David and Sue Carpenter certainly have the expertise to maximize the potential of Pankhurst's excellent vineyard.

✓ *Chardonnay* • *Classic red blend (Cabernet-Merlot)* • *Pinot Noir*

PETERSONS
Lower Hunter Valley
⭐⭐

Petersons went through a difficult patch in the early 1990s, but has returned to form, and even seems to be getting better with every new vintage.

✓ *Botrytis* (Sémillon) • *Cabernet Sauvignon* (Ian's Selection) • *Chardonnay* • *Sémillon* (Show Reserve) • *Shiraz* (Back Block, Glenesk, Glenesk Old Block Shiraz, Ian's Selection)

POET'S CORNER
Mudgee
⭐☆ⓥ

The history of Poet's Corner is a bit like a reverse takeover, albeit one that is now confined within one of Australia's largest wine groups. Poet's Corner is housed in the old Craigmoor building, which was established in 1858. At one time, Craigmoor was the only winery in Mudgee, but was taken over in 1983 by Montrose, which owned three vineyards in the area, one of them being Poet's Corner, whence the brand was born. Montrose was purchased in 1988 by Wyndham Estate, which was itself purchased in 1990 by Orlando, to form Orlando Wyndham. Thus it is that Poet's Corner, which grew out of Montrose, which took over Craigmoor, is now the primary brand in the group's Mudgee outpost, with the older, once more famous brands of Montrose and Craigmoor effectively its second labels. However, while the Montrose label might be

secondary, the quality of many of its wines most certainly is not.

✓ *Sémillon* (Henry Lawson) • *Shiraz* (Montrose Black)

POTHANA
Lower Hunter Valley
⭐⭐

The family-owned brand of well-travelled, former Lake's Folly winemaker David Hook.

✓ *Chardonnay* (Belford) • *Sémillon* (Belford) • *Shiraz*

RAVENSWORTH
Canberra District
⭐ⓥ

The personal brand of Bryan Martin, the assistant winemaker at Clonakilla. Martin is also the vineyard manager and a partner in Rosehill Vineyards, which is where these wines are sourced from. Although he's busy doing these three jobs, he seems to spend more time in the kitchen, cooking for any passing wine journalist he can drag off the street. Despite being a graduate of Charles Sturt University, with a Bachelor of Applied Science (Wine Science) and an Associate Degree in Applied Science (Wine Growing), his background is in the food and hospitality industry. When he's not cooking, Martin teaches food at various institutes including the Australian International Hotel School.

✓ *Marsanne* • *Shiraz*

ROSEMOUNT ESTATE
Upper Hunter Valley
⭐ⓥ

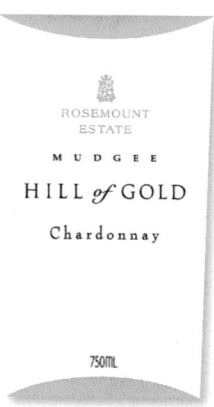

In February 2001 Rosemount merged with Southcorp and, for a while, Philip Shaw became chief winemaker, pushing to one side – and eventually out – John Duval, Penfolds' illustrious winemaker. It was Shaw who made Rosemount's reputation and maintained it even when production went stratospheric, so when he went, it left open the question of just how it might affect the future quality of this brand. However, the new winemaker, Matt Koch, has assisted Shaw since 1995, and there were so many outstanding wines that it was difficult to see how this brand

could fall apart at the seams. However, that is exactly what started to happen, and this has continued under the auspices of brewing giant Fosters, which took over Southcorp in 2005, ironically declaring not to repeat the mistakes of Southcorp's merger five years earlier. The quality potential remains high at Rosemount; if only the right business strategy could be found.

✓ *Cabernet Sauvignon* (Regional Showcase Coonawarra, Show Reserve Coonawarra) • *Chardonnay* (Diamond Label Unoaked, Show Reserve Cool Climate Release Robe) • *Classic Blend* (Show Reserve Traditional)

ROTHBURY ESTATE
Lower Hunter Valley
⭐⭐ⓥ

Once owned by the late Len Evans, who took the company public, and under his chairmanship it continued to produce wines of an extraordinarily high quality. Evans left in 1996, when Rothbury was taken over by Mildara Blass, now Beringer Blass. Quality is currently very high.

✓ *Chardonnay* (Brokenback) • *Merlot* (Neil McGuigan Series) • *Sémillon* (Brokenback, Neil McGuigan Series) • *Shiraz* (Brokenback)

TALGA
Canberra District
⭐☆

Established in 1998 by the Richard family, and son-in-law Ian Little. The Chardonnay is a rich, oaky, designer wine, whereas the firm tannins in the Shiraz make it a much more serious long-term prospect – although it should also appeal to the same wealthy segment of the market.

✓ *Chardonnay* • *Shiraz*

TOWER ESTATE
Lower Hunter Valley
⭐⭐ⓥ

Any joint-venture that involved the late Len Evans is bound to be noteworthy, and at Tower Estate, it is the relatively inexpensive price asked for such stunning quality that is so amazing.

✓ *Chardonnay* • *Riesling* • *Sémillon* • *Shiraz*

TULLOCH
Upper Hunter Valley
⭐⭐ⓥ

Tulloch was once one of the most traditional wineries in the Hunter Valley, but under Southcorp it was little more than a brand and was sold in 2002 to Inglewood Wines. Although Southcorp kept the quality generally good, with the occasional star performer, these wines have gone from good to great under Inglewood, with Jay Tulloch given a free hand as winemaker.

✓ *Verdelho*

KEITH TULLOCH
Lower Hunter Valley
⭐⭐

Eponymous brand established in 1997 by a former Lindemans and Rothbury Estate winemaker with a small, but expanding production. Five varietal wines made under the Per Diem label (Cabernet Sauvignon, Chardonnay, Merlot, Shiraz, and Verdelho) are produced exclusively for The Australian Wine Selectors club.

✓ *Chardonnay* • *Classic red blend* (Forres Blend) • *Sémillon* • *Shiraz* (Kester)

TYRRELL'S VINEYARDS
Lower Hunter Valley
⭐⭐

This long-established winery is still family-owned, and although in the 1990s some critics believed that Tyrrell's Chardonnay Vat 47 was not quite as outstanding as it was in the 1970s and 1980s, that was because the number of great Australian Chardonnay wines had increased, not because the quality of Vat 47 had dropped. It is still one of this country's exceptional white wines, although I have to say that what impresses me most here is the Sémillon, especially when aged in bottle. The Shee-Oak Chardonnay is unoaked. It refers to the name of the vineyard where the Chardonnay is grown, and it was so named because of the she-oak trees surrounding the vines. She-oak, or *Casuarina equisetifolia*, is not an oak as such, but an evergreen with red, termite-resistant wood.

✓ *Cabernet-Merlot* (Old Winery) • *Chardonnay* (Shee-Oak, Vat 47) • *Sémillon* (Belford, Lost Block, Steven's Reserve, Vat 1) • *Shiraz* (Old Winery, Vat 9)

WYNDHAM ESTATE WINES
Lower Hunter Valley
⭐☆ⓥ

Part of the French-owned Orlando Wyndham group since 1990, Wyndham Estate offers a great range of good-value wines, particularly under the Show Reserve label.

✓ *Cabernet Sauvignon* (Mudgee Show Reserve) • *Fortified* (George Wyndham Old Tawny Port) • *Sémillon* (Show Reserve)

VICTORIA

Although Victoria is the smallest of Australia's mainland states, it is second only to South Australia for the volume of wine produced, and is by far the most diverse in terms of cool-climate terroirs and the styles of premium-quality wine made.

THE WINES OF VICTORIA range from deep-coloured, cassis-flavoured Cabernet Sauvignon, to some surprisingly classy Pinot Noir, and from light and delicate aromatic whites, to rich, oaky, yet finely structured Chardonnay and Sémillon, as well as fortified and sparkling wines of the highest reputation. Victoria is one of Australia's oldest winemaking states – and the most famous when it comes to the country's classic fortified specialities, especially its rich and sticky liqueur Muscat and Tokay.

John Batman established Melbourne in 1834, and within four years, William Ryrie, a sheep farmer, planted the first Yarra Valley vineyard in a place that became known as Yering. The most important sequence of events in the viticultural history of the state began with the appointment of Swiss-born Charles La Trobe as Superintendent of Melbourne in 1839 and culminated in the arrival of 11 fellow Swiss *vignerons* from his home canton of Neufchâtel in 1846. They laid the foundation of Victoria's future wine industry when they settled in the Geelong district and planted vineyards around their homes.

GREAT DIVIDING RANGE, VICTORIA
Vines grow on the main upland areas of Victoria, a continuation of Eastern Australia's Great Dividing Range, which is up to 300 kilometres (190 miles) wide.

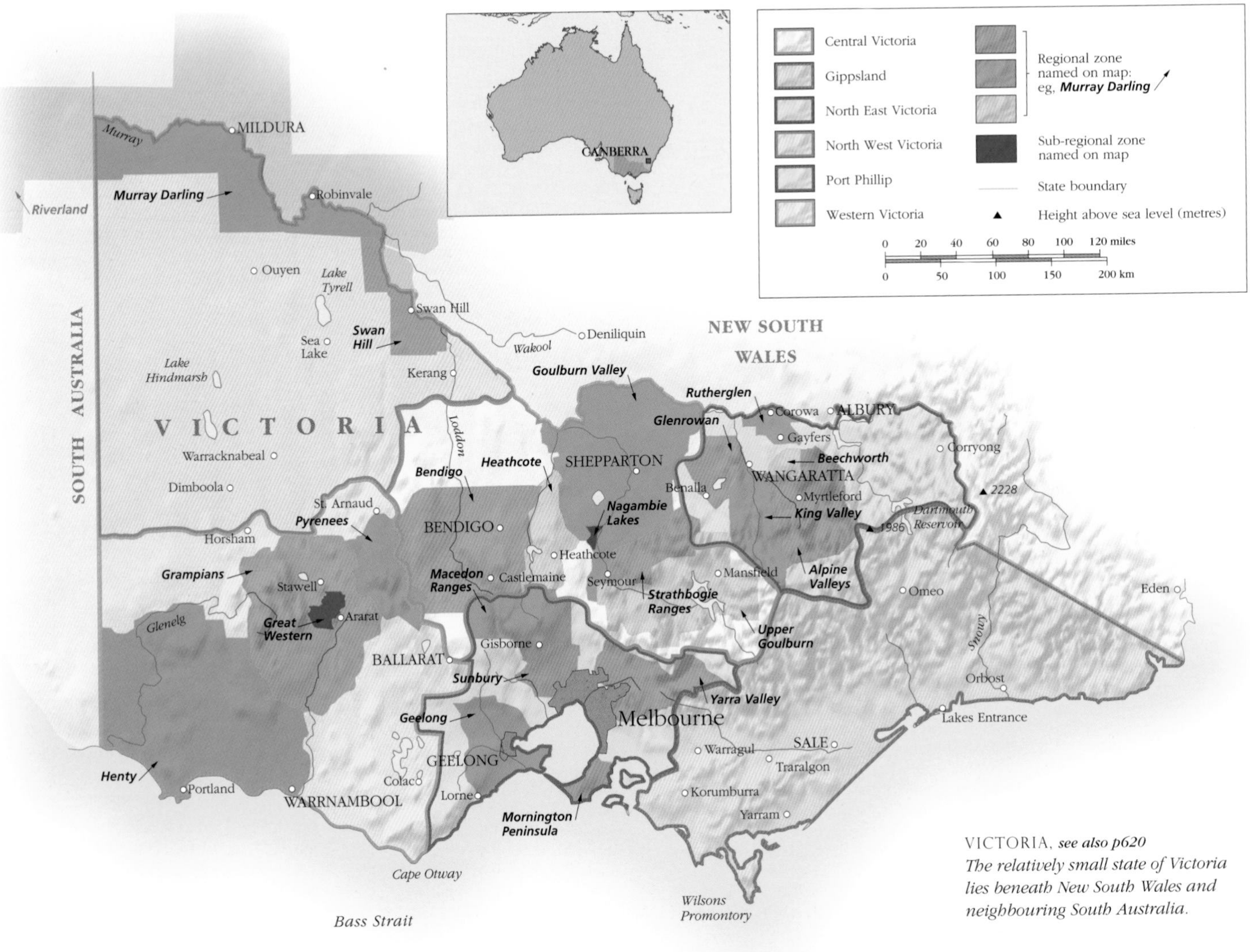

Map Legend

- Central Victoria
- Gippsland
- North East Victoria
- North West Victoria
- Port Phillip
- Western Victoria
- Regional zone named on map: eg, **Murray Darling**
- Sub-regional zone named on map
- State boundary
- ▲ Height above sea level (metres)

0   20   40   60   80   100   120 miles
0   50   100   150   200 km

VICTORIA, *see also p620*
The relatively small state of Victoria lies beneath New South Wales and neighbouring South Australia.

CHÂTEAU TAHBILK, GOULBURN VALLEY
This well-known Victorian winery's huge output consists of traditionally made wines. Its Cabernets can be very tannic, requiring at least 10 years in the bottle.

FACTORS AFFECTING TASTE AND QUALITY

LOCATION
Victoria is the smallest of Australia's mainland states, situated in the very southeastern corner of the continent.

CLIMATE
Climates are extremely varied, ranging from the hot continental conditions of northwest Victoria around Mildura, to the temperate coastal climes of the Yarra Valley.

ASPECT
Vines are grown on all types of land – from the flat or undulating low-lying valley plains, mostly producing vast quantities of basic-quality wines, to the steeper, sloping sites favoured for premium wines, where vineyards are planted to an altitude of 650 metres (2,150 feet).

SOIL
A wide variety of soils, ranging from the red loam of northeast Victoria that produces its famous fortified wines; through the sandy alluvial soils of the Murray Basin that produce mainly bulk wines; and the gravelly soil mixed with quartz and shale on a clay sub-soil found in the premium wine-producing Pyrenees area; to the rich, poorly drained, volcanic soils in Geelong.

VITICULTURE AND VINIFICATION

Victoria is the only Australian state to have been totally devastated by phylloxera (1875–81). So, unlike neighbouring South Australia, its vines all have to be grafted on to American rootstock. It generally utilizes high-quality wine-producing techniques. The northeast is traditionally dessert-wine country, but here, as elsewhere in Australia, winemakers have searched for cool-climate areas to expand the state's premium varietal industry since the 1970s. The famous traditional method sparkling wines of Victoria's Great Western region have suffered with competition from the new up-and-coming sparkling-wine areas such as the French-influenced Bendigo district to the east.

GRAPE VARIETIES
Primary varieties: Brown Muscat (Muscat Blanc à Petits Grains), Cabernet Sauvignon, Chardonnay, Marsanne, Merlot, Pinot Noir, Riesling, Sauvignon Blanc, Sémillon, Shiraz (Syrah) Tokay (Muscadelle)
Secondary varieties: Arneis, Barbera, Cabernet Franc, Carignan, Chasselas, Cinsault, Clare Riesling (Crouchen), Cortese, Dolcetto, Durif, Flora, Folle Blanche, Gamay, Gewürztraminer, Graciano, Grenache, Lagrein, Malbec, Mondeuse, Mourvèdre, Muscat Gordo Blanco (Muscat d'Alexandrie), Nebbiolo, Orange Muscat (Muscat Fleur d'Oranger), Petit Verdot, Pinot Gris, Pinot Meunier, Roussanne, Sangiovese, Tarrango, Tempranillo, Verduzzo, Viognier

STICKY STUFF

Victoria's fortified wines are world class, with Liqueur Muscat and Liqueur Tokay its supreme classics: great wines that know no peers. The older these wines are, the sweeter they are likely to be, in addition to being richer and more complex. Since many of these products are exported to Europe, where most of the terminology evolved, the same wine will be available bearing a different designation, thus the current status of these wines under EU regulations is also provided. Many of these wines are being shipped to Europe as "Australian Fortified Wine" or "Fortified Wine of Australia" qualified by acceptable terms such as "ruby" or "tawny", but it is illegal to use either the word "fortified" or "liqueur" on any wine in the US, so there are designation complications for that market that are even more difficult to generalize about.

Liqueur Muscat The most luscious of Australia's fortified wines, the best Liqueur Muscat can be like liquid Christmas cake. This wine is usually made from Brown Muscat (Muscat Blanc à Petits Grains), and has a minimum of 160 g/l of residual sugar. While it is well worth paying a premium for a step or two up on a producer's entry-level Liqueur Muscat, there is no need to be seduced by ultra-rare, super-expensive, extremely ancient bottlings, unless you just want a mind-blowing, tiny sip, as they are seldom drinkable in the ordinary sense. There are no EU restrictions on the naming of this product, but "liqueur" is not permitted for any wine in the USA, where this term is reserved for spirits, so Liqueur Muscat should be labelled as Muscat Australian Dessert Wine. In the USA, the sweeter versions may be labelled as Australian Dessert Wine. *See also* Classifications, *right*.

Liqueur Port Invariably made in a *rancio* style, to replicate a tawny rather than vintage or ruby Port character. Traditionally, Australian "port" grape varieties include Shiraz, Grenache and Mataro (Mourvèdre). Under EU-Australian agreements, the name Liqueur Port is due to be phased out. Although this was supposed to have happened by the end of 1997, it was not officially agreed until 2010. Australian fortified wines made in the Port style must now be labelled "Australian Vintage", "Australian Ruby", or "Australian Tawny". Technical restrictions include a minimum of 18% alcohol, and a maximum of 72 g/l of residual sugar. In the USA, the sweeter versions may be labelled as Australian Dessert Wine. *See also* Classifications, *below*, but note that they apply only to Australian Tawny.

Liqueur Sherry Traditionally, the most important grapes for Australian Sherry-style wines are Muscat, Palomino, and Pedro Ximenez. Until the EU phase-out date of 2010, it remained legal for Australian fortified wines to be labelled "Sherry", qualified or not, in Australia (and in any export market where this name is legally permitted as a generic style). As from 2010, the use of the term "Sherry" has been banned and has been replaced by "Australian Aperitif Wine" or "Apera", which should be qualified by Pale Dry (for *fino* style with under 10 g/l residual sugar), Medium Dry (for *amontillado* style with under 27 g/l sugar), Medium Sweet (for *oloroso* style with 28–72 g/l sugar), Sweet (over 72 g/l), and Cream (over 90 g/l). In the USA, the sweeter versions may be labelled as Australian Dessert Wine. Note that the classifications below do not apply to these "Sherry" styles.

Liqueur Tokay Australia's very own, unique fortified wine style, Liqueur Tokay is made exclusively from Muscadelle grapes and has between 150 and 220 g/l residual sugar. There are no restrictions under EU–Australian agreements, despite Hungary's membership of the EU, until 2010, when it was decided that these wines would be sold as Topaque, although this does not come into force until 2020. *See also* Classifications, *below*.

Classifications
The following age-based classifications apply only to Australian fortified wines:
  Classic: minimum 5 years
  Grand: minimum 10 years
  Rare: minimum 15 years

THE APPELLATIONS OF
VICTORIA

ALPINE VALLEYS
Most of the wineries and vineyards in the Alpine Valleys region are located in and around the upper reaches of the Ovens River, although vines grow as far north as the Kiewa Valley. This is a cool-climate region, with primarily Chardonnay, Sauvignon Blanc, Cabernet Sauvignon, Merlot, Pinot Noir, and Shiraz grapes growing on alluvial soils. The wines are ripe and well structured, although the Shiraz can be quite rustic.

BEECHWORTH
This small GI region within the North West Victoria zone is former gold-digging country, where Ned Kelly once plied his trade as Australia's most infamous "bushranger". Beechworth is located in the foothills of the Victorian Alps, at the northeastern edge of the Alpine Valleys, of which it is geographically a part, but Beechworth contains wineries of superstar quality, such as Giaconda, and thus it has been accorded its own regional status. The soils vary from fertile sandy alluvium on the Ovens Valley flood plain to granitic loam over decomposed gravel and clay at higher elevations,

and it is the latter that produces some of Australia's finest Chardonnay, not to mention some excellent Pinot Noir and Riesling. The size and structure of Giaconda's Chardonnay belie Beechworth's cool, sub-alpine, frosty climate. Fortified wine is a small but strong feature of this region.

BENDIGO

Situated about 160 kilometres (100 miles) northwest of Melbourne, this part of the Central Victoria zonal GI has a dry climate, although only some of its vines are irrigated. Bendigo is gold-mining country, and viticulture began here during the 1850s Gold Rush. The vineyards tend to be small and scattered over three main growing areas: the Granite Slopes to the southeast; Loddon Valley to the northwest; and Marong and Golden Waters to the southwest. Bendigo is primarily known for its menthol-eucalyptus-tasting red wines. The sandy loam over red clay, quartz, and ironstone soil is well suited to producing top-quality Shiraz, but Cabernet Sauvignon and Chardonnay can also excel. More recent plantings have even included such contrasting varietals as Sauvignon Blanc and Viognier. And, as Domaine Chandon (known as Green Point on export markets) has shown, the potential for premium-quality sparkling wines also exists.

CENTRAL VICTORIA

Also known as Victorian High Country, this zonal GI encompasses the regional GIs of Bendigo, Goulburn Valley, Heathcote, Strathbogie Ranges, and Upper Goulburn.

GEELONG

Southeast of Ballarat, facing Melbourne across Port Phillip Bay, the vineyards of this district fan beyond the town of Geelong itself. Viticulture was established by Swiss immigrants in the mid-1800s, but came to a halt in 1875, when phylloxera struck, and the Victorian government ordered the removal of all vines. Geelong began its viticultural revival in 1966, somewhat earlier than other rediscovered areas of Australia, when Nini and Daryl Sefton planted the Idyll vineyard. The cool climate and volcanic soil produce wines of fine acidity and varietal character, particularly from Chardonnay and Pinot Noir. Cabernet Sauvignon and Shiraz sometimes fare well. Bannockburn and Scotchman's Hill are the best producers.

GIPPSLAND

Sometimes referred to as Coastal Victoria, this vast zonal GI encompasses two relatively small areas known locally as East Gippsland and South Gippsland, but has expanded well beyond these boundaries to give some sort of common thread to 20-odd wineries. Most vineyards are located in and around the towns of Bairnsdale, Loch, and Foster on the South Gippsland Highway.

GLENROWAN

Part of the North East zone, this region was once better known outside Australia as Milawa, thanks to Brown Brothers, which used the name on its widely exported wines. Glenrowan has always, however, been more widely used by other winemakers. This is a classic dessert-wine area, but individual vineyards produce excellent Cabernet Sauvignon and other premium varietals, even Graciano. (Brown Brothers 1974 Milawa Graciano was still in truly amazing form in 2004.)

GOULBURN VALLEY

Sub-region:

Nagambie Lakes

Chateau Tahbilk (now known simply as Tahbilk) was the solitary exponent of fine wines in this traditional wine district 120 kilometres (75 miles) north of Melbourne, until the Mitchelton winery was established in 1969. Since then a number of new wineries have opened their doors and begun to attract attention. At the heart of this region, qualitatively, or at its southern tip, geographically, is Nagambie Lakes, which has its own, well-deserved GI. Beyond this sub-region, most Goulburn Valley vines are located to the north, in and around Mooroopna and Shepparton, but there are others further north at Katunga, to the east between Cobram and Yarrawonga, and to the west near Echuca.

The region's climate is warm and dry in summer, making it dependent on irrigation from the Goulburn River and aquifers. The wines are generally full-bodied, with Cabernet Sauvignon and Shiraz the best varieties, whether in their pure form or, more traditionally, blended together. Shiraz gets more attention than Cabernet Sauvignon these days, perhaps because of the Great Australian Shiraz Challenge, which has taken place here every year since 1995. Such an event obviously focuses attention on the locally grown Shiraz, although the competition is open to any Australian region. Chardonnay and Riesling can also be very good, and both Tahbilk and Mitchelton have produced excellent Marsanne.

GRAMPIANS

The famous old sparkling-wine district of Great Western has been renamed Grampians under the GI scheme. Although it is still best known for sparkling wines, the dropping of Great Western should at least allow the region's finest varietal, Shiraz, to shine without being lumbered by a name that is linked historically and indelibly to the connotation of fizz. Cabernet Sauvignon, Chardonnay, and Riesling can also be excellent. Top-performing wineries are Best's, Mount Langi Ghiran, and Seppelt.

HEATHCOTE

Formerly considered by many to be part of Bendigo, Heathcote has been recognized by Australia's GI system as a wine region in its own right since 2002. This is due, in part, to its reputation as a premium Shiraz-producing area, which is well deserved, and has been built up slowly over more than 25 years of often outstanding vintages from the likes of Jasper Hill. However, it is perhaps no coincidence that the influential critic Robert Parker awarded Wild Duck Creek Estate 1997 Duck Muck Shiraz a perfect 100-point score, which not only propelled its owner, David "Duck" Anderson, from obscurity to international fame overnight, but also reflected well on the potential of the entire locality. This assessment was responsible for the US discovering Australian Shiraz in general, and a GI of its own was the least that Heathcote deserved in the circumstances. The region sits on the north side of the Great Dividing Range at elevations between 160 to 320 metres (525 to 1,050 feet). The soil is a rich, red volcanic type known as Cambrian, the mineral content of which is said to favour the production of red wine varietals, particularly Shiraz.

HENTY

Formerly known as Drumborg, then Far South West and now a GI by the name of Henty, this remote region might have a changing identity, but is still best known for Seppelt's Drumborg winery. Henty takes its name from the Henty brothers, who in 1834 were the first to settle this part of the Portland Bay area, where they established a sheep station. In addition to the famous merino sheep, the Henty brothers also brought vines with them, plus "13 heifers, 5 pigs, 4 working bullocks, 2 turkeys, and 6 dogs". Grapes were more of an afterthought, and it seems that the idea of a vineyard literally withered on the vine. The earliest truly commercial viticultural operation was not set up until much later, when Seppelt established its Drumborg winery in the 1960s. The company had been looking for new supplies of grapes to furnish its growing production of sparkling wines, and the grapes from this area have been very useful components in many an Australian fizz blend ever since. The soil is volcanic and the climate so cool that some varieties did not ripen. It is surprising, therefore, that Cabernet Sauvignon and Merlot should be so successful here, but they can be excellent; Riesling and Pinot Noir are also very good. A number of other wineries have now opened up.

KING VALLEY

Until 1989 Brown Brothers were the sole buyers of grapes in King Valley, but the fruit has since been sold far and wide, and other wineries have been built here. It has now become a fully-fledged GI, but the boundaries were not finalized at the time of writing, thus the area depicted on the map should be considered as an approximate representation. Chardonnay, Riesling, and Cabernet are the most important varieties, but Barbera, Nebbiolo, and Sangiovese have shown the greatest potential. Sparkling wine is also produced.

MACEDON RANGES

A developing district within the Central Victoria region, Macedon (plain and simple) was once considered to include Sunbury, but that has since been established as a GI in its own right, and this region is now referred to as Macedon Ranges. The good folk of Melbourne flock to the Macedon Ranges in summer to escape the heat, thus it has the reputation of an "icy-cold" climate. Cool, maybe, but icy, I think not. The Macedon Ranges are certainly cool enough for some sparkling winemakers to source grapes from here. Chardonnay and Pinot Noir are also good, but a whole range of grapes grows well here, if the site is carefully selected to maximize the number of hours of sunshine.

MORNINGTON PENINSULA

After an early, but unsuccessful, start in the 1950s, a number of growers have established vineyards in this area overlooking Port Phillip Bay, south of Melbourne. Although only a handful established wineries initially, there are now more than 40

CRITTENDEN
ESTATE®

PINOT NOIR
MORNINGTON PENINSULA
2008

750ml

facilities in the area. Provided the vineyards are adequately protected from strong sea winds that whip up over the bay, Mornington Peninsula's cool, often wet, maritime climate shows great potential for first-class winemaking. Chardonnay and Pinot Noir are already exciting, with Viognier and Pinot Gris waiting in the wings. The red volcanic soils would seem to be ideal for premium Shiraz, and, to a lesser degree, Cabernet Sauvignon, Malbec, and Merlot.

MURRAY DARLING

This regional GI overlaps two zonal GIs: North West Victoria and Big Rivers, New South Wales. The region takes its name from the Murray and Darling rivers, two of Australia's great wine rivers. Further upstream is the Rutherglen area, while just downstream is Riverland. The Murray Darling region brings together several areas of mainly irrigated vineyards dotted along the banks of the middle section of the river. Vineyard plantings soared in the late 1990s, creating a major switch of emphasis from white to red, with some impressive and, frankly, unexpected results coming through.

NAGAMBIE LAKES

The Nagambie Lakes sub-region GI is part of the Goulburn Valley, where the Tahbilk and Mitchelton wineries are located. This is where the very best Goulburn Valley wines have traditionally been made. Its boundaries were determined on the basis of the Nagambie Lakes system, a large body of water made up of lakes, billabongs, lagoons, and streams of, and linked by, the Goulburn River. It is the only wine region in Australia where the climate is dramatically influenced by an inland water mass, which enables the vines to enjoy a milder, cooler climate than would otherwise be expected. This is a vivid illustration of man's role as the joker in the *terroir* pack, because these bodies of water are all man-made, as is the Goulburn River Weir, which created them, and was constructed in 1888 following a four-year drought (1877–81). Another factor in determining the Nagambie Lakes GI boundary was the rare soil type found in the area. Known as duplex 2.2, this soil is a red, sandy loam with a very high iron oxide content (hence the colour), over a gravelly-sandy alluvium deposited by the river system, and this is said to give a certain distinctive regional character to the wines.

NORTH EAST VICTORIA

This zonal GI encompasses the regional GIs of Alpine Valleys, Beechworth, Glenrowan, and Rutherglen.

NORTH WEST VICTORIA

This zonal GI encompasses the Victorian parts of the regional GIs of Murray Darling and Swan Hill.

PORT PHILLIP

This zonal GI encompasses the regional GIs of Geelong, Macedon Ranges, Mornington Peninsula, Sunbury, and Yarra Valley.

PYRENEES

Formerly known as the Avoca district, the vineyards around Mount Avoca, Redbank, and Moonambel are now called Pyrenees, although the former name will no doubt remain in use for a while. Pyrenees, the name of a nearby mountain range, was chosen by local wine growers as an expressive marketing "hook" upon which to "hang" their wines. By whatever name, this area was originally perceived to be red-wine country, making wines of a distinctive and attractive minty character. There was a time in the early 1990s when white wine and even sparkling wine were thought to be the region's best prospects, but the original perceptions have since been proven right. Shiraz, Cabernet Sauvignon, and Merlot are the outstanding wines, with Chardonnay, and perhaps Pinot Noir, on the next rung of quality.

RUTHERGLEN

Rutherglen was once considered by many to include also Glenrowan (or Milawa), but it has always been the heart of the North East region and the soul of Victoria's wine industry, and since 1997 its own boundaries have been determined by the GI process. Although there are other, arguably more exciting regions in Victoria, it remains the hub around which the entire state's most traditional viticultural activities revolve. Rutherglen comprises a collection of wineries and vineyards on the south bank of the Murray River, around the town of Rutherglen, and further south into the hinterland. This is Australia's greatest dessert-wine country, producing liqueur Muscats and Tokays that know no peers. However, in addition to these world-famous fortified wines, the cooler areas of Rutherglen have emerged as an innovative light wine-producing region. Chardonnay and Sémillon are clean, fresh, and vibrant; Gewürztraminer is performing relatively well; and Durif, Carignan, Shiraz, and Cabernet Sauvignon all show promise to one degree or another.

STRATHBOGIE RANGES

Better known in Australia than abroad, this region was first planted in 1968 by Alan Plunkett, whose natural inclination was to grow cool-climate varieties, such as Riesling and Gewürztraminer. In the 1990s Dominion Wines drew attention to the area by establishing its winery at Avenel. Others followed and, in recent years, the Strathbogie Ranges has developed a growing reputation as a source for sparkling-wine components and for crisp, fresh white wines of excellent fruit intensity from a number of boutique wineries. The vineyards are located at varying altitudes, ranging from 150 to 650 metres (500 to 2,130 feet). This, plus the diversity of soil types throughout the region, suggests there may be an untapped potential for numerous styles of wine beyond the grape varieties already cultivated, which include Chardonnay, Pinot Gris, Riesling, Sauvignon Blanc, Cabernet Franc, Cabernet Sauvignon, Merlot, and Pinot Noir.

SUNBURY

Sunbury is lower in altitude and much warmer in climate than the Macedon Ranges, which abut this region along the 400-metre (1,310-foot) contour line. It has alluvial soils on the plain and basalt-based loams on the slopes. Sunbury was lumped together with Macedon as part of the same region until it achieved its own GI in 1998. This status was deserved for historical reasons alone, Sunbury having been productive as a viticultural region as long ago as the 1860s. Indeed, it was Sunbury, not Macedon, that was established by the founders of Goona Warra in 1858 and Craiglee in 1864. Many Australians favour this region's Chardonnay and Shiraz, and these are definitely the best wines from its leading wine producer today, Craiglee. Other varieties grown include Sauvignon Blanc, Sémillon, Cabernet Sauvignon, and Pinot Noir. A number of new vineyards have been planted, and there are now 14 wineries in the region.

SWAN HILL

This regional GI overlaps New South Wales, extending to Kyalite, but most producers are located in Victoria. Swan Hill has a Mediterranean climate, with high temperatures and low summer rainfall, making viticulture dependent on irrigation from the Murray River. The region encompasses Brown Brothers' Mystic Park vineyard to the south, and a couple of other large wineries (Andrew Peace and R L Buller), but mainly comprises smaller boutique wineries. There are some very good red wines from Cabernet Franc, Cabernet Sauvignon, Shiraz, Durif, and Sangiovese; whites are less exciting, although Chardonnay and Riesling fare quite well. The Golden Mile Wine Trail runs from Goodnight in the north to Beverford in the south, with many of the wineries along the way offering lunch, as well as the inevitable cellar doors sales.

UPPER GOULBURN

South of the more famous Goulburn Valley region, this GI covers the upper reaches of the river. Upper Goulburn encompasses the Lake Eidon area, between Alexander and Mansfield, and is set against the backdrop of the snow-capped Australian Alps, where the river begins its journey. This region makes crisp Chardonnay, which is better used as a component for sparkling-wine production than as a still varietal wine, the best varieties for which are the more aromatic types, such as Riesling or Sauvignon Blanc. Some Gewürztraminer is also grown. Perhaps the best-known winery in this region is Delatite, just outside Mansfield.

WESTERN VICTORIA

This zonal GI encompasses the regional GIs of Grampians, Henty, and Pyrenees.

YARRA VALLEY

Considered by many as Australia's answer to Burgundy, this recently rediscovered wine region benefits not only from the enriching after-effect of earlier sheep farming, but also from a cool climate, a long growing season, relatively light yields, and some very talented winemakers. The vines grow on the grey-brown loams (to the south) and red volcanic soils (to the north). Viticulture began in 1837, when the three Ryrie brothers planted vines on their cattle ranch, Yering Station, and with the help of Swiss and German immigrants, Yering and two other wineries, St Huberts and Yeringberg, achieved an international reputation for the Yarra Valley. This region declined in the depression of the 1890s and the situation was exacerbated by the consumer shift to fortified wines, so that by the 1920s the only surviving winery was forced to close down.

Viticulture in the Yarra Valley was revived in the 1960s by medical doctors who anticipated that consumers would return to table wines. Dr John Middleton pioneered this revival when he established the Mount Mary vineyard. The latest and most successful wave of interest in producing Yarra Valley wines came in the late 1980s. Wine critic James Halliday was responsible for much of this after he established Coldstream Hills in 1985. It was Halliday more than anyone who made consumers believe in Yarra Valley Pinot Noir. It also helped that Moët & Chandon set up its Green Point/Domaine Chandon winery a few years later. Halliday has also produced some fine Chardonnay and Cabernet Sauvignon, but it was the Pinot Noir that caused the most excitement. Shiraz and Merlot are also very good and, of course, with the presence of Domaine Chandon, Yarrabank, and Devaux Yering Station, this is also sparkling-wine country.

THE WINE PRODUCERS OF

VICTORIA

ALL SAINTS
Rutherglen
★☆ⓥ

Established in 1864, All Saints was owned personally by the late Peter Brown of Brown Brothers fame, as was the nearby St Leonards winery.

✓ *Durif* (Carlyle) • *Fortified* (all Liqueur Muscats, all Tokays, Vintage Port, Old Tawny Port, Show Reserve Amontillado) • *Shiraz* (Carlyle)

ARMSTRONG VINEYARDS
Grampians
★★

Limited quantity, top-performing Shiraz from former Seppelt Great Western winemaker, Tony Royal.

✓ *Shiraz*

BALGOWNIE
Bendigo
★☆

Balgownie went through a patchy period in the early 1990s, but now seems to be pulling out of it as far as the reds are concerned. The whites are disappointing.

✓ *Cabernet Sauvignon* (Estate) • *Shiraz* (Estate)

BANNOCKBURN VINEYARDS
Geelong
★★

Winemaker Gary Farr's experience at Domaine Dujac in Burgundy shows through in the finesse of these wines, which are as appreciated in Europe as they are in Australia. The SRH Chardonnay and Serre Pinot Noir are ultra-premium limited releases.

✓ *Chardonnay* • *Classic red blend* (Cabernet-Merlot) • *Pinot Noir* • *Shiraz*

BASS PHILLIP
Gippsland
★★ⓥ

Various stunning Pinot Noir in minuscule quantities.

✓ *Pinot Noir*

BERRYS BRIDGE
Pyrenees
★☆ⓥ

Established in 1990, but sold grapes initially, with 1997 the first vintage, and intense Shiraz the best and most consistent wine so far.

✓ *Shiraz*

BEST'S WINES
Great Western
★★ⓥ

This historic winery boasts a large, superb range that includes many gems, such as the stunning Thomson Family Shiraz and the lovely zesty-fresh, lime-scented Riesling.

✓ *Cabernet Sauvignon* • *Chardonnay* • *Merlot* • *Riesling* • *Shiraz*

BINDI WINE GROWERS
Macedon Ranges
★★

Fast-rising Chardonnay and Pinot Noir specialist of stunning quality and individuality.

✓ *Chardonnay* • *Pinot Noir*

BLACKJACK VINEYARD
Bendigo
★

Blackjack Vineyard was named after an American sailor who caught gold fever in the 1850s and jumped ship, but this family-owned venture was established much more recently, in 1987. Everyday drinking Shiraz under the Chortle's Edge label.

✓ *Classic red blend* (Cabernet Merlot) • *Shiraz*

BLUE PYRENEES
Pyrenees
★

The original winemaker here was Frenchman Vincent Gere, who tended to make his sparkling wines on the sweet side until the 1990 vintage, when they became more classic in style. He was succeeded by Kim Hart, who placed most emphasis on still wines. Then Greg Dedman, the current winemaker, gradually raised quality all round, resulting in Blue Pyrenees being sold to a Sydney-based syndicate in 2002. Second wines are sold under Fiddlers Creek and Ghost Gum labels.

✓ *Cabernet Sauvignon* • *Chardonnay* • *Classic red blend* (Reserve Red) • *Shiraz* • *Sparkling wine* (Midnight Cuvée)

BROWN BROTHERS
King Valley

The size of this family-owned firm is deceptive until you visit Brown Brothers' so-called micro-vinification winery, which is bigger and better equipped than 70 per cent of the wineries I regularly visit, with so-called micro-vinification tanks that are like a battery of boutique wineries. Brown Brothers' experimental wines are thus as polished as any commercially produced wine, which explains why this is one of Australia's most innovative wine producers. One of Brown Brothers' experiments has been with the Spanish Graciano grape, and that has demonstrated incredible longevity, with a 1974 vintage blowing away every example of the "genuine thing" put up by Rioja wineries at the London wine trade fair in 2004. The Tarrango might not be a fine wine, but if you like Beaujolais, it is made in that style, only better than 90 per cent of wines bearing that appellation.

✓ *Botrytis* (Noble Riesling) • *Cabernet Sauvignon* (Patricia) • *Chardonnay* (Patricia) • *Classic red blend* (Shiraz Mondeuse Cabernet) • *Fortified* (Reserve Muscat, Very Old Tokay) • *Graciano* • *Shiraz* (Banksdale) • *Sparkling* (Patricia, Pinot Noir, and Chardonnay, Vintaged Pinot Chardonnay)

R L BULLER & SON
Rutherglen
★☆

This firm dates back to 1921, and also has a winery at Beverford in Swan Hill. The most consistent table wines are Cabernet Sauvignon (Beverford), Durif (Sails), Sémillon (Beverford), and Shiraz (Beverford), but you can buy better, and cheaper, elsewhere. Best advice is to concentrate on the beautiful fortified wines, and if you see any of the final release of the 1978 Vintage Port, make every effort to get your hands on it. Judged on Fortified alone, R L Buller would deserve two and a half stars.

✓ *Fortified* (Calliope Rare Liqueur Muscat, Calliope Rare Liqueur Tokay, Fine Old Muscat, Fine Old Tawny)

BY FARR
Geelong
★★☆

The personal label of Bannockburn's turbo-charged winemaker Gary Farr, from vines growing on the other side of the road to those of Bannockburn. So many puns could be made from "By Farr". Thankfully, none have so far, as the wine does all the talking.

✓ *Chardonnay* • *Pinot Noir* • *Shiraz*

CAMPBELLS WINERY
Rutherglen
★★

This is one fortified wine specialist that has expanded into varietal wines with brilliant success.

✓ *Durif* (The Barkly) • *Fortified* (Allen's Port, Isabella Liqueur Tokay, Liquid Gold Tokay, Merchant Prince Liqueur Muscat) • *Shiraz* (Bobbie Burns)

CHAMBERS
Rutherglen
★★

Bill Chambers is one of the all-time great producers of fortified wine. The Old Rare Muscat and Tokay have no peers.

✓ *Fortified* (all Liqueur Muscat, all Liqueur Tokay)

COFIELD
Rutherglen
★

Cofield specializes in small quantities of high-quality red fizz and produces a surprisingly good Merlot for Rutherglen.

✓ *Merlot* (Rutherglen) • *Shiraz* • *Sparkling* (Shiraz)

COLDSTREAM HILLS
Yarra Valley
★★

James Halliday, the doyen of Australia's wine writers, has sold this property to Southcorp, but is still involved with the winemaking on a consultancy basis. Coldstream is well known for beautiful Pinot Noir and classic Chardonnay, the Reserves of which are well worth the price for those with deep enough pockets. However, the Cabernet Sauvignon, and more recently, the Merlot have been the surprises, reflecting Halliday's penchant for length, elegance, and finesse in these Bordeaux varieties, rather than mere weight or punch.

✓ *Cabernet Sauvignon* • *Chardonnay* • *Merlot* • *Pinot Noir*

CRAIGLEE
Sunbury
★☆

This famous 19th-century, four-storey, bluestone winery was re-established in 1976 by Pat Carmody, who released his first wine, a 1980 Shiraz, in 1982.

✓ *Shiraz*

CRAWFORD RIVER
Western District
★★

This property was established in 1982 by John Thomson, who quickly built a reputation for Riesling, particularly in the botrytis style, but is also very consistent these days with Cabernet.

✓ *Cabernet Sauvignon • Classic red blend* (Cabernet Merlot) • *Classic white blend* (Sémillon Sauvignon Blanc) • *Riesling*

CRITTENDEN AT DROMANA
Mornington Peninsula
★☆ Ⓥ

Garry Crittenden no longer has any connection with Dromana Estate, the public company he founded, where his son Rollo is now chief winemaker. Nor does he have any involvement with any of Dromana Estate's labels, not even its top-performing Garry Crittenden "i" (for Italian) range. All this seems a bit strange, considering his new label is Crittenden at Dromana, and he has reclaimed the former Dromana Estate winery and vineyard. He had never sold these to the publicly quoted company, although the equipment inside the winery belonged to Dromana Estate, and this had to be relocated to his new facility at Tuerong (see Dromana Estate). He has always kept the Schinus brand separate from the public company, and continues with that, as well as playing on his reputation for Italian varietals by releasing Arneis, Barbera, Rosato, and Sangiovese under the Pinocchio label, while Crittenden at Dromana will focus on Pinot Noir and Chardonnay. It is a sure bet to recommend in general Crittenden's new wines, but too early to specify which will be the standouts. (If Michelin can do it with *their* stars, I surely can with mine!)

CURLEWIS WINERY
Geelong
★★

Established in 1998 by Rainer Brett, who has very quickly established an enviable reputation for great Pinot Noir. His Shiraz is pretty damn good too.

✓ *Pinot Noir • Shiraz*

CURLY FLAT
Macedon Ranges
★☆

Owners Phillip and Jeni Moraghan's production is relatively small, but specializes in Burgundian varietals, and the quality is outstanding. A new winery was built in 2002, and the old one was turned over to cellar sales. Second wines are sold under the Williams Crossing label.

✓ *Chardonnay • Pinot Noir*

DALWHINNIE
Pyrenees
★★

Intensely rich and well-structured wines are consistently produced from these vineyards adjacent to Taltarni.

✓ *Cabernet Sauvignon* (Moonambel) • *Chardonnay • Pinot Noir • Shiraz* (Moonambel)

DE BORTOLI
Yarra Valley
★★ Ⓥ

Riverina-based De Bortoli opened up this "posh" operation in one of Australia's most up-and-coming premium-quality wine regions in 1987. Over the years, it has gradually built up an outstanding reputation, helped in no small respect by the fact that it is personally run by Leanne de Bortoli, whose husband, Stephen Webber, was Lindemans' winemaker before taking up the post of the chief winemaker here. Second wines are sold under Gulf Station and Windy Peak labels.

✓ *Cabernet Sauvignon* (Yarra Valley) • *Chardonnay* (Gulf Station, Yarra Valley) • *Classic red blend* (Melba Barrel Select) • *Pinot Noir* (Gulf Station, Yarra Valley) • *Riesling* (Windy Peak, Yarra Valley) • *Rosé* (Cabernet) • *Shiraz* (GS Reserve)

DELATITE WINERY
Central Victorian High Country
★ Ⓥ

Situated on its own, in the Great Divide, Delatite has produced some very good value wines that always show rich, tangy fruit. This winery has a reputation for its Deadman's Hill Gewürztraminer.

✓ *Chardonnay • Classic red blend* (RJ Cabernet-Merlot) • *Pinot Noir • Riesling* (VS)

DIAMOND VALLEY VINEYARDS
Yarra Valley
★★

David Lance is well known for Pinot Noir of great intensity yet elegance,

but his other wines should not be overlooked.

✓ *Cabernet Sauvignon • Chardonnay • Classic red blend* (Cabernet-Merlot) • *Pinot Noir • Sémillon-Sauvignon*

DOMAINE CHANDON
Yarra Valley
★☆ Ⓥ

Moët & Chandon's Australian winery was set up later than its California venture, but quickly overtook it in quality. Much of the credit should go to Dr Tony Jordan, who ran the enterprise at that time, but even he will admit that, with sources stretching across an entire continent, he had a wider choice of quality components to draw on. Jordan left to take over at Wirra Wirra, but has returned to head all of LVMH's winemaking operations in Australia and New Zealand, including Western Australia's Cape Mentelle. The Rosé and Blanc de Noirs are both very good, and would be recommended under other producers, but I wanted to showcase the very best fizz produced here. Conversely, the non-vintage Brut still needs work. In 2004, Chandon became the first major producer to market a sparkling wine sealed by a crown-cap: Brut ZD (for Zero Dosage). A pure Chardonnay blend, the inaugural 2000 vintage was one of the few non-dosaged wines that could be consumed easily upon purchase, but this was achieved by the softness of the base wines, and I found myself struggling to drink more than one glassful. The wines are known on export markets as Green Point.

✓ *Chardonnay* (Reserve) • *Pinot Noir* (Reserve) • *Sparkling wine* (Blanc de Blancs, Cuvée Riche, Pinot Shiraz, Vintage Brut)

DOMINIQUE PORTET
Yarra Valley
★☆ Ⓥ

After 22 years as CEO at Taltarni, Dominique Portet left to set up his own venture in the Yarra Valley. So far the Heathcote Shiraz is the standout.

✓ *Cabernet Sauvignon* (Heathcote) • *Sauvignon Blanc • Shiraz* (Heathcote)

DROMANA ESTATE
Mornington Peninsula
★☆ Ⓥ

In 2004, this producer moved from Dromana to Tuerong, as founder Garry Crittenden reclaimed the former Dromana Estate winery and vineyard for his new label, Crittenden at Dromana. It was Crittenden who had established Dromana Estate in 1982, but when he took the company public in 2001, he retained ownership of the property on which the winery stood and its surrounding vineyards. He also kept the rights to the Schinus

label. He is no longer connected with the company (see Crittenden of Dromana), although his son Rollo is now its chief winemaker, being responsible not only for Dromana Estate, but also Mornington Estate, Yarra Valley Hills, and Garry Crittenden "i" (for Italian) labels. He is producing wines that are every bit as good his father's and he continues to improve. Director and shareholder David Traeger is the winemaker for Baptista, Broken River, and, of course, his eponymous brand.

✓ *Chardonnay* (Reserve) • *Dolcetto* (Garry Crittenden "i") • *Nebbiolo* (Garry Crittenden "i") • *Pinot Noir* (Estate, Reserve) • *Sangiovese* (Garry Crittenden "i") • *Shiraz* (Baptista)

EVELYN COUNTY ESTATE
Yarra Valley
★☆ Ⓥ

Everything here is design-driven – from the cellar door doubling as a Tony Simbert gallery, to the restaurant and label. Even the wines appear to be designed for elegance.

✓ *Botrytized* (Sticky Black Paddock Chardonnay) • *Chardonnay* (Black Paddock) • *Merlot* (Black Paddock) • *Pinot Noir* (Black Paddock)

GALLI ESTATE
Sunbury
★☆ Ⓥ

Established in 1997 by Pam and Lorenzo Galli, who have swiftly built up a formidable reputation.

✓ *Cabernet Sauvignon • Pinot Grigio • Shiraz*

GIACONDA
Beechworth
★★☆

Exquisitely crafted, highly sought-after wines, which only those on the mailing list have any chance of acquiring. The Pinot Noir is by far the best of an amazing range of wines.

✓ *Cabernet Sauvignon • Chardonnay • Classic white blend* (Les Deux) • *Pinot Noir • Roussanne* (Aeolia)

HANGING ROCK
Macedon Ranges
★

This was once the largest winery in the Macedon area, and specialized in bottle-fermented sparkling wine, but Shiraz is the best wine here. Although the Heathcote Shiraz is top of the range and certainly the best, the basic Victoria Shiraz can be very nearly as good at almost half the price.

✓ *Shiraz*

JASPER HILL
Heathcote
⑧★★☆

Not exactly known as the epitome of elegance, but there is no doubting the quality of Jasper Hill's biodynamic red wines in the big, muscular, complex style.

✓ *Classic red blend* (Emily's Paddock Shiraz-Cabernet Franc) • *Shiraz* (Georgia's Paddock)

JINDALEE ESTATE
Geelong
★★✦ Ⓥ

Established in 1997 by Vince and David Littoree, who own 570 hectares (1,400 acres) of vineyards in the Murray Darling region. The Jindalee label is for penny-pinchers, yet the Chardonnay can be very good indeed. The pricier Fettlers Rest label was launched in 2001, exclusively for estate-grown Geelong fruit.

✓ *Pinot Noir* (Fettlers Rest) • *Shiraz* (Fettlers Rest)

JINKS CREEK
Gippsland
★✦ Ⓥ

Although established in 1981, the winery was not built until 1992. Owner-winemaker Andrew Clark is a consultant viticulturist to 10 different vineyards, which gives him access to a wide range of fruit to supplement his own small Gippsland property. Winemaking practices include some wild yeast fermentations, no filtration, and a minimal sulphur regime.

✓ *Pinot Noir* (Fettlers Rest) • *Shiraz* (Heathcote, Longford Gippsland, Yarra Valley)

KARA KARA
Pyrenees
★✦ Ⓥ

At one time this winery seemed to be doing good things with Sauvignon Blanc, pure and blended, but excels today with its red wines.

✓ *Cabernet Sauvignon* • *Shiraz*

KINGS CREEK WINERY
Mornington Peninsula
★✦ Ⓥ

Some varietals are more consistent than others, but the Burgundian duo of Pinot Noir (particularly) and Chardonnay are always excellent quality.

✓ *Cabernet Sauvignon* • *Shiraz*

LILLYDALE VINEYARDS
Yarra Valley
★✦ Ⓥ

Established in 1975, Lillydale has been owned by McWilliam's since 1994. I always thought of Lillydale as being best for white wines, but under McWilliam's, the reds have outclassed everything except the elegantly rich and stylish Yarra Valley Chardonnay.

✓ *Chardonnay* • *Classic red blend* (Cabernet-Merlot) • *Shiraz*

LINDEMANS WINES
Murray Darling
★★✦ Ⓥ

This vast winery is now part of Southcorp and produces wine from almost everywhere, although its historic home in the Hunter Valley has been reduced to cellar-door sales only. The Karadoc winery in the Murray Darling region churns out copious quantities of very respectable, sub-A$10 wines, including the good-value Cawarra range and umpteen million of cases of Bin 65 Chardonnay, and would deserve a rating of no more than one star, and that would be for miraculous consistency, rather than quality *per se*. Lindemans' Coonawarra winery, which also makes the Padthaway wines, would, however, easily rate two stars, hence the compromise of one and a half. Even at Coonawarra, regionality has gradually been replaced by state-wide blends, ripping the heart and soul out of the Lindemans heritage. The real pity is that under Southcorp, Lindemans no longer produces a modern equivalent of its legendary Hunter Riesling, some 70-year-old examples of which are still in amazing condition. The message to corporate Southcorp must be to reverse the decline of regionality in general, and reintroduce some form of ultra-premium bottle-aged Hunter Sémillon in particular.

✓ *Cabernet Sauvignon* (St George) • *Chardonnay* (Padthaway) • *Classic red blend* (Limestone Ridge Shiraz-Cabernet, Pyrus Cabernet-Merlot-Cabernet Franc) • *Fortified* (Macquarie Tawny Port) • *Pinot Noir* (Padthaway) • *Shiraz* (Padthaway)

MERRICKS CREEK
Mornington Peninsula
★★★

Established in 1998 by Peter and Georgina Parker, who are reputed to have a ridiculously high-density, low-canopy vineyard planted with a single variety, Pinot Noir, but this couple are not completely mad. They are indeed Pinot purists, but most of the 2-hectare (3-acre) vineyard is planted with vines 1 metre apart, and rows a very generous 2.5 metres (8 feet) apart, with the canopy a good 2 metres (6.5 feet) high. However, a separate plot is planted with vines just 600 millimetres (2 feet) apart and row spacing at 1 metre (3.3 feet), with the fruiting wire just 20 centimetres (8 inches) above the ground – this plot must be frost-free. And only

half barking. The results are very impressive, with a helping hand from contract winemaker Nick Farr, who is the son of Pinot genius Gary (Bannockburn and By Farr), who acted as consultant viticulturist.

✓ *Pinot Noir* • *Sparkling wine* (Pinot Noir)

MERRICKS ESTATE
Mornington Peninsula
★★✦

Consistently stunning Shiraz. Owned by the Kefford family since 1977, with no connection to Merricks Creek above.

✓ *Shiraz*

MÉTIER WINES
Yarra Valley
★★★

Owner-winemaker Martin Williams is a Master of Wine with winemaking experience on three continents. He established Metier in 1995 and has achieved two and a half stars fame in a very short space of time with his single-vineyard masterpieces. Williams is also a partner in Master Winemakers, a premium contract winemaking business.

✓ *Chardonnay* (Trafford Vineyard) • *Classic red blends* (Manytrees Shiraz-Viognier) • *Pinot Noir* (Schoolhouse Vineyard, Trafford Vineyard)

MITCHELTON VINTNERS
Goulburn Valley
★★✦ Ⓥ

Part of the Lion Nathan wine division since its takeover of Petaluma. Innovative Rhône-style wines have added to Mitchelton's reputation as one of Australia's greatest value-for-money brands, although I find the whites such as Viognier and Airstrip (Marsanne-Roussanne-Viognier) too fat and soft.

✓ *Botrytis* (Blackwood Park Botrytis Riesling) • *Chardonnay* (Vineyard Series) • *Classic red blend* (Crescent Shiraz-Mourvèdre-Grenache) • *Merlot* (Chinaman's Ridge) • *Riesling* (Blackwood Park) • *Shiraz* (Print)

MONTALTO VINEYARDS
Mornington Peninsula
★★✦

Pinot Noir is definitely the standout at Montalto, which was established in 1998. Although the Pennon Hill range is effectively Montalto's entry-level label, some vintages of the Pennon Hill Pinot Noir are of such superb quality that they rank as one of the world's best bargains for this sought-after variety.

✓ *Chardonnay* • *Pinot Noir* • *Riesling*

MOOROODUC ESTATE
Mornington Peninsula
★★

Richard McIntyre's well-established estate has long been reputed for its

Chardonnay, but if anything, the Pinot Noir is even better.

✓ *Chardonnay* • *Pinot Noir* • *Riesling*

MORRIS WINES
Rutherglen
★★ Ⓥ

While the table wines are decent enough (many of them being made at the parent company's Jacob's Creek winery), no one visits Morris Wines to taste anything other than the fortifieds, the older and rarer blends of which are arguably the best of their type in the world. In fact, I was so eager not to miss an appointment to taste such nectar here in the early 1990s that I received an on-the-spot speeding fine of A$350 from Victoria's finest as I sped across the state line from New South Wales. The legendary Mick Morris was amazed at the size of the fine, asking what on earth I had done to deserve it, and I shall never forget that twinkle in his eye and the characteristic chuckle as I told him that my mind was so intent on getting to the winery that I hadn't realized that I had overtaken a police car in my haste!

✓ *Fortified* (entire range)

MOUNT AVOCA VINEYARD
Pyrenees
★

This winery was purchased by Barrington Estate in the Hunter Valley in 2002, and is currently performing better with red wines than white.

✓ *Cabernet Sauvignon* • *Classic red blend* (Arda's Choice) • *Merlot* • *Shiraz*

MOUNT BECKWORTH
Pyrenees
★✦ Ⓥ

Established in 1984, although I've only just come across these wines, perhaps because the grapes were sold in bulk, and wines under the Mount Beckworth label did not appear until much more recently.

✓ *Chardonnay* • *Pinot Noir* • *Shiraz*

MOUNT LANGI GHIRAN
Grampians
★★ Ⓥ

This winery and vineyards were purchased by the Rathbone Family Group in 2002, but former owner Trevor Mast has stayed on as winemaker. Mast produces rich, ripe, complex reds (particularly Shiraz), and increasingly exciting Riesling.

✓ *Cabernet Sauvignon* (Joanna) • *Classic red blend* (Billi Billi, Cabernet Sauvignon-Merlot) • *Riesling* • *Shiraz* (Cliff Edge)

MOUNT MARY VINEYARD
Yarra Valley
★★✦

Only small quantities of reds are made at Mount Mary, but these are outstanding with a well-deserved cult following.

Chardonnay • Classic red blend (Quintet) • Classic white blend (Triolet) • Pinot Noir

MURRINDINI
Central Victorian High Country
★★☆ V

Owner-winemaker Hugh Cuthbertson makes wines of an extraordinary consistency and quality from a tiny vineyard between the Yarra Valley and the Strathbogie Ranges.

Chardonnay • Classic red blend (Cabernets-Merlot)

NICHOLSON RIVER
Gippsland
★★

Great improvement over recent years from this well-established Gippsland producer. Second wines sold under the Mountview label.

Chardonnay • Classic red blend (The Nicholson) • Pinot Noir

OAKRIDGE
Yarra Yarra
★★

Stunning quality since the arrival of winemaker David Bicknell in 2001. The 864 Riesling is a manufactured icewine style, freezing the grapes in the winery, then pressing them in a refrigerated press!

Chardonnay (864, Yarra Valley) • Riesling (864) • Shiraz (864, Yarra Valley)

PARINGA ESTATE
Mornington Peninsula
★★

Established in 1985, Lindsay McCall's Paringa Estate is well entrenched as one of the "grands crus" of Mornington Peninsula.

Pinot Noir • Shiraz

PASSING CLOUDS
Bendigo
★★☆ V

Graeme Leith continues to produce classy, unirrigated red wines.

Classic red blend (Graeme's Blend, Angel's Bland) • Shiraz (Reserve)

PHILLIP ISLAND VINEYARD
Port Phillip
★★☆

Established in 1994 by David Lance of Diamond Valley fame, Phillip Island must be the only vineyard within spitting distance of penguins and a seal colony.

Chardonnay • Pinot Noir • Riesling

PONDALOWIE VINEYARDS
Bendigo
★★ V

Dominic and Krystina Morris have established Pondalowie Vineyards not only as the "grand cru" of

Bendigo, but also as one of the best wineries in Australia. Look out for the annually changing "Special Release" – I loved the delicious Sparkling Shiraz!

Classic red blend (Shiraz-Viognier, Vineyard Blend) • Fortified (Vintage Port) • Tempranillo (Mt Unwooded)

PORT PHILLIP ESTATE
Mornington Peninsula
★★☆

Established in 1987, this property was sold in 2000 to current incumbents Giorgio and Dianne Gjergja, who are making some stunning red wines.

Pinot Noir (Reserve) • Shiraz (Reserve)

PRINCE ALBERT
Geelong
★★☆ ◉

Bruce Hyett produces tiny quantities of highly acclaimed Pinot Noir.

Pinot Noir

PUNCH
Yarra Valley
★★

Instantly established as iconic Pinot Noir, Punch is produced in minuscule volumes by James and Claire Lance from exactly the same fruit as Diamond Valley White Label Pinot Noir (produced by David Lane).

Pinot Noir (Close Planted)

RED EDGE
Heathcote
★★

Named after the red volcanic soil of the vineyard purchased in 1994 by Peter and Judy Dredge – and I don't think it is a coincidence that it is also almost an anagram of their surname. The vineyard was planted in 1971 by Vert Vietman, who originally named it Red Hill. Although the Dredges have expanded the vineyard, they still have quite a lot of mature vines to work with – this shows through in the intensity of some of their wines.

Cabernet Sauvignon • Shiraz (Heathcote, Degree)

RED HILL ESTATE
Mornington Peninsula
★★

Described by the president of the Australian Winemakers Federation as the "best view of any vineyard in the world", no wonder Red Hill's restaurant is packed out. One of the peninsula's very best Pinot Noirs.

Chardonnay • Pinot Noir

ROCHFORD WINES
Yarra Valley
★★☆

Part of this enterprise was formerly known as Eyton on Yarra. It was taken over in 2002 by Rochford Wines, whose winemaker, David

Creed, coincidentally was a contract winemaker for Eyton on Yarra in 1993. The Rochford and Eyton wines have evolved into a three-tiered range, all under the Rochford label. The Rochford R Range is from the Macedon Ranges and represents those wines formerly sold as Rochford; the Rochford E Range is from Yarra Valley and is effectively the old Eyton wines; while the Rochford V Range is sourced from both wineries plus bought-in grapes and consequently sold under the broader Victoria GI.

Chardonnay (R) • Pinot Noir (R)

SCOTCHMAN'S HILL
Geelong
★ V

This winery is owned by David and Vivienne Browne, whose Burgundy-style specialist vineyard and winery overlook the Bellarine Peninsula and benefit from cool maritime breezes. Second wines sold under the Spray Farm label.

Chardonnay • Pinot Noir

SEPPELT GREAT WESTERN
Great Western
★★ V

Part of the Southcorp group, this legendary sparkling-wine producer makes everything from cheap but expertly made lime-and-lavender fizz under its most basic Great Western Brut label, through numerous exceptional-value, relatively inexpensive, genuinely premium *cuvées*, to the truly fine-quality, upmarket Salinger *cuvée*. And then there is the Show Sparkling Shiraz, which is one of Australia's icons: the biggest, brashest, and most brilliant of sparkling "Burgundies", even though its massive, concentrated blackcurrant-syrup fruit is too much for many to swallow more than half a glass. But it is definitely a "show" wine in the biggest of senses. And just because this winery has a well-deserved reputation for sparkling wine, it would be wrong to overlook some of Seppelt's exceptionally fine table wines. A two-star classification is not too high, because some individual wines, both with and without bubbles, would rate two and a half stars on their own.

Cabernet Sauvignon (Dorrien) • Chardonnay (Drumborg, Partalunga) • Pinot Noir (Drumborg, Sunday Creek) • Shiraz (Chalambar) • Riesling (Drumborg) • Sparkling (Blanc de Blancs, Original Sparkling Shiraz, Pinot Noir-Chardonnay, Salinger, Show Sparkling Shiraz, Sparkling Shiraz)

SEVILLE ESTATE
Yarra Valley
★★☆ V

This winery made its name on minuscule releases of its superb botrytized Riesling, but has been

owned by Brokenwood since 1997, and now concentrates on the more marketable premium varietals.

Chardonnay • Pinot Noir • Shiraz

SHADOWFAX
Geelong
★★★

Shadowfax: is it some pun on email? No, it's from *The Lord of the Rings*, in which Shadowfax was chief among horses. Deep and meaningful, then? No, I suspect it was just named by some Tolkien nutter. Shadowfax is not run by nutters, though. This ultra-modern and stylish winery, which is located in Werribee Park, has its own award-winning, luxury hotel and restaurant, The Mansion Hotel, and makes wines that are as lush and as manicured as its surroundings.

Cabernet Sauvignon (Yarra Valley) • Chardonnay • Pinot Noir • Shiraz (McLaren Vale) • Viognier (Adelaide Hills)

SHANTELL
Yarra Valley
★★☆

An underrated producer of fine white wines, Shantell has recently started to make excellent reds.

Cabernet Sauvignon • Chardonnay • Sémillon • Shiraz

STANTON & KILLEEN
Rutherglen
★★

Affectionately known as "Stomp It and Kill It", this famous old fortified wine producer also manages to make some excellent table wines.

Classic red blend (Shiraz Durif) • Fortified (entire Classic range, Grand Rutherglen Muscat) • Shiraz (Moodemere)

STONIER WINES
Mornington Peninsula
★★

Stonier has been owned by Lion Nathan since the takeover of Petaluma, but its Burgundy-style wines get even more stunning by the vintage under winemaker Geraldine McFaul, who has started specializing in the expression of single vineyards.

Entire range

TAHBILK
Goulburn Valley
★★☆ V

The oldest winery in Victoria was established in 1860, when it was known as Chateau Tahbilk, but dropped the pretension at the turn of the millennium. It still makes very traditional wines that always improve in bottle. Second wines are sold under the Dalfarras, Everyday Drinking, and Republic labels.

✓ *Cabernet Sauvignon • Marsanne • Riesling • Sémillon • Shiraz*

TALTARNI VINEYARDS
Pyrenees
★★☆

Taltarni is Aboriginal for "red earth", the soil in this vineyard being an iron-rich siliceous clay and thus red in colour. The wines have always been noticeably rich in extract, but they are no longer as austere, lean or – for reds – as tannic as they used to be under Dominique Portet (who now has his own label). The style has become more relaxed, and easier to access at a much earlier age. Clover Hill and Lalla Gulley are premium single-vineyard wines, while second wines are sold under the Fiddleback label.

✓ *Cabernet Sauvignon* (Taltarni) • *Chardonnay* (Lalla Gulley) • *Classic red blend* (Cephas) • *Merlot* (Taltarni) • *Sauvignon Blanc* (Fumé Blanc) • *Shiraz* (Taltarni) • *Sparkling* (Clover Hill, Taltarni Brut Taché)

TARRINGTON VINEYARDS
Henty
★★☆

Beautiful Burgundy-style Pinot Noir and refreshing unoaked Chardonnay.

✓ *Chardonnay • Pinot Noir*

TEN MINUTES BY TRACTOR
Yarra Valley
★★

You have to admire the ingenuity of such a name for a winery in country that thinks nothing of trucking grapes across several state lines. But it's not a gimmick. This venture is the combination of three separate family-owned vineyards (hence the three single-vineyard labels: Judd, McCutcheon, and Wallis), each of which is just 10 minutes by tractor from the other two. The wines are brilliant.

✓ *Chardonnay • Pinot Noir*

VIRGIN HILLS VINEYARDS
Macedon
★★

The creation of Hungarian-born Melbourne restaurateur Tom Lazar, this "one-wine-winery" has been one of Australia's hidden jewels for more than three decades. Lazar did not learn winemaking; he simply read a book, planted a vineyard, and made his wine. Virgin Hills has always consisted primarily of Cabernet Sauvignon, plus a dash of Syrah, Merlot, and Malbec. Lazar

used to maintain approximately 75 per cent Cabernet Sauvignon, but over the years this has varied between 60 and 85 per cent. When he retired, Mark Sheppard took over the winemaking, and continued in the Lazar fashion, making it one of the Australia's least-known, greatest wines. Sheppard left to join Vincorp, but returned when Vincorp owned Virgin Hills for a short while in 1998, after which it was purchased by Michael Hope, the current proprietor.

✓ *Virgin Hills*

WARRABILLA
Rutherglen
★★☆ 🅥

Great quality-price ratio from former All Saints owner-winemaker Alan Sutherland Smith.

✓ *Classic red blend* (Reserve Shiraz Durif) • *Durif* (Reserve) • *Fortified* (Reserve Muscat) • *Merlot* (Reserve) • *Shiraz* (Parola's Limited Release, Reserve)

WARRENMANG VINEYARD
Pyrenees
★ 🅥

The Grand Pyrenees does not indicate the nature of its blend on the label, but contains Merlot, Cabernet Franc, and Shiraz.

✓ *Cabernet Sauvignon • Chardonnay • Classic red blend* (Grand Pyrenees) • *Shiraz* (Puma)

WATER WHEEL
Bendigo
★ 🅥

Owner-winemaker Peter Cumming established this vineyard in 1972, and makes well-crafted wines at very reasonable prices, deserving its ★ rating on value alone.

✓ *Cabernet Sauvignon • Chardonnay*

WEDGETAIL ESTATE
Yarra Valley
★★☆ 🅥

This is a new one for me, although it was apparently established back in 1994. Superb Burgundian varietals, and although the quality of the Cabernet (Cabernet Sauvignon-Shiraz blend) is vulnerable to change of vintage, it does hit the spot when the weather is right.

✓ *Chardonnay • Classic white blend* (Cabernet) • *Riesling*

WILLOW CREEK
Mornington Peninsula
★

Willow Creek is housed in a historic building with magnificent views.

✓ *Cabernet Sauvignon • Chardonnay* (Tulum)

YARRA BURN
Yarra Junction
★★

Established in 1975, but owned by BRL Hardy since 1995, the Yarra Burn range has been revamped. The quality is up and is still improving. I used to favour the Bastard Hill *cuvées* of Chardonnay and Pinot Noir, but the straight Yarra Burn label is often as good nowadays, and sometimes even a little better!

✓ *Chardonnay • Pinot Noir • Shiraz • Sparkling* (Pinot Noir-Chardonnay-Pinot Meunier)

YARRA RIDGE
Yarra Valley
★ 🅥

Founded in 1982, but now owned by Beringer Blass, Yarra Ridge continues to make elegant red wines in a firm yet accessible style. Wines from other regions are sold under the Mount Tanglefoot range of the Yarra Ridge label.

✓ *Classic white blend* (Mount Tanglefoot Sémillon-Sauvignon Blanc) • *Pinot Noir*

YARRA VALLEY HILLS
Yarra Valley
★★☆ 🅥

Owner-winemaker Terry Hill has turned out some truly fine, relatively inexpensive wines since he established Yarra Valley Hills in 1993.

✓ *Pinot Noir • Riesling*

YARRA YARRA
Yarra Valley
★★

Tiny production of superbly expressive wines from a vineyard that is so good, they named it twice!

✓ *Classic red blend* (Cabernets) • *Classic white blend* (Sémillon-Sauvignon Blanc) • *Cabernet Sauvignon* (Reserve)

YARRA YERING
Yarra Valley
★★

The first in a number of Yarra-named wineries, Yarra Yering was founded in 1969 by New Zealand botanist Dr Bailey Carrodus, whose blended reds are legendary. Remarkably, Carrodus remained as the day-to-day winemaker until his death in 2008. Dry Red No.1 is Cabernet-based; Dry Red No.2 is Shiraz-based; Dry Red No.3 is Cabernet-Tempranillo.

✓ *Cabernet Sauvignon* (Young Vines) • *Classic red blend* (Dry Red No.1, Dry Red No.2) • *Merlot • Shiraz* (Underhill)

YELLOWGLEN VINEYARDS
Ballarat
★ 🅥

This operation was started by Australian Ian Home and *champenois* Dominique Landragin, but is now owned by Beringer Blass. The wines have always shown excellent potential and have improved enormously, especially since the early 1990s. The non-vintage Pinot Noir-Chardonnay is often superior to the vintaged Brut. Wines also sold under Home and Landragin label.

✓ *Sparkling* (Cuvée Victoria, Hargrave, Pinot Noir-Chardonnay)

YERING STATION
Yarra Valley
★★

Part of the Rathbone Family Group since 1996, Yering Station sells table wines under its own name, and sparkling wines under the Yarrabank label. Its most prestigious sparkling wine is the Tibault and Gillet Cuvée, but I have to go back to the 1995 and 1994 vintages to find the real class that this wine once had, and it is amazing that these old Australian bubblies have aged so gracefully.

✓ *Chardonnay* (Reserve) • *Classic red blend* (Reserve Shiraz-Viognier) • *Merlot • Pinot Noir* (Reserve) • *Sparkling* (Yarrabank)

YERINGBERG
Yarra Valley
★★

The oldest winery in the Yarra Valley, Yeringberg was established in 1862 by Guillaume, Baron de Pury, and re-established in 1969 by his grandson, Guillaume de Pury, who has consistently produced fine, sometimes exceptionally fine, wines. The Dry Red is a Bordeaux-style blend.

✓ *Chardonnay • Classic red blend* (Dry Red) • *Classic white blend* (Marsanne-Roussanne) • *Pinot Noir*

ZILZIE
Murray Darling
★ 🅥

A major supplier of grapes to Southcorp, the Forbes family established its own winery in 2000. With improving quality, and very reasonable prices, Zilzie is a name to watch. Second labels include Forbes Faily and Buloke Reserve.

✓ *Classic red blend* (Show Reserve GSM) • *Merlot* (Show Reserve) • *Tempranillo* (Buloke Reserve) • *Shiraz* (Show Reserve)

TASMANIA

Some local winemakers like to think of Tasmania as "the Champagne of the southern hemisphere". Although this island state does make some exceedingly fine sparkling wines, it really has much more to offer than that.

ALTHOUGH THIS IS REALLY A NEW WINE REGION, nine vines were planted here by William Bligh of HMS *Bounty* as early as 1788. They were planted at the eastern end of Adventure Bay on Bruny Island, which is much farther south than Tasmanian vines grow today, and not surprisingly, Bligh found they had not survived when he returned in 1791. The first true vineyard was established in 1823 at Prospect Farm by Bartholomew Broughton, an extraordinary convict who had been granted a pardon and eventually came to own a substantial amount of property. By 1827, the quality of his wines had prompted the *Colonial Times* to contrast them with those of Gregory Blaxland, whose Parramatta River vineyard near Sydney had already produced Australia's first exported and first medal-winning wine. The paper reported that a Dr Shewin, who had tasted Blaxland's

PIPERS BROOK VINEYARD, TASMANIA
This world famous winery dominates Pipers Brook, the most successful wine-producing district of Tasmania.

famous wine, remarked that by comparison Broughton's was "as far superior as fine Port to Blackstrap".

Such was the cruelty of Britain's penal system in the colonies that it took its toll on Broughton's lifespan. His successful attempt to be pardoned suggests that he probably suffered less than most convicts at the time, yet it was sufficient to cut short the luxury of his freedom. He died in 1828, aged 32. Captain Charles Swanston purchased Broughton's property, and by 1865 there were no fewer than 45 different varieties of vines flourishing at various sites on the island. Yet, by the end of the same decade, virtually all the vineyards had disappeared, although some gnarled vines of Broughton's 1823 vineyard can still be seen today in the New Town area of Hobart. This is Australia's second-oldest vineyard and Australia's oldest surviving vineyard, since any remains of Australia's very first vineyard are buried and forgotten under the concrete and asphalt of Sydney's great metropolis.

Except for an ephemeral resurgence in the 1880s, Tasmania's wine industry was non-existent until the renaissance of the 1950s, which was led by a Frenchman called Jean Miguet. Miguet was not a *vigneron* by profession; he came to Tasmania to work on the construction of a hydro-electric plant, but his new home at La Provence, north of Launceston, reminded him of his native Haute-Savoie and, since it was protected from ocean winds by trees, he believed that grapes might ripen there. In 1956 he cleared his bramble-strewn land and planted vines that grew successfully enough to encourage another European, Claudio Alcorso, to establish a vineyard on the Derwent River in 1958. Alcorso and his Moorilla Estate are still prospering, but after 15 years, ill-health forced Miguet to abandon his vineyard and return to France, where he sadly died from leukaemia in 1974.

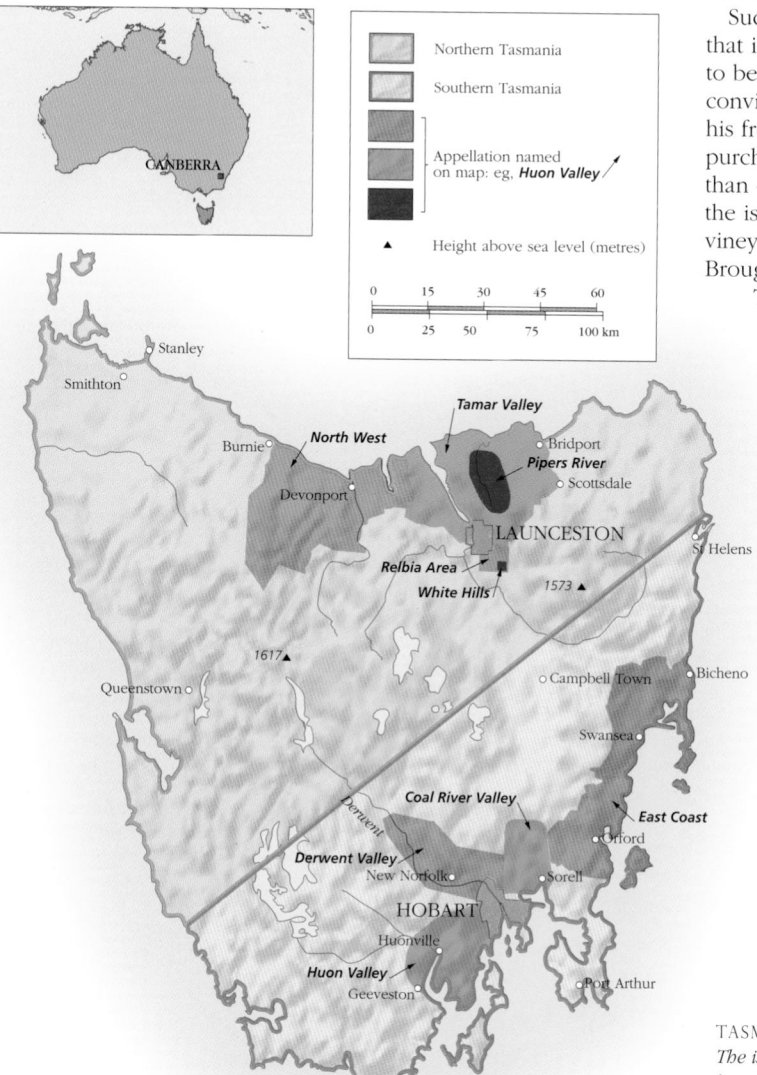

Northern Tasmania

Southern Tasmania

Appellation named on map: eg, *Huon Valley*

▲ Height above sea level (metres)

| 0 | 15 | 30 | 45 | 60 |
| 0 | 25 | 50 | 75 | 100 km |

Stanley
Smithton
North West
Burnie
Devonport
Tamar Valley
Bridport
Pipers River
Scottsdale
LAUNCESTON
Relbia Area
White Hills
1573 ▲
St Helens
1617 ▲
Queenstown
Campbell Town
Bicheno
Swansea
Coal River Valley
East Coast
Orford
Derwent Valley
New Norfolk
Sorell
HOBART
Huonville
Huon Valley
Geeveston
Port Arthur

CANBERRA

TASMANIA, *see also p620*
The island of Tasmania lies due south, on the same latitude as New Zealand's South Island. This area covers a wide variety of climates, terrains, and wines.

TREASURE ISLAND

The fact that the Australian wine industry is prepared to pay significantly more for sparkling-wine grapes, both Chardonnay and Pinot Noir, grown in Tasmania than anywhere else in the country illustrates the intrinsic superiority of this island for that style of wine. But Tasmania also produces some of Australia's best Pinot Noir; its Chardonnay has a minerality that is ideal for unoaked still wines (if producers use their best fruit); the off-dry Rieslings have more finesse than anything grown outside Germany's famed Mosel; and the Sauvignon Blancs are beginning to challenge those of Marlborough in New Zealand. This is quite a potential treasure trove.

CRAIGOW, CAMBRIDGE
Where once opium poppies mingled with orchard trees, Hobart heart surgeon Dr Barry Edwards has planted Pinot Noir, Riesling, Chardonnay, and Gewürztraminer.

FACTORS AFFECTING TASTE AND QUALITY

LOCATION
The island of Tasmania lies 160 kilometres (100 miles) due south of Victoria.

CLIMATE
Tasmania is significantly cooler than Victoria (*see* p630), with very similar conditions to Marlborough in New Zealand. However, the Tamar Valley and even the Coal River in the south are warmer and drier than parts of Victoria. The north is warmer and sunnier than the south of the island, but this is slightly compensated for by the lower-lying vineyards in the south. Tasmania does not have the propensity for drought that many wine regions on the mainland suffer from.

ASPECT
Vines are mostly grown on gentle slopes up to 210 metres (690 feet) high in the north but lower-lying in the south.

SOIL
Tasmania is famously clayey – over gravel in the north, more sandy and sandstone in the south.

VITICULTURE AND VINIFICATION
The harvest is approximately one week later in the south compared to the north of the island. With Richard Smart in residence at Tamar Ridge, the very latest viticultural technology and thinking are in practice here. High-tech equipment such as pressing in an inert-gas atmosphere can be found, but the deployment of technology is dependent on the size of the operation, and many wineries are very small.

GRAPE VARIETIES
Primary varieties: Chardonnay, Pinot Noir
Secondary varieties: Cabernet Franc, Cabernet Sauvignon, Gamay, Merlot, Pinot Gris, Pinot Meunier, Riesling, Sauvignon Blanc, Sémillon, Shiraz, Traminer

---

THE APPELLATIONS OF

TASMANIA

Note None of these regions has GI status at the time of writing.

COAL RIVER VALLEY
Centred around Richmond, Australia's finest Georgian village, the Coal River Valley is the warmest exception in the south, with temperatures in places matching those of the Tamar Valley in the north. This enables the production of some of Tasmania's most succulent Pinot Noir, as well as its raciest Riesling. It is also the only place in Tasmania where Cabernet Sauvignon and Merlot can work.

DERWENT VALLEY
Most vineyards are on the left bank of the Derwent River as it bends between Hobart and New Norfolk. Several varieties excel here, including Chardonnay and Pinot Noir in both still and sparkling formats.

EAST COAST
A large area with a few wineries around Moulting Lagoon, where sparkling wine and Pinot Noir excel.

HUON VALLEY
The most southerly of Tasmania's regions, sometimes called Huon and Channel. Pinot Noir and Riesling do well, and Elsewhere and No Regrets, in Glaziers Bay, are the best-performing wineries, with Yellow Point on the Great Bay side the latest Pinot Noir success.

NORTH WEST
This area south of Davenport is marginal in viticultural terms, although some Pinot Noir and sparkling wines have proved their worth.

NORTHERN TASMANIA
The north/south divide of this island's wine region has been taken from James Halliday's commonsense division of Tasmania. Generally, the north is warmer than Southern Tasmania, with higher altitude vineyards (190–210 metres [625–690 feet]).

PIPERS RIVER
The heart of the Tamar Valley, where Andrew Pirie launched Tasmania's first fine-wine hopes in 1974, reinforced by Roederer in 1980, when it invested in the Heemskerk vineyard to produce a premium sparkling wine called Jansz. Roederer later pulled out amid rumours that the grapes would not ripen! This was untrue, as the quality of Jansz today attests.

RELBIA AREA
An up-and-coming small wine region south of Launceston, where Josef Chromy and Tamar Ridge have both struck lucky.

SOUTHERN TASMANIA
Generally cooler than Southern Tasmania, with low-lying vineyards (50–175 metres [165–575 feet]).

TAMAR VALLEY
Tasmania's most important and most successful wine region, with the prime Pipers Brook district at is heart. Its many *terroirs* permit a diverse range of varieties.

WHITE HILLS
With its steep basalt and dolerite slopes, this mound gives an immediate sense of place. It has been the source of some of Pirie's award-winning Pinot Noir.

THE WINE PRODUCERS OF
TASMANIA

Note At least a third of this island's most successful medal-winning wines are made by or under the guidance of Julian Alcorso's Winemaking Tasmania. Frogmore Creek (formerly Hood winemaking services) also contract for 20 different labels, including many award-winning wines.

APOGEE
Lebrina

Andrew Pirie has gone back to the original single-vineyard concept that produced one of the world's greatest sparkling wines in 1995.

ARRAS

Not a winery as such, so no location, but one of Australia's greatest sparklers. *See* Bay of Fires.

BAY OF FIRES
Pipers River
★★★ **V**

Classy boutique wines from this outpost of the Hardy Wine Company, thanks to the petite but hugely talented Fran Austin.

✓ *Entire range*

BREAM CREEK
Bream Creek
★★

Fred Peacock's wines are a surprise and a delight, including beautifully ripe 2005 Cabernet Sauvignon.

✓ *Entire range*

CAMPANIA HILLS
Campania
★

The 2006 Unwooded Chardonnay was the first wine to show Tasmania's potential for a Chablis style, but more recent vintages are not as exciting.

✓ *Pinot Noir*

CHARTLEY ESTATE
Rowella
★★✩

Tiny even by boutique standards.

✓ *Riesling*

JOSEF CHROMY
Relbia
★★

Immaculate wines made in high-tech artisanal winery.

✓ *Entire range*

CLEMENS HILL
Cambridge
★★

Delicious, fruit-driven style.

✓ *Entire range*

CLOVER HILL
Lebrina
★★✩

Sparkling-wine releases since and including the 2006 vintage

have stepped up a gear in finesse.

✓ *Sparkling wine*

CRAIGOW
Cambridge
★★ **V**

Wines of exciting quality are produced here by Hobart surgeon Barry Edwards.

✓ *Pinot Noir • Riesling*

DOMAINE A
Campania
★★

Peter Althaus maintains the highest standards and is unremitting in his aim for a north European style from southern-hemisphere grapes.

✓ *Entire range*

ELSEWHERE VINEYARD
Glaziers Bay
★★✩ **V**

Superb Pinot Noir from the Huon Valley, and very good Riesling too.

✓ *Pinot Noir* (Bay of Eight) • *Riesling*

FREYCINET
Swansea
★★

Surprisingly big and beautiful Cabernet Sauvignon-Merlot and various other fine wines, including standout Radenti sparkling wine, Riesling, and Louis Chardonnay, but the exquisitely crafted Pinot Noir surpasses everything here.

✓ *Entire range*

FROGMORE CREEK
Cambridge
O★★

Owned by Tony Scherer of Tasmania and Jack Kidwiler of California, who have made some weird and wonderful wines over the years, from the only true wild ferment I have seen. (Normally the yeast resident in the winery itself dominates the fermentation after the first 2–3% of alcohol, but Frogmore puts the fermenting vessel in the vineyard itself!) The Riesling FGR (Forty Grams Residual) is stunning. The range includes the excellent 42°S label.

✓ *Entire range*

HOLM OAK
Rowella
★ **V**

First-rate Riesling.

✓ *Riesling*

JANSZ
Pipers Brook
★★

Now owned by Hill-Smith Family Vineyards, and under the careful eye of Natalie Fryar, these sparkling wines have more finesse than ever.

✓ *Entire range*

STEFANO LUBIANA
Granton
★★

Probably best known for his excellent sparkling wine, Stefano produces brilliant Pinot Noir, Chardonnay, and a whole lot more. Aims for finesse and minerality.

✓ *Entire range*

MEADOWBANK VINEYARD
Cambridge
★★✩

Classic black-cherry Pinot Noir from just north of Hobart, including the brilliant Henry James Pinot Noir.

✓ *Cabernet Sauvignon • Chardonnay* (Grace Elizabeth) • *Pinot Noir*

MILTON
Cranbrook
★

Boutique winery in dream location.

✓ *Pinot Noir • Riesling*

MOORILLA ESTATE
Berriedale
★★

This pioneering Tasmanian winery still produces wines.

✓ *Cabernet Sauvignon • Chardonnay • Riesling • Syrah*

NO REGRETS
Glaziers Bay
★★

An extremely promising start by Eric and Jette Phillips, who established this venture in 2000, just after they sold the nearby Elsewhere Vineyard.

✓ *Chardonnay • Classic white blend* (Triple S) • *Pinot Noir • Riesling • Sparkling* (Miss Otis)

PIPERS BROOK VINEYARD
Pipers Brook
★

This winery was taken over in 2001 by the Belgian-owned Kreglinger Australia, who have yet to convince me about their sparkling wines.

✓ *Chardonnay • Pinot Noir* (Reserve) • *Riesling*

PIRIE TASMANIA
Rosevears
★★

Soon to be sparkling wines only.

✓ *Entire range*

POOLEY WINES
Campania
★★

Previously called Cooinda, this winery has always produced award-winning Riesling, but its Pinot Noir may be even better.

✓ *Pinot Noir • Riesling*

PRESSING MATTERS
Hobart
★★✩

Owned by the irrepressible Greg Mellick, who is Tasmania's highest-ranking barrister, a major-general in the Australian Defence Force Reserves, and Cricket Australia's special investigator into corruption. He is also the only senior wine judge I've caught asleep during a live competition panel discussion!

✓ *Riesling*

PROVIDENCE VINEYARDS
Lalla
★★

Established as La Provence in 1956, with vines illegally removed from France, and smuggled into Tasmania.

✓ *Chardonnay • Pinot Noir*

ROSLYN ESTATE
Campania
★

One of the first Tasmanian wineries to make world-class Sauvignon Blanc.

✓ *Sauvignon Blanc*

STONEY RISE
Gravelly Beach
★★

Joe and Lou Holyman make great Pinot Noir, even in off-years.

✓ *Entire range*

TAMAR RIDGE
Kayena
★★

Purchased by Brown Brothers in 2010, Tamar Ridge is the largest vineyard owner and wine producer in Tasmania. With the winemaking foundations laid down by Andrew Pirie (since left) and Richard Smart as the on-site viticultural consultant (still contract), the best-practice regime here is as high as it gets. Tamar Ridge also own Coombend, Rosevears Estate, and Pirie Tasmania.

✓ *Entire range*

TWO BUD SPUR
Gardners Bay
★★ **V**

Great Pinot Noir by marine biologists Craig Mundy and Karen Miller.

✓ *Pinot Noir*

VELO
Legana
★★✩

Best by far for classic Chardonnay.

✓ *Chardonnay*

YELLOW POINT
Birchs Bay
★★

The Huon Valley's latest and fastest-rising Pinot Noir star.

✓ *Pinot Noir*

SOUTH AUSTRALIA

This is Australia's most productive and contradictory wine region, accounting for 42 per cent of the country's vineyards, and over 50 per cent of its total wine output, ranging from its cheapest to its most expensive wine.

THE BEGINNINGS OF THIS VAST MARKET GARDEN of grapes can be traced back to John Barton Hack, who planted vines at Chichester Gardens, North Adelaide, in 1837, but they were removed in 1840 in order to make way for urbanization. Meanwhile, in 1839, Hack had purchased a 1,600-hectare (4,000-acre) property near Mount Barker called Echunga Springs, where he also planted vines, producing his first wine in 1843, and sending a case to Queen Victoria the following year. Hack's Echunga Springs is generally thought to have produced the first wine in South Australia, although George Stevenson had established a vineyard in 1838 at North Adelaide, and so could have made wine at least one year before Hack, and possibly as

early as 1841. There is no documented evidence that he did or, at least, none that has surfaced. Nonetheless, it would be reasonable to assume that the records from this era are far from complete, because if Hack was indeed the first to make wine in 1843, how come, in the very same year, *The South Australian Vigneron* was published? Where would be the demand? Furthermore, the author of this work, George McEwin, is credited on the cover as "Gardener to George Stevenson". What is on record, however, is that Stevenson won a prize for his "Burgundy" at the South Australian Agricultural and Horticultural Show in 1845.

INCREASING REGIONAL DEFINITION

The paradox is that if consumers are asked what South Australia means to them as a winemaking state, they will probably say that it has a reputation for cheap wine, but ask them about Coonawarra, and they will say it is Australia's most famous, premium-quality wine region. Ask them about the Barossa Valley, and they will say that is where Australia's greatest Shiraz comes from. This state is an object lesson in the need to focus on regional definition. Only by increasing the regional definition

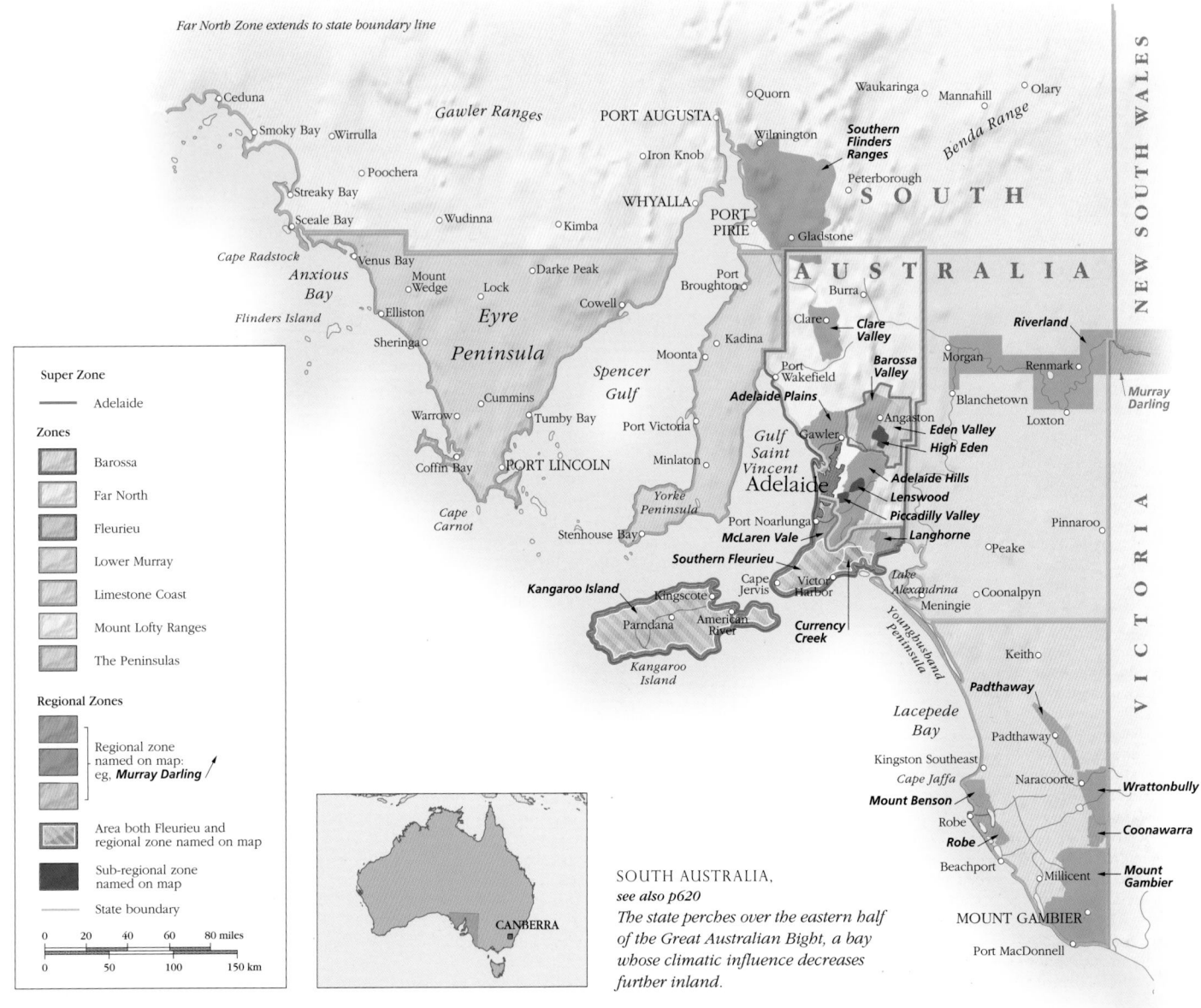

Super Zone

— Adelaide

Zones

■ Barossa
■ Far North
■ Fleurieu
■ Lower Murray
■ Limestone Coast
■ Mount Lofty Ranges
■ The Peninsulas

Regional Zones

Regional zone named on map: eg, **Murray Darling**

Area both Fleurieu and regional zone named on map

Sub-regional zone named on map

— State boundary

| 0 | 20 | 40 | 60 | 80 miles |
| 0 | 50 | 100 | 150 km |

CANBERRA

SOUTH AUSTRALIA, see also p620
The state perches over the eastern half of the Great Australian Bight, a bay whose climatic influence decreases further inland.

Far North Zone extends to state boundary line

FACTORS AFFECTING TASTE AND QUALITY

✴ LOCATION
This is the southern central part of the country, with Australia's five other mainland states to the east, north, and west, and half of the Great Australian Bight forming the coastline to the south.

☀ CLIMATE
The climate varies greatly, from the intensely hot continental conditions of the largely cask-wine producing Riverland area, through the less extreme but still hot and dry Barossa Valley, to the cooler but still dry Coonawarra region. Sea breezes reduce humidity in the plains around Adelaide, which receives low annual rainfall, as does the whole region.

⛰ ASPECT
Vines are grown on all types of land, from the flat coastal plain around Adelaide and flat interior Riverland district to the varied locations of the Barossa Valley, where vines are grown from the valley floor at 250 metres (820 feet), up to the slopes to a maximum of 600 metres (1,970 feet) at Pewsey Vale.

▦ SOIL
Soils are varied, ranging from sandy loam over red earth (*terra rossa*) on a limestone-marl sub-soil in the Adelaide and Riverland areas (the latter having suffered for some time from excess salinity), through variable sand, loam, and clay topsoils, over red-brown loam and clay sub-soils in the Barossa Valley, to the thin layer of weathered limestone, stained red by organic and mineral matter, over a thick limestone sub-soil in the Coonawarra area.

▦ VITICULTURE AND VINIFICATION
This varies enormously, from the bulk-production methods of the large modern wineries that churn out vast quantities of clean, well-made, inexpensive wine from grapes grown in Riverland's high-yielding irrigated vineyards, to the use of new oak on restricted yields of premium-quality varietals by top estate wineries in areas such as Coonawarra, the Barossa Valley, and the up-and-coming Padthaway or Wrattonbully districts, which produce some of Australia's greatest wines.

🍇 GRAPE VARIETIES
Primary varieties: Cabernet Franc, Cabernet Sauvignon, Chardonnay, Malbec, Merlot, Petit Verdot, Pinot Noir, Riesling, Sauvignon Blanc, Sémillon, Shiraz (Syrah)
Secondary varieties: Brown Muscat (Muscat Blanc à Petits Grains), Cinsault, Clare Riesling (Crouchen), Gewürztraminer, Grenache, Mourvèdre, Muscat Gordo Blanco (Muscat d'Alexandrie), Palomino, Pedro Ximénez, Ruby Cabernet, Sangiovese, Portugal (Tinto Amarella), Tokay (Muscadelle), Touriga (Touriga Nacional), Ugni Blanc

REMUAGE, BAROSSA VALLEY
Giant gyropalettes are indicative of the scale of the operation at the Southcorp-owned Barossa Valley cooperative.

within South Australia will its wine industry be recognized for its true quality and future potential.

It is already happening, as the Adelaide Hills, for example, brings a breath of cool air to the hot-climate image of this state. And within the Adelaide Hills, smaller areas such as the Piccadilly Valley manage to express the notion that specific and different *terroirs* can and do exist side by side. Even the Mount Lofty Ranges zonal GI, encompassing the Adelaide Hills and Clare Valley, expresses a difference. No two Rieslings are more intrinsically Australian than those from the Clare and Eden valleys, yet how could you mistake one for the other? With winemaking of consistently high standards from such outstanding producers as Grosset, the highly individual character and quality of sub-regions within the Clare Valley, such as Polish Hill, are starting to stand out. There are certainly plenty of top-notch producers in this state. How strange that South Australia should have such a generally inexpensive image when it produces some of Australia's finest and most expensive wines, from Grosset Polish Hill, to Henschke Hill of Grace, Rockford Black Shiraz, Petaluma Tiers Chardonnay, and, of course, Penfolds Grange.

THE APPELLATIONS OF

SOUTH AUSTRALIA

ADELAIDE GI
A superzonal GI that encompasses the regions of Barossa, Fleurieu, and the Mount Lofty Ranges.

ADELAIDE HILLS GI
Sub-regions:
Lenswood, Piccadilly Valley
Petaluma country. This hilly region is just 15 kilometres (9 miles) from the coast, overlooking Adelaide, the Adelaide Plains, and McLaren Vale. It has two sub-regions of its own, Lenswood and Piccadilly Valley, which are determined by differing temperatures and soil types. Along with Clare Valley and Adelaide Plains, this region is part of the much larger Mount Lofty Ranges GI. Although the Adelaide Hills have a Mediterranean climate, this is by far the coolest of all South Australian wine regions, being strongly influenced by elevation ranging from 350 to 700 metres (1,150 to 2,300 feet), and the winds that sweep across St Vincents Gulf. Undulating hills are interspersed with steep slopes, which drop into frost-prone gullies, creating many different kinds of *terroir* according to height, aspect, and the various soils, which range from (but are not restricted to) sandy alluvium on the valley floor, to yellow and red loams on the slopes. The first vines were planted here in the 1840s, but viticulture struggled for economic survival, finally succumbing to the Great Depression. Its revival finally came in the 1970s, when boutique wineries started to satisfy the demand of consumers who were switching from fortified to table wine. Chardonnay, Riesling, Pinot Noir, and bottle-fermented sparkling wines are now the classics here, with Cabernet Franc and Merlot faring better than Cabernet Sauvignon. Sauvignon Blanc and Sémillon are rising stars, with Sangiovese and the inevitable Shiraz showing promise.

ADELAIDE PLAINS GI
The Adelaide Plains is described by James Halliday as "one of the least appealing, most frequently visited regions in Australia". It is, as he also states, "laser-flat and searingly hot in summer". Little surprise, then, that there are very few wineries here, and those that do exist mostly source their grapes from elsewhere. However, extraordinarily fine wines can be made from vines growing in these furnace-like conditions, as illustrated by some of the wines produced by the top-performing Primo winery from Joe Grilli's Virginia vineyard. Part of the Adelaide Plains has long since been consumed by the city's sprawling suburbs, which now surround Penfolds' legendary Magill vineyard. The grapes from this vineyard used to be the base for Penfolds' remarkable Grange Hermitage, but they now go to make The Magill Estate.

BAROSSA GI
A zonal GI encompassing the Barossa Valley and Eden Valley regional GIs.

BAROSSA VALLEY GI
This district is the oldest and most important of South Australia's premium varietal areas. With a hot, dry climate, the vines mostly grow on flatlands at an altitude of 240 to 300 metres (800 to 1,000 feet), although in some areas the altitude rises to 550 metres (1,800 feet), and the vines are cooled by ocean breezes. The Barossa Valley is heavily dependent on irrigation, but boreholes are metered, and the amount of water that may be drawn is strictly regulated. Big, brash Shiraz is king in this region, although a significant volume of white wine is also produced.

Chardonnay, Sémillon, and Riesling dominate, and depending on the climate and the soil (which may be limestone, clay, or sand), these white wines can range from full bodied to surprisingly delicate.

CLARE VALLEY GI

Clare Valley is the most northerly vinegrowing district in South Australia and its climate is correspondingly hotter and drier. Many of the vineyards are not irrigated, however, and the result is a low yield of very intensely flavoured, big-bodied, often strapping wines. Riesling is the valley's most important variety and botrytis-affected wines are rich, fine, and mellifluous. Other good wines are Cabernet Sauvignon (often blended with Malbec or Shiraz), Sémillon, and Shiraz.

COONAWARRA GI

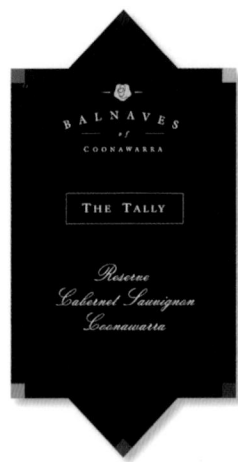

This famous district is the most southerly in South Australia. Coonawarra is Aboriginal for "wild honeysuckle"; it also happens to be easy on Anglo-Saxon tongues and this has been useful when it comes to marketing wine from the district in English-speaking countries. Consequently, this region achieved worldwide fame, which paradoxically held it back during the GI process, while other less well-known regions were demarcated relatively quickly. Everyone with the slightest chance of being considered part of Coonawarra wanted to be included within the boundaries, while the bureaucrats operating the GI scheme demonstrated little or no imagination; thus, it took eight years to settle all the disputes. The crux of the matter revolved around Coonawarra's red earth, or *terra rossa*. Black soil areas are interspersed among the *terra rossa* and these soils produce quite different wines, even though they share the same limestone sub-soil. The neatest solution would have been to have two appellations: a regional Coonawarra GI, within which there would be a sub-regional Coonawarra Terra Rossa GI. The Coonawarra ridge hardly stands out topographically, being just 59 metres (194 feet) above sea level, but it does stand out viticulturally, since the surrounding land is flat, frosty, and poorly drained. This, and the Mediterranean climate, which enjoys the cooling maritime influences off the Southern Ocean, make height-challenged Coonawarra superbly suited to viticulture, whether on black or red soils. It is just that those vineyards on *terra rossa* soils have historically been responsible for some of Australia's outstanding wines, particularly Cabernet Sauvignon. Vineyards on black soils can produce some very good wines, but those on *terra rossa* are demonstrably more expressive of their *terroir*. Cabernet Sauvignon might be king of the *terra*

rossa, but other varieties that perform well throughout Coonawarra include Shiraz, Petit Verdot, Pinot Noir, Malbec, and Merlot. Although Coonawarra is red wine country *par excellence*, successful white grapes include Chardonnay, Riesling, Sauvignon Blanc, and Sémillon.

CURRENCY CREEK GI

This regional GI is located on the Fleurieu Peninsula, extending from Port Elliot in the west to the shores of Lake Alexandrina in the east, and includes three islands: Hindmarsh, Mundoo, and Long Islands. The proximity to Lake Alexandrina, and the mouth of the Murray River moderates the hot Mediterranean climate, making the area suitable for viticulture. Grapes growing include Cabernet Sauvignon, Chardonnay, Sauvignon Blanc, and Shiraz.

EDEN VALLEY GI
Sub-region:
High Eden

The Eden Valley has a rockier, more acid soil than that found in the neighbouring Barossa Valley, with a cooler, much wetter climate. Vineyards are located at an altitude of 400–600 metres (1,300–2,000 feet) in the Mount Lofty Ranges, which form part of the Barossa Range. The Eden Valley GI is not a valley as such, but takes its name from the township of Eden Valley. While the pre-eminence of Henschke might suggest that the Eden Valley is world-class Shiraz country, that is very much due to one vineyard, Hill of Grace, and the 130-year-old Shiraz vines planted there. Eden Valley is best known for its quintessentially Australian (that is, limey) Riesling, and deservedly so. Chardonnay also fares well.

FAR NORTH GI

Apart from the Southern Flinders Ranges GI in the far south, the vast Far North zonal GI is very much a viticultural wilderness.

FLEURIEU GI

This zonal GI consists of the peninsula jutting out towards Kangaroo Island, and encompasses the regional GIs of Currency Creek, Kangaroo Island, Langhorne Creek, McLaren Vale, and Southern Fleurieu.

HIGH EDEN GI

So named because, unsurprisingly, this sub-regional GI is located at the highest point in Eden Valley, which also makes it one of the coolest and most windy areas. The terrain is hilly, and rugged, with poor sandy soils that are well suited to Chardonnay, Riesling, and Shiraz, as is the rest of the Eden Valley. Cabernet Sauvignon is also grown.

KANGAROO ISLAND GI

Located off the coast of South Australia, Kangaroo Island is renowned for its natural beauty, and an abundance of wildlife, including colonies of Australian sea lions, New Zealand fur seals, penguins, and the once-endangered Cape Barren goose. In recent years, Kangaroo Island has also been making a name for its Bordeaux-style blends. Most vines are grown on ruddy-coloured ironstone or sandy loam soils on the north side of the island, near Kingscote, where the maritime climate is marked by strong winds and moderate humidity. In addition to Bordeaux varieties, Chardonnay and Shiraz are also grown.

THE HARVEST, BAROSSA VALLEY
Many of the best premium varietal producers in South Australia have some sort of interest in the Barossa Valley, the state's most important wine area.

LANGHORNE CREEK GI

This once tiny, traditional area, located southeast of Adelaide on the Bremer River, has expanded rapidly since 1995, when Orlando started sourcing grapes from here for huge brands such as Jacob's Creek. This district was named after Alfred Langhorne, a cattle-herder from New South Wales, who arrived in 1841. The meagre annual rainfall of 35 centimetres (14 inches) means that the vineyards require irrigation. This area is reputed for its beefy reds and for its dessert wines.

LENSWOOD GI

This sub-regional GI is located north of Piccadilly, the other sub-region in the Adelaide Hills. The vines grow on steep slopes and benefit from a cool climate, but at 400 to 560 metres (1,300 to 1,840 feet), thus lower than those in Piccadilly (up to 710 metres, 2,330 feet), and do not experience quite the same snap of coldness. The grape varieties that excel are the same – Chardonnay and Pinot Noir – and the quality can be equally exciting.

LIMESTONE COAST GI

The naming of this zonal GI was a stroke of genius compared with all the hoo-ha over Coonawarra, when growers and bureaucrats alike could not see the wood for the trees. Not merely because Limestone Coast is so evocative of the one geological factor that links the regional GIs within its borders (Coonawarra, Mount Benson,

Padthaway, and Wrattonbully), but also because, rightly or wrongly, limestone is one of the few soils known by even the casual wine drinker to have a positive influence over the growing of grapes.

LOWER MURRAY GI

A zonal GI that encompasses the regional GI of Riverland.

McLAREN VALE GI

The rolling green hills of McLaren Vale's vineyards and orchards begin south of Adelaide and extend to south of Morphett Vale. With 56 centimetres (22 inches) of rain and a complex range of soils, including sand, sandy loam, limestone, red clay, and many forms of rich alluvium, there is great potential for quality in a range of styles from various grapes. This is perhaps why it is the most volatile wine district, attracting a lot of new talent, but also seeing wineries close or change hands. McLaren Vale produces big red wines of excellent quality from Shiraz and Cabernet Sauvignon (often blended with Merlot), with some increasingly fresh and vital white wines from Chardonnay, Sémillon, and Sauvignon Blanc. Fine dessert wines are also produced.

MOUNT LOFTY RANGES GI

This zonal GI encompasses the regional GIs of Adelaide Hills, Adelaide Plains, and Clare Valley.

PADTHAWAY GI

Once known as Keppoch, this area has been developed almost exclusively by the larger companies (Hardy's built Australia's largest winery for 20 years here in 1998). Provided the smaller businesses are not unreasonably prevented from buying land within the area, this should benefit all types of operation. The success of small ventures should be welcomed by the larger companies because it endorses the intrinsic quality potential of the district they are promoting.

THE PENINSULAS GI

If the Far North zonal GI is a massive viticultural wilderness above an imaginary line, then the Peninsulas is that part of South Australia to the south of the same line where hardly any wineries exist. It is not as if there is no scope for viticulture here. There are plenty of gently undulating hills, with the right aspect and altitude. The sub-soil is limestone, with everything from sandy-clayey loams to gravel for topsoil. There is even *terra rossa*. But there are only a couple of vineyards (Boston Bay and Decoline) in this zonal GI, and they are both confined to the Port Lincoln area on the Southern Eyre Peninsula.

PICCADILLY GI

Sub-region situated in the west of the Adelaide Hills GI, between Ashton and Bridgewater. The vines grow at altitudes of 400 to 710 metres (1,300 to 2,300 feet), benefiting from a very cool, wet climate, which stretches the ripening process, yielding grapes with naturally high tartaric acid levels. Chardonnay and Pinot Noir excel.

RIVERLAND GI

The wine areas that cluster around the Murray River in Victoria continue into Riverland, South Australia's irrigated answer to Riverina in New South Wales and Murray Darling in Victoria. Although a lot of cheap cask-wine is made in the Riverland district, rarely is a bad one encountered. Cabernet Sauvignon, Cabernet Sauvignon-Malbec, Chardonnay, and Riesling all fare well, and some relatively inexpensive wines are produced in the area.

SOUTHERN FLEURIEU GI

This region GI is located at the southern end of the Fleurieu Peninsula, where its gentle, undulating coastal country benefits from cooling winds coming from both the west and south, and vines grow in sandy loam and gravelly-ironstone soils. An up-and-coming area for small, boutique wineries, where Shiraz grows best, but other varieties include Cabernet Sauvignon, Malbec, Riesling, and Viognier.

SOUTHERN FLINDERS RANGES GI

Although the first grapes were grown here in the 1890s, it is only in the past 15 years that viticulture has become viable on a commercial scale, hence its regional GI status. This has been due to three factors: the so-called "Goyder's line of rainfall", which reduces demand on water supplies; an early harvest; and a ready market in the neighbouring Barossa and Clare valleys. The Southern Flinders Ranges are divided by "Goyder's line of rainfall", which was named after the surveyor George W Goyder, who first determined the "northernmost limits of feasible agriculture". Irrigation comes from underground water, but with an annual rainfall of 450–650 millimetres (17–25 inches), it is possible to grow grapes without it, which explains the focus on dry-grown, premium-quality grapes. The elevation extends from just 20 metres (65 feet) on the coast to 718 metres (2,355 feet) at Frypan Hill, but most vineyards are located on slopes at a height of 350 to 550 metres (1,150 to 1,800 feet), where the region's warm to hot climate is tempered by the cooling effects of altitude and winds crossing the gulf. The soils range from deep sandy loam on the coastal plains to the west of the Flinders Ranges, to deep loam over red clay to the east, around the Wild Dog Creek Land System, and more shallow, stony loam on the slopes. The best suited grapes are Cabernet Sauvignon, Merlot, and Shiraz.

WRATTONBULLY GI

Surprisingly easy to pronounce for Anglo-Saxon tongues, despite the peculiar name, perhaps because it is itself an Anglo-Saxon interpretation of the Aboriginal expression (for "a place of rising smoke signals"). Wrattonbully was not the original name for this region, sandwiched between Coonawarra and Padthaway. It was formerly known as Koppamurra, but there is a vineyard of that name in the area, and there were trademark problems in using it for a GI, thus it was decided to rename the region Wrattonbully, presumably to send out a signal. The first commercial vineyard was established in 1968, and by the 1990s most of Australia's biggest wine groups were sourcing fruit from here. The climate is very similar to that of Coonawarra, but its slightly higher aspect provides better air drainage, therefore a reduced risk of frost, and lower humidity, thus fewer cryptogamic disease problems. The sub-soil is limestone, of course, with various topsoils consisting of red-brown sandy and clayey loams, including some of the purest *terra rossa* soils, making this ideal *terroir* for Cabernet Sauvignon and Shiraz. Potentially, the reputation of Wrattonbully will be at least as great as Coonawarra's. We have barely begun to hear about these wines.

THE WINE PRODUCERS OF

SOUTH AUSTRALIA

TIM ADAMS
Clare Valley
★★Ⓥ

The Tim Adams style is very pure, deeply flavoured, and bursting with fruit, no wine more so than the fabulous, pure lime-juice Sémillon.

☑ *Classic red blend* (The Fergus) • *Sémillon* • *Shiraz* (Aberfeldy)

ANGOVE'S
Riverland
★Ⓥ

Most wines are fairly cheap and usually rack up a bronze medal at wine competitions, thus the odds are that even those not specifically recommended below can be relied on for above average quality and very good value.

☑ *Cabernet Sauvignon* (Sarnia Farm) • *Chardonnay* (Classic Reserve) • *Classic red blend* (Agincourt Cabernet Sauvignon-Malbec-Merlot, Butterfly Ridge Shiraz-Cabernet) • *Fortified* (Premium Port)

ANNIE'S LANE AT QUELLTALER ESTATE
Clare Valley
★★Ⓥ

The winemaker since 2000 for this precious part of the Beringer Blass empire has been the talented Caroline Dunn, who in 1999 became the first woman to win the coveted Jimmy Watson Trophy, and in 2001 was awarded the Dux of the inaugural Len Evans Wine tutorial.

☑ *Classic red blend* (Cabernet-Merlot, Shiraz-Grenache-Mourvèdre) • *Riesling* • *Shiraz*

ASHTON HILLS
Adelaide Hills
★★Ⓥ

Owner-winemaker Stephen George has honed his style into one of great elegance. Wines are also sold under the Galah label.

☑ *Chardonnay* • *Classic red blend* (Cabernet Merlot) • *Pinot Noir* • *Riesling* • *Shiraz* (Lone Star) • *Sparkling* (Salmon Brut)

BALNAVES OF COONAWARRA
Coonawarra
★★

Established in 1975 by Doug Balnaves, who sold his entire harvest as grapes until 1990, when he hired a contract winemaker to launch his own label. Quality and consistency surged upwards in 1996, when Balnaves of Coonawarra got its own brand-new winery, with

Wynns' former assistant winemaker Peter Bissell in charge.

✓ *Cabernet Sauvignon* • *Chardonnay* • *Classic red blend* (The Blend) • *Shiraz*

BAROSSA VALLEY ESTATE
Barossa Valley
★

Owned by BRL Hardy, Barossa Valley Estate continues to make E & E Black Pepper Shiraz, one of the biggest, oakiest sparkling Shiraz wines in the country from the low-yielding Barossa vineyards of Elmor Roehr and Elmore Schulz (whence the E & E). A recent addition to the output here is the E Minor range.

✓ *Classic red blend* (Monculta Cabernet Sauvignon-Merlot) • *Shiraz* • *Sparkling* (E & E Sparkling Shiraz)

BERRI ESTATES
Riverland
ⓥ

The merger between Thomas Hardy and Sons and the huge, Berri-Renmano winery formed BRL Hardy, and this cooperative winery, servicing some 850 private grape-growers, was absolutely essential for the growth of that group. However, despite this pivotal role, and although Berri Estates is Australia's largest winery, processing up to 163,000 tonnes (this record set in 2004), neither its Berri Estates, nor its Renmano brand contribute much to the wealth and grandeur of BRL Hardy today. Most wines are bag-in-the-box and very cheap, although well made for what they are.

BETHANY WINES
Barossa Valley
★⯪ⓥ

Bethany produces some big, chewy, and often incredibly jammy red wines.

✓ *Chardonnay* (Barrel Fermented) • *Classic red blend* (Cabernet-Merlot) • *Grenache* • *Shiraz* (GR 6 Reserve)

BOWEN ESTATE
Coonawarra
★★

Doug Bowen continues to produce some truly exceptional wines.

✓ *Cabernet Sauvignon* • *Classic red blend* (Cabernet-Merlot) • *Shiraz* (Ampleton)

BRAND'S OF COONAWARRA
Coonawarra
★★ⓥ

This winery is sometimes known as Brand's Laira, because of its famous Laira vineyard in Coonawarra's *terra rossa* heartland, the original part of which is planted with 110-year-old Shiraz vines. The Brand family did not purchase the Laira vineyard until 1946, and the first wine sold under the Brand's Laira label was not until the 1966 vintage. In 1990, McWilliams purchased 50 per cent of what was then known as Brand's Estate, buying up the other 50 per cent in 1994, retaining Jim and Bill Brand as winemakers. Jim Brand is still one of this winery's two winemakers. The old Laira Vineyard Shiraz is sold today as Stentiford Old Vines Reserve. Other fruit from the extended Laira vineyard is also found in the Patron's Reserve Cabernet Sauvignon.

✓ *Cabernet Sauvignon* (Patron's Reserve) • *Riesling* • *Shiraz* (Stentiford Old Vines Reserve)

BREMERTON WINES
Langhorne Creek
★⯪ⓥ

Established in 1988, but the fact that rapidly expanding production in recent years has been matched with either constant or improved quality is something that the Wilson family should be proud of.

✓ *Cabernet Sauvignon* (Walter's) • *Classic red blend* (Tamblyn) • *Shiraz* (Old Adam)

GRANT BURGE
Barossa Valley
★★⯪ⓥ

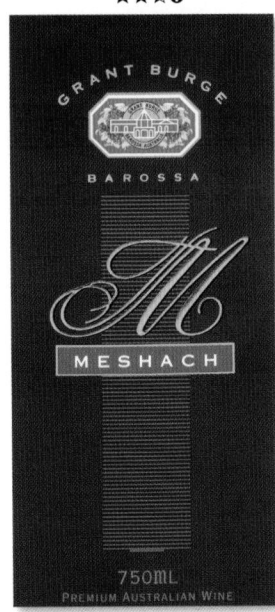

Owner-winemaker Grant Burge launched this venture in 1988. Since then, it has built up a reputation for richness, quality, and consistency, and he has not let his concentration lapse once. Grant Burge is probably best known for his icon Shiraz, Meshach, but the Filsell is probably just as outstanding at one-third the price, and there are numerous other wines, red and white, that are in a similar class. The Holy Trinity is a Grenache-Shiraz-Mourvèdre blend; MSJ2 is Shiraz-Cabernet; Balthasar is Shiraz-Viognier. The Lily Farm Frontignac is not a fortified wine, but is made in a wonderfully fresh, sweetish, late-harvest style.

✓ *Cabernet Sauvignon* (Cameron Vale) • *Chardonnay* (Summers) • *Classic red blend* (MSJ2, The Holy Trinity) • *Fortified* (20 Year Old Tawny) • *Frontignac* (Lily Farm) • *Riesling* (Thorn) • *Sémillon* (Barossa Vines, RBS2, Zerk) • *Shiraz* (Filsell, Meshach, Miamba)

LEO BURING
Eden Valley and Clare Valley
★★ⓥ

Orlando took over the Leo Buring winery (which now operates as Richmond Grove), but Southcorp bought the Leo Buring name. Although just one of Southcorp's many brands, Leo Buring remains one of Australia's foremost Riesling producers. Indeed, the range is now reduced to this one varietal, and just three versions of that. On the one hand, this is a tragic end to a once great winery, but on the other, as an exclusive Riesling brand, Leo Buring must rate a good two stars.

✓ *Entire range*

CARDINHAM ESTATE
Clare Valley
★⯪ⓥ

Although these vineyards have been established since 1980, the Smith family sold grapes, not wine, and they did not launch their own label until 2000, since when the wines have rapidly achieved a brilliant reputation.

✓ *Classic red blend* (Cabernet-Merlot) • *Sangiovese* • *Shiraz* (Standbrooke)

CHAIN OF PONDS
Adelaide Hills
★⯪

Zar Brooks, the young man who put a smile on the face of d'Arenberg, was hired as CEO to put his impish ideas to work here, before he moved onto stranger things (Stranger & Stranger actually, a brand consultancy firm).

✓ *Chardonnay* • *Pinot Noir* (Jerusalem Selection) • *Sémillon* (Adelaide Hills) • *Shiraz* (Grave's Gate)

CHAPEL HILL WINERY
McLaren Vale
★★

This Chapel Hill has no connection with the Australian-made wines of the same name from Hungary, but instead derives its name from the deconsecrated, 19th-century hilltop chapel which is used as its winery. In December 2000, Chapel Hill was purchased by the Swiss Schmidheiny family, which also owns Cuvaison Winery in California, as well as vineyards in Argentina and Switzerland.

✓ *Cabernet Sauvignon* • *Chardonnay* (Reserve, Unwooded) • *Classic red blend* (The Vicar) • *Shiraz* (McLaren Vale) • *Verdelho*

M CHAPOUTIER
Mount Benson
★★ⓥⓑ

This famous Rhône Valley *négociant* established its presence in Australia in 1998, when it purchased land at Mount Benson, and began planting. It now has 36 hectares (90 acres) of Shiraz, Marsanne, Viognier, and Cabernet Sauvignon, plus two joint ventures in Victoria: one with Jasper Hill at Heathcote, the other with Mount Langi Ghiran in the Grampians region. Mount Benson is biodynamic, as is Jasper Hill, but Mount Langi Ghiran is not at the time of writing. Chapoutier's Mount Benson Shiraz is not your typical Australian blockbuster, claiming only 13 per cent alcohol, with only 20 per cent new oak.

✓ *Entire range, now and in the future*

CLARENDON HILLS
McLaren Vale
★★⯪

Roman Bratasiuk strives for the biggest, most concentrated wines he can possibly extract from his old vines.

✓ *Grenache* (Romas Vineyard) • *Shiraz* (Piggott Range)

COCKATOO RIDGE
Barossa Valley
★ⓥ

Although the Cockatoo Ridge wine label has been around since 1991, this company was not established until 2002, when it was launched on the Australian stock exchange, and now occupies Hardy's former Siegersdorf winery, which was built in 1920. Cockatoo Ridge took over International Australian Vintners (formerly Andrew Garrett Vineyard Estates) in May 2004 and in the process acquired various labels, including the founder's eponymous brand Andrew Garrett (export only, confusingly almost exactly the same brand name as Garrett sold to Beringer Blass), Barossa Valley, Kelly's Promise (the Reserve restricted to the McLaren Vale fruit), Yarra Glen (Yarra Valley), Springwood Park (from various South Australian regions), and Ironwood.

✓ *Chardonnay* (Springwood Park) • *Classic red blend* (Yarra Glen Irma's Cabernet)

CORIOLE
McLaren Vale
★★

Full-throttle reds, including top-flight Shiraz and what was once the New World's best Sangiovese (still the same brilliant quality, but lots of top producers are now growing this and other Italian varieties). Redstone is a Shiraz-Cabernet blend, while Mary Kathleen is a Bordeaux-style blend.

✓ *Classic red blend* (Mary Kathleen, Redstone) • *Chenin Blanc* •

Nebbiolo • Sangiovese • Sémillon (especially the occasional Lalla Rookh) • *Shiraz*

CRABTREE OF WATERVALE
Clare Valley
★★ Ⓥ

Smallish, family-owned enterprise producing extraordinary-value, elegantly structured wines.

✓ *Grenache • Riesling • Shiraz*

CROSER
See Petaluma

D'ARENBERG WINES
McLaren Vale
★★★☆

The original vineyards were planted in the 1890s, and purchased in 1912 by teetotaller John Osborn, whose family has owned the business ever since. I have been tasting these wines since the 1970s, when the style of the reds was sort of dusty-dry, but could they age! The wines became more rounded in the 1980s, but the real revolution came in the 1990s, when the wines became more voluptuous. The 1990s also saw the arrival of Zar Brooks, whose marketing flair, and ability to dream up catchy names, woke this slumbering giant. All of d'Arenberg's Shiraz wines are stunning, but none more so than Dead Arm, which is a true Australian classic. Old Vine Shiraz and Footbolt Shiraz are almost in the same league, as is Sticks & Stones, the Rioja-style blend, and The Ironstone Pressings blend of Grenache, Mourvèdre, and Shiraz.

✓ *Botrytis* (Noble Riesling) • *Cabernet Sauvignon* (The Coppermine Road) • *Chardonnay* • *Classic red blend* (Bonsai Vine GSM, Sticks & Stones Tempranillo-Grenache, The Ironstone Pressings, The Laughing Magpie Shiraz-Viognier) • *Grenache* (The Custodian) • *Mourvèdre* (The Twentyeight Road) • *Shiraz*

ELDERTON
Barossa Valley
★★ Ⓥ

Established in 1984, Elderton has gained an enviable reputation for its high-quality, often highly oaked, wines since the early 1990s, with Cabernet Sauvignon king of this particular castle.

✓ *Cabernet Sauvignon* (Ashmead) •

Classic red blend (CSM) • *Merlot* • *Shiraz* (Command) • *Sparkling* (Pinot Pressings)

ELDRIDGE
Clare Valley
★★ Ⓥ

The quality from Leigh and Karen Eldridge gets better with each vintage. Surprisingly good Gamay.

✓ *Cabernet Sauvignon • Classic white blend* (Sémillon-Sauvignon Blanc) • *Gamay • Riesling* (Watervale) • *Shiraz* (Blue Chip)

GARTNER FAMILY VINEYARDS
Coonawarra
★★ Ⓥ

When you have over 400 hectares (1,000 acres), plus a shareholding in almost 200 hectares (500 acres) elsewhere, and supply other wineries with grapes, it's very easy to hold back something special for your own label.

✓ *Cabernet Sauvignon • Chardonnay • Shiraz*

GLAETZER WINES
Barossa Valley
★★

Brilliant Shiraz, both still and sparkling.

✓ *Shiraz • Sparkling* (Shiraz)

GROSSET
Clare Valley
★★★☆

Owner-winemaker Jeffrey Grosset is widely regarded as the king of Australian Riesling, but everything he produces is special. Gaia is a Bordeaux-style blend. Mesh is a Yalumba-Grosset collaboration.

✓ *Chardonnay* (Piccadilly) • *Classic red blend* (Gaia) • *Classic white blend* (Sémillon Sauvignon Blanc) • *Pinot Noir • Riesling* (Mesh, Polish Hill, Watervale)

HAAN WINES
Barossa Valley
★☆ Ⓥ

Established in 1993 by Hans and Fransien Haan. They are determined to make a name for their Merlot, thus have contracted James Irvine as winemaker.

✓ *Merlot • Sémillon • Viognier*

HAMILTON
McLaren Vale
★☆ Ⓥ

Richard Hamilton makes stunning wines, particularly reds. Hut Block Cabernets is a blend of Cabernet Sauvignon and Cabernet Franc. Hamilton also owns his late uncle's vineyard in Coonawarra, Leconfield.

✓ *Cabernet Sauvignon* (Hut Block) • *Classic red blend* (Hut Block Cabernets) • *Merlot* (Lot 148) • *Shiraz* (Gumpers' Block, Centurion 100 Year Old Vines)

HARDY'S
McLaren Vale
★★ Ⓥ

This large brand is the basis of the BRL Hardy group, which continues to produce a number of wines under various labels bearing the Hardy's name. This diverse selection ranges from penny-pinchers through penny-savers to premium-quality wines. Eileen Hardy Chardonnay (a wine named after the late, much-loved matriarch of the family for 40 years) consistently retains its reputation as one of Australia's very greatest wines.

✓ *Botrytis* (Padthaway Noble Riesling) • *Cabernet Sauvignon* (Padthaway, Thomas Hardy, Tintara) • *Chardonnay* (Eileen Hardy, Tintara) • *Fortified* (Ports: Show, Tall Ships, Tawny, Vintage, Whiskers Blake Tawny) • *Riesling* (Siegersdorf) • *Shiraz* (Eileen Hardy, Oomoo, Tintara) • *Sparkling* (Arras as from 1997 vintage, Banrock Station Sparkling Shiraz, Sir James, Nottage Hill, Omni)

HEGGIES VINEYARD
Eden Valley
★★

Part of Yalumba, this winery has always been known for its Riesling, but has started to produce a fine Merlot in recent years.

✓ *Merlot • Riesling*

HENRY'S DRIVE
Padthaway
★★

Established in 1998, Henry's Drive was "discovered" by US critic Robert Parker and has quickly gained a reputation as one of Australia's finest red-wine specialists.

✓ *Cabernet Sauvignon • Shiraz*

HENSCHKE
Eden Valley
★★★☆

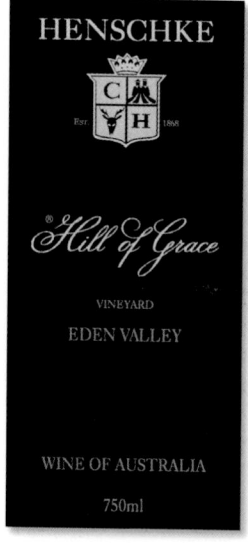

Founded in 1868, this is one of Australia's oldest and greatest wine-producing icons, with Hill of Grace Shiraz, and Cyril Henschke Cabernet Sauvignon lording it over the rest of the highly acclaimed range. Keyneton Estate used to be named Shiraz-Cabernet-Malbec, then Shiraz-Cabernet-Merlot, but is now labelled Euphonium, presumably to allow a certain varietal flexibility without advertising the fact. Henry's is a Shiraz-Grenache-Viognier blend, while Johann's Garden is a Grenache-Mourvèdre-Shiraz.

✓ *Cabernet Sauvignon* (Cyril Henschke) • *Chardonnay* (Crane's Eden Valley, Lenswood Croft) • *Classic red blend* (Keyneton Estate Euphonium, Henry's, Johann's Garden) • *Merlot* (Abbot's Prayer) • *Pinot Noir* (Giles) • *Riesling* (Green's Hill) • *Sémillon* (Julius Eden Valley, Louis Eden Valley) • *Shiraz* (Mount Edelstone, Hill of Grace)

HEWITSON
Adelaide
★★★☆

Dean Hewitson was a winemaker at Petaluma for 10 years, where he achieved the impossible by shining even in the bright light of Brian Croser. During his time at Petaluma, he completed a vintage at that company's subsidiary in Oregon, the Argyle Winery, three harvests in France, and picked up a Masters degree at UC Davis in California. Hewitson's speciality is to source grapes from very old, superbly sited vineyards in various regions. The Mourvèdre is the extreme example, coming from 160-year-old vines in Barossa.

✓ *Entire range*

HILLSTOWE
Adelaide Hills
★★ Ⓥ

Part of the Banksia group, thus now within the Lion Nathan portfolio.

✓ *Chardonnay* (Udy's Mill) • *Merlot* (The Pinchbowl) • *Shiraz* (Mary's Hundred)

HOLLICK WINES
Coonawarra
★ Ⓥ

Owner-viticulturist Ian Hollick set up his venture in 1983 and has produced some fresh, clean, well-focused wines, including a red Bordeaux-style blend that is simply sold by its Coonawarra appellation.

✓ *Cabernet Sauvignon* (Ravenswood) • *Chardonnay* (Reserve) • *Classic red blend* (Coonawarra Cabernet Sauvignon-Merlot)

INGOLDBY
McLaren Vale
★ Ⓥ

Now just another Beringer Blass brand, making mostly good-value wines, but with occasional standouts.

✓ *Cabernet Sauvignon* (McLaren Vale) • *Chardonnay* (McLaren Vale) • *Shiraz* (McLaren Vale Reserve)

IRVINE
Eden Valley
★★

Established in 1980 by the indefatigable James Irvine, whose name has become synonymous with Merlot. Cheaper wines sold under the Eden Crest range.

✓ *Classic red blend* (Eden Crest Merlot-Cabernet) • *Merlot* (James Irvine Grand Merlot)

JAMIESONS RUN
Coonawarra
★ Ⓥ

At one time, this was the most underrated brand in the Beringer Blass stable. It is not quite the treasure trove of inexpensive goodies it used to be, but can still come up with exceptional-value Chardonnay.

✓ *Classic red blend* (Winemakers Reserve Cabernet-Shiraz) • *Chardonnay*

JIM BARRY WINES
Clare Valley
★★ Ⓥ

Run by Mark and Peter, sons of the eponymous Jim Barry. Their top

Shiraz, The Armagh, is one of Australia's greatest wines. It is also one of the country's most expensive, and, at one-third of the price and almost as good quality as The Armagh, the McRae Wood Shiraz is better value. Virtually all other wines produced by Jim Barry are sold at bargain prices.

✓ *Cabernet Sauvignon* (McRae Wood) • *Chardonnay* (Unwooded) • *Fortified* (Old Walnut Tawny Port, Sentimental Bloke Port) • *Riesling* (Watervale) • *Shiraz* (Lodge Hill, McRae Wood, The Armagh)

KAESLER WINES
Barossa Valley
★★ Ⓥ

Toby and Treena Hauppauff have shone with Shiraz since purchasing the Kaesler vineyard in 1990, helped no doubt by a core of 120-year-old Shiraz vines. Now they are making top Cabernet Sauvignon.

✓ *Cabernet Sauvignon* • *Shiraz* (Old Vine, Stonehorse)

KATNOOK ESTATE
Coonawarra
★★

Part of the Wingara Group, which is majority-owned by Freixenet of Spain. With 330 hectares (815 acres) of vineyards in prime *terra rossa* soil, Katnook is an upmarket producer of intensely flavoured wines that display remarkable finesse, the very best being Cabernet Sauvignon, Shiraz, and Sauvignon Blanc. Between 1979 and 2005, Katnook wines won a remarkable 14 trophies, plus 110 gold, 243 silver, and 645 bronze medals; then they stopped counting. Expensive wines are sold under the Riddoch label. This should not be confused with Wynns' John Riddoch, although some Riddoch reds are of almost the same outstanding quality. The penny-pinching label Deakin Estate (Murray Darling) has effectively replaced Katnook's cheaper Sunnycliff range.

✓ *Cabernet Sauvignon* (including Riddoch) • *Merlot* • *Riesling* • *Sauvignon Blanc* • *Shiraz* (including Riddoch)

KAY BROTHERS
McLaren Vale
★★ Ⓥ

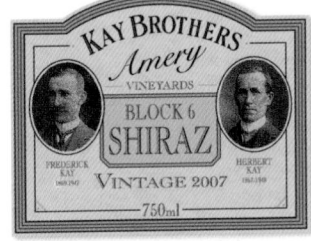

A fast-rising star, thanks not only to the blessing of critic Robert Parker, but also to a block of incredibly low-yielding Shiraz vines planted in 1897.

✓ *Merlot* • *Shiraz* (Block 6, Hillside)

KILIKANOON
Clare Valley
★★ Ⓥ

Kilikanoon has been the talk of the town since 2002, when its Riesling, Shiraz, and Cabernet Sauvignon walked away with six out of seven trophies at the Clare Valley Wine Show.

✓ *Cabernet Sauvignon* (Blocks Road) • *Grenache* (Prodigal) • *Riesling* (Mort's Block) • *Shiraz* (Covenant, Oracle)

KNAPPSTEIN
Clare Valley
★★ Ⓥ

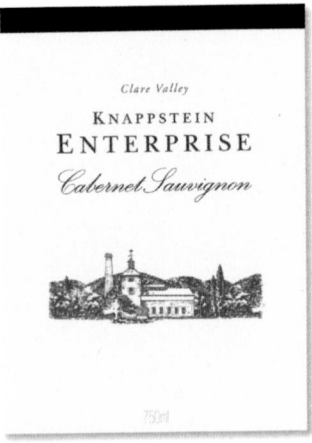

Part of Lion Nathan since the takeover of Petaluma. The wines continue going from strength to strength in the capable hands of Andrew Hardy, who trained under Brian Croser.

✓ *Cabernet Sauvignon* (Enterprise) • *Classic white blend* (Sauvignon Blanc-Sémillon) • *Riesling* (Hand Picked) • *Shiraz* (Enterprise) • *Sparkling* (Chainsaw Sparkling Shiraz)

KNAPPSTEIN LENSWOOD VINEYARD
Lenswood
★★★

Since selling off his original winery and vineyards to Petaluma, now owned by Lion Nathan, Tim Knappstein produces a fraction of his former output exclusively from his Lenswood vineyard in the Adelaide Hills, which he established in 1981. If anything, Knappstein's wines are more focused, and have greater finesse, than ever. The Palatine is a blend of Merlot, Malbec, and Cabernet Sauvignon.

✓ *Chardonnay* • *Classic red blend* (The Palatine) • *Pinot Noir* • *Sauvignon Blanc* • *Sémillon*

LEASINGHAM
Clare Valley
★★ Ⓥ

Part of the BRL Hardy group, Leasingham makes wines that offer outstanding quality and value. Bastion (sold on some export markets as Magnus) is a Shiraz-Cabernet blend, while Bin 56 is Cabernet-Malbec.

✓ *Cabernet Sauvignon* (Classic Clare) • *Classic red blend* (Bastion Shiraz Cabernet, Bin 56) • *Riesling* (Bin 7, Classic Clare) • *Shiraz* (Bin 61, Classic Clare, Domaine)

LECONFIELD
Coonawarra
★★ Ⓥ

Owned by Richard Hamilton (*see* Hamilton), whose uncle, Sydney Hamilton, established Leconfield in 1974.

✓ *Cabernet Sauvignon* • *Merlot* • *Shiraz*

PETER LEHMANN
Barossa Valley
★★ Ⓥ

Often underrated in Australia itself, Peter Lehmann's range of always excellent-value, mostly brilliant-quality wines is highly regarded on international markets. The Mentor is a Cabernet Sauvignon-Malbec-Shiraz blend, while The Seven Surveys is Mourvèdre-Shiraz-Grenache.

✓ *Cabernet Sauvignon* • *Chardonnay* (The Barossa) • *Classic red blend* (The Mentor, The Seven Surveys) • *Fortified* (The King) • *Riesling* (Reserve) • *Rosé* (Grenache) • *Sémillon* (Reserve, The Barossa) • *Shiraz* (Mudflat, Stonewall)

LINDEMANS WINES
Coonawarra

Although this is the best-performing part of Lindemans' current operations, it is impossible to subdivide the brand according to location, particularly when Southcorp is progressively dropping Lindemans' regionality in favour of state blends. Consequently, all this brand's best wines can be found in the Victoria section, where the overall score is cb, although the wines produced in Lindemans Coonawarra winery would easily rate cc at the moment. *See* Lindemans Wines, Victoria.

MAGLIERI OF MCLAREN VALE
McLaren Vale
★★

Part of Beringer Blass since 1999. These extraordinary bargain wines are at last finding their way into mainstream outlets on export markets.

✓ *Barbera* • *Cabernet Sauvignon* • *Nebbiolo* • *Sangiovese* • *Sémillon* • *Shiraz*

MAJELLA
Coonawarra
★★

The Lynn family had kept merino sheep for four generations, when in 1968 George and Pat Lynn decided to invest in vineyards. The first 10 years were less than successful, with 30 tonnes or more of grapes left to rot on the vines in some years due to low demand. In 1980, however, they entered into an agreement to supply Wynns, a relationship that lasted for over 20 years, giving the Lynns confidence to strike out on their own. Cabernet Sauvignon and Shiraz are the standout wines here. The Malleea is a Shiraz-Cabernet Sauvignon blend.

✓ *Cabernet Sauvignon* • *Classic red blend* (The Malleea) • *Shiraz* • *Sparkling* (Sparkling Shiraz)

MAXWELL WINES
McLaren Vale
★☆❶

Founded in 1979, this fairly well-established winery became an Aladdin's cave of wonderful vinous treasures in the 1990s, but has settled down to two absolute standouts.

✓ *Cabernet Sauvignon* (Lime Cave) • *Shiraz* (Ellen Street)

CHARLES MELTON
Barossa Valley
★★❶

Most famous for his Châteauneuf-du-Pape-type blend, cheekily named Nine Popes, but all the reds produced here are high-flyers, and Melton's sweet, seductive, sparkling Shiraz is regularly one of Australia's two or three finest. Rose of Virginia is a Grenache-Cabernet blend. If you want to see just how small, thus concentrated, a bunch of dry-farmed Shiraz is, then take a look at the website.

✓ *Cabernet Sauvignon* • *Classic red blend* (Nine Popes) • *Rosé* (Rose of Virginia) • *Shiraz*

GEOFF MERRILL
McLaren Vale
★☆❶

While Geoff Merrill was senior winemaker (1977–85) at Chateau Reynella, he started selling wines under his own name. He was appointed consultant red winemaker for Reynella's parent company, Thomas Hardy and Son, in 1985, but was actively searching for somewhere to make his own wines. That same year, Merrill came across the run-down Mount Hurtle Winery, which he purchased and restored, before leaving Hardy's in 1988 to concentrate on his own operation. At first, the emphasis was on the Mount Hurtle brand, but since 1993, when he took up the position as a consultant winemaker in Italy to UK supermarket Sainsbury and Gruppo Italiano Vini in Italy, the international fame of the moustachioed Merrill began to

outshine that of Mount Hurtle, thus it was inevitable that his eponymous brand would one day take centre stage. Merrill's style is for elegance and length over concentration and weight, with the occasional over-oaking the only significant chink in his armour. Virtually all the wines offer value for money to one degree or another. The one obvious exception being the stunningly beautiful, but horrendously expensive Henley Shiraz. Mount Hurtle survives, but as an exclusive brand for Liquorland.

✓ *Chardonnay* (Unwooded) • *Classic red blend* (Shiraz-Grenache-Mourvèdre) • *Classic white blend* (Sémillon-Chardonnay) • *Shiraz* (Henley, Reserve)

MIRANDA WINES
Barossa
★☆❶

Part of McGuigan Simeon since 2003, the origins of Miranda Wines date back to 1938, when Francesco Miranda arrived from Naples. There are three Miranda wineries, all producing and selling their own wines: the original and largest in Riverina, the latest (1998) in King Valley, and the best in Barossa. These wines are under-rated, but they picked up more than 2,500 national and international awards between 1995 and 2005 (when they stopped counting), so they must be doing something right. The single most medal-laden wine is Golden Botrytis from the Riverina winery, but most of Miranda's best wines are made in the Barossa, where the value is great, and the quality constantly improving. The Emu Plains Colombard-Chardonnay is not a classic white blend, but it is a deliciously fresh one! An inexpensive range of night-harvested wines is sold under the Firefly label.

✓ *Botrytis* (Botrytis Sémillon, Golden Botrytis) • *Cabernet Sauvignon* (High Country) • *Classic red blend* (Reserve Shiraz Cabernet) • *Riesling* (Eden Valley) • *Rosé* (White Shiraz) • *Shiraz* (Family Reserve Old Vine, The Drainings)

MITCHELL
Clare Valley
★☆❶

A small winery, Mitchell produces one of Australia's classic examples of Riesling.

✓ *Riesling* (Watervale) • *Shiraz* (Pepper Tree Vineyard)

MITOLO
Adelaide Plains
★★

Fast-rising star with award-winning wine made by Ben Glaetzer. The wines are mostly sourced from McLaren Vale, with (so far) one from the Barossa Valley.

✓ *Cabernet Sauvignon* (Serpico) • *Shiraz* (G.A.M., Savitar)

MOUNT HORROCKS
Clare Valley
★★

The quality and definition in style of these wines have really shone since the late 1990s, especially in the Riesling wines, which are world class. All Rieslings are highly recommended, but one – the Cordon Cut – should be explained. Its beautifully balanced sweet style is achieved by cutting, but leaving in place the cordon, which disconnects the grape clusters from the vine's metabolism, artificially inducing *passerillage*.

✓ *Classic red blend* (Cabernet-Merlot) • *Riesling* • *Sémillon*

MOUNTADAM VINEYARD
Eden Valley
★★

Recently purchased by LVMH, this estate produces wines that are rich, yet lean, and of excellent quality. They come from vineyards that once belonged to Adam Wynn, son of the founder of the almost legendary Wynns Coonawarra estate (now belonging to Southcorp). Adam Wynn is still very active in the day-to-day running of Mountadam. The Red is a Cabernet Sauvignon-Merlot blend. Other brands include David Wynn and Eden Ridge.

✓ *Classic red blend* (The Red) • *Pinot Noir* • *Riesling*

MURDOCK
Coonawarra
❓

I have not tasted the Cabernet Sauvignon from this producer (established 1998), but colleagues who have rave about its richness, ripeness, and elegance. To achieve elegance with richness and ripeness is, for me, the height of quality; thus, I feel obliged to pass on the recommendation of this fast-rising producer.

NEPENTHE VINEYARDS
Adelaide Hills
★★

In 1996 the Tweddall family became the second-ever vineyard owner to receive permission to build a winery in the Adelaide Hills (Petaluma being the first, almost 20 years earlier).

✓ *Chardonnay* • *Pinot Noir* • *Riesling*

NOON WINERY
McLaren Vale
★★

I don't know whether it's a trick of the mind, or if it really happened, but I have this memory of Drew Noon in 1991 at Cassegrain, where he was assistant winemaker, and he is telling me that he dropped the "e" from the end of his name because he didn't want to be "no one"! Since then, he has passed his Master of Wine examination, taken over his parents' winery, and caused

enough of a stir with his massive, super-ripe wine oddities to catch the attention of critic Robert Parker. Eclipse is a Grenache-Shiraz blend, and VP is a vintage port style.

✓ *Cabernet Sauvignon* (Reserve) • *Classic red wine* (Eclipse) • *Fortified* (VP) • *Shiraz* (Reserve)

O'LEARY WALKER
Clare Valley
★☆❶

David O'Leary and Nick Walker started this enterprise in 2001, and so far the Rieslings have been splendid.

✓ *Classic red blend* (Cabernet Sauvignon Merlot) • *Riesling* (Watervale) • *Sémillon* (Watervale)

ORLANDO
Barossa Valley
★★❶

Orlando in general, and Jacob's Creek in particular, have propelled the French-owned Orlando Wyndham group to become one of Australia's top four wine companies. But there is a big difference between the Jacob's Creek basic range at A$8 a bottle, and various top-performing Jacob's Creek Reserve wines at twice the price (and 10 times the bargain). Even in the basic range, there are vintages that have been so stunning that they have run away with gold medals at Capital Shows, and have even taken trophies or top golds, much to the embarrassment of some judges. I am not ashamed to say that I have been impressed by bottom-line Jacob's Creek wines such as the 2003 Grenache-Shiraz, 2000 Merlot, 1998 Shiraz-Cabernet, 2000 Sémillon-Sauvignon Blanc, 2000 and 2002 Riesling. Even Jacob's Creek Chardonnay (the very thought of which normally makes my mouth water for a decent beer) enjoyed a remarkable run of quality between the 1999 and 2002 vintages, outclassing the Reserve in the last two of those years. From launch in 1983 to 2005 (when they stopped counting), Jacob's Creek core range Riesling alone won 253 awards, including three trophies and 20 gold medals. The entire Jacob's Creek range has notched up 27 trophies and 169 golds, but is the wine the same everywhere? Is the same vintage of the same variety or blend exactly the same, not only in all parts of Australia, but on every market in the world? There is considerable variation in the awards, with supposedly the same wine winning a trophy and numerous golds, yet sometimes three times as many bronzes, but that happens to many other wines, and could equally be due to variation of judging panels or the precise stage at which the wines have developed in bottle when they are tasted. Until every wine at every competition is analysed, I do not suppose we will ever know. Note that JC below indicates Jacob's Creek.

✓ *Botrytis* (Sémillon) • *Cabernet Sauvignon* (Jacaranda Ridge, JC Reserve, St Hugo) • *Chardonnay* (JC Limited Release, Russet Ridge Coonawarra, St Hilary Padthaway) • *Classic red blend* (JC Grenache-Shiraz, JC Limited Release Shiraz-Cabernet) • *Riesling* (JC, JC Reserve) • *Shiraz* (Centenary Hill, JC Reserve, Lawson's Padthaway)

PARACOMBE
Adelaide Hills
★ ❤

Owner-viticulturist-winemaker Paul Drogemuller produces one of Australia's best-value Cabernet Franc wines.

✓ *Cabernet Franc* • *Chardonnay* • *Sauvignon Blanc*

PARKER ESTATE
Coonawarra
★★☆

Acquired by the Rathbone Family Group in 2004, who utilized the consulting services of Dr Andrew Pirie (*see* Pipers Brook, Tasmania) for a short while, the wines are now made by Peter Bissell of Balnaves. The estate's small, low-yielding vineyard produces super-premium wines, headed by First Growth, a blend of Cabernet Sauvignon and Merlot.

✓ *Cabernet Sauvignon* (Terra Rossa) • *Classic red blend* (Terra Rossa First Growth) • *Merlot* (Terra Rossa)

PAULETT'S
Clare Valley
★☆

I have always enjoyed Neil Paulett's beautifully focused white wines, and am now rapidly becoming impressed with some of his reds.

✓ *Classic red blend* (Cabernet-Merlot) • *Riesling* • *Sauvignon Blanc* • *Shiraz*

PENFOLDS WINES
Barossa Valley
★★★☆ ❤

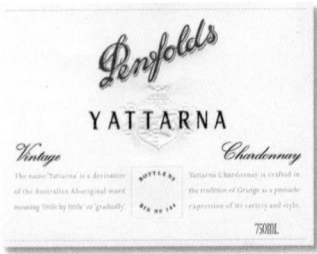

Penfolds' superb Grange (formerly Grange Hermitage) is Australia's most famous wine, created by the late and legendary Max Schubert, and through this single masterpiece Penfolds itself has become a living legend. Naturally enough, Grange is a very expensive product – the price of a Bordeaux *premier cru* – but other far less expensive Penfolds wines are miniature

masterpieces in their own right. However, some wines, such as Bin 707 and The Magill, have become very pricey (though nowhere near as expensive as Grange), and The Magill is, in terms of its origin, more Grange than Grange has ever been, being sourced entirely from the vineyard that many people once believed to be the sole source of Grange. It is now part of Southcorp. RWT stands for Red Wine Trial, only the trial has long since stopped, and the name has stuck. Positioned between Grange and Magill, RWT is a Shiraz of incredible finesse for its size. Bin 707 is positioned as the Cabernet Sauvignon equivalent of RWT. Bin 138 is a Barossa Valley Shiraz-Mourvèdre-Grenache. Bin 389 is a Cabernet-Shiraz. Rawson's Retreat is the penny-pinching, decent-value label, but for just a little more, Koonunga Hill offers far better value for money, and even has the occasional real standout. Penfolds' Clare Valley operation is certified organic.

✓ *Cabernet Sauvignon* (Bin 407, Bin 707) • *Chardonnay* (Bin 00A, Bin 98A, Yattarna) • *Classic red blend* (Bin 138, Bin 389) • *Fortified* (Grandfather Port) • *Riesling* (Eden Valley Reserve) • *Sémillon* (Adelaide Hills) • *Shiraz* (Grange, Kalimna Bin 28, Magill Estate, RWT)

PENLEY ESTATE
Coonawarra
★★

Established in 1988 by Kym Tolley (whose mother was a Penfold and father a Tolley, hence the cheekily named Pen-ley). Penley Estates leans towards Penfolds in style, as Kym's penchant is clearly for red wines, but he has also produced an excellent, rich, lush, toasty Chardonnay. However, Reserve and Phoenix Cabernet Sauvignons are the absolute standouts here.

✓ *Cabernet Sauvignon* • *Chardonnay* • *Classic red blend* (Shiraz-Cabernet) • *Sparkling* (Pinot Noir-Chardonnay)

PETALUMA
Adelaide Hills
★★★☆ ❤

This is still Brian Croser's domaine, even though Petaluma was the target of a hostile takeover by Lion Nathan. In the ensuing acrimony, Croser swore that he would not work for the new owner, but ended up in charge of Lion Nathan's entire wine group. Under Croser, Petaluma became a master of beautifully ripe, classically dry, top-quality Riesling that ages slowly and gracefully, and one of the best exponents of sparkling wine in the New World (*see* Argyle Winery, Oregon). Not to mention one of Australia's best Merlot wines, and a highly reputed Chardonnay too. Second wines are sold under Bridgewater Mill label.

✓ *Entire range*

PEWSEY VALE
Eden Valley
★★☆

Forget the Cabernet Sauvignon, there is only one reason to buy Pewsey Vale, and that is for its absolutely classic Eden Valley Riesling. Even the "basic" Riesling is superb, but The Contour is magnificent.

✓ *Riesling*

PIKES
Clare Valley
★★☆ ❤

Made by Neil Pike, formerly a winemaker at Mitchell, these excellent-quality red wines lean less on weight than subtlety and elegance to achieve complexity. The Luccio Red is a super-Tuscan-type blend of Sangiovese, Merlot, and Cabernet Sauvignon.

✓ *Classic red blend* (Luccio Red) • *Riesling* • *Shiraz*

PRIMO
Adelaide Plains
★★ ❤

I cannot think why I was not wildly enthusiastic about these wines in previous editions. Owner-winemaker Joe Grilli produces some truly excellent wines, including the exquisitely rich, creamy-cedary Joseph sparkling red, its cult following being easily justified by the fact that it is regularly one of Australia's top two or three sparkling red wines. Although the

best wines are sold under the Joseph label, don't ignore the basic Primo Estate white (La Biondina) and red (Il Briccone), which represent tremendous, everyday drinking value.

✓ *Botrytis* (Joseph La Magna Riesling) • *Classic red blend* (Il Briccone Shiraz-Sangiovese, Joseph Cabernet-Merlot) • *Colombard* (Il Biondina) • *Sparkling* (Joseph Red)

PUNTERS CORNER
Coonawarra
★★

This venture started life quite modestly in 1988, with 16 hectares (40 acres) of vineyards in Victoria and Coonawarra, but now amounts to more than 150 hectares (370 acres), virtually all in Coonawarra, including 12 hectares (30 acres) surrounding the Punters Corner cellar sales (the wines are made under contract elsewhere). The basic Shiraz is stunning, but pales in comparison with the Spartacus Reserve. The Cabernet is almost entirely Cabernet Sauvignon, with just 9 per cent (or thereabouts) of Merlot. Triple Crown is a blend of Cabernet Sauvignon, Shiraz, and Merlot.

✓ *Cabernet Sauvignon* • *Classic red blend* (Cabernet, Triple Crown) • *Shiraz*

RESCHKE WINES
Coonawarra
★★

The launch of the first wine, the 1998 Empyrean, caused something of a stir. First, because the asking price was A$100 for a wine with no track record. Second, because its big, porty character was praised to heaven and back by those who believe big is best. The next two vintages, however, saw a substantial drop down in alcohol level: virtually 1 per cent per year, so that by 2000 Empyrean was a Bordeaux-like 12.9 per cent alcohol. The wine is now more elegant, and possibly longer-lived, depending what you expect in a fully mature wine. The Vitulus is 100 per cent Cabernet Sauvignon, whereas the Empyrean has always included 10 per cent Merlot, but has also had 3 per cent Cabernet Franc since 1999 (thus remains with the limit of a so-called pure varietal, which may include up to 15 per cent of other grape varieties). The Taikurri is a blend of Cabernet Sauvignon, Merlot, Malbec, and Cabernet Franc.

✓ *Cabernet Sauvignon* (Empyrean, Vitulus) • *Classic red blend* (Taikurri) • *Shiraz*

REYNELLA
McLaren Vale
★★☆

Formerly known as Chateau Reynella, this historic winery dates from 1838, but has belonged to BRL Hardy and its previous incarnations since 1982. Only two, so-called super-premium wines are made, both with the emphasis on traditional methods. Fruit is favoured over oak, although the latter – both American and French – still plays a significant role.

✓ *Cabernet Sauvignon* (Basket Pressed) • *Fortified* (Vintage Port) • *Shiraz* (Basket Pressed)

ROCKFORD WINES
Barossa Valley
★★

The very traditional reds from low-yielding vines might be a bit soupy for some, but the Black Shiraz will be admired by anyone who enjoys Australia's wonderfully eccentric, show-style, sparkling Shiraz. Owner-winemaker Robert O'Callaghan has apparently made a number of one-off, single-vineyard Shiraz wines that are simply spectacular, but I have not yet tasted them.

✓ *Cabernet Sauvignon* (Rifle Range) • *Grenache* (Moppa Springs) • *Sémillon* (Local Growers) • *Shiraz* (Basket Press) • *Sparkling* (Black Shiraz)

ROSEMOUNT ESTATE
McLaren Vale

See Rosemount Estate, New South Wales.

ROUGE HOMME
Limestone Coast
Ⓥ

Southcorp sold off the winery of this Lindemans brand in 2002, but not the name, thus it really is just another brand, albeit a good-value one. Rouge Homme could throw the odd curved ball, such as the truly excellent 1997 Coonawarra Pinot Noir. How on earth did they manage that? Coonawarra is hardly Burgundy; in fact, it is one of the last places on earth any sane person would plant that variety. In recent years, however, the provenance of these wines has been widened to the Limestone Coast, while the range has been reduced to a mere five wines. The Cabernet Sauvignon used to be the most reliable Rouge Homme, and some vintages were extraordinarily good, but 1999 was the last produced, unless Southcorp changes its mind. That leaves the Cabernet Merlot and Shiraz Cabernet as the safest bets.

RYMILL
Coonawarra
★★

This property is owned and run by the descendants of John Riddoch, who planted the first Coonawarra vineyard in 1861. The MC2 is so named because it is a blend of Merlot and two Cabernets (Sauvignon and Franc), but it is also half of Einstein's famous formula, $E=mc^2$, which demonstrates that energy equals mass and, as nuclear fission scientists would discover 30-odd years later, a minuscule mass can equal fabulously large amount of energy in some circumstances, so maybe there is also a more mystical meaning behind this label?

✓ *Cabernet Sauvignon* • *Classic red blend* (MC^2) • *Shiraz*

ST HALLETT
Barossa Valley
★★

Part of Banksia, which was taken over by Lion Nathan in 2001, this long-established winery still makes splendidly rich wines. Indeed, the quality has deepened over the last few years. GST is a blend of Grenache, Shiraz, and Touriga. It is also a pun on GST (Goods Services Tax), but that's only 10 per cent of the story.

✓ *Cabernet Sauvignon* • *Classic red blend* (GST) • *Merlot* • *Riesling* (Eden Valley) • *Shiraz* (Blackwell, Old Block)

SALTRAM
Barossa Valley
★★

Saltram has refocused on its red wines, for which it was once justifiably famous, and is again today.

✓ *Cabernet Sauvignon* (Mamre Brook) • *Chardonnay* (Mamre Brook) • *Classic red blend* (Barossa Cabernet-Merlot) • *Shiraz* (Mamre Brook, No.1 Reserve, The Eighth Maker)

SEAVIEW WINERY
McLaren Vale
★☆Ⓥ

Now part of Southcorp, Seaview has the edge over its sister Seppelt brand with its entry-level wines, although Seppelt wins hands down in the premium category.

✓ *Sparkling* (Blanc de Blancs, Edwards & Chaffey, Pinot Noir-Chardonnay)

SEPPELT
Barossa Valley
★★★☆Ⓥ

Seppelt Great Western in Victoria is Southcorp's sparkling wine specialist, while this Seppelt, in Seppeltsfield of the Barossa Valley, is its fortified wine specialist. Even though part of a corporate empire, Seppelt remains as priceless a piece of Australia's wine history as it has ever been, and Southcorp has emphasized that by restricting this winery and cellars exclusively to fortified wine. Table wines used to be made here, but no longer – they are all sourced from Victoria. The entire range of Seppelt's fortified wine is recommended, none more so than the Para range of liqueur ports. Yet it is with these wines that I have my only quibble. Or, more accurately, with the bottles that contain the wines. Worst of all is the Para 100 Year Old Liqueur Port, vintages of which easily fetch between A$1,000 and A$2,000 a bottle, and is contained in a bottle that is a cross between a pretentious Cognac bottle and Mateus! What is wrong with a top-quality classic bottle shape?

✓ *Entire range*

SHAW & SMITH
Adelaide Hills
★★Ⓥ

This venture was set up in 1989 by Martin Shaw, who is well known for his flying winemaker activities, and Michael Hill-Smith, the first Australian to become a Master of Wine. After squatting at Petaluma for a decade, Shaw & Smith built their own high-tech winery at Balhannah in 2000.

✓ *Chardonnay* (M3) • *Sauvignon Blanc* • *Merlot* • *Shiraz*

SKILLOGALEE
Clare Valley
★☆Ⓥ

Owner-winemaker David Palmer produces increasingly stylish wines from his 60-hectare (150-acre) property, particularly the Riesling.

✓ *Classic red blend* (The Cabernets) • *Riesling* • *Shiraz*

TAPANAPPA WINES
Wrattonbully
❓

This must be one to watch: a partnership formed between Brian Croser, Champagne Bollinger (which was a major shareholder in Petaluma before the takeover by Lion Nathan), and Jean-Michel Cazes of Château Lynch-Bages in Bordeaux. This high-powered trio has purchased Koppamurra Vineyard in Wrattonbully. Tapanappa is named after a sandstone formation near Croser's beach house. Apparently it is an Aboriginal word meaning "stick to the path" – and a lot of people will be watching to see if they live up to this!

TATACHILLA
McLaren Vale
★★Ⓥ

Part of Banksia, which was taken over by Lion Nathan in 2001, this long-established winery has increased tremendously its already excellent quality and value over the last five years or so. Keystone is a Grenache-Shiraz blend, while Partners is Cabernet Sauvignon-Shiraz.

✓ *Cabernet Sauvignon* (McLaren Vale, Padthaway) • *Classic red blend* (Keystone, Partners) • *Merlot* (Adelaide Hills, Clarendon Vineyard) • *Shiraz* (Foundation, McLaren Vale) • *Sparkling* (Sparkling Malbec)

TAYLORS
Clare Vale
★★★☆Ⓥ

The basic Cabernet Sauvignon, Shiraz, and Riesling would probably be singled out at any other winery. They're not just some of the best bargains in Australia, but some of the country's greatest wines too. The St Andrews range is, however, in a different league, as is part of the relatively new Jaraman range. The best classic red blend is the Promised Land Shiraz-Cabernet, but it too cannot live in the company of those recommended below. Wines also sold under the Wakefield label (the Cabernet Sauvignon and Merlot can be brilliant).

✓ *Cabernet Sauvignon* (Jaraman, St Andrews) • *Chardonnay* (Jaraman) • *Riesling* (Jaraman, Clare, St Andrews) • *Shiraz* (St Andrews)

TOLLANA
Barossa Valley
★☆Ⓥ

Once entirely estate-produced, Tollana is now part of Southcorp, and I used to think this had not affected its identity, quality, or value, but is it my imagination or is this brand, which dates from 1888, disappearing before our very eyes? It is like watching a grand old ship steam into the horizon.

✓ *Botrytis* (Riesling) • *Cabernet Sauvignon* (Bin TR222) • *Shiraz* (Bin TR16)

TORBRECK
Barossa Valley
★★★☆Ⓥ

The antithesis of Tollana, Torbreck is relatively young (1994), privately owned, and all of a sudden making headlines (thanks in part to US critic Robert Parker's gushing accolades). Both RunRig and Descendant are

Shiraz-Viognier blends, but the former will set you back A$200–250, whereas the latter costs a mere A$125–150 – so what is the difference? Well, RunRig contains just 3 per cent of Viognier, compared to 8 per cent in Descendant. Furthermore, the Viognier is vinified separately for RunRig, whereas both grapes are crushed and fermented together for Descendant, which makes the cheaper wine (if it is possible to describe Descendant as cheaper) more classic in French terms. They are each from different vineyards, the Descendant vineyard having been planted from cuttings from RunRig, hence the name. Descendant spends 18 months in 2- to 3-year-old French oak, whereas RunRig is given 30 months in French oak, 60 per cent of which is new. The Steading is Grenache, Mataro (Mourvèdre), and Shiraz, while Cuvée Juveniles is a full-throttle, fruit-driven, unoaked blend of Grenache, Shiraz, and Mataro. Juveniles is all old vines, but best drunk as young and as fresh as possible. VMR is a Viognier, Marsanne, and Roussanne blend, with winning acidity balance. The Bothie is Torbeck's interpretation of a Muscat de Beaumes-de-Venise.

✓ *Classic red blend* (Cuvée Juveniles, Descendant, RunRig, The Steading) • *Classic white blend* (VMR) • *Grenache* (Les Amis) • *Fortified* (The Bothie) • *Shiraz* (The Factor, The Struie)

TURKEY FLAT
Barossa Valley
★★♥

Turkey Flat is a high-flying winery producing several exceptionally rich, lush, complex red wines from superbly sited vineyards, the core of which are over 150 years old. Butcher's Block is a blend of Mataro (Mourvèdre), Shiraz, and Grenache.

✓ *Cabernet Sauvignon* • *Classic red blend* (Butcher's Block) • *Classic white blend* (Marsanne Sémillon) • *Fortified* (Pedro Ximénez) • *Grenache Noir* • *Rosé* • *Shiraz*

GEOFF WEAVER
Adelaide Hills
★★♥

For four years Geoff Weaver was chief winemaker for the entire Hardys wine group, which effectively made him personally responsible for 10 per cent of Australia's entire wine production. Not the sort of pressure that many of us would want to endure for too long, so little surprise that he left to pursue his own small wine operation in 1992. He had in fact planted his vineyard at Lenswood 10 years earlier, so it was nicely matured, and wines had been made on a part-time basis since 1986. Weaver's vineyard was also history in the making, as it

was a pioneering venture into an untried region.

✓ *Chardonnay* • *Classic red blend* (Cabernet-Merlot) • *Pinot Noir* • *Riesling* • *Sauvignon Blanc*

WENDOUREE
Clare Valley
★★✦♥

One of Australia's icon wineries since the late 19th century. Wendouree's current CEO-winemaker, Tony Brady, has continued to produce some of this country's longest-lived reds since taking over in 1974. Shiraz is the jewel in Wendouree's crown, but given some bottle-age, Brady's wonderfully individual and expressive blended reds are near equals.

✓ *Cabernet Sauvignon* • *Classic red blend* (Shiraz-Malbec, Shiraz-Mataro, Cabernet Sauvignon-Malbec) • *Shiraz*

WIRRA WIRRA
McLaren Vale
★★

When Greg and Roger Trott took over Wirra Wirra in 1969, it was a wreck, literally. But the Trotts built it into a stylish winery making stylish wines, helped in the early days by that dynamic flying winemaker duo, Croser & Jordan (or should that be Jordan & Croser?). Croser returned for a stint as managing director, when he grew restless having achieved everything he had set out to do at Domaine Chandon, but returned to that fold when LVMH made him an offer he couldn't refuse. Whoever Greg Trott has had around the place, Wirra Wirra has always had an excellent reputation, but over the last few years the quality has become more exciting and deepened across the range.

✓ *Cabernet Sauvignon* (The Angelus) • *Chardonnay* • *Classic red blend* (Grenache-Shiraz) • *Fortified* (VP Vintage Fortified Shiraz) • *Grenache* (McLaren Vale) • *Shiraz* (Church Block, McLaren Vale, RSW)

WOLF BLASS
Barossa Valley
★✦♥

This company is now part of Beringer Blass, but its range is still huge and the wines are marketed as aggressively as ever. Wolf Blass wines are mostly graded according to the colour of their label, which works well enough, although the Yellow Label tends to be more cheap than cheerful these days (the last exception being the 1999 Yellow Label Cabernet Sauvignon, which really did punch above its weight). The Red Label is cheaper than the Yellow, and Eaglehawk cheaper still (but try the Riesling!). Contrary to what most people intuitively think, the pecking order after Yellow Label is Gold, Grey, Black, and, logically, at the very

top comes Platinum. It is this role reversal of what the colours really mean that has been the genius of Wolf Blass marketing, and no Australian winery is more marketing-driven than Wolf Blass, but its best wines have to be among the country's most prolific award-winners for this to work, and that has always been so. By 1990, the total number of awards that Wolf Blass had garnered stood at 2,575, including an amazing 135 trophies and no fewer than 712 gold medals. That was more than 20 years ago. Who knows what the total is nowadays, but I can safely say that at the upper end of the Wolf Blass range, the quality has never been better. The Grey Label, which has been around since 1967, has replaced the Brown Label, but I've retained the Brown Label recommendations as the wines will be around for some time to come.

✓ *Cabernet Sauvignon-Shiraz* (Black Label, Grey Label, Platinum Label, President's Selection) • *Classic red blend* (Black Label Cabernet Sauvignon-Shiraz, Grey Label Cabernet Sauvignon-Shiraz) • *Riesling* (Clare Valley, Eaglehawk, Gold Label, South Australia) • *Shiraz* (Brown Label, McLaren Vale Reserve, Platinum Label, President's Selection)

WOODSTOCK
McLaren Vale
★★✦

Doug and Mary Collett acquired a 10-hectare (25-acre), derelict vineyard and an old cottage named Woodstock in 1973. Apparently, the Townsend family had settled there in 1859, from Woodstock in Oxfordshire, England, which was the origin of the name. In fact I wrote the first and all successive editions of this encyclopedia in Witney, which is just a few miles from Woodstock. The Townsend name is still common in these parts. They are probably all distantly related to the original settlers of this property. The Colletts should try to get a local importer. The good folk of Woodstock would probably treat it as their house wine, making it as popular in its restaurants as Oxford Landing is in that city. Five Feet is a blend of Cabernet Sauvignon, Shiraz, Merlot, and Petit Verdot. The name supposedly comes from the wooden stocks found in English Woodstock, which had five holes for five feet – pull the other one!

✓ *Classic red blend* (Five Feet) • *Shiraz* (The Stocks)

WYNNS
Coonawarra
★✦♥

John Riddoch is supposed to be the top wine here, but, superb as it is, the straight Black Label Cabernet Sauvignon, although disappointingly thin during the 1980s, has been the epitome of elegance ever since, and, at half the price of John

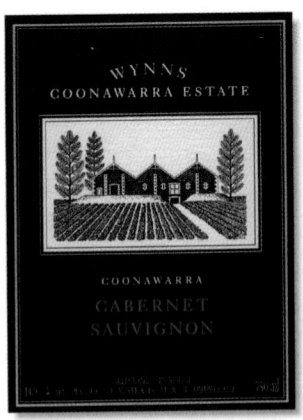

Riddoch, represents much better value. The Michael Shiraz in on a par with the John Riddoch, in terms of quality and price, but the basic Shiraz is not the equivalent of the Black Label Cabernet Sauvignon, neither is it meant to be, as its much cheaper price indicates. Wynns is part of Southcorp.

✓ *Cabernet Sauvignon* • *Chardonnay* • *Classic red blend* (Cabernet Shiraz-Merlot) • *Shiraz* • *Riesling*

YALUMBA
Barossa Valley
★★★✦

This winery produces a vast range of styles and qualities, both still and sparkling. The Reserve and The Signature are both blends of Cabernet Sauvignon and Shiraz. Mesh is a Yalumba-Grosset collaboration. Oxford Landing is its penny-pinching, entry-level brand, offering very good value for money. Yalumba also owns Heggies Vineyard in Eden Valley, and Nautilus in New Zealand.

✓ *Cabernet Sauvignon* (The Menzies) • *Chardonnay* (Adelaide Hills, Heggies) • *Classic red blend* (Barossa Valley Shiraz-Viognier, Hand Picked Mourvèdre-Grenache-Shiraz, The Reserve, The Signature) • *Fortified* (all Museum Release wines) • *Pinot Noir* (Adelaide Hills) • *Riesling* (Hand Picked Eden Valley, Mesh) • *Shiraz* (The Octavius) • *Sparkling* (Cuvée One, Cuvée Two, D since 1989, D Black, NV Jansz, vintaged Jansz since 1997) • *Viognier* (Eden Valley, The Virgilius Eden Valley)

ZEMA ESTATE
Coonawarra
★★✦♥

Established in 1982 by the Zema family, who currently cultivate 60 hectares (150 acres) of prime *terra rossa* land in Coonawarra. Cluny is a blend of Cabernet Sauvignon, Merlot, Cabernet Franc, and Malbec.

✓ *Cabernet Sauvignon* (Family Selection) • *Classic red blend* (Cluny) • *Shiraz* (Family Selection)

WESTERN AUSTRALIA

Much to the chagrin of winemakers in the rest of the country, Western Australia attracts a disproportionate amount of media attention for a state that possesses just 7 per cent of Australia's vineyards. But it is no coincidence that from that 7 per cent, Western Australia produces a mere 3 per cent of the grapes crushed.

WITHOUT WORLD-CLASS WINE REGIONS such as Margaret River, Western Australia could not produce world-class wines, but restricting yields enables those wines to stand out. Coonawarra might be Australia's most famous wine region, but South Australia is also a prolific producer of cheap wine. Apart from Western Australia, the only other state to harvest a smaller percentage of the country's crop than its vineyards represent is Victoria, and the best wines from that state's myriad top-performing wine regions also receive disproportionate publicity.

HOW IT ALL BEGAN
The vineyards of Western Australia were established in 1829, by either Thomas Waters or Captain John Septimus Roe. If the founder was Roe, he would not have made any wine; his vines were grown to produce table grapes and raisins. Waters, on the other hand, bought 8 hectares (20 acres) of land that was to become Olive Farm. Waters was a botanist who had learned his

VASSE FELIX WINERY
A modern pioneering vineyard in the Margaret River region, Australia's first appellation of origin, Vasse Felix still produces a fine Cabernet Sauvignon.

winemaking skills from Boers in South Africa. He arrived in Australia with numerous seeds and plants, and by 1842 was making and bartering wine. In 1835, King William IV granted over 3,000 hectares (7,400 acres) of Swan Valley land to one Henry Revett Bland, who sold it to a trio of British army officers. These

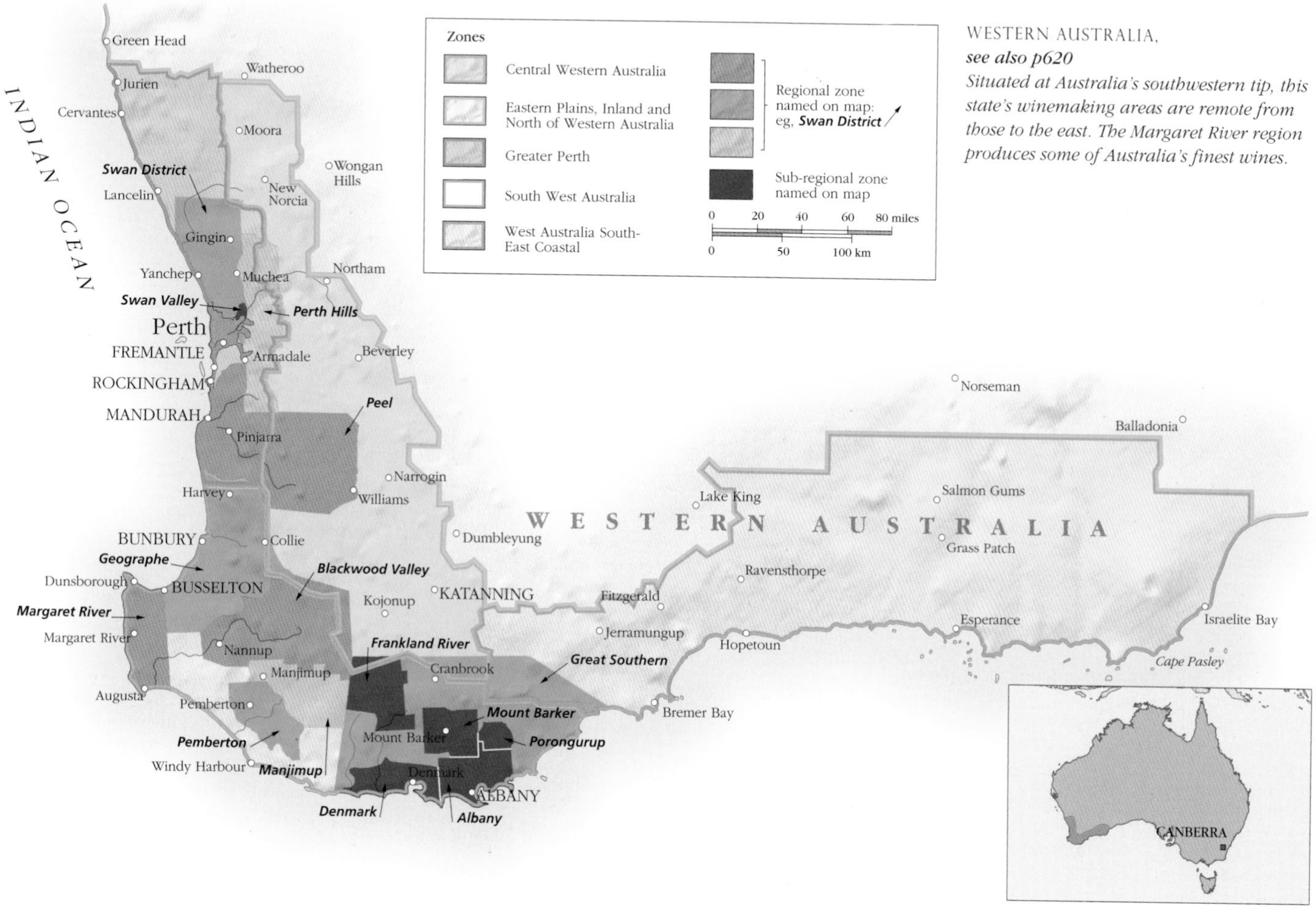

WESTERN AUSTRALIA,
see also p620
Situated at Australia's southwestern tip, this state's winemaking areas are remote from those to the east. The Margaret River region produces some of Australia's finest wines.

Map

Zones
- Central Western Australia
- Eastern Plains, Inland and North of Western Australia
- Greater Perth
- South West Australia
- West Australia South-East Coastal

Regional zone named on map: eg, *Swan District*

Sub-regional zone named on map

0 20 40 60 80 miles
0 50 100 km

INDIAN OCEAN

Green Head
Jurien
Watheroo
Cervantes
Moora
Swan District
Lancelin
Wongan Hills
New Norcia
Gingin
Northam
Yanchep
Muchea
Swan Valley
Perth Hills
Perth
FREMANTLE
Armadale
Beverley
ROCKINGHAM
MANDURAH
Peel
Pinjarra
Narrogin
Harvey
Williams
BUNBURY
Collie
Dumbleyung
Geographe
Blackwood Valley
Dunsborough
BUSSELTON
Kojonup
KATANNING
Margaret River
Fitzgerald
Margaret River
Nannup
Frankland River
Jerramungup
Augusta
Manjimup
Cranbrook
Great Southern
Pemberton
Mount Barker
Porongurup
Windy Harbour
Mount Barker
Denmark
ALBANY
Manjimup
Denmark
Albany

W E S T E R N   A U S T R A L I A
Norseman
Balladonia
Lake King
Salmon Gums
Grass Patch
Ravensthorpe
Esperance
Israelite Bay
Hopetoun
Cape Pasley
Bremer Bay

CANBERRA

SWAN VALLEY VINEYARDS
This flat plain belongs to one of the hottest winegrowing regions in the world, and the first of Western Australia's wine districts to be established.

FACTORS AFFECTING TASTE AND QUALITY

LOCATION
Western Australia's vine-growing areas sweep around the southwestern corner of Australia from Perth to Albany.

CLIMATE
This is very variable, from the long, very hot, dry summers and short, wet winters of the Swan Valley, one of the hottest winegrowing areas of the world, through the Mediterranean-type conditions of the Margaret River, with a higher rainfall and summer heat tempered by ocean breezes such as the "Fremantle Doctor" and "Albany Doctor", to the even cooler Lower Great Southern Area, which also has some light rainfall in summer. Ocean winds can exacerbate salinity problems and high coastal humidity helps with the development of botrytis.

ASPECT
Most vines are planted on the relatively flat coastal plain and river valley basins, but also on some rather more undulating, hilly areas, such as those around Denmark and Mount Barker near Albany in the south and east of the region. Vineyards generally grow at an altitude of between 90 and 250 metres (295 and 820 feet), but can be as high as 340 metres (1,115 feet) in the Blackwood Valley.

SOIL
Soils are fairly homogenous,

being mainly deep, free-draining, alluvial, sandy, gravelly, or clay loams over clay subsoils. Loam soils such as karri and marri are named after the gum trees that used to grow on them, and have significantly different properties. The Geographe area has a fine, white-grey topsoil called tuart sand, over a base of limestone with gravel in parts of the Margaret River.

VITICULTURE AND VINIFICATION
Drip irrigation is widespread because of the general lack of summer rain and the free-draining nature of the soil, although, ironically, winter water-logging due to clay subsoils is also a problem. Wide planting, mechanized harvesting, and the use of the most modern vinification techniques typify the area, which has generally concentrated on developing the cooler regions away from the Swan Valley in recent years. Well-equipped boutique wineries dominate the Margaret River wine regions.

GRAPE VARIETIES
Primary varieties: Cabernet Sauvignon, Chardonnay, Merlot, Riesling, Sauvignon Blanc, Sémillon, Shiraz (Syrah)
Secondary varieties: Cabernet Franc, Chenin Blanc, Malbec, Muscat Gordo Blanco (Muscat d'Alexandrie), Pinot Noir, Tokay (Muscadelle), Verdelho, Zinfandel

new owners, Messrs Lowis, Yule, and Houghton, were stationed in India, but Yule was despatched by the senior officer, Colonel Houghton, to run the property. Thus Houghton Wines, the first commercial winery in Western Australia, takes its name from a man who never set foot in the country.

The Swan Valley remained the hub of the state's wine industry and, with an influx of Europeans, all experienced in viticulture and

winemaking, the expertise of this industry grew. Gradually, Mount Barker evolved as a wine area, then Frankland, and last, but certainly not least, Margaret River. For most non-Australian wine drinkers, it is the last of these appellations that has provided the greatest excitement and pleasure. Neither the climate nor the soil of the Margaret River is special in itself, but combined they produce grapes of unparalleled purity and finesse.

THE APPELLATIONS OF
WESTERN AUSTRALIA

ALBANY GI
One of five sub-regional GIs within the Great Southern region, Albany has a Mediterranean climate that is moderated by sea breezes known locally as the "Albany Doctor". Soils suitable for viticulture are quite patchy, and mostly confined to the slopes. Pinot Noir has something of a reputation thanks, primarily, to Bill Wignall (Wignall Wines), but Cabernet Sauvignon, Chardonnay, and Sauvignon Blanc probably perform at least as well.

BLACKWOOD VALLEY GI
This GI is the least known and one of the newest of Western Australia's wine regions, sandwiched between Manjimup and Geographe. The first vineyard was Blackwood Crest, planted by Max

Fairbrass in 1976, and by 2004 there were over 50 vineyards and 10 wineries. The climate is Mediterranean, with dry summers and wet winters. Vines grow at an elevation of 100 to 340 metres (330 to 1,115 feet) on gravelly loam soils, which are thinner and more gravelly, with some red earths, on the steeper slopes. Cabernet Sauvignon is the most widely planted variety and the most successful, with Shiraz on the increase. Other grapes include Chardonnay, Riesling, Sauvignon Blanc, and Sémillon.

CENTRAL WESTERN AUSTRALIA GI
This zonal GI covers a vast area of the Darling Ranges, from the Great Southern GI to north of the

Swan District, but size is the only impressive aspect of what is currently a viticultural wasteland.

DENMARK GI
The newest sub-region within the Great Southern GI, Denmark is situated some 60 kilometres (37 miles) along the coast from Albany. With its wet winters and warm to hot summers, the ocean's moderating influence, and a mix of marri and karri loam soils, the focus here has quite rightly been on Chardonnay and Pinot Noir. Other varieties grown include Cabernet Franc, Cabernet Sauvignon, Sauvignon Blanc, Sémillon, and Shiraz. The etymological origin of this Denmark had nothing to do with the Scandinavian country, but was named after Dr Alexander Denmark, an English naval surgeon.

EASTERN PLAINS, INLAND AND NORTH OF WESTERN AUSTRALIA GI

Hardly rolls off the tongue, does it? I sincerely doubt that any wines will be sold under this zonal GI, which is the ultimate expression of bureaucratic logic, referring to all areas of Western Australia not already covered.

FRANKLAND RIVER GI

A small area on the western edge of the Great Southern zone, Frankland River was put on the map by Houghton. This GI is, however, something of a misnomer, as four rivers converge in this sub-region: the Frankland, Gordon, Kent, and Tone. The climate is more Continental than Mediterranean, and, unlike the other sub-regions of the Great Southern zone, Frankland River has virtually no maritime influence. Surprisingly crisp Rieslings are made here. It is also good for Cabernet Sauvignon. Other grapes grown include Chardonnay, Sauvignon Blanc, and Shiraz.

GEOGRAPHE GI

Formerly known as the Southwest Coastal Plains, this regional GI takes in the curve of land on Geographe Bay, where the somewhat Mediterranean climate is cooled and humidified by the Indian Ocean. The region extends inland, where it creeps eastward into the foothills of the Darling Range. Geographe has a limestone subsoil, and is dissected by four rivers, the Capel, Collie, Ferguson, and Harvey, which have deposited alluvial soils that have a much higher nutrient content than the deep sandy soils in the coastal areas. Chardonnay is perhaps the most successful variety, followed by Cabernet Sauvignon and Merlot, with Sémillon and Shiraz on the rise.

GREAT SOUTHERN GI

Sub-regions:

Albany, Denmark, Frankland River, Mount Barker, Porongurup

This regional GI is the coolest of Western Australia's viticultural areas, and, although it has similar climatic influences to Margaret River, it has a lower rainfall. The vineyards are scattered throughout a vast area, and mostly consist of Riesling, Cabernet Sauvignon, Shiraz, Malbec, Pinot Noir, and Chardonnay.

GREATER PERTH GI

This zonal GI encompasses the regional GIs of the Peel, Perth Hills, and Swan District.

MANJIMUP GI

This GI is immediately north of Pemberton, on the same latitude as the Margaret River. Manjimup GI finalization was delayed because some producers wanted to be part of Pemberton, but the two regions differ in both soils and climate. Manjimup is warmer, with more sunshine and less humidity, while the marri loam is less fertile, having more sand and gravel than Pemberton's karri loam. In addition to wines produced by local boutique wineries, the region also sells a lot of its fruit to other wineries in the state. Chardonnay is the most widely planted variety, but Cabernet Sauvignon and Merlot fare best. There is more hope than promise for Pinot Noir, even though Picardy, the region's top producer, makes excellent wines from this grape. Other grapes grown include Sauvignon Blanc and Verdelho.

MARGARET RIVER GI

This regional GI remains Australia's premier region for wine lovers who seek class and finesse, rather than weight and glory. Situated south of Perth, the Margaret River district attracted much attention in 1978 when it established Australia's first Appellation of Origin system. Like similar schemes, it was unsuccessful. The first vineyard was planted in the Margaret River area at Bunbury as long ago as 1890. However, it was a vineyard planted by Dr Tom Cullity at Vasse Felix in 1967 that was the first step in the Margaret River's journey to success. The region follows a ridge that runs along the coast from Cape Naturaliste to Cape Leeuwin in the south, with Margaret River flowing westward through its centre, while the Blackwood River flows southwest to Augusta. The land is undulating, with vines planted up to a maximum altitude of 90 metres (295 feet) on gravelly, sandy loams, with the majority of vineyards and wineries located in and around Wilyabrup. The warm maritime climate is cooled by ocean breezes, with most rain falling in autumn and winter. Relatively minor problems do exist in the area, notably powdery mildew, parrots, wind, and, most serious, dry summers. The powdery mildew seems to be under control, and the vineyard workers plant sunflowers to distract the parrots from the vines, while rye grass acts as a windbreak. A lot of vines experience water-stress, not a heat-related problem, but dry-summer induced, and one that is exacerbated by the wind factor. The greatness of Margaret River wines cannot be disputed. This quality of fruit is not bettered by any other Australian wine region. The best varieties are Cabernet Sauvignon, Chardonnay, Sauvignon Blanc, Sémillon, and Shiraz.

MOUNT BARKER GI

A sub-region of the Great Southern zonal GI, where vines enjoy a Mediterranean climate, and grow at altitudes of 180 to 250 metres (590 to 820 feet) on gravelly-sandy loams over gently undulating hills. Growers avoid the valley floors due to the salinity of their soils. Mount Barker has a reputation for its lime-laden Riesling, and elegant red wines from Cabernet Sauvignon and Shiraz. Pinot Noir has also won awards. Other varieties grown include Cabernet Franc, Chardonnay, Malbec, Merlot, Sauvignon Blanc, Sémillon, and Shiraz.

PEEL GI

This large region takes in the Peel Inlet just south of Mandurah, where the vines enjoy a Mediterranean climate that is cooled and moderated by this large body of water, backed up by the Indian Ocean, although this effect diminishes further inland. The soils are extremely diverse, and range from deep, free-draining tuart sand on the coast to sandy-alluvium on the plains, with marri-jarrah loams, yellow duplex soils, and gravel further inland. Although vines were planted at Pinjarra as early as 1857, and remained productive for 40 years, it was not until the 1970s that viticulture in this region underwent sustained development. Chenin Blanc and Shiraz are the primary varieties. Other grapes grown include Cabernet Sauvignon, Chardonnay, Merlot, Sémillon, Shiraz, and Verdelho.

PEMBERTON GI

This GI south of Manjimup is one of Western Australia's less consistent wine regions, but with vineyards established in the 1980s and 1990s, it is still a young area and the locals are still confident. Pemberton is commonly known as "Karri country" after its magnificent forests of Karri gum trees,

which give their name to the soil in which they grow. Karri loam is a deep, red, fertile soil that is too fertile for vines, causing excessive vigour problems, although growers overcome this by deliberate water-stressing and hard pruning to control the canopy. Pemberton was originally thought to be a Pinot Noir area, but Cabernet Sauvignon, Merlot, and Shiraz have been far more successful. Other varieties grown include Chardonnay, Sauvignon Blanc, Sémillon, and Verdelho.

PERTH HILLS GI

This regional GI is adjacent to the Swan Valley and consists of a strip of the lower slopes of the Darling Ranges. Although this area has a hot climate, it is higher and cooler than the Swan Valley, with grapes ripening some two weeks later. Cabernet Sauvignon and Chardonnay are the most successful grapes, with Chenin Blanc, Shiraz, and Pinot Noir the other primary varieties grown.

PORONGURUP GI

Set against a backdrop of the Porongurup Ranges, this picturesque region is one of five sub-regional GIs encompassed by the Great Southern region. The vines benefit from a Mediterranean climate, and grow on granite-based karri loam soils. The primary varieties are Cabernet Franc, Cabernet Sauvignon, Chardonnay, Merlot, Pinot Noir, Riesling, Sémillon, Shiraz, and Verdelho.

SOUTH WEST AUSTRALIA GI

This zonal GI encompasses the majority of Western Australia's most exciting wine areas, including the regional GIs of Blackwood Valley, Geographe, Great Southern, Manjimup, Margaret River, and Pemberton.

SWAN DISTRICT GI

Sub-region:

Swan Valley

This regional GI contains the Swan Valley itself, but also extends northwards from Perth, encompassing former unclassified areas such as Gingin and Moondah Brook.

SWAN VALLEY GI

This sub-regional GI is located northeast of Perth, and represents the heart and soul of the Swan District zone. The Swan Valley has the dubious distinction of being one of the hottest viticultural regions in the world. Partly because of this, and partly as a reaction to the phenomenal success of the Margaret River, several producers have deserted the area and the number of vineyards is shrinking. What was once the traditional centre of Western Australia's wine industry is now a waning force, although the best areas are cooled by the so-called "Fremantle Doctor" wind, allowing the old-fashioned, foursquare wines to be replaced by lighter and fresher styles. If the Swan Valley can claim to make any classic wine whatsoever, it has to be fortified wines made from the Muscat Gordo Blanco and Muscadelle grapes. Other important varieties include Cabernet Sauvignon, Chardonnay, Merlot, Sémillon, and Shiraz.

WEST AUSTRALIAN SOUTH EAST COASTAL GI

This zonal GI covers a large swathe of coastal area that lies immediately to the east of the Great Southern zone.

THE WINE PRODUCERS OF
WESTERN AUSTRALIA

ALKOOMI WINES
Frankland
★★Ⓥ

Sheep farmers Mervyn and Judy Lange established this venture in 1971, making their first wines five years later. They always used to produce fresh, fruity, and rich-flavoured wines that could be recommended with confidence, but were seldom special. However, since the mid-to-late 1990s the quality, style, and expressiveness have become ever more impressive. Blackbutt is a blend of Malbec, Cabernet Sauvignon, Cabernet Franc, and Merlot. Young, easy-drinking wines are sold under the Sutherlands label.

✓ *Cabernet Sauvignon* (Frankland River) • *Classic red blend* (Blackbutt) • *Riesling* (Frankland River) • *Sémillon* (Wandoo) • *Shiraz* (Jarrah)

AMBERLEY ESTATE
Margaret River
★Ⓥ

Eddie Price, a former chief winemaker at Brown Brothers, is the managing director and winemaker at Amberley, where most wines offer good value, but Shiraz excels.

✓ *Sémillon* (First Selection) • *Shiraz*

ASHBROOK ESTATE
Margaret River
★★Ⓥ

Great quality, and even better value.

✓ *Chardonnay* • *Classic red blend* (Cabernet-Merlot) • *Sémillon* • *Verdelho*

BROOKLAND VALLEY
Margaret River
★★Ⓥ◉

Malcolm and Deirdre Jones established Brookland Valley in 1984, with BRL Hardy purchasing a 50 per cent shareholding in 1997. Since then the quality has gone from good to excellent.

✓ *Chardonnay* • *Classic red blend*

(Cabernet-Merlot, Verse 1 Cabernet-Merlot) • *Classic white blend* (Verse 1 Sémillon-Sauvignon Blanc) • *Merlot* • *Sémillon* (Verse 1)

CAPE MENTELLE
Margaret River
★★★⁄Ⓥ

Referred to by locals as the "Mentelle asylum", this is where David Hohnen started his cult-driven empire, which included New Zealand's Cloudy Bay phenomenon. He retired in 2003, to be succeeded by Dr Tony Jordan, who now oversees all of LVMH's operations in Australia and New Zealand. The quality remains exemplary, showing an uncanny ability to straddle both Old and New World styles, respecting tradition, and understanding restraint and finesse, yet revealing the best of Margaret River's ripe fruit flavours. This is the legacy of Hohnen's own philosophy, and it even applies to the Zinfandel, which under Cape Mentelle boasts infinitely more finesse than many a California icon of this variety. Marmaduke is primarily Shiraz-Grenache-Mataro (Mourvèdre), with a little Merlot and Pinot Noir. Trinders is Cabernet Sauvignon and Merlot, with a little Cabernet Franc and Petit Verdot. Georgina is Sauvignon Blanc and Chardonnay, with a little Sémillon and Chenin Blanc. Wallcliffe is a blend of Sauvignon Blanc and Sémillon.

✓ *Cabernet Sauvignon* • *Chardonnay* • *Classic red blend* (Marmaduke, Trinders) • *Classic white blend* (Georgina, Sémillon-Sauvignon, Wallcliffe) • *Shiraz* • *Zinfandel*

CAPEL VALE WINES
Geographe
★⁄★

Owner Peter Pratten, a former radiologist, is the driving force behind this expanding brand, which is known for its delicious, vibrantly fruity wines.

✓ *Cabernet Sauvignon* • *Classic white blend* (Sauvignon Blanc-Sémillon) • *Merlot* (Howecroft) • *Riesling* (Whispering Hill) • *Shiraz* (Kinnaird, Mount Barker Trifecta)

CHATSFIELD
Mount Barker
★Ⓥ

Irish-born Dr Ken Lynch has a well-established record for producing easy-drinking wines, especially his ripe, peachy Riesling.

✓ *Cabernet Franc* (Soft Red) • *Chardonnay* • *Riesling* • *Shiraz*

CLAIRAULT
Margaret River
★⁄★ Ⓥ

The Martin family has expanded the vineyards, aiming to become biodynamic, and has taken the quality of the wines to new heights.

✓ *Cabernet Sauvignon* • *Chardonnay* • *Classic red blend* (Claddagh Reserve) • *Classic white blend* (Sémillon-Sauvignon Blanc) • *Riesling* • *Sémillon*

CULLEN WINES
Margaret River
★★★⁄◉

Di Cullen sadly passed away in 2003, leaving the winery that she

and her late husband Kevin established in 1966 in the hands of her youngest daughter, Vanya. She could not have left the business in safer hands. Vanya Cullen has been the winemaker since 1989, and makes an outstanding range of wines, which get better with every vintage. If winemakers of the stature of Dr Andrew Pirie are eager to subject themselves to a masterclass with her, it is little wonder that she was voted Australia's Winemaker of the Year in 2000. Cullen is an organic producer that is converting to biodynamic and, in 2006, became Australia's first carbon-neutral winery.

✓ *Entire range*

DEVIL'S LAIR
Margaret River
★★Ⓥ

Planted in 1981, and purchased by Southcorp in 1996, Devil's Lair takes it name from the nearby Devil's Lair cave, where the fossil remains of the so-called Tasmanian devil have been discovered. The Cabernets blend of Cabernet Sauvignon, Cabernet Franc, and Merlot is deep, dark, and yet finely structured, showing great potential. The Fifth Leg wines are more for ready drinking, but they are fine, elegant wines nonetheless.

✓ *Classic red blend* (Cabernet, Fifth Leg Red) • *Classic white blend* (Fifth Leg White)

EDWARDS WINES
Margaret River
★★

Sensational wines, particularly reds, from brothers Michael and Christo Edwards.

✓ *Entire range*

EVANS & TATE
Margaret River
★★⁄

This winery used to own vineyards in the Swan Valley, as well as the Margaret River, but it has sold off its Swan Valley holdings. In March 2003, Evans & Tate purchased the cash-strapped Cranswick Estates for A$100 million, but despite the latter's precarious financial situation, it fuelled Evans & Tate's profits by more than 40 per cent in the first year, and in excess of 70 per cent the second year. The best wines at Evans & Tate combine richness with finesse.

✔ *Cabernet-Merlot* (Barrique 61) •
Chardonnay • *Merlot* • *Sémillon*
• *Sémillon-Sauvignon* • *Shiraz*

FERMOY
ESTATE
Margaret River
★ **V**

The most consistent wines produced
at the Fermoy Estate now are
Chardonnay and Merlot. A new
range has been launched under
the Sentinel label, but has yet to
make its mark.

✔ *Chardonnay* • *Merlot*

FERNGROVE VINEYARDS
Great Southern
★☆ **V**

Murray Burton ordered the first
vines to be planted in 1996, and
now has over 400 hectares (1,000
acres) of vineyards, plus a brand-
new winery built in 1999. Since
then these wines have really
taken off, reaching orbit with
the 2002 Cossack Riesling, which
won a record seven trophies
and four golds.

✔ *Classic white blend* (Sémillon-
Sauvignon Blanc) • *Riesling*
(Cossack) • *Shiraz*

FLAMETREE
Margaret River
★★☆

Every wine this family-owned
winery has produced since its
start-up in 2007 has been jaw-
droppingly fabulous.

✔ *Entire range*

FLINDERS BAY
Margaret River
★ **V**

Established in 1995 as a joint
venture between two families, the
grape-growing Gillespies and wine-
retailing Irelands.

✔ *Classic white blend* (Pericles
Sauvignon-Sémillon Blanc) •
Merlot • *Shiraz*

FRANKLAND ESTATE
Frankland
★ **V**

Frankland Estate is best for its
blended red, which consists of
Cabernets, Merlot, and Malbec. It
is dedicated to the late Professor
Olmo, California's famous grape
breeder, not for creating varieties
such as Ruby Cabernet, but because
he was instrumental in selecting
areas of Frankland best suited to
viticulture in the early days of this
wine region. Olmo's Reward is a
blend of Cabernet Franc and Merlot
primarily, supported by Malbec,
Cabernet Sauvignon, and Petit
Verdot. Poison Hill refers to the
heartleaf plant growing there,
which is poisonous to sheep and
dogs, and thus was a threat to
early settlers.

✔ *Classic red blend* (Olmo's
Reward) • *Riesling* (Isolation
Bridge, Poison Hill)

GALAFREY
Great Southern
★ **V**

Anyone who names a winery after
the mythical planet of the Time
Lords in *Doctor Who* should be
locked up in a dark place –
preferably with a good supply
of Galafrey wines.

✔ *Cabernet Sauvignon* •
Chardonnay (Unoaked) • *Classic
white blend* (Galafrey Art Label
Semillon-Sauvignon Blanc) •
Riesling • *Shiraz*

GILBERTS
Great Southern
★★☆ **V**

The Gilberts have their wines made
by contract at Plantagenet, which
does a better job for them than it
does with its own wines, which are
good, but just not in the same
class. This is a classic demonstration
of the benefits of superior *terroir*.
Best known to an informed few for
their Riesling, which thrust the
Gilberts into the limelight when it
won Best of Show at the Qantas
West Australian Wine Show in both
2000 and 2001, the class of these
wines can also be seen throughout
the range.

✔ *Entire range*

GOUNDREY
WINES
Great Southern
★ **V**

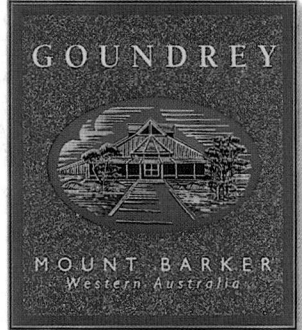

Owned by Perth-based US
millionaire Jack Bendat, who has
invested millions in Goundrey and
has been intent on driving sales
ever upwards, but only of late
does there seems to be a more
mature reflection as to increasing
consistency of quality.

✔ *Cabernet Sauvignon* (Reserve)
• *Chardonnay* (Unwooded) •
Chenin Blanc • *Shiraz* (Reserve)

GRALYN ESTATE
Margaret River
★★

The style leans more towards size
than finesse, but you cannot help
being seduced by the lush quality
of these wines.

✔ *Cabernet Sauvignon* • *Classic
red blend* (Shiraz-Cabernet)
• *Fortified* (Vintage Port) •
Shiraz (Old Vine)

HACKERSLEY
Geographe
★★ **V**

These wines have come a long way
in the short while since Hackersley
was established as a joint venture
between three families. The quality
far exceeds the reasonable prices
asked (so far), especially for such
a tiny production.

✔ *Cabernet Sauvignon* • *Merlot*
• *Shiraz*

HAPPS VINEYARD
Margaret River
★

Erl Happ makes several wines, all of
which are eminently drinkable, but
you can tell that he puts his heart
into his reds, of which Merlot is
the most highly regarded. Charles
Andreas is a blend of Cabernet
Sauvignon, Merlot, Cabernet Franc,
Malbec, and Petit Verdot.

✔ *Cabernet Franc* (Three Hills)
• *Classic red blend* (Charles
Andreas) • *Merlot* (Three Hills)

HIGHER PLANE
Margaret River
★☆

Venture by Craig and Cathie Smith
that has rapidly hit the heights.
Craig is a doctor (plastic surgeon),
which is almost *de rigueur* for
anyone starting a wine business
in this part of the world, and
Cathie has a Master of Business
in Wine Marketing. Winemaking
by Matt Wood.

✔ *Chardonnay* • *Classic red blend*
(Cabernet-Merlot) • *Merlot*

HOUGHTON WINES
Swan Valley
★★☆ **V**

Houghton wines are generally
underestimated because of the
winery's location in the under-
performing Swan Valley, its huge
production, and the fact that it
is part of the even more gigantic
BRL Hardy, but this winery is an
exemplary instance of how big can
be beautiful. Houghton's White
Burgundy (sold as HWB in the
EU) is a case in point: large-
production and inexpensive, yet an
award-winning wine of legendary
reputation. However, if you have
been impressed by the value of
White Burgundy, you should
try the White Burgundy Show
Reserve, which is released when
fully mature, and illustrates the
potential quality of a wine that is
mostly consumed within hours of
purchase. As for its content, White
Burgundy is primarily a blend of
Chardonnay, Chenin Blanc, and
Sémillon, with a mishmash of
other varieties, such as Verdelho,
Sauvignon Blanc, Muscadelle, etc.
These large-volume blends tend
to evolve hand-in-hand with the
development of Australia's vineyard
mix. My notes from almost 30 years
ago reveal that the 1981 was a
50/50 blend of Chenin Blanc and

Muscadelle. From the past to the
future: one day this wine will have
to be renamed, of course, as part
of Australia's trading agreement
with France. Top of the Houghton
hierarchy is Jack Mann, a super-
premium wine named after the late
and legendary winemaker, Jack
Mann MBE. Jack Mann is usually a
blend of Cabernet Sauvignon with
maybe Malbec one year, Shiraz
another. At one time it was a
blend that included both of those
ancillary varieties, and occasionally
it can be pure Cabernet Sauvignon
(1998, for example). The Crofters
is a blend of Cabernet Sauvignon
and Merlot.

✔ *Cabernet Sauvignon* (Margaret
River) • *Chardonnay*
(Pemberton) • *Classic red blend*
(Crofters, Jack Mann) • *Classic
white blend* (Sémillon-Sauvignon
Blanc, White Burgundy Show
Reserve) • *Riesling* (Frankland
River) • *Sauvignon Blanc*
(Pemberton) • *Shiraz* (Frankland)
• *Verdelho* (Show Reserve)

HOWARD PARK
Denmark
★★

Now owned by the Burch family,
who also have vineyards in
Margaret River, where they have
built a new winery that has taken
over some of the production. And
lest the high rating mislead anyone,
the production is very substantial
indeed. Entry-level wines are sold
under the Madfish label, of which
the Chardonnay, Sémillon-Sauvignon
Blanc, and Shiraz are all
recommended as strongly as the
Howard Park wines listed below.

✔ *Cabernet Sauvignon* •
Chardonnay • *Classic red blend*
(Cabernet Sauvignon-Merlot)
• *Pinot Noir* (Scotsdale) • *Riesling*
• *Shiraz* (Leston, Scotsdale)

KARRIVIEW
Great Southern
★★

Tiny production of expressive
Burgundian varietals.

✔ *Chardonnay* • *Pinot Noir*

KILLERBY
Margaret River
★☆

This winery's move to the Margaret River has coincided with a noticeable increase in quality.

✓ *Cabernet Sauvignon* • *Chardonnay* • *Shiraz*

LEEUWIN ESTATE
Margaret River
★★☆

Leeuwin Estate continues to produce lush, stylish, and very classy wines that belong with food.

✓ *Cabernet Sauvignon* (Art Series) • *Chardonnay* (Art Series) • *Classic red blend* (Prelude Vineyards Cabernet-Merlot) • *Classic white blend* (Sibblings Sauvignon Blanc-Sémillon) • *Pinot Noir* (Art Series) • *Riesling* (Art Series) • *Sauvignon Blanc* (Art Series)

LENTON BRAE
Margaret River
★★☆

Established in 1983 by Bruce Tomlinson, whose son Edward is the winemaker today.

✓ *Cabernet Sauvignon* • *Chardonnay* • *Classic red blend* (Cabernet-Merlot)

MERUM
Margaret River
★★

Tiny production of stunning Sémillon, and a beautiful Shiraz.

✓ *Sémillon* • *Shiraz*

MOONDAH BROOK
Swan District
★★Ⓥ

This brand belongs to BRL Hardy and its good value, fruit-driven wines are made at the Houghton winery.

✓ *Cabernet Sauvignon* • *Chardonnay* • *Chenin Blanc* • *Shiraz* • *Verdelho*

MOSS BROTHERS
Margaret River
★★Ⓥ

Established in 1984 by David Moss, who had been a viticulturist at Houghton and Moss Wood; Peter Moss, who actually built boutique wineries for a living; and Jane Moss, who graduated from

Roseworthy. With such experience, how could they fail? Well, they didn't, and Sémillon is this winery's flagship.

✓ *Classic red blend* (Cabernet Sauvignon-Merlot) • *Sémillon* • *Shiraz* • *Verdelho*

MOSS WOOD
Margaret River
★★

One of the very best Margaret River wineries, Moss Wood was the first in the area to perfect Pinot Noir, and arguably the best Sémillon outside the Hunter Valley.

✓ *Cabernet Sauvignon* (Glenmore Vineyard) • *Chardonnay* (Lefroy Brook Vineyard) • *Merlot* (Ribbon Vale) • *Pinot Noir* • *Sémillon*

PIERRO
Margaret River
★★☆

Mike Perkin, who is a genius with white wines, makes one of the best examples of Chardonnay in Margaret River. His LTC is a blend of Sémillon and Sauvignon Blanc.

✓ *Chardonnay* • *Classic red blend* (Cabernet-Merlot) • *Classic white blend* (LTC)

PLANTAGENET WINES
Great Southern
★★☆

A winery named after the shire in which it is situated, Plantagenet was the first to cultivate Mount Barker, and is the leading winery in the area today.

✓ *Cabernet Sauvignon* • *Chardonnay* • *Classic red blend* (Omrah Merlot-Cabernet) • *Pinot Noir* • *Riesling* • *Shiraz*

SANDALFORD
Margaret River
★★☆

A historic winery dating back to 1840, Sandalford was purchased in 1991 by Peter and Debra Prendiville, who have successfully resurrected this great old name.

✓ *Cabernet Sauvignon* (Premium) • *Classic white blend* (Premium Sémillon-Sauvignon Blanc) • *Fortified* (Sandalera) • *Riesling* • *Shiraz* (Premium) • *Verdelho*

SETTLERS RIDGE
Margaret River
★ⓋⓄ

Wayne and Kaye Nobbs purchased this 40-hectare (100-acre) property in 1994. Originally part of a dairy farm in the heart of the Margaret River region, its gravelly loam soils were immediately planted with vines, which yielded a first crop in 1997. Since then, Settlers Ridge organic wines have won more than 50 medals at wine shows.

✓ *Cabernet Sauvignon* • *Shiraz*

SMITHBROOK
Manjimup
★★☆

Owned by Lion Nathan since the takeover of Petaluma, who used the Pinot Noir for its Croser sparkling wine before it was dug up.

✓ *Cabernet Sauvignon* • *Classic red blend* (The Yilgarn) • *Merlot* • *Sauvignon Blanc*

SUCKFIZZLE
Margaret River
★★☆

The creation of two well-known Margaret River winemakers, Stuart Pym and Janice McDonald. The seemingly bizarre name was inspired by the Great Lord Suckfizzle from Rabelais's *Gargantua*, whereas the wines themselves are simply inspired.

✓ *Cabernet Sauvignon* • *Classic white blend* (Sauvignon Blanc-Sémillon) • *Muscat* (Stella Bella Pink) • *Sauvignon Blanc* (Stella Bella)

VASSE FELIX
Margaret River
★★☆

One of the Margaret River's pioneering wineries of the modern era, Vasse Felix's speciality has always been its long-lived Cabernet Sauvignons. It remains so today, although since the change of ownership, and the move to a new winery in 1999, they are softer and easier to drink at a younger age than they used to be. Heytesbury is a Cabernet-Shiraz blend. Classic Dry White is a Sémillon-Sauvignon Blanc blend.

✓ *Cabernet Sauvignon* • *Chardonnay* (Heytesbury) • *Classic red blend* (Heytesbury) • *Classic white blend* (Classic Dry White)

VOYAGER ESTATE
Margaret River
★★

This property was purchased in 1991 by the current owner, Michael Wright, the mining magnate.

✓ *Cabernet Sauvignon* (Tom Price) • *Chardonnay* • *Classic red blend* (Cabernet Sauvignon-Merlot) • *Classic white blend* (Sauvignon Blanc-Sémillon,

Tom Price Sémillon-Sauvignon Blanc) • *Shiraz*

WILLESPIE
Margaret River
★

Kevin Squance continues to produce fine-quality Verdelho, but the expressiveness of his red wines, especially the Shiraz, has improved dramatically, which is a revelation.

✓ *Cabernet Sauvignon* (Reserve) • *Classic red blend* (Cabernets) • *Shiraz* • *Verdelho*

WILLOW BRIDGE ESTATE
Geographe
★★Ⓥ

Established in 1997, when the Dewar family purchased this 180-hectare (445-acre) property in the Ferguson Valley. So far, they have planted 60 hectares (150 acres), producing some immediately impressive wines in the process.

✓ *Cabernet Sauvignon* (Reserve) • *Classic white blend* (Winemaker's Reserve Sémillon Sauvignon Blanc) • *Shiraz* (The Black Dog, Winemakers Reserve)

WOODY NOOK
Margaret River
☆

Neil Gallagher of Woody Nook has always made a lovely Cabernet Sauvignon, and is now starting to be noticed for his Sauvignon Blanc.

✓ *Cabernet Sauvignon* • *Sauvignon Blanc*

XANADU
Margaret River
★★☆

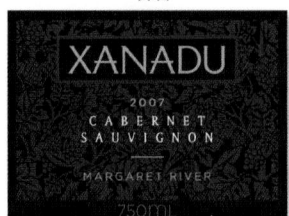

Formerly Chateau Xanadu, this ex-boutique winery has expanded its annual production to 100,000 cases. Secession is a blend of Sémillon, Sauvignon Blanc, Chenin Blanc, and Chardonnay. Wines are also sold under the following brands (top-quality wines): Chais Clarendon (Shiraz), and Normans (Adelaide Hills Chardonnay, Encounter Bay Cabernet Sauvignon, Old Vines Shiraz). The Lagan Estate is a blend of Cabernet Sauvignon, Merlot, and Cabernet Franc. Wines are also produced under the NXG label, which stands for Next Generations wines, although they have yet to make their mark.

✓ *Cabernet Franc* • *Cabernet Sauvignon* • *Chardonnay* • *Classic red blend* (Lagan Estate) • *Classic white blend* • *Merlot* • *Sémillon*

QUEENSLAND AND NORTHERN TERRITORY

These two states cover nearly half of Australia but contain less than 22 per cent of its population. Beyond Brisbane, Australia's third-largest city, the dusty outback is sparsely populated, yet there are at least two serious vine-growing areas, and both are in Queensland.

QUEENSLAND

For one of the last places on Earth where one might expect to find vineyards, Queensland, surprisingly, has 111 wineries. The first vineyard was established in the 1860s, either by the Raymont family at Alderley, just 8 kilometres (5 miles) from the centre of Brisbane, or by Samuel Basset in Romavilla in 1863. Most sources credit Raymont, but the exact date is unknown. Although some early award-winning fortified wines were produced by Basset in Romavilla, it was not until Shiraz was introduced to the Granite Belt in the mid-1960s that the quality generally began to reach acceptable standards. Summers are much cooler in Queensland's high-altitude Granite Belt than in many other, far more famous Australian regions, which explains why this state's wine industry is enjoying a revival. However, South Burnett, where the climate is more tropical, is Queensland's latest, fastest-growing wine region.

NORTHERN TERRITORY

An even less likely location for winemaking than Queensland is hard to imagine, but its western neighbour, Northern Territory, is such a place. Curiously, it is illegal to drink alcohol in a public place within 2 kilometres (1 mile) of a licensed bar, except, of course, inside one. Alice Springs was home to Chateau Hornsby and its 3 hectares (7.5 acres) of vineyards from 1977 until December 2002, and the story is too good to consign to the dustbin of history. (It was abandoned in 2002 only because Hornsby had to move closer to Sydney so that Helen, his partner, could have access to long-term medical treatment.) Chateau Hornsby had one great marketing idea: every year, he made the first *nouveau* in the world by harvesting Shiraz at one minute past midnight on 1 January – something impossible elsewhere. Combine that idea with Alice Spring's tourism, and it is surprising that nobody has picked up where Hornsby left off.

There is, however, one new kid on the Northern Territory block. Red Centre Wines, at Ti Tree, 194 kilometres (120 miles) north of Alice Springs, where John and Shirley Crayford produce a red wine and a fortified tawny from 2 hectares (5 acres) of vines. They also have 7 hectares (17 acres) of mango orchards, and from the look of their tin shed with "Shatto Mango" roughly daubed in red paint above the door, they are more into their mango wines, which are shipped as far as China and Singapore.

FACTORS AFFECTING TASTE AND QUALITY

LOCATION
Queensland is situated in the northeastern corner of Australia, with the Coral Sea to the east, and the Northern Territory, the north-central state, to the west.

CLIMATE
Annual rainfall at Roma is only 51 centimetres (20 inches), but the Granite Belt receives 79 centimetres (31 inches). Much of it tends to fall at vintage time and this can be a problem, but frost and hail pose a greater danger. Temperatures are high (similar to the Margaret River in Western Australia), but not unduly so, due to the tempering effect of altitude.

ASPECT
The altitude of Stanthorpe in the Granite Belt, where the surrounding vineyards lie between 750 and 940 metres (2,500 and 3,100 feet) above sea level, helps to temper the otherwise scorching summer heat in both areas. The vines here are generally grown in the hilly area, on sloping sites, whereas at South Burnett vines grow at 300–442 metres (990–1,459 feet) on more rolling countryside.

SOIL
The soils of Queensland are phylloxera-free. As the name suggests, they are granitic in the Granite Belt around Stanthorpe. South Burnett varies from red granitic-sand with basalt on the plains and terraces, to basalt-based soils, light sandy soils, red-coloured light, clayey soils, and heavier brown and black clayey soils elsewhere. The area around Alice Springs shares the same infertile, coarse, red, iron-rich sandy soil that is common to much of central Australia.

VITICULTURE AND VINIFICATION
Irrigation is necessary to produce wines near Alice Springs and, indeed, at Roma. The most modern technology is used in these areas to combat the problems of heat and oxidation. As a result, quite good wines are produced.

GRAPE VARIETIES
Primary varieties: Cabernet Sauvignon, Chardonnay, Riesling, Sauvignon Blanc, Sémillon, Shiraz (Syrah), Verdelho
Secondary varieties: Barbera, Cabernet Franc, Chambourcin, Chenin Blanc, Gamay, Malbec, Marsanne, Merlot, Mourvèdre, Muscat (Muscat Blanc à Petits Grains), Nebbiolo, Petit Verdot, Pinot Gris, Pinot Noir, Ruby Cabernet, Sangiovese, Sylvaner, Tarrango, Tempranillo, Touriga (Touriga Nacional), Viognier, Zinfandel

AN OUTBACK STATION IN ALICE SPRINGS
The hot, dry climate means irrigation is necessary for the area's red-sand soil, but there is an abundant supply of water underground.

THE APPELLATIONS OF
QUEENSLAND AND NORTHERN TERRITORY

GRANITE BELT GI

Italian immigrants and their families pioneered viticulture and winemaking in the 1920s, selling to relations and friends in the Italian cane-growing communities to the north, but the current boutique-based industry started in the 1960s, when Shiraz was planted. The vines here are grown in an area that surrounds the town of Ballandean, on an elevated granite plateau 240 kilometres (150 miles) west of Brisbane. It is the altitude of this district, between 790 and 1,000 metres (2,500 and 3,280 feet), that provides a sufficiently cool climate. Indeed, at Felsberg, located at an altitude of 850 metres (2,750 feet), the grapes sometimes struggle to ripen. As can be imagined, the soil is granitic, with Riesling the most suitable variety, although the most successful individual wine is, believe it or not, Ballandean's late-harvest Sylvaner. Other varieties that do well include Cabernet Sauvignon, Chardonnay, Sémillon, and Shiraz.

ROMA

Like Alice Springs, Roma is not a GI wine region, but viticulture in this hot and arid area of Queensland is almost equally as improbable, thus its inclusion as one of most bizarre locations to plant a vine. While this might not be classic wine country, there are some 25 hectares (62 acres) of vines, and the solitary wine estate, Romavilla, has not missed a vintage since 1866, which alone makes Roma worthy of mention. Indeed, there are not many producers in Australia's premium wine regions who can claim to have 140 consecutive vintages under their belt. If Roma is any sort of wine country, it is – or it is meant to be – fortified wine country, which is why I was so surprised to be greeted by a sign proclaiming "Welcome to Roma, Champagne Country", when I first visited the town. Apparently, in 1864 a certain Mayor Mitchell was so struck by Roma's resemblance to the Champagne area that he mentioned the fact in dispatches, and the description stuck. This can mean only one thing: that Mitchell had never visited Champagne in his life.

SOUTH BURNETT GI

For anyone who has followed the tiny, emerging wine industry in Queensland, it might come as a surprise to discover that South Burnett was the first official wine region in this state. Observers might be forgiven for expecting that honour would go to the Granite Belt, which is Queensland's oldest and most famous wine region, yet it received GI status in 2002, almost two years after South Burnett. Vineyards in this regional GI were established in the early 1990s, and currently stretch from Goomeri in the north, through the Murgon region to the Bunya Mountains, Kingaroy, and south to Nanango. Not surprisingly, the climate is hot, humid, and subtropical, with high rainfall during the growing season. There are various soil types – from red granitic-sandy soils on the plains and terraces, to basalt-based soils, light sandy soils, red-coloured, light clayey soils, and heavier brown and black clayey soils elsewhere. Grape varieties include Cabernet Sauvignon, Chardonnay, Merlot, Riesling, Sauvignon Blanc, Sémillon, and Shiraz.

THE WINE PRODUCERS OF
QUEENSLAND AND NORTHERN TERRITORY

ALBERT RIVER WINES
Tamborine
★✰Ⓥ

Established in 1998 but initially aided by bought-in fruit, the first pure Queensland wines were not produced until 2000. These wines are produced by the ubiquitous Peter Scudamore-Smith MW, who is contracted by a dozen or more wineries. Recent plantations include the Petit Manseng, which is rare in Australia but has demonstrated in Southwest France that it is capable of producing classy late-harvest wines. The first harvest here should be in 2012.

✓ *Classic red blend* (Shiraz-Viognier) • *Merlot*

BACK POCKET
Granite Belt
★✰

Owned by Mal Baisden and Lel Doon, who use the contract winemaking services of Peter Scudamore-Smith MW.

✓ *Tempranillo* (Castanets)

BALLANDEAN
Granite Belt
★✰Ⓥ

This family-owned winery is justly famous for its cane-cut late-harvest Sylvaner, but its other wines are among the best in the Granite Belt, with the vintages assuming an even greater consistency since 2000, when Dylan Rhymer took on the day-to-day winemaking responsibility.

✓ *Chardonnay* (Family Reserve) • *Classic red blend* (Generation 3) • *Fortified* (Liqueur Muscat) • *Shiraz* (Family Reserve) • *Sylvaner* (Late Harvest)

BARAMBAH RIDGE
South Burnett
★✰Ⓥ

Since this winery was purchased by Jane and Steve Wilson, who live on neighbouring property Barambah Station, the wines have begun to demonstrate the true potential of South Burnett, with consultant Peter Scudamore-Smith MW.

✓ *Chardonnay* (especially First Grid) • *Dessert wine* (Rack-Dried Sémillon) • *Shiraz*

BOIREANN
Granite Belt
★★

Although established in 1998, it has only been in the past few years that red-wine specialist Peter Stark has taken the Granite Belt to new heights. Will others follow?

✓ *Entire range*

ROBERT CHANNON
Granite Belt
★Ⓥ

Yet another winery that benefits from the services of consultant winemaker Peter Scudamore-Smith MW, Robert Channon goes to great lengths to ensure best practices throughout its vineyard, such as the installation of a permanent bird netting. The Verdelho still stands out.

✓ *Chardonnay* • *Pinot Gris* • *Verdelho*

CLOVELY ESTATE
South Burnett
★★Ⓥ

This ambitious 180-hectare (445-acre) project was established in 1997, and since then it has produced some of South Burnett's finest wines. It is owned by the Heading family, who wisely steered clear of hands-on management, electing instead to head-hunt a highly professional team to put the winery firmly on the map, which it has certainly done.

✓ *Botrytis* (Left Field Sémillon) • *Cabernet Sauvignon* (Reserve) • *Chardonnay* (Left Field, Reserve) • *Classic red blend* (Shiraz-Merlot-Cabernet) • *Petit Verdot* (Left Field) • *Sémillon* (Left Field) • *Shiraz* (Double Pruned)

GOLDEN GROVE ESTATE
Granite Belt
★★

The Costanzo family have lived here since the 1940s, when they established an orchard and fruit farm. The first vines, Shiraz, went in the ground in 1972, but a winery was not established until 1992, when Sam and Grace Costanzo quickly made a name for themselves. However, their son Ray has made even greater strides with a wide range of wines, including many curveballs, all terrifyingly good. In addition to excellent classics, such as the Shiraz from the first vines planted on this estate, Golden Grove produces some outstanding, more eclectic wines, such as Barbera, Durif, Malbec, Mourvèdre, and Tempranillo, plus an intriguing classic red blend of Tempranillo, Durif, and Barbera. As the range widens, the quality just gets better and better.

✓ *Entire range*

GRANITE RIDGE WINES
Granite Belt
★✰Ⓥ

Founded in 1995 by current owner-winemaker, Dennis Ferguson, who originally named this venture Denlana Ferguson Estate.

✓ *Shiraz* (Granite Rock)

HERITAGE WINES
Granite Belt
★✰Ⓥ

This nicely maturing operation was established in 1992 by Bryce and Paddy Kassulke, who rapidly made a reputation for themselves. Their son John Handy is now the winemaker, and he, too, has the habit of picking up awards.

✓ *Cabernet Sauvignon* (Reserve) • *Sémillon* • *Shiraz* (Patricia) • *Verdelho* (Reserve Blend)

JESTER HILL
Granite Belt
★✰

This winery was founded in 1993 by John and Genevieve Ashwell, who achieved a good reputation, particularly for Cabernet Sauvignon and Shiraz. Then, one day in March 2010, two motorcyclists, Michael and Ann Bourke, set off for the Granite Belt and came across Jester Hill. They loved the place but had no idea that they would be the new owners nine months down the line. John Ashwell remains as winemaker, and two main labels are the same: Touchstone for the premium wines, and Two Fools for a bit of fun –

apparently John and Genevieve used this name because you have to be fool to own a vineyard.

✓ *Cabernet Sauvignon* (Touchstone) • *Shiraz* (Touchstone) • *Sparkling wine* (Sparkling Shiraz)

KOMINOS WINES
Granite Belt

The Shiraz here has moved over the years from carbonic maceration to dense, often jammy richness.

✓ *Classic red blend* (Cabernet-Merlot) • *Dessert wine* (Botrytis Sémillon) • *Merlot* (Reserve)

MASON WINES
Granite Belt
★✰

The Mason family consistently produces some excellent wines from two former stone-fruit orchards.

✓ *Classic white blend* (Sémillon-Sauvignon Blanc) • *Petit Verdot*

PRESTON PEAK
Toowoomba
★Ⓥ

One of the more successful Queensland operations, Preston Peak draws on fruit from two different vineyards, the largest being at Devil's Elbow in the Granite Belt, where the winery is also located, but all other operations, including the cellar door, are at the Preston Vineyard near Toowoomba, with glorious views of Table Top Mountain, Lockyer Valley, and the Darling Downs.

✓ *Cabernet Sauvignon* (Leaf Series) • *Chardonnay* (Leaf Series) • *Petit Verdot* (Leaf Series) • *Sauvignon Blanc* (Leaf Series) • *Sémillon* (Leaf Series) • *Shiraz* (Reserve)

RAVENS CROFT WINES
Granite Belt
★★

Founded in 2002 by South African-born owner-winemaker Mark Ravenscroft, whose wines are as elegant as their presentation.

✓ *Petit Verdot* • *Verdelho*

RIMFIRE
MacLagan
★Ⓥ

Established in 1991 by the Connellan family, who have created a mysterious legend around a dry white wine called 1893. This supposedly comes from a vineyard propagated from a single 100-year-old vine found on their property, which they claim is "not listed on the Australian DNA grapevine database".

✓ *Classic red blend* (Cabernet Franc-Ruby Cabernet) • *Muscat* (Dry White) • *Verdelho*

RIVERSANDS VINEYARDS
St George
★Ⓥ

Established in 1990, and purchased by Alison and David Blacket in 1996, these vineyards are located on the banks of the Balbonne River

in the southwest of Queensland. The fortified wines are the best.

✓ *Fortified* (Golden Liqueur Muscat, Stirlings Reserve Red Liqueur Muscat)

ROBINSONS FAMILY
Granite Belt
★✰Ⓥ

John Robinson got his passion for wine when living in France, close to the Beaujolais region, then studied wine science at Riverina College under Brian Croser.

✓ *Cabernet Sauvignon*

ROMAVILLA WINERY
Roma
★✰

Established in 1863, Romavilla is a living reminder of Queensland's wine history. However, although the recommended fortified wines are rich and intense, with a big finish, there are few other wines of interest.

✓ *Chardonnay* (Reserve) • *Classic red blend* (Old Tawny Port, Very Old Liqueur Muscat, Very Old Tawny)

RUMBALARA VINEYARDS
Fletcher
★✰Ⓥ

Rumbalara is Aboriginal for "end of the rainbow". Established in 1974 by Bob and Una Gray, Rumbalara became an early award-winner, but its performance dropped off as newer and better vineyards sprang up across the Granite Belt. The Grays sold up to Mike and Bobbi Cragg in December 2002, and in recent years, these wines have made a splendid comeback.

✓ *Cabernet Sauvignon* • *Classic red blend* (Shiraz-Merlot-Cabernet Sauvignon) • *Merlot* • *Shiraz*

SIRROMET WINES
Mount Cotton
★★

Established by the Morris family in 1998, Sirromet's *avant-garde* 200-seat restaurant was recognized in 2004 with numerous awards, including Brisbane's Best Tourism Restaurant, Brisbane's Best Restaurant in a Winery, and Brisbane's Restaurant of the Year. Part of this success is due, no doubt, to its Brisbane-friendly location, just 30 minutes southeast of the city. But not only has the restaurant maintained its incredible reputation, but so have the wines, which have gone from excellent to world-class. Australia's leading wine authority James Halliday attributes this, at least in part, to Adam Chapman, whom he believes to be "the most skilled winemaker practising in Queensland". A good part must also be down to the location of Sirromet's 144 hectares (356 acres) of vineyards in and around the Ballandean area of the Granite Belt: St Jude's (22 hectares [54 acres] growing Shiraz,

Chardonnay, Verdelho, and Cabernet Sauvignon); The Night Sky (23 hectares [57 acres] of Pinot Gris, Verdelho, Chardonnay, and Viognier); and Seven Scenes (101 hectares [250 acres] in 40 separate blocks growing 17 grape varieties). Sirromet claims that Seven Scenes is Australia's highest-altitude vineyard and the source of many of its medal-winning wines.

✓ *Entire range*

SUMMIT ESTATE
Granite Belt
★★★

Granite Belt's "*grand cru*" operation was originally established by Bill Ryan, Tim Galligan, and Martin Millard, when they planted 0.8 hectares (2 acres) of Shiraz, Zinfandel, Malbec, Merlot, Pinot Noir, and Grenache. A state-of-the-art winery was built in 2005, and since then the winemaking has carefully moved towards gravity rather than pumps throughout the entire process. Now there are 17 hectares (42 acres) and 10 shareholders, and the aptly named Summit Estate has a reputation that is second to none in Queensland. The reds, in particular, perform well, being beautifully coloured with intense fruit and great length without any heaviness. The Alto Spanish Collection is an unusual but exciting Monastrell-based blend, with Grenache, Shiraz, Tempranillo, Cabernet Sauvignon, and Tannat.

SYMPHONY HILL WINES
Granite Belt
★★

Owned by the Macpherson family, who are obviously perfectionists, from the finesse of these wines. Top quality across the board.

✓ *Entire range*

TOBIN WINES
Granite Belt
★✰

This family-owned eponymous winery was established in 1964, and the Shiraz and Sémillon that went in over the first three years are the oldest surviving vines in the Granite Belt.

✓ *Cabernet Sauvignon* (Luella) • *Chardonnay* (Lily) • *Dessert wine* (Liqueur Muscat) • *Merlot* (Elliott) • *Shiraz* (Max)

WITCHES FALLS WINERY
North Tamborine
★✰

Jon Heslop produces some elegantly rich wines from selected Granite Belt fruit in his winery just northwest of Gold Coast.

✓ *Cabernet Sauvignon* (Prophecy Unfiltered) • *Chardonnay* (Prophecy Wild Ferment) • *Grenache* • *Marsanne* • *Merlot* (Prophecy) • *Shiraz* (Syrah)

NEW ZEALAND

New Zealand's isolation and cool, maritime climate make it the most exciting place on earth for wine, yet certain producers want to marginalize its most successful variety, Sauvignon Blanc. In the process they run the risk of ruining their unique reputation. While there is no doubt that New Zealand can and does produce top-class wines from numerous other grape varieties, only Sauvignon Blanc is undeniably a class apart from the same grape grown anywhere else in the world. No other country can make a similar claim for any other grape variety, and no other country has such an unassailable flagship for its wine industry. Why throw that away?

SOME PRODUCERS WOULD ALSO LIKE to build a fresh reputation based on, of all grapes, Chardonnay. I am not an "anything but Chardonnay" man, but this is the last grape that any region should specialize in. New Zealand's producers should, of course, continue to make the finest Chardonnay possible, but only as part of an increasing range of world class wines. Chardonnay's place is alongside Pinot Noir, various Bordeaux varieties, Riesling, sparkling wine, and promising new grapes such as Syrah. All of these add to the breadth and depth of New Zealand's reputation.

So why would anyone in this industry want to marginalize Sauvignon Blanc? Embarrassment! They feel uncomfortable that New Zealand should be so famous for a grape of such obvious,

MISSION VINEYARDS,
NORTH ISLAND
The Hawke's Bay winery has recently upgraded its wines.

NEW ZEALAND
Although South Island has a younger wine industry, it boasts a slightly more favourable growing climate than North Island, having lighter rainfall.

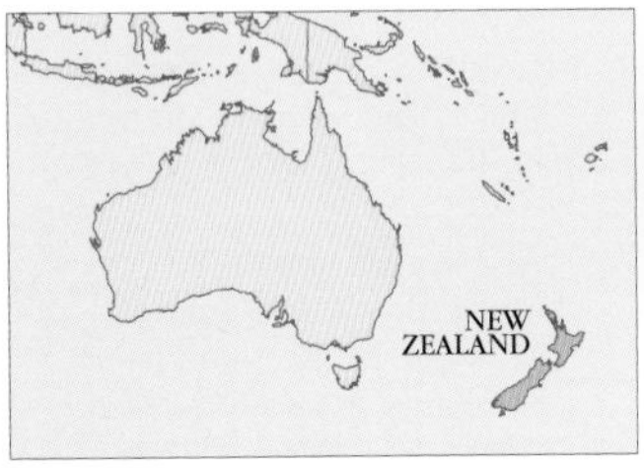

North Island wine zones

Northland
Sub-regions: ① Kaitaia, ② Kerikeri, ③ Whangarei

Auckland
Sub-regions: ① Clevedon, ② Great Barrier Island, ③ Henderson, ④ Huapai, ⑤ Kumeu, ⑥ Mahurangi, ⑦ Matakana, ⑧ Oratia, ⑨ Waiheke Island

Waikato
Sub-regions: ① Hamilton, ② Te Kauwhata

Bay of Plenty
Sub-regions: ① Galatea, ② Katikati, ③ Rotorua, ④ Tauranga, ⑤ Thornton, ⑥ Whakatane

Gisborne
Sub-regions: ① Hexton, ② Matawhero, ③ Ormond

Hawke's Bay
Sub-regions: ① Bay View, ② Eskdale, ③ Flaxmere, ④ Hastings, ⑤ Havelock North, ⑥ Mangatahi, ⑦ Te Awanga

Wellington
Sub-regions: ① Gladstone, ② Martinborough, ③ Masterton, ④ Otaki, ⑤ Te Horo

Wairarapa

South Island wine zones

Nelson
Sub-regions: ① Clifton, ② Golden Bay, ③ Motueka, ④ Nelson, ⑤ Richmond, ⑥ Upper Moutere, ⑦ Waimea Plains

Marlborough
Sub-regions: ① Awatere Valley, ② Blenheim, ③ Kaituna, ④ Koromiko, ⑤ Waihopai Valley, ⑥ Wairau Valley, ⑦ Woodbourne

Canterbury
Sub-regions: ① Banks Peninsula, ② Christchurch, ③ Omihi, ④ Waipara, ⑤ Weka Pass

Otago
Sub-regions: ① Alexandra, ② Bannockburn, ③ Bendigo, ④ Cromwell, ⑤ Dunstan, ⑥ Ettrick, ⑦ Gibbston, ⑧ Lake Hayes, ⑨ Wanaka, ⑩ Waitaki Valley

Central Otago

— Region boundary

▲ Height above sea level (metres)

0   50   100   150 miles

0   50   100   150   200   250   300 km

Kaitaia

WHANGAREI

NORTHLAND

AUCKLAND

Auckland

Thames

North Island

WAIKATO

Hamilton

Te Kuiti

ROTORUA   BAY OF PLENTY

Whakatane ▲1775

GISBORNE

GISBORNE

NEW PLYMOUTH

Taumarunui

Taupo

HAWKE'S BAY

TARANAKI

Taihape

NAPIER
HASTINGS

WANGANUI

MANAWATU
WANGANUI

Dannevirke

PACIFIC OCEAN

NELSON

Otaki

WELLINGTON

Wellington

Nelson

Blenheim

TASMAN

Westport

MARLBOROUGH

2227 ▲

Greymouth

WEST COAST

Kaikoura

2400 ▲

Rangiora

Christchurch

CANTERBURY

Haast

Ashburton

Fairlie

TIMARU

South Island

3764 ▲

3036 ▲

Milford Sound

Queenstown

Te Anau

Alexandra

Oamaru

OTAGO

SOUTHLAND

Dunedin

Gore

Balclutha

INVERCARGILL

Stewart Island

NEW ZEALAND

FACTORS AFFECTING TASTE AND QUALITY

LOCATION
With the exception of Waiheke Island, all of New Zealand's grape-growing areas are on its two principal islands, North Island and South Island, stretched over 1,600 kilometres (1,000 miles) between latitudes 36°S and 45°S. Central Otago is the most southerly location.

CLIMATE
North Island generally has a cool maritime climate, similar to that of Bordeaux in temperature but with much higher rainfall. The crucial autumn periods are rarely dry; heavy rains and high humidity lead to problems of grape damage and rot. South Island is significantly cooler, but sunnier and drier. Marlborough is South Island's warmest area, and often has the country's most hours of sunshine. Rainfall is variable. Using the California heat summation system, the most important viticultural areas in both islands are all Region 1.

ASPECT
Most vines are planted on flat or gently sloping land, and are easy to work. Some north-facing slopes have been planted in Auckland and Te Kauwhata; these provide better drainage and longer hours of intensive sunlight. Some steep vineyards are found in South Island's Central Otago district.

SOIL
Soils are varied, mostly clay or loam-based, often sandy or gravelly, with schistous loess over gravel in Central Otago, and volcanic subsoils in parts of Northland (Cottle Hill), and around Canterbury (Banks Peninsula).

VITICULTURE AND VINIFICATION
Harvests begin in March and April, six months ahead of wine regions in the northern hemisphere. Canopy management has totally transformed New Zealand's wines, especially its reds, which no longer possess the excessive pyrazines that once gave them an unwelcome, ever-present herbaceousness. Most winemakers have studied oenology in Australia, and done at least one *stage* in Europe. This straddling of Old and New World, tradition and technique, has helped shape New Zealand's wine reputation. Many producers have adopted screwcap bottles.

GRAPE VARIETIES
Primary varieties: Cabernet Sauvignon, Chardonnay, Merlot, Pinot Noir, Riesling, Sauvignon Blanc
Secondary varieties: Cabernet Franc, Chenin Blanc, Gewürztraminer, Malbec, Müller-Thurgau, Muscat (Muscat Blanc à Petits Grains), Pinotage, Pinot Gris, Sémillon, Syrah

COOPERS CREEK WINERY, NORTH ISLAND
Situated in the Huapai Valley, this winery produces exceptionally stylish wines. Talented North Island winemakers use both traditional and high-tech methods.

upfront character. They long to have a more complex, classier wine to fly the flag. But it is nothing to be ashamed of: it is a refreshing, pure, vibrantly fruity wine. Sauvignon Blanc is the ideal choice to open up wider markets, whereas a more complex, more expensive wine would be restrictive.

PAST, PRESENT, AND FUTURE

Up to the 1980s, Cooks, Corbans, and Montana dominated the New Zealand wine scene, and the most popular product was Müller-Thurgau sweetened-up with Süssreserve (now that was a wine to be embarrassed about). In 1987, Cooks took over Corbans, and both were consumed by Montana, then Sauvignon Blanc began its inexorable rise. Now Cooks and Corbans are little more than brand names without heart or soul, with wines that are seldom seen on export markets. And Montana itself has been taken over by the multinational drinks group Allied-Domecq.

Meanwhile, the number of individual wineries has ballooned from 100 in the mid-1980s to more than 700 in 2011. The range of varietals has blossomed in their wake, as boutique producers have sought something different with which to gain an edge. Nowhere has this been more evident than in red wine varieties. Just over 20 years ago, almost all of New Zealand's red wines were noted for their herbaceous flavours, a result of excessive vigour in the vineyard, but this has been eradicated through better canopy management. Bordeaux varieties are now old hat, Pinot Noir has become one of the country's hottest wines, and even Syrah is excelling.

After Montana and Nobilo, the largest wine producer is Villa Maria, followed by a number of fairly big, well-known wineries, but the majority of wineries are very small operations. The large range of New Zealand brands available even on export markets like the UK makes it hard to believe that Montana processes more

than half of the country's entire wine output. This is a heavy responsibility to bear, but one that rests lightly on Montana's shoulders, since it also produces many of the country's finest and best value wines. It is a role model that other large wine producers throughout the world should follow.

The future should be bright for New Zealand if it can accept Sauvignon Blanc as the gift it is and show restraint in yields, thereby consolidating quality, thus the reputation, of its wines. This consolidation begins in the vineyard, getting to grips with where each variety grows best, and within these areas, selecting a compact range of site-specific clones and rootstock. It also means looking up from the valley floor to the surrounding hills, which is where the future lies. I cannot imagine that anyone has stood on the hills surrounding Marlborough and not wondered whether the vines are in the right place. Obviously they are not badly sited because quality speaks for itself, but some pretty special wines could be made in those hills. Irrigation is the problem, but not an insurmountable one. Besides, potential pioneers should not be thinking in terms of the irrigation required to churn out valley-floor yields. That would be defeating the object.

There are only two blots on New Zealand's winescape: one is brand disorientation, the other is a lack of a verifiable appellation system. Brand disorientation is when wines blended from two or more countries are sold under the same brand name as pure New Zealand wines. This is particularly dangerous when the name in question is globally famous. If this practice is not restricted to entirely different, easily distinguishable brands, it could undermine New Zealand's reputation as a premium wine producer.

As for a lack of a verifiable appellation system, I do not refer to a draconian system like the French AOC, which dictates what must be grown, how the vines should be trained, and what the style of wine should be. I mean simply a system that can guarantee that what is on the label is what is in the bottle – essentially that the grapes are of the variety claimed and were grown in the area indicated. New Zealand's core regions of Auckland, Bay of Plenty, Gisborne, Hawke's Bay, Northland, Waikato, and Wellington on North Island, and Canterbury, Central Otago, Marlborough, and Nelson on South Island are defined by the Local Government Act of 1974. However, the geographical appellations of Certified Origin status announced in 1996, and mentioned in previous editions of this book, have not been implemented. This was to be the wine industry's interpretation of the Geographical Indications Act 1994, an umbrella law designed to guarantee the origin of numerous products, not just wine. Certified Origin should have been done and dusted long ago, but as one New Zealand wine official put it, "Let's just say it is very complicated, but I am hopeful of some action in the next year or so ... although I am not holding my breath." Complicated or not, the New Zealand wine industry must get its act together if it wants to steer clear of long-running boundary sagas like that in Coonawarra, Australia, and prevent a repeat of various labelling scandals. Particularly as the current definition of origin does not hold water, let alone wine. As the same official source confirmed: sub-regions "are not defined in any legislation", but "they can be used if the grapes are derived from the named place", yet "the boundaries of each such sub-region have not been defined" because they "are evolving over time as new vineyards are developed". And I thought the French were irrational.

NEUDORF VINEYARDS, SOUTH ISLAND
Neudorf Vineyards on South Island produces 2,000 cases annually from its 4.5 hectares (11 acres) of land.

RECENT NEW ZEALAND VINTAGES

2011 This was a large, slightly early harvest of very good quality.

2010 One of the greatest vintages on record.

2009 Good to very good quality on South Island, thanks to severe green pruning and dropping fruit, but it was one of the best red-wine vintages of the decade in Martinborough and Hawke's Bay.

2008 A difficult vintage on North Island, and a huge crop of only average quality on South Island.

2007 This small crop of excellent to great quality almost everywhere (Central Otago was merely good) was overshadowed at the time by the news that phylloxera had been found in Wairarapa (Wellington). With time, it is inevitable that phylloxera will spread – and with 25 per cent of New Zealand's vines ungrafted, it will mean a massive replanting programme.

THE APPELLATIONS OF

NEW ZEALAND

NEW ZEALAND

The New Zealand appellation is usually found on exported cask wines (bag-in-the-box) and inexpensive blended wines sold on the domestic market, such as Montana's Waimanu range and Corbans' White Label (if indeed the wine is from New Zealand at all!).

NORTH ISLAND

Supporting some 70 per cent of the population, North Island is where New Zealand's wine industry began and was confined to until 1973. North Island is technically an appellation in its own right, but seldom seen as such, although it has in the past been used by Azure Bay (Sauvignon Blanc-Sémillon).

AUCKLAND
Sub-regions

Brighams Creek, Clevedon, Drury, Glendene, Great Barrier Island, Henderson, Henderson Valley, Hobsonville, Huapai, Huapai Valley, Ihuamato, Karaka, Kumeu, Lincoln, Mahurangi, Mangatangi, Mangere, Matakana, Matua Valley,
Oneroa, Onetangi, Oratia, Pukekohe, Putiki Bay, Ranui, Riverhead, Riverlea, Sunnyvale, Swanson, Swanson Valley, Taupaki, Waiheke, Waiheke Island, Waimauku, Waitakere, Warkworth, West Auckland, Whitford, Woodhill

In the 1960s, a decade before the first vines were planted in Marlborough, Auckland possessed more than half of New Zealand's vineyards. Even though the area under vine has doubled over the past 10 years, Auckland possesses just 1.7 per cent of the country's vineyards today, such has been the rate of change throughout the rest of New Zealand. Despite this minuscule contribution in terms of vineyard land, Auckland remains the traditional centre of its wine industry, primarily because it houses the headquarters of the largest wine companies: Montana and Villa Maria both bottle wines here from all over the country. And despite growth elsewhere, Auckland still has more wineries than any other region.

Auckland's various wine districts produce some of the country's very finest wines. Clevedon's vineyards are sited on steep, north-facing hillsides, where Cabernet Sauvignon, Malbec, Merlot, Syrah, and even Montepulciano vines are low-yielding and mostly hand-picked. There is also a growing reputation for Chardonnay and Pinot Gris in dessert wine styles. In the 1960s, the Henderson-Oratia district in West Auckland was second only to Hawke's Bay as the country's largest wine producing region, and is still the centre of New Zealand's fortified wine industry. The Kumeu-Huapai district escapes some of the rain that falls on West Auckland, and has long been established as a source of premium varietal wines, including Chardonnay, Merlot, and Cabernet Sauvignon, although some wineries source their fruit from further south. Matakana-Mahurangi is located on the east coast to the north of Auckland. A small, but fast-growing area, it is known for its pinkish-red, iron-rich, granulated clay soil, upon which the local wineries have built a certain red wine reputation and are beginning to show promise for full, fruity white wines. Waiheke Island is much drier and sunnier than mainland Auckland, and is one of New Zealand's most exciting districts for Bordeaux-style reds. Tiny quantities of Cabernet-Merlot have been produced on Great Barrier Island, which is way out in the Pacific, well beyond Waiheke Island. Transport costs have prevented this island from developing a wine industry with any aspirations for a national reputation. Although John Mellars, the largest of Great Barrier Island's two vineyards, with just 1 hectare (2.5 acres) of vines, has managed to survive on local trade since his first crop in 1993.

BAY OF PLENTY
Sub-regions
Bethlehem, Galatea, Katikati, Murupara, Rotorua, Tauranga, Thornton, Whakatane

Known more for its dairy products than for wine, the Bay of Plenty is a very large region containing relatively few wineries, and even fewer vineyards, as most of the producers source their fruit from Hawke's Bay or elsewhere. The most famous names here are Morton Estate and Mills Reef, but only Covell Estate has any significant area under vine (7 hectares/17 acres and growing).

EAST COAST

This multi-regional appellation straddles the eastern coast of both North Island and South Island, which effectively encompasses 90 per cent of all the vines growing in New Zealand. It is used by high-volume wines where the brand name and flexibility of sourcing are more important than a specified provenance. Current users of the East Coast appellation include Azure Bay (Sauvignon Blanc-Sémillon), Babich (Chardonnay, Pinot Noir, and Pinotage), Montana (which owns the Azure brand, but also has an export-only East Coast range under the Montana label for Cabernet Sauvignon-Merlot, Chardonnay – usually Marlborough, Unwooded Chardonnay – usually Gisborne, and Pinotage), and Villa Maria (Gewürztraminer, Merlot-Cabernet, Müller-Thurgau).

GISBORNE
Sub-regions
Bushmere, Hexton, Makaraka, Makauri, Manutuke, Matawhero, Mohaka, Muhaka, Muriwai, Ormond, Ormond Valley, Patutahi, Te Araroa, Te Karaka, Tolaga Bay, Waihirere, Waimata, Wairoa

Gisborne is synonymous with Poverty Bay and has been dubbed "carafe country" due to its once-enormous yields of Müller-Thurgau. But Gisborne Müller-Thurgau has become uneconomic for even the cheapest bag-in-the-box wines (which are now mostly blended with imported wines). Consequently, the amount of Müller-Thurgau grown has dropped dramatically.

Now Chardonnay is the region's major grape variety but Gisborne still has a reputation as a source of blending fodder. Most vineyards are located on the plains either side of the Waipaoa River, and although the grape varieties grown have improved, this area is primarily flat and extremely fertile, thus it is inclined to churn out even the most classic of grapes at relatively high yields. Little wonder then that Gisborne regularly produces a higher tonnage of grapes than Hawke's Bay, despite having half the area under vine. There is no sense of place to most of the wines produced, since Gisborne Chardonnay averages over 100 hectolitres per hectare. It is, however, ideal for bulking out young, easy-drinking multi-regional blends, and this is one reason why only a small proportion ends up under the Gisborne appellation.

Another reason is the small number of wineries, although this is starting to change, having risen from 19 to 27 since 2007. In the hands of quality-conscious growers, even vineyards on the flats can produce expressive Chardonnay. With moves into the hills overlooking the plains, we can expect to see more individual, higher quality Gisborne Chardonnay in future years.

More than one-third of Gisborne's vines are in flat-as-a-pancake Patutahi. To the south is Manutuke, the region's oldest winegrowing district (1894), where some of Gisborne's rare red wine varietals can be found, including Malbec and Pinot Noir. White grapes vary from Chenin Blanc (probably Gisborne's best) to Chardonnay, Muscat, and Riesling. Prior to the Chardonnay boom, Gisborne's only premium varietal was Gewürztraminer from around Matawhero, on the opposite bank of the Waipaoa. Although this was and still is justly famous by New Zealand's standards, its rendition is more floral than spicy, and Gewürztraminer from Montana's Patutahi estate has been every bit as impressive. North of Matawhero, radiating out from the suburbs of Gisborne itself, the Makauri district runs either side of the Taruheru River into Makaraka and Bushmere. Makauri grows some of the region's better Müller-Thurgau, along with Muscat, Sémillon, and Merlot. On the other side of the plain, at the foot of the Hexton Hills, some of this bulk-blending region's more exotic varieties can be found, including Gewürztraminer, Malbec, Merlot, and Viognier. Creeping further northwest, around the edge of the foothills, is Waihirere, which is also referred to as the Golden Hills. This area has a reputation for Chardonnay, as does Ormond further north. Corbans' late, lamented Cottage Block Chardonnay came from the Benson Vineyard in the Ormond region. It is now called Whitmore Vineyard, and in good years the grapes go into the Montana "O" Ormond Estate Chardonnay. Gisborne's northernmost vines are found at Tiritiri Organic Vineyard, in the back of beyond, on the upper reaches of the Waimata River.

In conclusion, Gisborne is essentially white wine country, where loose-cluster grapes perform best. Varieties with tightly packed clusters run the risk of rot, while most red varieties (less than 10 per cent of all Gisborne vines) are difficult to ripen. This may change as more early-ripening clones of classic red wine varieties become available, and if growers plant a thirst-quenching cover-crop between the rows to mop up as much of the diluting rain as possible.

HAWKE'S BAY
Sub-regions
Bay View, Clive, Crownthorpe, Dartmoor, Dartmoor Valley, Eskdale, Fernhill, Flaxmere, Gimblett Road, Greenmeadows, Haumoana, Havelock North, Heretaunga, Hastings, Korokipo, Mangatahi, Maraekakahoe, Matapiro, Meeanee, Mere Road, Mt Erin, Napier, Ngatarawa, Ngaruroro, Ohiti, Ohiti Road, Okawa, Omarunui, Pakuratahi Valley, Puketapu, Roy's Hill, Sherenden, Swamp Road, Taradale, Te Awanga, Te Mata, Tuki Tuki, Tutaekuri, Twyford, Waiohiki, Wharerangi, Woodthorpe

Hawkes Bay or Hawke's Bay? As the *Encyclopaedia Britannica* and even official Hawke's Bay publications use both spellings, even on the same page, each name is obviously in common usage. But since Captain Cook named the bay after the First Lord of the Admiralty, Lord Hawke, it should really be Hawke's Bay with an apostrophe. Hawke's Bay is the driest wine region in the country and has the most diverse range of soils, including but not restricted to fine alluvium over greywacke gravel, hard-pan clays, heavy silts, sandy loams, sandy loams over clay, sandy silt loams over gravel, stones over gravel, and stony gravels. Hawke's Bay has always offered more potential for Cabernet Sauvignon and its derivative blends than Marlborough or any other New Zealand region, but it is wrong to class this region as red wine country, let alone the sole province of Bordeaux varieties. It is at least as exciting for Chardonnay, and a handful of producers compete even with Marlborough's best Sauvignon Blancs, albeit in a richer, fuller style.

The two most important grape varieties are Chardonnay and Merlot, but the complex matrix of soils, the differences in aspect, and local variations in climate open up Hawke's Bay to myriad different grape varieties, some of which are yet to be planted. Gimblett Road is only just finding its feet for polished Syrah that is neither Australian nor Rhône in style, and seems likely to eclipse the already heady reputation of this designated district's Cabernet Sauvignon and Chardonnay. Roy's Hill is synonymous with Gimblett Road, although geographically Gimblett Road is located at the foot of Roy's Hill. Gimblett Gravels is a memorable, descriptive appellation invented by a number of wineries to market the superior qualities of their Gimblett Road vineyards. Adjacent to Gimblett Road, to the southwest, is Ngatarawa. (The "g" in Maori names beginning "Ng" is silent, thus Ngatarawa is pronounced "na-ta-rawaa".) This region is also known as the Redmetal Triangle, because the free-draining gravel deposits are known locally as "red metals" due to their colour and metal content. However, what distinguishes Ngatarawa from the neighbouring Gimblett Road is the different water-retention capacity of the gravel subsoil. In Ngatarawa, the gravels retain more moisture, giving the area a slight edge in hotter years, whereas Gimblett Road has the advantage in cooler vintages. Ngatarawa reds are generally softer than those from Gimblett Road, with Merlot the best-suited variety. It is also well known for its botrytized whites.

Dartmoor Valley could be called the Tutaekuri Valley, as its vineyards are laid out along its banks and in its hinterland, over the hills behind Taradale, leading up to Woodthorpe and beyond. This is indeed Bordeaux country, favouring Cabernet Sauvignon on the lower reaches, and Merlot further upriver. Chardonnay also fares well, particularly on the upper reaches and at Swamp Road, north of Omahu, between the Ngaruroro and Tutaekuri rivers, and in the vineyards of Fernhill and Korokipo on the northern bank of the Tutaekuri. Eskdale is north of Napier, but the climate is cooler than the Hastings area due to sea breezes drawn up the Esk Valley, although nights can be warmer. Soils are relatively fertile, although more gravelly towards the coast, where the wines take on more finesse. Big, bold Bordeaux-type reds can be produced from Eskdale through the Esk Valley, and a little further south at Bay View. Sheltered by Te Mata Peak, the north-facing slopes of Te Mata's famous Coleraine vineyard at Havelock North, southeast of Hastings, are suntraps that have established over 30 years their ability to produce top-class Cabernet Sauvignon.

To the east is Te Awanga, a coastal block of vines from the northern suburbs of Te Wanga to the mouth of the Tukituki River, where some surprising big, bold Chardonnay and Bordeaux-style blends are grown. To the west of Ngatarawa, on the bend of the Ngaruroro River is Maraekakahoe, while further upriver and significantly cooler is the up-and-coming area of Mangatahi. Growers believe that Mangatahi's greater diurnal extremes of temperature will enable it to establish a reputation as Burgundy country, in both red and white formats. On the opposite, northern bank is the even newer Crownthorpe area, which is also known as Matapiro, and best suited to early-ripening varieties. Waipawa and Waipukurau are located at the centre of Hawke's Bay itself, but way off the established Hawke's Bay viticultural map, to the southwest of Maraekakahoe. These new winegrowing areas are distinctly cool, offering the promise of crisper white wines than Hawke's Bay has previously been known for, and with hopes for sparkling wines and Pinot Noir.

NORTHLAND
Sub-regions

Dargaville, Kaikohe, Kaitaia, Kerikeri, Kohukohu, Otaika, Raumanga, Ruakaka, Sweetwater, Te Hana, Whangarei

It was in Kerikeri, Northland, that Samuel Marsden planted New Zealand's first vines in 1819. Shortly after, in 1833, James Busby, the so-called father of Australian viticulture, settled at Waitangi, where two years later he established his own vineyard. Despite these auspicious beginnings, local winemaking dwindled to almost nothing until quite recently. Production has tripled over the past 15 years, but starting from a minuscule point. There are even now just seven wineries, and the vines planted do not represent even one per cent of the country's vineyards. Currently most vines are located in three districts: Kaitaia on the far northwest, the Bay of Islands (which contains the appellation Kaikohe and Kerikeri) in the northeast, and around Whangarei, Northland's largest city. These areas boast the country's warmest climate, hence Cabernet Sauvignon, Chardonnay, and Merlot are the three most widely planted varieties. But they

also have the highest rainfall and humidity, particularly on the west coast, and thus suffer fungal diseases and variations in yield. Sémillon, Pinot Gris, and Syrah are on the rise.

WAIKATO
Sub-regions

Cambridge, Hamilton, Karangahake, Mangatawhiri, Ngahinepouri, Ohaupo, Paeroa, Pokeno, Pukeroro, Tamahere, Te Kauwhata, Thames

Situated inland, south of Auckland, and dotted across various diverse locations, Waikato is more cow country than wine region. Indeed, the cows in this area are said to outnumber humans by five-to-one, which is why the region is known as Mooloo to the locals. It encompasses the Te Kauwhata district, where yields are lower, but the climate is hotter and more humid, thus making it more suitable for botrytized wines.

WELLINGTON
Sub-regions

East Taratahi, Gladstone, Kapiti, Longbush, Martinborough, Masterton, Otaki, Pirinoa, Ponatahi, Taratahi, Te Horo, Te Muna, Tuhitarata, Waingawa, Wairarapa

This region can be divided into two distinctly different viticultural districts: Te Horo, a two-winery district to the west of the Taraua Range, and Wairarapa, which encompasses among other areas Martinborough, Wellington's most important district. It is extraordinary to think that Martinborough was only of minor importance in the first edition of this book, as it rapidly achieved a name in the early 1990s as a potentially exciting area for Pinot Noir. This mantle has since been taken over by Central Otago, which has turned out to be no bad thing for Martinborough, since it has always been at least as good for Chardonnay as for Pinot Noir, and is probably the best place to grow Sauvignon Blanc on New Zealand's North Island. But it does not stop there, as its Rieslings are among the best in the country, not to mention its reputation for Pinot Gris and Gewürztraminer, although this is more in a New World context than objectively defined.

Just a few kilometres east of the town of Martinborough is Te Muna, an up-and-coming sub-district with great hopes for Pinot Noir, as evidenced by Larry McKenna's Escarpment vineyard. Craggy Range is also planting Sauvignon Blanc, Chardonnay, Pinot Gris, and Riesling in addition to Pinot Noir, and when all of its vineyards come on stream, such is its belief in Te Muna, it will double Martinborough's output. Other Wairarapa areas include East Taratahi, Gladstone, and Masterton. Gladstone is southwest of Masterton, north of Martinborough, where some the first

Wairarapa vines were planted. Gladstone and the nearby East Taratahi area are well suited to Riesling and Sauvignon Blanc in the main, whereas Pinot Noir is grown on the sunniest, north-facing slopes. This area is attracting a lot of interest; so too is Masterton itself, where the same varieties are planted, though many of the vineyards are really quite young.

SOUTH ISLAND

South Island has a much lower population than North Island and, due to transport difficulties, was not cultivated until 1973. It has quickly demonstrated exciting potential for premium varietals. Technically an appellation in its own right, it is seldom seen as such.

CANTERBURY
Sub-regions

Akaroa, Amberley, Banks Peninsula, Burnham, Christchurch, Coutts Island, Halswell, Kaiapoi, Kaituna Valley, Lansdowne, Larcomb, Lincoln, North Canterbury, Omihi, Omihi Hills, Omihi Valley, School Road, Selwyn, Swannanoa, Taitapu, Tram Road, Two Chain Road, Waikari, Waipara, Waipara Valley, Weka Pass, West Melton

Although the summer here can be as warm as in Marlborough, the autumn is cooler and overall temperatures are lower. At just 62 centimetres (24 inches), the annual rainfall is substantially lower than in Marlborough and less than half of that received in Auckland. Most vineyards are located on the plains surrounding Christchurch, New Zealand's third-largest city, or at Waipara, a coastal area to the north. Quality is less consistent than it used to be, but this region still promises more than it gives. Anyone who has driven from Marlborough to Queenstown and back again knows just how flat and boring the plains around Christchurch are. It is depressing, after driving through some of the world's most spectacular scenery. There are one or two interesting producers on the plains, where the most successful wines are Pinot Noir and Chardonnay in an elegant style, but the best wineries have vineyards elsewhere.

Winegrowing in this region began as early as 1840 on the Banks Peninsula, but it has been stop-start here ever since. With just one winery and 3 hectares (7 acres) of vines, production is negligible. Waipara is the one classic winemaking area in the Canterbury region, with a variety of soils, including clays, gravels, and, in the promising Waikari-Weka Pass area to the north, brilliant-white, hard limestone. This encourages a number of different grapes to be planted. Currently, Pinot Noir, Chardonnay, Sauvignon Blanc, and Riesling fare best, but other varieties include Pinot Gris, Sémillon, and Gewürztraminer. Even Cabernet Sauvignon and Merlot are grown.

CENTRAL OTAGO
Sub-regions

Alexandra, Ardgau Valley, Bannockburn, Bendigo, Central Otago, Cromwell, Dunstan, Earnscleugh, Ettrick, Gibbston, Hawea, Lake Hayes, Lowburn, Luggat, Omarama, Queenstown, Roxburgh, Tarras, Waitaki Valley, Wanaka

Otago is the authentic regional name, but because the vineyards are located inland, the term Central Otago has evolved, and is more commonly used in a viticultural context than Otago itself. Central Otago is the fastest-developing wine region in New Zealand, having grown 20-fold over the past 15 years, and is the hottest, hippest, coolest place in New Zealand for vineyard investors. The cause of all this activity is the grape variety being grown. Fifteen years ago, no one knew what they should be growing in Central Otago. In fact, so confused was the issue that local growers would lobby every passing wine journalist for his or her opinion. With heat summation well below the supposed minimum for ripening grapes of 1,000°C degree-days, the growers assumed that it must be white wine country; but what variety, and whether to plump for sparkling, nobody was quite sure. If anything, there was a tendency to think of playing it safe with German varieties. No one ever imagined Central Otago could be red wine country, let alone a potential home for Pinot Noir, the Holy Grail of all red wine grapes. But since Central Otago Pinot Noir took off in the late 1990s, there has been no stopping it. A lesson, perhaps, for all those "fruit salad" regions throughout the world: find the right grape and create a reputation, rather than trying to be all things to all consumers.

So, what makes Pinot Noir work in heat summation-challenged Central Otago? Well, heat is not everything, and summation does not take account of the beneficial effect of diurnal temperature difference. Warm daytimes ripen the fruit, but the cooler it is at night, the more acidity is preserved, yielding brighter, more vibrant fruit. In Central Otago, the difference between the highest daytime and lowest night-time temperatures can be as much as 30°C. Furthermore, the days this far south are long, with little cloud and low rainfall, thus exceptionally sunny and dry. At Bannockburn, in the heart of Central Otago's Pinot Noir country, the average annual precipitation is half that of rot-prone Burgundy. There are just 50 centimetres (20 inches) of rainfall, yet Milford Haven, only 120 kilometres (75 miles) away, can have over 850 centimetres (28 feet) in a single year. And finally, the schistous loess is a heavy-textured soil, which the Pinot likes, but schist tends to powder, rather than clay up, and thus provides excellent drainage. The fact that there is very little rot, due to low humidity (30 to 40 per cent), is just the icing on the cake, keeping the vineyards clean and free from the chemicals that are often used to combat cryptogamic diseases.

Although trial blocks of vines had been planted as far south as Alexandra in the 1950s, it was not until 1976 that Central Otago's first commercial vineyard, Rippon, was established in Wanaka. And it took another five years for the first commercial vineyards to be planted in what would become Pinot country, between Gibbston (Gibbston Valley, 1981) and Alexandra (Black Ridge, 1981). Wanaka represents just three per cent of Central Otago production and did not attract any other wineries until 1994, when Mount Maude started planting further north, halfway between Albert Town and Lake Hawea, and more recently when the Orpington Vineyard was established on the Ballantyne Road in Wanaka. Only time will tell whether these are just the first two in a last-minute rush. Alexandra is the most southerly established wine area in New Zealand; yet, counterintuitively, it is one of the warmest wine areas in Central Otago. Some claim it to be the very hottest, but it is an area of extremes. Whereas the sunny, north-facing sites are indeed among Central Otago's warmest, other parts are too cool for any sort of viticulture. By contrast, Gibbston is one of the coolest districts in the region, and its Pinot Noir wines are just beginning to shine. More than two-thirds of all the vines planted in Central Otago are found between Lowburn and the Cromwell Basin, including Bannockburn, the most intensively planted area in the region. It is much too early to make definitive

statements as to which Central Otago area is best, but based on the wines produced so far, the warm north-facing sites in Bannockburn are definitely leading the pack for Pinot Noir. Bendigo is located at the northern end of Lake Dunstan in the Cromwell Basin. No wineries exist as yet, but many Central Otago wineries own vineyards or purchase fruit from here. Bendigo is the warmest of all the Central Otago wine areas, and even grows Syrah. Lake Hayes is located at the junction for Arrowtown and it boasts some of New Zealand's highest vineyards, which can only be considered a gamble at this southerly latitude. Bendemere is its highest and coldest vineyard, off the heat-summation viability scale, somewhere in the low 800s, which must be scary, even for a hardened gambler. The most southerly vines are found in the Margaret-John Vineyards at Ettrick, 40 kilometres south of Alexandra.

MARLBOROUGH

Sub-regions

Awatere, Awatere Valley, Benmorven, Blenheim, Brancott, Brancott Valley, Conders Bend, Dillons Point, Dillons Point Road, Dog Point, Fairhall, Fairhall Valley, Hawkesbury, Kaituna, Koromiko, Lower Wairau, Marshlands, Omaka, Omaka Valley, Rarangi, Raupara, Renwick, Riverlands, Spring Creek, Waihopai, Waihopai Valley, Wairau, Wairau Valley, Woodbourne

Allan Scott planted the first vines here in 1973. At the time, Scott was opening up Montana's new Stoneleigh vineyard, but he set up his own winery and vineyards in 1990. Marlborough quickly became New Zealand's most famous wine region, and Marlborough Sauvignon Blanc its greatest asset. The part of Marlborough planted with vines is primarily the Wairau plains between the town of Blenheim and the Waihopai River. Protected by the Inland Kaikoura Range from cold, southerly winds, and by North Island from northeasterly winds, the combination of free-draining soils, abundant sunshine, cool nights, and a long growing season creates the ideal environment to produce wines that are marked by electrifyingly bright fruit flavours. Awatere Valley is located to the southeast, just over the Wither Hills, where grapes often take one or two weeks longer to ripen, and show intense flavour. The Lower Wairau and Spring Creek areas are immediately north of Blenheim, where irrigation is seldom necessary, and Sauvignon is giving way to Pinot Noir. Raupara is a warm, sheltered area west of Spring Creek, immediately north of the main Wairau plain, where the grapes are usually harvested first, with fruit-driven whites and some of Marlborough's ripest red wines. Vines have recently been planted north of the Wairau River, at the foot of the Richmond Range in Conders Bend, Kaituna, and further east, in areas that are becoming known for their Sauvignon Blanc and Pinot Noir. Benmorven, Brancott Valley, and Fairhall Valley are part of the Southern Valley, south of Raupara, nestling up to, but not yet climbing, the foothills. The climate is cooler and drier than

Raupara, allowing Riesling and, to a certain extent, Pinot Noir to compete with Chardonnay and Sauvignon Blanc. Further west is Omaka or Hawkesbury Valley, which includes Dog Point, where Pinot Noir shows promise, but frost can be a danger. Situated northeast of Blenheim, the up-and-coming areas of Marshlands and Rarangi are the closest to the sea, with vineyards on free-draining pea-gravel soils overlooking Cloudy Bay. This would be the obvious appellation name, although I think a certain winery might object. Koromiko is further north, along the Tuamarina River, but boasts only one producer, Johannishof, Marlborough's most northerly winery. Kaikoura Winery is Marlborough's most southerly winery, at Kaikoura, which is more famous for its seal colony than for vineyards, although there is a small block of vines.

NELSON

Sub-regions

Appleby, Atawhai, Brightwater, Burkes Bank, Clifton, Golden Bay, Hope, Lower Moutere, Mahara, Mariri, Motueka, Motueka Valley, Moutere, Nelson, Neudorf, Rabbit Island, Redwood Valley, Richmond, Ruby Bay, Stoke, Tasman, Upper Moutere, Waimea, Waimea Plains, Wakapuaka, Wakefield

Nelson is overshadowed by the fame of Marlborough, on the other side of Mount Richmond, but not because of any lack of quality potential. Nelson is known for its long warm summers, cool autumn nights, and for being one of the sunniest places in New Zealand. The only negative factor is rainfall, although that is nowhere near as high as in Auckland. The low profile has been due simply to there being no parcels of land of sufficient size available to attract any of New Zealand's larger wineries. Nelson has thus never benefited from any significant marketing. The high price of land has not helped either. However, over the past 15 years, the decline of Nelson's apple industry has resulted in many orchards being converted to vineyards, increasing the area under vine ninefold and quadrupling the number of wineries.

Many of Nelson's wineries, including most of the oldest established producers, are located on the Waimea plains to the east of Richmond, where rich, fruity wines are made. Similar wines are made to the south, at Brightwater, where most of the region's newest vineyards are located, and to the northwest, at Redwood Valley, which is used by Seifried Estate as a second label. Moutere runs north from Upper Moutere, on the edge of the Redwood Valley, to the southern outskirts of Motueka. Upper Moutere produces the more impressive wines, with a broad structure and a certain minerality of fruit, but most wines are marketed as Moutere plain and simple. The Motueka wine area north of Motueka itself is quite new, and capable of growing Sauvignon Blanc with an intense, passion-fruit flavour. Clifton and Golden Bay are well to the north of Motueka. Despite having produced wines in the late 19th century, it is generally considered much too wet for grape growing, but that did not stop David Heraud from establishing Waiwera Estate at Clifton in 1989. A few other brave souls have since followed his lead, such as Golden Bay Wines and Parr & Simpson Limestone Bay, both in Takaka.

THE WINE STYLES OF
NEW ZEALAND

BOTRYTIZED WINES

Botrytis, or noble rot, appears on an unpredictable basis throughout all of New Zealand's wine regions. The nearest that New Zealand has to a dedicated dessert-wine area is Te Kauwhata in Waikato, because of its high humidity. As such, it is a two-winery sub-district. The one producer that specializes in the style is Rongopai. Riesling is, without doubt, the premier grape for this style in New Zealand, producing wines of the most vivid flavour enhanced by a scintillating acidity to deliver a razor-sharp sweetness. Chardonnay is, surprisingly, the second most successful variety, a chance discovery after Hunters produced the first Botrytis Chardonnay in 1987. All peaches and cream, it stunned those lucky enough to taste it, and encouraged other New Zealanders to perfect this unusual wine. Botrytized Sémillon has yet to make its mark, but should do so now that less grassy clones are coming into production.

⌇— 1–15 years

🍷 *Dry River* (Botrytis Riesling) • *Fromm* (Auslese) • *Giesen* (Canterbury Late Harvest Riesling) • *Martinborough* (Late Harvest Riesling) • *Montana* (Virtu Noble Semillon) • *Rongopai* (Ultimo Late Harvest) • *Villa Maria* (Noble Reserve Riesling)

CABERNET FRANC

Increasingly popular as a pure varietal wine, Cabernet Franc has always been considered a useful component in classic red wine blends. Hawke's Bay is the best region, and Gimblett Road the best sub-district.

⌇— 2–5 years (up to 15 for exceptional wines)

🍷 *Clearview* • *Kim Crawford* (Wicken)

CABERNET SAUVIGNON
Pure and Blended

Not so long ago, New Zealand suffered from a reputation for green, aggressive red wines. It was white-wine country, and its cool climate was thought to be too cool to ripen such thick-skinned grapes as Cabernet Sauvignon. Today, however, almost every wine region in New Zealand has become a gold mine for rich, ripe red wines of the most serious and sensual quality. Even volume-selling brands such as Montana Cabernet Sauvignon are big, full, and spicy, with more quality and character than you can find in Bordeaux for twice the price. The most exciting Cabernet Sauvignon wines are produced by strict selection from top vineyards or crafted by smaller boutique wineries. Hawke's Bay is the best region, and Gimblett Road the best sub-district.

⌇— 2–5 years (up to 15 for exceptional wines)

🍷 *Craggy Range* (The Quarry) • *Firstland* (Cabernet-Merlot-Malbec) • *Goldwater Estate* (Cabernet-Merlot) • *Montana* (Tom) • *Stonyridge* (Larose) • *Te Mata* (Coleraine) • *Trinity Hill* (Gimblett Road) • *Vidal* (Joseph Soler) • *Villa Maria* (Reserve Cabernet Sauvignon-Merlot)

CHARDONNAY

The world's most widespread classic grape really does produce something special in New Zealand, which is why its cultivation has increased from 350

hectares (865 acres) in the late 1980s to more than 3,700 hectares (9,143 acres) today. It is generally less predictable, more expressive, and capable of a slower, more classic rate of maturation than its Australian equivalent. This is due not only to cooler climatic conditions, but also to hand-picking, whole-bunch pressing, a wider use of natural (local) yeast fermentation, and less obvious oak, although some producers can spoil the natural elegance of these wines by various permutations of malolactic fermentation and lees-contact that turn out too heavy-handed. There is more weight and complexity in Hawke's Bay, greater finesse in Marlborough, lusher qualities in Nelson, and more upfront fruit in Gisborne. Central Otago still has to establish its style.

⌇— 1–4 years

🍷 *Ata Rangi* (Craighall) • *Clearview* • *Kumeu River* (Maté's Vineyard) • *Matua Valley* (Ararimu) • *Morton Estate* (Coniglio) • *Neudorf* (Moutere) • *Nobilo* (Icon) • *Villa Maria* (Reserve Barrique Fermented Gisborne)

CHENIN BLANC

New Zealanders should be able to show South Africa that their country can produce far more exciting Chenin Blanc than the Cape can. But the variety has never been widely planted here, and what there is has been declining of late. Pity; it would be great if, after Sauvignon Blanc, New Zealand could demolish the reputation of the Loire's other famous white grape. An opportunity missed?

⌇— 1–3 years

🍷 *The Millton Vineyard* (Te Arai)

CLASSIC WHITE-WINE BLENDS

Classic white-wine blends are one of New Zealand's slowest-developing niches, yet ultimately they could prove to be one of its most rewarding. The most logical partner for Sauvignon is Sémillon, of course, although until recently the only Sémillon vines cultivated in New Zealand were aggressively aromatic and unsuited for blending unless used in a covert way to emphasize the character of a seemingly pure Sauvignon Blanc wine. For classic blends, however, where a more neutral base is required, New Zealand's traditional late-ripening Swiss clone is much too grassy. The popular Australian Chardonnay-Sémillon blend is not a common combination in New Zealand, where Chardonnay does not need to be crisped up, but Chardonnay and Chenin Blanc have proved to be surprisingly good bed-mates.

⌇— 1–3 years

🍷 *Pegasus Bay* (Sauvignon-Sémillon) • *Villa Maria* (Private Bin Chardonnay-Chenin)

GEWÜRZTRAMINER

This is one of New Zealand's potentially exciting niche wines. But the wrong vine stock, and little understanding of how to produce a classic dry Gewürztraminer with any real spice, results in typically wishy-washy wines, with rose-petal aromas and Turkish delight fruit. These are the best, but none of them truly excites me.

⌇— 1–3 years

🍷 *Dry River* • *Lawson's Dry Hills* • *Margrain* • *Montana* ("P" Patutahi)

SAUVIGNON BLANC GRAPES, CLOUDY BAY
Cloudy Bay makes one of Marlborough's greatest Sauvignon Blancs, and its cult following has benefited the reputation of the entire New Zealand wine industry.

MALBEC
Pure and Blended

Increasing at a rate similar to Syrah, Malbec does not have the same single-varietal cachet. It is judged more useful for its ability to add some mid-palate smoothness to a classic red wine blends. The pure Malbecs of Fromm and Mills Reef are exceptions. Hawke's Bay is the best region, and Gimblett Road the best sub-district.

🍷⤳ 2–8 years

🍷 *Esk Valley* (The Terraces) • *Fromm* (Reserve) • *Mills Reef* (Elspeth)

MERLOT
Pure and Blended

Fifteen years ago there was twice as much Cabernet Sauvignon growing in New Zealand as there was Merlot. Now the position has reversed, even though the area planted with Cabernet Sauvignon has increased eight-fold. Merlot is much more lush than any of the Cabernet varieties, but with a more European structure than California Merlot. Some wines, such as the Goldwater Esslin, are not made every year. Hawke's Bay is the best region, and Gimblett Road the best sub-district.

🍷⤳ 2–8 years

🍷 *Craggy Range* (Sophia) • *Esk Valley* (Reserve Merlot-Malbec-Cabernet Sauvignon) • *Matua* Valley (Bullrush) • *C J Pask* (Gimblett Road Reserve) • *Sacred Hill* (Brokenstone) • *Selaks* (Founders Reserve) • *Sileni* (EV) • *Trinity Hill* (Gimblett Road) • *Unison Vineyard* (Unison Selection)

PINOT GRIS

The most successful are closer to Pinot Grigio in style than to the spicy variety grown in Alsace, but it is distinctly superior Pinot Grigio, with more delicious, riper fruit.

🍷⤳ 1–3 years

🍷 *Ata Rangi* (Lismore) • *Chard Farm* • *Kim Crawford* (Boyzone) • *Dry River* • *Neudorf* (Moutere) • *Palliser Estate*

PINOT NOIR

The Holy Grail of all grapes was first thought to excel in Martinborough. Although some excellent Pinot Noir wines have been and still are being made there, it certainly has not turned out to be a second Burgundy. South Island has produced most of the best Pinot Noir wines on a consistent basis. First it was Nelson that showed the most promise, particularly from the likes of Neudorf, whose Moutere Pinot Noir rarely fails to please. Then it was Canterbury, followed by Marlborough and, most exciting of all, Central Otago. However, as far as outside observers are concerned, Central Otago made its name on the 1998 vintage, and that was the year of the El Niño-induced drought, after which the region has enjoyed a string of good vintages. We have to remember that Central Otago's heat summation generally defies the viticultural textbooks. There are reasons other than heat summation why viticulture does work this far south, but I think it only prudent that we see what sort of Pinot Noir this region can produce throughout a series of cool vintages before we declare Central Otago to be the southern hemisphere's Burgundy.

🍷⤳ 2–8 years

🍷 *Akarua* • *Ata Rangi* • *Craggy Range* (Te Muna) • *Felton Road* (Block 3, Block 5) • *Martinborough Vineyard* (Reserve) • *Neudorf* (Moutere) • *Two Paddocks* (The Last Chance)

RIESLING

Truly dry Riesling is still a minority product in New Zealand, where most renditions of this variety have some residual sugar, even if the result is not a distinctive sweetness. New Zealand Riesling seems to be generally crisper than its Australian counterpart, with more citrous finesse. It does not have the same simplistic lime fruit, and is not inclined to go petrolly very quickly either. In structure and style it leans closer to northern Europe, although not as close as the Riesling produced in Michigan or the Finger Lakes of the USA.

🍷⤳ 1–5 years

🍷 *Kim Crawford* • *Dry River* (Craighall) • *Felton Road* • *Framingham* • *Grove Mill* • *Hunter's* (Stoneburn) • *Montana* (Stoneleigh) • *Neudorf* (Dry Moutere) • *Palliser Estate* • *Pegasus Bay* (Aria)

SAUVIGNON BLANC

Why does New Zealand's Sauvignon Blanc have such vivaciously crisp and pure fruit character, while you have to scratch around to find any hint of fruit in most Loire versions of this wine? It is certainly not due to the use of a particularly expressive clone, as the clone in question is the UCD1, which was developed at the University of California, Davis; although it could be argued that the UCD1 has evolved into a more localized clone. All the most important volatile compounds responsible for this grape's aroma have been identified, but some are more abundant in New Zealand than anywhere else; and while others are not, they are invariably more intense. Why this should be so is unknown, other than that there are, no doubt, other odourless compounds that have a synergistic effect upon the more obviously aromatic ones. Denis Dubourdieu of Bordeaux University is convinced it is the uniqueness of New Zealand's soil and climate. Certainly this country in general, but Marlborough in particular, has the rare capability to ripen Sauvignon Blanc slowly to a near-perfect state, enabling a large number of wineries to produce very fresh wines with ripe gooseberry fruit and such an electrifying balance of mouth-watering acidity that the flavours can intensify as grapefruit or passion fruit. Asparagus and peas, especially canned peas, are unwanted characteristics. Since 2004, the Marlborough Wine

ATA RANGI, MARTINBOROUGH
This estate produces consistent Pinot Noir.

Research Centre has received a government grant of NZ$1.6 million (US$1.25 million) per annum to investigate the factors affecting the aroma and flavour profile of New Zealand Sauvignon Blanc and how the processes involved can be harnessed in the vineyard and during fermentation. This expenditure reflects the importance of New Zealand's flagship variety, the country's most widely cultivated grape, with almost 17,000 hectares (42,000 acres) planted, more than doubling in area since 2005. Sauvignon Blanc now represents over 60 per cent of all New Zealand wines and more than 80 per cent of its wine exports.

🍷⤳ 1–2 years (not older, unless you like the asparagus or tinned-peas character that quickly develops with bottle-age in these wines, particularly when from the ripest vintages)

🍷 *Cloudy Bay* • *Craggy Range* • *Kim Crawford* • *Hunter's* • *Isabel Estate* • *Koura* (Whalesback) • *Montana* (B Brancott) • *Nobilo* (Icon) • *Palliser Estate* • *Villa Maria*

SPARKLING WINES

At one time, Montana's Lindauer Brut and Rosé exemplified New Zealand's sparkling-wine industry. They are very good for creamy, easy-drinking fizzes made by the transfer method, but it took collaboration between Montana and Deutz to put this country on the bottle-fermented sparkling-wine map. However, it was *champenois* Daniel Le Brun who actually demonstrated Marlborough's true potential for serious sparkling wine. Le Brun's star shone so brightly in the early 1990s that he eclipsed even Montana. With the benefit of hindsight, however, we can see that his reputation was built on just three vintages: 1989, 1990, and 1991. It was the quality of these particular vintages and the speed with which Le Brun achieved this quality that grabbed the wine media's attention. Meanwhile, Cloudy Bay's Pelorus was slowly developing a cult following to match that of its Sauvignon Blanc. When Hunter's released its deliciously fresh and easy-drinking Miru Miru, the international wine press was willing to concede the potential of Kiwi fizz, even though the Hunter's Brut is the superior wine. Quartz Reef now promises to put Central Otago on the sparkling-wine map, although Marlborough still reigns supreme.

🍷⤳ 1–2 years (from purchase)

🍷 *Kim Crawford* (Rory) • *Hunter's* (Hunter's Brut, Miru Miru) • *Montana* (Lindauer Special Reserve, Deutz Blanc de Blancs) • *Cloudy* Bay (Pelorus) • *Quartz Reef* (Chauvet NV, Chauvet vintage)

SYRAH

This could be one of New Zealand's greatest wines. The quality of this grape has come a long way since the first commercial release of Stonecroft Syrah, the earliest vintages of which were tight and green. Hawke's Bay is definitely the right place for this variety, specifically in the Gimblett Road sub-district, where the Syrah grows dark and deep, developing a truly lush style that is set off by the classic cracked-peppercorn character. The best examples are neither Rhône nor Australian in style.

🍷⤳ 2–5 years (up to 15 for exceptional wines)

🍷 *Craggy Range* (Le Sol) • *Kingsley Estate* (Gimblett Gravels) • *Te Mata* (Bullnose) • *Trinity Hill* (Gimblett Road) • *Vidal* (Soler)

THE WINE PRODUCERS OF
NEW ZEALAND

AKARUA
Central Otago
★★ ⓥ

This Bannockburn winery produces beautiful Pinot Noir at relatively inexpensive prices. I purchased a case of the 2002 to lay down, but drank the lot and had to order another two cases! The Gullies, Akarua's entry-level Pinot Noir, is often better than most producers' top-of-the-line Pinot Noir.

✓ *Pinot Noir*

ALPHA DOMUS
Hawke's Bay
★★½

Sometimes the wines have too much of a fruit-accentuated style, both reds and whites. They are never unfriendly; they just try too hard. Reds have become quite big in recent vintages. Now is the time for this producer to start thinking more about finesse than size.

✓ *Classic red blend* (The Aviator, The Navigator) • *Chardonnay* (AD) • *Pinot Noir* • *Sauvignon Blanc* • *Sémillon* (Leonarda)

ALPINE PACIFIC WINES
Canterbury
★

Formerly known as Chancellor Estates, these Waipara wines are sold under The Hanmer Junction and Mount Cass labels.

✓ *Pinot Noir* (Mount Cass)

AMISFIELD
Central Otago
★½

Wines of impressive acidity from vineyards in the Pisa Range foothills, just north of Lowburn. Only Riesling disappoints.

✓ *Pinot Gris* • *Pinot Noir*

ATA RANGI
Martinborough
★★ ⓥ

Clive Paton consistently demonstrates that Martinborough can hack it with Central Otago's very best Pinot Noirs. He also makes one of Martinborough's best Chardonnays. I am currently reserving my opinion on Ata Rangi's Célèbre. Since it has moved away from Cabernet towards more Merlot, and increased its Syrah content, so it has become more blackcurrant and has displayed less complexity and finesse. Hopefully there is a swing back in the pipeline. Or maybe it's just a vintage thing?

✓ *Chardonnay* (Craighall) • *Pinot Gris* (Lismore) • *Pinot Noir*

BABICH
Henderson
★★

The entry-level varietal wines of this large producer have never been exciting, but the top-of-the-range Babich wines, such as Irongate and The Patriarch, always excel (they are two-star wines in their own right), and Babich's Marlborough wines have seen a recent climb in quality.

✓ *Classic red blend* (Irongate) • *Cabernet Sauvignon* (The Patriarch) • *Chardonnay* (Irongate, The Patriarch) • *Pinot Gris* (Marlborough) • *Sauvignon Blanc* (Cowslip Valley Marborough, Marlborough, Winemakers Reserve)

BALDHILLS
Central Otago

A young Pinot Noir and Pinot Gris vineyard with, it seems, excellent potential.

BANNOCK BRAE
Central Otago
★

Although its first vintage was in 2001, Bannock Brae has produced some excellent Pinot Noir, with plenty of ripe, creamy fruit, from its vineyard on the shore of Lake Dunstan. The entry-level Goldfields label is also recommended.

✓ *Pinot Noir*

BENFIELD & DELAMARE
Martinborough
★★½

Minuscule quantities of high quality Bordeaux-style blends produced in Martinborough's Pinot Noir country.

✓ *Classic red blend* (Merlot-Cabernet Sauvignon-Cabernet Franc)

BILANCIA
Hawke's Bay
★

Bilancia is Italian for balance. This is the personal label of Trinity Hill's winemaker, Warren Gibson, and his partner, Lorraine Leheny, who is Bilancia's winemaker. Some excellent wines have been made from purchased grapes since 1997, with Syrah from its own vineyard the following year, and Viognier in 2000.

✓ *Merlot* • *Syrah*

BLACK RIDGE
Central Otago
★

You can rely on good quality Pinot Noir and Chardonnay from this Alexandra vineyard, and sometimes Riesling. Owner Verdun Burgess even grows Cabernet Sauvignon because he was told it would never ripen. "Hey Verdun, bet you'll never grow truffles!"

✓ *Pinot Noir*

BLAKE FAMILY VINEYARD
Hawke's Bay
★★

Wine-loving San Francisco financier Mark Blake is a man on a mission: he wants to produce wine in the style of a great Bordeaux – not just a good Bordeaux or, indeed, an excellent Bordeaux, but a great Bordeaux. In 2002, he bought the 10-hectare (25-acre) Redd Gravels vineyard from Thornbury Wines, and he replanted it in 2002–03. A small amount of 2004 was produced by Doug Wisor, who died tragically young (*see* Craggy Range), but its superb quality is a fitting tribute to the talented winemaker. That vintage and the 2005, 2006, and 2007 have all been released to well-deserved rave reviews. Blake Family Vineyards Redd Gravels is a Merlot-based blend of great intensity balanced by a silky tannic structure that should see it through a couple of decades in bottle.

✓ *Classic red blend* (Redd Gravels)

BROOKFIELD
Napier
★★½

Impressive quality red wines, particularly in recent vintages.

✓ *Classic red blend* (Gold Label) • *Syrah* (Hillside)

CABLE BAY
Waiheke Island
★

It might seem strange that the best wine from this Waiheke Island producer is a very fine Marlborough Sauvignon Blanc, but even its Waiheke Merlot-Malbec-Cabernet is blended from various vineyards spread over the island. Winemakers Neil Culley and Briony Carnachan aim to produce the best wines they can, and they are not frightened to admit that this is not always achieved by restricting themselves to their own vineyards.

✓ *Sauvignon Blanc*

CAIRNBRAE
Marlborough
★★ ⚡ ⓥ

Purchased by Sacred Hill in 2001. The quality here remains high, and the value is even better.

✓ *Chardonnay* • *Riesling* (Late Harvest, Reserve) • *Sauvignon Blanc* (The Stones)

CANTERBURY HOUSE
Waipara

Michael Reid's ambitious project started in 1994, with the first wines produced in 1997. Early wines were disappointing, particularly the dodgy sparkling wine, but gradually the quality picked up, especially the Sauvignon Blanc. However, since the 2002 vintage, the quality at Canterbury House has been on a real roll under the helm of new winemaker Alan McCorkindale.

✓ *Chardonnay* (Reserve) • *Pinot Noir* • *Riesling* (Noble) • *Sauvignon Blanc*

CARRICK
Central Otago

This up-and-coming Bannockburn producer makes mainly Pinot Noir in a clean, rich, fruity, easy-drinking style.

✓ *Pinot Noir*

CELLIER LE BRUN
Marlborough
★

Daniel Le Brun has had no connection with his old company since 1996, when Allan McWilliams took over as winemaker and general manager. Allan has improved the quality of Cellier Le Brun's wines (confusingly sold under the Daniel Le Brun label) since the late-1990s. Second label wines are sold under Terrace Road brand.

✓ *Blanc de Blancs*

CENTRAL OTAGO WINE COMPANY
Central Otago

Affectionately known as CowCo, this bespoke winemaking company is owned by a group of investors, including actor Sam Neill and winemaker Dean Shaw. At the time of writing (2011), in addition to Two Paddocks, Dean also makes the wines for Dry Gulley, Kawarau Estate, Maharg, Mt Rosa, Nevis Bluff, Pisa Mooring, Rock 'n' Pillar, Sleeping Dogs, Surveyor Thomson Wines, Three Miners, and Torr Estate.

CHARD FARM
Central Otago
★

Owned by Rob Hay, one of the earliest viticultural pioneers this far south, Chard Farm enjoys a dramatic location. It is approached along a rough-hewn track that bends around a mountainside, with a steep gorge on one side and barely enough room to drive a car. Some wines still have a tendency to rapidly develop a canned-pea character, but Redgate Pinot Noir is a banker.

✓ *Pinot Gris* • *Pinot Noir* (Redgate) • *Riesling*

CLEARVIEW ESTATE
Hawke's Bay
★★⭒

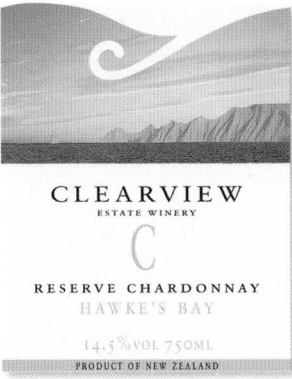

Unashamedly bold-flavoured wines from Tim Turvey, whose red wines have always benefited most from this approach. Some would claim the Chardonnay is one of New Zealand's very best. Production is set to rise due to a 55 per cent increase in vineyard holdings.

✓ *Cabernet Franc* • *Chardonnay* • *Classic red blend* (Merlot-Malbec, Old Olive Block)

CLIFFORD BAY
Marlborough
★

An instant success from its very first vintage (1997), Clifford Bay's white wines have seduced critics and customers alike. They now seem set to repeat the experience with their very own Pinot Noir, as from the 2003 vintage.

✓ *Chardonnay* • *Pinot Noir* • *Sauvignon Blanc*

CLOUDY BAY
Marlborough
★★★⭒

Cloudy Bay is a subsidiary of Cape Mentelle in Western Australia, which is now part of the French LVMH group. With 140 hectares (350 acres) supplying a fraction of its needs, even when newly planted vineyards come on stream, this is a big business. Yet it has developed the aura of a boutique winery, which has been essential to maintaining its perceived cult following and thus its relatively high prices (particularly on export markets). It has cleverly set up such a wide distribution for its Cloudy Bay Sauvignon Blanc that importers mail their clients saying, "Our allotment of seven cases has arrived," and it quickly sells out, giving the impression of a limited production. The Chardonnay is at least as good as the Sauvignon Blanc, but it is the latter that has made Cloudy Bay synonymous with Marlborough's marketing success. This is why the winery released its *barrique*-fermented Te Koko Sauvignon Blanc, rather than mess with the winning formula of its entry-level Sauvignon Blanc. I continue to have a strange, almost love-hate relationship with sparkling Pelorus. In tastings with other sparkling wines, I am invariably disappointed, finding it heavy by comparison, and lacking in finesse. Yet, whenever I order Pelorus in a restaurant, I am seldom disappointed. On its own, in the context of food, Pelorus is never heavy, and always has the finesse that is missing in the clinical ambience of a technical tasting. Sometimes it is the contradictory nature of a wine that makes it special.

✓ *Chardonnay* • *Pinot Noir* • *Sauvignon Blanc* • *Sparkling wine* (Pelorus)

COLLARDS
Henderson
★★⭒Ⓥ

This winery, founded by English horticulturist J W Collard in 1910, is still in family ownership. Brothers Bruce and Geoffrey Collard have maintained the winery's reputation for consistency across the range.

The wines have a rich vibrancy of fruit, notably the textbook Hawke's Bay Chardonnay, which displays a fine youthful complexity.

✓ *Chardonnay* (Hawke's Bay) • *Riesling* • *Sauvignon Blanc*

COOPERS CREEK
Huapai
★★Ⓥ

Despite a proliferation of silly names (Cat's Pee on a Gooseberry Bush Sauvignon, Fat Cat Chardonnay, etc), the winemaking here is very serious.

✓ *Chardonnay* (Swamp Reserve) • *Classic red blend* (Merlot-Cabernet Franc) • *Pinot Noir* (Glamour Puss, Marlborough) • *Riesling* (Hawke's Bay, Marlborough Late Harvest, Nelson) • *Sauvignon Blanc* (Marlborough)

COVELL ESTATE
Galatea
★Ⓑ

You have to be dedicated or mad, preferably both, to stick rigidly to a biodynamic regime. You also have to be dedicated or mad to plant a vineyard in the Bay of Plenty, where no one else has had the confidence to plant more than the odd acre of vines. Either way, Bob Covell makes a fine, steely, citrus-flavoured Riesling.

✓ *Riesling*

CRAGGY RANGE
Hawke's Bay
★★★⭒

The most ambitious wine project New Zealand has seen, the Craggy Range winery, with 285 hectares (700 acres) of vineyards, has so far cost US$36 million. It is owned by Terry Peabody, an American businessman who has lived in Australia for more than 35 years. The winery is a mix of technology and tradition, and finely tuned to produce single-vineyard wines. One of New Zealand's top viticulturists, Steve Smith MW, is in overall charge, and Rod Easthorpe has been appointed winemaker following the tragic sporting accident that took the life of the young and talented Doug Wisor. All the wines show great finesse, from Sauvignon Blanc to Syrah, and everything between. Red Rock is Craggy Range's great-value second label, with interesting wines such as The Underarm Syrah and Gravel Pit Red.

✓ *Entire range*

KIM CRAWFORD
Hawke's Bay
★★

One of New Zealand's most experienced, talented, and award-winning winemakers, Kim Crawford has had his own winery since 1996. It was purchased by the Vincor group, Crawford's Canadian

distributor, in 2004. The quality remains very good, and is climbing even higher. The Boyzone Pinot Gris has lovely fruit, but in true New World fashion, absolutely no spice.

✓ *Cabernet Franc* (Wicken) • *Chardonnay* (Tietjen, Unoaked) • *Classic red blend* (Tane) • *Pinot Gris* (Boyzone) • *Riesling* • *Sauvignon Blanc* • *Sparkling wine* (Rory)

CROSSROADS
Hawke's Bay
★★⭒

The flagship wine here is a classic red blend called Talisman. Crossroads is happy to confirm it is comprised of six different black grape varieties, but refuses to divulge what they are, which has piqued many a New Zealand critic. The Destination Series is an entry-level range of 10 upfront, easy-drinking varietal wines, after which comes the Reserve range, and the Collectors Edition. The future focus will be on Merlot, Cabernet-Merlot, Syrah, and Chardonnay. And, of course, Talisman, whatever that is.

✓ *Chardonnay* (Reserve) • *Pinot Noir* (Collectors Edition) • *Classic red blend* (Talisman)

DELEGAT'S
Henderson
★★⭒

The style is generally quite restrained, with more elegance than richness, but seldom lacking depth or length. Marlborough wines are sold under the Oyster Bay label.

✓ *Classic red blend* (Reserve Cabernet-Merlot) • *Merlot* (Reserve) • *Riesling* (Oyster Bay Botrytized) • *Sauvignon Blanc* (Oyster Bay)

DRY RIVER
Martinborough
★★

Neil McCallum sold Dry River to New York investment manager Julian Robertson and Napa Valley vineyard owner Reg Oliver (*see* Te Awa) in February 2003, but stayed on as winemaker. So, there is no real difference for the time being, except for Neil, who has NZ$11 million in his pocket and, as he does not have to waste time running a business, more time to fish. Neil is known for his Gewürztraminer and Pinot Gris, but I have yet to be impressed beyond New World norms (ie, the wines have no spice). He is, however, capable of producing one of New Zealand's most delicately perfumed dry Rieslings, his Pinot Noirs evolve beautifully, and his decadently rich botrytized wines are the stuff of legend.

✓ *Chardonnay* (Botrytized, Craighall) • *Gewürztraminer* • *Pinot Gris* • *Pinot Noir* • *Riesling* (Botrytized, Craighall) • *Syrah*

DRYLANDS
Marlborough
★ Ⓥ

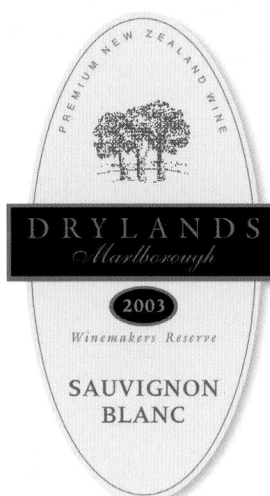

Selaks built this winery before the company was taken over by Nobilo, which itself was purchased by BRL Hardy, now part of Constellation, the world's largest wine-producing group. Easy-drinking reds; much finer whites.

⟋ *Riesling* (Winemakers Reserve) • *Sauvignon Blanc*

ESCARPMENT
Martinborough
★ ✩

If anyone put Martinborough Pinot Noir on the map, it was Larry McKenna, when he was the winemaker at Martinborough Vineyard. This is why his new venture (in partnership with the Kirby family) is so tantalizing for Martinborough Pinot Noir lovers.

⟋ *Pinot Noir*

ESK VALLEY
Hawke's Bay
★ ✩ Ⓥ

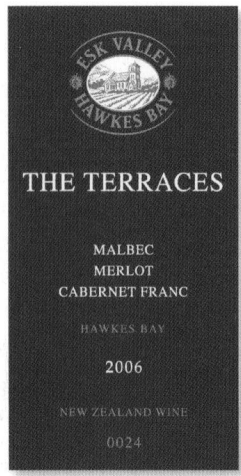

Esk Valley red wines have become increasingly impressive under the ownership of Villa Maria. The Terraces (Malbec-Merlot-Cabernet Franc) is one of New Zealand's most outstanding classic red blends.

⟋ *Classic red blend* (Merlot-Malbec-Cabernet Sauvignon, Merlot-Cabernet Sauvignon, The Terraces) • *Merlot* (Black Label) • *Verdelho*

FAIRHILL DOWNS
Marlborough
★

This vineyard has been planted since 1982, but the Small family did not sell their own wine until 1996. Since then they have developed a reputation for their bold fruit, balanced by crisp, ripe acidity. So vivid was the fruit in the 2003 Pinot Gris that it was almost Sauvignon Blanc-like!

⟋ *Pinot Gris* • *Sauvignon Blanc*

FELTON ROAD
Central Otago
★★★✩

This is the producer of New Zealand's greatest Pinot Noir, and a stunning medium-sweet Riesling. Other labels include Cornish Point (good value, easy-drinking Drystone Pinot Noir). The difference between Felton Road's top-performing Block 3 and Block 5 Pinot Noirs has more to do with the clones than the soil. These vineyards are organic/biodynamic in part, but are not certified as such.

⟋ *Chardonnay* • *Pinot Noir* (Block 3, Block 5) • *Riesling*

FIRSTLAND
Waikato
★★✩

Originally known as De Redcliffe, this Waikato winery now excels at red winemaking, which had previously been its weakest area. Firstland was purchased in 2002 by Ed Astor, a wealthy former publisher from the US, whose decision to take the wines off the New Zealand market and focus on exports has been remarkably successful in boosting the reputation of this winery.

⟋ *Cabernet Sauvignon* (Reserve) • *Classic red blend* • *Cabernet Sauvignon* (Cabernet-Merlot-Malbec) • *Sauvignon Blanc* (Marlborough)

FORREST ESTATE
Marlborough
★★✩

An interesting range of fine wines is produced here, especially the soft, classic Sauvignon Blanc.

⟋ *Classic red blend* (Cornerstone) • *Cabernet Sauvignon* (Cornerstone) • *Merlot* (Cornerstone) • *Riesling* (Botrytized, Late Harvest) • *Sauvignon Blanc*

FOXES ISLAND WINES
Marlborough
★

John Belsham, Hunter's former winemaker, went on to establish Raupara Vintners, a designer-wine

service that catered for the explosion of new labels for vineyards with no winery of their own in the 1990s. He now focuses on his own wines, which invariably show a preference for finesse over weight, size, and overused vinification techniques. John very much specializes in the two classic Burgundian grapes. My only criticism is that he was so darn good with Sauvignon Blanc, he should add that variety.

⟋ *Chardonnay* • *Pinot Noir*

FRAMINGHAM
Marlborough
★★✩ Ⓥ

Although Framingham produces a large and fascinating range of varietal wines, including a rare Montepulciano, its true speciality is Riesling in all its styles.

⟋ *Riesling* • *Sauvignon Blanc*

FROMM
Marlborough
★★✩

George and Ruth Fromm also own the George Fromm winery in Malans, Switzerland, where they currently live. The vineyards here are organic/biodynamic, but not certified as such. Winemaker Hätsch Kalberer believes in the minimum of intervention, regularly relying on wild yeasts and never filtering his red wines. Hätsch has carved out a cosy red-wine niche for Fromm, but his Riesling should not be overlooked, particularly the Auslese. All Fromm wines are sold under the La Strada label.

⟋ *Malbec* (Reserve) • *Pinot Noir* (Fromm Vineyard) • *Riesling* (Auslese) • *Syrah* (Reserve)

GIBBSTON VALLEY
Central Otago
★

Grant Taylor's Pinot Noirs are becoming increasingly fleshy, and this stylistic progression should continue as the new warmer vineyards in Alexandra and Bendigo come into production.

⟋ *Pinot Noir* (Reserve)

GIESEN
WINE ESTATE
Canterbury and Marlborough
★ ✩ Ⓥ

Once the most important winery in Canterbury, the Giesen brothers have invested so heavily in a Marlborough winery and vineyards that this is now their primary location.

⟋ *Pinot Noir* (Canterbury Reserve) • *Riesling* (Canterbury Reserve, Canterbury Late Harvest, Marlborough/Canterbury) • *Sauvignon Blanc* (Marlborough)

GLADSTONE
Wairarapa
✩

This small winery produced its first vintage in 1991, but the current owners took over in 1996. Some interesting reds, but intense Sauvignon is the best buy here.

⟋ *Sauvignon Blanc*

GOLDWATER ESTATE
Waiheke Island
★★★✩

Kim and Jeanette Goldwater produce one of New Zealand's greatest red wines, the Goldwater Cabernet-Merlot (sometimes with some Cabernet Franc). This is a wine of classic quality, which has the richness, finesse, longevity, and potential complexity to compete with the best wines that California, Australia, or Bordeaux can produce.

⟋ *Classic red blend* (Cabernet-Merlot) • *Merlot* (Esslin) • *Sauvignon Blanc* (New Dog)

GRAVITAS
Marlborough
★

This is a fast-rising star in Marlborough's brightly lit firmament, with intensely flavoured, expressive white wines produced by Brian Bicknell.

⟋ *Chardonnay* • *Sauvignon Blanc*

GREENHOUGH
Nelson
★✩

Established in 1991 by Andrew Greenhough and Jenny Wheeler, this small but growing vineyard produces wines that are brimming with fruit.

✓ *Chardonnay* (Hope Vineyard) •
Pinot Noir (Hope Vineyard) •
Riesling (Hope Vineyard) •
Sauvignon Blanc

GROVE MILL
Marlborough
★Ⓥ

Grove Mill is New Zealand's first
carbon-neutral winery, thanks in
part to its "smart cellar". This
involves energy-efficient technology
to draw cold night air into the
winery and high-performance
insulation to keep temperatures
low during the day. There is also
a heat-exchanger to supply the
entire complex with hot water.

✓ *Chardonnay* • *Riesling* •
Sauvignon Blanc

HARRIER RISE VINEYARD
Kumeu
★

The owner-winemaker is Tim
Harris, an Auckland lawyer and
Metro Magazine columnist.
When he established this red
wine specialist venture in 1986, he
called it Waitakere Road Vineyard,
and sold the wine under the
Harrier Rise Vineyard label. He
dropped the Waitakere Road
name in 1997.

✓ *Cabernet Franc* (Monza) • *Merlot*
(Bigney Coigne)

HERON'S FLIGHT
Matakana
★

David Hoskins and Mary Evans
used to make splendid Cabernet
Sauvignon, but they caught the
Italian bug and started trialling
Italian varieties in 1994. By 2004,
they had replaced all the French
varieties with Italian vines.

✓ *Sangiovese*

HERZOG
Marlborough
★☆

These wines might seem expensive,
but if a Michelin-starred restaurant
in a classic European wine region
sold the wine, its customers would
not blink at such prices. And that's
not an unreasonable comparison,
for while Hans Herzog makes the
wines, his wife Therese runs the
winery's restaurant, drawing on
her Michelin-starred experience
in Switzerland.

✓ *Classic red blend* (Spirit of
Marlborough) • *Montepulciano*

HIGHFIELD ESTATE
Marlborough
★

This Japanese-owned estate, with
its brightly coloured Tuscan-styled
winery and restaurant overlooking
the Omaka Valley, is perhaps best
known for its improving sparkling
wine, but rich, smooth Pinot Noir
is the most consistent style here.

✓ *Pinot Noir* • *Sauvignon Blanc* •
Sparkling wine (Elstree)

HUIA
Marlborough
☆

Claire and Mike Allan are white
wine specialists, making only
one red, a Pinot Noir. The
white wines are all hand-picked
and whole-bunch pressed,
which works particularly well
for Sauvignon Blanc and an
improving sparkling wine.

✓ *Sauvignon Blanc*

HUNTER'S
Marlborough
★★Ⓥ

This large, established, and
expanding winery is run by Jane
Hunter, a gifted viticulturist whose
medal-winning standards have
earned her an OBE, the respect
of her neighbours, and the very
first IWS Women in Wine Award.
Gary Duke is her longstanding
winemaker.

✓ *Chardonnay* • *Riesling*
(Stoneburn) • *Sauvignon Blanc*
(Flax Mill, Marlborough,
Winemaker's Selection) •
Sparkling wine (Hunter's,
Miru Miru)

HYPERION
Northland
☆

In Greek mythology, Hyperion was
one of the 12 Titans – the Titan of
light. I'm not quite sure what light
is shining out of John Crone's
winery, a former cowshed north
of Auckland, but of all his wines,
which are named after one Titan or
another, his Gaia Merlot is the one
that most deserves to be set free.

✓ *Merlot* (Gaia)

ISABEL ESTATE
Marlborough
★☆

This winery consistently produces
one of New Zealand's most
impressive Sauvignon Blancs. Watch
out for the occasional release of
Noble Sauvage, a botrytized version
of Marlborough's famous varietal.

✓ *Pinot Gris* • *Pinot Noir* •
Sauvignon Blanc

JACKSON ESTATE
Marlborough
★☆Ⓥ

At one time, Jackson Estate
consistently produced
Marlborough's greatest Sauvignon
Blanc. The quality is still just as
high, but a number of wineries
now make Sauvignon Blanc that is
at least as fine, and which of them
produce the best of the crop varies
from year to year. But Jackson
Estate excels in quality and value
throughout the range.

✓ *Chardonnay* • *Pinot Noir* •
Riesling • *Sauvignon Blanc*

KAHURANGI ESTATE
Nelson
★Ⓥ

This is the original Seifried winery
and 10.5-hectare (26-acre) vineyard.
It was sold in 1998 to the current
owners, Amanda and Greg Day,
who renamed it Kahurangi, which
is Maori for "treasured possession".
Kahurangi might be a new name,
but it boasts the oldest commercial
vineyard in the region. And with
a new 12-ha (30-acre) vineyard
just a kilometre away (on the
northwestern side of Upper
Moutere, planted in 2001),
production is expanding fast.

✓ *Chardonnay* • *Riesling* •
Sauvignon Blanc

KAITUNA VALLEY
Canterbury
★

Owner-winemakers Grant and
Helen Whelan specialize in Pinot
Noir and Chardonnay.

✓ *Pinot Noir*

KARAKA POINT
Auckland

Located on the Karaka Peninsula,
southwest of Auckland, this winery
is probably best known for its
Chardonnay and Syrah (sometimes
sold as Shiraz).

KAWARAU
Central Otago
★◉

A restaurant-winery in an idyllic
setting, with lovely, rich Pinot Noir.

✓ *Pinot Noir*

KEMBLEFIELD
Hawke's Bay
★Ⓥ

John Kemble produces excellent
Chardonnay and Merlot-Cabernet.
For a short while his 2001
Gewürztraminer showed some
spicy potential, but a second
tasting was disappointing, as
were later vintages.

✓ *Chardonnay* (The Distinction)
• *Classic red blend* (Merlot-
Cabernet)

KINGSLEY ESTATE
Hawke's Bay
Ⓑ★☆

Red-wine specialist Kingsley Tobin
is one of only a few organic
producers in Hawke's Bay.

✓ *Classic red blend* (Cabernet-
Malbec, Cabernet Sauvignon-
Merlot) • *Cabernet Sauvignon*
• *Merlot* • *Syrah*

KOURA BAY
Marlborough
★☆

The Whalesback was probably the
most delicious Sauvignon Blanc
produced in 2003. There might be
finer examples, but none that are
more delicious.

✓ *Sauvignon Blanc* (Whalesback)

KUMEU RIVER
Auckland
★★

Master of Wine Michael Brajkovich
regularly produces one of New
Zealand's greatest Chardonnays,
but his reds are just as good.
Excellent value, easy-drinking
wines are sold under the Kumeu
River Village label.

✓ *Chardonnay* (Maté's Vineyard) •
Classic red blend (Melba) • *Merlot*
• *Pinot Gris* • *Pinot Noir*

LAKE CHALICE
Marlborough
★❷Ⓥ

Lake Chalice opened its new
winery in 2004. Called South Pacific
Cellars, and sited at Riverlands for
logistic rather than viticultural
reasons, this is a clever joint
venture with Waipara Hills and
New Zealand Vineyards Ltd. It is
clever because it means that both
wineries can have a state-of-the-art
winery with economies of scale
and efficiencies that would not be
possible on an individual basis.
Top-of-the-range wines are sold
under the Platinum label.

✓ *Chardonnay* (Platinum F V) •
Sauvignon Blanc (Marlborough)

LAWSON'S DRY HILLS
Marlborough
★✫🅥

This winery is capable of producing intensely flavoured white wines. The Gewürztraminer is a bit too pretty-pretty, but highly regarded by New World standards. The Sauvignon Blanc is my favourite.

✓ *Chardonnay • Gewürztraminer • Riesling • Sauvignon Blanc*

LINCOLN
Henderson
✫

Most critics would put Lincoln's Chardonnay first, but I prefer the richer reds, with their minty finesse and fruitcake complexity. The Chardonnay Heritage Patricia is alarmingly overwhelmed by coconutty American oak.

✓ *Classic red blend* (Home Vineyards, Vintage Selection)

McCASHIN'S
Nelson
✫

When the McCashin family sold its famous Nelson brewery to Lion Breweries in 1999, it already had swapped horses, selling the first vintage (1998) of McCashin's wine, albeit from purchased grapes. Initially, wines were sourced from various different regions, but with the purchase of an established 40-hectare (100-acre) vineyard at Hope, this winery has begun to focus its efforts on Nelson.

✓ *Pinot Noir*

MAN O' WAR VINEYARDS
Waiheke Island
★✫

Although 60 hectares (150 acres) of vineyards were planted amid 4,500 hectares (11,120 acres) of rugged clifftop farmland on Waiheke in 1993, this family venture only came to international attention around 2005

✓ *Classic red blend* (Dreadnought, Ironclad)

MARGARET-JOHN
Central Otago
❓

John and Margaret May farm New Zealand's most southerly vineyard, at Ettrick, some 40 kilometres (25 miles) southeast of Alexandra.

MARGRAIN
Martinborough
★

This vineyard was planted in 1992 by Graham and Daryl Margrain, who made their first wine in 1995. In January 2000, they purchased the old Chifney vineyard. Margrain makes one of New Zealand's highest award-winning Gewürztraminers (by New World norms), but the Pinot Noir is the better wine.

✓ *Chardonnay • Gewürztraminer • Pinot Noir • Riesling* (Botrytis Selection)

MARTINBOROUGH VINEYARDS
Martinborough
★★

This winery's reputation was established by winemaker Larry McKenna, but his successor, Claire Mulholland (ex-Gibbston Valley), has proved more than a match.

✓ *Chardonnay • Pinot Noir* (Reserve) • *Riesling* (Jackson Block, Late Harvest)

MATAKANA ESTATE
Auckland
✫

The quality at Matakana's most successful winery has been steadily improving since 2001. Wines are also sold under the Goldridge Estate label.

✓ *Chardonnay* (Goldridge Premium Reserve) • *Pinot Gris* (Matakana)

MATARIKI
Hawke's Bay
★✫

Although owners John and Rosemary O'Connor planted this vineyard as long ago as 1981, they did not start making and selling wines until 1997. Their mission statement is to produce "fruit-driven wines of elegance and complexity" using a "hands-off" approach to viticulture, and a "hands-on" approach in the winery. It has proved to be a very successful winemaking philosophy.

✓ *Chardonnay • Classic red blend* (Quintology)• *Merlot • Sauvignon Blanc • Syrah*

MATAWHERO WINES
Gisborne
✫

Owner Denis Irwin was going to quit a few years ago, but ended up

selling just half of his vineyards and refocusing his operation entirely on Bordeaux and Burgundy varieties. Gewürztraminer used to be his most consistent wine, and many believed it was New Zealand's finest example of that grape. But that was a reputation built on success at international competitions in the 1970s, when expectations were very different. I will not mourn the fact that Denis has sold his Gewürztraminer vineyards. However, if he wanted to reinvent himself as a specialist in Bordeaux grapes, why not move to Hawke's Bay? It is because Denis Irwin never takes the easiest route. So why change now? He has always cropped at a low level, hand-harvested, and used natural yeasts to express the individual *terroir* of his product long before they became fashionable. Occasionally this has produced something stunning, but the results have been inconsistent, which is why I cannot recommend anything specific. You will have to suck it and see, and sometimes you will be very pleased.

MATUA VALLEY
Waimauku
★★

Owned by Beringer Blass since 2001, Matua Valley is located northwest of Auckland, but produces wine mainly from three other regions: Hawke's Bay, Gisborne, and Marlborough. This is a very large producer, with a high-tech winery that regularly produces a range of fine, expressive wines that are a pleasure to drink. The Ararimu label is reserved for Matua Valley's very best wines. At the other end of the price spectrum, the Settler Series concentrates on exceptional value, fruit-driven, entry-level wines. The Innovator series consists of commercial volumes of experimental wines. Excellent Marlborough wines are sold under the Shingle Peak label, and high quality, highly individual wines from the Ngatarawa triangle are sold under the Matheson Vineyard label.

✓ *Chardonnay* (Ararimu, Judd Estate) • *Classic red blend* (Ararimu Merlot-Cabernet Sauvignon) • *Grenache* (Innovator) • *Merlot* (Bullrush) • *Muscat* (Late Harvest) •

Pinot Noir (Wairarapa) • *Sauvignon Blanc* (Matheson Vineyard, Shingle Peak) • *Syrah* (Matheson Vineyard)

DOMAINE GEORGE MICHEL
Hawke's Bay
★🅥

Fine quality Chardonnay from a Beaujolais grower who now lives in New Zealand. There is also good Sauvignon and fairish Pinot Noir.

✓ *Chardonnay*

MILLS REEF
Hawke's Bay
★✫

Deliciously rich, fruity whites, and some stunning reds produced by father-and-son team Paddy and Tim Preston. Elspeth Preston, Paddy's mother, passed away in 2003 at the ripe old age of 94.

✓ *Classic red blend* (Elspeth) • *Malbec* (Elspeth) • *Merlot* (Elspeth) • *Syrah* (Elspeth)

THE MILLTON VINEYARD
Gisborne
★🅑

This biodynamic producer is justly famous for its award-winning, lightly botrytized, medium-sweet Opou Riesling. It also produces a stylish, barrel-fermented Chardonnay, and is appreciated locally for Chenin Blanc.

✓ *Chardonnay* (Essencia, Opou Vineyards) • *Chenin Blanc* (Te Arai) • *Pinot Noir* (Clos de Ste Anne)

MISSION ESTATE WINERY
Taradale
★🅥

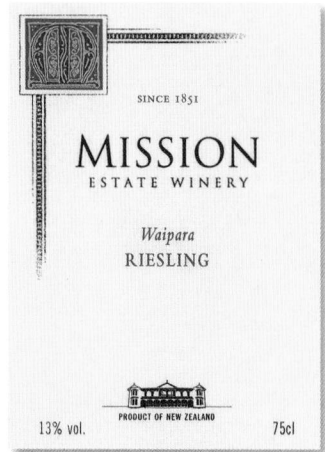

From a wine perspective, the Society of Mary fell into a rut until quite recently, which is understandable considering it has been making wine here for more than 150 years. Now things are on the move, the quality is improving, and the best wines are extremely good value.

✓ *Cabernet Sauvignon* (Reserve)
• *Chardonnay* (Reserve)
• *Riesling*

MORTON ESTATE
Bay of Plenty
★✩

Well known for its white wines, particularly Chardonnay, and especially Black Label and the top-of-the-range Coniglio, Morton Estate also produces some great red wines. Black Label is the premium range, but the quality of White Label wines is not to be sniffed at. Cheaper wines are sold under the Mill Road brand.

✓ *Classic red blend* (Black Label Merlot-Cabernet, White Label, The Mercure)
• *Chardonnay* (Black Label, Coniglio, Riverview) • *Sauvignon Blanc* (Stone Creek, White Label, Marlborough) • *Sparkling wine* (Black Label)

MT DIFFICULTY
Central Otago
★

With no fewer than six vineyards and a heap of experience in South Africa, Italy, and Oregon, a lot is expected from father-and-son team Robin and Matt Dicey. At the time of writing, Matt Dicey was also making wine for Alexandra Wine Company, Bannock Brae, and Mount Michael.

✓ *Pinot Noir*

MOUNT EDWARD
Central Otago
★

Owner-winemaker Alan Brady was the original proprietor of Gibbston Valley, where he was the first person to plant grapes in what is now the viticultural boom area of southern Central Otago. After selling his interest in Gibbston Valley, Brady set up this far smaller operation down the road, where he concentrates on producing rich, elegant Pinot Noir.

✓ *Pinot Noir*

MOUNT RILEY
Marlborough
★✩❤

This fast-expanding, fast-improving, award-winning winery has 100 hectares (250 acres) of vines spread over six vineyards, including the top-performing Seventeen Valley south of Blenheim.

✓ *Chardonnay* (Seventeen Valley) •
Pinot Noir (Seventeen Valley) •
Sauvignon Blanc

MOUNTFORD
Marlborough
★

Owners Michael and Buffy Eaton are attracting much well-deserved praise for the Pinot Noir and Chardonnay produced by their blind Taiwanese winemaker, Chung Pin Lin.

✓ *Pinot Noir*

MUDDY WATER
Waipara
★✩

Waipara is Maori for "muddy water", but there is nothing murky about the pure fruit in these wines. Belinda Gould's wines include Pinotage and the world's most southerly Syrah.

✓ *Chardonnay* • *Riesling* (James Hardwick, Unplugged)

MURDOCH JAMES
Martinborough
★

An up-and-coming, organic Martinborough producer, which now incorporates the old Blue Rock vineyard. An expanding range of wines includes Syrah and a rare, pure varietal Pinot Meunier.

However, the 2003 Sauvignon Blanc was so green, it was mean!

✓ *Pinot Noir* (Fraser)

NAUTILUS
Marlborough
★

Owned by the Australian Yalumba group, Nautilus is improving on all fronts. It has invested heavily in developing its Pinot Noir, which is showing progress, but the rich, ripe, Sauvignon Blanc is still its number-one wine. Wines are also sold under the Twin Islands second label.

✓ *Pinot Gris* • *Pinot Noir* • *Sauvignon Blanc* • *Sparkling wine* (Marlborough Brut)

NEUDORF VINEYARDS
Nelson
★★

I have always enjoyed Tim and Judy Finn's creamy, Burgundian-style wines – particularly the Pinot Noir, which now benefits from its own winery. New vineyards should increase production by 50 per cent.

✓ *Chardonnay* (Moutere) • *Pinot Gris* (Moutere) • *Pinot Noir* (Moutere) • *Riesling* (Dry Moutere, Late Harvest Moutere) • *Sauvignon Blanc*

MONTANA WINERIES
Auckland, Gisborne, Hawke's Bay, and Marlborough
★★❤

Although purchased by Allied-Domecq in 2001, and technically renamed Allied-Domecq Wines New Zealand in 2004, it is extremely doubtful that it will ever be known as anything other than Montana Wines. The company owns 3,000 hectares (7,400 acres) of vines, and accounts for 55 per cent of all New Zealand's wines, making it the largest wine producer in the country, yet remarkable quality and consistency exist at all price points. Church Road is Montana's high-tech Hawke's Bay boutique winery, producing wines that combine the restrained exuberance of cool-climate New World fruit with the classic Old World structure. The top wine produced at Church Road is "Tom", Montana's icon red wine.

Corbans has been consumed, and is little more than just another label, but the wines are nonetheless well made, representing excellent value. Although Cooks swallowed Corbans in 1987, it no longer exists as a brand, even though its prey still does.

The only mistake made by Montana is one that other New Zealand wine producers have also made in recent years, and that is to create an uncertainty of origin for some of its lesser brands: Copperfields, Jackman Ridge, Murray Ridge, Riverlands, Robard & Butler, and Timara. Another label, Longridge, is described by Montana as "one of New Zealand's classic boutique wine ranges", yet the wines are often multi-regional blends. There's nothing wrong with that, but it is hardly the definition of a boutique winery, especially in years when yields are low, and

BRANCOTT WINERY
Montana's Brancott Winery was the first established in Marlborough, and opened in 1976.

KAITUNA
Wetlands neighbour the Kaituna vineyard, planted in 2000 at the northern end of the Wairau Valley.

some Longridge wines are more than 50 per cent Chilean! All duly declared, but not boutique, not classic, and not New Zealand. Saints is another mishmash brand, with some regional varietals, a pure imported Shiraz, and a multinational Cabernet Sauvignon-Merlot. Oaklands is a cask wine (bag-in-the-box) brand, which was relaunched as a varietal cask wine range in 2002, and includes imported wines.

Other Montana brands include Aquila (sweet, carbonated fizz), Azure Bay, Bernadino (sweet, carbonated, multinational fizz), Blenheimer, Brightstone, Cellarmans, Chardon (sweet, carbonated, multinational, low-alcohol), Chasseur, Country, Diva (*cuve close* sparkling), Emerald Peak, Huntaway, Italiano (sweet, carbonated, multinational, low-alcohol), Liebestraum, Lindauer, Montel, Oaklands, Ridge Estate, Riverlea, St Arnaud, Seven Oaks, Sun Country, Velluto Rosso, Verde, Vineyard, Virtu, Waimanu, and Wohnsiedler. Ironically, since Allied-Domecq has purchased Montana, it is committed to selling Deutz Montana sparkling wines, although it owns Mumm and Perrier-Jouët!

✓ *Classic red blend* (Church Road, Tom) • *Cabernet Sauvignon* ("F" Fairhall, Marlborough) • *Chardonnay* (Church Road, Marlborough, "O" Ormand Estate, "R" Renwick Estate) • *Corbans* (Private Bin, Cottage Block) • *Gewürztraminer* ("P" Patutahi) • *Merlot* • *Pinot Noir* (Reserve, "T" Terraces) • *Riesling* (Reserve, Stoneleigh) • *Sauvignon Blanc* ("B" Brancott, Marlborough Reserve, Stoneleigh) • *Sémillon* (Virtu Noble) • *Sparkling Wines* (all Deutz *cuvées*, Lindauer Special Reserve)

NGA WAKA VINEYARD

Martinborough
★★

This is a small winery producing wines that boast intense, crisp fruit. All are now sealed by screwcap.

✓ *Riesling • Sauvignon Blanc*

NGATARAWA WINES

Hawke's Bay
★★

Founded by the Glazebrook family and Alwyn Corban in 1981. The Glazebrooks sold up in 1999, and Alwyn's cousin Brian Corban joined the company. This is a quality-conscious Hawke's Bay winery making its mark with distinctive red wines. But with the exception of Alwyn Riesling and Glazebrook Chardonnay, its whites are so understated that their subtlety is lost on me. Second wines are sold under the Stables brand.

✓ *Cabernet • Merlot* (Glazebrook) *• Chardonnay* (Glazebrook) *• Riesling* (Alwyn)

NO. 1 FAMILY ESTATE

Marlborough
★★

This brand is the result of Daniel Le Brun being unable to market wine under his own name for three years following the severing, in 1996, of his ties with Cellier Le Brun. In 1999, three years to the day after the split, Daniel cheekily opened up Le Brun Family Estate (since renamed No.1 Family Estate) around the corner. He produces three sparkling wines: Cuvée No.1 (non-vintage *blanc de blancs*), Cuvée Number Eight (non-vintage classic blend), and Cuvée Virginie (vintage classic blend).

✓ *Cuvée Number Eight*

NOBILO

Auckland
★

So much change in so little time. This was already a large wine producer before it purchased Selaks in 1998. That deal brought with it substantial additional vineyards, and the new Drylands winery in Marlborough, allowing Nobilo both

to increase production and to develop its premium wine range. A new publicly listed company was formed, attracting investment from Australian giant BRL Hardy. The Aussies liked what they saw, invested more in the company, then effectively took it over in 2000, when the Nobilo family exchanged its remaining shareholding in the old family firm for shares in BRL Hardy (and did very nicely out of that when BRL Hardy was itself taken over by Constellation Brands in 2003). Nobilo is now the second-largest wine producer in New Zealand. Nobilo's Icon has replaced Dixon Vineyard as the company's best Chardonnay. There is also an exciting Icon Marlborough Sauvignon Blanc, which is a welcome addition to the basic, but consistently excellent, Marlborough Sauvignon Blanc. Nobilo needs to improve its red wines, but the premium Icon range is obviously the one to watch. Other labels include Fall Harvest, Fernleaf, and the new Station Road brand.

✓ *Chardonnay* (Icon) *• Sauvignon Blanc* (Marlborough, Icon)

OKAHU ESTATE

Northland
✫

Established in 1984, Okahu Estate has started to earn more awards in recent years, so Monty Knight must be doing something right. Located 3.5 kilometres (2 miles) from Kaitaia on the road to Ahipara, at the southern end of the Ninety Mile Beach, this is the most northerly vineyard in New Zealand.

✓ *Cabernet* (Kaz) *• Chardonnay* (Clifton Proprietor's Reserve)

OLSSENS

Central Otago
★✫

A Bannockburn star in the making, with complex Pinot Noir and a Sauvignon Blanc that is way too delicious for this far south!

✓ *Pinot Noir* (Sleepjack Creek)

OMAKA SPRINGS

Marlborough
✫ Ⓥ

This estate is owned by Geoff and Robina Jensen, who were pioneers of the New Zealand olive industry, having planted 2,500 olive trees in 23 different varieties at Omaka Springs before venturing into the wine industry. They produce inexpensive, unpretentious wines from some 60 hectares (150 acres) of vineyards.

✓ *Sauvignon Blanc*

PALLISER ESTATE

Martinborough
★✫ Ⓥ

This is a substantial producer of consistently classy wines. Even those under second label Pencarrow show some finesse.

✓ *Chardonnay* (including Pencarrow) *Pinot Gris • Pinot Noir • Riesling • Sauvignon Blanc* (including Pencarrow)

C J PASK

Hawke's Bay
★★

Kate Radburnd continues to churn out a wide range of classic quality, richly flavoured wines. There are also good value, inexpensive wines sold under the Roy's Hill label.

✓ *Classic red blend* (Declaration, Gimblett Road Cabernet-Merlot) *• Chardonnay* (Gimblett Road) *• Merlot* (Gimblett Road Reserve, Reserve) *• Syrah* (Reserve)

PEGASUS BAY

Waipara
★★

The Donaldson family operate a very fine winery and restaurant south of Waipara. The style of wine produced is richly flavoured with a classic structure.

✓ *Chardonnay* (Finale) *• Classic red blend* (Cabernet-Merlot) *• Pinot Noir* (especially Prima Donna) *• Riesling* (Aria) *• Classic white blend* (Sauvignon-Sémillon)

PENINSULA ESTATE

Waiheke Island
✫

Brave or stupid, there is no doubting the viticultural risk taken by Doug Hamilton in planting this Cabernet-blend vineyard. It sticks out into the Pacific, exposed to salt-bearing sea breezes on three sides.

✓ *Classic red blend* (Island Red) *• Syrah* (Zeno)

PEREGRINE

Central Otago
★

Owned by Greg Hay, who helped his brother Rob establish Chard Farm before setting out on his own. Peregrine produces wines from grapes grown on the Wentworth Estates, under the banner "Wines with Altitude". Wentworth was set up as a cost-effective means of farming 30 hectares (75 acres) in an area close to Queenstown,

where the price of land is high. It effectively involves selling off plots of land to build houses surrounded by vines, which are then managed by Wentworth. It provides the householder with an income from the meticulously manicured vines around it, and Peregrine with the grapes it needs.

✓ *Pinot Noir • Riesling*

PROVIDENCE

Matakana
★

This is a small, export-oriented, red wine specialist, whose wine often costs an arm and a leg, but the price can vary considerably from country to country.

✓ *Classic red blend* (Merlot-Cabernet Franc-Malbec)

QUARTZ REEF

Central Otago
★★✫

This estate is owned by Rudi Bauer and Clotilde Chauvet (who also makes Champagne in Rilly-la-Montagne). Rudi and Clotilde met at Rippon in the early 1990s, when Rudi was the winemaker. Clotilde took over as Rippon's winemaker when Rudi moved south, but they kept in touch, eventually establishing Quartz Reef together in 1996. They have pioneered vineyards at Bendigo and produce excellent Pinot Noir and sparkling wine. Rudi made the wines for Two Paddocks until the Central Otago Wine Company was set up, and Dean Shaw (who worked for Rudi at Rippon) took over. Rudi's consultancy work has gradually given way as Quartz Reef has taken off, but at the time of writing he was still making wines for Northburn, Pisa Range, and Rockburn.

✓ *Pinot Noir* (Reserve) *• Sparkling wine*

RICHMOND PLAINS

Nelson
✫ Ⓞ

Also known as Holmes Brothers, this was the first vineyard on South Island to go organic.

✓ *Sauvignon Blanc* (Marlborough)

RIPPON
Wanaka
★

In 1974, against all advice, Lois and Rolfe Mills chose one of the most beautiful areas in the world to grow vines. They have certainly succeeded, although it took until 1989 to make their first commercial wine. Rippon is biodynamic, but not certified as such.

✓ *Pinot Noir* • *Riesling*

ROCKBURN
Central Otago
★

Greg Hay of Peregrine is the viticulturist, and Rudi Bauer of Quartz Reef the winemaker.

✓ *Pinot Noir*

RONGOPAI WINES
Te Kauwhata

The original Rongopai winery was established in 1932 by the Gordon family, and this continued until the death of Lou Gordon in 1954. The winery fell into disrepair until 1982, when it was resurrected by Dr Rainer Eschenbruch and Tom Van Dam from the nearby Te Kauwhata Viticultural Research Station. They produced the first new Rongopai wines in 1985, attracting instant acclaim for their botrytized wines. But Eschenbruch left in 1993, and Van Dam retired in 2001. The current owner, Scottish businessman Derek Reid, had invested in Rongopai since 1991. In 1995, he purchased the old viticultural research station, which has since become Rongopai's winery. Reid's Rongopai is no longer confined to producing stickies, although they still excel. The range includes dry whites, reds, and a port style. The only wine not produced is sparkling, although I wonder if the winemaker, Emmanuel Bollinger, has thought of bringing one out under his own label.

✓ *Chardonnay* (Ultimo) • *Dessert wine* (Ultimo Late Harvest)

SACRED HILL
Hawke's Bay
★☆

Since Sacred Hill produced its first wine in 1986, its reputation has been built on its vineyards in the Dartmoor Valley hills of Hawke's Bay. In 2001, the owners purchased Cairnbrae in Marlborough, and in addition to maintaining that brand, its vineyards now contribute to Sacred Hill's growing prestige, particularly its vibrantly fresh Sauvignon Blanc. Less expensive, early-drinking wines are sold under the Whitecliff label.

✓ *Chardonnay* (Rifleman's) • *Classic red blend* (Helmsman) • *Merlot* (Brokenstone) • *Riesling* (Halo Botrytis) • *Sauvignon Blanc* (Marlborough)

SAINT CLAIR
Marlborough
★★ⓥ

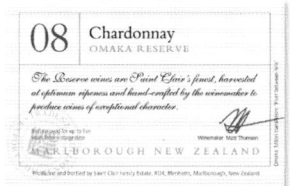

This is a large vineyard that consistently produces fresh, crisp, expressive whites, including one of New Zealand's best Sauvignon Blancs. There is also a rich, deliciously fresh, deep-flavoured, fruit-driven Merlot.

✓ *Chardonnay* (Omaka) • *Merlot* (Reserve) • *Riesling* • *Sauvignon Blanc*

ST HELENA
Canterbury
☆

The nation's oldest Pinot Noir vines are found at St Helena's vineyard near the Waimakirri River, which explains why this winery used to be one of New Zealand's leading Pinot Noir exponents. It was this winery that put Canterbury Pinot Noir on the map, with its legendary 1982 vintage. Those days are long gone, however. Although St Helena occasionally manages to produce excellent wines from this variety under the Reserve label, the consistency is no longer there.

✓ *Pinot Noir* (Reserve)

ST JÉRÔME
Henderson
★

The Ozich brothers have a well-deserved reputation for their Bordeaux-style blend, Matuka.

✓ *Classic red blend* (Matuka)

DANIEL SCHUSTER
Canterbury
★☆

Danny Schuster co-authored *Grape Growing & Winemaking: A Handbook for Cool Climates* (1973), which has encouraged many New Zealanders to give it a go.

✓ *Chardonnay* (Omihi Hills) • *Pinot Noir* (Omihi Hills)

ALLAN SCOTT
Marlborough
★☆

Allan Scott established Marlborough's very first vineyard in 1973, while working for Montana. He later became Corbans' chief viticulturist, but left to set up his own business in 1989. He produces a good, but not special, Pinot Noir, and has been persevering with a sparkling wine that frankly needs more finesse. But Scott truly excels at still white wines, which seem to have more fruit than wines from surrounding vineyards, particularly his Riesling.

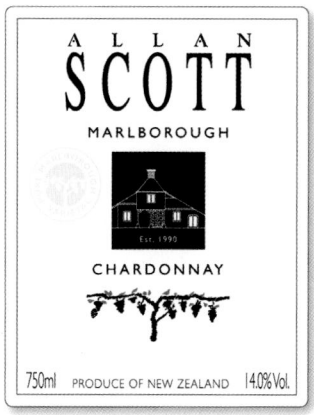

✓ *Chardonnay* • *Riesling* • *Sauvignon Blanc*

SEIFRIED ESTATE
Nelson
★☆ⓥ

Hermann Seifried's original winery and 10.5-hectare (26-acre) vineyard now belong to Amanda and Greg Day, who purchased and renamed it Kahurangi Estate in 1998. Two years earlier, the Seifried family had opened a brand new winery in closer proximity to most of its other vineyards, which now total 160 hectares (395 acres). Seifried always was Nelson's biggest wine producer, and still is. Consumers outside New Zealand will know these wines as Redwood Valley. Seifried is best for white wines, especially the superb botrytized Riesling and one of this country's better dry Rieslings.

✓ *Chardonnay* (Old Coach Road) • *Pinot Noir* • *Riesling* (Botrytis Dry Riesling)

SELAKS
Auckland
★★ⓥ

This has been the award-winning division of the Nobilo group since it was taken over by the group in 1998. Selaks continues to produce fine quality, stylish wines by the barrel-load, with its superb, fruity red wines now notching up as many successes as its crisp, refreshing whites.

✓ *Chardonnay* (Founders Reserve, Premium Selection) • *Merlot* (Founders Reserve) • *Riesling* (Founders Reserve Noble) • *Sauvignon Blanc* (Premium Selection) • *Syrah* (Founders Reserve)

SERESIN
Marlborough
★☆◉

The vines are all hand-tended, and some wines are fermented with wild yeasts. Winemaker Brian Bicknell is known for his flying winemaker exploits, but nothing he has made under contract compares with the wines from Seresin, some of which rank among the very best from Marlborough. The Seresin vineyard is certified organic. The Tatou and Raupo Creek vineyards were in the process of conversion at the time of writing, after which there are plans to go fully biodynamic. Future impetus will be towards polishing up the already impressive Pinot Noir.

✓ *Chardonnay* (Reserve) • *Pinot Gris* • *Pinot Noir* • *Riesling* • *Sauvignon Blanc* (Marama)

SHERWOOD ESTATE
Canterbury
☆

Confusingly, wines solely from Sherwood Estate's own vineyards are sold under the Clearwater Vineyards label, while those under the Sherwood Estate label include purchased fruit. Other labels include Stratum, an entry-level range.

✓ *Sauvignon Blanc*

SILENI
Hawke's Bay
★☆ⓥ

Since crushing its first crop in 1998, this winery has quickly built up a reputation for wines of style and finesse. Wines in the EV range are made only in exceptional vintages, while those in the Estate Selection are premium wines from Sileni's own vineyards. Entry-level wines are sold under the Cellar Selection label, and often represent exceptional value.

✓ *Chardonnay* (Estate Selection) • *Classic red blend* (Estate Selection Merlot-Cabernets) • *Merlot* (EV) • *Sémillon* (Estate Selection)

SLEEPING DOGS
Central Otago
★☆

Owned by film director Roger Donaldson, whose earliest work, *Sleeping Dogs* (1977), was the cornerstone of the New Zealand film industry. It gave his friend Sam Neill his first screen role. Donaldson's vineyard was the original other half of Two Paddocks, which he and Neill planted, but they are entirely separate operations.

However, they both share the same winemaker – Dean Shaw.

✓ *Pinot Noir*

SOLJANS
Auckland
⭐

Tony Soljans can sometimes go over the top with the amount of VA lift he gives to the fruit in his wines, but it works well when it is understated.

✓ *Cabernet-Merlot* (Estate) • *Port-style wine* (10-Year-Old Tawny)

SPENCER HILL
Nelson
⭐

This estate was established in the Upper Moutere area in 1992 by Philip and Sheryl Jones, whose first release was in 1994. Production in the initial years was tiny, with no wine whatsoever made in 1999. Production was moved to its current location in the Coastal Ridge, north of Nelson, in 2000. Other labels include Mariner Vineyards (from own vineyards plus purchased fruit), and Tasman Bay.

✓ *Chardonnay* • *Pinot Noir* • *Sauvignon Blanc* (Tasman Bay)

SPY VALLEY
Marlborough
⭐ⓥ

Owned by the Johnson family, Spy Valley is a name to watch out for. The name has its origins in the cold war: Spy Valley is what the locals have called the Waihopai Valley since the Americans built a listening station there. The grapes come from the 145-hectare (360-acre) Johnson Estate, which might sound vast for a relatively new winery, but the Johnsons have been growing for other wineries since 1992. Fresh, crisp, vibrantly fruity Sauvignon Blanc; sweet, ripe Pinot Noir; and classy Riesling are the best so far.

✓ *Chardonnay* • *Pinot Noir* • *Riesling* (Dry) • *Sauvignon Blanc*

STAETE LANDT
Marlborough
⭐ⓥ

From the beginning (in 1997), Ruud Maasdam and Dorien Vermaas have aimed to produce single-vineyard wines. All in fact come from the same 21-hectare (52-acre) vineyard but they have been selected on a parcel-by-parcel basis according to which combination of variety and rootstock grows best. If there are differences, they are effectively what the Burgundians would call *climats* (individual block or plots), and it would be a good idea to name them.

✓ *Pinot Noir* • *Sauvignon Blanc*

STONECROFT
Hawke's Bay
⭐

Alan Limmer pioneered Syrah in New Zealand, but his has lacked the

lush character of other, more successful Syrahs that have been released of late. New plantations might re-energize this wine in the future. Meanwhile, Limmer makes better Chardonnay, and a classic red blend (Cabernet-Syrah-Merlot) called Ruhani.

✓ *Chardonnay* • *Classic red blend* (Ruhani)

STONYRIDGE
Waiheke Island
⭐⭐⭐½

Since 1985, Stephen White has produced one of New Zealand's truly great red wines, Larose, which sells out within hours of being offered *en primeur* each year.

✓ *Classic red blend* (Larose)

STRATFORD WINES
Marlborough
⭐⭐½

This is the personal label of Margrain's winemaker, Strat Canning, who first produced these wines in 1997. His best wine is, without doubt, Pinot Noir, but Strat's wonderfully racy Riesling should not be overlooked.

✓ *Chardonnay* • *Pinot Noir* • *Riesling*

TE AWA
Hawke's Bay
⭐

Sold in December 2002 to New York investment manager Julian Robertson and Napa Valley vineyard owner Reg Oliver (*see* Dry River), Te Awa remains under the same day-to-day control, with viticulturist Gus Lawson in overall charge. Winemaker Jenny Dobson worked at Domaine Dujac in Burgundy for 18 months before going over to the opposition – Bordeaux – where she was appointed winemaker at Château Sénéjac. Zone 10 and Boundary are both two-star wines. Entry-level wines are sold under the Longlands label.

✓ *Cabernet Sauvignon* (Zone 10) • *Classic red blend* (Boundary)

TE KAIRANGA
Martinborough
⭐⭐½

With 100 hectares (250 acres) under vine, Te Kairanga is no boutique winery, but its rich, creamy Pinot Noir is the sort of impressive quality

expected from the smallest, top-performing producer. Second label wines are sold under the Castlepoint brand.

✓ *Chardonnay* • *Pinot Noir* • *Syrah*

TE MATA
Hawke's Bay
⭐⭐

Te Mata Estate was purchased in 1978 by John Buck, who with the help of winemaker Peter Cowley has fashioned two of the country's greatest red wines, Awatea and Coleraine. However, in some years Awatea and/or Coleraine are too attenuated to deserve top billing. If John and Peter believe in their *terroir*, they should acknowledge that it is not possible for the vineyard to provide a top class wine every year, and declassify when necessary. Other labels include the entry-level Rymer's Change range.

✓ *Chardonnay* (Castle Hill, Elston) • *Classic red blend* (Awatea, Coleraine, Woodthorpe Syrah-Viognier) • *Sauvignon Blanc* (Cape Crest, Castle Hill) • *Syrah* (Bullnose) • *Viognier* (Woodthorpe)

TE MOTU
Waiheke Island
⭐

The Te Motu vineyard is just 60 metres from Stonyridge Vineyard, where Larose, one of New Zealand's true icon wines is produced. Currently just one style is marketed, a Cabernet-Merlot (which also includes a little Cabernet Franc and Malbec), with the same style appearing under the second label (Dunleavy).

✓ *Classic red blend* (Te Motu)

TE WHARE RA
Marlborough
⭐

Established by Allen and Joyce Hogan in 1979, Te Whare Ra (Maori for "the house in the sun") became the first Marlborough vineyard to be planted after Montana had paved the way. The Hogans sold Te Whare Ra to Roger and Christine Smith in 1998, and the Smiths sold it on to the present owners, Jason and Anna Flowerday. A couple of years ago, I would have said it was still work in progress for the Flowerdays, but the wines

have started to come into their stride since the 2009 and 2010 vintages, especially the Rieslings.

✓ *Classic white blend* (Toru) • *Riesling* (Dry, Medium) • *Sauvignon Blanc* • *Syrah*

TORLESSE
Waipara
⭐

Established in 1987 by 20-odd grower-suppliers, Torlesse soon went into receivership. It re-emerged in 1990 as a new company that is now owned by several shareholders, also with vineyards dotted over Waipara. The spread of the vineyards should give winemakers Kym Rayner and Paul Hewett the opportunity to create a range of individual *terroir*-based wines, which is precisely their intention. So, watch this space. In the meantime, try the deliciously rich Sauvignon Blanc.

✓ *Sauvignon Blanc*

TRINITY HILL
Hawke's Bay
⭐⭐

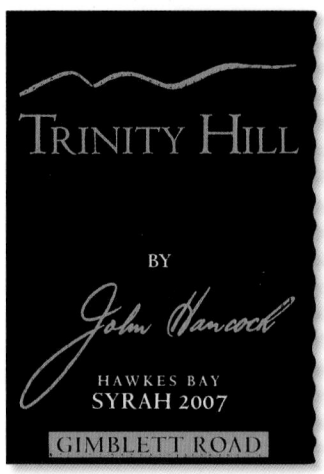

The trinity here consists of managing director John Hancock, who helped establish Morton Estate's reputation before setting up Trinity Hill; winemaker Warren Gibson, who assisted Hancock at Morton Estate; and viticulturist Michael Bell, who is a Gimblett Gravels expert, having tended the famed Irongate vineyard. The great thing about Hancock is that he insists on making beautiful wines even from grapes he dislikes, such as Sauvignon Blanc. However, Trinity Hill's most outstanding wines so far are Merlot and Syrah. The worst wine I could find at Trinity Hill was the High Country Pinot Noir, and that's a glugging wine full of strawberry fruit. The only thing I could fault it on was its straightforward, upfront, easy-drinking quality.

✓ *Cabernet Sauvignon* (Gimblett Road) • *Classic red blend* (Gimblett Road Cabernet Sauvignon-Merlot, Shepherds Croft Cabernet Sauvignon-Merlot, Shepherds Croft Merlot-Cabernet

Franc-Syrah) • *Merlot* (Gimblett Road) • *Riesling* (Wairarapa) • *Roussanne* • *Syrah* (Gimblett Road) • *Tempranillo*

TWO PADDOCKS
Gibbston Valley
★★☆

This estate is owned by actor Sam Neill, who lives in Central Otago and loves Pinot Noir. The original 2-hectare (5-acre) Two Paddocks on the Gibbston Back Road is so called because it was one of two neighbouring paddocks planted by Neill and friend Roger Donaldson in 1993. Donaldson has his own label (Sleeping Dogs), while Neill retains the name for the overall business, although this vineyard is now known as One Paddock. In 1998, Neill purchased Alex Paddocks in the Earnscleugh Valley, Alexandra, which is a warmer site, where 3 hectares (7 acres) have been planted. Alex Paddocks yielded its first crop in 2001, enabling the first truly *two-paddock* Two Paddocks to be produced that year. Then, in 2002, winemaker Dean Shaw made the stunning single-vineyard The Last Chance Pinot Noir. The latest addition has been Redbanks Paddock, also in the Earnscleugh Valley, but significantly warmer still. With potentially 25 hectares (60 acres) of vineyards, this is Neill's most ambitious project so far. Just a few acres have been planted, including a little Riesling, and he intends to expand the operation only as and when needs be. Since 2002, a soft, easy-drinking blend of all three paddocks has been produced under the Picnic Pinot Noir label.

✓ *Pinot Noir* (The Last Chance)

UNISON VINEYARD
Hawke's Bay
★★

Unison's high-density Gimblett Gravels vineyard produces just two reds, both of which blend Merlot, Cabernet Sauvignon, and Syrah. One is simply called Unison, the other Unison Selection. Both are brilliant. Now there is a refreshing rosé from the same varieties. This is a winery on the way up.

✓ *Classic red blend* (Unison, Unison Selection)

VALLI
Central Otago
★

This is the own label of Gibbston Valley's winemaker, Grant Taylor. It is named after a distant relative who emigrated to New Zealand in the 19th century. Taylor has two small vineyards at his disposal, one in Gibbston Valley, which is supposed to be better in cooler vintages, the other in Bannockburn, which excels in warmer years.

✓ *Pinot Noir* (Bannockburn Vineyard)

VAVASOUR
Marlborough
★★☆

Situated south of Blenheim, in the Awatere Valley, where the intense sun and dry winds are responsible for the intense fruit flavour of these well-structured wines. Excellent value wines are also sold under the Dashwood label.

✓ *Chardonnay* • *Pinot* Noir • *Sauvignon Blanc*

VIDAL
Hawke's Bay
★★☆Ⓥ

Vidal was founded by a Spaniard, Anthony Vidal, but is now owned by George Fistonich, the son of a Dalmatian immigrant and proprietor of Villa Maria. This winery consistently produces some of the most exciting red wines in the Hawke's Bay area. The whites often lack finesse, although they are usually very easy to drink, and Vidal produces one of New Zealand's better Gewürztraminers.

✓ *Classic red blend* (Reserve Merlot-Cabernet Sauvignon) • *Cabernet Sauvignon* (Joseph Soler, Reserve) • *Chardonnay* (Reserve) • *Sauvignon Blanc* (Estate) • *Syrah* (Soler)

VILLA MARIA
Auckland
★★Ⓥ

New Zealand's best all-round wine producer is the country's third-largest (after Montana and Nobilo), and the only one of the three that is still New Zealand-owned. Villa Maria has a vast range of wines that are all beautifully crafted to enhance fruit and finesse. Where oak is used, the touch is light and impeccably integrated. For such a large company to have the level of quality and consistency that Villa Maria has is pretty remarkable. But some of the kudos must go to Montana for chasing Villa Maria on quality and value at all price points,

despite its production being considerably larger still. The very best Villa Maria wines deserve two and a half stars. Full marks to proprietor George Fistonich, who converted the entire production to screwcap bottling.

✓ *Entire range*

VINO ALTO
Auckland
Ⓥ

I have not tasted these wines, but I am passing on high praise from Bob Campbell MW and other critics I respect in New Zealand. Any readers who are curious how Italian varieties and styles might work in New Zealand should start at Vino Alto, where Margaret and Enzo Bettio grow, among others, Arneis, Barbera, Corvina, Montepulciano, Nebbiolo, and Sangiovese. The Retico is, apparently, well worth seeking out as an example of a rare Amarone-style wine, made from grapes that have been dried on racks for two months prior to fermentation.

WAIPARA HILLS
Canterbury
★Ⓥ

An ambitious, young, up-and-coming venture that makes and sells wines from Canterbury and Marlborough, as well as Waipara.

✓ *Riesling*

WAIPARA SPRINGS
Waipara
★Ⓥ

Owned by the Moore family, who tend the vineyard, and the Grants, who make and sell the wines, Waipara Springs produces consistently fine-quality wines.

✓ *Chardonnay* (Lightly Oaked) • *Pinot Noir* (Reserve) • *Sauvignon Blanc*

WAIPARA WEST
Canterbury
★Ⓥ

This winery and vineyard is owned by a partnership called Tutton Sienko Hill. Paul Tutton is a London wine merchant, Olga Sienko is his wife, and Lindsay Hill is his sister-in-law, and the viticulturist who manages the Waipara West vineyard.

✓ *Chardonnay* • *Classic red blend* (Ram Paddock Red) • *Pinot Noir*

WAIRAU RIVER
Marlborough
★

Phil and Chris Rose have been growing grapes since 1978. In 1991, they decided to launch their own label, and now take the pick of the crop from their 125 hectares (310 acres) of vines spread over three vineyards. John Belsham (*see* Foxes Island Wines) has been the winemaker from the beginning.

✓ *Pinot Gris* • *Riesling* • *Sauvignon Blanc*

WEST BROOK
Auckland
★Ⓥ

Founded by Mick Ivicevich in 1937 in what was rural Henderson. The estate was surrounded on all sides by urban sprawl by 2000, when grandson Anthony Ivicevich moved West Brook to its present location in the Ararimu Valley. Top wines are sold under the Blue Ridge label.

✓ *Chardonnay* (Blue Ridge) • *Riesling* (Marlborough) • *Sauvignon Blanc* (Blue Ridge)

WHITEHAVEN
Marlborough
★★☆

Sensational Riesling and Sauvignon Blanc, particularly the Single Vineyard Reserve.

✓ *Chardonnay* • *Riesling* • *Sauvignon Blanc*

CHARLES WIFFEN
Marlborough
★Ⓥ

Charles Wiffen is based at Cheviot in North Canterbury, his vineyards are in Marlborough, and his wines are made in Auckland by Anthony Ivicevich of West Brook. Rieslings have been nothing less than stunning, especially the Late Harvest. Also very good are the Chardonnay and Sauvignon Blanc.

✓ *Chardonnay* • *Riesling* (Late Harvest) • *Sauvignon Blanc*

WITHER HILLS
Marlborough
★★☆Ⓥ

In 2002, Wither Hills winery was purchased by Lion Nathan, the brewing giant that owns Australia's Petaluma. The vineyards are in South Island's Marlborough region, but the winery is at Henderson, Auckland, on North Island.

✓ *Chardonnay* • *Pinot Noir* • *Sauvignon Blanc*

ASIA

Although there are more than 800 wineries spread over 15 Asian countries, China, Japan, and India are, by far, the continent's most important winemaking nations.

BALI

In 1994 Hatten Wines produced a rosé from Alphonse Lavallée table grapes. Local growers allow these grapes to crop as regularly as once a month, thus Hatten Rosé reached its 150th vintage by 2005! Hatten itself grows Chambourcin (on trial) and a Muscat-like variety called Belgia. The latter makes a semi-sweet, aromatic white wine called Alexandria, which won a bronze medal at the International Wine and Spirit Competition in the UK in 2003. Its winemaker, French-born Vincent Desplats, also makes two traditional method wines, a rosé called Jepun and a white called Tungjung.

⩗ *Hatten Wines* (Alexandria)

BHUTAN

Taltarni of Victoria, Australia, consults for a vineyard established in the early 1990s at Paro, at an altitude of 2,300 metres (7,500 feet).

BURMA

Myanmar Vineyard Estate was established in 1998 by Bert Morsbach at Loikaw, but moved in 1999 to Aythaya, where the vines grow on limestone slopes at 1,300 metres (4,265 feet). Varieties include Barbera, Cabernet Sauvignon, Chardonnay, Chenin Blanc, Dornfelder, Gewürztraminer, Muscat, Sauvignon Blanc, Sémillon, Syrah, and Tempranillo. Red, white, and rosé wines are sold under the Aythaya label.

KOREA

Korea has 16,000 hectares (40,000 acres) of vineyards, primarily for table grapes and dried fruit. Winemaking dates back at least 2,000 years, but it was traditionally from rice and aromatized with herbs for medicinal purposes. A grape-based cooperative winery was set up in 1993 by Yoon Byeong-tae to make wine under the Chateaumani label. More recently, Roh Chong-ku established the East of Eden winery in a mountainous area of Pongwha County. He is a strong believer in Sanmaru, the local *amurensis* vine, and is Korea's only producer of such a wine, sold as Empery Cupid Wild Grapes Wine.

KYRGYZSTAN

Situated between China and Kazakhstan, this country's vineyards amount to just 6,272 hectares (15,498 acres) and produce just over 20,000 hectolitres (222,000 cases) of wine.

TAJIKISTAN

There are more than 20 wineries in this central Asian state, most of which are found in Leninabad, Ghissar, and Vakhsh. In total, 32,000 hectares (79,070 acres) of vineyards produce 60,000 hectolitres (666,000 cases) of wine.

NEPAL

Isolated vineyards have been spotted at 2,750 metres (9,000 feet) near Jomsom in the Western District. Note that "Nepali wine" often seen on menus in Nepal, is not wine at all but merely the local mistranslation of *raksi*, a distilled rice liquor.

PHILIPPINES

Wine grapes have been grown at Ilcos and Cebu in the past, but no commercial wine production. Rice wine has been made here since before the Spanish conquistadors, according to local sources. Palm, coconut, and fruit wines also exist.

TAIWAN

Changhua County was known as the nation's wine-grape capital until 1999, when the state-run Taiwan Tobacco and Wine Bureau lost its monopoly status as the exclusive buyer of the entire grape harvest. The area of vines diminished, and numerous private wineries sprang up across the country. The area still has the greatest concentration of wine grapes, and the Erlin Township in Changhua has the highest concentration of wineries in Taiwan. In 2008, The Taiwan Wine Cellar was established by Changhua County Erlin Farmers' Association to showcase the variety of grape wines made in the county.

FACTORS AFFECTING TASTE AND QUALITY

LOCATION
One-third of the world!

CLIMATE
China Vineyards are classified as "humid micro-thermal cool", similar to those of Austria and Hungary, where continental conditions are influenced by great water masses, creating hot, damp summers and very cold, dry winters. **India** Hot with no real winter. Two harvests a year: one dry, one humid-monsoon (usually avoided). Altitude of Maharashtra and Dodballapur provides a relatively cool climate. **Japan** Extremes of climate: freezing winds in the winter, monsoon rains in spring and autumn, and typhoons in the summer. The temperature drops northwards; humidity rises southwards. The climate of Miyazaki Prefecture on Kyushu has been likened to that of Florida!

ASPECT
China Recent plantings have been on well-drained, south-facing slopes to overcome the earlier problem of high water-tables on the flatter sites. **India** Gentle east- and south-facing slopes at an altitude of 750m (2,460ft) in Narayangaon, and 600m (1,980ft) in Nasik and Dodballapur **Japan** On Honshu Island, the best vineyards are planted on the south-facing valley slopes around Kofu.

SOIL
China Generally alluvial. **India** Lime-rich soils at Narayangaon, sandy-clay loam at Nasik, and red-sandy loam at Dodballapur. **Japan** Predominantly acidic soils that are unsuitable for viticulture, except around Kofu, where the soil is gravelly and of volcanic origin.

VITICULTURE AND VINIFICATION
In tropical regions, such as Bali, the grape vines never winter, and up to 15 vintages can be harvested. **China** Big, new wineries in the western provinces of Xinjiang, Gansu, and Ningxia are responsible for most of this expansion. Export-orientated wineries are driving quality standards upwards and have had some remarkable success with super-premium wines, such as Dragon Seal's Syrah, but attempts to raise standards across the board are held back by high-yielding varieties that crop up to 150 hl/ha. **India** Vine training is moving from the Lenz Moser high system to more sophisticated high-trellis systems. **Japan** Recent developments have concentrated on the growing of top European varietals, and although this continues at an increasing pace, attention is also shifting to the Koshu grape. The biggest problem is still rain.

GRAPE VARIETIES
China Beichun, Cabernet Franc, Cabernet Sauvignon, Carignan, Chardonnay, Chasan, Chenin Blanc, Crystal, Gamay, Gewürztraminer, Grenache, Italian Riesling, Maru (Mare's Nipple), Marsanne, Merlot, Muscat d'Hambourg, Muscat à Petits Grains, Merlot, Pinot Noir, Rkatsiteli, Rose Honey, Saperavi, Sauvignon Blanc, Sémillon, Sylvaner, Syrah, Welschriesling **India** Bangalore Blue (Isabelle), Cabernet Sauvignon, Chardonnay, Karachi Gulabi (Muscat Hambourg), Pinot Noir, Ruby Red, Thompson Seedless, Ugni Blanc **Japan** Cabernet Sauvignon, Campbell's Early, Chardonnay, Delaware, Koshu, Merlot, Müller-Thurgau, Muscat Bailey, Riesling, Sémillon

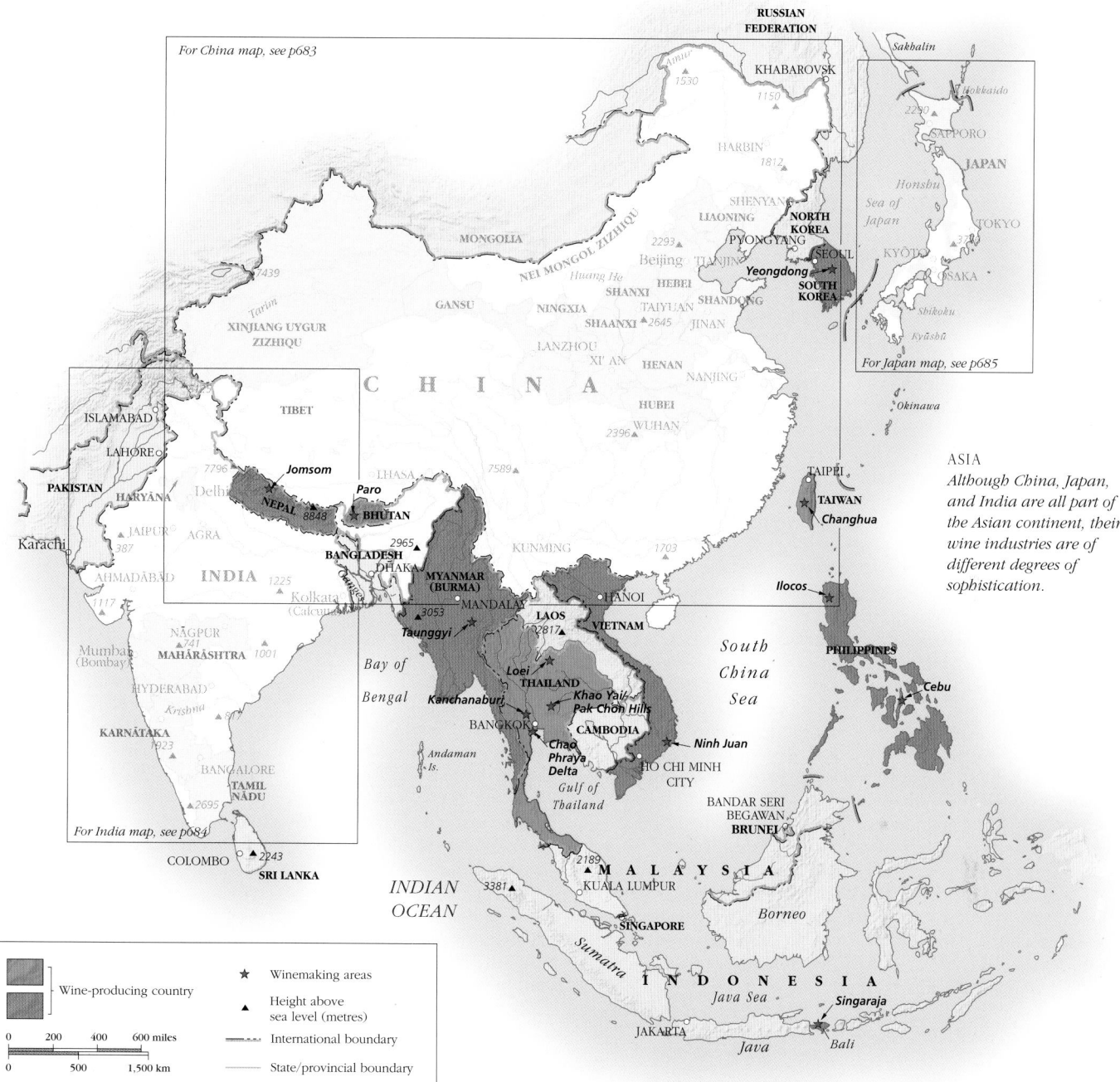

ASIA
Although China, Japan, and India are all part of the Asian continent, their wine industries are of different degrees of sophistication.

Map legend:
- Wine-producing country
- ★ Winemaking areas
- ▲ Height above sea level (metres)
- International boundary
- State/provincial boundary
- 0 200 400 600 miles
- 0 500 1,500 km

THAILAND

A 12-year viticultural study ordered by King Bhumibol in the mid-1970s experimented with more than 400 types of grapes from Australia, Germany, and the USA. In 1992, the Thai government officially allowed wine production, and in 1993 the country's first winery, Château de Loei, was established in the Phurua highlands of northeastern Thailand by the late Dr Chaijudh Karnasuta. Château de Loei has been followed by Shala One, Siam Winery, PB Valley Khao Yai, Granmonte, and Village Farm.

The Siam Winery released its first wine in 1997, but is already Thailand's biggest producer. Owned by the Yoovidhya family, its wines are marketed under the Chantemp and Monsoon labels. Grapes are grown on the famous "floating vineyards" around Damnoen Saduak in the Chao Phraya Delta. The vineyards do not actually float, but vines are grown on thin strips of land separated by canals, from which they are tended by growers in boats.

Shala One is located at King Amphur Dong Charoen in Pichit province and is best known for its Shiraz. The Khao Yai region, 175 kilometres (109 miles) northeast of Bangkok, is Thailand's most popular spot for vineyards: PB Valley Khao Yai; Village Farm, which sells wine under Château de Brumes and Village Thai labels; and Granmonte, Thailand's newest winery, are all located here.

✓ *Château de Loei* (Reserve Syrah) • *Granmonte* (Celebration Syrah, Unwooded Chenin Blanc-Colombard) • *Khao Yai Winery* (Pirom Khao Yai Reserve Tempranillo) • *Siam Winery* (Monsoon Valley Rosé)

UZBEKISTAN

There are numerous wineries in Bukhara, Samarkand, and Tashkent. Together, 100,000 hectares (247,000 acres) of vineyards produce just over 250,000 hectolitres (2.77 million cases) of wine, mostly high-strength reds, dessert wines, and sparkling wines.

VIETNAM

This country's first winery was the ill-fated Ninh Thuan joint-venture, established by Allied-Domecq in 1995. The potential was thought to be very high, since the Vietnamese were the first Asians to acquire a taste for wine. But the Vietnamese drink only Bordeaux, and tourists do not generally want to try Vietnamese wine.

CHINA

It is assumed that Chinese grape-winemaking (as opposed to rice-winemaking) began in 128 BC, when General Chang planted vinifera *seeds at the Imperial Palace in Chang An (now Xian), which is 1,000 kilometres (600 miles) south of Beijing.*

THE FIRST DOCUMENTED PROOF of wines, rather than vines, however, comes from AD 674, when a spectacular grape variety was sent to Emperor Tai-Tsung by a Turkish people known as the Yagbu. Called Mare's Nipple, this variety had purple grapes, with bunches up to 60 centimetres (2 feet) long, and the wine made from it was described as "fiery".

In 1892, Zhang Bishi, a Chinese businessman, brought cuttings of 10 *vinifera* grape varieties from Europe, and built the Zhang Yu Winery at Yantai in Shandong province. In 1910, a French priest opened a winery in Beijing called Shangyi (now Beijing Friendship Winery), and in 1914, a German company called Melchers set up a winery at Tsingtao (now Quindao) on the Shandong peninsula.

In more recent times, Rémy Martin was brought in to give expert technical assistance to the first Franco-Chinese joint venture. In 1980, this resulted in Dynasty, the first European-style wine produced in China, developed in conjunction with the Tianjin Winery. In 1987, the Pernod-Ricard group created the Dragon Seal brand in association with the Beijing Friendship Winery. This was more of a success and achieved much higher standards than Dynasty, but Pernod-Ricard pulled out of the venture in 2001, frustrated (so it was claimed) by a lack of profitability, although some market analysts saw this as part of China's policy to "localize" ownership. Certainly, there has been no fear of poor returns by the increasing number of international investments made in the Chinese wine industry in more recent years.

There are now more than 450 wineries in China, with 140 in the Yantai-Penglai district of Shandong alone, but many are small facilities. Most vineyards are either state-owned or cooperatives of several families in the same village. The area under vine has almost trebled since the late 1990s and currently stands at 486,000 hectares (1.2 million acres).

At first glance, it appears as if China has one-third more area under vine than the USA, but almost 80 per cent of its vines are table grapes, and a further 10 per cent are raisins. Only 10 per cent of China's vineyards produce wine, yet its wine production is still one and one half times the size of either South Africa or Germany, making it the seventh-largest wine-producing country in the world. More than 80 per cent of the production is red wine – not because China is red-wine

BODEGA LANGES, HEBEI
This 100 per cent Austrian-owned winery in the Hebei province has its own cooperage, where it makes all of its own barrels (3,500 per year) from Chinese oak grown in the Changbai mountains in the north of the country.

country, but because the Chinese are red-wine drinkers. So where are these wines, and are they any good? Virtually all Chinese wines are consumed locally, and the average quality is so dismal that they would not stand much chance against the most modest competition on international markets. Only a handful of Chinese wines are currently of interest, and it is the contrast between the number of world-class wines produced in South Africa or Germany and the paucity of recommendations on this page that illustrates the enormity of the task facing this country's wine industry. China has a mountain to climb before it becomes a world player on the winemaking scene, but it does have the potential to get there, in terms of both *terroir* and economic drive.

OPENING UP CHINA'S WINE REGIONS

Shandong has always been the hub of China's modern wine industry and developments in this province continue at a giddy pace. The latest joint-venture is between Château Lafite and China's largest state-owned investment company, who plant to produce the country's greatest wine in Penglai, an area that is already known locally as "China's Bordeaux". However, rot is a persistent problem on the east coast; consequently, expansion and new ventures have spread out beyond the Shandong heartland to central China, the far west, and the deep south. In central China, the rapidly rising star is the Shanxi Grace Winery, which was established in 1997 but quickly demonstrated the premium-quality potential of the central Shanxi Province. Expansion in the western Autonomous Region of Xinjiang and its neighbouring Gansu and Ningxia provinces has also been taking place at breakneck speed, with Suntime (Xintian) leading the way. This winery came from nowhere

GRACE VINEYARDS, SHANXI
This beautiful valley south of Taiyuan in Shanxi province is carpeted with vines grown by Grace Vineyards, one of China's most prestigious and highly successful wineries.

CHÂTEAU CHANGYU AFIP GLOBAL, HEBEI
The vines growing in Huailai Rongchen vineyard near Guanting Lake in Hebei province are Cabernet Sauvignon and belong to the Sino-French Château Changyu AFIP Global.

in 1998 to become one of the four largest wineries in China by 2003. In Gansu, the Mogao Winery has collaborated with Mihalis Boutaris of the Kir-Yianni in Naoussa, Greece, to plant the first Xinomavro vines in China. In Ningxia, the revitalized Yuquan Winery is now the Province's largest producer. Many major Shandong wineries now source grapes from these western provinces, particularly black grapes. The latest rush to plant has been in the Yunnan Province in the south, where vineyards have sprung up on 2-km- (1.2-mile-) high mountain plateaux close to the Vietnamese border. Three varieties have been growing here since the late 19th century, having been brought, supposedly, by French Christian missionaries – two black grapes: Honey Rose and Wild French; and one white: Crystal (possibly *labrusca*). New plantings are, however, of more traditional international varieties, such as Cabernet Sauvignon, Merlot, Grenache, and Chardonnay. Other interesting ventures include Bodega Langes (100% Austrian-owned in Changli, Hebei), Château Changyu AFIP Global (Disney meets Bordeaux, also in Hebei; Sino-French venture), and Château Changyu Golden Ice Wine Valley (another Changyu project involving 400 hectares (1,000 acres) of Vidal reserved exclusively for icewine; Sino-Canadian venture).

✓ *Dragon Seal* (Huailai Cabernet Sauvignon, Huailai Syrah) • *Shanxi Grace Vineyard* (Cabernet Franc)

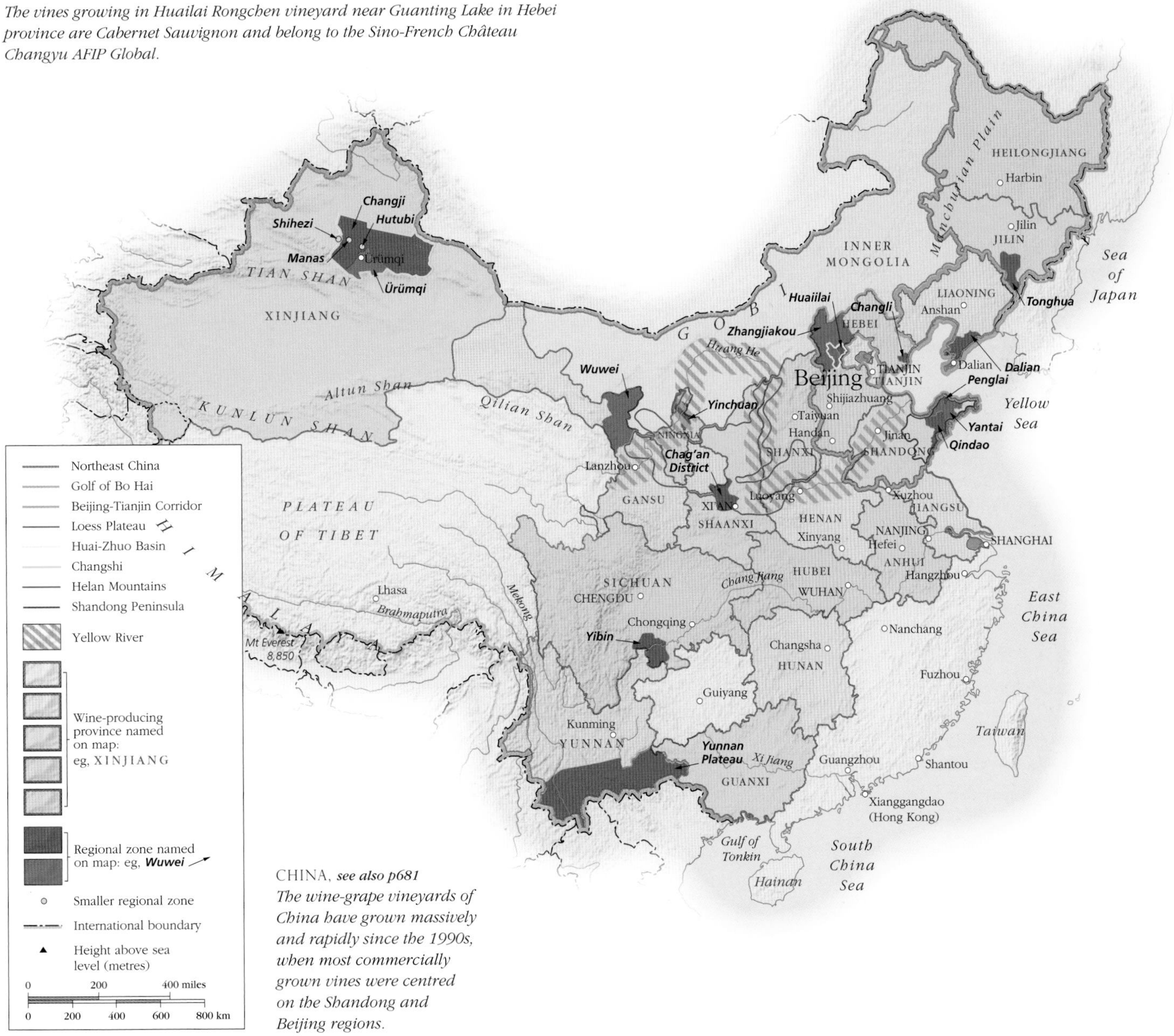

Map legend

- Northeast China
- Golf of Bo Hai
- Beijing-Tianjin Corridor
- Loess Plateau
- Huai-Zhuo Basin
- Changshi
- Helan Mountains
- Shandong Peninsula

Yellow River

Wine-producing province named on map: eg, XINJIANG

Regional zone named on map: eg, **Wuwei**

○ Smaller regional zone

── International boundary

▲ Height above sea level (metres)

0   200   400 miles
0 200 400 600 800 km

CHINA, *see also p681*
The wine-grape vineyards of China have grown massively and rapidly since the 1990s, when most commercially grown vines were centred on the Shandong and Beijing regions.

INDIA

The vine has been growing in India for more than 6,000 years, and the country now has 65,000 hectares (160,000 acres) of vineyards, 22,000 (54,000 acres) of which are wine grapes, producing 180,000 hectolitres (2 million cases). The industry has grown tenfold since the mid-1990s and now boasts more than 100 wineries, with 50-odd located in Maharashtra.

THE FAMOUS INDIAN MEDICAL TREATISES *Sasruta Samhita* and *Charaka Samhita*, written between 1356 BC and 1220 BC, mention the medicinal properties of grapes already growing in India, and specific grape varieties are named in *Arthashastra*, a treatise on political economy, once thought to have been written in the 4th century BC but now considered to date from the 2nd century AD. The first large-scale cultivation of grapes was by Persian invaders in about AD 1300, and they quickly spread the practice to the Aurangabad district of Maharashtra, so that by 1430 a Moorish trader by the name of Ibn Batuta reported having seen vineyards flourishing in the south of India.

So, viticulture is not new to this country, but in 1982 one man born of humble origins kick-started the modern Indian wine industry, when self-made multi-millionaire Sham Chougule asked Piper-Heidsieck to assist him in his quest to create a world-class sparkling wine. And so the Indage Vintners (formerly Champagne Indage) empire was born. Chougule convinced the English wine trade that the sparkling wines he was selling in the late-1980s were composed of 30 per cent Chardonnay and 70 per cent Ugni Blanc. I could not believe they were growing Chardonnay in India at that time, so I braved the Monsoon season to see for myself. I was truly amazed to find Chardonnay in his vineyard, but even more amazed to see that the vines were too young to crop at that juncture. I later found out from Raphael Brisbois, the French oenologist who made those wines, that they were all 100 per cent Thompson Seedless! A decision to expand rapidly in 2008 coincided with poor quality, and a 60 per cent drop in sales resulted in a wind-up order in 2009 issued by the High Court in Mumbai and has cast doubt over the survival of any of its brands. Chougule has, however, paved the way for Sula, Grover, and the other

classic varietal ventures that followed in this increasingly higher-quality, more sophisticated wine-producing country.

✓ *Big Banyan* (Bellissima, Chenin Blanc) • *Deccan Plateau* (Trivalli) • *Four Season* (Shiraz, Viognier) • *Fratelli* (Cabernet Sauvignon, Chenin Blanc) • *The Good Earth Company* (Sauvignon Blanc) • *Grover* (Cabernet Sauvignon-Shiraz, La Reserve Cabernet Sauvignon) • *Nine Hills* (Cabernet Sauvignon, Chenin Blanc, Sauvignon Blanc) • *Sula* (Dindori Reserve Shiraz) • *Vallonné* (Merlot) • *York Winery* (Chenin Blanc, Reserve Shiraz)

HARVESTING AT SULA VINEYARDS
This woman is harvesting at Nashik (or Nasik) in Maharashtra province, where Sula has opened India's first winery restaurant. The 50-seater Mediterranean-style diner is called Little Italy @ Sula.

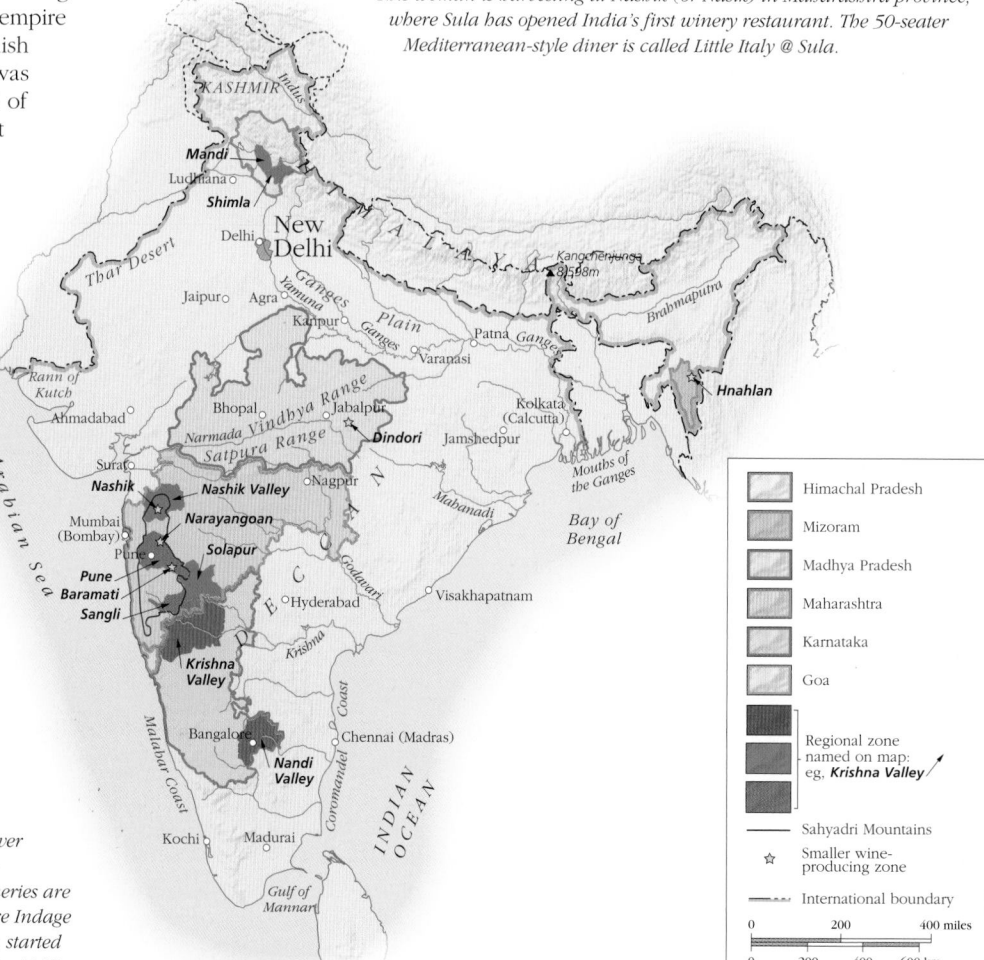

INDIA, *see also p681*
Although the vineyards of India cover 2,100 km (1,300 miles) of the sub-continent, most vineyards and wineries are in the Maharashtra province, where Indage Vintners, then Champagne Indage, started the modern Indian wine industry in 1982.

Himachal Pradesh

Mizoram

Madhya Pradesh

Maharashtra

Karnataka

Goa

Regional zone named on map: eg, *Krishna Valley*

Sahyadri Mountains

☆ Smaller wine-producing zone

International boundary

| 0 | 200 | 400 miles |
| 0 | 200 | 400 | 600 km |

JAPAN

Japanese wine production was first documented by the Portuguese in the 16th century, but it probably dates back to much earlier times.

IN THE 17TH CENTURY, under the all-powerful Tokugawa shogunate, which even controlled the emperor, Japanese wine virtually became extinct, and all things perceived as Christian or Western were condemned. Only after Yoshinobu, the last shogun, gave military and civil powers back to the emperor in 1867 were conditions right to rebuild Japan's wine industry. In 1875, the first commercial winery was established west of Tokyo in the Yamanashi district, which still accounts for 40 per cent of Japanese vineyards.

Due to this history, wine drinking was not felt to be natural in Japanese society, and it has been slow to take off, but Westernization led to a doubling of wine consumption throughout the 1980s, and it has doubled again since. This led the industry to improve quality and come clean on the provenance of its products. Once notorious for bottling imported bulk wine as "Produce of Japan", the industry now has a voluntary code that ensures the labelling of all imported wines as *yunyu san*, Japanese-fermented wines as *kokunai san*, and any blends of the two must be clearly indicated. This self-regulated system is adhered to by producers of any note, but *kokunai san* can still be fermented from imported grapes, grape juice, or concentrate.

Virtually all of Japan's best wines to date have been from classic grape varieties, mostly French (particularly Cabernet Sauvignon, Chardonnay, and Merlot), but there is renewed interest in Koshu, a variety this country has made its own. Though this grape originated in Asia Minor, arriving in China via the Silk Route and brought into Japan by Buddhists, it has been cultivated in the Yamanashi district since at least the 8th century. Until recently, the Koshu grape was used only to make sweet wine, or it would be lost in a blended "modern"-style wine. Since the turn of the millennium, however, some innovative Japanese producers have been honing a pure, dry style. Experimentation in production methods is going on, but the groundwork should first be sorted out, by selecting the best sites,

developing specialized clones, and reducing yields. When this is accomplished – and with Denis Dubourdieu, the world-renowned white-wine consultant from the University of Bordeaux working closely with Grace Wines, the largest producer of Koshu – it might even become Japan's flagship wine.

There are 200 commercial wineries in Japan; the largest are Chateau Mercian, Sapporo, and Suntory. Suntory operates four wineries (Yamanashi, Yamagata, Shiojiri in Nagano, and Seto in Okayama).

Ajima Budoshu (Chardonnay) • *Château Mercian* (Hokushin Reserve Chardonnay, Private Reserve Kikyogahara Merlot) • *Domaine Sogga* (Chardonnay) • *Grace* (Misawa Private Reserve Cabernet-Merlot, Misawa Private Reserve Koshu – for Koshu lovers only!) • *Hayashi Farm* (Kifugo, Kikyogahara Merlot) • *Kumamoto* (Night Harvest Chardonnay) • *Manns* (Solaris Chikumagawa Nagano Merlot) • *Okuizumo* (Shimane Chardonnay) • *Sapporo* (Grande Polaire Furusato Cabernet Sauvignon, Grande Polaire Nagano Furusato Vineyard Cabernet Sauvignon, Grande Polaire Yoichi Kifu) • *Suntory* (Tomi no Oka Cabernet Merlot, Tsutaishizaka Chardonnay) • *Tsuno* (Campbell's Early Rose)

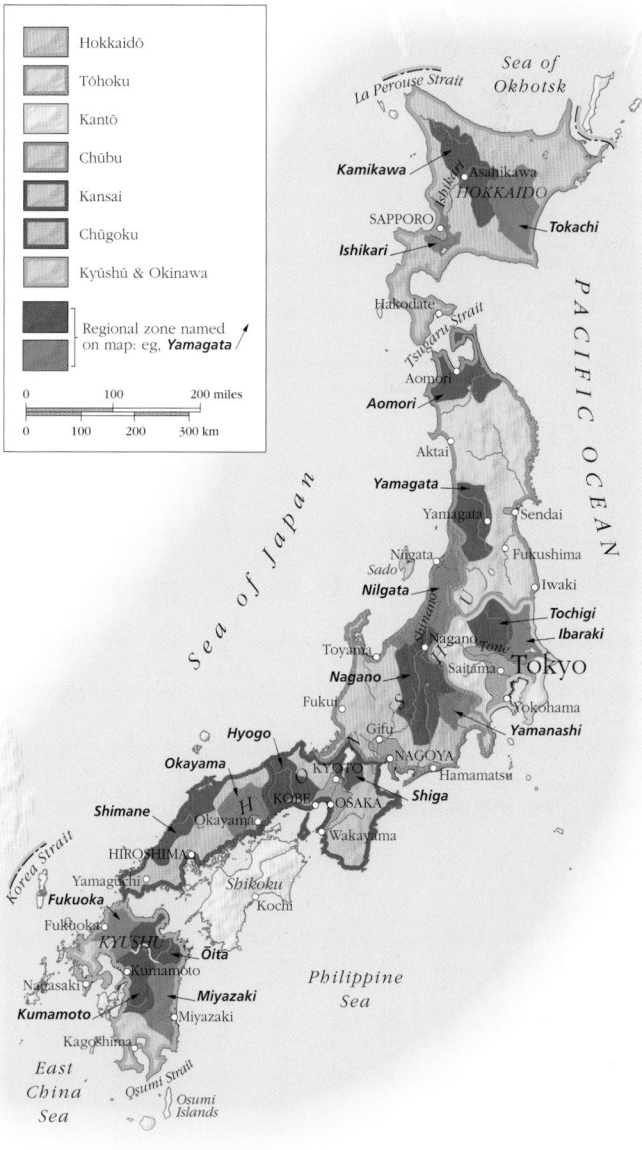

	Hokkaidō
	Tōhoku
	Kantō
	Chūbu
	Kansai
	Chūgoku
	Kyūshū & Okinawa

Regional zone named on map: eg, *Yamagata*

0   100   200 miles
0   100   200   300 km

JAPAN, *see also p681*

There are vineyards in almost every prefecture of Japan – from the north of Hokkaido, to Miyazaking in the south of Kyushu – but more than 40 per cent are still in Yamanashi, where Japan's first commercial winery opened in 1875.

A VINEYARD IN THE YAMANASHI-KEN DISTRICT, JAPAN
In the Yamanashi-Ken wine district, west of Tokyo on the island of Honshu, the vines are trained high on slightly sloping, south-facing slopes.

GUIDE TO GOOD VINTAGES

This chart provides a useful fingertip reference to the comparative performance of over 950 vintages, covering 28 different categories of wine. As with any vintage chart, the ratings should merely be seen as "betting odds". They express the likelihood of what might reasonably be expected from a wine of a given year and should not be used as a guide to buying specific wines. No blanket rating can highlight the many exceptions that exist in every vintage, although the higher the rating, the fewer the exceptions; quality and consistency do to some extent go hand in hand.

KEY TO VINTAGE RATINGS

90 – 100*	Excellent to superb
80 – 89	Good to very good
70 – 79	Average to good
60 – 69	Disappointing
40 – 59	Very bad
0 – 39	Disastrous

* No vintage can be accurately described as perfect, but those achieving a maximum score are truly great vintages.

Remember that some wines are not particularly enjoyable, nor even superior, in so-called great years. Such wines, which are normally light-bodied, aromatic whites that are best drunk while young, fresh, and grapey (eg, Muscat d'Alsace, German QbA, or Kabinett), favour vintages with ratings of between 70 and 85, or lower.

WINE CATEGORY	2010	2009	2008	2007	2006	2005	2004	2003	2002	2001	2000	1999	1998	1997	1996	1995	1994	1993	1992	1991	1990	1989
BORDEAUX – MÉDOC AND GRAVES	90	99	89	80	85	96	94	93	91	90	98	85	85	83	95	90	85	82	78	78	90	95
BORDEAUX – ST-ÉMILION and POMEROL	90	98	90	83	87	98	94	89	85	91	97	88	90	80	90	85	85	78	75	92	95
BORDEAUX – SAUTERNES and BARSAC	95	98	87	98	87	95	90	92	95	98	87	87	89	95	90	95	79	60	65	60	92	95
BURGUNDY – CÔTE D'OR – red	70	97	87	85	86	95	84	75	90	84	85	91	89	88	97	90	70	87	85	82	95	92
BURGUNDY – CÔTE D'OR – white	80	91	89	90	89	90	86	65	90	90	87	89	90	92	97	92	80	87	95	70	98	95
BURGUNDY – BEAUJOLAIS – red	88	97	84	85	88	92	80	90	85	80	87	88	83	85	90	85	90	85	92	85	90	90
CHAMPAGNE	86	90	88	84	84	84	86	50-85	90	35	85	86	90	85	90	90	70	87	85	80	95	89
ALSACE	89	90	70-85	87	70	89	87	65-90	88	90	85	85	85	90	60	90	87	85	80	75	95	90
LOIRE – sweet white	80-95	95	88	70-88	75	95	80	93	85	95	60	60	60	91	90	95	90	55	55	50	90	90
LOIRE – red	80-95	95	80	85	85	95	85	95	85	80	85	80	75	90	92	90	60	60	40	40	90	90
RHÔNE – NORTHERN RHÔNE	93	96	80	90	92	96	86	96	70	85	90	91	89	85	85	92	75	65	75	85	96	95
RHÔNE – SOUTHERN RHÔNE	93	92	85	95	90	96	90	93	55	89	92	88	95	70	85	90	80	80	75	70	90	95
GERMANY – MOSEL	89	91	90	92	85	96	91	85-97	92	90	80	87	75	90	85	92	92	94	92	88	100	98
GERMANY – RHINE	89	90	92	90	80	90	90	85-94	90	92	80	87	85	95	84	90	85	90	90	80	95	95
ITALY – BAROLO	89	90	92	92	95	86	96	90	75	96	90	95	94	92	96	90	88	85	75	80	93	95
ITALY – CHIANTI	89	90	90	91	94	85	93	89	75	91	87	92	85	93	80	88	90	85	75	80	90	65
SPAIN – RIOJA	92	90	87	85	87	95	95	80	70	93	85	84	80	85	75	87	95	87	85	85	78	85
PORTUGAL – VINTAGE PORT	89	85	87	95	70	80	88	94	70	86	95	75	80	90	–	88	95	–	85	95	–	–
US – CALIFORNIA – red	87	89	90	88	90	96	95	90	92	94	89	94	89	87	88	92	94	88	91	93	80	80
US – CALIFORNIA – white	88	90	87	88	90	96	90	90	91	90	89	90	89	88	88	90	88	89	92	85	80	82
US – PACIFIC NORTHWEST – red	89	80-90	94	88	90	85	89	88	93	89	90	95	92	85	90	88	88	87	89	85	85	85
US – PACIFIC NORTHWEST – white	84	90	94	80-88	90	82	84	85	90	90	90	90	88	85	90	85	75	69	85	85	88	80
AUSTRALIA – HUNTER VALLEY – red	88	89	70	88	90	95	82	98	70	70	88	80	90	65	95	85	70	90	65	95	80	85
AUSTRALIA – HUNTER VALLEY – white	88	91	75	87	88	90	89	98	95	85	88	80	90	65	95	85	85	90	75	90	75	90
AUSTRALIA – BAROSSA VALLEY – red	90	88	83	80	90	95	90	70	92	90	80	70-95	94	90	95	70	80	80	80	90	95	85
AUSTRALIA – BAROSSA VALLEY – white	90	90	88	80	90	90	86	70	88	75	85	80	90	90	95	80	80	70	80	90	90	70
AUSTRALIA – MARGARET RIVER – red	90	90	90	92	85	88	90	70	90	95	89	90	87	90	90	95	95	85	90	98	88	85
AUSTRALIA – MARGARET RIVER – white	90	90	90	92	95	89	87	70	90	90	88	85	85	85	95	93	93	85	88	86	85	88

LOW-RATED VINTAGES

These should be treated with extreme caution, but not ignored. Although wine investors buy only great vintages of blue-chip wines, the clever wine drinker makes a beeline for unfashionable vintages at a tasting and searches for the exceptions. This is because, no matter how successful the wine, if it comes from a modest year, it will be relatively inexpensive.

CLOSE-SCORING WINES

Obviously, the smaller the gap between two scores, the less difference one might expect in the quality of the wines, but many readers may think that to discriminate by as little as one point is to split hairs. Certainly, a one-point difference reveals no great divide but, on balance, it indicates which vintage has the edge.

UNRATED VINTAGES

It is impossible to rate generally undeclared vintages of Port and Champagne because the few wines released often prove to be truly exceptional anomalies. Take the Champagne vintage of 1951: this was one of the worst vintages in Champagne's history. According to almost everyone who remembers the harvest, no pure vintaged Champagnes were produced, yet my research has uncovered three. If I were to rank 1951 on the two I actually tasted (Clos des Goisses and Salon), it would be one of the finest vintages of the century, which is clearly nonsense. Port vintages pose a similar problem: should 1992 be judged on the basis of the superb Taylor's, by the handful of other good, but distinctly lesser, 1992s, or by the majority of shippers, who did not produce good enough wine to declare a vintage?

1988	1987	1986	1985	1984	1983	1982	1981	1980	1979	1978	1977	1976	PRE-1976 GREAT VINTAGES	
88	78	90	92	75	88	98	82	78	85	90	45	80	1975, 1970, 1961, 1953, 1949, 1945, 1929, 1928, 1900	**BORDEAUX** – MÉDOC AND GRAVES
88	75	85	92	65	85	98	82	75	85	80	45	80	1975, 1961, 1953, 1949, 1945, 1929, 1928, 1900	**BORDEAUX** – ST-ÉMILION and POMEROL
95	60	90	85	60	100	70	70	80	80	65	50	85	1975, 1962, 1959, 1955, 1949, 1947, 1945, 1937	**BORDEAUX** – SAUTERNES and BARSAC
98	70	78	100	70	88	80	75	60	75	85	40	88	1971, 1961, 1959, 1949, 1945, 1929, 1919, 1915	**BURGUNDY** – CÔTE D'OR – red
92	80	92	90	80	88	86	85	72	80	88	50	80	1962, 1928, 1921	**BURGUNDY** – CÔTE D'OR – white
85	78	85	90	70	90	72	74	55	60	90	55	90	1961, 1959, 1957, 1949, 1945, 1929	**BURGUNDY** – BEAUJOLAIS – red
90	–	80	95	–	90	92	90	70	90	80	–	90	1975, 1964, 1959, 1947, 1945, 1928, 1921, 1914	**CHAMPAGNE**
90	78	75	90	65	100	80	89	60	85	40	33	10	1975, 1971, 1969, 1961, 1959, 1953, 1949 1945, 1937, 1921	**ALSACE**
90	60	85	87	65	90	85	70	65	55	75	30	92	1975, 1971, 1969, 1961, 1959, 1949, 1945, 1921	**LOIRE** – sweet white
85	40	85	90	75	85	85	80	70	60	80	45	90	1975, 1969, 1961	**LOIRE** – red
95	88	86	95	70	98	92	75	78	81	100	50	85	1972, 1970, 1961	**RHÔNE** – NORTHERN RHÔNE
92	70	88	90	70	92	88	87	83	78	98	72	85	1972, 1970, 1967, 1961	**RHÔNE** – SOUTHERN RHÔNE
95	75	93	95	50	100	70	75	50	85	55	50	100	1975, 1973, 1971, 1969, 1959, 1953, 1949, 1945, 1921	**GERMANY** – MOSEL
90	78	93	95	50	98	73	75	50	88	55	50	98	1975, 1971, 1969, 1959, 1953, 1949, 1945, 1921	**GERMANY** – RHINE
95	88	82	95	55	90	95	80	60	85	100	40	80	1971, 1958, 1947, 1931, 1922	**ITALY** – BAROLO
90	83	80	93	60	85	90	80	70	85	88	75	40	1971, 1947, 1931, 1928, 1911	**ITALY** – CHIANTI
80	80	80	80	75	88	100	85	80	60	80	25	85	1970, 1968, 1964, 1962, 1942, 1934, 1924, 1920, 1916	**SPAIN** – RIOJA
–	–	–	95	–	95	80	–	85	–	80	99	–	1969, 1963, 1945, 1935, 1931, 1927, 1908	**PORTUGAL** – VINTAGE PORT
85	90	88	98	92	90	88	85	88	80	88	80	88	1974, 1970, 1968, 1951, 1946	**US** – CALIFORNIA – red
88	85	90	84	95	86	86	88	90	80	88	85	80	1974, 1970, 1967	**US** – CALIFORNIA – white
85	85	86	96	50	95	84	88	88	80	88	80	88	1975	**US** – PACIFIC NORTHWEST – red
80	85	90	96	70	95	83	80	87	80	88	80	88		**US** – PACIFIC NORTHWEST – white
80	88	95	90	80	90	80	80	90	98	80	80	70	1975, 1965	**AUSTRALIA** – HUNTER VALLEY – red
90	90	95	90	80	90	80	85	98	90	70	70	80	1967	**AUSTRALIA** – HUNTER VALLEY – white
85	80	88	95	95	70	90	85	80	92	70	80	90		**AUSTRALIA** – BAROSSA VALLEY – red
80	80	90	95	95	85	90	70	80	92	90	70	90		**AUSTRALIA** – BAROSSA VALLEY – white
88	88	88	90	80	80	90	85	80	80	70	90	45		**AUSTRALIA** – MARGARET RIVER – red
85	88	88	90	80	80	90	85	90	80	45	70	65		**AUSTRALIA** – MARGARET RIVER – white

MICROPEDIA

Terms that are explained more comprehensively within the main body of the book are accompanied by a cross-reference to the appropriate page. Terms that appear within a Micropedia entry and have their own separate entry appear set in bold type. For more tasting terms, *see* Tastes and Aromas, p77.

Key to abbreviations: Fr. = French; Ger. = German; Gr. = Greek; It. = Italian; Port. = Portuguese; Sp. = Spanish; S Afr. = South African.

ABC An acronym for "Anything But Cabernet" or "Anything But Chardonnay", ABC was a more-than-acceptable term when originally conceived by Randall Grahm of Bonny Doon. Grahm was selling Cabernet at the time, but saw it as a rut that every California winery was trapped in. He wanted to explore the quality potential of other grapes, particularly the Rhône varieties, but was severely restricted by the public demand for Cabernet and Chardonnay. While Cabernet walked off the shelf, Grahm had to work hard at selling the virtues of anything more exotic. Compelled to sell Cabernet to fund other activities, he came up with the ABC term. Everyone loved it when Grahm invented it. It has since been hijacked by inverted snobs and myopic critics, however, who have been zealots in their crusade to rid the world of two great wine grapes.

ABV Abbreviation for **alcohol** by volume.

AC (Port., Gr.) Short for *Adega Cooperativa* in Portugal and Agricultural Cooperative in Greece, or other titles denoting a local or regional cooperative in these countries.

ACCESSIBLE Literally that the wine is **easy** to approach, with no great barriers of **tannin**, **acidity**, or undeveloped **extract** to prevent enjoyment of drinking. This term is often used for young, fine-quality wine that will undoubtedly improve with age but whose tannins are **supple** and thus approachable.

ACETALDEHYDE The principal **aldehyde** in all wines, but found in much greater quantities in Sherry. In light, unfortified **table wines**, a small amount of acetaldehyde enhances the **bouquet**, but an excess is undesirable because it is unstable, halfway to complete **oxidation**, and evokes a **Sherry-like** smell.

ACETIC ACID The most important **volatile acid** found in wine, apart from **carbonic acid**. Small amounts of acetic acid contribute positively to the attractive flavour of a wine, but large quantities produce a taste of **vinegar**.

ACETIFICATION The production of **acetic acid** in a wine.

ACETOBACTER The **vinegar** *bacillus* (rod-shaped bacterium), which can cause **acetification**.

ACIDITY Essential for the life and vitality of all wines. Too much will make wine too **sharp** (not **sour** – that's a fault), but not enough will make it taste **flat** and dull, and the flavour will not last in the mouth. *See also* **Total acidity**; **pH**.

ACTIVE ACIDITY Acids contain positively charged hydrogen ions, the concentration of which determines the **total acidity** of a wine. The **pH** is the measure of the electrical charge of a given solution (positive **acidity** hydrogen buffered by negative alkalinity hydrogen ions). Thus the pH of a wine is a measure of its active acidity.

ADEGA (Port.) Cellar or winery. Often used as part of a firm's title.

AEROBIC Occurring in the presence of air.

AFTERTASTE A term for the flavour and **aroma** left in the mouth after the wine has been swallowed. When the aftertaste is attractive, it could be the reason why you prefer one wine to a similar wine with no particular aftertaste.

AGES GRACEFULLY Describes wine that retains **finesse** as it **matures** and that sometimes may even increase in finesse.

AGGLOMERATED CORK These **cork** stoppers are made of granulated cork, usually produced from the leftovers of the manufacture of natural cork closures. The granulated cork is washed and dried and mixed with a food-grade glue before being either individually injected into moulds or produced by extrusion (ie, a continuous "sausage" that is cut into individual corks).

AGGRESSIVE The opposite of **soft** and **smooth**.

ALBAN or **ALBANUM** An **ancient Roman wine** that rose to fame after the demise of **Falernum**, Alban was first mentioned by Dionysius of Halicarnassus and was usually consumed when 10 to 20 years old. Some sources claim it to be very sweet, while others believe it to be **sharp**, even **sour**. However, sweetness was a mark of a great wine in those days, so its fame would suggest that it was indeed very sweet.

ALBANY DOCTOR One of Western Australia's beneficially cooling sea breezes, the Albany Doctor provides similar relief to that of the famous **Fremantle Doctor**, only farther south and closer to the coast. *See also* **Canberra Doctor**.

ALBARIZA (Sp.) A white-surfaced soil formed by **diatomaceous** (decomposed deep-sea algae) deposits, which is found in the Sherry-producing area of Spain. *See also* Sherry Country, p379.

ALCOHOL In wine terms, this is **ethyl alcohol**; a colourless flammable liquid. Alcohol is essential to the flavour and **body** of **alcoholic** products; thus, a de-alcoholized wine is intrinsically difficult to perfect.

ALCOHOLIC This term is usually employed in a pejorative rather than a literal sense and implies that a wine has too much **alcohol** to be in **balance**.

ALDEHYDE The midway stage between an **alcohol** and an acid, formed during the **oxidation** of an alcohol. **Acetaldehyde** is the most important of the common wine aldehydes, and forms as wine alcohol oxidizes to become **acetic acid** (**vinegar**). Small amounts of acetaldehyde add to the **complexity** of a wine, but too much will make a **table wine** smell like Sherry.

ALDEHYDIC An excessive form of **oxidative**. *See* Acetaldehyde; Aldehyde.

ALLIER A famous type of **oak** used for barrelmaking from **Tronçais**, **Grosbois**, **Civrais**, **Dreuille**, or any other forest in the Allier *département* in the centre of France.

ALTE REBEN (Ger.) Old vines.

ALTEC The great **cork** hope that flopped. Launched by Sabaté in 1994, Altec was the first so-called technical cork specifically designed to combat **TCA**, the cause of **cork taint or corked wine**. Sabaté's researchers had found that TCA adheres to the woody part of the cork called lignin, which is relatively heavy, so they ground the cork into tiny granular pieces and removed the heavier lignin, then added polymer microspheres

to replicate the structural properties of the lignin and used a food-grade glue to form an **agglomerated cork**. Almost overnight, sales of Altec alone pushed Sabaté from a small-time cork producer to the world's number-two cork manufacturer, but in 2001 the *Wine Spectator* website published an investigative piece under the headline "Wineries Claim Alternative Cork Caused Widespread Taint Problems". This was the polar opposite of Altec's *raison d'être*, and it ended with legal action that was settled out of court in 2003. The details of the settlement have never been revealed, nor has Sabaté ever given a satisfactory explanation of what went wrong. However, with sales going from zero to 800 million a year, a number of industry insiders have suggested that the sourcing of raw materials went from a very high quality by a firm that was passionate about defeating TCA to such large and diverse volumes from various sources that quality control became impossible.

AMINO ACIDS Proteins formed by a combination of fruit **esters**, amino acids are found naturally in grapes and are both created and consumed during **fermentation** and **autolysis**. They are essential precursors to the **complexity** and **finesse** of a sparkling wine. *See also* **Maillard reactions**.

AMPELOGRAPHER An expert who studies, records, and identifies grapevines.

AMYLIC The peardrop, banana, or bubblegum **aromas** of amyl or isoamyl acetate, excessive amounts of which can be produced in white wines if the **fermentation** is conducted at a very low temperature, and in red wines made by **carbonic maceration**.

ANAEROBIC Occurring in the absence of oxygen. Most maturation processes that take place in a sealed bottle are considered to be anaerobic.

ANBAUGEBIET (Ger.) A wine region in Germany, such as Rheinpfalz or Mosel, that is divided into districts (**Bereiche**). All QbA and QmP wines must show their *Anbaugebiet* of origin on the label.

ANCIENT GREEK WINES The Greeks preferred sweet wines that were very high in **alcohol**, but they always diluted their wine, usually with three or four parts water, the intention of such a mix being to enjoy the aesthetic pleasure of the wine and to be intoxicated just enough to have the mind released from inhibition. At banquets, it was the *symposiarchos* (master of drinking) who decided the ratio of water to wine. The wine was always added to the water, never the water to the wine, a practice that developed from the earliest times when it was necessary to add wine to water, albeit in smaller proportions, as a "disinfectant" to protect against disease and to disguise any stagnant smell. This was particularly necessary on long voyages. In Homer's *Odyssey*, for example, a ratio of one part wine to 20 parts water is mentioned. *See* specific ancient Greek wines: **Anthosmias**; **Ariusian**; **Chian**; **Coan**; **Denthis**; **Eresos**; **Lesbian**; **Pramnian**; **Thasian** (or **Thasos**).

ANCIENT ROMAN WINES The Romans added herbs, spices, and resin to perfume their wines, a practice that was copied from the Egyptians. Like the Greeks, the Romans diluted their wine with water, although with just one or two parts water, which was considered barbaric by the Greeks, just as the Gauls, who drank wine undiluted, were regarded as barbaric by the Romans. *See* specific ancient Roman wines: **Alban**; **Caecuban**; **Caucinian**; **Conditum**; **Falernian**; **Falernum**; **Faustian**; **Formian** (or **Formianum**); **Gauran** (or **Gauranum**); **Lora**;

Mamertine (or Mamertinum); Marsic; Massicum; Mulsum; Passum; Praenestine (or Praenestinum); Privernatinum (or Privernian); Rhaetic (or Rhaeticum); Rhegium; Sorrentum (or Surrentine or Surrentinum); Setine (or Setinum); Statan; Tiburtine; Trifolian.

ANTHOCYANINS The second-most important group of **phenolic compounds** found in wine, anthocyanins are colour pigments located in the grapes' skins.

ANTHOSMIAS This **ancient Greek wine** was made "stronger with the fruit of new vines rather than of old" and **cut** with one part seawater to 50 parts wine.

ANTI-OXIDANT Any chemical that prevents grapes, **must**, or wine from **oxidizing**, such as **ascorbic acid** or sulphur dioxide (**SO₂**).

AOC (Fr.) *Appellation d'Origine Contrôlée* is the top rung in the French wine-quality system, although in practice it includes everything from the greatest French wines to the worst; thus, it is almost always better to buy an expensive *vin de pays* than a cheap AOC wine.

AOP (Fr.) Common abbreviation for *Appellation d'Origine Protégée*, the French-language version of the EU umbrella classification for all national quality-wine regimes, such as **AOC** in France, **DOC** in Italy, **DO** in Spain, etc. The English equivalent is PDO (Protected Denomination of Origin).

APERITIF Originally used exclusively to describe a beverage prescribed purely for laxative purposes, the term aperitif now describes any drink that is taken before a meal in order to stimulate the appetite.

APPELLATION Literally a name, this term is usually used to refer to an official geographically based designation for a wine. An appellation does not necessarily infer a whole bunch of rules dictating what must be grown and how, or what sort of wine must be made. That level of bureaucratic interference is purely a matter for each individual country; thus, countries such as France, Italy, Spain, and Portugal dictate these details, whereas the likes of Germany, the USA, and Australia do not.

APPELLATION D'ORIGINE CONTRÔLÉE See **AOC.**

AQUIFER A water-retaining geological formation into which rainfall from the surrounding area drains.

ARGON An expensive noble inert gas, superior to both nitrogen and **CO₂** for winemaking purposes, such as blanketing wines inside vats to prevent **oxidation**.

ARGONNE A well-known type of **oak** used for barrelmaking from a forest in the Ardennes *département* of northern France.

ARIUSIAN This **ancient Greek wine** was supposedly the best **Chian** wine.

AROMA This should really be confined to the fresh and fruity smells reminiscent of grapes, rather than the more winey or bottle-**mature** complexities of **bouquet**; but it is not always possible to use this word in its purest form – hence, aroma and bouquet may be thought of as being synonymous.

AROMATIC GRAPE VARIETIES The most aromatic classic varieties are Gewürztraminer, Muscat, and Riesling, and they are defined as such because when **ripe** they possess high levels of various **terpenes** in their skins. Although attractive when young, these terpenes take a few years in bottle to develop their full **varietal** potential.

AROMATIZED WINE Usually **fortified**, these wines are flavoured by as few as one, or as many as fifty, aromatic substances and range from bitter-sweet **vermouth** to Retsina. The various herbs, fruits, flowers, and other less-appetizing ingredients used include strawberries, orange peel, elderflowers, wormwood, quinine, and pine resin.

ASCORBIC ACID Otherwise known as Vitamin C, ascorbic acid is an **anti-oxidant**, which is often used in conjunction with sulphur. It has a more freshening effect than sulphur, which tends to dampen the aromatics in wine. It also enables less sulphur to be used in the **vinification** process. Not to be confused with **sorbic acid**.

ASEPTIC A particular characteristic of a substance such as **sorbic acid** or sulphur dioxide (**SO₂**) that can kill bacteria.

ASPECT The topography of a vineyard, including its altitude, the direction in which the vines face, and the angle of any slope.

ASPERSION A method of protecting vines from frost by spraying with water. *See* Combating frost (photograph and cation), p220.

ASSEMBLAGE (Fr.) A blend of base wines that creates the final *cuvée*.

ATA *See* Atypical ageing.

ATMOSPHERE A measure of atmospheric pressure: 1 atmosphere = 15 pounds per square inch. The average internal pressure of a bottle of Champagne is 6 atmospheres.

ATTACK A wine with good attack suggests one that is **complete** and readily presents its full armament of taste characteristics to the **palate**. The wine is likely to be youthful rather than **mature** and its attack augurs well for its future.

ATYPICAL AGEING or **ATA** Although first noticed in Germany in 1977, ATA was not so widely known in the global wine industry until about 1995, when viticultural researchers from Germany, Austria, and Switzerland began comparing notes. Wines affected by ATA are **thin** or **green** or unripe, with atypical **aromas** and a loss of **varietal** flavour. The worst cases develop a dirty-dishcloth, dirty-floorcloth, or mothball aroma. ATA is a phenomenon associated with vine stress during drought conditions, which restricts nitrogen uptake, increasing a plant hormone called indole acetic acid (IAA), which breaks down into aminoacetophenone and unpleasant smelling indoles (skatole being the worst offender). High levels of UV irradiation in the vineyard can have a similar effect. ATA can also have a naphthalene-like (mothball) smell.

AUSLESE (Ger.) A category of German **QmP** wine that is very sweet, made from late-harvested grapes, and may also contain some **botrytized grapes.**

AUSTERE This term is used to describe wine that lacks **fruit** and is dominated by harsh **acidity** and/or **tannin**.

AUTOLYSIS The enzymatic breakdown of **yeast** cells that increases the possibility of bacterial spoilage; the **autolytic** effect of ageing a wine on its **lees** is therefore undesirable in most wines, exceptions being those bottled **sur lie** (principally Muscadet) and sparkling wines.

AUTOLYTIC With the aroma of a freshly disgorged *brut*-style sparkling wine, which is not **yeasty** at all but has a flowery, often acacia-like **freshness**.

AWRI Common abbreviation for the Australian Wine Research Institute.

BACK-BLEND To blend fresh, unfermented grape juice into a **fully fermented** wine, with the aim of adding a certain fresh, **grapey** sweetness commonly associated with German wines. Synonymous with the German practice of adding *Süssreserve*.

BACKWARDS Describes a wine that is slow to develop (the opposite of **precocious**).

BAKED Applies to wines of high **alcoholic** content that give a sensory perception of grapes harvested in great heat – either from a hot country or from a classic wine area in a swelteringly hot year. This characteristic can be controlled to some extent by the following methods: early harvesting, night harvesting, rapid transport to the winery, and modern **cool-fermentation** techniques.

BALANCE Refers to the harmonious relationship between acids, **alcohol**, **fruit**, **tannin**, and other natural elements. If you have two similar wines but you definitely prefer one of them, its balance is likely to be one of the two determining factors (**length** being the other).

BAN DE VENDANGE (Fr.) Official regional start of grape-picking for the latest **vintage**.

BARREL-FERMENTED Some white wines are still traditionally fermented in **oak** barrels – new for top-quality Bordeaux, Burgundy, and premium **varietal** wines; old for middle-quality wines and top-quality Champagnes. New barrels impart oaky characteristics; the older the barrels, the less oaky and more **oxidative** the influence. Barrel-fermented wines have more complex **aromas** than wines that have simply been matured in wood. *See also* Stainless steel or oak?, p29.

BARRIQUE (Fr.) This literally means "barrel", but is used generically in English-speaking countries for any small **oak** cask and often denotes the use of new oak.

BASIC A marketing term for a quality category; *see* **Premium.**

BASIC TASTE There are only five known basic tastes: **bitterness**, **sourness** (or **acidity**), **sweetness**, saltiness, and umami. These are the only tastes we actually experience; all others are tastes that we smell through the **olfactory bulb**. *See* Olfactory bulb; Taste bud; Taste receptor.

BÂTONNAGE (Fr.) Lees-stirring. This practice is often carried out on **fine** wines made from relatively **neutral grape varieties**, such as Chardonnay, to instil some additional fullness, but it can easily be overdone. *Bâtonnage* should be "felt, not smelt" – you should never be able to pick up a wine and smell a leesy-*bâtonnage* **aroma**.

BAUMÉ (Fr.) A scale of measurement used to indicate the amount of sugar in grape **must.**

BEERENAUSLESE (Ger.) A category of German **QmP** wine that comes above *Auslese* but beneath *Trockenbeerenauslese* (TbA) and is made from **botrytized** grapes. It has more **finesse** and **elegance** than any other intensely sweet wine, with the possible exception of *Eiswein.*

BELLÊME Lesser-known type of **oak** used for barrelmaking, from a forest in the Orne *département* of Normandy.

BENCH or **BENCHLAND** The flat land between two slopes, this term describes a form of natural, rather than artificial, terrace.

BENTONITE This is a fine clay containing a volcanic ash derivative called montromillonite, which is a hydrated silicate of magnesium that activates a precipitation in wine when used as a **fining** agent.

BERCE Lesser-known type of **oak** used for barrelmaking, from a forest in the Sarthe *département* of the Loire Valley.

BEREICH (Ger.) A wine district in Germany, which contains smaller *Grosslagen* and is itself part of a larger *Anbaugebiet.*

BERTRANGE A well-known type of **oak** used for barrelmaking, from a small forest in the Nièvre *département* in the centre of France.

BIG VINTAGE, BIG YEAR These terms are usually applied to great years, because the exceptional weather conditions produce bigger (ie, **fuller** and **richer**) wines than normal. They may also be used literally to describe a year with a big crop.

BIG WINE This term describes a **full**-bodied wine with an exceptionally **rich** flavour.

BIODYNAMIC Wines produced biodynamically are grown without the aid of chemical or synthetic sprays or **fertilizers** and are vinified with natural **yeast** and the minimum use of **filtration**, sulphur dioxide (**SO₂**), and **chaptalization**. There are several competing organizations that certify biodynamic farming, but they all agree on one thing: to be biodynamic, you must first be certified **organic**. The essential difference between the two is the range of preparations sprayed on to the compost, soil, and vines in biodynamic vineyards.

BISCUITY A desirable aspect of **bouquet** that is found in some Champagnes – particularly in well-**matured**, Pinot-Noir-dominated blends (Chardonnay-dominated Champagnes tend to go **toasty**, although some top-quality Chardonnay Champagnes can slowly acquire a **creamy** biscuitiness).

BITE A very definite qualification of **grip**. Bite is usually a desirable characteristic, although an unpleasant bite is possible.

BITTERNESS One of the five **basic tastes**, bitterness may be an unpleasant aspect of a poorly made wine or an expected characteristic of an as-yet-undeveloped concentration of flavours that should, with **maturity**, become **rich** and delicious. The term is often applied to **tannin**.

BLACKSTRAP A derogatory term that originated when Port was an unsophisticated product, coloured by elderberries and very **coarse**.

BLANC DE BLANCS (Fr.) This literally means "white of whites", and describes a white wine made from white grapes. It is a term often, but not exclusively, used for sparkling wines.

BLANC DE NOIRS (Fr.) This literally means "white of blacks", and describes a white wine made from black grapes. It is a term that is often, but not exclusively, used for sparkling wines. In the New World, such wines usually have a tinge of pink (often no different from a fully fledged **rosé**), but a **classic** *blanc de noirs* should be as white as possible without artificial means.

BLIND, BLIND TASTING A winetasting at which the identity of the wines is unknown to the taster until after he or she has made notes and given scores. All competitive tastings are made blind.

BLOWZY An overblown and exaggerated fruity **aroma**, such as fruit jam, which may be attractive in a cheap wine, but would indicate a lack of **finesse** in a more expensive product.

BLUSH WINE A **rosé** wine that is probably cheap.

BOB An acronym for **buyer's own brand**, under which many retailers and restaurants sell wine of increasingly good value – particularly in the supermarket sector, in which the selection process has been increasingly honed to a fine art since the early 1980s.

BODEGA (Sp.) The Spanish equivalent of the Portuguese *adega* (ie, a cellar or winery).

BODY The impression of weight in the mouth, which is brought about by a combination of the fruit **extract** and **alcoholic** strength.

BOTA (Sp.) A Sherry butt (cask) with a capacity of between 600 and 650 litres.

BOTRYTIS A generic term for rot, but also often used as an abbreviation of *Botrytis cinerea*.

BOTRYTIS CINEREA The technically correct name for **noble rot** – the only rot that is welcomed by winemakers, particularly in sweet-wine areas, as it is responsible for the world's greatest sweet wines. *See also* Sauternes and Barsac, p143.

BOTRYTIZED GRAPES Literally "rotten grapes", but the term is commonly used for grapes that have been affected by *Botrytis cinerea*.

BOTTLE-AGE The length of time a wine spends in bottle before it is consumed. A wine that has good bottle-age is one that has sufficient time to **mature** properly. Bottle-ageing has a **mellowing** effect.

BOTTLE-AROMAS Synonymous with **tertiary aromas**, these are the mellowing **aromas**. In Riesling and Gewürztraminer, these are **richer** aromatics, since **terpenes** develop under **anaerobic** conditions. In sparkling wine, they are the **mellowing** complex aromas created after **disgorgement**, such as **toasty** and **biscuity**.

BOUQUET This should really be applied to the combination of smells directly attributable to a wine's **maturity** in bottle – thus "aroma" for grape-related smells and "bouquet" for maturation-related smells. But it is not always possible to use these words in their purest form – hence, aroma and bouquet may be considered synonymous.

BOURGEOIS (Fr.) *Cru bourgeois* is a Bordeaux **château** classification beneath *cru classé*.

BOURGOGNE 1. The wine of Burgundy. 2. A type of **oak** used for barrelmaking, from **Châtillon** or any other forest in the Burgundy region.

BREATHING A term used to describe the interaction between a wine and the air after a bottle has been opened and before it is drunk.

BREED The **finesse** of a wine that is due to the intrinsic quality of grape and **terroir** combined with the irrefutable skill and experience of a great winemaker.

BRETTANOMYCES A **genus** of **yeast** that can inhabit a winery or barrels that are sold from one winery to another. Brett (as it is commonly referred to) is a common spoilage organism that mainly, although not exclusively, affects red wines. It creates various **volatile phenols**, including ethyl-4-phenol, which is responsible for the Brett off-odours, such as the so-called sweaty saddles, barnyard, stables, and generally horsey smells.

BRUT (Fr.) Normally reserved for sparkling wines, *brut* literally means raw or bone dry. Even the driest wines, however, contain a little **residual sugar** (formerly 0–15 g/l residual sugar; now 0–12 g/l).

BRUT NATURE A style of Champagne that receives no *dosage*, *brut nature* should be enjoyed as soon as it is released, as it does not age well and is likely to become **oxidative**, possibly excessively oxidative. Furthermore, no Champagne without **residual sugar** can benefit from the potentially complex **aromas** created by Maillard reactions.

BURNT Synonymous with **baked**, and marginally uncomplimentary.

BUTT *See* Bota.

BUTTERSCOTCH An excessive form of **buttery**. Can come from time in **oak** but is usually from diacetyl produced by **malolactic**.

BUTTERY This is normally a **rich**, **fat**, and positively delicious character found in white wines, particularly those that have undergone **malolactic** fermentation.

BUYER'S OWN BRAND Often seen as the acronym **BOB**, this is a brand that belongs to the wine buyer, which could be a wine merchant, supermarket, or restaurant (the buyer is the seller as far as the consumer is concerned).

CA (Sp.) Short for *Cooperativa Agrícola* and other titles denoting a local or regional cooperative.

CAECUBAN Ancient Roman wine (Lazio coast) considered to be a First Growth around 70 BC, thus on a par with **Falernum** and **Setinum**, but had disappeared by the time of Pliny the Elder (AD 23–79). **Smoother** than Falernian, Caecuban was a sweet, strong, intoxicating white wine that turned "fire-coloured" as it aged.

CALENUM This **ancient Roman wine** was made from the Molle Calenum, a large grape that gave a light wine that was, according to Pliny, kinder on the stomach than **Falernian**.

CANBERRA DOCTOR An easterly evening wind from the coast that helps to cool Canberra, although it virtually blows itself out by the time it reaches Braidwood or Bungendore. *See also* **Albany Doctor** and **Fremantle Doctor**.

CANOPY The leafy area surrounding the vine.

CANOPY MANAGEMENT The vine's **canopy** is comprised of the collective arrangement of its shoots, leaves, and fruit. Ideally, a canopy will have most of its leaves well-exposed to sunlight, as this promotes fruit ripening through **photosynthesis**, and air circulation will be good, which provides the least favourable environmental conditions for the development of fungal diseases. References to an excessive or too-vigorous canopy imply that the ratio of leaves to fruit is too high, causing **herbaceous** flavours in the wines produced from such vines.

CANOPY MICROCLIMATE The climatic environment immediately surrounding the canopy of a vine.

CANTINA (It.) Winery.

CANTINA SOCIALE (It.) A grower's cooperative.

CAP The *manta*, or layer of skins that rises to the top of the vat during *cuvaison*.

CARAMEL An excessive form of **buttery**. Can come from time in **oak** but is usually from diacetyl produced by **malolactic**.

CARBON DIOXIDE *See* Carbonic gas.

CARBONATE A salt or **ester** of **carbonic acid**. Active or free carbonates increase the alkalinity of soil and are thus found in limestone soils, such as chalk.

CARBONIC ACID The correct term for carbon dioxide (CO_2) when it dissolves in the water content of wine (to become H_2CO_3). Although sometimes referred to as a **volatile acid**, it is held in equilibrium with the gas in its dissolved state and cannot be isolated in its pure form.

CARBONIC GAS Synonymous with carbon dioxide (CO_2), this gas is naturally produced during the **fermentation** process (when the sugar is converted into almost equal parts of **alcohol** and carbonic gas). It is normally allowed to escape during fermentation, although a tiny amount will always be present in its dissolved form (**carbonic acid**) in any wine, even a still one; otherwise, it would taste dull, **flat**, and lifeless. If the gas is prevented from escaping, the wine becomes sparkling.

CARBONIC MACERATION A generic term covering several methods of vinifying wine under the pressure of **carbonic gas**. Such wines, Beaujolais Nouveau being the archetypal example, are characterized by **amylic** aromas (peardrops, bubblegum, nail varnish). If this method is used for just a small part of a blend, however, it can lift the **fruit** and soften a wine without leaving such telltale **aromas**. *See also* Carbonic Maceration, p32.

CASEIN A milk protein sometimes used for **fining**.

CASK-FERMENTED *See* **barrel-fermented**.

CASSIS (Fr.) Literally "blackcurrant". If *cassis* is used by wine tasters in preference to "blackcurrant", it probably implies a **richer**, more concentrated, and viscous character.

CAUCINIAN An individual named site on the top slopes of the famous ancient Roman vineyard of **Falernum**.

CEDARWOOD A purely subjective word applied to a particular **bouquet** associated with the bottle-**maturity** of a wine previously stored or fermented in wood, usually **oak**.

CELLAR DOOR A sales point at a winery. This is often a sophisticated retail operation in the New World, with sales of wine accessories, books, and T-shirts as well as the wines. For small growers in the Old World, however, purchases are more-often-than-not conducted in the producer's kitchen!

CENTRIFUGAL FILTRATION Not **filtration** in the pure sense, but a process in which unwanted matter is separated from wine or grape juice by so-called "centrifugal force".

CÉPAGE (Fr.) Literally "grape variety", this is sometimes used on the label immediately prior to the variety, while in the plural format (*cépages*) it is used to refer to the **varietal** recipe of a particular *cuvée*.

CERAMIC FILTRATION An ultra-fine **depth filtration** that utilizes **perlite**.

CHAI, CHAIS (Fr.) Building(s) used for wine storage.

CHAPTALIZATION The addition of sugar to fresh grape juice in order to raise a wine's **alcoholic** potential. Theoretically it takes 1.7 kilograms of sugar per hectolitre of wine to raise its alcoholic strength by one per cent, but red wines actually require two kilograms to allow for evaporation during the *remontage*. The term is named after Antoine Chaptal, a brilliant chemist and technocrat who served under Napoleon as minister of the interior from 1800 to 1805 and instructed winegrowers on the advantages of adding sugar at pressing time.

CHARM This is a subjective term; if a wine charms, it appeals without attracting in an obvious fashion.

CHARMAT METHOD Invented in 1907 by Eugène Charmat, this is a bulk-production method of making inexpensive sparkling wine through a natural **second fermentation** inside a sealed vat. Also known as the tank method or *cuve close*.

CHÂTEAU (Fr.) Literally "castle" or "stately home". Whereas many château-bottled wines do actually come from magnificent buildings that could truly be described as châteaux, many are modest one-storey villas; some no more than specially built *cuveries*; and a few merely tin sheds! The legal connotation is the same as for any *domaine*-bottled wine.

CHÂTILLON A well-known type of **oak** used for barrelmaking, from any forest in the Burgundy region of France.

CHEESY This is a characteristic element in the **bouquet** of a very old Champagne, although other wines that have an extended contact with their **lees** – possibly those that have not been racked or **filtered** – may also possess it. It is probably caused by the production during **fermentation** of a very small amount of butyric acid that may later develop into an **ester** called ethyl butyrate.

CHESTNUT BARRELS Although chestnut is usually considered too porous and **tannic** for winemaking purposes and can colour a wine, barrels are made on a commercial basis from this wood. Most are produced by cooperages in Burgundy (by Billon in Beaune, Dargaud & Jaegle in Romanèche-Thorins, and Seguin Moreau in Chagny, for example) but seldom for Burgundian vintners. Some chestnut barrels are made in Portugal and Italy. Several wines specifically vinified in chestnut are made in Sardinia, principally from Vernaccia di Oristano and Cannonau (aka Grenache) grapes. A sparkling wine that undergoes its first fermentation in chestnut barrels is made from **organically** grown Xarel-lo near Sitges in Spain and sold under the Ancestral label. *See also* **Oak**.

CHEWY An extreme qualification of **meaty**.

CHIAN A "most delicious" **ancient Greek wine**, according to Virgil and Pliny, with the best Chian coming from Ariusium on the island of Chios. Probably the greatest Greek wine of antiquity; certainly the Romans believed this to be the case. According to mythology, it was Oinopion, son of Dionysus and founder of Chios, who had personally taught the Chians the art of making "black wine", which meant red wine but was described as black because a red wine looked black in the earthenware drinking vessels of the time.

CHIP-BUDDING A method of propagating vines in which a vine bud with a tiny wedge-shape of phloem (live bark) and xylem (inner wood) is inserted into a **rootstock** in an existing root system.

CHLOROSIS A vine disorder caused by mineral imbalance (too much active **lime**; not enough **iron** or magnesium) that is often called "green sickness".

CHOCOLATY, CHOCOLATE-BOX This is a subjective term often used to describe the odour and flavour of Cabernet Sauvignon or Pinot Noir wines. Sometimes "chocolate-box" is used to describe the **bouquet** of fairly **mature** Bordeaux. The fruity character of a wine may also be described as chocolaty in wines with a **pH** above 3.6.

CHRISTMAS CAKE A more intense version of the tasting term **fruitcake**. Commonly found in **maturing** Champagne, usually from a high percentage of Pinot Noir.

CIGAR-BOX A subjective term often applied to a certain complex **bouquet** in wines that have been matured in **oak** and have received good **bottle-age** (usually used in relation to red Bordeaux).

CITROUS, CITRUSSY This describes **aromas** and flavours of far greater **complexity** than mere lemony can suggest.

CIVRAIS Lesser-known type of **oak** used for barrelmaking, from a forest in the **Allier** *département* in the centre of France.

CLAIRET (Fr.) A wine that falls somewhere between a dark **rosé** and a light red wine.

CLARET An English term for a red Bordeaux wine. Etymologically, it has the same roots as the French term *clairet*.

CLASSIC, CLASSY These are both subjective words to convey an obvious impression of quality. These terms are applied to wines that not only portray the correct characteristics for their type and origin, but also possess the **finesse** and **style** indicative of top-quality wines.

CLASSICO (It.) This term may be used only for wines produced in the historic, or classic, area of an **appellation** – usually a small, hilly area at the centre of a **DOC**.

CLEAN A straightforward term applied to any wine devoid of unwanted or unnatural **undertones** of **aroma** and flavour.

CLIMAT (Fr.) A single plot of land with its own name, located within a specific vineyard. *See also Lieu-dit*.

CLONE A vine that has developed differently to other vines of the same variety due to a process of selection – either natural, as in the case of a vine adapting to local conditions, or artificial. *See also* Clones and cloning, p46.

CLOS (Fr.) Synonymous with *climat*, except that this plot of land is, or was, enclosed by walls.

CLOSED Refers to the **nose** or **palate** of a wine that fails to show much character (or "open"). It implies the wine has some qualities – even if "hidden" – that should open up as the wine develops in bottle.

CLOVES Often part of the complex **bouquet** found on a wine fermented or matured in **oak**, the **aroma** of cloves is actually caused by eugenic acid, which is created during the **toasting** of oak barrels.

CLOYING Describes the sickly and sticky character of a poor sweet wine, where the **finish** is heavy and often unclean.

CO₂ *See* **Carbonic gas**.

COAN An **ancient Greek wine** from the island of Kos, Coan was mixed with seawater, and the salty wine became all the rage in the 4th century BC, leading to the process being copied in various parts of Greece.

COARSE Applies to a "rough and ready" wine, not necessarily unpleasant but certainly not fine.

COATES LAW OF MATURITY Master of Wine Clive Coates claims that a wine remains at its **peak** for as long as it took to arrive at this point in its **maturity**. This law is infinitely variable according to both the wine and individual consumers. If you find a specific wine to your liking in, say, its fifth month, year, or decade, it will remain within the bounds of this taste profile until its tenth month, year, or decade. If you think about it, however, the Coates law of maturity has a logic – and whereas I

do not let it influence my optimal drinking recommendations in this book, I have yet to find an anomaly serious enough to debunk the theory.

COCONUTTY-OAK Coconutty **aromas** are produced by various **wood lactones** that are most commonly found in American **oak**.

COMMERCIAL A commercial wine is blended to a widely acceptable formula. At its worst it may be bland and inoffensive, at its best it will be fruity, **quaffable**, and uncomplicated.

COMPACT FRUIT This term suggests a good weight of **fruit** with a correct **balance** of **tannin** (if red) and **acidity** that is presented on the **nose** and **palate** in a distinct manner that is opposite to **open-knit**.

COMPIEGNE Lesser-known type of **oak** used for barrelmaking, from a forest in the Seine-et-Marne *département* of the Île de France.

COMPLETE Refers to a wine that has everything (**fruit**, **tannin**, **acidity**, **depth**, **length**, and so on) and thus feels satisfying in the mouth.

COMPLEXITY An overworked word that refers to many different nuances of smell or taste. Great wines in their youth may have a certain complexity, but it is only with **maturity** in bottle that a wine will achieve its full potential in terms of complexity.

CONCOCTION Usually a derogatory term, but can be used in a positive sense for a medley of flavours in an inexpensive wine.

CONDITUM Spiced **ancient Roman wine** that was sweetened with honey and contained laurel, mastic, saffron, date seeds, and dates soaked in wine.

COOKED Similar to **baked**, but may also imply the addition of grape concentrate to the wine during **fermentation**.

COOL A cool sensation in the mouth is usually attributed to menthol (as in peppermint). *See* **Heat**.

COOL-FERMENTED An obviously cool-fermented wine is very **fresh**, with simple **aromas** of apples, pears, and bananas.

CORK This material has been around since Roman times – or since the ancient Greek and Egyptian civilizations if we consider the sealing of amphorae with cork stoppers. The earliest post-Roman use of cork as a bottle stopper was in England in the 16th century, although the English did not start binning bottles until the 17th century, following the development of strong bottle glass. Prior to this, glass bottles stood upright and were little more than glorified carafes. Since bottles have been cellared on their side, which keeps the cork in contact with the wine, maintaining its elasticity and ensuring its seal, the humble cork has been the catalyst for our understanding of how wine **matures**. Corks can contribute **tannins** and **oak** characteristics to a wine, which is not surprising because cork is the bark of an oak tree (*Quercus suber*) and contains many of the same **phenolic compounds** and **volatile phenols**, including **vanillin**. Some critics view this as a natural part of a wine's maturation, while others point out that since its effect cannot be predicted, this phenomenon taints the wine the winemaker intended to bottle and must therefore be seen as a fault. Even putting that to one side, the oxygen ingress of a cork can vary by more than 1,000-fold, which fundamentally affects the maturation. As an **AWRI** study stated, if you put the same wine into 12 different bottles, sealed each one with a cork that is **TCA**-free, and left them for 10 years, you would still end up with 12 different wines! Although the incidence of **cork taint** has dramatically reduced from 8 per cent in the early 1990s to maybe 2 to 3 per cent by 2011, the more we know about cork, the more issues we find. *See also* **Agglomerated cork**; **Cork harvesting**; **Crown-cap**; **Diam**; **Screwcap**; **Synthetic closures**.

CORK HARVESTING Cork comes from the bark of the *Quercus suber*, an evergreen species of **oak** that can live for 200 to 250 years. It should be 20 or 25 years old before its first cork is harvested. Harvesting is conducted by removing the bark from the longest, straightest part of the trunk. This bark grows back and will be ready for harvesting every 7 to 12 years. The time between harvests may be affected by climatic conditions (eg, in hotter climes, it is possible to harvest at shorter intervals than in cooler climes), but essentially, the longer a tree is left between harvests, the thicker the bark; and the thicker the bark, the higher-quality cork it yields. The vast majority of cork trees are not part of a natural environment but have, like vines, been cultivated, with Portugal supplying half of the world's cork. The next major producer is Spain, after which, in order of importance (albeit on a much lower scale of production) come Algeria, Italy, Morocco, Tunisia, and France. In China, cork is produced to a small extent from *Quercus variabilis*, a deciduous oak found throughout Asia, but its potential yield is significantly lower than that of *Quercus suber*.

CORK TAINT or **CORKED WINE** This has been a recognized phenomenon since the late 17th century, but until the second half of the 20th century, wine was the preserve of the rich and privileged, so the problem was contained. Since the 1970s, however, the consumption of wine has been enjoyed by a much wider and larger customer base, and consequently the incidence of "corked wine" has become common knowledge. The cause of cork taint was first identified in 1981 by a Swiss research scientist, and by the 1990s its incidence had been quantified at such an alarmingly high percentage (8%) that a significant proportion of winemakers started looking for alternative closures. It was originally believed that a penicillin or aspergillus mould in the **cork** might be the cause of this taint, but such infections have always been extremely rare, which is why, in the late 1970s, Hans Tanner at the Wädenswil Research Institute was commissioned by Swiss winegrowers to discover the true cause. After several years of little progress, Tanner was helped by a colleague who was doing pioneering work with gas-chromatography and mass-spectrometry, and eventually he became the first person to determine that the cork taint was due to extremely low levels of various chloroanisoles, with 2,4,6-trichloroanisole (commonly referred to as **TCA**) the main culprit. Initially thought to be exclusively the unwanted by-product of sterilizing corks with chlorine, TCA has since been identified at source in cork oak trees, in **oak** barrels, wooden pallets, and wooden roofs. Other compounds that may also be responsible include **geosmin**, which gives beetroots (beets) their **earthy** taste and can be found in reservoir water.

CORRECT This word describes a wine with all the correct characteristics for its type and origin, but not necessarily an exciting wine.

CÔTE, CÔTES (Fr.) Slope(s) or hillside(s) of one contiguous slope or hill.

COTEAUX (Fr.) Slopes and hillsides in a hilly area, not contiguous.

COULURE (Fr.) A physiological disorder of the vine that occurs as a result of alternating periods of warm and cold, dry and wet conditions after bud-break. If this culminates in a flowering during which the weather is too sunny, the sap rushes past the **embryo bunches** to the shoot tips, causing a vigorous growth of foliage, but denying the clusters an adequate supply of essential nutrients. The barely formed berries thus dry up and drop to the ground.

COUPAGE (Fr.) Blending by cutting one wine with another.

CREAMY A subjective term used to convey the impression of a creamy flavour that may be indicative of the variety of grape or method of **vinification**. I tend to use this word in connection with the fruitiness or oakiness of a wine. Dr Tony Jordan believes that creaminess in a sparkling wine is probably a combination of the **finesse** of the *mousse* (created by the most minuscule of bubbles and their slow release) and an understated **malolactic** influence, the combined effect of which is picked up at the back of the throat on the **finish** of the wine, and this is most apparent in Chardonnay-based wines.

CREAMY-OAK A more subtle, lower-key version of the **vanilla-oak** character that is most probably derived from **wood lactones** during maturation in small **oak** barrels.

CRÉMANT (Fr.) Although traditionally ascribed to a Champagne with a low-pressure and a soft, **creamy** *mousse*, this term has now been phased out in Champagne as part of the bargain struck with other producers of French sparkling wines who have agreed to drop the term *méthode champenoise*. In return they have been exclusively permitted to use this old Champagne term to create their own **appellations**, such as Crémant de Bourgogne and Crémant d'Alsace.

CRISP A **clean** wine, with good **acidity** showing on the **finish**, yielding a refreshing, clean taste.

CROSS A vine that has been propagated by crossing two or more varieties within the same species (within *Vitis vinifera*, for example). In contrast, a **hybrid** is a cross between two or more varieties from more than one species.

CROSSFLOW FILTRATION A relatively new, high-speed form of micro-**filtration** in which the wine flows across (not through), a **membrane filter**, thus avoiding build-up.

CROWN-CAP The common beer-bottle cap, which is now widely used as the temporary closure while a sparkling wine undergoes its **second fermentation**.

CRU or **CRÛ** (Fr.) Literally means growth, as in *cru bourgeois* or *cru classé*.

CRU BOURGEOIS (Fr.) A non-classified **growth** of the Médoc.

CRU CLASSÉ (Fr.) An officially classified French vineyard.

CRUSH Grapes are often crushed so that the juice can **macerate** in the skins prior to and during **fermentation** – to obtain colour for red wines, and aromatic qualities for white wines. In the USA and Australia, "the crush" is synonymous with the harvest in general and with the crushing/pressing in particular.

CRYPTOGAMIC Refers to a fungus-based disease such as grey rot.

CS (It.) Short for *Cantina Sociale* and other titles denoting a local or regional cooperative.

CULTIVAR A term used mainly in South Africa for a cultivated variety of wine grape.

CUT 1. In blending, a wine of a specific character may be used to cut (mix with) a wine dominated by an opposite quality. This can range from a bland wine that is cut by a small quantity of very acidic wine, to a white wine that is cut with a little red wine to make a **rosé**, as in pink Champagne. The most severe form of cutting is also called stretching and involves diluting wine with water, an illegal practice. 2. A cut in pressing terms is a point at which the quality of juice changes, the term deriving from the days of old vertical presses when the lid of the press would be lifted and workers would cut up the compacted mass with sharp spades, piling it in the middle so that more juice may be extracted. 3. In matching food and wine, a wine with high **acidity** may be used to cut (**balance**) the **organoleptic** effect of grease from a grilled or fried dish or an oily fish, just

as the effervescence of a fine sparkling wine cuts the **creamy** texture of certain soups and sauces.

CUVAISON (Fr.) The **fermentation** period in red-wine production, during which the juice is kept in contact with its skins.

CUVE (Fr.) Vat; a *cuve* should not be confused with *cuvée*.

CUVE CLOSE (Fr.) A method of producing sparkling wine that involves a **second fermentation** in a vat. *Cuve close* is synonymous with the **Charmat method** or tank method.

CUVÉE (Fr.) This originally meant the wine of one *cuve* or vat but now refers to a specific blend or product that, in current commercial terms, will be from several vats.

CUVERIE, CUVIER (Fr.) The room or building housing the fermenting vats (*cuves*).

CV (Fr.) Short for *Coopérative de Vignerons* and various other titles that denote a local or regional cooperative.

DARNAY Lesser-known type of **oak** used for barrelmaking, from a forest in the **Vosges** *département* of northeastern France.

DEFINITION A wine with good definition is one that is not just **clean** with a correct **balance** but that also has a positive expression of its grape variety or origin.

DÉGORGEMENT (Fr.) *See* **Disgorgement**.

DÉGORGEMENT TARDIVE (Fr.) Late-disgorged. *See* **LD**.

DEGREE-DAYS *See* **Heat summation**.

DÉLESTAGE (Fr.) Commonly known to anglophile winemakers as "**rack** and return". *Délestage* is a process designed to produce softer red wines by reducing harsh **tannins** from the grape seeds, and is particularly successful in areas where unripe seeds are common due to uneven **ripening**. The basic *délestage* procedure starts after a cold soak of juice and skins. The juice is drawn off into a separate tank, allowing the **cap** to fall to the bottom of the first tank, where it is left to drain for several hours. During this time, many of the seeds are loosened from the pulp and can be caught by a **filter** that allows free passage to the draining juice, which also goes to the second tank. Once the cap has drained out, the drain is closed off, and the juice from the second tank is pumped back into the first tank, where it is mixed with cap. This process is repeated on a daily basis until all the seeds and their harsh tannins are removed.

DELICATE Describes the quieter characteristics of quality that give a wine **charm**.

DEMI-MUID (Fr.) A large oval barrel with a capacity of 300 litres (600 litres in Champagne).

DEMI-SEC (Fr.) This literally means "semi-dry" but such wines actually taste quite sweet (formerly 33–50 g/l **residual sugar** for sparkling wines in the EU; now 32–50 g/l).

DENDOMETER A very accurate device that measures the minute swelling and shrinkage of the vine trunk in response to water use. It can be used to control the amount of irrigation water taken up by the vine, rather than the amount that goes into the ground.

DENOMINAÇÃO DE ORIGEM CONTROLADA (Port.) *See* **DOC**.

DENOMINACIÓN DE ORIGEN (Sp.) *See* **DO**.

DENOMINACIÓN DE ORIGEN CALIFICADA (Sp.) *See* **DOCa**.

DENOMINAZIONE DI ORIGINE CONTROLLATA (It.) *See* **DOC**.

DENOMINAZIONE DI ORIGINE CONTROLLATA E GARANTITA (It.) *See* **DOCG**.

DENTHIS "Unfired" and "unboiled" **ancient Greek wine** from the western foothills of the Mount Taygetus region of Messinia that was described by the Greek poet Alkman as having *anthosmias*, or "the bouquet of flowers".

DÉPARTEMENT (Fr.) A French geopolitical region, geographically similar to a UK county but more geopolitically similar to a US state.

DEPTH This refers primarily to a wine's depth of flavour and secondarily to its depth of interest.

DEPTH FILTRATION The separation of solids from a liquid solely inside a **filtration** medium such as **kieselguhr** (*see* **Diatomaceous earth**). A rotary drum vacuum or plate-and-frame filter is commonly used.

DIAM A brand of so-called technical cork, Diam is an **agglomerated cork** comprised of tiny **cork** particles that have been cleaned and processed by super-critical CO_2 to remove all traces of **TCA**. No TCA has ever been found in these corks, but some winemakers believe they have a **scalping** effect on the **fruit**, though other winemakers swear by Diam.

DIATOMACEOUS EARTH Also known as kieselguhr, this is a fine, powdered, silaceous earth evolved from decomposed deep-sea algae called diatoms. *See also* **Perlite**; **Ceramic filtration**; **Polishing**.

DIRECT-PRODUCING HYBRID Also "direct producer" and "**hybrid direct producer**", this term dates back to 1880, when *vinifera* varieties were crossed with various native American species in an attempt to produce grapes with the character of the former from vines with the resistance to **phylloxera** of the latter, so that the phylloxera-infested vineyards of France could be replanted. This was one of the two approaches to overcome phylloxera and, ultimately, the least successful, since no direct-producing hybrid – then or now – has ever matched the quality of the classic varieties that have established the specific reputation of each famous winemaking area, whereas the alternative strategy of **grafting** those classic *vinifera* vines to American **rootstock** did.

DIRTY This applies to any wine with an unpleasant off-taste or off-smell, and is probably the result of poor **vinification** or bad bottling.

DISGORGEMENT This is part of the process of making a bottle-fermented sparkling wine such as Champagne. After **fermentation**, the **yeast** forms a deposit, which must be removed. To allow for this removal, the bottles are inverted in a freezing brine for just long enough for the sediment to form a semi-frozen slush that adheres to the neck of the bottle. This enables the bottle to be re-inverted without disturbing the wine. The temporary cap used to seal the bottle is removed and the internal pressure is sufficient to eject or "disgorge" the slush of sediment without losing very much wine at all. The wine is then topped up and a traditional Champagne **cork** is used to seal the bottle.

DISTINCTIVE Describes a wine with a positive character. All **fine wines** are distinctive to some degree or other, but not all distinctive wines are necessarily fine.

DIURNAL DIFFERENCE In **viticulture**, any reference to a diurnal or daily difference will invariably be a reference to temperature, comparing the highest daytime temperature with the lowest night-time temperature – the greater the difference, the better the grapes' **acidity** retention. There can be a wide diurnal difference in relatively cool wine areas, such as Champagne, as well as in essentially hot ones, such as Idaho.

DO (Sp.) This stands for Spain's *Denominación de Origen*, which is theoretically the equivalent of the French **AOC**.

DOBLE PASTA (Sp.) Red wines macerated with double the normal proportion of grape skins to juice during **fermentation**. *See also* Spanish Label Language, p362.

DOC (It., Port.) Short for Italy's *Denominazione di Origine Controllata* and Portugal's *Denominação de Origem Controlada*, which are theoretically the equivalent of the French **AOC**.

DOCa (Sp.) Abbreviation for Spain's *Denominación de Origen Calificada*, which is the equivalent of the Italian **DOCG**.

DOCG (It.) Italy's *Denominazione di Origine Controllata e Garantita* is theoretically one step above the French **AOC**. Ideally, it should be similar to, say, a *premier cru* or *grand cru* in Burgundy or a *cru classé* in Bordeaux, but in reality, it is almost as big a catch-all as Italy's *Denominazione di Origine Controllata* itself.

DOPPELSTÜCK (Ger.) A very large oval cask with a capacity of 2,400 litres.

DOSAGE (Fr.) Sugar added to a sparkling wine after **disgorgement**, the amounts of which are controlled by the terminology used on the label – **brut**, **demi-sec**, and so on.

DOUX (Fr.) Sweet, as applied to wines (50 g/l or more of **residual sugar** for sparkling wines in the EU).

DREUILLE Lesser-known type of **oak** used for barrelmaking, from a forest in the **Allier** *département* in the centre of France.

DRIP IRRIGATION Various forms exist, but at its most sophisticated, this is a computer-controlled watering system programmed with the vine's general water requirement and constantly amended by a continuous flow of data from soil sensors. The water is supplied literally drip-by-drip through a complex system of pipes with metered valves.

DRYING UP Describes a wine that has dried up and lost some of its **freshness** and **fruit** through ageing in the bottle. It may still be enjoyable, but remaining bottles should not be kept long.

DUPLEX SOILS So called when two contrasting soil textures are found layered, with a sharp divide between the two. Duplex soils usually consist of a coarse soil over a fine-grained soil, and are commonly found in Western Australia, where they are invariably sand over clay. They are categorized by colour (red, yellow, brown, dark, and grey duplex soils) based on the colour of the subsoil, not the topsoil.

DUSTY Akin to "peppery" in a red wine; a blurring of **varietal definition** in a white wine (in which case, it might be due to **TCA**).

EARTH FILTRATION This term can be synonymous with **depth filtration**.

EARTHY Describes a drying impression in the mouth. Some wines can be enjoyably earthy, but the finest-quality wines should be as **clean** as a whistle. When a wine is very earthy, it is usually due to a preponderance of **geosmin**, which can occur naturally in grapes, but in excess can give a wine a **corked** taste.

EASY This term is to a certain extent synonymous with **accessible**, but probably implies a cheaper, **value-for-money** wine, whereas "accessible" often applies to finer wines.

EASY TO DRINK or **EASY DRINKING** This is not the opposite of hard to drink; it is the opposite of a wine that you do not want to rush and similar, therefore, to a magazine or a page-turner of a book being "easy to read".

EAU-DE-VIE (Fr.) Literally, "water of life"; specifically, a grape-derived spirit.

EDELFÄULE (Ger.) The German term for **noble rot**; *see* **Botrytis cinerea**.

EDELKEUR (S Afr.) The South African term for noble rot; *see* **Botrytis cinerea**.

EDGE Almost, but not quite, synonymous with **grip**; wine can have an edge of **bitterness** or **tannin**. Edge usually implies that a wine has the

capacity to develop, while grip may be applied to a wine in various stages of development, including fully **mature** wine.

EDGY Synonymous with **nervy** or "nervous".

EGG WHITE A traditional **fining** agent that fines out negatively charged matter.

EINZELLAGE (Ger.) A single-vineyard wine area; the smallest geographical unit allowed under German wine law.

EISWEIN (Ger.) Originally a German concept but now used in the New World as well, this rare wine resulted from the tradition of leaving grapes on the vine in the hope of attracting *Botrytis cinerea*. The grapes are then frozen by frost or snow, harvested, and pressed while frozen. They are pressed while still frozen because the frozen ice rises to the top of the vat and it can be scraped off to leave a concentrated juice that produces a wine with a unique **balance** of sweetness, **acidity**, and **extract**.

ELEGANT A subjective term applied to wines that may also be termed "**stylish**" or "possessing **finesse**".

ELEVATED FRUIT Synonymous with **VA lift**.

ÉLEVÉ EN FÛTS DE CHÊNE (Fr.) Aged in **oak** barrels.

ELEVEUR, ÉLEVAGE (Fr.) Literally "bringing up" or "raising" the wine. Both terms refer to the traditional function of a *négociant*: namely to buy ready-made wines after the harvest and take care of them until they are ready to be bottled and sold. The task involves **racking** the wines and blending them into a marketable product as each house sees fit.

EMBRYO BUNCHES In spring, the vine develops little clusters of miniature green berries that will form a bloom a few weeks later. If a berry successfully flowers, it is capable of developing into a grape. The embryo bunch is, thus, an indication of the potential size of the crop.

EN PRIMEUR (Fr.) Classic wines such as Bordeaux are offered for sale *en primeur*, which is to say within a year of the harvest, before the final blending and bottling has taken place. For experienced buyers given the opportunity to taste, this is a calculated risk and the price should reflect this element of chance.

ENCÉPAGEMENT (Fr.) The relative proportions of the grape varieties in a blend.

ENOLOGIST, ENOLOGY (Am.) The American spelling of **oenologist**, **oenology**.

ENTRY-LEVEL WINE From the producer's point of view, this will be his cheapest, most basic quality of wine. From a critic's point of view, this will be the cheapest wine worth buying.

ENZYMES These are proteins produced by living organisms, which can be anything from human beings down to the most basic life forms, such as **yeast** cells. Enzymes function as catalysts for specific biochemical reactions, breaking down molecules, such as the **yeast enzymes** that break down molecules of sugar into molecules of **carbonic gas** and **alcohol** during **fermentation**. Or the enzymatic breakdown of the yeast cells themselves in the biochemical process of **autolysis**. In fact, enzymes play so many important and varying roles in the **vinification** process that some have been isolated and developed into commercial products to assist in basic tasks such as pressing and settling or to tweak a wine this way or that. Most commercial enzyme products are based on the following enzymes: *pectinase* (primarily assists **maceration** and clarification; used specifically for macerating or pressing of white juice, clarification of white juice, yeast autolysis, red colour extraction, red colour stability, and **filtration**); *cellulase* (primarily assists maceration and colour stability; used specifically for macerating or pressing of white juice, red colour extraction, and red colour stability); *hemicellulase* (primarily assists maceration and colour stability; used specifically for macerating or pressing of white juice, red colour extraction, and red colour stability); *glucanase* (primarily assists clarification; used specifically for macerating or pressing of white juice, red colour stability, and filtration, including filtration of botrytized wines); *glycosidase* (primarily assists maceration and colour stability; used specifically for macerating or pressing of white juice); *polygalacturonase* (used specifically for macerating or pressing of white juice, and filtration); *ß-glucosidase* (primarily assists clarification; used specifically to release bound **terpenes** in aromatic wines); *rhamnosidase* (used specifically to release bound terpenes in aromatic wines); *apiosidase* (used specifically to release bound terpenes in aromatic wines); *arabinofuransidase* (used specifically to release bound terpenes in aromatic wines); and *lysozyme* (used specifically to kill or control lactic bacteria). Some enzyme preparations (notably those extracted from moulds such as *Aspergillus niger* or *Trichoderma harzianum*) are so **aggressive** that they come with warnings not to use before pressing whites or fermenting reds. The enzymes in questions destroy grapeskin, creating a haze of solids so fine that they are either very difficult or impossible to remove. Some winemakers swear by commercial enzyme products; others view them as unnecessary tinkering.

ERESOS This **ancient Greek wine** was reputedly the best wine from Lesbos.

ESTERS Sweet-smelling compounds, formed during **fermentation** and throughout maturation, that contribute to a wine's **aroma** and **bouquet**.

ESTUFAGEM (Port.) The process whereby Madeira is heated in ovens called *estufas*, then cooled.

ETHANOIC ACID Synonymous with **acetic acid**.

ETHANOL Synonymous with **ethyl alcohol**.

ETHYL ALCOHOL This main **alcohol** in wine is so important in quantitative terms that to speak of a wine's alcohol is to refer purely to its ethyl alcohol content.

EU LOT NUMBER Proposed by an EC directive in 1989 and implemented by all member states of the Community by 1992, this Lot Number must be indicated on every bottle of wine produced in or sold to the EU. Should a wine have to be removed from general distribution for any reason, this code can save unnecessary waste by pinpointing the shipment involved.

EVERYDAY WINES These are inexpensive, **easy-drinking** wines.

EX-CELLARS Wines offered *en primeur* are usually purchased "ex-cellars"; the cost of shipping the wine to the importer's cellars is extra, on top of which any duty and taxes will be added.

EXPANSIVE Describes a wine that is **big**, but open and **accessible**.

EXPRESSIVE A wine that is expressive is true to its grape variety and area of origin.

EXTRA BRUT A very dry style of Champagne (0–6 g/l), of which only those with the maximum permitted *dosage* have any realistic chance of ageing smoothly, so it is best consumed on purchase.

EXTRA SEC Literally means "extra dry", but with between 12 and 17 g/l of **residual sugar** (formerly 12–20 g/l for sparkling wines in the EU), an *extra sec* Champagne can have a discernible hint of sweetness.

EXTRACT Sugar-free soluble solids that give **body** to a wine. The term covers everything from proteins and vitamins to **tannins**, calcium, and **iron**.

FALERNIAN An individual named site encompassing the best lower slopes of the famous ancient Roman vineyard of **Falernum**. This site

produced sweet white wines that were very high **alcohol** content, according to Pliny, who claimed that it is "the only wine that ignites when a flame is applied to it". *See* **Ancient Roman wines**; 121 BC in "A Chronology of Wine", p86.

FALERNUM Possibly the most well-known ancient Roman vineyard, Falernum was produced from Aminean grapes (known as Greco today) grown on the slopes of Mount Falernus in the Campanium hills. These slopes were sub-divided into three individually named sites: **Caucinian** (on the top slopes), **Faustian** (from the best mid-slopes), and **Falernian** (from the lower slopes). Falernum was a late-harvested white wine that was usually drunk at between 10 and 20 years of age, when it was amber-coloured. The most fashionable of all **ancient Roman wines**, Falernum was probably the first wine to experience such a heavy demand that the quality was noted to decrease as the volume produced increased. *See also* 121 BC in "A Chronology of Wine", p86.

FALL BRIGHT A liquid that becomes limpid after cloudy matter drops as sediment to the bottom of the vessel is said to fall bright.

FALL OVER A wine that goes past its **peak** and starts to decline at a relatively young age, and at a faster than normal rate, is said to fall over.

FARMYARDY In 1982, Anthony Hanson wrote "great Burgundy smells of shit", but whether just a touch of farmyard or a full-blown **manure** aroma, these mercaptan-derived **aromas** are no longer acceptable. *See* Manure in Tastes and Aromas, p80.

FAT A wine **full** in **body** and **extract**. It is good for any wine to have some fat, but fat in an unqualified sense can be derogatory and no wine should be too fat, as it will be **flabby** or too **blowzy**.

FATTY ACIDS A term sometimes used for **volatile acids**.

FAUSTIAN An individual named site encompassing the best mid-slopes of the famous ancient Roman vineyard of **Falernum**. These slopes were part on the estate of belonging to Faustus Cornelius Sulla, son of the dictator Sulla, the only man in history who successfully attacked and occupied both Athens and Rome. Many regarded Faustus to be the best **Falernum**. *See* **Ancient Roman wines**.

FEMININE A subjective term used to describe a wine with a preponderance of delicately attractive qualities, rather than weight or strength. Descibes a wine of striking beauty, grace, and **finesse**, with a silky texture and exquisite style.

FERMENTATION The biochemical process by which **enzymes** secreted by **yeast** cells convert sugar molecules into almost equal parts of **alcohol** and **carbonic gas**. *See also* Fermentation, p28.

FERTILIZER A chemical product used to enrich the soil with one or more of the three basic requirements for all plant life: potassium (for fruit development and general plant metabolism), phosphorus (for root development), and nitrogen (for leaf development). Technically the term also refers to **manure**, compost, and other natural means of soil enrichment.

FEUILLETTE (Fr.) A small Burgundian barrel with a capacity of 114 litres (132 litres in Chablis).

FIELD BLEND, FIELD MIX The best description I have seen for this is "a wine recipe planted in the ground". It is not a homogenous vineyard planted to a single grape variety (of which there may be several different **clones**), but a vineyard planted with a collection of grape varieties that reflect traditional Old World practices of several generations ago. The advantage is that if a disease or disorder affected one variety, the others would probably pull through unscathed. The disadvantage, however, is that the different varieties do not **ripen** at the same time; this was not a problem in the old days, however, since it was common practice

to make several *tries* or sweeps through the vineyards, picking only the ripe grapes and cutting out any rotten ones.

FILTER, FILTRATION The removal of suspended matter. There are four basic methods of filtration: **depth filtration** (also known as earth filtration); **pad filtration** (also known as sheet filtration), **membrane filtration** (also known as micro-porous filtration), and **crossflow filtration**. There is also **centrifugal filtration**, which is not filtration in the pure sense but achieves the same objective of removing unwanted particles suspended in wine or grape juice.

FINE WINES Quality wines, representing only a small percentage of all wines produced.

FINESSE That elusive, indescribable quality that separates a **fine wine** from those of lesser quality.

FINING The clarification of fresh grape juice or wine is often sped up by the use of various fining agents that operate by an electrolytic reaction to fine out oppositely charged matter. *See also* Fining, p29.

FINISH The quality, and a person's enjoyment, of a wine's **aftertaste**.

FIRM Refers to a certain amount of **grip**. A firm wine is a wine of good constitution, held up with a certain amount of **tannin** and **acidity**.

FIRST PRESSING The first pressing **yields** the sweetest, cleanest, clearest juice.

FIXED ACIDITY This is the **total acidity** less the **volatile acidity**.

FIXED SULPHUR The principal reason why SO_2 (sulphur dioxide) is added to grape juice and wine is to prevent **oxidation**, but only **free sulphur** can do this. Upon contact with wine, some SO_2 immediately combines with oxygen and other elements, such as sugars and acids, and is known as fixed or bound sulphur. What remains is free sulphur, capable of combining with molecules of oxygen at some future date.

FLABBY The opposite of **crisp**, referring to a wine lacking in **acidity** and consequently dull, weak, and **short**.

FLASH PASTEURIZATION A **sterilization** technique that should not be confused with full **pasteurization**. It involves subjecting the wine to a temperature of about 80°C (176°F) for between 30 and 60 seconds.

FLAT 1. A sparkling wine that has lost all of its *mousse*. 2. A term that is interchangeable with **flabby**, especially when referring to a lack of **acidity** on the **finish**.

FLESHY This term refers to a wine with plenty of **fruit** and **extract** and implies a certain underlying **firmness**.

FLOOD-IRRIGATED The crudest form of irrigation and the cheapest where water is readily available (such as from the Andes snow-melt in parts of Chile and Argentina). Sluice-gates are opened up, allowing water to flow into irrigation channels around and between rows of vines.

FLOR (Sp.) A scum-like **yeast** film that naturally occurs and floats on the surface of some Sherries as they mature in part-filled wooden butts. It is the *flor* that gives Fino Sherry its inimitable character.

FLURBEREINIGUNG (Ger.) A modern viticultural method of growing vines in rows that run vertically up and down slopes, rather than across in terraces.

FLYING WINEMAKER The concept of the flying winemaker was born in Australia, where due to the size of the country and the staggered picking dates, highly sought-after consultants Brian Croser (now Petaluma) and Tony Jordan (now Green Point) would hop by plane from harvest to harvest. Riding on the success of Australian wines in the UK market, other Australian wine wizards began to stretch their wings, flying in and out of everywhere from southern Italy to Slovakia, usually at the behest of British supermarkets. Like the spread of Chardonnay and Cabernet, the flying winemakers were at first welcomed by wine writers, then turned upon for standardizing wine wherever they went. The truth is that before the arrival of international grapes and international winemakers, the peasant cooperatives in these countries had no idea that they could even produce wines to compete on the international market. Now that they have established a certain standard with known grape varieties and modern technology, they are beginning to turn to their roots to see what indigenous varieties might have the potential to produce more **expressive** wines. Few winemakers do more flying than Moët & Chandon's Richard Geoffroy, but the term is usually attributed to the mercenaries of the trade, who work for a supermarket, a supplier to a supermarket, or more than one company. Well-known flying winemakers include Peter Bright, Nick Butler, Steve Donnelly, Michael Goundrey, Lynette Hudson, Jacques and François Lurton, Geoff Merril, Kym Milne, Martin Shaw, Brenden Smith, Adrian Wing, and John Worontschak. The late, famous Bordeaux professor Peynaud avoided the flying-winemaker tag, as has Ribereau-Gayon, despite the fact that they have each consulted for more companies in more countries over more years than the entire flock of flying winemakers listed above, perhaps because today's mercenaries have a more hands-on approach to their job than was traditional for consultants in the past.

FOLIAR FEEDS Plant nutrients that are sprayed directly onto, and are absorbed by, the foliage.

FONTAINBLEAU Lesser-known type of **oak** used for barrelmaking, from a forest in the Seine-et-Marne *département* of the Île de France.

FORMIAN or **FORMIANUM** An **ancient Roman wine** from the Gulf of Caieta, Formian was compared by Aelius Galenus (also known as Galen of Pergamon) to **Privernatinum** and **Rhegium** but was **richer** and earlier-developing. Athenaeus of Naucratis also compared it to those two wines, claiming Formian was **smoother** and that it matured more quickly.

FORTIFIED Fortification with pure **alcohol** (usually very strong grape spirit of 77 to 98 per cent) can take place either before **fermentation** (as in **Ratafia de Champagne** and **Pineau des Charentes**), during fermentation (as in Port and Muscat de Beaumes de Venise), or after fermentation (as in Sherry).

FOUDRE (Fr.) A large wooden cask or vat.

FOXY The very **distinctive**, highly perfumed character of certain indigenous American grape varieties that can be sickly sweet and **cloying** to unconditioned palates.

FREE-RUN JUICE See *Vin de goutte*.

FREE SULPHUR The active element of sulphur dioxide (SO_2) in wine, produced by free sulphur combining with intruding molecules of oxygen.

FREMANTLE DOCTOR Also known as the "Freo Doctor", this afternoon sea breeze brings a cooling relief to better parts of the Swan Valley in Western Australia. *See also* **Albany Doctor; Canberra Doctor**.

FRENCH PARADOX In 1991, Morley Safer, host of the CBS show *60 Minutes*, screened a programme about the so-called French paradox. This described how the high-cholesterol-consuming, high-**alcohol**-drinking, low-exercising French have a very low mortality rate from heart disease compared to health-conscious Americans, who have low-cholesterol diets, exercise frequently, and drink relatively little alcohol. Part of the explanation was attributed to the Mediterranean diet, in which milk plays a negligible role and wine – particularly red wine – a very important one. Although it is a complete food for the young, milk is unnatural for adults, who cannot digest it properly. The more milk an adult drinks (and Americans are particularly high consumers of milk), the greater the risk of cardiovascular disease, while three glasses of wine a day has a proven protective effect against cardiovascular disease. *See also* **Health benefits of wine**.

FRESH Describes wines that are **clean** and still vital with youth.

FRIABLE Term used to describe a soil structure that is crumbly or easily broken up.

FRIZZANTE (It.) Semi-sparkling.

FRIZZANTINO (It.) Very lightly sparkling, between still and semi-sparkling (ie, *perlant*).

FRUIT Wine is made from grapes and must therefore be 100 per cent fruit, yet a fruity flavour depends on the grapes used having the correct combination of **ripeness** and **acidity**.

FRUIT-BOMB The etymological origin of this term provides its own definition. The fruit in any wine described as a fruit-bomb will be super-**rich**, super-lush, and super-concentrated. California was probably the first to produce such wines, but the term was not coined at that juncture. The concept of a fruit-bomb first emerged on the Australian wine-competition circuit – for what variety originally, no one is sure, but it was soon applied to Pinot Noir more than any other wine. Having failed so miserably to achieve the basic **varietal character** of Pinot Noir, Australian wine producers and judges were happy for a short while in the early 1990s, when more and more Pinot Noir wines demonstrated this varietal purity. However, they soon got fed up with simple varietal Pinot Noir. Both the producers and judges wanted the right **structure** on which to hang that fruit and more **finesse** and potential **complexity**, but all they got was more fruit. There were successes, of course, but the harder most tried, the more of a caricature their Pinot Noir became. As an example of a fruit-bomb, somebody once wrote "think Jim Carrey rather than Jeremy Irons", and that's about as close as any analogy can get.

FRUITCAKE This is a subjective term for a wine that tastes, smells, or has the **complexity** of the mixed dried-fruit **richness** and spices found in fruitcake. Commonly found in **maturing** Champagne, usually from a high percentage of Pinot Noir.

FUDER (Ger.) A large oval cask with a capacity of 1,000 litres, more prevalent in Mosel areas than in those of the Rhine.

FULL This term usually refers to **body**, as in "full-bodied". However, a wine can be light in body yet full in flavour.

FULLY FERMENTED A wine that is allowed to complete its natural course of **fermentation** and so yield a totally dry wine.

FÛT (Fr.) A wooden cask, usually made of **oak**, in which wines are aged, or fermented and aged.

GARRIGUE (Fr.) A type of moorland found in Languedoc-Roussillon.

GAURAN or **GAURANUM** Ancient Roman wine produced a few kilometres west of Naples in the hills above Puteoli, the source of "Purpūra", the finest and most expensive dye of the ancient world. According to Athenaeus of Naucratis, "Gauran is both rare and excellent, besides being vigorous and **rich**." He also believed it to be **smoother** than either Praenestine or Tiburtine.

GELATINE A positively charged **fining** agent used for removing negatively charged suspended matter in wines, especially an excess of **tannin**.

GENERIC Describes a wine, usually blended, of a general **appellation**.

GENEROUS A generous wine gives its **fruit** freely on the **palate**; an ungenerous wine is likely to have little or no fruit and, probably, excess **tannin**. All wines should have some degree of generosity.

GENUS The botanical family *Ampelidaceae* has 10 *genera*, one of which, *Vitis*, through the sub-genus *Euvites*, contains the species *Vitis*

vinifera, to which all the famous winemaking grape varieties belong.

GEOSMIN A chemical compound sometimes found in wine; responsible for the characteristic earthiness of beetroot and the **earthy** taste of some potatoes.

GLASS CLOSURES *See* Vino-Lok.

GLUGGY Easy to guzzle.

GOOD GRIP A healthy **structure** of tannin supporting the **fruit** in a wine.

GOÛT DE TERROIR (Fr.) Literally translates as "taste of earth" but does not infer any sort of **earthy** taste. It denotes a combination of good **typicity** and "sense of place" – the essence of *terroir*.

GRAFT The joint between the **rootstock** and the scion of the **producer vine**.

GRAND CRU (Fr.) Literally "great growth". In regions such as Burgundy, where the term's use is strictly controlled, it has real meaning (in other words, the wine should be great relative to the quality of the year), but in other winemaking areas where there are no controls, it will mean little.

GRAND VIN (Fr.) Normally used in Bordeaux, this term applies to the main wine sold under the **château**'s famous name and it will have been produced from only the finest barrels. Wines excluded during this process go into second, third, and sometimes fourth wines that are sold under different labels.

GRANDE MARQUE (Fr.) Literally a great or famous brand. In the world of wine, the term *grande marque* is specific to Champagne and applies to members of the *Syndicat de Grandes Marques*, which include, of course, all the famous names.

GRAPEY This term may be applied to an **aroma** or flavour that is reminiscent of grapes rather than wine, and is a particular characteristic of German wines and wines made from various Muscat or Muscat-like grapes.

GRAPPA (It.) A rough spirit distilled from the grapeskins and stalks that are left after pressing, which are mixed with water and fermented.

GRASSY Often used to describe certain wines (commonly Colombard, Scheurebe, or Sauvignon Blanc) portraying a grassy type of **fruitiness**, usually through low **ripeness** (as opposed to under-ripeness, which would be **green**).

GREEN Young and tart, as in Vinho Verde. It can be either a derogatory term or simply a description of a youthful wine that might well improve.

GREEN PRUNING Pruning is a bit of a misnomer, as this is really a method of reducing **yields** by thinning out the potential crop when the grapes are green (unripe) by cutting off a certain percentage of the bunches, so that what remains achieves a quicker, greater, and more even **ripening**. Also called summer pruning.

GRIP This term applies to a **firm** wine with a positive **finish**. A wine showing grip on the finish indicates a certain **bite** of **acidity** in white wines and of tannin in red wines.

GRIPPY Good grippy **tannins** imply ripe tannins that have a nice tactile effect without seeming in the least **firm**, **harsh**, or **austere**.

GROSBOIS Lesser-known type of **oak** used for barrelmaking, from a forest in the **Allier** *département* in the centre of France.

GROSSLAGE (Ger.) A wine area in Germany that is part of a larger district or **Bereich**.

GROWTH *See* Cru.

GUTSY A wine **full** in body, **fruit**, **extract**, and – usually – **alcohol**. The term is normally applied to wines of fairly ordinary quality.

GUZZLY This term is synonymous with **gluggy**.

HALBFÜDER (Ger.) An oval cask with a capacity of 500 litres, more prevalent in Mosel areas than in those of the Rhine.

HALBSTÜCK (Ger.) An oval 600-litre cask.

HARD Indicates a certain severity, often due to excess **tannin** and possible **acidity**.

HARSH A more derogatory term than **coarse**.

HEALTH BENEFITS OF WINE Wine consumed in moderation flushes out the cholesterol and fatty substances that can build up inside the body's artery walls. It does this through the powerful **anti-oxidant** properties of various chemical compounds found naturally in wine (through contact with grapeskins), the most important of which are polyphenols such as procyanidins and rytoalexins such as reservatol. Most chloresterol in the body is carried around the body on LDLs (low density lipoproteins), which clog up the arteries. By contrast, HDLs (high density lipoproteins) do not clog up the arteries, but take the cholesterol straight to the liver, where it is processed out of the system. The anti-oxidants convert LDL into HDL, literally flushing away the cholesterol and other fatty substances. Together with **alcohol** itself, these anti-oxidants also act as an anti-coagulant on the blood, diminishing its clotting ability, which reduces the chances of a stroke by 50 per cent in contrast with non-drinkers. (However, I would be equally as dishonest as the neo-Prohibitionists who make phoney health-danger claims if I did not point out the one true health danger of moderate drinking that has recently come to light. In 2002, the *British Journal of Cancer* published a study demonstrating that a woman's risk of contracting breast cancer increases by 6 per cent if she consumes just one drink per day, and this rises to 32 per cent if she has three or four drinks per day. The report concludes that 4 per cent of all breast cancers are attributable to alcohol. However, it all balances out in the end. In a summary of this report, Dr Isabel dos Santos Silva of the International Agency for Research on Cancer wrote, "Alcohol intake … is likely to account, at present, for a small proportion of breast cancer cases in developed countries, but for women who drink moderately, its lifetime cardioprotective effects probably outweigh its health hazards." And as Dr Philip Norrie pointed out, ten times the number of women die from vascular disease than from breast cancer.)

HEAT The **hot** and **cool** sensations in the mouth are physiological experiences created when receptors on the tongue and in the throat are activated by compounds such as capsaicin (the hot sensation of chillies) and menthol (peppermint). Although these receptors have a direct neural link to the brain and are located close to receptors on the **taste buds**, they do not activate the **taste receptors** and are not therefore classified as tastes. They work independently from any **aromas** picked up by **olfaction**. (Menthol triggers its receptors even when applied directly to the tongue with the **olfactory bulb** fully occluded.)

HEAT SUMMATION A system of measuring the growth potential of vines in a specific area in terms of the environmental temperature, expressed in degree-days. A vine's vegetative cycle is activated only above a temperature of 10°C (50°F). The time during which these temperatures persist equates to the vine's growing season. To calculate the number of degree-days, the proportion of the daily mean temperature significant to the vine's growth – the daily mean minus the inactive 10°C (50°F) – is multiplied by the number of days of the growing season. For example, a growing season of 200 days with a daily mean temperature of 15°C (59°F) gives a heat summation of 1,000 degree-days Celsius (1,800 degree-days Fahrenheit) based on the following calculation: (15 - 10) x 200 = 1,000.

HECTARE A measurement of area; 1 hectare is equal to 10,000 square metres or 2.471 acres.

HERBACEOUS A green-leaf or white-currant characteristic that is usually associated with too much **vigour** in the vine's **canopy**, which can cause under-ripeness, resulting in excessive **pyrazine** content. A herbaceous quality can also be the result of aggressive extraction techniques employed for red wines fermented in stainless steel.

HERBAL, HERBAL-OAK These terms apply to wines matured in cask, but unlike **vanilla-oak**, **creamy-oak**, **smoky-oak**, and **spicy-oak**, their origin is unknown. A herbal character devoid of **oak** is usually derived from the **varietal character** of a grape and is common to many varieties.

HERBICIDE A weed-killer that is usually, but not necessarily, a highly toxic concoction of chemicals.

HIGH-DENSITY VINES Vines planted close together compete with each other to **yield** higher-quality fruit, but less of it per vine, than vines planted further apart. Initial planting costs are higher and more labour is required for pruning and other activities, but if the vineyard is in balance, the greater number of vines should produce the same overall volume per **hectare**, even though the output per vine is reduced. Quantity can therefore be maintained while significantly raising quality, although there is a threshold density which vineyards must reach before real benefits appear. For example, more than half the vineyards in the New World are planted at less than 2,000 vines per hectare (800 per acre) and 1,200 to 1,500 per hectare (485 to 600 per acre) is very common, whereas in Champagne, 6,666 vines per hectare (2,699 per acre) is the minimum allowed by law, 7,000 to 8,000 (2,830 to 3,240 per acre) the average, and 11,000 (4,450 per acre) possible. In pre-**phylloxera** times, it was something like 25,000 vines per hectare (10,000 per acre). Indeed, before California's vineyards were mechanized, the average density of vines was twice what it is now because every other row has been ripped up to allow entry for tractors. When Joseph Drouhin planted his vineyard in Oregon, he planted 7,450 vines per hectare and brought over French tractors that straddled the rows of vines, rather than going between them. All of a sudden, high-density vineyards entered the American vocabulary, although Drouhin did not consider them to be high density – merely a matter of course.

HIGH-TONE A term used in this book to describe elements of the bouquet that aspire to **elegance**, but that can become too exaggerated and be slightly reminiscent of **vermouth**.

HOGSHEAD A barrel with a capacity of between 300 and 315 litres, commonly found in Australia and New Zealand.

HOLLOW A wine that appears to lack any real flavour in the mouth compared to the promise shown on the **nose**. Usually due to a lack of **body**, **fruit**, or **acidity**.

HONEST Applied to any wine, but usually to one that is of a fairly basic quality, honest implies it is true in character and **typical** of its type and origin. It also implies that the wine does not give any indication of being **souped up** or mucked around with in any unlawful way. The use of the word honest is, however, a way of damning with faint praise for it does not suggest a wine of any special or truly memorable quality.

HONEYED Many wines develop a honeyed character through **bottle-age**, particularly sweet wines and more especially those with some **botrytis** character. However, some dry wines can also become honeyed, a **mature** Riesling being the classic example.

HORIZONTAL TASTING A tasting of different wines of the same style or **vintage**. A vertical tasting consists of different vintages of the same wine.

HOT 1. A hot sensation in the mouth is usually attributed to an imbalance between **fruit** and **alcohol** so that the latter dominates, or the searing effect (if the wine is dry) of spice-laden **terpene** aromatics on the **finish** of a Gewürztraminer. *See* Heat. 2. Synonym for **baked**.

HOUSE CLARET An unpretentious and not too expensive everyday-drinking red Bordeaux.

HYBRID A **cross** between two or more grape varieties from more than one species.

HYDROGEN SULPHIDE When hydrogen combines with sulphur dioxide (SO_2), the result is a smell of bad eggs. If this occurs prior to bottling and is dealt with immediately, it can be rectified. If allowed to progress, the hydrogen sulphide can develop into **mercaptans** and ruin the wine.

ICEWINE *See Eiswein*.

ICON WINE This category is above **ultra-premium** and will be priced in hundreds or thousands of dollars.

IGP (Fr.) Common abbreviation for *Indication Géographique Protégée*, the French language version of the EU umbrella classification encompassing *vins de pays* and other national equivalents. The English equivalent is PGI (Protected Geographical Indication).

INDICAÇÃO DE PROVENIÊNCIA REGULAMENTADA (Port.) *See* IPR.

INKY Can refer either to a wine's opacity of colour or to an inkiness of character indicating a deep flavour with plenty of **supple tannin**.

IPR (Port.) Short for *Indicação de Proveniência Regulamentada*, a Portuguese quality designation that falls between **DOC** and **VR**.

IRON This is found as a trace element in fresh grapes that have been grown in soils in which relatively substantial ferrous deposits are located. Wines from such sites may naturally contain a tiny amount of iron, which is barely perceptible on the **palate**. If there is too much iron, the flavour becomes medicinal. Above seven milligrams per litre for white and ten milligrams per litre for red, there is a danger of the wine going cloudy. But wines of such high iron levels should have been blue-fined prior to bottling (*see* **Fining**).

ISINGLASS A gelatinous **fining** agent obtained from the swim-bladder of freshwater fish and used to clear hazy, low-**tannin** wines.

JAMMY Commonly used to describe a **fat** and eminently drinkable red wine rich in **fruit**, if perhaps a bit contrived and lacking **elegance**.

JUG WINE California's mass-produced *vin de table*, synonymous with carafe wine.

JUPILLE A lesser-known type of **oak** used for barrelmaking, from a small forest in the Sarthe *département* of the Loire Valley.

KABINETT (Ger.) The first rung of predication in Germany's QmP range, one below *Spätlese*, and often drier than a QbA.

KIESELGUHR A form of **diatomaceous** earth.

LACTIC ACID The acid that develops in sour milk, and which is also created in wine during the **malolactic** fermentation.

LAGAR (Port.) A rectangular concrete receptacle in which people tread grapes.

LAID-BACK A term that has come into use since the arrival of California wines on the international scene in the early 1980s. It usually implies that a wine is very relaxed, **easy to drink**, and confident of its own quality.

LANDWEIN (Ger.) German equivalent of *vin de pays*.

LATE DISGORGED *See* LD.

LD A sparkling-wine term that stands for "late disgorged" and, paradoxically, means the same as "recently disgorged". The use of LD implies that the wine in question is of a mature **vintage** that has been kept on its **yeast** deposit for an extended period. *See also* **RD**.

LEACHING A term that may be used to refer to the deliberate removal of **tannin** from new **oak** by steaming – or when discussing certain aspects of soil, such as **pH**, that can be affected when **carbonates** are leached (removed) by rainwater.

LEES Sediment that accumulates in the bottom of a vat during the **fermentation** of a wine.

LEMONY Many dry and medium-sweet wines have a tangy, fruity **acidity** that is suggestive of lemons.

LENGTH A wine that has length is one whose flavour lingers in the mouth a long time after swallowing. If two wines taste the same, yet you definitely prefer one, but do not understand why, it is probably because the one you prefer has a greater length. *See also* **Balance.**

LESBIAN The sweet **ancient Greek wine** of Lesbos. *See also* **Eresos.**

LIE (Fr.) The French for **lees.** *See also Sur lie.*

LIEU-DIT (Fr.) A named site (plural: *lieux-dits*). This term is commonly used for wines of specific **growths** that do not have **grand cru** status.

LIGHT VINTAGE A light **vintage** or year produces relatively light wines. Not a great vintage, but not necessarily a bad one either.

LIME This is the **classic** character shared by both the Sémillon and Riesling grape varieties when grown in many areas of Australia, which explains why Sémillon from the Hunter Valley used to be sold as Hunter Riesling.

LIMOUSIN A famous type of **oak** used for barrelmaking, from any forest in the Haute-Vienne, Creuse, and Correze *départements* in the centre of France.

LINALOOL A compound found in some grapes, particularly the Muscat and Riesling varieties. It contributes to the peachy-flowery fragrance that is characteristic of Muscat wines.

LINGERING Normally applied to the **finish** of a wine – an **aftertaste** that literally lingers.

LIQUEUR DE DOSAGE Sugar dissolved in wine that is added to Champagne and other sparkling wines after **disgorgement** to produce various styles (**brut nature, extra brut, brut, extra sec, sec, demi-sec,** and **doux**), each depending on the amount of **residual sugar** in the final product.

LIQUEUR DE TIRAGE (Fr.) Bottling liqueur: the mix of wine, **yeast**, and sugar added to still Champagne to induce the *mousse*.

LIQUOREUX (Fr.) Literally "liqueur-like", this term is often applied to dessert wines of an unctuous quality. (Sometimes also "liquorous".)

LIQUORICE A quality often detected in Monbazillac, but may be found in any **rich**, sweet wine. The term refers to the concentration of flavours from heat-shrivelled grapes, rather than **botrytized** grapes.

LIVELINESS, LIVELY A term that usually implies a certain youthful freshness of **fruit** due to good **acidity** and a touch of **carbonic gas.**

LONGEVITY Potentially long-lived wines may owe their longevity to a significant content of **tannin**, **acidity**, alcohol, and/or sugar.

LORA This **ancient Roman wine** was effectively an undistilled form of *grappa*, having been produced from the cake of grapeskins left after pressing, which was then mixed with water. Bitter and **tannic**, Lora was further **cut** with water and given to slaves.

LUSCIOUS, LUSCIOUSNESS Almost synonymous with **voluptuous**, although more frequently used to describe an unctuous, sweet white wine than a succulently **rich** red.

MACERATION A term that is usually applied to the period during the **vinification** process when the fermenting juice is in contact with its skins. This process is traditionally used in red-winemaking, but it is on the increase for white wines utilizing **pre-fermentation maceration** techniques.

MACÉRATION CARBONIQUE The French term for **carbonic maceration.**

MACROCLIMATE Regional climate.

MADERIZED All Madeiras are maderized by the *estufagem*, in which the wines are slowly heated

in specially constructed ovens, and then by cooling them. This is undesirable in all wines except for certain Mediterranean wines that are deliberately made in a *rancio* style. Any ordinary, light, **table wine** that is maderized will often be erroneously diagnosed as **oxidized**, but there is a significant difference in the symptoms: maderized wines have a duller **nose**, have rarely any hint of the **Sherry**-like character of **acetaldehyde**, and are flatter on the **palate**. All colours and styles of wine are capable of maderizing and the likely cause is storage in bright sunlight or too much warmth.

MAILLARD REACTIONS Chemical interactions between **amino acids** created during **autolysis** and **residual sugar** added by **dosage**, which are responsible for many of the **mellow**, complex post-disgorgement aromas adored by drinkers of **mature** Champagne. Maillard reactions also play an important role in the **raisining** of grapes, and they occur in cooking as part of the caramelizing process that happens during the sealing of meat.

MALIC A tasting term that describes the green apple **aroma** and flavour found in some young wines due to the presence of **malic acid**, the dominant acid found in apples.

MALIC ACID A very strong-tasting acid that diminishes during the fruit's ripening process, but still persists in ripe grapes and, although reduced by **fermentation**, in wine too. The quantity of malic acid present in a wine may sometimes be considered too much, particularly in a red wine, and the smoothing effect of replacing it with just two-thirds the quantity of the much weaker **lactic acid** is often desirable. *See also* Malolactic fermentation, p29.

MALOLACTIC The malolactic **fermentation** is often termed a **secondary fermentation**, but it is not an **alcoholic** fermentation. It is an entirely different biochemical process that converts the hard **malic acid** of unripe grapes into soft **lactic acid** and **carbonic gas**. The level of malolactic contribution will vary according to the style of wine in question. It is essential for red wine but not for white, **rosé**, or sparkling – and malolactic for some white-wine varietals should be avoided altogether. Whatever the grape variety or style of wine, malolactic should never be immediately discernible. There is nothing so vulgar and clumsy in a wine as a nostril-full of diacetyl, whether it is **caramel**, **butterscotch**, or simply **buttery**. *See also* Malolactic fermentation, p29.

MAMERTINE or **MAMERTINUM** This **ancient Roman wine** from the northeastern tip of Sicily (roughly the same area as Faro **DOC** today) was the favourite of Julius Caesar.

MANURE A very extreme form of **farmyardy**.

MANNOPROTEIN Nitrogenous matter secreted from **yeast** during **autolysis**.

MANTA *See* **Cap**.

MARC 1. The residue of skins, pips, and stalks after pressing. 2. The name given to a four-tonne load of grapes in Champagne. 3. A rough brandy made from the residue of skins, pips, and stalks after pressing.

MARQUE A brand or make.

MARSIC An **ancient Roman wine** that was described as "very dry and wholesome".

MASSICUM An **ancient Roman wine** from the Naples area that was known for its **firm structure**.

MATURE, MATURITY Refers to a wine's development in bottle, as opposed to **ripe**, which describes the maturity of the grape itself.

MEAN An extreme qualification of **ungenerous**.

MEATY This term suggests a wine so **rich** in body and **extract** that the drinker feels almost able to chew it. Wines with a high **tannin** content are often meaty.

MELLOW Describes a wine that is **round** and nearing its **peak** of **maturity**.

MEMBRANE FILTRATION Use of a thin screen of biologically inert material, perforated with micro-sized pores that occupy 80 per cent of the membrane, to **filter** wine. Anything larger than these holes is denied passage when the wine is pumped through during **filtration**.

MERCAPTANS Methyl and ethyl alcohols can react with **hydrogen sulphide** to form mercaptans (sometimes referred to as thiols), foul-smelling compounds that are often impossible to remove and can ruin a wine. Mercaptans can smell of garlic, onion, burnt rubber, or stale cabbage.

MESOCLIMATE In strict scientific terms, mesoclimate is site climate, while **microclimate** is more specific.

METAL or **METALLIC** Some *terroir* can give a wine a distinctly metallic **finish**, particularly when produced from relatively **neutral grape varieties**, such as Chardonnay growing in the *lieu-dit* of Les Bionnes in Avize on the Côte des Blancs of Champagne.

METAYAGE The cultivation of land for a proprietor whereby the tenant receives a proportion of the crop produced in payment for his labours. This form of sharecropping dates back to Roman times and was recommended by Oliver de Serres in *Le Theatre d'Agriculture*, written in 1600, as a means of sharing the risk of winemaking.

MÉTHODE CHAMPENOISE (Fr.) The process in which an effervescence is produced through a **secondary fermentation** in the same bottle in which the wine is sold (in other words, not *transvasage*). This procedure is used for Champagne and other good-quality sparkling wines. In Europe, the term is forbidden on the label of any wine other than Champagne, which never uses it itself.

MÉTHODE GAILLAÇOISE (Fr.) A variant of *méthode rurale* involving **disgorgement**.

MÉTHODE RURALE (Fr.) The precursor of *méthode champenoise*, this method involves no **secondary fermentation**. The wine is bottled before the first **alcoholic** fermentation has finished, and **carbonic gas** is produced during the continuation of **fermentation** in the bottle. There is also no **disgorgement**.

METODO CHAMPENOIS (It.) Italian for *méthode champenoise*.

MICROCLIMATE Due to a combination of shelter, exposure, proximity to mountains and/or water mass, and other topographical features unique to a given area, a vineyard can enjoy (or be prone to) a specific microclimate that differs from the standard climate of the region as a whole. Technically, this is a **mesoclimate**, not a microclimate. Scientists refer to the conditions around just one or a handful of vines as a microclimate, but the variations recorded on such microscale are meaningless to non-scientists and, indeed, to any wine, no matter how tiny the vineyard might be. This is why "microclimate" is still in common usage for the environment of a single site.

MICRO-OXYGENATION This process involves the ultra-slow diffusion of oxygen throughout a wine from a device that is little more than a sophisticated version of those oxygenators you see bubbling away in aquariums, only the bubbles are virtually microscopic. It was lampooned by Jonathan Nossiter's film *Mondovino*, which gave the impression that world-famous consultant Michel Rolland advised most of his clients to use it. Although used primarily to soften harsh **tannins**, micro-oxygenation can also intensify colour by as much as 30 per cent by fixing colour molecules to tannin molecules that would otherwise be unfixed and drop out. Furthermore, it can remove stinky, **reductive** tank **aromas** and reduce **herbaceous** notes. Micro-oxygenation was devised in 1991 by Patrick Ducournau of Domaine Mouréou and Chapelle L'Enclos in Madiran, the home the Tannat grape, which is legendary for its harsh tannins.

MICRO-POROUS FILTRATION Synonymous with **membrane filtration**.

MICRO-VINIFICATION This technique involves **fermentation** in small, specialized vats, which are seldom bigger than a washing machine. The process is often used to make experimental wines. There are certain dynamics involved in fermentation that determine a minimum optimum size of vat, which is why home-brewers seldom make a **polished** product and why most wines made in research stations are dull.

MID-PALATE 1. The centre-top of your tongue. 2. A subjective term to describe the middle of the taste sensation when taking a mouthful of wine. It may be **hollow** if the wine is **thin** and lacking, or **full** if it is **rich** and satisfying.

MILLERANDAGE (Fr.) A physiological disorder of the vine that occurs after cold or wet weather at the time of the flowering. This makes fertilization very difficult, and consequently many berries fail to develop, remaining small and seedless even when the rest of the bunch is full-sized and **ripe**.

MILLÉSIME (Fr.) **Vintage** year. *See also Récolte*.

MILLÉSIMÉ (Fr.) Vintaged wine.

MINERALITY This tasting term causes controversy because it is impossible to taste minerals in a wine. Those who use it are often labelled snobs, but most experienced tasters understand what is meant by minerality in a wine, just as they understand what is meant by a **petrolly** Riesling, although there is no petrol in any wine, and everyone knows perfectly well that petrolly Riesling does not smell or taste like petrol. All specialist subjects have their own vocabulary as a necessity to convey ideas and opinions quickly. These vocabularies often contain words that seem contradictory or misleading to other people, but it is only when the subject is wine or some other aspect of culture or art that the users of such words are considered to be snobs. The hard sciences have some of the weirdest buzzwords, but no one ever accuses the users of those terms of being snobs. Snobbery has nothing to do with the use of words such as petrol or minerality to describe wine. It's simply a matter of communication and understanding. Minerality in wine has nothing to do with the saltiness of mineral waters. In fact, it leans more towards **bitterness** than saltiness, although it is not a **basic taste** and thus neither. Minerality is one of the opposites of fatness in a wine. It can be likened to a certain nervosity of **fruit** and always shows at its best and at its most in wines that are leaner, less **alcoholic**, and more acidic. In many ways, it is the absence of things or the absence of excesses that determines the existence of minerality, but a wine of good minerality is never one that is lacking. It's always a desirable characteristic. Pump up the fruit, and the minerality is overwhelmed. The more **oak** that is used, the more minerality is hidden. **Malolactic** kills minerality. Minerality is exceedingly difficult to describe with words; it has to be tasted to be understood, and understanding minerality is less of a revelation and more something that gradually dawns upon the individual.

MISTELLE (Fr.) Fresh grape juice that has been muted with **alcohol** before any **fermentation** can take place (ie, a VdL).

MOELLEUX (Fr.) Literally **soft** or **smooth**, this term implies a **rich**, medium-sweet style in most areas of France. In the Loire, however, it is used to indicate a truly rich, sweet **botrytis** wine, thereby distinguishing it from *demi-sec*.

MONOPOLE (Fr.) Denotes the single ownership of one vineyard.

MOUSSE (Fr.) The effervescence of a sparkling wine, which is best judged in the mouth because a wine may appear to be **flat** in one glass and vigorous in another due to the different surfaces. The bubbles of a good *mousse* should be small and persistent; the strength of effervescence depends on the style of wine.

MOUSSEUX (Fr.) Literally "sparkling".

MOUTH-FILL Literally meaning a wine that easily fills the mouth with a satisfying flavour. There is no holding back, but it does not quite imply anything too **upfront** or obvious.

MUID (Fr.) A large oval barrel with a capacity of 600 litres.

MULSUM Ancient Roman mixed drink consisting of wine (usually **Massicum** or **Falernian**) sweetened with honey, which was mixed in just before serving as an **aperitif**. It was often freely dispensed to lower classes at public events to solicit their political support. It may also, according to taste, have included myrrh, cassia, costum, malobathrum, nard, or pepper. See **Ancient Roman wines**.

MUST Unfermented or partly fermenting grape juice.

MUST WEIGHT The amount of sugar in ripe grapes or grape **must**.

MUSTUM Ancient Roman **concoction** containing partially fermented grape juice and **vinegar**. See **Ancient Roman wines**.

MUTAGE (Fr.) The addition of pure **alcohol** to a wine or to fresh grape juice either before **fermentation** can take place, as in the case of a *vin de liqueur* (VdL), or during fermentation, as in the case of a *vin doux naturel* (VDN). *See also* Mutage, p31.

MYTIC DIAM A Champagne-cork version of **Diam**.

NANOCLATE The environmental climate in the air cavities through the **canopy** and immediately above the leaves.

NÉGOCIANT (Fr.) Trader or merchant. The name is derived from the traditional practice of negotiating with growers (to buy wine) and wholesalers or customers (to sell it).

NÉGOCIANT-ÉLEVEUR (Fr.) A wine firm that buys in ready-made wines for *éleveur*. The wines are then blended and bottled under the *négociant*'s label.

NERVY, NERVOUS A subjective term usually applied to a dry white wine that is **firm** and vigorous, but not quite settled down.

NEUTRAL GRAPE VARIETIES Such grapes include virtually all the minor, nondescript varieties that produce bland tasting, low-quality wines, but also encompass better known varieties such as the Melon de Bourgogne, Aligoté, Pinot Blanc, Pinot Meunier, and even classics such as Chardonnay and Sémillon. The opposite of **aromatic grape varieties**, these are ideal for **oak**-maturation, bottling *sur lie*, and turning into fine sparkling wines because their characteristics are enhanced rather than hidden by these processes.

NEVERS A famous type of **oak** used for barrelmaking, from a forest in the **Nievre** *département* in the centre of France.

NIEVRE A type of **oak** used for barrelmaking, from **Nevers**, **Bertrange**, or any other forest in the Nievre *département* in the centre of France.

NOBLE ROT A condition caused by the fungus *Botrytis cinerea* under certain conditions.

NOSE The smell or odour of a wine, encompassing both **aroma** and **bouquet**.

OAK Many wines are fermented or aged in wooden casks and the most commonly used wood is oak.

There are two main categories of oak, French and American, and they are both used the world over. Although the French always use French oak, the greatest California wines are also usually made in French oak barrels. American oak is traditional in Spain, particularly Rioja, and Australia, although both these countries have a growing usage of French oak. Oak often gives a **vanilla** taste to wine because it contains a substance called **vanillin**, which also gives vanilla pods their vanilla **aroma**. French oak is perceived to be finer and more refined, while American oak is generally considered to have a more **upfront**, obvious character. This difference in character is due not to intrinsic qualities in the two types of oak (although American oak grows more quickly than French and has a bigger grain, which does have some influence), but to the traditional weathering of French oak in the open for several years, which **leaches** out the most volatile aromatics. American oak is kiln-dried (therefore not leached) and sawn (unlike French oak, which is split), which ruptures the grain, exposing the wine to the oak's most volatile elements in a relatively short time. If French oak were to be kiln-dried and sawn, and American weathered and split, I suspect our perception of the two forms of oak might well be reversed. American oak is often highly charred in the construction of a barrel (winemakers can order it lightly **toasted**, medium toasted, or highly charred), and this too has an effect, adding **caramel**, toffee, and **smoky**-toasty aromas to a wine. The toastiness in oak is different to any toastiness derived from the grape itself. Strangely, oak can produce a cedary taste, although this is probably confined to wines made from **spicy** black-grape varieties that are fermented and/or matured in relatively old wood. If you get a very strong impression of coconut, it's a good bet that the oak used was American. Oak barrels are very expensive to buy and labour intensive to work with, so if you find a very cheap wine with obvious oak character, it will inevitably be due to the use of oak chips or shavings, which are chucked into a huge, gleaming stainless-steel vat of wine. Cheating this may be, but it is legal, and if people like the taste of oak-aged wine, but cannot afford to pay much for a bottle, what is wrong with it? *See also* Stainless steel or oak?, p29.

OAK GRAIN The tightness of the **oak** grain is a measure of its quality for winemaking purposes. Strangely enough, the tighter the grain is, the more porous its wood will be. However, the rationale is simple enough because the more porous the wood, the greater the **micro-oxygenation** of the wine – hence, the softer the **tannins**. A compilation of various standards from around the world can be distilled into the following classification: very fine (less than 1.5 mm), fine (1.5–2 mm or 2.5 mm), medium-fine (2.5–3 mm or 3.5 mm), and wide (greater than 3 mm or 3.5 mm).

OECHSLE LEVEL (Ger.) A system of measuring the sugar content in grapes for wine categories in Germany and Austria.

OENOLOGIST, OENOLOGY Pronounced "enologist" and "enology" (and spelled this way in the USA). Oenology is the scientific study of wine. It is a branch of chemistry, but with practical consequences, hands-on production experience, and an understanding of **viticulture**.

OFF VINTAGE An off **vintage** or year is one in which many poor wines are produced due to adverse climatic conditions, such as very little sunshine during the summer, which can result in unripe grapes, and rain or humid heat at the harvest, which can result in rot. Generally an off vintage is a vintage to be avoided, but approach any opportunity to taste the wines with an open mind because there are always good wines made in every vintage, and they have to be sold at bargain prices if a vintage has a bad reputation.

OIDIUM A fungal disease of the vine that turns leaves powdery grey and dehydrates grapes.

OILY A subjective term meaning **fat** and viscous, and often also **flat** and **flabby**.

OLFACTION The sense of smell, much of which is perceived as taste. *See* How We Taste Smells, p73.

OLFACTORY BULB A sensory organ situated above the nose and between the eyes, the olfactory bulb provides us with not only the sense of smell but also much of what we interpret as taste.

OLOROSO (Sp.) A Sherry style, naturally dry but usually sweetened for export markets.

OPEN-KNIT An open and enjoyable **nose** or **palate**, usually found in a modest wine that is not capable of much development.

OPULENT Suggestive of a rather luxurious **varietal aroma**; very **rich**, but not quite **blowzy**.

ORGANIC WINES A generic term for wines made using the minimum amount of SO_2 (sulphur dioxide), from grapes grown without the use of chemical **fertilizers**, **pesticides**, or **herbicides**.

ORGANOLEPTIC Affecting a bodily organ or sense, usually that of taste or smell.

OSMOTIC PRESSURE When two solutions are separated by a semi-permeable membrane, water will leave the weaker solution for the more concentrated one in an endeavour to equalize the differing solution strengths. In winemaking, this is most commonly seen when **yeast** cells are put to work in grape juice with an exceptionally high sugar content. Since water accounts for 65 per cent of a yeast cell, osmotic pressure causes the water to escape through the semi-permeable cell membrane. The cell caves in (a phenomenon called plasmolysis), and the yeast dries up and eventually dies.

OVERTONE A dominating element of **nose** and **palate**; often one that is not directly attributable to the grape or wine.

OXIDATION, OXIDIZED These terms are ambiguous; as soon as grapes are pressed or crushed, oxidation sets in and the juice or wine will become oxidized to a certain and increasing extent. Oxidation is also an unavoidable part of **fermentation** and essential to the maturation process. In this case, however, in order not to mislead it is best to speak of a **mature** or, at the extreme, **oxidative** wine. This is because when the word oxidized is used, even among experts, it will invariably be in an extremely derogatory manner, to highlight the **Sherry-like** odour of a wine that is in a prematurely advanced stage of oxidation. In a totally oxidized wine, the **acetaldehyde** is converted to **acetic acid**, and the **aroma** turns to **vinegar**.

OXIDATIVE A wine that openly demonstrates the character of browning apple, raisins, or hazelnuts on the **nose** or **palate**. This can develop into an overtly **aldehydic** character when excessively oxidative. An oxidative style is legitimate for some wines, such as Champagne, that go through two major **reductive** processes (**second fermentation** and **autolysis**) but may be made deliberately oxidative (eg, Krug and Bollinger) or **reductive** (eg, Dom Pérignon, Pol Roger, Taittinger, *et al*). Some Champagnes are not necessarily made oxidative but become oxidative due to the use of low or no *dosage* and SO_2 (eg, Jacquesson).

PAD FILTRATION A filtration system utilizing a plate-and-frame **filter** with a series of cellulose, asbestos, or paper sheets through which wine is passed.

PALATE The flavour or taste of a wine.

PARTIAL ROOTZONE DRYING *See* PRD.

PASSERILLAGE (Fr.) Grapes without **noble rot** that are left on the vine become cut off from the plant's metabolic system as its sap withdraws into its roots. The warmth of the day, followed by the cold of the night, causes the grapes to dehydrate and concentrate in a process known as

passerillage. The sweet wine produced from these grapes is prized in certain areas. A *passerillage* wine from a hot autumn will be totally different to one from a cold autumn. **Roasted** is an excessive and quick form of *passerillage* caused by great heat, often at the height or end of summer, rather than the normal, drawn-out autumnal *passerillage*.

PASSITO (It.) The Italian equivalent of *passerillage*. *Passito* grapes are semi-dried, either outside – on the vine or on mats – or inside a warm building. This concentrates the pulp and produces strong, often sweet wines.

PASSUM Ancient Roman wine made from grapes left to **raisin** on the vine, the concept having been passed to the Romans from Carthage by the Phoenicians.

PASTEURIZATION A generic term for various methods of **stabilization** and **sterilization**.

PDO *See* AOP.

PEAK The ideal **maturity** of a wine. Those liking **fresher**, **crisper** wines will perceive an earlier peak in the same wine than drinkers who prefer mature wines. As a rule of thumb that applies to all extremes of taste, a wine will remain at its peak for as long as it took to reach it.

PEARDROP *See* Amylic; Carbonic maceration.

PEPPERY A term applied to young wines whose components are raw and not yet in harmony, sometimes quite fierce and **prickly** on the **nose**. It also describes the characteristic odour and flavour of southern French wines, particularly Grenache-based ones. Syrah can smell of freshly crushed black pepper, while white pepper is the character of great Grüner Veltliner. Young Ports and light red Riojas can also be very peppery.

PERFUME An agreeable scented quality of a wine's **bouquet**.

PERLANT (Fr.) Very slightly sparkling, less so than *crémant* and *pétillant*.

PERLITE A fine, powdery, light, lustrous substance of volcanic origin with **diatomaceous earth**-like properties When perlite is used for filtration, it is sometimes referred to as **ceramic filtration**.

PESTICIDE Literally a pest-killer, but more accurately a parasite-killer, the term pesticide implies a highly toxic concoction of chemicals capable of eradicating parasitic insects that attack the vine, including larvae, flies, moths, and spiders.

PÉTILLANCE, PÉTILLANT (Fr.) This term describes a wine with sufficient **carbonic gas** to create a light sparkle.

PETIT CHÂTEAU (Fr.) Literally "small castle", this term is applied to any wine **château** that is neither a *cru classé* nor a *cru bourgeois*.

PETROL, PETROLLY With some **bottle-age**, the finest Rieslings have a **vivid bouquet** that some call petrolly. This petrolly character has an affinity with various **zesty** and **citrussy** odours, but many lemony, citrussy, zesty smells are totally different from one another and the Riesling's petrolly character is both singular and unmistakable. As great Riesling matures, so it also develops a **honeyed** character, bringing a **classic**, honeyed-petrol **richness** to the wine.

pH A commonly used chemical abbreviation of "potential hydrogen-ion concentration", a measure of the **active acidity** or alkalinity of a liquid. It does not give any indication of the **total acidity** in a wine, but neither does the human **palate**. When we perceive the **acidity** in wine through taste, it is more closely associated with the pH than with the total acidity.

PHENOLS, PHENOLIC COMPOUNDS Compounds found in the skin, seeds, and stalks of grapes, the most common being **tannin** and **anthocyanins**.

PHOTOSYNTHESIS The process by which light energy is trapped by chorophyll, a green chemical in the leaves, and is converted into chemical energy in the form of glucose. This is then carried

around the plant in special tubes called phloem to grow shoots, leaves, flowers, and fruit.

PHYLLOXERA The vine louse *Phylloxera vastatrix*, which devastated the vineyards of Europe in the late 19th century, still infests the soils of nearly all the world's winegrowing regions. At the time, it was considered the greatest disaster in the history of wine, but with hindsight, it was a blessing in disguise. Before phylloxera arrived, many of Europe's greatest wine regions had gradually been devalued because of increased demand for their wines. This led to bulk-producing, inferior varieties being planted, and vineyards being extended into unsuitable lands. As phylloxera spread, it became apparent that every vine had to be **grafted** on to phylloxera-resistant American rootstock. This forced a much-needed rationalization, in which only the best sites in the classic regions were replanted and only noble vines were cultivated, a costly operation that vineyard owners in lesser areas could not afford. The grafting took France 50 years, and enabled the AOC system to be set up. It is hard to imagine what regional or **varietal** identities might now exist if phylloxera had not occurred.

PIPE (Port.) The most famous Portuguese barrel, a Douro pipe has a capacity of 550 litres.

PIQUANT 1. This term refers to a perfect knife-edge **balance** between sweetness and **acidity** that could well describe that found in the greatest Mosel *Kabinett*. 2. (Fr.) Usually applied to a pleasing white wine with positive underlying **fruit** and **acidity**.

PLAFOND LIMITÉ DE CLASSEMENT *See* PLC.

PLC *Plafond Limité de Classement*, a legalized form of cheating whereby producers of **AOC** wines are allowed to exceed the official maximum limit by as much as 20 per cent.

PLUM PUDDING A subjective term for a **rich** and **spicy** red wine; a more intense term than **Christmas cake**.

PLUMMY An **elegant**, juicy flavour and texture that resembles the fleshiness of plums.

POLISHED Describes a wine that has been skilfully crafted, leaving no rough edges. It is **smooth** and refined to drink.

POLISHING The very last, ultra-fine **filtration** of a wine, usually with **kieselguhr** (*see* Diatomaceous earth) or **perlite**. It is so called because it leaves the wine bright. Many high-quality wines are not **polished** because the process can wash out natural flavours.

POSCA A wine deliberately made to go **sour**, then mixed with water and given to soldiers and lower classes. Posca was occasionally sweetened with honey, and Roman legionnaires considered it refreshing.

POST-DISGORGEMENT AGEING The period between **disgorgement** and when the wine is consumed. With the sudden exposure to air after an extended period of ageing under **anaerobic** conditions, the development of a sparkling wine after disgorgement is very different from its development before.

POURRITURE NOBLE (Fr.) Noble rot, which is caused by the fungus *Botrytis cinerea* under certain conditions.

PRAENESTINE Ancient Roman wine (red) produced in Praeneste (now Palestrina) in Lazio.

PRAMNIAN Ancient Greek wine produced in several regions. Athenaeus of Naucratis suggested that Pramnian could be a generic name for a dark red wine of good quality and ageing potential.

PRD Partial rootzone drying, a clever way of fooling the vine into thinking that it is not being irrigated, when, in fact, it is. This is achieved by alternating irrigation between two separate parts of the root system. Part of the vine receives a carefully metered out **drip irrigation**, but the rest of the plant system is unaware of this and, not sensing the irrigation, believes that it is, in fact, experiencing a mild water stress. The vine thus diverts its metabolism (energy) from the leaves to the grape clusters, improving the quality of the fruit. When the water is drawn into the part of the vine that has shut down the metabolism of its leaves, this part of the vine reverses the metabolic process. This is the very time that the drip irrigation is switched to that side of the vine, as it has already accepted the water's presence. However, by turning off the irrigation to the other side of the vine, that side now believes it is experiencing a mild water stress, and it is its turn to divert the vine's metabolism from the leaves to the grape clusters. And so it goes on, drip feeding either side of a vine that perpetually experiences a mild state of water stress. This conserves water, and whilst it does not increase **yields** *per se*, it does produce better quality at normal yields.

PRECOCIOUS A wine that develops early.

PRE-FERMENTATION MACERATION The practice of **maceration** of juice in grape skins prior to **fermentation**, to enhance the **varietal character** of the wine. This maceration is usually carried out cold and is normally employed for **aromatic** white varieties but can be undertaken warm – or even quite hot for red wines.

PREMIER CRU (Fr.) Literally "First Growth", this term is of relevance only in those areas where it is controlled, such as in Burgundy and Champagne.

PREMIUM WINE A marketing term for a quality category. So-called premium or premium-quality wine is not as expensive as you might think and certainly not the top category of wine. *See also* **Super-premium wine; Ultra-premium wine; Icon wine**.

PRESS WINE *See* **Vin de presse**.

PRICKLE, PRICKLY This term describes a wine with residual **carbonic gas**, but with less than the light sparkle of a *pétillant* wine. This characteristic can be desirable in some **fresh** white and **rosé** wines, but it is usually taken as a sign of an undesirable **secondary fermentation** in red wines, although it is deliberately created in certain South African examples.

PRIMARY AROMAS These **aromas** are attributed to the grape. *See also* **Secondary aromas; Tertiary aromas**.

PRIVERNATINUM or **PRIVERNIAN** Ancient Roman **wine** that was light and pleasant, from the Volscian Hills in the south of Lazio. Athenaeus of Naucratis found Privernatinum to be thinner than **Rhegium**.

PRODUCER VINE Vines are usually **grafted** on to **phylloxera**-resistant **rootstock**, but the grapes produced are characteristic of the above-ground producer vine, or scion, which is normally a variety of *Vitis vinifera*.

PROTEIN HAZE Protein is present in all wines. Too much protein can react with **tannin** to cause a haze, in which case **bentonite** is usually used as a **fining** agent to remove it.

PUNCHEON A 450-litre barrel commonly found in Australia and New Zealand.

PVPP Abbreviation for polyvinylpolypyrrolidone, a **fining** agent used to remove compounds sensitive to browning from white wines.

PYRAZINES One of the most important groups of aromatic compounds found in grapes (especially methoxypyrazines), pyrazines typically have **green**, leafy, **grassy** characteristics through to bell-pepper, green-pea and asparagus. The more **herbaceous** pyrazine **aromas** are symptomatic of an excessively vigorous vine **canopy**, particularly in red wines. Although pyrazines become less abundant as grapes ripen, they are considered a vital element in the **varietal character** of Sauvignon Blanc.

QbA (Ger.) Germany's *Qualitätswein bestimmter Anbaugebiete* is the theoretical equivalent of the French **AOC**.

QmP (Ger.) The abbreviation for *Qualitätswein mit Prädikat*. Literally a "quality wine with predication", this term is used for any German wine above **QbA**, from **Kabinett** upwards. The predication carried by a QmP wine depends upon the level of ripeness of the grapes used in the wine.

QUAFFABLE, QUAFFING WINE An unpretentious wine that is enjoyable and **easy to drink**.

QUALITÄTSWEIN BESTIMMTER ANBAUGEBIETE *See* **QbA**.

QUALITÄTSWEIN MIT PRÄDIKAT *See* **QmP**.

QUERCUS The Latin for **oak** or oak tree, of which there are more than 600 species. Those of particular interest for wine include *Quercus alba* (American oak or white oak), *Quercus gariana* (sometimes called *Quercus garryana*, a tighter-grained American oak found in Oregon), *Quercus ilex* (Holm oak), *Quercus robur* (solitary oak trees, also known as *Quercus pdeunculata* or common oak, English oak, pedunculate oak, and truffle oak), *Quercus sessilis* (forest oak, longer and straighter trunk, also known as *Quercus petraea* or *Quercus sessiflora* or durmast oak, roble oak, sessile oak, steineiche oak and Welsh oak), *Quercus suber* (evergreen species of oak commonly known as cork oak, the bark of which is harvested for the cork industry), and *Quercus variabilis* (deciduous species of oak commonly known as Chinese cork oak). *See also* **Cork**.

QUINTA (Port.) A wine estate.

QUINTAL The equivalent of 100 kilograms. Argentina, Chile and other Spanish-speaking countries often talk about harvest **yields** in terms of quintales per **hectare**.

R2 A yeast strain (*Saccharomyces cerevisiae race bayanus*) discovered by Danish-born winemaker Peter Vinding-Diers.

RACKING The draining of a wine off its **lees** into a fresh cask or vat. *See also* Racking, p29.

RACY Often applied to wines of the Riesling grape. The term racy accurately suggests the **liveliness**, vitality, and **acidity** of this grape.

RAISIN 1. A dried Muscat grape (as opposed to a sultana, which is a dried Thompson Seedless grape, or a currant, which is a dried Zante grape). 2. Often used generically in winemaking for a grape that has shrivelled on the vine due to *passerillage*. 3. (Fr.) French for grape.

RANCIO Description of a *vin doux naturel* (**VDN**) stored in **oak** casks for at least two years, often with the barrels exposed to direct sunlight. This imparts a distinctive flavour that is popular in the Roussillon area of France.

RATAFIA A liqueur made by combining **marc** with grape juice, Ratafia de Champagne being the best known.

RD A sparkling-wine term that stands for "recently disgorged", the initials RD are the trademark of Champagne Bollinger. *See also* **LD**.

RECIOTO (It.) A strong, sweet wine made in Italy from *passito* grapes.

RÉCOLTANT (Fr.) Vineyard owner.

RÉCOLTE (Fr.) Harvest. *See also* **Millésime**.

REDOX The ageing process of wine was originally conceived as purely **oxidative**, but it was then discovered that when one substance in wine is **oxidized** (gains oxygen), another is reduced (loses oxygen). This is known as a reductive-oxidative, or redox reaction. **Organoleptically**, however, wines reveal either oxidative or **reductive** characters. In the presence of air, wine is prone to an oxidative character, but shut off from a supply of oxygen, reductive characteristics begin

to dominate; thus, the bouquet of **bottle-age** is a reductive one and the **aroma** of a **fresh**, young wine is more oxidative than reductive.

REDUCTIVE The less exposure it has to air, the more reductive a wine will be. Different as they are in basic character, Champagne (although there are some Champagnes that are deliberately made less reductive than others), Muscadet *sur lie*, and Beaujolais Nouveau are all examples of reductive, as opposed to **oxidative**, wines – from the vividly **autolytic** Champagne, through Muscadet *sur lie* with its barest hint of autolytic character, to the **amylic aroma** of Beaujolais Nouveau. A good contrast is Madeira, which is reductive, while Sherry is oxidative. The term is, however, abused, as many tasters use it to describe a fault, where the wine is heavily reduced.

REFRACTOMETER An optical device used to measure the sugar content of grapes when out in the field.

REMONTAGE (Fr.) Pumping wine over the **cap** (or *manta*) of skins during the **cuvaison** of red wine.

REMUAGE (Fr.) An intrinsic part of the *méthode champenoise*; deposits thrown off during **secondary fermentation** are eased down to the neck of the bottle and are then removed at **disgorgement**.

RESERVE WINES Still wines from previous vintages that are blended with the wines of one principal year to produce a **balanced** non-**vintage** Champagne.

RESIDUAL SUGAR The sweetness of a wine expressed in grams per litre (thus a 75 cl bottle will contain only three-quarter of the grams expressed). Even dry wines can have up to 2 grams of **unfermentable residual sugar** per litre.

RESIDUAL SWEETNESS In one sense, this is synonymous with **residual sugar**, but in another it infers the **basic taste** of sweetness, rather than grams of sweetness per litre – and a greater number of grams per litre does not necessarily translate as sweeter. With no more than 2 g/l of **unfermentable sugar**, the sugars present in all but so-called completely dry wine will be primarily glucose and fructose. Fructose is approximately twice as sweet as glucose, but as the residual sugar found in most wines is predominantly fructose, this is of little relevance. The only significant exception is the relative sweetness of sparkling wine made by different methods. For most sparkling wines the residual sugar is added via a **dosage**, which inverts to equal proportions fructose and glucose, whereas any residual sugar in a sparkling made by the rural method, or *méthode rurale* (see p37), will be exclusively fructose because it is literally the residue of the first fermentation. It follows, therefore, that a traditional-method sparkling wine with 8 g/l residual sugar (4 g fructose plus 4 g glucose) will be 25 per cent less sweet than a rural-method sparkling wine with 8 g of residual sugar (all fructose), providing everything else is equal in terms of both the wines and the taster.

RETICENT A wine that is holding back on its **nose** or **palate**, perhaps through youth, and may well develop with a little more **maturity**.

RHAETIC or **RHAETICUM** Sweet ancient Roman **wine** that was made from grapes grown near Verona. Suetonius claims that this wine was the favourite of Augustus, the first Roman emperor, while other writers attribute that honour to **Setine**.

RHEGIUM A light and pleasant **ancient Roman wine** from Rhegium (now Reggio di Calabria), **smoother** than that of **Sorrentum** and "fit to use after 15 years".

RICH, RICHNESS 1. A term used by Champagne producers for a sweeter style, such as **sec** or **demi-sec**. 2. A wine with **balanced** wealth of **fruit** and **depth** on the **palate**, and a good **finish**.

RIPASSO (It.) Re-**fermentation** of wine on the **lees**.

RIPE Grapes ripen; wines **mature**. However, the **fruit** and even the **acidity** in wine can be referred to as ripe. Tasters should be careful not to mistake a certain **residual sweetness** for ripeness.

RIPE ACIDITY The main acidic component in **ripe** grapes (**tartaric acid**) tastes refreshing and **fruity**, even in large proportions, whereas the main **acidity** in unripe grapes (**malic acid**) tastes **hard** and unpleasant.

ROASTED Describes the character of grapes subjected to the shrivelling or roasting on the vine (*passerillage*), due to excessive heat, rather than **noble rot**.

ROBUST A milder form of **aggressive**, which may frequently be applied to a **mature** product. A wine is robust by nature, rather than aggressive through youth.

ROOTSTOCK The lower rooting part of a **grafted** vine, usually **phylloxera**-resistant. *See* Rootstock, p45.

ROPP Common abbreviation for "roll-on pilfer-proof", a type of **screwcap**. *See also* **ROTE**.

ROSÉ This French term has become as anglicized for pink wine as rendezvous has for appointment. In most cases, a rosé is made by crushing black grapes and keeping the juice in contact with the grapeskins for a short while prior to pressing or by running off coloured juice (*saignée*). It will have no discernible **tannin** content. Champagne rosé is a rare case where the wine may be made by blending a little red wine into a white wine.

ROTE Common abbreviation for "roll-on tamper-evident", a type of **screwcap**. *See also* **ROPP**.

ROUND A wine that has rounded off all its edges of **tannin**, **acidity**, **extract**, and so on through **maturity** in bottle.

SACCHAROMETER A laboratory device used for measuring the sugar content of grape juice, based on specific gravity.

SAIGNÉE (Fr.) The process of drawing off surplus liquid from the fermenting vat in order to produce a **rosé** wine from the **free-run** juice. In cooler wine regions, this process may be used to produce a darker wine than would normally be possible from the remaining mass of grape pulp because the greater ratio of solids to liquid provides more colouring pigment.

SAINT-GERMAIN Lesser-known type of **oak** used for barrelmaking, from a forest in the Seine-et-Marne *département* of the Île de France.

SAINT HÉLÈNE Lesser-known type of **oak** used for barrelmaking, from a forest in the **Vosges** *département* of northeastern France.

SASSY Should be a less cringing version of the cheeky, audacious character found in a wine with bold, brash but not necessarily **big** flavour.

SCALP, SCALPED, SCALPING This refers to a flavour or **fruit** loss that could be due to **TCA**, which might be present at a level undetectable by the taster, but whose scalping effect is noticeable. If in doubt, open a second bottle to see if it does have more flavour or fruit.

SCHIRMECK Lesser-known type of **oak** used for barrelmaking, from a forest in the **Vosges** *département* of northeastern France.

SCION *See* Producer vine.

SCREWCAP Hated by some but loved by many, including the author of this encyclopedia, especially for wines to drink upon purchase and for wines of short- and medium-term ageing. It's a bit of a generalization, but the French do not like screwcaps, yet the long-skirted **Stelvin**, which was the world's first wine-specific screwcap and has thus become synonymous with the generic term screwcap in the wine industry, was invented by the French. *See also* **Crown-cap**; **Synthetic closures**.

SEC (Fr.) Dry. When applied to wine, this means without any sweetness, but it does not mean there is no **fruit**. Dry wines with plenty of very **ripe** fruit can sometimes seem so **rich** they may appear to have some sweetness.

SECOND or **SECONDARY FERMENTATION** The **fermentation** that occurs in bottle during the *méthode champenoise*. The term is sometimes also used, mistakenly, to refer to **malolactic** fermentation.

SECONDARY AROMAS Not so much "fermentation aromas" as some sources state, but more the aromas of a freshly fermented wine. **Fermentation** aromas suggest the smell of a fermentation, which would be considered a fault in a finished wine, as both primary and secondary aromas are found in commercially available wines. *See also* **Primary** aromas; **Tertiary** aromas.

SEKT (Ger.) Sparkling wine.

SELECTION DE GRAINS NOBLES (Fr.) In Alsace, a rare, intensely sweet, **botrytized** wine. Often abbreviated to SGN.

SEMI-CARBONIC MACERATION An adaption of the traditional **carbonic maceration** method of **fermentation**, in which whole bunches of grapes are placed in a vat that is then sealed while its air is displaced with CO_2.

SETINE or **SETINUM** This **ancient Roman wine** from grapes grown in the hills of Sitia is generally considered one of the great wines of antiquity because it was favoured by Augustus and most of his courtiers, although the Roman historian Gaius Suetonius Tranquillus claimed **Rhaetic** wine was the first Roman emperor's favourite wine.

SHARP This term applies to **acidity**, whereas **bitterness** applies to **tannin** and, sometimes, other natural solids. Immature wines may be sharp. However, if used by professional tasters, the term is usually a derogatory one. The opposite to sharp acidity is usually described as **ripe acidity**, which can make the **fruit** refreshingly tangy.

SHEET FILTRATION *See* **Pad filtration**.

SHERRY-LIKE This term refers to the odour of a wine in an advanced state of **oxidation**, which is undesirable in low-strength or unfortified wines. It is caused by excessive **acetaldehyde**.

SHORT Refers to a wine that may have a good **nose** and initial flavour, but falls short on the **finish**, its taste quickly disappearing after the wine has been swallowed.

SKIN-CONTACT The **maceration** of grape skins in **must** or fermenting wine can extract varying amounts of colouring pigments, **tannin**, and aromatic compounds.

SLAVONIAN OAK A type of **oak** used for barrelmaking, from forests in eastern Croatia.

SLEEK Synonymous with **smart** and **stylish**, sleek infers a focused, fault-free modern style.

SMART Synonymous with **sleek** and **stylish**, smart implies a focused, fault-free modern style.

SMOKINESS, SMOKY, SMOKY COMPLEXITY, SMOKY-OAK Some grapes have an inherent smoky character (particularly Syrah and Sauvignon Blanc). This charcter can also come from well-toasted **oak** casks, but may also indicate an unfiltered wine. Some talented winemakers do not **rack** their wines and sometimes do not **filter** them in a passionate bid to retain maximum character and create an individual and **expressive** wine.

SMOOTH The opposite of **aggressive** and more extreme than **round**.

SO₂ A commonly used chemical formula for sulphur dioxide, an **anti-oxidant** with **aseptic** (anti-bacterial) qualities that is used in the production of wine. It should not be noticeable in the finished product, but sometimes a whiff may be detected on recently bottled wine. A good swirl in the glass or a vigorous decanting should remove this trace

and after a few months in bottle it ought to disappear altogether of its own accord. The acrid odour of sulphur in a wine should, if detected, be akin to the smell of a recently extinguished match. If it has a rotten-egg **aroma**, the sulphur has been reduced to **hydrogen sulphide** and the wine may well have formed **mercaptans** that you will not be able to remove. *See also* The use of sulphur, p28.

SOFT Interchangeable with **smooth**, although it usually refers to the **fruit** on the **palate**, whereas smooth is more often applied to the **finish**. Softness is a very desirable quality, but "extremely soft" may be derogatory, implying a weak and **flabby** wine.

SOLERA (Sp.) A system of continually refreshing an established blend with a small amount of new wine (equivalent in proportion to the amount of the blend that has been extracted from the *solera*) to effect a wine of consistent quality and character. Some existing *soleras* were laid down in the 19th century, and whereas it would be true to say that every bottle of that *solera* sold today contains a little of that first **vintage**, it would not even be a teaspoon. You would have to measure it in molecules, but there would be infinitesimal amounts of each and every vintage from the date of its inception to the year before bottling. *See also* The *solera* blending system, p382.

SOLID This term is interchangeable with **firm**.

SOLUMOLOGICAL The science of soil and, in the context of wine, the relationship between specific soil types and vine varieties.

SORBIC ACID A **yeast**-inhibiting compound found in the berries of mountain ash, sorbic acid is sometimes added to sweet wines to prevent re-fermentation, but it can give a powerful geranium odour if the wine subsequently undergoes **malolactic** fermentation.

SORRENTUM, SURRENTINE, or **SURRENTINUM** The Pavie/Parker/Robinson of antiquity, Sorrentum is from the promontory forming the southern horn of the Bay of Naples. It divided opinion 200 years ago, when the poet Publius Papinius Statius ranked it as the equal of **Falernian**, yet Tiberius described it as "only **generous** vinegar", while his successor, Caligula, thought it "worthless"!

SOUPED UP, SOUPY Implies a wine has been blended with something **richer** or more **robust**. A wine may well be legitimately souped up, or use of the term could mean that the wine has been played around with. The wine might not be **correct**, but it could still be very enjoyable.

SOUR In purely scientific terms of **basic taste**, this is synonymous with **acidity**, but in wine-tasting terms it is definitely a negative, indicating something off, with **acetic acid** dominating.

SOUS MARQUE (Fr.) A **marque** under which wines, usually second-rate wines, are offloaded.

SOUTHERN-STYLE This term describes the obvious characteristics of a wine from the sunny south of France. For reds, it may be complimentary at an **honest** basic level, indicating a **full**-bodied, full-flavoured wine with a **peppery** character. For whites, it will probably be derogatory, implying a **flabby** wine with too much **alcohol** and too little **acidity** and **freshness**.

SOUTIRAGE (Fr.) Synonymous with **racking**.

SPARGING A process in which **carbonic gas** is introduced into a wine before bottling, often simply achieved through a valve in the pipe between the vat and the bottling line. *See also* Carbonation, p37.

SPÄTLESE (Ger.) A QmP wine that is one step above *Kabinett*, but one below *Auslese*. It is fairly sweet and made from late-picked grapes.

SPICY 1. A **varietal characteristic** of some grapes, such as Gewürztraminer. 2. An aspect of a complex **bouquet** or **palate**, probably derived from **bottle-age** after time spent in wood.

SPICY-OAK A subjective term describing complex **aromas** derived from **fermentation** or maturation in **oak** that can give the impression of various spices – usually "creamy" ones such as cinnamon or nutmeg – and that are enhanced by **bottle-age**.

SPRITZ, SPRITZIG (Ger.) Synonymous with *pétillant*.

SPUMANTE (It.) Fully sparkling.

STABILIZATION The process by which a heaving broth of biochemical activity becomes firmly fixed and not easily changed. Most wines are stablized by **tartrate** precipitation, **filtration**, **fining**, and the addition of SO_2 (sulphur dioxide).

STAGE (Fr.) A period of practical experience. It has long been traditional for vineyard owners to send their sons on a *stage* (internship) to a great château in Bordeaux. Now the *Bordelais* send their sons on similar *stages* to California and Australia.

STALKY 1. The **herbaceous**-tannic **varietal** **characteristic** of Cabernet grapes. 2. Applies literally to wines made from grapes which were pressed with their stalks. 3. Could be indicative of **cork taint** or **corked wine**.

STATAN According to Athenaeus of Naucratis, this was one of the best **ancient Roman wines**, resembling **Falernian** but "lighter and innocuous", leading us to suspect that inoffensive wines were preferable in those times.

STELVIN This brand of **screwcap** was developed specifically for wine in 1959 by La Bouchage Mecanique (a French firm later taken over by Pechiney), which effectively put a longer skirt on its existing Stelcap, a general-purpose closure. The product was initially called Stelcap-vin but was soon shortened to Stelvin.

STERILIZATION The ultimate sterilization of a very cheap, **commercial** wine may be **pasteurization** or flash pasteurization.

STICKIES Common parlance for very sweet wines, usually **fortified** or **botrytized**.

STRETCHED This term describes a wine that has been diluted or **cut** with water (or a significantly inferior wine), which is usually illegal in an official **appellation**. It can also refer to wine that has been produced from vines that have been "stretched" to **yield** a high volume of attenuated **fruit**.

STRUCTURE The structure of a wine is literally composed of its solids (**tannin**, **acidity**, sugar, and **extract** or density of **fruit** flavour) in **balance** with the **alcohol**, and how positively they form and feel in the mouth.

STÜCK (Ger.) A 1,200-litre oval cask.

STUCK FERMENTATION A stuck, literally halted, **fermentation** is always difficult to rekindle and, even when done successfully, the resultant wine can taste strangely bitter. The most common causes for a stuck fermentation are: 1. temperatures of 35°C (95°F) or above; 2. nutrient deficiency, which can cause **yeast** cells to die; 3. high sugar content, which results in high **osmotic pressure**, which can cause yeast cells to die.

STYLISH Describes wines possessing all the subjective qualities of **charm**, **elegance**, and **finesse**. A wine might have the "style" of a certain region or type, but this does not mean it is stylish. A wine is either stylish or it is not – it defies definition.

SUBTLE Although this description should mean a significant yet understated characteristic, it is often employed by wine snobs and frauds who taste a wine with a famous label and know that it should be special, but cannot detect anything exceptional. They need an ambiguous word to get out of the hole they have dug for themselves.

SULPHUR DIOXIDE See SO_2.

SUMMER PRUNING Synonymous with **green pruning**.

SUPER-PREMIUM WINE This category comes between **premium** and **ultra-premium wines** and may be priced at, say, $10–20.

SUPER-SECOND A term that evolved when Second-Growth (*deuxième cru*) châteaux, such as Palmer and Cos d'Estournel, started making wines that came close to First-Growth (*premier cru*) quality at a time when certain First Growths were not always performing well. The first super-second was Palmer 1961, although the term did not evolve until some time during the early 1980s.

SUPERTASTER A term that applies to those people who have more **taste buds** than the rest of us. However, contrary to what the name infers, being a so-called supertaster is more of a burden than a blessing when it comes to tasting wine because a supertaster is super-sensitive to **bitterness** and, consequently, finds even the softest **tannins** in the greatest red wines too bitter to enjoy. This super-sensitivity is thought to be a survival trait from our hunter-gatherer days, when the only instrument we had to avoid toxic foods was our palates, since the majority of the most poisonous substances are bitter to taste. *See* What Is a Supertaster?, p74.

SUPER-TUSCAN This term was coined in Italy in the 1980s for the Cabernet-boosted *vini da tavola* blends that were infinitely better and far more expensive than Tuscany's traditional Sangiovese-based wines. *See* Birth of the Super-Tuscans, p335.

SUPERVIN A **screwcap** developed by Auscap in Australia.

SUPPLE Describes a wine that is **easy to drink**, not necessarily **soft**, but the term suggests more ease than **round** does. With age, the **tannin** in wine is said to become supple.

SUPPLE TANNIN Tannins are generally perceived to be harsh and mouth-puckering, but the tannins in a **ripe** grape are **supple**, whereas those in an unripe grape are not.

SUR LIE (Fr.) Describes wines, usually Muscadet, that have been kept on their **lees** and have not been **racked** or **filtered** prior to bottling. Although this practice increases the possibility of bacterial infection, the risk is worth taking for those wines made from **neutral grape varieties**. In the wines of Muscadet, for example, this practice enhances the **fruit** of the normally bland Melon de Bourgogne grape and adds a **yeasty** dimension of **depth** that can give the flavour of a modest white Burgundy. It also avoids aeration and retains more of the **carbonic gas** created during **fermentation**, thereby imparting a certain **liveliness** and **freshness**.

SUREPURE A new South African process that uses light energy to purify wine. First deployed in the wine industry at the Franschhoek wine estate of L'Ormarins in 2009, SurePure used patented Turbulator technology to transmit ultraviolet energy (UV-C at 250–270 nm) to deactivate microbes, reducing the need to add **sulphur**.

SÜSSRESERVE (Ger.) Unfermented, fresh grape juice commonly used to sweeten German wines up to and including *Spätlese* level. It is also added to cheaper *Auslesen*. Use of *Süssreserve* is far superior to the traditional French method of sweetening wines, which utilizes grape concentrate instead of grape juice. *Süssreserve* provides a **fresh** and **grapey** character that is desirable in inexpensive medium-sweet wines.

SYNTHETIC CLOSURES The first commercially available synthetic **corks** were produced by companies such as Novembal (France) and Metal Box (UK), using an injection-moulded ethylene vinyl acetate polymer, which was insufficiently flexible to provide what would be regarded today as an acceptable quality of wine closure, due to an unacceptable level of oxygen ingress. The next level of technology, achieved in the early 1990s by companies such as Supremecorq and Integra, provided closures of greater flexibility and thus improved performance, yet they were still not a satisfactory alternative to cork, particularly for longer than a year or two in bottle. Finally, by

dropping the injection-moulded process, two-part closures such as Nomacorc and Neocork, which are comprised of an inner core produced by an extrusion process and sleeved in a softer and more flexible gasket or outer sleeve, managed to achieve a very satisfactory performance as an alternative to cork. The outer sleeve is so soft and flexible that, if used as a one-piece closure, it would be practically impossible to insert into a bottle and even harder to extract – but as an outer skin to the extruded inner core, it provides an almost perfect seal with the inside of the bottle. *See also* **Crown-cap**; **Screwcap**.

TABLE WINE A term that originally distinguished between a light, unfortified wine (which was generally the preserve of the dining table) and a **fortified** wine (which was served at other times, such as Sherry in the morning, Madeira at teatime, and even Port, which the men would retire with). The term *vin de table* was then usurped by the French wine regime, which cast it as the lowest of the low. Now the term has been replaced by *vin de France*.

TAFELWEIN (Ger.) **Table wine** or *vin de table*.

TALENTO (It.) Since March 1996, producers of Italian *méthode champenoise* wines may use the new term "Talento", which has been registered as a trademark by the Instituto Talento Metodo Classico – established in 1975 and formerly called the Instituto Spumante Classico Italiano. Talento is almost synonymous with the Spanish term Cava, although to be fully compatible it would have to assume the mantle of a **DOC** and to achieve that would require the mapping of all the areas of production. However, it will take all the *talento* they can muster to turn most Italian *spumante* **brut** into an international class of sparkling wine.

TANK METHOD *See* **Cuve close**.

TANNIC, TANNIN Tannins are various **phenolic** substances found naturally in wine that come from the skin, seeds, and stalks of grapes. They can also be picked up from **oak** casks, particularly new ones. Grape tannins can be divided into **ripe** and unripe, the former being most desirable. In a proper **balance**, however, both types are essential to the **structure** of red wines, in order to knit the many flavours together. Unripe tannins are not water-soluble and will remain harsh no matter how old the wine is, whereas ripe tannins are water-soluble, have a **suppleness** or, at most, a **grippy** feel from an early age, and will drop out as the wine **matures**. Ripe grape tannin softens with age, is vital to the structure of a serious red wine, and is useful in wines chosen to accompany food.

TART Refers to a noticeable **acidity** that is much more than **piquant** and very close to **sharp**.

TARTARIC ACID The **ripe acid** of grapes that increases slightly when the grapes increase in sugar during the *véraison*.

TARTRATES, TARTRATE CRYSTALS Deposits of **tartaric acid** look very much like sugar crystals at the bottom of a bottle and may be precipitated when a wine experiences low temperatures. Tartrates are also deposited simply through the process of time, although seldom in a still or sparkling wine that has spent several months in contact with its **lees**, as this produces a **mannoprotein** called MP32, which prevents the precipitation of tartrates. A fine deposit of glittering crystals can also be deposited on the base of a **cork** if it has been soaked in a sterilizing solution of metabisulphite prior to bottling. All are harmless. *See also* Cold stabilization, p30.

TASTE BUD We have approximately 10,000 taste buds, mostly on the tongue but also on the soft or upper palate, the insides of the cheeks, around the back of the throat, the upper throat, and even on the lips. As the name implies, these are bud-like protrusions, and they contain **taste receptors**, which detect only the **basic tastes** of bitterness, **sourness** (or acidity), **sweetness**, saltiness, and umami.

TASTE RECEPTOR In each **taste bud**, there are approximately 100 taste receptors; thus, we each have around one million taste receptors. There are many different types of taste receptor, including a number whose purpose is unknown or not fully understood, but essentially they all transmit the detection of a **basic taste** directly to the brain without any input from the **olfactory bulb**. Some taste receptors detect only **bitterness**, while others detect only **sourness** (acidity) or **sweetness** or saltiness or **umami**, but with 100 or so taste receptors in each taste bud, each taste bud has the ability to detect all basic tastes.

TASTEVIN (Fr.) A shallow, dimpled, silver cup used for tasting, primarily in Burgundy.

TbA (Ger.) A commonly used abbreviation of *Trockenbeerenauslese*, this category is for wines produced from individually picked, **botrytized grapes** that have been left on the vine to shrivel. The wine is golden-amber to amber in colour, intensely sweet, viscous, very complex and as different from *Beerenauslese* as that wine is from *Kabinett*.

TCA Short for trichloroanisole, the prime (but by no means only) culprit responsible for **corked** wines. TCA can be found in **oak** staves, wooden pallets, and winery beams, as well as in **cork**, so it is theoretically possible to find a "corked" wine in a bottle sealed with a **screwcap**!

TDN Common abbreviation for trimethyldihydronaphthalene, the active chemical compound responsible for the so-called **petrol** (kerosene, gasoline, or paraffin) **aroma** of bottle-matured Riesling. TDN develops through the degradation of beta carotene, an **anti-oxidant** that is itself derived from another anti-oxidant – lutein. The ratio of beta carotene to lutein is higher in Riesling than in any other white grape variety. Studies show that the lower the **pH** of a wine, the higher its potential for developing TDN, thus its propensity to develop in warmer climes. The longer it takes for the petrol aromas to emerge, the more **finesse** they have. Interestingly, **cork** absorbs 40 per cent of TDN, so **screwcaps** effectively preserve petrol aromas.

TEINTURIER A grape variety with coloured (red), as opposed to clear, juice.

TERPENES These compounds are responsible for some of the most powerful spice-laden and full-blown floral aromatics found in *vinifera* grapes, particularly varieties such as Gewürztraminer, Muscat, and Riesling. Terpenes and their derivatives (terpenoids) are present in wine in six forms: **terpenoid acids**, **terpenoid alcohols**, **terpenoid aldehydes**, **terpenoid esters**, and **terpenoid oxides**. All these terpenoids are derived from isopentenyl pyrophosphate (IPP), which is a five-carbon isoprenic; thus, terpenes are always multiples of five units (5, 10, 15, 20, etc), up to caratenoids (40), after which they are lumped together as polyisoprenoids. Although there are more than 400 naturally occurring terpenoid compounds in the plant world, only 44 have so far been found in grapes or wine, and of these, 18 or more possess some significant degree of influence over wine **aromas**. The six most important terpenoids are: citronellol, geraniol, hotrienol, **linalool**, nerol, and alpha-terpineol. As only free terpenes are odiferous and all free terpenes have to be present at above-threshold levels to have any aromatic effect, there is an enormous untapped aromatic potential in almost every wine produced, since a large proportion of terpenes are found in their bound form. However, bound terpenes can be freed by hydrolytic action via either acids or **enzymes**, and to a certain extent this happens naturally in the *véraison* of the grapes and **vinification** of the wine. To capitalize on this, wine laboratories all over the world have formulated various specialized enzymatic preparations to achieve the same ends but to a much greater extent. Some of the most experienced wine judges in Australia believe that enzyme treatments on Rieslings produce an unnatural, overly floral character. No studies have been made, as yet, to determine the veracity of such claims, and no similar accusations have been made against the use of enzymes for either Gewürztraminer or Muscat, but the practice of using enzyme preparations for this and other purposes remains controversial, not least because the purpose of enzymes is to break down molecules, and sometimes it is impossible to predict what they might do next. When referencing any terpenoid compound, you will find that many are found in the aromas of various flowers, fruits, spices, and herbs. This does not mean that each terpene will contribute all the aromas indicated to any specific wine; it might be just one or two aromas, or none of the above, or they might together create entirely different aromas. The range of aromas for which these compounds are responsible beyond the confines of grape and glass should, however, give readers some idea of the aromatic pathway down which each terpene can be found.

TERPENOID ACIDS The only terpenoid acid of interest as far as wine **terpenes** are concerned is geranic acid (found in Muscat and contributing to the **aroma** of cardom and peppermint).

TERPENOID ALCOHOLS By far the most prolific, influential, and important category of terpenoids found in wine, terpenoid alcohols are present in increasing quantities in grapes as they **ripen**: citronellol (found in garden rose, geranium, ginger, black pepper, basil, peppermint, and cardamom; also plays a supporting role to citronellal in the **aroma** of lemon eucalyptus); diendol (not aromatic in itself but breaks down into hotrienol and nerol oxide); eugenol (the most **herbal**-influenced, spice-laden aroma of all terpenoid alcohols; found in bay leaves, **cloves**, and allspice); farnesol (the only terpenoid important to grape and wine aroma that is not a monoterpene or single-carbon **terpene**; farnesol is a sesquiterpene [15 carbon atoms] alcohol that is found in linden oil and is a constituent of garden-rose aroma); geraniol (although found in nutmeg, ginger, basil, rosemary, sage, cardamom, and grapefruit, geraniol can bring elements of peach and orange to the Muscat aroma, for which it is one of three main aromatic constituents); hotrienol (the aroma of linden or lime tree, but at levels higher than 30 ug/l it is regarded as an indicator of premature ageing, probably due to poor storage conditions); linalool (or linalol; found in lavender, bergamot, jasmine, basil, rosemary, sage, star anise, cinnamon, cloves, nutmeg, coriander, cardamom, ginger, black pepper, and mandarin; one of the three terpene compounds principally responsible for Muscat aroma); nerol (found in orange blossom, ginger, basil, cardamom, mint, and mandarin; also one of the three terpene compounds principally responsible for the Muscat aroma); and a-terpineol (lilac and **lime**).

TERPENOID ALDEHYDES Just two of any importance as far as wine **terpenes** are concerned: citronellol (although found in ginger, black pepper, geranium, and peppermint, citronellol is overwhelmingly **lemony**-resinous in character, representing a minimum of 82 per cent of lemon eucalyptus oil); and geranial (cinnamon, **clove**, ginger, basil, and peppermint).

TERPENOID ESTERS Only two of any real importance as far as wine **terpenes** are concerned: geranyl acetate (found in lemongrass, coriander, nutmeg, cinnamon, peppermint, and, of course, geranium); and linalyl acetate (lavender, bergamot, jasmine, cinnamon, cardamom, bell pepper, basil, rosemary, sage, and peppermint).

TERPENOID OXIDES The three of most interest as far as wine **terpenes** are concerned are: linalool oxide (hay and pine; found mostly in white Muscat varieties); nerol oxide (an **oxidation** of nerol alcohol; sweet-fruity **aroma** found in Bulgarian rose); and rose oxide (found in Bulgarian rose but can also be **green**, geranium-like).

TERROIR (Fr.) This literally means "soil", but in a viticultural sense *terroir* refers in a more general way to a vineyard's whole growing environment, which also includes altitude, **aspect**, climate, and any other significant factors that may affect the life of a vine, and thereby the quality of the grapes it produces.

TERTIARY AROMAS Synonymous with **bottle**-aromas, these are the more **mellow aromas** that build up with age in the bottle. *See also* **Primary aromas**; **Secondary aromas**.

TÊTE DE CUVÉE (Fr.) The first flow of juice during the pressing of the grapes, and the cream of the *cuvée*. It is the easiest juice to extract and the highest in quality, with the best **balance** of acids, sugars, and minerals.

THASIAN or **THASOS** The wines of Thasos were mixed with honeyed dough and stored before straining and serving. Thasian was famous until the 2nd century BC, when production slowly deteriorated due to higher-volume, lower-quality wines produced in Rhodes, Knedos, Kos, and various Ionian coastal cities.

THIN A term used to describe a wine that is lacking in **body**, **fruit**, and other properties.

THIRD LEAF A term derived from the earliest French **AOC** laws that determined that wine should be made only from vines that have given their *troisième feuille*, which is to say their third vegetative cycle or third year. Many vines provide a small crop in their second year, and it is debatable whether any such crop should be entirely and immediately **green pruned**.

TIBURTINE A **thin ancient Roman wine**, Tiburtine "easily evaporates" and "matures in 10 years, but it is better when aged", according to Athenaeus of Naucratis. This statement, combined with the extremely old age at which the best Roman wines were generally consumed, implies that a 10-year-old wine was not considered "aged" in this period.

TIGHT A **firm** wine of good **extract** and possibly significant **tannin** that seems to be under tension, like a wound spring waiting to be released. Its potential is far more obvious than that of **reticent** or **closed** wines.

TIRAGE (Fr.) Bottling.

TOAST 1. A slow-developing, bottle-induced **aroma** commonly associated with Chardonnay, but that can develop in wines made from other grapes (including red wines). Toasty **bottle-aromas** are initially noticeable on the **aftertaste**, often with no indication on the **nose**. 2. A fast-developing **oak**-induced **aroma**. 3. Barrels are toasted during their construction to one of three grades: light or low, medium, and heavy or high.

TOBACCO A subjective **bouquet**/tasting term often applied to **oak**-matured wines, usually Bordeaux.

TONNELIER A cooper or barrelmaker.

TONNELLERIE A cooperage or barrel works.

TOTAL ACIDITY The total amount of **acidity** in a wine is usually measured in grams per litre and, because each acid is of a different strength, expressed either in terms of sulphuric or **tartaric acid**.

TRANSFER METHOD Synonym of *transvasage*.

TRANSVASAGE (Fr.) In what is also known as the transfer method, non-*méthode champenoise* sparkling wines undergo a **second fermentation** in bottle, and are then decanted, **filtered**, and re-bottled under pressure to maintain the *mousse*.

TRICHLOROANISOLE *See* TCA.

TRIE (Fr.) This term usually refers to the harvesting of selected over-ripe or **botrytized grapes** by numerous sweeps (*tries*) through the vineyard.

TRIFOLIAN According to Athenaeus of Naucratis, this **ancient Roman** wine apparently **matured** more slowly than **Sorrentum**, and critics of modern wine-speak should note that he considered it to be "more **earthy**".

TROCKENBEERENAUSLESE *See* TbA.

TRONÇAIS A famous type of **oak** used for barrelmaking, from a small forest in the **Allier** *département* in the centre of France.

TYPICAL Over-used, less-than-honest form of the term "**honest**".

TYPICITY A wine that shows good typicity is one that accurately reflects its grape variety or varieties, but it will be dependent on the person using this term to indicate whether it also encompasses a "sense of place". Typicity does not have to be confined to **varietal character**, but its meaning is not precise without further qualification.

UC (Fr.) Short for *Union Coopérative* or other titles denoting a local or regional cooperative.

UC DAVIS The University of California's **oenology** department at Davis.

ULLAGE (Fr.) 1. The space between the top of the wine and the head of the bottle or cask. An old bottle of wine with an *ullage* beneath the shoulder of the bottle is unlikely to be any good. 2. The practice of topping up wine in a barrel to keep it full and thereby prevent excessive **oxidation**.

ULTRA-PREMIUM WINE This category comes between **super-premium** and **icon wines** and may be priced at tens of dollars up to, say, $150.

UMAMI The fifth **basic taste** (after sweetness, **sourness**, **bitterness**, and saltiness – see The Taste, or "Palate", of a Wine, p73) is the Eastern concept of umami (meaning "deliciousness" and implying a satisfying taste of completeness), which is triggered by the **amino acid** glutamate, hence the use of monosodium glutamate as a taste enhancer in Chinese cuisine. The concept of umami as a basic taste is contested by some scientists, who argue that it is artificial and created out of a complex continuum of perceptions. Other scientists claim that this explains all basic tastes, including sweetness, **sourness**, bitterness, and saltiness. Yet others propose further basic taste sensations, such as the taste of free **fatty acids** and a **metallic** sensation. See What Is Umami?, p74.

UNDERTONE A subtle and supporting characteristic that does not dominate like an **overtone**. In a **fine wine**, a strong and simple overtone of youth can evolve into a **delicate** undertone with **maturity**, adding to a vast array of other nuances that give the wine **complexity**.

UNFERMENTABLE RESIDUAL SUGAR Even **fully fermented** dry wines can and usually do have a tiny amount of **residual sugar**, due to the presence of unfermentable sugars such as arabinose, rhamnose, ribose, and xylose. **Yeasts** are unable to convert these sugars, so there will be up to 2 g/l of residual sugar in the driest wines.

UNGENEROUS A wine that lacks generosity has little or no **fruit** and also far too much **tannin** (if red) or **acidity** for a correct and harmonious **balance**.

UNRIPE ACID Malic acid, as opposed to **tartaric acid** or **ripe acid**.

UPFRONT This term suggests a wine with an attractive, simple, immediately recognizable quality that says it all. Such a wine may initially be interesting, but it will not develop further and the last glass would say nothing more about its characteristics than the first.

UTA (Ger.) Acronym for *Untypischer Alterungs*, or atypical ageing (ATA).

UVAGGIO (It.) Wine that has been blended from various grape varieties.

VA The abbreviation for **volatile acidity**.

VA LIFT A winemaking "trick" whereby the **volatile acidity** is elevated to enhance the fruitiness of wine, but it is never allowed to rise anywhere near the level where the wine becomes unstable. Acceptable only in wines that are ready to drink, as this phenomenon does not improve with age.

VALUE FOR MONEY This is the difference between penny-saving and penny-pinching. True value for money exists at £50, $50, or whatever, just as much as it does at £5, $5, or whatever, and the decision whether to buy will depend on how deep your pocket is, not whether it is ten times better.

VANILLA, VANILLA-OAK Often used to describe the **nose** and sometimes the **palate** of an **oak**-aged wine, especially Rioja. It is the most basic and obvious of oak-induced characteristics.

VANILLIN An **aldehyde** with a vanilla **aroma** that is found naturally in **oak** to one degree or another.

VARIETAL, VARIETAL AROMA, VARIETAL CHARACTER The unique and **distinctive** character of a single grape variety as expressed in the wine it produces.

VC (Sp.) Short for *vino comarcal*, which literally means a "local wine" and can be compared to the *vin de pays* of France.

VdL A common abbreviation of *vin de liqueur*, a **fortified** wine that is normally muted with **alcohol** before **fermentation** can begin.

VdlT (Sp.) Short for *vino de la tierra*, which literally means a "country wine", but is closer to the VDQS of France than its *vin de pays*.

VDN A common abbreviation for *vin doux naturel*. This is, in fact, a **fortified** wine, such as Muscat de Beaumes de Venise, that has been muted during the **fermentation** process, after it has achieved a level of between 5 and 8 per cent **alcohol**.

VDQS A common abbreviation for *vin délimité de qualité supérieure*, a lapsed quality-control system below **AOC** but above *vin de pays*. VDQS is no longer in existence, but the definition will be retained in the Micropedia for historical reference.

VdT (It.) Short for *vino da tavola*.

VEGETAL A tasting term that can range from relatively neutral root vegetables, often **cooked**, through the more aromatic celeriac, to certain **herbaceous** notes, such as asparagus, bell pepper, and so on.

VENDANGE TARDIVE (Fr.) Late harvest.

VÉRAISON (Fr.) The ripening period, during which the grapes do not actually change very much in size, but do gain in colour (if black) and increase in sugar and **tartaric acid**, while at the same time decreasing in unripe **malic acid**.

VERMOUTH An aromatized wine. The name vermouth originates from *Wermut*, the German for wormwood, which is its principal ingredient. The earliest examples made in Germany in the 16th century were for local consumption only, the first commercial vermouth being Punt-é-Mes, created by Antonio Carpano of Turin in 1786. Traditionally, Italian vermouth is red and sweet, while French is white and dry, but both countries make both styles. Vermouth is made by blending very bland base wines (they are two or three years old and come from Apulia and Sicily in Italy and

Languedoc-Roussillon in France) with an extract of aromatic ingredients, then sweetening the blend with sugar and fortifying it with pure **alcohol**. Chambéry, a pale and delicately aromatic wine made in the Savoie, France, is the only vermouth with an official **appellation**.

VERTICAL TASTING *See* Horizontal tasting.

VIERTELSTÜCK (Ger.) A 300-litre oval cask.

VIGNERON (Fr.) Vineyard worker; often a vineyard owner.

VIGNOBLE (Fr.) Vineyard.

VIGOUR Although this term could easily apply to wine, it is invariably used when discussing the growth of a vine, and particularly of its **canopy**. In order to ripen grapes properly, a vine needs about 50 square centimetres (7.75 square inches) of leaf surface to every gram of **fruit**, but if a vine is too vigorous (termed "high vigour"), the grapes will have an over-**herbaceous** character, even when they are theoretically **ripe**.

VIN DE L'ANNÉE (Fr.) This term is synonymous with *vin primeur*.

VIN DE CAFÉ (Fr.) This category of French wine is sold by the carafe in cafés, bistros, and so on.

VIN DÉLIMITÉ DE QUALITÉ SUPÉRIEUR *See* VDQS.

VIN DOUX NATUREL *See* VDN.

VIN DE FRANCE This term has replaced *vin de table* as the lowest-quality wine in the French wine regime, but since these wines are now allowed to indicate grape variety and **vintage**, some producers have started selling interesting wines at this level. The effect has been to raise standards from the bottom up.

VIN DE GARDE (Fr.) Wine that is capable of significant improvement if it is allowed to age.

VIN DE GLACE (Fr.) French equivalent of *Eiswein*.

VIN DE GOUTTE (Fr.) Also called the free-run juice. In the case of white wine, this is the juice that runs free from the press before the actual pressing operation begins. With red wine, it is fermented wine drained off from the *manta*, or **cap**, before this is pressed.

VIN GRIS (Fr.) A delicate, pale version of **rosé**.

VIN JAUNE (Fr.) This is the famous "yellow wine" of the Jura that derives its name from its honey-gold colour that results from a deliberate **oxidation** beneath a **Sherry-like flor**. The result is similar to an aged Fino Sherry, although it is not **fortified**. *See also* The Jura, Bugey, and Savoie, p274.

VIN DE LIQUEUR *See* VdL.

VIN MOUSSEUX (Fr.) This literally means "sparkling wine" without any particular connotation of quality one way or the other. But because all fine sparkling wines in France utilize other terms, for all practical purposes it implies a cheap, low-quality product.

VIN NOUVEAU (Fr.) This term is synonymous with *vin primeur*.

VIN ORDINAIRE (Fr.) Literally "an ordinary wine", this term is most often applied to a French *vin de table*, although it can be used in a rather derogatory way to describe any wine from any country.

VIN DE PAILLE (Fr.) Literally "straw wine", a complex sweet wine produced by leaving late-picked grapes to dry and shrivel in the sun on straw mats. *See also* The Jura, Bugey, and Savoie, p274.

VIN DE PAYS (Fr.) A rustic style of country wine that is one step above *vin de table*, but one beneath VDQS. *See also* Vins de Pays and Vins de France, p298.

VIN DE PRESSE (Fr.) Very dark, **tannic**, red wine pressed out of the *manta*, or **cap**, after the *vin de goutte* has been drained off.

VIN PRIMEUR Young wine made to be drunk within the year in which it is produced. Beaujolais Primeur is the official designation of the most famous *vin primeur*, but export markets see it labelled as Beaujolais Nouveau most of the time.

VIN DE TABLE (Fr.) Literally "table wine", although not necessarily a direct translation of this term. It is used to describe the lowest level of wine in France and is not allowed to give either the grape variety or the area of origin on the label. In practice, it is likely to consist of various varieties from numerous areas that have been blended in bulk in order to produce a wine of consistent character, or lack thereof, as the case may be.

VIN D'UNE NUIT (Fr.) A rosé or very pale red wine that is allowed contact with the *manta*, or **cap**, for one night only.

VINEGAR Alcohol that has been oxidized into **acetic acid**.

VINEGAR FLY A synonym for the *Drosophila melanogaster*, or common fruit fly.

VINHO REGIONAL (Port.) *See* **VR**.

VINIFERA *See Vitis vinifera*.

VINIFICATION Far more than simply describing **fermentation**, vinification involves the entire process of making wine, from the moment the grapes are picked to the point at which the wine is finally bottled.

VINIMATIC This is an enclosed, rotating **fermentation** tank with blades fixed to the inner surface, that works on the same principle as a cement-mixer. Used initially to extract the maximum colour from the grape skins with the minimum **oxidation**, it is now being utilized for **pre-fermentation maceration**.

VINO COMARCAL (Sp.) *See* **VC**.

VINO-LOK A commercial glass-stopper alternative to **cork**, Vino-Lok utilizes a sealing ring made of DuPont Elvax, a registered ethylene vinyl acetate polymer. It is the click-on, click-off quality of this seal that sets it apart, making it not only tremendously easy to bottle wine but also effortless to reseal not just the bottle it comes with but many other bottles, too – so don't throw these closures away!

VINO DE MESA (Sp.) **Table wine**, *vin de table*.

VINO NOVELLO (It.) The same as *vin primeur*.

VINO DA TAVOLA (It.) *Vin de table*, table wine.

VINO DE LA TIERRA (Sp.) *See* **VdlT**.

VINOUS Of, or relating to, a characteristic of wine. When used to describe a wine, this term implies basic qualities only.

VINTAGE 1. A wine of one year. 2. Synonymous with harvest: a vintage wine is the wine of one year's harvest only (or at least 85 per cent* according to EU regulations) and the year may be anything from poor to exceptional. It is, for this reason, a misnomer to use the term vintage for the purpose of indicating a wine of special quality.

VISCOSITY Higher viscosity as expressed by rivulets gathering on the inside of a glass after swirling (known as "legs" or "tears") is a crude indicator of higher alcohol levels in a wine and, contrary to popular belief, has no bearing on the relative quality of a wine.

VITICULTURE Cultivation of the vine. Viticulture is to grapes what horticulture is to flowers.

VITIS The VITIS International Varietal Catalogue is a database comprised of the accepted international standard grape-variety names and their known synonyms.

VITIS VINIFERA A species covering all varieties of vines that provide classic winemaking grapes. *See also* The Wine Vine Tree, p45.

VITISPIRANE An aromatic compound that forms during bottle maturation, vitispirane can have a chrysanthemum bouquet, while trans-vitispirane is heavier, more exotic, and more fruity, even camphor-like.

VIVID The **fruit** in some wines can be so **fresh**, **ripe**, clean-cut, and **expressive** that it quickly gives a vivid impression of complete character in the mouth.

VOLATILE ACIDS These acids, sometimes called **fatty acids**, are capable of evaporating at low temperatures, hence the volatility. Too much volatile acidity is always a sign of instability, but small amounts actually play a significant role in the taste and **aroma** of a wine. Formic, butyric, and proprionic are all volatile acids that may be found in wine, but **acetic acid** and **carbonic acid** are the most important, and acetic acid is the one referred to when an experienced taster makes the comment "VA" or "Too much VA". The volatile **aroma** of acetic acid will be easily recognized by anyone who has ever made a sweet-and-sour sauce in Chinese cuisine or a *sauce diable* in French cuisine and has caught a whiff of **vinegar** evaporating over the heat.

VOLATILE PHENOLS Almost one-third of all French wines tested have volatile **phenols** above the level of perception, so they are clearly not always bad. Some volatile phenols such as ethyl-4-guaiacol (**smoky**-spicy **aroma**) and, to a lesser degree, vinyl-4-guaiacol (carnation aroma) can actually contribute attractive elements to a wine's bouquet. However, volatile phenols are generally considered to be faults, and the amount of ethyl and vinyl phenols present in a wine is increased by harsh methods of pressing (particularly the use of continuous presses), insufficient settling, use of particular strains of **yeast**, and, to a lesser extent, increased **skin-contact**. Ethyl-4-phenol is responsible for the so-called Brett off-aromas (stables, horsey, sweaty-saddles – *see Brettanomyces*), while vinyl-4-phenol has a Band-Aid (sticking plaster) off-**aroma**.

VOLUPTUOUS A term used to describe a succulently **rich** wine, often a red wine, which has a seductive, mouth-filling flavour. *See also* **Luscious**.

VOSGES 1. A mountain range bordering and sheltering the Alsace region of France. 2. A well-known type of **oak** used for barrelmaking, from **Darnay**, **Saint Hélène**, **Schirmeck**, or any other forest in the Vosges *département* of eastern France.

VQPRD (Fr.) Common abbreviation for *vin de qualité produit dans une région délimité*, the French language version of the lapsed EU umbrella classification encompassing national quality wine regimes, such as **AOC**, **DOC**, etc. QWPSR, or "quality wine produced in a specified region", is the English equivalent. VQPRD has now replaced by **AOP**.

VR (Port.) The abbreviation for *vinho regional*, the lowest rung in Portugal's **appellation** system. A VR can be compared to the regional *vin de pays* category in France.

WARM, WARMTH Terms suggestive of a good-flavoured red wine with a high **alcoholic** content; if these terms are used with an accompanying description of cedary or **creamy**, they can mean well matured in **oak**.

WATER IMMERSION A fairly recent barrelmaking process whereby the **oak** staves are rinsed prior to **cooperage** (whereas soaking barrels in water following cooperage is a long-established practice). According to a review of the chemical and sensory profile of water-immersion barrels published by *Practical Vineyard & Winery* in the November/December 2010 issue, water immersion is said to have a significant impact on refining the flavour profile, making the oak influence more subtle, resulting in more **elegant** wines.

WATERSHED A term used for an area where water drains into a river system, lake, or some other body of water.

WATERY An extreme qualification of **thin**.

WEISSHERBST (Ger.) A single-variety rosé wine produced from black grapes only.

WET FEET *Vinifera* vines famously do not like "wet feet" – that is, they do not respond well to being grown in areas where water accumulates. Some varieties, even closely related varieties, are even more sensitive to this than others, such as Sauvignon Gris, which is not as resilient to water accumulation as Sauvignon Blanc.

WINE The fermented juice of grapes, as opposed to "fruit wine", which may be made from other fruits.

WINE DIAMONDS A euphemistic synonym for tartrate crystals.

WINE LAKE A common term for the EU surplus of low-quality **table wine**.

WINKLER SCALE A term synonymous with the **heat-summation** system.

WOOD LACTONES These are various **esters** that are picked up from new **oak**; they may be the source of certain **creamy-oak** and coconutty characteristics.

WOOD-MATURED This term normally refers to a wine that has been aged in new **oak**.

YEAST A kind of fungus that is absolutely vital in all winemaking. Yeast cells excrete a number of **yeast enzymes**, some 22 of which are necessary to complete the chain reaction that is known as **fermentation**. *See also* Yeast the Fermenter, p28.

YEAST ENZYMES Each yeast **enzyme** acts as a catalyst for one particular activity in the **fermentation** process and is specific for that one task only.

YEASTY This is not a complimentary term for most wines, although a yeasty bouquet can sometimes be desirable in a good-quality sparkling wine, especially if it is young. However, a simple yeastiness does not convey the **finesse** that the **aromas** of certain yeast products can, such as bread dough, bready, or brioche.

YIELD 1. The quantity of grapes produced from a given area of land. 2. How much juice is pressed from this quantity of grapes. Wine people in Europe measure yield in hl/ha (hectolitres per **hectare** – a hectolitre equals 1,000 litres), referring to how much juice has been extracted from the grapes harvested from a specific area of land. This is fine when the amount of juice that can be pressed from grapes is controlled by European-type **appellation** systems, but in the New World, where this seldom happens, they tend to talk in terms of tons per acre. It can be difficult trying to make exact conversions in the field, particularly after a heavy tasting session, when even the size of a ton or gallon can become quite elusive. This is why, as a rough guide, I multiply the tons or divide the hectolitres by 20 to convert one to the other. This is based on the average extraction rates for both California and Australia, which makes it a good rule-of-thumb. Be aware that white wines can benefit from higher yields than reds (although sweet wines should have the lowest yields of all) and that sparkling wines can get away with relatively high yields. For example, Sauternes averages 25 hl/ha, Bordeaux 50 hl/ha, and Champagne 80 hl/ha.

ZESTY A **lively** characteristic that is suggestive of a **zippy** tactile impression combined, maybe, with a **distinctive** hint of **citrus aroma**.

ZING, ZINGY, ZIP, ZIPPY Terms that are all indicative of something that is notable for being refreshing, **lively**, and vital in character, resulting from a high **balance** of ripe fruit **acidity** in the wine.

ZYGOSACCHAROMYCES BAILII A so-called spoilage **yeast** that can generate a flocculant deposit in **wine**.

ZYMASE An **enzyme** involved in the conversion of sugar into **alcohol**.

ZYMOLOGY The science of **fermentation**.

INDEX

ACKNOWLEDGMENTS

AUTHOR'S ACKNOWLEDGMENTS (2011, 5th edition)
Special thanks go to David Tombesi-Walton and Simon Murrell of Sands Publishing
Solutions, with whom I have worked for several years – not just on *The Sotheby's®
Wine Encyclopedia* but other publishing projects, too. I have nothing but admiration
for David's editorial skills, not least his nigh-mystical ability to decipher my mark-ups,
which even I have great difficulty understanding by the time the proofs are sent to
me for checking. Simon's art skills are so legendary that he ended up carrying out
virtually all of the map revisions, including all those of radically improved design,
enlisting the cartographers only where brand-new maps or extended areas of
existing maps were needed. However, new maps and extensions were essential
for this major revise, and, as ever, I have Tom Coulson and Martin Darlison of
Encompass Graphics to thank for providing those.

My gratitude to Lyn Parry for her invaluable assistance in structuring the list
of grape varieties and synonyms for the vastly expanded ABC of Grape Varieties
is such that I have mentioned her in the Introduction.

There are always too many colleagues and friends to name in the international wine
trade who have helped coordinate my trips around the world, supplied or confirmed
technical information, and assisted in determining the boundaries of wine regions that
have never been mapped until now, let alone the hundreds of wineries that shipped
samples for tasting in the final phase of compiling this edition. However, special
thanks must go to Michael Schmidt, Tim James, Yannick Joseph, Yves Bénard, and
Cécile Mathiaud, followed by Adam Montefiore, Robert Gorak, Mary-Irene Triantafillou
Pitsaki, Nico Manessis, Evangelos Gerovassiliou, Christopher Parker, David Creighton,
Dr Patrick McGovern, Dr Ron Jackson, Chris Skyrme, Laura Rylance, Dr Richard Smart,
Denis Gastin, Daniel Milmo, Martin Hinterleitner, Dr Jasenka Piljac Zegarac, Srdjan
Zitkovic, Visooth Lohitnavy, Silvia Baratta, Françoise Peretti, and Eberhard Eisch,
with no apologies whatsoever for any twisted arms or broken legs left in my wake!

PHOTOGRAPHIC CREDITS
t = top, b = bottom, l = left, r = right, c = centre
akg-images: 85 tr, 86 tr, 87 tl, 87 tr, 89 cr. **Alamy Images:** Mike Booth 88 bl; Peter Eastland
494; Norma Joseph 88 t; Lou Linwei 682 t; Mary Evans Picture Library 89 bl. **Ancient Art &
Architecture Collection** 86 bl. **The Art Archive:** Gianni Dagli Orti 84. **Bildagentur Mauritius:**
Koch 429; Rossenbach 425. **Anthony Blake:** 203 t, 426. **Harry Baker:** 24 tl. **Bonny Doon:** Alex
Krause 27. **Bernard Breuer:** 425 t, 425 b. **Michail Busselle:** 137. **Camel Valley:** 34, 462. **Cephas:**
Nigel Blythe 64 tr, 54 tl, 60 br, 436, 437, 685; Andy Christodolo 52 tr, 404, 408, 607, 609, 669;
Kevin Judd 60 tr, 640, 668; Clay McLachlan 684; Alain Proust 512; Mick Rock 18 t, 29, 47,
92, 110, 111, 112, 129, 138 bl, 172 t, 172 b, 185 t, 185 b, 187 r, 191, 197 b, 197, 208, 210, 214,
215, 234, 241, 261, 263, 298, 312, 314, 324, 326, 327, 347, 349, 353, 361, 372, 377, 379, 380,
392, 394, 412, 434, 435 t, 435 b, 442 t, 496 b, 496 t, 458, 510, 570, 585, 624; Ted Stefanski 540.
Champagne Bureau: 24 br, 25 tl. **Champagne Pommery:** 216. **Chateau d'Esclans:** 33 tr, 293.
Chateau Haut-Brion: 142 bl. **CIVC Epernay:** 220, 217 b. **Click Chicago:** Peter Fronk 534, 576,
586; John Lawlor 537; Chuck O'Rear 537. **Stephanie Colasanti:** 400. **Bruce Coleman / Herbert
Kranwetter:** 395. **Bruce Coleman / Sandro Prato:** 528. **Corbis:** Peter Adams / JAI 402;
Atlantide Phototravel 343; Michael Freeman 86 br; Franck Guiziou / Hemis 275 br;
Lehmann, Herbert / the food passionates 481; Lehmann, Jörg / the food passionates 275 bl;
John Miller / Robert Harding World Imagery 456; Charles O'Rear 2, 12, 618; Ryan Pyle
682 b; Siffert, Hans-Peter / the food passionates 100; Anneliese Villiger 1; Jim Wark /
Monsoon / Photolibrary 530; Stefan Wermuth / Reuters 94–95. **Andy Crawford:** 38, 39 b, 40.
Patrick Eagar: 17 r, 175 t, 246, 247, 653. **Food and Wine from France:** 25 br. **French
Government Tourist Office:** 274. **Getty Images:** Danita Delimont 683; Travel Ink 503. **Sonia
Halliday:** 505. **Horizon:** Milton Wordley 644. **Denis Hughes-Gilbey:** 25 cr, 252 b. **Imagebank:**
S Barbosa 608. **Impact:** Pamla Toler 663, 664. **Landscape Only:** Charlie Waite 335 t, 335 b.
Mentzendorff: 384, 385. **David Murray / Jules Felmes:** 30. **Nyetimber:** 93 tl, 459. **Ian O'Leary:**
75, 76. **Courtesy of the Penn Museum** 85 cl. **Pipers Brook Vineyard:** 639. **Janet Price:** 138 br,
156 t, 156 b, 175 b, 180, 181 t, 181 b, 197, 236, 264 t, 264 b, 611, 621, 622, 631 t, 643 t.
Quinto do Centro: 33 tl, 388. **Ridgeview:** 465. **Riedel:** 70, 71. **Louis Roederer:** 219.
Philippe Roy: 98, 99. **Saratoga County Historian's Office** 86 cr. **Scope:** Jean-Luc Barde 211,
279; Jacques Guillard 252 t; Michel Guillard 24 tr, 24 bl, 25 bl, 104 b, 108 t, 126, 130 t,
130 b, 134, 138 tr, 138 cr, 143 tr, 144 t, 293; Jacques Sierpinski 285; Jean-Daniel Sudres
25 tr. **Sands Publishing Solutions:** Simon Murrell 69. **Norbert Schiller:** 508, 509. **Sotheby's:** 10,
11. Tokaj Disznókő: Zoltán Gávai 474 **Tom Stevenson:** 18 b, 143 bl, 143 br, 144 b, 473, 507.
Tony Stone: 654; Fritz Prenzl 659. **TopFoto.co.uk:** The Granger Collection 91 bl.
US Patent and Trademark Office 90. **Visionbank:** Colin Maher 117, 145. **Willmes:** 26.
Jon Wyand: 9 tl, 317, 428, 532 b, 549, 563, 570 b. **Ysios** 358. **Zefa:** Armstrong 555;
Eigen 442 b; Fotostudio 483; Harlicek 448; W H Mueller 14 tr; K Oster 417;
Haro Schumacher 526. **Dacotah Rennau:** 736 (photograph of author).
All other images © dkimages.com

ILLUSTRATION CREDITS
Vinification artworks by Patrick Mulrey; all other illustrations by Kuo Kang Chen.

JACKET IMAGES
Front: Gunter Marx ©Dorling Kindersley;
back and spine (t): Alex Havret © Dorling Kindersley;
spine (b) © Dorling Kindersley / Rough Guides.

DORLING KINDERSLEY WOULD ALSO LIKE TO THANK:
Nishi Bhasin, Manjari Rathi, Pooja Huria, Pramod Pant, Nain Rawat, Mukta Arora,
Archna Sharma, and Tina Joseph (for digital content management); Caroline Reed
(for editorial assistance); Margaret Parrish (for US editorial consultancy).

TOM STEVENSON

*Tom Stevenson has been writing about wine for
more than 35 years. He is the author of 23 critically
acclaimed books and winner of 32 literary awards
– including Wine Writer of the Year three times and
The Wine Literary Award, America's only lifetime
achievement award for wine writers. In 2011, he
was elected to the Wine Writers' Hall of Fame by the
Wine Media Guild of New York. He has a regular
column in* The World of Fine Wine *and has judged
at wine competitions in the USA, France, Germany,
Greece, Australia, and the UK, where he chairs the
panels for Champagne and Alsace at the
Decanter* World Wine Awards.

*Tom's books have been published internationally
by more than 50 publishers and, in total, have been
translated into over 25 languages. He has specialized
in Champagne since embarking on a six-year
research project that culminated in the publication
of* Champagne *(Sotheby's Publications, 1986).
In 1998, his* Christie's World Encyclopedia of
Champagne & Sparkling Wine *(Absolute Press) was
the first book to publish a 17th-century document
proving that the English invented the so-called*
méthode champenoise *six years before Dom
Pérignon set foot in Hautvillers. This revelation
ensured the book made history as the only wine book
to warrant a leader in any UK national newspaper
(*The Guardian, *14 October 1998). Tom's other
consuming passion is Alsace, and in 1993* The Wines
of Alsace *(Faber & Faber) duly appeared to universal
plaudits, winning two awards, including the Veuve
Clicquot Best Wine Book of the Year in the USA.*

Tom is best known, however, as the author of
The Sotheby's® Wine Encyclopedia, *which
Dorling Kindersley has published continuously
since 1988 and which has sold more than
600,000 copies in 14 major languages.*